楷書 해서로 쉽게 배울 수 있는 故事成語 고사성어 100

저자 著者 김영배 金榮培

솔과학

읽어두기

1. 기초 획과 점의 표현에 있어 운필법과 순서를 표시하여 초학자가 쉽게 익힐 수 있도록 하였다.
2. 한자어는 한글과 병기하여 읽기 편하게 하였다.
3. 고사성어 100은 대중성과 활용성, 실용성을 기준으로 선정하였다.
4. 창작 작품을 예시하여 초학자의 창작 기회를 제공하고자 하였다.

해서楷書로 쉽게 배울 수 있는 고사성어 100
故事成語

目 次

1. 해서의 의의意義

서예의 뜻과 서체

서예는 붓을 포함한 유사한 도구를 사용하여 쇠 · 돌 · 나무 · 비단 · 종이 · 뼈 등 다양한 바탕에 자기의 생각을 글씨 또는 그림의 형태로 풀어내는 예술이다. 한편, 작품을 보고 글씨의 아름다움을 느끼는 것은 글자의 형태, 점과 획, 필세筆勢[글씨의 획에 드러난 기세], 결구結構[글씨의 짜임새], 간가間架[점과 획, 획과 획 사이] 등 장법章法[대장법:전체 작품에서 글자와 행간의 관계. 소장법:한 글자에서 점획의 안배나 한 글자와 몇 글자의 배치]이 뛰어나고 먹을 사용하는 데 있어 진하고 흐린 먹을 적절히 사용하여 붓을 운용할 때 강약强弱의 조절 속에서 시각적으로 조형적 미감을 자아낸다.

글씨는 점 · 획으로 이루어져 있으며, 붓의 운필에 따라 점 · 획의 생명력이 달라진다. 송나라의 소식蘇軾은 글씨 획을 인체에 비교하여 신神 · 기氣 · 골骨 · 육肉 · 혈血 등이 있어야 생명력이 있다고 말했다.

서체의 변화로 보면, 전서篆書 · 예서隷書 · 초서草書 · 해서楷書 · 행서行書 등으로 변하여 왔다. 서체는 갑골문 이후 정체正體와 초체草體의 두 갈래로 나뉘어 발전하였다.

청나라 시기의 유희재劉熙載는 『예개藝概 · 서개書概』에서 "서체는 두 가지 종류가 있다. 전서篆書 · 예서隷書 · 해서楷書를 모두 자세히 알 수 있는 정적靜的인 글씨이고, 또 하나는 행서行書와 초서草書이며 모두 간략簡略하고 동적動的인 글씨이다."라 하여 정체正體와 초체草體로 분류하였다. 초체는 비교적 개인적인 목적에서 사용되었고, 정체는 각각 시대별로 국가에서 공식적으로 사용되었다.

해서楷書[1)]의 변천

중국 후한後漢 말기부터 사용되기 시작한 해서楷書는 장회관張懷瓘이 『서단書斷』의 팔분八分[=예서]을 설명하는 부분에서 "해서楷書라는 용어의 해자楷字는 법식法式 · 모模[본보기]와 같은 뜻이다." 라고 풀이하였다. 또 허신의 『설문해자說文解字』에서는 나무인데, 공자묘孔子墓를 둘러싸고 있는 나무이다.[2)] 라고 하여 표준으로 삼을 만한 서체라는 의미를 가지고 있다. 『진서晉書 · 위항전衛恒傳』에는 상곡사람 왕차중王次仲이 처음 해서를 만들었다.[3)] 라고 되어 있다. 해서楷書는 정해正楷 · 진서眞書[4)] · 정서正書라고 부르는데 예서隷書로부터 획을 간단하게 줄이고 가로 획은 평평하게 하고 세로획은 수직으로 점점 변화되어 왔다. 다른 해설을 보면, "형체는 방정하고 필획은 평직으로 되어 있으니 해서의 본보기라고 할 수 있다."[5)] 해서는 한나라 말기에 만들어져서 지금까지 오랜 세월 동안 쓰여지고 있는 서체이다. 해서는 한나라 예서의 법을 이어 받고 형체미적 발전을 가져왔다. 그 특징은 점 · 획이나 형태가 간결하고 명확한 간가間架 · 결구結構가 정돈된 서체이다. 따라서 가장 쓰기 쉽고, 읽기 쉬우며 실용적인 글씨로 중요한 서체가 되었다. 그 결과도 엄정嚴正하고 정제整齊되어 침착沈着 부동미不動美가 강하게 나타난다.

해서의 명칭은 당나라 시기까지는 진서眞書 · 정서正書 · 예서隷書 · 금예今隷 · 장정서章程書 등 여러 명칭이 있었으며, 송나라 시대 이후 해서로 불렀다. 위진남북조魏晉南北朝와 수당隋唐시대에는 해서를 한예漢隷와 구분하지 않고 예서隷書라는 이름으로 해서楷書와 행서行書 모두를 지칭하기도 하였으며 또 한예漢隷를 팔분八分, 행서行書를 예서隷書로 부르는 등 해서의 명칭과 개념이 확립되지 않았다.

삼국시기까지 해서를 발전시킨 조위曹魏시기의 종요鍾繇를 들 수 있다. 그의 해서는 〈천계직표薦季直表〉 · 〈하첩표賀捷表〉 · 〈선시표宣示表〉 등을 들 수 있다.

호소석胡小石은 『서예략론書藝略論』에서 "종요의 해서는 예서의 필세筆勢와 자세字勢를 가지고 있으며 왕희지는 종요를 계승하였으나 예서의 필세와 형세를 모두 버렸다."라고 하여 왕희지 해서에 중요한 역할을 한 것으로 나타난다.

동진東晉의 왕희지王羲之는 종요鍾繇 서예를 이어받아 남조南朝에서 크게 유행하였으며, 북조北朝에서도 안정된 정치체제가 구축된 후 한화漢化 정책으로 남쪽의 문화를 받아들였으며 남조南朝에서 사용되고 있는 해서를 공식 서체로 사용하였다. 남조南朝에서는 비를 세우지 못하게 하는 전통 때문에 비각에 새긴 해서는 그 수가 적으나 북조北朝에서는 해서를 사용하여 묘지墓誌 · 조상기造像記 · 마애磨崖 · 석비石碑 등의 수많은 서예 작품을 남기고 있다. 북조의 해서는 질박하고 웅장하며 강건한 미감을 특성으로 하고 남조南朝시기는 단아하고 수려한 미감과 함께 예술성이 가장 뛰어나다고 평가된다. 당나라시대에는 해서가 진晉나라 시기 해서나 북위北魏나라 시기 해서와 구별되는 가장 큰 특징은 서예가 작품의 개성보다는 법칙을 중시하고 규범화되어 있는 것이다. 그 후 당唐나라 초당初唐 4대가인 구양순歐陽詢, 우세남虞世南, 저수량褚遂良, 설직薛稷 등과 성당盛唐시기 안진경顔眞卿, 중당中唐시기 유공권柳公權 등의 활약으로 해서가 완성되어 서예 풍이 다채롭고 성대하게 되었다. 그러나 어떤 의미에서는 지나친 규범성으로 말미암아 심미적 특징이 통일되어 작품과 작가의 개성이 표현되지 못하였기 때문에 진晉나라 해서나 위魏나라 해서에 비하여 예술성이 뒤지고 있다고 할 수 있다.

송나라에서 청나라시기까지 해서는 문서를 기록하거나 과거 시험에 답안을 쓰기 위하여 공부하는 대상으로 쓰였다. 원나라와 명나라시기의 대각체臺閣體[6] 청나라시기의 관각체館閣體로 자리 잡은 해서는 인쇄를 대신하는 수단이었다. 그러나 청나라후기 쇠와 돌에 새겨진 문자나 그림을 연구하는 학문과 문자가 생겨난 원리를 연구하는 학문 등이 성행하여 금석학자와 서예가들은 점차 쇠와 돌에 새겨진 서예의 아름다움에 눈을 뜨게 되어 비학파碑學派가 생겨나 금석서예를 가르치고 배웠으며 북위北魏해서와 전서와 예서를 임서臨書하고 창작하는 대상으로 삼았다.

세 종류의 해서

해서는 북위해北魏楷 [북위체北魏體]와 당해唐楷 중 구양순歐陽詢체와 안진경顔眞卿체로 나누어서 설명하겠다.

북위해서北魏楷書[=육조六朝[7] 해서楷書]

위진남북조魏晉南北朝시기는 해서가 발전하고 성숙되었던 시기라고 할 수 있다. 당시의 정치상황은 매우 혼란스러운 전란시기였기에 소식消息과 군령軍令을 급히 발포發布하면서, 필획이 많은 형태의 예서에 비해 해서가 필획이 적고 쓰기에 편리하여 유행하게 되었다. 나라의 혼란함으로 인해 글씨도 안정되지 못한 글씨가 유행하던 시기이다. 창의성 있는 작품을 제작해야 하는 작가 입장에서는 완벽하지 못한 글씨 속에 자기의 마음을 불어넣어 새로운 자기만의 작품을 만들 수 있는 좋은 기회를 제공할 수 있는 것이 장점이다.

강유위의 『광예주쌍즙廣藝舟雙楫』에서 북위체北魏體의 10가지 아름다움[8] 대해 이렇게 말했다. 첫째, 정신의 힘이 웅건하고 강하다. 둘째, 기상이 순박하고 화목하다. 셋째, 필법이 뛰어나다. 넷째, 점획이 준엄하

장맹룡비(張猛龍碑)

고 두텁다. 다섯째, 필의와 형태가 특이하고 자유롭다. 여섯째, 정신이 날아 움직인다. 일곱째, 흥취가 무르익어 만족할 만하다. 여덟째, 골법이 통달하다. 아홉째, 결구가 자연스럽다. 열째, 피와 살이 풍성하고 아름답다. 육조시기의 모범이 되는 글씨중 하나인 〈장맹용비張猛龍碑〉에 대하여 알아보면, 당시 불교가 성행하였지만, 장맹용張猛龍은 유교를 선양하였다. 이 장맹룡의 덕을 기리는 송덕비頌德碑이다. 이 글씨는 당나라시기의 구양순歐陽詢이 영향을 받았다고 할 수 있다. 굵은 획과 가는 획을 적절히 안배하여 방필方筆의 강건하고 씩씩한 필세와 부드러운 맛을 함께 지니고 있으며 풍부한 변화가 있다. 이 비음碑陰의 서체의 포치布置와 결구는 자유스러워 글씨의 크기도 들쭉날쭉한 형세를 하고 있으면서도 조화를 이루고 있어 서민적인 풍토가 느껴지는 형태를 추구하고 있다. 행서 필의를 가미하고 있어 해서 중에 초서라고 불러도 무리가 없을 것이다. 또한 태세의 변화와 글씨 크기의 변화 등이 자연스럽기 때문에 무궁무진한 창작의 세계를 열 수 있는 소재를 제공한다. 비양碑陽은 정제됨 속에서 방원方圓의 변화를 추구하고 있어 해서의 모범이라 할 수 있다.

북위체北魏體의 특징은 필기筆氣가 혼후[渾厚 : 화기가 있고 인정이 두터움]하고, 의태[意態 : 마음의 상태]는 질탕[跌宕 : 한껏 흐트러져 방탕에 가까움]하며, 길고 짧으며 크고 작음이 그 형태에 따라 분항포백分行布白에 있어 묘妙를 다하였으되 정제한 가운데에서 변화하고 방평方平한 속에 기굴[奇堀:글씨의 획과 형태가 남다르게 특이하고 기이]함을 갖추고 있어 훌륭하다. 북위체는 해서의 발전시기로서 위로는 종요 · 왕희지을 잇고 아래로 수隋 · 당唐을 열었으니, 당에 이르러 해서는 완전히 성숙되었다.

중국서예 4대 해서楷書의 대가 4체를 살펴보면, 당나라 초기 구양순歐陽詢[구양순체][9] · 당나라 중기 안진경顔真卿[안진경체][10] · 당나라 유공권柳公權[유체][11] · 원나라의 조맹부趙孟頫[송설체][12]이다. 이 중 당나라의 구양순의 〈구성궁예천명九成宮醴泉名〉과 〈안진경의 안근례비顔勤禮碑〉를 예를 들어 보겠다.

구성궁예천명(九成宮醴泉銘)

구성궁예천명九成宮醴泉銘

구양순(557~641), 자는 신본信本, 지금의 호남성湖南省 장사長沙사람이며, 벼슬은 수나라의 태상박사太常博士와 당나라의 태자율갱령太字率更令 했다. 그의 글씨는 해서를 가장 잘 썼으며, 필력이 뛰어나고 결구結構가 특이하여 후대사람이 이르기를 '구체歐體' 라고 한다.

그가 쓴 구성궁예천명九成宮醴泉銘[구양순 76세때 쓴 글씨]은 황제의 명령에 의해 쓴 작품으로 글자의 형태는 크고 단정하고 엄정하여 해서로서의 기본 조건을 모두 다 충족시키고 있다. 이 비碑는 결체에 여유가 있고 용필도 자유자재하여 빼어난 점은, 꺾거나 휘는 데서 붓이 나가다가 멈추고 그대로 자연스럽게 거둔다.

안근례비顔勤禮碑

해서의 창안자인 안진경顔眞卿(709~785)은 字는 청신淸臣이고 호는 응방應方이다. 그리고 안근례顔勤禮는 안진경의 증조부로서 자字는 경敬이다. 안진경은 정원원년貞元元年(785) 77세때 사망하였는데, 만년晩年에 이르러서는 그 서예의 명성은 더욱 높았다.

안근례비(顔勤禮碑)

안진경은 왕희지 왕헌지 부자의 필법을 이어 후대에 최고의 영향을 준 서예가이다. 그의 서예학습은 처음에는 '초성草聖' 장욱張旭에게 배웠고, 후에는 초당 4대가에게 큰 영향을 받았지만, 고법古法을 변화시켜 초당 서풍과 다른 서풍을 일으켰다. 특히 행서는 전서와 주문籒文을 취해 다른 서예가와 달리 획이 단단하면서도 살이 풍부한 속에 마르지 않은 골력을 얻고, 금석기와 고상한 인품이 더해져서 기운생동氣韻生動한 글씨를 썼다.

---

1) 法式；典範.『禮記 · 儒行』今世行之, 後世以爲楷.
2)『說文』木也, 孔子塚蓋樹之者.
『淮南子 · 草木訓』, 楷木生孔子塚上, 其幹枝疎而不屈, 以質得其直也.
清 段玉裁,『說文解字注』楷木也. 孔子塚蓋樹之者. 皇覽云. 塚塋中樹以百數. 皆異種. 傳言弟子各持 其方樹來種之. 按楷亦方樹之一也. 儒行曰.今世行之.後世以爲楷. 楷, 法式也. 楷之言稽我稽古. 而後世又於此焉稽也. 從木. 皆聲. 苦駭切. 十五部. 以下言木名. 故先之以孔塚所樹.
3)『진서晉書 · 위항전衛恒傳』.上穀王次仲, 始作楷法.
4) 真書: 今隸 · 楷書 · 正書로 칭한다. 한나라 말기에 나왔다. 한나라시기의 波磔을 변화시키고, 鉤趯을 더하여서 만들어 냈다. 魏나라 鍾繇로부터 晉나라 王羲之는 體勢를 변화시켜서 法則을 만들었다. 隸書와 楷書를 완전히 분류하여 다른 서체를 만들었다. 鍾繇의『賀克捷表』·『墓田丙舍』, 王羲之의『樂毅論』·『黃庭經』·『東方朔畫贊』등 해서 최고작품이라고 할 만하다.
5)『辭海』, 形體方正, 筆畫平直, 可作楷模.
6) 臺閣體: 명 · 청나라의 묵색이 짙고 글씨 크기가 고른 네모반듯하고 깔끔한 서체
7) 六朝: 삼국의 吳 · 東晋 · 南朝의 宋 · 齊 · 梁 · 陳을 뜻함.
8) 康有爲의『廣藝舟雙楫』,「十六宗 第16」, 有十美. 一曰魄力雄強, 二曰氣象渾穆, 三曰筆法跳越, 四曰點畫峻厚, 五曰意態奇逸, 六曰精神飛動, 七曰興趣酣足, 八曰骨法洞達, 九曰結構天成, 十曰血肉豐美.
9) 歐陽詢(557~641), 字信本, 潭州臨湘(今湖南長沙)人.
10) 顔真卿(709~785), 字 清臣, 京兆萬年人, 祖籍唐琅琊臨沂(今山東臨沂). 秘書監顔師古五世從孫 · 司徒顔杲卿從弟, 唐代名臣, 書法家.
11) 柳公權(778~865), 字 誠懸, 京兆華原(今陝西銅川市)人.唐代著名書法家 · 詩人.
12) 趙孟頫(1254~1322), 字 子昂, 號 松雪道人 · 水晶宮道人 · 鷗波, 浙江吳興(今浙江湖州)人.南宋末至元初著名書法家 · 畫家 · 詩人, 宋太祖趙匡胤十一世孫 · 秦王趙德芳嫡派子孫.

2. 기초획

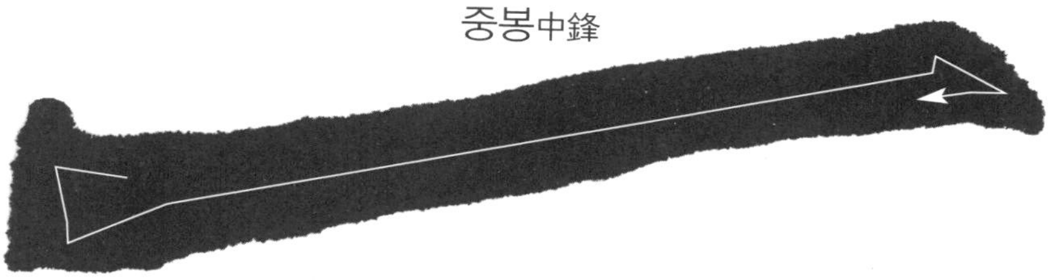

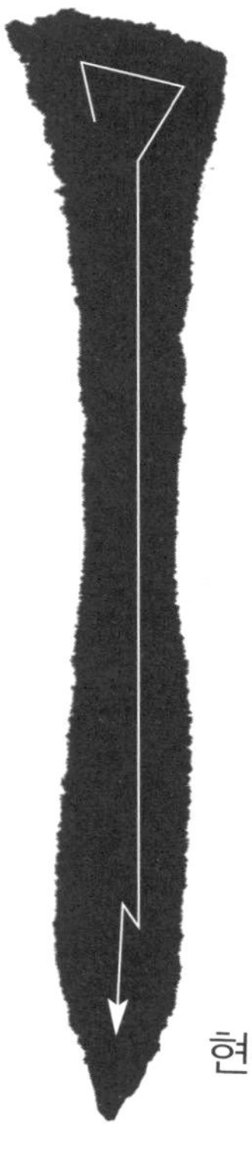

기필起筆(낙필落筆) : 점과 획을 운필할 때 붓 끝을 종이 위에 대는 동작을 말한다.
행필行筆 : 기필 후 점과 획을 운필하여 나아가는 모습을 말한다.
역입逆入 : 점과 획을 운필할 때 붓이 오른쪽에서 왼쪽으로 들어가서 오른쪽으로 운필하는 방법이다.
회봉回鋒 : 수필收筆 할 때에 붓을 거두어들인다.
수필收筆 : 필획의 끝부분에 이르러 마무리할 때의 용필 방법을 말한다.
삼절三折 : 붓을 운필 할 때 멈추었다가 호를 모았다가 가는 모습이다.
수로垂露 : 세로획의 끝부분에 이르렀을 때 필봉을 드러내지 않고 붓을 머물러 위로 향하여 에워싸듯이 거두어 이슬이 맺힌 모양 같이 보이는 것.
현침懸針 : 세로획의 끝부분에 이르렀을 때 필봉을 드러내서 마치 바늘이 매달린 것 같은 모습이다.
중봉中鋒 : 정봉正鋒이라고도 하며, 편봉과 서로 대칭된다. 운필을 할 때 획 속에 봉鋒이 지나간 자리가 중앙에 있는 것을 말한다.

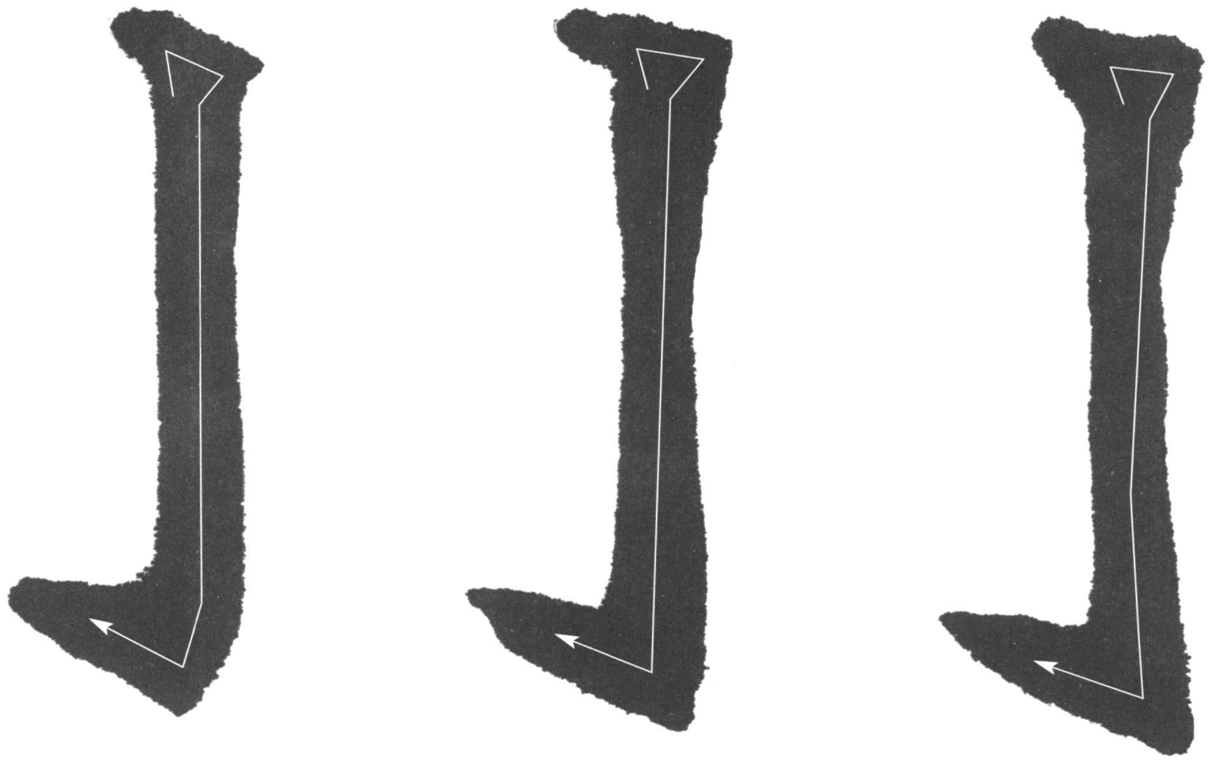

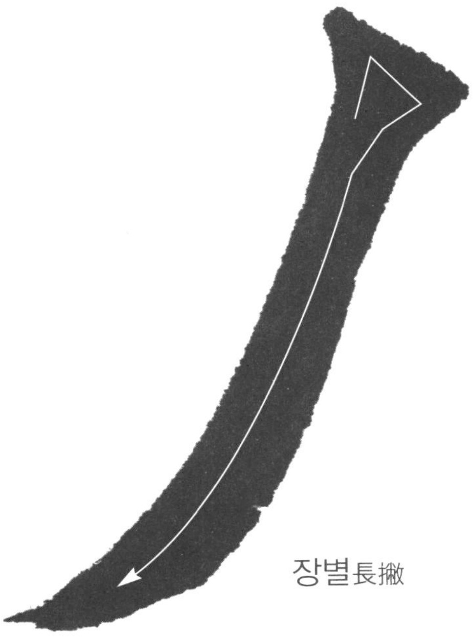

장별長撇

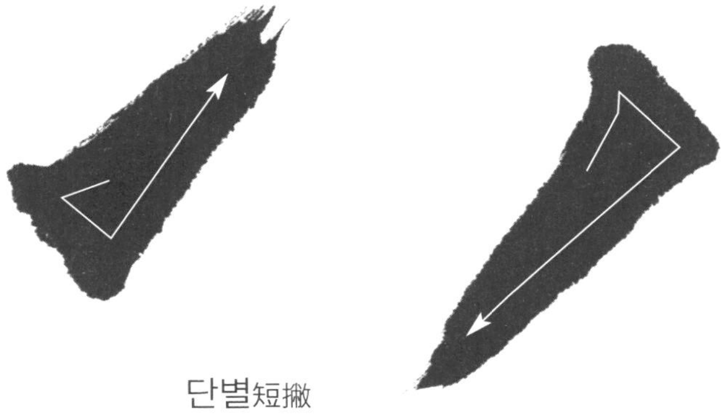

단별短撇

3. 영자팔법永字八法

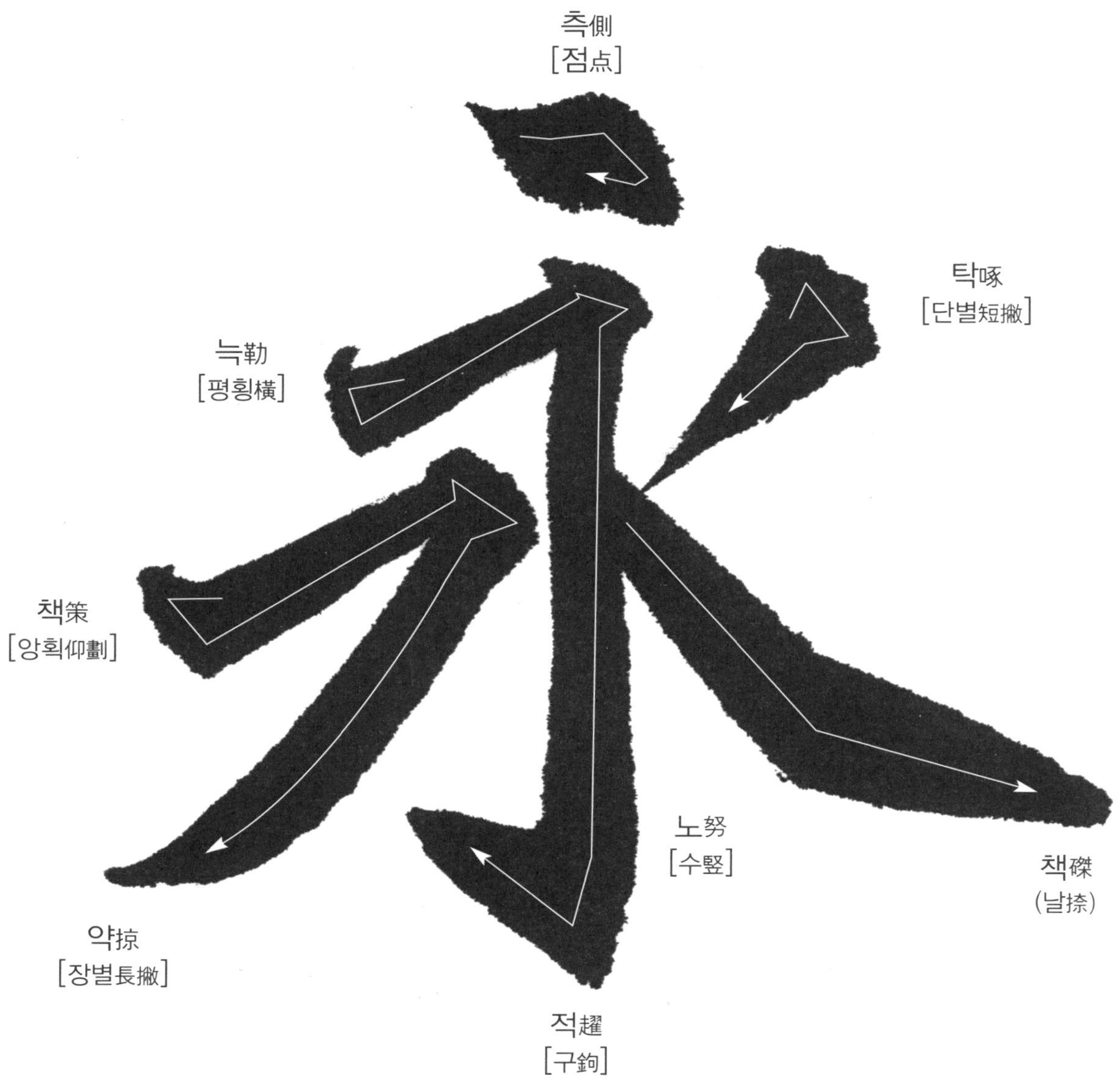

영자팔법永字八法은 서예 획의 종류 여덟 가지를 길 영永 자를 통해 설명한 것이다.
후한시대의 채옹이 처음 고안했다고도 한다.

1. 측(側) – 점획[점点] : 기울어 있는 점.
2. 늑(勒) – 가로획[늑勒] : 가로 긋는 획의 시작부분인 진흙에 말발굽 형태의 모양을 말한다.
3. 노(努) – 세로획[수竪] : 세로로 내려 긋는 획인데, 마치 활을 힘껏 당길 때의 형세形勢와 같다고 하여 노弩라고도 한다.
4. 적(趯) – 갈고리 획[구鉤] : 붓을 누른 다음 갑자기 튀게 하면서 힘을 붓 끝에 집중시킨다.
5. 책(策) – 오른쪽의 위로 쳐다보는 왼쪽의 윗 획으로 채찍을 치는 필세筆勢이다.
6. 약(掠) – [장별長撇] : 길게 왼쪽으로 삐친 획이다.
7. 탁(啄) – [단별短撇] 짧은 왼 삐침: 오른쪽 위에서 왼쪽으로 짧게 삐친 획으로 새가 모이를 쪼을 때의 부리 모습과 비슷하다.
8. 책(磔) – 파임[날捺] : 붓을 역입逆入하여 붓털을 펴서 서서히 진행시키다 끝에 와서 거두어 세웠다가 반복하면서 붓 끝을 모으며 뺀다.

4. 기초자基礎字 설명

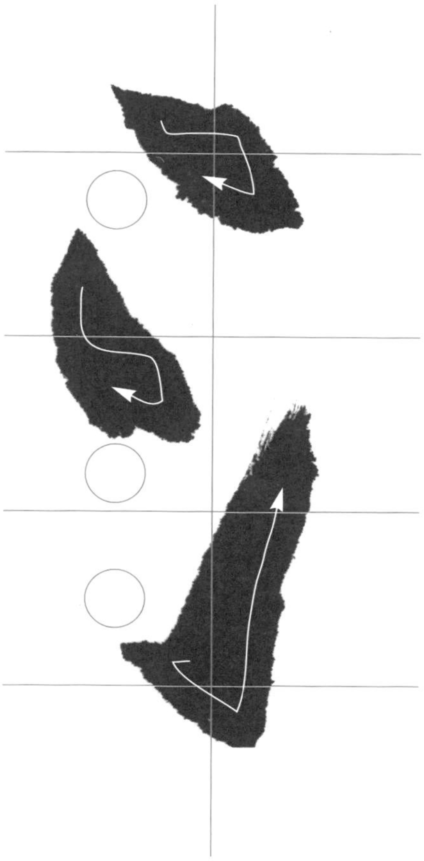

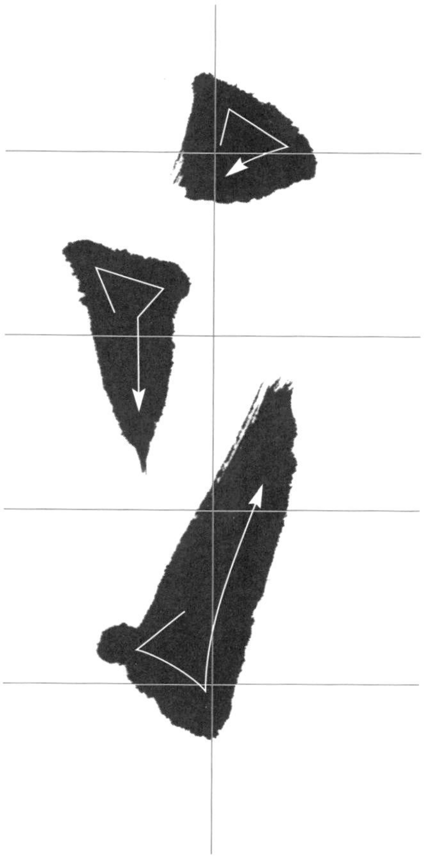

물 수 水

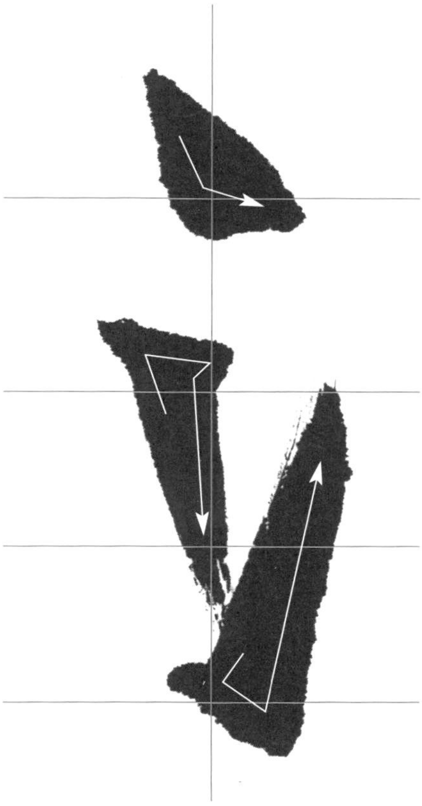

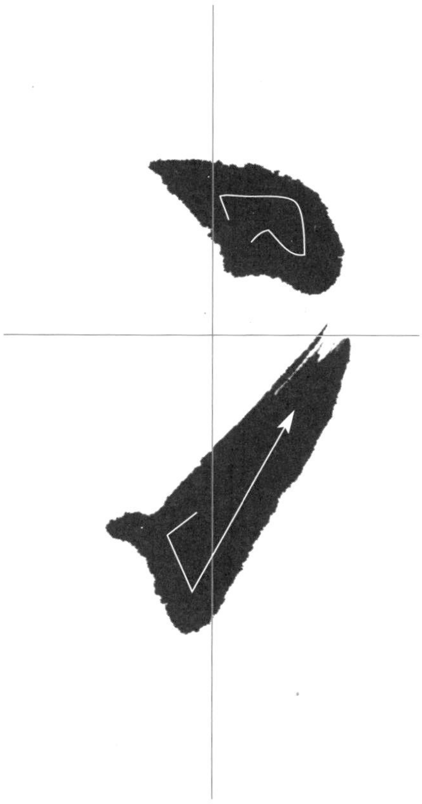

얼음 빙 氷, 冰

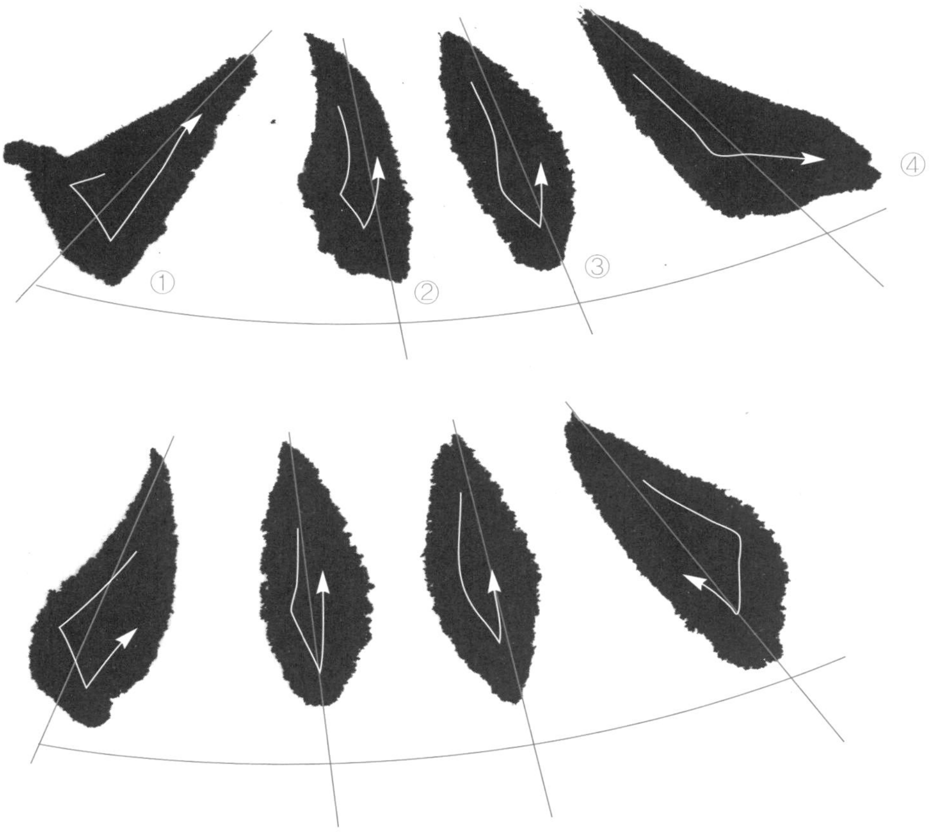

불화 火

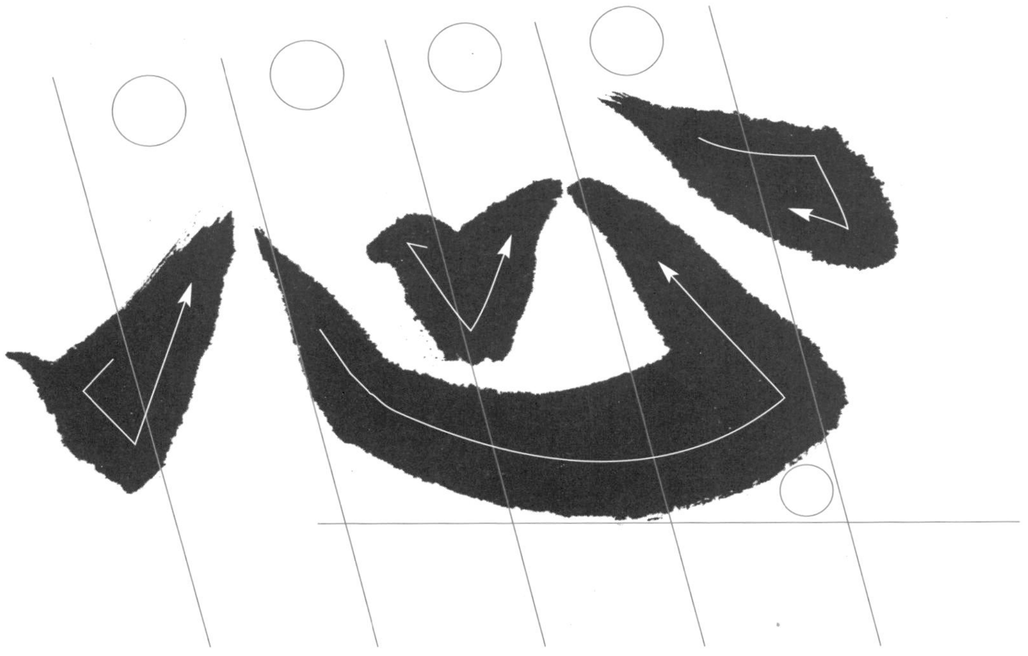

마음 심 心, 忄

고을 읍, 아첨할 압 邑(阝:우측)

새 을 乙

아들 자 子

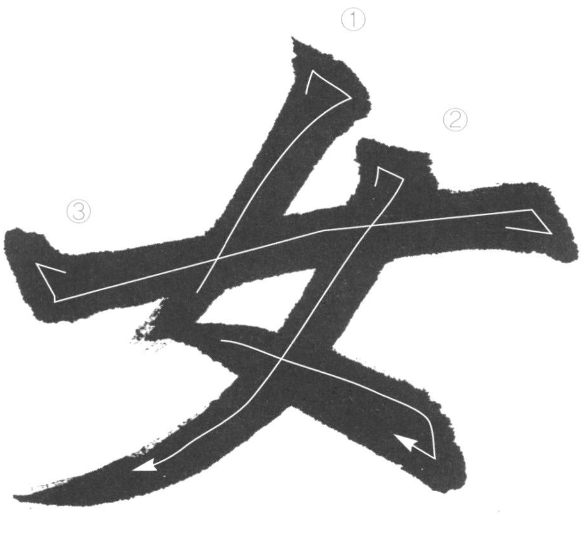

여자 여 女

나무 목 木

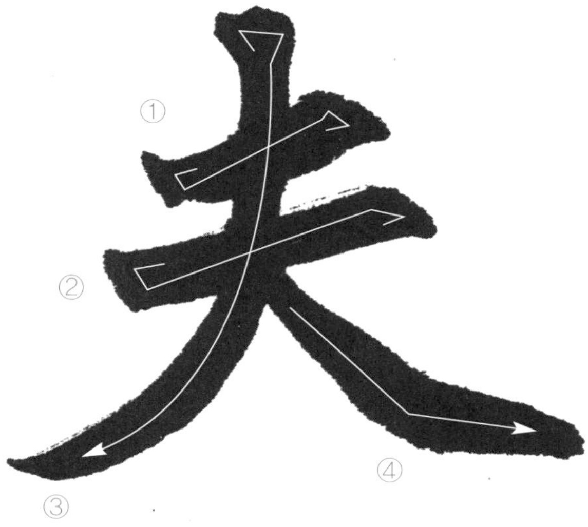

사내 부, 지아비 부 夫

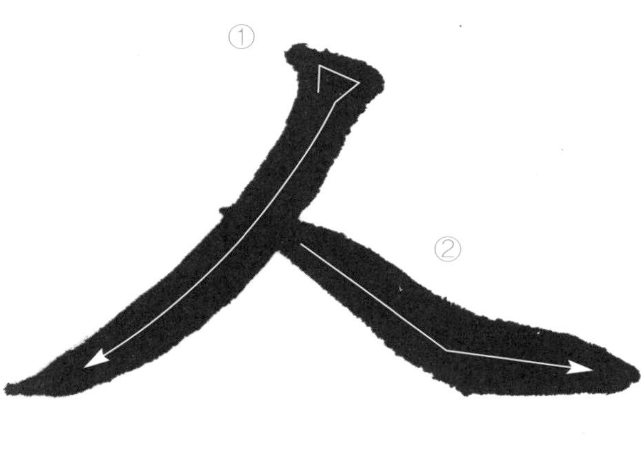

사람 인 人(亻)

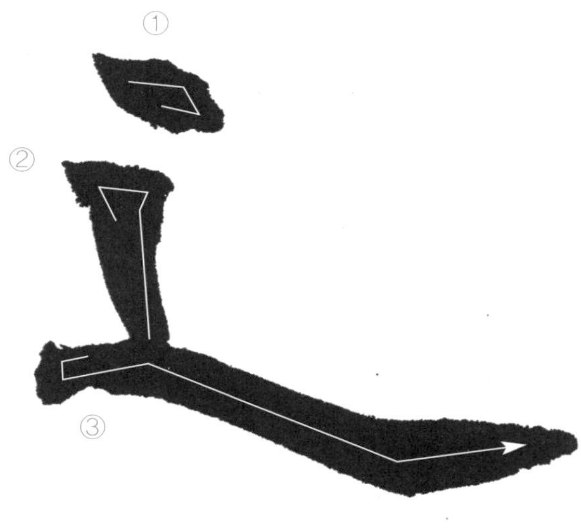

쉬엄쉬엄 갈 착 辵(辶)

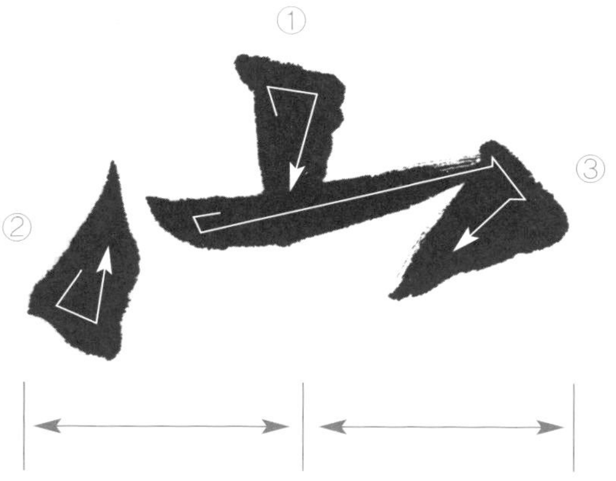

집 면 宀

보일 시, 땅귀신 기 示

창 과 戈

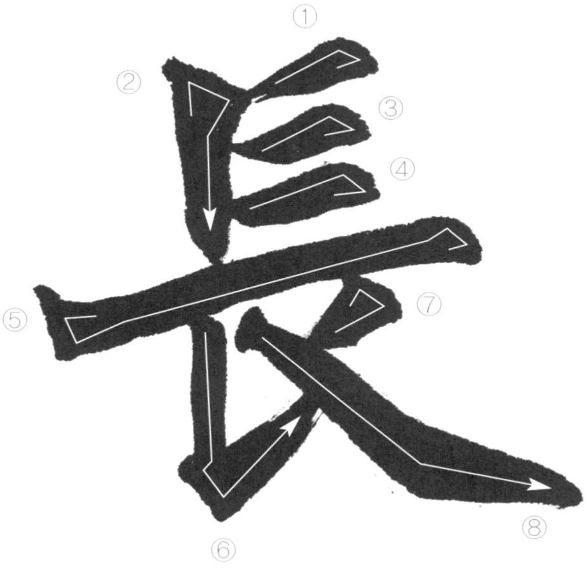

길 장, 어른 장 長

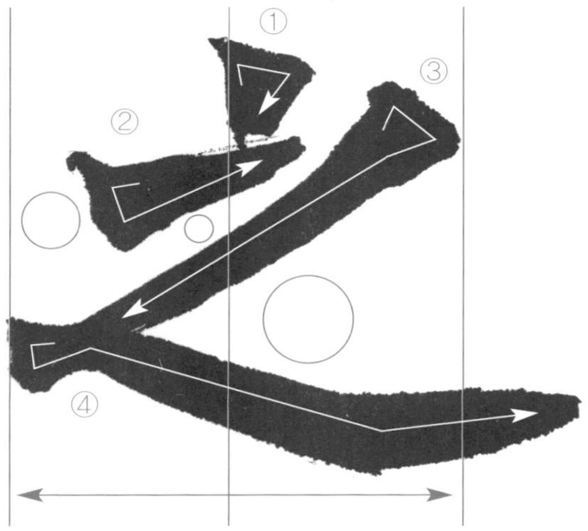

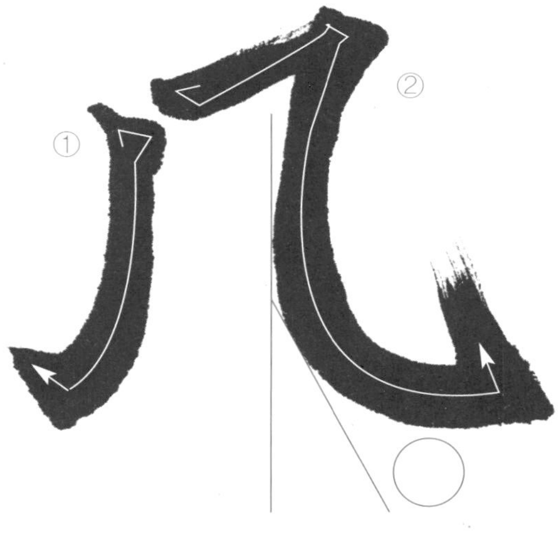

갈 지 之

안석 궤, 몇 기, 무릇 범 几

고을 주 州

하품 흠 欠

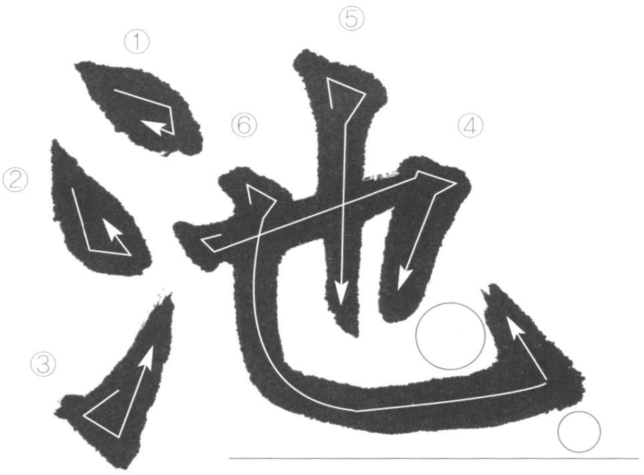

못 지, 강이름 타, 제기할 철 池

날 일 日

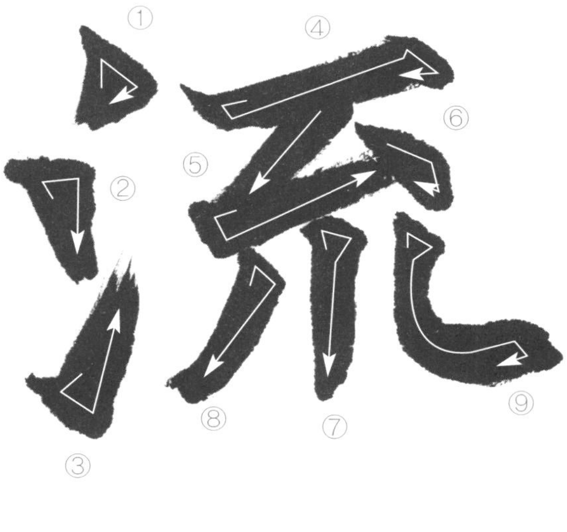

흐를 류 流

어조사 호 乎

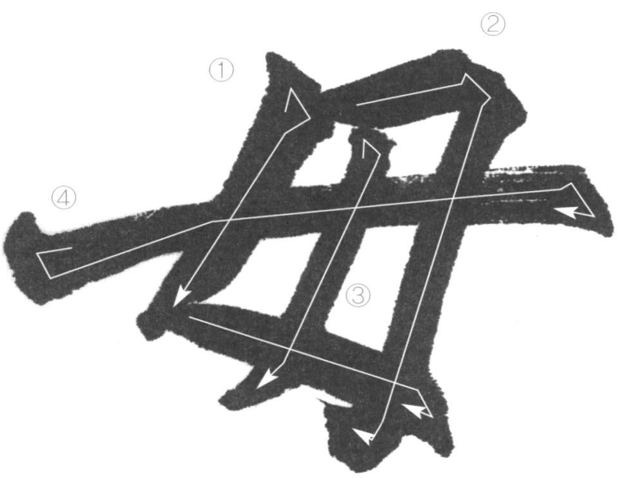

관직이름 무, 말 무, 없을 무 毋

기운 기, 빌 걸[乞과 同字] 气

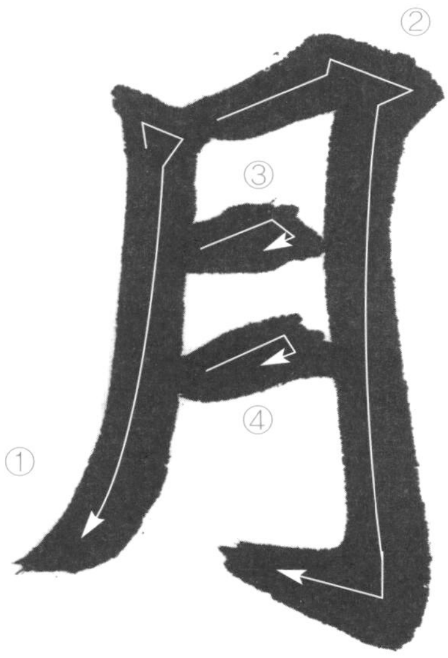

달 월 月

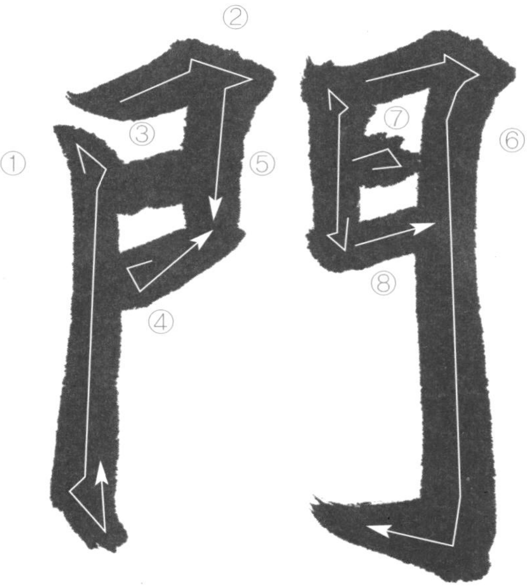

문 문 門

해서楷書로 쉽게 배울 수 있는 고사성어 100

故事成語

참고자료: 고사성어 발췌 : 전광진 『선생님 한 책』 LBH교육출판사, 2012.

목차目次

① 산[山]을 좋아하고[樂]물[水]을 좋아함[樂]。 ② 산이나 강 같은 자연을 즐기고 좋아함。

① 백년[百年]을 내다보는 큰[大] 계획[計劃]。 ② 먼 장래에 대한 장기 계획。

① 마음[心]으로 지은[作] 것이 삼일[三日]밖에 못 감。 ② 결심이 오래 가지 못함。

① 괴로움[苦]을 함께[同]하고 즐거움[樂]도 함께[同] 함。 ② 괴로움과 즐거움도 함께 함。

① 천리[千里] 길도 멀다고[遠] 여기지 아니함。 ② 먼 길을 기꺼이 달려감。

不 아닐 불

遠 멀 원

千 일천 천

里 마을 리

人 사람 인

命 목숨 명

在 있을 재

天 하늘 천

① 사람[人]의 목숨[命]은 하늘[天]에 달려 있음[在]。 ② 사람이 오래 살거나 일찍 죽는 것은 다 하늘의 뜻이라는 말。

① 꽃[花]이 핀 아침[朝]과 달[月]이 뜨는 저녁[夕]。 ② 「경치가 좋은 시절」을 이르는 말。

① 하늘[천]을 공경[恭敬]하고 사람[人]을 사랑[愛]함。 ② 하늘이 내린 운명을 달게 받고 남들을 사랑하며 사이좋게 지냄。

① 오랜 세월[萬古]이 지나도록 변[變]하지 않음[不]。 ② 영원히 변하지 아니함。「진리」를 형용한 말로 많이 쓰임。

① 무엇이든지 다 통[通]하여 알지[知] 못하는[不] 것이 없음[無]。 ② 무엇이든지 환히 잘 앎。

① 한[二] 가지를 들으면[聞] 열[十] 가지를 미루어 앎[知]。② 사고력과 추리력이 매우 빼어남。

聞 들을 문

一 한 일

知 알 지

十 열 십

北 북녘 북

窓 창문 창

三 석 삼

友 벗 우

① 서재의 북[北]쪽 창[窓]에 있는 세[三] 벗[友]。② 「거문고、술、시[詩]」를 일컬음。

① 자기 분수[分數]를 편안[便安]하게 여기며 만족[滿足]할 줄 앎[知]。 ② 자기의 분수에 맞게 살며 만족스럽게 잘 삶。

安 편안할 안

分 나눌 분

知 알 지

足 넉넉할 족

雨 비 우

順 순조로울 순

風 바람 풍

調 고를 조

① 비[雨]와 바람[風]이 순조[順調]로움。 ② 농사에 알맞게 기후가 순조로움。

① 마음[心]으로부터[以] 마음[心]을 전함[傳]。② 서로 마음이 잘 통함。

① 사물[事物]의 이치를 바로잡아[格] 높은 지식[知識]에 이름[致]。② 주자학에서 「사물의 본질이나 이치를 끝까지 연구하여 후천적인 지식을 닦음」을 이르고、양명학에서 「자기 생각의 잘못을 바로잡고 선천적인 양지[養志]를 닦음」을 이름。

① 가르치고[敎] 배우는[學] 일이 서로[相] 자라게[長] 함。 ② 가르치고 배우는 것이 서로 도움이 됨。 ③ 가르치면서 배우고, 배우면서 가르친다。

① 묻지[問] 않아도[不] 가[可]히 알[知] 수 있음。 ② 스스로 잘 알 수 있음。

① 눈앞의 이익[利益]을 보면[見] 의리[義理]를 먼저 생각[思]함。 ② 의리를 중요하게 여김。

① 풀[草]을 묶어[結] 은혜[恩惠]에 보답[報]함。 ② 죽어서도 혼령이 되어서라도 은혜를 잊지 않고 갚음。

① 세상[世上]을 다스리고[經] 백성[民]을 구제[救濟]함。 ② 백성의 살림을 잘 보살펴 줌。

① 권세[權勢]는 십년[十年]을 가지 못함[不]。 ② 아무리 높은 권세라도 오래 가지 못함。

① 공[功]을 따져 보아[論] 알맞은 상[賞]을 내림[行]。 ② 공로에 따라 상을 줌。

① 많으면[多] 많을수록[多] 더욱[益] 좋음[善]。 ② 양적으로 많으면 좋음。

① 등잔[燈盞]의 불[火]과 가히 친[親]하게 할 만함。
② 가을밤이면 날씨가 서늘하여 등불을 밝혀 글 읽기에 알맞음。「가을」을 형용한 말로 많이 쓰임。

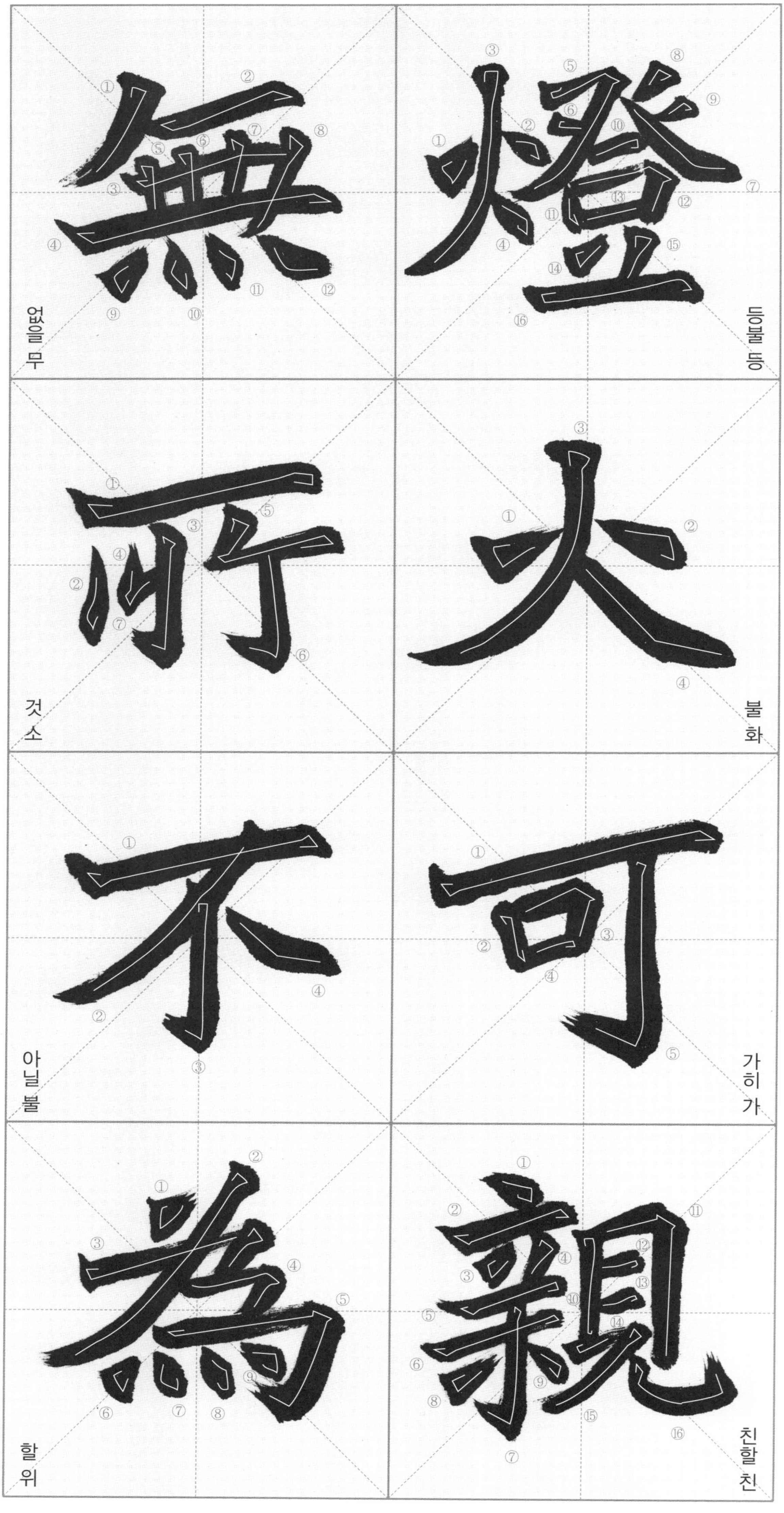

① 못[不] 할[爲] 것[所]이 아무 것도 없음[無]。
② 하지 못하는 일이 없음。

① 널리[博] 배우고[學] 많이[多] 앎[識]。 ② 학문이 넓고 아는 것이 많음。

① 수없이 많은[百] 싸움[戰]을 치른 노련[老鍊]한 장수[將帥]。 ② 세상일을 많이 겪어서 여러 가지 일로 능란한 사람。

① 부유[富裕]함과 귀[貴]함은 하늘[天]의 뜻에 달려 있음[在]。 ② 사람의 힘으로 부귀를 어찌할 수 없음。

① 공이 있는 자에게는 믿을 만하게[信] 상[賞]을 주고、 죄가 있는 사람에게는 반드시[必] 벌[罰]을 줌。

② 상과 벌을 공정하고 엄중하게 하는 일을 이르는 말。

① 실재[實在]의 일[事]에서 올바름[是]을 찾아냄[求]。② 사실에 토대를 두어 진리를 탐구하는 일。
③ 정확한 고증을 바탕으로 하는 과학적·객관적 학문 태도。

① 가난함[貧]을 편안[便安]하게 여기며 사람의 도리[道理]를 즐겨[樂] 지킴。② 가난함에도 불구하고 사람의 도리를 잘 함。

① 옛것[故]을 익히고 새것[新]을 앎[知]。 ② 옛것을 앎으로써 새것을 앎。

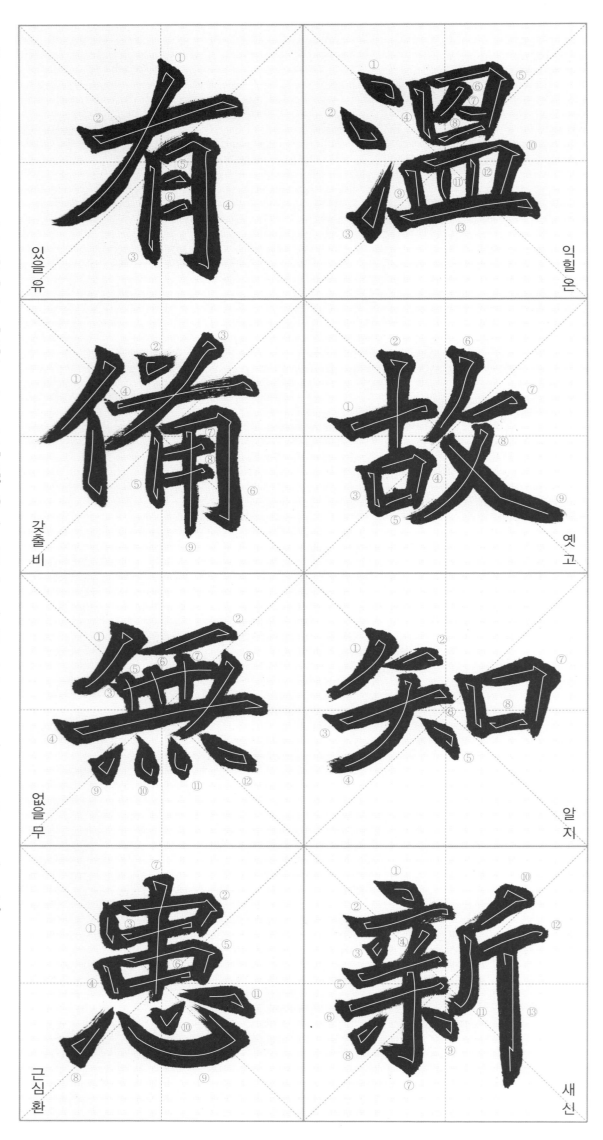

溫 익힐 온

故 옛 고

知 알 지

新 새 신

有 있을 유

備 갖출 비

無 없을 무

患 근심 환

① 준비[準備]가 되어 있으면[有] 근심[患]할 것이 없음[無]。 ② 사전에 준비가 돼 있으면 걱정할 일이 생기지 아니함。

① 원인[原因]에 대한 결과[結果]가 마땅히[應] 갚아짐[報]。 ② 과거 또는 전생에 지은 일에 대한 결과로、 뒷날의 吉凶禍福이 주어짐。

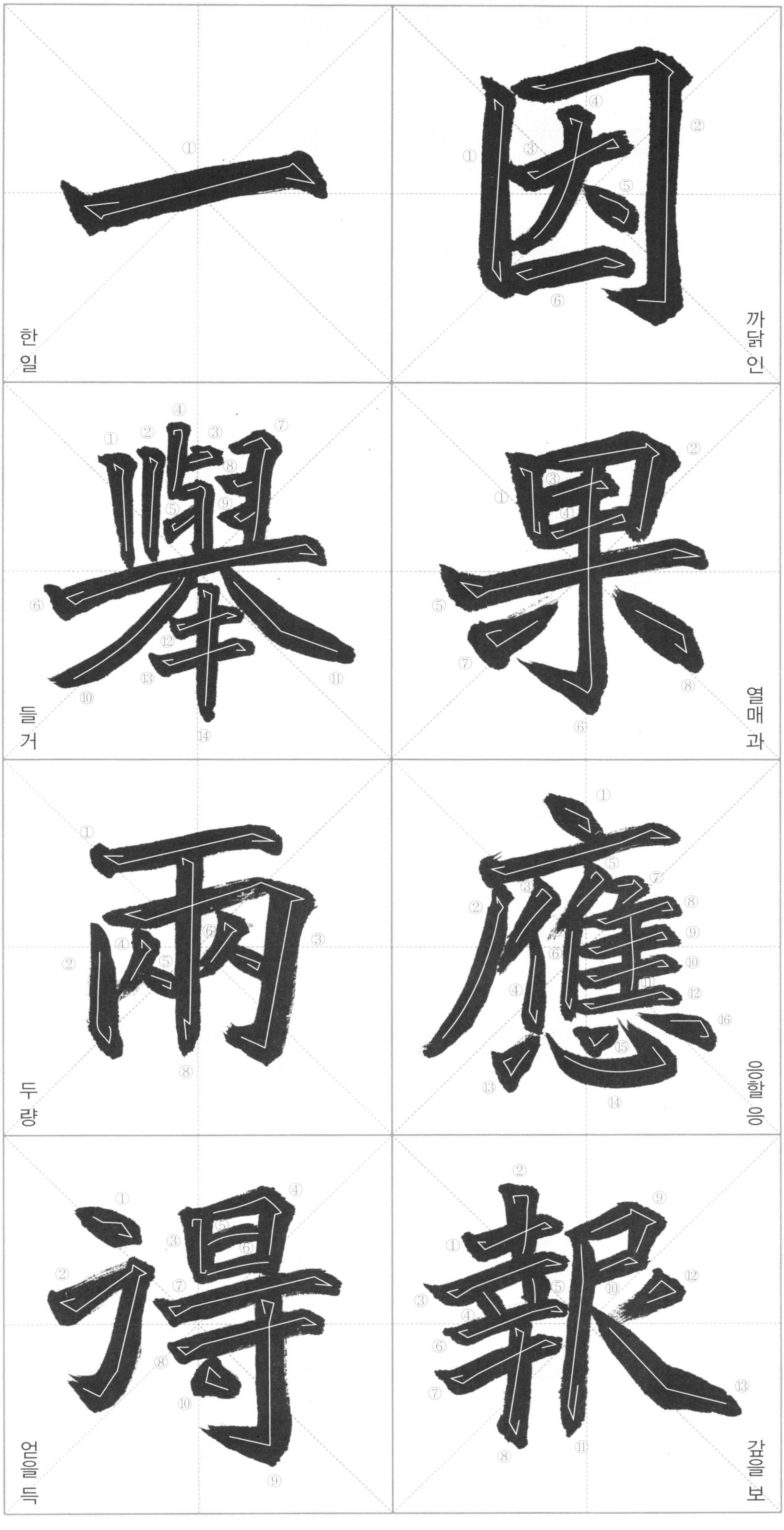

① 한[一] 번 움직여서[擧] 두[兩] 가지를 얻음[得]。 ② 한 번의 노력으로 두 가지 효과를 거둠。

① 날[日]마다 뜻을 이루고[就] 달[月]마다 나아감[將]。 ② 발전이 빠르고 성취가 많음。

① 스스로[自] 굳세게[强] 되기 위하여 쉬지[息] 않고[不] 노력함。 ② 게으름을 피지 않고 스스로 열심히 노력함。

竹馬故友

① 대나무[竹]로 만든 말[馬]을 타고 함께 놀던 오랜[故] 친구[友]。 ② 어릴 때부터 놀며 자란 벗。

至誠感天

① 지극[至極]한 정성[精誠]이 있으면 하늘[天]도 감동[感動]함。 ② 지극한 정성으로 일을 하면 남들이 도와 줌。

① 편안[便安]하게 살[居] 때 앞으로 닥칠 위험[危險]을 미리 생각함[思]。
② 미래의 일이나 위험을 미리 대비함。

① 하늘[天]을 공경[恭敬]하고 백성[民]을 위한 일을 부지런히[勤] 힘씀。
② 하늘이 부여한 사명을 경건하게 받아들이고 백성을 위하여 부지런히 노력함。

① 쓴[苦] 것이 다하면[盡] 단[甘] 것이 옴[來]. ② 고생 끝에 즐거운 일이 생김.

苦 쓸 고

盡 다할 진

甘 달 감

來 올 래

① 임금[君]과 신하[臣下] 간에는 의리[義理]가 있어야[有] 함. ② 임금과 신하 사이의 도리는 의리에 있음.

君 임금 군

臣 신하 신

有 있을 유

義 옳을 의

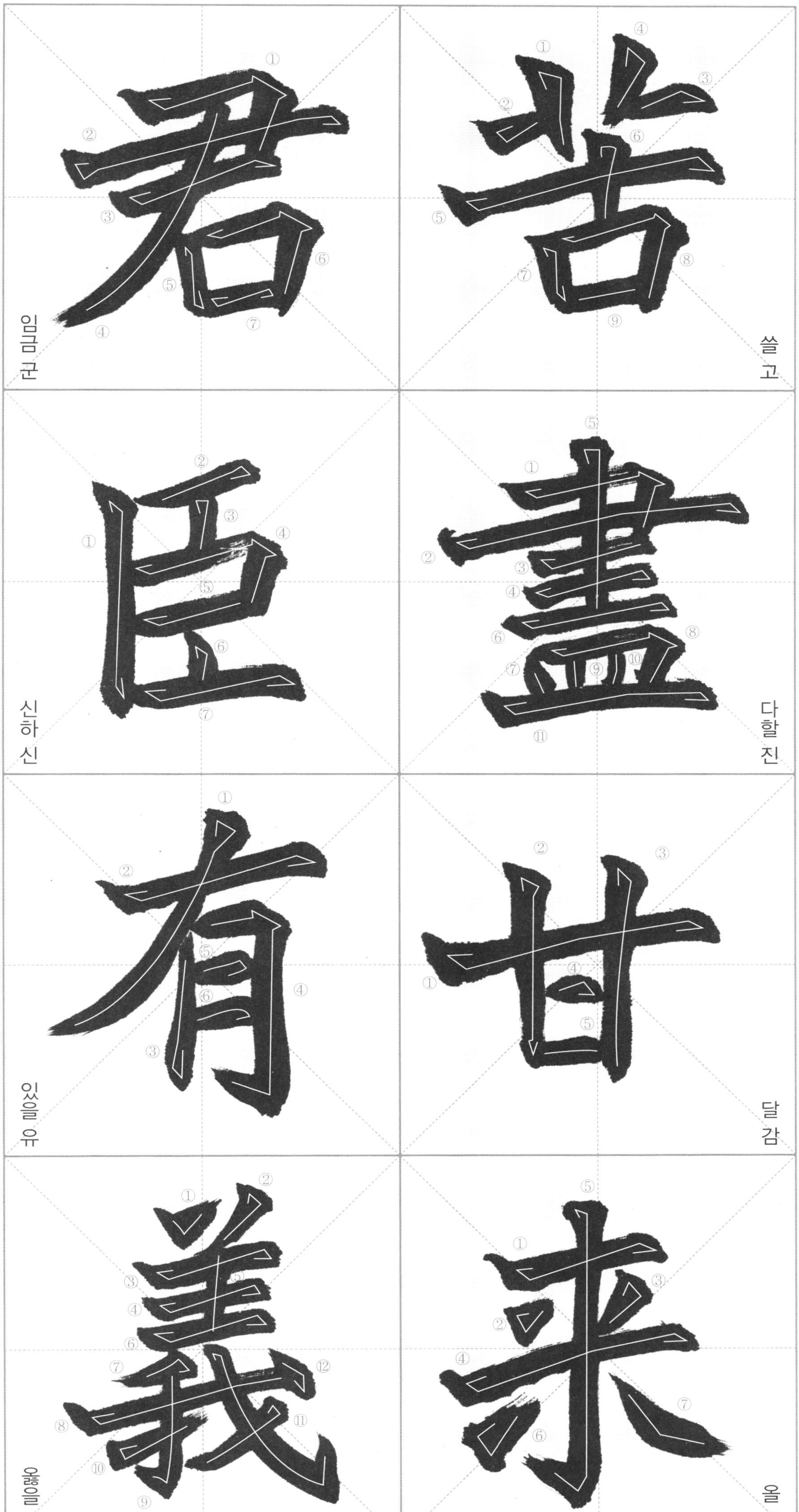

① 금[金]이나 옥[玉] 같은 법률의 조목[科]과 조항[條]。
② 소중히 여기고 꼭 지켜야 할 법률이나 규정。 또는 절대적인 것으로 여기어 지키는 규칙이나 교훈。

① 가지가 축축 늘어질 정도로 키가 큰[長] 소나무[松]。 ② 매우 크고 우뚝하게 잘 자란 소나무。

① 밝은[明] 거울[鏡]이 될 만큼 고요하게 멈추어[止] 있는 물[水]. ② 맑고 고요한 심경[心境].

明 밝을 명

鏡 거울 경

止 그칠 지

水 물 수

① 책을 널리[博] 많이 보고[覽] 잘[强] 기억[記憶] 함. ② 독서를 많이 하여 아는 것이 많음.

博 넓을 박

覽 볼 람

强 강할 강

記 기록할 기

① 많은[百] 사람들[家]이 다투어[爭] 울어댐[鳴]。 ② 많은 학자나 문화인 등이 자기의 학설이나 주장을 자유롭게 발표 논쟁、토론하는 일。

① 백[百] 번 꺾여도[折] 굽히지[屈] 않음[不]。 ② 어떠한 어려움에도 굽히지 않음。

① 모든 일[事]은 반드시[必] 바른[正] 길로 돌아감[歸]。 ② 일의 잘잘못이 언젠가는 밝혀져서 올바른 데로 돌아감。

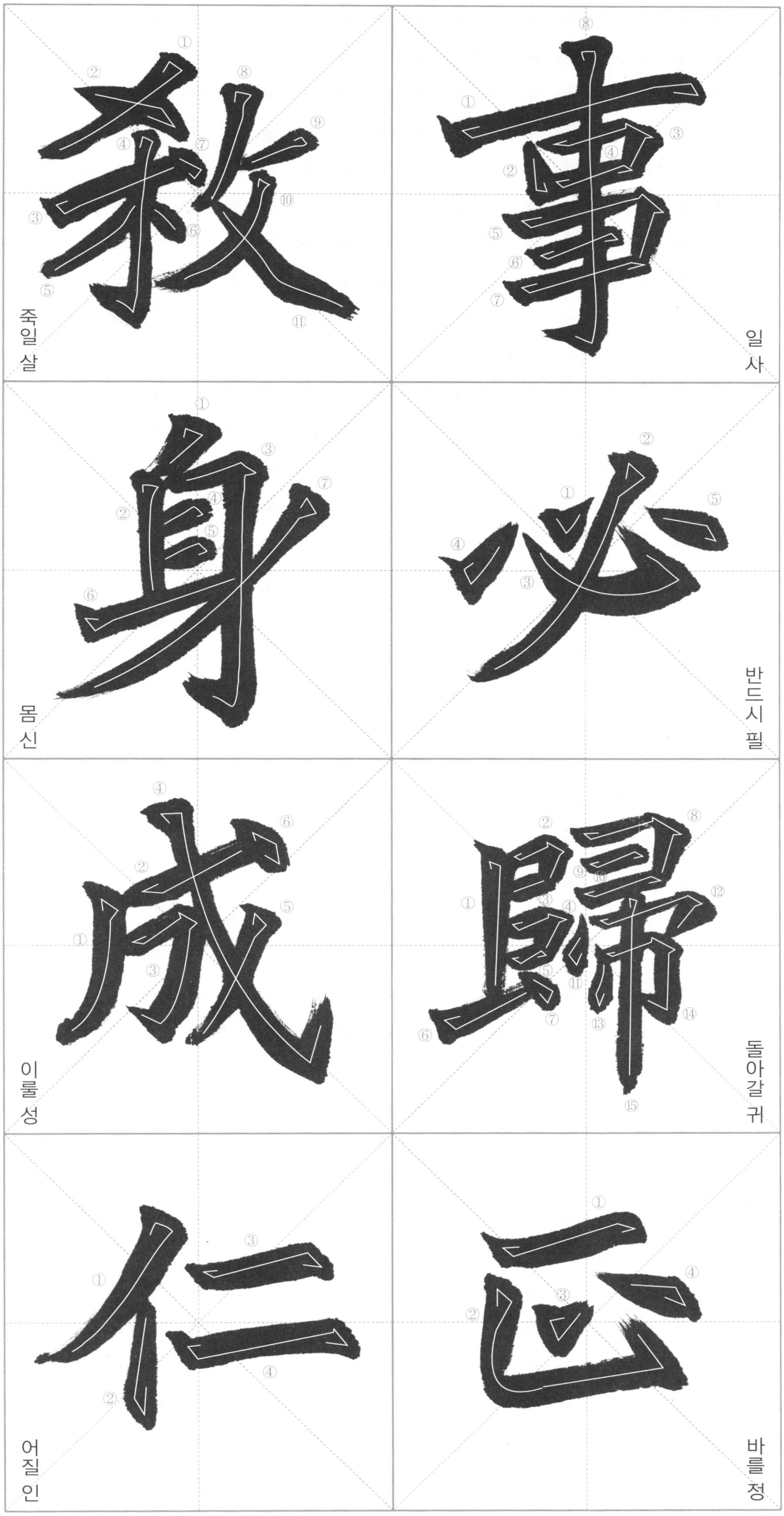

① 자신의 몸[身]을 죽여[殺] 인[仁]을 이룸[成]。 ② 옳은 일을 위해 자기의 몸을 바침。

① 공[公] 적인 일을 먼저[先]하고 사사로운[私] 일은 뒤[後]로 미룸。② 자기 일은 뒤로 미루고 공적인 일을 먼저 함。

① 묵은해[舊]를 보내고[送] 새해[新]를 맞이함[迎]。② 새로운 마음으로 새해를 맞이함。

① 중국 당나라 때 관리를 등용하는 시험에서 인물평가의 기준으로 삼았던 몸가짐[身]·말씨[言]·글씨[書]·판단[判斷]의 네 가지.
② 인물을 선택하는 데 적용한 네 가지 조건∷ 신수·말씨·문필·판단력[출처 『唐書』].

身 몸 신

言 말씀 언

書 쓸 서

判 판단할 판

藥 약 약

房 방 방

甘 달 감

草 풀 초

① 한약방[韓藥房]에서 어떤 처방이나 다 들어가는 감초[甘草].
② 「모임마다 불쑥불쑥 잘 나타나는 사람」, 또는 「흔하게 보이는 물건」을 비유하는 말.

① 옥[玉] 같이 귀한 골격[骨格]과 신선[神仙] 같은 풍채[風采]。 ② 귀티가 나고 신선 같이 깔끔한 풍채。

① 15분[一刻] 같이 짧은 시간도 천금[千金]과 같이 귀중함。 ② 짧은 시간도 귀하게 여겨 헛되이 보내지 않아야 함。

① 충성[忠誠]을 다하여서[盡] 나라[國]의 은혜를 갚음[報]。 ② 나라를 위하여 충성을 다함。

盡 다할 진

忠 충성 충

報 갚을 보

國 나라 국

天 하늘 천

生 날 생

緣 인연 연

分 나눌 분

① 하늘[天]에서 생겨난[生] 이 연분[緣分]。 ② 하늘이 맺어준 인연。

① 잘못[過]을 고치어[改] 착한[善] 마음으로 바꿈[遷]。 ② 허물을 고치고 옳은 길로 들어섬。

① 마음이 굳고[堅] 참을성[忍]이 있어서 뽑히지[拔] 아니함[不]。 ② 마음이 굳어 흔들리지 아니함。

① 지나침은[過] 미치지[及] 못함[不]과 같음[猶]。 ② 중용[中庸]이 중요함을 이르는 말。

① 나라[國]가 태평[太平]하고 백성[民]이 편안함[便安]。 ② 나라가 태평하고 국민의 생활이 넉넉함。

① 자기[自己]의 욕심을 이기고[克] 예의[禮義] 바르게 되돌아[復] 옴。 ② 지나친 욕심을 누르고 예의범절을 갖춤。

① 쇠[金]와 같이 단단하고 난초[蘭]같이 향기롭게 맺은[계] 사이。 ② 단단하고 향기로운 벗 사이의 우정。

金蘭之交 · 水魚之交 · 斷金之交 · 布衣之交 · 莫逆之友 · 知己之友 · 金石之交

① 비단[錦]으로 만든 옷[衣]을 입고 고향[故鄕]에 돌아 옴[還]。 ② 「성공하여 고향으로 돌아옴」을 비유하는 말。

① 운이 좋고[吉] 나쁨[凶]과 재앙[禍]과 복[福]。 ② 「운수」를 풀어서 달리 이르는 말。

① 짜던 베틀[機]의 날을 끊어[斷] 훈계[訓戒] 함. ② 「중도에 포기하면 헛일임」을 비유하여 이르는 말.

끊을 단

斷

베틀 기

機

어조사 지

之

경계할 계

戒

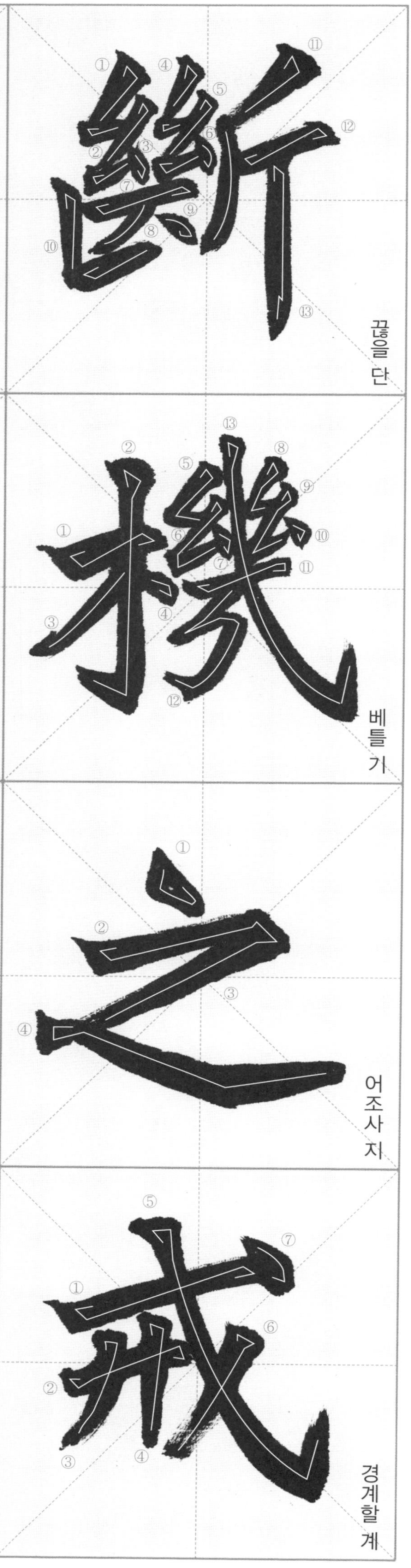

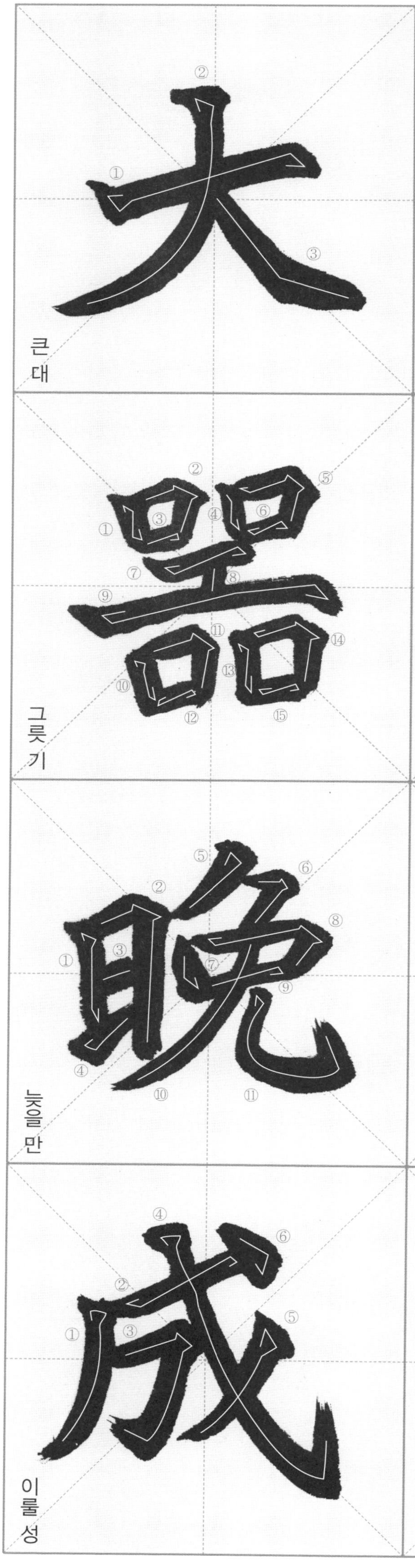

① 큰[大] 그릇[器]을 만들자면 시간이 오래 걸려 늦게[晚] 이루어짐[成].
② 「크게 될 사람은 성공이 늦음」을 비유하여 이르는 말. [출처 『老子』].

큰 대

大

그릇 기

器

늦을 만

晚

이룰 성

成

① 높은[高] 자리에 오르려면[登] 자기[自己]부터 낮춰야[卑] 함。 ② 「지위가 높아질수록 자신을 낮춤」을 이르는 말。

① 한없이 넓은[萬頃] 호수의 푸른[蒼] 물결[波]。 ② 넓은 바다나 호수의 아름다운 물결。

① 사심[私心]을 버리고[滅] 공공[公共]의 일을 받듦[奉]. ② 공무[公務]를 함에 있어 개인적인 마음을 버림.

멸 없앨 滅

사 사사로울 私

봉 받들 奉

공 여럿 公

① 무릉[武陵]에서 복숭아[桃] 꽃잎이 흘러내려오는 근원지[根源地]. ② 「세상과 따로 떨어진 별천지」를 비유하는 말.

무 굳셀 武

릉 언덕 陵

도 복숭아나무 桃

원 근원 源

① 자기보다 아래[下]인 사람에게 묻는[問] 일을 부끄러워하지[恥] 아니함[不]。 ② 자기보다 못한 사람에게도 물어볼 정도로 마음을 열고 지냄。

不 아닐 불

恥 부끄러울 치

下 아래 하

問 물을 문

不 아닐 불

偏 치우칠 편

不 아닐 부

黨 무리 당

① 어느 한쪽으로 치우치지[偏] 아니하고[不] 어느 한 편과 무리[黨] 짓지 아니함[不]。 ② 어느 편으로 치우치지 않고 매우 공정함。

先

먼저 선

見

볼 견

之

어조사 지

明

밝을 명

壽

목숨 수

福

복 복

康

편안할 강

寧

편안할 녕

① 앞일을 먼저[先] 내다보는[見] 밝은[明] 지혜. ② 닥쳐올 일을 미리 아는 슬기로움.

① 오래 살고[壽] 복[福]을 누리며 건강[健康]하고 편안함[寧]. ② 건강하게 오래 삶.

① 손[手]에서 책[卷]을 놓지[釋] 않음[不]。 ② 늘 책을 들고 지냄。 ③ 독서를 매우 좋아함。

① 몸[身]을 닦고[修]、 그런 후에 집[家]을 다스림[齊]。 ② 자기 수양을 하고 집안을 잘 돌봄。

① 깊이[深] 생각하고[思] 푹 익을[熟] 정도로 충분히 생각[考]함。 ② 신중을 기하여 곰곰이 생각함。

① 처지[處地]를 바꾸어[易] 그것[之]을 생각함[思]。 ② 상대편의 처지에서 생각해 봄。

① 향기[芳]가 백대[百世]에 걸쳐 흐름[流]。 ② 꽃다운 이름이 후세에 길이 전함。

① 하나[一]의 이치로써[以] 모든 것[之]을 꿰뚫음[관]。 ② 하나의 이치로 모든 것을 꿰뚫음。

① 어떤 시기[時機]가 닥치면[臨] 그에 부응[副應]하여 변화[變化]함。 ② 그때그때의 형편에 따라 알맞게 일을 처리함。

臨 임할 림

機 시기 기

應 응할 응

變 변할 변

立 설 립

身 몸 신

揚 드러낼 양

名 이름 명

① 입신[立身]하여 이름[名]을 세상에 날림[揚]。 ② 출세하여 세상에 이름을 떨침。

① 재화[災禍]가 바뀌어[轉] 도리어 복[福]이 됨[爲]。 ② 위기를 극복하여 좋은 기회가 됨。

옮길 전

재화 화

할 위

복 복

① 낮[晝]에는 밭을 갈고[耕] 밤[夜]에는 글을 읽음[讀]。 ② 어려운 여건 속에서도 꿋꿋이 공부함。

낮 주

밭갈 경

밤 야

읽을 독

① 다른[他] 산[山]의 돌[石]。 ② 다른 사람의 별 것 아닌 언행이 자기의 덕을 닦는 데 도움이 됨。 다른 산에 있는 하찮은 돌이라도 자기의 옥을 가는 데 도움이 된다는 말이 『詩經』에 나온다。

① 사악[邪惡]한 것을 깨뜨리고[破] 올바른[正] 것을 드러냄[顯]。
② 사견[私見]과 사도[邪道]를 깨고 정법[正法]을 드러내는 일。 삼론종의 근본 교의이다。

① 바르고 큰[浩] 그러한[然] 모양의 기운[氣運]。 ② 하늘과 땅 사이에 가득 찬 넓고 큰 원기。 ③ 한량없이 넓고 거침없이 큰 기개。

① 기쁨[喜]과 노여움[怒]과 슬픔[哀]과 즐거움[樂]。 ② 사람의 온갖 감정。

① 착한[善] 일을 권장[勸奬]하고 악[惡]한 일을 징계[懲戒]함。 ② 착한 사람을 높이고 악한 사람을 벌함。

① 벗[朋=友] 사이는 믿음[信]이 있어야함[有]。 ② 친구사이에 지켜야할 도리。 즉、「믿음」을 말한다。

① 풍류[騷]를 읊는 사람[人]과 먹[墨]을 다루는 사람[客]。 ② 시인과 서예가、화가 등 풍류를 아는 사람을 통칭하는 말。

① 화[禍]를 멀리하고[遠] 복[福]을 불러들임[召]。 ② 화를 물리치고 복을 안음。

① 바람[風]을 읊고[吟] 달[月]을 가지고 놂[弄]。 ② 자연에 대해 시를 짓고 흥취를 자아내며 즐김。

① 반딧불[螢]과 눈[雪] 빛 아래에서 공부하여 세운 공[功]。 ② 등불을 밝힐 수 없을 정도로 가난한 생활에서도 고생을 무릅쓰고 학문을 닦은 보람。

① 널리[弘] 많은 사람들[人間]을 이롭게[益] 함。② 세상의 모든 사람들을 도와 줌。단군의 건국이념。

① 푸른[靑] 색은 쪽[藍] 풀에서[於] 나왔음[出]。② 「제자나 후배가 스승이나 선배보다 나음」을 비유하여 이르는 말。「푸른 물감을 쪽 풀에서 채취했는데, 그것이 쪽 풀보다 더 푸르다」[靑出於藍, 以靑於藍] 이라는 말이 『荀子』[권학편勸學篇]。

해서楷書로 쉽게 배울 수 있는 고사성어 100
故事成語

창작작품

아정여경我靜如鏡

『육기시집陸機詩集』: 거울처럼 고요하다.

秋風唯苦吟世路少知音
窓外三更雨燈前萬里心
戊戌大暑錄崔致遠詩 青耘金榮培

최치원崔致遠 추야우중秋夜雨中

추풍유고음秋風唯苦吟 세로소지음世路少知音
창외삼경우窓外三更雨 등전만리심燈前萬里心

쓸쓸한 가을바람에 괴로이 읊조리니
세상에 내 마음을 아는 이 드물구나
창밖에는 깊은 밤에 비가 내리는데
등불 앞에 만리 고국 그리는 마음이로다

허즉의리래거虛則義理來居

『채근담菜根譚』 마음을 비워야 의리가 와서 머문다.

통명학사효달치도通明學事曉達治道

「정명도程明道」 밝게 학문에 통하여 크게 다스리는 도를 밝힌다.

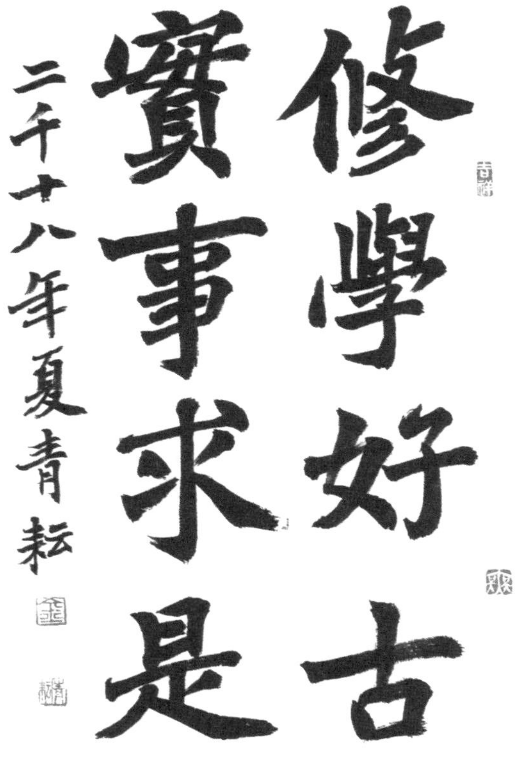

수학호고실사구시修學好古實事求是

『후한서後漢書 · 하간헌왕덕전河間獻王德傳』
학문을 닦고 옛 것을 좋아했는데, 실제 사실에 입각해서 올바름을 구하였다.

源遠之水旱亦不竭
戊戌大暑
青耘

원원지수한역불갈源遠之水旱亦不竭

「용비어천가」샘이 깊은 물은 가뭄에도 마르지 않는다.

採藥忽迷路
千峰秋葉裏
山僧汲水歸
林末茶烟起
錄李珥詩山中 青耘

이이李珥 산중山中

채약홀미로採藥忽迷路 약을 캐다 홀연 길을 잃었는데
천봉추엽리千峰秋葉裏 첩첩 산들 단풍 옷 입고 섰네
산승급수귀山僧汲水歸 산승이 물을 길어 돌아가니
임말다연기林末茶烟起 수풀 끝에 차 끓이는 연기가 솔솔.

德不孤
青耘書

得其樂
青耘金榮培

덕불고德不孤

『논어論語 · 이인里仁』 子曰 **德不孤** 必有隣
덕은 외롭지 않음.

득기락得其樂　마음에 맞는 즐거움을 얻다.

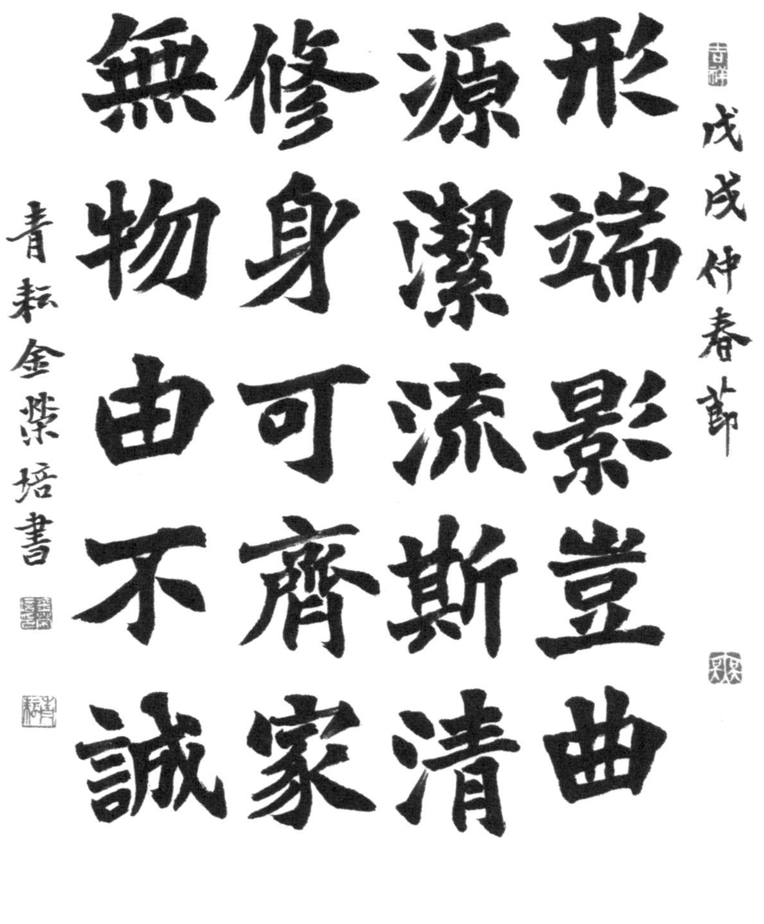
形端影豈曲
源潔流斯清
修身可齊家
無物由不誠
戊戌仲春節
青耘金榮培書

이색李穡
시자손일편示子孫一篇

형단영기곡 形端影豈曲
원결류사청 源潔流斯清
수신가제가 修身可齊家
무물유불성 無物由不誠

모습이 단정한데
그림자가 어찌 굽으랴
근원이 맑으면
물줄기도 맑은 것을
자신을 잘 닦아야
집안을 다스리니
성실하지 않고서
이루어지는 것은 없다네.

영수가복永受嘉福

오래도록 아름다운 복을 받는다.

통어천지자덕야通於天地者德也
행어만물자도야行於萬物者道也

『장자莊子 · 천지天地』
천지에 통하는 것이 덕이요 만물에 행하여지는 것이 도이다.

입춘대길건양다경立春大吉建陽多慶

봄이 시작되니 크게 길하고, 땅의 모든 것이
경사스러운 일이 많이 일어나기를 바란다.

독립獨立

나라나 단체가 완전한 자주권을 가짐.

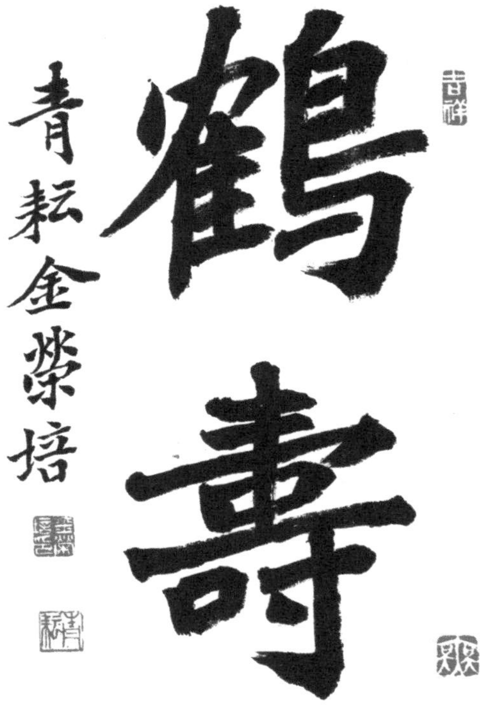

학수鶴壽　　학과 같이 장수하기를 기원하는 말.

독락獨樂　　홀로 즐기다.

내직이외곡內直而外曲

『장자莊子 · 인간세人間世』
속마음은 강직하게 지니고 밖으로는 부드럽게 하라.

장생무극長生無極

『초연수焦延壽 · 초씨역림焦氏易林』
끝이 없이 오랜 삶.

渭水雄誇遇聖君
桐江奇事動星文
何如寂寞溪雲裏
魚鳥相親遠世紛
丙子夏至節錄李退溪先生詩 青耘金榮培

이황李滉　소천조어小川釣魚

위수웅과우성군渭水雄誇遇聖君
동강기사동성문桐江奇事動星文
하여적막계운리何如寂寞溪雲裏
어조상친원세분魚鳥相親遠世紛

위수의 성대한 일 성군을 만났고
동강의 기이한 일 별빛을 움직였지
어떠한가 고요히 시내 구름 속에서
어조와 벗하며 세속을 어지러움을 멀리하도다.

山不在高有仙則名水不在
深有龍則靈斯是陋室惟吾
德馨苔痕上階綠草色入簾
青談笑有鴻儒往來無白丁可
以調素琴閱金經無絲竹之亂
耳無案牘之勞形南陽諸葛
廬西蜀子雲亭孔子云何陋
之有 癸巳雨夏 青耘 金榮培

「누실명陋室銘(누추한 집)」 − 유우석劉禹錫, 『고문관지古文觀止 권7卷7』

山不在高 有仙則名 水不在深 有龍則靈 斯是陋室 惟吾德馨 苔痕上階綠 草色入簾青 談笑有鴻儒 往來
無白丁 可以調素琴 閱金經 無絲竹之亂耳 無案牘之勞形 南陽諸葛廬 西蜀子雲亭 孔子云 何陋之有

산이 높아서가 아니라 신선이 있으면 명산이요. 물이 깊음에 있는 것이 아니라 용이 있으면 신령스럽
다네. 이곳은 누추한 집이나 오직 나의 덕으로 향이 난다네. 이끼 흔적 계단위에 푸르고 풀빛은 주렴
으로 들어와 푸르네. 좋은 얘기 나누는 선비는 있는데, 오가는 평민은 없으며 거문고를 타고 불경을
본다네. 음악소린 귀를 어지럽히지 않고, 관청의 문서로 몸을 수고롭게 하지 않는 것이 남양 제갈량의
초가집이나 서촉 양자운의 정자와 같으니 공자께서는, "무슨 누추함이 있겠는가?"라 하셨네.

戊戌仲夏節 青耘 金榮培

博學篤志

박학독지博學篤志

『논어論語·자장子張』
널리 배우고 뜻을 독실하게 하다.

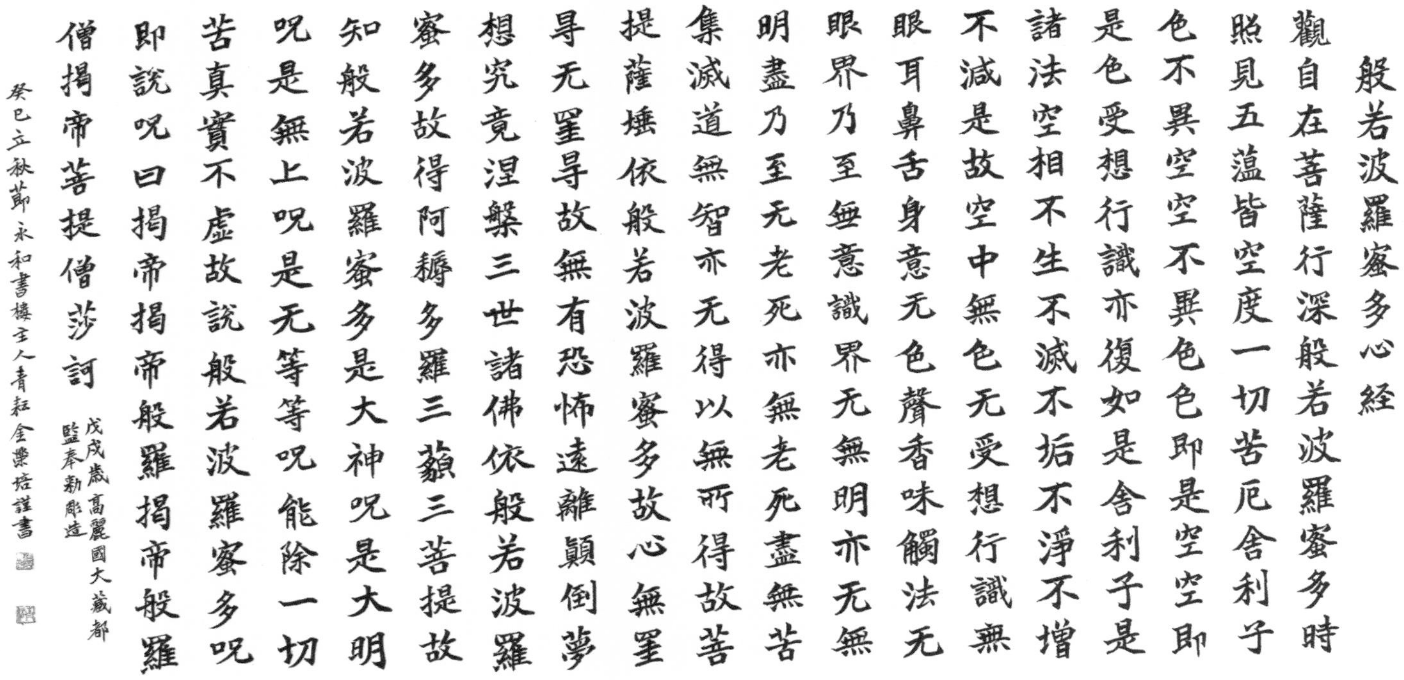

반야심경般若心經

觀自在菩薩行深般若波羅蜜多時照見五蘊皆空度一切苦厄舍利子色不異空空不異色色卽是空空卽是色受想行識亦復如是舍利子是諸法空相不生不滅不垢不淨不增不減是故空中無色無受想行識無眼耳鼻舌身意無色聲香味觸法無眼界乃至無意識界無無明亦無無明盡乃至無老死亦無老死盡無苦集滅道無智亦無得以無所得故菩提薩埵依般若波羅蜜多故心無罣碍無罣碍故無有恐怖遠離顚倒夢想究竟涅槃三世諸佛依般若波羅蜜多故得阿耨多羅三藐三菩提故知般若波羅蜜多是大神呪是大明呪是無上呪是無等等呪能除一切苦眞實不虛故說般若波羅蜜多呪卽說呪曰揭諦揭諦波羅揭諦波羅僧揭諦菩提娑婆訶

관자재보살이 깊은 반야바라밀다를 행할 때, 오온이 공한 것을 비추어 보고 온갖 고통에서 건너느니라. 사리자여! 색이 공과 다르지 않고 공이 색과 다르지 않으며, 색이 곧 공이요 공이 곧 색이니, 수상행식도 그러하니라. 사리자여! 모든 법은 공하여 나지도 멸하지도 않으며, 더럽지도 깨끗하지도 않으며, 늘지도 줄지도 않느니라. 그러므로 공 가운데는 색이 없고 수상행식도 없으며, 안이비설신의도 없고, 색성향미촉법도 없으며, 눈의 경계도 의식의 경계까지도 없고, 무명도 무명이 다함까지도 없으며, 늙고 죽음도 늙고 죽음이 다함까지도 없고, 고집멸도도 없으며, 지혜도 얻음도 없느니라. 얻을 것이 없는 까닭에 보살은 반야바라밀다를 의지하므로 마음에 걸림이 없고 걸림이 없으므로 두려움이 없어서, 뒤바뀐 헛된 생각을 멀리 떠나 완전한 열반에 들어가며, 삼세의 모든 부처님도 반야바라밀다를 의지하므로 최상의 깨달음을 얻느니라. 반야바라밀다는 가장 신비하고 밝은 주문이며 위없는 주문이며 무엇과도 견줄 수 없는 주문이니, 온갖 괴로움을 없애고 진실하여 허망하지 않음을 알지니라. 이제 반야바라밀다주를 말하리라. 아제아제 바라아제 바라승아제 모지 사바하.

주경야송書耕夜誦

『위서魏書 · 최광전崔光傳』: 낮에는 일하고 밤에는 공부한다.

독서좌운석고금잡송풍
讀書坐雲石鼓琴雜松風

「엽옹葉顒」 글을 읽으며
운석雲石에 앉아 있고
거문고를 타며
송풍松風을 쏘인다.

想究竟涅槃三世諸佛依般若波羅
蜜多故得阿耨多羅三藐三菩提故
知般若波羅蜜多是大神呪是大明
呪是無上呪是無等等呪能除一切
苦真實不虛故說般若波羅蜜多呪
即說呪曰揭帝揭帝般羅揭帝般羅

저자약력

김 영 배 金榮培

· 호 : 청운靑耘, 영화서루永和書樓
· 주소 : (우 03132) 서울시 종로구 돈화문로11가길 59
(익선동,현대뜨레비앙)
· 전화 : 02-747-9636(사무실) · 010-8751-9636(핸드폰)
· http://cafe.daum.net/yhmyh청운서예전각연구실
· http://blog.naver.com/younghwa9636
· E-mail : younghwa9636@hanmail.net

| 학력 |

· 2002 경기대전통예술대학원(서예전공)
· 2012 성균관대일반대학원유학과 철학박사(동양미학)

| 경력 |

· 1988~1999 제7회 대한민국미술대전[입선7회, 특선1회] 한국미술협회
· 1991~2000 동아미술대전[입선6회, 특선] 동아일보사
· 1992~2001 한국서예청년작가 초대작가(예술의 전당 서예박물관)
· 2003, 2010, 2017 대한민국미술대전 심사위원 역임(한국미술협회)
· 2002~2012 한국전각협회 사무국장 역임 / (2012~현,이사)
· 2003~2017 경기대 · 동방대학원대학교 · 성균관대 · 수원대 · 숙명여대
성신여대 · 춘천교대 외래교수 역임
· 2007~ 중국서령인사 명예사원(전각)
· 2011 대한민국 제5대 국새모형인문부문 심사위원 역임
· 2013 명인제13-1003-21호 서예한문전각부문(한국예총)
· 현) 중국호남제일사범학원객좌교수 · 세종대회화과 강사

해서楷書로 쉽게 배울 수 있는 고사성어 100
故事成語

초판 인쇄 2019년 5월 20일
2쇄 인쇄 2023년 9월 25일
2쇄 발행 2023년 10월 5일

지은이 김영배
펴낸이 김재광
펴낸곳 솔과학
영 업 최희선
등 록 제10-140호 1997년 2월 22일
주 소 서울특별시 마포구 독막로 295번지 302호(염리동 삼부골든타워)
전 화 02)714-8655
팩 스 02)711-4656
E-mail solkwahak@hanmail.net

ISBN 979-11-87124-54-2 (03640)

값 12,000원

ingenious	독창적인, 정교한	ingenuous	솔직한, 숨김없는
inhabit	살다, 거주하다	inhibit	억제하다, ~하지 못하게 하다
instigate	선동하다, 부추기다	investigate	조사하다, 수사하다
intend	의도하다, 의미하다	intent	몰두하는, 의도
invaluable	매우 귀중한	valueless	하찮은, 가치 없는
invent	발명하다	invert	뒤집다, 도치시키다
irrigate	물을 대다, 관개하다	irritate	짜증나게 하다, 자극하다
label	표, 라벨을 붙이다	labo(u)r	노동, 노동의
lay	놓다, (알을) 낳다	lie	눕다, 거짓말하다, 거짓말
lead	이끌다, 납	lid	뚜껑
lessen	줄이다, 줄다	lesson	수업, 교훈
level	정도, 수준, 평평한	lever	지레, 지렛대로 움직이다
literal	문자 그대로의	literate	글을 읽고 쓸 줄 아는
literary	문학의, 문학적인	literacy	글을 읽고 쓸 줄 아는 능력
loose	느슨한, 헐렁한	lose	잃다, 지다
mass	덩어리, 대규모의	mess	엉망진창인 상태
mean	뜻하다, 비열한	means	수단, 방법
mediation	조정, 중재	meditation	명상, 심사숙고
meld	섞이다, 섞다	melt	녹다, 녹이다
miner	광부	minor	적은, 미성년자, 부전공
momentary	순간적인, 잠깐의	momentous	중대한
moss	이끼	moth	나방
mound	언덕, 무더기	mount	오르다, 증가하다
neural	신경(계통)의	neutral	중립의
noble	고결한, 귀족	novel	소설, 새로운
numeral	숫자, 수사	numerous	많은
objective	목적, 객관적인	objection	이의, 반대
odd	이상한, 홀수의	odds	가능성, 역경
own	소유하다, 자신의	owe	빚지고 있다
pare	벗기다, 깎다	pear	배
peak	절정, 정점, 봉우리	peek	훔쳐 보다
peel	벗기다, 껍질	pill	알약
persevere	버티다, 이겨내다	preserve	보존하다
personal	개인의, 개인적인	personnel	직원의, 직원
phase	단계, 시기	phrase	구, 구절
poem	시	poet	시인
pole	막대기, 극	pore	구멍
politic	현명한, 신중한	political	정치적인, 정당의
pray	기도하다	prey	먹이, 사냥감
principal	주요한, (단체의) 장	principle	원리, 원칙
probe	조사하다, 조사	prove	입증하다, 증명하다
propel	나아가게 하다	proper	적절한, 정당한
qualify	자격을 얻다, 자격을 주다	quantify	양을 나타내다, 수량화하다
quota	한도, 몫	quote	인용하다
raise	올리다, 일으키다	rise	오르다, 증가
real	진짜의, 현실적인	rear	뒤쪽, 뒤쪽의
reality	현실, 실재	realty	부동산, 물적 재산
require	필요하다, 요구하다	inquire	묻다, 조사하다
respectable	존경할 만한, 훌륭한	respective	각자의, 각각의
responsible	책임이 있는	responsive	즉각 반응하는
role	역할	roll	통, 구르다
rot	썩다, 썩히다	rote	암기
royal	왕실의, 왕의	loyal	충성스러운
sail	항해하다, 돛	sale	판매, 매출, 영업
sand	모래, 모래사장	send	보내다, 발송하다
saw	톱, 톱질하다	sew	바느질하다, (바느질로) 만들다
scrap	조각, 폐기하다	scrape	긁다, 긁기
sensible	분별 있는, 합리적인	sensitive	민감한, 예민한
sole	유일한, 단 하나의	sore	아픈, 상처
soul	영혼, 정신, 마음	sour	신, 상하다
successful	성공한, 성공적인	successive	연속하는
sympathy	동정, 연민, 공감	empathy	감정 이입, 공감
vague	모호한, 애매한	vogue	유행
vain	헛된, 하찮은	vein	정맥, 혈관
virtual	사실상의, 가상의	virtue	미덕, 덕
wonder	궁금해하다, 놀라움	wander	돌아다니다

KB205931

aboard	탑승하여, 배 위로	**abroad**	해외에(서)
access	접근[접속]하다, 접근	**assess**	평가하다, 재다
adapt	적응시키다, 적응하다	**adopt**	채택하다, 입양하다
addiction	중독	**addition**	추가, 덧셈
aesthetic	미학의, 미(美)의	**authentic**	진짜의, 진정한
affect	영향을 미치다, 감정	**effect**	가져오다, 결과, 영향, 효과
alley	골목	**ally**	동맹국, 협력자, 지지하다
annual	매년의, 연간의	**annul**	취소하다
appeal	매력, 간청	**appear**	나타나다, ~인 것 같다
arise	생기다, 발생하다	**arouse**	불러일으키다
artificial	인공의, 인위적인	**artistic**	예술적인
assault	폭행, 공격, 괴롭히다	**assort**	분류하다, 구분하다
bald	대머리인	**bold**	대담한, 용감한
barrel	통, 배럴	**barren**	척박한, 황량한
beat	이기다, 때리다	**bit**	조금, 약간
beside	~의 옆에	**besides**	게다가, ~이외에도
borrow	빌리다, 차용하다	**burrow**	굴을 파다
breadth	폭, 넓이	**breath**	숨, 호흡
bribe	뇌물, 뇌물을 주다	**bride**	신부
cancel	취소하다, 무효화하다	**cancer**	암
cite	인용하다, 예로 들다	**site**	장소, (인터넷) 사이트
cloth	옷감, 직물, 천	**clothes**	옷, 의복
clown	광대	**crown**	왕관, 왕위에 앉히다
coast	해안, 해변, 연안	**cost**	값, (값·비용이) ~이다
collect	모으다, 수집하다	**correct**	맞는, 옳은, 바로잡다
command	명령, 명령하다	**commend**	칭찬하다, 추천하다
competent	유능한, 적격인	**competitive**	경쟁의
complement	보충하다, 보충	**compliment**	칭찬하다, 칭찬
confident	자신 있는	**confidential**	비밀의, 기밀의
confirm	확인하다, 승인하다	**conform**	따르다, 순응하다

conscience	양심	**conscious**	의식하는
considerable	상당한, 중요한	**considerate**	사려 깊은
council	의회, 협의회	**counsel**	조언, 상담을 하다
curb	억제하다, 억제	**curve**	곡선, 곡선을 이루다
daily	매일 일어나는, 일일	**dairy**	낙농업, 유제품의
dedicate	바치다, 헌신하다	**delicate**	연약한, 섬세한
deep	깊은, 깊이	**dip**	살짝 담그다, 내려가다
deprive	빼앗다	**derive**	끌어내다, 얻다, 유래하다
desert	사막, 버리다	**dessert**	디저트, 후식
devote	바치다, 헌신하다	**devout**	독실한
die	죽다, 사망하다	**dye**	염색하다
discreet	신중한, 분별 있는	**discrete**	분리된, 별개의
distinct	별개의, 뚜렷한	**instinct**	본능, 직감
emigrate	이주하다, 이민	**immigrate**	이민 오다, 와서 살다
emphasize	강조하다, 역설하다	**empathize**	공감하다, 감정 이입하다
ethical	윤리[도덕]의	**ethnic(al)**	민족의
expand	확장하다, 확대되다	**expend**	(돈·시간을) 쓰다
extend	확장하다, 연장하다	**extent**	정도, 크기
fail	실패하다, ~하지 못하다	**fair**	타당한, 공정하게, 박람회
fertile	비옥한, 다산의	**futile**	헛된, 쓸데없는
find	찾다, 발견하다	**found**	설립하다, 기초를 쌓다
firm	회사, 딱딱한	**form**	종류, 유형, 형성되다
flesh	살, 과육	**fresh**	신선한, 생생한
fury	분노, 격분	**furry**	털로 덮인, 털 같은
garage	차고, 주차장	**garbage**	쓰레기(장)
greed	탐욕, 식탐	**grid**	격자무늬, 격자판
imaginable	상상할 수 있는	**imaginary**	가상적인
immense	엄청난, 어마어마한	**immerse**	담그다, ~에 몰두하다
imply	암시하다, 내포하다	**infer**	추론하다, 유추하다
industrial	산업의, 공업의	**industrious**	근면한, 부지런한

정답표

01 글의 목적 파악
문제편 p.007 해설편 p.002

01 ①	02 ⑤	03 ⑤	04 ④	05 ③
06 ⑤	07 ③	08 ②	09 ③	10 ⑤
11 ①	12 ②	13 ①	14 ②	15 ②
16 ②	17 ①			

02 심경·분위기 파악
문제편 p.018 해설편 p.012

01 ①	02 ①	03 ②	04 ①	05 ①
06 ①	07 ①	08 ①	09 ①	10 ⑤
11 ⑤	12 ②	13 ②	14 ①	15 ②
16 ②	17 ⑤	18 ①	19 ②	

03 필자의 주장
문제편 p.028 해설편 p.024

01 ②	02 ③	03 ②	04 ②	05 ①
06 ②	07 ⑤	08 ③	09 ⑤	10 ⑤
11 ②	12 ⑤	13 ④	14 ②	15 ⑤
16 ④	17 ⑤	18 ①	19 ②	20 ⑤

04 의미 추론
문제편 p.040 해설편 p.038

01 ④	02 ⑤	03 ⑤	04 ①	05 ③
06 ③	07 ③	08 ⑤	09 ④	10 ①
11 ⑤	12 ④	13 ④	14 ①	15 ①

05 요지 추론
문제편 p.050 해설편 p.051

01 ⑤	02 ⑤	03 ①	04 ③	05 ③
06 ①	07 ⑤	08 ④	09 ②	10 ③
11 ③	12 ⑤	13 ⑤	14 ②	15 ④
16 ①	17 ②	18 ④	19 ⑤	

06 주제 추론
문제편 p.061 해설편 p.065

01 ②	02 ③	03 ②	04 ③	05 ⑤
06 ③	07 ②	08 ⑤	09 ⑤	10 ②
11 ④	12 ④	13 ⑤	14 ⑤	15 ⑤
16 ⑤	17 ④	18 ①	19 ⑤	20 ②
21 ②				

07 제목 추론
문제편 p.074 해설편 p.082

01 ④	02 ⑤	03 ②	04 ③	05 ①
06 ①	07 ③	08 ⑤	09 ③	10 ②
11 ③	12 ②	13 ③	14 ②	15 ③
16 ④	17 ②	18 ①	19 ⑤	20 ③
21 ①	22 ③	23 ⑤	24 ④	25 ④

08 도표의 이해
문제편 p.089 해설편 p.102

01 ④	02 ③	03 ③	04 ④	05 ⑤
06 ⑤	07 ④	08 ④	09 ④	10 ④
11 ③	12 ③	13 ③	14 ③	15 ③
16 ④	17 ⑤	18 ③	19 ④	

09 내용 일치 파악
문제편 p.101 해설편 p.114

01 ③	02 ④	03 ③	04 ④	05 ⑤
06 ⑤	07 ③	08 ④	09 ②	10 ④
11 ③	12 ④	13 ④	14 ④	15 ③
16 ④	17 ⑤	18 ④		

10 안내문
문제편 p.112 해설편 p.126

01 ⑤	02 ④	03 ③	04 ④	05 ⑤
06 ④	07 ⑤	08 ⑤	09 ⑤	10 ④
11 ④	12 ④	13 ③	14 ⑤	15 ④
16 ⑤	17 ③	18 ④	19 ③	20 ③
21 ④	22 ②	23 ④	24 ②	25 ③
26 ④	27 ④	28 ③	29 ④	30 ⑤
31 ③	32 ⑤	33 ④		

11 빈칸 추론(1)-어휘, 짧은 어구
문제편 p.132 해설편 p.137

01 ①	02 ②	03 ①	04 ①	05 ②
06 ③	07 ①	08 ②	09 ①	10 ①
11 ①	12 ③	13 ①	14 ①	15 ④
16 ③	17 ④	18 ①	19 ②	20 ⑤
21 ②	22 ④	23 ①	24 ②	25 ②
26 ②	27 ④	28 ②	29 ①	30 ③
31 ①	32 ③	33 ①		

12 빈칸 추론(2)-긴 어구, 문장
문제편 p.149 해설편 p.164

01 ①	02 ①	03 ③	04 ①	05 ③
06 ④	07 ③	08 ④	09 ③	10 ②
11 ①	12 ⑤	13 ③	14 ②	15 ④
16 ④	17 ②	18 ⑤	19 ④	20 ①
21 ①	22 ②	23 ②	24 ①	25 ④
26 ④	27 ③	28 ①	29 ①	30 ②
31 ①	32 ⑤	33 ①	34 ②	35 ②
36 ③	37 ⑤	38 ②	39 ⑤	40 ①
41 ⑤	42 ②	43 ②	44 ③	45 ④
46 ③	47 ①	48 ②	49 ①	50 ⑤

13 무관한 문장 찾기
문제편 p.176 해설편 p.209

01 ③	02 ④	03 ④	04 ③	05 ④
06 ④	07 ③	08 ④	09 ③	10 ④
11 ④	12 ③	13 ④	14 ④	15 ③
16 ③	17 ③	18 ③	19 ③	

14 문장 배열
문제편 p.185 해설편 p.223

01 ②	02 ⑤	03 ②	04 ②	05 ③
06 ②	07 ③	08 ③	09 ⑤	10 ④
11 ⑤	12 ④	13 ⑤	14 ④	15 ③
16 ⑤	17 ③	18 ⑤	19 ②	20 ⑤
21 ④	22 ⑤	23 ②	24 ⑤	25 ①
26 ②	27 ③	28 ②	29 ②	30 ③
31 ⑤	32 ②	33 ③	34 ⑤	35 ⑤
36 ③	37 ②	38 ③	39 ⑤	40 ②
41 ②	42 ③	43 ⑤	44 ③	

15 주어진 문장 위치 파악
문제편 p.209 해설편 p.260

01 ④	02 ④	03 ④	04 ④	05 ③
06 ②	07 ③	08 ④	09 ④	10 ③
11 ③	12 ④	13 ③	14 ④	15 ④
16 ④	17 ⑤	18 ⑤	19 ⑤	20 ④
21 ①	22 ③	23 ④	24 ③	25 ⑤
26 ⑤	27 ⑤	28 ③	29 ③	30 ⑤
31 ③	32 ①	33 ③	34 ③	35 ②
36 ①	37 ③	38 ④	39 ③	40 ②
41 ④	42 ③	43 ②	44 ④	

16 문단 요약
문제편 p.233 해설편 p.294

01 ②	02 ①	03 ①	04 ①	05 ②
06 ①	07 ②	08 ①	09 ①	10 ①
11 ①	12 ②	13 ①	14 ①	15 ①
16 ④	17 ①	18 ①	19 ⑤	20 ①

17 장문의 이해-단일지문
문제편 p.245 해설편 p.313

01 ②	02 ③	03 ④	04 ⑤	05 ①
06 ⑤	07 ⑤	08 ⑤	09 ①	10 ④
11 ①	12 ⑤	13 ③	14 ④	15 ①
16 ④	17 ③	18 ④	19 ③	20 ②
21 ⑤	22 ⑤	23 ⑤	24 ⑤	25 ②
26 ③	27 ⑤	28 ④	29 ②	30 ④
31 ①	32 ⑤	33 ②	34 ①	35 ①
36 ③	37 ①	38 ⑤	39 ①	40 ⑤
41 ①	42 ④	43 ①	44 ⑤	45 ①
46 ④				

18 장문의 이해-복합지문
문제편 p.270 해설편 p.341

01 ②	02 ⑤	03 ⑤	04 ④	05 ④
06 ⑤	07 ⑤	08 ⑤	09 ④	10 ④
11 ⑤	12 ③	13 ⑤	14 ④	15 ②
16 ②	17 ③	18 ⑤	19 ④	20 ③
21 ③	22 ③	23 ②	24 ②	25 ③
26 ④	27 ③	28 ③	29 ⑤	30 ⑤
31 ⑤	32 ④	33 ⑤	34 ④	35 ②
36 ③	37 ③	38 ⑤	39 ④	40 ②
41 ③	42 ④	43 ③	44 ⑤	45 ⑤
46 ④	47 ④	48 ②	49 ②	50 ③
51 ③	52 ②	53 ③	54 ③	

1회 20분 미니모의고사
문제편 p.288 해설편 p.365

01 ①	02 ⑤	03 ①	04 ③	05 ④
06 ④	07 ⑤	08 ②	09 ⑤	10 ③
11 ④	12 ②			

2회 20분 미니모의고사
문제편 p.294 해설편 p.374

01 ②	02 ②	03 ①	04 ⑤	05 ④
06 ②	07 ③	08 ①	09 ②	10 ⑤
11 ④	12 ②			

3회 20분 미니모의고사
문제편 p.299 해설편 p.382

01 ③	02 ①	03 ②	04 ④	05 ⑤
06 ③	07 ⑤	08 ②	09 ⑤	10 ①
11 ③	12 ③			

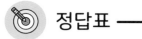

정답표

01 글의 목적 파악
문제편 p.007 해설편 p.002

01 ①	02 ⑤	03 ⑤	04 ④	05 ③
06 ⑤	07 ③	08 ②	09 ③	10 ⑤
11 ①	12 ②	13 ①	14 ②	15 ②
16 ②	17 ①			

02 심경·분위기 파악
문제편 p.018 해설편 p.012

01 ①	02 ①	03 ②	04 ①	05 ①
06 ①	07 ①	08 ①	09 ①	10 ⑤
11 ⑤	12 ②	13 ②	14 ①	15 ②
16 ②	17 ⑤	18 ①	19 ②	

03 필자의 주장
문제편 p.028 해설편 p.024

01 ②	02 ③	03 ②	04 ②	05 ①
06 ②	07 ⑤	08 ③	09 ⑤	10 ⑤
11 ②	12 ⑤	13 ④	14 ②	15 ⑤
16 ④	17 ⑤	18 ①	19 ②	20 ⑤

04 의미 추론
문제편 p.040 해설편 p.038

01 ④	02 ⑤	03 ⑤	04 ①	05 ③
06 ③	07 ③	08 ⑤	09 ④	10 ①
11 ⑤	12 ④	13 ④	14 ①	15 ①

05 요지 추론
문제편 p.050 해설편 p.051

01 ⑤	02 ⑤	03 ①	04 ③	05 ③
06 ①	07 ⑤	08 ④	09 ②	10 ③
11 ③	12 ⑤	13 ⑤	14 ②	15 ④
16 ①	17 ②	18 ④	19 ⑤	

06 주제 추론
문제편 p.061 해설편 p.065

01 ②	02 ③	03 ②	04 ③	05 ⑤
06 ③	07 ②	08 ⑤	09 ⑤	10 ②
11 ④	12 ④	13 ⑤	14 ⑤	15 ⑤
16 ⑤	17 ④	18 ①	19 ⑤	20 ②
21 ②				

07 제목 추론
문제편 p.074 해설편 p.082

01 ④	02 ⑤	03 ②	04 ③	05 ①
06 ①	07 ③	08 ⑤	09 ③	10 ②
11 ③	12 ②	13 ③	14 ②	15 ③
16 ④	17 ②	18 ①	19 ⑤	20 ③
21 ①	22 ③	23 ⑤	24 ④	25 ④

08 도표의 이해
문제편 p.089 해설편 p.102

01 ④	02 ③	03 ③	04 ④	05 ⑤
06 ⑤	07 ④	08 ④	09 ④	10 ④
11 ③	12 ③	13 ③	14 ③	15 ③
16 ④	17 ⑤	18 ③	19 ④	

09 내용 일치 파악
문제편 p.101 해설편 p.114

01 ③	02 ④	03 ③	04 ④	05 ⑤
06 ⑤	07 ③	08 ④	09 ②	10 ④
11 ③	12 ④	13 ④	14 ④	15 ③
16 ④	17 ⑤	18 ④		

10 안내문
문제편 p.112 해설편 p.126

01 ⑤	02 ④	03 ③	04 ④	05 ⑤
06 ④	07 ⑤	08 ⑤	09 ⑤	10 ④
11 ④	12 ④	13 ③	14 ⑤	15 ④
16 ⑤	17 ③	18 ④	19 ③	20 ③
21 ④	22 ②	23 ④	24 ②	25 ③
26 ④	27 ④	28 ③	29 ④	30 ⑤
31 ③	32 ⑤	33 ④		

11 빈칸 추론(1)-어휘, 짧은 어구
문제편 p.132 해설편 p.137

01 ①	02 ②	03 ①	04 ①	05 ②
06 ③	07 ①	08 ②	09 ①	10 ①
11 ①	12 ③	13 ①	14 ①	15 ④
16 ③	17 ④	18 ①	19 ②	20 ⑤
21 ②	22 ④	23 ①	24 ②	25 ②
26 ②	27 ④	28 ②	29 ①	30 ③
31 ①	32 ③	33 ①		

12 빈칸 추론(2)-긴 어구, 문장
문제편 p.149 해설편 p.164

01 ①	02 ①	03 ③	04 ①	05 ③
06 ④	07 ③	08 ④	09 ③	10 ②
11 ①	12 ⑤	13 ③	14 ②	15 ④
16 ④	17 ②	18 ⑤	19 ④	20 ①
21 ①	22 ②	23 ②	24 ①	25 ④
26 ④	27 ③	28 ①	29 ①	30 ②
31 ①	32 ⑤	33 ①	34 ②	35 ②
36 ③	37 ⑤	38 ②	39 ⑤	40 ①
41 ⑤	42 ②	43 ②	44 ③	45 ④
46 ③	47 ①	48 ②	49 ①	50 ⑤

13 무관한 문장 찾기
문제편 p.176 해설편 p.209

01 ③	02 ④	03 ④	04 ③	05 ④
06 ④	07 ③	08 ④	09 ③	10 ④
11 ④	12 ③	13 ④	14 ④	15 ③
16 ③	17 ③	18 ③	19 ③	

14 문장 배열
문제편 p.185 해설편 p.223

01 ②	02 ⑤	03 ②	04 ②	05 ③
06 ②	07 ③	08 ③	09 ⑤	10 ④
11 ⑤	12 ④	13 ⑤	14 ④	15 ③
16 ⑤	17 ③	18 ⑤	19 ②	20 ⑤
21 ④	22 ⑤	23 ②	24 ⑤	25 ①
26 ②	27 ③	28 ②	29 ②	30 ③
31 ⑤	32 ②	33 ③	34 ⑤	35 ⑤
36 ③	37 ②	38 ③	39 ⑤	40 ②
41 ②	42 ③	43 ⑤	44 ③	

15 주어진 문장 위치 파악
문제편 p.209 해설편 p.260

01 ④	02 ④	03 ④	04 ④	05 ③
06 ②	07 ③	08 ④	09 ④	10 ③
11 ③	12 ④	13 ③	14 ④	15 ④
16 ④	17 ⑤	18 ⑤	19 ⑤	20 ④
21 ①	22 ③	23 ④	24 ③	25 ⑤
26 ⑤	27 ⑤	28 ③	29 ③	30 ⑤
31 ③	32 ①	33 ③	34 ③	35 ②
36 ①	37 ③	38 ④	39 ③	40 ②
41 ④	42 ③	43 ②	44 ④	

16 문단 요약
문제편 p.233 해설편 p.294

01 ②	02 ①	03 ①	04 ①	05 ②
06 ①	07 ②	08 ①	09 ①	10 ①
11 ①	12 ②	13 ①	14 ①	15 ①
16 ④	17 ①	18 ①	19 ⑤	20 ①

17 장문의 이해-단일지문
문제편 p.245 해설편 p.313

01 ②	02 ③	03 ④	04 ⑤	05 ①
06 ⑤	07 ⑤	08 ⑤	09 ①	10 ④
11 ①	12 ⑤	13 ③	14 ④	15 ①
16 ④	17 ③	18 ④	19 ③	20 ②
21 ⑤	22 ⑤	23 ⑤	24 ⑤	25 ②
26 ③	27 ⑤	28 ④	29 ②	30 ④
31 ①	32 ⑤	33 ②	34 ①	35 ①
36 ③	37 ①	38 ⑤	39 ①	40 ⑤
41 ①	42 ④	43 ①	44 ⑤	45 ①
46 ④				

18 장문의 이해-복합지문
문제편 p.270 해설편 p.341

01 ②	02 ⑤	03 ⑤	04 ④	05 ④
06 ⑤	07 ⑤	08 ⑤	09 ④	10 ④
11 ⑤	12 ③	13 ⑤	14 ④	15 ②
16 ②	17 ③	18 ⑤	19 ④	20 ③
21 ③	22 ③	23 ②	24 ②	25 ③
26 ④	27 ③	28 ③	29 ⑤	30 ⑤
31 ⑤	32 ④	33 ⑤	34 ④	35 ②
36 ③	37 ③	38 ⑤	39 ④	40 ②
41 ③	42 ④	43 ③	44 ⑤	45 ⑤
46 ④	47 ④	48 ②	49 ②	50 ③
51 ③	52 ②	53 ③	54 ③	

1회 20분 미니모의고사
문제편 p.288 해설편 p.365

01 ①	02 ⑤	03 ①	04 ③	05 ④
06 ④	07 ⑤	08 ②	09 ⑤	10 ③
11 ④	12 ②			

2회 20분 미니모의고사
문제편 p.294 해설편 p.374

01 ②	02 ②	03 ①	04 ⑤	05 ④
06 ②	07 ③	08 ①	09 ②	10 ⑤
11 ④	12 ②			

3회 20분 미니모의고사
문제편 p.299 해설편 p.382

01 ③	02 ①	03 ②	04 ④	05 ⑤
06 ③	07 ⑤	08 ②	09 ⑤	10 ①
11 ③	12 ③			

MOTHERTONGUE
마더텅출판사
since1999.4.1.

2025 마더텅 전국연합 학력평가 기출문제집 고2 영어 독해

전국연합 학력평가와 학교 시험에 자주 출제되는 유형을
철저히 분석하여 적용한 유형별 기출문제집!
2025 교육과정에 맞는 영어 독해 전 유형 수록!

- 영어 1등급, 30일 완성을 위한 ① 학습계획표 ② 문제풀이 제한시간 ③ DAY인덱스
- 직독직해 훈련을 위한 자세한 끊어읽기 해설
- 지문의 이해를 돕는 친절한 첨삭 해설 및 어법 풀이

특별 무료 제공

| 유형별 TIP 및 최신 1개년 수능 대표예제 해설강의
| 전 문항 문제풀이 동영상 강의
| 전국연합 학력평가와 학교 내신 대비를 위한 20분 미니모의고사 3회분 수록
| 교육부 선정 필수 암기 어휘 2200개와 교재에서 배운 어휘를 수록한 <WORD BOOK> 및 단어시험지 한글(HWP)파일
| 필수 암기 어휘 2200개 중 최신 1개년 시행 학력평가에 나온 <적중 단어 466>

문항구성표

[마더텅 전국연합 학력평가 기출문제집 고2 영어 독해]는
총 552문항을 유형별로 나누어 수록하였습니다.

1) 2022~2024(2022년~2024년 9월) 시행 최신 3개년 고2 전국연합 학력평가 독해 유형 전 문항
2) 2016~2021 시행 고2 전국연합 학력평가 중 2025 교육과정에 맞는 우수 문항

연도별 문항구성표

* 최신 경향 반영하여 '연결어구', '지칭 추론' 유형은 삭제하였습니다.

시행연도	3월	6월	9월	11월	연도별 문항 수
2024	26	26	26	-	78
2023	26	26	26	26	104
2022	26	26	26	26	104
2021	21	17	20	22	80
2020	15	11	15	18	59
2019	14	14	15	12	55
2018	5	9	11	9	34
2017	4	3	5	6	18
2016	-	7	8	5	20
총 수록 문항 수					552

목차

20분 미니모의고사

30일 완성 학습계획표

- 마더텅 수능기출문제집을 100% 활용할 수 있도록 도와주는 학습계획표입니다. 계획표를 활용하여 학습 일정을 계획하고 자신의 성적을 체크해 보세요. 꼭 30일 완성을 목표로 하지 않더라도, 스스로 학습 현황을 체크하면서 공부하는 습관은 문제집을 끝까지 푸는 데 도움을 줍니다.
- 날짜별로 정해진 분량에 맞춰 공부하고 학습 결과를 기록합니다.
- 계획은 도중에 틀어질 수 있습니다. 하지만 계획을 세우고 지키는 과정은 그 자체로 효율적인 학습에 큰 도움이 됩니다. 학습 중 계획이 변경될 경우에 대비해 마더텅 홈페이지에서 학습계획표 PDF 파일을 제공하고 있습니다.

2025 **마더텅 전국연합 학력평가 기출문제집**
고2 영어 독해

Day	학습 내용	성취도				
		100%	99~75%	74~50%	49~25%	24~0%
01일차	01 글의 목적 파악 01~17번 02 심경·분위기 파악 01~15번					
02일차	02 심경·분위기 파악 16~19번 03 필자의 주장 01~20번 04 의미 추론 01~04번					
03일차	04 의미 추론 05~15번 05 요지 추론 01~04번					
04일차	05 요지 추론 05~19번 06 주제 추론 01~04번					
05일차	06 주제 추론 05~21번					
06일차	07 제목 추론 01~18번					
07일차	07 제목 추론 19~25번 08 도표의 이해 01~12번					
08일차	08 도표의 이해 13~19번 09 내용 일치 파악 01~14번					
09일차	09 내용 일치 파악 15~18번 10 안내문 01~28번					
10일차	10 안내문 29~33번 11 빈칸 추론(1) 01~12번					
11일차	11 빈칸 추론(1) 13~24번					
12일차	11 빈칸 추론(1) 25~33번 12 빈칸 추론(2) 01~06번					
13일차	12 빈칸 추론(2) 07~18번					
14일차	12 빈칸 추론(2) 19~30번					
15일차	12 빈칸 추론(2) 31~42번					
16일차	12 빈칸 추론(2) 43~50번 13 무관한 문장 찾기 01~08번					
17일차	13 무관한 문장 찾기 09~19번 14 문장 배열 01~06번					
18일차	14 문장 배열 07~20번					
19일차	14 문장 배열 21~34번					
20일차	14 문장 배열 35~44번 15 주어진 문장 위치 파악 01~04번					
21일차	15 주어진 문장 위치 파악 05~18번					
22일차	15 주어진 문장 위치 파악 19~32번					
23일차	15 주어진 문장 위치 파악 33~44번 16 문단 요약 01~02번					
24일차	16 문단 요약 03~16번					
25일차	16 문단 요약 17~20번 17 장문의 이해-단일지문 01~10번					
26일차	17 장문의 이해-단일지문 11~24번					
27일차	17 장문의 이해-단일지문 25~38번					
28일차	17 장문의 이해-단일지문 39~46번 18 장문의 이해-복합지문 01~09번					
29일차	18 장문의 이해-복합지문 10~30번					
30일차	18 장문의 이해-복합지문 31~54번					

취약한 유형 파악하기

※ 유형별로 맞은 문항 번호에는 O, 틀린 문항 번호에는 X 표시해 보세요.
취약한 유형의 문제를 파악하고, TIP 강의를 통해 해당 유형을 공부해 보세요.

01 글의 목적 파악	p7		p8		p9		p10		p11		p12		p13		p14		p15			
	1	2	3	4	5	6	7	8	9	10	11	12	13	14	15	16	17			
02 심경·분위기 파악	p18		p19			p20			p21			p22		p23		p24		p25		
	1	2	3	4	5	6	7	8	9	10	11	12	13	14	15	16	17	18	19	
03 필자의 주장	p28		p29		p30		p31		p32		p33		p34		p35		p36		p37	
	1	2	3	4	5	6	7	8	9	10	11	12	13	14	15	16	17	18	19	20
04 의미 추론	p40		p41		p42		p43		p44		p45		p46		p47					
	1	2	3	4	5	6	7	8	9	10	11	12	13	14	15					
05 요지 추론	p50		p51		p52			p53		p54		p55		p56		p57		p58		
	1	2	3	4	5	6	7	8	9	10	11	12	13	14	15	16	17	18	19	
06 주제 추론	p61		p62		p63		p64		p65		p66		p67		p68		p69		p70	
	1	2	3	4	5	6	7	8	9	10	11	12	13	14	15	16	17	18	19	20
	p71																			
	21																			
07 제목 추론	p74		p75		p76		p77		p78		p79		p80		p81		p82		p83	
	1	2	3	4	5	6	7	8	9	10	11	12	13	14	15	16	17	18	19	20
	p84		p85		p86															
	21	22	23	24	25															
08 도표의 이해	p89		p90		p91		p92		p93		p94		p95		p96		p97		p98	
	1	2	3	4	5	6	7	8	9	10	11	12	13	14	15	16	17	18	19	
09 내용 일치 파악	p101		p102		p103		p104		p105		p106		p107		p108		p109			
	1	2	3	4	5	6	7	8	9	10	11	12	13	14	15	16	17	18		
10 안내문	p112		p113		p114		p115		p116		p117		p118		p119		p120		p121	
	1	2	3	4	5	6	7	8	9	10	11	12	13	14	15	16	17	18	19	20
	p122		p123		p124		p125		p126		p127		p128							
	21	22	23	24	25	26	27	28	29	30	31	32	33							
11 빈칸 추론(1)-어휘, 짧은 어구	p132		p133		p134		p135		p136		p137		p138		p139		p140		p141	
	1	2	3	4	5	6	7	8	9	10	11	12	13	14	15	16	17	18	19	20
	p142		p143		p144		p145		p146		p147		p148							
	21	22	23	24	25	26	27	28	29	30	31	32	33							
12 빈칸 추론(2)-긴 어구, 문장	p149		p150		p151		p152		p153		p154		p155		p156		p157		p158	
	1	2	3	4	5	6	7	8	9	10	11	12	13	14	15	16	17	18	19	20
	p159		p160		p161		p162		p163		p164		p165		p166		p167		p168	
	21	22	23	24	25	26	27	28	29	30	31	32	33	34	35	36	37	38	39	40
	p169		p170		p171		p172		p173											
	41	42	43	44	45	46	47	48	49	50										
13 무관한 문장 찾기	p176		p177			p178			p179			p180			p181			p182		
	1	2	3	4	5	6	7	8	9	10	11	12	13	14	15	16	17	18	19	
14 문장 배열	p185		p186		p187		p188		p189		p190		p191		p192		p193		p194	
	1	2	3	4	5	6	7	8	9	10	11	12	13	14	15	16	17	18	19	20
	p195		p196		p197		p198		p199		p200		p201		p202		p203		p204	
	21	22	23	24	25	26	27	28	29	30	31	32	33	34	35	36	37	38	39	40
	p205		p206																	
	41	42	43	44																
15 주어진 문장 위치 파악	p209		p210		p211		p212		p213		p214		p215		p216		p217		p218	
	1	2	3	4	5	6	7	8	9	10	11	12	13	14	15	16	17	18	19	20
	p219		p220		p221		p222		p223		p224		p225		p226		p227		p228	
	21	22	23	24	25	26	27	28	29	30	31	32	33	34	35	36	37	38	39	40
	p229		p230																	
	41	42	43	44																
16 문단 요약	p233		p234		p235		p236		p237		p238		p239		p240		p241		p242	
	1	2	3	4	5	6	7	8	9	10	11	12	13	14	15	16	17	18	19	20
17 장문의 이해-단일지문	p245		p246		p247		p248		p249		p250		p251		p252		p253		p254	
	1	2	3	4	5	6	7	8	9	10	11	12	13	14	15	16	17	18	19	20
	p255		p256		p257		p258		p259		p260		p261		p262		p263		p264	
	21	22	23	24	25	26	27	28	29	30	31	32	33	34	35	36	37	38	39	40
	p265		p266		p267															
	41	42	43	44	45	46														
18 장문의 이해-복합지문	p270			p271			p272			p273			p274			p275				
	1	2	3	4	5	6	7	8	9	10	11	12	13	14	15	16	17	18		
	p276			p277			p278			p279			p280			p281				
	19	20	21	22	23	24	25	26	27	28	29	30	31	32	33	34	35	36		
	p282			p283			p284			p285			p286			p287				
	37	38	39	40	41	42	43	44	45	46	47	48	49	50	51	52	53	54		

유형 TIP

01. 글의 목적 파악

글이 전달하고자 하는 것, 즉 글쓴이의 입장이나 글의 중심 생각을 파악함. 주제가 확실히 드러나지 않는 경우가 있고, 핵심어와 내용 전체를 종합해서 선택지의 상위어와 연결 짓는 능력이 요구됨.

유형 TIP 25BR2T_CH01 대표 예제 25BR2E_CH01

유형 공략법

1) 글의 종류를 파악한다.

편지글, 안내문, 광고글, 불평이나 불만을 표현하는 글

2) 편지글의 경우, 편지를 쓴 사람과 편지를 받는 사람과의 관계를 파악한다.

광고글, 안내문의 형식도 있지만 대개는 편지글로 되어 있기 때문에 중요함.

3) 글의 흐름 전환에 주의한다.

But, However 등 반전, 역접의 연결사가 있는지를 확인해야 함.

4) 목적을 나타내는 근거를 파악한다.

to V(~하기 위해서), so that, in order that, in order to V, so as to V, for the purpose of, for the sake of

I would like to V, I want to V, I am asking you to V/for, we hope that…

5) 선택지의 '~하려고' 부분에 초점을 맞추어 읽는다.

필수 암기 어휘와 표현

1) 빈출 어휘

accept 수락하다	advertise 광고하다	advise 충고하다	apologize 사과하다
appeal 호소하다	apply 신청[지원]하다	appreciate 감사하다	blame 비난하다
cancel 취소하다	complain 불평하다	confirm 확인하다	congratulate 축하하다
consult 자문을 구하다	criticize 비판하다	decline 거절하다	demand 요구하다
encourage 격려하다	forgive 용서하다	greet 인사하다	guide 안내하다
inform 알리다	inquire 문의하다	introduce 소개하다	invite 초대하다
notify 통지하다	offer 제안하다	order 주문하다	permit 허가하다
persuade 설득하다	praise 칭찬하다	protest 항의하다	recommend 추천하다
refuse 거절하다	reject 거절하다	remind 상기시키다	report 보고하다
reproach 비난하다	request 요청하다	suggest 제안하다	warn 경고하다

2) 목적별로 자주 쓰이는 표현

감사	appreciate, I'm grateful, contribution, commitment, recognition, acknowledgement, hard work, successful, invaluable
충고, 조언	advise, recommend, suggest, need, have to V, you'd better, you should, you may be able to V, be sure to V, how/what about
거절	decline, refuse, reject, I am afraid, not appropriate, yet, not interested at this moment, regret, for later use
요구, 촉구	ask, call for, request, require, demand, must, have to V, should, would like to V
경고, 항의	complain, criticize, suffer, warn, afraid, disappointed, dissatisfied, unfair, harmful, damaging, alarming, getting serious, run out of, caution, danger, problem

글의 목적 파악 대표 예제 - 2024학년도 수능 18번

다음 글의 목적으로 가장 적절한 것은?

(1) I'm Charlie Reeves, manager of Toon Skills Company. (2) If you're interested in new webtoon-making skills and techniques, this post is for you. (3) This year, we've launched special online courses, which contain a variety of contents about webtoon production. (4) Each course consists of ten units that help improve your drawing and story-telling skills. (5) Moreover, these courses are designed to suit any level, from beginner to advanced. (6) It costs $45 for one course, and you can watch your course as many times as you want for six months. (7) Our courses with talented and experienced instructors will open up a new world of creativity for you. (8) It's time to start creating your webtoon world at https://webtoonskills.com.

✔ 웹툰 제작 온라인 강좌를 홍보하려고 문장(3)
② 웹툰 작가 채용 정보를 제공하려고
③ 신작 웹툰 공개 일정을 공지하려고
④ 웹툰 창작 대회에 출품을 권유하려고
⑤ 기초적인 웹툰 제작 방법을 설명하려고

STEP 1 글의 종류를 파악한다.

→ 홍보하는 글임.

STEP 2 홍보하는 글의 경우, 홍보 대상을 파악한다.

→ Toon Skills 회사의 경영자가 웹툰 제작에 관한 온라인 강좌를 소개함.

STEP 3 목적을 나타내는 근거를 파악한다.

→ 문장 (3)의 'we've launched ~' 에서 글의 목적을 드러내고 있음.

STEP 4 선택지의 '~하려고' 부분에 초점을 맞추어 읽는다.

→ 선택지 ①이 문장 (3)에 맞게 '홍보하려고'로 기술되어 있으므로 정답임.

전문 해석

(1) 저는 Toon Skills 회사의 경영자인 Charlie Reeves입니다. (2) 만약 여러분이 새 웹툰 제작 기술과 기법에 관심이 있다면, 이 게시글은 여러분을 위한 것입니다. (3) 올해, 저희는 특별한 온라인 강좌를 시작했고, 그것들은 웹툰 제작에 관한 다양한 내용을 포함합니다. (4) 각각의 강좌는 여러분의 그리기와 스토리텔링 기술을 향상하는 것을 돕는 열 개의 단원으로 구성됩니다. (5) 게다가, 이 강좌는 초급부터 고급까지 어떤 수준에도 적합하도록 고안되어 있습니다. (6) 한 강좌당 45달러의 비용이 들고, 여러분은 여러분의 강좌를 6개월 동안 원하는 만큼 여러 번 볼 수 있습니다. (7) 재능이 있고 능숙한 강사들이 있는 저희의 강좌는 여러분에게 창의력의 새로운 세상을 열어줄 것입니다. (8) https://webtoonskills.com에서 여러분의 웹툰 세상을 만들기 시작할 시간입니다.

중요 어휘

□ launch 통 시작하다, 출시하다 / 명 개시, 출시
□ consist of ~로 구성되다
□ be designed to V ~하도록 고안되다
□ suit 통 적합하다, 맞다
□ advanced 형 고급의, 진보한, 선진의
□ talented 형 재능이 있는
□ experienced 형 능숙한, 경험이 많은
□ it is time to V ~할 시간이다

자세한 해설지 QR→
자세한해설-CH01

01 글의 목적 파악

동영상 강의
25BR2_CH01

01 ⏲ 50초

★☆☆ 2021년 3월 18번

다음 글의 목적으로 가장 적절한 것은?

My name is Anthony Thompson and I am writing on behalf of the residents' association. Our recycling program has been working well thanks to your participation. However, a problem has recently occurred that needs your attention. Because there is no given day for recycling, residents are putting their recycling out at any time. This makes the recycling area messy, which requires extra labor and cost. To deal with this problem, the residents' association has decided on a day to recycle. I would like to let you know that you can put out your recycling on Wednesdays only. I am sure it will make our apartment complex look much more pleasant. Thank you in advance for your cooperation.

① 재활용품 배출 허용 요일을 알리려고
② 쓰레기 분리배출의 필요성을 설명하려고
③ 쓰레기 분리배출 후 주변 정리를 부탁하려고
④ 입주민 대표 선출 결과를 공지하려고
⑤ 쓰레기장 재정비 비용을 청구하려고

02 ⏲ 50초

★☆☆ 2021년 6월 18번

다음 글의 목적으로 가장 적절한 것은?

Send

Dear animal lovers,

I am writing on behalf of the Protect Animal Organization. Our organization was founded on the belief that all animals should be respected and treated with kindness, and must be protected by law. Over the past 20 years, we have provided lost animals with protection, new homes, and sometimes health care. Currently, our animal shelter is full, and we need your help to build a new shelter. We are seeking donations in any amount. Every dollar raised goes to building homes for animals in need. You can donate to us online at www.protectanimal.org. Thank you for considering supporting us.

Sincerely,
Stella Anderson

① 사무실을 빌려준 것에 대해 감사하려고
② 동물 병원 설립의 필요성을 주장하려고
③ 새롭게 시행되는 동물 보호법에 대해 설명하려고
④ 동물 보호 단체의 봉사 활동 프로그램을 안내하려고
⑤ 새로운 동물 보호소를 짓기 위한 기부를 요청하려고

정답과 해설 : 01 002 02 002

03 ⏱ 50초

★☆☆ 2022년 6월 18번

다음 글의 목적으로 가장 적절한 것은?

Dear Ms. Stevens,

My name is Peter Watson, and I'm the manager of the Springton Library. Our storytelling program has been so well-attended that we are planning to expand the program to 6 days each week. This means that we need to recruit more volunteers to read to the children. People still talk about the week you filled in for us when one of our volunteers couldn't come. You really brought those stories to life! So, would you be willing to read to the preschoolers for an hour, from 10 to 11 a.m. every Friday? I hope you will take this opportunity to let more children hear your voice. We are looking forward to your positive reply.

Best regards,
Peter Watson

① 도서관의 운영 시간 연장을 제안하려고
② 봉사 활동 시간이 변경된 것을 안내하려고
③ 독서 토론 수업에 참여할 아동을 모집하려고
④ 봉사 활동에 참여하지 못하게 된 것을 사과하려고
⑤ 책 읽어 주기 자원봉사에 참여해 줄 것을 요청하려고

04 ⏱ 50초

★☆☆ 2022년 9월 18번

다음 글의 목적으로 가장 적절한 것은?

Dear Customer Service,

I am writing in regard to my magazine subscription. Currently, I have just over a year to go on my subscription to *Economy Tomorrow* and would like to continue my subscription as I have enjoyed the magazine for many years. Unfortunately, due to my bad eyesight, I have trouble reading your magazine. My doctor has told me that I need to look for large print magazines and books. I'd like to know whether there's a large print version of your magazine. Please contact me if this is something you offer. Thank you for your time. I look forward to hearing from you soon.

Sincerely,
Martin Gray

① 잡지 기삿거리를 제보하려고
② 구독 기간 변경을 신청하려고
③ 구독료 인상에 대해 항의하려고
④ 잡지의 큰 글자판이 있는지 문의하려고
⑤ 잡지 기사 내용에 대한 정정을 요구하려고

정답과 해설 : 03 003 04 003

05 ⓘ 50초

★☆☆ 2022년 11월 18번

다음 글의 목적으로 가장 적절한 것은?

Dear local business owners,

My name is Carol Williams, president of the student council at Yellowstone High School. We are hosting our annual quiz night on March 30 and plan to give prizes to the winning team. However, this event won't be possible without the support of local businesses who provide valuable products and services. Would you be willing to donate a gift certificate that we can use as a prize? We would be grateful for any amount on the certificate. In exchange for your generosity, we would place an advertisement for your business on our answer sheets. Thank you for taking time to read this letter and consider our request. If you'd like to donate or need more information, please call or email me. I look forward to hearing from you soon.

Carol Williams

① 행사 홍보물 게시가 가능한지를 문의하려고
② 학교 퀴즈 행사에 사용할 물품 제작을 의뢰하려고
③ 우승 상품으로 사용할 상품권을 기부해 줄 것을 요청하려고
④ 학교 행사로 예상되는 소음 발생에 대해 양해를 구하려고
⑤ 퀴즈 행사 개최를 위한 장소 사용 허가를 받으려고

06 ⓘ 50초

★☆☆ 2023년 9월 18번

다음 글의 목적으로 가장 적절한 것은?

To whom it may concern,

I would like to draw your attention to a problem that frequently occurs with the No. 35 buses. There is a bus stop about halfway along Fenny Road, at which the No. 35 buses are supposed to stop. It would appear, however, that some of your drivers are either unaware of this bus stop or for some reason choose to ignore it, driving past even though the buses are not full. I would be grateful if you could remind your drivers that this bus stop exists and that they should be prepared to stop at it. I look forward to seeing an improvement in this service soon.

Yours faithfully,
John Williams

① 버스 운전기사 채용 계획을 문의하려고
② 버스 정류장의 위치 변경을 요청하려고
③ 도로 공사로 인한 소음에 대해 항의하려고
④ 출퇴근 시간의 버스 배차 간격 단축을 제안하려고
⑤ 버스 정류장 무정차 통과에 대한 시정을 요구하려고

정답과 해설 : 05 004 06 004

07 ⓒ 50초

★☆☆
2019년 9월 18번

다음 글의 목적으로 가장 적절한 것은?

To whom it may concern,

We are students from St. Andrew's College who are currently taking a Media Studies class that requires us to film a short video. We would like to film at Sunbury Park on November 14th, 2019, from 9 a.m. to 3 p.m. After looking for several days to find good locations, we decided on filming at Sunbury because it is not overly populated during this time of day. Our team will not cause any issues to public services or other park visitors. We would therefore like to request permission to film at Sunbury Park at the time above. If you need to contact our Media Studies teacher, Damien Matthews, for further information, he can be reached at damien@st_andrews.ac.uk.

Yours faithfully,
Taylor Johnson & Chloe Moore

① 영화제 참가 방법을 문의하려고
② 공원 주변 차량 통제를 건의하려고
③ 공원에서의 촬영 허가를 요청하려고
④ 영상 편집 강좌 이수 여부를 확인하려고
⑤ 촬영으로 인한 불편 사항에 대해 항의하려고

08 ⓒ 50초

★☆☆
2023년 3월 18번

다음 글의 목적으로 가장 적절한 것은?

It was a pleasure meeting you at your gallery last week. I appreciate your effort to select and exhibit diverse artwork. As I mentioned, I greatly admire Robert D. Parker's paintings, which emphasize the beauty of nature. Over the past few days, I have been researching and learning about Robert D. Parker's online viewing room through your gallery's website. I'm especially interested in purchasing the painting that depicts the horizon, titled *Sunrise*. I would like to know if the piece is still available for purchase. It would be a great pleasure to house this wonderful piece of art. I look forward to your reply to this inquiry.

① 좋아하는 화가와의 만남을 요청하려고
② 미술 작품의 구매 가능 여부를 문의하려고
③ 소장 중인 미술 작품의 감정을 의뢰하려고
④ 미술 작품의 소유자 변경 내역을 확인하려고
⑤ 기획 중인 전시회에 참여하는 화가를 홍보하려고

정답과 해설 : 07 005 08 005

09 ⓢ 50초

★☆☆ 2022년 3월 18번

다음 글의 목적으로 가장 적절한 것은?

As I explained on the telephone, I don't want to take my two children by myself on a train trip to visit my parents in Springfield this Saturday since it is the same day the Riverside Warriors will play the Greenville Trojans in the National Soccer Championship. I would really appreciate it, therefore, if you could change my tickets to the following weekend (April 23). I fully appreciate that the original, special-offer ticket was non-exchangeable, but I did not know about the soccer match when I booked the tickets and I would be really grateful if you could do this for me. Thank you in advance.

① 특가로 제공되는 기차표를 구매하려고
② 축구 경기 입장권의 환불을 요구하려고
③ 다른 날짜로 기차표 변경을 요청하려고
④ 기차표 예약이 가능한 날짜를 알아보려고
⑤ 축구 경기 날짜가 연기되었는지를 확인하려고

10 ⓢ 50초

★☆☆ 2018년 9월 18번

다음 글의 목적으로 가장 적절한 것은?

Dear Mr. Terry Walter,

I am the principal of Springfield Public School. As you know, Springfield Public School is located at the intersection of First Street and Pine Street. The safety of our children is at risk largely due to the disregard for speed limits by motorists traveling along Pine Street. I have regularly witnessed vehicles traveling far in excess of the speed limit on Pine Street. Additionally, parents have expressed concern for the safety of their children who must cross Pine Street. For these reasons, we are requesting the installation of speed bumps on Pine Street. I know that one of your missions, as well as ours, is to ensure that our young people are afforded a safe and secure environment to and from school each day. I anticipate that your approval of this request will greatly improve the safety of our children.

Sincerely,
Emma Hudson

① 과속 차량 특별 단속 실시를 촉구하려고
② 교차로 교통신호 체계 개선을 건의하려고
③ 학생 대상 교통안전교육 강의를 부탁하려고
④ 제한속도 규정 표지판 교체 시기를 안내하려고
⑤ 학교 주변 도로에 과속방지턱 설치를 요청하려고

정답과 해설 : 09 006 10 007

11 ⓛ 50초

★☆☆ 2021년 9월 18번

다음 글의 목적으로 가장 적절한 것은?

Dear parents and students of Douglas School,

As you know, our school was built over 150 years ago. While we are proud of our school's history, the facilities are not exactly what they should be for modern schooling. Thanks to a generous donation to the school foundation, we will be able to start renovating those parts of our campus that have become outdated. We hope this will help provide our students with the best education possible. I'm writing to inform you that the auditorium will be the first building closed for repairs. Students will not be able to use the auditorium for about one month while the repairs are taking place. We hope that you will understand how this brief inconvenience will encourage community-wide benefits for years to come.

Sincerely,
Vice Principal Kyla Andrews

① 수리로 인한 강당 폐쇄를 안내하려고
② 캠퍼스 투어 프로그램 일정을 조정하려고
③ 강당 사용을 위한 신청 방법을 공지하려고
④ 강당 신축을 위한 기금 모금 행사를 홍보하려고
⑤ 집짓기 행사에 참여할 자원 봉사자를 모집하려고

12 ⓛ 50초

★☆☆ 2021년 11월 18번

다음 글의 목적으로 가장 적절한 것은?

To whom it may concern,

I am a parent of a high school student who takes the 145 bus to commute to Clarkson High School. This is the only public transport available from our area and is used by many students. Recently, I heard that the city council is planning to discontinue this service. My husband and I start work early in the morning and this makes it impossible for us to drop our son off at school. It would take him nearly an hour to walk to school and there is a lot of traffic in the morning, so I do not consider it safe to bike. This matter will place many families, including ours, under a lot of stress. As a resident of Sunnyville, I think such a plan is unacceptable. I urge the council to listen to the concerns of the community.

Sincerely,
Lucy Jackson

① 버스 노선 변경에 항의하려고
② 버스 운행 중단 계획에 반대하려고
③ 버스 배차 간격 조정을 요청하려고
④ 자전거 전용 도로 설치를 건의하려고
⑤ 통학로 안전 관리 강화를 촉구하려고

정답과 해설 : 11 007 12 008

13 ⓒ 50초

★☆☆ 2023년 6월 18번

다음 글의 목적으로 가장 적절한 것은?

Dear parents,

Regular attendance at school is essential in maximizing student potential. Recently, we've become concerned about the number of unapproved absences across all grades. I would like to further clarify that your role as a parent is to approve any school absence. Parents must provide an explanation for absences to the school within 7 days from the first day of any period of absence. Where an explanation has not been received within the 7-day time frame, the school will record the absence as unjustified on the student's record. Please ensure that you go to the parent portal site and register the reason any time your child is absent. Please approve all absences, so that your child will not be at a disadvantage. Many thanks for your cooperation.

Sincerely,
Natalie Brown, Vice Principal

① 자녀의 결석 사유를 등록해 줄 것을 요청하려고
② 학교 홈페이지의 일시적 운영 중단을 공지하려고
③ 자녀가 지각하지 않도록 부모의 지도를 당부하려고
④ 방과 후 프로그램에 대한 부모의 관심을 독려하려고
⑤ 인정 결석은 최대 7일까지 허용된다는 것을 안내하려고

14 ⓒ 50초

★☆☆ 2023년 11월 18번

다음 글의 목적으로 가장 적절한 것은?

To whom it may concern,

I am writing to inform you of an ongoing noise issue that I am experiencing. My apartment faces the basketball courts of the community center. While I fully support the community center's services, I am constantly being disrupted by individuals playing basketball late at night. Many nights, I struggle to fall asleep because I can hear people bouncing balls and shouting on the basketball courts well after 11 p.m.. Could you restrict the time the basketball court is open to before 9 p.m.? I'm sure I'm not the only person in the neighborhood that is affected by this noise issue. I appreciate your assistance.

Sincerely,
Ian Baldwin

① 체육관의 바닥 교체 공사를 요구하려고
② 농구 코트의 운영 시간 제한을 요청하려고
③ 문화 센터 시설의 대관 날짜를 변경하려고
④ 건강 증진 프로그램 신청 방법을 문의하려고
⑤ 지역 내 체육 시설의 증설 가능 여부를 확인하려고

정답과 해설 : 13 008 14 009

15 ⓒ 50초

★☆☆ 2024년 3월 18번

다음 글의 목적으로 가장 적절한 것은?

Dear Art Crafts People of Greenville,

For the annual Crafts Fair on May 25 from 1 p.m. to 6 p.m., the Greenville Community Center is providing booth spaces to rent as in previous years. To reserve your space, please visit our website and complete a registration form by April 20. The rental fee is $50. All the money we receive from rental fees goes to support upcoming activities throughout the year. We expect all available spaces to be fully booked soon, so don't get left out. We hope to see you at the fair.

① 지역 예술가를 위한 정기 후원을 요청하려고
② 공예품 박람회의 부스 예약을 안내하려고
③ 대여 물품의 반환 방법을 설명하려고
④ 지역 예술가가 만든 물품을 홍보하려고
⑤ 지역 행사 일정의 변경 사항을 공지하려고

16 ⓒ 50초

★☆☆ 2024년 6월 18번

다음 글의 목적으로 가장 적절한 것은?

Dear Residents,

My name is Kari Patterson, and I'm the manager of the River View Apartments. It's time to take advantage of the sunny weather to make our community more beautiful. On Saturday, July 13 at 9 a.m., residents will meet in the north parking lot. We will divide into teams to plant flowers and small trees, pull weeds, and put colorful decorations on the lawn. Please join us for this year's Gardening Day, and remember no special skills or tools are required. Last year, we had a great time working together, so come out and make this year's event even better!

Warm regards,
Kari Patterson

① 아파트 내 정원 조성에 대한 의견을 수렴하려고
② 정원가꾸기 날 행사에 참여할 것을 독려하려고
③ 쓰레기를 지정된 장소에 버릴 것을 당부하려고
④ 지하 주차장 공사 일정에 대해 공지하려고
⑤ 정원박람회 개최 날짜 변경을 안내하려고

정답과 해설 : 15 010 16 010

17 ⓘ 50초

★☆☆ 2024년 9월 18번

다음 글의 목적으로 가장 적절한 것은?

To whom it may concern,

My name is Peter Jackson and I am thinking of applying for the Advanced Licensed Counselor Program that the university provides. I found that the certification for 100 hours of counseling experience is required for the application. However, I do not think I could possibly complete the required counseling experience by the current deadline. So, if possible, I kindly request an extension of the deadline until the end of this summer vacation. I am actively working on obtaining the certification, and I am sure I will be able to submit it by then. I understand the importance of following the application process, and would greatly appreciate your consideration of this request. I look forward to your response.

Sincerely,
Peter Jackson

① 상담 경력 증명서의 제출 기한 연장을 요청하려고
② 서류 심사 결과 발표의 지연에 대해 항의하려고
③ 전문 상담 강좌의 추가 개설을 제안하려고
④ 대학의 편의 시설 확충을 건의하려고
⑤ 대학 진학 상담 예약을 취소하려고

정답과 해설 : 17 011

유형 TIP

02. 심경·분위기 파악

지문의 상황이나 사건을 토대로 분위기를 파악해서 답을 찾아야 함. 제시된 이야기 속의 주인공이 어떤 상황에 처해 있는지, 달라진 상황에 따라 심경이 어떻게 변화했는지에 초점을 맞추어야 함.

유형 TIP 25BR2T_CH02
대표 예제 25BR2E_CH02

유형 공략법

1) 지문의 전체적인 흐름과 분위기를 파악한다.

지엽적인 내용에 초점을 맞춘 선택지를 고르지 않도록 주의해야 함.

2) 감정이나 분위기를 나타내는 표현을 유의해서 읽는다.

감정을 표현하는 형용사가 직접 등장하지 않더라도, 간접적으로 분위기나 심경을 묘사하는 표현을 놓치지 않아야 함.

3) 선택지의 단어가 긍정적인 의미인지 부정적인 의미인지 파악하고 정답을 고른다.

필수 암기 어휘와 표현

1) 심경

긍정적	grateful 감사하는, joyous 즐거운, comfortable 편안한, convinced 확신하는, exhilarated 유쾌한, impressed 감명받은, satisfied 만족스러운, amused 즐거워하는, determined 결의에 찬, gratified 만족한, excited 신난, 흥미진진한, fascinated 매혹된, contented 만족한, encouraged 고무된, pleased 기쁜, relaxed 편안해진, relieved 안도하는, sympathetic 동정적인, 공감하는, touched 감동한, anticipating 고대하는
부정적	afraid 두려운, angry 화난, disappointed 실망한, annoyed 짜증난, envious 부러운, embarrassed 당혹스러운, nervous 불안한, sorrowful 슬픈, anxious 근심스러운, ashamed 부끄러운, upset 불쾌한, frustrated 좌절감을 느끼는, worried 걱정하는, concerned 염려하는, scared 겁먹은, alarmed 불안해하는, astonished 놀란, confused 혼란스러운, jealous 질투하는, guilty 가책을 느끼는, depressed 우울한, desperate 절박한, devastated 망연자실한, discouraged 낙담한, cynical 냉소적인, terrified 겁먹은, horrified 무서운, dissatisfied 불만족하는, disturbed 동요한, exhausted 지친, indignant 분개한, irritated 신경질이 난, melancholy 우울한, miserable 비참한, puzzled 당황한, frightened 겁을 먹은, indifferent 무관심한, regretful 후회하는, skeptical 회의적인, bored 지루한

2) 분위기

awesome 굉장한, 멋진	awful 끔찍한	tense 긴장한	monotonous 단조로운
lively 활기찬	horrible 끔찍한	despairing 절망적인	tedious 지루한
dynamic 역동적인	scary 무서운	grave 심각한	pastoral 평화로운
moving 감동적인	urgent 긴급한, 다급한	disappointing 실망스러운	wearisome 지루한
romantic 낭만적인	frightening 두려운	mysterious 신비한	gloomy 음울한
festive 즐거운, 흥겨운	solemn 엄숙한	spectacular 장관을 이루는	melancholy 우울한

심경·분위기 파악 대표 예제 - 2024학년도 수능 19번

다음 글에 드러난 David의 심경 변화로 가장 적절한 것은?

(1) David was starting a new job in Vancouver, and he was waiting for his bus. (2) He kept looking back and forth between his watch and the direction the bus would come from. (3) He thought, "My bus isn't here yet. I can't be late on my first day." (4) David couldn't feel at ease. (5) When he looked up again, he saw a different bus coming that was going right to his work. (6) The bus stopped in front of him and opened its door. (7) He got on the bus thinking, "Phew! Luckily, this bus came just in time so I won't be late." (8) He leaned back on an unoccupied seat in the bus and took a deep breath, finally able to relax.

✓ nervous → relieved (- / +)
② lonely → hopeful (- / +)
③ pleased → confused (+ / -)
④ indifferent → delighted (- / +)
⑤ bored → thrilled (- / +)

STEP 1 지문의 전체적인 흐름과 분위기를 파악한다.

→ David가 새로 출근하게 되어 버스를 기다리는 일상을 다루고 있는 일화 성격의 글임.

STEP 2 감정이나 분위기를 나타내는 표현을 유의해서 읽는다.

→ 문장 (2)부터 (4)까지는 David가 오지 않는 버스를 초조하게 기다리고 있는데, 특히 문장 (4)에 'couldn't feel at ease'가 있는 것으로 보아 부정적인 감정인 것을 알 수 있음. 이후 문장 (5)부터 (8)을 통해 직장으로 향하는 다른 버스가 도착해서 David가 안심했음을 알 수 있으며, 특히 문장 (8)의 'finally able to relax'에서 이 점이 확실하게 드러남.

STEP 3 선택지의 단어가 긍정적인 의미인지 부정적인 의미인지 파악하고 정답을 고른다.

→ 보기 ①, ②, ④, ⑤는 부정적인 감정에서 긍정적인 감정으로 바뀌는 선택지임. 문장 (4)의 '마음을 놓을 수 없었다'라는 표현을 통해 'nervous'가 적절함을 알 수 있고, 문장 (8)의 '마침내 안심할 수 있었다'라는 표현을 보아 'relieved'가 적절하므로 정답은 ①임.

전문 해석

(1) David는 Vancouver에서 새로운 일을 시작할 예정이었고, 그는 자신이 탈 버스를 기다리고 있었다. (2) 그는 계속 자신의 시계와 그 버스가 올 방향 사이를 왔다 갔다 하며 보고 있었다. (3) 그는 "내가 탈 버스가 아직 여기 안 왔군. 난 첫날부터 늦을 수는 없어."라고 생각했다. (4) David는 마음을 놓을 수 없었다. (5) 그가 다시 올려다보았을 때, 그는 자신의 직장으로 바로 가는 다른 버스가 오고 있는 것을 보았다. (6) 그 버스는 그의 앞에서 멈췄고 문을 열었다. (7) 그는 "휴! 다행히 내가 늦지 않도록 이 버스가 딱 맞춰서 왔네."라고 생각하면서 그 버스에 탔다. (8) 그는 버스에서 비어 있는 좌석에 등을 기대며 심호흡을 했고, 마침내 안심할 수 있었다.

중요 어휘

- □ **keep V-ing** 계속 ~하다
- □ **back and forth** 왔다 갔다 하며, 앞뒤로
- □ **feel at ease** 마음을 놓다, 안심하다
- □ **luckily** 부 다행히, 운 좋게
- □ **just in time** 딱 맞춰서, 때마침, 알맞은 때에
- □ **lean** 동 기대다
- □ **unoccupied** 형 비어 있는, 점령되지 않은

자세한 해설지 QR➜

자세한해설-CH02

02 심경·분위기 파악

동영상 강의

25BR2_CH02

01

50초

★☆☆

2021년 6월 19번

다음 글에 드러난 Dave의 심경 변화로 가장 적절한 것은?

Dave sat up on his surfboard and looked around. He was the last person in the water that afternoon. Suddenly something out toward the horizon caught his eye and his heart froze. It was every surfer's worst nightmare — the fin of a shark. And it was no more than 20 meters away! He turned his board toward the beach and started kicking his way to the shore. Shivering, he gripped his board tighter and kicked harder. 'I'm going to be okay,' he thought to himself. 'I need to let go of the fear.' Five minutes of terror that felt like a lifetime passed before he was on dry land again. Dave sat on the beach and caught his breath. His mind was at ease. He was safe. He let out a contented sigh as the sun started setting behind the waves.

♦ fin: 지느러미

① scared → relieved
② indifferent → proud
③ amazed → horrified
④ hopeful → worried
⑤ ashamed → grateful

02

50초

★☆☆

2022년 6월 19번

다음 글에 드러난 'I'의 심경 변화로 가장 적절한 것은?

I walked up to the little dark brown door and knocked. Nobody answered. I pushed on the door carefully. When the door swung open with a rusty creak, a man was standing in a back corner of the room. My hands flew over my mouth as I started to scream. He was just standing there, watching me! As my heart continued to race, I saw that he had also put his hands over his mouth. Wait a minute... It was a mirror! I took a deep breath and walked past a table to the old mirror that stood in the back of the room. I felt my heartbeat returning to normal, and calmly looked at my reflection in the mirror.

① terrified → relieved
② hopeful → nervous
③ confident → anxious
④ annoyed → grateful
⑤ disappointed → thrilled

정답과 해설 : 01 012 02 012

03 ⓒ 50초

★☆☆
2018년 3월 19번

다음 글에 드러난 'I'의 심경 변화로 가장 적절한 것은?

On December 6th, I arrived at University Hospital in Cleveland at 10:00 a.m. I went through the process of admissions. I grew anxious because the time for surgery was drawing closer. I was directed to the waiting area, where I remained until my name was called. I had a few hours of waiting time. I just kept praying. At some point in my ongoing prayer process, before my name was called, in the midst of the chaos, an unbelievable peace embraced me. All my fear disappeared! An unbelievable peace overrode my emotions. My physical body relaxed in the comfort provided, and I looked forward to getting the surgery over with and working hard at recovery.

① cheerful → sad
② worried → relieved
③ angry → ashamed
④ jealous → thankful
⑤ hopeful → disappointed

04 ⓒ 50초

★☆☆
2020년 11월 19번

다음 글에 드러난 Ryan의 심경 변화로 가장 적절한 것은?

Ryan, an eleven-year-old boy, ran home as fast as he could. Finally, summer break had started! When he entered the house, his mom was standing in front of the refrigerator, waiting for him. She told him to pack his bags. Ryan's heart soared like a balloon. *Pack for what? Are we going to Disneyland?* He couldn't remember the last time his parents had taken him on a vacation. His eyes beamed. "You're spending the summer with uncle Tim and aunt Gina." Ryan groaned. "The whole summer?" "Yes, the whole summer." The anticipation he had felt disappeared in a flash. For three whole miserable weeks, he would be on his aunt and uncle's farm. He sighed.

① excited → disappointed
② furious → regretful
③ irritated → satisfied
④ nervous → relaxed
⑤ pleased → jealous

05 ⓒ 50초

★☆☆
2021년 11월 19번

다음 글에 드러난 Ted의 심경 변화로 가장 적절한 것은?

One Friday afternoon, Ted was called to the vice president of human resources. Ted sat down, beaming in anticipation. Today was the big day and this meeting would mark a turning point in his career! Ted felt sure that it was for his promotion and that the vice president would make him the marketing manager. "Ted, there is no easy way to say this." Ted suddenly realized this meeting wasn't going to be as he expected. Ted's mind went blank. The vice president continued, "Ted, I know you've desperately wanted this promotion, but we decided Mike is more suitable." Ted just sat there, frozen. He felt as if he had been hit by a truck. *Don't panic*. All he was able to do was repeat that sentence over and over to himself.

① hopeful → shocked
② relaxed → lonely
③ ashamed → relieved
④ indifferent → upset
⑤ embarrassed → pleased

정답과 해설 : 03 013 04 013 05 014

06 ⓒ 50초

★☆☆ 2022년 3월 19번

다음 글에 드러난 'I'의 심경으로 가장 적절한 것은?

Hours later — when my back aches from sitting, my hair is styled and dry, and my almost invisible makeup has been applied — Ash tells me it's time to change into my dress. We've been waiting until the last minute, afraid any refreshments I eat might accidentally fall onto it and stain it. There's only thirty minutes left until the show starts, and the nerves that have been torturing Ash seem to have escaped her, choosing a new victim in me. My palms are sweating, and I have butterflies in my stomach. Nearly all the models are ready, some of them already dressed in their nineteenth-century costumes. Ash tightens my corset.

① tense and nervous
② proud and confident
③ relieved and pleased
④ indifferent and bored
⑤ irritated and disappointed

07 ⓒ 50초

★☆☆ 2022년 11월 19번

다음 글에 드러난 'I'의 심경 변화로 가장 적절한 것은?

Dan and I were supposed to make a presentation that day. Right after the class started, my phone buzzed. It was a text from Dan saying, "I can't make it on time. There's been a car accident on the road!" I almost fainted. 'What should I do?' Dan didn't show up before our turn, and soon I was standing in front of the whole class. I managed to finish my portion, and my mind went blank for a few seconds, wondering what to do. 'Hold yourself together!' I quickly came to my senses and worked through Dan's part of the presentation as best as I could. After a few moments, I finished the entire presentation on my own. Only then did the tension vanish. I could see our professor's beaming face.

① panicked → relieved
② sorrowful → indifferent
③ sympathetic → content
④ jealous → delighted
⑤ confused → humiliated

08 ⓒ 50초

★☆☆ 2023년 6월 19번

다음 글에 드러난 Ester의 심경 변화로 가장 적절한 것은?

Ester stood up as soon as she heard the hum of a hover engine outside. "Mail," she shouted and ran down the third set of stairs and swung open the door. It was pouring now, but she ran out into the rain. She was facing the mailbox. There was a single, unopened letter inside. She was sure this must be what she was eagerly waiting for. Without hesitation, she tore open the envelope. She pulled out the paper and unfolded it. The letter said, 'Thank you for applying to our company. We would like to invite you to our internship program. We look forward to seeing you soon.' She jumped up and down and looked down at the letter again. She couldn't wait to tell this news to her family.

① anticipating → excited
② confident → ashamed
③ curious → embarrassed
④ surprised → confused
⑤ indifferent → grateful

정답과 해설 : 06 015 07 015 08 016

09 ⓘ 50초

★☆☆ 2023년 9월 19번

다음 글에 드러난 'I'의 심경 변화로 가장 적절한 것은?

My 10-year-old appeared, in desperate need of a quarter. "A quarter? What on earth do you need a quarter for?" My tone bordered on irritation. I didn't want to be bothered with such a trivial demand. "There's a garage sale up the street, and there's something I just gotta have! It only costs a quarter. Please?" I placed a quarter in my son's hand. Moments later, a little voice said, "Here, Mommy, this is for you." I glanced down at the hands of my little son and saw a four-inch cream-colored statue of two small children hugging one another. Inscribed at their feet were words that read *It starts with 'L' ends with 'E' and in between are 'O' and 'V*.' As I watched him race back to the garage sale, I smiled with a heart full of happiness. That 25-cent garage sale purchase brought me a lot of joy.

◆ quarter: 25센트 동전 ◆◆ inscribe: 새기다

① annoyed → delighted ② ashamed → relieved
③ excited → confused ④ scared → confident
⑤ indifferent → jealous

10 ⓘ 50초

★☆☆ 2019년 6월 19번

다음 글에 드러난 Rowe의 심경 변화로 가장 적절한 것은?

Rowe jumps for joy when he finds a cave because he loves being in places where so few have ventured. At the entrance he keeps taking photos with his cell phone to show off his new adventure later. Coming to a stop on a rock a few meters from the entrance, he sees the icy cave's glittering view. He says, "Incredibly beautiful!" stretching his hand out to touch the icy wall. Suddenly, his footing gives way and he slides down into the darkness. He looks up and sees a crack of light about 20 meters above him. 'Phone for help,' he thinks. But he realizes there's no service this far underground. He tries to move upward but he can't. He calls out, "Is anyone there?" There's no answer.

① delighted → grateful
② disappointed → ashamed
③ indifferent → regretful
④ bored → frightened
⑤ excited → desperate

11 ⓘ 50초

★☆☆ 2019년 11월 19번

다음 글에 드러난 'I'의 심경 변화로 가장 적절한 것은?

One night, my family was having a party with a couple from another city who had two daughters. The girls were just a few years older than I, and I played lots of fun games together with them. The father of the family had an amusing, jolly, witty character, and I had a memorable night full of laughter and joy. While we laughed, joked, and had our dinner, the TV suddenly broadcast an air attack, and a screeching siren started to scream, announcing the "red" situation. We all stopped dinner, and we squeezed into the basement. The siren kept screaming and the roar of planes was heard in the sky. The terror of war was overwhelming. Shivering with fear, I murmured a panicked prayer that this desperate situation would end quickly.

① indifferent → satisfied ② relaxed → envious
③ frustrated → relieved ④ excited → bored
⑤ pleased → terrified

정답과 해설 : 09 016 10 017 11 018

12 ⓒ 50초

★☆☆ 2022년 9월 19번

다음 글에 드러난 'I'의 심경 변화로 가장 적절한 것은?

There was no choice next morning but to turn in my private reminiscence of Belleville. Two days passed before Mr. Fleagle returned the graded papers, and he returned everyone's but mine. I was anxiously expecting for a command to report to Mr. Fleagle immediately after school for discipline when I saw him lift my paper from his desk and rap for the class's attention. "Now, boys," he said, "I want to read you an essay. This is titled 'The Art of Eating Spaghetti.'" And he started to read. My words! He was reading *my words* out loud to the entire class. What's more, the entire class was listening attentively. Then somebody laughed, then the entire class was laughing, and not in contempt and ridicule, but with openhearted enjoyment. I did my best to avoid showing pleasure, but what I was feeling was pure ecstasy at this startling demonstration that my words had the power to make people laugh.

♦ reminiscence: 회상

① relieved → scared
② nervous → delighted
③ bored → confident
④ satisfied → depressed
⑤ confused → ashamed

13 ⓒ 50초

★☆☆ 2023년 3월 19번

다음 글에 드러난 Isabel의 심경 변화로 가장 적절한 것은?

On opening day, Isabel arrives at the cafe very early with nervous anticipation. She looks around the cafe, but she can't shake off the feeling that something is missing. As she sets out cups, spoons, and plates, Isabel's doubts grow. She looks around, trying to imagine what else she could do to make the cafe perfect, but nothing comes to mind. Then, in a sudden burst of inspiration, Isabel grabs her paintbrush and transforms the blank walls into landscapes, adding flowers and trees. As she paints, her doubts begin to fade. Looking at her handiwork, which is beautifully done, she is certain that the cafe will be a success. 'Now, success is not exactly guaranteed,' she thinks to herself, 'but I'll definitely get there.'

① calm → surprised
② doubtful → confident
③ envious → delighted
④ grateful → frightened
⑤ indifferent → uneasy

정답과 해설 : 12 018 13 019

14 ⓒ 60초

★★☆ 2018년 6월 20번

다음 글에 드러난 Masami의 심경 변화로 가장 적절한 것은?

While backpacking through Costa Rica, Masami found herself in a bad situation. She had lost all of her belongings, and had only $5 in cash. To make matters worse, because of a recent tropical storm, all telephone and Internet services were down. She had no way to get money, so decided to go knocking door to door, explaining that she needed a place to stay until she could contact her family back in Japan to send her some money. Everybody told her they had no space or extra food and pointed her in the direction of the next house. It was already dark when she arrived at a small roadside restaurant. The owner of the restaurant heard her story and really empathized. Much to her delight, Masami was invited in. The owner gave her some food, and allowed her to stay there until she could contact her parents.

① desperate → relieved
② gloomy → irritated
③ jealous → delighted
④ excited → worried
⑤ indifferent → curious

15 ⓒ 60초

★★☆ 2019년 3월 19번

다음 글에 드러난 'I'의 심경 변화로 가장 적절한 것은?

Something inside told me that by now someone had discovered my escape. It chilled me greatly to think that they would capture me and take me back to that awful place. So, I decided to walk only at night until I was far from the town. After three nights' walking, I felt sure that they had stopped chasing me. I found a deserted cottage and walked into it. Tired, I lay down on the floor and fell asleep. I awoke to the sound of a far away church clock, softly ringing seven times and noticed that the sun was slowly rising. As I stepped outside, my heart began to pound with anticipation and longing. The thought that I could meet Evelyn soon lightened my walk.

① moved → nervous
② fearful → hopeful
③ lonely → annoyed
④ sympathetic → amused
⑤ sorrowful → frightened

정답과 해설 : 14 020 15 020

16 ⓒ 50초

★☆☆ 2023년 11월 19번

다음 글에 드러난 Chaske의 심경 변화로 가장 적절한 것은?

Chaske, a Cherokee boy, was sitting on a tree stump. As a rite of passage for youths in his tribe, Chaske had to survive one night in the forest wearing a blindfold, not knowing he was observed by his father. After the sunset, Chaske could hear all kinds of noises. The wind blew the grass and shook his stump. A sense of dread swept through his body. *What if wild beasts are looking at me? I can't stand this!* Just as he was about to take off the blindfold to run away, a voice came in from somewhere. "I'm here around you. Don't give up, and complete your mission." It was his father's voice. *He has been watching me from nearby!* With just the presence of his father, the boy regained stability. What panicked him awfully a moment ago vanished into thin air.

① nervous → doubtful
② horrified → relieved
③ disappointed → curious
④ ashamed → frightened
⑤ bored → delighted

17 ⓒ 50초

★☆☆ 2024년 3월 19번

다음 글에 드러난 Sarah의 심경 변화로 가장 적절한 것은?

Sarah, a young artist with a love for painting, entered a local art contest. As she looked at the amazing artworks made by others, her confidence dropped. She quietly thought, 'I might not win an award.' The moment of judgment arrived, and the judges began announcing winners one by one. It wasn't until the end that she heard her name. The head of the judges said, "Congratulations, Sarah Parker! You won first prize. We loved the uniqueness of your work." Sarah was overcome with joy, and she couldn't stop smiling. This experience meant more than just winning; it confirmed her identity as an artist.

① hopeful → regretful
② relieved → grateful
③ excited → disappointed
④ depressed → frightened
⑤ discouraged → delighted

정답과 해설 : 16 021 17 022

18 ⓒ 50초

★☆☆
2024년 6월 19번

다음 글에 드러난 Emma의 심경 변화로 가장 적절한 것은?

It was the championship race. Emma was the final runner on her relay team. She anxiously waited in her spot for her teammate to pass her the baton. Emma wasn't sure she could perform her role without making a mistake. Her hands shook as she thought, "What if I drop the baton?" She felt her heart rate increasing as her teammate approached. But as she started running, she received the baton smoothly. In the final 10 meters, she passed two other runners and crossed the finish line in first place! She raised her hands in the air, and a huge smile came across her face. As her teammates hugged her, she shouted, "We did it!" All of her hard training had been worth it.

① nervous → excited
② doubtful → regretful
③ confident → upset
④ hopeful → disappointed
⑤ indifferent → amused

19 ⓒ 50초

★☆☆
2024년 9월 19번

다음 글에 드러난 'I'의 심경 변화로 가장 적절한 것은?

The passport control line was short and the inspectors looked relaxed; except the inspector at my window. He seemed to want to model the seriousness of the task at hand for the other inspectors. Maybe that's why I felt uneasy when he studied my passport more carefully than I expected. "You were here in September," he said. "Why are you back so soon?" "I came in September to prepare to return this month," I replied with a trembling voice, considering if I missed any Italian regulations. "For how long?" he asked. "One month, this time," I answered truthfully. I knew it was not against the rules to stay in Italy for three months. "Enjoy your stay," he finally said, as he stamped my passport. Whew! As I walked away, the burden I had carried, even though I did nothing wrong, vanished into the air. My shoulders, once weighed down, now stretched out with comfort.

① angry → ashamed
② nervous → relieved
③ bored → grateful
④ curious → frightened
⑤ hopeful → disappointed

정답과 해설 : 18 022 19 023

유형 TIP

03. 필자의 주장

필자가 강력하게 전달하고자 하는 중심 내용과 개인적인 견해를 파악해서 답을 찾아야 함.
선택지가 한글로 제시되는 유형임.

유형 TIP 25BR2T_CH03 대표 예제 25BR2E_CH03

유형 공략법

1) 문장의 형태와 지문 속의 단서에 주목한다.

주로 명령문이나 비교 구문, 강조 구문, 연결사, 당위의 표현, '중요한, 필수적인'의 의미를 나타내는 형용사 등으로 주장임을 나타냄.

2) 선택지의 내용에 유의한다.

합리적이고 일반적인 선택지, 지문과 부분적으로 일치하는 선택지는 오답인 경우가 많으므로 주의해야 함.
선택지가 지문의 중심 내용 및 전체 내용을 잘 반영해야 정답이 될 수 있음.

필수 암기 어휘와 표현

1) '당위/필요/제안'을 나타내는 표현

당위	should, must, have to V, ought to V, insist, obligatory, mandatory, cannot ~ without, may well, make sure
필요	need to V, it is necessary, it is essential, necessity
제안	it is time to V/for, suggest, would like, had better, important, desirable, might as well

2) '중요한, 필수적인'의 의미를 지닌 형용사

important, significant, crucial, critical, vital, key, essential, necessary, primary

3) 연결사 및 중요 표현

역접/대조	however, but, (and) yet, instead (of), rather, on the other hand, by[in] contrast, in contrast to, conversely, on the contrary, whereas, while, meanwhile, at the same time
양보	though, although, even if[though], still, nevertheless, nonetheless, even so, notwithstanding, despite (that), in spite of, having said that, that (being) said, granting that, admitting that, after all
요약	in short, shortly, in brief, briefly, in sum, to summarize, to sum up, to put it simply, in a word, on the whole, overall
재진술	that is (to say), in other words, namely, to put it another way, stated another way, i.e.
강조	indeed, above all, especially, of course, in particular, in fact, in effect, in reality, in truth, truly, actually, as a matter of fact, most important, more importantly, the thing is, it is clear that, no doubt, never, not at all, in the first place, most of all, certainly, (for) sure, surely, apparently, obviously
조건	if, once, given (that), unless, otherwise, if not, or else, in case of[that], in the event of[that], as[so] long as, suppose (that), supposing (that), provided (that), providing (that)

필자의 주장 대표 예제 - 2024학년도 수능 20번

다음 글에서 필자가 주장하는 바로 가장 적절한 것은?

(1) Values alone do not create and build culture. (2) Living your values only some of the time does not contribute to the creation and maintenance of culture. (3) Changing values into behaviors is only half the battle. (4) Certainly, this is a step in the right direction, but those behaviors must then be shared and distributed widely throughout the organization, along with a clear and concise description of what is expected. (5) It is not enough to simply talk about it. (6) It is critical to have a visual representation of the specific behaviors that leaders and all people managers can use to coach their people. (7) Just like a sports team has a playbook with specific plays designed to help them perform well and win, your company should have a playbook with the key shifts needed to transform your culture into action and turn your values into winning behaviors.

① 조직 문화 혁신을 위해서 모든 구성원이 공유할 핵심 가치를 정립해야 한다.
② 조직 구성원의 행동을 변화시키려면 지도자는 명확한 가치관을 가져야 한다.
③ 조직 내 문화가 공유되기 위해서 구성원의 자발적 행동이 뒷받침되어야 한다.
④ 조직의 핵심 가치 실현을 위해 구성원 간의 지속적인 의사소통이 필수적이다.
✔ 조직의 문화 형성에는 가치를 반영한 행동의 공유를 위한 명시적 지침이 필요하다. 문장(6)

STEP 1 문장의 형태와 지문 속의 단서에 주목한다.

→ '~을 해야한다' 또는 '~이 중요하다'라는 당위성을 표현하는 단서에 주목해야 하는데, 문장 (6)에서 시각적으로 특정한 행동을 표현하는 것이 중요하다고 언급함. 이는 ⑤의 '명시적 지침'에 해당함.

→ 문장 (7)에서 회사가 플레이 북을 가져야 한다는 말을 통해 주장의 단서를 확인할 수 있으므로 정답은 ⑤임.

STEP 2 선택지의 내용에 유의한다.

①: 조직의 가치를 정립하는 것만으로는 충분하지 않으므로 적절하지 않음.
②: 지도자가 명확한 가치관을 가져야 한다는 것보다도 그 가치관을 표현하는 것이 중요하다고 했으므로 적절하지 않음.
③: 조직 내 문화 공유를 위한 구성원의 자발적 행동은 언급되지 않음.
④: 조직의 핵심 가치 실현을 위한 구성원 간의 의사소통의 중요성은 언급되지 않음.

전문 해석

(1) 가치만으로는 문화를 만들거나 형성할 수 없다. (2) 가끔씩만 가치에 따라 생활하는 것은 문화의 형성과 유지에 기여하지 않는다. (3) 가치를 행동으로 바꾸는 것은 겨우 고비를 넘긴 것이다. (4) 분명히, 이것은 올바른 방향으로 나아가는 한 걸음이지만, 그 다음에 그러한 행동은 기대되는 것에 대한 명확하고 간결한 기술과 함께 조직 전체로 널리 공유되고 퍼져야 한다. (5) 단지 그것(기대되는 것)에 대해 이야기하는 것은 충분하지 않다. (6) 지도자와 모든 인사 담당자들이 자신들의 사람들(조직원들)을 지도하기 위해서 사용할 수 있는 특정 행동에 대한 시각적 표현을 가지는 것(특정 행동을 시각적으로 표현하는 것)이 대단히 중요하다. (7) 스포츠 팀이 그들이 잘 수행하고 이기는 것을 돕도록 고안된 구체적인 플레이를 포함한 플레이 북을 갖고 있는 것처럼, 여러분의 회사는 여러분의 문화를 행동으로 변화시키고 여러분의 가치를 이기는 행동으로 바꾸는 데 필요한 핵심적인 변화를 포함한 플레이 북을 가져야 한다.

중요 어휘

- □ contribute to N ~에 기여하다
- □ maintenance 명 유지
- □ be half the battle 고비를 넘기다
- □ distribute 동 퍼뜨리다, 나누어 주다, 유통하다
- □ concise 형 간결한, 축약된
- □ description 명 기술, 서술, 묘사
- □ representation 명 표현, 재현, 묘사
- □ people manager 인사 담당자
- □ playbook 명 플레이 북(팀의 공수 작전을 그림과 함께 기록한 책)
- □ key 형 핵심적인, 가장 중요한
- □ shift 명 변화, 교대 근무 / 동 바꾸다
- □ transform A into B A를 B로 변화시키다[바꾸어 놓다]

자세한 해설지 QR→
자세한해설-CH03

03 필자의 주장

동영상 강의

25BR2_CH03

01 ⓛ 50초

★☆☆
2021년 9월 20번

다음 글에서 필자가 주장하는 바로 가장 적절한 것은?

Without guidance from their teacher, students will not embark on a journey of personal development that recognizes the value of cooperation. Left to their own devices, they will instinctively become increasingly competitive with each other. They will compare scores, reports, and feedback within the classroom environment — just as they do in the sporting arena. We don't need to teach our students about winners and losers. The playground and the media do that for them. However, we do need to teach them that there is more to life than winning and about the skills they need for successful cooperation. A group working together successfully requires individuals with a multitude of social skills, as well as a high level of interpersonal awareness. While some students inherently bring a natural understanding of these skills with them, they are always in the minority. To bring cooperation between peers into your classroom, you need to teach these skills consciously and carefully, and nurture them continuously throughout the school years.

① 학생의 참여가 활발한 수업 방법을 개발해야 한다.
② 학생에게 성공적인 협동을 위한 기술을 가르쳐야 한다.
③ 학생의 의견을 존중하는 학교 분위기를 조성해야 한다.
④ 학생의 전인적 발달을 위해 체육활동을 강화해야 한다.
⑤ 정보를 올바르게 선별하도록 미디어 교육을 실시해야 한다.

02 ⓛ 50초

★☆☆
2022년 3월 20번

다음 글에서 필자가 주장하는 바로 가장 적절한 것은?

Though we are marching toward a more global society, various ethnic groups traditionally do things quite differently, and a fresh perspective is valuable in creating an open-minded child. Extensive multicultural experience makes kids more creative (measured by how many ideas they can come up with and by association skills) and allows them to capture unconventional ideas from other cultures to expand on their own ideas. As a parent, you should expose your children to other cultures as often as possible. If you can, travel with your child to other countries; live there if possible. If neither is possible, there are lots of things you can do at home, such as exploring local festivals, borrowing library books about other cultures, and cooking foods from different cultures at your house.

① 자녀가 전통문화를 자랑스럽게 여기게 해야 한다.
② 자녀가 주어진 문제를 깊이 있게 탐구하도록 이끌어야 한다.
③ 자녀가 다른 문화를 가능한 한 자주 접할 수 있게 해야 한다.
④ 창의성 발달을 위해 자녀의 실수에 대해 너그러워야 한다.
⑤ 경험한 것을 돌이켜 볼 시간을 자녀에게 주어야 한다.

정답과 해설 : 01 024 02 024

03 ⓒ 50초

★☆☆ 2022년 6월 20번

다음 글에서 필자가 주장하는 바로 가장 적절한 것은?

In the rush towards individual achievement and recognition, the majority of those who make it forget their humble beginnings. They often forget those who helped them on their way up. If you forget where you came from, if you neglect those who were there for you when things were tough and slow, then your success is valueless. No one can make it up there without the help of others. There are parents, friends, advisers, and coaches that help. You need to be grateful to all of those who helped you. Gratitude is the glue that keeps you connected to others. It is the bridge that keeps you connected with those who were there for you in the past and who are likely to be there in the end. Relationships and the way you treat others determine your real success.

① 원만한 인간관계를 위하여 사고의 유연성을 길러야 한다.
② 성공에 도움을 준 사람들에게 감사하는 마음을 가져야 한다.
③ 자신의 분야에서 성공하기 위해서는 경험의 폭을 넓혀야 한다.
④ 원하는 직업을 갖기 위해서는 다른 사람의 조언을 경청해야 한다.
⑤ 타인의 시선을 의식하지 않고 부단히 새로운 일에 도전해야 한다.

04 ⓒ 50초

★☆☆ 2019년 11월 20번

다음 글에서 필자가 주장하는 바로 가장 적절한 것은?

Over the years, memory has been given a bad name. It has been associated with rote learning and cramming information into your brain. Educators have said that understanding is the key to learning, but how can you understand something if you can't remember it? We have all had this experience: we recognize and understand information but can't recall it when we need it. For example, how many jokes do you know? You've probably heard thousands, but you can only recall about four or five right now. There is a big difference between remembering your four jokes and recognizing or understanding thousands. Understanding doesn't create use: only when you can instantly recall what you understand, and practice using your remembered understanding, do you achieve mastery. Memory means storing what you have learned; otherwise, why would we bother learning in the first place?

① 창의력 신장을 학습 활동의 목표로 삼아야 한다.
② 배운 것을 활용하기 위해서는 내용을 기억해야 한다.
③ 기억력 저하를 예방하기 위해 자신의 일상을 기록해야 한다.
④ 자연스러운 분위기를 만들 수 있는 농담을 알고 있어야 한다.
⑤ 학습 의욕을 유지하기 위해서는 실천 가능한 계획을 세워야 한다.

정답과 해설 : 03 025 04 026

05 ⏱ 50초

★☆☆ 2022년 9월 20번

다음 글에서 필자가 주장하는 바로 가장 적절한 것은?

We usually take time out only when we really need to switch off, and when this happens we are often overtired, sick, and in need of recuperation. Me time is complicated by negative associations with escapism, guilt, and regret as well as overwhelm, stress, and fatigue. All these negative connotations mean we tend to steer clear of it. Well, I am about to change your perception of the importance of me time, to persuade you that you should view it as vital for your health and wellbeing. Take this as permission to set aside some time for yourself! Our need for time in which to do what we choose is increasingly urgent in an overconnected, overwhelmed, and overstimulated world.

◆ recuperation: 회복

① 나를 위한 시간의 중요성을 인식해야 한다.
② 자신의 잘못을 성찰하는 자세를 가져야 한다.
③ 어려운 일이라고 해서 처음부터 회피해서는 안 된다.
④ 사회의 건강과 행복을 위하여 타인과 연대해야 한다.
⑤ 급변하는 사회에서 가치 판단을 신속하게 할 수 있어야 한다.

06 ⏱ 50초

★☆☆ 2023년 6월 20번

다음 글에서 필자가 주장하는 바로 가장 적절한 것은?

The introduction of new technologies clearly has both positive and negative impacts for sustainable development. Good management of technological resources needs to take them fully into account. Technological developments in sectors such as nuclear energy and agriculture provide examples of how not only environmental benefits but also risks to the environment or human health can accompany technological advances. New technologies have profound social impacts as well. Since the industrial revolution, technological advances have changed the nature of skills needed in workplaces, creating certain types of jobs and destroying others, with impacts on employment patterns. New technologies need to be assessed for their full potential impacts, both positive and negative.

① 기술 혁신을 저해하는 과도한 법률적 규제를 완화해야 한다.
② 기술의 도입으로 인한 잠재적인 영향들을 충분히 고려해야 한다.
③ 혁신적 농업 기술을 적용할 때는 환경적인 측면을 검토해야 한다.
④ 기술 진보가 가져온 일자리 위협에 대한 대비책을 마련해야 한다.
⑤ 기술 발전을 위해서는 혁신적 사고와 창의성이 뒷받침되어야 한다.

정답과 해설 : 05 026 06 027

07 ⓒ 50초

★☆☆ 2020년 11월 20번

다음 글에서 필자가 주장하는 바로 가장 적절한 것은?

When trying to convince someone to change their mind, most people try to lay out a logical argument, or make a passionate plea as to why their view is right and the other person's opinion is wrong. But when you think about it, you'll realize that this doesn't often work. As soon as someone figures out that you are on a mission to change their mind, the metaphorical shutters go down. You'll have better luck if you ask well-chosen, open-ended questions that let someone challenge their own assumptions. We tend to approve of an idea if we thought of it first — or at least, if we *think* we thought of it first. Therefore, encouraging someone to question their own worldview will often yield better results than trying to force them into accepting your opinion as fact. Ask someone well-chosen questions to look at their own views from another angle, and this might trigger fresh insights.

① 타인의 신뢰를 얻기 위해서는 일관된 행동을 보여 주어라.
② 협상을 잘하기 위해 질문에 담긴 상대방의 의도를 파악하라.
③ 논쟁을 잘하려면 자신의 가치관에서 벗어나려는 시도를 하라.
④ 원만한 대인 관계를 유지하려면 상대를 배려하는 태도를 갖춰라.
⑤ 설득하고자 할 때 상대방이 스스로 관점을 돌아보게 하는 질문을 하라.

08 ⓒ 50초

★☆☆ 2021년 11월 20번

다음 글에서 필자가 주장하는 바로 가장 적절한 것은?

In 2003, British Airways made an announcement that they would no longer be able to operate the London to New York Concorde flight twice a day because it was starting to prove uneconomical. Well, the sales for the flight on this route increased the very next day. There was nothing that changed about the route or the service offered by the airlines. Merely because it became a scarce resource, the demand for it increased. If you are interested in persuading people, then the principle of scarcity can be effectively used. If you are a salesperson trying to increase the sales of a certain product, then you must not merely point out the benefits the customer can derive from the said product, but also point out its uniqueness and what they will miss out on if they don't purchase the product soon. In selling, you should keep in mind that the more limited something is, the more desirable it becomes.

① 상품 판매 시 실현 가능한 판매 목표를 설정해야 한다.
② 판매를 촉진하기 위해서는 가격 경쟁력을 갖추어야 한다.
③ 효과적인 판매를 위해서는 상품의 희소성을 강조해야 한다.
④ 고객의 신뢰를 얻기 위해서는 일관된 태도를 유지해야 한다.
⑤ 고객의 특성에 맞춰 다양한 판매 전략을 수립하고 적용해야 한다.

정답과 해설 : 07 028 08 028

09 ⓒ 50초

★☆☆ 2023년 9월 20번

다음 글에서 필자가 주장하는 바로 가장 적절한 것은?

Managers frequently try to play psychologist, to "figure out" why an employee has acted in a certain way. Empathizing with employees in order to understand their point of view can be very helpful. However, when dealing with a problem area, in particular, remember that it is not the person who is bad, but the actions exhibited on the job. Avoid making suggestions to employees about personal traits they should change; instead suggest more acceptable ways of performing. For example, instead of focusing on a person's "unreliability," a manager might focus on the fact that the employee "has been late to work seven times this month." It is difficult for employees to change who they are; it is usually much easier for them to change how they act.

① 직원의 개인적 성향을 고려하여 업무를 배정하라.
② 업무 효율성 향상을 위해 직원의 자율성을 존중하라.
③ 조직의 안정을 위해 직원의 심리 상태를 수시로 확인하라.
④ 직원의 업무상 고충을 이해하기 위해 직원과 적극적으로 소통하라.
⑤ 문제를 보이는 직원에게 인격적 특성보다는 행동 방식에 대해 제안하라.

10 ⓒ 50초

★☆☆ 2023년 3월 20번

다음 글에서 필자가 주장하는 바로 가장 적절한 것은?

The more people have to do unwanted things the more chances are that they create unpleasant environment for themselves and others. If you hate the thing you do but have to do it nonetheless, you have choice between hating the thing and accepting that it needs to be done. Either way you will do it. Doing it from place of hatred will develop hatred towards the self and others around you; doing it from the place of acceptance will create compassion towards the self and allow for opportunities to find a more suitable way of accomplishing the task. If you decide to accept the fact that your task has to be done, start from recognising that your situation is a gift from life; this will help you to see it as a lesson in acceptance.

① 창의력을 기르려면 익숙한 환경에서 벗어나야 한다.
② 상대방의 무리한 요구는 최대한 분명하게 거절해야 한다.
③ 주어진 과업을 정확하게 파악한 후에 일을 시작해야 한다.
④ 효율적으로 일을 처리하기 위해 좋아하는 일부터 해야 한다.
⑤ 원치 않는 일을 해야만 할 때 수용적인 태도를 갖춰야 한다.

정답과 해설 : 09 029 10 030

11 ⓒ 60초

★★☆ 2017년 3월 23번

다음 글에서 필자가 주장하는 바로 가장 적절한 것은?

Children sometimes see and say things to please adults; teachers must realize this and the power it implies. Teachers who prefer that children see beauty as they themselves do are not encouraging a sense of aesthetics in children. They are fostering uniformity and obedience. Only children who choose and evaluate for themselves can truly develop their own aesthetic taste. Just as becoming literate is a basic goal of education, one of the key goals of all creative early childhood programs is to help young children develop the ability to speak freely about their own attitudes, feelings, and ideas about art. Each child has a right to a personal choice of beauty, joy, and wonder. Aesthetic development takes place in secure settings free of competition and adult judgment.

◆ aesthetics: 미학(美學)

① 아동의 정서 발달을 위해 미술 교육 시간을 늘려야 한다.
② 아동이 스스로 미적 감각을 기를 수 있게 해 주어야 한다.
③ 아동 미술 교육은 다른 과목과 통합적으로 실시해야 한다.
④ 아동의 창의성을 평가할 때 미적인 감각도 포함해야 한다.
⑤ 아동 미술 교육은 감상보다 창작에 더 비중을 두어야 한다.

12 ⓒ 60초

★★☆ 2018년 9월 21번

다음 글에서 필자가 주장하는 바로 가장 적절한 것은?

What we need in education is not measurement, accountability, or standards. While these can be useful tools for improvement, they should hardly occupy center stage. Our focus should instead be on making sure we are giving our youth an education that is going to arm them to save humanity. We are faced with unprecedented perils, and these perils are multiplying and pushing at our collective gates. We should be bolstering curriculum that helps young people mature into ethical adults who feel a responsibility to the global community. Without this sense of responsibility we have seen that many talented individuals give in to their greed and pride, and this destroys economies, ecosystems, and entire species. While we certainly should not abandon efforts to develop standards in different content areas, and also strengthen the STEM subjects, we need to take seriously our need for an education centered on global responsibility. If we don't, we risk extinction.

◆ bolster: 강화하다

① 융합 교육 강화를 위한 정책을 조속히 수립해야 한다.
② 학생 자치활동을 통해 민주 시민 의식을 함양해야 한다.
③ 교육은 미래 산업에 대비한 인재 육성에 앞장서야 한다.
④ 급변하는 미래에 대비하기 위해 교육과정을 다양화해야 한다.
⑤ 교육은 지구 공동체에 책임감을 가진 도덕적 인간을 길러내야 한다.

정답과 해설 : 11 030 12 031

13 ⓒ 60초

★★☆ 2018년 11월 20번

다음 글에서 필자가 주장하는 바로 가장 적절한 것은?

Breaks are necessary to revive your energy levels and recharge your mental stamina, but they shouldn't be taken carelessly. If you've planned your schedule effectively, you should already have scheduled breaks at appropriate times throughout the day, so any other breaks in the midst of ongoing work hours are unwarranted. While scheduled breaks keep you on track by being strategic, re-energizing methods of self-reinforcement, unscheduled breaks derail you from your goal, as they offer you opportunities to procrastinate by making you feel as if you've got "free time." Taking unscheduled breaks is a sure-fire way to fall into the procrastination trap. You may rationalize that you're only getting a cup of coffee to keep yourself alert, but in reality, you're just trying to avoid having to work on a task at your desk. So to prevent procrastination, commit to having no random breaks instead.

♦ derail: 벗어나게 하다 ♦♦ procrastinate: 미루다

① 적절한 휴식을 통해 업무 스트레스로부터 벗어나야 한다.
② 효율적인 업무 처리를 위해 과업을 미루는 습관을 버려야 한다.
③ 능력에 맞게 업무를 배분함으로써 노동 생산성을 높여야 한다.
④ 일의 지연을 막으려면 계획되지 않은 휴식을 취하지 말아야 한다.
⑤ 일을 처리하는 속도를 높이려면 쾌적한 업무 환경을 조성해야 한다.

14 ⓒ 60초

★★☆ 2021년 3월 20번

다음 글에서 필자가 주장하는 바로 가장 적절한 것은?

No matter what your situation, whether you are an insider or an outsider, you need to become the voice that challenges yesterday's answers. Think about the characteristics that make outsiders valuable to an organization. They are the people who have the perspective to see problems that the insiders are too close to really notice. They are the ones who have the freedom to point out these problems and criticize them without risking their job or their career. Part of adopting an outsider mentality is forcing yourself to look around your organization with this disassociated, less emotional perspective. If you didn't know your coworkers and feel bonded to them by your shared experiences, what would you think of them? You may not have the job security or confidence to speak your mind to management, but you can make these "outsider" assessments of your organization on your own and use what you determine to advance your career.

① 조직 내의 의사소통이 원활한지 수시로 살피라.
② 외부자의 관점으로 자기 조직을 비판적으로 바라보라.
③ 관심사의 공유를 통해 직장 동료와의 관계를 개선하라.
④ 과거의 성공에 도취되어 자기 계발을 소홀히 하지 말라.
⑤ 동료의 실수를 비판하기보다는 먼저 이해하려고 노력하라.

정답과 해설 : 13 032 14 032

15 ⓒ 60초

★★☆ 2019년 3월 20번

다음 글에서 필자가 주장하는 바로 가장 적절한 것은?

I am sure you have heard something like, "You can do anything you want, if you just persist long and hard enough." Perhaps you have even made a similar assertion to motivate someone to try harder. Of course, words like these sound good, but surely they cannot be true. Few of us can become the professional athlete, entertainer, or movie star we would like to be. Environmental, physical, and psychological factors limit our potential and narrow the range of things we can do with our lives. "Trying harder" cannot substitute for talent, equipment, and method, but this should not lead to despair. Rather, we should attempt to become the best we can be within our limitations. We try to find our niche. By the time we reach employment age, there is a finite range of jobs we can perform effectively.

♦ assertion: 주장, 단언 ♦♦ niche: 적소(適所)

① 수입보다는 적성을 고려해 직업을 선택해야 한다.
② 성공하려면 다양한 분야에서 경험을 쌓아야 한다.
③ 장래의 모습을 그리며 인생의 계획을 세워야 한다.
④ 자신의 재능과 역량을 스스로 제한해서는 안 된다.
⑤ 자신의 한계 내에서 최고가 되려고 시도해야 한다.

16 ⓒ 70초

★★★ 2022년 11월 20번

다음 글에서 필자가 주장하는 바로 가장 적절한 것은?

Clarity in an organization keeps everyone working in one accord and energizes key leadership components like trust and transparency. No matter who or what is being assessed in your organization, what they are being assessed on must be clear and the people must be aware of it. If individuals in your organization are assessed without knowing what they are being assessed on, it can cause mistrust and move your organization away from clarity. For your organization to be productive, cohesive, and successful, trust is essential. Failure to have trust in your organization will have a negative effect on the results of any assessment. It will also significantly hinder the growth of your organization. To conduct accurate assessments, trust is a must — which comes through clarity. In turn, assessments help you see clearer, which then empowers your organization to reach optimal success.

① 조직이 구성원에게 제공하는 보상은 즉각적이어야 한다.
② 조직의 발전을 위해 구성원은 동료의 능력을 신뢰해야 한다.
③ 조직 내 구성원의 능력에 맞는 명확한 목표를 설정해야 한다.
④ 조직의 신뢰 형성을 위해 구성원에 대한 평가 요소가 명확해야 한다.
⑤ 구성원의 의견 수용을 위해 신뢰에 기반한 조직 문화가 구축되어야 한다.

정답과 해설 : 15 033 16 034

17 ⓒ 50초

★☆☆ 2023년 11월 20번

다음 글에서 필자가 주장하는 바로 가장 적절한 것은?

Agriculture includes a range of activities such as planting, harvesting, fertilizing, pest management, raising animals, and distributing food and agricultural products. It is one of the oldest and most essential human activities, dating back thousands of years, and has played a critical role in the development of human civilizations, allowing people to create stable food supplies and settle in one place. Today, agriculture remains a vital industry that feeds the world's population, supports rural communities, and provides raw materials for other industries. However, agriculture faces numerous challenges such as climate change, water scarcity, soil degradation, and biodiversity loss. As the world's population continues to grow, it is essential to find sustainable solutions to address the challenges facing agriculture and ensure the continued production of food and other agricultural products.

① 토양의 질을 개선하기 위해 친환경 농법의 연구와 개발이 필요하다.
② 세계 인구의 증가에 대응하기 위해 농산물 품종의 다양화가 필요하다.
③ 기후 변화에 대한 지속 가능한 대책은 경제적 관점에서 고려되어야 한다.
④ 다른 산업 분야와의 공동 연구를 통해 상품성을 가진 농작물을 개발해야 한다.
⑤ 농업이 직면한 문제 해결 및 식량과 농산물의 지속적 생산을 위한 방안이 필요하다.

18 ⓒ 50초

★☆☆ 2024년 3월 20번

다음 글에서 필자가 주장하는 바로 가장 적절한 것은?

Too many times people, especially in today's generation, expect things to just happen overnight. When we have these false expectations, it tends to discourage us from continuing to move forward. Because this is a high tech society, everything we want has to be within the parameters of our comfort and convenience. If it doesn't happen fast enough, we're tempted to lose interest. So many people don't want to take the time it requires to be successful. Success is not a matter of mere desire; you should develop patience in order to achieve it. Have you fallen prey to impatience? Great things take time to build.

♦ parameter: 매개 변수, 제한

① 성공하기 위해서는 인내심을 길러야 한다.
② 안락함을 추구하기보다 한계에 도전해야 한다.
③ 사회 변화의 속도에 맞춰 빠르게 대응해야 한다.
④ 기회를 기다리기보다 능동적으로 행동해야 한다.
⑤ 흥미를 잃지 않으려면 자신이 좋아하는 일을 해야 한다.

정답과 해설 : 17 035 18 035

19 ⓛ 50초

★☆☆
2024년 6월 20번

다음 글에서 필자가 주장하는 바로 가장 적절한 것은?

Most people resist the idea of a true self-estimate, probably because they fear it might mean downgrading some of their beliefs about who they are and what they're capable of. As Goethe's maxim goes, it is a great failing "to see yourself as more than you are." How could you really be considered self-aware if you refuse to consider your weaknesses? Don't fear self-assessment because you're worried you might have to admit some things about yourself. The second half of Goethe's maxim is important too. He states that it is equally damaging to "value yourself at less than your true worth." We underestimate our capabilities just as much and just as dangerously as we overestimate other abilities. Cultivate the ability to judge yourself accurately and honestly. Look inward to discern what you're capable of and what it will take to unlock that potential.

♦ maxim: 격언

① 주관적 기준으로 타인을 평가하는 것을 피해야 한다.
② 정확하고 정직하게 자신을 평가하는 능력을 길러야 한다.
③ 자신이 가진 잠재력을 믿고 다양한 분야에 도전해야 한다.
④ 다른 사람과 비교하기보다는 자신의 성장에 주목해야 한다.
⑤ 문제를 해결하기 위해 근본 원인을 정확하게 분석해야 한다.

20 ⓛ 50초

★☆☆
2024년 9월 20번

다음 글에서 필자가 주장하는 바로 가장 적절한 것은?

Merely convincing your children that worry is senseless and that they would be more content if they didn't worry isn't going to stop them from worrying. For some reason, young people seem to believe that worry is a fact of life over which they have little or no control. Consequently, they don't even try to stop. Therefore, you need to convince them that worry, like guilt and fear, is nothing more than an emotion, and like all emotions, is subject to the power of the will. Tell them that they can eliminate worry from their lives by simply refusing to attend to it. Explain to them that if they refuse to act worried regardless of how they feel, they will eventually stop feeling worried and will begin to experience the contentment that accompanies a worry-free life.

① 아이가 죄책감과 책임감을 구분하도록 가르쳐야 한다.
② 아이가 스스로 불안의 원인을 찾도록 도와주어야 한다.
③ 아이의 감정에 공감하고 있음을 구체적으로 표현해야 한다.
④ 부모로서 느끼는 감정에 관해 아이와 솔직하게 대화해야 한다.
⑤ 아이에게 자기 의지로 걱정을 멈출 수 있음을 알려주어야 한다.

정답과 해설 : 19 036 20 036

유형TIP

04. 의미 추론

유형 TIP 대표 예제

25BR2T_CH04 25BR2E_CH04

제시되는 지문 자체가 어려운 편이고, 밑줄 친 부분에 주로 비유적인 표현이 사용되기 때문에 난이도가 높은 유형임.

유형 공략법

1) 지문의 주제와 전반적인 내용**을 파악한다.**
주제, 필자의 의도 등을 파악하면 밑줄 친 부분의 의미를 찾는 것이 수월해짐.

2) 밑줄 친 부분을 빈칸으로 바라보고 **빈칸에 들어가야 할 내용을** 주제와 연관**시켜 추론한다.**
밑줄 친 부분이 포함된 문장과 주제를 고려했을 때 밑줄 친 부분이 어떤 내용이어야 할지를 생각하는 것이 밑줄 친 부분의 비유적이고 함축적인 의미를 알아내려고 하는 것보다 수월함.

3) **지문의** 주제와 무관한 선택지는 과감히 제거**한다.**

4) **고른 정답을 밑줄 친 표현 자리에 넣었을 때,** 글의 흐름이 매끄러운지를 확인**한다.**

필수 암기 어휘와 표현

주제의 위치를 보여 주는 표현

의견/주장	I believe, I think, in my opinion, be aware of
중요성/필요성/당위성	need to V, must, have to V, should, important, necessary, essential
역접/대조	however, but, (and) yet, instead (of), rather, on the other hand, by[in] contrast, in contrast to, conversely, on the contrary, whereas, while, meanwhile, at the same time
양보	though, although, even if[though], still, nevertheless, nonetheless, even so, notwithstanding, despite (that), in spite of, having said that, that (being) said, granting that, admitting that
요약	in short, shortly, in brief, briefly, in sum, to summarize, to sum up, to put it simply, in a word, on the whole, overall
재진술	that is (to say), in other words, namely, to put it another way, stated another way, i.e.
강조	indeed, above all, especially, of course, in particular, in fact, in effect, in reality, in truth, truly, actually, as a matter of fact, most important, more importantly, the thing is, it is clear that, no doubt, never, not at all, in the first place, most of all, certainly, (for) sure, surely, apparently, obviously
조건	if, once, given (that), unless, otherwise, if not, or else, in case of[that], in the event of[that], as[so] long as, suppose (that), supposing (that), provided (that), providing (that)

의미 추론 대표 예제 - 2024학년도 수능 21번

밑줄 친 a nonstick frying pan이 다음 글에서 의미하는 바로 가장 적절한 것은? 3점

(1) How you focus your attention plays a critical role in how you deal with stress. (2) Scattered attention harms your ability to let go of stress, because even though your attention is scattered, it is narrowly focused, for you are able to fixate only on the stressful parts of your experience. (3) When your attentional spotlight is widened, you can more easily let go of stress. (4) You can put in perspective many more aspects of any situation and not get locked into one part that ties you down to superficial and anxiety-provoking levels of attention. (5) A narrow focus heightens the stress level of each experience, but a widened focus turns down the stress level because you're better able to put each situation into a broader perspective. (6) One anxiety-provoking detail is less important than the bigger picture. (7) It's like transforming yourself into a nonstick frying pan. (8) You can still fry an egg, but the egg won't stick to the pan.

* provoke: 유발시키다

① never being confronted with any stressful experiences in daily life
② broadening one's perspective to identify the cause of stress
③ rarely confining one's attention to positive aspects of an experience
④ having a larger view of an experience beyond its stressful aspects
⑤ taking stress into account as the source of developing a wide view

STEP 1 지문의 주제와 전반적인 내용을 파악한다.

→ 주의를 집중하는 방식이 스트레스에 대처하는 방식에 결정적인 역할을 한다는 것이 지문의 주제임.

STEP 2 밑줄 친 부분을 빈칸으로 바라보고 빈칸에 들어가야 할 내용을 주제와 연관시켜 추론한다.

→ 문장 (5)에서 더 넓어진 초점을 가질 때 더 넓은 관점을 통해 스트레스에 더 잘 대처할 수 있다고 했고, 이것이 곧 글의 주제와 연결되어 있음. 이를 바탕으로 밑줄 친 문장이 포함된 문장 (7)에서 자기 자신을 무엇으로 변화시키는지를 확인해야 함.

STEP 3 지문의 주제와 무관한 선택지는 과감히 제거한다.

①: 일상에서 스트레스가 많은 어떤 경험을 직면하지 않는다는 내용은 언급되지 않음.
②: 스트레스의 원인을 확인하기 위한 내용은 언급되지 않음.
③: 경험의 긍정적인 측면에만 주의를 국한시키는 내용은 글의 주제에서 벗어남.
⑤: 넓은 관점을 발전시키기 위해 스트레스를 그 원천으로 고려한다는 내용은 글의 주제에서 벗어남.

STEP 4 고른 정답을 밑줄 친 표현 자리에 넣었을 때, 글의 흐름이 매끄러운지를 확인한다.

④: 'stick(달라붙다)'이라는 표현은 문장 (4)에서 말한 '피상적이고 불안을 유발하는 주의 수준에 얽맨다'라는 의미임. 따라서 밑줄 친 표현처럼 'nonstick(달라붙지 않는다)'이라고 하면 스트레스를 넘어 더 큰 관점을 가지는 것을 의미하므로 ④가 적절함.

전문 해석

(1) 여러분이 주의를 집중하는 방식은 여러분이 스트레스에 대처하는 방식에 결정적인 역할을 한다. (2) 분산된 주의는 스트레스를 해소하는 여러분의 능력을 손상시키는데, 왜냐하면 여러분의 주의가 분산되어 있더라도 여러분은 여러분의 경험에서 스트레스가 많은 부분에만 집착할 수 있으므로 그것(여러분의 주의)은 좁게 집중되기 때문이다. (3) 여러분의 주의의 집중이 넓어질 때 여러분은 더 쉽게 스트레스를 해소할 수 있다. (4) 여러분은 어떤 상황이든 더 많은 측면을 균형 있게 볼 수 있고 피상적이고 불안을 유발하는 주의 수준에 여러분을 얽매는 한 부분에 갇히지 않을 수 있다. (5) 좁은 초점은 각 경험의 스트레스 수준을 높이지만 넓어진 초점은 여러분이 각 상황을 더 넓은 관점으로 더 잘 볼 수 있기 때문에 스트레스 수준을 낮춘다. (6) 불안을 유발하는 하나의 세부 사항은 더 큰 그림보다 덜 중요하다. (7) 그것은 여러분 스스로를 달라붙지 않는 프라이팬(어떤 경험에 대해 그것의 스트레스가 많은 측면을 넘어서는 더 큰 관점을 가지는 것)으로 변화시키는 것과 같다. (8) 여러분은 여전히 계란을 부칠 수 있지만 그 계란은 팬에 달라붙지 않을 것이다.

중요 어휘

□ critical 형 결정적인, 중요한
□ scattered 형 분산된, 흩어진
□ let go of ~을 해소하다[놓아주다]
□ narrowly 부 좁게, 가까스로
□ fixate on ~에 집착하다
□ attentional 형 주의의
□ widen 동 넓히다, 넓어지다
□ put A in perspective A를 균형 있게 보다
□ lock 동 가두다, 잠그다 / 명 자물쇠
□ tie A down to A를 ~에 얽매다[가두다]
□ superficial 형 피상적인, 표면상의
□ heighten 동 높이다, 증가시키다
□ turn down 낮추다, 거절하다
□ transform 동 변화시키다, 변형시키다
□ nonstick 형 달라붙지 않는
□ fry 동 부치다, 굽다, 튀기다
□ stick 동 달라붙다, 찌르다 / 명 막대기
□ identify 동 확인하다, 동일시하다
□ confine 동 국한시키다, 감금하다
□ take A into account A를 고려하다

자세한 해설지 QR→

자세한해설-CH04

DAY 02
04 의미 추론

동영상 강의

258R2_CH04

01 ⓒ 120초

★★☆ 2022년 3월 21번

밑줄 친 *Fish is Fish*-style assimilation이 다음 글에서 의미하는 바로 가장 적절한 것은? [3점]

Studies by Vosniado and Brewer illustrate *Fish is Fish*-style assimilation in the context of young children's thinking about the earth. They worked with children who believed that the earth is flat (because this fit their experiences) and attempted to help them understand that, in fact, it is spherical. When told it is round, children often pictured the earth as a pancake rather than as a sphere. If they were then told that it is round like a sphere, they interpreted the new information about a spherical earth within their flat-earth view by picturing a pancake-like flat surface inside or on top of a sphere, with humans standing on top of the pancake. The model of the earth that they had developed — and that helped them explain how they could stand or walk upon its surface — did not fit the model of a spherical earth. Like the story *Fish is Fish*, where a fish imagines everything on land to be fish-like, everything the children heard was incorporated into their preexisting views.

① established knowledge is questioned and criticized
② novel views are always favored over existing ones
③ all one's claims are evaluated based on others' opinions
④ new information is interpreted within one's own views
⑤ new theories are established through experiments

02 ⓒ 120초

★★☆ 2022년 9월 21번

밑줄 친 the innocent messenger who falls before a firing line이 다음 글에서 의미하는 바로 가장 적절한 것은? [3점]

Perhaps worse than attempting to get the bad news out of the way is attempting to soften it or simply not address it at all. This "Mum Effect" — a term coined by psychologists Sidney Rosen and Abraham Tesser in the early 1970s — happens because people want to avoid becoming the target of others' negative emotions. We all have the opportunity to lead change, yet it often requires of us the courage to deliver bad news to our superiors. We don't want to be the innocent messenger who falls before a firing line. When our survival instincts kick in, they can override our courage until the truth of a situation gets watered down. "The Mum Effect and the resulting filtering can have devastating effects in a steep hierarchy," writes Robert Sutton, an organizational psychologist. "What starts out as bad news becomes happier and happier as it travels up the ranks — because after each boss hears the news from his or her subordinates, he or she makes it sound a bit less bad before passing it up the chain."

① the employee being criticized for being silent
② the peacemaker who pursues non-violent solutions
③ the negotiator who looks for a mutual understanding
④ the subordinate who wants to get attention from the boss
⑤ the person who gets the blame for reporting unpleasant news

정답과 해설 : 01 038 02 038

03 ⓘ 120초

★★☆ 2019년 9월 21번

밑줄 친 the omnivore's paradox가 다음 글에서 의미하는 바로 가장 적절한 것은?

Humans are omnivorous, meaning that they can consume and digest a wide selection of plants and animals found in their surroundings. The primary advantage to this is that they can adapt to nearly all earthly environments. The disadvantage is that no single food provides the nutrition necessary for survival. Humans must be flexible enough to eat a variety of items sufficient for physical growth and maintenance, yet cautious enough not to randomly ingest foods that are physiologically harmful and, possibly, fatal. This dilemma, the need to experiment combined with the need for conservatism, is known as the omnivore's paradox. It results in two contradictory psychological impulses regarding diet. The first is an attraction to new foods; the second is a preference for familiar foods.

① irony of wanting but disliking nutritious food
② conflict between vegetarians and meat eaters
③ sacrificing quality of food for quantity of food
④ difficulty in judging whether something is edible
⑤ need to be both flexible and cautious about foods

04 ⓘ 120초

★★☆ 2022년 6월 21번

밑줄 친 'give away the house'가 다음 글에서 의미하는 바로 가장 적절한 것은? [3점]

For companies interested in delighting customers, exceptional value and service become part of the overall company culture. For example, year after year, Pazano ranks at or near the top of the hospitality industry in terms of customer satisfaction. The company's passion for satisfying customers is summed up in its credo, which promises that its luxury hotels will deliver a truly memorable experience. Although a customer-centered firm seeks to deliver high customer satisfaction relative to competitors, it does not attempt to *maximize* customer satisfaction. A company can always increase customer satisfaction by lowering its price or increasing its services. But this may result in lower profits. Thus, the purpose of marketing is to generate customer value profitably. This requires a very delicate balance: the marketer must continue to generate more customer value and satisfaction but not 'give away the house'.

◆ credo: 신조

① risk the company's profitability
② overlook a competitor's strengths
③ hurt the reputation of the company
④ generate more customer complaints
⑤ abandon customer-oriented marketing

정답과 해설 : 03 039 04 040

05 ⓘ 120초

★★☆ 2022년 11월 21번

밑줄 친 "eating my problems for breakfast"가 다음 글에서 의미하는 바로 가장 적절한 것은?

Research in the science of peak performance and motivation points to the fact that different tasks should ideally be matched to our energy level. For example, analytical tasks are best accomplished when our energy is high and we are free from distractions and able to focus. I generally wake up energized. Over the years, I have consistently stuck to the habit of "eating my problems for breakfast." I'm someone who tends to overthink different scenarios and conversations that haven't happened yet. When I procrastinate on talking with an unhappy client or dealing with an unpleasant email, I find I waste too much emotional energy during the day. It's as if the task hangs over my head, and I'll spend more time worrying about it, talking about it, and avoiding it, than it would actually take to just take care of it. So for me, it'll always be the first thing I get done. If you know you are not a morning person, be strategic about scheduling your difficult work later in the day.

♦ procrastinate: 미루다

① thinking of breakfast as fuel for the day
② trying to reflect on pleasant events from yesterday
③ handling the most demanding tasks while full of energy
④ spending the morning time improving my physical health
⑤ preparing at night to avoid decision making in the morning

06 ⓘ 120초

★★☆ 2023년 9월 21번

밑줄 친 forward "thinking"이 다음 글에서 의미하는 바로 가장 적절한 것은?

I suspect fungi are a little more forward "thinking" than their larger partners. Among trees, each species fights other species. Let's assume the beeches native to Central Europe could emerge victorious in most forests there. Would this really be an advantage? What would happen if a new pathogen came along that infected most of the beeches and killed them? In that case, wouldn't it be more advantageous if there were a certain number of other species around — oaks, maples, or firs — that would continue to grow and provide the shade needed for a new generation of young beeches to sprout and grow up? Diversity provides security for ancient forests. Because fungi are also very dependent on stable conditions, they support other species underground and protect them from complete collapse to ensure that one species of tree doesn't manage to dominate.

♦ fungus: 균류, 곰팡이류 (*pl.* fungi)
♦♦ beech: 너도밤나무 ♦♦♦ pathogen: 병원균

① responsible for the invasion of foreign species
② eager to support the dominance of one species
③ aware that diversity leads to the stability of forests
④ indifferent to helping forests regenerate after collapse
⑤ careful that their territories are not occupied by other species

정답과 해설 : 05 041 06 042

07 ⏱ 120초

★★☆
2023년 3월 21번

밑줄 친 helping move the needle forward가 다음 글에서 의미하는 바로 가장 적절한 것은? 3점

Everyone's heard the expression *don't let the perfect become the enemy of the good*. If you want to get over an obstacle so that your idea can become the solution-based policy you've long dreamed of, you can't have an all-or-nothing mentality. You have to be willing to alter your idea and let others influence its outcome. You have to be okay with the outcome being a little different, even a little *less*, than you wanted. Say you're pushing for a clean water act. Even if what emerges isn't as well-funded as you wished, or doesn't match how you originally conceived the bill, you'll have still succeeded in ensuring that kids in troubled areas have access to clean water. That's what counts, that *they* will be safer because of your idea and your effort. Is it perfect? No. Is there more work to be done? Absolutely. But in almost every case, helping move the needle forward is vastly better than not helping at all.

① spending time and money on celebrating perfection
② suggesting cost-saving strategies for a good cause
③ making a difference as best as the situation allows
④ checking your resources before altering the original goal
⑤ collecting donations to help the education of poor children

08 ⏱ 130초

★★★
2020년 11월 21번

밑줄 친 turns the life stories of these scientists from lead to gold가 다음 글에서 의미하는 바로 가장 적절한 것은? 3점

In school, there's one curriculum, one right way to study science, and one right formula that spits out the correct answer on a standardized test. Textbooks with grand titles like *The Principles of Physics* magically reveal "the principles" in three hundred pages. An authority figure then steps up to the lectern to feed us "the truth." As theoretical physicist David Gross explained in his Nobel lecture, textbooks often ignore the many alternate paths that people wandered down, the many false clues they followed, the many misconceptions they had. We learn about Newton's "laws" — as if they arrived by a grand divine visitation or a stroke of genius — but not the years he spent exploring, revising, and changing them. The laws that Newton failed to establish — most notably his experiments in alchemy, which attempted, and spectacularly failed, to turn lead into gold — don't make the cut as part of the one-dimensional story told in physics classrooms. Instead, our education system turns the life stories of these scientists from lead to gold.

♦ lectern: 강의대 ♦♦ alchemy: 연금술

① discovers the valuable relationships between scientists
② emphasizes difficulties in establishing new scientific theories
③ mixes the various stories of great scientists across the world
④ focuses more on the scientists' work than their personal lives
⑤ reveals only the scientists' success ignoring their processes and errors

정답과 해설 : 07 043 08 044

09 ⓒ 130초

★★★ 2023년 6월 21번

밑줄 친 have entirely lost our marbles가 다음 글에서 의미하는 바로 가장 적절한 것은? 3점

North America's native cuisine met the same unfortunate fate as its native people, save for a few relics like the Thanksgiving turkey. Certainly, we still have regional specialties, but the Carolina barbecue will almost certainly have California tomatoes in its sauce, and the Louisiana gumbo is just as likely to contain Indonesian farmed shrimp. If either of these shows up on a fast-food menu with lots of added fats or HFCS, we seem unable either to discern or resist the corruption. We have yet to come up with a strong set of generalized norms, passed down through families, for savoring and sensibly consuming what our land and climate give us. We have, instead, a string of fad diets convulsing our bookstores and bellies, one after another, at the scale of the national best seller. Nine out of ten nutritionists view this as evidence that we have entirely lost our marbles.

♦ relic: 전해 내려오는 풍속
♦♦ HFCS: 액상 과당 ♦♦♦ convulse: 큰 소동을 일으키다

① have utterly disrupted our complex food supply chain
② have vividly witnessed the rebirth of our classic recipes
③ have completely denied ourselves access to healthy food
④ have become totally confused about our distinctive food identity
⑤ have fully recognized the cultural significance of our local foods

10 ⓒ 130초 최고오답률

★★★ 2019년 11월 21번

밑줄 친 the democratization of business financing이 다음 글에서 의미하는 바로 가장 적절한 것은?

Crowdfunding is a new and more collaborative way to secure funding for projects. It can be used in different ways such as requesting donations for a worthy cause anywhere in the world and generating funding for a project with the contributors then becoming partners in the project. In essence, crowdfunding is the fusion of social networking and venture capitalism. In just the same way as social networks have rewritten the conventional rules about how people communicate and interact with each other, crowdfunding in all its variations has the potential to rewrite the rules on how businesses and other projects get funded in the future. Crowdfunding can be viewed as the democratization of business financing. Instead of restricting capital sourcing and allocation to a relatively small and fixed minority, crowdfunding empowers everyone connected to the Internet to access both the collective wisdom and the pocket money of everyone else who connects to the Internet.

① More people can be involved in funding a business.
② More people will participate in developing new products.
③ Crowdfunding can reinforce the conventional way of financing.
④ Crowdfunding keeps social networking from facilitating funding.
⑤ The Internet helps employees of a company interact with each other.

정답과 해설 : 09045 10045

11 ⓒ 130초 최고오답률

★★★ 2020년 6월 21번

밑줄 친 constantly wearing masks가 다음 글에서 의미하는 바로 가장 적절한 것은? 3점

Over the centuries various writers and thinkers, looking at humans from an outside perspective, have been struck by the theatrical quality of social life. The most famous quote expressing this comes from Shakespeare: "All the world's a stage, / And all the men and women merely players; / They have their exits and their entrances, / And one man in his time plays many parts." If the theater and actors were traditionally represented by the image of masks, writers such as Shakespeare are implying that all of us are constantly wearing masks. Some people are better actors than others. Evil types such as Iago in the play *Othello* are able to conceal their hostile intentions behind a friendly smile. Others are able to act with more confidence and bravado — they often become leaders. People with excellent acting skills can better navigate our complex social environments and get ahead.

◆ bravado: 허세

① protecting our faces from harmful external forces
② performing on stage to show off our acting skills
③ feeling confident by beating others in competition
④ doing completely the opposite of what others expect
⑤ adjusting our behavior based on the social context given

12 ⓒ 130초

★★★ 2023년 11월 21번

밑줄 친 be more than just sugar on the tongue이 다음 글에서 의미하는 바로 가장 적절한 것은? 3점

The arts and aesthetics offer emotional connection to the full range of human experience. "The arts can be more than just sugar on the tongue," Anjan Chatterjee, a professor at the University of Pennsylvania, says. "In art, when there's something challenging, which can also be uncomfortable, this discomfort, if we're willing to engage with it, offers the possibility of some change, some transformation. That can also be a powerful aesthetic experience." The arts, in this way, become vehicles to contend with ideas and concepts that are difficult and uncomfortable otherwise. When Picasso painted his masterpiece *Guernica* in 1937, he captured the heartbreaking and cruel nature of war, and offered the world a way to consider the universal suffering caused by the Spanish Civil War. When Lorraine Hansberry wrote her play *A Raisin in the Sun*, she gave us a powerful story of people struggling with racism, discrimination, and the pursuit of the American dream while also offering a touching portrait of family life.

① play a role in relieving psychological anxiety
② enlighten us about the absoluteness of beauty
③ conceal the artist's cultural and ethnic traditions
④ embrace a variety of experiences beyond pleasure
⑤ distort the viewers' accurate understanding of history

정답과 해설 : 11 046 12 047

13 ⓒ 130초

★★★
2024년 3월 21번

밑줄 친 <u>we were still taping bricks to accelerators</u>가 다음 글에서 의미하는 바로 가장 적절한 것은? [3점]

If you had wanted to create a "self-driving" car in the 1950s, your best option might have been to strap a brick to the accelerator. Yes, the vehicle would have been able to move forward on its own, but it could not slow down, stop, or turn to avoid barriers. Obviously not ideal. But does that mean the entire concept of the self-driving car is not worth pursuing? No, it only means that at the time we did not yet have the tools we now possess to help enable vehicles to operate both autonomously and safely. This once-distant dream now seems within our reach. It is much the same story in medicine. Two decades ago, <u>we were still taping bricks to accelerators</u>. Today, we are approaching the point where we can begin to bring some appropriate technology to bear in ways that advance our understanding of patients as unique individuals. In fact, many patients are already wearing devices that monitor their conditions in real time, which allows doctors to talk to their patients in a specific, refined, and feedback-driven way that was not even possible a decade ago.

◆ strap: 끈으로 묶다 ◆◆ autonomously: 자율적으로

① the importance of medical education was overlooked
② self-driving cars enabled patients to move around freely
③ the devices for safe driving were unavailable at that time
④ lack of advanced tools posed a challenge in understanding patients
⑤ appropriate technologies led to success in developing a new medicine

14 ⓒ 120초

★★☆
2024년 6월 21번

밑줄 친 <u>"Slavery resides under marble and gold."</u>가 다음 글에서 의미하는 바로 가장 적절한 것은? [3점]

Take a look at some of the most powerful, rich, and famous people in the world. Ignore the trappings of their success and what they're able to buy. Look instead at what they're forced to trade in return — look at what success has cost them. Mostly? Freedom. Their work demands they wear a suit. Their success depends on attending certain parties, kissing up to people they don't like. It will require — inevitably — realizing they are unable to say what they actually think. Worse, it demands that they become a different type of person or do bad things. Sure, it might pay well — but they haven't truly examined the transaction. As Seneca put it, <u>"Slavery resides under marble and gold."</u> Too many successful people are prisoners in jails of their own making. Is that what you want? Is that what you're working hard toward? Let's hope not.

◆ trappings: 장식

① Your success requires you to act in ways you don't want to.
② Fame cannot be achieved without the help of others.
③ Comparing yourself to others makes you miserable.
④ Hard labor guarantees glory and happiness in the future.
⑤ There exists freedom in the appearance of your success.

정답과 해설 : 13 048 14 049

15 ⏱ 120초

★★☆
2024년 9월 21번

밑줄 친 Build a jazz band가 다음 글에서 의미하는 바로 가장 적절한 것은?

In today's information age, in many companies and on many teams, the objective is no longer error prevention and replicability. On the contrary, it's creativity, speed, and keenness. In the industrial era, the goal was to minimize variation. But in creative companies today, maximizing variation is more essential. In these situations, the biggest risk isn't making a mistake or losing consistency; it's failing to attract top talent, to invent new products, or to change direction quickly when the environment shifts. Consistency and repeatability are more likely to suppress fresh thinking than to bring your company profit. A lot of little mistakes, while sometimes painful, help the organization learn quickly and are a critical part of the innovation cycle. In these situations, rules and process are no longer the best answer. A symphony isn't what you're going for. Leave the conductor and the sheet music behind. Build a jazz band instead.

① Foster variation within an organization.
② Limit the scope of variability in businesses.
③ Invent a new way of minimizing risk-taking.
④ Promote teamwork to forecast upcoming changes.
⑤ Share innovations over a sufficient period of time.

정답과 해설 : 15 050

유형 TIP

05. 요지 추론

필자가 전달하려고 하는 중심 내용을 한 문장으로 표현한 것을 고르는 유형
정답은 해당 지문의 중심 내용을 잘 요약한 것을 골라야 함.

유형 TIP 25BR2T_CH05 대표 예제 25BR2E_CH05

유형 공략법

1) 지문의 흐름을 파악한다.
연결사와 강조 표현 등에 주목하여 지문의 주제문과 핵심 문장을 찾아야 함.

2) 선택지의 내용에 유의한다.
합리적이고 일반적인 선택지, 지문과 부분적으로 일치하는 선택지는 오답인 경우가 많으므로 주의해야 함.
선택지가 지문의 중심 내용 및 전체 내용을 잘 반영해야 정답이 될 수 있음.

필수 암기 어휘와 표현

1) 주장하거나 내용을 강조하는 표현

당위	must, have to V, ought to V, should
주장/의견	I believe, I feel, I insist, I think, in my opinion, as for me
제안/권유	I suggest, had better, it is good to V
필요/중요	need to V, it is necessary to V, it is important to V

2) 연결사 및 중요 표현

역접/대조	however, but, (and) yet, instead (of), rather, on the other hand, by[in] contrast, in contrast to, conversely, on the contrary, whereas, while, meanwhile, at the same time
양보	though, although, even if[though], still, nevertheless, nonetheless, even so, notwithstanding, despite (that), in spite of, having said that, that (being) said, granting that, admitting that, after all
요약	in short, shortly, in brief, briefly, in sum, to summarize, to sum up, to put it simply, in a word, on the whole, overall
재진술	that is (to say), in other words, namely, to put it another way, stated another way, i.e.
강조	indeed, above all, especially, of course, in particular, in fact, in effect, in reality, in truth, truly, actually, as a matter of fact, most important, more importantly, the thing is, it is clear that, no doubt, never, not at all, in the first place, most of all, certainly, (for) sure, surely, apparently, obviously
조건	if, once, given (that), unless, otherwise, if not, or else, in case of[that], in the event of[that], as[so] long as, suppose (that), supposing (that), provided (that), providing (that)

요지 추론 대표 예제 - 2024학년도 수능 22번

다음 글의 요지로 가장 적절한 것은?

(1) Being able to prioritize your responses allows you to connect more deeply with individual customers, be it a one-off interaction around a particularly delightful or upsetting experience, or the development of a longer-term relationship with a significantly influential individual within your customer base. (2) If you've ever posted a favorable comment — or any comment, for that matter — about a brand, product or service, think about what it would feel like if you were personally acknowledged by the brand manager, for example, as a result. (3) In general, people post because they have something to say — and because they want to be recognized for having said it. (4) In particular, when people post positive comments they are expressions of appreciation for the experience that led to the post. (5) While a compliment to the person standing next to you is typically answered with a response like "Thank You," the sad fact is that most brand compliments go unanswered. (6) These are lost opportunities to understand what drove the compliments and create a solid fan based on them.

* compliment: 칭찬

✔ 고객과의 관계 증진을 위해 고객의 브랜드 칭찬에 응답하는 것은 중요하다.

② 고객의 피드백을 면밀히 분석함으로써 브랜드의 성공 가능성을 높일 수 있다.

③ 신속한 고객 응대를 통해서 고객의 긍정적인 반응을 이끌어 낼 수 있다.

④ 브랜드 매니저에게는 고객의 부정적인 의견을 수용하는 태도가 요구된다.

⑤ 고객의 의견을 경청하는 것은 브랜드의 새로운 이미지 창출에 도움이 된다.

STEP 1 지문의 흐름을 파악한다.

→ 문장 (1)에서 고객에 대한 응답의 우선순위를 두는 것을 언급하며 글의 중심 소재를 소개함. 문장 (3), (4)는 고객이 일반적인 의견을 제시하는 이유를 언급하며, 이 글의 키워드가 고객의 일반적인 의견임을 나타내고 있음. 문장 (5)와 (6)에서는 고객의 칭찬에 응답하지 못하는 것의 결과를 이야기함. 따라서 이 글의 요지는 고객과의 관계 증진을 위해 고객의 칭찬에 응답하는 것이 중요하다는 것임.

STEP 2 선택지의 내용에 유의한다.

②: 고객의 피드백을 분석하는 내용이 언급되지 않았음.
③: 고객 응대의 신속함이 고객의 긍정적인 반응을 이끌어낸다는 내용은 언급되지 않음.
④: 브랜드 매니저가 취해야 할 태도는 언급되지 않음.
⑤: 브랜드의 새로운 이미지 창출에 대해 언급되지 않음.

전문 해석

(1) 여러분의 응답에 우선순위를 매길 수 있는 것은, 그것이 특별히 기쁘거나 화가 나는 경험에 대한 단 한 번의 상호 작용이든, 혹은 여러분의 고객층 내에 상당히 영향력 있는 개인과의 더 장기적인 관계의 발전이든 간에, 여러분이 각각의 고객과 더 깊이 연결되게 한다. (2) 만약 여러분이 어떤 브랜드, 제품 또는 서비스에 대한 호의적인 의견, 혹은 그 문제에 대한 아무 의견을 게시한 적이 있다면, 예를 들어, 그 결과, 여러분이 그 브랜드 관리자에게 개인적으로 인정을 받는다면 어떤 기분일지 생각해 보아라. (3) 일반적으로, 사람들은 그들이 말할 것이 있기 때문에, 그리고 그들이 그것을 말한 것에 대해 인정받고 싶기 때문에 (의견을) 게시한다. (4) 특히, 사람들이 긍정적인 의견을 게시할 때 그것은 그 게시물로 이끈 경험에 대한 감사의 표현이다. (5) 여러분의 옆에 서 있는 사람에 대한 칭찬은 보통 '감사합니다'와 같은 응답으로 대답을 받지만, 슬픈 사실은 대부분의 브랜드 칭찬은 대답을 받지 못한다는 것이다. (6) 이는 무엇이 그 칭찬을 이끌어 냈는지 이해하고 그것들을 바탕으로 확고한 팬을 만들 놓쳐버린 기회이다(기회를 놓쳐버린 것이다).

중요 어휘

- □ prioritize 동 우선순위를 매기다
- □ allow A to V A가 ~하게 하다
- □ one-off 형 단 한 번의
- □ significantly 부 상당히
- □ customer base 고객층
- □ post 동 게시하다, 올리다, 발송하다 / 명 우편(물)
- □ favorable 형 호의적인, 유리한
- □ acknowledge 동 인정하다, 감사를 표하다
- □ recognize 동 인정하다, 알아보다
- □ appreciation 명 감사, 공감, 감상
- □ compliment 명 칭찬
- □ unanswered 형 대답이 없는
- □ lost 형 놓쳐버린, 잃어버린
- □ solid 형 확고한, 단단한

자세한 해설지 QR→

자세한해설-CH05

05 요지 추론

동영상 강의

25BR2_CH05

01 ⓒ 80초

★☆☆ 2021년 6월 22번

다음 글의 요지로 가장 적절한 것은?

When it comes to the decision to get more exercise, you are setting goals that are similar to running a half marathon with very little training! You make a decision to buy a gym membership and decide to spend an hour at the gym every day. Well, you might stick to that for a day or two, but chances are you won't be able to continue to meet that commitment in the long term. If, however, you make a commitment to go jogging for a few minutes a day or add a few sit-ups to your daily routine before bed, then you are far more likely to stick to your decision and to create a habit that offers you long-term results. The key is to start small. Small habits lead to long-term success.

① 상황에 따른 유연한 태도가 목표 달성에 효과적이다.
② 올바른 식습관과 규칙적인 운동이 건강 유지에 도움이 된다.
③ 나쁜 습관을 고치기 위해서는 장기적인 계획이 필수적이다.
④ 꿈을 이루기 위해서는 원대한 목표를 세우는 것이 중요하다.
⑤ 장기적인 성공을 위해 작은 습관부터 시작하는 것이 필요하다.

02 ⓒ 80초

★☆☆ 2021년 11월 22번

다음 글의 요지로 가장 적절한 것은?

Who is this person? This is the question all stories ask. It emerges first at the ignition point. When the initial change strikes, the protagonist overreacts or behaves in an otherwise unexpected way. We sit up, suddenly attentive. *Who is this person who behaves like this?* The question then re-emerges every time the protagonist is challenged by the plot and compelled to make a choice. Everywhere in the narrative that the question is present, the reader or viewer will likely be engaged. Where the question is absent, and the events of drama move out of its narrative beam, they are at risk of becoming detached — perhaps even bored. If there's a single secret to storytelling then I believe it's this. *Who is this person?* Or, from the perspective of the character, *Who am I?* It's the definition of drama. It is its electricity, its heartbeat, its fire.

♦ ignition: 발화 ♦♦ protagonist: 주인공

① 독자의 공감을 얻기 위해 구체적인 인물 묘사가 중요하다.
② 이야기의 줄거리를 단순화시키는 것이 독자의 이해를 높인다.
③ 거리를 두고 주인공의 상황을 객관적으로 바라볼 필요가 있다.
④ 주인공의 역경과 행복이 적절히 섞여야 이야기가 흥미로워진다.
⑤ 주인공에 대한 지속적인 궁금증 유발이 독자의 몰입을 도와준다.

정답과 해설 : 01 051 02 051

03 ⓒ 80초

★☆☆ 2022년 6월 22번

다음 글의 요지로 가장 적절한 것은?

The problem with simply adopting any popular method of parenting is that it ignores the most important variable in the equation: the uniqueness of your child. So, rather than insist that one style of parenting will work with every child, we might take a page from the gardener's handbook. Just as the gardener accepts, without question or resistance, the plant's requirements and provides the right conditions each plant needs to grow and flourish, so, too, do we parents need to custom-design our parenting to fit the natural needs of each individual child. Although that may seem difficult, it is possible. Once we understand who our children really are, we can begin to figure out how to make changes in our parenting style to be more positive and accepting of each child we've been blessed to parent.

♦ equation: 방정식

① 자녀의 특성에 맞는 개별화된 양육이 필요하다.
② 식물을 키우는 것이 자녀의 창의성 발달에 도움이 된다.
③ 정서적 교감은 자녀의 바람직한 인격 형성에 필수적이다.
④ 자녀에게 타인을 존중하는 태도를 가르치는 것이 중요하다.
⑤ 전문가에 의해 검증된 양육 방식을 따르는 것이 바람직하다.

04 ⓒ 80초

★☆☆ 2020년 9월 22번

다음 글의 요지로 가장 적절한 것은?

The psychology professor Dr. Kelly Lambert's research explains that keeping what she calls the "effort-driven rewards circuit" well engaged helps you deal with challenges in the environment around you or in your emotional life more effectively and efficiently. Doing hands-on activities that produce results you can see and touch — such as knitting a scarf, cooking from scratch, or tending a garden — fuels the reward circuit so that it functions optimally. She argues that the documented increase in depression among Americans may be directly correlated with the decline of purposeful physical activity. When we work with our hands, it increases the release of the neurochemicals dopamine and serotonin, both responsible for generating positive emotions. She also explains that working with our hands gives us a greater sense of control over our environment and more connection to the world around us. All of which contributes to a reduction in stress and anxiety and builds resilience against the onset of depression.

① 긍정적인 감정은 타인에게 쉽게 전이된다.
② 감정 조절은 대인 관계 능력의 핵심 요소이다.
③ 수작업 활동은 정신 건강에 도움을 줄 수 있다.
④ 과도한 신체활동은 호르몬 분비의 불균형을 초래한다.
⑤ 취미 활동을 통해 여러 분야의 사람들을 만날 수 있다.

정답과 해설 : 03 052 04 053

05 ⓒ 80초

★☆☆ 2020년 11월 22번

다음 글의 요지로 가장 적절한 것은?

The vast majority of companies, schools, and organizations measure and reward "high performance" in terms of individual metrics such as sales numbers, résumé accolades, and test scores. The problem with this approach is that it is based on a belief we thought science had fully confirmed: that we live in a world of "survival of the fittest." It teaches us that those with the *best* grades, or the *most* impressive résumé, or the *highest* point score, will be the ONLY ones to succeed. The formula is simple: be better and smarter and more creative than everyone else, and you will be successful. But this formula is inaccurate. Thanks to new research, we now know that achieving our highest potential is not about survival of the fittest but survival of the best fit. In other words, success is not just about how creative or smart or driven you are, but how well you are able to connect with, contribute to, and benefit from the ecosystem of people around you.

♦ accolade: 수상, 표창

① 효율적인 업무 배분은 조직의 생산성을 향상시킨다.
② 유연한 사고방식은 원활한 의사소통에 도움이 된다.
③ 사람들과 잘 어울려 일하는 능력이 성공을 가능하게 한다.
④ 비판적 사고 능력은 정확성을 추구하는 태도에서 출발한다.
⑤ 치열한 경쟁 사회에서 최고의 실력을 갖추는 것이 필수적이다.

06 ⓒ 80초

★☆☆ 2021년 9월 22번

다음 글의 요지로 가장 적절한 것은?

Too many officials in troubled cities wrongly imagine that they can lead their city back to its former glories with some massive construction project — a new stadium or light rail system, a convention center, or a housing project. With very few exceptions, no public policy can slow the tidal forces of urban change. We mustn't ignore the needs of the poor people who live in the Rust Belt, but public policy should help poor *people*, not poor places. Shiny new real estate may dress up a declining city, but it doesn't solve its underlying problems. The hallmark of declining cities is that they have *too much* housing and infrastructure relative to the strength of their economies. With all that supply of structure and so little demand, it makes no sense to use public money to build more supply. The folly of building-centric urban renewal reminds us that cities aren't structures; cities are people.

① 도시 재생을 위한 공공정책은 건설보다 사람에 중점을 두어야 한다.
② 대중 교통 이용이 편리하도록 도시 교통 체계를 구축해야 한다.
③ 사회기반시설 확충을 통해 지역 경제를 활성화해야 한다.
④ 에너지를 절감할 수 있는 친환경 건물을 설계해야 한다.
⑤ 문화유산 보존을 우선하는 도시 계획을 수립해야 한다.

07 ⓒ 80초

★☆☆ 2022년 3월 22번

다음 글의 요지로 가장 적절한 것은?

Advice from a friend or family member is the most well-meaning of all, but it's not the best way to match yourself with a new habit. While hot yoga may have changed your friend's life, does that mean it's the right practice for you? We all have friends who *swear* their new habit of getting up at 4:30 a.m. changed their lives and that we have to do it. I don't doubt that getting up super early changes people's lives, sometimes in good ways and sometimes not. But be cautious: You don't know if this habit will actually make your life better, especially if it means you get less sleep. So yes, you can try what worked for your friend, but don't beat yourself up if your friend's answer doesn't change you in the same way. All of these approaches involve guessing and chance. And that's not a good way to strive for change in your life.

① 한번 잘못 들인 습관은 바로잡기가 어렵다.
② 꾸준한 반복을 통해 올바른 습관을 들일 수 있다.
③ 친구나 가족의 조언은 항상 귀담아들을 필요가 있다.
④ 사소하더라도 좋은 습관을 들이면 인생이 바뀔 수 있다.
⑤ 타인에게 유익했던 습관이 자신에게는 효과가 없을 수 있다.

정답과 해설 : 05 053 06 054 07 055

08 ⓒ 80초

★☆☆ 2022년 11월 22번

다음 글의 요지로 가장 적절한 것은?

In one study, when researchers suggested that a date was associated with a new beginning (such as "the first day of spring"), students viewed it as a more attractive time to kick-start goal pursuit than when researchers presented it as an unremarkable day (such as "the third Thursday in March"). Whether it was starting a new gym habit or spending less time on social media, when the date that researchers suggested was associated with a new beginning, more students wanted to begin changes right then. And more recent research by a different team found that similar benefits were achieved by showing goal seekers modified weekly calendars. When calendars depicted the current day (either Monday or Sunday) as the first day of the week, people reported feeling more motivated to make immediate progress on their goals.

① 새로운 시작을 하기 전에 장기적인 계획을 세우는 것이 바람직하다.
② 자신이 해야 할 일을 일정표에 표시하는 것이 목표 달성에 효과적이다.
③ 문제 행동을 개선하기 위해 원인이 되는 요소를 파악할 필요가 있다.
④ 날짜가 시작이라는 의미와 관련지어질 때 목표 추구에 강한 동기가 부여된다.
⑤ 상세한 일정표를 작성하는 것은 여러 목표를 동시에 달성하는 데 도움이 된다.

09 ⓒ 80초

★☆☆ 2022년 9월 22번

다음 글의 요지로 가장 적절한 것은?

Most parents think that if our child would just "behave," we could stay calm as parents. The truth is that managing our own emotions and actions is what allows us to feel peaceful as parents. Ultimately we can't control our children or the obstacles they will face — but we can always control our own actions. Parenting isn't about what our child does, but about how we respond. In fact, most of what we call parenting doesn't take place between a parent and child but within the parent. When a storm brews, a parent's response will either calm it or trigger a full-scale tsunami. Staying calm enough to respond constructively to all that childish behavior — and the stormy emotions behind it — requires that we grow, too. If we can use those times when our buttons get pushed to reflect, not just react, we can notice when we lose equilibrium and steer ourselves back on track. This inner growth is the hardest work there is, but it's what enables you to become a more peaceful parent, one day at a time.

① 자녀의 행동 변화를 위해 부모의 즉각적인 반응이 필요하다.
② 부모의 내적 성장을 통한 평정심 유지가 양육에 중요하다.
③ 부모는 자녀가 감정을 다스릴 수 있게 도와주어야 한다.
④ 부모와 자녀는 건설적인 의견을 나눌 수 있어야 한다.
⑤ 바람직한 양육은 자녀에게 모범을 보이는 것이다.

정답과 해설 : 08 055 09 056

10 ⓒ 80초

★☆☆ 2016년 9월 21번

다음 글의 요지로 가장 적절한 것은?

Some organizations may be reluctant to facilitate their employees' participation in volunteer activities. They may believe it's none of their business: if employees want to do volunteer activity, they can make their own arrangements and do so on their own time. Corporations also may be concerned about allocating the resources needed to set up such programs, or perhaps they fear that facilitating employees' engagement elsewhere may weaken their commitment to the organization or their jobs. Not to worry on that last point: research shows that participating in corporate volunteer activity heightens rather than weakens employees' organizational commitment, in part because people feel a sense of self-worth when they do the good deeds that their organizations made it easier for them to do.

① 기업의 사회 봉사활동은 기업 이미지를 긍정적으로 만든다.
② 성과에 따른 적절한 보상은 직원의 만족도를 향상시킨다.
③ 직원의 봉사활동을 지원하는 것은 회사에 도움이 된다.
④ 기업은 자선 단체에 대한 후원을 확대할 필요가 있다.
⑤ 자기 계발과 회사 업무 간의 균형이 중요하다.

11 ⓒ 90초

★★☆ 2021년 3월 22번

다음 글의 요지로 가장 적절한 것은?

Fears of damaging ecosystems are based on the sound conservationist principle that we should aim to minimize the disruption we cause, but there is a risk that this principle may be confused with the old idea of a 'balance of nature.' This supposes a perfect order of nature that will seek to maintain itself and that we should not change. It is a romantic, not to say idyllic, notion, but deeply misleading because it supposes a static condition. Ecosystems are dynamic, and although some may endure, apparently unchanged, for periods that are long in comparison with the human lifespan, they must and do change eventually. Species come and go, climates change, plant and animal communities adapt to altered circumstances, and when examined in fine detail such adaptation and consequent change can be seen to be taking place constantly. The 'balance of nature' is a myth. Our planet is dynamic, and so are the arrangements by which its inhabitants live together.

♦ idyllic: 목가적인

① 생물 다양성이 높은 생태계가 기후 변화에 더 잘 적응한다.
② 인간의 부적절한 개입은 자연의 균형을 깨뜨린다.
③ 자연은 정적이지 않고 역동적으로 계속 변한다.
④ 모든 생물은 적자생존의 원칙에 순응하기 마련이다.
⑤ 동식물은 상호 경쟁을 통해 생태계의 균형을 이룬다.

정답과 해설 : 10 057 11 057

12 ⓒ 90초

★★☆ 2020년 6월 22번

다음 글의 요지로 가장 적절한 것은?

Personal blind spots are areas that are visible to others but not to you. The developmental challenge of blind spots is that you don't know what you don't know. Like that area in the side mirror of your car where you can't see that truck in the lane next to you, personal blind spots can easily be overlooked because you are completely unaware of their presence. They can be equally dangerous as well. That truck you don't see? It's really there! So are your blind spots. Just because you don't see them, doesn't mean they can't run you over. This is where you need to enlist the help of others. You have to develop a crew of special people, people who are willing to hold up that mirror, who not only know you well enough to see that truck, but who also care enough about you to let you know that it's there.

① 모르는 부분을 인정하고 질문하는 것이 중요하다.
② 폭넓은 인간관계는 성공에 결정적인 영향을 미친다.
③ 자기발전은 실수를 기회로 만드는 능력에서 비롯된다.
④ 주변에 관심을 가지고 타인을 도와주는 것이 바람직하다.
⑤ 자신의 맹점을 인지하도록 도와줄 수 있는 사람이 필요하다.

13 ⓒ 90초

★★☆ 2023년 3월 22번

다음 글의 요지로 가장 적절한 것은?

Brands that fail to grow and develop lose their relevance. Think about the person you knew who was once on the fast track at your company, who is either no longer with the firm or, worse yet, appears to have hit a plateau in his or her career. Assuming he or she did not make an ambitious move, more often than not, this individual is a victim of having failed to stay relevant and embrace the advances in his or her industry. Think about the impact personal computing technology had on the first wave of executive leadership exposed to the technology. Those who embraced the technology were able to integrate it into their work styles and excel. Those who were resistant many times found few opportunities to advance their careers and in many cases were ultimately let go through early retirement for failure to stay relevant and update their skills.

♦ hit a plateau: 정체기에 들다

① 다양한 업종의 경력이 있으면 구직 활동에 유리하다.
② 직원의 다양한 능력을 활용하면 업계를 주도할 수 있다.
③ 기술이 발전함에 따라 단순 반복 업무가 사라지고 있다.
④ 자신의 약점을 인정하면 동료들로부터 도움을 얻기 쉽다.
⑤ 변화를 받아들이지 못하면 업계에서의 적합성을 잃게 된다.

정답과 해설 : 12 058 13 059

14 ⓒ 90초

★★☆ 2023년 6월 22번

다음 글의 요지로 가장 적절한 것은?

Perhaps, the advent of Artificial Intelligence (AI) in the workplace may bode well for Emotional Intelligence (EI). As AI gains momentum and replaces people in jobs at every level, predictions are, there will be a premium placed on people who have high ability in EI. The emotional messages people send and respond to while interacting are, at this point, far beyond the ability of AI programs to mimic. As we get further into the age of the smart machine, it is likely that sensing and managing emotions will remain one type of intelligence that puzzles AI. This means people and jobs involving EI are safe from being taken over by machines. In a survey, almost three out of four executives see EI as a "must-have" skill for the workplace in the future as the automatizing of routine tasks bumps up against the impossibility of creating effective AI for activities that require emotional skill.

♦ bode: ~의 징조가 되다 ♦♦ momentum: 추진력

① 감성 지능의 결여는 직장 내 대인 관계 갈등을 심화시킨다.
② 미래의 직장에서는 감성 지능의 가치가 더욱 높아질 것이다.
③ 미래 사회에서는 감성 지능을 갖춘 기계가 보편화될 것이다.
④ 미래에는 대부분의 직장 업무를 인공 지능이 대신할 것이다.
⑤ 인간과 인공 지능 간의 상호 작용은 감성 지능의 발달을 저해한다.

15 ⓒ 100초

★★★ 2023년 9월 22번

다음 글의 요지로 가장 적절한 것은?

It's remarkable that positive fantasies help us relax to such an extent that it shows up in physiological tests. If you want to unwind, you can take some deep breaths, get a massage, or go for a walk — but you can also try simply closing your eyes and fantasizing about some future outcome that you might enjoy. But what about when your objective is to make your wish a reality? The *last* thing you want to be is relaxed. You want to be energized enough to get off the couch and lose those pounds or find that job or study for that test, and you want to be motivated enough to stay engaged even when the inevitable obstacles or challenges arise. The principle of "Dream it. Wish it. Do it." does not hold true, and now we know why: in dreaming it, you undercut the energy you need to do it. You put yourself in a temporary state of complete happiness, calmness — and inactivity.

♦ physiological: 생리학적인

① 과도한 목표 지향적 태도는 삶의 만족감을 떨어뜨린다.
② 긍정적 자세로 역경을 극복할 때 잠재 능력이 발휘된다.
③ 편안함을 느끼는 상황에서 자기 개선에 대한 동기가 생긴다.
④ 낙관적인 상상은 소망을 실현하는 데 필요한 동력을 약화시킨다.
⑤ 막연한 목표보다는 명확하고 구체적인 목표가 실현 가능성이 크다.

정답과 해설 : 14 060 15 060

16 ⏱ 80초

★☆☆
2023년 11월 22번

다음 글의 요지로 가장 적절한 것은?

Many historians have pointed to the significance of accurate time measurement to Western economic progress. The French historian Jacques Le Goff called the birth of the public mechanical clock a turning point in Western society. Until the late Middle Ages, people had sun or water clocks, which did not play any meaningful role in business activities. Market openings and activities started with the sunrise and typically ended at noon when the sun was at its peak. But when the first public mechanical clocks were introduced and spread across European cities, market times were set by the stroke of the hour. Public clocks thus greatly contributed to public life and work by providing a new concept of time that was easy for everyone to understand. This, in turn, helped facilitate trade and commerce. Interactions and transactions between consumers, retailers, and wholesalers became less irregular. Important town meetings began to follow the pace of the clock, allowing people to better plan their time and allocate resources in a more efficient manner.

① 공공 시계는 서양 사회의 경제적 진보에 영향을 미쳤다.
② 서양에서 생산된 시계는 세계적으로 정교함을 인정받았다.
③ 서양의 시계는 교역을 통해 전파되어 세계적으로 대중화되었다.
④ 기계 시계의 발명은 다른 측량 장비들의 개발에 도움을 주었다.
⑤ 중세 시대의 시계 발명은 자연법칙을 이해하는 데 큰 전환점이 되었다.

17 ⏱ 100초

★★★
2024년 3월 22번

다음 글의 요지로 가장 적절한 것은?

We tend to overrate the impact of new technologies in part because older technologies have become absorbed into the furniture of our lives, so as to be almost invisible. Take the baby bottle. Here is a simple implement that has transformed a fundamental human experience for vast numbers of infants and mothers, yet it finds no place in our histories of technology. This technology might be thought of as a classic time-shifting device, as it enables mothers to exercise more control over the timing of feeding. It can also function to save time, as bottle feeding allows for someone else to substitute for the mother's time. Potentially, therefore, it has huge implications for the management of time in everyday life, yet it is entirely overlooked in discussions of high-speed society.

① 새로운 기술은 효율적인 시간 관리에 도움이 된다.
② 새로운 기술에 비해 기존 기술의 영향력이 간과되고 있다.
③ 현대 사회의 새로운 기술이 양육자의 역할을 대체하고 있다.
④ 새로운 기술의 사용을 장려하는 사회적 인식이 요구된다.
⑤ 기존 기술의 활용은 새로운 기술의 개발에 도움이 된다.

정답과 해설 : 16 061 17 062

18 ⏱ 80초

★☆☆ 2024년 6월 22번

다음 글의 요지로 가장 적절한 것은?

If a firm is going to be saved by the government, it might be easier to concentrate on lobbying the government for more money rather than taking the harder decision of restructuring the company to be able to be profitable and viable in the long term. This is an example of something known as moral hazard — when government support alters the decisions firms take. For example, if governments rescue banks who get into difficulty, as they did during the credit crisis of 2007–08, this could encourage banks to take greater risks in the future because they know there is a possibility that governments will intervene if they lose money. Although the government rescue may be well intended, it can negatively affect the behavior of banks, encouraging risky and poor decision making.

♦ viable: 성장할 수 있는

① 기업에 대한 정부의 지원이 새로운 기술의 도입을 촉진한다.
② 현명한 소비자들은 윤리적 기업의 제품을 선택하는 경향이 있다.
③ 정부와 기업은 협력으로 사회적 문제의 해결책을 모색할 수 있다.
④ 정부의 구제는 기업의 의사 결정에 부정적인 영향을 미칠 수 있다.
⑤ 합리적 의사 결정은 다양한 대안에 대한 평가를 통해 이루어진다.

19 ⏱ 80초

★☆☆ 2024년 9월 22번

다음 글의 요지로 가장 적절한 것은?

Any new or threatening situation may require us to make decisions and this requires information. So important is communication during a disaster that normal social barriers are often lowered. We will talk to strangers in a way we would never consider normally. Even relatively low grade disruption of our life such as a fire drill or a very late train seems to give us the permission to break normal etiquette and talk to strangers. The more important an event to a particular public, the more detailed and urgent the requirement for news becomes. Without an authoritative source of facts, whether that is a newspaper or trusted broadcast station, rumours often run riot. Rumours start because people believe their group to be in danger and so, although the rumour is unproven, feel they should pass it on. For example, if a worker heard that their employer's business was doing badly and people were going to be made redundant, they would pass that information on to colleagues.

♦ redundant: (일시) 해고된

① 소수에 의한 정보 독점은 합리적 의사 결정을 방해한다.
② 대중의 지속적 관심이 뉴스의 공정성을 향상시킬 수 있다.
③ 위기에 처한 사람은 권위 있는 전문가의 의견을 구하려고 한다.
④ 소문은 유사한 성향을 지닌 사람들 사이에서 더 빠르게 퍼진다.
⑤ 위기 상황에서는 확인되지 않은 정보라도 전달하려는 경향이 크다.

정답과 해설 : 18 063 19 063

유형 TIP

06. 주제 추론

글의 중심 생각과 필자의 입장 등을 요약한 것이 곧 글의 주제가 됨.
글의 주제를 파악하는 것은 다른 영어 독해 유형을 푸는 데 바탕이 됨.

유형 TIP 대표 예제

25BR2T_CH06 25BR2E_CH06

유형 공략법

1) 반복되는 내용과 주제의 위치를 보여 주는 표현에 주목하여 주제를 파악한다.

글에서는 반복되는 내용이 곧 주제임.
연결사 등 주제의 위치를 보여 주는 표현을 활용한 문장이 주제문일 확률이 높음.

2) 지나치게 포괄적이거나 지엽적인 선택지에 주의한다.

정답은 지문의 내용을 모두 포함해야 함.
교묘하게 지문의 핵심 어구를 포함한 듯 보이는 선택지를 선택하지 않도록 주의해야 함.

필수 암기 어휘와 표현

1) 주제의 위치를 보여 주는 표현

의견/주장	I believe, I think, in my opinion, be aware of
중요성/필요성/당위성	need to V, must, have to V, should, important, necessary, essential
역접/대조	however, but, (and) yet, instead (of), rather, on the other hand, by[in] contrast, in contrast to, conversely, on the contrary, whereas, while, meanwhile, at the same time
양보	though, although, even if[though], still, nevertheless, nonetheless, even so, notwithstanding, despite (that), in spite of, having said that, that (being) said, granting that, admitting that
요약	in short, shortly, in brief, briefly, in sum, to summarize, to sum up, to put it simply, in a word, on the whole, overall
재진술	that is (to say), in other words, namely, to put it another way, stated another way, i.e.
강조	indeed, above all, especially, of course, in particular, in fact, in effect, in reality, in truth, truly, actually, as a matter of fact, most important, more importantly, the thing is, it is clear that, no doubt, never, not at all, in the first place, most of all, certainly, (for) sure, surely, apparently, obviously
조건	if, once, given (that), unless, otherwise, if not, or else, in case of[that], in the event of[that], as[so] long as, suppose (that), supposing (that), provided (that), providing (that)

2) 선택지에서 많이 나오는 표현

a way to V ~하는 방법	shortcomings of ~의 단점	classification 분류	variety 다양성
how to V ~하는 방법	importance of ~의 중요성	difference 차이점	advance 진보, 향상
origin of ~의 유래	significance of ~의 중요성	simplicity 단순함	reduction 감소
the role of ~의 역할	need for ~에 대한 필요	technique 기술	convenience 편의성
effect of ~의 효과	advantage of ~의 장점	alternative 대안	capacity 능력, 수용력
causes of ~의 원인	characteristics of ~의 특징	behavior 행동	condition 조건
limitations of ~의 한계	the relation of ~의 관계	trend 경향	contrast 대조
difficulties in ~의 어려움	distinguishing 특색 있는	tendency 경향	quality 특질, 품질
necessity of ~의 필요성	demand 요구, 수요	promotion 촉진	recommendation 권장, 추천
the purpose of ~의 목적	development 발전	benefit 이점	indicator 지표, 척도

주제 추론 대표 예제 - 2024학년도 수능 23번

다음 글의 주제로 가장 적절한 것은?

(1) Managers of natural resources typically face market incentives that provide financial rewards for exploitation. (2) For example, owners of forest lands have a market incentive to cut down trees rather than manage the forest for carbon capture, wildlife habitat, flood protection, and other ecosystem services. (3) These services provide the owner with no financial benefits, and thus are unlikely to influence management decisions. (4) But the economic benefits provided by these services, based on their non-market values, may exceed the economic value of the timber. (5) For example, a United Nations initiative has estimated that the economic benefits of ecosystem services provided by tropical forests, including climate regulation, water purification, and erosion prevention, are over three times greater per hectare than the market benefits. (6) Thus cutting down the trees is economically inefficient, and markets are not sending the correct "signal" to favor ecosystem services over extractive uses.

* exploitation: 이용 ** timber: 목재

① necessity of calculating the market values of ecosystem services

✔ significance of weighing forest resources' non-market values

③ impact of using forest resources to maximize financial benefits

④ merits of balancing forests' market and non-market values

⑤ ways of increasing the efficiency of managing natural resources

STEP 1 반복되는 내용과 주제의 위치를 보여 주는 표현에 주목하여 주제를 파악한다.

→ 삼림 지대의 생태계 서비스라는 비시장 가치가 크다는 것을 설명하는 글로, 문장 (4)에서 역접의 연결사 'But'을 활용하여 일반적 통념과는 달리 생태계 서비스라는 비시장 가치의 경제적 이익이 시장 가치의 경제적 이익을 능가할 수 있다는 가능성을 제시함.

→ 내용을 요약하여 제시하는 연결사 'Thus'를 활용하여 비시장 가치의 경제적 이익과 효율성을 요약하는 문장 (6)의 내용도 이 글의 주제와 연관되어 있음.

STEP 2 지나치게 포괄적이거나 지엽적인 선택지에 주의한다.

①: 생태계 서비스의 시장 가치는 언급되었으나, 가치를 산출하는 것의 필요성 자체는 언급되지 않음.

③: 삼림 자원을 이용하는 이유가 재정적 이익을 극대화하기 위함이라는 내용은 언급되지 않음.

④: 삼림 지대를 예시로 들고 있으나, 시장 가치와 비시장 가치 사이의 균형과 그 장점은 언급되지 않음.

⑤: 천연자원 관리와 관련된 내용은 언급되지 않음.

전문 해석

(1) 천연자원 관리자는 일반적으로 이용에 대한 재정적인 보상을 제공하는 시장 유인에 직면한다. (2) 예를 들어, 삼림 지대의 소유자는 탄소 포집, 야생 동물 서식지, 홍수 방지, 그리고 다른 생태계 서비스를 위해 숲을 관리하기보다는 나무를 베어 낼 시장 유인을 가진다. (3) 이러한 (생태계) 서비스는 소유자에게 어떠한 재정적 이익도 제공하지 않고, 그러므로 관리 결정에 영향을 미칠 것 같지 않다. (4) 그러나 이러한 서비스에 의해 제공되는 경제적 이익은, 그것의 비시장 가치에 근거하여, 목재의 경제적 가치를 넘어설 수도 있다. (5) 예를 들어, 국제 연합의 한 계획은, 기후 조절, 물 정화, 그리고 침식 방지를 포함하여, 열대림에 의해 제공되는 생태계 서비스의 경제적 이익이 시장 이익보다 헥타르당 세 배 이상 더 크다고 추정했다. (6) 그러므로 나무를 베는 것은 경제적으로 비효율적이며, 시장은 (천연자원을) 추출하는 이용보다 생태계 서비스를 선호하게 하는 올바른 '신호'를 보내지 않고 있다.

- carbon capture(탄소 포집): 화석연료 사용 시 발생하는 이산화 탄소를 모으는 기술

중요 어휘

- □ natural resource 천연자원
- □ face 동 직면하다, 마주하다
- □ incentive 명 유인, 동기, 장려책
- □ exploitation 명 (부당한) 이용, 착취, 개발
- □ wildlife 명 야생 동물
- □ habitat 명 서식지
- □ flood 명 홍수
- □ financial 형 재정적인, 금융의
- □ exceed 동 넘어서다, 초과하다
- □ timber 명 목재
- □ initiative 명 계획, 진취성, 주도권
- □ tropical forest 열대림
- □ purification 명 정화
- □ erosion 명 침식, 부식
- □ hectare 명 헥타르(땅 면적의 단위, 1헥타르=10,000m²)
- □ favor A over B B보다 A를 선호하다
- □ extractive 형 추출하는, 채취하는
- □ calculate 동 산출하다, 계산하다
- □ weigh 동 따져 보다, 무게를 달다
- □ merit 명 장점, 가치, 훌륭함
- □ balance A and B A와 B의 균형을 이루다

자세한 해설지 QR→

자세한해설-CH06

06 주제 추론

동영상 강의

25BR2_CH06

01 ⓒ 80초

★☆☆
2021년 6월 23번

다음 글의 주제로 가장 적절한 것은?

Creativity is a step further on from imagination. Imagination can be an entirely private process of internal consciousness. You might be lying motionless on your bed in a fever of imagination and no one would ever know. Private imaginings may have no outcomes in the world at all. Creativity does. Being creative involves doing something. It would be odd to describe as creative someone who never did anything. To call somebody creative suggests they are actively producing something in a deliberate way. People are not creative in the abstract; they are creative in something: in mathematics, in engineering, in writing, in music, in business, in whatever. Creativity involves putting your imagination to work. In a sense, creativity is applied imagination.

① the various meanings of imagination
② creativity as the realization of imagination
③ factors which make imaginative people attractive
④ the necessity of art education to enhance creativity
⑤ effects of a creative attitude on academic achievement

02 ⓒ 80초

★☆☆
2021년 11월 23번

다음 글의 주제로 가장 적절한 것은?

Shutter speed refers to the speed of a camera shutter. In behavior profiling, it refers to the speed of the eyelid. When we blink, we reveal more than just blink rate. Changes in the speed of the eyelid can indicate important information; shutter speed is a measurement of fear. Think of an animal that has a reputation for being fearful. A Chihuahua might come to mind. In mammals, because of evolution, our eyelids will speed up to minimize the amount of time that we can't see an approaching predator. The greater the degree of fear an animal is experiencing, the more the animal is concerned with an approaching predator. In an attempt to keep the eyes open as much as possible, the eyelids involuntarily speed up. Speed, when it comes to behavior, almost always equals fear. In humans, if we experience fear about something, our eyelids will do the same thing as the Chihuahua; they will close and open more quickly.

◆ eyelid: 눈꺼풀

① eye contact as a way to frighten others
② fast blinking as a symptom of eye fatigue
③ blink speed as a significant indicator of fear
④ fast eye movement as proof of predatory instinct
⑤ blink rate as a difference between humans and animals

정답과 해설 : 01 065 02 065

03 ⓒ 80초

★☆☆
2022년 9월 23번

다음 글의 주제로 가장 적절한 것은?

We have already seen that learning is much more efficient when done at regular intervals: rather than cramming an entire lesson into one day, we are better off spreading out the learning. The reason is simple: every night, our brain consolidates what it has learned during the day. This is one of the most important neuroscience discoveries of the last thirty years: sleep is not just a period of inactivity or a garbage collection of the waste products that the brain accumulated while we were awake. Quite the contrary: while we sleep, our brain remains active; it runs a specific algorithm that replays the important events it recorded during the previous day and gradually transfers them into a more efficient compartment of our memory.

♦ consolidate: 통합 정리하다

① how to get an adequate amount of sleep
② the role that sleep plays in the learning process
③ a new method of stimulating engagement in learning
④ an effective way to keep your mind alert and active
⑤ the side effects of certain medications on brain function

04 ⓒ 90초

★★☆
2019년 11월 23번

다음 글의 주제로 가장 적절한 것은?

Our world today is comparatively harmless. We don't have to be careful every moment that a tiger is behind us. We do not have to worry about starving. Our dangers today are, for example, high blood pressure or diabetes. To be clear, we have a Stone Age brain that lives in a modern world. Because of this, many situations are considered a threat by our brains, although they are harmless to our survival. In the past, danger meant we either had to flee or fight. If we have an appointment but are stuck in a traffic jam, that does not really threaten our lives. However, our brain considers this a danger. That is the point. There is no danger, but our brain rates it as such. If we have an unpleasant conversation with our partner, it does not threaten our lives, and we do not have to flee or fight. The danger is an illusion. Our Stone Age brain sees a mortal danger that is not there.

① the role of instinct in deciding to flee or fight
② benefits of danger perception for humans' survival
③ our perception of harmless situations as threatening
④ the human brain's evolution for telling friend from foe
⑤ primitive people's ways of quickly dealing with dangers

정답과 해설 : 03 066 04 067

05 ⏱ 90초

★★☆
2023년 3월 23번

다음 글의 주제로 가장 적절한 것은?

What consequences of eating too many grapes and other sweet fruit could there possibly be for our brains? A few large studies have helped to shed some light. In one, higher fruit intake in older, cognitively healthy adults was linked with less volume in the hippocampus. This finding was unusual, since people who eat more fruit usually display the benefits associated with a healthy diet. In this study, however, the researchers isolated various components of the subjects' diets and found that fruit didn't seem to be doing their memory centers any favors. Another study from the Mayo Clinic saw a similar inverse relationship between fruit intake and volume of the cortex, the large outer layer of the brain. Researchers in the latter study noted that excessive consumption of high-sugar fruit (such as mangoes, bananas, and pineapples) may cause metabolic and cognitive problems as much as processed carbs do.

* hippocampus: (대뇌 측두엽의) 해마 ** carb: 탄수화물 식품

① benefits of eating whole fruit on the brain health
② universal preference for sweet fruit among children
③ types of brain exercises enhancing long-term memory
④ nutritional differences between fruit and processed carbs
⑤ negative effect of fruit overconsumption on the cognitive brain

06 ⏱ 90초

★★☆
2018년 9월 22번

다음 글의 주제로 가장 적절한 것은?

Although we don't know the full neurological effects of digital technologies on young children's development, we do know that all screen time is not created equal. For example, reading an e-book, videoconferencing with grandma, or showing your child a picture you just took of them is not the same as the passive, television-watching screen time that concerns many parents and educators. So, rather than focusing on *how much* children are interacting with screens, parents and educators are turning their focus instead to *what* children are interacting with and *who* is talking with them about their experiences. Though parents may be tempted to hand a child a screen and walk away, guiding children's media experiences helps them build important 21st Century skills, such as critical thinking and media literacy.

① the predictors of children's screen media addiction
② reasons for children's preference for screen media
③ importance of what experiences kids have with screens
④ effects of the amount of screen time on kids' social skills
⑤ necessity of parental control on children's physical activities

07

⏱ 90초 ★★☆ 2022년 6월 23번

다음 글의 주제로 가장 적절한 것은?

In the movie *Groundhog Day*, a weatherman played by Bill Murray is forced to re-live a single day over and over again. Confronted with this seemingly endless loop, he eventually rebels against living through the same day the same way twice. He learns French, becomes a great pianist, befriends his neighbors, helps the poor. Why do we cheer him on? Because we don't want perfect predictability, even if what's on repeat is appealing. Surprise engages us. It allows us to escape autopilot. It keeps us awake to our experience. In fact, the neurotransmitter systems involved in reward are tied to the level of surprise: rewards delivered at regular, predictable times yield a lot less activity in the brain than the same rewards delivered at random unpredictable times. Surprise gratifies.

♦ loop: 고리 ♦♦ neurotransmitter: 신경전달물질

① considerations in learning foreign languages
② people's inclination towards unpredictability
③ hidden devices to make a movie plot unexpected
④ positive effects of routine on human brain function
⑤ danger of predicting the future based on the present

08

⏱ 90초 ★★☆ 2023년 9월 23번

다음 글의 주제로 가장 적절한 것은?

If cooking is as central to human identity, biology, and culture as the biological anthropologist Richard Wrangham suggests, it stands to reason that the decline of cooking in our time would have serious consequences for modern life, and so it has. Are they all bad? Not at all. The outsourcing of much of the work of cooking to corporations has relieved women of what has traditionally been their exclusive responsibility for feeding the family, making it easier for them to work outside the home and have careers. It has headed off many of the domestic conflicts that such a large shift in gender roles and family dynamics was bound to spark. It has relieved other pressures in the household, including longer workdays and overscheduled children, and saved us time that we can now invest in other pursuits. It has also allowed us to diversify our diets substantially, making it possible even for people with no cooking skills and little money to enjoy a whole different cuisine. All that's required is a microwave.

① current trends in commercial cooking equipment
② environmental impacts of shifts in dietary patterns
③ cost-effective ways to cook healthy meals at home
④ reasons behind the decline of the food service industry
⑤ benefits of reduced domestic cooking duties through outsourcing

정답과 해설 : 07 069 08 070

09 ⓒ 90초

★★☆ 2016년 9월 23번

다음 글의 주제로 가장 적절한 것은?

The cultural ideas spread by empire were seldom the exclusive creation of the ruling elite. Since the imperial vision tends to be universal and inclusive, it was relatively easy for imperial elites to adopt ideas, norms, and traditions from wherever they found them, rather than to stick to a single rigid tradition. While some emperors sought to purify their cultures and return to what they viewed as their roots, for the most part empires have produced hybrid civilizations that absorbed much from their subject peoples. The imperial culture of Rome was Greek almost as much as Roman. Imperial Mongol culture was a Chinese copycat. In the imperial United States, an American president of Kenyan blood can eat Italian pizza while watching his favorite film, *Lawrence of Arabia*, a British epic about the Arab rebellion against the Turks.

♦ hybrid: 잡종의, 합성의

① reasons for the collapse of great empires
② severe moral corruption of imperial elites
③ distinct differences among ancient empires
④ impacts of ancient Rome on Western culture
⑤ integrative characteristics of empire civilizations

10 ⓒ 90초

★★☆ 2022년 11월 23번

다음 글의 주제로 가장 적절한 것은?

Native Americans often sang and danced in preparation for launching an attack. The emotional and neurochemical excitement that resulted from this preparatory singing gave them stamina to carry out their attacks. What may have begun as an unconscious, uncontrolled act — rushing their victims with singing and beating drums in a frenzy — could have become a strategy as the victors saw firsthand the effect their actions had on those they were attacking. Although war dances risk warning an enemy of an upcoming attack, the arousal and synchronizing benefits for the attackers may compensate for the loss of surprise. Humans who sang, danced, and marched may have enjoyed a strong advantage on the battlefield as well as intimidated enemies who witnessed such a spectacle. Nineteenth-and twentieth-century Germans feared no one more than the Scots — the bagpipes and drums were disturbing in their sheer loudness and visual spectacle.

♦ frenzy: 격분 ♦♦ synchronize: 동시에 움직이게 하다

① cultural differences in honoring war victims
② benefits of utilizing sound and motion in warfare
③ functions of music in preventing or resolving conflicts
④ strategies of analyzing an enemy's vulnerable points in war
⑤ effects of religious dances on lowering anxiety on the battlefield

11 ⏱ 100초

★★★
2021년 3월 23번

다음 글의 주제로 가장 적절한 것은?

Before the modern scientific era, creativity was attributed to a superhuman force; all novel ideas originated with the gods. After all, how could a person create something that did not exist before the divine act of creation? In fact, the Latin meaning of the verb "inspire" is "to breathe into," reflecting the belief that creative inspiration was similar to the moment in creation when God first breathed life into man. Plato argued that the poet was possessed by divine inspiration, and Plotin wrote that art could only be beautiful if it descended from God. The artist's job was not to imitate nature but rather to reveal the sacred and transcendent qualities of nature. Art could only be a pale imitation of the perfection of the world of ideas. Greek artists did not blindly imitate what they saw in reality; instead they tried to represent the pure, true forms underlying reality, resulting in a sort of compromise between abstraction and accuracy.

◆ transcendent: 초월적인

① conflicting views on the role of artists
② positive effects of imitation on creativity
③ contribution of art to sharing religious beliefs
④ gods as a source of creativity in the pre-modern era
⑤ collaboration between philosophy and art in ancient times

12 ⏱ 100초

★★★
2019년 9월 23번

다음 글의 주제로 가장 적절한 것은?

The original idea of a patent, remember, was not to reward inventors with monopoly profits, but to encourage them to share their inventions. A certain amount of intellectual property law is plainly necessary to achieve this. But it has gone too far. Most patents are now as much about defending monopoly and discouraging rivals as about sharing ideas. And that disrupts innovation. Many firms use patents as barriers to entry, suing upstart innovators who trespass on their intellectual property even on the way to some other goal. In the years before World War I, aircraft makers tied each other up in patent lawsuits and slowed down innovation until the US government stepped in. Much the same has happened with smartphones and biotechnology today. New entrants have to fight their way through "patent thickets" if they are to build on existing technologies to make new ones.

◆ trespass: 침해하다

① side effects of anti-monopoly laws
② ways to protect intellectual property
③ requirements for applying for a patent
④ patent law abuse that hinders innovation
⑤ resources needed for technological innovation

정답과 해설 : 11 072 12 073

13 ⏱ 100초

★★★
2021년 9월 23번

다음 글의 주제로 가장 적절한 것은?

Many marine species including oysters, marsh grasses, and fish were deliberately introduced for food or for erosion control, with little knowledge of the impacts they could have. Fish and shellfish have been intentionally introduced all over the world for aquaculture, providing food and jobs, but they can escape and become a threat to native species, ecosystem function, or livelihoods. Atlantic salmon are reared in ocean net-pens in Washington State and British Columbia. Many escape each year, and they have been recovered in both saltwater and freshwater in Washington State, British Columbia, and Alaska. Recreational fishing can also spread invasive species. Bait worms from Maine are popular throughout the country. They are commonly packed in seaweed which contains many other organisms. If the seaweed is discarded, it or the organisms on it can colonize new areas. Fishing boots, recreational boats, and trailers can pick up organisms at one location and move them elsewhere.

♦ aquaculture: 양식(업)

① benefits of recreational ocean fishing
② ways to maintain marine biodiversity
③ potential value of the ocean for ecotourism
④ contribution of ocean farming to food supply
⑤ human influence on the spread of invasive species

14 ⏱ 100초

★★★
2018년 6월 21번

다음 글의 주제로 가장 적절한 것은?

The development of writing was pioneered not by gossips, storytellers, or poets, but by accountants. The earliest writing system has its roots in the Neolithic period, when humans first began to switch from hunting and gathering to a settled lifestyle based on agriculture. This shift began around 9500 B.C. in a region known as the Fertile Crescent, which stretches from modern-day Egypt, up to southeastern Turkey, and down again to the border between Iraq and Iran. Writing seems to have evolved in this region from the custom of using small clay pieces to account for transactions involving agricultural goods such as grain, sheep, and cattle. The first written documents, which come from the Mesopotamian city of Uruk and date back to around 3400 B.C., record amounts of bread, payment of taxes, and other transactions using simple symbols and marks on clay tablets.

♦ transaction: 거래

① various tools to improve agricultural production
② regional differences in using the writing system
③ ways to store agricultural goods in ancient cities
④ changed lifestyles based on agricultural development
⑤ early writing as a means of recording economic activities

정답과 해설 : 13 074 14 075

15 ⓘ 100초

★★★ 2019년 6월 23번

다음 글의 주제로 가장 적절한 것은?

In this world, being smart or competent isn't enough. People sometimes don't recognize talent when they see it. Their vision is clouded by the first impression we give and that can lose us the job we want, or the relationship we want. The way we present ourselves can speak more eloquently of the skills we bring to the table, if we actively cultivate that presentation. Nobody likes to be crossed off the list before being given the opportunity to show others who they are. Being able to tell your story from the moment you meet other people is a skill that must be actively cultivated, in order to send the message that you're someone to be considered and the right person for the position. For that reason, it's important that we all learn how to say the appropriate things in the right way and to present ourselves in a way that appeals to other people — tailoring a great first impression.

♦ eloquently: 설득력 있게

① difficulty of presenting yourself in public
② risks of judging others based on first impressions
③ factors keeping you from making great impressions
④ strategies that help improve your presentation skills
⑤ necessity of developing the way you show yourself

16 ⓘ 100초

★★★ 2022년 3월 23번

다음 글의 주제로 가장 적절한 것은?

Individual human beings differ from one another physically in a multitude of visible and invisible ways. If races — as most people define them — are real biological entities, then people of African ancestry would share a wide variety of traits while people of European ancestry would share a wide variety of *different* traits. But once we add traits that are less visible than skin coloration, hair texture, and the like, we find that the people we identify as "the same race" are less and less like one another and more and more like people we identify as "different races." Add to this point that the physical features used to identify a person as a representative of some race (e.g. skin coloration) are continuously variable, so that one cannot say where "brown skin" becomes "white skin." Although the physical differences themselves are real, the way we use physical differences to classify people into discrete races is a cultural construction.

♦ entity: 실체 ♦♦ discrete: 별개의

① causes of physical variations among different races
② cultural differences between various races
③ social policies to overcome racism
④ importance of environmental factors in evolution
⑤ misconception about race as a biological construct

정답과 해설 : 15 075 16 076

17 ⓒ 100초

★★★ 2023년 6월 23번

다음 글의 주제로 가장 적절한 것은? [3점]

Education must focus on the trunk of the tree of knowledge, revealing the ways in which the branches, twigs, and leaves all emerge from a common core. Tools for thinking stem from this core, providing a common language with which practitioners in different fields may share their experience of the process of innovation and discover links between their creative activities. When the same terms are employed across the curriculum, students begin to link different subjects and classes. If they practice abstracting in writing class, if they work on abstracting in painting or drawing class, and if, in all cases, they call it abstracting, they begin to understand how to think beyond disciplinary boundaries. They see how to transform their thoughts from one mode of conception and expression to another. Linking the disciplines comes naturally when the terms and tools are presented as part of a universal imagination.

① difficulties in finding meaningful links between disciplines
② drawbacks of applying a common language to various fields
③ effects of diversifying the curriculum on students' creativity
④ necessity of using a common language to integrate the curriculum
⑤ usefulness of turning abstract thoughts into concrete expressions

18 ⓒ 90초

★★☆ 2023년 11월 23번

다음 글의 주제로 가장 적절한 것은?

Sylvan Goldman invented the shopping cart and introduced it in his stores in 1937. It was an excellent device that would make it easy for shoppers to buy as much as they wanted without getting tired or seeking others' help. But Goldman discovered that in spite of his repeated advertisements and explanations, he could not persuade his shoppers to use the wheeled carts. Men were reluctant because they thought they would appear weak if they pushed such carts instead of carrying their shopping. Women wouldn't touch them because the carts reminded them of baby carriages. It was only a few elderly shoppers who used them. That made the carts even less attractive to the majority of the shoppers. Then Goldman hit upon an idea. He hired several models, men and women, of different ages and asked them to wheel the carts in the store and shop. A young woman employee standing near the entrance told the regular shoppers, 'Look, everyone is using the carts. Why don't you?' That was the turning point. A few shills disguised as regular shoppers easily accomplished what logic, explanations, and advertisements failed to do. Within a few weeks shoppers readily accepted those carts.

* shill: 바람잡이

① persuasive power of peer behavior
② methods to help consumers shop less
③ innovative ways to reduce waste in retail
④ hidden nature of human beings to support materialism
⑤ importance of a store layout based on customer needs

DAY 05 06 주제 추론

정답과 해설 : 17 077 18 078

19 ⓒ 100초

★★★ 2024년 3월 23번

다음 글의 주제로 가장 적절한 것은?

Empathy is frequently listed as one of the most desired skills in an employer or employee, although without specifying exactly what is meant by *empathy*. Some businesses stress cognitive empathy, emphasizing the need for leaders to understand the perspective of employees and customers when negotiating deals and making decisions. Others stress affective empathy and empathic concern, emphasizing the ability of leaders to gain trust from employees and customers by treating them with real concern and compassion. When some consultants argue that successful companies foster empathy, what that translates to is that companies should conduct good market research. In other words, an "empathic" company understands the needs and wants of its customers and seeks to fulfill those needs and wants. When some people speak of design with empathy, what that translates to is that companies should take into account the specific needs of different populations — the blind, the deaf, the elderly, non-English speakers, the color-blind, and so on — when designing products.

♦ empathy: 공감, 공감 능력 ♦♦ compassion: 동정심

① diverse benefits of good market research
② negative factors in making business decisions
③ difficulties in designing products with empathic concern
④ efforts to build cognitive empathy among employees
⑤ different interpretations of empathy in business

20 ⓒ 80초

★☆☆ 2024년 6월 23번

다음 글의 주제로 가장 적절한 것은?

If there is little or no diversity of views, and all scientists see, think, and question the world in a similar way, then they will not, as a community, be as objective as they maintain they are, or at least aspire to be. The solution is that there should be far greater diversity in the practice of science: in gender, ethnicity, and social and cultural backgrounds. Science works because it is carried out by people who pursue their curiosity about the natural world and test their and each other's ideas from as many varied perspectives and angles as possible. When science is done by a diverse group of people, and if consensus builds up about a particular area of scientific knowledge, then we can have more confidence in its objectivity and truth.

♦ consensus: 일치

① value of acquiring scientific knowledge through trial and error
② necessity of various perspectives in practicing science
③ benefits of building good relationships among scientists
④ curiosity as a key factor in designing experiments
⑤ importance of specialization in scientific research

정답과 해설 : 19 079 20 080

21 ⓒ 90초

★★☆
2024년 9월 23번

다음 글의 주제로 가장 적절한 것은?

People seem to recognize that the arts are cultural activities that draw on (or react against) certain cultural traditions, certain shared understanding, and certain values and ideas that are characteristic of the time and place in which the art is created. In the case of science, however, opinions differ. Some scientists, like the great biologist J. B. S. Haldane, see science in a similar light — as a historical activity that occurs in a particular time and place, and that needs to be understood within that context. Others, however, see science as a purely "objective" pursuit, uninfluenced by the cultural viewpoint and values of those who create it. In describing this view of science, philosopher Hugh Lacey speaks of the belief that there is an underlying order of the world which is simply there to be discovered — the world of pure "fact" stripped of any link with value. The aim of science according to this view is to represent this world of pure "fact", independently of any relationship it might bear contingently to human practices and experiences.

◆ contingently: 혹여라도

① misconceptions on how experimental data should be measured
② views on whether science is free from cultural context or not
③ ways for minimizing cultural bias in scientific pursuits
④ challenges in achieving objectivity in scientific studies
⑤ functions of science in analyzing cultural phenomena

DAY 05
06 주제 추론

정답과 해설 : 21 080

유형 TIP

07. 제목 추론

주제 추론 유형과 유사하나 주제를 간결하고 포괄적으로 나타낸 것을 정답으로 찾아야 함.
지문의 핵심어와 제목 선택지의 핵심어가 다르거나, 내용이 은유적으로 표현되는 경우도 있음.

유형 TIP 대표 예제

25BR2T_CH07 25BR2E_CH07

유형 공략법

1) 반복되는 내용과 주제의 위치를 보여 주는 표현에 주목하여 주제를 파악한다.

글에서는 반복되는 내용이 곧 주제임.
연결사 등 주제 위치를 보여 주는 표현을 활용한 문장이 주제문일 확률이 높음.

2) 선택지의 비유적이고 함축적인 표현에 주의한다.

3) 지나치게 포괄적이거나 지엽적인 선택지에 주의한다.

정답은 지문의 내용을 모두 포함해야 함.
교묘하게 지문의 핵심 어구를 포함한 듯 보이는 선택지를 선택하지 않도록 주의해야 함.

필수 암기 어휘와 표현

연결사 및 중요 표현

역접/대조	however, but, (and) yet, instead (of), rather, on the other hand, by[in] contrast, in contrast to, conversely, on the contrary, whereas, while, meanwhile, at the same time
양보	though, although, even if[though], still, nevertheless, nonetheless, even so, notwithstanding, despite (that), in spite of, having said that, that (being) said, granting that, admitting that, after all
요약	in short, shortly, in brief, briefly, in sum, to summarize, to sum up, to put it simply, in a word, on the whole, overall
재진술	that is (to say), in other words, namely, to put it another way, stated another way, i.e.
강조	indeed, above all, especially, of course, in particular, in fact, in effect, in reality, in truth, truly, actually, as a matter of fact, most important, more importantly, the thing is, it is clear that, no doubt, never, not at all, in the first place, most of all, certainly, (for) sure, surely, apparently, obviously
조건	if, once, given (that), unless, otherwise, if not, or else, in case of[that], in the event of[that], as[so] long as, suppose (that), supposing (that), provided (that), providing (that)

제목 추론 대표 예제 - 2024학년도 수능 24번

다음 글의 제목으로 가장 적절한 것은? 3점

(1) The concept of overtourism rests on a particular assumption about people and places common in tourism studies and the social sciences in general. (2) Both are seen as clearly defined and demarcated. (3) People are framed as bounded social actors either playing the role of hosts or guests. (4) Places, in a similar way, are treated as stable containers with clear boundaries. (5) Hence, places can be full of tourists and thus suffer from overtourism. (6) But what does it mean for a place to be full of people? (7) Indeed, there are examples of particular attractions that have limited capacity and where there is actually no room for more visitors. (8) This is not least the case with some man-made constructions such as the Eiffel Tower. (9) However, with places such as cities, regions or even whole countries being promoted as destinations and described as victims of overtourism, things become more complex. (10) What is excessive or out of proportion is highly relative and might be more related to other aspects than physical capacity, such as natural degradation and economic leakages (not to mention politics and local power dynamics).

* demarcate: 경계를 정하다

① The Solutions to Overtourism: From Complex to Simple
② What Makes Popular Destinations Attractive to Visitors?
③ Are Tourist Attractions Winners or Losers of Overtourism?
④ The Severity of Overtourism: Much Worse than Imagined
✔ Overtourism: Not Simply a Matter of People and Places

STEP 1 반복되는 내용과 주제의 위치를 보여 주는 표현에 주목하여 주제를 파악한다.

→ 문장 (1)부터 (5)까지 과잉 관광의 개념에 적용되는 인간과 장소라는 두 요소를 설명한 이후, 문장 (6)과 (9)에서 각각 주의를 환기하는 'But'과 'However'를 활용하여 장소에 사람이 많다는 '과잉 관광'의 의미에 대한 이슈를 제기하고, 이어서 문장 (10)을 통해 과잉 관광에는 장소에 사람이 많다는 것 이외에 다른 요인도 있음을 재차 강조하고 있음. 따라서 과잉 관광이 물리적 수용 능력 말고도 다른 것과 관련 있다는 것이 이 글의 주제임.

STEP 2 지나치게 포괄적이거나 지엽적인 선택지에 주의한다.

①: 과잉 관광을 해결하자는 취지의 글이 아님.
②: 인기 있는 목적지의 매력적인 요소가 무엇인지를 분석하는 글이 아님.
③: 과잉 관광으로 관광 명소가 혜택을 보는지 안 보는지에 대한 언급은 없음.
④: 과잉 관광의 부정적인 측면을 강조한 내용은 없음.

전문 해석

(1) 과잉 관광의 개념은 관광학 및 사회 과학 전반에서 흔한 사람과 장소에 대한 특정한 가정에 기초한다. (2) (사람과 장소) 둘 다 명확히 정의되고 경계가 정해져 있는 것으로 여겨진다. (3) 사람은 주인 또는 손님 둘 중 하나의 역할을 하는 경계가 확실한 사회적 행위자로 표현된다. (4) 유사한 방식으로, 장소는 명확한 경계를 가진 안정적인 용기(容器)로 취급된다. (5) 따라서, 장소는 관광객으로 가득 찰 수 있으며 그래서 과잉 관광으로 고통받을 수 있다. (6) 그러나 장소가 사람으로 꽉 차 있다는 것은 무엇을 의미하는가? (7) 사실, 제한된 수용 능력을 가지고 더 많은 방문객을 위한 공간이 실제로 없는 특정 명소의 사례가 있다. (8) 이는 특히 에펠탑과 같은 일부 인공 건축물의 경우이다. (9) 그러나, 여행의 목적지로 홍보되고 과잉 관광의 피해자로 묘사되는 도시, 지역 또는 심지어 국가 전체와 같은 장소의 경우, 상황은 더 복잡해진다. (10) 과도하거나 균형이 안 맞는 것은 매우 상대적이며 물리적 수용 능력보다는 자연적인 질적 저하와 경제적 유출(정치와 지역 권력 역학은 말할 것도 없고)과 같은 다른 측면과 더 관련이 있을 수도 있다.
- overtourism(과잉 관광): 지역 규모에 비해 너무 많은 관광객이 오는 현상

중요 어휘

- □ rest on ~에 기초하다[의거하다]
- □ see A as B A를 B로 여기다
- □ demarcate 동 경계를 정하다
- □ frame 동 표현하다, 틀을 씌우다
- □ bounded 형 경계가 확실한
- □ container 명 용기, 그릇, (화물 수송용) 컨테이너
- □ attraction 명 (관광) 명소, 매력
- □ capacity 명 수용 능력, 용량, (타고난) 능력
- □ not least 특히
- □ construction 명 건축(물), 구조(물)
- □ destination 명 (여행의) 목적지
- □ victim 명 피해자, 희생자
- □ things 명 상황, 형편
- □ excessive 형 과도한, 지나친
- □ out of proportion 균형이 안 맞는
- □ degradation 명 (질적) 저하
- □ leakage 명 유출, 누출, 누수
- □ not to mention ~는 말할 것도 없고
- □ dynamics 명 (단수 취급) 역학, 역학 관계

자세한 해설지 QR→
자세한해설-CH07

07 제목 추론

동영상 강의

25BR2_CH07

01 ⓒ 80초

★☆☆ 2020년 3월 24번

다음 글의 제목으로 가장 적절한 것은?

If a food contains more sugar than any other ingredient, government regulations require that sugar be listed first on the label. But if a food contains several different kinds of sweeteners, they can be listed separately, which pushes each one farther down the list. This requirement has led the food industry to put in three different sources of sugar so that they don't have to say the food has that much sugar. So sugar doesn't appear first. Whatever the true motive, ingredient labeling still does not fully convey the amount of sugar being added to food, certainly not in a language that's easy for consumers to understand. A world-famous cereal brand's label, for example, indicates that the cereal has 11 grams of sugar per serving. But nowhere does it tell consumers that more than one-third of the box contains added sugar.

① Artificial Sweeteners: Good or Bad?
② Consumer Benefits of Ingredient Labeling
③ Sugar: An Energy Booster for Your Brain
④ Truth About Sugar Hidden in Food Labels
⑤ What Should We Do to Reduce Sugar Intake?

02 ⓒ 90초

★★☆ 2019년 9월 24번

다음 글의 제목으로 가장 적절한 것은?

The earliest challenges and contests to solve important problems in mathematics date back to the sixteenth and seventeenth centuries. Some of these problems have continued to challenge mathematicians until modern times. For example, Pierre de Fermat issued a set of mathematical challenges in 1657, many on prime numbers and divisibility. The solution to what is now known as Fermat's Last Theorem was not established until the late 1990s by Andrew Wiles. David Hilbert, a German mathematician, identified 23 unsolved problems in 1900 with the hope that these problems would be solved in the twenty-first century. Although some of the problems were solved, others remain unsolved to this day. More recently, in 2000, the Clay Mathematics Institute named seven mathematical problems that had not been solved with the hope that they could be solved in the twenty-first century. A $1 million prize will be awarded for solving each of these seven problems.

① Glory in the Past, Ugliness in the Present
② Doubt: What Leads to Unexpected Findings
③ Formulas in Math Solve Problems in Other Areas
④ Unknown Geniuses Achieving the Greatest Things
⑤ Unsolved Math Problems Passed to Future Generations

정답과 해설 : 01 082 02 082

03 ⏲ 90초

★★☆ 2019년 11월 24번

다음 글의 제목으로 가장 적절한 것은?

There has been a general belief that sport is a way of reducing violence. Anthropologist Richard Sipes tests this notion in a classic study of the relationship between sport and violence. Focusing on what he calls "combative sports," those sports including actual body contact between opponents or simulated warfare, he hypothesizes that if sport is an alternative to violence, then one would expect to find an inverse correlation between the popularity of combative sports and the frequency and intensity of warfare. In other words, the more combative sports (e.g., football, boxing) the less likely warfare. Using the Human Relations Area Files and a sample of 20 societies, Sipes tests the hypothesis and discovers a significant relationship between combative sports and violence, but a direct one, not the inverse correlation of his hypothesis. According to Sipes' analysis, the more pervasive and popular combative sports are in a society, the more likely that society is to engage in war. So, Sipes draws the obvious conclusion that combative sports are not alternatives to war but rather are reflections of the same aggressive impulses in human society.

① Is There a Distinction among Combative Sports?
② Combative Sports Mirror Human Aggressiveness
③ Never Let Your Aggressive Impulses Consume You!
④ International Conflicts: Creating New Military Alliances
⑤ Combative Sports Are More Common among the Oppressed

04 ⏲ 90초

★★☆ 2020년 6월 24번

다음 글의 제목으로 가장 적절한 것은?

Many inventions were invented thousands of years ago so it can be difficult to know their exact origins. Sometimes scientists discover a model of an early invention and from this model they can accurately tell us how old it is and where it came from. However, there is always the possibility that in the future other scientists will discover an even older model of the same invention in a different part of the world. In fact, we are forever discovering the history of ancient inventions. An example of this is the invention of pottery. For many years archaeologists believed that pottery was first invented in the Near East (around modern Iran) where they had found pots dating back to 9,000 B.C. In the 1960s, however, older pots from 10,000 B.C. were found on Honshu Island, Japan. There is always a possibility that in the future archaeologists will find even older pots somewhere else.

① How Can You Tell Original from Fake?
② Exploring the Materials of Ancient Pottery
③ Origin of Inventions: Never-Ending Journey
④ Learn from the Past, Change for the Better
⑤ Science as a Driving Force for Human Civilization

DAY 06 07 제목 추론

정답과 해설 : 03 083 04 084

05 ⓒ 90초

★★☆ 2021년 3월 24번

다음 글의 제목으로 가장 적절한 것은?

Some beginning researchers mistakenly believe that a good hypothesis is one that is guaranteed to be right (e.g., *alcohol will slow down reaction time*). However, if we already know your hypothesis is true before you test it, testing your hypothesis won't tell us anything new. Remember, research is supposed to produce *new* knowledge. To get new knowledge, you, as a researcher-explorer, need to leave the safety of the shore (established facts) and venture into uncharted waters (as Einstein said, "If we knew what we were doing, it would not be called research, would it?"). If your predictions about what will happen in these uncharted waters are wrong, that's okay: Scientists are allowed to make mistakes (as Bates said, "Research is the process of going up alleys to see if they are blind"). Indeed, scientists often learn more from predictions that do not turn out than from those that do.

♦ uncharted waters: 미개척 영역

① Researchers, Don't Be Afraid to Be Wrong
② Hypotheses Are Different from Wild Guesses
③ Why Researchers Are Reluctant to Share Their Data
④ One Small Mistake Can Ruin Your Whole Research
⑤ Why Hard Facts Don't Change Our Minds

06 ⓒ 90초

★★☆ 2022년 6월 24번

다음 글의 제목으로 가장 적절한 것은?

A building is an inanimate object, but it is not an inarticulate one. Even the simplest house always makes a statement, one expressed in brick and stone, in wood and glass, rather than in words — but no less loud and obvious. When we see a rusting trailer surrounded by weeds and abandoned cars, or a brand-new mini-mansion with a high wall, we instantly get a message. In both of these cases, though in different accents, it is "Stay Out of Here." It is not only houses, of course, that communicate with us. All kinds of buildings — churches, museums, schools, hospitals, restaurants, and offices — speak to us silently. Sometimes the statement is deliberate. A store or restaurant can be designed so that it welcomes mostly low-income or high-income customers. Buildings tell us what to think and how to act, though we may not register their messages consciously.

♦ inarticulate: 표현을 제대로 하지 못하는

① Buildings Do Talk in Their Own Ways!
② Design of Buildings Starts from Nature
③ Language of Buildings: Too Vague to Grasp
④ Which Is More Important, Safety or Beauty?
⑤ How Do Architects Attach Emotions to Buildings?

정답과 해설 : 05 085 06 085

07 ⓒ 90초

★★☆ 2023년 9월 24번

다음 글의 제목으로 가장 적절한 것은?

As you may already know, what and how you buy can be political. To whom do you want to give your money? Which companies and corporations do you value and respect? Be mindful about every purchase by carefully researching the corporations that are taking our money to decide if they deserve our support. Do they have a record of polluting the environment, or do they have fair-trade practices and an end-of-life plan for the products they make? Are they committed to bringing about good in the world? For instance, my family has found a company producing recycled, plastic-packaging-free toilet paper with a social conscience. They contribute 50 percent of their profits to the construction of toilets around the world, and we're genuinely happy to spend our money on this special toilet paper each month. Remember that the corporate world is built on consumers, so as a consumer you have the power to vote with your wallet and encourage companies to embrace healthier and more sustainable practices with every purchase you choose to make.

① Green Businesses: Are They Really Green?
② Fair Trade Does Not Always Appeal to Consumers
③ Buy Consciously, Make Companies Do the Right Things
④ Do Voters Have a Powerful Impact on Economic Policy?
⑤ The Secret to Saving Your Money: Record Your Spending

08 ⓒ 90초

★★☆ 2017년 11월 22번

다음 글의 제목으로 가장 적절한 것은?

Katherine Schreiber and Leslie Sim, experts on exercise addiction, recognized that smartwatches and fitness trackers have probably inspired sedentary people to take up exercise, and encouraged people who aren't very active to exercise more consistently. But they were convinced the devices were also quite dangerous. Schreiber explained that focusing on numbers separates people from being in tune with their body. Exercising becomes mindless, which is 'the goal' of addiction. This 'goal' that she mentioned is a sort of automatic mindlessness, the outsourcing of decision making to a device. She recently sustained a stress fracture in her foot because she refused to listen to her overworked body, instead continuing to run toward an unreasonable workout target. Schreiber has suffered from addictive exercise tendencies, and vows not to use wearable tech when she works out.

♦ sedentary: 주로 앉아서 지내는

① Get out of Your Chair If You Want to Stay Fit
② Addiction: Another Name for Unbreakable Habit
③ Don't Respond Mindlessly to Stressful Situations
④ It's Time to Use Advanced Technology for a Better Life
⑤ Setting a Workout Goal with Technology Isn't Always Right

정답과 해설 : 07 086 08 087

09 ⏱ 90초

★★☆ 2019년 6월 24번

다음 글의 제목으로 가장 적절한 것은?

Take the choice of which kind of soup to buy. There's too much data here for you to struggle with: calories, price, salt content, taste, packaging, and so on. If you were a robot, you'd be stuck here all day trying to make a decision, with no obvious way to trade off which details matter more. To land on a choice, you need a summary of some sort. And that's what the feedback from your body is able to give you. Thinking about your budget might make your palms sweat, or your mouth might water thinking about the last time you consumed the chicken noodle soup, or noting the excessive creaminess of the other soup might give you a stomachache. You simulate your experience with one soup, and then the other. Your bodily experience helps your brain to quickly place a value on soup A, and another on soup B, allowing you to tip the balance in one direction or the other. You don't just extract the data from the soup cans, you feel the data.

① You Are What You Eat!
② Bodily Feedback Can Fool You
③ What to Eat? Your Body Will Tell You!
④ The More Choices, the Better Outcomes
⑤ Read Information on Food Labels Carefully

10 ⏱ 90초

★★☆ 2020년 11월 24번

다음 글의 제목으로 가장 적절한 것은?

In government, in law, in culture, and in routine everyday interaction beyond family and immediate neighbours, a widely understood and clearly formulated language is a great aid to mutual confidence. When dealing with property, with contracts, or even just with the routine exchange of goods and services, concepts and descriptions need to be as precise and unambiguous as possible, otherwise misunderstandings will arise. If full communication with a potential counterparty in a deal is not possible, then uncertainty and probably a measure of distrust will remain. As economic life became more complex in the later Middle Ages, the need for fuller and more precise communication was accentuated. A shared language facilitated clarification and possibly settlement of any disputes. In international trade also the use of a precise and well-formulated language aided the process of translation. The Silk Road could only function at all because translators were always available at interchange points.

♦ accentuate: 강조하다

① Earn Trust with Reliable Goods Rather Than with Words!
② Linguistic Precision: A Key to Successful Economic Transactions
③ Difficulties in Overcoming Language Barriers and Distrust in Trade
④ The More the Economy Grows, the More Complex the World Gets
⑤ Excessive Confidence: The Biggest Reason for Miscommunication

정답과 해설 : 09 088 10 088

11 ⓒ 90초

★★☆ 2017년 6월 23번

다음 글의 제목으로 가장 적절한 것은?

Numbers were invented to describe precise amounts: three teeth, seven days, twelve goats. When quantities are large, however, we do not use numbers in a precise way. We approximate using a 'round number' as a place mark. It is easier and more convenient. When we say, for example, that there were a hundred people at the market, we don't mean that there were exactly one hundred people there. And when we say that the universe is 13.7 billion years old, we don't mean exactly 13,700,000,000; we mean give or take a few hundred million years. Big numbers are understood approximately, small ones precisely, and these two systems interact uneasily. It is clear nonsense to say that next year the universe will be '13.7 billion and one' years old. It will remain 13.7 billion years old for the rest of our lives.

① Mystery in Inventing Numbers
② Numbers: The Mirror of Precision
③ Flexibility Allowed in Big Numbers
④ How Numbers Manipulate Our Lives
⑤ Don't Use Round Numbers in Science!

12 ⓒ 90초

★★☆ 2018년 6월 22번

다음 글의 제목으로 가장 적절한 것은?

Why do you go to the library? For books, yes — and you like books because they tell stories. You hope to get lost in a story or be transported into someone else's life. At one type of library, you can do just that — even though there's not a single book. At a Human Library, people with unique life stories volunteer to be the "books." For a certain amount of time, you can ask them questions and listen to their stories, which are as fascinating and inspiring as any you can find in a book. Many of the stories have to do with some kind of stereotype. You can speak with a refugee, a soldier suffering from PTSD, and a homeless person. The Human Library encourages people to challenge their own existing notions — to truly get to know, and learn from, someone they might otherwise make quick judgements about.

◆ PTSD(Post Traumatic Stress Disorder): 외상 후 스트레스 장애

① Useful Books for Learning Languages
② The Place Where People Are the Books
③ Library: Starting Point for Your Academic Research
④ How to Choose People in the Human Library
⑤ What a Touching Story of a Booklover!

정답과 해설 : 11 089 12 090

13 ⓒ 90초

★★☆ 2021년 6월 24번

다음 글의 제목으로 가장 적절한 것은?

News reporters are taught to start their stories with the most important information. The first sentence, called the lead, contains the most essential elements of the story. A good lead can convey a lot of information. After the lead, information is presented in decreasing order of importance. Journalists call this the "inverted pyramid" structure — the most important information (the widest part of the pyramid) is at the top. The inverted pyramid is great for readers. No matter what the reader's attention span — whether she reads only the lead or the entire story — the inverted pyramid maximizes the information she gets. Think of the alternative: If news stories were written like mysteries with a dramatic payoff at the end, then readers who broke off in mid-story would miss the point. Imagine waiting until the last sentence of a story to find out who won the presidential election or the Super Bowl.

♦ inverted: 거꾸로 된

① Inverted Pyramid: Logically Impossible Structure
② Curiosity Is What Makes Readers Keep Reading
③ Where to Put Key Points in News Writing
④ The More Information, the Less Attention
⑤ Readers, Tell the Facts from the Fakes!

14 ⓒ 90초

★★☆ 2021년 11월 24번

다음 글의 제목으로 가장 적절한 것은?

The free market has liberated people in a way that Marxism never could. What is more, as A. O. Hirschman, the Harvard economic historian, showed in his classic study *The Passions and the Interests*, the market was seen by Enlightenment thinkers Adam Smith, David Hume, and Montesquieu as a powerful solution to one of humanity's greatest traditional weaknesses: violence. When two nations meet, said Montesquieu, they can do one of two things: they can wage war or they can trade. If they wage war, both are likely to lose in the long run. If they trade, both will gain. That, of course, was the logic behind the establishment of the European Union: to lock together the destinies of its nations, especially France and Germany, in such a way that they would have an overwhelming interest not to wage war again as they had done to such devastating cost in the first half of the twentieth century.

♦ Marxism: 마르크스주의

① Trade War: A Reflection of Human's Innate Violence
② Free Market: Winning Together over Losing Together
③ New Economic Framework Stabilizes the Free Market
④ Violence Is the Invisible Hand That Disrupts Capitalism!
⑤ How Are Governments Involved in Controlling the Market?

정답과 해설 : 13091 14091

15 ⓒ 90초

★★☆ 2022년 3월 24번

다음 글의 제목으로 가장 적절한 것은?

The realization of human domination over the environment began in the late 1700s with the industrial revolution. Advances in manufacturing transformed societies and economies while producing significant impacts on the environment. American society became structured on multiple industries' capitalistic goals as the development of the steam engine led to the mechanized production of goods in mass quantities. Rural agricultural communities with economies based on handmade goods and agriculture were abandoned for life in urban cities with large factories based on an economy of industrialized manufacturing. Innovations in the production of textiles, iron, and steel provided increased profits to private companies. Simultaneously, those industries exerted authority over the environment and began dumping hazardous by-products in public lands and waterways.

① Strategies for Industrial Innovations
② Urbanization: A Road to a Better Life
③ Industrial Development Hurt the Environment
④ Technology: A Key to Sustainable Development
⑤ The Driving Force of Capitalism Was Not Greed

16 ⓒ 90초

★★☆ 2023년 3월 24번

다음 글의 제목으로 가장 적절한 것은?

Winning turns on a self-conscious awareness that others are watching. It's a lot easier to move under the radar when no one knows you and no one is paying attention. You can mess up and be rough and get dirty because no one even knows you're there. But as soon as you start to win, and others start to notice, you're suddenly aware that you're being observed. You're being judged. You worry that others will discover your flaws and weaknesses, and you start hiding your true personality, so you can be a good role model and good citizen and a leader that others can respect. There is nothing wrong with that. But if you do it at the expense of being who you really are, making decisions that please others instead of pleasing yourself, you're not going to be in that position very long. When you start apologizing for who you are, you stop growing and you stop winning. Permanently.

① Stop Judging Others to Win the Race of Life
② Why Disappointment Hurts More than Criticism
③ Winning vs. Losing: A Dangerously Misleading Mindset
④ Winners in a Trap: Too Self-Conscious to Be Themselves
⑤ Is Honesty the Best Policy to Turn Enemies into Friends?

DAY 06 07 제목 추론

정답과 해설 : 15 092 16 093

17 ⓒ 90초

★★☆ 2022년 11월 24번

다음 글의 제목으로 가장 적절한 것은?

The recent "cycling as a lifestyle" craze has expressed itself in an increase in the number of active cyclists and in growth of cycling club membership in several European, American, Australian and Asian urban areas. It has also been accompanied by a symbolic reinterpretation of the bicycle. After the bicycle had been associated with poverty for many years, expensive recreational bicycles or recreationally-inspired commuting bicycles have suddenly become aspirational products in urban environments. In present times, cycling has become an activity which is also performed for its demonstrative value, its role in identity construction and its effectiveness in impressing others and signaling social status. To a certain extent, cycling has turned into a symbolic marker of the well-off. Obviously, value-laden consumption behavior is by no means limited to cycling. However, the link with identity construction and conspicuous consumption has become particularly manifest in the case of cycling.

♦ conspicuous: 눈에 잘 띄는

① Cycling Contributes to a City's Atmosphere and Identity
② The Rise of Cycling: A New Status Symbol of City Dwellers
③ Cycling Is Wealth-Building but Worsens Social Inequality
④ How to Encourage and Sustain the Bicycle Craze in Urban Areas
⑤ Expanding Bike Lane Networks Can Lead to More Inclusive Cities

18 ⓒ 100초

★★★ 2022년 9월 24번

다음 글의 제목으로 가장 적절한 것은? [3점]

From the earliest times, healthcare services have been recognized to have two equal aspects, namely clinical care and public healthcare. In classical Greek mythology, the god of medicine, Asklepios, had two daughters, Hygiea and Panacea. The former was the goddess of preventive health and wellness, or hygiene, and the latter the goddess of treatment and curing. In modern times, the societal ascendancy of medical professionalism has caused treatment of sick patients to overshadow those preventive healthcare services provided by the less heroic figures of sanitary engineers, biologists, and governmental public health officers. Nevertheless, the quality of health that human populations enjoy is attributable less to surgical dexterity, innovative pharmaceutical products, and bioengineered devices than to the availability of public sanitation, sewage management, and services which control the pollution of the air, drinking water, urban noise, and food for human consumption. The human right to the highest attainable standard of health depends on public healthcare services no less than on the skills and equipment of doctors and hospitals.

♦ ascendancy: 우세 ♦♦ dexterity: 기민함

① Public Healthcare: A Co-Star, Not a Supporting Actor
② The Historical Development of Medicine and Surgery
③ Clinical Care Controversies: What You Don't Know
④ The Massive Similarities Between Different Mythologies
⑤ Initiatives Opening up Health Innovation Around the World

정답과 해설 : 17 094 18 095

19 ⓘ 100초

★★★ 2023년 6월 24번

다음 글의 제목으로 가장 적절한 것은?

New words and expressions emerge continually in response to new situations, ideas and feelings. *The Oxford English Dictionary* publishes supplements of new words and expressions that have entered the language. Some people deplore this kind of thing and see it as a drift from correct English. But it was only in the eighteenth century that any attempt was made to formalize spelling and punctuation of English at all. The language we speak in the twenty-first century would be virtually unintelligible to Shakespeare, and so would his way of speaking to us. Alvin Toffler estimated that Shakespeare would probably only understand about 250,000 of the 450,000 words in general use in the English language now. In other words, so to speak, if Shakespeare were to materialize in London today he would understand, on average, only five out of every nine words in our vocabulary.

♦ deplore: 한탄하다

① Original Meanings of Words Fade with Time
② Dictionary: A Gradual Continuation of the Past
③ Literature: The Driving Force Behind New Words
④ How Can We Bridge the Ever-Widening Language Gap?
⑤ Language Evolution Makes Even Shakespeare Semi-literate!

20 ⓘ 100초

★★★ 2017년 9월 24번

다음 글의 제목으로 가장 적절한 것은?

In 1947, when the Dead Sea Scrolls were discovered, archaeologists set a finder's fee for each new document. Instead of lots of extra scrolls being found, they were simply torn apart to increase the reward. Similarly, in China in the nineteenth century, an incentive was offered for finding dinosaur bones. Farmers located a few on their land, broke them into pieces, and made a lot of money. Modern incentives are no better: Company boards promise bonuses for achieved targets. And what happens? Managers invest more energy in trying to lower the targets than in growing the business. People respond to incentives by doing what is in their best interests. What is noteworthy is, first, how quickly and radically people's behavior changes when incentives come into play, and second, the fact that people respond to the incentives themselves, and not the higher intentions behind them.

♦ scroll: 두루마리

① Relive the Glory of the Golden Past
② How Selfishness Weakens Teamwork
③ Rewards Work Against Original Purposes
④ Non-material Incentives: Superior Motivators
⑤ Cultural Heritage Becomes Tourism Booster!

정답과 해설 : 19 096 20 096

21 ⓒ 100초

★★★ 2018년 6월 23번

다음 글의 제목으로 가장 적절한 것은?

We create a picture of the world using the examples that most easily come to mind. This is foolish, of course, because in reality, things don't happen more frequently just because we can imagine them more easily. Thanks to this prejudice, we travel through life with an incorrect risk map in our heads. Thus, we overestimate the risk of being the victims of a plane crash, a car accident, or a murder. And we underestimate the risk of dying from less spectacular means, such as diabetes or stomach cancer. The chances of bomb attacks are much rarer than we think, and the chances of suffering depression are much higher. We attach too much likelihood to spectacular, flashy, or loud outcomes. Anything silent or invisible we downgrade in our minds. Our brains imagine impressive outcomes more readily than ordinary ones.

① We Weigh Dramatic Things More!
② Brains Think Logically, Not Emotionally
③ Our Brains' Preference for Positive Images
④ How Can People Overcome Their Prejudices?
⑤ The Way to Reduce Errors in Risk Analysis

22 ⓒ 100초

★★★ 2023년 11월 24번

다음 글의 제목으로 가장 적절한 것은?

In response to human-like care robots, critics might charge that human-robot interactions create moral hazards for dementia patients. Even if deception is sometimes allowed when it serves worthy goals, should it be allowed for vulnerable users? Just as children on the autism spectrum with robot companions might be easily fooled into thinking of robots as friends, older adults with cognitive deficits might be. According to Alexis Elder, a professor at UMD, robots are *false* friends, inferior to true friendship. Reasoning along similar lines, John Sullins, a professor at Sonoma State University, holds that robots should "remain iconic or cartoonish so that they are easily distinguished as synthetic even by unsophisticated users." At least then no one is fooled. Making robots clearly fake also avoids the so-called "uncanny valley," where robots are perceived as scary because they so closely resemble us, but not quite. Other critics of robot deception argue that when care recipients are deceived into thinking that robots care, this crosses a line and violates human *dignity*.

♦ dementia: 치매 ♦♦ autism: 자폐성

① The Importance of Protecting Human Dignity
② Robots Can't Surpass Human Beings in Nursing Jobs
③ Why Robots for Vulnerable People Should Look Like Robots
④ Can Robots Learn Ethical Behavior Through Human Interaction?
⑤ Healthcare Robots: Opening the Era of Online Medical Checkups

정답과 해설 : 21 097 22 098

23 ⓒ 80초

★☆☆ 2024년 3월 24번

다음 글의 제목으로 가장 적절한 것은?

The most prevalent problem kids report is that they feel like they need to be accessible at all times. Because technology allows for it, they feel an obligation. It's easy for most of us to relate — you probably feel the same pressure in your own life! It is really challenging to deal with the fact that we're human and can't always respond instantly. For a teen or tween who's still learning the ins and outs of social interactions, it's even worse. Here's how this behavior plays out sometimes: Your child texts one of his friends, and the friend doesn't text back right away. Now it's easy for your child to think, "This person doesn't want to be my friend anymore!" So he texts again, and again, and again — "blowing up their phone." This can be stress-inducing and even read as aggressive. But you can see how easily this could happen.

◆ tween: (10 ~ 12세 사이의) 십대 초반의 아동

① From Symbols to Bytes: History of Communication
② Parents' Desire to Keep Their Children Within Reach
③ Building Trust: The Key to Ideal Human Relationships
④ The Positive Role of Digital Technology in Teen Friendships
⑤ Connected but Stressed: Challenges for Kids in the Digital Era

24 ⓒ 90초

★★☆ 2024년 6월 24번

다음 글의 제목으로 가장 적절한 것은?

We tend to break up time into units, such as weeks, months, and seasons; in a series of studies among farmers in India and students in North America, psychologists found that if a deadline is on the other side of a "break" — such as in the New Year — we're more likely to see it as remote, and, as a result, be less ready to jump into action. What you need to do in that situation is find another way to think about the timeframe. For example, if it's November and the deadline is in January, it's better to tell yourself you have to get it done "this winter" rather than "next year." The best approach is to view deadlines as a challenge that you have to meet within a period that's imminent. That way the stress is more manageable, and you have a better chance of starting — and therefore finishing — in good time.

◆ imminent: 임박한

① Delayed Deadlines: No Hurries, No Worries
② How Stress Affects Your Perception of Time
③ Why Do We Manage Our Tasks Worse in Winter?
④ Trick Your Mind to Get Your Work Done in Time
⑤ The Sooner You Start, The More Errors You Make

정답과 해설 : 23 099 24 100

25 ⏱ 90초

★★☆
2024년 9월 24번

다음 글의 제목으로 가장 적절한 것은?

Mental development consists of individuals increasingly mastering social codes and signals themselves, which they can master only in social situations with the support of more competent individuals, typically adults. In this sense, mental development consists of internalizing social patterns and gradually becoming a responsible actor among other responsible actors. In Denmark, the age of criminal responsibility is 15 years, which means that we then say that people have developed sufficient mental maturity to be accountable for their actions at this point. And at the age of 18 people are given the right to vote and are thereby formally included in the basic democratic process. I do not know whether these age boundaries are optimal, but it is clear that mental development takes place at different rates for different individuals, and depends especially on the social and family environment they have been given. Therefore, having formal limits for responsibility from a specific age that apply to everyone is a somewhat questionable practice. But the question, of course, is whether it can be done any differently.

① Adult Influence Is Key to Child Development
② How Can Social Codes Limit People's Cognition?
③ Democracy Grows Only with Responsible Youth
④ Setting Responsibilities Based on Age: Is It Appropriate?
⑤ Aging: A Possible Obstacle to Consistent Personal Growth

정답과 해설 : 25 101

유형 TIP

08. 도표의 이해

도표를 빠르고 정확하게 해석하여 그 내용을 영어로 표현하는 능력이 요구됨.
지문에 쓰이는 증감, 비교, 배수 등 수치 표현을 이해해야 함.

유형 TIP 25BR2T_CH08
대표 예제 25BR2E_CH08

유형 공략법

1) 도표의 제목과 지문의 첫 문장을 먼저 확인**한다.**
무엇에 관한 내용인지를 파악할 수 있는 정보가 도표의 제목과 지문의 첫 문장에 포함되어 있음.

2) 도표의 가로축, 세로축, 범례**를 확인한다.**
이 내용을 확인하면 어떤 것을 비교하고 있는지, 어떤 수치에 주목해야 하는지를 알 수 있음.

3) 선택지의 내용과 도표를 대조**하여 확인한다.**

4) 수치와 관련된 표현**에 주의하여 읽는다.**
가장 높거나 낮은 수치, 가장 큰 차이 등 특징적인 수치에 주목해야 함.

필수 암기 어휘와 표현

1) 도표와 관련된 표현

증가	increase, rise, add to, go up, grow, multiply, soar, surge, skyrocket, reach its peak
감소	decrease, diminish, decline, reduce, go down, drop, fall, plunge, plummet
비교	outnumber, surpass, remain, unchanged, match, be equal to
수	double, triple, quadruple, two thirds, a quarter, three-quarters, one and a half, the number of
비율	rate, ratio, portion, proportion, (percentage) share, account for, constitute, make up, hold
추이	gradually, steadily, continuously, constantly, consistently, dramatically, enormously, slightly, rapidly, sharply, steeply, significantly, progressively, periodically, overall
순위	A is preceded by B, followed by A, lead, rank/come+서수사, top five, first place, second most favored
기타	sum, average, tendency, profit, sales, revenue, loss, expenditure

2) 수치와 관련된 표현

최상급/비교급/원급 표현	최상급 – (the) most/least 형/부 혹은 (the) 형/부+-est 비교급 – more/less 형/부 than 혹은 형/부+-er than 원급 – (긍정) A as 형/부 as B (부정) A not as[so] 형/부 as B
배수사 표현	배수사(twice(=two times), three times…) + as 형/부 as ('as 형/부 as' 자리에 '비교급 than' 사용 가능) (참고) twice, half를 쓸 경우에는 비교급 than 사용 불가 배수사+정관사+명사: 명사의 ~배
분수 표현	분자는 기수, 분모는 서수로 표현 / 분자가 2 이상인 경우 분모를 복수형으로 (예) 1/3 = one-third, 3/5 = three-fifths
비율 표현	percentage(퍼센트, %): 백분율 percentage point(퍼센트포인트, %p): 두 백분율 값의 차이를 나타내는 단위

도표의 이해 대표 예제 - 2024학년도 수능 25번

다음 도표의 내용과 일치하지 않는 것은?

Percentages of Respondents Who Sometimes or Often Actively Avoided News in Five Countries in 2017, 2019, and 2022

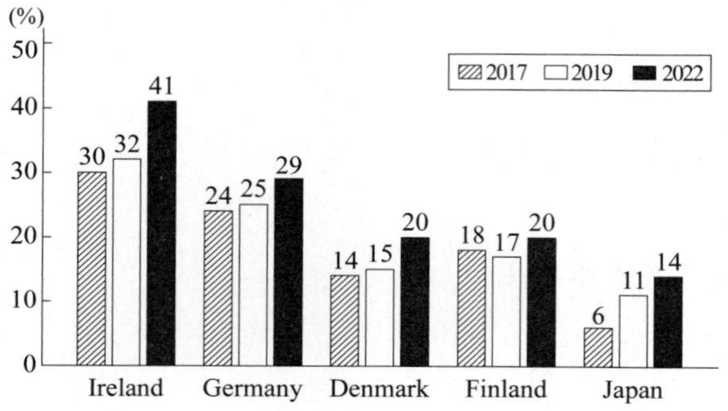

(1) The above graph shows the percentages of the respondents in five countries who sometimes or often actively avoided news in 2017, 2019, and 2022. ①(2) For each of the three years, Ireland showed the highest percentage of the respondents who sometimes or often actively avoided news, among the countries in the graph. ②(3) In Germany, the percentage of the respondents who sometimes or often actively avoided news was less than 30% in each of the three years. ③(4) In Denmark, the percentage of the respondents who sometimes or often actively avoided news in 2019 was higher than that in 2017 but lower than that in 2022. ④(5) In Finland, the percentage of the respondents who sometimes or often actively avoided news in 2019 was lower than that in 2017, which was also true for Japan. ⑤(6) In Japan, the percentage of the respondents who sometimes or often actively avoided news did not exceed 15% in each of the three years.

STEP 1 도표의 제목과 지문의 첫 문장을 먼저 확인한다.

→ 뉴스를 피했던 응답자들의 비율을 국가 및 연도별로 비교하는 내용임을 알 수 있음.

STEP 2 도표의 가로축, 세로축, 범례를 확인한다.

→ 다섯 개의 국가를 세 개의 연도로 나누어 각 국가의 연도별로 뉴스를 피하는 사람의 비율을 제시하고 있음.

STEP 3 선택지의 내용과 도표를 대조하여 확인한다.

①: 각 연도별 아일랜드의 비율 → 2017(30%), 2019(32%), 2022(41%) ∴ 세 연도 모두 아일랜드의 비율이 가장 높음.
②: 각 연도별 독일의 비율 → 2017(24%), 2019(25%), 2022(29%) ∴ 세 연도 모두 독일의 비율은 30%보다 적음.
③: 각 연도별 덴마크의 비율 → 2017(14%) < 2019(15%) < 2022(20%)
④: 각 연도별 핀란드의 비율 → 2017(18%) > 2019(17%) / 각 연도별 일본의 비율 → 2017(6%) < 2019(11%)
∴ 핀란드의 비율 양상과 일본의 비율 양상이 서로 다르므로 ④가 도표와 일치하지 않음.
⑤: 각 연도별 일본의 비율 → 2017(6%), 2019(11%), 2022(14%) ∴ 세 연도 모두 일본의 비율은 15%보다 적음.

전문 해석

(1) 위 그래프는 2017년, 2019년, 그리고 2022년에 5개의 국가에서 때때로 또는 자주 적극적으로 뉴스를 피했던 응답자들의 비율을 보여 준다. ①(2) 세 해 각각에 대해, 아일랜드는 그래프에 있는 국가들 중에서 때때로 또는 자주 적극적으로 뉴스를 피했던 응답자들의 가장 높은 비율을 보였다. ②(3) 독일에서, 때때로 또는 자주 적극적으로 뉴스를 피했던 응답자들의 비율은 세 해 각각에서 30%보다 적었다. ③(4) 덴마크에서, 2019년에 때때로 또는 자주 적극적으로 뉴스를 피했던 응답자들의 비율은 2017년의 그것(때때로 또는 자주 적극적으로 뉴스를 피했던 응답자들의 비율)보다 더 높았지만, 2022년의 그것(때때로 또는 자주 적극적으로 뉴스를 피했던 응답자들의 비율)보다 더 낮았다. ④(5) 핀란드에서, 2019년에 때때로 또는 자주 적극적으로 뉴스를 피했던 응답자들의 비율은 2017년의 그것(때때로 또는 자주 적극적으로 뉴스를 피했던 응답자들의 비율)보다 더 낮았고, 그것은 일본도 마찬가지였다(→ 마찬가지가 아니었다). ⑤(6) 일본에서, 때때로 또는 자주 적극적으로 뉴스를 피했던 응답자들의 비율은 세 해 각각에서 15%를 넘지 않았다.

중요 어휘

- □ respondent 명 응답자
- □ actively 부 적극적으로
- □ avoid 동 피하다
- □ exceed 동 넘다, 넘어서다

자세한 해설지 QR→
자세한해설-CH08

참고) 각 도표의 특징

막대그래프	값의 크기를 막대의 길이로 표현한 그래프로 상대적인 수량을 나타낼 때 흔히 사용된다. 시간적인 변화보다는 특정 시점에서의 수량을 상호 비교하고자 할 경우에 주로 사용된다.
꺾은선그래프	수량을 점으로 표시하고 그 점들을 선으로 이은 그래프로 시간에 따른 자료의 추세를 나타내는 데 주로 쓰인다.
원그래프	원 전체를 100%로 보고 각 부분의 비율을 원의 부채꼴 면적으로 표현한 그래프이다. 전체와 부분, 부분과 부분의 비율을 볼 때 사용한다.

08 도표의 이해

동영상 강의

25BR2_CH08

01 ⓒ 80초

★☆☆ 2021년 6월 25번

다음 표의 내용과 일치하지 않는 것은?

Top Seven Natural Gas Producing Countries Worldwide

(unit: billion cubic meters)

2014			2018		
Rank	Country	Amount	Rank	Country	Amount
1	The United States	729	1	The United States	863
2	Russia	610	2	Russia	725
3	Iran	172	3	Iran	248
4	Canada	161	4	Qatar	181
5	Qatar	160	5	China	176
6	China	132	6	Canada	172
7	Norway	108	7	Australia	131

The table above shows the top seven natural gas producing countries worldwide in 2014 and 2018. ① The United States, Russia, and Iran were the top three natural gas producing countries in both 2014 and 2018. ② In 2014 and 2018 respectively, the gap of the amount of natural gas production between Russia and Iran was larger than 400 billion cubic meters. ③ Canada ranked lower in 2018 than in 2014 even though the amount of natural gas produced in Canada increased. ④ Between 2014 and 2018, the increase in natural gas production in China was more than three times that in Qatar. ⑤ Australia, which was not included among the top seven natural gas producing countries in 2014, ranked seventh in 2018.

02 ⓒ 80초

★☆☆ 2021년 11월 25번

다음 표의 내용과 일치하지 않는 것은?

Share of Respondents Familiar with/Engaged in E-Sports in 2020

Country	Familiarity (%)	Engagement (%)
China	72	47
Denmark	67	10
Indonesia	57	40
U.S.	34	8
Spain	33	17
UAE	26	19
Iraq	26	16

The above table shows the share of respondents familiar with or engaged in e-sports in selected countries in 2020. ① Among the countries in the table, China was the country with the highest percentage both in e-sports familiarity and in e-sports engagement. ② When it comes to e-sports familiarity, Denmark showed a higher percentage than Indonesia, but the percentage of e-sports engagement in Denmark was lower than Indonesia's. ③ The percentage of U.S. respondents familiar with e-sports was higher than that of Spanish respondents, and with e-sports engagement, the percentage in the U.S. was more than twice that of Spain. ④ While the percentage of e-sports familiarity in Spain was higher than that in the UAE, the percentage of e-sports engagement in Spain was two percentage points lower than that in the UAE. ⑤ As for e-sports familiarity, among the selected countries, the UAE and Iraq showed the lowest percentage, where fewer than a third of respondents in each country were familiar with e-sports.

정답과 해설 : 01 102 02 102

03 ⓒ 80초

★☆☆ 2022년 9월 25번

다음 도표의 내용과 일치하지 않는 것은?

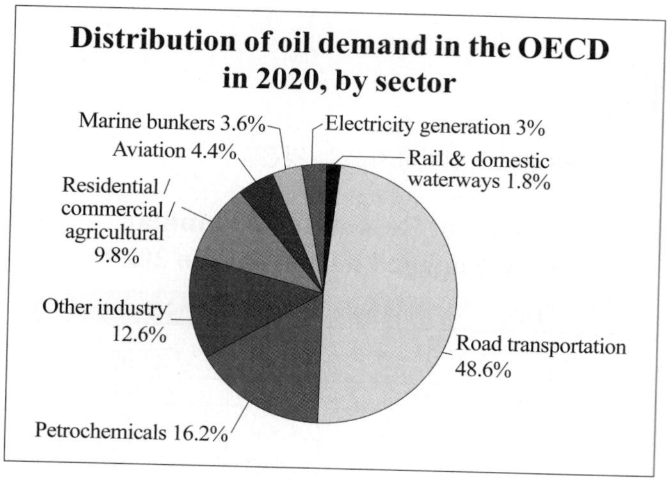

The above graph shows the distribution of oil demand by sector in the OECD in 2020. ① The Road transportation sector, which took up 48.6%, was the greatest oil demanding sector in the OECD member states. ② The percentage of oil demand in the Petrochemicals sector was one-third that of the Road transportation sector. ③ The difference in oil demand between the Other industry sector and the Petrochemicals sector was smaller than the difference in oil demand between the Aviation sector and the Electricity generation sector. ④ The oil demand in the Residential, commercial and agricultural sector took up 9.8% of all oil demand in the OECD, which was the fourth largest among all the sectors. ⑤ The percentage of oil demand in the Marine bunkers sector was twice that of the oil demand in the Rail & domestic waterways sector.

04 ⓒ 80초

★☆☆ 2023년 6월 25번

다음 도표의 내용과 일치하지 않는 것은?

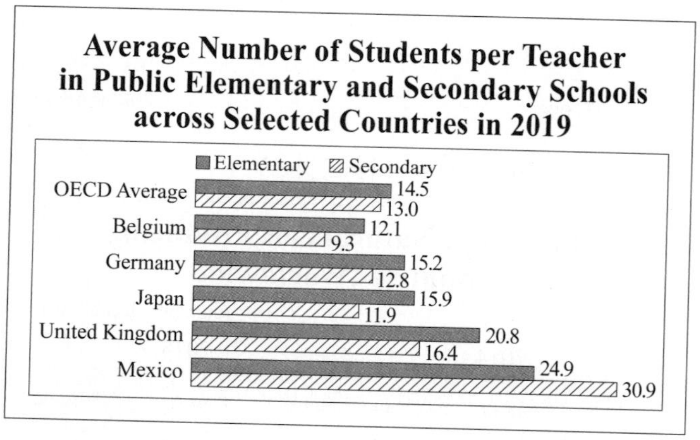

The graph above shows the average number of students per teacher in public elementary and secondary schools across selected countries in 2019. ① Belgium was the only country with a smaller number of students per teacher than the OECD average in both public elementary and secondary schools. ② In both public elementary and secondary schools, the average number of students per teacher was the largest in Mexico. ③ In public elementary schools, there was a smaller number of students per teacher on average in Germany than in Japan, whereas the reverse was true in public secondary schools. ④ The average number of students per teacher in public secondary schools in Germany was less than half that in the United Kingdom. ⑤ Of the five countries, Mexico was the only country with more students per teacher in public secondary schools than in public elementary schools.

정답과 해설 : 03 103 04 103

05 ⓒ 80초

★☆☆ 2023년 9월 25번

다음 도표의 내용과 일치하지 않는 것은?

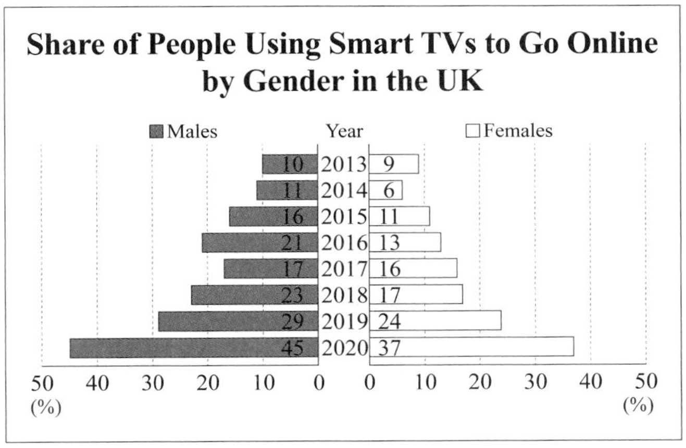

The graph above shows the findings of a survey on the use of smart TVs to go online in the UK from 2013 to 2020, by gender. ① In each year from 2013 to 2020, the percentage of male respondents who used smart TVs to access the Internet was higher than that of female respondents. ② The percentage gap between the two genders was the largest in 2016 and in 2020, which both had an 8 percentage point difference. ③ In 2020, the percentage of respondents who reported using smart TVs to go online was higher than 30% for both males and females. ④ For male respondents, 2017 was the only year that saw a decrease in the percentage of those accessing the Internet via smart TVs compared to the previous year, during the given period. ⑤ In 2014, the percentage of females using smart TVs to access the Internet was the lowest during the given period at 6%, and it was still below 10% in 2015.

06 ⓒ 80초

★☆☆ 2017년 11월 24번

다음 도표의 내용과 일치하지 않는 것은?

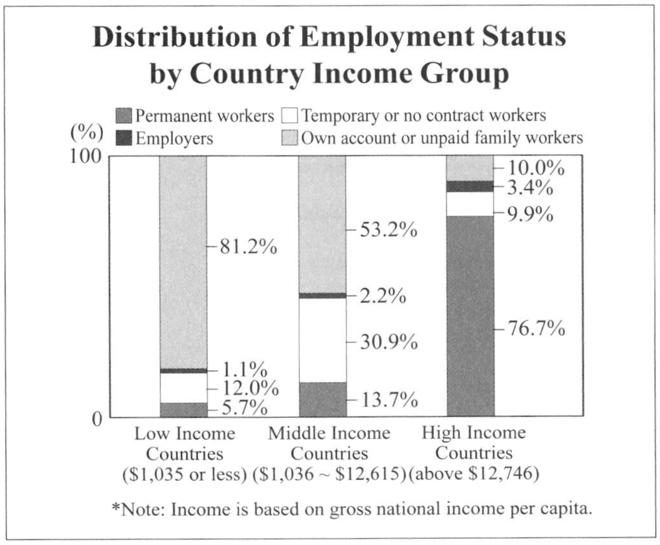

The above graph shows the distribution of employment status by country income group. ① In low income countries, the largest employment status group was own account or unpaid family workers, followed by temporary or no contract workers, permanent workers, and employers. ② In middle income countries, although own account or unpaid family workers comprised the largest employment status group, their proportion was 28 percentage points lower than that of low income countries. ③ The proportion of temporary or no contract workers in middle income countries was more than twice that of permanent workers in middle income countries. ④ In high income countries, employers accounted for 3.4%, which was larger than the proportion of employers in each of the other two country income groups, respectively. ⑤ The smallest percentage point gap between permanent workers and temporary or no contract workers was found in high income countries.

DAY 07 08 도표의 이해

정답과 해설 : 05 104 06 105

07 ⓒ 80초

★☆☆ 2022년 3월 25번

다음 도표의 내용과 일치하지 않는 것은?

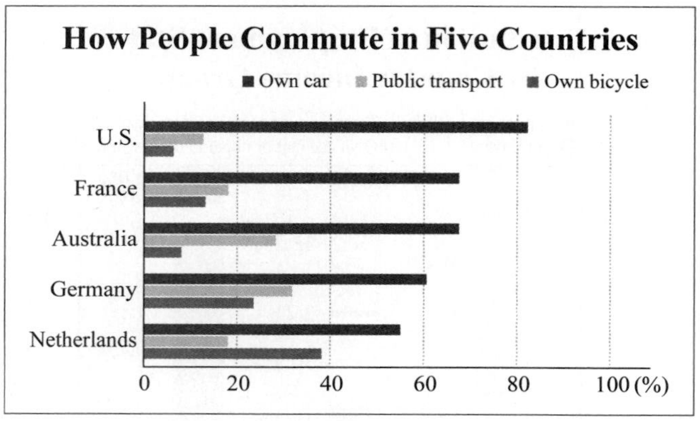

The above graph shows which modes of transportation people use for their daily commute to work, school, or university in five selected countries. ① In each of the five countries, the percentage of commuters using their own car is the highest among all three modes of transportation. ② The U.S. has the highest percentage of commuters using their own car among the five countries, but it has the lowest percentages for the other two modes of transportation. ③ Public transport is the second most popular mode of transportation in all the countries except for the Netherlands. ④ Among the five countries, France has the biggest gap between the percentage of commuters using their own car and that of commuters using public transport. ⑤ In terms of commuters using public transport, Germany leads all of the countries, immediately followed by Australia.

08 ⓒ 80초

★☆☆ 2018년 9월 24번

다음 도표의 내용과 일치하지 않는 것은?

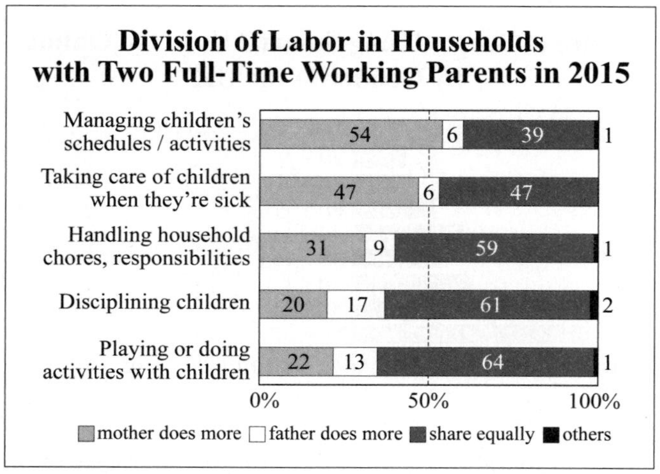

The graph above shows the division of labor in households where both parents work full-time in 2015. ① The percentage of "mother does more" households in every category is higher than that of "father does more" households. ② While the category with the highest percentage of "mother does more" households is "Managing children's schedules / activities," the category with the highest percentage of "father does more" households is "Disciplining children." ③ When it comes to taking care of children when they're sick, the percentage of "mother does more" households is the same as that of "share equally" households. ④ The percentage of "share equally" households is over two times higher than that of "mother does more" households in three categories. ⑤ The category that shows the highest percentage of "share equally" households is "Playing or doing activities with children," followed by the category "Disciplining children."

정답과 해설 : 07 105 08 106

09 ⓒ 80초

★☆☆ 2019년 3월 24번

다음 도표의 내용과 일치하지 않는 것은?

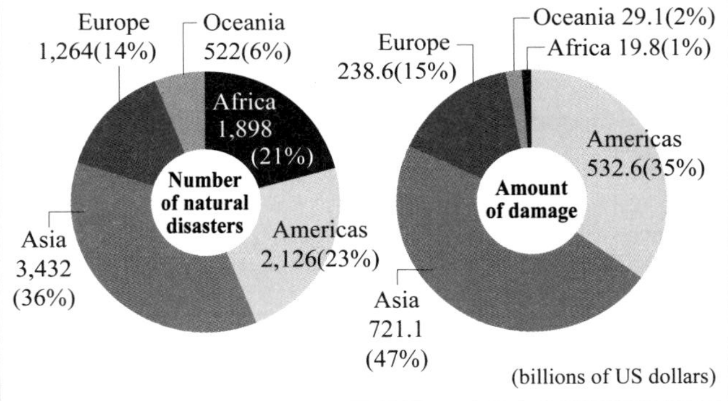

The two pie charts above show the number of natural disasters and the amount of damage by region in 2014. ① The number of natural disasters in Asia was the largest of all five regions and accounted for 36 percent, which was more than twice the percentage of Europe. ② Americas had the second largest number of natural disasters, taking up 23 percent. ③ The number of natural disasters in Oceania was the smallest and less than a third of that in Africa. ④ The amount of damage in Asia was the largest and more than the combined amount of Americas and Europe. ⑤ Africa had the least amount of damage even though it ranked third in the number of natural disasters.

10 ⓒ 80초

★☆☆ 2019년 11월 25번

다음 표의 내용과 일치하지 않는 것은?

Jobs in Renewable Energy Technology in 2014 and 2015

Year of 2014		Year of 2015	
Renewable Energy Technology	Jobs (thousands)	Renewable Energy Technology	Jobs (thousands)
Solar Photovoltaic	2,495	Solar Photovoltaic	2,772
Liquid Biofuels	1,788	Liquid Biofuels	1,678
Wind Power	1,027	Wind Power	1,081
Biomass	822	Solar Heating/Cooling	939
Solar Heating/Cooling	764	Biomass	822
Biogas	381	Biogas	382
Small Hydropower	209	Small Hydropower	204
Geothermal Energy	154	Geothermal Energy	160
Total	7,600	Total	8,000

• Note: Figures may not add to total shown because of rounding.

The tables above show the number of jobs in renewable energy technology around the world in 2014 and 2015. ① The total number of jobs was larger in 2015 than in 2014. ② In both years, solar photovoltaic had the largest number of jobs, and the number of jobs increased in 2015. ③ The rank of liquid biofuels remained the same in both years though the number of jobs decreased in 2015. ④ Solar heating/cooling ranked higher in 2015 than in 2014, but still had fewer than 900 thousand jobs. ⑤ Among the lowest three ranks in 2014, only small hydropower showed a decrease in the number of jobs in 2015.

정답과 해설 : 09 107 10 107

11 ⓒ 80초

★☆☆ 2020년 11월 25번

다음 도표의 내용과 일치하지 않는 것은?

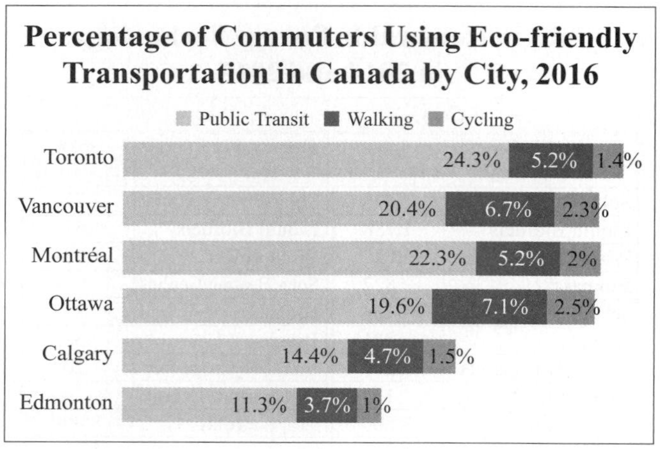

The above graph shows the percentage of commuters using eco-friendly transportation to get to work in six large cities in Canada in 2016. ① For all six given cities, the percentage of people who commuted by public transit was the highest, while the percentage of people who commuted by cycling was the lowest. ② The percentages of people who commuted by walking were the same in both Toronto and Montréal even though the percentages of people who commuted by public transit in those two cities were different. ③ In Vancouver, the percentage of people who commuted by public transit was over ten times higher than that of people who commuted by cycling. ④ Even though Ottawa ranked fourth in the percentage of people who commuted by public transit, this city was in first place in the percentage of people who commuted by walking or cycling. ⑤ Compared with Calgary, Edmonton recorded lower percentages for all three given types of eco-friendly transportation.

12 ⓒ 80초

★☆☆ 2022년 6월 25번

다음 도표의 내용과 일치하지 않는 것은?

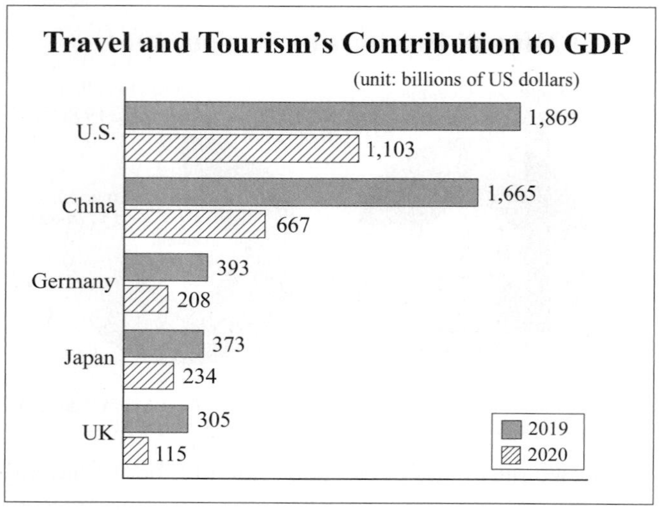

The above graph shows travel and tourism's contribution to GDP for each of the five countries in 2019 and in 2020. ① In all five countries, travel and tourism's contribution to GDP in 2020 decreased compared to the previous year. ② Both in 2019 and in 2020, the U.S. showed the largest contribution of travel and tourism to GDP among the five countries, followed by China. ③ In China, travel and tourism's contribution to GDP in 2020 was less than a third that in 2019. ④ In 2019, Germany showed a larger contribution of travel and tourism to GDP than Japan, whereas the reverse was true in 2020. ⑤ In 2020, the UK was the only country where the contribution of travel and tourism to GDP was less than $200 billion.

정답과 해설 : 11 108 12 108

13 ⓒ 80초

★☆☆ 2023년 3월 25번

다음 도표의 내용과 일치하지 않는 것은?

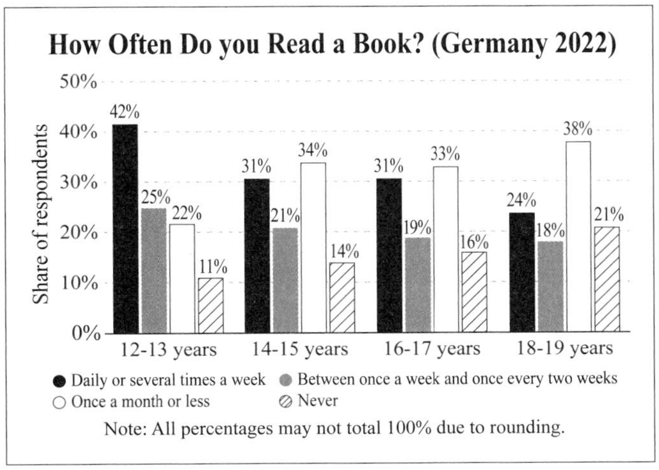

The above graph shows how often German children and young adults read books in 2022 according to age groups. ① In each age group except 12 to 13-year-olds, those who said they read books once a month or less accounted for the largest proportion. ② Of the 12 to 13-year-old group, 42% stated they read daily or several times a week, which was the highest share within that group. ③ In the 14 to 15-year-old group, the percentage of teenagers who read daily or several times a week was three times higher than that of those who never read a book in the same age group. ④ In the 16 to 17-year-old group, those who read between once a week and once every two weeks were less than 20%. ⑤ More than one fifth of the age group of 18 to 19 years responded that they never read any book.

14 ⓒ 90초

★★☆ 2021년 3월 25번

다음 도표의 내용과 일치하지 않는 것은?

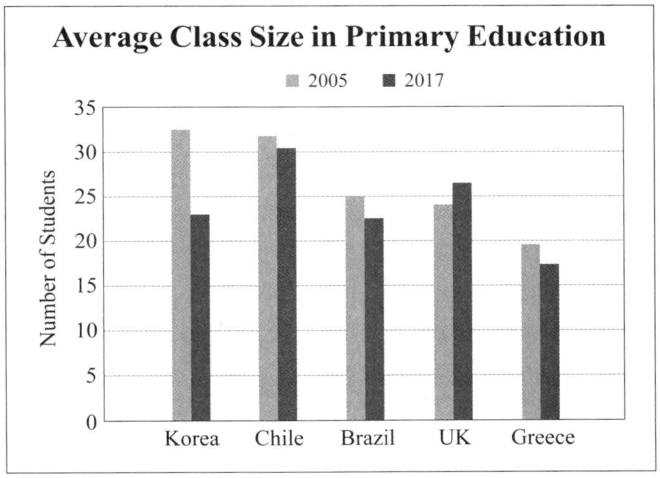

The above graph shows the average class size in primary education of five countries in 2005 and 2017. ① In every country except the UK, the average class size in 2017 decreased compared to that in 2005. ② In 2005, Korea's average class size was the largest of all the countries, with more than 30 students in a class. ③ In 2017, however, Chile's average class size was the largest of all the countries, with fewer than 30 students in a class. ④ In 2005, the average class size in Brazil was larger than that in the UK, whereas the reverse was true in 2017. ⑤ In Greece, the average class size was fewer than 20 students in a class in both 2005 and 2017.

정답과 해설 : 13 109 14 109

15 ⓒ 90초

★★☆ 2022년 11월 25번

다음 도표의 내용과 일치하지 않는 것은?

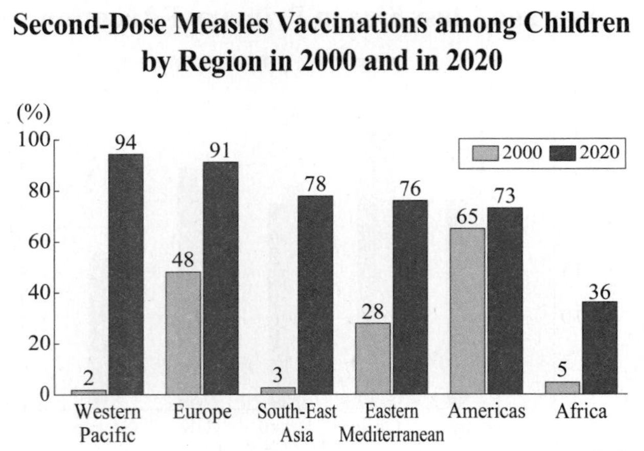

* measles: 홍역

The graph above shows the percentage of children who received second-dose measles vaccinations in six regions in 2000 and in 2020. ① The percentage of vaccinated children in the Western Pacific was lower than that of Europe in 2000, but the vaccination percentage in 2020 of the Western Pacific exceeded that of Europe by 3 percentage points. ② Among all regions, South-East Asia achieved the second biggest increase in its percentage of vaccinated children over the two decades, and it ranked third in the percentage of vaccinated children among the six regions in 2020. ③ In the Eastern Mediterranean, the percentage of vaccinated children more than doubled from 2000 to 2020, but did not exceed that of the Americas in either year. ④ The percentage of vaccinated children in the Americas was the highest among the six regions in 2000, but it increased the least of all regions over the two decades. ⑤ In Africa, the percentage of children who received the vaccine in 2020 was more than seven times higher than in 2000, but was still the lowest among the six regions in 2020.

16 ⓒ 80초

★☆☆ 2023년 11월 25번

다음 도표의 내용과 일치하지 않는 것은?

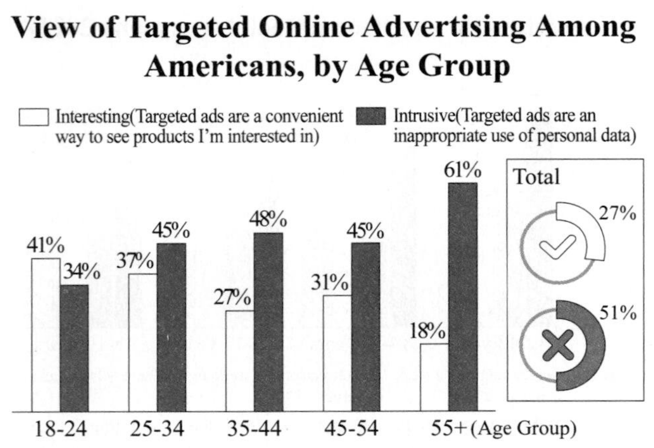

Conducted on May 1, 2019 (missing percentages to 100%: "don't know")

The graph above shows the results of a 2019 survey on the views of American age groups on targeted online advertising. ① In total, while 51% of the respondents said targeted ads were intrusive, 27% said they were interesting. ② The percentage of respondents who believed that targeted ads were interesting was the highest in the age group of 18 to 24. ③ The percentage of respondents aged 25 to 34 who said that targeted ads were intrusive was the same as that of respondents aged 45 to 54 who said the same. ④ Among all age groups, the gap between respondents who said targeted ads were interesting and those who believed them to be intrusive was the largest in the 35-to-44 age group. ⑤ The age group of 55 and above was the only group where the percentage of respondents who believed targeted ads were intrusive was more than 50%.

17 ⓒ 80초

★☆☆ 2024년 3월 25번

다음 도표의 내용과 일치하지 않는 것은?

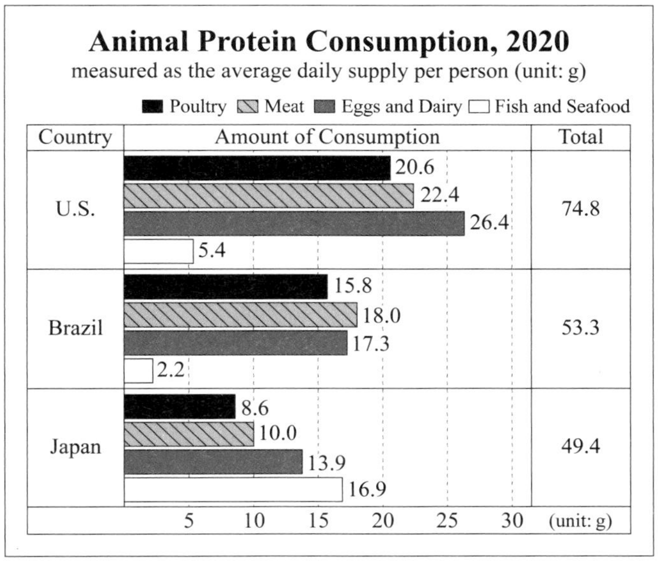

The graph above shows the animal protein consumption measured as the average daily supply per person in three different countries in 2020. ① The U.S. showed the largest amount of total animal protein consumption per person among the three countries. ② Eggs and Dairy was the top animal protein consumption source among four categories in the U.S., followed by Meat and Poultry at 22.4g and 20.6g, respectively. ③ Unlike the U.S., Brazil consumed the most animal protein from Meat, with Eggs and Dairy being the second most. ④ Japan had less than 50g of the total animal protein consumption per person, which was the smallest among the three countries. ⑤ Fish and Seafood, which was the least consumed animal protein consumption source in the U.S. and Brazil, ranked the second highest in Japan.

18 ⓒ 80초

★☆☆ 2024년 6월 25번

다음 도표의 내용과 일치하지 않는 것은?

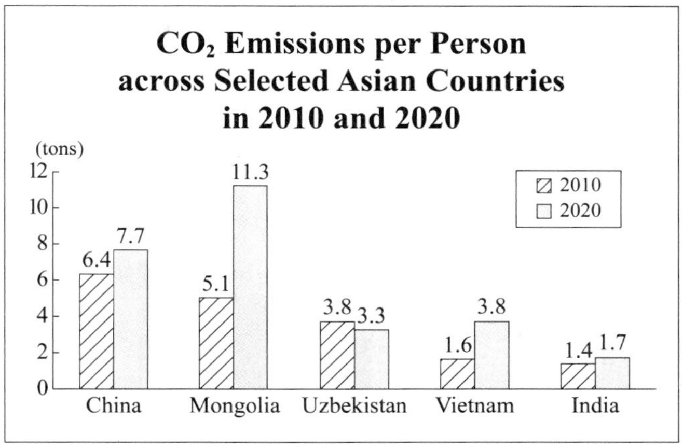

The graph above shows the amount of CO_2 emissions per person across selected Asian countries in 2010 and 2020. ① All the countries except Uzbekistan had a greater amount of CO_2 emissions per person in 2020 than that in 2010. ② In 2010, the amount of CO_2 emissions per person of China was the largest among the five countries, followed by that of Mongolia. ③ However, in 2020, Mongolia surpassed China in terms of the amount of CO_2 emissions per person, with the amount of Mongolia more than twice that of China. ④ In 2010, Uzbekistan produced a larger amount of CO_2 emissions per person than Vietnam, while the opposite was true in 2020. ⑤ Among the five countries, India was the only one where the amount of CO_2 emissions per person was less than 2 tons in 2020.

정답과 해설 : 17 111 18 112

19 ⓒ 80초

★☆☆
2024년 9월 25번

다음 도표의 내용과 일치하지 않는 것은?

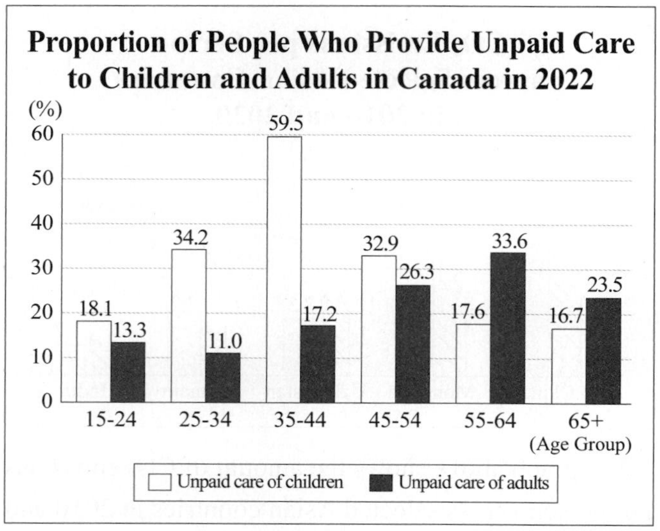

The graph above shows the percentage of people who provided unpaid care to children and adults by age group in Canada in 2022. ① Notably, the 35–44 group had the highest percentage of individuals providing unpaid care to children, reaching 59.5%. ② However, the highest percentage of individuals providing unpaid care to adults was found in the 55–64 group. ③ Compared to the 25–34 group, the 15–24 group had a lower percentage of individuals providing unpaid care to children and a higher percentage of individuals providing unpaid care to adults. ④ The percentage of people providing unpaid care to adults in the 45–54 group was more than twice as high as that in the 35–44 group. ⑤ The 55–64 group and the 65 and older group showed a similar percentage of individuals providing unpaid care to children, with a difference of less than 1 percentage point.

정답과 해설 : 19 113

유형TIP

09. 내용 일치 파악

선택지가 한글로 제시되어 정답률이 높은 유형
지문의 내용이 선택지와 일치하는지 여부를 파악하면 됨.

유형 TIP 25BR2T_CH09 대표 예제 25BR2E_CH09

유형 공략법

1) 선택지와 지문을 함께 읽어서 **시간을 절약한다.**
선택지의 순서는 지문에서 제시되는 내용의 순서와 일치함.

2) 선택지와 글의 내용을 정확하게 비교**한다.**
지문의 내용과 선택지의 앞부분은 같지만 뒷부분이 틀린 경우도 있으니 주의해야 함.

3) **자신의 배경지식, 상식 등을 배제하고** 지문 속의 정보만을 바탕으로 **정답을 찾는다.**

필수 암기 어휘와 표현

1) 빈출 표현

수량	single, double, plural, some, any, a few, a little, many, much, half, a number of, a lot
정도	excessive, affluent, enough, lack, compact, scattered, deep, shallow, breathtaking, simple, complicated, complex, legendary, impressive, trivial, precise, accurate, exact, inevitable, superior, inferior, relatively, absolutely, rare, common
범주	every, widespread, most, almost, nearly, local, global, including, except for, regardless
상태, 성질	similar, different, endangered, safe, secure, dangerous, legal, progressive, conservative, mild, hard, careless, intelligent, elegant, stable, disastrous
거리, 형태	near, far, close, distant, oval, round, circle, rectangular, curved, straight, -shaped
크기, 폭	big, large, small, wide, broad, narrow, major, minor, tiny, magnificent, vast, limited
부정	few, little, hardly, barely, scarcely, rarely, seldom
부분부정	not+전체를 나타내는 단어(all, every, both), not always, not necessarily, not entirely
전체부정	no, not ~ any, nobody, none, neither, never, anything but, far from, beyond, the last+명사

2) 주의해야 하는 어휘

bad	나쁜, 틀린	badly	서투르게, 대단히, 몹시
bare	① 벌거벗은 ② 빈	barely	① 간신히, 겨우 ② 거의 ~않다 ③ 빈약하게
close	① 가까운 ② 빽빽한	closely	① 접근하여 ② 자세히 ③ 밀접하게
dear	① 친애하는 ② 소중한 ③ 비싼	dearly	몹시, 극진히, 비싼 대가를 치르고
deep	① 깊은 ② 난해한	deeply	① 깊이 ② 철저히 ③ 강렬하게
hard	① 굳은, 단단한 ② 곤란한, 어려운 ③ 열심인 ① 굳게, 단단히 ② 열심히 ③ 몹시	hardly	거의 ~않다, 조금도 ~않다
high	① 높은 ② 상류의, 고위의 ③ 비싼 ① 높게, 높이 ② 고가로, 비싸게	highly	① 고귀하게 ② 크게, 대단히 ③ 높이 평가하여
late	① 늦은, 지각한 ② 이전의 ① 늦게, 뒤늦게 ② 밤이 늦도록	lately	요즈음, 최근에

내용 일치 파악 대표 예제 - 2024학년도 수능 26번

Charles H. Townes에 관한 다음 글의 내용과 일치하지 않는 것은?

(1) Charles H. Townes, one of the most influential American physicists, was born in South Carolina. (2) In his childhood, he grew up on a farm, studying the stars in the sky. (3) He earned his doctoral degree from the California Institute of Technology in 1939, and then he took a job at Bell Labs in New York City. (4) After World War II, he became an associate professor of physics at Columbia University. (5) In 1958, Townes and his co-researcher proposed the concept of the laser. (6) Laser technology won quick acceptance in industry and research. (7) He received the Nobel Prize in Physics in 1964. (8) He was also involved in Project Apollo, the moon landing project. (9) His contribution is priceless because the Internet and all digital media would be unimaginable without the laser.

① 어린 시절에 농장에서 성장하였다. 문장(2)
② 박사 학위를 ~~받기 전에~~ (받은 후에) Bell Labs에서 일했다. 문장(3)
③ 1958년에 레이저의 개념을 제안하였다. 문장(5)
④ 1964년에 노벨 물리학상을 수상하였다. 문장(7)
⑤ 달 착륙 프로젝트에 관여하였다. 문장(8)

STEP 1 선택지와 글의 내용을 정확하게 비교한다.

① - 문장(2): 어린 시절 농장에서 성장함.
② - 문장(3): 박사 학위를 받은 후에 Bell Labs에서 일함.
③ - 문장(5): 1958년에 레이저의 개념을 제안함.
④ - 문장(7): 1964년에 노벨 물리학상을 수상함.
⑤ - 문장(8): 달 착륙 프로젝트인 Project Apollo에 관여했음.

전문 해석

(1) 가장 영향력 있는 미국 물리학자 중 한 명인 Charles H. Townes는 South Carolina에서 태어났다. (2) 그의 어린 시절에, 그는 하늘의 별들을 공부하며 농장에서 성장했다. (3) 그는 1939년에 California 공과 대학에서 박사 학위를 받았고, 그런 다음 그는 뉴욕시에 있는 Bell Labs에 취직했다. (4) 제2차 세계대전 후에, 그는 Columbia 대학교에서 물리학 부교수가 되었다. (5) 1958년에, Townes와 그의 동료 연구원은 레이저의 개념을 제안했다. (6) 레이저 기술은 산업과 연구에서 빠른 승인을 얻었다. (7) 그는 1964년에 노벨 물리학상을 받았다. (8) 그는 또한 달 착륙 프로젝트인 Project Apollo에 관여했다. (9) 인터넷과 모든 디지털 매체는 레이저 없이는 상상도 할 수 없기 때문에 그의 기여는 아주 귀중하다.

중요 어휘

- □ **influential** 형 영향력 있는, 영향력이 큰
- □ **take a job** 취직하다
- □ **associate professor** 명 부교수
- □ **propose** 동 제안하다, 제시하다
- □ **be involved in** ~에 관여하다[개입되다]
- □ **landing** 명 착륙, 상륙
- □ **contribution** 명 기여, 기부
- □ **priceless** 형 아주 귀중한, 값을 매길 수 없는
- □ **unimaginable** 형 상상도 할 수 없는, 생각조차 못 하는

자세한 해설지 QR➔
자세한해설-CH09

09 내용 일치 파악

동영상 강의

25BR2_CH09

01 ⓒ 80초

★☆☆ 2021년 3월 28번

Ingrid Bergman에 관한 다음 글의 내용과 일치하지 않는 것은?

Ingrid Bergman was born in Stockholm, Sweden on August 29, 1915. Her mother was German and her father Swedish. Her mother died when she was three, and her father passed away when she was 12. Eventually she was brought up by her Uncle Otto and Aunt Hulda. She was interested in acting from an early age. When she was 17, she attended the Royal Dramatic Theater School in Stockholm. She made her debut on the stage but was more interested in working in films. In the early 1940s, she gained star status in Hollywood, playing many roles as the heroine of the film. Bergman was considered to have tremendous acting talent, an angelic natural beauty and the willingness to work hard to get the best out of films. She was fluent in five languages and appeared in a range of films, plays and TV productions.

① 어머니는 독일인이었고 아버지는 스웨덴인이었다.
② 17세에 Royal Dramatic Theater School에 다녔다.
③ 영화를 통해 데뷔했으나 연극에 더 관심이 있었다.
④ 1940년대 초에 할리우드에서 스타의 지위를 얻었다.
⑤ 다섯 개의 언어에 유창했다.

02 ⓒ 80초

★☆☆ 2021년 11월 26번

John Bowlby에 관한 다음 글의 내용과 일치하지 않는 것은?

John Bowlby, British developmental psychologist and psychiatrist, was born in 1907, to an upper-middle-class family. His father, who was a member of the King's medical staff, was often absent. Bowlby was cared for primarily by a nanny and did not spend much time with his mother, as was customary at that time for his class. Bowlby was sent to a boarding school at the age of seven. He later recalled this as being traumatic to his development. This experience, however, proved to have a large impact on Bowlby, whose work focused on children's development. Following his father's suggestion, Bowlby enrolled at Trinity College, Cambridge to study medicine, but by his third year, he changed his focus to psychology. During the 1950s, Bowlby briefly worked as a mental health consultant for the World Health Organization. His attachment theory has been described as the dominant approach to understanding early social development.

① 아버지는 왕의 의료진의 일원이었다.
② 어머니와 많은 시간을 보내지 못했다.
③ 기숙 학교로 보내진 것이 성장에 있어 충격적인 일이었다.
④ Trinity 대학에 심리학을 공부하기 위해 입학했다.
⑤ 세계 보건 기구에서 정신 건강 자문 위원으로 일했다.

정답과 해설 : 01 114 02 114

03 ⓒ 80초

★☆☆ 2022년 3월 28번

Gordon Parks에 관한 다음 글의 내용과 일치하지 않는 것은?

Gordon Parks was a photographer, author, film director, and musician. He documented the everyday lives of African Americans at a time when few people outside the black community were familiar with their lives. Parks was born the youngest of 15 children and grew up on his family's farm. After the death of his mother, he went to live with a sister in Minnesota. Parks eventually dropped out of school and worked at various jobs. His interest in photography was inspired by a photo-essay he read about migrant farm workers. After he moved to Chicago, Parks began taking photos of poor African Americans. In 1949, he became the first African American to be a staff photographer for *Life* magazine. He also wrote music pieces in his life and in 1956 the Vienna Orchestra performed a piano concerto he wrote. Parks was an inspiring artist until he died in 2006.

① 15명의 자녀 중 막내로 태어났다.
② 어머니가 돌아가신 후 Minnesota에 있는 누나와 살러 갔다.
③ 학교를 중퇴하지 않고 다양한 일자리에서 일했다.
④ *Life* 지의 사진 기자가 된 최초의 아프리카계 미국인이었다.
⑤ 그가 작곡한 피아노 협주곡을 1956년에 Vienna Orchestra가 연주했다.

04 ⓒ 80초

★☆☆ 2022년 6월 26번

monarch butterfly에 관한 다음 글의 내용과 일치하지 않는 것은?

The monarch butterfly has lovely bright colors splashed on its wings. The wings have white spots on the outer margins. The hind wings are rounded, and they are lighter in color than the front wings. The body is black with white spots. The mother butterfly lays only one egg on the underside of milkweed leaves, which hatches about three to five days later. The monarch loves to fly around in the warm sunshine, from March through October, all across the United States. The monarch cannot survive the cold winter temperatures of the northern states. So, it very wisely migrates from the northern states to the south, and hibernates. The monarch is the only insect that can fly more than four thousand kilometers to a warmer climate.

♦ hibernate: 동면하다

① 날개의 바깥 가장자리에 흰 점이 있다.
② 뒷날개는 앞날개보다 색이 더 밝다.
③ 알은 약 3일에서 5일 후에 부화한다.
④ 북부 주의 추운 겨울 기온에 잘 버틴다.
⑤ 4천 킬로미터 넘게 날 수 있다.

정답과 해설 : 03 115 04 116

05 ⓒ 80초

★☆☆ 2022년 9월 26번

Carl-Gustaf Rossby에 관한 다음 글의 내용과 일치하지 않는 것은?

Carl-Gustaf Rossby was one of a group of notable Scandinavian researchers who worked with the Norwegian meteorologist Vilhelm Bjerknes at the University of Bergen. While growing up in Stockholm, Rossby received a traditional education. He earned a degree in mathematical physics at the University of Stockholm in 1918, but after hearing a lecture by Bjerknes, and apparently bored with Stockholm, he moved to the newly established Geophysical Institute in Bergen. In 1925, Rossby received a scholarship from the Sweden-America Foundation to go to the United States, where he joined the United States Weather Bureau. Based in part on his practical experience in weather forecasting, Rossby had become a supporter of the "polar front theory," which explains the cyclonic circulation that develops at the boundary between warm and cold air masses. In 1947, Rossby accepted the chair of the Institute of Meteorology, which had been set up for him at the University of Stockholm, where he remained until his death ten years later.

① Stockholm에서 성장하면서 전통적인 교육을 받았다.
② University of Stockholm에서 수리 물리학 학위를 받았다.
③ 1925년에 장학금을 받았다.
④ polar front theory를 지지했다.
⑤ University of Stockholm에 마련된 직책을 거절했다.

06 ⓒ 80초

★☆☆ 2022년 11월 26번

Janaki Ammal에 관한 다음 글의 내용과 일치하지 않는 것은?

Janaki Ammal, one of India's most notable scientists, was born in 1897, and was expected to wed through an arranged marriage. Despite living at a time when literacy among women in India was less than one percent, she decided to reject tradition and attend college. In 1924, she went to the U.S. and eventually received a doctorate in botany from the University of Michigan. Ammal contributed to the development of the sweetest sugarcane variety in the world. She moved to England where she co-authored the *Chromosome Atlas of Cultivated Plants*. Following a series of famines, she returned to India to help increase food production at the request of the Prime Minister. However, Ammal disagreed with the deforestation taking place in an effort to grow more food. She became an advocate for the preservation of native plants and successfully saved the Silent Valley from the construction of a hydroelectric dam.

① 관습을 따르지 않고 대학에 입학하기로 결심했다.
② 세계에서 가장 단 사탕수수 품종 개발에 기여했다.
③ *Chromosome Atlas of Cultivated Plants*를 공동 집필했다.
④ 식량 생산을 증가시키는 데 도움을 주기 위해 인도로 돌아갔다.
⑤ 수력 발전 댐의 건설로부터 Silent Valley를 지키는 데 실패했다.

정답과 해설 : 05 116 06 117

07 ⏱ 80초

★☆☆ 2023년 9월 26번

Camille Flammarion에 관한 다음 글의 내용과 일치하지 않는 것은?

Camille Flammarion was born at Montigny-le-Roi, France. He became interested in astronomy at an early age, and when he was only sixteen he wrote a book on the origin of the world. The manuscript was not published at the time, but it came to the attention of Urbain Le Verrier, the director of the Paris Observatory. He became an assistant to Le Verrier in 1858 and worked as a calculator. At nineteen, he wrote another book called *The Plurality of Inhabited Worlds*, in which he passionately claimed that life exists outside the planet Earth. His most successful work, *Popular Astronomy*, was published in 1880, and eventually sold 130,000 copies. With his own funds, he built an observatory at Juvisy and spent May to November of each year there. In 1887, he founded the French Astronomical Society and served as editor of its monthly publication.

♦ observatory: 천문대

① 어린 나이에 천문학에 흥미가 생겼다.
② 1858년에 Le Verrier의 조수가 되었다.
③ 19세에 쓴 책에서 외계 생명체의 존재를 부인했다.
④ 자신의 자금으로 Juvisy에 천문대를 세웠다.
⑤ French Astronomical Society를 설립했다.

08 ⏱ 80초

★☆☆ 2019년 11월 26번

Lotte Laserstein에 관한 다음 글의 내용과 일치하지 않는 것은?

Lotte Laserstein was born into a Jewish family in East Prussia. One of her relatives ran a private painting school, which allowed Lotte to learn painting and drawing at a young age. Later, she earned admission to the Berlin Academy of Arts and completed her master studies as one of the first women in the school. In 1928 her career skyrocketed as she gained widespread recognition, but after the seizure of power by the Nazi Party, she was forbidden to exhibit her artwork in Germany. In 1937 she emigrated to Sweden. She continued to work in Sweden but never recaptured the fame she had enjoyed before. In her work, Lotte repeatedly portrayed Gertrud Rose, her closest friend. To Lotte, she embodied the type of the "New Woman" and was so represented.

① 어린 나이에 회화와 소묘를 배웠다.
② Berlin Academy of Arts에 입학 허가를 받았다.
③ 나치당의 권력 장악 이후 독일에서 작품 전시를 금지당했다.
④ 이전에 누렸던 명성을 스웨덴에서 되찾았다.
⑤ 가장 가까운 친구인 Gertrud Rose를 그렸다.

정답과 해설 : 07 118 08 118

09 ⓒ 80초

★☆☆ 2020년 11월 26번

Alice Coachman에 관한 다음 글의 내용과 일치하지 않는 것은?

Alice Coachman was born in 1923, in Albany, Georgia, U.S.A. Since she was unable to access athletic training facilities because of the racism of the time, she trained using what was available to her, running barefoot along the dirt roads near her home and using homemade equipment to practice her jumping. Her talent in track and field was noticeable as early as elementary school. Coachman kept practicing hard and gained attention with her achievements in several competitions during her time in high school and college. In the 1948 London Olympics, Coachman competed in the high jump, reaching 5 feet, 6.5 inches, setting both an Olympic and an American record. This accomplishment made her the first black woman to win an Olympic gold medal. She is in nine different Halls of Fame, including the U.S. Olympic Hall of Fame. Coachman died in 2014, at the age of 90 in Georgia after she had dedicated her life to education.

① 집 근처에서 맨발로 달리며 훈련했다.
② 육상 경기에서의 재능을 고등학교 때부터 보였다.
③ 런던 올림픽에서 높이뛰기 올림픽 기록과 미국 기록을 세웠다.
④ 흑인 여성 최초로 올림픽 금메달리스트가 되었다.
⑤ 9개의 명예의 전당에 올랐다.

10 ⓒ 80초

★☆☆ 2023년 3월 26번

Julia Margaret Cameron에 관한 다음 글의 내용과 일치하지 않는 것은?

British photographer Julia Margaret Cameron is considered one of the greatest portrait photographers of the 19th century. Born in Calcutta, India, into a British family, Cameron was educated in France. Given a camera as a gift by her daughter in December 1863, she quickly and energetically devoted herself to the art of photography. She cleared out a chicken coop and converted it into studio space where she began to work as a photographer. Cameron made illustrative studio photographs, convincing friends and family members to pose for photographs, fitting them in theatrical costumes and carefully composing them into scenes. Criticized for her so-called bad technique by art critics in her own time, she ignored convention and experimented with composition and focus. Later critics appreciated her valuing of spiritual depth over technical perfection and now consider her portraits to be among the finest expressions of the artistic possibilities of the medium.

◆ chicken coop: 닭장

① 인도에서 태어나고 프랑스에서 교육받았다.
② 딸로부터 카메라를 선물로 받았다.
③ 친구들과 가족 구성원에게 연극 의상을 입히고 촬영했다.
④ 능숙한 사진 기술로 자기 시대 예술 비평가에게 인정받았다.
⑤ 정신적 깊이에 가치를 둔 점을 훗날 높이 평가받았다.

정답과 해설 : 09 119 10 119

11 ⓒ 80초

★☆☆ 2017년 3월 25번

Victor Frankl에 관한 다음 글의 내용과 일치하지 않는 것은?

Victor Frankl, a famous psychiatrist, remained head of the neurology department at the Vienna Policlinic Hospital for twenty-five years. He wrote more than thirty books for both professionals and general readers. He met with politicians, world leaders such as Pope Paul VI, philosophers, students, teachers, and numerous individuals who had read and been inspired by his books. He lectured widely in Europe, the Americas, Australia, Asia, and Africa; and held professorships at Harvard, Stanford, and the University of Pittsburgh. Even in his nineties, Frankl continued to engage in dialogue with visitors from all over the world and to respond personally to some of the hundreds of letters he received every week. Twenty-nine universities awarded him honorary degrees, and the American Psychiatric Association honored him with the Oskar Pfister Award.

♦ neurology: 신경(병)학

① 전문가와 일반 독자를 위한 책을 30권 넘게 썼다.
② 자신의 책에 영감을 받은 많은 사람들을 만났다.
③ 대학교에서 강연을 했지만 교수직은 맡지 않았다.
④ 90대에도 방문객과의 대화를 계속했다.
⑤ 29개의 대학교에서 명예 학위를 받았다.

12 ⓒ 80초

★☆☆ 2017년 11월 25번

Francis Crick에 관한 다음 글의 내용과 일치하지 않는 것은?

Francis Crick, the Nobel Prize-winning codiscoverer of the structure of the DNA molecule, was born in Northampton, England in 1916. He attended University College London, where he studied physics, graduating with a Bachelor of Science degree in 1937. He soon began conducting research toward a Ph.D., but his path was interrupted by the outbreak of World War Ⅱ. During the war, he was involved in naval weapons research, working on the development of magnetic and acoustic mines. After the war, Dr. R. V. Jones, the head of Britain's wartime scientific intelligence, asked Crick to continue the work, but Crick decided to continue his studies, this time in biology. In 1951, Crick met James Watson, a young American biologist, at the Strangeways Research Laboratory. They formed a collaborative working relationship solving the mysteries of the structure of DNA.

① University College London에서 물리학을 공부했다.
② 제2차 세계대전의 발발로 박사 학위를 위한 연구가 중단됐다.
③ 전쟁 중 해군 무기 연구에 참여했다.
④ Dr. R. V. Jones의 요청으로 전공을 생물학으로 바꿨다.
⑤ James Watson과 함께 DNA 구조의 비밀을 푸는 일을 했다.

정답과 해설 : 11 120 12 121

13 ⏱ 80초

★☆☆ 2021년 9월 26번

Patricia Bath에 관한 다음 글의 내용과 일치하지 않는 것은?

Patricia Bath spent her life advocating for eye health. Born in 1942, she was raised in the Harlem area of New York City. She graduated from Howard University's College of Medicine in 1968. It was during her time as a medical intern that she saw that many poor people and Black people were becoming blind because of the lack of eye care. She decided to concentrate on ophthalmology, which is the branch of medicine that works with eye diseases and disorders. As her career progressed, Bath taught students in medical schools and trained other doctors. In 1976, she co-founded the American Institute for the Prevention of Blindness (AiPB) with the basic principle that "eyesight is a basic human right." In the 1980s, Bath began researching the use of lasers in eye treatments. Her research led to her becoming the first African-American female doctor to receive a patent for a medical device.

① 뉴욕 시의 Harlem 지역에서 성장했다.
② 1968년에 의과 대학을 졸업했다.
③ 의과 대학에서 학생을 가르쳤다.
④ 1976년에 AiPB를 단독으로 설립했다.
⑤ 의료 장비 특허를 받았다.

14 ⏱ 80초

★☆☆ 2023년 6월 26번

John Ray에 관한 다음 글의 내용과 일치하지 않는 것은?

Born in 1627 in Black Notley, Essex, England, John Ray was the son of the village blacksmith. At 16, he went to Cambridge University, where he studied widely and lectured on topics from Greek to mathematics, before joining the priesthood in 1660. To recover from an illness in 1650, he had taken to nature walks and developed an interest in botany. Accompanied by his wealthy student and supporter Francis Willughby, Ray toured Britain and Europe in the 1660s, studying and collecting plants and animals. He married Margaret Oakley in 1673 and, after leaving Willughby's household, lived quietly in Black Notley to the age of 77. He spent his later years studying samples in order to assemble plant and animal catalogues. He wrote more than twenty works on theology and his travels, as well as on plants and their form and function.

♦ theology: 신학

① 마을 대장장이의 아들이었다.
② 성직자의 길로 들어서기 전 Cambridge 대학에 다녔다.
③ 병에서 회복하기 위해 자연을 산책하기 시작했다.
④ Francis Willughby에게 후원받아 홀로 유럽을 여행하였다.
⑤ 동식물의 목록을 만들기 위해 표본을 연구하며 말년을 보냈다.

DAY 08 09 내용 일치 파악

15 ⓒ 80초

★☆☆ 2023년 11월 26번

Maggie L. Walker에 관한 다음 글의 내용과 일치하지 않는 것은?

Maggie L. Walker achieved national prominence as a businesswoman and community leader. She was among the earliest Black students to attend newly-established public schools for African Americans. After graduating, she worked as a teacher for three years at the Valley School, where she had studied. In the early 1900s, Virginia banks owned by white bankers were unwilling to do business with African American organizations or individuals. The racial discrimination by white bankers drove her to study banking and financial laws. She established a newspaper to promote closer communication between the charitable organization she belonged to and the public. Soon after, she founded the St. Luke Penny Savings Bank, which survived the Great Depression and merged with two other banks. It thrived as the oldest continually African American-operated bank until 2009. Walker achieved successes with the vision to make improvements in the way of life for African Americans.

① 아프리카계 미국인을 위해 설립된 학교에 다녔다.
② 졸업 후 자신이 공부했던 학교에서 교사로 일했다.
③ 인종 차별로 인해 은행 금융법 공부를 시작할 수 없었다.
④ 자선 단체와 대중 간의 소통을 장려하고자 신문사를 설립했다.
⑤ 그녀가 설립한 은행은 대공황에서 살아남아 다른 은행들과 합병했다.

16 ⓒ 80초

★☆☆ 2024년 3월 26번

Theodore von Kármán에 관한 다음 글의 내용과 일치하지 않는 것은?

Theodore von Kármán, a Hungarian-American engineer, was one of the greatest minds of the twentieth century. He was born in Hungary and at an early age, he showed a talent for math and science. In 1908, he received a doctoral degree in engineering at the University of Göttingen in Germany. In the 1920s, he began traveling as a lecturer and consultant to industry. He was invited to the United States to advise engineers on the design of a wind tunnel at California Institute of Technology (Caltech). He became the director of the Guggenheim Aeronautical Laboratory at Caltech in 1930. Later, he was awarded the National Medal of Science for his leadership in science and engineering.

① 어린 시절 수학과 과학에 재능을 보였다.
② University of Göttingen에서 공학 박사 학위를 받았다.
③ 1920년대에 강연자 겸 자문 위원으로 다니기 시작했다.
④ Caltech의 공학자를 초청하여 조언을 구했다.
⑤ National Medal of Science를 받았다.

정답과 해설 : 15 123 16 123

17 ⓒ 80초

★☆☆ 2024년 6월 26번

Henry David Thoreau에 관한 다음 글의 내용과 일치하지 않는 것은?

Henry David Thoreau was born in Concord, Massachusetts in 1817. When he was 16, he entered Harvard College. After graduating, Thoreau worked as a schoolteacher but he quit after two weeks. In June of 1838 he set up a school with his brother John. However, he had hopes of becoming a nature poet. In 1845, he moved into a small self-built house near Walden Pond. At Walden, Thoreau did an incredible amount of reading. The journal he wrote there became the source of his most famous book, *Walden*. In his later life, Thoreau traveled to the Maine woods, to Cape Cod, and to Canada. At the age of 43, he ended his travels and returned to Concord. Although his works were not widely read during his lifetime, he never stopped writing, and his works fill 20 volumes.

① 졸업한 후에 교사로 일했다.
② 자연 시인이 되기를 희망했다.
③ Walden에서 엄청난 양의 독서를 했다.
④ 43세에 여행을 마치고 Concord로 돌아왔다.
⑤ 그의 작품은 그의 일생 동안 널리 읽혔다.

18 ⓒ 80초

★☆☆ 2024년 9월 26번

Charles Elton에 관한 다음 글의 내용과 일치하지 않는 것은?

Born in the English city of Liverpool, Charles Elton studied zoology under Julian Huxley at Oxford University from 1918 to 1922. After graduating, he began teaching as a part-time instructor and had a long and distinguished teaching career at Oxford from 1922 to 1967. After a series of arctic expeditions with Huxley, he worked with a fur-collecting and trading company as a biological consultant, and examined the company's records to study animal populations. In 1927, he wrote his first and most important book, *Animal Ecology*, in which he demonstrated the nature of food chains and cycles. In 1932, he helped establish the Bureau of Animal Population at Oxford. In the same year he became the editor of the new *Journal of Animal Ecology*. Throughout his career, Elton wrote six books and played a major role in shaping the modern science of ecology.

① 대학에서 동물학을 공부했다.
② 대학 졸업 후 가르치는 일을 시작했다.
③ 생물학 컨설턴트로서 한 회사와 함께 일했다.
④ 마지막으로 쓴 저서는 *Animal Ecology*였다.
⑤ 1932년에 *Journal of Animal Ecology*의 편집자가 되었다.

정답과 해설 : 17 124 18 125

유형TIP

10. 안내문

정보를 전달하는 글 외에도 표나 그림을 포함하며, 선택지가 한글로 제시되어 정답률이 높은 유형
대회나 행사의 안내문이 주로 출제되며, 간혹 기사문이나 광고문과 같은 실용문이 실리기도 함.

유형 TIP 25BR2T_CH10 대표 예제 25BR2E_CH10

유형 공략법

1) 문제에서 무엇을 묻는지와 지문이 어떤 종류의 글인지를 확인해야 한다.
내용 일치인지 불일치인지 헷갈리지 않게 주의해야 함.
대회, 행사 등의 안내문, 설명서 등 지문이 어떤 종류의 글인지를 파악해야 함.

2) 선택지를 먼저 읽는다.

3) 선택지를 토대로 확인해야 할 사항이 무엇인지를 파악하고 안내문에서 그 내용을 찾는다.

필수 암기 어휘와 표현

공통	주최 host, hold, take place / 장소 online ↔ on site, indoors ↔ outdoors 준비 사항 preparations, will be provided(will not be provided) 요구 사항 requirements, be required 입장/입장비 admission, enter, ticket, pass 등록/등록비 register, sign up for, registration, fee, tuition/participation/registration fee, payment, full payment 기타 비용 관련 insurance, rental fee, discount, free of charge 취소 및 환불 cancel, cancellation policy, cancellation fee, refund, refund policy 예약 reservation / 주차 parking, parking lot, parking fee, free parking 공지 note / 추가 정보 details, additional information / 질문/문의 사항 questions, inquiries 연락 visit our website, please email us, please contact us, feel free to contact us
대회	대회 contest, competition / 참가 participate, participant, enter, entry, entrant 참가 자격 be open to 제출 submit, submission, upload / 출품작 entry, work / 마감 기한 deadline 평가 judging/evaluation criteria / 결과 발표 notify, notification, announce, be posted 순위 1st/first, 2nd/second, 3rd/third place / 상 prize, gift certificate 수상자 winner, winning+N / 수여 award
설명서	설명서 manual, instructions / 제품 product, device feature, description, function, caution 사용 operate, operation, use, battery, charge
수업/워크숍	수업/워크숍 class, workshop / 수준 level, beginner 인원 제한 Spaces are limited. The class size is limited.
장소	장소 location, tour, on site / 스케줄 tour schedule, tour timetable 기타 restroom, parking / 선착순 first come, first served/seated
행사	행사 event, occasion, annual event, camp, festival, EXPO / 활동 activities, program 자선/기부 행사 charity, local charity, donation event, donation, donate, donor

안내문 대표 예제 - 2024학년도 수능 27번

Turtle Island Boat Tour에 관한 다음 안내문의 내용과 일치하지 않는 것은?

(1) **Turtle Island Boat Tour**

(2) The fantastic Turtle Island Boat Tour invites you to the beautiful sea world.

(3) **Dates:** From June 1 to August 31, 2024

(4) **Tour Times**

Weekdays	1 p.m. – 5 p.m.
Weekends	9 a.m. – 1 p.m.
	1 p.m. – 5 p.m.

(5) ※ Each tour lasts four hours.

(6) **Tickets & Booking**

(7) • $50 per person for each tour

(8) (Only those aged 17 and over can participate.)

(9) • Bookings must be completed no later than 2 days before the day of the tour.

(10) • No refunds after the departure time

(11) • Each tour group size is limited to 10 participants.

(12) **Activities**

(13) • Snorkeling with a professional diver

(14) • Feeding tropical fish

(15) ※ Feel free to explore our website, www.snorkelingti.com.

① 주말에는 하루에 두 번 운영된다. 문장(4)

② 17세 이상만 참가할 수 있다. 문장(8)

③ ~~당일~~ 예약이 가능하다. 문장(9)
관광 당일 이틀 전까지

④ 출발 시간 이후에는 환불이 불가능하다. 문장(10)

⑤ 전문 다이버와 함께 하는 스노클링 활동이 있다. 문장(13)

STEP 1 문제에서 무엇을 묻는지와 지문이 어떤 종류의 글인지를 확인해야 한다.

→ 안내문의 내용과 일치하지 '않는' 선택지를 찾아야 함.

→ 거북섬 보트 관광을 공지하는 글임.

STEP 2 선택지를 토대로 확인해야 할 사항이 무엇인지를 파악하고 안내문에서 그 내용을 찾는다.

① 주말에는 몇 번 운영되는가?

→ 문장(4): 주말(weekends)에는 하루에 두 번 운영됨.

② 참가 가능한 나이는?

→ 문장(8): 오직 17세 이상만(only those aged 17 and over) 참가할 수 있음.

③ 당일 예약이 가능한가?

→ 문장(9): 관광 당일 이틀 전(2 days before the day of the tour)까지 예약되어야 함.

④ 출발 시간 이후 환불이 가능한가?

→ 문장(10): 출발 시간 이후에는 환불이 불가능(no refunds)함.

⑤ 전문 다이버와 함께 하는 활동이 있는가?

→ 문장(13): 전문(professional) 다이버와 함께하는 스노클링(snorkeling) 활동이 있음.

전문 해석

(1) 거북섬 보트 관광

(2) 환상적인 거북섬 보트 관광은 아름다운 바다 세계로 여러분을 초대합니다.

(3) 날짜: 2024년 6월 1일부터 8월 31일까지

(4) 관광 시간

평일	오후 1시~오후 5시
주말	오전 9시~오후 1시
	오후 1시~오후 5시

(5) ※ 각 관광은 4시간 동안 계속됩니다.

(6) 표와 예약

(7) • 각 관광별 인당 50달러

(8) (오직 17세 이상만 참가할 수 있습니다.)

(9) • 예약은 늦어도 관광 당일 이틀 전까지 완료되어야 합니다.

(10) • 출발 시간 이후 환불 불가

(11) • 각 관광단의 규모는 10명의 참가자로 제한됩니다.

(12) 활동

(13) • 전문 다이버와 함께하는 스노클링

(14) • 열대어에게 먹이 주기

(15) ※ 저희의 웹사이트 www.snorkelingti.com을 편하게 살펴보세요.

중요 어휘

□ last 동 계속되다, 지속되다
□ booking 명 예약
□ complete 동 완료하다, 끝마치다 / 형 완전한
□ no later than 늦어도 ~까지
□ departure 명 출발, 떠남
□ feed 동 먹이를 주다
□ tropical 형 열대의
□ feel free to V 편하게 ~하다, 마음대로 ~하다
□ explore 동 살피다, 탐험하다

자세한 해설지 QR→ 자세한해설-CH10

DAY 09 10 안내문

10 안내문

동영상 강의

25BR2_CH10

01 ⓢ 50초

★☆☆ 2020년 11월 27번

Zero Waste Day 2020에 관한 다음 안내문의 내용과 일치하지 않는 것은?

Zero Waste Day 2020

Zero Waste Day (ZWD) 2020 is an opportunity for you to clean out your attic and donate items for reuse.

When & Where:

First Saturday in November (November 7, 2020), 9:00 a.m. – 12:00 p.m. (rain or shine)

At 400 Union Square

Accepted Items:

• **Wearable clothes / shoes**
All sizes of clothes and shoes MUST BE DRY.

• **Bedding (pillows, blankets, or mattress covers)**
Worn or torn is fine, but no oil stains are allowed.

• **Electronics (computers, laptops, or cell phones)**
All data on the device must be deleted.

Note: If an item isn't accepted, please be prepared to take it home. There is no place for you to drop off garbage.

ZWD is open to ALL!

For more information, please visit www.zwd.org.

① 우천 시에도 행사가 예정대로 진행된다.
② 의류와 신발은 건조된 상태의 것만 받는다.
③ 헤지거나 찢어진 침구류도 기부가 가능하다.
④ 전자 기기에 저장된 모든 정보는 삭제되어야 한다.
⑤ 기부 물품 접수가 거절되면 현장에서 버릴 수 있다.

02 ⓢ 50초

★☆☆ 2021년 11월 27번

The Great Pumpkin Roll에 관한 다음 안내문의 내용과 일치하지 않는 것은?

The Great Pumpkin Roll

Let's race pumpkins by rolling them down a hill! How far will they go across the road?

□ **Date**: The last Sunday of May, 2021
□ **Location**: Branford Hill in the town of Goomeri
□ **Registration Fee**: $10 for adults, $2 for teens
□ **Rules**
• The participant who rolls their pumpkin farthest wins.
• Pumpkins must be at least 15 cm in width.
• Participants must roll pumpkins only using an underarm action.
• Each participant has only one opportunity to roll a pumpkin.
□ **Prizes**
• $1,000 for the person whose pumpkin lands in the Lucky Spot (If more than one participant lands their pumpkin in the Lucky Spot, the money will be divided equally.)
• $500 for the adult champion and $200 for the teen champion

Please visit www.goomeripumpkinfestival.com.

① 2021년 5월의 마지막 일요일에 열린다.
② 경기에 사용하는 호박의 최소 너비에 제한이 있다.
③ 참가자는 팔을 아래로 내려 호박을 굴려야 한다.
④ 참가자에게 호박을 굴릴 수 있는 기회를 여러 번 준다.
⑤ Lucky Spot에 호박을 넣은 모두가 상금을 균등하게 나눠 갖는다.

정답과 해설 : 01 126 02 126

03 ⓒ 50초

★☆☆ 2022년 6월 27번

2022 Korean Speech Contest에 관한 다음 안내문의 내용과 일치하지 않는 것은?

2022 Korean Speech Contest

Are you a foreign student who wants to show off your Korean? Make your own video sharing your experiences in Korea.

- **Theme**: "My Experiences While Staying in Korea"
- **Video Submission Deadline**: September 5th
- **Prizes**
  - 1st place: $100 and traditional Korean tea
  - 2nd place: $50 and a traditional Korean doll
- **Details**
  - Your name must be mentioned at the beginning of the video.
  - Your video must be between 3 to 5 minutes.
  - Please email your video file to k-speech@kcontest.com.

① 한국에서 지내는 동안의 경험을 주제로 한다.
② 영상 제출 마감일은 9월 5일이다.
③ 1등에게는 상금과 한국 전통 인형이 주어진다.
④ 영상 도입부에 이름이 언급되어야 한다.
⑤ 이메일로 영상 파일을 보내야 한다.

04 ⓒ 50초

★☆☆ 2022년 9월 27번

The Colchester Zoo Charity Race에 관한 다음 안내문의 내용과 일치하지 않는 것은?

The Colchester Zoo Charity Race

Join us for a charity event to help endangered species.
You will be running through Colchester Zoo, home to over 260 species!

Date: Sunday, Sep. 25th, 2022

Time: 9:00 a.m. – 11:00 a.m.

Registration Fee: $50
- Registration fee includes a free pass to the zoo, food and drinks, and official photos.
- Register at www.info.colchesters.com.

Course Length: 10km
- Every runner will run 1km of the race through the zoo before going out to the main road.

Other Information
- Only the runners who complete the race will receive a medal at the finish line.
- Event T-shirts can be purchased at the zoo.

① 2시간 동안 진행된다.
② 등록비에는 음식과 음료가 포함된다.
③ 코스 길이는 10km이다.
④ 모든 참가자는 메달을 받는다.
⑤ 행사 티셔츠는 동물원에서 구입할 수 있다.

정답과 해설 : 03 126 04 127

05 ⓒ 50초

★☆☆ 2022년 3월 26번

2022 Bluehill Virtual Gala에 관한 다음 안내문의 내용과 일치하지 않는 것은?

2022 Bluehill Virtual Gala

You're invited to the 2022 Bluehill Virtual Gala hosted by the Bluehill Community Center. We'll have an online party to raise funds for our charity programs! Because we can't gather together in person this year, we are joining together virtually.

- Our Virtual Gala is on April 2 from 6 p.m. to 8 p.m.
- It will include musical performances, special lectures, and live auctions!
- Our MC will be Edward Jones, the famous actor from *A Good Neighbor*.

Everyone is welcome. This event will stream for free!
To join the party,
simply visit www.bluehillgala.org.

① 자선 프로그램 기금 마련을 위한 온라인 파티이다.
② 4월 2일 오후 6시부터 8시까지 진행된다.
③ 음악 공연과 특별 강연, 라이브 경매가 있을 것이다.
④ 배우 Edward Jones가 사회를 볼 것이다.
⑤ 유료로 스트리밍될 것이다.

06 ⓒ 50초

★☆☆ 2022년 11월 27번

2022 Strawberry Festival에 관한 다음 안내문의 내용과 일치하지 않는 것은?

2022 Strawberry Festival

Join us for a fun family festival. This year, we are back to hosting an in-person event in Berry Square!

□ **Date**: November 26, 2022 (11:00 a.m. – 5:00 p.m.)

□ **Tickets**: $20 per person
(Children 6 and under are FREE.)

□ **Special Events**

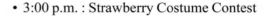

- 11:00 a.m. : Baking Class for Kids
- 1:00 p.m. : Strawberry Pie-Eating Contest
- 3:00 p.m. : Strawberry Costume Contest

□ **Note**
- The parking fee is $5 and includes tram service to the ticket booth.
- If you are interested in volunteering, complete an application form and email it to manager@strawberryfestival.org.

① 올해는 대면 행사로 개최된다.
② 6세 이하의 어린이에게는 입장료를 받지 않는다.
③ 딸기파이 먹기 대회가 오후에 열린다.
④ 매표소로 가는 트램 서비스는 주차비에 포함되지 않는다.
⑤ 자원봉사에 관심이 있다면 신청서를 이메일로 보내야 한다.

정답과 해설 : 05 127 06 127

07 ⓒ 50초

★☆☆ 2023년 3월 27번

Have a Good Night App에 관한 다음 안내문의 내용과 일치하지 않는 것은?

Have a Good Night App

This smart app helps you have a refreshing sleep!

FEATURES

■ **Sounds for Sleep**

– Providing relaxing sounds for sleep

■ **Sleep Recorder**

– Recording sounds such as coughing or snoring while sleeping

■ **Sleep Pattern Tracker**

– Checking and analyzing the user's sleep pattern

■ **Stress-Free Alarm Tones**

– Adjusting alarm tones to the user's sleep pattern

PRICE

■ **Basic version**: Free

■ **Premium version (extra soundtracks)**: $30 per year

Click HERE to Download the App!

① 수면을 위한 편안한 소리를 제공한다.
② 자는 동안 기침이나 코를 고는 소리를 녹음한다.
③ 이용자의 수면 패턴을 확인하고 분석한다.
④ 수면 패턴에 따라 알람음을 조정한다.
⑤ 기본 버전은 1년에 30달러이다.

08 ⓒ 50초

★☆☆ 2023년 3월 28번

2023 Online Talent Show에 관한 다음 안내문의 내용과 일치하는 것은?

2023 Online Talent Show

Show off your amazing talents!

■ **Categories**: singing, dancing, playing instruments

■ **How to Enter**

– Record a 3-minute video of your talent and send it to talent@westhigh.edu.
– Submit the entry between March 27 and March 31.

■ **How We Select a Winner**

1. All the videos will be uploaded on the school website on April 5.
2. Students and teachers will vote for their favorite video.
3. The video that receives the most votes will win.

* The winning video will be played at the school festival.

For more information, please visit www.westhigh.edu.

① 참가 부문은 노래와 춤을 포함한 네 가지이다.
② 비디오의 길이에는 제한이 없다.
③ 제출 기간은 3월 27일부터 7일 동안이다.
④ 학생들만 우승작 선정 투표에 참여할 수 있다.
⑤ 우승한 비디오는 학교 축제에서 상영될 것이다.

DAY 09 10 안내문

정답과 해설 : 07 128 08 128

09 ⏱ 50초

★☆☆ 2023년 6월 27번

Peace Marathon Festival에 관한 다음 안내문의 내용과 일치하지 않는 것은?

Peace Marathon Festival

The Peace Marathon Festival will be held to promote world peace and share compassion for people in need. Join us to enjoy running and make a better world.

When & Where
- Sunday, September 3, 2023 (Start time: 10 a.m.)
- Civic Stadium

Participation Fee & Qualification
- Full & Half: $30 (20 years or older)
- 10 km & 5 km: $15 (No age limit)

Registration
- The number of participants is limited to 1,000. (First come, first served.)
- Online only at ipmarathon.com

Notes
- Souvenirs and medals will be given to all participants.
- Changing rooms will be available at no charge.
- Water will be provided every 2.5 km and at the finish line.

① 출발 시각은 오전 10시이다.
② 5 킬로미터 코스는 참가에 나이 제한이 없다.
③ 참가자는 선착순 1,000명으로 제한된다.
④ 모든 참가자들에게 기념품과 메달이 주어진다.
⑤ 물은 결승선에서만 제공된다.

10 ⏱ 50초

★☆☆ 2023년 9월 27번

Roselands Virtual Sports Day에 관한 다음 안내문의 내용과 일치하지 않는 것은?

Roselands Virtual Sports Day

Roselands Virtual Sports Day is an athletic competition that you can participate in from anywhere.

When: October 16th – 22nd, 2023

How the event works
- There are 10 challenges in total.
- You can see videos explaining each challenge on our school website.
- The more challenges you complete, the more points you will gain for your class.
- The class with the most points will get a prize.
- Parents and teachers can also participate.

How to submit your entry
- Email us videos of you completing the challenges at virtualsportsday@roselands.com.
- The size of the video file must not exceed 500MB.

① 10월 16일부터 22일까지 열린다.
② 총 10개의 도전 과제가 있다.
③ 학교 웹사이트에서 도전 과제를 설명하는 영상을 볼 수 있다.
④ 학부모와 교사는 참여할 수 없다.
⑤ 제출할 영상파일 용량이 500MB를 초과하면 안 된다.

정답과 해설 : 09 128 10 128

11 ⓒ 50초

★☆☆ 2022년 3월 27번

Woodside Clay Workshop에 관한 다음 안내문의 내용과 일치하는 것은?

Woodside Clay Workshop

7 p.m. Thursday March 31, 2022
7 p.m. Thursday April 7, 2022

This is a two-session workshop for adults. In the first session, you will learn the basics of clay and create unique ceramic pendants. In the second session, you will decorate the pieces before we glaze and fire them. Your pendants will be ready to be picked up from April 14.

– This workshop is suitable for beginners, so no experience is necessary.
– Fee: £25 (including all materials, instruction and a glass of wine)
– There are limited spaces, so book early. Advance bookings only.

For more information, visit our website at www.woodsideclay.co.uk.

* glaze: 유약을 바르다

① 목요일 오전에 진행된다.
② 어린이를 대상으로 한다.
③ 두 번째 시간에 펜던트를 찾아갈 수 있다.
④ 모든 재료가 참가비에 포함된다.
⑤ 사전 예약을 받지 않는다.

12 ⓒ 50초

★☆☆ 2020년 9월 27번

2020 Game-Coding Workshop에 관한 다음 안내문의 내용과 일치하지 <u>않는</u> 것은?

2020 Game-Coding Workshop

Turn your children's love for computer games into a skill. This game-coding workshop will teach them to use block-based coding software to create their own games!

□ **Date & Time**
- Saturday, December 12th, 1:00 pm to 3:00 pm

□ **Registration**
- Closes Friday, November 27th
- Participation fee is $30 (free for Lansing Kids Club members).
- Sign up in person at Kid's Coding Center or online at www.lanskidscoding.com.

□ **Requirements**
- Open only to children 9 to 12 years old
- Laptops will not be provided. Participants must bring their own.
- No prior coding knowledge is required.

Please visit our website for more information.

① 토요일 오후에 진행된다.
② Lansing 키즈 클럽 회원은 참가비가 무료이다.
③ 온라인 등록이 가능하다.
④ 참가자들에게 노트북 컴퓨터가 제공된다.
⑤ 코딩에 대한 사전 지식이 필요 없다.

13 ⓒ 50초

★☆☆ 2020년 11월 28번

Sign Language Class에 관한 다음 안내문의 내용과 일치하는 것은?

Sign Language Class

If you've ever considered studying sign language, our class is one of the best ways to do it! The class is open to people of all ages, but all children must be accompanied by an adult.

Class Schedule

- Where: Coorparoo Community Center
- When: September – October, 2020 (7:00 p.m. – 9:00 p.m.)

Levels

- Class #1 (Monday and Tuesday)
  – No previous sign language experience is required.
- Class #2 (Wednesday and Thursday)
  – Knowledge of at least 1,000 signs is required.

Note

- Tuition is $100.
- We do not provide refunds unless class is cancelled due to low registration.
- Registration is available only online and before August 31.

Visit our website at www.CRsignlgs.com.

① 어린이들도 어른 동반 없이 참여할 수 있다.
② 수업은 주 3일 진행된다.
③ 수화 경험이 없어도 참여할 수 있는 수업이 있다.
④ 환불은 예외 없이 불가능하다.
⑤ 현장 등록이 가능하다.

14 ⓒ 50초

★☆☆ 2021년 3월 26번

Grey County 2021 Job Fair에 관한 다음 안내문의 내용과 일치하는 것은?

Grey County 2021 Job Fair

April 28, 2:00 p.m. – 6:00 p.m.
Bayshore Community Center

Businesses across Grey County can now register for a booth at the 2021 Job Fair. Last year's was the largest ever held in this area with more than 80 employers and over 1,000 job seekers. This year, we're moving to an even larger location with plenty of space for all attendees.

– Registration Fee: $80
– Registration Deadline: April 14, 6:00 p.m.

Enhanced Services to Employers

- 5 m × 5 m booth
- Free wifi
- Employer-only lounge and refreshments

For more information,
visit www.greycountyjobfair.org.

① 행사 진행 시간은 6시간이다.
② 작년보다 더 좁은 장소에서 열린다.
③ 등록 마감일은 4월 28일이다.
④ 가로세로 각각 10m인 부스가 제공된다.
⑤ 고용주 전용 라운지와 다과가 제공된다.

정답과 해설 : 13 129 14 130

15 ⏱ 50초

★☆☆ 2022년 6월 28번

EZ Portable Photo Printer 사용에 관한 다음 안내문의 내용과 일치하는 것은?

EZ Portable Photo Printer User Manual

Note on LED Indicator
- White: Power on
- Red: Battery charging

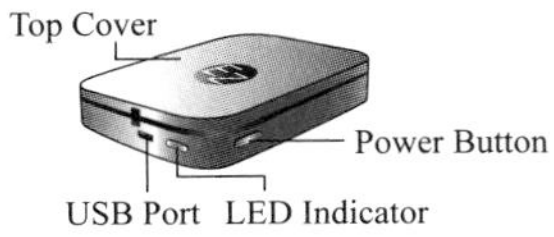

How to Operate
- Press the power button to turn the printer on.
- Press the power button twice to turn the printer off.
- To charge the battery, connect the cable to the USB port. It takes 60 – 90 minutes for a full charge.
- To connect to the printer wirelessly, download the 'EZ Printer App' on your mobile device.

How to Load Photo Paper
- Lift the printer's top cover.
- Insert the photo paper with any logos facing downward.

① LED 표시기의 흰색은 충전 중임을 나타낸다.
② 전원 버튼을 한 번 누르면 전원이 꺼진다.
③ 배터리가 완전히 충전되는 데 2시간 이상 걸린다.
④ 무선 연결을 위해 앱을 다운로드해야 한다.
⑤ 인화지를 로고가 위로 향하도록 넣어야 한다.

16 ⏱ 50초

★☆☆ 2022년 11월 28번

Maple Spring Light Art Exhibition에 관한 다음 안내문의 내용과 일치하는 것은?

Maple Spring Light Art Exhibition

The Maple Spring Light Art Exhibition will illuminate you, with a route surrounded by light artwork. Admire the beautiful light artwork as you walk through Maple Spring.

□ **Date**: December 1 – 31, 2022
(closed on the 2nd and 4th Monday of the month)
□ **Time**: 7 p.m. – 11 p.m.
□ **Entrance Fee**: $5 per person
□ **Exhibition Route**: alongside the Bow River in central Maple Spring
(Only digital maps of the route are available.)
- Souvenirs will be available on site and online.
- Local residents can get a 10% discount off the entrance fee.

Please visit www.maplespringlight.com for more information.

① 매주 월요일은 운영하지 않는다.
② 밤 11시 이후에도 입장이 가능하다.
③ 관람 경로가 담긴 지도는 종이로만 제공한다.
④ 기념품은 현장에서만 구매 가능하다.
⑤ 지역 주민은 입장료의 10% 할인을 받을 수 있다.

정답과 해설 : 15 130 16 131

17 ⓒ 50초

★☆☆ 2023년 6월 28번

Out to Lunch에 관한 다음 안내문의 내용과 일치하는 것은?

Out to Lunch

Do you want to enjoy an afternoon with tasty food and great music? 'Out to Lunch' is the perfect event to meet your needs! Come and enjoy this event held in Caras Park in downtown Missoula!

Dates & Times

• Every Wednesday in June, 12 p.m. – 3 p.m.

Highlights

• 10% discount at all food trucks including Diamond Ice Cream
• Live music performance of the new group Cello Brigade
• Face-painting and water balloon fight for kids

Notices

• Bring your own lawn chairs and blankets.
• Dispose of your waste properly.
• Drinking alcoholic beverages is strictly banned.

① 일 년 내내 수요일마다 열리는 행사이다.
② 푸드 트럭에서는 가격을 20% 할인해 준다.
③ 라이브 음악 공연이 마련되어 있다.
④ 개인 의자와 담요를 가지고 올 수 없다.
⑤ 주류를 포함한 음료를 마실 수 있다.

18 ⓒ 50초

★☆☆ 2023년 9월 28번

Back-to-school Giveaway Event에 관한 다음 안내문의 내용과 일치하는 것은?

Back-to-school Giveaway Event

The City of Easton will host a free back-to-school giveaway event. Join us for this fun event to help children of all ages prepare to go back to school after summer vacation.

When: Saturday, September 2nd,
9 a.m. – 11 a.m.

Location: City of Easton Central Park
(This event will be held rain or shine.)

Participation requirements

• Open to City of Easton residents only
• Must bring a valid ID

Note

• 500 backpacks will be given out on a first-come, first-served basis.
• A parent or a guardian must come with their child to receive the backpack.

For more information, call the City Council at 612–248–6633.

① 토요일 오후에 진행된다.
② 우천 시에는 취소된다.
③ Easton시 주민이 아니어도 참여할 수 있다.
④ 가방 500개가 선착순으로 배부될 것이다.
⑤ 부모 또는 보호자만 와도 가방을 받을 수 있다.

정답과 해설 : 17 131 18 131

19 ⓒ 50초

★☆☆
2018년 9월 27번

A Midsummer Night's Dream Audition에 관한 다음 안내문의 내용과 일치하지 않는 것은?

A Midsummer Night's Dream Audition

a musical adaptation of the William Shakespeare play

We are looking for dancers for the musical *A Midsummer Night's Dream* that will open at the Elliot Arts Center in the spring of 2019.

• When:
– Saturday, Dec. 15, 2018
(9 a.m. until 6 p.m.)
– Sunday, Dec. 16, 2018
(9 a.m. until 11 a.m.)
• Where: Studio Vahn

Requirement
• a modern / ballet dance background
• ability to sing preferred
• no prior stage experience required

Registration
• If you are interested in auditioning, email us at casting@studiovahn.com.
• Please include in your email:
– a completed application form with current photos
– a signed guardian consent form (only teens)
• All applications must be received by Friday, Nov. 30, 2018.

For more information,
visit www.studiovahn.com.

① 2019년 봄에 있을 공연을 위한 무용수들을 모집한다.
② 일요일은 오전 오디션만 가능하다.
③ 이전 무대 경험이 요구된다.
④ 십 대 참가자는 보호자의 동의서를 제출해야 한다.
⑤ 신청 마감일은 2018년 11월 30일이다.

20 ⓒ 50초

★☆☆
2019년 6월 27번

Flying Apron Cookery School Classes에 관한 다음 안내문의 내용과 일치하지 않는 것은?

Flying Apron Cookery School Classes

Enjoy a variety of classes in our beautiful cooking school kitchen!

Class
• French Meals: 5th July
• British Brunch: 12th July
• Taste of Mexico: 19th July

Time: 7:30 pm to 9:30 pm
Fee: $50 per person per class
(including the cost of all the ingredients)

* Each class requires a minimum of 4 participants and a maximum of 10.
* Participants can't get a refund once their class starts.
* After class, participants can take home all recipes and the meals they cooked.

① 영국식 브런치 강좌는 7월 12일에 열린다.
② 수업료에 모든 재료비가 포함되어 있다.
③ 참가 인원이 10명 이상이어야 강좌가 개설된다.
④ 각 수업이 시작되면 환불을 받을 수 없다.
⑤ 요리한 음식은 수업 이후 집으로 가져갈 수 있다.

DAY 09
10 안내문

21 ⓢ 50초

★☆☆
2021년 11월 28번

Plogging Event에 관한 다음 안내문의 내용과 일치하는 것은?

Plogging Event

Have you heard of Plogging? It comes from the Swedish word for pick up, "plocka upp" and is a combination of jogging and picking up litter. In 2016, it started in Sweden and has recently come to the UK, becoming a new movement for saving nature.

When & Where

- 9 a.m. on the first Monday of each month
- Outside the ETNA Centre, East Twickenham

What to Prepare

- Just bring your running shoes, and we will provide all the other equipment.
- There is no fee to participate, but you are welcome to donate toward our conservation work.

※ No reservations are necessary to participate.

For more information,
visit www.environmenttrust.org.

① 2016년에 영국에서 시작되었다.
② 매달 첫 번째 일요일 오전 9시에 열린다.
③ 운동화를 포함한 장비들이 지급된다.
④ 참가비는 무료이다.
⑤ 참가하려면 예약이 필요하다.

22 ⓢ 50초

★☆☆
2022년 9월 28번

7-Day Story Writing Competition에 관한 다음 안내문의 내용과 일치하는 것은?

7-Day Story Writing Competition

Is writing your talent? This is the stage for you.

When: From Monday, Dec. 5th to Sunday, Dec. 11th, 2022

Age: 17 and over

Content

- All participants will write about the same topic.
- You will be randomly assigned one of 12 literary genres for your story.
- You'll have exactly 7 days to write and submit your story.

Submission

- Only one entry per person
- You can revise and resubmit your entry until the deadline.

Prize

- We will choose 12 finalists, one from each genre, and the 12 entries will be published online and shared via social media.
- From the 12 finalists, one overall winner will be chosen and awarded $500.

※ To register and for more information, visit our website at www.7challenge_globestory.com.

① 17세 미만 누구나 참여할 수 있다.
② 참가자들은 동일한 주제에 대하여 글을 쓴다.
③ 참가자들은 12가지 문학 장르 중 하나를 선택할 수 있다.
④ 1인당 출품작을 최대 3편까지 제출할 수 있다.
⑤ 결승 진출자 전원에게 상금이 수여된다.

정답과 해설 : 21 132 22 133

23 ⓒ 50초

★☆☆ 2019년 9월 28번

Mini Beam Projector 사용에 관한 다음 안내문의 내용과 일치하는 것은?

Mini Beam Projector

– Instructions –

LED Power Indicator

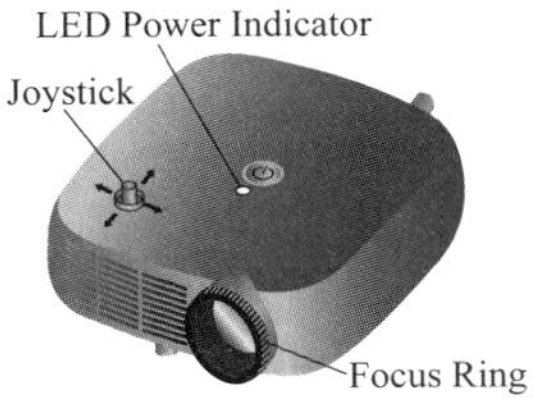

- **Red:** Power standby state
- **Green:** Projector on and operating

How to Operate

- In standby mode, press the power button once to turn the projector on.
- Press the power button twice to turn the projector off.
- Adjust the volume level by moving the joystick left or right.
- Adjust the focus of the image by rotating the focus ring.

Connecting a USB Device

Connect a USB device to the USB port of the projector to enjoy your content files. You cannot write data to or delete data from the USB device.

① 전원표시기의 녹색은 대기 상태임을 나타낸다.
② 전원 버튼을 한 번 누르면 전원이 꺼진다.
③ 조이스틱을 위아래로 움직여 음량을 조절한다.
④ 포커스 링을 돌려서 이미지의 초점을 맞춘다.
⑤ USB 장치에 있는 데이터를 삭제할 수 있다.

24 ⓒ 50초

★☆☆ 2020년 3월 28번

Bright Cat Toy에 관한 다음 안내문의 내용과 일치하는 것은?

Bright Cat Toy

Attract your cat's attention and satisfy their hunting instincts with a unique electronic cat toy.

Key Benefits

- The feather appears randomly in the 6 holes.
- Feathers can be exchanged easily.
- It automatically stops running after 8 minutes.
- It is fully charged in 30 minutes via USB-cable, and it runs for 5 hours.

How to Use

- Short press the button to power on/off the device.
- Long press the button to change feathers.

What's in the Box

- Bright Cat Toy: 1 piece
- Feather: 2 pieces (1 installed, 1 extra)

① 구멍에서 정해진 순서대로 깃털이 나온다.
② 8분 후에 자동으로 작동을 멈춘다.
③ 완전히 충전하는 데 5시간이 걸린다.
④ 켜거나 끄려면 버튼을 길게 눌러야 한다.
⑤ 총 세 개의 깃털이 제공된다.

25 ⏱ 50초

★☆☆ 2021년 3월 27번

The Riverside Escape에 관한 다음 안내문의 내용과 일치하지 않는 것은?

The Riverside Escape

The Riverside Escape is a city-wide escape game played on your smartphone. We turn the city of Riverside into a giant escape game wherein teams must race around the city completing challenges without getting caught.

How to Play

- Get your ticket — one ticket per team of up to 6 players.
- Choose the start date for the game. We will send you detailed information via email before your date of choice.
- Arrive at the start location and start anytime you want on the day.
- Score as many points as possible by answering the puzzles while moving around the city.

Opening Times

March 1, 2021 – May 31, 2021
Monday – Sunday, 10:00 – 20:00

Ticket Price

$50 per ticket (This price may change on a daily basis.)

Come join us for an escape adventure!

① 도시 전역에서 벌어지는 탈출 게임이다.
② 최대 여섯 명으로 구성된 팀당 티켓 한 장을 사야 한다.
③ 선택한 게임 시작일 이전에 전화로 상세한 정보를 알려 준다.
④ 2021년 3월 1일부터 세 달간 열린다.
⑤ 티켓 가격은 매일 달라질 수 있다.

26 ⏱ 50초

★☆☆ 2023년 11월 27번

2024 Youth Tennis Camp에 관한 다음 안내문의 내용과 일치하지 않는 것은?

2024 Youth Tennis Camp

2024 Youth Tennis Camp is where your child can get instruction from qualified tennis players at indoor tennis courts. It will provide fundamental tennis skills to your children!

Who: Ages 13 to 18
When: January 15 – 18, 2024
Monday to Thursday, 9:00 a.m. – 12:00 p.m.
Registration Fee: $100(lunch included)

Cancellation Policy

- 5 days before the class: 100% refund
- 1 – 4 days before the class: 50% refund
- On the day of the class and afterwards: No refund

Note

- No outside food is allowed.
- Participants must bring their own tennis equipment.

Registration is ONLY available online and will start on December 16. Visit our website at www.ytc2024.com to register.

① 자격을 가진 테니스 선수가 지도한다.
② 금요일에는 강습이 없다.
③ 등록비에는 점심 식사가 포함된다.
④ 강습 당일 취소 시 환불받을 수 있다.
⑤ 참가자들은 테니스 장비를 가져와야 한다.

정답과 해설 : 25 134 26 134

27 ⓒ 50초

★☆☆ 2023년 11월 28번

Cherrywood High School's T-shirt Design Contest에 관한 다음 안내문의 내용과 일치하는 것은?

Cherrywood High School's T-shirt Design Contest

Help us to design our new school shirts! A panel of student council members will select the winning design. Take this chance at being the designer for the new school T-shirt. This contest is open to all students!

Submission Deadline: 16:00 on December 22, 2023

Winner Announcement Date: December 29, 2023

Location for Submissions: Art Teacher's Office

Contest Rules

- Sketch your design on a piece of plain paper.
- Write your student number and name on your paper.
- Include the school name and logo in your design.
- Max of 4 colors can be used.

Good luck and thanks for your participation!

① 교사들이 수상 디자인을 선정할 예정이다.
② 수상자 발표일은 제출 마감일 다음 날이다.
③ 출품작은 학생회실에 제출해야 한다.
④ 종이에 자신의 학번과 이름을 써야 한다.
⑤ 사용 가능한 색상 수에 제한이 없다.

28 ⓒ 50초

★☆☆ 2024년 3월 27번

Basic Latte Art Class에 관한 다음 안내문의 내용과 일치하지 않는 것은?

Basic Latte Art Class

Make perfect lattes and present them in the most beautiful way! In this class, you will learn how to steam and pour milk. You will make three latte art designs on your own: heart, tulip, and leaf.

Date: April 27, 2024
Time: 9 a.m. – 1 p.m.
Place: Camefort Community Center

Registration & Fee

- Register online at www.camefortcc.com, from April 22 to April 24.
- $60 per person (cost of ingredients included)

Note

- Dairy alternatives will be available for non-milk drinkers.
- Students can get a 10% discount.

① 세 가지 라떼 아트 디자인을 직접 만들 것이다.
② 수업은 4시간 동안 진행된다.
③ 등록은 4월 24일부터 시작된다.
④ 비용에 재료비가 포함되어 있다.
⑤ 우유를 마시지 않는 사람은 대체 유제품을 사용할 수 있다.

정답과 해설 : 27 135 28 135

29 ⓒ 50초

★☆☆
2024년 3월 28번

Family Night-hiking Event에 관한 다음 안내문의 내용과 일치하는 것은?

Family Night-hiking Event

Join us for a fun-filled night of hiking and family bonding!

Date: Saturday, May 4
Time: 6 p.m. – 9 p.m.
Location: Skyline Preserve
Cost
- Adults: $20
- Children under 19: $10

Guidelines
- Children must be accompanied by legal guardians.
- Bring a flashlight and a bottle of water.
- Follow the instructions of the guides at all times.

Registration
- Visit www.familyhiking.com and register by April 26.
- A free first aid kit is provided for all who register by April 12.

① 토요일과 일요일 이틀간 진행된다.
② 오후 5시에 시작된다.
③ 어른과 어린이의 참가비는 같다.
④ 어린이는 법적 보호자를 동반해야 한다.
⑤ 추첨을 통해 구급상자가 무료로 제공된다.

30 ⓒ 50초

★☆☆
2024년 6월 27번

2024 Future Engineers Camp에 관한 다음 안내문의 내용과 일치하지 <u>않는</u> 것은?

2024 Future Engineers Camp

Calling all young creators! Join us at Southside Maker Space to explore the wonders of engineering with exciting activities.

Date: Saturday, July 20 & Sunday, July 21
Time: 10 a.m. – 4 p.m.
Ages: 14 to 16
Participation Fee: $100

Day 1 – Robotics Workshop
- Learn basic coding skills.
- Work in teams to build mini-robots.

Day 2 – Flying Challenge
- Make and test toy airplanes.
- Participate in an airplane flying race.

Notes
- Lunch is included in the participation fee.
- All tools and materials for the projects are provided.

For more information, please visit www.southsidemaker.com.

① 오전 10시부터 오후 4시까지 진행된다.
② 참가비는 100달러이다.
③ 기본적인 코딩 기술을 배운다.
④ 장난감 비행기를 만들고 테스트한다.
⑤ 점심 식사는 참가비에 포함되지 않는다.

정답과 해설 : 29 135 30 135

31 ⓒ 50초

★☆☆
2024년 6월 28번

Taste the City에 관한 다음 안내문의 내용과 일치하는 것은?

Taste the City

Experience Jamestown's diverse and delicious food culture all in one place. Enjoy tasty treats, and discover new restaurants!

When & Where

- September 6th – 8th (10 a.m. – 9 p.m.)
- Grand Park

Highlights
- 30 kinds of food samples provided by local restaurants
- Live music performances each evening
- Cooking classes with experienced chefs

Entry Tickets
- Adult: $15
- Child: $10

※ No pre-reservations necessary, just show up and enjoy.

① 9월 6일부터 일주일 동안 열린다.
② 라이브 음악 공연이 하루 종일 진행된다.
③ 숙련된 요리사들과의 요리 수업이 있다.
④ 어른과 아이의 입장권 가격은 동일하다.
⑤ 사전 예약이 필요하다.

32 ⓒ 50초

★☆☆
2024년 9월 27번

Clifton Fall Clean-up Day 2024에 관한 다음 안내문의 내용과 일치하지 않는 것은?

Clifton Fall Clean-up Day 2024

Join us for this annual event to clean up the fallen leaves in Central Park, and enjoy meeting your neighbors!

When: Sunday, October 20th, 1 p.m. – 3 p.m.

Details
- Clean-up will be done in groups of 10 people based on age.
- After the clean-up, you can enjoy a casual gathering with neighbors.
- Food trucks will be set up for your gathering.

Notes
- A T-shirt with the event's logo will be provided as a gift.
- You'll be supplied with cleaning materials, such as bags and gloves, so you don't have to bring them.

We're looking forward to seeing you there!

① 매년 열리는 행사이다.
② 10명씩 조를 이루어 청소할 것이다.
③ 푸드 트럭이 설치될 것이다.
④ 행사 로고가 있는 티셔츠가 제공될 것이다.
⑤ 청소 도구를 가져와야 한다.

정답과 해설 : 31 136 32 136

33 ⏱ 50초 ★☆☆ 2024년 9월 28번

Sustainable Fashion Festival 2024에 관한 다음 안내문의 내용과 일치하는 것은?

Sustainable Fashion Festival 2024

Sustainable Fashion Festival 2024 is coming! Be inspired and learn how to live sustainably while looking fabulous.

When & Where
- Friday, September 13th, 5 p.m. – 9 p.m.
- Aimes Community Center

Tickets: $20 for early birds / $25 at the door
(Early purchase discount ends two days before the event.)

Programs
- Marketplace for sustainable products: You can sell or buy new, vintage, or upcycled clothing.
- Talks from eco-fashion experts on fashion's sustainable future
- Clothing exchange: You can exchange 5 or fewer items.
- Runway showcase of sustainable designs

※ To sell your sustainable products at our marketplace, registration is required in advance.

Contact us on social media for more information.

① 금요일 오전에 진행된다.
② 티켓 조기 구매 할인은 행사 사흘 전 종료된다.
③ 장터에서 새 의류를 구입할 수 없다.
④ 5개 이하의 의류 물품을 교환할 수 있다.
⑤ 사전 등록 없이도 지속 가능 제품을 판매할 수 있다.

정답과 해설 : 33 136

유형 TIP

11. 빈칸 추론(1) & 12. 빈칸 추론(2)

기출문제에서 고난도 유형에 속하며 배점이 높음.
지문의 내용에 대한 전체적인 이해도를 바탕으로 논리력과 추론 능력이 함께 요구됨.

유형 TIP 대표 예제

25BR2T_CH11 25BR2E_CH11

유형 공략법

1) 빈칸이 포함된 문장을 먼저 읽는다.

빈칸이 있는 문장을 먼저 읽고 빈칸 해결을 위해 지문에서 어떤 정보를 얻어야 하는지 생각해야 함.

2) 지문의 주제를 파악한다.

지문의 논리 구조를 먼저 파악하고, 빈칸의 내용을 유추해 보아야 함. 빈칸은 주로 주제나 지문의 핵심 내용을 포함하기 때문임.

3) 빈칸은 핵심 내용을 포함하지만 다른 말로 표현되어 있다(paraphrase).

빈칸에는 주제 또는 주제와 밀접한 관련이 있는 세부 사항이 들어감.
보통 유의어를 사용하거나 문장 구조를 바꾸어서 다른 말로 표현함(paraphrase).

4) 지문의 주제를 기준으로 오답 선택지를 소거한다.

선택지가 지엽적이지는 않은지, 글의 주제나 소재와 연관성이 있는지를 파악해야 함.
선택지를 읽을 때 아래의 경우에 부합한다면 오답일 확률이 높음.
① 주제와 반대되는 선택지
② 소재와 무관한, 단순히 지문에 들어간 단어에만 집중한 선택지
③ 지문의 소재와는 맞으나 주제와는 맞지 않는 단어를 포함한 선택지

필수 암기 어휘와 표현

Paraphrase에 사용될 수 있는 유의어

diversity	variety, multiplicity, heterogeneity, difference, distinction
imagination	vision, fantasy, creativity, ingenuity, invention
object	thing, stuff, entity, being / purpose, aim, goal, target
popular	common, general, prevailing, prevalent, fashionable, favorite
accurate	precise, correct, exact, strict, right
subject	명 topic, content, issue, matter / 형 dependent, subordinate
experience	undergo, encounter, go through, face, feel, taste
abstract	theoretical, conceptual, notional, hypothetical
fit	adapt, adjust, accommodate, suit, conform to
abuse	misuse, mistreat, damage, harm, insult
convert	transform, change, turn, alter, modify
acknowledge	admit, allow, accept, concede, grant, recognize
provide	supply, give, offer, furnish, equip, serve
eliminate	remove, discard, get rid of, dispose of
find	discover, find out, spot, detect, learn

빈칸 추론(1) 대표 예제 - 2024학년도 수능 31번

다음 빈칸에 들어갈 말로 가장 적절한 것은?

(1) Over the last decade the attention given to how children learn to read has foregrounded the nature of *textuality*, and of the different, interrelated ways in which readers of all ages make texts mean. (2) 'Reading' now applies to a greater number of representational forms than at any time in the past: pictures, maps, screens, design graphics and photographs are all regarded as text. (3) In addition to the innovations made possible in picture books by new printing processes, design features also predominate in other kinds, such as books of poetry and information texts. (4) Thus, reading becomes a more complicated kind of interpretation than it was when children's attention was focused on the printed text, with sketches or pictures as an adjunct. (5) Children now learn from a picture book that words and illustrations complement and enhance each other. (6) Reading is not simply ________________. (7) Even in the easiest texts, what a sentence 'says' is often not what it means.

* adjunct: 부속물

① knowledge acquisition
✔ word recognition
③ imaginative play
④ subjective interpretation
⑤ image mapping

STEP 1 빈칸이 포함된 문장을 먼저 읽는다.

→ 읽기는 단순히 어떤 것이 아님.
→ 빈칸 앞의 표현 'not simply'를 통해 빈칸에는 주제와 반대되는 내용이 들어간다는 것을 알 수 있음.

STEP 2 지문의 주제를 파악한다.

→ 읽기의 대상이 되는 것이 다양한 매체가 되어 복잡한 해석을 필요로 한다는 것이 글의 주제임.
→ 문장 (2)에서 그림, 지도, 화면, 디자인 그래픽, 사진도 모두 텍스트로 간주된다고 함. 그래서 문장 (5)에서 이제 아이들이 글과 삽화가 보완적인 관계임을 알게 된 것처럼, 문장 (4)의 내용대로 읽기가 더 복잡한 해석을 요구한다고 함.
→ 그러므로 읽기의 과정은 단지 쓰인 글을 읽고 해석하는 것이 아님.

STEP 3 빈칸은 핵심 내용을 포함하지만 다른 말로 표현되어 있다.

→ 문장 (7)의 'what a sentence 'says' is often not what it means'가 문장 (6)의 'not simply word recognition'으로 다르게 표현되어 있음.

STEP 4 지문의 주제를 기준으로 오답 선택지를 소거한다.

→ 읽기가 단순히 글자를 인식하는 데서 그치지 않는다는 것이 이 글의 주제임. 지식 습득(knowledge acquisition), 상상 놀이(imaginative play), 주관적인 해석(subjective interpretation), 이미지 매핑(image mapping)은 이러한 주제에서 벗어나는 내용이므로 정답이 될 수 없음.

전문 해석

(1) 지난 10년 동안 아이들이 읽기를 배우는 방법에 주어진 관심은 '텍스트성'의 본질과 모든 연령의 독자들이 텍스트가 의미를 가지도록 만드는 다양한 상호 연관된 방식의 본질을 특히 중시해 왔다. (2) 이제 '읽기'는 과거의 그 어느 때보다 더 많은 재현의 형식에 적용되는데, 즉, 그림, 지도, 화면, 디자인 그래픽, 그리고 사진은 모두 텍스트로 간주된다. (3) 새로운 인쇄 과정으로 인해 그림책에서 가능해진 혁신 외에도, 디자인 특징은 또한 시집과 정보 텍스트와 같은 다른 종류에서도 두드러진다. (4) 그러므로, 읽기는 부속물로 스케치나 그림을 가진 인쇄된 텍스트에 아이들의 주의가 집중되었을 때 그랬던 것보다 더 복잡한 종류의 해석이 된다. (5) 아이들은 이제 그림책에서 글과 삽화가 서로를 보완하고 향상한다는 것을 배운다. (6) 읽기는 단순히 단어 인식이 아니다. (7) 심지어 가장 쉬운 텍스트에서조차 종종 문장이 '말하는' 바가 그것이 의미하는 바는 아니다.

중요 어휘

□ decade 명 10년
□ foreground 동 특히 중시하다, 전면에 놓다
□ nature 명 본질, 자연
□ textuality 명 텍스트성
□ interrelated 형 상호 연관된, 서로 관계가 있는
□ mean 동 의미를 가지다
□ a number of 많은, 다수의
□ representational 형 재현의, 표상의, 대표의
□ form 명 형식, 방식 / 동 형성하다
□ regard A as B A를 B로 간주하다[여기다]
□ feature 명 특징, 특성
□ predominate 동 두드러지다, 우위를 차지하다
□ complicated 형 복잡한, 어려운
□ interpretation 명 해석, 설명, 이해
□ adjunct 명 부속물, 부가물
□ illustration 명 삽화
□ complement 동 보완[보충]하다 / 명 보완물, 보충물
□ enhance 동 향상시키다, 강화하다
□ recognition 명 인식, 인정
□ acquisition 명 획득, 습득
□ imaginative 형 상상의, 창의적인
□ subjective 형 주관적인

자세한 해설지 QR→
자세한해설-CH11

빈칸 추론(2) 대표 예제 - 2024학년도 수능 32번

다음 빈칸에 들어갈 말로 가장 적절한 것은?

(1) A musical score within any film can add an additional layer to the film text, which goes beyond simply imitating the action viewed. (2) In films that tell of futuristic worlds, composers, much like sound designers, have added freedom to create a world that is unknown and new to the viewer. (3) However, unlike sound designers, composers often shy away from creating unique pieces that reflect these new worlds and often present musical scores that possess familiar structures and cadences. (4) While it is possible that this may interfere with creativity and a sense of space and time, it in fact ______________________. (5) Through recognizable scores, visions of the future or a galaxy far, far away can be placed within a recognizable context. (6) Such familiarity allows the viewer to be placed in a comfortable space so that the film may then lead the viewer to what is an unfamiliar, but acceptable vision of a world different from their own.

* score: 악보 ** cadence: (율동적인) 박자

① frees the plot of its familiarity
✔ aids in viewer access to the film
③ adds to an exotic musical experience
④ orients audiences to the film's theme
⑤ inspires viewers to think more deeply

STEP 1 빈칸이 포함된 문장을 먼저 읽는다.

→ 문장 (4)의 전반부는 익숙한 구조의 음악은 영화의 창의성과 시공간의 감각을 방해할 수도 있다고 말함.

→ 후반부에서는 이에 반하여(while) 음악이 '실제로(in fact)' 어떠한 역할을 하는지가 담겨야 함.

STEP 2 지문의 주제를 파악한다.

→ 영화 음악이 영화 내에서 하는 역할을 설명하는 것이 이 글의 주제임.

→ 문장 (1)과 (2)에서 영화 음악은 영화 텍스트에 부합하여 영화에 새롭고 추가적인 층을 더할 수 있다고 함. 그러나 문장 (3)은 영화가 새로운 세계를 만들어도 그 영화에 들어가는 음악은 익숙한 형태를 취한다고 이야기함. 문장 (5)와 (6)은 친숙한 음악으로 미래나 먼 은하의 장면을 이해 가능한 맥락으로 이끌고 관객으로 하여금 자신의 것이 아닌 세상을 이해할 수 있게 한다고 설명함.

→ 영화 음악은 익숙함으로 관객을 이해시키는 역할을 함.

STEP 3 빈칸은 핵심 내용을 포함하지만 다른 말로 표현되어 있다.

→ 문장 (4)에 들어갈 'aids in viewer access to the film'이 문장 (5)의 'can be placed within a recognizable context'로 다르게 표현되어 있음.

STEP 4 지문의 주제를 기준으로 오답 선택지를 소거한다.

(1) 주제와 반대되는 선택지

①: 문장 (5)에서 음악은 낯선 영화를 관객이 알아볼 수 있는 맥락으로 끌고 올 수 있다고 설명함. 따라서 줄거리에서 친숙함을 없앤다(frees)는 것은 글의 주제와 반대되므로 ①은 정답이 될 수 없음.

(2) 소재와 무관한, 단순히 지문에 들어간 단어에만 집중한 선택지

③: 영화 음악이 영화에 추가적인 층을 '더한다'고는 했으나, 이것은 이국적인(exotic) 음악 경험을 '더한다'는 것과는 무관함. ③은 단순히 'add'라는 단어만 활용한 선택지임.

(3) 지문의 소재와는 맞으나 주제와는 맞지 않는 단어를 포함한 선택지

④: 영화가 글의 주요 소재는 맞으나 음악이 관객을 영화의 주제로 향하게 하는(orients) 것은 글의 소재를 확대 해석한 것임. 따라서 ④는 지문의 소재와는 맞으나 주제와는 맞지 않는 선택지임.

⑤: 관객들이 더 깊이 생각할 수 있게 영감을 준다(inspires)는 것은 영화를 계속 생각하게 만든다는 내용으로 지문 내에서 언급된 바가 없으므로 주제에 맞지 않는 선택지임.

전문 해석

(1) 어떤 영화 내에서든 음악은 영화 텍스트에 추가적인 층을 더할 수 있는데, 이는 보이는 연기를 단순히 모방하는 것을 넘어선다. (2) 미래 세계에 대해 이야기하는 영화에서, 작곡가들은 사운드 디자이너와 거의 마찬가지로 관객에게 알려지지 않은 새로운 세계를 창조할 수 있는 자유를 더해 왔다. (3) 그러나, 사운드 디자이너와 달리 작곡가들은 흔히 이러한 새로운 세계를 반영하는 독특한 작품을 만드는 것을 피하고 흔히 익숙한 구조와 박자를 가진 음악을 제시한다. (4) 이것이 창의성과 시공간의 감각을 방해할 수 있다는 가능성이 있지만, 실제로 그것은 영화에 대한 관객의 접근을 돕는다. (5) 알아볼 수 있는 음악을 통해, 미래 또는 아주 멀리 떨어진 은하의 장면은 알아볼 수 있는 맥락 안에 놓일 수 있다. (6) 이러한 친숙함은 그리하여 영화가 관객을 그들 자신의 것(세계)과 다른 세계에 관한 낯설지만 수용 가능한 장면으로 이끌 수 있도록 편안한 공간에 관객을 놓이게 한다.

중요 어휘

- □ score 명 (영화·연극의) 음악 (작품), 악보
- □ layer 명 층, 막, 단계
- □ simply 부 단순히, 간단히
- □ imitate 동 모방하다, 흉내 내다
- □ action 명 연기, 동작
- □ futuristic 형 미래의, 미래에 관한
- □ shy away from ~을 피하다
- □ piece 명 작품 (한 점)
- □ cadence 명 박자, 운율
- □ interfere with ~을 방해하다
- □ aid 동 돕다, 지원하다
- □ recognizable 형 (쉽게) 알아볼 수 있는
- □ vision 명 장면, 광경
- □ galaxy 명 은하
- □ familiarity 명 친숙함, 익숙함
- □ free A of B A에서 B를 없애다
- □ plot 명 줄거리, 구성
- □ orient A to B A를 B로 향하게 하다

자세한 해설지 QR→
자세한해설-CH12

11 빈칸 추론(1)-어휘, 짧은 어구

동영상 강의

25BR2_CH11

01 ⓒ 120초

★★☆ 2021년 6월 31번

다음 빈칸에 들어갈 말로 가장 적절한 것은?

The tendency for one purchase to lead to another one has a name: the Diderot Effect. The Diderot Effect states that obtaining a new possession often creates a spiral of consumption that leads to additional purchases. You can spot this pattern everywhere. You buy a dress and have to get new shoes and earrings to match. You buy a toy for your child and soon find yourself purchasing all of the accessories that go with it. It's a chain reaction of purchases. Many human behaviors follow this cycle. You often decide what to do next based on what you have just finished doing. Going to the bathroom leads to washing and drying your hands, which reminds you that you need to put the dirty towels in the laundry, so you add laundry detergent to the shopping list, and so on. No behavior happens in ________________. Each action becomes a cue that triggers the next behavior.

① isolation
② comfort
③ observation
④ fairness
⑤ harmony

02 ⓒ 120초

★★☆ 2022년 11월 31번

다음 빈칸에 들어갈 말로 가장 적절한 것은?

No learning is possible without an error signal. Organisms only learn when events violate their expectations. In other words, surprise is one of the fundamental drivers of learning. Imagine hearing a series of identical notes, AAAAA. Each note draws out a response in the auditory areas of your brain — but as the notes repeat, those responses progressively decrease. This is called "adaptation," a deceptively simple phenomenon that shows that your brain is learning to anticipate the next event. Suddenly, the note changes: AAAAA#. Your primary auditory cortex immediately shows a strong surprise reaction: not only does the adaptation fade away, but additional neurons begin to vigorously fire in response to the unexpected sound. And it is not just repetition that leads to adaptation: what matters is whether the notes are ________________. For instance, if you hear an alternating set of notes, such as ABABA, your brain gets used to this alternation, and the activity in your auditory areas again decreases. This time, however, it is an unexpected repetition, such as ABABB, that triggers a surprise response.

① audible
② predictable
③ objective
④ countable
⑤ recorded

정답과 해설 : 01 137 02 137

03 ⏱ 120초

★★☆ 2023년 6월 31번

다음 빈칸에 들어갈 말로 가장 적절한 것은?

In the course of his research on business strategy and the environment, Michael Porter noticed a peculiar pattern: Businesses seemed to be profiting from regulation. He also discovered that the stricter regulations were prompting more ________________ than the weaker ones. The Dutch flower industry provides an illustration. For many years, the companies producing Holland's world-renowned tulips and other cut flowers were also contaminating the country's water and soil with fertilizers and pesticides. In 1991, the Dutch government adopted a policy designed to cut pesticide use in half by 2000 — a goal they ultimately achieved. Facing increasingly strict regulation, greenhouse growers realized they had to develop new methods if they were going to maintain product quality with fewer pesticides. In response, they shifted to a cultivation method that circulates water in closed-loop systems and grows flowers in a rock wool substrate. The new system not only reduced the pollution released into the environment; it also increased profits by giving companies greater control over growing conditions.

♦ substrate: 배양판

① innovation ② resistance
③ fairness ④ neglect
⑤ unity

04 ⏱ 120초

★★☆ 2021년 3월 31번

다음 빈칸에 들어갈 말로 가장 적절한 것은? 3점

Even the most respectable of all musical institutions, the symphony orchestra, carries inside its DNA the legacy of the ________________. The various instruments in the orchestra can be traced back to these primitive origins — their earliest forms were made either from the animal (horn, hide, gut, bone) or the weapons employed in bringing the animal under control (stick, bow). Are we wrong to hear this history in the music itself, in the formidable aggression and awe-inspiring assertiveness of those monumental symphonies that remain the core repertoire of the world's leading orchestras? Listening to Beethoven, Brahms, Mahler, Bruckner, Berlioz, Tchaikovsky, Shostakovich, and other great composers, I can easily summon up images of bands of men starting to chase animals, using sound as a source and symbol of dominance, an expression of the will to predatory power.

♦ legacy: 유산 ♦♦ formidable: 강력한

① hunt ② law ③ charity
④ remedy ⑤ dance

정답과 해설 : 03 138 04 139

05 ⏱ 120초

★★☆ 2021년 9월 31번

다음 빈칸에 들어갈 말로 가장 적절한 것은?

________________ works as a general mechanism for the mind, in many ways and across many different areas of life. For example, Brian Wansink, author of *Mindless Eating*, showed that it can also affect our waistlines. We decide how much to eat not simply as a function of how much food we actually consume, but by a comparison to its alternatives. Say we have to choose between three burgers on a menu, at 8, 10, and 12 ounces. We are likely to pick the 10-ounce burger and be perfectly satisfied at the end of the meal. But if our options are instead 10, 12, and 14 ounces, we are likely again to choose the middle one, and again feel equally happy and satisfied with the 12-ounce burger at the end of the meal, even though we ate more, which we did not need in order to get our daily nourishment or in order to feel full.

① Originality ② Relativity
③ Visualization ④ Imitation
⑤ Forgetfulness

06 ⏱ 120초

★★☆ 2022년 9월 31번

다음 빈칸에 들어갈 말로 가장 적절한 것은? [3점]

It is not the peasant's goal to produce the highest possible time-averaged crop yield, averaged over many years. If your time-averaged yield is marvelously high as a result of the combination of nine great years and one year of crop failure, you will still starve to death in that one year of crop failure before you can look back to congratulate yourself on your great time-averaged yield. Instead, the peasant's aim is to make sure to produce a yield above the starvation level in every single year, even though the time-averaged yield may not be highest. That's why ________________ may make sense. If you have just one big field, no matter how good it is on the average, you will starve when the inevitable occasional year arrives in which your one field has a low yield. But if you have many different fields, varying independently of each other, then in any given year some of your fields will produce well even when your other fields are producing poorly.

① land leveling ② weed trimming
③ field scattering ④ organic farming
⑤ soil fertilization

정답과 해설 : 05 140 06 140

07 ⏱ 120초

★★☆ 2021년 11월 31번

다음 빈칸에 들어갈 말로 가장 적절한 것은?

The elements any particular animal needs are relatively predictable. They are predictable based on the past: what an animal's ancestors needed is likely to be what that animal also needs. ________________, therefore, can be hardwired. Consider sodium (Na). The bodies of terrestrial vertebrates, including those of mammals, tend to have a concentration of sodium nearly fifty times that of the primary producers on land, plants. This is, in part, because vertebrates evolved in the sea and so evolved cells dependent upon the ingredients that were common in the sea, including sodium. To remedy the difference between their needs for sodium and that available in plants, herbivores can eat fifty times more plant material than they otherwise need (and eliminate the excess). Or they can seek out other sources of sodium. The salt taste receptor rewards animals for doing the latter, seeking out salt in order to satisfy their great need.

* terrestrial: 육생의 ** vertebrate: 척추동물 *** herbivore: 초식 동물

① Taste preferences
② Hunting strategies
③ Migration patterns
④ Protective instincts
⑤ Periodic starvations

08 ⏱ 130초

★★★ 2017년 9월 31번

다음 빈칸에 들어갈 말로 가장 적절한 것은? 3점

We are the CEOs of our own lives. We work hard to urge ourselves to get up and go to work and do what we must do day after day. We also try to encourage the people working for and with us, those who are doing business with us, and even those who regulate us. We do this in our personal lives, too: From a very young age, kids try to persuade their parents to do things for them ("Dad, I'm too scared to do this!") with varying degrees of success. As adults, we try to encourage our significant others to do things for us ("Sweetie, I had such a stressful day today, can you please put the kids to bed and do the dishes?"). We attempt to get our kids to clean up their rooms. We try to induce our neighbors to help out with a neighborhood party. Whatever our official job descriptions, we are all part-time ________________.

① judges ② motivators
③ inventors ④ analysts
⑤ observers

DAY 10 11 빈칸 추론(1)

정답과 해설 : 07 141 08 142

09 ⓒ 130초

★★★ 2020년 3월 31번

다음 빈칸에 들어갈 말로 가장 적절한 것은? 3점

When he was dying, the contemporary Buddhist teacher Dainin Katagiri wrote a remarkable book called *Returning to Silence*. Life, he wrote, "is a dangerous situation." It is the weakness of life that makes it precious; his words are filled with the very fact of his own life passing away. "The china bowl is beautiful because sooner or later it will break.... The life of the bowl is always existing in a dangerous situation." Such is our struggle: this unstable beauty. This inevitable wound. We forget — how easily we forget — that love and loss are intimate companions, that we love the real flower so much more than the plastic one and love the cast of twilight across a mountainside lasting only a moment. It is this very ______________ that opens our hearts.

① fragility ② stability
③ harmony ④ satisfaction
⑤ diversity

10 ⓒ 130초

★★★ 2020년 9월 34번

다음 빈칸에 들어갈 말로 가장 적절한 것은? 3점

In the current landscape, social enterprises tend to rely either on grant capital (e.g., grants, donations, or project funding) or commercial financing products (e.g., bank loans). Ironically, many social enterprises at the same time report of significant drawbacks related to each of these two forms of financing. Many social enterprises are for instance reluctant to make use of traditional commercial finance products, fearing that they might not be able to pay back the loans. In addition, a significant number of social enterprise leaders report that relying too much on grant funding can be a risky strategy since individual grants are time limited and are not reliable in the long term. Grant funding can also lower the incentive for leaders and employees to professionalize the business aspects, thus leading to unhealthy business behavior. In other words, there seems to be a substantial need among social enterprises for ______________________________.

◆ grant: (정부나 단체에서 주는) 보조금

① alternatives to the traditional forms of financing
② guidelines for promoting employee welfare
③ measures to protect employees' privacy
④ departments for better customer service
⑤ incentives to significantly increase productivity

정답과 해설 : 09 143 10 143

11 ⏱ 130초

★★★
2021년 11월 32번

다음 빈칸에 들어갈 말로 가장 적절한 것은? 3점

We might think that our gut instinct is just an inner feeling — a secret interior voice — but in fact it is shaped by a perception of something visible around us, such as a facial expression or a visual inconsistency so fleeting that often we're not even aware we've noticed it. Psychologists now think of this moment as a 'visual matching game'. So a stressed, rushed or tired person is more likely to resort to this visual matching. When they see a situation in front of them, they quickly match it to a sea of past experiences stored in a mental knowledge bank and then, based on a match, they assign meaning to the information in front of them. The brain then sends a signal to the gut, which has many hundreds of nerve cells. So the visceral feeling we get in the pit of our stomach and the butterflies we feel are a(n) ______________________.

♦ gut: 직감, 창자 ♦♦ visceral: 본능적인

① result of our cognitive processing system
② instance of discarding negative memories
③ mechanism of overcoming our internal conflicts
④ visual representation of our emotional vulnerability
⑤ concrete signal of miscommunication within the brain

12 ⏱ 130초

★★★
2022년 6월 31번

다음 빈칸에 들어갈 말로 가장 적절한 것은?

Followers can be defined by their position as subordinates or by their behavior of going along with leaders' wishes. But followers also have power to lead. Followers empower leaders as well as vice versa. This has led some leadership analysts like Ronald Heifetz to avoid using the word *followers* and refer to the others in a power relationship as "citizens" or "constituents." Heifetz is correct that too simple a view of followers can produce misunderstanding. In modern life, most people wind up being both leaders and followers, and the categories can become quite ______________. Our behavior as followers changes as our objectives change. If I trust your judgment in music more than my own, I may follow your lead on which concert we attend (even though you may be formally my subordinate in position). But if I am an expert on fishing, you may follow my lead on where we fish, regardless of our formal positions or the fact that I followed your lead on concerts yesterday.

♦ vice versa: 반대로, 거꾸로

① rigid
② unfair
③ fluid
④ stable
⑤ apparent

DAY 10
11 빈칸 추론(1)

정답과 해설 : 11 144 12 145

13 ⓒ 130초

★★★ 2022년 9월 33번

다음 빈칸에 들어갈 말로 가장 적절한 것은?

As well as making sense of events through narratives, historians in the ancient world established the tradition of history as a(n) ____________________. The history writing of Livy or Tacitus, for instance, was in part designed to examine the behavior of heroes and villains, meditating on the strengths and weaknesses in the characters of emperors and generals, providing exemplars for the virtuous to imitate or avoid. This continues to be one of the functions of history. French chronicler Jean Froissart said he had written his accounts of chivalrous knights fighting in the Hundred Years' War "so that brave men should be inspired thereby to follow such examples." Today, historical studies of Lincoln, Churchill, Gandhi, or Martin Luther King, Jr. perform the same function.

♦ chivalrous: 기사도적인

① source of moral lessons and reflections
② record of the rise and fall of empires
③ war against violence and oppression
④ means of mediating conflict
⑤ integral part of innovation

14 ⓒ 130초

★★★ 2023년 9월 31번

다음 빈칸에 들어갈 말로 가장 적절한 것은? 3점

Rebels may think they're rebels, but clever marketers influence them just like the rest of us. Saying, "Everyone is doing it" may turn some people off from an idea. These people will look for alternatives, which (if cleverly planned) can be exactly what a marketer or persuader wants you to believe. If I want you to consider an idea, and know you strongly reject popular opinion in favor of maintaining your independence and uniqueness, I would present the majority option first, which you would reject in favor of my actual preference. We are often tricked when we try to maintain a position of defiance. People use this ____________________ to make us "independently" choose an option which suits their purposes. Some brands have taken full effect of our defiance towards the mainstream and positioned themselves as rebels; which has created even stronger brand loyalty.

♦ defiance: 반항

① reversal
② imitation
③ repetition
④ conformity
⑤ collaboration

정답과 해설 : 13 146 14 146

15 ⓒ 130초

★★★
2018년 11월 31번

다음 빈칸에 들어갈 말로 가장 적절한 것은? 3점

A good many scientists and artists have noticed the ________________ of creativity. At the Sixteenth Nobel Conference, held in 1980, scientists, musicians, and philosophers all agreed, to quote Freeman Dyson, that "the analogies between science and art are very good as long as you are talking about the creation and the performance. The creation is certainly very analogous. The aesthetic pleasure of the craftsmanship of performance is also very strong in science." A few years later, at another multidisciplinary conference, physicist Murray Gell-Mann found that "everybody agrees on where ideas come from. We had a seminar here, about ten years ago, including several painters, a poet, a couple of writers, and the physicists. Everybody agrees on how it works. All of these people, whether they are doing artistic work or scientific work, are trying to solve a problem."

① formality
② objectivity
③ complexity
④ universality
⑤ uncertainty

16 ⓒ 130초

★★★
2023년 6월 33번

다음 빈칸에 들어갈 말로 가장 적절한 것은? 3점

In adolescence many of us had the experience of falling under the sway of a great book or writer. We became entranced by the novel ideas in the book, and because we were so open to influence, these early encounters with exciting ideas sank deeply into our minds and became part of our own thought processes, affecting us decades after we absorbed them. Such influences enriched our mental landscape, and in fact our intelligence depends on the ability to absorb the lessons and ideas of those who are older and wiser. Just as the body tightens with age, however, so does the mind. And just as our sense of weakness and vulnerability motivated the desire to learn, so does our creeping sense of superiority slowly close us off to new ideas and influences. Some may advocate that we all become more skeptical in the modern world, but in fact a far greater danger comes from ________________________ that burdens us as individuals as we get older, and seems to be burdening our culture in general.

♦ entrance: 매료시키다

① the high dependence on others
② the obsession with our inferiority
③ the increasing closing of the mind
④ the misconception about our psychology
⑤ the self-destructive pattern of behavior

정답과 해설 : 15 147 16 148

17 ⏱ 130초

★★★ 2018년 9월 31번

다음 빈칸에 들어갈 말로 가장 적절한 것은? [3점]

Online environments vary widely in how easily you can save whatever happens there, what I call its *recordability* and *preservability*. Even though the design, activities, and membership of social media might change over time, the content of what people posted usually remains intact. Email, video, audio, and text messages can be saved. When perfect preservation is possible, time has been suspended. Whenever you want, you can go back to reexamine those events from the past. In other situations, ______________ slips between our fingers, even challenging our reality testing about whether something existed at all, as when an email that we seem to remember receiving mysteriously disappears from our inbox. The slightest accidental tap of the finger can send an otherwise everlasting document into nothingness.

① scarcity
② creativity
③ acceleration
④ permanency
⑤ mysteriousness

18 ⏱ 130초 최고오답률

★★★ 2021년 9월 32번

다음 빈칸에 들어갈 말로 가장 적절한 것은?

Philosophical activity is based on the ______________________________. The philosopher's thirst for knowledge is shown through attempts to find better answers to questions even if those answers are never found. At the same time, a philosopher also knows that being too sure can hinder the discovery of other and better possibilities. In a philosophical dialogue, the participants are aware that there are things they do not know or understand. The goal of the dialogue is to arrive at a conception that one did not know or understand beforehand. In traditional schools, where philosophy is not present, students often work with factual questions, they learn specific content listed in the curriculum, and they are not required to solve philosophical problems. However, we know that awareness of what one does not know can be a good way to acquire knowledge. Knowledge and understanding are developed through thinking and talking. Putting things into words makes things clearer. Therefore, students must not be afraid of saying something wrong or talking without first being sure that they are right.

① recognition of ignorance
② emphasis on self-assurance
③ conformity to established values
④ achievements of ancient thinkers
⑤ comprehension of natural phenomena

정답과 해설 : 17 149 18 149

19 ⓒ 130초 최고오답률 ★★★ 2022년 3월 31번

다음 빈칸에 들어갈 말로 가장 적절한 것은?

Around the boss, you will always find people coming across as friends, good subordinates, or even great sympathizers. But some do not truly belong. One day, an incident will blow their cover, and then you will know where they truly belong. When it is all cosy and safe, they will be there, loitering the corridors and fawning at the slightest opportunity. But as soon as difficulties arrive, they are the first to be found missing. And difficult times are the true test of ______________. Dr. Martin Luther King said, "The ultimate test of a man is not where he stands in moments of comfort and convenience, but where he stands at times of challenge and controversy." And so be careful of friends who are always eager to take from you but reluctant to give back even in their little ways. If they lack the commitment to sail with you through difficult weather, then they are more likely to abandon your ship when it stops.

* loiter: 서성거리다 ** fawn: 알랑거리다

① leadership ② loyalty ③ creativity
④ intelligence ⑤ independence

20 ⓒ 130초 최고오답률 ★★★ 2018년 6월 34번

다음 빈칸에 들어갈 말로 가장 적절한 것은? 3점

Appreciating ______________________________ can correct our false notions of how we see the world. People love heroes. Individuals are given credit for major breakthroughs. Marie Curie is treated as if she worked alone to discover radioactivity and Newton as if he discovered the laws of motion by himself. The truth is that in the real world, nobody operates alone. Scientists not only have labs with students who contribute critical ideas, but also have colleagues who are doing similar work, thinking similar thoughts, and without whom the scientist would get nowhere. And then there are other scientists who are working on different problems, sometimes in different fields, but nevertheless set the stage through their own findings and ideas. Once we start understanding that knowledge isn't all in the head, that it's shared within a community, our heroes change. Instead of focusing on the individual, we begin to focus on a larger group.

* radioactivity: 방사능

① the process of trial and error
② the changeable patterns of nature
③ the academic superiority of scholars
④ the diversity of scientific theories
⑤ the collective nature of knowledge

정답과 해설 : 19 150 20 151

21 ⏲ 130초 최고오답률 ★★★ 2019년 6월 31번

다음 빈칸에 들어갈 말로 가장 적절한 것은? 3점

Psychologists Leon Festinger, Stanley Schachter, and sociologist Kurt Back began to wonder how friendships form. Why do some strangers build lasting friendships, while others struggle to get past basic platitudes? Some experts explained that friendship formation could be traced to infancy, where children acquired the values, beliefs, and attitudes that would bind or separate them later in life. But Festinger, Schachter, and Back pursued a different theory. The researchers believed that ________________ was the key to friendship formation; that "friendships are likely to develop on the basis of brief and passive contacts made going to and from home or walking about the neighborhood." In their view, it wasn't so much that people with similar attitudes became friends, but rather that people who passed each other during the day tended to become friends and so came to adopt similar attitudes over time.

* platitude: 상투적인 말

① shared value
② physical space
③ conscious effort
④ similar character
⑤ psychological support

22 ⏲ 130초 최고오답률 ★★★ 2021년 3월 32번

다음 빈칸에 들어갈 말로 가장 적절한 것은?

Our brains have evolved to remember unexpected events because basic survival depends on the ability to perceive causes and predict effects. If the brain predicts one event and experiences another, the unusualness will be especially interesting and will be encoded accordingly. Neurologist and classroom teacher Judith Willis has claimed that surprise in the classroom is one of the most effective ways of teaching with brain stimulation in mind. If students are exposed to new experiences via demonstrations or through the unexpected enthusiasm of their teachers or peers, they will be much more likely to connect with the information that follows. Willis has written that encouraging active discovery in the classroom allows students to interact with new information, moving it beyond working memory to be processed in the frontal lobe, which is devoted to advanced cognitive functioning. ________________ sets us up for learning by directing attention, providing stimulation to developing perceptual systems, and feeding curious and exploratory behavior.

* frontal lobe: (대뇌의) 전두엽

① Awareness of social responsibility
② Memorization of historical facts
③ Competition with rivals
④ Preference for novelty
⑤ Fear of failure

정답과 해설 : 21 152 22 153

23 ⏱ 130초 최고오답률 ★★★ 2022년 6월 33번

다음 빈칸에 들어갈 말로 가장 적절한 것은? 3점

What is unusual about journalism as a profession is ______________________. In theory, practitioners in the classic professions, like medicine or the clergy, contain the means of production in their heads and hands, and therefore do not have to work for a company or an employer. They can draw their income directly from their clients or patients. Because the professionals hold knowledge, moreover, their clients are dependent on them. Journalists hold knowledge, but it is not theoretical in nature; one might argue that the public depends on journalists in the same way that patients depend on doctors, but in practice a journalist can serve the public usually only by working for a news organization, which can fire her or him at will. Journalists' income depends not on the public, but on the employing news organization, which often derives the large majority of its revenue from advertisers.

① its lack of independence
② the constant search for truth
③ the disregard of public opinion
④ its balance of income and faith
⑤ its overconfidence in its social influence

24 ⏱ 130초 최고오답률 ★★★ 2019년 9월 31번

다음 빈칸에 들어갈 말로 가장 적절한 것은? 3점

Children develop the capacity for solitude in the presence of an attentive other. Consider the silences that fall when you take a young boy on a quiet walk in nature. The child comes to feel increasingly aware of what it is to be alone in nature, supported by being "with" someone who is introducing him to this experience. Gradually, the child takes walks alone. Or imagine a mother giving her two-year-old daughter a bath, allowing the girl's reverie with her bath toys as she makes up stories and learns to be alone with her thoughts, all the while knowing her mother is present and available to her. Gradually, the bath, taken alone, is a time when the child is comfortable with her imagination. ______________ enables solitude.

* reverie: 공상

① Hardship ② Attachment
③ Creativity ④ Compliment
⑤ Responsibility

정답과 해설 : 23 154 24 154

25 ⓒ 130초 최고오답률

★★★ 2020년 11월 31번

다음 빈칸에 들어갈 말로 가장 적절한 것은?

Over 4.5 billion years ago, the Earth's primordial atmosphere was probably largely water vapour, carbon dioxide, sulfur dioxide and nitrogen. The appearance and subsequent evolution of exceedingly primitive living organisms (bacteria-like microbes and simple single-celled plants) began to change the atmosphere, liberating oxygen and breaking down carbon dioxide and sulfur dioxide. This made it possible for higher organisms to develop. When the earliest known plant cells with nuclei evolved about 2 billion years ago, the atmosphere seems to have had only about 1 percent of its present content of oxygen. With the emergence of the first land plants, about 500 million years ago, oxygen reached about one-third of its present concentration. It had risen to almost its present level by about 370 million years ago, when animals first spread on to land. Today's atmosphere is thus not just a requirement to sustain life as we know it — it is also ____________________.

♦ primordial: 원시의 ♦♦ sulfur dioxide: 이산화황

① a barrier to evolution
② a consequence of life
③ a record of primitive culture
④ a sign of the constancy of nature
⑤ a reason for cooperation among species

26 ⓒ 130초 최고오답률

★★★ 2021년 6월 32번

다음 빈칸에 들어갈 말로 가장 적절한 것은? 3점

While leaders often face enormous pressures to make decisions quickly, premature decisions are the leading cause of decision failure. This is primarily because leaders respond to the superficial issue of a decision rather than taking the time to explore the underlying issues. Bob Carlson is a good example of a leader ____________________ in the face of diverse issues. In the economic downturn of early 2001, Reell Precision Manufacturing faced a 30 percent drop in revenues. Some members of the senior leadership team favored layoffs and some favored salary reductions. While it would have been easy to push for a decision or call for a vote in order to ease the tension of the economic pressures, as co-CEO, Bob Carlson helped the team work together and examine all of the issues. The team finally agreed on salary reductions, knowing that, to the best of their ability, they had thoroughly examined the implications of both possible decisions.

♦ revenue: 총수입 ♦♦ implication: 영향

① justifying layoffs
② exercising patience
③ increasing employment
④ sticking to his opinions
⑤ training unskilled members

정답과 해설 : 25 155 26 156

27 ⏱ 130초 최고오답률

★★★ 2023년 3월 31번

다음 빈칸에 들어갈 말로 가장 적절한 것은?

Free play is nature's means of teaching children that they are not ______________. In play, away from adults, children really do have control and can practice asserting it. In free play, children learn to make their own decisions, solve their own problems, create and follow rules, and get along with others as equals rather than as obedient or rebellious subordinates. In active outdoor play, children deliberately dose themselves with moderate amounts of fear and they thereby learn how to control not only their bodies, but also their fear. In social play children learn how to negotiate with others, how to please others, and how to manage and overcome the anger that can arise from conflicts. None of these lessons can be taught through verbal means; they can be learned only through experience, which free play provides.

◆ rebellious: 반항적인

① noisy
② sociable
③ complicated
④ helpless
⑤ selective

28 ⏱ 130초 최고오답률

★★★ 2018년 3월 31번

다음 빈칸에 들어갈 말로 가장 적절한 것은?

Most importantly, money needs to be ______________ in a predictable way. Precious metals have been desirable as money across the millennia not only because they have intrinsic beauty but also because they exist in fixed quantities. Gold and silver enter society at the rate at which they are discovered and mined; additional precious metals cannot be produced, at least not cheaply. Commodities like rice and tobacco can be grown, but that still takes time and resources. A dictator like Zimbabwe's Robert Mugabe could not order the government to produce 100 trillion tons of rice. He was able to produce and distribute trillions of new Zimbabwe dollars, which is why they eventually became more valuable as toilet paper than currency.

◆ intrinsic: 내재적인

① invested
② scarce
③ transferred
④ divisible
⑤ deposited

정답과 해설 : 27 157 28 158

29 ⓣ 130초

★★★ 2023년 11월 31번

다음 빈칸에 들어갈 말로 가장 적절한 것은? [3점]

Coincidence that is statistically impossible seems to us like an irrational event, and some define it as a miracle. But, as Montaigne has said, "the origin of a miracle is in our ______________, at the level of our knowledge of nature, and not in nature itself." Glorious miracles have been later on discovered to be obedience to the laws of nature or a technological development that was not widely known at the time. As the German poet, Goethe, phrased it: "Things that are *mysterious* are *not* yet *miracles*." The miracle assumes the intervention of a "higher power" in its occurrence that is beyond human capability to grasp. Yet there are methodical and simple ways to "cause a miracle" without divine revelation and inspiration. Instead of checking it out, investigating and finding the source of the event, we define it as a miracle. The miracle, then, is the excuse of those who are too lazy to think.

♦ revelation: 계시

① ignorance ② flexibility
③ excellence ④ satisfaction
⑤ exaggeration

30 ⓣ 120초

★★☆ 2024년 3월 31번

다음 빈칸에 들어갈 말로 가장 적절한 것은?

Dancers often push themselves to the limits of their physical capabilities. But that push is misguided if it is directed toward accomplishing something physically impossible. For instance, a tall dancer with long feet may wish to perform repetitive vertical jumps to fast music, pointing his feet while in the air and lowering his heels to the floor between jumps. That may be impossible no matter how strong the dancer is. But a short-footed dancer may have no trouble! Another dancer may be struggling to complete a half-turn in the air. Understanding the connection between a rapid turn rate and the alignment of the body close to the rotation axis tells her how to accomplish her turn successfully. In both of these cases, understanding and working within the ______________ imposed by nature and described by physical laws allows dancers to work efficiently, minimizing potential risk of injury.

♦ alignment: 정렬 ♦♦ rotation axis: 회전축

① habits ② cultures
③ constraints ④ hostilities
⑤ moralities

정답과 해설 : 29 159 30 160

31 ⏱ 120초

★★☆ 2024년 6월 31번

다음 빈칸에 들어갈 말로 가장 적절한 것은?

We collect stamps, coins, vintage cars even when they serve no practical purpose. The post office doesn't accept the old stamps, the banks don't take old coins, and the vintage cars are no longer allowed on the road. These are all side issues; the attraction is that they are in ________________. In one study, students were asked to arrange ten posters in order of attractiveness — with the agreement that afterward they could keep one poster as a reward for their participation. Five minutes later, they were told that the poster with the third highest rating was no longer available. Then they were asked to judge all ten from scratch. The poster that was no longer available was suddenly classified as the most beautiful. In psychology, this phenomenon is called *reactance*: when we are deprived of an option, we suddenly deem it more attractive.

① short supply ② good shape
③ current use ④ great excess
⑤ constant production

32 ⏱ 130초 최고오답률

★★★ 2024년 9월 31번

다음 빈칸에 들어갈 말로 가장 적절한 것은? 3점

When we get an unfavorable outcome, in some ways the *last* thing we want to hear is that the process was fair. As outraging as the combination of an unfavorable outcome and an unfair process is, this combination also brings with it a consolation prize: the possibility of attributing the bad outcome to something other than ourselves. We may reassure ourselves by believing that our bad outcome had little to do with us and everything to do with the unfair process. If the process is fair, however, we cannot nearly as easily ________________ the outcome; we got what we got "fair and square." When the process is fair we believe that our outcome is deserved, which is another way of saying that there must have been something about ourselves (what we did or who we are) that caused the outcome.

♦ consolation: 위로

① expect ② diversify
③ externalize ④ generate
⑤ overestimate

정답과 해설 : 31 161 32 161

33 ⓒ 130초

★★★
2024년 9월 32번

다음 빈칸에 들어갈 말로 가장 적절한 것은? [3점]

The well-known American ethnologist Alfred Louis Kroeber made a rich and in-depth study of women's evening dress in the West, stretching back about three centuries and using reproductions of engravings. Having adjusted the dimensions of these plates due to their diverse origins, he was able to analyse the constant elements in fashion features and to come up with a study that was neither intuitive nor approximate, but precise, mathematical and statistical. He reduced women's clothing to a certain number of features: length and size of the skirt, size and depth of the neckline, height of the waistline. He demonstrated unambiguously that fashion is ______________________ which is not located at the level of annual variations but on the scale of history. For practically 300 years, women's dress was subject to a very precise periodic cycle: forms reach the furthest point in their variations every fifty years. If, at any one moment, skirts are at their longest, fifty years later they will be at their shortest; thus skirts become long again fifty years after being short and a hundred years after being long.

♦ engraving: 판화 ♦♦ dimension: 크기

① a profoundly regular phenomenon
② a practical and progressive trend
③ an intentionally created art form
④ a socially influenced tradition
⑤ a swiftly occurring event

정답과 해설 : 33 162

12 빈칸 추론(2)-긴 어구, 문장

01 120초

★★☆ 2021년 9월 33번

다음 빈칸에 들어갈 말로 가장 적절한 것은? 3점

The most powerful emotional experiences are those that bring joy, inspiration, and the kind of love that makes suffering bearable. These emotional experiences are the result of choices and behaviors that result in our feeling happy. When we look at happiness through a spiritual filter, we realize that it does not mean the absence of pain or heartache. Sitting with a sick or injured child, every parent gets to know the profound joy that bubbles over when a son or daughter begins to heal. This is a simple example of how we can be flooded with happiness that becomes more intense as we contrast it with previous suffering. Experiences such as this go into the chemical archives of the limbic system. Each time you experience true happiness, the stored emotions are activated as you are flooded with even deeper joy than you remembered. Your spiritual genes are, in a sense, ______________________.

* limbic system: 변연계(인체의 기본적인 감정·욕구 등을 관장하는 신경계)

① your biological treasure map to joy
② your hidden key to lasting friendships
③ a mirror showing your unique personality
④ a facilitator for communication with others
⑤ a barrier to looking back to your joyful childhood

02 120초

★★☆ 2022년 11월 32번

다음 빈칸에 들어갈 말로 가장 적절한 것은?

The connectedness of the global economic market makes it vulnerable to potential "infection." A financial failure can make its way from borrowers to banks to insurers, spreading like a flu. However, there are unexpected characteristics when it comes to such infection in the market. Infection can occur even without any contact. A bank might become insolvent even without having any of its investments fail. ______________________________ to financial markets, just as cascading failures due to bad investments. If we all woke up tomorrow and believed that Bank X would be insolvent, then it would become insolvent. In fact, it would be enough for us to fear that others believed that Bank X was going to fail, or just to fear our collective fear! We might all even know that Bank X was well-managed with healthy investments, but if we expected others to pull their money out, then we would fear being the last to pull our money out. Financial distress can be self-fulfilling and is a particularly troublesome aspect of financial markets.

* insolvent: 지급 불능의, 파산한 ** cascading: 연속된

① Fear and uncertainty can be damaging
② Unaffordable personal loans may pose a risk
③ Ignorance about legal restrictions may matter
④ Accurate knowledge of investors can be poisonous
⑤ Strong connections between banks can create a scare

정답과 해설 : 01 164 02 164

03 ⓒ 120초

★★☆
2016년 11월 32번

다음 빈칸에 들어갈 말로 가장 적절한 것은? [3점]

The Neanderthals would have faced a problem when it was daylight: the light quality is much poorer at high latitudes and this would have meant that they couldn't see things in the distance so well. For a hunter, this is a serious problem, because you really don't want to make the mistake of not noticing the mother rhinoceros hiding in a dark corner of the forest edge when trying to spear her calf. Living under low light conditions places a much heavier premium on vision than most researchers imagine. The evolutionary response to low light levels is ______________________. It is the familiar principle from conventional star-gazing telescopes: under the dim lighting of the night sky, a larger mirror allows you to gather more of the light from whatever you want to look at. By the same token, a larger retina allows you to receive more light to compensate for poor light levels.

① to get big enough to frighten animals
② to move their habitats to lower latitudes
③ to increase the size of the visual processing system
④ to develop auditory sense rather than visual system
⑤ to focus our attention on what we perceive to be the threat

04 ⓒ 120초

★★☆
2019년 9월 34번

다음 빈칸에 들어갈 말로 가장 적절한 것은? [3점]

If you want to use the inclined plane to help you move an object (and who wouldn't?), then you have to move the object over a longer distance to get to the desired height than if you had started from directly below and moved upward. This is probably already clear to you from a lifetime of stair climbing. Consider all the stairs you climb compared to the actual height you reach from where you started. This height is always less than the distance you climbed in stairs. In other words, ______________________ to reach the intended height. Now, if we were to pass on the stairs altogether and simply climb straight up to your destination (from directly below it), it would be a shorter climb for sure, but the needed force to do so would be greater. Therefore, we have stairs in our homes rather than ladders.

◆ inclined plane: (경)사면

① more distance in stairs is traded for less force
② a ladder should be positioned at a steep angle
③ the distance needs to be measured precisely
④ an object's weight has to be reduced
⑤ slopes are often preferred to stairs

정답과 해설 : 03 165 04 166

05 ⓒ 120초

★★☆ 2020년 11월 32번

다음 빈칸에 들어갈 말로 가장 적절한 것은?

One of the primary ways by which music is able to take on significance in our inner world is by the way it interacts with memory. Memories associated with important emotions tend to be more deeply embedded in our memory than other events. Emotional memories are more likely to be vividly remembered and are more likely to be recalled with the passing of time than neutral memories. Since music can be extremely emotionally evocative, key life events can be emotionally heightened by the presence of music, ensuring that memories of the event become deeply encoded. Retrieval of those memories is then enhanced by contextual effects, in which a recreation of a similar context to that in which the memories were encoded can facilitate their retrieval. Thus, ____________________ can activate intensely vivid memories of the event.

♦ evocative: 불러일으키는 ♦♦ retrieval: 회복

① analyzing memories of the event thoroughly
② increasing storage space for recalling the event
③ re-hearing the same music associated with the event
④ reconstructing the event in the absence of background music
⑤ enhancing musical competence to deliver emotional messages

06 ⓒ 120초

★★☆ 2022년 3월 32번

다음 빈칸에 들어갈 말로 가장 적절한 것은?

When you're driving a car, your memory of how to operate the vehicle comes from one set of brain cells; the memory of how to navigate the streets to get to your destination springs from another set of neurons; the memory of driving rules and following street signs originates from another family of brain cells; and the thoughts and feelings you have about the driving experience itself, including any close calls with other cars, come from yet another group of cells. You do not have conscious awareness of all these separate mental plays and cognitive neural firings, yet they somehow work together in beautiful harmony to synthesize your overall experience. In fact, we don't even know the real difference between how we remember and how we think. But, we do know they are strongly intertwined. That is why truly improving memory can never simply be about using memory tricks, although they can be helpful in strengthening certain components of memory. Here's the bottom line: To improve and preserve memory at the cognitive level, you have to ____________________.

♦ close call: 위기일발 ♦♦ intertwine: 뒤얽히게 하다

① keep your body and mind healthy
② calm your mind in stressful times
③ concentrate on one thing at a time
④ work on all functions of your brain
⑤ share what you learn with other people

정답과 해설 : 05 167 06 168

07 ⓒ 120초

★★☆ 2022년 9월 34번

다음 빈칸에 들어갈 말로 가장 적절한 것은?

Psychologist Christopher Bryan finds that when we ________________, people evaluate choices differently. His team was able to cut cheating in half: instead of "Please don't cheat," they changed the appeal to "Please don't be a cheater." When you're urged not to cheat, you can do it and still see an ethical person in the mirror. But when you're told not to be a cheater, the act casts a shadow; immorality is tied to your identity, making the behavior much less attractive. Cheating is an isolated action that gets evaluated with the logic of consequence: Can I get away with it? Being a cheater evokes a sense of self, triggering the logic of appropriateness: What kind of person am I, and who do I want to be? In light of this evidence, Bryan suggests that we should embrace nouns more thoughtfully. "Don't Drink and Drive" could be rephrased as: "Don't Be a Drunk Driver." The same thinking can be applied to originality. When a child draws a picture, instead of calling the artwork creative, we can say "You are creative."

① ignore what experts say
② keep a close eye on the situation
③ shift our emphasis from behavior to character
④ focus on appealing to emotion rather than reason
⑤ place more importance on the individual instead of the group

08 ⓒ 130초

★★★ 2020년 6월 34번

다음 빈칸에 들어갈 말로 가장 적절한 것은? [3점]

The availability heuristic refers to a common mistake that our brains make by assuming that the instances or examples that come to mind easily are also the most important or prevalent. It shows that we make our decisions based on the recency of events. We often misjudge the frequency and magnitude of the events that have happened recently because of the limitations of our memories. According to Harvard professor, Max Bazerman, managers conducting performance appraisals often fall victim to the availability heuristic. The recency of events highly influences a supervisor's opinion during performance appraisals. Managers give more weight to performance during the three months prior to the evaluation than to the previous nine months of the evaluation period because ________________. The availability heuristic is influenced by the ease of recall or retrievability of information of some event. Ease of recall suggests that if something is more easily recalled in your memory, you think that it will occur with a high probability.

* appraisal: 평가 ** retrievability: 회복력

① there is little reliable data about workers
② the frequent contacts help the relationship
③ they want to evaluate employees objectively
④ the recent instances dominate their memories
⑤ distorted data have no impact on the evaluation

정답과 해설 : 07 168 08 169

09 ⓒ 130초

★★★
2021년 11월 33번

다음 빈칸에 들어갈 말로 가장 적절한 것은? 3점

When it comes to climates in the interior areas of continents, mountains ______________________. A great example of this can be seen along the West Coast of the United States. Air moving from the Pacific Ocean toward the land usually has a great deal of moisture in it. When this humid air moves across the land, it encounters the Coast Range Mountains. As the air moves up and over the mountains, it begins to cool, which causes precipitation on the windward side of the mountains. Once the air moves down the opposite side of the mountains (called the leeward side) it has lost a great deal of moisture. The air continues to move and then hits the even higher Sierra Nevada mountain range. This second uplift causes most of the remaining moisture to fall out of the air, so by the time it reaches the leeward side of the Sierras, the air is extremely dry. The result is that much of the state of Nevada is a desert.

① increase annual rainfall in dry regions
② prevent drastic changes in air temperature
③ play a huge role in stopping the flow of moisture
④ change wind speed as air ascends and descends them
⑤ equalize the amount of moisture of surrounding land areas

10 ⓒ 130초

★★★
2023년 3월 32번

다음 빈칸에 들어갈 말로 가장 적절한 것은?

Many early dot-com investors focused almost entirely on revenue growth instead of net income. Many early dot-com companies earned most of their revenue from selling advertising space on their Web sites. To boost reported revenue, some sites began exchanging ad space. Company A would put an ad for its Web site on company B's Web site, and company B would put an ad for its Web site on company A's Web site. No money ever changed hands, but each company recorded revenue (for the value of the space that it gave up on its site) and expense (for the value of its ad that it placed on the other company's site). This practice did little to boost net income and ______________________ — but it did boost *reported* revenue. This practice was quickly put to an end because accountants felt that it did not meet the criteria of the revenue recognition principle.

* revenue: 수익 ** net income: 순이익

① simplified the Web design process
② resulted in no additional cash inflow
③ decreased the salaries of the employees
④ intensified competition among companies
⑤ triggered conflicts on the content of Web ads

정답과 해설 : 09 170 10 171

11 ⓒ 130초

★★★ 2023년 3월 33번

다음 빈칸에 들어갈 말로 가장 적절한 것은? [3점]

Scholars of myth have long argued that myth gives structure and meaning to human life; that meaning is amplified when a myth evolves into a world. A virtual world's ability to fulfill needs grows when lots and lots of people believe in the world. Conversely, a virtual world cannot be long sustained by a mere handful of adherents. Consider the difference between a global sport and a game I invent with my nine friends and play regularly. My game might be a great game, one that is completely immersive, one that consumes all of my group's time and attention. If its reach is limited to the ten of us, though, then it's ultimately just a weird hobby, and it has limited social function. For a virtual world to provide lasting, wide-ranging value, its participants must ____________________. When that threshold is reached, psychological value can turn into wide-ranging social value.

* adherent: 추종자 ** threshold: 기준점

① be a large enough group to be considered a society
② have historical evidence to make it worth believing
③ apply their individual values to all of their affairs
④ follow a strict order to enhance their self-esteem
⑤ get approval in light of the religious value system

12 ⓒ 130초

★★★ 2017년 11월 33번

다음 빈칸에 들어갈 말로 가장 적절한 것은? [3점]

Veblen goods are named after Thorstein Veblen, a US economist who formulated the theory of "conspicuous consumption". They are strange because demand for them increases as their price rises. According to Veblen, these goods must signal high status. A willingness to pay higher prices is due to a desire to advertise wealth rather than to acquire better quality. A true Veblen good, therefore, should not be noticeably higher quality than the lower-priced equivalents. If the price falls so much that ____________________, the rich will stop buying it. There is much evidence of this behavior in the markets for luxury cars, champagne, watches, and certain clothing labels. A reduction in prices might see a temporary increase in sales for the seller, but then sales will begin to fall.

* conspicuous: 과시적인

① the government starts to get involved in the industry
② manufacturers finally decide not to supply the market
③ the law of supply and demand does not work anymore
④ there is no quality competition remaining in the market
⑤ it is no longer high enough to exclude the less well off

정답과 해설 : 11 172 12 173

13 ⓒ 130초

★★★ 2022년 3월 33번

다음 빈칸에 들어갈 말로 가장 적절한 것은? 3점

According to many philosophers, there is a purely logical reason why science will never be able to explain everything. For in order to explain something, whatever it is, we need to invoke something else. But what explains the second thing? To illustrate, recall that Newton explained a diverse range of phenomena using his law of gravity. But what explains the law of gravity itself? If someone asks *why* all bodies exert a gravitational attraction on each other, what should we tell them? Newton had no answer to this question. In Newtonian science the law of gravity was a fundamental principle: it explained other things, but could not itself be explained. The moral generalizes. However much the science of the future can explain, the explanations it gives will have to make use of certain fundamental laws and principles. Since nothing can explain itself, it follows that at least some of these laws and principles ______________________.

◆ invoke: 언급하다

① govern human's relationship with nature
② are based on objective observations
③ will themselves remain unexplained
④ will be compared with other theories
⑤ are difficult to use to explain phenomena

14 ⓒ 130초

★★★ 2022년 3월 34번

다음 빈칸에 들어갈 말로 가장 적절한 것은? 3점

In one example of the important role of laughter in social contexts, Devereux and Ginsburg examined frequency of laughter in matched pairs of strangers or friends who watched a humorous video together compared to those who watched it alone. The time individuals spent laughing was nearly twice as frequent in pairs as when alone. Frequency of laughing was only slightly shorter for friends than strangers. According to Devereux and Ginsburg, laughing with strangers served to create a social bond that made each person in the pair feel comfortable. This explanation is supported by the fact that in their stranger condition, when one person laughed, the other was likely to laugh as well. Interestingly, the three social conditions (alone, paired with a stranger, or paired with a friend) did not differ in their ratings of funniness of the video or of feelings of happiness or anxiousness. This finding implies that their frequency of laughter was not because we find things funnier when we are with others but instead we ______________________.

① have similar tastes in comedy and humor
② are using laughter to connect with others
③ are reluctant to reveal our innermost feelings
④ focus on the content rather than the situation
⑤ feel more comfortable around others than alone

정답과 해설 : 13 174 14 174

15 ⓒ 130초

★★★
2023년 3월 34번

다음 빈칸에 들어갈 말로 가장 적절한 것은? [3점]

It seems natural to describe certain environmental conditions as 'extreme', 'harsh', 'benign' or 'stressful'. It may seem obvious when conditions are 'extreme': the midday heat of a desert, the cold of an Antarctic winter, the salinity of the Great Salt Lake. But this only means that these conditions are extreme *for us*, given our particular physiological characteristics and tolerances. To a cactus there is nothing extreme about the desert conditions in which cacti have evolved; nor are the icy lands of Antarctica an extreme environment for penguins. It is lazy and dangerous for the ecologist to assume that ____________________. Rather, the ecologist should try to gain a worm's-eye or plant's-eye view of the environment: to see the world as others see it. Emotive words like harsh and benign, even relativities such as hot and cold, should be used by ecologists only with care.

♦ benign: 온화한 ♦♦ salinity: 염도

① complex organisms are superior to simple ones
② technologies help us survive extreme environments
③ ecological diversity is supported by extreme environments
④ all other organisms sense the environment in the way we do
⑤ species adapt to environmental changes in predictable ways

16 ⓒ 130초

★★★
2023년 9월 32번

다음 빈칸에 들어갈 말로 가장 적절한 것은? [3점]

A typical soap opera creates an abstract world, in which a highly complex web of relationships connects fictional characters that exist first only in the minds of the program's creators and are then recreated in the minds of the viewer. If you were to think about how much human psychology, law, and even everyday physics the viewer must know in order to follow and speculate about the plot, you would discover it is considerable — at least as much as the knowledge required to follow and speculate about a piece of modern mathematics, and in most cases, much more. Yet viewers follow soap operas with ease. How are they able to cope with such abstraction? Because, of course, the abstraction ____________________. The characters in a soap opera and the relationships between them are very much like the real people and relationships we experience every day. The abstraction of a soap opera is only a step removed from the real world. The mental "training" required to follow a soap opera is provided by our everyday lives.

♦ soap opera: 드라마, 연속극

① is separated from the dramatic contents
② is a reflection of our unrealistic desires
③ demonstrates our poor taste in TV shows
④ is built on an extremely familiar framework
⑤ indicates that unnecessary details are hidden

정답과 해설 : 15 175 16 176

17 ⏱ 130초

★★★ 2018년 9월 34번

다음 빈칸에 들어갈 말로 가장 적절한 것은? [3점]

For many centuries European science, and knowledge in general, was recorded in Latin — a language that no one spoke any longer and that had to be learned in schools. Very few individuals, probably less than one percent, had the means to study Latin enough to read books in that language and therefore to participate in the intellectual discourse of the times. Moreover, few people had access to books, which were handwritten, scarce, and expensive. The great explosion of scientific creativity in Europe was certainly helped by the sudden spread of information brought about by Gutenberg's use of movable type in printing and by the legitimation of everyday languages, which rapidly replaced Latin as the medium of discourse. In sixteenth-century Europe it became much easier to make a creative contribution not necessarily because more creative individuals were born then than in previous centuries or because social supports became more favorable, but because ________________________.

① the number of rich people increased
② information became more widely accessible
③ people were able to learn Latin more easily
④ education provided equal opportunities for all
⑤ new methods of scientific research were introduced

18 ⏱ 130초 최고오답률

★★★ 2020년 11월 34번

다음 빈칸에 들어갈 말로 가장 적절한 것은? [3점]

In the modern world, we look for certainty in uncertain places. We search for order in chaos, the right answer in ambiguity, and conviction in complexity. "We spend far more time and effort on trying to control the world," best-selling writer Yuval Noah Harari says, "than on trying to understand it." We look for the easy-to-follow formula. Over time, we ________________________. Our approach reminds me of the classic story of the drunk man searching for his keys under a street lamp at night. He knows he lost his keys somewhere on the dark side of the street but looks for them underneath the lamp, because that's where the light is. Our yearning for certainty leads us to pursue seemingly safe solutions — by looking for our keys under street lamps. Instead of taking the risky walk into the dark, we stay within our current state, however inferior it may be.

① weigh the pros and cons of our actions
② develop the patience to bear ambiguity
③ enjoy adventure rather than settle down
④ gain insight from solving complex problems
⑤ lose our ability to interact with the unknown

정답과 해설 : 17 177 18 178

19 ⓒ 130초

★★★ 2021년 3월 34번

다음 빈칸에 들어갈 말로 가장 적절한 것은? [3점]

Even companies that sell physical products to make profit are forced by their boards and investors to reconsider their underlying motives and to collect as much data as possible from consumers. Supermarkets no longer make all their money selling their produce and manufactured goods. They give you loyalty cards with which they track your purchasing behaviors precisely. Then supermarkets sell this purchasing behavior to marketing analytics companies. The marketing analytics companies perform machine learning procedures, slicing the data in new ways, and resell behavioral data back to product manufacturers as marketing insights. When data and machine learning become currencies of value in a capitalist system, then every company's natural tendency is to maximize its ability to conduct surveillance on its own customers because ____________________.

♦ surveillance: 관찰, 감시

① its success relies on the number of its innovative products
② more customers come through word-of-mouth marketing
③ it has come to realize the importance of offline stores
④ the customers are themselves the new value-creation devices
⑤ questions are raised on the effectiveness of the capitalist system

20 ⓒ 130초

★★★ 2022년 9월 32번

다음 빈칸에 들어갈 말로 가장 적절한 것은?

There are several reasons why support may not be effective. One possible reason is that receiving help could be a blow to self-esteem. A recent study by Christopher Burke and Jessica Goren at Lehigh University examined this possibility. According to the threat to self-esteem model, help can be perceived as supportive and loving, or it can be seen as threatening if that help is interpreted as implying incompetence. According to Burke and Goren, support is especially likely to be seen as threatening if it is in an area that is self-relevant or self-defining — that is, in an area where your own success and achievement are especially important. Receiving help with a self-relevant task can ____________________, and this can undermine the potential positive effects of the help. For example, if your self-concept rests, in part, on your great cooking ability, it may be a blow to your ego when a friend helps you prepare a meal for guests because it suggests that you're not the master chef you thought you were.

① make you feel bad about yourself
② improve your ability to deal with challenges
③ be seen as a way of asking for another favor
④ trick you into thinking that you were successful
⑤ discourage the person trying to model your behavior

정답과 해설 : 19 179 20 180

21 ⏱ 130초

★★★
2022년 11월 33번

다음 빈칸에 들어갈 말로 가장 적절한 것은?

Negative numbers are a lot more abstract than positive numbers — you can't see negative 4 cookies and you certainly can't eat them — but you can think about them, and you *have to*, in all aspects of daily life, from debts to contending with freezing temperatures and parking garages. Still, many of us haven't quite made peace with negative numbers. People have invented all sorts of funny little mental strategies to ______________________. On mutual fund statements, losses (negative numbers) are printed in red or stuck in parentheses with no negative sign to be found. The history books tell us that Julius Caesar was born in 100 B.C., not -100. The underground levels in a parking garage often have designations like B1 and B2. Temperatures are one of the few exceptions: folks do say, especially here in Ithaca, New York, that it's -5 degrees outside, though even then, many prefer to say 5 below zero. There's something about that negative sign that just looks so unpleasant.

♦ parentheses: 괄호

① sidestep the dreaded negative sign
② resolve stock market uncertainties
③ compensate for complicated calculating processes
④ unify the systems of expressing numbers below zero
⑤ face the truth that subtraction can create negative numbers

22 ⏱ 130초

★★★
2022년 11월 34번

다음 빈칸에 들어갈 말로 가장 적절한 것은? 3점

Observational studies of humans cannot be properly controlled. Humans live different lifestyles and in different environments. Thus, they are insufficiently homogeneous to be suitable experimental subjects. These *confounding factors* undermine our ability to draw sound causal conclusions from human epidemiological surveys. Confounding factors are variables (known or unknown) that make it difficult for epidemiologists to ______________________. For example, Taubes argued that since many people who drink also smoke, researchers have difficulty determining the link between alcohol consumption and cancer. Similarly, researchers in the famous Framingham study identified a significant correlation between coffee drinking and coronary heart disease. However, most of this correlation disappeared once researchers corrected for the fact that many coffee drinkers also smoke. If the confounding factors are known, it is often possible to correct for them. However, if they are unknown, they will undermine the reliability of the causal conclusions we draw from epidemiological surveys.

♦ homogeneous: 동질적인 ♦♦ epidemiological: 역학의

① distort the interpretation of the medical research results
② isolate the effects of the specific variable being studied
③ conceal the purpose of their research from subjects
④ conduct observational studies in an ethical way
⑤ refrain from intervening in their experiments

DAY 14
12 빈칸 추론 (2)

정답과 해설 : 21 180 22 181

23 ⓒ 130초

★★★ 2017년 9월 33번

다음 빈칸에 들어갈 말로 가장 적절한 것은? [3점]

One of the most curious paintings of the Renaissance is a careful depiction of a weedy patch of ground by Albrecht Dürer. Dürer extracts design and harmony from an apparently random collection of weeds and grasses that we would normally not think twice to look at. By taking such an ordinary thing, he is able to convey his artistry in a pure form. In a similar way, scientists often ______________________ when trying to understand the essence of a problem. Studying relatively simple systems avoids unnecessary complications, and can allow deeper insights to be obtained. This is particularly true when we are trying to understand something as problematic as our ability to learn. Human reactions are so complex that they can be difficult to interpret objectively. It sometimes helps to step back and consider how more modest creatures, like bacteria or weeds, deal with the challenges they face.

① depend on personal experience
② choose to study humble subjects
③ work in close cooperation with one another
④ look for solutions to problems from the past
⑤ test a hypothesis through lots of experiments

24 ⓒ 130초

★★★ 2019년 3월 34번

다음 빈칸에 들어갈 말로 가장 적절한 것은? [3점]

Credit arrangements of one kind or another have existed in all known human cultures. The problem in previous eras was not that no one had the idea or knew how to use it. It was that people seldom wanted to extend much credit because they didn't trust that the future would be better than the present. They generally believed that times past had been better than their own times and that the future would be worse. To put that in economic terms, they believed that the total amount of wealth was limited. People therefore considered it a bad bet to assume that they would be producing more wealth ten years down the line. Business looked like a zero-sum game. Of course, the profits of one particular bakery might rise, but only at the expense of the bakery next door. The king of England might enrich himself, but only by robbing the king of France. You could cut the pie in many different ways, but ______________________.

◆ credit arrangement: 신용 거래

① it never got any bigger
② its value changed in time
③ it made everybody wealthier
④ there always was another pie
⑤ everyone could get an even share of it

정답과 해설 : 23 182 24 183

25 ⏱ 130초

★★★ 2019년 6월 33번

다음 빈칸에 들어갈 말로 가장 적절한 것은? 3점

At the pharmaceutical giant Merck, CEO Kenneth Frazier decided to motivate his executives to take a more active role in leading innovation and change. He asked them to do something radical: generate ideas that would put Merck out of business. For the next two hours, the executives worked in groups, pretending to be one of Merck's top competitors. Energy soared as they developed ideas for drugs that would crush theirs and key markets they had missed. Then, their challenge was to reverse their roles and figure out how to defend against these threats. This "kill the company" exercise is powerful because ____________________. When deliberating about innovation opportunities, the leaders weren't inclined to take risks. When they considered how their competitors could put them out of business, they realized that it was a risk not to innovate. The urgency of innovation was apparent.

* crush: 짓밟다 ** deliberate: 심사숙고하다

① the unknown is more helpful than the negative
② it highlights the progress they've already made
③ it is not irrational but is consumer-based practice
④ it reframes a gain-framed activity in terms of losses
⑤ they discuss how well it fits their profit-sharing plans

26 ⏱ 130초 최고오답률

★★★ 2020년 6월 33번

다음 빈칸에 들어갈 말로 가장 적절한 것은? 3점

Sociologists have proven that people bring their own views and values to the culture they encounter; books, TV programs, movies, and music may affect everyone, but they affect different people in different ways. In a study, Neil Vidmar and Milton Rokeach showed episodes of the sitcom *All in the Family* to viewers with a range of different views on race. The show centers on a character named Archie Bunker, an intolerant bigot who often gets into fights with his more progressive family members. Vidmar and Rokeach found that viewers who didn't share Archie Bunker's views thought the show was very funny in the way it made fun of Archie's absurd racism — in fact, this was the producers' intention. On the other hand, though, viewers who were themselves bigots thought Archie Bunker was the hero of the show and that the producers meant to make fun of his foolish family! This demonstrates why it's a mistake to assume that a certain cultural product ____________________.

* bigot: 고집쟁이

① can provide many valuable views
② reflects the idea of the sociologists
③ forms prejudices to certain characters
④ will have the same effect on everyone
⑤ might resolve social conflicts among people

정답과 해설 : 25 184 26 185

27 ⏱ 130초

★★★
2023년 6월 32번

다음 빈칸에 들어갈 말로 가장 적절한 것은? [3점]

It's hard to pay more for the speedy but highly skilled person, simply because there's less effort being observed. Two researchers once did a study in which they asked people how much they would pay for data recovery. They found that people would pay a little more for a greater quantity of rescued data, but what they were most sensitive to was the number of hours the technician worked. When the data recovery took only a few minutes, willingness to pay was low, but when it took more than a week to recover the same amount of data, people were willing to pay much more. Think about it: They were willing to pay more for the slower service with the same outcome. Fundamentally, when we ____________________________, we're paying for incompetence. Although it is actually irrational, we *feel* more rational, and more comfortable, paying for incompetence.

① prefer money to time
② ignore the hours put in
③ value effort over outcome
④ can't stand any malfunction
⑤ are biased toward the quality

28 ⏱ 130초 〈최고오답률〉

★★★
2018년 3월 34번

다음 빈칸에 들어갈 말로 가장 적절한 것은? [3점]

When the late Theodore Roosevelt came back from Africa, just after he left the White House in 1909, he made his first public appearance at Madison Square Garden. Before he would agree to make the appearance, he carefully arranged for nearly one thousand *paid applauders* to be scattered throughout the audience to applaud his entrance on the platform. For more than 15 minutes, these paid hand-clappers made the place ring with their enthusiasm. The rest of the audience took up the suggestion and joined in for another quarter hour. The newspaper men present were literally swept off their feet by the tremendous applause given the American hero, and his name was emblazoned across the headlines of the newspapers in letters two inches high. Roosevelt ____________________________.

♦ emblazon: 선명히 새기다

① understood and made intelligent use of personal promotion
② made public policies that were beneficial to his people
③ knew when was the right time for him to leave office
④ saw the well-being of his supporters as the top priority
⑤ didn't appear before the public in an arranged setting

정답과 해설 : 27 186 28 187

29 ⏲ 130초 최고오답률

★★★ 2019년 9월 33번

다음 빈칸에 들어갈 말로 가장 적절한 것은? [3점]

New technology tends to come from new ventures — startups. From the Founding Fathers in politics to the Royal Society in science to Fairchild Semiconductor's "traitorous eight" in business, small groups of people bound together by a sense of mission have changed the world for the better. The easiest explanation for this is negative: it's hard to develop new things in big organizations, and it's even harder to do it by yourself. Bureaucratic hierarchies move slowly, and entrenched interests shy away from risk. In the most dysfunctional organizations, signaling that work is being done becomes a better strategy for career advancement than actually doing work. At the other extreme, a lone genius might create a classic work of art or literature, but he could never create an entire industry. Startups operate on the principle that you need to work with other people to get stuff done, but you also need to ______________________________.

♦ entrenched: 굳어진

① stay small enough so that you actually can
② give yourself challenges as often as possible
③ outperform rival businesses in other countries
④ employ the efficient system of big enterprises
⑤ control the organization with consistent policies

30 ⏲ 130초 최고오답률

★★★ 2019년 11월 34번

다음 빈칸에 들어갈 말로 가장 적절한 것은? [3점]

Attitude has been conceptualized into four main components: affective (feelings of liking or disliking), cognitive (beliefs and evaluation of those beliefs), behavioral intention (a statement of how one would behave in a certain situation), and behavior. Public attitudes toward a wildlife species and its management are generated based on the interaction of those components. In forming our attitudes toward wolves, people strive to keep their affective components of attitude consistent with their cognitive component. For example, I could dislike wolves; I believe they have killed people (cognitive belief), and having people killed is of course bad (evaluation of belief). The behavioral intention that could result from this is to support a wolf control program and actual behavior may be a history of shooting wolves. In this example, ______________________________, producing a negative overall attitude toward wolves.

① attitude drives the various forms of belief
② all aspects of attitude are consistent with each other
③ cognitive components of attitude outweigh affective ones
④ the components of attitude are not simultaneously evaluated
⑤ our biased attitudes get in the way of preserving biodiversity

정답과 해설 : 29 188 30 189

31 ⏱ 130초 최고오답률

★★★
2021년 9월 34번

다음 빈칸에 들어갈 말로 가장 적절한 것은? [3점]

Deep-fried foods are tastier than bland foods, and children and adults develop a taste for such foods. Fatty foods cause the brain to release oxytocin, a powerful hormone with a calming, antistress, and relaxing influence, said to be the opposite of adrenaline, into the blood stream; hence the term "comfort foods." We may even be genetically programmed to eat too much. For thousands of years, food was very scarce. Food, along with salt, carbs, and fat, was hard to get, and the more you got, the better. All of these things are necessary nutrients in the human diet, and when their availability was limited, you could never get too much. People also had to hunt down animals or gather plants for their food, and that took a lot of calories. It's different these days. We have food at every turn — lots of those fast-food places and grocery stores with carry-out food. But that ingrained "caveman mentality" says that we can't ever get too much to eat. So craving for "unhealthy" food may ________________.

① actually be our body's attempt to stay healthy
② ultimately lead to harm to the ecosystem
③ dramatically reduce our overall appetite
④ simply be the result of a modern lifestyle
⑤ partly strengthen our preference for fresh food

32 ⏱ 130초

★★★
2022년 6월 32번

다음 빈칸에 들어갈 말로 가장 적절한 것은?

Color is an interpretation of wavelengths, one that only exists internally. And it gets stranger, because the wavelengths we're talking about involve only what we call "visible light", a spectrum of wavelengths that runs from red to violet. But visible light constitutes only a tiny fraction of the electromagnetic spectrum — less than one ten-trillionth of it. All the rest of the spectrum — including radio waves, microwaves, X-rays, gamma rays, cell phone conversations, wi-fi, and so on — all of this is flowing through us right now, and we're completely unaware of it. This is because we don't have any specialized biological receptors to pick up on these signals from other parts of the spectrum. The slice of reality that we can see is ________________.

* electromagnetic: 전자기의 ** receptor: 수용체

① hindered by other wavelengths
② derived from our imagination
③ perceived through all senses
④ filtered by our stereotypes
⑤ limited by our biology

정답과 해설 : 31 190 32 191

33 ⓒ 130초 최고오답률

★★★ 2022년 6월 34번

다음 빈칸에 들어갈 말로 가장 적절한 것은? 3점

In most of the world, capitalism and free markets are accepted today as constituting the best system for allocating economic resources and encouraging economic output. Nations have tried other systems, such as socialism and communism, but in many cases they have either switched wholesale to or adopted aspects of free markets. Despite the widespread acceptance of the free-market system, ______________________. Government involvement takes many forms, ranging from the enactment and enforcement of laws and regulations to direct participation in the economy through entities like the U.S.'s mortgage agencies. Perhaps the most important form of government involvement, however, comes in the attempts of central banks and national treasuries to control and affect the ups and downs of economic cycles.

♦ enactment: (법률의) 제정 ♦♦ entity: 실체

① markets are rarely left entirely free
② governments are reluctant to intervene
③ supply and demand are not always balanced
④ economic inequality continues to get worse
⑤ competition does not guarantee the maximum profit

34 ⓒ 130초

★★★ 2023년 9월 34번

다음 빈칸에 들어갈 말로 가장 적절한 것은? 3점

Much of human thought is designed to screen out information and to sort the rest into a manageable condition. The inflow of data from our senses could create an overwhelming chaos, especially given the enormous amount of information available in culture and society. Out of all the sensory impressions and possible information, it is vital to find a small amount that is most relevant to our individual needs and to organize that into a usable stock of knowledge. Expectancies accomplish some of this work, helping to screen out information that is irrelevant to what is expected, and focusing our attention on clear contradictions. The processes of learning and memory ______________________. People notice only a part of the world around them. Then, only a fraction of what they notice gets processed and stored into memory. And only part of what gets committed to memory can be retrieved.

♦ retrieve: 생각해 내다

① tend to favor learners with great social skills
② are marked by a steady elimination of information
③ require an external aid to support our memory capacity
④ are determined by the accuracy of incoming information
⑤ are facilitated by embracing chaotic situations as they are

정답과 해설 : 33 191 34 192

35 ⓒ 130초 최고오답률

★★★ 2019년 3월 32번

다음 빈칸에 들어갈 말로 가장 적절한 것은? [3점]

Sometimes a person is acclaimed as "the greatest" because ______________________. For example, violinist Jan Kubelik was acclaimed as "the greatest" during his first tour of the United States, but when impresario Sol Hurok brought him back to the United States in 1923, several people thought that he had slipped a little. However, Sol Elman, the father of violinist Mischa Elman, thought differently. He said, "My dear friends, Kubelik played the Paganini concerto tonight as splendidly as ever he did. Today you have a different standard. You have Elman, Heifetz, and the rest. All of you have developed and grown in artistry, technique, and, above all, in knowledge and appreciation. The point is: you know more; not that Kubelik plays less well."

♦ acclaim: 칭송하다 ♦♦ impresario: 기획자, 단장

① there are moments of inspiration
② there is little basis for comparison
③ he or she longs to be such a person
④ other people recognize his or her efforts
⑤ he or she was born with great artistic talent

36 ⓒ 130초 최고오답률

★★★ 2020년 9월 32번

다음 빈칸에 들어갈 말로 가장 적절한 것은? [3점]

When we are emotionally charged, we often use anger to hide our more primary and deeper emotions, such as sadness and fear, which doesn't allow for true resolution to occur. Separating yourself from an emotionally upsetting situation gives you the space you need to better understand what you are truly feeling so you can more clearly articulate your emotions in a logical and less emotional way. A time-out also helps ______________________. When confronted with situations that don't allow us to deal with our emotions or that cause us to suppress them, we may transfer those feelings to other people or situations at a later point. For instance, if you had a bad day at work, you may suppress your feelings at the office, only to find that you release them by getting into a fight with your kids or spouse when you get home later that evening. Clearly, your anger didn't originate at home, but you released it there. When you take the appropriate time to digest and analyze your feelings, you can mitigate hurting or upsetting other people who have nothing to do with the situation.

♦ mitigate: 완화하다

① restrain your curiosity
② mask your true emotions
③ spare innocent bystanders
④ provoke emotional behavior
⑤ establish unhealthy relationships

정답과 해설 : 35 193 36 194

37 ⏲ 130초 최고오답률

★★★ 2023년 6월 34번

다음 빈칸에 들어갈 말로 가장 적절한 것은? 3점

Many people look for safety and security in popular thinking. They figure that if a lot of people are doing something, then it must be right. It must be a good idea. If most people accept it, then it probably represents fairness, equality, compassion, and sensitivity, right? Not necessarily. Popular thinking said the earth was the center of the universe, yet Copernicus studied the stars and planets and proved mathematically that the earth and the other planets in our solar system revolved around the sun. Popular thinking said surgery didn't require clean instruments, yet Joseph Lister studied the high death rates in hospitals and introduced antiseptic practices that immediately saved lives. Popular thinking said that women shouldn't have the right to vote, yet people like Emmeline Pankhurst and Susan B. Anthony fought for and won that right. We must always remember __________________________. People may say that there's safety in numbers, but that's not always true.

♦ antiseptic: 멸균의

① majority rule should be founded on fairness
② the crowd is generally going in the right direction
③ the roles of leaders and followers can change at any time
④ people behave in a different fashion to others around them
⑤ there is a huge difference between acceptance and intelligence

38 ⏲ 130초 최고오답률

★★★ 2023년 9월 33번

다음 빈칸에 들어갈 말로 가장 적절한 것은? 3점

As always happens with natural selection, bats and their prey have __________________________ for millions of years. It's believed that hearing in moths arose specifically in response to the threat of being eaten by bats. (Not all insects can hear.) Over millions of years, moths have evolved the ability to detect sounds at ever higher frequencies, and, as they have, the frequencies of bats' vocalizations have risen, too. Some moth species have also evolved scales on their wings and a fur-like coat on their bodies; both act as "acoustic camouflage," by absorbing sound waves in the frequencies emitted by bats, thereby preventing those sound waves from bouncing back. The B-2 bomber and other "stealth" aircraft have fuselages made of materials that do something similar with radar beams.

♦ frequency: 주파수 ♦♦ camouflage: 위장 ♦♦♦ fuselage: (비행기의) 기체

① been in a fierce war over scarce food sources
② been engaged in a life-or-death sensory arms race
③ invented weapons that are not part of their bodies
④ evolved to cope with other noise-producing wildlife
⑤ adapted to flying in night skies absent of any lights

정답과 해설 : 37 195 38 196

39 ⏲ 130초 최고오답률

★★★ 2021년 11월 34번

다음 빈칸에 들어갈 말로 가장 적절한 것은? [3점]

One vivid example of how ____________________ is given by Dan Ariely in his book *Predictably Irrational*. He tells the story of a day care center in Israel that decided to fine parents who arrived late to pick up their children, in the hope that this would discourage them from doing so. In fact, the exact opposite happened. Before the imposition of fines, parents felt guilty about arriving late, and guilt was effective in ensuring that only a few did so. Once a fine was introduced, it seems that in the minds of the parents the entire scenario was changed from a social contract to a market one. Essentially, they were paying for the center to look after their children after hours. Some parents thought it worth the price, and the rate of late arrivals increased. Significantly, once the center abandoned the fines and went back to the previous arrangement, late arrivals remained at the high level they had reached during the period of the fines.

① people can put aside their interests for the common good
② changing an existing agreement can cause a sense of guilt
③ imposing a fine can compensate for broken social contracts
④ social bonds can be insufficient to change people's behavior
⑤ a market mindset can transform and undermine an institution

40 ⏲ 130초 최고오답률

★★★ 2023년 11월 32번

다음 빈칸에 들어갈 말로 가장 적절한 것은? [3점]

Information encountered after an event can influence subsequent remembering. External information can easily integrate into a witness's memory, especially if the event was poorly encoded or the memory is from a distant event, in which case time and forgetting have degraded the original memory. With reduced information available in memory with which to confirm the validity of post-event misinformation, it is less likely that ____________________. Instead, especially when it fits the witness's current thinking and can be used to create a story that makes sense to him or her, it may be integrated as part of the original experience. This process can be explicit (i.e., the witness knows it is happening), but it is often unconscious. That is, the witness might find himself or herself thinking about the event differently without awareness. Over time, the witness may not even know the source of information that led to the (new) memory. Sources of misinformation in forensic contexts can be encountered anywhere, from discussions with other witnesses to social media searches to multiple interviews with investigators or other legal professionals, and even in court.

* forensic: 법정의

① this new information will be rejected
② people will deny the experience of forgetting
③ interference between conflicting data will occur
④ the unconscious will be involved in the recall process
⑤ a recent event will last longer in memory than a distant one

정답과 해설 : 39 197 40 198

41 ⓒ 130초 최고오답률

★★★ 2023년 11월 33번

다음 빈칸에 들어갈 말로 가장 적절한 것은? 3점

Correlations are powerful because the insights they offer are relatively clear. These insights are often covered up when we bring causality back into the picture. For instance, a used-car dealer supplied data to statisticians to predict which of the vehicles available for purchase at an auction were likely to have problems. A correlation analysis showed that orange-colored cars were far less likely to have defects. Even as we read this, we already think about why it might be so: Are orange-colored car owners likely to be car enthusiasts and take better care of their vehicles? Or, is it because orange-colored cars are more noticeable on the road and therefore less likely to be in accidents, so they're in better condition when resold? Quickly we are caught in a web of competing causal hypotheses. But our attempts to illuminate things this way only make them cloudier. Correlations exist; we can show them mathematically. We can't easily do the same for causal links. So we would do well to ________________________.

① stay away from simply accepting the data as they are
② point out every phenomenon in light of cause and effect
③ apply a psychological approach to color preferences
④ admit that correlations are within the framework of causality
⑤ hold off from trying to explain the reason behind the correlations

42 ⓒ 130초

★★★ 2023년 11월 34번

다음 빈칸에 들어갈 말로 가장 적절한 것은?

Most mice in the wild are eaten or die before their life span of two years is over. They die from *external causes*, such as disease, starvation, or predators, not due to *internal causes*, such as aging. That is why nature has made mice to live, on average, for no longer than two years. Now we have arrived at an important point: The average life span of an animal species, or the rate at which it ages, is determined by ________________________. That explains why a bat can live to be 30 years old. In contrast to mice, bats can fly, which is why they can escape from danger much faster. Thanks to their wings, bats can also cover longer distances and are better able to find food. Every genetic change in the past that made it possible for a bat to live longer was useful, because bats are much better able than mice to flee from danger, find food, and survive.

① the distance that migrating species can travel for their survival
② the average time that this animal species can survive in the wild
③ the amount of energy that members of the species expend in a day
④ the extent to which this species is able to protect its source of food
⑤ the maximum size of the habitat in which it and its neighbors coexist

DAY 15 12 빈칸 추론(2)

정답과 해설 : 41 199 42 200

43 ⓒ 120초

★★☆ 2024년 3월 32번

다음 빈칸에 들어갈 말로 가장 적절한 것은?

We must explore the relationship between children's film production and consumption habits. The term "children's film" implies ownership by children — *their* cinema — but films supposedly made for children have always been ________________, particularly in commercial cinemas. The considerable crossover in audience composition for children's films can be shown by the fact that, in 2007, eleven Danish children's and youth films attracted 59 per cent of theatrical admissions, and in 2014, German children's films comprised seven out of the top twenty films at the national box office. This phenomenon corresponds with a broader, international embrace of what is seemingly children's culture among audiences of diverse ages. The old prejudice that children's film is some other realm, separate from (and forever subordinate to) a more legitimate cinema for adults is not supported by the realities of consumption: children's film is at the heart of contemporary popular culture.

♦ subordinate: 하위의

① centered on giving moral lessons
② consumed by audiences of all ages
③ appreciated through an artistic view
④ produced by inexperienced directors
⑤ separated from the cinema for adults

44 ⓒ 130초

★★★ 2024년 3월 33번

다음 빈칸에 들어갈 말로 가장 적절한 것은? [3점]

Beethoven's drive to create something novel is a reflection of his state of curiosity. Our brains experience a sense of reward when we create something new in the process of exploring something uncertain, such as a musical phrase that we've never played or heard before. When our curiosity leads to something novel, the resulting reward brings us a sense of pleasure. A number of investigators have modeled how curiosity influences musical composition. In the case of Beethoven, computer modeling focused on the thirty-two piano sonatas written after age thirteen revealed that the musical patterns found in all of Beethoven's music decreased in later sonatas, while novel patterns, including patterns that were unique to a particular sonata, increased. In other words, Beethoven's music ________________ as his curiosity drove the exploration of new musical ideas. Curiosity is a powerful driver of human creativity.

♦ sonata: 악곡의 한 형식

① had more standardized patterns
② obtained more public popularity
③ became less predictable over time
④ reflected his unstable mental state
⑤ attracted less attention from the critics

정답과 해설 : 43 201 44 202

45 ⓒ 130초 최고오답률

★★★ 2024년 3월 34번

다음 빈칸에 들어갈 말로 가장 적절한 것은? 3점

Technologists are always on the lookout for quantifiable metrics. Measurable inputs to a model are their lifeblood, and like a social scientist, a technologist needs to identify concrete measures, or "proxies," for assessing progress. This need for quantifiable proxies produces a bias toward measuring things that are easy to quantify. But simple metrics can take us further away from the important goals we really care about, which may require complicated metrics or be extremely difficult, or perhaps impossible, to reduce to any measure. And when we have imperfect or bad proxies, we can easily fall under the illusion that we are solving for a good end without actually making genuine progress toward a worthy solution. The problem of proxies results in technologists frequently ______________________. As the saying goes, "Not everything that counts can be counted, and not everything that can be counted counts."

♦ metric: 측정 기준

① regarding continuous progress as a valid solution
② prioritizing short-term goals over long-term visions
③ mistaking a personal bias for an established theory
④ substituting what is measurable for what is meaningful
⑤ focusing more on possible risks than concrete measures

46 ⓒ 120초

★★☆ 2024년 6월 32번

다음 빈칸에 들어갈 말로 가장 적절한 것은?

If we've invested in something that hasn't repaid us — be it money in a failing venture, or time in an unhappy relationship — we find it very difficult to walk away. This is the sunk cost fallacy. Our instinct is to continue investing money or time as we hope that our investment will prove to be worthwhile in the end. Giving up would mean acknowledging that we've wasted something we can't get back, and that thought is so painful that we prefer to avoid it if we can. The problem, of course, is that if something really is a bad bet, then staying with it simply increases the amount we lose. Rather than walk away from a bad five-year relationship, for example, we turn it into a bad 10-year relationship; rather than accept that we've lost a thousand dollars, we lay down another thousand and lose that too. In the end, by delaying the pain of admitting our problem, we only add to it. Sometimes we just have to ______________.

① reduce profit
② offer rewards
③ cut our losses
④ stick to the plan
⑤ pay off our debt

정답과 해설 : 45 203 46 204

47 ⏱ 130초

★★★ 2024년 6월 33번

다음 빈칸에 들어갈 말로 가장 적절한 것은? [3점]

On our little world, light travels, for all practical purposes, instantaneously. If a lightbulb is glowing, then of course it's physically where we see it, shining away. We reach out our hand and touch it: It's there all right, and unpleasantly hot. If the filament fails, then the light goes out. We don't see it in the same place, glowing, illuminating the room years after the bulb breaks and it's removed from its socket. The very notion seems nonsensical. But if we're far enough away, an entire sun can go out and we'll continue to see it shining brightly; we won't learn of its death, it may be, for ages to come — in fact, for how long it takes light, which travels fast but not infinitely fast, to cross the intervening vastness. The immense distances to the stars and the galaxies mean that we ________________________.

♦ instantaneously: 순간적으로 ♦♦ intervene: 사이에 들다

① see everything in space in the past
② can predict when our sun will go out
③ lack evidence of life on other planets
④ rely on the sun as a measure of time
⑤ can witness the death of a star as it dies

48 ⏱ 130초

★★★ 2024년 6월 34번

다음 빈칸에 들어갈 말로 가장 적절한 것은? [3점]

Financial markets do more than take capital from the rich and lend it to everyone else. They enable each of us to smooth consumption over our lifetimes, which is a fancy way of saying that we don't have to spend income at the same time we earn it. Shakespeare may have admonished us to be neither borrowers nor lenders; the fact is that most of us will be both at some point. If we lived in an agrarian society, we would have to eat our crops reasonably soon after the harvest or find some way to store them. Financial markets are a more sophisticated way of managing the harvest. We can spend income now that we have not yet earned — as by borrowing for college or a home — or we can earn income now and spend it later, as by saving for retirement. The important point is that ________________________, allowing us much more flexibility in life.

♦ admonish: 권고하다 ♦♦ agrarian: 농업(농민)의

① we can ignore the complexity of financial markets
② earning income has been divorced from spending it
③ financial markets can regulate our impulses
④ we sell our crops as soon as we harvest them
⑤ managing working hours has become easier than ever

정답과 해설 : 47 204 48 205

49 ⏱ 120초

★★☆ 2024년 9월 33번

다음 빈칸에 들어갈 말로 가장 적절한 것은? 3점

Over the last few centuries, humanity's collective prosperity has skyrocketed, as technological progress has made us far wealthier than ever before. To share out those riches, almost all societies have settled upon the market mechanism, rewarding people in various ways for the work that they do and the things that they own. But rising inequality, itself often driven by technology, has started to put that mechanism under strain. Today, markets already provide immense rewards to some people but leave many others with very little. And now, technological unemployment threatens to become a more radical version of the same story, taking place in the particular market we rely upon the most: the labor market. As that market begins to break down, more and more people will be in danger of ______________________.

① not receiving a share of society's prosperity at all
② making too large of an investment in new areas
③ not fully comprehending technological terms
④ unconsciously wasting the rewards from their work
⑤ not realizing the reason to raise their cost of living

50 ⏱ 130초

★★★ 2024년 9월 34번

다음 빈칸에 들어갈 말로 가장 적절한 것은? 3점

It's often said that those who can't do, teach. It would be more accurate to say that those who can do, can't teach the basics. A great deal of expert knowledge is implicit, not explicit. The further you progress toward mastery, ______________________. Experiments show that skilled golfers and wine aficionados have a hard time describing their putting and tasting techniques — even asking them to explain their approaches is enough to interfere with their performance, so they often stay on autopilot. When I first saw an elite diver do four and a half somersaults, I asked how he managed to spin so fast. His answer: "Just go up in a ball." Experts often have an intuitive understanding of a route, but they struggle to clearly express all the steps to take. Their brain dump is partially filled with garbage.

♦ aficionado: 애호가 ♦♦ somersault: 공중제비

① the greater efforts you have to put into your work
② the smaller number of strategies you use to solve problems
③ the less you tend to show off your excellent skills to others
④ the more detail-oriented you are likely to be for task completion
⑤ the less conscious awareness you often have of the fundamentals

정답과 해설 : 49 206 50 207

유형 TIP

13. 무관한 문장 찾기

지문의 논리적 구조 및 문맥을 파악하는 능력과 어휘력이 요구됨.
지문을 구성하는 문장이 서로 유기적으로 연결되어 있는지, 통일성이 있는지를 확인해야 함.

유형 TIP 25BR2T_CH13 대표 예제 25BR2E_CH13

유형 공략법

1) 지문의 전개 방식과 주제를 파악한다.

2) 지시 대명사, 정관사, 연결사 등의 단서를 통해 글의 연결성을 확인한다.

단서들을 앞 문장과 연결시켜 해석하며 문장이 서로 유기적으로 연결되는지 확인함.

3) 주제에서 벗어나는 문장을 고르고, 그 문장을 제외한 나머지 내용이 통일성이 있는지를 확인한다.

정답 문장을 제외하면 앞뒤 문장이 자연스럽게 연결됨.

이 유형에서 자주 하는 실수

1) 글의 통일성이나 연결성에 주목하지 않고 문장을 해석만 하는 경우
2) 주제와 관련 있는 듯한 단어라고 착각하여 그 단어에만 주목하는 경우
3) 지시 대명사, 정관사, 연결사 등에 큰 주의를 기울이지 않는 경우
4) 앞에서 언급된 내용과 다른 측면에서 접근한 문장이라 무관하다고 생각하는 경우
5) 너무 포괄적이거나 구체적인 진술임에도 글의 소재나 주제를 포함하는 문장이라고 넘어가는 경우

필수 암기 어휘와 표현

연결사 및 중요 표현

지시어	인칭 대명사	(주격) it, they (소유격) its, their 예 It was a great idea, They'd rather put money and time, Their notions
	지시 대명사/형용사	this, that, these, those 예 This illustrates that, That's why, From this perspective, in this way
	정관사	the + 앞에서 언급된 명사 예 ~ when forget-me-nots form their seeds. The seeds are designed to make ~ Rechard Taylor defined determinism ~ . The determinist, then, assumes that ~ The best archival decisions about art ~ . The best decisions ~
기타		such, given, along/as with + 앞에서 언급된 명사 예 in such conditions, given that choice, along with those grains, as with links

역접/대조	however, but, (and) yet, instead (of), rather, on the other hand, by[in] contrast, in contrast to, conversely, on the contrary, whereas, while, meanwhile, at the same time
양보	though, although, even if[though], still, nevertheless, nonetheless, even so, notwithstanding, despite (that), in spite of, having said that, that (being) said, granting that, admitting that, after all
요약	in short, shortly, in brief, briefly, in sum, to summarize, to sum up, to put it simply, in a word, on the whole, overall
재진술	that is (to say), in other words, namely, to put it another way, stated another way, i.e.
강조	indeed, above all, especially, of course, in particular, in fact, in effect, in reality, in truth, truly, actually, as a matter of fact, most important, more importantly, the thing is, it is clear that, no doubt, never, not at all, in the first place, most of all, certainly, (for) sure, surely, apparently, obviously
조건	if, once, given (that), unless, otherwise, if not, or else, in case of[that], in the event of[that], as[so] long as, suppose (that), supposing (that), provided (that), providing (that)

무관한 문장 찾기 대표 예제 - 2024학년도 수능 35번

다음 글에서 전체 흐름과 관계 없는 문장은?

(1) Speaking fast is a high-risk proposition. (2) It's nearly impossible to maintain the ideal conditions to be persuasive, well-spoken, and effective when the mouth is traveling well over the speed limit. ①(3) Although we'd like to think that our minds are sharp enough to always make good decisions with the greatest efficiency, they just aren't. ②(4) In reality, the brain arrives at an intersection of four or five possible things to say and sits idling for a couple of seconds, considering the options. ③(5) Making a good decision helps you speak faster because it provides you with more time to come up with your responses. ④(6) When the brain stops sending navigational instructions back to the mouth and the mouth is moving too fast to pause, that's when you get a verbal fender bender, otherwise known as filler. ⑤(7) *Um*, *ah*, *you know*, and *like* are what your mouth does when it has nowhere to go.

STEP 1 지문의 전개 방식과 주제를 파악한다.

→ 빠르게 말하는 것은 위험성이 높다는 언급을 시작으로, 그로 인한 위험성을 예시로 들어 설명함.

STEP 2 지시 대명사, 정관사, 연결사 등의 단서를 통해 글의 연결성을 확인한다.

문장(3): 우리가 항상 가장 큰 효율로 좋은 결정을 내릴 수 있다고 생각하더라도 사실 그렇지 않다는 내용은 문장 (2)의 이상적인 조건을 유지하는 것이 거의 불가능하다는 것과 이어짐.
문장(4): 실제로 빨리 말했을 때 나타나는 뇌의 반응은 문장 (2)의 빨리 말할 때의 반응이 이상적일 거라 생각하지만 실제로는 그렇지 않다는 내용과 연결됨.
문장(6): 너무 빨리 말하려고 해서 생기는 반응을 '필러(filler)'라고 부른다는 것은 문장 (4)의 뇌의 빈둥거리는 반응과 이어짐.
문장(7): '*Um, ah, you know,* and *like*'는 '필러(filler)'의 예시임.

STEP 3 주제에서 벗어나는 문장을 고르고, 그 문장을 제외한 나머지 내용이 통일성이 있는지를 확인한다.

→ 문장(5): 지문 전체적으로 빨리 말했을 때 생기는 반응이 이상적이지 않다는 것을 바탕으로 전개됨. 문장 (5)는 좋은 결정을 내리는 것이 말을 더 빨리 하도록 돕는다고 언급하고, 이는 빨리 말하는 것을 부정적으로 바라보는 지문의 주제와 상반됨. 또한, 문장 (4)의 뇌의 빈둥거리는 반응과 문장 (6), (7)의 필러를 설명하는 내용으로 전개되는 흐름과도 어울리지 않음.

전문 해석

(1) 빠르게 말하는 것은 위험성이 높은 일이다. (2) 입이 제한 속도를 훨씬 넘어서 움직일 때, 설득력 있고, 말을 잘하며, 효과적인 이상적 조건을 유지하는 것은 거의 불가능하다. ①(3) 비록 우리가 우리의 정신이 항상 최고의 효율로 좋은 결정을 내릴 수 있을 정도로 예리하다고 생각하고 싶겠지만, 그것(우리의 정신)은 정말 그렇지 않다. ②(4) 실제로, 뇌는 말할 가능성이 있는 것들 네다섯 가지가 있는 교차 지점에 도달하고 나서는 선택지를 고려하면서 몇 초 동안 빈둥거리며 앉아있다. ③(5) 좋은 결정을 내리는 것은 여러분이 더 빠르게 말하도록 돕는데, 왜냐하면 그것이 여러분에게 (여러분의) 응답을 생각해 낼 수 있는 더 많은 시간을 제공하기 때문이다. ④(6) 뇌가 입에 항해 지시를 다시 보내는 것을 멈추고도 입이 너무 빨리 움직여서 멈출 수 없을 때, 그때가 여러분이 다르게는 필러라고도 알려진 가벼운 언어적 사고를 겪는 때이다. ⑤(7) '음, 아, 알다시피, 그러니까'는 여러분의 입이 갈 곳이 없을 때 하는 것이다.

중요 어휘

- □ proposition 명 일, 문제, 제의
- □ persuasive 형 설득력 있는
- □ well-spoken 형 말을 잘하는
- □ speed limit 명 제한 속도
- □ intersection 명 교차 지점, 교차로
- □ idle 동 빈둥거리다 / 형 게으른
- □ come up with ~를 생각해 내다[고안하다]
- □ navigational 형 항해의, 항공의
- □ instruction 명 지시, 지도
- □ verbal 형 언어적인, 언어의, 말로 된
- □ fender bender 명 (자동차의) 가벼운 사고
- □ otherwise 부 다르게는, 그렇지 않으면

자세한 해설지 QR➔
자세한해설-CH13

13 무관한 문장 찾기

동영상 강의

25BR2_CH13

01 ⏲ 90초

★★☆
2021년 6월 35번

다음 글에서 전체 흐름과 관계 없는 문장은?

An interesting phenomenon that arose from social media is the concept of *social proof*. It's easier for a person to accept new values or ideas when they see that others have already done so. ① If the person they see accepting the new idea happens to be a friend, then social proof has even more power by exerting peer pressure as well as relying on the trust that people put in the judgments of their close friends. ② For example, a video about some issue may be controversial on its own but more credible if it got thousands of *likes*. ③ When expressing feelings of liking to friends, you can express them using nonverbal cues such as facial expressions. ④ If a friend recommends the video to you, in many cases, the credibility of the idea it presents will rise in direct proportion to the trust you place in the friend recommending the video. ⑤ This is the power of social media and part of the reason why videos or "posts" can become "viral."

♦ exert: 발휘하다 ♦♦ viral: 바이러스성의, 입소문이 나는

02 ⏲ 90초

★★☆
2022년 6월 35번

다음 글에서 전체 흐름과 관계 없는 문장은?

Inflationary risk refers to uncertainty regarding the future real value of one's investments. Say, for instance, that you hold $100 in a bank account that has no fees and accrues no interest. If left untouched there will always be $100 in that bank account. ① If you keep that money in the bank for a year, during which inflation is 100 percent, you've still got $100. ② Only now, if you take it out and put it in your wallet, you'll only be able to purchase half the goods you could have bought a year ago. ③ In other words, if inflation increases faster than the amount of interest you are earning, this will decrease the purchasing power of your investments over time. ④ It would be very useful to know in advance what would happen to your firm's total revenue if you increased your product's price. ⑤ That's why we differentiate between nominal value and real value.

♦ accrue: 생기다 ♦♦ nominal: 명목의, 액면(상)의

정답과 해설 : 01 209 02 209

03 ⏱ 90초

★★☆
2019년 3월 35번

다음 글에서 전체 흐름과 관계 없는 문장은?

When we were infants, we were tuned in to the signals from our body that told us when to eat and when to stop. We had an instinctive awareness of what foods and how much food our body needed. ① As we grew older this inner wisdom became lost in a bewildering host of outer voices that told us how we should eat. ② We received conflicting messages from our parents, from our peers, and from scientific research. ③ These messages created a confusion of desires, impulses, and aversions that have made us unable to just eat and to eat just enough. ④ They have helped us see things in our right perspectives, thus having an insight into the world. ⑤ If we are to return to a healthy and balanced relationship with food, it is essential that we learn to turn our awareness inward and to hear again what our body is always telling us.

♦ aversion: 반감, 혐오

04 ⏱ 90초

★★☆
2021년 3월 35번

다음 글에서 전체 흐름과 관계 없는 문장은?

Academics, politicians, marketers and others have in the past debated whether or not it is ethically correct to market products and services directly to young consumers. ① This is also a dilemma for psychologists who have questioned whether they ought to help advertisers manipulate children into purchasing more products they have seen advertised. ② Advertisers have admitted to taking advantage of the fact that it is easy to make children feel that they are losers if they do not own the 'right' products. ③ When products become more popular, more competitors enter the marketplace and marketers lower their marketing costs to remain competitive. ④ Clever advertising informs children that they will be viewed by their peers in an unfavorable way if they do not have the products that are advertised, thereby playing on their emotional vulnerabilities. ⑤ The constant feelings of inadequateness created by advertising have been suggested to contribute to children becoming fixated with instant gratification and beliefs that material possessions are important.

♦ fixated: 집착하는 ♦♦ gratification: 만족(감)

05 ⏱ 90초

★★☆
2022년 9월 35번

다음 글에서 전체 흐름과 관계 없는 문장은?

Taking a stand is important because you become a beacon for those individuals who are your people, your tribe, and your audience. ① When you raise your viewpoint up like a flag, people know where to find you; it becomes a rallying point. ② Displaying your perspective lets prospective (and current) customers know that you don't just sell your products or services. ③ The best marketing is never just about selling a product or service, but about taking a stand — showing an audience why they should believe in what you're marketing enough to want it at any cost, simply because they agree with what you're doing. ④ If you want to retain your existing customers, you need to create ways that a customer can feel like another member of the team, participating in the process of product development. ⑤ Products can be changed or adjusted if they aren't functioning, but rallying points align with the values and meaning behind what you do.

♦ beacon: 횃불 ♦♦ rallying point: 집합 지점

정답과 해설 : 03 210 04 211 05 211

06 ⓒ 90초

★★☆
2018년 11월 35번

다음 글에서 전체 흐름과 관계 없는 문장은?

Hygge, a term that comes from Danish, is both a noun and a verb and does not have a direct translation into English. The closest word would have to be *coziness*, but that doesn't really do it justice. ① While *hygge* is centered around cozy activities, it also includes a mental state of well-being and togetherness. ② It's a holistic approach to deliberately creating intimacy, connection, and warmth with ourselves and those around us. ③ When we *hygge*, we make a conscious decision to find joy in the simple things. ④ The joy in the simple things, such as making a home-cooked meal, has been removed because we perceive them as difficult and time-consuming. ⑤ For example, lighting candles and drinking wine with a close friend you haven't seen in a while, or sprawling out on a blanket while having a relaxing picnic in the park with a circle of your loved ones in the summertime can both be *hygge*.

♦ holistic: 전체론적인

07 ⓒ 90초

★★☆
2021년 9월 35번

다음 글에서 전체 흐름과 관계 없는 문장은?

Nurses hold a pivotal position in the mental health care structure and are placed at the centre of the communication network, partly because of their high degree of contact with patients, but also because they have well-developed relationships with other professionals. ① Because of this, nurses play a crucial role in interdisciplinary communication. ② They have a mediating role between the various groups of professionals and the patient and carer. ③ Mental healthcare professionals are legally bound to protect the privacy of their patients, so they may be, rather than unwilling, unable to talk about care needs. ④ This involves translating communication between groups into language that is acceptable and comprehensible to people who have different ways of understanding mental health problems. ⑤ This is a highly sensitive and skilled task, requiring a high level of attention to alternative views and a high level of understanding of communication.

08 ⓒ 90초

★★☆
2022년 3월 35번

다음 글에서 전체 흐름과 관계 없는 문장은?

Today's "digital natives" have grown up immersed in digital technologies and possess the technical aptitude to utilize the powers of their devices fully. ① But although they know which apps to use or which websites to visit, they do not necessarily understand the workings behind the touch screen. ② People need technological literacy if they are to understand machines' mechanics and uses. ③ In much the same way as factory workers a hundred years ago needed to understand the basic structures of engines, we need to understand the elemental principles behind our devices. ④ The lifespan of devices depends on the quality of software operating them as well as the structure of hardware. ⑤ This empowers us to deploy software and hardware to their fullest utility, maximizing our powers to achieve and create.

♦ deploy: 사용하다

정답과 해설 : 06 212 07 213 08 213

09 ⓒ 90초

★★☆
2023년 3월 35번

다음 글에서 전체 흐름과 관계 없는 문장은?

Human processes differ from rational processes in their outcome. A process is *rational* if it always does the right thing based on the current information, given an ideal performance measure. In short, rational processes go by the book and assume that the book is actually correct. ① Human processes involve instinct, intuition, and other variables that don't necessarily reflect the book and may not even consider the existing data. ② As an example, the rational way to drive a car is to always follow the laws. ③ Likewise, pedestrian crossing signs vary depending on the country with differing appearances of a person crossing the street. ④ However, traffic isn't rational; if you follow the laws precisely, you end up stuck somewhere because other drivers aren't following the laws precisely. ⑤ To be successful, a self-driving car must therefore act humanly, rather than rationally.

10 ⓒ 90초

★★☆
2023년 6월 35번

다음 글에서 전체 흐름과 관계 없는 문장은?

Before getting licensed to drive a cab in London, a person has to pass an incredibly difficult test with an intimidating name — "The Knowledge." ① The test involves memorizing the layout of more than 20,000 streets in the Greater London area — a feat that involves an incredible amount of memory resources. ② In fact, fewer than 50 percent of the people who sign up for taxi driver training pass the test, even after spending two or three years studying for it! ③ And as it turns out, the brains of London cabbies are different from non-cab-driving humans in ways that reflect their herculean memory efforts. ④ In other words, they must hold a full driving license, issued by the Driver and Vehicle Licensing Authority, for at least a year. ⑤ In fact, the part of the brain that has been most frequently associated with spatial memory, the tail of the sea horse-shaped brain region called the hippocampus, is *bigger* than average in these taxi drivers.

♦ herculean: 초인적인 ♦♦ hippocampus: 해마

11 ⓒ 100초

★★★
2019년 6월 35번

다음 글에서 전체 흐름과 관계 없는 문장은?

People often assume erroneously that if a Hadza adult of Tanzania does not know how to solve an algebraic equation, then he must be less intelligent than we are. ① Yet there is no evidence to suggest that people from some cultures are fast learners and people from others are slow learners. ② The study of comparative cultures has taught us that people in different cultures learn different cultural content (attitudes, values, ideas, and behavioral patterns) and that they accomplish this with similar efficiency. ③ The traditional Hadza hunter has not learned algebra because such knowledge would not particularly enhance his adaptation to life in the East African grasslands. ④ Consequently, he failed to adapt to the environment of the grasslands because he lacked survival skills. ⑤ However, he would know how to track a wounded bush buck that he has not seen for three days and where to find groundwater.

♦ algebraic equation: 대수 방정식 ♦♦ bush buck: 부시벅(아프리카 영양)

정답과 해설 : 09 214 10 215 11 215

12 ⓒ 100초

★★★
2020년 9월 35번

다음 글에서 전체 흐름과 관계 없는 문장은?

The major oceans are all interconnected, so that their geographical boundaries are less clear than those of the continents. As a result, their biotas show fewer clear differences than those on land. ① The oceans themselves are continually moving because the water within each ocean basin slowly rotates. ② These moving waters carry marine organisms from place to place, and also help the dispersal of their young or larvae. ③ In other words, coastal ocean currents not only move animals much less often than expected, but they also trap animals within near-shore regions. ④ Furthermore, the gradients between the environments of different areas of ocean water mass are very gradual and often extend over wide areas that are inhabited by a great variety of organisms of differing ecological tolerances. ⑤ There are no firm boundaries within the open oceans although there may be barriers to the movement of organisms.

♦ biota: 생물 군집 ♦♦ gradient: 변화도

13 ⓒ 100초

★★★
2021년 11월 35번

다음 글에서 전체 흐름과 관계 없는 문장은?

There is a pervasive idea in Western culture that humans are essentially rational, skillfully sorting fact from fiction, and, ultimately, arriving at timeless truths about the world. ① This line of thinking holds that humans follow the rules of logic, calculate probabilities accurately, and make decisions about the world that are perfectly informed by all available information. ② Conversely, failures to make effective and well-informed decisions are often attributed to failures of human reasoning — resulting, say, from psychological disorders or cognitive biases. ③ In this picture, whether we succeed or fail turns out to be a matter of whether individual humans are rational and intelligent. ④ Our ability to make a reasonable decision has more to do with our social interactions than our individual psychology. ⑤ And so, if we want to achieve better outcomes — truer beliefs, better decisions — we need to focus on improving individual human reasoning.

♦ pervasive: 널리 스며 있는

14 ⓒ 100초

★★★
2022년 11월 35번

다음 글에서 전체 흐름과 관계 없는 문장은?

Of all the human emotions, none is trickier or more elusive than envy. It is very difficult to actually discern the envy that motivates people's actions. ① The reason for this elusiveness is simple: we almost never directly express the envy we are feeling. ② Envy entails the admission to ourselves that we are inferior to another person in something we value. ③ Not only is it painful to admit this inferiority, but it is even worse for others to see that we are feeling this. ④ Envy can cause illness because people with envy can cast the "evil eye" on someone they envy, even unwittingly, or the envious person can become ill from the emotion. ⑤ And so almost as soon as we experience the initial feelings of envy, we are motivated to disguise it to ourselves — it is not envy we feel but unfairness at the distribution of goods or attention, resentment at this unfairness, even anger.

♦ elusive: 이해하기 어려운

정답과 해설 : 12 216 13 216 14 217

15 ⓒ 100초

★★★ 2023년 9월 35번

다음 글에서 전체 흐름과 관계 없는 문장은?

The irony of early democracy in Europe is that it thrived and prospered precisely because European rulers for a very long time were remarkably weak. ① For more than a millennium after the fall of Rome, European rulers lacked the ability to assess what their people were producing and to levy substantial taxes based on this. ② The most striking way to illustrate European weakness is to show how little revenue they collected. ③ For this reason, tax collectors in Europe were able to collect a huge amount of revenue and therefore had a great influence on how society should function. ④ Europeans would eventually develop strong systems of revenue collection, but it took them an awfully long time to do so. ⑤ In medieval times, and for part of the early modern era, Chinese emperors and Muslim caliphs were able to extract much more of economic production than any European ruler with the exception of small city-states.

♦ levy: 부과하다 ♦♦ caliph: 칼리프(과거 이슬람 국가의 통치자)

16 ⓒ 90초

★★☆ 2023년 11월 35번

다음 글에서 전체 흐름과 관계 없는 문장은? 3점

Moral excellence, according to Aristotle, is the result of habit and repetition, though modern science would also suggest that it may have an innate, genetic component. ① This means that moral excellence will be broadly set early in our lives, which is why the question of how early to teach it is so important. ② Freud suggested that we don't change our personality much after age five or thereabouts, but as in many other things, Freud was wrong. ③ A person of moral excellence cannot help doing good — it is as natural as the change of seasons or the rotation of the planets. ④ Recent psychological research shows that personality traits stabilize around age thirty in both men and women and regardless of ethnicity as the human brain continues to develop, both neuroanatomically and in terms of cognitive skills, until the mid-twenties. ⑤ The advantage of this new understanding is that we can be a bit more optimistic than Aristotle and Freud about being able to teach moral excellence.

♦ neuroanatomically: 신경 해부학적으로

17 ⓒ 90초

★★☆ 2024년 3월 35번

다음 글에서 전체 흐름과 관계 없는 문장은?

We are the only species that seasons its food, deliberately altering it with the highly flavored plant parts we call herbs and spices. It's quite possible that our taste for spices has an evolutionary root. ① Many spices have antibacterial properties — in fact, common seasonings such as garlic, onion, and oregano inhibit the growth of almost every bacterium tested. ② And the cultures that make the heaviest use of spices — think of the garlic and black pepper of Thai food, the ginger and coriander of India, the chili peppers of Mexico — come from warmer climates, where bacterial spoilage is a bigger issue. ③ The changing climate can have a significant impact on the production and availability of spices, influencing their growth patterns and ultimately affecting global spice markets. ④ In contrast, the most lightly spiced cuisines — those of Scandinavia and northern Europe — are from cooler climates. ⑤ Our uniquely human attention to flavor, in this case the flavor of spices, turns out to have arisen as a matter of life and death.

♦ cuisine: 요리(법)

정답과 해설 : 15 218 16 219 17 219

18 ⓒ 90초

★★☆ 2024년 6월 35번

다음 글에서 전체 흐름과 관계 없는 문장은?

As the old joke goes: "Software, free. User manual, $10,000." But it's no joke. A couple of high-profile companies make their living selling instruction and paid support for free software. The copy of code, being mere bits, is free. The lines of free code become valuable to you only through support and guidance. ① A lot of medical and genetic information will go this route in the coming decades. ② Right now getting a full copy of all your DNA is very expensive ($10,000), but soon it won't be. ③ The public exposure of people's personal genetic information will undoubtedly cause serious legal and ethical problems. ④ The price is dropping so fast, it will be $100 soon, and then the next year insurance companies will offer to sequence you for free. ⑤ When a copy of your sequence costs nothing, the interpretation of what it means, what you can do about it, and how to use it — the manual for your genes — will be expensive.

♦ sequence: (유전자) 배열 순서를 밝히다

19 ⓒ 90초

★★☆ 2024년 9월 35번

다음 글에서 전체 흐름과 관계 없는 문장은?

Minimal processing can be one of the best ways to keep original flavors and taste, without any need to add artificial flavoring or additives, or too much salt. This would also be the efficient way to keep most nutrients, especially the most sensitive ones such as many vitamins and anti-oxidants. ① Milling of cereals is one of the most harsh processes which dramatically affect nutrient content. ② While grains are naturally very rich in micronutrients, anti-oxidants and fiber (i.e. in wholemeal flour or flakes), milling usually removes the vast majority of minerals, vitamins and fibers to raise white flour. ③ To increase grain production, the use of chemical fertilizers should be minimized, and insect-resistant grain varieties should be developed. ④ Such a spoilage of key nutrients and fiber is no longer acceptable in the context of a sustainable diet aiming at an optimal nutrient density and health protection. ⑤ In contrast, fermentation of various foodstuffs or germination of grains are traditional, locally accessible, low-energy and highly nutritious processes of sounded interest.

♦ fermentation: 발효 ♦♦ germination: 발아

정답과 해설 : 18 220 19 221

유형TIP

14. 문장 배열

주어진 글 뒤에 이어질 내용을 논리적으로, 순서에 맞게 배열하는 유형
선후 관계, 인과 관계 등의 논리에 기반한 판단 능력이 요구됨.

유형 TIP 25BR2T_CH14
대표 예제 25BR2E_CH14

유형 공략법

1) 주어진 글을 바탕으로 지문의 소재와 내용을 대략적으로 파악**한다.**

2) 각 문단의 첫 번째 문장**을 읽고 주어진 글 다음에 올 수 있는 문장을 찾는다.**
시간의 흐름, 질문-대답, 문제 제기-해결책 등의 논리 구조를 따라야 함.
지시 대명사, 정관사, 연결사 등의 단서에 주목하여 올바른 순서대로 문단을 배열해야 함.

3) **위와 같은 방법으로 나머지 문단도 순서대로 연결한다.**

필수 암기 어휘와 표현

연결사 및 중요 표현

지시어	인칭 대명사	(주격) it, they (소유격) its, their 예 It was a great idea, They'd rather put money and time, Their notions
	지시 대명사/형용사	this, that, these, those 예 This illustrates that, That's why, From this perspective, in this way
	정관사	the + 앞에서 언급된 명사 예 ~ when forget-me-nots form their seeds. The seeds are designed to make ~ Rechard Taylor defined determinism ~ . The determinist, then, assumes that ~ The best archival decisions about art ~ . The best decisions ~
기타		such, given, along[as] with + 앞에서 언급된 명사 예 in such conditions, given that choice, along with those grains, as with links

시간/순서	then, after, afterwards, subsequently, later, next, finally, lastly, earlier, recently, now, during, while, meanwhile, in the meantime, at the same time, simultaneously, suddenly, immediately, soon, as soon as, once, upon[on] V-ing, by the time, at that time, at that moment
예시	for example, for instance, to illustrate, to demonstrate, as an example, as[for] an illustration, specifically, e.g.
첨가	also, besides, moreover, furthermore, what is[what's] more, in addition (to), additionally, adding to, plus, as well, too, after all, similarly, likewise, what's worse, to make matters worse
인과	(원인) because, since, for, as, now (that), seeing (that), on account of, due to (결과) so, so that, thus, therefore, hence, as a result, as a consequence, in turn, accordingly, consequently, thereby, for this reason, as such, lead to, result in
결론	in the end, at last, ultimately, eventually, finally, in conclusion, to conclude, in the final[last/ultimate] analysis, it follows that, the bottom line is that

문장 배열 대표 예제 - 2024학년도 수능 36번

주어진 글 다음에 이어질 글의 순서로 가장 적절한 것은?

> (1) Negotiation can be defined as an attempt to explore and reconcile conflicting positions in order to reach an acceptable outcome.

(A) (2) Areas of difference can and do frequently remain, and will perhaps be the subject of future negotiations, or indeed remain irreconcilable. (3) In those instances in which the parties have highly antagonistic or polarised relations, the process is likely to be dominated by the exposition, very often in public, of the areas of conflict.

(B) (4) In these and sometimes other forms of negotiation, negotiation serves functions other than reconciling conflicting interests. (5) These will include delay, publicity, diverting attention or seeking intelligence about the other party and its negotiating position.

(C) (6) Whatever the nature of the outcome, which may actually favour one party more than another, the purpose of negotiation is the identification of areas of common interest and conflict. (7) In this sense, depending on the intentions of the parties, the areas of common interest may be clarified, refined and given negotiated form and substance.

* reconcile: 화해시키다 ** antagonistic: 적대적인

*** exposition: 설명

① (A) — (C) — (B)
② (B) — (A) — (C)
③ (B) — (C) — (A)
④ (C) — (A) — (B) ✔
⑤ (C) — (B) — (A)

STEP 1 주어진 글을 바탕으로 지문의 소재와 내용을 대략적으로 파악한다.

→ 협상의 정의를 제시하여 협상의 목적이 무엇인지를 추측할 수 있음.

STEP 2 각 문단의 첫 번째 문장을 읽고 주어진 글 다음에 올 수 있는 문장을 찾는다.

→ 주어진 글은 협상의 정의를 제시하며 협상이 수용 가능한 결과에 도달하기 위한 시도라고 함. 이어지는 문장은 수용 가능한 결과가 무엇인지 설명하는 쪽으로 전개될 것임을 추측할 수 있음. 따라서 주어진 글 다음으로 the outcome(=문장 (1)의 an acceptable outcome)을 포함한 (C)가 옴.

STEP 3 위와 같은 방법으로 나머지 문단도 순서대로 연결한다.

(C) → (A): (C)에서 공동 이익과 갈등 영역의 식별이 협상의 목적임을 이야기한 후 먼저 '공동 이익이 있는 영역(the areas of common interest)'은 명확해지고 다듬어져 협상의 형식과 실체가 된다고 함. (C)에 이어서 '차이의 영역(Areas of difference)'은 계속 남아서 다른 협상의 대상이 된다고 설명하며 서로 반대되는 개념을 제시하는 (A)가 오는 것이 자연스러움.

(A) → (B): (A)에서 언급하고 있는 당사자들이 적대적이고 양극화된 상황에서 진행되는 협상이 (B)의 첫 문장에서 '이러한(these)' 형태의 협상으로 지칭되어 있으므로, (A) 다음에는 (B)가 와야 함.

전문 해석

(1) 협상은 수용 가능한 결과에 도달하기 위해 상반된 입장을 탐색하고 조정하려는 시도로 정의될 수 있다.

(C) (6) 실제로 다른 당사자보다 한쪽 당사자에게 더 유리할 수도 있는, 그 결과의 본질이 무엇이든, 협상의 목적은 공동 이익과 갈등 영역의 식별이다. (7) 이러한 의미에서, 당사자들의 의사에 따라 공동 이익이 있는 영역은 명확해지고 다듬어지며, 협상된 형식과 실체가 부여될 수도 있다.

(A) (2) 차이의 영역은 남아 있을 수 있고 정말로 흔히 남아 있으며, 어쩌면 향후 협상의 대상이 되거나, 혹은 실제로 타협할 수 없는 상태로 남아 있을 것이다. (3) 당사자들이 매우 적대적이거나 양극화된 관계를 맺고 있는 그러한 경우에, 그 과정은 갈등 영역에 대한, 매우 흔히 공개적인, 설명에 의해 지배될 가능성이 높다.

(B) (4) 이러한 형태의 협상과 때로는 다른 형태의 협상에서, 협상은 상충하는 이해관계를 조정하는 것과는 다른 기능을 수행한다. (5) 이것들은 지연, 홍보, 관심을 돌리거나 상대방과 그쪽의 협상 입장에 대한 정보를 찾는 것을 포함할 것이다.

중요 어휘

- □ negotiation 명 협상, 교섭
- □ attempt 명 시도 / 통 시도하다
- □ explore 통 탐색하다, 탐구하다
- □ reconcile 통 조정하다, 화해시키다
- □ conflicting 형 상반되는, 모순되는
- □ outcome 명 결과, 성과
- □ favour 통 ~에게 유리하다, 편애하다 / 명 호의
- □ party 명 당사자, 정당, 모임
- □ interest 명 이익, 이해관계
- □ clarify 통 명확히 하다
- □ refine 통 다듬다, 정제하다
- □ substance 명 실체, 본질, 물질
- □ irreconcilable 형 타협할 수 없는
- □ highly 부 매우
- □ antagonistic 형 적대적인, 반대의
- □ polarise 통 양극화시키다, 양극화되다
- □ dominate 통 지배하다, 우위를 차지하다
- □ exposition 명 설명, 해설, 전시회
- □ function 명 기능 / 통 기능하다, 작용하다
- □ delay 명 지연, 연기 / 통 미루다, 연기하다
- □ publicity 명 홍보, 광고
- □ divert 통 (방향을) 돌리다, 우회시키다
- □ intelligence 명 정보, 기밀, 지능

자세한 해설지 QR→ 자세한해설-CH14

동영상 강의 25BR2_CH14

01

120초 ★★☆ 2020년 9월 36번

주어진 글 다음에 이어질 글의 순서로 가장 적절한 것은?

> When a change in the environment occurs, there is a relative increase or decrease in the rate at which the neurons fire, which is how intensity is coded. Furthermore, relativity operates to calibrate our sensations.

(A) Although both hands are now in the same water, one feels that it is colder and the other feels warmer because of the relative change from prior experience. This process, called *adaptation*, is one of the organizing principles operating throughout the central nervous system.

(B) For example, if you place one hand in hot water and the other in iced water for some time before immersing them both into lukewarm water, you will experience conflicting sensations of temperature because of the relative change in the receptors registering hot and cold.

(C) It explains why you can't see well inside a dark room if you have come in from a sunny day. Your eyes have to become accustomed to the new level of luminance. Adaptation explains why apples taste sour after eating sweet chocolate and why traffic seems louder in the city if you normally live in the country.

♦ calibrate: 조정하다 ♦♦ luminance: (빛의) 밝기

① (A) — (C) — (B)
② (B) — (A) — (C)
③ (B) — (C) — (A)
④ (C) — (A) — (B)
⑤ (C) — (B) — (A)

02

120초 ★★☆ 2021년 3월 36번

주어진 글 다음에 이어질 글의 순서로 가장 적절한 것은? 3점

> Once we recognize the false-cause issue, we see it everywhere. For example, a recent long-term study of University of Toronto medical students concluded that medical school class presidents lived an average of 2.4 years less than other medical school graduates.

(A) Perhaps this extra stress, and the corresponding lack of social and relaxation time — rather than being class president per se — contributes to lower life expectancy. If so, the real lesson of the study is that we should all relax a little and not let our work take over our lives.

(B) Probably not. Just because being class president is correlated with shorter life expectancy does not mean that it *causes* shorter life expectancy. In fact, it seems likely that the sort of person who becomes medical school class president is, on average, extremely hard-working, serious, and ambitious.

(C) At first glance, this seemed to imply that being a medical school class president is bad for you. Does this mean that you should avoid being medical school class president at all costs?

♦ per se: 그 자체로

① (A) — (C) — (B)
② (B) — (A) — (C)
③ (B) — (C) — (A)
④ (C) — (A) — (B)
⑤ (C) — (B) — (A)

DAY 17 14 문장 배열

정답과 해설 : 01 223 02 223

03 ⏱ 120초

★★☆ 2023년 6월 36번

주어진 글 다음에 이어질 글의 순서로 가장 적절한 것은?

> When evaluating a policy, people tend to concentrate on how the policy will fix some particular problem while ignoring or downplaying other effects it may have. Economists often refer to this situation as *The Law of Unintended Consequences*.

(A) But an unintended consequence is that the jobs of some autoworkers will be lost to foreign competition. Why? The tariff that protects steelworkers raises the price of the steel that domestic automobile makers need to build their cars.

(B) For instance, suppose that you impose a tariff on imported steel in order to protect the jobs of domestic steelworkers. If you impose a high enough tariff, their jobs will indeed be protected from competition by foreign steel companies.

(C) As a result, domestic automobile manufacturers have to raise the prices of their cars, making them relatively less attractive than foreign cars. Raising prices tends to reduce domestic car sales, so some domestic autoworkers lose their jobs.

① (A) — (C) — (B)
② (B) — (A) — (C)
③ (B) — (C) — (A)
④ (C) — (A) — (B)
⑤ (C) — (B) — (A)

04 ⏱ 120초

★★☆ 2018년 9월 35번

주어진 글 다음에 이어질 글의 순서로 가장 적절한 것은?

> Calling your pants "blue jeans" almost seems redundant because practically all denim is blue. While jeans are probably the most versatile pants in your wardrobe, blue actually isn't a particularly neutral color.

(A) The natural indigo dye used in the first jeans, on the other hand, would stick only to the outside of the threads. When the indigo-dyed denim is washed, tiny amounts of that dye get washed away, and the thread comes with them.

(B) Ever wonder why it's the most commonly used hue? Blue was the chosen color for denim because of the chemical properties of blue dye. Most dyes will permeate fabric in hot temperatures, making the color stick.

(C) The more denim was washed, the softer it would get, eventually achieving that worn-in, made-just-for-me feeling you probably get with your favorite jeans. That softness made jeans the trousers of choice for laborers.

♦ hue: 색상 ♦♦ permeate: 스며[배어]들다

① (A) — (C) — (B)
② (B) — (A) — (C)
③ (B) — (C) — (A)
④ (C) — (A) — (B)
⑤ (C) — (B) — (A)

정답과 해설 : 03 224 04 225

05 120초

★★☆ 2021년 6월 37번

주어진 글 다음에 이어질 글의 순서로 가장 적절한 것은?

> In one survey, 61 percent of Americans said that they supported the government spending more on 'assistance to the poor'.

(A) Therefore, the framing of a question can heavily influence the answer in many ways, which matters if your aim is to obtain a 'true measure' of what people think. And next time you hear a politician say 'surveys prove that the majority of the people agree with me', be very wary.

(B) But when the same population was asked whether they supported spending more government money on 'welfare', only 21 percent were in favour. In other words, if you ask people about individual welfare programmes — such as giving financial help to people who have long-term illnesses and paying for school meals for families with low income — people are broadly in favour of them.

(C) But if you ask about 'welfare' — which refers to those exact same programmes that you've just listed — they're against it. The word 'welfare' has negative connotations, perhaps because of the way many politicians and newspapers portray it.

* wary: 조심성 있는 ** connotation: 함축

① (A) — (C) — (B) ② (B) — (A) — (C)
③ (B) — (C) — (A) ④ (C) — (A) — (B)
⑤ (C) — (B) — (A)

06 120초

★★☆ 2021년 11월 36번

주어진 글 다음에 이어질 글의 순서로 가장 적절한 것은?

> Regarding food production, under the British government, there was a different conception of responsibility from that of French government. In France, the responsibility for producing good food lay with the producers.

(A) It would be unfair to interfere with the shopkeeper's right to make money. In the 1840s, a patent was granted for a machine designed for making fake coffee beans out of chicory, using the same technology that went into manufacturing bullets.

(B) The state would police their activities and, if they should fail, would punish them for neglecting the interests of its citizens. By contrast, the British government — except in extreme cases — placed most of the responsibility with the individual consumers.

(C) This machine was clearly designed for the purposes of swindling, and yet the government allowed it. A machine for forging money would never have been licensed, so why this? As one consumer complained, the British system of government was weighted against the consumer in favour of the swindler.

* swindle: 사기 치다 ** forge: 위조하다

① (A) — (C) — (B) ② (B) — (A) — (C)
③ (B) — (C) — (A) ④ (C) — (A) — (B)
⑤ (C) — (B) — (A)

정답과 해설 : 05 226 06 227

07 ⏱ 120초

★★☆ 2022년 6월 37번

주어진 글 다음에 이어질 글의 순서로 가장 적절한 것은? 3점

> One interesting feature of network markets is that "history matters." A famous example is the QWERTY keyboard used with your computer.

(A) Replacing the QWERTY keyboard with a more efficient design would have been both expensive and difficult to coordinate. Thus, the placement of the letters stays with the obsolete QWERTY on today's English-language keyboards.

(B) You might wonder why this particular configuration of keys, with its awkward placement of the letters, became the standard. The QWERTY keyboard in the 19th century was developed in the era of manual typewriters with physical keys.

(C) The keyboard was designed to keep frequently used keys (like E and O) physically separated in order to prevent them from jamming. By the time the technology for electronic typing evolved, millions of people had already learned to type on millions of QWERTY typewriters.

♦obsolete: 구식의 ♦♦configuration: 배열

① (A) — (C) — (B) ② (B) — (A) — (C)
③ (B) — (C) — (A) ④ (C) — (A) — (B)
⑤ (C) — (B) — (A)

08 ⏱ 120초

★★☆ 2023년 3월 37번

주어진 글 다음에 이어질 글의 순서로 가장 적절한 것은? 3점

> A common but incorrect assumption is that we are creatures of reason when, in fact, we are creatures of both reason and emotion. We cannot get by on reason alone since any reason always eventually leads to a feeling. Should I get a wholegrain cereal or a chocolate cereal?

(A) These deep-seated values, feelings, and emotions we have are rarely a result of reasoning, but can certainly be influenced by reasoning. We have values, feelings, and emotions before we begin to reason and long before we begin to reason effectively.

(B) I can list all the reasons I want, but the reasons have to be based on something. For example, if my goal is to eat healthy, I can choose the wholegrain cereal, but what is my reason for wanting to be healthy?

(C) I can list more and more reasons such as wanting to live longer, spending more quality time with loved ones, etc., but what are the reasons for those reasons? You should be able to see by now that reasons are ultimately based on non-reason such as values, feelings, or emotions.

① (A) — (C) — (B) ② (B) — (A) — (C)
③ (B) — (C) — (A) ④ (C) — (A) — (B)
⑤ (C) — (B) — (A)

정답과 해설 : 07 227 08 228

09 ⓒ 120초

★★☆ 2020년 9월 37번

주어진 글 다음에 이어질 글의 순서로 가장 적절한 것은?

> When an important change takes place in your life, observe your response. If you resist accepting the change it is because you are afraid; afraid of losing something.

(A) To learn to let go, to not cling and allow the flow of the river, is to live without resistances; being the creators of constructive changes that bring about improvements and widen our horizons.

(B) In life, all these things come and go and then others appear, which will also go. It is like a river in constant movement. If we try to stop the flow, we create a dam; the water stagnates and causes a pressure which accumulates inside us.

(C) Perhaps you might lose your position, property, possession, or money. The change might mean that you lose privileges or prestige. Perhaps with the change you lose the closeness of a person or a place.

♦ stagnate: (물이) 고이다

① (A) — (C) — (B)　② (B) — (A) — (C)
③ (B) — (C) — (A)　④ (C) — (A) — (B)
⑤ (C) — (B) — (A)

10 ⓒ 120초

★★☆ 2020년 11월 36번

주어진 글 다음에 이어질 글의 순서로 가장 적절한 것은?

> Mark Granovetter examined the extent to which information about jobs flowed through weak versus strong ties among a group of people.

(A) This means that they might have information that is most relevant to us, but it also means that it is information to which we may already be exposed. In contrast, our weaker relationships are often with people who are more distant both geographically and demographically.

(B) Their information is more novel. Even though we talk to these people less frequently, we have so many weak ties that they end up being a sizable source of information, especially of information to which we don't otherwise have access.

(C) He found that only a sixth of jobs that came via the network were from strong ties, with the rest coming via medium or weak ties; and with more than a quarter coming via weak ties. Strong ties can be more homophilistic. Our closest friends are often those who are most like us.

♦ demographically: 인구통계학적으로
♦♦ homophilistic: 동족친화적인

① (A) — (C) — (B)　② (B) — (A) — (C)
③ (B) — (C) — (A)　④ (C) — (A) — (B)
⑤ (C) — (B) — (A)

정답과 해설 : 09 229 10 230

11 ⓘ 120초

★★☆ 2018년 11월 37번

주어진 글 다음에 이어질 글의 순서로 가장 적절한 것은? [3점]

> Some fad diets might have you running a caloric deficit, and while this might encourage weight loss, it has no effect on improving body composition, and it could actually result in a loss of muscle mass.

(A) Timing is also important. By eating the right combinations of these key macronutrients at strategic intervals throughout the day, we can help our bodies heal and grow even faster.

(B) Your body also needs the right balance of key macronutrients to heal and grow stronger. These macronutrients, which include protein, carbohydrates, and healthy fats, can help your body maximize its ability to repair, rebuild, and grow stronger.

(C) Calorie restriction can also cause your metabolism to slow down, and significantly reduce energy levels. Controlling caloric intake to deliver the proper amount of calories so that the body has the energy it needs to function and heal is the only proper approach.

* fad: (일시적인) 유행 ** macronutrient: 다량 영양소

① (A) — (C) — (B) ② (B) — (A) — (C)
③ (B) — (C) — (A) ④ (C) — (A) — (B)
⑤ (C) — (B) — (A)

12 ⓘ 120초

★★☆ 2019년 11월 37번

주어진 글 다음에 이어질 글의 순서로 가장 적절한 것은? [3점]

> Like the physiological discoveries of the late nineteenth century, today's biological breakthrough has fundamentally altered our understanding of how the human organism works and will change medical practice fundamentally and thoroughly.

(A) Remember the scientific method, which you probably first learned about back in elementary school? It has a long and difficult process of observation, hypothesis, experiment, testing, modifying, retesting, and retesting again and again and again.

(B) That's how science works, and the breakthrough understanding of the relationship between our genes and chronic disease happened in just that way, building on the work of scientists from decades — even centuries — ago. In fact, it is still happening; the story continues to unfold as the research presses on.

(C) The word "breakthrough," however, seems to imply in many people's minds an amazing, unprecedented revelation that, in an instant, makes everything clear. Science doesn't actually work that way.

① (A) — (C) — (B) ② (B) — (A) — (C)
③ (B) — (C) — (A) ④ (C) — (A) — (B)
⑤ (C) — (B) — (A)

정답과 해설 : 11 231 12 231

13 ⏱ 120초

★★☆ 2020년 11월 37번

주어진 글 다음에 이어질 글의 순서로 가장 적절한 것은? [3점]

When we think of culture, we first think of human cultures, of *our* culture. We think of computers, airplanes, fashions, teams, and pop stars. For most of human cultural history, none of those things existed.

(A) Sadly, this remains true as the final tribal peoples get overwhelmed by those who value money above humanity. We are living in their end times and, to varying extents, we're all contributing to those endings. Ultimately our values may even prove self-defeating.

(B) They held extensive knowledge, knew deep secrets of their lands and creatures. And they experienced rich and rewarding lives; we know so because when their ways were threatened, they fought to hold on to them, to the death.

(C) For hundreds of thousands of years, no human culture had a tool with moving parts. Well into the twentieth century, various human foraging cultures retained tools of stone, wood, and bone. We might pity human hunter-gatherers for their stuck simplicity, but we would be making a mistake.

♦ forage: 수렵 채집하다

① (A) — (C) — (B)
② (B) — (A) — (C)
③ (B) — (C) — (A)
④ (C) — (A) — (B)
⑤ (C) — (B) — (A)

14 ⏱ 120초

★★☆ 2022년 9월 36번

주어진 글 다음에 이어질 글의 순서로 가장 적절한 것은?

If DNA were the only thing that mattered, there would be no particular reason to build meaningful social programs to pour good experiences into children and protect them from bad experiences.

(A) This number came as a surprise to biologists: given the complexity of the brain and the body, it had been assumed that hundreds of thousands of genes would be required.

(B) So how does the massively complicated brain, with its eighty-six billion neurons, get built from such a small recipe book? The answer relies on a clever strategy implemented by the genome: build incompletely and let world experience refine.

(C) But brains require the right kind of environment if they are to correctly develop. When the first draft of the Human Genome Project came to completion at the turn of the millennium, one of the great surprises was that humans have only about twenty thousand genes.

① (A) — (C) — (B)
② (B) — (A) — (C)
③ (B) — (C) — (A)
④ (C) — (A) — (B)
⑤ (C) — (B) — (A)

정답과 해설: 13 232 14 233

15 ⏱ 120초

★★☆ 2023년 6월 37번

주어진 글 다음에 이어질 글의 순서로 가장 적절한 것은?

> Species that are found in only one area are called endemic species and are especially vulnerable to extinction.

(A) But warmer air from global climate change caused these clouds to rise, depriving the forests of moisture, and the habitat for the golden toad and many other species dried up. The golden toad appears to be one of the first victims of climate change caused largely by global warming.

(B) They exist on islands and in other unique small areas, especially in tropical rain forests where most species are highly specialized. One example is the brilliantly colored golden toad once found only in a small area of lush rain forests in Costa Rica's mountainous region.

(C) Despite living in the country's well-protected Monteverde Cloud Forest Reserve, by 1989, the golden toad had apparently become extinct. Much of the moisture that supported its rain forest habitat came in the form of moisture-laden clouds blowing in from the Caribbean Sea.

♦ lush: 무성한, 우거진

① (A) — (C) — (B)
② (B) — (A) — (C)
③ (B) — (C) — (A)
④ (C) — (A) — (B)
⑤ (C) — (B) — (A)

16 ⏱ 130초

★★★ 2020년 3월 36번

주어진 글 다음에 이어질 글의 순서로 가장 적절한 것은? 3점

> Habits create the foundation for mastery. In chess, it is only after the basic movements of the pieces have become automatic that a player can focus on the next level of the game. Each chunk of information that is memorized opens up the mental space for more effortful thinking.

(A) You fall into mindless repetition. It becomes easier to let mistakes slide. When you can do it "good enough" automatically, you stop thinking about how to do it better.

(B) However, the benefits of habits come at a cost. At first, each repetition develops fluency, speed, and skill. But then, as a habit becomes automatic, you become less sensitive to feedback.

(C) This is true for anything you attempt. When you know the simple movements so well that you can perform them without thinking, you are free to pay attention to more advanced details. In this way, habits are the backbone of any pursuit of excellence.

① (A) — (C) — (B)
② (B) — (A) — (C)
③ (B) — (C) — (A)
④ (C) — (A) — (B)
⑤ (C) — (B) — (A)

정답과 해설 : 15 234 16 235

17 ⏱ 130초

★★★ 2021년 9월 37번

주어진 글 다음에 이어질 글의 순서로 가장 적절한 것은? 3점

> Heat is lost at the surface, so the more surface area you have relative to volume, the harder you must work to stay warm. That means that little creatures have to produce heat more rapidly than large creatures.

(A) Despite the vast differences in heart rates, nearly all mammals have about 800 million heartbeats in them if they live an average life. The exception is humans. We pass 800 million heartbeats after twenty-five years, and just keep on going for another fifty years and 1.6 billion heartbeats or so.

(B) They must therefore lead completely different lifestyles. An elephant's heart beats just thirty times a minute, a human's sixty, a cow's between fifty and eighty, but a mouse's beats six hundred times a minute — ten times a second. Every day, just to survive, the mouse must eat about 50 percent of its own body weight.

(C) We humans, by contrast, need to consume only about 2 percent of our body weight to supply our energy requirements. One area where animals are curiously uniform is with the number of heartbeats they have in a lifetime.

① (A) — (C) — (B) ② (B) — (A) — (C)
③ (B) — (C) — (A) ④ (C) — (A) — (B)
⑤ (C) — (B) — (A)

18 ⏱ 130초

★★★ 2021년 11월 37번

주어진 글 다음에 이어질 글의 순서로 가장 적절한 것은? 3점

> Because we are told that the planet is doomed, we do not register the growing number of scientific studies demonstrating the resilience of other species. For instance, climate-driven disturbances are affecting the world's coastal marine ecosystems more frequently and with greater intensity.

(A) Similarly, kelp forests hammered by intense El Niño water-temperature increases recovered within five years. By studying these "bright spots," situations where ecosystems persist even in the face of major climatic impacts, we can learn what management strategies help to minimize destructive forces and nurture resilience.

(B) In a region in Western Australia, for instance, up to 90 percent of live coral was lost when ocean water temperatures rose, causing what scientists call coral bleaching. Yet in some sections of the reef surface, 44 percent of the corals recovered within twelve years.

(C) This is a global problem that demands urgent action. Yet, as detailed in a 2017 paper in *BioScience*, there are also instances where marine ecosystems show remarkable resilience to acute climatic events.

* doomed: 운이 다한
** resilience: 회복력 *** kelp: 켈프(해초의 일종)

① (A) — (C) — (B) ② (B) — (A) — (C)
③ (B) — (C) — (A) ④ (C) — (A) — (B)
⑤ (C) — (B) — (A)

DAY 18 14 문장 배열

정답과 해설 : 17 235 18 236

19 ⏱ 130초

★★★ 2022년 3월 36번

주어진 글 다음에 이어질 글의 순서로 가장 적절한 것은?

> The ancient Greeks used to describe two very different ways of thinking — *logos* and *mythos*. *Logos* roughly referred to the world of the logical, the empirical, the scientific.

(A) But lots of scholars then and now — including many anthropologists, sociologists and philosophers today — see a more complicated picture, where *mythos* and *logos* are intertwined and interdependent. Science itself, according to this view, relies on stories.

(B) *Mythos* referred to the world of dreams, storytelling and symbols. Like many rationalists today, some philosophers of Greece prized *logos* and looked down at *mythos*. Logic and reason, they concluded, make us modern; storytelling and mythmaking are primitive.

(C) The frames and metaphors we use to understand the world shape the scientific discoveries we make; they even shape what we see. When our frames and metaphors change, the world itself is transformed. The Copernican Revolution involved more than just scientific calculation; it involved a new story about the place of Earth in the universe.

♦ empirical: 경험적인

① (A) — (C) — (B)
② (B) — (A) — (C)
③ (B) — (C) — (A)
④ (C) — (A) — (B)
⑤ (C) — (B) — (A)

20 ⏱ 130초

★★★ 2022년 6월 36번

주어진 글 다음에 이어질 글의 순서로 가장 적절한 것은?

> Touch receptors are spread over all parts of the body, but they are not spread evenly. Most of the touch receptors are found in your fingertips, tongue, and lips.

(A) But if the fingers are spread far apart, you can feel them individually. Yet if the person does the same thing on the back of your hand (with your eyes closed, so that you don't see how many fingers are being used), you probably will be able to tell easily, even when the fingers are close together.

(B) You can test this for yourself. Have someone poke you in the back with one, two, or three fingers and try to guess how many fingers the person used. If the fingers are close together, you will probably think it was only one.

(C) On the tip of each of your fingers, for example, there are about five thousand separate touch receptors. In other parts of the body there are far fewer. In the skin of your back, the touch receptors may be as much as 2 inches apart.

① (A) — (C) — (B)
② (B) — (A) — (C)
③ (B) — (C) — (A)
④ (C) — (A) — (B)
⑤ (C) — (B) — (A)

정답과 해설 : 19 237 20 238

21 ⏱ 130초

★★★
2023년 3월 36번

주어진 글 다음에 이어질 글의 순서로 가장 적절한 것은?

> Like positive habits, bad habits exist on a continuum of easy-to-change and hard-to-change.

(A) But this kind of language (and the approaches it spawns) frames these challenges in a way that isn't helpful or effective. I specifically hope we will stop using this phrase: "break a habit." This language misguides people. The word "break" sets the wrong expectation for how you get rid of a bad habit.

(B) This word implies that if you input a lot of force in one moment, the habit will be gone. However, that rarely works, because you usually cannot get rid of an unwanted habit by applying force one time.

(C) When you get toward the "hard" end of the spectrum, note the language you hear — *breaking* bad habits and *battling* addiction. It's as if an unwanted behavior is a nefarious villain to be aggressively defeated.

♦ spawn: 낳다 ♦♦ nefarious: 사악한

① (A) — (C) — (B)
② (B) — (A) — (C)
③ (B) — (C) — (A)
④ (C) — (A) — (B)
⑤ (C) — (B) — (A)

22 ⏱ 130초

★★★
2019년 6월 36번

주어진 글 다음에 이어질 글의 순서로 가장 적절한 것은?

> Without money, people could only barter. Many of us barter to a small extent, when we return favors.

(A) There is no need to find someone who wants what you have to trade; you simply pay for your goods with money. The seller can then take the money and buy from someone else. Money is transferable and deferrable — the seller can hold on to it and buy when the time is right.

(B) What would happen if you wanted a loaf of bread and all you had to trade was your new car? Barter depends on the double coincidence of wants, where not only does the other person happen to have what I want, but I also have what he wants. Money solves all these problems.

(C) A man might offer to mend his neighbor's broken door in return for a few hours of babysitting, for instance. Yet it is hard to imagine these personal exchanges working on a larger scale.

♦ barter: 물물 교환(하다)

① (A) — (C) — (B)
② (B) — (A) — (C)
③ (B) — (C) — (A)
④ (C) — (A) — (B)
⑤ (C) — (B) — (A)

정답과 해설 : 21 239 22 240

23 ⓒ 130초

★★★
2022년 9월 37번

주어진 글 다음에 이어질 글의 순서로 가장 적절한 것은? [3점]

> One benefit of reasons and arguments is that they can foster humility. If two people disagree without arguing, all they do is yell at each other. No progress is made.

(A) That is one way to achieve humility — on one side at least. Another possibility is that neither argument is refuted. Both have a degree of reason on their side. Even if neither person involved is convinced by the other's argument, both can still come to appreciate the opposing view.

(B) Both still think that they are right. In contrast, if both sides give arguments that articulate reasons for their positions, then new possibilities open up. One of the arguments gets refuted — that is, it is shown to fail. In that case, the person who depended on the refuted argument learns that he needs to change his view.

(C) They also realize that, even if they have some truth, they do not have the whole truth. They can gain humility when they recognize and appreciate the reasons against their own view.

* humility: 겸손 ** articulate: 분명히 말하다

① (A) — (C) — (B)
② (B) — (A) — (C)
③ (B) — (C) — (A)
④ (C) — (A) — (B)
⑤ (C) — (B) — (A)

24 ⓒ 130초

★★★
2016년 9월 39번

주어진 글 다음에 이어질 글의 순서로 가장 적절한 것은? [3점]

> The foragers' secret of success, which protected them from starvation and malnutrition, was their varied diet. Farmers tend to eat a very limited and unbalanced diet.

(A) The peasant's ancient ancestor, the forager, may have eaten berries and mushrooms for breakfast; fruits and snails for lunch; and rabbit steak with wild onions for dinner. Tomorrow's menu might have been completely different. This variety ensured that the ancient foragers received all the necessary nutrients.

(B) The typical peasant in traditional China ate rice for breakfast, rice for lunch, and rice for dinner. If she was lucky, she could expect to eat the same on the following day. By contrast, ancient foragers regularly ate dozens of different foodstuffs.

(C) Especially in pre-modern times, most of the calories feeding an agricultural population came from a single crop — such as wheat, potatoes, or rice — that lacks some of the vitamins, minerals, and other nutritional materials humans need.

* forager: 수렵 채집 생활인

① (A) — (C) — (B)
② (B) — (A) — (C)
③ (B) — (C) — (A)
④ (C) — (A) — (B)
⑤ (C) — (B) — (A)

정답과 해설 : 23 240 24 241

25 ⓒ 130초

★★★ 2016년 11월 37번

주어진 글 다음에 이어질 글의 순서로 가장 적절한 것은? [3점]

> For years business leaders and politicians have portrayed environmental protection and jobs as mutually exclusive.

(A) Pollution control, protection of natural areas and endangered species, and limits on use of nonrenewable resources, they claim, will choke the economy and throw people out of work. Ecological economists dispute this claim, however.

(B) Recycling, for instance, makes more new jobs than extracting raw materials. This doesn't necessarily mean that recycled goods are more expensive than those from raw resources. We're simply substituting labor in the recycling center for energy and huge machines used to extract new materials in remote places.

(C) Their studies show that only 0.1 percent of all large-scale layoffs in the United States in recent years were due to government regulations. Environmental protection, they argue, not only is necessary for a healthy economic system, but it actually creates jobs and stimulates business.

① (A) — (C) — (B)
② (B) — (A) — (C)
③ (B) — (C) — (A)
④ (C) — (A) — (B)
⑤ (C) — (B) — (A)

26 ⓒ 130초 최고오답률

★★★ 2018년 11월 36번

주어진 글 다음에 이어질 글의 순서로 가장 적절한 것은?

> During the late 1800s, printing became cheaper and faster, leading to an explosion in the number of newspapers and magazines and the increased use of images in these publications.

(A) This "yellow journalism" sometimes took the form of gossip about public figures, as well as about socialites who considered themselves private figures, and even about those who were not part of high society but had found themselves involved in a scandal, crime, or tragedy that journalists thought would sell papers.

(B) Photographs, as well as woodcuts and engravings of them, appeared in newspapers and magazines. The increased number of newspapers and magazines created greater competition — driving some papers to print more salacious articles to attract readers.

(C) Gossip was of course nothing new, but the rise of mass media in the form of widely distributed newspapers and magazines meant that gossip moved from limited (often oral only) distribution to wide, printed dissemination.

♦ engraving: 판화 ♦♦ salacious: 외설스러운
♦♦♦ dissemination: 보급

① (A) — (C) — (B)
② (B) — (A) — (C)
③ (B) — (C) — (A)
④ (C) — (A) — (B)
⑤ (C) — (B) — (A)

정답과 해설 : 25 242 26 243

27 ⏱ 130초

★★★ 2019년 6월 37번

주어진 글 다음에 이어질 글의 순서로 가장 적절한 것은? [3점]

> Brain research provides a framework for understanding how the brain processes and internalizes athletic skills.

(A) This internalization transfers the swing from a consciously controlled left-brain function to a more intuitive or automatic right-brain function. This description, despite being an oversimplification of the actual processes involved, serves as a model for the interaction between conscious and unconscious actions in the brain, as it learns to perfect an athletic skill.

(B) In practicing a complex movement such as a golf swing, we experiment with different grips, positions and swing movements, analyzing each in terms of the results it yields. This is a conscious, left-brain process.

(C) Once we identify those elements of the swing that produce the desired results, we rehearse them over and over again in an attempt to record them permanently in "muscle memory." In this way, we internalize the swing as a kinesthetic feeling that we trust to recreate the desired swing on demand.

♦ kinesthetic: 운동 감각의

① (A) — (C) — (B)
② (B) — (A) — (C)
③ (B) — (C) — (A)
④ (C) — (A) — (B)
⑤ (C) — (B) — (A)

28 ⏱ 130초 〈최고오답률〉

★★★ 2020년 3월 37번

주어진 글 다음에 이어질 글의 순서로 가장 적절한 것은? [3점]

> Regardless of whether the people existing after agriculture were happier, healthier, or neither, it is undeniable that there were more of them. Agriculture both supports and requires more people to grow the crops that sustain them.

(A) And a larger population doesn't just mean increasing the size of everything, like buying a bigger box of cereal for a larger family. It brings qualitative changes in the way people live.

(B) Estimates vary, of course, but evidence points to an increase in the human population from 1–5 million people worldwide to a few hundred million once agriculture had become established.

(C) For example, more people means more kinds of diseases, particularly when those people are sedentary. Those groups of people can also store food for long periods, which creates a society with haves and have-nots.

♦ sedentary: 한 곳에 정착해 있는

① (A) — (C) — (B)
② (B) — (A) — (C)
③ (B) — (C) — (A)
④ (C) — (A) — (B)
⑤ (C) — (B) — (A)

정답과 해설 : 27 244 28 244

29 ⏱ 130초

★★★ 2021년 3월 37번

주어진 글 다음에 이어질 글의 순서로 가장 적절한 것은?

> We commonly argue about the fairness of taxation — whether this or that tax will fall more heavily on the rich or the poor.

(A) Taxes on tobacco, alcohol, and casinos are called "sin taxes" because they seek to discourage activities considered harmful or undesirable. Such taxes express society's disapproval of these activities by raising the cost of engaging in them. Proposals to tax sugary sodas (to combat obesity) or carbon emissions (to address climate change) likewise seek to change norms and shape behavior.

(B) But the expressive dimension of taxation goes beyond debates about fairness, to the moral judgements societies make about which activities are worthy of honor and recognition, and which ones should be discouraged. Sometimes, these judgements are explicit.

(C) Not all taxes have this aim. We do not tax income to express disapproval of paid employment or to discourage people from engaging in it. Nor is a general sales tax intended as a deterrent to buying things. These are simply ways of raising revenue.

* deterrent: 억제책

① (A) — (C) — (B)
② (B) — (A) — (C)
③ (B) — (C) — (A)
④ (C) — (A) — (B)
⑤ (C) — (B) — (A)

30 ⏱ 130초

★★★ 2023년 9월 37번

주어진 글 다음에 이어질 글의 순서로 가장 적절한 것은? [3점]

> Architects might say a machine can never design an innovative or impressive building because a computer cannot be "creative." Yet consider the Elbphilharmonie, a new concert hall in Hamburg, which contains a remarkably beautiful auditorium composed of ten thousand interlocking acoustic panels.

(A) Are these systems behaving "creatively"? No, they are using lots of processing power to blindly generate varied possible designs, working in a very different way from a human being.

(B) It is the sort of space that makes one instinctively think that only a human being — and a human with a remarkably refined creative sensibility, at that — could design something so aesthetically impressive. Yet the auditorium was, in fact, designed algorithmically, using a technique known as "parametric design."

(C) The architects gave the system a set of criteria, and it generated a set of possible designs for the architects to choose from. Similar software has been used to design lightweight bicycle frames and sturdier chairs, among much else.

* aesthetically: 미적으로 ** sturdy: 튼튼한, 견고한

① (A) — (C) — (B)
② (B) — (A) — (C)
③ (B) — (C) — (A)
④ (C) — (A) — (B)
⑤ (C) — (B) — (A)

DAY 19 14 문장 배열

정답과 해설 : 29 245 30 246

31 ⏱ 130초

★★★ 2020년 6월 37번

주어진 글 다음에 이어질 글의 순서로 가장 적절한 것은? [3점]

> Since we know we can't completely eliminate our biases, we need to try to limit the harmful impacts they can have on the objectivity and rationality of our decisions and judgments.

(A) If it did, we can move on and make an objective and informed decision. If it didn't, we can try the same strategy again or implement a new one until we are ready to make a rational judgment.

(B) Then we can choose an appropriate de-biasing strategy to combat it. After we have implemented a strategy, we should check in again to see if it worked in the way we had hoped.

(C) It is important that we are aware when one of our cognitive biases is activated and make a conscious choice to overcome that bias. We need to be aware of the impact the bias has on our decision making process and our life.

① (A) — (C) — (B) ② (B) — (A) — (C)
③ (B) — (C) — (A) ④ (C) — (A) — (B)
⑤ (C) — (B) — (A)

32 ⏱ 130초

★★★ 2022년 11월 36번

주어진 글 다음에 이어질 글의 순서로 가장 적절한 것은?

> The right to be forgotten is a right distinct from but related to a right to privacy. The right to privacy is, among other things, the right for information traditionally regarded as protected or personal not to be revealed.

(A) One motivation for such a right is to allow individuals to move on with their lives and not be defined by a specific event or period in their lives. For example, it has long been recognized in some countries, such as the UK and France, that even past criminal convictions should eventually be "spent" and not continue to affect a person's life.

(B) The right to be forgotten, in contrast, can be applied to information that has been in the public domain. The right to be forgotten broadly includes the right of an individual not to be forever defined by information from a specific point in time.

(C) Despite the reason for supporting the right to be forgotten, the right to be forgotten can sometimes come into conflict with other rights. For example, formal exceptions are sometimes made for security or public health reasons.

① (A) — (C) — (B) ② (B) — (A) — (C)
③ (B) — (C) — (A) ④ (C) — (A) — (B)
⑤ (C) — (B) — (A)

정답과 해설 : 31 247 32 248

33 ⏱ 130초 최고오답률

★★★ 2022년 11월 37번

주어진 글 다음에 이어질 글의 순서로 가장 적절한 것은? 3점

> To an economist who succeeds in figuring out a person's preference structure — understanding whether the satisfaction gained from consuming one good is greater than that of another — explaining behavior in terms of changes in underlying likes and dislikes is usually highly problematic.

(A) When income rises, for example, people want more children (or, as you will see later, more satisfaction derived from children), even if their inherent desire for children stays the same.

(B) To argue, for instance, that the baby boom and then the baby bust resulted from an increase and then a decrease in the public's inherent taste for children, rather than a change in relative prices against a background of stable preferences, places a social scientist in an unsound position.

(C) In economics, such an argument about birth rates would be equivalent to saying that a rise and fall in mortality could be attributed to an increase in the inherent desire change for death. For an economist, changes in income and prices, rather than changes in tastes, affect birth rates.

① (A) — (C) — (B)　② (B) — (A) — (C)
③ (B) — (C) — (A)　④ (C) — (A) — (B)
⑤ (C) — (B) — (A)

34 ⏱ 130초 최고오답률

★★★ 2023년 9월 36번

주어진 글 다음에 이어질 글의 순서로 가장 적절한 것은?

> If you drive down a busy street, you will find many competing businesses, often right next to one another. For example, in most places a consumer in search of a quick meal has many choices, and more fast-food restaurants appear all the time.

(A) Yes, costs rise, but consumers also gain information to help make purchasing decisions. Consumers also benefit from added variety, and we all get a product that's pretty close to our vision of a perfect good — and no other market structure delivers that outcome.

(B) However, this misconception doesn't account for why firms advertise. In markets where competitors sell slightly differentiated products, advertising enables firms to inform their customers about new products and services.

(C) These competing firms advertise heavily. The temptation is to see advertising as driving up the price of a product without any benefit to the consumer.

① (A) — (C) — (B)　② (B) — (A) — (C)
③ (B) — (C) — (A)　④ (C) — (A) — (B)
⑤ (C) — (B) — (A)

DAY 19 14 문장 배열

정답과 해설 : 33 249 34 249

35 ⓒ 130초 최고오답률 ★★★ 2021년 6월 36번

주어진 글 다음에 이어질 글의 순서로 가장 적절한 것은?

> Consider the story of two men quarreling in a library. One wants the window open and the other wants it closed. They argue back and forth about how much to leave it open: a crack, halfway, or three-quarters of the way.

(A) The librarian could not have invented the solution she did if she had focused only on the two men's stated positions of wanting the window open or closed. Instead, she looked to their underlying interests of fresh air and no draft.

(B) After thinking a minute, she opens wide a window in the next room, bringing in fresh air without a draft. This story is typical of many negotiations. Since the parties' problem appears to be a conflict of positions, they naturally tend to talk about positions — and often reach an impasse.

(C) No solution satisfies them both. Enter the librarian. She asks one why he wants the window open: "To get some fresh air." She asks the other why he wants it closed: "To avoid a draft."

♦ draft: 외풍 ♦♦ impasse: 막다름

① (A) — (C) — (B)
② (B) — (A) — (C)
③ (B) — (C) — (A)
④ (C) — (A) — (B)
⑤ (C) — (B) — (A)

36 ⓒ 130초 최고오답률 ★★★ 2022년 3월 37번

주어진 글 다음에 이어질 글의 순서로 가장 적절한 것은?

> There is no doubt that the length of some literary works is overwhelming. Reading or translating a work in class, hour after hour, week after week, can be such a boring experience that many students never want to open a foreign language book again.

(A) Moreover, there are some literary features that cannot be adequately illustrated by a short excerpt: the development of plot or character, for instance, with the gradual involvement of the reader that this implies; or the unfolding of a complex theme through the juxtaposition of contrasting views.

(B) Extracts provide one type of solution. The advantages are obvious: reading a series of passages from different works produces more variety in the classroom, so that the teacher has a greater chance of avoiding monotony, while still giving learners a taste at least of an author's special flavour.

(C) On the other hand, a student who is only exposed to 'bite-sized chunks' will never have the satisfaction of knowing the overall pattern of a book, which is after all the satisfaction most of us seek when we read something in our own language.

♦ excerpt: 발췌 ♦♦ juxtaposition: 병치

① (A) — (C) — (B)
② (B) — (A) — (C)
③ (B) — (C) — (A)
④ (C) — (A) — (B)
⑤ (C) — (B) — (A)

정답과 해설 : 35 250 36 251

37 ⏲ 120초

★★☆
2023년 11월 36번

주어진 글 다음에 이어질 글의 순서로 가장 적절한 것은?

> The size of a species is not accidental. It's a fine-tuned interaction between a species and the world it inhabits. Over large periods of time, size fluctuations have often signalled significant changes in the environment.

(A) But we are beginning to see changes in this trend. Scientists have discovered that many animals are shrinking. Around the world, species in every category have been found to be getting smaller, and one major cause appears to be the heat.

(B) Generally speaking, over the last five hundred million years, the trend has been towards animals getting larger. It's particularly notable in marine animals, whose average body size has increased 150-fold in this time.

(C) Animals living in the Italian Alps, for example, have seen temperatures rise by three to four degrees Celsius since the 1980s. To avoid overheating, chamois goats now spend more of their days resting rather than searching for food, and as a result, in just a few decades, the new generations of chamois are 25 percent smaller.

① (A) — (C) — (B)
② (B) — (A) — (C)
③ (B) — (C) — (A)
④ (C) — (A) — (B)
⑤ (C) — (B) — (A)

38 ⏲ 130초

★★★
2023년 11월 37번

주어진 글 다음에 이어질 글의 순서로 가장 적절한 것은? 3점

> For a long time, random sampling was a good shortcut. It made analysis of large data problems possible in the pre-digital era.

(A) There is no need to focus at the beginning, since collecting all the information makes it possible to do that afterwards. Because rays from the entire light field are included, it is closer to all the data. As a result, the information is more "reuseable" than ordinary pictures, where the photographer has to decide what to focus on before she presses the shutter.

(B) But much as converting a digital image or song into a smaller file results in loss of data, information is lost when sampling. Having the full (or close to the full) dataset provides a lot more freedom to explore, to look at the data from different angles or to look closer at certain aspects of it.

(C) A fitting example may be the light-field camera, which captures not just a single plane of light, as with conventional cameras, but rays from the entire light field, some 11 million of them. The photographers can decide later which element of an image to focus on in the digital file.

① (A) — (C) — (B)
② (B) — (A) — (C)
③ (B) — (C) — (A)
④ (C) — (A) — (B)
⑤ (C) — (B) — (A)

정답과 해설 : 37 252 38 253

39 ⏱ 130초

★★★ 2024년 3월 36번

주어진 글 다음에 이어질 글의 순서로 가장 적절한 것은? [3점]

Development of the human body from a single cell provides many examples of the structural richness that is possible when the repeated production of random variation is combined with nonrandom selection.

(A) Those in the right place that make the right connections are stimulated, and those that don't are eliminated. This process is much like sculpting. A natural consequence of the strategy is great variability from individual to individual at the cell and molecular levels, even though large-scale structures are quite similar.

(B) The survivors serve to produce new cells that undergo further rounds of selection. Except in the immune system, cells and extensions of cells are not genetically selected during development, but rather, are positionally selected.

(C) All phases of body development from embryo to adult exhibit random activities at the cellular level, and body formation depends on the new possibilities generated by these activities coupled with selection of those outcomes that satisfy previously built-in criteria. Always new structure is based on old structure, and at every stage selection favors some cells and eliminates others.

♦molecular: 분자의 ♦♦embryo: 배아

① (A) — (C) — (B)
② (B) — (A) — (C)
③ (B) — (C) — (A)
④ (C) — (A) — (B)
⑤ (C) — (B) — (A)

40 ⏱ 130초

★★★ 2024년 3월 37번

주어진 글 다음에 이어질 글의 순서로 가장 적절한 것은? [3점]

In order to bring the ever-increasing costs of home care for elderly and needy persons under control, managers of home care providers have introduced management systems.

(A) This, in the view of managers, has contributed to the resolution of the problem. The home care workers, on the other hand, may perceive their work not as a set of separate tasks to be performed as efficiently as possible, but as a service to be provided to a client with whom they may have developed a relationship.

(B) These systems specify tasks of home care workers and the time and budget available to perform these tasks. Electronic reporting systems require home care workers to report on their activities and the time spent, thus making the distribution of time and money visible and, in the perception of managers, controllable.

(C) This includes having conversations with clients and enquiring about the person's well-being. Restricted time and the requirement to report may be perceived as obstacles that make it impossible to deliver the service that is needed. If the management systems are too rigid, this may result in home care workers becoming overloaded and demotivated.

① (A) — (C) — (B)
② (B) — (A) — (C)
③ (B) — (C) — (A)
④ (C) — (A) — (B)
⑤ (C) — (B) — (A)

정답과 해설 : 39 254 40 255

41 ⓒ 120초

★★☆ 2024년 6월 36번

주어진 글 다음에 이어질 글의 순서로 가장 적절한 것은?

> Brains are expensive in terms of energy. Twenty percent of the calories we consume are used to power the brain.

(A) By directing your attention, they perform tricks with their hands in full view. Their actions should give away the game, but they can rest assured that your brain processes only small bits of the visual scene.

(B) So brains try to operate in the most energy-efficient way possible, and that means processing only the minimum amount of information from our senses that we need to navigate the world. Neuroscientists weren't the first to discover that fixing your gaze on something is no guarantee of seeing it. Magicians figured this out long ago.

(C) This all helps to explain the prevalence of traffic accidents in which drivers hit pedestrians in plain view, or collide with cars directly in front of them. In many of these cases, the eyes are pointed in the right direction, but the brain isn't seeing what's really out there.

♦ prevalence: 널리 행하여짐 ♦♦ pedestrian: 보행자 ♦♦♦ collide: 충돌하다

① (A) — (C) — (B)
② (B) — (A) — (C)
③ (B) — (C) — (A)
④ (C) — (A) — (B)
⑤ (C) — (B) — (A)

42 ⓒ 130초

★★★ 2024년 6월 37번

주어진 글 다음에 이어질 글의 순서로 가장 적절한 것은? [3점]

> Buying a television is current consumption. It makes us happy today but does nothing to make us richer tomorrow. Yes, money spent on a television keeps workers employed at the television factory.

(A) The crucial difference between these scenarios is that a college education makes a young person more productive for the rest of his or her life; a sports car does not. Thus, college tuition is an investment; buying a sports car is consumption.

(B) But if the same money were invested, it would create jobs somewhere else, say for scientists in a laboratory or workers on a construction site, while also making us richer in the long run.

(C) Think about college as an example. Sending students to college creates jobs for professors. Using the same money to buy fancy sports cars for high school graduates would create jobs for auto workers.

① (A) — (C) — (B)
② (B) — (A) — (C)
③ (B) — (C) — (A)
④ (C) — (A) — (B)
⑤ (C) — (B) — (A)

정답과 해설 : 41 256 42 257

43 ⓒ 120초

★★☆ 2024년 9월 36번

주어진 글 다음에 이어질 글의 순서로 가장 적절한 것은?

> It would seem obvious that the more competent someone is, the more we will like that person. By "competence," I mean a cluster of qualities: smartness, the ability to get things done, wise decisions, etc.

(A) If this were true, we might like people more if they reveal some evidence of fallibility. For example, if your friend is a brilliant mathematician, superb athlete, and gourmet cook, you might like him or her better if, every once in a while, they screwed up.

(B) One possibility is that, although we like to be around competent people, those who are *too* competent make us uncomfortable. They may seem unapproachable, distant, superhuman — and make us look bad (and feel worse) by comparison.

(C) We stand a better chance of doing well at our life tasks if we surround ourselves with people who know what they're doing and have a lot to teach us. But the research evidence is paradoxical: In problem-solving groups, the participants who are considered the most competent and have the best ideas tend not to be the ones who are best liked. Why?

♦ fallibility: 실수를 저지르기 쉬움

① (A) — (C) — (B)
② (B) — (A) — (C)
③ (B) — (C) — (A)
④ (C) — (A) — (B)
⑤ (C) — (B) — (A)

44 ⓒ 120초

★★☆ 2024년 9월 37번

주어진 글 다음에 이어질 글의 순서로 가장 적절한 것은? 3점

> A computational algorithm that takes input data and generates some output from it doesn't really embody any notion of meaning. Certainly, such a computation does not generally have as its purpose its own survival and well-being.

(A) Some bees might not bother to make the journey, considering it not worthwhile. The input, such as it is, is processed in the light of the organism's own internal states and history; there is nothing prescriptive about its effects.

(B) It does not, in general, assign value to the inputs. Compare, for example, a computer algorithm with the waggle dance of the honeybee, by which means a foraging bee conveys to others in the hive information about the source of food (such as nectar) it has located.

(C) The "dance" — a series of stylized movements on the comb — shows the bees how far away the food is and in which direction. But this input does not simply program other bees to go out and look for it. Rather, they evaluate this information, comparing it with their own knowledge of the surroundings.

♦ forage: 먹이를 찾아다니다 ♦♦ comb: 벌집

① (A) — (C) — (B)
② (B) — (A) — (C)
③ (B) — (C) — (A)
④ (C) — (A) — (B)
⑤ (C) — (B) — (A)

정답과 해설 : 43 258 44 258

유형 TIP

15. 주어진 문장 위치 파악

주어진 문장이 제시된 지문의 어느 위치에 들어가야 적절한지를 파악하는 유형
글의 통일성, 일관성, 논리성에 대한 이해력과 흐름을 파악하는 능력이 요구됨.

유형 TIP 25BR2T_CH15 대표 예제 25BR2E_CH15

유형 공략법

1) 주어진 문장을 읽으면서 대명사, 연결사 등의 단서가 있는지 가장 먼저 확인한다.
이와 같은 표현이 문장이 들어가야 할 위치에 대한 단서임.
지시어가 무엇을 가리키는지, 연결사로 어떻게 글의 흐름이 전환되는지를 염두에 두고 글을 읽어야 함.

2) 주어진 문장을 제외하고 글을 읽을 때, 문장과 문장 간의 흐름이 끊기는 부분을 찾는다.
대명사, 연결사 등에서 글의 앞뒤 흐름이 자연스럽지 못하다는 것을 알 수 있음.
위와 같은 것들로 알 수 없다면, 주어진 문장을 재진술(보편적인 내용, 구체적인 내용, 예시를 드는 내용 등)하는 문장을 찾아 앞뒤 둘 중 자연스러운 곳에 넣는다.

3) 들어갈 위치를 찾았다면, 그 위치에 문장을 넣어 다시 읽어 보고 글에 통일성이 있는지를 확인한다.

필수 암기 어휘와 표현

연결사 및 중요 표현

지시어	인칭 대명사	(주격) it, they (소유격) its, their 예 It was a great idea, They'd rather put money and time, Their notions
	지시 대명사/형용사	this, that, these, those 예 This illustrates that, That's why, From this perspective, in this way
	정관사	the + 앞에서 언급된 명사 예 ~ when forget-me-nots form their seeds. The seeds are designed to make ~ Rechard Taylor defined determinism ~ . The determinist, then, assumes that ~ The best archival decisions about art ~ . The best decisions ~
기타		such, given, along/as with + 앞에서 언급된 명사 예 in such conditions, given that choice, along with those grains, as with links

시간/순서	then, after, afterwards, subsequently, later, next, finally, lastly, earlier, recently, now, during, while, meanwhile, in the meantime, at the same time, simultaneously, suddenly, immediately, soon, as soon as, once, upon[on] V-ing, by the time, at that time, at that moment
예시	for example, for instance, to illustrate, to demonstrate, as an example, as[for] an illustration, specifically, e.g.
첨가	also, besides, moreover, furthermore, what is[what's] more, in addition (to), additionally, adding to, plus, as well, too, after all, similarly, likewise, what's worse, to make matters worse
인과	(원인) because, since, for, as, now (that), seeing (that), on account of, due to (결과) so, so that, thus, therefore, hence, as a result, as a consequence, in turn, accordingly, consequently, thereby, for this reason, as such, lead to, result in
결론	in the end, at last, ultimately, eventually, finally, in conclusion, to conclude, in the final[last/ultimate] analysis, it follows that, the bottom line is that

DAY 20 15 주어진 문장 위치 파악

주어진 문장 위치 파악 대표 예제 - 2024학년도 수능 38번

글의 흐름으로 보아, 주어진 문장이 들어가기에 가장 적절한 곳은?

> (1) Yes, some contests are seen as world class, such as identification of the Higgs particle or the development of high temperature superconductors.

(2) Science is sometimes described as a winner-take-all contest, meaning that there are no rewards for being second or third. (3) This is an extreme view of the nature of scientific contests. (①) (4) Even those who describe scientific contests in such a way note that it is a somewhat inaccurate description, given that replication and verification have social value and are common in science. (②) (5) It is also inaccurate to the extent that it suggests that only a handful of contests exist. (✓) (6) But many other contests have multiple parts, and the number of such contests may be increasing. (④) (7) By way of example, for many years it was thought that there would be "one" cure for cancer, but it is now realized that cancer takes multiple forms and that multiple approaches are needed to provide a cure. (⑤) (8) There won't be one winner — there will be many.

* replication: 반복 ** verification: 입증

STEP 1 주어진 문장을 읽으면서 대명사, 연결사 등의 단서가 있는지 가장 먼저 확인한다.

→ 주어진 문장이 '일부 대회(some contests)'는 세계적 수준으로 여겨진다고 언급한 것으로 보아, '일부 대회'가 가리키는 것이 무엇인지를 파악하는 것이 중요함.

STEP 2 주어진 문장을 제외하고 글을 읽을 때, 문장과 문장 간의 흐름이 끊기는 부분을 찾는다.

→ 문장 (5)의 오직 소수의 대회만이 존재한다고 시사하는 것이 부정확하다는 내용은 문장 (6)에서 다양한 요소가 있는 많은 다른 대회가 있다는 내용과 자연스럽게 이어지는데, 문장 (6)에는 역접의 접속사 'But'이 있어 연결이 자연스럽지 않고 흐름이 끊김.

→ 문장 (1)의 일부 대회(some contests)는 문장 (5)의 승자가 독식하는 '오직 소수의 대회(a handful of contests)'에 상응하는 표현임. 그리고 문장 (6)은 다른 많은 과학 대회에는 다양한 요소가 있고, 그런 대회의 수가 늘고 있다는 내용을 역접의 접속사로 다시 제시함. 따라서 주어진 문장 (1)은 문장 (5)와 (6) 사이인 ③에 와야 함.

STEP 3 들어갈 위치를 찾았다면, 그 위치에 문장을 넣어 다시 읽어 보고 글에 통일성이 있는지를 확인한다.

문장(5): 오직 소수의 대회만이 존재한다는 생각도 부정확함.
문장(1): 물론 세계적 수준으로 여겨지는 일부 대회도 있음.
문장(6): 그러나 다양한 요소가 있는 다른 대회도 많고, 그러한 대회의 수는 증가하고 있을지도 모름.
∴ 문장 (6)의 내용은 문장 (1)을 반박하는 것이므로, 주어진 문장 (1)은 문장 (6) 앞에 오는 것이 자연스러움.

전문 해석

(2) 과학은 때때로 승자 독식 대회로 묘사되는데, 이는 2등이나 3등인 것에는 보상이 없다는 것을 의미한다. (3) 이것은 과학 대회의 본질에 대한 극단적인 시각이다. ① (4) 과학 대회를 그런 식으로 묘사하는 사람들조차도, 반복과 입증이 사회적 가치가 있고 과학에서 흔한 것임을 고려하면, 그것이 다소 부정확한 설명이라고 지적한다. ② (5) 오직 소수의 대회만이 존재한다는 것을 시사할 경우 그것은 또한 부정확하다. ③ (1) 물론, 힉스 입자 검증이나 고온의 초전도체 개발과 같은 일부 대회는 세계적 수준으로 여겨진다. (6) 하지만 많은 다른 대회는 다양한 요소가 있고, 그러한 대회의 수는 증가하고 있을지도 모른다. ④ (7) 예를 들어, 수년 동안 암에 대한 '하나의' 치료법이 있을 것이라고 생각되었지만, 이제는 암은 다양한 형태를 취하고 치료법을 제공하기 위해 다양한 접근법이 필요하다고 인식된다. ⑤ (8) 승자는 한 명이 아니라 많을 것이다.

중요 어휘

- □ **extreme** 형 극단적인, 심각한
- □ **nature** 명 본질, 성질
- □ **note** 동 지적하다, 주목하다
- □ **somewhat** 부 다소, 어느 정도
- □ **inaccurate** 형 부정확한, 잘못된
- □ **description** 명 설명, 묘사
- □ **replication** 명 반복, 복제
- □ **verification** 명 입증, 증명
- □ **to the extent that** ~할 경우(에는), ~할 정도로
- □ **a handful of** 소수의
- □ **identification** 명 검증, 확인
- □ **particle** 명 입자
- □ **superconductor** 명 (물리) 초전도체
- □ **multiple** 형 다양한, 많은
- □ **part** 명 요소, 부분

자세한 해설지 QR→

자세한해설-CH15

15 주어진 문장 위치 파악

동영상 강의

25BR2_CH15

01 ⏱ 120초

★★☆ 2020년 3월 39번

글의 흐름으로 보아, 주어진 문장이 들어가기에 가장 적절한 곳은? 3점

> In some cases, their brains had ceased to function altogether.

Of all the medical achievements of the 1960s, the most widely known was the first heart transplant, performed by the South African surgeon Christiaan Barnard in 1967. (①) The patient's death 18 days later did not weaken the spirits of those who welcomed a new era of medicine. (②) The ability to perform heart transplants was linked to the development of respirators, which had been introduced to hospitals in the 1950s. (③) Respirators could save many lives, but not all those whose hearts kept beating ever recovered any other significant functions. (④) The realization that such patients could be a source of organs for transplantation led to the setting up of the Harvard Brain Death Committee, and to its recommendation that the absence of all "discernible central nervous system activity" should be "a new criterion for death". (⑤) The recommendation has since been adopted, with some modifications, almost everywhere.

⧫ respirator: 인공호흡기
⧫⧫ discernible: 식별 가능한 ⧫⧫⧫ criterion: 기준

02 ⏱ 120초

★★☆ 2021년 6월 38번

글의 흐름으로 보아, 주어진 문장이 들어가기에 가장 적절한 곳은? 3점

> However, transfer of one kind of risk often means inheriting another kind.

Risk often arises from uncertainty about how to approach a problem or situation. (①) One way to avoid such risk is to contract with a party who is experienced and knows how to do it. (②) For example, to minimize the financial risk associated with the capital cost of tooling and equipment for production of a large, complex system, a manufacturer might subcontract the production of the system's major components to suppliers familiar with those components. (③) This relieves the manufacturer of the financial risk associated with the tooling and equipment to produce these components. (④) For example, subcontracting work for the components puts the manufacturer in the position of relying on outsiders, which increases the risks associated with quality control, scheduling, and the performance of the end-item system. (⑤) But these risks often can be reduced through careful management of the suppliers.

⧫ subcontract: 하청을 주다(일감을 다른 사람에게 맡기다)

정답과 해설 : 01 260 02 260

03 ⓒ 120초

★★☆ 2019년 9월 38번

글의 흐름으로 보아, 주어진 문장이 들어가기에 가장 적절한 곳은?

> In much the same way, an array of technological, political, economic, cultural, and linguistic factors can exist and create a similar kind of pull or drag or friction.

Open international online access is understood using the metaphor "flat earth." It represents a world where information moves across the globe as easily as a hockey puck seems to slide across an ice rink's flat surface. (①) This framework, however, can be misleading — especially if we extend the metaphor. (②) As anyone who has crossed an ice rink can confirm, just because the surface of the rink appears flat and open does not necessarily mean that surface is smooth or even. (③) Rather, such surfaces tend to be covered by a wide array of dips and cracks and bumps that create a certain degree of pull or drag or friction on any object moving across it. (④) They affect how smoothly or directly information can move from point to point in global cyberspace. (⑤) Thus, while the earth might appear to be increasingly flat from the perspective of international online communication, it is far from frictionless.

04 ⓒ 120초

★★☆ 2020년 11월 38번

글의 흐름으로 보아, 주어진 문장이 들어가기에 가장 적절한 곳은?

> But the flowing takes time, and if your speed of impact is too great, the water won't be able to flow away fast enough, and so it pushes back at you.

Liquids are destructive. Foams feel soft because they are easily compressed; if you jump on to a foam mattress, you'll feel it give beneath you. (①) Liquids don't do this; instead they flow. (②) You see this in a river, or when you turn on a tap, or if you use a spoon to stir your coffee. (③) When you jump off a diving board and hit a body of water, the water has to flow away from you. (④) It's that force that stings your skin as you belly-flop into a pool, and makes falling into water from a great height like landing on concrete. (⑤) The incompressibility of water is also why waves can have such deadly power, and in the case of tsunamis, why they can destroy buildings and cities, tossing cars around easily.

♦ compress: 압축하다 ♦♦ give: (힘을 받아) 휘다

정답과 해설 : 03 261 04 262

05 ⏱ 120초

★★☆ 2021년 11월 39번

글의 흐름으로 보아, 주어진 문장이 들어가기에 가장 적절한 곳은? 3점

> In full light, seedlings reduce the amount of energy they allocate to stem elongation.

Scientists who have observed plants growing in the dark have found that they are vastly different in appearance, form, and function from those grown in the light. (①) This is true even when the plants in the different light conditions are genetically identical and are grown under identical conditions of temperature, water, and nutrient level. (②) Seedlings grown in the dark limit the amount of energy going to organs that do not function at full capacity in the dark, like cotyledons and roots, and instead initiate elongation of the seedling stem to propel the plant out of darkness. (③) The energy is directed to expanding their leaves and developing extensive root systems. (④) This is a good example of phenotypic plasticity. (⑤) The seedling adapts to distinct environmental conditions by modifying its form and the underlying metabolic and biochemical processes.

◆ elongation: 연장
◆◆ cotyledon: 떡잎 ◆◆◆ phenotypic plasticity: 표현형 적응성

06 ⏱ 130초

★★★ 2022년 6월 39번

글의 흐름으로 보아, 주어진 문장이 들어가기에 가장 적절한 곳은?

> But by the 1970s, psychologists realized there was no such thing as a general "creativity quotient."

The holy grail of the first wave of creativity research was a personality test to measure general creativity ability, in the same way that IQ measured general intelligence. (①) A person's creativity score should tell us his or her creative potential in any field of endeavor, just like an IQ score is not limited to physics, math, or literature. (②) Creative people aren't creative in a general, universal way; they're creative in a specific sphere of activity, a particular domain. (③) We don't expect a creative scientist to also be a gifted painter. (④) A creative violinist may not be a creative conductor, and a creative conductor may not be very good at composing new works. (⑤) Psychologists now know that creativity is domain specific.

◆ quotient: 지수 ◆◆ holy grail: 궁극적 목표

DAY 21
15 주어진 문장 위치 파악

정답과 해설 : 05 262 06 263

07 ⏱ 130초

★★★
2022년 9월 38번

글의 흐름으로 보아, 주어진 문장이 들어가기에 가장 적절한 곳은? 3점

> However, the capacity to produce skin pigments is inherited.

Adaptation involves changes in a population, with characteristics that are passed from one generation to the next. This is different from acclimation — an individual organism's changes in response to an altered environment. (①) For example, if you spend the summer outside, you may acclimate to the sunlight: your skin will increase its concentration of dark pigments that protect you from the sun. (②) This is a temporary change, and you won't pass the temporary change on to future generations. (③) For populations living in intensely sunny environments, individuals with a good ability to produce skin pigments are more likely to thrive, or to survive, than people with a poor ability to produce pigments, and that trait becomes increasingly common in subsequent generations. (④) If you look around, you can find countless examples of adaptation. (⑤) The distinctive long neck of a giraffe, for example, developed as individuals that happened to have longer necks had an advantage in feeding on the leaves of tall trees.

♦ pigment: 색소

08 ⏱ 130초

★★★
2023년 6월 38번

글의 흐름으로 보아, 주어진 문장이 들어가기에 가장 적절한 곳은?

> Rather, we have to create a situation that doesn't actually occur in the real world.

The fundamental nature of the experimental method is manipulation and control. Scientists manipulate a variable of interest, and see if there's a difference. At the same time, they attempt to control for the potential effects of all other variables. The importance of controlled experiments in identifying the underlying causes of events cannot be overstated. (①) In the real-uncontrolled-world, variables are often correlated. (②) For example, people who take vitamin supplements may have different eating and exercise habits than people who don't take vitamins. (③) As a result, if we want to study the health effects of vitamins, we can't merely observe the real world, since any of these factors (the vitamins, diet, or exercise) may affect health. (④) That's just what scientific experiments do. (⑤) They try to separate the naturally occurring relationship in the world by manipulating one specific variable at a time, while holding everything else constant.

정답과 해설 : 07 264 08 265

09 ⏱ 130초

★★★ 2023년 9월 38번

글의 흐름으로 보아, 주어진 문장이 들어가기에 가장 적절한 곳은?

You don't sit back and speculate about the meaning of life when you are stressed.

The brain is a high-energy consumer of glucose, which is its fuel. Although the brain accounts for merely 3 percent of a person's body weight, it consumes 20 percent of the available fuel. (①) Your brain can't store fuel, however, so it has to "pay as it goes." (②) Since your brain is incredibly adaptive, it economizes its fuel resources. (③) Thus, during a period of high stress, it shifts away from the analysis of the nuances of a situation to a singular and fixed focus on the stressful situation at hand. (④) Instead, you devote all your energy to trying to figure out what action to take. (⑤) Sometimes, however, this shift from the higher-thinking parts of the brain to the automatic and reflexive parts of the brain can lead you to do something too quickly, without thinking.

♦ glucose: 포도당

10 ⏱ 130초

★★★ 2017년 6월 38번

글의 흐름으로 보아, 주어진 문장이 들어가기에 가장 적절한 곳은?

If this goes on for any length of time the reactions in our cells cannot continue and we die.

It is vitally important that wherever we go and whatever we do the body temperature is maintained at the temperature at which our enzymes work best. It is not the temperature at the surface of the body which matters. (①) It is the temperature deep inside the body which must be kept stable. (②) At only a few degrees above or below normal body temperature our enzymes cannot function properly. (③) All sorts of things can affect internal body temperature, including heat generated in the muscles during exercise, fevers caused by disease, and the external temperature. (④) We can control our temperature in lots of ways: we can change our clothing, the way we behave and how active we are. (⑤) But we also have an internal control mechanism: when we get too hot we start to sweat.

♦ enzyme: 효소

정답과 해설 : 09 266 10 266

11 ⏱ 130초

★★★
2019년 3월 39번

글의 흐름으로 보아, 주어진 문장이 들어가기에 가장 적절한 곳은? 3점

> Rather, it is the air moving through a small hole into a closed container, as a result of air being blown out of the container by a fan on the inside.

Hubert Cecil Booth is often credited with inventing the first powered mobile vacuum cleaner. (①) In fact, he only claimed to be the first to coin the term "vacuum cleaner" for devices of this nature, which may explain why he is so credited. (②) As we all know, the term "vacuum" is an inappropriate name, because there exists no vacuum in a vacuum cleaner. (③) But I suppose a "rapid air movement in a closed container to create suction" cleaner would not sound as scientific or be as handy a name. (④) Anyway, we are stuck with it historically, and it is hard to find any references to "vacuum" prior to Booth. (⑤) Interestingly, Booth himself did not use the term "vacuum" when he filed a provisional specification describing in general terms his intended invention.

♦ provisional specification: 임시 제품 설명서

12 ⏱ 130초

★★★
2022년 6월 38번

글의 흐름으로 보아, 주어진 문장이 들어가기에 가장 적절한 곳은? 3점

> This temperature is of the surface of the star, the part of the star which is emitting the light that can be seen.

One way of measuring temperature occurs if an object is hot enough to visibly glow, such as a metal poker that has been left in a fire. (①) The color of a glowing object is related to its temperature: as the temperature rises, the object is first red and then orange, and finally it gets white, the "hottest" color. (②) The relation between temperature and the color of a glowing object is useful to astronomers. (③) The color of stars is related to their temperature, and since people cannot as yet travel the great distances to the stars and measure their temperature in a more precise way, astronomers rely on their color. (④) The interior of the star is at a much higher temperature, though it is concealed. (⑤) But the information obtained from the color of the star is still useful.

정답과 해설 : 11 267 12 268

13 ⓒ 130초

★★★ 2022년 9월 39번

글의 흐름으로 보아, 주어진 문장이 들어가기에 가장 적절한 곳은?

> This inequality produces the necessary conditions for the operation of a huge, global-scale engine that takes on heat in the tropics and gives it off in the polar regions.

On any day of the year, the tropics and the hemisphere that is experiencing its warm season receive much more solar radiation than do the polar regions and the colder hemisphere. (①) Averaged over the course of the year, the tropics and latitudes up to about 40° receive more total heat than they lose by radiation. (②) Latitudes above 40° receive less total heat than they lose by radiation. (③) Its working fluid is the atmosphere, especially the moisture it contains. (④) Air is heated over the warm earth of the tropics, expands, rises, and flows away both northward and southward at high altitudes, cooling as it goes. (⑤) It descends and flows toward the equator again from more northerly and southerly latitudes.

♦ latitude: 위도

14 ⓒ 130초

★★★ 2023년 3월 39번

글의 흐름으로 보아, 주어진 문장이 들어가기에 가장 적절한 곳은? 3점

> For others, whose creativity is more focused on methods and technique, creativity may lead to solutions that drastically reduce the work necessary to solve a problem.

Creativity can have an effect on productivity. Creativity leads some individuals to recognize problems that others do not see, but which may be very difficult. (①) Charles Darwin's approach to the speciation problem is a good example of this; he chose a very difficult and tangled problem, speciation, which led him into a long period of data collection and deliberation. (②) This choice of problem did not allow for a quick attack or a simple experiment. (③) In such cases creativity may actually decrease productivity (as measured by publication counts) because effort is focused on difficult problems. (④) We can see an example in the development of the polymerase chain reaction (PCR) which enables us to amplify small pieces of DNA in a short time. (⑤) This type of creativity might reduce the number of steps or substitute steps that are less likely to fail, thus increasing productivity.

♦ speciation: 종(種) 분화
♦♦ polymerase chain reaction: 중합 효소 연쇄 반응

정답과 해설 : 13 268 14 269

15 ⓒ 130초

★★★
2023년 9월 39번

글의 흐름으로 보아, 주어진 문장이 들어가기에 가장 적절한 곳은? 3점

> It is, however, noteworthy that although engagement drives job performance, job performance also drives engagement.

Much research has been carried out on the causes of engagement, an issue that is important from both a theoretical and practical standpoint: identifying the drivers of work engagement may enable us to manipulate or influence it. (①) The causes of engagement fall into two major camps: situational and personal. (②) The most influential situational causes are job resources, feedback and leadership, the latter, of course, being responsible for job resources and feedback. (③) Indeed, leaders influence engagement by giving their employees honest and constructive feedback on their performance, and by providing them with the necessary resources that enable them to perform their job well. (④) In other words, when employees are able to do their jobs well — to the point that they match or exceed their own expectations and ambitions — they will engage more, be proud of their achievements, and find work more meaningful. (⑤) This is especially evident when people are employed in jobs that align with their values.

♦ align with: ~과 일치하다

16 ⓒ 130초

★★★
2018년 11월 39번

글의 흐름으로 보아, 주어진 문장이 들어가기에 가장 적절한 곳은? 3점

> Even though there may be a logically easy set of procedures to follow, it's still an emotional battle to change your habits and introduce new, uncomfortable behaviors that you are not used to.

Charisma is eminently learnable and teachable, and in many ways, it follows one of Newton's famed laws of motion: *For every action, there is an equal and opposite reaction*. (①) That is to say that all of charisma and human interaction is a set of signals and cues that lead to other signals and cues, and there is a science to deciphering which signals and cues work the most in your favor. (②) In other words, charisma can often be simplified as a checklist of what to do at what time. (③) However, it will require brief forays out of your comfort zone. (④) I like to say that it's just a matter of using muscles that have long been dormant. (⑤) It will take some time to warm them up, but it's only through practice and action that you will achieve your desired goal.

♦ decipher: 판독하다 ♦♦ foray: 시도
♦♦♦ dormant: 활동을 중단한

정답과 해설 : 15 270 16 271

17 ⓒ 130초

★★★ 2021년 3월 38번

글의 흐름으로 보아, 주어진 문장이 들어가기에 가장 적절한 곳은? 3점

> However, some types of beliefs cannot be tested for truth because we cannot get external evidence in our lifetimes (such as a belief that the Earth will stop spinning on its axis by the year 9999 or that there is life on a planet 100-million light-years away).

Most beliefs — but not all — are open to tests of verification. This means that beliefs can be tested to see if they are correct or false. (①) Beliefs can be verified or falsified with objective criteria external to the person. (②) There are people who believe the Earth is flat and not a sphere. (③) Because we have objective evidence that the Earth is in fact a sphere, the flat Earth belief can be shown to be false. (④) Also, the belief that it will rain tomorrow can be tested for truth by waiting until tomorrow and seeing whether it rains or not. (⑤) Also, meta-physical beliefs (such as the existence and nature of a god) present considerable challenges in generating evidence that everyone is willing to use as a truth criterion.

♦ verification: 검증, 확인 ♦♦ falsify: 거짓임을 입증하다

18 ⓒ 130초

★★★ 2021년 9월 39번

글의 흐름으로 보아, 주어진 문장이 들어가기에 가장 적절한 곳은? 3점

> There isn't really a way for us to pick up smaller pieces of debris such as bits of paint and metal.

The United Nations asks that all companies remove their satellites from orbit within 25 years after the end of their mission. This is tricky to enforce, though, because satellites can (and often do) fail. (①) To tackle this problem, several companies around the world have come up with novel solutions. (②) These include removing dead satellites from orbit and dragging them back into the atmosphere, where they will burn up. (③) Ways we could do this include using a harpoon to grab a satellite, catching it in a huge net, using magnets to grab it, or even firing lasers to heat up the satellite, increasing its atmospheric drag so that it falls out of orbit. (④) However, these methods are only useful for large satellites orbiting Earth. (⑤) We just have to wait for them to naturally re-enter Earth's atmosphere.

♦ harpoon: 작살

정답과 해설 : 17 271 18 272

19 ⓒ 130초

★★★
2021년 11월 38번

글의 흐름으로 보아, 주어진 문장이 들어가기에 가장 적절한 곳은? 3점

> But this is a short-lived effect, and in the long run, people find such sounds too bright.

Brightness of sounds means much energy in higher frequencies, which can be calculated from the sounds easily. A violin has many more overtones compared to a flute and sounds brighter. (①) An oboe is brighter than a classical guitar, and a crash cymbal brighter than a double bass. (②) This is obvious, and indeed people like brightness. (③) One reason is that it makes sound subjectively louder, which is part of the loudness war in modern electronic music, and in the classical music of the 19th century. (④) All sound engineers know that if they play back a track to a musician that just has recorded this track and add some higher frequencies, the musician will immediately like the track much better. (⑤) So it is wise not to play back such a track with too much brightness, as it normally takes quite some time to convince the musician that less brightness serves his music better in the end.

20 ⓒ 130초

★★★
2017년 11월 39번

글의 흐름으로 보아, 주어진 문장이 들어가기에 가장 적절한 곳은?

> However, some say that a freer flow of capital has raised the risk of financial instability.

The liberalization of capital markets, where funds for investment can be borrowed, has been an important contributor to the pace of globalization. Since the 1970s there has been a trend towards a freer flow of capital across borders. (①) Current economic theory suggests that this should aid development. (②) Developing countries have limited domestic savings with which to invest in growth, and liberalization allows them to tap into a global pool of funds. (③) A global capital market also allows investors greater scope to manage and spread their risks. (④) The East Asian crisis of the late 1990s came in the wake of this kind of liberalization. (⑤) Without a strong financial system and a sound regulatory environment, capital market globalization can sow the seeds of instability in economies rather than growth.

정답과 해설 : 19 273 20 274

21 ⏱ 130초

★★★ 2018년 6월 37번

글의 흐름으로 보아, 주어진 문장이 들어가기에 가장 적절한 곳은? 3점

> Thinking of an internal cause for a person's behaviour is easy — the strict teacher is a stubborn person, the devoted parents just love their kids.

You may be wondering why people prefer to prioritize internal disposition over external situations when seeking causes to explain behaviour. One answer is simplicity. (①) In contrast, situational explanations can be complex. (②) Perhaps the teacher appears stubborn because she's seen the consequences of not trying hard in generations of students and wants to develop self-discipline in them. (③) Perhaps the parents who're boasting of the achievements of their children are anxious about their failures, and conscious of the cost of their school fees. (④) These situational factors require knowledge, insight, and time to think through. (⑤) Whereas, jumping to a dispositional attribution is far easier.

◆ disposition: 성질, 기질

22 ⏱ 130초 최고오답률

★★★ 2019년 6월 39번

글의 흐름으로 보아, 주어진 문장이 들어가기에 가장 적절한 곳은? 3점

> The most profitable information likely comes through network connections that provide "inside" information.

You're probably already starting to see the tremendous value of network analysis for businesspeople. (①) In the business world, information is money: a tip about anything from a cheap supplier to a competitor's marketing campaign to an under-the-table merger discussion can inform strategic decisions that might yield millions of dollars in profits. (②) You might catch it on TV or in the newspaper, but that's information everyone knows. (③) And it isn't just information that travels through network connections — it's influence as well. (④) If you have a connection at another company, you can possibly ask your connection to push that company to do business with yours, to avoid a competitor, or to hold off on the launch of a product. (⑤) So clearly, any businessperson wants to increase their personal network.

◆ merger: 합병

정답과 해설 : 21 274 22 275

23 ⓢ 130초

★★★ 2020년 9월 38번

글의 흐름으로 보아, 주어진 문장이 들어가기에 가장 적절한 곳은? 3점

> In terms of the overall value of an automobile, you can't drive without tires, but you can drive without cup holders and a portable technology dock.

Some resources, decisions, or activities are *important* (highly valuable on average) while others are *pivotal* (small changes make a big difference). Consider how two components of a car relate to a consumer's purchase decision: tires and interior design. Which adds more value on average? The tires. (①) They are essential to the car's ability to move, and they impact both safety and performance. (②) Yet tires generally do not influence purchase decisions because safety standards guarantee that all tires will be very safe and reliable. (③) Differences in interior features — optimal sound system, portable technology docks, number and location of cup holders — likely have far more effect on the consumer's buying decision. (④) Interior features, however, clearly have a greater impact on the purchase decision. (⑤) In our language, the tires are important, but the interior design is pivotal.

24 ⓢ 130초 최고오답률

★★★ 2021년 9월 38번

글의 흐름으로 보아, 주어진 문장이 들어가기에 가장 적절한 곳은?

> It is possible to argue, for example, that, today, the influence of books is vastly overshadowed by that of television.

Interest in ideology in children's literature arises from a belief that children's literary texts are culturally formative, and of massive importance educationally, intellectually, and socially. (①) Perhaps more than any other texts, they reflect society as it wishes to be, as it wishes to be seen, and as it unconsciously reveals itself to be, at least to writers. (②) Clearly, literature is not the only socialising agent in the life of children, even among the media. (③) There is, however, a considerable degree of interaction between the two media. (④) Many so-called children's literary classics are televised, and the resultant new book editions strongly suggest that viewing can encourage subsequent reading. (⑤) Similarly, some television series for children are published in book form.

♦ resultant: 그 결과로 생긴

정답과 해설 : 23276 24277

25 ⓒ 130초

★★★
2022년 3월 38번

글의 흐름으로 보아, 주어진 문장이 들어가기에 가장 적절한 곳은?

> For instance, the revolutionary ideas that earned Einstein his Nobel Prize — concerning the special theory of relativity and the photoelectric effect — appeared as papers in the *Annalen der Physik*.

In the early stages of modern science, scientists communicated their creative ideas largely by publishing books. (①) This modus operandi is illustrated not only by Newton's *Principia*, but also by Copernicus' *On the Revolutions of the Heavenly Spheres*, Kepler's *The Harmonies of the World*, and Galileo's *Dialogues Concerning the Two New Sciences*. (②) With the advent of scientific periodicals, such as the *Transactions of the Royal Society of London*, books gradually yielded ground to the technical journal article as the chief form of scientific communication. (③) Of course, books were not abandoned altogether, as Darwin's *Origin of Species* shows. (④) Even so, it eventually became possible for scientists to establish a reputation for their creative contributions without publishing a single book-length treatment of their ideas. (⑤) His status as one of the greatest scientists of all time does not depend on the publication of a single book.

◆ photoelectric effect: 광전 효과

◆◆ modus operandi: 작업 방식[절차]

26 ⓒ 130초

★★★
2022년 3월 39번

글의 흐름으로 보아, 주어진 문장이 들어가기에 가장 적절한 곳은? 3점

> Although sport clubs and leagues may have a fixed supply schedule, it is possible to increase the number of consumers who watch.

A supply schedule refers to the ability of a business to change their production rates to meet the demand of consumers. Some businesses are able to increase their production level quickly in order to meet increased demand. However, sporting clubs have a fixed, or inflexible (inelastic) production capacity. (①) They have what is known as a fixed supply schedule. (②) It is worth noting that this is not the case for sales of clothing, equipment, memberships and memorabilia. (③) But clubs and teams can only play a certain number of times during their season. (④) If fans and members are unable to get into a venue, that revenue is lost forever. (⑤) For example, the supply of a sport product can be increased by providing more seats, changing the venue, extending the playing season or even through new television, radio or Internet distribution.

◆ memorabilia: 기념품 ◆◆ venue: 경기장

정답과 해설 : 25 277 26 278

27 ⏲ 130초

★★★
2022년 11월 38번

글의 흐름으로 보아, 주어진 문장이 들어가기에 가장 적절한 곳은?

> It does this by making your taste buds perceive these flavors as bad and even disgusting.

In the natural world, if an animal consumes a plant with enough antinutrients to make it feel unwell, it won't eat that plant again. Intuitively, animals also know to stay away from these plants. Years of evolution and information being passed down created this innate intelligence. (①) This "intuition," though, is not just seen in animals. (②) Have you ever wondered why most children hate vegetables? (③) Dr. Steven Gundry justifies this as part of our genetic programming, our inner intelligence. (④) Since many vegetables are full of antinutrients, your body tries to keep you away from them while you are still fragile and in development. (⑤) As you grow and your body becomes stronger enough to tolerate these antinutrients, suddenly they no longer taste as bad as before.

♦ taste bud: 미뢰(味蕾)

28 ⏲ 130초 최고오답률

★★★
2022년 11월 39번

글의 흐름으로 보아, 주어진 문장이 들어가기에 가장 적절한 곳은? 3점

> However, the rigidity of rock means that land rises and falls with the tides by a much smaller amount than water, which is why we notice only the ocean tides.

The difference in the Moon's gravitational pull on different parts of our planet effectively creates a "stretching force." (①) It makes our planet slightly stretched out along the line of sight to the Moon and slightly compressed along a line perpendicular to that. (②) The tidal stretching caused by the Moon's gravity affects our entire planet, including both land and water, inside and out. (③) The stretching also explains why there are generally *two* high tides (and two low tides) in the ocean each day. (④) Because Earth is stretched much like a rubber band, the oceans bulge out both on the side facing toward the Moon and on the side facing away from the Moon. (⑤) As Earth rotates, we are carried through both of these tidal bulges each day, so we have high tide when we are in each of the two bulges and low tide at the midpoints in between.

♦ rigidity: 단단함
♦♦ perpendicular: 직각을 이루는 ♦♦♦ bulge: 팽창하다

정답과 해설 : 27 279 28 280

29 ⏱ 130초

★★★ 2023년 6월 39번

글의 흐름으로 보아, 주어진 문장이 들어가기에 가장 적절한 곳은?

> These healthful, non-nutritive compounds in plants provide color and function to the plant and add to the health of the human body.

Why do people in the Mediterranean live longer and have a lower incidence of disease? Some people say it's because of what they eat. Their diet is full of fresh fruits, fish, vegetables, whole grains, and nuts. Individuals in these cultures drink red wine and use great amounts of olive oil. Why is that food pattern healthy? (①) One reason is that they are eating a palette of colors. (②) More and more research is surfacing that shows us the benefits of the thousands of colorful "phytochemicals" (*phyto*=plant) that exist in foods. (③) Each color connects to a particular compound that serves a specific function in the body. (④) For example, if you don't eat purple foods, you are probably missing out on anthocyanins, important brain protection compounds. (⑤) Similarly, if you avoid green-colored foods, you may be lacking chlorophyll, a plant antioxidant that guards your cells from damage.

♦ antioxidant: 산화 방지제

30 ⏱ 130초 최고오답률

★★★ 2016년 6월 38번

글의 흐름으로 보아, 주어진 문장이 들어가기에 가장 적절한 곳은? [3점]

> Nevertheless, the productivity gap tends to widen because men dominate the use of the new equipment and modern agricultural methods.

In primitive agricultural systems, the difference in productivity between male and female agricultural labor is roughly proportional to the difference in physical strength. (①) As agriculture becomes less dependent upon human muscular power, the difference in labor productivity between the two genders might be expected to narrow. (②) However, this is far from being so. (③) It is usually the men who learn to operate new types of equipment while women continue to work with old hand tools. (④) With the introduction of improved agricultural equipment, there is less need for male muscular strength. (⑤) Thus, in the course of agricultural development, women's labor productivity remains unchanged compared to men's.

♦ proportional: 비례하는

DAY 22
15 주어진 문장 위치 파악

정답과 해설 : 29 281 30 281

31 ⓒ 130초 최고오답률

★★★
2018년 11월 38번

글의 흐름으로 보아, 주어진 문장이 들어가기에 가장 적절한 곳은?

> However, living off big game in the era before refrigeration meant humans had to endure alternating periods of feast and famine.

The problem of amino acid deficiency is not unique to the modern world by any means. (①) Preindustrial humanity probably dealt with protein and amino acid insufficiency on a regular basis. (②) Sure, large hunted animals such as mammoths provided protein and amino acids aplenty. (③) Droughts, forest fires, superstorms, and ice ages led to long stretches of difficult conditions, and starvation was a constant threat. (④) The human inability to synthesize such basic things as amino acids certainly worsened those crises and made surviving on whatever was available that much harder. (⑤) During a famine, it's not the lack of calories that is the ultimate cause of death; it's the lack of proteins and the essential amino acids they provide.

◆ synthesize: 합성하다

32 ⓒ 130초 최고오답률

★★★
2020년 6월 39번

글의 흐름으로 보아, 주어진 문장이 들어가기에 가장 적절한 곳은? 3점

> We have a continual desire to communicate our feelings and yet at the same time the need to conceal them for proper social functioning.

For hundreds of thousands of years our hunter-gatherer ancestors could survive only by constantly communicating with one another through nonverbal cues. Developed over so much time, before the invention of language, that is how the human face became so expressive, and gestures so elaborate. (①) With these counterforces battling inside us, we cannot completely control what we communicate. (②) Our real feelings continually leak out in the form of gestures, tones of voice, facial expressions, and posture. (③) We are not trained, however, to pay attention to people's nonverbal cues. (④) By sheer habit, we fixate on the words people say, while also thinking about what we'll say next. (⑤) What this means is that we are using only a small percentage of the potential social skills we all possess.

◆ counterforce: 반대 세력 ◆◆ sheer: 순전한

정답과 해설 : 31 282 32 283

33 ⏱ 130초 최고오답률

★★★
2020년 9월 39번

글의 흐름으로 보아, 주어진 문장이 들어가기에 가장 적절한 곳은? 3점

> When an overall silence appears on beats 4 and 13, it is not because each musician is thinking, "On beats 4 and 13, I will rest."

In the West, an individual composer writes the music long before it is performed. The patterns and melodies we hear are pre-planned and intended. (①) Some African tribal music, however, results from collaboration by the players on the spur of the moment. (②) The patterns heard, whether they are the silences when all players rest on a beat or the accented beats when all play together, are not planned but serendipitous. (③) Rather, it occurs randomly as the patterns of all the players converge upon a simultaneous rest. (④) The musicians are probably as surprised as their listeners to hear the silences at beats 4 and 13. (⑤) Surely that surprise is one of the joys tribal musicians experience in making their music.

♦ serendipitous: 우연히 얻은 ♦♦ converge: 한데 모아지다

34 ⏱ 130초 최고오답률

★★★
2021년 3월 39번

글의 흐름으로 보아, 주어진 문장이 들어가기에 가장 적절한 곳은?

> But the necessary and useful instinct to generalize can distort our world view.

Everyone automatically categorizes and generalizes all the time. Unconsciously. It is not a question of being prejudiced or enlightened. Categories are absolutely necessary for us to function. (①) They give structure to our thoughts. (②) Imagine if we saw every item and every scenario as truly unique — we would not even have a language to describe the world around us. (③) It can make us mistakenly group together things, or people, or countries that are actually very different. (④) It can make us assume everything or everyone in one category is similar. (⑤) And, maybe, most unfortunate of all, it can make us jump to conclusions about a whole category based on a few, or even just one, unusual example.

정답과 해설 : 33 283 34 284

35 ⓒ 130초 최고오답률

★★★ 2023년 3월 38번

글의 흐름으로 보아, 주어진 문장이 들어가기에 가장 적절한 곳은?

> In the electric organ the muscle cells are connected in larger chunks, which makes the total current intensity larger than in ordinary muscles.

Electric communication is mainly known in fish. The electric signals are produced in special electric organs. When the signal is discharged the electric organ will be negatively loaded compared to the head and an electric field is created around the fish. (①) A weak electric current is created also in ordinary muscle cells when they contract. (②) The fish varies the signals by changing the form of the electric field or the frequency of discharging. (③) The system is only working over small distances, about one to two meters. (④) This is an advantage since the species using the signal system often live in large groups with several other species. (⑤) If many fish send out signals at the same time, the short range decreases the risk of interference.

36 ⓒ 130초 최고오답률

★★★ 2019년 9월 39번

글의 흐름으로 보아, 주어진 문장이 들어가기에 가장 적절한 곳은? 3점

> Attitudes and values, however, are subjective to begin with, and therefore they are easily altered to fit our ever-changing circumstances and goals.

In physics, the principle of relativity requires that all equations describing the laws of physics have the same form regardless of inertial frames of reference. The formulas should appear identical to any two observers and to the same observer in a different time and space. (①) Thus, the same task can be viewed as boring one moment and engaging the next. (②) Divorce, unemployment, and cancer can seem devastating to one person but be perceived as an opportunity for growth by another person, depending on whether or not the person is married, employed, and healthy. (③) It is not only beliefs, attitudes, and values that are subjective. (④) Our brains comfortably change our perceptions of the physical world to suit our needs. (⑤) We will never see the same event and stimuli in exactly the same way at different times.

♦ inertial frame of reference: 관성좌표계

정답과 해설 : 35 285 36 286

37 ⓒ 130초

★★★
2023년 11월 38번

글의 흐름으로 보아, 주어진 문장이 들어가기에 가장 적절한 곳은?

> We must reexamine this stereotype, however, as it doesn't always hold true.

Introverted leaders do have to overcome the strong cultural presumption that extroverts are more effective leaders. (①) Although the population splits into almost equal parts between introverts and extroverts, more than 96 percent of managers and executives are extroverted. (②) In a study done in 2006, 65 percent of senior corporate executives viewed introversion as a barrier to leadership. (③) Regent University found that a desire to be of service to others and to empower them to grow, which is more common among introverts than extroverts, is a key factor in becoming a leader and retaining leadership. (④) So-called servant leadership, dating back to ancient philosophical literature, adheres to the belief that a company's goals are best achieved by helping workers or customers achieve their goals. (⑤) Such leaders do not seek attention but rather want to shine a light on others' wins and achievements; servant leadership requires humility, but that humility ultimately pays off.

♦ humility: 겸손

38 ⓒ 130초

★★★
2023년 11월 39번

글의 흐름으로 보아, 주어진 문장이 들어가기에 가장 적절한 곳은?

> However, contrary to the trend of the past several decades, in many new situations that are occurring today, allowing for imprecision — for messiness — may be a positive feature, not a shortcoming.

By the nineteenth century, France had developed a system of precisely defined units of measurement to capture space, time, and more, and had begun to get other nations to adopt the same standards. (①) Just half a century later, in the 1920s, the discoveries of quantum mechanics forever destroyed the dream of comprehensive and perfect measurement. (②) And yet, outside a relatively small circle of physicists, the mindset of humankind's drive to flawlessly measure continued among engineers and scientists. (③) In the world of business it even expanded, as the precision-oriented sciences of mathematics and statistics began to influence all areas of commerce. (④) As a tradeoff for relaxing the standards of allowable errors, one can get a hold of much more data. (⑤) It isn't just that "more is better than some," but that, in fact, sometimes "more is greater than better."

정답과 해설 : 37 286 38 287

39 ⏱ 130초

★★★ 2024년 3월 38번

글의 흐름으로 보아, 주어진 문장이 들어가기에 가장 적절한 곳은? [3점]

> However, there are many lines of evidence to suggest that vagrancy can, on rare occasions, dramatically alter the fate of populations, species or even whole ecosystems.

It is a common assumption that most vagrant birds are ultimately doomed, aside from the rare cases where individuals are able to reorientate and return to their normal ranges. (①) In turn, it is also commonly assumed that vagrancy itself is a relatively unimportant biological phenomenon. (②) This is undoubtedly true for the majority of cases, as the most likely outcome of any given vagrancy event is that the individual will fail to find enough resources, and/or be exposed to inhospitable environmental conditions, and perish. (③) Despite being infrequent, these events can be extremely important when viewed at the timescales over which ecological and evolutionary processes unfold. (④) The most profound consequences of vagrancy relate to the establishment of new breeding sites, new migration routes and wintering locations. (⑤) Each of these can occur through different mechanisms, and at different frequencies, and they each have their own unique importance.

♦ vagrancy: 무리에서 떨어져 헤맴 ♦♦ doomed: 죽을 운명의 ♦♦♦ inhospitable: 살기 힘든

40 ⏱ 130초 〔최고오답률〕

★★★ 2024년 3월 39번

글의 흐름으로 보아, 주어진 문장이 들어가기에 가장 적절한 곳은?

> Only then are they able to act quickly in accordance with their internalized expertise and evidence-based experience.

Intuition can be great, but it ought to be hard-earned. (①) Experts, for example, are able to think on their feet because they've invested thousands of hours in learning and practice: their intuition has become data-driven. (②) Yet most people are not experts, though they often think they are. (③) Most of us, especially when we interact with others on social media, act with expert-like speed and conviction, offering a wide range of opinions on global crises, without the substance of knowledge that supports it. (④) And thanks to AI, which ensures that our messages are delivered to an audience more inclined to believing it, our delusions of expertise can be reinforced by our personal filter bubble. (⑤) We have an interesting tendency to find people more open-minded, rational, and sensible when they think just like us.

♦ intuition: 직관 ♦♦ delusion: 착각

정답과 해설 : 39 288 40 289

41 ⏲ 130초

★★★
2024년 6월 38번

글의 흐름으로 보아, 주어진 문장이 들어가기에 가장 적절한 곳은?

> But the Net doesn't just connect us with businesses; it connects us with one another.

The Net differs from most of the mass media it replaces in an obvious and very important way: it's bidirectional. (①) We can send messages through the network as well as receive them, which has made the system all the more useful. (②) The ability to exchange information online, to upload as well as download, has turned the Net into a thoroughfare for business and commerce. (③) With a few clicks, people can search virtual catalogues, place orders, track shipments, and update information in corporate databases. (④) It's a personal broadcasting medium as well as a commercial one. (⑤) Millions of people use it to distribute their own digital creations, in the form of blogs, videos, photos, songs, and podcasts, as well as to critique, edit, or otherwise modify the creations of others.

♦ bidirectional: 두 방향으로 작용하는 ♦♦ thoroughfare: 통로

42 ⏲ 130초

★★★
2024년 6월 39번

글의 흐름으로 보아, 주어진 문장이 들어가기에 가장 적절한 곳은?

> Instead, automation created hundreds of millions of jobs in entirely new fields.

Imagine that seven out of ten working Americans got fired tomorrow. What would they all do? It's hard to believe you'd have an economy at all if you gave pink slips to more than half the labor force. But that is what the industrial revolution did to the workforce of the early 19th century. Two hundred years ago, 70 percent of American workers lived on the farm. (①) Today automation has eliminated all but 1 percent of their jobs, replacing them with machines. (②) But the displaced workers did not sit idle. (③) Those who once farmed were now manning the factories that manufactured farm equipment, cars, and other industrial products. (④) Since then, wave upon wave of new occupations have arrived — appliance repair person, food chemist, photographer, web designer — each building on previous automation. (⑤) Today, the vast majority of us are doing jobs that no farmer from the 1800s could have imagined.

♦ pink slip: 해고 통지서

정답과 해설 : 41 290 42 291

43 ⏱ 120초

★★☆
2024년 9월 38번

글의 흐름으로 보아, 주어진 문장이 들어가기에 가장 적절한 곳은?

> But there are also important differences between the two types of contagion.

There are deep similarities between viral contagion and behavioral contagion. (①) For example, people in close or extended proximity to others infected by a virus are themselves more likely to become infected, just as people are more likely to drink excessively when they spend more time in the company of heavy drinkers. (②) One is that visibility promotes behavioral contagion but inhibits the spread of infectious diseases. (③) Solar panels that are visible from the street, for instance, are more likely to stimulate neighboring installations. (④) In contrast, we try to avoid others who are visibly ill. (⑤) Another important difference is that whereas viral contagion is almost always a bad thing, behavioral contagion is sometimes negative — as in the case of smoking — but sometimes positive, as in the case of solar installations.

♦ contagion: 전염

44 ⏱ 120초

★★☆
2024년 9월 39번

글의 흐름으로 보아, 주어진 문장이 들어가기에 가장 적절한 곳은? [3점]

> Real hibernation involves profound unconsciousness and a dramatic fall in body temperature — often to around 32 degrees Fahrenheit.

Sleep is clearly about more than just resting. One curious fact is that animals that are hibernating also have periods of sleep. It comes as a surprise to most of us, but hibernation and sleep are not the same thing at all, at least not from a neurological and metabolic perspective. (①) Hibernating is more like being anesthetized: the subject is unconscious but not actually asleep. (②) So a hibernating animal needs to get a few hours of conventional sleep each day within the larger unconsciousness. (③) A further surprise to most of us is that bears, the most famous of wintry sleepers, don't actually hibernate. (④) By this definition, bears don't hibernate, because their body temperature stays near normal and they are easily awakened. (⑤) Their winter sleeps are more accurately called a state of torpor.

♦ hibernation: 동면
♦♦ anesthetize: 마취시키다 ♦♦♦ torpor: 휴면

정답과 해설 : 43 291 44 292

유형TIP

16. 문단 요약

주어진 글의 내용을 토대로, 글의 요지나 결론을 요약한 요약문에 적절한 어휘를 넣는 유형
요지를 파악하는 능력뿐만 아니라 어휘력도 요구됨.

유형 TIP 25BR2T_CH16
대표 예제 25BR2E_CH16

유형 공략법

1) 요약문을 가장 먼저 읽는다.
지문의 내용을 대략적으로 파악하고 어떤 부분에 주목해야 하는지 알 수 있음.

2) **지문의** 전체적인 내용을 파악**한다.**
주제문이나 지문의 핵심 어휘를 찾으면 내용 파악이 더 쉬워짐. 내용 일부분만 해석하고 이해하면 오답을 고를 확률이 높아지므로 주의해야 함.

3) 반복해서 나오는 어휘 또는 어구**가** 지문 전체의 내용을 아우르는지를 확인**한다.**
반복 어구는 곧 요약문의 빈칸에 들어갈 정답과 깊게 연관되어 있음. 선택지에서 비슷한 어휘를 찾고, 그 어휘를 요약문에 넣었을 때 지문의 내용을 제대로 반영했는지를 확인해야 함.

4) **유의어를 비롯하여** 어휘력**을 높인다.**
선택지에 제시되는 어휘는 지문에 언급된 어휘를 그대로 쓰지 않음. 유의어를 사용해 다른 말로 바꾸어 표현되는(paraphrase) 경우가 많으니 어휘력을 기르는 것이 도움이 됨.

필수 암기 어휘와 표현

Paraphrase에 사용될 수 있는 유의어

accept	agree, approve, admit, acknowledge	adjust	adapt, change, alter, modify, accustom oneself to
affect	impact, influence, concern, have an impact[effect] on, act on	analysis	examination, investigation, review, scrutiny
assure	make certain, ensure, confirm, guarantee	avoid	prevent, stop, refrain from, frustrate, avert
criticize	blame, censure, condemn, denounce, find fault with, put down, reproach, rebuke	contribute	help, support, assist, benefit / give, provide, donate
delay	postpone, defer, put off, suspend, hold up	convince	persuade, encourage, prevail on[upon], satisfy, induce, make believe
demand	request, require, call for, expect	defend	protect, guard, shield, cover, shelter, stand up for
emphasize	stress, highlight, underline, give priority to	depend on[upon]	be determined by / rely on, count on, trust
identify	notice, recognize, distinguish, tell, spot	encourage	inspire, cheer / promote, foster / persuade, convince
marginal	insignificant, minor, small, peripheral	justify	explain, support, defend, uphold, maintain
offend	distress, upset, outrage, hurt, insult	observe	watch, witness, distinguish, notice / follow, obey, comply with, abide by, conform to
render	make / provide, give / represent, perform	progress	development, advance, advancement, progression
sacrifice	offer, give up, let go, abandon	promising	hopeful, encouraging, bright, auspicious, propitious
valid	sound, rational, reasonable, logical, fair, just	sensible	wise, intelligent, rational, reasonable, judicious

문단 요약 대표 예제 - 2024학년도 수능 40번

다음 글의 내용을 한 문장으로 요약하고자 한다. 빈칸 (A)와 (B)에 들어갈 말로 가장 적절한 것은?

(1) Even those with average talent can produce notable work in the various sciences, so long as they do not try to embrace all of them at once. (2) Instead, they should concentrate attention on one subject after another (that is, in different periods of time), although later work will weaken earlier attainments in the other spheres. (3) This amounts to saying that the brain adapts to universal science in *time* but not in *space*. (4) In fact, even those with great abilities proceed in this way. (5) Thus, when we are astonished by someone with publications in different scientific fields, realize that each topic was explored during a specific period of time. (6) Knowledge gained earlier certainly will not have disappeared from the mind of the author, but it will have become simplified by condensing into formulas or greatly abbreviated symbols. (7) Thus, sufficient space remains for the perception and learning of new images on the cerebral blackboard.

* condense: 응축하다 ** cerebral: 대뇌의

⬇

(8) Exploring one scientific subject after another ___(A)___ remarkable work across the sciences, as the previously gained knowledge is retained in simplified forms within the brain, which ___(B)___ room for new learning.

(A)		(B)
✔ enables	……	leaves
② challenges	……	spares
③ delays	……	creates
④ requires	……	removes
⑤ invites	……	diminishes

STEP 1 요약문을 가장 먼저 읽는다.

→ (A)와 (B) 모두 동사로 제시되어 있음. 한 과학 주제를 탐구한 후 다른 주제를 탐구하는 것이 놀라운 작업과 어떤(=(A)) 연관성이 있는지, 그리고 새로운 학습을 위한 공간을 어떻게(=(B)) 하는지를 글에서 파악해야 함.

STEP 2 지문의 전체적인 내용을 파악한다.

→ 과학 주제의 탐구를 설명하는 글로, 문장 (1)부터 (4)까지는 능력과 상관없이 누구든 과학 주제를 탐구할 때 한 주제를 끝낸 후 다음 주제로 차례차례 넘어간다고 서술함. 문장 (5)부터 (7)까지는 한 주제가 시간을 가지고 탐구되어야 획득된 지식이 응축되어 남고 다른 주제를 탐구하기 위한 공간이 충분히 생긴다고 설명함. 따라서 이 두 내용을 적절하게 요약하는 것이 중요함.

STEP 3 반복해서 나오는 어휘 또는 어구가 지문 전체의 내용을 아우르는지를 확인한다.

→ 문장 (1)의 'notable work in the various sciences'와 문장 (2)의 'should concentrate attention on one subject after another'를 통해 한 주제를 탐구한 후 다른 주제를 탐구하는 것이 놀라운 성과를 만든다는 내용이 등장함. 따라서 (A)에는 'enables'가 와야 함.

→ 문장 (6)의 'condensing into formulas or greatly abbreviated symbols', 문장 (7)의 'sufficient space remains'를 통해 탐구된 주제는 뇌에서 축약된 형태로 저장되어 다른 주제를 탐구하기 위한 충분한 공간이 남는다는 내용이 등장함. 이를 통해 (B)에는 새로 배운 내용을 위한 공간이 충분히 '남아있다'는 말이 적절하므로, 'leaves'가 와야 함.

전문 해석

(1) 평균적인 재능을 가진 사람이라도 그들이 과학 분야 전부를 한번에 포용하려고 하지 않는 한 다양한 과학 분야에서 주목할 만한 성과를 낼 수 있다. (2) 대신, 나중의 작업이 다른 영역에 있는 이전의 성취를 약화할 것이더라도, 그들은 한 주제 다음에 다른 주제로 (즉, 서로 다른 기간에) 주의를 집중해야 한다. (3) 이는 뇌가 보편적인 과학에 '시간'적으로는 적응하지만 '공간'적으로는 적응하지 못한다고 말하는 것과 같다. (4) 사실, 뛰어난 능력을 가진 사람도 이런 식으로 나아간다. (5) 따라서, 우리가 서로 다른 과학 분야의 출판물을 가진 누군가에게 놀랄 때, 각 주제가 특정 기간 동안 탐구되었다는 것을 인식하라. (6) 이전에 얻은 지식은 저자의 마음에서 분명 사라지지 않을 것이지만, 공식이나 크게 축약된 기호로 응축되어 단순화될 것이다. (7) 따라서, 대뇌 칠판에는 새로운 이미지의 인식과 학습을 위한 충분한 공간이 남아 있다.

⬇

(8) 하나의 과학 주제를 탐구한 후에 다른 것을 탐구하는 것은 (여러) 과학 분야들을 가로지르는(여러 분야의 과학 전반에 걸친) 놀라운 작업을 (A)가능하게 하는데, 이전에 얻은 지식이 뇌 안에서 단순화된 형태로 유지되고, 이는 새로운 학습을 위한 공간을 (B)남겨 두기 때문이다.

중요 어휘

- □ notable 형 주목할 만한
- □ work 명 성과, 작업, 업무, 일
- □ so[as] long as ~하는 한
- □ embrace 동 포용하다, 받아들이다
- □ attainment 명 성취, 달성
- □ sphere 명 영역, 구(球)
- □ universal 형 보편적인, 일반적인
- □ proceed 동 나아가다, 진행하다
- □ astonish 동 놀라게 하다
- □ publication 명 출판물
- □ formula 명 공식
- □ abbreviated 형 축약된, 줄여 쓴
- □ perception 명 인식
- □ cerebral 형 대뇌의
- □ retain 동 유지하다

자세한 해설지 QR→

자세한해설-CH16

16 문단 요약

01 ⏱ 110초

★☆☆ 2021년 9월 40번

다음 글의 내용을 한 문장으로 요약하고자 한다. 빈칸 (A)와 (B)에 들어갈 말로 가장 적절한 것은?

Music is used to mold customer experience and behavior. A study was conducted that explored what impact it has on employees. Results from the study indicate that participants who listen to rhythmic music were inclined to cooperate more irrespective of factors like age, gender, and academic background, compared to those who listened to less rhythmic music. This positive boost in the participants' willingness to cooperate was induced regardless of whether they liked the music or not. When people are in a more positive state of mind, they tend to become more agreeable and creative, while those on the opposite spectrum tend to focus on their individual problems rather than giving attention to solving group problems. The rhythm of music has a strong pull on people's behavior. This is because when people listen to music with a steady pulse, they tend to match their actions to the beat. This translates to better teamwork when making decisions because everyone is following one tempo.

⬇

According to the study, the music played in workplaces can lead employees to be ___(A)___ because the beat of the music creates a ___(B)___ for working.

(A)		(B)
① uncomfortable	……	competitive mood
② cooperative	……	shared rhythm
③ distracted	……	shared rhythm
④ attentive	……	competitive mood
⑤ indifferent	……	disturbing pattern

02 ⏱ 120초

★★☆ 2021년 11월 40번

다음 글의 내용을 한 문장으로 요약하고자 한다. 빈칸 (A)와 (B)에 들어갈 말로 가장 적절한 것은?

In a study, Guy Mayraz, a behavioral economist, showed his experimental subjects graphs of a price rising and falling over time. The graphs were actually of past changes in the stock market, but Mayraz told people that the graphs showed recent changes in the price of wheat. He asked each person to predict where the price would move next — and offered them a reward if their forecasts came true. But Mayraz had also divided his participants into two categories, "farmers" and "bakers". Farmers would be paid extra if wheat prices were high. Bakers would earn a bonus if wheat was cheap. So the subjects might earn two separate payments: one for an accurate forecast, and a bonus if the price of wheat moved in their direction. Mayraz found that the prospect of the bonus influenced the forecast itself. The farmers hoped and *predicted* that the price of wheat would rise. The bakers hoped for — and predicted — the opposite. They let their hopes influence their reasoning.

⬇

When participants were asked to predict the price change of wheat, their ___(A)___ for where the price would go, which was determined by the group they belonged to, ___(B)___ their predictions.

(A)		(B)
① wish	……	affected
② wish	……	contradicted
③ disregard	……	restricted
④ disregard	……	changed
⑤ assurance	……	realized

정답과 해설 : 01 294 02 294

03 ⏱ 120초

★★☆ 2018년 3월 40번

다음 글의 내용을 한 문장으로 요약하고자 한다. 빈칸 (A)와 (B)에 들어갈 말로 가장 적절한 것은?

Despite all the talk of how weak intentions are in the face of habits, it's worth emphasizing that much of the time even our strong habits do follow our intentions. We are mostly doing what we intend to do, even though it's happening automatically. This probably goes for many habits: although we perform them without bringing the intention to consciousness, the habits still line up with our original intentions. Even better, our automatic, unconscious habits can keep us safe even when our conscious mind is distracted. We look both ways before crossing the road despite thinking about a rather depressing holiday we took in Brazil, and we put oven gloves on before reaching into the oven despite being preoccupied about whether the cabbage is overcooked. In both cases, our goal of keeping ourselves alive and unburnt is served by our automatic, unconscious habits.

⬇

The habitual acts we automatically do are related to our ____(A)____ and these acts can be helpful in keeping us from ____(B)____ in our lives.

(A)		(B)
① intention	……	danger
② intention	……	ignorance
③ mood	……	danger
④ experience	……	laziness
⑤ experience	……	ignorance

04 ⏱ 120초

★★☆ 2019년 11월 40번

다음 글의 내용을 한 문장으로 요약하고자 한다. 빈칸 (A)와 (B)에 들어갈 말로 가장 적절한 것은?

Psychologist John Bargh did an experiment showing human perception and behavior can be influenced by external factors. He told a bunch of healthy undergraduates that he was testing their language abilities. He presented them with a list of words and asked them to create a coherent sentence from it. One of the lists was "DOWN SAT LONELY THE MAN WRINKLED BITTERLY THE WITH FACE OLD". "Bitterly, the lonely old man with the wrinkled face sat down" is one possible solution. But this was no linguistics test. Bargh was interested in how long it took the students to leave the lab and walk down the hall after they were exposed to the words. What he found was extraordinary. Those students who had been exposed to an "elderly" mix of words took almost 40 percent longer to walk down the hall than those who had been exposed to "random" words. Some students even walked with their shoulders bent forwards, dragging their feet as they left, as if they were 50 years older than they actually were.

⬇

In an experiment about human perception and behavior, participants who experienced ____(A)____ to words related to "elderly" showed pace, and some of them even showed posture, ____(B)____ to what the words suggested.

(A)		(B)
① exposure	……	corresponding
② resistance	……	irrelevant
③ exposure	……	contrary
④ resistance	……	similar
⑤ preference	……	comparable

정답과 해설 : 03 295 04 296

05 ⏱ 120초

★★☆ 2022년 9월 40번

다음 글의 내용을 한 문장으로 요약하고자 한다. 빈칸 (A)와 (B)에 들어갈 말로 가장 적절한 것은? [3점]

Greenwashing involves misleading a consumer into thinking a good or service is more environmentally friendly than it really is. Greenwashing ranges from making environmental claims required by law, and therefore irrelevant (CFC-free for example), to puffery (exaggerating environmental claims) to fraud. Researchers have shown that claims on products are often too vague or misleading. Some products are labeled "chemical-free," when the fact is everything contains chemicals, including plants and animals. Products with the highest number of misleading or unverifiable claims were laundry detergents, household cleaners, and paints. Environmental advocates agree there is still a long way to go to ensure shoppers are adequately informed about the environmental impact of the products they buy. The most common reason for greenwashing is to attract environmentally conscious consumers. Many consumers do not find out about the false claims until after the purchase. Therefore, greenwashing may increase sales in the short term. However, this strategy can seriously backfire when consumers find out they are being deceived.

* CFC: 염화불화탄소 ** fraud: 사기

⬇

While greenwashing might bring a company profits ___(A)___ by deceiving environmentally conscious consumers, the company will face serious trouble when the consumers figure out they were ___(B)___.

(A)		(B)
① permanently	……	manipulated
② temporarily	……	misinformed
③ momentarily	……	advocated
④ ultimately	……	underestimated
⑤ consistently	……	analyzed

06 ⏱ 120초

★★☆ 2019년 6월 40번

다음 글의 내용을 한 문장으로 요약하고자 한다. 빈칸 (A)와 (B)에 들어갈 말로 가장 적절한 것은?

Intergroup contact is more likely to reduce stereotyping and create favorable attitudes if it is backed by social norms that promote equality among groups. If the norms support openness, friendliness, and mutual respect, the contact has a greater chance of changing attitudes and reducing prejudice than if they do not. Institutionally supported intergroup contact — that is, contact sanctioned by an outside authority or by established customs — is more likely to produce positive changes than unsupported contact. Without institutional support, members of an in-group may be reluctant to interact with outsiders because they feel doing so is deviant or simply inappropriate. With the presence of institutional support, however, contact between groups is more likely to be seen as appropriate, expected, and worthwhile. For instance, with respect to desegregation in elementary schools, there is evidence that students were more highly motivated and learned more in classes conducted by teachers (that is, authority figures) who supported rather than opposed desegregation.

* sanction: 승인하다 ** desegregation: 인종 차별 폐지

⬇

Backed by social norms that pursue intergroup equality, intergroup contact tends to weaken ___(A)___ more, especially when it is led by ___(B)___ support.

(A)		(B)
① bias	……	organizational
② bias	……	individualized
③ bias	……	financial
④ balance	……	organizational
⑤ balance	……	individualized

DAY 24 16 문단 요약

정답과 해설 : 05 297 06 298

07 ⓒ 120초

★★☆ 2022년 6월 40번

다음 글의 내용을 한 문장으로 요약하고자 한다. 빈칸 (A)와 (B)에 들어갈 말로 가장 적절한 것은?

The great irony of performance psychology is that it teaches each sportsman to believe, as far as he is able, that he will win. No man doubts. No man indulges his inner skepticism. That is the logic of sports psychology. But only one man *can* win. That is the logic of sport. Note the difference between a scientist and an athlete. Doubt is a scientist's stock in trade. Progress is made by focusing on the evidence that refutes a theory and by improving the theory accordingly. Skepticism is the rocket fuel of scientific advance. But doubt, to an athlete, is poison. Progress is made by ignoring the evidence; it is about creating a mindset that is immune to doubt and uncertainty. Just to reiterate: From a rational perspective, this is nothing less than crazy. Why should an athlete convince himself he will win when he knows that there is every possibility he will lose? Because, to win, one must proportion one's belief, not to the evidence, but to whatever the mind can usefully get away with.

♦reiterate: 되풀이하다

⬇

Unlike scientists whose ___(A)___ attitude is needed to make scientific progress, sports psychology says that to succeed, athletes must ___(B)___ feelings of uncertainty about whether they can win.

(A)		(B)
① confident	……	keep
② skeptical	……	eliminate
③ arrogant	……	express
④ critical	……	keep
⑤ stubborn	……	eliminate

08 ⓒ 120초

★★☆ 2023년 3월 40번

다음 글의 내용을 한 문장으로 요약하고자 한다. 빈칸 (A)와 (B)에 들어갈 말로 가장 적절한 것은?

A young child may be puzzled when asked to distinguish between the directions of right and left. But that same child may have no difficulty in determining the directions of up and down or back and front. Scientists propose that this occurs because, although we experience three dimensions, only two had a strong influence on our evolution: the vertical dimension as defined by gravity and, in mobile species, the front/back dimension as defined by the positioning of sensory and feeding mechanisms. These influence our perception of vertical versus horizontal, far versus close, and the search for dangers from above (such as an eagle) or below (such as a snake). However, the left-right axis is not as relevant in nature. A bear is equally dangerous from its left or the right side, but not if it is upside down. In fact, when observing a scene containing plants, animals, and man-made objects such as cars or street signs, we can only tell when left and right have been inverted if we observe those artificial items.

♦axis: 축

⬇

Having affected the evolution of our ___(A)___ perception, vertical and front/back dimensions are easily perceived, but the left-right axis, which is not ___(B)___ in nature, doesn't come instantly to us.

(A)		(B)
① spatial	……	significant
② spatial	……	scarce
③ auditory	……	different
④ cultural	……	accessible
⑤ cultural	……	desirable

정답과 해설 : 07299 08300

09 ⏱ 120초

★★☆ 2023년 6월 40번

다음 글의 내용을 한 문장으로 요약하고자 한다. 빈칸 (A)와 (B)에 들어갈 말로 가장 적절한 것은?

People behave in highly predictable ways when they experience certain thoughts. When they agree, they nod their heads. So far, no surprise, but according to an area of research known as "proprioceptive psychology," the process also works in reverse. Get people to behave in a certain way and you cause them to have certain thoughts. The idea was initially controversial, but fortunately it was supported by a compelling experiment. Participants in a study were asked to fixate on various products moving across a large computer screen and then indicate whether the items appealed to them. Some of the items moved vertically (causing the participants to nod their heads while watching), and others moved horizontally (resulting in a side-to-side head movement). Participants preferred vertically moving products without being aware that their "yes" and "no" head movements had played a key role in their decisions.

⬇

In one study, participants responded ___(A)___ to products on a computer screen when they moved their heads up and down, which showed that their decisions were unconsciously influenced by their ___(B)___.

	(A)		(B)
①	favorably	……	behavior
②	favorably	……	instinct
③	unfavorably	……	feeling
④	unfavorably	……	gesture
⑤	irrationally	……	prejudice

10 ⏱ 130초

★★★ 2020년 11월 40번

다음 글의 내용을 한 문장으로 요약하고자 한다. 빈칸 (A)와 (B)에 들어갈 말로 가장 적절한 것은?

In 2011, Micah Edelson and his colleagues conducted an interesting experiment about external factors of memory manipulation. In their experiment, participants were shown a two minute documentary film and then asked a series of questions about the video. Directly after viewing the videos, participants made few errors in their responses and were correctly able to recall the details. Four days later, they could still remember the details and didn't allow their memories to be swayed when they were presented with any false information about the film. This changed, however, when participants were shown fake responses about the film made by other participants. Upon seeing the incorrect answers of others, participants were also drawn toward the wrong answers themselves. Even after they found out that the other answers had been fabricated and didn't have anything to do with the documentary, it was too late. The participants were no longer able to distinguish between truth and fiction. They had already modified their memories to fit the group.

⬇

According to the experiment, when participants were given false information itself, their memories remained ___(A)___, but their memories were ___(B)___ when they were exposed to other participants' fake responses.

	(A)		(B)
①	stable	……	falsified
②	fragile	……	modified
③	stable	……	intensified
④	fragile	……	solidified
⑤	concrete	……	maintained

11 ⏱ 130초

★★★ 2020년 9월 40번

다음 글의 내용을 한 문장으로 요약하고자 한다. 빈칸 (A)와 (B)에 들어갈 말로 가장 적절한 것은?

Some researchers at Sheffield University recruited 129 hobbyists to look at how the time spent on their hobbies shaped their work life. To begin with, the team measured the seriousness of each participant's hobby, asking them to rate their agreement with statements like "I regularly train for this activity," and also assessed how similar the demands of their job and hobby were. Then, each month for seven months, participants recorded how many hours they had dedicated to their activity, and completed a scale measuring their belief in their ability to effectively do their job, or their "self-efficacy." The researchers found that when participants spent longer than normal doing their leisure activity, their belief in their ability to perform their job increased. But this was only the case when they had a serious hobby that was dissimilar to their job. When their hobby was both serious and similar to their job, then spending more time on it actually decreased their self-efficacy.

⬇

Research suggests that spending more time on serious hobbies can boost ____(A)____ at work if the hobbies and the job are sufficiently ____(B)____.

	(A)		(B)
①	confidence	……	different
②	productivity	……	connected
③	relationships	……	balanced
④	creativity	……	separate
⑤	dedication	……	similar

12 ⏱ 130초

★★★ 2019년 9월 40번

다음 글의 내용을 한 문장으로 요약하고자 한다. 빈칸 (A)와 (B)에 들어갈 말로 가장 적절한 것은?

When we see an adorable creature, we must fight an overwhelming urge to squeeze that cuteness. And pinch it, and cuddle it, and maybe even bite it. This is a perfectly normal psychological tick — an oxymoron called "cute aggression" — and even though it sounds cruel, it's not about causing harm at all. In fact, strangely enough, this compulsion may actually make us more caring. The first study to look at cute aggression in the human brain has now revealed that this is a complex neurological response, involving several parts of the brain. The researchers propose that cute aggression may stop us from becoming so emotionally overloaded that we are unable to look after things that are super cute. "Cute aggression may serve as a tempering mechanism that allows us to function and actually take care of something we might first perceive as overwhelmingly cute," explains the lead author, Stavropoulos.

♦ oxymoron: 모순 어법

⬇

According to research, cute aggression may act as a neurological response to ____(A)____ excessive emotions and make us ____(B)____ for cute creatures.

	(A)		(B)
①	evaluate	……	care
②	regulate	……	care
③	accept	……	search
④	induce	……	search
⑤	display	……	speak

정답과 해설 : 11 303 12 304

13 ⓒ 130초

★★★
2023년 9월 40번

다음 글의 내용을 한 문장으로 요약하고자 한다. 빈칸 (A)와 (B)에 들어갈 말로 가장 적절한 것은?

In 2006, researchers conducted a study on the motivations for helping after the September 11th terrorist attacks against the United States. In the study, they found that individuals who gave money, blood, goods, or other forms of assistance because of other-focused motives (giving to reduce another's discomfort) were almost four times more likely to still be giving support one year later than those whose original motivation was to reduce personal distress. This effect likely stems from differences in emotional arousal. The events of September 11th emotionally affected people throughout the United States. Those who gave to reduce their own distress reduced their emotional arousal with their initial gift, discharging that emotional distress. However, those who gave to reduce others' distress did not stop empathizing with victims who continued to struggle long after the attacks.

♦ distress: (정신적) 고통 ♦♦ arousal: 자극

⬇

A study found that the act of giving was less likely to be ___(A)___ when driven by self-centered motives rather than by other-focused motives, possibly because of the ___(B)___ in emotional arousal.

(A)		(B)
① sustained	……	decline
② sustained	……	maximization
③ indirect	……	variation
④ discouraged	……	reduction
⑤ discouraged	……	increase

14 ⓒ 130초

★★★
2022년 3월 40번

다음 글의 내용을 한 문장으로 요약하고자 한다. 빈칸 (A)와 (B)에 들어갈 말로 가장 적절한 것은?

Distance is a reliable indicator of the relationship between two people. Strangers stand further apart than do acquaintances, acquaintances stand further apart than friends, and friends stand further apart than romantic partners. Sometimes, of course, these rules are violated. Recall the last time you rode 20 stories in an elevator packed with total strangers. The sardine-like experience no doubt made the situation a bit uncomfortable. With your physical space violated, you may have tried to create "psychological" space by avoiding eye contact, focusing instead on the elevator buttons. By reducing closeness in one nonverbal channel (eye contact), one can compensate for unwanted closeness in another channel (proximity). Similarly, if you are talking with someone who is seated several feet away at a large table, you are likely to maintain constant eye contact — something you might feel uncomfortable doing if you were standing next to each other.

♦ sardine-like: 승객이 빽빽이 들어찬 ♦♦ proximity: 근접성

⬇

Physical distance between people is ___(A)___ by relationship status, but when the distance is not appropriate, people ___(B)___ their nonverbal communication to establish a comfortable psychological distance.

(A)		(B)
① determined	……	adjust
② concealed	……	interpret
③ influenced	……	ignore
④ predicted	……	stop
⑤ measured	……	decrease

DAY 24 16 문단 요약

정답과 해설 : 13 305 14 306

15 ⓒ 130초

★★★ 2022년 11월 40번

다음 글의 내용을 한 문장으로 요약하고자 한다. 빈칸 (A)와 (B)에 들어갈 말로 가장 적절한 것은? 3점

A study investigated the economic cost of prejudice based on blind assumptions. Researchers gave a group of Danish teenagers the choice of working with one of two people. The teenager had never met either of them. One of the people had a name that suggested they were from a similar ethnic or religious background to the teenager. The other had a name that suggested they were from a different ethnic or religious background. The study showed that the teenagers were prepared to earn an average of 8% less if they could work with someone they thought came from the same ethnic or religious background. And this prejudice was evident among teenagers with ethnic majority names as well as those with ethnic minority names. The teenagers were blindly making assumptions about the race of their potential colleagues. They then applied prejudice to those assumptions, to the point where they actually allowed that prejudice to reduce *their own* potential income. The job required the two teenagers to work together for just *90 minutes*.

⬇

A study in which teenagers expressed a(n) ___(A)___ to work with someone of a similar background, even at a financial cost to themselves, suggests that an assumption-based prejudice can ___(B)___ rational economic behavior.

(A)		(B)
① preference	……	outweigh
② hesitation	……	reinforce
③ preference	……	strengthen
④ hesitation	……	overwhelm
⑤ inability	……	underlie

16 ⓒ 130초 최고오답률

★★★ 2021년 3월 40번

다음 글의 내용을 한 문장으로 요약하고자 한다. 빈칸 (A)와 (B)에 들어갈 말로 가장 적절한 것은?

At the University of Iowa, students were briefly shown numbers that they had to memorize. Then they were offered the choice of either a fruit salad or a chocolate cake. When the number the students memorized was seven digits long, 63% of them chose the cake. When the number they were asked to remember had just two digits, however, 59% opted for the fruit salad. Our reflective brains know that the fruit salad is better for our health, but our reflexive brains desire that soft, fattening chocolate cake. If the reflective brain is busy figuring something else out — like trying to remember a seven-digit number — then impulse can easily win. On the other hand, if we're not thinking too hard about something else (with only a minor distraction like memorizing two digits), then the reflective system can deny the emotional impulse of the reflexive side.

♦ reflective: 숙고하는 ♦♦ reflexive: 반사적인

⬇

According to the above experiment, the ___(A)___ intellective load on the brain leads the reflexive side of the brain to become ___(B)___.

(A)		(B)
① limited	……	powerful
② limited	……	divided
③ varied	……	passive
④ increased	……	dominant
⑤ increased	……	weakened

정답과 해설 : 15 307 16 308

17 ⏱ 120초

★★☆ 2023년 11월 40번

다음 글의 내용을 한 문장으로 요약하고자 한다. 빈칸 (A)와 (B)에 들어갈 말로 가장 적절한 것은?

Multiple laboratory studies show that cooperative people tend to receive social advantages from others. One way to demonstrate this is to give people the opportunity to act positively or negatively toward contributors. For example, Pat Barclay, a professor at the University of Guelph, had participants play a cooperative game where people could contribute money toward a group fund which helped all group members, and then allowed participants to give money to other participants based on their reputations. People who contributed more to the group fund were given responsibility for more money than people who contributed less. Similar results have been found by other researchers. People who contribute toward their groups are also chosen more often as interaction partners, preferred as leaders, rated as more desirable partners for long-term relationships, and are perceived to be trustworthy and have high social status. Uncooperative people tend to receive verbal criticism or even more severe punishment.

⬇

Studies suggest that individuals who act with ___(A)___ toward their communities are more likely to be viewed as deserving of ___(B)___ by members of that community than those who don't.

(A)		(B)
① generosity	……	benefit
② hostility	……	support
③ generosity	……	humiliation
④ hostility	……	hospitality
⑤ tolerance	……	dishonor

18 ⏱ 130초

★★★ 2024년 3월 40번

다음 글의 내용을 한 문장으로 요약하고자 한다. 빈칸 (A)와 (B)에 들어갈 말로 가장 적절한 것은?

The fast-growing, tremendous amount of data, collected and stored in large and numerous data repositories, has far exceeded our human ability for understanding without powerful tools. As a result, data collected in large data repositories become "data tombs" — data archives that are hardly visited. Important decisions are often made based not on the information-rich data stored in data repositories but rather on a decision maker's instinct, simply because the decision maker does not have the tools to extract the valuable knowledge hidden in the vast amounts of data. Efforts have been made to develop expert system and knowledge-based technologies, which typically rely on users or domain experts to *manually* input knowledge into knowledge bases. However, this procedure is likely to cause biases and errors and is extremely costly and time consuming. The widening gap between data and information calls for the systematic development of tools that can turn data tombs into "golden nuggets" of knowledge.

♦ repository: 저장소 ♦♦ golden nugget: 금괴

⬇

As the vast amounts of data stored in repositories ___(A)___ human understanding, effective tools to ___(B)___ valuable knowledge are required for better decision-making.

(A)		(B)
① overwhelm	……	obtain
② overwhelm	……	exchange
③ enhance	……	apply
④ enhance	……	discover
⑤ fulfill	……	access

DAY 25 16 문단 요약

정답과 해설 : 17 309 18 310

19 ⏱ 130초

★★★ 2024년 6월 40번

다음 글의 내용을 한 문장으로 요약하고자 한다. 빈칸 (A)와 (B)에 들어갈 말로 가장 적절한 것은?

Many things spark *envy*: ownership, status, health, youth, talent, popularity, beauty. It is often confused with jealousy because the physical reactions are identical. The difference: the subject of *envy* is a thing (status, money, health etc.). The subject of jealousy is the behaviour of a third person. *Envy* needs two people. Jealousy, on the other hand, requires three: Peter is jealous of Sam because the beautiful girl next door rings him instead. Paradoxically, with envy we direct resentments toward those who are most similar to us in age, career and residence. We don't envy businesspeople from the century before last. We don't envy millionaires on the other side of the globe. As a writer, I don't envy musicians, managers or dentists, but other writers. As a CEO you envy other, bigger CEOs. As a supermodel you envy more successful supermodels. Aristotle knew this: 'Potters envy potters.'

⬇

Jealousy involves three parties, focusing on the ____(A)____ of a third person, whereas envy involves two individuals whose personal circumstances are most ____(B)____, with one person resenting the other.

(A)		(B)
① actions	······	different
② possessions	······	unique
③ goals	······	ordinary
④ possessions	······	favorable
⑤ actions	······	alike

20 ⏱ 120초

★★☆ 2024년 9월 40번

다음 글의 내용을 한 문장으로 요약하고자 한다. 빈칸 (A)와 (B)에 들어갈 말로 가장 적절한 것은?

The concern about how we appear to others can be seen in children, though work by the psychologist Ervin Staub suggests that the effect may vary with age. In a study where children heard another child in distress, young children (kindergarten through second grade) were more likely to help the child in distress when with another child than when alone. But for older children — in fourth and sixth grade — the effect reversed: they were less likely to help a child in distress when they were with a peer than when they were alone. Staub suggested that younger children might feel more comfortable acting when they have the company of a peer, whereas older children might feel more concern about being judged by their peers and fear feeling embarrassed by overreacting. Staub noted that "older children seemed to discuss the distress sounds less and to react to them less openly than younger children." In other words, the older children were deliberately putting on a poker face in front of their peers.

⬇

The study suggests that, contrary to younger children, older children are less likely to help those in distress in the ____(A)____ of others because they care more about how they are ____(B)____.

(A)		(B)
① presence	······	evaluated
② presence	······	motivated
③ absence	······	viewed
④ absence	······	assisted
⑤ audience	······	trained

정답과 해설 : 19 311 20 312

유형 TIP

17. 장문의 이해-단일지문

긴 글을 읽고, 제목 추론이나 빈칸 추론, 어휘 추론 문제 중 두 문제가 출제됨.
지문의 길이가 길어졌으므로, 그에 상응하는 종합적인 사고력과 빠른 독해력이 요구됨.

유형 TIP 25BR2T_CH17 대표 예제 25BR2E_CH17

유형 공략법

1) 지문을 읽기 전에 문제부터 확인한다.

어떤 부분에 초점을 맞추어 읽어야 하는지, 지문에서 어떤 정보를 파악해야 하는지를 먼저 알고 있어야 함.

2) 앞에서 연습했던 문제 풀이를 각 문제에 적용하여 문제를 해결한다.

유형이 다르면 접근 방식도 달라져야 하는 만큼 충분한 연습이 필요함. 최근 41번은 제목 추론, 42번은 어휘 추론 유형으로 출제되고 있음.

① 제목 추론

반복되는 내용과 주제의 위치를 보여 주는 표현에 주목하여 주제를 파악한다.
선택지의 비유적이고 함축적인 표현에 주의한다.
지나치게 포괄적이거나 지엽적인 선택지에 주의한다.

② 어휘 추론

앞뒤 맥락을 살펴보고 해당 어휘가 적절한지 판단한다.
반의어 관계에 있는 단어들을 알아 두는 것이 도움이 된다.

필수 암기 어휘와 표현

기출 및 필수 암기 반의어

형용사/부사	above 위에 – below 아래에, abstract 추상적인 – obvious 분명한, ample 풍부한 – scanty 빈약한, backward 뒤의 – forward 앞의, blunt/dull 무딘 – keen/sharp 날카로운, careless 부주의한 – careful 조심하는, close 가까운 – distant 먼, coarse 거친 – fine 고운, complete/full 완전한 – incomplete 불완전한, complex 복잡한 – simple 간단한, constant 변함없는 – variable 변하기 쉬운, crooked/curved 구부러진 – straight 곧은, crucial/critical 중대한 – secondary/minor 부차적인, deep 깊은 – shallow 얕은, different 다른 – similar 비슷한/identical 동일한, easy 쉬운 – hard/difficult 어려운, external 외부의 – internal 내부의, finite 한정된 – infinite 무한한, flexible/fluid 융통성 있는 – inflexible/rigid 융통성 없는, imprecise 부정확한 – precise 정확한, invalid/void 무효의 – valid 유효한, gradual 점진적인 – dramatic 극적인, limited 제한된 – unlimited 무제한의, minimum 아주 적은·최소의 – maximum 최대한의/massive 대량의, natural 자연의·자연스러운 – artificial 인공의·인위적인, objective 객관적인 – subjective 주관적인, perfect 완벽한 – imperfect 불완전한, plentiful/abundant 풍부한 – scarce 부족한, positive 긍정적인 – negative 부정적인, promising 유망한 – unpromising 가망 없는, proper/appropriate 적절한 – improper/inappropriate 적절하지 않은, random 무작위의 – systematical 체계적, slight 약간의 – huge 막대한, static 정적인 – dynamic 역동적인, unfamiliar 낯선·잘 모르는 – familiar 익숙한·잘 아는, upward 상향하는 – downward 하향하는, useful 유용한 – useless 쓸모없는, willing 기꺼이 하는 – reluctant 마지못해 하는, vague 모호한 – distinct 뚜렷한
동사	accelerate 가속화하다 – slow down 속도를 줄이다, accept 받아들이다 – reject 거부하다/avoid 피하다, add 더하다 – subtract 빼다, ascend 올라가다 – descend 내려가다, assert 주장하다 – deny 부인하다, attach 붙이다 – detach 떼다, bend 굽히다 – straighten 똑바르게 하다, block 막다 – help 돕다, conceal 감추다 – reveal 드러내다, decrease 감소하다 – increase 증가하다, degrade 저하시키다 – upgrade/improve 개선하다, disappoint 실망시키다 – satisfy 만족시키다, disregard/ignore 무시하다 – respect 존중하다, enhance 향상시키다 – limit 제한하다, exclude 배제하다 – include 포함하다, exhaust 고갈시키다 – conserve 보존하다, extend 넓히다 – reduce 줄이다, integrate 통합하다 – separate 분리하다, oppose 반대하다 – support 지지하다, promote 촉진하다 – disrupt 방해하다, raise 올리다 – lower 내리다, relieve 완화하다 – compound 악화시키다, start 시작하다 – stop 멈추다
명사	bottom 맨 아래 – top 맨 위, consistency 일관성 – inconsistency 일관성 없음·모순, discord 불화 – harmony 조화, elimination 제거 – accumulation 축적, immobility 부동성 – mobility 유동성·이동성, lack 부족 – sufficiency 충분, part 부분 – whole 전체, uncertainty 불확실성 – certainty 확실성, uniformity 획일성 – variety 다양성

DAY 25 17 장문의 이해 – 단일지문

장문의 이해-단일지문 대표 예제 - 2024학년도 수능 41~42번

다음 글을 읽고, 물음에 답하시오.

(1) One way to avoid contributing to overhyping a story would be to say nothing. (2) However, that is not a realistic option for scientists who feel a strong sense of responsibility to inform the public and policymakers and/or to offer suggestions. (3) Speaking with members of the media has **(a)** advantages in getting a message out and perhaps receiving favorable recognition, but it runs the risk of misinterpretations, the need for repeated clarifications, and entanglement in never-ending controversy. (4) Hence, the decision of whether to speak with the media tends to be highly individualized. (5) Decades ago, it was **(b)** unusual for Earth scientists to have results that were of interest to the media, and consequently few media contacts were expected or encouraged. (6) In the 1970s, the few scientists who spoke frequently with the media were often **(c)** criticized by their fellow scientists for having done so. (7) The situation now is quite different, as many scientists feel a responsibility to speak out because of the importance of global warming and related issues, and many reporters share these feelings. (8) In addition, many scientists are finding that they **(d)** enjoy the media attention and the public recognition that comes with it. (9) At the same time, other scientists continue to resist speaking with reporters, thereby preserving more time for their science and **(e)** running the risk of being misquoted and the other unpleasantries associated with media coverage.

* overhype: 과대광고하다 ** entanglement: 얽힘

41. 윗글의 제목으로 가장 적절한 것은?

① The Troubling Relationship Between Scientists and the Media
✔ A Scientist's Choice: To Be Exposed to the Media or Not?
③ Scientists! Be Cautious When Talking to the Media
④ The Dilemma over Scientific Truth and Media Attention
⑤ Who Are Responsible for Climate Issues, Scientists or the Media?

42. 밑줄 친 (a) ~ (e) 중에서 문맥상 낱말의 쓰임이 적절하지 않은 것은?

① (a) ② (b) ③ (c) ④ (d) ✔ (e)

STEP 1 제목 추론

1) 반복되는 내용과 주제의 위치를 보여 주는 표현에 주목하여 주제를 파악한다.

→ 문장 (1)에서 과대광고에 기여하는 것을 피하는 방법은 아무 말도 하지 않는 것이라고 했지만, 문장 (2)는 현실적으로 과학자들이 많은 사람들을 대상으로 말을 하지 않을 수 없다는 것을 언급함. 문장 (3)은 과학자가 매체와 대화하는 것은 성과를 인정받는 등의 장점도 있지만 논쟁에 얽힐 위험성 등의 단점도 있다는 것을 지적함. 문장 (4)에서는 매체와 대화 여부는 개인화되어 있음을 밝힘.

2) 지나치게 포괄적이거나 지엽적인 선택지에 주의한다.

①: 글의 내용은 과학자가 매체에 노출되는 것과 관련되어 있지만 과학자와 매체 사이의 불편한 관계를 설명하지는 않음.

③: 매체에 이야기할 때 과학자가 가져야 할 태도만 이야기하는 것은 전체적인 내용을 아우르지 못하는 지엽적인 선택지임.

④: 글의 내용은 매체의 관심을 얻기 위해 과학적 진실을 은폐하거나 조작하는 데에서 오는 딜레마와는 무관함.

⑤: 기후 문제는 매체와 접촉하는 과학자들의 예시로 글에서 언급되었을 뿐이므로, 지엽적인 선택지임.

STEP 2 어휘 추론

1) 앞뒤 맥락을 살펴보고 해당 어휘가 적절한지 판단한다.

(a): 문장 (3)에서 매체를 통해 과학자가 메시지를 알리고 인정을 받는다는 내용은 매체 접촉으로 과학자가 얻는 '이점(advantages)'에 해당함.

(b): 수십 년 전에는 매체 접촉이 거의 기대되지 않았으므로, 과학자가 매체에게 흥미로운 결과물을 갖는 것은 '드문(unusual)' 일임.

(c): 문장 (5)에 따르면 매체 접촉은 장려되지 않았으므로, 매체와 자주 이야기한 과학자는 동료들에게 '비난을 받았음(criticized)'을 추론할 수 있음.

(d): 문장 (7)에서 현재는 이전과는 다르게 과학자가 공개적으로 발언해야 한다고 언급했으므로, 이제는 매체에 접촉하는 것과 그로 인한 대중의 관심을 '즐긴다(enjoy)'는 것이 적절함.

(e): 문장 (3)에서 언급한 대로, 매체 접촉은 장점도 있지만 계속 해명해야 하고 오해를 불러일으킬 수 있다는 단점도 있음. 따라서 매체 보도와 관련된 불쾌한 일을 겪을 위험을 '감수하는(running)' 것이 아니라 '피하고자(avoiding)' 매체 접촉을 꺼려하는 과학자들도 있다고 해야 적절함.

전문 해석

(1) 이야기를 과대광고하는 데 기여하는 것을 피하는 한 가지 방법은 아무 말도 하지 않는 것이다. (2) 그러나 그것은 대중과 정책 담당자에게 알리고(알리거나) 제안을 제공해야 한다는 강한 책임감을 느끼는 과학자들에게 현실적인 선택지가 아니다. (3) 매체 구성원들과 이야기하는 것은 메시지를 알리고 어쩌면 우호적인 인정을 받는 것에서 (a)이점을 가지지만 그것은 오해, 반복적인 해명의 필요 그리고 끝나지 않는 논쟁에 얽힘의 위험이 있다. (4) 이런 이유로 매체와 이야기할지에 대한 결정은 매우 개인화된 경향이 있다. (5) 수십 년 전, 지구 과학자들이 매체에게 흥미로운 결과를 가지는 것은 (b)드물었고 결과적으로 매체 접촉은 거의 기대되거나 장려되지 않았다. (6) 1970년대에, 매체와 자주 이야기했던 극소수의 과학자들은 그렇게 했다는 이유로 자신들의 동료 과학자들에게 종종 (c)비난을 받았다. (7) 현재의 상황은 꽤 다른데, 지구 온난화 및 관련 문제들의 중요성으로 인해 많은 과학자들이 공개적으로 말해야 한다는 책임감을 느끼며, 많은 기자들이 이러한 느낌을 공유하기 때문이다. (8) 게다가, 많은 과학자들은 자신들이 매체 관심과 그에 따라오는 대중의 인정을 (d)즐긴다는 것을 발견하고 있다. (9) 동시에, 다른 과학자들은 기자들과 이야기하기를 계속해서 거부하는데, 그렇게 함으로써 자신들의 과학을 위한 더 많은 시간을 지키고 잘못 인용될 위험과 매체 보도와 관련된 다른 불쾌한 사건들을 (e)감수한다(→ 피한다).

중요 어휘

- □ overhype 동 과대광고하다
- □ realistic 형 현실적인
- □ option 명 선택지
- □ inform 동 알리다
- □ policymaker 명 정책 담당자[입안자]
- □ media 명 매체 (medium의 복수형)
- □ favorable 형 우호적인
- □ recognition 명 인정, 인식
- □ run the risk (of) (~의) 위험이 있다, 위험을 감수하다
- □ misinterpretation 명 오해
- □ clarification 명 해명, 설명
- □ entanglement 명 얽힘, 복잡한 관계
- □ controversy 명 논쟁, 논란
- □ hence 부 이런 이유로, 그러므로
- □ highly 부 매우, 몹시
- □ individualize 동 개인화하다, 개별화하다
- □ consequently 부 결과적으로
- □ criticize 동 비난하다, 비판하다
- □ fellow 명 동료
- □ speak out 공개적으로 말하다
- □ thereby 부 그렇게 함으로써
- □ preserve 동 지키다, 보존하다
- □ misquote 동 잘못 인용하다
- □ unpleasantry 명 불쾌한 사건
- □ associate 동 관련시키다, 연관 짓다, 연상하다
- □ coverage 명 보도

자세한 해설지 QR→
자세한해설-CH17

17 장문의 이해-단일지문

동영상 강의

25BR2_CH17

01~02 : 230초

[01~02] 다음 글을 읽고, 물음에 답하시오.

In this day and age, it is difficult to imagine our lives without email. But how often do we consider the environmental impact of these virtual messages? At first glance, digital messages appear to **(a)** save resources. Unlike traditional letters, no paper or stamps are needed; nothing has to be packaged or transported. Many of us tend to assume that using email requires little more than the electricity used to power our computers. It's easy to **(b)** overlook the invisible energy usage involved in running the network — particularly when it comes to sending and storing data.

Every single email in every single inbox in the world is stored on a server. The incredible quantity of data requires huge server farms — gigantic centres with millions of computers which store and transmit information. These servers consume **(c)** minimum amounts of energy, 24 hours a day, and require countless litres of water, or air conditioning systems, for cooling. The more messages we send, receive and store, the **(d)** more servers are needed — which means more energy consumed, and more carbon emissions. Clearly, sending and receiving electronic messages in an environmentally conscious manner is by no means enough to stop climate change. But with a few careful, mindful changes, **(e)** unnecessary CO_2 emissions can easily be avoided.

01

★☆☆ 2021년 9월 41번

윗글의 제목으로 가장 적절한 것은?

① Recycling Makes Your Life Even Better
② Eco-friendly Use of Email Saves the Earth
③ Traditional Letters: The Bridge Between Us
④ Email Servers: Records of Past and Present
⑤ Technicians Looking for Alternative Energy

02

★☆☆ 2021년 9월 42번

밑줄 친 (a) ~ (e) 중에서 문맥상 낱말의 쓰임이 적절하지 않은 것은?

① (a) ② (b) ③ (c) ④ (d) ⑤ (e)

정답과 해설 : 01~02 313

ⓘ 03~04 : 240초

[03~04] 다음 글을 읽고, 물음에 답하시오.

Paralysis by analysis is a state of overthinking and analyzing a particular problem, but you still end up not making a decision. One famous ancient fable of the fox and the cat explains this situation of paralysis by analysis in the simplest way. In the story, the fox and the cat discuss how many ways they have to escape their hunters. Cat quickly climbs a tree. Fox, on the other hand, begins to analyze all the ways to escape that he knows. But unable to decide which one would be the best, he **(a)** fails to act and gets caught by the dogs. This story perfectly illustrates the analysis paralysis phenomenon: the **(b)** inability to act or decide due to overthinking about available alternatives. People experience that although they start with a good intention to find a solution to a problem, they often analyze indefinitely about various factors that might lead to wrong decisions. They don't feel satisfied with the available information and think they still need **(c)** more data to perfect their decision. Most often this situation of paralysis by analysis **(d)** arises when somebody is afraid of making an erroneous decision that can lead to potential catastrophic consequences: it might impact their careers or their organizations' productivity. So that's why people are generally **(e)** confident in making decisions that involve huge stakes.

♦ paralysis: 마비 ♦♦ stakes: (계획 · 행동 등의 성공 여부에) 걸려 있는 것

03

★★☆
2021년 6월 41번

윗글의 제목으로 가장 적절한 것은?

① Best Ways to Keep You from Overthinking
② Overthinking or Overdoing: Which Is Worse?
③ Costs and Benefits of Having Various Alternatives
④ Overthinking: A Barrier to Effective Decision-making
⑤ Trapped in Moral Dilemma: Harmful for Your Survival

04

★★☆
2021년 6월 42번

밑줄 친 (a) ~ (e) 중에서 문맥상 낱말의 쓰임이 적절하지 않은 것은? [3점]

① (a) ② (b) ③ (c) ④ (d) ⑤ (e)

정답과 해설 : 03~04 314

05~06 : 240초

[05~06] 다음 글을 읽고, 물음에 답하시오.

Evolutionary biologists believe sociability drove the evolution of our complex brains. Fossil evidence shows that as far back as 130,000 years ago, it was not **(a)** unusual for *Homo sapiens* to travel more than a hundred and fifty miles to trade, share food and, no doubt, gossip. Unlike the Neanderthals, their social groups extended far beyond their own families. Remembering all those **(b)** connections, who was related to whom, and where they lived required considerable processing power.

It also required wayfinding savvy. Imagine trying to **(c)** maintain a social network across tens or hundreds of square miles of Palaeolithic wilderness. You couldn't send a text message to your friends to find out where they were — you had to go out and visit them, remember where you last saw them or imagine where they might have gone. To do this, you needed navigation skills, spatial awareness, a sense of direction, the ability to store maps of the landscape in your mind and the motivation to travel around. Canadian anthropologist Ariane Burke believes that our ancestors **(d)** developed all these attributes while trying to keep in touch with their neighbours. Eventually, our brains became primed for wayfinding. Meanwhile the Neanderthals, who didn't travel as far, never fostered a spatial skill set; despite being sophisticated hunters, well adapted to the cold and able to see in the dark, they went extinct. In the prehistoric badlands, nothing was more **(e)** useless than a circle of friends.

◆ savvy: 요령, 지식 ◆◆ Palaeolithic: 구석기 시대의

05

★★☆ 2020년 11월 41번

윗글의 제목으로 가장 적절한 것은?

① Social Networks: An Evolutionary Advantage
② Our Brain Forced Us to Stay Close to Our Family!
③ How We Split from Our Way and Kept Going on My Way
④ Why Do Some People Have Difficulty in Social Relationships?
⑤ Being Connected to Each Other Leads to Communicative Skills

06

★★☆ 2020년 11월 42번

밑줄 친 (a) ~ (e) 중에서 문맥상 낱말의 쓰임이 적절하지 않은 것은? 3점

① (a) ② (b) ③ (c) ④ (d) ⑤ (e)

정답과 해설 : 05~06 315

⏱ 07~08 : 240초

[07~08] 다음 글을 읽고, 물음에 답하시오.

Events or experiences that are out of ordinary tend to be remembered better because there is nothing competing with them when your brain tries to access them from its storehouse of remembered events. In other words, the reason it can be **(a)** difficult to remember what you ate for breakfast two Thursdays ago is that there was probably nothing special about that Thursday or that particular breakfast — consequently, all your breakfast memories combine together into a sort of generic impression of a breakfast. Your memory **(b)** merges similar events not only because it's more efficient to do so, but also because this is fundamental to how we learn things — our brains extract abstract rules that tie experiences together.

This is especially true for things that are **(c)** routine. If your breakfast is always the same — cereal with milk, a glass of orange juice, and a cup of coffee for instance — there is no easy way for your brain to extract the details from one particular breakfast. Ironically, then, for behaviors that are routinized, you can remember the generic content of the behavior (such as the things you ate, since you always eat the same thing), but **(d)** particulars to that one instance can be very difficult to call up (such as the sound of a garbage truck going by or a bird that passed by your window) *unless* they were especially distinctive. On the other hand, if you did something unique that broke your routine — perhaps you had leftover pizza for breakfast and spilled tomato sauce on your dress shirt — you are **(e)** less likely to remember it.

07

★★★
2023년 6월 41번

윗글의 제목으로 가장 적절한 것은?

① Repetition Makes Your Memory Sharp!
② How Does Your Memory Get Distorted?
③ What to Consider in Routinizing Your Work
④ Merging Experiences: Key to Remembering Details
⑤ The More Unique Events, the More Vivid Recollection

08

★★☆
2023년 6월 42번

밑줄 친 (a) ~ (e) 중에서 문맥상 낱말의 쓰임이 적절하지 않은 것은?

① (a) ② (b) ③ (c) ④ (d) ⑤ (e)

정답과 해설 : 07~08 316

Ⓛ 09~10 : 240초

[09~10] 다음 글을 읽고, 물음에 답하시오.

U.S. commercial aviation has long had an extremely effective system for encouraging pilots to submit reports of errors. The program has resulted in numerous improvements to aviation safety. It wasn't easy to establish: pilots had severe self-induced social pressures against **(a)** admitting to errors. Moreover, to whom would they report them? Certainly not to their employers. Not even to the Federal Aviation Authority (FAA), for then they would probably be punished. The solution was to let the National Aeronautics and Space Administration (NASA) set up a **(b)** voluntary accident reporting system whereby pilots could submit semi-anonymous reports of errors they had made or observed in others.

Once NASA personnel had acquired the necessary information, they would **(c)** detach the contact information from the report and mail it back to the pilot. This meant that NASA no longer knew who had reported the error, which made it impossible for the airline companies or the FAA (which enforced penalties against errors) to find out who had **(d)** rejected the report. If the FAA had independently noticed the error and tried to invoke a civil penalty or certificate suspension, the receipt of self-report automatically exempted the pilot from punishment. When a sufficient number of similar errors had been collected, NASA would analyze them and issue reports and recommendations to the airlines and to the FAA. These reports also helped the pilots realize that their error reports were **(e)** valuable tools for increasing safety.

09

★★☆
2020년 9월 41번

윗글의 제목으로 가장 적절한 것은?

① Aviation Safety Built on Anonymous Reports
② More Flexible Manuals Mean Ignored Safety
③ Great Inventions from Unexpected Mistakes
④ Controversies over New Safety Regulations
⑤ Who Is Innovating Technology in the Air?

10

★★★
2020년 9월 42번

밑줄 친 (a) ~ (e) 중에서 문맥상 낱말의 쓰임이 적절하지 않은 것은? [3점]

① (a) ② (b) ③ (c) ④ (d) ⑤ (e)

정답과 해설 : 09~10 317

⏲ 11~12 : 240초

[11~12] 다음 글을 읽고, 물음에 답하시오.

In England in the 1680s, it was unusual to live to the age of fifty. This was a period when knowledge was not spread **(a)** widely, there were few books and most people could not read. As a consequence, knowledge passed down through the oral traditions of stories and shared experiences. And since older people had accumulated more knowledge, the social norm was that to be over fifty was to be wise. This social perception of age began to shift with the advent of new technologies such as the printing press. Over time, as more books were printed, literacy **(b)** increased, and the oral traditions of knowledge transfer began to fade. With the fading of oral traditions, the wisdom of the old became less important and as a consequence being over fifty was no longer seen as **(c)** signifying wisdom.

We are living in a period when the gap between chronological and biological age is changing fast and where social norms are struggling to **(d)** adapt. In a video produced by the AARP (formerly the American Association of Retired Persons), young people were asked to do various activities 'just like an old person'. When older people joined them in the video, the gap between the stereotype and the older people's actual behaviour was **(e)** unnoticeable. It is clear that in today's world our social norms need to be updated quickly.

11

★★☆
2023년 9월 41번

윗글의 제목으로 가장 적절한 것은?

① Our Social Norms on Aging: An Ongoing Evolution
② The Power of Oral Tradition in the Modern World
③ Generational Differences: Not As Big As You Think
④ There's More to Aging than What the Media Shows
⑤ How Well You Age Depends on Your Views of Aging

12

★★☆
2023년 9월 42번

밑줄 친 (a) ~ (e) 중에서 문맥상 낱말의 쓰임이 적절하지 않은 것은? [3점]

① (a) ② (b) ③ (c) ④ (d) ⑤ (e)

정답과 해설 : 11~12 318

13~14 : 250초

[13~14] 다음 글을 읽고, 물음에 답하시오.

We're creatures who live and die by the energy stores we've built up in our bodies. Navigating the world is a difficult job that requires moving around and using a lot of brainpower — an energy-expensive endeavor. When we make correct **(a)** predictions, that saves energy. When you know that edible bugs can be found beneath certain types of rocks, it saves turning over *all* the rocks. The better we predict, the less energy it costs us. Repetition makes us more confident in our forecasts and more efficient in our actions. So there's something **(b)** appealing about predictability.

But if our brains are going to all this effort to make the world predictable, that begs the question: if we love predictability so much, why don't we, for example, just replace our televisions with machines that emit a rhythmic beep twenty-four hours a day, predictably? The answer is that there's a problem with a **(c)** lack of surprise. The better we understand something, the less effort we put into thinking about it. Familiarity **(d)** reduces indifference. Repetition suppression sets in and our attention diminishes. This is why — no matter how much you enjoyed watching the World Series — you aren't going to be satisfied watching that same game over and over. Although predictability is reassuring, the brain strives to **(e)** incorporate new facts into its model of the world. It always seeks novelty.

13

★★☆ 2019년 11월 41번

윗글의 제목으로 가장 적절한 것은?

① Why Are Television Reruns Still Popular?
② Predictability Is Something Not to Be Feared!
③ What Really Satisfies Our Brain: Familiarity or Novelty
④ Repetition Gives Us Expertise at the Expense of Creativity
⑤ Our Hunter-Gatherer Ancestors Were Smart in Saving Energy

14

★★★ 2019년 11월 42번

밑줄 친 (a) ~ (e) 중에서 문맥상 낱말의 쓰임이 적절하지 않은 것은? [3점]

① (a) ② (b) ③ (c) ④ (d) ⑤ (e)

정답과 해설 : 13~14 319

🕓 15~16 : 250초

[15~16] 다음 글을 읽고, 물음에 답하시오.

In 2000, James Kuklinski of the University of Illinois led an influential experiment in which more than 1,000 Illinois residents were asked questions about welfare. More than half indicated that they were confident that their answers were correct — but in fact, only three percent of the people got more than half of the questions right. Perhaps more disturbingly, the ones who were the *most* confident they were right were generally the ones who knew the least about the topic. Kuklinski calls this sort of response the "I know I'm right" syndrome. "It implies not only that most people will resist correcting their factual beliefs," he wrote, "but also that the very people who most need to correct them will be least likely to do so."

How can we have things so wrong and be so sure that we're right? Part of the answer lies in the way our brains are wired. Generally, people tend to seek ________________. There is a substantial body of psychological research showing that people tend to interpret information with an eye toward reinforcing their preexisting views. If we believe something about the world, we are more likely to passively accept as truth any information that confirms our beliefs, and actively dismiss information that doesn't. This is known as "motivated reasoning." Whether or not the consistent information is accurate, we might accept it as fact, as confirmation of our beliefs. This makes us more confident in said beliefs, and even less likely to entertain facts that contradict them.

15

★★☆ 2018년 9월 41번

윗글의 제목으로 가장 적절한 것은?

① Belief Wins Over Fact
② Still Judge by Appearance?
③ All You Need Is Motivation
④ Facilitate Rational Reasoning
⑤ Correct Errors at the Right Time

16

★★★ 2018년 9월 42번

윗글의 빈칸에 들어갈 말로 가장 적절한 것은? 3점

① diversity ② accuracy ③ popularity
④ consistency ⑤ collaboration

정답과 해설 : 15~16 320

17~18 : 250초

[17~18] 다음 글을 읽고, 물음에 답하시오.

Stories populate our lives. If you are not a fan of stories, you might imagine that the best world is a world without them, where we can only see the facts in front of us. But to do this is to **(a)** deny how our brains work, how they are *designed* to work. Evolution has given us minds that are alert to stories and suggestion because, through many hundreds of thousands of years of natural selection, minds that can attend to stories have been more **(b)** successful at passing on their owners' genes.

Think about what happens, for example, when animals face one another in conflict. They rarely plunge into battle right away. No, they first try to **(c)** signal in all kinds of ways what the *outcome* of the battle is going to be. They puff up their chests, they roar, and they bare their fangs. Animals evolved to attend to stories and signals because these turn out to be an efficient way to navigate the world. If you and I were a pair of lions on the Serengeti, and we were trying to decide the strongest lion, it would be most **(d)** sensible — for both of us — to plunge straight into a conflict. It is far better for each of us to make a show of strength, to tell *the story* of how our victory is inevitable. If one of those stories is much more **(e)** convincing than the other, we might be able to agree on the outcome without actually having the fight.

♦ fang: 송곳니

17

★★★ 2021년 11월 41번

윗글의 제목으로 가장 적절한 것은?

① The Light and Dark Sides of Storytelling
② How to Interpret Various Signals of Animals
③ Why Are We Built to Pay Attention to Stories?
④ Story: A Game Changer for Overturning a Losing Battle
⑤ Evolution: A History of Human's Coexistence with Animals

18

★★★ 2021년 11월 42번

밑줄 친 (a) ~ (e) 중에서 문맥상 낱말의 쓰임이 적절하지 않은 것은?

① (a) ② (b) ③ (c) ④ (d) ⑤ (e)

정답과 해설 : 17~18 322

Ⓒ 19~20 : 250초

[19~20] 다음 글을 읽고, 물음에 답하시오.

A neuropsychologist, Michael Gazzaniga conducted a study that shows that our brains **(a)** excel at creating coherent (but not necessarily true) stories that deceive us. In the study, split-brain patients were shown an image such that it was visible to only their left eye and asked to select a related card with their left hand. Left-eye vision and left-side body movement are controlled by the right hemisphere. In a split-brain patient, the connection between the right and left hemispheres has been broken, meaning no information can cross from one hemisphere to the other. Therefore, in this experiment, the right hemisphere was doing all of the work, and the left hemisphere was **(b)** aware of what was happening.

Gazzaniga then asked participants why they chose the card that they did. Because language is processed and generated in the left hemisphere, the left hemisphere is required to respond. However, because of the experiment's design, only the right hemisphere knew why the participant selected the card. As a result, Gazzaniga expected the participants to be **(c)** silent when asked to answer the question. But instead, every subject fabricated a response. The left hemisphere was being asked to provide a **(d)** rationalization for a behavior done by the right hemisphere. The left hemisphere didn't know the answer. But that didn't keep it from fabricating an answer. That answer, however, had no basis in reality. Now if this study had been limited to split-brain patients, it would be interesting but not very **(e)** relevant to us. It turns out split-brain patients aren't the only ones who fabricate reasons. We all do it. We all need a coherent story about ourselves, and when information in that story is missing, our brains simply fill in the details.

♦ coherent: 일관성 있는

19

★★★
2022년 11월 41번

윗글의 제목으로 가장 적절한 것은?

① Which Side of the Brain Do We Tend to Use More?
② How Our Brain's Hemispheres Interact in Storytelling
③ The Deceptive Brain: Insights from a Split-Brain Patient Study
④ To Be Creative, Activate Both Hemispheres of Your Brain!
⑤ The Dominance of the Left Brain in Image Processing

20

★★★
2022년 11월 42번

밑줄 친 (a) ~ (e) 중에서 문맥상 낱말의 쓰임이 적절하지 않은 것은? [3점]

① (a) ② (b) ③ (c) ④ (d) ⑤ (e)

정답과 해설 : 19~20 323

21~22 : 250초

[21~22] 다음 글을 읽고, 물음에 답하시오.

We lose our words. *Intelligence* once meant more than what any artificial intelligence does. It used to include sensibility, sensitivity, awareness, reason, wit, etc. And yet we readily call machines intelligent now. *Affective* is another word that once meant a lot more than what any machine can deliver. Yet we have become used to describing machines that portray emotional states or can sense our emotional states as exemplars of "affective computing." These new meanings become our new normal, and we forget other meanings. We have to struggle to recapture lost language, lost meanings, and perhaps, in time, lost experiences.

At one conference I attended, the robots were called "caring machines," and when I objected, I was told we were using this word not because the robots care but because they will take care of us. The conference participants believed caring is a behavior, a function, not a feeling. They seemed puzzled: Why did I care so much about semantics? What's wrong with me?

It is natural for words to change their meaning over time and with new circumstances. *Intelligence* and *affective* have changed their meaning to ______________ what machines can do. But now the words *caring, friend, companionship,* and *conversation*?

A lot is at stake in these words. They are not yet lost. We need to remember these words and this conversation before we don't know how to have it. Or before we think we can have it with a machine.

♦ semantics: (언어학의 일종인) 의미론

21

★★☆ 2016년 9월 41번

윗글의 제목으로 가장 적절한 것은?

① What's Lost When a Language Dies
② Artificial Intelligence: Good or Evil?
③ Will Robots Care for You in the Future?
④ Harmony Between Humans and Machines
⑤ Beware of Losing the Meaning of Words

22

최고오답률

★★★ 2016년 9월 42번

윗글의 빈칸에 들어갈 말로 가장 적절한 것은? 3점

① praise
② monitor
③ conceal
④ restrict
⑤ accommodate

DAY 26 17 장문의 이해-단일지문

정답과 해설 : 21~22 324

Ⓛ 23~24 : 250초

[23~24] 다음 글을 읽고, 물음에 답하시오.

A new study published in *Science* reveals that people generally approve of driverless, or autonomous, cars programmed to sacrifice their passengers in order to save pedestrians, but these same people are not enthusiastic about riding in such autonomous vehicles (AVs) themselves. In six online surveys of U.S. residents conducted in 2015, researchers asked participants how they would want their AVs to behave. The scenarios involved in the surveys varied in the number of pedestrian and passenger lives that could be saved, among other factors. For example, participants were asked whether it would be more moral for AVs to sacrifice one passenger rather than kill 10 pedestrians. Survey participants said that AVs should be programmed to be utilitarian and to minimize harm to pedestrians, a position that would put the safety of those outside the vehicle ahead of the driver and passengers' safety. The same respondents, however, said they prefer to buy cars that protect them and their passengers, especially if family members are involved. This suggests that if both self-protective and utilitarian AVs were allowed on the market, few people would be willing to ride in the latter — even though they would prefer others to do so. The ________________, which illustrates an ethical tension between the good of the individual and that of the public, persisted across a wide range of survey scenarios analyzed.

♦ utilitarian: 공리적인

23

★★☆ 2017년 9월 41번

윗글의 제목으로 가장 적절한 것은?

① Will AVs Finally End Car Accidents?
② How Driverless Cars Cause Unemployment
③ Safety Measures Required for Driverless Cars
④ Putting Safety First: A New Trend in Car Industry
⑤ The Dilemma: AVs to Save Passengers or Pedestrians?

24

최고오답률

★★★ 2017년 9월 42번

윗글의 빈칸에 들어갈 말로 가장 적절한 것은? 3점

① guilt
② inferiority
③ pessimism
④ ignorance
⑤ inconsistency

정답과 해설 : 23~24 325

⏱ 25~26 : 250초

[25~26] 다음 글을 읽고, 물음에 답하시오.

One cannot take for granted that the findings of any given study will have validity. Consider a situation where an investigator is studying deviant behavior. In particular, she is investigating the extent to which cheating by college students occurs on exams. Reasoning that it is more **(a)** difficult for people monitoring an exam to keep students under surveillance in large classes than in smaller ones, she hypothesizes that a higher rate of cheating will occur on exams in large classes than in small. To test this hypothesis, she collects data on cheating in both large classes and small ones and then analyzes the data. Her results show that **(b)** more cheating per student occurs in the larger classes. Thus, the data apparently **(c)** reject the investigator's research hypothesis. A few days later, however, a colleague points out that all the large classes in her study used multiple-choice exams, whereas all the small classes used short answer and essay exams. The investigator immediately realizes that an extraneous variable (exam format) is interfering with the independent variable (class size) and may be operating as a **(d)** cause in her data. The apparent support for her research hypothesis may be nothing more than an artifact. Perhaps the true effect is that more cheating occurs on multiple-choice exams than on essay exams, regardless of class **(e)** size.

♦ validity: 타당도 ♦♦ surveillance: 감독 ♦♦♦ artifact: 가공물

25

★★★ 2019년 6월 41번

윗글의 제목으로 가장 적절한 것은?

① Investigator's Attitude: Subjective vs. Objective
② Research Error from Wrong Experimental Design
③ Test Your Hypothesis to Obtain Academic Support
④ Limitations of Multiple-choice Exams in Large Classes
⑤ Is There Any Way to Discourage Students from Cheating?

26

★★★ 2019년 6월 42번

밑줄 친 (a) ~ (e) 중에서 문맥상 낱말의 쓰임이 적절하지 않은 것은?

① (a) ② (b) ③ (c) ④ (d) ⑤ (e)

정답과 해설 : 25~26 326

ⓒ 27~28 : 250초

[27~28] 다음 글을 읽고, 물음에 답하시오.

Common sense suggests that discussion with others who express different opinions should produce more moderate attitudes for everyone in the group. Surprisingly, this is not always the case. In group polarization, a period of discussion pushes group members to take more extreme positions in the direction that they were already inclined to prefer. Group polarization does not **(a)** reverse the direction of attitudes, but rather accentuates the attitudes held at the beginning. Two pressures appear to push individuals to take more extreme positions following a group discussion. First, conformity and desire for affiliation contribute to group polarization. If the majority of a group is leaning in a particular direction, what could be a better way of fitting in than **(b)** agreeing with that majority, and maybe even taking its argument one step farther? There is also a tendency for like-minded people to affiliate with one another, which can provide **(c)** reinforcement for existing opinions, increase people's confidence in those opinions, lead to the discovery of new reasons for those opinions and counterarguments to opposing views, and reduce exposure to conflicting ideas. Second, exposure to discussion on a topic introduces new reasons for **(d)** changing an attitude. If you are already opposed to gun control and you listen to additional arguments supporting your position, you might end up more **(e)** opposed than you were originally.

♦ accentuate: 강화하다 ♦♦ affiliation: 소속

27

★★★
2022년 6월 41번

윗글의 제목으로 가장 적절한 것은?

① Have More Companions and Perform Better!
② Group Competition: Not Necessarily Harmful
③ Exposure to New Ideas Weakens Group Identity
④ Sharing Ideas: The Surest Way to Foster Creativity
⑤ Black Gets Darker, White Gets Brighter in Group Discussion

28

★★★
2022년 6월 42번

밑줄 친 (a) ~ (e) 중에서 문맥상 낱말의 쓰임이 적절하지 않은 것은? [3점]

① (a) ② (b) ③ (c) ④ (d) ⑤ (e)

정답과 해설 : 27~28 327

⏱ 29~30 : 250초

[29~30] 다음 글을 읽고, 물음에 답하시오.

Unlike coins and dice, humans have memories and do care about wins and losses. Still, the probability of a hit in baseball does not **(a)** increase just because a player has not had one lately. Four outs in a row may have been bad luck, line drives hit straight into fielders' gloves. This bad luck does not **(b)** ensure good luck the next time at bat. If it is not bad luck, then a physical problem may be causing the player to do poorly. Either way, a baseball player who had four outs in a row is not due for a hit, nor is a player who made four hits in a row due for an out. If anything, a player with four hits in a row is probably a **(c)** better batter than the player who made four outs in a row.

Likewise, missed field goals need not be balanced by successes. A poor performance may simply suggest that the kicker is not very good. Being rejected for jobs does not make a job offer more likely. If anything, the evidence is mounting that this person is not qualified or interviews poorly. Not having a fire does not increase the chances of a fire — it may just be the mark of a **(d)** careless homeowner who does not put paper or cloth near a stove, put metal in the microwave, leave home with the stove on, or fall asleep smoking cigarettes. Every safe airplane trip does not increase the chances that the next trip will be a **(e)** crash.

29

★★★
2019년 3월 41번

윗글의 제목으로 가장 적절한 것은?

① Go with the Crowd
② Chance Is Only Chance
③ Misfortune: A Blessing in Disguise
④ Strike the Iron While It Is Hot
⑤ No Rain from Loud Thunder

30 최고오답률

★★★
2019년 3월 42번

밑줄 친 (a) ~ (e) 중에서 문맥상 낱말의 쓰임이 적절하지 않은 것은?

① (a) ② (b) ③ (c) ④ (d) ⑤ (e)

정답과 해설 : 29~30 329

ⓘ 31~32 : 250초

[31~32] 다음 글을 읽고, 물음에 답하시오.

The driver of FOMO (the fear of missing out) is the social pressure to be at the right place with the right people, whether it's from a sense of duty or just trying to get ahead, we feel **(a)** obligated to attend certain events for work, for family and for friends. This pressure from society combined with FOMO can wear us down. According to a recent survey, 70 percent of employees admit that when they take a vacation, they still don't **(b)** disconnect from work. Our digital habits, which include constantly checking emails, and social media timelines, have become so firmly established, it is nearly impossible to simply enjoy the moment, along with the people with whom we are sharing these moments.

JOMO (the joy of missing out) is the emotionally intelligent antidote to FOMO and is essentially about being present and being **(c)** content with where you are at in life. You do not need to compare your life to others but instead, practice tuning out the background noise of the "shoulds" and "wants" and learn to let go of worrying whether you are doing something wrong. JOMO allows us to live life in the slow lane, to appreciate human connections, to be **(d)** intentional with our time, to practice saying "no," to give ourselves "tech-free breaks," and to give ourselves permission to acknowledge where we are and to feel emotions. Instead of constantly trying to keep up with the rest of society, JOMO allows us to be who we are in the present moment. When you **(e)** activate that competitive and anxious space in your brain, you have so much more time, energy, and emotion to conquer your true priorities.

♦ antidote: 해독제

31 최고오답률

★★★
2022년 9월 41번

윗글의 제목으로 가장 적절한 것은?

① Missing Out Has Its Benefits
② JOMO: Another Form of Self-Deception
③ How to Catch up with Digital Technology
④ Being Isolated from Others Makes You Lonely
⑤ Using Social Media Wisely: The Dos and Don'ts

32 최고오답률

★★★
2022년 9월 42번

밑줄 친 (a) ~ (e) 중에서 문맥상 낱말의 쓰임이 적절하지 않은 것은?

① (a) ② (b) ③ (c) ④ (d) ⑤ (e)

정답과 해설 : 31~32 330

🕓 33~34 : 250초

[33~34] 다음 글을 읽고, 물음에 답하시오.

While complex, blockchains exhibit a set of core characteristics, which flow from the technology's reliance on a peer-to-peer network, public-private key cryptography, and consensus mechanisms. Blockchains are disintermediated and transnational. They are resilient and resistant to change, and enable people to store nonrepudiable data, pseudonymously, in a transparent manner. Most — if not all — blockchain-based networks feature market-based or game-theoretical mechanisms for reaching consensus, which can be used to coordinate people or machines. These characteristics, when combined, enable the deployment of autonomous software and explain why blockchains serve as a powerful new tool to facilitate economic and social activity that otherwise would be difficult to achieve.

At the same time, these characteristics represent the technology's greatest ________________. The disintermediated and transnational nature of blockchains makes the technology difficult to govern and makes it difficult to implement changes to a blockchain's underlying software protocol. Because blockchains are pseudonymous and have a tamper-resistant data structure supported by decentralized consensus mechanisms, they can be used to coordinate socially unacceptable or criminal conduct, including conduct facilitated by autonomous software programs. Moreover, because blockchains are transparent and traceable, they are prone to being co-opted by governments or corporations, transforming the technology into a powerful tool for surveillance and control.

♦cryptography: 암호화 기법 ♦♦pseudonymous: 유사 익명성의

33

★★★ 2018년 11월 41번

윗글의 제목으로 가장 적절한 것은?

① A Brief History of Blockchain Technology
② Blockchain Technology Is a Double-Edged Sword
③ Blockchain: The Greatest Economic Breakthrough Ever
④ Why Are People Wild About Blockchain-Based Digital Money?
⑤ Pros & Cons of Government Regulation of Blockchain Technology

34 최고오답률

★★★ 2018년 11월 42번

윗글의 빈칸에 들어갈 말로 가장 적절한 것은? 3점

① limitations ② stereotypes
③ impacts ④ innovations
⑤ possibilities

DAY 27

17 장문의 이해 - 단일지문

정답과 해설 : 33~34 331

35~36 : 250초

[35~36] 다음 글을 읽고, 물음에 답하시오.

Creative people aren't all cut from the same cloth. They have **(a)** varying levels of maturity and sensitivity. They have different approaches to work. And they're each motivated by different things. Managing people is about being aware of their unique personalities. It's also about empathy and adaptability, and knowing how the things you do and say will be interpreted and adapting accordingly. Who you are and what you say may not be the **(b)** same from one person to the next. For instance, if you're asking someone to work a second weekend in a row, or telling them they aren't getting that deserved promotion just yet, you need to bear in mind the **(c)** group. Vincent will have a very different reaction to the news than Emily, and they will each be more receptive to the news if it's bundled with different things. Perhaps that promotion news will land **(d)** easier if Vincent is given a few extra vacation days for the holidays, while you can promise Emily a bigger promotion a year from now. Consider each person's complex positive and negative personality traits, their life circumstances, and their mindset in the moment when deciding what to say and how to say it. Personal connection, compassion, and an individualized management style are **(e)** key to drawing consistent, rock star-level work out of everyone.

35

★★★ 2023년 3월 41번

윗글의 제목으로 가장 적절한 것은?

① Know Each Person to Guarantee Best Performance
② Flexible Hours: An Appealing Working Condition
③ Talk to Employees More Often in Hard Times
④ How Empathy and Recognition Are Different
⑤ Why Creativity Suffers in Competition

36

최고오답률

★★★ 2023년 3월 42번

밑줄 친 (a) ~ (e) 중에서 문맥상 낱말의 쓰임이 적절하지 않은 것은?

① (a) ② (b) ③ (c) ④ (d) ⑤ (e)

정답과 해설 : 35~36 332

37~38 : 250초

[37~38] 다음 글을 읽고, 물음에 답하시오.

Being able to have a good fight doesn't just make us more civil; it also develops our creative muscles. In a classic study, highly creative architects were more likely than their technically competent but less original peers to come from homes with **(a)** plenty of friction. They often grew up in households that were "tense but secure," as psychologist Robert Albert notes: "The creative person-to-be comes from a family that is anything but **(b)** harmonious." The parents weren't physically or verbally abusive, but they didn't shy away from conflict, either. Instead of telling their children to be seen but not heard, they **(c)** encouraged them to stand up for themselves. The kids learned to dish it out — and take it. That's exactly what happened to Wilbur and Orville Wright, who invented the airplane.

When the Wright brothers said they thought together, what they really meant is that they fought together. When they were solving problems, they had arguments that lasted not just for hours but for weeks and months at a time. They didn't have such **(d)** ceaseless fights because they were angry. They kept quarreling because they enjoyed it and learned from the experience. "I like scrapping with Orv," Wilbur reflected. As you'll see, it was one of their most passionate and prolonged arguments that led them to **(e)** support a critical assumption that had prevented humans from soaring through the skies.

◆ dish it out: 남을 비판하다 ◆◆ scrap with: ~과 다투다

37

★★☆ 2022년 3월 41번

윗글의 제목으로 가장 적절한 것은?

① The Power of Constructive Conflict
② Lighten Tense Moments with Humor
③ Strategies to Cope with Family Stress
④ Compromise: A Key to Resolving Conflict
⑤ Rivalry Between Brothers: A Serious Crisis

38

최고오답률

★★★ 2022년 3월 42번

밑줄 친 (a) ~ (e) 중에서 문맥상 낱말의 쓰임이 적절하지 않은 것은? 3점

① (a) ② (b) ③ (c) ④ (d) ⑤ (e)

DAY 27

17 장문의 이해 - 단일지문

정답과 해설 : 37~38 334

⏱ 39~40 : 240초

[39~40] 다음 글을 읽고, 물음에 답하시오.

In Western society, many music performance settings make a clear distinction between performers and audience members: the performers are the "doers" and those in the audience take a decidedly passive role. The performance space itself may further **(a)** reinforce the distinction with a physical separation between the stage and audience seating. Perhaps because this distinction is so common, audiences seem to greatly value opportunities to have special "access" to performers that affords understanding about performers' style of music. Some performing musicians have won great approval by regularly **(b)** incorporating "audience participation" into their concerts. Whether by leading a sing-along activity or teaching a rhythm to be clapped at certain points, including audience members in the music making can **(c)** boost the level of engagement and enjoyment for all involved. Performers who are uncomfortable leading audience participation can still connect with the audience simply by giving a special glimpse of the performer **(d)** perspective. It is quite common in classical music to provide audiences with program notes. Typically, this text in a program gives background information about pieces of music being performed and perhaps biographical information about historically significant composers. What may be of more interest to audience members is background information about the very performers who are onstage, including an explanation of why they have chosen the music they are presenting. Such insight can make audience members feel **(e)** distant to the musicians onstage, both metaphorically and emotionally. This connection will likely enhance the expressive and communicative experience.

39

★★★
2023년 11월 41번

윗글의 제목으로 가장 적절한 것은?

① Bridge the Divide and Get the Audience Involved
② Musical Composition Reflects the Musician's Experience
③ Why a Performer's Style Changes with Each Performance
④ Understanding Performers on Stage: An Audience's Responsibility
⑤ The Effect of Theater Facilities on the Success of a Performance

40

★★☆
2023년 11월 42번

밑줄 친 (a) ~ (e) 중에서 문맥상 낱말의 쓰임이 적절하지 않은 것은?

① (a) ② (b) ③ (c) ④ (d) ⑤ (e)

정답과 해설 : 39~40 335

◷ 41~42 : 240초

[41~42] 다음 글을 읽고, 물음에 답하시오.

It's untrue that teens can focus on two things at once — what they're doing is shifting their attention from one task to another. In this digital age, teens wire their brains to make these shifts very quickly, but they are still, like everyone else, paying attention to one thing at a time, sequentially. Common sense tells us multitasking should **(a)** increase brain activity, but Carnegie Mellon University scientists using the latest brain imaging technology find it doesn't. As a matter of fact, they discovered that multitasking actually decreases brain activity. Neither task is done as well as if each were performed **(b)** individually. Fractions of a second are lost every time we make a switch, and a person's interrupted task can take 50 percent **(c)** longer to finish, with 50 percent more errors. Turns out the latest brain research **(d)** contradicts the old advice "one thing at a time."

It's not that kids can't do some tasks simultaneously. But if two tasks are performed at once, one of them has to be familiar. Our brains perform a familiar task on "automatic pilot" while really paying attention to the other one. That's why insurance companies consider talking on a cell phone and driving to be as **(e)** dangerous as driving while drunk — it's the driving that goes on "automatic pilot" while the conversation really holds our attention. Our kids may be living in the Information Age but our brains have not been redesigned yet.

41

★☆☆ 2024년 3월 41번

윗글의 제목으로 가장 적절한 것은?

① Multitasking Unveiled: What Really Happens in Teens' Brains
② Optimal Ways to Expand the Attention Span of Teens
③ Unknown Approaches to Enhance Brain Development
④ Multitasking for a Balanced Life in a Busy World
⑤ How to Build Automaticity in Performing Tasks

42

★★★ 2024년 3월 42번

밑줄 친 (a) ~ (e) 중에서 문맥상 낱말의 쓰임이 적절하지 않은 것은?

① (a) ② (b) ③ (c) ④ (d) ⑤ (e)

정답과 해설 : 41~42 336

Ⓛ 43~44 : 250초

[43~44] 다음 글을 읽고, 물음에 답하시오.

We have biases that support our biases! If we're partial to one option — perhaps because it's more memorable, or framed to minimize loss, or seemingly consistent with a promising pattern — we tend to search for information that will **(a)** justify choosing that option. On the one hand, it's sensible to make choices that we can defend with data and a list of reasons. On the other hand, if we're not careful, we're **(b)** likely to conduct an imbalanced analysis, falling prey to a cluster of errors collectively known as "confirmation biases."

For example, nearly all companies include classic "tell me about yourself" job interviews as part of the hiring process, and many rely on these interviews alone to evaluate applicants. But it turns out that traditional interviews are actually one of the **(c)** least useful tools for predicting an employee's future success. This is because interviewers often subconsciously make up their minds about interviewees based on their first few moments of interaction and spend the rest of the interview cherry-picking evidence and phrasing their questions to **(d)** confirm that initial impression: "I see here you left a good position at your previous job. You must be pretty ambitious, right?" versus "You must not have been very committed, huh?" This means that interviewers can be prone to **(e)** noticing significant information that would clearly indicate whether this candidate was actually the best person to hire. More structured approaches, like obtaining samples of a candidate's work or asking how he would respond to difficult hypothetical situations, are dramatically better at assessing future success, with a nearly threefold advantage over traditional interviews.

43

★★☆ 2024년 6월 41번

윗글의 제목으로 가장 적절한 것은?

① Bias Trap: How Our Preconceptions Mislead Us
② Utilize the Power of Similar Personality Types!
③ More Information Adds Up to Worse Choices
④ Why Are You Persuaded by Others' Perspectives?
⑤ Interviews: The Fairest Judgment for All Applicants

44

최고오답률

★★★ 2024년 6월 42번

밑줄 친 (a) ~ (e) 중에서 문맥상 낱말의 쓰임이 적절하지 않은 것은? 3점

① (a) ② (b) ③ (c) ④ (d) ⑤ (e)

정답과 해설 : 43~44 337

45~46 : 240초

[45~46] 다음 글을 읽고, 물음에 답하시오.

What makes questioning authority so hard? The **(a)** difficulties start in childhood, when parents — the first and most powerful authority figures — show children "the way things are." This is a necessary element of learning language and socialization, and certainly most things learned in early childhood are **(b)** noncontroversial: the English alphabet starts with A and ends with Z, the numbers 1 through 10 come before the numbers 11 through 20, and so on. Children, however, will spontaneously question things that are quite obvious to adults and even to older kids. The word "why?" becomes a challenge, as in, "Why is the sky blue?" Answers such as "because it just is" or "because I say so" tell children that they must unquestioningly **(c)** accept what authorities say "just because," and children who persist in their questioning are likely to find themselves dismissed or yelled at for "bothering" adults with "meaningless" or "unimportant" questions. But these questions are in fact perfectly **(d)** unreasonable. Why is the sky blue? Many adults do not themselves know the answer. And who says the sky's color needs to be called "blue," anyway? How do we know that what one person calls "blue" is the same color that another calls "blue"? The scientific answers come from physics, but those are not the answers that children are seeking. They are trying to understand the world, and no matter how **(e)** irritating the repeated questions may become to stressed and time-pressed parents, it is important to take them seriously to encourage kids to question authority to think for themselves.

45

★★☆
2024년 9월 41번

윗글의 제목으로 가장 적절한 것은?

① Things Plain to You Aren't to Children: Let Them Question
② Children's Complaints: Should Parents Accept All of Them?
③ Want More Challenges? They'll Make Your Energy Dry Up!
④ Authority Has Hidden Power to Nurture Children's Morality
⑤ Answering Is More Crucial than Questioning for Quick Learning

46

★★☆
2024년 9월 42번

밑줄 친 (a) ~ (e) 중에서 문맥상 낱말의 쓰임이 적절하지 않은 것은?

① (a) ② (b) ③ (c) ④ (d) ⑤ (e)

DAY 28
17 장문의 이해 - 단일지문

정답과 해설 : 45~46 339

유형TIP

18. 장문의 이해-복합지문

장문의 이해-단일지문 유형보다 더 긴 지문이 제시되지만 난이도는 더 낮음.
한 지문에 주로 단락 배열, 지칭 추론, 내용 일치 파악, 총 세 가지의 질문이 출제됨.

유형 TIP 25BR2T_CH18
대표 예제 25BR2E_CH18

유형 공략법

1) 내용 일치 파악: 선택지와 글의 내용을 정확하게 비교한다.
지문의 내용과 선택지의 앞부분은 같지만 뒷부분이 틀린 경우도 있으니 주의해야 함.
내용 일치 파악 문제의 선택지를 통해 내용을 대략적으로 파악할 수 있음.

2) 단락 배열: 단락 순서 배열과 관련된 근거를 찾는다.
시간의 흐름, 공간의 이동, 이야기 속 등장인물의 첫 등장, 연결사, 지시어, 대명사 등에 주목해야 함. 특히 지문이 이야기 형식으로 전개되므로 시간과 공간의 변화에 초점을 맞추어 읽는 것이 좋음.

3) 지칭 추론: 글의 흐름을 놓치지 않도록 주의해야 한다.
(a)~(e) 중에 가리키는 대상이 다른 것을 찾는 유형임. 지문 내에서 처음 등장하는 대상이나 인물에 표시하면서 읽으면 정답 파악에 도움이 됨.

장문의 이해-복합지문 대표 예제 - 2024학년도 수능 43~45번

다음 글을 읽고, 물음에 답하시오.

(A)

(1) Emma and Clara stood side by side on the beach road, with their eyes fixed on the boundless ocean. (2) The breathtaking scene that surrounded them was beyond description. (3) Just after sunrise, they finished their preparations for the bicycle ride along the beach road. (4) Emma turned to Clara with a question, "Do you think this will be your favorite ride ever?" (5) Clara's face lit up with a bright smile as she nodded. (6) "Definitely! **(a)** I can't wait to ride while watching those beautiful waves!"

(B)

(1) When they reached their destination, Emma and Clara stopped their bikes. (2) Emma approached Clara, saying "Bicycle riding is unlike swimming, isn't it?" (3) Clara answered with a smile, "Quite similar, actually. (4) Just like swimming, riding makes me feel truly alive." (5) She added, "It shows **(b)** me what it means to live while facing life's tough challenges." (6) Emma nodded in agreement and suggested, "Your first beach bike ride was a great success. (7) How about coming back next summer?" (8) Clara replied with delight, "With **(c)** you, absolutely!"

(C)

(1) Clara used to be a talented swimmer, but she had to give up her dream of becoming an Olympic medalist in swimming because of shoulder injuries. (2) Yet she responded to the hardship in a constructive way. (3) After years of hard training, she made an incredible recovery and found a new passion for bike riding. (4) Emma saw how the painful past made her maturer and how it made **(d)** her stronger in the end. (5) One hour later, Clara, riding ahead of Emma, turned back and shouted, "Look at the white cliff!"

(D)

(1) Emma and Clara jumped on their bikes and started to pedal toward the white cliff where the beach road ended. (2) Speeding up and enjoying the wide blue sea, Emma couldn't hide her excitement and exclaimed, "Clara, the view is amazing!" (3) Clara's silence, however, seemed to say that she was lost in her thoughts. (4) Emma understood the meaning of her silence. (5) Watching Clara riding beside her, Emma thought about Clara's past tragedy, which **(e)** she now seemed to have overcome.

43. 주어진 글 (A)에 이어질 내용을 순서에 맞게 배열한 것으로 가장 적절한 것은?

① (B) – (D) – (C)　② (C) – (B) – (D)
③ (C) – (D) – (B)　④ (D) – (B) – (C)
✓ (D) – (C) – (B)

44. 밑줄 친 (a) ~ (e) 중에서 가리키는 대상이 나머지 넷과 다른 것은?

① (a)　② (b)　✓ (c)　④ (d)　⑤ (e)

45. 윗글의 내용으로 적절하지 않은 것은?

① Emma와 Clara는 자전거 탈 준비를 일출 직후에 마쳤다. 문장(A-3)
② Clara는 자전거 타기와 수영이 꽤 비슷하다고 말했다. 문장(B-3)
✓ Clara는 올림픽 수영 경기에서 메달을 땄다. 문장(C-1) 따지 못했다
④ Emma와 Clara는 자전거를 타고 하얀 절벽 쪽으로 갔다. 문장(D-1)
⑤ Emma는 Clara의 침묵의 의미를 이해했다. 문장(D-4)

STEP 1 내용 일치 파악: 선택지와 글의 내용을 정확하게 비교한다.
① - 문장(A-3): Emma와 Clara는 자전거 탈 준비를 일출 직후에 함.
② - 문장(B-3): Clara는 자전거 타기와 수영이 꽤 비슷하다고 말함.
③ - 문장(C-1): Clara는 올림픽 수영 경기에서 메달을 따지 못했음.
④ - 문장(D-1): Emma와 Clara는 자전거를 타고 하얀 절벽 쪽으로 감.
⑤ - 문장(D-4): Emma는 Clara의 침묵의 의미를 이해함.

STEP 2 단락 배열: 단락 순서 배열과 관련된 근거를 찾는다.
(A) → (D): (A-3)에서 Emma와 Clara는 해변 도로를 따라 자전거를 탈 준비를 마쳤고, (D-1)에서 자전거를 타고 하얀 절벽까지 갔다고 했으므로 (A) 다음에 (D)가 오는 것이 적절함.
(D) → (C): (D-4)와 (D-5)에서 Clara가 침묵하자 Emma는 그 이유가 Clara의 과거의 비극적인 사건 때문임을 알아차렸고, (C-1)에서 Clara가 과거에 겪은 사건이 언급되었으므로 (D) 다음에 (C)가 오는 것이 적절함.
(C) → (B): (C-5)에서 Clara가 Emma에게 하얀 절벽에 거의 도착했다고 외쳤고, (B-1)에서 두 사람이 목적지인 하얀 절벽에 도착했다는 언급이 있으므로 (C) 다음에 (B)가 오는 것이 적절함.

STEP 3 지칭 추론: 글의 흐름을 놓치지 않도록 주의해야 한다.
(B-7)에서 Emma가 Clara에게 질문을 하고, (B-8)에서 Clara가 대답하고 있으므로 'you'는 Emma를 가리킴. 나머지는 모두 Clara를 가리킴.

전문 해석

(A) (1) Emma와 Clara는 그들의 시선을 끝없는 바다에 고정한 채 해변 도로에 나란히 서 있었다. (2) 그들을 둘러싼 숨이 멎는 듯한 광경은 말로 형용할 수 없었다. (3) 일출 직후, 그들은 해변 도로를 따라 자전거를 탈 준비를 마쳤다. (4) Emma가 Clara를 향해 돌아서서 물었다. "이번이 지금껏 너의 최고의 라이딩이 될 거라고 생각하니?" (5) Clara가 고개를 끄덕일 때 그녀의 얼굴이 환한 미소로 밝아졌다. (6) "물론이지! (a)나(Clara)는 저 아름다운 파도를 보면서 빨리 자전거를 타고 싶어!"

(D) (1) Emma와 Clara는 그들의 자전거에 올라타서 해변 도로가 끝나는 하얀 절벽을 향해 페달을 밟기 시작했다. (2) 속도를 높이고 넓고 푸른 바다를 즐기며, Emma는 자신의 흥분을 숨기지 못하고 "Clara, 경치가 굉장해!"라고 소리쳤다. (3) 그러나 Clara의 침묵은 그녀가 사색에 잠겨 있다고 말하는 듯했다. (4) Emma는 그녀의 침묵의 의미를 이해했다. (5) 자신의 옆에서 Clara가 자전거를 타는 것을 보면서, Emma는 Clara의 지난 비극에 대해 생각했는데, 이제는 (e)그녀(Clara)가 그것을 극복한 듯 보였다.

(C) (1) Clara는 재능 있는 수영 선수였지만, 어깨 부상 때문에 올림픽 수영 메달리스트가 되겠다는 자신의 꿈을 포기해야 했다. (2) 그러나 그녀는 건설적인 방식으로 고난에 대응했다. (3) 수년의 힘든 훈련 후에, 그녀는 믿기지 않을 정도의 회복을 이뤘고 자전거 타기에 대한 새로운 열정을 발견했다. (4) Emma는 고통스러운 과거가 어떻게 그녀(Clara)를 더 성숙해지게 만들었는지, 그리고 그것이 결국 어떻게 (d)그녀(Clara)를 더 강하게 만들었는지를 보았다. (5) 한 시간 후에, Clara는 Emma의 앞에서 자전거를 타다가 뒤를 돌아보며 "저 하얀 절벽을 봐!"라고 소리쳤다.

(B) (1) 그들이 목적지에 도착했을 때, Emma와 Clara는 자전거를 멈추었다. (2) Emma는 Clara에게 다가가 "자전거 타기는 수영과 달라, 그렇지 않니?"라고 말했다. (3) Clara는 웃으며 대답했다, "사실, 꽤나 비슷해. (4) 꼭 수영처럼 자전거 타기는 내가 진정으로 살아 있다고 느끼게 만들어 줘." (5) "그것은 (b)나(Clara)에게 삶의 힘든 도전에 직면하면서 산다는 것이 무엇을 의미하는지를 보여 줘."라고 그녀는 덧붙였다. (6) Emma는 동의하며 고개를 끄덕이고 제안했다, "너의 첫 번째 해변 자전거 타기는 엄청난 성공이었어. (7) 내년 여름에 다시 오는 게 어때?" (8) Clara는 "(c)너(Emma)와 함께라면, 물론이지!"라고 기쁘게 대답했다.

중요 어휘

- □ side by side 나란히
- □ boundless 형 끝없는, 무한한
- □ breathtaking 형 숨이 멎는 듯한, 깜짝 놀랄 만한
- □ beyond description 말로 형용할 수 없는
- □ light up with ~으로 밝아지다 [빛이 나다]
- □ nod 동 고개를 끄덕이다
- □ can't wait to V 빨리 ~하고 싶다, ~하기를 기대하다
- □ exclaim 동 소리치다, 외치다
- □ silence 명 침묵, 고요
- □ be lost in thought 사색에 잠기다, 골똘히 생각하다
- □ beside 전 ~ 옆에, ~에 비해
- □ past 형 지난, 이전의 / 명 과거
- □ tragedy 명 비극
- □ injury 명 부상
- □ respond to N ~에 대응하다
- □ hardship 명 고난, 어려움
- □ constructive 형 건설적인
- □ mature 형 성숙한, 어른스러운
- □ in the end 결국, 마침내
- □ unlike 전 ~과 다른
- □ agreement 명 동의, 합의

자세한 해설지 QR→
자세한해설-CH18

18 장문의 이해-복합지문

동영상 강의 25BR2_CH18

01~03 : 230초

[01~03] 다음 글을 읽고, 물음에 답하시오.

(A)

Victor applied for the position of office cleaner at a very big company. The manager interviewed him, then gave him a test: cleaning, stocking, and supplying designated facility areas. After observing what **(a)** <u>he</u> was doing, the manager said, "You are hired. Give me your email address, and I'll send you some documents to fill out."

(B)

(b) <u>He</u> then sold the tomatoes in a door to door round. In two hours, he succeeded to double his capital. He repeated the operation three times and returned home with 60 dollars. Victor realized that he could survive by this way, and started to go every day earlier, and returned late. Thus, **(c)** <u>his</u> money doubled or tripled each day. Shortly later, he bought a cart, then a truck, and then he had his own fleet of delivery vehicles.

(C)

Victor replied, "I don't have a computer, nor an email." "I'm sorry," said the manager. And he added, "If you don't have an email, how do you intend to do this job? This job requires you to have an email address. I can't hire you." Victor left with no hope at all. **(d)** <u>He</u> didn't know what to do, with only 10 dollars in his pocket. He then decided to go to the supermarket and bought a 10kg box of tomatoes.

(D)

Several years later, Victor's company became the biggest food company in his city. He started to plan his family's future, and decided to get a life insurance. He called an insurance broker. When the conversation was concluded, **(e)** <u>he</u> asked him his email. Victor replied: "I don't have an email." The broker replied curiously, "You don't have an email, and yet have succeeded to build an empire. Do you imagine what you could have been if you had an email?" He thought for a while, and replied, "An office cleaner!"

01

★☆☆ 2021년 6월 43번

주어진 글 (A)에 이어질 내용을 순서에 맞게 배열한 것으로 가장 적절한 것은?

① (B) — (D) — (C)
② (C) — (B) — (D)
③ (C) — (D) — (B)
④ (D) — (B) — (C)
⑤ (D) — (C) — (B)

02

★☆☆ 2021년 6월 44번

밑줄 친 (a) ~ (e) 중에서 가리키는 대상이 나머지 넷과 <u>다른</u> 것은?

① (a) ② (b) ③ (c) ④ (d) ⑤ (e)

03

★☆☆ 2021년 6월 45번

윗글의 Victor에 관한 내용으로 적절하지 <u>않은</u> 것은?

① 사무실 청소부 자리에 지원하였다.
② 2시간 만에 자본금을 두 배로 만들었다.
③ 슈퍼마켓에 가서 토마토를 샀다.
④ 그의 회사는 도시에서 가장 큰 식품 회사가 되었다.
⑤ 이메일이 있다고 보험 중개인에게 답했다.

정답과 해설 : 01~03 341

⏱ 04~06 : 230초

[04~06] 다음 글을 읽고, 물음에 답하시오.

(A)

There once lived a girl named Melanie. She wanted to be a ballet dancer. One day, Melanie's mother saw her dancing with the flawless steps and enthusiasm of a ballerina. "Isn't it strange? Melanie is dancing so well without any formal training!" her mother said. "I must get **(a)** her professional lessons to help her polish her skill."

(B)

Disappointed, they returned home, tears rolling down Melanie's cheeks. With her confidence and ego hurt, Melanie never danced again. **(b)** She completed her studies and became a schoolteacher. One day, the ballet instructor at her school was running late, and Melanie was asked to keep an eye on the class so that they wouldn't roam around the school. Once inside the ballet room, she couldn't control herself. She taught the students some steps and kept on dancing for some time. Unaware of time or the people around her, **(c)** she was lost in her own little world of dancing.

(C)

Just then, the ballet instructor entered the classroom and was surprised to see Melanie's incredible skill. "What a performance!" the instructor said with a sparkle in her eyes. Melanie was embarrassed to see the instructor in front of her. "Sorry, Ma'am!" she said. "For what?" the instructor asked. "You are a true ballerina!" The instructor invited Melanie to accompany **(d)** her to a ballet training center, and Melanie has never stopped dancing since. Today, she is a world-renowned ballet dancer.

(D)

The following day, Melanie accompanied her mother to a local dance institute. Upon meeting the dance teacher, Mr. Edler, her mother requested to admit Melanie to his institute. The teacher asked Melanie to audition. **(e)** She was happy and showed him some of her favorite dance steps. However, he wasn't interested in her dance. He was busy with other tasks in the dance room. "You can leave now! The girl is just average. Don't let her waste her time aspiring to be a dancer," he said. Melanie and her mother were shocked to hear this.

04

★☆☆ 2021년 9월 43번

주어진 글 (A)에 이어질 내용을 순서에 맞게 배열한 것으로 가장 적절한 것은?

① (B) — (D) — (C)
② (C) — (B) — (D)
③ (C) — (D) — (B)
④ (D) — (B) — (C)
⑤ (D) — (C) — (B)

05

★★☆ 2021년 9월 44번

밑줄 친 (a) ~ (e) 중에서 가리키는 대상이 나머지 넷과 다른 것은?

① (a) ② (b) ③ (c) ④ (d) ⑤ (e)

06

★☆☆ 2021년 9월 45번

윗글의 내용으로 적절하지 않은 것은?

① 엄마는 Melanie가 발레리나의 열정을 가지고 춤추는 것을 보았다.
② Melanie는 학생들에게 스텝을 가르쳤다.
③ Melanie는 세계적으로 유명한 발레 댄서이다.
④ Melanie는 지역 댄스 학원에 엄마와 동행했다.
⑤ Mr. Edler는 Melanie의 춤에 관심을 보였다.

정답과 해설 : 04~06 342

ⓛ 07~09 : 230초

[07~09] 다음 글을 읽고, 물음에 답하시오.

(A)

The basketball felt like it belonged in Chanel's hands even though it was only a practice game. She decided not to pass the ball to her twin sister, Vasha. Instead, **(a)** she stopped, jumped, and shot the ball toward the basket, but it bounced off the backboard. Chanel could see that her teammates were disappointed. The other team got the ball and soon scored, ending the game.

(B)

The next day, Chanel played in the championship game against a rival school. It was an intense game and the score was tied when Chanel was passed the ball by Vasha, with ten seconds left in the game. **(b)** She leaped into the air and shot the ball. It went straight into the basket! Chanel's last shot had made her team the champions. Vasha and all her other teammates cheered for her.

(C)

At first, Chanel did not like practicing with Vasha because every time Vasha shot the ball, it went in. But whenever it was Chanel's turn, she missed. **(c)** She got frustrated at not making a shot. "Don't give up!" Vasha shouted after each missed shot. After twelve misses in a row, her thirteenth shot went in and she screamed, "I finally did it!" Her twin said, "I knew **(d)** you could! Now let's keep practicing!"

(D)

When the practice game ended, Chanel felt her eyes sting with tears. "It's okay," Vasha said in a comforting voice. Chanel appreciated her, but Vasha wasn't making her feel any better. Vasha wanted to help her twin improve. She invited her twin to practice with **(e)** her. After school, they got their basketball and started practicing their basketball shots.

07

★☆☆
2022년 11월 43번

주어진 글 (A)에 이어질 내용을 순서에 맞게 배열한 것으로 가장 적절한 것은?

① (B) — (D) — (C)
② (C) — (B) — (D)
③ (C) — (D) — (B)
④ (D) — (B) — (C)
⑤ (D) — (C) — (B)

08

★★☆
2022년 11월 44번

밑줄 친 (a) ~ (e) 중에서 가리키는 대상이 나머지 넷과 다른 것은?

① (a) ② (b) ③ (c) ④ (d) ⑤ (e)

09

★☆☆
2022년 11월 45번

윗글의 Chanel에 관한 내용으로 적절하지 않은 것은?

① 연습 경기 중에 팀원들의 실망한 모습을 보았다.
② 라이벌 학교와의 챔피언십 경기에 출전했다.
③ 팀을 우승시키는 마지막 슛을 성공했다.
④ 슛 연습에서 연이은 실패 후에 12번째 슛이 들어갔다.
⑤ 방과 후에 농구 슛을 연습하기 시작했다.

정답과 해설 : 07~09 343

⏲ 10~12 : 230초

[10~12] 다음 글을 읽고, 물음에 답하시오.

(A)

A businessman boarded a flight. Arriving at his seat, he greeted his travel companions: a middle-aged woman sitting at the window, and a little boy sitting in the aisle seat. After putting his bag in the overhead bin, he took his place between them. After the flight took off, he began a conversation with the little boy. He appeared to be about the same age as **(a)** his son and was busy with a coloring book.

(B)

As the plane rose and fell several times, people got nervous and sat up in their seats. The man was also nervous and grabbing **(b)** his seat as tightly as he could. Meanwhile, the little boy was sitting quietly beside **(c)** him. His coloring book and crayons were put away neatly in the seat pocket in front of him, and his hands were calmly resting on his legs. Incredibly, he didn't seem worried at all.

(C)

Then, suddenly, the turbulence ended. The pilot apologized for the bumpy ride and announced that they would be landing soon. As the plane began its descent, the man said to the little boy, "You are just a little boy, but **(d)** I have never met a braver person in all my life! Tell me, how is it that you remained so calm while all of us adults were so afraid?" Looking him in the eyes, he said, "My father is the pilot, and he's taking me home."

♦ turbulence: 난기류

(D)

He asked the boy a few usual questions, such as his age, his hobbies, as well as his favorite animal. He found it strange that such a young boy would be traveling alone, so he decided to keep an eye on **(e)** him to make sure he was okay. About an hour into the flight, the plane suddenly began experiencing turbulence. The pilot told everyone to fasten their seat belts and remain calm, as they had encountered rough weather.

10

★☆☆ 2022년 6월 43번

주어진 글 (A)에 이어질 내용을 순서에 맞게 배열한 것으로 가장 적절한 것은?

① (B) — (D) — (C)
② (C) — (B) — (D)
③ (C) — (D) — (B)
④ (D) — (B) — (C)
⑤ (D) — (C) — (B)

11

★☆☆ 2022년 6월 44번

밑줄 친 (a) ~ (e) 중에서 가리키는 대상이 나머지 넷과 다른 것은?

① (a) ② (b) ③ (c) ④ (d) ⑤ (e)

12

★☆☆ 2022년 6월 45번

윗글의 내용으로 적절하지 않은 것은?

① 사업가는 중년 여성과 소년 사이에 앉았다.
② 비행기가 오르락내리락하자 사람들은 긴장했다.
③ 소년은 색칠 공부 책과 크레용을 가방에 넣었다.
④ 소년은 자신의 아버지가 조종사라고 말했다.
⑤ 조종사는 사람들에게 안전벨트를 매고 침착하라고 말했다.

정답과 해설 : 10~12 344

⏲ 13~15 : 230초

[13~15] 다음 글을 읽고, 물음에 답하시오.

(A)

Once upon a time there lived a poor but cheerful shoemaker. He was so happy, he sang all day long. The children loved to stand around his window to listen to **(a)** him. Next door to the shoemaker lived a rich man. He used to sit up all night to count his gold. In the morning, he went to bed, but he could not sleep because of the sound of the shoemaker's singing.

(B)

He could not sleep, or work, or sing — and, worst of all, the children no longer came to see **(b)** him. At last, the shoemaker felt so unhappy that he seized his bag of gold and ran next door to the rich man. "Please take back your gold," he said. "The worry of it is making me ill, and I have lost all of my friends. I would rather be a poor shoemaker, as I was before." And so the shoemaker was happy again and sang all day at his work.

(C)

There was so much there that the shoemaker was afraid to let it out of his sight. So he took it to bed with him. But he could not sleep for worrying about it. Very early in the morning, he got up and brought his gold down from the bedroom. He had decided to hide it up the chimney instead. But he was still uneasy, and in a little while he dug a hole in the garden and buried his bag of gold in it. It was no use trying to work. **(c)** He was too worried about the safety of his gold. And as for singing, he was too miserable to utter a note.

(D)

One day, **(d)** he thought of a way of stopping the singing. He wrote a letter to the shoemaker asking him to visit. The shoemaker came at once, and to his surprise the rich man gave him a bag of gold. When he got home again, the shoemaker opened the bag. **(e)** He had never seen so much gold before! When he sat down at his bench and began, carefully, to count it, the children watched through the window.

13

★☆☆ 2021년 3월 43번

주어진 글 (A)에 이어질 내용을 순서에 맞게 배열한 것으로 가장 적절한 것은?

① (B) — (D) — (C)
② (C) — (B) — (D)
③ (C) — (D) — (B)
④ (D) — (B) — (C)
⑤ (D) — (C) — (B)

14

★☆☆ 2021년 3월 44번

밑줄 친 (a) ~ (e) 중에서 가리키는 대상이 나머지 넷과 다른 것은?

① (a) ② (b) ③ (c) ④ (d) ⑤ (e)

15

★☆☆ 2021년 3월 45번

윗글의 shoemaker에 관한 내용으로 적절하지 않은 것은?

① 그의 노래로 인해 옆집 사람이 잠을 잘 수 없었다.
② 예전처럼 가난하게 살고 싶지 않다고 말했다.
③ 정원에 구멍을 파고 금화가 든 가방을 묻었다.
④ 부자가 보낸 편지에 즉시 그를 만나러 갔다.
⑤ 금화를 셀 때 아이들이 그 모습을 봤다.

정답과 해설 : 13~15 346

16~18 : 230초

[16~18] 다음 글을 읽고, 물음에 답하시오.

(A)

John was a sensitive boy. Even his hair was ticklish. When breeze touched his hair he would burst out laughing. And when this ticklish laughter started, no one could make him stop. John's laughter was so contagious that when John started feeling ticklish, everyone ended up in endless laughter. He tried everything to control his ticklishness: wearing a thousand different hats, using ultra strong hairsprays, and shaving his head. But nothing worked. One day he met a clown in the street. The clown was very old and could hardly walk, but when he saw John in tears, he went to cheer **(a)** him up.

♦ ticklish: 간지럼을 타는

(B)

All were full of children who were sick, or orphaned, children with very serious problems. But as soon as they saw the clown, their faces changed completely and lit up with a smile. That day was even more special, because in every show John's contagious laughter would end up making the kids laugh a lot. The old clown winked at **(b)** him and said "Now do you see what a serious job it is? That's why I can't retire, even at my age."

(C)

It didn't take long to make John laugh, and they started to talk. John told **(c)** him about his ticklish problem. Then he asked the clown how such an old man could carry on being a clown. "I have no one to replace me," said the clown, "and I have a very serious job to do." And then he took John to many hospitals, shelters, and schools.

(D)

And he added, "Not everyone could do it. He or she has to have a special gift for laughter." This said, the wind again set off John's ticklishness and **(d)** his laughter. After a while, John decided to replace the old clown. From that day onward, the fact that John was different actually made **(e)** him happy, thanks to his special gift.

16

★☆☆
2022년 3월 43번

주어진 글 (A)에 이어질 내용을 순서에 맞게 배열한 것으로 가장 적절한 것은?

① (B) — (D) — (C)
② (C) — (B) — (D)
③ (C) — (D) — (B)
④ (D) — (B) — (C)
⑤ (D) — (C) — (B)

17

★★☆
2022년 3월 44번

밑줄 친 (a) ~ (e) 중에서 가리키는 대상이 나머지 넷과 다른 것은?

① (a) ② (b) ③ (c) ④ (d) ⑤ (e)

18

★☆☆
2022년 3월 45번

윗글의 John에 관한 내용으로 적절하지 않은 것은?

① 간지럼을 타지 않으려고 온갖 시도를 했다.
② 전염성 있는 웃음으로 아이들을 많이 웃게 했다.
③ 광대에게 그렇게 늙어서도 어떻게 계속 일할 수 있는지 물었다.
④ 광대와 함께 여러 병원과 보호 시설, 학교에 갔다.
⑤ 광대의 뒤를 잇지 않기로 했다.

정답과 해설 : 16~18 347

⏱ 19~21 : 230초

[19~21] 다음 글을 읽고, 물음에 답하시오.

(A)

There was a very wealthy man who was bothered by severe eye pain. He consulted many doctors and was treated by several of them. He did not stop consulting a galaxy of medical experts; he was heavily medicated and underwent hundreds of injections. However, the pain persisted and was worse than before. At last, **(a)** he heard about a monk who was famous for treating patients with his condition. Within a few days, the monk was called for by the suffering man. ♦ monk: 수도사

(B)

In a few days everything around **(b)** that man was green. The wealthy man made sure that nothing around him could be any other colour. When the monk came to visit him after a few days, the wealthy man's servants ran with buckets of green paint and poured them all over him because he was wearing red clothes. **(c)** He asked the servants why they did that.

(C)

They replied, "We can't let our master see any other colour." Hearing this, the monk laughed and said "If only you had purchased a pair of green glasses for just a few dollars, you could have saved these walls, trees, pots, and everything else and you could have saved a large share of **(d)** his fortune. You cannot paint the whole world green."

(D)

The monk understood the wealthy man's problem and said that for some time **(e)** he should concentrate only on green colours and not let his eyes see any other colours. The wealthy man thought it was a strange prescription, but he was desperate and decided to try it. He got together a group of painters and purchased barrels of green paint and ordered that every object he was likely to see be painted green just as the monk had suggested.

19

★☆☆
2022년 9월 43번

주어진 글 (A)에 이어질 내용을 순서에 맞게 배열한 것으로 가장 적절한 것은?

① (B) — (D) — (C)
② (C) — (B) — (D)
③ (C) — (D) — (B)
④ (D) — (B) — (C)
⑤ (D) — (C) — (B)

20

★★☆
2022년 9월 44번

밑줄 친 (a) ~ (e) 중에서 가리키는 대상이 나머지 넷과 다른 것은?

① (a) ② (b) ③ (c) ④ (d) ⑤ (e)

21

★☆☆
2022년 9월 45번

윗글의 내용으로 적절하지 않은 것은?

① 부자는 눈 통증으로 여러 명의 의사에게 치료받았다.
② 수도사는 붉은 옷을 입고 부자를 다시 찾아갔다.
③ 하인들은 녹색 안경을 구입했다.
④ 부자는 수도사의 처방이 이상하다고 생각했다.
⑤ 부자는 주변을 모두 녹색으로 칠하게 했다.

정답과 해설 : 19~21 348

⏱ 22~24 : 230초

[22~24] 다음 글을 읽고, 물음에 답하시오.

(A)

When Jack was a young man in his early twenties during the 1960s, he had tried to work in his father's insurance business, as was expected of him. His two older brothers fit in easily and seemed to enjoy their work. But Jack was bored with the insurance industry. "It was worse than being bored," he said. "I felt like I was dying inside." Jack felt drawn to hair styling and dreamed of owning a hair shop with a lively environment. He was sure that **(a)** he would enjoy the creative and social aspects of it and that he'd be successful.

(B)

Jack understood that his father feared adoption, in this case especially because the child was of a different racial background than their family. Jack and Michele risked rejection and went ahead with the adoption. It took years but eventually Jack's father loved the little girl and accepted **(b)** his son's independent choices. Jack realized that, although he often felt fear and still does, he has always had courage. In fact, courage was the scaffolding around which **(c)** he had built richness into his life.

♦ scaffolding: 발판

(C)

When he was twenty-six, Jack approached his father and expressed his intentions of leaving the business to become a hairstylist. As Jack anticipated, his father raged and accused Jack of being selfish, ungrateful, and unmanly. In the face of his father's fury, Jack felt confusion and fear. His resolve became weak. But then a force filled **(d)** his chest and he stood firm in his decision. In following his path, Jack not only ran three flourishing hair shops, but also helped his clients experience their inner beauty by listening and encouraging them when they faced dark times.

(D)

His love for his work led to donating time and talent at nursing homes, which in turn led to becoming a hospice volunteer, and eventually to starting fundraising efforts for the hospice program in his community. And all this laid a strong stepping stone for another courageous move in his life. When, after having two healthy children of their own, Jack and his wife, Michele, decided to bring an orphaned child into their family, **(e)** his father threatened to disown them.

22

★☆☆ 2023년 9월 43번

주어진 글 (A)에 이어질 내용을 순서에 맞게 배열한 것으로 가장 적절한 것은?

① (B) — (D) — (C)
② (C) — (B) — (D)
③ (C) — (D) — (B)
④ (D) — (B) — (C)
⑤ (D) — (C) — (B)

23

★★☆ 2023년 9월 44번

밑줄 친 (a) ~ (e) 중에서 가리키는 대상이 나머지 넷과 다른 것은?

① (a) ② (b) ③ (c) ④ (d) ⑤ (e)

24

★☆☆ 2023년 9월 45번

윗글의 Jack에 관한 내용으로 적절하지 않은 것은?

① 두 형은 자신들의 일을 즐기는 것으로 보였다.
② 아버지의 반대로 입양을 포기했다.
③ 아버지에게 회사를 떠나겠다는 의사를 밝혔다.
④ 세 개의 번창하는 미용실을 운영했다.
⑤ 지역사회에서 모금 운동을 시작했다.

정답과 해설 : 22~24 349

Ⓛ 25~27 : 240초

[25~27] 다음 글을 읽고, 물음에 답하시오.

(A)

Eight-year-old Yolanda went to her grandmother's and proudly announced that she was going to be very successful when she grew up and asked her grandmother if she could give her any tips on how to achieve this. The grandmother nodded, took the girl by the hand, and walked **(a)** her to a nearby plant nursery. There, the two of them chose and purchased two small trees.

(B)

The grandmother smiled and said, "Remember this, and you will be successful in whatever you do: If you choose the safe option all of your life, you will never grow. But if you are willing to face the world with all of its challenges, you will learn from those challenges and grow to achieve great heights." Yolanda looked up at the tall tree, took a deep breath, and nodded **(b)** her head, realizing that her wise grandmother was right.

(C)

They returned home and planted one of them in the back yard and planted the other tree in a pot and kept it indoors. Then her grandmother asked her which of the trees **(c)** she thought would be more successful in the future. Yolanda thought for a moment and said the indoor tree would be more successful because it was protected and safe, while the outdoor tree had to cope with the elements. Her grandmother shrugged and said, "We'll see." Her grandmother took good care of both trees.

♦ elements: 악천후

(D)

In a few years, Yolanda, now a teenager, came to visit her grandmother again. Yolanda reminded her that **(d)** she had never really answered her question from when she was a little girl about how she could become successful when she grew up. The grandmother showed Yolanda the indoor tree and then took **(e)** her outside to have a look at the towering tree outside. "Which one is greater?" the grandmother asked. Yolanda replied, "The outside one. But that doesn't make sense; it had to cope with many more challenges than the one inside."

25

★★☆
2020년 3월 43번

주어진 글 (A)에 이어질 내용을 순서에 맞게 배열한 것으로 가장 적절한 것은?

① (B) — (D) — (C)
② (C) — (B) — (D)
③ (C) — (D) — (B)
④ (D) — (B) — (C)
⑤ (D) — (C) — (B)

26

★★☆
2020년 3월 44번

밑줄 친 (a) ~ (e) 중에서 가리키는 대상이 나머지 넷과 다른 것은?

① (a) ② (b) ③ (c) ④ (d) ⑤ (e)

27

★☆☆
2020년 3월 45번

윗글의 내용으로 적절하지 않은 것은?

① Yolanda는 자신이 크게 성공할 것이라고 자랑스럽게 말했다.
② 할머니는 역경으로부터 배울 수 있다고 말했다.
③ Yolanda는 집 밖에 심은 나무가 더 잘 자랄 거라고 말했다.
④ 할머니는 두 나무를 정성스럽게 돌보았다.
⑤ Yolanda는 십 대가 되어 할머니를 다시 방문했다.

정답과 해설 : 25~27 351

⏱ 28~30 : 240초

[28~30] 다음 글을 읽고, 물음에 답하시오.

(A)

It was an unbearably hot Chicago day when the emergency call came over the radio for Jacob's firefighting crew to handle a fire in a downtown apartment building. When they arrived, the roaring fire was spreading through the whole building. Jacob thought it was already looking pretty hopeless. But suddenly, a woman came running up to **(a)** him yelling at the top of her lungs, "My baby, my Kris is on the fifth floor!"

(B)

The tense crowd below broke into cheers as they saw Jacob emerge from the building with the boy. Holding Kris against **(b)** his chest, Jacob could feel the boy's heart pounding, and when he coughed from the smoke, Jacob knew Kris would survive. Paramedics tended to the boy while Jacob himself fell to the ground. Two weeks after the rescue, two people visited Jacob at the station — Kris and his mother. They came to thank him and told him they were forever in his debt.

♦ paramedic: 응급 구조대원

(C)

Her desperate and urgent voice made Jacob decide to enter the building instantly. He made his way up to the fifth floor with another firefighter. By the time they made it up to the fifth floor, the fire had grown so fierce, neither could see more than a few feet in front of them. Jacob's partner looked at him and gave him the thumbs-down. As a fireman, **(c)** he knew his partner was right, but he just kept seeing that mother's face in his head.

(D)

Impulsively, Jacob ran down the hall without his partner, disappearing into the flames. As flames shot out of the apartment like fireballs **(d)** he could see a little boy lying on the floor in just about the only spot that wasn't on fire. He didn't even have time to figure out if he was alive or dead. He just grabbed **(e)** him and rushed out. Jacob and the boy cleared the fifth floor landing just as the fireman could hear the sound of the floor above collapsing.

28

★☆☆
2019년 9월 43번

주어진 글 (A)에 이어질 내용을 순서에 맞게 배열한 것으로 가장 적절한 것은?

① (B) — (D) — (C)
② (C) — (B) — (D)
③ (C) — (D) — (B)
④ (D) — (B) — (C)
⑤ (D) — (C) — (B)

29

★★☆
2019년 9월 44번

밑줄 친 (a) ~ (e) 중에서 가리키는 대상이 나머지 넷과 다른 것은?

① (a) ② (b) ③ (c) ④ (d) ⑤ (e)

30

★★☆
2019년 9월 45번

윗글의 내용으로 적절하지 않은 것은?

① 불이 건물 전체로 퍼지고 있었다.
② Kris와 엄마는 소방서에 방문했다.
③ Jacob은 동료와 함께 5층으로 올라갔다.
④ 소년은 불이 붙지 않은 바닥에 누워 있었다.
⑤ Jacob은 소년을 발견한 즉시 생사를 확인했다.

정답과 해설 : 28~30 352

Ⓛ 31~33 : 240초

[31~33] 다음 글을 읽고, 물음에 답하시오.

(A)

It was a hot day in early fall. Wylder was heading to the school field for his first training. He had just joined the team with five other students after a successful tryout. Approaching the field, **(a)** <u>he</u> saw players getting ready, pulling up their socks and strapping on shin guards. But they weren't together. New players were sitting in the shade by the garage, while the others were standing in the sun by the right pole. Then Coach McGraw came and watched the players.

♦ shin: 정강이

(B)

'Wow,' thought Wylder. From his new location on the grass, he stretched out his legs. He liked what he was hearing. A new sense of team spirit came across **(b)** <u>him</u>, a deeper sense of connection. It was encouraging to hear Coach talk about this, to see him face the challenge head-on. Now his speech was over. The players got up and started walking on the field to warm up. "Good job, Coach. That was good," Wylder said to McGraw in a low voice as he walked past him, keeping **(c)** <u>his</u> eyes down out of respect.

(C)

McGraw continued to point, calling each player out, until he was satisfied with the rearrangement. "Okay, this is how it's going to be," he began. "We need to learn how to trust and work with each other. This is how a team plays. This is how I want you to be on and off the field: together." The players looked at each other. Almost immediately, McGraw noticed a change in their postures and faces. **(d)** <u>He</u> saw some of them starting to smile.

(D)

Coach McGraw, too, saw the pattern — new kids and others grouping separately. 'This has to change,' he thought. He wanted a winning team. To do that, he needed to build relationships. "I want you guys to come over here in the middle and sit," he called the players as he walked over. "You!" McGraw roared, pointing at Wylder. "Come here onto the field and sit. And Jonny! You sit over there!" He started pointing, making sure they mixed together. Wylder realized what Coach was trying to do, so **(e)** <u>he</u> hopped onto the field.

31

★★☆
2023년 3월 43번

주어진 글 (A)에 이어질 내용을 순서에 맞게 배열한 것으로 가장 적절한 것은?

① (B) — (D) — (C)
② (C) — (B) — (D)
③ (C) — (D) — (B)
④ (D) — (B) — (C)
⑤ (D) — (C) — (B)

32

★★☆
2023년 3월 44번

밑줄 친 (a) ~ (e) 중에서 가리키는 대상이 나머지 넷과 <u>다른</u> 것은?

① (a) ② (b) ③ (c) ④ (d) ⑤ (e)

33

★☆☆
2023년 3월 45번

윗글의 내용으로 적절하지 <u>않은</u> 것은?

① Wylder는 다섯 명의 다른 학생과 팀에 합류했다.
② Wylder는 잔디 위의 새로운 자리에서 다리를 쭉 폈다.
③ McGraw는 재배열이 마음에 들 때까지 선수들을 불러냈다.
④ McGraw는 선수들의 자세와 얼굴의 변화를 알아차렸다.
⑤ McGraw는 선수들에게 운동장 밖으로 나가라고 말했다.

정답과 해설 : 31~33 353

⏲ 34~36 : 240초

[34~36] 다음 글을 읽고, 물음에 답하시오.

(A)

Henrietta is one of the greatest "queens of song." She had to go through a severe struggle before **(a)** she attained the enviable position as the greatest singer Germany had produced. At the beginning of her career she was hissed off a Vienna stage by the friends of her rival, Amelia. But in spite of this defeat, Henrietta endured until all Europe was at her feet.

♦ hiss off: 야유하여 쫓아내다

(B)

The answer was, "That's my mother, Amelia Steininger. She used to be a great singer, but she lost her voice, and she cried so much about it that now **(b)** she can't see anymore." Henrietta inquired their address and then told the child, "Tell your mother an old acquaintance will call on her this afternoon." She searched out their place and undertook the care of both mother and daughter. At her request, a skilled doctor tried to restore Amelia's sight, but it was in vain.

(C)

But Henrietta's kindness to **(c)** her former rival did not stop here. The next week she gave a benefit concert for the poor woman, and it was said that on that occasion Henrietta sang as **(d)** she had never sung before. And who can doubt that with the applause of that vast audience there was mingled the applause of the angels in heaven who rejoice over the good deeds of those below?

(D)

Many years later, when Henrietta was at the height of her fame, one day she was riding through the streets of Berlin. Soon she came across a little girl leading a blind woman. She was touched by the woman's helplessness, and she impulsively beckoned the child to **(e)** her, saying "Come here, my child. Who is that you are leading by the hand?"

34

★★☆ 2023년 6월 43번

주어진 글 (A)에 이어질 내용을 순서에 맞게 배열한 것으로 가장 적절한 것은?

① (B) — (D) — (C)
② (C) — (B) — (D)
③ (C) — (D) — (B)
④ (D) — (B) — (C)
⑤ (D) — (C) — (B)

35

★★☆ 2023년 6월 44번

밑줄 친 (a) ~ (e) 중에서 가리키는 대상이 나머지 넷과 다른 것은?

① (a) ② (b) ③ (c) ④ (d) ⑤ (e)

36

★☆☆ 2023년 6월 45번

윗글의 내용으로 적절하지 않은 것은?

① Amelia와 Henrietta는 라이벌 관계였다.
② Henrietta는 모녀의 거처를 찾아내서 그들을 돌보았다.
③ 숙련된 의사가 Amelia의 시력을 회복시켰다.
④ 불쌍한 여성을 위해 Henrietta는 자선 콘서트를 열었다.
⑤ Henrietta는 눈먼 여성을 데리고 가는 여자 아이와 마주쳤다.

정답과 해설 : 34~36 355

Ⓒ 37~39 : 240초

[37~39] 다음 글을 읽고, 물음에 답하시오.

(A)

Maria Sutton was a social worker in a place where the average income was very low. Many of Maria's clients had lost their jobs when the coal industry in a nearby town collapsed. Every Christmas season, knowing how much children loved presents at Christmas, Maria tried to arrange a special visit from Santa Claus for one family. Alice, the seven-year-old daughter of Maria, was very enthusiastic about helping with **(a)** her mother's Christmas event.

(B)

On Christmas Eve, Maria and Alice visited Karen's house with Christmas gifts. When Karen opened the door, Maria and Alice wished the astonished woman a merry Christmas. Then Alice began to unload the gifts from the car, handing them to Karen one by one. Karen laughed in disbelief, and said she hoped she would one day be able to do something similar for someone else in need. On her way home, Maria said to Alice, "God multiplied **(b)** your gift."

(C)

This year's lucky family was a 25-year-old mother named Karen and her 3-year-old son, who she was raising by herself. However, things went wrong. Two weeks before Christmas Day, a representative from a local organization called Maria to say that the aid she had requested for Karen had fallen through. No Santa Claus. No presents. Maria saw the cheer disappear from Alice's face at the news. After hearing this, **(c)** she ran to her room.

(D)

When Alice returned, her face was set with determination. She counted out the coins from her piggy bank: $4.30. "Mom," she told Maria, "**(d)** I know it's not much. But maybe this will buy a present for the kid." Maria gave her daughter a lovely hug. The next day, Maria told her coworkers about her daughter's latest project. To **(e)** her surprise, staff members began to open their purses. The story of Alice's gift had spread beyond Maria's office, and Maria was able to raise $300 — plenty for a Christmas gift for Karen and her son.

37

★★☆ 2020년 6월 43번

주어진 글 (A)에 이어질 내용을 순서에 맞게 배열한 것으로 가장 적절한 것은?

① (B) — (D) — (C)
② (C) — (B) — (D)
③ (C) — (D) — (B)
④ (D) — (B) — (C)
⑤ (D) — (C) — (B)

38

★★☆ 2020년 6월 44번

밑줄 친 (a) ~ (e) 중에서 가리키는 대상이 나머지 넷과 다른 것은?

① (a) ② (b) ③ (c) ④ (d) ⑤ (e)

39

★☆☆ 2020년 6월 45번

윗글의 내용으로 적절하지 않은 것은?

① Maria는 평균 소득이 매우 낮은 지역의 사회복지사였다.
② 크리스마스 전날 Karen은 선물을 받았다.
③ Karen은 세 살 된 아들을 키우고 있었다.
④ Maria는 지역 단체 대표의 연락을 받지 못했다.
⑤ Maria는 300달러를 모금할 수 있었다.

정답과 해설 : 37~39 356

⏱ 40~42 : 250초

[40~42] 다음 글을 읽고, 물음에 답하시오.

(A)

Is it possible that two words can change someone's day, someone's life? What if those same two words could change the world? Well, Cheryl Rice is on a quest to find out. This quest accidentally began in November, 2016 in a grocery store. **(a)** She was standing in the checkout line behind a woman who looked to be in her 60's. When it was the woman's turn to pay, the cashier greeted her by name and asked her how she was doing.

♦ quest: 탐색

(B)

As Cheryl walked into the parking lot, she spotted the woman returning her shopping cart, and she remembered something in her purse that could help her. She approached the woman and said, "Excuse me, I couldn't help overhearing what you said to the cashier. It sounds like you're going through a really hard time right now. I'm so sorry. I'd like to give you something." And (b) she handed her a small card.

(C)

The woman looked down, shook her head and said, "Not so good. My husband just lost his job. I don't know how I'm going to get through the holidays." Then **(c)** she gave the cashier some food stamps. Cheryl's heart ached. She wanted to help but didn't know how. "Should I offer to pay for her groceries, ask for her husband's resume?" She did nothing — yet. And the woman left the store.

♦ food stamp: 구호 대상자용 식량 카드

(D)

When the woman read the card's only two words, she began to cry. And through her tears, she said, "You have no idea how much this means to me." **(d)** She was a little startled by her reply. Having never done anything like this before, Cheryl hadn't anticipated the reaction she might receive. All **(e)** she could think to respond was, "Oh, my. Would it be OK to give you a hug?" After they embraced, she walked back to her car and began to cry too. The words on the card? "You Matter."

40

★★☆
2018년 6월 43번

주어진 글 (A)에 이어질 내용을 순서에 맞게 배열한 것으로 가장 적절한 것은?

① (B) — (D) — (C)
② (C) — (B) — (D)
③ (C) — (D) — (B)
④ (D) — (B) — (C)
⑤ (D) — (C) — (B)

41

★★★
2018년 6월 44번

밑줄 친 (a) ~ (e) 중에서 가리키는 대상이 나머지 넷과 다른 것은?

① (a) ② (b) ③ (c) ④ (d) ⑤ (e)

42

★★★
2018년 6월 45번

윗글의 Cheryl Rice에 관한 내용으로 적절하지 않은 것은?

① 계산대 줄에 서 있었다.
② 대화를 우연히 엿들었다고 말했다.
③ 작은 카드를 건넸다.
④ 식료품 구입비를 대신 지불했다.
⑤ 차로 돌아와서 울었다.

정답과 해설 : 40~42 358

Ⓛ 43~45 : 240초

[43~45] 다음 글을 읽고, 물음에 답하시오.

(A)

Once upon a time, two brothers, Robert and James, who lived on neighboring farms fell into conflict. It was the first serious fight in 40 years of farming side by side. It began with a small misunderstanding and it grew into a major argument, and finally it exploded into an exchange of bitter words followed by weeks of silence. One morning there was a knock on Robert's door. **(a)** He opened it to find a carpenter with a toolbox.

(B)

The two brothers stood awkwardly for a moment, but soon met on the bridge and shook hands. They saw the carpenter leaving with his toolbox. "No, wait! Stay a few more days." Robert told him. "Thank you for **(b)** your invitation. But I need to go build more bridges. Don't forget. The fence leads to isolation and the bridge to openness," said carpenter. The two brothers nodded at the carpenter's words.

(C)

Looking at Robert, the carpenter said, "I'm looking for a few days' work. Do **(c)** you have anything to repair?" "I have nothing to be repaired, but I have a job for you. Look across the creek at that farm. Last week, my younger brother James took his bulldozer and put that creek in the meadow between us. Well, **(d)** I will do even worse. I want you to build me an 8-foot tall fence which will block him from seeing my place," said Robert. The carpenter seemed to understand the situation.

(D)

Robert prepared all the materials the carpenter needed. The next day, Robert left to work on another farm, so he couldn't watch the carpenter for some days. When Robert returned and saw the carpenter's work, his jaw dropped. Instead of a fence, the carpenter had built a bridge that stretched from one side of the creek to the other. His brother was walking over, waving **(e)** his hand in the air. Robert laughed and said to the carpenter, "You really can fix anything."

43

★☆☆
2023년 11월 43번

주어진 글 (A)에 이어질 내용을 순서에 맞게 배열한 것으로 가장 적절한 것은?

① (B) — (C) — (D)
② (C) — (B) — (D)
③ (C) — (D) — (B)
④ (D) — (B) — (C)
⑤ (D) — (C) — (B)

44

★★☆
2023년 11월 44번

밑줄 친 (a) ~ (e) 중에서 가리키는 대상이 나머지 넷과 다른 것은?

① (a) ② (b) ③ (c) ④ (d) ⑤ (e)

45

★☆☆
2023년 11월 45번

윗글의 내용으로 적절하지 않은 것은?

① Robert와 James는 40년간 나란히 농사를 지었다.
② Robert는 떠나려는 목수에게 더 머무르라고 말했다.
③ James는 불도저로 초원에 샛강을 만들었다.
④ Robert는 목수가 필요로 하는 재료들을 준비해 주었다.
⑤ 목수는 샛강에 다리 대신 울타리를 설치했다.

정답과 해설 : 43~45 359

ⓒ 46~48 : 230초

[46~48] 다음 글을 읽고, 물음에 답하시오.

(A)

Christine was a cat owner who loved her furry companion, Leo. One morning, she noticed that Leo was not feeling well. Concerned for her beloved cat, Christine decided to take him to the animal hospital. As she always brought Leo to this hospital, she was certain that the vet knew well about Leo. **(a)** She desperately hoped Leo got the necessary care as soon as possible.

(B)

"I'll call **(b)** you with updates as soon as we know anything," said the vet. Throughout the day, Christine anxiously awaited news about Leo. Later that day, the phone rang and it was the vet. "The tests revealed a minor infection. Leo needs some medication and rest, but he'll be back to his playful self soon." Relieved to hear the news, Christine rushed back to the animal hospital to pick up Leo.

(C)

The vet provided detailed instructions on how to administer the medication and shared tips for a speedy recovery. Back at home, Christine created a comfortable space for Leo to rest and heal. **(c)** She patted him with love and attention, ensuring that he would recover in no time. As the days passed, Leo gradually regained his strength and playful spirit.

(D)

The waiting room was filled with other pet owners. Finally, it was Leo's turn to see the vet. Christine watched as the vet gently examined him. The vet said, "**(d)** I think Leo has a minor infection." "Infection? Will he be okay?" asked Christine. "We need to do some tests to see if he is infected. But for the tests, it's best for Leo to stay here," replied the vet. It was heartbreaking for Christine to leave Leo at the animal hospital, but **(e)** she had to accept it was for the best.

46

★☆☆
2024년 3월 43번

주어진 글 (A)에 이어질 내용을 순서에 맞게 배열한 것으로 가장 적절한 것은?

① (B) — (D) — (C)
② (C) — (B) — (D)
③ (C) — (D) — (B)
④ (D) — (B) — (C)
⑤ (D) — (C) — (B)

47

★☆☆
2024년 3월 44번

밑줄 친 (a) ~ (e) 중에서 가리키는 대상이 나머지 넷과 다른 것은?

① (a) ② (b) ③ (c) ④ (d) ⑤ (e)

48

★★☆
2024년 3월 45번

윗글의 내용으로 적절하지 않은 것은?

① Christine은 수의사가 Leo에 대해 잘 알고 있을 거라고 확신했다.
② Christine은 병원을 방문한 다음 날 수의사의 전화를 받았다.
③ 수의사는 Leo의 빠른 회복을 위한 조언을 했다.
④ 대기실은 다른 반려동물의 주인들로 꽉 차 있었다.
⑤ Leo의 감염 여부를 알기 위해 검사를 할 필요가 있었다.

정답과 해설 : 46~48 360

⌚ 49~51 : 240초

[49~51] 다음 글을 읽고, 물음에 답하시오.

(A)

On Saturday morning, Todd and his 5-year-old daughter Ava walked out of the store with the groceries they had just purchased. As they pushed their grocery cart through the parking lot, they saw a red car pulling into the space next to their pick-up truck. A young man named Greg was driving. "That's a cool car," Ava said to her dad. **(a)** He agreed and looked at Greg, who finished parking and opened his door.

(B)

By this time, Greg had already pulled one thin wheel out of his car and attached it to the frame. He was now pulling a second wheel out when he looked up and saw Todd standing near him. Todd said, "Hi there! Have a great weekend!" Greg seemed a bit surprised, but replied by wishing **(b)** him a great weekend too. Then Greg added, "Thanks for letting me have my independence." "Of course," Todd said.

(C)

As Todd finished loading his groceries, Greg's door remained open. Todd noticed Greg didn't get out of his car. But he was pulling something from his car. He put a metal frame on the ground beside his door. Remaining in the driver's seat, he then reached back into **(c)** his car to grab something else. Todd realized what he was doing and considered whether **(d)** he should try to help him. After a moment, he decided to approach Greg.

(D)

After Todd and Ava climbed into their truck, Ava became curious. So she asked why **(e)** he didn't offer to help the man with his wheelchair. Todd said, "Why do you insist on brushing your teeth without my help?" She answered, "Because I know how to!" He said, "And the man knows how to put together his wheelchair." Ava understood that sometimes the best way to help someone is to not help at all.

49

★★☆ 2024년 6월 43번

주어진 글 (A)에 이어질 내용을 순서에 맞게 배열한 것으로 가장 적절한 것은?

① (B) — (D) — (C)
② (C) — (B) — (D)
③ (C) — (D) — (B)
④ (D) — (B) — (C)
⑤ (D) — (C) — (B)

50

★★☆ 2024년 6월 44번

밑줄 친 (a) ~ (e) 중에서 가리키는 대상이 나머지 넷과 다른 것은?

① (a) ② (b) ③ (c) ④ (d) ⑤ (e)

51

★☆☆ 2024년 6월 45번

윗글의 내용으로 적절하지 않은 것은?

① Ava는 차가 멋지다고 말했다.
② Greg는 얇은 바퀴를 프레임에 끼웠다.
③ Greg는 휠체어를 꺼내준 것에 감사하다고 말했다.
④ Todd는 Greg가 차에서 내리지 않은 것을 알아차렸다.
⑤ Ava는 트럭에 오른 후 호기심이 생겼다.

정답과 해설 : 49~51 362

⏲ 52~54 : 230초

[52~54] 다음 글을 읽고, 물음에 답하시오.

(A)

My two girls grew up without challenges with respect to development and social interaction. My son Benjamin, however, was quite delayed. He struggled through his childhood, not fitting in with the other children and wondering what he was doing wrong at every turn. He was teased by the other children and frowned upon by a number of unsympathetic adults. But his Grade 1 teacher was a wonderful, caring person who took the time to ask why Benjamin behaved the way **(a)** he did.

(B)

I suspected the teacher had paid for it out of his own pocket. It was a story-board book with a place for a photo. On each page there was an outline of an animal and a hole so that the face in the photo appeared to be the face of the animal. Wondering if Benjamin would really be interested in the book, I brought it home. He loved it! Through that book, he saw that **(b)** he could be anything he wanted to be: a cat, an octopus, a dinosaur — even a frog!

(C)

The teacher was determined to understand Benjamin and to accept him as he was. One day he came home with a note from his teacher. He suggested I go to the school library. They were having a sale, and **(c)** he thought my son would like one of the books. I couldn't go for a couple of days and was concerned I'd missed the opportunity. When I finally went to the school, his teacher told me that the sale had ended but that the library had saved the book for my little boy.

(D)

Benjamin joyfully embarked on an imaginative journey through the book, and little did we know, it laid the groundwork for his future successes. And thankfully, his teacher had taken the time to observe and understand **(d)** him and had discovered a way to help him reach out of his own world and join ours through a story-board book. My son later became a child actor and performed for seven years with a Toronto casting agency. **(e)** He is now a published author who writes fantasy and science-fiction! Who would have guessed?

52

★☆☆ 2024년 9월 43번

주어진 글 (A)에 이어질 내용을 순서에 맞게 배열한 것으로 가장 적절한 것은?

① (B) — (D) — (C)
② (C) — (B) — (D)
③ (C) — (D) — (B)
④ (D) — (B) — (C)
⑤ (D) — (C) — (B)

53

★☆☆ 2024년 9월 44번

밑줄 친 (a) ~ (e) 중에서 가리키는 대상이 나머지 넷과 다른 것은?

① (a) ② (b) ③ (c) ④ (d) ⑤ (e)

54

★☆☆ 2024년 9월 45번

윗글의 내용으로 적절하지 않은 것은?

① Benjamin은 어린 시절 다른 아이들과 잘 어울리지 않았다.
② 'I'는 선생님이 책값을 지불했다고 짐작했다.
③ Benjamin은 'I'가 가져온 책을 좋아하지 않았다.
④ 선생님은 'I'에게 학교 도서관에 방문할 것을 제안했다.
⑤ Benjamin은 아역 배우가 되었다.

정답과 해설 : 52~54 363

1회 20분 미니모의고사

날짜 월 일 요일
시간 : ~ :

동영상 강의
25BR2_CH19

01

★☆☆
2020년 9월 18번

다음 글의 목적으로 가장 적절한 것은?

Dear Residents,

We truly value and appreciate all of our residents, including those with pets. We believe that allowing people to live with their pets enriches their lives. While we encourage you to enjoy your pets, we also want to ensure that you do not do so at the expense of your neighbors or your community. We have received reports that some residents have been disturbed by noise from dogs barking. Excessive barking by dogs disrupts everyone within hearing, particularly those who are elderly or sick or who have small children. We kindly ask that you keep your dogs' noise levels to a minimum. Thank you for your assistance with this.

Regards,
Conway Forest Apartments Management Office

① 반려견이 짖는 소리를 최소화 해줄 것을 요청하려고
② 아파트 내 반려동물 출입 가능 구역을 안내하려고
③ 아파트 공사로 인한 소음 발생에 대해 사과하려고
④ 반려견 대소변 관련 민원처리 결과를 공지하려고
⑤ 반려동물과 외출 시 목줄 사용을 당부하려고

02

★★☆
2017년 3월 20번

다음 글의 요지로 가장 적절한 것은?

Much has been written and said about positive self-talk — for example, repeating to ourselves "I am wonderful" when we feel down, "I am strong" when going through a difficult time, or "I am getting better every day in every way" each morning in front of the mirror. The evidence that this sort of pep talk works is weak, and there are psychologists who suggest that it can actually hurt more than it can help. Little, unfortunately, has been written about *real self-talk*, acknowledging honestly what we are feeling at a given point. When feeling down, saying "I am really sad" or "I feel so torn" — to ourselves or to someone we trust — is much more helpful than declaring "I am tough" or "I am happy."

* pep talk: 격려의 말

① 타인에 대한 비난은 자신의 감정도 상하게 한다.
② 우울할 때 자신에게 하는 격려의 말은 큰 힘이 된다.
③ 자아 성찰은 타인의 조언을 받는 것보다 효과적이다.
④ 가까운 사이일수록 말과 행동을 조심할 필요가 있다.
⑤ 자신이 느끼는 감정을 솔직히 인정하는 것이 도움이 된다.

정답과 해설 : 01 365 02 365

03

★★☆ 2016년 11월 21번

다음 글의 제목으로 가장 적절한 것은?

We have constructed so many large reservoirs to hold water, and they are located primarily in the Northern Hemisphere rather than randomly around the globe. As a result, enough of Earth's mass has shifted to speed up its rotation. Currently, 88 huge reservoirs hold some 10 trillion tons of water. Before the reservoirs were built, this water was located in the ocean, which has most of its mass in the Southern Hemisphere. The effect is like a whirling skater who pulls her arms in to turn faster. Because natural factors in the environment, such as the pull of tides, are gradually slowing Earth's rotation, the human influence is accidentally working against the natural rate of deceleration. The shift in Earth's mass has also changed the location of the axis on which Earth rotates.

① Reservoir Effect: Unintended Change in Earth's Rotation
② Why Figure Skaters Spin Faster with Their Arms in
③ Factors Affecting the Location of Reservoirs
④ Eco-Friendly Water Holding Method
⑤ What Makes Earth Rotate Slower?

04

★★★ 2020년 9월 29번

다음 글의 밑줄 친 부분 중, 어법상 틀린 것은? 3점

All social interactions require some common ground upon which the involved parties can coordinate their behavior. In the interdependent groups ① in which humans and other primates live, individuals must have even greater common ground to establish and maintain social relationships. This common ground is morality. This is why morality often is defined as a shared set of standards for ② judging right and wrong in the conduct of social relationships. No matter how it is conceptualized — whether as trustworthiness, cooperation, justice, or caring — morality ③ to be always about the treatment of people in social relationships. This is likely why there is surprising agreement across a wide range of perspectives ④ that a shared sense of morality is necessary to social relations. Evolutionary biologists, sociologists, and philosophers all seem to agree with social psychologists that the interdependent relationships within groups that humans depend on ⑤ are not possible without a shared morality.

정답과 해설 : 03 366 04 366

05

★★★
2019년 9월 30번

다음 글의 밑줄 친 부분 중, 문맥상 낱말의 쓰임이 적절하지 않은 것은? [3점]

A champion of free speech and religious toleration, Voltaire was a controversial figure. He is, for instance, supposed to have declared, "I hate what you say, but will defend to the death your right to say it," a powerful ① defense of the idea that even views that you despise deserve to be heard. In eighteenth-century Europe, however, the Catholic Church strictly ② controlled what could be published. Many of Voltaire's plays and books were censored and burned in public, and he was even imprisoned in the Bastille in Paris because he had ③ insulted a powerful aristocrat. But none of this stopped him challenging the prejudices and pretensions of those around him. In his short philosophical novel, *Candide*, he completely ④ supported the kind of religious optimism about humanity and the universe that other contemporary thinkers had expressed, and he did it in such an entertaining way that the book became an instant bestseller. Wisely, Voltaire left his name ⑤ off the title page, otherwise its publication would have landed him in prison again for making fun of religious beliefs.

06

★☆☆
2018년 3월 26번

Science Showcase Video Contest에 관한 다음 안내문의 내용과 일치하지 않는 것은?

Science Showcase Video Contest

Create a video that effectively communicates a specific aspect of science and is informative for a broad public audience. Videos should be submitted between June 1 and August 31. Winners will be announced in early October.

Up to $2,000 in Prize Money

Guidelines:

- One or two entries per individual
- Submit the following to sciencesshowcase@kmail.com:
  - the title of your video
  - your name and phone number
  - a download link to your video
- No restrictions on style of video

For more information, please visit our website: www.scienceshowcase.org.

① 8월 31일까지 영상물을 제출해야 한다.
② 수상자는 10월 초에 발표한다.
③ 상금은 2,000달러까지 수여된다.
④ 출품작은 1인당 한 편으로 제한된다.
⑤ 영상물의 형식에는 제한이 없다.

정답과 해설 : 05 368 06 369

07

★☆☆
2020년 3월 25번

다음 도표의 내용과 일치하지 않는 것은?

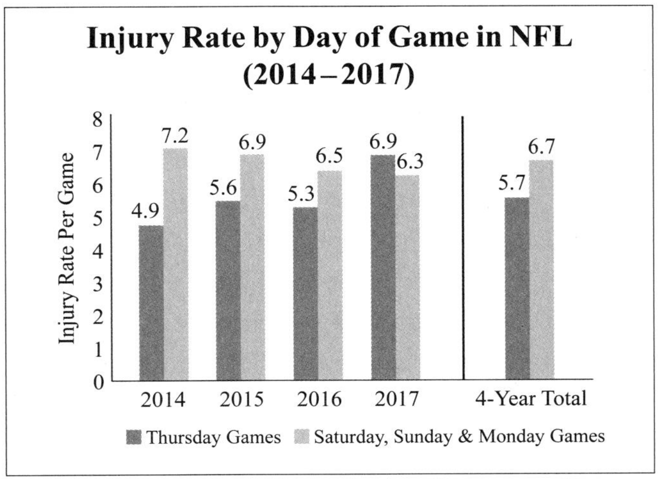

The above graph shows the injury rate by day of game in the National Football League (NFL) from 2014 to 2017. ① The injury rate of Thursday games was the lowest in 2014 and the highest in 2017. ② The injury rate of Saturday, Sunday and Monday games decreased steadily from 2014 to 2017. ③ In all the years except 2017, the injury rate of Thursday games was lower than that of Saturday, Sunday and Monday games. ④ The gap between the injury rate of Thursday games and that of Saturday, Sunday and Monday games was the largest in 2014 and the smallest in 2017. ⑤ In two years out of the four, the injury rate of Thursday games was higher than that of the 4-year total.

08

★★★
2019년 3월 33번

다음 빈칸에 들어갈 말로 가장 적절한 것은? 3점

Theseus was a great hero to the people of Athens. When he returned home after a war, the ship that had carried him and his men was so treasured that the townspeople preserved it for years and years, replacing its old, rotten planks with new pieces of wood. The question Plutarch asks philosophers is this: is the repaired ship still the same ship that Theseus had sailed? Removing one plank and replacing it might not make a difference, but can that still be true once all the planks have been replaced? Some philosophers argue that the ship must be ______________________. But if this is true, then as the ship got pushed around during its journey and lost small pieces, it would already have stopped being the ship of Theseus.

◆ plank: 널빤지

① the reminder of victory
② the sum of all its parts
③ fit for the intended use
④ the property of the country
⑤ around for a long period of time

1회 20분 미니모의고사

정답과 해설 : 07 369 08 370

09 최고오답률

★★★
2020년 3월 34번

다음 빈칸에 들어갈 말로 가장 적절한 것은? [3점]

The growing field of genetics is showing us what many scientists have suspected for years — ______________________. This information helps us better understand that genes are under our control and not something we must obey. Consider identical twins; both individuals are given the same genes. In mid-life, one twin develops cancer, and the other lives a long healthy life without cancer. A specific gene instructed one twin to develop cancer, but in the other the same gene did not initiate the disease. One possibility is that the healthy twin had a diet that turned off the cancer gene — the same gene that instructed the other person to get sick. For many years, scientists have recognized other environmental factors, such as chemical toxins (tobacco for example), can contribute to cancer through their actions on genes. The notion that food has a specific influence on gene expression is relatively new.

① identical twins have the same genetic makeup
② our preference for food is influenced by genes
③ balanced diet is essential for our mental health
④ genetic engineering can cure some fatal diseases
⑤ foods can immediately influence the genetic blueprint

10

★★☆
2017년 6월 39번

다음 글에서 전체 흐름과 관계 없는 문장은?

Food shortages caused by global warming could force as many as 1 billion people to leave their homes by 2050, according to the Earth Institute, a New York-based aid agency. ① Hardest hit may be Africa, which could lose two-thirds of its cropland due to desertification, which occurs when the land loses its ability to produce vegetation and turns into deserts. ② Although many scientists expect climate change to result in more rainfall, some areas could experience droughts because rainfall is sporadic or falls in concentrations in some places but misses others. ③ Having an adequate farming system helps farmers overcome long-term droughts. ④ Also, desertification could occur because warmer temperatures draw moisture out of the soil. ⑤ When regions can no longer produce food, people will be forced to move to other areas, making them "climate refugees."

♦ sporadic: 산발적인

정답과 해설 : 09 370 10 371

[11~12] 다음 글을 읽고, 물음에 답하시오.

Animal studies have dealt with the distances creatures may keep between themselves and members of other species. These distances determine the functioning of the so-called 'flight or fight' mechanism. As an animal senses what it considers to be a predator approaching within its 'flight' distance, it will quite simply run away. The distance at which this happens is amazingly **(a)** consistent, and Hediger, a Swiss biologist, claimed to have measured it remarkably precisely for some of the species that he studied. Naturally, it varies from species to species, and usually the larger the animal the **(b)** shorter its flight distance. I have had to use a long focus lens to take photographs of giraffes, which have very large flight distances. By contrast, I have several times nearly stepped on a squirrel in my garden before it drew attention to itself by suddenly escaping! We can only assume that this **(c)** variation in distance matches the animal's own assessment of its ability to accelerate and run.

The 'fight' distance is always **(d)** smaller than the flight distance. If a perceived predator approaches within the flight distance but the animal is trapped by obstacles or other predators and cannot **(e)** flee, it must stand its ground. Eventually, however, attack becomes the best form of defence, and so the trapped animal will turn and fight.

11

★★☆
2020년 3월 41번

윗글의 제목으로 가장 적절한 것은?

① How Animals Migrate Without Getting Lost
② Flight or Fight Mechanism: Still in Our Brain
③ Why the Size Matters in the Survival of Animals
④ Distances: A Determining Factor for Flight or Attack
⑤ Competition for Food Between Large and Small Animals

12

★★★
2020년 3월 42번

밑줄 친 (a) ~ (e) 중에서 문맥상 낱말의 쓰임이 적절하지 않은 것은?

① (a) ② (b) ③ (c) ④ (d) ⑤ (e)

1회 20분 미니모의고사

정답과 해설 : 11~12 372

2회 20분 미니모의고사

날짜 월 일 요일
시간 : ~ :

동영상 강의
25BR2_CH20

01

★★☆
2020년 3월 23번

다음 글의 주제로 가장 적절한 것은?

In addition to the varied forms that recreation may take, it also meets a wide range of individual needs and interests. Many participants take part in recreation as a form of relaxation and release from work pressures or other tensions. Often they may be passive spectators of entertainment provided by television, movies, or other forms of electronic amusement. However, other significant play motivations are based on the need to express creativity, discover hidden talents, or pursue excellence in varied forms of personal expression. For some participants, active, competitive recreation may offer a channel for releasing hostility and aggression or for struggling against others or the environment in adventurous, high-risk activities. Others enjoy recreation that is highly social and provides the opportunity for making new friends or cooperating with others in group settings.

① effects of recreational participation on memory
② various motivations for recreational participation
③ importance of balance between work and leisure
④ social factors promoting the recreation movement
⑤ economic trends affecting recreational participation

02

★★☆
2019년 6월 21번

다음 글에서 필자가 주장하는 바로 가장 적절한 것은?

If you are feeling overwhelmed by the amount of responsibility that you have to deal with in your own life or your own home, you are going to have to figure out a way that you can balance out these responsibilities. For example, is there somebody that you can turn to to tell them that you have too much on your plate and you are feeling too overwhelmed by these responsibilities? If you can find somebody and divide up the labor so that you don't feel so overwhelmed by everything that you are doing, all you have to do sometimes is to ask for help and your life will feel that much better. Many times people will surprise you with their willingness to help you out, so never assume that other people don't care about your stress. Let them know honestly how you are feeling and allow yourself some opportunities to avoid responsibility and give yourself a chance to relax.

① 자신이 맡은 일에 책임감을 가지고 끝까지 완수하라.
② 책임지고 할 일이 많을 때 타인에게 도움을 요청하라.
③ 업무 효율성을 높이기 위해 스트레스를 잘 관리하라.
④ 주어진 시간을 잘 활용하기 위해 일의 우선순위를 정하라.
⑤ 갈등을 원만하게 해결하기 위해 다양한 의견에 귀를 기울여라.

정답과 해설 : 01 374 02 374

03

★★★ 2020년 9월 21번

밑줄 친 got "colder"가 다음 글에서 의미하는 바로 가장 적절한 것은? [3점]

If creators knew when they were on their way to fashioning a masterpiece, their work would progress only forward: they would halt their idea-generation efforts as they struck gold. But in fact, they backtrack, returning to versions that they had earlier discarded as inadequate. In Beethoven's most celebrated work, the Fifth Symphony, he scrapped the conclusion of the first movement because it felt too short, only to come back to it later. Had Beethoven been able to distinguish an extraordinary from an ordinary work, he would have accepted his composition immediately as a hit. When Picasso was painting his famous *Guernica* in protest of fascism, he produced 79 different drawings. Many of the images in the painting were based on his early sketches, not the later variations. If Picasso could judge his creations as he produced them, he would get consistently "warmer" and use the later drawings. But in reality, it was just as common that he got "colder."

① moved away from the desired outcome
② lost his reputation due to public criticism
③ became unwilling to follow new art trends
④ appreciated others' artwork with less enthusiasm
⑤ imitated masters' styles rather than creating his own

04

★★★ 2016년 11월 28번

다음 글의 밑줄 친 부분 중, 어법상 틀린 것은? [3점]

Why do we often feel that others are paying more attention to us than they really are? The spotlight effect means seeing ourselves at center stage, thus intuitively overestimating the extent ① to which others' attention is aimed at us. Timothy Lawson explored the spotlight effect by having college students ② change into a sweatshirt with a big popular logo on the front before meeting a group of peers. Nearly 40 percent of them ③ were sure the other students would remember what the shirt said, but only 10 percent actually did. Most observers did not even notice ④ that the students changed sweatshirts after leaving the room for a few minutes. In another experiment, even noticeable clothes, such as a T-shirt with singer Barry Manilow on it, ⑤ provoking only 23 percent of observers to notice — far fewer than the 50 percent estimated by the students sporting the 1970s soft rock singer on their chests.

♦ sport: 자랑해 보이다

2회 20분 미니모의고사

정답과 해설 : 03 375 04 376

05 최고오답률

★★★ 2016년 6월 34번

다음 빈칸에 들어갈 말로 가장 적절한 것은? 3점

There is no known cure for the ills of ownership. As Adam Smith said, ownership is woven into our lives. But being aware of it might help. Everywhere around us we see the temptation to improve the quality of our lives by buying a larger home, a second car, a new dishwasher, a lawn mower, and so on. But, once we upgrade our possessions we have a very hard time going back down. Ownership simply changes our perspective. Suddenly, moving backward to our pre-ownership state is a loss, one that we cannot accept. And so, while moving up in life, we fall into the fantasy that ____________________, but in reality, it's unlikely. Downgrading to a smaller home, for instance, is experienced as a loss, it is psychologically painful, and we are willing to make all kinds of sacrifices in order to avoid such losses.

① purchasing a house is always profitable
② everyone can improve their quality of life
③ we are able to deal with the loss of faith
④ we can always return to the previous state
⑤ we are willing to sacrifice our pleasure for honor

06

★★★ 2016년 9월 31번

다음 빈칸에 들어갈 말로 가장 적절한 것은?

Changing our food habits is one of the hardest things we can do, because the impulses governing our preferences are often hidden, even from ourselves. And yet adjusting what you eat is entirely possible. We do it all the time. Were this not the case, the food companies that launch new products each year would be wasting their money. After the fall of the Berlin Wall, housewives from East and West Germany tried each other's food products for the first time in decades. It didn't take long for those from the East to realize that they preferred Western yogurt to their own. Equally, those from the West discovered a liking for the honey and vanilla wafer biscuits of the East. From both sides of the wall, these German housewives showed a remarkable ____________ in their food preferences.

① simplicity ② flexibility ③ difference
④ resistance ⑤ consistency

07

★★☆ 2020년 6월 35번

다음 글에서 전체 흐름과 관계 없는 문장은?

Marketing management is concerned not only with finding and increasing demand but also with changing or even reducing it. For example, Uluru (Ayers Rock) might have too many tourists wanting to climb it, and Daintree National Park in North Queensland can become overcrowded in the tourist season. ① Power companies sometimes have trouble meeting demand during peak usage periods. ② In these and other cases of excess demand, the needed marketing task, called demarketing, is to reduce demand temporarily or permanently. ③ Efforts should be made to compensate for the losses caused by the increase in supply. ④ The aim of demarketing is not to completely destroy demand, but only to reduce or shift it to another time, or even another product. ⑤ Thus, marketing management seeks to affect the level, timing, and nature of demand in a way that helps the organisation achieve its objectives.

정답과 해설 : 05 377 06 377 07 378

08

★★★
2017년 11월 40번

다음 글의 내용을 한 문장으로 요약하고자 한다. 빈칸 (A)와 (B)에 들어갈 말로 가장 적절한 것은? 3점

Power distance is the term used to refer to how widely an unequal distribution of power is accepted by the members of a culture. It relates to the degree to which the less powerful members of a society accept their inequality in power and consider it the norm. In cultures with high acceptance of power distance (e.g., India, Brazil, Greece, Mexico, and the Philippines), people are not viewed as equals, and everyone has a clearly defined or allocated place in the social hierarchy. In cultures with low acceptance of power distance (e.g., Finland, Norway, New Zealand, and Israel), people believe inequality should be minimal, and a hierarchical division is viewed as one of convenience only. In these cultures, there is more fluidity within the social hierarchy, and it is relatively easy for individuals to move up the social hierarchy based on their individual efforts and achievements.

⬇

Unlike cultures with high acceptance of power distance, where members are more ___(A)___ to accept inequality, cultures with low acceptance of power distance allow more ___(B)___ within the social hierarchy.

(A)		(B)
① willing	......	mobility
② willing	......	assistance
③ reluctant	......	resistance
④ reluctant	......	flexibility
⑤ afraid	......	openness

09

★★★
2021년 9월 36번

주어진 글 다음에 이어질 글의 순서로 가장 적절한 것은? 3점

When trying to sustain an independent ethos, cultures face a problem of critical mass. No single individual, acting on his or her own, can produce an ethos.

(A) They manage this feat through a combination of trade, to support their way of life, and geographic isolation. The Inuit occupy remote territory, removed from major population centers of Canada. If cross-cultural contact were to become sufficiently close, the Inuit ethos would disappear.

(B) Rather, an ethos results from the interdependent acts of many individuals. This cluster of produced meaning may require some degree of insulation from larger and wealthier outside forces. The Canadian Inuit maintain their own ethos, even though they number no more than twenty-four thousand.

(C) Distinct cultural groups of similar size do not, in the long run, persist in downtown Toronto, Canada, where they come in contact with many outside influences and pursue essentially Western paths for their lives.

* ethos: 민족(사회) 정신 ** insulation: 단절

① (A) — (C) — (B)
② (B) — (A) — (C)
③ (B) — (C) — (A)
④ (C) — (A) — (B)
⑤ (C) — (B) — (A)

2회 20분 미니모의고사

정답과 해설 : 08 379 09 379

[10~12] 다음 글을 읽고, 물음에 답하시오.

(A)

Once upon a time there was a king of Armenia, who, being of a curious turn of mind and in need of some change, sent **(a)** <u>his</u> men throughout the land to make the following proclamation: "Hear this! Whatever man among you can prove himself the most outrageous liar in Armenia shall receive an apple made of pure gold from the hands of His Majesty the King!"

(B)

"You are a perfect liar, sir!" exclaimed the king. "I owe you no money!" "A perfect liar am I?" said the poor man. "Then give me the golden apple!" The king, realizing that the man was trying to trick him, said, "No, no! You are not a liar!" "Then give me the pot of gold you owe me, sire," said the man. The king saw the dilemma. **(b)** <u>He</u> handed over the golden apple.

(C)

The king was beginning to grow tired of **(c)** <u>his</u> new sport and was thinking of calling the whole contest off without declaring a winner. Then there appeared before him a poor, ragged man, carrying a large sack over **(d)** <u>his</u> shoulder. "What can I do for you?" asked His Majesty. "Sire!" said the poor man, slightly bewildered. "Surely you remember? You owe me a pot of gold, and I have come to collect it."

(D)

People began to swarm to the palace from every town and village in the country, people of all ranks and conditions, princes, merchants, farmers, priests, rich and poor, tall and short, fat and thin. There was no lack of liars in the land, and each one told his tale to the king. None of those lies, however, convinced the king that **(e)** <u>he</u> had listened to the best one.

10

★★☆
2019년 3월 43번

주어진 글 (A)에 이어질 내용을 순서에 맞게 배열한 것으로 가장 적절한 것은?

① (B) — (D) — (C)
② (C) — (B) — (D)
③ (C) — (D) — (B)
④ (D) — (B) — (C)
⑤ (D) — (C) — (B)

11

★★☆
2019년 3월 44번

밑줄 친 (a) ~ (e) 중에서 가리키는 대상이 나머지 넷과 <u>다른</u> 것은?

① (a) ② (b) ③ (c) ④ (d) ⑤ (e)

12

★★☆
2019년 3월 45번

윗글의 내용으로 적절하지 <u>않은</u> 것은?

① 왕은 아르메니아 최고의 거짓말쟁이를 찾으려 했다.
② 왕이 가난한 남자에게 황금 한 항아리를 하사했다.
③ 왕은 승자를 발표하지 않고 대회를 중단하려고 했다.
④ 가난한 남자가 커다란 자루를 메고 왕 앞에 나타났다.
⑤ 온갖 부류의 사람들이 궁궐로 모여들기 시작했다.

정답과 해설 : 10~12 380

01

★☆☆
2019년 3월 18번

다음 글의 목적으로 가장 적절한 것은?

Dear Mr. Spencer,

I will have lived in this apartment for ten years as of this coming April. I have enjoyed living here and hope to continue doing so. When I first moved into the Greenfield Apartments, I was told that the apartment had been recently painted. Since that time, I have never touched the walls or the ceiling. Looking around over the past month has made me realize how old and dull the paint has become. I would like to update the apartment with a new coat of paint. I understand that this would be at my own expense, and that I must get permission to do so as per the lease agreement. Please advise at your earliest convenience.

Sincerely,
Howard James

♦ as per: ~에 따라서

① 아파트 안전 진단 결과를 통보하려고
② 아파트 임대차 계약 연장을 논의하려고
③ 아파트 도색 작업에 대한 허락을 받으려고
④ 아파트 수리 비용 부담에 대해 상의하려고
⑤ 아파트 도색에 대한 설문 결과를 알려 주려고

02

★☆☆
2017년 3월 19번

다음 글에 드러난 'I'의 심경 변화로 가장 적절한 것은?

I rode my bicycle alone from work on the very quiet road of my hometown. Suddenly, I noticed a man with long hair secretly riding behind me. I felt my heart jump. I quickened my legs pushing the pedals, hoping to ride faster. He kept following me through the dark, across the field. At last, I got home and tried to reach the bell. The man reached for me. I turned my head around and saw the oddest face in the world. From deep in his throat, I heard him say, "Excuse me, you dropped your bag," giving the bag back to me. I couldn't say anything, but was full of shame and regret for misunderstanding him.

① scared → embarrassed
② worried → proud
③ excited → disappointed
④ happy → concerned
⑤ bored → moved

정답과 해설 : 01 382 02 382

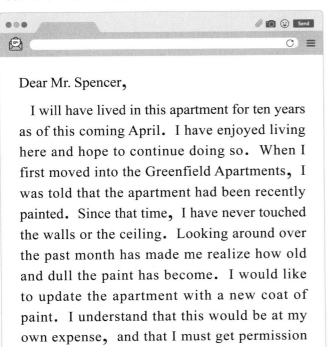

03

★★☆ 2016년 9월 24번

다음 글의 제목으로 가장 적절한 것은?

People who communicate to others about themselves rather freely, who are frank and open, who express their views, opinions, knowledge, and feelings freely, and who share their knowledge and personal experiences with others can be considered as the self-disclosing type. These people constantly communicate with others and make an impact on them. This communication or self-disclosure helps in generating data and such an individual has more of an open and public self than private self. Without an optimal amount of self-disclosure we deny an opportunity for others to know us and for ourselves to get appropriate feedback. People who don't communicate openly are private individuals who may have difficulty discovering themselves fully. At least it is difficult for them to see themselves fully through the eyes of others and also they make limited impact on others.

① Why We Fear Self-disclosure
② Open Yourself Up for Yourself
③ How to Be Honest Without Being Harsh
④ Don't Underestimate the Power of Feedback
⑤ Confidence: A Key to Effective Communication

04 최고오답률

★★★ 2016년 9월 28번

다음 글의 밑줄 친 부분 중, 어법상 틀린 것은? [3점]

Before the washing machine was invented, people used washboards to scrub, or they carried their laundry to riverbanks and streams, ① where they beat and rubbed it against rocks. Such backbreaking labor is still commonplace in parts of the world, but for most homeowners the work is now done by a machine that ② automatically regulates water temperature, measures out the detergent, washes, rinses, and spin-dries. With ③ its electrical and mechanical system, the washing machine is one of the most technologically advanced examples of a large household appliance. It not only cleans clothes, but it ④ is so with far less water, detergent, and energy than washing by hand requires. ⑤ Compared with the old washers that squeezed out excess water by feeding clothes through rollers, modern washers are indeed an electrical-mechanical phenomenon.

정답과 해설 : 03 383 04 383

05

★★★
2016년 6월 36번

주어진 글 다음에 이어질 글의 순서로 가장 적절한 것은?

> To learn about the nature and location of memory, scientists in the 1940s began their search for memory in the most obvious place: within the cells of our brains — our neurons.

(A) These interconnected webs are intricately involved in our memories. The memory the rats had of the maze was spread throughout their brains. Whenever the scientists cut out a piece, they damaged only a small portion of the involved connections.

(B) Researchers eventually turned their search for memories to the wiring between neurons rather than within the cells themselves. Each of the hundred billion neurons in our brains is connected to seven thousand other neurons, in a dense web of nerve fibers.

(C) They cut out parts of rats' brains, trying to make them forget a maze, and found that it didn't matter what part of the brain they chose; the rats never forgot. In 1950, the researchers gave up, concluding that memory must be somewhere else.

◆ maze: 미로

① (A) — (C) — (B)
② (B) — (A) — (C)
③ (B) — (C) — (A)
④ (C) — (A) — (B)
⑤ (C) — (B) — (A)

06

★☆☆
2020년 3월 26번

Christiaan Huygens에 관한 다음 글의 내용과 일치하지 <u>않는</u> 것은?

Dutch mathematician and astronomer Christiaan Huygens was born in The Hague in 1629. He studied law and mathematics at his university, and then devoted some time to his own research, initially in mathematics but then also in optics, working on telescopes and grinding his own lenses. Huygens visited England several times, and met Isaac Newton in 1689. In addition to his work on light, Huygens had studied forces and motion, but he did not accept Newton's law of universal gravitation. Huygens' wide-ranging achievements included some of the most accurate clocks of his time, the result of his work on pendulums. His astronomical work, carried out using his own telescopes, included the discovery of Titan, the largest of Saturn's moons, and the first correct description of Saturn's rings.

◆ pendulum: 시계추

① 대학에서 법과 수학을 공부했다.
② 1689년에 뉴턴을 만났다.
③ 뉴턴의 만유인력 법칙을 받아들였다.
④ 당대의 가장 정확한 시계 중 몇몇이 업적에 포함되었다.
⑤ 자신의 망원경을 사용하여 천문학 연구를 수행했다.

정답과 해설 : 05 384 06 385

07

★★★ 2018년 9월 38번

글의 흐름으로 보아, 주어진 문장이 들어가기에 가장 적절한 곳은?

> This allows the solids to carry the waves more easily and efficiently, resulting in a louder sound.

Tap your finger on the surface of a wooden table or desk, and observe the loudness of the sound you hear. Then, place your ear flat on top of the table or desk. (①) With your finger about one foot away from your ear, tap the table top and observe the loudness of the sound you hear again. (②) The volume of the sound you hear with your ear on the desk is much louder than with it off the desk. (③) Sound waves are capable of traveling through many solid materials as well as through air. (④) Solids, like wood for example, transfer the sound waves much better than air typically does because the molecules in a solid substance are much closer and more tightly packed together than they are in air. (⑤) The density of the air itself also plays a determining factor in the loudness of sound waves passing through it.

♦ molecule: 분자

08

★★★ 2016년 6월 32번

다음 빈칸에 들어갈 말로 가장 적절한 것은? [3점]

Although people most commonly think of persuasion as deep processing, it is actually shallow processing that is the more common way to influence behavior. For example, Facebook started inserting advertisements in the middle of users' webpages. Many users didn't like this change and, on principle, refused to click on the ads. However, this approach displays a fundamental misunderstanding of the psychology behind the ads. The truth is that Facebook never expected anyone to click on the ads. All the company wants is to expose you to those product brands and images. The more times you're exposed to something, in general, the more you like it. Everyone is influenced by ______________________. So, even though you can ignore the ads, by simply being in front of your eyes, they're doing their work.

① others' opinions on the ads
② the familiarity of an image
③ their loyalty to a specific brand
④ false information on the Internet
⑤ the deep processing of information

정답과 해설 : 07 386 08 386

09 최고오답률

★★★ 2016년 6월 33번

다음 빈칸에 들어갈 말로 가장 적절한 것은? 3점

In science, we can never really prove that a theory is true. All we can do in science is use evidence to reject a hypothesis. Experiments never directly prove that a theory is right; all they can do is provide indirect support by rejecting all the other theories until ______________. For example, sometimes you hear people say things like 'evolution is only a theory: science has never proved it.' Well, that's true, but only in the sense that science never proves that any theory is positively true. But the theory of evolution has assembled an enormous amount of convincing data proving that other competing theories are false. So though it hasn't been proved, overwhelmingly, evolution is the best theory that we have to explain the data we have.

① scientists admit to using false data
② researchers document their methods
③ people go back to their original hypothesis
④ the theories can be explained in words
⑤ only one likely theory remains

10

★★★ 2016년 11월 40번

다음 글의 내용을 한 문장으로 요약하고자 한다. 빈칸 (A)와 (B)에 들어갈 말로 가장 적절한 것은? 3점

Inappropriate precision means giving information or figures to a greater degree of apparent accuracy than suits the context. For example, advertisers often use the results of surveys to prove what they say about their products. Sometimes they claim a level of precision not based reliably on evidence. So, if a company selling washing powder claims 95.45% of British adults agree that this powder washes whiter than any other, then this level of precision is clearly inappropriate. It is unlikely that all British adults were surveyed, so the results are based only on a sample and not the whole population. At best the company should be claiming that over 95% of *those asked* agreed that their powder washes whiter than any other. Even if the whole population had been surveyed, to have given the result to two decimal points would have been absurd. The effect is to propose a high degree of scientific precision in the research. Frequently, however, inappropriate precision is an attempt to mask the unscientific nature of a study.

◆ decimal point: 소수점

⬇

Advertisers often give us information with a(n) ___(A)___ precision, but it can be considered as an intention to conceal the lack of ___(B)___ of their research.

	(A)		(B)
①	excessive	……	reliability
②	excessive	……	popularity
③	sufficient	……	investment
④	reasonable	……	integrity
⑤	reasonable	……	availability

3회 20분 미니모의고사

정답과 해설 : 09 387 10 388

[11~12] 다음 글을 읽고, 물음에 답하시오.

Eye-blocking is a nonverbal behavior that can occur when we feel threatened or don't like what we see. Squinting and closing or shielding our eyes are actions that have evolved to protect the brain from seeing undesirable images. As an investigator, I used eye-blocking behaviors to assist in the arson investigation of a tragic hotel fire in Puerto Rico. A security guard came under immediate suspicion because the blaze broke out in an area where he was assigned. One of the ways we determined he had nothing to do with starting the fire was by asking him some specific questions as to where he was before the fire, at the time of the fire, and whether or not he set the fire. After each question I observed his face for any telltale signs of eye-blocking behavior. He blocked his eyes only when questioned about where he was when the fire started. Oddly, in contrast, he did not seem troubled by the question, "Did you set the fire?" This told me the real issue was his ________________ at the time of the fire. He was questioned further by the investigators and eventually admitted to leaving his post to visit his girlfriend, who also worked at the hotel. Unfortunately, while he was gone, the arsonists entered the area he should have been guarding and started the fire. In this case, the guard's eye-blocking behavior gave us the insight we needed to pursue a line of questioning that eventually broke the case open.

♦ arson: 방화(죄)

11

★★★
2016년 6월 41번

윗글의 제목으로 가장 적절한 것은?

① Why Did the Man Set the Fire?
② Factors Interrupting Eye-blocking
③ Eye-blocking Reveals Hidden Information
④ Strategies to Hide Eye-blocking Behaviors
⑤ Hiring a Security Guard to Protect a Building

12

★★★
2016년 6월 42번

윗글의 빈칸에 들어갈 말로 가장 적절한 것은? 3점

① emotion ② judgment ③ location
④ safety ⑤ reaction

정답과 해설 : 11~12 389

적중 단어 466

교재 WORD BOOK <교육부 선정 필수 암기 어휘 2200> 중 고2 2023년 11월, 2024년 3월, 6월, 9월 학력평가에 출제된 단어들을 선별하였습니다.

단어	뜻
able	a. ~할 수 있는, 재능 있는
accept	v. 받아들이다, 수락하다
access	n. 입장, 접속 / v. 접근하다
accident	n. 사고, 재해
accompany	v. 동반하다, 동행하다
accomplish	v. 완수하다, 성취하다
accurate	a. 정확한, 정밀한
achieve	v. 달성하다, 잘 해내다
admit	v. 인정하다, ~에 들어갈 수 있다
advance	n. 전진 / v. 나아가게 하다, 나아가다
advantage	n. 유리한 점 / v. 유리하게 하다
affect	v. 영향을 미치다, 발생하다
allow	v. 허락하다, 인정하다
alter	v. 바꾸다, 바뀌다
although	conj. ~이긴 하지만
among	prep. ~에 둘러싸여, ~의 가운데에
amount	n. 총액 / v. ~에 달하다
analysis	n. 분석 연구
angle	n. 각도 / v. 각을 이루다
annual	a. 매년의 / n. 연감
appear	v. ~인 것 같다, 나타나다
apply	v. 지원하다, 쓰다
appreciate	v. 진가를 알아보다
approach	v. 다가가다 / n. 접근법
appropriate	a. 적절한 / v. 도용하다
argue	v. 언쟁을 하다, 주장하다
asleep	a. 잠이 든, 자고 있는
assess	v. 평가하다, 가늠하다
assume	v. 가정하다
attend	v. 참석하다, 주의를 기울이다
attention	n. 주의
attract	v. 마음을 끌다, 매혹하다
audience	n. 청중, 관중
available	a. 구할[이용할] 수 있는, 쓸모 있는
average	a. 평균의 / n. 평균 v. 평균 ~이 되다
avoid	v. 방지하다, 막다
background	n. 배경, 경력
barrier	n. 장벽 / v. 방책으로 둘러싸다
behavio(u)r	n. 처신, 행동
belief	n. 신념, 확신
benefit	n. 혜택 / v. 유익하다, 이득을 보다
bias	n. 편견 / v. 편견을 갖게 하다
bit	n. 조금, 약간
blow	v. 불다, 치다 n. 한줄기 바람, 세게 때림
bore	v. 지루하게 하다, 구멍을 뚫다 n. 지겨운 사람, 구멍
brain	n. 뇌 / v. 머리를 내리치다
broadcast	v. 방송하다 / n. 방송 a. 방송의 / ad. 널리
career	n. 직업 / v. 달리다, 질주하다
cart	n. 수레 / v. 운반하다
category	n. 범주, 부문
cause	n. 원인 / v. 야기하다
century	n. 100년, 세기
challenge	n. 도전 v. 도전하다, 이의를 제기하다
climate	n. 기후, 지역
cluster	n. 무리 v. 무리를 이루다, 떼를 짓게 하다
code	n. 암호 / v. 부호로 처리하다
comfort	n. 안락 / v. 위로하다
comfortable	a. 편한, 쾌적한
commerce	n. 무역, 통상
common	a. 흔한 / n. 공유지
communication	n. 의사소통, 통신
community	n. 주민, 지역 사회
companion	n. 동반자 / v. 동행하다
complete	a. 완벽한 v. 완전[완벽]하게 만들다
concept	n. 개념, 관념
concern	v. 관계하다, 관련되다 / n. 걱정
conduct	v. 행동하다, 지휘하다 / n. 행동
confirm	v. 사실임을 보여주다, 확인해 주다
connect	v. 잇다, 이어지다
consider	v. 고려하다, 잘 생각해 보다
consistent	a. 한결같은, 일관된
constant	a. 끊임없는 / n. 정수
consume	v. 소비하다, 소비되다
consumption	n. 소비, 소모
contest	n. 대회 / v. 경쟁을 벌이다
context	n. 맥락, 전후 사정
continue	v. 계속하다, 계속되다
contrary	a. 다른 / n. 반대 / ad. 반대로
contrast	n. 대조 / v. 대조하다, 대조를 이루다
contribute	v. 기부하다, 기증하다
corporate	a. 기업의, 회사의
create	v. 창조하다, 창조적인 일을 하다
critic	n. 비평가, 평론가
crucial	a. 중대한, 결정적인
curiosity	n. 호기심, 진기함
curious	a. 궁금한, 알고 싶어 하는
current	a. 현재의 / n. 흐름, 전류
data	n. (datum의 복수형) 자료, 정보
deal	v. 다루다, 나누어 주다 / n. 거래
decade	n. 10년, 10권
degree	n. 도, 정도
delay	n. 지연 / v. 연기하다, 지체하다
delight	n. 기쁨 / v. 기쁨을 주다, 기뻐하다
demonstrate	v. 입증하다, 시위를 하다
depend	v. 의존하다, 의지하다
desire	n. 욕구 / v. 바라다
detail	n. 세부 사항 / v. 상세히 알리다
determine	v. 알아내다, 결정하다
develop	v. 성장[발달]시키다, 성장[발달]하다
device	n. 장치, 기구
differ	v. 다르다, 상이하다
different	a. 다른, 차이가 나는
direct	a. 직접적인 / ad. 직행으로 v. 향하게 하다, 지도하다
disappoint	v. 실망시키다, 좌절시키다
discount	n. 할인 / v. 할인하다 a. 할인 판매의
disease	n. 병, 질병
distance	n. 거리 / v. 거리를 두다
distinguish	v. 구별하다, 판별하다
diverse	a. 다양한, 다른
divide	v. 나누다, 나뉘다 / n. 분할
due	a. ~로 인한
each	pron. 각각 / a. 각각의 / ad. 각각에
earn	v. 벌다, (수익 등을) 올리다
easy	a. 쉬운 / ad. 조심해서
effect	n. 영향 / v. 가져오다
effective	a. 효과적인, 실질적인

efficient	a. 능률적인, 효율적인
effort	n. 노력, 분투
element	n. 요소, 성분
eliminate	v. 없애다, 제거하다
else	a. 또[그 밖의] 다른 / ad. 그 밖에
embrace	v. 껴안다, 서로 껴안다 / n. 포옹
encourage	v. 격려하다, 용기를 북돋우다
engineer	n. 기사 / v. 기사로 일하다
enhance	v. 높이다, 올리다
enjoy	v. 즐기다, 즐거운 시간을 보내다
entire	a. 전체의 / n. 전부
environment	n. 환경, 주위
equipment	n. 장비, 용품
era	n. 연대, 시대
error	n. 실수, 오류
especially	ad. 특히, 특별히
essential	a. 필수적인 / n. 필수[기본]적인 것
establish	v. 설립하다, 수립하다
ethical	a. 윤리적인, 도덕상의
evaluate	v. 평가하다, 감정하다
even	ad. ~도 / a. 평평한
event	n. 사건, 일
ever	ad. 언제든, 한번이라도
evidence	n. 증거 / v. 입증하다
examine	v. 조사하다, 심리하다
excellent	a. 훌륭한, 탁월한
except	prep. ~을 제외하고는 conj. ~라는 점만 제외하면 v. 제외하다
exchange	n. 교환 / v. 교환하다, 교체하다
excite	v. 흥분시키다, 초조하게 만들다
exist	v. 존재하다, 실재하다
expand	v. 확대하다, 확대되다
expect	v. 예상하다, 생각하다
experience	n. 경험 / v. 경험하다
experiment	n. 실험 / v. 실험하다
expert	n. 전문가 / a. 전문가의
explain	v. 설명하다, 이유가 되다
explicit	a. 분명한, 명쾌한
explore	v. 탐험하다, 탐사하다
factor	n. 요인 / v. 인수 분해하다
fair	a. 공정한 / ad. 공정하게 / n. 박람회
false	a. 틀린, 사실이 아닌
famous	a. 유명한, 이름난
fear	n. 공포 / v. 두려워하다
feature	n. 특색 / v. 특징으로 삼다
fee	n. 요금 / v. 요금을 지불하다
feed	v. 음식을 먹이다, 먹이를 먹다 n. 먹이
few	a. 많지 않은 / pron. 소수
figure	n. 수치 / v. 판단하다
flavo(u)r	n. 맛 / v. 맛[풍미]을 더하다
follow	v. 따라가다, 뒤따라가다 n. 뒤따르기
forever	ad. 영원히 / n. 영원
forward	ad. 앞으로 / a. 앞으로 가는 v. 보내다 / n. 포워드
foster	v. 조성하다 / a. 수양-
function	n. 기능 / v. 기능하다
fundamental	a. 근본적인 / n. 근본
gap	n. 틈, 구멍
generate	v. 발생시키다, 만들어 내다
generation	n. 사람들, 세대
genetic	a. 유전의, 유전학의
graph	n. 그래프 / v. 그래프로 나타내다
grateful	a. 고마워하는, 감사하는
half	n. 반 / a. 반의 / ad. 절반 정도로
happen	v. 일어나다, 발생하다
harvest	n. 수확 / v. 수확하다, 추수하다
hazard	n. 위험 v. 틀릴 셈치고 제안[추측]하다
health	n. 건강, 건강 상태
hear	v. 듣다, 전해 듣다
hire	v. 고용하다, 고용되다 / n. 고용
huge	a. 막대한, 엄청난
immense	a. 엄청난, 어마어마한
importance	n. 중요성, 중대성
important	a. 중요한, 소중한
include	v. 포함하다, 함유하다
increase	v. 증가시키다, 인상되다 / n. 증가
individual	a. 각각의 / n. 개인
industry	n. 산업, 공업
infect	v. 감염시키다, 전염시키다
influence	n. 영향 v. 영향을 주다, 감화를 주다
inhibit	v. 억제하다, 저해하다
input	n. 투입 / v. 입력하다 a. 입력 장치의
instance	n. 사례 / v. ~을 예로 들다
instead	ad. 대신에
instinct	n. 본능, 본성
insurance	n. 보험 / a. 보험의
interest	n. 관심 / v. 관심[흥미]을 끌다
internal	a. 안의, 내부의
interview	n. 면접 v. 면접을 보다, 인터뷰를 하다
invent	v. 발명하다, 고안하다
invest	v. 투자하다, 돈을 쓰다
involve	v. 수반하다, 포함하다
journal	n. 신문, 잡지
judge	n. 판사 / v. 재판하다
knowledge	n. 지식, 학문
lab(oratory)	n. 실험실 / a. 실험실의
labo(u)r	n. 노동 / a. 노동자의 v. 노동하다, 상세히 설명하다
lack	n. 부족 / v. 부족하다
law	n. 법, 법률
lay	v. 놓다, 알을 낳다 / n. 위치
lead	v. 안내하다, 앞장서서 가다 n. 이끌기, 납
leaf	n. 잎, 나뭇잎
leave	v. 떠나다, 출발하다 / n. 허락, 허가
legal	a. 법률의 / n. 법률 요건
let	v. 두다, 세가 놓이다 / n. 임대
level	n. 평평함 / a. 평평한 ad. 평평하게 / v. 평평하게 하다
limit	n. 한계 / v. 제한하다
link	n. 관련 / v. 연결하다, 관련되다
list	n. 목록 / v. 목록[명단]을 작성하다
local	a. 장소의 / n. 지역 주민
lose	v. 잃어버리다, 지다
loss	n. 분실, 상실
lot	n. 추첨 / ad. 훨씬 v. 구분하다, 제비 뽑기를 하다
major	a. 큰[많은] 쪽의 / n. 소령 v. 전공하다
majority	n. 대다수, 대부분
manage	v. 간신히 ~하다, 살아 나가다
material	n. 재료 / a. 물질의
matter	n. 문제 / v. 중요하다
mean	v. 의미하다 / a. 비열한, 중간의 n. 수단
measure	v. 측정하다, 측량하다 / n. 조치

2025 마더텅
전국연합 학력평가 기출문제집
고2 영어 독해
WORD BOOK

MOTHERTONGUE
마더텅출판사
since1999.4.1.

2025 마더텅 전국연합 학력평가 기출문제집
고2 영어 독해 WORD BOOK

2025 마더텅 전국연합 학력평가 기출문제집 고2 영어 독해 WORD BOOK은
교육부 선정 필수 암기 어휘 2200개와 교재에 수록된 독해 기출 문제 총 552문항**에 대한 어휘가**
문제편의 문항 구성 순으로 수록되어 있습니다.

WORD BOOK 목차

※ WORD BOOK 30일 완성 학습계획표가 1페이지에 수록되어 있습니다.

※ 학습계획표를 활용하여 학습 일정을 계획하고 규칙적으로 단어를 암기해 보세요.

※ 날짜별로 정해진 분량에 맞춰 단어를 암기하고 자신이 완벽하게 단어를 암기했는지 체크해 보세요.

※ 스스로 학습 현황을 체크하면서 공부하는 습관은 문제집을 끝까지 푸는 데 도움을 줍니다.

WORD BOOK 30일 완성

Step 1 단어를 외울 때는 소리 내어 읽으면서 영어 단어와 한글 뜻을 여러 번 쓰세요.
Step 2 영어 단어와 한글 뜻을 모두 외운 다음 단어의 왼쪽 네모 상자에 체크하세요.
Step 3 외우지 못한 단어는 영어 단어와 한글 뜻을 여러 번 쓰세요.
Step 4 모든 네모 상자에 체크가 될 때까지 어휘 암기를 반복하세요.

Day	학습 내용	페이지	1회독	2회독	3회독
1일차	교육부 선정 필수 암기 어휘 2200	2			
2일차		3			
3일차		4			
4일차		5			
5일차		6			
6일차		7			
7일차		8			
8일차		9			
9일차		10			
10일차		11			
11일차		12			
12일차		13			
13일차		14			
14일차		복습			
15일차	마더텅 기출문제집 수록 어휘	15~18			
16일차		19~22			
17일차		23~26			
18일차		27~30			
19일차		복습			
20일차		31~34			
21일차		35~38			
22일차		39~42			
23일차		43~46			
24일차		복습			
25일차		47~49			
26일차		50~52			
27일차		53~55			
28일차		56~57			
29일차		58~59			
30일차		복습			

교육부 선정 필수 암기 어휘 2200

☐ **abandon**	v. 버리다 n. 방종
☐ **able**	a. ~할 수 있는, 재능 있는
☐ **aboard**	ad. prep. 탄, 탑승한
☐ **abound**	v. 아주 많다, 풍부하다
☐ **abroad**	ad. 해외에, 해외로
☐ **absent**	a. 결석한 v. 결석하다
☐ **absolute**	a. 완전한 n. 절대적인 것
☐ **absorb**	v. 흡수하다, 빨아들이다
☐ **abstract**	a. 추상적인 n. 추상화 v. 추출하다
☐ **absurd**	a. 우스꽝스러운 n. 불합리
☐ **abundant**	a. 풍부한, 아주 많은
☐ **abuse**	n. 남용 v. 남용하다
☐ **academy**	n. 학교, 학술원
☐ **accelerate**	v. 속도를 높이다, 가속화되다
☐ **accent**	n. 말씨 v. 강조하다
☐ **accept**	v. 받아들이다, 수락하다
☐ **access**	n. 입장, 접속 v. 접근하다
☐ **accident**	n. 사고, 재해
☐ **accommodate**	v. 공간을 제공하다, 수용하다
☐ **accompany**	v. 동반하다, 동행하다
☐ **accomplish**	v. 완수하다, 성취하다
☐ **accord**	n. 일치 v. 일치시키다, 일치하다
☐ **account**	n. 계좌 v. 간주하다, 설명하다
☐ **accumulate**	v. 모으다, 늘어나다
☐ **accurate**	a. 정확한, 정밀한
☐ **accuse**	v. 고발[비난]하다, 혐의를 제기하다
☐ **ache**	v. 아프다 n. 아픔
☐ **achieve**	v. 달성하다, 잘 해내다
☐ **acid**	n. 산(酸) a. 산성(酸性)의
☐ **acknowledge**	v. 인정하다
☐ **acquire**	v. 습득하다, 얻다
☐ **acquisition**	n. 습득, 획득
☐ **adapt**	v. 맞추다, 익숙해지다
☐ **addict**	n. 중독자 v. ~에 빠지게 하다
☐ **adequate**	a. 충분한, 적절한
☐ **adjust**	v. 조정하다, 적응하다
☐ **administer**	v. 관리하다, 집행하다
☐ **administration**	n. 관리, 경영
☐ **admire**	v. 존경하다, 감탄하다
☐ **admission**	n. 입장, 들어감
☐ **admit**	v. 인정하다, 들어가게 하다
☐ **adolescent**	n. 청소년 a. 청소년기의
☐ **adopt**	v. 입양하다, 채택하다
☐ **advance**	n. 전진 v. 나아가게 하다, 나아가다
☐ **advantage**	n. 유리한 점 v. 유리하게 하다
☐ **adventure**	n. 모험, 모험심
☐ **adverse**	a. 부정적인, 불리한
☐ **advertize / advertise**	v. 광고하다, 알리다
☐ **advice**	n. 조언, 충고
☐ **advise**	v. 조언하다, 의논하다
☐ **advocate**	v. 지지하다 n. 옹호자
☐ **aesthetic**	a. 심미적 n. 미적 특질
☐ **affair**	n. 일, 문제
☐ **affect**	v. 영향을 미치다, 발생하다
☐ **affection**	n. 애착, 보살핌
☐ **afford**	v. 여유[형편]가 되다, ~할 수 있다
☐ **agency**	n. 대리점, 대행사
☐ **agenda**	n. 의제, 안건
☐ **agent**	n. 대리인, 중개상
☐ **aggress**	v. 공격하다
☐ **aggressive**	a. 공격적인
☐ **agriculture**	n. 농업, 농사
☐ **aid**	n. 원조 v. 돕다
☐ **aim**	n. 목적 v. 목표로 하다
☐ **airline**	n. 항공사, 정기 항공로
☐ **airport**	n. 공항
☐ **alarm**	n. 불안, 경보기 v. 불안하게 만들다
☐ **alert**	a. 기민한 v. 알리다 n. 경계
☐ **alien**	a. 생경한 n. 외국인 체류자 v. 양도하다
☐ **alike**	a. 비슷한 ad. 비슷하게
☐ **alive**	a. 살아 있는, 넘치는
☐ **allocate**	v. 할당하다, 분배하다
☐ **allow**	v. 허락하다, 인정하다
☐ **ally**	n. 동맹국 v. 동맹하다
☐ **alongside**	prep. ~ 옆에 ad. 나란히
☐ **aloud**	ad. 소리 내어, 큰소리로
☐ **alter**	v. 바꾸다, 바뀌다
☐ **alternate**	a. 번갈아 생기는 v. 번갈아 나오게 만들다
☐ **alternative**	n. 대안 a. 대체 가능한
☐ **although**	conj. ~이긴 하지만
☐ **altogether**	ad. 완전히, 전적으로
☐ **amaze**	v. 놀라게 하다
☐ **ambassador**	n. 대사, 사절
☐ **ambition**	n. 야망 v. 열망하다
☐ **ambitious**	a. 야심 있는, 야망을 가진
☐ **ambulance**	n. 구급차
☐ **among**	prep. ~에 둘러싸여, ~의 가운데에
☐ **amount**	n. 총액 v. ~에 달하다
☐ **amuse**	v. 즐겁게 하다, 웃기다
☐ **analysis**	n. 분석 연구
☐ **analyze / analyse**	v. 분석하다, 분해하다
☐ **anchor**	n. 닻, 진행자 v. 닻을 내리다, 정박하다
☐ **ancient**	a. 고대의 n. 고대인
☐ **angel**	n. 천사, 천사 같은 사람
☐ **anger**	n. 화 v. 화나게 하다
☐ **angle**	n. 각도 v. 향하게 하다
☐ **anniversary**	n. 기념일 a. 해마다의
☐ **announce**	v. 발표하다, 알리다
☐ **annoy**	v. 짜증나게 하다, 귀찮게 하다
☐ **annual**	a. 매년의 n. 연감
☐ **ant**	n. 개미
☐ **anticipate**	v. 예상하다, 예기하다
☐ **anxiety**	n. 불안(감), 염려
☐ **anxious**	a. 불안해하는, 염려하는
☐ **apart**	ad. 떨어져, 따로
☐ **apology**	n. 사과, 사죄
☐ **apparent**	a. 분명한, 명백한
☐ **appeal**	n. 간청, 매력 v. 호소하다
☐ **appear**	v. ~인 것 같다, 나타나다
☐ **applicant**	n. 지원자, 신청자
☐ **apply**	v. 지원하다, 쓰다
☐ **appoint**	v. 임명하다, 지명하다
☐ **appreciate**	v. 진가를 알아보다
☐ **approach**	v. 다가가다 n. 접근법
☐ **appropriate**	a. 적절한 v. 도용하다
☐ **approve**	v. 찬성하다
☐ **approximate**	a. 거의 정확한 v. 비슷하다, 가깝다
☐ **architect**	n. 건축가, 건축 기사
☐ **architecture**	n. 건축, 건축학
☐ **argue**	v. 언쟁을 하다, 주장하다
☐ **arise**	v. 생기다, 발생하다
☐ **army**	n. 군대, 육군
☐ **arrange**	v. 마련하다, 처리하다
☐ **arrest**	v. 체포하다, 심장이 멎다 n. 체포, 저지
☐ **arrow**	n. 화살, 화살표
☐ **article**	n. 글, 기사
☐ **artifice**	n. 책략, 계략
☐ **artificial**	a. 인공의, 인조의
☐ **aside**	ad. 한쪽으로 n. 방백
☐ **asleep**	a. 잠이 든, 자고 있는
☐ **aspect**	n. 측면, 양상
☐ **aspire**	v. 열망하다, 염원하다
☐ **assault**	n. 폭행(죄) v. 폭행하다
☐ **assemble**	v. 모이다, 모으다
☐ **assert**	v. 주장하다
☐ **assess**	v. 평가하다, 가늠하다
☐ **asset**	n. 자산, 이점
☐ **assign**	v. 맡기다, 선임하다, 양도하다
☐ **assignment**	n. 과제, 임무
☐ **assist**	v. 돕다, 어시스트하다 n. 원조
☐ **assistant**	n. 조수 a. 보조하는
☐ **associate**	v. 연상하다 a. 제휴한 n. 동료
☐ **assume**	v. 가정하다
☐ **assure**	v. 장담하다, 확언하다
☐ **astonish**	v. 깜짝 놀라게 하다
☐ **athlete**	n. (운동) 선수
☐ **atmosphere**	n. 대기, 공기
☐ **atom**	n. 원자, 미립자
☐ **attach**	v. 붙이다, 연관되다
☐ **attack**	n. 공격, 폭행 v. 공격하다, 폭행하다
☐ **attempt**	n. 시도 v. 시도하다
☐ **attend**	v. 참석하다, 주의를 기울이다
☐ **attention**	n. 주의
☐ **attitude**	n. 태도, 마음가짐
☐ **attract**	v. 마음을 끌다, 매혹하다
☐ **attribute**	v. 결과로 보다 n. 자질
☐ **auction**	n. 경매 v. 경매로 팔다
☐ **audience**	n. 청중, 관중
☐ **authentic**	a. 진본인, 진품인
☐ **author**	n. 작가 v. 쓰다
☐ **automatic**	a. 자동의 n. 자동 권총[소총]
☐ **avail**	v. 도움이 되다, 쓸모가 있다 n. 소용
☐ **available**	a. 구할[이용할] 수 있는, 쓸모 있는
☐ **average**	a. 평균의 n. 평균 v. 평균 ~이 되다
☐ **avoid**	v. 방지하다, 막다
☐ **await**	v. 기다리다, 대기하다
☐ **awake**	a. 잠들지 않은 v. 깨다, 각성시키다
☐ **award**	n. 상 v. 주다, 수여하다
☐ **aware**	a. 알고 있는, 의식[자각]하고 있는
☐ **awe**	n. 경외감 v. 경외심을 갖게 하다
☐ **awful**	a. 끔찍한 ad. 되게
☐ **awkward**	a. 어색한, 곤란한
☐ **background**	n. 배경, 경력
☐ **bacon**	n. 베이컨
☐ **balance**	n. 균형 v. 균형을 유지하다
☐ **balloon**	n. 풍선 v. 부풀다, 부풀게 하다
☐ **ban**	v. 금지하다 n. 금지
☐ **band**	n. 밴드 v. 띠를 두르다
☐ **bang**	v. 쾅하고 치다 n. 쾅(하는 소리)
☐ **bankrupt**	a. 파산한 n. 파산자 v. 파산시키다
☐ **bar**	v. 빗장을 지르다, (길을) 막다[차단하다] prep. ~을 제외하고
☐ **bare**	a. 벌거벗은, 노출된 v. 벌거벗기다, 드러내다
☐ **bargain**	n. 싸게 사는 물건 v. 협상[흥정]하다
☐ **bark**	n. 나무껍질, 짖는 소리 v. 껍질을 벗기다, 짖다
☐ **barrier**	n. 장벽 v. 방책으로 둘러싸다
☐ **basis**	n. 근거, 이유
☐ **battery**	n. 건전지, 배터리
☐ **battle**	n. 전투 v. 싸우다
☐ **bay**	n. 만(灣), 구역, 구간
☐ **beam**	n. 빛줄기, 광선 v. 활짝 웃다, 보내다
☐ **bean**	n. 콩
☐ **beard**	n. (턱)수염
☐ **beast**	n. 짐승, 야수
☐ **beat**	v. 두드리다 n. 고동 a. 녹초가 된
☐ **beer**	n. 맥주, 맥주 한 잔
☐ **beg**	v. 간청하다, 애원하다
☐ **behalf**	n. 이익, 이로움
☐ **behave**	v. 처신하다, 예의 바르게 행동하다

☐ behavio(u)r	n. 처신, 행동
☐ belief	n. 신념, 확신
☐ belong	v. 속하다, 소속하다
☐ bench	n. 벤치 v. 벤치를 놓다
☐ bend	v. 굽히다, 숙이다 n. 굽이, 굽은 곳
☐ beneath	prep. 아래[밑]에 ad. 아래쪽에
☐ benefit	n. 혜택 v. 유익하다, 이득을 보다
☐ bet	v. 돈을 걸다 n. 내기
☐ betray	v. 넘겨주다, 배반하다
☐ beyond	prep. ~ 저편에 ad. 건너편에
☐ bias	n. 편견 v. 편견을 갖게 하다
☐ billion	n. 10억 a. 10억의
☐ bin	n. 쓰레기통 v. 상자에 넣다
☐ bind	v. 묶다, 굳다 n. 곤경
☐ biography	n. 전기, 일대기
☐ biology	n. 생물학, 생명 작용
☐ bit	n. 조금, 약간
☐ bite	v. 물다 n. 물기
☐ bitter	a. 격렬한 n. 쓴맛
☐ blame	v. ~을 탓하다 n. 책임
☐ blank	a. 빈 n. 빈칸 v. 비우다, 멍해지다
☐ blanket	n. 담요 a. 전반적인 v. 뒤덮다
☐ blast	n. 폭발 v. 폭발시키다, 폭발하다
☐ blend	v. 섞다, 섞이다 n. 혼합
☐ bless	v. 가호를 빌다
☐ blind	a. 눈이 먼 v. 눈이 멀게 만들다
☐ blink	v. (눈을) 깜박이다 n. 눈을 깜박거림
☐ block	n. 덩어리 v. 막다
☐ blonde	a. 금발인 n. 금발 머리 여자
☐ bloom	n. 꽃 v. 꽃을 피우다
☐ blossom	n. 꽃 v. 꽃이 피다
☐ blow	v. 불다, 치다 n. 한줄기 바람, 세게 때림, 개화
☐ boil	v. 끓다, 끓이다 n. 끓음
☐ bold	a. 용감한 n. 볼드체
☐ bomb	n. 폭탄 v. 폭격하다, 질주하다
☐ bond	n. 끈 v. 접착시키다, 유대감을 형성하다
☐ boom	n. 쾅[탕] 하는 소리 v. 쾅[탕] 하는 소리를 내다
☐ boost	v. 신장시키다 n. 격려
☐ boot	n. 부츠 v. 세게 차다, 부팅되다
☐ border	n. 국경[경계] v. 접하다, 인접하다
☐ bore	v. 지루하게 하다, 구멍을 뚫다 n. 지겨운 사람, 구멍
☐ boss	n. 상관 v. 지휘하다 a. 아주 좋은
☐ bother	v. 신경 쓰다, 귀찮게 하다 n. 성가심
☐ bounce	v. 튀다, 튀기다 n. (공 등이) 튐
☐ boundary	n. 경계(선), 한계
☐ bow	v. 절하다, (허리를) 굽히다, 활처럼 휘다 n. 절, 활
☐ bowl	n. 그릇, 통, 공 v. 공을 굴리다
☐ brain	n. 뇌, 지능 v. 머리를 내리치다
☐ brake	n. 브레이크 v. 브레이크를 밟다
☐ branch	n. 나뭇가지 v. 가지를 뻗다, 갈라지다, 가르다
☐ brand	n. 상표 v. 낙인을 찍다
☐ breast	n. 유방, 가슴 v. 가슴으로 밀다
☐ breath	n. 숨, 호흡
☐ breathe	v. 호흡하다, 숨을 쉬다
☐ breed	v. 새끼를 낳다, 사육하다 n. 품종
☐ breeze	n. 산들바람 v. 거침없이 움직이다
☐ brick	n. 벽돌, 블록
☐ brief	a. 짧은 n. 개요 v. 알려주다
☐ brilliant	a. 아주 밝은, 눈부신
☐ broad	a. 넓은, 광범위한
☐ broadcast	v. 방송하다 n. 방송 a. 방송의 ad. 널리
☐ brutal	a. 잔혹한, 악랄한
☐ brute	n. 짐승, 짐승 같은 인간 a. 횡포한
☐ bubble	n. 거품 v. 거품이 일다, 거품을 일으키다
☐ budget	n. 예산 v. 예산을 세우다 a. 저가의
☐ bug	n. 벌레 v. 도청장치를 달다
☐ bulk	n. 대부분, 규모 v. 부피가 커지다
☐ bull	n. 황소, 수컷
☐ bully	n. 괴롭히는 사람 v. 괴롭히다
☐ bump	v. 부딪치다 n. 쿵
☐ bunch	n. 다발 v. 다발로 묶다
☐ bundle	n. 꾸러미 v. 마구 밀어 넣다, 짐을 꾸리다
☐ burden	n. 부담, 짐 v. 부담[짐]을 지우다
☐ burst	v. 터지다, 터뜨리다
☐ bury	v. 묻다, 매장하다
☐ bush	n. 관목, 덤불
☐ butcher	n. 정육점 주인 v. 잔인하게 살해하다
☐ buzz	v. 윙윙거리다 n. 윙윙거림
☐ cable	n. 굵은 밧줄 v. 전보를 보내다
☐ cage	n. (짐승의) 우리 v. 우리에 넣다
☐ calculate	v. 계산하다, 산출하다
☐ calculator	n. 계산기
☐ calendar	n. 달력, 일정표
☐ calm	a. 침착한 v. 진정시키다 n. 평온
☐ cancel	v. 취소하다 n. 취소
☐ cancer	n. 암, 해악
☐ candidate	n. 입후보자, 후보(자)
☐ canvas	n. 캔버스 천, 화폭
☐ capable	a. ~을 할 수 있는, 유능한
☐ cape	n. 망토, 곶, 갑
☐ capital	n. 수도 a. 주요한
☐ captain	n. 선장 v. 통솔하다
☐ capture	v. 붙잡다 n. 생포
☐ career	n. 직업, 경력 v. 달리다, 질주하다
☐ carpet	n. 카펫 v. 카펫을 깔다
☐ cart	n. 수레 v. 운반하다
☐ carve	v. 조각하다, 새기다, 고기를 잘라 내다
☐ cast	v. 던지다, 배역을 정 하다 n. 출연자들
☐ castle	n. 성 v. 성을 쌓다
☐ catalog(ue)	n. 목록 v. 목록을 만들다
☐ category	n. 범주, 부문
☐ cater	v. 음식을 공급하다, 부응하다
☐ cattle	n. 소, 들소
☐ causal	a. 원인의, 원인이 되는
☐ cause	n. 원인 v. ~을 야기하다
☐ caution	n. 조심, 신중, 주의 v. 경고하다
☐ cave	n. 굴, 동굴 v. 굴을 파다, 함몰하다
☐ cease	v. 중단시키다, 중단되다
☐ ceiling	n. 천장, 최고 한도
☐ celebrate	v. 기념하다, 축배를 들다
☐ celebrity	n. 유명 인사, 명사
☐ cell	n. 세포
☐ censor	n. 검열관 v. 검열하다
☐ century	n. 100년, 세기
☐ certificate	n. 증서 v. 증명서를 주다
☐ chain	n. 사슬 v. (사슬로) 묶다
☐ chairman	n. 의장, 회장
☐ challenge	n. 도전 v. 도전하다, 이의를 제기하다
☐ chamber	n. 회관 v. 방에 가두다 a. 실내악의
☐ champion	n. 챔피언 a. 우승한 v. 싸우다
☐ channel	n. 채널 v. (돈·감정·생각 등을) (~에) 쏟다
☐ chaos	n. 혼돈, 혼란
☐ character	n. 성격, 기질
☐ characteristic	a. 특유의 n. 특징
☐ charge	n. 요금 v. 청구하다
☐ charity	n. 자선[구호] 단체, 자선
☐ charm	n. 매력 v. 매혹하다, 매력을 가지다
☐ chart	n. 도표 v. 기록하다
☐ chase	v. 뒤쫓다, 추적하다 n. 추적
☐ chat	v. 담소[이야기]를 나누다 n. 담소
☐ cheek	n. 볼 v. 무례[뻔뻔] 하게 말하다
☐ cheer	n. 환호(성) v. 환호하다, 기운이 나다
☐ chef	n. 요리사, 주방장
☐ chemical	a. 화학의 n. 화학 물질
☐ chest	n. 가슴, 흉부
☐ chew	v. 씹다 n. 씹기
☐ chief	a. 주된 n. 우두머리
☐ chill	n. 냉기 v. 차게 식히다, 차게 식다 a. 쌀쌀한
☐ chin	n. 턱 v. 턱걸이를 하다
☐ chip	n. 이가 빠진 흔적 v. 이가 빠지다
☐ choice	n. 선택 a. 아주 좋은
☐ choir	n. 합창단 v. 합창하다
☐ chop	v. 자르다 n. 자르기
☐ chorus	n. 후렴 v. 합창을 하다
☐ chronic	a. 만성적인, 장기간에 걸친
☐ cigarette	n. 담배, 궐련
☐ cinema	n. 영화관, 극장
☐ circulate	v. 순환시키다, 순환하다
☐ circumstance	n. 환경, 상황
☐ cite	v. 예를 들다, 언급하다
☐ citizen	n. 시민, 주민
☐ civil	a. 시민의, 민간의
☐ claim	v. 주장하다 n. 주장
☐ clap	v. 박수를 치다 n. 박수
☐ clash	n. 충돌 v. 맞붙다
☐ clause	n. 절, 조항
☐ clay	n. 점토 v. 점토를 바르다
☐ clerk	n. 직원 v. 직원으로 일하다
☐ click	v. 찰칵하는 소리를 내다 n. 찰칵하는 소리
☐ client	n. 의뢰인, 고객
☐ cliff	n. 절벽, 낭떠러지
☐ climate	n. 기후, 지역
☐ cling	v. 꼭 붙잡다, 매달리다
☐ clinic	n. 병원, 병동
☐ clip	n. 핀, 자르기 v. 클립[핀]으로 고정 하다, 잘라내다
☐ clue	n. 단서 v. 암시를 주다
☐ cluster	n. 무리 v. 무리를 이루다, 떼를 짓게 하다
☐ coach	n. 코치 v. 지도하다
☐ coal	n. 석탄, 석탄 조각
☐ coast	n. 해안 v. 관성으로 나아가다
☐ code	n. 암호 v. 부호로 처리하다
☐ coin	n. 동전 v. 만들다
☐ coincide	v. 동시에 일어나다, 일치하다
☐ collaborate	v. 협력하다, 공동으로 작업하다
☐ collapse	v. 붕괴되다, 접다 n. 실패
☐ collar	n. 옷깃 v. 붙잡다
☐ colleague	n. 동료
☐ colony	n. 식민지, 식민지 이민단
☐ column	n. 기둥, 원주
☐ combat	n. 싸움 v. 싸우다, 전투하다

□ **combine** v. 결합하다, 결합되다 n. 연합체
□ **comedy** n. 코미디, 희극
□ **comfort** n. 안락 v. 위로하다
□ **comfortable** a. 편한, 쾌적한
□ **command** n. 명령 v. 명령하다
□ **comment** n. 논평 v. 논평하다
□ **commerce** n. 무역, 통상, 상업
□ **commission** n. 위원회 v. 의뢰하다
□ **commit** v. 저지르다, 전념하다
□ **committee** n. 위원회
□ **commodity** n. 상품, 물품
□ **common** a. 흔한 n. 공유지
□ **communicate** v. (생각 등을) 전하다, 연락을 주고받다
□ **communication** n. 의사소통, 통신
□ **communist** n. 공산주의자 a. 공산주의(자)의
□ **community** n. 주민, 지역 사회
□ **companion** n. 동반자 v. 동행하다
□ **compare** v. 비교하다, 필적하다 n. 비교
□ **compatible** a. 호환이 되는, 양립될 수 있는
□ **compel** v. 강요하다, 강제하다
□ **compensate** v. 보상하다, 보상금을 주다
□ **compete** v. 경쟁하다, 겨루다
□ **competent** a. 유능한, 능숙한
□ **compile** v. 엮다, 편집하다
□ **complain** v. 불평하다, 투덜대다
□ **complement** v. 보완하다 n. 보완물
□ **complete** a. 완벽한 v. 완전[완벽]하게 만들다
□ **complex** a. 복잡한 n. 복합 건물
□ **complexity** n. 복잡성, 복잡함
□ **complicate** v. 복잡하게 만들다 a. 복잡한
□ **component** n. 요소 a. 구성하고 있는
□ **compose** v. 구성하다, 글을 쓰다
□ **compound** n. 혼합물 a. 합성의 v. 섞다
□ **comprehend** v. 이해하다, 알다
□ **comprehensive** a. 포괄적인
□ **comprise** v. ~으로 이뤄지다, 구성하다
□ **compromise** n. 타협 v. 타협하다, 양보하다
□ **conceal** v. 감추다, 숨기다
□ **conceive** v. 생각하다, 이해하다
□ **concentrate** v. 집중시키다, 집중하다 n. 농축물
□ **concept** n. 개념, 관념
□ **concern** v. 관련되다, 걱정시키다 n. 걱정
□ **concert** n. 음악회 v. 협력하다
□ **conclude** v. 결론을 내리다, 말을 끝맺다
□ **concrete** a. 콘크리트로 된, 구체적인 n. 콘크리트 v. 콘크리트를 바르다
□ **condemn** v. 규탄하다, 비난하다
□ **conduct** v. 행동하다, 지휘하다 n. 행동
□ **confer** v. 상의하다, 수여하다
□ **confess** v. 자백하다, 고백하다
□ **confide** v. 털어놓다, 신뢰하다
□ **confident** a. 자신감 있는
□ **confine** v. 국한시키다, 인접하다 n. 경계
□ **confirm** v. 사실임을 보여주다, 확인해 주다
□ **conflict** n. 충돌 v. 상충하다
□ **conform** v. 따르다, 일치시키다
□ **confront** v. 닥치다, 맞서다
□ **confuse** v. 혼란시키다, 혼동하다
□ **congress** n. 회의, 의회
□ **connect** v. 잇다, 이어지다
□ **conscience** n. 양심, 가책
□ **conscious** a. 의식하는, 자각하는
□ **consent** n. 동의 v. 동의하다
□ **conserve** v. 아끼다, 보존하다 n. 과일 설탕 조림
□ **consider** v. 고려하다, 잘 생각해 보다
□ **consist** v. 되어 있다, 이루어져 있다
□ **consistent** a. 한결같은, 일관된
□ **constant** a. 끊임없는 n. 정수
□ **constitute** v. ~이 되다, 구성하다
□ **constitution** n. 헌법, 체질, 구성
□ **constrain** v. ~하게 만들다, 강요하다
□ **construct** v. 건설하다 n. 구성 개념
□ **construction** n. 건설, 공사
□ **consult** v. 상담하다, 상의하다
□ **consume** v. 소비하다, 소비되다
□ **consumer** n. 소비자
□ **consumption** n. 소비, 소모
□ **contact** n. 닿음 v. 접촉시키다, 접촉하다
□ **contain** v. 포함하다, 함유하다
□ **contemporary** a. 동시대의, 현대의 n. 동시대인
□ **contend** v. 주장하다, 논쟁하다
□ **content** n. 내용(물), 만족(감) a. 만족하는 v. 만족시키다
□ **contest** n. 대회 v. 경쟁을 벌이다
□ **context** n. 맥락, 전후 사정
□ **continent** n. 대륙, 육지 a. 자제하는, 절제하는
□ **continue** v. 계속하다, 계속되다
□ **contract** n. 계약 v. 계약하다, 줄다
□ **contradict** v. 부정하다, 모순되다
□ **contrary** a. 다른 n. 반대 ad. 반대로
□ **contrast** n. 대조 v. 대조하다, 대조를 이루다
□ **contribute** v. 기부하다, 기증하다
□ **controversy** n. 논란, 논쟁
□ **convene** v. 소집하다, 회합하다
□ **convenient** a. 편리한, 간편한
□ **convention** n. 관습, 관례
□ **conversation** n. 대화, 담화
□ **converse** v. 대화를 나누다 n. 담화, 정반대 a. 반대의
□ **convert** v. 전환시키다, 전환되다 n. 개종자
□ **convey** v. 전달하다, 전하다
□ **convict** v. 유죄를 선고하다 n. 죄수
□ **convince** v. 납득시키다, 확신시키다
□ **cooperate** v. 협력하다, 합동하다
□ **coordinate** v. 조직화하다 a. 동격의
□ **cop** n. 경찰관, 체포 v. 붙잡다, 체포하다
□ **cope** v. 대처하다, 대응하다
□ **copy** n. 복사 v. 복사하다
□ **copyright** n. 저작권 a. 저작권 보호를 받는 v. 저작권을 보호하다
□ **cord** n. 끈 v. 끈으로 묶다
□ **core** n. 중심, 속 a. 핵심적인 v. 가운데를 파내다
□ **corn** n. 곡식 v. 작은 알갱이로 만들다
□ **corporate** a. 기업의, 회사의
□ **corporation** n. 기업, 회사
□ **correct** a. 맞는 v. 바로잡다
□ **correspond** v. 일치하다, 부합하다
□ **corridor** n. 복도, 회랑
□ **corrupt** a. 부패한 v. 부패하게 만들다, 부패하다
□ **costume** n. 의상 v. 의상을 입히다
□ **cottage** n. 작은 집, 오두막집
□ **cotton** n. 목화, 면직물
□ **cough** v. 기침하다 n. 기침
□ **council** n. 의회, 회의
□ **counsel** n. 조언 v. 상담을 하다
□ **count** v. 세다 n. 셈
□ **counter** n. 계산대, 판매대
□ **counterpart** n. 상대, 대응 관계에 있는 사람[것]
□ **countryside** n. 시골 지역, 전원 지대
□ **county** n. 자치주
□ **coupon** n. 쿠폰, 할인권
□ **courage** n. 용기, 담력
□ **crack** v. 갈라지다 n. 금
□ **craft** n. (수)공예 v. 공예품을 만들다
□ **crash** n. 사고 v. 충돌하다
□ **crawl** v. 기다, 자주 드나들다 n. 기어가기
□ **craze** n. 대유행 v. 미치게 하다
□ **crazy** a. 정상이 아닌 n. 미치광이
□ **create** v. 창조하다, 창조적인 일을 하다
□ **creature** n. 생물, 생명이 있는 존재
□ **credible** a. 믿을 수 있는, 신뢰할 수 있는
□ **credit** n. 신용 거래 v. 입금하다 a. 신용 거래의
□ **creep** v. 살금살금 움직이다, 기다
□ **crew** n. 승무원 v. 승무원을 하다
□ **crime** n. 범죄, 범행
□ **criminal** a. 범죄의 n. 범인, 범죄자
□ **crisis** n. 위기, 최악의 고비
□ **crisp** a. 바삭바삭한 n. 감자칩 v. 바삭바삭하게 만들다
□ **criterion** n. 기준
□ **critic** n. 비평가, 평론가
□ **criticism** n. 비판, 비난
□ **criticize / criticise** v. 비판하다, 비난하다
□ **crop** n. (농)작물 v. 심다
□ **crowd** n. 사람들, 군중 v. 가득 메우다, 떼 지어 모이다
□ **crown** n. 왕관 v. 왕관을 씌우다
□ **crucial** a. 중대한, 결정적인
□ **cruel** a. 잔혹한, 잔인한
□ **cruise** n. 유람선 여행 v. 유람선을 타고 다니다
□ **crush** v. 으스러뜨리다, 잔뜩 몰려들다 n. 잔뜩 몰려든 군중
□ **crystal** n. 결정체 a. 수정의
□ **cultivate** v. 경작하다, 일구다
□ **cure** v. 낫게 하다, 병이 낫다 n. 치유(법)
□ **curiosity** n. 호기심, 진기함
□ **curious** a. 궁금한, 알고 싶어 하는
□ **curl** v. 곱슬곱슬하다 n. 곱슬곱슬한 머리카락
□ **currency** n. 통화, 통용
□ **current** a. 현재의 n. 흐름, 전류
□ **curriculum** n. 교육[교과] 과정, 이수 과정
□ **curry** n. 카레 v. 카레 요리를 하다
□ **curse** n. 욕(설) v. 욕을 하다
□ **curve** n. 곡선 v. 곡선으로 나아가다
□ **custody** n. 양육권, 보호
□ **custom** n. 관습 a. 주문 제작의
□ **cute** a. 귀여운, 매력적인
□ **cycle** n. 자전거 v. 자전거를 타다, 순환시키다
□ **cyclist** n. 자전거 타는 사람
□ **cynical** a. 냉소적인, 비꼬는
□ **dairy** n. 낙농장 a. 유제품의
□ **damage** n. 손상 v. 손상을 주다, 손상되다
□ **damp** a. 축축한 n. 축축한 상태 v. 축축하게 하다
□ **dare** v. 감히 ~하다 n. 모험
□ **darling** n. 여보 a. 가장 사랑하는
□ **dash** n. 돌진 v. 서둘러 가다
□ **data** n. (*sing.* datum) 자료, 정보
□ **database** n. 데이터베이스
□ **datum** n. 자료, 정보
□ **dawn** n. 새벽 v. 밝다
□ **deal** v. 다루다, 나누어 주다 n. 거래
□ **debate** n. 토론 v. 토론하다
□ **debt** n. 빚, 부채

☐ **decade** n. 10년, 10권
☐ **decay** n. 부패 v. 부패하다, 부패시키다
☐ **decent** a. 괜찮은, 제대로 된
☐ **deck** n. 갑판 v. 꾸미다
☐ **declare** v. 선언하다, 신고하다
☐ **declension** n. 기울어짐
☐ **decline** n. 감소 v. 줄어들다, 거절하다
☐ **decorate** v. 장식하다, 꾸미다
☐ **decrease** v. 줄다, 줄이다 n. 감소
☐ **dedicate** v. 바치다, 전념하다
☐ **defeat** v. 패배시키다 n. 패배
☐ **defend** v. 방어하다, 수비하다
☐ **defendant** n. 피고 a. 피고의
☐ **defense / defence** n. 방어, 옹호
☐ **deficiency** n. 결핍, 부족
☐ **deficit** n. 적자, 부족액
☐ **define** v. 정의하다, 규정하다
☐ **definite** a. 확실한 n. 확실한 것[사람]
☐ **degree** n. 도, 정도
☐ **delay** n. 지연 v. 연기하다, 지체하다
☐ **delegate** n. 대표 v. 위임하다, 선정하다
☐ **delete** v. 삭제하다, 지우다
☐ **deliberate** a. 고의의 v. 숙고하다
☐ **delicate** a. 연약한, 다치기 쉬운
☐ **delight** n. 기쁨 v. 기쁨을 주다, 기뻐하다
☐ **deliver** v. 배달하다, 출산하다
☐ **demand** n. 요구 v. 요구하다, 필요로 하다
☐ **democracy** n. 민주주의, 민주 국가
☐ **democrat** n. 민주주의자, 민주주의 옹호자
☐ **demon** n. 악령, 악마
☐ **demonstrate** v. 입증하다, 시위를 하다
☐ **dense** a. 빽빽한, 밀집한
☐ **dentist** n. 치과 의사, 치과
☐ **deny** v. 부인하다, 부정하다
☐ **depart** v. 떠나다, 출발하다
☐ **department** n. 부서, 부처
☐ **departure** n. 떠남, 출발
☐ **depend** v. 의존하다, 의지하다
☐ **dependence** n. 의존, 의지
☐ **depict** v. 그리다, 표현하다
☐ **deposit** n. 착수금 v. 두다, 침전되다
☐ **depress** v. 우울하게 만들다
☐ **deprive** v. 빼앗다, 박탈하다
☐ **derive** v. 얻다, 유래하다
☐ **descend** v. 내려오다, 내려가다
☐ **describe** v. 말하다, 서술하다
☐ **description** n. 서술, 기술
☐ **desert** n. 사막 v. 버리다
☐ **deserve** v. ~할[받을] 만하다
☐ **designate** v. 지정하다 a. 지명된
☐ **desire** n. 욕구 v. 바라다
☐ **despair** n. 절망 v. 절망하다
☐ **desperate** a. 자포자기한
☐ **despite** prep. ~에도 불구하고 n. 무례
☐ **destination** n. 목적지, 도착지

☐ **destine** v. 미리 정해 두다, 운명 짓다
☐ **destiny** n. 운명, 숙명
☐ **destroy** v. 파괴하다, 말살하다
☐ **destruct** a. 파괴용의 n. 자폭 v. 자폭시키다, 자폭하다
☐ **destruction** n. 파괴, 파멸
☐ **detach** v. 떼어내다, 분리되다
☐ **detail** n. 세부 사항 v. 상세히 알리다
☐ **detect** v. 발견하다, 알아내다
☐ **determine** v. 알아내다, 결정하다
☐ **develop** v. 성장[발달]시키다, 성장[발달]하다
☐ **device** n. 장치, 기구
☐ **devil** n. 악마, 악령
☐ **devise** v. 창안하다
☐ **devote** v. 바치다, 쏟다
☐ **diabetes** n. 당뇨병
☐ **diary** n. 수첩, 메모장
☐ **dictate** v. 받아쓰게 하다 n. 명령
☐ **dictionary** n. 사전 a. 사전의
☐ **diet** n. 식사, 식습관 v. 다이어트를 하다
☐ **differ** v. 다르다, 상이하다
☐ **different** a. 다른, 차이가 나는
☐ **dig** v. 파다, 뒤지다 n. 쿡 찌름
☐ **dignity** n. 위엄, 품위
☐ **dimension** n. 크기, 치수
☐ **diminish** v. 줄어들다, 줄이다
☐ **dine** v. 식사를 하다, 식사를 대접하다
☐ **dip** v. 살짝 담그다, 내려가다 n. 담그기
☐ **diplomat** n. 외교관, 외교[사교]에 능한 사람
☐ **direct** a. 직접적인 v. 향하게 하다, 지도하다 ad. 직행으로
☐ **dirt** n. 먼지, 때
☐ **dirty** a. 더러운 v. 더럽히다, 더러워지다
☐ **disabled** a. 장애를 가진
☐ **disadvantage** n. 불리한 점 v. 불리하게 하다
☐ **disappear** v. 보이지 않게 되다, 사라지다
☐ **disappoint** v. 실망시키다, 좌절시키다
☐ **disaster** n. 참사, 재난
☐ **disc** n. 동글납작한 판 v. 음반에 녹음하다
☐ **discharge** v. 해방시키다, (기체·액체가) 흐르다 n. 방출
☐ **discipline** n. 규율 v. 훈육하다
☐ **discount** n. 할인 v. 할인하다 a. 할인 판매의
☐ **discourage** v. 막다, 말리다
☐ **discourse** n. 담론 v. 담화하다
☐ **discriminate** v. 식별하다, 구별하다 a. 식별된
☐ **disease** n. 병, 질병
☐ **disgust** n. 혐오감 v. 혐오감을 유발하다

☐ **dish** n. 접시 v. 접시에 담다, 오목해지다
☐ **dismiss** v. 해고하다, 해산하다 n. 해산
☐ **disorder** n. 엉망 v. 어지럽히다
☐ **display** v. 전시하다 n. 전시, 진열
☐ **dispose** v. 배열하다, 처리하다, 일의 성패를 결정하다
☐ **dispute** n. 분쟁 v. 반박하다, 논쟁하다
☐ **disrupt** v. 방해하다 a. 분열된
☐ **distance** n. 거리 v. 거리를 두다
☐ **distinct** a. 뚜렷한, 분명한
☐ **distinguish** v. 구별하다, 판별하다
☐ **distort** v. 비틀다, 왜곡하다, 일그러뜨리다
☐ **distract** v. 집중이 안 되게 하다, 산만하게 하다
☐ **distribute** v. 나누어 주다, 분배하다
☐ **district** n. 지구, 지역 v. 구역으로 나누다
☐ **disturb** v. 방해하다, 건드리다
☐ **dive** v. 뛰어들다 n. 뛰어들기
☐ **diverse** a. 다양한, 다른
☐ **divide** v. 나누다, 나뉘다 n. 분할
☐ **divine** a. 신성한 v. 알다
☐ **divorce** n. 이혼 v. 이혼하다
☐ **document** n. 서류 v. 기록하다
☐ **dolphin** n. 돌고래
☐ **domain** n. 영역, 분야
☐ **domestic** a. 국내의 n. 가정부
☐ **dominant** a. 우세한 n. 주요[우세]한 것
☐ **dominate** v. 지배하다, 우위를 차지하다
☐ **donate** v. 기부하다
☐ **dose** n. 복용량 v. 투약하다, 약을 복용하다
☐ **dot** n. 점 v. 점을 찍다, 여기저기 흩어 놓다
☐ **doubt** n. 의심 v. 의심하다
☐ **dozen** n. 12개짜리 한 묶음 a. 십 여개의
☐ **draft** n. 원고 a. 초안의 v. 초안[원고]을 작성하다
☐ **drag** v. 끌다
☐ **drain** v. 물을 빼내다, 물이 빠지다 n. 배수관
☐ **drama** n. 희곡, 각본
☐ **dread** v. 몹시 무서워하다 n. 두려움 a. 두려운
☐ **drill** n. 드릴 v. 구멍을 뚫다, 반복 연습[훈련]을 하다
☐ **drown** v. 익사시키다, 물에 빠져 죽다
☐ **drug** n. 약물 v. 약물을 투여하다
☐ **dual** a. 둘의, 이중의
☐ **due** a. ~로 인한
☐ **dull** a. 따분한, 흐릿한 v. 둔하게 하다, 둔해지다
☐ **dump** v. 버리다, 떨어지다 n. 폐기장
☐ **dust** n. 흙먼지 v. 먼지를 털다

☐ **duty** n. 의무, 본분
☐ **dwell** v. 살다 n. 운전 정지
☐ **dynamic** n. 역학 a. 정력적인
☐ **each** pron. 각각 a. 각각의 ad. 각각에
☐ **eager** a. 열렬한, 간절히 바라는
☐ **earn** v. 벌다, (수익 등을) 올리다
☐ **ease** n. 쉬움, 편안함 v. 편하게 해 주다, 편해지다
☐ **easy** a. 쉬운 ad. 느긋하게
☐ **economy** n. 경제, 경기
☐ **edge** n. 끝 v. 테두리를 두르다, 조금씩 움직이다
☐ **edit** v. 수정하다, 편집하다 n. 편집
☐ **educate** v. 교육하다, 가르치다
☐ **effect** n. 영향 v. 가져오다
☐ **effective** a. 효과적인, 실질적인
☐ **efficient** a. 능률적인, 효율적인
☐ **effort** n. 노력, 분투
☐ **either** pron. 어느 하나 a. 어느 하나의 ad. ~도 또한
☐ **elaborate** a. 정교한 v. 자세히 설명하다
☐ **elect** v. 선출하다 a. 당선된
☐ **electric** a. 전기의 n. 전기 장치
☐ **electronic** a. 전자의, 전자 공학의
☐ **elegant** a. 우아한, 품위 있는
☐ **element** n. 요소, 성분
☐ **elementary** a. 초보의, 초급의
☐ **elevate** v. 올리다, 들어올리다
☐ **elevator** n. 엘리베이터, 승강기
☐ **eliminate** v. 없애다, 제거하다
☐ **elite** n. 엘리트 a. 엘리트의
☐ **else** a. 또[그 밖의] 다른 ad. 그 밖에
☐ **embarrass** v. 당황스럽게 만들다, 어색하게 하다
☐ **embassy** n. 대사관
☐ **embrace** v. 껴안다, 받아들이다 n. 포옹
☐ **emerge** v. 나오다, 모습을 드러내다
☐ **emergence** n. 나타남, 출현
☐ **emergency** n. 비상 a. 비상시를 위한
☐ **emission** n. 배출, 방사
☐ **emit** v. 내다, 내뿜다
☐ **emotion** n. 감정, 정서
☐ **emphasis** n. 강조, 역점
☐ **emphasize** v. 강조하다, 두드러지게 하다
☐ **empire** n. 제국, 거대 기업
☐ **employ** v. 고용하다 n. 고용
☐ **empty** a. 빈 v. 비우다, 비게 되다
☐ **encounter** v. (우연히) 만나다 n. 만남, 조우
☐ **encourage** v. 격려하다, 용기를 북돋우다
☐ **endure** v. 참다, 견뎌내다
☐ **enemy** n. 적, 장애물
☐ **enforce** v. 집행하다, 실행하다
☐ **engage** v. 관여하게 하다, 고용되다, 약속하다

☐ engine	n. 엔진, 기관
☐ engineer	n. 기사 v. 기사로 일하다
☐ enhance	v. 높이다, 올리다
☐ enjoy	v. 즐기다, 즐거운 시간을 보내다
☐ enormous	a. 막대한, 거대한
☐ enrol(l)	v. 명부에 올리다, 입학하다
☐ enterprise	n. 기업, 회사
☐ entertain	v. 즐겁게 하다, 접대하다
☐ enthusiastic	a. 열렬한, 열광적인
☐ entire	a. 전체의 n. 전부
☐ entitle	v. 자격[권리]을 주다, 제목을 붙이다
☐ entry	n. 들어감, 입장
☐ envelope	n. 봉투, 덮개
☐ environ	v. 둘러싸다, 에워싸다
☐ environment	n. 환경, 주위
☐ envy	n. 부러움 v. 부러워하다
☐ equal	a. 동일한 n. 동등한 사람[것] v. ~과 같다
☐ equip	v. 장비를 갖추다
☐ equipment	n. 장비, 용품
☐ era	n. 연대, 시대
☐ erase	v. 지워 버리다, 없애다
☐ eraser	n. 지우개, 지우는 사람
☐ erect	a. 똑바로 선 v. 건립하다, 똑바로 서다
☐ err	v. 실수하다, 잘못하다
☐ error	n. 실수, 오류
☐ escape	v. 달아나다, 피하다 n. 탈출
☐ especial	a. 특별한, 각별한
☐ especially	ad. 특히, 특별히
☐ essay	n. 수필 v. 시도하다
☐ essence	n. 본질, 정수
☐ essential	a. 필수적인 n. 필수[기본]적인 것
☐ establish	v. 설립하다, 수립하다
☐ estate	n. 사유지, 토지
☐ estimate	n. 추정 v. 추정하다
☐ ethic	n. 윤리, 도덕
☐ ethical	a. 윤리적인, 도덕상의
☐ ethnic	a. 민족의 n. 소수 민족
☐ evacuate	v. 대피시키다, 대피하다
☐ evaluate	v. 평가하다, 감정하다
☐ even	ad. ~마저 a. 평평한
☐ event	n. 사건, 일
☐ eventually	ad. 결국, 마침내
☐ ever	ad. 언제든, 한번이라도
☐ evidence	n. 증거 v. 입증하다
☐ evil	a. 사악한 n. 악
☐ evitable	a. 피할 수 있는
☐ evolution	n. 진화, 발전
☐ evolve	v. 발달[진전]하다, 진화시키다
☐ exact	a. 정확한 v. 요구하다
☐ exaggerate	v. 과장하다, 과장해서 말하다
☐ exam	n. 시험, 검사
☐ examination	n. 시험, 조사
☐ examine	v. 조사하다, 심리하다
☐ exceed	v. 넘다, 도를 넘다
☐ excel	v. 뛰어나다, 능가하다
☐ excellent	a. 훌륭한, 탁월한
☐ except	prep. ~을 제외하고는 conj. ~라는 점만 제외하면 v. 제외하다
☐ excess	n. 지나침 a. 초과한
☐ exchange	n. 교환 v. 교환하다, 교체하다
☐ excite	v. 흥분시키다, 초조하게 만들다
☐ exclude	v. 제외하다, 배제하다
☐ exclusive	a. 독점적인 n. 독점 기사
☐ excuse	n. 변명 v. 용서하다
☐ executive	n. 경영 간부 a. 경영의
☐ exhaust	v. 기진맥진하게 만들다 n. 배출
☐ exhibit	v. 전시하다, 전시회를 하다 n. 전시품
☐ exist	v. 존재하다, 실재하다
☐ exit	n. 출구 v. 나가다
☐ exotic	a. 외국의 n. 외래품
☐ expand	v. 확대하다, 확대되다
☐ expect	v. 예상하다, 생각하다
☐ expense	n. 돈, 비용
☐ expensive	a. 비싼, 돈이 많이 드는
☐ experience	n. 경험 v. 경험하다
☐ experiment	n. 실험 v. 실험하다
☐ expert	n. 전문가 a. 전문가의
☐ expertise	n. 전문 지식[기술]
☐ explain	v. 설명하다, 이유가 되다
☐ explicit	a. 분명한, 명쾌한
☐ explode	v. 폭발시키다, 폭발하다
☐ explore	v. 탐험하다, 탐사하다
☐ export	v. 수출하다 n. 수출 a. 수출의
☐ expose	v. 드러내다 n. 폭로
☐ express	v. 나타내다 a. 급행의 ad. 급행으로 n. 급행열차
☐ extend	v. 늘리다, 이어지다
☐ extent	n. 정도, 한도
☐ external	a. 외부의 n. 외부
☐ extinct	a. 멸종된, 더 이상 존재하지 않는
☐ extra	a. 추가의 ad. 추가로 n. 추가되는 것
☐ extract	n. 발췌 v. 추출하다
☐ extraordinary	a. 기이한, 놀라운
☐ extreme	a. 극도의 n. 극단
☐ eyebrow	n. 눈썹
☐ fabric	n. 직물, 천
☐ facilitate	v. 가능하게 하다, 용이하게 하다
☐ facility	n. 시설, 기관
☐ factor	n. 요인 v. 인수 분해하다
☐ factory	n. 공장 a. 공장의
☐ faculty	n. 능력, 재능
☐ fade	v. 바래다, 희미하게 만들다
☐ faint	a. 희미한 v. 실신하다 n. 실신
☐ fair	a. 공정한 ad. 공정하게 n. 박람회
☐ faith	n. 믿음, 신뢰
☐ false	a. 틀린, 사실이 아닌
☐ fame	n. 명성 v. 명성을 떨치다
☐ familiar	a. 익숙한 n. 친구
☐ famous	a. 유명한, 이름난
☐ fancy	v. 상상하다 n. 상상 a. 상상의
☐ fantastic	a. 환상적인, 기막히게 좋은
☐ fare	n. 요금 v. 되어가다
☐ fascinate	v. 매료하다, 매혹하다
☐ fashion	n. 유행 v. 만들다, 빚다
☐ fasten	v. 매다, 채워지다
☐ fatal	a. 죽음을 초래하는, 치명적인
☐ fate	n. 운 v. 운명 짓다
☐ fault	n. 잘못 v. 나무라다
☐ favo(u)r	n. 호의 v. 호의를 보이다
☐ fear	n. 공포 v. 두려워하다
☐ feature	n. 특색 v. 특징으로 삼다
☐ federal	a. 연방의 n. 연방주의자
☐ fee	n. 요금 v. 요금을 지불하다
☐ feed	v. 음식을 먹이다, 먹이를 먹다 n. 먹이
☐ fellow	n. 사나이 a. 동료의
☐ female	a. 여자의 n. 여자
☐ fence	n. 울타리 v. 울타리를 치다, 펜싱을 하다
☐ ferry	n. 연락선 v. 나르다, 배로 건너다
☐ fertile	a. 기름진, 비옥한
☐ fever	n. 열, 발열
☐ few	a. 많지 않은 pron. 소수
☐ fiber / fibre	n. 섬유, 섬유소
☐ fiction	n. 소설, 허구
☐ fierce	a. 사나운, 험악한
☐ figure	n. 수치 v. 판단하다
☐ filter	n. 여과기 v. 여과하다, 걸러지다
☐ final	a. 마지막의 n. 결승전
☐ finance	n. 재원 v. 자금을 대다, 재정을 처리하다
☐ finite	a. 한정된 n. 유한
☐ firm	n. 회사 a. 단단한 ad. 단단하게 v. 단단하게 하다
☐ fit	a. 알맞은 v. 맞다 n. 맞는 것
☐ flag	n. 기 v. 기를 게양하다, 신호로 정지시키다
☐ flame	n. 불길 v. 활활 타오르다, 불길을 쏘다
☐ flash	v. 비치다, 비추다 n. 섬광 a. 눈이 부신
☐ flat	a. 평평한 n. 평평한 부분 ad. 평평하게 v. 평평하게 하다
☐ flavo(u)r	n. 맛 v. 맛[풍미]을 더하다
☐ flaw	n. 흠 v. 흠[금]이 생기게 하다
☐ flee	v. 달아나다, 도망하다
☐ flesh	n. 살 v. 살에 찌르다, 살이 붙다
☐ flexible	a. 신축성 있는, 융통성 있는
☐ flight	n. 비행, 항공편 v. 떼지어 날다, 쏘다
☐ flip	v. 톡 던지다[튕기다], 튕겨지다 n. 톡 던지기[튕기기]
☐ float	v. 뜨다, 띄우다 n. 장식 차량
☐ flock	n. 떼 v. 떼를 짓다
☐ flood	n. 홍수 v. 물에 잠기게 하다, 물에 잠기다
☐ flourish	v. 번창하다, 휘두르다
☐ flow	n. 흐름 v. 흐르다, 흘리다
☐ flush	v. 붉어지다, 물을 내리다 n. 홍조
☐ fog	n. 안개 v. 안개로 뒤덮이다
☐ fold	v. 접다, 망하다 n. 접힌 부분
☐ folk	n. 사람들 a. 민속의
☐ follow	v. (뒤)따라가다 n. 뒤따르기
☐ fond	a. 좋아하는, 애정을 느끼는
☐ forbid	v. 금하다, 허락하지 않다
☐ force	n. 물리력 v. 강요하다
☐ forecast	n. 예측 v. 예측하다
☐ forehead	n. 이마, 앞부분
☐ foreign	a. 외국의, 대외의
☐ forever	ad. 영원히 n. 영원
☐ forgive	v. 용서하다, 탕감하다
☐ format	n. 구성 방식 v. 포맷[서식]을 만들다
☐ former	a. 이전의, 옛날의 n. 제작자, 형성자
☐ formula	n. 공식, 화학식
☐ forth	ad. ~에서 멀리, 앞으로
☐ fortunate	a. 운 좋은, 다행한
☐ fortune	n. 운, 행운
☐ forward	ad. 앞으로 a. 앞으로 가는 v. 보내다 n. 포워드
☐ foster	v. 조성하다 a. 수양-
☐ found	v. 설립하다, 세우다
☐ foundation	n. 토대, 기초
☐ fountain	n. 분수, 분수처럼 뿜어져 나오는 것
☐ fraction	n. 부분, 일부
☐ frame	n. 틀 v. 틀에 넣다, 구상하다, 만들다
☐ framework	n. 뼈대, 골조
☐ frankly	ad. 솔직히, 노골적으로
☐ freeze	v. 얼다, 동결시키다 n. 한파
☐ frequent	a. 잦은 v. 자주 다니다
☐ fright	n. 공포, 놀람
☐ frog	n. 개구리 v. 개구리를 잡다
☐ frost	n. 서리 v. 서리가 내리다
☐ frown	v. 눈살을 찌푸리다 n. 찌푸림
☐ frustrate	v. 좌절감을 주다, 좌절하다

- □ fry v. 튀기다, 새까맣게 타다 n. 튀김
- □ fuel n. 연료 v. 연료를 공급하다
- □ fulfil v. 실현하다, 성취하다
- □ function n. 기능 v. 기능하다
- □ fund n. 자금 v. 자금[기금]을 대다
- □ fundamental a. 근본적인 n. 근본
- □ funeral n. 장례식 a. 장례식의
- □ fur n. 털 a. 모피의
- □ furious a. 몹시 화가 난, 격노한
- □ furnish v. 비치하다, 제공하다
- □ furniture n. 가구, 비품
- □ furthermore ad. 뿐만 아니라, 더욱이
- □ fury n. 격노, 격분
- □ fuse n. 퓨즈 v. 퓨즈가 끊어지다
- □ gain v. 얻다, 나아지다 n. 이익
- □ gallery n. 미술관, 화랑
- □ gamble v. 도박하다, 모험하다 n. 도박, 모험
- □ gang n. 범죄 조직, 패거리 v. 집단을 이루다
- □ gap n. 틈, 구멍
- □ garage n. 차고 v. 차고에 넣다
- □ gasoline / petrol n. 가솔린, 휘발유
- □ gate n. 문 v. 문을 달다
- □ gather v. 모으다, 쌓이다
- □ gaze v. 응시하다 n. 응시
- □ gear n. 기어 v. 기어를 넣다, 서로 맞물리다
- □ gender n. 성, 성별
- □ gene n. 유전자, 유전 인자
- □ general a. 일반적인 n. 장군 v. 장군으로서 지휘하다
- □ generate v. 발생시키다, 만들어 내다
- □ generation n. 사람들, 세대
- □ generous a. 후한, 아끼지 않는
- □ genetic a. 유전의, 유전학의
- □ genius n. 천재성, 천재
- □ gentle a. 온화한 v. 길들이다 n. 구더기
- □ genuine a. 진짜의, 진품의
- □ geography n. 지리학, 지리
- □ geology n. 지질학
- □ gesture n. 몸짓 v. 몸짓으로 가리키다
- □ ghost n. 유령 v. 대필하다
- □ giant n. 거인 a. 엄청나게 큰
- □ gift n. 선물 v. 부여하다
- □ giraffe n. 기린, 기린자리
- □ glance v. 힐끗 보다 n. 힐끗 보기
- □ glare v. 노려보다 n. 눈부심
- □ global a. 지구의, 세계적인
- □ globe n. 지구본, 구체 v. 공 모양으로 만들다
- □ glory n. 영광, 영예
- □ glove n. 장갑 v. 장갑을 끼다
- □ glow v. 빛나다, 타다 n. 불빛
- □ glue n. 접착제 v. 접착제를 바르다
- □ goat n. 염소, 염소자리
- □ golf n. 골프 v. 골프를 치다
- □ gorgeous a. 아주 멋진, 훌륭한
- □ govern v. 다스리다, 통치하다
- □ government n. 정부, 정권
- □ grab v. 붙잡다 n. 붙잡으려고 함
- □ grace n. 우아함 v. 꾸미다
- □ grade n. 품질, 등급, 성적 v. 나누다, ~의 등급이다
- □ gradual a. 점진적인, 서서히 일어나는
- □ graduate n. 졸업생 v. 졸업하다 a. 졸업생의
- □ grain n. 곡물, 낟알
- □ grand a. 웅장한 n. 1,000달러[파운드]
- □ grant v. 승인하다 n. 보조금
- □ graph n. 그래프 v. 그래프로 나타내다
- □ graphic a. 그래프로 나타내는 n. 그래픽 아트 작품
- □ grasp v. 꽉 잡다, 꽉 잡다 n. 꽉 쥐기
- □ grateful a. 고마워하는, 감사하는
- □ grave n. 무덤, 묘 a. 심각한 v. 새기다, 조각하다
- □ greed n. 탐욕, 욕심
- □ greet v. 맞다, 환영하다
- □ grief n. 비탄, 비통
- □ grip n. 꽉 붙잡음 v. 꽉 잡다, 움켜잡다
- □ grocery n. 식료품점, 식료품 판매업
- □ gross a. 총체의 ad. 모두 n. 총체
- □ guarantee n. 굳은 약속, 보증 v. 약속하다
- □ guard n. 경비원 v. 지키다, 경계하다
- □ guardian n. 수호자, 보호자
- □ guest n. 손님 v. 게스트로 참여하다
- □ guide n. 안내(서), 안내인 v. 안내하여 데려가다
- □ guideline n. 지침, 가이드라인
- □ guilt n. 유죄(임), 책임
- □ guilty a. 유죄의, 책임이 있는
- □ gulf n. 만(灣) v. 집어삼키다
- □ gun n. 총 v. 총으로 쏘다
- □ gym(nasium) n. 체육관, 체육
- □ habitat n. 서식지, 환경
- □ half n. 반 a. 반의 ad. 절반 정도로
- □ hall n. 현관, 복도
- □ halt v. 멈추다, 세우다, 주저하다 n. 멈춤
- □ hammer n. 망치 v. 망치로 치다
- □ handicap n. 장애 v. 불리하게 만들다
- □ handle v. 만지다, 손을 사용하다 n. 손잡이
- □ handsome a. 멋진, 잘생긴
- □ happen v. 일어나다, 발생하다
- □ harbo(u)r n. 항구, 피난처 v. 숨겨 주다, 숨다
- □ harm n. 해 v. 해치다
- □ harmonious a. 사이가 좋은, 화목한
- □ harmony n. 조화, 화합
- □ harsh a. 가혹한, 냉혹한
- □ harvest n. 수확 v. 수확하다, 추수하다
- □ haunt v. 나타나다, 출몰하다 n. 자주 가는 곳
- □ hazard n. 위험 v. 틀릴 셈치고 제안[추측]하다
- □ headache n. 두통, 머리가 아픔
- □ headquarters n. 본부, 본사
- □ heal v. 치유하다, 낫다
- □ health n. 건강, 건강 상태
- □ healthy a. 건강한, 건강에 좋은
- □ hear v. 듣다, 전해 듣다
- □ heaven n. 천국, 천당
- □ heel n. 발뒤꿈치, 경사 v. 기울다
- □ height n. 높이, 고도
- □ heir n. 상속인 v. 상속하다
- □ helicopter n. 헬리콥터 v. 헬리콥터로 가다
- □ hell n. 지옥, 지옥 같은 곳
- □ hence ad. 이런 이유로, 따라서
- □ heritage n. 유산, 전통
- □ hesitate v. 주저하다, 망설이다
- □ hide v. 숨기다, 숨다 n. 은신처
- □ hierarchy n. 계급, 계층
- □ highlight v. 강조하다 n. 하이라이트
- □ highway n. 고속도로 a. 노상에 출몰하는
- □ hint n. 힌트 v. 암시하다
- □ hire v. 고용하다, 고용되다 n. 고용
- □ hole n. 구멍, 구덩이 v. 구멍을 뚫다
- □ holy a. 신성한 n. 신성한 것[곳]
- □ honey n. 벌꿀 a. 벌꿀의 v. 달게 하다
- □ hono(u)r n. 존경, 명예 v. 존경하다
- □ hook n. 갈고리 v. 갈고리로 걸다
- □ horizon n. 수평선, 지평선
- □ horror n. 공포(감), 경악
- □ host n. 주인, 무리, 떼 v. 주최하다
- □ hostile a. 적대적인, 적의를 가진
- □ hotel n. 호텔
- □ household n. 가정 a. 가정의
- □ hug v. 껴안다 n. 껴안기
- □ huge a. 막대한, 엄청난
- □ humo(u)r n. 유머 v. 비위를 맞춰 주다
- □ hunger n. 굶주림 v. 갈망하다, 굶주리게 하다
- □ hungry a. 배고픈, 굶주리는
- □ hurt v. 다치게 하다, 아프다 a. 다친 n. 상처
- □ hut n. 오두막 v. 오두막에 서 묵다[살다]
- □ hypothesis n. 가설, 전제
- □ ideal a. 이상적인 n. 이상
- □ identical a. 동일한, 똑같은
- □ identify v. 확인하다, 동일시하다
- □ identity n. 동일성, 독자성, 신분
- □ ideology n. 이데올로기, 이념
- □ ignore v. 무시하다, 못 본 척하다
- □ ill a. 아픈 ad. 나쁘게 n. 문제
- □ illude v. 속이다, 헷갈리게 하다
- □ illusion n. 오해, 착각
- □ illustrate v. 삽화를 넣다, 예시를 들다
- □ imagine v. 상상하다, 그리다
- □ imitate v. 모방하다, 본뜨다
- □ immediate a. 즉각적인, 당면한
- □ immense a. 엄청난, 어마어마한
- □ immigrate v. 이주해 오다, 이주시키다
- □ immune a. 면역성이 있는 n. 면역자
- □ impact n. 영향 v. 영향[충격]을 주다
- □ imperial a. 제국의, 황제의
- □ implement v. 시행하다 n. 도구
- □ imply v. 나타내다, 암시하다
- □ import n. 수입품 v. 중요하다
- □ importance n. 중요성, 중대성
- □ important a. 중요한, 소중한
- □ impose v. 도입하다, 부과하다
- □ impress v. 깊은 인상을 주다 n. 인상
- □ improve v. 개선하다, 좋아지다
- □ incentive n. 장려(책), 자극 a. 장려하는
- □ incident n. 일 a. 일어나기 쉬운
- □ incline v. 기울어지게 하다 n. 경사
- □ include v. 포함하다, 함유하다
- □ income n. 소득, 수입
- □ incorporate v. 창립하다, 포함하다 a. 사업체의
- □ increase v. 증가시키다, 인상되다 n. 증가
- □ incredible a. 믿을 수 없는, 믿기 힘든
- □ indeed ad. 정말, 확실히
- □ independent a. 독립된
- □ index n. 색인 v. 색인을 만들다
- □ indicate v. 나타내다, 보여주다
- □ individual a. 각각의 n. 개인
- □ induce v. 설득하다, 권유하다
- □ industry n. 산업, 공업
- □ inevitable a. 불가피한 n. 필연적인 것
- □ infant n. 유아 a. 유아용의
- □ infect v. 감염시키다, 전염시키다
- □ infer v. 추론하다, 추측하다
- □ inference n. 추론, 추측
- □ inflate v. 부풀리다, 팽창하다
- □ influence n. 영향 v. 영향을 주다, 감화를 주다

☐ **inform** v. 알리다, 정보를 제공하다
☐ **ingredient** n. 재료, 성분
☐ **inhabit** v. 살다, 거주하다
☐ **inherent** a. 고유의, 본래의
☐ **inhibit** v. 억제하다, 저해하다
☐ **initial** a. 처음의 n. 머리글자
☐ **inject** v. 주입하다, 주사하다
☐ **injure** v. 다치게 하다, 부상을 입히다
☐ **inn** n. 여인숙, 여관
☐ **innocent** a. 죄가 없는 n. 순결한 사람
☐ **innovate** v. 혁신하다, 획기적으로 하다
☐ **input** n. 투입 v. 입력하다 a. 입력 장치의
☐ **inquire / enquire** v. 묻다, 문의하다
☐ **insect** n. 곤충 a. 곤충의
☐ **insert** v. 끼우다 n. 삽입 광고
☐ **insight** n. 통찰력, 식견
☐ **insist** v. 고집하다, 우기다
☐ **inspect** v. 점검하다, 검사하다
☐ **inspire** v. 고무하다, 영감을 주다
☐ **install** v. 설치하다, 설비하다
☐ **instance** n. 사례 v. ~을 예로 들다
☐ **instant** a. 즉각적인 n. 순간
☐ **instead** ad. 대신에
☐ **instinct** n. 본능, 본성
☐ **institute** n. 기관 v. 도입하다
☐ **institution** n. 기관, 단체
☐ **instruct** v. 가르치다, 교육하다
☐ **instrument** n. 기구, 도구
☐ **insult** v. 모욕하다 n. 모욕
☐ **insurance** n. 보험 a. 보험의
☐ **insure** v. 보험에 들다
☐ **integrate** v. 통합시키다, 통합되다 a. 통합된
☐ **intellect** n. 지적 능력, 지성
☐ **intellectual** a. 지능의 n. 지식인
☐ **intelligent** a. 총명한, 똑똑한
☐ **intend** v. 의도하다
☐ **intense** a. 극심한, 극도의
☐ **intent** a. 집중된 n. 의향
☐ **intention** n. 의사, 의도
☐ **interest** n. 관심 v. 관심[흥미]을 끌다
☐ **interfere** v. 간섭하다, 참견하다
☐ **interior** n. 내부 a. 내부의
☐ **intermediate** a. 중간의 n. 중간에 있는 것
☐ **internal** a. 안의, 내부의
☐ **interpret** v. 설명하다, 통역하다
☐ **interrupt** v. 방해하다, 중단하다 n. 중단하기
☐ **interval** n. 간격, 사이
☐ **intervene** v. 개입하다, 중재하다
☐ **interview** n. 면접 v. 면접을 보다, 인터뷰를 하다
☐ **intimate** a. 친한 n. 절친한 친구 v. 넌지시 알리다
☐ **intrigue** v. 흥미를 불러일으키다, 모의하다 n. 모의
☐ **invade** v. 침입하다, 침략하다
☐ **invent** v. 발명하다, 고안하다

☐ **inventor** n. 발명가, 고안자
☐ **invest** v. 투자하다, 돈을 쓰다
☐ **investigate** v. 조사하다, 수사하다
☐ **involve** v. 수반하다, 포함하다
☐ **iron** n. 철 a. 철의 v. 다리미질을 하다
☐ **irony** n. 아이러니, 역설 a. 철의, 쇠로 만든
☐ **irritate** v. 짜증나게 하다, 짜증을 내다, 무효로 하다
☐ **island** n. 섬 a. 섬의
☐ **isolate** v. 격리하다 n. 고립된 것[사람] a. 고립된
☐ **item** n. 항목 v. 항목별로 쓰다
☐ **jail** n. 교도소 v. 투옥하다
☐ **jar** n. 병, 단지
☐ **jaw** n. 턱 v. 지껄이다
☐ **jeans** n. 청바지
☐ **jog** v. 조깅하다, 살짝 치다[밀다] n. 조깅, 울퉁불퉁함
☐ **joint** a. 공동의 n. 관절 v. 접합하다, 연결되다
☐ **joke** n. 농담 v. 농담하다, 놀리다
☐ **journal** n. 신문, 잡지
☐ **journey** n. 여행 v. 여행하다
☐ **joy** n. 기쁨 v. 기뻐하다, 기쁘게 하다
☐ **judge** n. 판사 v. 재판하다
☐ **junior** a. 손아래의 n. 손아래 사람
☐ **jury** n. 배심원단 v. 심사하다 a. 임시의, 응급의
☐ **justice** n. 정의, 공평성
☐ **keen** a. 간절히 ~하고 싶은
☐ **kit** n. 조립용품 세트
☐ **knee** n. 무릎 v. 무릎으로 치다, 무릎을 꿇다
☐ **knight** n. (중세의) 기사
☐ **knock** v. 두드리다 n. 두드림
☐ **knot** n. 매듭 v. 매다, 매듭을 짓다
☐ **knowledge** n. 지식, 학문
☐ **lab(oratory)** n. 실험실 a. 실험실의
☐ **label** n. 상표 v. 상표를 붙이다
☐ **labo(u)r** n. 노동 v. 노동하다, 상세히 설명하다 a. 노동자의
☐ **lack** n. 부족 v. 부족하다
☐ **ladder** n. 사다리 v. 사다리를 오르다
☐ **lamb** n. 새끼 양 v. 양이 새끼를 낳다
☐ **lamp** n. 등 v. 비추다, 빛나다
☐ **landscape** n. 풍경 v. 조경을 하다
☐ **lane** n. 길, 도로
☐ **language** n. 언어, 말
☐ **lap** n. 무릎 v. 싸다, 겹쳐지다
☐ **latter** a. 후자의 n. 후자
☐ **laugh** v. 웃다, 웃으며 ~하다 n. 웃음
☐ **launch** v. 시작하다, 착수하다 n. 개시, 론치

☐ **laundry** n. 세탁물, 세탁
☐ **law** n. 법, 법률
☐ **lawn** n. 잔디밭, 잔디 구장
☐ **lawyer** n. 변호사, 법률가
☐ **lay** v. 놓다, 알을 낳다
☐ **layer** n. 층 v. 층으로 놓다, 층을 이루다
☐ **lead** v. 안내하다, 앞장서서 가다 n. 이끌기, 납
☐ **leaf** n. 잎, 나뭇잎
☐ **league** n. 리그, 연합
☐ **leak** v. 새게 하다, 누설되다 n. 새는 곳
☐ **lean** v. 기울다, 기울이다 n. 기울기 a. 여윈
☐ **leap** v. 뛰다, 뛰어넘다 n. 뛰기
☐ **lease** n. 임대차 계약 v. 임대하다
☐ **leather** n. 가죽 v. 가죽을 씌우다 a. 가죽의
☐ **leave** v. 떠나다, 출발하다 n. 허락, 허가
☐ **lecture** n. 강의 v. 강의하다
☐ **legal** a. 법률의 n. 법률 요건
☐ **legend** n. 전설, 신화
☐ **legislate** v. 법률을 제정하다
☐ **legitimate** a. 정당한 v. 정당화하다
☐ **leisure** n. 여가 a. 한가한
☐ **lemon** n. 레몬 a. 레몬 색의
☐ **lend** v. 빌려주다, 대여하다
☐ **let** v. 두다, 세를 주다 n. 임대
☐ **level** n. 평평함 a. 평평한 ad. 평평하게 v. 평평하게 하다
☐ **liberal** a. 자유주의의 n. 자유주의자
☐ **liberty** n. 자유, 해방
☐ **license / licence** n. 허가, 면허 v. 허가하다
☐ **lid** n. 뚜껑, 덮개
☐ **lift** v. 들어올리다, 들리다 n. 승강기
☐ **likewise** ad. 똑같이, 비슷하게
☐ **limit** n. 한계 v. 제한하다
☐ **linguistic** a. 말의, 언어의
☐ **link** n. 관련 v. 연결하다, 관련되다
☐ **liquid** n. 액체 a. 액체 형태의
☐ **list** n. 목록 v. 목록[명단]을 작성하다
☐ **literature** n. 문학, 문예
☐ **livingroom** n. 거실
☐ **load** n. 짐 v. 짐을 싣다
☐ **loan** n. 대출 v. 빌려주다
☐ **local** a. 장소의 n. 지역 주민
☐ **locate** v. 위치하게 하다, 정착하다
☐ **lock** v. 잠그다, 고정되다 n. 자물쇠
☐ **log** n. 통나무 v. 일지에 기록하다, 벌목하다
☐ **logic** n. 논리, 타당성
☐ **lone** a. 혼자인, 단독의
☐ **loose** a. 느슨한 v. 느슨하게 하다, 풀리다
☐ **lose** v. 잃어버리다, 지다

☐ **loss** n. 분실, 상실
☐ **lot** n. 추첨 v. 구분하다, 제비 뽑기를 하다 ad. 훨씬
☐ **loud** a. (소리가) 큰 ad. 크게
☐ **loyal** a. 충성스러운, 충직한 n. 충신, 애국자
☐ **lump** n. 덩어리 a. 덩어리의 v. 한 덩어리로 하다
☐ **luxury** n. 호화로움 a. 고급의
☐ **machine** n. 기계 v. 기계로 만들다 a. 기계의
☐ **magazine** n. 잡지, 프로그램
☐ **magic** n. 마법 a. 마법의
☐ **magnet** n. 자석, 자철
☐ **magnificent** a. 장려한, 장엄한
☐ **main** a. 주된 n. 본관
☐ **maintain** v. 지속[계속]하다, 유지하다
☐ **major** a. 큰[많은] 쪽의 n. 소령 v. 전공하다
☐ **majority** n. 대다수, 대부분
☐ **male** a. 남자의 n. 남자
☐ **manage** v. 간신히 ~하다, 살아 나가다
☐ **manifest** v. 표현하다, 나타나다 a. 분명한
☐ **manipulate** v. 조종하다, 기계를 다루다
☐ **manner** n. 방식, 방법
☐ **manufacture** v. 제조하다, 생산하다 n. 제조
☐ **margin** n. 여백 v. 가장자리를 붙이다
☐ **marine** a. 바다의 n. 해병대
☐ **mark** n. 표시 v. 표시하다, 자국이 나다
☐ **marvel** n. 경이로운 일 v. 경탄하다
☐ **mask** n. 마스크 v. 감추다, 가면을 쓰다
☐ **mass** n. 덩어리 a. 대량의 v. 많이 모으다
☐ **master** n. 주인 a. 주요한 v. 정복하다
☐ **match** n. 성냥, 경기 v. 필적하다, 조화되다
☐ **mate** n. 친구 v. 짝지어주다, 짝짓기를 하다
☐ **material** n. 재료 a. 물질의
☐ **matter** n. 문제 v. 중요하다
☐ **mature** a. 어른스러운, 숙성된 v. 어른이 되다, 성숙하게 하다
☐ **maximum** a. 최대의 n. 최대
☐ **maybe** ad. 어쩌면, 아마
☐ **mayor** n. 시장, 단체장
☐ **meal** n. 식사 v. 식사하다
☐ **mean** v. 의미하다 a. 비열한, 중간의 n. 수단
☐ **meanwhile** ad. 그 동안에, 그 사이에
☐ **measure** v. 측정하다, 측량하다 n. 조치
☐ **mechanic** n. 정비공, 기계공
☐ **mechanism** n. 기계 장치, 기구
☐ **media** n. (*sing.* medium), 매체
☐ **mediate** v. 조정하다, 중재하다 a. 중개의

- □ **medical** a. 의학의 n. 의학도
- □ **medicine** n. 약 v. 약을 먹이다
- □ **medieval** a. 중세의, 중세식의
- □ **medium** a. 중간의 n. 매체
- □ **melon** n. 멜론, 참외
- □ **melt** v. 녹다, 녹이다 n. 용해
- □ **mental** a. 정신의 n. 정신병 환자
- □ **mention** v. 말하다 n. 언급
- □ **menu** n. 메뉴, 식단표
- □ **merchant** n. 상인 a. 상인의
- □ **mere** a. 겨우 ~의 n. 작은 호수
- □ **merge** v. 합병하다, 통합되다
- □ **merit** n. 가치 v. 받을 만하다, 공덕을 쌓다
- □ **mess** n. 엉망인 상태 v. 지저분하게 만들다
- □ **message** n. 전갈 v. 메시지를 보내다
- □ **metal** n. 금속 v. 자갈을 깔다
- □ **method** n. 방법, 방식
- □ **metropolitan** a. 대도시의 n. 대도시[수도] 거주자
- □ **microphone** n. 마이크(로폰), 송화기
- □ **microwave** n. 전자레인지 v. 전자레인지에 요리하다
- □ **migrant** n. 이주자 a. 이주하는
- □ **migrate** v. 이동하다, 이동[이주]시키다
- □ **mild** a. 가벼운, 순한, 온화한
- □ **military** a. 군의 n. 군인
- □ **mill** n. 방앗간 v. 갈다, 제분기를 쓰다
- □ **million** n. 100만 a. 100만의
- □ **mine** n. 광산 v. 채굴하다
- □ **miner** n. 광부, 광산 노동자
- □ **mineral** n. 광물(질) a. 광물의
- □ **minimal** a. 아주 적은, 최소의
- □ **minimum** a. 최소의 n. 최소
- □ **ministry** n. 부처, 내각
- □ **minor** a. 작은 n. 미성년자
- □ **minute** n. 분 a. 급조한, 미세한, 세심한
- □ **miracle** n. 기적, 기적 같은 일
- □ **mirror** n. 거울 v. 잘 보여주다
- □ **missile** n. 미사일 a. 던질 수 있는
- □ **mission** n. 임무 v. 파견하다
- □ **mix** v. 섞다, 섞이다 n. 혼합체
- □ **mobile** a. 이동하는 n. 움직이는 조각
- □ **mock** v. 놀리다 a. 거짓된 n. 놀려대기
- □ **mode** n. 방식, 방법
- □ **moderate** a. 보통의 v. 완화되다
- □ **modern** a. 현대의, 근대의
- □ **modest** a. 그리 대단하지 않은, 보통의, 겸손한
- □ **modify** v. 수정하다, 변경되다
- □ **moist** a. 촉촉한, 습기가 있는
- □ **moisture** n. 수분, 습기
- □ **molecule** n. 분자, 미립자
- □ **moment** n. 잠깐, 잠시
- □ **monitor** n. 화면 v. 추적 관찰하다
- □ **monster** n. 괴물 a. 엄청나게 큰
- □ **monument** n. 기념비 v. 기념비를 세우다
- □ **mood** n. 기분, 감정
- □ **moral** a. 도덕의 n. 도덕
- □ **moreover** ad. 게다가, 더욱이
- □ **mortal** a. 언젠가는 반드시 죽는 n. 사람 ad. 매우
- □ **motion** n. 운동, 움직임 v. 동작을 해 보이다
- □ **motive** n. 동기 a. 움직이게 하는 v. 동기를 주다
- □ **motor** n. 모터 v. 자동차로 가다
- □ **mount** v. 오르다 n. 오르기, 산, 언덕
- □ **mud** n. 진흙 v. 진흙투성이로 만들다
- □ **multiple** a. 많은 n. 배수
- □ **murder** n. 살인(죄) v. 살해하다
- □ **muscle** n. 근육 v. 힘으로 밀고 나아가다
- □ **museum** n. 박물관, 미술관
- □ **mushroom** n. 버섯 a. 버섯의 v. 급속히 생기다
- □ **mutual** a. 상호간의, 서로의
- □ **mystery** n. 수수께끼, 미스터리
- □ **myth** n. 신화, 근거 없는 믿음
- □ **nail** n. 손톱 v. 못으로 박다
- □ **naive** a. 순진한, 순진해 빠진
- □ **naked** a. 벌거벗은
- □ **narrate** v. 이야기하다, 말하다
- □ **narrow** a. 좁은 v. 좁아지다, 좁히다
- □ **nasty** a. 끔찍한, 형편없는
- □ **native** a. 출생지의 n. 태생인 사람
- □ **navy** n. 해군, 짙은 남색
- □ **neat** a. 정돈된, 단정한
- □ **necessary** a. 필요한 n. 없어서는 안 되는 것
- □ **needle** n. 바늘 v. 바느질하다 a. 마음 졸이게 하는
- □ **negate** v. 무효화하다
- □ **negative** a. 부정적인 n. 부정 v. 거부하다
- □ **neglect** v. 소홀히 하다 n. 소홀
- □ **negotiate** v. 협상하다, 성사시키다
- □ **neighbo(u)r** n. 이웃 a. 이웃의 v. 이웃하다
- □ **neither** a. pron. (둘 중의) 어느 것도 ~ 아니다
- □ **nephew** n. 조카
- □ **nerve** n. 신경 v. 힘을 북돋우다
- □ **nervous** a. 불안해하는, 초조해하는
- □ **nest** n. 둥지 v. 둥지에 넣다
- □ **net** n. 그물 a. 그물의 v. 그물로 잡다
- □ **network** n. 망 v. 통신망을 구축하다
- □ **neutral** a. 중립적인 n. 중립
- □ **nevertheless** ad. 그렇기는 하지만
- □ **nightmare** n. 악몽, 가위눌림
- □ **noble** a. 고결한 n. 고귀한 사람, 귀족
- □ **nod** v. 끄덕이다 n. 끄덕임
- □ **noise** n. 잡음 v. 퍼뜨리다
- □ **nominate** v. 지명하다, 출마하다
- □ **none** pron. 아무도 ~ 않다
- □ **nonetheless** ad. 그렇기는 하지만
- □ **noon** n. 정오, 한낮
- □ **nor** conj. ~도 (또한) 아니다[없다]
- □ **norm** n. 표준, 일반적인 것
- □ **normal** a. 보통의 n. 보통
- □ **notice** n. 주목 v. 알아차리다
- □ **novel** n. 소설 a. 새로운
- □ **nowadays** ad. 요즈음에는 n. 요즈음
- □ **nowhere** ad. 아무데도 ~없이 n. 아무데도 아닌 곳
- □ **nuclear** a. 핵의 n. 핵 에너지
- □ **numerous** a. 많은, 무수한
- □ **nut** n. 견과 v. 너트로 죄다
- □ **oak** n. 오크 a. 오크의
- □ **obey** v. 복종하다, 순종하다
- □ **object** n. 물건 v. 반대하다
- □ **objective** n. 목표 a. 객관적인
- □ **oblige** v. 강요하다, 호의를 베풀다
- □ **observe** v. 보다, 관찰하다
- □ **obsess** v. 사로잡다, 강박감을 갖다
- □ **obtain** v. 얻다, 존재하다
- □ **obvious** a. 분명한, 명백한
- □ **occasion** n. 경우 v. 원인이 되다
- □ **occupation** n. 직업, 일
- □ **occupy** v. 차지하다, 점유하다
- □ **occur** v. 일어나다, 발생하다
- □ **occurrence** n. 발생, 존재
- □ **ocean** n. 대양, 바다
- □ **odd** a. 이상한, 홀수의 n. 자투리
- □ **offend** v. 기분을 상하게 하다, 범죄를 저지르다
- □ **offer** v. 제의하다, 제안하다 n. 제의
- □ **officer** n. 장교 v. 장교를 배치하다
- □ **once** ad. 한 번 conj. 일단 ~하면
- □ **opera** n. 오페라
- □ **operate** v. 작동하다, 조작하다
- □ **opinion** n. 의견, 생각
- □ **opportune** a. 좋은, 적절한
- □ **opportunity** n. 기회, 호기
- □ **oppose** v. 반대하다, 저항하다
- □ **opt** v. 선택하다, 선정하다
- □ **optimist** n. 낙천주의자, 낙관론자
- □ **option** n. 선택, 선택할 수 있는 것
- □ **oral** a. 구두의 n. 구두시험
- □ **orbit** n. 궤도 v. 궤도를 돌다, 선회하다
- □ **orchestra** n. 오케스트라
- □ **order** n. 순서 v. 명령하다
- □ **ordinary** a. 보통의 n. 보통의 상태
- □ **organ** n. 장기, 기관
- □ **organic** a. 유기농의
- □ **organize / organise** v. 준비하다, 조직화되다
- □ **orient** v. (동쪽으로) 향하게 하다[향하다] a. 동쪽의 n. 동쪽, 동양
- □ **orientation** n. 방향, 성향
- □ **origin** n. 기원, 근원
- □ **original** a. 원래의 n. 원본
- □ **other** a. 다른 pron. 다른 사람[것] ad. ~ 외에
- □ **otherwise** ad. 그렇지 않으면[않았다면]
- □ **ought** ~해야 하다 n. 의무
- □ **outcome** n. 결과, 성과
- □ **outline** n. 개요 v. 개요를 서술하다
- □ **output** n. 생산량 v. 생산하다
- □ **outrage** n. 격분 v. 격분하게 만들다
- □ **outstanding** a. 뛰어난, 걸출한
- □ **oven** n. 오븐, 가마
- □ **overall** a. 전체의 ad. 전부 n. 작업복
- □ **overcome** v. 극복하다, 이기다
- □ **overhead** ad. 머리 위에[로] a. 머리 위의
- □ **overlap** v. 겹치다, 겹쳐지다 n. 겹침
- □ **overlook** v. 못 보고 넘어가다 n. 간과
- □ **overnight** ad. 밤사이에 a. 야간의 v. 하룻밤을 지내다
- □ **oversea(s)** a. 해외의 ad. 바다 건너 n. 외국
- □ **overwhelm** v. 휩싸다, 압도하다
- □ **owe** v. 빚지고 있다, 빚이 있다
- □ **own** a. 자기 자신의 v. 소유하다
- □ **pace** n. 속도 v. 서성거리다
- □ **pack** v. 짐을 싸다 n. 꾸러미
- □ **pad** n. 패드 v. 패드[보호대/완충재]를 대다
- □ **pain** n. 고통 v. 아프게 하다, 아프다
- □ **pair** n. 쌍 v. 짝 지우다, 한 쌍이 되다
- □ **palace** n. 궁전, 왕실
- □ **pale** a. 창백한 v. 창백해지다, 창백하게 하다
- □ **palm** n. 손바닥, 야자수
- □ **pan** n. 냄비 v. 혹평하다
- □ **panel** n. 판 v. 판으로 덮다
- □ **panic** n. 극심한 공포 a. 공황적인 v. 공황을 일으키다
- □ **parade** n. 행렬 v. 뽐내며 걷다, 줄지어 행진시키다
- □ **paragraph** n. 단락 v. 단락으로 나누다, 짧은 기사를 쓰다
- □ **parallel** a. 평행한 n. 평행선 ad. 평행하여 v. 평행하다
- □ **pardon** v. 사면하다 n. 용서

☐ **parliament** n. 의회, 국회
☐ **participate** v. 참가하다, 참여하다
☐ **particle** n. 입자, 조각
☐ **particular** a. 특정한 n. 자세한 사항
☐ **particularly** ad. 특히, 특별히
☐ **passage** n. 통로 v. 나아가다
☐ **passenger** n. 승객, 여객
☐ **passion** n. 열정 v. 열정을 느끼다
☐ **passport** n. 여권, 열쇠
☐ **past** a. 지나간 n. 과거 prep. ~을 지나서 ad. 지나가서
☐ **pat** v. 가볍게 두드리다 n. 가볍게 두드리기
☐ **patch** n. 부분 v. 덧대다
☐ **patent** n. 특허 a. 특허의 v. 특허를 받다
☐ **path** n. 길, 방향
☐ **patient** n. 환자 a. 참을성 있는
☐ **pattern** n. 무늬 v. 무늬를 만들다
☐ **pause** v. 멈추다, 정지시키다 n. 멈춤
☐ **pave** v. 포장하다 n. 포장 도로
☐ **peace** n. 평화, 평온
☐ **peaceful** a. 평화적인, 비폭력적인
☐ **peak** n. 절정 v. 절정에 달하다 a. 절정기의
☐ **pear** n. 배, 배나무
☐ **peasant** n. 소작인 a. 소작인의
☐ **peel** v. 껍질을 벗기다[깎다], 껍질이 벗겨지다 n. 껍질
☐ **peer** n. 또래 v. ~에 필적하다, 유심히 보다
☐ **penalty** n. 처벌, 형벌
☐ **pepper** n. 후추 v. 후추를 뿌리다
☐ **per** prep. ~에 대하여, ~마다
☐ **perceive** v. 감지하다, 인지하다
☐ **perception** n. 지각, 자각
☐ **perfect** a. 완벽한 v. 완벽하게 하다
☐ **perform** v. 행하다, 작동하다
☐ **perhaps** ad. 아마 n. 우연한 일
☐ **period** n. 기간 a. 시대의
☐ **permanent** a. 영구적인 n. 파마
☐ **permit** v. 허용하다 n. 허가증
☐ **persist** v. 집요하게 계속하다
☐ **person** n. 사람, 개인
☐ **personality** n. 성격, 인격
☐ **perspective** n. 관점 a. 원근법에 의한
☐ **persuade** v. 설득하다, 설득하여 ~하게 하다
☐ **pet** n. 반려동물 v. 특별히 귀여워하다
☐ **phase** n. 단계 v. 단계적으로 하다
☐ **phenomenon** n. 현상, 경이로운 사람[것]
☐ **philosophy** n. 철학, 인생관
☐ **photo(graph)** n. 사진 v. 사진을 찍다

☐ **phrase** n. (문법) 구(句) v. 표현하다
☐ **physical** a. 육체의 n. 건강 검진
☐ **physics** n. 물리학
☐ **picnic** n. 소풍 v. 소풍을 가다
☐ **pie** n. 파이
☐ **piece** n. 조각 v. 이어서 붙이다
☐ **pile** n. 쌓아 올린 것 v. 쌓다, 모이다
☐ **pill** n. 알약
☐ **pin** n. 핀 v. 핀으로 꽂다
☐ **pinch** v. 꼬집다, 너무 끼다 n. 꼬집기
☐ **pine** n. 소나무, 솔 v. 애타게 그리워하다
☐ **pioneer** n. 개척자 v. 개척하다 a. 개척자의
☐ **pipe** n. 관 v. 관을 통해 보내다, 피리를 불다
☐ **pitch** n. 던지기 v. 던지다
☐ **pity** n. 연민 v. 애석해 하다
☐ **plain** a. 분명한 n. 평원 ad. 분명히
☐ **plane** n. 비행기 a. 평면인 v. 대패로 깎다, 활공하다
☐ **planet** n. 행성, 지구
☐ **plant** n. 식물, 공장 v. 심다
☐ **plate** n. 접시 v. 도금하다
☐ **platform** n. 플랫폼 v. 단을 설치하다
☐ **plenty** n. 많음 a. 많은 ad. 많이
☐ **plot** n. 음모, 작은 땅 v. 음모하다, 구획하다
☐ **plus** prep. ~을 더하여 n. 플러스 부호(+) conj. 더욱이 v. 더하다
☐ **pocket** n. 호주머니 v. 호주머니에 넣다 a. 호주머니에 넣을 수 있는
☐ **poem** n. 시
☐ **poet** n. 시인
☐ **poison** n. 독 a. 유독한 v. 독을 넣다
☐ **polar** a. 극의, 극지의
☐ **pole** n. 극, 극지, 막대기
☐ **policy** n. 정책, 방침, 보험 증권
☐ **polish** n. 광택제 v. 닦다, 윤을 내다
☐ **polite** a. 예의 바른, 공손한
☐ **politics** n. 정치, 정치학
☐ **poll** n. 여론 조사 v. 득표하다, 투표하다
☐ **pollute** v. 오염시키다, 더럽히다
☐ **pond** n. 연못 v. 못을 만들다, 고이다
☐ **pool** n. 수영장 v. 물웅덩이를 만들다
☐ **pop** n. 펑 하는 소리 v. 펑 하는 소리가 나다
☐ **popular** a. 인기 있는, 일반적인
☐ **populate** v. 살다, 거주하다
☐ **population** n. 인구, 주민
☐ **pork** n. 돼지고기

☐ **port** n. 항구, 항구 도시
☐ **portion** n. 부분 v. 나누다
☐ **portrait** n. 초상화, 인물 사진
☐ **pose** v. 제기하다, 포즈를 취하다 n. 포즈
☐ **posit** v. 놓다 n. 놓여 있는 것
☐ **position** n. 위치 v. 놓다
☐ **positive** a. 긍정적인 n. 현실
☐ **possess** v. 소유하다, 지니고 있다
☐ **possible** a. 가능한 n. 가능성
☐ **post** n. 우편, 기둥 v. 붙이다
☐ **poster** n. 포스터 v. 포스터[벽보]를 붙이다
☐ **pot** n. 냄비 v. 통에 넣다, 쏘다
☐ **potential** a. 가능성이 있는 n. 가능성
☐ **pour** v. 붓다, 흘러나오다 n. 유출
☐ **powder** n. 가루 v. 가루로 만들다
☐ **practical** a. 현실[실질]적인 n. 실기 시험
☐ **practice / practise** n. 연습 v. 연습하다
☐ **praise** n. 칭찬 v. 칭찬하다
☐ **pray** v. 기도하다, 빌다
☐ **preach** v. 설교하다, 전도하다 n. 설교
☐ **precede** v. 앞서다, 선행하다
☐ **precise** a. 정확한, 정밀한
☐ **predator** n. 포식자, 포식 동물
☐ **predict** v. 예측하다, 예견하다
☐ **prefer** v. ~을 (더) 좋아하다, 선호하다
☐ **pregnant** a. 임신한, 그득한
☐ **prejudice** n. 편견 v. 편견을 갖게 하다
☐ **premium** n. 보험료 a. 우수한
☐ **prepare** v. 준비하다, 대비하다
☐ **prescribe** v. 처방을 내리다, 처방하다
☐ **presence** n. 출석, 참석
☐ **preserve** v. 보호하다, 저장하다 n. 전유물
☐ **preside** v. 주재하다, 주도하다
☐ **president** n. 대통령, 의장
☐ **press** n. 신문, 언론 v. 누르다, 밀다
☐ **presume** v. 추정하다, 가정하다
☐ **pretend** v. ~인 척하다 a. 가짜의
☐ **prevail** v. 만연하다, 우세하다
☐ **prevent** v. 막다, 방해하다
☐ **previous** a. 이전의, 앞의
☐ **prey** n. 먹이 v. 잡아먹다
☐ **price** n. 값 v. 값을 매기다
☐ **pride** n. 자랑스러움 v. 자랑스러워하다
☐ **priest** n. 성직자 v. 성직자로 임명하다
☐ **primary** a. 주된 n. 예비 선거
☐ **prime** a. 주된 n. 한창때
☐ **primitive** a. 원시의, 원시 사회의
☐ **principal** a. 주요한 n. 우두머리
☐ **principle** n. 원칙, 주의

☐ **prior** a. 이전의, 앞의
☐ **prison** n. 교도소 v. 감금하다
☐ **privacy** n. 혼자 있는 상태, 사생활
☐ **private** a. 사유의 n. 병사
☐ **privilege** n. 특권 v. 특권을 주다
☐ **prize** n. 상 v. 소중히 하다
☐ **probable** a. 있을 것 같은 n. 일어날 듯한 사건
☐ **probably** ad. 아마, 십중팔구는
☐ **procedure** n. 절차, 방법
☐ **proceed** v. 계속 진행하다, 계속하다
☐ **process** n. 과정 v. 가공[처리]하다, 행진하다
☐ **produce** v. 생산하다, 산출하다 n. 생산물[품]
☐ **profession** n. 직업, 직종
☐ **professor** n. 교수, 교사
☐ **profile** n. 옆얼굴(의 윤곽), 개요 v. 윤곽을 그리다
☐ **profit** n. 이익 v. 이익을 주다
☐ **profound** a. 엄청난 n. 깊음
☐ **progress** n. 진전 v. 진전을 보이다
☐ **prohibit** v. 금하다, 금지하다
☐ **prominent** a. 중요한, 유명한
☐ **promise** v. 약속하다 n. 약속
☐ **promote** v. 촉진하다, 고취하다
☐ **prompt** a. 즉각적인 v. 촉발하다 n. 자극[촉발]하는 것
☐ **pronounce** v. 발음하다, 의견을 말하다
☐ **pronunciation** n. 발음, 발음 표기
☐ **proof** n. 입증 a. 견딜 수 있는 v. 방수[방염] 처리를 하다
☐ **proper** a. 적절한, 적당한
☐ **property** n. 재산, 소유물
☐ **proportion** n. 부분 v. 할당하다
☐ **propose** v. 제안하다, 제의하다
☐ **prospect** n. 가망 v. 탐사하다
☐ **prosper** v. 번영하다, 번영하게 하다
☐ **protect** v. 보호하다, 지키다
☐ **protein** n. 단백질 a. 단백질의
☐ **protest** n. 항의 v. 항의[반대]하다
☐ **proud** a. 자랑스러워하는, 자랑스러운
☐ **prove** v. 증명하다, 드러나다
☐ **provide** v. 제공하다, 공급하다
☐ **province** n. 주(州), 도(道)
☐ **provoke** v. 유발하다, 야기하다
☐ **psychology** n. 심리학, 심리 (상태)
☐ **pub** n. 퍼브(대중적 술집)
☐ **public** a. 일반인의, 공공의 n. 일반 사람들
☐ **publish** v. 출판하다
☐ **publisher** n. 출판인, 발행인
☐ **pull** v. 끌다, 당기다 n. 끌기
☐ **pump** n. 펌프 v. 퍼 올리다
☐ **punch** v. 주먹으로 치다 n. 치기
☐ **punish** v. 처벌하다, 응징하다
☐ **pupil** n. 학생, 눈동자, 동공

□ purchase n. 구입 v. 구입하다
□ pure a. 순수한, 깨끗한
□ purple a. 자주색의 n. 자주색 v. 자주색이 되게 하다
□ purpose n. 목적 v. 작정하다
□ pursue v. 추구하다, 쫓아가다
□ puzzle n. 퍼즐 v. 당황하게 하다, 당황하다
□ qualify v. 자격을 주다, 출전할 자격이 있다
□ quality n. 질 a. 고급의
□ quantity n. 양, 수량
□ quarter n. 4분의 1 v. 4등분 하다 a. 4분의 1의
□ questionnaire n. 설문지
□ quit v. 그만두다 a. 자유로운 n. 놓아주기, 사직
□ quite ad. 꽤, 제법
□ quote v. 인용하다 n. 인용문
□ rage n. 격렬한 분노 v. 몹시 화를 내다
□ rail n. 난간 v. 난간으로 둘러싸다, 기차여행을 하다
□ rainbow n. 무지개
□ raise v. 들어올리다 n. 올리기
□ rally n. 집회 v. 결집시키다, 모이다
□ random a. 닥치는 대로의 n. 닥치는 대로 하기
□ range n. 범위 v. 배열하다, (양·크기 등이) 일정한 범위) 이다
□ rank n. 지위 v. 매기다, 차지하다
□ rapid a. 빠른 n. 급류
□ rare a. 드문, 희귀한, 설익은
□ rat n. 쥐 v. 쥐를 잡다
□ rate n. 속도 v. 평가하다, 평가되다
□ rather ad. 오히려, 꽤
□ rational a. 합리적인, 이성적인
□ raw a. 익히지 않은 n. 찰과상
□ reach v. 이르다, 뻗다 n. 거리
□ react v. 반응하다, 반응을 보이다
□ real a. 현실적인 ad. 정말 n. 현실
□ realize / realise v. 깨닫다, 실현하다
□ rear n. 뒤 a. 후방의 ad. 후방에서 v. 기르다
□ reason n. 이유 v. 논하다, 판단하다
□ reasonable a. 타당한, 사리에 맞는
□ rebel n. 반역자 v. 반란을 일으키다
□ receipt n. 영수증
□ receive v. 받다, 손님을 맞이하다
□ recent a. 최근의 n. 현세
□ reception n. 접수처, 프런트
□ recipe n. 조리법, 요리법

□ recognize v. 알아보다, 서약서를 제출하다
□ recommend v. 추천하다, 천거하다
□ record n. 기록 v. 기록하다 a. 기록적인
□ recover v. 되찾다, 회복되다
□ recruit v. 모집하다, 보충하다 n. 신병
□ recycle v. 재활용하다, 재생하다
□ reduce v. 줄이다, 줄다
□ refer v. 조회하다, 조회시키다
□ refine v. 정제하다, 순수해지다
□ reflect v. 반사하다, 비추다
□ reform v. 개혁하다, 개심하다 n. 개혁
□ refrigerate v. 식히다, 차가워지다
□ refrigerator n. 냉장고, 냉각 장치
□ refuse v. 거절하다, 거부하다
□ regard v. 여기다, 주시하다 n. 관심
□ region n. 지방, 지역
□ register v. 등록하다 n. 기록부
□ regret v. 후회하다 n. 후회
□ regular a. 규칙적인 n. 단골손님 ad. 규칙적으로
□ regulate v. 규제하다, 통제하다
□ reinforce v. 강화하다 n. 보강물
□ reject v. 거부하다 n. 불합격품
□ relate v. 관련시키다, 관계가 있다
□ relation n. 관계, 사이
□ relationship n. 관계, 친족 관계
□ relative n. 친척 a. 비교상의
□ relax v. 편하게 하다, 휴식을 취하다
□ release v. 풀어 주다 n. 석방
□ relevant a. 관련 있는, 적절한
□ relief n. 안도, 안심
□ relieve v. 없애 주다, 완화하다
□ religion n. 종교, 종파
□ reluctant a. 꺼리는, 마음 내키지 않는
□ rely v. 의지하다, 의존하다
□ remain v. 남다 n. 나머지
□ remark n. 말 v. 말하다, 알아채다
□ remedy n. 해결책 v. 치료하다
□ remind v. 상기시키다, 생각나게 하다
□ remote a. 외진 n. 현장 중계 ad. 멀리 떨어져
□ remove v. 치우다, 이동하다 n. 이동
□ rent n. 집세 v. 세내다
□ repair v. 수리하다 n. 수리
□ repeat v. 반복하다, 되풀이되다 n. 반복
□ replace v. 대신하다, 대체하다
□ reply v. 대답하다 n. 대답
□ report v. 발표하다, 보고하다 n. 보고(서)
□ represent v. 나타내다, 상징하다
□ republic n. 공화국, -계
□ reputation n. 평판, 명성

□ request n. 요청 v. 요청하다
□ require v. 필요하다, 필요로 하다
□ rescue v. 구조하다 n. 구조 a. 구조의
□ research n. 연구 v. 연구하다
□ resemble v. 닮다, 비슷하다
□ reserve v. 예약하다 n. 비축 a. 예비의
□ reside v. 살다, 거주하다
□ resident n. 거주자 a. 거주하는
□ resign v. 사임하다, 사직하다
□ resist v. 저항하다 n. 방염제
□ resolve v. 해결하다, 결심하다 n. 결심
□ resort n. 휴양지 v. 의지하다
□ resource n. 자원 v. 자원을 제공하다
□ respect n. 존경(심) v. 존경하다
□ respective a. 각자의, 각각의
□ respond v. 대답하다, 응답하다 n. 벽기둥
□ responsible a. 책임지고 있는, 책임이 있는
□ rest n. 휴식, 나머지 v. 쉬다, 쉬게 하다, (여전히·계속) ~이다
□ restore v. 회복시키다, 되찾게 하다
□ restrain v. 저지하다, 제지하다
□ restrict v. 제한하다, 한정하다
□ result n. 결과 v. 발생하다
□ resume v. 다시 시작하다 n. 개요, 요약, 이력서
□ retail n. 소매 a. 소매의 v. 소매하다 ad. 소매로
□ retain v. 유지하다, 보유하다
□ retire v. 은퇴하다, 퇴직시키다
□ retreat v. 후퇴하다, 후퇴시키다 n. 후퇴
□ reveal v. 밝히다 n. 계시
□ revenge n. 복수 v. 복수하다
□ reverse v. 뒤바꾸다, 뒤바뀌다 n. (정)반대 a. (정)반대의
□ review n. 검토 v. 재검토하다, 논평하다
□ revise v. 변경하다 n. 수정판
□ revive v. 의식을 되찾다, 회복시키다
□ revolution n. 혁명, 변혁
□ reward n. 보상 v. 보상하다, 보답하다
□ rhythm n. 리듬, 율동
□ rice n. 쌀 v. 으깨다
□ rid v. 없애다, 제거하다
□ ride v. 타다, 타고 가다 n. 타기, 탈 것
□ ridicule n. 조롱 v. 조롱하다
□ ridiculous a. 웃기는, 우스운
□ riot n. 폭동 v. 폭동[소동]을 일으키다
□ rise n. 오름 v. 일어나다, 올리다
□ risk n. 위험 v. 위태롭게 하다

□ rival n. 경쟁자 a. 경쟁하는 v. 경쟁하다
□ roar v. 으르렁거리다, 큰 소리로 말하다 n. 으르렁거림
□ roast v. 굽다, 구워지다 n. 구운 고기 a. 구운
□ rob v. 빼앗다, 도둑질을 하다
□ rocket n. 로켓 v. 로켓탄으로 공격하다, 치솟다
□ rod n. 막대, 장대
□ role n. 역할, 임무
□ roll n. 통 v. 구르다, 굴리다
□ romantic a. 로맨틱한
□ roof n. 지붕 v. 지붕을 덮다
□ root n. 뿌리 a. 뿌리의 v. 뿌리를 내리다
□ rope n. 밧줄 v. 밧줄로 묶다
□ rot v. 썩다, 썩히다 n. 썩음
□ rough a. 고르지 않은 n. 러프 ad. 거칠게 v. 거칠게 하다
□ round a. 둥근 ad. 둥글게 n. 둥근 모양 v. 둥글게 하다
□ route n. 길 v. 보내다
□ routine n. 일 a. 정례적인
□ row n. 열, (노) 젓기, 소란 v. 줄세우다, 노를 젓다, 꾸짖다
□ royal a. 왕의 n. 왕족
□ rub v. 문지르다, 마찰되다 n. 문지르기
□ rubber n. 고무 a. 고무로 만든
□ rude a. 무례한, 버릇 없는
□ ruin v. 망치다, 폐허가 되다 n. 붕괴
□ rule n. 규칙 v. 지배하다
□ rumo(u)r n. 소문 v. 소문을 내다
□ rural a. 시골의, 지방의
□ rush v. 급속히 움직이다 n. 급작스러운 움직임
□ sack n. 부대, 약탈 v. 해고하다, 약탈하다
□ sacred a. 성스러운, 신성한
□ sacrifice n. 희생 v. 희생하다
□ sail v. 항해하다, 조종하다 n. 돛
□ salary n. 급여 a. 급여를 받는 v. 급여를 주다
□ sample n. 견본 a. 견본의 v. 맛보다
□ satellite n. 위성 a. (인공)위성의
□ satisfy v. 만족시키다, 충족시키다
□ sauce n. 소스 v. 소스를 치다
□ scale n. 규모, 저울, 비늘 v. 오르다, 비례하다, 무게가 ~이다, 비늘을 벗기다
□ scan v. 살피다 n. 정밀 검사
□ scandal n. 추문 v. 비방하다
□ scarce a. 부족한 ad. 겨우
□ scare v. 겁먹게 하다 n. 놀람 a. 두려워하게 하는
□ scarf n. 스카프 v. 스카프를 두르다

□ scatter	v. (흩)뿌리다, 흩어지다 n. 흩뿌리기
□ scene	n. 현장, 장면
□ schedule	n. 스케줄 v. 일정을 잡다
□ scheme	n. 계획 v. 책략을 꾸미다
□ scholar	n. 학자, 장학생
□ scope	n. 기회, 여지 v. 샅샅이 살피다
□ scramble	v. 몸을 움직이다 n. 기어오르기
□ scratch	v. 긁다 n. 긁기
□ scream	v. 비명을 지르다 n. 비명
□ screen	n. 화면 v. 가리다, 상영되다
□ screw	n. 나사[못] v. 나사로 고정시키다, (나사가) 돌다
□ sculpt	v. 조각하다, 새기다
□ sculpture	n. 조각품 v. 조각하다
□ seal	v. 봉하다 n. 직인, 바다표범
□ search	n. 찾기 v. 찾다, 수색하다
□ seat	n. 자리 v. 앉히다, 의자에 앉다
□ secret	a. 비밀의 n. 비밀
□ secretary	n. 비서, 서기
□ section	n. 부분 v. 구분하다
□ sector	n. 부문, 구역 v. 부채꼴로 분할하다
□ secure	a. 안심하는 v. 안전하게 지키다
□ seed	n. 씨 v. 씨를 뿌리다 a. 씨의
□ seek	v. 찾다, 구하다
□ seem	v. ~인 것처럼 보이다
□ seize	v. 와락[꽉] 붙잡다, 잡다
□ select	v. 선발하다 a. 엄선된 n. 고급품
□ self	n. 모습, 본모습
□ senior	a. 손위의 n. 연장자
□ sensation	n. 느낌, 감각
□ sense	n. 감각 v. 감지하다
□ sensible	a. 분별 있는, 합리적인
□ sentence	n. 문장 v. 선고하다
□ sentiment	n. 정서, 감정
□ separate	a. 분리된 v. 분리되다, 나누다
□ sequence	n. 연속 v. 차례로 배열하다
□ series	n. 연속, 연쇄
□ serious	a. 심각한, 중대한
□ serve	v. 일하다, 시중들다 n. 서브 (넣기)
□ session	n. 시간, 기간
□ settle	v. 해결하다, 합의하다
□ several	a. 몇몇의 pron. 몇몇
□ severe	a. 극심한, 심각한
□ sew	v. 만들다, 바느질하다
□ shade	n. 그늘 v. 그늘지게 하다
□ shadow	n. 그림자 v. 그림자를 드리우다
□ shake	v. 흔들리다, 뒤흔들다 n. 흔들기
□ shall	(미래) ~일 것이다, (의지) ~할 것이다
□ shallow	a. 얕은 n. 얕은 곳 v. 얕게 하다, 얕아지다 ad. 얕게
□ shame	n. 수치심 v. 창피스럽게 하다
□ shape	n. 모양 v. 모양[형태]으로 만들다, 구체화되다
□ share	v. 나누다, 함께 나누다[하다] n. 몫
□ sharp	a. 날카로운 ad. 날카롭게 n. 날카로운 것
□ shave	v. 면도하다, 깎다 n. 면도
□ sheep	n. 양
□ sheet	n. 시트 v. 시트를 깔다
□ shelf	n. 선반, 책꽂이
□ shell	n. 껍데기 v. 껍데기를 벗기다
□ shelter	n. 대피(처), 보호소 v. 보호하다, 피하다
□ shift	v. 옮기다, 바꾸다 n. 변화
□ shine	v. 빛나다, 비추다 n. 윤(기)
□ shock	n. 충격 v. 충격을 주다
□ shoot	v. 쏘다 n. 사격
□ shore	n. 기슭, 해안, 지주 v. 지주를 받치다
□ shoulder	n. 어깨 v. 짊어지다, 어깨로 밀어 헤치며 나아가다
□ shout	v. 외치다, 큰 소리로 말하다 n. 외침
□ shower	n. 소나기 v. 소나기로 적시다
□ shut	v. 닫다, 닫히다 a. 닫힌
□ sigh	v. 한숨을 쉬다, 한숨 쉬며 말하다 n. 한숨
□ sight	n. 시력 v. 갑자기 보다, 겨냥하다 a. 처음 보는
□ sign	n. 징후 v. 서명하다
□ significant	a. 중요한, 의미 있는
□ silent	a. 말을 안 하는, 침묵하는
□ silly	a. 어리석은 n. 바보
□ silver	n. 은 a. 은의
□ similar	a. 비슷한 n. 유사물
□ simple	a. 간단한 n. 어수룩한 사람
□ simulate	v. ~한 체하다 a. 흉내낸
□ simultaneous	a. 동시의, 동시에 일어나는
□ sin	n. 죄 v. 죄를 짓다
□ since	prep. ~부터 conj. ~한 이후로
□ single	a. 단 하나의 n. 하나 ad. 혼자서
□ sink	v. 가라앉다, 침몰시키다 n. 싱크대
□ site	n. 위치 v. 위치시키다
□ situate	v. 두다, 위치시키다
□ situation	n. 상황, 처지
□ skill	n. 기량, 솜씨
□ skip	v. 깡충깡충 뛰다, 뛰어넘다 n. 깡충깡충 뛰기
□ slave	n. 노예 a. 노예의
□ slice	n. 조각 v. 썰다, 얇게 자르다
□ slide	v. 미끄러지다 n. 미끄러짐
□ slight	a. 약간의 n. 무시 v. 무시하다
□ slim	a. 날씬한 v. 살을 빼다
□ slip	v. 미끄러지다, 놓아주다 n. 실수
□ slope	n. 비탈 v. 경사지다 a. 경사진
□ smart	a. 맵시 좋은, 영리한 v. 욱신거리다 n. 욱신거림
□ smash	v. 박살내다, 부딪치다 n. 박살내기
□ smoke	n. 연기 v. 피우다, 흡연을 하다
□ smooth	a. 매끈한 ad. 평탄하게 v. 매끈하게 하다
□ snack	n. 간단한 식사 v. 식사를 간단히 하다
□ snake	n. 뱀 v. 꿈틀거리다
□ snap	v. 딱 하고 부러뜨리다 n. 찰칵 하는 소리 a. 성급한
□ sneak	v. 살금살금 가다 n. 몰래 하기
□ soak	v. (액체 속에) 잠그다, 잠기다 n. (액체 속에) 잠그기
□ soap	n. 비누 v. 비누칠을 하다
□ social	a. 사회의 n. 사교 파티
□ society	n. 사회, 집단
□ sociology	n. 사회학
□ soil	n. 토양, 더럽히기 v. 더럽히다, 얼룩지다
□ soldier	n. 군인 v. 군인이 되다
□ sole	a. 유일한, 단 하나의 n. 발바닥
□ solid	a. 단단한 n. 고체 ad. 일치하여
□ solve	v. 해결[타결]하다, 풀다
□ somewhat	ad. 어느 정도 n. 조금
□ soon	ad. 곧, 머지않아
□ sophisticate	v. 궤변을 부리다 n. 안식이 높은 사람
□ sore	a. 아픈 n. 상처 ad. 몹시
□ sort	n. 종류 v. 분류하다, 조화되다
□ soul	n. 영혼, 혼
□ sour	a. 신 n. 신맛
□ source	n. 원천 v. 구입하다
□ span	n. 기간 v. (얼마의 기간에) 걸치다
□ spare	a. 남는 n. 여분 v. 할애하다, 절약하다
□ spark	n. 불꽃 v. (불꽃을) 튀기다, 불꽃이 튀다
□ special	a. 특수한 n. 특별한 것
□ species	n. 종(種: 생물 분류의 기초 단위)
□ specific	a. 구체적인 n. 특성
□ spectacle	n. 장관, 광경
□ spectrum	n. 스펙트럼, 빛띠
□ speech	n. 연설, 담화
□ spell	v. 철자를 말하다[쓰다] n. 주문
□ spend	v. 쓰다, 낭비하다 n. 비용
□ sphere	n. 구(球)
□ spill	v. 흐르다, 흘리다 n. 흘림
□ spin	v. 돌다, 회전시키다 n. 회전
□ spirit	n. 정신 v. 기운을 북돋우다
□ spit	v. 뱉다, 침을 뱉다 n. 침
□ splash	v. 튀다, 끼얹다 n. (물 등을) 튀김
□ split	v. 나누다, 나뉘다 n. 분할 a. 분할된
□ spoil	v. 망치다, 상하다 n. 약탈품
□ sponsor	n. 광고주 v. 광고주[스폰서]가 되다
□ spot	n. 점 v. 점을 찍다, 더럽혀지다 a. 즉석의
□ spouse	n. 배우자 v. 결혼하다
□ spray	n. 물보라, 잔가지 v. 물보라를 일으키다
□ spread	v. 펼치다, 펼쳐지다 n. 확산
□ spy	n. 스파이 v. 스파이 활동[노릇]을 하다, 알아채다
□ square	a. 정사각형 모양의 n. 정사각형
□ squeeze	v. (손가락으로 꼭) 짜다, 압착되다 n. (꼭) 짜기
□ stable	a. 안정된 n. 안정성, 마구간
□ stack	n. 더미 v. 쌓다, 쌓이다
□ stage	n. 단계 a. 무대의
□ stain	v. 얼룩지게 하다, 더러워지다 n. 얼룩
□ stairs	n. 계단
□ stamp	n. 우표 v. 구르다, 쿵쾅거리며 걷다
□ standard	n. 표준, 기준 a. 일반적인
□ stare	v. 빤히 쳐다보다, 응시하다 n. 응시
□ starve	v. 굶주리다, 굶기다
□ state	n. 상태 a. 국가의 v. 말하다
□ station	n. 역 v. 배치하다
□ statistic	n. 통계 a. 통계의
□ statue	n. 조각상, 조상(彫像)
□ status	n. 신분, 자격
□ steady	a. 꾸준한 v. 균형을 잡다 ad. 흔들림 없이
□ steal	v. 훔치다, 도둑질하다 n. 훔치기
□ steam	n. 김 v. 김[증기]을 내뿜다, 찌다
□ steel	n. 강철 v. 강철을 입히다
□ steep	a. 가파른 n. 가파른 곳

☐ **stem** n. 줄기 v. 줄기를 떼어내다, 일어나다, (흐름을) 막다
☐ **step** n. 걸음 v. 걷다, 디디다
☐ **stick** n. 나뭇가지, 찌르기 v. 막대기로 받치다, 찌르다
☐ **stiff** a. 뻣뻣한 ad. 몹시 n. 시체 v. 속이다
☐ **still** ad. 아직도 a. 가만히 있는 n. 고요 v. 고요[잠잠]하게 하다
☐ **stimulate** v. 자극하다, 격려가 되다
☐ **stir** v. 젓다, 약간 움직이다[흔들리다] n. 동요
☐ **stitch** n. (바느질에서) 땀 v. 바느질하다
☐ **stock** n. 재고품 v. (가게에 상품을 갖춰 두고) 있다 a. 재고가 있는
☐ **stomach** n. 위 v. 즐기다
☐ **storm** n. 폭풍 v. 기습하다, 급습하다
☐ **stove** n. 스토브 v. 스토브로 데우다
☐ **straight** ad. 똑바로 a. 곧은 n. 똑바름
☐ **strain** n. 부담, 종족, 혈통 v. 혹사하다, 안간힘을 쓰다
☐ **strange** a. 이상한 ad. 이상하게
☐ **strategy** n. 계획, 전략
☐ **stream** n. 개울 v. 흐르다, 흘리다
☐ **stress** n. 스트레스 v. 강조하다, 스트레스를 받다
☐ **stretch** v. 늘이다, 늘어나다 n. 뻗은 지역
☐ **strict** a. 엄한, 엄격한
☐ **strike** v. 치다, 두드리다 n. 파업
☐ **string** n. 끈 v. 묶다, 줄지어 늘어서다 a. 줄로 된
☐ **strip** v. 벗기다, 옷을 벗다 n. 가느다란 조각
☐ **stripe** n. 줄무늬 v. 줄무늬를 넣다
☐ **stroke** n. 치기, 쓰다듬기 v. 선[획]을 긋다, 어루만지다
☐ **structure** n. 구조 v. 조직하다
☐ **struggle** v. 투쟁하다 n. 투쟁
☐ **studio** n. 스튜디오, 영화 촬영소
☐ **stuff** n. 것[것들] v. 채워 넣다, 잔뜩 먹다
☐ **subject** n. 주제 a. ~될 수 있는 v. 지배하에 두다
☐ **subjective** a. 주관적인, 마음속에 존재하는
☐ **submarine** n. 잠수함 a. 바다 속의
☐ **submission** n. 항복, 굴복
☐ **submit** v. 제출하다, 항복하다
☐ **subscribe** v. 구독하다, 기부하다
☐ **substance** n. 물질, 실체
☐ **substantial** a. 상당한 n. 실체[실질]적인 것

☐ **substitute** n. 대리인 a. 대리의 v. 교체하다, 대신하다
☐ **subtle** a. 미묘한, 감지하기 힘든
☐ **suburb** n. 교외, 시외
☐ **succeed** v. 성공하다, 뒤를 잇다
☐ **success** n. 성공, 성과
☐ **such** a. 그런 pron. 그런 사람[것](들)
☐ **suck** v. 빨다, 빨아 먹다 n. 빨기
☐ **sudden** a. 갑작스러운 ad. 갑자기 n. 돌연
☐ **suffer** v. 시달리다, 겪다
☐ **suffice** v. (~에) 충분하다
☐ **sufficient** a. 충분한 n. 충분(한 양)
☐ **suggest** v. 제안하다, 제의하다
☐ **suicide** n. 자살 v. 자살하다, 죽이다
☐ **suit** n. 정장 v. 편리하다
☐ **suite** n. 스위트룸, (가구) 세트
☐ **sum** n. 액수, 총합 v. 합하다, 합[합계]이 ~이 되다
☐ **summary** n. 요약 a. 간략한
☐ **summit** n. (산의) 정상 v. 정상 회담에 참석하다
☐ **super** a. 대단한 ad. 특별히 n. 건물 관리인
☐ **superb** a. 최고의, 최상의
☐ **superior** a. 우수한 n. 상관
☐ **supervise** v. 감독하다, 지휘하다
☐ **supper** n. 저녁, 야식
☐ **supplement** n. 보충(물) v. 보충하다
☐ **supply** n. 공급(량) v. 공급하다 a. 보급의
☐ **support** v. 지지하다 n. 지지
☐ **suppose** v. 생각하다, 추정하다
☐ **surface** n. 표면 a. 표면의
☐ **surgery** n. 외과, 수술
☐ **surprise** n. 뜻밖의 일 v. 놀라게 하다
☐ **surrender** v. 항복하다, 포기하다 n. 항복
☐ **surround** v. 둘러싸다 n. 가장자리
☐ **survey** n. 조사 v. 살피다, 측량하다
☐ **survive** v. 살아남다, 견뎌 내다
☐ **suspect** v. 의심하다 n. 혐의자 a. 의심스러운
☐ **suspend** v. 매달다, 정지하다
☐ **sustain** v. 유지하다, 살아가게 하다
☐ **swallow** v. 삼키다 n. 삼키기, 제비
☐ **swear** v. 맹세하다, 욕을 하다 n. 서약, 선서, 욕설
☐ **sweat** n. 땀 v. 땀을 흘리다
☐ **sweater** n. 스웨터, 땀 흘리는 사람[것]
☐ **sweep** v. 쓸다 n. 쓸기
☐ **sweet** a. 달콤한 n. 단 것
☐ **swell** v. 붓다, 붓게 하다 n. 팽창

☐ **swift** a. 신속한 ad. 빠르게 n. 칼새
☐ **swing** v. 흔들리다, 흔들다 n. 흔들기
☐ **switch** n. 스위치 v. 바꾸다, 바뀌다
☐ **symbol** n. 상징(물) v. 상징을 이용하다
☐ **sympathy** n. 동정, 연민
☐ **symphony** n. 교향곡, 심포니
☐ **symptom** n. 증상, 증후
☐ **system** n. 제도, 체제
☐ **tackle** v. 씨름하다, 태클하다 n. 태클
☐ **tag** n. 꼬리표 v. 꼬리표를 붙이다, 따라다니다
☐ **tale** n. 이야기, 소설
☐ **talent** n. 재주, 재능
☐ **tank** n. 탱크
☐ **tap** v. 톡톡 두드리다 n. 두드리기, 수도꼭지
☐ **target** n. 목표 v. 목표[표적]로 삼다
☐ **task** n. 일 v. 일을 부과하다
☐ **tax** n. 세금 v. 세금을 부과하다
☐ **tea** n. 찻잎, 차 v. 차를 마시다, 차를 대접하다
☐ **tear** v. 찢다, 찢어지다 n. 찢어진 곳, 눈물
☐ **tease** v. 놀리다, 집적거리다
☐ **technique / technic** n. 기법, 기술
☐ **technology** n. 기술, 기계
☐ **teenage** a. 십 대의 n. 10대
☐ **telegraph** n. 전신 v. 전보를 치다, 신호하다
☐ **temperature** n. 온도, 기온
☐ **temple** n. 신전, 사원, 관자놀이
☐ **temporary** a. 일시적인 n. 임시 고용인
☐ **tempt** v. 유혹하다, 부추기다
☐ **tenant** n. 세입자 v. 임차해서 살다, 살다
☐ **tend** v. 경향이 있다, 돌보다, 보살피다
☐ **tender** a. 상냥한 n. 제출 v. 제출하다
☐ **tense** a. 긴장한 v. 긴장시키다
☐ **term** n. 용어 v. 칭하다
☐ **terminal** n. 공항 터미널 a. 말기의
☐ **terminate** v. 끝나다, 끝내다 a. 유한의
☐ **terrace** n. 테라스 v. 테라스를 만들다
☐ **terrible** a. 끔찍한, 소름 끼치는
☐ **terrific** a. 아주 좋은, 멋진
☐ **territory** n. 영토, 영지
☐ **terror** n. 공포, 두려움
☐ **terrorist** n. 테러리스트, 테러범
☐ **text** n. 본문 v. 문자를 보내다
☐ **theater / theatre** n. 공연장, 극장
☐ **theme** n. 주제 a. 특정한 주제를 가진

☐ **then** ad. 그때, 그 다음에 a. 당시의 n. 그때
☐ **theory** n. 이론, 학설
☐ **therapy** n. 치료, 요법
☐ **therefore** ad. 그러므로, 그러니
☐ **thick** a. 두꺼운 ad. 두껍게 n. 가장 굵은[두꺼운] 부분
☐ **thief** n. 도둑, 절도범
☐ **thin** a. 얇은 ad. 얇게 v. 얇게 만들다, 얇아지다
☐ **thorough** a. 빈틈없는, 철두철미한
☐ **though** conj. (비록) ~이긴 하지만 ad. 그렇지만
☐ **thousand** n. 1000 a. 1000의
☐ **thread** n. 실 v. 실을 꿰다, 뚫고 나아가다
☐ **threat** n. 협박, 위협
☐ **thrill** n. 황홀감, 전율 v. 열광시키다, 열광하다
☐ **throat** n. 목구멍 v. ~에 홈을 파다
☐ **through** prep. ~을 통해 ad. 지나서 a. 직통의
☐ **throw** v. 던지다 n. 던지기
☐ **thumb** n. 엄지손가락 v. 차를 얻어 타다
☐ **thus** ad. 이렇게 하여, 이와 같이
☐ **tick** v. 째깍거리다 n. 째깍째깍 하는 소리
☐ **tide** n. 조수 v. 조수처럼 흐르다, 일어나다
☐ **tidy** a. 깔끔한 v. 정돈하다 n. 정리함
☐ **tie** v. 묶다, 묶이다 n. 넥타이
☐ **tight** a. 단단한 ad. 단단히
☐ **till** prep. conj. ~까지
☐ **timber** n. 수목 v. 나무를 벌채하다 a. 목재로 된
☐ **tin** n. 주석 a. 주석의 v. 주석을 입히다
☐ **tiny** a. 아주 작은[적은], 조그마한
☐ **tip** n. (뾰족한) 끝, 조언, 기울이기 v. 끝에 달다, 팁을 주다, 기울이다
☐ **tissue** n. 조직 v. 화장지로 닦아내다
☐ **title** n. 제목 v. 제목[표제]을 붙이다
☐ **toast** n. 토스트, 건배 v. 굽다, 구워지다, 건배하다
☐ **toe** n. 발가락 v. 발끝을 대다, 발끝을 움직이다
☐ **toilet** n. 변기(통), 화장실
☐ **tone** n. 어조, 음색 v. 탄력 있게 만들다, 어울리다
☐ **tongue** n. 혀
☐ **tool** n. 연장, 도구 v. (차를) 몰다
☐ **topic** n. 화제, 주제
☐ **torture** n. 고문 v. 고문하다

☐ toss	v. 던지다, 뒤척이다 n. 동전 던지기
☐ total	a. 총 n. 합계 v. 합계[총] ~이 되다
☐ tough	a. 힘든
☐ tour	n. 여행 v. 여행하다
☐ toward(s)	prep. (어떤 방향) 쪽으로 a. 임박한
☐ towel	n. 수건 v. 수건으로 닦다
☐ tower	n. 탑, 고는 사람[것] v. 높이 솟다
☐ toxic	a. 유독한 n. 유독 화학 약품
☐ trace	v. 추적하다, 거슬러 올라가다 n. 자취
☐ trade	n. 거래 v. 거래하다, 매매하다
☐ tradition	n. 전통, 관습
☐ traffic	n. 교통(량) v. 매매하다
☐ tragic	a. 비극적인 n. 비극적 요소
☐ trail	n. 자국 v. 끌다, 끌리다
☐ transact	v. 거래하다, 사무를 보다
☐ transfer	v. 옮기다, 갈아타다 n. 옮김, 이동
☐ transform	v. 변형시키다, 변형되다 n. 변환
☐ transition	n. 이행, 전환
☐ translate	v. 번역하다
☐ transmit	v. 보내다 v. 자손에게 전해지다
☐ transport	n. 수송 v. 수송하다
☐ transportation	n. 수송, 운송
☐ trap	n. 덫 v. 가두다, 덫을 놓다
☐ tray	n. 쟁반, 상자
☐ treasure	n. 보물 v. 대단히 귀하게 여기다
☐ treat	v. 대하다, 다루다 n. 대접
☐ treaty	n. 조약, 협정
☐ tremendous	a. 엄청난 ad. 굉장히
☐ trend	n. 동향 v. 향해 있다
☐ triangle	n. 삼각형, 트라이앵글
☐ tribe	n. 부족, 종족
☐ trick	n. 속임수 v. 속이다 a. 교묘한
☐ trigger	n. 방아쇠 v. 촉발시키다, 방아쇠를 당기다
☐ trim	v. 다듬다 n. 다듬기 a. 잘 가꾼
☐ triumph	n. 승리 v. 승리를 거두다, 정복하다
☐ troop	n. 병력 v. 무리[떼]를 지어 가다, 수송하다
☐ trouble	n. 문제 v. 괴롭히다, 걱정하다
☐ trunk	n. 몸통 a. 주요한
☐ trust	n. 신뢰 v. 신뢰하다, 신임하다
☐ truth	n. 사실, 진상
☐ tube	n. 관 v. 관을 달다
☐ tune	n. 곡 v. 악기를 조율하다
☐ tunnel	n. 터널 v. 터널[굴]을 뚫다
☐ turnover	n. 거래액, 전환, 전복 a. 접어서 접힌
☐ twin	n. 쌍둥이 v. 자매 관계를 맺다 a. 쌍둥이의
☐ twist	v. 휘다, 비틀리다 n. 비틀기
☐ ultimate	a. 궁극적인 n. 극치
☐ unaware	a. 알지 못하는, 모르는
☐ undergo	v. 겪다, 경험하다
☐ underlie	v. ~의 밑에[아래에] 있다, 기저를 이루다
☐ undermine	v. ~의 밑을 파다, 기반을 약화시키다
☐ undertake	v. 착수하다, 증인이 되다
☐ uniform	n. 제복 a. 획일적인
☐ unify	v. 통합하다, 통일하다
☐ union	n. 노동 조합, 조합
☐ unique	a. 유일무이한 n. 유일한[독특한] 사람[것]
☐ unit	n. 구성 단위, 한 개
☐ unite	v. 통합시키다, 연합하다
☐ universe	n. 우주, 은하계
☐ university	n. 대학, 전(全) 대학생
☐ unless	conj. ~하지 않는 한, ~이 아닌 한
☐ unprecedented	a. 전례가 없는, 미증유의
☐ until	prep. ~(때)까지
☐ update	v. 갱신하다 n. 갱신
☐ upper	a. 더 위에 있는 n. 윗부분
☐ upset	v. 속상하게 만들다 a. 속상한
☐ upward(s)	a. 위쪽을 향한 ad. 위쪽을 향해서
☐ urban	a. 도시의, 도회지의
☐ urge	v. 강력히 권고하다, 주장하다 n. 욕구
☐ urgent	a. 긴급한, 시급한
☐ utilize / utilise	v. 활용하다, 이용하다
☐ utter	a. 완전한, 순전한 v. 말하다
☐ vacate	v. 비우다, 사직하다
☐ vacation	n. 방학 v. 휴가를 보내다
☐ vaccine	n. 백신
☐ vacuum	n. 진공 a. 진공의 v. 진공청소기로 청소하다
☐ vague	a. 모호한, 애매한
☐ valid	a. 유효한, 정당한
☐ valley	n. 계곡, 골짜기
☐ value	n. 가치 v. 소중하게 생각하다
☐ van	n. 밴, 선두, 전위
☐ vanish	v. 사라지다, 숨기다 n. 소음(消音)
☐ various	a. 여러 가지의, 각양각색의
☐ vary	v. 서로 다르다, 다르게 하다
☐ vast	a. 방대한 n. 광대함
☐ vehicle	n. 차량, 탈것
☐ venture	n. 벤처 v. 감행하다
☐ verb	n. 동사
☐ verbal	a. 언어의 n. 동사류
☐ verse	n. 운문 v. 시로 표현하다, 정통하다, 숙달하다
☐ version	n. -판, -본
☐ versus	prep. ~ 대(對), ~에 비해
☐ vertical	a. 수직의 n. 수직선
☐ vessel	n. 배, 선박
☐ veterinarian	n. 수의사
☐ via	prep. ~을 경유하여 [거쳐], ~을 통하여
☐ vice	n. 악, 악덕, 대리(자) a. 대리의 prep. ~ 대신에
☐ victim	n. 피해자, 희생자
☐ victory	n. 승리, 정복
☐ view	n. 견해 v. 여기다
☐ vigor	n. 정력, 힘
☐ vigorous	a. 활발한, 격렬한
☐ villa	n. 휴가용 주택, 별장
☐ village	n. 마을, 부락
☐ violent	a. 폭력적인, 난폭한
☐ virgin	n. 미경험자 a. 원래[자연] 그대로의
☐ virtual	a. 사실상의, 실질상의
☐ virtue	n. 선, 선행
☐ virus	n. 바이러스, 병원체
☐ visible	a. 보이는 n. 눈에 보이는 것
☐ vision	n. 시력 v. 환영으로 보다
☐ visual	a. 시각의 n. 시각 자료
☐ vital	a. 필수적인 n. 생명 유지 필수 기관
☐ vivid	a. 뚜렷한, 생생한
☐ vocabulary	n. 어휘, 용어
☐ vocation	n. 천직, 소명
☐ volume	n. 용량, 용적
☐ volunteer	n. 자원 봉사자 v. 자원하다 a. 자원의
☐ vote	n. 표 v. 투표하다, 선출하다
☐ wage	n. 임금, 급료 v. 벌이다, 다투다
☐ wander	v. 거닐다, 돌아다니다 n. 거닐기
☐ warehouse	n. 창고 v. 창고에 보관하다
☐ warn	v. 경고하다, 주의를 주다
☐ warrant	n. 영장 v. 정당[타당]하게 만들다
☐ waste	v. 낭비하다, 낭비되다 n. 낭비, 쓰레기 a. 버려진
☐ wave	n. 파도 v. 흔들다
☐ weak	a. 약한, 힘이 없는
☐ wealth	n. 재물, 재산
☐ weapon	n. 무기, 병기
☐ weave	v. 직물을 짜다, 엮어지다 n. 짜는[엮는] 법
☐ weed	n. 잡초 v. 잡초를 뽑다
☐ weigh	v. 무게[체중]가 ~이다 n. 무게 달기
☐ weird	a. 기이한 n. 운명
☐ welfare	n. 안녕, 행복
☐ whale	n. 고래
☐ wheat	n. 밀, 소맥
☐ wheel	n. 바퀴 v. 밀다, 선회하다
☐ whereas	conj. ~에 반하여, n. (공문서의) 전문
☐ whether	conj. ~인지 (아닌지), ~이든 (아니든)
☐ which	a. 어느 pron. 어느 것
☐ while	conj. ~하는 동안에 n. 잠깐 v. (시간을) 보내다
☐ whip	n. 채찍 v. 채찍질[매질]하다, 갑자기 움직이다
☐ whisper	v. 속삭이다 n. 속삭임
☐ whistle	n. 호루라기 v. 휘파람으로 불다
☐ whole	a. 전체의 n. 완전체
☐ wicked	a. 못된 n. 악인
☐ wide	a. 넓은 ad. 널리 n. 표적을 벗어난 것
☐ wild	a. 야생의 n. 자연 ad. 난폭하게
☐ wing	n. 날개 v. 날다, 날아가다
☐ wipe	v. 닦다, 지우다 n. 닦기
☐ wire	n. 철사 v. 전선을 연결하다, 전보를 치다
☐ wise	a. 지혜로운 v. 알리다
☐ wit	n. 기지, 재치
☐ withdraw	v. 빼내다, 물러나다
☐ within	prep. ~ 이내에 ad. 내부에서
☐ without	prep. ~ 없이 ad. ~ 없이 n. 밖 conj. ~하지 않으면
☐ witness	n. 목격자 v. 목격하다, 증언하다
☐ wonder	v. 궁금하다, 놀라다 n. 경탄, 경이(로운 것)
☐ wool	n. 양털
☐ worship	n. 예배, 숭배 v. 예배하다
☐ worth	a. ~의 가치가 있는 n. 어치[짜리]
☐ would	(will의 과거형) ~일[할] 것이다
☐ wound	n. 상처 v. 상처[부상]를 입히다, 상처를 입다
☐ wrap	v. 싸다, 몸을 감싸다 n. 숄, 포장지
☐ wreck	n. 난파선 v. 파괴시키다, 난파하다
☐ yell	v. 소리치다 n. 고함
☐ yet	ad. 아직 conj. 그렇지만
☐ yield	v. (수익 등을) 내다, 굴복하다 n. 산출
☐ zebra	n. 얼룩말
☐ zero	n. 0 a. 0의
☐ zone	n. 지역

01
- on behalf of ~을 대표하여
- resident 명사 입주민
- association 명사 조합, 협회
- recycle 동사 재활용하다, 재사용하다
- participation 명사 참여
- given 형용사 정해진 / 전치사 ~을 고려해 볼 때
- put out (쓰레기 등을 집 밖으로) 내놓다
- require 동사 필요로 하다
- extra 형용사 추가의
- decide on ~을 결정하다
- apartment complex 아파트 단지
- cooperation 명사 협조

02
- on behalf of ~을 대표하여, ~을 대신하여
- found 동사 설립하다
- treat 동사 대우하다, 대하다
- lost 형용사 길 잃은
- care 명사 관리, 돌봄, 보살핌
- shelter 명사 보호소, 주거지
- seek 동사 구하다, 찾다
- donation 명사 기부(금)
- raise 동사 (자금을) 모금하다, 모으다
- in need 도움이 필요한, 어려움에 처한

03
- well-attended 형용사 많은 사람들이 참석한
- expand 동사 확대하다
- recruit 동사 모집하다
- bring A to life A에게 생명을 불어넣다
- fill in for ~을 대신하다, 대신해서 일해 주다
- preschooler 명사 미취학 아동
- look forward to N/V-ing ~을 기다리다[고대하다]

04
- in/with regard to ~와 관련하여
- subscription 명사 구독, 구독료
- have trouble V-ing ~하는 데 어려움이 있다

05
- student council 학생회
- valuable 형용사 유용한, 귀중한, 값비싼
- be willing to V 흔쾌히 ~하다, 기꺼이 ~하다
- donate 동사 기부하다
- gift certificate 명사 상품권
- generosity 명사 관대함, 너그러움

06
- frequently 부사 자주, 빈번히
- be supposed to V ~하기로 되어있다
- be unaware of ~을 인식하지 못하다
- ignore 동사 무시하다
- remind 동사 상기시키다, 생각나게 하다
- improvement 명사 개선, 향상

07
- require A to V A에게 ~할 것을 요구하다
- decide on V-ing ~하기로 결정하다
- populated 형용사 붐비는, 사람이 많은
- request 동사 요청하다, 요구하다
- permission 명사 허가, 허락

08
- pleasure 명사 즐거운 일, 즐거움
- appreciate 동사 감사하다, 인정하다
- exhibit 동사 전시하다
- diverse 형용사 다양한
- mention 동사 언급하다, 말하다
- admire 동사 존경하다, 찬양하다
- emphasize 동사 강조하다
- viewing 명사 감상, (바라)보기, TV 시청
- be interested in ~에 관심이 있다
- purchase 동사 구매하다 / 명사 구매
- depict 동사 묘사하다, 그리다
- horizon 명사 지평선, 수평선
- A be titled B A는 B라고 제목이 붙여지다
- sunrise 명사 일출, 해돋이
- piece 명사 (예술) 작품
- available 형용사 유효한, 이용 가능한
- house 동사 소장하다, 보관하다, 집에 들이다
- inquiry 명사 문의, 질문

09
- by oneself 혼자
- following 형용사 다음의
- special-offer 특가로 제공되는
- non-exchangeable 교환할 수 없는
- match 명사 경기
- book 동사 예약하다
- grateful 형용사 감사하는
- in advance 미리, 사전에

10
- intersection 명사 교차로, 교차점, 사거리
- be at risk 위험하다
- largely 부사 주로, 대개
- disregard 명사 무시, 경시 / 동사 무시하다, 경시하다
- regularly 부사 자주, 종종
- witness 동사 목격하다, 보다 / 명사 목격자
- concern 명사 우려, 걱정 / 동사 걱정하다, 염려하다
- request 동사 요청하다, 간청하다 / 명사 요청, 요구, 간청
- installation 명사 설치, 설비
- speed bump 명사 과속방지턱
- secure 형용사 위험 없는, 안심하는 / 동사 안전하게 하다
- anticipate 동사 기대하다, 고대하다

11
- schooling 명사 학교 교육
- generous 형용사 후한, 넉넉한
- foundation 명사 재단, 토대
- renovate 동사 보수하다, 수리하다
- outdated 형용사 구식인
- inform 동사 알리다
- community-wide 지역 사회 전체의

12
- concern 동사 관련되다, 우려하게 만들다 / 명사 우려, 염려, 관심사
- commute 동사 통학하다, 통근하다
- public transport(=public transportation) 명사 대중교통
- council 명사 의회
- discontinue 동사 중단하다, 그만하다
- drop A off A를 데려다주다
- traffic 명사 교통(량), 운항, 수송
- bike 동사 자전거를 타다
- place 동사 (특정한 상황에) 처하게 하다, 놓다
- unacceptable 형용사 받아들이기 어려운
- urge 동사 촉구하다, 강력히 권고하다

13
- regular 형용사 규칙적인, 정기적인
- attendance 명사 출석, 참석
- essential 형용사 필수적인, 아주 중요한
- maximize 동사 극대화하다
- potential 명사 잠재력, 가능성
- concerned 형용사 걱정하는, 우려하는
- the number of A A의 수
- unapproved 형용사 승인되지 않은, 허가되지 않은
- absence 명사 결석, 결근
- clarify 동사 분명히 하다, 확실히 하다
- approve 동사 승인하다, 허가하다
- time frame 명사 기간
- unjustified 형용사 정당하지 않은
- register 동사 등록하다, 기재하다
- absent 형용사 결석한, 결근한
- at a disadvantage 불이익에 처하여, 불리한 처지에

14
- ongoing 형용사 (계속) 진행 중인, 발달 중인 / 명사 전진
- face 동사 ~을 마주보다, 향하다, 직면하다
- disrupt 동사 방해하다, 피해를 주다
- struggle 동사 애쓰다, 분투하다
- well 부사 훨씬, 아주, 상당히
- neighborhood 명사 근처, 인근, 이웃

15
- craft 명사 공예, 기술
- annual 형용사 연례의, 매년의
- fair 명사 박람회 / 형용사 공평한, 공정한
- reserve 동사 예약하다, 보유하다
- registration form 신청서
- rental 명사 대여, 임대 / 형용사 대여의, 임대의
- throughout the year 연중, 일년 내내

16
- resident 명사 주민, 투숙객 / 형용사 거주하는

문제편 : p.007~014 | 정답과 해설 : p.002~011

☐ take advantage of ~을 이용하다[활용하다]
☐ weed 명사 잡초 / 동사 잡초를 뽑다
☐ lawn 명사 잔디, 잔디밭

17
☐ apply 동사 지원하다, 신청하다
☐ certification 명사 증명서
☐ counseling 명사 상담, 조언
☐ application 명사 지원, 적용
☐ deadline 명사 마감 기한, 마감일
☐ extension 명사 연장, 확대
☐ actively 부사 열심히, 적극적으로
☐ obtain 동사 얻다, 구하다
☐ consideration 명사 고려, 사려, 숙고

02. 심경·분위기 파악

01
☐ sit up 고쳐 앉다
☐ catch someone's eye ~의 눈에 띄다[눈길을 사로잡다]
☐ freeze 동사 얼어붙다, 얼리다
☐ fin 명사 지느러미
☐ shiver 동사 (흥분·공포 등으로) 떨다
☐ grip 동사 꽉 붙잡다
☐ think to oneself 마음속으로 생각하다
☐ let go of ~을 떨쳐버리다[놓다]
☐ lifetime 명사 평생
☐ catch one's breath 숨을 돌리다
☐ at ease 마음이 편안한, 마음이 편안하게
☐ let out 내쉬다, (신음·울음소리 등을) 내다
☐ contented 형용사 만족스러운
☐ sigh 명사 한숨

02
☐ swing 동사 흔들리다 (swing-swung-swung)
☐ rusty 형용사 녹슨
☐ creak 명사 삐걱거리는 소리
☐ scream 동사 소리 지르다, 비명을 지르다
☐ race 동사 (심장이) 요동치다, 경주하다
☐ wait a minute/second/moment 잠깐, 가만 있자(방금 무언가를 알아챘거나 기억이 났을 때 하는 말)
☐ reflection 명사 (거울 등에 비친) 모습, 상
☐ relieved 형용사 안도하는, 안심한
☐ thrilled 형용사 (너무 좋아서) 아주 흥분한, 황홀해하는

03
☐ anxious 형용사 불안한, 걱정하는
☐ remain 동사 머무르다, 남아있다
☐ ongoing 형용사 계속하고 있는
☐ chaos 명사 혼돈, 혼란
☐ embrace 동사 감싸 안다, 껴안다
☐ override 동사 ~을 압도하다, ~의 위를 덮다

04
☐ refrigerator 명사 냉장고
☐ pack 동사 (짐을) 싸다, 포장하다
☐ soar 동사 날아오르다, 치솟다
☐ beam 동사 반짝거리다, 빛나다 / 명사 광선
☐ groan 동사 (불만·고통으로) 신음 소리를 내다, 투덜거리다
☐ anticipation 명사 기대, 예상
☐ in a flash 눈 깜짝할 새에, 즉시, 순식간에
☐ miserable 형용사 괴로운, 불행한, 비참한

05
☐ vice president 명사 부사장, 부통령
☐ human resources 명사 (회사의) 인사과, 인적 자원
☐ beam 동사 밝게 웃다 / 명사 광선
☐ mark 동사 찍다, 표시하다
☐ turning point 명사 전환점
☐ promotion 명사 승진, 홍보
☐ go blank (머릿속이) 하얘지다, (마음이) 텅 비다
☐ desperately 부사 간절히, 필사적으로
☐ panic 동사 당황하다, 겁에 질려 어쩔 줄을 모르다 (panic-panicked-panicked)

06
☐ ache 동사 아프다
☐ apply 동사 바르다, 신청하다, 적용하다
☐ refreshments 명사 (복수형으로) 다과
☐ accidentally 부사 우연히
☐ stain 동사 얼룩지게 하다, 더럽히다
☐ nerves 명사 (복수형으로) 초조함, 날카로운 신경
☐ torture 동사 괴롭히다
☐ victim 명사 희생자
☐ have butterflies in one's stomach 안절부절못하다
☐ tense 형용사 긴장한, 긴박한
☐ indifferent 형용사 무관심한
☐ irritated 형용사 짜증이 난

07
☐ be supposed to V ~하기로 예정되어 있다
☐ make a presentation 발표하다
☐ make it (모임 등에) 가다, 성공하다, 해내다
☐ on time 제시간에, 정각에
☐ faint 동사 기절하다, 정신이 아찔해지다 / 형용사 희미한
☐ show up 나타나다
☐ manage to V 겨우 ~해내다
☐ come to one's senses 정신을 차리다, 의식을 회복하다
☐ tension 명사 긴장감
☐ vanish 동사 사라지다
☐ beaming 형용사 웃음을 띤, 밝게 빛나는

08
☐ as soon as ~하자마자
☐ hum 명사 웅웅거리는 소리
☐ pour 동사 (비가) 마구 쏟아지다
☐ eagerly 부사 간절히, 열심히
☐ hesitation 명사 망설임, 주저
☐ unfold 동사 펼치다, 펴다
☐ apply 동사 지원하다, 신청하다, 적용하다

09
☐ tone 명사 말투
☐ border on ~에 아주 가깝다
☐ irritation 명사 짜증
☐ trivial 형용사 사소한
☐ garage sale 명사 (자택 차고에서 하는) 중고 물품 세일
☐ glance down 흘깃 내려다보다
☐ inscribe 동사 (비석·종이 등에) 새기다, 파다
☐ in between 사이에, 중간에

10
☐ venture 동사 (위험을 무릅쓰고) 가다, 모험하다 / 명사 모험, 벤처 (사업)
☐ show off 자랑하다
☐ glittering 형용사 반짝이는, 빛나는
☐ stretch out 뻗다
☐ footing 명사 발디딤, 입장, 기초
☐ give way 무너지다, 항복하다
☐ slide 동사 미끄러지다
☐ crack 명사 틈, 흠 / 동사 금이 가다, 부수다
☐ phone 동사 전화를 걸다 / 명사 전화

11
☐ jolly 형용사 유쾌한
☐ witty 형용사 재치 있는
☐ broadcast 동사 알리다, 방송하다 (broadcast-broadcast(ed)-broadcast(ed))
☐ screeching 형용사 날카로운, 끽 소리를 내는
☐ squeeze 동사 비집고 들어가다, (쥐어서) 짜다
☐ basement 명사 지하실, 지하
☐ roar 명사 굉음
☐ terror 명사 공포, 두려움, 테러
☐ overwhelming 형용사 압도적인, 대항할 수 없는
☐ shiver 동사 (몸을) 떨다 / 명사 전율
☐ murmur 동사 중얼거리다, 속삭이다
☐ desperate 형용사 절망적인, 자포자기한

12
☐ private 형용사 개인적인
☐ grade 동사 채점하다 / 명사 등급, 학년
☐ but(=except) 전치사 ~ 외에, ~을 제외하고
☐ anxiously 부사 초조하게
☐ expect 동사 기다리다, 기대하다, 예상하다
☐ discipline 명사 벌, 훈육, 규율
☐ rap 동사 두드리다
☐ attentively 부사 주의 깊게
☐ contempt 명사 경멸, 무시
☐ ridicule 명사 조소 / 동사 비웃다
☐ openhearted 형용사 숨김없는, 솔직한
☐ ecstasy 명사 환희, 황홀경
☐ startling 형용사 놀라운
☐ demonstration 명사 입증, 시연, 시위

13
☐ opening day 개업일, 개장일
☐ anticipation 명사 기대, 예상
☐ shake off ~을 떨쳐버리다, 털어내다

문제편 : p.015~022 정답과 해설 : p.011~020

set out	~을 진열하다, 정리하다
doubt	명사 의구심, 의심
come to mind	생각나다, 생각이 떠오르다
burst	명사 폭발
inspiration	명사 영감
transform A into B	A를 B로 바꾸다
landscape	명사 풍경화, 풍경
fade	동사 사라지다, 희미해지다
handiwork	명사 작품, 일
guarantee	동사 보장하다, 약속하다 / 명사 보장, 품질 보증서
think to oneself	마음속으로 생각하다, 조용히 생각하다
definitely	부사 분명히, 확실히

14

to make matters worse	설상가상으로
recent	형용사 최근의
tropical	형용사 열대의, 열대 지방의
be down	중지되다, 고장이 나다
in the direction of	~의 방향으로

15

inside	형용사 마음속의, 안의 / 부사 마음속으로, 안에
chill	동사 오싹하게 만들다, 춥게 만들다 / 명사 오한, 한기
awful	형용사 끔찍한, 지독한
feel sure	~을 확신하다
deserted	형용사 사람이 없는, 버림받은
cottage	명사 오두막집, 작은 집
pound	동사 뛰다, 두드리다
anticipation	명사 기대, 예상
longing	명사 갈망, 열망
lighten	동사 가볍게 해주다, 밝아지다

16

stump	명사 그루터기 / 동사 쿵쿵거리며 걷다
rite of passage	통과 의례
youth	명사 청년, 젊음
tribe	명사 부족, 종족
blindfold	명사 눈가리개
observe	동사 지켜보다, 관찰하다
all kinds of	온갖 종류의
beast	명사 짐승, 야수
stand	동사 견디다, 참다
mission	명사 임무, 사절단
presence	명사 존재, 있음
regain	동사 되찾다, 회복하다
stability	명사 안정, 안정성
panic	동사 겁에 질리게 하다 (panic-panicked-panicked) / 명사 공포, 공황
vanish	동사 사라지다, 없어지다

17

enter	동사 참가하다, 들어가다
judgment	명사 심사, 판단
one by one	한 명씩, 하나씩
head	명사 (단체의) 장, 머리 / 동사 ~로 향하다
uniqueness	명사 독특함, 특이함
be overcome with	~에 휩싸이다
more than just	단순히 ~ 이상의
confirm	동사 확인해 주다, 확인하다
identity	명사 정체성

18

championship	명사 결승전, 선수권
final	형용사 마지막의, 최종의 / 명사 결승전, 기말고사
runner	명사 주자, 경주마
relay	명사 계주 / 동사 중계하다
perform	동사 수행하다, 연주[공연]하다
heart rate	심박수
training	명사 훈련, 교육

19

passport control	여권 심사, 출입국 관리
inspector	명사 심사관, 감독관
at hand	당면한, (거리가) 가까운
uneasy	형용사 불안한, 걱정되는
study	동사 살피다, 검토하다
trembling	형용사 떨리는, 전율하는 / 명사 떨림, 전율
regulation	명사 규정, 규제
truthfully	부사 정직하게, 진실하게
burden	명사 부담, 짐
vanish	동사 사라지다, 없어지다
weigh A down	A를 짓누르다

03. 필자의 주장

01

guidance	명사 지도
embark on	~에 착수하다
cooperation	명사 협동
leave (one) to (one's) own devices	(제멋대로 하게) 내버려 두다
arena	명사 경기장
interpersonal	형용사 대인 관계의
awareness	명사 인식
inherently	부사 선천적으로
minority	명사 소수
peer	명사 또래
consciously	부사 의식적으로
nurture	동사 육성하다, 양육하다

02

march	동사 나아가다, 행진하다
ethnic	형용사 민족의
fresh	형용사 새로운, 신선한
perspective	명사 관점
valuable	형용사 가치가 있는, 귀중한
open-minded	형용사 개방적인, 마음이 열린
extensive	형용사 광범위한, 아주 넓은
come up with	~을 떠올리다
association	명사 연상, 관련
capture	동사 포착하다, 붙잡다
unconventional	형용사 관습에 얽매이지 않는, 색다른
expose A to B	A를 B에 접하게 하다, 노출시키다
explore	동사 탐방하다, 탐험하다, 탐구하다

03

rush	명사 질주, 혼잡 / 동사 급히 움직이다, 재촉하다, 돌진하다
individual	형용사 개인의, 각각의 / 명사 개인
achievement	명사 성취
recognition	명사 인정, 인식
make it	성공하다, 시간 맞춰 가다
humble	형용사 초라한, 시시한, 겸손한
be on one's way up	성공으로 가는 과정에 있다, 성공 가도를 달리다
neglect	동사 소홀히 하다, 방치하다
grateful	형용사 감사하는, 고마워하는
gratitude	명사 감사, 고마움
be likely to V	~할 것 같다, ~할 가능성이 높다
determine	동사 결정하다

04

give A a bad name	A에게 오명을 씌우다
associate	동사 결부시키다, 연관시키다
rote	명사 (내용을 이해하지 못하는) 기계적 암기
cram	동사 억지로 쑤셔 넣다, 벼락치기하다
recall	동사 기억해 내다, 상기하다
instantly	부사 즉각적으로, 바로
achieve	동사 (목표 등에) 이르다, 달성하다
mastery	명사 경지, 숙달

05

take time out	쉬다
recuperation	명사 회복
complicate	동사 복잡하게 만들다
association	명사 연상, 연계, 협회
escapism	명사 현실 도피
overwhelm	동사 압도하다
fatigue	명사 피로감
connotation	명사 함축
steer clear of	~을 피하다
be about to V	이제[막] ~하려고 하다
perception	명사 인식, 통찰력
view A as B	A를 B로 간주하다
vital	형용사 필수적인, 활력이 넘치는
permission	명사 허락
set aside	따로 떼어 두다, 곁에 두다, 확보하다
urgent	형용사 긴급한, 다급해하는
overstimulate	동사 지나치게 자극하다

06

introduction	명사 도입, 소개
have an impact	영향을 가지다[미치다]
sustainable	형용사 (환경 파괴 없이) 지속 가능한
management	명사 관리, 경영

문제편 : p.023~030 | 정답과 해설 : p.020~028

- ☐ resource — 명사 자원, 재원
- ☐ take A into account — A를 고려하다
- ☐ sector — 명사 분야, 부문
- ☐ nuclear energy — 명사 원자력, 핵에너지
- ☐ agriculture — 명사 농업
- ☐ not only A but also B — A뿐만 아니라 B도
- ☐ benefit — 명사 이익, 이점 / 동사 혜택을 주다, 이익을 보다
- ☐ risk — 명사 위험, 위험 요인 / 동사 ~를 감수하다, 무릅쓰다
- ☐ accompany — 동사 수반하다, 동반하다
- ☐ advance — 명사 발전, 진보
- ☐ profound — 형용사 심오한, 깊은
- ☐ as well — 또한, 역시
- ☐ revolution — 명사 혁명, 변혁, 회전, 공전
- ☐ nature — 명사 본질, 본성
- ☐ destroy — 동사 없애다, 파괴하다
- ☐ assess — 동사 평가하다
- ☐ potential — 형용사 잠재적인 / 명사 잠재력

07

- ☐ convince — 동사 설득하다, 납득시키다
- ☐ lay out — ~을 펼치다[제시하다]
- ☐ logical — 형용사 논리적인, 타당한
- ☐ plea — 명사 항변, 애원, 간청
- ☐ mission — 명사 임무, 사명
- ☐ metaphorical — 형용사 은유적인, 비유적인
- ☐ open-ended — 형용사 다양한 대답이 가능한, 열린 결말의
- ☐ question — 명사 질문, 의문 / 동사 의문을 갖다
- ☐ challenge — 동사 (진실·정당성 등을) 의심하다, 이의를 제기하다, 도전하다
- ☐ assumption — 명사 가정, 추정
- ☐ tend to V — ~하려는 경향이 있다
- ☐ approve of — ~을 인정하다[승인하다]
- ☐ yield — 동사 (결과·이익을) 가져오다, 양보하다
- ☐ trigger — 동사 유발하다, 작동시키다
- ☐ insight — 명사 통찰력, 이해

08

- ☐ make an announcement — 발표하다, 공표하다
- ☐ operate — 동사 운항하다, 작동하다
- ☐ flight — 명사 항공편, 비행
- ☐ uneconomical — 형용사 경제성이 없는, 비경제적인
- ☐ sale — 명사 판매
- ☐ route — 명사 노선, 길
- ☐ scarcity — 명사 희소성, 부족, 결핍
- ☐ point out — 강조하다, 지적하다, 가리키다
- ☐ derive A from B — B로부터 A를 얻다
- ☐ uniqueness — 명사 유일함, 고유성
- ☐ miss out on — ~를 놓치게 되다[놓치다]
- ☐ keep in mind — 명심하다
- ☐ limited — 형용사 한정적인, 제한된
- ☐ desirable — 형용사 가치 있는, 바람직한

09

- ☐ manager — 명사 관리자, 경영자
- ☐ psychologist — 명사 심리학자
- ☐ empathize — 동사 공감하다, 감정 이입하다
- ☐ point of view — 명사 관점, 견해
- ☐ exhibit — 동사 보이다, 나타내다, 전시하다
- ☐ trait — 명사 (성격상의) 특성, 특색
- ☐ unreliability — 명사 신뢰할 수 없음

10

- ☐ unwanted — 형용사 원치 않는, 불필요한
- ☐ unpleasant — 형용사 불편한, 불친절한
- ☐ nonetheless — 부사 그럼에도 (불구하고)
- ☐ hatred — 명사 증오, 혐오
- ☐ acceptance — 명사 수용, 동의, 수락
- ☐ compassion — 명사 연민, 동정
- ☐ suitable — 형용사 적합한, 알맞은
- ☐ accomplish — 동사 성취하다

11

- ☐ please — 동사 즐겁게 하다
- ☐ realize — 동사 이해하다, (명확히) 파악하다
- ☐ imply — 동사 암시하다
- ☐ prefer — 동사 선호하다
- ☐ foster — 동사 조장하다
- ☐ uniformity — 명사 획일성
- ☐ obedience — 명사 복종
- ☐ evaluate — 동사 평가하다
- ☐ for oneself — 스스로
- ☐ aesthetic — 형용사 미적인
- ☐ taste — 명사 취향, 맛
- ☐ literate — 형용사 글을 읽고 쓸 줄 아는
- ☐ key — 형용사 핵심적인 / 명사 열쇠
- ☐ attitude — 명사 태도
- ☐ right — 명사 권리 / 형용사 옳은, 바른, 오른쪽의
- ☐ wonder — 명사 경이 / 동사 궁금해하다
- ☐ take place — (일·사건이) 일어나다[발생하다]
- ☐ setting — 명사 환경
- ☐ competition — 명사 경쟁
- ☐ judgment — 명사 판단

12

- ☐ accountability — 명사 책임, 책무(성)
- ☐ occupy — 동사 차지하다, 점유하다
- ☐ center — 명사 중심(부), 핵심 / 동사 (~에) 중점을 두다, 집중시키다
- ☐ make sure — 확실히 하다, 명확히 하다
- ☐ arm — 동사 준비시키다, 무장시키다 / 명사 팔
- ☐ humanity — 명사 인류, 인간(성)
- ☐ unprecedented — 형용사 전례 없는, 유례없는
- ☐ peril — 명사 위기, 위험
- ☐ collective — 형용사 공동체의, 집단의
- ☐ bolster — 동사 강화하다, 개선하다
- ☐ mature — 동사 성숙하다, 잘 익히다 / 형용사 성숙한, 분별력 있는
- ☐ ethical — 형용사 도덕적인, 윤리의
- ☐ give in to — ~에 굴복하다
- ☐ greed — 명사 탐욕, 욕심
- ☐ ecosystem — 명사 생태(계)
- ☐ extinction — 명사 멸종, 소멸

13

- ☐ break — 명사 휴식, 휴가
- ☐ revive — 동사 회복시키다, 되살리다
- ☐ recharge — 동사 재충전하다
- ☐ appropriate — 형용사 적절한, 알맞은
- ☐ in the midst of — ~(하는) 중에, 한창일 때
- ☐ ongoing — 형용사 진행 중인
- ☐ unwarranted — 형용사 불필요한, 부적절한
- ☐ on track — 순조롭게 진행되는, 정상 궤도에 있는
- ☐ strategic — 형용사 전략적인
- ☐ self-reinforcement — 명사 자기 강화
- ☐ procrastinate — 동사 미루다
- ☐ sure-fire — 형용사 확실한, 틀림없는
- ☐ rationalize — 동사 합리화하다
- ☐ alert — 형용사 정신이 맑은[초롱초롱한] / 동사 알리다
- ☐ avoid V-ing — ~하는 것을 (회)피하다
- ☐ commit to V-ing — (~하겠다고) 약속하다, 맹세하다

14

- ☐ outsider — 명사 외부자
- ☐ challenge — 동사 이의를 제기하다 / 명사 도전, 문제
- ☐ characteristic — 명사 특성
- ☐ perspective — 명사 관점
- ☐ point out — ~을 지적하다
- ☐ criticize — 동사 비판하다
- ☐ risk — 동사 위태롭게 하다 / 명사 위험
- ☐ adopt — 동사 채택하다, 입양하다
- ☐ mentality — 명사 사고방식
- ☐ disassociate — 동사 분리시키다
- ☐ bond — 동사 결속시키다, 유대감을 형성하다 / 명사 유대
- ☐ job security — 직업 안정성, 고용보장
- ☐ management — 명사 경영진
- ☐ assessment — 명사 평가
- ☐ on one's own — 독자적으로
- ☐ determine — 동사 알아내다, 결정하다
- ☐ advance — 동사 발전시키다 / 명사 발전, 진전

15

- ☐ persist — 동사 지속하다, 고집하다
- ☐ motivate — 동사 자극하다, 동기부여를 하다
- ☐ sound — 동사 ~하게 들리다, ~인 것 같다 / 명사 소리
- ☐ few — 형용사 거의 없는, 극소수의
- ☐ substitute — 동사 대체하다, 바꾸다
- ☐ despair — 명사 체념, 절망
- ☐ employment — 명사 취업, 고용
- ☐ finite — 형용사 한정된, 유한한

16

- ☐ clarity — 명사 명확성
- ☐ accord — 명사 조화, 일치
- ☐ component — 명사 요소, 부품
- ☐ transparency — 명사 투명성

문제편 : p.031~035 정답과 해설 : p.028~035

- assess 동사 평가하다
- mistrust 명사 불신 / 동사 불신하다
- move A away from A를 ~에서 멀어지게 하다
- cohesive 형용사 응집력이 있는, 결합력이 있는
- assessment 명사 평가
- hinder 동사 방해하다, 막다
- conduct 동사 수행하다, 행동하다
- empower 동사 ~할 수 있도록 하다, 권한을 주다
- optimal 형용사 최적의

17

- a range of 다양한
- fertilize 동사 비료를 주다
- pest 명사 해충, 유해 동물, 성가신 사람(물건)
- distribute 동사 유통하다, 분배하다
- essential 형용사 필수적인, 근본적인 / 명사 핵심 사항(요점)
- critical 형용사 중요한, 중대한, 비판적인
- civilization 명사 문명 (사회), 전 세계 (사람들)
- stable 형용사 안정적인, 차분한 / 명사 마구간
- settle 동사 정착하다, 해결하다
- vital 형용사 필수적인, 생명 유지와 관련된
- rural 형용사 지방의, 시골의
- raw material 원자재
- scarcity 명사 부족, 결핍, 희소성
- degradation 명사 (질의) 저하, 악화
- biodiversity 명사 생물 다양성
- sustainable 형용사 지속 가능한
- address 동사 (문제 등을) 다루다, 고심하다

18

- generation 명사 세대, 시대
- overnight 부사 하룻밤 사이에
- discourage 동사 막다, 방해하다, 낙담시키다
- high tech 첨단 기술
- parameter 명사 한도, 제한, 매개 변수
- tempt 동사 유혹하다
- matter 명사 문제, 일 / 동사 중요하다
- fall prey to N ~의 먹이가 되다, ~에 굴복하다
- impatience 명사 조바심, 성급함

19

- resist 동사 저항하다, 반대하다, 참다, 견디다
- self-estimate 자기 평가
- downgrade 동사 낮추다, 격하시키다, 훼손시키다
- capable 형용사 할 수 있는, 유능한
- maxim 명사 격언, 금언
- self-aware 형용사 자기를 인식하는, 자각하는
- refuse 동사 거부하다, 거절하다
- self-assessment 명사 자기 평가
- the second half 후반부, 하반기
- underestimate 동사 과소평가하다
- overestimate 동사 과대평가하다
- cultivate 동사 기르다, 경작하다, 재배하다, 구축하다
- discern 동사 파악하다, 알아차리다, 포착하다
- unlock 동사 열다, (비밀을) 드러내다

20

- merely 부사 그저, 한낱
- convince 동사 설득하다, 확신시키다
- senseless 형용사 무의미한, 의식을 잃은
- content 형용사 만족한 / 명사 내용물
- consequently 부사 결과적으로
- guilt 명사 죄책감, 유죄
- be subject to A A의 지배를 받다
- will 명사 의지, 유언장
- eliminate 동사 없애다, 탈락시키다
- refuse 동사 ~하려고 하지 않다, ~을 거부하다
- attend 동사 주의를 기울이다
- contentment 명사 만족감, 자족감
- accompany 동사 동반하다, 동행하다

04. 의미 추론

01

- assimilation 명사 동화(同化), 흡수
- fit 동사 일치하다, 맞다
- spherical 형용사 구형의, 구 모양의
- picture 동사 상상하다, 묘사하다
- sphere 명사 구
- surface 명사 표면
- incorporate into ~에 통합시키다
- preexisting 형용사 기존의, 이전부터 존재하는
- question 동사 ~에 의문을 갖다, 이의를 제기하다
- novel 형용사 새로운 / 명사 소설
- favor A over B A를 B보다 선호하다
- existing 형용사 기존의

02

- get A out of the way A를 먼저 처리하고 넘어가다
- soften 동사 완화하다, 누그러뜨리다
- address 동사 다루다
- coin 동사 (새로운 단어를) 만들다
- superior 명사 상사 / 형용사 우수한, 우월한
- innocent 형용사 무고한, 순진한
- messenger 명사 전령, 전달자
- firing line 명사 사선, 방화선, 최전방 부대
- kick in 발동하다
- override 동사 무효화하다, 기각하다
- water down 희석시키다, 약화시키다
- devastating 형용사 파괴적인
- steep 형용사 가파른, 급격한
- rank 명사 단계, 지위, 서열
- subordinate 명사 부하 / 형용사 종속된, 부차적인
- peacemaker 명사 중재자
- negotiator 명사 협상가
- blame 명사 책임, 비난 / 동사 비난하다

03

- omnivorous 형용사 잡식성의, 아무거나 먹는
- surroundings 명사 (항상 복수) 주위 환경
- earthly 형용사 지구상의, 세속적인
- sufficient 형용사 충분한, 넉넉한
- maintenance 명사 유지, 보수
- cautious 형용사 신중한, 조심스러운
- ingest 동사 섭취하다, 삼키다
- physiologically 부사 생리학적으로
- fatal 형용사 치명적인, 죽음을 초래하는
- conservatism 명사 현상 유지, 보수주의
- omnivore 명사 잡식 동물
- paradox 명사 역설, 모순(된 말)
- contradictory 형용사 모순적인, 자가당착의
- impulse 명사 충동, 자극
- attraction 명사 끌림, 매력, 명소
- edible 형용사 식용의, 먹을 수 있는

04

- delight 동사 즐겁게 하다, 기쁨을 주다 / 명사 기쁨
- exceptional 형용사 뛰어난, 우수한, 이례적인
- hospitality industry (호텔, 식당 등의) 서비스업
- sum up 요약하다
- credo 명사 신조
- deliver 동사 제공하다, 배달하다
- seek to V ~하고자 하다, ~하려고 하다
- relative to ~대비, ~에 비례하여, ~에 관하여
- maximize 동사 최대화하다
- delicate 형용사 미묘한, 섬세한
- give away 거저 주다
- risk 동사 ~을 걸다, 위태롭게 하다
- profitability 명사 수익성
- overlook 동사 간과하다, 못 보고 넘어가다
- reputation 명사 평판, 명성
- abandon 동사 버리다, 포기하다

05

- peak 형용사 최고의 / 명사 절정, 정점
- ideally 부사 이상적으로
- analytical 형용사 분석적인
- distraction 명사 집중을 방해하는 것, 오락 활동
- stick to ~을 고수하다
- overthink 동사 너무 많이 생각하다
- emotional 형용사 감정적인
- hang over one's head 뇌리에서 떠나지 않다
- strategic 형용사 전략적인
- schedule 동사 일정을 짜다 / 명사 일정

06

- suspect 동사 짐작하다, 생각하다, 의심하다
- fungi 명사 균류 (fungus의 복수형)
- species 명사 (생물 분류 단위인) 종
- assume 동사 가정하다, 추측하다
- native 형용사 태생의, 토착의
- victorious 형용사 승리를 거둔, 승리한
- advantage 명사 이점, 장점
- come along 나타나다, 생겨나다
- infect 동사 감염시키다
- advantageous 형용사 유리한, 이로운
- generation 명사 세대

문제편 : p.036~042 | 정답과 해설 : p.035~043

- sprout (동사) 싹을 틔우다 / (명사) 새싹
- diversity (명사) 다양성
- security (명사) 안전(성)
- ancient (형용사) 오래된, 고대의
- dependent (형용사) 의존하는
- stable (형용사) 안정적인, 견실한
- condition (명사) 조건, 상황
- protect A from B A를 B로부터 보호하다
- complete (형용사) 완전한 / (동사) 완성하다
- collapse (명사) 붕괴 / (동사) 붕괴하다
- manage to V 어떻게든[간신히] ~해내다

07

- expression (명사) 표현, 표출
- enemy (명사) 적, 장애물
- get over ~을 극복하다, ~을 넘다
- obstacle (명사) 장애물, 방해(물)
- policy (명사) 방책, 정책
- mentality (명사) 사고방식
- alter (동사) 바꾸다, 변하다
- influence (동사) 영향을 미치다 / (명사) 영향(력)
- outcome (명사) 결과
- push for ~을 추진하다, ~을 요구하다
- emerge (동사) 나타나다, 나오다
- well-funded (형용사) 자금이 충분하게 지원된
- conceive (동사) 고안하다, 생각하다
- bill (명사) 법안, 고지서, 지폐
- ensure (동사) (반드시) ~하게 하다, 보장하다
- have access to N ~에 접근하다
- count (동사) 중요하다, 세다
- needle (명사) 바늘
- vastly (부사) 훨씬, 대단히, 엄청나게

08

- formula (명사) 공식, 방식
- standardize (동사) 표준화하다, 획일화하다
- grand (형용사) 웅대한, 대단한
- principle (명사) 원리, 원칙
- physics (명사) 물리학
- authority figure 권위자
- lectern (명사) 강의대, 연설대
- alternate (형용사) 다른, 대안이 되는
- misconception (명사) 오해, 잘못된 생각
- divine (형용사) 신성한, 신이 내려 주신
- visitation (명사) 방문
- revise (동사) 개정하다, 변경하다
- establish (동사) 확립하다, 제정하다, 입증하다
- alchemy (명사) 연금술
- spectacularly (부사) 장대하게, 극적으로, 굉장히
- lead (명사) 납
- one-dimensional (형용사) 일차원적인, 깊이 없는, 표면적인

09

- unfortunate (형용사) 불행한
- save for ~을 제외하고
- regional (형용사) 지역의, 지방의
- specialty (명사) (지역) 특산물, 전공
- show up 나타나다
- discern (동사) 식별하다, 알아차리다
- resist (동사) 저항하다, 반대하다
- corruption (명사) 변질, 변형, 부패
- come up with ~을 내놓다, ~을 찾아내다
- norm (명사) 기준, 표준
- savor (동사) 맛보다, 맛이 나다
- sensibly (부사) 현명하게
- consume (동사) 소비하다, 섭취하다
- fad (명사) (일시적인) 유행
- convulse (동사) 큰 소동을 일으키다
- scale (명사) 규모, 범위
- nutritionist (명사) 영양학자
- marbles (명사) (흔히 복수형으로) 분별, 이성, 대리석
- utterly (부사) 완전히, 아주, 철저하게

10

- collaborative (형용사) 협력적인, 공동의
- secure (동사) 확보하다, 안전하게 지키다
- cause (명사) 목적, 명분, 이유 / (동사) 유발하다
- contributor (명사) 기부자, 기여자
- fusion (명사) 결합, 융합
- capitalism (명사) 자본주의
- conventional (형용사) 전통적인, 관습적인
- variation (명사) 변주, 변이, 변화
- democratization (명사) 민주화
- restrict (동사) 한정하다, 제한하다
- allocation (명사) 배분, 할당
- empower (동사) ~할 수 있게 하다(=enable), 권한을 주다
- collective (형용사) 집단의, 공동의
- reinforce (동사) 강화하다
- keep A from V-ing A가 ~하는 것을 막다
- facilitate (동사) 용이하게 하다, 촉진하다

11

- thinker (명사) 사상가, 사색가
- perspective (명사) 관점, 시각
- strike (동사) ~와 마주하다, ~에 충돌하다 (strike-struck-struck)
- theatrical (형용사) 연극적인, 연극의
- quality (명사) 속성, 품질
- quote (명사) 명언, 인용문
- express (동사) 나타내다, 표현하다
- represent (동사) 표현하다, 대표하다
- imply (동사) 암시하다, 의미하다
- constantly (부사) 끊임없이, 항상
- conceal (동사) 숨기다, 감추다
- hostile (형용사) 적대적인, 강력히 반대하는
- bravado (명사) 허세 / (동사) 허세를 부리다
- get ahead 앞서가다, 출세하다

12

- aesthetics (명사) (단수 취급) 미학
- challenging (형용사) 도전적인, 저항[항의]하는, 어려움을 주는
- discomfort (명사) 불편, 불쾌
- engage with ~에 관여하다, ~을 다루다
- transformation (명사) 변형, 변화, 변질
- vehicle (명사) 수단, 매개체, 차량
- contend with ~와 싸우다[다투다]
- masterpiece (명사) 걸작, 명작
- cruel (형용사) 잔인한, 잔혹한, 고통스러운
- struggling with ~로 분투하다, ~하느라 애쓰다
- discrimination (명사) 차별, 구별
- portrait (명사) 묘사, 초상화
- relieve (동사) 완화하다, 덜다, 안도하게 하다
- enlighten (동사) 일깨우다, 이해시키다, 계몽하다
- embrace (동사) 포괄하다, 아우르다, 포옹하다

13

- strap A to B B에 A를 끈으로 묶다
- accelerator (명사) 가속 페달, 가속 장치
- vehicle (명사) 자동차, 차량
- on one's own 스스로
- barrier (명사) 장애물, 장벽
- be worth V-ing ~할 가치가 있다
- possess (동사) 가지다, 소유하다
- operate (동사) 작동하다, 운영하다
- autonomously (부사) 자율적으로, 독자적으로
- within one's reach ~의 손이 미치는 곳에
- approach (동사) ~에 접근하다, 다가가다
- appropriate (형용사) 적절한
- advance (동사) 증진시키다, 향상시키다
- device (명사) 장치, 기구
- monitor (동사) 관찰하다, 감시하다
- condition (명사) (건강) 상태
- in real time 실시간으로
- refined (형용사) 정제된, 세련된

14

- in return 대가로, 답례로
- depend on ~에 달려 있다, ~에 의존하다
- kiss up 아첨하다, 아부하다
- inevitably (부사) 필연적으로, 불가피하게
- examine (동사) 고찰하다, 검토하다
- transaction (명사) 거래, 매매
- slavery (명사) 노예, 노예제도
- reside (동사) 살다, 거주하다
- marble (명사) 대리석, 구슬
- jail (명사) 감옥, 교도소
- fame (명사) 명성, 인기
- miserable (형용사) 비참한, 불행한
- glory (명사) 영광

15

- objective (명사) 목표 / (형용사) 객관적인
- no longer 더 이상 ~이 아닌
- prevention (명사) 방지, 예방
- replicability (명사) 반복 가능성, 복제 가능성
- keenness (명사) 명민함, 날카로움
- variation (명사) 변화, 변형
- consistency (명사) 일관성, 한결같음
- talent (명사) 재능 있는 사람, 재능, 장기

문제편 : p.043~047 정답과 해설 : p.043~050

suppress	동사 짓누르다, 억압하다
process	명사 과정, 절차
conductor	명사 지휘자
foster	동사 장려하다, 조성하다
scope	명사 범위, 기회, 여지
variability	명사 변동성, 가변성
forecast	동사 예측하다, 예보하다

05. 요지 추론

01

decision	명사 결심, 판단
training	명사 훈련, 교육, 연수
stick to	~을 고수하다[지키다]
be able to V	~을 할 수 있다
meet	동사 지키다, 충족시키다, 만나다
commitment	명사 약속, 전념, 헌신
sit-up	명사 윗몸 일으키기

02

ignition	명사 발화(불이 일어나거나 타기 시작함), 점화(불을 붙이거나 켬)
initial	형용사 처음의, 초기의
strike	동사 발생하다, 부딪치다, 때리다
protagonist	명사 주인공
overreact	동사 과민 반응하다
attentive	형용사 주의를 기울이는
challenge	동사 도전하다, 이의를 제기하다
narrative	명사 이야기, 묘사 / 형용사 이야기의
present	형용사 존재하는, 현재의 / 동사 주다, 제시하다 / 명사 선물, 현재
engage	동사 몰입시키다, 몰두시키다, 끌어들이다
absent	형용사 부재하는, 결석한
beam	명사 빛줄기, 기둥, 환한 미소 / 동사 활짝 웃다, 비추다
at risk of	~할 위험에 처한
detach	동사 분리하다, 떼다

03

adopt	동사 채택하다, 입양하다, 취하다
parenting	명사 양육, 육아
variable	명사 변수 / 형용사 가변적인
equation	명사 방정식
insist	동사 주장하다
resistance	명사 거부감, 저항
flourish	동사 번성하다, 잘 자라다, 번창하다
custom-design	동사 맞춤 설계하다
natural	형용사 타고난, 자연의, 자연스러운
bless	동사 축복하다

04

psychology	명사 심리학, 심리 (상태)
circuit	명사 회로, 순환
hands-on	형용사 수작업의, 실천하는
from scratch	처음부터, 무(無)에서부터
tend	동사 손질하다, 돌보다
optimally	부사 최적으로, 최선으로
document	동사 ~을 문서에 기록하다
be correlated with	~와 관련이 있다
purposeful	형용사 의도적인, 목적이 있는
neurochemical	명사 신경 화학 물질 / 형용사 신경 화학의
be responsible for	~을 담당하다, ~에 대한 책임을 지다
reduction	명사 감소
resilience	명사 회복력, 탄성
onset	명사 발병, 시작

05

organization	명사 조직, 단체
measure	동사 측정하다, 평가하다 / 명사 기준, 척도
performance	명사 성과, 성능, 수행
in terms of	~의 관점에서, ~에 관하여
individual	형용사 개인의, 별개의 / 명사 개인
metric	명사 측정 기준
résumé	명사 이력(서), 개요
accolade	명사 수상, 표창
approach	명사 접근(법) / 동사 접근하다
confirm	동사 입증하다, 확인하다
impressive	형용사 인상적인, 감명 깊은
formula	명사 공식, 방식
potential	명사 잠재력, 가능성 / 형용사 잠재적인, 가능성 있는
driven	형용사 열의가 있는, 의욕이 넘치는
ecosystem	명사 생태계

06

troubled	형용사 (장소·상황·시기가) 문제가 있는, (사람이) 걱정하는
glory	명사 영광
massive	형용사 대규모의, 거대한
housing	명사 주택, 주택 공급
public policy	공공 정책
urban	형용사 도시의
real estate	명사 부동산
dress up	~을 꾸미다
declining	형용사 쇠퇴하는
underlying	형용사 기저에 있는, 근본적인
hallmark	명사 특징
infrastructure	명사 기반시설
structure	명사 건축물, 구조물, 구조
make sense	의미가 있다, 타당하다
public money	공공 자금
folly	명사 어리석음
centric	형용사 중심의
renewal	명사 재생, 부활, 갱신
remind	동사 상기시키다

07

well-meaning	형용사 좋은 뜻에서 하는, 선의의
match	동사 (필요에) 맞추다, 일치하다, 필적하다
practice	명사 습관, 버릇
swear	동사 확언하다, 맹세하다
doubt	동사 의심하다 / 명사 의심, 의혹
cautious	형용사 주의 깊은, 신중한
beat oneself up	자책하다
approach	명사 접근법 / 동사 다가가다
involve	동사 포함하다, 수반하다, 관련시키다
chance	명사 우연, 가능성, 기회
strive for	~을 위해 노력하다

08

be associated with	~과 관련이 있다
attractive	형용사 매력적인
kick-start	동사 시작하다, 시동을 걸다
pursuit	명사 추구
unremarkable	형용사 평범한, 특별할 것 없는
modified	형용사 수정된
depict	동사 표현하다, 묘사하다
motivated	형용사 동기 부여가 된
immediate	형용사 즉각적인
progress	명사 진전

09

behave	동사 예의 바르게 행동하다, 올바르게 처신하다
obstacle	명사 장애물, 장애
parenting	명사 양육, 육아
brew	동사 (폭풍우 등이) 일어나려고 하다, 태동하다
constructively	부사 건설적으로
use A to V	A를 ~하는 데 사용하다
reflect	동사 반성하다, 곰곰이 생각하다, 비추다
equilibrium	명사 (마음의) 평정, 평형
steer	동사 나아가다, 이끌다, 조종하다

10

be reluctant to V	~하는 것을 꺼리다
facilitate	동사 촉진하다, 용이하게 하다
be concerned about	~에 대해 걱정하다
allocate	동사 할당하다
resource	명사 자원
engagement	명사 관여, 참여
commitment	명사 헌신, 전념
heighten	동사 향상시키다
self-worth	명사 자부심, 자아 존중감
deed	명사 행위, 위업

11

sound	형용사 건전한, 정상적인
conservationist	명사 환경 보호주의자
principle	명사 원칙, 원리
disruption	명사 파괴, 붕괴
suppose	동사 전제로 하다, 가정하다
not to say	~라고까지는 할 수 없어도, ~는 아니더라도
idyllic	형용사 목가적인
notion	명사 개념, 생각
misleading	형용사 오해의 소지가 있는, 잘못 인도하는
endure	동사 지속되다, 견디다

- apparently 부사 겉보기에는
- in comparison with ~와 비교하면
- consequent 형용사 결과적인
- myth 명사 잘못된 통념, 근거 없는 믿음
- arrangement 명사 방식, 배열, 준비
- inhabitant 명사 서식자, 주민

12
- blind spot 명사 맹점
- visible 형용사 (눈에) 보이는, 가시적인
- developmental 형용사 발달상의
- challenge 명사 어려움, 도전
- overlook 동사 간과하다, 눈감아 주다
- unaware 형용사 인지하지 못하는
- presence 명사 존재, 출석
- run over ~을 (차로) 치다
- enlist 동사 요청하다, 입대하다
- be willing to V 기꺼이 ~하다

13
- relevance 명사 적합성, 타당성, 관련성
- fast track 승진 가도, 빠른 길
- hit a plateau 정체기에 들다, 안정기에 들다
- ambitious 형용사 야심에 찬
- victim 명사 희생자, 피해자
- embrace 동사 포용하다, 껴안다
- advance 명사 발전, 증가 / 동사 발전시키다, 증진되다
- executive leadership 경영 지도자
- expose 동사 노출시키다, 드러내다, 폭로하다
- integrate 동사 흡수하다, 통합하다
- excel 동사 탁월하다, 뛰어나다
- resistant 형용사 저항하는, 잘 견디는
- ultimately 부사 결국, 궁극적으로
- let A go A를 놓다[풀어 주다, 해고하다]
- retirement 명사 은퇴, 퇴직

14
- advent 명사 출현, 도래
- bode 동사 ~의 징조가 되다, 조짐이다
- momentum 명사 추진력, 가속도
- prediction 명사 예측, 예견
- premium 명사 프리미엄, 상, 장려금
- mimic 동사 모방하다, 흉내내다
- age 명사 시대, 나이
- puzzle 동사 당혹스럽게 하다, 어쩔 줄 모르게 하다
- take over 장악하다, 인수하다
- executive 명사 임원, 간부
- automatize 동사 자동화하다
- bump up 부딪히다

15
- remarkable 형용사 주목할 만한, 놀라운
- fantasy 명사 상상, 환상
- to such an extent that ~할 정도로, ~일 경우에
- unwind 동사 긴장을 풀다, (감은 것을) 풀다
- fantasize 동사 상상하다, 공상하다
- outcome 명사 결과
- objective 명사 목표, 목적 / 형용사 객관적인
- energize 동사 동력을 공급하다, 활기를 북돋우다
- get off 일어나다, 떠나다, 벗어나다, 내리다
- engaged 형용사 몰두하고 있는, 바쁜, 약혼한
- inevitable 형용사 피할 수 없는, 필연적인
- obstacle 명사 장애물, 방해물
- undercut 동사 약화시키다, 싸게 팔다
- temporary 형용사 일시적인, 임시의
- inactivity 명사 무기력, 무활동

16
- point to N ~을 시사하다[암시하다]
- significance 명사 중요성, 의의, 의미
- accurate 형용사 정확한, 정밀한
- measurement 명사 측정, 측량
- Western 형용사 서구의, 서양의
- progress 명사 발전, 진보 / 동사 발전하다, 진보하다
- mechanical 형용사 기계의, 자동의
- turning point 명사 전환점
- Middle Ages 명사 중세 시대
- sunrise 명사 일출
- peak 명사 최고점, 정점, (산의) 정상 / 동사 절정에 이르다
- stroke 명사 (시계가) 울리는 소리, 치기, 뇌졸중 / 동사 쓰다듬다
- concept 명사 개념, 구상, 발상
- commerce 명사 상업, 무역
- transaction 명사 거래, 매매, 처리 (과정)
- retailer 명사 소매업자
- wholesaler 명사 도매업자
- pace 명사 속도, 페이스
- allocate 동사 분배하다, 할당하다

17
- tend to V ~하는 경향이 있다
- overrate 동사 과대평가하다
- impact 명사 영향, 효과
- in part 부분적으로는
- older 형용사 기존의, 이전의
- absorbed 형용사 흡수된, 합병된
- invisible 형용사 눈에 띄지[보이지] 않는
- implement 명사 도구, 기구 / 동사 시행하다
- transform 동사 바꾸다, 전환시키다
- fundamental 형용사 근본적인, 본질적인
- infant 명사 영유아
- classic 형용사 전형적인, 대표적인
- device 명사 장치, 기구
- enable A to V A가 ~할 수 있게 하다
- exercise 동사 발휘하다, 행사하다
- function to V ~하는 기능을 하다
- feeding 명사 (아기의) 수유, 먹이 주기
- substitute for A A를 대신하다
- implication 명사 영향, 결과
- management 명사 관리, 경영
- overlook 동사 간과하다, 못 보고 넘어가다
- discussion 명사 담론, 논의, 토론

18
- firm 명사 기업, 회사 / 형용사 단단한, 확고한
- concentrate on ~에 집중하다
- lobby 동사 로비를 하다 / 명사 로비
- restructure 동사 구조 조정하다, 재구성하다
- profitable 형용사 수익성 있는, 이득이 되는
- viable 형용사 성장할 수 있는, 실행 가능한
- moral 형용사 도덕적인 / 명사 교훈
- hazard 명사 위험 / 동사 ~을 위태롭게 하다
- alter 동사 바꾸다, 달라지다
- rescue 동사 구제하다, 구조하다
- credit 명사 신용, 신뢰, 명성 / 동사 믿다, 신용하다
- crisis 명사 위기, 최악의 고비
- intervene 동사 개입하다, 끼어들다
- lose money 손해를 보다

19
- threatening 형용사 위협적인, 위협을 주는
- disaster 명사 재난, 재앙
- barrier 명사 장벽, 장애물
- relatively 부사 비교적, 상대적으로
- disruption 명사 혼란, 방해, 지장
- fire drill 명사 소방 훈련
- permission 명사 허용, 허가
- detailed 형용사 상세한, 자세한
- urgent 형용사 긴박한, 시급한
- authoritative 형용사 믿을 만한, 권위 있는
- rumour 명사 소문, 루머
- run riot 제멋대로 뻗어 나가다, 마구 날뛰다
- unproven 형용사 입증[증명]되지 않은
- pass A on to B A를 B에 전달하다[넘겨주다]
- redundant 형용사 해고된, 불필요한
- colleague 명사 (같은 직장의) 동료

06. 주제 추론

01
- creativity 명사 창의성
- further on 더 나아가서, 더 앞으로
- imagination 명사 상상력
- entirely 부사 전적으로, 오로지
- internal 형용사 내적인, 내부의
- consciousness 명사 의식, 자각
- motionless 형용사 움직이지 않는
- in a fever of ~의 흥분 속에서, 열광하여
- outcome 명사 결과
- involve 동사 수반하다, 포함하다
- deliberate 형용사 의도적인
- abstract 형용사 추상적인
- applied 형용사 적용된, 응용의
- realization 명사 실현

문제편 : p.055~061 정답과 해설 : p.058~065

02

- ☐ refer to ~을 지칭하다[언급하다]
- ☐ eyelid [명사] 눈꺼풀
- ☐ blink [동사] 눈을 깜빡이다 / [명사] 눈 깜빡임
- ☐ rate [명사] 비율, 속도, 요금 / [동사] 평가하다
- ☐ indicate [동사] 나타내다, 가리키다
- ☐ measurement [명사] 척도, 측정, 치수
- ☐ reputation [명사] 평판, 명성
- ☐ fearful [형용사] 겁이 많은, 걱정하는, 무서운
- ☐ come to (one's) mind (~에게) 생각나다, 생각이 떠오르다
- ☐ approach [동사] 다가오다, 다가가다
- ☐ predator [명사] 포식자
- ☐ be concerned with ~에 대해 걱정하다
- ☐ in an attempt to V ~하려는 시도로
- ☐ involuntarily [부사] 무의식적으로, 자기도 모르게
- ☐ equal [동사] ~와 같다[맞먹다] / [형용사] 동일한, 평등한
- ☐ symptom [명사] 증상, 징후, 조짐
- ☐ fatigue [명사] 피로
- ☐ indicator [명사] 지표
- ☐ instinct [명사] 본능

03

- ☐ interval [명사] 간격, 사이
- ☐ cram [동사] 벼락치기로 공부하다, 쑤셔 넣다
- ☐ be better off (~하는 편이) 더 낫다
- ☐ consolidate [동사] 통합 정리하다, 굳히다
- ☐ inactivity [명사] 무활동, 정지
- ☐ waste [형용사] 쓸모가 없어진 / [동사] 낭비하다
- ☐ accumulate [동사] 축적하다, 모으다
- ☐ awake [형용사] 깨어 있는
- ☐ compartment [명사] 구획, 칸, 객실
- ☐ adequate [형용사] 적절한, 충분한
- ☐ stimulate [동사] 자극하다, 흥분시키다
- ☐ engagement [명사] 참여, 약속
- ☐ alert [형용사] 기민한, 경계하는
- ☐ medication [명사] 약물 (치료)

04

- ☐ comparatively [부사] 비교적(으로), 상대적(으로)
- ☐ starving [명사] 굶주림, 기아
- ☐ diabetes [명사] 당뇨병
- ☐ to be clear 정확히 하자면, 명백히 말하자면
- ☐ flee [동사] 도망치다, 달아나다
- ☐ appointment [명사] (업무적인) 약속, (병원 등의) 예약
- ☐ stuck [형용사] 갇힌, 꼼짝 못 하는
- ☐ traffic jam [명사] 교통 체증
- ☐ rate A (as) B A를 B로 여기다[평가하다]
- ☐ illusion [명사] 착각, 오해
- ☐ mortal [형용사] 치명적인, 죽음을 면할 수 없는

05

- ☐ consequence [명사] 결과
- ☐ possibly [부사] 과연, 아마, 혹시
- ☐ shed [동사] 밝히다, 비추다 (shed-shed-shed)
- ☐ light [명사] (새로운) 사실[발견]
- ☐ intake [명사] 섭취, 흡입
- ☐ cognitively [부사] 인지적으로
- ☐ link [동사] 연결시키다, 관련되다 / [명사] 연결, 관계
- ☐ volume [명사] 크기, 부피
- ☐ finding [명사] (조사·연구 등의) 결과, 발견
- ☐ isolate [동사] 분리하다, 고립시키다
- ☐ component [명사] 구성 요소
- ☐ memory center 기억 중추
- ☐ favor [명사] 도움, 호의, 부탁
- ☐ inverse [형용사] 반대의, 역의
- ☐ cortex [명사] (대뇌) 피질
- ☐ latter [형용사] 후자의, 마지막의 / [명사] 후자, 마지막 것
- ☐ excessive [형용사] 과도한
- ☐ consumption [명사] 섭취, 소비
- ☐ metabolic [형용사] 신진대사의
- ☐ cognitive [형용사] 인지의
- ☐ processed [형용사] 가공된

06

- ☐ neurological [형용사] 신경학적인, 신경학상의
- ☐ passive [형용사] 수동적인, 간접적인
- ☐ interact with ~와 상호 작용하다
- ☐ critical thinking [명사] 비판적 사고
- ☐ predictor [명사] 예측 변수, 요인
- ☐ addiction [명사] 중독
- ☐ preference [명사] 선호, 애호
- ☐ parental [형용사] 부모의, 아버지[어머니]의

07

- ☐ confront [동사] 직면하다, 닥치다, 맞서다
- ☐ endless [형용사] 끝이 없는, 무한한
- ☐ loop [명사] 고리
- ☐ rebel [동사] 저항하다, 반란을 일으키다 / [명사] 저항 세력
- ☐ live through ~을 겪다
- ☐ befriend [동사] ~와 친구가 되다
- ☐ cheer on ~을 응원하다
- ☐ predictability [명사] 예측 가능성
- ☐ engage [동사] 끌어들이다, 사로잡다, 고용하다
- ☐ escape [동사] ~을 벗어나다, 도망가다
- ☐ awake to ~을 인식하다[알아차리다]
- ☐ be involved in ~에 관련된
- ☐ tie [동사] 관련시키다, 구속하다, 묶다 / [명사] 구속, 유대
- ☐ yield [동사] 산출하다 / [명사] 산출량(수확량), 총수익
- ☐ gratify [동사] 만족감을 주다, 충족시키다
- ☐ inclination [명사] 성향, ~하는 경향

08

- ☐ anthropologist [명사] 인류학자
- ☐ consequence [명사] 결과, 중요함
- ☐ relieve [동사] 해방시키다, 덜어 주다
- ☐ exclusive [형용사] 한정된, 독점적인, 배타적인
- ☐ head off ~을 막다[저지하다], ~을 회피하다
- ☐ dynamics [명사] 역학, 역학 관계, 원동력
- ☐ be bound to V 틀림없이[반드시] ~하다
- ☐ pressure [명사] 고난, 곤란, 압박, 압력
- ☐ pursuit [명사] (시간과 에너지를 들여 하는) 일, 활동, 추구
- ☐ diversify [동사] 다양[다각]화하다, 다양해지다
- ☐ substantially [부사] 상당히, 많이, 주로, 대체로
- ☐ cuisine [명사] 요리

09

- ☐ seldom [부사] 거의 ~ 아닌
- ☐ exclusive [형용사] 독점적인
- ☐ imperial [형용사] 제국의, 제국적인
- ☐ inclusive [형용사] 포괄적인, 폭넓은
- ☐ rigid [형용사] 엄격한, 융통성 없는
- ☐ emperor [명사] 황제
- ☐ subject [형용사] 지배를 받는, 종속된 / [명사] 주제, 과목
- ☐ epic [명사] 장편 서사 (영화), 서사시
- ☐ rebellion [명사] 저항, 반란
- ☐ collapse [명사] 몰락, 붕괴
- ☐ integrative [형용사] 통합적인, 통합하는

10

- ☐ preparation [명사] 준비, 대비
- ☐ launch [동사] 개시하다, 시작하다
- ☐ preparatory [형용사] 준비의, 준비를 위한
- ☐ stamina [명사] 힘, 체력
- ☐ carry out 수행하다
- ☐ unconscious [형용사] 무의식적인
- ☐ rush [동사] 공격하다, 덤벼들다, 서두르다
- ☐ victim [명사] 희생자, 피해자
- ☐ frenzy [명사] 격분, 광란
- ☐ strategy [명사] 전략, 전술
- ☐ firsthand [부사] 직접, 바로
- ☐ upcoming [형용사] 곧 있을, 다가오는
- ☐ arousal [명사] 자극
- ☐ synchronize [동사] 동시에 움직이게 하다
- ☐ compensate for ~을 보상해 주다
- ☐ march [동사] 행진하다 / [명사] 행진
- ☐ intimidate [동사] 겁먹게 하다, 위협하다
- ☐ spectacle [명사] 장관, 구경거리
- ☐ sheer [형용사] 순전한, 순수한
- ☐ honor [동사] 기리다 / [명사] 명예
- ☐ utilize [동사] 활용하다
- ☐ warfare [명사] 전쟁, 전투
- ☐ vulnerable [형용사] 취약한, 상처받기 쉬운

11

- ☐ modern [형용사] 근대의, 현대의
- ☐ superhuman [형용사] 초인적인
- ☐ novel [형용사] 새로운
- ☐ originate [동사] 유래하다
- ☐ divine [형용사] 신(神)의, 신(神)이 내린
- ☐ inspire [동사] 영감을 주다
- ☐ reflect [동사] 반영하다
- ☐ possess [동사] 사로잡다, 소유하다
- ☐ descend [동사] 내려오다
- ☐ imitate [동사] 모방하다

□ sacred 형용사 신성한
□ transcendent 형용사 초월적인
□ pale imitation 어설프게 흉내 낸 것
□ blindly 부사 맹목적으로
□ underlying 형용사 기저를 이루는
□ compromise 명사 타협, 절충
□ abstraction 명사 추상, 관념
□ accuracy 명사 정확성

12

□ patent 명사 특허(권), 특허증
□ monopoly 명사 독점, 독차지
□ intellectual property 명사 지적 재산
□ plainly 부사 명백히, 솔직히
□ defend 동사 지키다, 방어하다
□ discourage 동사 단념시키다, 낙담시키다
□ disrupt 동사 방해하다, 지장을 주다
□ firm 명사 회사 / 형용사 딱딱한, 확고한
□ barrier 명사 장벽, 장애물
□ sue 동사 고소하다, 소송을 제기하다
□ upstart 형용사 신흥의, 벼락부자인
□ trespass 동사 침해하다 / 명사 무단출입
□ tie A up in B (다른 일을 할 수 없게) A를 B로 묶어 놓다
□ lawsuit 명사 소송, 고소
□ entrant 명사 참가자, 신입자
□ thicket 명사 덤불, 복잡하게 얽힌 것
□ side effect 명사 부작용
□ hinder 동사 방해하다, 저지하다

13

□ oyster 명사 굴
□ marsh 명사 습지
□ deliberately 부사 의도적으로, 신중하게
□ erosion 명사 침식, 부식
□ aquaculture 명사 (수산) 양식
□ livelihood 명사 생계
□ rear 동사 기르다
□ recover 동사 재발견하다, 되찾다, 회복하다
□ recreational 형용사 여가용의, 오락의
□ invasive 형용사 침입의, 침략적인
□ discard 동사 버리다, 폐기하다
□ colonize 동사 군락을 이루다, 식민지로 만들다
□ biodiversity 명사 생물 다양성
□ ecotourism 명사 생태 관광

14

□ pioneer 동사 개척하다 / 명사 개척자
□ have one's roots in ~에 뿌리를 두다, ~을 근거로 두다
□ settled 형용사 정착한, 자리를 잡은, 안정적인, 안정된
□ fertile 형용사 (토양이) 비옥한, 기름진
□ crescent 명사 초승달 (모양)
□ evolve 동사 발달하다, 진전시키다
□ transaction 명사 거래, 계약
□ grain 명사 곡물
□ date back to (시기가) ~까지 거슬러 올라가다
□ payment of taxes 납세
□ clay tablet 점토판
□ regional 형용사 지역(별)의, 지역적인

15

□ competent 형용사 능력이 있는, 능숙한, 충분한
□ talent 명사 재능, 장기
□ cloud 동사 흐리다, 어두워지다 / 명사 구름
□ bring to the table 기여하다, 제시하다, 제공하다
□ actively 부사 적극적으로, 활발히
□ cultivate 동사 계발하다, 기르다, 경작하다
□ be crossed off the list 목록에서 지워지다, 제명되다
□ appeal 동사 매력적이다, 관심을 끌다, 호소하다 / 명사 매력, 호소
□ tailor 동사 (목적에 맞게) 만들다, 맞추다, 재단하다

16

□ differ from ~와 다르다
□ race 명사 인종
□ biological 형용사 생물학적인, 생물학의
□ entity 명사 실체, 독립체
□ ancestry 명사 혈통, 가계
□ identify 동사 식별하다
□ representative 명사 전형, 표본 / 형용사 전형적인, 대표하는
□ variable 형용사 변할 수 있는 / 명사 변수
□ classify 동사 분류하다
□ discrete 형용사 별개의
□ construction 명사 구성(물), 건축물, 공사
□ variation 명사 차이, 변형
□ overcome 동사 극복하다, 이기다
□ racism 명사 인종 차별주의, 인종 차별 행위
□ evolution 명사 진화, 발전
□ misconception 명사 오해
□ construct 명사 구성(물), 구조물 / 동사 구성하다, 건설하다

17

□ trunk 명사 (나무) 줄기, 몸통, 여행용 큰 가방
□ reveal 동사 밝히다, 드러내다, 폭로하다
□ twig 명사 잔가지
□ emerge 동사 나오다, 드러나다, 생겨나다
□ stem from ~에서 비롯되다[유래하다]
□ employ 동사 사용하다, 고용하다
□ disciplinary 형용사 학문의, 교과의, 훈계의, 징계의
□ universal 형용사 보편적인, 일반적인
□ drawback 명사 문제점, 약점, 결점
□ integrate 동사 통합하다
□ concrete 형용사 구체적인, 콘크리트로 만든

18

□ seek 동사 구하다, 찾다
□ in spite of ~에도 불구하고
□ explanation 명사 설명, 이유, 해명
□ persuade 동사 설득하다, 납득시키다
□ wheeled 형용사 바퀴 달린, 바퀴로 움직이는
□ reluctant 형용사 꺼리는, 마지못한, 주저하는
□ majority 명사 대다수, 가장 많은 수
□ hit upon[on] ~을 (우연히) 떠올리다[생각해 내다]
□ wheel 동사 (바퀴 달린 것을) 밀다, 끌다, 운전하다
□ disguise 동사 위장하다, 변장[가장]하다, 숨기다 / 명사 변장
□ accomplish 동사 달성하다, 해내다, 완수하다
□ logic 명사 논리, 타당성
□ readily 부사 기꺼이, 선뜻, 쉽게

19

□ empathy 명사 공감, 감정 이입
□ list 동사 (목록에) 언급하다, 열거하다 / 명사 목록
□ desired 형용사 바라는, 훌륭한
□ specify 동사 (구체적으로) 명시하다
□ stress 동사 강조하다, 강세를 두다
□ emphasize 동사 강조하다, 역설하다, 두드러지게 하다
□ perspective 명사 관점, 시각
□ negotiate 동사 협상하다, 교섭하다
□ affective 형용사 정서적인, 감정적인
□ concern 명사 관심, 배려, 염려
□ compassion 명사 동정심, 연민
□ foster 동사 기르다, 양육하다
□ translate 동사 (특정하게) 의미하다, 번역하다
□ fulfill 동사 충족하다, (의무 등을) 다하다
□ take A into account A를 고려하다
□ interpretation 명사 해석, 이해, 설명

20

□ diversity 명사 다양성, 포괄성
□ question 동사 ~에 의문을 제기하다 / 명사 질문
□ objective 형용사 객관적인, 사실에 기초한 / 명사 목적
□ maintain 동사 주장하다, 유지하다, 부양하다
□ aspire 동사 열망하다, 갈망하다
□ practice 명사 실행 / 동사 실행하다
□ ethnicity 명사 민족성
□ carry out ~을 수행[실시]하다
□ pursue 동사 추구하다, 추적하다
□ curiosity 명사 호기심
□ test 동사 검증하다, 검사하다
□ varied 형용사 다양한
□ angle 명사 각도, 관점
□ diverse 형용사 다양한, 여러 가지의
□ consensus 명사 의견 일치, 합의
□ build up 확립되다, 개발하다, 높이다
□ particular 형용사 특정한, 특별한, 까다로운
□ confidence 명사 자신감, 확신
□ objectivity 명사 객관성

21

□ recognize 동사 인식하다, 인지하다
□ draw on ~에 기반하다, ~을 이용하다
□ react against ~에 반하다[반발하다]
□ be characteristic of ~에 특유한, ~의 특징을 나타내는

문제편 : p.066~071 정답과 해설 : p.073~081

☐	differ	동사 (의견이) 다르다
☐	biologist	명사 생물학자
☐	light	명사 관점, 견해, 빛
☐	historical	형용사 역사적인, 역사와 관련된
☐	occur	동사 발생하다, 일어나다
☐	context	명사 맥락, 문맥
☐	purely	부사 완전히, 순전히
☐	objective	형용사 객관적인 / 명사 목적, 목표
☐	pursuit	명사 일, 연구, 추구
☐	uninfluenced	형용사 영향을 받지 않은
☐	viewpoint	명사 관점, 견해
☐	speak of	~에 대해 말하다
☐	underlying	형용사 근본적인, 근원적인, 기저의
☐	stripped of	~가 없는
☐	aim	명사 목표, 목적 / 동사 겨냥하다
☐	represent	동사 표현하다, 나타내다
☐	independently of	~와 별개로[관계 없이]
☐	bear	동사 (관계 등을) 맺다, 참다, 견디다
☐	contingently	부사 혹여라도, 우연히, 경우에 따라서
☐	practice	명사 관습, 관행, 연습, 실행 / 동사 연습하다

07. 제목 추론

01

☐	contain	동사 함유하다, 포함하다
☐	ingredient	명사 성분, 재료
☐	regulation	명사 규제, 규정
☐	require	동사 요구하다, 필요로 하다
☐	list	동사 (표·명부 등에) 기재하다, 기입하다
☐	sweetener	명사 감미료
☐	separately	부사 따로따로, 개별적으로
☐	requirement	명사 요건, 필요조건
☐	motive	명사 동기 / 동사 동기를 부여하다
☐	convey	동사 전달하다, 운반하다
☐	indicate	동사 표시하다, 나타내다, 가리키다
☐	serving	명사 1인분

02

☐	challenge	명사 도전 (과제), 난제 / 동사 도전하다, 이의를 제기하다
☐	date back to	(시기가) ~까지 거슬러 올라가다
☐	issue	동사 발표하다, 발행하다 / 명사 쟁점, 문제
☐	mathematical	형용사 수학적인, 수리적인, 아주 정확한
☐	prime number	명사 (수학에서의) 소수
☐	divisibility	명사 가분성, 나누어떨어짐
☐	establish	동사 입증하다, 확립하다
☐	identify	동사 식별해 내다, 확인하다
☐	name	동사 (정확히) 지정하다, 밝히다, 명명하다

03

☐	violence	명사 폭력, 폭행
☐	anthropologist	명사 인류학자
☐	notion	명사 개념, 생각
☐	combative	형용사 전투적인, 금방이라도 싸울 듯한
☐	opponent	명사 경쟁자, 상대방
☐	simulate	동사 모의하다, 시뮬레이션하다
☐	warfare	명사 전투, 전쟁
☐	hypothesize	동사 가설을 세우다
☐	alternative	명사 대체물, 대안
☐	inverse	형용사 역의, 반대의 / 명사 역
☐	correlation	명사 상관관계, 연관성
☐	frequency	명사 빈도, 주파수
☐	intensity	명사 강도, 세기
☐	hypothesis	명사 가설, 가정, 추측
☐	significant	형용사 유의미한, 상당한, 중요한
☐	pervasive	형용사 만연한, 스며드는
☐	be likely to V	~할 가능성이 있다, ~하기 쉽다
☐	engage in	~에 참여하다, 종사하다
☐	reflection	명사 반영, 반사, 반성
☐	aggressive	형용사 공격적인, 싸우기를 좋아하는
☐	impulse	명사 충동, 충격

04

☐	invention	명사 발명품, 발명
☐	origin	명사 기원, 출처
☐	accurately	부사 정확히, 정밀하게
☐	pottery	명사 도자기
☐	archaeologist	명사 고고학자
☐	date back to	~로 거슬러 올라가다
☐	tell A from B	A와 B를 구별하다
☐	material	명사 재료 / 형용사 물질의
☐	driving force	추진력
☐	civilization	명사 문명

05

☐	mistakenly	부사 잘못하여, 틀리게
☐	hypothesis	명사 가설 (복수형 hypotheses)
☐	guarantee	동사 보장하다
☐	slow down	~을 둔화시키다
☐	shore	명사 해변
☐	established facts	기정 사실
☐	venture into	~로 과감히 들어가 보다
☐	uncharted waters	미개척 영역
☐	prediction	명사 예측
☐	alley	명사 골목길
☐	blind	형용사 막다른, 눈이 먼
☐	reluctant	형용사 주저하는, 꺼리는
☐	hard	형용사 확실한, 엄연한

06

☐	inanimate	형용사 무생물의
☐	inarticulate	형용사 표현을 제대로 하지 못하는, 불분명한
☐	statement	명사 진술, 성명
☐	obvious	형용사 명확한, 분명한
☐	rust	동사 녹슬다 / 명사 녹
☐	trailer	명사 트레일러 (하우스)
☐	accent	명사 억양, 말씨
☐	deliberate	형용사 의도적인, 신중한
☐	income	명사 소득, 수입
☐	register	동사 알아차리다, 등록하다
☐	consciously	부사 의식적으로
☐	vague	형용사 모호한, 희미한
☐	grasp	동사 파악하다, 움켜잡다

07

☐	political	형용사 정치적인
☐	corporation	명사 기업, 회사, 법인
☐	mindful	형용사 주의를 기울이는, 유념하는
☐	deserve	동사 ~할 자격이 있다, ~을 받을 만하다
☐	pollute	동사 오염시키다
☐	fair-trade	형용사 공정 거래의
☐	practice	명사 관행, 실행, 연습
☐	be committed to N	~에 헌신하다, 전념하다
☐	bring about	~을 가져오다[야기하다]
☐	good	명사 이득, 행복, 선(善)
☐	conscience	명사 양심, 가책
☐	contribute A to B	A를 B에 기부하다[기증하다]
☐	genuinely	부사 정말로, 진심으로
☐	embrace	동사 받아들이다, 수용하다
☐	consciously	부사 의식적으로

08

☐	sedentary	형용사 주로 앉아서 지내는
☐	consistently	부사 지속적으로
☐	convinced	형용사 확신하는, 신념이 있는
☐	mindless	형용사 아무 생각이 없는, 분별력이 없는
☐	outsource	동사 (작업·생산을) 위탁하다, 위임하다
☐	sustain	동사 (상처를) 입다, 당하다
☐	fracture	명사 골절, 균열, 금
☐	overworked	형용사 혹사당하는
☐	unreasonable	형용사 지나친, 터무니없는
☐	fit	형용사 건강한, 적합한, 알맞은 / 동사 (모양·크기 등이) 맞다
☐	advanced	형용사 진보한

09

☐	struggle	동사 고심하다, 분투하다
☐	content	명사 함유량, 내용물
☐	trade off	균형을 잡다, 교환하다
☐	land on	~에 이르다, 착륙하다
☐	note	동사 알아차리다, 주목하다
☐	excessive	형용사 지나친, 과도한
☐	creaminess	명사 느끼함, 크림 같음
☐	simulate	동사 시뮬레이션하다, 가장하다
☐	bodily	형용사 신체적인, 몸의
☐	place a value on	~에 가치를 두다, 부여하다
☐	tip	동사 기울이다, 뒤집어 엎다

10

☐	government	명사 정치(통치) 체제, 정부
☐	routine	형용사 일상적인, 틀에 박힌 / 명사 일상
☐	immediate	형용사 가까운, 인접한, 즉각적인
☐	formulate	동사 표현하다, 말하다, 만들어 내다
☐	aid	명사 도움, 지원 / 동사 돕다, 거들다
☐	mutual	형용사 상호의, 서로 간의
☐	confidence	명사 신뢰, 확신, 자신감
☐	property	명사 재산, 소유물

문제편 : p.074~078 정답과 해설 : p.082~089

- contract — 명사 계약 / 동사 계약하다, 수축하다
- unambiguous — 형용사 모호하지 않은, 분명한
- counterparty — 명사 (거래의) 상대방, 당사자
- a measure of — 어느 정도의, 일정량의
- distrust — 명사 불신 / 동사 불신하다
- accentuate — 동사 강조하다, 악센트를 붙이다
- facilitate — 동사 용이하게 하다, 촉진하다
- clarification — 명사 명확화, 설명
- settlement — 명사 해결, 합의, 정착
- dispute — 명사 분쟁, 논쟁
- translation — 명사 통역, 번역
- reliable — 형용사 믿을 수 있는, 신뢰할 만한
- linguistic — 형용사 언어적인, 말의
- transaction — 명사 거래, 매매
- excessive — 형용사 과도한, 지나친

11

- approximate — 동사 어림잡다
- round — 형용사 어림의, 대략의
- uneasily — 부사 불안하게, 불편하게
- nonsense — 명사 터무니없는 생각, 터무니없는 말
- mirror — 명사 반영, 거울
- flexibility — 명사 유연성, 융통성
- manipulate — 동사 조종하다, 다루다

12

- transport — 동사 (다른 장소·상황에 있는) 느낌이 들게 하다, 이동시키다, 수송하다
- fascinating — 형용사 매력적인, 대단히 흥미로운
- inspiring — 형용사 감동적인, 고무적인
- have to do with — ~과 관련이 있다
- stereotype — 명사 고정 관념
- existing — 형용사 기존의
- notion — 명사 생각, 관념

13

- story — 명사 기사, 이야기
- essential — 형용사 필수적인, 본질적인
- element — 명사 요소, 성분
- convey — 동사 전달하다, 운반하다
- present — 동사 제시하다, 보여주다
- inverted — 형용사 거꾸로 된, 반대의
- attention span — 주의 지속 시간, 주의 집중 범위
- maximize — 동사 극대화하다, 최대한 활용하다
- alternative — 명사 대안 / 형용사 대체 가능한
- mystery — 명사 미스터리, 추리물
- payoff — 명사 결말, (급여) 지불
- break off — (갑자기) 멈추다, 중단하다
- presidential election — 대통령 선거
- tell A from B — A를 B와 구별하다[구분하다]

14

- liberate — 동사 자유롭게 하다, 해방시키다
- classic — 형용사 대표적인, 일류의
- thinker — 명사 사상가
- wage — 동사 (전쟁·전투를) 벌이다
- in the long run — 장기적으로, 결국에는
- trade — 동사 거래를 하다 / 명사 거래, 무역
- gain — 동사 이득을 얻다, ~을 얻게 되다
- establishment — 명사 설립
- overwhelming — 형용사 저항할 수 없는, 압도적인
- interest — 명사 이해관계, 이익
- devastating — 형용사 (대단히) 파괴적인, 엄청나게 충격적인
- innate — 형용사 타고난, 선천적인
- framework — 명사 체제, 틀
- stabilize — 동사 안정시키다
- disrupt — 동사 방해하다

15

- realization — 명사 실현, 깨달음
- domination — 명사 지배, 우세
- structure — 동사 구축하다, 조직화하다
- capitalistic — 형용사 자본주의적인
- rural — 형용사 시골의, 지방의
- agricultural — 형용사 농업의, 농경의
- abandon — 동사 버리다, 포기하다
- textile — 명사 직물, 옷감
- steel — 명사 철강(업)
- exert — 동사 행사하다, 가하다
- dump — 동사 내버리다, 떠넘기다
- by-product — 명사 부산물, 부작용
- waterway — 명사 수로, 항로
- urbanization — 명사 도시화
- greed — 명사 탐욕

16

- self-conscious — 형용사 자의식 과잉의, 남의 시선을 의식하는
- awareness — 명사 인식, 자각
- under the radar — 눈에 띄지 않게, 몰래
- mess up — 망치다
- rough — 형용사 난폭한, 거친, 대략적인
- observe — 동사 관찰하다, 준수하다
- judge — 동사 평가하다, 판단하다 / 명사 판사
- flaw — 명사 결함, 흠, 금
- at the expense of — ~을 희생하면서, ~을 잃어가며
- please — 동사 만족시키다, 기쁘게 하다
- permanently — 부사 영원히

17

- craze — 명사 열풍, 대유행
- reinterpretation — 명사 재해석
- associated with — ~와 관련된
- poverty — 명사 가난, 빈곤, 부족
- aspirational — 형용사 열망하는, 동경의 대상인
- demonstrative — 형용사 드러내 놓고 표현하는, 숨기지 않는
- signal — 동사 (어떤 일이 있거나 있을 것임을) 암시하다, 시사하다, 신호를 보내다
- well-off — 형용사 부유한, 유복한
- value-laden — 형용사 가치 판단적인, 개인적 의견에 영향을 받는
- by no means — 결코 ~이 아닌
- conspicuous — 형용사 과시적인, 눈에 잘 띄는, 튀는, 뚜렷한
- manifest — 형용사 분명한 / 동사 분명해지다, 나타내다, 드러내 보이다
- dweller — 명사 거주자, 주민
- inclusive — 형용사 포괄적인, 폭넓은

18

- healthcare — 명사 의료, 건강 관리
- namely — 부사 다시 말해, 즉
- clinical — 형용사 임상의
- medicine — 명사 의술, 의학
- preventive — 형용사 예방적인, 예방을 위한
- wellness — 명사 건강 (관리)
- hygiene — 명사 위생
- societal — 형용사 사회적인
- ascendancy — 명사 우세, 우위, 지배권
- professionalism — 명사 전문성, 뛰어난 기량
- overshadow — 동사 가리다, 그늘지게 하다
- heroic — 형용사 영웅적인, 영웅의
- sanitary — 형용사 위생의, 깨끗한
- be attributable to N — ~에 기인하다
- surgical — 형용사 외과적인, 수술의
- dexterity — 명사 기민함, 솜씨
- pharmaceutical — 형용사 제약의, 약학의
- sanitation — 명사 위생 시설
- sewage — 명사 하수, 오물
- attainable — 형용사 달성할 수 있는, 이룰 수 있는
- controversy — 명사 논란
- initiative — 명사 계획, 주도권, 결단력

19

- emerge — 동사 생기다, 부상하다, 드러나다
- supplement — 명사 추가[보충]분, 증보판
- deplore — 동사 한탄하다, 애통해 하다
- drift — 명사 표류, 이동
- formalize — 동사 공식화하다
- punctuation — 명사 구두법
- virtually — 부사 사실상, 거의, 가상으로
- unintelligible — 형용사 이해할 수 없는
- materialize — 동사 나타나다, 구체화하다
- fade — 동사 사라지다, (색이) 바래다, 희미해지다

20

- archaeologist — 명사 고고학자
- finder — 명사 발견한 사람
- fee — 명사 사례(금), 보수 / 명사 요금
- torn — 형용사 찢어진
- incentive — 명사 보상(금), 장려(금)
- make money — 돈을 벌다
- achieved — 형용사 달성된, 이룬
- noteworthy — 형용사 주목할 만한
- radically — 부사 급격하게, 급진적으로
- relive — 동사 (상상 속에서) 다시 체험하다
- non-material — 형용사 비물질적인
- superior — 형용사 보다 더 우수한
- heritage — 명사 유산

문제편 : p.079~083 정답과 해설 : p.089~097

21

- foolish 형용사 어리석은
- in reality 현실에서
- prejudice 명사 편견
- victim 명사 희생자
- spectacular 형용사 극적인, 장관을 이루는
- stomach cancer 위암
- chance 명사 가능성
- depression 명사 우울증
- flashy 형용사 현란한, 화려하게 치장한
- outcome 명사 결과
- invisible 형용사 보이지 않는
- downgrade 동사 평가 절하하다, (중요성이나 가치를) 떨어뜨리다
- readily 부사 쉽게

22

- response 명사 반응, 회신
- charge 동사 비난하다, 청구하다
- moral hazard 도덕적 위험, 도덕적 해이
- dementia 명사 치매
- deception 명사 속임수, 기만
- serve 동사 달성하다, 기여하다, 봉사하다
- vulnerable 형용사 취약한, 연약한
- autism 명사 자폐성, 자폐증
- companion 명사 친구, 동반자
- cognitive 형용사 인지의, 인식의
- deficit 명사 결함, 결손, 적자
- inferior to N ~보다 열등한
- reason 동사 판단하다, 사고하다 / 명사 이성, 이유
- line 명사 입장, 선
- iconic 형용사 상징적인, 우상의
- cartoonish 형용사 만화 같은
- synthetic 형용사 가짜의, 합성의
- unsophisticated 형용사 순진한, 단순한
- uncanny 형용사 불쾌한, 이상한
- recipient 명사 받는 사람, 수령인
- violate 동사 침해하다, 위반하다
- dignity 명사 존엄성, 위엄
- surpass 동사 능가하다, 뛰어넘다
- ethical 형용사 윤리적인, 도덕적인
- era 명사 시대
- medical checkup 건강 검진

23

- prevalent 형용사 일반적인, 널리 퍼져 있는
- report 동사 이야기하다, 전하다, 알리다
- accessible 형용사 연락될 수 있는, 접근하기 쉬운
- obligation 명사 의무감, 의무
- respond 동사 응답하다, 반응하다
- instantly 부사 즉시, 즉각
- teen 명사 십 대(13~19세)
- tween 명사 십 대 초반의 아동(10~12세)
- ins and outs 세부적인 것, 구석구석
- play out 나타나다, (점진적으로 일이) 벌어지다
- text 동사 문자 메시지를 보내다 / 명사 본문, 글
- blow up 폭파하다, 터뜨리다
- induce 동사 유발하다, 유도하다
- aggressive 형용사 공격적인, 대단히 적극적인
- symbol 명사 상징, 기호
- byte 명사 바이트(컴퓨터의 8비트에 해당)
- within reach 가까이에, 손이 닿는 곳에
- ideal 형용사 이상적인, 가장 알맞은

24

- tend to V ~하는 경향이 있다
- break up A into B A를 B로 나누다
- a series of 일련의
- psychologist 명사 심리학자
- deadline 명사 마감일, 기한
- break 명사 단절, 중단
- be likely to V ~할 가능성이 있다
- remote 형용사 멀리 떨어진, 먼
- be ready to V ~할 준비가 되다
- jump into action 행동으로 옮기다
- timeframe 명사 시간 틀, 기간
- get A done A를 끝내다[끝마치다]
- approach 명사 접근법
- view A as B A를 B로 여기다
- meet a challenge 도전에 대처하다
- imminent 형용사 임박한, 목전의
- manageable 형용사 관리될 수 있는

25

- mental 형용사 정신의, 마음의
- consist of ~으로 구성되다[이루어지다]
- individual 명사 개인 / 형용사 개인적인
- increasingly 부사 점점 더, 갈수록 더
- master 동사 숙달하다 / 명사 주인
- code 명사 규범, 규칙
- competent 형용사 유능한, 능숙한
- internalize 동사 내면화하다, 자기 것으로 하다
- gradually 부사 점진적으로, 점차
- actor 명사 행위자, 배우
- criminal 형용사 형사의, 범죄의 / 명사 범죄자
- sufficient 형용사 충분한, 흡족한
- maturity 명사 성숙, 원숙
- be accountable for ~에 (대한) 책임을 지다
- right 명사 권리, 오른쪽 / 형용사 올바른
- thereby 부사 그럼으로써, 그것 때문에
- formally 부사 공식적으로, 격식을 갖추어
- democratic 형용사 민주의, 민주적인
- boundary 명사 경계(선), 분계(선)
- optimal 형용사 최적의, 최선의
- take place 일어나다, 개최되다
- rate 명사 속도, 비율 / 동사 평가하다
- apply to A A에 적용되다
- somewhat 부사 다소, 어느 정도
- questionable 형용사 의문스러운, 미심쩍은

01

- natural gas 천연가스
- respectively 부사 각각
- billion 명사 10억
- cubic meter 세제곱미터
- rank 동사 기록하다, (순위를) 차지하다

02

- respondent 명사 응답자
- be familiar with ~에 친숙하다
- be engaged in ~에 참여하다, ~에 종사하다
- familiarity 명사 친숙(도)
- engagement 명사 참여(도)
- when it comes to N/V-ing ~에 있어서, ~에 관한 한
- as for ~에 있어서, ~에 대해 말하자면

03

- distribution 명사 분포, 분배
- sector 명사 부문, 분야
- petrochemical 명사 석유화학제품 / 형용사 석유화학의
- aviation 명사 항공(술)
- residential 형용사 주거의, 주택에 관한
- agricultural 형용사 농업의, 농사의
- marine 형용사 해양의, 해상의
- bunker 명사 (배의) 연료 (창고), 저장고
- domestic 형용사 국내의, 가정용의
- waterway 명사 수로, 항로

04

- average 형용사 평균의, 보통의 / 명사 평균, 평균 수준
- public 형용사 공립의, 공공의, 대중의
- elementary 형용사 초등의, 초급의, 기본적인, 근본적인
- secondary 형용사 중등 교육[학교]의, 이차적인, 부수적인
- whereas 접속사 반면에
- reverse 명사 (정)반대, 뒷면 / 동사 뒤바꾸다, 반전시키다, 뒤집다

05

- findings 명사 (연구) 결과
- access 동사 (컴퓨터에) 접속하다, ~에 접근하다
- given 형용사 주어진, 제시된

06

- distribution 명사 분포, 분배
- employment status 고용 상태
- A be followed by B B가 A의 뒤를 잇다
- temporary 형용사 임시의, 일시적인
- no contract worker 무계약직 직원
- permanent worker 정규직 직원
- comprise 동사 차지하다, 구성하다
- proportion 명사 비율

문제편 : p.084~091 | 정답과 해설 : p.097~105

07
- [ ] mode of transportation 교통수단
- [ ] commute 명사 통근 / 동사 통근하다
- [ ] in terms of ~의 경우에는, ~에 관하여
- [ ] lead 동사 앞서다, 이끌다

08
- [ ] household 명사 가정
- [ ] manage 동사 관리하다, 감독하다, 간신히 ~하다
- [ ] discipline 동사 훈육하다 / 명사 훈육, 규율

09
- [ ] disaster 명사 재해, 재난
- [ ] account for (비율을) 차지하다, 점유하다
- [ ] take up (공간·비율을) 차지하다

10
- [ ] renewable 형용사 재생 가능한
- [ ] biofuel 명사 바이오 연료
- [ ] hydropower 명사 수력 발전

11
- [ ] commuter 명사 통근자
- [ ] transportation 명사 교통(수단), 운송
- [ ] public transit 대중교통
- [ ] rank 동사 (순위를) 차지하다 / 명사 지위, 계급

12
- [ ] tourism 명사 관광, 관광업
- [ ] contribution 명사 기여
- [ ] compared to ~와 비교하여
- [ ] previous 형용사 전의, 이전의
- [ ] reverse 명사 반대 / 형용사 반대의 / 동사 뒤바꾸다

13
- [ ] except 전치사 ~을 제외하고
- [ ] proportion 명사 비율
- [ ] state 동사 말하다, 진술하다 / 명사 상태
- [ ] round 동사 반올림하다

14
- [ ] primary education 초등 교육
- [ ] whereas 접속사 그러나 (사실은), ~에 반하여
- [ ] reverse 명사 반대, 역

15
- [ ] dose 명사 1회분, 복용량
- [ ] measles 명사 홍역
- [ ] vaccination 명사 백신 접종
- [ ] vaccinate 동사 백신 접종을 하다
- [ ] Mediterranean 명사 지중해 / 형용사 지중해의
- [ ] decade 명사 10년

16
- [ ] targeted advertising 표적 광고
- [ ] intrusive 형용사 거슬리는, 침입하는
- [ ] convenient 형용사 편리한, 간편한
- [ ] inappropriate 형용사 부적절한, 알맞지 않은
- [ ] conduct 동사 수행하다, 행동하다

17
- [ ] protein 명사 단백질
- [ ] consumption 명사 섭취(량), 소비(량)
- [ ] measure 동사 측정하다, 재다
- [ ] average 형용사 평균의, 보통의
- [ ] daily 형용사 일일의, 매일의
- [ ] supply 명사 공급량, 비축량
- [ ] poultry 명사 가금류
- [ ] respectively 부사 각각
- [ ] consume 동사 섭취하다, 소비하다

18
- [ ] emission 명사 (빛·열·가스 등의) 배출, 배출물, 배기가스
- [ ] except 전치사 ~을 제외하고 / 접속사 ~라는 점만 제외하면
- [ ] surpass 동사 능가하다, 뛰어넘다
- [ ] in terms of ~에 있어서, ~에 관하여
- [ ] opposite 명사 반대(되는 사람·것) / 형용사 반대편의, 정반대의

19
- [ ] unpaid 형용사 무급의, 무보수의
- [ ] care 명사 돌봄, 보살핌
- [ ] notably 부사 특히
- [ ] individual 명사 사람, 개인
- [ ] reach 동사 ~에 달하다[이르다]
- [ ] compared to A A에 비해, A와 비교하여

09. 내용 일치 파악

01
- [ ] pass away 돌아가시다, 사망하다
- [ ] bring A up A를 기르다, 양육하다
- [ ] attend 동사 (~에) 다니다, 참석하다
- [ ] status 명사 지위, 상태
- [ ] tremendous 형용사 엄청난, 굉장한
- [ ] angelic 형용사 천사 같은
- [ ] willingness 명사 의지, 의사
- [ ] be fluent in ~에 유창하다
- [ ] a range of 다양한

02
- [ ] psychiatrist 명사 정신과 의사
- [ ] class 명사 계급, 계층
- [ ] absent 형용사 집을 비운, 부재한, 결석한
- [ ] care for ~을 돌보다[보살피다]
- [ ] primarily 부사 주로
- [ ] customary 형용사 관례적인, 습관적인
- [ ] boarding school 명사 기숙 학교
- [ ] recall 동사 회상하다, 기억해 내다
- [ ] traumatic 형용사 충격적인, 정신적 외상의
- [ ] development 명사 성장, 발달
- [ ] prove to V ~으로 판명되다[드러나다]
- [ ] enroll 동사 입학하다, 등록하다
- [ ] briefly 부사 잠시, 간단히
- [ ] consultant 명사 자문 위원, 상담가
- [ ] dominant 형용사 지배적인, 우세한

03
- [ ] document 동사 기록하다 / 명사 문서
- [ ] eventually 부사 결국
- [ ] drop out of school 학교를 중퇴하다
- [ ] migrant 명사 떠돌이, 이주자
- [ ] concerto 명사 협주곡
- [ ] inspiring 형용사 영감을 주는

04
- [ ] monarch 명사 제왕, 군주
- [ ] margin 명사 가장자리, 차이
- [ ] hind 형용사 뒤의
- [ ] hatch 동사 부화하다
- [ ] survive 동사 ~에서 살아남다
- [ ] migrate 동사 이주하다
- [ ] hibernate 동사 동면하다

05
- [ ] notable 형용사 저명한, 유명한
- [ ] meteorologist 명사 기상학자
- [ ] apparently 부사 짐작하건대, 듣자[보아] 하니
- [ ] practical 형용사 실질적인, 실용적인
- [ ] cyclonic circulation 명사 저기압성 순환
- [ ] warm air mass 온난 기단
- [ ] cold air mass 한랭 기단

06
- [ ] notable 형용사 유명한, 주목할 만한
- [ ] wed 동사 결혼하다
- [ ] arranged marriage 중매 결혼
- [ ] literacy 명사 식자율, 읽고 쓸 줄 아는 능력
- [ ] reject 동사 거부하다, 받아들이지 않다
- [ ] doctorate 명사 박사 학위
- [ ] botany 명사 식물학
- [ ] sugarcane 명사 사탕수수
- [ ] variety 명사 품종, 다양성, 변화
- [ ] co-author 동사 ~을 공동 집필하다 / 명사 공동 저자
- [ ] chromosome 명사 염색체
- [ ] atlas 명사 지도책, 도해집
- [ ] famine 명사 기근
- [ ] Prime Minister 명사 수상
- [ ] deforestation 명사 삼림 벌채
- [ ] advocate 명사 옹호자, 변호사
- [ ] hydroelectric 형용사 수력 발전의

07
- [ ] astronomy 명사 천문학
- [ ] origin 명사 기원, 유래
- [ ] manuscript 명사 원고
- [ ] attention 명사 관심, 주의
- [ ] director 명사 관리자, 감독
- [ ] assistant 명사 조수, 보조자
- [ ] calculator 명사 계산원, 계산기
- [ ] passionately 부사 열정적으로
- [ ] copy 명사 (책을 세는 단위) 부, 사본
- [ ] publication 명사 간행물, 출판

08
- [ ] run 동사 운영하다, 관리하다, 달리다

문제편 : p.092~104 | 정답과 해설 : p.105~119

- [ ] skyrocket 동사 급상승하다, 급등하다
- [ ] recognition 명사 인정, 인식
- [ ] seizure 명사 장악, 점령
- [ ] exhibit 동사 전시하다, 보이다
- [ ] emigrate 동사 이주하다, 이민 가다
- [ ] recapture 동사 되찾다, 탈환하다
- [ ] portray 동사 그리다, 묘사하다
- [ ] embody 동사 구체화하다, 형상화하다, 구현하다
- [ ] type 명사 (표)상, 전형, 본보기
- [ ] represent 동사 표현하다, 나타내다, 대표하다

09

- [ ] access 동사 이용하다, 접근하다
- [ ] athletic 형용사 운동의, 운동선수의
- [ ] facility 명사 시설, 기관
- [ ] racism 명사 인종 차별
- [ ] barefoot 부사 맨발로 / 형용사 맨발의
- [ ] equipment 명사 장비, 설비
- [ ] noticeable 형용사 눈에 띄는, 주목할 만한
- [ ] achievement 명사 성취, 업적
- [ ] competition 명사 대회, 경기, 경쟁
- [ ] compete in ~에 출전하다[참가하다]
- [ ] set a record 기록을 세우다
- [ ] accomplishment 명사 성과, 업적
- [ ] dedicate A to B A를 B에 바치다[헌신하다]

10

- [ ] portrait 명사 인물 사진, 초상화
- [ ] born into (~인 가정)에서 태어난
- [ ] devote oneself to N/V-ing ~에 열중하다[헌신하다]
- [ ] convert 동사 바꾸다, 전환시키다
- [ ] convince A to V A가 ~하도록 설득하다[납득시키다]
- [ ] fit 동사 (옷을) 입히다, (모양·크기가) 맞다
- [ ] theatrical 형용사 연극의
- [ ] costume 명사 의상, 복장
- [ ] compose 동사 구성하다, 작곡하다
- [ ] so-called 형용사 소위, 이른바
- [ ] convention 명사 관습, 전통, 대회
- [ ] critic 명사 비평가
- [ ] composition 명사 구도, 구성, 작품, 작곡
- [ ] appreciate 동사 높이 평가하다, 진가를 인정하다
- [ ] value 동사 가치를 두다 / 명사 가치
- [ ] spiritual 형용사 정신적인
- [ ] depth 명사 깊이
- [ ] medium 명사 표현 수단, 매체 (media의 단수형)

11

- [ ] psychiatrist 명사 정신과 의사
- [ ] neurology 명사 신경학
- [ ] politician 명사 정치인
- [ ] pope 명사 교황
- [ ] numerous 형용사 수많은
- [ ] lecture 동사 강연하다
- [ ] widely 부사 널리
- [ ] hold 동사 (직장·직무에) 재직하다
- [ ] professorship 명사 교수직

- [ ] award 동사 수여하다 / 명사 상
- [ ] honorary 형용사 (학위·지위 등) 명예의
- [ ] association 명사 (협)회
- [ ] honor 동사 수여하다 / 명사 명예, 명성

12

- [ ] codiscoverer 명사 공동 발견자
- [ ] conduct 동사 (연구 등을) 하다, 행동하다
- [ ] outbreak 명사 (전쟁 등의) 발발, 시작
- [ ] magnetic 형용사 자기(장)의, 자석의
- [ ] acoustic 형용사 음향의, 청각의
- [ ] wartime 형용사 전시의(전쟁 중의)
- [ ] intelligence 명사 정보, 기밀, 정보요원들
- [ ] collaborative 형용사 공동의

13

- [ ] advocate 동사 옹호하다, 지지하다
- [ ] ophthalmology 명사 안과학
- [ ] branch 명사 분야, 부서
- [ ] disorder 명사 (신체 기능의) 장애, 엉망, 무질서
- [ ] treatment 명사 치료, 처치, 대우
- [ ] patent 명사 특허

14

- [ ] blacksmith 명사 대장장이
- [ ] widely 부사 폭넓게, 널리
- [ ] priesthood 명사 사제직, 성직
- [ ] illness 명사 병, 질환
- [ ] take to N ~하기 시작하다
- [ ] botany 명사 식물학
- [ ] accompany 동사 ~와 동행하다[동반하다]
- [ ] household 명사 집안, 가정
- [ ] sample 명사 표본, 샘플
- [ ] assemble 동사 정리하다, 조립하다
- [ ] catalogue 명사 목록, 카탈로그
- [ ] work 명사 저서, 작품
- [ ] theology 명사 신학

15

- [ ] prominence 명사 명성, 유명함, 두드러짐
- [ ] own 동사 소유하다 / 형용사 ~ 자신의
- [ ] be unwilling to V ~하는 것을 꺼리다
- [ ] racial discrimination 인종 차별
- [ ] drive A to V A가 ~하게 만들다
- [ ] charitable 형용사 자선의, 자비로운
- [ ] found 동사 설립하다 (found-founded-founded)
- [ ] merge 동사 합병하다, 통합하다
- [ ] thrive 동사 번창하다, 번영하다

16

- [ ] mind 명사 지성인, 마음, 정신
- [ ] doctoral degree 박사 학위
- [ ] engineering 명사 공학, 공학 기술
- [ ] travel 동사 다니다, 이동하다, 여행하다
- [ ] consultant 명사 자문 위원, 상담가
- [ ] advise 동사 조언하다, 충고하다, (정식으로) 알리다

17

- [ ] quit 동사 그만두다, (살던 곳을) 떠나다 (quit-quit-quit)
- [ ] set up 세우다, 건립하다, 설치하다 (set-set-set)
- [ ] pond 명사 연못
- [ ] incredible 형용사 엄청난, 놀랄만한, 대단한
- [ ] journal 명사 저널, 일기
- [ ] volume 명사 (전집 따위의) 권, 책, (~의) 양

18

- [ ] zoology 명사 동물학
- [ ] instructor 명사 강사, 교사
- [ ] distinguished 형용사 훌륭한, 뛰어난
- [ ] career 명사 경력, 직업
- [ ] a series of 일련의
- [ ] arctic 형용사 북극의
- [ ] expedition 명사 탐험, 원정
- [ ] fur 명사 모피, 털
- [ ] biological 형용사 생물학의
- [ ] consultant 명사 컨설턴트, 고문
- [ ] examine 동사 검토하다, 살펴보다
- [ ] population 명사 개체군, 개체수
- [ ] demonstrate 동사 설명하다, 입증하다
- [ ] nature 명사 본질, 특질
- [ ] food chain 명사 먹이 사슬
- [ ] establish 동사 설립하다, 확립하다
- [ ] editor 명사 편집자
- [ ] shape 동사 형성하다, 구체화하다

10. 안내문

01

- [ ] attic 명사 다락방
- [ ] donate 동사 기부하다, 기증하다
- [ ] reuse 명사 재사용 / 동사 재사용하다
- [ ] wearable 형용사 입을 수 있는 / 명사 의복
- [ ] bedding 명사 침구류
- [ ] stain 명사 얼룩, 오염
- [ ] drop off 버리다

02

- [ ] width 명사 너비, 폭
- [ ] underarm 형용사 팔을 아래로 내린 / 부사 팔을 아래로 내려서
- [ ] land 동사 안착하다, 안착시키다, 착륙하다 / 명사 육지, 땅
- [ ] divide 동사 분배하다, 나누다 / 명사 분할, 분배
- [ ] equally 부사 균등하게, 똑같이, 마찬가지로
- [ ] champion 명사 우승자

03

- [ ] speech 명사 말하기, 연설
- [ ] show off 뽐내다, 으스대다, 자랑하다
- [ ] submission 명사 제출, 굴복
- [ ] mention 동사 언급하다, 거론하다

04

- [ ] endangered 형용사 멸종 위기의
- [ ] species 명사 종

08 09 10 안내문

문제편 : p.105~113 정답과 해설 : p.119~127

- registration fee 명사 등록비

05
- virtual 형용사 가상의
- gala 명사 행사, 축제
- host 동사 주최하다
- virtually 부사 가상으로, 거의, 사실상
- auction 명사 경매

06
- in-person 형용사 대면의, 직접
- tram 명사 트램, 전차
- application 명사 신청(서)

07
- refreshing 형용사 상쾌한, 상쾌함을 주는
- feature 명사 특징 / 동사 특별히 포함하다
- coughing 명사 기침
- snoring 명사 코 고는 소리
- adjust 동사 조정하다, 조절하다

08
- talent 명사 재능
- show off 뽐내다, 자랑하다
- instrument 명사 악기, 기구
- submit 동사 제출하다
- entry 명사 참가작

09
- promote 동사 장려하다, 촉진하다, 홍보하다, 승진하다
- compassion 명사 온정, 동정, 연민
- qualification 명사 자격, 자질
- registration 명사 등록, 기재

10
- virtual 형용사 가상의, 사실상의
- athletic 형용사 운동의, 운동 경기의
- complete 동사 완성하다, 끝내다 / 형용사 완전한
- submit 동사 제출하다
- entry 명사 출품작
- exceed 동사 초과하다, 넘다

11
- clay 명사 점토, 찰흙
- ceramic 형용사 도자기의 / 명사 도자기
- glaze 동사 유약을 바르다 / 명사 유약
- be suitable for ~에게 적합하다
- fee 명사 참가비, 요금, 사례금
- instruction 명사 강습, 설명, 지시

12
- turn A into B A를 B로 바꾸다
- in person 직접

13
- sign language 명사 수화
- consider 동사 고려하다, 검토하다
- be accompanied by ~을 동반하다, 동행하다
- previous 형용사 이전의, 사전의
- tuition 명사 수업료, 수업
- available 형용사 가능한, 이용할 수 있는

14
- county 명사 카운티, 군(郡)
- job fair 채용 박람회
- register 동사 등록하다
- job seeker 구직자
- attendee 명사 참가자
- enhance 동사 향상하다
- refreshment 명사 (주로 복수) 다과

15
- manual 명사 설명서, 안내서 / 형용사 수동의
- note 명사 유의 사항, 메모
- indicator 명사 표시기, 지표
- charge 동사 충전하다, 청구하다
- operate 동사 작동시키다, 조작하다
- wirelessly 부사 무선으로
- load 동사 (카메라 등의 장비에 필름 등을) 넣다, (짐을) 싣다
- lift 동사 들어 올리다, 올리다
- insert 동사 넣다, 끼우다
- face 동사 향하다, 직면하다
- downward 부사 아래로, 아래쪽으로

16
- illuminate 동사 비추다, 밝히다
- route 명사 경로, 길
- surround 동사 둘러싸다, 에워싸다
- admire 동사 감탄하다, 존경하다
- souvenir 명사 기념품

17
- need 명사 요구, 필요, 욕구
- dispose of ~을 처리하다, 없애다
- properly 부사 올바르게, 적절히
- beverage 명사 음료
- strictly 부사 엄격하게
- ban 동사 금지하다

18
- back-to-school 형용사 신학기의
- giveaway 명사 경품, 증정품
- host 동사 개최하다, 주최하다 / 명사 주인
- rain or shine 날씨에 관계없이, 비가 오든 화창하든
- resident 명사 주민, 거주자
- valid 형용사 유효한, 타당한
- first-come, first-served 선착순

19
- adaptation 명사 각색, 적응
- play 명사 연극, 희곡, 놀이 / 동사 (연극·영화 등에서) 연기하다, 배역을 맡다, 놀다
- look for ~을 찾다, 구하다, 바라다, 기대하다
- background 명사 경력, 전력, 배경, 배후 사정, 사전 지식
- preferred 형용사 우대되는, 우선되는
- completed 형용사 완성된, 완전한
- signed 형용사 서명된, 합의된

20
- cookery 명사 요리(법)
- a variety of 여러 가지의
- ingredient 명사 재료
- refund 명사 환불(금) / 동사 환불하다

21
- come from ~에서 오다, ~에서 생겨나다
- combination 명사 결합, 조합
- pick up 줍다, 치우다, 정리하다
- litter 명사 쓰레기 / 동사 (쓰레기 등을) 버리다
- movement 명사 (조직적으로 벌이는) 운동, (몸·신체 부위의) 움직임
- equipment 명사 (불가산 명사) 장비들
- be welcome to V ~해도 좋다
- donate 동사 기부하다
- conservation 명사 (자연) 보호, 보존
- reservation 명사 예약

22
- assign 동사 배정하다, 부과하다
- literary 형용사 문학의
- submit 동사 제출하다, 항복하다
- submission 명사 제출, 항복
- entry 명사 출품작
- revise 동사 수정하다
- finalist 명사 결승 진출자
- via 전치사 (특정 시스템 등을) 통하여
- overall 형용사 전체의, 종합적인

23
- indicator 명사 표시기, 지표
- standby 명사 대기, 대역 / 형용사 대기의, 대역의
- adjust 동사 조절하다, 적응하다
- focus 명사 초점, 주목 / 동사 초점을 맞추다, 집중하다
- port 명사 포트(기기 접속 단자), 항구

24
- attract 동사 끌다
- attention 명사 주의, 관심
- instinct 명사 본능
- via 전치사 ~을 통해
- extra 명사 여분 / 형용사 여분의, 추가의

25
- escape 명사 탈출 / 동사 탈출하다
- city-wide 형용사 도시 전역의
- turn A into B A를 B로 바꾸다
- wherein 그곳에서
- race 동사 질주하다, 경주하다
- challenge 명사 도전 과제, 큰 문제
- location 명사 지점, 장소
- on a daily basis 매일
- adventure 명사 모험, 모험심

26
- indoor 형용사 실내의, 실내용의
- cancellation 명사 취소, 무효화
- policy 명사 정책, 방침
- afterwards 부사 이후, 나중에

문제편 : p.114~124 정답과 해설 : p.127~134

27

- panel — 명사 위원단, 패널
- student council — 명사 학생회, 학생 자치위원회
- deadline — 명사 마감 기한, 마감 시간
- announcement — 명사 발표, 공고

28

- pour — 동사 따르다, 붓다
- on one's own — 스스로, 혼자 힘으로
- dairy — 명사 유제품 / 형용사 유제품의
- alternative — 형용사 대체의 / 명사 대체품, 대안
- available — 형용사 사용[이용]할 수 있는

29

- bonding — 명사 유대, 긴밀한 유대
- preserve — 명사 보호 구역 / 동사 보존하다, 보호하다
- legal — 형용사 법적인, 합법적인
- guardian — 명사 보호자, 후견인
- first aid kit — 구급상자

30

- explore — 동사 탐구하다, 탐험하다
- wonder — 명사 경이로움 / 동사 궁금해하다
- engineering — 명사 공학 기술
- robotics — 명사 로봇 공학

31

- diverse — 형용사 다양한, 다른
- highlight — 명사 주요 사항, 하이라이트, 가장 흥미로운 부분 / 동사 강조하다
- local — 형용사 현지의, 지역의 / 명사 현지인
- chef — 명사 요리사, 주방장
- entry — 명사 입장

32

- clean-up — 명사 청소
- annual — 형용사 연례의, 매년의
- casual — 형용사 (관계가) 가벼운, 격식을 차리지 않는
- gathering — 명사 모임, 집회, 수집
- material — 명사 도구, 재료

33

- sustainable — 형용사 (환경 파괴 없이) 지속 가능한, 지탱할 수 있는
- inspire — 동사 영감을 주다, 고무[격려]하다
- fabulous — 형용사 멋진, 믿어지지 않는, 엄청난
- marketplace — 명사 장터, 시장
- upcycle — 동사 (재활용품을) 업사이클하다, 더 나은 것으로 만들다
- talk — 명사 강연, 연설, 이야기
- in advance — 사전에, 미리, 선지급으로

11. 빈칸 추론(1)-어휘, 짧은 어구

01

- tendency — 명사 경향, 추세
- purchase — 명사 구매 / 동사 구매하다
- obtain — 동사 얻다, 입수하다
- possession — 명사 소유물
- spiral — 명사 소용돌이, 나선
- consumption — 명사 소비
- spot — 동사 발견하다 / 명사 점, 곳
- go with — ~와 어울리다
- chain reaction — 연쇄 반응
- remind — 동사 상기시키다
- detergent — 명사 세제
- isolation — 명사 고립 (상태)
- trigger — 동사 유발하다

02

- violate — 동사 거스르다, 위반하다, 어기다
- expectation — 명사 기대, 예상
- fundamental — 형용사 근본적인, 본질적인, 필수적인
- a series of — 일련의
- identical — 형용사 동일한, 똑같은
- note — 명사 음, 음표, 메모
- auditory — 형용사 청각의, 귀의
- progressively — 부사 점진적으로, 꾸준히, 계속해서
- adaptation — 명사 적응, 각색
- deceptively — 부사 현혹될 정도로, 속여서
- anticipate — 동사 예상하다, 예측하다, 기대하다
- primary — 형용사 1차의, 첫 번째의, 주요한, 기본적인
- cortex — 명사 피질
- fade away — 사라지다
- vigorously — 부사 힘차게, 활발하게, 격렬하게
- fire — 동사 발화하다, 점화되다, 해고하다
- matter — 동사 중요하다, 문제 되다 / 명사 문제, 물질
- alternating — 형용사 교차의, 교대의
- trigger — 동사 일으키다, 촉발시키다 / 명사 방아쇠

03

- peculiar — 형용사 독특한, 기이한
- profit — 동사 이익을 얻다[주다] / 명사 이익, 수익
- regulation — 명사 규제, 규정
- illustration — 명사 예시, 실례
- world-renowned — 형용사 세계적으로 유명한
- cut flowers — 절화, 잘라 낸 꽃을 이용할 목적으로 재배되는 화훼
- contaminate — 동사 오염시키다, 더럽히다
- fertilizer — 명사 비료
- pesticide — 명사 농약, 살충제
- adopt — 동사 채택하다, 입양하다
- be designed to V — ~하도록 고안되다
- cut A in half — A를 절반으로 줄이다
- ultimately — 부사 결국, 궁극적으로
- face — 동사 ~에 직면하다[맞서다]
- strict — 형용사 엄격한, 엄한
- method — 명사 방법, 수단
- maintain — 동사 유지하다, 지속하다
- in response — 대응으로, 반응으로
- shift — 동사 전환하다, 바뀌다
- cultivation — 명사 재배, 경작
- circulate — 동사 순환시키다
- loop — 명사 루프, 고리, 순환
- substrate — 명사 배양판
- release — 동사 배출하다, 방출하다

04

- respectable — 형용사 훌륭한, 존경할 만한
- institution — 명사 단체, 기관, 협회
- carry — 동사 (특징을) 지니다[갖다], 나르다
- trace back to — ~로 거슬러 올라가다
- primitive — 형용사 원시적인
- hide — 명사 가죽 / 동사 숨기다
- gut — 명사 내장
- formidable — 형용사 강력한, 어마어마한
- aggression — 명사 공격(성)
- awe-inspiring — 형용사 경외감을 자아내는
- assertiveness — 명사 당당함, 자기주장
- summon up — ~을 떠올리다[불러일으키다]
- band — 명사 무리
- dominance — 명사 지배, 우월함
- predatory — 형용사 공격적인, 포식동물 같은

05

- relativity — 명사 상대성
- mechanism — 명사 메커니즘(어떤 대상의 작동 원리나 구조)
- waistline — 명사 허리둘레
- function — 명사 함수, 기능
- consume — 동사 소비하다
- comparison — 명사 비교
- alternative — 명사 대안 / 형용사 대체 가능한
- nourishment — 명사 영양분, 음식물

06

- peasant — 명사 농부, 소작농
- crop — 명사 농작물, 수확량
- yield — 명사 생산량, 산출 / 동사 생산하다, 양보하다
- marvelously — 부사 엄청나게, 놀라울 만큼
- starve — 동사 굶주리다
- congratulate A on B — B에 대해 A(사람)를 축하하다
- level — 명사 수준 / 동사 평평하게 하다
- scatter — 동사 흩어지게 만들다, 흩어지다
- inevitable — 형용사 피할 수 없는
- occasional — 형용사 이따금의, 가끔의
- vary — 동사 서로 다르다, 달라지다
- weed — 명사 잡초 / 동사 잡초를 뽑다
- trim — 동사 다듬다, 손질하다
- organic — 형용사 유기농의, 유기체에서 만들어진
- fertilize — 동사 비료를 주다, 수정시키다

07

- need — 동사 필요로 하다 / 명사 욕구, 필요
- hardwired — 형용사 타고난
- terrestrial — 형용사 육생의, 지구의
- vertebrate — 명사 척추동물
- mammal — 명사 포유동물, 포유류
- concentration — 명사 농도, 집중
- evolve — 동사 진화하다, 진화시키다
- dependent — 형용사 의존적인
- ingredient — 명사 성분, 구성 요소

문제편 : p.125~135 | 정답과 해설 : p.135~142

☐ remedy 동사 해결하다, 고치다 / 명사 약, 치료
☐ herbivore 명사 초식 동물
☐ eliminate 동사 배설하다, 제거하다
☐ excess 명사 초과분, 과잉
☐ seek out 찾아다니다
☐ receptor 명사 수용기
☐ reward 동사 보상하다 / 명사 보상(금)
☐ periodic 형용사 주기적인
☐ starvation 명사 굶주림, 기아

08

☐ regulate 동사 통제하다, 규제하다
☐ varying 형용사 가지각색의, 바뀌는, 변화하는
☐ induce 동사 유도하다
☐ part-time 형용사 시간제의

09

☐ contemporary 형용사 현대의, 동시대의
☐ remarkable 형용사 주목할 만한, 놀라운
☐ unstable 형용사 불안정한
☐ inevitable 형용사 불가피한, 필연적인
☐ intimate 형용사 친밀한, 사적인
☐ companion 명사 동반자
☐ fragility 명사 연약함, 부서지기 쉬움

10

☐ landscape 명사 상황, 풍경
☐ enterprise 명사 기업, 회사
☐ grant 명사 보조금 / 동사 주다, 승인하다
☐ capital 명사 자본(금), 수도
☐ commercial 형용사 상업의 / 명사 광고 (방송)
☐ financing 명사 금융, 자금 조달
☐ loan 명사 대출(금) / 동사 대출하다, 빌려주다
☐ significant 형용사 중대한, 상당한
☐ drawback 명사 문제점, 결점
☐ make use of ~을 이용하다, 사용하다
☐ pay back 상환하다, 되갚다
☐ incentive 명사 동기, 장려책
☐ professionalize 동사 전문화하다, 직업화하다
☐ unhealthy 형용사 불건전한, 건강하지 않은
☐ substantial 형용사 상당한, 중대한, 실질적인
☐ alternative 명사 대안 / 형용사 대안이 되는, 대체 가능한

11

☐ gut (instinct) 명사 직감, 창자
☐ perception 명사 인식, 지각
☐ inconsistency 명사 불일치
☐ fleeting 형용사 순식간의, 잠깐 동안의
☐ match 동사 연결시키다, 연결하다, 어울리다 / 명사 연결, 일치하는 것
☐ resort to N/V-ing ~에 의존하다
☐ assign 동사 부여하다, 맡기다, 할당하다
☐ visceral 형용사 본능적인, 강한 감정에 따른
☐ pit of one's stomach (긴장감 따위를 느끼게 되는) 배 속
☐ butterflies 명사 (복수형) 긴장감, 불안한 마음
☐ discard 동사 버리다

☐ vulnerability 명사 취약성
☐ concrete 형용사 구체적인

12

☐ define 동사 정의하다
☐ subordinate 명사 부하 / 형용사 종속된, 부수적인
☐ go along with ~을 따르다, ~에 동의하다, 동조하다
☐ empower 동사 힘·권한을 주다
☐ vice versa 부사 반대로, 거꾸로
☐ analyst 명사 분석가
☐ constituent 명사 구성원, 구성 성분, 유권자
☐ wind up V-ing(=end up V-ing) 결국 ~하게 되다
☐ fluid 형용사 유동적인
☐ objective 명사 목표, 목적 / 형용사 객관적인
☐ follow one's lead ~을 따르다, ~의 주도를 따르다
☐ attend 동사 참석하다
☐ expert 명사 전문가 / 형용사 전문가의
☐ regardless of ~와 관계없이, 상관없이
☐ rigid 형용사 엄격한, 뻣뻣한
☐ stable 형용사 안정된, 안정적인
☐ apparent 형용사 분명한, 명백한

13

☐ make sense of ~을 이해하다
☐ narrative 명사 이야기, 서사
☐ reflection 명사 성찰, 반영
☐ examine 동사 살펴보다, 조사하다, 검사하다
☐ meditate 동사 숙고하다, 명상하다
☐ emperor 명사 황제
☐ general 명사 장군
☐ exemplar 명사 본보기, 모범, 표본
☐ virtuous 형용사 도덕적인
☐ imitate 동사 모방하다
☐ chronicler 명사 연대기 학자
☐ account 명사 이야기, 설명, 계좌 / 동사 간주하다
☐ chivalrous 형용사 기사도적인, 예의 바른
☐ historical 형용사 역사적인
☐ the rise and fall 흥망성쇠
☐ oppression 명사 억압, 탄압
☐ means 명사 수단
☐ mediate 동사 중재하다, 조정하다
☐ integral 형용사 필수적인

14

☐ rebel 명사 반항자, 반역자
☐ turn A off A를 흥미를 잃게 만들다
☐ alternative 명사 대안, 양자택일 / 형용사 대체 가능한, 양자택일의
☐ persuader 명사 설득자
☐ independence 명사 독립성
☐ uniqueness 명사 유일성
☐ present 동사 제시하다
☐ preference 명사 선호
☐ trick 동사 속이다
☐ defiance 명사 반항, 저항
☐ suit 동사 맞다, 적합하다

☐ mainstream 명사 주류(主流)

15

☐ a good many 상당히 많은, 꽤 많은
☐ universality 명사 보편성, 일반성
☐ conference 명사 학회, 회의
☐ hold 동사 개최하다, 열다, 잡다
☐ quote 동사 인용하다, 전달하다
☐ analogy 명사 유사성, 비유
☐ performance 명사 행위, 실행
☐ analogous 형용사 유사한, 비슷한
☐ aesthetic 형용사 심미적인, 미학적인
☐ craftsmanship 명사 장인 정신, 솜씨, 기예
☐ multidisciplinary 형용사 여러 학문 분야에 걸친, 다학적인

16

☐ under the sway of ~의 영향 아래, ~의 지배 아래
☐ entrance 동사 매료시키다, 황홀하게 하다 / 명사 입장
☐ encounter 명사 만남 / 동사 만나다, 직면하다
☐ enrich 동사 풍부하게 하다, 부유하게 하다
☐ landscape 명사 풍경
☐ intelligence 명사 지성, 지능
☐ vulnerability 명사 취약성, 상처받기 쉬움
☐ creeping 형용사 슬며시 접근하는, 서서히 진행되는
☐ superiority 명사 우월성
☐ close off 동사 차단시키다, 폐쇄시키다
☐ advocate 동사 주장하다, 지지하다 / 명사 대변인, 옹호자
☐ skeptical 형용사 회의적인, 의심 많은
☐ burden 동사 부담을 주다 / 명사 짐, 부담

17

☐ vary in ~이 다양하다, 여러 가지다
☐ recordability 명사 기록 가능성
☐ preservability 명사 저장 가능성
☐ intact 형용사 온전한, 전혀 다치지 않은
☐ preservation 명사 보존, 보호
☐ suspend 동사 멈추다, 중단하다
☐ reexamine 동사 다시 돌아보다, 재검토하다
☐ slip 동사 빠져나가다, 미끄러지다 / 명사 실수
☐ testing 명사 검증, 시험
☐ mysteriously 부사 불가사의하게, 미궁 속에
☐ accidental 형용사 우발적인, 우연한
☐ everlasting 형용사 영원히 존재하는, 변치 않는

18

☐ philosophical 형용사 철학적인
☐ recognition 명사 인식
☐ ignorance 명사 무지
☐ hinder 동사 방해하다
☐ conception 명사 개념, 구상, 이해
☐ beforehand 부사 미리
☐ work with ~을 공부 대상으로 하다, ~와 함께 일하다
☐ acquire 동사 얻다
☐ self-assurance 명사 자신(감)
☐ conformity 명사 순응, 따름
☐ thinker 명사 사상가, 생각하는 사람

문제편 : p.135~140 정답과 해설 : p.142~150

comprehension 명사 이해력

19

- come across as ~라는 인상을 주다
- subordinate 명사 부하, 하급자 / 형용사 종속된, 부수적인
- sympathizer 명사 동조자, 지지자
- belong 동사 속하다
- cover 명사 위장 / 동사 씌우다, 가리다
- cosy(=cozy) 형용사 편안한, 아늑한
- loiter 동사 서성거리다
- corridor 명사 복도
- fawn 동사 알랑거리다
- test 명사 시험대, 시험
- loyalty 명사 충성심
- challenge 명사 도전, 문제, 어려움 / 동사 도전하다, 이의를 제기하다
- controversy 명사 논쟁
- be eager to V ~을 열망하다
- reluctant 형용사 꺼리는, 주저하는
- commitment 명사 헌신, 약속

20

- appreciate 동사 이해하다, 감사하다, 감상하다
- notion 명사 개념, 생각
- give credit for ~에 대한 공로를 인정하다
- breakthrough 명사 획기적 발견, 돌파구
- treat 동사 간주하다, 다루다, 치료하다, 고치다
- operate 동사 일하다, 움직이다, 작용하다
- get/go nowhere 아무런 성과를 얻지 못하다
- trial and error 명사 시행착오
- superiority 명사 우월성
- collective 형용사 집단적인, 집단의

21

- lasting 형용사 지속적인, 영속적인
- struggle 동사 어려움을 겪다, 애쓰다, 발버둥치다 / 명사 발버둥질, 노력
- be traced to ~으로 거슬러 올라가다
- infancy 명사 유아기
- bind 동사 단결시키다, 묶다
- pursue 동사 추구하다, 추적하다
- brief 형용사 짧은, 간단한
- passive 형용사 수동적인, 소극적인
- adopt 동사 취하다, 채택하다, 입양하다

22

- evolve 동사 진화하다, 발달하다
- perceive 동사 인식하다, 감지하다
- unusualness 명사 특이함, 특이성
- encode 동사 (정보를 특정한 형식으로) 입력하다
- neurologist 명사 신경학자
- with A in mind A를 염두에 두고, 고려하여
- stimulation 명사 자극
- expose 동사 노출하다
- demonstration 명사 실연, 직접 보여 줌
- enthusiasm 명사 열의, 열성
- working memory 작업 기억
- devote 동사 전념하다, 전념하다, 헌신하다
- perceptual 형용사 지각의
- feed 동사 충족하다, 먹이를 주다
- exploratory 형용사 탐구적인

23

- profession 명사 직업, 전문직
- practitioner 명사 전문직 종사자(특히 의사, 변호사)
- clergy 명사 성직자(들)
- means 명사 (복수형으로) 수단, 방법
- draw 동사 끌어내다, 추첨하다, 인출하다, 비기다
- in nature 본질적으로
- in practice 실제로
- serve 동사 ~에게 봉사하다, 도움이 되다, 제공하다
- fire 동사 해고하다, 발사하다
- at will 마음대로
- derive 동사 (이익·즐거움 등을) 얻다, 끌어내다, ~에서 유래하다
- revenue 명사 수익, 수입
- disregard 명사 무시 / 동사 무시하다
- public opinion 명사 여론
- overconfidence 명사 과신, 지나친 자신

24

- capacity 명사 능력, 용량
- solitude 명사 혼자 있음, 고독
- in the presence of ~가 있을 때, ~의 앞에서
- attentive 형용사 관심을 가져주는, 주의를 기울이는, 배려하는
- fall 동사 (어둠·침묵 등이) 찾아오다, 떨어지다
- increasingly 부사 점점 더, 갈수록 더
- gradually 부사 점차, 서서히
- reverie 명사 공상
- all the while 내내, 그동안 쭉
- available 형용사 시간을 낼 수 있는, 이용할 수 있는
- attachment 명사 애착, 부착
- enable 동사 ~을 가능하게 하다

25

- primordial 형용사 원시의, 원시적인
- largely 부사 대체로, 주로
- water vapo(u)r 명사 수증기
- carbon dioxide 명사 이산화탄소
- sulfur dioxide 명사 이산화황
- nitrogen 명사 질소
- appearance 명사 출현, 출연, 외모
- subsequent 형용사 그 후의, 뒤이은
- exceedingly 부사 극히, 몹시, 대단히
- primitive 형용사 원시적인, 발달되지 않은
- organism 명사 생물체, 유기체, 생물
- microbe 명사 미생물
- liberate 동사 (화합물에서) 유리(遊離)시키다, 해방하다
- nuclei 명사 핵 (nucleus의 복수형)
- content 명사 함량, 내용, 목차
- emergence 명사 출현, 등장
- concentration 명사 농도, 집중
- requirement 명사 필요조건, 필수품
- sustain 동사 유지하다, 지속하다, 견디다
- constancy 명사 불변성, 충성

26

- enormous 형용사 거대한
- premature 형용사 섣부른, 시기상조의
- superficial 형용사 피상적인
- underlying 형용사 근원적인
- exercise 동사 발휘하다, 행사하다, 운동하다
- patience 명사 인내심
- diverse 형용사 다양한
- downturn 명사 침체, 하락
- favor 동사 선호하다
- layoff 명사 해고
- salary 명사 임금
- push for ~을 계속 요구하다, 추진하다
- call for ~을 요청하다
- ease 동사 완화하다
- tension 명사 긴장
- examine 동사 검토하다, 검사하다
- thoroughly 부사 철저하게
- implication 명사 영향, 암시

27

- means 명사 (복수형으로) 수단, 방법, 방도
- assert 동사 행사하다, 주장하다, 확고히 하다
- get along with ~와 잘 지내다
- equal 명사 동등한 사람 / 형용사 동일한, 평등한
- obedient 형용사 복종하는, 말을 잘 듣는, 순종적인
- rebellious 형용사 (규칙·일반 통념 등에 대해) 반항적인
- subordinate 명사 부하, 하급자 / 형용사 종속된, 부차적인
- deliberately 부사 의도적으로, 고의로, 신중하게
- dose 동사 (약 등을) 주다, 투여하다 / 명사 1회 복용량
- moderate 형용사 적정한, 적당한, 보통의, 중간의
- thereby 부사 그렇게 함으로써, 그것 때문에
- negotiate 동사 협상하다, 성사시키다, 타결하다
- please 동사 기쁘게 하다, 만족시키다
- overcome 동사 극복하다 (overcome-overcame-overcome)
- arise 동사 생기다, 발생하다, (무엇의 결과로) 유발되다 (arise-arose-arisen)
- lesson 명사 교훈, 가르침
- verbal 형용사 언어적인, 언어의

28

- predictable 형용사 예측할 수 있는, 예측 가능한
- precious 형용사 귀중한, 귀한
- desirable 형용사 바람직한, 가치 있는
- intrinsic 형용사 내재적인, 본질적인
- fixed 형용사 고정된
- commodity 명사 상품, 생산물
- dictator 명사 독재자
- currency 명사 통화, 화폐

문제편 : p.141~145 | 정답과 해설 : p.150~159

29

- [ ] coincidence 명사 우연, 우연의 일치
- [ ] statistically 부사 통계적으로, 통계학상으로
- [ ] irrational 형용사 비이성적인, 불합리한
- [ ] glorious 형용사 영광스러운, 영예로운
- [ ] obedience 명사 순응, 복종
- [ ] phrase 동사 표현하다 / 명사 구, 구절
- [ ] mysterious 형용사 신비한, 이해하기 힘든
- [ ] assume 동사 가정하다, 전제하다, 추정하다
- [ ] intervention 명사 개입, 간섭
- [ ] occurrence 명사 발생, 존재, 나타남
- [ ] capability 명사 능력, 역량
- [ ] grasp 동사 이해하다, 파악하다, 손에 꽉 잡다
- [ ] methodical 형용사 체계적인, 꼼꼼한
- [ ] divine 형용사 신의, 신적인
- [ ] inspiration 명사 영감, 영감을 주는 사람[것]
- [ ] check out 확인하다, 대출하다
- [ ] investigate 동사 조사하다, 연구하다
- [ ] source 명사 근원, 출처
- [ ] excuse 명사 변명, 핑계 / 동사 용서하다

30

- [ ] limit 명사 한계, 한도 / 동사 제한하다
- [ ] capability 명사 능력, 역량
- [ ] push 동사 밀어붙이다, 압박하다
- [ ] misguide 동사 잘못 이해하다, 오도하다
- [ ] direct 동사 향하다 / 형용사 직접적인
- [ ] repetitive 형용사 반복적인, 반복되는
- [ ] vertical 형용사 수직의, 세로의
- [ ] point 동사 뾰족하게 하다, 가리키다
- [ ] heel 명사 발뒤꿈치, 뒤꿈치
- [ ] rapid 형용사 빠른, 민첩한, 서두르는
- [ ] rate 명사 속도, 비율
- [ ] alignment 명사 정렬, 가지런함
- [ ] rotation axis 명사 회전축
- [ ] constraint 명사 제약, 통제
- [ ] impose 동사 (강제로) 주다, 부과하다
- [ ] minimize 동사 최소화하다, 축소하다
- [ ] potential 형용사 잠재적인 / 명사 가능성, 잠재력
- [ ] injury 명사 부상, 상처
- [ ] hostility 명사 적대감, 적의
- [ ] morality 명사 도덕, 도덕성

31

- [ ] stamp 명사 우표 / 동사 발을 구르다
- [ ] serve 동사 도움이 되다, 수행하다, 제공하다
- [ ] practical 형용사 실용적인, 현실적인
- [ ] side 형용사 부수적인 / 명사 면, 쪽
- [ ] attraction 명사 매력, 끌림
- [ ] short 형용사 부족한, 짧은
- [ ] arrange 동사 배열하다, 정리하다
- [ ] agreement 명사 합의, 동의
- [ ] rating 명사 평가, 순위
- [ ] classify 동사 분류하다, 구분하다
- [ ] be deprived of ~을 빼앗기다
- [ ] deem 동사 (~로) 여기다[생각하다]
- [ ] excess 명사 과잉, 초과

32

- [ ] unfavorable 형용사 불리한, 호의적이 아닌
- [ ] outcome 명사 결과, 성과
- [ ] outrage 동사 분노를 일으키다 / 명사 격분, 격노
- [ ] combination 명사 조합
- [ ] consolation 명사 위로, 위안
- [ ] prize 명사 상, 포상
- [ ] attribute A to B A를 B의 탓으로 돌리다
- [ ] reassure 동사 안심시키다
- [ ] not nearly 결코 ~가 아닌
- [ ] externalize 동사 외적 원인으로 돌리다, 외면화하다
- [ ] fair and square 정정당당하게
- [ ] deserve 동사 ~을 받을 만하다, 누릴 자격이 있다

33

- [ ] ethnologist 명사 민족학자
- [ ] in-depth 형용사 심층적인, 철저하고 상세한
- [ ] stretch back ~으로 거슬러 올라가다
- [ ] century 명사 1세기, 100년
- [ ] reproduction 명사 복제(품), 재생산, 번식
- [ ] engraving 명사 판화, 조각(술)
- [ ] dimension 명사 크기, 규모, 차원
- [ ] plate 명사 판, 접시
- [ ] diverse 형용사 다양한, 다른, 별개의
- [ ] origin 명사 기원, 출신
- [ ] analyse 동사 분석하다, 조사하다
- [ ] constant 형용사 일정한, 끊임없는
- [ ] element 명사 요소, 성분
- [ ] intuitive 형용사 직관적인, 직감에 의한
- [ ] approximate 형용사 대략적인, 근사치인
- [ ] precise 형용사 정확한, 정밀한
- [ ] statistical 형용사 통계적인
- [ ] reduce A to B A를 B로 정리하다
- [ ] unambiguously 부사 분명하게
- [ ] profoundly 부사 완전히, 매우, 깊이
- [ ] scale 명사 척도, 규모, 등급
- [ ] practically 부사 거의, 사실상
- [ ] be subject to A A의 영향을 받다
- [ ] periodic 형용사 주기적인, 시대의, 간헐적인

12. 빈칸 추론(2)-긴 어구, 문장

01

- [ ] inspiration 명사 영감
- [ ] bearable 형용사 견딜 수 있는
- [ ] result in ~로 이끌다[야기하다]
- [ ] spiritual 형용사 정신적인
- [ ] absence 명사 부재, 없음, 결석
- [ ] heartache 명사 심적 고통
- [ ] get to know 알게 되다
- [ ] profound 형용사 심오한
- [ ] bubble over (흥분·열광 등이) 벅차오르다
- [ ] be flooded with ~로 넘쳐나다
- [ ] contrast A with B A와 B를 대조하다[대비시키다]
- [ ] archive 명사 기록 보관소
- [ ] limbic system 변연계
- [ ] biological 형용사 생물학적(인), 생물학의
- [ ] lasting 형용사 지속되는, 영속적인
- [ ] facilitator 명사 촉진제, 조력자
- [ ] barrier 명사 장벽

02

- [ ] vulnerable 형용사 취약한
- [ ] potential 형용사 잠재적인, 가능성이 있는 / 명사 잠재력
- [ ] infection 명사 감염, 전염
- [ ] make one's way 나아가다, 가다, 출세하다
- [ ] insurer 명사 보증인, 보험업자
- [ ] contact 명사 접촉, 연락
- [ ] insolvent 형용사 지급 불능의, 파산한
- [ ] cascading 형용사 연속적인, 폭포와 같은
- [ ] collective 형용사 집단적인, 공동의
- [ ] distress 명사 고통, 괴로움
- [ ] self-fulfilling 형용사 자기 충족적인, 자기 달성적인
- [ ] troublesome 형용사 골치 아픈, 성가신
- [ ] aspect 명사 측면

03

- [ ] latitude 명사 위도
- [ ] rhinoceros 명사 코뿔소
- [ ] edge 명사 언저리, 가장자리
- [ ] spear 동사 창으로 찍다
- [ ] calf 명사 (소·고래 등의) 새끼
- [ ] processing 명사 처리 (과정)
- [ ] principle 명사 원리
- [ ] conventional 형용사 일반적인, 전통적인
- [ ] dim 형용사 희미한
- [ ] retina 명사 망막
- [ ] compensate for ~을 보완하다[보상하다]
- [ ] auditory 형용사 청각의

04

- [ ] inclined plane 경사면
- [ ] desired 형용사 바라던, 희망했던
- [ ] lifetime 명사 평생, 일생, 생애
- [ ] trade for ~으로[와] 교환하다
- [ ] intended 형용사 목표한, 의도된
- [ ] steep 형용사 가파른
- [ ] precisely 부사 정확하게, 신중하게
- [ ] slope 명사 경사지, 경사면

05

- [ ] primary 형용사 주요한, 최초의, 근본적인
- [ ] take on (특성·특질 등을) 띠다
- [ ] significance 명사 중요성, 의의
- [ ] embed 동사 (마음·기억 등에) 새기다, 박아 넣다
- [ ] vividly 부사 생생히, 선명하게
- [ ] recall 동사 기억해 내다, 상기하다
- [ ] neutral 형용사 중립적인, 감정을 자제하는

문제편 : p.146~151 정답과 해설 : p.159~167

heighten	동사 고조시키다, 증가시키다
presence	명사 존재, 출석
ensure	동사 확실하게 하다, 보증하다
encode	동사 암호화하다, 부호화하다
retrieval	명사 회복, 복구
context	명사 맥락, 전후 관계
facilitate	동사 촉진시키다, 용이하게 하다
reconstruct	동사 재구성하다, 재건하다
absence	명사 부재, 결석, 없음
competence	명사 역량, 적성

06

navigate	동사 주행하다, 항해하다, 길을 찾다
destination	명사 목적지, 도착지
spring	동사 (갑자기) 발생하다, 일어나다
neuron	명사 신경 세포
originate from	~으로부터 생기다
close call	아슬아슬한 상황, 위기일발
yet another	또 다른, 잇따라
conscious	형용사 의식적인
cognitive	형용사 인지의
neural	형용사 신경(계)의
synthesize	동사 종합하다, 합성하다
intertwine	동사 뒤얽다, 엮다
bottom line	명사 요점, 핵심
work on	~을 작동시키다, ~에 노력을 들이다

07

emphasis	명사 중점, 강조
character	명사 품성, 인격
appeal	명사 호소 / 동사 호소하다
urge	동사 강요하다, 강력히 권고하다 / 명사 욕구, 충동
cast	동사 (그림자를) 드리우다, 던지다
immorality	명사 비도덕성
get away with	(나쁜 짓을 하고) 들키지 않다, 그냥 넘어가다
evoke	동사 (감정·기억·이미지 등을) 환기하다, 불러일으키다
trigger	동사 촉발하다 / 명사 방아쇠
appropriateness	명사 적절함, 타당성
in light of	~에 비추어 볼 때, ~을 고려하면
embrace	동사 받아들이다, 포용하다
rephrase	동사 바꿔 말하다
originality	명사 독창성, 창의성

08

availability	명사 가용성, 유용성
heuristic	명사 휴리스틱, (자기) 발견적 방법
prevalent	형용사 널리 퍼져 있는, 일반적인
recency	명사 최신성, 새로움
frequency	명사 빈도, 주파수
magnitude	명사 규모, 중요도
appraisal	명사 평가, 감정
fall victim to	~의 희생양이 되다, ~에 희생되다
supervisor	명사 관리자, 감독관
give weight to	~에 비중을 두다, ~을 중요시하다
dominate	동사 지배하다, 가장 두드러지다
ease	명사 용이함, 쉬움
retrievability	명사 회복력, 복구 가능성
probability	명사 확률, 가능성
distorted	형용사 왜곡된, 비뚤어진

09

interior	형용사 내륙의, 내부의 / 명사 내부
continent	명사 대륙
play a role in V-ing	~하는 데 역할을 하다
moisture	명사 수분, 습기
humid	형용사 습한
encounter	동사 ~와 마주치다
precipitation	명사 강수, 강수량
windward	형용사 풍상측(風上側)의, 바람이 불어오는 쪽의
leeward	형용사 풍하측(風下側)의, 바람이 불어가는 쪽의
uplift	명사 상승, 증가, 희망
rainfall	명사 강우(량)
drastic	형용사 급격한, 극단적인
ascend	동사 상승하다, 올라가다
descend	동사 하강하다, 내려오다
equalize	동사 균등하게 하다

10

revenue	명사 수익
net income	명사 순수익
earn	동사 (돈을) 벌다, 얻다
boost	동사 증가시키다, 밀어올리다
exchange	동사 교환하다, 맞바꾸다
change hands	주인이 바뀌다
give up	~을 내어주다, ~을 포기하다
expense	명사 비용, 지출
practice	명사 관행, 관례, 연습, 실습
result in	~을 야기하다, 결과적으로 ~이 되다
additional	형용사 추가적인, 부가적인
inflow	명사 유입
be put to an end	종결되다, 종료되다
accountant	명사 회계사
meet	동사 충족시키다, 부합하다
criteria	명사 기준 (criterion의 복수형)
recognition	명사 인식, 인정
principle	명사 원칙, 원리
intensify	동사 심해지다, 격렬해지다, 강화하다
trigger	동사 유발하다, 촉발하다

11

scholar	명사 학자, 장학생
myth	명사 신화
argue	동사 주장하다, 다투다
amplify	동사 증폭시키다, 확대하다
virtual	형용사 가상의, 허상의
fulfill	동사 충족시키다, 실현하다
need	명사 욕구, 필요
conversely	부사 반대로, 거꾸로
sustain	동사 지속하다, 유지하다
a handful of	소수의, 한 줌의
adherent	명사 지지자, 추종자
immersive	형용사 몰입하게 하는
consume	동사 소모하다, 소비하다, 섭취하다
reach	명사 범위 / 동사 ~에 도달하다
though	부사 그러나, 그렇지만 / 접속사 ~이긴 하지만
limited	형용사 제한된, 한정된
A be considered B	A는 B로 여겨지다
threshold	명사 기준점, 한계점
psychological	형용사 심리적인

12

formulate	동사 만들어 내다
conspicuous	형용사 과시적인, 눈에 잘 띄는
status	명사 (사회적) 지위, 신분, 상태, 정세
willingness	명사 기꺼이 ~하는 마음
noticeably	부사 두드러지게, 현저히
equivalent	명사 동등한 물건, 등가물
well off	부유한, 잘사는
reduction	명사 하락, 감소
temporary	형용사 일시적인
get involved in	~에 관여하다
supply	동사 공급하다 / 명사 공급

13

philosopher	명사 철학자
purely	부사 순전히, 순수하게
invoke	동사 언급하다, 호소하다
to illustrate	예를 들면
recall	동사 떠올리다, 상기하다
diverse	형용사 다양한
phenomena	명사 현상 (phenomenon의 복수형)
body	명사 물체
exert A on B	B에 A를 행사하다[가하다]
gravitational attraction	중력
moral	명사 교훈 / 형용사 도덕적인
generalize	동사 일반화하다
make use of	~을 이용하다

14

examine	동사 조사하다
frequency	명사 빈도, 주파수
match	동사 짝을 짓다, 어울리다
slightly	부사 약간
serve to V	~하는 역할을 하다, ~하는 데 도움이 되다
bond	명사 유대 / 동사 유대감을 형성하다
rating	명사 평가, 순위, 등급
anxiousness	명사 불안감
imply	동사 의미하다
reluctant	형용사 꺼리는
innermost	형용사 가장 내밀한, 가장 안쪽의

15

extreme	형용사 극단적인, 극심한 / 명사 극도, 극단
harsh	형용사 혹독한, 가혹한
benign	형용사 온화한, 상냥한
obvious	형용사 명백한, 분명한

문제편 : p.151~156 | 정답과 해설 : p.168~176

☐ midday 명사 한낮, 정오
☐ Antarctic 형용사 남극의
☐ salinity 명사 염도, 염분
☐ physiological 형용사 생리(학)적인
☐ tolerance 명사 내성, 관용
☐ cactus 명사 선인장 (복수형 cacti)
☐ ecologist 명사 생태학자, 생태 운동가
☐ organism 명사 유기체, 생물(체)
☐ relativity 명사 상대성, 관계 있음

16

☐ typical 형용사 전형적인, 보통의
☐ soap opera 명사 연속극, 드라마
☐ abstract 형용사 추상적인
☐ complex 형용사 복잡한, 복합의
☐ fictional 형용사 허구의, 소설의
☐ psychology 명사 심리학
☐ physics 명사 물리학
☐ speculate 동사 추측하다, 사색하다
☐ considerable 형용사 상당한, 많은
☐ with ease 쉽게
☐ cope with ~에 대처하다, ~을 다루다
☐ abstraction 명사 추상(적 개념)
☐ extremely 부사 아주, 극도로
☐ familiar 형용사 친숙한, 익숙한
☐ framework 명사 틀
☐ removed 형용사 떨어져 있는, 동떨어진

17

☐ intellectual discourse 지적 담론
☐ scarce 형용사 희귀한, 드문
☐ bring about 야기하다, 초래하다
☐ movable 형용사 가동의, 움직일 수 있는
☐ printing 명사 인쇄술, 인쇄
☐ legitimation 명사 합법화, 합법적 인정
☐ everyday language 일상어
☐ favorable 형용사 호의적인, 긍정적인
☐ accessible 형용사 접근 가능한, 접근할 수 있는

18

☐ order 명사 질서, 순서
☐ chaos 명사 혼란, 혼돈
☐ ambiguity 명사 모호함, 불명확함
☐ conviction 명사 확신, 신념, 유죄 판결
☐ complexity 명사 복잡함, 복잡한 것
☐ formula 명사 공식, 방식
☐ interact 동사 상호 작용하다, 교류하다
☐ approach 명사 접근(법) / 동사 접근하다
☐ remind A of B A에게 B를 상기시키다
☐ underneath 전치사 ~의 아래에(서), ~의 밑에
☐ yearning 명사 열망, 동경, 간절함
☐ pursue 동사 추구하다, 쫓다
☐ seemingly 부사 겉보기에, 외견상으로
☐ risky 형용사 위험한, 무모한, 모험적인
☐ current 형용사 현재의, 지금의 / 명사 흐름, 경향

☐ state 명사 상태, 형편
☐ inferior 형용사 열악한, 열등한
☐ weigh 동사 따져 보다, ~의 무게를 달다, 무게가 ~이다
☐ patience 명사 인내심, 끈기
☐ settle down 정착하다, 몰두하다
☐ insight 명사 통찰력, 식견

19

☐ physical 형용사 실체가 있는, 물질적인, 신체의
☐ board 명사 이사회, 판자
☐ investor 명사 투자자
☐ underlying 형용사 근본적인, (다른 것의) 밑에 있는
☐ motive 명사 동기, 이유
☐ consumer 명사 소비자
☐ produce 명사 농산물, 생산물
☐ manufacture 동사 제조하다, 제작하다
☐ loyalty card 고객 우대 카드
☐ purchasing behavior 구매 행동
☐ analytics 명사 분석, 분석 정보
☐ slice 동사 쪼개다, 나누다, 가르다, 얇게 베다
☐ insight 명사 통찰력, 식견
☐ currency 명사 통화, 통용
☐ capitalist 형용사 자본주의적인
☐ conduct 동사 하다, 처리하다 / 명사 행동, 태도
☐ surveillance 명사 관찰, 감시
☐ device 명사 장치, 방법, 기기
☐ innovative 형용사 혁신적인, 획기적인
☐ word-of-mouth 형용사 입소문의, 구전의
☐ effectiveness 명사 효율성, 유효성

20

☐ blow 명사 타격, 충격
☐ supportive 형용사 협력적인, 지원하는
☐ threatening 형용사 위협적인, 협박하는
☐ imply 동사 암시하다
☐ incompetence 명사 무능함
☐ undermine 동사 손상시키다
☐ rest on ~에 달려 있다[놓여 있다]
☐ suggest 동사 암시하다, 제안하다

21

☐ negative 형용사 음수의, 마이너스의, 부정적인
☐ abstract 형용사 추상적인, 관념적인
☐ positive 형용사 양수의, 플러스의, 긍정적인
☐ contend with ~와 씨름하다[다투다]
☐ make peace with ~와 화해하다
☐ sidestep 동사 피하다, 회피하다
☐ dreaded 형용사 두려운, 무서운
☐ statement 명사 (사업) 보고서, 계산서, 진술, 성명
☐ parentheses 명사 괄호 (parenthesis의 복수형)
☐ designation 명사 명칭, 호칭, 지명, 지정
☐ exception 명사 예외, 제외
☐ folks 명사 (주로 복수형) 사람들
☐ resolve 동사 해소하다, 결심하다
☐ stock market 명사 주식 시장

☐ compensate 동사 보완하다, 보상하다
☐ unify 동사 통일[통합]하다
☐ subtraction 명사 뺄셈, 삭감, 공제

22

☐ observational 형용사 관찰의, 감시의
☐ homogeneous 형용사 동질적인, 동종의
☐ suitable 형용사 적절한, 적합한
☐ subject 명사 (연구) 대상, 주제, 과목
☐ confounding factor 교란 변수
☐ undermine 동사 손상시키다, 약화시키다
☐ draw 동사 도출하다, 끌다
☐ sound 형용사 타당한, 건전한
☐ causal 형용사 인과 관계의
☐ conclusion 명사 결론, 결말
☐ epidemiological 형용사 역학의
☐ variable 명사 변수 / 형용사 가변적인
☐ epidemiologist 명사 역학자
☐ isolate 동사 분리하다, 격리하다
☐ determine 동사 결정짓다, 알아내다
☐ consumption 명사 섭취, 소비
☐ correlation 명사 상관관계
☐ coronary 형용사 관상 동맥의
☐ correct for 수정하다, 교정하다
☐ reliability 명사 신뢰성
☐ distort 동사 왜곡하다, 비틀다
☐ interpretation 명사 해석, 이해
☐ conceal 동사 숨기다, 감추다
☐ conduct 동사 수행하다, 시행하다
☐ refrain 동사 억제하다, 삼가다
☐ intervene 동사 간섭하다, 개입하다

23

☐ depiction 명사 묘사, 서술
☐ weedy 형용사 잡초가 무성한
☐ extract A from B B로부터 A를 끌어내다[추출하다]
☐ ordinary 형용사 평범한
☐ convey 동사 전달하다
☐ artistry 명사 예술적 재능
☐ humble 형용사 보잘것없는, 미천한, 겸손한
☐ relatively 부사 비교적, 상대적으로
☐ complication 명사 복잡함
☐ problematic 형용사 해결하기 어려운, 문제가 있는
☐ modest 형용사 별것 아닌, 겸손한, 신중한
☐ hypothesis 명사 가설, 추정
☐ experiment 명사 (과학적인) 실험

24

☐ arrangement 명사 거래, 협정, 합의
☐ extend credit 신용 거래를 하다, 외상을 주다
☐ bet 명사 (도박이나 내기에서의) 선택, 추측
☐ enrich 동사 부유하게 만들다, 풍요롭게 하다
☐ rob 동사 약탈하다, 도둑질하다
☐ in time 곧, 이윽고

25

☐ pharmaceutical 형용사 제약의, 약학의

문제편 : p.156~161 정답과 해설 : p.176~185

□	executive	명사 임원, 경영진
□	innovation	명사 혁신, 쇄신
□	radical	형용사 급진적인, 근본적인
□	soar	동사 급증하다, 솟구치다
□	crush	동사 짓밟다, 밀어넣다
□	reverse	동사 (뒤)바꾸다, 뒤집다
□	defend	동사 방어하다, 옹호하다
□	reframe	동사 재구조화하다, 다시 구성하다
□	in terms of	~의 관점에서, (~이라는) 면에서
□	be inclined to V	~하고 싶어하다, ~하는 경향이 있다
□	take a risk	위험을 감수하다
□	urgency	명사 긴급(함), 절박
□	apparent	형용사 명백한, 분명한

26

□	sociologist	명사 사회학자
□	encounter	동사 직면하다, 마주치다
□	a range of	다양한
□	center on	~을 중심으로 하다
□	intolerant	형용사 편협한, 옹졸한, 견딜 수 없는
□	bigot	명사 고집쟁이, 편견이 아주 심한 사람
□	progressive	형용사 진보적인, 점진적인
□	make fun of	조롱하다, 비웃다
□	absurd	형용사 터무니없는, 말도 안 되는
□	intention	명사 의도, 목적
□	demonstrate	동사 입증하다, 보여주다
□	prejudice	명사 편견 / 동사 편견을 갖게 하다
□	resolve	동사 해결하다, 결심하다

27

□	observe	동사 관찰하다, 목격하다
□	ask A B	A에게 B를 묻다
□	recovery	명사 복구, 회복
□	quantity	명사 양
□	rescue	동사 구하다, 구제하다
□	sensitive	형용사 민감한, 예민한
□	the number of A	A의 수
□	willingness	명사 의사, 의지, 기꺼이 하려는 마음
□	be willing to V	기꺼이 ~하다, ~하기를 불사하다
□	outcome	명사 결과, 성과
□	value A over B	B보다 A를 중시하다[선호하다]
□	incompetence	명사 무능함
□	irrational	형용사 비합리적인, 비이성적인
□	rational	형용사 합리적인, 이성적인
□	prefer A to B	B보다 A를 선호하다
□	malfunction	명사 기능 불량, 오작동 / 동사 제대로 작동하지 않다

28

□	late	형용사 고(故), 이미 사망한, 늦은
□	arrange	동사 ~을 준비하다, 계획을 짜다, 정리하다, 배열하다
□	applauder	명사 박수치는 사람, 성원을 보내는 사람
□	scatter	동사 흩어지게 만들다, 흩뿌리다
□	applaud	동사 박수갈채를 보내다
□	platform	명사 연단, 강단, (기차역의) 플랫폼
□	take up	(제의 등을) 받아들이다
□	literally	부사 문자 그대로, 말 그대로
□	sweep off one's feet	(~의) 마음을 사로잡다
□	tremendous	형용사 엄청난
□	applause	명사 박수(갈채)
□	emblazon	동사 선명히 새기다
□	make use of	~을 활용하다[이용하다]
□	promotion	명사 홍보 (활동), 승진
□	priority	명사 우선 사항

29

□	venture	명사 벤처 (기업), 모험 / 동사 (위험을 무릅쓰고) 가다, 하다
□	startup	명사 스타트업, 신규 업체
□	traitorous	형용사 반역적인, 배반하는
□	bound together by	~으로 굳게 맺어진
□	sense of mission	사명감
□	bureaucratic	형용사 관료주의적인
□	hierarchy	명사 계급 제도, 체계
□	entrenched	형용사 굳어진, 확립된, 견고한
□	shy away from	~을 피하다
□	dysfunctional	형용사 제대로 기능하지 않는, 고장 난
□	classic	형용사 최고 수준의, 전형적인
□	principle	명사 원칙, 원리
□	outperform	동사 능가하다, 더 나은 결과를 내다

30

□	attitude	명사 태도, 자세
□	conceptualize	동사 개념화하다
□	component	명사 요소, 부품
□	affective	형용사 정서적인
□	cognitive	형용사 인지적인
□	intention	명사 의도, 목적
□	wildlife	명사 야생 동물
□	strive	동사 노력하다, 경쟁하다
□	consistent	형용사 일관된, 변함없는
□	outweigh	동사 ~보다 더 크다
□	simultaneously	부사 동시에, 일제히
□	biased	형용사 편향된, ~에 더 치중하는
□	preserve	동사 보존하다, 보호하다
□	biodiversity	명사 생물의 다양성

31

□	bland	형용사 (맛이) 자극적이지 않은, 특징 없는
□	relaxing	형용사 긴장을 완화시키는, 느긋한
□	blood stream	혈류
□	hence	부사 이런 이유로
□	comfort	명사 위안, 편안함 / 동사 위로하다
□	genetically	부사 유전적으로, 유전학적으로
□	scarce	형용사 부족한, 드문
□	along with	~와 더불어, ~와 마찬가지로
□	carbs	명사 탄수화물 (식품)
□	at every turn	도처에, 어디에서나, 언제나
□	carry-out	명사 포장 음식, 포장 음식 전문점
□	ingrained	형용사 뿌리 깊은, 깊이 몸에 밴
□	caveman	명사 원시인, 혈거인(동굴 속에 사는 사람)
□	mentality	명사 사고방식
□	craving	명사 갈망, 열망
□	attempt	명사 시도 / 동사 시도하다
□	ultimately	부사 궁극적으로
□	appetite	명사 식욕
□	preference	명사 선호

32

□	interpretation	명사 해석
□	wavelength	명사 파장
□	internally	부사 내부에서
□	constitute	동사 구성하다
□	fraction	명사 일부, 부분
□	trillion	1조
□	be unaware of	~을 알지 못하다
□	specialized	형용사 특별한
□	biological	형용사 생물학적인, 생물학의
□	receptor	명사 수용체
□	pick up on	~을 포착하다[이해하다, 알아차리다]
□	slice	명사 단면, 조각 / 동사 썰다
□	biology	명사 생명 작용(활동), 생물학
□	hinder	동사 방해하다, 저해하다
□	be derived from	~에서 파생되다[유래하다]
□	stereotype	명사 고정 관념

33

□	constitute	동사 구성하다, (단체를) 설립하다
□	allocate	동사 분배하다
□	output	명사 생산(량)
□	wholesale	부사 완전히, 대규모로 / 형용사 도매의, 대규모의 / 명사 도매
□	adopt	동사 (사상·의견·정책 등을) 받아들이다, 채택하다, 입양하다
□	widespread	형용사 광범위한
□	acceptance	명사 수용, 동의
□	involvement	명사 개입
□	range from A to B	A에서부터 B까지 이르다
□	enactment	명사 (법률의) 제정
□	enforcement	명사 집행
□	regulation	명사 규정, 규제
□	entity	명사 실체, 독립체
□	mortgage	명사 담보, (담보) 대출(금)
□	agency	명사 기관, 대리점, 단체
□	attempt	명사 시도
□	treasury	명사 재무기관, 금고
□	ups and downs	흥망성쇠
□	intervene	동사 개입하다

34

□	screen out	~을 걸러내다[차단하다]
□	sort	동사 분류하다 / 명사 종류
□	manageable	형용사 관리할 수 있는, 다루기 쉬운
□	inflow	명사 유입
□	chaos	명사 혼란, 혼돈
□	sensory	형용사 감각의
□	impression	명사 인상, 감명
□	vital	형용사 중요한

문제편 : p.161~165 | 정답과 해설 : p.185~193

- ☐ relevant 형용사 관련 있는, 적절한
- ☐ organize 동사 정리하다, 관리하다
- ☐ usable 형용사 사용할 수 있는, 편리한
- ☐ expectancy 명사 예상, 기대
- ☐ contradiction 명사 모순, 부정
- ☐ mark 동사 특징짓다, 표시하다 / 명사 점수, 표시
- ☐ steady 형용사 꾸준한, 확고한
- ☐ elimination 명사 제거, 삭제
- ☐ fraction 명사 일부, 부분
- ☐ process 동사 처리하다, 가공하다 / 명사 과정, 절차
- ☐ commit 동사 (기억·처리 등에) 넘기다[맡기다], (죄를) 범하다, 약속하다
- ☐ retrieve 동사 상기하다, 되찾다

35

- ☐ acclaim A (as B) A를 (B로) 칭송하다
- ☐ comparison 명사 비교, 비유
- ☐ impresario 명사 (극장 등의) 기획자, 단장
- ☐ slip 동사 실력이 떨어지다, 전락하다
- ☐ concerto 명사 협주곡, 콘체르토
- ☐ splendidly 부사 훌륭하게, 화려하게
- ☐ standard 명사 기준, 표준
- ☐ artistry 명사 예술성, 예술적 기교
- ☐ appreciation 명사 감상력, 음미, 비평
- ☐ inspiration 명사 영감, 창조적 자극

36

- ☐ charge 동사 (감정을) 흥분시키다, (요금 등을) 청구하다
- ☐ primary 형용사 원초적인, 주요한
- ☐ resolution 명사 해결책, 결단력
- ☐ articulate 동사 (분명히) 표현하다, 설명하다
- ☐ spare 동사 구하다, 살려주다 / 형용사 여분의
- ☐ innocent 형용사 무고한, 죄가 없는
- ☐ bystander 명사 구경꾼, 목격자, 행인
- ☐ be confronted with ~에 직면하다
- ☐ suppress 동사 억누르다, 진압하다
- ☐ mitigate 동사 완화시키다, 경감시키다
- ☐ have nothing to do with ~와 (전혀) 관련이 없다
- ☐ restrain 동사 억제하다, 저지하다
- ☐ provoke 동사 유발하다, 화나게 하다

37

- ☐ figure 동사 (~라고) 생각하다, 판단하다
- ☐ compassion 명사 동정심, 연민
- ☐ sensitivity 명사 민감성, 세심함
- ☐ revolve 동사 돌다, 회전하다
- ☐ antiseptic 형용사 멸균의
- ☐ practice 명사 (변호사나 의사 등 전문직의) 일, 업무, 관습, 연습
- ☐ win 동사 쟁취하다, 이기다
- ☐ be founded on ~에 기초하다[기반을 두다]
- ☐ follower 명사 팔로워, 추종자

38

- ☐ natural selection 명사 자연 선택, 자연 도태
- ☐ prey 명사 먹잇감, 피해자
- ☐ be engaged in ~에 참여[종사]하다
- ☐ life-or-death 형용사 생사가 걸린, 목숨을 건
- ☐ sensory 형용사 감각의
- ☐ arms race 명사 군비 경쟁
- ☐ moth 명사 나방
- ☐ in response to N ~에 대한 반응으로
- ☐ threat 명사 위협, 협박 / 동사 위협하다
- ☐ detect 동사 감지하다, 발견하다
- ☐ frequency 명사 주파수, 빈도
- ☐ vocalization 명사 발성
- ☐ scale 명사 비늘, 규모
- ☐ coat 명사 외피, 외투
- ☐ acoustic 형용사 음향의, 청각의
- ☐ camouflage 명사 위장 / 동사 위장하다
- ☐ absorb 동사 흡수하다, 빨아들이다
- ☐ emit 동사 방출하다, 내뿜다
- ☐ bounce back 되돌아가다
- ☐ bomber 명사 폭격기, 폭파범
- ☐ aircraft 명사 항공기
- ☐ fuselage 명사 (비행기의) 기체[동체]
- ☐ scarce 형용사 부족한, 드문

39

- ☐ vivid 형용사 생생한, 선명한
- ☐ mindset 명사 사고방식
- ☐ transform 동사 변질시키다, 변형시키다
- ☐ undermine 동사 훼손시키다, 약화시키다
- ☐ institution 명사 관습, 제도, 기관
- ☐ day care center 어린이집
- ☐ fine 동사 벌금을 부과하다 / 명사 벌금
- ☐ discourage A from V-ing A가 ~하는 것을 막다
- ☐ imposition 명사 부과, 시행, 도입
- ☐ guilt 명사 죄책감, 유죄
- ☐ ensure 동사 확실히 하다, 보장하다
- ☐ look after ~을 돌보다
- ☐ after hours 근무시간 후에
- ☐ abandon 동사 그만두다, 버리다
- ☐ arrangement 명사 방식, 합의
- ☐ put aside (감정·의견 차이 등을) 제쳐놓다[무시하다]
- ☐ common good 공익
- ☐ compensate 동사 보상하다
- ☐ bond 명사 유대(감)

40

- ☐ encounter 동사 마주치다, 직면하다 / 명사 만남
- ☐ subsequent 형용사 이후의, 그 다음의, 차후의
- ☐ external 형용사 외부의, 겉면의
- ☐ integrate 동사 통합시키다, 통합되다
- ☐ witness 명사 목격자 / 동사 목격하다
- ☐ poorly 부사 불충분하게, 안 좋게
- ☐ encode 동사 부호화하다, 암호로 만들다, 표현하다
- ☐ distant 형용사 먼, (멀리) 떨어져 있는
- ☐ degrade 동사 저하시키다, 분해하다
- ☐ validity 명사 유효성, 타당성
- ☐ make sense 말이 되다, 이해하다
- ☐ explicit 형용사 명시적인, 명백한
- ☐ unconscious 형용사 무의식적인, 의식을 잃은
- ☐ awareness 명사 의식, 관심
- ☐ misinformation 명사 잘못된 정보
- ☐ forensic 형용사 법정의, 법의학적인
- ☐ discussion 명사 토론, 논의
- ☐ investigator 명사 조사관, 수사관
- ☐ legal 형용사 법의, 법적인, 합법적인
- ☐ interference 명사 간섭, 개입, 방해

41

- ☐ correlation 명사 상관관계, 연관성
- ☐ insight 명사 통찰력, 이해
- ☐ relatively 부사 비교적, 상대적으로
- ☐ cover up 완전히 가리다, 은폐하다
- ☐ causality 명사 인과 관계
- ☐ used-car dealer 중고차 매매인
- ☐ supply 동사 제공하다, 공급하다
- ☐ statistician 명사 통계학자
- ☐ auction 명사 경매 / 동사 경매하다
- ☐ defect 명사 결함, 단점, 흠
- ☐ enthusiast 명사 애호가, 열광적인 팬
- ☐ noticeable 형용사 눈에 띄는, 뚜렷한
- ☐ causal 형용사 인과의, 원인이 되는
- ☐ hypothesis 명사 가설 (복수형 hypotheses)
- ☐ illuminate 동사 설명하다, 분명히 하다, 밝히다
- ☐ cloudy 형용사 흐린, 탁한
- ☐ causal link 인과 관계
- ☐ hold off 보류하다, 미루다
- ☐ approach 명사 접근 / 동사 접근하다
- ☐ framework 명사 틀, 뼈대

42

- ☐ life span 수명
- ☐ external 형용사 외부적인, 외부의
- ☐ starvation 명사 굶주림, 기아
- ☐ predator 명사 포식자
- ☐ internal 형용사 내부적인, 체내의, 내면의
- ☐ cover 동사 (거리를) 이동하다, 다루다, 취재하다
- ☐ genetic 형용사 유전적인, 유전학의
- ☐ flee 동사 도망치다 (flee-fled-fled)
- ☐ expend 명사 소비하다, (시간·노력 등을) 들이다

43

- ☐ production 명사 (영화·연극 등의) 제작, 생산, 생산량
- ☐ consumption 명사 소비, 소비량
- ☐ imply 동사 암시하다, 의미하다, 함축하다
- ☐ supposedly 부사 소위, 이른바, 아마도
- ☐ commercial 형용사 상업의, 상업적인, 이윤을 낳는
- ☐ considerable 형용사 상당한, 많은
- ☐ composition 명사 구성, 구성 요소, 작곡
- ☐ admission 명사 입장, 가입, 입장료
- ☐ comprise 동사 차지하다, ~으로 이루어지다, 구성하다

문제편 : p.166~170 정답과 해설 : p.193~202

correspond with ~와 일치하다[부합하다]
diverse 형용사 다양한, 여러 가지의
prejudice 명사 편견, 선입관
realm 명사 영역, 범위
subordinate 형용사 하위의, 종속된 / 명사 부하 직원
legitimate 형용사 제대로 된, 합리적인, 적법한
contemporary 형용사 현대의, 당대의, 동시대의

44
drive 명사 욕구, 추진력 / 동사 운전하다, 이끌다
novel 형용사 새로운 / 명사 소설
reflection 명사 반영, 반사, (거울에 비친) 모습
state 명사 상태, 국가, 주(州)
curiosity 명사 호기심, 진기함, 진기한 것
musical phrase 악절
investigator 명사 연구자, 조사관
composition 명사 작곡, 구성
driver 명사 원동력, 운전사

45
technologist 명사 기술자
be on the lookout for ~을 찾다[살피다], ~에 주의를 기울이다
quantifiable 형용사 정량화할 수 있는, 수량화할 수 있는
measurable 형용사 측정 가능한
input 명사 입력, 투입 / 동사 입력하다
lifeblood 명사 생명줄
identify 동사 확인하다, 동일시하다
concrete 형용사 구체적인, 단단한 / 명사 콘크리트
assess 동사 평가하다, 할당하다, 부과하다
bias 명사 편향, 편견
complicated 형용사 복잡한, 어려운
fall under ~에 빠지다
illusion 명사 착각, 환상, 환각
end 명사 목적, 결말
genuine 형용사 진정한, 진짜의, 진실된
worthy 형용사 가치 있는
count 동사 중요하다, (숫자를) 세다
regard A as B A를 B로 고려하다[보다]
valid 형용사 타당한, 유효한
prioritize 동사 우선시하다, 우선순위를 매기다
short-term 형용사 단기적인
long-term 형용사 장기적인
mistake A for B A를 B로 착각하다[오해하다]
established 형용사 기존의, 확립된

46
invest 동사 투자하다, 출자하다
repay 동사 보답하다, 상환하다
venture 명사 (벤처) 사업, (사업상의) 모험
sunk cost 매몰 비용(회수할 수 없는 비용)
fallacy 명사 오류, 틀린 생각
instinct 명사 본능, 타고난 소질
acknowledge 동사 인정하다
get back 되찾다, 돌아오다
add to N ~에 보태다[더하다]
offer 동사 제안하다, 권하다
reward 명사 보상 / 동사 보상하다
pay off 갚다, 청산하다, 도움이 되다
debt 명사 빚, 부채

47
for all practical purposes 실제로는, 사실상
instantaneously 부사 순간적으로, 즉시
lightbulb 명사 전구
unpleasantly 부사 불쾌할 정도로, 불쾌하게
illuminate 동사 (빛을) 비추다, 빛나다
remove 동사 제거하다, 옮기다
notion 명사 생각, 개념
nonsensical 형용사 말이 안되는, 터무니없는
sun 명사 항성, 태양
infinitely 부사 무한히, 한없이
intervening 형용사 사이에 있는[오는]
vastness 명사 광대함, 방대함
immense 형용사 엄청난
galaxy 명사 은하

48
financial 형용사 금융의, 재정의
capital 명사 자본(금), 수도
lend 동사 (돈을) 빌려주다, 대출하다, 부여하다
enable A to V A가 ~하는 것을 가능하게 하다
smooth 동사 원활하게 하다, 매끄럽게 하다
consumption 명사 소비
income 명사 소득, 수입
earn 동사 벌다, 얻다
admonish 동사 충고하다, 권고하다, 꾸짖다
lender 명사 빌려주는 사람
agrarian 형용사 농경의, 농업의
crop 명사 (농)작물
reasonably 부사 합리적으로, 상당히, 꽤
harvest 명사 수확, 추수 / 동사 수확하다, 추수하다
store 동사 저장하다, 보관하다
sophisticated 형용사 정교화된, 복잡한
manage 동사 관리하다, 운영하다
retirement 명사 은퇴, 퇴직
divorce 동사 분리시키다, 이혼하다
flexibility 명사 유연성, 융통성
impulse 명사 충동, 자극

49
collective 형용사 집합적인, 공동의
prosperity 명사 부, 번영, 번창
skyrocket 동사 급증하다, 급등하다
progress 명사 발전, 진행
share out 나누다, 분배하다
riches 명사 (복수형으로) 부, 재물
settle upon 채택하다, 결정하다
reward 동사 보상하다 / 명사 보상
inequality 명사 불평등, 불균등
drive 동사 생기다, 몰아붙이다, 운전하다
put A under strain A에 부담을 주다
immense 형용사 막대한, 엄청난
threaten 동사 ~할 우려가 있다, 위협하다
radical 형용사 급진적인, 근본적인
labor market 노동 시장
break down 무너지다, 고장나다
share 명사 몫, 지분 / 동사 공유하다
comprehend 동사 이해하다, 포함하다
term 명사 용어, 말, 학기
cost of living 생활비

50
accurate 형용사 정확한, 정밀한
a great deal of 많은, 다량의
expert 형용사 전문적인, 숙련된 / 명사 전문가
implicit 형용사 암시적인, 내포된
explicit 형용사 명시적인, 분명한
mastery 명사 숙련, 숙달
conscious 형용사 의식적인, 의도적인
awareness 명사 인식, 의식, 관심
fundamental 명사 (주로 복수로) 기본 (원칙) / 형용사 근본적인, 핵심적인
skilled 형용사 숙련된, 노련한
aficionado 명사 애호가, 매니아
approach 명사 접근 방식 / 동사 다가가다
interfere with ~을 방해하다
performance 명사 수행, 공연
autopilot 명사 자동 조종
somersault 명사 공중제비
intuitive 형용사 직관적인, 직감에 의한
understanding 명사 지식, 이해
route 명사 방법, 길, 경로
partially 부사 부분적으로, 불완전하게

13. 무관한 문장 찾기

01
phenomenon 명사 현상
arise 동사 생겨나다, 발생하다
happen to V 우연히 ~하다
exert 동사 (영향력 등을) 행사하다, 가하다
peer 명사 또래
rely on ~에 의존하다
controversial 형용사 논란이 되는
credible 형용사 신뢰할 수 있는, 믿을 만한
nonverbal 형용사 비언어적인
cue 명사 신호, 암시
credibility 명사 신뢰도, 신뢰성
in direct proportion to ~에 정비례하여
viral 형용사 입소문이 나는, 바이러스성의

02
inflationary 형용사 인플레이션에 관한, 인플레이션의
refer to ~와 관련 있다, ~을 참고하다
investment 명사 투자, 투자액

account	명사 계좌, 설명, 해석
fee	명사 수수료, 요금
accrue	동사 생기다, 누적되다, 축적되다
interest	명사 이자, 관심, 흥미
untouched	형용사 (본래) 그대로의, 훼손되지 않은
purchase	동사 구매하다, 구입하다 / 명사 구매, 구입
earn	동사 받다, (일을 하여 돈을) 벌다, 얻다
in advance	미리
revenue	명사 수입, 수익
differentiate	동사 구별하다, 구분 짓다
nominal	형용사 명목의, 액면(상)의

03

instinctive	형용사 본능적인, 무의식적인
awareness	명사 인식, 관심
wisdom	명사 지혜, 현명
bewildering	형용사 갈피를 못 잡게 하는, 어리둥절하게 만드는
a host of	다수의
conflicting	형용사 상충되는, 모순되는
confusion	명사 혼란
impulse	명사 충동, 충격
aversion	명사 혐오감
insight	명사 통찰력, 이해

04

academic	명사 대학 교수 / 형용사 학업의, 학문의
politician	명사 정치인, 정치가
ethically	부사 윤리적으로
manipulate	동사 조종하다, 다루다
admit to N/V-ing	~을 인정하다
peer	명사 또래 (집단)
unfavorable	형용사 부정적인, 호의적이지 않은
play on	(감정 등을) 이용하다
vulnerability	명사 취약성, 연약성
inadequateness	명사 불충분함, 부적절함
fixated	형용사 집착하는
gratification	명사 만족(감)
material	형용사 물질적인 / 명사 재료
possession	명사 소유물, 소유

05

stand	명사 입장, 태도
beacon	명사 횃불
tribe	명사 부족, 집단
rallying point	집합 지점
perspective	명사 관점, 시각, 전망
prospective	형용사 장래의, 유망한, 다가오는
at any cost	어떠한 비용을 지불하더라도
retain	동사 유지하다, 간직하다
align	동사 같은 선상에 있다, 나란하다, ~을 조정하다

06

term	명사 용어, 말, 학기
translation	명사 번역, 통역
coziness	명사 아늑함, 편안함
do A justice	A를 제대로 다루다[표현하다]
togetherness	명사 연대감, 단란함
deliberately	부사 의도적으로, 고의적으로
intimacy	명사 친밀감, 친교
connection	명사 유대감, 연결
conscious	형용사 의식적인, 의도적인
perceive	동사 인식하다, 여기다
sprawl	동사 팔다리를 쭉 펴고 눕다, 마구 뻗다
circle	명사 무리, 집단

07

hold a position	위치[지위]를 차지하다
pivotal	형용사 중추적인, 중요한
degree	명사 정도
professional	명사 전문가 / 형용사 직업의, 전문적인
interdisciplinary	형용사 학제 간의
mediate	동사 중재하다, 조정하다
carer	명사 보호자, 간병인
unwilling	형용사 꺼리는, 싫어하는
comprehensible	형용사 이해 가능한
alternative	형용사 대안적인, 대체 가능한

08

immerse	동사 몰입하다, 몰두하다
aptitude	명사 소질, 재능
utilize	동사 활용하다
not necessarily	반드시 ~은 아닌
mechanics	명사 역학, 기계학
structure	명사 구조 / 동사 조직하다, 구조화하다
elemental	형용사 기본적인, 본질적인
lifespan	명사 수명
empower	동사 ~할 능력을 주다, 권한을 주다
deploy	동사 (효율적으로) 사용하다
utility	명사 유용성, 쓸모가 있음

09

differ from	~과 다르다
outcome	명사 결과
rational	형용사 이성적인, 합리적인
measure	명사 척도, 측정 / 동사 재다, 측정하다
go by A	A를 따르다
assume	동사 가정하다, 추정하다
instinct	명사 본능, 타고난 소질
intuition	명사 직관, 직감
variable	명사 변수 / 형용사 변동이 심한
pedestrian	명사 보행자 / 형용사 도보의, 보행자의
appearance	명사 모습, 모양, 출현
humanly	부사 인간적으로

10

license	동사 면허를 내주다
intimidating	형용사 위협적인, 겁을 주는
layout	명사 구획, 배치
feat	명사 재주, 위업
sign up	등록하다, 참가하다
cabbie	명사 택시 기사
herculean	형용사 초인적인, 큰 힘이 드는
spatial memory	공간 기억
sea horse	명사 해마
hippocampus	명사 (뇌의) 해마

11

assume	동사 추정하다, 생각하다
erroneously	부사 잘못(되게), 틀리게
comparative	형용사 비교의, 상대적인
efficiency	명사 효율, 능률
enhance	동사 향상시키다
track	동사 추적하다 / 명사 길, 발자국

12

boundary	명사 경계(선), 한계(선)
continent	명사 대륙, 육지
basin	명사 분지, 유역, 양푼
rotate	동사 회전하다, 순환하다
organism	명사 생물, 유기체
dispersal	명사 분산, 확산
larvae	명사 유충 (larva의 복수형)
coastal	형용사 연안의, 해안의
ocean current	해류(海流)
trap	동사 가두다 / 명사 덫, 함정
near-shore	형용사 연안의
gradient	명사 변화도, 경사도
extend over	~에 걸쳐있다
inhabit	동사 서식하다, 거주하다
tolerance	명사 내성, 관용
firm	형용사 확실한, 단단한

13

pervasive	형용사 널리 스며 있는, 널리 퍼진
rational	형용사 이성적인, 합리적인
sort	동사 가려내다, 분류하다
timeless	형용사 영원한, 변치 않는
hold	동사 주장하다, 간주하다
probability	명사 가능성, 확률
conversely	부사 반대로, 역으로
reasoning	명사 사고
result from	~에서 비롯되다, ~이 원인이다
disorder	명사 장애, 영망
cognitive	형용사 인지적인, 인식의
bias	명사 편견
picture	명사 상황
turn out to be A	A로 판명되다
reasonable	형용사 이성적인, 타당한
have to do with	~와 관련이 있다

14

tricky	형용사 까다로운, 곤란한
elusive	형용사 이해하기 어려운, 회피하는
envy	명사 질투, 부러움 / 동사 시기하다, 질투하다, 부러워하다
discern	동사 알아차리다, 식별하다
motivate	동사 자극하다, 동기를 부여하다
elusiveness	명사 모호함, 이해하기 어려움
entail	동사 수반하다

문제편 : p.177~180 정답과 해설 : p.210~218

☐	admission	명사 인정, 가입
☐	inferior	형용사 열등한, 하위의
☐	cast	동사 (시선·미소 등을) 보내다[던지다], (그림자를) 드리우다
☐	unwittingly	부사 무의식적으로, 무심코
☐	envious	형용사 질투심이 강한, 부러워하는
☐	disguise	동사 감추다, 변장하다
☐	resentment	명사 분개, 억울함
☐	anger	명사 분노, 화

15

☐	democracy	명사 민주주의, 민주 국가, 평등
☐	thrive	동사 번성[번영]하다, 잘 자라다
☐	prosper	동사 번영[번창]하다, 성공하다
☐	precisely	부사 정확히, 바로, 꼭
☐	remarkably	부사 현저하게, 주목할 만하게
☐	assess	동사 평가하다, 재다
☐	levy	동사 부과하다, 징수하다 / 명사 (세금의) 추가 부담금
☐	substantial	형용사 상당한, 크고 튼튼한
☐	striking	형용사 눈에 띄는, 두드러진
☐	revenue	명사 세입, 수입
☐	function	동사 기능하다 / 명사 기능, 행사
☐	awfully	부사 지독하게, 정말, 몹시
☐	extract	동사 얻다, 추출하다 / 명사 추출물

16

☐	moral	형용사 도덕적인, 도덕과 관련된
☐	excellence	명사 우수성, 탁월함, 뛰어남
☐	innate	형용사 선천적인, 타고난
☐	genetic	형용사 유전적인, 유전학의
☐	component	명사 (구성) 요소, 부품
☐	thereabouts	부사 그 무렵에, 대략, 그 근처[부근]에서
☐	rotation	명사 (천체의) 자전, 회전
☐	personality	명사 성격, 인격, 개성
☐	trait	명사 (성격상의) 특성, 이목구비, 인상
☐	stabilize	동사 안정되다, 안정시키다
☐	ethnicity	명사 민족, 민족성
☐	in terms of	~의 면에서, ~에 관하여
☐	cognitive	형용사 인지의, 인식의
☐	optimistic	형용사 낙관적인, 낙관하는

17

☐	species	명사 종, 인종
☐	season	동사 양념하다 / 명사 계절
☐	deliberately	부사 의도적으로, 고의로
☐	alter	동사 바꾸다, 변경하다
☐	highly	부사 강하게, 매우
☐	flavor	동사 맛을 내다 / 명사 맛
☐	spice	명사 향신료 / 동사 향신료를 사용하다
☐	evolutionary	형용사 진화적인, 진화의
☐	antibacterial	형용사 항균의, 항균성의
☐	property	명사 속성, 재산
☐	inhibit	동사 저해하다, 방해하다, 억제하다
☐	bacterium	명사 박테리아 (복수형 bacteria)
☐	coriander	명사 고수
☐	spoilage	명사 부패, 손상
☐	ultimately	부사 궁극적으로, 결국
☐	uniquely	부사 독특히, 유례없이
☐	turn out	~로 드러나다
☐	arise	동사 생겨나다, 발생하다 (arise-arose-arisen)

18

☐	high-profile	형용사 세간의 이목을 끄는
☐	make one's living	돈을 벌다, 생계를 유지하다
☐	instruction	명사 지침, 설명
☐	paid	형용사 유료의, 유급의
☐	support	명사 지원 / 동사 지원하다
☐	copy	명사 사본 / 동사 복사하다, 베끼다
☐	mere	형용사 단지, 단순한
☐	valuable	형용사 가치 있는, 유용한
☐	guidance	명사 안내, 지도, 유도
☐	medical	형용사 의료의, 의학의
☐	genetic	형용사 유전의, 유전학의
☐	route	명사 경로, 노선
☐	coming	형용사 다가오는, 다음의 / 명사 시작, 도래
☐	decade	명사 10년
☐	exposure	명사 노출, 폭로
☐	undoubtedly	부사 의심할 여지 없이, 틀림없이
☐	legal	형용사 법적인, 법률과 관련된
☐	ethical	형용사 윤리적인, 도덕적인
☐	insurance	명사 보험, 보험금
☐	sequence	동사 (유전자의) 배열 순서를 밝히다 / 명사 배열, 순서
☐	for free	무료로
☐	cost	동사 ~의 비용이 들다 / 명사 비용, 값
☐	interpretation	명사 설명, 해석

19

☐	minimal	형용사 최소한의, 아주 적은
☐	artificial	형용사 인공의, 인위적인
☐	additive	명사 첨가물, 첨가제
☐	nutrient	명사 영양소, 영양분
☐	anti-oxidant	명사 항산화 물질
☐	mill	동사 제분하다, 갈다 / 명사 방앗간, 제분소
☐	cereal	명사 곡물, 곡류
☐	harsh	형용사 가혹한, 혹독한, 눈에 거슬리는
☐	dramatically	부사 크게, 극적으로
☐	content	명사 함량, 함유량, 내용물
☐	fiber	명사 섬유질, 성질, 내구성
☐	flakes	명사 플레이크(낟알을 얇게 으깬 식품)
☐	fertilizer	명사 비료, 거름
☐	resistant	형용사 ~에 강한, 저항력 있는
☐	variety	명사 품종, 다양성
☐	spoilage	명사 (음식·식품의) 손상, 부패
☐	sustainable	형용사 지속 가능한
☐	aim	동사 ~을 목표로 하다 / 명사 목적, 목표
☐	optimal	형용사 최적의, 최선의
☐	density	명사 밀도, 농도
☐	foodstuff	명사 식품, 식량
☐	sound	동사 알리다, 울리다

14. 문장 배열

01

☐	relative	형용사 상대적인, 비교상의
☐	fire	동사 발화하다, 발포하다
☐	intensity	명사 강도, 세기
☐	code	동사 부호화하다, 암호화하다
☐	operate	동사 작용하다, 작동하다
☐	calibrate	동사 조정하다, 눈금을 매기다
☐	sensation	명사 감각, 느낌
☐	immerse	동사 담그다, 몰두하게 하다
☐	lukewarm	형용사 미지근한, 미온의
☐	conflict	동사 상충하다 / 명사 갈등
☐	receptor	명사 감각 기관, 수용체
☐	register	동사 인식하다, (온도를) 가리키다
☐	adaptation	명사 (생리학) 순응, 적응
☐	central nervous system	명사 중추 신경계
☐	become(=be) accustomed to	~에 적응하다[익숙하다]
☐	luminance	명사 (빛의) 밝기

02

☐	recognize	동사 인식하다, 알아보다
☐	medical school	의과 대학
☐	president	명사 대표, 회장, 대통령
☐	at first glance	언뜻 보기에는, 처음에는
☐	imply	동사 의미하다, 넌지시 나타내다
☐	at all costs	무슨 수를 써서라도
☐	A be correlated with B	A가 B와 연관성이 있다
☐	life expectancy	기대 수명
☐	hard-working	형용사 근면한
☐	ambitious	형용사 야망을 가진, 야심 있는
☐	corresponding	형용사 (~에) 상응하는, 해당하는
☐	relaxation	명사 휴식
☐	contribute to	~의 원인이 되다
☐	take over	~을 장악하다

03

☐	downplay	동사 경시하다, 얕보다
☐	unintended	형용사 의도하지 않은, 고의가 아닌
☐	consequence	명사 결과
☐	tariff	명사 관세
☐	import	동사 수입하다
☐	steel	명사 철강
☐	steelworker	명사 철강 노동자
☐	foreign	형용사 외국의
☐	autoworker	명사 자동차 제조 노동자
☐	manufacturer	명사 제조업체
☐	relatively	부사 상대적으로
☐	attractive	형용사 매력적인
☐	sale	명사 판매, 매출(량)

04

☐	redundant	형용사 (표현이) 불필요한, 장황한

문제편 : p.181~186 정답과 해설 : p.218~226

- practically [부사] 실제로, 사실상
- versatile [형용사] 다용도인, 활용도가 높은
- wardrobe [명사] 옷장
- neutral [형용사] 무난한, 중간색의, 중립적인, 중성의
- hue [명사] 색상, 색조
- property [명사] 특성, 속성, 재산, 부동산
- dye [명사] 염료, 염색제 / [동사] 염색하다
- permeate [동사] 스며들다, 침투하다
- stick to ~에 들러붙다[달라붙다], 고수하다, 계속하다
- eventually [부사] 결국(엔), 마침내
- achieve [동사] 얻다, 성취하다
- trousers [명사] 바지 (한 벌)
- laborer [명사] 노동자

05

- spend [동사] (돈을) 쓰다, (시간을) 보내다
- assistance [명사] 지원, 도움
- welfare [명사] 복지, 후생
- in favo(u)r (of) ~을 찬성하는, ~을 마음에 들어하는
- broadly [부사] 대체로, 대략(적으로)
- refer to ~을 나타내다[지칭하다]
- connotation [명사] 함축(된 의미)
- portray [동사] 묘사하다, 보여주다
- framing [명사] 구성, 틀, 뼈대
- measure [명사] 척도, 측정
- wary [형용사] 조심하는, 경계하는

06

- lie [동사] 있다, 놓여 있다 (lie-lay-lain)
- police [동사] 감시하다, 치안을 유지하다
- neglect [동사] 등한시하다, 방치하다, 무시하다
- interfere [동사] 침해하다, 간섭하다
- patent [명사] 특허 / [형용사] 특허의
- grant [동사] 승인하다, 허락하다
- bullet [명사] 총알
- swindle [동사] 사기 치다
- forge [동사] 위조하다
- license [동사] 허가하다 / [명사] 면허
- weighted [형용사] (한쪽에 유·불리하게) 치우친, 편중된
- in favour of(=in favor of) ~의 이익이 되도록, ~을 위하여

07

- matter [동사] 중요하다, 문제가 되다
- wonder [동사] 의아해하다, 궁금해하다
- configuration [명사] 배열
- awkward [형용사] 어색한, 곤란한, 불편한
- placement [명사] 배치
- standard [명사] 표준
- era [명사] 시대
- manual [형용사] 수동의 / [명사] 설명서
- physical [형용사] 물리적인, 신체의
- jam [동사] (기계에 무엇이) 걸리다, 작동하지 못하게 되다 / [명사] (기계에 무엇이) 걸림, 고장
- evolve [동사] 발전하다, 진화하다
- efficient [형용사] 효율적인, 능률적인
- coordinate [동사] 조정하다, 조직화하다
- obsolete [형용사] 구식의, 더 이상 쓸모가 없는

08

- assumption [명사] 가정, 추정
- creature [명사] 피조물, 생물
- reason [명사] 이성, 이유 / [동사] 추론하다, 판단하다
- get by on ~으로 살아가다
- list [동사] 열거하다, 목록을 작성하다 / [명사] 목록
- be based on ~에 근거하다[기초하다]
- deep-seated [형용사] 뿌리 깊은, 고질적인
- rarely [부사] 거의 ~하지 않는
- certainly [부사] 분명히, 틀림없이
- influence [동사] 영향을 주다

09

- observe [동사] 관찰하다, 목격하다
- resist [동사] 저항하다, 반대하다
- property [명사] 재산, 소유물, 부동산
- possession [명사] 소유물, 재산
- privilege [명사] 특권, 특혜
- prestige [명사] 위신, 명망
- constant [형용사] 끊임없는, 변함없는
- stagnate [동사] (물이) 고이다, 침체되다
- accumulate [동사] 누적되다, 축적되다
- cling [동사] 매달리다, 고수하다
- resistance [명사] 저항, 반대
- bring about 가져오다, 초래하다
- widen [동사] 넓히다, 키우다
- horizon [명사] 시야, 수평선

10

- examine [동사] 조사하다, 검사하다
- extent [명사] 정도, 범위
- tie [명사] 유대 관계 / [동사] 묶다
- via [전치사] ~을 통해(=through)
- quarter [명사] 4분의 1, 분기(3개월)
- homophilistic [형용사] 동족 친화적인
- relevant [형용사] 의미 있는, 관련된
- expose [동사] 접하게 하다, 노출시키다
- in contrast 대조적으로
- distant [형용사] 멀리 떨어져 있는, 원격의
- geographically [부사] 지리(학)적으로
- demographically [부사] 인구 통계학적으로
- novel [형용사] 새로운, 진기한 / [명사] 소설
- frequently [부사] 빈번하게, 자주
- end up V-ing 결국 ~하게 되다
- sizable [형용사] 엄청난 (크기의), 꽤 큰
- otherwise [부사] 다른 방법으로, 그게 아니면

11

- deficit [명사] 부족, 적자
- composition [명사] 성분, 구성
- result in ~을 초래하다, (그 결과) ~이 되다
- mass [명사] (질)량, 크기
- restriction [명사] 제한, 제약, 구속
- metabolism [명사] 신진대사
- significantly [부사] 현저히, 상당히
- intake [명사] 섭취, 흡입
- function [동사] (제대로) 기능하다, 작용하다 / [명사] 기능, 작용
- key [형용사] 필수의, 핵심의 / [명사] 열쇠, 비결
- carbohydrate [명사] 탄수화물
- combination [명사] 조합(물), 결합(물)
- strategic [형용사] 전략적인, 전략상 중요한
- interval [명사] 간격, (중간) 휴식 시간

12

- physiological [형용사] 생리학적인, 생리적인
- breakthrough [명사] 획기적인 발견, 돌파구
- fundamentally [부사] 근본적으로, 완전히
- alter [동사] 바꾸다, 변하다
- organism [명사] 유기체, 생물
- practice [명사] 행위, 관행
- thoroughly [부사] 완전히, 철저히
- imply [동사] 의미하다, 암시하다
- unprecedented [형용사] 전례 없는
- revelation [명사] 발견, 폭로
- method [명사] 방법, 방식, 수단
- observation [명사] 관찰, 의견
- hypothesis [명사] 가설, 추측
- modify [동사] 수정하다, 수식하다
- gene [명사] 유전자
- chronic [형용사] 만성적인
- build on ~을 기반으로 하다, ~을 발판으로 삼다
- unfold [동사] 펼쳐지다, 퍼지다

13

- forage [동사] 수렵 채집하다
- retain [동사] 보유하다, 가지다, 유지하다
- pity [동사] 불쌍히 여기다, 동정하다 / [명사] 동정, 유감
- hunter-gatherer [명사] 수렵 채집인
- stuck [형용사] 꽉 막힌, 갇힌, 꼼짝 못하는
- simplicity [명사] 단순함, 간단함
- extensive [형용사] 광범위한, 넓은
- rewarding [형용사] 보람있는, 가치 있는
- threatened [형용사] 위협당한, 협박당한
- hold on to ~을 고수하다[지키다]
- remain [동사] 여전히 ~이다, 남다, 머무르다
- overwhelm [동사] 제압하다, 압도하다
- humanity [명사] 인간성
- contribute [동사] 기여하다, 공헌하다
- prove [동사] 증명하다, 판명되다, 알려지다
- self-defeating [형용사] (행위·계획·논의 등이 예상과는 달리) 자멸적인

14

- matter [동사] 중요하다
- require [동사] 필요로 하다, 요구하다
- draft [명사] 초안, 원고 / [동사] 초안을 작성하다

문제편 : p.187~191 정답과 해설 : p.226~234

- [ ] completion 명사 완성, 완료
- [ ] millennium 명사 새천년
- [ ] gene 명사 유전자
- [ ] assume 동사 추정하다
- [ ] massively 부사 엄청나게, 대량으로
- [ ] complicated 형용사 복잡한
- [ ] rely on ~에 있다[의존하다]
- [ ] implement 동사 실행하다
- [ ] refine 동사 정교하게 다듬다, 개선하다

15

- [ ] species 명사 (분류상의) 종
- [ ] endemic 형용사 (한 지역의) 토착의, 토종의, 고유의
- [ ] vulnerable 형용사 취약한, 저항력이 없는
- [ ] extinction 명사 멸종
- [ ] tropical 형용사 열대의, 열대 지방의
- [ ] rain forest 명사 (열대) 우림
- [ ] specialized 형용사 특수화된, 분화된
- [ ] brilliantly 부사 번쩍거리게, 눈부시게
- [ ] lush 형용사 푸르게 우거진, 무성한
- [ ] mountainous 형용사 산악의, 산이 많은
- [ ] apparently 부사 외관상, 보아하니
- [ ] extinct 형용사 멸종된, 사라진
- [ ] habitat 명사 서식지, 자생지
- [ ] moisture-laden 형용사 습기를 실은[머금은]
- [ ] laden 형용사 (짐을) 실은, (~을) 잔뜩 실은, (~이) 가득한
- [ ] cause A to V A가 ~하게 하다
- [ ] victim 명사 희생양, 희생자

16

- [ ] foundation 명사 기반, 기초, 토대
- [ ] mastery 명사 숙달, 통달
- [ ] chunk 명사 덩어리, 많은 양
- [ ] effortful 형용사 노력을 요하는, 노력이 필요한
- [ ] be free to V 자유롭게 ~하다, 마음껏 ~하다
- [ ] backbone 명사 근간, 중추
- [ ] pursuit 명사 추구, 추격
- [ ] excellence 명사 탁월함, 뛰어남
- [ ] come at a cost 대가가 따르다
- [ ] fluency 명사 유창함
- [ ] sensitive 형용사 민감한, 세심한
- [ ] mindless 형용사 머리를 쓸 필요가 없는, 무심한
- [ ] let A slide A를 내버려두다[소홀히 하다]

17

- [ ] surface area 표면적
- [ ] relative to ~에 비례하여
- [ ] volume 명사 체적
- [ ] creature 명사 생물, 사람
- [ ] lead 동사 이끌다, 살아가다
- [ ] curiously 부사 기묘하게도, 지독하게
- [ ] uniform 형용사 획일적인 / 명사 유니폼
- [ ] vast 형용사 막대한, 어마어마한
- [ ] heart rate 심장 박동 수
- [ ] pass 동사 넘다, 지나가다

18

- [ ] doomed 형용사 운이 다한
- [ ] register 동사 기억하다(주로 부정문에서 쓰임), 등록하다
- [ ] demonstrate 동사 증명하다, 행동으로 보여 주다
- [ ] resilience 명사 회복력
- [ ] disturbance 명사 교란, 방해, 소란
- [ ] intensity 명사 강도
- [ ] urgent 형용사 긴급한, 시급한
- [ ] detail 동사 자세히 설명하다, 상술하다
- [ ] remarkable 형용사 놀라운, 놀랄 만한
- [ ] acute 형용사 극심한, 예민한
- [ ] coral 명사 산호
- [ ] bleaching 명사 백화, 표백
- [ ] reef 명사 암초
- [ ] hammer 동사 강타하다 / 명사 망치
- [ ] persist 동사 지속되다, 계속하다
- [ ] destructive 형용사 파괴적인
- [ ] nurture 동사 키우다, 양육하다, 육성하다

19

- [ ] roughly 부사 대략, 거의, 거칠게
- [ ] refer to ~을 지칭하다, ~에 돌리다
- [ ] empirical 형용사 경험적인
- [ ] rationalist 명사 합리주의자
- [ ] prize 동사 높이 평가하다, 소중하게 여기다 / 명사 상
- [ ] look down at/on ~을 경시하다
- [ ] primitive 형용사 원시적인
- [ ] scholar 명사 학자
- [ ] anthropologist 명사 인류학자
- [ ] see 동사 이해하다, 보다
- [ ] picture 명사 상황 (파악)
- [ ] intertwine 동사 뒤얽히다, 밀접하게 관련되다
- [ ] interdependent 형용사 상호 의존적인, 서로 의존하는
- [ ] frame 명사 (생각의) 틀
- [ ] metaphor 명사 은유, 비유
- [ ] shape 동사 형성하다 / 명사 모양, 형태
- [ ] involve 동사 포함하다, 관련시키다

20

- [ ] receptor 명사 수용체
- [ ] spread 동사 퍼뜨리다, 펼치다, 바르다 (spread-spread-spread)
- [ ] evenly 부사 골고루, 고르게, 균등하게
- [ ] tip 명사 끝(부분), 조언
- [ ] apart 부사 떨어져, 따로, 산산이
- [ ] poke 동사 (쿡) 찌르다, (머리·손가락·막대기 등을) 내밀다
- [ ] close 형용사 가까운 / 동사 (눈을) 감다, (문을) 닫다
- [ ] tell 동사 구별하다, 말하다

21

- [ ] continuum 명사 연속체
- [ ] get toward ~에 가까워지다
- [ ] note 동사 ~에 주목하다, 언급하다 / 명사 메모, 쪽지
- [ ] unwanted 형용사 바람직하지 않은, 원치 않는, 반갑지 않은
- [ ] nefarious 형용사 사악한, 비도덕적인, 범죄의
- [ ] aggressively 부사 격렬하게, 공격적으로
- [ ] spawn 동사 (어떤 결과 상황을) 낳다
- [ ] frame 동사 틀을 씌우다 / 명사 틀, 액자, 뼈대
- [ ] specifically 부사 특히, 분명히, 명확하게
- [ ] misguide 동사 잘못 인도하다, 잘못된 길로 이끌다
- [ ] expectation 명사 기대, 예상
- [ ] get rid of 없애다, 제거하다
- [ ] imply 동사 암시하다, 의미하다
- [ ] input 동사 가하다, 투입하다 / 명사 입력, 조언, 투입
- [ ] apply 동사 (손·발 등으로) 힘을 가하다, 적용하다, 신청하다, (연고를) 바르다

22

- [ ] barter 동사 물물 교환하다 / 명사 물물 교환
- [ ] extent 명사 규모, 정도
- [ ] mend 동사 수리하다, 고치다
- [ ] in return for ~에 대한 보답으로
- [ ] coincidence 명사 부합, 동시 발생, 우연의 일치
- [ ] goods 명사 상품, 재산, 소유물
- [ ] transferable 형용사 이동이 가능한, 양도할 수 있는
- [ ] deferrable 형용사 연기할 수 있는, 유예 가능한
- [ ] hold on to ~을 계속 보유하다, 고수하다[지키다]

23

- [ ] argument 명사 주장, 논쟁, 논의
- [ ] foster 동사 기르다, 조성하다
- [ ] humility 명사 겸손
- [ ] disagree 동사 의견이 다르다, 동의하지 않다
- [ ] yell 동사 고함을 지르다, 외치다
- [ ] still 부사 여전히, 그럼에도 불구하고, 아직
- [ ] articulate 동사 분명히 말하다 / 형용사 분명한
- [ ] refute 동사 반박하다, 부인하다
- [ ] come to V ~하게 되다
- [ ] appreciate 동사 이해하다, 인정하다, 고마워하다
- [ ] recognize 동사 인식하다, 알아보다

24

- [ ] forager 명사 수렵 채집인
- [ ] starvation 명사 굶주림
- [ ] malnutrition 명사 영양실조
- [ ] varied 형용사 다양한, 갖가지의
- [ ] unbalanced 형용사 불균형한
- [ ] pre-modern 형용사 근대 이전의, 전근대적인
- [ ] single 형용사 단일의, 하나의
- [ ] crop 명사 농작물
- [ ] wheat 명사 밀
- [ ] peasant 명사 농부, 소작농
- [ ] by contrast 대조적으로
- [ ] regularly 부사 규칙적으로, 정기적으로
- [ ] dozens of 수십 가지의, 많은
- [ ] ancestor 명사 조상
- [ ] snail 명사 달팽이
- [ ] wild onion 명사 달래
- [ ] ensure 동사 보장해주다, 확실하게 하다

문제편 : p.192~196 | 정답과 해설 : p.234~242

25

- portray [동사] 묘사하다
- protection [명사] 보호
- mutually [부사] 상호 간에, 서로
- exclusive [형용사] 배타적인, 독점적인
- pollution [명사] 오염, 공해
- endangered [형용사] 멸종 위기에 처한, 위험에 처한
- claim [동사] 주장하다 / [명사] 주장, 의견
- choke [동사] 질식시키다, 목을 조르다
- throw A out of work A를 실직시키다
- ecological [형용사] 생태의
- economist [명사] 경제학자
- dispute [동사] ~에 대해 이의를 제기하다, 반박하다
- layoff [명사] 해고
- argue [동사] 주장하다, 언쟁하다, (말로) 다투다
- raw [형용사] 원자재의, 가공되지 않은
- recycled [형용사] 재활용된
- substitute A for B B를 A로 대체하다
- remote [형용사] 먼, 원격의

26

- printing [명사] 인쇄술, 인쇄
- explosion [명사] 폭발적인 증가, 폭발
- publication [명사] 출판물, 간행물
- woodcut [명사] 목판화
- competition [명사] 경쟁, 대회, 시합
- attract [동사] 유인하다, 끌어당기다, 매혹하다
- journalism [명사] 저널리즘 (기사거리를 모으고 기사를 쓰는 일)
- public figure 유명 인사, 공인
- socialite [명사] 사교계 명사
- private figure 사인, 일반인(공인이 아닌 사람)
- distributed [형용사] 배포[분포]되는, 광범위한
- move [동사] 바뀌다, 움직이다 / [명사] 변화, 이동
- oral [형용사] (입에서) 입으로 전해지는, 구두의

27

- framework [명사] 틀, 뼈대
- internalize [동사] 내면화하다, 습득하다
- athletic [형용사] 운동의, 체육의
- yield [동사] 산출하다, 항복하다, 양보하다
- conscious [형용사] 의식적인, 의식하는
- rehearse [동사] 연습하다, 시연하다
- in an attempt to V ~하기 위하여, ~하려는 시도로
- kinesthetic [형용사] 운동 감각(성)의
- on demand 필요로 하는 즉시, 요구만 있으면 (언제든지)
- intuitive [형용사] 직관적인, 직관에 의한
- oversimplification [명사] 지나친 단순화[간소화]
- model [명사] 본보기, 모범

28

- agriculture [명사] 농업
- undeniable [형용사] 부인할 수 없는, 명백한
- sustain [동사] 살아가게 하다, 지탱하다
- estimate [명사] 추정치, 견적 / [동사] 추정하다
- vary [동사] 다양하다, 달라지다
- evidence [명사] 증거, 흔적
- population [명사] 인구
- establish [동사] 확립하다, 설립하다
- qualitative [형용사] 질적인, 성질상의
- sedentary [형용사] 한곳에 머물러 사는, 앉아서 하는

29

- fairness [명사] 공정성
- taxation [명사] 과세, 조세
- expressive [형용사] 표현적인, ~을 나타내는
- dimension [명사] 차원, 규모
- moral [형용사] 도덕적인, 도의적인
- honor [명사] 명예, 영광
- recognition [명사] 인정, 인식
- discourage [동사] 억제하다, 막다, 좌절시키다
- explicit [형용사] 노골적인, 명백한
- undesirable [형용사] 바람직하지 않은, 달갑지 않은
- disapproval [명사] 반감, 못마땅함
- engage in ~에 참여하다
- sugary [형용사] 설탕이 든
- carbon emission 탄소 배출
- address [동사] (문제를) 다루다, 처리하다
- norm [명사] 규범, 표준
- shape [동사] 형성하다, (어떤) 형태로 만들다
- income [명사] 소득, 수입
- paid employment 유급 고용
- deterrent [명사] 억제책, 억제력
- revenue [명사] 세수, 세입

30

- innovative [형용사] 혁신적인, 획기적인
- impressive [형용사] 인상적인, 강한 인상을 주는
- remarkably [부사] 놀랍도록, 두드러지게
- auditorium [명사] 강당, 관객석
- interlock [동사] 서로 맞물리다
- acoustic [형용사] 음향의, 청각의
- instinctively [부사] 본능적으로, 직관적으로
- refined [형용사] 세련된, 정제된
- sensibility [명사] 감수성, 감성, 감각
- at that 그것도, 게다가
- criteria [명사] 기준 (criterion의 복수형)
- generate [동사] 만들어 내다, 발생시키다
- sturdy [형용사] 튼튼한, 견고한 (sturdy-sturdier-sturdiest)
- blindly [부사] 무턱대고, 맹목적으로

31

- eliminate [동사] 제거하다, 삭제하다
- bias [명사] 편견, 편향
- have an impact on ~에 영향을 미치다
- objectivity [명사] 객관성
- rationality [명사] 합리성
- cognitive [형용사] 인지적인, 인지의
- conscious [형용사] 의식적인, 의도적인
- overcome [동사] 극복하다
- appropriate [형용사] 적절한, 적합한
- combat [동사] ~와 맞서다, 싸우다
- implement [동사] 실행하다
- informed [형용사] 정보에 기반한, 교양 있는
- rational [형용사] 합리적인, 이성적인

32

- right [명사] 권리 / [형용사] 옳은, 오른쪽의
- distinct [형용사] 구별되는, (전혀) 다른
- related [형용사] 관련이 있는, 관련된
- be regarded as ~이라고 여겨지다
- reveal [동사] 공개하다, 폭로하다
- apply A to B A를 B에 적용하다
- domain [명사] 영역, 분야
- criminal [형용사] 범죄의 / [명사] 범인
- conviction [명사] 유죄 판결
- come into conflict 충돌하다, 싸우다

33

- succeed in V-ing ~하는 것에 성공하다
- preference [명사] 선호(도), 애호
- satisfaction [명사] 만족(감)
- consume [동사] 소비하다, 섭취하다
- underlying [형용사] 기저에 있는, 근본적인
- baby bust 출생률의 급락
- inherent [형용사] 내재적인, 고유의
- taste [명사] 기호, 취향 / [동사] 맛보다
- relative [형용사] 상대적인, 관계있는 / [명사] 친척
- stable [형용사] 변동이 없는, 안정적인
- unsound [형용사] 불안정한, 견고하지 못한, 건강하지 않은
- argument [명사] 주장, 논거, 논쟁
- equivalent [형용사] 같은, 동등한
- rise [명사] 상승 / [동사] 증가하다, 오르다 (rise-rose-risen)
- mortality [명사] 사망률
- be attributed to ~에 기인하다, ~의 덕분으로 여겨지다
- derived from ~에서 얻어진

34

- compete [동사] 경쟁하다, (~와) 겨루다
- temptation [명사] 유혹
- drive up (값 등을) 끌어올리다
- benefit [명사] 혜택, 이익, 이득 / [동사] 혜택을 얻다, 도움이 되다
- misconception [명사] 오해, 잘못된 생각
- account for ~을 설명하다, 차지하다
- competitor [명사] 경쟁자
- differentiate [동사] 차별하다, 구별하다
- enable A to V A가 ~할 수 있게 하다
- inform A about B A에게 B를 알리다[통지하다]
- variety [명사] 다양성, 변화, 종류
- vision [명사] 상상, 환상, 시력
- deliver [동사] (결과를) 내놓다[산출하다], 배달하다

35

- quarrel [동사] 싸우다, 다투다
- back and forth 주고받으며, 왔다갔다
- librarian [명사] 사서

문제편 : p.197~202 | 정답과 해설 : p.242~251

- draft 명사 외풍, 원고, 초안
- negotiation 명사 협상, 절충
- party 명사 당사자, 단체
- impasse 명사 교착 상태, 막다름
- state 동사 언급하다, 진술하다
- underlying 형용사 근원적인, 근본적인
- interest 명사 이해관계

36
- overwhelming 형용사 압도적인, 너무도 강력한
- work 명사 작품, 일
- extract 명사 발췌(본), 초록 / 동사 추출하다
- monotony 명사 단조로움
- flavour(=flavor) 명사 묘미, 특징, 풍미
- chunk 명사 토막, 덩어리
- adequately 부사 충분히
- illustrate 동사 설명하다, 예증하다
- excerpt 명사 발췌
- plot 명사 줄거리, 음모
- gradual 형용사 점진적인, 완만한
- involvement 명사 몰입, 몰두, 관련, 개입
- imply 동사 내포하다, 암시하다
- unfold 동사 (이야기·사태 등을) 전개하다, 펼치다
- juxtaposition 명사 병치
- contrasting 형용사 대조적인, 대비되는

37
- accidental 형용사 우연한, 돌발적인
- fine-tuned 형용사 미세 조정이 된
- inhabit 동사 살다, 거주하다, 서식하다
- fluctuation 명사 변동, (사람·마음의) 동요, 흥망
- signal 동사 나타내다, 시사하다, 암시하다 / 명사 신호
- significant 형용사 상당한, 중요한
- notable 형용사 두드러지는, 눈에 띄는, 주목할 만한
- shrink 동사 작아지다, 줄어들다, 수축하다
- major 형용사 주요한, 중대한
- overheat 동사 과열되다, 과열하다

38
- random 형용사 무작위의, 임의로
- sampling 명사 (표본, 견본의) 추출(법)
- shortcut 명사 지름길, 손쉬운 방법
- analysis 명사 분석, 분석 연구
- convert 동사 변환[전환]시키다, 개조하다
- fitting 형용사 적당한, 적절한
- plane 명사 평면, 수평면, 비행기
- as with ~와 마찬가지로
- conventional 형용사 기존의, 전통적인
- element 명사 요소, 성분

39
- cell 명사 세포
- structural 형용사 구조적인, 구조상의
- richness 명사 풍부함, 부유함
- random 형용사 무작위적인, 임의의
- variation 명사 변이, 변형, 변주곡
- phase 명사 단계, 국면, (천체의) 상
- exhibit 동사 보여 주다, 전시하다
- cellular 형용사 세포의, 휴대 전화의
- formation 명사 형성, 구성
- couple 동사 결합하다
- previously 부사 이전에, 미리
- built-in 형용사 확립된, 붙박이의, 타고난, 고유의
- criteria 명사 기준 (단수형 criterion)
- favor 동사 선호하다 / 명사 부탁, 우호
- serve to V ~하는 역할을 하다
- undergo 동사 거치다, 겪다
- round 명사 과정, (정기적으로 진행되는 일의) 한 차례 / 형용사 둥근
- immune 형용사 면역의, 면역이 된
- extension 명사 확장, 확대
- genetically 부사 유전적으로
- positionally 부사 위치에 의해, 위치적으로
- stimulate 동사 활성화하다, 자극하다
- sculpt 동사 조각하다
- consequence 명사 결과
- variability 명사 변이성, 가변성, 변동성

40
- needy 형용사 빈곤한, 궁핍한, 어려운
- bring A under control A를 통제하다[제어하다]
- specify 동사 (구체적으로) 명시하다
- available 형용사 사용 가능한, 이용할 수 있는
- distribution 명사 분배, 분포
- contribute to A A에 기여하다
- resolution 명사 해결, 결의안, 결심
- perceive 동사 인식하다, 여기다
- enquire 동사 묻다, 문의하다
- obstacle 명사 장애물, 장애
- rigid 형용사 엄격한, 융통성 없는
- demotivate 동사 의욕을 잃게 하다

41
- in terms of ~의 측면[관점]에서
- consume 동사 소비하다, 소모하다
- operate 동사 작동되다, 움직이다
- process 동사 처리하다 / 명사 과정, 절차
- navigate 동사 항해하다, 길을 찾다
- neuroscientist 명사 신경과학자
- fix one's gaze on ~에 시선을 고정하다, ~을 응시하다
- gaze 명사 시선, 눈길, 응시
- direct one's attention (to A) (A로) ~의 주의를 끌다[~의 눈길을 돌리다]
- perform 동사 행하다, 수행하다
- in full view 다 보이는 데서, 바로 앞에서
- give away ~을 누설하다[폭로하다], ~을 나눠주다
- game 명사 속임수, 계략
- assure 동사 확신하다, 납득하다, 보장하다
- visual 형용사 시각적인, 시각의
- prevalence 명사 널리 행하여짐, 보급, 유포
- pedestrian 명사 보행자
- collide with ~와 충돌하다

42
- current 형용사 현재의, 지금의
- consumption 명사 소비, 소모(량)
- invest 동사 투자하다, 쏟다, 부여하다
- laboratory 명사 실험실
- construction site 건설 현장
- graduate 명사 졸업생 / 동사 졸업하다
- crucial 형용사 중대한, 결정적인
- productive 형용사 생산적인, 결실이 있는
- tuition 명사 등록금, 수업료
- investment 명사 투자

43
- obvious 형용사 명백한, 확실한
- competent 형용사 능력 있는, 능숙한, 권한이 있는
- competence 명사 능력, 능숙함, 권한, 기능
- cluster 명사 무리, (작은 열매의) 송이 / 동사 무리를 이루다
- stand a chance of V-ing ~할 가능성이 있다
- paradoxical 형용사 역설적인, 모순된
- unapproachable 형용사 접근할 수 없는
- distant 형용사 먼, 동떨어진
- by comparison 그에 비해
- superb 형용사 최고의, 최상의
- gourmet 형용사 미식의
- screw up 망치다, 엉망으로 만들다
- (every) once in a while 가끔, 이따금

44
- computational 형용사 컴퓨터를 사용한
- generate 동사 생성하다, 발생시키다
- embody 동사 구현하다, 상징하다, 포함하다
- notion 명사 개념, 관념, 생각
- computation 명사 계산, 계량, 평가
- survival 명사 생존, 유물
- assign 동사 부여하다, 맡기다
- means 명사 수단, 방법, (개인이 가진) 돈, 수입
- forage 동사 먹이를 찾다
- convey 동사 알려주다, 전달하다
- nectar 명사 (꽃의) 꿀
- locate 동사 ~의 위치를 찾아내다
- stylize 동사 양식화하다
- comb 명사 벌집, 빗
- evaluate 동사 평가하다, ~의 수치를 구하다
- bother 동사 일부러 ~하다
- such as it is 대단한 것은 못되지만
- in the light of ~을 고려하여, ~에 비추어
- organism 명사 유기체
- prescriptive 형용사 규정하는, 규범적인

15. 주어진 문장 위치 파악

01
- transplant 명사 이식 / 동사 이식하다
- surgeon 명사 외과 의사
- era 명사 시대

문제편 : p.202~209 | 정답과 해설 : p.251~260

- respirator 명사 인공호흡기, 방독 마스크
- function 명사 기능 / 동사 기능하다
- cease 동사 중단하다, 그치다
- committee 명사 위원회
- discernible 형용사 식별 가능한, 알아볼 수 있는
- nervous 형용사 신경의, 불안해하는
- criterion 명사 기준, 척도 (복수형 criteria)
- adopt 동사 받아들이다, 채택하다
- modification 명사 수정, 변경

02
- risk 명사 위험, 위험 요소
- uncertainty 명사 불확실성
- contract 동사 계약하다, 수축하다
- party 명사 당사자, 정당
- minimize 동사 최소화하다
- associated with ~와 관련된
- capital cost 자본 비용
- tooling 명사 세공, 연장을 쓰는 일
- manufacturer 명사 제조(업)자, 생산 회사
- subcontract 동사 하청을 주다
- major 형용사 주요한, 중대한, 심각한
- component 명사 부품, (구성) 요소
- supplier 명사 공급(업)자, 공급 회사
- transfer 명사 이전, 이동 / 동사 이동하다
- inherit 동사 이어받다, 상속받다
- end-item 명사 완제품

03
- metaphor 명사 은유, 비유
- represent 동사 나타내다, 대표하다
- hockey puck 하키 퍽(아이스하키에서 공처럼 치는 고무 원반)
- confirm 동사 확인하다, 확정하다
- even 형용사 고른, 평평한
- an array of(= a wide array of) 다수의
- dip 명사 움푹 팬 부분
- crack 명사 (갈라져 생긴) 금
- bump 명사 요철, 튀어나온 부분
- drag 명사 저항력, 방해물 / 동사 끌다
- friction 명사 마찰력, (의견) 충돌
- linguistic 형용사 언어적인, 언어(학)의
- perspective 명사 관점, 시각
- frictionless 형용사 마찰이 없는

04
- destructive 형용사 파괴적인, 해를 끼치는
- compress 동사 압축하다, 꾹 누르다
- give 동사 (힘을 받아) 휘어지다, 구부러지다 / 명사 탄력성, 신축성
- tap 명사 수도꼭지 / 동사 가볍게 두드리다
- stir 동사 젓다, 섞다
- a body of 많은 양의
- impact 명사 충돌, 충격, 영향
- force 명사 힘, 군대 / 동사 강요하다, 강제하다
- sting 동사 얼얼하게 하다, 따끔따끔하게 하다

- belly-flop 동사 배로 수면을 치며 떨어지다
- height 명사 높이, 키, 고도
- concrete 명사 콘크리트 / 형용사 콘크리트로 된, 구체적인
- incompressibility 명사 비(非)압축성
- deadly 형용사 치명적인, 위험한
- in the case of ~의 경우에
- toss 동사 던지다, 토스하다

05
- vastly 부사 상당히, 굉장히, 대단히
- function 명사 기능 / 동사 기능하다
- identical 형용사 동일한
- seedling 명사 묘목
- organ 명사 기관, 장기
- capacity 명사 능력, 용량
- initiate 동사 시작하다, 착수시키다
- elongation 명사 연장
- propel 동사 나아가게 하다, 몰고 가다
- allocate 동사 배분하다, 할당하다
- adapt 동사 적응하다, 맞추다
- distinct 형용사 별개의, 분명한
- underlying 형용사 근원적인, 근본적인
- metabolic 형용사 신진대사의

06
- holy grail 궁극적 목표
- general 형용사 전반적인, 일반적인
- intelligence 명사 지능
- endeavor 명사 노력, 시도, 애씀 / 동사 노력하다, 시도하다
- quotient 명사 지수, (나눗셈에서) 몫
- universal 형용사 보편적인
- specific 형용사 특정한
- sphere 명사 범위, 영역, 구(체)
- particular 형용사 특정한
- domain 명사 영역
- gifted 형용사 재능 있는, 타고난
- conductor 명사 지휘자
- compose 동사 작곡하다, 구성하다

07
- involve 동사 수반하다, 포함하다, 관련시키다
- population 명사 개체군, 개체수, 인구
- organism 명사 유기체, 생물체
- in response to ~에 (반)응하여
- alter 동사 변하다, 달라지다, 바꾸다
- acclimate(=acclimatize) 동사 순응하다, (장소·기후 등에) 익숙해지다
- concentration 명사 농도, 집중
- pigment 명사 색소, 안료
- temporary 형용사 일시적인, 임시의
- pass A on to B A에게 B를 물려주다
- inherit 동사 유전으로 이어받다, 상속하다
- thrive 동사 번영하다, 번창하다
- trait 명사 특징, 특성, 특색
- subsequent 형용사 다음의, 차후의

- countless 형용사 수많은, 무수한
- distinctive 형용사 특유의, 독특한
- happen to V 우연히 ~하다
- have an advantage in ~하는 데 유리하다

08
- fundamental 형용사 근본적인, 핵심적인, 필수적인
- manipulation 명사 조작, 속임수
- variable 명사 변수 / 형용사 변하기 쉬운, 가변성의
- attempt to V ~하려고 시도하다
- potential 형용사 잠재적인, 가능성이 있는 / 명사 가능성, 잠재력
- underlying 형용사 근본적인, 근원적인, 기저에 있는
- correlated 형용사 상관관계가 있는
- vitamin supplements 비타민 보충제
- merely 부사 단지, 그저, 한낱
- observe 동사 관찰하다, 준수하다

09
- glucose 명사 포도당
- fuel 명사 연료, 동력 에너지원
- account for ~을 차지하다, ~을 설명하다
- adaptive 형용사 적응력이 있는, 적응할 수 있는
- economize 동사 절약하다, 아끼다
- shift 동사 이동하다, 옮기다 / 명사 이동, 변경, 교대 근무 시간
- nuance 명사 미묘한 차이, 뉘앙스
- singular 형용사 단일한, 단수형의
- at hand 당면한, 머지않아
- sit back 편안히 앉다
- speculate 동사 사색하다, 추측하다
- reflexive 형용사 반사적인

10
- vitally 부사 매우 중요하게, 필수적으로
- wherever 접속사 어디에(로) ~하든지, 어디든지
- whatever 접속사 무엇을 ~하든지, 무엇이든지
- properly 부사 제대로, 적절하게
- internal 형용사 내부의, 내부적인
- fever 명사 (신체의 병으로 인한) 열
- external 형용사 외부의, 외부적인

11
- be credited with ~라고 인정받다, 명성을 얻다
- mobile 형용사 이동식의, 기동성 있는
- vacuum cleaner 명사 진공청소기
- coin 동사 (새로운 낱말·어구를) 만들다 / 명사 동전, 주화
- nature 명사 특징, 본질, 자연, 천성
- on the inside 내부의, 안에
- suction 명사 흡입력, 흡입
- handy 형용사 편리한, 유용한
- be stuck with ~을 떨쳐버리지 못하다
- reference 명사 언급, 참조
- file 동사 제출하다, 발송하다 / 명사 파일
- provisional 형용사 임시의, 임시적인
- specification 명사 (제품) 설명서, 사양

문제편 : p.209~214 정답과 해설 : p.260~267

- [ ] intended 형용사 의도된, 계획된

12
- [ ] temperature 명사 온도
- [ ] visibly 부사 눈에 띄게, 분명히
- [ ] glow 동사 빛나다, 타오르다 / 명사 불빛, 홍조
- [ ] poker 명사 부지깽이, 찌르는 사람, 포커
- [ ] measure 동사 측정하다 / 명사 단위, 척도, 조치
- [ ] precise 형용사 정확한
- [ ] rely on ~에 의존하다
- [ ] surface 명사 표면
- [ ] emit 동사 방출하다, 내뿜다
- [ ] interior 명사 내부 / 형용사 내부의
- [ ] conceal 동사 숨기다, 감추다
- [ ] obtain 동사 얻다, 구하다

13
- [ ] hemisphere 명사 (지구 또는 뇌의) 반구
- [ ] solar 형용사 태양의
- [ ] radiation 명사 복사열, 방사선
- [ ] over/in the course of ~중, ~동안
- [ ] latitude 명사 위도, 지역
- [ ] inequality 명사 불균형
- [ ] operation 명사 작동
- [ ] take on 받다, (일 등을) 맡다
- [ ] give off (열·냄새·빛 등을) 방출하다
- [ ] working fluid 작동유
- [ ] atmosphere 명사 대기, 분위기
- [ ] moisture 명사 수분, 습기
- [ ] earth 명사 땅, 지구
- [ ] flow away 흐르다
- [ ] altitude 명사 고도
- [ ] descend 동사 하강하다, 내려오다
- [ ] equator 명사 적도
- [ ] northerly 형용사 북쪽의, 북쪽에 있는
- [ ] southerly 형용사 남쪽의, 남쪽에 있는

14
- [ ] have an effect on ~에 영향을 미치다
- [ ] productivity 명사 생산성
- [ ] lead A to V A가 ~하도록 이끌다
- [ ] individual 명사 개인 / 형용사 각각의
- [ ] speciation 명사 종 분화, 종 형성
- [ ] tangled 형용사 뒤얽힌, 엉켜 있는, 복잡한
- [ ] deliberation 명사 심사숙고, 신중함
- [ ] attack 명사 착수, 개시, 공격
- [ ] measure 동사 측정하다, 재다 / 명사 조치, 양
- [ ] publication 명사 출판(물)
- [ ] method 명사 방법, 방식
- [ ] lead to A A로 이어지다
- [ ] drastically 부사 극적으로, 급격히
- [ ] enable A to V A가 ~할 수 있게 하다
- [ ] amplify 동사 증폭시키다, 확대하다
- [ ] the number of ~의 수
- [ ] substitute 동사 대체하다, 교체하다

15
- [ ] carry out ~을 수행하다
- [ ] cause 명사 원인
- [ ] engagement 명사 몰입, 참여, 약속, 약혼
- [ ] theoretical 형용사 이론적인
- [ ] practical 형용사 실제적인, 실용적인
- [ ] standpoint 명사 관점, 견지
- [ ] identify 동사 알아내다, 발견하다
- [ ] driver 명사 동기, 동인, 추진 요인
- [ ] manipulate 동사 조작하다, 조종하다
- [ ] fall into ~으로 나뉘다
- [ ] camp 명사 입장, 견해, 진영, 측
- [ ] responsible 형용사 책임이 있는
- [ ] constructive 형용사 건설적인
- [ ] performance 명사 수행, 성과
- [ ] noteworthy 형용사 주목할 만한
- [ ] match 동사 ~에 부합하다, 일치하다
- [ ] exceed 동사 ~을 능가하다, 넘어서다
- [ ] evident 형용사 분명한, 명백한
- [ ] be employed in ~에 종사하다

16
- [ ] charisma 명사 카리스마, 통솔력
- [ ] eminently 부사 (긍정적인 의미에서) 분명히, 대단히
- [ ] famed 형용사 유명한, 널리 알려진
- [ ] action 명사 작용, 행동
- [ ] reaction 명사 반작용, 반응
- [ ] that is to say 즉, 다시 말해서
- [ ] interaction 명사 상호 작용
- [ ] cue 명사 단서, 신호
- [ ] in one's favor ~에게 유리하게, ~를 위하여
- [ ] procedure 명사 절차, 방법
- [ ] be used to ~에 익숙하다

17
- [ ] verification 명사 검증, 확인, 증명
- [ ] verify 동사 진실임을 입증하다, 확인하다
- [ ] falsify 동사 거짓임을 입증하다
- [ ] objective 형용사 객관적인
- [ ] external 형용사 외부의
- [ ] sphere 명사 구, 둥근 물체
- [ ] evidence 명사 증거
- [ ] lifetime 명사 일생
- [ ] spin 동사 회전하다
- [ ] axis 명사 축
- [ ] meta-physical 형용사 형이상학의
- [ ] existence 명사 존재
- [ ] present 동사 야기하다, 주다
- [ ] considerable 형용사 상당한
- [ ] challenge 명사 도전, 문제 / 동사 도전하다
- [ ] generate 동사 만들어 내다, 발생시키다
- [ ] be willing to V 기꺼이 ~하다

18
- [ ] satellite 명사 (인공)위성
- [ ] orbit 명사 궤도 / 동사 궤도를 돌다
- [ ] tricky 형용사 까다로운, 교활한
- [ ] enforce 동사 시행하다, 강요하다
- [ ] tackle 동사 해결하다, (문제 상황과) 씨름하다
- [ ] come up with ~를 내놓다, 생각해 내다
- [ ] novel 형용사 새로운 / 명사 소설
- [ ] drag 동사 끌다 / 명사 항력
- [ ] atmosphere 명사 대기(권), 분위기
- [ ] burn up 다 타버리다, 몹시 열이 나다
- [ ] fire 동사 발사하다, 불을 붙이다, 해고하다
- [ ] heat up 가열하다, 뜨거워지다
- [ ] atmospheric 형용사 대기의
- [ ] pick up ~을 수거하다, 집다, 획득하다
- [ ] debris 명사 잔해물, 쓰레기

19
- [ ] frequency 명사 주파수
- [ ] calculate 동사 계산하다, 산출하다
- [ ] obvious 형용사 명백한
- [ ] indeed 부사 실제로, 정말
- [ ] subjectively 부사 주관적으로
- [ ] play back 틀어 주다
- [ ] track 명사 곡, 길
- [ ] short-lived 형용사 일시적인, 오래가지 못하는
- [ ] in the long run 장기적으로, 결국
- [ ] convince 동사 납득시키다, 설득시키다
- [ ] serve 동사 도움이 되다, 기여하다, 제공하다

20
- [ ] liberalization 명사 자유화
- [ ] capital 형용사 자본의, 주요한, 대문자의 / 명사 자본, 수도, 대문자
- [ ] fund 명사 자금, 기금
- [ ] investment 명사 (시간·노력 등의) 투자
- [ ] contributor 명사 기여 요인, 공헌자
- [ ] domestic 형용사 국내의, 가정의, 애완용의
- [ ] tap into ~을 이용하다, 사용하다
- [ ] scope 명사 기회, 여지, 범위
- [ ] manage 동사 관리하다, 경영하다, 간신히 ~하다
- [ ] spread 동사 분산시키다, 펼치다
- [ ] instability 명사 (경제적·심리적) 불안정성
- [ ] crisis 명사 위기, 최악의 고비 (복수형 crises)
- [ ] in the wake of ~의 결과로, ~에 뒤이어
- [ ] sound 형용사 올바른, 건강한
- [ ] regulatory 형용사 규제의
- [ ] seed 명사 (사건의) 원인, 근원, 씨앗

21
- [ ] prioritize 동사 우선시하다
- [ ] disposition 명사 (타고난) 기질, 성격
- [ ] seek 동사 찾다, (추)구하다
- [ ] strict 형용사 엄격한
- [ ] stubborn 형용사 완고한, 고집이 센
- [ ] devoted 형용사 헌신적인
- [ ] self-discipline 명사 자기 훈련(자제력), 자기 수양
- [ ] boast of ~을 자랑하다, 뽐내다
- [ ] think through (문제에 대해) 충분히 생각하다
- [ ] whereas 접속사 반면에

문제편 : p.214~219 | 정답과 해설 : p.268~275

- [ ] dispositional 형용사 (타고난) 기질의, 성향의
- [ ] attribution 명사 귀인(원인을 돌림)

22
- [ ] tremendous 형용사 엄청난, 굉장한
- [ ] supplier 명사 공급자, 공급 회사
- [ ] under-the-table (거래 등이) 비밀리의, 내밀의
- [ ] merger 명사 (조직체·기업체의) 합병
- [ ] inform 동사 ~에 영향을 미치다, 알려주다
- [ ] yield 동사 산출하다, 항복하다, 양도하다
- [ ] catch 동사 얻다, 보다, 잡다
- [ ] profitable 형용사 수익성이 있는, 이득이 되는
- [ ] likely 부사 아마 / 형용사 ~할 것 같은, 적당한
- [ ] hold off on A A를 연기하다, 미루다

23
- [ ] pivotal 형용사 중추적인, 중심이 되는
- [ ] component 명사 (구성) 요소, 부품, 성분
- [ ] guarantee 동사 보장하다 / 명사 보증
- [ ] reliable 형용사 믿을 만한, 신뢰할 수 있는
- [ ] optimal 형용사 최적의, 최선의
- [ ] portable 형용사 휴대용의, 이동식의
- [ ] have an effect/impact on ~에 영향을 미치다
- [ ] overall 형용사 전반적인 / 부사 전반적으로
- [ ] automobile 명사 자동차

24
- [ ] ideology 명사 이데올로기, 이념
- [ ] literature 명사 문학 (작품)
- [ ] literary 형용사 문학의, 문학적인
- [ ] formative 형용사 형성되는, 형성에 중요한
- [ ] unconsciously 부사 무의식적으로
- [ ] socialise(=socialize) 동사 사회화하다, 어울리다
- [ ] vastly 부사 크게, 막대하게
- [ ] overshadow 동사 가리다, 그림자를 드리우다
- [ ] considerable 형용사 상당한, 중요한
- [ ] interaction 명사 상호 작용
- [ ] televise 동사 텔레비전으로 방영하다
- [ ] resultant 형용사 그 결과로 생긴
- [ ] subsequent 형용사 그 후의, 다음의
- [ ] publish 동사 출판하다, 발표하다

25
- [ ] communicate 동사 전달하다, 소통하다
- [ ] advent 명사 출현
- [ ] periodical 명사 정기 간행물
- [ ] yield 동사 (자리를) 내주다, 양도하다, 포기하다
- [ ] yield ground to ~에게 내주다
- [ ] journal 명사 학술지, 신문
- [ ] chief 형용사 주요한, 최고의 / 명사 최고위자, 우두머리
- [ ] abandon 동사 버리다
- [ ] altogether 부사 완전히, 총, 전체적으로 보아
- [ ] reputation 명사 명성, 평판
- [ ] contribution 명사 기여, 공헌
- [ ] treatment 명사 다룸, 논의, 취급, 치료
- [ ] revolutionary 형용사 혁명적인
- [ ] paper 명사 논문, 종이, 신문
- [ ] depend on ~에 달려 있다, ~에 의존하다
- [ ] publication 명사 출간

26
- [ ] supply 명사 공급 / 동사 공급하다, 제공하다
- [ ] meet 동사 충족하다, 만나다
- [ ] demand 명사 수요 / 동사 요구하다
- [ ] fixed 형용사 고정된
- [ ] inflexible 형용사 유연하지 못한
- [ ] inelastic 형용사 비탄력적인, 고정적인
- [ ] note 동사 주목하다, 언급하다
- [ ] memorabilia 명사 기념품, 수집품
- [ ] venue 명사 (콘서트·스포츠 경기·회담 등의) 장소
- [ ] revenue 명사 수익, 수입
- [ ] distribution 명사 배급, 배포

27
- [ ] consume 동사 섭취하다, 소모하다
- [ ] antinutrient 명사 항영양소
- [ ] intuitively 부사 직관적으로, 직감적으로
- [ ] evolution 명사 진화, 발전
- [ ] pass A down A를 전해주다[물려주다]
- [ ] intelligence 명사 지능, 정보
- [ ] intuition 명사 직관, 직감
- [ ] justify 동사 정당화하다, 해명하다
- [ ] genetic 형용사 유전적인, 유전(학)의
- [ ] keep A away from B A를 B로부터 멀리하다
- [ ] fragile 형용사 연약한, 부서지기 쉬운
- [ ] taste bud 명사 미뢰(味蕾), 맛봉오리
- [ ] perceive 동사 인식하다, 인지하다
- [ ] disgusting 형용사 역겨운, 혐오스러운
- [ ] tolerate 동사 견디다, 참다, 용인하다

28
- [ ] gravitational pull 중력
- [ ] stretch 동사 잡아 늘이다, 늘이다
- [ ] compress 동사 누르다, 눌리다, 압축하다
- [ ] perpendicular 형용사 직각을 이루는, 수직적인
- [ ] tidal 형용사 조수의
- [ ] rigidity 명사 단단함, 엄격
- [ ] high tide 명사 만조(밀물)
- [ ] low tide 명사 간조(썰물)
- [ ] rubber band 명사 고무줄
- [ ] bulge 동사 부풀다 / 명사 팽창

29
- [ ] incidence 명사 발생률, 영향 범위
- [ ] surface 동사 표면화되다, 나타나다 / 명사 표면, 지면
- [ ] phytochemical 명사 (식물 속에 함유된) 식물 화학물질
- [ ] compound 명사 화합물, 복합체 / 형용사 합성의
- [ ] lack 동사 부족하다 / 명사 부족, 결핍
- [ ] chlorophyll 명사 엽록소
- [ ] antioxidant 명사 산화 방지제, 방부제

30
- [ ] primitive 형용사 원시의, 소박한, 구식의
- [ ] roughly 부사 대략적으로, 거의
- [ ] proportional 형용사 비례하는
- [ ] physical 형용사 물리적인, 신체적인
- [ ] muscular 형용사 근육의
- [ ] far from 전혀 ~이 아닌
- [ ] gap 명사 격차
- [ ] agricultural 형용사 농업의
- [ ] thus 부사 그러므로, 따라서
- [ ] in the course of ~동안, ~하는 중에
- [ ] unchanged 형용사 그대로인, 변하지 않은

31
- [ ] acid 명사 산, 신맛이 나는 것 / 형용사 신맛이 나는
- [ ] deficiency 명사 결핍, 부족
- [ ] preindustrial 형용사 산업화 이전의
- [ ] deal with ~에 대처하다, 해결하다 (deal-dealt-dealt)
- [ ] insufficiency 명사 불충분, 부족
- [ ] aplenty 부사 많이 / 형용사 많은
- [ ] live off ~에 의지해서 살다
- [ ] refrigeration 명사 냉장 (보관), 냉동 (보존)
- [ ] endure 동사 견디다, 참다
- [ ] alternating 형용사 번갈아 오는, 교차하는
- [ ] famine 명사 기근, 굶주림
- [ ] starvation 명사 굶주림, 기아
- [ ] crisis 명사 위기 (복수형 crises)
- [ ] survive on ~을 먹으며 목숨을 부지하다
- [ ] ultimate 형용사 근본적인, 궁극적인

32
- [ ] nonverbal 형용사 비언어적인
- [ ] cue 명사 신호, 단서
- [ ] elaborate 형용사 정교한, 정성을 들인
- [ ] conceal 동사 숨기다, 감추다
- [ ] proper 형용사 적절한, 제대로 된
- [ ] counterforce 명사 상충하는 힘, 반대 세력
- [ ] leak out 새어 나오다, 누출되다
- [ ] posture 명사 자세, 태도
- [ ] sheer 형용사 순전한, 완전한
- [ ] fixate 동사 집착하다, ~을 고정시키다
- [ ] potential 형용사 잠재적인, 가능성이 있는

33
- [ ] composer 명사 작곡가
- [ ] tribal 형용사 부족의, 종족의
- [ ] collaboration 명사 협연, 공동 작업, 협력
- [ ] on the spur of the moment 즉흥적으로, 충동적으로
- [ ] silence 명사 휴지(休止), 침묵, 고요
- [ ] accented 형용사 강세가 있는
- [ ] serendipitous 형용사 우연히 얻은, 우연히 발견한
- [ ] converge 동사 (한데) 모아지다, 집중되다
- [ ] simultaneous 형용사 동시의, 동시에 일어나는

34
- [ ] categorize 동사 분류하다

문제편 : p.219~225 | 정답과 해설 : p.275~285

- generalize 동사 일반화하다
- unconsciously 부사 무의식적으로
- prejudiced 형용사 편견을 가진
- enlightened 형용사 계몽된
- function 동사 (제대로) 활동하다, 기능하다
- instinct 명사 본능
- distort 동사 왜곡하다
- jump to a conclusion 성급하게 결론을 내리다

35

- electric 형용사 전기의, 전기를 이용하는
- organ 명사 기관, 장기
- discharge 동사 방출하다, 해고하다
- negatively 부사 음전하로, 부정적으로
- load 동사 (전하를) 띠다, 짐을 싣다
- electric field 전기장
- electric current 전류
- contract 동사 수축하다, 줄어들다, 계약하다 / 명사 계약
- chunk 명사 덩어리, 상당히 많은 양
- intensity 명사 강도, 강렬함
- frequency 명사 주파수, 빈도
- range 명사 범위, 다양성 / 동사 범위가 ~에 이르다
- interference 명사 간섭, 전파 방해, 개입

36

- relativity 명사 상대성 (이론), 상호 의존성
- equation 명사 방정식, 등식
- inertial 형용사 관성의, 관성에 의한
- formula 명사 공식, 제조법
- identical 형용사 동일한
- subjective 형용사 주관적인, 개인적인
- alter 동사 바꾸다, 변하다
- ever-changing 형용사 늘 변화하는
- engaging 형용사 매력적인, 호감이 가는
- devastating 형용사 엄청나게 충격적인, 파괴적인
- perceive 동사 여기다, 감지하다
- stimuli 명사 자극 (stimulus의 복수형)

37

- introverted 형용사 내향적인, 내성적인
- presumption 명사 억측, 추정
- extrovert 명사 외향적인 사람
- population 명사 인구, 주민
- split 동사 나뉘다, 분열되다 / 명사 분열, 분화, 분할
- introvert 명사 내향적인 사람
- executive 명사 경영 간부, 경영진 / 형용사 경영의, 행정의
- extroverted 형용사 외향적인, 사교적인
- corporate 형용사 기업의, 법인의
- introversion 명사 내향성
- barrier 명사 장애물, 장벽
- reexamine 동사 재검토하다, 재검사하다
- stereotype 명사 고정 관념
- be of service to N ~에게 도움이 되다

- empower 동사 ~에게 (…하는 능력을) 부여하다, 할 수 있게 하다, 권한을 주다
- retain 동사 유지하다, 보유하다
- adhere to N ~을 고수하다
- humility 명사 겸손, 겸양
- pay off 결실을 맺다, 성공하다, 성과를 올리다

38

- measurement 명사 측정, 측량
- capture 동사 포착하다, 포획하다, 사로잡다
- adopt 동사 채택하다, 입양하다
- standard 명사 기준, 규범
- quantum mechanics 양자 역학
- comprehensive 형용사 포괄적인, 종합적인
- outside 전치사 ~을 제외하고, 빼고, 넘어서 / 명사 바깥쪽
- drive 명사 추진력, 투지 / 동사 ~하게 만들다
- flawlessly 부사 완벽하게, 흠 없이
- oriented 형용사 ~을 지향하는
- commerce 명사 상업, 무역
- shortcoming 명사 단점, 결점
- tradeoff 명사 교환, 거래

39

- assumption 명사 가정, 추정
- doomed 형용사 죽을 운명의, 불운한
- reorientate 동사 방향을 다시 잡다
- undoubtedly 부사 의심할 여지 없이
- inhospitable 형용사 살기 힘든, 황량한, 불친절한
- perish 동사 죽다, 소멸되다
- infrequent 형용사 드문, 흔하지 않은
- timescale 명사 시간, 기간
- unfold 동사 진행되다, 밝혀지다, 펼쳐지다
- profound 형용사 중대한, 중요한, 심오한
- migration 명사 이동, 이주

40

- intuition 명사 직관, 직감
- hard-earned 형용사 애써서 얻은, 힘들게 얻은
- expert 명사 전문가 / 형용사 전문가의
- on one's feet 즉각적으로, 즉흥적으로
- invest 동사 투자하다, 투입하다, 쏟다
- practice 명사 실천, 연습
- in accordance with ~에 따라서, ~에 부합되게
- internalize 동사 내재화하다, 내면화하다
- expertise 명사 전문 지식
- conviction 명사 확신, 신념
- substance 명사 실체, 본질, 물질
- AI(=artificial intelligence) 명사 인공 지능
- ensure 동사 확실히 하다, 보장하다
- deliver 동사 전달하다, 배달하다
- inclined 형용사 ~하는 성향이 있는, (~을) 하고 싶은
- delusion 명사 착각, 망상
- reinforce 동사 강화하다, 보강하다

- tendency 명사 경향, 기질
- open-minded 형용사 개방적인, 마음이 열린
- rational 형용사 합리적인, 이성적인
- sensible 형용사 분별 있는, 합리적인

41

- obvious 형용사 분명한, 명백한
- bidirectional 형용사 두 방향으로 작용하는
- thoroughfare 명사 통로, 주요[간선] 도로
- commerce 명사 상거래, 무역, 상업
- track 동사 추적하다 / 명사 길, 자국
- shipment 명사 배송, 수송품, 적하물
- corporate 형용사 기업의, 법인의
- medium 명사 매체, 수단 (복수형 media)
- distribute 동사 배포하다, 분배하다
- modify 동사 수정하다, 바꾸다, 조정하다

42

- fire 동사 해고하다
- pink slip 해고 통지서
- labor force 노동력
- the industrial revolution 산업혁명
- workforce 명사 노동력, 노동자
- automation 명사 자동화
- eliminate 동사 제거하다, 없애다
- replace 동사 대체[대신]하다, 제자리에 놓다
- displaced 형용사 쫓겨난, 추방된
- idle 형용사 한가한, 나태한
- farm 동사 농사를 짓다, (동물을) 기르다 / 명사 농장
- man 동사 (어떤 장소에서) 일하다, ~에 인원을 배치하다
- manufacture 동사 제조하다, 생산하다
- occupation 명사 직업, 점령 (기간)
- appliance 명사 가전제품
- chemist 명사 화학자

43

- contagion 명사 전염, 감염
- viral 형용사 바이러스성의
- proximity 명사 가까움, 근접
- excessively 부사 과도하게
- in the company of ~와 함께
- inhibit 동사 막다, 억제하다
- stimulate 동사 자극하다, 촉진시키다
- installation 명사 설치, 설비
- whereas 접속사 반면에

44

- curious 형용사 호기심을 끄는, 이상한
- hibernate 동사 동면하다, 칩거하다
- hibernation 명사 동면
- neurological 형용사 신경학적인
- metabolic 형용사 신진대사적인
- anesthetize 동사 마취시키다, 마비시키다
- subject 명사 대상, 과목, 국민 / 형용사 ~될 수 있는, 종속된
- unconscious 형용사 의식이 없는, 무의식의

문제편 : p.226~230 | 정답과 해설 : p.285~293

- conventional 형용사 전형적인, 틀에 박힌
- unconsciousness 명사 무의식, 인사불성
- involve 동사 수반하다, 포함하다
- profound 형용사 깊은, 심오한
- dramatic 형용사 급격한, 극적인
- fall 명사 하락, 추락
- temperature 명사 온도, 기온
- degree 명사 (온도의 단위인) 도
- Fahrenheit 형용사 화씨의
- definition 명사 정의, 의미, 선명도
- awaken 동사 (잠에서) 깨우다
- accurately 부사 정확하게
- state 명사 상태, 양상
- torpor 명사 휴면 (상태), 무기력

16. 문단 요약

01

- mold 동사 형성하다, 주조하다 / 명사 거푸집
- conduct 동사 수행하다, 행동하다
- have an impact on ~에 영향을 미치다
- be inclined to V ~하는 경향이 있다
- irrespective of ~와 관계없이
- boost 명사 촉진제, 부양책 / 동사 북돋우다, 신장시키다
- induce 동사 야기하다, 유발하다
- regardless of ~와 무관하게
- agreeable 형용사 쾌활한, 선뜻 동의하는
- pull 명사 영향력, 매력, 끌어당기는 힘 / 동사 끌다, 당기다
- pulse 명사 리듬, 박자
- translate 동사 변환되다, 변환하다

02

- behavioral economist 행동 경제학자
- subject 명사 실험 대상자, 주제 / 형용사 ~될 수 있는, ~을 받아야 하는
- stock market 명사 주식 시장
- reward 명사 보상 / 동사 보상하다
- forecast 명사 예측, 예보 / 동사 예측하다
- come true 실현되다, 이루어지다
- payment 명사 보상, 보답, 지불
- prospect 명사 기대, 가능성, 예상
- reasoning 명사 추론, 추리
- belong to ~에 속하다
- contradict 동사 모순되다, 반박하다
- disregard 명사 무시, 묵살
- restrict 동사 제한하다, 방해하다
- assurance 명사 확언, 장담

03

- go for ~에 해당되다, ~에도 마찬가지다
- line up with ~에 동조하다, ~와 함께 작용하다
- unconscious 형용사 무의식적인
- conscious 형용사 의식하고 있는, 의식적인
- distract 동사 산만하게 하다, 정신없게 하다
- depressing 형용사 울적한, 우울한
- preoccupied 형용사 몰두한, 열중한, 선점된
- overcooked 형용사 지나치게 익은, 너무 익힌
- habitual 형용사 습관적인
- helpful 형용사 도움이 되는

04

- perception 명사 지각, 인식
- external 형용사 외부의, 겉의
- undergraduate 명사 대학생, 학부생
- coherent 형용사 (이야기가) 말이 되는, 이치에 맞는
- wrinkled 형용사 주름진, 쭈글쭈글한
- bitterly 부사 씁쓸하게, 비통하게
- linguistics 명사 언어학
- extraordinary 형용사 놀라운, 비범한
- bend 동사 구부리다, 휘다
- corresponding 형용사 일치하는, 상응하는
- suggest 동사 암시하다, 제안하다
- irrelevant 형용사 무관한, 상관없는
- comparable 형용사 유사한, 필적하는

05

- mislead A into V-ing A를 ~하도록 현혹하다, 오도하다
- good 명사 (주로 복수형) 재화
- puffery 명사 과대 광고, 과장된 칭찬
- exaggerate 동사 과장하다, 부풀리다
- fraud 명사 사기, 엉터리
- vague 형용사 모호한, 희미한
- label A (as) B A를 B라고 표기하다
- unverifiable 형용사 증명할 수 없는
- detergent 명사 세제
- advocate 명사 옹호자, 지지자 / 동사 옹호하다
- informed 형용사 정보를 알고 있는, 잘 아는
- conscious 형용사 (형용사/부사 뒤) 특별한 관심이 있는
- backfire 동사 역효과를 낳다
- deceive 동사 기만하다, 속이다
- figure out 알아내다
- misinform 동사 잘못된 정보를 주다
- permanently 부사 영구적으로
- manipulate 동사 조종하다, 다루다
- momentarily 부사 잠깐, 일시적으로

06

- intergroup 형용사 집단 간의, 그룹 사이의
- stereotyping 명사 고정 관념 형성, 정형화
- back 동사 뒷받침하다, 후원하다
- prejudice 명사 편견, 선입관
- institutionally 부사 제도적으로
- sanction 동사 승인하다, 허가하다 / 명사 허가
- established 형용사 기존의, 확립된, 인정된
- custom 명사 관습, 관행
- in-group 명사 (사회학) 내집단(개인이 소속되어 공동체 의식을 느끼는 집단)
- deviant 형용사 일탈적인, 규범에서 벗어난
- worthwhile 형용사 가치 있는, 훌륭한
- with respect to ~과 관련해서, ~에 대해
- desegregation 명사 인종 차별 폐지
- conduct 동사 지도하다, 지휘하다, 실시하다
- figure 명사 인물, 사람

07

- able 형용사 능력이 있는, 재능 있는
- doubt 동사 의심하다 / 명사 의심
- indulge 동사 ~에 빠지다, 마음껏 하다
- skepticism 명사 회의(감), 회의론
- stock in trade 일상적인 업무, 상투적인 것, 장사 수단
- progress 명사 진보 / 동사 나아가다
- refute 동사 반박하다
- accordingly 부사 그에 따라, 그래서
- advance 명사 진보, 발전, 전진
- mindset 명사 사고방식
- be immune to ~에 영향을 받지 않는, ~에 면역이 된
- uncertainty 명사 불확실성
- reiterate 동사 되풀이하다, 반복하다
- rational 형용사 이성적인
- proportion 동사 할당하다, ~에 적합하게 하다 / 명사 부분, 비율
- get away with ~을 (잘) 해내다, (벌 등을) 모면하다

08

- puzzled 형용사 당황하는, 어리둥절한
- distinguish 동사 구분하다, 구별하다
- direction 명사 쪽, 방향
- propose 동사 주장하다, 제안하다
- dimension 명사 차원, 규모, 치수
- vertical 형용사 수직의 / 명사 수직
- gravity 명사 중력
- mobile 형용사 이동하는, 움직임이 자유로운
- species 명사 (생물 분류의) 종
- position 동사 배치하다 / 명사 위치, 자리
- sensory 형용사 감각의
- versus 전치사 대(對), ~에 비해
- horizontal 명사 수평 / 형용사 수평의
- relevant 형용사 중요한, 유의미한, 관련된, 적절한
- upside down 부사 뒤집혀, 거꾸로
- man-made 형용사 사람이 만든, 인공적인
- tell 동사 구별하다, 알다
- invert 동사 뒤집다, 거꾸로 하다
- artificial 형용사 인공적인
- spatial 형용사 공간적인
- instantly 부사 즉시, 즉각적으로

09

- highly 부사 굉장히, 매우
- nod 동사 (고개를) 끄덕이다
- area 명사 분야, 구역, 지역
- proprioceptive 형용사 고유 수용의, 자기 수용의
- in reverse 역으로, 반대로
- initially 부사 처음에
- controversial 형용사 논란의 여지가 있는
- compelling 형용사 설득력 있는, 강력한
- fixate 동사 고정하다, 응시하다

문제편 : p.233~237 정답과 해설 : p.294~302

☐ indicate	[동사] 나타내다, 내비치다
☐ appeal	[동사] 매력적이다, 호소하다
☐ vertically	[부사] 수직으로
☐ horizontally	[부사] 수평으로
☐ result in	~하는 결과를 낳다, 초래하다
☐ favorably	[부사] 호의적으로
☐ unfavorably	[부사] 부정적으로, 호의적이지 않게

10

☐ colleague	[명사] (업무상의) 동료, 동업자
☐ conduct	[동사] (특정한 활동을) 하다, 지휘하다, 안내하다 / [명사] 행위, 지도, 수행
☐ external	[형용사] 외부의, 밖의
☐ manipulation	[명사] 조작, 손을 씀
☐ recall	[동사] 기억해 내다, 상기하다
☐ sway	[동사] 흔들다, 동요시키다 / [명사] 흔들림, 동요
☐ present	[동사] 제시하다, 보여주다 / [형용사] 현재의, (출석해) 있는
☐ fabricate	[동사] 조작하다, 제작하다
☐ distinguish between A and B	A와 B를 구별하다
☐ modify	[동사] 수정하다, 바꾸다

11

☐ recruit	[동사] 모집하다, 채용하다
☐ hobbyist	[명사] 취미에 열정적인 사람
☐ shape	[동사] 형성하다 / [명사] 형태, 모양
☐ seriousness	[명사] 진지함, 심각함
☐ assess	[동사] 평가하다, 가늠하다
☐ demand	[명사] 요구 (사항), 수요
☐ dedicate to	~에 전념하다, 헌신하다
☐ scale	[명사] 평가표, 규모
☐ dissimilar	[형용사] 다른, 닮지 않은
☐ boost	[동사] 북돋우다 / [명사] 격려, 증가
☐ sufficiently	[부사] 충분히

12

☐ adorable	[형용사] 사랑스러운
☐ overwhelming	[형용사] 엄청난, 압도적인
☐ squeeze	[동사] 꽉 쥐다, 짜내다
☐ pinch	[동사] 꼬집다
☐ cuddle	[동사] 꼭 껴안다
☐ oxymoron	[명사] 모순 어법
☐ aggression	[명사] 공격성
☐ cruel	[형용사] 잔인한, 잔혹한
☐ compulsion	[명사] 충동, 강요
☐ reveal	[동사] 밝히다, 드러내다
☐ neurological	[형용사] 신경학적인, 신경의
☐ overloaded	[형용사] 과부하된
☐ temper	[동사] 조절하다, 경감하다
☐ perceive A as B	A를 B로 여기다

13

☐ goods	[명사] 물품, 재화, 상품
☐ discomfort	[명사] 고통, 불편
☐ be likely to V	~할 가능성이 있다
☐ distress	[명사] 고통, 곤란, 고난
☐ likely	[부사] 아마
☐ stem from	~에서 유래하다
☐ arousal	[명사] 자극, 각성
☐ initial	[형용사] 초기의, 처음의
☐ empathize	[동사] 공감하다, 감정 이입하다
☐ struggle	[동사] 고군분투하다
☐ self-centered	[형용사] 자기중심의

14

☐ indicator	[명사] 지표
☐ acquaintance	[명사] 지인, 아는 사람
☐ violate	[동사] 위반하다, 침범하다
☐ packed	[형용사] 가득 찬
☐ channel	[명사] 채널(정보의 전달 경로)
☐ compensate for	~을 상쇄하다[보상하다]
☐ proximity	[명사] 근접성
☐ constant	[형용사] 계속적인
☐ adjust	[동사] 조절하다, 적응하다
☐ conceal	[동사] 감추다, 숨기다

15

☐ prejudice	[명사] 선입견, 편견 / [동사] 편견을 갖게 하다
☐ blind	[형용사] 맹목적인, 눈이 먼
☐ assumption	[명사] 가정, 추정
☐ ethnic	[형용사] 인종적인, 인종의
☐ religious	[형용사] 종교적인, 종교의
☐ earn	[동사] (돈을) 벌다, 얻다
☐ evident	[형용사] 분명한, 눈에 띄는
☐ make an assumption	가정을 하다, 추정을 내리다
☐ race	[명사] 인종, 민족, 경주
☐ potential	[형용사] 잠재적인, 가능성이 있는 / [명사] 가능성, 잠재력
☐ apply	[동사] 적용하다, 신청하다, 지원하다
☐ rational	[형용사] 이성적인, 합리적인
☐ outweigh	[동사] ~보다 더 중요하다, ~보다 무겁다

16

☐ briefly	[부사] 잠시, 짧게
☐ memorize	[동사] 암기하다
☐ digit	[명사] 자릿수
☐ opt	[동사] 선택하다
☐ reflective	[형용사] 숙고하는
☐ reflexive	[형용사] 반사적인
☐ impulse	[명사] (마음의) 충동
☐ distraction	[명사] 방해, 주의를 산만하게 하는 것
☐ intellective	[형용사] 지적인
☐ load	[명사] 부담, 무거운 짐

17

☐ cooperative	[형용사] 협력적인, 협동적인
☐ demonstrate	[동사] 증명하다, 보여 주다
☐ contribute	[동사] 기부하다, 기여하다
☐ fund	[명사] 기금, 자금
☐ reputation	[명사] 평판, 명성
☐ responsibility	[명사] 책임, 의무
☐ rate	[동사] 평가하다, 여기다
☐ desirable	[형용사] 바람직한, 탐나는
☐ perceive	[동사] 인식하다, 인지하다
☐ trustworthy	[형용사] 신뢰할 수 있는, 믿을 수 있는
☐ status	[명사] 지위, 신분
☐ verbal	[형용사] 언어의, 말로 하는
☐ severe	[형용사] 심한, 심각한, 엄격한
☐ deserve	[동사] ~을 누릴 자격이 있다[받을 만하다]

18

☐ fast-growing	[형용사] 빠르게 증가하는, 빨리 성장하는
☐ tremendous	[형용사] 엄청난, 굉장한
☐ store	[동사] 저장하다, 보관하다
☐ repository	[명사] 저장소, 보관소
☐ exceed	[동사] 넘어서다, 초과하다
☐ tomb	[명사] 무덤
☐ archive	[명사] (기록) 보관소
☐ instinct	[명사] 직감, 본능
☐ extract	[동사] 추출하다, 뽑다, 얻다
☐ domain	[명사] 분야, 영역, 범위
☐ manually	[부사] 수동으로, 손으로
☐ bias	[명사] 편견, 성향
☐ costly	[형용사] 비용이 많이 드는, 대가가 큰
☐ widen	[동사] 벌어지다, 넓어지다
☐ gap	[명사] 격차, 차이
☐ systematic	[형용사] 체계적인, 조직적인
☐ golden nugget	금괴
☐ overwhelm	[동사] 압도하다, 제압하다
☐ obtain	[동사] 얻다, 구하다

19

☐ spark	[동사] 촉발하다 / [명사] 불꽃
☐ ownership	[명사] 소유, 소유권
☐ confuse	[동사] 혼란시키다, 당황하게 하다
☐ identical	[형용사] 동일한, 똑같은
☐ subject	[명사] 대상, 주제, 과목
☐ ring	[동사] 전화하다 / [명사] 반지
☐ paradoxically	[부사] 역설적으로
☐ resentment	[명사] 분노, 분개
☐ residence	[명사] 거주지, 주택
☐ potter	[명사] 도공, 도예가
☐ party	[명사] 당사자, 정당, 잔치
☐ resent	[동사] 분개하다, 분노하다

20

☐ concern	[명사] 걱정, 우려, 관심사
☐ psychologist	[명사] 심리학자
☐ suggest	[동사] 시사하다, (넌지시) 말하다, 제안하다
☐ effect	[명사] 영향, 결과
☐ vary	[동사] 다르다, 다양하다
☐ in distress	곤경에 처한, 고통받는
☐ reverse	[동사] 뒤바뀌다, 반대로 되다
☐ peer	[명사] 또래
☐ feel comfortable V-ing	~하는 데 편안함을 느끼다
☐ judge	[동사] 판단하다, 평가하다
☐ embarrassed	[형용사] 창피한, 부끄러운
☐ overreact	[동사] 과잉 반응하다
☐ note	[동사] 언급하다, 주목하다
☐ openly	[부사] 공개적으로, 공공연히

- [ ] deliberately 부사 고의적으로, 의도적으로
- [ ] put on a poker face 무표정한 얼굴을 하다
- [ ] contrary to A A와 상반되게, A에 반해서
- [ ] evaluate 동사 평가하다, 감정하다

17. 장문의 이해-단일지문

01~02
- [ ] impact 명사 영향, 충격
- [ ] virtual 형용사 가상의, 사실상의
- [ ] at first glance 언뜻 보기에는
- [ ] overlook 동사 간과하다, 못 보고 넘어가다
- [ ] invisible 형용사 보이지 않는, 무형의
- [ ] run 동사 실행하다, 운영하다, 관리하다
- [ ] incredible 형용사 엄청난, 믿을 수 없는
- [ ] gigantic 형용사 거대한
- [ ] transmit 동사 전송하다, 송신하다
- [ ] countless 형용사 셀 수 없이 많은, 무수한
- [ ] carbon 명사 탄소
- [ ] emission 명사 배출, 배출물, 배기가스
- [ ] conscious 형용사 의식하는, 자각하는, 의도적인
- [ ] manner 명사 방식, 태도, 예의
- [ ] by no means 결코 ~가 아닌
- [ ] mindful 형용사 신중한, 의식하는, 유념하는

03~04
- [ ] paralysis 명사 마비
- [ ] analysis 명사 분석
- [ ] overthink 동사 지나치게 생각하다
- [ ] end up V-ing 결국 ~하게 되다
- [ ] ancient 형용사 고대의
- [ ] fable 명사 우화
- [ ] illustrate 동사 설명하다
- [ ] phenomenon 명사 현상
- [ ] inability 명사 할 수 없는 것, 무능
- [ ] available 형용사 이용 가능한
- [ ] alternative 명사 대안
- [ ] indefinitely 부사 무한히, 무기한으로
- [ ] arise 동사 발생하다
- [ ] erroneous 형용사 잘못된
- [ ] catastrophic 형용사 재앙적인, 큰 재해의
- [ ] consequence 명사 결과
- [ ] stake 명사 이해관계

05~06
- [ ] evolutionary 형용사 진화의, 진화론에 의한
- [ ] sociability 명사 사교성, 친목
- [ ] gossip 동사 잡담을 하다, 험담을 퍼뜨리다 / 명사 소문, 잡담
- [ ] considerable 형용사 상당한, 많은
- [ ] wayfinding 명사 길 찾기, 길 안내 표지
- [ ] savvy 명사 요령, 지식
- [ ] Palaeolithic 형용사 구석기 시대의
- [ ] wilderness 명사 황야
- [ ] spatial 형용사 공간의, 공간적인
- [ ] awareness 명사 인식, 의식
- [ ] landscape 명사 풍경, 경관
- [ ] anthropologist 명사 인류학자
- [ ] attribute 명사 특징, 특성 / 동사 원인으로 여기다
- [ ] prime 동사 준비하다 / 명사 전성기, 한창때 / 형용사 주요한, 최상의
- [ ] foster 동사 발전시키다, 조장하다
- [ ] sophisticated 형용사 수준 높은, 정교한, 복잡한
- [ ] extinct 형용사 멸종한, 사라진
- [ ] badlands 명사 불모지, 황무지
- [ ] split 동사 분열되다, 가르다, 쪼개다
- [ ] communicative 형용사 의사 전달의, 이야기하기 좋아하는

07~08
- [ ] storehouse 명사 창고, 저장소
- [ ] consequently 부사 결과적으로
- [ ] generic 형용사 일반적인, 포괄적인
- [ ] impression 명사 인상, 감명
- [ ] merge 동사 합치다, 합병하다
- [ ] fundamental 형용사 핵심적인, 근본적인
- [ ] extract 동사 추출하다, 뽑다
- [ ] abstract 형용사 추상적인, 관념적인
- [ ] tie 동사 묶다 / 명사 넥타이, 끈
- [ ] routine 형용사 일상적인 / 명사 일상
- [ ] ironically 부사 모순적으로, 역설적이게도
- [ ] routinize 동사 일상화하다
- [ ] particulars 명사 (주로 복수형) 세부 사항
- [ ] call up 상기하다, (힘·용기 등을) 불러일으키다
- [ ] distinctive 형용사 특이한, 독특한

09~10
- [ ] commercial 형용사 민간(용)의, 상업적인, 이윤을 추구하는
- [ ] aviation 명사 항공기 산업, 항공(술)
- [ ] improvement 명사 개선(점)
- [ ] self-induced 형용사 스스로 만들어 낸, 저절로 생긴
- [ ] admit 동사 인정하다, 허가하다
- [ ] employer 명사 고용주
- [ ] federal 형용사 연방의
- [ ] voluntary 형용사 자발적인, 자원한
- [ ] semi-anonymous 형용사 반(半) 익명의
- [ ] personnel 명사 인사부, 직원
- [ ] acquire 동사 얻다, 습득하다
- [ ] detach 동사 떼어내다, 분리하다
- [ ] reject 동사 거절하다
- [ ] invoke 동사 (법·규칙 등을) 적용하다, 들먹이다
- [ ] civil penalty 민사 처벌
- [ ] suspension 명사 정지, 보류
- [ ] exempt 동사 면제해 주다 / 형용사 면제된
- [ ] issue 동사 발급하다

11~12
- [ ] oral 형용사 구전의, 구두의
- [ ] accumulate 동사 축적하다, 모으다
- [ ] norm 명사 규범, 기준
- [ ] shift 동사 변하다, 이동하다 / 명사 변화, 이동
- [ ] advent 명사 출현, 도래
- [ ] printing press 명사 인쇄기
- [ ] literacy 명사 문해력, 글을 읽고 쓰는 능력
- [ ] transfer 명사 전달, 전송 / 동사 전달하다, 갈아타다
- [ ] fade 동사 사라지다, 희미해지다
- [ ] signify 동사 의미하다, 중요하다
- [ ] chronological age 명사 실제 연령, 실제 나이
- [ ] biological age 명사 생물학적 연령
- [ ] formerly 부사 이전에
- [ ] stereotype 명사 고정 관념

13~14
- [ ] navigate 동사 항해하다, 길을 찾다
- [ ] brainpower 명사 지력, 지능
- [ ] endeavor 명사 노력 / 동사 노력하다, 애쓰다
- [ ] edible 형용사 먹을 수 있는, 식용의
- [ ] appealing 형용사 매력적인, 호소하는
- [ ] predictability 명사 예측 가능성
- [ ] go to the effort to V ~하기 위해 노력을 들이다
- [ ] emit 동사 내다, 내뿜다
- [ ] rhythmic 형용사 주기적인, 리드미컬한
- [ ] familiarity 명사 친숙함, 익숙함
- [ ] indifference 명사 무관심, 무심
- [ ] suppression 명사 억제, 진압
- [ ] diminish 동사 감소하다, 줄어들다
- [ ] reassuring 형용사 안도감을 주는, 안심시키는
- [ ] incorporate A into B A를 B에 포함시키다
- [ ] novelty 명사 참신함, 새로움
- [ ] rerun 명사 재방송, 재시합 / 동사 재방송하다
- [ ] expertise 명사 전문성, 전문적 지식
- [ ] at the expense of ~의 대가로, ~을 희생하여

15~16
- [ ] resident 명사 거주자
- [ ] welfare 명사 복지, 후생
- [ ] indicate 동사 말하다, 나타내다, 보여 주다
- [ ] disturbingly 부사 충격적인 것은, 불안하게 하여
- [ ] syndrome 명사 증후군, 일련의 증상
- [ ] factual 형용사 사실적인, 사실에 기반을 둔
- [ ] lie 동사 (어떤 상태로) 있다, 놓여 있다
- [ ] substantial 형용사 상당한
- [ ] reinforce 동사 강화하다, 보강하다
- [ ] preexist 동사 기존에 존재하다
- [ ] passively 부사 소극적으로, 수동적으로
- [ ] dismiss 동사 무시하다, 묵살하다
- [ ] reasoning 명사 합리화, 추론
- [ ] consistent 형용사 일관성 있는, 한결같은
- [ ] contradict 동사 모순되다, 부정하다
- [ ] facilitate 동사 가능하게 하다, 용이하게 하다
- [ ] rational 형용사 이성적인, 합리적인

17~18
- [ ] populate 동사 거주하다, 살다
- [ ] deny 동사 부인하다
- [ ] alert 형용사 주의를 기울이는, 민감한

문제편 : p.245~253 정답과 해설 : p.313~323

☐ suggestion	[명사] 암시, 제안
☐ attend	[동사] 주의를 기울이다, 참석하다
☐ pass on	물려주다, 넘겨주다
☐ plunge into	~에 뛰어들다, 빠지다
☐ signal	[동사] 신호를 보내다, 암시하다 / [명사] 신호
☐ outcome	[명사] 결과
☐ puff up	(잔뜩) 부풀리다, 부어오르다
☐ roar	[동사] 포효하다, 으르렁거리다
☐ bare	[동사] 드러내다, 폭로하다
☐ fang	[명사] 송곳니
☐ navigate	[동사] 항해하다, 길을 찾다
☐ sensible	[형용사] 분별 있는, 합리적인
☐ inevitable	[형용사] 불가피한, 필연적인
☐ convincing	[형용사] 설득력 있는, 확실한
☐ game changer	전환점, 승부수
☐ overturn	[동사] 뒤집다, 번복시키다
☐ coexistence	[명사] 공존

19~20

☐ neuropsychologist	[명사] 신경 심리학자
☐ conduct	[동사] 수행하다, 지휘하다 / [명사] 행동
☐ excel	[동사] 탁월하다, 뛰어나다
☐ coherent	[형용사] 일관성 있는, 응집성의
☐ deceive	[동사] 속이다, 기만하다
☐ split	[명사] 분할, 분열 / [동사] 나누다, 분열시키다
☐ visible	[형용사] 보이는, 알아볼 수 있는, 뚜렷한
☐ be aware of	~을 알다, ~을 알아 차리다
☐ process	[동사] 처리하다, 가공하다 / [명사] 과정
☐ silent	[형용사] 침묵하는, 조용한
☐ subject	[명사] 피실험자, 과목, 대상
☐ fabricate	[동사] 꾸며 내다, 날조하다
☐ rationalization	[명사] (이론적) 설명, 합리화
☐ basis	[명사] 근거, 기준, 기초
☐ turn out	드러나다, 밝혀지다, 나타나다
☐ fill in	~을 채우다, ~을 대신하다

21~22

☐ artificial	[형용사] 인공의
☐ sensibility	[명사] 감각
☐ sensitivity	[명사] 감성
☐ awareness	[명사] 인지
☐ reason	[명사] 이성, 이유
☐ wit	[명사] 재치
☐ readily	[부사] 주저 없이, 손쉽게
☐ affective	[형용사] 감성적인
☐ exemplar	[명사] 전형, 모범
☐ normal	[명사] 표준, 정상 / [형용사] 보통의, 정상적인
☐ recapture	[동사] 되찾다
☐ in time	조만간, 이윽고
☐ caring	[형용사] 돌보는 / [명사] 돌보는 것
☐ object	[동사] 이의를 제기하다, 반대하다 / [명사] 물건, 물체
☐ puzzled	[형용사] 당황스러운, 어리둥절한
☐ semantics	[명사] (언어학에서) 의미론

☐ companionship	[명사] 우정, 동지애
☐ at stake	위태로운, 위기에 처한

23~24

☐ autonomous	[형용사] 자율의, 자율적인
☐ pedestrian	[명사] 보행자
☐ behave	[동사] (기계 등이) 작동하다, 움직이다, (특정한 방식으로) 행동하다
☐ vary	[동사] 달리 하다, 변화를 주다, 다르다, 변하다
☐ factor	[명사] 요인
☐ utilitarian	[형용사] 공리적인, 실리적인
☐ put A ahead of B	A를 B보다 우선시하다
☐ self-protective	[형용사] 자기방어적인
☐ latter	[명사] 후자, (나열된 것들 중에서) 마지막 / [형용사] 후자의, 마지막의
☐ ethical	[형용사] 윤리적인, 윤리의
☐ tension	[명사] 긴장
☐ good	[명사] 이익, 가치, 선 / [형용사] 좋은

25~26

☐ take for granted	당연하게 생각하다, 받아들이다
☐ findings	[명사] (주로 복수형) (연구) 결과
☐ deviant	[형용사] 일탈적인, 벗어난
☐ extent	[명사] 정도, 규모
☐ monitor	[동사] 감독하다, 감시하다
☐ surveillance	[명사] 감독, 감시
☐ hypothesize	[동사] 가설을 세우다, 제기하다
☐ analyze	[동사] 분석하다, 검토하다
☐ apparently	[부사] 명백히, 겉보기에
☐ multiple-choice	[형용사] 선다형(객관식)의
☐ extraneous	[형용사] 외부의, 관련 없는
☐ variable	[명사] 변수, 변인
☐ interfere	[동사] 방해하다, 간섭하다
☐ artifact	[명사] 가공물, 인공물

27~28

☐ common sense	[명사] 상식
☐ moderate	[형용사] (생각·태도 등이) 온건한, 중간의 / [동사] 누그러지다, 완화하다
☐ polarization	[명사] 양극화(서로 점점 더 달라지고 멀어짐)
☐ be inclined to V	~하는 경향이 있다
☐ reverse	[동사] 뒤집다
☐ accentuate	[동사] 강화하다, 강조하다
☐ hold	[동사] (태도·생각·의견 등을) 가지다, 지니다 (hold-held-held)
☐ conformity	[명사] 순응
☐ affiliation	[명사] 소속
☐ lean	[동사] 기울다, ~에 기대다 (lean-leaned/leant-leaned/leant)
☐ like-minded	[형용사] 같은 생각을 가진, 생각이 비슷한
☐ affiliate	[동사] 뭉치다, 가입하다, ~와 제휴하다
☐ reinforcement	[명사] 강화
☐ counterargument	[명사] 반론
☐ opposing	[형용사] 상반되는, 대립하는
☐ be opposed to	~에 반대하다
☐ companion	[명사] 동료, 동반자
☐ foster	[동사] 기르다, 촉진하다

29~30

☐ care about	~에 관심을 가지다
☐ probability of a hit	타율(야구에서 안타 수를 타격 수로 나눈 백분율)
☐ lately	[부사] 최근에, 얼마 전에
☐ in a row	연이어, 잇달아
☐ ensure	[동사] 보장하다, 반드시 ~하게[이게] 하다
☐ due for	~할 예정인
☐ rejected	[형용사] 거부당하는, 거절된
☐ mount	[동사] 증가하다, 올라가다
☐ qualified	[형용사] 자격이 있는
☐ chances	[명사] (주로 복수형) 가능성, 확률
☐ crash	[명사] (자동차 충돌, 항공기 추락) 사고 / [동사] 충돌하다, 폭락하다

31~32

☐ driver	[명사] 동인(어떤 사태를 일으키거나 변화시키는 데 작용하는 직접적인 원인)
☐ sense of duty	의무감
☐ obligate	[동사] 의무를 지우다
☐ wear down	지치게 하다, 약화시키다
☐ disconnect	[동사] 단절되다, 연락을 끊다
☐ intelligent	[형용사] 현명한, 지적인
☐ antidote	[명사] 해독제
☐ content	[형용사] 만족하는
☐ tune out	(잡음을) 무시하다
☐ let go of	버리다, ~을 손에서 놓다
☐ appreciate	[동사] 이해하다, 고마워하다
☐ intentional	[형용사] 의도적인
☐ keep up with	~을 따라잡다
☐ activate	[동사] 활성화하다, 작동시키다
☐ competitive	[형용사] 경쟁적인, 경쟁력 있는
☐ anxious	[형용사] 걱정스러운, 불안해하는
☐ priority	[명사] 우선순위
☐ deception	[명사] 기만, 사기
☐ catch up with	~을 따라잡다

33~34

☐ exhibit	[동사] 보이다, 드러내다, 전시하다
☐ peer-to-peer	[형용사] 개인 간의, P2P 방식의
☐ consensus	[명사] 합의, 일치된 의견
☐ disintermediated	[형용사] 탈중개적인, 금융기관의 중개를 벗어난
☐ transnational	[형용사] 초국가적인, 다국적의
☐ resilient	[형용사] 회복 탄력성이 있는, 탄력적인
☐ nonrepudiable	[형용사] 부인방지성의, 거부할 수 없는
☐ transparent	[형용사] 투명한, 정직한
☐ game-theoretical	게임 이론적인
☐ deployment	[명사] 배치, 동원
☐ autonomous	[형용사] 자동화된, 자립적인
☐ facilitate	[동사] 촉진하다, 용이하게 하다
☐ implement	[동사] 시행하다, 이행하다
☐ underlying	[형용사] 기본적인, 기초의, 기저의
☐ protocol	[명사] 프로토콜, 협정
☐ tamper-resistant	[형용사] 위조 방지의, 변경 저항적인
☐ decentralized	[형용사] 분산적인, 분권화된
☐ be prone to V-ing	~하기 쉽다, ~의 경향이 있다

문제편 : p.254~261 | 정답과 해설 : p.323~332

co-opt	[동사] 마음대로 사용하다, 억지로 끌어들이다
surveillance	[명사] 감시, 감독
double-edged	[형용사] 양날의, 이중적인
breakthrough	[명사] 돌파구
pros & cons	찬반 의견, 장단점
regulation	[명사] 규제, 통제

35~36

cut from the same cloth	같은 부류인, 비슷한
varying	[형용사] 다양한, 변화하는
maturity	[명사] 성숙도, 성숙함
sensitivity	[명사] 민감성, 세심함, 예민함
approach	[명사] 접근법 / [동사] 접근하다
motivate	[동사] 동기를 부여하다
be aware of	~을 알다, 알아차리다
unique	[형용사] 고유한, 독특한
personality	[명사] 성격, 개성
empathy	[명사] 공감, 감정 이입
adaptability	[명사] 적응성, 융통성
interpret	[동사] 해석하다, 설명하다, 통역하다
adapt	[동사] 맞추다, 적응하다
accordingly	[부사] 그에 따라, 따라서
in a row	연속하여, 연이어, 이어서
deserved	[형용사] 마땅한, 응당한
just yet	지금 당장으로서는 (~ 않다)
promotion	[명사] 승진, 홍보, 판촉 행사
bear in mind	(~을) 유념하다, 기억하다, 명심하다
receptive	[형용사] 수용적인, 잘 받아 들이는
bundle	[동사] 묶다 / [명사] 묶음, 꾸러미
complex	[형용사] 복잡한, 합성의 / [명사] 복합 건물
trait	[명사] 특징, 특성
circumstances	[명사] (주로 복수형) 상황
mindset	[명사] 사고방식
compassion	[명사] 동감, 연민
draw	[동사] 끌어내다, 당기다, 그리다
consistent	[형용사] 일관적인, 꾸준한
appealing	[형용사] 매력적인, 호소하는

37~38

civil	[형용사] 정중한, 예의 바른, 시민의
original	[형용사] 독창적인, 원래의
friction	[명사] 충돌, 불화, 마찰
tense	[형용사] 긴장감이 있는, 긴장된, (상황 등이) 긴박한
harmonious	[형용사] 화목한, 조화로운
verbally	[부사] 언어적으로, 말로
abusive	[형용사] 학대하는
shy away from	~을 피하다
stand up for	~의 입장을 내세우다, 지지(옹호)하다
dish it out	남을 비판하다
argument	[명사] 논쟁, 말다툼, 주장
ceaseless	[형용사] 끊임없는
quarrel	[동사] 싸우다, 말다툼하다
scrap with	~과 다투다
prolonged	[형용사] 장기적인
prevent A from V-ing	A를 ~하지 못하게 막다
soar	[동사] 날아오르다
constructive	[형용사] 건설적인
compromise	[명사] 타협 / [동사] 타협하다, ~을 위태롭게 하다

39~40

setting	[명사] 상황, 배경
distinction	[명사] 구분, 분리
decidedly	[부사] 분명히, 확실히
passive	[형용사] 수동적인, 소극적인
reinforce	[동사] (감정·생각 등을) 강화하다, (구조 등을) 보강하다
physical	[형용사] 물리적인, 신체적인
separation	[명사] 분리, 구분
greatly	[부사] 크게, 매우, 대단히
value	[동사] 가치를 부여하다, 소중히 여기다 / [명사] 가치
afford	[동사] 제공하다, ~을 지불할 수 있다
approval	[명사] 호응, 찬성
incorporate	[동사] 포함하다, 합병하다 / [명사] 회사
sing-along	[명사] 함께 노래 부르기
boost	[동사] 높이다, 향상하다
engagement	[명사] 참여, 몰입
glimpse	[명사] 흘끗 봄 / [동사] 흘끗 보다
perspective	[명사] 관점, 시각
biographical	[형용사] 전기적인, 전기체의
significant	[형용사] 중요한, 상당한
onstage	[형용사] 무대 위의, 관객 앞에서의
insight	[명사] 통찰, 통찰력
metaphorically	[부사] 비유적으로, 은유로
likely	[부사] 아마 / [형용사] 그럴듯한
enhance	[동사] 향상시키다, 높이다
expressive	[형용사] 표현하는, 나타내는

41~42

at once	동시에, 한꺼번에
shift	[동사] 전환하다 / [명사] 전환, 변화
attention	[명사] 주의, 관심
sequentially	[부사] 순차적으로, 연속하여
latest	[형용사] 최신의, 최근의
as a matter of fact	사실은
perform	[동사] 수행하다, 실시하다
individually	[부사] 개별적으로, 각각 따로
fraction	[명사] 아주 조금, 파편
switch	[명사] 전환 / [동사] 전환하다
interrupt	[동사] 중단시키다, 방해하다
contradict	[동사] 반박하다, 부정하다
advice	[명사] 조언, 충고
simultaneously	[부사] 동시에
familiar	[형용사] 익숙한, 친숙한
automatic pilot	자동 조종
insurance	[명사] 보험
consider A to V	A가 ~하다고 간주하다[여기다]
redesign	[동사] 재설계하다

43~44

bias	[명사] 편견, 편향
partial	[형용사] 편향된, 편파적인, 부분적인
promising	[형용사] 유망한, 촉망되는
justify	[동사] 정당화하다, 옹호하다
conduct	[동사] 수행하다, 지휘하다 / [명사] 행동, 경영
cluster	[명사] 덩어리, 군집, 무리
collectively	[부사] 총체적으로, 집합적으로
confirmation bias	[명사] 확증 편향
evaluate	[동사] 평가하다, 어림하다
subconsciously	[부사] 잠재의식적으로
cherry-pick	[동사] 선별하다, 신중히 선택하다
be prone to N	~하기 쉽다
threefold	[형용사] 세 배의

45~46

authority	[명사] 권위, 권위자, 지휘권
childhood	[명사] 유년 시절, 어린 시절
figure	[명사] 인물, 사람, 수치, 계산, 도형
element	[명사] 요소, 성분
socialization	[명사] 사회화
noncontroversial	[형용사] 논쟁의 여지가 없는
spontaneously	[부사] 즉흥적으로, 자발적으로
obvious	[형용사] 명백한, 분명한
unquestioningly	[부사] 의심 없이, 의문을 품지 않고
persist	[동사] 지속하다, 고집하다
dismiss	[동사] 쫓아내다, 물리치다, 해고하다
bother	[동사] ~을 성가시게 하다, 괴롭히다
meaningless	[형용사] 무의미한, 의미 없는
unreasonable	[형용사] 비합리적인, 부당한
physics	[명사] 물리학
seek	[동사] 찾다, 구하다, 추구하다
irritating	[형용사] 짜증스러운, 귀찮은
time-pressed	[형용사] 시간에 쫓기는
seriously	[부사] 진지하게, 진심으로
plain	[형용사] 명백한, 분명한, 소박한, 무늬가 없는

18. 장문의 이해-복합지문

01~03

apply for	~에 지원하다
stock	[동사] (재고를) 채우다 / [명사] 재고
designated	[형용사] 지정된
fill out	작성하다
require	[동사] 요구하다, 필요로 하다
door to door	집집마다
capital	[명사] 자본금
operation	[명사] 작업
fleet	[명사] 무리, 함대
insurance broker	보험 중개인
empire	[명사] 제국

04~06

flawless	[형용사] 흠이 없는
enthusiasm	[명사] 열정

문제편 : p.262~271 정답과 해설 : p.332~343

- [ ] polish 동사 연마하다, 윤을 내다
- [ ] accompany 동사 동행하다, 동반하다
- [ ] institute 명사 학원, 기관
- [ ] admit 동사 받아들이다, 들어가게 하다
- [ ] aspire 동사 열망하다
- [ ] ego 명사 자부심, 자아
- [ ] roam 동사 배회하다
- [ ] unaware of ~을 인식하지 못하는
- [ ] be lost in ~에 빠져 있다
- [ ] sparkle 명사 반짝임 / 동사 반짝이다
- [ ] world-renowned 세계적으로 유명한

07~09

- [ ] bounce 동사 튀다
- [ ] backboard 명사 (농구 골대의) 백보드
- [ ] sting 동사 따끔거리다, 쏘다, 찌르다
- [ ] frustrated 형용사 좌절감을 느끼는
- [ ] scream 동사 외치다, 소리치다
- [ ] intense 형용사 치열한, 극심한
- [ ] tie 동사 동점이 되다, 묶다
- [ ] leap 동사 뛰어오르다
- [ ] cheer 동사 환호하다

10~12

- [ ] board 동사 (비행기·배·차 등에) 탑승하다
- [ ] flight 명사 비행기, 항공편
- [ ] greet 동사 ~와 인사를 나누다, 환영하다
- [ ] companion 명사 동반자, 동행, 친구
- [ ] aisle seat 통로 쪽 좌석
- [ ] overhead bin 머리 위 짐칸
- [ ] take off 이륙하다
- [ ] keep an eye on ~를 지켜보다[주시하다]
- [ ] turbulence 명사 난기류, 격동
- [ ] fasten one's seatbelt 안전벨트를 매다
- [ ] rough weather 악천후
- [ ] bumpy 형용사 험난한, 울퉁불퉁한
- [ ] land 동사 착륙하다, 내려앉다
- [ ] descent 명사 하강, 내려오기

13~15

- [ ] at once 즉시, 당장
- [ ] out of one's sight ~의 시야에서 벗어나는, ~에게 보이지 않는 곳에
- [ ] chimney 명사 굴뚝
- [ ] uneasy 형용사 불안한
- [ ] in a little while 잠시 후에
- [ ] as for ~에 관해서라면
- [ ] miserable 형용사 몹시 불행한, 비참한
- [ ] utter 동사 (목소리를) 내다, 말하다
- [ ] seize 동사 움켜쥐다

16~18

- [ ] ticklish 형용사 간지럼을 타는
- [ ] burst out 터뜨리다, 갑자기 ~하기 시작하다
- [ ] contagious 형용사 전염성이 있는
- [ ] end up (in) N/V-ing 결국 ~하게 되다
- [ ] control 동사 억제하다, 조절하다
- [ ] shave 동사 밀다
- [ ] clown 명사 광대
- [ ] carry on N/V-ing ~을 계속하다
- [ ] replace 동사 ~을 대신하다, ~의 뒤를 잇다
- [ ] shelter 명사 보호 시설, 피난처
- [ ] orphan 동사 고아가 되게 하다
- [ ] light up 밝아지다, 환해지다 (light-lighted/lit-lighted/lit)
- [ ] retire 동사 은퇴하다
- [ ] set A off A를 터지게 하다

19~21

- [ ] severe 형용사 심한, 가혹한
- [ ] consult 동사 상담하다
- [ ] a galaxy of 수많은
- [ ] medicate 동사 약을 투여하다
- [ ] undergo 동사 받다, 겪다
- [ ] injection 명사 주사, 투입
- [ ] persist 동사 지속되다
- [ ] monk 명사 수도사
- [ ] call for 불러들이다, ~를 데리러 가다
- [ ] prescription 명사 처방(전)
- [ ] desperate 형용사 절박한, 필사적인
- [ ] barrel 명사 통
- [ ] servant 명사 하인
- [ ] bucket 명사 통, 양동이
- [ ] fortune 명사 재산, 운

22~24

- [ ] insurance 명사 보험
- [ ] lively 형용사 활기찬, 생기 있는 / 부사 활발하게
- [ ] aspect 명사 측면, 양상
- [ ] intention 명사 의사, 의도
- [ ] anticipate 동사 예상하다, 기대하다
- [ ] rage 동사 몹시 화를 내다 / 명사 격렬한 분노
- [ ] ungrateful 형용사 배은망덕한, 감사할 줄 모르는
- [ ] fury 명사 분노, 격분
- [ ] resolve 명사 (단호한) 결심 / 동사 결심하다, 해결하다
- [ ] flourishing 형용사 번창하는, 무성한
- [ ] orphan 동사 고아로 만들다 / 명사 고아
- [ ] disown 동사 의절하다, 자기 것이 아니라고 말하다
- [ ] adoption 명사 입양, 채택
- [ ] courage 명사 용기
- [ ] scaffolding 명사 발판, (건축 공사장의) 비계

25~27

- [ ] take A by the hand A의 손을 잡다
- [ ] nursery 명사 묘목장
- [ ] indoors 부사 실내에(서)
- [ ] outdoor 형용사 집 밖의, 실외의
- [ ] cope with ~을 이겨내다, ~에 대처하다
- [ ] elements 명사 (복수형) 악천후
- [ ] shrug 동사 어깨를 으쓱하다
- [ ] remind 동사 상기시키다, 일깨워주다
- [ ] towering 형용사 높이 솟은
- [ ] all of one's life 평생
- [ ] be willing to V 기꺼이 ~하다
- [ ] face 동사 맞서다

28~30

- [ ] unbearably 부사 참을 수 없을 정도로
- [ ] handle a fire 화재를 진압하다
- [ ] downtown 형용사 도심지의 / 부사 도심지에서
- [ ] roaring 형용사 맹렬히 타오르는, 으르렁거리는
- [ ] at the top of one's lungs 큰 소리로, 소리 지르며
- [ ] desperate 형용사 절박한, 절망적인
- [ ] urgent 형용사 다급한, 촉박한
- [ ] make one's way 나아가다, 출세하다
- [ ] fierce 형용사 격렬한, 사나운
- [ ] impulsively 부사 충동적으로
- [ ] collapse 동사 무너지다, 좌절하다
- [ ] break into ~하기 시작하다, 침입하다
- [ ] emerge from ~에서 나오다, 벗어나다
- [ ] tend to N ~을 돌보다
- [ ] be in one's debt ~에게 고마운 마음을 지니고 있다

31~33

- [ ] head 동사 (특정 방향으로) 향하다
- [ ] training 명사 훈련, 연수
- [ ] tryout 명사 적격 시험, 예선
- [ ] approach 동사 가까워지다, 다가가다
- [ ] shin 명사 정강이
- [ ] shade 명사 그늘, 응달
- [ ] in the sun 양지에
- [ ] pole 명사 기둥, 막대기
- [ ] group 동사 무리를 짓다, 모으다
- [ ] roar 동사 고함치다, 외치다, 으르렁거리다
- [ ] call A out A를 불러내다
- [ ] rearrangement 명사 재배열, 재정리
- [ ] posture 명사 자세, 태도
- [ ] sense of connection 연대감
- [ ] head-on 부사 정면으로, 정통으로

34~36

- [ ] struggle 명사 시련, 투쟁, 싸움 / 동사 고군분투하다, 힘겹게 나아가다
- [ ] attain 동사 도달하다, 이루다, 획득하다
- [ ] enviable 형용사 부러워하는, 선망의 대상이 되는
- [ ] hiss off 야유하여 ~을 퇴장시키다
- [ ] defeat 명사 좌절, 패배 / 동사 패배시키다, 이기다
- [ ] endure 동사 견디다, 참다, 오래가다
- [ ] come across (우연히) 마주치다, 발견하다
- [ ] helplessness 명사 무력함, 난감함
- [ ] impulsively 부사 충동적으로
- [ ] beckon 동사 오라고 손짓하다, 손짓으로 부르다
- [ ] acquaintance 명사 지인, 친분, 지식
- [ ] call on 방문하다, 요청하다, 촉구하다
- [ ] restore 동사 회복시키다, 되찾게 하다, 복원하다
- [ ] in vain 허사가 되어, 헛되이

문제편 : p.272~281 정답과 해설 : p.343~356

- [ ] applause [명사] 박수
- [ ] vast [형용사] 어마어마한, 방대한, 막대한
- [ ] mingle [동사] 섞(이)다, 어우러지다, 사람들과 어울리다
- [ ] rejoice over ~에 크게 기뻐하다

37~39

- [ ] social worker 사회복지사
- [ ] income [명사] 소득, 수입
- [ ] coal [명사] 석탄
- [ ] collapse [동사] 붕괴되다
- [ ] arrange [동사] 계획하다, 배치하다, 정리하다
- [ ] enthusiastic [형용사] 열정적인
- [ ] raise [동사] 키우다, 모금하다
- [ ] representative [명사] 대표 / [형용사] 대표적인
- [ ] aid [명사] 지원, 도움
- [ ] fall through 실패하다, 잘 안되다
- [ ] cheer [명사] 생기, 환호 / [동사] 환호하다
- [ ] determination [명사] 결의, 결심
- [ ] astonished [형용사] 깜짝 놀란
- [ ] unload [동사] (짐을) 내리다
- [ ] multiply [동사] 늘리다, 증가시키다, 곱하다

40~42

- [ ] on a quest 탐색 중인
- [ ] get through ~을 견디다, ~에 닿다
- [ ] ache [동사] (머리·마음 등이) 아프다
- [ ] spot [동사] 발견하다 / [명사] 얼룩, 점
- [ ] cannot help V-ing ~하지 않을 수 없다
- [ ] overhear [동사] 엿듣다
- [ ] go through ~을 겪다, (시간을) 보내다
- [ ] hand A B A에게 B를 건네다
- [ ] startled [형용사] 놀란
- [ ] anticipate [동사] 예상하다, 기대하다
- [ ] respond [동사] 반응하다, 응답하다
- [ ] embrace [동사] 껴안다, (생각·제안을) 받아들이다

43~45

- [ ] neighboring [형용사] 가까운, 이웃의, 인접한
- [ ] conflict [명사] 갈등, 충돌 / [동사] 상충하다
- [ ] misunderstanding [명사] 오해, 착오
- [ ] argument [명사] 논쟁, 주장
- [ ] explode [동사] 폭발하다, 터지다
- [ ] bitter [형용사] 심한, 쓴, 격렬한
- [ ] carpenter [명사] 목수
- [ ] creek [명사] 샛강, 개울
- [ ] meadow [명사] 초원, 목초지
- [ ] fence [명사] 울타리 / [동사] 울타리를 치다
- [ ] jaw [명사] 입, 턱
- [ ] awkwardly [부사] 어색하게, 서투르게
- [ ] isolation [명사] 고립, 분리, 격리
- [ ] openness [명사] 관대함, 솔직함

46~48

- [ ] furry [형용사] 털북숭이의, 털로 덮인
- [ ] companion [명사] 반려, 동반자, 친구
- [ ] vet(=veterinarian) [명사] 수의사
- [ ] examine [동사] 진찰하다, 검사하다
- [ ] infection [명사] 감염, 전염병
- [ ] reply [동사] 대답하다, 답장을 보내다
- [ ] anxiously [부사] 초조하게, 걱정스레
- [ ] medication [명사] 약물[약] (치료)
- [ ] playful [형용사] 장난기 넘치는, 장난기 많은
- [ ] self [명사] (평소) 모습, 본모습, 자신
- [ ] instruction [명사] 설명, 지시
- [ ] administer [동사] (약을) 투여하다, 관리하다, 운영하다
- [ ] recovery [명사] 회복, 되찾음
- [ ] pat [동사] 쓰다듬다, 토닥거리다
- [ ] ensure [동사] (반드시) ~하게 하다, 보장하다
- [ ] spirit [명사] 활기, 정신

49~51

- [ ] grocery [명사] 식료품, 식료품 잡화점
- [ ] metal [명사] 금속
- [ ] driver's seat 운전석
- [ ] grab [동사] 잡다, 움켜잡다
- [ ] wheel [명사] 바퀴, (자동차의) 핸들
- [ ] independence [명사] 독립성, 독립심
- [ ] insist on ~을 고집하다[주장하다]
- [ ] put together 조립하다, 만들다
- [ ] at all (부정문에서) 전혀, 조금도, 조금이라도

52~54

- [ ] interaction [명사] 상호 작용
- [ ] delay [동사] 지체시키다, 지연시키다 / [명사] 지체, 지연
- [ ] fit in with ~와 어울리다
- [ ] at every turn 언제나, 어디서나
- [ ] tease [동사] 괴롭히다, 놀리다
- [ ] frown upon ~에 눈살을 찌푸리다
- [ ] unsympathetic [형용사] 인정 없는, 매정한
- [ ] caring [형용사] 친절한, 배려하는, 보살피는
- [ ] suspect [동사] 짐작하다, 의심하다
- [ ] pay out of one's own pocket 자비로 지불하다
- [ ] outline [명사] 윤곽, 개요 / [동사] 윤곽을 그리다
- [ ] joyfully [부사] 즐겁게, 기쁘게
- [ ] embark on ~을 시작하다[착수하다]
- [ ] imaginative [형용사] 상상의, 창의적인
- [ ] groundwork [명사] 토대, 초석, 기초
- [ ] observe [동사] 관찰하다, (의견 등을) 말하다, 준수하다
- [ ] publish [동사] 출판하다, 발행하다

1회 20분 미니모의고사

01

- [ ] enrich [동사] 풍요롭게 하다
- [ ] at the expense of ~을 희생하면서, ~에 폐를 끼치면서
- [ ] disturb [동사] 방해하다, 건드리다
- [ ] excessive [형용사] 과도한, 지나친
- [ ] disrupt [동사] 방해하다, 지장을 주다

02

- [ ] pep talk 격려의 말
- [ ] suggest [동사] 시사하다, 암시하다, 제안하다
- [ ] given [형용사] 주어진
- [ ] torn [형용사] (마음이) 아픈, 슬픈
- [ ] declare [동사] (분명히) 말하다, 단언하다
- [ ] tough [형용사] 강한, 굳센

03

- [ ] reservoir [명사] 저수지
- [ ] mass [명사] 질량, 덩어리
- [ ] shift [동사] 이동하다 / [명사] 이동, 변화
- [ ] whirling [형용사] 회전하는
- [ ] gradually [부사] 점차, 점진적으로
- [ ] deceleration [명사] 감속
- [ ] unintended [형용사] 의도치 않은

04

- [ ] interaction [명사] 상호 작용
- [ ] common ground [명사] (사회 관계·논의·상호 이해 등의) 공통되는 기반, (관심·견해 따위의) 일치점
- [ ] involved [형용사] 관련된, 복잡한
- [ ] party [명사] 당사자, 단체, 정당, 파티
- [ ] coordinate [동사] 조정하다
- [ ] interdependent [형용사] 상호 의존적인
- [ ] primate [명사] 영장류
- [ ] establish [동사] (관계를) 맺다, (건물이나 체계를) 확립하다
- [ ] morality [명사] 도덕성
- [ ] define A as B A를 B로 정의하다[규정하다]
- [ ] conduct [명사] 행위
- [ ] conceptualize [동사] 개념화하다
- [ ] trustworthiness [명사] 신뢰성, 믿을 수 있음
- [ ] cooperation [명사] 협력
- [ ] justice [명사] 정의
- [ ] caring [명사] 배려, 보살핌
- [ ] treatment [명사] 대우, 취급
- [ ] agreement [명사] 합의
- [ ] a wide range of 광범위한
- [ ] perspective [명사] 시각, 관점
- [ ] evolutionary [형용사] 진화의
- [ ] depend on ~에 의존[의지]하다, ~을 믿다

05

- [ ] champion [명사] 옹호자
- [ ] free speech [명사] 언론의 자유
- [ ] religious [형용사] 종교적인, 종교의
- [ ] toleration [명사] 관용
- [ ] controversial [형용사] 논란이 많은
- [ ] figure [명사] 인물
- [ ] be supposed to V ~하다고 여겨지다[생각되다]
- [ ] declare [동사] 말하다, 선언하다
- [ ] defend to death 사력을 다해 옹호하다
- [ ] right [명사] 권리
- [ ] defense [명사] 변론, 변호, 방어
- [ ] view [명사] 의견, 견해
- [ ] despise [동사] 경멸하다
- [ ] deserve to V ~할 만하다, ~할 자격이 있다
- [ ] strictly [부사] 엄격히
- [ ] control [동사] 통제하다

문제편 : p.282~290 정답과 해설 : p.356~369

☐ publish 동사 출판하다
☐ play 명사 희곡, 각본, 연극
☐ censor 동사 검열하다
☐ in public 공개적으로
☐ imprison 동사 수감하다, 가두다
☐ insult 동사 모욕하다
☐ aristocrat 명사 귀족, 특권 계급의 사람
☐ challenge 동사 도전하다
☐ prejudice 명사 편견, 선입관
☐ pretension 명사 가식, 허세
☐ philosophical 형용사 철학의, 철학에 관련된
☐ novel 명사 소설
☐ support 동사 지지하다
☐ undermine 동사 훼손하다
☐ optimism 명사 낙관론, 낙관주의
☐ humanity 명사 인류
☐ contemporary 형용사 당대의, 동시대의
☐ thinker 명사 사상가
☐ express 동사 표명하다, 표현하다
☐ entertaining 형용사 재미있는
☐ instant 형용사 즉시의, 즉각적인
☐ leave A off B 동사 B에서 A를 빼다
☐ publication 명사 출판
☐ land 동사 두다, 빠트리다, 도착시키다
☐ make fun of ~을 조롱하다
☐ belief 명사 신념

06

☐ showcase 명사 쇼케이스, 공개 행사 / 동사 소개하다
☐ effectively 부사 효과적으로
☐ communicate 동사 전달하다, 전하다
☐ aspect 명사 측면, 양상
☐ informative 형용사 유용한 정보를 주는, 유익한
☐ prize money 명사 상금
☐ guideline 명사 지침, 가이드라인
☐ restriction 명사 제한, 규제

07

☐ injury rate 부상률
☐ steadily 부사 꾸준하게

08

☐ home 부사 고향에, 집에
☐ man 명사 부하, 남자
☐ treasured 형용사 소중히[귀하게] 여겨지는
☐ preserve 동사 보존하다, 지키다
☐ replace 동사 교체하다, 대체하다
☐ rotten 형용사 썩은, 부패한
☐ plank 명사 나무 판자, 널빤지
☐ philosopher 명사 철학자
☐ repair 동사 수리하다, 고치다
☐ sum 명사 총합, 전부
☐ journey 명사 여정, 여행

09

☐ genetics 명사 유전학
☐ suspect 동사 의심하다
☐ blueprint 명사 청사진, 설계도
☐ identical 형용사 일란성의, 동일한
☐ develop 동사 (병에) 걸리다, 발달시키다
☐ instruct 동사 명령하다, 지시하다
☐ initiate 동사 일으키다, 시작하다
☐ diet 명사 식사, 식습관
☐ toxin 명사 독소
☐ contribute to ~의 원인이 되다, ~에 기여하다
☐ notion 명사 생각, 개념
☐ relatively 부사 비교적, 상대적으로
☐ makeup 명사 구성, 구조, 화장
☐ fatal 형용사 치명적인

10

☐ shortage 명사 부족
☐ force 동사 ~하게 만들다, 강요하다
☐ aid 명사 구호, 원조
☐ agency 명사 기관
☐ cropland 명사 경작지
☐ desertification 명사 사막화
☐ vegetation 명사 초목, 식물
☐ rainfall 명사 비, 강우
☐ drought 명사 가뭄
☐ in concentration 집중하여
☐ farming 명사 농업, 농사
☐ overcome 동사 극복하다
☐ moisture 명사 습기

11~12

☐ so-called 형용사 소위, 이른바
☐ flight 명사 도주, 도망
☐ mechanism 명사 메커니즘, 방법
☐ predator 명사 포식자, 포식 동물
☐ consistent 형용사 일관적인
☐ remarkably 부사 놀라울 만큼, 상당히
☐ precisely 부사 정확하게
☐ draw 동사 끌다, 당기다, 그리다
☐ assume 동사 추정하다, 가정하다
☐ variation 명사 차이, 변화
☐ assessment 명사 평가
☐ accelerate 동사 속도를 높이다, 빨라지다
☐ perceive 동사 인식하다
☐ trap 동사 가두다 / 명사 덫, 함정
☐ flee 동사 달아나다, 도망하다
☐ stand one's ground 물러나지 않고 버티다
☐ migrate 동사 이동하다, 이주하다

2회 20분 미니모의고사

01

☐ meet 동사 충족시키다, 만족시키다
☐ need 명사 욕구 / 동사 필요로 하다
☐ take part in ~에 참여하다
☐ relaxation 명사 휴식, 완화
☐ release 명사 분출구, 해방, 방출 / 동사 방출하다
☐ tension 명사 긴장
☐ passive 형용사 수동적인, 소극적인
☐ spectator 명사 구경꾼, 방관자, 관중
☐ channel 명사 통로, 경로
☐ hostility 명사 적대감, 적의
☐ aggression 명사 공격성
☐ cooperate 동사 협동하다, 협력하다
☐ setting 명사 환경, 설정

02

☐ overwhelmed 형용사 압도된, 벅찬
☐ responsibility 명사 책임, 의무
☐ deal with ~을 처리하다, 다루다
☐ figure out ~을 알아내다, 계산하다
☐ balance out 균형을 잡다
☐ turn to ~에 의지하다
☐ divide up 분담하다, 갈리다
☐ willingness to V 기꺼이 ~ 하려는 마음
☐ assume 동사 추정하다, 당연하다고 여기다
☐ opportunity 명사 기회

03

☐ on one's way to V-ing/N ~하는 중에, ~로 가는 길에
☐ fashion 동사 만들어 내다
☐ masterpiece 명사 걸작, 대표작
☐ halt 동사 멈추다 / 명사 중단
☐ strike 동사 (금광·석유 등을) 발견하다
☐ backtrack 동사 되짚어가다, 철회하다
☐ discard 동사 폐기하다, 버리다
☐ celebrated 형용사 유명한
☐ scrap 동사 폐기하다, 버리다
☐ movement 명사 (음악 작품의) 악장
☐ distinguish A from B A와 B를 구분하다
☐ extraordinary 형용사 비범한, 특별한
☐ in protest of ~에 저항하여
☐ variation 명사 변형물, 변화
☐ creation 명사 (예술) 작품, 창조
☐ consistently 부사 일관적으로, 지속적으로
☐ reputation 명사 명성, 평판
☐ criticism 명사 비난, 비판
☐ appreciate 동사 감상하다, 감사하다, 인정하다

04

☐ pay attention to ~에 주목하다
☐ spotlight effect 조명 효과
☐ intuitively 부사 직관적으로
☐ overestimate 동사 과대평가하다
☐ be aimed at ~에게 향해 있다, ~을 목표로 하다
☐ peer 명사 또래, 동료
☐ nearly 부사 거의
☐ noticeable 형용사 매우 눈에 띄는
☐ provoke 동사 자극하다

05

☐ cure 명사 치료(법) / 동사 치료하다
☐ ownership 명사 소유(권)

☐ be woven into ~에 스며들어 있다
☐ be aware of ~을 알고 있다
☐ perspective 명사 관점, 견해
☐ loss 명사 손실, 손해, 상실, 패배
☐ downgrade 동사 (질이나 수준을) 낮추다
☐ sacrifice 명사 희생 / 동사 희생하다

06

☐ impulse 명사 충동, 욕구
☐ govern 동사 지배하다, 통치하다
☐ launch 동사 출시하다, (우주선 등을) 발사하다
☐ liking 명사 선호, 좋아함
☐ remarkable 형용사 놀랄 만한

07

☐ be concerned with ~와 관련이 있다
☐ demand 명사 수요 / 동사 요구하다
☐ overcrowded 형용사 과도하게 붐비는, 초만원인
☐ meet 동사 충족시키다, 만족시키다
☐ peak 형용사 최대의, 최고의 / 명사 최고조, 절정
☐ usage 명사 사용, 용법
☐ excess 형용사 과도한, 여분의 / 명사 과다, 과잉
☐ temporarily 부사 일시적으로, 임시로
☐ permanently 부사 영구적으로
☐ compensate for ~를 보상하다, (부족한 부분을) 메꾸다
☐ supply 명사 공급 / 동사 공급하다, 제공하다
☐ nature 명사 특징, 본성
☐ objective 명사 목적, 목표 / 형용사 객관적인

08

☐ refer to ~을 나타내다[언급하다], ~을 참고하다
☐ unequal 형용사 불평등한
☐ inequality 명사 불평등, 불균등
☐ norm 명사 일반적인 것, 표준
☐ acceptance 명사 수용, 인정
☐ allocate 동사 할당하다
☐ hierarchy 명사 (회사나 조직 내의) 계급, 계층
☐ hierarchical 형용사 계급의, 계층의
☐ convenience 명사 편의, 편리
☐ fluidity 명사 유동성, 흐름

09

☐ sustain 동사 지속시키다
☐ independent 형용사 독립적인, 독립된
☐ ethos 명사 민족(사회)정신
☐ rather 부사 오히려, 차라리
☐ interdependent 형용사 상호 의존적인
☐ cluster 명사 군집, 무리 / 동사 무리를 이루다
☐ require 동사 필요로 하다, 요구하다
☐ insulation 명사 단절, 단열
☐ number 동사 총 ~이 되다 / 명사 수
☐ feat 명사 위업
☐ geographic 형용사 지리적인, 지리학의
☐ remote 형용사 외딴, 외진
☐ territory 명사 영토, 지역

☐ sufficiently 부사 충분히
☐ distinct 형용사 뚜렷이 다른, 별개의
☐ in the long run 결국에는
☐ persist 동사 지속되다
☐ in contact with ~과 접촉하는
☐ pursue 동사 추구하다
☐ essentially 부사 본질적으로

10~12

☐ once upon a time (이야기를 시작할 때) 옛날 옛적에
☐ a ~ turn of mind ~한 성격, 사고방식
☐ proclamation 명사 포고, 선언
☐ outrageous 형용사 터무니없는, 충격적인
☐ swarm 동사 몰려들다, 떼지어 다니다
☐ prince 명사 제후, 영주, 왕자
☐ no lack of ~이 가득한, 많은
☐ convince 동사 설득하다, 납득시키다
☐ sport 명사 장난, 오락, 스포츠
☐ call off 중단하다, 철회하다
☐ sire 명사 폐하, 전하
☐ bewildered 형용사 당혹스러워하는, 어리둥절한
☐ collect 동사 (빚·세금을) 받다, 수금하다, 모으다
☐ exclaim 동사 소리치다, 외치다
☐ dilemma 명사 딜레마, 진퇴양난의 상황

3회 20분 미니모의고사

01

☐ ceiling 명사 천장
☐ dull 형용사 흐린, 무딘
☐ coat of paint 페인트칠
☐ at one's own expense ~의 자비 부담인, 사비로
☐ permission 명사 허락, 승인
☐ lease agreement 임대차 계약
☐ advise 동사 알려주다, 조언하다
☐ at one's earliest convenience 가능한 한 빨리, 되도록 일찍

02

☐ secretly 부사 몰래
☐ quicken 동사 더 빠르게 하다
☐ reach 동사 손을 뻗다
☐ throat 명사 목구멍
☐ shame 명사 부끄러움
☐ regret 명사 후회
☐ misunderstand 동사 오해하다

03

☐ frank 형용사 솔직한
☐ constantly 부사 지속적으로, 꾸준히
☐ self-disclosure 명사 자기 개방
☐ generate 동사 만들어내다, 생성하다
☐ public 형용사 공개적인, 개방적인
☐ private 형용사 사적인, 비공개의
☐ deny 동사 거절하다, 거부하다
☐ openly 부사 개방적으로
☐ fully 부사 완전히, 완전하게

☐ harsh 형용사 가혹한, 냉혹한
☐ underestimate 동사 과소평가하다

04

☐ washboard 명사 빨래판
☐ scrub 동사 비벼 빨다
☐ stream 명사 개울, 시내
☐ backbreaking 형용사 매우 힘든, (체력을) 소모시키는
☐ commonplace 형용사 흔히 일어나는, 아주 흔한
☐ automatically 부사 자동적으로, 기계적으로
☐ regulate 동사 조절하다, 조정하다
☐ measure out ~을 덜어내다[떼어내다]
☐ rinse 동사 헹구다, (비누 성분을) 씻어내다
☐ household appliance 가전제품
☐ excess 형용사 초과한, 과도한
☐ indeed 부사 정말로, 참으로
☐ phenomenon 명사 경이로운 물건, 진기한 물건

05

☐ obvious 형용사 명백한, 분명한
☐ cell 명사 세포
☐ maze 명사 미로
☐ somewhere else 어딘가 다른 곳에
☐ eventually 부사 결국, 마침내
☐ wiring 명사 연결, 배선
☐ dense 형용사 빽빽한, 조밀한
☐ nerve 명사 신경
☐ fiber 명사 섬유(질)
☐ interconnected 형용사 상호 연결된
☐ intricately 부사 복잡하게

06

☐ mathematician 명사 수학자
☐ astronomer 명사 천문학자
☐ devote 동사 바치다, 헌신하다
☐ initially 부사 처음에
☐ optics 명사 광학
☐ telescope 명사 망원경
☐ grind 동사 갈다 (grind-ground-ground)
☐ universal gravitation 명사 만유인력
☐ wide-ranging 형용사 광범위한
☐ achievement 명사 업적, 성취
☐ pendulum 명사 (시계)추, 진자
☐ astronomical 형용사 천문학의
☐ discovery 명사 발견
☐ moon 명사 위성, 달
☐ description 명사 묘사, 설명

07

☐ tap 동사 두드리다, 치다 / 명사 두드리는 소리
☐ observe 동사 관찰하다, 지켜보다
☐ flat 부사 바싹, 납작하게 / 형용사 평평한, 납작한
☐ typically 부사 전형적으로, 일반적으로
☐ substance 명사 물질, 본질, 핵심
☐ solid 명사 고체 / 형용사 고체의, 단단한, 견고한

문제편 : p.296~302 정답과 해설 : p.377~386

- density 명사 밀도, 농도
- play 동사 작용하다, 놀이를 하다 / 명사 놀이
- determining 형용사 결정적인

08

- persuasion 명사 설득
- processing 명사 사고 과정, 처리
- shallow 형용사 얕은, 얄팍한
- on principle 기본적으로
- fundamental 형용사 기본적인, 근본적인
- in general 일반적으로
- loyalty to ~에 대한 충성

09

- reject 동사 기각하다, 거부하다
- hypothesis 명사 가설 (hypotheses의 단수형)
- indirect 형용사 간접적인
- positively 부사 확실히, 분명히, 긍정적으로
- assemble 동사 모으다, 수집하다
- competing 형용사 경쟁하는, 대립되는
- overwhelmingly 부사 압도적으로

10

- precision 명사 정밀성
- apparent 형용사 명백한, 분명한
- suit 동사 적절하다, 들어맞다 / 명사 정장
- context 명사 상황, 문맥
- prove 동사 (사실임을) 입증하다
- absurd 형용사 터무니없는
- propose 동사 의도하다, 제안하다
- intention 명사 의도
- conceal 동사 숨기다
- lack 명사 부족, 결핍

11~12

- nonverbal 형용사 비언어적인
- squint 동사 눈을 가늘게 뜨다, 눈을 찡그리다
- shield 동사 가리다, 보호하다 / 명사 방패
- evolve 동사 진화하다, 발전하다
- undesirable 형용사 원하지 않는, 달갑지 않은
- assist in ~을 돕다
- arson 명사 방화(죄)
- suspicion 명사 용의, 혐의, 의혹
- blaze 명사 (대형) 화재, 불길
- break out (전쟁 등 안 좋은 일이) 발생하다, 일어나다
- assign 동사 배정하다, 할당하다
- determine 동사 밝히다, 알아내다
- as to ~에 관해, ~에 대해서
- observe 동사 관찰하다, 주시하다
- telltale 형용사 숨길 수 없는
- block 동사 (시야 등을) 가리다
- oddly 부사 희한하게도, 이상하게도
- troubled 형용사 불안해하는, 걱정하는
- eventually 부사 마침내, 결국
- post 명사 자리, 위치
- arsonist 명사 방화범
- insight 명사 통찰(력), 이해
- pursue 동사 계속하다, 추구하다

문제편 : p.302~304 | 정답과 해설 : p.386~390

▶ **Don't hesitate to V :** 주저하지 마라
Please **don't hesitate to apply** for this volunteer work at our charity soccer match.
자선 축구 경기의 자원봉사 활동에 **지원하는 데 주저하지 마십시오.**
출처: 2024학년도 대학수학능력시험 01번

▶ **get into an argument :** 말다툼을 하게 되다
Tiffany and I **got into an argument** at school.
Tiffany와 제가 학교에서 **말다툼을 했어요.**
출처: 2024학년도 대학수학능력시험 02번

▶ **cut A off :** (말 등을) 끊다
That's why when somebody's talking, you shouldn't **cut them off.**
그래서 누군가 말할 때는 **그들의 말을 끊**지 말아야 한단다.
출처: 2024학년도 대학수학능력시험 02번

▶ **experience trouble V-ing :** ~하는 데 어려움을 겪다
But recently, more and more people are **experiencing trouble falling** asleep.
하지만 최근에 점점 더 많은 사람들이 잠드**는 데 어려움을 겪고 있습니다.**
출처: 2024학년도 대학수학능력시험 03번

▶ **eye-catching :** 눈길을 끄는
And isn't that striped tablecloth really **eye-catching?**
그리고 저 줄무늬 식탁보는 정말로 **눈길을 끌**지 않나요?
출처: 2024학년도 대학수학능력시험 04번

▶ **bother :** 괴롭히다, 귀찮게 하다
Then, are your allergy symptoms **bother**ing you again?
그럼, 알레르기 증상이 또 너를 **괴롭히는 거**야?
출처: 2024학년도 대학수학능력시험 07번

▶ **make it :** 성공하다, 도착하다
I'm afraid I can't **make it** this time.
미안하지만 이번에는 **갈 수** 없어.
출처: 2024학년도 대학수학능력시험 12번

▶ **look forward to V-ing :** ~하기를 기대하다
That's too bad. I was **look**ing **forward to seeing** you there.
아쉽다. 나는 거기서 너를 **보기를 기대하고 있**었어.
출처: 2024학년도 대학수학능력시험 12번

▶ **put A off :** 미루다, 연기하다
You make me think of my old passion to be a painter, but I **put it off** for too long.
당신은 화가가 되고 싶다는 저의 오랜 열정에 대해 생각하게 만드시지만, 저는 너무 오랫동안 **그것을 미뤘어요.**
출처: 2024학년도 대학수학능력시험 13번

▶ **hold :** 가지고 있다, 중단하다
Oh, there's one copy left there, but unfortunately we can't **hold** it for you.
오, 거기에 한 권이 남아 있는데 유감스럽게도 저희가 고객님을 위해 그것을 **예약해 드릴** 수는 없네요.
출처: 2024학년도 대학수학능력시험 14번

▶ **make sure :** 반드시 ~하다
make sure you visit our school library to submit your application.
신청서를 제출하기 위해 **반드시** 학교 도서관을 방문해 주십시오.
출처: 2023학년도 대학수학능력시험 01번

▶ **rich in :** ~이 풍부한
It said apple peels are **rich in** vitamins and minerals, so they moisturize our skin and enhance skin glow.
사과 껍질은 비타민과 미네랄**이 풍부해서**, 피부에 수분을 공급하고 피부 광채를 향상시킨다고 했어요.
출처: 2023학년도 대학수학능력시험 02번

▶ **It seems ~ :** ~인[한] 것 같다
It seems to include useful information.
유용한 정보를 포함하고 있는 **것 같아**.
출처: 2023학년도 대학수학능력시험 04번

▶ **remind A of B :** A에게 B에 대해 다시 한 번 알려주다
We need to **remind** our loyal customers **of** the event.
우리는 단골 고객들에게 행사에 대해 **다시 한 번 알려 줘야** 해요.
출처: 2023학년도 대학수학능력시험 05번

▶ **What about ~? :** ~은 어때?
What about the live music**?**
라이브 음악**은 어때요?**
출처: 2023학년도 대학수학능력시험 05번

▶ **be scheduled to V :** ~할 예정이다
I'**m scheduled to** shoot your school's graduation photos on Wednesday, November 23rd.
11월 23일 수요일에 선생님 학교의 졸업 사진을 촬영**할 예정이에요**.
출처: 2023학년도 대학수학능력시험 08번

▶ **in stock :** 재고가 있는
These are the ones we have **in stock**.
이것들은 **재고가 있는** 것들이에요.
출처: 2023학년도 대학수학능력시험 10번

▶ **be willing to V :** ~할 의향이 있는
How much **are** you **willing to** spend?
얼마를 쓰실 **의향이 있으신가요**?
출처: 2023학년도 대학수학능력시험 10번

▶ **fair :** 박람회; 공정한
Our son said he's going to a career **fair** and asked if we can come along.
우리 아들이 직업 **박람회**에 갈 거라고 우리가 함께 갈 수 있는지 물어봤어요.
출처: 2023학년도 대학수학능력시험 12번

▶ **have trouble with :** ~으로 곤란을 겪다
Is there anything specific you're **having trouble with**?
특별히 **곤란한 일이 있**는 거니?
출처: 2023학년도 대학수학능력시험 13번

▶ **for no reason :** 이유 없이, 공연히
Does your dog chew up your shoes or bark **for no reason** at times?
당신의 개가 당신의 신발을 씹거나 때때로 **이유 없이** 짖나요?
출처: 2022학년도 대학수학능력시험 01번

▶ **what do you think about[of]? :** ~에 대해 어떻게 생각해?
What do you think about the balloons next to the welcome banner**?**
환영 현수막 옆에 있는 풍선들**에 대해 어떻게 생각해?**
출처: 2022학년도 대학수학능력시험 04번

▶ **I guess (that) ~ :** ~이라고 생각하다
Oh, then **I guess** you have to study for the science quiz, right?
오, 그럼 과학 퀴즈를 위한 공부를 해야 **하는구나**, 그렇지?
출처: 2022학년도 대학수학능력시험 07번

▶ **on one's way to :** ~으로 가는 길[도중]에
Actually, I'm **on my way to** volunteer at the school library.
사실, 학교 도서관에 자원봉사를 하**러 가는 중**이야.
출처: 2022학년도 대학수학능력시험 07번

▶ **for free :** 무료로, 공짜로
We'll also give out a children's science magazine **for free**.
저희는 또한 어린이 과학 잡지를 **무료로** 나눠드릴 것입니다.
출처: 2022학년도 대학수학능력시험 09번

▶ **in advance :** 미리
There's no admission fee, but to participate, you must register **in advance**.
입장료는 없지만, 참가하시려면, **미리** 등록하셔야 합니다.
출처: 2022학년도 대학수학능력시험 09번

▶ **available :** 이용 가능한
Oh, only these rooms are **available**.
오, 이 룸들만 **이용 가능하**구나.
출처: 2022학년도 대학수학능력시험 10번

▶ **enough to V :** ~하기에 충분히 …한
We need a room big **enough to** accommodate six of us.
우리 6명을 수용**할 만큼 충분히** 큰 룸이 필요해.
출처: 2022학년도 대학수학능력시험 10번

▶ **since :** ~ 때문에, ~한 이래로
Since we're meeting for two hours, I don't think we can spend more than $20 per hour.
우리는 두 시간 동안 만나기로 했**기 때문에**, 시간당 20달러 이상은 쓸 수 없을 것 같아.
출처: 2022학년도 대학수학능력시험 10번

▶ **beyond :** ~을 초과한, ~을 뛰어넘는
It's **beyond** our budget.
그것은 우리의 예산을 **초과해**.
출처: 2022학년도 대학수학능력시험 10번

▶ **look up at :** ~을 올려다보다
Oh, so you went outdoors to **look up at** stars.
오, 그럼 별**을 올려다보**기 위해서 야외로 나갔겠구나.
출처: 2021학년도 대학수학능력시험 02번

▶ **become familiar with :** ~에 친숙해지다
And I think it helped my son **become familiar with** mathematical concepts.
그리고 그것은 내 아들이 수학 개념**에 친숙해지**도록 도와준 것 같아.
출처: 2021학년도 대학수학능력시험 02번

▶ **get used to N/V-ing :** ~에 익숙해지다
I think looking at stars is a good way for kids to **get used to** mathematical concepts.
별을 보는 것은 아이들이 수학 개념**에 익숙해지**는 좋은 방법인 것 같아.
출처: 2021학년도 대학수학능력시험 02번

▶ **be honored to V :** ~하게 되어 영광으로 생각하다
I'**m honored to** interview the person who designed the school I'm attending.
제가 다니는 학교를 설계하신 분을 인터뷰**하게 되어 영광으로 생각해요**.
출처: 2021학년도 대학수학능력시험 03번

▶ **fill A up with B :** A를 B로 가득 채우다
We're going to **fill** those **up with** donations of toys and books.
저희는 그것들**을** 장난감과 책 기증품들**로 가득 채울** 거예요.
출처: 2021학년도 대학수학능력시험 04번

▶ **need to V :** ~해야 한다
It was founded to deliver the message that we **need to** admit our failures to truly succeed.
그곳은 우리가 진정으로 성공하기 위해서는 우리의 실패를 인정**해야 한다**는 메시지를 전달하기 위해 설립되었어.
출처: 2021학년도 대학수학능력시험 08번

▶ **advance to :** ~에 진출하다
We had the most applicants in the history of this competition, and only 10 participants will **advance to** the final round.
이 대회의 역사상 가장 많은 지원자들이 있었으며, 오직 10명의 참가자들만 결선**에 진출할** 것입니다.
출처: 2021학년도 대학수학능력시험 09번

▶ **be about to V :** ~할 예정이다
You cannot park here because we'**re about to** close off this section of the parking lot.
저희가 주차장의 이 구획을 폐쇄**할 예정이**기 때문에 여기에 주차하실 수 없습니다.
출처: 2021학년도 대학수학능력시험 12번

▶ **be out of :** ~이 없다
We'**re out of** this model right now.
지금 당장은 이 모델**이 없어요**.
출처: 2021학년도 대학수학능력시험 13번

▶ **break down :** 고장 나다
My washing machine **broke down** yesterday.
제 세탁기가 어제 **고장 났어요**.
출처: 2021학년도 대학수학능력시험 13번

▶ **inform A of B :** A에게 B에 대해 알리다
We'd like to **inform** you **of** the special events going on through this weekend.
여러분**께** 이번 주말 동안 진행되는 특별 행사들**에 대해 알려드리고자** 합니다.
출처: 2020학년도 대학수학능력시험 03번

▶ **have something to do with :** ~과 관련이 있다
I didn't know how we sleep **has something to do with** digestion.
나는 우리가 잠을 자는 방식이 소화**와 관련이 있는** 줄은 몰랐어.
출처: 2020학년도 대학수학능력시험 04번

▶ **must have p.p. :** ~했음이 틀림없다
It **must have been** very difficult to get a reservation because our party is on December 24th.
우리 파티가 12월 24일이기 때문에 예약하는 게 매우 어려**웠음이 틀림없어**.
출처: 2020학년도 대학수학능력시험 10번

▶ **take a look at :** ~을 보다
Okay, Mr. White. Let's **take a look at** the flight schedule. 좋아요, White 씨. 비행기 시간표**를 봐요**.
출처: 2020학년도 대학수학능력시험 12번

▶ **share A with B :** B와 A를 공유하다
Yeah. You can **share** ideas **with** others in the group about the book you're reading.
그래. 네가 읽고 있는 책에 대해서 모임 내의 다른 사람들**과** 생각**을 공유할** 수 있어.
출처: 2020학년도 대학수학능력시험 14번

▶ **take care of :** ~을 챙겨주다, 돌보다, 다루다, 처리하다
Until now his mother has always **taken care of** his travel bag, so he doesn't have any experience preparing it himself. 지금까지 그의 어머니가 그의 여행 가방**을** 항상 **챙겨주**어서, 그는 그것을 직접 준비한 경험이 없다.
출처: 2020학년도 대학수학능력시험 15번

▶ **have access to :** ~을 이용[접근, 출입]할 수 있다
How did people send mail before they **had access to** cars and trains?
사람들은 그들이 자동차와 기차를 **이용할 수 있**기 전에 어떻게 우편물을 보냈을까요?
출처: 2020학년도 대학수학능력시험 16~17번

▶ **due to N :** ~ 때문에
Once again, today's game has been canceled **due to** heavy rain.
다시 한 번 말씀드리지만, 오늘의 경기는 폭우 **때문에** 취소되었습니다.
출처: 2019학년도 대학수학능력시험 03번

▶ **be supposed to V :** ~하기로 되어 있다
Today's baseball game **was supposed to** begin in twenty minutes.
오늘의 야구 경기는 20분 후에 시작**하기로 되어 있었습니다**.
출처: 2019학년도 대학수학능력시험 03번

Tip 원래는 무엇을 하기로 되어 있었으나, 계획에 변경이 생겼음을 말할 때 많이 사용돼요!

▶ **According to + N :** ~에 따르면
According to the forecast, the weather will only get worse.
일기예보**에 따르면**, 날씨가 더 나빠질 뿐입니다.
출처: 2019학년도 대학수학능력시험 03번

영어 고득점 공부 방법

박재인 님 2023 마더텅 제7기 성적우수 장학생 동상
서울시 영동일고등학교
가톨릭관동대학교 의학과 합격
2024학년도 수능 화학Ⅰ 1등급(표준 점수 69)
사용 교재 **까만책** 국어 문학, 국어 독서, 국어 언어와 매체, 수학Ⅰ, 수학Ⅱ, 미적분, 화학Ⅰ, 생명과학Ⅱ 노란책 영어 영역

오답 정리가 중요

저는 마더텅 미니모의고사 영어 영역으로 공부하며 오답 정리를 확실하게 활용했습니다. 오답을 다시 보는 것의 중요성은 널리 알려져 있습니다. 그러나 오답 노트를 만드는 데에는 많은 시간이 소요될 수 있습니다. 따라서 저는 틀린 문제를 따로 정리하지 않고 책상이나 벽에 붙여놓은 후, 주기적으로 다시 푸는 방식을 택했습니다. 매주 한 번씩 틀린 문제들을 다시 푸는 것으로, 소중한 시간을 많이 소모하지 않으면서도 오답을 공부할 수 있었습니다.

박병준 님 2023 마더텅 제7기 성적우수 장학생 동상
화성시 이산고등학교
충북대학교 수의예과 합격
2024학년도 수능 영어 영역 1등급
사용 교재 **까만책** 영어 어법·어휘, 화학Ⅰ, 지구과학Ⅰ

1. 단어 암기가 가장 중요!

어휘 문제를 푼 후에는 단순히 답을 찾는 것이 아니라 모르는 어휘의 뜻을 찾아 익히는 것이 효과적입니다. 이렇게 하면 어휘력을 향상시키는 데 도움이 됩니다.

2. 모든 선지의 어법 확인

어법 문제의 경우에도 답을 바로 찾는 것뿐만 아니라 다른 선지들의 어법을 확인하여 다양한 문법을 접할 수 있도록 노력해야 합니다. 어법 문제를 푸는 경우에는 실전 모의고사만을 계속 푸는 것이 아니라 어법 하나마다 최대의 효율을 내며 공부하는 것이 중요합니다.

3. 듣기 시간 활용

어법 문제를 듣기 시간에 푸는 경우 주변이 조용하지 않을 때에도 풀 수 있도록 연습하는 것이 도움이 될 수 있습니다.

이다은 님 2023 마더텅 제7기 성적우수 장학생 동상
구미시 경북외국어고등학교
경희대학교 무역학과 합격
2024학년도 수능 영어 영역 1등급
사용 교재 **까만책** 국어 독서, 국어 문학, 영어 독해, 한국지리, 세계지리
빨간책 국어 영역, 수학 영역, 영어 영역, 한국지리, 세계지리 노란책 영어 영역

“ D-30 매일 1회씩 풀기 ”

마더텅 수능기출 모의고사는 실전 감각을 키우기 위해 수능 전 1-2달 동안 매일 푸는 연습을 했습니다. 하루에 정해진 양을 다 풀고 맞힌 문제더라도 답을 찾는 데 어려움이 있었거나, 헷갈렸던 선지는 표시해두고 채점 후 해설집을 활용하여 꼼꼼히 체크했습니다. 문제집 위쪽에 적힌 시간을 최대한 지키려고 노력하니 빠르고 정확하게 푸는 연습이 되어 실제 수능 때 시간이 넉넉히 남았습니다.

백종헌 님 2023 마더텅 제7기 성적우수 장학생 동상
용인시 대지고등학교
홍익대학교 경영학부 합격
2024학년도 수능 영어 영역 1등급
사용 교재 **까만책** 영어 독해, 사회·문화, 생활과 윤리

수능을 준비하면서는 무조건 많이 풀어보는 방식으로 공부했습니다. 아무래도 실전 감각을 유지하기 위한 용도이다 보니, 풀 수 있는 만큼 풀고, 헷갈리는 선지나 지문에는 체크를 한 뒤 해설을 보고 알게 된 내용을 문제집에 적어 놓는 식이었습니다. 이런 것들이 쌓이다 보니 자연스럽게 영어 감도 잡고, 실력도 올랐습니다.

박은빈 님 2023 마더텅 제7기 성적우수 장학생 동상
서울시 도선고등학교
고려대학교 경영대학 합격
2024학년도 수능 영어 영역 1등급
사용 교재 **까만책** 생활과 윤리, 사회문화 **빨간책** 영어 영역

학습계획표 활용하기

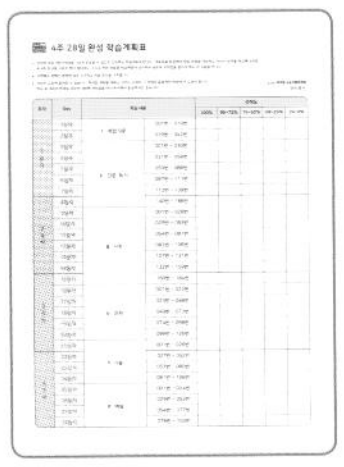

마더텅의 학습계획표를 따라가면 한 달 안에 문제집을 완료할 수 있어서 공부를 길게 끌지 않고 진행할 수 있었습니다. 계획표를 통해 매일 하나씩 문제를 풀었는데, 이렇게 하니 어느새 모든 문제를 해결할 수 있었습니다.

주혜린 님 2023 마더텅 제7기 성적우수 장학생 동상
서울시 서초고등학교
경북대학교 약학과 합격
2024학년도 수능 영어 영역 1등급
사용 교재 **까만책** 수학 영역, 생명과학Ⅰ, 지구과학Ⅰ **빨간책** 국어 영역, 수학 영역, 영어 영역

영어의 경우 절대평가가 되면서 공부를 등한시하는 학생들이 많아졌습니다. 그러나 영어는 공부를 소홀히할 경우 실력이 빠르게 떨어질 수 있기에 꾸준한 학습을 목표로 삼았습니다. 다른 과목에 시간을 많이 투자해야 할 때는 하루에 30분이라도 꼭 영어를 공부할 수 있도록 했습니다. 특히 듣기 시간에 틈틈이 문제를 푸는 연습은 시험 시간 내에 문제를 해결하는 데 큰 도움이 되었습니다.

MOTHERTONGUE
마더텅출판사
since1999.4.1.

www.toptutor.co.kr

2025 마더텅 전국연합 학력평가 기출문제집

고2 영어 독해 WORD BOOK

mechanism	n. 기계 장치, 기구
media	n. (medium의 복수형) 매체
medical	a. 의학의 / n. 의학도
mental	a. 정신의 / n. 정신병 환자
mere	a. 겨우 ~의 / n. 작은 호수
message	n. 전갈 / v. 메시지를 보내다
million	n. 100만 / a. 100만의
modern	a. 현대의, 근대의
moment	n. 잠깐, 잠시
moral	a. 도덕의 / n. 도덕
necessary	a. 필요한 / n. 없어서는 안 되는 것
negative	a. 부정적인 / n. 부정 / v. 거부하다
neighbo(u)r	n. 이웃 / a. 이웃의 / v. 이웃하다
neither	a. / pron. (둘 중의) 어느 것도 ~ 아니다
nervous	a. 불안해하는, 초조해하는
nor	conj. ~도 (또한) 아니다[없다]
normal	a. 보통의 / n. 보통
notice	n. 주목 / v. 알아차리다
numerous	a. 많은, 무수한
objective	n. 목표 / a. 객관적인
observe	v. 보다, 관찰하다
obtain	v. 얻다, 존재하다
obvious	a. 분명한, 명백한
occur	v. 일어나다, 발생하다
offer	v. 제의하다, 제안하다 / n. 제의
once	ad. 한 번 / conj. 일단 ~하면
operate	v. 작동하다, 조작하다
opinion	n. 의견, 생각
opportunity	n. 기회, 호기
option	n. 선택, 선택할 수 있는 것
order	n. 순서 / v. 명령하다
ordinary	a. 보통의 / n. 보통의 상태
origin	n. 기원, 근원
original	a. 원래의 / n. 원본
other	a. 다른 / pron. 다른 사람[것] ad. ~ 외에
otherwise	ad. 그렇지 않으면[않았다면]
outcome	n. 결과, 성과
overcome	v. 극복하다, 이기다
own	a. 자기 자신의 / v. 소유하다
panel	n. 판 / v. 판으로 덮다
particular	a. 특정한 / n. 자세한 사항
particularly	ad. 특히, 특별히
past	a. 지나간 / n. 과거 prep. 지나서 / ad. 지나서
patient	n. 환자 / a. 참을성 있는
pattern	n. 무늬 / v. 무늬를 만들다
peer	n. 또래 / v. 필적하다, 유심히 보다
per	prep. ~에 대하여, ~마다
perceive	v. 감지하다, 인지하다
perception	n. 지각, 자각
perfect	a. 완벽한 / v. 완벽하게 하다
perform	v. 행하다, 작동하다
perhaps	ad. 아마 / n. 우연한 일
period	n. 기간 / a. 시대의
person	n. 사람, 개인
personality	n. 성격, 인격
perspective	n. 관점 / a. 원근법에 의한
persuade	v. 설득하다, 설득하여 ~하게 하다
phenomenon	n. 현상, 경이로운 사람[것]
photo(graph)	n. 사진 / v. 사진을 찍다
phrase	n. (문법) 구(句) / v. 표현하다
physical	a. 육체의 / n. 건강 검진
plain	a. 분명한 / n. 평원 / ad. 분명히
planet	n. 행성, 지구
plant	n. 식물 / v. 심다
poet	n. 시인
population	n. 인구, 주민
positive	a. 긍정적인, 명확한 / n. 현실
possible	a. 가능한 / n. 가능성
potential	a. 가능성이 있는 / n. 가능성
practical	a. 현실[실질]적인 / n. 실기 시험
practice / practise	n. 연습 / v. 연습하다
predict	v. 예측하다, 예견하다
prefer	v. ~을 (더) 좋아하다, 선호하다
prepare	v. 준비하다, 대비하다
presence	n. 출석, 참석
previous	a. 이전의, 앞의
prey	n. 먹이 / v. 잡아먹다
prize	n. 상 / v. 소중히 하다
probably	ad. 아마, 십중팔구는
process	n. 과정 v. 가공[처리]하다, 행진하다
produce	v. 생산하다, 산출하다 n. 생산물[품]
professor	n. 교수, 교사
profit	n. 이익 / v. 이익을 주다
profound	a. 엄청난 / n. 깊음
progress	n. 진전 / v. 진전을 보이다
promote	v. 촉진하다, 고취하다
provide	v. 제공하다, 공급하다
public	a. 일반인의 / n. 일반 사람들
purchase	n. 구입 / v. 구입하다
purpose	n. 목적 / v. 작정하다
quite	ad. 꽤, 제법
raise	v. 들어올리다 / n. 올리기
random	a. 닥치는 대로의 n. 닥치는 대로 하기
range	n. 범위 v. 배열하다, (양·크기 등이 일정한 범위) 이다
rate	n. 속도 / v. 평가하다, 평가되다
rather	ad. 오히려, 꽤
reach	v. 이르다, 뻗다 / n. 거리
real	a. 현실적인 / ad. 정말 / n. 현실
reason	n. 이유 / v. 논하다, 판단하다
receive	v. 받다, 손님을 맞이하다
reduce	v. 줄이다, 줄다
reflect	v. 반사하다, 비추다
refuse	v. 거절하다, 거부하다
regard	v. 여기다, 주시하다 / n. 관심
register	v. 등록하다 / n. 기록부
regular	a. 규칙적인 / n. 단골손님 ad. 규칙적으로
reinforce	v. 강화하다 / n. 보강물
relationship	n. 관계, 친족 관계
relax	v. 편하게 하다, 휴식을 취하다
relieve	v. 없애 주다, 완화하다
rely	v. 의지하다, 의존하다
remain	v. 남다 / n. 나머지
remove	v. 치우다, 이동하다 / n. 이동
repair	v. 수리하다 / n. 수리
repeat	v. 반복하다, 되풀이되다 / n. 반복
reply	v. 대답하다 / n. 대답
require	v. 필요하다, 필요로 하다
research	n. 연구 / v. 연구하다
resource	n. 자원 / v. 자원을 제공하다
respond	v. 대답하다, 응답하다 / n. 벽기둥

rest	n. 휴식, 나머지 v. 쉬다, 쉬게 하다, (여전히·계속) ~이다
restrict	v. 제한하다, 한정하다
result	n. 결과 / v. 발생하다
reveal	v. 밝히다 / n. 계시
reward	n. 보상 / v. 보상하다, 보답하다
risk	n. 위험 / v. 위태롭게 하다
role	n. 역할, 임무
route	n. 길 / v. 보내다
rule	n. 규칙 / v. 지배하다
scale	n. 규모, 저울, 비늘 v. 오르다, 비례하다, 무게가 ~이다, 비늘을 벗기다
search	n. 찾기 / v. 찾다, 수색하다
seat	n. 자리 / v. 앉히다, 의자에 앉다
seek	v. 찾다, 구하다
seem	v. ~인 것처럼 보이다
select	v. 선발하다 / a. 엄선된 / n. 고급품
self	n. 모습, 본모습
sense	n. 감각 / v. 감지하다
sensible	a. 분별 있는, 합리적인
series	n. 연속, 연쇄
serious	a. 심각한, 중대한
serve	v. 일하다, 시중들다 / n. 서브
settle	v. 해결하다, 합의하다
shake	v. 흔들리다, 뒤흔들다 / n. 흔들기
shall	(미래) ~일 것이다, (의지) ~할 것이다
share	v. 나누다, 함께 나누다[하다] n. 몫
shift	v. 옮기다, 바꾸다 / n. 변화
shout	v. 외치다, 큰 소리로 말하다 / n. 외침
significant	a. 중요한, 의미 있는
similar	a. 비슷한 / n. 유사물
simple	a. 간단한 / n. 어수룩한 사람
since	prep. ~부터 / conj. ~한 이후로
single	a. 단 하나의 / n. 하나 / ad. 혼자서
site	n. 위치 / v. 위치시키다
situation	n. 상황, 처지
skill	n. 기량, 솜씨
social	a. 사회의 / n. 사교 파티
society	n. 사회, 집단
soon	ad. 곧, 머지않아
source	n. 원천 / v. 구입하다
span	n. 기간 / v. (얼마의 기간에) 걸치다
special	a. 특수한 / n. 특별한 것
species	n. 종(種: 생물 분류의 기초 단위)
specific	a. 구체적인 / n. 특성
spend	v. 쓰다, 낭비하다 / n. 비용
spread	v. 펼치다, 펼쳐지다 / n. 확산
stage	n. 단계 / a. 무대의
stamp	n. 우표 / v. 구르다, 쿵쾅거리며 걷다
state	n. 상태 / a. 국가의 / v. 말하다
status	n. 신분, 자격
still	ad. 아직도 / a. 가만히 있는 n. 고요 / v. 고요[잠잠]하게 하다
stimulate	v. 자극하다, 격려가 되다
strategy	n. 계획, 전략
stress	n. 스트레스 v. 강조하다, 스트레스를 받다
stretch	v. 늘이다, 늘어나다 / n. 뻗은 지역
structure	n. 구조 / v. 조직하다
struggle	v. 투쟁하다 / n. 투쟁
subject	n. 주제 / a. ~될 수 있는 v. 지배하에 두다
success	n. 성공, 성과
such	a. 그런 / pron. 그런 사람[것](들)
suggest	v. 제안하다, 제의하다
supply	n. 공급(량) / v. 공급하다 / a. 보급의
support	v. 지지하다 / n. 지지
surprise	n. 뜻밖의 일 / v. 놀라게 하다
system	n. 제도, 체제
talent	n. 재주, 재능
task	n. 일 / v. 일을 부과하다
technology	n. 기술, 기계
temperature	n. 온도, 기온
tend	v. 경향이 있다, 돌보다, 보살피다
term	n. 용어 / v. 칭하다
text	n. 본문 / v. 문자를 보내다
then	ad. 그때 / a. 당시의 / n. 그때
therefore	ad. 그러므로, 그러니
thin	a. 얇은 / ad. 얇게 v. 얇게 만들다, 얇아지다
though	conj. (비록) ~이긴 하지만 ad. 그렇지만
thousand	n. 1000 / a. 1000의
through	prep. ~을 통해 ad. 지나서 / a. 직통의
thus	ad. 이렇게 하여, 이와 같이
tool	n. 연장, 도구 / v. 천천히 몰다
total	a. 총 / n. 합계 v. 합계[총] ~이 되다
toward(s)	prep. (어떤 방향) 쪽으로 a. 임박한
trade	n. 거래 / v. 거래하다, 매매하다
tradition	n. 전통, 관습
treat	v. 대하다, 다루다 / n. 대접
trend	n. 동향 / v. 향해 있다
trust	n. 신뢰 / v. 신뢰하다, 신임하다
unique	a. 유일무이한 n. 유일한[독특한] 사람[것]
unit	n. 구성 단위, 한 개
university	n. 대학, 대학생
until	prep. ~(때)까지
update	v. 갱신하다 / n. 갱신
value	n. 가치 / v. 소중하게 생각하다
vanish	v. 사라지다, 숨기다 / n. 소음(消音)
various	a. 여러 가지의, 각양각색의
vary	v. 서로 다르다, 다르게 하다
vast	a. 방대한 / n. 광대함
vehicle	n. 차량, 탈것
view	n. 견해 / v. 여기다
visible	a. 보이는 / n. 눈에 보이는 것
vision	n. 시력 / v. 환영으로 보다
waste	v. 낭비하다, 낭비되다 n. 낭비 / a. 버려진
wheel	n. 바퀴 / v. 밀다, 선회하다
whereas	conj. ~에 반하여 / n. 서두, 전문
whether	conj. ~인지 (아닌지), ~이든 (아니든)
which	a. 어느 / pron. 어느 것
within	prep. ~ 이내에 / ad. 내부에서
without	prep. ~ 없이 / ad. ~ 없이 n. 밖 / conj. ~하지 않으면
witness	n. 목격자 / v. 목격하다, 증언하다
wonder	v. 궁금하다, 놀라다 / n. 경탄
worth	a. ~의 가치가 있는 / n. 어치[짜리]
would	will의 과거형, ~일[할] 것이다
yet	ad. 아직 / conj. 그렇지만

정답표

01 글의 목적 파악
문제편 p.007 해설편 p.002

01 ①	02 ⑤	03 ⑤	04 ④	05 ③
06 ⑤	07 ③	08 ②	09 ③	10 ⑤
11 ①	12 ②	13 ①	14 ②	15 ②
16 ②	17 ①			

02 심경·분위기 파악
문제편 p.018 해설편 p.012

01 ①	02 ①	03 ②	04 ①	05 ①
06 ①	07 ①	08 ①	09 ①	10 ⑤
11 ⑤	12 ②	13 ②	14 ①	15 ②
16 ②	17 ⑤	18 ①	19 ②	

03 필자의 주장
문제편 p.028 해설편 p.024

01 ②	02 ③	03 ②	04 ②	05 ①
06 ②	07 ⑤	08 ③	09 ⑤	10 ⑤
11 ②	12 ⑤	13 ④	14 ②	15 ⑤
16 ④	17 ⑤	18 ①	19 ②	20 ⑤

04 의미 추론
문제편 p.040 해설편 p.038

01 ④	02 ⑤	03 ⑤	04 ①	05 ③
06 ③	07 ③	08 ⑤	09 ④	10 ①
11 ⑤	12 ④	13 ④	14 ①	15 ①

05 요지 추론
문제편 p.050 해설편 p.051

01 ⑤	02 ⑤	03 ①	04 ③	05 ③
06 ①	07 ⑤	08 ④	09 ②	10 ③
11 ③	12 ⑤	13 ⑤	14 ②	15 ④
16 ①	17 ②	18 ④	19 ⑤	

06 주제 추론
문제편 p.061 해설편 p.065

01 ②	02 ③	03 ②	04 ③	05 ⑤
06 ③	07 ②	08 ⑤	09 ⑤	10 ②
11 ④	12 ④	13 ⑤	14 ⑤	15 ⑤
16 ⑤	17 ④	18 ①	19 ⑤	20 ②
21 ②				

07 제목 추론
문제편 p.074 해설편 p.082

01 ④	02 ⑤	03 ②	04 ③	05 ①
06 ①	07 ③	08 ⑤	09 ③	10 ②
11 ③	12 ②	13 ③	14 ②	15 ③
16 ④	17 ②	18 ①	19 ⑤	20 ③
21 ①	22 ③	23 ⑤	24 ④	25 ④

08 도표의 이해
문제편 p.089 해설편 p.102

01 ④	02 ③	03 ③	04 ④	05 ⑤
06 ⑤	07 ④	08 ④	09 ④	10 ④
11 ③	12 ③	13 ③	14 ③	15 ③
16 ④	17 ⑤	18 ③	19 ④	

09 내용 일치 파악
문제편 p.101 해설편 p.114

01 ③	02 ④	03 ③	04 ④	05 ⑤
06 ⑤	07 ③	08 ④	09 ②	10 ④
11 ③	12 ④	13 ④	14 ④	15 ③
16 ④	17 ⑤	18 ④		

10 안내문
문제편 p.112 해설편 p.126

01 ⑤	02 ④	03 ③	04 ④	05 ⑤
06 ④	07 ⑤	08 ⑤	09 ⑤	10 ④
11 ④	12 ④	13 ③	14 ⑤	15 ④
16 ⑤	17 ③	18 ④	19 ③	20 ③
21 ④	22 ②	23 ④	24 ②	25 ③
26 ④	27 ④	28 ③	29 ④	30 ⑤
31 ③	32 ⑤	33 ④		

11 빈칸 추론(1)-어휘, 짧은 어구
문제편 p.132 해설편 p.137

01 ①	02 ②	03 ①	04 ①	05 ②
06 ③	07 ①	08 ②	09 ①	10 ①
11 ①	12 ③	13 ①	14 ①	15 ④
16 ③	17 ④	18 ①	19 ②	20 ⑤
21 ②	22 ④	23 ①	24 ②	25 ②
26 ②	27 ④	28 ②	29 ①	30 ③
31 ①	32 ③	33 ①		

12 빈칸 추론(2)-긴 어구, 문장
문제편 p.149 해설편 p.164

01 ①	02 ①	03 ③	04 ①	05 ③
06 ④	07 ③	08 ④	09 ③	10 ②
11 ①	12 ⑤	13 ③	14 ②	15 ④
16 ④	17 ②	18 ⑤	19 ④	20 ①
21 ①	22 ②	23 ②	24 ①	25 ④
26 ④	27 ③	28 ①	29 ①	30 ②
31 ①	32 ⑤	33 ①	34 ②	35 ②
36 ③	37 ⑤	38 ②	39 ⑤	40 ①
41 ⑤	42 ②	43 ②	44 ③	45 ④
46 ③	47 ①	48 ②	49 ①	50 ⑤

13 무관한 문장 찾기
문제편 p.176 해설편 p.209

01 ③	02 ④	03 ④	04 ③	05 ④
06 ④	07 ③	08 ④	09 ③	10 ④
11 ④	12 ③	13 ④	14 ④	15 ③
16 ③	17 ③	18 ③	19 ③	

14 문장 배열
문제편 p.185 해설편 p.223

01 ②	02 ⑤	03 ②	04 ②	05 ③
06 ②	07 ③	08 ③	09 ⑤	10 ④
11 ⑤	12 ④	13 ⑤	14 ④	15 ③
16 ⑤	17 ③	18 ⑤	19 ②	20 ⑤
21 ④	22 ⑤	23 ②	24 ⑤	25 ①
26 ②	27 ③	28 ②	29 ②	30 ③
31 ⑤	32 ②	33 ③	34 ⑤	35 ⑤
36 ③	37 ②	38 ③	39 ⑤	40 ②
41 ②	42 ③	43 ⑤	44 ③	

15 주어진 문장 위치 파악
문제편 p.209 해설편 p.260

01 ④	02 ④	03 ④	04 ④	05 ③
06 ②	07 ③	08 ④	09 ④	10 ③
11 ③	12 ④	13 ③	14 ④	15 ④
16 ④	17 ⑤	18 ⑤	19 ⑤	20 ④
21 ①	22 ③	23 ④	24 ③	25 ⑤
26 ⑤	27 ⑤	28 ③	29 ③	30 ⑤
31 ③	32 ①	33 ③	34 ③	35 ②
36 ①	37 ③	38 ④	39 ③	40 ②
41 ④	42 ③	43 ②	44 ④	

16 문단 요약
문제편 p.233 해설편 p.294

01 ②	02 ①	03 ①	04 ①	05 ②
06 ①	07 ②	08 ①	09 ①	10 ①
11 ①	12 ②	13 ①	14 ①	15 ①
16 ④	17 ①	18 ①	19 ⑤	20 ①

17 장문의 이해-단일지문
문제편 p.245 해설편 p.313

01 ②	02 ③	03 ④	04 ⑤	05 ①
06 ⑤	07 ⑤	08 ⑤	09 ①	10 ④
11 ①	12 ⑤	13 ③	14 ④	15 ①
16 ④	17 ③	18 ④	19 ③	20 ②
21 ⑤	22 ⑤	23 ⑤	24 ⑤	25 ②
26 ③	27 ⑤	28 ④	29 ②	30 ④
31 ①	32 ⑤	33 ②	34 ①	35 ①
36 ③	37 ①	38 ⑤	39 ①	40 ⑤
41 ①	42 ④	43 ①	44 ⑤	45 ①
46 ④				

18 장문의 이해-복합지문
문제편 p.270 해설편 p.341

01 ②	02 ⑤	03 ⑤	04 ④	05 ④
06 ⑤	07 ⑤	08 ⑤	09 ④	10 ④
11 ⑤	12 ③	13 ⑤	14 ④	15 ②
16 ②	17 ③	18 ⑤	19 ④	20 ③
21 ③	22 ③	23 ②	24 ②	25 ③
26 ④	27 ③	28 ③	29 ⑤	30 ⑤
31 ⑤	32 ④	33 ⑤	34 ④	35 ②
36 ③	37 ③	38 ⑤	39 ④	40 ②
41 ③	42 ④	43 ③	44 ⑤	45 ⑤
46 ④	47 ④	48 ②	49 ②	50 ③
51 ③	52 ②	53 ③	54 ③	

1회 20분 미니모의고사
문제편 p.288 해설편 p.365

01 ①	02 ⑤	03 ①	04 ③	05 ④
06 ④	07 ⑤	08 ②	09 ⑤	10 ③
11 ④	12 ②			

2회 20분 미니모의고사
문제편 p.294 해설편 p.374

01 ②	02 ②	03 ①	04 ⑤	05 ④
06 ②	07 ③	08 ①	09 ②	10 ⑤
11 ④	12 ②			

3회 20분 미니모의고사
문제편 p.299 해설편 p.382

01 ③	02 ①	03 ②	04 ④	05 ⑤
06 ③	07 ⑤	08 ②	09 ⑤	10 ①
11 ③	12 ③			

9차 개정판 2쇄 2025년 1월 20일 (초판 1쇄 발행일 2016년 1월 7일) **발행처** (주)마더텅 **발행인** 문숙영 **책임 편집** 정다혜, 성현영
STAFF 김보란, 마혜진, 손유민, 윤은채, 조해라 **문항 선별** 정태은 / 김석화(수원여고), 문명기(문명기영어학원)
해설 집필 김효원, 오승연, 오정연, 유지원, 신다을, 신준기, 마더텅 편집부 / 김남경, 김채린, 박예은, 이수나, 이재은
교정 정태은, 정은주, 김미경(정이조영어학원 동작), 김지안 (압구정정보강북영어학원), 윤장환(세화여고), 이지언(상일여고), 황윤영(세화여고) / 김양현(성남외고), 김세영, 장신혜(TNT ACADEMY) **해설 감수** 정태은, 김석화(수원여고), 김진희(마더텅영어), 김태욱(대치상상학원), 오현진(대치동 새움학원), 최주영(마더텅영어), 강산(EBS 영어) / 조유정(분당영덕여고), 권수란 **입력 대조** 김효원, 류도이, 이윤정, 오승연, 오정연 / 심재선
디자인 김연실, 양은선 **인디자인 편집** 박미란 / 박수경, 전제연, 허문희 **컷** 박수빈, 곽원영
제작 이주영 **홍보** 정반석 **주소** 서울시 금천구 가마산로 96, 708호 **등록번호** 제1-2423호(1999년 1월 8일)

2025 마더텅
전국연합 학력평가 기출문제집
고2 영어 독해
정답과 해설편

MOTHERTONGUE
마더텅출판사
since1999.4.1.

정답표

01 글의 목적 파악
문제편 p.007 해설편 p.002

01 ①	02 ⑤	03 ⑤	04 ④	05 ③
06 ⑤	07 ③	08 ②	09 ③	10 ⑤
11 ①	12 ②	13 ①	14 ②	15 ②
16 ②	17 ①			

02 심경·분위기 파악
문제편 p.018 해설편 p.012

01 ①	02 ①	03 ②	04 ①	05 ①
06 ①	07 ①	08 ①	09 ①	10 ⑤
11 ⑤	12 ②	13 ②	14 ①	15 ②
16 ②	17 ⑤	18 ①	19 ②	

03 필자의 주장
문제편 p.028 해설편 p.024

01 ②	02 ③	03 ②	04 ②	05 ①
06 ②	07 ⑤	08 ③	09 ⑤	10 ⑤
11 ②	12 ⑤	13 ④	14 ②	15 ⑤
16 ④	17 ⑤	18 ①	19 ②	20 ⑤

04 의미 추론
문제편 p.040 해설편 p.038

01 ④	02 ⑤	03 ⑤	04 ①	05 ③
06 ③	07 ③	08 ⑤	09 ④	10 ①
11 ⑤	12 ④	13 ④	14 ①	15 ①

05 요지 추론
문제편 p.050 해설편 p.051

01 ⑤	02 ⑤	03 ①	04 ③	05 ③
06 ①	07 ⑤	08 ④	09 ②	10 ③
11 ③	12 ⑤	13 ⑤	14 ②	15 ④
16 ①	17 ②	18 ④	19 ⑤	

06 주제 추론
문제편 p.061 해설편 p.065

01 ②	02 ③	03 ②	04 ③	05 ⑤
06 ③	07 ②	08 ⑤	09 ⑤	10 ②
11 ④	12 ④	13 ⑤	14 ⑤	15 ⑤
16 ⑤	17 ④	18 ①	19 ⑤	20 ②
21 ②				

07 제목 추론
문제편 p.074 해설편 p.082

01 ④	02 ⑤	03 ②	04 ③	05 ①
06 ①	07 ③	08 ⑤	09 ③	10 ②
11 ③	12 ②	13 ③	14 ②	15 ③
16 ④	17 ②	18 ①	19 ⑤	20 ③
21 ①	22 ③	23 ⑤	24 ④	25 ④

08 도표의 이해
문제편 p.089 해설편 p.102

01 ④	02 ③	03 ③	04 ④	05 ⑤
06 ⑤	07 ④	08 ④	09 ④	10 ④
11 ③	12 ③	13 ③	14 ③	15 ③
16 ④	17 ⑤	18 ③	19 ④	

09 내용 일치 파악
문제편 p.101 해설편 p.114

01 ③	02 ④	03 ③	04 ④	05 ⑤
06 ⑤	07 ③	08 ④	09 ②	10 ④
11 ③	12 ④	13 ④	14 ④	15 ③
16 ④	17 ⑤	18 ④		

10 안내문
문제편 p.112 해설편 p.126

01 ⑤	02 ④	03 ③	04 ④	05 ⑤
06 ④	07 ⑤	08 ⑤	09 ⑤	10 ④
11 ④	12 ④	13 ③	14 ⑤	15 ④
16 ⑤	17 ③	18 ④	19 ③	20 ③
21 ④	22 ②	23 ④	24 ②	25 ③
26 ④	27 ④	28 ③	29 ④	30 ⑤
31 ③	32 ⑤	33 ④		

11 빈칸 추론(1)-어휘, 짧은 어구
문제편 p.132 해설편 p.137

01 ①	02 ②	03 ①	04 ①	05 ②
06 ③	07 ①	08 ②	09 ①	10 ①
11 ①	12 ③	13 ①	14 ①	15 ④
16 ③	17 ④	18 ①	19 ②	20 ⑤
21 ②	22 ④	23 ①	24 ②	25 ②
26 ②	27 ④	28 ②	29 ①	30 ③
31 ①	32 ③	33 ①		

12 빈칸 추론(2)-긴 어구, 문장
문제편 p.149 해설편 p.164

01 ①	02 ①	03 ③	04 ①	05 ③
06 ④	07 ③	08 ④	09 ③	10 ②
11 ①	12 ⑤	13 ③	14 ②	15 ④
16 ④	17 ②	18 ⑤	19 ④	20 ①
21 ①	22 ②	23 ②	24 ①	25 ④
26 ④	27 ③	28 ①	29 ①	30 ②
31 ①	32 ⑤	33 ①	34 ②	35 ②
36 ③	37 ⑤	38 ②	39 ⑤	40 ①
41 ⑤	42 ②	43 ②	44 ③	45 ④
46 ③	47 ①	48 ②	49 ①	50 ⑤

13 무관한 문장 찾기
문제편 p.176 해설편 p.209

01 ③	02 ④	03 ④	04 ③	05 ④
06 ④	07 ③	08 ④	09 ③	10 ④
11 ④	12 ③	13 ④	14 ④	15 ③
16 ③	17 ③	18 ③	19 ③	

14 문장 배열
문제편 p.185 해설편 p.223

01 ②	02 ⑤	03 ②	04 ②	05 ③
06 ②	07 ③	08 ③	09 ⑤	10 ④
11 ⑤	12 ④	13 ⑤	14 ④	15 ③
16 ⑤	17 ③	18 ⑤	19 ②	20 ⑤
21 ④	22 ⑤	23 ②	24 ⑤	25 ①
26 ②	27 ③	28 ②	29 ②	30 ③
31 ⑤	32 ②	33 ③	34 ⑤	35 ⑤
36 ③	37 ②	38 ③	39 ⑤	40 ②
41 ②	42 ③	43 ⑤	44 ③	

15 주어진 문장 위치 파악
문제편 p.209 해설편 p.260

01 ④	02 ④	03 ④	04 ④	05 ③
06 ②	07 ③	08 ④	09 ④	10 ③
11 ③	12 ④	13 ③	14 ④	15 ④
16 ④	17 ⑤	18 ⑤	19 ⑤	20 ④
21 ①	22 ③	23 ④	24 ③	25 ⑤
26 ⑤	27 ⑤	28 ③	29 ③	30 ⑤
31 ③	32 ①	33 ③	34 ③	35 ②
36 ①	37 ③	38 ④	39 ③	40 ②
41 ④	42 ③	43 ②	44 ④	

16 문단 요약
문제편 p.233 해설편 p.294

01 ②	02 ①	03 ①	04 ①	05 ②
06 ①	07 ②	08 ①	09 ①	10 ①
11 ①	12 ②	13 ①	14 ①	15 ①
16 ④	17 ①	18 ①	19 ⑤	20 ①

17 장문의 이해-단일지문
문제편 p.245 해설편 p.313

01 ②	02 ③	03 ④	04 ⑤	05 ①
06 ⑤	07 ⑤	08 ⑤	09 ①	10 ④
11 ①	12 ⑤	13 ③	14 ④	15 ①
16 ④	17 ③	18 ④	19 ③	20 ②
21 ⑤	22 ⑤	23 ⑤	24 ⑤	25 ②
26 ③	27 ⑤	28 ④	29 ②	30 ④
31 ①	32 ⑤	33 ②	34 ①	35 ①
36 ③	37 ①	38 ⑤	39 ①	40 ⑤
41 ①	42 ④	43 ①	44 ⑤	45 ①
46 ④				

18 장문의 이해-복합지문
문제편 p.270 해설편 p.341

01 ②	02 ⑤	03 ⑤	04 ④	05 ④
06 ⑤	07 ⑤	08 ⑤	09 ④	10 ④
11 ⑤	12 ③	13 ⑤	14 ④	15 ②
16 ②	17 ③	18 ⑤	19 ④	20 ③
21 ③	22 ③	23 ②	24 ②	25 ③
26 ④	27 ③	28 ③	29 ⑤	30 ⑤
31 ⑤	32 ④	33 ⑤	34 ④	35 ②
36 ③	37 ③	38 ⑤	39 ④	40 ②
41 ③	42 ④	43 ③	44 ⑤	45 ⑤
46 ④	47 ④	48 ②	49 ②	50 ③
51 ③	52 ②	53 ③	54 ③	

1회 20분 미니모의고사
문제편 p.288 해설편 p.365

01 ①	02 ⑤	03 ①	04 ③	05 ④
06 ④	07 ⑤	08 ②	09 ⑤	10 ③
11 ④	12 ②			

2회 20분 미니모의고사
문제편 p.294 해설편 p.374

01 ②	02 ②	03 ①	04 ⑤	05 ④
06 ②	07 ③	08 ①	09 ②	10 ⑤
11 ④	12 ②			

3회 20분 미니모의고사
문제편 p.299 해설편 p.382

01 ③	02 ①	03 ②	04 ④	05 ⑤
06 ③	07 ⑤	08 ②	09 ⑤	10 ①
11 ③	12 ③			

2025 마더텅
전국연합 학력평가 기출문제집
고2 영어 독해
정답과 해설편

첨삭해설 이해를 위한 문법 용어

S **주어** (Subject)	'-은/는/이/가'에 해당되는 말로 **동사**의 **주체**가 되는 말	
O **목적어** (Object)	'-을/를'에 해당되는 말로 **동사**의 **대상**(동작이 가해지는)이 되는 말	
C **보어** (Complement)	주어 또는 목적어를 **보충 설명**해주는 요소	
	1) S·C **주격 보어** (Subjective Complement)	**주어**를 보충 설명하는 말
	2) O·C **목적격 보어** (Objective Complement)	**목적어**를 보충 설명하는 말
V **동사** (Verb)	**동작, 상태, 성질**을 나타내는 말 1) be동사 vs. 일반동사 - **be동사**: 상태와 성질을 나타내는 동사 - **일반동사**: be동사를 뺀 나머지 동작을 나타내는 동사 2) 조동사 vs. 본동사 - **조동사**: 본동사를 도와주는 동사 본동사에 시제나 태(수동/능동)의 의미를 더하는 역할을 함. - **본동사**: 문장에 하나뿐인, 조동사의 도움을 받는 주요 동사 3) 자동사 vs. 타동사 - **자동사**: 목적어가 불필요한 동사 - **타동사**: 목적어가 필요한 동사	

문제편 p.007

01 글의 목적 파악

01 2021년 3월 18번 (정답률 95%) 정답 ①

[지문 끊어 읽기] 재활용품 배출 허용 요일

(1) My name is Anthony Thompson / and I am writing /
제 이름은 Anthony Thompson입니다 / 그리고 저는 쓰고 있습니다 /
on behalf of the residents' association.
입주민 조합을 대표하여

(2) Our recycling program has been working well /
우리의 재활용 프로그램은 잘 운영되고 있습니다 /
thanks to your participation.
여러분의 참여 덕분에

(3) However, / a problem has recently occurred /
선행사
그런데 / 문제가 최근에 생겼습니다 /
that needs your attention.
주격 관계대명사
여러분의 관심이 필요한

(4) Because there is no given day for recycling, /
재활용을 위해 정해진 날이 없어서 /
residents are putting their recycling out / at any time.
입주민들은 자신들의 재활용품을 내놓습니다 / 아무 때나

(5) This makes the recycling area messy, /
이것이 재활용 구역을 어지럽힙니다 /
which requires extra labor and cost.
관계대명사 계속적 용법
그리고 그것은 추가 노동과 비용을 필요로 합니다

힌트 이 문장에서 which는 앞의 comma(,)와 함께 쓰여 관계대명사의 계속적 용법임을 알 수 있음. 이것은 관계대명사 앞의 문장 전체를 부연 설명하는 역할을 하며, 이때 관계대명사로 that을 쓸 수 없음.

(6) To deal with this problem, /
부사적 용법(~하기 위해서)
이 문제를 처리하기 위해서 /
the residents' association has decided / on a day to recycle.
입주민 조합은 결정했습니다 / 재활용하는 날을

(7) I would like to let you know / that you can put out your recycling /
저는 여러분께 알려드리고 싶습니다 / 여러분은 여러분의 재활용품을 내놓을 수 있다는 것을 /
on Wednesdays only. 정답 단서
수요일에만

(8) I am sure / it will make our apartment complex /
사역V O
저는 확신합니다 / 그것이 우리 아파트 단지를 만들 것이라고 /
look much more pleasant.
O.C(동사원형)
훨씬 더 쾌적해 보이게

(9) Thank you in advance / for your cooperation.
미리 감사드립니다 / 여러분의 협조에

[전문 해석]

(1)제 이름은 Anthony Thompson이고 저는 입주민 조합을 대표하여 (글을) 쓰고 있습니다. (2)우리의 재활용 프로그램은 여러분의 참여 덕분에 잘 운영되고 있습니다. (3)그런데 최근에 여러분의 관심이 필요한 문제가 생겼습니다. (4)재활용을 위해 정해진 날이 없어서 입주민들은 아무 때나 자신들의 재활용품을 내놓습니다. (5)이것이 재활용 구역을 어지럽히고, 그것은 추가 노동과 비용을 필요로 합니다. (6)이 문제를 처리하기 위해서 입주민 조합은 재활용하는 날을 결정했습니다. (7)저는 여러분께 여러분은 수요일에만 여러분의 재활용품을 내놓을 수 있다는 것을 알려드리고 싶습니다. (8)저는 그것이 우리 아파트 단지를 훨씬 더 쾌적해 보이게 만들 것이라고 확신합니다. (9)여러분의 협조에 미리 감사드립니다.

[정답 확인]

다음 글의 목적으로 가장 적절한 것은?

✔ 재활용품(recycling) 배출 허용 요일을 알리려고 문장(7)
② 쓰레기 분리배출(put out your recycling)의 필요성을 설명하려고
③ 쓰레기 분리배출 후 주변 정리(arrangement)를 부탁하려고
④ 입주민(resident) 대표 선출 결과를 공지하려고
⑤ 쓰레기장 재정비 비용(cost)을 청구하려고

[중요 어휘]

□ on behalf of	~을 대표하여
□ resident	명사 입주민
□ association	명사 조합, 협회
□ recycle	동사 재활용하다, 재사용하다
□ participation	명사 참여
□ given	형용사 정해진 / 전치사 ~을 고려해 볼 때
□ put out	(쓰레기 등을 집 밖으로) 내놓다
□ require	동사 필요로 하다
□ extra	형용사 추가의
□ decide on	~을 결정하다
□ apartment complex	아파트 단지
□ cooperation	명사 협조

02 2021년 6월 18번 (정답률 95%) 정답 ⑤

[지문 끊어 읽기] 새로운 동물 보호소를 위한 기부

(1) Dear animal lovers,
동물 애호가들께

(2) I am writing / on behalf of the Protect Animal Organization.
저는 쓰고 있습니다 / Protect Animal Organization을 대표해서

(3) Our organization was founded / on the belief /
저희 단체는 설립되었습니다 / 믿음으로 /
that all animals should be respected and treated with kindness, /
모든 동물들이 존중받고 친절함으로 대우받아야 한다는 /
and must be protected by law.
그리고 법에 의해 보호되어야 한다는

힌트 'that'은 선행사 'the belief'의 동격의 접속사로 어떠한 믿음인지 설명함.

(4) Over the past 20 years, / we have provided / lost animals /
provide A with B: A에게 B를 제공하다
지난 20년간 / 저희는 제공해 왔습니다 / 길 잃은 동물들에게 /
with protection, new homes, and sometimes health care.
보호, 새로운 집, 그리고 때로는 건강 관리를

(5) Currently, / our animal shelter is full, /
현재 / 저희의 동물 보호소는 가득 찼습니다 /
and we need your help / to build a new shelter. 정답 단서
그리고 저희는 당신의 도움이 필요합니다 / 새로운 보호소를 짓기 위해

(6) We are seeking donations / in any amount. 정답 단서
저희는 기부금을 구하고 있습니다 / 어떤 액수든

(7) Every dollar raised / goes to building homes / for animals in need.
S V
모금된 모든 돈은 / 집을 짓는 데 쓰입니다 / 도움이 필요한 동물들을 위한

(8) You can donate to us online / at www.protectanimal.org.
당신은 온라인으로 저희에게 기부할 수 있습니다 / www.protectanimal.org에서

(9) Thank you for considering / supporting us.
고려해 주셔서 감사합니다 / 저희를 지원해 줄 것을

힌트 consider는 동명사를 목적어로 취하는 동사이기 때문에 support에 ing가 붙었고, consider 역시 전치사 for의 목적어이므로 ing가 붙음.

(10) Sincerely, Stella Anderson
진심을 담아, Stella Anderson (드림)

[전문 해석]

(1)동물 애호가들께,
(2)저는 Protect Animal Organization을 대표해서 (글을) 쓰고 있습니다. (3)저희 단체는 모든 동물들이 존중받고 친절함으로 대우받아야 하며, 법에 의해 보호되어야 한다는 믿음으로 설립되었습니다. (4)지난 20년간, 저희는 길 잃은 동물들에게 보호, 새로운 집, 그리고 때로는 건강 관리를 제공해 왔습니다. (5)현재, 저희의 동물 보호소는 가득 찼고, (그래서) 저희는 새로운 보호소를 짓기 위해 당신의 도움이 필요합니다. (6)저희는 어떤 액수든 기부금을 구하고 있습니다. (7)모금된 모든 돈은 도움이 필요한 동물들을 위한 집을 짓는 데 쓰입니다. (8)당신은 www.protectanimal.org에서 온라인으로 저희에게 기부할 수 있습니다. (9)저희를 지원해 줄 것을 고려해 주셔서 감사합니다.
(10)진심을 담아, Stella Anderson (드림)

[정답 확인]

다음 글의 목적으로 가장 적절한 것은?

① 사무실(office)을 빌려준 것에 대해 감사하려고
② 동물 병원 설립(foundation)의 필요성을 주장하려고
③ 새롭게 시행되는 동물 보호법(animal protection law)에 대해 설명하려고
④ 동물 보호 단체의 봉사 활동(voluntary work) 프로그램을 안내하려고
✔ 새로운 동물 보호소를 짓기 위한 기부(donation)를 요청하려고 문장(5), (6)

[중요 어휘]

☐ **on behalf of**	~을 대표하여, ~을 대신하여
☐ **found**	동사 설립하다
☐ **treat**	동사 대우하다, 대하다
☐ **lost**	형용사 길 잃은
☐ **care**	명사 관리, 돌봄, 보살핌
☐ **shelter**	명사 보호소, 주거지
☐ **seek**	동사 구하다, 찾다
☐ **donation**	명사 기부(금)
☐ **raise**	동사 (자금을) 모금하다, 모으다
☐ **in need**	도움이 필요한, 어려움에 처한

03 2022년 6월 18번 (정답률 95%)

정답 ⑤

[지문 끊어 읽기] 자원봉사자 모집

(1) Dear Ms. Stevens,
Stevens 씨께

(2) My name is Peter Watson, /
제 이름은 Peter Watson입니다 /
and I'm the manager of the Springton Library.
그리고 저는 Springton 도서관의 관리자입니다

(3) Our storytelling program has been so well-attended /
우리의 스토리텔링 프로그램에 매우 많은 분들이 참석해주셨습니다 /
that we are planning to expand the program / to 6 days each week.
so ~ that ⋯ : 너무 ~해서 ⋯하다
그래서 우리는 프로그램을 확대하는 것을 계획 중입니다 / 주 6일로

(4) This means / [that we need to recruit more volunteers /
명사절 접속사
이것은 의미합니다 / 우리가 자원봉사자를 더 많이 모집해야 할 필요가 있음을 /
to read to the children]. 정답단서 자원봉사자가 더 많이 필요하다는 목적을 드러내고 있음.
형용사적 용법 [ ]: means의 목적어절
아이들에게 책을 읽어 줄

(5) People still talk / about the week / you filled in for us /
선행사 관계부사절(when 생략)
사람들은 아직도 이야기합니다 / 일주일에 대해 / 당신이 우리를 대신한 /
when one of our volunteers couldn't come.
자원봉사자 중 한 명이 올 수 없었을 때

(6) You really brought those stories to life!
당신은 정말 그 이야기들에 생명을 불어넣었죠

(7) So, / would you be willing to read / to the preschoolers /
그런 이유로 / 당신은 책을 읽어 줄 의향이 있으십니까 / 미취학 아동들에게 /
for an hour, / from 10 to 11 a.m. / every Friday? 정답단서
한 시간 동안 / 오전 10시부터 11시까지 / 매주 금요일
아동들에게 책을 읽어 주는 봉사 활동을 할 의향이 있는지 묻고 있음.

(8) I hope / [you will take this opportunity /
저는 바랍니다 / 당신이 이 기회를 받아들이길 /
부사적 용법(결과)
to let more children hear your voice]. [ ]: hope의 목적어절
사역V O O.C
그래서 더 많은 아이들이 당신의 목소리를 듣게 되길

(9) We are looking forward to your positive reply.
우리는 당신의 긍정적인 답변을 기다리고 있습니다

(10) Best regards, Peter Watson
Peter Watson 드림

[전문 해석]

(1)Stevens 씨께,
(2)제 이름은 Peter Watson이고, 저는 Springton 도서관의 관리자입니다. (3)우리의 스토리텔링 프로그램에 매우 많은 분들이 참석해주셔서 우리는 프로그램을 주 6일로 확대하는 것을 계획 중입니다. (4)이것은 우리가 아이들에게 책을 읽어 줄 자원봉사자를 더 많이 모집해야 할 필요가 있음을 의미합니다. (5)사람들은 자원봉사자 중 한 명이 올 수 없었을 때 당신이 우리를 대신한 일주일에 대해 아직도 이야기합니다. (6)당신은 정말 그 이야기들에 생명을 불어넣었죠! (7)그런 이유로, 매주 금요일 오전 10시부터 11시까지 한 시간 동안 미취학 아동들에게 책을 읽어 줄 의향이 있으십니까? (8)당신이 이 기회를 받아들여서 더 많은 아이들이 당신의 목소리를 듣게 되길 바랍니다. (9)우리는 당신의 긍정적인 답변을 기다리고 있습니다.
(10)Peter Watson 드림

[정답 확인]

다음 글의 목적으로 가장 적절한 것은?

① 도서관의 운영 시간 연장(extension)을 제안하려고
② 봉사 활동 시간이 변경된(be changed) 것을 안내하려고
③ 독서 토론 수업에 참여할 아동을 모집하려고(recruit)
④ 봉사 활동에 참여하지 못하게 된 것을 사과하려고(apologize)
✔ 책 읽어 주기 자원봉사에 참여해 줄 것을 요청하려고(request) 문장(4), (7)

[중요 어휘]

☐ **well-attended**	형용사 많은 사람들이 참석한
☐ **expand**	동사 확대하다
☐ **recruit**	동사 모집하다
☐ **bring A to life**	A에게 생명을 불어넣다
☐ **fill in for**	~을 대신하다, 대신해서 일해 주다
☐ **preschooler**	명사 미취학 아동
☐ **look forward to N/V-ing**	~을 기다리다[고대하다]

04 2022년 9월 18번 (정답률 95%)

정답 ④

[지문 끊어 읽기] 큰 글자판의 잡지

(1) Dear Customer Service,
고객 서비스팀께

(2) I am writing / in regard to my magazine subscription.
저는 글을 씁니다 / 저의 잡지 구독과 관련하여

(3) Currently, / I have just over a year to go /
현재 / 저는 일 년 조금 넘게 남아 있습니다 /
on my subscription to *Economy Tomorrow* /
저의 *Economy Tomorrow* 구독이 /
and would like to continue my subscription /
그리고 구독을 계속하고 싶습니다 /
as I have enjoyed the magazine for many years.
~때문에(접속사)
저는 수년간 잡지를 즐겨왔기 때문에

(4) Unfortunately, / due to my bad eyesight, /
안타깝게도 / 저의 좋지 않은 시력 때문에 /
I have trouble reading your magazine.
저는 귀사의 잡지를 읽는 데 어려움이 있습니다

(5) My doctor has told me /
4형식V I.O
저의 의사는 저에게 말했습니다 /
[that I need to look for large print magazines and books].
[ ]: D.O(목적어절)
제가 큰 글자의 잡지와 책을 찾아봐야 할 필요가 있다고

(6) I'd like to know /
저는 알고 싶습니다 /
whether there's a large print version of your magazine. 주제문
귀사 잡지의 큰 글자판이 있는지를
잡지의 큰 글자판이 있는지를 알고 싶어함.

(7) Please contact me / if this is something you offer.
저에게 연락 부탁드립니다 / 만약 이것이 귀사가 제공하는 것이라면

(8) Thank you for your time.
시간 내주셔서 감사합니다

(9) I look forward to hearing / from you soon.
저는 들을 수 있기를 기대합니다 / 곧 귀사로부터

(10) Sincerely, Martin Gray
Martin Gray 드림

[전문 해석]

(1)고객 서비스팀께,
(2)저는 잡지 구독과 관련하여 글을 씁니다. (3)현재 저의 *Economy Tomorrow* 구독이 일 년 조금 넘게 남아 있는데, 저는 수년간 귀사의 잡지를 즐겨왔기 때문에 구독을 계속하고 싶습니다. (4)안타깝게도, 저의 좋지 않은 시력 때문에 귀사의 잡지를 읽는 데 어려움이 있습니다. (5)저의 의사는 제가 큰 글자의 잡지와 책을 찾아봐야 할 필요가 있다고 말했습니다. (6)저는 귀사 잡지의 큰 글자판이 있는지 알고 싶습니다. (7)만약 이것이 귀사가 제공하는 것이라면 저에게 연락 부탁드립니다. (8)시간 내주셔서 감사합니다. (9)곧 귀사로부터의 (소식을) 들을 수 있기를 기대합니다.
(10)Martin Gray 드림

[정답 확인]

다음 글의 목적으로 가장 적절한 것은?
① 잡지(magazine) 기삿거리를 제보하려고
② 구독(subscription) 기간 변경을 신청하려고
③ 구독료 인상에 대해 항의하려고(complain)
✔④ 잡지의 큰 글자판이 있는지 문의하려고(inquire) 문장(6)
⑤ 잡지 기사 내용에 대한 정정을 요구하려고(request)

[중요 어휘]

☐ **in/with regard to**	~와 관련하여
☐ **subscription**	명사 구독, 구독료
☐ **have trouble V-ing**	~하는 데 어려움이 있다

05 2022년 11월 18번 (정답률 95%) 정답 ③

[지문 끊어 읽기] 학교 행사를 위한 상품권 기부 요청

(1) Dear local business owners,
지역 상점 주인분들께

(2) My name is Carol Williams, /
제 이름은 Carol Williams입니다 /
president of the student council at Yellowstone High School.
Yellowstone 고등학교의 학생회장인

힌트 여기서 사용된 현재진행형은 가까운 미래를 나타내기 위해 사용되었음. 현재 시제나 현재진행 시제는 가까운 미래에 예정된 일을 표현할 때 사용될 수 있음.

(3) We are hosting our annual quiz night /
우리는 연례 퀴즈의 밤을 개최할 것입니다 /
on March 30 / and plan to give prizes / to the winning team.
명사적 용법
3월 30일에 / 그리고 상품을 제공할 계획입니다 / 우승팀에게

(4) However, / this event won't be possible /
그러나 / 이 행사는 불가능할 것입니다 /
without the support of local businesses /
선행사
지역 상점의 후원 없이는 /
[who provide valuable products and services]. [ ]: 주격 관계대명사절
유용한 상품들과 서비스를 제공해 주는

힌트 business가 셀 수 있는 명사일 때는 '상점, 사업체, 회사'라는 뜻임. 여기서는 선행사로, 관계대명사 who가 이끄는 관계절의 수식을 받고 있음.

(5) Would you be willing to donate a gift certificate /
선행사
흔쾌히 상품권을 기부해 주실 수 있으십니까 /
that we can use as a prize? 정답 단서 지역 상점 주인들에게 상품권 기부를 요청하고 있음.
목적격 관계대명사절
우리가 상품으로 사용할

(6) We would be grateful / for any amount on the certificate.
우리는 감사히 여길 것입니다 / 어떤 액수의 상품권이든

(7) In exchange for your generosity, /
귀하의 관대함에 대한 대가로 /
we would place an advertisement for your business /
우리는 귀하의 사업 광고를 싣겠습니다 /
on our answer sheets.
우리의 답안지에

(8) Thank you for taking time / to read this letter /
병렬①
시간을 할애해 주셔서 감사합니다 / 이 편지를 읽는 데 /
and consider our request.
병렬②(to 생략)
그리고 우리의 요청을 고려하는 데

(9) If you'd like to donate or need more information, /
만약 귀하께서 기부하기를 원하시거나 더 많은 정보를 필요로 하신다면 /
please call or email me.
저에게 전화나 이메일을 주십시오

(10) I look forward to hearing from you soon.
look forward to V-ing: ~하기를 기대하다
곧 귀하로부터 소식을 듣기를 기대하겠습니다

(11) Carol Williams
Carol Williams 드림

[전문 해석]

(1)지역 상점 주인분들께,
(2)제 이름은 Carol Williams이고, Yellowstone 고등학교의 학생회장입니다. (3)우리는 3월 30일에 연례 퀴즈의 밤을 개최할 것이고, 우승팀에게 상품을 제공할 계획입니다. (4)그러나 이 행사는 유용한 상품들과 서비스를 제공해 주는 지역 상점의 후원 없이는 불가능할 것입니다. (5)우리가 상품으로 사용할 상품권을 흔쾌히 기부해 주실 수 있으십니까? (6)우리는 어떤 액수의 상품권이든 감사히 여길 것입니다. (7)귀하의 관대함에 대한 대가로 우리의 답안지에 귀하의 사업 광고를 싣겠습니다. (8)이 편지를 읽고 우리의 요청을 고려하는 데 시간을 할애해 주셔서 감사합니다. (9)만약 귀하께서 기부하기를 원하시거나 더 많은 정보를 필요로 하신다면, 저에게 전화나 이메일을 주십시오. (10)곧 귀하로부터 소식을 듣기를 기대하겠습니다.
(11)Carol Williams 드림

[정답 확인]

다음 글의 목적으로 가장 적절한 것은?
① 행사 홍보물 게시가 가능한지를 문의하려고
② 학교 퀴즈 행사에 사용할 물품 제작을 의뢰하려고
✔③ 우승 상품으로 사용할 상품권(gift certificate)을 기부해 줄 것을 요청하려고 문장(5)
④ 학교 행사로 예상되는 소음 발생에 대해 양해를 구하려고(excuse)
⑤ 퀴즈 행사 개최를 위한 장소 사용 허가를 받으려고(get permission)

[중요 어휘]

☐ **student council**	학생회
☐ **valuable**	형용사 유용한, 귀중한, 값비싼
☐ **be willing to V**	흔쾌히 ~하다, 기꺼이 ~하다
☐ **donate**	동사 기부하다
☐ **gift certificate**	명사 상품권
☐ **generosity**	명사 관대함, 너그러움

06 2023년 9월 18번 (정답률 95%) 정답 ⑤

[지문 끊어 읽기] 버스 정류장 무정차 통과 시정 요구

(1) To whom it may concern,
관계자분께

(2) I would like to draw your attention to a problem /
저는 당신께서 한 문제에 주목해 주셨으면 합니다 / 선행사
that frequently occurs with the No. 35 buses.
35번 버스에서 자주 발생하는 주격 관계대명사절

(3) There is a bus stop / about halfway along Fenny Road, /
버스 정류장이 있습니다 / Fenny Road를 따라 중간쯤에 /
at which the No. 35 buses are supposed to stop.
그리고 그곳에서 35번 버스가 정차하기로 되어 있습니다

힌트 at which(전치사+관계대명사)는 관계부사 where로 바꿔 쓸 수 있으며, 콤마 뒤에 이어져 계속적 용법으로 사용됨. at which가 이끄는 관계사절은 앞에 나온 'a bus stop'을 보충 설명함.

(4) It would appear, / however, /
형식상의 주어
~인 것처럼 보입니다 / 하지만 /

[that some of your drivers are either unaware of this bus stop /
S V'①
당신의 운전기사들 중 일부가 이 버스 정류장을 인식하지 못한다 /
or for some reason choose to ignore it, /
V'②
혹은 어떤 이유에서인지 그것을 무시하기로 선택한다 /
driving past / even though the buses are not full]. [ ]: 내용상의 주어
분사구문(=and they drive ~)
지나쳐가면서 / 버스가 꽉 차지 않았음에도

힌트 'either A or B'는 'A 혹은 B'를 나타내며, either가 부사이므로 동사 are과 보어 unaware 사이에 위치함.

(5) I would be grateful / if you could remind your drivers /
저는 감사하겠습니다 / 당신이 당신의 운전기사들에게 상기시켜 주신다면 /
that this bus stop exists /
병렬①
이 버스 정류장이 존재한다는 것을 /
and that they should be prepared to stop at it. 정답 단서 버스 기사들이 정류장에 정차하게끔 상기시켜 달라고 요구함.
병렬②
그리고 그들이 그곳에 정차할 준비가 되어 있어야 한다는 것을

(6) I look forward to seeing an improvement in this service soon.
저는 곧 이 서비스의 개선을 보기를 기대합니다

(7) Yours faithfully, John Williams
진심을 담아, John Williams 드림

[전문 해석]

(1)관계자분께,
(2)저는 당신께서 35번 버스에서 자주 발생하는 한 문제에 주목해 주셨으면 합니다. (3)Fenny Road를 따라 중간쯤에 버스 정류장이 있고, 그곳에서 35번 버스가 정차하기로 되어 있습니다. (4)하지만 당신의 운전기사들 중 일부가 이 버스 정류장을 인식하지 못하거나 어떤 이유에서인지 그것을 무시하기로 선택한 것처럼 보이며, 버스가 꽉 차지 않았음에도 지나쳐갑니다. (5)저는 당신이 당신의 운전기사들에게 이 버스 정류장이 존재한다는 것과 그들이 그곳에 정차할 준비가 되어 있어야 한다는 것을 상기시켜 주신다면 감사하겠습니다. (6)저는 곧 이 서비스의 개선을 보기를 기대합니다.
(7)진심을 담아, John Williams 드림

[정답 확인]

다음 글의 목적으로 가장 적절한 것은?
① 버스 운전기사(bus driver) 채용 계획을 문의하려고
② 버스 정류장(bus stop)의 위치 변경을 요청하려고
③ 도로 공사(road construction)로 인한 소음에 대해 항의하려고
④ 출퇴근 시간의 버스 배차 간격 단축을 제안하려고(suggest)
✔ 버스 정류장 무정차 통과에 대한 시정을 요구하려고(request) 문장(5)

[중요 어휘]

□ **frequently**	부사 자주, 빈번히
□ **be supposed to V**	~하기로 되어있다
□ **be unaware of**	~을 인식하지 못하다
□ **ignore**	동사 무시하다
□ **remind**	동사 상기시키다, 생각나게 하다
□ **improvement**	명사 개선, 향상

07 2019년 9월 18번 (정답률 90%) 정답 ③

[지문 끊어 읽기] 공원에서의 촬영 허가

(1) To whom it may concern,
관계자님께

(2) We are students from St. Andrew's College /
저희는 St. Andrew's 대학의 학생들입니다 /
who are currently taking a Media Studies class /
미디어 연구 강좌를 현재 수강하고 있는 /
that requires us to film a short video.
저희에게 단편 영상을 촬영할 것을 요구하는

(3) We would like to film at Sunbury Park /
저희는 Sunbury 공원에서 촬영하고 싶습니다 /
on November 14th, 2019, / from 9 a.m. to 3 p.m.
2019년 11월 14일에 / 오전 9시부터 오후 3시까지

(4) After looking for several days / to find good locations, /
며칠 동안 둘러본 후 / 좋은 장소를 찾기 위해 /
we decided on filming at Sunbury /
저희는 Sunbury에서 촬영하기로 결정했습니다 /
because it is not overly populated / during this time of day.
그곳이 지나치게 붐비지 않기 때문에 / 하루 중 이 시간 동안

(5) Our team will not cause any issues /
저희 팀은 어떠한 문제도 일으키지 않을 것입니다 /
to public services or other park visitors.
공공 서비스나 다른 공원 방문객들에게

(6) We would therefore like to request permission /
그러므로 저희는 허가를 요청하고 싶습니다 /
to film at Sunbury Park / at the time above. 주제문
Sunbury 공원에서 촬영하기 위한 / 위 시간에

(7) If you need to contact our Media Studies teacher, Damien Matthews, /
미디어 연구 선생님이신 Damien Matthews에게 연락할 필요가 있으시다면 /
for further information, /
추가적인 정보를 위해 /
he can be reached at damien@st_andrews.ac.uk.
그는 damien@st_andrews.ac.uk로 연락받으실 수 있습니다

(8) Yours faithfully, Taylor Johnson & Chloe Moore
Taylor Johnson과 Chloe Moore (드림)

[전문 해석]

(1)관계자님께,
(2)저희는 저희에게 단편 영상을 촬영할 것을 요구하는 미디어 연구 강좌를 현재 수강하고 있는 St. Andrew's 대학의 학생들입니다. (3)저희는 2019년 11월 14일에, 오전 9시부터 오후 3시까지 Sunbury 공원에서 촬영하고 싶습니다. (4)좋은 장소를 찾기 위해 며칠 동안 둘러본 후, 저희는 하루 중 이 시간 동안 그곳이 지나치게 붐비지 않기 때문에 Sunbury에서 촬영하기로 결정했습니다. (5)저희 팀은 공공 서비스나 다른 공원 방문객들에게 어떠한 문제도 일으키지 않을 것입니다. (6)그러므로 저희는 위 시간에 Sunbury 공원에서 촬영하기 위한 허가를 요청하고 싶습니다. (7)추가적인 정보를 위해, 미디어 연구 (강좌의) 선생님이신 Damien Matthews에게 연락할 필요가 있으시다면, 그는 damien@st_andrews.ac.uk로 연락받으실 수 있습니다.
(8)Taylor Johnson과 Chloe Moore (드림)

[정답 확인]

다음 글의 목적으로 가장 적절한 것은?
① 영화제 참가(participation) 방법을 문의하려고
② 공원 주변 차량 통제(control)를 건의하려고
✔ 공원에서의 촬영 허가(permission)를 요청하려고 문장(6)
④ 영상 편집 강좌 이수 여부를 확인하려고
⑤ 촬영으로 인한 불편 사항에 대해 항의하려고(complain)

[중요 어휘]

□ **require A to V**	A에게 ~할 것을 요구하다
□ **decide on V-ing**	~하기로 결정하다
□ **populated**	형용사 붐비는, 사람이 많은
□ **request**	동사 요청하다, 요구하다
□ **permission**	명사 허가, 허락

08 2023년 3월 18번 (정답률 90%) 정답 ②

[지문 끊어 읽기] 미술 작품 구매

(1) It was a pleasure / meeting you at your gallery last week.
형식상의 주어 내용상의 주어(동명사구)
즐거운 일이었습니다 / 지난 주에 귀하의 미술관에서 귀하를 만난 것은

(2) I appreciate your effort / to select and exhibit diverse artwork.
형용사적 용법
저는 귀하의 노력에 감사드립니다 / 다양한 미술 작품을 선정하고 전시하고자 한

(3) As I mentioned, / I greatly admire Robert D. Parker's paintings, /
선행사
제가 언급했듯이 / 저는 Robert D. Parker의 그림을 대단히 존경합니다 /
which emphasize the beauty of nature.
주격 관계대명사(계속적 용법)
그런데 그것은 자연의 아름다움을 강조합니다

(4) Over the past few days, / I have been researching and learning /
지난 며칠에 걸쳐 / 저는 조사하고 공부해 오고 있습니다 /
about Robert D. Parker's online viewing room /
Robert D. Parker의 온라인 감상 공간에 관해 /
through your gallery's website.
귀하의 미술관 웹사이트를 통해

(5) I'm especially interested / in purchasing the painting /
저는 특히 관심이 있습니다 / 그림을 구매하는 것에 / 선행사
that depicts the horizon, / titled *Sunrise*.
주격 관계대명사
지평선을 묘사하는 / '일출'이라는 제목의

힌트 밑줄 친 부분은 앞에 나온 명사 the painting을 수식하는 과거분사구로, titled 앞에 '주격 관계대명사+be동사'가 생략된 것으로도 볼 수 있음.

(6) I would like to know / [if the piece is still available for purchase].
would like to V: ~하고 싶다 [ ]: if 명사절(~인지 아닌지)
저는 알고 싶습니다 / 그 작품이 여전히 구매가 유효한지를

정답 단서 Robert D. Parker의 '일출(*Sunrise*)'이라는 작품을 구매할 수 있는지 묻고 있음.

(7) It would be a great pleasure /
형식상의 주어
대단히 기쁜 일일 것입니다 /
to house this wonderful piece of art.
내용상의 주어(to부정사구)
이 멋진 미술 작품을 소장하는 것은

(8) I look forward to your reply to this inquiry.
저는 이 문의에 대한 귀하의 답변을 고대하고 있겠습니다

[전문 해석]

(1)지난 주에 귀하의 미술관에서 귀하를 만난 것은 즐거운 일이었습니다. (2)저는 다양한 미술 작품을 선정하고 전시하고자 한 귀하의 노력에 감사드립니다. (3)제가 언급했듯이, 저는 Robert D. Parker의 그림을 대단히 존경하는데, 그것은 자연의 아름다움을 강조합니다. (4)지난 며칠에 걸쳐, 저는 귀하의 미술관 웹사이트를 통해 Robert D. Parker의 온라인 감상 공간에 관해 조사하고 공부해 오고 있습니다. (5)저는 '일출'이라는 제목의, 지평선을 묘사하는 그림을 구매하는 것에 특히 관심이 있습니다. (6)저는 그 작품이 여전히 구매가 유효한지를 알고 싶습니다. (7)이 멋진 미술 작품을 소장하는 것은 대단히 기쁜 일일 것입니다. (8)저는 이 문의에 대한 귀하의 답변을 고대하고 있겠습니다.

[정답 확인]

다음 글의 목적으로 가장 적절한 것은?

① 좋아하는 화가와의 만남(meeting)을 요청하려고
② 미술 작품(piece of art)의 구매(purchase) 가능 여부를 문의하려고 문장(6)
③ 소장 중인 미술 작품의 감정(appraisal)을 의뢰하려고
④ 미술 작품의 소유자(owner) 변경 내역을 확인하려고
⑤ 기획 중인 전시회(exhibition)에 참여하는 화가를 홍보하려고

[중요 어휘]

□ **pleasure**	명사 즐거운 일, 즐거움
□ **appreciate**	동사 감사하다, 인정하다
□ **exhibit**	동사 전시하다
□ **diverse**	형용사 다양한
□ **mention**	동사 언급하다, 말하다
□ **admire**	동사 존경하다, 찬양하다
□ **emphasize**	동사 강조하다
□ **viewing**	명사 감상, (바라)보기, TV 시청
□ **be interested in**	~에 관심이 있다
□ **purchase**	동사 구매하다 / 명사 구매
□ **depict**	동사 묘사하다, 그리다
□ **horizon**	명사 지평선, 수평선
□ **A be titled B**	A는 B라고 제목이 붙여지다
□ **sunrise**	명사 일출, 해돋이
□ **piece**	명사 (예술) 작품
□ **available**	형용사 유효한, 이용 가능한
□ **house**	동사 소장하다, 보관하다, 집에 들이다
□ **inquiry**	명사 문의, 질문

09 2022년 3월 18번 (정답률 85%) 정답 ③

[지문 끊어 읽기] 축구 경기로 인한 기차표 변경 요청

(1) As I explained on the telephone, / I don't want /
전화로 설명드렸듯이 / 저는 하고 싶지 않습니다 /
to take my two children by myself on a train trip /
명사적 용법
혼자 두 아이를 데리고 기차 여행을 /
to visit my parents in Springfield this Saturday /
부사적 용법(목적)
이번 주 토요일에 Springfield에 사시는 저희 부모님을 뵈러 /
since it is the same day the Riverside Warriors will play the
=this Saturday
힌트 the same day 뒤에 관계부사 when이 생략되어 있음. 'the Riverside Warriors ~ Soccer Championship'은 the same day를 수식하는 관계부사절임.
Greenville Trojans /
그날이 Riverside Warriors가 Greenville Trojans와 시합할 날과 같은 날이어서 /
in the National Soccer Championship.
전국 축구 선수권 대회에서

(2) I would really appreciate it, / therefore, /
저는 정말 감사하겠습니다 / 그래서 /
if you could change my tickets / to the following weekend (April 23).
제 기차표를 바꿔 주시면 / 다음 주말(4월 23일)로

정답 단서 기차표를 다음 주말로 바꿔줄 것을 요청함.

(3) I fully appreciate /
저는 잘 압니다 /
that the original, special-offer ticket was non-exchangeable, /
명사절 접속사
특가로 제공되는 원래 기차표는 교환할 수 없다는 것을 /
but I did not know about the soccer match /
하지만 저는 축구 경기에 관해 알지 못했습니다 /
when I booked the tickets / and I would be really grateful /
기차표를 예매할 당시에는 / 그래서 저는 정말 감사하겠습니다 /
if you could do this for me.
저를 위해 이렇게 해 주시면

(4) Thank you in advance.
미리 감사드립니다

[전문 해석]

(1)전화로 설명드렸듯이, 이번 주 토요일이 전국 축구 선수권 대회에서 Riverside Warriors가 Greenville Trojans와 시합할 날과 같은 날이어서 그날 Springfield에 사시는 저희 부모님을 뵈러 혼자 두 아이를 데리고 기차 여행을 하고 싶지 않습니다. (2)그래서 제 기차표를 다음 주말(4월 23일)로 바꿔 주시면 정말 감사하겠습니다. (3)특가로 제공되는 원래 기차표는 교환할 수 없다는 것을 잘 알지만, 기차표를 예매할 당시에는 축구 경기에 관해 알지 못했으니 저를 위해 이렇게 해 주시면 정말 감사하겠습니다. (4)미리 감사드립니다.

[정답 확인]

다음 글의 목적으로 가장 적절한 것은?

① 특가로 제공되는 기차표를 구매하려고(purchase)
② 축구 경기 입장권의 환불(refund)을 요구하려고(require)
③ 다른 날짜로 기차표 변경을 요청하려고(request) 문장(2)
④ 기차표 예약(booking)이 가능한 날짜를 알아보려고
⑤ 축구 경기 날짜가 연기되었는지를(be postponed) 확인하려고

[중요 어휘]

□ **by oneself**	혼자
□ **following**	형용사 다음의
□ **special-offer**	특가로 제공되는
□ **non-exchangeable**	교환할 수 없는
□ **match**	명사 경기
□ **book**	동사 예약하다
□ **grateful**	형용사 감사하는
□ **in advance**	미리, 사전에

10 2018년 9월 18번 (정답률 85%) 정답 ⑤

[지문 끊어 읽기] 학교 주변 도로의 과속방지턱 설치

(1) Dear Mr. Terry Walter,
친애하는 Terry Walter 씨께

(2) I am the principal of Springfield Public School.
저는 Springfield 공립학교의 교장입니다

(3) As you know, / Springfield Public School is located /
아시는 바와 같이 / Springfield 공립학교는 위치하고 있습니다 /
at the intersection of First Street and Pine Street.
First Street과 Pine Street의 교차로에

(4) The safety of our children is at risk /
우리 아이들의 안전이 위험합니다 /
largely due to the disregard for speed limits /
주로 제한속도 무시로 인해 /
by motorists traveling along Pine Street. 정답단서
Pine Street을 따라 달리는 자동차 운전자들의

(5) I have regularly witnessed vehicles /
저는 차량들을 자주 목격해왔습니다 /
traveling far in excess of the speed limit on Pine Street.
Pine Street에서 제한속도를 훨씬 초과하여 달리는

(6) Additionally, / parents have expressed concern for the safety /
덧붙여 / 학부모님들은 안전에 대해 우려를 나타내고 계십니다 /
of their children who must cross Pine Street.
Pine Street을 건너야만 하는 자녀들의

(7) For these reasons, / we are requesting /
이러한 까닭으로 / 우리는 요청합니다 /
the installation of speed bumps on Pine Street. 주제문
Pine Street에 과속방지턱 설치를

힌트 문장 (7)의 'we are requesting ~'은 편지를 쓴 이의 부탁이 나타나는 표현이므로 여기에 글의 목적이 드러남.

(8) I know / that one of your missions, / as well as ours, /
저는 알고 있습니다 / 당신의 임무들 중 하나가 / 우리의 임무와 마찬가지로 /
is to ensure that our young people are afforded /
우리의 어린아이들이 제공받도록 보장하는 것이라고 /
a safe and secure environment to and from school each day.
매일 안전하고 위험 없는 등하교 환경을

(9) I anticipate / that your approval of this request /
저는 기대합니다 / 이러한 요청에 대한 당신의 승인이 /
will greatly improve the safety of our children.
우리 아이들의 안전을 크게 향상시킬 것이라고

(10) Sincerely, Emma Hudson
진심을 담아, Emma Hudson (드림)

[전문 해석]

(1)친애하는 Terry Walter 씨께,
(2)저는 Springfield 공립학교의 교장입니다. (3)아시는 바와 같이, Springfield 공립학교는 First Street과 Pine Street의 교차로에 위치하고 있습니다. (4)주로 Pine Street을 따라 달리는 자동차 운전자들의 제한속도 무시로 인해 우리 아이들의 안전이 위험합니다. (5)저는 Pine Street에서 제한속도를 훨씬 초과하여 달리는 차량들을 자주 목격해왔습니다. (6)덧붙여, 학부모님들은 Pine Street을 건너야만 하는 자녀들의 안전에 대해 우려를 나타내고 계십니다. (7)이러한 까닭으로, 우리는 Pine Street에 과속방지턱 설치를 요청합니다. (8)저는 당신의 임무들 중 하나가 우리의 임무와 마찬가지로, 우리의 어린아이들이 매일 안전하고 위험 없는 등하교 환경을 제공받도록 보장하는 것이라고 알고 있습니다. (9)저는 이러한 요청에 대한 당신의 승인이 우리 아이들의 안전을 크게 향상시킬 것이라고 기대합니다.
(10)진심을 담아, Emma Hudson (드림)

[정답 확인]

다음 글의 목적으로 가장 적절한 것은?

① 과속 차량(vehicles) 특별 단속 실시를 촉구하려고
② 교차로(intersection) 교통신호 체계 개선을 건의하려고
③ 학생 대상 교통안전(safety)교육 강의를 부탁하려고
④ 제한속도(speed limit) 규정 표지판 교체 시기를 안내하려고
✔ 학교 주변 도로에 과속방지턱(speed bumps) 설치를 요청하려고 문장(7)

[중요 어휘]

□ intersection	명사 교차로, 교차점, 사거리
□ be at risk	위험하다
□ largely	부사 주로, 대개
□ disregard	명사 무시, 경시 / 동사 무시하다, 경시하다
□ regularly	부사 자주, 종종
□ witness	동사 목격하다, 보다 / 명사 목격자
□ concern	명사 우려, 걱정 / 동사 걱정하다, 염려하다
□ request	동사 요청하다, 간청하다 / 명사 요청, 요구, 간청
□ installation	명사 설치, 설비
□ speed bump	명사 과속방지턱
□ secure	형용사 위험 없는, 안심하는 / 동사 안전하게 하다
□ anticipate	동사 기대하다, 고대하다

11 2021년 9월 18번 (정답률 85%) 정답 ①

[지문 끊어 읽기] 수리로 인한 강당 폐쇄

(1) Dear parents and students of Douglas School,
Douglas School의 학부모님 및 학생들께

(2) As you know, / our school was built over 150 years ago.
여러분도 아시다시피 / 우리 학교는 150여 년 전에 지어졌습니다.

(3) While we are proud of our school's history, /
우리는 우리 학교의 역사가 자랑스럽긴 하지만 /
the facilities are not exactly /
시설이 꼭 ~은 아닙니다 /
what they should be for modern schooling.
현대의 학교 교육에 맞는 것

힌트 not exactly는 부분부정으로 '꼭 ~은 아니다'로 해석됨.

(4) Thanks to a generous donation to the school foundation, /
학교 재단으로의 후한 기부 덕분에 /
we will be able to start renovating /
우리는 보수하는 것을 시작할 수 있을 것입니다 /
those parts of our campus / that have become outdated.
우리 캠퍼스의 그러한 부분들을 / 구식이 된

힌트 provide A with B : A에게 B를 제공하다

(5) We hope / this will help provide our students /
우리는 바랍니다 / 이것이 우리 학생들에게 제공하는 데에 도움을 주기를 /
with the best education possible.
가능한 한 최고의 교육을

(6) I'm writing to inform you /
4형식V I·O
저는 여러분에게 알리기 위해 쓰고 있습니다 /
that the auditorium will be the first building / closed for repairs. 정답단서
D·O
강당이 첫 번째 건물이 될 것이라는 점을 / 수리를 위해 폐쇄되는

(7) Students will not be able to use the auditorium /
학생들은 강당을 사용할 수 없을 것입니다 /
for about one month / while the repairs are taking place.
한 달 정도 / 수리가 진행되는 동안

(8) We hope that you will understand /
여러분이 이해해 주기를 바랍니다 /
how this brief inconvenience will encourage /
이 짧은 불편함이 어떻게 장려할 것인지 /
community-wide benefits / for years to come.
지역 사회 전체의 혜택을 / 향후 몇 년 동안

(9) Sincerely, Vice Principal Kyla Andrews
진심을 담아, 교감 Kyla Andrews (드림)

[전문 해석]

(1)Douglas School의 학부모님 및 학생들께,
(2)여러분도 아시다시피 우리 학교는 150여 년 전에 지어졌습니다. (3)우리는 우리 학교의 역사가 자랑스럽긴 하지만, 시설이 현대의 학교 교육에 꼭 맞는 것은 아닙니다. (4)학교 재단으

로의 후한 기부 덕분에, 우리는 구식이 된 우리 캠퍼스의 (그러한) 부분들을 보수하는 것을 시작할 수 있을 것입니다. (5)우리는 이것(보수)이 우리 학생들에게 가능한 한 최고의 교육을 제공하는 데에 도움을 주기를 바랍니다. (6)저는 여러분에게 강당이 수리를 위해 폐쇄되는 첫 번째 건물이 될 것이라는 점을 알리기 위해 (이 편지를) 쓰고 있습니다. (7)학생들은 수리가 진행되는 동안 한 달 정도 강당을 사용할 수 없을 것입니다. (8)이 짧은 불편함이 향후 몇 년 동안 지역 사회 전체의 혜택을 어떻게 장려할 것인지 여러분이 이해해 주기를 바랍니다. (9)진심을 담아, 교감 Kyla Andrews (드림)

[정답 확인]

다음 글의 목적으로 가장 적절한 것은?

✔ 수리(repairs)로 인한 강당 폐쇄를 안내하려고 문장(6)
② 캠퍼스(campus) 투어 프로그램 일정을 조정하려고
③ 강당(auditorium) 사용을 위한 신청 방법을 공지하려고
④ 강당 신축을 위한 기금 모금(fundraising) 행사를 홍보하려고
⑤ 집짓기 행사에 참여할 자원 봉사자(volunteer)를 모집하려고

[중요 어휘]

☐ **schooling**	명사 학교 교육
☐ **generous**	형용사 후한, 넉넉한
☐ **foundation**	명사 재단, 토대
☐ **renovate**	동사 보수하다, 수리하다
☐ **outdated**	형용사 구식인
☐ **inform**	동사 알리다
☐ **community-wide**	지역 사회 전체의

12 2021년 11월 18번 (정답률 85%) 정답 ②

[지문 끊어 읽기] 버스 중단 계획에 대한 반대

(1) To whom it may concern,
관계자분께

(2) I am a parent of a high school student /
저는 고등학생의 부모입니다 / 선행사
who takes the 145 bus / to commute to Clarkson High School.
주격 관계대명사절 부사적 용법(목적)
145번 버스를 타는 / Clarkson 고등학교로 통학하기 위해

(3) This is the only public transport / available from our area /
V① =The 145 bus 주격 관계대명사+be동사 생략
이것은 유일한 대중교통입니다 / 우리 지역에서 이용할 수 있는 /
and is used by many students.
V②
그리고 많은 학생들에 의해 이용됩니다

(4) Recently, / I heard /
최근 / 저는 들었습니다 /
that the city council is planning / to discontinue this service. 정답단서 시 의회가 145번 버스 서비스 중단을 계획하고 있음.
명사절 접속사 명사적 용법
시 의회가 계획하고 있다고 / 이 서비스를 중단하는 것을

(5) My husband and I start work early in the morning /
제 남편과 저는 아침 일찍 일을 시작합니다 /
and this makes it impossible /
5형식V 형식상의 목적어 O·C
그리고 이 점이 불가능하게 합니다 /
for us to drop our son off at school.
의미상 주어 내용상의 목적어
저희가 아들을 학교에 데려다주는 것을

(6) It would take him nearly an hour to walk to school /
=our son
그가 학교에 걸어가는 데는 거의 한 시간이 걸릴 것입니다 /
and there is a lot of traffic in the morning, /
그리고 아침에는 교통량이 많습니다 /
so I do not consider it / safe to bike.
형식상의 목적어 O·C 내용상의 목적어
그래서 저는 생각하지 않습니다 / 자전거를 타는 것이 안전하다고

힌트 'consider+목적어+목적격 보어'는 '~을 …로/…라고 생각하다, 여기다'라는 뜻을 지닌 구문임. 여기서 'to bike'는 내용상의 목적어, 'it'은 형식상의 목적어이고 형용사 'safe'는 목적격 보어임.

(7) This matter will place many families, /
이런 문제점은 많은 가족들을 처하게 할 것입니다 /
including ours, / under a lot of stress.
소유대명사(=our family)
저희를 포함한 / 엄청난 곤경에

(8) As a resident of Sunnyville, /
Sunnyville의 거주자로서 /
I think / such a plan is unacceptable. 정답단서 시 의회의 145번 버스 중단 계획을 받아들이기 어려움.
저는 생각합니다 / 그러한 계획을 받아들이기 어렵다고

(9) I urge / the council to listen to the concerns of the community.
5형식V O O·C
저는 촉구하는 바입니다 / 의회가 지역 사회의 우려를 경청할 것을

(10) Sincerely, Lucy Jackson
Lucy Jackson 드림

[전문 해석]

(1)관계자분께,
(2)저는 Clarkson 고등학교로 통학하기 위해 145번 버스를 타는 고등학생의 부모입니다. (3)이것은 우리 지역에서 이용할 수 있는 유일한 대중교통이며 많은 학생들에 의해 이용됩니다. (4)최근 저는 시 의회가 이 서비스를 중단하는 것을 계획하고 있다고 들었습니다. (5)제 남편과 저는 아침 일찍 일을 시작하며, 이 점이 저희가 아들을 학교에 데려다주는 것을 불가능하게 합니다. (6)제 아들이 학교에 걸어가는 데는 거의 한 시간이 걸릴 것이며 아침에는 교통량이 많아서 저는 자전거를 타는 것이 안전하다고 생각하지 않습니다. (7)이런 문제점은 저희를 포함한 많은 가족들을 엄청난 곤경에 처하게 할 것입니다. (8)Sunnyville의 거주자로서 저는 그러한 계획을 받아들이기 어렵다고 생각합니다. (9)저는 의회가 지역 사회의 우려를 경청할 것을 촉구하는 바입니다.
(10)Lucy Jackson 드림

[정답 확인]

다음 글의 목적으로 가장 적절한 것은?

① 버스 노선 변경에 항의하려고(object to)
✔ 버스 운행 중단(discontinuation) 계획에 반대하려고(oppose) 문장(4), (8)
③ 버스 배차 간격 조정을 요청하려고(request)
④ 자전거 전용 도로 설치(installation)를 건의하려고(suggest)
⑤ 통학로 안전 관리 강화를 촉구하려고(urge)

[중요 어휘]

☐ **concern**	동사 관련되다, 우려하게 만들다 / 명사 우려, 염려, 관심사
☐ **commute**	동사 통학하다, 통근하다
☐ **public transport (=public transportation)**	명사 대중교통
☐ **council**	명사 의회
☐ **discontinue**	동사 중단하다, 그만하다
☐ **drop A off**	A를 데려다주다
☐ **traffic**	명사 교통(량), 운항, 수송
☐ **bike**	동사 자전거를 타다
☐ **place**	동사 (특정한 상황에) 처하게 하다, 놓다
☐ **unacceptable**	형용사 받아들이기 어려운
☐ **urge**	동사 촉구하다, 강력히 권고하다

13 2023년 6월 18번 (정답률 80%) 정답 ①

[지문 끊어 읽기] 자녀의 결석 사유 등록

(1) Dear parents,
친애하는 학부모님께

(2) Regular attendance at school is essential /
학교에 규칙적인 출석은 필수적입니다 /
in maximizing student potential.
전치사 V-ing
학생의 잠재력을 극대화하는 데 있어

(3) Recently, / we've become concerned /
현재완료(have p.p.)
최근에 / 저희는 걱정하게 되었습니다 /

about the number of unapproved absences / across all grades.
~의 수
승인되지 않은 결석 수에 대해 / 전 학년에 걸친

(4) I would like to further clarify /
would like to V: ~하고 싶다
저는 더욱 분명히 하고 싶습니다 /
[that your role as a parent is to approve any school absence].
[ ]: that 명사절 명사적 용법(~하는 것)
학부모로서의 귀하의 역할이 어떠한 학교 결석이든 승인하는 것임을

(5) Parents must provide an explanation for absences /
학부모들은 결석에 대한 설명을 제공하셔야 합니다 /
to the school / within 7 days /
학교에 / 7일 이내에 /
from the first day of any period of absence. 정답 단서 자녀가 학교에 결석한 첫날로부터 7일 이내에 학부모들은 결석 사유를 제공해야 함.
어떠한 결석 기간이든 그 첫날로부터

(6) Where an explanation has not been received /
상황 부사절 접속사: ~한 경우에
설명이 주어지지 않은 경우에 /
within the 7-day time frame, / the school will record the absence /
7일의 기간 이내에 / 학교는 그 결석을 기록할 것입니다 /
as unjustified / on the student's record. 정답 단서 7일 이내에 결석 사유를 받지 못하면 학생의 결석은 학생부에 정당하지 않은 결석으로 기록됨.
정당하지 않은 것으로 / 학생부에

(7) Please ensure / [that you go to the parent portal site /
병렬①
확실히 해 주십시오 / 귀하가 학부모 포털 사이트에 가는 것을 /
and register the reason /
병렬②
그래서 사유를 등록하는 것을 /
any time your child is absent]. 주제문 자녀가 결석할 경우 학부모 포털 사이트에 들어가 결석 사유를 반드시 등록해 달라고 당부하고 있음.
귀하의 자녀가 결석하는 어느 때든 [ ]: that 명사절

힌트 밑줄 친 부분은 '(at) any time (when) your child is absent'의 의미로, 「any time+주어+동사」는 '~가 …하는 어느 때든, ~가 …하는 때마다'라고 해석됨.

(8) Please approve all absences, /
모든 결석을 승인해 주십시오 /
so that your child will not be at a disadvantage.
so that: ~하도록
귀하의 자녀가 불이익에 처하지 않도록

(9) Many thanks for your cooperation.
귀하의 협조에 대단히 감사드립니다

(10) Sincerely, Natalie Brown, Vice Principal
진심을 담아, 교감 Natalie Brown

[전문 해석]

(1)친애하는 학부모님께,
(2)학생의 잠재력을 극대화하는 데 있어 학교에 규칙적인 출석은 필수적입니다. (3)최근에, 저희는 전 학년에 걸친 승인되지 않은 결석 수에 대해 걱정하게 되었습니다. (4)저는 학부모로서의 귀하의 역할이 어떠한 학교 결석이든 승인하는 것임을 더욱 분명히 하고 싶습니다. (5)학부모들은 어떠한 결석 기간이든 그 첫날로부터 7일 이내에 학교에 결석에 대한 설명을 제공하셔야 합니다. (6)7일의 기간 이내에 설명이 주어지지 않은 경우에, 학교는 학생부에 그 결석을 정당하지 않은 것으로 기록할 것입니다. (7)귀하의 자녀가 결석하는 어느 때든 귀하가 학부모 포털 사이트에 가서 사유를 등록하는 것을 확실히 해 주십시오. (8)귀하의 자녀가 불이익에 처하지 않도록, 모든 결석을 승인해 주십시오. (9)귀하의 협조에 대단히 감사드립니다.
(10)진심을 담아, 교감 Natalie Brown

[정답 확인]

다음 글의 목적으로 가장 적절한 것은?
✔ 자녀의 결석(absence) 사유를 등록해 줄 것을 요청하려고 문장(7)
② 학교 홈페이지(school website)의 일시적 운영 중단을 공지하려고
③ 자녀가 지각하지 않도록 부모의 지도(guidance)를 당부하려고
④ 방과 후(after-school) 프로그램에 대한 부모의 관심(attention)을 독려하려고
⑤ 인정 결석은 최대 7일까지 허용된다(be allowed)는 것을 안내하려고

[중요 어휘]

□ regular	형용사 규칙적인, 정기적인
□ attendance	명사 출석, 참석
□ essential	형용사 필수적인, 아주 중요한
□ maximize	동사 극대화하다
□ potential	명사 잠재력, 가능성
□ concerned	형용사 걱정하는, 우려하는
□ the number of A	A의 수
□ unapproved	형용사 승인되지 않은, 허가되지 않은
□ absence	명사 결석, 결근
□ clarify	동사 분명히 하다, 확실히 하다
□ approve	동사 승인하다, 허가하다
□ time frame	명사 기간
□ unjustified	형용사 정당하지 않은
□ register	동사 등록하다, 기재하다
□ absent	형용사 결석한, 결근한
□ at a disadvantage	불이익에 처하여, 불리한 처지에

14 2023년 11월 18번 (정답률 100%) 정답 ②

[지문 끊어 읽기] 농구 코트 소음 문제

(1) To whom it may concern,
관계자분께

(2) I am writing to inform you of an ongoing noise issue /
선행사
저는 귀하께 계속 진행 중인 소음 문제에 대해 알려 드리기 위해 글을 쓰고 있습니다 /
that I am experiencing.
목적격 관계대명사절
제가 겪고 있는

힌트 inform A of B: A에게 B에 대해 알리다

(3) My apartment faces the basketball courts of the community center.
저의 아파트는 문화 센터의 농구 코트를 마주보고 있습니다

(4) While I fully support the community center's services, /
저는 문화 센터의 서비스를 전적으로 지지하지만 /
I am constantly being disrupted by individuals /
저는 사람들에 의해 지속적으로 방해받고 있습니다 /
playing basketball late at night.
밤늦게 농구를 하는

힌트 be being p.p.: 현재 진행 수동태

(5) Many nights, / I struggle to fall asleep / because I can hear /
지각V
많은 밤마다 / 저는 잠들기 위해 애씁니다 / 저는 들을 수 있기 때문입니다 /
people bouncing balls and shouting on the basketball courts /
O O·C① O·C②
사람들이 농구 코트에서 공을 튀기고 소리 지르는 것을 /
well after 11 p.m..
오후 11시 훨씬 이후에도

힌트 restrict A to B: A를 B로 제한하다

(6) Could you restrict the time / the basketball court is open /
귀하께서는 시간을 제한해 주실 수 있으신가요 / 농구 코트가 열리는 /
to before 9 p.m.? 정답 단서 농구 코트 운영 시간을 오후 9시 이전으로 제한해 줄 것을 요청함.
오후 9시 이전으로

(7) I'm sure / I'm not the only person in the neighborhood /
선행사
저는 확신합니다 / 제가 근처에서 유일한 사람이 아님을 /
that is affected by this noise issue.
주격 관계대명사절
이 소음 문제에 의해 영향을 받는

힌트 선행사에 the only가 있으므로 주격 관계대명사로 that이 사용되었음. 'I'm not the only person that ~'은 '내가 ~인 유일한 사람이 아니다'라는 뜻으로, '나만 그런 것이 아니라 다른 사람들도 그렇다'라는 의미를 강조한 표현임.

(8) I appreciate your assistance.
귀하의 도움에 감사드립니다

(9) Sincerely, Ian Baldwin
진심을 담아, Ian Baldwin

[전문 해석]

(1)관계자분께,
(2)저는 귀하께 제가 겪고 있는 계속 진행 중인 소음 문제에 대해 알려 드리기 위해 글을 쓰고 있습니다. (3)저의 아파트는 문화 센터의 농구 코트를 마주보고 있습니다. (4)저는 문화 센터의 서비스를 전적으로 지지하지만, 밤늦게 농구를 하는 사람들에 의해 지속적으로 방해받고 있습니다. (5)많은 밤마다, 오후 11시 훨씬 이후에도 사람들이 농구 코트에서 공을 튀기고 소

리 지르는 것을 들을 수 있기 때문에 저는 잠들기 위해 애씁니다. (6)귀하께서는 농구 코트가 열리는 시간을 오후 9시 이전으로 제한해 주실 수 있으신가요? (7)저는 제가 근처에서 이 소음 문제에 의해 영향을 받는 유일한 사람이 아님을 확신합니다. (8)귀하의 도움에 감사드립니다.
(9)진심을 담아, Ian Baldwin

[정답 확인]

다음 글의 목적으로 가장 적절한 것은?

① 체육관(gym)의 바닥 교체 공사를 요구하려고
✔ 농구 코트의 운영 시간 제한(restriction)을 요청하려고 문장(6)
③ 문화 센터(community center) 시설의 대관 날짜를 변경하려고
④ 건강 증진(health promotion) 프로그램 신청 방법을 문의하려고
⑤ 지역 내 체육 시설(sports facilities)의 증설 가능 여부를 확인하려고

[중요 어휘]

☐ **ongoing**	형용사 (계속) 진행 중인, 발달 중인 / 명사 전진
☐ **face**	동사 ~을 마주보다, 향하다, 직면하다
☐ **disrupt**	동사 방해하다, 피해를 주다
☐ **struggle**	동사 애쓰다, 분투하다
☐ **well**	부사 훨씬, 아주, 상당히
☐ **neighborhood**	명사 근처, 인근, 이웃

15 2024년 3월 18번 (정답률 90%)

정답 ②

[지문 끊어 읽기] 공예품 박람회 부스 예약

(1) Dear Art Crafts People of Greenville,
친애하는 Greenville의 공예가들에게

(2) For the annual Crafts Fair / on May 25 from 1 p.m. to 6 p.m., /
연례 공예품 박람회를 위해서 / 5월 25일 오후 1시부터 6시까지 열리는 /
the Greenville Community Center is providing booth spaces to rent / 형용사적 용법
Greenville 문화 센터에서는 대여할 수 있는 부스 공간을 제공합니다 /
as in previous years. 정답 단서 공예품 박람회를 위한 부스 대여를 안내하고 있음.
지난 몇 년간처럼

(3) To reserve your space, /
부사적 용법(목적)
여러분의 공간을 예약하려면 /
please visit our website and complete a registration form /
저희 웹사이트를 방문하여 신청서를 작성하시기 바랍니다 /
by April 20. 정답 단서 부스 예약 방법을 안내함.
4월 20일까지

(4) The rental fee is $50.
대여 요금은 50달러입니다

(5) All the money we receive from rental fees /
S, 선행사 목적격 관계대명사절
저희가 대여 요금으로 받는 모든 돈은 /
goes to support upcoming activities throughout the year.
V
연중 예정된 활동을 지원하는 데 사용됩니다

힌트 all available spaces가 '예약되는' 것이므로 to부정사가 수동형인 to be booked로 사용됨.

(6) We expect all available spaces to be fully booked soon, /
expect A to V: A가 ~할 것으로 예상하다
저희는 모든 이용할 수 있는 공간이 곧 전부 예약될 것으로 예상합니다 /
so don't get left out.
그러니 놓치지 마세요

(7) We hope to see you at the fair.
저희는 박람회에서 여러분을 뵙기를 바랍니다

[전문 해석]

(1)친애하는 Greenville의 공예가들에게,
(2)5월 25일 오후 1시부터 6시까지 열리는 연례 공예품 박람회를 위해서, Greenville 문화 센터에서는 지난 몇 년간처럼 대여할 수 있는 부스 공간을 제공합니다. (3)여러분의 공간을 예약하려면 저희 웹사이트를 방문하여 4월 20일까지 신청서를 작성하시기 바랍니다. (4)대여 요금은 50달러입니다. (5)저희가 대여 요금으로 받는 모든 돈은 연중 예정된 활동을 지원하는 데 사용됩니다. (6)저희는 모든 이용할 수 있는 공간이 곧 전부 예약될 것으로 예상하니 놓치지 마세요. (7)저희는 박람회에서 여러분을 뵙기를 바랍니다.

[정답 확인]

다음 글의 목적으로 가장 적절한 것은?

① 지역 예술가(local artist)를 위한 정기 후원을 요청하려고
✔ 공예품 박람회(crafts fair)의 부스 예약을 안내하려고 문장(2), (3)
③ 대여 물품의 반환(return) 방법을 설명하려고
④ 지역 예술가가 만든 물품을 홍보하려고(promote)
⑤ 지역 행사 일정의 변경 사항을 공지하려고(notify)

[중요 어휘]

☐ **craft**	명사 공예, 기술
☐ **annual**	형용사 연례의, 매년의
☐ **fair**	명사 박람회 / 형용사 공평한, 공정한
☐ **reserve**	동사 예약하다, 보유하다
☐ **registration form**	신청서
☐ **rental**	명사 대여, 임대 / 형용사 대여의, 임대의
☐ **throughout the year**	연중, 일년 내내

16 2024년 6월 18번 (정답률 95%)

정답 ②

[지문 끊어 읽기] 정원가꾸기의 날

(1) Dear Residents,
주민 여러분께

(2) My name is Kari Patterson, /
제 이름은 Kari Patterson입니다 /
and I'm the manager of the River View Apartments.
그리고 저는 River View 아파트의 관리인입니다

(3) It's time to take advantage of the sunny weather /
형용사적 용법
화창한 날씨를 이용할 때입니다 /
to make our community more beautiful.
부사적 용법, 5형식V O O·C
우리의 공동체를 더 아름답게 만들기 위해

(4) On Saturday, July 13 at 9 a.m., /
7월 13일 토요일 오전 9시에 /
residents will meet in the north parking lot.
주민들은 북쪽 주차장에서 만날 것입니다

(5) We will divide into teams / to plant flowers and small trees, /
병렬①(부사적 용법)
우리는 팀으로 나뉠 것입니다 / 꽃과 작은 나무들을 심기 위해 /
pull weeds, / and put colorful decorations on the lawn.
병렬②(to 생략) 병렬③(to 생략)
잡초를 뽑고 / 그리고 잔디에 다채로운 장식을 하기 위해 정답 단서 주민들끼리 팀을 나누어 식물을 심고 잡초를 뽑고 잔디를 장식할 것임.

(6) Please join us for this year's Gardening Day, / 정답 단서 올해의 정원가꾸기 날에 참여하기를 요청함.
V①
올해의 정원가꾸기 날에 저희와 함께해 주세요 /
and remember no special skills or tools are required.
V②
그리고 특별한 기술이나 도구는 필요하지 않다는 것을 기억하세요

(7) Last year, / we had a great time working together, /
작년에 / 우리는 함께 일하며 좋은 시간을 보냈습니다 /
so come out and make this year's event even better!
5형식V O 비교급 강조 O·C
그러니 오셔서 올해의 행사를 더 멋지게 만들어 주세요

(8) Warm regards, Kari Patterson
따뜻한 마음을 담아, Kari Patterson

[전문 해석]

(1)주민 여러분께,
(2)제 이름은 Kari Patterson이고 저는 River View 아파트의 관리인입니다. (3)우리의 공동체를 더 아름답게 만들기 위해 화창한 날씨를 이용할 때입니다. (4)7월 13일 토요일 오전 9시에 주민들은 북쪽 주차장에서 만날 것입니다. (5)우리는 꽃과 작은 나무들을 심고, 잡초를 뽑고, 잔디에 다채로운 장식을 하기 위해 팀으로 나뉠 것입니다. (6)올해의 정원가꾸기 날에 저희와

함께해 주시고, 특별한 기술이나 도구는 필요하지 않다는 것을 기억하세요. (7)작년에 우리는 함께 일하며 좋은 시간을 보냈으니 오셔서 올해의 행사를 더 멋지게 만들어 주세요!
(8)따뜻한 마음을 담아, Kari Patterson

[정답 확인]

다음 글의 목적으로 가장 적절한 것은?

① 아파트 내 정원 조성에 대한 의견(opinion)을 수렴하려고
✔ 정원가꾸기 날(Gardening Day) 행사에 참여할(join) 것을 독려하려고 문장(6)
③ 쓰레기(trash)를 지정된 장소에 버릴 것을 당부하려고
④ 지하 주차장 공사(construction) 일정에 대해 공지하려고
⑤ 정원박람회(garden fair) 개최 날짜 변경을 안내하려고

[중요 어휘]

□ **resident**	명사 주민, 투숙객 / 형용사 거주하는
□ **take advantage of**	~을 이용하다[활용하다]
□ **weed**	명사 잡초 / 동사 잡초를 뽑다
□ **lawn**	명사 잔디, 잔디밭

17 2024년 9월 18번 (정답률 95%) 정답 ①

[지문 끊어 읽기] 증명서 제출 기한 연장 요청

(1) To whom it may concern,
관계자분께

(2) My name is Peter Jackson /
저의 이름은 Peter Jackson입니다 /
and I am thinking of applying for the Advanced Licensed Counselor Program / (선행사)
그리고 저는 Advanced Licensed Counselor Program에 지원하는 것을 생각하고 있습니다 /
[that the university provides]. [ ]: 목적격 관계대명사절
대학교에서 제공하는

(3) I found /
저는 알게 되었습니다 /
[that the certification for 100 hours of counseling experience / (S')
100시간의 상담 경력 증명서가 /
is required / for the application]. [ ]: found의 목적어절
V'(수동태)
필요하다는 것을 / 지원을 위해

(4) However, / I do not think /
하지만 / 저는 생각하지 않습니다 /
[I could possibly complete the required counseling experience /
제가 아마도 필요한 상담 경력을 완료할 수 있을 거라고 /
by the current deadline]. [ ]: think의 목적어절(명사절 접속사 that 생략)
현재 마감 기한까지

(5) So, if possible, / I kindly request an extension of the deadline /
삽입절
그래서 가능하시다면 / 저는 마감 기한의 연장을 정중하게 요청합니다 /
until the end of this summer vacation. 정답단서 여름 방학 말까지 마감 기한의 연장을 요청함.
이번 여름 방학 말까지

(6) I am actively working on obtaining the certification, /
저는 증명서를 얻으려고 열심히 노력하고 있습니다 /
and I am sure / [I will be able to submit it by then]. [ ]: 목적어절 (명사절 접속사 that 생략)
그리고 저는 확신합니다 / 제가 그때까지 그것을 제출할 수 있을 것이라고

(7) I understand the importance of following the application process, /
V①
저는 지원 과정을 따르는 것의 중요성을 이해합니다 /
and would greatly appreciate your consideration of this request.
V②
그리고 이 요청에 대한 귀하의 고려에 대단히 감사하겠습니다

(8) I look forward to your response.
저는 귀하의 회신을 기다리겠습니다

(9) Sincerely, Peter Jackson
진심을 담아, Peter Jackson 드림

[전문 해석]

(1)관계자분께,
(2)저의 이름은 Peter Jackson이고, 저는 대학교에서 제공하는 Advanced Licensed Counselor Program에 지원하는 것을 생각하고 있습니다. (3)저는 지원을 위해 100시간의 상담 경력 증명서가 필요하다는 것을 알게 되었습니다. (4)하지만 저는 현재 마감 기한까지 제가 아마도 필요한 상담 경력을 완료할 수 있을 거라고 생각하지 않습니다. (5)그래서 가능하시다면, 저는 이번 여름 방학 말까지 마감 기한의 연장을 정중하게 요청합니다. (6)저는 증명서를 얻으려고 열심히 노력하고 있고, 제가 그때까지 그것을 제출할 수 있을 것이라고 확신합니다. (7)저는 지원 과정을 따르는 것의 중요성을 이해하며, 이 요청에 대한 귀하의 고려에 대단히 감사하겠습니다. (8)저는 귀하의 회신을 기다리겠습니다.
(9)진심을 담아, Peter Jackson 드림

[정답 확인]

다음 글의 목적으로 가장 적절한 것은?

✔ 상담 경력 증명서(certification)의 제출 기한 연장(extension)을 요청하려고 문장(5)
② 서류 심사 결과 발표의 지연에 대해 항의하려고(complain)
③ 전문 상담(counseling) 강좌의 추가 개설을 제안하려고
④ 대학의 편의 시설 확충(expansion)을 건의하려고
⑤ 대학 진학 상담 예약(appointment)을 취소하려고

[중요 어휘]

□ **apply**	동사 지원하다, 신청하다
□ **certification**	명사 증명서
□ **counseling**	명사 상담, 조언
□ **application**	명사 지원, 적용
□ **deadline**	명사 마감 기한, 마감일
□ **extension**	명사 연장, 확대
□ **actively**	부사 열심히, 적극적으로
□ **obtain**	동사 얻다, 구하다
□ **consideration**	명사 고려, 사려, 숙고

02 심경·분위기 파악

01 2021년 6월 19번 (정답률 95%) 정답 ①

[지문 끊어 읽기] 상어의 출현

(1) Dave sat up / on his surfboard / and looked around.
Dave는 고쳐 앉았다 / 자신의 서핑보드 위에서 / 그리고 둘러보았다

(2) He was the last person / in the water / that afternoon.
그는 마지막 사람이었다 / 물에 있던 / 그날 오후

(3) Suddenly something / out toward the horizon / caught his eye /
S① V①
갑자기 무언가가 / 수평선 위쪽으로 / 그의 눈에 띄었다 /
and his heart froze. 정답 단서
S② V②
그리고 그의 심장은 얼어붙었다

(4) It was every surfer's worst nightmare / — the fin of a shark. 정답 단서
그것은 모든 서퍼들의 최악의 악몽이었다 / 상어의 지느러미

(5) And it was no more than 20 meters away!
=only
그리고 그것은 불과 20미터밖에 떨어져 있지 않았다

(6) He turned his board / toward the beach /
그는 그의 보드를 돌렸다 / 해변을 향해 /
and started kicking his way to the shore.
그리고 해안가 쪽으로 발차기를 시작했다

(7) Shivering, / he gripped his board tighter / and kicked harder.
분사구문(=As he shivered)
떨면서 / 그는 그의 보드를 더 단단히 붙잡았다 / 그리고 더 강하게 발차기를 했다

(8) 'I'm going to be okay,' / he thought to himself.
'나는 괜찮을 거야.' / 그는 마음속으로 생각했다

(9) 'I need to let go of the fear.'
'나는 두려움을 떨쳐버릴 필요가 있어.'

(10) Five minutes of terror / that felt like a lifetime / passed /
S(선행사) 주격 관계대명사절 V
공포의 5분이 / 평생처럼 느껴졌던 / 지나갔다 /
before he was on dry land again.
그가 육지 위에 다시 있기 전에

(11) Dave sat on the beach / and caught his breath.
Dave는 해변에 앉았다 / 그리고 숨을 돌렸다

(12) His mind was at ease. 정답 단서
그의 마음은 편안했다

(13) He was safe.
그는 안전했다

(14) He let out a contented sigh / 정답 단서
그는 만족스러운 한숨을 내쉬었다 /
as the sun started setting / behind the waves.
태양이 저물기 시작할 때 / 파도 뒤로

[전문 해석]

(1)Dave는 자신의 서핑보드 위에서 (자세를) 고쳐 앉았고 (주위를) 둘러보았다. (2)그는 그날 오후 물에 있던 마지막 사람이었다. (3)수평선 위쪽으로 갑자기 무언가가 그의 눈에 띄었고 그의 심장은 얼어붙었다. (4)그것은 모든 서퍼들의 최악의 악몽인 상어의 지느러미였다. (5)그리고 그것은 불과 20미터밖에 떨어져 있지 않았다! (6)그는 그의 보드를 해변을 향해 돌렸고 해안가 쪽으로 발차기를 시작했다. (7)(몸을) 떨면서, 그는 그의 보드를 더 단단히 붙잡았고 더 강하게 발차기를 했다. (8)그는 마음속으로 '나는 괜찮을 거야.'라고 생각했다. (9)'나는 두려움을 떨쳐버릴 필요가 있어.' (10)그가 육지 위에 다시 있기(도착하기) 전에 평생처럼 느껴졌던 공포의 5분이 지나갔다. (11)Dave는 해변에 앉았고 숨을 돌렸다. (12)그의 마음은 편안했다. (13)그는 안전했다. (14)태양이 파도 뒤로 저물기 시작할 때 그는 만족스러운 한숨을 내쉬었다.

[정답 확인]

다음 글에 드러난 Dave의 심경 변화로 가장 적절한 것은?

① scared → relieved 겁먹은 → 안도하는
② indifferent → proud 무관심한 → 자랑스러워하는
③ amazed → horrified 놀란 → 겁에 질린
④ hopeful → worried 희망에 찬 → 걱정하는
⑤ ashamed → grateful 부끄러운 → 고마워하는

[중요 어휘]

☐ sit up	고쳐 앉다
☐ catch someone's eye	~의 눈에 띄다[눈길을 사로잡다]
☐ freeze	동사 얼어붙다, 얼리다
☐ fin	명사 지느러미
☐ shiver	동사 (흥분·공포 등으로) 떨다
☐ grip	동사 꽉 붙잡다
☐ think to oneself	마음속으로 생각하다
☐ let go of	~을 떨쳐버리다[놓다]
☐ lifetime	명사 평생
☐ catch one's breath	숨을 돌리다
☐ at ease	마음이 편안한, 마음이 편안하게
☐ let out	내쉬다, (신음·울음소리 등을) 내다
☐ contented	형용사 만족스러운
☐ sigh	명사 한숨

02 2022년 6월 19번 (정답률 95%) 정답 ①

[지문 끊어 읽기] 거울 속의 나와 마주친 경험

(1) I walked up / to the little dark brown door / and knocked.
나는 걸어갔다 / 작고 짙은 갈색 문으로 / 그리고 문을 두드렸다

(2) Nobody answered.
아무도 대답이 없었다

(3) I pushed on the door carefully.
나는 조심스럽게 그 문을 밀었다

(4) When the door swung open / with a rusty creak, /
그 문이 휙 열렸을 때 / 녹슬어서 삐걱거리는 소리와 함께 /
a man was standing / in a back corner of the room.
한 남자가 서 있었다 / 그 방의 뒤쪽 구석에

(5) My hands flew over my mouth /
두 손을 입에 갖다 댔다 /
as I started to scream. 정답 단서 놀라서 소리를 지르고 두 손을 입에 갖다 댐.
나는 소리 지르기 시작하며

힌트 flew는 동사 fly의 과거형으로 보통 '날다, 날아가다'의 의미로 쓰임. 여기서 '두 손이 내 입에 날아가다'는 두 손을 내 입에 갖다 댄 것을 의미함.

(6) He was just standing there, / watching me!
분사구문
그는 거기 서 있었다 / 나를 지켜보면서

(7) As my heart continued to race, / I saw /
내 심장이 계속 요동칠 때 / 나는 보았다 /
[that he had also put his hands over his mouth]. [ ]: saw의 목적어절
과거완료
그 역시 두 손을 그의 입 위로 올린 것을

(8) Wait a minute...
잠깐

(9) It was a mirror!
그것은 거울이었다

(10) I took a deep breath / and walked past a table /
나는 심호흡을 했다 / 그리고 테이블을 지나 걸어갔다 /
to the old mirror / [that stood in the back of the room].
선행사 [ ]: 주격 관계대명사절
오래된 거울로 / 방 뒤쪽에 세워져 있는

(11) I felt my heartbeat returning to normal, /
V①(지각V) O O.C
나는 심장 박동이 정상으로 돌아오는 것을 느꼈다 /
and calmly looked at my reflection / in the mirror. 정답 단서
V②
그리고 차분하게 내 모습을 바라보았다 / 거울 속

힌트 지각동사(feel)가 5형식 문장의 동사로 쓰였을 때, 목적격 보어로는 현재분사(returning)나 동사원형이 쓰임.

심장 박동이 다시 돌아오고 차분해짐.

[전문 해석]

(1)나는 작고 짙은 갈색 문으로 걸어가서 문을 두드렸다. (2)아무도 대답이 없었다. (3)나는 조심스럽게 그 문을 밀었다. (4)녹슬어서 삐걱거리는 소리와 함께 그 문이 휙 열렸을 때, 한 남자가 그 방의 뒤쪽 구석에 서 있었다. (5)나는 소리 지르기 시작하며 두 손을 입에 갖다 댔다. (6)그는 나를 지켜보면서, 거기 서 있었다! (7)내 심장이 계속 요동칠 때, 나는 그 역시 두 손을 그의 입 위로 올린 것을 보았다. (8)잠깐... (9)그것은 거울이었다! (10)나는 심호흡을 하고 테이블을 지나 방 뒤쪽에 세워져 있는 오래된 거울로 걸어갔다. (11)나는 심장 박동이 정상으로 돌아오는 것을 느꼈고, 차분하게 거울 속 내 모습을 바라보았다.

[정답 확인]

다음 글에 드러난 'I'의 심경 변화로 가장 적절한 것은?

✔ terrified → relieved
무서운 → 안도하는
② hopeful → nervous
희망에 찬 → 불안해하는
③ confident → anxious
자신감 있는 → 불안해하는
④ annoyed → grateful
짜증이 난 → 감사하는
⑤ disappointed → thrilled
실망한 → 아주 흥분한

[중요 어휘]

□ **swing**	동사 흔들리다 (swing-swung-swung)
□ **rusty**	형용사 녹슨
□ **creak**	명사 삐걱거리는 소리
□ **scream**	동사 소리 지르다, 비명을 지르다
□ **race**	동사 (심장이) 요동치다, 경주하다
□ **wait a minute/ second/moment**	잠깐, 가만 있자(방금 무언가를 알아챘거나 기억이 났을 때 하는 말)
□ **reflection**	명사 (거울 등에 비친) 모습, 상
□ **relieved**	형용사 안도하는, 안심한
□ **thrilled**	형용사 (너무 좋아서) 아주 흥분한, 황홀해하는

핵심 문장 (3)에서는 불안한 감정이 드러나 있지만, 문장 (7) 이후에 공포가 사라지고 마음이 평온해진 것을 파악하면 쉽게 정답을 고를 수 있음.

03 2018년 3월 19번 (정답률 90%) 정답 ②

[지문 끊어 읽기] 수술 시간 대기

(1) On December 6th, /
12월 6일에 /
I arrived at University Hospital in Cleveland / at 10:00 a.m.
나는 Cleveland에 있는 대학 병원에 도착했다 / 오전 10시에

(2) I went through the process of admissions.
나는 입원 절차를 끝냈다

(3) I grew anxious / 정답 단서
나는 점점 불안해졌다 /
because the time for surgery was drawing closer.
수술 시간이 가까워지고 있었기 때문에

(4) I was directed to the waiting area, / where I remained /
나는 대기 장소로 안내되었고 / 그곳에서 머물렀다 /
until my name was called.
내 이름이 불릴 때까지

(5) I had a few hours of waiting time.
나는 몇 시간의 대기 시간을 가졌다

(6) I just kept praying.
나는 단지 계속해서 기도할 뿐이었다

(7) At some point in my ongoing prayer process, /
내가 기도를 계속하고 있던 어느 시점에 /
before my name was called, / in the midst of the chaos, /
내 이름이 불리기 전 / 혼돈의 한가운데에서 /
an unbelievable peace embraced me. 정답 단서
믿을 수 없을 정도의 평화가 나를 감싸 안았다

(8) All my fear disappeared! 정답 단서
나의 모든 공포가 사라졌다

(9) An unbelievable peace overrode my emotions.
믿을 수 없을 정도의 평화가 내 감정들을 압도했다

(10) My physical body relaxed in the comfort provided, /
나의 육체는 주어진 평안 속에서 긴장을 풀었다 /
and I looked forward / to getting the surgery over with /
그리고 나는 고대했다 / 수술을 끝마치기를 /
and working hard at recovery.
그리고 회복에 힘쓰기를

[전문 해석]

(1)12월 6일 오전 10시에 나는 Cleveland에 있는 대학 병원에 도착했다. (2)나는 입원 절차를 끝냈다. (3)나는 수술 시간이 가까워지고 있었기 때문에 점점 불안해졌다. (4)나는 대기 장소로 안내되었고, 그곳에서 내 이름이 불릴 때까지 머물렀다. (5)나는 몇 시간의 대기 시간을 가졌다. (6)나는 단지 계속해서 기도할 뿐이었다. (7)내가 기도를 계속하고 있던 어느 시점에, 내 이름이 불리기 전 혼돈의 한가운데에서 믿을 수 없을 정도의 평화가 나를 감싸 안았다. (8)나의 모든 공포가 사라졌다! (9)믿을 수 없을 정도의 평화가 내 감정들(공포)을 압도했다. (10)나의 육체는 주어진 평안 속에서 긴장을 풀었고, 나는 수술을 끝마치고 회복에 힘쓰기를 고대했다(즐거운 마음으로 기다렸다).

[정답 확인]

다음 글에 드러난 'I'의 심경 변화로 가장 적절한 것은?

① cheerful → sad
쾌활한 → 슬픈
✔ worried → relieved
걱정되는 → 안도하는
③ angry → ashamed
화난 → 부끄러운
④ jealous → thankful
질투하는 → 고마워하는
⑤ hopeful → disappointed
희망찬 → 실망한

[중요 어휘]

□ **anxious**	형용사 불안한, 걱정하는
□ **remain**	동사 머무르다, 남아있다
□ **ongoing**	형용사 계속하고 있는
□ **chaos**	명사 혼돈, 혼란
□ **embrace**	동사 감싸 안다, 껴안다
□ **override**	동사 ~을 압도하다, ~의 위를 덮다

04 2020년 11월 19번 (정답률 90%) 정답 ①

[지문 끊어 읽기] 여름 방학의 시작

(1) Ryan, an eleven-year-old boy, / ran home / as fast as he could.
11세 소년 Ryan은 / 집으로 달려갔다 / 가능한 한 빨리

(2) Finally, / summer break had started!
마침내 / 여름 방학이 시작됐다

(3) When he entered the house, / his mom was standing /
그가 집으로 들어갔을 때 / 그의 엄마는 서 있었다 /
in front of the refrigerator, / waiting for him.
냉장고 앞에 / 그를 기다리면서

(4) She told him / to pack his bags.
그녀는 그에게 말했다 / 가방을 싸라고

(5) Ryan's heart soared / like a balloon. 정답 단서
Ryan의 심장은 날아올랐다 / 풍선처럼

(6) *Pack for what?*
'왜 가방을 싸지?'

(7) *Are we going to Disneyland?*
'우리가 디즈니랜드에 가는 걸까?'

(8) He couldn't remember /
그는 기억할 수 없었다 /
the last time his parents had taken him on a vacation.
마지막으로 그의 부모님이 자신을 데리고 휴가를 갔던 때를

(9) His eyes beamed.
그의 눈이 반짝거렸다

(10) "You're spending the summer / with uncle Tim and aunt Gina."
너는 여름을 보내게 될 거야 / Tim 삼촌과 Gina 숙모와 함께

(11) Ryan groaned. 정답 단서
Ryan은 신음 소리를 냈다

(12) "The whole summer?"
"여름 내내요?"

(13) "Yes, the whole summer."
"그래, 여름 내내."

(14) The anticipation / he had felt / disappeared in a flash. 정답 단서
S V
기대는 / 그가 느꼈었던 / 눈 깜짝할 새에 사라졌다

(15) For three whole miserable weeks, /
괴로운 3주 동안 내내 /
he would be on his aunt and uncle's farm.
그는 그의 숙모와 삼촌의 농장에 있게 될 것이다

(16) He sighed.
그는 한숨을 쉬었다

[전문 해석]

(1)11세 소년 Ryan은 가능한 한 빨리 집으로 달려갔다. (2)마침내, 여름 방학이 시작됐다! (3)그가 집으로 들어갔을 때, 그의 엄마는 냉장고 앞에 서서 그를 기다리고 있었다. (4)그녀는 그에게 가방을 싸라고 말했다. (5)Ryan의 심장은 풍선처럼 날아올랐다. (6)'왜 가방을 싸지?' (7)'우리가 디즈니랜드에 가는 걸까?' (8)그는 마지막으로 그의 부모님이 자신을 데리고 휴가를 갔던 때를 기억할 수 없었다. (9)그의 눈이 반짝거렸다. (10)"너는 Tim 삼촌과 Gina 숙모와 함께 여름을 보내게 될 거야." (11)Ryan은 신음 소리를 냈다. (12)"여름 내내요?" (13)"그래, 여름 내내." (14)그가 느꼈었던 기대는 눈 깜짝할 새에 사라졌다. (15)괴로운 3주 동안 내내, 그는 그의 숙모와 삼촌의 농장에 있게 될 것이다. (16)그는 한숨을 쉬었다.

[정답 확인]

다음 글에 드러난 Ryan의 심경 변화로 가장 적절한 것은?

✔ excited → disappointed
신이 난 → 실망한
② furious → regretful
몹시 화가 난 → 후회하는
③ irritated → satisfied
짜증이 난 → 만족한
④ nervous → relaxed
긴장한 → 편안한
⑤ pleased → jealous
기쁜 → 질투하는

[중요 어휘]

□ **refrigerator**	명사 냉장고
□ **pack**	동사 (짐을) 싸다, 포장하다
□ **soar**	동사 날아오르다, 치솟다
□ **beam**	동사 반짝거리다, 빛나다 / 명사 광선
□ **groan**	동사 (불만·고통으로) 신음 소리를 내다, 투덜거리다
□ **anticipation**	명사 기대, 예상
□ **in a flash**	눈 깜짝할 새에, 즉시, 순식간에
□ **miserable**	형용사 괴로운, 불행한, 비참한

05 2021년 11월 19번 (정답률 90%) 정답 ①

[지문 끊어 읽기] 승진 실패로 인한 충격

(1) One Friday afternoon, / Ted was called /
어느 금요일 오후 / Ted는 호출되었다 /
to the vice president of human resources.
인사과의 부사장에게

(2) Ted sat down, / beaming in anticipation. 정답 단서 Ted는 기대감에 차 웃으며 앉음.
분사구문(동시동작)
Ted는 앉았다 / 기대감에 차 밝게 웃으며

(3) Today was the big day /
오늘은 중요한 날이었다 /
and this meeting would mark a turning point / in his career!
그리고 이 만남은 전환점을 찍게 될 것이었다 / 그의 경력에 있어

(4) Ted felt sure / that it was for his promotion /
=this meeting
명사절 접속사①
Ted는 확신했다 / 이것이 자신의 승진을 위한 자리라고 /
and that the vice president would make him /
명사절 접속사② 5형식V O
그리고 부사장이 자신을 만들어줄 것이라고 /
the marketing manager.
O·C
마케팅 매니저로

(5) "Ted, / there is no easy way / to say this."
Ted / 쉽지는 않네요 / 이런 말을 하기가

(6) Ted suddenly realized / [this meeting wasn't going to be /
Ted는 돌연 깨달았다 / 이 만남이 되지는 않을 것임을 /
as he expected]. [ ]: realized의 목적어절(명사절 접속사 that 생략)
접속사
자신이 예상했던 대로

(7) Ted's mind went blank.
2형식V S·C
Ted의 머릿속이 하얘졌다

(8) The vice president continued,
부사장은 계속해서 말을 이어 나갔다

(9) "Ted, / I know / you've desperately wanted this promotion, /
Ted / 저는 알고 있습니다 / 당신이 이번 승진을 간절히 원해왔다는 것을 /
but we decided / Mike is more suitable."
하지만 우리는 결정했습니다 / Mike가 더 적합하다고

(10) Ted just sat there, / frozen.
Ted는 그저 그곳에 앉아 있었다 / 얼어붙은 채

힌트 분사구문 'being frozen'에서 'being'이 생략된 형태이며, 분사구문의 주어는 주절의 주어인 Ted와 동일하여 생략됨.

(11) He felt / as if he had been hit by a truck. 정답 단서 Ted는 트럭에 치인 것 같은 충격을 느낌.
그는 기분이었다 / 마치 트럭에 치인 것 같은

힌트 as if 가정법 과거완료가 쓰인 문장으로, 'as if/though+S+had p.p.'의 형태로 쓸 수 있음. '마치 ~이었던 것과 같은'으로 해석하며 주절의 시제보다 전에 있던 상황을 가정함.

(12) *Don't panic.*
'당황하지 말자.'

(13) All he was able to do / was repeat that sentence /
대명사S 목적격 관계대명사절 V
그가 할 수 있었던 전부라고는 / 그 문장을 되풀이하는 것뿐이었다 /
over and over to himself.
계속해서 자신에게

힌트 to부정사의 명사적 용법에 해당하며 문장에서 주격 보어 역할을 함. 주어 자리에 'all/what/the only thing/the first thing+S+V'가 오고 동사가 be동사인 경우, 주격 보어로 오는 to 부정사의 'to'가 생략될 수 있음.

[전문 해석]

(1)어느 금요일 오후, Ted는 인사과의 부사장에게 호출되었다. (2)Ted는 기대감에 차 밝게 웃으며 앉았다. (3)오늘은 중요한 날이었으며, 이 만남은 그의 경력에 있어 전환점을 찍게 될 것이었다! (4)Ted는 이것이 자신의 승진을 위한 자리이며, 부사장이 자신을 마케팅 매니저로 만들어줄 것이라고 확신했다. (5)"Ted, 이런 말을 하기가 쉽지는 않네요." (6)Ted는 돌연 이 만남이 자신이 예상했던 대로 되지는 않을 것임을 깨달았다. (7)Ted의 머릿속이 하얘졌다. (8)부사장은 계속해서 말을 이어 나갔다. (9)"Ted, 당신이 이번 승진을 간절히 원해 왔다는 것을 알고 있지만, 우리는 Mike가 더 적합하다고 결정했습니다." (10)Ted는 얼어붙은 채 그저 그곳에 앉아 있었다. (11)그는 마치 트럭에 치인 것 같은 기분이었다. (12)'당황하지 말자.' (13)그가 할 수 있었던 전부라고는 그 문장을 계속해서 자신에게 되풀이하는 것뿐이었다.

[정답 확인]

다음 글에 드러난 Ted의 심경 변화로 가장 적절한 것은?

✔ hopeful → shocked
기대하는 → 충격을 받은
② relaxed → lonely
여유 있는 → 외로운
③ ashamed → relieved
부끄러운 → 안심한
④ indifferent → upset
무관심한 → 속상한
⑤ embarrassed → pleased
당황스러운 → 기쁜

[중요 어휘]

□ vice president	명사 부사장, 부통령
□ human resources	명사 (회사의) 인사과, 인적 자원
□ beam	동사 밝게 웃다 / 명사 광선
□ mark	동사 찍다, 표시하다
□ turning point	명사 전환점
□ promotion	명사 승진, 홍보
□ go blank	(머릿속이) 하얘지다, (마음이) 텅 비다
□ desperately	부사 간절히, 필사적으로
□ panic	동사 당황하다, 겁에 질려 어쩔 줄을 모르다 (panic-panicked-panicked)

06 2022년 3월 19번 (정답률 90%)

정답 ①

[지문 끊어 읽기] 쇼 준비하기

(1) Hours later / — when my back aches from sitting, /
몇 시간 후에 / 앉아 있어서 허리가 아플 때 /

my hair is styled and dry, /
머리는 모양이 잡혀서 마를 때 /

and my almost invisible makeup has been applied — /
그리고 거의 보이지 않는 화장을 했을 때 /

Ash tells me [it's time to change into my dress]. [ ]: D·O(명사절 접속사 that 생략)
4형식V I·O it's time to V: ~할 시간이다
Ash는 나에게 드레스로 갈아입을 시간이라고 말한다

(2) We've been waiting until the last minute, /
우리는 마지막 순간까지 기다리고 있었다 /

afraid [any refreshments I eat might accidentally fall onto it and stain it]. [ ]: 명사절(접속사 that 생략)
=dress =dress
내가 먹는 다과가 우연히 드레스에 떨어져 얼룩지게 할까 두려워

힌트 형용사 afraid 앞에 being이 생략된 분사구문임. 또한 afraid 뒤에 of+명사나 that절이 오면 '(어떤 일이 있을까 봐) 두려운, 걱정하는'이라는 뜻임. 원문은 'We've been waiting until the last minute, because we've been afraid that any refreshments I eat might accidentally fall onto it and stain it.'임.

(3) There's only thirty minutes left / until the show starts, /
30분밖에 남지 않았다 / 쇼가 시작될 때까지 /

and the nerves that have been torturing Ash /
S(선행사) 주격 관계대명사절
그리고 Ash를 괴롭히던 초조함이 /

seem to have escaped her, /
V
그녀에게서 빠져나온 것 같다 /

힌트 완료부정사 to have p.p.는 부정사의 시제가 주절의 시제보다 과거인 경우 사용함. 초조함이 그녀에게서 빠져나온 것(escape)이 그렇게 보이는 것(seem)보다 먼저 일어난 일이므로 to have p.p. 형태로 쓰임.

choosing a new victim in me.
분사구문(연속동작)
그리고 새로운 희생자로 나를 선택한 것 같다

정답 단서 쇼가 시작될 때까지 얼마 남지 않자 초조해했던 Ash처럼 '나'도 초조해지기 시작함.

정답 단서 '나'는 손바닥에서 땀이 날 정도로 긴장되고 안절부절못함.

(4) My palms are sweating, / and I have butterflies in my stomach.
내 손바닥에서 땀이 나고 있다 / 그리고 나는 안절부절못한다

(5) Nearly all the models are ready, /
거의 모든 모델이 준비가 되었다 /

some of them already dressed /
그리고 일부 모델은 이미 입고 있다 /

in their nineteenth-century costumes.
그들의 19세기 복장을

힌트 being이 생략된 분사구문임. 주절의 동사와 주어가 같지 않으므로 주어(some of them)를 생략하지 않았음. 'and some of them are dressed ~'으로 바꿔 생각하면 이해가 쉬움.

(6) Ash tightens my corset.
Ash가 내 코르셋을 조인다

[전문 해석]

(1)몇 시간 후에, 앉아 있어서 허리가 아프고, 머리는 모양이 잡혀서 마르고, 거의 보이지 않는 화장을 했을 때, Ash는 나에게 드레스로 갈아입을 시간이라고 말한다. (2)내가 먹는 다과가 우연히 드레스에 떨어져 얼룩지게 할까 두려워 우리는 마지막 순간까지 기다리고 있었다. (3)쇼가 시작될 때까지 30분밖에 남지 않았고 Ash를 괴롭히던 초조함이 그녀에게서 빠져나와 새로운 희생자로 나를 선택한 것 같다. (4)내 손바닥에서 땀이 나고 있고, 나는 안절부절못한다. (5)거의 모든 모델이 준비가 되었고, 일부 모델은 이미 19세기 복장을 입고 있다. (6)Ash가 내 코르셋을 조인다.

[정답 확인]

다음 글에 드러난 'I'의 심경으로 가장 적절한 것은?

✔ tense and nervous 긴장하고 불안해하는
② proud and confident 자랑스럽고 자신감 있는
③ relieved and pleased 안도하고 기쁜
④ indifferent and bored 무관심하고 지루한
⑤ irritated and disappointed 짜증이 나고 실망한

[중요 어휘]

□ ache	동사 아프다
□ apply	동사 바르다, 신청하다, 적용하다
□ refreshments	명사 (복수형으로) 다과
□ accidentally	부사 우연히
□ stain	동사 얼룩지게 하다, 더럽히다
□ nerves	명사 (복수형으로) 초조함, 날카로운 신경
□ torture	동사 괴롭히다
□ victim	명사 희생자
□ have butterflies in one's stomach	안절부절못하다
□ tense	형용사 긴장한, 긴박한
□ indifferent	형용사 무관심한
□ irritated	형용사 짜증이 난

07 2022년 11월 19번 (정답률 90%)

정답 ①

[지문 끊어 읽기] 홀로 전체 발표를 하게 된 일

(1) Dan and I were supposed to make a presentation / that day.
Dan과 나는 발표를 하기로 예정되어 있었다 / 그날

(2) Right after the class started, / my phone buzzed.
수업이 시작된 직후에 / 나의 전화기가 울렸다

(3) It was a text from Dan / saying, / "I can't make it on time. /
그것은 Dan으로부터 온 문자 메시지였다 / ~라고 하는 / 나는 제시간에 갈 수 없어 /

There's been a car accident / on the road!"
차 사고가 있었어 / 도로에서

(4) I almost fainted. 정답 단서 제시간에 올 수 없다는 Dan의 문자 메시지를 받은 'I'는 기절할 뻔했음.
나는 거의 기절할 뻔했다

(5) 'What should I do?'
'어떻게 해야 하지?'

(6) Dan didn't show up / before our turn, /
Dan은 나타나지 않았다 / 우리의 차례 전에 /

and soon I was standing / in front of the whole class.
그리고 곧 나는 서 있었다 / 전체 학생들 앞에

(7) I managed to finish my portion, / and my mind went blank /
나는 겨우 내 몫을 다 끝냈다 / 그리고 나의 정신은 멍해졌다 /

for a few seconds, / wondering what to do.
몇 초간 / 무엇을 해야 할지 생각하면서 분사구문-동시동작

(8) 'Hold yourself together!'
'정신 차려!'

(9) I quickly came to my senses /
병렬①
나는 재빨리 정신을 차렸다 /

and worked through Dan's part of the presentation /
병렬②
그리고 Dan의 발표 부분을 해 나갔다 /

as best as I could.
내가 할 수 있는 최선을 다해

(10) After a few moments, / I finished the entire presentation /
잠시 후 / 나는 전체 발표를 끝냈다 /

on my own.
혼자서

힌트 Only 부사구가 문두에 위치할 때 주어와 동사의 도치가 일어남. 이때 동사가 일반동사인 경우, 조동사 'do/does/did'가 주어 앞으로 도치되며 일반동사는 동사원형의 형태를 취하게 됨. 지문 전체의 시제가 과거이기 때문에 조동사 did가 쓰임.

(11) Only then / did the tension vanish. 정답 단서 혼자서 발표를 다 마친 후에야 긴장감이 사라짐.
그제서야 / 긴장감이 사라졌다

(12) I could see our professor's beaming face.
나는 우리 교수님의 웃음을 띤 얼굴을 볼 수 있었다

[전문 해석]

(1)그날, Dan과 나는 발표를 하기로 예정되어 있었다. (2)수업이 시작된 직후에 나의 전화가 울렸다. (3)그것은 "나는 제시간에 갈 수 없어. 도로에서 차 사고가 있었어!"라고 하는 Dan으로부터 온 문자 메시지였다. (4)나는 거의 기절할 뻔했다. (5)'어떻게 해야 하지?' (6)Dan은 우리의 차례 전에 나타나지 않았고, 곧 나는 전체 학생들 앞에 서 있었다. (7)나는 겨우 내 몫을 다 끝냈고, 무엇을 해야 할지 생각하면서 나의 정신은 몇 초간 멍해졌다. (8)'정신 차려!' (9)나는 재빨리 정신을 차렸고 Dan의 발표 부분을 내가 할 수 있는 최선을 다해 해 나갔다. (10)잠시 후, 나는 혼자서 전체 발표를 끝냈다. (11)그제서야 긴장감이 사라졌다. (12)나는 우리 교수님의 웃음을 띤 얼굴을 볼 수 있었다.

[정답 확인]

다음 글에 드러난 'I'의 심경 변화로 가장 적절한 것은?

✔ panicked → relieved
당황한 → 안심한
② sorrowful → indifferent
슬픈 → 무관심한
③ sympathetic → content
호의적인 → 만족하는
④ jealous → delighted
질투하는 → 기쁜
⑤ confused → humiliated
혼란스러운 → 굴욕적인

[중요 어휘]

☐ **be supposed to V**	~하기로 예정되어 있다
☐ **make a presentation**	발표하다
☐ **make it**	(모임 등에) 가다, 성공하다, 해내다
☐ **on time**	제시간에, 정각에
☐ **faint**	동사 기절하다, 정신이 아찔해지다 / 형용사 희미한
☐ **show up**	나타나다
☐ **manage to V**	겨우 ~해내다
☐ **come to one's senses**	정신을 차리다, 의식을 회복하다
☐ **tension**	명사 긴장감
☐ **vanish**	동사 사라지다
☐ **beaming**	형용사 웃음을 띤, 밝게 빛나는

08 2023년 6월 19번 (정답률 90%)

정답 ①

[지문 끊어 읽기] 인턴십 합격

(1) Ester stood up /
Ester는 일어났다 /
as soon as she heard the hum of a hover engine outside.
그녀가 밖에서 호버 엔진의 웅웅거리는 소리를 듣자마자

(2) "Mail," she shouted / and ran down the third set of stairs /
그녀는 "편지."라고 소리쳤다 / 그리고 세 층계를 뛰어 내려갔다 /
and swung open the door.
그리고 문을 확 열었다

(3) It was pouring now, / but she ran out into the rain.
이제는 비가 마구 쏟아지고 있었다 / 하지만 그녀는 빗속으로 달려 나갔다

(4) She was facing the mailbox.
그녀는 우편함을 마주하고 있었다

(5) There was a single, unopened letter inside.
안에는 뜯지 않은 편지 한 통이 있었다

(6) She was sure / this must be [what she was eagerly waiting for]. 정답 단서 간절히 기다리던 편지가 도착한 것임이 분명함.
그녀는 확신했다 / 이것이 그녀가 간절히 기다렸던 것이 틀림없다고
[ ]: S·C(선행사를 포함한 관계대명사절)

(7) Without hesitation, / she tore open the envelope.
망설임 없이 / 그녀는 봉투를 뜯어 열었다

(8) She pulled out the paper / and unfolded it. (=the paper)
그녀는 종이를 꺼냈다 / 그리고 그것을 펼쳤다

(9) The letter said, / 'Thank you for applying to our company.
편지에 쓰이길 / 우리 회사에 지원해 주셔서 감사합니다

(10) We would like to invite you / to our internship program.
우리는 당신을 초대하고 싶습니다 / 우리의 인턴십 프로그램에

(11) We look forward to seeing you soon.'
우리는 곧 당신을 보길 기대합니다

(12) She jumped up and down / and looked down at the letter again.
그녀는 펄쩍 뛰었다 / 그리고 편지를 다시 내려보았다

(13) She couldn't wait to tell this news to her family. 정답 단서 가족들에게 인턴십에 합격했다는 소식을 빨리 알리고 싶어함.
그녀는 가족에게 이 소식을 빨리 말하고 싶었다

[전문 해석]

(1)Ester는 밖에서 호버 엔진의 웅웅거리는 소리를 듣자마자 일어났다. (2)그녀는 "편지."라고 소리치며 세 층계를 뛰어 내려갔고 문을 확 열었다. (3)이제는 비가 마구 쏟아지고 있었지만, 그녀는 빗속으로 달려 나갔다. (4)그녀는 우편함을 마주하고 있었다. (5)안에는 뜯지 않은 편지 한 통이 있었다. (6)그녀는 이것이 그녀가 간절히 기다렸던 것이 틀림없다고 확신했다. (7)망설임 없이 그녀는 봉투를 뜯어 열었다. (8)그녀는 종이를 꺼내 펼쳤다. (9)편지에 쓰이길, '우리 회사에 지원해 주셔서 감사합니다. (10)우리는 당신을 우리의 인턴십 프로그램에 초대하고 싶습니다. (11)우리는 곧 당신을 보길 기대합니다.' (12)그녀는 펄쩍 뛰며 편지를 다시 내려보았다. (13)그녀는 가족에게 이 소식을 빨리 말하고 싶었다.

[정답 확인]

다음 글에 드러난 Ester의 심경 변화로 가장 적절한 것은?

✔ anticipating → excited
기대하는 → 신이 난
② confident → ashamed
자신감 있는 → 부끄러운
③ curious → embarrassed
호기심 있는 → 당황한
④ surprised → confused
놀란 → 혼란스러운
⑤ indifferent → grateful
무관심한 → 감사하는

[중요 어휘]

☐ **as soon as**	~하자마자
☐ **hum**	명사 웅웅거리는 소리
☐ **pour**	동사 (비가) 마구 쏟아지다
☐ **eagerly**	부사 간절히, 열심히
☐ **hesitation**	명사 망설임, 주저
☐ **unfold**	동사 펼치다, 펴다
☐ **apply**	동사 지원하다, 신청하다, 적용하다

09 2023년 9월 19번 (정답률 90%)

정답 ①

[지문 끊어 읽기] 아들과 25센트 동전

(1) My 10-year-old appeared, / in desperate need of a quarter.
나의 열 살짜리 아이가 나타났다 / 25센트 동전을 절실히 필요로 하며

(2) "A quarter? / What on earth do you need a quarter for?" (on earth: 의문사 강조)
25센트 동전 / 너는 25센트 동전이 도대체 무엇 때문에 필요하니

(3) My tone bordered on irritation. 정답 단서 '나'의 말투는 짜증에 가까움.
나의 말투는 짜증에 아주 가까웠다

(4) I didn't want to be bothered / with such a trivial demand.
나는 방해받고 싶지 않았다 / 그런 사소한 요구에

(5) "There's a garage sale up the street, /
거리 위쪽에서 중고 물품 세일을 해요 /
and there's something I just gotta have!
그런데 제가 꼭 사야할 게 있어요

(6) It only costs a quarter. / Please?"
25센트밖에 안 해요 / 네

(7) I placed a quarter in my son's hand.
나는 아들의 손에 25센트 동전을 쥐여 주었다

(8) Moments later, / a little voice said, /
잠시 후 / 작은 목소리로 말했다 /
"Here, Mommy, this is for you."
"여기요, 엄마, 이건 엄마를 위한 거예요."

(9) I glanced down at the hands of my little son /
나는 내 어린 아들의 손을 흘깃 내려다보았다 /
and saw a four-inch cream-colored statue /
그리고 4인치짜리 크림색의 조각상을 보았다 /
of two small children hugging one another.
두 어린아이들이 서로 껴안고 있는

(10) Inscribed at their feet were words /
그들의 발밑에는 말이 새겨져 있었다 / S(선행사)
[that read *It starts with 'L' ends with 'E' and in between are 'O' and 'V.'*] [ ]: 주격 관계대명사절
'L'로 시작하여 'E'로 끝나고 그 사이에 'O'와 'V'가 있다'라는

힌트 관계대명사절의 수식을 받는 주어 words 이하가 주어이며 보어가 문두로 나가면서 주어와 술어가 도치됨.

(11) As I watched him race back to the garage sale, /
나는 그가 중고 물품 세일로 서둘러 돌아가는 모습을 바라보며 /
I smiled with a heart full of happiness. 정답 단서
나는 행복이 가득한 마음으로 미소를 지었다

아이가 중고 물품 세일 행사로 돌아가는 모습을 보며 '나'는 행복함에 미소를 지음.

(12) That 25-cent garage sale purchase / brought me a lot of joy.
S 4형식V I·O D·O
그 25센트짜리 중고 물품 세일 구매는 / 내게 큰 기쁨을 가져왔다

[전문 해석]

(1)나의 열 살짜리 아이가 25센트 동전을 절실히 필요로 하며 나타났다. (2)"25센트 동전? 너는 25센트 동전이 도대체 무엇 때문에 필요하니?" (3)나의 말투는 짜증에 아주 가까웠다. (4)나는 그런 사소한 요구에 방해받고 싶지 않았다. (5)"거리 위쪽에서 중고 물품 세일을 하는데, 제가 꼭 사야할 게 있어요! (6)25센트밖에 안 해요. 네?" (7)나는 아들의 손에 25센트 동전을 쥐여 주었다. (8)잠시 후, 작은 목소리로 말했다, "여기요, 엄마, 이건 엄마를 위한 거예요." (9)나는 내 어린 아들의 손을 흘깃 내려다보았고 두 어린아이들이 서로 껴안고 있는 4인치짜리 크림색의 조각상을 보았다. (10)그들의 발밑에는 "'L'로 시작하여 'E'로 끝나고 그 사이에 'O'와 'V'가 있다'라는 말이 새겨져 있었다. (11)나는 그가 중고 물품 세일 (행사)로 서둘러 돌아가는 모습을 바라보며, 나는 행복이 가득한 마음으로 미소를 지었다. (12)그 25센트짜리 중고 물품 세일 구매는 내게 큰 기쁨을 가져왔다.

[정답 확인]

다음 글에 드러난 'I'의 심경 변화로 가장 적절한 것은?

✔ annoyed → delighted
짜증이 난 → 기쁜
② ashamed → relieved
부끄러운 → 안도하는
③ excited → confused
신이 난 → 혼란스러운
④ scared → confident
무서워하는 → 자신감 있는
⑤ indifferent → jealous
무관심한 → 질투하는

[중요 어휘]

□ **tone**	명사 말투
□ **border on**	~에 아주 가깝다
□ **irritation**	명사 짜증
□ **trivial**	형용사 사소한
□ **garage sale**	명사 (자택 차고에서 하는) 중고 물품 세일
□ **glance down**	흘깃 내려다보다
□ **inscribe**	동사 (비석·종이 등에) 새기다, 파다
□ **in between**	사이에, 중간에

문제편 p.021

핵심 글의 분위기와 심경을 파악하는 문제의 답을 찾을 때는, 주어진 상황 묘사에 집중하면서 장면을 상상해 보는 것이 좋음. 여기서는 현장감을 주려고 시제도 현재형으로 쓰고 있음.

10 2019년 6월 19번 (정답률 85%)

정답 ⑤

[지문 끊어 읽기] 얼음 동굴에서의 사고

정답 단서

(1) Rowe jumps for joy / when he finds a cave / because he loves /
Rowe는 기뻐 날뛴다 / 그가 동굴을 찾을 때 / 그가 좋아하기 때문에 /
being in places / where so few have ventured.
장소에 있는 것을 / 거의 아무도 가보지 못한

(2) At the entrance / he keeps taking photos / with his cell phone /
keep V-ing: 계속해서 ~하다
입구에서 / 그는 계속해서 사진을 찍는다 / 그의 휴대폰으로 /
to show off / his new adventure / later.
자랑하기 위해 / 그의 새로운 모험을 / 나중에

(3) Coming to a stop / on a rock / a few meters from the entrance, /
멈춰서 / 바위에 / 입구로부터 몇 미터 떨어진 /
he sees / the icy cave's glittering view.
그는 본다 / 얼음 동굴의 반짝이는 경치를

(4) He says, / "Incredibly beautiful!" /
그는 말한다 / "믿을 수 없을 정도로 아름다워!" /
stretching his hand out / to touch the icy wall.
그의 손을 뻗으며 / 얼음벽을 만지기 위해

(5) Suddenly, / his footing gives way /
갑자기 / 그의 발디딤이 무너진다 /
and he slides down / into the darkness.
그리고 그는 미끄러져 내려간다 / 어둠 속으로

(6) He looks up / and sees a crack of light /
그는 올려다본다 / 그리고 한 틈의 빛을 본다 /
about 20 meters above him.
그보다 약 20미터 위에 있는

(7) 'Phone for help,' / he thinks.
'전화로 도움을 요청하자.' / 그는 생각한다

(8) But he realizes / there's no service / this far underground.
하지만 그는 알아차린다 / 서비스가 없다는 것을 / 이렇게 깊은 지하에서는

(9) He tries to move upward / but he can't. 정답 단서
그는 위쪽으로 움직이려고 노력한다 / 하지만 그는 할 수 없다

(10) He calls out, / "Is anyone there?" 정답 단서
그는 외친다 / "거기 누구 있어요?"

(11) There's no answer.
아무런 대답이 없다

[전문 해석]

(1)Rowe는 거의 아무도 가보지 못한 장소에 있는 것을 좋아하기 때문에 (그가) 동굴을 찾을 때 기뻐 날뛴다. (2)입구에서 그는 나중에 그의 새로운 모험을 자랑하기 위해 그의 휴대폰으로 계속해서 사진을 찍는다. (3)입구로부터 몇 미터 떨어진 바위에 멈춰서, 그는 얼음 동굴의 반짝이는 경치를 본다. (4)그는 얼음벽을 만지기 위해 그의 손을 뻗으며 "믿을 수 없을 정도로 아름다워!"라고 말한다. (5)갑자기 그의 발디딤이 무너지고(그는 발을 헛디디고) 그는 어둠 속으로 미끄러져 내려간다. (6)그는 올려다보고 그보다 약 20미터 위에 있는 한 틈의 빛을 본다. (7)'전화로 도움을 요청하자.'라고 그는 생각한다. (8)하지만 그는 이렇게 깊은 지하에서는 서비스가 없다는(전화 신호가 잡히지 않는다는) 것을 알아차린다. (9)그는 위쪽으로 움직이려고 노력하지만 할 수 없다. (10)그는 "거기 누구 있어요?"라고 외친다. (11)아무런 대답이 없다.

[정답 확인]

다음 글에 드러난 Rowe의 심경 변화로 가장 적절한 것은?

① delighted → grateful
기뻐하는 → 감사하는
② disappointed → ashamed
실망한 → 부끄러운
③ indifferent → regretful
무관심한 → 후회하는
④ bored → frightened
지루해하는 → 겁먹은
✔ excited → desperate
들뜬 → 절망적인

[중요 어휘]

□ venture	동사 (위험을 무릅쓰고) 가다, 모험하다 / 명사 모험, 벤처 (사업)
□ show off	자랑하다
□ glittering	형용사 반짝이는, 빛나는
□ stretch out	뻗다
□ footing	명사 발디딤, 입장, 기초
□ give way	무너지다, 항복하다
□ slide	동사 미끄러지다
□ crack	명사 틈, 흠 / 동사 금이 가다, 부수다
□ phone	동사 전화를 걸다 / 명사 전화

핵심 지문의 전반부와 후반부에서 각각 일어나는 사건을 분리해서 파악하고, 심정을 드러내는 단어에 주목하며 독해하면 답을 빠르게 찾아낼 수 있음. 전반부에서 'I'는 유쾌한 파티를 즐기고 있었는데, 후반부에서는 갑작스러운 공습으로 전쟁이 시작되면서 두려움에 떠는 모습이 드러남.

11 2019년 11월 19번 (정답률 85%)

정답 ⑤

[지문 끊어 읽기] 전쟁의 발발

(1) One night, my family was having a party /
어느 날 밤 우리 가족은 파티를 하고 있었다 /
with a couple from another city / who had two daughters.
다른 도시에서 온 부부와 / 두 명의 딸이 있는

(2) The girls were just a few years older than I, /
그 소녀들은 나보다 단지 몇 살 더 많았다 /
and I played lots of fun games / together with them.
그리고 나는 많은 재미있는 게임을 했다 / 그들과 함께

(3) The father of the family had / an amusing, jolly, witty character, /
그 가족의 아버지는 갖고 있었다 / 재미있고, 유쾌하며, 재치 있는 성격을 /
and I had a memorable night / full of laughter and joy. 정답 단서
그리고 나는 잊지 못할 밤을 보냈다 / 웃음과 기쁨으로 가득한

힌트 밑줄 친 부분은 a memorable night를 수식하며, '주격 관계대명사 + be동사(which was)'가 생략된 것임.

(4) While we laughed, joked, and had our dinner, /
우리가 웃고 농담하며 우리의 저녁을 먹는 동안 /
the TV suddenly broadcast an air attack, /
TV는 갑자기 공습을 알렸다 /
and a screeching siren started to scream, /
그리고 날카로운 사이렌이 울리기 시작했다 /
announcing the "red" situation.
'적색' 상황을 알리면서

힌트 밑줄 친 부분은 '~하면서'라는 동시 동작을 뜻하는 분사구문으로, announcing의 의미상의 주어는 a screeching siren임.

(5) We all stopped dinner, / and we squeezed into the basement.
우리는 모두 저녁 식사를 멈추었다 / 그리고 지하실로 비집고 들어갔다

(6) The siren kept screaming /
사이렌은 계속 울렸다 /
and the roar of planes was heard / in the sky.
그리고 비행기의 굉음이 들렸다 / 하늘에서

(7) The terror of war was overwhelming. 정답 단서
전쟁의 공포는 압도적이었다

(8) Shivering with fear, / I murmured a panicked prayer /
분사구문(~하면서)
두려움에 떨면서 / 나는 겁에 질린 기도를 중얼거렸다 /
that this desperate situation would end quickly. 정답 단서
이 절망적인 상황이 빨리 끝나게 해달라는

[전문 해석]

(1)어느 날 밤, 우리 가족은 다른 도시에서 온, 두 명의 딸이 있는 부부와 파티를 하고 있었다. (2)그 소녀들은 나보다 단지 몇 살 더 많았고, 나는 그들과 함께 많은 재미있는 게임을 했다. (3)그 가족의 아버지는 재미있고, 유쾌하며, 재치 있는 성격을 갖고 있었고, 나는 웃음과 기쁨으로 가득한 잊지 못할 밤을 보냈다. (4)우리가 웃고 농담하며 우리의 저녁을 먹는 동안 TV는 갑자기 공습을 알렸고, 날카로운 사이렌이 '적색' 상황을 알리면서 울리기 시작했다. (5)우리는 모두 저녁 식사를 멈추었고, 지하실로 비집고 들어갔다. (6)사이렌은 계속 울렸고 하늘에서 비행기의 굉음이 들렸다. (7)전쟁의 공포는 압도적이었다. (8)두려움에 떨면서, 나는 이 절망적인 상황이 빨리 끝나게 해달라는 겁에 질린 기도를 중얼거렸다.

[정답 확인]

다음 글에 드러난 'I'의 심경 변화로 가장 적절한 것은?

① indifferent → satisfied 무관심한 → 만족한
② relaxed → envious 안도한 → 부러워하는
③ frustrated → relieved 절망한 → 안심한
④ excited → bored 신이 난 → 지루한
⑤ pleased → terrified 즐거운 → 무서워하는 ✔

[중요 어휘]

□ jolly	형용사 유쾌한
□ witty	형용사 재치 있는
□ broadcast	동사 알리다, 방송하다 (broadcast-broadcast(ed)-broadcast(ed))
□ screeching	형용사 날카로운, 끽 소리를 내는
□ squeeze	동사 비집고 들어가다, (쥐어서) 짜다
□ basement	명사 지하실, 지하
□ roar	명사 굉음
□ terror	명사 공포, 두려움, 테러
□ overwhelming	형용사 압도적인, 대항할 수 없는
□ shiver	동사 (몸을) 떨다 / 명사 전율
□ murmur	동사 중얼거리다, 속삭이다
□ desperate	형용사 절망적인, 자포자기한

12 2022년 9월 19번 (정답률 85%)

정답 ②

[지문 끊어 읽기] '나'의 글이 가진 힘

(1) There was no choice / next morning /
~할 수밖에 없었다 / 다음 날 아침 /
but to turn in my private reminiscence of Belleville.
Belleville에 대한 나의 개인적인 회상을 제출할

힌트 (have) no choice but to V: ~할 수밖에 없다, 어쩔 수 없이 ~하다 =cannot help + V-ing =cannot but + 동사원형 =cannot help but + 동사원형

(2) Two days passed /
이틀이 흘렀다 /
before Mr. Fleagle returned the graded papers, /
Fleagle 선생님이 채점된 과제들을 돌려주기 전에 /
and he returned everyone's but mine.
=everyone's graded papers 전치사
그리고 그는 내 것을 제외하고 모든 사람들의 과제를 돌려주었다

(3) I was anxiously expecting / 정답 단서 Fleagle 선생님으로부터 과제를 돌려받지 못해 불안하고 초조함.
나는 초조하게 기다리고 있었다 /
for a command to report to Mr. Fleagle /
Fleagle 선생님에게 찾아오라는 지시를 /
immediately after school for discipline /
학교 끝나고 즉시 벌을 받으러 /
when I saw / him lift my paper from his desk /
지각V O O·C①
내가 보았을 때 / 그가 그의 책상에서 내 과제를 집어 드는 것을 /
and rap for the class's attention.
O·C②
그리고 학생들의 주목을 끌기 위해 두드리는 것을

(4) "Now, boys," / he said, / "I want to read you an essay.
"자, 여러분," / 그가 말했다 / 나는 여러분에게 글 한 편을 읽어주고 싶습니다

(5) This is titled / 'The Art of Eating Spaghetti.'"
이 글의 제목은 / '스파게티를 먹는 예술'입니다

(6) And he started to read.
그리고 그는 읽기 시작했다

(7) My words!
내 글을

(8) He was reading *my words* out loud / to the entire class.
그는 '내 글'을 크게 소리 내어 읽어주고 있었다 / 온 학생들에게

(9) What's more, / the entire class was listening attentively.
더욱이 / 온 학생들이 주의 깊게 듣고 있었다

(10) Then somebody laughed, / then the entire class was laughing, /
그 후 누군가가 웃었다 / 그러자 온 학생들이 웃고 있었다 /
and not in contempt and ridicule, /
not A but B
경멸이나 조소가 아니라 /
but with openhearted enjoyment.
숨김없는 즐거움으로

(11) I did my best / to avoid showing pleasure, /
S① V①
나는 최선을 다했다 / 기쁨을 드러내는 것을 피하려고 /
but what I was feeling was pure ecstasy / 정답 단서 학급 친구들이 자신의 글을 듣고 즐겁게 웃었다는 것에 기쁨을 느낌.
S② V②
하지만 내가 느낀 것은 순수한 환희였다 /
at this startling demonstration / that my words had the power /
이 놀라운 입증에 대한 / 내 글이 힘을 가졌다는 /
to make people laugh.
형용사적 용법
사람들을 웃게 만드는

[전문 해석]

(1)다음 날 아침 Belleville에 대한 나의 개인적인 회상을 제출할 수밖에 없었다. (2)Fleagle 선생님이 채점된 과제들을 돌려주기 전에 이틀이 흘렀고, 그는 내 것을 제외하고 모든 사람들의 과제를 돌려주었다. (3)나는 Fleagle 선생님이 그의 책상에서 내 과제를 집어 들고 학생들의 주목을 끌기 위해 두드리는 것을 보았을 때, 나는 학교 끝나고 즉시 벌을 받으러 그에게 찾아오라는 지시를 초조하게 기다리고 있었다. (4)그가 말했다. "자, 여러분, 나는 여러분에게 글 한 편을 읽어주고 싶습니다. (5)이 글의 제목은 '스파게티를 먹는 예술'입니다." (6)그리고 그는 읽기 시작했다. (7)내 글을! (8)그는 '내 글'을 온 학생들에게 크게 소리 내어 읽어주고 있었다. (9)더욱이, 온 학생들이 주의 깊게 듣고 있었다. (10)그 후 누군가가 웃었고, 그러자 온 학생들이 경멸이나 조소가 아니라, 숨김없는 즐거움으로 웃고 있었다. (11)나는 기쁨을 드러내는 것을 피하려고 최선을 다했지만, 내가 느낀 것은 내 글이 사람들을 웃게 만드는 힘을 가졌다는 이 놀라운 입증에 대한 순수한 환희였다.

[정답 확인]

다음 글에 드러난 'I'의 심경 변화로 가장 적절한 것은?

① relieved → scared
안도한 → 무서워하는
② ✔ nervous → delighted
불안해하는 → 기뻐하는
③ bored → confident
지루한 → 자신 있는
④ satisfied → depressed
만족한 → 우울한
⑤ confused → ashamed
혼란스러운 → 부끄러운

[중요 어휘]

□ **private**	형용사 개인적인
□ **grade**	동사 채점하다 / 명사 등급, 학년
□ **but(=except)**	전치사 ~ 외에, ~을 제외하고
□ **anxiously**	부사 초조하게
□ **expect**	동사 기다리다, 기대하다, 예상하다
□ **discipline**	명사 벌, 훈육, 규율
□ **rap**	동사 두드리다
□ **attentively**	부사 주의 깊게
□ **contempt**	명사 경멸, 무시
□ **ridicule**	명사 조소 / 동사 비웃다
□ **openhearted**	형용사 숨김없는, 솔직한
□ **ecstasy**	명사 환희, 황홀경
□ **startling**	형용사 놀라운
□ **demonstration**	명사 입증, 시연, 시위

13 2023년 3월 19번 (정답률 80%) 정답 ②

[지문 끊어 읽기] 카페 개업식

(1) On opening day, / Isabel arrives at the cafe very early /
개업일에 / Isabel은 카페에 아주 일찍 도착한다 /
with nervous anticipation. 정답 단서 카페 개업일에 Isabel은 초조한 기대를 가짐.
초조한 기대를 가지고

(2) She looks around the cafe, / but she can't shake off the feeling /
그녀는 카페를 둘러본다 / 하지만 그녀는 느낌을 떨쳐 낼 수가 없다 /
that something is missing. 정답 단서 카페를 둘러보던 Isabel은 무언가 부족하다는 느낌을 받음.
동격의 that절(the feeling과 동격)
무언가가 빠졌다는

(3) As she sets out cups, spoons, and plates, / Isabel's doubts grow. 정답 단서 의구심이 점점 커짐.
그녀가 컵, 숟가락, 그리고 접시를 진열함에 따라 / Isabel의 의구심은 커진다

(4) She looks around, / [trying to imagine /
try to V: ~하려고 애쓰다[노력하다]
그녀는 주변을 둘러본다 / 상상하기 위해 애쓰면서 /
what else she could do / to make the cafe perfect], / [ ]: 분사구문(~하면서)
의문사 5형식V O O·C(형용사)
그녀가 다른 무엇을 할 수 있는지를 / 카페를 완벽하게 만들기 위해서 /
but nothing comes to mind.
하지만 그 무엇도 생각나지 않는다

(5) Then, / in a sudden burst of inspiration, /
그러더니 / 갑작스러운 영감의 폭발 속에서 /
Isabel grabs her paintbrush /
S V①
Isabel은 그녀의 붓을 쥔다 /
and transforms the blank walls into landscapes, /
V②
그리고 텅 빈 벽을 풍경화로 바꾼다 /
adding flowers and trees.
분사구문(~하면서)
꽃과 나무를 더하면서

(6) As she paints, / her doubts begin to fade. 정답 단서 텅 빈 벽을 풍경화로 채우면서 무언가 부족하다는 의구심이 사라지기 시작함.
그녀가 그림을 그리면서 / 그녀의 의구심은 사라지기 시작한다

(7) [Looking at her handiwork, / which is beautifully done], /
[ ]: 분사구문 선행사 주격 관계대명사
그녀의 작품을 바라보면서 / 아름답게 완성된 /
she is certain / that the cafe will be a success. 정답 단서 벽에 완성된 자신의 작품을 바라보면서, 성공을 확신함.
그녀는 확신한다 / 카페가 성공작이 될 것이라고

(8) 'Now, success is not exactly guaranteed,' /
'자, 성공이 확실히 보장되지는 않았어' /
she thinks to herself, / 'but I'll definitely get there.'
재귀대명사
그녀는 마음속으로 생각한다 / '하지만 나는 분명 그곳에 도달할 거야.'

[중요 구문]

(4) She looks around, [trying to imagine [what else she could do to make the cafe perfect]], but nothing comes to mind.
S① V① [ ]: 분사구문 [ ]: imagine의 목적어 부사적 용법 S② V②

[전문 해석]

(1)개업일에, Isabel은 초조한 기대를 가지고 카페에 아주 일찍 도착한다. (2)그녀는 카페를 둘러보지만, 그녀는 무언가가 빠졌다는 느낌을 떨쳐 낼 수가 없다. (3)그녀가 컵, 숟가락, 그리고 접시를 진열함에 따라, Isabel의 의구심은 커진다. (4)그녀는 카페를 완벽하게 만들기 위해서 그녀가 다른 무엇을 할 수 있는지를 상상하기 위해 애쓰면서 주변을 둘러보지만, 그 무엇도 생각나지 않는다. (5)그러더니, 갑작스러운 영감의 폭발 속에서, Isabel은 그녀의 붓을 쥐고, 꽃과 나무를 더하면서 텅 빈 벽을 풍경화로 바꾼다. (6)그녀가 그림을 그리면서, 그녀의 의구심은 사라지기 시작한다. (7)아름답게 완성된 그녀의 작품을 바라보면서, 그녀는 카페가 성공작이 될 것이라고 확신한다. (8)그녀는 마음속으로 생각한다. '자, 성공이 확실히 보장되지는 않았어. 하지만 나는 분명 그곳에 도달할 거야.'

[정답 확인]

다음 글에 드러난 Isabel의 심경 변화로 가장 적절한 것은?

① calm → surprised 차분한 → 놀란
✔ doubtful → confident 확신이 없는 → 확신하는
③ envious → delighted 부러워하는 → 아주 기뻐하는
④ grateful → frightened 감사하는 → 무서워하는
⑤ indifferent → uneasy 무관심한 → 불안한

[중요 어휘]

☐ **opening day**	개업일, 개장일
☐ **anticipation**	명사 기대, 예상
☐ **shake off**	~을 떨쳐버리다, 털어내다
☐ **set out**	~을 진열하다, 정리하다
☐ **doubt**	명사 의구심, 의심
☐ **come to mind**	생각나다, 생각이 떠오르다
☐ **burst**	명사 폭발
☐ **inspiration**	명사 영감
☐ **transform A into B**	A를 B로 바꾸다
☐ **landscape**	명사 풍경화, 풍경
☐ **fade**	동사 사라지다, 희미해지다
☐ **handiwork**	명사 작품, 일
☐ **guarantee**	동사 보장하다, 약속하다 / 명사 보장, 품질 보증서
☐ **think to oneself**	마음속으로 생각하다, 조용히 생각하다
☐ **definitely**	부사 분명히, 확실히

14 2018년 6월 20번 (정답률 75%) 정답 ①

[지문 끊어 읽기] 배낭여행 중 일어난 일

(1) While backpacking through Costa Rica, /
Costa Rica를 지나 배낭여행을 하면서 /
Masami found herself in a bad situation. 정답단서
Masami는 자신이 좋지 않은 상황에 처해있다는 것을 깨달았다

(2) She had lost all of her belongings, / and had only $5 in cash.
그녀는 그녀의 모든 소지품을 잃어버렸다 / 그리고 단지 현금 5달러만을 가지고 있었다

(3) To make matters worse, (정답단서) / because of a recent tropical storm, /
설상가상으로 / 최근의 열대 폭풍우 때문에 /
all telephone and Internet services were down.
모든 전화와 인터넷 서비스가 중지되었다

(4) She had no way to get money, / 정답단서
그녀는 돈을 구할 방법이 없었다 /
so decided to go knocking door to door, /
그래서 집집마다 문을 두드리러 가기로 결정했다 /
explaining that she needed a place to stay /
머무를 장소가 필요하다는 것을 설명하면서 /
until she could contact her family back in Japan /
그녀가 일본에 있는 그녀의 가족들에게 연락을 할 수 있을 때까지 /
to send her some money.
그녀에게 약간의 돈을 보내달라고

(5) Everybody told her / they had no space or extra food /
모두들 그녀에게 말했다 / 그들은 장소나 여분의 음식이 없다고 /
and pointed her in the direction of the next house.
그리고 그녀에게 옆집 방향을 가리켰다

(6) It was already dark /
이미 어두워져 있었다 /
when she arrived at a small roadside restaurant.
그녀가 길가의 작은 식당에 도착했을 때는

(7) The owner of the restaurant heard her story /
식당의 주인은 그녀의 이야기를 들었다 /
and really empathized.
그리고 진정으로 공감했다

(8) Much to her delight, / Masami was invited in. 정답단서
매우 기쁘게도 / Masami는 안으로 초대받았다

(9) The owner gave her some food, /
주인은 그녀에게 약간의 음식을 주었다 /
and allowed her to stay there / until she could contact her parents.
그리고 그곳에 머무르게 해주었다 / 그녀가 그녀의 부모님에게 연락을 할 수 있을 때까지

[전문 해석]

(1)Costa Rica(코스타리카)를 지나 배낭여행을 하면서, Masami는 자신이 좋지 않은 상황에 처해있다는 것을 깨달았다. (2)그녀는 그녀의 모든 소지품을 잃어버렸고, 단지 현금 5달러만을 가지고 있었다. (3)설상가상으로, 최근의 열대 폭풍우 때문에 모든 전화와 인터넷 서비스가 중지되었다. (4)그녀는 돈을 구할 방법이 없어서(없었기 때문에), 그녀가 일본에 있는 그녀의 가족들에게 약간의 돈을 보내달라고 연락을 할 수 있을 때까지 머무를 장소가 필요하다는 것을 설명하면서 집집마다 문을 두드리러 가기로 결정했다. (5)모두들 그녀에게 그들은 (머무를 수 있는) 장소나 여분의 음식이 없다고 말하며 옆집 방향을 가리켰다. (6)그녀가 길가의 작은 식당에 도착했을 때는 (날이) 이미 어두워져 있었다. (7)식당의 주인은 그녀의 이야기를 들었고 진정으로 공감했다. (8)매우 기쁘게도, Masami는 안으로 초대받았다. (9)(식당) 주인은 그녀에게 약간의 음식을 주었고, 그녀가 그녀의 부모님에게 연락을 할 수 있을 때까지 그곳에 머무르게 해주었다.

[정답 확인]

다음 글에 드러난 Masami의 심경 변화로 가장 적절한 것은?

✔ desperate → relieved 절망적인 → 안도하는
② gloomy → irritated 우울한 → 짜증이 난
③ jealous → delighted 질투하는 → 기뻐하는
④ excited → worried 들뜬 → 걱정하는
⑤ indifferent → curious 무관심한 → 궁금해하는

✱중요 초반부터 '좋지 않은 상황'에 놓여 있음을 밝힌 후, 설상가상으로(To make matters worse) 상황이 더 악화된 '절망적인' 상태에서 식당 주인으로부터 따뜻한 대접을 받아 '안도하게' 되었음.

[중요 어휘]

☐ **to make matters worse**	설상가상으로
☐ **recent**	형용사 최근의
☐ **tropical**	형용사 열대의, 열대 지방의
☐ **be down**	중지되다, 고장이 나다
☐ **in the direction of**	~의 방향으로

핵심 글의 전반부에서 화자는 누군가에게 붙잡힐 것을 걱정하고 있지만, 문장 (8) 이후부터는 희망에 가득 차 있음.

15 2019년 3월 19번 (정답률 75%) 정답 ②

[지문 끊어 읽기] 탈출 후 여정

(1) Something inside told me / that by now /
(told: 과거시제)
마음속의 무언가가 나에게 말했다 / 지금쯤 이미 /
someone had discovered my escape.
(had discovered: 과거완료시제)
누군가 나의 탈출을 발견했을 것이라고

힌트 '누군가 발견했을' 시점은 마음속의 무언가가 '말했던' 시점보다 과거이므로 '과거완료(had p.p.)' 시제를 썼음.

(2) It chilled me greatly / [to think / [that they would capture me /
(It: 형식상의 주어) ([ ]: think의 목적어절(that ~ place))
나를 몹시 오싹하게 만들었다 / 생각하는 것은 / 그들이 나를 붙잡을 것이라고 /
and take me back / to that awful place]]. 정답단서
그리고 나를 다시 데리고 갈 것이라고 / 그 끔찍한 곳으로 ([ ]: 내용상의 주어)

(3) So, / I decided to walk / only at night /
그래서 / 나는 걷기로 결정했다 / 밤에만 /
until I was far from the town.
내가 그 도시로부터 멀어질 때까지는

(4) After three nights' walking, /
사흘 밤의 걷기 후 /
I felt sure / that they had stopped chasing me.
(felt: 과거시제) (had stopped: 과거완료시제)
나는 확신했다 / 그들이 나를 추적하는 것을 중단했다는 것을

힌트 stop 다음에는 to부정사와 V-ing 둘 다 올 수 있지만, to부정사가 올 때에는 stop의 목적어로 오는 것이 아니라 '~하기 위해서'라는 뜻의 부사적 용법으로 옴. 예를 들어, I stopped chasing은 '추적하는 것을 멈췄다'라는 의미이고, I stopped to chase는 '추적하기 위해서 멈췄다'라는 의미임.

(5) I found a deserted cottage / and walked into it.
나는 사람이 없는 오두막집을 발견했다 / 그리고 그 안으로 걸어 들어갔다

(6) Tired, / I lay down / on the floor / and fell asleep.
분사구문-이유(~해서)
피로하여 / 나는 누웠다 / 바닥에 / 그리고 잠들었다

(7) I awoke / to the sound / of a far away church clock, /
V①
나는 잠에서 깼다 / 소리에 / 멀리 떨어진 교회 시계의 /
softly ringing seven times /
부드럽게 일곱 번 울리는 /
and noticed / that the sun was slowly rising.
V②
그리고 알아차렸다 / 천천히 해가 떠오르고 있음을

(8) As I stepped outside, / my heart began to pound /
내가 밖으로 나갔을 때 / 나의 심장이 뛰기 시작했다 /
with anticipation and longing. 정답 단서
기대와 갈망으로

(9) The thought / that I could meet Evelyn soon /
S 동격의 that
그 생각은 / 머지않아 내가 Evelyn을 만날 수 있다는 /
lightened my walk. 정답 단서
V
나의 걸음을 가볍게 해주었다

[전문 해석]

(1)지금쯤 이미 누군가 나의 탈출을 발견했을 것이라고 마음속의 무언가가 나에게 말했다(생각이 내 마음속에 떠올랐다). (2)그들이 나를 붙잡고 다시 그 끔찍한 곳으로 데리고 갈 것이라고 생각하는 것은 나를 몹시 오싹하게 만들었다(생각하니 오싹해졌다). (3)그래서, 나는 내가 그 도시로부터 멀어질 때까지는 밤에만 걷기로 결정했다. (4)사흘 밤의 걷기 후(사흘 밤을 걷고 나니), 나는 그들이 나를 추적하는 것을 중단했다는 것을 확신했다. (5)나는 사람이 없는 오두막집을 발견하고 그 안으로 걸어 들어갔다. (6)피로하여(피로한 나머지), 나는 바닥에 누워 잠들었다. (7)나는 부드럽게 일곱 번 울리는 멀리 떨어진 교회 시계의 소리에 잠에서 깨었고 천천히 해가 떠오르고 있음을 알아차렸다. (8)(내가) 밖으로 나갔을 때, 나의 심장이 기대와 갈망으로 뛰기 시작했다. (9)머지않아 내가 Evelyn을 만날 수 있다는 그 생각은 나의 걸음을 가볍게 해주었다.

[정답 확인]

다음 글에 드러난 'I'의 심경 변화로 가장 적절한 것은?

① moved → nervous
감동한 → 불안해하는
✔ fearful → hopeful
걱정하는 → 희망에 찬
③ lonely → annoyed
외로운 → 짜증이 난
④ sympathetic → amused
동정하는 → 재미있어 하는
⑤ sorrowful → frightened
슬픈 → 겁먹은

[중요 어휘]

□ **inside**	형용사 마음속의, 안의 / 부사 마음속으로, 안에
□ **chill**	동사 오싹하게 만들다, 춥게 만들다 / 명사 오한, 한기
□ **awful**	형용사 끔찍한, 지독한
□ **feel sure**	~을 확신하다
□ **deserted**	형용사 사람이 없는, 버림받은
□ **cottage**	명사 오두막집, 작은 집
□ **pound**	동사 뛰다, 두드리다
□ **anticipation**	명사 기대, 예상
□ **longing**	명사 갈망, 열망
□ **lighten**	동사 가볍게 해주다, 밝아지다

16 2023년 11월 19번 (정답률 90%) 정답 ②

[지문 끊어 읽기] 체로키족의 통과 의례

(1) Chaske, / a Cherokee boy, / was sitting on a tree stump.
=
Chaske는 / 체로키족 소년인 / 나무 그루터기에 앉아 있었다

(2) As a rite of passage for youths / in his tribe, /
청년들에 대한 통과 의례로 / 그의 부족에서 /
Chaske had to survive one night in the forest /
Chaske는 숲속에서 하룻밤을 살아남아야 했다 /
wearing a blindfold, /
분사구문(부대상황)
눈가리개를 쓰고 /
[not knowing / he was observed by his father]. [ ]: 분사구문(부대상황)
knowing의 목적어절(that 생략)
모른 채로 / 자신의 아버지가 지켜보는 것을

(3) After the sunset, / Chaske could hear all kinds of noises.
해가 지고 난 후에 / Chaske는 온갖 종류의 소리를 들을 수 있었다

(4) The wind blew the grass / and shook his stump.
V① V②
바람이 풀을 날렸다 / 그리고 그의 그루터기를 흔들었다

(5) A sense of dread swept through his body. 정답 단서 눈을 가린 채로 두려워함.
두려움이 그의 몸을 휩쓸었다

(6) *What if wild beasts are looking at me?*
'만약 야생 짐승들이 나를 바라보고 있으면 어떡하지?'

힌트 What if + S + V(현재시제) ~?: 만약 ~라면 어떡하지?(단순 조건에 대한 결과)
What if + S + V(과거시제) ~?: 만약 ~라면 어떻게 될까?(화자의 바람, 상상 등에 대한 조건)

(7) *I can't stand this!*
'나는 이것을 견딜 수가 없어!'

(8) Just as he was about to take off the blindfold / to run away, /
be about to V: 막 ~하려고 하다 부사적 용법(목적)
그가 눈가리개를 막 벗으려고 했을 때 / 도망가기 위해 /
a voice came in from somewhere.
어디선가 목소리가 들려왔다

(9) "I'm here around you.
내가 여기 네 곁에 있어

(10) Don't give up, / and complete your mission."
포기하지 말아라 / 그리고 너의 임무를 완수해라

(11) It was his father's voice.
그것은 아버지의 목소리였다

(12) *He has been watching me from nearby!*
have been V-ing: 현재완료진행
'그가 근처에서 나를 지켜보고 계셨구나!'

정답 단서 아버지의 목소리를 듣고 안정을 되찾음.

(13) With just the presence of his father, / the boy regained stability.
아버지의 존재만으로도 / 소년은 안정을 되찾았다

(14) [What panicked him awfully a moment ago] / [ ]: S
선행사를 포함한 관계대명사
조금 전까지 그를 끔찍하게 겁에 질리게 했던 것이 /
vanished into thin air.
V
흔적도 없이 사라졌다

힌트 into thin air: 흔적도 없이, 온데간데없이

[전문 해석]

(1)체로키족 소년인 Chaske는 나무 그루터기에 앉아 있었다. (2)그의 부족에서 청년들에 대한 통과 의례로, Chaske는 자신의 아버지가 지켜보는 것을 모른 채로 눈가리개를 쓰고 숲속에서 하룻밤을 살아남아야 했다. (3)해가 지고 난 후에, Chaske는 온갖 종류의 소리를 들을 수 있었다. (4)바람이 풀을 날렸고 그의 그루터기를 흔들었다. (5)두려움이 그의 몸을 휩쓸었다. (6)'만약 야생 짐승들이 나를 바라보고 있으면 어떡하지? (7)나는 이것을 견딜 수가 없어!' (8)그가 도망가기 위해 눈가리개를 막 벗으려고 했을 때, 어디선가 목소리가 들려왔다. (9)"내가 여기 네 곁에 있어. (10)포기하지 말고 너의 임무를 완수해라." (11)그것은 아버지의 목소리였다. (12)'그가 근처에서 나를 지켜보고 계셨구나!' (13)아버지의 존재만으로도 소년은 안정을 되찾았다. (14)조금 전까지 그를 끔찍하게 겁에 질리게 했던 것이 흔적도 없이 사라졌다.
- Cherokee(체로키족): 북아메리카 남동부에 거주하던 원주민 민족

[정답 확인]

다음 글에 드러난 Chaske의 심경 변화로 가장 적절한 것은?

① nervous → doubtful
불안해 하는 → 의심을 품은
✔ horrified → relieved
겁에 질린 → 안도한
③ disappointed → curious
실망한 → 호기심이 많은
④ ashamed → frightened
부끄러운 → 겁먹은
⑤ bored → delighted
지루한 → 기쁜

[중요 어휘]

☐ stump	명사 그루터기 / 동사 쿵쿵거리며 걷다
☐ rite of passage	통과 의례
☐ youth	명사 청년, 젊음
☐ tribe	명사 부족, 종족
☐ blindfold	명사 눈가리개
☐ observe	동사 지켜보다, 관찰하다
☐ all kinds of	온갖 종류의
☐ beast	명사 짐승, 야수
☐ stand	동사 견디다, 참다
☐ mission	명사 임무, 사절단
☐ presence	명사 존재, 있음
☐ regain	동사 되찾다, 회복하다
☐ stability	명사 안정, 안정성
☐ panic	동사 겁에 질리게 하다 (panic-panicked-panicked) / 명사 공포, 공황
☐ vanish	동사 사라지다, 없어지다

17 2024년 3월 19번 (정답률 90%)

정답 ⑤

[지문 끊어 읽기] 미술 대회 우승

(1) Sarah, a young artist with a love for painting, /
S =
그림 그리기를 좋아하는 젊은 예술가인 Sarah는 /
entered a local art contest.
V
지역 미술 대회에 참가했다

(2) As she looked at the amazing artworks made by others, /
과거분사구
그녀가 다른 사람들에 의해 만들어진 엄청난 예술 작품들을 보았을 때 /
her confidence dropped. 정답단서 Sarah는 다른 사람들이 만든 예술 작품을 보고 자신감이 하락함.
그녀의 자신감은 하락했다

(3) She quietly thought, / 'I might not win an award.'
그녀는 조용히 생각했다 / '나는 상을 받지 못할 수도 있겠다.'

(4) The moment of judgment arrived, /
심사의 순간이 다가왔다 /
and the judges began announcing winners one by one.
그리고 심사위원들은 한 명씩 수상자를 발표하기 시작했다

(5) It wasn't until the end that she heard her name.
그녀는 마지막에서야 자신의 이름을 들었다

힌트 'She didn't hear her name until the end.'라는 의미의 문장에서 '~해서야 …하다'라는 not until 구문을 이용하여 'it is[was] ~ that 강조구문'으로 바꾼 문장으로, it was와 that 사이에 강조하고자 하는 not until the end를 삽입한 형태임. 'It is not until ~ that S V' 구문은 '~에서야 S가 V하다'라고 해석함.

(6) The head of the judges said, /
심사위원장이 말했다 /
"Congratulations, Sarah Parker! /
축하합니다, Sarah Parker /
You won first prize. / We loved the uniqueness of your work."
당신이 1등을 수상했습니다 / 우리는 당신 작품의 독특함이 정말 좋았습니다

(7) Sarah was overcome with joy, /
Sarah는 기쁨에 휩싸였다 /
and she couldn't stop smiling. 정답단서 Sarah는 기쁨에 휩싸여 미소를 멈출 수 없었음.
그리고 그녀는 미소를 멈출 수 없었다

힌트 stop V-ing: ~하는 것을 멈추다
stop to V: ~하기 위해 (하던 것을) 멈추다

(8) This experience meant more than just winning; /
이 경험은 단순한 수상 이상을 의미했다 /
it confirmed her identity as an artist.
이것은 예술가로서 그녀의 정체성을 확인해 주었다

[전문 해석]

(1)그림 그리기를 좋아하는 젊은 예술가인 Sarah는 지역 미술 대회에 참가했다. (2)그녀가 다른 사람들에 의해 만들어진 엄청난 예술 작품들을 보았을 때, 그녀의 자신감은 하락했다. (3)그녀는 '나는 상을 받지 못할 수도 있겠다.'라고 조용히 생각했다. (4)심사의 순간이 다가왔고, 심사위원들은 한 명씩 수상자를 발표하기 시작했다. (5)그녀는 마지막에서야 자신의 이름을 들었다. (6)심사위원장이 "축하합니다, Sarah Parker! 당신이 1등을 수상했습니다. 우리는 당신 작품의 독특함이 정말 좋았습니다."라고 말했다. (7)Sarah는 기쁨에 휩싸였고 그녀는 미소를 멈출 수 없었다. (8)이 경험은 단순한 수상 이상을 의미했는데, 이것은 예술가로서 그녀의 정체성을 확인해 주었다.

[정답 확인]

다음 글에 드러난 Sarah의 심경 변화로 가장 적절한 것은?

① hopeful → regretful
희망에 찬 → 후회하는
② relieved → grateful
안도하는 → 감사해 하는
③ excited → disappointed
신난 → 실망한
④ depressed → frightened
우울한 → 겁먹은
⑤ discouraged → delighted (✔)
낙담한 → 기쁜

[중요 어휘]

☐ enter	동사 참가하다, 들어가다
☐ judgment	명사 심사, 판단
☐ one by one	한 명씩, 하나씩
☐ head	명사 (단체의) 장, 머리 / 동사 ~로 향하다
☐ uniqueness	명사 독특함, 특이함
☐ be overcome with	~에 휩싸이다
☐ more than just	단순히 ~ 이상의
☐ confirm	동사 확인해 주다, 확인하다
☐ identity	명사 정체성

18 2024년 6월 19번 (정답률 95%)

정답 ①

[지문 끊어 읽기] 계주 결승전 우승

(1) It was the championship race.
결승전 경주였다

(2) Emma was the final runner / on her relay team.
Emma는 마지막 주자였다 / 그녀의 계주 팀의

(3) She anxiously waited in her spot /
그녀는 그녀의 자리에서 초조하게 기다렸다 /
for her teammate to pass her the baton.
to부정사의 의미상의 주어
그녀의 팀 동료가 그녀에게 바통을 건네는 것을

(4) Emma wasn't sure / [she could perform her role] / [ ]: 명사절(접속사 that 생략)
Emma는 확신하지 못했다 / 그녀가 자신의 역할을 수행할 수 있을지 /
without making a mistake.
실수를 하지 않고

(5) Her hands shook / as she thought, / "What if I drop the baton?"
그녀의 손이 떨렸다 / 그녀가 생각하면서 / "만약 내가 바통을 떨어뜨리면 어떡하지?"

(6) She felt her heart rate increasing /
지각V O O.C(V-ing)
그녀는 심박수가 증가하는 것을 느꼈다 /
as her teammate approached. 정답단서 계주 마지막 주자인 Emma는 긴장한 모습을 보임.
그녀의 팀 동료가 다가올수록

힌트 지각동사의 목적격 보어로 원형부정사, 현재분사, 과거분사가 올. 현재분사가 올 경우 능동과 진행의 의미가, 과거분사가 올 경우에는 수동의 의미를 나타냄. 문장 (6)은 심박수가 증가하고 있다는 진행의 의미를 강조하여 현재분사를 씀.

(7) But as she started running, / she received the baton smoothly.
하지만 그녀가 달리기 시작하자 / 그녀는 순조롭게 바통을 받았다

(8) In the final 10 meters, / she passed two other runners /
S V①
마지막 10미터에서 / 그녀는 두 명의 다른 주자를 제쳤다 /
and crossed the finish line / in first place!
V②
그리고 결승선을 통과했다 / 1위로

(9) She raised her hands in the air, /
그녀는 두 손을 하늘로 치켜들었다 /
and a huge smile came across her face. 정답단서 Emma는 끝내 1등으로 결승선을 통과하고 기뻐함.
그리고 큰 미소가 그녀의 얼굴에 떠올랐다

(10) As her teammates hugged her, / she shouted, / "We did it!"
팀 동료들이 그녀를 안아주었을 때 / 그녀는 외쳤다 / "우리가 해냈어!"

(11) All of her hard training had been worth it.
그녀의 모든 힘든 훈련이 그럴 만한 가치가 있었다

힌트 훈련은 경주에서 이긴 것보다 이전에 있었던 일이므로 과거완료 시제를 사용함.

[전문 해석]

(1)결승전 경주였다. (2)Emma는 그녀의 계주 팀의 마지막 주자였다. (3)그녀는 그녀의 자리에서 팀 동료가 그녀에게 바통을 건네는 것을 초조하게 기다렸다. (4)Emma는 그녀가 실수를 하지 않고 자신의 역할을 수행할 수 있을지 확신하지 못했다. (5)"만약 내가 바통을 떨어뜨리면 어떡하지?"라고 생각하면서 그녀의 손이 떨렸다. (6)그녀는 그녀의 팀 동료가 다가올수록 심박수가 증가하는 것을 느꼈다. (7)하지만 그녀가 달리기 시작하자, 그녀는 순조롭게 바통을 받았다. (8)마지막 10미터에서, 그녀는 두 명의 다른 주자를 제치고 1위로 결승선을 통과했다! (9)그녀는 두 손을 하늘로 치켜들었고, 큰 미소가 그녀의 얼굴에 떠올랐다. (10)팀 동료들이 그녀를 안아주었을 때, 그녀는 "우리가 해냈어!"라고 외쳤다. (11)그녀의 모든 힘든 훈련이 그럴 만한 가치가 있었다.

[정답 확인]

다음 글에 드러난 Emma의 심경 변화로 가장 적절한 것은?

✔ nervous → excited 긴장한 → 신이 난
② doubtful → regretful 의심하는 → 후회하는
③ confident → upset 자신감 있는 → 속상한
④ hopeful → disappointed 희망에 찬 → 실망한
⑤ indifferent → amused 무관심한 → 재미있어 하는

[중요 어휘]

□ **championship**	명사 결승전, 선수권
□ **final**	형용사 마지막의, 최종의 / 명사 결승전, 기말고사
□ **runner**	명사 주자, 경주마
□ **relay**	명사 계주 / 동사 중계하다
□ **perform**	동사 수행하다, 연주[공연]하다
□ **heart rate**	심박수
□ **training**	명사 훈련, 교육

19 2024년 9월 19번 (정답률 95%) 정답 ②

[지문 끊어 읽기] 여권 심사

(1) The passport control line was short /
S① V①
여권 심사 줄은 짧았다 /
and the inspectors looked relaxed; /
S② V②
그리고 심사관들은 관대해 보였다 /

힌트 look+형용사: ~하게 보이다

except the inspector at my window.
내 창구의 심사관은 예외였다

(2) He seemed to want to model /
그는 모범을 보이고 싶은 것처럼 보였다 /
the seriousness of the task at hand / for the other inspectors.
당면한 업무의 심각성에 대해 / 다른 심사관들에게

(3) Maybe that's why I felt uneasy / 정답 단서 '나'는 심사관을 보고 불안감을 느끼고 있음.
아마 그것이 내가 불안하다고 느꼈던 이유이다 /
when he studied my passport more carefully / than I expected.
그가 내 여권을 더 꼼꼼히 살펴볼 때 / 내가 예상했던 것보다

(4) "You were here in September," / he said.
"당신은 9월에 여기 계셨네요." / 그가 말했다

(5) "Why are you back so soon?"
"당신은 왜 이렇게 빨리 돌아오셨나요?"

(6) "I came in September / to prepare to return this month," /
부사적 용법(목적) 명사적 용법(목적어)
저는 9월에 왔었어요 / 이번 달에 돌아올 것을 준비하려고 /
I replied with a trembling voice, / 정답 단서 심사관의 질문에 '나'는 떨리는 목소리로 대답함.
나는 떨리는 목소리로 대답했다 /
[considering if I missed any Italian regulations]. [ ]: 분사구문
명사절 접속사(~인지 아닌지)
내가 이탈리아의 어떤 규정을 놓친 건 아닌지 생각하면서

(7) "For how long?"/ he asked.
"얼마나 오래요?" / 그가 물었다

(8) "One month, this time," / I answered truthfully.
"이번에는 한 달이요." / 나는 정직하게 대답했다

(9) I knew / it was against the rules /
형식상의 주어
나는 알고 있었다 / 규정에 어긋나지 않는다는 것을 /
[to stay in Italy for three months]. [ ]: 내용상의 주어
이탈리아에 세 달 동안 체류하는 것이

(10) "Enjoy your stay," / he finally said, / as he stamped my passport.
접속사(~하면서)
"즐거운 여행 되세요." / 그가 마침내 말했다 / 그가 내 여권에 도장을 찍으면서

(11) Whew!
휴

(12) As I walked away, / the burden I had carried, /
S, 선행사 목적격 관계대명사절(관계대명사 생략)
내가 걸어나갈 때 / 내가 짊어지고 있던 부담이 /
even though I did nothing wrong, / vanished into the air. 정답 단서 '내'가 짊어지고 있던 부담(=심사관 앞에서 느꼈던 불안감)이 허공으로 사라짐.
V
나는 아무 잘못도 하지 않았음에도 불구하고 / 허공으로 사라졌다

(13) My shoulders, / once weighed down, /
내 어깨는 / 한때 짓눌렸던 / 삽입구(which were 생략)
now stretched out with comfort. 정답 단서 '나'의 짓눌렸던 어깨가 편안함으로 쭉 펴지게 됨.
이제 편안함과 함께 쭉 펴졌다

[전문 해석]

(1)여권 심사 줄은 짧았고 심사관들은 관대해 보였는데, 내 창구의 심사관은 예외였다. (2)그는 다른 심사관들에게 당면한 업무의 심각성에 대해 모범을 보이고 싶은 것처럼 보였다. (3)아마 그것이 내가 예상했던 것보다 그가 내 여권을 더 꼼꼼히 살펴볼 때 내가 불안하다고 느꼈던 이유이다. (4)"당신은 9월에 여기 계셨네요."라고 그가 말했다. (5)"당신은 왜 이렇게 빨리 돌아오셨나요?" (6)나는 내가 이탈리아의 어떤 규정을 놓친 건 아닌지 생각하면서 "저는 이번 달에 돌아올 것을 준비하려고 9월에 왔었어요."라고 떨리는 목소리로 대답했다. (7)"얼마나 오래요?"라고 그가 물었다. (8)"이번에는 한 달이요."라고 나는 정직하게 대답했다. (9)나는 이탈리아에 세 달 동안 체류하는 것이 규정에 어긋나지 않는다는 것을 알고 있었다. (10)"즐거운 여행 되세요."라고 그가 마침내 내 여권에 도장을 찍으면서 말했다. (11)휴! (12)내가 걸어나갈 때, 나는 아무 잘못도 하지 않았음에도 불구하고, 내가 짊어지고 있던 부담이 허공으로 사라졌다. (13)한때 짓눌렸던 내 어깨는 이제 편안함과 함께 쭉 펴졌다.

[정답 확인]

다음 글에 드러난 'I'의 심경 변화로 가장 적절한 것은?

① angry → ashamed 화가 난 → 부끄러운
✔ nervous → relieved 긴장한 → 편안한
③ bored → grateful 지루한 → 감사하는
④ curious → frightened 궁금해하는 → 무서워하는
⑤ hopeful → disappointed 희망에 찬 → 실망한

[중요 어휘]

□ **passport control**	여권 심사, 출입국 관리
□ **inspector**	명사 심사관, 감독관
□ **at hand**	당면한, (거리가) 가까운
□ **uneasy**	형용사 불안한, 걱정되는
□ **study**	동사 살피다, 검토하다
□ **trembling**	형용사 떨리는, 전율하는 / 명사 떨림, 전율
□ **regulation**	명사 규정, 규제
□ **truthfully**	부사 정직하게, 진실하게
□ **burden**	명사 부담, 짐
□ **vanish**	동사 사라지다, 없어지다
□ **weigh A down**	A를 짓누르다

문제편 p.028

03 필자의 주장

01 2021년 9월 20번 (정답률 95%) 정답 ②

[지문 끊어 읽기] 성공적인 협동을 위한 기술

(1) Without guidance from their teacher, /
그들의 선생님의 지도 없이 /
students will not embark on /
학생들은 ~에 착수하지 않을 것이다 /
a journey of personal development /
개인적 발달의 여정 / 선행사
that recognizes the value of cooperation.
주격 관계대명사
협동의 가치를 인정하는

(2) Left to their own devices, /
분사구문(Being 생략)
그들이 제멋대로 하게 내버려 두어지면 /
they will instinctively become increasingly competitive /
그들은 본능적으로 점점 더 경쟁적이게 될 것이다 /
with each other.
서로

(3) They will compare / scores, reports, and feedback /
그들은 비교할 것이다 / 점수, 성적표, 그리고 피드백을 /
within the classroom environment / — just as they do /
교실 환경 내에서 / 그들이 하는 것처럼 /
in the sporting arena.
스포츠 경기장에서

(4) We don't need to teach our students / about winners and losers.
우리는 우리 학생들에게 가르칠 필요가 없다 / 승자와 패자에 대해

(5) The playground and the media do that / for them.
운동장과 미디어가 그것을 한다 / 그들을 위해

(6) However, / we do need to teach them /
강조의 조동사
하지만 / 우리는 그들에게 정말로 가르칠 필요가 있다 /
that there is more to life / than winning /
삶에는 더 많은 것이 있다는 것을 / 이기는 것보다 /
and about the skills / they need for successful cooperation.
선행사 목적격 관계대명사절
그리고 기술들에 대해서 / 그들이 성공적인 협동을 위해 필요한

(7) A group working together successfully /
S 현재분사
함께 성공적으로 일하는 집단은 /
requires individuals / with a multitude of social skills, /
V
개인들을 필요로 한다 / 많은 사회적 기술을 가진 /
as well as a high level of interpersonal awareness.
A as well as B: B뿐 아니라 A
높은 수준의 대인 관계 인식뿐만 아니라

(8) While some students inherently bring /
일부 학생들은 선천적으로 가져오긴 하지만 /
a natural understanding of these skills with them, /
이러한 기술들의 자연스러운 이해를 /
they are always in the minority.
그들은 항상 소수이다

(9) To bring cooperation between peers / into your classroom, /
또래들 사이의 협동을 가져오기 위해서 / 당신의 교실에 /
you need to teach these skills / consciously and carefully, /
병렬①
당신은 이러한 기술들을 가르칠 필요가 있다 / 의식적으로 그리고 주의 깊게 / 주제문
and nurture them continuously / throughout the school years.
병렬②(to 생략)
그리고 그것들을 계속해서 육성할 필요가 있다 / 학창시절 내내

[전문 해석]

(1)그들의 선생님의 지도 없이, 학생들은 협동의 가치를 인정하는 개인적 발달의 여정에 착수하지 않을 것이다. (2)그들이 제멋대로 하게 내버려 두어지면, 그들은 본능적으로 서로 점점 더 경쟁적이게 될 것이다. (3)그들은 그들이 스포츠 경기장에서 하는 것처럼 교실 환경 내에서 점수, 성적표, 그리고 피드백을 비교할 것이다. (4)우리는 우리 학생들에게 승자와 패자에 대해 가르칠 필요가 없다. (5)운동장과 미디어가 그들을 위해 그것(승자와 패자에 대해 가르치는 것)을 한다. (6)하지만 우리는 그들에게 삶에는 이기는 것보다 더 많은 것이 있다는 것과 그들이 성공적인 협동을 위해 필요한 기술들에 대해서 정말로 가르칠 필요가 있다. (7)함께 성공적으로 일하는 집단은 높은 수준의 대인 관계 인식뿐만 아니라 많은 사회적 기술을 가진 개인들을 필요로 한다. (8)일부 학생들은 이러한 기술들의 자연스러운 이해를 선천적으로 가져오긴 하지만, 그들은 항상 소수이다. (9)당신의 교실에 또래들 사이의 협동을 가져오기 위해서, 당신은 의식적으로 그리고 주의 깊게 이러한 기술들을 가르치고 학창시절 내내 그것(기술)들을 계속해서 육성할 필요가 있다.

[정답 확인]

다음 글에서 필자가 주장하는 바로 가장 적절한 것은?

① 학생의 참여(participation)가 활발한 수업 방법을 개발해야 한다.
② 학생에게 성공적인 협동(successful cooperation)을 위한 기술을 가르쳐야 한다. 문장(9)
③ 학생의 의견을 존중하는(respect) 학교 분위기를 조성해야 한다.
④ 학생의 전인적 발달(development)을 위해 체육활동을 강화해야 한다.
⑤ 정보를 올바르게 선별하도록 미디어(media) 교육을 실시해야 한다.

[중요 어휘]

☐ guidance	명사 지도
☐ embark on	~에 착수하다
☐ cooperation	명사 협동
☐ leave (one) to (one's) own devices	(제멋대로 하게) 내버려 두다
☐ arena	명사 경기장
☐ interpersonal	형용사 대인 관계의
☐ awareness	명사 인식
☐ inherently	부사 선천적으로
☐ minority	명사 소수
☐ peer	명사 또래
☐ consciously	부사 의식적으로
☐ nurture	동사 육성하다, 양육하다

02 2022년 3월 20번 (정답률 95%) 정답 ③

[지문 끊어 읽기] 자녀 교육에 있어 다문화 경험의 필요성

(1) Though we are marching toward a more global society, /
부사절 접속사(양보)
우리는 더 글로벌한 사회로 나아가고 있지만 /
various ethnic groups traditionally do things quite differently, /
다양한 민족 집단들은 전통적으로 상당히 다르게 일을 하고 있다 /
and a fresh perspective is valuable /
그래서 새로운 관점이 가치가 있다 /
in creating an open-minded child.
개방적인 아이를 만드는 데

(2) Extensive multicultural experience makes kids more creative /
광범위한 다문화 경험은 아이들을 더 창의적으로 만든다 / V① O O·C
(measured / by how many ideas they can come up with /
측정됨 / 얼마나 많은 생각을 떠올릴 수 있는지로 / 병렬①
and by association skills) /
병렬②
그리고 연상 능력으로 /

힌트 괄호 안의 'measured ~ by association skills'는 계속적 용법의 관계대명사절임. 앞 문장 전체를 선행사로 취하며 과거분사 'measured' 앞에 'which is'가 생략됨. 관계대명사 'which'는 계속적 용법으로 사용 시 앞 문장의 일부나 전체를 선행사로 취할 수 있음.

and allows them to capture unconventional ideas / 정답 단서
V② O(=kids) O·C
그리고 그들이 관습에 얽매이지 않는 생각을 포착할 수 있게 한다 /
from other cultures / to expand on their own ideas.
부사적 용법(목적)
다른 문화로부터 / 아이 자신의 생각을 확장하기 위해

광범위한 다문화 경험은 아이들을 더 창의적으로 만들고 관습에 얽매이지 않는 생각을 포착할 수 있게 함.

★중요 필자는 광범위한 다문화 경험이 아이의 창의성에 도움을 주기 때문에 부모는 자녀가 가능한 한 자주 다른 문화를 접하게 해야 한다고 이야기하고 있음. 이를 위해 부모가 할 수 있는 일의 구체적인 예시들이 주제문 이후에 나열되어 있음.

(3) As a parent, /
부모로서 /
you should expose your children to other cultures /
당신은 자녀가 다른 문화를 접하게 해야 한다 /
as often as possible. 주제문
as+원급+as possible: 가능한 한 ~하게
가능한 한 자주

부모로서 자녀가 다른 문화를 가능한 한 자주 접하도록 하는 것이 중요하다고 강조함.

(4) If you can, / travel with your child to other countries; /
할 수 있다면 / 자녀와 다른 나라로 여행하라 /
live there if possible.
가능하면
그리고 가능하면 거기서 살라

힌트 세미콜론(;)은 두 문장을 이어 주는 접속사 역할을 할 수 있음. 맥락에 맞는 적절한 접속사를 넣어서 해석하면 되는데 본문의 경우 '그리고(and)'를 넣어서 해석하는 게 자연스러움.

(5) If neither is possible, /
대명사(어느 것도 ~아니다)
어느 것도 가능하지 않다면 /
there are lots of things you can do at home, /
선행사 목적격 관계대명사 생략
본국에서 당신이 할 수 있는 일이 많다 /
such as exploring local festivals, /
병렬①
지역 축제 탐방하기와 같이 /
borrowing library books about other cultures, /
병렬②
다른 문화에 대한 도서관 책 빌리기 /
and cooking foods from different cultures at your house.
병렬③
그리고 집에서 다른 문화의 음식 요리하기

[전문 해석]

(1)우리는 더 글로벌한 사회로 나아가고 있지만, 다양한 민족 집단들은 전통적으로 상당히 다르게 일을 하고 있어, 개방적인 아이를 만드는 데 새로운 관점이 가치가 있다. (2)광범위한 다문화 경험은 아이를 더 창의적으로 만들고 (얼마나 많은 생각을 떠올릴 수 있는지와 연상 능력으로 측정됨) 아이 자신의 생각을 확장하기 위해 다른 문화로부터 그들이 관습에 얽매이지 않는 생각을 포착할 수 있게 한다. (3)부모로서 자녀가 다른 문화를 가능한 한 자주 접하게 해야 한다. (4)할 수 있다면 자녀와 다른 나라로 여행하고, 가능하면 거기서 살라. (5)어느 것도 가능하지 않다면, 지역 축제 탐방하기와 다른 문화에 대한 도서관 책 빌리기, 집에서 다른 문화의 음식 요리하기와 같이 본국에서 할 수 있는 일이 많다.

[정답 확인]

다음 글에서 필자가 주장하는 바로 가장 적절한 것은?

① 자녀가 전통문화를 자랑스럽게 여기게(be proud of) 해야 한다.
② 자녀가 주어진 문제를 깊이 있게 탐구하도록(explore) 이끌어야 한다.
✔ 자녀가 다른 문화를 가능한 한 자주 접할(be exposed) 수 있게 해야 한다. 문장(3)
④ 창의성(creativity) 발달을 위해 자녀의 실수에 대해 너그러워야(generous) 한다.
⑤ 경험한 것을 돌이켜 볼 시간을 자녀에게 주어야 한다.

[중요 어휘]

□ **march**	동사 나아가다, 행진하다
□ **ethnic**	형용사 민족의
□ **fresh**	형용사 새로운, 신선한
□ **perspective**	명사 관점
□ **valuable**	형용사 가치가 있는, 귀중한
□ **open-minded**	형용사 개방적인, 마음이 열린
□ **extensive**	형용사 광범위한, 아주 넓은
□ **come up with**	~을 떠올리다
□ **association**	명사 연상, 관련
□ **capture**	동사 포착하다, 붙잡다
□ **unconventional**	형용사 관습에 얽매이지 않는, 색다른
□ **expose A to B**	A를 B에 접하게 하다, 노출시키다
□ **explore**	동사 탐방하다, 탐험하다, 탐구하다

03 2022년 6월 20번 (정답률 95%) 정답 ②

[지문 끊어 읽기] 성공을 도와준 사람들에게 감사하는 태도

(1) In the rush / towards individual achievement and recognition, /
질주 속에서 / 개인의 성취와 인정을 향한 /
[the majority of those who make it] / [ ]: S
선행사 주격 관계대명사절
성공한 사람들의 대다수는 /
forget their humble beginnings.
V
그들의 초라했던 시작을 잊는다

힌트 'the majority of (~의 대다수)'는 of 뒤에 오는 명사에 따라 동사의 수를 일치시킴. 위 문장에서는 the majority of those로 복수 명사가 왔기 때문에 복수 동사(forget)를 사용함.

(2) They often forget those / who helped them / on their way up.
선행사 주격 관계대명사절
그들은 종종 사람들을 잊는다 / 자신을 도와준 / 성공으로 가는 과정에서

(3) If you forget where you came from, / if you neglect those /
간접의문문 선행사
당신이 어디서 왔는지 잊어버린다면 / 당신이 사람들을 소홀히 한다면 /
[who were there for you / when things were tough and slow], /
곁에 있어 준 / 상황이 힘들고 진척이 없을 때 / [ ]: 주격 관계대명사절
then your success is valueless. 정답 단서 성공이 가치 있으려면, 상황이 힘들었을 때 도와준 사람들을 소홀히 해서는 안 된다는 필자의 주장이 드러남.
당신의 성공은 가치가 없다

(4) No one can make it up there / without the help of others.
아무도 성공할 수 없다 / 다른 사람의 도움 없이는

(5) There are parents, friends, advisers, and coaches / that help.
선행사 주격 관계대명사절
부모님, 친구, 조언자, 코치들이 있다 / 도움을 주는

주제문 도와준 사람들에게 감사해야 한다고 함.

(6) You need to be grateful / to all of those / who helped you.
선행사 주격 관계대명사절
당신은 감사할 필요가 있다 / 사람들 모두에게 / 당신을 도와준

(7) Gratitude is the glue / [that keeps you connected to others].
[ ]: 주격 관계대명사절
선행사 5형식V O O.C
감사는 접착제이다 / 당신과 다른 사람들을 연결해 주는

(8) It is the bridge / [that keeps you connected with those /
=gratitude 선행사 [ ]: 주격 관계대명사절 선행사
그것은 다리이다 / 사람들과 당신을 계속해서 연결해 주는 /
who were there for you in the past /
주격 관계대명사절①
당신을 위해 과거에 곁에 있었던 /
and who are likely to be there in the end].
주격 관계대명사절②
그리고 마지막에도 곁에 있을 것 같은

힌트 문장 (8)은 2형식 문장으로, 보어 자리에 있는 the bridge가 선행사가 되어 주격 관계대명사절을 이끎. 이 주격 관계대명사절 안에 전치사 with의 목적어 those를 수식하는 주격 관계대명사절 2개가 and로 병렬을 이루고 있음. 주격 관계대명사절 안의 동사는 선행사와 수 일치를 하는데, 선행사 the bridge는 단수 명사이므로 단수 동사 keeps를, 선행사 those는 복수 명사이므로 복수 동사 were, are을 취함.

(9) [Relationships / and the way you treat others] /
[ ]: S
관계 / 그리고 당신이 다른 사람들을 대하는 방식이 /
determine your real success.
V
당신의 진정한 성공을 결정한다

[전문 해석]

(1)개인의 성취와 인정을 향한 질주 속에서, 성공한 사람들의 대다수는 그들의 초라했던 시작을 잊는다. (2)그들은 종종 성공으로 가는 과정에서 자신을 도와준 사람들을 잊는다. (3)당신이 어디서 왔는지 잊어버리고, 상황이 힘들고 진척이 없을 때 곁에 있어 준 사람들을 소홀히 한다면, 당신의 성공은 가치가 없다. (4)아무도 다른 사람의 도움 없이는 성공할 수 없다. (5)도움을 주는 부모님, 친구, 조언자, 코치들이 있다. (6)당신은 당신을 도와준 사람들 모두에게 감사할 필요가 있다. (7)감사는 당신과 다른 사람들을 연결해 주는 접착제이다. (8)그것은 당신을 위해 과거에 곁에 있었고 마지막에도 곁에 있을 것 같은 사람들과 당신을 계속해서 연결해 주는 다리이다. (9)관계와 당신이 다른 사람들을 대하는 방식이 당신의 진정한 성공을 결정한다.

[정답 확인]

다음 글에서 필자가 주장하는 바로 가장 적절한 것은?

① 원만한 인간관계를 위하여 사고의 유연성(flexibility)을 길러야 한다.
✔ 성공에 도움을 준 사람들에게 감사하는(grateful) 마음을 가져야 한다. 문장(6)
③ 자신의 분야에서 성공하기 위해서는 경험의 폭을 넓혀야(broaden) 한다.
④ 원하는 직업을 갖기 위해서는 다른 사람의 조언(advice)을 경청해야 한다.
⑤ 타인의 시선을 의식하지 않고 부단히 새로운 일에 도전해야 한다.

[중요 어휘]

□ **rush**	명사 질주, 혼잡 / 동사 급히 움직이다, 재촉하다, 돌진하다
□ **individual**	형용사 개인의, 각각의 / 명사 개인
□ **achievement**	명사 성취
□ **recognition**	명사 인정, 인식
□ **make it**	성공하다, 시간 맞춰 가다
□ **humble**	형용사 초라한, 시시한, 겸손한
□ **be on one's way up**	성공으로 가는 과정에 있다, 성공 가도를 달리다

□ neglect	동사 소홀히 하다, 방치하다
□ grateful	형용사 감사하는, 고마워하는
□ gratitude	명사 감사, 고마움
□ be likely to V	~할 것 같다, ~할 가능성이 높다
□ determine	동사 결정하다

핵심 정보를 이해(understand)하는 것뿐만 아니라, 필요할 때 정보를 즉각적으로 기억해내어(recall) 활용할(use) 수 있는 것이 중요하다고 설명하고 있음. 이는 주제문인 문장 (8)에서도 잘 드러남.

04 2019년 11월 20번 (정답률 90%) 정답 ②

[지문 끊어 읽기] 배운 것을 활용하는 방법

(1) Over the years, / memory has been given a bad name.
여러 해 동안 / 기억은 오명을 받아왔다

힌트 'give I·O(~에게) D·O(~을)'의 수동태 문장으로, 4형식 동사는 목적어가 2개이기 때문에 수동태로 바뀌어도 동사 다음에 여전히 목적어가 하나 남음.

(2) It has been associated / with rote learning /
그것은 결부되어 왔다 / 기계적 암기 학습과 /
and cramming information / into your brain.
그리고 정보를 억지로 쑤셔 넣는 것과 / 당신의 뇌에

(3) Educators have said / that understanding is the key to learning, /
교육자들은 말해왔다 / 이해가 학습의 핵심이라고 /
but how can you understand something /
하지만 어떻게 당신이 어떤 것을 이해할 수 있겠는가 /
if you can't remember it?
당신이 그것을 기억해 내지 못한다면

(4) We have all had this experience: /
현재완료시제(have+p.p.)
우리는 모두 이러한 경험을 해본 적이 있다 /
we recognize and understand information /
우리는 정보를 인식하고 이해한다 /
but can't recall it / when we need it.
하지만 그것을 기억해 내지 못한다 / 우리가 그것을 필요로 할 때

(5) For example, / how many jokes do you know?
예를 들어 / 당신은 얼마나 많은 농담을 알고 있는가

(6) You've probably heard thousands, / but you can only recall /
당신은 아마도 수천 개를 들어왔을 것이다 / 하지만 당신은 겨우 기억해 낼 수 있다 /
about four or five / right now.
약 네다섯 개만을 / 지금 당장

(7) There is a big difference / between /
큰 차이가 있다 / ~ 사이에는 /
remembering your four jokes /
당신의 농담 네 개를 기억하는 것 /
and recognizing or understanding thousands. 정답 단서
그리고 수천 개를 인식하거나 이해하는 것

(8) Understanding doesn't create use: /
이해는 활용을 만들어 내지 않는다 /
only when you can instantly recall /
조동사 동사원형①
오직 당신이 즉각적으로 기억해 낼 수 있을 때에만 /
what you understand, / and practice /
동사원형②
당신이 이해한 것을 / 그리고 행할 수 있을 때에만 /
using your remembered understanding, /
당신의 기억된 이해를 활용하는 것을 /
do you achieve mastery. 주제문
당신은 경지에 이른다

힌트 practice는 목적어로 동명사를 취하는 3형식 동사이기 때문에 using이 왔음. 여기서 your remembered understanding은 using의 목적어임.

힌트 'mean to V(~하는 것을 의도하다)'와 'mean V-ing(~하는 것을 의미하다)'를 구분해야 함.

(9) Memory means storing / what you have learned; /
기억은 저장하는 것을 의미한다 / 당신이 배운 것을 /
otherwise, / why would we bother learning / in the first place?
그렇지 않다면 / 우리는 왜 배우려고 애를 쓰는가 / 애초에

힌트 bother은 목적어로 동명사와 to부정사를 모두 취할 수 있고, '~하려고 애를 쓰다'라는 의미임.

[중요 구문]

(8) ~ [only when you can instantly recall ~, and practice ~],
only+when부사절
do you achieve mastery.
도치(do동사+S+동사원형)

힌트 부정어가 문두로 가면 주어와 동사가 도치되듯이, only가 문두로 가면 '주절'의 주어와 동사가 도치됨. when이 이끄는 절은 only와 한 덩어리인 부사절이므로 주어와 동사의 도치가 부사절 when이 아니라 주절 'do you achieve mastery'에서 일어난 것임.

[전문 해석]

(1)여러 해 동안, 기억은 오명을 받아왔다. (2)그것은 기계적 암기 학습, 그리고 당신의 뇌에 정보를 억지로 쑤셔 넣는 것과 결부되어 왔다. (3)교육자들은 이해가 학습의 핵심이라고 말해왔지만, 당신이 어떤 것을 기억해 내지 못한다면 어떻게 (당신이) 그것을 이해할 수 있겠는가? (4)우리는 모두 이러한 경험을 해본 적이 있다. 우리는 정보를 인식하고 이해하지만, 우리가 그것을 필요로 할 때 그것을 기억해 내지 못한다. (5)예를 들어, 당신은 얼마나 많은 농담을 알고 있는가? (6)당신은 아마도 수천 개를 들어왔을 것이지만, 지금 당장 겨우 약 네다섯 개만을 기억해 낼 수 있다. (7)당신의 농담 네 개를 기억하는 것과 (농담) 수천 개를 인식하거나 이해하는 것 사이에는 큰 차이가 있다. (8)이해는 활용을 만들어 내지 않는다. 오직 당신이 이해한 것을 즉각적으로 기억해 낼 수 있고, 당신의 기억된 이해를 활용하는 것을 행할 수 있을 때에만, 당신은 경지에 이른다. (9)기억은 당신이 배운 것을 저장하는 것을 의미하는데, 그렇지 않다면, 애초에 우리는 왜 배우려고 애를 쓰는가?

[정답 확인]

다음 글에서 필자가 주장하는 바로 가장 적절한 것은?

① 창의력 신장을 학습(learning) 활동의 목표로 삼아야 한다.
② 배운 것을 활용하기(use) 위해서는 내용을 기억해야(recall) 한다. 문장(8)
③ 기억력 저하를 예방하기 위해 자신의 일상을 기록해야(record) 한다.
④ 자연스러운 분위기를 만들 수 있는 농담(joke)을 알고 있어야 한다.
⑤ 학습 의욕을 유지하기 위해서는 실천 가능한 계획(plan)을 세워야 한다.

[중요 어휘]

□ give A a bad name	A에게 오명을 씌우다
□ associate	동사 결부시키다, 연관시키다
□ rote	명사 (내용을 이해하지 못하는) 기계적 암기
□ cram	동사 억지로 쑤셔 넣다, 벼락치기하다
□ recall	동사 기억해 내다, 상기하다
□ instantly	부사 즉각적으로, 바로
□ achieve	동사 (목표 등에) 이르다, 달성하다
□ mastery	명사 경지, 숙달

05 2022년 9월 20번 (정답률 90%) 정답 ①

[지문 끊어 읽기] 나를 위한 시간의 중요성

(1) We usually take time out / only when we really need to switch off, /
우리는 보통 쉰다 / 우리가 정말로 스위치를 꺼야 할 때만 /
and when this happens /
그리고 이러한 상황이 발생할 때 /
we are often overtired, sick, and in need of recuperation.
우리는 종종 지나치게 피곤하거나 아프거나 회복을 필요로 한다

(2) Me time is complicated / 정답 단서 Me time(나를 위한 시간)이 지문에 계속 반복되므로 이 글의 키워드임을 알 수 있음.
나를 위한 시간은 복잡해진다 /
by negative associations / with escapism, guilt, and regret /
부정적인 연상에 의해 / 현실 도피, 죄책감, 후회와의 /
as well as overwhelm, stress, and fatigue.
B as well as A: A뿐만 아니라 B도
압도하다, 스트레스, 피로감뿐만 아니라

(3) All these negative connotations mean /
이러한 모든 부정적인 함축은 의미한다 /
[we tend to steer clear of it]. [ ]: mean의 목적어절
=me time
우리가 그것을 피하려는 경향이 있음을

(4) Well, I am about to change /
자, 나는 이제 바꾸려고 한다 / 병렬①
your perception of the importance of me time, /
나를 위한 시간의 중요성에 관한 당신의 인식을 /
4형식V
to persuade you / [that you should view it /
병렬② I·O =me time
당신을 설득하려고 한다 / 당신이 그것을 간주해야 한다고 /
as vital for your health and wellbeing]. 주제문 나를 위한 시간을 부정적으로 인식하는 것이 아니라 건강과 행복에 필수적인 것으로 인식을 바꿔야 한다고 주장함.
당신의 건강과 행복에 필수적인 것으로 [ ]: D·O(목적어절)

=me time
(5) Take this as permission / to set aside some time for yourself!
이것을 허락으로 삼아라 / 당신 자신을 위하여 일부 시간을 따로 떼어 두도록 하는

(6) Our need for time / in which to do what we choose /
S 형용사적 용법
시간에 대한 우리의 필요는 / 우리가 선택한 것을 할 수 있는 /
is increasingly urgent /
V
점점 긴급해지고 있다 /
in an overconnected, overwhelmed, and overstimulated world.
지나치게 연결되고 압도적이고 지나치게 자극적인 세상에서

힌트 선행사 'time'을 '전치사+관계대명사'인 'in which'가 꾸며주는 형태임. 밑줄 친 부분은 'time to do what we choose in'으로도 바꿀 수 있음.

[전문 해석]

(1)우리는 보통 정말로 스위치를 꺼야 할 때만 쉬고, 이러한 상황이 발생할 때 우리는 종종 지나치게 피곤하거나 아프거나 회복을 필요로 한다. (2)나를 위한 시간은 '압도하다, 스트레스, 피로감'뿐만 아니라 '현실 도피, 죄책감, 후회'와의 부정적인 연상에 의해 복잡해진다. (3)이러한 모든 부정적인 함축은 우리가 나를 위한 시간을 피하려는 경향이 있음을 의미한다. (4)자, 나는 이제 나를 위한 시간의 중요성에 관한 당신의 인식을 바꾸고, 당신이 그것을 당신의 건강과 행복에 필수적인 것으로 간주해야 한다고 설득하려고 한다. (5)이것을 당신 자신을 위하여 일부 시간을 따로 떼어 두도록 하는 허락으로 삼아라! (6)우리가 선택한 것을 할 수 있는 시간에 대한 필요는 지나치게 연결되고 압도적이고 지나치게 자극적인 세상에서 점점 긴급해지고 있다.

[정답 확인]

다음 글에서 필자가 주장하는 바로 가장 적절한 것은?

① 나를 위한 시간의 중요성(importance)을 인식해야(perceive) 한다. 문장(4)
② 자신의 잘못을 성찰하는 자세를 가져야 한다.
③ 어려운 일이라고 해서 처음부터 회피해서는(steer clear of) 안 된다.
④ 사회의 건강과 행복(wellbeing)을 위하여 타인과 연대해야 한다.
⑤ 급변하는 사회에서 가치 판단을 신속하게 할 수 있어야 한다.

[중요 어휘]

□ take time out	쉬다
□ recuperation	명사 회복
□ complicate	동사 복잡하게 만들다
□ association	명사 연상, 연계, 협회
□ escapism	명사 현실 도피
□ overwhelm	동사 압도하다
□ fatigue	명사 피로감
□ connotation	명사 함축
□ steer clear of	~을 피하다
□ be about to V	이제[막] ~하려고 하다
□ perception	명사 인식, 통찰력
□ view A as B	A를 B로 간주하다
□ vital	형용사 필수적인, 활력이 넘치는
□ permission	명사 허락
□ set aside	따로 떼어 두다, 곁에 두다, 확보하다
□ urgent	형용사 긴급한, 다급해하는
□ overstimulate	동사 지나치게 자극하다

06 2023년 6월 20번 (정답률 90%) 정답 ②

[지문 끊어 읽기] 새로운 기술의 잠재적 영향들에 대한 충분한 고려

(1) The introduction of new technologies /
새로운 기술의 도입은 /
clearly has both positive and negative impacts /
분명히 긍정적인 영향과 부정적인 영향 모두를 가진다 /
for sustainable development. 정답단서 새로운 기술의 도입은 지속 가능한 발전에 긍정적 영향과 부정적 영향 모두를 가질 수 있음.
지속 가능한 발전에

중요 문장 (2)의 them은 문장 (1)의 both positive and negative impacts를 의미함. 즉, 문장 (2)는 기술 자원을 적절하게 관리하려면 새로운 기술의 도입이 지속 가능한 발전에 미치는 긍정적 영향과 부정적 영향 모두를 충분히 고려할 필요가 있다는 의미임.

(2) Good management of technological resources /
기술 자원의 적절한 관리는 /
needs to take them fully into account. 정답단서 기술 자원을 적절하게 관리하려면 기술이 가지는 긍정적 영향과 부정적 영향 모두를 충분히 고려해야 함.
그것들을 충분히 고려하는 것을 필요로 한다

(3) Technological developments / 중요 원자력 기술이 인간의 건강에 위험할 수 있으나 기술적 발전을 수반할 수 있는 것처럼, 기술은 긍정적인 측면과 부정적인 측면 모두를 가지고 있음.
기술적 발전들은 / S
in sectors such as nuclear energy and agriculture /
원자력과 농업과 같은 분야에서의 /
provide examples /
V O
사례들을 제공한다 /
of [how not only environmental benefits /
어떻게 환경적 이익들뿐만 아니라 /
but also risks to the environment or human health /
환경 또는 인간의 건강에 대한 위험들도 /
can accompany technological advances]. [ ]: 간접의문문
기술적 발전을 수반할 수 있는지

힌트 how가 이끄는 긴 간접의문문이 명사절로서 전치사 of의 목적어 역할을 함. 이때 간접의문문의 어순은 '의문사(how)+S+V'이며, 주어는 'not only A but also B (A뿐만 아니라 B도)'의 구조를 취함.

(4) New technologies / have profound social impacts / as well.
새로운 기술들은 / 심오한 사회적인 영향을 가지고 있다 / 또한

(5) Since the industrial revolution, / 중요 문장 (5)는 문장 (4)에서 언급한 '기술이 사회에까지 심오한 영향력을 가지는' 구체적인 사례임.
~이래로
산업 혁명 이래로 /
technological advances have changed /
기술적 발전들은 변화시켰다 / 현재완료(계속)
the nature of skills needed in workplaces, /
과거분사구
직장에서 요구되는 기술의 본질을 /
=other (types of) jobs
creating certain types of jobs / and destroying others, /
특정 종류의 일자리들을 만들어 냈다 / 그리고 다른 것들은 없애 버렸다 /
with impacts on employment patterns.
고용 패턴에 영향을 주면서

힌트 앞 문장의 내용에 이어지는 결과를 나타내는 분사구문으로, 주절의 주어인 technological advances가 동작의 주체이므로 각각 현재분사 creating과 destroying이 사용되었음.

(6) New technologies need to be assessed /
새로운 기술들은 평가될 필요가 있다 /
for their full potential impacts, /
그것들의 모든 잠재적 영향들에 대해 /
both positive and negative. 주제문 새로운 기술은 긍정적인 것이든 부정적인 것이든 그것이 가지는 모든 잠재적인 영향들에 대해 평가되어야 함.
긍정적이고 부정적인

중요 앞에 나온 '그것들의 모든 잠재적 영향들(their full potential impacts)'에 대한 부연 설명으로, 문장 (6)은 긍정적 영향과 부정적 영향을 모두 고려하여 새로운 기술들을 평가할 필요가 있다는 의미임.

[전문 해석]

(1)새로운 기술의 도입은 분명히 지속 가능한 발전에 긍정적인 영향과 부정적인 영향 모두를 가진다. (2)기술 자원의 적절한 관리는 그것들을 충분히 고려하는 것을 필요로 한다. (3)원자력과 농업과 같은 분야에서의 기술적 발전들은 어떻게 환경적 이익들뿐만 아니라 환경 또는 인간의 건강에 대한 위험들도 기술적 발전을 수반할 수 있는지에 대한 사례들을 제공한다. (4)새로운 기술들은 또한 심오한 사회적인 영향을 가지고 있다. (5)산업 혁명 이래로, 기술적 발전들은 직장에서 요구되는 기술의 본질을 변화시켜, 고용 패턴에 영향을 주면서 특정 종류의 일자리들을 만들어 내고 다른 것들은 없애 버렸다. (6)새로운 기술들은 긍정적이고 부정적인, 그것들의 모든 잠재적 영향들에 대해 평가될 필요가 있다.

[정답 확인]

다음 글에서 필자가 주장하는 바로 가장 적절한 것은?

① 기술 혁신을 저해하는 과도한 법률적 규제(legal regulations)를 완화해야 한다.
② 기술의 도입으로 인한 잠재적인 영향들(potential impacts)을 충분히 고려해야(take fully into account) 한다. 문장(6)
③ 혁신적 농업 기술(innovative agricultural technologies)을 적용할 때는 환경적인(environmental) 측면을 검토해야 한다.
④ 기술 진보가 가져온 일자리 위협(a job threat)에 대한 대비책을 마련해야 한다.
⑤ 기술 발전을 위해서는 혁신적 사고(innovative thinking)와 창의성이 뒷받침되어야 한다.

[중요 어휘]

□ introduction	명사 도입, 소개
□ have an impact	영향을 가지다[미치다]
□ sustainable	형용사 (환경 파괴 없이) 지속 가능한
□ management	명사 관리, 경영
□ resource	명사 자원, 재원
□ take A into account	A를 고려하다
□ sector	명사 분야, 부문
□ nuclear energy	명사 원자력, 핵에너지

문제편 p.031

□ agriculture	명사 농업
□ not only A but also B	A뿐만 아니라 B도
□ benefit	명사 이익, 이점 / 동사 혜택을 주다, 이익을 보다
□ risk	명사 위험, 위험 요인 / 동사 ~를 감수하다, 무릅쓰다
□ accompany	동사 수반하다, 동반하다
□ advance	명사 발전, 진보
□ profound	형용사 심오한, 깊은
□ as well	또한, 역시
□ revolution	명사 혁명, 변혁, 회전, 공전
□ nature	명사 본질, 본성
□ destroy	동사 없애다, 파괴하다
□ assess	동사 평가하다
□ potential	형용사 잠재적인 / 명사 잠재력

07 2020년 11월 20번 (정답률 85%) 정답 ⑤

[지문 끊어 읽기] 설득하기에 좋은 질문

(1) When trying to convince someone / to change their mind, /
누군가에게 설득하려고 할 때 / 그들의 마음을 바꾸도록 /
most people try to lay out a logical argument, /
대부분의 사람들은 논리적 주장을 펼치려고 한다 /
or make a passionate plea / as to why their view is right /
~에 대해
또는 열정적인 항변을 한다 / 왜 자신의 관점이 옳은지에 대해 /
and the other person's opinion is wrong.
그리고 왜 다른 사람의 의견이 틀린지에 대해

(2) But / when you think about it, / you'll realize /
하지만 / 당신이 그것에 대해 생각해 보면 / 당신은 깨달을 것이다 /
that this doesn't often work.
이것이 종종 효과가 없다는 것을

(3) As soon as someone figures out / that you are on a mission /
누군가가 알아차리자마자 / 당신이 임무를 띠고 있다는 것을 /
to change their mind, / the metaphorical shutters go down.
자신의 마음을 바꾸려는 / 은유적인 셔터는 내려간다

(4) You'll have better luck /
당신은 더 좋은 운이 따를 것이다 /
if you ask well-chosen, open-ended questions /
만약 당신이 잘 선택된, 다양한 대답이 가능한 질문을 한다면 /
that let someone challenge their own assumptions. 정답단서
사역V O O·C(동사원형)
누군가가 자기 자신의 가정을 의심하도록 하는

(5) We tend to approve of an idea / if we thought of it first /
우리는 어떤 견해를 인정하려는 경향이 있다 / 우리가 그것을 먼저 생각해 냈을 때 /
— or at least, / if we *think* / we thought of it first.
혹은 최소한 / 우리가 '생각'할 때 / 우리가 그것을 먼저 생각해 냈다고

힌트 if는 '~라면'이라는 조건절이지만, 해석할 때에는 '~할 때, ~할 경우' 등으로 자연스러운 해석이 가능함.

(6) Therefore, /
그러므로 /
encouraging someone / to question their own worldview /
S(비교대상①)
누군가에게 장려하는 것은 / 자기 자신의 세계관에 의문을 갖도록 /
will often yield better results /
종종 더 나은 결과를 가져올 것이다 /
than trying to force them / into accepting your opinion as fact.
비교대상②
그들에게 강요하려고 하는 것보다 / 당신의 의견을 사실로 받아들이도록

힌트 동명사구인 주어의 비교대상이 than 이후 병렬구조로 동명사구가 왔음.

(7) Ask someone well-chosen questions /
누군가에게 잘 선택된 질문을 하라 /
to look at their own views / from another angle, / 주제문
자기 자신의 관점을 바라보도록 / 다른 각도에서 /
and this might trigger fresh insights.
그러면 이것은 새로운 통찰력을 유발할 것이다

[전문 해석]

(1)누군가에게 (그들의) 마음을 바꾸도록 설득하려고 할 때, 대부분의 사람들은 논리적 주장을 펼치려고 하거나 왜 자신의 관점이 옳고 다른 사람의 의견이 틀린지에 대해 열정적인 항변을 한다. (2)하지만 당신이 그것에 대해 생각해 보면, 당신은 이것이 종종 효과가 없다는 것을 깨달을 것이다. (3)누군가가 당신이 자신의 마음을 바꾸려는 임무를 띠고 있다는 것을 알아차리자마자, 은유적인 (마음의) 셔터는 내려간다. (4)만약 당신이 누군가가 자기 자신의 가정(의 정당성)을 의심하도록 하는 잘 선택된, 다양한 대답이 가능한 질문을 한다면 당신은 더 좋은 운이 따를 것이다. (5)우리는 우리가 어떤 견해를 먼저 생각해 냈을 때, 혹은 최소한 우리가 그것을 먼저 생각해 냈다고 '생각'할 때, 그것을 인정하려는 경향이 있다. (6)그러므로 누군가에게 자기 자신의 세계관에 의문을 갖도록 장려하는 것은 당신의 의견을 사실로 받아들이도록 그들에게 강요하려고 하는 것보다 종종 더 나은 결과를 가져올 것이다. (7)누군가에게 자기 자신의 관점을 다른 각도에서 바라보도록 잘 선택된 질문을 하라. 그러면 이것은 새로운 통찰력을 유발할 것이다.

[정답 확인]

다음 글에서 필자가 주장하는 바로 가장 적절한 것은?

① 타인의 신뢰를 얻기 위해서는 일관된(consistent) 행동을 보여 주어라.
② 협상을 잘하기 위해 질문에 담긴 상대방의 의도(intention)를 파악하라.
③ 논쟁(argument)을 잘하려면 자신의 가치관에서 벗어나려는 시도를 하라.
④ 원만한 대인 관계를 유지하려면(maintain) 상대방을 배려하는 태도를 갖춰라.
⑤ 설득하고자 할 때 상대방이 스스로 관점을 돌아보게 하는 질문(question)을 하라. 문장(7)

[중요 어휘]

□ convince	동사 설득하다, 납득시키다
□ lay out	~을 펼치다[제시하다]
□ logical	형용사 논리적인, 타당한
□ plea	명사 항변, 애원, 간청
□ mission	명사 임무, 사명
□ metaphorical	형용사 은유적인, 비유적인
□ open-ended	형용사 다양한 대답이 가능한, 열린 결말의
□ question	명사 질문, 의문 / 동사 의문을 갖다
□ challenge	동사 (진실·정당성 등을) 의심하다, 이의를 제기하다, 도전하다
□ assumption	명사 가정, 추정
□ tend to V	~하려는 경향이 있다
□ approve of	~을 인정하다[승인하다]
□ yield	동사 (결과·이익을) 가져오다, 양보하다
□ trigger	동사 유발하다, 작동시키다
□ insight	명사 통찰력, 이해

08 2021년 11월 20번 (정답률 85%) 정답 ③

[지문 끊어 읽기] 상품의 희소성

(1) In 2003, / British Airways made an announcement /
2003년에 / 영국 항공은 발표했다 /
that they would no longer be able to operate /
동격의 that(=an announcement)
자신들이 더 이상 운항할 수 없을 것이라고 /
the London to New York Concorde flight / twice a day /
런던에서 뉴욕까지 가는 콩코드 항공편을 / 하루에 두 번 /
because it was starting to prove / uneconomical.
=the London~a day 2형식V S·C
왜냐하면 그것이 드러나기 시작하고 있었기 때문이었다 / 경제성이 없는 것으로

(2) Well, / the sales for the flight on this route / increased /
S V
그런데 / 이 노선의 항공편 판매가 / 증가했다 /
the very next day.
바로 다음 날

힌트 부사 'very'는 최상급 또는 'best, last, next, first, same'을 강조할 때 사용되기도 하며 이때에는 '바로, 정말로'라는 뜻임.

(3) There was nothing /
아무것도 없었다 / 선행사

[that changed about the route or the service /
노선이나 서비스에 있어서 달라진 것은 /
offered by the airlines]. [ ]: 주격 관계대명사절
주격 관계대명사+be동사 생략
항공사에 의해 제공되는

힌트 'American Airlines(아메리칸 항공), Delta Air Lines(델타 항공)'와 같이 항공사명은 일반적으로 'airlines'라는 복수형을 사용하고 단수 취급함. 따라서 'the airlines'는 앞서 언급된 'British Airways'를 가리키는 것으로 볼 수 있음.

(4) Merely because it became a scarce resource, /
단지 그것이 부족한 자원이 되었기 때문에 /
the demand for it increased. 정답 단서 부족한(희소한) 자원이 되었다는 사실만으로 수요가 증가함.
그것에 대한 수요가 증가했다

(5) If you are interested in persuading people, /
만약에 여러분이 사람들을 설득하는 데에 관심이 있다면 /
then the principle of scarcity can be effectively used. 정답 단서 희소성의 원리를 사용하면 사람들을 효과적으로 설득할 수 있음.
희소성의 원리가 효과적으로 사용될 수 있다

(6) If you are a salesperson /
만약 여러분이 판매원이라면 /
trying to increase the sales of a certain product, /
특정 상품의 판매를 증가시키려 노력하는 /
then you must not merely point out the benefits /
not merely A but also B: A뿐만 아니라 B 또한 / 선행사
여러분은 단지 혜택을 강조할 뿐만이 아니라 /
the customer can derive from the said product, /
목적격 관계대명사 생략
고객이 언급된 상품으로부터 얻을 수 있는 /
but also point out its uniqueness / 정답 단서 특정 상품의 판매를 증가시키려면 그것의 유일함(희소성)을 강조해야 함.
O①
그것의 유일함을 또한 강조해야만 한다 /
and [what they will miss out on /
그리고 그들이 무엇을 놓치게 될 것인지를 /
if they don't purchase the product soon]. [ ]: O②(의문사 what이 이끄는 명사절)
만약에 그들이 그 상품을 빨리 구매하지 않는다면

(7) In selling, / you should keep in mind /
판매에 있어 / 여러분은 명심해야 한다 /
that the more limited something is, /
명사절 접속사
무언가가 더 한정적일수록 /
the more desirable it becomes. 주제문 판매에 있어 무언가가 더 한정적일수록(희소성이 높을수록) 그것은 더 가치있게 된다는 것을 강조하고 있음.
그것이 더 가치 있게 된다는 것을

힌트 'the 비교급 S V, the 비교급 S V' 구문으로 '더 ~할수록 더 …하다'라는 뜻임.

[전문 해석]

(1)2003년에 영국 항공은 자신들이 더 이상 런던에서 뉴욕까지 가는 콩코드 항공편을 하루에 두 번 운항할 수 없을 것이라고 발표했는데, 왜냐하면 그것이 경제성이 없는 것으로 드러나기 시작하고 있었기 때문이었다. (2)그런데 바로 다음 날 이 노선의 항공편 판매가 증가했다. (3)노선이나 항공사에 의해 제공되는 서비스에 있어서 달라진 것은 아무것도 없었다. (4)단지 그것이 부족한 자원이 되었기 때문에 그것에 대한 수요가 증가했다. (5)만약에 여러분이 사람들을 설득하는 데에 관심이 있다면, 희소성의 원리가 효과적으로 사용될 수 있다. (6)만약 여러분이 특정 상품의 판매를 증가시키려 노력하는 판매원이라면, 여러분은 단지 고객이 언급된 상품으로부터 얻을 수 있는 혜택을 강조할 뿐만이 아니라 그것의 유일함과 만약에 그들이 그 상품을 빨리 구매하지 않는다면 그들이 무엇을 놓치게 될 것인지를 또한 강조해야만 한다. (7)판매에 있어 여러분은 무언가가 더 한정적일수록 그것이 더 가치 있게 된다는 것을 명심해야 한다.

[정답 확인]

다음 글에서 필자가 주장하는 바로 가장 적절한 것은?

① 상품 판매 시 실현 가능한 판매 목표를 설정해야(set a goal) 한다.
② 판매를 촉진하기(promote) 위해서는 가격 경쟁력을 갖추어야 한다.
③ 효과적인 판매를 위해서는 상품의 희소성(scarcity)을 강조해야(point out) 한다. 문장(7)
④ 고객의 신뢰를 얻기 위해서는 일관된 태도를 유지해야(maintain) 한다.
⑤ 고객의 특성에 맞춰 다양한 판매 전략(strategy)을 수립하고 적용해야 한다.

[중요 어휘]

☐ make an announcement	발표하다, 공표하다
☐ operate	동사 운항하다, 작동하다
☐ flight	명사 항공편, 비행
☐ uneconomical	형용사 경제성이 없는, 비경제적인
☐ sale	명사 판매
☐ route	명사 노선, 길
☐ scarcity	명사 희소성, 부족, 결핍
☐ point out	강조하다, 지적하다, 가리키다
☐ derive A from B	B로부터 A를 얻다
☐ uniqueness	명사 유일함, 고유성
☐ miss out on	~를 놓치게 되다[놓치다]
☐ keep in mind	명심하다
☐ limited	형용사 한정적인, 제한된
☐ desirable	형용사 가치 있는, 바람직한

09 2023년 9월 20번 (정답률 85%) 정답 ⑤

[지문 끊어 읽기] 관리자가 직원의 행동을 바꾸는 방식

(1) Managers frequently try to play psychologist, / to "figure out" /
관리자들은 심리학자 역할을 하려고 자주 노력한다 / '파악하기' 위해 / 부사적 용법(목적)
why an employee has acted in a certain way.
직원이 왜 특정한 방식으로 행동했는지를

(2) [Empathizing with employees /
[ ]: S
직원들과 공감하는 것은 /
in order to understand their point of view] / can be very helpful.
그들의 관점을 이해하기 위해 / 매우 도움이 될 수 있다

(3) However, / when dealing with a problem area, in particular, /
하지만 / 특히 문제 영역을 다룰 때 /
=a problem area
remember / [that it is not the person who is bad, /
not A but B: A가 아니라 B
기억하라 / 그것은 잘하지 못하는 사람이 아니라 /
but the actions exhibited on the job]. [ ]: 목적어절(remember의 목적어)
과거분사구
근무 중에 보여지는 행동이라는 것을

(4) Avoid making suggestions to employees /
직원들에게 제안하는 것을 피하라 /
about personal traits they should change; / instead /
선행사 목적격 관계대명사절
그들이 바꿔야 할 인격적 특성에 대해 / 대신에 /
suggest more acceptable ways of performing. 주제문 직원의 행동을 바꿀 방법을 직원에게 제시해야 함.
더 수용 가능한 수행 방법을 제안하라

(5) For example, / instead of focusing on a person's "unreliability," /
예를 들어 / 어떤 사람의 '신뢰할 수 없음'에 초점을 맞추는 대신 /
a manager might focus on the fact /
관리자는 사실에 초점을 맞출 수도 있을 것이다 / =
[that the employee "has been late to work seven times this month."]
그 직원이 '이번 달에 회사에 일곱 번 지각했다'는

(6) It is difficult / for employees to change who they are; /
형식상의 주어① 의미상의 주어① 내용상의 주어①
어렵다 / 직원들은 자신이 어떤 사람인지를 바꾸기는 /
it is usually much easier / for them to change how they act. 정답 단서 사람 자체를 바꾸는 것보다 행동을 바꾸는 것이 더 쉬움.
형식상의 주어② 의미상의 주어② 내용상의 주어②
일반적으로 훨씬 더 쉽다 / 그들이 자신이 행동하는 방식을 바꾸기는

✶중요 문장 (5)에서 든 예시처럼, 사람 자체의 됨됨이를 지적하는 것보다 그 사람이 바꾸었으면 하는 행동과 그것을 바꿀 방법을 제시하는 것이 좋다고 했음. 그러므로 행동 방식을 제안하는 것에 관한 내용을 담은 선택지가 정답이 됨.

[전문 해석]

(1)관리자들은 직원이 왜 특정한 방식으로 행동했는지를 '파악하기' 위해 심리학자 역할을 하려고 자주 노력한다. (2)그들의 관점을 이해하기 위해 직원들과 공감하는 것은 매우 도움이 될 수 있다. (3)하지만 특히 문제 영역을 다룰 때, 그것은 잘하지 못하는 사람이 아니라 근무 중에 보여지는 행동이라는 것을 기억하라. (4)직원들에게 그들이 바꿔야 할 인격적 특성에 대해 제안하는 것을 피하고, 대신에 더 수용 가능한 수행 방법을 제안하라. (5)예를 들어, 관리자는 어떤 사람의 '신뢰할 수 없음'에 초점을 맞추는 대신, 그 직원이 '이번 달에 회사에 일곱 번 지각했다'는 사실에 초점을 맞출 수도 있을 것이다. (6)직원들은 자신이 어떤 사람인지를 바꾸기는 어렵지만, 일반적으로 자신이 행동하는 방식을 바꾸기는 훨씬 더 쉽다.

[정답 확인]

다음 글에서 필자가 주장하는 바로 가장 적절한 것은?

① 직원의 개인적 성향(personal disposition)을 고려하여 업무를 배정하라.
② 업무 효율성 향상을 위해 직원의 자율성(autonomy)을 존중하라.

③ 조직의 안정을 위해 직원의 심리 상태(mental state)를 수시로 확인하라.
④ 직원의 업무상 고충을 이해하기 위해 직원과 적극적으로 소통하라(communicate).
✔ 문제를 보이는 직원에게 인격적 특성(personal trait)보다는 행동 방식에 대해 제안하라. 문장(4)

[중요 어휘]

☐ manager	명사 관리자, 경영자
☐ psychologist	명사 심리학자
☐ empathize	동사 공감하다, 감정 이입하다
☐ point of view	명사 관점, 견해
☐ exhibit	동사 보이다, 나타내다, 전시하다
☐ trait	명사 (성격상의) 특성, 특색
☐ unreliability	명사 신뢰할 수 없음

10 2023년 3월 20번 (정답률 80%)

정답 ⑤

[지문 끊어 읽기] 부정적 상황에 대한 수용적인 태도

(1) The more people have to do unwanted things /
the 비교급
더 많은 사람들이 원치 않는 일을 해야 할수록 /
the more chances are / that they create unpleasant environment /
the 비교급: 더 ~할수록, 더 …하다
가능성이 더 크다 / 그들이 불편한 환경을 만들 /
for themselves and others. 정답 단서 원치 않는 일을 할 때 불편한 환경이 만들어질 가능성이 높다는 문제 상황을 제시함.
자신과 다른 사람들에게

(2) If you hate the thing you do / but have to do it nonetheless, /
=the thing
만약 여러분이 하는 일이 싫다면 / 하지만 그럼에도 그것을 해야 한다면 /
you have choice / between hating the thing /
병렬①
여러분은 선택지가 있다 / 그것을 싫어하는 것과 ~ 사이에 /
and accepting that it needs to be done.
병렬② 접속사
그것이 완료될 필요가 있다는 것을 받아들이는 것

힌트 between A and B는 'A와 B 사이에'라는 의미로 A와 B에 전치사 between의 목적어인 동명사 hating과 accepting이 쓰임.

(3) Either way you will do it.
어느 쪽이든 여러분은 그것을 할 것이다

(4) Doing it from place of hatred /
S
증오의 자리에서 그것을 하는 것은 /
will develop hatred towards the self and others around you; /
V
자신과 주변 사람들을 향해 증오를 키울 것이다 /
doing it from the place of acceptance /
S'
수용의 자리에서 그것을 하는 것은 /
will create compassion towards the self /
V'①
자신에 대한 연민을 만들 것이다 /
and allow for opportunities /
V'②(will 생략)
그리고 기회를 가능케 할 것이다 /
to find a more suitable way / of accomplishing the task. 정답 단서
형용사적 용법
더 적합한 방법을 발견할 / 그 과업을 성취할

수용의 자리에서 원치 않는 일을 한다면 그 과업을 성취할 방법을 찾을 기회가 생긴다고 함.

(5) If you decide to accept the fact / that your task has to be done, /
동격의 접속사
만약 여러분이 사실을 받아들이기로 결정한다면 / 여러분의 과업이 완료되어야 한다는 /
start from recognising / that your situation is a gift from life; /
접속사
인식하는 것부터 시작하라 / 여러분의 상황이 삶의 선물이라는 것을 /
this will help you to see it / as a lesson in acceptance. 주제문
이는 여러분이 그것을 바라보게끔 도울 것이다 / 수용의 교훈으로

원치 않는 과업을 하기로 했다면 그 상황을 선물이라고 받아들이라는 필자의 주장을 알 수 있음.

[전문 해석]

(1)더 많은 사람들이 원치 않는 일을 해야 할수록 그들이 자신과 다른 사람들에게 불편한 환경을 만들 가능성이 더 크다. (2)만약 여러분이 하는 일이 싫지만 그럼에도 그것을 해야 한다면, 여러분은 그것을 싫어하는 것과 그것이 완료될 필요가 있다는 것을 받아들이는 것 사이에 선택지가 있다. (3)어느 쪽이든 여러분은 그것을 할 것이다. (4)증오의 자리에서 그것을 하는 것은 자신과 주변 사람들을 향해 증오를 키울 것이다. 반면에 수용의 자리에서 그것을 하는 것은 자신에 대한 연민을 만들고 그 과업을 성취할 더 적합한 방법을 발견할 기회를 가능케 할 것이다. (5)만약 여러분의 과업이 완료되어야 한다는 사실을 받아들이기로 결정한다면, 여러분의 상황이 삶의 선물이라는 것을 인식하는 것부터 시작하라. (그러면) 이는 여러분이 그것을 수용의 교훈으로 바라보게끔 도울 것이다.

[정답 확인]

다음 글에서 필자가 주장하는 바로 가장 적절한 것은?

① 창의력을 기르려면 익숙한 환경에서 벗어나야(get away) 한다.
② 상대방의 무리한 요구는 최대한 분명하게 거절해야(reject) 한다.
③ 주어진 과업을 정확하게 파악한(figure out) 후에 일을 시작해야 한다.
④ 효율적으로 일을 처리하기(handle) 위해 좋아하는 일부터 해야 한다.
✔ 원치 않는 일을 해야만 할 때 수용적인(acceptive) 태도를 갖춰야 한다. 문장(5)

[중요 어휘]

☐ unwanted	형용사 원치 않는, 불필요한
☐ unpleasant	형용사 불편한, 불친절한
☐ nonetheless	부사 그럼에도 (불구하고)
☐ hatred	명사 증오, 혐오
☐ acceptance	명사 수용, 동의, 수락
☐ compassion	명사 연민, 동정
☐ suitable	형용사 적합한, 알맞은
☐ accomplish	동사 성취하다

11 2017년 3월 23번 (정답률 75%)

정답 ②

[지문 끊어 읽기] 아동의 미적 감각을 기르는 방법

(1) Children sometimes see and say things to please adults; /
아이들은 때때로 어른들을 즐겁게 하려고 여러 것들을 보고 말한다 /
teachers must realize this and the power it implies.
교사들은 이 사실과 그것이 암시하는 힘을 이해해야 한다

(2) Teachers who prefer /
선호하는 교사들은 /
that children see beauty as they themselves do /
그들 자신들이 하는 대로 아이들이 미를 보기를 /
are not encouraging a sense of aesthetics in children.
아이들의 미적 감각을 북돋우지 못하고 있다

(3) They are fostering uniformity and obedience.
그들은 획일성과 복종을 조장하고 있는 것이다

(4) Only children who choose and evaluate for themselves /
오직 스스로 선택하고 평가하는 아이들만이 /
can truly develop their own aesthetic taste. 주제문
진정으로 그들 자신의 미적 취향을 발전시킬 수 있다

✶ 중요 문장 (4)에서 Only와 for themselves라는 표현은 문장 (2)의 teachers와 대비하여 미적 감각 발달의 주체가 children임을 강조함.

(5) Just as becoming literate is a basic goal of education, /
글을 읽고 쓸 줄 알게 되는 것이 교육의 기본 목표인 것처럼 /
one of the key goals of all creative early childhood programs /
모든 창의적인 유아기 프로그램들의 핵심 목표 중 하나는 /
is to help young children develop the ability /
어린아이들이 능력을 발전시키도록 돕는 것이다 /
to speak freely about their own attitudes, feelings, and ideas about art.
미술에 관한 자기의 태도, 감정 그리고 아이디어에 관하여 자유롭게 말할 수 있는

(6) Each child has a right /
각각의 아이는 권리를 가지고 있다 /
to a personal choice of beauty, joy, and wonder.
미, 기쁨, 그리고 경이에 대한 개인적인 선택에 대해서

(7) Aesthetic development takes place in secure settings /
미적 발달은 안전한 환경에서 일어난다 /
free of competition and adult judgment.
경쟁과 어른의 판단이 없는

[전문 해석]

(1)아이들은 때때로 어른들을 즐겁게 하려고 여러 것들을 보고 말한다. 교사들은 이 사실과 그것이 암시하는 힘을 이해해야 한다. (2)그들 자신들이 하는(보는) 대로 아이들이 미(美)를 보기를 선호하는 교사들은 아이들의 미적 감각을 북돋우지 못하고 있다. (3)그들은 획일성과 복종을 조장하고 있는 것이다. (4)오직 스스로 선택하고 평가하는 아이들만이 진정으로 그들 자신의 미적 취향을 발전시킬 수 있다. (5)글을 읽고 쓸 줄 알게 되는 것이 교육의 기본 목표인 것처럼, 모든 창의적인 유아기 프로그램들의 핵심 목표 중 하나는 어린아이들이 미술에 관한 자기의 태도, 감정 그리고 아이디어에 관하여 자유롭게 말할 수 있는 능력을 발전시키도록 돕는 것이다. (6)각각의 아이는 미, 기쁨, 그리고 경이에 대한 개인적인 선택에 대해서 권리를 가지고 있다(개인적인 선택권을 가지고 있다). (7)미적 발달은 경쟁과 어른의 판단이 없는(경쟁과 어른의 판단에서 벗어난) 안전한 환경에서 일어난다.

[정답 확인]

다음 글에서 필자가 주장하는 바로 가장 적절한 것은?

① 아동의 정서 발달(emotional development)을 위해 미술 교육 시간을 늘려야 한다.
✔ 아동이 스스로 미적 감각(a sense of aesthetics)을 기를 수 있게 해 주어야 한다. 문장(4)
③ 아동 미술 교육(education)은 다른 과목과 통합적으로 실시해야 한다.
④ 아동의 창의성(creativity)을 평가할 때 미적인 감각도 포함해야 한다.
⑤ 아동 미술 교육(education)은 감상보다 창작에 더 비중을 두어야 한다.

★ **중요** 아이들의 미적 감각 발달에 방해가 되는 요소인 경쟁과 어른(교사)의 판단을 제시하고 미, 기쁨, 경이에 대한 아이들의 권리를 언급하면서까지 필자가 주장하고 싶은 것은 아이들의 '자율성'임. 이것이 정답에서는 '스스로'라는 말로 풀어 제시되었음.

[중요 어휘]

□ **please**	동사 즐겁게 하다
□ **realize**	동사 이해하다, (명확히) 파악하다
□ **imply**	동사 암시하다
□ **prefer**	동사 선호하다
□ **foster**	동사 조장하다
□ **uniformity**	명사 획일성
□ **obedience**	명사 복종
□ **evaluate**	동사 평가하다
□ **for oneself**	스스로
□ **aesthetic**	형용사 미적인
□ **taste**	명사 취향, 맛
□ **literate**	형용사 글을 읽고 쓸 줄 아는
□ **key**	형용사 핵심적인 / 명사 열쇠
□ **attitude**	명사 태도
□ **right**	명사 권리 / 형용사 옳은, 바른, 오른쪽의
□ **wonder**	명사 경이 / 동사 궁금해하다
□ **take place**	(일·사건이) 일어나다[발생하다]
□ **setting**	명사 환경
□ **competition**	명사 경쟁
□ **judgment**	명사 판단

핵심 지문 전반에 걸쳐서 education, responsibility, global과 같은 단어가 반복해서 나오고 있음. 이를 통해 필자가 주장하고자 하는 바가 교육, 책임 그리고 지구와 관련된 것임을 알 수 있음.

12 2018년 9월 21번 (정답률 75%) 정답 ⑤

[지문 끊어 읽기] 교육의 역할

(1) What we need in education /
교육에서 우리가 필요로 하는 것은 /
is not measurement, accountability, or standards.
측정, 책임, 또는 기준이 아니다

(2) While these can be useful tools for improvement, /
이러한 것들은 향상을 위한 유용한 도구가 될 수 있지만 /
they should hardly occupy center stage.
그것들이 주요한 역할을 완전히 차지하지는 않아야 한다

(3) Our focus should instead be on making sure /
그 대신에 우리의 초점은 확실히 하는 데 있어야 한다 /
we are giving our youth an education /
우리가 우리의 젊은이들에게 교육을 제공하고 있다는 것을 /
that is going to arm them / to save humanity.
그들을 준비시킬 / 인류를 지키도록

(4) We are faced with unprecedented perils, /
우리는 전례 없는 위기에 직면해 있다 /
and these perils are multiplying /
그리고 이러한 위기들은 증가하고 있다 /
and pushing at our collective gates.
그리고 우리 공동체의 문을 밀어붙이고 있다

(5) We should be bolstering curriculum /
우리는 교육과정을 강화해야 한다 /
that helps young people mature into ethical adults /
젊은이들이 도덕적인 어른으로 성숙하는 것을 도와줄 /
who feel a responsibility to the global community. 주제문
지구 공동체에 책임감을 느끼는

(6) Without this sense of responsibility / we have seen /
이러한 책임감 없이 / 우리는 목격해왔다 /
that many talented individuals give in to their greed and pride, /
재능이 있는 많은 개인들이 그들의 탐욕과 자만심에 굴복하는 것을 /
and this destroys economies, ecosystems, and entire species.
그리고 이것이 경제, 생태계 그리고 종 전체를 파괴하는 것을

(7) While we certainly should not abandon efforts /
우리는 분명 노력을 그만두어서는 안 되지만 /
to develop standards in different content areas, /
다양한 내용 영역에서 기준을 개발하는 /
and also strengthen the STEM subjects, /
그리고 또한 STEM 과목들을 강화하는 /
we need to take seriously / our need for an education /
우리는 심각하게 받아들일 필요가 있다 / 교육에 대한 우리의 필요성을 /
centered on global responsibility.
국제적인 책임감에 중점을 둔

(8) If we don't, / we risk extinction.
만약 우리가 그렇게 하지 않으면 / 우리는 멸종의 위험에 처한다

[전문 해석]

(1)교육에서 우리가 필요로 하는 것은 측정, (학업 성적에 대한) 책임, 또는 기준이 아니다. (2)이러한 것들은 향상을 위한 유용한 도구가 될 수 있지만, 그것들이 주요한 역할을 완전히 차지하지는 않아야 한다(차지해서는 안 된다). (3)그 대신에, 우리의 초점은 우리가 우리의 젊은이들에게 인류를 지키도록 그들을 준비시킬 교육을 제공하고 있다는 것을 확실히 하는 데 있어야 한다. (4)우리는 전례 없는 위기에 직면해 있고, 이러한 위기들은 증가하고 있으며 우리 공동체의 문을 밀어붙이고 있다(생존을 위협하고 있다). (5)우리는 젊은이들이 지구 공동체에 책임감을 느끼는 도덕적인 어른으로 성숙하는(성장하는) 것을 도와줄 교육과정을 (계속) 강화해야 한다. (6)이러한 책임감 없이 우리는 재능이 있는 많은 개인들이 그들의 탐욕과 자만심에 굴복하는 것, 그리고 이것이 경제, 생태계 그리고 종 전체를 파괴하는 것을 목격해왔다. (7)우리는 분명 다양한 내용 영역에서 기준을 개발하고 또한 STEM(Science, Technology, Engineering, Mathematics) 과목들을 강화하는 노력을 그만두어서는 안 되지만, 우리는 국제적인 책임감에 중점을 둔 교육에 대한 우리의 필요성을 심각하게 받아들일 필요가 있다. (8)만약 우리가 그렇게 하지 않으면, 우리는 멸종의 위험에 처한다(처하게 된다).

- STEM subjects(STEM 과목): 산업 및 기업계의 기초가 되는 Science(과학), Technology(기술), Engineering(공학), Mathematics(수학)의 4가지 과목을 이르는 말로, 현재 미국 교육 과정에서 중요시되고 있는 과목들이다.

[정답 확인]

다음 글에서 필자가 주장하는 바로 가장 적절한 것은?

① 융합 교육 강화(strengthen)를 위한 정책을 조속히 수립해야 한다.
② 학생 자치활동을 통해 민주 시민 의식(democratic civic awareness)을 함양해야 한다.
③ 교육(education)은 미래 산업에 대비한 인재 육성에 앞장서야 한다.
④ 급변하는 미래에 대비하기 위해 교육과정(curriculum)을 다양화해야 한다.
✔ 교육은 지구 공동체에 책임감(responsibility to the global community)을 가진 도덕적(ethical) 인간을 길러내야 한다. 문장(5)

[중요 어휘]

□ **accountability**	명사 책임, 책무(성)
□ **occupy**	동사 차지하다, 점유하다
□ **center**	명사 중심(부), 핵심 / 동사 (~에) 중점을 두다, 집중시키다
□ **make sure**	확실히 하다, 명확히 하다

문제편 p.034

☐ **arm**	동사 준비시키다, 무장시키다 / 명사 팔
☐ **humanity**	명사 인류, 인간(성)
☐ **unprecedented**	형용사 전례 없는, 유례없는
☐ **peril**	명사 위기, 위험
☐ **collective**	형용사 공동체의, 집단의
☐ **bolster**	동사 강화하다, 개선하다
☐ **mature**	동사 성숙하다, 잘 익히다 / 형용사 성숙한, 분별력 있는
☐ **ethical**	형용사 도덕적인, 윤리의
☐ **give in to**	~에 굴복하다
☐ **greed**	명사 탐욕, 욕심
☐ **ecosystem**	명사 생태(계)
☐ **extinction**	명사 멸종, 소멸

13 2018년 11월 20번 (정답률 75%) 정답 ④

[지문 끊어 읽기] 일의 지연을 막는 방법

(1) Breaks are necessary / to revive your energy levels /
병렬①
휴식들은 필요하다 / 당신의 에너지 수준을 회복시키기 위해 /
and recharge your mental stamina, /
병렬②
그리고 당신의 정신적인 체력을 재충전하기 위해 /
but they shouldn't be taken carelessly.
=breaks
하지만 그것들은 부주의하게 취해져서는 안 된다

(2) If you've planned your schedule effectively, /
만약 당신이 당신의 일정을 효과적으로 계획했다면 /
you should already have scheduled breaks /
당신은 이미 계획된 휴식들을 가지고 있을 것이다 /
at appropriate times / throughout the day, /
적절한 시간에 / 그날 하루 전체를 통틀어 /
so any other breaks / in the midst of ongoing work hours /
그러므로 어떤 다른 휴식도 / 진행 중인 업무 시간 중에 /
are unwarranted.
불필요하다

(3) While scheduled breaks keep you on track /
S'
계획된 휴식들은 당신이 순조롭게 일하도록 하지만 /
by being strategic, re-energizing methods of self-reinforcement, /
자기 강화의 전략적인 재충전 방법이 됨으로써 /
unscheduled breaks derail you / from your goal, /
S
계획되지 않은 휴식들은 당신을 벗어나게 한다 / 당신의 목표로부터 /
as they offer you / opportunities to procrastinate /
4형식V' I·O D·O
그들은 당신에게 제공하기 때문에 / 미룰 기회를 /
by making you feel / as if you've got "free time."
사역V(V-ing) O 동사원형
당신을 느끼게 만들어서 / 당신이 '자유 시간'이 있는 것처럼

힌트 'keep A on track'은 'A를 선로(올바른 길) 안에 둔다'는 의미이므로, '순조롭게 일하게 한다'는 의미가 있는데, 이는 '(레일 바깥으로) 벗어나게 하다'라는 의미의 derail과 대조를 이룸.

(4) Taking unscheduled breaks / is a sure-fire way /
계획되지 않은 휴식들을 취하는 것은 / 확실한 방법이다 /
to fall into the procrastination trap.
미루는 습관의 덫에 빠지는

(5) You may rationalize / that you're only getting a cup of coffee /
당신은 합리화할 수도 있다 / 당신이 그저 커피 한 잔을 마시려는 것이라고 /
to keep yourself alert, / but in reality, /
당신 자신의 정신을 맑게 유지하기 위해 / 하지만 실제로는 /
you're just trying to avoid / having to work on a task /
당신은 그저 피하려고 노력하고 있을 뿐이다 / 과업을 해야 한다는 것을 /
at your desk.
당신 책상 위에 있는

(6) So to prevent procrastination, /
결론
그러므로 미루는 것을 막기 위해서는 /
commit to having no random breaks instead. 주제문
대신에 어떠한 임의의 휴식도 취하지 않겠다고 약속하라

힌트 'procrastination'은 '미루는 습관(버릇), 미루기, (일의) 지연' 등으로 문맥에 따라서 다양하게 해석됨.

[전문 해석]

(1)휴식들은 당신의 에너지 수준을 회복시키고 당신의 정신적인 체력을 재충전하기 위해 필요하지만, (그것들은) 부주의하게 취해져서는 안 된다. (2)만약 당신이 당신의 일정을 효과적으로 계획했다면, 당신은 이미 그날 하루 전체를 통틀어 적절한 시간에 계획된 휴식들을 가지고 있을 것이므로, 진행 중인 업무 시간 중에 어떤 다른 휴식도 불필요하다. (3)계획된 휴식들은 자기 강화의 전략적인 재충전 방법이 됨으로써 당신이 순조롭게 일하도록 하지만, 계획되지 않은 휴식들은 당신을 (당신이) '자유 시간'이 있는 것처럼 느끼게 만들어서 (일을) 미룰 기회를 당신에게 제공하기 때문에 당신을 당신의 목표로부터 벗어나게 한다. (4)계획되지 않은 휴식들을 취하는 것은 미루는 습관의 덫에 빠지는 확실한 방법이다. (5)당신은 당신이 그저 (당신 자신의) 정신을 맑게 유지하기 위해 커피 한 잔을 마시려는 것이라고 합리화할 수도 있지만, 실제로는 당신은 그저 당신 책상 위에 있는 과업을 해야 한다는 것(사실)을 피하려고 노력하고 있을 뿐이다. (6)그러므로 미루는 것을 막기 위해서는(미루지 않기 위해서는), 대신에 어떠한 임의의 휴식도 취하지 않겠다고 약속하라.

[정답 확인]

✶중요 본문의 내용에 따르면 ②도 틀린 주장은 아니지만, 필자가 강조하려는 점은 '미루는 습관을 피하려면 임의로 휴식 시간을 가지면 안 된다는 것'임.

다음 글에서 필자가 주장하는 바로 가장 적절한 것은?

① 적절한 휴식(breaks)을 통해 업무 스트레스로부터 벗어나야 한다.
② 효율적인 업무 처리를 위해 과업을 미루는 습관(procrastination)을 버려야 한다.
③ 능력에 맞게 업무를 배분함으로써 노동 생산성(productivity)을 높여야 한다.
✔④ 일의 지연을 막으려면 계획되지 않은(unscheduled) 휴식을 취하지 말아야 한다. 문장(6)
⑤ 일을 처리하는 속도를 높이려면 쾌적한 업무 환경(environment)을 조성해야 한다.

[중요 어휘]

☐ **break**	명사 휴식, 휴가
☐ **revive**	동사 회복시키다, 되살리다
☐ **recharge**	동사 재충전하다
☐ **appropriate**	형용사 적절한, 알맞은
☐ **in the midst of**	~(하는) 중에, 한창일 때
☐ **ongoing**	형용사 진행 중인
☐ **unwarranted**	형용사 불필요한, 부적절한
☐ **on track**	순조롭게 진행되는, 정상 궤도에 있는
☐ **strategic**	형용사 전략적인
☐ **self-reinforcement**	명사 자기 강화
☐ **procrastinate**	동사 미루다
☐ **sure-fire**	형용사 확실한, 틀림없는
☐ **rationalize**	동사 합리화하다
☐ **alert**	형용사 정신이 맑은[초롱초롱한] / 동사 알리다
☐ **avoid V-ing**	~하는 것을 (회)피하다
☐ **commit to V-ing**	(~하겠다고) 약속하다, 맹세하다

핵심 외부자의 특징을 설명하면서 외부자의 관점으로 조직을 평가할 것을 주장하는 글임. 글에서 반복하여 지칭하고 있는 키워드를 찾는다면 주장을 쉽게 추론할 수 있음.

14 2021년 3월 20번 (정답률 75%) 정답 ②

[지문 끊어 읽기] 외부자의 관점과 조직 평가

(1) No matter what your situation, /
여러분의 상황이 어떠하든 /
whether you are an insider or an outsider, /
여러분이 내부자이든 외부자이든 /
you need to become the voice /
선행사
여러분은 목소리가 될 필요가 있다 /
that challenges yesterday's answers. 주제문
주격 관계대명사
어제의 정답에 이의를 제기하는

(2) Think about the characteristics / that make outsiders valuable /
특성들에 관해 생각해 보라 / 외부자를 가치 있게 만드는 /
to an organization.
조직에

(3) They are the people / who have the perspective /
그들은 사람들이다 / 관점을 가진 /

힌트 that이 이끄는 관계대명사절에서 notice의 목적어가 없으므로 that이 목적격 관계대명사로 쓰였음을 알 수 있음.

to see problems / that the insiders are too close to really notice.
too ~ to V(너무 ~해서 V할 수 없다)
문제들을 볼 수 있는 / 내부자가 너무 가까이 있어서 정말 알아차릴 수 없는

(4) They are the ones / who have the freedom /
그들은 사람들이다 / 자유를 가진 /
to point out these problems / and criticize them /
병렬① 병렬②
이런 문제들을 지적할 / 그리고 그것들을 비판할 /
without risking their job or their career.
자신의 일자리나 자신의 경력을 위태롭게 하지 않고

힌트 'to point'와 '(to) criticize'는 병렬 구조인데 criticize 앞에 반복되는 to가 생략됨. 둘 다 'the freedom'을 수식하는 형용사적 용법으로 쓰임.

(5) Part of adopting an outsider mentality / 정답 단서
외부자의 사고방식을 채택하는 것의 일부는 /
is forcing yourself / to look around your organization /
V O O·C(to V)
여러분 스스로가 ~하게 만드는 것이다 / 여러분의 조직을 둘러보게 /
with this disassociated, less emotional perspective.
이렇게 분리된, 덜 감정적인 관점으로

(6) If you didn't know your coworkers / and feel bonded to them /
병렬① 병렬②
여러분이 자신의 동료를 모른다면 / 그리고 그들에게 결속되어 있다고 느끼지 않는다면 /
by your shared experiences, / what would you think of them?
여러분의 공유된 경험에 의해 / 여러분은 그들에 관해 어떻게 생각하겠는가

(7) You may not have the job security or confidence /
여러분이 직업 안정성이나 확신을 갖고 있지 않을지도 모른다 /
to speak your mind to management, /
형용사적 용법(~할)
자신의 생각을 경영진에게 말할 /
정답 단서
but you can make these "outsider" assessments of your organization /
병렬①
하지만 여러분은 자신의 조직에 관해 이런 '외부자의' 평가를 할 수 있다 /
on your own / and use what you determine /
병렬②
독자적으로 / 그리고 여러분이 알아낸 것을 이용할 수 있다 /
to advance your career.
부사적 용법(~하기 위해)
자신의 경력을 발전시키기 위해

[전문 해석]

(1)여러분의 상황이 어떠하든, 여러분이 내부자이든 외부자이든, 여러분은 어제의 정답에 이의를 제기하는 목소리가 될 필요가 있다. (2)외부자를 조직에 가치 있게 만드는 특성들에 관해 생각해 보라. (3)그들은 내부자가 너무 가까이 있어서 (내부자의 위치에서는) 정말 알아차릴 수 없는 문제들을 볼 수 있는 관점을 가진 사람들이다. (4)그들은 자신의 일자리나 자신의 경력을 위태롭게 하지 않고 이런 문제들을 지적하고 그것들을 비판할 자유를 가진 사람들이다. (5)외부자의 사고방식을 채택하는 것의 일부는 이렇게 분리된, 덜 감정적인 관점으로 여러분 스스로가 조직을 둘러보게 만드는 것이다. (6)여러분이 자신의 동료를 모르고 여러분의 공유된 경험에 의해 그들에게 결속되어 있다고 느끼지 않는다면, 여러분은 그들에 관해 어떻게 생각하겠는가? (7)여러분이 자신의 생각을 경영진에게 말할 직업 안정성이나 확신을 갖고 있지 않을지도 모르지만, 여러분은 자신의 조직에 관해 이런 '외부자의' 평가를 독자적으로 할 수 있고 여러분이 알아낸 것을 자신의 경력을 발전시키기 위해 이용할 수 있다.

[정답 확인]

다음 글에서 필자가 주장하는 바로 가장 적절한 것은?

① 조직(organization) 내의 의사소통이 원활한지 수시로 살피라.
✔ 외부자(outsider)의 관점으로 자기 조직을 비판적으로 바라보라. 문장(1)
③ 관심사의 공유를 통해 직장 동료(coworker)와의 관계를 개선하라.
④ 과거의 성공(success)에 도취되어 자기 계발을 소홀히 하지 말라.
⑤ 동료의 실수를 비판하기(criticize)보다는 먼저 이해하려고 노력하라.

[중요 어휘]

□ **outsider**	명사 외부자
□ **challenge**	동사 이의를 제기하다 / 명사 도전, 문제
□ **characteristic**	명사 특성
□ **perspective**	명사 관점
□ **point out**	~을 지적하다
□ **criticize**	동사 비판하다
□ **risk**	동사 위태롭게 하다 / 명사 위험
□ **adopt**	동사 채택하다, 입양하다
□ **mentality**	명사 사고방식
□ **disassociate**	동사 분리시키다
□ **bond**	동사 결속시키다, 유대감을 형성하다 / 명사 유대
□ **job security**	직업 안정성, 고용보장
□ **management**	명사 경영진
□ **assessment**	명사 평가
□ **on one's own**	독자적으로
□ **determine**	동사 알아내다, 결정하다
□ **advance**	동사 발전시키다 / 명사 발전, 진전

15 2019년 3월 20번 (정답률 70%) 정답 ⑤

[지문 끊어 읽기] 한계를 극복하는 방법

(1) I am sure / you have heard something like, /
나는 확신한다 / 당신이 ~와 같은 것을 들어본 적이 있을 것이라고 /
"You can do anything you want, / if you just persist /
당신은 당신이 원하는 그 무엇이든 할 수 있다 / 만약 당신이 지속하기만 한다면 /
long and hard enough."
충분히 오랫동안 그리고 열심히

힌트 enough는 부사를 꾸며줄 경우에는 부사 뒤에 위치하는 반면, enough food와 같이 명사를 수식하는 경우에는 명사보다 앞에 위치함.

(2) Perhaps you have even made a similar assertion /
아마 당신은 심지어 비슷한 주장을 했을지도 모른다 /
to motivate someone / to try harder.
누군가를 자극하기 위해 / 더 열심히 노력하도록

(3) Of course, / words like these sound good, /
S 감각V(2형식)+형용사
물론 / 이와 같은 말들은 좋게 들린다 /
but surely they cannot be true.
그러나 확실히 그것들은 사실일 수가 없다

힌트 few와 a few는 둘 다 셀 수 있는 경우에 사용되고 둘 다 '별로 없다'라는 의미이지만, few가 '거의 없는'이라는 부정적인 의미인 반면, a few는 '(그래도) 약간이라도 있는'이라는 긍정적인 의미로 쓰임.

(4) Few of us can become /
우리 중에 ~가 될 수 있는 사람은 거의 없다 /
the professional athlete, entertainer, or movie star /
프로 운동선수, 연예인, 또는 인기 영화배우 /
we would like to be.
우리가 되고 싶어하는

(5) Environmental, physical, and psychological factors limit our potential /
S V①
환경적, 신체적, 그리고 심리적 요인들은 우리의 잠재력을 제한한다 /
and narrow the range / of things we can do with our lives.
V②
그리고 범위를 한정한다 / 우리가 우리의 인생에서 할 수 있는 것들의

(6) "Trying harder" cannot substitute /
'더 열심히 노력하는 것'이 대체할 수는 없다 /
for talent, equipment, and method, /
재능, 장비, 그리고 방법을 /
but this should not lead to despair.
그러나 이것이 체념으로 이어져서는 안 된다

(7) Rather, we should attempt / to become the best we can be /
오히려 우리는 시도해야 한다 / 우리가 될 수 있는 최고가 되려고 /
within our limitations. 주제문
우리의 한계 내에서

(8) We try to find / our niche.
우리는 찾으려 노력한다 / 우리의 적소를

(9) By the time we reach employment age, /
우리가 취업 연령에 도달할 무렵에는 /
there is a finite range of jobs / we can perform effectively.
한정된 범위의 직업들이 있다 / 우리가 효과적으로 수행할 수 있는

[전문 해석]

(1)나는 당신이 "만약 당신이 충분히 오랫동안 그리고 열심히 (노력을) 지속하기만 한다면, 당신은 당신이 원하는 그 무엇이든 할 수 있다."와 같은 것을 들어본 적이 있을 것이라고 확신한

다. (2)아마 당신은 심지어 누군가를 더 열심히 노력하도록 자극하기 위해 비슷한 주장을 했을지도 모른다. (3)물론, 이와 같은 말들은 좋게 들리지만, 확실히 그것들은 사실일 수가 없다. (4)우리 중에 우리가 되고 싶어하는 프로 운동선수, 연예인, 또는 인기 영화배우가 될 수 있는 사람은 거의 없다. (5)환경적, 신체적, 그리고 심리적 요인들은 우리의 잠재력을 제한하고, 우리가 우리의 인생에서 할 수 있는 것들의 범위를 한정한다. (6)'더 열심히 노력하는 것'이 재능, 장비, 그리고 방법을 대체할 수는 없지만, 이것이 체념으로 이어져서는 안 된다. (7)오히려, 우리는 우리의 한계 내에서 우리가 될 수 있는 최고가 되려고 시도해야 한다. (8)우리는 우리의 적소(우리에게 꼭 맞는 역할)를 찾으려 노력한다. (9)우리가 취업 연령에 도달할 무렵에는, 우리가 효과적으로 수행할 수 있는 한정된 범위의 직업들이 있다(우리는 한정된 범위의 직무들만을 효과적으로 수행할 수 있을 뿐이다).

[정답 확인]

다음 글에서 필자가 주장하는 바로 가장 적절한 것은?

① 수입(income)보다는 적성(aptitude)을 고려해 직업을 선택해야 한다.
② 성공하려면 다양한 분야(field)에서 경험(experience)을 쌓아야 한다.
③ 장래의 모습을 그리며 인생의 계획(plan)을 세워야 한다.
④ 자신의 재능(talent)과 역량을 스스로 제한해서는(limit) 안 된다.
✔ 자신의 한계(limitation) 내에서 최고가 되려고 시도해야(attempt) 한다. 문장(7)

★중요 전체적으로 limitation에 관한 이야기를 하고 있어서 오해하기 쉽지만, 이 글은 주어진 한계를 인정하고 그 안에서 최대한 노력하라는 내용을 담고 있음.

[중요 어휘]

☐ persist	동사 지속하다, 고집하다
☐ motivate	동사 자극하다, 동기부여를 하다
☐ sound	동사 ~하게 들리다, ~인 것 같다 / 명사 소리
☐ few	형용사 거의 없는, 극소수의
☐ substitute	동사 대체하다, 바꾸다
☐ despair	명사 체념, 절망
☐ employment	명사 취업, 고용
☐ finite	형용사 한정된, 유한한

16 2022년 11월 20번 (정답률 55%)

정답 ④

[지문 끊어 읽기] 조직 평가의 신뢰와 명확성

(1) Clarity in an organization /
S
조직에서의 명확성은 /
keeps everyone working in one accord /
V①(5형식) O O·C
모두가 계속 조화롭게 일하게 한다 /
and energizes key leadership components /
V②(3형식) O
그리고 핵심적인 리더십 요소에 활력을 준다 /
like trust and transparency. 정답단서 조직 내 화합과 리더십에 영향을 미치는 명확성에 대해 언급함.
전치사
신뢰와 투명성 같은

(2) No matter who or what is being assessed in your organization, /
여러분의 조직에서 누가 또는 무엇이 평가되고 있는지 간에 /
[what they are being assessed on] /
[ ]: S①(간접의문문)
그들이 무엇에 대해 평가되고 있는지는 /
must be clear / and the people must be aware of it.
S②
분명해야 한다 / 그리고 사람들은 그것을 알고 있어야 한다

힌트 no matter who(누가 ~하더라도), no matter what(무엇이 ~하더라도)은 복합관계대명사인 whoever와 whatever로 바꿔 쓸 수 있음. whoever와 whatever는 명사절과 부사절로 쓰이는데, 여기서는 양보의 부사절로 쓰임.

(3) If individuals in your organization are assessed /
만약 여러분의 조직에 있는 개개인들이 평가된다면 /
without knowing what they are being assessed on, /
간접의문문
그들이 무엇에 대해 평가되고 있는지를 알지 못한 채로 /
it can cause mistrust /
병렬①
그것은 불신을 초래할 수 있다 /
and move your organization away from clarity.
병렬②
그리고 여러분의 조직을 명확성으로부터 멀어지게 할 수 있다

(4) For your organization to be productive, cohesive, and successful, /
to부정사의 의미상의 주어 부사적 용법(목적)
여러분의 조직이 생산적이고 응집력이 있고 성공적이기 위해서는 /
trust is essential.
신뢰가 필수적이다

(5) Failure to have trust in your organization /
failure to V: ~하지 못함
여러분의 조직에 대한 신뢰를 갖지 못하는 것은 /
will have a negative effect / on the results of any assessment.
부정적인 영향을 끼칠 것이다 / 어떤 평가의 결과에도

(6) It will also significantly hinder / the growth of your organization.
그것은 또한 상당히 방해할 것이다 / 여러분의 조직의 성장을

(7) To conduct accurate assessments, / trust is a must /
부사적 용법(목적) 선행사
정확한 평가를 수행하기 위해 / 신뢰는 필수적인 것이다 /
— which comes through clarity. 정답단서 조직원의 평가에 신뢰는 필수적이고 그 신뢰는 명확성에서 나옴.
주격 관계대명사
그것은 명확성으로부터 온다

힌트 이 문장에서 관계대명사 which는 계속적 용법으로 사용되었는데, 이때 'assessments ~ clearer' 전체를 선행사이자, 관계대명사절의 주어로 받아 단수 동사 empowers가 쓰였음.

(8) In turn, / [assessments help you see clearer], /
[ ]: 선행사 5형식V O O·C(동사원형/to V)
결국 / 평가는 여러분이 더 분명하게 볼 수 있도록 도와주는데 /
which then empowers your organization to reach optimal success.
주격 관계대명사(계속적 용법) 5형식V O O·C(to V)
그것은 그러고 나서 여러분의 조직이 최적의 성공에 도달하도록 해 준다

[전문 해석]

(1)조직에서의 명확성은 모두가 계속 조화롭게 일하게 하고 신뢰와 투명성 같은 핵심적인 리더십 요소에 활력을 준다. (2)여러분의 조직에서 누가 또는 무엇이 평가되고 있는지 간에 그들이 무엇에 대해 평가되고 있는지는 분명해야 하고 사람들은 그것을 알고 있어야 한다. (3)만약 여러분의 조직에 있는 개개인들이 그들이 무엇에 대해 평가되고 있는지를 알지 못한 채로 평가된다면, 그것은 불신을 초래하고 여러분의 조직을 명확성으로부터 멀어지게 할 수 있다. (4)여러분의 조직이 생산적이고 응집력이 있고 성공적이기 위해서는 신뢰가 필수적이다. (5)여러분의 조직에 대한 신뢰를 갖지 못하는 것은 어떤 평가의 결과에도 부정적인 영향을 끼칠 것이다. (6)그것은 또한 여러분의 조직의 성장을 상당히 방해할 것이다. (7)정확한 평가를 수행하기 위해 신뢰는 필수적인 것이고, 그것은 명확성으로부터 온다. (8)결국 평가는 여러분이 더 분명하게 볼 수 있도록 도와주는데, 그것은 그러고 나서 여러분의 조직이 최적의 성공에 도달하도록 해 준다.

[정답 확인]

다음 글에서 필자가 주장하는 바로 가장 적절한 것은?

① 조직이 구성원에게 제공하는 보상(reward)은 즉각적이어야 한다.
② 조직의 발전을 위해 구성원은 동료의 능력(co-worker's capability)을 신뢰해야 한다.
③ 조직 내 구성원의 능력에 맞는 명확한 목표(clear goal)를 설정해야 한다.
✔ 조직의 신뢰 형성을 위해 구성원에 대한 평가 요소가 명확해야(clarify) 한다. 문장(7)
⑤ 구성원의 의견 수용을 위해 신뢰에 기반한 조직 문화(organizational culture)가 구축되어야 한다.

[문제 풀이]

이 글은 조직 평가에서 중요한 신뢰가 조직의 명확성에 기인한다는 내용이다. 문장 (1)에서 명확성이 조직이 조화롭게 일하게 하고 리더십의 핵심적인 요소에 필요하다고 언급한 뒤, 이어서 평가 요소에는 신뢰가 필수적이라는 내용이 계속해서 나온다. 이에 대해 문장 (7)에서 조직 평가에 있어 신뢰가 필수적이고 그 신뢰는 명확성에서 나온다고 하며 평가의 명확성이 조직으로 하여금 최적의 성공에 도달하도록 해준다며 글을 마무리한다. 따라서 필자가 주장하는 바로 가장 적절한 것은 ④이다.

[중요 어휘]

☐ clarity	명사 명확성
☐ accord	명사 조화, 일치
☐ component	명사 요소, 부품
☐ transparency	명사 투명성
☐ assess	동사 평가하다
☐ mistrust	명사 불신 / 동사 불신하다
☐ move A away from	A를 ~에서 멀어지게 하다
☐ cohesive	형용사 응집력이 있는, 결합력이 있는
☐ assessment	명사 평가
☐ hinder	동사 방해하다, 막다
☐ conduct	동사 수행하다, 행동하다

☐ empower	동사 ~할 수 있도록 하다, 권한을 주다
☐ optimal	형용사 최적의

17 2023년 11월 20번 (정답률 90%) 정답 ⑤

[지문 끊어 읽기] 농업이 직면한 문제

(1) Agriculture includes a range of activities /
농업은 다양한 활동들을 포함한다 /
such as planting, harvesting, fertilizing, pest management, raising animals, and distributing food and agricultural products.
파종, 수확, 비료 주기, 해충 관리, 동물 사육, 그리고 식량 및 농산물 유통과 같은

(2) It is one of the oldest and most essential human activities, / (V①, =Agriculture)
그것은 가장 오래되고 가장 필수적인 인간 활동 중 하나이다 /
[dating back thousands of years], / [ ]: 분사구문
수천 년 전으로 거슬러 올라가는 /
and has played a critical role in the development of human civilizations, / (V②)
그리고 인류 문명의 발전에 중요한 역할을 해왔다 /
[allowing people to create stable food supplies and settle in one place]. [ ]: 분사구문 (5형식V', O', O·C①(to V), O·C②)
사람들이 안정적인 식량 공급을 창출하고 한곳에 정착할 수 있게 하였다

(3) Today, / agriculture remains a vital industry / (선행사)
오늘날 / 농업은 필수적인 산업으로 남아 있다 /
[that feeds the world's population, / (병렬①)
세계 인구를 먹여 살리는 /
supports rural communities, / (병렬②)
지방 공동체를 지원하는 /
and provides raw materials for other industries]. [ ]: 주격 관계대명사절 (병렬③)
그리고 다른 산업에 원자재를 공급하는

힌트 'provide B for A'는 'A에게 B를 공급하다'라고 해석하며, 'provide A with B(A에게 B를 공급하다)'로 바꾸어 쓸 수도 있음.

(4) However, / agriculture faces numerous challenges /
그러나 / 농업은 수많은 문제에 직면하고 있다 /
such as climate change, water scarcity, soil degradation, and biodiversity loss. **정답 단서** 농업은 여러 문제에 직면하고 있음.
기후 변화, 물 부족, 토질 저하, 그리고 생물 다양성 손실과 같은

(5) As the world's population continues to grow, /
세계 인구가 계속 증가함에 따라 /
it is essential [to find sustainable solutions / (형식상의 주어, [ ]: 내용상의 주어)
지속 가능한 해결책을 찾는 것이 필수적이다 /
to address the challenges facing agriculture / (현재분사구)
농업이 직면한 문제를 다루는 /
and ensure the continued production of food and other agricultural products]. **정답 단서** 농업이 직면한 문제를 해결하고 지속적인 농산물 생산을 위한 해결책을 찾아야 함.
그리고 식량과 다른 농산물의 지속적인 생산을 보장할

힌트 'to address'와 '(to) ensure'은 and를 중심으로 병렬로 연결된 to부정사로, ensure 앞의 to는 생략되어 있음. 앞에 나오는 명사 solutions를 수식하는 형용사적 용법으로 해석하면 자연스러움.

[전문 해석]

(1)농업은 파종, 수확, 비료 주기, 해충 관리, 동물 사육, 그리고 식량 및 농산물 유통과 같은 다양한 활동들을 포함한다. (2)그것은 수천 년 전으로 거슬러 올라가는 가장 오래되고 가장 필수적인 인간 활동 중 하나이고, 인류 문명의 발전에 중요한 역할을 해왔으며, 사람들이 안정적인 식량 공급을 창출하고 한곳에 정착할 수 있게 하였다. (3)오늘날, 농업은 세계 인구를 먹여 살리고 지방 공동체를 지원하며 다른 산업에 원자재를 공급하는 필수적인 산업으로 남아 있다. (4)그러나, 농업은 기후 변화, 물 부족, 토질 저하, 그리고 생물 다양성 손실과 같은 수많은 문제에 직면하고 있다. (5)세계 인구가 계속 증가함에 따라, 농업이 직면한 문제를 다루고 식량과 다른 농산물의 지속적인 생산을 보장할 지속 가능한 해결책을 찾는 것이 필수적이다.

[정답 확인]

다음 글에서 필자가 주장하는 바로 가장 적절한 것은?

① 토양의 질을 개선하기 위해 친환경(eco-friendly) 농법의 연구와 개발이 필요하다.
② 세계 인구의 증가에 대응하기 위해 농산물 품종의 다양화(diversification)가 필요하다.
③ 기후 변화에 대한 지속 가능한 대책(sustainable solutions)은 경제적 관점에서 고려되어야 한다.
④ 다른 산업 분야와의 공동 연구(collaboration)를 통해 상품성을 가진 농작물을 개발해야 한다.
⑤ ✔ 농업이 직면한 문제 해결 및 식량과 농산물의 지속적 생산(continued production)을 위한 방안이 필요하다. 문장(5)

[중요 어휘]

☐ a range of	다양한
☐ fertilize	동사 비료를 주다
☐ pest	명사 해충, 유해 동물, 성가신 사람(물건)
☐ distribute	동사 유통하다, 분배하다
☐ essential	형용사 필수적인, 근본적인 / 명사 핵심 사항(요점)
☐ critical	형용사 중요한, 중대한, 비판적인
☐ civilization	명사 문명 (사회), 전 세계 (사람들)
☐ stable	형용사 안정적인, 차분한 / 명사 마구간
☐ settle	동사 정착하다, 해결하다
☐ vital	형용사 필수적인, 생명 유지와 관련된
☐ rural	형용사 지방의, 시골의
☐ raw material	원자재
☐ scarcity	명사 부족, 결핍, 희소성
☐ degradation	명사 (질의) 저하, 악화
☐ biodiversity	명사 생물 다양성
☐ sustainable	형용사 지속 가능한
☐ address	동사 (문제 등을) 다루다, 고심하다

18 2024년 3월 20번 (정답률 85%) 정답 ①

[지문 끊어 읽기] 성공을 위한 인내심

(1) Too many times / people, / especially in today's generation, /
너무나 많은 경우에 / 사람들은 / 특히 오늘날의 세대에서 /
expect things to just happen overnight. (5형식V, O, O·C(to V))
일이 하룻밤 사이에 그냥 일어나기를 기대한다

★중요 어떤 일이 하룻밤 사이에 일어나기를 기대하는 것이 헛된 것이라고 이야기하므로 필자의 주장은 그 반대인 일을 이루는 데 시간과 인내가 필요하다는 내용일 것을 예상할 수 있음.

(2) When we have these false expectations, /
우리가 이런 헛된 기대를 가질 때 /
it tends to discourage us from continuing to move forward.
이것은 우리가 계속해서 앞으로 나아가는 것을 막는 경향이 있다

힌트 'discourage A from V-ing'는 'A가 ~하는 것을 막다'라는 의미로, 'keep, prevent, ban, forbid, hinder' 등으로 바꾸어 사용할 수 있음.

(3) Because this is a high tech society, / everything we want / (S)
지금은 첨단 기술 사회이기 때문에 / 우리가 원하는 모든 것은 /
has to be within the parameters of our comfort and convenience. (V)
우리의 편안함과 편리함이라는 한도 내에 있어야 한다

힌트 선행사 everything 뒤에 목적격 관계대명사 that이 생략된 형태임.

(4) If it doesn't happen fast enough, / we're tempted to lose interest. (=everything we want)
그것이 충분히 빠르게 일어나지 않으면 / 우리는 흥미를 잃도록 유혹받는다

(5) So many people don't want to take the time / (선행사)
그래서 많은 사람들이 시간을 들이기를 원하지 않는다 /
it requires to be successful. (목적격 관계대명사절)
성공하는 데 필요한

(6) Success is not a matter of mere desire; /
성공은 단순한 욕망의 문제가 아니다 /
you should develop patience / in order to achieve it. **주제문** 성공을 이루기 위해 인내심을 길러야 함. (=success)
여러분은 인내심을 길러야 한다 / 그것을 이루기 위해

(7) Have you fallen prey to impatience? (현재완료(경험))
여러분은 조바심의 먹이가 되어본 적이 있는가

(8) Great things take time to build. (형용사적 용법)
위대한 일들은 이루는 데 시간이 걸린다

[전문 해석]

(1)너무나 많은 경우에 특히 오늘날의 세대에서 사람들은 일이 하룻밤 사이에 그냥 일어나기를 기대한다. (2)우리가 이런 헛된 기대를 가질 때, 이것은 우리가 계속해서 앞으로 나아가는 것을 막는 경향이 있다. (3)지금은 첨단 기술 사회이기 때문에 우리가 원하는 모든 것은 우리의 편안함과 편리함이라는 한도 내에 있어야 한다. (4)그것이 충분히 빠르게 일어나지 않으면 우리는 흥미를 잃도록 유혹받는다. (5)그래서 많은 사람들이 성공하는 데 필요한 시간을 들이기를 원하지 않는다. (6)성공은 단순한 욕망의 문제가 아니므로, 여러분은 그것을 이루기 위해 인내심을 길러야 한다. (7)여러분은 조바심의 먹이가 되어본 적이 있는가? (8)위대한 일들은 이루는 데 시간이 걸린다.

[정답 확인]

다음 글에서 필자가 주장하는 바로 가장 적절한 것은?

✔ 성공하기 위해서는 인내심(patience)을 길러야 한다. 문장(6)
② 안락함(comfort)을 추구하기보다 한계에 도전해야 한다.
③ 사회 변화의 속도에 맞춰 빠르게(swiftly) 대응해야 한다.
④ 기회(opportunity)를 기다리기보다 능동적으로 행동해야 한다.
⑤ 흥미를 잃지(lose interest) 않으려면 자신이 좋아하는 일을 해야 한다.

[중요 어휘]

☐ generation	명사 세대, 시대
☐ overnight	부사 하룻밤 사이에
☐ discourage	동사 막다, 방해하다, 낙담시키다
☐ high tech	첨단 기술
☐ parameter	명사 한도, 제한, 매개 변수
☐ tempt	동사 유혹하다
☐ matter	명사 문제, 일 / 동사 중요하다
☐ fall prey to N	~의 먹이가 되다, ~에 굴복하다
☐ impatience	명사 조바심, 성급함

19 2024년 6월 20번 (정답률 80%)

정답 ②

[지문 끊어 읽기] 자신에 대한 객관적인 평가

(1) Most people resist the idea of a true self-estimate, /
대부분의 사람들은 진정한 자기 평가에 대한 생각에 저항한다 /
probably because they fear /
아마도 그들이 두려워하기 때문이다 /
[it might mean downgrading some of their beliefs /
=a true self-estimate
그것이 그들의 믿음 일부를 낮추는 것을 의미할지도 모른다고 /
about who they are and what they're capable of]. [ ]: fear의 목적어절
그들이 누구인지 그리고 그들이 무엇을 할 수 있는지에 대한

힌트 문장 (1)의 'who'와 'what'은 관계대명사가 아닌 의문사이므로, 의문사의 의미를 살려 '누구'와 '무엇'으로 해석함. 의문사절은 about의 목적어 역할을 하는 명사절이며 병렬로 연결되어 있음.

(2) As Goethe's maxim goes, / it is a great failing /
괴테의 격언처럼 / 큰 실수이다 / 형식상의 주어
"to see yourself / as more than you are." 정답 단서 자신을 과대평가하는 것은 피해야 함.
내용상의 주어
너 자신을 보는 것은 / 현재 너의 모습 이상으로

(3) How could you really be considered self-aware /
be considered 형용사: ~는 …하다고 여겨지다
여러분은 어떻게 진정으로 자기를 인식하고 있다고 여겨질 수 있을까 /
if you refuse to consider your weaknesses?
여러분이 자신의 약점을 생각하는 것을 거부한다면

★중요 자신의 약점이나 단점까지도 인정해야 자신에 대해 제대로 알 수 있다는 의미임.

(4) Don't fear self-assessment / because you're worried /
자기 평가를 두려워하지 마라 / 여러분이 걱정하기 때문에 /
[you might have to admit / some things about yourself].
여러분이 인정해야 할지도 모른다는 것을 / 자신에 대한 어떤 것들을 [ ]: 명사절(접속사 that 생략)

(5) The second half of Goethe's maxim is important too.
괴테의 격언의 후반부도 역시 중요하다

(6) He states / that it is equally damaging /
형식상의 주어
그는 주장한다 / 동일하게 해롭다고 /
[to "value yourself / at less than your true worth]." 정답 단서
자신을 평가하는 것이 / 여러분의 진정한 가치보다 덜하다고 [ ]: 내용상의 주어 자신을 과소평가하는 것도 해로움.

(7) We underestimate our capabilities /
우리는 우리의 능력을 과소평가한다 /
just as much and just as dangerously /
많이 그리고 위험하게 /
as we overestimate other abilities.
우리가 다른 능력을 과대평가하는 것만큼

힌트 '~만큼 …한'이라는 뜻의 'as+형용사/부사+as'가 병렬로 연결되어 있음.

(8) Cultivate the ability / to judge yourself accurately and honestly.
형용사적 용법
능력을 길러라 / 여러분 자신을 정확하고 정직하게 판단하는
주제문 자신을 정확하고 정직하게 판단할 줄 알아야 함.

(9) Look inward to discern / what you're capable of /
부사적 용법(목적)
파악하기 위해 내면을 들여다보라 / 여러분이 할 수 있는 것을 /
and what it will take to unlock that potential.
그리고 그 잠재력을 열기 위해 필요한 것을

힌트 병렬로 연결된 what절은 discern의 목적어절이자 선행사를 포함한 관계대명사절임.

[전문 해석]

(1)대부분의 사람들은 진정한 자기 평가에 대한 생각에 저항하는데, 아마도 그것이 그들이 누구인지, 그리고 그들이 무엇을 할 수 있는지에 대한 그들의 믿음 일부를 낮추는 것을 의미할지도 모른다고 두려워하기 때문이다. (2)괴테의 격언처럼, "너 자신을 현재 너의 모습 이상으로 보는 것"은 큰 실수이다. (3)여러분이 자신의 약점을 생각하는 것을 거부한다면 어떻게 진정으로 자기를 인식하고 있다고 여겨질 수 있을까? (4)자신에 대한 어떤 것들을 여러분이 인정해야 할지도 모른다는 것을 걱정하기 때문에 자기 평가를 두려워하지 마라. (5)괴테의 격언의 후반부도 역시 중요하다. (6)그는 "여러분의 진정한 가치보다 덜하다고 자신을 평가하는 것"이 동일하게 해롭다고 주장한다. (7)우리는 다른 능력을 과대평가하는 것만큼 많이 그리고 위험하게 우리의 능력을 과소평가한다. (8)여러분 자신을 정확하고 정직하게 판단하는 능력을 길러라. (9)여러분이 할 수 있는 것과 그 잠재력을 열기(발휘하기) 위해 필요한 것을 파악하기 위해 내면을 들여다보라.

[정답 확인]

다음 글에서 필자가 주장하는 바로 가장 적절한 것은?

① 주관적(subjective) 기준으로 타인을 평가하는 것을 피해야(avoid) 한다.
✔ 정확하고(accurately) 정직하게(honestly) 자신을 평가하는 능력을 길러야(cultivate) 한다. 문장(8)
③ 자신이 가진 잠재력(potential)을 믿고 다양한 분야에 도전해야 한다.
④ 다른 사람과 비교하기(compare)보다는 자신의 성장(growth)에 주목해야 한다.
⑤ 문제를 해결하기 위해 근본 원인을 정확하게 분석해야(analyze) 한다.

[중요 어휘]

☐ resist	동사 저항하다, 반대하다, 참다, 견디다
☐ self-estimate	자기 평가
☐ downgrade	동사 낮추다, 격하시키다, 훼손시키다
☐ capable	형용사 할 수 있는, 유능한
☐ maxim	명사 격언, 금언
☐ self-aware	형용사 자기를 인식하는, 자각하는
☐ refuse	동사 거부하다, 거절하다
☐ self-assessment	명사 자기 평가
☐ the second half	후반부, 하반기
☐ underestimate	동사 과소평가하다
☐ overestimate	동사 과대평가하다
☐ cultivate	동사 기르다, 경작하다, 재배하다, 구축하다
☐ discern	동사 파악하다, 알아차리다, 포착하다
☐ unlock	동사 열다, (비밀을) 드러내다

20 2024년 9월 20번 (정답률 95%)

정답 ⑤

[지문 끊어 읽기] 걱정 없는 삶

(1) Merely convincing your children /
S(4형식V, 동명사) I·O
그저 여러분의 아이들을 설득하는 것만으로는 /
[that worry is senseless] /
걱정이 무의미하다고 / [ ]: D·O①(명사절)
and [that they would be more content / if they didn't worry] /
그리고 그들이 더 만족할 것이라고 / 그들이 걱정하지 않는다면 / [ ]: D·O②

힌트 동명사 convincing이 주어인 문장으로, convincing부터 didn't worry까지가 주어부에 해당함. convince는 4형식 동사로 간접목적어(I·O)와 직접목적어(D·O)를 가지는데, convince가 4형식으로 사용될 때는 직접목적어로 that절을 사용함. 여기서 두 개의 that절은 and에 의해 병렬로 연결된 것을 확인할 수 있음.

힌트 「if+S'+동사의 과거형, S+조동사 과거형+동사원형」 구조의 가정법 과거 구문임.

isn't going to stop them from worrying.
V =your children
그들이 걱정하는 것을 멈추게 하지 않을 것이다

힌트 'stop A from V-ing'는 'A가 ~하는 것을 멈추다'라는 의미로, 'prevent, prohibit, keep, ban, hinder' 등의 동사들도 같은 구조로 사용될 수 있음.

(2) For some reason, / young people seem to believe /
어떤 이유로 / 아이들은 믿는 것 같다 /
that worry is a fact of life /
접속사 선행사
걱정이 삶의 사실이라고 /
[over which they have little or no control]. [ ]: 전치사+목적격 관계대명사절
그들이 거의 통제할 수 없거나 아예 통제할 수 없는

힌트 little+셀 수 없는 명사: 거의 없는 / a little+셀 수 없는 명사: 약간의

정답 단서 아이들이 걱정은 통제할 수 없는 것이라고 믿고 있음.

(3) Consequently, / they don't even try to stop.
=young people
결과적으로 / 그들은 멈추려고 노력하지도 않는다

(4) Therefore, / you need to convince them / [that worry, /
S V 4형식V(to V) I·O(=young people) S'
따라서 / 여러분은 그들을 설득할 필요가 있다 / 걱정이 /
like guilt and fear, / is nothing more than an emotion, /
V'① ~에 지나지 않는
죄책감과 두려움처럼 / 어떤 감정에 지나지 않는다고 /
and like all emotions, / is subject to the power of the will]. [ ]: D·O 주제문
V'②
그리고 모든 감정과 같이 / 의지의 힘에 지배를 받는다고

걱정은 어떤 감정에 지나지 않으며, 자기 의지로 걱정을 지배할 수 있음.

(5) Tell them / [that they can eliminate worry from their lives /
4형식V I·O(=young people) 접속사
그들에게 전하라 / 그들이 자신의 삶으로부터 걱정을 없앨 수 있다는 것을 /
by simply refusing to attend to it]. [ ]: D·O
by V-ing: ~함으로써 =worry
단순히 그것에 주의를 기울이려고 하지 않음으로써

힌트 explain은 목적어를 취하는 3형식 동사인데, 길이가 긴 that절이 목적어로 왔기 때문에 부사구 to them과 도치되었음.

(6) Explain to them / [that if they refuse to act worried /
=young people
그들에게 설명하라 / 만약 그들이 걱정하며 행동하는 것을 거부한다면 /
regardless of how they feel, /
간접의문문
자신이 어떻게 느끼는지와 상관없이 /
they will eventually stop feeling worried /
S' V'①
그들은 결국 걱정하는 것을 멈출 것이다 /
and will begin to experience the contentment /
V'② 선행사
그리고 만족감을 경험하기 시작할 것이다 /
that accompanies a worry-free life]. [ ]: Explain의 목적어절
주격 관계대명사절
걱정 없는 삶을 동반하는

[전문 해석]

(1)걱정은 무의미하고 그들(아이들)이 걱정하지 않는다면 그들이 더 만족할 것이라고 그저 여러분의 아이들을 설득하는 것만으로는 그들이 걱정하는 것을 멈추게 하지 않을 것이다. (2)어떤 이유로, 아이들은 걱정이 그들이 거의 통제할 수 없거나 아예 통제할 수 없는 삶의 사실이라고 믿는 것 같다. (3)결과적으로, 그들은 멈추려고 노력하지도 않는다. (4)따라서, 여러분은 걱정이 죄책감과 두려움처럼 어떤 감정에 지나지 않고, 모든 감정과 같이 의지의 힘에 지배를 받는다고 그들을 설득할 필요가 있다. (5)그들에게 단순히 걱정에 주의를 기울이려고 하지 않음으로써 그들이 자신의 삶으로부터 걱정을 없앨 수 있다는 것을 전하라. (6)그들에게 만약 자신이 어떻게 느끼는지와 상관없이 걱정하며 행동하는 것을 거부한다면, 그들은 결국 걱정하는 것을 멈추고 걱정 없는 삶을 동반하는 만족감을 경험하기 시작할 것이라고 설명하라.

[정답 확인]

다음 글에서 필자가 주장하는 바로 가장 적절한 것은?

① 아이가 죄책감(guilt)과 책임감(responsibility)을 구분하도록 가르쳐야 한다.
② 아이가 스스로 불안(anxiety)의 원인을 찾도록 도와주어야 한다.
③ 아이의 감정에 공감하고(empathize) 있음을 구체적으로 표현해야 한다.
④ 부모로서 느끼는 감정(emotions)에 관해 아이와 솔직하게 대화해야 한다.
⑤ (✓) 아이에게 자기 의지(will)로 걱정(worry)을 멈출 수 있음을 알려주어야 한다. 문장(4)

[중요 어휘]

□ **merely**	부사 그저, 한낱
□ **convince**	동사 설득하다, 확신시키다
□ **senseless**	형용사 무의미한, 의식을 잃은
□ **content**	형용사 만족한 / 명사 내용물
□ **consequently**	부사 결과적으로
□ **guilt**	명사 죄책감, 유죄
□ **be subject to A**	A의 지배를 받다
□ **will**	명사 의지, 유언장
□ **eliminate**	동사 없애다, 탈락시키다
□ **refuse**	동사 ~하려고 하지 않다, ~을 거부하다
□ **attend**	동사 주의를 기울이다
□ **contentment**	명사 만족감, 자족감
□ **accompany**	동사 동반하다, 동행하다

04 의미 추론

01 2022년 3월 21번 (정답률 75%) 정답 ④

[지문 끊어 읽기] 아이들의 새로운 정보의 해석 방식

(1) Studies by Vosniado and Brewer /
Vosniado와 Brewer의 연구는 /
illustrate *Fish is Fish*-style assimilation /
*Fish is Fish*식의 동화를 보여 준다 /
in the context of young children's thinking / about the earth.
어린아이들이 가진 생각의 맥락에서 / 지구에 관한

(2) They worked with children / (병렬①, 선행사)
그들은 아이들을 대상으로 연구했다 /
[who believed that the earth is flat / (명사절 접속사)
지구가 평평하다고 믿는 /
(because this fit their experiences)] / [ ]: 주격 관계대명사절
(이것이 그들의 경험과 일치하기 때문에) /
and attempted to help them understand / (병렬②, 5형식V, O, O·C)
그리고 그들이 이해하도록 도우려고 시도했다 /
that, in fact, it is spherical. (명사절 접속사, =the earth)
사실은 그것이 구형이라는 것을

힌트 종속절의 주어와 주절의 주어가 동일할 경우 종속절에서 '주어+be동사'는 생략 가능함. 본문의 경우 종속절의 주어와 주절의 주어가 children으로 동일하므로 when이 이끄는 종속절에서 'they(=children) were'이 생략됨. 혹은 분사구문에서 being이 생략된 형태로도 볼 수 있음.

(3) When told it is round, / children often pictured the earth /
그것이 둥글다고 들으면 / 아이들은 흔히 지구를 상상했다 /
as a pancake / rather than as a sphere. 정답 단서 (병렬①, 병렬②)
팬케이크와 같이 / 구보다는

아이들은 지구가 둥글다는 말을 들으면 팬케이크 같은 모양을 상상함.

힌트 A rather than B 구문으로 여기서 A와 B는 병렬을 이뤄야 함. 본문의 경우 'as+명사' 구조가 반복되고 있음.

(4) If they were then told / that it is round like a sphere, / (=the earth, 명사절 접속사)
그런 다음 그들이 들으면 / 그것이 구처럼 둥글다고 /
they interpreted the new information /
그들은 새로운 정보를 해석했다 /
about a spherical earth / within their flat-earth view / 정답 단서
구형의 지구에 관한 / 그들의 평평한 지구라는 관점 안에서 /

아이들은 지구가 구처럼 둥글다는 새로운 정보를 기존의 관점 안에서 해석함.

by picturing a pancake-like flat surface /
팬케이크처럼 평평한 표면을 상상함으로써 /
inside or on top of a sphere, /
구의 안쪽이나 위쪽에 있는 /
with humans standing on top of the pancake.
사람들이 팬케이크 위에 서 있으면서

힌트 'with+명사+분사'는 분사구문의 일종으로 주절과 동시에 일어나거나 연속적인 동작·상태를 나타냄. 명사와 분사의 관계가 능동이면 현재분사를, 수동이면 과거분사를 씀.

(5) The model of the earth / that they had developed / (S, 선행사; 목적격 관계대명사절)
지구의 모형은 / 그들이 개발한 /
— and [that helped them explain / (5형식V, O, O·C)
그리고 그들이 설명하는 데 도움이 된 /
how they could stand or walk / upon its surface] — / [ ]: 주격 관계대명사절 (간접의문문(explain의 목적어))
자신들이 어떻게 서 있거나 걸을 수 있는지를 / 그것의 표면 위에서 /
did not fit the model / of a spherical earth. (V, 동격의 of)
모형과 일치하지 않았다 / 구형의 지구라는

힌트 문장 중간에 대시(—)를 이용하여 삽입된 주격 관계대명사로, 앞에 있는 'that'과 마찬가지로 The model of the earth를 선행사로 가짐.

(6) Like the story *Fish is Fish*, / (선행사)
*Fish is Fish*의 이야기처럼 /
[where a fish imagines everything on land to be fish-like], /
물고기가 육지에 있는 모든 것이 물고기 같다고 상상한다는 / [ ]: 관계부사절
everything the children heard / was incorporated / (S, 선행사; 목적격 관계대명사절; V)
아이들이 들은 모든 것은 / 통합되었다 /
into their preexisting views. 정답 단서
그들의 기존 관점에

아이들이 들은 모든 것은 기존 관점에 통합됨.

힌트 imagine은 5형식 동사로 사용될 수 있음. 목적격 보어 자리에 형용사가 올 경우 to be가 생략될 수 있지만 본문은 생략되지 않은 형태임.

[전문 해석]

(1)Vosniado와 Brewer의 연구는 지구에 관한 어린아이들이 가진 생각의 맥락에서 *Fish is Fish*식의 동화(새로운 정보는 개인의 관점 안에서 해석된다)를 보여 준다. (2)그들은 지구가 평평하다고 믿는 아이들을 (이것이 그들의 경험과 일치하기 때문에) 대상으로 연구했고 사실은 지구가 구형이라는 것을 그들이 이해하도록 도우려고 시도했다. (3)지구가 둥글다는 말을 들으면 아이들은 흔히 지구를 구의 형태보다는 팬케이크와 같다고 상상했다. (4)그런 다음 지구가 구처럼 둥글다는 말을 들으면 그들은 팬케이크처럼 평평한 표면이 구의 안쪽이나 위쪽에 있으며 사람들이 팬케이크 위에 서 있는 것을 상상함으로써 자신들의 평평한 지구라는 관점 안에서 구형의 지구에 관한 새로운 정보를 해석했다. (5)자신들이 어떻게 지구의 표면에 서 있거나 걸을 수 있는지를 설명하는 데 도움이 된 그들이 개발한 지구의 모형은 구형의 지구라는 모형과 일치하지 않았다. (6)물고기가 육지의 모든 것을 물고기와 닮은 것으로 상상한다는 *Fish is Fish*의 이야기처럼, 아이들이 들은 모든 것은 그들의 기존 관점에 통합되었다.

- Fish is Fish(물고기는 물고기야!): 네덜란드의 어린이책 작가이자 일러스트레이터인 레오 리오니의 동화책임. 연못에서 물고기와 올챙이가 함께 성장하는데 올챙이는 개구리가 되어 바깥 세상 이야기를 해주고, 물고기는 상상하던 물 밖으로 나오지만 숨을 쉴 수 없어 이를 개구리가 구해준다는 내용임.

[정답 확인]

밑줄 친 *Fish is Fish*-style assimilation이 다음 글에서 의미하는 바로 가장 적절한 것은?

① established knowledge is questioned and criticized
확립된 지식에 의문을 갖고 비판한다
② novel views are always favored over existing ones
새로운 관점은 항상 기존의 관점보다 선호된다
③ all one's claims are evaluated based on others' opinions
개인의 모든 주장은 타인의 견해에 기반하여 평가된다
④ new information is interpreted within one's own views ✔
새로운 정보는 개인의 관점 안에서 해석된다
⑤ new theories are established through experiments
새로운 이론은 실험을 통해 확립된다

[중요 어휘]

□ assimilation	명사 동화(同化), 흡수
□ fit	동사 일치하다, 맞다
□ spherical	형용사 구형의, 구 모양의
□ picture	동사 상상하다, 묘사하다
□ sphere	명사 구
□ surface	명사 표면
□ incorporate into	~에 통합시키다
□ preexisting	형용사 기존의, 이전부터 존재하는
□ question	동사 ~에 의문을 갖다, 이의를 제기하다
□ novel	형용사 새로운 / 명사 소설
□ favor A over B	A를 B보다 선호하다
□ existing	형용사 기존의

02 2022년 9월 21번 (정답률 70%) 정답 ⑤

[지문 끊어 읽기] 침묵 효과

(1) Perhaps worse / (S·C)
아마도 더 나쁜 것은 /
than attempting to get the bad news out of the way /
나쁜 소식부터 먼저 이야기하고 넘어가려고 하는 것보다 /
is attempting to soften it / or simply not address it at all. (V, 동명사S)
그것을 완화하려고 하는 것이다 / 혹은 전혀 다루지 않으려고 하는 것이다

힌트 강조를 위해 주격 보어구 'worse than attempting to get the bad news out of the way'가 문두로 나가며 주어와 동사의 도치가 일어남.

(2) This "Mum Effect" / (S)
이 '침묵 효과'는 /
— a term coined by psychologists Sidney Rosen and Abraham Tesser in the early 1970s — /
1970년대 초반에 심리학자인 Sidney Rosen과 Abraham Tesser가 만든 용어인 /
happens / because people want to avoid becoming the target / (V)
발생한다 / 사람들이 표적이 되는 것을 피하고 싶기 때문에 /

of others' negative emotions. 정답 단서 사람들은 다른 사람들의 부정적 감정의 표적이 되는 것을 피하고 싶어함.
다른 사람들의 부정적인 감정의

(3) We all have the opportunity to lead change, /
형용사적 용법
우리 모두는 변화를 이끌 기회를 가지고 있다 /
yet it often [requires of us the courage /
그러나 그것은 종종 우리에게 용기를 요구한다 /
to deliver bad news to our superiors]. 정답 단서 상사에게 나쁜 소식을 전달하는 것은 용기가 필요한 쉽지 않은 일임.
형용사적 용법
우리의 상사에게 나쁜 소식을 전달할

힌트 'require A of B(B에게 A를 요구하다)'에서 A(the courage to deliver bad news to our superiors)가 너무 길어서 of us 뒤로 이동한 형태임.

(4) We don't want to be the innocent messenger /
선행사
우리는 무고한 전령이 되고 싶어 하지는 않는다 /
[who falls before a firing line].
사선 앞에서 쓰러지는 [ ]: 주격 관계대명사절

✶중요 문장 (2)에서 사람들은 다른 사람의 부정적 감정의 표적이 되는 걸 피하고 싶어 한다고 언급하고, 문장 (3)에서 상사에게 나쁜 소식을 전달하는 것은 용기가 필요한 일이라고 함. 따라서 문맥상 밑줄 친 부분은 '나쁜 소식을 전달함으로써 부정적 감정의 표적이 되는 것'을 의미한다고 유추할 수 있음.

(5) When our survival instincts kick in, /
우리의 생존 본능이 발동하면 /
they can override our courage /
그것은 우리의 용기를 무효로 할 수 있다 /
until the truth of a situation gets watered down.
어떤 상황의 진상이 희석될 때까지

힌트 '비난받을 처지에 있다'라는 뜻의 be in the firing line을 응용한 표현으로, 여기서는 '비난받을 처지에 놓이게 되는'이라고 이해하면 됨.

(6) "The Mum Effect and the resulting filtering /
침묵 효과와 그로 인해 발생하는 여과는 /
can have devastating effects / in a steep hierarchy," /
파괴적인 결과를 가져올 수 있다 / 가파른 위계 관계에서 /
writes Robert Sutton, an organizational psychologist.
조직 심리학자 Robert Sutton이 말한다

✶중요 문장 (1)에서 언급한 '나쁜 소식을 완화하거나 전혀 다루지 않으려고 하는 것'을 의미한다고 볼 수 있음.

(7) "What starts out as bad news / becomes happier and happier /
S(=선행사 포함 관계대명사) V
나쁜 소식으로 시작한 것이 / 점점 더 좋아진다 /
as it travels up the ranks /
접속사(~할수록)
그것이 단계를 올라갈수록 /
— because after each boss hears the news /
그 이유는 각 단계의 상사가 그 소식을 듣고 나서 /
from his or her subordinates, /
자신의 부하 직원으로부터 /
he or she makes it sound a bit less bad /
S 형식V O O·C
그 사람은 그것을 다소 덜 나쁘게 들리도록 만들기 때문이다 /
before passing it up the chain."
그것이 다음 단계로 넘어가기 전에

힌트 '비교급 and 비교급'은 '점점 더 ~한'이라는 뜻임.

[전문 해석]

(1)아마도 나쁜 소식부터 먼저 이야기하고 넘어가려고 하는 것보다 더 나쁜 것은 그것을 완화하거나 전혀 다루지 않으려고 하는 것이다. (2)1970년대 초반에 심리학자인 Sidney Rosen과 Abraham Tesser가 만든 용어인 이 '침묵 효과'는 사람들이 다른 사람들의 부정적인 감정의 표적이 되는 것을 피하고 싶기 때문에 발생한다. (3)우리 모두는 변화를 이끌 기회를 가지고 있으나, 그것은 종종 우리에게 우리의 상사에게 나쁜 소식을 전달할 용기를 요구한다. (4)우리는 사선 앞에서 쓰러지는 무고한 전령(불쾌한 소식을 전하는 데 책임을 지는 사람)이 되고 싶어 하지는 않는다. (5)우리의 생존 본능이 발동하면, 그것은 어떤 상황의 진상이 희석될 때까지 우리의 용기를 무효로 할 수 있다. (6)"침묵 효과와 그로 인해 발생하는 여과는 가파른 위계 관계에서 파괴적인 결과를 가져올 수 있다."라고 조직 심리학자 Robert Sutton이 말한다. (7)"나쁜 소식으로 시작한 것이 단계를 올라갈수록 점점 더 좋아진다. 그 이유는 각 단계의 상사가 자신의 부하 직원으로부터 그 소식을 듣고 나서 다음 단계로 넘어가기 전에 그것을 다소 덜 나쁘게 들리도록 만들기 때문이다."

[정답 확인]

밑줄 친 the innocent messenger who falls before a firing line이 다음 글에서 의미하는 바로 가장 적절한 것은?

① the employee being criticized for being silent
침묵하기 때문에 비난받는 직원
② the peacemaker who pursues non-violent solutions
비폭력적인 해결책을 추구하는 중재자
③ the negotiator who looks for a mutual understanding
상호 이해를 기대하는 협상가
④ the subordinate who wants to get attention from the boss
상사의 관심을 얻고자 하는 부하
✔ the person who gets the blame for reporting unpleasant news
불쾌한 소식을 전하는 데 책임을 지는 사람

[중요 어휘]

□ get A out of the way	A를 먼저 처리하고 넘어가다
□ soften	동사 완화하다, 누그러뜨리다
□ address	동사 다루다
□ coin	동사 (새로운 단어를) 만들다
□ superior	명사 상사 / 형용사 우수한, 우월한
□ innocent	형용사 무고한, 순진한
□ messenger	명사 전령, 전달자
□ firing line	명사 사선, 방화선, 최전방 부대
□ kick in	발동하다
□ override	동사 무효화하다, 기각하다
□ water down	희석시키다, 약화시키다
□ devastating	형용사 파괴적인
□ steep	형용사 가파른, 급격한
□ rank	명사 단계, 지위, 서열
□ subordinate	명사 부하 / 형용사 종속된, 부차적인
□ peacemaker	명사 중재자
□ negotiator	명사 협상가
□ blame	명사 책임, 비난 / 동사 비난하다

03 2019년 9월 21번 (정답률 65%) 정답 ⑤

[지문 끊어 읽기] 잡식 동물의 역설

(1) Humans are omnivorous, /
인간은 잡식성이다 /
meaning that they can consume and digest /
그리고 이것은 그들이 먹고 소화할 수 있다는 것을 뜻한다 /
a wide selection of plants and animals /
다양한 종류의 식물과 동물을 /
found in their surroundings.
그들의 주위 환경에서 발견되는

(2) The primary advantage to this / is that they can adapt /
이것의 주요한 이점은 / 그들이 적응할 수 있다는 것이다 /
to nearly all earthly environments.
지구상의 거의 모든 환경에

(3) The disadvantage / is that no single food provides the nutrition /
단점은 / 어떤 단 한 가지의 음식만으로는 영양분을 공급하지 못한다는 것이다 /
necessary for survival.
생존에 필요한

(4) Humans must be flexible enough / to eat a variety of items /
S·C①
인간은 충분히 융통성이 있어야 한다 / 다양한 대상을 먹을 만큼 /
sufficient for physical growth and maintenance, /
신체적인 성장과 유지에 충분할 /
yet cautious enough / not to randomly ingest foods /
S·C②
하지만 충분히 신중해야 한다 / 음식을 임의로 섭취하지 않을 만큼 /
that are physiologically harmful and, possibly, fatal. 정답 단서
생리학적으로 해가 되고 어쩌면 치명적일

(5) This dilemma, / [the need to experiment /
S [ ]: The dilemma와 동격
이 딜레마는 / 즉 시도하고자 하는 욕구는 /
combined with the need for conservatism], /
과거분사구
현상 유지에 대한 욕구와 결합되어 /
is known as the omnivore's paradox.
V
잡식 동물의 역설이라고 알려져 있다

✶중요 이 문장에서 'experiment'는 인간이 잡식성이기 때문에 다양한 것을 먹고자 하는 욕구가 있음을 드러내고, 'conservatism'은 어떤 것이 자신에게 해가 될지 모르니 무턱대고 먹지 않으려고 하는, 일종의 보수적인 경향성을 나타내는 말임.

힌트 'result in'은 '~라는 결과를 낳다' 혹은 '(결과적으로) ~을 야기하다'라는 뜻임. 'result from'은 '(결과가) ~로부터 비롯되다'의 의미로, 정반대의 뜻임.

(6) It results in / two contradictory psychological impulses /
그것은 결과를 낳는다 / 두 가지의 모순적인 심리적 충동이라는 /
regarding diet.
식사와 관련된

(7) The first is an attraction to new foods; /
첫 번째는 새로운 음식으로의 끌림이다 /
the second is a preference for familiar foods.
두 번째는 익숙한 음식에 대한 선호이다

[전문 해석]

(1)인간은 잡식성인데, 이것은 그들이 (그들의) 주위 환경에서 발견되는 다양한 종류의 식물과 동물을 먹고 소화할 수 있다는 것을 뜻한다. (2)이것(잡식성인 것)의 주요한 이점은 그들(인간들)이 지구상의 거의 모든 환경에 적응할 수 있다는 것이다. (3)단점은 어떤 단 한 가지의 음식만으로는 생존에 필요한 영양분을 공급하지 못한다는 것이다. (4)인간은 신체적인 성장과 유지(를 하기)에 충분할 다양한 대상(음식)을 먹을 만큼 충분히 융통성이 있어야 하지만, 생리학적으로 해가 되고, 어쩌면, 치명적일 음식을 임의로 섭취하지 않을 만큼 충분히 신중해야 한다. (5)이 딜레마, 즉 현상 유지에 대한(현상을 유지하고자 하는) 욕구와 결합되어 (새로운 음식을) 시도하고자 하는 욕구는, 잡식 동물의 역설(음식에 대해 융통성이 있는 동시에 신중해야 할 필요)이라고 알려져 있다. (6)그것은 식사와 관련된 두 가지의 모순적인 심리적 충동이라는 결과를 낳는다(충동으로 이어진다). (7)첫 번째는 새로운 음식으로의 끌림(새로운 음식에 끌리는 것)이다. 두 번째는 익숙한 음식에 대한 선호(익숙한 음식을 선호하는 것)이다.

[정답 확인]

밑줄 친 the omnivore's paradox가 다음 글에서 의미하는 바로 가장 적절한 것은?

① irony of wanting but disliking nutritious food
영양가 있는 음식을 원하지만 싫어하는 모순
② conflict between vegetarians and meat eaters
채식주의자와 육식하는 사람들 사이의 갈등
③ sacrificing quality of food for quantity of food
음식의 양을 위해 음식의 질을 희생하는 것
④ difficulty in judging whether something is edible
어떤 것이 식용인지 아닌지를 판단하는 것의 어려움
✔ need to be both flexible and cautious about foods
음식에 대해 융통성이 있는 동시에 신중해야 할 필요

★중요 'the omnivore's paradox'가 무엇인지 파악하려면 문장 (4)를 놓쳐서는 안 됨. 보기 ⑤는 문장 (4)의 'flexible'이나 'cautious' 등의 단어가 그대로 들어가 있는 데다가, 이 문장을 압축해 놓았음.

[문제 풀이]

이 글에서는 인간이 잡식성이기 때문에 생기는 역설을 설명하고 있다. 인간은 무엇이든 먹을 수 있지만, 음식 한 종류만 먹고는 생존할 수 없기 때문에 다양한 음식을 섭취해야만 한다. 문장 (4)와 (5)에서 언급했듯, 다양한 음식을 섭취하려는 것은 기존의 선호나 행동에서 더 나아가야 하는 융통성을 필요로 한다. 그러나 어떤 것이 해가 되거나 치명적인지는 먹어보지 않으면 알 수가 없으니 신중해야 한다는 것을 역설이라 설명한 것이다. 따라서 ⑤가 정답이다.

[오답 풀이]

① - 본문에서도 음식의 영양을 언급하긴 했으나, 영양가 있는 음식에 대한 좋고 싫음이나 욕구는 말하고자 하는 바와 거리가 있는 데다가 언급된 바가 없으므로 정답이 될 수 없다.
④ - 어떤 것이 식용인지 아닌지를 판단하는 것은 본문 내에서 음식이 치명적일 수도 있으니 신중해야 한다고 부분적으로만 언급되었을 뿐, 주어진 어구를 충분히 설명하지는 못한다.

[중요 어휘]

□ omnivorous	형용사 잡식성의, 아무거나 먹는
□ surroundings	명사 (항상 복수) 주위 환경
□ earthly	형용사 지구상의, 세속적인
□ sufficient	형용사 충분한, 넉넉한
□ maintenance	명사 유지, 보수
□ cautious	형용사 신중한, 조심스러운
□ ingest	동사 섭취하다, 삼키다
□ physiologically	부사 생리학적으로
□ fatal	형용사 치명적인, 죽음을 초래하는
□ conservatism	명사 현상 유지, 보수주의
□ omnivore	명사 잡식 동물
□ paradox	명사 역설, 모순(된 말)
□ contradictory	형용사 모순적인, 자가당착의
□ impulse	명사 충동, 자극
□ attraction	명사 끌림, 매력, 명소
□ edible	형용사 식용의, 먹을 수 있는

04 2022년 6월 21번 (정답률 65%)

정답 ①

[지문 끊어 읽기]

고객 만족을 위한 마케팅

(1) For companies / interested in delighting customers, /
주격 관계대명사+be동사 생략
기업들에게 / 고객들을 즐겁게 하는 데 관심이 있는 /
exceptional value and service become part of the overall company culture.
2형식V S.C
뛰어난 가치와 서비스는 기업 문화 전반의 일부가 된다

(2) For example, / year after year, / Pazano ranks /
예를 들어 / 해마다 / Pazano는 차지한다 /
at or near the top / of the hospitality industry /
최상위 또는 상위권을 / 서비스업 중 /
in terms of customer satisfaction.
고객 만족이라는 측면에서

(3) The company's passion / for satisfying customers /
S
그 기업의 열정은 / 고객을 만족시키기 위한 /
is summed up in its credo, / which promises /
V 선행사 계속적 용법(=and it~)
그것의 신조에 요약되어 있다 / 그리고 이는 약속한다 /
[that its luxury hotels will deliver / a truly memorable experience].
명사절 접속사 [ ]: promises의 목적어절
그것의 고급 호텔이 제공할 것을 / 진정으로 기억될 만한 경험을

(4) Although a customer-centered firm seeks to deliver /
고객 중심 기업은 제공하고자 하지만 /
high customer satisfaction / relative to competitors, /
높은 고객 만족을 / 경쟁사 대비 /
it does not attempt to *maximize* / customer satisfaction. 정답단서
그것은 '최대화'하려고 시도하지는 않는다 / 고객 만족을
고객 중심 기업은 상대적으로 높은 고객 만족을 제공하고자 하지만 고객 만족을 최대화하려고 하지는 않음.

(5) A company can always increase customer satisfaction /
기업은 고객 만족을 항상 높일 수 있다 /
by lowering its price / or increasing its services.
병렬① 병렬②
그것의 가격을 낮춤으로써 / 혹은 그것의 서비스를 증진시킴으로써

힌트 'result in+결과'는 '~로 이어지다, ~을 야기하다'의 의미로, 'result from+원인'과 구분해야 함.

(6) But this may result in lower profits. 정답단서
=문장 (5)
하지만 이것은 더 낮은 이윤으로 이어질지도 모른다
기업이 고객 만족을 '최대화'하려고 하지 않는 이유는 고객에게 제공하는 서비스의 가격을 낮추거나 서비스를 증진시키는 것이 기업 입장에서는 더 낮은 이윤으로 이어질 수 있기 때문임.

(7) Thus, / the purpose of marketing /
따라서 / 마케팅의 목적은 /
is to generate customer value profitably. 정답단서
명사적 용법(S.C)
수익을 내면서 고객 가치를 창출하는 것이다
그래서 마케팅은 수익을 내면서 고객 가치를 창출하는 것을 목적으로 함.

(8) This requires a very delicate balance: /
이것은 매우 미묘한 균형을 필요로 한다 /
the marketer must continue to generate /
마케팅 담당자는 계속해서 창출해야 한다 /
more customer value and satisfaction /
더 많은 고객 가치와 만족을 /
but not 'give away the house'.
하지만 '집을 거저나 다름없이 팔아서는' 안 된다

힌트 'continue'와 'not give away'가 병렬로 이어져 있음. 'not' 앞에 'must'가 생략되었다는 것에 유의해야 함.

[전문 해석]

(1)고객들을 즐겁게 하는 데 관심이 있는 기업들에게, 뛰어난 가치와 서비스는 기업 문화 전반의 일부가 된다. (2)예를 들어, 해마다, 고객 만족이라는 측면에서 Pazano는 서비스업 중 최상위 또는 상위권을 차지한다. (3)고객을 만족시키기 위한 그 기업의 열정은 그것의 신조에 요약되어 있고, 이는 그 기업의 고급 호텔이 진정으로 기억될 만한 경험을 제공할 것을 약속한다. (4)고객 중심 기업은 경쟁사 대비 높은 고객 만족을 제공하고자 하지만, 그것은 고객 만족을 '최대화'하려고 시도하지는 않는다. (5)기업은 가격을 낮추거나 서비스를 증진시킴으로써 고객 만족을 항상 높일 수 있다. (6)하지만 이것은 더 낮은 이윤으로 이어질지도 모른다. (7)따라서, 마케팅의 목적은 수익을 내면서 고객 가치를 창출하는 것이다. (8)이것은 매우 미묘한 균

형을 필요로 한다. 마케팅 담당자는 더 많은 고객 가치와 만족을 계속해서 창출해야 하지만 '집을 거저나 다름없이 팔아서는(기업의 수익성을 걸어서는)' 안 된다.

[정답 확인]

밑줄 친 'give away the house'가 다음 글에서 의미하는 바로 가장 적절한 것은?

✔ risk the company's profitability
기업의 수익성을 걸어서는
② overlook a competitor's strengths
경쟁사의 강점을 간과해서는
③ hurt the reputation of the company
기업의 평판을 해쳐서는
④ generate more customer complaints
고객의 불만을 더 야기해서는
⑤ abandon customer-oriented marketing
고객 중심의 마케팅을 버려서는

[문제 풀이]

이 글은 기업이 고객 만족을 위해 어떻게 마케팅을 해야 하는지에 대해 설명한다. 기업은 고객 만족도를 높이고자 한다. 그런데 고객 만족도를 항상 높게 유지하기 위해서는 제공하는 서비스의 가격을 낮추거나 서비스를 증진시켜야 한다. 기업의 목적은 수익인데, 앞서 말한 방식을 택하면 낮은 이윤을 얻을 수밖에 없다. 따라서 마케팅은 고객 만족과 이윤 추구 사이의 균형을 유지해야 한다. 밑줄 친 부분은 이러한 내용을 요약하여 기업이 수익성을 포기해서는 안 된다는 내용을 의미해야 하므로 정답은 ①이다.

[중요 어휘]

☐ **delight**	동사 즐겁게 하다, 기쁨을 주다 / 명사 기쁨
☐ **exceptional**	형용사 뛰어난, 우수한, 이례적인
☐ **hospitality industry**	(호텔, 식당 등의) 서비스업
☐ **sum up**	요약하다
☐ **credo**	명사 신조
☐ **deliver**	동사 제공하다, 배달하다
☐ **seek to V**	~하고자 하다, ~하려고 하다
☐ **relative to**	~대비, ~에 비례하여, ~에 관하여
☐ **maximize**	동사 최대화하다
☐ **delicate**	형용사 미묘한, 섬세한
☐ **give away**	거저 주다
☐ **risk**	동사 ~을 걸다, 위태롭게 하다
☐ **profitability**	명사 수익성
☐ **overlook**	동사 간과하다, 못 보고 넘어가다
☐ **reputation**	명사 평판, 명성
☐ **abandon**	동사 버리다, 포기하다

05 2022년 11월 21번 (정답률 65%) 정답 ③

[지문 끊어 읽기] 에너지가 많을 때 힘든 일을 처리하는 습관

(1) Research in the science of peak performance and motivation / (S)
최고의 수행과 동기 부여에 대한 과학 연구는 /
points to the fact / (V)
사실을 지적한다 /
that [different tasks should ideally be matched / (동격의 접속사)
각각의 일이 이상적으로 맞춰져야 한다는 /
to our energy level].
우리의 에너지 수준에

(2) For example, / analytical tasks are best accomplished /
예를 들어 / 분석적인 일은 가장 잘 수행된다 /
when our energy is high / and we are free from distractions /
우리의 에너지가 높을 때 / 그리고 우리가 집중을 방해하는 것들이 없을 때 /
and able to focus.
그리고 집중할 수 있을 때
힌트 able to 앞에 반복되는 we are이 생략됨. 원래 문장은 we are able to focus임.

(3) I generally wake up energized.
나는 보통 활기찬 상태로 일어난다

(4) Over the years, / I have consistently stuck to / (현재완료)
몇 년 동안 / 나는 꾸준히 고수해 왔다 /
the habit of "eating my problems for breakfast."
'아침 식사로 나의 문제를 먹는' 습관을

(5) I'm someone / (선행사①)
나는 사람이다 /
who tends to overthink different scenarios and conversations / (주격 관계대명사, 선행사②)
다양한 시나리오와 대화를 너무 많이 생각하는 경향이 있는 /
that haven't happened yet. (주격 관계대명사)
아직 일어나지 않은

(6) When I procrastinate / on talking with an unhappy client / (병렬①)
내가 미룰 때 / 불만족스러워 하는 고객과 이야기하는 것을 /
or dealing with an unpleasant email, / (병렬②)
또는 불쾌한 이메일을 처리하는 것을 /
I find I waste too much emotional energy / during the day.
나는 내가 너무 많은 감정적인 에너지를 낭비한다고 생각한다 / 낮 동안에

(7) It's as if the task hangs over my head, /
마치 그 일이 뇌리에서 떠나지 않는 것 같다 /
and I'll spend more time worrying about it, / (병렬①)
그리고 나는 더 많은 시간을 그것에 대해 걱정하며 보낼 것이다 /
talking about it, / and avoiding it, / (병렬②, 병렬③)
그것에 대해 이야기하는 데 / 그리고 그것을 피하는 데 /
than it would actually take / to just take care of it.
실제로 걸리는 것보다 / 그것을 단지 처리하는 데

(8) So for me, / it'll always be the first thing / I get done. 정답 단서 (=the task)
그래서 나에게는 / 그것이 항상 첫 번째 일이 될 것이다 / 내가 끝내는
나는 힘든 일을 첫 번째로 끝냄.
힌트 선행사 the first thing과 I get done 사이에 목적격 관계대명사 that이 생략되어 있음.

(9) If you know / you are not a morning person, / be strategic /
만약 여러분이 안다면 / 자신이 아침형 인간이 아니라는 것을 / 전략을 세우라 /
about scheduling your difficult work / later in the day. 정답 단서
여러분의 어려운 일을 하도록 일정을 짜는 것에 대한 / 오후 늦은 시간에
자신이 에너지가 많은 시간에 어려운 일을 하라고 조언함.

[전문 해석]

(1)최고의 수행과 동기 부여에 대한 과학 연구는 각각의 일이 우리의 에너지 수준에 이상적으로 맞춰져야 한다는 사실을 지적한다. (2)예를 들어, 분석적인 일은 우리의 에너지가 높고 집중을 방해하는 것들이 없으며 집중할 수 있을 때 가장 잘 수행된다. (3)나는 보통 활기찬 상태로 일어난다. (4)몇 년 동안 나는 '아침 식사로 나의 문제를 먹는'(에너지가 가득할 동안 대부분의 힘든 일들을 처리하는 것) 습관을 꾸준히 고수해 왔다. (5)나는 아직 일어나지 않은 다양한 시나리오와 대화를 너무 많이 생각하는 경향이 있는 사람이다. (6)불만족스러워 하는 고객과 이야기하거나 불쾌한 이메일을 처리하는 것을 미룰 때, 나는 내가 낮 동안에 너무 많은 감정적인 에너지를 낭비한다고 생각한다. (7)마치 그 일이 뇌리에서 떠나지 않는 것 같고, 나는 그것을 단지 처리하는 데 실제로 걸리는 것보다 더 많은 시간을 그것에 대해 걱정하고, 그것에 대해 이야기하고 그리고 그것을 피하는 데 보낼 것이다. (8)그래서 나에게는 그것이 항상 내가 끝내는 첫 번째 일이 될 것이다. (9)만약 여러분이 자신이 아침형 인간이 아니라는 것을 안다면, 여러분의 어려운 일을 오후 늦은 시간에 하도록 일정을 짜는 것에 대한 전략을 세우라.

[정답 확인]

밑줄 친 "eating my problems for breakfast"가 다음 글에서 의미하는 바로 가장 적절한 것은?

① thinking of breakfast as fuel for the day
아침 식사를 하루를 위한 연료로 생각하는 것
② trying to reflect on pleasant events from yesterday
어제의 즐거운 일들을 되돌아보려고 노력하는 것
✔ handling the most demanding tasks while full of energy
에너지가 가득할 동안 가장 힘든 일들을 처리하는 것
④ spending the morning time improving my physical health
나의 신체적 건강을 향상시키면서 아침 시간을 보내는 것

⑤ preparing at night to avoid decision making in the morning
아침에 의사 결정하는 것을 피하기 위해 밤에 준비하는 것

[문제 풀이]

본문은 일이 우리의 에너지 수준에 이상적으로 맞춰져야 한다는 사실을 보여 준다. 문장 (2)에 따르면 분석적인 일은 에너지가 높고 집중이 잘 되는 때에 잘 수행된다고 하는데, 문장 (3)에서 필자는 일어날 때 보통 활기찬 상태라고 한다. 이 활기찬 상태와 대조적으로 처리해야 할 힘든 일을 나중으로 미룰 때, 필자는 실제로 그 일을 처리하는 시간보다 그것을 걱정하고, 이야기하고, 피하는 데에 더 많은 시간을 보내며 낮 동안에 감정적으로 많은 에너지를 낭비한다고 한다. 그래서 문장 (8)에서 필자는 그것(힘든 일)이 가장 첫 번째로 끝내는 일이 될 것이라고 말하고 있다. 따라서 밑줄 친 부분의 '아침'은 '에너지가 높을 때'를 의미하며, '문제를 먹는'다는 것은 '힘든 일을 처리한다'라는 뜻임을 알 수 있다. 따라서 정답은 ③이다.

[중요 어휘]

☐ peak	형용사 최고의 / 명사 절정, 정점
☐ ideally	부사 이상적으로
☐ analytical	형용사 분석적인
☐ distraction	명사 집중을 방해하는 것, 오락 활동
☐ stick to	~을 고수하다
☐ overthink	동사 너무 많이 생각하다
☐ emotional	형용사 감정적인
☐ hang over one's head	뇌리에서 떠나지 않다
☐ strategic	형용사 전략적인
☐ schedule	동사 일정을 짜다 / 명사 일정

06 2023년 9월 21번 (정답률 65%)

정답 ③

[지문 끊어 읽기]

숲의 다양성을 지키는 균류

(1) I suspect / [fungi are a little more forward "thinking" /
나는 짐작한다 / 균류가 약간 더 앞서 '생각한다'고 /
than their larger partners]. [ ]: 명사절(접속사 that 생략)
자신의 더 큰 상대보다

(2) Among trees, / each species fights other species.
S V O
나무들 사이에서 / 각 종들은 다른 종들과 싸운다 /

(3) Let's assume / [the beeches native to Central Europe /
S'
가정해 보자 / 중부 유럽 태생의 너도밤나무가 /
could emerge victorious / in most forests there]. [ ]: 명사절(접속사 that 생략)
V'
승리를 거둘 수 있다고 / 그곳의 숲 대부분에서

(4) Would this really be an advantage?
이것은 정말로 이점일까

힌트 문장 (5)와 (6)은 가정법 과거 구문이 사용되었는데, if절에 과거시제 동사(각각 came/were)가 사용되었고, 주절에는 '조동사 과거형+동사원형(각각 would happen/wouldn't, be)'이 쓰였음. (가정법 과거: If+S'+과거V' ~, S+조동사 과거형+동사원형 ~)

(5) What would happen / if a new pathogen came along /
선행사
무슨 일이 발생할까 / 만약 새로운 병원균이 나타난다면 /
[that infected most of the beeches and killed them]?
병렬① [ ]: 주격 관계대명사절 병렬②
너도밤나무의 대부분을 감염시켜 그것들을 죽이는

(6) In that case, / wouldn't it be more advantageous /
그런 경우에 / 더 유리하지 않을까 /
if there were a certain number of other species around /
일정한 수의 다른 종들이 주변에 있다면 / 선행사
— oaks, maples, or firs — /
참나무, 단풍나무 또는 전나무 /
that would continue to grow and provide the shade / [needed /
주격 관계대명사 병렬① 병렬② [ ]: 과거분사구
계속 자라나서 그늘을 제공해 줄 / 필요로 되는 /
for a new generation of young beeches /
새로운 세대의 어린 너도밤나무들이 /
to sprout and grow up]?
싹을 틔우고 자라나기 위해

힌트 to부정사의 부사적 용법인 to sprout and grow up의 의미상의 주어임.

(7) Diversity provides security / for ancient forests. 정답 단서 다양성은 오래된 숲에 안전을 제공함.
S V O
다양성은 안전을 제공한다 / 오래된 숲에

(8) Because fungi are also very dependent on stable conditions, /
균류는 또한 안정적인 조건에 매우 의존적이기 때문에 /
they support other species underground /
V①
그것들은 땅속에서 다른 종들을 지원한다 /
and protect them from complete collapse / to ensure /
V② =other species 부사적 용법(~하기 위해)
그리고 그것들을 완전한 붕괴로부터 보호한다 / 확실히 하기 위해 /
[that one species of tree doesn't manage to dominate]. 정답 단서
[ ]: that 명사절 S' V' O'
한 종의 나무가 어떻게든 우세해지지 않도록
균류는 어느 한 종의 나무가 우세해지지 않도록 땅속에서 다른 종들을 지원하고 그것들의 완전한 붕괴를 막음.

[전문 해석]

(1)나는 균류가 자신의 더 큰 상대보다 약간 더 앞서 '생각한다'(다양성이 숲의 안정으로 이어진다는 것을 알고 있는)고 짐작한다. (2)나무들 사이에서, 각 종들은 다른 종들과 싸운다. (3)중부 유럽 태생의 너도밤나무가 그곳의 숲 대부분에서 승리를 거둘 수 있다고 가정해 보자. (4)이것은 정말로 이점일까? (5)만약 너도밤나무의 대부분을 감염시켜 그것들을 죽이는 새로운 병원균이 나타난다면 무슨 일이 발생할까? (6)그런 경우에, 계속 자라나서 새로운 세대의 어린 너도밤나무들이 싹을 틔우고 자라나기 위해 필요로 되는 그늘을 제공해 줄 참나무, 단풍나무 또는 전나무와 같이 일정한 수의 다른 종들이 주변에 있다면 더 유리하지 않을까? (7)다양성은 오래된 숲에 안전을 제공한다. (8)균류는 또한 안정적인 조건에 매우 의존적이기 때문에, 그것들은 한 종의 나무가 어떻게든 우세해지지 않도록 확실히 하기 위해 땅속에서 다른 종들을 지원하고 그것들을 완전한 붕괴로부터 보호한다.

[정답 확인]

밑줄 친 forward "thinking"이 다음 글에서 의미하는 바로 가장 적절한 것은?

① responsible for the invasion of foreign species
외래종의 침입에 책임이 있는
② eager to support the dominance of one species
한 종의 우세함을 지지하는 데 열심인
✔③ aware that diversity leads to the stability of forests
다양성이 숲의 안정으로 이어진다는 것을 알고 있는
④ indifferent to helping forests regenerate after collapse
붕괴 후에 숲이 재생되는 것을 돕는 것에 무관심한
⑤ careful that their territories are not occupied by other species
그들의 영토가 다른 종들에 의해 점령되지 않도록 조심하는

[문제 풀이]

문맥상 문장 (1)의 '자신의 더 큰 상대(their larger partners)'는 나무들을 의미하므로, 지문을 통해 균류가 어떤 점에서 나무들보다 더 큰 혜안을 가지고 있는지를 추론해야 한다. 문장 (2)~(6)은 다른 종들과의 경쟁에서 우위를 점하게 된 너도밤나무가 병원균에 감염되어 대부분 사라지는 상황을 가정하면서, 겉보기에는 유리해 보이는 상황이 실제로는 그렇지 않음을 설명하고 있다. 즉, 문장 (7)을 통해 알 수 있듯이, 오래된 숲에 더 중요한 것은 한 종이 우세하기보다는 '다양성'이 보존되는 것이다. 그런데 문장 (8)에 따르면 '균류(fungi)'는 마치 이러한 사실을 알기라도 하는 듯 땅속에서 다른 종들을 지원하고 그것들의 완전한 붕괴를 막음으로써 숲의 다양성을 유지하고 있다. 따라서 밑줄 친 forward "thinking"이 의미하는 바로 가장 적절한 것은 ③이다.

[중요 어휘]

☐ suspect	동사 짐작하다, 생각하다, 의심하다
☐ fungi	명사 균류 (fungus의 복수형)
☐ species	명사 (생물 분류 단위인) 종
☐ assume	동사 가정하다, 추측하다
☐ native	형용사 태생의, 토착의
☐ victorious	형용사 승리를 거둔, 승리한
☐ advantage	명사 이점, 장점
☐ come along	나타나다, 생겨나다
☐ infect	동사 감염시키다
☐ advantageous	형용사 유리한, 이로운
☐ generation	명사 세대
☐ sprout	동사 싹을 틔우다 / 명사 새싹

□	**diversity**	명사 다양성
□	**security**	명사 안전(성)
□	**ancient**	형용사 오래된, 고대의
□	**dependent**	형용사 의존하는
□	**stable**	형용사 안정적인, 견실한
□	**condition**	명사 조건, 상황
□	**protect A from B**	A를 B로부터 보호하다
□	**complete**	형용사 완전한 / 동사 완성하다
□	**collapse**	명사 붕괴 / 동사 붕괴하다
□	**manage to V**	어떻게든[간신히] ~해내다

● 지문 구조도

주장

(1) 균류(fungi)는 자신의 더 큰 상대(=나무)보다 약간 더 앞서 생각함.

↓

근거

(2)~(4) 만약 여러 나무 종들이 싸우는 상황에서, 너도밤나무(beeches)가 승리를 거둔(emerge victorious)다면, 이는 이점이 될까?

(5) (어느 한 종이 우세한 상황에서) 그 종을 감염시켜(infect) 죽이는(kill) 새로운 병원균(a new pathogen)이 나타날 수 있음.
(6) 한 종이 우세한 것보다는, 새로운 세대(a new generation)의 어린 나무들이 자라나도록(grow up) 도와줄 다른 종들(other species)이 주변에 있는 것이 더 유리할(more advantageous) 수 있음.
↓
(7) 오래된 숲에 안전(security)을 제공하는 것은 '다양성(diversity)'임.

← (8) 균류는 땅속에서 다른 종들을 지원하고(support) 다른 종들을 완전한 붕괴로부터 보호하여(protect) 어느 한 종의 나무가 우세하지(dominate) 않게 함. (=다양성에 기여함)

07 2023년 3월 21번 (정답률 60%) 정답 ③

[지문 끊어 읽기] 문제해결을 위한 사고방식

(1) Everyone's heard the expression /
모두 표현을 들어 본 적이 있다 /
don't let the perfect become the enemy of the good.
'완벽함이 괜찮음의 적이 되게 두지 말라'는

(2) If you want to get over an obstacle /
(If: 조건절 접속사)
여러분이 장애물을 극복하고 싶다면 /
so that your idea can become the solution-based policy /
(so that: ~하도록, ~하기 위해 / policy: 선행사)
여러분의 아이디어가 해결을 기반으로 한 방책이 될 수 있도록 /
you've long dreamed of, /
(목적격 관계대명사절)
여러분이 오랫동안 꿈꿔 왔던 /
you can't have an all-or-nothing mentality. 정답 단서 전부 아니면 전무라고 여기는 사고방식은 문제 해결에 도움이 되지 않음.
여러분은 전부 아니면 전무라고 여기는 사고방식을 가져서는 안 된다

(3) You have to be willing to alter your idea /
(be willing to V: 기꺼이 ~하다)
여러분은 기꺼이 여러분의 아이디어를 바꾸어야 한다 /
and let others influence its outcome.
(let: 5형식V / others: O / influence: O·C)
그리고 다른 사람이 그것의 결과에 영향을 미치도록 해야 한다

(4) You have to be okay / with the outcome being a little different, /
여러분은 괜찮다고 여겨야 한다 / 결과가 조금 달라도 /
even a little *less*, / than you wanted.
심지어 조금 '못'하여도 / 여러분이 원했던 것과

(5) Say / you're pushing for a clean water act.
가정해보자 / 여러분이 수질 오염 방지법을 추진하고 있다고

(6) Even if what emerges isn't as well-funded as you wished, /
(what emerges: S' / isn't: V'①)
비록 나타난 것이 여러분이 원했던 만큼의 자금이 충분하게 지원되지 않더라도 /
or doesn't match how you originally conceived the bill, /
(doesn't match: V'② / how ~: 선행사 the way가 생략된 관계부사절)
또는 여러분이 처음에 그 법안을 고안한 방식과 일치하지 않더라도 /
you'll have still succeeded /
여러분은 여전히 성공해 있을 것이다 /
in ensuring [that kids in troubled areas have access to clean water].
([ ]: 명사절(ensuring의 목적어절))
힘든 지역의 아이들이 깨끗한 물에 접근하도록 하는 데
힌트 동격의 접속사 that으로, 앞에서 나온 내용을 다시 설명해주고 있음. 힘든 지역의 아이들이 깨끗한 물에 접근하도록 했다는 것, 즉 여러분 덕분에 그들이 더 안전하리라는 것이 중요하다는 의미임.

(7) That's what counts, / that *they* will be safer /
중요한 것이다 / '그들'이 더 안전하리라는 것이 /
because of your idea and your effort. 정답 단서 아이디어와 노력 덕분에 아이들은 더 안전할 것이라는 것이 중요함.
여러분의 아이디어와 노력 덕분에
★중요 수질 오염 방지법을 추진하여 나타난 결과가 어떻든, 아이디어를 내고 노력하는 과정을 통해 아이들이 깨끗한 물에 접근할 수 있게 하여 안전을 보장한다는 점에서 성공한 것임. 즉, 주어진 상황에서 최선의 행동을 한다면 결과가 완벽하지 않아도 성공했다고 할 수 있음.

(8) Is it perfect? / No.
완벽한가 / 아니다

(9) Is there more work / to be done? / Absolutely.
일이 더 있는가 / 해야 할 / 당연하다

(10) But in almost every case, /
하지만 거의 모든 경우에 /
helping move the needle forward is vastly better /
(helping move the needle forward: 동명사S / is: V)
바늘을 앞으로 이동시키는 것을 돕는 것이 훨씬 더 낫다 /
than not helping at all.
전혀 돕지 않는 것보다

[전문 해석]

(1)모두 '완벽함이 괜찮음의 적이 되게 두지 말라'는 표현을 들어 본 적이 있다. (2)여러분이 장애물을 극복해서 여러분의 아이디어가 여러분이 오랫동안 꿈꿔 왔던, 해결을 기반으로 한 방책이 될 수 있도록 하고 싶다면, 전부 아니면 전무라고 여기는 사고방식을 가져서는 안 된다. (3)여러분은 기꺼이 여러분의 아이디어를 바꾸고 다른 사람이 그것의 결과에 영향을 미치도록 해야 한다. (4)여러분은 결과가 여러분이 원했던 것과 조금 다르거나, 심지어 조금 '못'하여도 괜찮다고 여겨야 한다. (5)여러분이 수질 오염 방지법을 추진하고 있다고 가정해보자. (6)비록 나타난 것이 여러분이 원했던 만큼의 자금이 충분하게 지원되지 않거나, 여러분이 처음에 그 법안을 고안한 방식과 일치하지 않더라도, 여러분은 힘든 지역의 아이들이 깨끗한 물에 접근하도록 하는 데 여전히 성공해 있을 것이다. (7)여러분의 아이디어와 노력 덕분에 '그들'이 더 안전하리라는 것이 중요한 것이다. (8)완벽한가? 아니다. (9)해야 할 일이 더 있는가? 당연하다. (10)하지만 거의 모든 경우에, 바늘을 앞으로 이동시키는 것을 돕는 것(상황이 허락하는 한 최선의 변화를 만들기)이 전혀 돕지 않는 것보다 훨씬 더 낫다.

[정답 확인]

밑줄 친 helping move the needle forward가 다음 글에서 의미하는 바로 가장 적절한 것은?

① spending time and money on celebrating perfection
완벽을 축하하는 데 시간과 돈을 소비하기
② suggesting cost-saving strategies for a good cause
좋은 목적을 위한 비용 절감 전략 제안하기
✔③ making a difference as best as the situation allows
상황이 허락하는 한 최선의 변화를 만들기
④ checking your resources before altering the original goal
원래의 목표를 바꾸기 전에 자원을 확인하기
⑤ collecting donations to help the education of poor children
가난한 어린이들의 교육을 돕기 위한 기부금 모으기

[문제 풀이]

이 지문은 문제 해결에 있어서 완벽을 추구하는 것보다 주어진 상황에서 최선을 다하고자 하는 사고방식이 더 낫다고 설명하는 글이다. 이에 대한 예시로 수질 오염 방지법을 추진하는 상황을 가정하고, 아이디어를 내고 노력했다면 결과가 좀 부족하더라도 힘든 지역의 아이들이 깨끗한 물에 접근하도록 하는 데 여전히 성공할 것이라고 설명한다. 따라서 '바늘을 앞으로 이동시키는 것을 돕는 것'은 결과가 미미해 보이더라도 포기하지 않고 할 수 있는 것을 하는 것을 의미하며, 이는 '상황이 허락하는 한 최선의 변화를 만드는 것'이라고 할 수 있다. 따라서 정답은 ③이다.

[중요 어휘]

□	**expression**	명사 표현, 표출
□	**enemy**	명사 적, 장애물
□	**get over**	~을 극복하다, ~을 넘다

□ obstacle	명사 장애물, 방해(물)
□ policy	명사 방책, 정책
□ mentality	명사 사고방식
□ alter	동사 바꾸다, 변하다
□ influence	동사 영향을 미치다 / 명사 영향(력)
□ outcome	명사 결과
□ push for	~을 추진하다, ~을 요구하다
□ emerge	동사 나타나다, 나오다
□ well-funded	형용사 자금이 충분하게 지원된
□ conceive	동사 고안하다, 생각하다
□ bill	명사 법안, 고지서, 지폐
□ ensure	동사 (반드시) ~하게 하다, 보장하다
□ have access to N	~에 접근하다
□ count	동사 중요하다, 세다
□ needle	명사 바늘
□ vastly	부사 훨씬, 대단히, 엄청나게

핵심 교육과정은 성공적인 과학적 발견의 결과만을 다룰 뿐, 그 과정에서 과학자들이 경험한 수많은 실패는 다루지 않는다는 내용의 글임. 밑줄 친 문장의 납과 금이 과학자들의 이야기와 관련해서 각각 무엇을 비유하는지를 파악하면 답을 찾을 수 있음.

08 2020년 11월 21번 (정답률 55%)

정답 ⑤

[지문 끊어 읽기] 과학자들의 실패를 다루지 않는 교육과정

(1) In school, / there's one curriculum, /
학교에는 / 하나의 교육과정이 있다 /
one right way / to study science, / and one right formula /
하나의 올바른 방식 / 과학을 공부하는 / 그리고 하나의 올바른 공식 /
that spits out the correct answer / on a standardized test.
정답을 내뱉는 / 표준화된 시험에서

(2) Textbooks / with grand titles / like *The Principles of Physics* /
교과서들은 / 웅대한 제목을 가진 / '물리학의 원리'와 같은 /
magically reveal "the principles" / in three hundred pages.
'그 원리들'을 마법처럼 드러내 보인다 / 300페이지로

(3) An authority figure then / steps up to the lectern /
그러고 나서 권위자는 / 강의대에 올라선다 /
to feed us "the truth."
우리에게 '진실'을 알려 주기 위해서

(4) As theoretical physicist David Gross explained /
이론 물리학자 David Gross가 설명했듯이 /
in his Nobel lecture, / textbooks often ignore /
그의 노벨상 강연에서 / 교과서들은 종종 무시한다 /
the many alternate paths / that people wandered down, /
많은 다른 경로들을 / 사람들이 헤매고 다닌 /
the many false clues / they followed, /
많은 잘못된 단서들을 / 그들이 따랐던 /
the many misconceptions / they had.
많은 오해들을 / 그들이 가졌던

(5) We learn / about Newton's "laws" / — as if they arrived /
우리는 배운다 / 뉴턴의 '법칙들'에 대해서 / 마치 그것들이 찾아온 것처럼 /
by a grand divine visitation or a stroke of genius — /
대단한 신성한 방문이나 천재적 솜씨로 /
but not the years / he spent /
=not (about) the years
하지만 오랜 시간들은 아니다 / 그가 보낸 /
exploring, revising, and changing them. 정답 단서
그것들을 탐구하고, 개정하고, 변경하면서

힌트 문자 그대로 해석하면 '천재의 충격, 천재의 타격'으로 풀이될 수 있는데, 어떤 문제를 해결할 수 있는 '기발한 생각'과 같은 것을 가리키는 표현으로 '천재적 솜씨' 정도로 해석될 수 있음.

(6) The laws / that Newton failed to establish /
법칙들은 / 뉴턴이 확립하는 데 실패했던 /
— most notably / his experiments in alchemy, /
가장 유명하기로는 / 연금술에서의 그의 실험들은 /
which attempted, and spectacularly failed, /
병렬① 병렬②
시도했으나 장대하게 실패했던 /
to turn lead into gold — / don't make the cut /
attempted와 failed의 목적어
납을 금으로 바꾸는 것을 / 선택되지 못한다 /
as part of the one-dimensional story /
일차원적인 이야기의 일부로 /
told in physics classrooms.
물리학 수업에서 언급되는

힌트 make the cut은 어떤 목표를 달성하거나 대회에서 본선에 진출하는 것을 뜻함. 본문에서는 과학자들의 여러 실험과 이론 중에 수업 시간에 다루는 공식적인 이야기로 선택되는 것을 이 표현으로 나타냈음.

(7) Instead, / our education system /
대신에 / 우리의 교육 시스템은 /
turns the life stories of these scientists / from lead to gold.
이 과학자들의 인생 이야기를 바꾼다 / 납에서 금으로

[전문 해석]

(1)학교에는 하나의 교육과정, 과학을 공부하는 하나의 올바른 방식, 그리고 표준화된 시험에서 정답을 내뱉는 하나의 올바른 공식이 있다. (2)'물리학의 원리'와 같은 웅대한 제목을 가진 교과서들은 300페이지로 '그 원리들'을 마법처럼 드러내 보인다. (3)그러고 나서 권위자는 우리에게 '진실'을 알려 주기 위해서 강의대에 올라선다. (4)이론 물리학자 David Gross가 그의 노벨상 강연에서 설명했듯이, 교과서들은 사람들이 헤매고 다닌 많은 다른 경로들, 그들이 따랐던 많은 잘못된 단서들, 그들이 가졌던 많은 오해들을 종종 무시한다. (5)우리는 뉴턴의 '법칙들'에 대해서 마치 그것들이 대단한 신성한 방문이나 천재적 솜씨로 찾아온 것처럼 배우지만, 그가 그것들을 탐구하고, 개정하고, 변경하면서 보낸 시간들은 아니다(시행착오에 대해서는 배우지 않는다). (6)뉴턴이 확립하는 데 실패했던 법칙들, 가장 유명하기로는 납을 금으로 바꾸는 것을 시도했으나 장대하게 실패했던 연금술에서의 그의 실험들은, 물리학 수업에서 언급되는 일차원적인 이야기의 일부로 선택되지 못한다. (7)대신에, 우리의 교육 시스템은 이 과학자들의 인생 이야기를 납에서 금으로 바꾼다(과학자들의 과정과 오류들은 무시하면서 그들의 성공만을 드러내 보인다).

[정답 확인]

밑줄 친 turns the life stories of these scientists from lead to gold가 다음 글에서 의미하는 바로 가장 적절한 것은?

① discovers the valuable relationships between scientists
과학자들 사이의 귀중한 관계를 발견한다
② emphasizes difficulties in establishing new scientific theories
새로운 과학 이론을 확립하는 것의 어려움을 강조한다
③ mixes the various stories of great scientists across the world
전 세계의 위대한 과학자들의 다양한 이야기를 섞는다
④ focuses more on the scientists' work than their personal lives
과학자들의 개인적인 삶보다 그들의 업적에 더 초점을 둔다
⑤ reveals only the scientists' success ignoring their processes and errors
과학자들의 과정과 오류들은 무시하면서 그들의 성공만을 드러내 보인다

[문제 풀이]

본문은 학교의 공식적인 교육과정에서 과학자들이 겪었던 시행착오들과 실패가 전혀 다루어지지 않는다고 주장한다. 예를 들어, 그 유명한 뉴턴조차 납을 금으로 바꾸는 연금술 실험에서 보기 좋게 실패한 바 있으나, 실제 물리학 수업에서 그러한 이야기는 다루어지지 않는다. 이러한 맥락에서, 교육 시스템이 과학자들의 이야기를 '납에서 금으로' 바꾼다는 문장 (7)의 내용은 현 교육 시스템이 과학자들의 성공적인 발견에만 초점을 맞춤으로써 그들을 실제보다 위대해 보이게 만든다는 의미이므로, 정답은 ⑤이다.

[중요 어휘]

□ formula	명사 공식, 방식
□ standardize	동사 표준화하다, 획일화하다
□ grand	형용사 웅대한, 대단한
□ principle	명사 원리, 원칙
□ physics	명사 물리학
□ authority figure	권위자
□ lectern	명사 강의대, 연설대
□ alternate	형용사 다른, 대안이 되는
□ misconception	명사 오해, 잘못된 생각
□ divine	형용사 신성한, 신이 내려 주신
□ visitation	명사 방문
□ revise	동사 개정하다, 변경하다
□ establish	동사 확립하다, 제정하다, 입증하다
□ alchemy	명사 연금술

☐ **spectacularly**	부사 장대하게, 극적으로, 굉장히
☐ **lead**	명사 납
☐ **one-dimensional**	형용사 일차원적인, 깊이 없는, 표면적인

09 2023년 6월 21번 (정답률 55%) 정답 ④

[지문 끊어 읽기] 토착 요리의 정체성 혼란

(1) North America's native cuisine met the same unfortunate fate /
북아메리카의 토착 요리는 같은 불행한 운명을 맞이했다 /
as its native people, / save for a few relics /
(its: =North America's, save for: ~을 제외하고)
그곳의 원주민들처럼 / 몇 가지 전해 내려오는 풍속을 제외하고 /
like the Thanksgiving turkey.
추수감사절 칠면조와 같은

(2) Certainly, / we still have regional specialties, /
확실히 / 우리는 여전히 지역 특산물을 가지고 있다 /
but the Carolina barbecue will almost certainly have California tomatoes in its sauce, /
(its: =the Carolina barbecue's)
하지만 캐롤리나 바비큐는 거의 확실히 캘리포니아 토마토를 소스에 넣을 것이다 /
and the Louisiana gumbo is just as likely to contain Indonesian farmed shrimp.
그리고 루이지애나 검보도 마찬가지로 인도네시아 양식 새우를 포함할 것이다

(3) If either of these shows up on a fast-food menu /
(these: =the Carolina barbecue and the Louisiana gumbo)
만약 이들 중 하나가 패스트푸드 메뉴에 나타난다면 /
with lots of added fats or HFCS, /
지방이나 액상과당이 많이 첨가되어 /
we seem unable either to discern or resist the corruption. 정답 단서 (토착 음식이 변형되더라도 우리는 그 변화를 알아차리거나 거부할 수 없음.)
우리는 그 변질을 식별하거나 저항할 수 없을 것 같다

(4) We have yet to come up with a strong set of generalized norms, /
우리는 강력한 일반화된 기준을 아직 내놓지 못했다 /
passed down through families, /
가계를 통해 내려오는 /
for savoring and sensibly consuming /
(savoring: 병렬①(3형식V), consuming: 병렬②(3형식V))
맛보고 현명하게 소비하기 위해 /
[what our land and climate give us]. 정답 단서 (우리 지역에서 나는 식재료를 맛보고 소비하는 데 있어 대대로 내려오는 기준을 갖지 못함.)
([ ]: O(선행사를 포함한 관계대명사절))
우리의 땅과 기후가 우리에게 주는 것을

(5) We have, instead, a string of fad diets /
대신 우리는 일련의 유행 식단을 가지고 있다 /
convulsing our bookstores and bellies, / one after another, /
(convulsing: 현재분사)
우리의 서점과 배에 큰 소동을 일으키는 / 연이어 /
at the scale of the national best seller. 정답 단서 (전국적으로 유행하는 식단에 따라 우리의 식단은 변화함.)
전국적인 베스트셀러의 규모로

(6) Nine out of ten nutritionists view this /
10명 중 9명의 영양학자들은 이것을 본다 /
as evidence [that we have entirely lost our marbles]. ([ ]: evidence와 동격)
우리가 완전히 우리의 분별력을 잃었다는 증거로

[전문 해석]

(1)추수감사절 칠면조와 같은 몇 가지 전해 내려오는 풍속을 제외하고, 북아메리카의 토착 요리는 그곳의 원주민들처럼 같은 불행한 운명을 맞이했다. (2)확실히, 우리는 여전히 지역 특산물을 가지고 있지만, 캐롤리나 바비큐는 거의 확실히 캘리포니아 토마토를 소스에 넣을 것이고, 루이지애나 검보도 마찬가지로 인도네시아 양식 새우를 포함할 것이다. (3)만약 이들 중 하나가 지방이나 액상과당이 많이 첨가되어 패스트푸드 메뉴에 나타난다면, 우리는 그 변질을 식별하거나 저항할 수 없을 것 같다. (4)우리는 우리의 땅과 기후가 우리에게 주는 것을 맛보고 현명하게 소비하기 위해, 가계를 통해 내려오는 강력한 일반화된 기준을 아직 내놓지 못했다. (5)대신, 우리는 전국적인 베스트셀러의 규모로 연이어 서점과 배에 큰 소동을 일으키는 일련의 유행 식단을 가지고 있다. (6)10명 중 9명의 영양학자들은 이것을 우리가 완전히 우리의 분별력을 잃었다(우리의 독특한 음식 정체성에 대해 완전히 혼란스러워졌다)는 증거로 본다.

[정답 확인]

밑줄 친 have entirely lost our marbles가 다음 글에서 의미하는 바로 가장 적절한 것은?

① have utterly disrupted our complex food supply chain
우리의 복잡한 식품 공급망을 완전히 파괴했다
② have vividly witnessed the rebirth of our classic recipes
우리의 전통 요리법의 재탄생을 생생하게 목격했다
③ have completely denied ourselves access to healthy food
건강한 음식에 대한 접근을 우리 스스로 완전히 거부했다
✔④ have become totally confused about our distinctive food identity
우리의 독특한 음식 정체성에 대해 완전히 혼란스러워졌다
⑤ have fully recognized the cultural significance of our local foods
우리의 지역 음식의 문화적 중요성을 완전히 인식했다

[문제 풀이]

이 글은 토착 요리의 정체성 혼란에 대해 설명하는 내용이다. 마지막 문장의 밑줄 친 부분은 영양학자들이 보는 증거로 우리가 분별력을 완전히 잃었다는 것이다. 앞서 토착 요리에서 지역 특산물이 아닌 다른 지역의 것을 사용한다는 것과 변형이 되더라도 우리가 이를 알아차리지 못하고, 전통적인 요리 방식에 관한 일반화된 기준이 아직 없고 우리는 전국적인 유행에 따라 식단을 가진다는 것이다. 이를 통해 토착 요리에 대한 우리의 가치관이 무분별함을 알 수 있다. 따라서 밑줄 친 부분의 의미로 가장 적절한 것은 ④ 'have become totally confused about our distinctive food identity(우리의 독특한 음식 정체성에 대해 완전히 혼란스러워졌다)'이다.

[중요 어휘]

☐ **unfortunate**	형용사 불행한
☐ **save for**	~을 제외하고
☐ **regional**	형용사 지역의, 지방의
☐ **specialty**	명사 (지역) 특산물, 전공
☐ **show up**	나타나다
☐ **discern**	동사 식별하다, 알아차리다
☐ **resist**	동사 저항하다, 반대하다
☐ **corruption**	명사 변질, 변형, 부패
☐ **come up with**	~을 내놓다, ~을 찾아내다
☐ **norm**	명사 기준, 표준
☐ **savor**	동사 맛보다, 맛이 나다
☐ **sensibly**	부사 현명하게
☐ **consume**	동사 소비하다, 섭취하다
☐ **fad**	명사 (일시적인) 유행
☐ **convulse**	동사 큰 소동을 일으키다
☐ **scale**	명사 규모, 범위
☐ **nutritionist**	명사 영양학자
☐ **marbles**	명사 (흔히 복수형으로) 분별, 이성, 대리석
☐ **utterly**	부사 완전히, 아주, 철저하게

핵심 인터넷을 통해 불특정 다수로부터 자금을 조달하는 'crowd(군중)-funding(자금)'에 대한 글임. 밑줄 친 부분은 크라우드 펀딩을 '기업 자금 조달의 민주화'라고 표현하고 있으므로, 지문을 통해 크라우드 펀딩의 전반적 특성을 파악한 뒤 밑줄 친 부분이 의미하는 바를 추론할 것.

10 2019년 11월 21번 (정답률 40%) 정답 ①

[지문 끊어 읽기] 크라우드 펀딩

(1) Crowdfunding is a new and more collaborative way /
크라우드 펀딩은 새롭고 더 협력적인 방법이다 /
to secure funding for projects.
프로젝트의 자금을 확보하는

(2) It can be used in different ways /
그것은 여러 가지 방식들로 이용될 수 있다 /
such as requesting donations / for a worthy cause /
(requesting: 병렬①)
기부를 요청하는 것과 같이 / 가치 있는 목적을 위해 /
anywhere in the world / and generating funding / for a project /
(generating: 병렬②)
세계 어디에서든 / 그리고 자금을 만들어내는 것 / 프로젝트를 위한 /

with the contributors / then becoming partners in the project.
기부자들과 함께 / 이후 프로젝트의 파트너가 될

(3) In essence, / crowdfunding is the fusion /
본질적으로 / 크라우드 펀딩은 결합이다 /
of social networking and venture capitalism.
소셜 네트워킹과 벤처 자본주의의

(4) In just the same way /
정확히 동일한 방식으로 /
as social networks have rewritten the conventional rules /
소셜 네트워크가 전통적인 규칙을 다시 쓴 것과 /
about how people communicate and interact with each other, /
사람들이 서로 어떻게 소통하고 상호작용하는지에 대해 /
crowdfunding / in all its variations / has the potential /
크라우드 펀딩은 / 다양한 형태의 / 잠재력을 가진다 /
to rewrite the rules /
규칙을 다시 쓸 /
on how businesses and other projects get funded / in the future.
기업들과 그 밖의 프로젝트들이 어떻게 자금을 얻는지에 대한 / 미래에

힌트 in all its variations는 직역하면 '그것의 모든 변주 속에서'이지만, 문장 (2)에서 크라우드 펀딩이 여러 가지 방식들로 이용될 수 있다고 했으므로, 문맥상 '다양한 형태의'라고 해석할 수 있음.

(5) Crowdfunding can be viewed /
크라우드 펀딩은 간주될 수 있다 /
as the democratization of business financing.
기업 자금 조달의 민주화로

힌트 'view A as B(A를 B로 간주하다)'를 수동태로 바꾼 문장임. 목적어였던 A가 수동태 문장의 주어로 나오면서 동사는 'be viewed'의 형태로 바뀌고 'as B'는 그대로 남아 지금의 문장 형태가 되었음.

(6) Instead of restricting capital sourcing and allocation /
자본의 조달과 배분을 한정하는 것 대신에 /
to a relatively small and fixed minority, /
비교적 소규모의 고정된 소수로 /
crowdfunding empowers everyone connected to the Internet
to access /
크라우드 펀딩은 인터넷에 연결된 모든 사람들이 접근할 수 있게 해준다 /
both the collective wisdom and the pocket money /
집단 지성과 적은 돈에 /
of everyone else / who connects to the Internet. 정답단서
다른 모든 사람들의 / 인터넷에 접속하는

힌트 여기서 empowers는 enables와 같은 뜻으로, 'empower (=enable) A to V'는 'A가 ~할 수 있게 해주다'라는 의미의 5형식 구문임.

[전문 해석]

(1)크라우드 펀딩은 프로젝트의 자금을 확보하는 새롭고 더 협력적인 방법이다. (2)그것은 가치 있는 목적을 위해 세계 어디에서든 기부를 요청하는 것, 그리고 이후 프로젝트의 파트너가 될 기부자들과 함께 프로젝트를 위한 자금을 만들어내는 것과 같이, 여러 가지 방식들로 이용될 수 있다. (3)본질적으로, 크라우드 펀딩은 소셜 네트워킹과 벤처 자본주의의 결합이다. (4)사람들이 서로 어떻게 소통하고 상호작용하는지에 대해 소셜 네트워크가 전통적인 규칙을 다시 쓴 것과 정확히 동일한 방식으로, 다양한 형태의 크라우드 펀딩은 기업들과 그 밖의 프로젝트들이 미래에 어떻게 자금을 얻는지에 대한 규칙을 다시 쓸 잠재력을 가진다. (5)크라우드 펀딩은 기업 자금 조달의 민주화(더 많은 사람들이 기업 자금 조달에 연관될 수 있다)로 간주될 수 있다. (6)자본의 조달과 배분을 비교적 소규모의 고정된 소수로 한정하는 것 대신에, 크라우드 펀딩은 인터넷에 연결된 모든 사람들이 인터넷에 접속하는 다른 모든 사람들의 집단 지성과 적은 돈에 접근할 수 있게 해준다.

[정답 확인]

밑줄 친 the democratization of business financing이 다음 글에서 의미하는 바로 가장 적절한 것은?

✔ More people can be involved in funding a business.
더 많은 사람들이 기업 자금 조달에 연관될 수 있다.
② More people will participate in developing new products.
더 많은 사람들이 새 상품을 개발하는 데 참여할 것이다.
③ Crowdfunding can reinforce the conventional way of financing.
크라우드 펀딩은 자금 조달의 전통적인 방법을 강화할 수 있다.
④ Crowdfunding keeps social networking from facilitating funding.
크라우드 펀딩은 소셜 네트워킹이 자금 조달을 용이하게 하는 것을 막는다.
⑤ The Internet helps employees of a company interact with each other.
인터넷은 회사의 직원들이 서로 소통하도록 돕는다.

[문제 풀이]

크라우드 펀딩은 많은 사람들에게서 프로젝트의 자금을 조달하는 방법이다. 지문에서는 크라우드 펀딩의 특성 중, 'a relatively small and fixed minority'에 해당하는 소수의 투자자들에게서 큰 돈을 받는 것이 아니라 더 많은 사람들에게서 각각 적은 돈을 받는다는 점에 주목한다. 즉, 'democratization'이란 문장 (6)에서 설명하듯 소수가 아닌 다양한 사람들에게서 수평적인 방식으로 기업 자금을 받는 것을 의미하므로 답은 ①이다.

[중요 어휘]

□ collaborative	형용사 협력적인, 공동의
□ secure	동사 확보하다, 안전하게 지키다
□ cause	명사 목적, 명분, 이유 / 동사 유발하다
□ contributor	명사 기부자, 기여자
□ fusion	명사 결합, 융합
□ capitalism	명사 자본주의
□ conventional	형용사 전통적인, 관습적인
□ variation	명사 변주, 변이, 변화
□ democratization	명사 민주화
□ restrict	동사 한정하다, 제한하다
□ allocation	명사 배분, 할당
□ empower	동사 ~할 수 있게 하다(=enable), 권한을 주다
□ collective	형용사 집단의, 공동의
□ reinforce	동사 강화하다
□ keep A from V-ing	A가 ~하는 것을 막다
□ facilitate	동사 용이하게 하다, 촉진하다

핵심 유명한 극작가인 셰익스피어가 한 말에 빗대어 인간의 사회적 삶에 연극적인 속성이 있음을 설명하는 글임. 비유를 활용하고 있다는 점을 잘 이해해야 글에서 말하고자 하는 바를 헷갈리지 않고 파악할 수 있음.

11 2020년 6월 21번 (정답률 40%)

정답 ⑤

[지문 끊어 읽기] 인간의 사회적 삶 속 연극적 속성

(1) Over the centuries /
수 세기에 걸쳐 /
various writers and thinkers, /
여러 작가와 사상가들은 /
looking at humans from an outside perspective, /
외부의 관점에서 인간들을 바라보며 /
have been struck / by the theatrical quality of social life.
마주해왔다 / 사회적 삶의 연극적 속성과

힌트 문장의 주어는 'various writers and thinkers'이고, 동사는 'have been struck'임. 주어와 동사의 사이에 분사구문이 삽입되어 있는 구조임.

(2) The most famous quote / expressing this /
가장 유명한 명언은 / 이것을 나타내는 /
comes from Shakespeare: / "All the world's a stage, /
셰익스피어에게서 비롯된다 / 모든 세상은 무대이다 /
And all the men and women merely players; /
그리고 모든 남성과 여성은 단지 배우일 뿐이다 /
They have their exits and their entrances, /
그들은 자신의 퇴장과 입장이 있다 /
And one man in his time plays many parts."
그리고 한 인간은 그의 일생 동안 다양한 역할을 연기한다

(3) If the theater and actors were traditionally represented /
만약 연극과 배우들이 전통적으로 표현된다면 /
by the image of masks, /
가면의 이미지에 의해 /
writers such as Shakespeare are implying /
셰익스피어와 같은 작가들은 암시하고 있다 /
that all of us are constantly wearing masks.
우리 모두가 끊임없이 가면을 쓰고 있다는 것을

(4) Some people are better actors than others.
어떤 사람들은 다른 사람들보다 더 나은 배우이다

(5) Evil types / such as Iago / in the play *Othello* /
악역들은 / Iago와 같은 / 연극 <Othello> 속 /
are able to conceal their hostile intentions /
자신들의 적대적인 의도를 숨길 수 있다 /
behind a friendly smile.
친근한 미소 뒤에

(6) Others are able to act / with more confidence and bravado /
다른 사람들은 연기를 할 수 있다 / 더 많은 자신감과 허세를 가지고 /

— they often become leaders.
그들은 주로 리더가 된다

(7) People with excellent acting skills /
훌륭한 연기력을 가지고 있는 사람들은 /
can better navigate our complex social environments /
우리의 복잡한 사회적 환경을 더 잘 헤쳐 나갈 수 있다 /
and get ahead. 정답단서
그리고 앞서갈 수 있다

[전문 해석]

(1)수 세기에 걸쳐, 여러 작가와 사상가들은 외부의 관점에서 인간들을 바라보며 사회적 삶의 연극적 속성과 마주해왔다. (2)이것을 나타내는 가장 유명한 명언은 셰익스피어에게서 비롯된다. "모든 세상은 무대이고, 모든 남성과 여성은 단지 배우일 뿐이다. 그들은 자신의 퇴장과 입장이 있고, 한 인간은 그의 일생 동안 다양한 역할을 연기한다." (3)만약 연극과 배우들이 가면의 이미지에 의해 전통적으로 표현된다면, 셰익스피어와 같은 작가들은 우리 모두가 끊임없이 가면을 쓰고 있다는(주어진 사회적 상황에 따라 우리의 행동을 조절한다는) 것을 암시하고 있(는 것이)다. (4)어떤 사람들은 다른 사람들보다 더 나은 배우이다. (5)연극 〈Othello(오셀로)〉 속 Iago(이아고)와 같은 악역들은 자신들의 적대적인 의도를 친근한 미소 뒤에 숨길 수 있다. (6)다른 사람들은 더 많은 자신감과 허세를 가지고 연기를 할 수 있고, 그들은 주로 리더가 된다. (7)훌륭한 연기력을 가지고 있는 사람들은 우리의 복잡한 사회적 환경을 더 잘 헤쳐 나갈 수 있고 앞서갈 수 있다.
- Othello(오셀로): 영국의 세계적인 극작가이자 시인인 셰익스피어의 4대 비극 중 하나로, 오셀로가 악인 Iago(이아고)에게 속아 선량한 아내 데스데모나를 의심하게 된다는 내용이다.

[정답 확인]

밑줄 친 constantly wearing masks가 다음 글에서 의미하는 바로 가장 적절한 것은?
① protecting our faces from harmful external forces
해로운 외부의 힘으로부터 우리의 얼굴을 보호한다는
② performing on stage to show off our acting skills
우리의 연기력을 자랑하기 위해 무대 위에서 공연한다는
③ feeling confident by beating others in competition
경쟁에서 다른 사람들을 이김으로써 자신감을 느낀다는
④ doing completely the opposite of what others expect
다른 사람들이 기대한 것과 완전히 반대로 행동한다는
✔⑤ adjusting our behavior based on the social context given
주어진 사회적 상황에 따라 우리의 행동을 조절한다는

[문제 풀이]

사람들은 자신의 일생 동안 다양한 역할을 연기하며 살아간다는 셰익스피어의 말을 인용하면서, 사회적 상황에 따라 적절하게 대처하는 능력을 훌륭한 연기력에 비유하는 글이다. 구체적으로, 악역이 적대적 의도를 친근한 미소 뒤에 숨긴다는 문장 (5)의 내용이나, 자신감과 허세를 가지고 연기하여 리더가 된다는 문장 (6)의 내용은 모두, 겉으로 드러나는 행동을 조절함으로써 각자가 처한 사회적 환경에 대처하는 것이라 할 수 있다. 따라서 밑줄 친 부분이 의미하는 바로 가장 적절한 것은 ⑤이다.

[오답 풀이]

② - 문장 (7)에도 제시되어 있는 연기력(acting skills)이라는 어구가 선택지 ②에 그대로 나와 있고 글 전반적으로 연극 또는 연기와 관련된 표현이 많아서 헷갈릴 수 있으나, 본문은 연기 자체에 대한 글이 아니라 사회적 상황에 따른 행동을 연기에 빗대어 표현한 글이다. 따라서 무대에서 연기한다는 내용을 담고 있는 ②는 정답이 될 수 없다.

[중요 어휘]

☐ thinker	명사 사상가, 사색가
☐ perspective	명사 관점, 시각
☐ strike	동사 ~와 마주하다, ~에 충돌하다 (strike-struck-struck)
☐ theatrical	형용사 연극적인, 연극의
☐ quality	명사 속성, 품질
☐ quote	명사 명언, 인용문
☐ express	동사 나타내다, 표현하다
☐ represent	동사 표현하다, 대표하다
☐ imply	동사 암시하다, 의미하다
☐ constantly	부사 끊임없이, 항상
☐ conceal	동사 숨기다, 감추다
☐ hostile	형용사 적대적인, 강력히 반대하는
☐ bravado	명사 허세 / 동사 허세를 부리다
☐ get ahead	앞서가다, 출세하다

12 2023년 11월 21번 (정답률 55%) 정답 ④

[지문 끊어 읽기] 예술을 통한 다양한 경험

(1) The arts and aesthetics offer emotional connection /
예술과 미학은 정서적인 연결을 제공한다 /
to the full range of human experience. 정답단서 예술은 다양한 인간 경험에 대한 정서적인 연결을 제공함.
다양한 인간 경험에 대한

(2) "The arts can be more than just sugar on the tongue," /
"예술은 단순히 혀 위의 설탕 그 이상이 될 수 있다." /
Anjan Chatterjee, a professor at the University of Pennsylvania, says.
Pennsylvania 대학교의 교수인 Anjan Chatterjee는 말한다

(3) "In art, / when there's something challenging, /
예술에서 / 무언가 도전적인 것이 있을 때 /
which can also be uncomfortable, / this discomfort, /
계속적 용법 S
그리고 그것이 또한 불편할 수 있을 때 / 이 불편은 /
[if we're willing to engage with it], / [ ]: 삽입절
만약 우리가 기꺼이 그것에 관여하려 한다면 /
offers the possibility of some change, some transformation.
V
어떤 변화, 어떤 변형의 가능성을 제공한다

(4) That can also be a powerful aesthetic experience."
그것은 또한 강력한 미적 경험이 될 수 있다

(5) The arts, / in this way, / become vehicles /
예술은 / 이러한 방식으로 / 수단이 된다 /
to contend with ideas and concepts /
형용사적 용법 선행사
아이디어 및 개념들과 싸우는 /
[that are difficult and uncomfortable otherwise]. 정답단서
그렇지 않았더라면 어렵고 불편한 [ ]: 주격 관계대명사절 예술은 어렵고 불편한 아이디어와 싸우는 수단이 됨.

(6) When Picasso painted his masterpiece *Guernica* in 1937, /
Picasso가 1937년에 그의 걸작 *Guernica*를 그렸을 때 /
he captured [the heartbreaking and cruel nature of war], / [ ]: O
V①
그는 가슴 아프고 잔인한 전쟁의 본질을 포착했다 /
and offered the world /
V②(4형식V) I·O
그리고 세상에 제공했다 /
[a way to consider the universal suffering /
형용사적 용법
보편적인 고통을 숙고할 방법을 /
caused by the Spanish Civil War]. [ ]: D·O
스페인 내전으로 초래된

(7) When Lorraine Hansberry wrote her play *A Raisin in the Sun*, /
Lorraine Hansberry가 그녀의 희곡 *A Raisin in the Sun*을 썼을 때 /
she gave us [a powerful story of people /
4형식V I·O
그녀는 우리에게 사람들의 강력한 이야기를 전해 주었다 /
struggling with racism, discrimination, and the pursuit of the American dream] / [ ]: D·O
인종 차별, 차별, 그리고 아메리칸 드림의 추구로 분투하는 /
[while also offering a touching portrait of family life]. [ ]: 분사구문(동시동작)
또한 가정 생활에 대한 감동적인 묘사를 제공하면서

[전문 해석]

(1)예술과 미학은 다양한 인간 경험에 대한 정서적인 연결을 제공한다. (2)Pennsylvania 대학교의 교수인 Anjan Chatterjee는 "예술은 단순히 혀 위의 설탕 그 이상이 될(기쁨 이상의 다양한 경험들을 포괄할) 수 있다."라고 말한다. (3)"예술에서, 무언가 도전적인 것이 있고 그것이 또한 불편할 수 있을 때, 이 불편은 만약 우리가 기꺼이 그것에 관여하려 한다면 어떤 변화, 어떤 변형의 가능성을 제공한다. (4)그것은 또한 강력한 미적 경험이 될 수 있다." (5)이러한 방

문제편 p.046

식으로, 예술은 그렇지 않았더라면 어렵고 불편한 아이디어 및 개념들과 싸우는 수단이 된다. (6)Picasso가 1937년에 그의 걸작 *Guernica*를 그렸을 때, 그는 가슴 아프고 잔인한 전쟁의 본질을 포착했고, 스페인 내전으로 초래된 보편적인 고통을 숙고할 방법을 세상에 제공했다. (7)Lorraine Hansberry가 그녀의 희곡 *A Raisin in the Sun*을 썼을 때, 그녀는 또한 가정 생활에 대한 감동적인 묘사를 제공하면서 인종 차별, 차별, 그리고 아메리칸 드림의 추구로 분투하는 사람들의 강력한 이야기를 전해 주었다.

[정답 확인]

밑줄 친 be more than just sugar on the tongue이 다음 글에서 의미하는 바로 가장 적절한 것은?

① play a role in relieving psychological anxiety
심리적 불안을 완화하는 데 역할을 할
② enlighten us about the absoluteness of beauty
우리에게 아름다움의 절대성에 대해 일깨워줄
③ conceal the artist's cultural and ethnic traditions
예술가의 문화적, 인종적 전통을 숨길
④ ✔ embrace a variety of experiences beyond pleasure
기쁨 이상의 다양한 경험들을 포괄할
⑤ distort the viewers' accurate understanding of history
역사에 대한 관람자의 정확한 이해를 왜곡할

[문제 풀이]

이 지문은 예술의 기능에 대해서 설명하는 글이다. 문장 (1)에서 예술은 다양한 인간 경험에 대한 정서적인 연결을 제공한다고 언급되며, 문장 (5)에서는 예술이 어렵고 불편한 아이디어를 다룰 수 있는 수단이라고 설명한다. 또한, 문장 (6), (7)에서는 Picasso와 Lorraine Hansberry의 작품을 예로 들며 예술에 고통이나 차별과 같은 경험이 포함될 수 있음을 보여준다. 따라서 예술은 단순히 사람들에게 기쁨을 주는 '혀 위의 설탕(sugar on the tongue)'이 아니라 그 이상으로 다양한 경험을 제공하는 것으로 볼 수 있으므로 적절한 답은 ④이다.

[중요 어휘]

☐ aesthetics	명사 (단수 취급) 미학
☐ challenging	형용사 도전적인, 저항[항의]하는, 어려움을 주는
☐ discomfort	명사 불편, 불쾌
☐ engage with	~에 관여하다, ~을 다루다
☐ transformation	명사 변형, 변화, 변질
☐ vehicle	명사 수단, 매개체, 차량
☐ contend with	~와 싸우다[다투다]
☐ masterpiece	명사 걸작, 명작
☐ cruel	형용사 잔인한, 잔혹한, 고통스러운
☐ struggle with	~로 분투하다, ~하느라 애쓰다
☐ discrimination	명사 차별, 구별
☐ portrait	명사 묘사, 초상화
☐ relieve	동사 완화하다, 덜다, 안도하게 하다
☐ enlighten	동사 일깨우다, 이해시키다, 계몽하다
☐ embrace	동사 포괄하다, 아우르다, 포옹하다

13 2024년 3월 21번 (정답률 55%) 정답 ④

[지문 끊어 읽기] 자율 주행 자동차와 의료 분야의 발전 과정

(1) If you had wanted to create a "self-driving" car in the 1950s, /
만약 여러분이 1950년대에 '자율 주행' 자동차를 만들고 싶었다면 /
your best option might have been /
S V
여러분의 가장 좋은 선택은 ~이었을 것이다 /
힌트 가정법 과거완료인 「If+S'+had p.p. ~, S+조동사 과거형+have p.p. ~」가 사용된 문장으로, 과거 사실의 반대 상황을 가정함.
[to strap a brick to the accelerator]. [ ]: S·C
가속 페달에 벽돌을 끈으로 묶는 것
정답 단서 만약 1950년대에 '자율 주행' 자동차를 만들고자 했다면, 가속 페달에 벽돌을 끈으로 묶는 다소 원시적인 방법이 사용되었을 것임.

(2) Yes, /
물론 /
the vehicle would have been able to move forward on its own, /
would have p.p.: ~이었을 것이다
그 자동차는 스스로 앞으로 나아갈 수 있었을 것이다 /
but it could not slow down, stop, or turn to avoid barriers.
병렬① 병렬② 병렬③ 부사적 용법(목적)
하지만 그것은 속도를 줄이거나, 멈추거나, 또는 장애물을 피하기 위해 방향을 바꿀 수는 없었다

(3) Obviously not ideal.
분명히 이상적이지 않다

(4) But does that mean / [the entire concept of the self-driving car /
=문장(2) 내용
그러나 그것이 의미하는가 / 자율 주행 자동차라는 전체 개념이 /
is not worth pursuing]? [ ]: mean의 목적어절(접속사 that 생략)
추구할 만한 가치가 없다는 것을

(5) No, / it only means /
아니다 / 그것은 단지 의미한다 /
that at the time we did not yet have the tools we now possess /
선행사 목적격 관계대명사절
우리가 지금은 가지고 있는 도구를 그 당시에는 우리가 아직 가지고 있지 않았다는 것을 /
to help enable vehicles to operate /
형용사적 용법
자동차가 작동될 수 있도록 돕는 /
힌트 1)「help+동사원형/to V」: ~하도록 돕다 2)「enable A to V」: A가 ~할 수 있게 하다
both autonomously and safely.
자율적이고도 안전하게
정답 단서 1950년대에는 지금처럼 자동차를 자율적이고도 안전하게 작동될 수 있게 하는 도구를 가지고 있지 않았기에 자율 주행 자동차의 모습이 이상적이지는 않았음.

(6) This once-distant dream / now seems within our reach.
한때는 멀기만 했던 이 꿈이 / 이제는 우리의 손이 미치는 곳에 있는 것처럼 보인다

(7) It is much the same story / in medicine.
거의 마찬가지인
그것은 거의 마찬가지의 이야기이다 / 의학에서도
정답 단서 의학도 자율 주행 자동차의 사례와 거의 마찬가지임.

(8) Two decades ago, / we were still taping bricks to accelerators.
20년 전에 / 우리는 여전히 가속 페달에 벽돌을 테이프로 묶고 있었다
정답 단서 20년 전에, 의학에서는 1950년대의 자율 주행 자동차와 같은 원시적인 방법이 사용되었음.

(9) Today, / we are approaching the point / where we can begin /
선행사 관계부사
오늘날 / 우리는 지점에 접근하고 있다 / 우리가 시작할 수 있는 /
to bring some appropriate technology to bear /
bring A to bear: A를 도입[적용]하다
몇몇 적절한 기술을 도입하는 것을 /
in ways [that advance our understanding of patients /
선행사 [ ]: 주격 관계대명사절
환자에 대한 우리의 이해를 증진시키는 방식으로 /
as unique individuals].
고유한 개인으로서
정답 단서 20년 전과 달리 오늘날은 우리가 환자를 고유한 개인으로서 이해할 수 있게 하는 적절한 기술을 이용할 수 있게 되었음.

(10) In fact, / many patients are already wearing devices /
선행사
사실 / 많은 환자가 이미 장치들을 착용하고 있다 /
[that monitor their conditions in real time], / [ ]: 주격 관계대명사절
그들의 상태를 실시간으로 관찰하는 /
which allows doctors to talk to their patients /
allow A to V: A가 ~하도록 하다
그리고 이는 의사가 자신의 환자에게 말할 수 있도록 해준다 /
힌트 앞 절의 내용을 선행사로 가지는 계속적 용법의 관계대명사로, '접속사(and)+대명사(it)'로 바꿀 수 있음.
in a specific, refined, and feedback-driven way /
선행사
구체적이고, 정제되었으며 피드백을 기반으로 하는 방식으로 /
[that was not even possible a decade ago]. [ ]: 주격 관계대명사절
10년 전에는 심지어 가능하지도 않았던

[전문 해석]

(1)만약 여러분이 1950년대에 '자율 주행' 자동차를 만들고 싶었다면, 여러분의 가장 좋은 선택은 가속 페달에 벽돌을 끈으로 묶는 것이었을 것이다. (2)물론, 그 자동차는 스스로 앞으로 나아갈 수 있었겠지만, 그것은 속도를 줄이거나, 멈추거나, 또는 장애물을 피하기 위해 방향을 바꿀 수는 없었다. (3)(이는) 분명히 이상적이지 않다. (4)그러나 그것이 자율 주행 자동차라는 전체 개념이 추구할 만한 가치가 없다는 것을 의미하는가? (5)아니다, 그것은 단지 우리가 지금은 가지고 있는, 자동차가 자율적이고도 안전하게 작동될 수 있도록 돕는 도구를 그 당시에는 우리가 아직 가지고 있지 않았다는 것을 의미한다. (6)한때는 멀기만 했던 이 꿈이 이제는 우리의 손이 미치는 곳에 있는 것처럼 보인다. (7)그것은 의학에서도 거의 마찬가지의 이야기이다. (8)20년 전에, 우리는 여전히 가속 페달에 벽돌을 테이프로 묶고 있었다(진보된 도구의 결핍이 환자를 이해하는 데 어려움을 제기했다). (9)오늘날, 우리는 고유한 개인으로서 환자에 대한 우리의 이해를(우리가 환자를 고유한 개인으로서 이해하는 것을) 증진시키는 방식으로 몇몇 적절한 기술을 도입하는 것을 시작할 수 있는 지점에 접근하고 있다. (10)사실, 많은 환자가 이미 그들의 상태를 실시간으로 관찰하는 장치들을 착용하고 있으며, 이는 의사가 10년 전에는 심지어 가능하지도 않았던 구체적이고, 정제되었으며 피드백을 기반으로 하는 방식으로 자신의 환자에게 말할 수 있도록 해준다.

[정답 확인]

밑줄 친 we were still taping bricks to accelerators가 다음 글에서 의미하는 바로 가장 적절한 것은?

① the importance of medical education was overlooked
의학 교육의 중요성이 간과되었다
② self-driving cars enabled patients to move around freely
자율 주행 자동차들은 환자가 자유롭게 돌아다닐 수 있도록 했다
③ the devices for safe driving were unavailable at that time
안전 주행을 위한 장치들이 그 당시에는 이용 불가능했다
✔ lack of advanced tools posed a challenge in understanding patients
진보된 도구의 결핍이 환자를 이해하는 데 어려움을 제기했다
⑤ appropriate technologies led to success in developing a new medicine
적절한 기술들이 새로운 약을 개발하는 데 있어 성공으로 이어졌다

[문제 풀이]

'의료 분야의 발전 과정'을 '자율 주행 자동차의 발전 과정'에 빗대어 설명한 글이다. 글쓴이는 '가속 페달에 벽돌을 끈으로 묶었던' 과거 자율 주행 자동차의 방식이 오늘날 자동차를 자율적이고도 안전하게 운행할 수 있게 하는 방식으로 발전한 것처럼, 의료 분야에서도 '가속 페달에 벽돌을 테이프로 묶는 것'과 같았던 20년 전의 방식이 향상된 도구와 기술을 바탕으로 환자 개개인을 맞춤형으로 더 효과적으로 이해할 수 있는 방식으로 발전되었다고 설명한다. 즉, 문장 (8)의 밑줄 친 부분은 진보된 도구가 존재하지 않았던 '이상적이지 않은(not ideal)' 과거의 의료 상황을 나타내므로, 밑줄 친 부분이 의미하는 바로 가장 적절한 것은 ④이다.

[중요 어휘]

□ strap A to B	B에 A를 끈으로 묶다
□ accelerator	명사 가속 페달, 가속 장치
□ vehicle	명사 자동차, 차량
□ on one's own	스스로
□ barrier	명사 장애물, 장벽
□ be worth V-ing	~할 가치가 있다
□ possess	동사 가지다, 소유하다
□ operate	동사 작동하다, 운영하다
□ autonomously	부사 자율적으로, 독자적으로
□ within one's reach	~의 손이 미치는 곳에
□ approach	동사 ~에 접근하다, 다가가다
□ appropriate	형용사 적절한
□ advance	동사 증진시키다, 향상시키다
□ device	명사 장치, 기구
□ monitor	동사 관찰하다, 감시하다
□ condition	명사 (건강) 상태
□ in real time	실시간으로
□ refined	형용사 정제된, 세련된

14 2024년 6월 21번 (정답률 70%) 정답 ①

[지문 끊어 읽기]

(1) Take a look /
살펴봐라 /
at some of the most powerful, rich, and famous people in the world.
세계에서 가장 영향력 있고, 부유하며, 유명한 사람들 중 몇몇을

(2) Ignore / the trappings of their success /
무시해라 / 그들의 성공의 장식을 / 병렬①
and what they're able to buy.
병렬②
그리고 그들이 살 수 있는 것을

(3) Look instead / at what they're forced to trade in return /
A be forced to V: A가 ~하도록 강요받다
대신에 봐라 / 그들이 대가로 맞바꾸도록 강요받았던 것을 /
— look at what success has cost them. 정답 단서 성공한 사람들은 성공의 대가로 무언가를 맞바꿈.
성공이 그들에게 치르게 한 것을 봐라

(4) Mostly? / Freedom.
대부분은 / 자유이다

(5) Their work demands / they wear a suit.
명사절(접속사 that 생략)
그들의 업무는 요구한다 / 그들이 정장을 입는 것을

힌트 '주장, 제안, 명령, 요구 등'을 나타내는 동사 뒤에 오는 that절에서 당위성을 나타내는 조동사 should가 쓰이나, 많은 경우 생략되어 주어 다음에 바로 동사원형이 쓰이는 것을 볼 수 있음. 이 문장에서도 'they should wear'에서 조동사 should가 생략되었음.

(6) Their success depends / on attending certain parties, /
그들의 성공은 달려 있다 / 특정 파티에 참석하는 것에 /
kissing up to people they don't like.
선행사 ↑ 목적격 관계대명사 생략
그들이 좋아하지 않는 사람들에게 아첨하는 것에

(7) It will require / — inevitably — /
=success
그것은 요구할 것이다 / 필연적으로 /
realizing [they are unable to say / what they actually think].
[ ]: realizing의 목적어절(that 생략) say의 목적어(선행사를 포함한 관계대명사절)
그들이 말할 수 없다는 사실을 깨닫는 것을 / 그들이 실제로 생각하는 것을

힌트 동사 require의 목적어로 to부정사와 동명사가 올 수 있는데, 이 문장에서는 동명사 realizing이 왔음. 이는 약간의 뉘앙스 차이는 있지만 'It will require them to realize ~'와 비슷함.

(8) Worse, / it demands /
더 나쁜 것은 / 그것은 요구한다 /
[that they become a different type of person / or do bad things].
그들이 다른 유형의 사람이 되도록 / 혹은 부당한 일을 하도록
[ ]: 명사절(demands의 목적어절)

정답 단서 성공은 다른 유형의 사람이 되거나 부당한 일을 하도록 요구함.

★중요 문장 (6)~(8)은 성공과 자유를 교환하여 행동에 제약이 생기는 상황을 제시함.

(9) Sure, / it might pay well /
물론 / 그것은 많은 보수를 줄지도 모른다 /
— but they haven't truly examined the transaction.
그러나 그들은 그 거래를 제대로 고찰한 적이 없다

(10) As Seneca put it, / "Slavery resides under marble and gold."
Seneca가 말했듯이 / "대리석과 황금 아래에 노예가 산다."

★중요 대리석과 황금은 성공으로 얻을 수 있는 이익을 가리키고, 노예는 자유를 잃은 사람을 의미함. 따라서 '많은 이익을 가져다준 성공은 우리 행동에서 자유를 앗아가는 결과를 가져온다'라는 의미로 해석할 수 있음.

(11) Too many successful people are prisoners /
너무 많은 성공한 사람들은 죄수들이다 /
in jails of their own making.
그들이 스스로 만든 감옥의

(12) Is that [what you want]? [ ]: 선행사를 포함한 관계대명사절
그것이 당신이 원하는 것인가

(13) Is that [what you're working hard toward]? [ ]: 선행사를 포함한 관계대명사절
그것이 당신이 목표로 하여 열심히 일하고 있는 것인가

(14) Let's hope not.
그렇지 않기를 바라자

[전문 해석]

(1)세계에서 가장 영향력 있고, 부유하며, 유명한 사람들 중 몇몇을 살펴봐라. (2)그들의 성공의 장식과 그들이 살 수 있는 것을 무시해라. (3)대신에 그들이 대가로 맞바꾸도록 강요받았던 것을 봐라. 성공이 그들에게 치르게 한 것을 봐라. (4)대부분은? 자유이다. (5)그들의 업무는 그들이 정장을 입는 것을 요구한다. (6)그들의 성공은 특정 파티에 참석하고, 그들이 좋아하지 않는 사람들에게 아첨하는 것에 달려 있다. (7)그것은 필연적으로 그들이 실제로 생각하는 것을 말할 수 없다는 사실을 깨닫는 것을 요구할 것이다. (8)더 나쁜 것은, 그것은 그들이 다른 유형의 사람이 되거나 부당한 일을 하도록 요구한다. (9)물론, 그것은 많은 보수를 줄지도 모른다. 그러나 그들은 그 거래를 제대로 고찰한 적이 없다. (10)Seneca가 말했듯이, "대리석과 황금 아래에 노예가 산다."(성공은 당신이 원하지 않는 방식으로 행동하길 요구한다.) (11)너무 많은 성공한 사람들은 그들이 스스로 만든 감옥의 죄수들이다. (12)그것이 당신이 원하는 것인가? (13)그것이 당신이 목표로 하여 열심히 일하고 있는 것인가? (14)그렇지 않기를 바라자.

[정답 확인]

밑줄 친 "Slavery resides under marble and gold."가 다음 글에서 의미하는 바로 가장 적절한 것은?

✔ Your success requires you to act in ways you don't want to.
성공은 당신이 원하지 않는 방식으로 행동하길 요구한다.
② Fame cannot be achieved without the help of others.
명성은 다른 사람들의 도움 없이는 얻을 수 없다.
③ Comparing yourself to others makes you miserable.
다른 사람과 자신을 비교하는 것은 당신을 비참하게 만든다.
④ Hard labor guarantees glory and happiness in the future.
열심히 일하는 것은 미래의 영광과 행복을 보장한다.
⑤ There exists freedom in the appearance of your success.
성공의 겉모습에는 자유가 존재한다.

문제편 p.047

[중요 어휘]

☐ in return	대가로, 답례로
☐ depend on	~에 달려 있다, ~에 의존하다
☐ kiss up	아첨하다, 아부하다
☐ inevitably	부사 필연적으로, 불가피하게
☐ examine	동사 고찰하다, 검토하다
☐ transaction	명사 거래, 매매
☐ slavery	명사 노예, 노예제도
☐ reside	동사 살다, 거주하다
☐ marble	명사 대리석, 구슬
☐ jail	명사 감옥, 교도소
☐ fame	명사 명성, 인기
☐ miserable	형용사 비참한, 불행한
☐ glory	명사 영광

15 2024년 9월 21번 (정답률 65%) 정답 ①

[지문 끊어 읽기] 정보화 시대 조직 내의 변화

(1) In today's information age, /
오늘날 정보화 시대에는 /
in many companies and on many teams, /
많은 기업과 팀에서 /
the objective is no longer error prevention and replicability.
목표는 더 이상 오류 방지와 반복 가능성이 아니다

(2) On the contrary, / it's creativity, speed, and keenness.
=the objective
반대로 / 그것은 창의성, 속도, 그리고 명민함이다

(3) In the industrial era, / the goal was to minimize variation.
산업화 시대에서 / 목표는 변화를 최소화하는 것이었다 S·C

(4) But in creative companies today, /
그러나 오늘날의 창의적 기업에서는 /
maximizing variation is more essential.
S, 동명사 V
변화를 극대화하는 것이 더 필수적이다

(5) In these situations, / the biggest risk isn't making a mistake /
이러한 상황에서 / 가장 큰 위험은 실수를 하는 것이 아니다 / 병렬①
or losing consistency;
병렬②
혹은 일관성을 잃는 것이

(6) it's failing / to attract top talent, /
=the biggest risk 병렬①(명사적 용법)
그것은 실패하는 것이다 / 가장 재능이 있는 사람을 끌어들이는 것에 /
to invent new products, / or to change direction quickly /
병렬② 병렬③
새로운 제품을 만드는 것에 / 혹은 방향을 빠르게 바꾸는 것에 /
when the environment shifts. 정답 단서 오늘날 기업에서 가장 큰 위험은 가장 재능 있는 사람을 끌어들이고 새로운 것을 받아들이는 것에 실패하는 것임.
상황이 변할 때

(7) Consistency and repeatability are more likely /
일관성과 반복 가능성은 가능성이 더 높다 / 정답 단서 일관성과 반복 가능성은 창의성을 억압할 가능성이 높음.
to suppress fresh thinking / than to bring your company profit.
병렬① 병렬②(4형식V) I·O D·O
새로운 생각을 짓누를 / 여러분의 회사에 이익을 가지고 오기보다는

(8) A lot of little mistakes, / while sometimes painful, /
S
많은 작은 실수는 / 때때로 고통스러우나 / 힌트 부사절 'while they are sometimes painful'에서 주절의 주어와 같은 것을 가리키는 종속절의 주어인 they와 be동사가 생략되었음.
help the organization learn quickly /
V①(5형식V) O O·C
조직이 빠르게 배우기를 돕는다 /
and are a critical part of the innovation cycle.
V②
그리고 혁신 주기의 중요한 부분이다

(9) In these situations, /
이러한 상황 속에서 /
rules and process are no longer the best answer.
규칙과 과정은 더 이상 최선의 답이 아니다

(10) A symphony isn't [what you're going for]. [ ]: S·C(선행사를 포함한 관계대명사절)
교향악단은 여러분이 추구하는 것이 아니다

(11) Leave the conductor and the sheet music behind. 힌트 leave A behind : A를 뒤에 남기다
지휘자와 악보는 뒤에 남겨 두어라

(12) Build a jazz band instead.
대신에 재즈 밴드를 결성하라

[전문 해석]

(1)오늘날 정보화 시대에는, 많은 기업과 팀에서 목표는 더 이상 오류 방지와 반복 가능성이 아니다. (2)반대로, 그것은 창의성, 속도, 그리고 명민함이다. (3)산업화 시대에서, 목표는 변화를 최소화하는 것이었다. (4)그러나 오늘날의 창의적 기업에서는, 변화를 극대화하는 것이 더 필수적이다. (5)이러한 상황에서, 가장 큰 위험은 실수를 하는 것 혹은 일관성을 잃는 것이 아니다. (6)그것은 가장 재능이 있는 사람을 끌어들이는 것, 새로운 제품을 만드는 것, 혹은 상황이 변할 때 방향을 빠르게 바꾸는 것에 실패하는 것이다. (7)일관성과 반복 가능성은 여러분의 회사에 이익을 가지고 오기보다는 새로운 생각을 짓누를 가능성이 더 높다. (8)많은 작은 실수는 때때로 고통스러우나, 조직이 빠르게 배우기를 돕고 혁신 주기의 중요한 부분이다. (9)이러한 상황 속에서, 규칙과 과정은 더 이상 최선의 답이 아니다. (10)교향악단은 여러분이 추구하는 것이 아니다. (11)지휘자와 악보는 뒤에 남겨 두어라. (12)대신에 재즈 밴드를 결성하라(조직 내에서 변화를 장려하라).

[정답 확인]

밑줄 친 Build a jazz band가 다음 글에서 의미하는 바로 가장 적절한 것은?

✔ Foster variation within an organization.
조직 내에서 변화를 장려하라.
② Limit the scope of variability in businesses.
사업에서 변동성의 범위를 제한하라.
③ Invent a new way of minimizing risk-taking.
위험을 감수하는 것을 최소화하는 새로운 방법을 발명하라.
④ Promote teamwork to forecast upcoming changes.
팀워크를 증진하여 다가오는 변화를 예측하라.
⑤ Share innovations over a sufficient period of time.
충분한 기간 동안 혁신을 공유하라.

[문제 풀이]

시대의 변화에 따라 기업과 팀의 목표에 변화가 생긴다. 문장 (1), (2)에 따르면, 정보화 시대에 들어서자 많은 기업과 팀이 창의성, 속도, 그리고 명민함을 추구하기 시작했다. 문장 (3), (4)에서는 기업들이 산업화 시대와는 정반대로 변화를 극대화하는 것을 필수로 보고 있다고 한다. 문장 (5)~(8)에 따르면 일관성과 반복 가능성은 창의적인 생각을 막으므로 많은 작은 실수를 감수하고 새로운 도전을 시도하는 것이 오히려 조직이 빠르게 변화하도록 돕고 혁신 주기의 중요한 부분이라고 주장한다. 다시 말해, '재즈 밴드를 결성하라'는 것은 정해진 틀인 지휘자와 악보라는 일관성과 반복 가능성에서 벗어나 변화를 장려하라는 의미로 이해할 수 있다. 따라서 정답은 ①이다.

[중요 어휘]

☐ objective	명사 목표 / 형용사 객관적인
☐ no longer	더 이상 ~이 아닌
☐ prevention	명사 방지, 예방
☐ replicability	명사 반복 가능성, 복제 가능성
☐ keenness	명사 명민함, 날카로움
☐ variation	명사 변화, 변형
☐ consistency	명사 일관성, 한결같음
☐ talent	명사 재능 있는 사람, 재능, 장기
☐ suppress	동사 짓누르다, 억압하다
☐ process	명사 과정, 절차
☐ conductor	명사 지휘자
☐ foster	동사 장려하다, 조성하다
☐ scope	명사 범위, 기회, 여지
☐ variability	명사 변동성, 가변성
☐ forecast	동사 예측하다, 예보하다

05 요지 추론

01 2021년 6월 22번 (정답률 95%)

정답 ⑤

[지문 끊어 읽기] 장기적인 습관을 만드는 방법

(1) When it comes to the decision / to get more exercise, /
결심에 대해 말하자면 / 더 많은 운동을 하겠다는 / 형용사적 용법
you are setting goals / that are similar /
선행사 / 주격 관계대명사
당신은 목표를 세우고 있다 / 비슷한 /
to running a half marathon / with very little training!
하프 마라톤을 뛰는 것과 / 아주 적은 훈련을 하고

(2) You make a decision / to buy a gym membership /
형용사적 용법
당신은 결심을 한다 / 헬스장 회원권을 사기로 /
and decide to spend an hour / at the gym every day.
그리고 한 시간을 보내겠다고 결정한다 / 매일 헬스장에서

(3) Well, / you might stick to that / for a day or two, /
글쎄 / 당신은 그것을 고수할지도 모른다 / 하루나 이틀 정도 /
but chances are / you won't be able to continue /
하지만 가능성이 있다 / 당신이 계속할 수 없을 /
to meet that commitment / in the long term.
그 약속을 지키는 것을 / 장기적으로

힌트 '(The) chances are (that) ~'은 숙어와 같이 굳어진 표현으로, '~할 가능성이 있다', '아마 ~일 것이다' 등의 의미로 쓰임.

(4) If, however, you make a commitment /
그러나 만약 당신이 약속한다면 /
to go jogging for a few minutes a day /
하루에 몇 분씩 조깅을 하기로 /
or add a few sit-ups to your daily routine before bed, /
혹은 자기 전에 당신의 일상에 윗몸 일으키기 몇 개를 추가하기로 /
then you are far more likely / to stick to your decision /
그렇다면 당신은 가능성이 훨씬 더 높다 / 당신의 결심을 고수할 /
and to create a habit / that offers you long-term results.
선행사 / 주격 관계대명사
그리고 습관을 만들 / 당신에게 장기적인 결과를 주는

(5) The key is / to start small.
핵심은 ~이다 / 작게 시작하는 것

(6) Small habits lead to long-term success. 주제문
작은 습관이 장기적인 성공으로 이어진다

[중요 구문]

(4) If, ~, you make a commitment [to go jogging ~] or [(to) add a few sit-ups ~], then you are ~ likely [to stick to your decision] and [to create a habit ~ results].
병렬① 병렬② / 병렬'① 병렬'②

힌트 If절 안에서 등위접속사 or를 중심으로 to부정사로 묶인 동사 go와 add가 앞뒤로 병렬되었고, 주절 안에서는 등위접속사 and를 중심으로 to부정사인 to stick과 to create가 병렬되어 있음.

[전문 해석]

(1)더 많은 운동을 하겠다는 결심에 대해 말하자면, 당신은 아주 적은 훈련을 하고(거의 훈련을 하지 않고) 하프 마라톤을 뛰는 것과 비슷한 목표를 세우고 있다! (2)당신은 헬스장 회원권을 사기로 결심을 하고 매일 헬스장에서 한 시간을 보내겠다고 결정한다. (3)글쎄, 당신은 그것(결심)을 하루나 이틀 정도 고수할지도 모르지만, 당신이 장기적으로 그 약속을 지키는 것을 계속할 수 없을 가능성이 있다. (4)그러나 만약 당신이 하루에 몇 분씩 조깅을 하거나 자기 전에 당신의 일상에 윗몸 일으키기 몇 개를 추가하기로 약속한다면, 당신은 당신의 결심을 고수하고 당신에게 장기적인 결과를 주는 습관을 만들 가능성이 훨씬 더 높다. (5)핵심은 작게(작은 것부터) 시작하는 것이다. (6)작은 습관이 장기적인 성공으로 이어진다.

[정답 확인]

다음 글의 요지로 가장 적절한 것은?

① 상황에 따른 유연한(flexible) 태도가 목표 달성에 효과적이다.
② 올바른 식습관과 규칙적인(regular) 운동이 건강 유지에 도움이 된다.
③ 나쁜 습관을 고치기(amend) 위해서는 장기적인 계획이 필수적이다.
④ 꿈을 이루기 위해서는 원대한 목표(goal)를 세우는 것이 중요하다.
✔ 장기적인(long-term) 성공을 위해 작은 습관부터 시작하는 것이 필요하다.

[중요 어휘]

□ decision	명사 결심, 판단
□ training	명사 훈련, 교육, 연수
□ stick to	~을 고수하다[지키다]
□ be able to V	~을 할 수 있다
□ meet	동사 지키다, 충족시키다, 만나다
□ commitment	명사 약속, 전념, 헌신
□ sit-up	명사 윗몸 일으키기

02 2021년 11월 22번 (정답률 90%)

정답 ⑤

[지문 끊어 읽기] 독자를 몰입시키는 질문

(1) *Who is this person?*
'이 사람은 누구인가?'

(2) This is the question / all stories ask.
목적격 관계대명사 생략
이것은 질문이다 / 모든 이야기가 물어보는

(3) It emerges first / at the ignition point.
=the question
그것은 가장 먼저 나타난다 / 발화 지점에서

★중요 발화 지점(ignition point)이란 불이 붙어 타기 시작하는 최저 온도로, 여기서는 문장 (4)의 '처음의 변화(the initial change)'가 발생하는 시점을 발화 지점에 비유하여 표현함.

(4) When the initial change strikes, / the protagonist overreacts /
처음의 변화가 발생할 때 / 주인공은 과민 반응한다 /
or behaves in an otherwise unexpected way.
삽입
혹은 그렇지 않으면 예상치 못한 방식으로 행동한다

힌트 연속 동작을 나타내는 분사구문으로 원래는 'and we are suddenly attentive'에서 접속사 'and'와 주절과 공통된 주어인 'we'가 생략되고 be동사는 현재분사형인 being으로 변형되었지만 생략되었음.

(5) We sit up, / suddenly attentive. 정답 단서
우리는 일어나 앉는다 / 그리고 갑자기 주의를 기울인다

우리는 변화에 대한 주인공의 반응을 궁금해하며 주의를 기울이게 됨.

(6) *Who is this person / who behaves like this?*
선행사 / 주격 관계대명사절
이 사람은 누구인가 / 이렇게 행동하는

(7) The question then re-emerges / 정답 단서
그러고 나서 그 질문은 다시 나타난다 /
[every time the protagonist is challenged by the plot /
p.p.①
주인공이 줄거리에 도전받을 때마다 /
and compelled to make a choice].
p.p.② [ ]: 부사절(=each time/whenever~)
그리고 선택을 하도록 강요받을 때마다

주인공이 도전받거나 선택을 하도록 강요받을 때마다 독자 또는 시청자는 '이 사람은 누구인가' 라고 질문하게 됨.

힌트 'compel A to V(A가 ~하도록 강요하다)'라는 5형식 구문의 수동태 형태임. 주어 compel the protagonist to make a choice로 바꾸어 생각하면 이해하기 쉬움.

(8) Everywhere in the narrative / that the question is present, /
선행사 / 관계부사절
이야기의 모든 곳에서 / 그 질문이 존재하는 /
the reader or viewer will likely be engaged.
독자 또는 시청자는 몰입하게 될 것이다 주제문

힌트 선행사가 everywhere, nowhere, somewhere 등일 때 관계부사 where 대신 that을 씀.

이야기를 읽거나 시청하면서 '이 사람은 누구인가'라는 질문이 생길 때마다 독자 또는 시청자는 몰입하게 됨.

(9) Where the question is absent, /
접속사(~하는 곳에서)
그 질문이 부재하는 곳에서 /
and the events of drama move out of its narrative beam, /
그리고 드라마의 사건들이 이야기의 빛줄기에서 벗어나는 곳에서 /
they are at risk of becoming detached / — perhaps even bored.
그들은 분리될 위험에 놓인다 / 그리고 심지어는 지루해질 위험에 처할 수도 있다

힌트 perhaps (they are at risk of becoming) even bored에서 반복되는 부분이 생략됨. 참고로 be at risk of N/V-ing는 '주어가 ~할 위험에 처하다'라는 뜻임.

(10) If there's a single secret to storytelling /
만약 이야기하기에 한 가지 비밀이 있다면 /
then I believe / it's this.
목적어절(명사절 접속사 that 생략)
그렇다면 나는 믿는다 / 그것이 이것이라고

★중요 문장 (11)의 내용을 가리킴. 문장 (10) 전체는 '이 사람은 누구인가?', '나는 누구인가?' 등의 질문을 자아내는 것이 이야기하기(storytelling)에 있어서 중요하다는 뜻이며 문장 (12)에서 언급하듯이 이것이 곧 드라마의 정의임.

(11) *Who is this person?* / Or, /
'이 사람은 누구인가?' / 또는 /
from the perspective of the character, / *Who am I?*
등장인물의 관점에서 / '나는 누구인가?'

(12) It's the definition of drama.
그것이 드라마의 정의이다

(13) It is its electricity, its heartbeat, its fire.
그것이 드라마의 전기이고 심장 박동이자 불이다

정답과 해설
05 요지 추론

문제편 p.051

[전문 해석]

(1)'이 사람은 누구인가?' (2)이것은 모든 이야기가 물어보는 질문이다. (3)그것은 발화 지점에서 가장 먼저 나타난다. (4)처음의 변화가 발생할 때 주인공은 과민 반응하거나 그렇지 않으면 예상치 못한 방식으로 행동한다. (5)우리는 일어나 앉아 갑자기 주의를 기울인다. (6)'이렇게 행동하는 이 사람은 누구인가?' (7)그러고 나서 그 질문은 주인공이 줄거리에 도전받고 선택을 하도록 강요받을 때마다 다시 나타난다. (8)그 질문이 존재하는 이야기의 모든 곳에서 독자 또는 시청자는 몰입하게 될 것이다. (9)그 질문이 부재하고 드라마의 사건들이 이야기의 빛줄기에서 벗어나는 곳에서 그들은 분리될 위험에 놓이고, 심지어는 지루해질 위험에 처할 수도 있다. (10)만약 이야기하기에 한 가지 비밀이 있다면 나는 그것이 이것이라고 믿는다. (11)'이 사람은 누구인가?' 또는 등장인물의 관점에서 '나는 누구인가?' (12)그것이 드라마의 정의이다. (13)그것이 드라마의 전기이고 심장 박동이자 불이다.

[정답 확인]

다음 글의 요지로 가장 적절한 것은?

① 독자의 공감을 얻기 위해 구체적인 인물 묘사(portrayal)가 중요하다.
② 이야기의 줄거리(plot)를 단순화시키는(simplify) 것이 독자의 이해를 높인다.
③ 거리를 두고 주인공(protagonist)의 상황(circumstance)을 객관적으로 바라볼 필요가 있다.
④ 주인공의 역경(adversity)과 행복이 적절히 섞여야 이야기(narrative)가 흥미로워진다.
✔ 주인공에 대한 지속적인 궁금증(curiosity) 유발이 독자의 몰입을 도와준다.

[중요 어휘]

☐ ignition	명사 발화(불이 일어나거나 타기 시작함), 점화(불을 붙이거나 켬)
☐ initial	형용사 처음의, 초기의
☐ strike	동사 발생하다, 부딪치다, 때리다
☐ protagonist	명사 주인공
☐ overreact	동사 과민 반응하다
☐ attentive	형용사 주의를 기울이는
☐ challenge	동사 도전하다, 이의를 제기하다
☐ narrative	명사 이야기, 묘사 / 형용사 이야기의
☐ present	형용사 존재하는, 현재의 / 동사 주다, 제시하다 / 명사 선물, 현재
☐ engage	동사 몰입시키다, 몰두시키다, 끌어들이다
☐ absent	형용사 부재하는, 결석한
☐ beam	명사 빛줄기, 기둥, 환한 미소 / 동사 활짝 웃다, 비추다
☐ at risk of	~할 위험에 처한
☐ detach	동사 분리하다, 떼다

03 2022년 6월 22번 (정답률 90%)

정답 ①

[지문 끊어 읽기] 아이에게 맞는 양육 방식

(1) The problem with simply adopting any popular method of parenting /
S 전치사 동명사
대중적인 양육법을 단순히 채택하는 것의 문제는 /

is that it ignores the most important variable in the equation: /
V 명사절 접속사
그것이 방정식의 가장 중요한 변수를 무시한다는 것이다 /

the uniqueness of your child.
자녀의 독특함

힌트 콜론은 앞 내용에 대한 부연 설명을 하기 위해 쓰임. 이 문장에서는 'the most important variable in the equation'이 무엇인지 구체적으로 설명하기 위해 콜론이 쓰였고 'the uniqueness of your child'가 그 설명에 해당함.

(2) So, / rather than insist /
그래서 / 주장하기보다는 / 병렬①

힌트 A rather than B는 'B보다는 A'로 해석하며, 본문에서 A(take)는 주절의 동사이며 rather than B(insist) 부분이 문두로 나와있음. A와 B에는 동일한 품사가 와야 함.

that one style of parenting will work with every child, /
명사절 접속사
한 가지 양육 방식이 모든 아이들에게 효과가 있을 것이라고 /

we might take a page from the gardener's handbook.
병렬②
우리는 정원사의 안내서 일부를 참고할 수도 있다

(3) Just as the gardener accepts, /
접속사(~처럼) S' V'①
정원사가 받아들이는 것처럼 /

힌트 「(just) as+S'+V', so+조동사(do동사/be동사 등)+S+V」 형태의 문장으로, 'S'가 V'하는 것처럼 S도 V하다'라는 의미임. 이때 so 뒷부분은 주어와 동사가 도치될 수 있음. 여기서는 주어와 동사의 도치를 위해 조동사 do가 주어 앞에 쓰였음. 정원사가 각각의 식물에게 알맞은 방식으로 식물을 기르듯, 부모도 각각의 아이들에게 알맞은 방식으로 아이들을 양육해야 한다는 내용을 강조하고 있음.

without question or resistance, /
의문이나 거부감 없이 /

the plant's requirements / and provides the right conditions /
O'① V'② O'②(선행사)
식물의 요구 사항을 / 그리고 적절한 조건을 제공하는 것처럼 /

[each plant needs to grow and flourish], /
[ ]: 목적격 관계대명사절 부사적 용법(목적)
각각의 식물이 자라고 번성하기 위해 필요한 /

so, too, do we parents / need to custom-design our parenting /
부사 조동사 S V
우리 부모도 역시 / 양육을 맞춤 설계할 필요가 있다 /

to fit the natural needs of each individual child. **정답 단서** 부모는 각각의 아이들에게 알맞은 양육 방식을 맞춤 설계할 필요가 있다고 함.
아이들 개개인의 타고난 욕구에 맞는

(4) Although that may seem difficult, / it is possible.
그것이 어려워 보일지 모르지만 / 가능하다

(5) Once we understand who our children really are, /
명사절(간접의문문)
일단 우리가 우리 아이들이 진정 어떤 아이인지를 알게 되면 /

we can begin to figure out /
우리는 알아내기 시작할 수 있다 /

how to make changes in our parenting style /
의문사+to부정사(=의문사+S+should+V)
양육 방식에 변화를 줄 방법을 /

to be more positive and accepting of each child /
부사적 용법(목적) 선행사
아이에게 보다 긍정적이고 수용적이도록 /

[we've been blessed to parent]. [ ]: 목적격 관계대명사절
우리가 양육하도록 축복받은

[전문 해석]

(1)대중적인 양육법을 단순히 채택하는 것의 문제는 그것이 방정식의 가장 중요한 변수, 즉 자녀의 독특함을 무시한다는 것이다. (2)그래서, 한 가지 양육 방식이 모든 아이들에게 효과가 있을 것이라고 주장하기보다는, 우리는 정원사의 안내서 일부를 참고할 수도 있다. (3)정원사가 의문이나 거부감 없이 식물의 요구 사항을 받아들이고 각각의 식물이 자라고 번성하기 위해 필요한 적절한 조건을 제공하는 것처럼, 우리 부모도 역시 아이들 개개인의 타고난 욕구에 맞는 양육을 맞춤 설계할 필요가 있다. (4)그것이 어려워 보일지 모르지만, 가능하다. (5)일단 우리가 우리 아이들이 진정 어떤 아이인지를 알게 되면, 우리가 양육하도록 축복받은 아이에게 보다 긍정적이고 수용적이도록 양육 방식에 변화를 줄 방법을 알아내기 시작할 수 있다.

[정답 확인]

다음 글의 요지로 가장 적절한 것은?

✔ 자녀의 특성에 맞는 개별화된(individualized) 양육이 필요하다.
② 식물을 키우는 것이 자녀의 창의성(creativity) 발달에 도움이 된다.
③ 정서적 교감은 자녀의 바람직한 인격 형성에 필수적(necessary)이다.
④ 자녀에게 타인을 존중하는 태도(attitude)를 가르치는 것이 중요하다.
⑤ 전문가에 의해 검증된 양육 방식(parenting style)을 따르는 것이 바람직하다.

[중요 어휘]

☐ adopt	동사 채택하다, 입양하다, 취하다
☐ parenting	명사 양육, 육아
☐ variable	명사 변수 / 형용사 가변적인
☐ equation	명사 방정식
☐ insist	동사 주장하다
☐ resistance	명사 거부감, 저항
☐ flourish	동사 번성하다, 잘 자라다, 번창하다
☐ custom-design	동사 맞춤 설계하다
☐ natural	형용사 타고난, 자연의, 자연스러운
☐ bless	동사 축복하다

📍핵심 이 글은 보상 회로가 우울증과 같은 정신 질환을 회복시킬 수 있으며, 수작업 활동을 통해 보상 회로를 작동시킬 수 있다고 말하고 있음.

04 2020년 9월 22번 (정답률 85%) 정답 ③

[지문 끊어 읽기] 수작업 활동이 정신 건강에 미치는 영향

(1) The psychology professor Dr. Kelly Lambert's research /
심리학 교수인 Kelly Lambert 박사의 연구는 /
explains that / keeping /
~라고 설명한다 / 유지하는 것이 /
what she calls the "effort-driven rewards circuit" /
그녀가 '노력 주도 보상 회로'라고 부르는 것을 /
well engaged / helps you deal with challenges /
잘 작동되는 상태로 / 당신이 도전을 다루도록 돕는다 /
in the environment around you / or in your emotional life /
당신 주변의 환경에서의 / 혹은 당신의 감정적인 삶에서의 /
more effectively and efficiently. 정답 단서
더 효과적이고 효율적으로

힌트 'engage'는 '사용하다(occupy)'라는 의미를 내포하기 때문에 밑줄 친 부분도 '노력 주도 보상 회로'가 잘 사용되는 상태를 표현하기 위해 '잘 작동되는 상태로'라고 해석했음.

(2) Doing hands-on activities / 정답 단서
동명사S
수작업 활동을 하는 것은 /
that produce results / you can see and touch /
결과를 낳는 / 당신이 보고 만질 수 있는 /
— such as knitting a scarf, cooking from scratch, or tending a garden — /
스카프를 뜨거나, 처음부터 요리하거나, 혹은 정원을 손질하는 것과 같이 /
fuels the reward circuit / so that it functions optimally.
V
보상 회로를 부추긴다 / 그것이 최적으로 기능하도록

(3) She argues that / the documented increase / in depression /
그녀는 ~라고 주장한다 / 문서에 기록된 증가가 / 우울증의 /
among Americans / may be directly correlated /
미국인들 사이의 / 직접적으로 관련이 있을 수도 있다 /
with the decline / of purposeful physical activity.
감소와 / 의도적인 신체활동의

(4) When we work with our hands, / it increases the release /
우리가 우리의 손으로 작업할 때 / 그것은 방출을 증가시킨다 /
of the neurochemicals dopamine and serotonin, /
신경 화학 물질인 도파민과 세로토닌의 /
both responsible for generating positive emotions.
그리고 둘 다 긍정적인 감정을 발생시키는 것을 담당한다

힌트 밑줄 친 부분은 분사구문으로, 'both'는 앞에 나온 도파민과 세로토닌을 받은 분사구문의 주어이고, 'both' 뒤에 현재분사인 'being'이 생략되어 형용사구인 'responsible for ~'이 남은 것임.

(5) She also explains / that working with our hands gives us /
접속사 S' 4형식V' I·O'
그녀는 또한 설명한다 / 우리의 손으로 작업하는 것이 우리에게 제공한다고 /
a greater sense of control / over our environment /
더 큰 통제 감각을 / 우리의 환경에 대한 /
and more connection / to the world around us.
그리고 더 많은 연결을 / 우리 주변 세계와의

힌트 밑줄 친 부분은 gives의 직접목적어로, 접속사 and로 병렬 연결되어 있음.

(6) All of which / contributes to a reduction / in stress and anxiety /
이 모든 것이 / 감소에 기여한다 / 스트레스와 불안의 /
and builds resilience / against the onset of depression. 정답 단서
그리고 회복력을 길러준다 / 우울증의 발병에 대한

[중요 구문]

힌트 explains의 목적어인 that 명사절 안에 keeping이 이끄는 긴 동명사구가 주어로 왔음. 여기서 keep은 5형식 동사로 쓰였는데, (what she calls ~)가 keep의 목적어, well engaged가 목적격 보어임.

(1) ~ Dr. Kelly Lambert's research explains [that keeping (what she calls ~) well engaged helps you deal with challenges ~].
S' / 5형식V' O' O·C'(동사원형)

[전문 해석]

(1)심리학 교수인 Kelly Lambert 박사의 연구는 그녀가 '노력 주도 보상 회로'라고 부르는 것을 잘 작동되는 상태로 유지하는 것이 당신이 당신 주변의 환경이나 감정적인 삶에서의 도전을 더 효과적이고 효율적으로 다루도록 돕는다고 설명한다. (2)스카프를 뜨거나, 처음부터 요리하거나, 혹은 정원을 손질하는 것과 같이 당신이 보고 만질 수 있는 결과를 낳는 수작업 활동을 하는 것은 그것(보상 회로)이 최적으로 기능하도록 보상 회로를 부추긴다. (3)그녀는 문서에 기록된 미국인들 사이의 우울증 증가가 의도적인 신체활동의 감소와 직접적으로 관련이 있을 수도 있다고 주장한다. (4)우리가 손으로 작업할 때, 그것(보상 회로)은 신경 화학 물질인 도파민과 세로토닌의 방출(분비)을 증가시키고, (그것들은) 둘 다 긍정적인 감정을 발생시키는 것을 담당한다. (5)그녀는 또한 우리의 손으로 작업하는 것이 우리에게 환경에 대한 더 큰 통제 감각과 우리 주변 세계와의 더 많은 연결을 제공한다고 설명한다. (6)이 모든 것이 스트레스와 불안의 감소에 기여하고 우울증의 발병에 대한 회복력을 길러준다.

- dopamine(도파민): 뇌 조직 내의 흥분을 전달하는 물질로, 인간이 성취감, 쾌락 등을 느끼게 해주어 동기를 부여한다.
- serotonin(세로토닌): 혈액이 응고할 때 혈관 수축 작용을 하는 물질로, 인간의 감정을 조절하고 행복감을 느낄 수 있도록 해준다.

[정답 확인]

다음 글의 요지로 가장 적절한 것은?

① 긍정적인 감정(positive emotions)은 타인에게 쉽게 전이된다.
② 감정 조절은 대인 관계 능력의 핵심 요소이다.
③ 수작업 활동(hands-on activities)은 정신 건강에 도움을 줄 수 있다.
④ 과도한 신체활동(physical activity)은 호르몬 분비의 불균형을 초래한다.
⑤ 취미 활동을 통해 여러 분야의 사람들을 만날 수 있다.

[중요 어휘]

☐ psychology	명사 심리학, 심리 (상태)
☐ circuit	명사 회로, 순환
☐ hands-on	형용사 수작업의, 실천하는
☐ from scratch	처음부터, 무(無)에서부터
☐ tend	동사 손질하다, 돌보다
☐ optimally	부사 최적으로, 최선으로
☐ document	동사 ~을 문서에 기록하다
☐ be correlated with	~와 관련이 있다
☐ purposeful	형용사 의도적인, 목적이 있는
☐ neurochemical	명사 신경 화학 물질 / 형용사 신경 화학의
☐ be responsible for	~을 담당하다, ~에 대한 책임을 지다
☐ reduction	명사 감소
☐ resilience	명사 회복력, 탄성
☐ onset	명사 발병, 시작

05 2020년 11월 22번 (정답률 85%) 정답 ③

[지문 끊어 읽기] 성공에 필요한 능력

힌트 the+vast(막대한, 어마어마한)+majority(다수) =대부분, 대다수

(1) The vast majority / of companies, schools, and organizations /
대부분은 / 회사, 학교, 조직의 /
measure and reward "high performance" /
'높은 성과'를 측정하고 보상한다 /
in terms of individual metrics /
개인의 측정 기준의 관점에서 /
such as sales numbers, résumé accolades, and test scores.
판매 수치, 수상 이력, 시험 성적과 같은

(2) The problem with this approach / is /
이 접근법의 문제는 / ~이다 /
that it is based on a belief / [we thought /
접속사 선행사 삽입절
그것이 믿음을 기반으로 한다는 것 / 우리가 생각했던 /
science had fully confirmed:] / [ ]: 목적격 관계대명사절
과학이 완전히 입증했다고 /
that we live in a world of "survival of the fittest."
우리가 '가장 잘 적응하는 자의 생존'의 세계에 살고 있다는

(3) It teaches us [that /
4형식V I·O
그것은 우리에게 ~라고 가르친다 /
those with the *best* grades, or the *most* impressive résumé,
S'
or the *highest* point score, /
'최고의' 성적, '가장' 인상적인 이력서, 혹은 '가장 높은' 점수를 가진 사람들이 /
will be the ONLY ones to succeed]. [ ]: D·O(명사절)
V' 형용사적 용법
성공하는 '유일한' 사람들일 것이다

(4) The formula is simple: / be better and smarter and more creative /
그 공식은 간단하다 / 더 낫고 더 똑똑하고 더 창의적이게 되어라 /
than everyone else, / and you will be successful.
다른 누구보다 / 그러면 당신은 성공할 것이다

(5) But this formula is inaccurate.
그러나 이 공식은 정확하지 않다

(6) Thanks to new research, / we now know /
새로운 연구 덕분에 / 우리는 이제 안다 /
that achieving our highest potential /
우리의 잠재력을 최대한 발휘한다는 것이 /
is not about survival of the fittest / but survival of the best fit.
가장 잘 적응하는 자의 생존에 관한 것이 아니라 / 가장 잘 어울리는 자의 생존에 관한 것임을

힌트 형용사 'fit(딱 들어맞는, 적합한, 어울리는)'의 최상급에 관사 'the'를 붙여 각각 'the fittest/the best fit'이라는 두 개의 표현이 소개되고 있음. 뒤따르는 문장 (7)의 내용을 통해, 전자는 '가장 잘 적응하는 사람', 후자는 '가장 잘 어울리는 사람'이라는 의미임을 유추할 수 있음.

(7) In other words, / success is not just about /
다시 말해서 / 성공은 단지 ~에 관한 것이 아니라 /
how creative or smart or driven you are, /
당신이 얼마나 창의적이고, 똑똑하고, 혹은 열의가 있는지 /
but how well you are able to connect with, contribute to, and benefit from /
병렬① 병렬② 병렬③
당신이 얼마나 잘 관계를 맺고, 기여하고, 이익을 얻을 수 있는지에 관한 것이다 /
the ecosystem of people around you. 주제문
당신 주변에 있는 사람들의 생태계와

[중요 구문]

(7) In other words, success is
not just about [how creative or smart or driven you are],
but (about) [how well you are able to ~ people around you].

힌트 문장 (7)은 'not A but B' 구문으로, 'about+[how+형/부+S+V]' 형태의 두 개의 전치사구가 각각 A와 B 자리에 왔음.

[전문 해석]

(1)회사, 학교, 조직의 대부분은 판매 수치, 수상 이력, 시험 성적과 같은 개인의 측정 기준의 관점에서 '높은 성과'를 측정하고 보상한다. (2)이 접근법의 문제는 그것이 우리가 과학이 완전히 입증했다고 생각했던 믿음, 즉 우리가 '가장 잘 적응하는 자의 생존(적자생존)'의 세계에 살고 있다는 믿음을 기반으로 한다는 것이다. (3)그것은 우리에게 '최고의' 성적, '가장' 인상적인 이력서, 혹은 '가장 높은' 점수를 가진 사람들이 성공하는 '유일한' 사람들일 것이라고 가르친다. (4)그 공식은 간단하다. 다른 누구보다 더 낫고 더 똑똑하고 더 창의적이게 되면 당신은 성공할 것이다. (5)그러나 이 공식은 정확하지 않다. (6)새로운 연구 덕분에 우리는 이제 우리의 잠재력을 최대한 발휘한다는 것이 가장 잘 적응하는 자의 생존이 아니라 가장 잘 어울리는 자의 생존에 관한 것임을 안다. (7)다시 말해서, 성공은 단지 당신이 얼마나 창의적이고, 똑똑하고, 혹은 열의가 있는지에 관한 것이 아니라, 당신이 당신 주변에 있는 사람들의 생태계와 얼마나 잘 관계를 맺고, (그것에) 기여하고, (그것으로부터) 이익을 얻을 수 있는지에 관한 것이다.

[정답 확인]

다음 글의 요지로 가장 적절한 것은?
① 효율적인 업무 배분(distribution)은 조직의 생산성을 향상시킨다.
② 유연한 사고방식은 원활한 의사소통(communication)에 도움이 된다.
✔ 사람들과 잘 어울려(fit) 일하는 능력이 성공을 가능하게 한다.
④ 비판적(critical) 사고 능력은 정확성을 추구하는 태도에서 출발한다.
⑤ 치열한 경쟁 사회에서 최고의 실력(skill)을 갖추는 것이 필수적이다.

[중요 어휘]

□ **organization**	명사 조직, 단체
□ **measure**	동사 측정하다, 평가하다 / 명사 기준, 척도
□ **performance**	명사 성과, 성능, 수행
□ **in terms of**	~의 관점에서, ~에 관하여
□ **individual**	형용사 개인의, 별개의 / 명사 개인
□ **metric**	명사 측정 기준
□ **résumé**	명사 이력(서), 개요
□ **accolade**	명사 수상, 표창
□ **approach**	명사 접근(법) / 동사 접근하다
□ **confirm**	동사 입증하다, 확인하다
□ **impressive**	형용사 인상적인, 감명 깊은
□ **formula**	명사 공식, 방식
□ **potential**	명사 잠재력, 가능성 / 형용사 잠재적인, 가능성 있는
□ **driven**	형용사 열의가 있는, 의욕이 넘치는
□ **ecosystem**	명사 생태계

핵심 건물 중심의 기존 공공 정책을 비판하고 도시 재생을 위해서는 사람들에 중점을 둔 공공 정책을 수립해야 한다는 것을 강조하는 글로, 마지막에 이러한 주장을 명확하게 제시함.

06 2021년 9월 22번 (정답률 85%) 정답 ①

[지문 끊어 읽기] 도시 재생을 위한 공공 정책

(1) Too many officials in troubled cities / wrongly imagine /
문제가 있는 도시의 너무 많은 공무원들은 / 잘못 상상한다 /
that they can lead their city back to its former glories /
명사절 접속사
그들이 그들의 도시를 이전의 영광으로 되돌릴 수 있다고 /
with some massive construction project /
대규모 건설 프로젝트를 통해 /
— a new stadium or light rail system, a convention center, or a housing project.
새로운 경기장 또는 경전철 시스템, 컨벤션 센터, 또는 주택 프로젝트와 같은

힌트 'no + 명사구'가 주어인 경우 '어떤 (명사구)도 (동사)하지 않다'로 해석함.

(2) With very few exceptions, / no public policy can slow /
거의 예외 없이 / 어떤 공공 정책도 늦출 수 없다 /
the tidal forces of urban change.
도시 변화의 조석력을

힌트 tidal force의 사전적 의미는 '조석력'인데, 조수 차이를 일으키는 힘을 말함. 이 문장에서는 밀물과 썰물과 같이 어떤 양상이 변화하는 거스를 수 없는 '흐름'으로 자연스럽게 해석할 수 있음.

(3) We mustn't ignore the needs of the poor people /
우리는 가난한 사람들의 요구를 무시하면 안 된다 / 선행사
who live in the Rust Belt, /
주격 관계대명사
Rust Belt에 사는 /
but public policy should help poor *people*, / not poor places.
하지만 공공 정책은 가난한 '사람들'을 도와야 한다 / 가난한 지역이 아닌

(4) Shiny new real estate / may dress up a declining city, /
반짝이는 새로운 부동산은 / 쇠퇴하는 도시를 꾸밀 수는 있다 /
but it doesn't solve / its underlying problems.
=underlying problems of a declining city
하지만 이것은 해결하지는 않는다 / 그것의 기저에 있는 문제를

(5) The hallmark of declining cities /
쇠퇴하는 도시들의 특징은 /
is that they have *too much* housing and infrastructure /
V 명사절 접속사(S·C)
그것들이 '너무 많은' 주택과 기반 시설을 가지고 있다는 것이다 /
relative to the strength of their economies.
그것들의 경제력에 비해서

힌트 전치사 with는 보통 '~와 함께', '~을 이용해서', '~한 상태에서' 등으로 해석되지만 여기서는 '~ 때문에', '~로 인해'로 해석하면 자연스러움.

(6) With all that supply of structure and so little demand, /
건축물의 그 모든 공급과 너무 적은 수요 때문에 /
it makes no sense / [to use public money / to build more supply].
형식상의 주어 [ ]: 내용상의 주어 부사적 용법(목적)
의미가 없다 / 공공 자금을 사용하는 것은 / 더 많은 공급을 만들어 내기 위해

(7) The folly of building-centric urban renewal /
건물 중심의 도시 재생의 어리석음은 /
reminds us / that cities aren't structures; cities are people. 주제문
4형식V I·O D·O
우리에게 상기시킨다 / 도시는 건축물이 아니라 사람이라는 것을

[전문 해석]

(1)문제가 있는 도시의 너무 많은 공무원들은 새로운 경기장 또는 경전철 시스템, 컨벤션 센터, 또는 (저소득층을 위한) 주택 프로젝트와 같은 대규모 건설 프로젝트를 통해 그들의 도시를 이전의 영광으로 되돌릴 수 있다고 잘못 상상한다. (2)거의 예외 없이 어떤 공공 정책도 도시 변화의 조석력(흐름)을 늦출 수 없다. (3)우리는 Rust Belt에 사는 가난한 사람들의 요구를 무시하면 안 되지만 공공 정책은 가난한 지역이 아닌 가난한 '사람들'을 도와야 한다. (4)반짝이는 새로운 부동산은 쇠퇴하는 도시를 꾸밀 수는 있지만 이것은 그것(쇠퇴하는 도시)의 기저에 있는 문제를 해결하지는 않는다. (5)쇠퇴하는 도시들의 특징은 그것(쇠퇴하는 도시)들이 (그것들의) 경제력에 비해서 '너무 많은' 주택과 기반 시설을 가지고 있다는 것이다. (6)건축물의 그 모든 공급과 너무 적은 수요 때문에, 더 많은 공급을 만들어 내기 위해 공공 자금을 사용하는 것은 의미가 없다. (7)건물 중심의 도시 재생의 어리석음은 우리에게 도시는 건축물이 아니라 사람이라는 것을 상기시킨다.
- Rust Belt(러스트 벨트): 미국 북부의 쇠락한 공업지대

[정답 확인]

다음 글의 요지로 가장 적절한 것은?
✔ 도시 재생을 위한 공공정책(public policy)은 건설보다 사람에 중점을 두어야 한다.
② 대중 교통 이용이 편리하도록 도시 교통 체계(transportation system)를 구축해야 한다.
③ 사회기반시설(infrastructure) 확충을 통해 지역 경제를 활성화해야 한다.

④ 에너지를 절감할 수 있는 친환경 건물(green building)을 설계해야 한다.
⑤ 문화유산 보존(conservation)을 우선하는 도시 계획을 수립해야 한다.

[중요 어휘]

□ troubled	형용사 (장소·상황·시기가) 문제가 있는, (사람이) 걱정하는
□ glory	명사 영광
□ massive	형용사 대규모의, 거대한
□ housing	명사 주택, 주택 공급
□ public policy	공공 정책
□ urban	형용사 도시의
□ real estate	부동산
□ dress up	~을 꾸미다
□ declining	형용사 쇠퇴하는
□ underlying	형용사 기저에 있는, 근본적인
□ hallmark	명사 특징
□ infrastructure	명사 기반시설
□ structure	명사 건축물, 구조물, 구조
□ make sense	의미가 있다, 타당하다
□ public money	공공 자금
□ folly	명사 어리석음
□ centric	형용사 중심의
□ renewal	명사 재생, 부활, 갱신
□ remind	동사 상기시키다

07 2022년 3월 22번 (정답률 85%) 정답 ⑤

[지문 끊어 읽기] 각자에게 맞는 습관

(1) Advice from a friend or family member /
S
친구나 가족의 조언은 /
is the most well-meaning of all, /
V
모든 것 중에서 가장 좋은 뜻에서 하는 말이다 /
but it's not the best way / [to match yourself / with a new habit].
형식상의 주어 [ ]: 내용상의 주어
하지만 최선의 방법은 아니다 / 자신을 맞추는 것은 / 새로운 습관에

(2) While hot yoga may have changed your friend's life, /
핫 요가가 여러분 친구의 삶을 바꿔 놓았을지 모르지만 /
does that mean / it's the right practice for you?
그것이 의미할까 / 그것이 여러분에게 맞는 습관임을

힌트 조동사+have+p.p.는 과거 사실에 대한 추측, 후회, 확신 등을 나타냄. may have p.p.: ~했을지(도) 모른다(추측) / should have p.p.: ~했어야 했다(후회) / must have p.p.: ~했음이 틀림없다(확신) / cannot have p.p.: ~했을 리가 없다(확신)

(3) We all have friends / [who swear /
선행사 [ ]: 주격 관계대명사절
우리 모두에게는 친구들이 있다 / '확언하는' /
their new habit of getting up at 4:30 a.m. changed their lives /
S'① V'①
새벽 4시 30분에 일어나는 그들의 새로운 습관이 자신의 삶을 바꿨다고 /
and that we have to do it].
S'② V'② =their new habit
그리고 우리가 그렇게 해야 한다고

힌트 swear의 목적어 역할을 하는 that이 이끄는 명사절이 등위접속사 and를 중심으로 연결되어 있는데, 첫 번째 that절에서는 that이 생략되어 있음. 즉, '(that) their new habit of getting up at 4:30 a.m. changed their lives and that we have to do it.'의 형태임.

(4) I don't doubt /
나는 의심하지 않는다 /
that getting up super early changes people's lives, /
명사절 접속사
엄청 일찍 일어나는 것이 사람들의 삶을 바꾼다는 것을 /
sometimes in good ways / and sometimes not.
때로는 좋은 방식으로 / 그리고 때로는 그렇지 않게

힌트 등위접속사 and를 중심으로 2개의 구가 연결되어 있는데 'and sometimes not in good ways'에서 반복되는 in good ways가 생략됨.

(5) But be cautious: / You don't know /
그러나 주의하라 / 여러분은 알 수 없다 /
if this habit will actually make your life better, /
5형식V O O·C
이 습관이 실제로 여러분의 삶을 더 낫게 만들지 /
정답 단서 친구가 추천하는 습관이 삶을 더 낫게 만들지는 알 수 없다고 하고 있음.
especially if it means you get less sleep.
그것이 특히 여러분이 잠을 더 적게 자는 것을 의미한다면

힌트 첫 번째 if절은 know의 목적어 역할을 하는 명사절로, '~인지 아닌지'로 해석되고, 두 번째 if절은 주절에 종속되는 부사절로, '만약 ~이라면'으로 해석됨.

(6) So yes, / you can try /
그러니 / 여러분은 시도해 볼 수 있다 /
what worked for your friend, / but don't beat yourself up /
관계대명사 what이 이끄는 명사절
여러분의 친구에게 효과가 있었던 것을 / 하지만 자책하지 말라 /
if your friend's answer doesn't change you / in the same way.
친구의 정답이 여러분을 바꾸지 않는다고 해서 / 똑같은 방식으로
정답 단서 친구에게 효과가 있었던 것이 자신에게는 효과가 없다고 해서 자책하지 말라고 하고 있음.

(7) All of these approaches /
이 모든 접근법은 /
involve guessing and chance.
추측과 우연을 포함한다

(8) And that's not a good way / to strive for change in your life.
형용사적 용법
그리고 그것은 좋은 방법은 아니다 / 여러분 삶의 변화를 위해 노력하는

[전문 해석]

(1)친구나 가족의 조언은 모든 것 중에서 가장 좋은 뜻에서 하는 말이지만, 새로운 습관에 자신을 맞추는 것은 최선의 방법은 아니다. (2)핫 요가가 여러분 친구의 삶을 바꿔 놓았을지 모르지만, 그것이 여러분에게 맞는 습관임을 의미할까? (3)우리 모두에게는 새벽 4시 30분에 일어나는 새로운 습관이 자신의 삶을 바꿨고 우리가 그렇게 해야 한다고 '확언하는' 친구들이 있다. (4)나는 엄청 일찍 일어나는 것이 사람들의 삶을 때로는 좋은 방식으로, 때로는 그렇지 않게 바꾼다는 것을 의심하지 않는다. (5)그러나 주의하라. 이 습관이 특히 잠을 더 적게 자는 것을 의미한다면, 그것이 실제로 여러분의 삶을 더 낫게 만들지는 알 수 없다. (6)그러니, 친구에게 효과가 있었던 것을 시도해 볼 수 있지만, 친구의 정답이 여러분을 똑같은 방식으로 바꾸지 않는다고 해서 자책하지 말라. (7)이 모든 접근법은 추측과 우연을 포함한다. (8)그리고 그것은 여러분 삶의 변화를 위해 노력하는 좋은 방법은 아니다.

[정답 확인]

다음 글의 요지로 가장 적절한 것은?
① 한번 잘못 들인 습관(habit)은 바로잡기가 어렵다.
② 꾸준한 반복(repetition)을 통해 올바른 습관을 들일 수 있다.
③ 친구나 가족의 조언(advice)은 항상 귀담아들을 필요가 있다.
④ 사소하더라도 좋은 습관을 들이면 인생이 바뀔 수 있다.
✔ 타인에게 유익했던(beneficial) 습관이 자신에게는 효과가 없을 수 있다.

[중요 어휘]

□ well-meaning	형용사 좋은 뜻에서 하는, 선의의
□ match	동사 (필요에) 맞추다, 일치하다, 필적하다
□ practice	명사 습관, 버릇
□ swear	동사 확언하다, 맹세하다
□ doubt	동사 의심하다 / 명사 의심, 의혹
□ cautious	형용사 주의 깊은, 신중한
□ beat oneself up	자책하다
□ approach	명사 접근법 / 동사 다가가다
□ involve	동사 포함하다, 수반하다, 관련시키다
□ chance	명사 우연, 가능성, 기회
□ strive for	~을 위해 노력하다

08 2022년 11월 22번 (정답률 85%) 정답 ④

[지문 끊어 읽기] 시작과 관련된 날짜와 목표 추구 동기

(1) In one study, / when researchers suggested /
한 연구에서 / 연구자들이 제시했을 때 /
that a date was associated with a new beginning (such as "the first day of spring"), /
어떤 날짜가 새 시작('봄의 첫 번째 날'처럼)과 관련이 있다고 /
students viewed it as a more attractive time /
학생들은 그것을 더 매력적인 때로 보았다 /
to kick-start goal pursuit / than when researchers presented it /
형용사적 용법
목표 추구를 시작하기에 / 연구자들이 그것을 제시했을 때보다 /
as an unremarkable day (such as "the third Thursday in March").
평범한 날('3월의 세 번째 목요일'처럼)로

(2) Whether it was starting a new gym habit /
S·C①(동명사)
그것이 새로운 운동 습관을 시작하는 것이든 /
or spending less time on social media, /
S·C②(동명사)
혹은 소셜 미디어에 시간을 덜 쓰는 것이든 /
when the date that researchers suggested /
선행사 목적격 관계대명사절
연구자들이 제시하는 날짜가 ~일 때 /
was associated with a new beginning, /
새로운 시작과 관련될 /
more students wanted to begin changes / right then. 정답 단서
더 많은 학생들이 변화를 시작하기를 원했다 / 바로 그때

새로운 시작과 관련된 날짜가 제시될 때, 더 많은 학생들이 변화를 시작하기를 원함.

(3) And more recent research by a different team found /
S V
그리고 다른 팀에 의한 더 최근의 연구는 알아냈다 /
that similar benefits were achieved /
비슷한 이점들이 얻어졌다는 것을 /
by showing goal seekers modified weekly calendars.
4형식V I·O D·O
목표를 추구하는 사람들에게 수정된 주간 일정표를 보여 줌으로써

(4) When calendars depicted the current day (either Monday or Sunday) /
달력이 오늘을 (월요일이든 일요일이든) 표현했을 때 /
as the first day of the week, /
한 주의 첫날로 /
people reported feeling more motivated /
사람들은 더욱 동기 부여가 되는 것을 느낀다고 보고했다 /
to make immediate progress on their goals.
그들의 목표에 대한 즉각적인 진전을 이루는 데

[전문 해석]

(1)한 연구에서 연구자들이 어떤 날짜가 새 시작('봄의 첫 번째 날'처럼)과 관련이 있다고 제시했을 때, 학생들은 연구자들이 그것을 평범한 날('3월의 세 번째 목요일'처럼)로 제시했을 때보다 그것을 목표 추구를 시작하기에 더 매력적인 때로 보았다. (2)그것이 새로운 운동 습관을 시작하는 것이든 혹은 소셜 미디어에 시간을 덜 쓰는 것이든, 연구자들이 제시하는 날짜가 새로운 시작과 관련될 때 더 많은 학생들이 바로 그때 변화를 시작하기를 원했다. (3)그리고 다른 팀에 의한 더 최근의 연구는 목표를 추구하는 사람들에게 수정된 주간 일정표를 보여 줌으로써 비슷한 이점들이 얻어졌다는 것을 알아냈다. (4)달력이 오늘을 (월요일이든 일요일이든) 한 주의 첫날로 표현했을 때, 사람들은 그들의 목표에 대한 즉각적인 진전을 이루는 데 더욱 동기 부여가 되는 것을 느낀다고 보고했다.

[정답 확인]

다음 글의 요지로 가장 적절한 것은?

① 새로운 시작을 하기 전에 장기적인(long-term) 계획을 세우는 것이 바람직하다.
② 자신이 해야 할 일을 일정표에 표시하는 것이 목표 달성에 효과적이다.
③ 문제 행동을 개선하기 위해 원인이 되는 요소를 파악할 필요가 있다.
✔ 날짜가 시작이라는 의미와 관련지어질 때 목표 추구(goal pursuit)에 강한 동기가 부여된다.
⑤ 상세한 일정표(calendar)를 작성하는 것은 여러 목표를 동시에 달성하는 데 도움이 된다.

[중요 어휘]

□ be associated with	~과 관련이 있다
□ attractive	형용사 매력적인
□ kick-start	동사 시작하다, 시동을 걸다
□ pursuit	명사 추구
□ unremarkable	형용사 평범한, 특별할 것 없는
□ modified	형용사 수정된
□ depict	동사 표현하다, 묘사하다
□ motivated	형용사 동기 부여가 된
□ immediate	형용사 즉각적인
□ progress	명사 진전

09 2022년 9월 22번 (정답률 80%) 정답 ②

[지문 끊어 읽기] 양육을 위한 부모의 내적 성장

(1) Most parents think / that if our child would just "behave," /
대부분의 부모들은 생각한다 / 자신들의 자녀가 그저 '예의 바르게 행동하면' /
we could stay calm as parents.
부모로서 침착함을 유지할 수 있다고

(2) The truth is / that managing our own emotions and actions /
동명사S'
진실은 ~이다 / 우리의 감정과 행동을 관리하는 것이 /
is what allows us to feel peaceful / as parents.
V' 5형식V O O·C(to V)
우리가 평안함을 느끼도록 허락한다 / 부모로서

(3) Ultimately / we can't control /
궁극적으로 / 우리는 통제할 수 없다 /
our children or the obstacles they will face /
선행사 목적격 관계대명사절
우리의 자녀나 그들이 마주할 장애물을 /
— but we can always control / our own actions.
하지만 우리는 항상 통제할 수 있다 / 우리 자신의 행동은

(4) Parenting isn't about what our child does, /
양육은 우리 자녀가 무엇을 하는지에 대한 것이 아니라 /
but about how we respond.
우리가 어떻게 반응하는지에 대한 것이다

힌트 'not A but B' 구문으로 'A가 아니라 B'로 해석하며 B를 강조함. not이 문장 (4)에서는 is, (5)에서는 does와 결합된 형태로 쓰인 것에 주의할 것.

(5) In fact, / most of what we call parenting /
S
사실 / 우리가 양육이라고 부르는 것의 대부분은 /
doesn't take place between a parent and child /
V
부모와 자녀 사이에서 발생하는 것이 아니라 /
but within the parent.
부모 안에서 발생한다

(6) When a storm brews, / a parent's response will either calm it /
폭풍이 일어나려고 할 때 / 부모의 반응은 그것을 잠재울 것이다 /
or trigger a full-scale tsunami.
혹은 최대치의 해일을 유발할 것이다

(7) Staying calm enough to respond constructively /
동명사S
건설적으로 반응할 수 있을 만큼 충분히 침착함을 유지하는 것은 /
to all that childish behavior /
그 모든 아이 같은 행동에 /
— and the stormy emotions behind it — /
그리고 그 이면의 폭풍 같은 감정에 /
requires that we grow, too. 정답 단서
V
우리 역시 성장하는 것을 필요로 한다

아이의 행동과 감정에 건설적으로 반응할 수 있을 정도로 평정심을 유지하기 위해서는 부모가 성장해야 함.

힌트 요구, 주장, 제안, 필요, 명령 등을 나타내는 동사·형용사·명사 뒤의 that절 내용이 '당위성(~해야 한다)'을 의미할 경우 that절의 동사는 '(should)+동사원형'의 형태를 취함. 따라서 여기서 we와 grow 사이에 should가 생략되어 있음.

(8) If we can use those times / [when our buttons get pushed] /
[ ]: 관계부사절
만약 우리가 그 시간들을 사용할 수 있다면 / 우리를 화나게 하는 /
to reflect, not just react, /
단지 반응하는 데가 아니라 반성하는 데 /
we can notice when we lose equilibrium /
병렬①
우리는 우리가 언제 평정심을 잃는지 알아차릴 수 있다 /
and steer ourselves back on track.
병렬②
그리고 다시 제자리로 돌아갈 수 있다

힌트 'push one's buttons'는 '~을 화나게 하다'라는 뜻의 숙어 표현임. 따라서 밑줄 친 부분은 '우리를 화나게 하는'이라고 해석할 수 있음.

(9) This inner growth is the hardest work there is, /
이러한 내면의 성장은 가장 힘든 일이다 /
but it's what enables you to become a more peaceful parent, /
5형식V O O·C(to V)
하지만 그것은 당신이 더욱 평안한 부모가 될 수 있도록 해준다 /
one day at a time. 정답 단서
하루하루

부모의 내면이 성장하면 평안함을 유지할 수 있음.

[전문 해석]

(1)대부분의 부모들은 자신들의 자녀가 그저 '예의 바르게 행동하면' 부모로서 침착함을 유지할 수 있다고 생각한다. (2)진실은 우리의 감정과 행동을 관리하는 것이 우리가 부모로서 평안함을 느끼도록 허락한다는 것이다. (3)궁극적으로 우리는 우리의 자녀나 그들이 마주할 장애

물을 통제할 수 없지만 우리 자신의 행동은 항상 통제할 수 있다. (4)양육은 우리 자녀가 무엇을 하는지에 대한 것이 아니라 우리가 어떻게 반응하는지에 대한 것이다. (5)사실, 우리가 양육이라고 부르는 것의 대부분은 부모와 자녀 사이에서 발생하는 것이 아니라 부모 안에서 발생한다. (6)폭풍이 일어나려고 할 때, 부모의 반응은 그것을 잠재우거나 최대치의 해일을 유발할 것이다. (7)그 모든 아이 같은 행동과 그 이면의 폭풍 같은 감정에 건설적으로 반응할 수 있을 만큼 충분히 침착함을 유지하는 것은 우리 역시 성장하는 것을 필요로 한다. (8)만약 우리가 우리를 화나게 하는 그 시간들을 단지 반응하는 데가 아니라 반성하는 데 사용할 수 있다면, 우리는 우리가 언제 평정심을 잃는지 알아차릴 수 있고 다시 제자리로 돌아갈 수 있다. (9)이러한 내면의 성장은 가장 힘든 일이지만, 그것은 당신이 하루하루 더욱 평안한 부모가 될 수 있도록 해준다.

[정답 확인]

다음 글의 요지로 가장 적절한 것은?

① 자녀의 행동 변화를 위해 부모의 즉각적인 반응(response)이 필요하다.
② 부모의 내적 성장(inner growth)을 통한 평정심(equilibrium) 유지가 양육에 중요하다. ✔
③ 부모는 자녀가 감정을 다스릴 수 있게 도와주어야 한다.
④ 부모와 자녀는 건설적인(constructive) 의견을 나눌 수 있어야 한다.
⑤ 바람직한 양육(parenting)은 자녀에게 모범을 보이는 것이다.

[중요 어휘]

☐ **behave**	동사 예의 바르게 행동하다, 올바르게 처신하다
☐ **obstacle**	명사 장애물, 장애
☐ **parenting**	명사 양육, 육아
☐ **brew**	동사 (폭풍우 등이) 일어나려고 하다, 태동하다
☐ **constructively**	부사 건설적으로
☐ **use A to V**	A를 ~하는 데 사용하다
☐ **reflect**	동사 반성하다, 곰곰이 생각하다, 비추다
☐ **equilibrium**	명사 (마음의) 평정, 평형
☐ **steer**	동사 나아가다, 이끌다, 조종하다

핵심 직원의 봉사활동에 대한 기업의 입장을 다룬 글로, 봉사활동 장려를 꺼리는 일반적 견해와는 달리 봉사활동이 오히려 조직에 대한 헌신을 향상시킨다는 견해가 문장 (4)에 나옴.

10 2016년 9월 21번 (정답률 80%) 정답 ③

[지문 끊어 읽기] 직원의 봉사활동 지원의 장점

(1) Some organizations may be reluctant to facilitate /
어떤 조직은 촉진하는 것을 꺼릴지도 모른다 /
their employees' participation in volunteer activities.
그들의 직원들의 자원봉사 활동 참여를

(2) They may believe / it's none of their business: /
그들은 생각할지도 모른다 / 그것이 그들의 일과는 무관하다고 /
if employees want to do volunteer activity, /
만약 직원들이 자원봉사 활동을 하기를 원한다면 /
they can make their own arrangements and do so /
그들은 그들 스스로 준비하고 그렇게 할 수 있다 /
on their own time.
그들 자신의 시간에

(3) Corporations also may be concerned /
또한 기업들은 걱정할지도 모른다 /
about allocating the resources /
자원을 할당하는 것에 대해 /
needed to set up such programs, / or perhaps they fear /
그러한 프로그램을 준비하는 데 요구되는 / 또는 아마도 그들은 두려워할지도 모른다 /
that facilitating employees' engagement elsewhere /
다른 곳에 직원들의 관여를 촉진하는 것이 /
may weaken their commitment / to the organization or their jobs.
그들의 헌신을 약화시킬 수도 있다는 점을 / 조직이나 그들의 업무에 대한

(4) Not to worry on that last point: / research shows /
그 마지막 사항에 대해서는 걱정할 것 없다 / 연구는 보여준다 /
that participating in corporate volunteer activity heightens /
기업의 자원봉사 활동에 참여하는 것이 향상시킨다는 것을 /
rather than weakens employees' organizational commitment, /
직원들의 조직에 대한 헌신을 약화시키기보다는 /
in part because people feel a sense of self-worth /
사람들이 자부심을 느낀다는 부분적인 이유 때문에 /
when they do the good deeds /
그들이 선행을 할 때 /
that their organizations made it easier for them to do. 주제문
그들의 조직이 그들이 하기 쉽게 만들어준

★중요 A rather than B 구문인 heightens rather than weakens에서 내용이 전환됨.

[전문 해석]

(1)어떤 조직은 직원들의 자원봉사 활동 참여를 촉진하는 것을 꺼릴지도 모른다. (2)그들은 그것(직원의 자원봉사 활동)이 그들의 일과는 무관하다고 생각할지도 모르는데, (그 생각에 따르면) 만약 직원들이 자원봉사 활동을 하기를 원한다면, 그들 자신의 시간에(개인적인 시간을 들여) 스스로 준비하고 그렇게 (자원봉사 활동을) 할 수 있다. (3)또한 기업들은 그러한 프로그램을 준비하는 데 요구되는 자원을 할당하는 것에 대해 걱정할지도 모르고, 또는 아마도 그들(기업들)은 (조직이나 업무가 아닌) 다른 곳에 직원들의 관여를 촉진하는 것이 조직이나 업무에 대한 그들의 헌신을 약화시킬 수도 있다는 점을 두려워할지도 모른다. (4)그 마지막 사항에 대해서는 걱정할 것 없다. 연구는 그들(사람들)의 조직이 하기 쉽게 만들어준 선행을 할 때(조직이 봉사활동을 장려한다면) 사람들이 자부심을 느낀다는 부분적인 이유 때문에, 기업의 자원봉사 활동에 참여하는 것이 직원들의 조직에 대한 헌신을 약화시키기보다는 향상시킨다는 것을 보여준다.

[정답 확인]

다음 글의 요지로 가장 적절한 것은?

① 기업의 사회 봉사활동은 기업 이미지를 긍정적(positive)으로 만든다.
② 성과에 따른 적절한 보상은 직원의 만족도를 향상시킨다(heighten).
③ 직원의 봉사활동(volunteer activity)을 지원하는 것은 회사에 도움이 된다. ✔
④ 기업은(corporation) 자선 단체에 대한 후원을 확대할 필요가 있다.
⑤ 자기 계발과 회사 업무 간의 균형(balance)이 중요하다.

[중요 어휘]

☐ **be reluctant to V**	~하는 것을 꺼리다
☐ **facilitate**	동사 촉진하다, 용이하게 하다
☐ **be concerned about**	~에 대해 걱정하다
☐ **allocate**	동사 할당하다
☐ **resource**	명사 자원
☐ **engagement**	명사 관여, 참여
☐ **commitment**	명사 헌신, 전념
☐ **heighten**	동사 향상시키다
☐ **self-worth**	명사 자부심, 자아 존중감
☐ **deed**	명사 행위, 위업

핵심 사람들로부터 널리 받아들여지던 통념을 비판하는 글임. '자연의 균형'이라는 기존의 개념에서는 자연을 완벽하고 전혀 변하지 않는 것으로 보고 있는데, 이 글에서는 그것이 잘못된 인식이고 결국 자연은 끊임없이 변화한다는 주장을 펼치고 있음.

11 2021년 3월 22번 (정답률 75%) 정답 ③

[지문 끊어 읽기] 자연의 역동성

(1) Fears of damaging ecosystems /
생태계를 손상하는 것에 대한 두려움은 /
are based on the sound conservationist principle /
건전한 환경 보호주의자 원칙을 바탕으로 한다 /
that we should aim to minimize the disruption / we cause, /
동격의 that(=principle) / 목적격 관계대명사절
우리가 파괴를 최소화하는 것을 목표로 해야 한다는 / 우리가 초래하는 /
but there is a risk / that this principle may be confused /
동격의 that(=a risk)
하지만 위험이 있다 / 이 원칙이 혼동될지도 모른다는 /
with the old idea of a 'balance of nature.'
'자연의 균형'이라는 오래된 생각과

(2) This supposes a perfect order of nature /
=a balance of nature
이것은 완벽한 자연의 질서를 전제로 한다 /
that will seek to maintain itself / and that we should not change.
그 자체를 유지하려고 노력하는 / 그리고 우리가 바꾸어서는 안 되는

힌트 'a perfect order of nature'라는 하나의 선행사를 수식하는 관계대명사절이 두 개 이어지는 문장으로, 첫 번째 that은 주격 관계대명사이고, 이어지는 두 번째 that은 목적격 관계대명사임.

(3) It is a romantic, not to say idyllic, notion, /
삽입구
그것은 목가적이라고까지는 할 수 없어도 낭만적인 개념이다 /
but deeply misleading / because it supposes a static condition.
하지만 매우 오해의 소지가 있다 / 그것이 정적인 상태를 전제로 하기 때문에

(4) Ecosystems are dynamic, / and although some may endure, /
생태계는 역동적이다 / 그리고 일부는 지속될지도 모르지만 /
apparently unchanged, / for periods that are long /
겉보기에 변하지 않은 채로 / 오랜 기간 동안 / 주격 관계대명사절
in comparison with the human lifespan, /
인간의 수명과 비교하면 /
they must and do change eventually. 정답 단서
조동사(강조)
그것들은 결국 변할 것임에 틀림없고 정말 변한다

(5) Species come and go, / climates change, /
생물종들은 생겨났다 사라진다 / 기후는 변화한다 /
plant and animal communities adapt to altered circumstances, /
동식물 군집은 달라진 환경에 적응한다 /
and when examined in fine detail /
그리고 아주 상세하게 검토해 보면 /
such adaptation and consequent change /
그런 적응과 결과적인 변화는 /
can be seen to be taking place constantly. 정답 단서
항상 일어나고 있는 것으로 보일 수 있다

(6) The 'balance of nature' is a myth.
'자연의 균형'은 잘못된 통념이다

(7) Our planet is dynamic, / and so are the arrangements / 정답 단서
우리의 지구는 역동적이다 / 그리고 방식도 그러하다 /
by which its inhabitants live together.
그것의 서식자들이 함께 사는

[전문 해석]

(1)생태계를 손상하는 것에 대한 두려움은 우리가 초래하는 (환경) 파괴를 최소화하는 것을 목표로 해야 한다는 건전한 환경 보호주의자 원칙을 바탕으로 하지만, 이 원칙이 '자연의 균형'이라는 오래된 생각과 혼동될지도 모른다는 위험이 있다. (2)이것(자연의 균형)은 그 자체를 유지하려고 노력하고 우리가 바꾸어서는 안 되는 완벽한 자연의 질서를 전제로 한다. (3)그것은 목가적이라고까지는 할 수 없어도 낭만적인 개념이지만, 그것이 정적인 상태를 전제로 하기 때문에 매우 오해의 소지가 있다. (4)생태계는 역동적이고, 일부는 겉보기에 변하지 않은 채로 인간의 수명과 비교하면 오랜 기간 동안 지속될지도 모르지만, 그것들은 결국 변할 것임에 틀림없고 정말 변한다. (5)생물종들은 생겨났다 사라지고, 기후는 변화하며, 동식물 군집은 달라진 환경에 적응하는데, 아주 상세하게 검토해 보면 그런 적응과 결과적인 변화는 항상 일어나고 있는 것으로 보일 수 있다. (6)'자연의 균형'은 잘못된 통념이다. (7)우리의 지구는 역동적이고, 그것(지구)의 서식자들이 함께 사는 방식도 그러하다.

[정답 확인]

다음 글의 요지로 가장 적절한 것은?

① 생물 다양성(biodiversity)이 높은 생태계가 기후 변화에 더 잘 적응한다.
② 인간의 부적절한 개입(intervention)은 자연의 균형을 깨뜨린다.
③ 자연은 정적(static)이지 않고 역동적(dynamic)으로 계속 변한다. ✔
④ 모든 생물은 적자생존(survival of the fittest)의 원칙에 순응하기 마련이다.
⑤ 동식물은 상호 경쟁(mutual competition)을 통해 생태계의 균형을 이룬다.

[중요 어휘]

□ sound	형용사 건전한, 정상적인
□ conservationist	명사 환경 보호주의자
□ principle	명사 원칙, 원리
□ disruption	명사 파괴, 붕괴
□ suppose	동사 전제로 하다, 가정하다
□ not to say	~라고까지는 할 수 없어도, ~는 아니더라도
□ idyllic	형용사 목가적인
□ notion	명사 개념, 생각
□ misleading	형용사 오해의 소지가 있는, 잘못 인도하는
□ endure	동사 지속되다, 견디다
□ apparently	부사 겉보기에는
□ in comparison with	~와 비교하면
□ consequent	형용사 결과적인
□ myth	명사 잘못된 통념, 근거 없는 믿음
□ arrangement	명사 방식, 배열, 준비

□ **inhabitant** 명사 서식자, 주민

핵심 개인의 맹점이란 자신에게는 보이지 않지만 남에게는 보이는 부분을 의미하는데, 본문은 개인의 맹점을 사이드 미러의 한 부분에 비유하고 있음. 사이드 미러로는 보이지 않는 옆 차선의 트럭처럼 맹점은 눈에 보이지 않아 간과되기 쉽고 위험하기 때문에, 우리는 그것을 인지하기 위해 다른 사람들의 도움이 필요하다고 말하고 있음.

12 2020년 6월 22번 (정답률 70%) 정답 ⑤

[지문 끊어 읽기] 맹점에 대한 인지 방법

(1) Personal blind spots are areas /
개인의 맹점은 부분이다 /
that are visible to others / but not to you.
다른 사람들에게는 보이는 / 하지만 당신에게는 그렇지 않은

(2) The developmental challenge / of blind spots /
S
발달상의 어려움은 / 맹점의 /
is that you don't know / what you don't know.
V
당신이 모른다는 것이다 / 당신이 무엇을 모르는지

힌트 이 문장에서 what은 '무엇'을 뜻하는 의문사로 쓰여서 know의 목적어절을 이끌고 있음.

(3) Like that area / in the side mirror of your car /
선행사
그 영역처럼 / 당신 차의 사이드 미러의 /
where you can't see that truck / in the lane next to you, /
관계부사
당신이 트럭을 볼 수 없는 / 당신 옆 차선에 있는 /
personal blind spots / can easily be overlooked /
개인의 맹점은 / 쉽게 간과될 수 있다 /
because you are completely unaware / of their presence.
당신이 완전히 인지하지 못하기 때문에 / 그것들의 존재를

(4) They can be equally dangerous / as well.
그것들은 똑같이 위험할 수 있다 / 또한

(5) That truck / you don't see? / It's really there!
그 트럭 / 당신이 보지 않는 / 그것은 정말 거기에 있다

(6) So are your blind spots.
당신의 맹점도 마찬가지다

힌트 'so + 동사 + 주어'는 '~도 마찬가지다'라는 의미로 쓰인 도치 구문임. 풀어 쓰면 'Your blind spots are (really there), too.'임.

(7) Just because you don't see them, / doesn't mean /
당신이 그것들을 보지 않는다고 해서 / 의미하는 것은 아니다 /
they can't run you over.
그것들이 당신을 칠 수 없다는 것을

(8) This is / where you need to enlist / the help of others. 정답 단서
관계부사(선행사 생략)
이것이 ~이다 / 당신이 요청할 필요가 있는 상황 / 다른 사람들의 도움을

(9) You have to develop / a crew of special people, /
당신은 만들어야 한다 / 특별한 사람들의 무리를 /
people / who are willing to hold up that mirror, /
사람들 / 기꺼이 그 거울을 들 /
who not only know you well enough / to see that truck, /
당신을 충분히 잘 알 뿐만 아니라 / 그 트럭을 볼 수 있을 만큼 /
but who also care enough about you / to let you know /
또한 당신을 충분히 아끼는 / 당신에게 알려 줄 만큼 /
that it's there. 주제문
그것이 거기에 있다는 것을

[중요 구문]

힌트 주격 관계대명사절에서 'not only A but also B(A할 뿐만 아니라 또한 B하다)' 구문이 사용되었음. 따라서 '당신을 잘 알 뿐만 아니라 또한 아끼는 사람'이라고 해석됨.

(9) You have to develop a crew of special people, people [who are willing to ~, who not only know ~, but who also care ~].
(= 선행사, 주격 관계대명사①, 주격 관계대명사②, 주격 관계대명사③)

[전문 해석]

(1)개인의 맹점은 다른 사람들에게는 보이지만 당신에게는 보이지 않는 부분이다. (2)맹점의 (맹점이 지닌) 발달상의 어려움은 당신이 무엇을 모르는지 모른다는 것이다. (3)당신이 당신 옆 차선에 있는 트럭을 볼 수 없는, 당신 차의 사이드 미러의 그 영역처럼 개인의 맹점은 당신이 그것들의 존재를 완전히 인지하지 못하기 때문에 쉽게 간과될 수 있다. (4)그것들은 또한 똑같이 위험할 수 있다. (5)당신이 보지 않는(못하는) 그 트럭? 그것은 정말 거기에 있다! (6)당신의 맹점도 마찬가지다. (7)당신이 그것들을 보지 않는다고(못한다고) 해서 그것들이 당신을 칠 수 없다는 것을 의미하는 것은 아니다. (8)이것이 당신이 다른 사람들의 도움을 요청할 필요가 있는 상황이다. (9)당신은 특별한 사람들, 즉 기꺼이 그 거울을 들고 그 트럭(당신의 맹

점)을 볼 수 있을 만큼 당신을 충분히 잘 알 뿐만 아니라 또한 그것이 거기에 있다는 것을 당신에게 알려 줄 만큼 당신을 충분히 아끼는 사람들의 무리를 만들어야 한다.

[정답 확인]

다음 글의 요지로 가장 적절한 것은?

① 모르는 부분을 인정하고 질문하는(question) 것이 중요하다.
② 폭넓은 인간관계는 성공(success)에 결정적인 영향을 미친다.
③ 자기발전은 실수를 기회(opportunity)로 만드는 능력에서 비롯된다.
④ 주변에 관심을 가지고 타인을 도와주는 것이 바람직(desirable)하다.
✔ 자신의 맹점(blind spot)을 인지(aware)하도록 도와줄 수 있는 사람이 필요하다.

[중요 어휘]

☐ **blind spot**	명사 맹점
☐ **visible**	형용사 (눈에) 보이는, 가시적인
☐ **developmental**	형용사 발달상의
☐ **challenge**	명사 어려움, 도전
☐ **overlook**	동사 간과하다, 눈감아 주다
☐ **unaware**	형용사 인지하지 못하는
☐ **presence**	명사 존재, 출석
☐ **run over**	~을 (차로) 치다
☐ **enlist**	동사 요청하다, 입대하다
☐ **be willing to V**	기꺼이 ~하다

13 2023년 3월 22번 (정답률 65%) 정답 ⑤

[지문 끊어 읽기] 변화와 브랜드의 적합성

(1) Brands that fail to grow and develop / lose their relevance. 정답 단서 성장과 발전에 실패한 브랜드는 적합성을 잃게 됨.
S(=선행사) 주격 관계대명사 V
성장과 발전에 실패한 브랜드는 / 그들의 적합성을 잃는다

(2) Think about the person you knew /
선행사 목적격 관계대명사절
여러분이 알던 사람을 생각해 보라 /
who was once on the fast track at your company, /
주격 관계대명사①
한때 여러분의 회사에서 승진 가도에 있었던 /
who is either no longer with the firm / or, worse yet, /
주격 관계대명사② either A or B: A이거나 B인
더 이상 회사에 있지 않는 / 혹은 더 나쁘게는 /
appears to have hit a plateau in his or her career.
그 사람의 경력의 정체기에 든 것으로 보이는

힌트 the person을 수식하는 관계사절이 여러 개 연결되어 있음. 우선 목적격 관계대명사가 생략된 you knew가 the person을 수식하여 '여러분이 알던 사람'이라는 의미가 됨. 이어서 그 사람이 구체적으로 어떤 사람인지가 주격 관계대명사 who로 연결된 관계사절에서 설명되어 있음. 첫 번째 who절의 시제는 과거이므로 예전에는 잘나갔었다는 내용이며, 두 번째 who절은 현재 시제로 부정적인 내용이 이어지므로 여기서 who 앞의 콤마는 역접, 대조의 의미를 가짐. 마지막에 완료부정사 to have hit이 쓰인 것은 '정체기에 든 것'이 appears보다 과거에 일어났던 일이기 때문임.

(3) Assuming he or she did not make an ambitious move, /
그 사람이 야심에 찬 행동을 하지 않았다고 가정하면 /
more often than not, / this individual is a victim /
대개 / 이 사람은 희생자이다 /
of having failed to stay relevant and embrace the advances /
병렬① 병렬②(to 생략)
적합성을 유지하고 발전을 포용하는 데 실패한 /
in his or her industry. 정답 단서 야심에 찬 행동을 하지 않는다면, 업계에서 적합성을 잃고 발전하지 못하게 됨.
그 사람의 업계에서

(4) Think about the impact /
선행사
영향에 대해 생각해 보라 /
[personal computing technology had /
개인용 컴퓨터 사용 기술이 미친 /
on the first wave of executive leadership /
첫 물결의 경영 지도자에게 /
exposed to the technology]. [ ]: 목적격 관계대명사절
과거분사구
그 기술에 노출된

힌트 '~에 영향을 주다'라는 표현은 have an impact on임. 여기서는 목적격 관계대명사가 생략되어 있고, 목적어 the impact가 선행사이기 때문에 had 뒤에 on이 바로 이어지는 형태가 됨.

(5) Those who embraced the technology /
S(=선행사) 주격 관계대명사
기술을 포용한 이들은 /
were able to integrate it into their work styles / and excel.
병렬① 병렬②(to 생략)
그것을 그들의 작업 스타일에 흡수할 수 있었다 / 그리고 탁월할 수 있었다

(6) Those who were resistant many times /
S(=선행사) 주격 관계대명사
여러 번 저항한 이들은 /
found few opportunities to advance their careers /
형용사적 용법
그들의 경력을 발전시키기 위한 기회를 거의 찾을 수 없었다 /
and in many cases / were ultimately let go /
V
그리고 많은 경우 / 결국 사라지게 되었다 /
through early retirement /
이른 은퇴를 통해 /
for failure to stay relevant and update their skills. 정답 단서 기술에 저항한 이들은 경력 발전의 기회를 얻지 못하고, 기술 갱신 및 적합성 유지에 실패하여 업계에서 도태됨.
병렬①(형용사적 용법) 병렬②(to 생략)
적합성을 유지하고 그들의 기술을 새롭게 하는 데 실패하여

[전문 해석]

(1)성장과 발전에 실패한 브랜드는 그들의 적합성을 잃는다. (2)한때 여러분의 회사에서 승진 가도에 있었는데, 더 이상 회사에 있지 않거나, 더 나쁘게는 경력의 정체기에 든 것으로 보이는 여러분이 알던 사람을 생각해 보라. (3)그 사람이 야심에 찬 행동을 하지 않았다고 가정하면, 대개 이 사람은 그 사람의 업계에서 적합성을 유지하고 발전을 포용하는 데 실패한 희생자이다. (4)개인용 컴퓨터 사용 기술이 그 기술에 노출된 첫 물결의 경영 지도자에게 미친 영향에 대해 생각해 보라. (5)기술을 포용한 이들은 그것을 그들의 작업 스타일에 흡수하여 탁월할 수 있었다. (6)여러 번 저항한 이들은 그들의 경력을 발전시키기 위한 기회를 거의 찾을 수 없었고, 많은 경우 적합성을 유지하고 그들의 기술을 새롭게 하는 데 실패하여 이른 은퇴를 통해 결국 사라지게 되었다.

[정답 확인]

다음 글의 요지로 가장 적절한 것은?

① 다양한 업종의 경력(career)이 있으면 구직 활동에 유리하다.
② 직원의 다양한 능력을 활용하면 업계를 주도할(lead) 수 있다.
③ 기술이 발전함에 따라 단순 반복 업무(simple repetitive work)가 사라지고 있다.
④ 자신의 약점(weakness)을 인정하면 동료들로부터 도움을 얻기 쉽다.
✔ 변화를 받아들이지 못하면 업계에서의 적합성(relevance)을 잃게 된다.

[문제 풀이]

이 지문은 변화에 적응하지 못하고 성장과 발전의 기회를 놓친 브랜드는 적합성을 잃어 업계에서 유지되지 못한다고 설명하는 글이다. 이에 대해 우선 직장 동료의 경우를 예로 들고 있는데, 그 사람이 야심에 찬 행동을 하지 않는다면, 즉 변화를 받아들이려 하지 않는다면, 업계에서 적합성을 잃는다고 설명한다. 두 번째 예시로는 개인용 컴퓨터 사용 기술의 도입에 대한 상반된 반응을 제시한다. 먼저, 기술을 포용한 경우에는 작업 스타일에 기술을 적용하여 탁월한 성과를 낸다. 하지만 기술에 저항한 경우에는 경력 발전의 기회를 얻지 못하고 적합성을 잃어 업계에서 도태된다. 즉, 변화를 받아들이지 못하는 브랜드는 업계에서 적합성을 잃게 된다. 따라서 정답은 ⑤이다.

[중요 어휘]

☐ **relevance**	명사 적합성, 타당성, 관련성
☐ **fast track**	승진 가도, 빠른 길
☐ **hit a plateau**	정체기에 들다, 안정기에 들다
☐ **ambitious**	형용사 야심에 찬
☐ **victim**	명사 희생자, 피해자
☐ **embrace**	동사 포용하다, 껴안다
☐ **advance**	명사 발전, 증가 / 동사 발전시키다, 증진되다
☐ **executive leadership**	경영 지도자
☐ **expose**	동사 노출시키다, 드러내다, 폭로하다
☐ **integrate**	동사 흡수하다, 통합하다
☐ **excel**	동사 탁월하다, 뛰어나다
☐ **resistant**	형용사 저항하는, 잘 견디는
☐ **ultimately**	부사 결국, 궁극적으로
☐ **let A go**	A를 놓다[풀어 주다, 해고하다]
☐ **retirement**	명사 은퇴, 퇴직

정답과 해설 05 요지 추론

14 2023년 6월 22번 (정답률 65%) 정답 ②

[지문 끊어 읽기] 감성 지능의 가치

(1) Perhaps, /
아마도 /
the advent of Artificial Intelligence (AI) in the workplace /
직장에서 인공 지능(AI)의 출현은 /
may bode well / for Emotional Intelligence (EI).
좋은 징조가 될 수 있다 / 감성 지능(EI)에

(2) As AI gains momentum /
AI가 추진력을 받으면서 /
and replaces people in jobs at every level, /
그리고 모든 수준의 일자리에서 사람들을 대신하면서 /
predictions are, / there will be a premium / placed on people /
예측이 있다 / 프리미엄이 있을 것이라는 / 사람들에게 주어지는 / 선행사
[who have high ability in EI]. 정답단서 높은 EI 능력을 가진 사람들이 이득을 보게 될 것임.
높은 EI 능력을 가진 [ ]: 주격 관계대명사절

(3) The emotional messages /
S, 선행사
감정적인 메시지들은 /
[people send and respond to while interacting] /
사람들이 상호 작용하는 동안 보내고 반응하는 / [ ]: 목적격 관계대명사절(관계대명사 생략)
are, at this point, / far beyond the ability of AI programs to mimic.
V 형용사적 용법
이러한 점에서 ~이다 / AI 프로그램의 모방하는 능력을 훨씬 넘어선다

(4) As we get further / into the age of the smart machine, /
우리가 더 접어들수록 / 스마트 기기의 시대로 /
it is likely / that sensing and managing emotions will remain /
S'(V-ing) V'
가능성이 있다 / 감정을 감지하고 관리하는 것은 남을 /
one type of intelligence [that puzzles AI].
선행사 [ ]: 주격 관계대명사절
AI를 당혹스럽게 하는 지능의 한 유형으로

(5) This means / [people and jobs involving EI are safe /
S' V'
이것은 의미한다 / EI와 관련된 사람들과 직업들이 안전하다는 것을 /
from being taken over by machines]. [ ]: 목적어절(접속사 that 생략)
기계에 의해 장악되는 것으로부터

(6) In a survey, / almost three out of four executives /
한 설문 조사에서 / 임원 네 명 중 세 명 정도가 /
see EI as a "must-have" skill / for the workplace in the future /
EI를 '필수' 기술이라고 여긴다 / 미래 직장의 / 정답단서 EI가 미래 직장에서 필수적인 것이라 여겨짐.
as the automatizing of routine tasks bumps up /
접속사
일상적인 업무의 자동화가 부딪히면서 /
against the impossibility of creating effective AI /
효과적인 AI를 만드는 것의 불가능에 /
for activities [that require emotional skill].
선행사 [ ]: 주격 관계대명사절
정서적 기술이 필요한 활동을 위해

[전문 해석]

(1)아마도, 직장에서 인공 지능(AI)의 출현은 감성 지능(EI)에 좋은 징조가 될 수 있다. (2)AI가 추진력을 받고 모든 수준의 일자리에서 사람들을 대신하면서, 높은 EI 능력을 가진 사람들에게 주어지는 프리미엄이 있을 것이라는 예측이 있다. (3)이러한 점에서, 사람들이 상호 작용하는 동안 보내고 반응하는 감정적인 메시지들은 AI 프로그램의 모방하는 능력을 훨씬 넘어선다. (4)우리가 스마트 기기의 시대로 더 접어들수록, 감정을 감지하고 관리하는 것은 AI를 당혹스럽게 하는 지능의 한 유형으로 남을 가능성이 있다. (5)이것은 EI와 관련된 사람들과 직업들이 기계에 의해 장악되는 것으로부터 안전하다는 것을 의미한다. (6)한 설문 조사에서, 일상적인 업무의 자동화가 정서적 기술이 필요한 활동을 위해 효과적인 AI를 만드는 것의 불가능에 부딪히면서, 임원 네 명 중 세 명 정도가 EI를 미래 직장의 '필수' 기술이라고 여긴다.

[정답 확인]

다음 글의 요지로 가장 적절한 것은?

① 감성 지능(Emotional Intelligence)의 결여는 직장 내 대인 관계 갈등을 심화시킨다.
② 미래의 직장에서는 감성 지능의 가치가 더욱 높아질(become more valuable) 것이다.
③ 미래 사회에서는 감성 지능을 갖춘 기계가 보편화될(be generalized) 것이다.
④ 미래에는 대부분의 직장 업무를 인공 지능이 대신할(replace) 것이다.
⑤ 인간과 인공 지능 간의 상호 작용(interaction)은 감성 지능의 발달을 저해한다.

[문제 풀이]

이 글은 AI의 발달로 감성 지능(EI)의 중요성이 증가한다는 것을 시작으로, AI가 따라오지 못하는 유형의 지능이 바로 감성 지능임을 설명한다. 높은 EI 능력을 가진 사람들은 기계에 장악되지 않을 것이며, 한 조사에서 회사의 임원들의 대부분이 EI가 미래 직장에서 필수적인 기술이 될 것이라 했다. 이러한 내용을 토대로 하여, 글의 요지로 미래 직장에서 감성 지능의 가치가 높아질 것임을 추론할 수 있다. 따라서 정답은 ②이다.

[중요 어휘]

□ **advent**	명사 출현, 도래
□ **bode**	동사 ~의 징조가 되다[조짐이다]
□ **momentum**	명사 추진력, 가속도
□ **prediction**	명사 예측, 예견
□ **premium**	명사 프리미엄, 상, 장려금
□ **mimic**	동사 모방하다, 흉내 내다
□ **age**	명사 시대, 나이
□ **puzzle**	동사 당혹스럽게 하다, 어쩔 줄 모르게 하다
□ **take over**	장악하다, 인수하다
□ **executive**	명사 임원, 간부
□ **automatize**	동사 자동화하다
□ **bump up**	부딪히다

15 2023년 9월 22번 (정답률 50%) 정답 ④

[지문 끊어 읽기] 낙관적인 상상의 역기능

(1) It's remarkable / [that positive fantasies help us relax /
형식상의 주어 [ ]: 내용상의 주어 준사역V' O' O·C'(동사원형)
주목할 만하다 / 낙관적인 상상이 우리가 진정하는 데 도움이 된다는 것은 /
to such an extent / that it shows up in physiological tests].
~할 정도로 / 그것이 생리학적인 검사에서 나타나는

(2) If you want to unwind, /
만약 당신이 긴장을 풀고 싶다면 /
you can take some deep breaths, get a massage, or go for a walk /
병렬① 병렬② 병렬③
당신은 심호흡을 할 수 있고, 마사지를 받을 수 있으며 또는 산책을 갈 수도 있다 /
— but you can also try simply closing your eyes /
병렬①
그러나 당신은 또한 단순히 눈을 감아볼 수 있다 /
and fantasizing about some future outcome /
병렬② 선행사
그리고 어떤 미래 결과에 대해 상상해 볼 /
[that you might enjoy]. [ ]: 목적격 관계대명사절
당신이 즐길

(3) But what about /
그러나 어떤가 /
when your objective is [to make your wish a reality]? [ ]: S·C
5형식V' O' O·C'
당신의 목표가 당신의 소원을 현실로 만드는 것인 경우는

(4) The *last* thing you want to be / is relaxed.
당신이 바라는 '마지막' 일은 / 긴장이 풀리는 것이다

(5) You want to be energized enough /
당신은 충분히 동력을 공급받고 싶다 /
to get off the couch and lose those pounds /
병렬① 병렬②
소파에서 일어나 체중을 감량할 만큼 /
or find that job or study for that test, /
병렬③ 병렬④
또는 일자리를 찾거나 시험을 위해 공부할 만큼 /
and you want to be motivated enough to stay engaged /
그리고 당신은 계속 몰두할 만큼 충분히 동기 부여를 받고 싶어 한다 /
even when the inevitable obstacles or challenges arise.
피할 수 없는 장애물이나 과제가 나타나는 때에도

힌트 'enough+to V' 구문으로 '~할 만큼[정도로] 충분히'라는 뜻임. 이 문장의 두 개의 절 모두에서 enough to 구문이 사용되었는데, 첫 번째 enough to 이하에 4개의 동사구가 병렬로 연결되어 있으며 to get off 이외의 나머지 동사구는 동사 앞에 to가 생략되어 있음.

(6) The principle of "Dream it. Wish it. Do it." / does not hold true, /
S
'꿈꿔라. 소망하라. 하라.'라는 원칙은 / 사실이 아니다 /

and now we know why: /
그리고 이제 우리는 이유를 안다 /

in dreaming it, / you undercut the energy / you need to do it. 정답 단서 '꿈꿔라. 소망하라. 하라.'는 우리가 꿈을 꾸면서 그것을 실행할 에너지를 약화시키기 때문에 사실이 아님.
그것을 꿈꾸면서 / 당신은 에너지를 약화시킨다 / 당신이 그것을 하기 위해 필요한

힌트 선행사 the energy 뒤에 목적격 관계대명사(that/which)가 생략된 형태이며, to do it은 목적을 나타내는 to부정사의 부사적 용법으로 쓰임.

(7) You put yourself in a temporary state /
당신은 스스로를 일시적인 상태에 빠지게 한다 /

of complete happiness, calmness — and inactivity. 정답 단서 당신은 자신을 일시적으로 완전한 행복, 침착, 무기력의 상태로 놓음.
완전한 행복, 침착 그리고 무기력의

[전문 해석]

(1)낙관적인 상상이 생리학적인 검사에서 나타날 정도로 우리가 진정하는 데 도움이 된다는 것은 주목할 만하다. (2)만약 당신이 긴장을 풀고 싶다면 당신은 심호흡을 할 수 있고, 마사지를 받을 수 있으며 또는 산책을 갈 수도 있다. 그러나 당신은 또한 단순히 눈을 감고 당신이 즐길 어떤 미래 결과에 대해 상상해 볼 수도 있다. (3)그러나 당신의 목표가 당신의 소원을 현실로 만드는 것인 경우는 어떤가? (4)당신이 바라는 '마지막' 일은 긴장이 풀리는 것이다(당신은 긴장이 풀리는 것을 가장 바라지 않는다). (5)당신은 소파에서 일어나 체중을 감량할 만큼 또는 일자리를 찾거나 시험을 위해 공부할 만큼 충분히 동력을 공급받고 싶고, 피할 수 없는 장애물이나 과제가 나타나는 때에도 당신은 계속 몰두할 만큼 충분히 동기 부여를 받고 싶어 한다. (6)'꿈꿔라. 소망하라. 하라.'라는 원칙은 사실이 아니고, 이제 우리는 이유를 안다. 그것을 꿈꾸면서, 당신은 그것을 하기 위해 필요한 에너지를 약화시킨다. (7)당신은 스스로를 완전한 행복, 침착, 그리고 무기력의 일시적인 상태에 빠지게 한다.

[정답 확인]

다음 글의 요지로 가장 적절한 것은?

① 과도한 목표 지향적(goal-oriented) 태도는 삶의 만족감(satisfaction)을 떨어뜨린다.
② 긍정적 자세로 역경을 극복할 때 잠재 능력(potential ability)이 발휘된다.
③ 편안함을 느끼는 상황에서 자기 개선에 대한 동기(motivation)가 생긴다.
✔ 낙관적인(positive) 상상은 소망을 실현하는 데 필요한 동력을 약화시킨다(undercut).
⑤ 막연한 목표보다는 명확하고 구체적인 목표가 실현 가능성이 크다.

[문제 풀이]

이 글은 낙관적인 상상이 꿈을 이루는 동력을 약화시킨다는 내용이다. 글에 따르면 낙관적인 상상은 우리를 진정시킬 수 있기 때문에 목표를 이루기 위한 동기 부여가 잘 되지 않고 필요한 에너지를 약화시켜 결국에는 무기력의 상태가 된다고 말한다. 따라서 글의 요지로 가장 적절한 것은 ④이다.

[중요 어휘]

☐ remarkable	형용사 주목할 만한, 놀라운
☐ fantasy	명사 상상, 환상
☐ to such an extent that	~할 정도로, ~일 경우에
☐ unwind	동사 긴장을 풀다, (감은 것을) 풀다
☐ fantasize	동사 상상하다, 공상하다
☐ outcome	명사 결과
☐ objective	명사 목표, 목적 / 형용사 객관적인
☐ energize	동사 동력을 공급하다, 활기를 북돋우다
☐ get off	일어나다, 떠나다, 벗어나다, 내리다
☐ engaged	형용사 몰두하고 있는, 바쁜, 약혼한
☐ inevitable	형용사 피할 수 없는, 필연적인
☐ obstacle	명사 장애물, 방해물
☐ undercut	동사 약화시키다, 싸게 팔다
☐ temporary	형용사 일시적인, 임시의
☐ inactivity	명사 무기력, 무활동

16 2023년 11월 22번 (정답률 85%) 정답 ①

[지문 끊어 읽기] 공공 기계 시계

(1) Many historians have pointed to the significance of accurate time measurement /
현재완료
많은 역사가들은 정확한 시간 측정의 중요성을 시사해왔다 /

to Western economic progress. 정답 단서 많은 역사가들이 서양의 경제 발전에서 정확한 시간 측정의 중요성을 시사함.
서구 경제 발전에서

(2) The French historian Jacques Le Goff called /
프랑스 역사가 Jacques Le Goff는 불렀다 / 5형식V

the birth of the public mechanical clock /
공공 기계 시계의 탄생을 / O

a turning point in Western society.
서구 사회의 전환점이라고 O·C

(3) Until the late Middle Ages, / people had sun or water clocks, /
중세 시대 후기까지 / 사람들은 해시계나 물시계를 가지고 있었다 / 선행사

which did not play any meaningful role in business activities.
주격 관계대명사(계속적 용법)
그런데 그것은 경제 활동에서 어떤 의미 있는 역할도 하지 못했다

(4) Market openings and activities started with the sunrise /
시장 개장과 활동은 일출과 함께 시작했다 / V①

and typically ended at noon / when the sun was at its peak.
V② 선행사 관계부사절
그리고 보통 정오에 끝났다 / 해가 그 최고점에 이르는

(5) But when the first public mechanical clocks were introduced /
그러나 최초의 공공 기계 시계가 도입되었을 때 / 수동태①

and spread across European cities, /
수동태②(were 생략)
그리고 유럽 도시들 전역으로 퍼졌을 때 /

market times were set / by the stroke of the hour.
시장 시간은 정해졌다 / 시각을 알리는 소리에 의해

(6) Public clocks thus / greatly contributed to public life and work /
따라서 공공 시계는 / 공공의 삶과 일에 크게 기여했다 /

by providing a new concept of time /
선행사
시간의 새로운 개념을 제공함으로써 /

that was easy for everyone to understand.
모두가 이해하기 쉬운 주격 관계대명사절

힌트 for everyone은 to부정사의 의미상의 주어이고, to understand가 관계사절의 내용상의 주어에 해당함. 형식상의 주어 it 자리에 주격 관계대명사 that이 쓰인 구조임.

공공 시계의 등장으로 모두가 이해할 수 있는 시간의 새로운 개념이 생겨났고, 이것이 무역과 상업을 촉진하도록 도왔음.

(7) This, in turn, / helped facilitate trade and commerce. 정답 단서
그 결과 이것은 / 무역과 상업을 촉진하도록 도왔다

(8) [Interactions and transactions between consumers, retailers, and wholesalers] / [ ]:S
소비자, 소매업자, 그리고 도매업자 사이의 상호 작용과 거래는 /

became less irregular.
V
덜 불규칙해졌다

(9) Important town meetings began to follow the pace of the clock, /
중요한 마을 회의들은 시계의 속도를 따르기 시작했다 /

[allowing people to better plan their time /
5형식V O O·C, 병렬①
사람들이 자신의 시간을 더 잘 계획하도록 허락하면서 /

and allocate resources in a more efficient manner]. [ ]: 분사구문
병렬②(to 생략)
그리고 더 효율적인 방식으로 자원을 분배하도록

[전문 해석]

(1)많은 역사가들은 서구 경제 발전에서 정확한 시간 측정의 중요성을 시사해왔다. (2)프랑스 역사가 Jacques Le Goff는 공공 기계 시계의 탄생을 서구 사회의 전환점이라고 불렀다. (3)중세 시대 후기까지, 사람들은 해시계나 물시계를 가지고 있었는데, 그것은 경제 활동에서 어떤 의미 있는 역할도 하지 못했다. (4)시장 개장과 활동은 일출과 함께 시작했고 보통 해가 그 최고점에 이르는 정오에 끝났다. (5)그러나 최초의 공공 기계 시계가 도입되고 유럽 도시들 전역으로 퍼졌을 때, 시장 시간은 시각을 알리는 소리에 의해 정해졌다. (6)따라서 공공 시계는 모두가 이해하기 쉬운 시간의 새로운 개념을 제공함으로써 공공의 삶과 일에 크게 기여했다. (7)그 결과, 이것은 무역과 상업을 촉진하도록 도왔다. (8)소비자, 소매업자, 그리고 도매업자 사이의 상호 작용과 거래는 덜 불규칙해졌다. (9)중요한 마을 회의들은 시계의 속도를 따르기 시작했고, 이것은 사람들이 자신의 시간을 더 잘 계획하고 더 효율적인 방식으로 자원을 분배하도록 허락했다.

[정답 확인]

다음 글의 요지로 가장 적절한 것은?

✔ 공공 시계(public clock)는 서양 사회의 경제적 진보(economic progress)에 영향을 미쳤다.

② 서양에서 생산된 시계는 세계적으로 정교함(elaboration)을 인정받았다.
③ 서양의 시계는 교역(trade)을 통해 전파되어 세계적으로 대중화되었다.
④ 기계 시계의 발명은 다른 측량 장비들(measure equipment)의 개발에 도움을 주었다.
⑤ 중세 시대의 시계 발명은 자연법칙을 이해하는 데 큰 전환점(turning point)이 되었다.

[중요 어휘]

□ **point to N**	~을 시사하다[암시하다]
□ **significance**	명사 중요성, 의의, 의미
□ **accurate**	형용사 정확한, 정밀한
□ **measurement**	명사 측정, 측량
□ **Western**	형용사 서구의, 서양의
□ **progress**	명사 발전, 진보 / 동사 발전하다, 진보하다
□ **mechanical**	형용사 기계의, 자동의
□ **turning point**	명사 전환점
□ **Middle Ages**	명사 중세 시대
□ **sunrise**	명사 일출
□ **peak**	명사 최고점, 정점, (산의) 정상 / 동사 절정에 이르다
□ **stroke**	명사 (시계가) 울리는 소리, 치기, 뇌졸중 / 동사 쓰다듬다
□ **concept**	명사 개념, 구상, 발상
□ **commerce**	명사 상업, 무역
□ **transaction**	명사 거래, 매매, 처리 (과정)
□ **retailer**	명사 소매업자
□ **wholesaler**	명사 도매업자
□ **pace**	명사 속도, 페이스
□ **allocate**	동사 분배하다, 할당하다

17 2024년 3월 22번 (정답률 55%) 정답 ②

[지문 끊어 읽기] 과소평가되는 기존의 기술들

(1) We tend to overrate / the impact of new technologies /
우리는 과대평가하는 경향이 있다 / 새로운 기술의 영향을 /
in part because older technologies have become absorbed /
부분적으로는 기존의 기술이 흡수되었기 때문이다 /
into the furniture of our lives, /
우리 삶의 일부로 /
so as to be almost invisible. 정답 단서
거의 눈에 띄지 않을 정도로

힌트 밑줄 친 furniture은 문자 그대로 '가구'를 의미한다기보다는 가구와 같이 일상생활에서 너무나 익숙해져 거의 눈에 띄지 않는 상태를 비유적으로 표현한 것임.

'기존의 기술'은 거의 눈에 띄지 않을 정도로 우리 삶의 일부로 흡수되었음.

(2) Take the baby bottle.
젖병을 예로 들어보자

(3) Here is a simple implement /
V① S①(=the baby bottle), 선행사
여기 단순한 도구가 있다 /
[that has transformed a fundamental human experience /
인간의 근본적인 경험을 바꾼 /
for vast numbers of infants and mothers], / [ ]: 주격 관계대명사절
수많은 영유아와 엄마에 대해 /
yet it finds no place / in our histories of technology. 정답 단서
V② S②(=the baby bottle)
그러나 그것은 자리를 찾지 못한다 / 기술의 역사에서

문장 (1)의 예시로 젖병은 인간의 경험에 큰 변화를 가져왔지만 기술의 역사에서는 크게 주목받지 못했음.

(4) This technology /
이 기술은 /
might be thought of as a classic time-shifting device, /
전형적인 시간을 조절하는 장치로 여겨질지도 모른다 /
as it enables mothers [to exercise more control /
=because 5형식V O
왜냐하면 그것은 엄마들이 더 많은 통제력을 발휘할 수 있게 하기 때문이다 /
over the timing of feeding]. [ ]: O·C(to부정사구)
수유 시간에 대해

힌트 「think of A as B(A를 B로 여기다)」의 수동형인 「A+be thought of+as B(A는 B로 여겨지다)」의 구조임. think of를 'see/consider/view'로 바꿀 수 있음.

(5) It can also function to save time, / as bottle feeding allows /
부사적 용법(목적) =because
그것은 또한 시간을 절약하는 기능을 할 수 있다 / 왜냐하면 젖병 수유는 허락하기 때문이다 /
for someone else / to substitute for the mother's time.
다른 누군가가 / 엄마의 시간을 대신하는 것을

★중요 '젖병'은 문장 (1)에서 말한 '기존의 기술(older technologies)'의 일종으로, 문장 (2)~(6)은 젖병이 인간의 삶에 큰 영향을 미쳤음에도 불구하고 고속 사회의 새로운 기술에 비해 주목을 받지 못했음을 일관적으로 설명함.

(6) Potentially, therefore, / it has huge implications /
따라서 잠재적으로 / 그것은 큰 영향을 가진다 /
for the management of time in everyday life, /
일상생활의 시간 관리에 /
yet it is entirely overlooked / in discussions of high-speed society.
하지만 그것은 완전히 간과되고 있다 / 고속 사회의 담론에서 정답 단서

'젖병'은 일상생활의 시간 관리에 잠재적으로 큰 영향을 미치지만, 사회적 담론에서는 완전히 간과되고 있음.

[중요 구문]

(1) ~ older technologies have become absorbed into the furniture of our lives, so as to be almost invisible.
2형식V S·C(형용사)

→ ~ older technologies have become so absorbed into the furniture of our lives that they are almost invisible.
「so ~ that 구문」

힌트 밑줄 친 부분은 문맥상 「so ~ as to V(너무 ~해서 …하다)」의 의미로서, 「so ~ that+S+V(너무 ~해서 …하다)」 구문으로 바꾸어 나타낼 수 있음.

[전문 해석]

(1)우리는 새로운 기술의 영향을 과대평가하는 경향이 있는데, 부분적으로는 기존의 기술이 거의 눈에 띄지 않을 정도로 우리 삶의 일부로 흡수되었기 때문이다. (2)젖병을 예로 들어보자. (3)여기 수많은 영유아와 엄마에 대해 인간의 근본적인 경험을 바꾼 단순한 도구가 있으나 그것은 기술의 역사에서 자리를 찾지 못한다. (4)이 기술은 전형적인 시간을 조절하는 장치로 여겨질지도 모르는데, 왜냐하면 그것은 엄마들이 수유 시간에 대해 더 많은 통제력을 발휘할 수 있게 하기 때문이다. (5)그것은 또한 시간을 절약하는 기능을 할 수 있는데, 왜냐하면 젖병 수유는 다른 누군가가 엄마의 시간을 대신하는 것을 허락하기 때문이다. (6)따라서 잠재적으로 그것은 일상생활의 시간 관리에 큰 영향을 가지지만, 그것은 고속 사회의 담론에서 완전히 간과되고 있다.

[정답 확인]

다음 글의 요지로 가장 적절한 것은?
① 새로운 기술은 효율적인 시간 관리(time management)에 도움이 된다.
② 새로운 기술에 비해 기존 기술의 영향력이 간과되고(be overlooked) 있다.
③ 현대 사회의 새로운 기술이 양육자(caregiver)의 역할을 대체하고(substitute) 있다.
④ 새로운 기술의 사용을 장려하는(encourage) 사회적 인식(social perception)이 요구된다.
⑤ 기존 기술의 활용은 새로운 기술의 개발(development of new technologies)에 도움이 된다.

[문제 풀이]

문장 (1)은 기존의 기술이 일상에 흡수되어 거의 눈에 띄지 않는 탓에 새로운 기술의 영향이 과대평가되는 경향이 있다는 내용으로, 본문은 기존의 기술에 해당하는 젖병의 사례를 통해 '기존의 기술의 영향력이 과소평가되고 있다'고 주장한다. 즉, 문장 (2)~(6)에 따르면 젖병은 엄마의 수유 시간 관리를 통제할 수 있게 됨으로써 시간을 조절할 수 있게 되어 영유아와 엄마의 삶에 큰 영향력을 미쳤지만, 젖병이 '기술의 역사에서 자리를 찾지 못한다'라고 말하는 문장 (3)과 젖병이 일상생활의 시간 관리에 큰 영향을 미쳤지만 이러한 점이 '고속 사회의 담론에서 완전히 간과되고 있다'라고 말하는 문장 (6)의 내용을 통해, 기존의 기술이 가지는 영향력이 과소평가되고 있음을 추론할 수 있다. 따라서 글의 요지로 가장 적절한 것은 ②이다.

[중요 어휘]

□ **tend to V**	~하는 경향이 있다
□ **overrate**	동사 과대평가하다
□ **impact**	명사 영향, 효과
□ **in part**	부분적으로는
□ **older**	형용사 기존의, 이전의
□ **absorbed**	형용사 흡수된, 합병된
□ **invisible**	형용사 눈에 띄지[보이지] 않는
□ **implement**	명사 도구, 기구 / 동사 시행하다
□ **transform**	동사 바꾸다, 전환시키다
□ **fundamental**	형용사 근본적인, 본질적인
□ **infant**	명사 영유아

- classic — 형용사 전형적인, 대표적인
- device — 명사 장치, 기구
- enable A to V — A가 ~할 수 있게 하다
- exercise — 동사 발휘하다, 행사하다
- function to V — ~하는 기능을 하다
- feeding — 명사 (아기의) 수유, 먹이 주기
- substitute for A — A를 대신하다
- implication — 명사 영향, 결과
- management — 명사 관리, 경영
- overlook — 동사 간과하다, 못 보고 넘어가다
- discussion — 명사 담론, 논의, 토론

18 2024년 6월 22번 (정답률 90%) 정답 ④

[지문 끊어 읽기] 기업의 도덕적 위험

(1) If a firm is going to be saved by the government, /
기업이 정부로부터 구제받으려면 /
it might be easier / [to concentrate on lobbying the government /
형식상의 주어 / [ ]: 내용상의 주어
더 쉬울지도 모른다 / 정부에 로비하는 것에 집중하는 것이 /
for more money] /
더 많은 돈을 받기 위해 /
rather than taking the harder decision of restructuring the company /
회사를 구조 조정하는 어려운 결정을 내리는 것보다 /
to be able to be profitable and viable in the long term.
부사적 용법
장기적으로 수익성이 나고 성장할 수 있도록

(2) This is an example of something / known as moral hazard /
이것은 ~의 한 예이다 / 도덕적 위험이라고 알려진 / 현재분사구
— when government support alters the decisions firms take.
정부의 지원이 기업이 내리는 결정을 바꾸는 때 / 선행사 / 목적격 관계대명사절 (관계대명사 생략)

(3) For example, /
예를 들어 /
if governments rescue banks who get into difficulty, /
선행사 / 주격 관계대명사절
만약 정부가 어려움에 처한 은행을 구제한다면 /
=rescued
as they did during the credit crisis of 2007-08, /
=governments
2007~08년 신용 위기 때 그들이 그랬던 것처럼 / ★중요 정부가 은행을 구제하는 것을 가리킴.
this could encourage banks to take greater risks in the future /
이것은 은행이 미래에 더 큰 위험을 감수하도록 조장할 수 있다 /
because they know / [there is a possibility /
=banks
왜냐하면 그들이 알기 때문이다 / 가능성이 있다는 것을 /
that governments will intervene / if they lose money]. [ ]: know의 목적어절 (접속사 that 생략)
정부가 개입할 / 그들이 손해를 보는 경우 / =banks

(4) Although the government rescue may be well intended, /
정부의 구제가 좋은 의도일지라도 /
it can negatively affect the behavior of banks, /
=the government rescue
그것은 은행의 행동에 부정적인 영향을 미칠 수 있다 / [ ]: 분사구문(결과)
[encouraging risky and poor decision making]. 정답 단서
그리고 위험하고 형편없는 의사 결정을 조장할 수 있다
정부의 구제가 은행의 의사 결정에 부정적인 영향을 미칠 수 있음.

[전문 해석]

(1)기업이 정부로부터 구제받으려면, 장기적으로 수익성이 나고 성장할 수 있도록 회사를 구조 조정하는 어려운 결정을 내리는 것보다 더 많은 돈을 받기 위해 정부에 로비하는 것에 집중하는 것이 더 쉬울지도 모른다. (2)이것은 도덕적 위험이라고 알려진 것의 한 예로, 정부의 지원이 기업이 내리는 결정을 바꾸는 때이다. (3)예를 들어, 2007~08년 신용 위기 때 그들이 그랬던 것처럼, 만약 정부가 어려움에 처한 은행을 구제한다면, 이것은 은행이 미래에 더 큰 위험을 감수하도록 조장할 수 있는데, 왜냐하면 그들이 손해를 보는 경우 정부가 개입할 가능성이 있다는 것을 그들이 알기 때문이다. (4)정부의 구제가 좋은 의도일지라도, 그것은 은행의 행동에 부정적인 영향을 미칠 수 있고, 위험하고 형편없는 의사 결정을 조장할 수 있다.

[정답 확인]

다음 글의 요지로 가장 적절한 것은?

① 기업(firm)에 대한 정부의 지원이 새로운 기술의 도입을 촉진한다.
② 현명한 소비자들은 윤리적(ethical) 기업의 제품을 선택하는 경향이 있다.
③ 정부(government)와 기업은 협력(cooperation)으로 사회적 문제의 해결책을 모색할 수 있다.
✔ 정부의 구제(rescue)는 기업의 의사 결정(decision making)에 부정적인 영향을 미칠 수 있다.
⑤ 합리적(rational) 의사 결정은 다양한 대안에 대한 평가를 통해 이루어진다.

[중요 어휘]

- firm — 명사 기업, 회사 / 형용사 단단한, 확고한
- concentrate on — ~에 집중하다
- lobby — 동사 로비를 하다 / 명사 로비
- restructure — 동사 구조 조정하다, 재구성하다
- profitable — 형용사 수익성 있는, 이득이 되는
- viable — 형용사 성장할 수 있는, 실행 가능한
- moral — 형용사 도덕적인 / 명사 교훈
- hazard — 명사 위험 / 동사 ~을 위태롭게 하다
- alter — 동사 바꾸다, 달라지다
- rescue — 동사 구제하다, 구조하다
- credit — 명사 신용, 신뢰, 명성 / 동사 믿다, 신용하다
- crisis — 명사 위기, 최악의 고비
- intervene — 동사 개입하다, 끼어들다
- lose money — 손해를 보다

19 2024년 9월 22번 (정답률 90%) 정답 ⑤

[지문 끊어 읽기] 위기 상황에서의 정보 전달

(1) Any new or threatening situation /
S①
어떤 새롭거나 위협적인 상황은 / 정답 단서 긴박한 상황에서는 결정을 내리기 위한 정보가 필요함.
may require us to make decisions / and this requires information.
V①(5형식V) O O·C S② V②
우리가 결정을 내릴 것을 요구할 수도 있다 / 그리고 이것은 정보를 요구한다

(2) So important is communication during a disaster /
V S
재난 상황 중에는 소통이 매우 중요해서 /
that normal social barriers are often lowered.
보통의 사회적 장벽이 자주 낮아진다
힌트 '너무 ~해서 …하다'라는 의미의 'so ~ that …' 구문이 쓰였고, 보어인 'So important'가 문두에 강조되어 쓰이면서 주어와 동사의 도치가 일어남.

(3) We will talk to strangers /
우리는 낯선 사람에게 말을 걸 것이다 /
in a way we would never consider normally.
선행사 / 목적격 관계대명사절(관계대명사 생략)
우리가 보통은 전혀 고려하지 않을 방식으로
힌트 선행사 'a way'를 수식하는 관계사절 안에서 consider의 목적어가 없는 것으로 보아 목적격 관계대명사가 생략된 관계대명사절임을 알 수 있음.

(4) Even relatively low grade disruption of our life /
S
우리 삶에서의 비교적 낮은 수준의 혼란조차도 /
such as a fire drill or a very late train /
소방 훈련이나 매우 연착된 기차와 같은 /
seems to give us the permission / to break normal etiquette /
V 병렬①
우리에게 허용해 주는 것처럼 보인다 / 보통의 에티켓을 어기는 것을 /
and talk to strangers.
병렬②(to 생략)
그리고 낯선 사람에게 말을 거는 것을
힌트 '~할수록 …하다'라는 의미인 'the 비교급 S+V, the 비교급 S+V' 구문이 쓰였으며, 이때 be동사는 생략이 가능하므로 an event to a particular public 다음에 is가 생략된 것을 알 수 있음.

(5) The more important an event to a particular public, /
어떠한 사건이 특정 사람들에게 중요할수록 /
the more detailed and urgent the requirement for news becomes.
소식에 대한 요구가 더 상세하고 긴박해진다

(6) Without an authoritative source of facts, /
사실에 대한 믿을 만한 출처 없이 /

문제편 p.058

[whether that is a newspaper or trusted broadcast station], /
지시대명사 [ ]: 부사절(양보)
그것이 신문이든 신뢰할 만한 방송국이든 /
rumours often run riot.
소문은 자주 제멋대로 뻗어 나간다

(7) Rumours start /
소문은 시작된다 /
because people believe their group to be in danger /
V'①(5형식V) O' O·C'
사람들이 자신의 집단이 위험에 처해 있다고 여기기 때문에 /
and so, / although the rumour is unproven, /
삽입절
그래서 / 그 소문이 입증되지 않았음에도 불구하고 /
=the rumour
feel [they should pass it on]. 정답단서 위급 상황에서 사람들은 정보에 대한 사실 확인 없이 정보를 전달하려는 경향이 있음.
V'② [ ]: feel의 목적어절(명사절 접속사 that 생략)
그들이 이것을 전달해야 한다고 생각한다

(8) For example, / if a worker heard /
예를 들어 / 한 근로자가 들으면 /
that their employer's business was doing badly /
접속사
그의 고용주의 사업이 잘 안 된다고 /
and people were going to be made redundant, /
그리고 사람들이 해고될 것이라고 /
they would pass that information on to colleagues.
지시형용사
그들은 그 정보를 동료들에게 전달할 것이다

힌트 5형식 동사 make는 목적격 보어로 형용사나 명사를 가질 수 있는데, 이 문장은 수동태로 쓰여 목적어인 people이 주어로, 목적격 보어인 redundant는 made 뒤에 남아 있음.

[전문 해석]

(1)어떤 새롭거나 위협적인 상황은 우리가 결정을 내릴 것을 요구할 수도 있고 이것(결정을 내리는 것)은 정보를 요구한다. (2)재난 상황 중에는 소통이 매우 중요해서 보통의 사회적 장벽이 자주 낮아진다. (3)우리는 우리가 보통은 전혀 고려하지 않을 방식으로 낯선 사람에게 말을 걸 것이다. (4)소방 훈련이나 매우 연착된 기차와 같은 우리 삶에서의 비교적 낮은 수준의 혼란조차도 보통의 에티켓을 어기고 낯선 사람에게 말을 거는 것을 허용해 주는 것처럼 보인다. (5)어떠한 사건이 특정 사람들에게 중요할수록, 소식에 대한 요구가 더 상세하고 긴박해진다. (6)그것이 신문이든 신뢰할 만한 방송국이든, 사실에 대한 믿을 만한 출처 없이, 소문은 자주 제멋대로 뻗어 나간다. (7)소문은 사람들이 자신의 집단이 위험에 처해 있다고 여기기 때문에, 그 소문이 입증되지 않았음에도 불구하고, 그들이 이것을 전달해야 한다고 생각하기 때문에 시작된다. (8)예를 들어, 한 근로자가 그의 고용주의 사업이 잘 안 되고 사람들이 해고될 것이라고 들으면, 그들은 그 정보를 동료들에게 전달할 것이다.

[정답 확인]

다음 글의 요지로 가장 적절한 것은?

① 소수(minority)에 의한 정보 독점은 합리적(reasonable) 의사 결정을 방해한다.
② 대중(public)의 지속적 관심이 뉴스의 공정성(impartiality)을 향상시킬 수 있다.
③ 위기에 처한 사람은 권위 있는(authoritative) 전문가의 의견을 구하려고 한다.
④ 소문(rumour)은 유사한 성향을 지닌 사람들 사이에서 더 빠르게(rapidly) 퍼진다.
✔ 위기 상황에서는 확인되지 않은 정보라도 전달하려는(pass on) 경향이 크다.

[중요 어휘]

□ **threatening**	형용사 위협적인, 위협을 주는
□ **disaster**	명사 재난, 재앙
□ **barrier**	명사 장벽, 장애물
□ **relatively**	부사 비교적, 상대적으로
□ **disruption**	명사 혼란, 방해, 지장
□ **fire drill**	명사 소방 훈련
□ **permission**	명사 허용, 허가
□ **detailed**	형용사 상세한, 자세한
□ **urgent**	형용사 긴박한, 시급한
□ **authoritative**	형용사 믿을 만한, 권위 있는
□ **rumour**	명사 소문, 루머
□ **run riot**	제멋대로 뻗어 나가다, 마구 날뛰다
□ **unproven**	형용사 입증[증명]되지 않은
□ **pass A on to B**	A를 B에 전달하다[넘겨주다]
□ **redundant**	형용사 해고된, 불필요한
□ **colleague**	명사 (같은 직장의) 동료

06 주제 추론

01 2021년 6월 23번 (정답률 85%) 정답 ②

[지문 끊어 읽기] 상상력과 창의성의 관계

(1) Creativity is a step further on / from imagination.
창의성은 한 단계 더 나아간 것이다 / 상상력으로부터

(2) Imagination can be /
상상력은 ~일 수 있다 /
an entirely private process / of internal consciousness.
전적으로 사적인 과정 / 내적 의식의

(3) You might be lying motionless / on your bed /
당신은 움직임 없이 누워있을지도 모른다 / 당신의 침대 위에 /
in a fever of imagination / and no one would ever know.
상상력의 흥분 속에서 / 그리고 어느 누구도 알지 못할 것이다

힌트 여기서 lie는 뒤에 보어가 와야 완전해지는 불완전 자동사(2형식 동사)이고, 형용사만을 보어로 취함. (lie-lay-lain, lying)

(4) Private imaginings may have no outcomes / in the world / at all.
사적인 상상력들은 어떤 결과도 가지고 있지 않을지도 모른다 / 이 세상에서 / 전혀

(5) Creativity does.
창의성은 그렇다

힌트 대동사인 does는 문장 (4)의 have no outcomes와 대비되어 has outcomes를 의미함. 즉 사적인 상상력은 결과를 가지고 있지 않지만(문장 (4)), 창의성은 결과를 가진다는 의미임(문장 (5)).

(6) Being creative / involves doing something.
창의적인 것은 / 무언가 하는 것을 수반한다

(7) It would be odd / [to describe as creative /
형식상의 주어 [ ]: 내용상의 주어
이상할 것이다 / 창의적이라고 묘사하는 것은 /
someone who never did anything].
어떤 것도 절대로 하지 않았던 사람을

힌트 describe의 목적어로, 'describe+목적어+as+보어' 형태에서 목적어가 길어서 문장의 맨 뒤로 빠진 경우임.

(8) To call somebody creative / suggests /
명사적 용법(~하는 것)
누군가를 창의적이라고 부르는 것은 / 암시한다 /
they are actively producing something / in a deliberate way.
그들이 어떤 것을 적극적으로 만들어 내고 있다는 것을 / 의도적인 방식으로

힌트 suggests 뒤에 명사절 목적어를 이끄는 접속사 that이 생략됨. that절을 목적어로 취하는 동사는 대표적으로 know, think, believe, assume, suggest, recommend 등이 있음.

(9) People are not creative / in the abstract; /
the + 형용사: ~인(한) 것
사람들은 창의적이지 않다 / 추상적인 것에서는 /
they are creative in something: /
그들은 어떤 것에서 창의적이다 /
in mathematics, in engineering, in writing, in music, in business, in whatever.
수학에서, 공학에서, 글쓰기에서, 음악에서, 사업에서, 무엇에서든지

(10) Creativity involves / putting your imagination to work. 정답 단서
put ~ to work: ~을 작동시키다
창의성은 수반한다 / 당신의 상상력을 작동시키는 것을

(11) In a sense, / creativity is applied imagination. 정답 단서
어떤 면에서 / 창의성은 적용된 상상력이다

★중요 '적용된, 응용된'이라는 뜻의 applied는 상상력이 실제로 발현되어 현실에 구체화된 것을 가리킴. 이는 정답 ②의 realization으로 표현할 수 있음.

[전문 해석]

(1)창의성은 상상력으로부터 한 단계 더 나아간 것이다. (2)상상력은 내적 의식의 전적으로 사적인 과정일 수 있다. (3)당신은 상상력의 흥분 속에서 당신의 침대 위에 움직임 없이 누워있을지도 모르고 어느 누구도 (그런 사실을) 알지 못할 것이다. (4)사적인 상상력들은 이 세상에서 전혀 어떤 결과도 가지고 있지 않을지도 모른다. (5)창의성은 그렇다(결과를 가진다). (6)창의적인 것은 무언가 하는 것을 수반한다. (7)어떤 것도 절대로 하지 않았던 사람을 창의적이라고 묘사하는 것은 이상할 것이다. (8)누군가를 창의적이라고 부르는 것은 그들이 의도적인 방식으로 어떤 것을 적극적으로 만들어 내고 있다는 것을 암시한다. (9)사람들은 추상적인 것에서는 창의적이지 않다. 그들은 어떤 것에서 창의적이다. (예를 들면) 수학에서, 공학에서, 글쓰기에서, 음악에서, 사업에서, 무엇에서든지. (10)창의성은 당신의 상상력을 작동시키는 것을 수반한다. (11)어떤 면에서, 창의성은 적용된 상상력이다.

[정답 확인]

다음 글의 주제로 가장 적절한 것은?

① the various meanings of imagination
상상력의 다양한 의미들
✔② creativity as the realization of imagination
상상력의 실현으로서의 창의성
③ factors which make imaginative people attractive
상상력이 풍부한 사람들을 매력적으로 만드는 요인들
④ the necessity of art education to enhance creativity
창의성을 기르기 위한 예술 교육의 필요성
⑤ effects of a creative attitude on academic achievement
학업 성취에 관한 창의적인 태도의 효과

[문제 풀이]

지문에 따르면 상상력은 오로지 개인적인 내적 영역에 머무르지만, 창의성은 현실 세계에서 구체적인 결과물을 낸다는 차이점이 있다. 즉 창의성은 상상력에서 그치지 않고 의도적인 방식으로 어떤 것을 적극적으로 만들어 내고 상상력을 작동시켜 결과물을 만들어 내는 것이다. 그러므로 답은 ②다.

[중요 어휘]

creativity	명사 창의성
further on	더 나아가서, 더 앞으로
imagination	명사 상상력
entirely	부사 전적으로, 오로지
internal	형용사 내적인, 내부의
consciousness	명사 의식, 자각
motionless	형용사 움직이지 않는
in a fever of	~의 흥분 속에서, 열광하여
outcome	명사 결과
involve	동사 수반하다, 포함하다
deliberate	형용사 의도적인
abstract	형용사 추상적인
applied	형용사 적용된, 응용의
realization	명사 실현

02 2021년 11월 23번 (정답률 85%) 정답 ③

[지문 끊어 읽기] 눈 깜빡임 속도의 의미

(1) Shutter speed refers to the speed of a camera shutter.
셔터 속도는 카메라 셔터의 속도를 지칭한다

(2) In behavior profiling, / it refers to the speed of the eyelid.
=shutter speed
행동 프로파일링에서는 / 그것은 눈꺼풀의 속도를 지칭한다

(3) When we blink, / we reveal more / than just blink rate.
우리가 눈을 깜빡일 때 / 우리는 더 많은 것을 드러낸다 / 단지 눈 깜빡임의 비율보다

(4) Changes in the speed of the eyelid /
눈꺼풀 속도의 변화는 /
can indicate important information; /
중요한 정보를 나타낼 수 있다 /
shutter speed is a measurement of fear. 정답 단서 눈꺼풀의 속도는 두려움의 척도임.
셔터 속도가 두려움의 척도이다

(5) Think of an animal / [that has a reputation for being fearful].
선행사 [ ]: 주격 관계대명사절
동물을 생각해 보라 / 겁이 많다는 평판이 있는

(6) A Chihuahua might come to mind.
치와와가 생각날지도 모른다

(7) In mammals, / because of evolution, / our eyelids will speed up /
포유동물의 경우 / 진화 때문에 / 우리의 눈꺼풀은 속도를 높일 것이다 /
to minimize the amount of time /
부사적 용법(목적) 선행사
시간의 양을 최소로 하기 위하여 /
[that we can't see an approaching predator].
[ ]: 관계부사절
우리가 다가오는 포식자를 볼 수 없는

문제편 p.062

힌트 'the 비교급 S V, the 비교급 S V' 구문으로 '더 ~할수록, 더 …하다'라는 뜻을 가짐. 이때 비교급 자리에는 형용사/부사의 비교급이 옴.

(8) The greater the degree of fear an animal is experiencing, /
동물이 경험하고 있는 두려움의 정도가 더 클수록 /
the more the animal is concerned with an approaching predator.
그 동물은 다가오는 포식자에 대해 더 걱정한다

(9) In an attempt to keep the eyes open / as much as possible, /
5형식V O O·C =가능한 한 많이
눈을 뜨고 있으려는 시도로 / 가능한 한 많이 /
the eyelids involuntarily speed up.
눈꺼풀은 무의식적으로 속도를 높인다

(10) Speed, / when it comes to behavior, /
속도는 / 행동에 관한 한 / =~에 관한 한
almost always equals fear. 정답 단서 행동에 있어 눈 깜빡임의 속도는 거의 두려움과 같음.
거의 항상 두려움과 같다

(11) In humans, / if we experience fear about something, /
인간의 경우 / 만약 우리가 무언가에 대한 두려움을 경험한다면 /
our eyelids will do the same thing as the Chihuahua;
우리의 눈꺼풀은 치와와와 똑같은 행동을 할 것이다

힌트 세미콜론(;)은 마침표 대신 사용할 수 있으며 세미콜론의 앞뒤 문장 또는 절이 서로 밀접한 연관이 있음을 보여 줌.

(12) they will close and open more quickly.
그것들은 더 빠르게 닫히고 열릴 것이다

[전문 해석]

(1)셔터 속도는 카메라 셔터의 속도를 지칭한다. (2)행동 프로파일링에서는 그것은 눈꺼풀의 속도를 지칭한다. (3)우리가 눈을 깜빡일 때 우리는 단지 눈 깜빡임의 비율보다 더 많은 것을 드러낸다. (4)눈꺼풀 속도의 변화는 중요한 정보를 나타내는데, 즉 셔터 속도가 두려움의 척도라는 것이다. (5)겁이 많다는 평판이 있는 동물을 생각해 보라. (6)치와와가 생각날지도 모른다. (7)포유동물의 경우 진화 때문에, 우리가 다가오는 포식자를 볼 수 없는 시간의 양을 최소로 하기 위하여 우리의 눈꺼풀은 속도를 높일 것이다. (8)동물이 경험하고 있는 두려움의 정도가 더 클수록 그 동물은 다가오는 포식자에 대해 더 걱정한다. (9)가능한 한 많이 눈을 뜨고 있으려는 시도로 눈꺼풀은 무의식적으로 속도를 높인다. (10)행동에 관한 한 속도는 거의 항상 두려움과 같다. (11)인간의 경우 만약 우리가 무언가에 대한 두려움을 경험한다면, 우리의 눈꺼풀은 치와와와 똑같은 행동을 할 것이다. (12)즉 그것들은 더 빠르게 닫히고 열릴 것이다.
- profiling(프로파일링): 어떤 개인의 심리적, 행동적 특성을 분석함으로써 특정 상황이나 영역에서의 행동을 예상하는 것

[정답 확인]

다음 글의 주제로 가장 적절한 것은?

① eye contact as a way to frighten others
다른 이들을 겁먹게 만들기 위한 방법으로서 눈맞춤
② fast blinking as a symptom of eye fatigue
눈 피로의 증상으로서 빠른 눈 깜빡임
✔ blink speed as a significant indicator of fear
두려움의 중요한 지표로서 눈 깜빡임 속도
④ fast eye movement as proof of predatory instinct
포식 본능의 증거로서 빠른 눈동자 움직임
⑤ blink rate as a difference between humans and animals
인간과 동물 사이의 차이로서 눈 깜빡임 속도

[중요 어휘]

□ **refer to**	~을 지칭하다[언급하다]
□ **eyelid**	명사 눈꺼풀
□ **blink**	동사 눈을 깜빡이다 / 명사 눈 깜빡임
□ **rate**	명사 비율, 속도, 요금 / 동사 평가하다
□ **indicate**	동사 나타내다, 가리키다
□ **measurement**	명사 척도, 측정, 치수
□ **reputation**	명사 평판, 명성
□ **fearful**	형용사 겁이 많은, 걱정하는, 무서운
□ **come to (one's) mind**	(~에게) 생각나다, 생각이 떠오르다
□ **approach**	동사 다가오다, 다가가다
□ **predator**	명사 포식자
□ **be concerned with**	~에 대해 걱정하다
□ **in an attempt to V**	~하려는 시도로
□ **involuntarily**	부사 무의식적으로, 자기도 모르게
□ **equal**	동사 ~와 같다[맞먹다] / 형용사 동일한, 평등한
□ **symptom**	명사 증상, 징후, 조짐
□ **fatigue**	명사 피로
□ **indicator**	명사 지표
□ **instinct**	명사 본능

03 2022년 9월 23번 (정답률 80%) 정답 ②

[지문 끊어 읽기] 학습에서 수면의 역할

(1) We have already seen / [that learning is much more efficient /
우리는 이미 보았다 / 학습이 훨씬 더 효율적이라는 것을 /
when done at regular intervals]:
규칙적인 간격으로 행해질 때 [ ]: 명사절(목적어)

힌트 접속사 'when'을 남긴 분사구문으로, 본래 부사절은 'when learning is done ~'의 형태임. 주절의 주어와 부사절의 주어가 같아 'learning'이 생략되었음. 또 분사구문에서는 'being'이 종종 생략되므로 밑줄 친 부분에서도 생략되어 'when done'만 남음.

(2) rather than cramming an entire lesson into one day, /
하루에 한 단원 전체를 벼락치기로 공부하는 것보다 /
we are better off spreading out the learning.
우리는 학습을 나누어 하는 편이 더 낫다

(3) The reason is simple:
이유는 간단하다

(4) every night, / our brain consolidates /
매일 밤 / 우리의 뇌는 통합 정리한다 /
what it has learned during the day. 주제문 매일 밤 뇌는 배운 내용을 통합 정리함.
선행사를 포함한 관계대명사
낮 동안에 배운 것을

(5) This is one of the most important neuroscience discoveries /
이것은 가장 중요한 신경 과학 발견 중 하나이다 /
of the last thirty years:
지난 30년간

(6) sleep is not just a period of inactivity /
병렬①
수면은 그저 무활동의 시간이 아니다 /
or a garbage collection of the waste products /
병렬② 선행사
혹은 쓸모가 없어진 결과물들의 쓰레기 수거의 시간이 아니다 /
that the brain accumulated while we were awake.
목적격 관계대명사
우리가 깨어있는 동안 뇌가 축적한

(7) Quite the contrary:
오히려 그 정반대다

(8) while we sleep, / our brain remains active; 정답 단서 자는 동안에도 뇌는 계속 활동하고 있음.
우리가 자는 동안 / 뇌는 계속 활동적인 채로 있다

(9) it runs a specific algorithm / that replays the important events /
선행사 주격 관계대명사 V'①
그것은 특정한 알고리즘을 작동시킨다 / 중요한 사건들을 재상영하는 /
it recorded during the previous day /
그것이 그 전날 동안 기록한 /
and gradually transfers them /
V'②
그리고 점진적으로 그것들을 이동시키는 /
into a more efficient compartment of our memory. 정답 단서 수면 중에도 학습에 영향을 미치는 뇌의 역할에 대해 구체적으로 설명함.
우리 기억의 더 효율적인 구획으로

[전문 해석]

(1)우리는 학습이 규칙적인 간격으로 행해질 때 훨씬 더 효율적이라는 것을 이미 보았다. (2)하루에 한 단원 전체를 벼락치기로 공부하는 것보다 우리는 학습을 나누어 하는 편이 더 낫다. (3)이유는 간단하다. (4)우리의 뇌는 매일 밤 낮 동안에 배운 것을 통합 정리한다. (5)이것은 지난 30년간 가장 중요한 신경 과학 발견 중 하나이다. (6)수면은 그저 무활동 혹은 우리가 깨어있는 동안 뇌가 축적한 쓸모가 없어진 결과물들의 쓰레기 수거의 시간이 아니다. (7)오히려 그 정반대다. (8)우리가 자는 동안 뇌는 계속 활동적인 채로 있다. (9)뇌는 그 전날 동안 기록한 중요한 사건들을 재상영하고 점진적으로 그것들을 우리 기억의 더 효율적인 구획으로 이동시키는 특정한 알고리즘을 작동시킨다.

[정답 확인]

다음 글의 주제로 가장 적절한 것은?

① how to get an adequate amount of sleep
적절한 양의 수면을 취하는 방법
② the role that sleep plays in the learning process (✔)
학습 과정 중 수면이 하는 역할
③ a new method of stimulating engagement in learning
학습 참여를 자극하는 새로운 방법
④ an effective way to keep your mind alert and active
정신을 기민하고 활동적으로 유지하는 효과적인 방법
⑤ the side effects of certain medications on brain function
뇌 기능에 대한 특정 약물의 부작용

[중요 어휘]

☐ **interval**	명사 간격, 사이
☐ **cram**	동사 벼락치기로 공부하다, 쑤셔 넣다
☐ **be better off**	(~하는 편이) 더 낫다
☐ **consolidate**	동사 통합 정리하다, 굳히다
☐ **inactivity**	명사 무활동, 정지
☐ **waste**	형용사 쓸모가 없어진 / 동사 낭비하다
☐ **accumulate**	동사 축적하다, 모으다
☐ **awake**	형용사 깨어 있는
☐ **compartment**	명사 구획, 칸, 객실
☐ **adequate**	형용사 적절한, 충분한
☐ **stimulate**	동사 자극하다, 흥분시키다
☐ **engagement**	명사 참여, 약속
☐ **alert**	형용사 기민한, 경계하는
☐ **medication**	명사 약물 (치료)

핵심 글의 전반부에서 오래 전 석기 시대에는 생명을 위협하는 상황이 곳곳에 도사리고 있어 인간의 뇌가 생존을 위해 이러한 위험을 인식하도록 진화했다는 내용이 제시됨. 글의 후반부에서는 더 이상 그렇게 위험하지는 않은 오늘날에도 약간의 스트레스를 받는 상황이 발생하면, 뇌는 그것을 생명을 위협하는 상황으로 인식한다는 내용을 설명함.

04 2019년 11월 23번 (정답률 75%) 정답 ③

[지문 끊어 읽기] 무해한 상황에 대한 뇌의 인지

(1) Our world today is comparatively harmless.
오늘날 우리의 세계는 비교적 무해하다

(2) We don't have to be careful every moment /
우리는 매 순간 주의할 필요가 없다 /
that a tiger is behind us.
호랑이가 우리의 뒤에 있는지

힌트 don't have to V =don't need to V =need not V'는 모두 '~할 필요가 없다'라는 의미임.

(3) We do not have to worry / about starving.
우리는 걱정할 필요가 없다 / 굶주림에 대해

(4) Our dangers today are, / for example, /
오늘날 우리의 위험은 ~이다 / 예를 들어 /
high blood pressure or diabetes.
고혈압이나 당뇨병

(5) To be clear, / we have a Stone Age brain /
정확히 하자면 / 우리는 석기 시대의 뇌를 가지고 있다 /
that lives in a modern world.
현대 세계에 사는

중요 우리가 살아가는 세계가 더 이상 우리의 생명에 위협적이지 않음에도 불구하고, 우리의 뇌는 여전히 위협이 아닌 것들을 위협으로 인식한다는 점에서, 필자는 우리의 뇌를 '석기 시대의 뇌'라고 비유적으로 표현함.

(6) Because of this, /
이 때문에 /
many situations are considered a threat / by our brains, /
많은 상황들은 위협으로 간주된다 / 우리의 뇌에 의해 /
although they are harmless / to our survival. 정답 단서
그것들이 무해함에도 불구하고 / 우리의 생존에

힌트 either A or B는 'A 또는 B (둘 중에 하나)'라고 해석함. 여기서는, fight 앞에 'had to'가 생략되었음.

(7) In the past, / danger meant / we either had to flee or fight.
과거에는 / 위험이 의미했다 / 우리가 도망치거나 싸워야만 한다는 것을

(8) If we have an appointment / but are stuck in a traffic jam, /
만약 우리가 약속이 있다면 / 그런데 교통 체증에 갇혀 있다면 /
that does not really threaten our lives.
그것이 실제로 우리의 생명을 위협하지는 않는다

(9) However, our brain considers this a danger.
5형식V O O·C
그러나 우리의 뇌는 이것을 위협으로 간주한다

(10) That is the point.
그것이 핵심이다

중요 문장 (11)에서 it은 '약속에 늦는 것', such는 위험 또는 위협을 가리킴. 즉, '약속에 늦는 것'이 위험하다고는 볼 수 없지만 우리의 뇌는 위험으로 인식한다는 의미임.

(11) There is no danger, / but our brain rates it / as such. 정답 단서
위험은 없다 / 하지만 우리의 뇌는 그것을 여긴다 / 그러한 것으로

(12) If we have an unpleasant conversation / with our partner, /
만약 우리가 불쾌한 대화를 나눈다면 / 우리의 파트너와 /
it does not threaten our lives, / and we do not have to flee or fight.
그것은 우리의 생명을 위협하지 않는다 / 그리고 우리는 도망치거나 싸울 필요가 없다

(13) The danger is an illusion.
그 위험은 착각이다

(14) Our Stone Age brain sees a mortal danger / that is not there.
우리의 석기 시대의 뇌는 치명적인 위험을 본다 / 존재하지 않는

[전문 해석]

(1)오늘날 우리의 세계는 비교적 무해하다. (2)우리는 호랑이가 우리의 뒤에 있는지 매 순간 주의할 필요가 없다. (3)우리는 굶주림에 대해 걱정할 필요가 없다. (4)예를 들어 오늘날 우리의 위험은 고혈압이나 당뇨병이다. (5)정확히 하자면 우리는 현대 세계에 사는 석기 시대의 뇌를 가지고 있다. (6)이 때문에 많은 상황들은 그것들이 우리의 생존에 무해함에도 불구하고 우리의 뇌에 의해 위협으로 간주된다. (7)과거에는 위험이 우리가 도망치거나 싸워야만 한다는 것을 의미했다. (8)만약 우리가 약속이 있는데 교통 체증에 갇혀 있다면 그것이 실제로 우리의 생명을 위협하지는 않는다. (9)그러나 우리의 뇌는 이것을 위험으로 간주한다. (10)그것이 핵심이다. (11)위험은 없지만 우리의 뇌는 그것을 그러한 것(위험)으로 여긴다. (12)만약 우리가 파트너와 불쾌한 대화를 나눈다면 그것은 우리의 생명을 위협하지 않으며 우리는 도망치거나 싸울 필요가 없다. (13)그 위험은 착각이다. (14)우리의 석기 시대의 뇌는 존재하지 않는 치명적인 위험을 본다.

[정답 확인]

다음 글의 주제로 가장 적절한 것은?

① the role of instinct in deciding to flee or fight
도망칠지 또는 싸울지 결정하는 데 있어 본능의 역할
② benefits of danger perception for humans' survival
인간의 생존을 위한 위험 인지의 이점
③ our perception of harmless situations as threatening (✔)
무해한 상황을 위협으로 (인식하는) 우리의 인지
④ the human brain's evolution for telling friend from foe
우리 편과 적을 구별하기 위한 인간 뇌의 진화
⑤ primitive people's ways of quickly dealing with dangers
위험에 빠르게 대처하는 원시인들의 방법

[중요 어휘]

☐ **comparatively**	부사 비교적(으로), 상대적(으로)
☐ **starving**	명사 굶주림, 기아
☐ **diabetes**	명사 당뇨병
☐ **to be clear**	정확히 하자면, 명백히 말하자면
☐ **flee**	동사 도망치다, 달아나다
☐ **appointment**	명사 (업무적인) 약속, (병원 등의) 예약
☐ **stuck**	형용사 갇힌, 꼼짝 못 하는
☐ **traffic jam**	명사 교통 체증
☐ **rate A (as) B**	A를 B로 여기다[평가하다]
☐ **illusion**	명사 착각, 오해
☐ **mortal**	형용사 치명적인, 죽음을 면할 수 없는

정답과 해설 06 주제 추론

문제편 p.063

05 2023년 3월 23번 (정답률 75%) 정답 ⑤

[지문 끊어 읽기] 과도한 과일 섭취가 뇌에 미치는 부정적 영향

(1) What consequences /
어떤 결과가 /
of eating too many grapes and other sweet fruit /
포도와 다른 단 과일을 너무 많이 먹는 것의 /
could there possibly be / for our brains?
과연 있을까 / 우리 뇌에

(2) A few large studies have helped / to shed some light.
S V O(명사적 용법)
몇 개의 대규모 연구들은 도왔다 / 어떤 새로운 사실을 밝혀내는 것을

(3) In one, /
한 연구에서 /
higher fruit intake in older, cognitively healthy adults /
S
나이가 더 많고 인지적으로 건강한 성인들의 더 높은 과일 섭취가 /
was linked with less volume in the hippocampus. 정답 단서
V
해마의 더 작은 크기와 연결되었다

(나이가 많고 인지적으로 건강한 어른들의 높은 과일 섭취는 해마의 작은 크기와 연결됨.)

★중요 해마는 대뇌의 양쪽 측두엽에 위치한 기관으로 기억과 관련됨. 해마나 대뇌 피질이 '작아진다'는 것은 기능이 일부 손상된다는 의미로 보면 됨. 따라서 예로 든 두 연구는 과도한 과일 섭취의 부정적인 영향을 보여줌.

(4) This finding was unusual, / since people who eat more fruit /
S', 선행사 주격 관계대명사절
그 연구 결과는 특이하다 / 왜냐하면 과일을 더 많이 먹는 사람들이 /
usually display the benefits / associated with a healthy diet.
V' O'
보통 이점을 보이기 때문이다 / 건강한 식단과 관련된

(5) In this study, / however, /
이 연구에서 / 그러나 /
the researchers isolated various components of the subjects' diets /
V①
연구자들은 피험자들의 식단의 다양한 구성 요소들을 분리했다 /
and found /
V②
그리고 발견했다 /
[that fruit didn't seem to be doing their memory centers any favors].
과일은 그들의 기억 중추에 어떤 도움도 주지 않는 것처럼 보인다는 것을 [ ]: O(접속사 that이 이끄는 명사절)

★중요 문장 (3)에서 제시된 연구에서 나이가 많고 인지적으로 건강한 성인의 높은 과일 섭취가 해마의 더 작은 크기와 연결된다고 함. 보통 과일을 더 많이 먹는 사람일수록 건강한 식단과 관련된 이점을 보인다고 알려져 있기 때문에 이 연구 결과는 특이하다고 문장 (4)에서 말함. 또한, 문장 (5)에서 연구자들이 피험자들의 식단을 분리해보니 과일이 기억 중추에 어떤 도움도 주지 않는 것처럼 보인다는 것을 발견함.

(6) Another study from the Mayo Clinic /
S
Mayo Clinic에서 한 또 다른 연구도 /
saw a similar inverse relationship /
V
비슷한 반대의 관계를 보였다 /
between fruit intake and volume of the cortex, /
과일 섭취와 대뇌 피질의 크기 사이의 /
the large outer layer of the brain.
뇌의 큰 바깥층인

★중요 문장 (6)에서 또 다른 연구에서도 과일 섭취와 대뇌 피질 크기 사이의 반대 관계를 보였음을 언급하고, 문장 (7)에서는 당이 높은 과일의 과도한 섭취가 신진대사와 인지 문제를 유발할 수 있다고 확인함.

(7) Researchers in the latter study noted /
후자의 연구에서 연구자들은 주목했다 /
that excessive consumption of high-sugar fruit /
S'
당이 높은 과일의 과도한 섭취가 /
(such as mangoes, bananas, and pineapples) /
(망고, 바나나, 파인애플과 같은) /
may cause metabolic and cognitive problems /
V'
신진대사 문제와 인지 문제를 유발할 수 있다는 것에 /
as much as processed carbs do. 정답 단서
가공된 탄수화물 식품이 그러한 만큼

(당이 높은 과일의 과다한 섭취는 인지 문제를 유발할 수 있음.)

힌트 일반동사를 대신하는 대동사 do는 이 문장에서 cause를 대신하여 쓰임. 대동사 do를 쓸 때에는 대신해주는 일반동사의 수나 시제에 일치하여 do/does/did로 씀.

[전문 해석]

(1)포도와 다른 단 과일을 너무 많이 먹는 것이 과연 우리 뇌에 어떤 결과를 미칠까? (2)몇 개의 대규모 연구들은 어떤 새로운 사실을 밝혀내는 것을 도왔다. (3)한 연구에서, 나이가 더 많고 인지적으로 건강한 성인들의 더 높은 과일 섭취가 해마의 더 작은 크기와 연결되었다. (4)그 연구 결과는 특이한데, 왜냐하면 과일을 더 많이 먹는 사람들이 보통 건강한 식단과 관련된 이점을 보이기 때문이다. (5)그러나 이 연구에서, 연구자들은 피험자들의 식단의 다양한 구성 요소들을 분리했고 과일은 그들의 기억 중추에 어떤 도움도 주지 않는 것처럼 보인다는 것을 발견했다. (6)Mayo Clinic에서 한 또 다른 연구도 과일 섭취와 뇌의 큰 바깥층인 대뇌 피질의 크기 사이의 비슷한 반대의 관계를 보였다. (7)후자의 연구에서 연구자들은 (망고, 바나나, 파인애플과 같은) 당이 높은 과일의 과도한 섭취가 가공된 탄수화물 식품이 그러한 만큼 신진대사 문제와 인지 문제를 유발할 수 있다는 것에 주목했다.

[정답 확인]

다음 글의 주제로 가장 적절한 것은?

① benefits of eating whole fruit on the brain health
과일을 통째로 먹는 것이 뇌 건강에 주는 이점
② universal preference for sweet fruit among children
아이들 사이에서 단 과일에 대한 보편적인 선호
③ types of brain exercises enhancing long-term memory
장기 기억을 향상하는 뇌 운동의 유형
④ nutritional differences between fruit and processed carbs
과일과 가공된 탄수화물 식품 사이의 영양적인 차이
✔⑤ negative effect of fruit overconsumption on the cognitive brain
과일의 과도한 섭취가 인지적인 뇌에 미치는 부정적 영향

[중요 어휘]

□ consequence	명사 결과
□ possibly	부사 과연, 아마, 혹시
□ shed	동사 밝히다, 비추다 (shed-shed-shed)
□ light	명사 (새로운) 사실[발견]
□ intake	명사 섭취, 흡입
□ cognitively	부사 인지적으로
□ link	동사 연결시키다, 관련되다 / 명사 연결, 관계
□ volume	명사 크기, 부피
□ finding	명사 (조사·연구 등의) 결과, 발견
□ isolate	동사 분리하다, 고립시키다
□ component	명사 구성 요소
□ memory center	기억 중추
□ favor	명사 도움, 호의, 부탁
□ inverse	형용사 반대의, 역의
□ cortex	명사 (대뇌) 피질
□ latter	형용사 후자의, 마지막의 / 명사 후자, 마지막 것
□ excessive	형용사 과도한
□ consumption	명사 섭취, 소비
□ metabolic	형용사 신진대사의
□ cognitive	형용사 인지의
□ processed	형용사 가공된

06 2018년 9월 22번 (정답률 70%) 정답 ③

[지문 끊어 읽기] 아이들의 스크린에 대한 경험

(1) Although we don't know /
비록 우리는 알지 못하지만 /
the full neurological effects of digital technologies on young children's development, /
디지털 기술들이 어린아이들의 발달에 미치는 모든 신경학적인 영향들을 /
we do know / that all screen time is not created equal.
우리는 분명히 알고 있다 / 모든 스크린 타임이 동등하게 만들어지지 않는다는 것을

(2) For example, /
예를 들어 /
reading an e-book, videoconferencing with grandma, /
전자책을 읽는 것, 할머니와 화상 통화를 하는 것은 /
or showing your child a picture you just took of them /
또는 당신이 방금 찍은 그들의 사진을 당신의 아이에게 보여주는 것은 /
is not the same as / the passive, television-watching screen time /
~와 같지 않다 / 수동적인 TV 시청 스크린 타임과 /
that concerns many parents and educators.
많은 부모들과 교육자들을 걱정시키는

(3) So, / rather than focusing /
그래서 / 초점을 맞추기보다 /
on *how much* children are interacting with screens, /
'얼마나' 아이들이 스크린과 상호작용을 하고 있는가에 /

parents and educators are turning their focus instead /
그 대신에 부모들과 교육자들은 그들의 초점을 돌리고 있다 /

to *what* children are interacting with /
아이들이 '무엇'과 상호작용을 하고 있는가로 /

and *who* is talking with them about their experiences. 주제문
그리고 그들의 경험들에 관하여 '누구'와 이야기하고 있는가로

(4) Though parents may be tempted /
부모들은 ~하고 싶을지도 모르지만 /

to hand a child a screen and walk away, /
아이에게 스크린을 건네주고 떠나 버리고 /

guiding children's media experiences /
아이들의 미디어 경험들을 안내해 주는 것은 /

helps them build important 21st Century skills, / 정답단서
그들이 21세기의 중요한 역량들을 기르는 데 도움을 준다 /

such as critical thinking and media literacy.
비판적 사고와 정보 해독력과 같은

[전문 해석]

(1)비록 우리는 디지털 기술들이 어린아이들의 발달에 미치는 모든 신경학적인 영향들을 알지 못하지만, 우리는 모든 스크린 타임이 동등하게 만들어지지 않는다는 것을 분명히 알고 있다. (2)예를 들어 전자책을 읽는 것, 할머니와 화상 통화를 하는 것, 또는 당신이 방금 찍은 그들(자녀)의 사진을 당신의 아이에게 보여주는 것은 많은 부모들과 교육자들을 걱정시키는, 수동적인 TV 시청 스크린 타임과 같지 않다. (3)그래서 부모들과 교육자들은 '얼마나' 아이들이 스크린과 상호작용을 하고 있는가에 초점을 맞추기보다, 그 대신에 아이들이 '무엇'과 상호작용을 하고 있는가 그리고 그들의 경험들에 관하여 '누구'와 이야기하고 있는가로 그들의 초점을 돌리고 있다. (4)부모들은 아이에게 스크린을 건네주고 떠나 버리고 싶을지도 모르지만, 아이들의 미디어 경험들을 안내해 주는 것은 그들이 비판적 사고와 정보 해독력과 같은 21세기의 중요한 역량들을 기르는 데 도움을 준다.

- media literacy(정보 해독력): 미디어 접근, 내용 분석, 메시지 평가, 자기표현 및 대화로서의 미디어 창출 능력에 관한 것으로, 교육에서는 미디어의 영향을 이해하고 비판적으로 받아들이며 창조하는 능력을 기르는 것을 목표로 한다. 현대 정보사회에서 미디어 교육은 글을 읽고 쓰는 것을 가르치는 것과 마찬가지로 교과과정의 하나로 포함되어 있다.

[정답 확인]

다음 글의 주제로 가장 적절한 것은?

① the predictors of children's screen media addiction
아이들의 스크린 미디어 중독 예측 변수

② reasons for children's preference for screen media
스크린 미디어에 대한 아이들의 선호 이유

✔ importance of what experiences kids have with screens
아이들이 스크린과 어떤 경험을 가지고 있는가의 중요성

④ effects of the amount of screen time on kids' social skills
스크린 타임의 양이 아이들의 사회성 기술(사교 능력)에 미치는 영향

⑤ necessity of parental control on children's physical activities
아이들의 신체 활동에 있어서 부모의 통제의 필요성

★중요 지문에 스크린 미디어에 관한 내용들이 담겨 있지만, 아이들이 스크린 미디어에 중독된 이유에 대해서는 설명하지 않음.

★중요 지문에서 부모의 통제가 필요하다고 하는 부분은 아이들의 신체 활동이 아니라 아이들의 미디어 경험에 있어서 필요하다고 말한 것임. 문장 (4)를 보면 바로 알 수 있음.

[중요 어휘]

☐ **neurological**	형용사	신경학적인, 신경학상의
☐ **passive**	형용사	수동적인, 간접적인
☐ **interact with**		~와 상호작용하다
☐ **critical thinking**	명사	비판적 사고
☐ **predictor**	명사	예측 변수, 요인
☐ **addiction**	명사	중독
☐ **preference**	명사	선호, 애호
☐ **parental**	형용사	부모의, 아버지[어머니]의

07 2022년 6월 23번 (정답률 70%)

정답 ②

[지문 끊어 읽기] 예측 불가능성

(1) In the movie *Groundhog Day*, /
영화 *Groundhog Day*에서 /

a weatherman played by Bill Murray /
(과거분사구)
Bill Murray가 연기한 기상 캐스터는 /

문제편 p.064

힌트 5형식 구문 'force A to V(A를 ~하도록 하다/강요하다)'의 수동태 형태인 A be forced to V는 보통 'A가 ~해야 한다, A가 ~하도록 강요당하다'라고 해석함. 여기서 A는 'a weatherman'임.

is forced to re-live a single day / over and over again.
하루를 다시 살아야 한다 / 반복해서

(2) [Confronted with this seemingly endless loop], /
[ ]: 분사구문(Being 생략)
끝이 없어 보이는 이 고리에 직면하여 /

he eventually rebels / against living through the same day /
그는 결국 저항한다 / 같은 날을 겪는 것에 /

the same way twice.
같은 방식으로 두 번

(3) He learns French, / becomes a great pianist, /
V① V②
그는 프랑스어를 배운다 / 위대한 피아노 연주자가 된다 /

befriends his neighbors, / helps the poor.
V③ V④
그의 이웃들과 친구가 된다 / 가난한 사람들을 도와준다

힌트 'the+형용사'는 복수 보통 명사의 역할을 할 수 있음. 따라서 본문의 'the poor'는 '가난한 사람들'로 해석됨.

(4) Why do we cheer him on?
우리는 왜 그를 응원하는가

(5) Because we don't want perfect predictability, /
우리는 완벽한 예측 가능성은 원하지 않기 때문이다 /

even if what's on repeat is appealing. 주제문
S'(명사절) V' S·C'
반복되는 것이 매력적일지라도

반복되는 것이 매력적일지라도, 우리는 완벽한 예측 가능성은 원하지 않는다고 함. 즉, 우리는 예측 불가능성에 더 이끌린다고 할 수 있음.

(6) Surprise engages us.
놀라움은 우리를 끌어들인다

(7) It allows us to escape autopilot.
5형식V O O·C
그것은 우리를 자동 조종 장치에서 벗어나게 한다

(8) It keeps us awake to our experience.
5형식V O O·C
그것은 우리가 우리의 경험을 계속 인식하게 한다

(9) In fact, / the neurotransmitter systems involved in reward /
S 주격 관계대명사+be동사(which are) 생략
실제로 / 보상과 관련된 신경 전달 물질 체계는 /

are tied to the level of surprise:
V
놀라움의 수준과 관련이 있다

(10) rewards delivered at regular, predictable times /
S
규칙적이고 예측 가능한 때에 전달되는 보상은 /

yield a lot less activity in the brain / than the same rewards /
V
뇌에서 훨씬 적은 활동을 산출한다 / 동일한 보상보다 /

delivered at random unpredictable times. 정답단서
무작위의 예측 불가능한 때에 전달되는

무작위로 예측 불가능한 때에 전달되는 보상이 뇌에서 보다 많은 활동을 산출한다고 함.

(11) Surprise gratifies. 정답단서
1형식V
놀라움은 만족감을 준다

예측 불가능성으로부터 야기되는 놀라움은 우리에게 만족감을 준다고 함.

[전문 해석]

(1)영화 *Groundhog Day*에서, Bill Murray가 연기한 기상 캐스터는 하루를 반복해서 다시 살아야 한다. (2)끝이 없어 보이는 이 고리에 직면하여, 그는 결국 같은 날을 같은 방식으로 두 번 사는 것에 저항한다. (3)그는 프랑스어를 배우고, 위대한 피아노 연주자가 되고, 이웃들과 친구가 되고, 가난한 사람들을 도와준다. (4)우리는 왜 그를 응원하는가? (5)왜냐하면 반복되는 것이 매력적일지라도, 우리가 완벽한 예측 가능성은 원하지 않기 때문이다. (6)놀라움은 우리를 끌어들인다. (7)그것은 우리를 자동 조종 장치에서 벗어나게 한다. (8)그것은 우리가 우리의 경험을 계속 인식하게 한다. (9)실제로, 보상과 관련된 신경 전달 물질 체계는 놀라움의 수준과 관련이 있다. (10)규칙적이고, 예측 가능한 때에 전달되는 보상은 무작위의 예측 불가능한 때에 전달되는 동일한 보상보다 뇌에서 훨씬 적은 활동을 산출한다. (11)놀라움은 만족감을 준다.

[정답 확인]

다음 글의 주제로 가장 적절한 것은?

① considerations in learning foreign languages
외국어 학습에서의 고려 사항

✔ people's inclination towards unpredictability
예측 불가능성에 대한 사람들의 성향

문제편 p.064

③ hidden devices to make a movie plot unexpected
영화 줄거리를 예상치 못하게 만드는 숨겨진 장치
④ positive effects of routine on human brain function
루틴이 인간의 뇌 기능에 미치는 긍정적인 영향
⑤ danger of predicting the future based on the present
현재를 바탕으로 미래를 예측하는 것의 위험성

[문제 풀이]

이 지문은 예측 불가능성을 선호하는 우리의 성향에 대한 글이다. 문장 (1)~(5)에서 반복되는 하루지만 처음과는 다른 방식으로 살아가는 인물을 우리가 응원하게 되는 이유는 바로 '예측 불가능성' 때문이라고 한다. 이어지는 문장 (6)~(11)에서 우리가 예측 불가능성으로 인한 놀라움을 매력적으로 느낀다고 하는데, 이에 대한 근거로 무작위의 예측 불가능한 때에 전달되는 보상이 뇌에서 보다 많은 활동을 산출한다는 것을 제시한다. 따라서 정답은 ②이다.

[중요 어휘]

□ confront	동사 직면하다, 닥치다, 맞서다
□ endless	형용사 끝이 없는, 무한한
□ loop	명사 고리
□ rebel	동사 저항하다, 반란을 일으키다 / 명사 저항 세력
□ live through	~을 겪다
□ befriend	동사 ~와 친구가 되다
□ cheer on	~을 응원하다
□ predictability	명사 예측 가능성
□ engage	동사 끌어들이다, 사로잡다, 고용하다
□ escape	동사 ~을 벗어나다, 도망가다
□ awake to	~을 인식하다[알아차리다]
□ be involved in	~에 관련된
□ tie	동사 관련시키다, 구속하다, 묶다 / 명사 구속, 유대
□ yield	동사 산출하다 / 명사 산출량(수확량), 총수익
□ gratify	동사 만족감을 주다, 충족시키다
□ inclination	명사 성향, ~하는 경향

08 2023년 9월 23번 (정답률 70%) 정답 ⑤

[지문 끊어 읽기] 요리 감소의 긍정적 결과

(1) If cooking is as central to human identity, biology, and culture /
요리가 인간 정체성, 생물학, 그리고 문화에 중요하다면 /
as the biological anthropologist Richard Wrangham suggests, /
생물인류학자 Richard Wrangham이 말하는 것만큼 /
it stands [to reason /
형식상의 주어 [ ]: 내용상의 주어
당연하다 /
힌트 'it stands to reason (that) S V'는 '~은 당연하다, ~은 당연한 이치이다'라는 뜻으로, that은 생략이 가능함.
[that the decline of cooking in our time /
[ ]: 명사절(reason의 목적어)
우리 시대에서의 요리 감소가 /
would have serious consequences / for modern life]], /
심각한 결과를 초래할 것이다 / 현대 생활에 /
and so it has.
=has had serious consequences
그리고 실제로 그래왔다

(2) Are they all bad?
그것들이 모두 나쁜가

(3) Not at all.
전혀 그렇지 않다

(4) The outsourcing of much of the work of cooking to corporations /
요리하는 일의 많은 부분을 기업에게 아웃소싱하는 것은 /
has relieved women /
여성들을 해방시켰다 /
of what has traditionally been their exclusive responsibility /
=the thing which
전통적으로 그들의 한정된 책임이었던 것에서 /
for feeding the family, /
가족들을 먹이는 /
[making it easier /
형식상의 목적어
더 쉽게 했다 /
정답 단서 아웃소싱을 통해 요리할 책임에서 해방시키는 것은 여성들에게 경제적 활동을 할 수 있는 기회를 줌.
for them [to work outside the home and have careers]]. [ ]: 분사구문(making ~ careers)
의미상의 주어 병렬① [ ]: 내용상의 목적어 병렬②(to 생략)
그들이 집 밖에서 일하고 직업을 가지는 것을

(5) It has headed off many of the domestic conflicts /
그것은 많은 가정 내 갈등을 막아냈다 /
[that such a large shift in gender roles and family dynamics /
성 역할과 가족 역학에서의 그렇게 큰 변화가 /
was bound to spark]. [ ]: 목적격 관계대명사절
틀림없이 촉발하였을

(6) It has relieved other pressures in the household, /
병렬①
그것은 가정의 다른 고난을 덜어 주었다 /
including longer workdays and overscheduled children, /
~을 포함하여(전치사)
더 긴 근무일과 바쁜 자녀들을 포함하여 /
and saved us time /
병렬② 선행사
그리고 시간을 절약해 주었다 /
힌트 이 that은 관계부사 when을 대신하여 사용되었으며 선행사 time을 수식함.
that we can now invest in other pursuits. 정답 단서 아웃소싱은 사람들이 다양한 일에 시간을 투자할 수 있도록 만들어 줌.
이제 우리가 다른 일에 투자할 수 있는

(7) It has also allowed us to diversify our diets substantially, /
그것은 또한 우리가 자신의 식단을 상당히 다양화하도록 해 주었다 /
making it possible /
형식상의 목적어
가능하게 만들었다 /
even for people with no cooking skills and little money /
to부정사의 의미상의 주어
요리 기술이 없고 돈이 거의 없는 사람들조차 /
to enjoy a whole different cuisine. 정답 단서 아웃소싱은 기술적, 경제적 한계에 상관없이 모든 사람들이 다양한 요리를 즐길 수 있도록 함.
내용상의 목적어
완전히 색다른 요리를 즐기는 것을

(8) All that's required / is a microwave.
필요한 것은 / 전자레인지뿐이다

[전문 해석]

(1)생물인류학자 Richard Wrangham이 말하는 것만큼 요리가 인간 정체성, 생물학, 그리고 문화에 중요하다면, 우리 시대에서의 요리 감소가 현대 생활에 심각한 결과를 초래할 것임은 당연하고, 실제로 그래왔다. (2)그것들이 모두 나쁜가? (3)전혀 그렇지 않다. (4)요리하는 일의 많은 부분을 기업에게 아웃소싱하는 것은 전통적으로 여성들의 한정된, 가족들을 먹이는 책임이었던 것에서 여성들을 해방시켰으며 그들이 집 밖에서 일하고 직업을 가지는 것을 더 쉽게 했다. (5)그것은 성 역할과 가족 역학에서의 그렇게 큰 변화가 틀림없이 촉발하였을 많은 가정 내 갈등을 막아냈다. (6)그것은 더 긴 근무일과 바쁜 자녀들을 포함하여 가정의 다른 고난을 덜어 주었으며, 이제 우리가 다른 일에 투자할 수 있는 시간을 절약해 주었다. (7)그것은 또한 우리가 자신의 식단을 상당히 다양화하도록 해 주었으며, 요리 기술이 없고 돈이 거의 없는 사람들조차 완전히 색다른 요리를 즐기는 것을 가능하게 만들었다. (8)필요한 것은 전자레인지뿐이다.

- outsourcing(아웃소싱): 기업이나 기관이 비용 절감과 효율 극대화를 목적으로 기업 업무의 일부를 외부에 위탁하여 처리하는 방식

[정답 확인]

다음 글의 주제로 가장 적절한 것은?

① current trends in commercial cooking equipment
상업용 요리 도구에서의 현재 경향
② environmental impacts of shifts in dietary patterns
식사 양식 변화의 환경적인 영향
③ cost-effective ways to cook healthy meals at home
집에서 건강한 식사를 요리하기 위한 비용 효율적인 방법
④ reasons behind the decline of the food service industry
음식 서비스 산업 쇠퇴 이면의 이유
⑤ benefits of reduced domestic cooking duties through outsourcing
아웃소싱을 통해 줄어든 가정의 요리 의무에서의 혜택

[문제 풀이]

문장 (1)은 생물인류학자 Richard Wrangham의 주장을 필두로 사회의 통념을 언급하고, 문장 (2)를 통해 주제를 환기하면서 문장 (3)에서부터 화자가 말하고자 하는 바를 드러낸다. 문장 (4)~(7)은 요리를 해야 하는 책임을 기업에게 아웃소싱하면서 발생하는 긍정적인 영향에 대해서 언급하는데, 그에 대한 예시로 시간 절약, 여성에게 주어진 경제적 자립 기회, 그리고 다양한 요리를 경험할 수 있는 기회를 들어 자신의 주장을 뒷받침한다. 따라서, 이 모든 내용을 함축하는 ⑤가 정답이다.

[중요 어휘]

□ **anthropologist**	명사 인류학자
□ **consequence**	명사 결과, 중요함
□ **relieve**	동사 해방시키다, 덜어 주다
□ **exclusive**	형용사 한정된, 독점적인, 배타적인
□ **head off**	~을 막다[저지하다], ~을 회피하다
□ **dynamics**	명사 역학, 역학 관계, 원동력
□ **be bound to V**	틀림없이[반드시] ~하다
□ **pressure**	명사 고난, 곤란, 압박, 압력
□ **pursuit**	명사 (시간과 에너지를 들여 하는) 일, 활동, 추구
□ **diversify**	동사 다양[다각]화하다, 다양해지다
□ **substantially**	부사 상당히, 많이, 주로, 대체로
□ **cuisine**	명사 요리

핵심 제국의 문화적 특징은 제국의 시각이 가진 특징과 일맥상통하기 때문에 배타적이기보다는 다른 문화를 적극 받아들여 혼성 문명을 만들어낸다는 것을 로마와 미국을 예로 들어 설명하는 글임.

09 2016년 9월 23번 (정답률 60%) 정답 ⑤

[지문 끊어 읽기] 제국 문명의 통합적 특징

(1) The cultural ideas spread by empire /
제국에 의해 퍼뜨려진 문화적 개념들은 /
were seldom the exclusive creation of the ruling elite.
거의 지배 계층의 독점적인 창조물이 아니었다

(2) Since the imperial vision tends to be universal and inclusive, /
제국의 시각은 보편적이고 포괄적인 경향이 있기 때문에 /
it was relatively easy for imperial elites /
제국의 지배 계층에게 상대적으로 쉬웠다 /
to adopt ideas, norms, and traditions /
개념, 규범, 전통을 채택하는 것은 /
from wherever they found them, /
그들이 그것들을 발견한 곳이 어디든 그곳에서 /
rather than to stick to a single rigid tradition. 주제문
하나의 엄격한 전통을 고수하는 것보다

(3) While some emperors sought / to purify their cultures /
일부 황제들이 노력했지만 / 자신들의 문화를 정화하려고 /
and return / to what they viewed as their roots, /
그리고 돌아가려고 / 그들이 자신들의 뿌리라고 여겼던 것으로 /
for the most part / empires have produced hybrid civilizations /
대부분 / 제국들은 혼성 문명을 만들어냈다 /
that absorbed much from their subject peoples. 정답 단서
자신들의 피지배 민족들로부터 많은 것을 흡수한

(4) The imperial culture of Rome was Greek /
로마의 제국 문화는 그리스식이었다 /
almost as much as Roman.
거의 로마식 못지않게

(5) Imperial Mongol culture was a Chinese copycat.
몽고 제국의 문화는 중국의 복사판이었다

(6) In the imperial United States, /
미국 제국에서 /
an American president of Kenyan blood / can eat Italian pizza /
케냐 혈통의 미국 대통령은 / 이탈리아 피자를 먹을 수 있다 /
while watching his favorite film, *Lawrence of Arabia*, /
자신이 좋아하는 영화인 〈Lawrence of Arabia〉를 보며 /
a British epic / about the Arab rebellion against the Turks.
영국의 장편 서사 / 튀르크족에 대항하는 아랍의 저항에 관한

[전문 해석]

(1)제국에 의해 퍼뜨려진 문화적 개념들은 거의 지배 계층의 독점적인 창조물이 아니었다. (2)제국의 시각은 보편적이고 포괄적인 경향이 있기 때문에, 그들(제국의 지배 계층)이 그것들(개념, 규범, 전통)을 발견한 곳이 어디든 그곳에서 개념, 규범, 전통을 채택하는 것은 (제국의 지배 계층에게) 하나의 엄격한 전통을 고수하는 것보다 상대적으로 쉬웠다. (3)일부 황제들이 자신들의 문화를 정화하고 자신들의 뿌리라고 여겼던 것으로 돌아가려고 노력했지만 대부분 제국들은 자신들의 피지배 민족들로부터 많은 것을 흡수한 혼성 문명을 만들어냈다. (4)로마의 제국 문화는 거의 로마식 못지않게 그리스식이었다. (5)몽고 제국의 문화는 중국 (문화)의 복사판이었다. (6)(현재 제국과 같이 강대국인) 미국 제국에서 케냐 혈통의 미국 대통령(Barack Obama를 칭함)은 자신이 좋아하는, 튀르크족에 대항하는 아랍의 저항에 관한 영국의 장편 서사 영화인 〈Lawrence of Arabia(아라비아의 로렌스)〉를 보며 이탈리아 피자를 먹을 수 있다.

- 〈Lawrence of Arabia(아라비아의 로렌스)〉: 1962년 개봉한 영화로 1차 세계대전 기간 동안 아랍 민족의 독립에 적극 참여했던 영국군 장교 T.E. 로렌스의 실화를 바탕으로 한 영화이다.

[정답 확인]

다음 글의 주제로 가장 적절한 것은?

① reasons for the collapse of great empires
위대한 제국이 몰락한 이유
② severe moral corruption of imperial elites
제국 지배계층의 극심한 도덕적 부패
③ distinct differences among ancient empires
고대 제국들 간의 뚜렷한 차이점
④ impacts of ancient Rome on Western culture
서구 문화에 고대 로마가 끼친 영향
⑤ integrative characteristics of empire civilizations
제국 문명의 통합적인 특징들

중요 문장 (2)의 universal and inclusive, 문장 (3)의 absorbed, 문장 (5)의 copycat 등에서 정답의 integrative의 의미를 찾아볼 수 있음.

[중요 어휘]

□ **seldom**	부사 거의 ~ 아닌
□ **exclusive**	형용사 독점적인
□ **imperial**	형용사 제국의, 제국적인
□ **inclusive**	형용사 포괄적인, 폭넓은
□ **rigid**	형용사 엄격한, 융통성 없는
□ **emperor**	명사 황제
□ **subject**	형용사 지배를 받는, 종속된 / 명사 주제, 과목
□ **epic**	명사 장편 서사 (영화), 서사시
□ **rebellion**	명사 저항, 반란
□ **collapse**	명사 몰락, 붕괴
□ **integrative**	형용사 통합적인, 통합하는

10 2022년 11월 23번 (정답률 60%) 정답 ②

[지문 끊어 읽기] 전쟁에서 활용되는 소리와 동작

(1) Native Americans often sang and danced /
북미 원주민들은 종종 노래를 불렀고 춤을 췄다 /
in preparation for launching an attack.
공격을 개시하기 위한 준비로

(2) The emotional and neurochemical excitement /
(선행사)
감정적이고 신경 화학적인 흥분 상태가 /
[that resulted from this preparatory singing] /
[ ]: 주격 관계대명사절
이러한 준비의 노래에서 야기된 /
gave them stamina / to carry out their attacks.
(형용사적 용법)
힘을 그들에게 제공했다 / 그들의 공격을 수행하기 위한

힌트 'result from'은 '~에서 야기되다, 기인하다'라는 뜻으로 'from' 이후에 원인이 나옴. 반대의 상황을 나타내는 '~의 결과가 되다'라는 뜻의 'result in'은 'in' 이후에 결과가 나오므로 유의할 것.

(3) What may have begun as an unconscious, uncontrolled act /
무의식적이고 억제되지 않는 행동으로서 시작했을지도 모르는 것 /
— rushing their victims /
그들의 희생자를 공격하는 것은 /
with singing and beating drums in a frenzy — /
격분하여 노래를 부르고 북을 치는 것으로 /
could have become a strategy / 정답 단서 노래를 부르고 북을 치는 것이 전쟁터에서 전략이 되었을지도 모름.
전략이 되었을 수도 있다 /

힌트 '조동사(may, could)+have p.p.'는 과거 사실에 대한 추측을 나타내고 조동사의 의미를 살려서, 'may[could]+have p.p.'는 '~했을지도 모른다'로 해석됨.

as the victors saw firsthand / the effect [their actions had /
선행사
승리자들이 직접 목격하면서 / 자신들의 행동이 미치는 영향을 /
on those they were attacking]. [ ]: 목적격 관계대명사절(목적격 관계대명사 생략)
선행사 목적격 관계대명사 생략
그들이 공격하고 있는 사람들에게

(4) Although war dances risk warning an enemy /
비록 전쟁의 춤이 적에게 경고하는 위험을 감수하는 것임에도 불구하고 /
of an upcoming attack, /
곧 있을 공격을 /
the arousal and synchronizing benefits for the attackers /
공격자들에게 주는 자극과 동시에 움직이게 하는 이점이 /
may compensate for the loss of surprise. 정답 단서 전쟁 중 추는 춤이 주는 이점을 설명함.
기습의 상실을 보상해 줄 수 있다

(5) Humans who sang, danced, and marched /
S(선행사) 주격 관계대명사
노래하고, 춤추고, 행진했던 사람들은 /
may have enjoyed a strong advantage on the battlefield / 정답 단서 노래, 춤, 행진이 전쟁터에서 큰 역할을 함.
병렬①
전쟁터에서 강한 우세를 누렸을지도 모른다 /
as well as intimidated enemies /
병렬②(may have 생략) 선행사
적들을 겁먹게 했을 뿐만 아니라 /
who witnessed such a spectacle.
주격 관계대명사
그러한 장관을 목격한

(6) Nineteenth-and twentieth-century Germans feared no one /
19세기와 20세기의 독일인들은 두려워한 사람이 아무도 없었다 /
more than the Scots /
스코틀랜드인들보다 /
— the bagpipes and drums were disturbing /
백파이프와 북이 교란시켰다 /
in their sheer loudness and visual spectacle.
순전한 시끄러움과 시각적인 장관으로

힌트 해석에 다소 어려움이 있을 수 있으나, 'feared no one'을 먼저 해석하고 그 후에 'more than the Scots'를 해석하면 됨. '두려워한 사람이 없었다 / 스코틀랜드인들보다'는 결국 '스코틀랜드인들보다 두려워한 사람은 아무도 없었다, 즉 스코틀랜드인들을 가장 두려워했다'라는 최상의 의미로 해석할 수 있음.

[전문 해석]

(1)북미 원주민들은 공격을 개시하기 위한 준비로 종종 노래를 불렀고 춤을 췄다. (2)이러한 준비의 노래에서 야기된 감정적이고 신경 화학적인 흥분 상태가 그들의 공격을 수행하기 위한 힘을 그들에게 제공했다. (3)무의식적이고 억제되지 않는 행동으로서 시작했을지도 모르는 것, 즉 격분하여 노래를 부르고 북을 치는 것으로 그들의 희생자를 공격하는 것은 승리자들이 그들이 공격하고 있는 사람들에게 자신들의 행동이 미치는 영향을 직접 목격하면서 전략이 되었을 수도 있다. (4)비록 전쟁의 춤이 적에게 곧 있을 공격을 경고하는 위험을 감수하는 것임에도 불구하고, 공격자들에게 주는 자극과 동시에 움직이게 하는 이점이 기습의 상실을 보상해 줄 수 있다. (5)노래하고, 춤추고, 행진했던 사람들은 그러한 장관을 목격한 적들을 겁먹게 했을 뿐만 아니라 전쟁터에서 강한 우세를 누렸을지도 모른다. (6)19세기와 20세기의 독일인들은 스코틀랜드인들을 가장 두려워했는데, 백파이프와 북이 순전한 시끄러움과 시각적인 장관으로 교란시켰다.

[정답 확인]

다음 글의 주제로 가장 적절한 것은?

① cultural differences in honoring war victims
전쟁 희생자를 기리는 것의 문화적 차이
✔② benefits of utilizing sound and motion in warfare
전쟁에서 소리와 동작을 활용하는 것의 이점
③ functions of music in preventing or resolving conflicts
갈등을 예방하거나 해결하는 데 있어 음악의 기능
④ strategies of analyzing an enemy's vulnerable points in war
전쟁에서 적의 취약점을 분석하는 전략
⑤ effects of religious dances on lowering anxiety on the battlefield
전쟁터에서 불안을 낮추는 종교적인 춤의 영향

[문제 풀이]

지문은 전쟁터에서 노래와 춤, 북 소리 등이 가진 영향에 대해 설명한다. 처음에는 큰 의미 없이 그런 행동을 취했을지 모르나, 전쟁 진행 중 이러한 행동은 상대가 겁을 먹게 하고 공격하는 이들의 정서적 자극(사기 증진)을 주었기 때문에 효과적이었다. 전쟁에서 노래나 악기와 같은 소리, 무용이나 행진 등의 동작은 곧 효과적인 전술 전략이 되었다는 내용이 반복적으로 지문 안에서 제시되고 있다. 따라서 이 글의 주제는 ②이다.

[중요 어휘]

□ **preparation**	명사 준비, 대비
□ **launch**	동사 개시하다, 시작하다
□ **preparatory**	형용사 준비의, 준비를 위한
□ **stamina**	명사 힘, 체력
□ **carry out**	수행하다
□ **unconscious**	형용사 무의식적인
□ **rush**	동사 공격하다, 덤벼들다, 서두르다
□ **victim**	명사 희생자, 피해자
□ **frenzy**	명사 격분, 광란
□ **strategy**	명사 전략, 전술
□ **firsthand**	부사 직접, 바로
□ **upcoming**	형용사 곧 있을, 다가오는
□ **arousal**	명사 자극
□ **synchronize**	동사 동시에 움직이게 하다
□ **compensate for**	~을 보상해 주다
□ **march**	동사 행진하다 / 명사 행진
□ **intimidate**	동사 겁먹게 하다, 위협하다
□ **spectacle**	명사 장관, 구경거리
□ **sheer**	형용사 순전한, 순수한
□ **honor**	동사 기리다 / 명사 명예
□ **utilize**	동사 활용하다
□ **warfare**	명사 전쟁, 전투
□ **vulnerable**	형용사 취약한, 상처받기 쉬운

핵심 주제문이 첫 문장에 드러나 있고, 주제를 부연 설명하기 위한 특별한 예시가 추가되어 있는 전형적인 두괄식 지문임.

11 2021년 3월 23번 (정답률 55%) 정답 ④

[지문 끊어 읽기] 전근대적 시대의 창의성의 원천

(1) Before the modern scientific era, / creativity was attributed /
근대의 과학적인 시대 이전에 / 창의성은 기인한 것으로 여겨졌다 /
to a superhuman force; / all novel ideas originated /
초인적인 힘에 / 모든 새로운 생각은 유래했다 /
with the gods. 정답 단서
신에게서

힌트 'A be attributed to B'는 'attribute A to B: A의 원인을 B로 돌리다'의 수동태 문장으로, 'A가 B에 기인한 것으로 여겨지다'로 해석될 수 있음.

(2) After all, / how could a person create /
결국 / 어떻게 인간이 만들 수 있었겠는가 /
something that did not exist / before the divine act of creation?
주격 관계대명사절
존재하지 않았던 것을 / 신의 창조 행위 이전에

(3) In fact, / the Latin meaning of the verb "inspire" /
사실 / '영감을 주다'라는 동사의 라틴어 의미는 /
is "to breathe into," / [reflecting the belief /
[ ]: 분사구문
'숨결을 불어넣다'이다 / 믿음을 반영한다 /
that creative inspiration was similar / to the moment in creation / 정답 단서
접속사(=the belief, 동격)
창의적 영감은 비슷했다는 / 창조의 순간과 /
when God first breathed life / into man].
신이 처음에 생명을 불어 넣었을 때 / 인간에게

(4) Plato argued / that the poet was possessed /
플라톤은 주장했다 / 시인은 사로잡혔다고 /
by divine inspiration, / and Plotin wrote /
신이 내린 영감에 / 그리고 플로티노스는 썼다 /
that art could only be beautiful / if it descended from God.
예술은 아름다울 수 있다고 / 그것이 신으로부터 내려온 경우에만

(5) The artist's job / was not to imitate nature /
예술가의 일은 / 자연을 모방하는 것이 아니라 /
but rather to reveal /
오히려 드러내는 것이었다 /
the sacred and transcendent qualities of nature.
자연의 신성하고 초월적인 특성을

힌트 'not A but B(A가 아니라 B)'의 상관접속사의 형태로 사용되고 있음. 둘 다 뒤에 to부정사가 쓰인 것에 유의해야 함.

(6) Art could only be a pale imitation / of the perfection /
예술은 어설프게 흉내 낸 것에 불과한 것일 수 있다 / 완벽함을 /
of the world of ideas.
관념 세계의

(7) Greek artists did not blindly imitate / what they saw in reality;
그리스의 예술가들은 맹목적으로 모방하지 않았다 / 그들이 현실에서 본 것을

힌트 관계대명사인 what이 이끄는 명사절로, what은 선행사를 내포하고 있으므로 '~하는(한) 것'이라고 해석이 되며, what이 이끄는 명사절 전체가 imitate의 목적어로 쓰임.

(8) instead they tried to represent /
그 대신 그들은 나타내려고 애썼다 /
the pure, true forms / underlying reality, /
순수하고 진정한 형태를 / 현실의 기저를 이루는 /
[resulting in a sort of compromise /
[ ]: 분사구문
그 결과 일종의 타협을 야기했다 /
between abstraction and accuracy].
추상과 정확성 간에

[전문 해석]

(1)근대의 과학적인 시대 이전에 창의성은 초인적인 힘에 기인한 것으로 여겨졌는데, 모든 새로운 생각은 신에게서 유래했다(고 여겨졌다). (2)결국 신의 창조 행위 이전에 존재하지 않았던 것을 어떻게 인간이 만들 수 있었겠는가? (3)사실, '영감을 주다'라는 동사의 라틴어 의미는 '숨결을 불어넣다'이고 창의적 영감은 신이 처음에 인간에게 생명을 불어 넣었을 때 창조의 순간과 비슷했다는 믿음을 반영한다. (4)플라톤은 시인은 신이 내린 영감에 사로잡혔다고 주장했고, 플로티노스는 예술은 그것이 신으로부터 내려온 경우에만 아름다울 수 있다고 썼다. (5)예술가의 일은 자연을 모방하는 것이 아니라 오히려 자연의 신성하고 초월적인 특성을 드러내는 것이었다. (6)예술은 관념(이데아) 세계의 완벽함을 어설프게 흉내 낸 것에 불과한 것일 수 있다. (7)그리스의 예술가들은 그들이 현실에서 본 것을 맹목적으로 모방하지 않았다. (8)그 대신 그들은 현실의 기저를 이루는 순수하고 진정한 형태를 나타내려고 애썼는데, 그 결과 추상과 정확성 간에 일종의 타협을 야기했다.

[정답 확인]

다음 글의 주제로 가장 적절한 것은?

① conflicting views on the role of artists
예술가의 역할에 관한 상충하는 견해들
② positive effects of imitation on creativity
모방이 창의성에 미치는 긍정적인 영향
③ contribution of art to sharing religious beliefs
종교적 믿음을 공유하는 것에 대한 예술의 기여
✔ gods as a source of creativity in the pre-modern era
전근대적인 시대에 창의성의 원천으로서의 신
⑤ collaboration between philosophy and art in ancient times
고대에 철학과 예술 간의 협력

[문제 풀이]

근대 시대 이전, 창의성은 초인적인 힘, 즉 신에게서 유래했다는 주제의 글로 본문은 첫 문장에서 주제문을 제시한 뒤 창의적 영감은 신으로부터 내려왔다는 플라톤과 플로티노스의 주장을 예로 들고 있다. 나아가 예술가는 관념(이데아)의 완벽함을 어설프게 흉내 내고자 했기 때문에, 추상과 정확성 간에 일종의 타협도 하게 되었다고 한다. 따라서 본문의 주제는 ④가 적절하다.

[중요 어휘]

☐ **modern**	형용사 근대의, 현대의
☐ **superhuman**	형용사 초인적인
☐ **novel**	형용사 새로운
☐ **originate**	동사 유래하다
☐ **divine**	형용사 신(神)의, 신(神)이 내린
☐ **inspire**	동사 영감을 주다
☐ **reflect**	동사 반영하다
☐ **possess**	동사 사로잡다, 소유하다
☐ **descend**	동사 내려오다
☐ **imitate**	동사 모방하다
☐ **sacred**	형용사 신성한
☐ **transcendent**	형용사 초월적인
☐ **pale imitation**	어설프게 흉내 낸 것
☐ **blindly**	부사 맹목적으로
☐ **underlying**	형용사 기저를 이루는
☐ **compromise**	명사 타협, 절충
☐ **abstraction**	명사 추상, 관념
☐ **accuracy**	명사 정확성

핵심 발명품을 공유함으로써 혁신을 장려하려는 특허권의 본래 목적과는 달리 기술과 이윤을 독점하여 오히려 혁신을 저해하는 방향으로 악용되고 있음을 지적한 글임.

12 2019년 9월 23번 (정답률 55%) 정답 ④

[지문 끊어 읽기] 혁신을 방해하는 특허법 악용

(1) The original idea of a patent, / remember, /
특허권의 본래 목적은 / 명심하라 /
was not to reward inventors / with monopoly profits, /
not A but B
발명가들에게 보상하는 것이 아니었다 / 독점 이윤으로 /
but to encourage them / to share their inventions.
그러나 그들을 권장하는 것이었다 / 그들의 발명들을 공유하도록

(2) A certain amount of intellectual property law /
어느 정도의 지적 재산법은 /
is plainly necessary / to achieve this.
명백히 필요하다 / 이것을 이루기 위해

(3) But it has gone too far.
하지만 그것은 도를 넘었다

(4) Most patents / are now as much about defending monopoly /
as much A as B: B만큼이나 A한
대부분의 특허권은 / 이제 독점을 지키는 것에 관한 것이다 /
and discouraging rivals / as about sharing ideas.
그리고 경쟁자들을 단념시키는 것에 관한 것이다 / 아이디어를 공유하는 것만큼이나

(5) And that disrupts innovation. 정답 단서
그리고 그것은 혁신을 방해한다

(6) Many firms use patents / as barriers to entry, /
많은 회사들은 특허권을 사용한다 / 진입 장벽으로 /
suing upstart innovators /
그리고 신흥 혁신가들을 고소한다 /
who trespass on their intellectual property /
그들의 지적 재산을 침해하는 /
even on the way to some other goal.
심지어 어떤 다른 목표로 향하고 있는

힌트 suing으로 시작하는 종속절은 접속사(and)와 주어(they=many firms)가 생략되고 동사가 V-ing로 변한 분사구문임. 분사구문의 주어는 주절의 주어와 동일할 경우에 생략할 수 있음.

(7) In the years before World War I, /
제1차 세계 대전 이전 몇 년 동안 /
aircraft makers tied each other up / in patent lawsuits /
항공기 제조사들은 서로를 묶어 놓았다 / 특허권 소송들로 /
and slowed down innovation / until the US government stepped in.
그리고 혁신을 늦추었다 / 미국 정부가 개입할 때까지

(8) Much the same has happened /
거의 동일한 일이 일어나고 있다 /
with smartphones and biotechnology / today.
스마트폰과 생명 공학에서도 / 오늘날

(9) New entrants have to fight their way /
새로운 참가자들은 싸워 나아가야 한다 /
through "patent thickets" /
'특허권 덤불'을 헤쳐 /
if they are to build on existing technologies / to make new ones. 정답 단서
be to V: ~하고자 하다, ~할 의도이다
그들이 기존의 기술을 기반으로 하고자 한다면 / 새로운 것을 만들기 위해

중요 특허권을 덤불에 비유한 것으로 보아, 덤불이 길을 가는 데 방해되는 것처럼, 특허권도 새로운 기술을 만들려는 신흥 혁신가들의 발목을 잡는다는 것을 유추할 수 있음.

[전문 해석]

(1)특허권의 본래 목적은 발명가들에게 독점 이윤으로 보상하는 것이 아니라 그들이 그들의 발명들을 공유하도록 권장하는 것임을 명심하라. (2)어느 정도의 지적 재산법은 이것(발명의 공유)을 이루기 위해 명백히 필요하다. (3)하지만 그것은 도를 넘었다. (4)대부분의 특허권은 이제 아이디어를 공유하는 것만큼이나 독점을 지키고 경쟁자들을 단념시키는 것에 관한 것이다. (5)그리고 그것은 혁신을 방해한다. (6)많은 회사들은 특허권을 진입 장벽으로 사용하며, 심지어 어떤 다른 목표로 향하고 있는, 그들의 지적 재산을 침해하는 신흥 혁신가들을 고

정답과 해설
06 주제 추론

소한다. (7)제1차 세계 대전 이전 몇 년 동안 항공기 제조사들은 특허권 소송들로 서로를 묶어 놓았으며(서로의 발목을 잡았으며) 미국 정부가 개입할 때까지 혁신을 늦추었다. (8)오늘날 스마트폰과 생명 공학 (분야)에서도 거의 동일한 일이 일어나고 있다. (9)새로운 참가자들은 (업계에 처음 진입한 사람들은) 그들이 새로운 기술을 만들기 위해 기존의 것을 기반으로 하고자 한다면, '특허권 덤불'을 헤쳐 (싸워) 나아가야 한다.

- World War I(제1차 세계 대전, 1914년~1918년): 오스트리아가 세르비아에 선전 포고하며 유럽을 중심으로 일어난 국제 전쟁
- biotechnology(생명 공학): 생물의 특성을 인위적으로 변형시켜서 인간에게 이로운 것을 만드는 기술

[정답 확인]

다음 글의 주제로 가장 적절한 것은?

① side effects of anti-monopoly laws
독점 금지법의 부작용
② ways to protect intellectual property
지적 재산을 보호하는 방법
③ requirements for applying for a patent
특허권 신청 요건들
✔ patent law abuse that hinders innovation
혁신을 방해하는 특허법 악용
⑤ resources needed for technological innovation
기술 혁신에 필요한 자원

[문제 풀이]

지문은 특허권이 원래 발명의 공유를 권장하기 위해서 만들어졌으나, 이제는 발명을 독점하고 있는 사람들에 의해 이윤 추구의 수단으로 악용되고 있다고 설명한다. 문장 (6)~(9)에서 제시된 신흥 혁신가들을 고소하여 진입 장벽을 형성하는 것, 제1차 세계 대전 당시 특허권 소송들로 인한 혁신의 저해, 스마트폰과 생명 공학 분야에서의 '특허권 덤불' 등은 모두 특허권이 변질되어 악용되는 구체적인 사례들로, 필자는 이와 같은 악용 사례들을 통해 특허권이 오히려 혁신에 방해가 되는 현실을 문제로 지적하고 있다. 따라서 지문의 주제로는 ④가 가장 적절하다.

[중요 어휘]

□ patent	명사 특허(권), 특허증
□ monopoly	명사 독점, 독차지
□ intellectual property	명사 지적 재산
□ plainly	부사 명백히, 솔직히
□ defend	동사 지키다, 방어하다
□ discourage	동사 단념시키다, 낙담시키다
□ disrupt	동사 방해하다, 지장을 주다
□ firm	명사 회사 / 형용사 딱딱한, 확고한
□ barrier	명사 장벽, 장애물
□ sue	동사 고소하다, 소송을 제기하다
□ upstart	형용사 신흥의, 벼락부자인
□ trespass	동사 침해하다 / 명사 무단출입
□ tie A up in B	(다른 일을 할 수 없게) A를 B로 묶어 놓다
□ lawsuit	명사 소송, 고소
□ entrant	명사 참가자, 신입자
□ thicket	명사 덤불, 복잡하게 얽힌 것
□ side effect	명사 부작용
□ hinder	동사 방해하다, 저지하다

핵심 인간의 어떤 행위들이 해양 침입종의 전파를 야기했는지, 그리고 그 행위가 해양 생태에 어떤 영향을 불러왔는지에 주목해야 함.

13 2021년 9월 23번 (정답률 55%) 정답 ⑤

[지문 끊어 읽기] 침입종의 전파에 대한 인간의 영향

(1) Many marine species /
많은 해양 종들은 /
including oysters, marsh grasses, and fish /
굴, 습지 풀, 그리고 물고기를 포함한 / 정답 단서
were deliberately introduced / for food or for erosion control, /
의도적으로 도입되었다 / 식량이나 침식 방지를 위해 /
with little knowledge of the impacts / they could have.
영향에 대한 지식이 거의 없는 상태에서 / 그것들이 미칠 수 있는

(2) Fish and shellfish have been intentionally introduced / 정답 단서
어패류는 의도적으로 도입되었다 /
all over the world / for aquaculture, /
전 세계에 / 양식을 위해 /
[providing food and jobs], / but they can escape /
[ ]: 분사구문(결과) 병렬①
음식과 일자리를 제공했다 / 그러나 그것들은 탈출할 수 있다 /
and become a threat to native species, ecosystem function,
병렬②
or livelihoods.
그리고 토착종, 생태계 기능, 또는 생계에 위협이 될 수 있다

(3) Atlantic salmon are reared / in ocean net-pens / 정답 단서
대서양 연어는 길러진다 / 해양 그물 어장에서 /
in Washington State and British Columbia.
워싱턴주와 브리티시컬럼비아주의

(4) Many escape each year, / and they have been recovered /
매년 많은 연어가 탈출한다 / 그리고 그것들은 재발견된다 /
in both saltwater and freshwater /
해수와 담수 모두에서 /
in Washington State, British Columbia, and Alaska.
워싱턴주, 브리티시컬럼비아주, 그리고 알래스카주의

(5) Recreational fishing can also spread invasive species. 정답 단서
여가용 낚시 또한 침입종을 전파시킬 수 있다

(6) Bait worms from Maine are popular throughout the country.
메인주의 미끼용 벌레들은 전국적으로 인기가 있다

(7) They are commonly packed in seaweed /
선행사
그것들은 보통 해초에 싸여 있다 /
which contains many other organisms.
주격 관계대명사
많은 다른 유기체들을 포함하는

(8) If the seaweed is discarded, / it or the organisms on it /
만약 해초가 버려지면 / 그것이나 그것 위에 있는 유기체들은 / S
can colonize new areas.
V
새로운 영역에서 군락을 이룰 수 있다

(9) Fishing boots, recreational boats, and trailers /
낚시용 장화, 여가용 보트, 그리고 트레일러는 / 정답 단서
can pick up organisms at one location / and move them elsewhere.
유기체들을 한 장소에서 집어 올릴 수 있다 / 그리고 그것들을 다른 곳으로 옮길 수 있다

[전문 해석]

(1)굴, 습지 풀, 그리고 물고기를 포함한 많은 해양 종들은 그것들이 미칠 수 있는 영향에 대한 지식이 거의 없는 상태에서 식량이나 침식 방지를 위해 의도적으로 도입되었다. (2)어패류는 양식을 위해 전 세계에 의도적으로 도입되어 음식과 일자리를 제공했지만, 그것들은 탈출해서 토착종, 생태계 기능, 또는 생계에 위협이 될 수 있다. (3)대서양 연어는 워싱턴주와 브리티시컬럼비아주의 해양 그물 어장에서 길러진다. (4)매년 많은 연어가 탈출하며, 그것들은 워싱턴주, 브리티시컬럼비아주, 그리고 알래스카주의 해수와 담수 모두에서 재발견된다. (5)여가용 낚시 또한 침입종을 전파시킬 수 있다. (6)메인주의 미끼용 벌레들은 전국적으로 인기가 있다. (7)그것들은 보통 많은 다른 유기체들을 포함하는 해초에 싸여 있다. (8)만약 해초가 버려지면, 그것(해초)이나 그것 위에 있는 유기체들은 새로운 영역에서 군락을 이룰 수 있다. (9)낚시용 장화, 여가용 보트, 그리고 트레일러는 유기체들을 한 장소에서 집어 올려 다른 곳으로 옮길 수 있다.

[정답 확인]

다음 글의 주제로 가장 적절한 것은?

① benefits of recreational ocean fishing
여가용 해양 낚시의 이점
② ways to maintain marine biodiversity
해양 생물 다양성을 유지하기 위한 방법
③ potential value of the ocean for ecotourism
생태 관광을 위한 해양의 잠재적 가치

④ contribution of ocean farming to food supply
식품 공급에 대한 해양 농업의 기여
⑤ human influence on the spread of invasive species
침입종의 전파에 대한 인간의 영향

[중요 어휘]

□ oyster	명사 굴
□ marsh	명사 습지
□ deliberately	부사 의도적으로, 신중하게
□ erosion	명사 침식, 부식
□ aquaculture	명사 (수산) 양식
□ livelihood	명사 생계
□ rear	동사 기르다
□ recover	동사 재발견하다, 되찾다, 회복하다
□ recreational	형용사 여가용의, 오락의
□ invasive	형용사 침입의, 침략적인
□ discard	동사 버리다, 폐기하다
□ colonize	동사 군락을 이루다, 식민지로 만들다
□ biodiversity	명사 생물 다양성
□ ecotourism	명사 생태 관광

핵심 주제를 첫 문장에서 제시한 두괄식 구조로, 여러 사례를 들어 내용을 상세히 설명하는 글임.

14 2018년 6월 21번 (정답률 50%) 정답 ⑤

[지문 끊어 읽기] 초기의 글쓰기의 역할

(1) The development of writing was pioneered /
쓰기의 발달은 개척되었다 /
not by gossips, storytellers, or poets, / but by accountants. 주제문
수다쟁이들, 이야기꾼들, 혹은 시인들에 의해서가 아니라 / 회계사들에 의해서

(2) The earliest writing system has its roots in the Neolithic period, /
가장 초기의 쓰기 체계는 신석기 시대에 뿌리를 두고 있다 /
when humans first began to switch /
그때 인간은 처음으로 전환하기 시작했다 /
from hunting and gathering to a settled lifestyle /
수렵과 채집에서 정착 생활 방식으로 /
based on agriculture.
농업에 기초한

(3) This shift began around 9500 B.C. /
이러한 변화는 기원전 9500년경에 시작되었다 /
in a region known as the Fertile Crescent, /
비옥한 초승달 지대라고 알려진 지역에서 /
which stretches from modern-day Egypt, /
이곳은 현대의 이집트로부터 뻗어 있다 /
up to southeastern Turkey, /
튀르키예 남동부까지 /
and down again to the border between Iraq and Iran.
그리고 거기에다가 아래로는 이라크와 이란 사이의 국경까지

(4) Writing seems to have evolved in this region /
쓰기는 이 지역에서 발달해온 것으로 보인다 /
from the custom of using small clay pieces /
작은 점토 조각을 사용하는 관습으로부터 /
to account for transactions involving agricultural goods /
농산품에 관련된 거래를 기록하기 위해 /
such as grain, sheep, and cattle. 정답 단서
곡물, 양, 그리고 소와 같은

★중요 문장 (4)의 account for transactions involving agricultural goods는 정답에서 recording economic activities로 표현되었음.

(5) The first written documents, /
최초로 쓰인 문서는 /
which come from the Mesopotamian city of Uruk /
메소포타미아 도시 Uruk에서 나온 /
and date back to around 3400 B.C., /
그리고 기원전 3400년경까지 거슬러 올라가는 /
record amounts of bread, payment of taxes, and other transactions / 정답 단서
빵의 양, 납세, 그리고 다른 거래들을 기록하고 있다 /
using simple symbols and marks / on clay tablets.
간단한 부호와 표시를 사용하여 / 점토판에

[전문 해석]

(1)쓰기의 발달은 수다쟁이들, 이야기꾼들, 혹은 시인들에 의해서가 아니라 회계사들에 의해서 개척되었다. (2)가장 초기의 쓰기 체계는 신석기 시대에 뿌리를 두고 있는데, 그때 인간은 처음으로 수렵과 채집에서 농업에 기초한 정착 생활 방식으로 전환하기 시작했다. (3)이러한 변화는 기원전 9500년경에 비옥한 초승달 지대라고 알려진 지역에서 시작되었는데, 이곳은 현대의 이집트로부터 튀르키예 남동부까지, 그리고 거기에다가 아래로는 이라크와 이란 사이의 국경까지 뻗어 있다. (4)쓰기는 이 지역에서 곡물, 양, 그리고 소와 같은 농산품에 관련된 거래를 기록하기 위해 작은 점토 조각을 사용하는 관습으로부터 발달해온 것으로 보인다. (5)메소포타미아 도시 Uruk(우루크)에서 나오고(발견되고) 기원전 3400년경까지 거슬러 올라가는 최초로 쓰인 문서는 빵의 양, 납세, 그리고 다른 거래들을 간단한 부호와 표시를 사용하여 점토판에 기록하고 있다.

- Neolithic period(신석기 시대, 기원전 8000년경~기원전 2000년경): 선사시대의 시기 구분상 인간이 간석기를 생활도구로 사용한 시대. 후빙기의 시작과 더불어 구석기 시대의 수렵과 채집 위주의 이동 생활에서, 인간이 최초로 원시농경과 목축에 의한 식량생산을 하게 되면서 안정된 정착 생활로의 생활 방식의 변화가 일어난 시기
- Fertile Crescent(비옥한 초승달 지대): 최초의 농경문화 발상지. 문명의 기초를 이루었던 세 개의 강이 흐르고 있어 토지가 매우 비옥하였으며 과거 메소포타미아 지역으로부터 시작하여 현재의 튀르키예, 이란, 이라크를 거쳐 이집트까지의 방대한 지역에 이르는 초승달 모양의 지대
- Mesopotamia(메소포타미아): 서아시아 티그리스강과 유프라테스강 사이의 지역 일대를 가리키는 명칭으로 현재의 이라크를 중심으로 시리아의 북동부, 이란의 남서부를 포함하는 지역
- Uruk(우루크): 이라크의 남동부, 유프라테스강 부근에 있는 수메르의 도시 유적

[정답 확인]

다음 글의 주제로 가장 적절한 것은?

① various tools to improve agricultural production
농업 생산량을 향상시키기 위한 다양한 도구(농기구)들
② regional differences in using the writing system
쓰기 체계 사용에 있어서 지역별 차이점
③ ways to store agricultural goods in ancient cities
고대 도시에서 농산품을 보관하는 방법들
④ changed lifestyles based on agricultural development
농업 발달에 근거하여 변화한 생활 방식
⑤ early writing as a means of recording economic activities
경제 활동을 기록하는 수단으로서의 초기의 글쓰기

[중요 어휘]

□ pioneer	동사 개척하다 / 명사 개척자
□ have one's roots in	~에 뿌리를 두다, ~을 근거로 두다
□ settled	형용사 정착한, 자리를 잡은, 안정적인, 안정된
□ fertile	형용사 (토양이) 비옥한, 기름진
□ crescent	명사 초승달 (모양)
□ evolve	동사 발달하다, 진전시키다
□ transaction	명사 거래, 계약
□ grain	명사 곡물
□ date back to	(시기가) ~까지 거슬러 올라가다
□ payment of taxes	납세
□ clay tablet	점토판
□ regional	형용사 지역(별)의, 지역적인

핵심 문장 (4)의 presentation, 문장 (6)의 tell your story를 보면 지문이 자기 자신을 보여주는 것에 대해 이야기하는 것을 알 수가 있고, 문장 (6)의 actively cultivated와 문장 (7)의 learn을 보아 지문은 자기 자신을 보여주는 방법을 계발해야 한다고 강조하고 있음.

15 2019년 6월 23번 (정답률 50%) 정답 ⑤

[지문 끊어 읽기] 자신을 보여주는 방식에 대한 계발

(1) In this world, / being smart or competent isn't enough.
이 세상에서 / 똑똑하거나 능력이 있는 것은 충분하지가 않다

(2) People sometimes don't recognize talent / when they see it.
때때로 사람들은 재능을 알아보지 못한다 / 그들이 그것을 볼 때

(3) Their vision is clouded / by the first impression we give /
그들의 시야는 흐려진다 / 우리가 주는 첫인상에 의해서 /

and that can lose us / the job we want, /
그리고 그것은 우리를 잃게 할 수 있다 / 우리가 원하는 직업을 /
or the relationship we want.
아니면 우리가 원하는 관계를

(4) The way / we present ourselves /
방식은 / 우리가 우리 자신을 보여주는 /
can speak more eloquently / of the skills /
더 설득력 있게 말해줄 수 있다 / 기술들에 대해 /
we bring to the table, / if we actively cultivate that presentation.
우리가 기여할 / 만약 우리가 그러한 보여주기를 적극적으로 계발한다면

✱중요 문장 (4)는 나를 보여주는 방식을 잘 계발하면 내가 가진 기량들을 상대방에게 더 효과적으로 어필할 수 있다는 의미임. 여기서 the skills는 문장 (2)의 talent와 같은 맥락으로, 우리가 기여(제공)할 수 있는, 우리가 가진 기술, 재능 및 능력을 의미함.

(5) Nobody likes to be crossed off the list /
아무도 목록에서 지워지고 싶어하지 않는다 /
before being given the opportunity / to show others /
기회가 주어지기도 전에 / 다른 사람들에게 보여줄 /
who they are.
그들이 누구인지

(6) Being able to tell your story /
당신의 이야기를 할 수 있다는 것은 /
from the moment you meet other people /
당신이 다른 사람들을 만나는 그 순간부터 /
is a skill / that must be actively cultivated, /
기술이다 / 적극적으로 계발되어야 하는 /
in order to send the message /
메시지를 보내기 위해 /
that you're someone to be considered /
당신이 고려되어야 할 누군가라는 /
and the right person for the position.
그리고 그 직책에 적합한 사람이라는

(7) For that reason, / it's important / that we all learn /
그러한 이유로 / 중요하다 / 우리 모두가 배우는 것이 /
how to say the appropriate things / in the right way /
병렬①
적절한 것을 말하는 법을 / 올바른 방식으로 /
and to present ourselves / in a way that appeals to other people /
병렬②
그리고 우리 자신을 보여주는 법을 / 다른 사람들에게 매력적인 방식으로 /
— tailoring a great first impression. 주제문
훌륭한 첫인상을 만들면서

[전문 해석]

(1)이 세상에서 똑똑하거나 능력이 있는 것은 충분하지가 않다. (2)때때로 사람들은 재능을 볼 때 그것을 알아보지 못한다. (3)그들의 시야는 우리가 주는 첫인상에 의해서 흐려지며 그것(흐려진 시야)은 우리가 원하는 직업이나 관계를 잃게 할 수 있다. (4)우리가 우리 자신을 보여주는 방식은 만약 우리가 그러한 보여주기를 적극적으로 계발한다면, 우리가 기여할 (우리의) 기술들에 대해 더 설득력 있게 말해줄 수 있다. (5)아무도 그들(자신)이 누구인지 다른 사람들에게 보여줄 기회가 주어지기도 전에 목록에서 지워지고 싶어 하지 않는다. (6)당신이 다른 사람들을 만나는 그 순간부터 당신의 이야기를 할 수 있다는 것은 당신이 (채용을 위해) 고려되어야 할 누군가이며 그 직책에 적합한 사람이라는 메시지를 보내기 위해 적극적으로 계발되어야만 하는 기술이다. (7)그러한 이유로 우리 모두가 올바른 방식으로 적절한 것을 말하는 법과 다른 사람들에게 훌륭한 첫인상을 만들면서 매력적인 방식으로 우리 자신을 보여주는 법을 배우는 것이 중요하다.

[정답 확인]

다음 글의 주제로 가장 적절한 것은?

① difficulty of presenting yourself in public
사람들이 있는 데서 당신 자신을 보여주는 것의 어려움
② risks of judging others based on first impressions
첫인상에 근거하여 남을 판단하는 것의 위험성
③ factors keeping you from making great impressions
당신이 좋은 인상을 만들지 못하게 하는 요인들
④ strategies that help improve your presentation skills
당신의 보여주기 기술을 향상시키게 도와주는 전략들
✔ necessity of developing the way you show yourself
당신이 당신 자신을 보여주는 방식을 계발하는 것의 필요성

✱중요 지문에 자신을 보여주는 방식을 나아지게 할 수 있는 방법들이 제시되긴 하지만, 지문의 요점은 이 보여주는 방식을 계발하는 것에 대한 중요성을 말하고 있음.

[문제 풀이]

본문은 아무리 똑똑하고 능력이 있는 사람이라도 자신이 가진 재능과 기술을 상대방에게 보여주지 못한다면 원하는 직업이나 관계를 잃을 수도 있다고 말하고 있다. 올바른 방식으로 적절한 것을 말하고, 다른 사람에게 자신을 매력적인 방식으로 보일 수 있는 보여주기(presenting) 기술을 계발해야 한다고 주장한다. 따라서 정답은 ⑤이다.

[중요 어휘]

☐ **competent**	형용사 능력이 있는, 능숙한, 충분한
☐ **talent**	명사 재능, 장기
☐ **cloud**	동사 흐리다, 어두워지다 / 명사 구름
☐ **bring to the table**	기여하다, 제시하다, 제공하다
☐ **actively**	부사 적극적으로, 활발히
☐ **cultivate**	동사 계발하다, 기르다, 경작하다
☐ **be crossed off the list**	목록에서 지워지다, 제명되다
☐ **appeal**	동사 매력적이다, 관심을 끌다, 호소하다 / 명사 매력, 호소
☐ **tailor**	동사 (목적에 맞게) 만들다, 맞추다, 재단하다

16 2022년 3월 23번 (정답률 40%) 정답 ⑤

[지문 끊어 읽기] 허구적인 생물학적 인종 개념

(1) Individual human beings differ / from one another physically /
인간 개개인은 다르다 / 신체적으로 서로 /
in a multitude of visible and invisible ways.
눈에 보이고 눈에 보이지 않는 여러 가지 면에서

(2) If races / — as most people define them — /
만약 인종이 / 대부분의 사람이 그것을 정의하듯이 / =races
are real biological entities, /
정말 생물학적 실체라면 /
then people of African ancestry would share a wide variety of traits /
아프리카계 혈통인 사람들은 매우 다양한 특성을 공유할 것이다 /
while people of European ancestry would share a wide variety of *different* traits.
한편 유럽계 혈통인 사람들은 매우 다양한 '다른' 특성을 공유할 것이다

(3) But once we add traits /
선행사
하지만 우리가 특성들을 추가해 보면 /
[that are less visible than skin coloration, hair texture, and the like], / [ ]: 주격 관계대명사절
피부색, 머릿결 같은 것들보다 눈에 덜 보이는 /
we find / that the people we identify as "the same race" /
명사절 접속사 S'
우리는 알게 된다 / 우리가 '같은 인종'이라고 식별하는 사람들이 /
are less and less like one another /
V'
서로 점점 덜 닮았다는 것을 /
and more and more like people / we identify as "different races."
그리고 사람들과 더욱더 닮았다는 것을 / 우리가 '다른 인종'이라고 식별하는

정답 단서 눈에 덜 보이는 특성들을 보면, 같은 인종의 사람들끼리보다는 서로 다른 인종의 사람들끼리 더 닮았다는 것을 알게 된다고 하고 있음.

힌트 'the physical features'부터 문장 끝까지는 모두 add의 목적어로 명사절 접속사 that이 이끌고 있음. 'A를 B에 추가하다'라는 add A to B에서 목적어에 해당하는 A 부분이 길어서 문장의 맨 끝으로 이동함.

(4) Add to this point /
이 점에 추가해 보라 /
that the physical features [used to identify a person as a representative of some race] / [ ]: 주격 관계대명사절
명사절 접속사 S'(=선행사) identify A as B: A를 B라고 식별하다
어떤 사람을 어떤 인종의 전형이라고 식별하는 데 사용되는 신체적 특성이 /
(e.g. skin coloration) /
(예를 들어, 피부색) /
are continuously variable, / 정답 단서
V'
지속적으로 변할 수 있다는 것을 /
so that one cannot say /
그래서 사람은 말할 수 없다는 것을 /
where "brown skin" becomes "white skin."
어디서 '갈색 피부'가 '흰 피부'가 되는지를

정답 단서 특정 인종의 전형적인 신체적 특성은 지속적으로 변하므로 신체적 특성을 이용하여 인종을 분류하는 것은 잘못된 방법임을 말하고 있음.

힌트 so that 앞에 comma(,)가 있으면 결과의 부사절을 이끄는 접속사로 '그래서, 그 결과'를 의미하는 접속사 so와 의미가 같음. 목적의 부사절을 이끄는 접속사 so that과 혼동하지 않도록 유의할 것.

(5) Although the physical differences themselves are real, /
비록 신체적 차이 그 자체가 실재하더라도 /

the way [we use physical differences /
S(=선행사) [ ]: 관계부사절
우리가 신체적 차이를 사용하는 방식은 /

to classify people into discrete races] /
부사적 용법(목적)
사람들을 별개의 인종으로 분류하기 위해 /

is a cultural construction. 주제문 신체적 차이가 실재하더라도 신체적 차이를 사용하여 인종을 분류하는 것은 문화적 구성이라고 함.
V
문화적 구성이다

[전문 해석]

(1)인간 개개인은 눈에 보이고 눈에 보이지 않는 여러 가지 면에서 신체적으로 서로 다르다. (2)대부분의 사람이 인종을 정의하듯이, 그것이 정말 생물학적 실체라면, 아프리카계 혈통인 사람들은 매우 다양한 특성을 공유하는 한편, 유럽계 혈통인 사람들은 매우 다양한 '다른' 특성을 공유할 것이다. (3)하지만 우리가 피부색, 머릿결 같은 것들보다 눈에 덜 보이는 특성들을 추가해 보면, 우리가 '같은 인종'이라고 식별하는 사람들이 서로 점점 덜 닮았고 우리가 '다른 인종'이라고 식별하는 사람들과 더욱더 닮았다는 것을 알게 된다. (4)어떤 사람을 어떤 인종의 전형이라고 식별하는 데 사용되는 신체적 특성(예를 들어, 피부색)이 지속적으로 변할 수 있어서 어디서 '갈색 피부'가 '흰 피부'가 되는지를 말할 수 없는 것을 이 점에 추가해 보라. (5)비록 신체적 차이 그 자체가 실재하더라도, 사람들을 별개의 인종으로 분류하기 위해 우리가 신체적 차이를 사용하는 방식은 문화적 구성이다.

[정답 확인]

다음 글의 주제로 가장 적절한 것은?

① causes of physical variations among different races
다른 인종 간 신체적 차이의 원인
② cultural differences between various races
다양한 인종 간의 문화 차이
③ social policies to overcome racism
인종 차별주의를 극복하기 위한 사회 정책
④ importance of environmental factors in evolution
진화에 있어서 환경적 요인의 중요성
⑤ misconception about race as a biological construct
생물학적 구성물로서의 인종에 대한 오해

[문제 풀이]

이 지문은 신체적 차이에 기반한 인종 개념은 사실은 문화적으로 구성된 것임을 설명하는 글이다. 문장 (1)과 (3)에 따르면 인간 개개인은 눈에 보이고, 눈에 보이지 않는 여러 가지 면에서 서로 신체적으로 다른데, 눈에 덜 보이는 특성에선 '같은 인종'의 사람들이 서로 덜 닮았고, '다른 인종'의 사람들이 더 닮았다고 한다. 덧붙여 문장 (4)에서 피부색과 같이 인종을 식별하는 데 사용되는 신체적 특성은 지속적으로 변해서 다른 인종으로 분류되는 지점을 정의하기 힘들다며 눈에 보이는 특성만으로 인종을 분류하는 것의 문제점을 지적하고 있다. 이어서 문장 (5)에서 신체적 차이가 실재한다고 해도 눈에 보이는 특성들로 인종을 분류하는 방식 자체는 문화적 구성임을 다시 한번 짚어주고 있다. 따라서 정답은 ⑤이다.

[오답 풀이]

① - 본문은 인종에 대해 우리가 오해하고 있는 것이 무엇인지 설명할 뿐 인종 간 신체적 차이가 나는 원인에 대한 이야기는 언급하지 않았으므로 ①은 오답이다.

[중요 어휘]

□ **differ from**	~와 다르다
□ **race**	명사 인종
□ **biological**	형용사 생물학적인, 생물학의
□ **entity**	명사 실체, 독립체
□ **ancestry**	명사 혈통, 가계
□ **identify**	동사 식별하다
□ **representative**	명사 전형, 표본 / 형용사 전형적인, 대표하는
□ **variable**	형용사 변할 수 있는 / 명사 변수
□ **classify**	동사 분류하다
□ **discrete**	형용사 별개의
□ **construction**	명사 구성(물), 건축물, 공사
□ **variation**	명사 차이, 변형
□ **overcome**	동사 극복하다, 이기다
□ **racism**	명사 인종 차별주의, 인종 차별 행위
□ **evolution**	명사 진화, 발전
□ **misconception**	명사 오해
□ **construct**	명사 구성(물), 구조물 / 동사 구성하다, 건설하다

17 2023년 6월 23번 (정답률 35%) 정답 ④

[지문 끊어 읽기] 교육에서의 공통 언어

(1) Education must focus on the trunk of the tree of knowledge, /
교육은 지식의 나무 줄기에 초점을 맞춰야 한다 /
[revealing the ways /
방식을 밝히면서 /
in which the branches, twigs, and leaves all emerge /
전치사+관계대명사
나뭇가지, 잔가지, 그리고 잎이 모두 나오는 /
from a common core]. [ ]: 분사구문
공통의 핵심에서

(2) Tools for thinking stem from this core, /
사고를 위한 도구는 이 핵심에서 비롯된다 / =a common core
[providing a common language / 정답 단서 공통 언어를 통해 공통의 핵심에서 사고를 위한 도구가 비롯됨.
공통 언어를 제공하면서 /
with which practitioners in different fields /
전치사+관계대명사
다양한 분야의 실무자들이 /
may share their experience of the process of innovation /
병렬①
혁신 과정에 대한 그들의 경험을 공유할 수 있는 /
and discover links between their creative activities]. [ ]: 분사구문
병렬②(may 생략)
그리고 그들의 창의적 활동 사이의 연결 고리를 발견할 수 있는

(3) When the same terms are employed / across the curriculum, /
동일한 용어가 사용될 때 / 교육 과정 전반에 걸쳐 /
students begin to link different subjects and classes. 정답 단서
학생들은 서로 다른 과목들과 수업들을 연결하기 시작한다 학생들은 교육 과정 전반에서 동일한 용어, 즉 공통 언어가 사용될 때 각각의 과목들을 연결하기 시작함.

(4) If they practice abstracting in writing class, /
그들이 글쓰기 수업에서 추상을 연습한다면 /
if they work on abstracting in painting or drawing class, /
그들이 회화나 그림 그리기 수업에서 추상을 연습한다면 /
and if, in all cases, they call it abstracting, /
그리고 모든 경우에 그들이 그것을 추상이라고 칭한다면 /
they begin to understand /
그들은 이해하기 시작한다 /
how to think beyond disciplinary boundaries. 정답 단서 각각 다른 수업에서 '추상'이라는 공통된 용어를 학습한 학생들은 학문의 경계를 넘어 사고하는 방법을 이해하기 시작함.
의문사+to V(=의문사+S should V)
어떻게 학문의 경계를 넘어 사고하는지

(5) They see how to transform their thoughts /
그들은 그들의 생각을 어떻게 바꾸는지 알게 된다 /
from one mode of conception and expression to another.
하나의 개념과 표현 방식에서 다른 방식으로

(6) Linking the disciplines comes naturally /
학문들을 연결하는 것은 자연스럽게 이루어진다 /
when the terms and tools are presented /
용어들과 도구들이 제시될 때 /
as part of a universal imagination.
보편적 상상력의 일부로

[전문 해석]

(1)교육은 나뭇가지, 잔가지, 그리고 잎이 모두 공통의 핵심에서 나오는 방식을 밝히면서, 지식의 나무 줄기에 초점을 맞춰야 한다. (2)다양한 분야의 실무자들이 혁신 과정에 대한 그들의 경험을 공유하고 그들의 창의적 활동 사이의 연결 고리를 발견할 수 있는 공통 언어를 제공하면서, 사고를 위한 도구는 이 핵심에서 비롯된다. (3)교육 과정 전반에 걸쳐 동일한 용어가 사용될 때, 학생들은 서로 다른 과목들과 수업들을 연결하기 시작한다. (4)그들이 글쓰기 수업에서 추상을 연습하고, 회화나 그림 그리기 수업에서 추상을 연습하고, 그리고 모든 경우에 그들이 그것을 추상이라고 칭한다면, 그들은 어떻게 학문의 경계를 넘어 사고하는지 이해하기 시작한다. (5)그들은 그들의 생각을 어떻게 하나의 개념과 표현 방식에서 다른 방식으로 바꾸

는지 알게 된다. (6)용어들과 도구들이 보편적 상상력의 일부로 제시될 때, 학문들을 연결하는 것은 자연스럽게 이루어진다.

[정답 확인]

다음 글의 주제로 가장 적절한 것은?

① difficulties in finding meaningful links between disciplines
학문 간의 의미 있는 연결을 찾아내는 것의 어려움

② drawbacks of applying a common language to various fields
다양한 분야에 공통 언어를 적용하는 것의 문제점

③ effects of diversifying the curriculum on students' creativity
교육 과정 다양화가 학생들의 창의력에 미치는 영향

✔④ necessity of using a common language to integrate the curriculum
교육 과정을 통합하기 위해 공통 언어를 사용하는 것의 필요성

⑤ usefulness of turning abstract thoughts into concrete expressions
추상적인 생각을 구체적인 표현으로 전환하는 것의 유용성

[문제 풀이]

이 지문은 공통의 핵심을 강조하는 교육 방식으로 학문 간 통합을 달성할 수 있다고 설명하는 글이다. 문장 (2)에 따르면 다양한 분야의 실무자들은 공통 언어라는 공통의 핵심을 통해 혁신 과정에 대한 경험 공유 및 창의적 활동 간의 연결 고리를 발견한다. 이와 같은 맥락으로 문장 (3)에서는 학생들이 교육 과정 전반에서의 동일한 용어, 즉 공통 언어를 통해 각 과목들을 연결한다고 설명한다. 이에 대해 문장 (4)에서는 공통 언어로서 '추상'을 예시로 설명하고 있고, 문장 (5)~(6)에서 공통 언어를 통해 사고의 전환이 이루어져 학문 간 통합이 달성될 수 있다고 설명한다. 다시 말해, 교육 과정을 통합하기 위해서는 공통 언어의 사용이 필요하다고 설명하고 있으므로 정답은 ④이다.

[오답 풀이]

③ - 본문에서는 학문들을 연결하는 것, 즉 교육 과정의 통합에 대해 이야기하고 있으며, 이는 교육 과정 전반에서 공통 언어를 사용하여 학생들의 사고를 전환함으로써 가능하다. 교육 과정 다양화는 통합과는 반대되는 내용이므로 ③은 정답이 될 수 없다.

[중요 어휘]

☐ **trunk**	명사 (나무) 줄기, 몸통, 여행용 큰 가방
☐ **reveal**	동사 밝히다, 드러내다, 폭로하다
☐ **twig**	명사 잔가지
☐ **emerge**	동사 나오다, 드러나다, 생겨나다
☐ **stem from**	~에서 비롯되다[유래하다]
☐ **employ**	동사 사용하다, 고용하다
☐ **disciplinary**	형용사 학문의, 교과의, 훈계의, 징계의
☐ **universal**	형용사 보편적인, 일반적인
☐ **drawback**	명사 문제점, 약점, 결점
☐ **integrate**	동사 통합하다
☐ **concrete**	형용사 구체적인, 콘크리트로 만든

18 2023년 11월 23번 (정답률 70%) 정답 ①

[지문 끊어 읽기] 동료 행동의 설득력

(1) Sylvan Goldman invented the shopping cart /
V①
Sylvan Goldman은 쇼핑 카트를 발명했다 /
and introduced it in his stores / in 1937.
V②
그리고 자신의 가게들에 그것을 도입했다 / 1937년에

(2) It was an excellent device / [that would make it easy /
=the shopping cart 선행사 형식상의 목적어
그것은 훌륭한 장치였다 / 쉽게 만들어 준 /
for shoppers to buy as much as they wanted /
to부정사의 의미상의 주어 내용상의 목적어
쇼핑객들이 자신들이 원하는 만큼 구매하는 것을 /
without getting tired or seeking others' help]. [ ]: 주격 관계대명사절
V-ing① V-ing②
지치거나 다른 사람들의 도움을 구하는 것 없이

(3) But Goldman discovered /
하지만 Goldman은 발견했다 /
[that in spite of his repeated advertisements and explanations, /
=despite
자신의 반복적인 광고와 설명에도 불구하고 / 정답 단서 설명과 광고만으로는 원하는 행동을 하도록 사람들을 유도하는 것은 어려움.
he could not persuade his shoppers / to use the wheeled carts].
그는 쇼핑객들에게 설득할 수 없다는 것을 / 바퀴 달린 카트를 사용하도록 [ ]: discovered의 목적어절

(4) Men were reluctant /
남성들은 꺼렸다 /
because they thought [they would appear weak /
그들은 자신들이 약해 보일 것이라고 생각했기 때문에 /
if they pushed such carts / instead of carrying their shopping].
V-ing
만약 그들이 그런 카트를 민다면 / 자신들의 쇼핑한 물건을 들고 다니는 것 대신에

힌트 동사 thought의 목적어에 해당하는 절로서, 접속사 that이 생략되었음. 'that'이 이끄는 명사절이 목적어로 쓰였을 경우에는 생략이 가능함.

(5) Women wouldn't touch them /
여성들은 그것들에 손을 대려 하지 않았다 /
because the carts reminded them of baby carriages.
카트들이 그들에게 유아차를 연상시켰기 때문에

힌트 remind A of B : A에게 B를 연상[상기]시키다

(6) It was only a few elderly shoppers /
오직 소수의 노인 쇼핑객들뿐이었다 /
who used them.
=the wheeled carts
그것들을 사용하는 사람들은

힌트 「It is ~ that[who] …」 강조구문으로, '…한 것은 바로 ~이다'라고 해석되며 be동사와 that 사이에 오는 표현을 강조함. 이 문장에서는 'only a few elderly shoppers'를 강조하고 있는데, 강조하는 대상이 '사람'이면 that을 who로 바꾸어 쓸 수 있음. 해당 구문은 It was와 who를 없애더라도 완전한 문장을 이룸.

(7) That made the carts even less attractive /
=문장(6) 비교급 강조
그것이 카트들을 훨씬 덜 매력적으로 만들었다 /
to the majority of the shoppers.
대다수의 쇼핑객들에게

(8) Then Goldman hit upon an idea.
그때 Goldman은 한 아이디어를 떠올렸다

(9) He hired several models, men and women, of different ages /
V①
그는 몇몇 다른 연령대의 남성과 여성 모델을 고용했다 /
and asked them to wheel the carts / in the store and shop. 정답 단서
V②(5형식V) O O.C
그리고 그들에게 카트들을 밀도록 요청했다 / 상점과 매장에서

정답 단서 모델을 고용해서 사람들이 같은 행동을 하도록 유도함.

(10) A young woman employee / standing near the entrance /
S 현재분사구
한 젊은 여성 직원이 / 입구 근처에 서 있던 /
told the regular shoppers, / 'Look, everyone is using the carts. /
V
일반 쇼핑객들에게 말했다 / 보세요, 모든 사람들이 카트를 사용하고 있습니다 /
Why don't you?'
해 보는 게 어떠세요

(11) That was the turning point.
그것이 전환점이었다

(12) A few shills / disguised as regular shoppers /
S 과거분사구
몇몇 바람잡이들이 / 일반 쇼핑객으로 위장한 /
easily accomplished /
쉽게 달성했다 /
what logic, explanations, and advertisements failed to do. 정답 단서
선행사를 포함한 관계대명사
논리, 설명, 그리고 광고들이 하지 못했던 것을

정답 단서 단순한 광고나 설명보다는 주변 사람들의 행동이 더욱 설득력 있음.

(13) Within a few weeks / shoppers readily accepted those carts.
몇 주 만에 / 쇼핑객들은 그 카트를 기꺼이 받아들였다

[전문 해석]

(1)Sylvan Goldman은 쇼핑 카트를 발명했고 1937년에 자신의 가게들에 그것을 도입했다. (2)그것은 쇼핑객들이 지치거나 다른 사람들의 도움을 구하는 것 없이 자신들이 원하는 만큼 구매하는 것을 쉽게 만들어 준 훌륭한 장치였다. (3)하지만 Goldman은 자신의 반복적인 광고와 설명에도 불구하고, 쇼핑객들에게 바퀴 달린 카트를 사용하도록 설득할 수 없다는 것을 발견했다. (4)남성들은 만약 그들이 자신들의 쇼핑한 물건을 들고 다니는 것 대신에 그런 카트를 민다면 자신들이 약해 보일 것이라고 생각했기 때문에 꺼렸다. (5)여성들은 카트들이 그들에게 유아차를 연상시켰기 때문에 그것들에 손을 대려 하지 않았다. (6)그것들을 사용하는 사람들은 오직 소수의 노인 쇼핑객들뿐이었다. (7)그것이 대다수의 쇼핑객들에게 카트들을 훨씬 덜 매력적으로 만들었다. (8)그때 Goldman은 한 아이디어를 떠올렸다. (9)그는 몇몇 다른 연령대의 남성과 여성 모델을 고용해서 그들에게 상점과 매장에서 카트들을 밀도록 요청했다. (10)입구 근처에 서 있던 한 젊은 여성 직원이 일반 쇼핑객들에게 '보세요, 모든 사람들이 카트

를 사용하고 있습니다. 해 보는 게 어떠세요?'라고 말했다. (11)그것이 전환점이었다. (12)일반 쇼핑객으로 위장한 몇몇 바람잡이들이 논리, 설명, 그리고 광고들이 하지 못했던 것을 쉽게 달성했다. (13)몇 주 만에 쇼핑객들은 그 카트를 기꺼이 받아들였다.

[정답 확인]

다음 글의 주제로 가장 적절한 것은?

✔ persuasive power of peer behavior
동료 행동의 설득력
② methods to help consumers shop less
고객들이 쇼핑을 덜 하도록 돕는 법
③ innovative ways to reduce waste in retail
소매상에서 쓰레기를 줄이는 획기적인 방법
④ hidden nature of human beings to support materialism
물질만능주의를 지지하는 사람들의 숨겨진 본성
⑤ importance of a store layout based on customer needs
고객 요구를 기반으로 한 상점 배치의 중요성

[중요 어휘]

□ **seek**	동사 구하다, 찾다
□ **in spite of**	~에도 불구하고
□ **explanation**	명사 설명, 이유, 해명
□ **persuade**	동사 설득하다, 납득시키다
□ **wheeled**	형용사 바퀴 달린, 바퀴로 움직이는
□ **reluctant**	형용사 꺼리는, 마지못한, 주저하는
□ **majority**	명사 대다수, 가장 많은 수
□ **hit upon[on]**	~을 (우연히) 떠올리다[생각해 내다]
□ **wheel**	동사 (바퀴 달린 것을) 밀다, 끌다, 운전하다
□ **disguise**	동사 위장하다, 변장[가장]하다, 숨기다 / 명사 변장
□ **accomplish**	동사 달성하다, 해내다, 완수하다
□ **logic**	명사 논리, 타당성
□ **readily**	부사 기꺼이, 선뜻, 쉽게

19 2024년 3월 23번 (정답률 45%) 정답 ⑤

[지문 끊어 읽기] 사업상 공감의 다양한 해석

(1) Empathy is frequently listed /
공감은 목록에 종종 언급된다 /
as one of the most desired skills in an employer or employee, /
전치사(~로)
고용주나 직원에게 가장 바라는 기술 중 하나로 /
although without specifying exactly /
정확히 명시하지는 않지만 /
힌트 접속사 'although' 뒤에 'it(=empathy) is'가 생략된 형태로, 바로 뒤에 '전치사 without+V-ing'의 부사구가 연결되어 있음.
[what is meant by *empathy*]. [ ]: 명사절(specifying의 목적어)
'공감'이 무엇을 의미하는지

(2) Some businesses stress cognitive empathy, /
일부 기업은 인지적 공감을 강조한다 /
[emphasizing the need /
필요성을 강조하며 /
for leaders to understand the perspective of employees
to부정사의 의미상의 주어 형용사적 용법
and customers /
리더가 직원과 고객의 관점을 이해할 /
when negotiating deals and making decisions]. 정답 단서 공감은 리더의 인지적 공감을 의미함.
병렬①(분사구문) 병렬② [ ]: 분사구문(동시동작)
거래를 협상하고 결정을 내릴 때

(3) Others stress affective empathy and empathic concern, /
=Other businesses
다른 기업은 정서적 공감과 공감적 관심을 강조한다 /
[emphasizing the ability of leaders /
리더의 능력을 강조하며 /
to gain trust from employees and customers /
형용사적 용법
직원과 고객의 신뢰를 얻는 /
by treating them with real concern and compassion]. 정답 단서 공감은 정서적 공감, 공감적 관심을 의미하기도 함.
[ ]: 분사구문(동시동작)
진정한 관심과 동정심으로 그들을 대함으로써

(4) When some consultants argue /
일부 자문 위원이 주장할 때 /
힌트 'argue that ~'은 '~을 (해야 한다고) 주장하다'라는 의미로 당위성을 표현함. 이때 that절에는 should가 사용되지만 생략이 가능함.
that successful companies foster empathy, /
성공하는 기업은 공감 능력을 길러야 한다고 /
what that translates to is /
S V
그것이 의미하는 바는 ~이다 /
힌트 문장 (4)와 (6)의 'what that translates to'는 선행사를 포함한 관계대명사 what이 'to'의 목적격으로 쓰여 what 뒤에 불완전한 구조가 이어짐. 'that'은 문장 (4)에서는 'successful ~ empathy'를, 문장 (6)에서는 'design with empathy'를 가리켜 (성공적인 기업이) 공감 능력을 기르는 것을 의미함.
[that companies should conduct good market research]. 정답 단서 공감은 기업의 시장 조사 수행 결과와도 관련이 있음.
접속사 [ ]: 명사절(주격 보어)
기업이 시장 조사를 잘 수행해야 한다는 것

(5) In other words, / an "empathic" company understands /
V①
다시 말해 / '공감하는' 기업은 이해한다 /
the needs and wants of its customers /
고객의 필요와 요구를 /
and seeks to fulfill those needs and wants.
V②
그리고 그 필요와 요구를 충족시키려고 노력한다

(6) When some people speak of design with empathy, /
일부 사람들이 공감을 담은 디자인을 말할 때 /
what that translates to is /
S V
그것이 의미하는 바는 ~이다 /
[that companies should take into account /
회사가 고려해야 한다는 것 /
the specific needs of different populations] / [ ]: 명사절(주격 보어)
각양각색의 사람들의 구체적인 필요 사항을 /
— the blind, the deaf, the elderly, non-English speakers, the color-blind, and so on — /
시각 장애인, 청각 장애인, 노인, 비영어권 화자, 색맹 등 /
when designing products.
제품을 디자인할 때

[전문 해석]

(1)'공감'이 무엇을 의미하는지 정확히 명시하지는 않지만, 공감은 고용주나 직원에게 가장 바라는 기술 중 하나로 목록에 종종 언급된다. (2)일부 기업은 리더가 거래를 협상하고 결정을 내릴 때 직원과 고객의 관점을 이해할 필요성을 강조하며 인지적 공감을 강조한다. (3)다른 기업은 진정한 관심과 동정심으로 직원과 고객을 대함으로써 그들의 신뢰를 얻는 리더의 능력을 강조하며 정서적 공감과 공감적 관심을 강조한다. (4)일부 자문 위원이 성공하는 기업은 공감 능력을 길러야 한다고 주장할 때, 그것이 의미하는 바는 기업이 시장 조사를 잘 수행해야 한다는 것이다. (5)다시 말해, '공감하는' 기업은 고객의 필요와 요구를 이해하고, 그 필요와 요구를 충족시키려고 노력한다. (6)일부 사람들이 공감을 담은 디자인을 말할 때, 그것이 의미하는 바는 회사가 제품을 디자인할 때 시각 장애인, 청각 장애인, 노인, 비영어권 화자, 색맹 등 각양각색의 사람들의 구체적인 필요 사항을 고려해야 한다는 것이다.

[정답 확인]

다음 글의 주제로 가장 적절한 것은?

① diverse benefits of good market research
좋은 시장 조사의 다양한 이점
② negative factors in making business decisions
사업상의 결정을 내리는 데 있어서 부정적 요소
③ difficulties in designing products with empathic concern
공감적 관심을 가지고 제품을 디자인하는 것의 어려움
④ efforts to build cognitive empathy among employees
직원들 간의 인지적 공감을 형성하기 위한 노력
✔ different interpretations of empathy in business
사업상의 공감에 대한 다양한 해석

[문제 풀이]

지문은 사업에서 기본적인 자질로 일컬어지는 '공감'에 대해 설명하며, 이것이 어떤 하나의 개념으로 통합되지 않음을 언급한다. 문장 (2)부터 글의 마지막까지는 모두 공감의 다양한 측면을 보여 준다. 문장 (2)는 리더의 자질로서 직원과 고객의 관점을 이해하는 공감, 즉 '인지적 공감'에 대한 내용이다. 이와 유사하게 문장 (3)은 리더의 '정서적 공감', '공감적 관심'으로 대표되는 관심과 동정심을 언급한다. 문장 (4)부터 (6)까지는 시장 조사, 즉 고객의 필요와 요구를 이해하는 공감을 담은 디자인을 예시로 들어 설명한다. 이처럼 공감은 사업상 다

양하게 해석될 수 있다는 내용의 주제를 정답으로 골라야 한다. 따라서 정답은 ⑤ 'different interpretations of empathy in business(사업상의 공감에 대한 다양한 해석)'이다.

[오답 풀이]

④ - 지문은 다양하게 해석될 여지가 있는 공감에 대해 설명하고 있으므로, ④와 같이 직원들 간의 인지적 공감을 형성한다는 것은 지문의 일부만을 담고 있다. 따라서 ④는 정답이 될 수 없다.

[중요 어휘]

☐ **empathy**	명사 공감, 감정 이입
☐ **list**	동사 (목록에) 언급하다, 열거하다 / 명사 목록
☐ **desired**	형용사 바라는, 훌륭한
☐ **specify**	동사 (구체적으로) 명시하다
☐ **stress**	동사 강조하다, 강세를 두다
☐ **emphasize**	동사 강조하다, 역설하다, 두드러지게 하다
☐ **perspective**	명사 관점, 시각
☐ **negotiate**	동사 협상하다, 교섭하다
☐ **affective**	형용사 정서적인, 감정적인
☐ **concern**	명사 관심, 배려, 염려
☐ **compassion**	명사 동정심, 연민
☐ **foster**	동사 기르다, 양육하다
☐ **translate**	동사 (특정하게) 의미하다, 번역하다
☐ **fulfill**	동사 충족하다, (의무 등을) 다하다
☐ **take A into account**	A를 고려하다
☐ **interpretation**	명사 해석, 이해, 설명

20 2024년 6월 23번 (정답률 85%) 정답 ②

[지문 끊어 읽기] 과학에서 다양한 관점들의 중요성

(1) If there is little or no diversity of views, /
만약 견해의 다양성이 거의 없거나 전혀 없다면 /
and all scientists see, think, and question the world in a similar way, /
그리고 모든 과학자들이 비슷한 방식으로 세상을 보고, 생각하고, 의문을 제기한다면 /
then they will not, as a community, be as objective / 정답 단서
(삽입구)
그러면 그들은 하나의 공동체로서 객관적이지 않을 것이다 /
as they maintain they are, / or at least aspire to be.
(S' V'① 명사절(that 생략) V'②)
그들이 자신들이 그러하다고 주장하는 만큼 / 혹은 최소한 그러기를 열망하는 만큼

힌트 「as+원급(형/부)+as+A (A만큼 ~한[하게])」의 원급 비교 문장으로서, 문장 (1)에는 형용사의 원급인 objective(객관적인)가 사용되었음.

정답 단서: 과학자들 사이에 견해의 다양성이 거의 없거나 전혀 없다면, 그들은 객관성을 잃게 될 것임.

힌트 밑줄 친 부분은 모두 be동사 형태의 대동사로서, 각각 'are objective', 'be objective'를 의미함.

(2) The solution is / [that there should be far greater diversity /
(S V 비교급 강조)
해결책은 ~이다 / 훨씬 더 많은 다양성이 있어야 한다는 것 /
in the practice of science]: / 주제문
과학의 실행에 있어 / [ ]: S·C(that 명사절)
in gender, ethnicity, and social and cultural backgrounds.
성별, 민족성, 그리고 사회적 문화적 배경에 있어서

주제문: 과학의 실행에 있어, 훨씬 더 많은 다양성이 있어야 함.

(3) Science works / because it is carried out / by people /
과학은 작동한다 / 그것이 수행되기 때문에 / 사람들에 의해서 / (선행사)
[who pursue their curiosity about the natural world /
(병렬① [ ]: 주격 관계대명사절)
자연 세계에 대한 그들의 호기심을 추구하는 /
and test their and each other's ideas /
(병렬②)
그리고 그들의 그리고 서로의 아이디어를 검증하는 /
from as many varied perspectives and angles as possible]. 정답 단서
가능한 한 많은 다양한 관점과 각도에서

힌트 「as+원급(형/부)+as possible (가능한 한 ~한[하게])」의 원급 비교 표현으로서, more이나 most가 아닌 원급 many가 사용되었음에 유의해야 함.

정답 단서: 과학은 자연 세계에 대한 호기심을 가지고 서로의 아이디어를 가능한 한 많은 다양한 관점과 각도에서 검증하는 사람들이 있기 때문에 작동함.

(4) [When science is done / by a diverse group of people], /
과학이 행해질 때 / 다양한 집단의 사람들에 의해 / [ ]: 부사절(조건)①
and [if consensus builds up /
그리고 만약 의견 일치가 확립된다면 /
about a particular area of scientific knowledge], /
과학 지식의 특정 영역에 대하여 / [ ]: 부사절(조건)②
then we can have more confidence / in its objectivity and truth. 정답 단서
그러면 우리는 더 큰 자신감을 가질 수 있다 / 그것의 객관성과 진실성에 있어

정답 단서: 과학이 다양한 집단의 사람들에 의해 행해지고 그들 사이의 의견 일치가 확립될 때, 비로소 그것의 객관성과 진실성을 자신할 수 있게 됨.

[전문 해석]

(1)만약 견해의 다양성이 거의 없거나 전혀 없고, 모든 과학자들이 비슷한 방식으로 세상을 보고, 생각하고, 의문을 제기한다면, 그러면 그들은 하나의 공동체로서 그들이 자신들이 그러하다고 주장하거나 최소한 그러기를 열망하는 만큼 객관적이지 않을 것이다. (2)해결책은 과학의 실행에 있어 훨씬 더 많은 다양성이 있어야 한다는 것이다. 즉 성별, 민족성, 그리고 사회적 문화적 배경에 있어서 (더 많은 다양성이 있어야 한다). (3)과학은 그것이 자연 세계에 대한 그들의 호기심을 추구하고 가능한 한 많은 다양한 관점과 각도에서 그들의 그리고 서로의 아이디어를 검증하는 사람들에 의해서 수행되기 때문에 작동한다. (4)과학이 다양한 집단의 사람들에 의해 행해질 때, 그리고 만약 과학 지식의 특정 영역에 대하여 의견 일치가 확립된다면, 그러면 우리는 그것의 객관성과 진실성에 있어 더 큰 자신감을 가질 수 있다.

[정답 확인]

다음 글의 주제로 가장 적절한 것은?

① value of acquiring scientific knowledge through trial and error
시행착오를 통해 과학적 지식을 습득하는 것의 가치
✔② necessity of various perspectives in practicing science
과학을 실행함에 있어 다양한 관점들의 필요성
③ benefits of building good relationships among scientists
과학자들 간에 좋은 관계를 형성하는 것의 이점
④ curiosity as a key factor in designing experiments
실험을 설계하는 데 있어 핵심 요소로서의 호기심
⑤ importance of specialization in scientific research
과학적 연구에서 전문화의 중요성

[중요 어휘]

☐ **diversity**	명사 다양성, 포괄성
☐ **question**	동사 ~에 의문을 제기하다 / 명사 질문
☐ **objective**	형용사 객관적인, 사실에 기초한 / 명사 목적
☐ **maintain**	동사 주장하다, 유지하다, 부양하다
☐ **aspire**	동사 열망하다, 갈망하다
☐ **practice**	명사 실행 / 동사 실행하다
☐ **ethnicity**	명사 민족성
☐ **carry out**	~을 수행[실시]하다
☐ **pursue**	동사 추구하다, 추적하다
☐ **curiosity**	명사 호기심
☐ **test**	동사 검증하다, 검사하다
☐ **varied**	형용사 다양한
☐ **angle**	명사 각도, 관점
☐ **diverse**	형용사 다양한, 여러 가지의
☐ **consensus**	명사 의견 일치, 합의
☐ **build up**	확립되다, 개발하다, 높이다
☐ **particular**	형용사 특정한, 특별한, 까다로운
☐ **confidence**	명사 자신감, 확신
☐ **objectivity**	명사 객관성

21 2024년 9월 23번 (정답률 75%) 정답 ②

[지문 끊어 읽기] 과학에 대한 두 가지 견해

(1) People seem to recognize / that the arts are cultural activities /
(접속사 선행사①)
사람들은 인식하는 것처럼 보인다 / 예술이 문화적인 활동이라고 /
[that draw on (or react against) certain cultural traditions, certain shared understanding, and certain values and ideas / (선행사②)
특정한 문화적 전통, 특정한 공유된 이해, 그리고 특정한 가치와 생각에 기반한(또는 그에 반하는) /
[that are characteristic of the time and place] / [ ]: 주격 관계대명사절②(that are ~ place)
시기와 장소에 특유한 / (선행사③)
in which the art is created]. [ ]: 주격 관계대명사절①(that draw ~ created)
(전치사+목적격 관계대명사절③)
예술이 창작된

힌트 한 문장 내에서 '선행사+관계대명사절'이 세 번이나 등장하여 수식 관계를 잘 파악해야 하는 문장임. 각 요소에 달려 있는 번호(①~③)끼리 잘 짝지어 관계를 확인할 것.

(2) In the case of science, however, / opinions differ.
그러나 과학의 경우에 / 의견이 다르다

(3) Some scientists, like the great biologist J. B. S. Haldane, /
위대한 생물학자 J. B. S. Haldane과 같은 몇몇 과학자들은 /
see science in a similar light /
비슷한 관점에서 과학을 본다 /
— as a historical activity /
역사적인 활동으로 /
that occurs in a particular time and place, /
특정한 시기와 장소에서 발생하는 /
and that needs to be understood within that context.
그리고 그 맥락 안에서 이해될 필요가 있는

힌트 부정대명사 'Some ~', 'Others ~'는 '일부는 ~', '또 다른 일부는 ~'이라는 뜻으로, 두 개 이상의 집단에서 상반된 의견이 있음을 나타내는 의미로 사용함.

정답 단서 어떤 과학자들은 과학을 특정한 시기와 장소에서 발생하고 그 맥락 안에서 이해될 필요가 있는 역사적인 활동으로 봄.

(4) Others, however, / see science as a purely "objective" pursuit, /
그러나 다른 이들은 / 과학을 완전히 '객관적인' 일로 본다 /
[uninfluenced by the cultural viewpoint and values of those /
사람들의 문화적인 관점과 가치에 의해 영향을 받지 않는 /
who create it].
그것을 창조한

[ ]: 과거분사구

정답 단서 반면 다른 사람들은 과학을 문화적인 관점이나 가치에 영향을 받지 않는 객관적인 일로 봄.

(5) In describing this view of science, /
과학에 대한 이러한 관점을 묘사하는 데 있어 /
philosopher Hugh Lacey speaks of the belief /
철학자 Hugh Lacey는 믿음에 대해 말한다 /
[that there is an underlying order of the world /
세계의 근본적인 질서가 있다는 /
[which is simply there to be discovered] /
그저 거기에 있어서 발견되는 /
— the world of pure "fact" / stripped of any link with value].
완전한 '사실'의 세계 / 가치와 어떤 연결 고리도 없는

[ ]: 주격 관계대명사절 / 부사적 용법(결과) / 과거분사구 / [ ]: the belief와 동격

(6) The aim of science / according to this view /
과학의 목표는 / 이 관점에 따라 /
is to represent this world of pure "fact", /
이 완전한 '사실'의 세계를 표현하는 것이다 /
independently of any relationship / [it might bear contingently /
어떠한 관계와도 별개로 / 그것이 혹여라도 맺을 수도 있는 /
to human practices and experiences].
인간의 관습 및 경험과

[ ]: 목적격 관계대명사절(관계대명사 생략)

[전문 해석]

(1)사람들은 예술이 창작된 시기와 장소에 특유한 특정한 문화적 전통, 특정한 공유된 이해, 그리고 특정한 가치와 생각에 기반한(또는 그에 반하는) 문화적인 활동이라고 인식하는 것처럼 보인다. (2)그러나 과학의 경우에 의견이 다르다. (3)위대한 생물학자 J. B. S. Haldane과 같은 몇몇 과학자들은 비슷한 관점에서 과학을 보는데, 특정한 시기와 장소에서 발생하고 그 맥락 안에서 이해될 필요가 있는 역사적인 활동으로 본다는 것이다. (4)그러나 다른 이들은 과학을 그것을 창조한 사람들의 문화적인 관점과 가치에 의해 영향을 받지 않는 완전히 '객관적인' 일로 본다. (5)과학에 대한 이러한 관점을 묘사하는 데 있어, 철학자 Hugh Lacey는 그저 거기에 있어서 발견되는 세계의 근본적인 질서가 있다는 믿음에 대해 말하는데, 이것은 가치와 어떤 연결 고리도 없는 완전한 '사실'의 세계이다. (6)이 관점에 따라 과학의 목표는 그것이 인간의 관습 및 경험과 혹여라도 맺을 수도 있는 어떠한 관계와도 별개로 완전한 '사실'의 세계를 표현하는 것이다.

[정답 확인]

다음 글의 주제로 가장 적절한 것은?

① misconceptions on how experimental data should be measured
실험 데이터가 어떻게 측정되어야 하는지에 대한 오해
✔ views on whether science is free from cultural context or not
과학이 문화적 맥락에서 자유로운지 아닌지에 대한 관점
③ ways for minimizing cultural bias in scientific pursuits
과학 연구에서 문화적 편견을 최소화하는 방법
④ challenges in achieving objectivity in scientific studies
과학 연구에서 객관성을 성취하는 데의 어려움
⑤ functions of science in analyzing cultural phenomena
문화적 현상을 분석하는 데 있어 과학의 기능

[중요 어휘]

recognize	동사 인식하다, 인지하다
draw on	~에 기반하다, ~을 이용하다
react against	~에 반하다[반발하다]
be characteristic of	~에 특유한, ~의 특징을 나타내는
differ	동사 (의견이) 다르다
biologist	명사 생물학자
light	명사 관점, 견해, 빛
historical	형용사 역사적인, 역사와 관련된
occur	동사 발생하다, 일어나다
context	명사 맥락, 문맥
purely	부사 완전히, 순전히
objective	형용사 객관적인 / 명사 목적, 목표
pursuit	명사 일, 연구, 추구
uninfluenced	형용사 영향을 받지 않은
viewpoint	명사 관점, 견해
speak of	~에 대해 말하다
underlying	형용사 근본적인, 근원적인, 기저의
stripped of	~가 없는
aim	명사 목표, 목적 / 동사 겨냥하다
represent	동사 표현하다, 나타내다
independently of	~와 별개로[관계없이]
bear	동사 (관계 등을) 맺다, 참다, 견디다
contingently	부사 혹여라도, 우연히, 경우에 따라서
practice	명사 관습, 관행, 연습, 실행 / 동사 연습하다

문제편 p.074

07 제목 추론

01 2020년 3월 24번 (정답률 85%)

정답 ④

[지문 끊어 읽기]

식품 라벨에 숨겨진 설탕에 관한 진실

(1) If a food contains more sugar / than any other ingredient, /
어떤 식품이 설탕을 더 많이 함유하고 있으면 / 다른 어떤 성분보다 /
government regulations require /
정부 규제는 요구한다 /
that sugar be listed first on the label.
설탕이 라벨에 첫 번째로 기재될 것을

힌트 '~할 것을 요구/요청하다'라는 뜻의 'require(요구/요청동사) that S (should) V' 구문임. 여기에선 should가 생략되었으니 V에는 동사원형의 형태가 와야 하므로 'be'가 온 것임.

(2) But if a food contains several different kinds of sweeteners, /
그러나 어떤 식품이 몇몇의 다양한 종류의 감미료를 함유하고 있으면 /
they can be listed separately, /
그것들은 따로따로 기재될 수 있다 /
which pushes each one / farther down the list.
계속적 용법의 관계대명사
그런데 그것은 각각을 밀어 내린다 / 목록에서 더 아래로

(3) This requirement has led the food industry to put in three different sources of sugar /
5형식V O O·C(to V)
이 요건은 식품 업계가 세 가지의 다른 당의 원료를 넣게 해 왔다 /
so that they don't have to say / the food has that much sugar.
접속사 역할
그들이 말할 필요가 없도록 / 그 식품이 그렇게 많은 설탕을 포함하고 있다고

(4) So sugar doesn't appear first. 정답 단서
따라서 설탕은 첫 번째로 나오지 않는다

(5) Whatever the true motive, /
진짜 동기가 무엇이든지 간에 /
ingredient labeling still does not fully convey /
성분 표시는 여전히 완전하게 전달하지 못한다 /
the amount of sugar being added to food, / 주제문
식품에 첨가되어 있는 설탕의 양을 /
certainly not in a language /
선행사
확실히 언어로 되어 있지 않다 /
that's easy for consumers to understand.
주격 관계대명사 의미상의 주어 부사적 용법(형용사 수식)
소비자가 이해하기 쉬운

(6) A world-famous cereal brand's label, / for example, /
세계적으로 유명한 시리얼 브랜드의 라벨은 / 예를 들어 /
indicates / that the cereal has 11 grams of sugar per serving.
표시한다 / 그 시리얼이 1인분당 11그램의 설탕을 함유하고 있다고

(7) But nowhere does it tell consumers /
하지만 어디에서도 소비자들에게 말해주지 않는다 /
that more than one-third of the box /
상자의 3분의 1 이상이 /
contains added sugar.
첨가당을 함유하고 있다고

힌트 부정어구 'nowhere'을 강조하기 위해 부정어구를 문두에 위치시키고, 주어와 동사를 도치시킨 문장임. 동사로 'tell'이라는 일반동사가 왔으므로 '부정어구+조동사 do+S+V'의 형태가 되었음. be동사가 오는 경우에는 '부정어구+be동사+S'의 형태가 됨.

[전문 해석]

(1)어떤 식품이 다른 어떤 성분보다 설탕을 더 많이 함유하고 있으면, 정부 규제는 설탕이 라벨에 첫 번째로 기재될 것을 요구한다. (2)그러나 어떤 식품이 몇몇의 다양한 종류의 감미료를 함유하고 있으면, 그것들은 따로따로 기재될 수 있는데, 그것은 각각(의 감미료)를 목록에서 더 아래로 밀어 내린다. (3)이 요건은 식품 업계가 그 식품이 그렇게 많은 설탕을 포함하고 있다고 그들이 말할 필요가 없도록 세 가지의 다른 당의 원료를 (식품에) 넣게 해 왔다. (4)따라서 설탕은 (라벨에서) 첫 번째로 나오지 않는다. (5)진짜 동기가 무엇이든지 간에, 성분 표시는 여전히 식품에 첨가되어 있는 설탕의 양을 완전하게 전달하지 못하고, 확실히 소비자가 이해하기 쉬운 언어로 되어 있지 않다. (6)예를 들어, 세계적으로 유명한 시리얼 브랜드의 라벨은 그 시리얼이 1인분당 11그램의 설탕을 함유하고 있다고 표시한다. (7)하지만 어디에서도 (시리얼) 상자의 3분의 1 이상이 첨가당을 함유하고 있다고 소비자들에게 말해주지 않는다.

[정답 확인]

다음 글의 제목으로 가장 적절한 것은?

① Artificial Sweeteners: Good or Bad?
인공적인 감미료: 좋을까 아니면 나쁠까?
② Consumer Benefits of Ingredient Labeling
성분 표시로 얻는 소비자 이익
③ Sugar: An Energy Booster for Your Brain
설탕: 당신의 뇌를 위한 에너지 촉진제
④ Truth About Sugar Hidden in Food Labels
식품 라벨에 숨겨진 설탕에 관한 진실
⑤ What Should We Do to Reduce Sugar Intake?
설탕 섭취를 줄이기 위해 우리는 무엇을 해야 하는가?

[중요 어휘]

☐ contain	동사 함유하다, 포함하다
☐ ingredient	명사 성분, 재료
☐ regulation	명사 규제, 규정
☐ require	동사 요구하다, 필요로 하다
☐ list	동사 (표·명부 등에) 기재하다, 기입하다
☐ sweetener	명사 감미료
☐ separately	부사 따로따로, 개별적으로
☐ requirement	명사 요건, 필요조건
☐ motive	명사 동기 / 동사 동기를 부여하다
☐ convey	동사 전달하다, 운반하다
☐ indicate	동사 표시하다, 나타내다, 가리키다
☐ serving	명사 1인분

02 2019년 9월 24번 (정답률 75%)

정답 ⑤

[지문 끊어 읽기]

풀리지 않은 수학 문제들

(1) The earliest challenges and contests /
가장 초기의 도전들과 경쟁들은 /
to solve important problems in mathematics /
수학에서 중요한 문제들을 풀어내려는 /
date back / to the sixteenth and seventeenth centuries.
거슬러 올라간다 / 16세기와 17세기까지

(2) Some of these problems /
이 문제들 중 몇몇은 /
have continued to challenge mathematicians / until modern times.
수학자들에게 계속해서 도전해 오고 있다 / 현대까지도

(3) For example, /
예를 들어 /
Pierre de Fermat issued a set of mathematical challenges /
피에르 드 페르마는 일련의 수학적 도전 과제들을 발표했다 /
in 1657, / many on prime numbers and divisibility.
1657년에 / 다수가 소수와 가분성에 관한 것

힌트 a set of mathematical challenges를 부연 설명하고 있음. 여기서 전치사 on은 about의 의미임.

힌트 '가분성'이란 수학에서 0이 아닌 어떤 정수로 나누어떨어지는 것을 말함.

(4) The solution /
해답은 /
to what is now known as Fermat's Last Theorem /
오늘날 페르마의 마지막 정리라고 알려진 것에 대한 /
was not established until the late 1990s / by Andrew Wiles.
1990년대 후반에서야 입증되었다 / Andrew Wiles에 의해

힌트 「not A until B」: B하고 나서야 비로소 A이다
=It is[was] not until B that A
=Not until B+be동사[do/조동사]+A
=A only after B

(5) David Hilbert, a German mathematician, /
독일의 수학자 David Hilbert는 /
identified 23 unsolved problems / in 1900 / with the hope /
23개의 풀리지 않은 문제들을 식별해 냈다 / 1900년에 / 희망을 가지고 /
that these problems would be solved / in the twenty-first century.
이 문제들이 풀릴 것이라는 / 21세기에는

(6) Although some of the problems were solved, /
비록 그 문제들 중 일부는 해결되었으나 /

others remain unsolved / to this day.
나머지들은 여전히 풀리지 않은 채 남아 있다 / 오늘날까지도

(7) More recently, in 2000, /
더 최근인 2000년에는 /
the Clay Mathematics Institute named seven mathematical problems / (과거시제)
클레이 수학 연구소가 7가지 수학적 문제들을 지정했다 /
that had not been solved / with the hope / (과거완료(수동))
풀리지 않았던 / 희망을 가지고 /
that they could be solved in the twenty-first century. 정답 단서
21세기에는 그것들이 풀릴 것이라는

(8) A $1 million prize will be awarded /
100만 달러의 상금이 주어질 것이다 /
for solving each of these seven problems. 정답 단서
이 7개의 문제를 해결하는 것에 대해 각각

[전문 해석]

(1)수학에서 중요한 문제들을 풀어내려는 가장 초기의 도전들과 경쟁들은 16세기와 17세기까지 거슬러 올라간다. (2)이 (어려운) 문제들 중 몇몇은 현대까지도 수학자들에게 계속해서 도전해 오고 있다. (3)예를 들어 피에르 드 페르마는 1657년에 일련의 수학적 도전 과제들을 발표했는데, (그것들 중) 다수가 소수와 가분성에 관한 것(이었다). (4)오늘날 페르마의 마지막 정리라고 알려진 것에 대한 해답은 Andrew Wiles에 의해 1990년대 후반에서야 입증되었다. (5)독일의 수학자 David Hilbert는 (아직 풀리지 않은) 이 문제들이 21세기에는 풀릴 것이라는 희망을 가지고, 1900년에 23개의 풀리지 않은 문제들을 식별해 냈다. (6)비록 그 문제들 중 일부는 해결되었으나, 나머지들은 오늘날까지도 여전히 풀리지 않은 채 남아 있다. (7)더 최근인 2000년에는 클레이 수학 연구소가 21세기에는 그것들이 풀릴 것이라는 희망을 가지고, (그 당시까지) 풀리지 않았던 7가지 수학적 문제들을 지정했다. (8)이 7개의 문제를 해결하는 것에 대해 각각 100만 달러의 상금이 주어질 것이다.

- Fermat's Last Theorem(페르마의 마지막 정리): 'n이 3 이상의 정수일 때, $x^n+y^n=z^n$을 만족시키는 정수 x, y, z는 존재하지 않는다'는 명제로, 17세기 프랑스 수학자 피에르 드 페르마가 그의 책 귀퉁이에 적어 놓은 이후 약 350년간 풀리지 않는 난제로 남아 있었으며, 1990년대 후반 최종적으로 Andrew Wiles에 의해 증명되었다.
- Clay Mathematics Institute(클레이 수학 연구소, CMI): 수학의 발전과 전파를 목적으로 한 미국 매사추세츠주에 있는 비영리 재단. 새로운 밀레니엄을 기념하여 2000년 5월 24일에 오랫동안 풀리지 않은 7가지 수학적 문제들을 '밀레니엄 문제'로 지정하고 문제당 100만 달러의 상금을 내걸었다.

[정답 확인]

다음 글의 제목으로 가장 적절한 것은?

① Glory in the Past, Ugliness in the Present
과거의 영광, 현재의 추한 모습
② Doubt: What Leads to Unexpected Findings
의구심: 예기치 못한 발견으로 이끄는 것
③ Formulas in Math Solve Problems in Other Areas
수학 공식들이 다른 영역의 문제들을 해결한다
④ Unknown Geniuses Achieving the Greatest Things
가장 위대한 일들을 해 내는 무명의 천재들
✔⑤ Unsolved Math Problems Passed to Future Generations
미래 세대에 건네진 풀리지 않은 수학 문제들

[중요 어휘]

□ challenge	명사 도전 (과제), 난제 / 동사 도전하다, 이의를 제기하다
□ date back to	(시기가) ~까지 거슬러 올라가다
□ issue	동사 발표하다, 발행하다 / 명사 쟁점, 문제
□ mathematical	형용사 수학적인, 수리적인, 아주 정확한
□ prime number	명사 (수학에서의) 소수
□ divisibility	명사 가분성, 나누어떨어짐
□ establish	동사 입증하다, 확립하다
□ identify	동사 식별해 내다, 확인하다
□ name	동사 (정확히) 지정하다, 밝히다, 명명하다

문제편 p.075

03 2019년 11월 24번 (정답률 75%)

핵심 지문의 초반에서 일반적인 믿음(general belief)이나 상식 등을 먼저 언급하면, 그 이후에 그것과 상반되는 내용이 전개되는 경우가 많음.
이 지문에서도 스포츠가 폭력을 감소시킨다는 일반적인 믿음을 먼저 제시하고, 실제로는 그와 반대로 전투적 스포츠가 인기 있는 사회에서는 전쟁 또한 자주 발생했다는 내용의 연구를 소개하고 있음.

정답 ②

[지문 끊어 읽기] 전투적 스포츠와 인간의 공격성

(1) There has been a general belief / that sport is a way /
일반적인 믿음이 있어왔다 / 스포츠가 하나의 방법이라는 /
of reducing violence.
폭력을 감소시키는

(2) Anthropologist Richard Sipes tests this notion /
인류학자 Richard Sipes는 이 개념을 검증한다 /
in a classic study of the relationship / between sport and violence.
관계에 대한 고전적인 연구에서 / 스포츠와 폭력의

(3) Focusing on what he calls "combative sports," / those sports / (= 동격)
그가 '전투적 스포츠'라고 부르는 것에 초점을 맞추면서 / 그러한 스포츠들 /
including actual body contact between opponents or simulated warfare, / (병렬① 병렬②)
경쟁자들 사이의 실제 신체 접촉이나 모의 전투를 포함하는 /
he hypothesizes / that if sport is an alternative to violence, /
그는 가설을 세운다 / 만일 스포츠가 폭력의 대체물이라면 /
then one would expect to find an inverse correlation /
우리가 역 상관관계를 찾을 것을 기대할 수 있을 것이라고 /
between the popularity of combative sports /
전투적 스포츠의 인기 /
and the frequency and intensity of warfare.
그리고 전투의 빈도 및 강도 사이에서

★중요 문장 (3)에서 언급된 '역 상관관계'를 문장 (4)에서는 전투적 스포츠가 증가할 때 전투 가능성이 감소한다고 풀어서 설명하고 있음.

(4) In other words, / the more combative sports / (the 비교급)
다시 말해 / 전투적 스포츠가 더 많을수록 /
(e.g., football, boxing) / the less likely warfare. (the 비교급)
(예를 들어 축구, 권투) / 전투는 더 적을 것이다

(5) Using the Human Relations Area Files and a sample of 20 societies, /
Human Relations Area Files와 20개 사회의 표본을 이용하여 /
Sipes tests the hypothesis /
Sipes는 그 가설을 검증한다 /
and discovers a significant relationship /
그리고 유의미한 관계를 발견한다 /
between combative sports and violence, /
전투적 스포츠와 폭력 사이의 /
but a direct one, / not the inverse correlation of his hypothesis. 정답 단서 (=correlation)
직접적인 상관관계를 / 그의 가설에서의 역 상관관계가 아닌

힌트 'but ~, not ~'은 'not A(명사) but B(명사)'의 명사구로, 'a significant relationship(유의미한 관계)'의 동격임. 다만 여기서는 'but B, not A'로 순서가 바뀌어 쓰였음.

(6) According to Sipes' analysis, /
Sipes의 분석에 따르면 /
the more pervasive and popular combative sports are /
전투적 스포츠가 더 만연하고 인기가 많을수록 /
in a society, / the more likely that society is / to engage in war. (지시형용사)
한 사회에서 / 그 사회는 가능성이 더 크다 / 전쟁에 참여할

(7) So, Sipes draws the obvious conclusion /
그러므로 Sipes는 분명한 결론을 도출해낸다 /
that combative sports are not alternatives to war / (S' V'①)
전투적 스포츠가 전쟁의 대체물이 아니라는 /
but rather are reflections of the same aggressive impulses / (V'②)
오히려 동일한 공격적인 충동의 반영이라는 /
in human society. 주제문
인간 사회의

힌트 원칙적으로, 2개의 문장을 연결하기 위해서는 접속사 1개가 반드시 필요하지만, 'The 비교급 (S V), the 비교급 (S V)' 구문은 문장과 문장의 연결임에도 불구하고 접속사 없이 '~할수록 …하다'라는 의미를 가지는 특수한 구문임.

[중요 구문]

(6) ①: Combative sports are more pervasive and popular in a society. (S V 비교급)
②: That society is more likely to engage in war. (S V 비교급)
⇒ **The** more pervasive and popular combative sports are in a society, **the** more likely that society is to engage in war.

문제편 p.075

[전문 해석]

(1)스포츠가 폭력을 감소시키는 하나의 방법이라는 일반적인 믿음이 있어왔다. (2)인류학자 Richard Sipes는 스포츠와 폭력의 관계에 대한 고전적인 연구에서 이 개념을 검증한다. (3)그가 (소위) '전투적 스포츠'라고 부르는 것, 즉 경쟁자들 사이의 실제 신체 접촉이나 모의 전투를 포함하는 그러한 스포츠들에 초점을 맞추면서, 그는 만일 스포츠가 폭력의 대체물이라면 (우리가) 전투적 스포츠의 인기와 전투의 빈도 및 강도 사이에서 역 상관관계를 찾을 것을 기대할 수 있을 것이라고 가설을 세운다. (4)다시 말해 전투적 스포츠(예를 들어 축구, 권투)가 더 많을수록, 전투는 더 적을 것이다. (5)Human Relations Area Files와 20개 사회의 표본을 이용하여 Sipes는 그 가설을 검증하고 전투적 스포츠와 폭력 사이의 유의미한 관계, (단) 그의 가설에서의 역 상관관계가 아닌 직접적인 상관관계를 발견한다. (6)Sipes의 분석에 따르면 전투적 스포츠가 한 사회에서 더 만연하고 인기가 많을수록, 그 사회는 전쟁에 참여할 가능성이 더 크다. (7)그러므로 Sipes는 전투적 스포츠가 전쟁의 대체물이 아니라 오히려 인간 사회의 동일한 공격적인 충동의 반영이라는 분명한 결론을 도출해낸다.

- Human Relations Area Files(HRAF): 비교문화 관련 연구들을 지원하고 풍부한 연구 자료 및 교수 학습 자료를 제공하는 국제적 비영리기관으로, 미국 코네티컷주에 위치해 있다. 회원뿐만 아니라 비회원을 위한 데이터베이스를 따로 구축하여 개방하고 있다.

[정답 확인]

다음 글의 제목으로 가장 적절한 것은?

① Is There a Distinction among Combative Sports?
전투적 스포츠들 사이에 차이가 있는가?

✔ Combative Sports Mirror Human Aggressiveness
전투적 스포츠는 인간의 공격성을 반영한다

③ Never Let Your Aggressive Impulses Consume You!
절대 당신의 공격적인 충동이 당신을 집어삼키지 않도록 하라!

④ International Conflicts: Creating New Military Alliances
국제 분쟁: 새로운 군사 동맹의 형성

⑤ Combative Sports Are More Common among the Oppressed
전투적 스포츠는 탄압받는 이들 사이에서 더 흔하다

[중요 어휘]

☐ violence	명사 폭력, 폭행
☐ anthropologist	명사 인류학자
☐ notion	명사 개념, 생각
☐ combative	형용사 전투적인, 금방이라도 싸울 듯한
☐ opponent	명사 경쟁자, 상대방
☐ simulate	동사 모의하다, 시뮬레이션하다
☐ warfare	명사 전투, 전쟁
☐ hypothesize	동사 가설을 세우다
☐ alternative	명사 대체물, 대안
☐ inverse	형용사 역의, 반대의 / 명사 역
☐ correlation	명사 상관관계, 연관성
☐ frequency	명사 빈도, 주파수
☐ intensity	명사 강도, 세기
☐ hypothesis	명사 가설, 가정, 추측
☐ significant	형용사 유의미한, 상당한, 중요한
☐ pervasive	형용사 만연한, 스며드는
☐ be likely to V	~할 가능성이 있다, ~하기 쉽다
☐ engage in	~에 참여하다, 종사하다
☐ reflection	명사 반영, 반사, 반성
☐ aggressive	형용사 공격적인, 싸우기를 좋아하는
☐ impulse	명사 충동, 충격

핵심 고대 발명품들의 역사가 계속 새로 발견되고 있다는 내용의 글로, 도자기를 예시로 들고 있음. 제목을 추론하는 문제는 글의 주제를 간결하고 분명하게 담은 선택지를 고르면 됨.

04

2020년 6월 24번 (정답률 75%) 정답 ③

[지문 끊어 읽기] 발명품의 기원

(1) Many inventions were invented / thousands of years ago /
많은 발명품들은 발명되었다 / 수천 년 전에 /
so it can be difficult / to know their exact origins.
(it: 형식상의 주어, to know their exact origins: 내용상의 주어)
따라서 어려울 수 있다 / 그것들의 정확한 기원을 아는 것은

(2) Sometimes scientists discover a model of an early invention /
때때로 과학자들은 초기 발명품의 모형을 발견한다 /
and from this model / they can accurately tell us /
그리고 이 모형으로부터 / 그들은 우리에게 정확히 말해 줄 수 있다 /
how old it is / and where it came from.
그것이 얼마나 오래되었는지를 / 그리고 그것이 어디에서 왔는지를

힌트 tell의 직접목적어로 의문사절이 온 형태임. 의문사가 이끄는 절의 어순은 '의문사 (+형용사)+주어+동사'임.

(3) However, / there is always the possibility /
그러나 / 가능성이 항상 존재한다 /
[that in the future other scientists will discover /
미래에 다른 과학자들이 발견할 /
an even older model of the same invention /
똑같은 발명품의 훨씬 더 오래된 모형을 /
in a different part of the world]. [ ]: the possibility와 동격
세계의 다른 곳에서

(4) In fact, / we are forever discovering /
사실 / 우리는 끊임없이 발견하고 있다 /
the history of ancient inventions. 주제문
고대 발명품들의 역사를

(5) An example of this / is the invention of pottery.
이것의 한 예가 / 도자기라는 발명품이다

(6) For many years / archaeologists believed /
수년 동안 / 고고학자들은 믿었다 /
that pottery was first invented in the Near East /
(that: 접속사, the Near East: 선행사)
근동지역에서 도자기가 처음 발명되었다고 /
(around modern Iran) / where they had found pots /
(where: 관계부사(장소))
(현대의 이란 근처) / 그들이 도자기를 발견했던 /
dating back to 9,000 B.C.
기원전 9,000년으로 거슬러 올라가는

(7) In the 1960s, / however, / older pots from 10,000 B.C. /
1960년대에 / 하지만 / 기원전 10,000년으로부터의 더 오래된 도자기들이 /
were found on Honshu Island, Japan.
일본의 혼슈섬에서 발견되었다

(8) There is always a possibility /
가능성은 언제나 존재한다 /
that in the future archaeologists will find /
(that: a possibility와 동격)
미래에 고고학자들이 발견할 /
even older pots somewhere else.
다른 어딘가에서 훨씬 더 오래된 도자기를

[전문 해석]

(1)많은 발명품들은 수천 년 전에 발명되어서 그것들의 정확한 기원을 아는 것은 어려울 수 있다. (2)때때로 과학자들은 초기 발명품의 모형을 발견하고 이 모형으로부터 (그들은) 그것이 얼마나 오래되었고 어디에서 왔는지를 우리에게 정확히 말해 줄 수 있다. (3)그러나 미래에 다른 과학자들이 세계의 다른 곳에서 똑같은 발명품의 훨씬 더 오래된 모형을 발견할 가능성이 항상 존재한다. (4)사실 우리는 고대 발명품들의 역사를 끊임없이 발견하고 있다. (5)이것의 한 예가 도자기라는 발명품이다. (6)수년 동안 고고학자들은 그들이 기원전 9,000년으로 거슬러 올라가는 도자기를 발견했던 근동지역(현대의 이란 근처)에서 도자기가 처음 발명되었다고 믿었다. (7)하지만 1960년대에 기원전 10,000년(으로부터)의 더 오래된 도자기들이 일본의 혼슈섬에서 발견되었다. (8)미래에 고고학자들이 다른 어딘가에서 훨씬 더 오래된 도자기를 발견할 가능성은 언제나 존재한다.

[정답 확인]

다음 글의 제목으로 가장 적절한 것은?

① How Can You Tell Original from Fake?
당신은 어떻게 원본과 모조품을 구별할 수 있는가?

② Exploring the Materials of Ancient Pottery
고대 도자기의 재료를 탐구하기

✔ Origin of Inventions: Never-Ending Journey
발명품의 기원: 끝나지 않는 여정

④ Learn from the Past, Change for the Better
과거로부터 배우고, 더 나은 것을 위해 변화하라

⑤ Science as a Driving Force for Human Civilization
인간 문명의 추진력으로서의 과학

[중요 어휘]

invention	명사 발명품, 발명
origin	명사 기원, 출처
accurately	부사 정확히, 정밀하게
pottery	명사 도자기
archaeologist	명사 고고학자
date back to	~로 거슬러 올라가다
tell A from B	A와 B를 구별하다
material	명사 재료 / 형용사 물질의
driving force	추진력
civilization	명사 문명

05 2021년 3월 24번 (정답률 75%)

정답 ①

[지문 끊어 읽기] 연구자의 요건

(1) Some beginning researchers mistakenly believe /
일부 처음 시작하는 연구자들은 잘못 믿는다 /
that a good hypothesis is one / that is guaranteed to be right /
접속사 / 주격 관계대명사
좋은 가설은 가설이라고 / 옳다는 것이 보장된 /
(e.g., *alcohol will slow down reaction time*).
(예를 들면 '알코올은 반응 시간을 둔화시킬 것이다')

(2) However, / if we already know / your hypothesis is true /
하지만 / 이미 우리가 알고 있다면 / 당신의 가설이 사실이라고 /
before you test it, / testing your hypothesis /
당신이 그것을 검사해 보기 전에 / 당신의 가설을 검사하는 것은 /
won't tell us anything new.
우리에게 아무런 새로운 것도 말해 주지 않을 것이다

(3) Remember, / research is supposed to produce *new* knowledge.
기억하라 / 연구란 '새로운' 지식을 생산해야 한다는 것을

(4) To get new knowledge, / you, as a researcher-explorer, /
부사적 용법(~하기 위해서)
새로운 지식을 얻기 위해서 / 연구자이자 탐험가로서 당신은 /
need to leave the safety of the shore (established facts) /
병렬①
해변의 안전함(기정 사실)을 떠날 필요가 있다 /
and venture into uncharted waters / 주제문
병렬②
그리고 미개척 영역으로 과감히 들어가 볼 필요가 있다 /
(as Einstein said, / "If we knew what we were doing, /
아인슈타인이 말했듯이 / 우리가 무엇을 하고 있는지 안다면 /
it would not be called research, would it?").
그것은 연구라고 불리지 않을 것이다, 그렇지

(5) If your predictions /
S'
당신의 예측이 /
about what will happen in these uncharted waters /
간접의문문: 전치사의 목적어
이런 미개척 영역에서 무엇이 일어날 것인지에 관한 /
are wrong, / that's okay: 정답 단서
V'
틀린다면 / 그것은 괜찮다

(6) Scientists are allowed to make mistakes /
과학자는 실수를 저지르는 것이 허용되어 있다 /
(as Bates said, / "Research is the process of going up alleys /
Bates가 말했듯이 / 연구는 골목길을 올라가 보는 과정이다 /
to see if they are blind").
=alleys
그것들이 막혀 있는지 보려고

(7) Indeed, / scientists often learn more from predictions /
정말로 / 과학자는 예측들로부터 종종 더 많이 배운다 /
that do not turn out / than from those that do.
주격 관계대명사절
결과를 내지 않는 / 결과를 내는 예측들보다는

힌트 those는 앞에 나온 predictions를 지칭하는 대명사, do는 turn out을 대신하는 대동사임.

[전문 해석]

(1)일부 처음 시작하는 연구자들은 좋은 가설은 옳다는 것이 보장된 가설이라고 잘못 믿는다(예를 들면, '알코올은 반응 시간을 둔화시킬 것이다'). (2)하지만 당신이 가설을 검사해 보기 전에 그것이 사실이라고 이미 우리가 알고 있다면 당신의 가설을 검사하는 것은 우리에게 아무런 새로운 것도 말해 주지 않을 것이다. (3)연구란 '새로운' 지식을 생산해야 한다는 것을 기억하라. (4)새로운 지식을 얻기 위해서 연구자이자 탐험가로서 당신은 해변의 안전함(기정 사실)을 떠나 미개척 영역으로 과감히 들어가 볼 필요가 있다(아인슈타인이 말했듯이, "우리가 무엇을 하고 있는지 안다면, 그것은 연구라고 불리지 않을 것이다, 그렇지?"). (5)이런 미개척 영역에서 무엇이 일어날 것인지에 관한 당신의 예측이 틀린다면 그것은 괜찮다. (6)과학자는 실수를 저지르는 것이 허용되어 있다(Bates가 말했듯이, "연구는 골목길이 막혀 있는지 보려고(막다른 길인지 보려고) 골목길을 올라가 보는 과정이다."). (7)정말로 과학자는 결과를 내는 예측들보다는 결과를 내지 않는 예측들로부터 종종 더 많이 배운다.

[정답 확인]

다음 글의 제목으로 가장 적절한 것은?

✔ Researchers, Don't Be Afraid to Be Wrong
연구자여, 틀리는 것을 두려워 말라
② Hypotheses Are Different from Wild Guesses
가설은 터무니없는 추측과 다르다
③ Why Researchers Are Reluctant to Share Their Data
연구자가 정보 공유를 주저하는 이유
④ One Small Mistake Can Ruin Your Whole Research
하나의 작은 실수가 여러분의 연구 전체를 망칠 수 있다
⑤ Why Hard Facts Don't Change Our Minds
확실한 사실이 우리의 생각을 바꾸지 않는 이유

[중요 어휘]

mistakenly	부사 잘못하여, 틀리게
hypothesis	명사 가설 (복수형 hypotheses)
guarantee	동사 보장하다
slow down	~을 둔화시키다
shore	명사 해변
established facts	기정 사실
venture into	~로 과감히 들어가 보다
uncharted waters	미개척 영역
prediction	명사 예측
alley	명사 골목길
blind	형용사 막다른, 눈이 먼
reluctant	형용사 주저하는, 꺼리는
hard	형용사 확실한, 엄연한

06 2022년 6월 24번 (정답률 75%)

정답 ①

[지문 끊어 읽기] 건물이 전하는 메시지

(1) A building is an inanimate object, /
건물은 무생물이다 /
but it is not an inarticulate one.
하지만 표현을 제대로 하지 못하는 사물은 아니다

힌트 대명사 one은 앞에 나온 a(n)+가산 명사를 대신할 수 있음. 본문에서 one은 object를 대신함.

힌트 'even+최상급'은 양보의 의미를 가져 '아무리 ~라도, 아무리 ~한 것일지라도'라고 해석함.

(2) Even the simplest house always makes a statement, /
아무리 단순한 집이라도 항상 진술을 한다 /
one expressed in brick and stone, in wood and glass, /
=a statement
벽돌과 돌, 나무와 유리로 표현되는 진술 /
단순한 집도 건물의 구성 요소에 따라 말을 전함.
rather than in words / — but no less loud and obvious. 정답 단서
말보다 / 하지만 꽤 크고 명확하다

힌트 'A no less ~ than B'는 'A는 B와 마찬가지로 ~하다, A는 B 못지않게 ~하다'라는 뜻으로 여기서는 obvious 뒤에 'than in words'가 생략되었다고 보면 됨.

(3) When we see a rusting trailer /
병렬①
우리가 녹슨 트레일러를 볼 때 /
surrounded by weeds and abandoned cars, /
잡초와 버려진 자동차로 둘러싸인 /

or a brand-new mini-mansion with a high wall, /
병렬②
혹은 높은 벽을 가진 아주 새로운 소형 저택을 /
we instantly get a message.
우리는 즉시 메시지를 받는다

(4) In both of these cases, / though in different accents, /
이 두 경우 모두 / 비록 다른 억양이지만 /
it is "Stay Out of Here."
=the message
그것은 "여기에 들어오지 마시오."이다

힌트 종속절 'though the message is in different accents'가 분사구문 'though being in different accents'로 바뀐 후 being은 생략되고 접속사 though는 남아 있는 형태임.

(5) It is not only houses, / of course, / that communicate with us.
it is ~ that 강조구문
집뿐만이 아니다 / 물론 / 우리와 소통하는 것은

(6) All kinds of buildings /
모든 종류의 건물들이 /
— churches, museums, schools, hospitals, restaurants, and offices — /
교회, 박물관, 학교, 병원, 식당, 사무실 등 /
speak to us silently. 정답 단서 집을 비롯한 모든 종류의 건물이 말을 전함.
우리에게 조용히 말한다

(7) Sometimes the statement is deliberate.
때때로 그 진술은 의도적이다

(8) A store or restaurant can be designed /
가게나 식당은 설계될 수 있다 /
so that it welcomes /
그것이 맞이하기 위해서 /
mostly low-income or high-income customers.
주로 저소득층 또는 고소득층 고객을

힌트 'so that+S+V'는 'S가 V하기 위해서'라는 의미로, 'in order to V'와 같은 의미임. 이 경우에는 so that절의 주어가 주절의 주어와 같으므로, 따로 의미상의 주어 없이 'to welcome'으로 치환할 수 있음.

힌트 A or B 구조의 명사구를 대명사로 받을 때 단수 취급함. 따라서 so that절에서 a store or restaurant를 대신할 때 단수인 대명사 it을 사용함.

(9) Buildings tell us / what to think and how to act, /
4형식V I·O D·O
건물들은 우리에게 알려 준다 / 무엇을 생각하고 어떻게 행동해야 하는지를 /
though we may not register their messages consciously. 정답 단서
우리가 그들의 메시지를 의식적으로 알아차리지 않더라도

건물은 건물이 가진 특징으로 메시지를 전달하며 우리는 그것을 받아들임.

중요 건물은 표지판과 같은 직접적인 단어로 메시지를 전달하기보다는 건물이 지니는 특성을 바탕으로 메시지를 전달하며 문장 (3), (4), (8)을 통해 이에 대한 예시를 확인할 수 있음.

[전문 해석]

(1)건물은 무생물이지만, 표현을 제대로 하지 못하는 사물은 아니다. (2)아무리 단순한 집이라도 항상 진술을 하는데, 그것은 말보다 벽돌과 돌, 나무와 유리로 표현되지만 꽤 크고 명확하다. (3)잡초와 버려진 자동차로 둘러싸인 녹슨 트레일러나 높은 벽을 가진 아주 새로운 소형 저택을 볼 때, 우리는 즉시 메시지를 받는다. (4)이 두 경우 모두, 비록 다른 억양이지만, 그것은 "여기에 들어오지 마시오."이다. (5)물론 우리와 소통하는 것은 집뿐만이 아니다. (6)교회, 박물관, 학교, 병원, 식당, 사무실 등 모든 종류의 건물들이 우리에게 조용히 말한다. (7)때때로 그 진술은 의도적이다. (8)가게나 식당은 주로 저소득층 또는 고소득층 고객을 맞이하기 위해서 설계될 수 있다. (9)건물들은 우리가 그들의 메시지를 의식적으로 알아차리지 않더라도 우리에게 무엇을 생각하고 어떻게 행동해야 하는지를 알려 준다.

[정답 확인]

다음 글의 제목으로 가장 적절한 것은?

✔ Buildings Do Talk in Their Own Ways!
건물은 그들만의 방식으로 정말로 말을 한다!
② Design of Buildings Starts from Nature
건물의 디자인은 자연으로부터 시작한다
③ Language of Buildings: Too Vague to Grasp
건물의 언어: 파악하기에는 너무 모호하다
④ Which Is More Important, Safety or Beauty?
무엇이 더 중요한가, 안전 혹은 아름다움?
⑤ How Do Architects Attach Emotions to Buildings?
어떻게 건축가들이 건물에 감정을 담는가?

[중요 어휘]

☐ **inanimate**	형용사 무생물의
☐ **inarticulate**	형용사 표현을 제대로 하지 못하는, 불분명한
☐ **statement**	명사 진술, 성명
☐ **obvious**	형용사 명확한, 분명한
☐ **rust**	동사 녹슬다 / 명사 녹
☐ **trailer**	명사 트레일러 (하우스)
☐ **accent**	명사 억양, 말씨
☐ **deliberate**	형용사 의도적인, 신중한
☐ **income**	명사 소득, 수입
☐ **register**	동사 알아차리다, 등록하다
☐ **consciously**	부사 의식적으로
☐ **vague**	형용사 모호한, 희미한
☐ **grasp**	동사 파악하다, 움켜잡다

07 2023년 9월 24번 (정답률 75%) 정답 ③

[지문 끊어 읽기] 기업을 변화시키는 소비자의 힘

(1) As you may already know, /
당신이 이미 알고 있겠지만 /
what and how you buy / can be political.
당신이 무엇을 어떻게 구매하는지는 / 정치적일 수 있다

힌트 what과 how가 이끄는 의문사절이 주어에 병렬 관계로 온 형태임. 명사절로 쓰인 의문사절의 어순은 '의문사+S+V'임.

(2) To whom / do you want to give your money?
누구에게 / 당신은 돈을 주고 싶은가

(3) Which companies and corporations / do you value and respect?
어떤 회사와 기업을 / 당신은 가치 있게 여기고 존중하는가

(4) Be mindful about every purchase /
모든 구매에 주의를 기울여라 /
by carefully researching the corporations /
선행사
기업들을 면밀히 조사함으로써 /
that are taking our money /
주격 관계대명사절
우리의 돈을 가져가는 /
to decide if they deserve our support. 정답 단서 소비자는 올바른 기업을 선택하도록 주의해서 구매해야 함.
부사적 용법(목적) 명사절 접속사: ~인지 아닌지
그들이 우리의 지원을 받을 자격이 있는지 아닌지를 결정하기 위해

(5) Do they have a record of polluting the environment, /
그들은 환경을 오염시킨 기록이 있는가 /
or do they have fair-trade practices and an end-of-life plan /
아니면 그들은 공정 거래 관행과 제품 수명 종료 계획이 있는가 /
for the products they make?
그들이 만드는 제품에 대한

(6) Are they committed / to bringing about good in the world?
전치사 동명사
그들은 헌신하고 있는가 / 세상에 이득을 가져오는 것에

(7) For instance, / my family has found a company /
예를 들어 / 우리 가족은 한 회사를 발견했다 /
[producing recycled, plastic-packaging-free toilet paper /
재활용된, 플라스틱 포장이 없는 화장지를 생산하는 /
with a social conscience].
사회적 양심을 가지고

(8) They contribute 50 percent of their profits /
그들은 수익의 50%를 기부한다 /
to the construction of toilets around the world, /
전 세계의 화장실 건설에 /
and we're genuinely happy to spend our money /
부사적 용법(감정의 원인)
그리고 우리는 돈을 쓸 수 있어서 정말로 기쁘다 /
on this special toilet paper each month.
매달 이 특별한 화장지에

(9) Remember / that the corporate world is built on consumers, /
명사절 접속사
기억하라 / 기업의 세계는 소비자를 기반으로 한다는 것을 /
so as a consumer / you have the power /
그러므로 소비자로서 / 당신은 힘을 가지고 있다 /
to vote with your wallet /
병렬①
지갑으로 투표할 /

and encourage companies to embrace healthier and more
병렬②(to 생략)
sustainable practices /
그리고 회사들이 더 건강하고 더 지속 가능한 관행을 받아들이도록 장려할 /
with every purchase you choose to make. 정답 단서 소비자는 구매를 통해 회사들이 건강하고 지속 가능한 관행을 따르도록 만드는 힘을 가지고 있음.
당신이 선택하는 모든 구매를 통해

[전문 해석]

(1)당신이 이미 알고 있겠지만, 당신이 무엇을 어떻게 구매하는지는 정치적일 수 있다. (2)당신은 누구에게 돈을 주고 싶은가? (3)당신은 어떤 회사와 기업을 가치 있게 여기고 존중하는가? (4)기업들이 우리의 지원을 받을 자격이 있는지를 결정하기 위해 우리의 돈을 가져가는 기업들을 면밀히 조사함으로써 모든 구매에 주의를 기울여라. (5)그들은 환경을 오염시킨 기록이 있는가, 아니면 그들은 그들이 만드는 제품에 대한 공정 거래 관행과 제품 수명 종료 계획이 있는가? (6)그들은 세상에 이득을 가져오는 것에 헌신하고 있는가? (7)예를 들어, 우리 가족은 사회적 양심을 가지고 재활용된, 플라스틱 포장이 없는 화장지를 생산하는 한 회사를 발견했다. (8)그들은 수익의 50%를 전 세계의 화장실 건설에 기부하고 우리는 매달 이 특별한 화장지에 돈을 쓸 수 있어서 정말로 기쁘다. (9)기업의 세계는 소비자를 기반으로 하므로, 소비자로서 당신은 당신이 선택하는 모든 구매를 통해 지갑으로 투표하고 회사들이 더 건강하고 더 지속 가능한 관행을 받아들이도록 장려할 힘을 가지고 있다는 것을 기억하라.

[정답 확인]

다음 글의 제목으로 가장 적절한 것은?

① Green Businesses: Are They Really Green?
친환경 사업: 그것들은 정말로 친환경적일까?
② Fair Trade Does Not Always Appeal to Consumers
공정한 거래가 언제나 소비자에게 매력적인 것은 아니다
✔③ Buy Consciously, Make Companies Do the Right Things
의식적으로 구매하라, 회사들이 올바른 일을 하도록 만들어라
④ Do Voters Have a Powerful Impact on Economic Policy?
유권자들은 경제 정책에 강력한 영향을 미치는가?
⑤ The Secret to Saving Your Money: Record Your Spending
돈을 절약하는 비결: 당신의 지출을 기록하라

[중요 어휘]

☐ **political**	형용사 정치적인
☐ **corporation**	명사 기업, 회사, 법인
☐ **mindful**	형용사 주의를 기울이는, 유념하는
☐ **deserve**	동사 ~할 자격이 있다, ~을 받을 만하다
☐ **pollute**	동사 오염시키다
☐ **fair-trade**	형용사 공정 거래의
☐ **practice**	명사 관행, 실행, 연습
☐ **be committed to N**	~에 헌신하다[전념하다]
☐ **bring about**	~을 가져오다[야기하다]
☐ **good**	명사 이득, 행복, 선(善)
☐ **conscience**	명사 양심, 가책
☐ **contribute A to B**	A를 B에 기부하다[기증하다]
☐ **genuinely**	부사 정말로, 진심으로
☐ **embrace**	동사 받아들이다, 수용하다
☐ **consciously**	부사 의식적으로

08 2017년 11월 22번 (정답률 70%) 정답 ⑤

[지문 끊어 읽기] 과학기술을 이용한 운동 목표의 맹점

(1) Katherine Schreiber and Leslie Sim, experts on exercise addiction, /
운동 중독에 관한 전문가인 Katherine Schreiber와 Leslie Sim은 /
recognized /
인정했다 /
that smartwatches and fitness trackers have probably inspired sedentary people /
스마트워치와 건강 추적기가 아마도 주로 앉아서 지내는 사람들이 ~하도록 격려해왔을 것이라고 /
to take up exercise, /
운동을 시작하도록 /
and encouraged people who aren't very active /
그리고 별로 활동적이지 않은 사람들을 장려해왔을 것이라고 /
to exercise more consistently.
더 지속적으로 운동하도록

(2) But / they were convinced /
그러나 / 그들은 확신했다 /
the devices were also quite dangerous. 정답 단서
그 장치들이 또한 상당히 위험하다고
✶중요 전자 장치 덕분에 운동을 하지 않던 사람들이 운동을 하게 되었지만 이 글은 이로 인한 부정적인 면을 주목하고 있음을 문장 (2)에서 확인할 수 있음.

(3) Schreiber explained / that focusing on numbers /
Schreiber는 설명했다 / 숫자에 집중하는 것이 /
separates people / from being in tune with their body. 정답 단서
사람들을 분리시킨다고 / 그들의 신체와 조화를 이루는 것으로부터

(4) Exercising becomes mindless, / which is 'the goal' of addiction.
운동하는 것이 아무 생각이 없는 상태가 된다 / 그리고 그것이 중독의 '목표'이다

(5) This 'goal' that she mentioned /
그녀가 언급한 이 '목표'는 /
is a sort of automatic mindlessness, / 정답 단서
일종의 무의식적인 무분별함이다 /
the outsourcing of decision making to a device.
장치에 의사 결정을 위탁하는 것

(6) She recently sustained a stress fracture in her foot /
그녀는 최근 그녀의 발에 피로 골절을 입었다 /
because she refused to listen to her overworked body, /
그녀는 혹사당하는 몸에 귀 기울이는 것을 거부했기 때문에 /
instead continuing to run /
대신 계속해서 달렸기 때문에 /
toward an unreasonable workout target. 정답 단서
지나친 운동 목표를 향하여

(7) Schreiber has suffered from addictive exercise tendencies, /
Schreiber는 중독적인 운동 성향으로 고통을 겪어왔다 /
and vows not to use wearable tech / when she works out.
그리고 웨어러블 기술을 사용하지 않기로 맹세한다 / 그녀가 운동할 때

[전문 해석]

(1)운동 중독에 관한 전문가인 Katherine Schreiber와 Leslie Sim은 스마트워치와 건강 추적기가 아마도 주로 앉아서 지내는 사람들이 운동을 시작하도록 격려해왔을 것이고, 별로 활동적이지 않은 사람들을 더 지속적으로 운동하도록 장려해왔을 것이라고 인정했다. (2)그러나 그들은 그 장치들이 또한 상당히 위험하다고 확신했다. (3)Schreiber는 숫자에 집중하는 것이 사람들을 그들의 신체와 조화를 이루는 것으로부터 분리시킨다고 설명했다. (4)운동하는 것이 아무 생각이 없는 상태가 되고 그것이 중독의 '목표'이다. (5)그녀가 언급한 이 '목표'는 일종의 무의식적인 무분별함, 즉 장치에 의사 결정을 위탁하는(맡기는) 것이다. (6)그녀는 혹사당하는 몸에 귀 기울이는 것을 거부했고, 대신 지나친 운동 목표를 향하여 계속해서 달렸기 때문에 최근 그녀의 발에 피로 골절을 입었다. (7)Schreiber는 중독적인 운동 성향으로 고통을 겪어왔고, 운동할 때 웨어러블 기술을(기계를) 사용하지 않기로 맹세한다.
- wearable device(웨어러블 디바이스): '입을 수 있는 기기'라는 뜻으로 몸에 부착하거나 착용하여 사용하는 전자장치이다. 대표적인 웨어러블 디바이스로는 스마트워치와 VR안경 등이 있다.
- smart watch(스마트워치): 무선통신 기능을 갖춘 손목시계로 블루투스와 와이파이로 스마트폰·스마트패드 등과 연동되며 통화는 물론 문자와 날씨 등 간단한 정보를 얻을 수 있다.

[정답 확인]

다음 글의 제목으로 가장 적절한 것은?

① Get out of Your Chair If You Want to Stay Fit
당신이 건강을 지키기를 원한다면 의자에서 벗어나라(일어나라)
② Addiction: Another Name for Unbreakable Habit
중독: 깨뜨릴 수 없는(바뀔 수 없는) 습관의 또 다른 이름
③ Don't Respond Mindlessly to Stressful Situations
스트레스가 많은 상황에 생각 없이 대처하지 마라
④ It's Time to Use Advanced Technology for a Better Life
더 나은 삶을 위해 진보한 기술을 사용할 때이다
✔⑤ Setting a Workout Goal with Technology Isn't Always Right
과학기술(웨어러블 기계)과 함께 운동 목표를 정하는 것이 항상 옳지만은 않다

[중요 어휘]

☐ **sedentary**	형용사 주로 앉아서 지내는

문제편 p.078

□ consistently	부사 지속적으로
□ convinced	형용사 확신하는, 신념이 있는
□ mindless	형용사 아무 생각이 없는, 분별력이 없는
□ outsource	동사 (작업·생산을) 위탁하다, 위임하다
□ sustain	동사 (상처를) 입다, 당하다
□ fracture	명사 골절, 균열, 금
□ overworked	형용사 혹사당하는
□ unreasonable	형용사 지나친, 터무니없는
□ fit	형용사 건강한, 적합한, 알맞은 / 동사 (모양·크기 등이) 맞다
□ advanced	형용사 진보한

09 2019년 6월 24번 (정답률 70%) 정답 ③

[지문 끊어 읽기] 신체로부터의 피드백

(1) Take the choice of / which kind of soup to buy.
~에 대한 선택을 하라 / 어떤 종류의 수프를 살 것인지

(2) There's too much data here / for you to struggle with: /
여기에는 너무 많은 자료가 있다 / 당신이 고심해야 할 /
calories, price, salt content, taste, packaging, and so on.
칼로리, 가격, 소금 함유량, 맛, 포장, 그리고 기타 등등

(3) If you were a robot, / you'd be stuck here all day /
(S' 과거V' — 가정법 과거; S 조동사 과거형 V(동사원형))
만약 당신이 로봇이라면 / 당신은 하루 종일 여기에 매여있을 것이다 /
trying to make a decision, / with no obvious way to trade off /
결정하려 애쓰면서 / 균형을 잡을 분명한 방법이 없는 채로 /
which details matter more.
어떤 세부 사항이 더 중요한지에 대해

(4) To land on a choice, / you need a summary / of some sort. 정답 단서
선택에 이르기 위해서 / 당신은 요약이 필요하다 / 일종의

(5) And that's / what the feedback from your body is able to give you. 정답 단서
그리고 그것은 ~이다 / 당신의 신체로부터 나오는 피드백이 당신에게 줄 수 있는 것

(6) Thinking about your budget /
당신의 예산에 관해 생각하는 것은 /
might make your palms sweat, /
당신의 손바닥에 땀이 나게 할지도 모른다 /
or your mouth might water / thinking about /
또는 당신의 입은 군침을 흘릴지도 모른다 / ~에 관해 생각하면서 /
the last time you consumed the chicken noodle soup, /
지난번 당신이 치킨 누들 수프를 먹었을 때 /
or noting the excessive creaminess / of the other soup /
또는 지나친 느끼함을 알아차리는 것은 / 또 다른 수프의 /
might give you a stomachache.
당신에게 복통을 일으킬지도 모른다

★중요 우리가 어떤 수프를 먹을지 선택하기 위해서는 요약된 정보가 필요한데, 신체로부터 나오는 피드백이 그러한 정보를 줄 수 있다고 이야기함.

(7) You simulate your experience / with one soup, /
당신은 당신의 경험을 시뮬레이션한다 / 하나의 수프로 /
and then the other.
그러고 나서 또 다른 것으로

(8) Your bodily experience / helps your brain to quickly place /
(help A to V: A가 ~하는 것을 돕다)
당신의 신체적 경험은 / 당신의 뇌가 재빠르게 ~를 두는 것을 돕는다 /
a value on soup A, / and another on soup B, /
A수프에 하나의 가치를 / 그리고 B수프에 또 다른 것을 /
[allowing you to tip the balance / in one direction or the other].
당신이 균형을 기울이게 해준다 / 한쪽으로 또는 다른 쪽으로 [ ]: 분사구문(결과)

(9) You don't just extract the data / from the soup cans, /
당신은 단지 자료를 추출하는 것이 아니다 / 수프 캔으로부터 /
you feel the data.
당신은 자료를 느낀다

[중요 구문]

(6) [Thinking about your budget might make your palms sweat], or [your mouth might water thinking about the last time you consumed ~], or [noting ~ might give you a stomachache].
(동명사: S① V① / S② V② 분사구문(동시동작) / 동명사: S③ V③)

[전문 해석]

(1)어떤 종류의 수프를 살 것인지에 대한 선택을 하라. (2)여기에는 칼로리, 가격, 소금 함유량, 맛, 포장, 그리고 기타 등등 당신이 고심해야 할 너무 많은 자료가 있다. (3)만약 당신이 로봇이라면, 당신은 어떤 세부 사항이 더 중요한지에 대해 균형을 잡을 분명한 방법이 없는 채로 (어떤 수프를 살 것인지) 결정하려 애쓰면서 하루 종일 여기에 매여있을 것이다. (4)선택에 이르기 위해서 당신은 일종의 요약이(요약된 정보가) 필요하다. (5)그리고 그것(요약된 정보)은 당신의 신체로부터 나오는 피드백이 당신에게 줄 수 있는 것이다. (6)당신의 예산에 관해 생각하는 것은 당신의 손바닥에 땀이 나게 할지도 모르고, (또는) 당신의 입은 지난번 당신이 치킨 누들 수프를 먹었을 때에 관해 생각하면서 군침을 흘릴지도 모르며, (또는) 또 다른 수프의 지나친 느끼함을 알아차리는 것은 당신에게 복통을 일으킬지도 모른다. (7)당신은 하나의 수프로, 그러고 나서 또 다른 것(수프)으로 당신의 경험을 시뮬레이션한다. (8)당신의 신체적 경험은 당신의 뇌가 재빠르게 A수프에 하나의 가치를, 그리고 B수프에 또 다른 것(가치)을 두는 것을 도우며, (그 결과) 당신이 한쪽으로 또는 다른 쪽으로 균형을 기울이게(어느 한쪽으로 마음을 쏟게) 해준다. (9)당신은 단지 수프 캔으로부터 자료를 추출하는 것이 아니라 자료를 느낀다(느끼는 것이다).

[정답 확인]

다음 글의 제목으로 가장 적절한 것은?

① You Are What You Eat!
당신이 먹는 것이 곧 당신이다(먹는 것을 보면 그 사람을 알 수 있다)!
② Bodily Feedback Can Fool You
신체의 피드백은 당신을 속일 수 있다
✔③ What to Eat? Your Body Will Tell You!
무엇을 먹을 것인가? 당신의 신체가 당신에게 말해줄 것이다!
④ The More Choices, the Better Outcomes
더 많은 선택, 더 나은 결과
⑤ Read Information on Food Labels Carefully
식품 라벨의 정보를 주의 깊게 읽어라

[중요 어휘]

□ struggle	동사 고심하다, 분투하다
□ content	명사 함유량, 내용물
□ trade off	균형을 잡다, 교환하다
□ land on	~에 이르다, 착륙하다
□ note	동사 알아차리다, 주목하다
□ excessive	형용사 지나친, 과도한
□ creaminess	명사 느끼함, 크림 같음
□ simulate	동사 시뮬레이션하다, 가장하다
□ bodily	형용사 신체적인, 몸의
□ place a value on	~에 가치를 두다, 부여하다
□ tip	동사 기울이다, 뒤집어 엎다

10 2020년 11월 24번 (정답률 70%) 정답 ②

[지문 끊어 읽기] 언어적 정확성의 장점

(1) In government, / in law, / in culture, /
정치 체제에서 / 법에서 / 문화에서 /
and in routine everyday interaction /
그리고 일상적인 매일의 상호 작용에서 /
beyond family and immediate neighbours, /
가족 및 가까운 이웃을 넘어서는 /
a widely understood and clearly formulated language /
폭넓게 이해되고 확실하게 표현된 언어가 /
is a great aid / to mutual confidence. 정답 단서
굉장한 도움이 된다 / 상호 신뢰에

(2) When dealing / with property, / with contracts, /
다룰 때 / 재산을 / 계약을 /
or even just with the routine exchange of goods and services, /
혹은 심지어 단순히 상품과 서비스의 일상적인 교환을 /
concepts and descriptions /
개념과 설명은 /
need to be as precise and unambiguous as possible, / 정답단서
as 형용사/부사 as possible: 가능한 한 ~한/~하게
가능한 한 정확하고 모호하지 않아야 한다 /
otherwise misunderstandings will arise.
그렇지 않으면 오해가 생길 것이다

(3) If full communication / with a potential counterparty /
만약 완전한 의사소통이 / 잠재적 상대방과의 /
in a deal / is not possible, /
거래에서 / 가능하지 않다면 /
then uncertainty and probably a measure of distrust / will remain.
그렇다면 불확실성과 아마도 어느 정도의 불신이 / 남게 될 것이다

(4) As economic life became more complex /
경제 생활이 더 복잡해지면서 /
in the later Middle Ages, / the need /
중세 시대 후반에 / 필요가 /
for fuller and more precise communication / was accentuated. 정답단서
더욱 완전하고 더욱 정확한 의사소통에 대한 / 강조되었다

(5) A shared language / facilitated /
공유된 언어는 / 용이하게 했다 /
clarification and possibly settlement of any disputes.
병렬① 병렬②
명확화와 아마도 어떤 분쟁의 해결을

(6) In international trade also /
국제 무역에서도 또한 /
the use of a precise and well-formulated language / 정답단서
정확하고 잘 표현된 언어의 사용은 /
aided the process of translation.
통역의 과정을 도왔다

(7) The Silk Road / could only function at all /
실크로드는 / 그나마 기능할 수 있었다 /
because translators were always available / at interchange points.
통역가들이 항상 이용 가능했기 때문에 / 교환 지점에서

[전문 해석]

(1)정치 체제에서, 법에서, 문화에서, 그리고 가족 및 가까운 이웃을 넘어서는 일상적인 매일의 상호 작용에서, 폭넓게 이해되고 확실하게 표현된 언어가 상호 신뢰에 굉장한 도움이 된다. (2)재산, 계약, 혹은 심지어 단순히 상품과 서비스의 일상적인 교환을 다룰 때 개념과 설명은 가능한 한 정확하고 모호하지 않아야 하며, 그렇지 않으면 오해가 생길 것이다. (3)만약 거래에서 잠재적 상대방과의 완전한 의사소통이 가능하지 않다면, (그렇다면) 불확실성과 아마도 어느 정도의 불신이 남게 될 것이다. (4)중세 시대 후반에 경제 생활이 더 복잡해지면서 더욱 완전하고 더욱 정확한 의사소통에 대한 필요가 강조되었다. (5)공유된 언어는 (의사소통의) 명확화와 아마도 어떤 분쟁의 해결을 용이하게 했다. (6)국제 무역에서도 또한 정확하고 잘 표현된 언어의 사용은 통역의 과정을 도왔다. (7)실크로드는 교환 지점에서 통역가들이 항상 이용 가능했기 때문에 그나마 기능할 수 있었다.

[정답 확인]

다음 글의 제목으로 가장 적절한 것은?

① Earn Trust with Reliable Goods Rather Than with Words!
말보다는 믿을 수 있는 상품으로 신뢰를 얻자!
✔② Linguistic Precision: A Key to Successful Economic Transactions
언어적 정확성: 성공적인 경제적 거래의 비결
③ Difficulties in Overcoming Language Barriers and Distrust in Trade
언어 장벽을 극복하는 어려움과 거래에서의 불신
④ The More the Economy Grows, the More Complex the World Gets
경제가 더 성장할수록, 세상은 더 복잡해진다
⑤ Excessive Confidence: The Biggest Reason for Miscommunication
과도한 신뢰: 잘못된 의사소통의 가장 큰 원인

[중요 어휘]

□ government	명사 정치(통치) 체제, 정부
□ routine	형용사 일상적인, 틀에 박힌 / 명사 일상
□ immediate	형용사 가까운, 인접한, 즉각적인
□ formulate	동사 표현하다, 말하다, 만들어 내다
□ aid	명사 도움, 지원 / 동사 돕다, 거들다
□ mutual	형용사 상호의, 서로 간의
□ confidence	명사 신뢰, 확신, 자신감
□ property	명사 재산, 소유물
□ contract	명사 계약 / 동사 계약하다, 수축하다
□ unambiguous	형용사 모호하지 않은, 분명한
□ counterparty	명사 (거래의) 상대방, 당사자
□ a measure of	어느 정도의, 일정량의
□ distrust	명사 불신 / 동사 불신하다
□ accentuate	동사 강조하다, 악센트를 붙이다
□ facilitate	동사 용이하게 하다, 촉진하다
□ clarification	명사 명확화, 설명
□ settlement	명사 해결, 합의, 정착
□ dispute	명사 분쟁, 논쟁
□ translation	명사 통역, 번역
□ reliable	형용사 믿을 수 있는, 신뢰할 만한
□ linguistic	형용사 언어적인, 말의
□ transaction	명사 거래, 매매
□ excessive	형용사 과도한, 지나친

핵심 숫자는 정확한 양을 기술하기 위해 발명되었다는 내용으로 글을 시작한 후, 문장 (2)의 however로 내용을 전환하여, 양이 많을 때에는 정확한 숫자보다 어림수를 사용하는 것이 더 쉽고 편리하다는 요지를 드러냄.

11 2017년 6월 23번 (정답률 65%) 정답 ③

[지문 끊어 읽기] 큰 숫자에서 허용된 유연성

(1) Numbers were invented to describe precise amounts: /
숫자는 정확한 양을 기술하기 위해 발명되었다 /
three teeth, seven days, twelve goats.
치아 3개, 7일, 염소 12마리

(2) When quantities are large, / however, /
양이 많을 때 / 그러나 /
we do not use numbers in a precise way. 정답단서
우리는 숫자를 정확한 방법으로 사용하지 않는다

(3) We approximate using a 'round number' / as a place mark. 주제문
우리는 '어림수'를 사용하여 어림잡는다 / 장소 표시처럼

(4) It is easier and more convenient. 정답단서
그것은 더 쉽고 더 편리하다

(5) When we say, / for example, /
우리가 말할 때 / 예를 들어 /
that there were a hundred people at the market, /
시장에 100명의 사람들이 있었다고 /
we don't mean /
우리는 의미하지는 않는다 /
that there were exactly one hundred people there.
그곳에 정확히 100명의 사람이 있었다는 것을

(6) And when we say / that the universe is 13.7 billion years old, /
그리고 우리가 말할 때 / 우주의 나이는 137억 년이라고 /
we don't mean exactly 13,700,000,000; /
우리는 정확히 13,700,000,000을 의미하지 않는다 /
we mean give or take a few hundred million years.
우리는 몇 억 년을 더하거나 뺀 대략을 의미한다

(7) Big numbers are understood approximately, /
큰 숫자들은 대강 이해된다 /
small ones precisely, / and these two systems interact uneasily.
작은 숫자들은 정확히 이해된다 / 그리고 이러한 두 체계는 불안하게 상호 작용을 한다

(8) It is clear nonsense to say /
말하는 것은 완전히 터무니없는 생각이다 /
that next year the universe will be '13.7 billion and one' years old.
내년에 우주가 '137억 1'년이라고

(9) It will remain 13.7 billion years old / for the rest of our lives.
그것은 계속 137억 년일 것이다 / 우리의 삶의 나머지 동안

[전문 해석]

(1)숫자는 치아 3개, 7일, 염소 12마리 같은 정확한 양을 기술하기 위해 발명되었다. (2)그러나, 양이 많을 때 우리는 숫자를 정확한 방법으로 사용하지 않는다. (3)우리는 '어림수'를 장소 표시처럼 사용하여 (그 수치를) 어림잡는다. (4)그것은 더 쉽고 더 편리하다. (5)예를 들어, 우리가 시장에 100명의 사람들이 있었다고 말할 때 우리는 그곳에 정확히 100명의 사람이 있었다는 것을 의미하지는 않는다. (6)그리고 우리가 우주의 나이는 137억 년이라고 말할 때 우리는 정확히 13,700,000,000을 의미하지는 않는다. 우리는 몇 억 년을 더하거나 뺀 대략(적인 나이)을 의미한다. (7)큰 숫자들은 대강 이해되고 작은 숫자들은 정확히 이해되며 이러한 두 체계는 불안하게 상호 작용을 한다. (8)내년에 우주가 '137억 1'년이라고 말하는 것은 완전히 터무니없는 생각이다. (9)우리의 삶의 나머지 동안(우리의 남은 생애 동안) 그것은 계속 137억 년일 것이다.

- place mark(장소 표시): 지도 위에 특정 장소의 위치를 나타내는 표시

[정답 확인]

다음 글의 제목으로 가장 적절한 것은?

① Mystery in Inventing Numbers
숫자 발명의 미스터리
② Numbers: The Mirror of Precision
숫자: 정확성의 반영
✔ Flexibility Allowed in Big Numbers
큰 숫자에서 허용된 유연성
④ How Numbers Manipulate Our Lives
어떻게 숫자는 우리의 삶을 조종하는가
⑤ Don't Use Round Numbers in Science!
과학에서 어림수를 사용하지 마라!

✶중요 문장 (2)의 quantities are large, (5)의 a hundred people, (6)의 13.7 billion 등의 예시가 정답에서 Big Numbers로 표현됨.

[중요 어휘]

□ approximate	동사 어림잡다
□ round	형용사 어림의, 대략의
□ uneasily	부사 불안하게, 불편하게
□ nonsense	명사 터무니없는 생각, 터무니없는 말
□ mirror	명사 반영, 거울
□ flexibility	명사 유연성, 융통성
□ manipulate	동사 조종하다, 다루다

핵심 두 번째 문장을 주제로 오해하기 쉬운 글인데 글의 주제는 문장 (4) 이후부터 등장하며, '책은 없지만 사람들이 자기 이야기를 들려주며 책의 역할을 하는 도서관에 대한 소개'임.

12 2018년 6월 22번 (정답률 65%)

정답 ②

[지문 끊어 읽기]

사람들이 책이 되는 곳

(1) Why do you go to the library?
당신은 왜 도서관에 가는가

(2) For books, yes / — and you like books / because they tell stories.
그렇다 책 때문이다 / 그리고 당신은 책을 좋아한다 / 그것들이 이야기를 들려주기 때문에

(3) You hope to / get lost in a story /
당신은 희망한다 / 어떤 이야기 속에서 길을 잃기를 /
or be transported into someone else's life.
또는 다른 사람의 삶 속에 있는 느낌이 들기를

(4) At one type of library, / you can do just that /
한 형태의 도서관에서는 / 당신은 정말 그렇게 할 수 있다 /
— even though there's not a single book.
비록 책이 단 한 권도 없지만

(5) At a Human Library, / people with unique life stories volunteer /
Human Library에서는 / 특별한 인생 이야기를 가진 사람들이 자진한다 /
to be the "books." 정답 단서
'책'이 되기를

(6) For a certain amount of time, /
어느 정도의 시간 동안 /
you can ask them questions / and listen to their stories, /
당신은 그들에게 질문할 수 있다 / 그리고 그들의 이야기를 들을 수 있다 /
which are as fascinating and inspiring /
그런데 그것은 아주 매력적이고 감동적이다 /
as any you can find in a book. 정답 단서
당신이 그 어느 책에서 발견할 수 있는 것 못지않게

(7) Many of the stories / have to do with some kind of stereotype.
그 이야기들 중 많은 것들은 / 일종의 어떤 고정 관념과 관련이 있다

(8) You can speak /
당신은 이야기할 수 있다 /
with a refugee, a soldier suffering from PTSD, and a homeless person.
피난민, 외상 후 스트레스 장애로 고통 받는 군인, 그리고 집이 없는 사람과

(9) The Human Library encourages people /
Human Library는 사람들을 장려한다 /
to challenge their own existing notions /
기존에 그들이 갖고 있던 자신들의 생각에 도전하도록 /
— to truly get to know, and learn from, /
진정으로 알게 되고 배우도록 /
someone they might otherwise make quick judgements about.
그렇지 않았다면 섣부른 판단을 내렸을지 모르는 누군가에 대해

[전문 해석]

(1)당신은 왜 도서관에 가는가? (2)그렇다, 책 때문이다. 그리고 책들이 이야기를 들려주기 때문에 당신은 그것들을 좋아한다. (3)당신은 어떤 이야기 속에서 길을 잃거나(이야기에 몰입하거나) 다른 사람의 삶 속에 있는 느낌이 들기를(다른 사람의 삶을 살아보기를) 희망한다. (4)한 (어떤) 형태의 도서관에서는 비록 (그곳에는) 책이 단 한 권도 없지만 당신은 정말 그렇게(어떤 이야기에 몰입하거나 다른 사람의 삶 속에 들어가는 것을) 할 수 있다. (5)Human Library에서는 특별한 인생 이야기를 가진 사람들이 '책'이 되기를 자진한다. (6)어느 정도의 시간 동안 당신은 그들에게 질문할 수 있고 그들의 이야기를 들을 수 있는데, 그것은 당신이 그 어느 책에서 발견할 수 있는 것 못지않게 아주 매력적이고 감동적이다. (7)그 이야기들 중 많은 것들은 일종의 어떤 고정 관념과 관련이 있다. (8)당신은 피난민, 외상 후 스트레스 장애로 고통 받는 군인, 그리고 집이 없는 사람(노숙자)과 이야기할 수 있다. (9)Human Library는 사람들이 기존에 갖고 있던 자신들의 생각에 도전하도록 장려하는데, 그렇지 않았다면 섣부른 판단을 내렸을지 모르는 누군가에 대해 진정으로 알게 되고 (그 누군가로부터) 배우도록 한다.

- PTSD(외상 후 스트레스 장애): Post Traumatic Stress Disorder의 약어로 생명을 위협할 정도의 극심한 스트레스(정신적 외상)를 겪고 나서 경험하는 심리적인 병을 말한다.

[정답 확인]

다음 글의 제목으로 가장 적절한 것은?

① Useful Books for Learning Languages
언어를 배우는 데 유용한 책
✔ The Place Where People Are the Books
사람들이 책이 되는 곳
③ Library: Starting Point for Your Academic Research
도서관: 당신의 학문적인 연구를 위한 출발점
④ How to Choose People in the Human Library
Human Library에서 사람들을 선택하는 법
⑤ What a Touching Story of a Booklover!
애서가(책벌레)에 관한 감동적인 이야기!

✶중요 'Human Library'에는 특별한 경험을 하거나 소외되어 편견의 대상이 되었을지도 모를 사람들의 이야기가 있다고 소개하지만 그 대상을 어떻게 선정하는지는 지문에서 중요한 내용이 아님.

[문제 풀이]

지문에서는 사람들이 도서관에 가는 이유가 책을 통해 이야기에 몰입하거나 다른 사람들의 삶 속으로 들어가길 원해서라고 하며, 책 없이도 그런 경험이 가능한 Human Library를 소개하고 있다. 이곳에서는 특별한 인생 이야기를 지닌 사람들이 자신의 이야기를 들려주고 사람들로부터 질문을 받기도 하면서 책의 역할을 대신한다. 따라서 정답은 ②이다.

[중요 어휘]

□ transport	동사 (다른 장소·상황에 있는) 느낌이 들게 하다, 이동시키다, 수송하다
□ fascinating	형용사 매력적인, 대단히 흥미로운
□ inspiring	형용사 감동적인, 고무적인

have to do with	~과 관련이 있다
☐	stereotype	[명사] 고정 관념
☐	existing	[형용사] 기존의
☐	notion	[명사] 생각, 관념

13 2021년 6월 24번 (정답률 65%) 정답 ③

[지문 끊어 읽기] 뉴스 기사 작성의 요령

(1) News reporters are taught / to start their stories /
뉴스 보도 기자들은 배운다 / 그들의 기사를 시작하도록 /

with the most important information.
가장 중요한 정보로

(2) The first sentence, / called the lead, /
힌트 삽입구로, 앞의 'The first sentence'를 수식함. '불린다'는 수동의 의미를 포함하므로 과거분사가 사용되었으며, 'which is'가 생략되었다고 보아도 됨.
첫 번째 문장은 / 첫머리라고 불리는 /

contains the most essential elements of the story. [정답 단서]
기사의 가장 필수적인 요소를 포함한다

(3) A good lead / can convey a lot of information.
좋은 첫머리는 / 많은 정보를 전달할 수 있다

(4) After the lead, / information is presented /
첫머리 다음으로 / 정보는 제시된다 /

in decreasing order of importance.
중요도가 감소하는 순서로

(5) Journalists call this the "inverted pyramid" structure /
call A B: A를 B라고 부르다
언론인들은 이것을 '거꾸로 된 피라미드' 구조라고 부른다 /

— the most important information /
가장 중요한 정보가 /

(the widest part of the pyramid) / is at the top.
(피라미드의 가장 넓은 부분인) / 제일 위에 있는

(6) The inverted pyramid is great / for readers.
거꾸로 된 피라미드는 아주 좋다 / 독자들에게
힌트 목적격 관계대명사인 which/that이 생략된 목적격 관계대명사절로, 선행사 the information을 꾸며주는 역할을 함.

(7) No matter what the reader's attention span /
독자의 주의 지속 시간이 어떻든 간에 /
— whether she reads only the lead / or the entire story /
병렬① / 병렬②
그녀가 첫머리만 읽든지 / 아니면 기사 전체를 읽든지 /
[정답 단서]
— the inverted pyramid maximizes the information / she gets.
거꾸로 된 피라미드는 정보를 극대화한다 / 그녀가 얻는

(8) Think of the alternative: / If news stories were written /
대안을 생각해 보자 / 만약 보도 기사가 쓰였다면 /

like mysteries with a dramatic payoff / at the end, /
극적인 결말이 있는 미스터리처럼 / 마지막에 /

then readers / who broke off in mid-story / would miss the point.
S↑ S V
그렇다면 독자들은 / 기사 중간에 멈춘 / 요점을 놓칠 것이다

(9) Imagine waiting / until the last sentence of a story /
기다리는 것을 상상해 보아라 / 기사의 마지막 문장까지 /

to find out / who won the presidential election /
의문사 / 병렬①
힌트 선거에서 당선되는 것, 대회에서 우승하는 것 모두 동사 'win'을 사용하여 표현하므로 문장 (9)에서는 간단히 'or'로 연결되어 있음.
알아내기 위해 / 누가 대통령 선거에 당선되었는지 /

or the Super Bowl.
병렬②
혹은 슈퍼볼에서 우승했는지

[중요 구문] **힌트** 현재 일어나지 않은 일을 가정하고 있으므로 가정법 과거를 사용함. 가정법 과거 형태는 'If+S'+동사의 과거형 ~, S+조동사 과거형+동사원형'이며, if절의 be동사는 인칭 상관없이 'were'이 됨.

(8) ~ If news stories were written ~, then readers ~ would miss ~.
S' 동사의 과거형 S 조동사 과거형 동사원형

[전문 해석]

(1)뉴스 보도 기자들은 그들의 기사를 가장 중요한 정보로 시작하도록 배운다. (2)첫머리라고 불리는 첫 번째 문장은 기사의 가장 필수적인 요소를 포함한다. (3)좋은 첫머리는 많은 정보를 전달할 수 있다. (4)첫머리 다음으로, 정보는 중요도가 감소하는 순서로 제시된다. (5)언론인들은 이것을 (피라미드의 가장 넓은 부분인) 가장 중요한 정보가 제일 위에 있는 '거꾸로

된 피라미드' 구조라고 부른다. (6)거꾸로 된 피라미드는 독자들에게 아주 좋다. (7)독자가 첫머리만 읽든지 아니면 기사 전체를 읽든지, 그녀의 주의 지속 시간(집중할 수 있는 시간)이 어떻든 간에, 거꾸로 된 피라미드는 그녀가 얻는 정보를 극대화한다. (8)대안(다른 방식)을 생각해 보자. 만약 보도 기사가 마지막에 극적인 결말이 있는 미스터리처럼 쓰였다면, 그렇다면 기사 중간에 (읽는 것을) 멈춘 독자들은 요점을 놓칠 것이다. (9)누가 대통령 선거에 당선되었는지 혹은 슈퍼볼에서 우승했는지 알아내기 위해 기사의 마지막 문장까지 (읽으며) 기다리는 것을 상상해 보아라.

- lead(첫머리, 리드): 정보 제공이 목적인 일반적인 스트레이트 기사의 맨 앞에 육하원칙을 바탕으로 요지를 추려서 쓴 문장을 말함.
- Super Bowl(슈퍼볼): 미국의 미식축구 리그 NFL(National Football League)의 결승전. 미국에서 가장 큰 스포츠 행사인 만큼 중계료, 광고비 등이 화제가 되기도 함.

[정답 확인]

다음 글의 제목으로 가장 적절한 것은?

① Inverted Pyramid: Logically Impossible Structure
거꾸로 된 피라미드: 논리적으로 불가능한 구조
② Curiosity Is What Makes Readers Keep Reading
호기심이 바로 독자들이 계속 읽게 만드는 것이다
③ Where to Put Key Points in News Writing ✔
뉴스 기사 작성 시 요점을 어디에 두어야 하는가
④ The More Information, the Less Attention
정보가 더 많을수록 주목도는 더 떨어진다
⑤ Readers, Tell the Facts from the Fakes!
독자들이여, 가짜와 사실을 구별하라!

[문제 풀이]

뉴스 보도 기사를 쓸 때의 주의점에 대해 설명하는 글이다. 기사의 첫 번째 문장이 보도하고자 하는 내용의 가장 필수적인 요소를 포함해야 한다는 것을 문장 (2)에서 강조하며, 순차적으로 덜 중요한 정보를 배치한다는 내용이 문장 (4)에서 언급된다. 본문은 이것이 'inverted pyramid structure(거꾸로 된 피라미드 구조)'이며, 이러한 구조로 기사가 쓰이지 않는다면 정보 전달이 극대화되지 않는다는 점을 예시를 들어 강조한다. 따라서 기사에서 요점이 되는 내용, 즉 필수적인 요소를 어디에 배치해야 좋은가에 대한 글이므로, 이 내용을 모두 포함하는 ③이 정답이다.

[중요 어휘]

☐	story	[명사] 기사, 이야기
☐	essential	[형용사] 필수적인, 본질적인
☐	element	[명사] 요소, 성분
☐	convey	[동사] 전달하다, 운반하다
☐	present	[동사] 제시하다, 보여주다
☐	inverted	[형용사] 거꾸로 된, 반대의
☐	attention span	주의 지속 시간, 주의 집중 범위
☐	maximize	[동사] 극대화하다, 최대한 활용하다
☐	alternative	[명사] 대안 / [형용사] 대체 가능한
☐	mystery	[명사] 미스터리, 추리물
☐	payoff	[명사] 결말, (급여) 지불
☐	break off	(갑자기) 멈추다, 중단하다
☐	presidential election	대통령 선거
☐	tell A from B	A를 B와 구별하다[구분하다]

14 2021년 11월 24번 (정답률 65%) 정답 ②

[지문 끊어 읽기] 자유 시장을 통한 폭력의 해결

(1) The free market has liberated people /
자유 시장은 사람들을 자유롭게 해 왔다 /
힌트 'way'가 선행사일 때, 관계부사로 'how'가 올 수 없으므로 관계부사 'that'이 왔음.
in a way that Marxism never could.
마르크스주의가 결코 할 수 없었던 방식으로

(2) What is more, /
게다가 /
as A. O. Hirschman, the Harvard economic historian, /
접속사 =
하버드 대학 경제 역사학자인 A. O. Hirschman이 /

showed in his classic study *The Passions and the Interests*, /
V
자신의 대표적 연구인 *The Passions and the Interests*에서 보여 주었듯이 /

the market was seen /
S(=the free market) V
시장은 여겨졌다 /

힌트 'see A as B(A를 B로 여기다)' 구문이 수동태로 바뀐 형태임. 'Enlightenment thinkers saw the market as a powerful solution to ~'로 바꿔서 생각하면 이해하기 쉬움.

by Enlightenment thinkers Adam Smith, David Hume, and Montesquieu /
계몽주의 사상가들인 Adam Smith, David Hume 그리고 Montesquieu에 의해 /

as a powerful solution /
강력한 해결책으로 /

to one of humanity's greatest traditional weaknesses: / violence.
인류의 가장 큰 전통적 약점들 중 하나에 대한 / 폭력

정답 단서 자유 시장은 인류의 가장 큰 약점 중 하나인 '폭력'에 대한 해결책으로 여겨짐.

(3) When two nations meet, / said Montesquieu, /
두 국가가 만날 때 / Montesquieu가 말했던 바로는 /

they can do one of two things: / they can wage war /
그들은 두 가지 중 하나를 할 수 있다 / 그들은 전쟁을 벌일 수 있다 /

or they can trade.
혹은 그들은 거래를 할 수 있다

(4) If they wage war, / both are likely to lose / in the long run. 정답 단서
만약 그들이 전쟁을 벌인다면 / 둘 다 손해를 볼 가능성이 있다 / 장기적으로

두 국가가 전쟁을 벌이면 장기적으로 두 국가 모두 손해를 입음.

(5) If they trade, / both will gain. 정답 단서
만약 그들이 거래를 한다면 / 둘 다 이득을 얻을 것이다

두 국가가 전쟁 대신 거래를 하면 두 국가 모두 이득을 얻을 수 있음.

(6) That, / of course, /
그것이 / 물론 / 삽입

was the logic / behind the establishment of the European Union:
논리였다 / 유럽 연합의 설립 이면에 있는

힌트 :(콜론)은 앞에 나온 특정 내용을 부연 설명하거나 강조할 때 사용할 수 있음. 본문의 경우 'the logic behind the establishment of the European Union(유럽 연합의 설립 이면에 있는 논리)'에 대한 구체적인 내용을 콜론 뒤에서 설명하고 있음.

(7) to lock together the destinies of its nations, /
그것의 국가들의 운명을 한데 묶었다 / =the European Union's

especially France and Germany, / in such a way /
특히 프랑스와 독일 / 그렇게 함으로써 /

that they would have an overwhelming interest /
그들은 저항할 수 없는 이해관계를 가졌을 것이다 /

not to wage war again /
부사적 용법(목적)
다시는 전쟁을 벌이지 않도록 /

as they had done to such devastating cost /
그들이 너무나도 파괴적인 대가를 치르며 그랬었던 것처럼 /

in the first half of the twentieth century.
20세기 전반에

힌트 'in such a way that'은 '그렇게 함으로써 ~하다'라는 뜻으로 'such a way'는 방법을, that절 이하는 결과를 나타냄.

★중요 여기서 말하는 'an overwhelming interest(저항할 수 없는 이해관계)'란 연합함으로써 얻는 이익이 전쟁을 벌이는 것보다 압도적으로 좋기 때문에 전쟁보다 연합을 선택할 수밖에 없는 것을 말함.

힌트 'to one's cost'는 '대가를 치르며'라는 뜻임. 이 문장에서는 'one's' 자리에 'such devastating'이 들어와 명사 'cost'를 수식하고 있음.

[전문 해석]

(1)자유 시장은 마르크스주의가 결코 할 수 없었던 방식으로 사람들을 자유롭게 해 왔다. (2)게다가 하버드 대학 경제 역사학자인 A. O. Hirschman이 자신의 대표적 연구인 *The Passions and the Interests*에서 보여 주었듯이, 시장은 계몽주의 사상가들인 Adam Smith, David Hume 그리고 Montesquieu에 의해 인류의 가장 큰 전통적 약점들 중 하나인 폭력에 대한 강력한 해결책으로 여겨졌다. (3)Montesquieu가 말했던 바로는 두 국가가 만날 때 그들은 두 가지 중 하나를 할 수 있는데, 즉 그들은 전쟁을 벌이거나 거래를 할 수 있다. (4)만약 그들이 전쟁을 벌인다면, 둘 다 장기적으로 손해를 볼 가능성이 있다. (5)만약 그들이 거래를 한다면, 둘 다 이득을 얻을 것이다. (6)물론 그것이 유럽 연합의 설립 이면에 있는 논리였다. (7)즉 그것의 국가들, 특히 프랑스와 독일의 운명을 한데 묶었는데 그렇게 함으로써 그들이 20세기 전반에 너무나도 파괴적인 대가를 치르며 그랬었던 것처럼 다시는 전쟁을 벌이지 않도록 그들은 저항할 수 없는 이해관계를 가졌을 것이다.

- free market(자유 시장): 시장 활동에 대한 국가의 간섭이 배제된, 즉 개인의 경제 활동의 자유가 최대한으로 보장된 시장
- Enlightenment(계몽주의): 18세기에 프랑스와 독일을 기점으로 유럽 전역에 유행했던 사상. 이성의 힘과 인류의 무한한 진보를 믿으며 구습(舊習)을 타파하고자 했음.
- capitalism(자본주의): 사유 재산제에 바탕을 두고 이윤 획득을 위해 상품의 생산과 소비가 이루어지는 경제 체제

[정답 확인]

다음 글의 제목으로 가장 적절한 것은?

① Trade War: A Reflection of Human's Innate Violence
무역 전쟁: 인간의 타고난 폭력의 반영
✔② Free Market: Winning Together over Losing Together
자유 시장: 함께 지는 것보다 함께 이기는 것
③ New Economic Framework Stabilizes the Free Market
새로운 경제 체제가 자유 시장을 안정시킨다
④ Violence Is the Invisible Hand That Disrupts Capitalism!
폭력은 자본주의를 방해하는 보이지 않는 손이다!
⑤ How Are Governments Involved in Controlling the Market?
정부는 시장을 통제하는 데 어떻게 관여하는가?

[문제 풀이]

자유 시장이 국가 간 전쟁과 폭력을 해결하는 방식에 대한 글이다. Montesquieu에 따르면 두 국가가 만났을 때 전쟁을 선택하면 둘 다 장기적으로 큰 손해를 보는 반면, 자유 시장의 방식으로 거래를 하면 둘 다 이득을 얻을 수 있다. 이렇게 자유 시장은 양측의 이해관계를 한데 묶어 전쟁을 억제했는데 이는 곧 유럽 연합의 설립 배경이 되기도 했다. 지문 전반에 걸쳐 자유 시장이 서로 다른 두 국가에게 이득이 된다는 것을 반복적으로 설명하고 있으므로 글의 제목으로는 자유 시장의 특징을 나타내는 ②가 적절하다.

[중요 어휘]

□ liberate	동사 자유롭게 하다, 해방시키다
□ classic	형용사 대표적인, 일류의
□ thinker	명사 사상가
□ wage	동사 (전쟁·전투를) 벌이다
□ in the long run	장기적으로, 결국에는
□ trade	동사 거래를 하다 / 명사 거래, 무역
□ gain	동사 이득을 얻다, ~을 얻게 되다
□ establishment	명사 설립
□ overwhelming	형용사 저항할 수 없는, 압도적인
□ interest	명사 이해관계, 이익
□ devastating	형용사 (대단히) 파괴적인, 엄청나게 충격적인
□ innate	형용사 타고난, 선천적인
□ framework	명사 체제, 틀
□ stabilize	동사 안정시키다
□ disrupt	동사 방해하다

15 2022년 3월 24번 (정답률 65%) 정답 ③

[지문 끊어 읽기] 환경을 해치는 제조업 발달

(1) The realization of human domination over the environment /
S
인간의 환경 지배 실현은 /

began in the late 1700s / with the industrial revolution.
V
1700년대 후반에 시작되었다 / 산업 혁명과 함께

(2) Advances in manufacturing /
제조업의 발달은 /

transformed societies and economies /
사회와 경제를 변화시켰다 /

while producing significant impacts / on the environment. 정답 단서
중대한 영향을 미치면서 / 환경에

힌트 접속사의 의미를 살리기 위해 접속사를 생략하지 않은 분사구문임.

제조업의 발달이 환경에 중대한 영향을 미침.

(3) American society became structured /
미국 사회는 구축되었다 /

on multiple industries' capitalistic goals /
여러 산업의 자본주의적 목표에 따라 /

as the development of the steam engine led /
접속사(~하면서)
증기 기관의 발달이 이어지면서 /

to the mechanized production of goods / in mass quantities.
기계화된 상품의 생산으로 / 대량의

(4) Rural agricultural communities /
시골의 농업 사회는 / S

with economies based on handmade goods and agriculture /
수제 상품과 농업에 기반을 둔 경제를 가진 /

were abandoned / for life in urban cities with large factories /
V
버려졌다 / 대규모 공장이 있는 도시에서의 삶을 위해 /

based on an economy of industrialized manufacturing.
산업화된 제조업 경제를 기반으로 한

(5) Innovations / in the production of textiles, iron, and steel /
S
혁신은 / 직물, 철, 철강 생산에서의 /
provided increased profits / to private companies.
V
증가된 이윤을 제공했다 / 사기업에

(6) Simultaneously, / those industries exerted authority /
병렬①
동시에 / 그런 산업들은 권력을 행사했다 /
over the environment /
환경에 /
and began dumping hazardous by-products /
병렬②
그리고 유해한 부산물을 내버리기 시작했다 /
in public lands and waterways. 정답 단서 직물, 철, 철강 생산 등의 제조업 기반 산업들이 공공 토지와 수로에 유해한 부산물을 내버리기 시작함. 문장 (2)에서 말한 영향(impact)이 부정적인 영향이라는 것을 알 수 있음.
공공 토지와 수로에

[전문 해석]

(1)인간의 환경 지배 실현은 1700년대 후반 산업 혁명과 함께 시작되었다. (2)제조업의 발달은 환경에 중대한 영향을 미치면서 사회와 경제를 변화시켰다. (3)증기 기관의 발달이 기계화된 상품의 대량 생산으로 이어지면서 미국 사회는 여러 산업의 자본주의적 목표에 따라 구축되었다. (4)수제 상품과 농업에 기반을 둔 경제를 가진 시골의 농업 사회는 산업화된 제조업 경제를 기반으로 한 대규모 공장이 있는 도시에서의 삶을 위해 버려졌다. (5)직물, 철, 철강 생산에서의 혁신은 사기업의 이윤을 증가시켰다. (6)동시에, 그런 산업들은 환경에 권력을 행사하였고 공공 토지와 수로에 유해한 부산물을 내버리기 시작했다.

[정답 확인]

다음 글의 제목으로 가장 적절한 것은?

① Strategies for Industrial Innovations
산업 혁신을 위한 전략
② Urbanization: A Road to a Better Life
도시화: 더 나은 삶으로 가는 길
③ Industrial Development Hurt the Environment (✔)
산업 발달이 환경을 해쳤다
④ Technology: A Key to Sustainable Development
기술: 지속 가능한 발전의 열쇠
⑤ The Driving Force of Capitalism Was Not Greed
자본주의의 원동력은 탐욕이 아니었다

[문제 풀이]

필자는 산업 혁명과 함께 인간이 환경에 행사하는 영향력이 커졌음을 지적한다. 제조업 기반 산업이 중심이 되면서 농업 중심의 시골 사회는 도시보다 뒷전이 되었다. 또한 제조 과정 중 생기는 유해한 부산물이 공공 토지와 수로 등에 버려졌는데, 이러한 현상은 결국 산업 발달이 환경에 악영향을 끼치는 결과를 낳았음을 시사한다. 따라서 이 글의 제목으로 ③ 'Industrial Development Hurt the Environment(산업 발달이 환경을 해쳤다)'가 적절하다.

[중요 어휘]

□ **realization**	명사 실현, 깨달음
□ **domination**	명사 지배, 우세
□ **structure**	동사 구축하다, 조직화하다
□ **capitalistic**	형용사 자본주의적인
□ **rural**	형용사 시골의, 지방의
□ **agricultural**	형용사 농업의, 농경의
□ **abandon**	동사 버리다, 포기하다
□ **textile**	명사 직물, 옷감
□ **steel**	명사 철강(업)
□ **exert**	동사 행사하다, 가하다
□ **dump**	동사 내버리다, 떠넘기다
□ **by-product**	명사 부산물, 부작용
□ **waterway**	명사 수로, 항로
□ **urbanization**	명사 도시화
□ **greed**	명사 탐욕

16 2023년 3월 24번 (정답률 65%) 정답 ④

[지문 끊어 읽기] 승리와 타인의 시선에 대한 자의식 과잉

(1) Winning turns on a self-conscious awareness /
승리는 자의식 과잉의 인식을 촉발한다 /
that others are watching. 정답 단서 승리는 다른 이들이 보고 있다는 자의식 과잉의 인식을 촉발함.
동격의 접속사
다른 이들이 보고 있다는

(2) It's a lot easier / to move under the radar /
형식상의 주어 내용상의 주어
훨씬 더 쉽다 / 눈에 띄지 않게 움직이는 것은 /
when no one knows you / and no one is paying attention.
아무도 여러분을 모를 때 / 그리고 아무도 주의를 기울이고 있지 않을 때

(3) You can mess up and be rough and get dirty /
병렬① 병렬② 병렬③
여러분은 망치고 난폭해지고 더러워질 수 있다 /
because no one even knows you're there.
아무도 여러분이 그곳에 있다는 것조차 모르기 때문에

(4) But as soon as you start to win, / and others start to notice, /
병렬① 병렬②
그러나 여러분이 승리하기 시작하자마자 / 그리고 다른 사람들이 알아차리기 시작하자마자 /
you're suddenly aware / that you're being observed.
여러분은 갑자기 인식한다 / 여러분이 관찰되고 있다는 것을

(5) You're being judged.
여러분은 평가되고 있다

(6) You worry / that others will discover your flaws and weaknesses, /
여러분은 걱정한다 / 다른 사람들이 여러분의 결함과 약점을 발견할까 봐 /
and you start hiding your true personality, /
그리고 여러분은 여러분의 진정한 성격을 숨기기 시작한다 /
so you can be a good role model and good citizen /
여러분이 좋은 본보기이자 좋은 시민이 될 수 있도록 /
and a leader that others can respect.
선행사 목적격 관계대명사
그리고 다른 사람들이 존경하는 지도자가

(7) There is nothing wrong with that.
그것이 잘못된 것은 아니다

(8) But if you do it / at the expense of being who you really are, /
그러나 여러분이 그렇게 한다면 / 자신의 진정한 모습이 되는 것을 희생하면서 /
making decisions that please others /
선행사 주격 관계대명사
다른 사람들을 만족시키는 결정을 하면서 /
instead of pleasing yourself, /
여러분 스스로를 만족시키는 것 대신에 /
you're not going to be in that position very long. 정답 단서 여러분의 진짜 모습이 되는 것을 희생하면서 다른 사람들을 만족시키는 결정을 한다면 승리의 위치에 길게 있지는 못할 것임.
여러분은 그 위치에 그리 오래 있지는 못할 것이다

(9) When you start apologizing / for who you are, /
여러분이 사과하기 시작할 때 / 여러분이 누구인지에 대해 /
you stop growing / and you stop winning.
여러분은 성장하기를 멈춘다 / 그리고 여러분은 승리하기를 멈춘다
힌트 stop + V-ing: ~하는 것을 멈추다
stop + to V: ~하기 위해 멈추다

(10) Permanently.
영원히

[전문 해석]

(1)승리는 다른 이들이 보고 있다는 자의식 과잉의 인식을 촉발한다. (2)아무도 여러분을 모르고 아무도 주의를 기울이고 있지 않을 때 눈에 띄지 않게 움직이는 것은 훨씬 더 쉽다. (3)아무도 여러분이 그곳에 있다는 것조차 모르기 때문에 여러분은 망치고 난폭해지고 더러워질 수 있다. (4)그러나 여러분이 승리하기 시작하고 다른 사람들이 알아차리기 시작하자마자, 여러분은 갑자기 관찰되고 있다는 것을 인식한다. (5)여러분은 평가되고 있다. (6)여러분은 다른 사람들이 여러분의 결함과 약점을 발견할까 봐 걱정하고, 여러분이 좋은 본보기이자 좋은 시민이고 다른 사람들이 존경하는 지도자가 될 수 있도록 여러분의 진정한 성격을 숨기기 시작한다. (7)그것이 잘못된 것은 아니다. (8)그러나 여러분 스스로를 만족시키는 것 대신에 다른 사람들을 만족시키는 결정을 하며 자신의 진정한 모습이 되는 것을 희생하면서 그렇게 한다면, 여러분은 그 위치에 그리 오래 있지는 못할 것이다. (9)여러분이 누구인지에 대해 사과하기 시작할 때, 여러분은 성장하기를 멈추고 승리하기를 멈춘다. (10)영원히.

정답과 해설 07 제목 추론

[정답 확인]

다음 글의 제목으로 가장 적절한 것은?

① Stop Judging Others to Win the Race of Life
삶의 경주에서 승리하기 위해 다른 사람들을 판단하는 것을 멈춰라
② Why Disappointment Hurts More than Criticism
왜 실망이 비판보다 더 상처를 많이 주는가
③ Winning vs. Losing: A Dangerously Misleading Mindset
승리 대 패배: 위험하게 오도하는 사고방식
✔ Winners in a Trap: Too Self-Conscious to Be Themselves
덫에 걸린 승리자들: 자기 자신이 되기에 너무 자의식 과잉인
⑤ Is Honesty the Best Policy to Turn Enemies into Friends?
적을 친구로 돌리기에 정직이 가장 좋은 방책인가?

[문제 풀이]

본문에 따르면, 승리는 다른 사람들이 자신을 보고 있다는 자의식 과잉의 인식을 촉발한다. 아무도 보지 않을 때는 망치고 난폭해지고 더러워질 수 있지만, 여러분이 승리하기 시작하면서 다른 사람들을 인식하게 되고 자신의 진짜 모습을 숨기게 된다. 그것이 잘못된 것은 아니지만, 자신의 본모습대로 행동하지 않으면서 다른 사람들을 만족시키기 위해 행동하는 것은 승리를 지속시키지 않는다. 따라서 승리자들이 자신의 본래 모습대로 있기에는 지나치게 자의식이 강해져서 마치 덫에 걸린 듯하다는 내용의 ④가 적절하다.

[중요 어휘]

☐ **self-conscious**	[형용사] 자의식 과잉의, 남의 시선을 의식하는
☐ **awareness**	[명사] 인식, 자각
☐ **under the radar**	눈에 띄지 않게, 몰래
☐ **mess up**	망치다
☐ **rough**	[형용사] 난폭한, 거친, 대략적인
☐ **observe**	[동사] 관찰하다, 준수하다
☐ **judge**	[동사] 평가하다, 판단하다 / [명사] 판사
☐ **flaw**	[명사] 결함, 흠, 금
☐ **at the expense of**	~을 희생하면서, ~을 잃어가며
☐ **please**	[동사] 만족시키다, 기쁘게 하다
☐ **permanently**	[부사] 영원히

17 2022년 11월 24번 (정답률 60%) 정답 ②

[지문 끊어 읽기] 자전거 타기의 상징적 재해석

(1) The recent "cycling as a lifestyle" craze /
최근의 '생활 양식으로서의 자전거 타기' 열풍은 /
has expressed itself / in an increase /
나타났다 / 증가로 /
in the number of active cyclists /
적극적으로 자전거를 타는 사람들 수의 /
and in growth of cycling club membership /
그리고 자전거 타기 클럽 회원의 성장으로 /
in several European, American, Australian and Asian urban areas.
몇몇 유럽, 미국, 호주 그리고 아시아 도시 지역에서

힌트 'the number of'는 '~의 수'라는 뜻으로, of 뒤에는 복수명사가 옴. 하지만 'the number'가 수 자체를 의미하므로 단수 취급을 함. 'a number of'는 '몇몇의, 많은'이라는 뜻을 가지며 of 뒤에 복수명사가 오는 것은 동일하지만 복수 취급 함.

(2) It has also been accompanied /
=The recent ~ craze
그것은 또한 동반되어 왔다 /
by a symbolic reinterpretation of the bicycle. [정답 단서] 자전거 타기가 본래의 여가 활동과 다르게 상징으로 변화함.
자전거의 상징적인 재해석과

(3) After the bicycle had been associated with poverty for many years, /
자전거가 수년 동안 가난과 연관되었던 이후로 /
expensive recreational bicycles /
비싼 여가용 자전거는 /
or recreationally-inspired commuting bicycles /
혹은 여가용으로부터 영감을 받은 통근용 자전거는 /
have suddenly become aspirational products /
갑자기 열망의 상품이 되었다 /
in urban environments.
도시 환경에서

(4) In present times, / cycling has become an activity /
현재 / 자전거 타기는 활동이 되었다 / ↑선행사
[which is also performed / for its demonstrative value, /
[ ]: 주격 관계대명사절 병렬①(전치사 for의 목적어)
수행되기도 하는 / 그것의 드러내 놓고 표현하는 가치를 위해 /
its role in identity construction /
병렬②(전치사 for의 목적어)
정체성 형성에 있어서의 그것의 역할을 위해 /
and its effectiveness / in impressing others /
병렬③(전치사 for의 목적어) 병렬①'(전치사 in의 목적어, 동명사)
그리고 그것의 효과를 위해 / 타인에게 깊은 인상을 주는 것에 있어서의 /
and signaling social status]. [정답 단서] 자전거 타기는 가치 표현 및 정체성 형성의 역할을 수행하기도 하지만 깊은 인상을 남기는 것과 사회적 지위 암시의 역할 또한 수행함.
병렬②'(전치사 in의 목적어, 동명사)
그리고 사회적 지위를 암시하는 것에 있어서의

(5) To a certain extent, / cycling has turned /
어느 정도는 / 자전거 타기는 바뀌었다 /
into a symbolic marker of the well-off.
부유한 사람들의 상징적 표시로

(6) Obviously, / value-laden consumption behavior /
분명히 / 가치 판단적인 소비 행위는 /
is by no means limited to cycling.
결코 ~이 아닌
결코 자전거 타기에 한정되지 않는다

(7) However, /
그러나 /
the link with identity construction and conspicuous consumption /
정체성 형성과 과시적인 소비와의 관련성은 /
has become particularly manifest / in the case of cycling.
특히 분명해졌다 / 자전거 타기의 경우에

[전문 해석]

(1)최근의 '생활 양식으로서의 자전거 타기' 열풍은 몇몇 유럽, 미국, 호주 그리고 아시아 도시 지역에서 적극적으로 자전거를 타는 사람들 수의 증가와 자전거 타기 클럽 회원의 성장으로 나타났다. (2)그것은 또한 자전거의 상징적인 재해석과 동반되어 왔다. (3)자전거가 수년 동안 가난과 연관되었던 이후로, 비싼 여가용 자전거 혹은 여가용으로부터 영감을 받은 통근용 자전거는 도시 환경에서 갑자기 열망의 상품이 되었다. (4)현재 자전거 타기는 그것의 드러내 놓고 표현하는 가치, 정체성 형성에 있어서의 그것의 역할, 그리고 타인에게 깊은 인상을 주고 사회적 지위를 암시하는 것에 있어서의 그것의 효과를 위해 수행되기도 하는 활동이 되었다. (5)어느 정도는, 자전거 타기가 부유한 사람들의 상징적 표시로 바뀌었다. (6)분명히, 가치 판단적인 소비 행위는 결코 자전거 타기에 한정되지 않는다. (7)그러나 정체성 형성과 과시적인 소비와의 관련성은 자전거 타기의 경우에 특히 분명해졌다.

[정답 확인]

다음 글의 제목으로 가장 적절한 것은?

① Cycling Contributes to a City's Atmosphere and Identity
자전거 타기는 도시의 분위기 그리고 정체성에 기여한다
✔ The Rise of Cycling: A New Status Symbol of City Dwellers
자전거 타기의 부상: 도시 거주자들의 새로운 지위적 상징
③ Cycling Is Wealth-Building but Worsens Social Inequality
자전거 타기는 부를 축적하지만 사회적 불평등을 악화시킨다
④ How to Encourage and Sustain the Bicycle Craze in Urban Areas
도시 지역에서 자전거 열풍을 독려하고 유지시키는 방법
⑤ Expanding Bike Lane Networks Can Lead to More Inclusive Cities
자전거 도로 연결망 확장은 더 포괄적인 도시로 이끌 수 있다

[문제 풀이]

'생활 양식으로서의 자전거 타기' 열풍은 유럽, 미국, 호주, 아시아의 몇몇 도시 지역에서 열풍을 일으키면서 자전거를 타는 사람들의 수가 증가함과 동시에 의미가 변형되기 시작했다. 일종의 가난의 상징이었던 자전거가 값비싼 여가용의 등장으로 열망의 대상이 되고, 그에 따라 가치와 개인의 정체성 형성에도 영향을 미칠 뿐만 아니라 사회적 지위를 암시하고 소비자들은 사람들의 선망을 받을 수 있게 되었다. 이러한 소비가 부를 과시하는 새로운 지표가 되었다는 내용과 일맥상통하므로 ②가 적절하다.

[중요 어휘]

☐ **craze**	[명사] 열풍, 대유행
☐ **reinterpretation**	[명사] 재해석

- associated with ~와 관련된
- poverty 명사 가난, 빈곤, 부족
- aspirational 형용사 열망하는, 동경의 대상인
- demonstrative 형용사 드러내 놓고 표현하는, 숨기지 않는
- signal 동사 (어떤 일이 있거나 있을 것임을) 암시하다, 시사하다, 신호를 보내다
- well-off 형용사 부유한, 유복한
- value-laden 형용사 가치 판단적인, 개인적 의견에 영향을 받는
- by no means 결코 ~이 아닌
- conspicuous 형용사 과시적인, 눈에 잘 띄는, 튀는, 뚜렷한
- manifest 형용사 분명한 / 동사 분명해지다, 나타내다, 드러내 보이다
- dweller 명사 거주자, 주민
- inclusive 형용사 포괄적인, 폭넓은

18 2022년 9월 24번 (정답률 55%) 정답 ①

[지문 끊어 읽기] 공공 의료

(1) From the earliest times, /
가장 초기 시대부터 /
healthcare services have been recognized /
의료 서비스는 인식되어 왔다 /
to have two equal aspects, /
두 개의 동일한 측면을 지닌다고 /
namely clinical care and public healthcare. 정답단서 고대에도 의료 서비스는 임상 치료와 공공 의료로 나뉘어 인식됨.
다시 말해 임상 치료와 공공 의료라는

(2) In classical Greek mythology, /
고대 그리스 신화에서 /
the god of medicine, Asklepios, had two daughters, /
의술의 신인 Asklepios는 딸이 두 명 있었다 /
Hygiea and Panacea.
Hygiea와 Panacea라는

(3) The former was the goddess /
전자는 여신이었다 /
of preventive health and wellness, or hygiene, /
예방적 건강과 건강 관리, 즉 위생의 /
and the latter the goddess / of treatment and curing.
그리고 후자는 여신이었다 / 치료와 치유의

힌트 and 앞뒤로 동일한 형태의 문장이 반복되어, the latter와 the goddess 사이에 be동사 'was'가 생략됨.

(4) In modern times, /
현대에 /
the societal ascendancy of medical professionalism /
의료 전문성의 사회적 우세는 /
has caused treatment of sick patients /
5형식V O
아픈 환자들의 치료를 만들어왔다 /
to overshadow those preventive healthcare services /
O·C
그러한 예방적인 의료 서비스를 가리도록 /
[provided by the less heroic figures /
덜 영웅적인 인물들에 의해 제공되는 /
of sanitary engineers, biologists, and governmental public health officers]. [ ]: healthcare services 수식
위생 공학자, 생물학자, 정부 공공 보건 공무원과 같은

(5) Nevertheless, /
그럼에도 불구하고 /
the quality of health that human populations enjoy /
S
인간이 누리는 건강의 질은 /
is attributable less to surgical dexterity, innovative pharmaceutical products, and bioengineered devices /
V
외과적 기민함, 혁신적인 제약 제품, 그리고 생체 공학적 기기에 덜 기인한다 /
than to the availability of public sanitation, sewage management, and services /
선행사
공공 위생 시설의 이용 가능성, 하수 관리, 그리고 서비스들보다 /
which control the pollution of the air, drinking water, urban noise,
주격 관계대명사
and food for human consumption. 정답단서 공공 의료 서비스가 사람들의 건강의 질에 큰 영향을 끼침.
대기 오염, 식수, 도시 소음, 그리고 인간이 소비하는 음식을 관리하는

(6) The human right / to the highest attainable standard of health /
S
인간의 권리는 / 달성할 수 있는 가장 높은 수준의 건강에 대한 /
depends on public healthcare services / 정답단서 공공 의료 서비스는 인간의 높은 수준의 건강을 달성하게 함.
V
공공 의료 서비스에 달려 있다 /
no less than on the skills and equipment of doctors and hospitals.
의사와 병원의 기술과 장비에 못지않게

힌트 'no less than'은 '~에 못지않게'라는 뜻으로 긍정적인 어감을 내포함. '겨우 ~인, ~밖에 되지 않는'이라는 의미를 가진 'no more than'과 헷갈리지 않도록 유의할 것.

[전문 해석]

(1)가장 초기 시대부터 의료 서비스는 두 개의 동일한 측면, 다시 말해 임상 치료와 공공 의료라는 측면을 지닌다고 인식되어 왔다. (2)고대 그리스 신화에서 의술의 신인 Asklepios는 Hygiea와 Panacea라는 딸이 두 명 있었다. (3)전자는 예방적 건강과 건강 관리, 즉 위생의 여신이었고, 후자는 치료와 치유의 여신이었다. (4)현대에, 의료 전문성의 사회적 우세는 아픈 환자들의 치료가 위생 공학자, 생물학자, 정부 공공 보건 공무원과 같은 덜 영웅적인 인물들에 의해 제공되는 그러한 예방적인 의료 서비스를 가리도록 만들어왔다. (5)그럼에도 불구하고 인간이 누리는 건강의 질은 공공 위생 시설의 이용 가능성, 하수 관리, 그리고 대기 오염, 식수, 도시 소음, 그리고 인간이 소비하는 음식을 관리하는 서비스들보다 외과적 기민함, 혁신적인 제약 제품, 그리고 생체 공학적 기기에 덜 기인한다. (6)달성할 수 있는 가장 높은 수준의 건강에 대한 인간의 권리는 의사와 병원의 기술과 장비에 못지않게 공공 의료 서비스에 달려 있다.

[정답 확인]

다음 글의 제목으로 가장 적절한 것은?

✔① Public Healthcare: A Co-Star, Not a Supporting Actor
공공 의료: 조연이 아닌 공동 주연
② The Historical Development of Medicine and Surgery
의료와 수술의 역사적인 발전
③ Clinical Care Controversies: What You Don't Know
임상 치료 논란: 당신이 모르는 것
④ The Massive Similarities Between Different Mythologies
다른 신화들 사이의 엄청난 유사점
⑤ Initiatives Opening up Health Innovation Around the World
전 세계의 건강 혁신을 여는 계획

[문제 풀이]

의료 서비스는 고대부터 임상 치료와 공공 의료 제공으로 나뉘어 인식되어 왔는데, 현대에는 예방적인 공공 의료 서비스가 임상 치료에 비해 덜 중요하게 여겨진다. 그렇지만 문장 (5)와 (6)은 공공 위생 시설이나 하수 관리 등의 공공 의료 서비스가 없다면 높은 수준의 건강을 달성할 수 없음을 짚는다. 지문은 결국 의료 서비스에서 공공 의료가 가지는 중요성에 대해 말하고 있으므로, 제목은 이 내용을 포함해야 한다. 따라서 정답은 공공 의료도 큰 의미가 있다는 것을 'co-star'로 표현한 ①이다.

[중요 어휘]

- healthcare 명사 의료, 건강 관리
- namely 부사 다시 말해, 즉
- clinical 형용사 임상의
- medicine 명사 의술, 의학
- preventive 형용사 예방적인, 예방을 위한
- wellness 명사 건강 (관리)
- hygiene 명사 위생
- societal 형용사 사회적인
- ascendancy 명사 우세, 우위, 지배권
- professionalism 명사 전문성, 뛰어난 기량
- overshadow 동사 가리다, 그늘지게 하다
- heroic 형용사 영웅적인, 영웅의
- sanitary 형용사 위생의, 깨끗한
- be attributable to N ~에 기인하다
- surgical 형용사 외과적인, 수술의

문제편 p.083

- [ ] **dexterity** 명사 기민함, 솜씨
- [ ] **pharmaceutical** 형용사 제약의, 약학의
- [ ] **sanitation** 명사 위생 시설
- [ ] **sewage** 명사 하수, 오물
- [ ] **attainable** 형용사 달성할 수 있는, 이룰 수 있는
- [ ] **controversy** 명사 논란
- [ ] **initiative** 명사 계획, 주도권, 결단력

19 2023년 6월 24번 (정답률 55%) 정답 ⑤

[지문 끊어 읽기] 언어의 진화

(1) New words and expressions emerge continually /
새로운 단어와 표현은 끊임없이 생긴다 /
in response to new situations, ideas and feelings. 정답단서 새로운 단어와 표현은 새로운 상황, 아이디어, 감정에 반응하여 계속 생겨남.
새로운 상황, 아이디어와 감정에 반응하여

(2) *The Oxford English Dictionary* publishes /
'Oxford 영어 사전'은 출판한다 /
supplements of new words and expressions / 선행사
새로운 단어와 표현의 추가분을 /
that have entered the language. 주격 관계대명사절
그 언어에 등장한

(3) Some people deplore this kind of thing / 병렬①
어떤 사람들은 이런 종류의 일을 한탄한다 /
and see it as a drift from correct English. 병렬②
그리고 이것을 올바른 영어로부터의 표류로 본다

힌트 'It+be동사+강조 대상+that+나머지 부분'의 강조 구문으로, 원래 문장은 'Any attempt was made to formalize spelling and punctuation of English at all only in the eighteenth century'이나, 'only in the eighteenth century'를 강조하기 위해 문장 (4)의 형태로 씀.

(4) But it was only in the eighteenth century /
그러나 불과 18세기이다 /
that any attempt was made /
시도가 이루어진 것은 /
to formalize spelling and punctuation of English at all.
영어의 철자와 구두법을 조금이라도 공식화하려는

힌트 'to formalize'는 명사를 수식하는 형용사적 용법으로, 원래 'any attempt to formalize ~ at all was made'에서 to부정사 부분이 길기 때문에 동사 뒤에 위치하게 되었음.

힌트 선행사 the language 뒤에 목적격 관계대명사 which 혹은 that이 생략된 형태임.

(5) [The language we speak in the twenty-first century] / [ ]: S①
21세기에 우리가 말하는 언어는 /
would be virtually unintelligible to Shakespeare, / V①
Shakespeare에게는 사실상 이해하기 어려울 것이다 /
and so would his way of speaking to us. V② S② 정답단서 Shakespeare는 21세기에 우리가 사용하는 언어를 이해할 수 없고, 우리도 Shakespeare가 말하는 언어를 이해할 수 없음.
그리고 그가 말하는 방식은 우리에게도 그럴 것이다

힌트 앞에 언급된 내용에 대해 '~도 역시 그렇다'는 의미를 나타낼 때, 'so+조동사[be동사/대동사do]+주어'로 쓸 수 있음. 앞 문장에서 사용된 조동사 'would'를 쓰고 반복되는 'be virtually unintelligible'은 생략됨.

(6) Alvin Toffler estimated /
Alvin Toffler는 추정했다 /
[that Shakespeare would probably only understand about 250,000 of the 450,000 words /
Shakespeare가 아마도 450,000개의 단어 중에서 약 250,000개의 단어만 이해할 것이라고 /
in general use in the English language now]. [ ]: estimated의 목적어(명사절)
현재 영어에서 일반적으로 사용되는

(7) In other words, / so to speak, /
다시 말해서 / 말하자면 /
if Shakespeare were to materialize in London today /
만약 Shakespeare가 오늘날 런던에 나타난다면 /
he would understand, / on average, /
그는 이해할 것이다 / 평균적으로 /
only five out of every nine words in our vocabulary. 정답단서 오늘날 런던에 Shakespeare가 나타난다면, 그는 우리 어휘의 9개 단어당 5개 정도, 즉 절반 정도만 이해할 것임.
우리 어휘에 있는 9개의 단어당 5개의 단어만

힌트 'If+S'+were to+V' ~, S+조동사의 과거+V'는 실현 가능성이 희박함을 강조하는 가정법 미래임.

[전문 해석]

(1)새로운 단어와 표현은 새로운 상황, 아이디어와 감정에 반응하여 끊임없이 생긴다. (2)'Oxford 영어 사전'은 그 언어에 등장한 새로운 단어와 표현의 추가분을 출판한다. (3)어떤 사람들은 이런 종류의 일을 한탄하고 이것을 올바른 영어로부터의 표류로 본다. (4)그러나 영어의 철자와 구두법을 조금이라도 공식화하려는 시도가 이루어진 것은 불과 18세기이다. (5)21세기에 우리가 말하는 언어는 Shakespeare에게는 사실상 이해하기 어려울 것이고 그가 말하는 방식은 우리에게도 그럴 것이다. (6)Alvin Toffler는 Shakespeare가 아마도 현재 영어에서 일반적으로 사용되는 450,000개의 단어 중에서 약 250,000개의 단어만 이해할 것이라고 추정했다. (7)다시 말해서, 말하자면, 만약 Shakespeare가 오늘날 런던에 나타난다면, 그는 평균적으로 우리 어휘에 있는 9개의 단어당 5개의 단어만 이해할 것이다.

- Shakespeare(셰익스피어, 1564년~1616년): 16세기에 활동한 영국의 극작가이자 시인

[정답 확인]

다음 글의 제목으로 가장 적절한 것은?

① Original Meanings of Words Fade with Time
단어의 원래 의미는 시간과 함께 사라진다
② Dictionary: A Gradual Continuation of the Past
사전: 과거의 점진적인 지속
③ Literature: The Driving Force Behind New Words
문학: 새로운 단어 뒤의 원동력
④ How Can We Bridge the Ever-Widening Language Gap?
어떻게 우리가 계속 넓어지는 언어 차이를 메울 수 있을까?
✔ Language Evolution Makes Even Shakespeare Semi-literate!
언어 진화는 Shakespeare조차 반문맹으로 만든다!

[문제 풀이]

문장 (1)~(2)에 따르면, 새로운 상황, 아이디어, 감정에 대한 새로운 단어와 표현이 계속 만들어지고 이러한 새로운 단어와 표현의 추가분들은 사전에 담긴다. 이를 올바른 언어에서 벗어난 쓰임이라며 못마땅하게 여기는 사람도 있지만, 이처럼 언어를 공식화하려는 시도는 18세기가 되어서야 나타났으며, 문장 (5)~(7)에서 Shakespeare와 우리 시대의 단어 차이를 예로 들며 새로운 단어와 표현의 등장으로 언어는 계속 변화해왔음을 강조한다. 특히 마지막 문장에 따르면 Shakespeare는 오늘날 영어에서 사용되는 어휘의 절반만을 이해할 수 있을 것이라고 하므로, 글의 제목으로는 언어가 진화함에 따라 Shakespeare조차 반문맹으로, 즉 언어를 반만 이해하는 사람으로 만든다는 ⑤가 적절하다.

[중요 어휘]

- [ ] **emerge** 동사 생기다, 부상하다, 드러나다
- [ ] **supplement** 명사 추가[보충]분, 증보판
- [ ] **deplore** 동사 한탄하다, 애통해 하다
- [ ] **drift** 명사 표류, 이동
- [ ] **formalize** 동사 공식화하다
- [ ] **punctuation** 명사 구두법
- [ ] **virtually** 부사 사실상, 거의, 가상으로
- [ ] **unintelligible** 형용사 이해할 수 없는
- [ ] **materialize** 동사 나타나다, 구체화하다
- [ ] **fade** 동사 사라지다, (색이) 바래다, 희미해지다

핵심 이 글에서 중점적으로 다루고자 하는 것은 현대의 보상금인데, 이를 위해 문장 (1)에서 문장 (4)까지 사해 사본과 중국의 공룡 뼈 발견 등 다양한 예시를 먼저 언급했음.

20 2017년 9월 24번 (정답률 50%) 정답 ③

[지문 끊어 읽기] 보상금의 역효과

(1) In 1947, / 정답단서
1947년 /
when the Dead Sea Scrolls were discovered, /
사해 사본이 발견되었을 때 /
archaeologists set a finder's fee for each new document.
고고학자들은 새로운 문서마다 발견한 사람에 대한 사례금을 정했다

★중요 새로운 문서가 발견될 때마다 사례금을 지급했기 때문에, 두루마리를 찢어서 여러 조각으로 만들어 중복으로 사례금을 탔다는 의미임.

(2) Instead of lots of extra scrolls being found, /
추가의 많은 두루마리가 발견되는 대신에 /
they were simply torn apart / to increase the reward.
그것들은 그저 갈기갈기 찢어졌다 / 사례금을 늘리기 위해

(3) Similarly, / in China in the nineteenth century, / 정답단서
유사하게 / 19세기 중국에서는 /
an incentive was offered for finding dinosaur bones.
공룡의 뼈를 발견하는 것에 대해 보상금이 주어졌다

(4) Farmers located a few on their land, /
농부들은 그들의 토지에서 몇 개를 찾아냈다 /
broke them into pieces, / and made a lot of money.
그것들을 조각들로 부쉈다 / 그리고 많은 돈을 벌었다

(5) Modern incentives are no better: / 정답단서
현대의 보상금도 더 나을 것이 없다 /
Company boards promise bonuses for achieved targets.
회사의 이사회는 달성된 목표에 대해 보너스를 약속한다

(6) And what happens?
그리고 무슨 일이 일어나는가

(7) Managers invest more energy /
관리자들은 더 많은 에너지를 쏟는다 /
in trying to lower the targets / than in growing the business.
목표를 낮추는 것에 / 사업을 키우는 것보다

(8) People respond to incentives /
사람들은 보상금에 반응한다 /
by doing what is in their best interests. 주제문
그들에게 가장 이익이 되는 것을 함으로써

(9) What is noteworthy is, first, /
주목할 만한 것은 첫째로 ~이다 /
how quickly and radically people's behavior changes /
사람들의 행동이 얼마나 빠르고 급격하게 변화하는가 /
when incentives come into play, / and second, the fact /
보상금이 시행될 때 / 그리고 두 번째로는 사실이다 /
that people respond to the incentives themselves, /
사람들이 보상금 그 자체에 반응한다는 /
and not the higher intentions behind them. 정답단서
그것들의 이면에 있는 더 높은 차원의 의도가 아닌

[전문 해석]

(1)1947년 사해 사본이 발견되었을 때, 고고학자들은 각각의 새로운 문서마다 발견한 사람에 대한 사례금을 정했다. (2)추가의 많은 두루마리가 발견되는 대신에 사례금을 늘리기 위해 그것들(두루마리)은 그저 갈기갈기 찢어졌다. (3)(이와) 유사하게 19세기 중국에서는 공룡의 뼈를 발견하는 것에 대해 보상금이 주어졌다. (4)농부들은 그들의 토지에서 몇 개를 찾아내어 그것들(공룡의 뼈)을 조각들로 부수고 많은 돈을 벌었다. (5)현대의 보상금도 더 나을 것이 없다. 회사의 이사회는 달성된 목표에 대해 보너스를 (주겠다고) 약속한다. (6)그리고 무슨 일이 일어나는가? (7)관리자들은 사업을 키우는 것보다 목표를 낮추는 것에 더 많은 에너지를 쏟는다. (8)사람들은 그들에게 가장 이익이 되는 것을 함으로써 보상금에 반응한다. (9)주목할 만한 것은 첫째로 보상금이 시행될 때 사람들의 행동이 얼마나 빠르고 급격하게 변화하는가이며, 두 번째로는 사람들이 그것들(보상금)의 이면에 있는 더 높은 차원의 의도가 아닌 보상금 그 자체에 반응한다는 사실이다.

- Dead Sea Scrolls(사해 사본): 사해 문서. 사해 북서부의 쿰란 동굴에서 발견된 히브리어 등으로 쓰인 성서 사본
- Dead Sea(사해): 이스라엘과 요르단 사이에 있는 소금물 호수로, 염분이 해수보다도 훨씬 높아 생물이 살지 못하여 사해(죽은 바다)라는 이름이 붙음.

[정답 확인]

다음 글의 제목으로 가장 적절한 것은?

① Relive the Glory of the Golden Past
소중한 과거의 영광을 다시 체험하라
② How Selfishness Weakens Teamwork
이기적임(이기적인 것)이 공동 작업을 어떻게 약화시키는가
✔ Rewards Work Against Original Purposes
보상금은 원래의 목적에 반대로 작용한다
④ Non-material Incentives: Superior Motivators
비물질적인 장려금: 보다 더 우수한 동기를 부여하는 것
⑤ Cultural Heritage Becomes Tourism Booster!
문화유산은 관광 촉진제가 된다!

✶중요 선택지 ③의 Original Purposes가 뜻하는 바를 문장 (7)에서는 growing the business로, 문장 (9)에서는 the higher intentions behind them으로 표현함.

[문제 풀이]

본문은 어떤 일에 대한 보상금은 사람들이 최상의 결과를 내도록 일을 하게끔 동기를 부여하기 위해 주어지지만, 사실상 사람들은 보상금, 즉 돈에 반응할 뿐이라는 것을 여러 가지 예를 들어 설명한다. 즉, 보상금을 내걸면 사람들이 자신의 이익에 더 몰두하면서 오히려 보상금을 설정하면서 의도했던 목표는 무시되는 결과를 낳는 것이다. 그러므로 이 글의 제목으로 적절한 것은 ③ 'Rewards Work Against Original Purposes(보상금은 원래의 목적에 반대로 작용한다)'이다.

[중요 어휘]

□ archaeologist	명사 고고학자
□ finder	명사 발견한 사람
□ fee	명사 사례(금), 보수 / 명사 요금
□ torn	형용사 찢어진
□ incentive	명사 보상(금), 장려(금)
□ make money	돈을 벌다
□ achieved	형용사 달성된, 이룬
□ noteworthy	형용사 주목할 만한
□ radically	부사 급격하게, 급진적으로
□ relive	동사 (상상 속에서) 다시 체험하다
□ non-material	형용사 비물질적인
□ superior	형용사 보다 더 우수한
□ heritage	명사 유산

21 2018년 6월 23번 (정답률 50%) 정답 ①

[지문 끊어 읽기] 극적인 일들에 대한 집중

(1) We create a picture of the world / using the examples /
우리는 세상에 대한 그림을 만들어 낸다 / 예시들을 이용하여 /
that most easily come to mind.
가장 쉽게 떠오르는

(2) This is foolish, / of course, / because in reality, /
이것은 어리석다 / 물론 / 왜냐하면 현실에서 /
things don't happen more frequently /
사건들은 더 자주 발생하지는 않기 때문이다 /
just because we can imagine them more easily.
단지 우리가 그것들을 더 쉽게 상상할 수 있다는 이유로

(3) Thanks to this prejudice, / we travel through life /
이 편견 때문에 / 우리는 삶을 여행한다 /
with an incorrect risk map in our heads.
우리의 머릿속에 있는 부정확한 위험 지도를 가지고

(4) Thus, we overestimate /
따라서 우리는 과대평가한다 /
the risk of being the victims of a plane crash, a car accident, or a murder. 정답단서
비행기 추락, 자동차 사고, 또는 살인의 희생자가 될 위험성을

(5) And we underestimate /
그리고 우리는 과소평가한다 /
the risk of dying from less spectacular means, /
덜 극적인 방법으로 죽을 위험성을 /
such as diabetes or stomach cancer.
당뇨병이나 위암과 같은

(6) The chances of bomb attacks / are much rarer than we think, /
폭탄 공격의 가능성은 / 우리가 생각하는 것보다 훨씬 더 희박하다 /
and the chances of suffering depression / are much higher.
그리고 우울증으로 고통 받을 가능성은 / 훨씬 더 높다

(7) We attach too much likelihood /
우리는 지나치게 많은 가능성을 부여한다 /
to spectacular, flashy, or loud outcomes. 주제문
극적이고 현란하며 요란한 결과에

✶중요 사람들이 실제로 발병 위험이 높은 질병을 과소평가하고 극적인 사건이나 사고에 더 많은 가능성을 부여한다는 문장 (7)이 힌트임.

(8) Anything silent or invisible / we downgrade in our minds.
조용하거나 보이지 않는 것은 / 우리는 마음속에서 평가 절하한다

(9) Our brains imagine impressive outcomes more readily /
우리의 뇌는 인상적인 결과를 더 쉽게 상상한다 /
than ordinary ones. 정답단서
평범한 것보다

문제편 p.084

[전문 해석]

(1)우리는 가장 쉽게 떠오르는 예시들을 이용하여 세상에 대한 그림을 만들어 낸다. (2)물론 이것은 어리석은데, 왜냐하면 현실에서 사건들은 단지 우리가 그것들(사건들)을 더 쉽게 상상할 수 있다는 이유로 더 자주 발생하지는 않기 때문이다. (3)이 편견 때문에 우리는 우리의 머릿속에 있는 부정확한 위험 지도를 가지고 삶을 여행한다. (4)따라서 우리는 (우리가) 비행기 추락, 자동차 사고, 또는 살인의 희생자가 될 위험성을 과대평가한다. (5)그리고 우리는 당뇨병이나 위암과 같은 덜 극적인 방법으로 죽을 위험성을 과소평가한다. (6)폭탄 공격의 가능성은 우리가 생각하는 것보다 훨씬 더 희박하고, 우울증으로 고통 받을 가능성은 훨씬 더 높다. (7)우리는 극적이고 현란하며 요란한 결과에 지나치게 많은 가능성을 부여한다. (8)우리는 마음속에서 조용하거나 보이지 않는 것은 평가 절하한다. (9)우리의 뇌는 평범한 것보다 인상적인 결과를 더 쉽게 상상한다.

[정답 확인]

다음 글의 제목으로 가장 적절한 것은?

✔ We Weigh Dramatic Things More!
우리는 극적인 일들을 더 많이 중시한다!
② Brains Think Logically, Not Emotionally
뇌는 감정적이 아니라 논리적으로 생각한다
③ Our Brains' Preference for Positive Images
긍정적인 이미지에 대한 우리 뇌의 선호
④ How Can People Overcome Their Prejudices?
사람들은 어떻게 그들의 편견을 극복할 수 있을까?
⑤ The Way to Reduce Errors in Risk Analysis
위험 분석에서 오류를 줄이는 방법

[문제 풀이]

사람들은 당뇨병, 위암, 우울증과 같이 실제로 발병 위험이 높지만 극적이지 않은 일들은 과소평가하고, 비행기 추락, 자동차 사고, 살인, 폭탄 공격과 같이 발생 위험성이 더 낮지만 극적인 사건들을 과대평가하는 경향이 있다고 한다. 이와 같이 사람들이 눈에 띄는 현란한 결과를 더 잘 떠올리고 여기에 더 많은 가능성을 부여한다는 내용으로 보아 가장 적절한 제목은 ① 'We Weigh Dramatic Things More!(우리는 극적인 일들을 더 많이 중시한다!)'이다.

[중요 어휘]

힌트 명사 chance는 '기회'의 의미로 가장 많이 쓰이지만 문장 (6)에서와 같이 '가능성'이라는 뜻도 지니는데, the chances of bomb attacks는 '폭탄 공격의 가능성'이라는 뜻임.

□ foolish	형용사 어리석은
□ in reality	현실에서
□ prejudice	명사 편견
□ victim	명사 희생자
□ spectacular	형용사 극적인, 장관을 이루는
□ stomach cancer	위암
□ chance	명사 가능성
□ depression	명사 우울증
□ flashy	형용사 현란한, 화려하게 치장한
□ outcome	명사 결과
□ invisible	형용사 보이지 않는
□ downgrade	동사 평가 절하하다, (중요성이나 가치를) 떨어뜨리다
□ readily	부사 쉽게

22 2023년 11월 24번 (정답률 55%) 정답 ③

[지문 끊어 읽기] 돌봄 로봇이 인간을 닮지 않아야 하는 이유

(1) In response to human-like care robots, / critics might charge /
인간을 닮은 돌봄 로봇들에 대한 반응으로 / 비평가들은 비난할지도 모른다 /
[that human-robot interactions create moral hazards /
인간-로봇의 상호 작용이 도덕적 위험을 만들어 낸다고 /
for dementia patients]. [ ]: 명사절(charge의 목적어절)
치매 환자들에게

(2) Even if deception is sometimes allowed /
속임수가 때때로 허용된다고 하더라도 /
when it serves worthy goals, /
그것이 가치 있는 목표를 달성할 때 /
should it be allowed for vulnerable users? 정답 단서 인간을 닮은 로봇이 취약한 사용자에게 사용되는 것에 문제를 제기함.
취약한 사용자들에게 그것이 허용되어야 할까

(3) Just as / children on the autism spectrum /
S'
~와 마찬가지로 / 자폐성 스펙트럼을 가진 아이들이 /
with robot companions / might be easily fooled /
V'
로봇 친구가 있는 / 쉽게 속을 수 있다 /
힌트 think of A as B : A를 B로 간주하다
into thinking of robots as friends, /
로봇을 친구로 생각하도록 /
힌트 동어 반복을 피하기 위해 be 이후에는 앞에서 언급한 'easily fooled ~ friends'가 생략되어 있음. 'fool A into N/V-ing'는 'A를 속여서 ~하게 만들다'라는 표현으로, 여기서는 수동태로 쓰여서 'A be fooled into N/V-ing'로 'A가 ~하도록 속다, A가 속아서 ~하다'라는 의미가 됨.
older adults with cognitive deficits might be.
S V
인지 결함을 가진 노인들도 그럴 수 있다

(4) According to Alexis Elder, / a professor at UMD, /
=
Alexis Elder에 따르면 / UMD의 교수인 /
robots are *false* friends, / inferior to true friendship.
로봇은 '가짜' 친구이다 / 진정한 우정보다 열등한

(5) [Reasoning along similar lines], / [ ]: 분사구문
비슷한 입장에서 판단하자면 /
John Sullins, / a professor at Sonoma State University, / holds /
S = V
John Sullins는 / Sonoma 주립 대학교 교수인 / 주장한다 /
[that robots should "remain iconic or cartoonish /
로봇이 상징적이거나 만화같이 남아 있어야 한다고 /
so that they are easily distinguished as synthetic /
~하도록, ~하기 위해
그것들이 가짜로 쉽게 구별될 수 있도록 /
even by unsophisticated users."] [ ]: 명사절(holds의 목적어절)
심지어 순진한 사용자들에 의해서도

(6) At least then / no one is fooled.
그러면 적어도 / 아무도 속지 않는다

(7) Making robots clearly fake /
S
로봇을 명백히 가짜로 만드는 것은 /
also avoids the so-called "uncanny valley," /
V 선행사
또한 소위 말하는 '불쾌한 골짜기'를 피하게 한다 /
[where robots are perceived as scary] /
로봇이 무섭다고 인지되는 / [ ]: 관계부사절
로봇을 가짜처럼 보이게 만드는 것의 또 다른 이점을 소개함.
because they so closely resemble us, / but not quite. 정답 단서
그들이 우리와 아주 가깝게 닮았기 때문에 / 완전히는 아니지만

(8) Other critics of robot deception argue /
로봇 속임수에 대한 다른 비평가들은 주장한다 /
[that when care recipients are deceived into thinking /
돌봄을 받는 사람들이 생각하도록 속을 때 /
that robots care, / this crosses a line /
thinking의 목적어절 S' V'①
로봇이 돌봐 준다고 / 이것은 선을 넘는다고 /
and violates human *dignity*]. 정답 단서 돌봄 로봇이 가짜처럼 보이지 않을 때의 문제를 계속해서 제기함.
V'② [ ]: 명사절(argue의 목적어절)
그리고 인간의 '존엄성'을 침해한다고

[전문 해석]

(1)인간을 닮은 돌봄 로봇들에 대한 반응으로, 비평가들은 인간-로봇의 상호 작용이 치매 환자들에게 도덕적 위험을 만들어 낸다고 비난할지도 모른다. (2)속임수가 가치 있는 목표를 달성할 때 때때로 허용된다고 하더라도, 취약한 사용자들에게 그것이 허용되어야 할까? (3)로봇 친구가 있는 자폐성 스펙트럼을 가진 아이들이 로봇을 친구로 생각하도록 쉽게 속을 수 있는 것과 마찬가지로, 인지 결함을 가진 노인들도 그럴 수 있다. (4)UMD의 교수인 Alexis Elder에 따르면, 로봇은 진정한 우정보다 열등한 '가짜' 친구이다. (5)비슷한 입장에서 판단하자면, Sonoma 주립 대학교 교수인 John Sullins는 로봇이 '심지어 순진한 사용자들에 의해서도 그것들이 가짜로 쉽게 구별될 수 있도록 상징적이거나 만화같이 남아 있어야 한다.'라고 주장한다. (6)그러면 적어도 아무도 속지 않는다. (7)로봇을 명백히 가짜로 만드는 것은 또한 로봇이 완전히는 아니지만 그들이 우리와 아주 가깝게 닮았기 때문에 무섭다고 인지되는, 소위 말하는 '불쾌한 골짜기'를 피하게 한다. (8)로봇 속임수에 대한 다른 비평가들은 돌봄을 받는 사람들이 로봇이 돌봐 준다고 생각하도록 속을 때, 이것은 선을 넘고 인간의 '존엄성'을 침해한다고 주장한다.

- uncanny valley(불쾌한 골짜기): 일본의 로봇공학자 모리 마사히로가 제안한 용어. 로봇이 인간과 비슷해지면서 호감도가 상승하다가 불완전하게 닮은 지점에서는 호감도가 갑자기 급격하게 떨어지는 현상을 그래프로 나타내면 골짜기처럼 보이기 때문에 이런 이름을 갖게 됨.

문제편 p.085

[정답 확인]

다음 글의 제목으로 가장 적절한 것은?

① The Importance of Protecting Human Dignity
인간 존엄성 보호의 중요성
② Robots Can't Surpass Human Beings in Nursing Jobs
로봇은 간호 업무에서 인간을 능가할 수 없다
✔ Why Robots for Vulnerable People Should Look Like Robots
왜 취약한 사람을 위한 로봇이 로봇처럼 생겨야 하는가
④ Can Robots Learn Ethical Behavior Through Human Interaction?
로봇이 인간 상호 작용을 통해 윤리적 행동을 배울 수 있는가?
⑤ Healthcare Robots: Opening the Era of Online Medical Checkups
의료 로봇: 온라인 건강 검진의 시대를 열다

[문제 풀이]

지문은 요양이나 돌봄을 위한 로봇이 인간처럼 생겨서는 안 된다는 것을 주요한 내용으로 삼는다. 필자는 치매 환자 등이 돌봄 로봇을 친구라고 쉽게 받아들이는 것을 경계해야 한다는 점을 들며, 로봇이 진짜 사람이 아니라 '가짜'임을 누구나 쉽게 구분할 수 있도록 생겨야 한다고 주장한다. 이를 통해 로봇이 인간을 닮아 무섭다고 느끼게 만드는 '불쾌한 골짜기'를 피할 수 있고, '로봇이 돌본다'라고 착각함으로써 생기는 인간의 존엄성 침해 문제도 해결할 수 있다고 한다. 따라서 이러한 내용을 담은 ③ 'Why Robots for Vulnerable People Should Look Like Robots(왜 취약한 사람을 위한 로봇이 로봇처럼 생겨야 하는가)'가 제목으로 적절하다.

[중요 어휘]

☐ **response**	명사 반응, 회신
☐ **charge**	동사 비난하다, 청구하다
☐ **moral hazard**	도덕적 위험, 도덕적 해이
☐ **dementia**	명사 치매
☐ **deception**	명사 속임수, 기만
☐ **serve**	동사 달성하다, 기여하다, 봉사하다
☐ **vulnerable**	형용사 취약한, 연약한
☐ **autism**	명사 자폐성, 자폐증
☐ **companion**	명사 친구, 동반자
☐ **cognitive**	형용사 인지의, 인식의
☐ **deficit**	명사 결함, 결손, 적자
☐ **inferior to N**	~보다 열등한
☐ **reason**	동사 판단하다, 사고하다 / 명사 이성, 이유
☐ **line**	명사 입장, 선
☐ **iconic**	형용사 상징적인, 우상의
☐ **cartoonish**	형용사 만화 같은
☐ **synthetic**	형용사 가짜의, 합성의
☐ **unsophisticated**	형용사 순진한, 단순한
☐ **uncanny**	형용사 불쾌한, 이상한
☐ **recipient**	명사 받는 사람, 수령인
☐ **violate**	동사 침해하다, 위반하다
☐ **dignity**	명사 존엄성, 위엄
☐ **surpass**	동사 능가하다, 뛰어넘다
☐ **ethical**	형용사 윤리적인, 도덕적인
☐ **era**	명사 시대
☐ **medical checkup**	건강 검진

23 2024년 3월 24번 (정답률 80%) 정답 ⑤

[지문 끊어 읽기] 디지털 시대의 의사 소통

(1) The most prevalent problem kids report is / [that they feel like / they need to be accessible at all times].
선행사 / 목적격 관계대명사 생략 / [ ]: 명사절(주격 보어)
아이들이 이야기하는 가장 일반적인 문제는 ~이다 / 그들이 느낀다는 것 / 그들이 항상 연락될 수 있어야 한다고

(2) Because technology allows for it, / they feel an obligation. 정답 단서
★중요 여기서 it은 앞 문장의 '항상 연락이 가능한 상태를 유지하는 것'을 의미함.
기술이 그것을 허용하기 때문에 / 그들은 의무감을 느낀다
아이들은 기술로 인해 항상 연락이 가능한 상황에 부담감을 느낌.

(3) It's easy for most of us to relate /
형식상의 주어 / 의미상의 주어 / 내용상의 주어
우리 대부분은 공감하기 쉽다 /
— you probably feel the same pressure / in your own life!
아마 여러분도 같은 압박을 느낄 것이다 / 자신의 삶에서

(4) It is really challenging / [to deal with the fact / that we're human and can't always respond instantly]. 정답 단서
형식상의 주어 / [ ]: 내용상의 주어
매우 힘들다 / 사실을 대처하는 것은 / 우리가 인간이고 항상 즉시 응답할 수 없다는
그래서 즉각적으로 응답할 수 없는 상황이 있다는 것을 받아들이기 힘들어함.

(5) For a teen or tween / [who's still learning the ins and outs / of social interactions], / it's even worse.
선행사 / [ ]: 주격 관계대명사절
십 대나 십 대 초반의 아동에게 / 아직 세부적인 것들을 배우고 있는 / 사회적 상호 작용의 / 상황은 훨씬 더 심각하다

(6) Here's how this behavior plays out sometimes: /
관계부사(=the way)
때때로 이 행동이 나타나는 방식은 다음과 같다 /
Your child texts one of his friends, /
여러분의 자녀가 자신의 친구 중 한 명에게 문자를 보낸다 /
and the friend doesn't text back right away.
그리고 그 친구가 즉시 답장을 보내지 않는다

(7) Now it's easy for your child [to think, / "This person doesn't want to be my friend anymore!"]
형식상의 주어 / 의미상의 주어 / [ ]: 내용상의 주어
이제 여러분의 자녀는 생각하기 쉽다 / "얘는 더 이상 내 친구가 되고 싶어 하지 않는구나!"

(8) So he texts again, and again, and again / — "blowing up their phone."
그래서 그는 다시, 다시, 그리고 또 다시 문자를 보낸다 / '전화기를 폭파하는 것'이다

(9) This can be stress-inducing / and even read as aggressive. 정답 단서
병렬① / 병렬②(과거분사)
이것은 스트레스를 유발할 수 있다 / 그리고 심지어 공격적인 것으로 읽힐 수 있다
답장을 바라며 계속해서 연락하는 것은 부정적인 결과를 낳음.

(10) But you can see / [how easily this could happen].
[ ]: see의 목적어절
하지만 여러분은 알 수 있다 / 이것이 얼마나 쉽게 일어날 수 있는지

★중요 디지털 시대를 사는 십 대에게 즉각적인 소통이 이루어지지 않는 것은 불안감을 줌. 문장 (5)에서 언급했듯이, 십 대는 사회적 상호 작용을 아직 배우고 있는 중이라 상대의 입장을 제대로 파악하지 못함. 이러한 상황이 반복되는 것은 흔한 일이고, 그로 인해 스트레스를 받는 등 부정적인 결과로 이어진다는 것이 이 글의 주된 내용임.

[전문 해석]

(1)아이들이 이야기하는 가장 일반적인 문제는 그들이 항상 연락될 수 있어야 한다고 느낀다는 것이다. (2)기술이 그것을 허용하기 때문에, 그들은 의무감을 느낀다. (3)우리 대부분은 공감하기 쉬운데, 아마 여러분도 자신의 삶에서 같은 압박을 느낄 것이다! (4)우리가 인간이고 항상 즉시 응답할 수 없다는 사실을 대처하는 것은 매우 힘들다. (5)아직 사회적 상호 작용의 세부적인 것들을 배우고 있는 십 대나 십 대 초반의 아동에게 상황은 훨씬 더 심각하다. (6)때때로 이 행동이 나타나는 방식은 다음과 같은데, 여러분의 자녀가 자신의 친구 중 한 명에게 문자를 보내고, 그 친구가 즉시 답장을 보내지 않는다고 하자. (7)이제 여러분의 자녀는 "얘는 더 이상 내 친구가 되고 싶어 하지 않는구나!"라고 생각하기 쉽다. (8)그래서 그는 다시, 다시, 그리고 또 다시 문자를 보내서 결국 '전화기를 폭파하는 것'이다. (9)이것은 스트레스를 유발할 수 있고, 심지어 공격적인 것으로 읽힐 수 있다. (10)하지만 여러분은 이것이 얼마나 쉽게 일어날 수 있는지 알 수 있다.

[정답 확인]

다음 글의 제목으로 가장 적절한 것은?

① From Symbols to Bytes: History of Communication
상징에서 바이트까지: 의사소통의 역사
② Parents' Desire to Keep Their Children Within Reach
자녀를 가까이에 두려는 부모의 욕망
③ Building Trust: The Key to Ideal Human Relationships
신뢰 형성하기: 이상적인 인간 관계의 핵심
④ The Positive Role of Digital Technology in Teen Friendships
십 대 우정에서의 디지털 기술의 긍정적인 역할
✔ Connected but Stressed: Challenges for Kids in the Digital Era
연결되었지만 스트레스를 받는다: 디지털 시대 속 아이들의 과제

문제편 p.085

[중요 어휘]

☐ prevalent	형용사 일반적인, 널리 퍼져 있는
☐ report	동사 이야기하다, 전하다, 알리다
☐ accessible	형용사 연락될 수 있는, 접근하기 쉬운
☐ obligation	명사 의무감, 의무
☐ respond	동사 응답하다, 반응하다
☐ instantly	부사 즉시, 즉각
☐ teen	명사 십 대(13~19세)
☐ tween	명사 십 대 초반의 아동(10~12세)
☐ ins and outs	세부적인 것, 구석구석
☐ play out	나타나다, (점진적으로 일이) 벌어지다
☐ text	동사 문자 메시지를 보내다 / 명사 본문, 글
☐ blow up	폭파하다, 터뜨리다
☐ induce	동사 유발하다, 유도하다
☐ aggressive	형용사 공격적인, 대단히 적극적인
☐ symbol	명사 상징, 기호
☐ byte	명사 바이트(컴퓨터의 8비트에 해당)
☐ within reach	가까이에, 손이 닿는 곳에
☐ ideal	형용사 이상적인, 가장 알맞은

24 2024년 6월 24번 (정답률 75%) 정답 ④

[지문 끊어 읽기] 마감일에 대한 인식 재설정하기

(1) We tend to break up time into units, /
우리는 시간을 단위로 나누는 경향이 있다 /
[such as weeks, months, and seasons]; /
주, 월, 계절과 같은 / [ ]: 수식어구
in a series of studies among farmers in India and students in North America, /
병렬① 병렬②
인도의 농부들과 북미의 학생들 사이의 일련의 연구에서 /
psychologists found /
심리학자들은 발견했다 /
[that if a deadline is on the other side of a "break" /
마감일이 '단절'의 반대편에 있는 경우에 /
— such as in the New Year — /
새해와 같이 /
we're more likely to see it as remote, /
병렬① =deadline
우리는 그것을 멀리 떨어진 것으로 여길 가능성이 더 크다 /
and, as a result, / be less ready to jump into action]. [ ]: 명사절(found의 목적어절)
병렬②
그리고 결과적으로 / 행동으로 옮길 준비를 덜 할

✶중요 break는 '단절, 중단'이라는 뜻으로, '주/월/계절' 등이 나누어지는 경계를 의미함. 즉, 12월 31일을 기점으로 올해와 새해가 구분될 때, 12월 31일은 '단절(break)'에 해당하고, '단절의 반대편(the other side of a "break")'이란 12월 31일 너머에 있는 '새해(the New Year)'를 의미할 것임.

(2) What you need to do in that situation /
S(관계대명사절)
그러한 상황에서 여러분이 해야 할 일은 /
is [find another way / to think about the timeframe]. [ ]: S·C
V 형용사적 용법
또 다른 방식을 찾는 것이다 / 그 시간 틀에 대해 생각하는

힌트 주어로 사용된 what절 내에 일반동사가 do가 쓰여서 주격 보어에 해당하는 'to find ~'에서 to를 생략함. to가 없어도 의미 전달이 명확하므로 생략이 가능함.

(3) For example, /
예를 들어 /
✶중요 마감일이 '단절의 반대편'인 next year(내년)일 경우 행동을 미루게 될 수 있음. 따라서 문장 (3)은 마감일이 내년 1월이라 하더라도 실제로는 일을 this winter(이번 겨울)까지 끝내는 것으로 생각해야 한다고 주장함.
if it's November and the deadline is in January, /
만약 지금이 11월이고 마감일이 1월이라면 /
it's better / [to tell yourself /
형식상의 주어 [ ]: 내용상의 주어
더 낫다 / 당신 스스로에게 말하는 것이 /
you have to get it done "this winter" / rather than "next year."]
당신이 그것을 '이번 겨울'에 끝내야 한다고 / '내년'보다는

정답 단서 만약 지금이 11월이고 마감일이 1월이라면, '내년'이 아닌 '이번 겨울' 내로 일을 끝내야 한다고 생각하는 편이 좋음.

(4) The best approach / is to view deadlines as a challenge /
선행사
최고의 접근법은 / 마감일을 도전으로 여기는 것이다 /
[that you have to meet /
[ ]: 목적격 관계대명사절
당신이 대처해야 하는 /
within a period that's imminent].
선행사 주격 관계대명사절
임박한 기간 내에

✶중요 '임박한 기간'이란, 문장 (3)에서의 'this winter(이번 겨울)'에 상응함.

정답 단서 마감일을 임박한 기간 내에 대처해야 하는 도전으로 여겨야 함.

(5) That way / the stress is more manageable, /
그런 방식으로 / 스트레스는 더 잘 관리될 수 있다 /
and you have a better chance of starting /
그리고 여러분은 시작할 더 나은 가능성을 가진다 / 동명사①
— and therefore finishing — / in good time.
동명사② 미리미리, 일찍이
그리고 그에 따라 끝낼 / 미리미리

정답 단서 마감일을 임박한 기간 내에 대응해야 할 도전으로 여기면, 스트레스를 더 효율적으로 관리하고 일을 미리미리 시작해서 끝낼 수 있음.

[중요 구문]

(3) ~, it's better [to tell yourself you have to get it done ~ "next year."]
S(형식상의 주어) 4형식V I·O D·O(접속사 that 생략) [ ]: 내용상의 주어

힌트 생략된 의미상의 주어와 행위(tell)의 대상이 모두 'you'임. 주어와 목적어가 같은 경우 목적어 자리에 인칭대명사 목적격 대신 재귀대명사를 씀.

힌트 get이 5형식 동사로 쓰인 'get+O+O·C'의 구조임. 목적어인 it이 의미하는 바는 맥락상 문장 (1)에서 언급된 '마감일이 '단절'의 반대편에 있는 (일인) 경우'임. 일은 동작(do)의 대상으로, 목적어와 목적격 보어의 관계가 수동이므로 목적격 보어에 과거분사 형태의 done을 씀.

[전문 해석]

(1)우리는 시간을 주, 월, 계절과 같은 단위로 나누는 경향이 있다. 인도의 농부들과 북미의 학생들 사이의(대상으로 한) 일련의 연구에서, 심리학자들은 마감일이 새해와 같이 '단절'의 반대편에 있는 경우에 우리는 그것을 멀리 떨어진 것으로 여기고, 결과적으로 행동으로 옮길 준비를 덜 할 가능성이 더 크다는 것을 발견했다. (2)그러한 상황에서 여러분이 해야 할 일은 그 시간 틀에 대해 생각하는 또 다른 방식을 찾는 것이다. (3)예를 들어, 만약 지금이 11월이고 마감일이 1월이라면, 여러분이 그것을 '내년'보다는 '이번 겨울'에 끝내야 한다고 여러분 스스로에게 말하는 것이 더 낫다. (4)최고의 접근법은 마감일을 임박한 기간 내에 여러분이 대처해야 하는 도전으로 여기는 것이다. (5)그런 방식으로, 스트레스는 더 잘 관리될 수 있으며, 여러분은 미리미리 (일을) 시작하고 그에 따라 끝낼 더 나은 가능성을 가진다.

[정답 확인]

다음 글의 제목으로 가장 적절한 것은?

① Delayed Deadlines: No Hurries, No Worries
지연된 마감일: 서두르지 말고, 걱정하지 말자
② How Stress Affects Your Perception of Time
스트레스가 당신의 시간 인식에 영향을 미치는 방법
③ Why Do We Manage Our Tasks Worse in Winter?
왜 우리는 겨울에 우리의 일을 더 못할까?
✔ Trick Your Mind to Get Your Work Done in Time
당신의 마음을 속여 제시간에 일을 끝내라
⑤ The Sooner You Start, The More Errors You Make
당신이 더 일찍 시작할수록, 당신은 더 많은 오류를 만든다

[중요 어휘]

☐ tend to V	~하는 경향이 있다
☐ break up A into B	A를 B로 나누다
☐ a series of	일련의
☐ psychologist	명사 심리학자
☐ deadline	명사 마감일, 기한
☐ break	명사 단절, 중단
☐ be likely to V	~할 가능성이 있다
☐ remote	형용사 멀리 떨어진, 먼
☐ be ready to V	~할 준비가 되다
☐ jump into action	행동으로 옮기다
☐ timeframe	명사 시간 틀, 기간
☐ get A done	A를 끝내다[끝마치다]
☐ approach	명사 접근법
☐ view A as B	A를 B로 여기다
☐ meet a challenge	도전에 대처하다
☐ imminent	형용사 임박한, 목전의
☐ manageable	형용사 관리될 수 있는

2024년 9월 24번 (정답률 75%) 정답 ④

[지문 끊어 읽기] 정신 발달과 연령 경계

(1) Mental development consists /
정신 발달은 구성된다 /

of individuals increasingly mastering social codes and signals
themselves, /
개인들이 그들 스스로 사회적 규범과 신호를 점점 더 숙달하는 것으로 /
선행사

[which they can master only in social situations /
그런데 그들은 이를 오직 사회적 상황에서만 숙달할 수 있다 /

with the support of more competent individuals, typically adults].
더 유능한 개인들, 일반적으로 어른들의 도움을 받는
[]: 목적격 관계대명사절(계속적 용법)

🔒힌트 individuals는 동명사 mastering의 의미상의 주어로, 동명사의 의미상의 주어는 동명사가 하는 행동의 주체임. 의미상의 주어가 대명사인 경우에는 주로 소유격이나 목적격의 형태로 나타나고 명사인 경우에는 명사가 그대로 쓰임.

(2) In this sense, / mental development consists /
이러한 면에서 / 정신 발달은 구성된다 /

of internalizing social patterns /
병렬①
사회적 양식을 내면화하는 것으로 /

and gradually becoming a responsible actor /
병렬②
그리고 점진적으로 책임감 있는 행위자가 되는 것으로 /

among other responsible actors.
책임감 있는 다른 행위자들 사이에서

🔒힌트 관계대명사 앞에 콤마(,)가 있을 경우 관계대명사의 계속적 용법임. 선행사가 구나 절 등의 일부 또는 전체일 때 계속적 용법의 관계대명사 which가 사용되며, 이는 and it으로 바꾸어 이해할 수 있음. 이 문장에서 선행사는 앞 문장 전체를 가리킴.

(3) In Denmark, / the age of criminal responsibility is 15 years, /
덴마크에서 / 형사 책임 연령은 15살이다 /

[which means / that we then say /
접속사
이것은 의미한다 / 그러면 우리가 말하는 것을 /

that people have developed sufficient mental maturity /
접속사
사람들이 충분한 정신적 성숙을 발현시켰다고 /

to be accountable for their actions at this point]. 정답단서
형용사적 용법
이 시점에서 자신의 행동에 책임을 질
[]: 관계사절(선행사=앞 문장 전체)

덴마크에서 범죄에 대한 책임을 지기 시작하는 연령은 15살이고, 이는 자신의 행동에 책임을 질 정신적 성숙을 발현시켰다고 사람들이 생각함을 의미함.

(4) And at the age of 18 / people are given the right to vote /
부사구 S V①(수동태)
그리고 18세에 / 사람들은 투표할 권리를 받는다 /
형용사적 용법

and are thereby formally included /
V②
그리고 그럼으로써 공식적으로 포함된다 /

in the basic democratic process.
기본적인 민주 절차에

🔒힌트 문장 (5)와 (7)의 whether은 모두 명사절을 이끄는 접속사로 쓰였는데, 문장 (5)의 명사절은 know의 목적어 역할을 하고, 문장 (7)의 명사절은 주격 보어 역할을 하고 있음.

(5) I do not know / [whether these age boundaries are optimal], /
명사절 접속사(~인지 아닌지)
나는 모른다 / 이러한 연령 경계가 최적인지 아닌지 /

but it is clear / [that mental development takes place /
형식상의 주어 병렬①
하지만 분명하다 / 정신 발달이 일어난다는 것은 /

at different rates for different individuals, /
서로 다른 개인들에게 다른 속도로 /

and depends especially on the social and family environment /
병렬② 선행사
그리고 특히 사회와 가족 환경에 달려 있다는 것은 /

they have been given]. []: 내용상의 주어
목적격 관계대명사절(관계대명사 생략)
그들에게 주어진

(6) Therefore, / [having formal limits for responsibility /
따라서 / 책임에 대한 공식적인 제한을 두는 것은 ↑ 선행사

from a specific age / that apply to everyone] / []: 동명사S
특정 연령부터 / 모든 사람에게 적용되는 / 주격 관계대명사절

is a somewhat questionable practice. 정답단서
V
다소 의문스러운 관행이다

필자는 특정 연령부터 책임에 대한 공식적인 제한을 두는 것을 모든 사람에게 적용시키는 관행에 의문을 가짐.

(7) But the question, of course, /
S 삽입구
그러나 물론 문제는 /

🔒힌트 이 문장에서 any는 differently를 수식하는 부사로, '조금이나마', '다소나마'의 의미로 해석할 수 있음.

is [whether it can be done any differently].
V 명사절 접속사(~인지 아닌지)
그것이 조금이나마 다르게 행해질 수 있는지 아닌지이다

[전문 해석]

(1)정신 발달은 개인들이 그들 스스로 사회적 규범과 신호를 점점 더 숙달하는 것으로 구성되는데, 그들은 이를 더 유능한 개인들, 일반적으로 어른들의 도움을 받는 사회적 상황에서만 숙달할 수 있다. (2)이러한 면에서, 정신 발달은 사회적 양식을 내면화하는 것과 책임감 있는 다른 행위자들 사이에서 점진적으로 책임감 있는 행위자가 되는 것으로 구성된다. (3)덴마크에서 형사 책임 연령은 15살인데, 이것은 그러면 우리가 사람들이 이 시점에서 자신의 행동에 책임을 질 충분한 정신적 성숙을 발현시켰다고 말하는 것을 의미한다. (4)그리고 18세에 사람들은 투표할 권리를 받고 그럼으로써 공식적으로 기본적인 민주 절차에 포함된다. (5)나는 이러한 연령 경계가 최적인지 아닌지 모르지만, 정신 발달이 서로 다른 개인들에게 다른 속도로 일어나고 특히 그들에게 주어진 사회와 가족 환경에 달려 있다는 것은 분명하다. (6)따라서 특정 연령부터 모든 사람에게 적용되는 책임에 대한 공식적인 제한을 두는 것은 다소 의문스러운 관행이다. (7)그러나 물론 문제는 그것이 조금이나마 다르게 행해질 수 있는지 아닌지이다.

[정답 확인]

다음 글의 제목으로 가장 적절한 것은?

① Adult Influence Is Key to Child Development
어른의 영향력은 아동 발달에서 핵심이다

② How Can Social Codes Limit People's Cognition?
어떻게 사회적 규범이 사람들의 인지를 제한하는가?

③ Democracy Grows Only with Responsible Youth
민주주의는 오직 책임감 있는 청년들과 함께 성장한다

✔ Setting Responsibilities Based on Age: Is It Appropriate?
연령에 기반한 책임 설정: 이것이 적절한가?

⑤ Aging: A Possible Obstacle to Consistent Personal Growth
노화: 지속적인 개인 성장에 대해 가능한 장애물

[중요 어휘]

☐ mental	형용사	정신의, 마음의
☐ consist of		~으로 구성되다[이루어지다]
☐ individual	명사 개인 / 형용사	개인적인
☐ increasingly	부사	점점 더, 갈수록 더
☐ master	동사 숙달하다 / 명사	주인
☐ code	명사	규범, 규칙
☐ competent	형용사	유능한, 능숙한
☐ internalize	동사	내면화하다, 자기 것으로 하다
☐ gradually	부사	점진적으로, 점차
☐ actor	명사	행위자, 배우
☐ criminal	형용사 형사의, 범죄의 / 명사	범죄자
☐ sufficient	형용사	충분한, 흡족한
☐ maturity	명사	성숙, 원숙
☐ be accountable for		~에 (대한) 책임을 지다
☐ right	명사 권리, 오른쪽 / 형용사	올바른
☐ thereby	부사	그럼으로써, 그것 때문에
☐ formally	부사	공식적으로, 격식을 갖추어
☐ democratic	형용사	민주의, 민주적인
☐ boundary	명사	경계(선), 분계(선)
☐ optimal	형용사	최적의, 최선의
☐ take place		일어나다, 개최되다
☐ rate	명사 속도, 비율 / 동사	평가하다
☐ apply to A		A에 적용되다
☐ somewhat	부사	다소, 어느 정도
☐ questionable	형용사	의문스러운, 미심쩍은

문제편 p.089

08 도표의 이해

01 2021년 6월 25번 (정답률 90%) 정답 ④

[지문 끊어 읽기] 천연가스 생산 국가

(1) The table above shows /
위 표는 보여준다 /
the top seven natural gas producing countries worldwide /
전 세계의 천연가스 생산 상위 7개 국가를 /
in 2014 and 2018.
2014년과 2018년에

① (2) The United States, Russia, and Iran /
미국, 러시아, 이란은 /
were the top three natural gas producing countries /
상위 3개 천연가스 생산 국가였다 /
in both 2014 and 2018.
2014년과 2018년 모두

② (3) In 2014 and 2018 respectively, /
2014년과 2018년 각각 /
the gap of the amount of natural gas production /
S
천연가스 생산량의 차이는 /
between Russia and Iran /
러시아와 이란 간의 /
was larger than 400 billion cubic meters.
V
4000억 세제곱미터보다 더 컸다

③ (4) Canada ranked lower in 2018 / than in 2014 /
캐나다는 2018년에 더 낮은 순위를 기록했다 / 2014년보다 /
even though the amount of natural gas produced in Canada increased.
S 과거분사구
V
비록 캐나다에서 생산된 천연가스 양은 증가했지만

★중요 표에서 2014년과 2018년 사이 중국의 천연가스 증가량은 44(billion cubic meters)이고, 카타르의 천연가스 증가량은 21(billion cubic meters)이므로 중국의 천연가스 증가량은 카타르의 2배가 넘음. 같은 순위에 있는 다른 국가나 C로 시작하는 Canada와 헷갈리지 않도록 주의할 것.

④ (5) Between 2014 and 2018, /
2014년과 2018년 사이 /
the increase in natural gas production in China /
S
중국의 천연가스 생산량의 증가는 /
was more than three times that in Qatar.
V
카타르의 그것의 3배 이상이었다

힌트 관계사절이 콤마를 사이에 두고 삽입되어, 주어인 Australia를 수식함.

⑤ (6) Australia, / which was not included /
S
호주는 / 포함되지 않았던 /
among the top seven natural gas producing countries in 2014, /
2014년 상위 7개 천연가스 생산 국가에 /
ranked seventh in 2018.
V
2018년에 7위를 기록했다

[전문 해석]

(1)위 표는 2014년과 2018년에 전 세계의 천연가스 생산 상위 7개 국가를 보여준다. ①(2)미국, 러시아, 이란은 2014년과 2018년 모두 상위 3개 천연가스 생산 국가였다. ②(3)2014년과 2018년 각각, 러시아와 이란 간의 천연가스 생산량 차이는 4000억 세제곱미터보다 더 컸다. ③(4)비록 캐나다에서 생산된 천연가스 양은 증가했지만 캐나다는 2014년보다 2018년에 더 낮은 순위를 기록했다. ④(5)2014년과 2018년 사이 중국의 천연가스 생산량의 증가는 카타르의 그것(천연가스 생산량의 증가)의 3배 이상이었다(→ 3배에 미치지 못했다). ⑤(6)2014년 상위 7개 천연가스 생산 국가에 포함되지 않았던 호주는 2018년에 7위를 기록했다.

[정답 확인]

다음 표의 내용과 일치하지 않는 것은?

Top Seven Natural Gas Producing Countries Worldwide
전 세계의 천연가스 생산 상위 7개 국가

(unit: billion cubic meters)
(단위: 10억 세제곱미터)

	2014			2018			
	순위 Rank	국가 Country	양 Amount	순위 Rank	국가 Country	양 Amount	
미국	1	The United States	729	1	The United States	863	미국
러시아	2	Russia	610	2	Russia	725	러시아
이란	3	Iran	172	3	Iran	248	이란
캐나다	4	Canada	161	4	Qatar	181	카타르
카타르	5	Qatar	160	5	China	176	중국
중국	6	China	132	6	Canada	172	캐나다
노르웨이	7	Norway	108	7	Australia	131	호주

[중요 어휘]

□ natural gas	천연가스
□ respectively	부사 각각
□ billion	명사 10억
□ cubic meter	세제곱미터
□ rank	동사 기록하다, (순위를) 차지하다

02 2021년 11월 25번 (정답률 90%) 정답 ③

[지문 끊어 읽기] 국가별 e-스포츠 친숙도 및 참여도

(1) The above table shows / the share of respondents /
위 표는 보여 준다 / 응답자들의 비율을 /
familiar with or engaged in e-sports /
e-스포츠에 친숙하거나 참여하는 /
in selected countries in 2020.
과거분사
2020년에 선택된 나라들에서

힌트 '주격 관계대명사+be동사(who are)'가 생략되어 있는 주격 관계대명사절로 선행사 respondents를 수식함. 'familiar with'와 'engaged in'이 등위접속사 or로 병렬 연결되어 있으며, 전치사 with와 in의 목적어는 동일하게 e-sports임.

① (2) Among the countries in the table, /
표 안의 나라들 중 /
China was the country with the highest percentage /
중국은 가장 높은 비율을 가진 나라였다 /
both in e-sports familiarity and in e-sports engagement.
e-스포츠 친숙도와 e-스포츠 참여도 모두에서

중국은 e-스포츠 친숙도와 e-스포츠 참여도 모두에서 가장 높은 비율을 가졌음.

② (3) When it comes to e-sports familiarity, /
e-스포츠 친숙도에 있어서 /
Denmark showed a higher percentage than Indonesia, /
덴마크가 인도네시아보다 더 높은 비율을 보였다 /
but the percentage of e-sports engagement in Denmark was lower than Indonesia's.
뒤에 percentage of e-sports engagement 생략
그러나 덴마크의 e-스포츠 참여도 비율은 인도네시아보다 더 낮았다

덴마크의 e-스포츠 친숙도 비율은 인도네시아보다 더 높았던 반면, e-스포츠 참여도 비율은 인도네시아보다 더 낮았음.

★중요 표에 따르면 e-스포츠 참여도는 미국이 8%, 스페인은 17%임. 미국의 비율은 스페인의 비율의 절반인 8.5%보다 적었다고 보는 것이 옳음.

③ (4) The percentage of U.S. respondents / familiar with e-sports /
미국 응답자들의 비율은 / e-스포츠에 친숙한 /
was higher than that of Spanish respondents, /
=the percentage
스페인 응답자들의 그것보다 더 높았다 /
and with e-sports engagement, /
그리고 e-스포츠 참여도에 있어서 /
the percentage in the U.S. was more than twice that of Spain.
미국의 비율은 스페인의 그것의 두 배보다 더 많았다 =the percentage

힌트 '배수사(e.g. twice, three times)+정관사+명사'는 '명사의 ~배'라는 뜻임. 원래 'twice the percentage of Spain'인데, 반복되는 the percentage를 지시대명사 that으로 바꾼 것임.

④ (5) While the percentage of e-sports familiarity in Spain was higher than that in the UAE, /
=the percentage of e-sports familiarity
스페인의 e-스포츠 친숙도 비율은 아랍 에미리트 연방의 그것보다 더 높았지만 /
the percentage of e-sports engagement in Spain /
스페인의 e-스포츠 참여도 비율은 /
was two percentage points lower than that in the UAE.
=the percentage of e-sports engagement
아랍 에미리트 연방의 그것보다 2퍼센트포인트 더 낮았다

스페인의 e-스포츠 친숙도 비율은 아랍 에미리트 연방보다 더 높았음. 반면 스페인의 e-스포츠 참여도 비율은 17%로, 19%였던 아랍 에미리트 연방보다 2퍼센트포인트 더 낮았음.

⑤ (6) As for e-sports familiarity, / among the selected countries, /
e-스포츠 친숙도에 있어서 / 선택된 나라들 중 /

the UAE and Iraq showed the lowest percentage, /
아랍 에미리트 연방과 이라크는 가장 낮은 비율을 보였다 /

where fewer than a third of respondents in each country /
관계부사(계속적 용법)
그리고 그곳에서 각 나라의 3분의 1보다 적은 응답자들이 /

were familiar with e-sports.
e-스포츠에 친숙했다

e-스포츠 친숙도 비율이 가장 낮았던 나라는 아랍 에미리트 연방과 이라크임. 또한 두 나라의 친숙도 비율인 26%는 응답자들의 3분의 1인 약 33%보다 적은 수치임.

[전문 해석]

(1)위 표는 2020년에 선택된 나라들에서 e-스포츠에 친숙하거나 참여하는 응답자들의 비율을 보여 준다. ①(2)표 안의 나라들 중, 중국은 e-스포츠 친숙도와 e-스포츠 참여도 모두에서 가장 높은 비율을 가진 나라였다. ②(3)e-스포츠 친숙도에 있어서, 덴마크가 인도네시아보다 더 높은 비율을 보였으나, 덴마크의 e-스포츠 참여도 비율은 인도네시아(e-스포츠 참여도 비율)보다 더 낮았다. ③(4)e-스포츠에 친숙한 미국 응답자들의 비율은 스페인 응답자들의 그것(비율)보다 더 높았고, e-스포츠 참여도에 있어서 미국의 비율은 스페인의 그것(비율)의 두 배보다 더 많았다(→ 절반보다 적었다). ④(5)스페인의 e-스포츠 친숙도 비율은 아랍 에미리트 연방의 그것(e-스포츠 친숙도 비율)보다 더 높았지만, 스페인의 e-스포츠 참여도 비율은 아랍 에미리트 연방의 그것(e-스포츠 참여도 비율)보다 2퍼센트포인트 더 낮았다. ⑤(6)e-스포츠 친숙도에 있어서, 선택된 나라들 중, 아랍 에미리트 연방과 이라크는 가장 낮은 비율을 보였고, 그곳에서 각 나라의 3분의 1보다 적은 응답자들이 e-스포츠에 친숙했다.

[정답 확인]

다음 표의 내용과 일치하지 않는 것은?

Share of Respondents Familiar with/Engaged in E-Sports in 2020 2020년 e-스포츠에 친숙하거나 참여하는 응답자들의 비율

	Country (국가)	Familiarity (%) (친숙도 (%))	Engagement (%) (참여도 (%))
중국	China	72	47
덴마크	Denmark	67	10
인도네시아	Indonesia	57	40
미국	U.S.	34	8
스페인	Spain	33	17
아랍 에미리트 연방	UAE	26	19
이라크	Iraq	26	16

[중요 어휘]

□ **respondent**	명사 응답자
□ **be familiar with**	~에 친숙하다
□ **be engaged in**	~에 참여하다, ~에 종사하다
□ **familiarity**	명사 친숙(도)
□ **engagement**	명사 참여(도)
□ **when it comes to N/V-ing**	~에 있어서, ~에 관한 한
□ **as for**	~에 있어서, ~에 대해 말하자면

03 2022년 9월 25번 (정답률 90%) 정답 ③

[지문 끊어 읽기] OECD에서의 부문별 원유 수요

(1) The above graph shows /
위 그래프는 보여준다 /

the distribution of oil demand by sector / in the OECD in 2020.
부문별 원유 수요에 따른 분포를 / 2020년 OECD에서의

① (2) The Road transportation sector, / which took up 48.6%, /
도로 교통 부문은 / 48.6%를 차지하는데 /

was the greatest oil demanding sector /
가장 큰 원유 수요 부문이었다 /

in the OECD member states.
OECD 회원국들에서

도로 교통 부문의 원유 수요의 비율은 48.6%로 가장 큰 비율을 차지함.

② (3) The percentage of oil demand in the Petrochemicals sector /
석유화학제품 부문의 원유 수요의 비율은 /

was one-third /
3분의 1이었다 /

that of the Road transportation sector.
=the percentage of oil demand
도로 교통 부문의 그것의

석유화학제품 부문의 원유 수요의 비율은 16.2%로 도로 교통 부문의 원유 수요의 비율인 48.6%의 3분의 1임.

③ (4) The difference in oil demand /
원유 수요 차이는 /

✱중요 3.6%p인 기타 산업 부문과 석유화학제품 부문 사이의 원유 수요 차이가 1.4%p인 항공 부문과 전기 생성 부문 사이의 원유 수요 차이보다 더 큼.

between the Other industry sector and the Petrochemicals sector /
기타 산업 부문과 석유화학제품 부문 사이의 /

was smaller than the difference in oil demand /
원유 수요 차이보다 더 작았다 /

between the Aviation sector and the Electricity generation sector.
항공 부문과 전기 생성 부문 사이의

④ (5) The oil demand in the Residential, commercial and agricultural sector /
주거, 상업, 그리고 농업 부문의 원유 수요는 /

took up 9.8% of all oil demand in the OECD, /
OECD의 총 원유 수요의 9.8%를 차지했다 /

which was the fourth largest among all the sectors.
계속적 용법
그런데 이는 전체 부문 중 네 번째로 컸다

주거, 상업, 농업 부문의 원유 수요의 비율은 도로 교통 부문, 석유화학제품 부문, 기타 산업 부문에 뒤이어 네 번째로 큼.

⑤ (6) The percentage of oil demand in the Marine bunkers sector /
해양 연료 부문의 원유 수요의 비율은 /

was twice / that of the oil demand /
=the percentage
두 배였다 / 원유 수요의 그것의 /

in the Rail & domestic waterways sector.
철도와 국내 수로 부문의

해양 연료 부문의 원유 수요의 비율은 3.6%로, 철도와 국내 수로 부문의 원유 수요의 비율인 1.8%의 두 배임.

[전문 해석]

(1)위 그래프는 2020년 OECD에서의 부문별 원유 수요에 따른 분포를 보여준다. ①(2)도로 교통 부문은 48.6%를 차지하는데, 이는 OECD 회원국들에서 가장 큰 원유 수요 부문이었다. ②(3)석유화학제품 부문의 원유 수요의 비율은 도로 교통 부문의 그것(원유 수요의 비율)의 3분의 1이었다. ③(4)기타 산업 부문과 석유화학제품 부문 사이의 원유 수요 차이는 항공 부문과 전기 생성 부문 사이의 원유 수요 차이보다 더 작았다(→ 더 컸다). ④(5)주거, 상업, 그리고 농업 부문의 원유 수요는 OECD의 총 원유 수요의 9.8%를 차지했는데, 이는 전체 부문 중 네 번째로 컸다. ⑤(6)해양 연료 부문의 원유 수요의 비율은 철도와 국내 수로 부문의 원유 수요의 그것(비율)의 두 배였다.

[정답 확인]

다음 도표의 내용과 일치하지 않는 것은?

2020년 OECD에서의 부문별 원유 수요에 따른 분포
Distribution of oil demand in the OECD in 2020, by sector

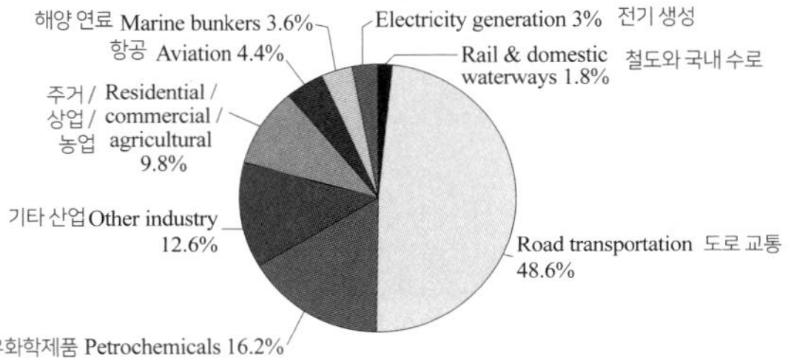

[중요 어휘]

□ **distribution**	명사 분포, 분배
□ **sector**	명사 부문, 분야
□ **petrochemical**	명사 석유화학제품 / 형용사 석유화학의
□ **aviation**	명사 항공(술)
□ **residential**	형용사 주거의, 주택에 관한
□ **agricultural**	형용사 농업의, 농사의
□ **marine**	형용사 해양의, 해상의
□ **bunker**	명사 (배의) 연료 (창고), 저장고
□ **domestic**	형용사 국내의, 가정용의
□ **waterway**	명사 수로, 항로

04 2023년 6월 25번 (정답률 90%) 정답 ④

[지문 끊어 읽기] 교사 1인당 평균 학생 수

(1) The graph above shows the average number of students per teacher /
위 도표는 교사 1인당 평균 학생 수를 보여 준다 /

in public elementary and secondary schools /
공립 초등학교와 중등학교의 /
across selected countries / in 2019.
선정된 국가들의 / 2019년에

①(2) Belgium was the only country /
벨기에는 유일한 국가였다 /
with a smaller number of students per teacher /
교사 1인당 적은 학생 수를 가진 /
than the OECD average /
OECD 평균보다 /
in both public elementary and secondary schools.
공립 초등학교와 중등학교 모두에서

벨기에에는 초등학교와 중등학교 모두 교사 1인당 학생 수가 OECD 평균보다 작은 수치를 보이는 유일한 국가임.

②(3) In both public elementary and secondary schools, /
공립 초등학교와 중등학교 모두에서 /
the average number of students per teacher /
교사 1인당 평균 학생 수가 /
was the largest in Mexico.
멕시코에서 가장 많았다

공립 초등학교와 중등학교 모두에서 교사 1인당 평균 학생 수가 가장 많은 국가는 멕시코임.

③(4) In public elementary schools, /
공립 초등학교에서 /
there was a smaller number of students per teacher on average in Germany /
독일에서의 교사 1인당 평균 학생 수가 더 적다 /
than in Japan, / whereas the reverse was true /
일본보다 / 반면에 그 반대였다 /
in public secondary schools.
공립 중등학교에서

힌트 동어 반복은 생략이 가능하므로 'in Japan' 앞에는 'the number of students per teacher on average'가 생략되어 있음.

공립 초등학교에서의 평균 학생 수는 독일이 15.2명, 일본은 15.9명으로 독일이 일본보다 적지만, 중등학교의 경우에는 독일이 12.8명, 일본이 11.9명으로 독일이 일본보다 평균 학생 수가 더 많음.

④(5) The average number of students per teacher /
교사 1인당 평균 학생 수는 /
in public secondary schools in Germany /
독일의 공립 중등학교에서의 /
was less than half that in the United Kingdom.
=the average number ~ in public secondary schools
영국의 그것의 절반보다 적었다

✶중요 공립 중등학교 교사 1인당 평균 학생 수는 독일이 12.8명, 영국은 16.4명임. 영국의 절반은 8.2명이므로 독일(12.8명)이 영국의 절반(8.2명)보다 많음. 도표에 따르면 중등학교 기준 독일과 영국의 평균 학생 수는 약 1.28배 차이가 남.

⑤(6) Of the five countries, / Mexico was the only country /
다섯 국가들 중에 / 멕시코는 유일한 국가였다 /
with more students per teacher in public secondary schools /
공립 중등학교에서 교사 1인당 더 많은 학생 수를 가진 /
than in public elementary schools.
공립 초등학교보다

다섯 국가들 중 멕시코를 제외한 나머지 네 개의 국가들은 교사 1인당 평균 학생 수가 모두 공립 중등학교보다 초등학교에서 더 많은 반면 멕시코만 공립 초등학교보다 중등학교에서 학생 수가 더 많았음.

[전문 해석]

(1)위 도표는 2019년 선정된 국가들의 공립 초등학교와 중등학교의 교사 1인당 평균 학생 수를 보여 준다. ①(2)벨기에는 공립 초등학교와 중등학교 모두에서 OECD 평균보다 교사 1인당 적은 학생 수를 가진 유일한 국가였다. ②(3)공립 초등학교와 중등학교 모두에서, 교사 1인당 평균 학생 수가 멕시코에서 가장 많았다. ③(4)공립 초등학교에서 독일에서의 교사 1인당 평균 학생 수가 일본보다 더 적었던 반면에, 공립 중등학교에서는 그 반대였다. ④(5)독일의 공립 중등학교에서의 교사 1인당 평균 학생 수는 영국의 교사 1인당 평균 학생 수의 절반보다 적었다(→ 많았다). ⑤(6)다섯 국가들 중에, 멕시코는 공립 초등학교보다 공립 중등학교에서 교사 1인당 더 많은 학생 수를 가진 유일한 국가였다.

[정답 확인]

다음 도표의 내용과 일치하지 않는 것은?

2019년 선정된 국가들의 공립 초등학교와 중등학교 교사 1인당 평균 학생 수

Average Number of Students per Teacher in Public Elementary and Secondary Schools across Selected Countries in 2019

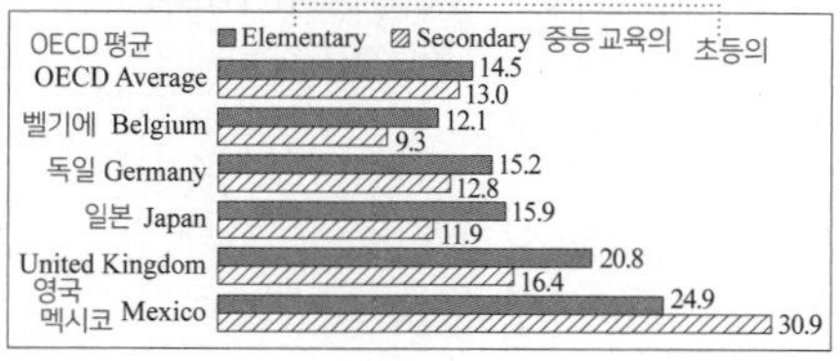

[중요 어휘]

□ **average**	형용사 평균의, 보통의 / 명사 평균, 평균 수준
□ **public**	형용사 공립의, 공공의, 대중의
□ **elementary**	형용사 초등의, 초급의, 기본적인, 근본적인
□ **secondary**	형용사 중등 교육[학교]의, 이차적인, 부수적인
□ **whereas**	접속사 반면에
□ **reverse**	명사 (정)반대, 뒷면 / 동사 뒤바꾸다, 반전시키다, 뒤집다

05 2023년 9월 25번 (정답률 90%) 정답 ⑤

[지문 끊어 읽기] 스마트 TV로 온라인에 접속하는 영국인의 남녀 비율

(1) The graph above shows the findings of a survey /
S V O
위 그래프는 설문 조사 결과를 보여 준다 /
on the use of smart TVs to go online / in the UK /
형용사적 용법
온라인에 접속하기 위한 스마트 TV 사용의 / 영국에서 /
from 2013 to 2020, / by gender.
2013년부터 2020년까지 / 성별에 따라

①(2) In each year from 2013 to 2020, /
2013년에서 2020년까지 매년 /
[the percentage of male respondents /
선행사
남성 응답자들의 비율은 /
who used smart TVs / to access the Internet] / [ ]:S
주격 관계대명사 부사적 용법(목적)
스마트 TV를 사용한 / 인터넷에 접속하기 위해 /
was higher / than that of female respondents.
V =the percentage
더 높았다 / 여성 응답자들의 그것보다

2013년에서 2020년까지 매년 남성 응답자들의 비율이 여성 응답자들의 비율보다 더 높음.

②(3) The percentage gap between the two genders was the largest /
두 성별 간 비율 격차는 가장 컸다 /
in 2016 and in 2020, /
2016년과 2020년에 /
which both had an 8 percentage point difference.
주격 관계대명사(계속적 용법)
그리고 이것들은 둘 다 8퍼센트포인트 차이를 가지고 있었다

남성과 여성 응답자 간 비율 격차는 2016년에 8퍼센트포인트(=21-13), 2020년에도 8퍼센트포인트(=45-37)로 두 해 모두 격차가 가장 컸음.

③(4) In 2020, / the percentage of respondents /
선행사
2020년에 / 응답자들의 비율은 /
who reported using smart TVs to go online /
주격 관계대명사
온라인에 접속하기 위해 스마트 TV를 사용한다고 보고한 /
was higher than 30% / for both males and females.
30퍼센트보다 더 높았다 / 남성과 여성 둘 다에서

2020년에 남성 응답자와 여성 응답자의 비율은 각각 45퍼센트와 37퍼센트로 모두 30퍼센트보다 높음.

④(5) For male respondents, / 2017 was the only year /
남성 응답자의 경우에 / 2017년은 유일한 해였다 /
that saw a decrease / in the percentage of those /
감소를 보인 / 사람들의 비율에 있어 /
accessing the Internet via smart TVs /
스마트 TV를 통해 인터넷에 접속하는 /
compared to the previous year, / during the given period.
전년도와 비교했을 때 / 주어진 기간 동안에

그래프 좌측의 남성 응답자들의 비율을 보면, 제시된 기간 중 유일하게 2017년도에 전년도(2016년)보다 낮은 비율을 보임.

⑤(6) In 2014, / the percentage of females /
2014년에 / 여성들의 비율은 /
using smart TVs to access the Internet /
인터넷에 접속하기 위해 스마트 TV를 사용한 /
was the lowest / during the given period /
가장 낮았다 / 주어진 기간 동안에 /
at 6%, / and it was still below 10% in 2015.
=the percentage of females ~ the Internet
6퍼센트로 / 그리고 그것은 2015년에 여전히 10퍼센트 미만이었다

✶중요 2014년에 스마트 TV로 인터넷에 접속한 여성 응답자들의 비율은 6퍼센트로 주어진 기간 중에 가장 낮은 비율을 기록했지만, 2015년에는 11퍼센트로 10퍼센트보다 높은 비율을 기록함.

[전문 해석]

(1)위 그래프는 2013년부터 2020년까지 영국에서 온라인에 접속하기 위한 스마트 TV 사용의 설문 조사 결과를 성별에 따라 보여 준다. ①(2)2013년에서 2020년까지 매년, 인터넷에

접속하기 위해 스마트 TV를 사용한 남성 응답자들의 비율은 여성 응답자들의 비율보다 더 높았다. ②(3)두 성별 간 비율 격차는 2016년과 2020년에 가장 컸으며, 이것들은 둘 다 8퍼센트포인트 차이를 가지고 있었다. ③(4)2020년에, 온라인에 접속하기 위해 스마트 TV를 사용한다고 보고한 응답자들의 비율은 남성과 여성 둘 다에서 30퍼센트보다 더 높았다. ④(5)남성 응답자의 경우에, 주어진 기간 동안에 2017년은 전년도와 비교했을 때 스마트 TV를 통해 인터넷에 접속하는 사람들의 비율에 있어 감소를 보인 유일한 해였다. ⑤(6)2014년에, 인터넷에 접속하기 위해 스마트 TV를 사용한 여성들의 비율은 6퍼센트로 주어진 기간 동안에 가장 낮았고, 그것은 2015년에 여전히 10퍼센트 미만이었다(→ 10퍼센트 이상이었다).

[정답 확인]

다음 도표의 내용과 일치하지 않는 것은?

영국에서 온라인에 접속하기 위해 스마트 TV를 사용하는 사람들의 성별에 따른 비율

Share of People Using Smart TVs to Go Online by Gender in the UK

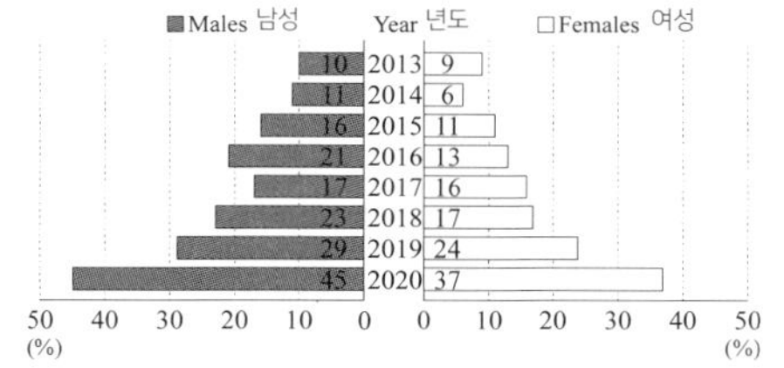

[중요 어휘]

☐ **findings**	명사 (연구) 결과
☐ **access**	동사 (컴퓨터에) 접속하다, ~에 접근하다
☐ **given**	형용사 주어진, 제시된

06 2017년 11월 24번 (정답률 85%) 정답 ⑤

[지문 끊어 읽기] 국가 소득 집단별 고용 상태

(1) The above graph shows / the distribution of employment status /
위의 그래프는 보여준다 / 고용 상태의 분포를 /
by country income group.
국가 소득 집단별로

①(2) In low income countries, / the largest employment status group /
저소득 국가들에서 / 가장 큰 고용 상태 집단은 /
was own account or unpaid family workers, /
자영업자 또는 무급 가족 종사자였다 /
followed by temporary or no contract workers, permanent workers, and employers.
그리고 임시 또는 무계약직 직원, 정규직 직원 그리고 고용주가 그 뒤를 이었다

②(3) In middle income countries, /
중간 소득 국가들에서 /
although own account or unpaid family workers comprised the largest employment status group, /
비록 자영업자나 무급 가족 종사자들이 가장 큰 고용 상태 집단을 차지했지만 /
their proportion was 28 percentage points lower /
그들의 비율은 28퍼센트포인트 더 낮았다 /
than that of low income countries.
저소득 국가들의 그것보다

③(4) The proportion of temporary or no contract workers /
임시 또는 무계약직 직원들의 비율은 /
in middle income countries /
중간 소득 국가에서 /
was more than twice that of permanent workers /
정규직 직원의 그것의 두 배 이상이었다 /
in middle income countries.
중간 소득 국가에서의

④(5) In high income countries, / employers accounted for 3.4%, /
고소득 국가에서 / 고용주는 3.4퍼센트를 차지했다 /
which was larger than the proportion of employers /
계속적 용법
그런데 이는 고용주의 비율보다 더 컸다 /
in each of the other two country income groups, / respectively.
나머지 다른 두 국가 소득 집단 각각에서의 / 각각

⑤(6) The smallest percentage point gap /
가장 작은 퍼센트포인트 차이는 /
between permanent workers and temporary or no contract workers /
정규직 직원과 임시 또는 무계약직 직원 사이의 /
was found in high income countries.
고소득 국가들에서 발견되었다

✶중요 도표 문제에서는 수치, 높낮이, 많고 적음을 항상 '반대'로 표현한 오답에 주목해야 하는데 이 문제는 high와 low를 바꿔 쓴 경우임.

[전문 해석]

(1)위의 그래프는 국가 소득 집단별로 고용 상태의 분포를 보여준다. ①(2)저소득 국가들에서, 가장 큰 고용 상태 집단은 자영업자 또는 무급 가족 종사자였고, 임시 또는 무계약직 직원, 정규직 직원 그리고 고용주가 (순서대로) 그 뒤를 이었다. ②(3)중간 소득 국가들에서, 비록 자영업자나 무급 가족 종사자들이 가장 큰 고용 상태 집단을 차지했지만, 그들의 비율은 저소득 국가들의 그것(비율)보다 28퍼센트포인트나 더 낮았다. ③(4)중간 소득 국가에서 임시 또는 무계약직 직원들의 비율은 중간 소득 국가에서의 정규직 직원의 그것(비율)의 두 배 이상이었다. ④(5)고소득 국가에서 고용주는 3.4퍼센트를 차지했는데, 이는 나머지 다른 두 국가 소득 집단 각각에서의 고용주의 비율보다 각각 더 컸다. ⑤(6)정규직 직원과 임시 또는 무계약직 직원 사이의 가장 작은 퍼센트포인트 차이는 고소득 국가들에서(→ 저소득 국가들에서) 발견되었다.

- own account worker(자영업자): 근로자를 1인 이상 고용하고 있거나 근로자를 고용하지 않고 자기 혼자 또는 1인 이상 파트너와 함께 사업하는 사람
- unpaid family worker(무급 가족 종사자): 자영업자의 가족이나 친인척으로서 임금을 받지 않고 해당 사업체 정규 근로시간의 3분의 1 이상을 종사하는 사람

[정답 확인]

다음 도표의 내용과 일치하지 않는 것은?

Distribution of Employment Status by Country Income Group 국가 소득 집단별 고용 상태의 분포

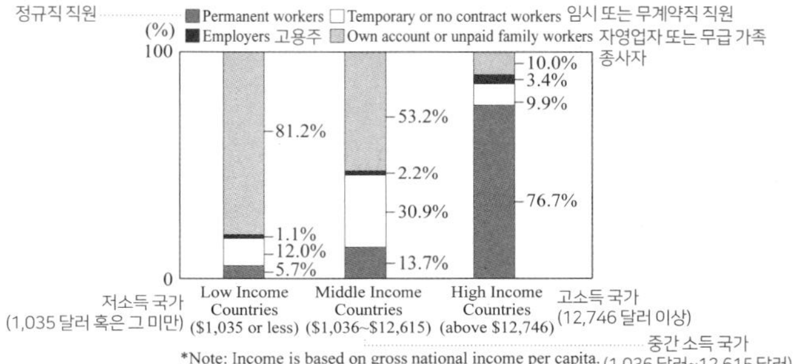

*Note: Income is based on gross national income per capita.
비고: 소득은 1인당 국민총소득을 기준으로 한다.

[중요 어휘]

☐ **distribution**	명사 분포, 분배
☐ **employment status**	고용 상태
☐ **A be followed by B**	B가 A의 뒤를 잇다
☐ **temporary**	형용사 임시의, 일시적인
☐ **no contract worker**	무계약직 직원
☐ **permanent worker**	정규직 직원
☐ **comprise**	동사 차지하다, 구성하다
☐ **proportion**	명사 비율

07 2022년 3월 25번 (정답률 85%) 정답 ④

[지문 끊어 읽기] 다섯 국가에서의 통근 방법

(1) The above graph shows /
위 그래프는 보여 준다 /
which modes of transportation people use /
명사절(간접의문문)
사람들이 어떤 교통수단을 이용하는지 /
for their daily commute to work, school, or university /
직장, 학교, 또는 대학교로 매일 통근을 위해 /
in five selected countries.
선택된 5개국에서

문제편 p.092

① (2) In each of the five countries, /
5개국 각각에서 /
the percentage of commuters using their own car /
자가용을 이용하는 통근자의 비율이 /
is the highest / among all three modes of transportation.
가장 높다 / 세 가지 교통수단 중

그래프에 제시된 모든 국가에서 자가용을 이용하는 비율이 가장 높았음.

② (3) The U.S. has the highest percentage of commuters using their own car /
미국은 자가용을 이용하는 통근자의 비율이 가장 높다 /
among the five countries, /
5개국 중에서 /
but it has the lowest percentages for the other two modes of transportation.
하지만 다른 두 교통수단의 비율은 가장 낮다

미국은 자가용을 이용하는 통근자의 비율이 가장 높았지만 대중교통과 자전거에 있어서는 가장 낮은 비율을 보여주었음.

③ (4) Public transport is the second most popular mode of transportation /
대중교통은 두 번째로 인기 있는 교통수단이다 /
in all the countries / except for the Netherlands.
모든 국가에서 / 네덜란드를 제외한

미국, 프랑스, 오스트레일리아, 독일에서는 대중교통이 두 번째로 인기 있는 교통수단이며, 네덜란드에서는 대중교통이 자가용과 자전거 다음으로 세 번째로 인기가 있었음.

④ (5) Among the five countries, / France has the biggest gap /
5개국 중에서 / 프랑스가 차이가 가장 크다 /
between [the percentage of commuters using their own car] [ ]: 병렬①
자가용을 이용하는 통근자의 비율 / 현재분사구
and [that of commuters using public transport]. [ ]: 병렬②
=the percentage 현재분사구
그리고 대중교통을 이용하는 통근자의 그것 간의

★중요 자가용을 이용하는 통근자와 대중교통을 이용하는 통근자의 비율 차이는 프랑스가 아닌 미국이 약 65% 차이로 가장 큼.

⑤ (6) In terms of commuters using public transport, /
대중교통을 이용하는 통근자의 경우에는 / 현재분사구
Germany leads all of the countries, /
독일이 모든 나라를 앞선다 /
immediately followed by Australia.
바로 그다음이 오스트레일리아이다

대중교통을 이용하는 통근자의 비율이 가장 높았던 곳은 독일이며, 그 다음은 오스트레일리아임.

힌트 앞에 being이 생략된 분사구문으로 원래 문장은 'and it(=Germany) is immediately followed ~'라고 볼 수 있음. 'A be followed by B'는 'A가 먼저 오고 뒤이어 B가 오는 순서'라는 것을 기억할 것.

[전문 해석]

(1)위 그래프는 선택된 5개국에서 사람들이 직장, 학교, 또는 대학교로 매일 통근을 위해 어떤 교통수단을 이용하는지 보여 준다. ①(2)5개국 각각에서 자가용을 이용하는 통근자의 비율이 세 가지 교통수단 중 가장 높다. ②(3)미국은 5개국 중에서 자가용을 이용하는 통근자의 비율이 가장 높지만, 다른 두 교통수단의 비율은 가장 낮다. ③(4)네덜란드를 제외한 모든 국가에서 대중교통은 두 번째로 인기 있는 교통수단이다. ④(5)5개국 중에서, 프랑스(→ 미국)가 자가용을 이용하는 통근자의 비율과 대중교통을 이용하는 통근자의 그것(비율) 간의 차이가 가장 크다. ⑤(6)대중교통을 이용하는 통근자의 경우에는, 독일이 모든 나라를 앞서고 바로 그다음이 오스트레일리아이다.

[정답 확인]

다음 도표의 내용과 일치하지 않는 것은?

다섯 국가에서 사람들이 통근하는 방법
How People Commute in Five Countries

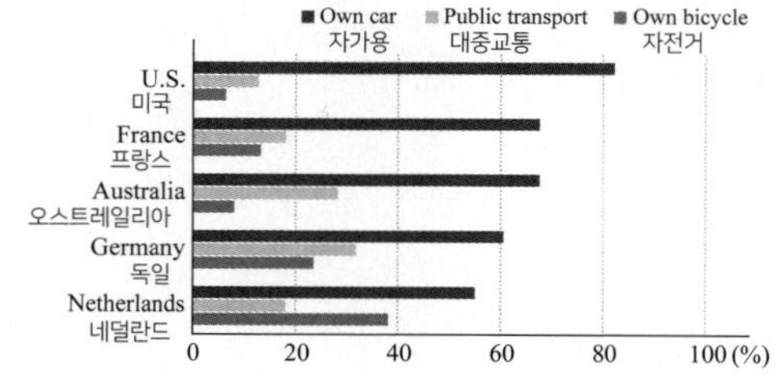

[중요 어휘]

☐ **mode of transportation**	교통수단
☐ **commute**	명사 통근 / 동사 통근하다
☐ **in terms of**	~의 경우에는, ~에 관하여
☐ **lead**	동사 앞서다, 이끌다

핵심 각각의 항목별로 비율을 비교할 때는 몇 개의 항목에서 몇 배씩 차이가 나는지 꼼꼼히 살펴봐야 함.

08 2018년 9월 24번 (정답률 80%) 정답 ④

[지문 끊어 읽기] 맞벌이 부부 가정의 노동 분담

(1) The graph above shows / the division of labor in households /
위 도표는 보여준다 / 가정의 노동 분담을 / 선행사
[where both parents work full-time / in 2015]. [ ]: 관계부사절
부모가 둘 다 전업으로 근무하는 / 2015년에

① (2) The percentage of "mother does more" households /
'엄마가 더 많이 하는' 가정의 비율은 /
in every category / is higher /
모든 항목에서 / 더 높다 /
than that of "father does more" households.
'아빠가 더 많이 하는' 가정의 그것보다

② (3) While the category with the highest percentage /
가장 높은 비율의 항목이 ~인 반면에 /
of "mother does more" households /
'엄마가 더 많이 하는' 가정의 /
is "Managing children's schedules/activities," /
'아이들의 일정/활동 관리하기'인 /
the category with the highest percentage /
가장 높은 비율의 항목은 /
of "father does more" households / is "Disciplining children."
'아빠가 더 많이 하는' 가정의 / '아이들을 훈육하기'이다

③ (4) When it comes to taking care of children / when they're sick, /
아이들을 돌보는 것에 관해서는 / 그들이 아플 때 /
the percentage of "mother does more" households /
'엄마가 더 많이 하는' 가정의 비율이 /
is the same as that of "share equally" households.
'동일하게 분담하는' 가정의 그것과 같다

④ (5) The percentage of "share equally" households /
'동일하게 분담하는' 가정의 비율은 /
is over two times higher /
두 배 이상 더 높다 /
than that of "mother does more" households / in three categories.
'엄마가 더 많이 하는' 가정의 그것보다 / 세 개의 항목에서

★중요 '동일하게 분담하는' 가정의 비율이 '엄마가 더 많이 하는' 가정의 비율보다 두 배 이상 더 높은 항목은 '아이들을 훈육하기'(20x2<61)와 '아이들과 놀아주기 또는 활동하기'(22x2<64) 두 항목뿐임.

⑤ (6) The category /
항목은 /
[that shows the highest percentage of "share equally" households] /
'동일하게 분담하는' 가정의 가장 높은 비율을 보여주는 /
is "Playing or doing activities with children," /
'아이들과 놀아주기 또는 활동하기'이다 /
followed by the category "Disciplining children."
그리고 뒤이어 '아이들을 훈육하기' 항목이다

힌트 비율이 높은 순으로 순위를 설명할 때, 'followed by'라는 표현을 사용하기도 함. 예를 들어 'A followed by B'이면 A가 B보다 비율이 높다는 것을 의미함. A가 순위상 앞이고 B의 추격을 받는다고 생각하면 이해하기 쉬움.

[전문 해석]

(1)위 도표는 2015년에 부모가 둘 다 전업으로 근무하는 가정의 노동 분담을 보여준다. ①(2)모든 항목에서 '엄마가 (집안일을) 더 많이 하는' 가정의 비율은 '아빠가 (집안일을) 더 많이 하는' 가정의 그것(비율)보다 더 높다. ②(3)'엄마가 (집안일을) 더 많이 하는' 가정의 가장 높은 비율의 항목이 '아이들의 일정/활동 관리하기'인 반면에, '아빠가 (집안일을) 더 많이 하는' 가정의 가장 높은 비율의 항목은 '아이들을 훈육하기'이다. ③(4)그들(아이들)이 아플 때, 아이들을 돌보는 것에 관해서는, '엄마가 (집안일을) 더 많이 하는' 가정의 비율이 '(집안일을) 동일하게 분담하는' 가정의 그것(비율)과 같다. ④(5)'(집안일을) 동일하게 분담하는' 가정의 비율은 '엄마가 (집안일을) 더 많이 하는' 가정의 그것(비율)보다 세 개의 항목에서(→ 두 개의 항목에서) 두 배 이상 더 높다. ⑤(6)'(집안일을) 동일하게 분담하는' 가정의 가장 높은 비율을 보여주는 항목은 '아이들과 놀아주기 또는 활동하기'이고, 뒤이어(그 다음으로 높은 비율을 보여주는 항목은) '아이들을 훈육하기' 항목이다.

Left column

[정답 확인]

다음 도표의 내용과 일치하지 않는 것은?
2015년의 부모 둘 다 전업으로 근무하는 가정의 노동 분담

Division of Labor in Households with Two Full-Time Working Parents in 2015

아이들의 일정/활동 관리하기 Managing children's schedules / activities	54	6	39	1
아이들이 아플 때 돌보기 Taking care of children when they're sick	47	6	47	
집안일과 책임 처리하기 Handling household chores, responsibilities	31	9	59	1
아이들을 훈육하기 Disciplining children	20	17	61	2
아이들과 놀아주기 또는 활동하기 Playing or doing activities with children	22	13	64	1

0% 50% 100%

■mother does more □father does more ■share equally □others
엄마가 더 많이 하는 아빠가 더 많이 하는 동일하게 분담하는 그 외

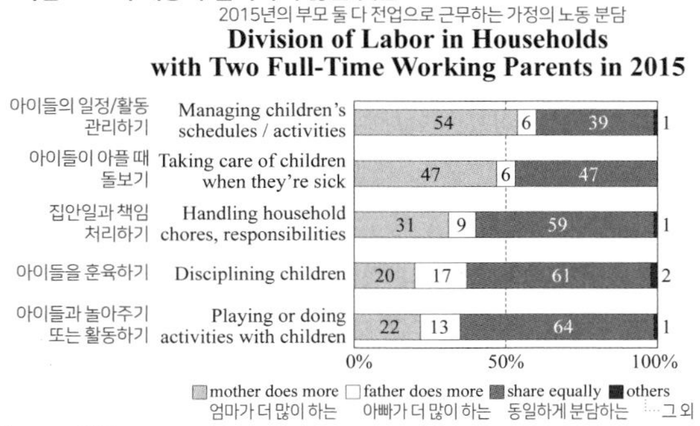

[중요 어휘]

☐ **household** [명사] 가정
☐ **manage** [동사] 관리하다, 감독하다, 간신히 ~하다
☐ **discipline** [동사] 훈육하다 / [명사] 훈육, 규율

📍**핵심** 지역별 자연재해 횟수와 피해액을 비교하는 글임. 도표 두 개가 제시되고 있으니, 각 문장에서 설명하고 있는 도표가 둘 중 어느 것인지 헷갈리지 않도록 주의해야 함.

09 2019년 3월 24번 (정답률 80%) 정답 ④

[지문 끊어 읽기] 지역별 자연재해 횟수와 피해액

(1) The two pie charts above show / the number of natural disasters /
위에 있는 두 원형 차트는 보여준다 / 자연재해 횟수를 /
and the amount of damage / by region / in 2014.
그리고 피해액을 / 지역별 / 2014년의

①(2) The number of natural disasters in Asia /
아시아의 자연재해 횟수는 /
was the largest of all five regions /
전체 다섯 지역들 중 가장 많았다 /
and accounted for 36 percent, /
그리고 36%를 차지했다 /
which was more than twice / the percentage of Europe.
계속적 용법
그런데 이는 두 배가 넘었다 / 유럽의 비율의

🔒**힌트** 'The number of+복수명사'는 명사의 수에 초점을 두어 단수 동사와 함께 씀. 반면, 'A number of+복수명사'는 많이 있다는 상태에 초점을 맞추기 때문에 복수 동사로 받음.

②(3) Americas had / the second largest number of natural disasters, /
아메리카는 가졌다 / 두 번째로 많은 자연재해 횟수를 /
taking up 23 percent.
23%를 차지하면서

🔒**힌트** America를 본문에서처럼 복수형으로 쓸 경우, 북아메리카와 남아메리카 대륙을 모두 아우르는 표현이 됨.

③(4) The number of natural disasters in Oceania /
오세아니아의 자연재해 횟수가 /
was the smallest / and less than a third / of that in Africa.
가장 적었다 / 그리고 3분의 1보다 더 적었다 / 아프리카의 그것의 =the number of natural disasters

④(5) The amount of damage in Asia / was the largest /
아시아의 피해액이 / 가장 컸다 /
and more than the combined amount /
그리고 총계액보다 더 많았다 /
of Americas and Europe.
아메리카와 유럽의

★**중요** 아시아의 피해액이 가장 컸던 것은 맞지만, 아메리카와 유럽의 총계액이 전체의 50%를 차지하는 반면 아시아의 피해액은 47%로 더 적은(less) 비율을 보임.

⑤(6) Africa had / the least amount of damage /
아프리카는 가졌다 / 가장 적은 피해액을 /
even though it ranked third / in the number of natural disasters.
비록 그것이 3위를 차지했지만 / 자연재해 횟수에서

[전문 해석]

(1)위에 있는 두 원형 차트는 2014년의 지역별 자연재해 횟수와 피해액을 보여준다. ①(2)아시아의 자연재해 횟수는 전체 다섯 지역들 중 가장 많았고 (총) 36%를 차지했는데, 이는 유럽의 비율의 두 배가 넘었다. ②(3)아메리카는 23%를 차지하면서, 두 번째로 많은 자연재해 횟수를 가졌다(기록했다). ③(4)오세아니아의 자연재해 횟수가 가장 적었으며, 아프리카의 그것(자연재해 횟수)의 3분의 1보다 더 적었다. ④(5)아시아의 피해액이 가장 컸으며, 아메리카와 유럽의 총계액보다 더 많았다(→ 더 적었다). ⑤(6)아프리카는 비록 (그것이) 자연재해 횟수에서 3위를 차지했지만, 가장 적은 피해액을 가졌다(기록했다).

Right column

[정답 확인]

다음 도표의 내용과 일치하지 않는 것은?

Natural Disasters by Region, 2014 2014년의 지역별 자연재해

유럽 Europe 1,264(14%)
오세아니아 Oceania 522(6%)
Africa 1,898 (21%) 아프리카
Number of natural disasters
아메리카 Americas 2,126(23%)
아시아 Asia 3,432 (36%)
자연재해 횟수

유럽 Europe 238.6(15%)
Oceania 29.1(2%) 오세아니아
Africa 19.8(1%) 아프리카
Americas 아메리카 532.6(35%)
Amount of damage
Asia 아시아 721.1 (47%)
피해액
(billions of US dollars) (10억 달러)

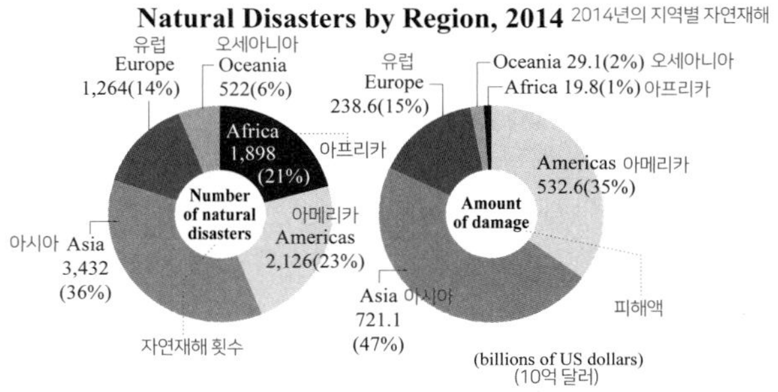

[중요 어휘]

☐ **disaster** [명사] 재해, 재난
☐ **account for** (비율을) 차지하다, 점유하다
☐ **take up** (공간·비율을) 차지하다

10 2019년 11월 25번 (정답률 80%) 정답 ④

[지문 끊어 읽기] 전 세계 재생 가능 에너지 기술의 일자리 수

(1) The tables above show / the number of jobs /
위의 표들은 보여준다 / 일자리 수를 /
in renewable energy technology / around the world /
재생 가능 에너지 기술에서의 / 전 세계의 /
in 2014 and 2015.
2014년과 2015년의

①(2) The total number of jobs was larger in 2015 / than in 2014.
전체 일자리 수는 2015년에 더 많았다 / 2014년보다

②(3) In both years, /
두 해 모두 /
solar photovoltaic had the largest number of jobs, /
태양광 발전이 가장 많은 일자리 수를 가졌다 /
and the number of jobs increased in 2015.
그리고 2015년에 일자리 수는 증가했다

🔒**힌트** 하나의 지문 안에서 태양광 발전(solar photovoltaic)이나 태양열 냉난방(solar heating/cooling) 등 비슷해 보이는 용어들이 사용되고 있기 때문에 헷갈리지 않도록 주의해야 함.

③(4) The rank of liquid biofuels remained the same /
액체 바이오 연료의 순위는 동일함을 유지했다 /
in both years / though the number of jobs decreased in 2015.
두 해 모두 / 비록 2015년에 일자리 수는 감소했지만

④(5) Solar heating/cooling ranked higher in 2015 / than in 2014, /
태양열 냉난방은 2015년에 더 높은 순위에 올랐다 / 2014년보다 /
but still had fewer / than 900 thousand jobs.
그러나 여전히 더 적은 수를 가졌다 / 90만 개의 일자리보다

★**중요** 태양열 냉난방은 2014년 5위, 2015년 4위를 기록했으므로 문장 (5)의 전반부 내용은 주어진 표와 일치하지만 문장 (5)의 후반부가 주어진 내용과 일치하지 않는데, 2015년에는 93만 9천(939 thousands)개의 일자리가 있었기 때문임. 이처럼 일부분은 주어진 지문과 일치하고, 일부분은 일치하지 않는 선택지를 주의해야 함.

⑤(6) Among the lowest three ranks in 2014, /
2014년 가장 낮은 세 개 순위 중에서 /
only small hydropower showed /
오직 소규모 수력 발전만이 보였다 /
a decrease in the number of jobs in 2015.
2015년 일자리 수에서의 감소를

[전문 해석]

(1)위의 표들은 2014년과 2015년 전 세계 재생 가능 에너지 기술(분야)에서의 일자리 수를 보여준다. ①(2)전체 일자리 수는 2014년보다 2015년에 더 많았다. ②(3)두 해 모두 태양광 발전이 가장 많은 일자리 수를 가졌고, 2015년에 일자리 수는 증가했다. ③(4)비록 2015년에 (액체 바이오 연료의) 일자리 수는 감소했지만, 액체 바이오 연료의 순위는 두 해 모두 동일함을 유지했다. ④(5)태양열 냉난방은 2014년보다 2015년에 더 높은 순위에 올랐으나, 여전히 90만 개의 일자리보다 더 적은(→ 더 많은) 수를 가졌다. ⑤(6)2014년 가장 낮은 세 개 순위 중에서 오직 소규모 수력 발전만이 2015년 일자리 수에서의 감소를 보였다.

- renewable energy(재생 가능 에너지): 태양광, 태양열, 풍력, 비, 파도, 지열 등과 같이 자연을 활용할 수 있어 재생 가능한 자원으로부터 발생된 에너지

정답과 해설
08

[정답 확인]

다음 표의 내용과 일치하지 않는 것은?

Jobs in Renewable Energy Technology in 2014 and 2015 2014년과 2015년의 재생 가능 에너지 기술에서의 일자리

	Year of 2014 2014년		Year of 2015 2015년		
재생 가능 에너지 기술	Renewable Energy Technology	Jobs (thousands)	Renewable Energy Technology	Jobs (thousands)	일자리(1,000)
태양광 발전	Solar Photovoltaic	2,495	Solar Photovoltaic	2,772	태양광 발전
액체 바이오 연료	Liquid Biofuels	1,788	Liquid Biofuels	1,678	액체 바이오 연료
풍력	Wind Power	1,027	Wind Power	1,081	풍력
바이오 매스	Biomass	822	Solar Heating/Cooling	939	태양열 냉난방
태양열 냉난방	Solar Heating/Cooling	764	Biomass	822	바이오 매스
생물 가스	Biogas	381	Biogas	382	생물 가스
소규모 수력	Small Hydropower	209	Small Hydropower	204	소규모 수력
지열 에너지	Geothermal Energy	154	Geothermal Energy	160	지열 에너지
총합	Total	7,600	Total	8,000	총합

• Note: Figures may not add to total shown because of rounding.
비고: 반올림으로 인해 수치가 총합으로 합계되지 않을 수 있다.

[중요 어휘]

- ☐ **renewable** 형용사 재생 가능한
- ☐ **biofuel** 명사 바이오 연료
- ☐ **hydropower** 명사 수력 발전

11 2020년 11월 25번 (정답률 80%) 정답 ③

[지문 끊어 읽기] 캐나다의 친환경 교통수단 이용 통근자 비율

(1) The above graph shows /
위 도표는 보여준다 /
the percentage of commuters / using eco-friendly transportation /
통근자의 비율을 / 친환경 교통수단을 이용한 / 현재분사구
to get to work / in six large cities in Canada / in 2016.
출근하기 위해 / 캐나다의 6개 대도시에서 / 2016년에

① (2) For all six given cities, / the percentage of people /
주어진 6개의 도시 모두에서 / 사람들의 비율이 / 선행사
[who commuted by public transit] / was the highest, /
대중교통으로 통근한 / 가장 높았다 / [ ]: 주격 관계대명사절
while the percentage of people / [who commuted by cycling] /
반면 사람들의 비율은 / 자전거로 통근한 / 선행사 [ ]: 주격 관계대명사절
was the lowest.
가장 낮았다

② (3) The percentages of people / who commuted by walking /
사람들의 비율은 / 도보로 통근한 /
were the same / in both Toronto and Montréal /
같았다 / 토론토와 몬트리올 모두에서 /
even though the percentages of people /
비록 사람들의 비율은 /
who commuted by public transit / in those two cities /
대중교통으로 통근한 / 그 두 도시에서 / =Toronto and Montréal
were different.
달랐지만

③ (4) In Vancouver, / the percentage of people /
밴쿠버에서 / 사람들의 비율은 /
who commuted by public transit / was over ten times higher /
대중교통으로 통근한 / 10배 넘게 더 높았다 /
than that of people / who commuted by cycling.
=the percentage
사람들의 비율보다 / 자전거로 통근한

✶중요 도표에서 밴쿠버를 보면, 대중교통으로 통근한 사람들의 비율은 20.4%이고, 자전거로 통근한 사람들의 비율은 2.3%이므로 10배(23%)에는 미치지 못함.

④ (5) Even though Ottawa ranked fourth /
비록 오타와는 4위를 차지했지만 /
in the percentage of people / who commuted by public transit, /
사람들의 비율에서 / 대중교통으로 통근한 /
this city was in first place / in the percentage of people /
이 도시는 1위를 했다 / 사람들의 비율에서 /
who commuted by walking or cycling.
도보 혹은 자전거로 통근한

⑤ (6) Compared with Calgary, / Edmonton recorded lower percentages /
분사구문(수동)
캘거리와 비교하면 / 에드먼턴이 더 낮은 비율을 기록했다 /

for all three given types of eco-friendly transportation.
주어진 세 가지 유형의 친환경 교통수단 모두에서

[전문 해석]

(1)위 도표는 2016년에 캐나다의 6개 대도시에서 출근하기 위해 친환경 교통수단을 이용한 통근자의 비율을 보여준다. ①(2)주어진 6개의 도시 모두에서 대중교통으로 통근한 사람들의 비율이 가장 높았고, 반면 자전거로 통근한 사람들의 비율은 가장 낮았다. ②(3)비록 그 두 도시(토론토와 몬트리올)에서 대중교통으로 통근한 사람들의 비율은 달랐지만, 토론토와 몬트리올 모두에서 도보로 통근한 사람들의 비율은 같았다. ③(4)밴쿠버에서 대중교통으로 통근한 사람들의 비율은 자전거로 통근한 사람들의 비율보다 10배 넘게 더 높았다(→ 10배에는 미치지 못했다). ④(5)비록 오타와는 대중교통으로 통근한 사람들의 비율에서 4위를 차지했지만, 이 도시는 도보 혹은 자전거로 통근한 사람들의 비율에서 1위를 했다. ⑤(6)캘거리와 비교하면 에드먼턴이 주어진 세 가지 유형의 친환경 교통수단 모두에서 더 낮은 비율을 기록했다.

[정답 확인]

다음 도표의 내용과 일치하지 않는 것은?

2016년 캐나다의 도시별 친환경 교통수단을 이용하는 통근자의 비율
Percentage of Commuters Using Eco-friendly Transportation in Canada by City, 2016

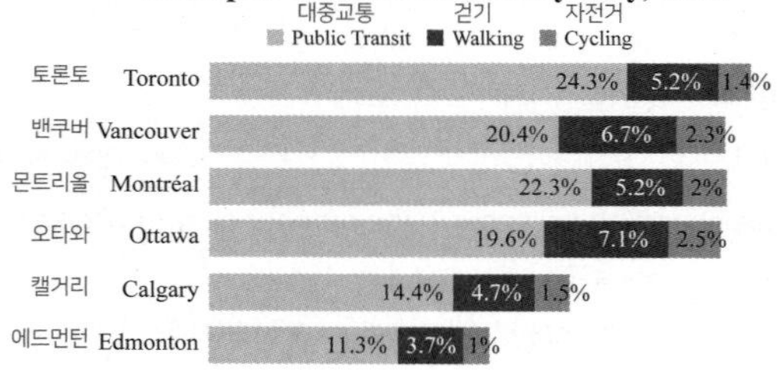

[중요 어휘]

- ☐ **commuter** 명사 통근자
- ☐ **transportation** 명사 교통(수단), 운송
- ☐ **public transit** 대중교통
- ☐ **rank** 동사 (순위를) 차지하다 / 명사 지위, 계급

12 2022년 6월 25번 (정답률 80%) 정답 ③

[지문 끊어 읽기] GDP에 대한 여행 및 관광의 기여

(1) The above graph shows /
위 그래프는 보여 준다 /
travel and tourism's contribution to GDP /
GDP에 대한 여행 및 관광의 기여를 /
for each of the five countries in 2019 and in 2020.
2019년과 2020년 5개국 각각의

① (2) In all five countries, /
5개국 모두에서 /
travel and tourism's contribution to GDP in 2020 /
2020년에 GDP에 대한 여행 및 관광의 기여는 /
decreased / compared to the previous year.
감소하였다 / 전년과 비교하여

5개국 모두 2019년과 비교하여 2020년 GDP에 대한 여행 및 관광의 기여가 감소함.

② (3) Both in 2019 and in 2020, /
2019년과 2020년 모두에서 /
the U.S. showed the largest contribution /
미국이 가장 큰 기여를 나타냈다 /
of travel and tourism to GDP /
GDP에 대한 여행 및 관광의 /
among the five countries, / followed by China.
5개국 중 / 그리고 중국이 그 뒤를 이었다

2019년과 2020년 모두 GDP에 대한 여행 및 관광의 기여가 가장 큰 국가는 미국이고 그 다음이 중국임.

힌트 being이 생략된 분사구문으로, 'and it(=the U.S.) was followed ~'로 바꿔 생각할 수 있음.

③ (4) In China, /
중국에서 /
travel and tourism's contribution to GDP in 2020 /
2020년에 GDP에 대한 여행 및 관광의 기여는 /
was less than a third that in 2019.
2019년의 그것의 3분의 1 미만이었다

✶중요 중국의 GDP에 대한 여행 및 관광의 기여는 2019년에는 16,650억 달러이고, 2020년에는 6,670억 달러임. 16,650의 3분의 1은 5,550이므로, 6,670은 16,650의 3분의 1보다 큰 수치임.

힌트 '배수사+the+명사'는 '명사의 몇 배'로 해석하는데, 본문에서는 배수사로 분수인 a third(1/3)가, 'the+명사'로는 the travel and tourism's contribution to GDP를 가리키는 대명사 that이 사용되었음.

④(5) In 2019, / Germany showed a larger contribution / 독일과 일본의 GDP에 대한 여행 및 관광의 기여를 비교하면 2019년에는 일본보다 독일이, 2020년에는 독일보다 일본이 더 큼.
2019년에 / 독일은 더 큰 기여를 나타냈다 /
of travel and tourism to GDP / than Japan, /
GDP에 대한 여행 및 관광의 / 일본보다 /
whereas the reverse was true in 2020.
반면에 2020년에는 그 반대였다

⑤(6) In 2020, / the UK was the only country / 2020년 영국의 GDP에 대한 여행 및 관광의 기여는 1,150억 달러로 2,000억 달러 미만이며, 나머지 국가는 모두 2,000억 달러보다 높음.
2020년에는 / 영국이 유일한 국가였다 / 선행사
where the contribution of travel and tourism to GDP /
관계부사(=in which)
GDP에 대한 여행 및 관광의 기여가 /
was less than $200 billion.
2,000억 달러 미만인

[전문 해석]

(1)위 그래프는 2019년과 2020년 5개국 각각의 GDP에 대한 여행 및 관광의 기여를 보여 준다. ①(2)5개국 모두에서, 2020년에 GDP에 대한 여행 및 관광의 기여는 전년과 비교하여 감소하였다. ②(3)2019년과 2020년 모두에서, 5개국 중 미국이 GDP에 대한 여행 및 관광의 기여가 가장 큰 것으로 나타났고, 중국이 그 뒤를 이었다. ③(4)중국에서, 2020년에 GDP에 대한 여행 및 관광의 기여는 2019년의 그것의 3분의 1 미만(→ 초과)이었다. ④(5)2019년에, 독일은 GDP에 대한 여행 및 관광의 기여가 일본보다 더 큰 것으로 나타난 반면, 2020년에는 그 반대였다. ⑤(6)2020년에는, 영국이 GDP에 대한 여행 및 관광의 기여가 2,000억 달러 미만인 유일한 국가였다.
- GDP(Gross Domestic Product, 국내 총생산): 한 나라의 영역 내에서 가계, 기업, 정부 등 모든 경제 주체가 일정 기간 동안 생산한 재화 및 서비스의 부가 가치를 시장 가격으로 평가하여 합산한 것

[정답 확인]

다음 도표의 내용과 일치하지 않는 것은?

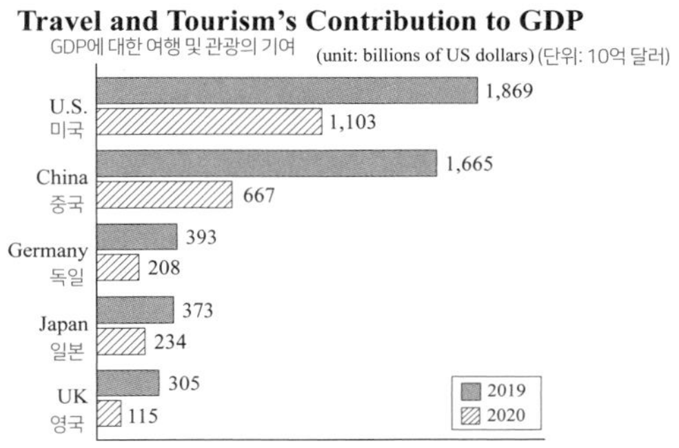

[중요 어휘]

☐ **tourism**	명사 관광, 관광업
☐ **contribution**	명사 기여
☐ **compared to**	~와 비교하여
☐ **previous**	형용사 전의, 이전의
☐ **reverse**	명사 반대 / 형용사 반대의 / 동사 뒤바꾸다

13 2023년 3월 25번 (정답률 80%) 정답 ③

[지문 끊어 읽기] 독일 어린이와 청소년의 독서 빈도

(1) The above graph shows /
위 그래프는 보여 준다 /
how often German children and young adults read books /
독일 어린이와 청소년들이 책을 얼마나 자주 읽었는지를 /
in 2022 / according to age groups.
2022년에 / 연령 집단에 따라

①(2) In each age group / except 12 to 13-year-olds, /
각각의 연령 집단에서 / 12세에서 13세를 제외한 /
those [who said they read books once a month or less] /
S(=선행사) [ ]: 주격 관계대명사절
한 달에 한 번 또는 그 미만으로 책을 읽었다고 말한 이들이 /
accounted for the largest proportion.
V
가장 많은 비율을 차지했다
12세에서 13세 연령 집단에서는 매일 또는 일주일에 여러 번 책을 읽는 이들의 비율이 가장 높았고, 다른 연령 집단에서는 한 달에 한 번 또는 그 미만으로 책을 읽는 이들의 비율이 각각 34%, 33%, 38%로 가장 높았음.

②(3) Of the 12 to 13-year-old group, / 12세에서 13세 집단의 42%가 매일 또는 일주일에 여러 번 책을 읽었으며, 그 집단 내에서 가장 높은 비율을 차지함.
12세에서 13세 집단에서 /
42% stated they read daily or several times a week, /
42%는 매일 또는 일주일에 여러 번 책을 읽었다고 말했다 /
which was the highest share within that group.
계속적 용법
이는 그 집단 내에서 가장 높은 비중이었다

③(4) In the 14 to 15-year-old group, / the percentage of teenagers /
14세에서 15세 집단에서 / 10대의 비율은 / S 선행사
[who read daily or several times a week] /
매일 또는 일주일에 여러 번 책을 읽은 / [ ]: 주격 관계대명사절
was three times higher / than that of those /
V =the percentage 선행사
3배 더 높았다 / 이들의 비율보다 /
[who never read a book in the same age group].
같은 연령 집단에서 책을 전혀 읽지 않은 [ ]: 주격 관계대명사절
✶중요 14세에서 15세 집단에서 매일 또는 일주일에 여러 번 책을 읽은 이들의 비율은 31%이고, 책을 전혀 읽지 않은 이들의 비율은 14%로 2배보다 조금 더 높음.

④(5) In the 16 to 17-year-old group, / 16세에서 17세 집단에서 일주일에 한 번에서 2주에 한 번 책을 읽은 이들이 19%로 20%보다 더 낮았음.
16세에서 17세 집단에서 /
those who read between once a week and once every two weeks /
1주에 한 번에서 2주에 한 번 책을 읽은 이들이 /
were less than 20%.
20%보다 더 낮았다

⑤(6) More than one fifth / of the age group of 18 to 19 years /
5분의 1보다 많은 수가 / 18세에서 19세의 연령 집단의 /
responded that they never read any book.
그들은 전혀 책을 읽지 않았다고 응답했다
18세에서 19세 집단에서 책을 전혀 읽지 않았다고 응답한 이들의 비율은 21%이고, 이는 5분의 1인 20%보다 많음.

[전문 해석]

(1)위 그래프는 2022년에 독일 어린이와 청소년들이 책을 얼마나 자주 읽었는지를 연령 집단에 따라 보여 준다. ①(2)12세에서 13세를 제외한 각각의 연령 집단에서 한 달에 한 번 또는 그 미만으로 책을 읽었다고 말한 이들이 가장 많은 비율을 차지했다. ②(3)12세에서 13세 집단에서 42%는 매일 또는 일주일에 여러 번 책을 읽었다고 말했는데, 이는 그 집단 내에서 가장 높은 비중이었다. ③(4)14세에서 15세 집단에서 매일 또는 일주일에 여러 번 책을 읽은 10대의 비율은 같은 연령 집단에서 책을 전혀 읽지 않은 이들의 비율보다 3배 더 높았다(→ 2배보다 더 높았다). ④(5)16세에서 17세 집단에서 1주에 한 번에서 2주에 한 번 책을 읽은 이들이 20%보다 더 낮았다. ⑤(6)18세에서 19세의 연령 집단의 5분의 1보다 많은 수가 전혀 책을 읽지 않았다고 응답했다.

[정답 확인]

다음 도표의 내용과 일치하지 않는 것은?

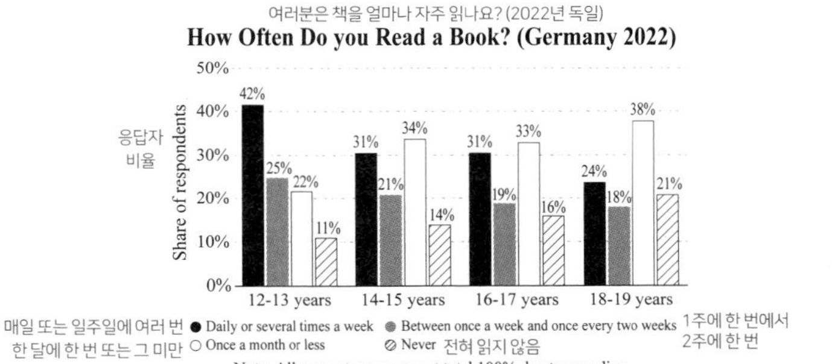

Note: All percentages may not total 100% due to rounding.
참고: 모든 비율은 반올림으로 인해 총 100%가 아닐 수 있음.

[중요 어휘]

☐ **except**	전치사 ~을 제외하고
☐ **proportion**	명사 비율
☐ **state**	동사 말하다, 진술하다 / 명사 상태
☐ **round**	동사 반올림하다

14 2021년 3월 25번 (정답률 75%) 정답 ③

[지문 끊어 읽기] 초등 교육에서의 평균 학급 크기

(1) The above graph shows the average class size /
위의 그래프는 평균 학급 크기를 보여 준다 /
in primary education of five countries / in 2005 and 2017.
다섯 국가의 초등 교육에서 / 2005년과 2017년에

문제편 p.096

①(2) In every country / except the UK, /
모든 국가에서 / 영국을 제외한 /
the average class size in 2017 decreased /
2017년에 평균 학급 크기는 줄어들었다 /
compared to that in 2005.
=the average class size
2005년에 그것에 비해

②(3) In 2005, /
2005년에 /
Korea's average class size was the largest of all the countries, /
한국의 평균 학급 크기는 모든 국가 중에서 가장 컸다 /
with more than 30 students / in a class.
30명보다 많은 학생들로 / 한 학급당

③(4) In 2017, / however, /
2017년에 / 그러나 /
Chile's average class size was the largest of all the countries, /
칠레의 평균 학급 크기는 모든 국가 중에서 가장 컸다 /
with fewer than 30 students / in a class.
30명보다 적은 학생들로 / 한 학급당

✶중요 도표에서 2017년 칠레의 평균 학급 크기는 한 학급당 30명보다 많음. 따라서 문장 (4)에는 fewer than 30 students가 아닌 more than 30 students가 오는 것이 적절함.

④(5) In 2005, / the average class size in Brazil was larger /
2005년에 / 브라질의 평균 학급 크기는 더 컸다 /
than that in the UK, / whereas the reverse was true / in 2017.
=the average class size
영국의 그것보다 / 그러나 그 반대가 사실이었다 / 2017년에는

⑤(6) In Greece, / the average class size was fewer /
그리스에서 / 평균 학급 크기가 더 작았다 /
than 20 students / in a class / in both 2005 and 2017.
학생 20명보다 / 한 학급당 / 2005년과 2017년 둘 다에

[전문 해석]

(1)위의 그래프는 2005년과 2017년에 다섯 국가의 초등 교육에서 평균 학급 크기를 보여 준다. ①(2)영국을 제외한 모든 국가에서 2017년에 평균 학급 크기는 2005년에 그것(평균 학급 크기)에 비해 줄어들었다. ②(3)2005년에 한국의 평균 학급 크기는 한 학급당 30명보다 많은 학생들로 모든 국가 중에서 가장 컸다. ③(4)그러나 2017년에 칠레의 평균 학급 크기는 한 학급당 30명보다 적은(→ 많은) 학생들로 모든 국가 중에서 가장 컸다. ④(5)2005년에 브라질의 평균 학급 크기는 영국의 그것(평균 학급 크기)보다 더 컸으나, 2017년에는 그 반대가 사실이었다. ⑤(6)그리스에서 2005년과 2017년 둘 다에 평균 학급 크기가 한 학급당 학생 20명보다 더 작았다.

[정답 확인]

다음 도표의 내용과 일치하지 않는 것은?

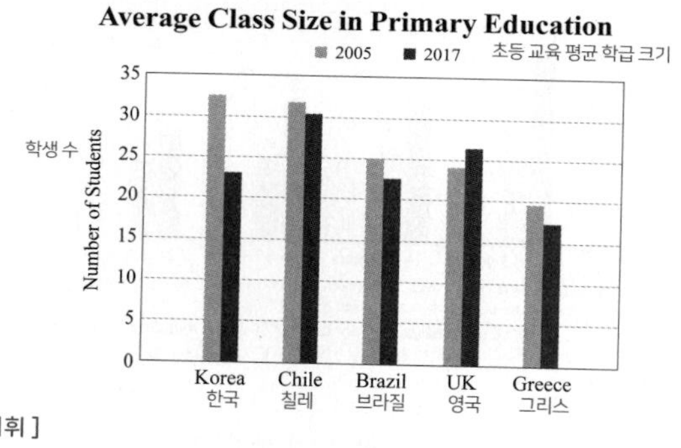

[중요 어휘]

☐ **primary education**	초등 교육
☐ **whereas**	접속사 그러나 (사실은), ~에 반하여
☐ **reverse**	명사 반대, 역

15 2022년 11월 25번 (정답률 75%)

정답 ③

[지문 끊어 읽기]

지역별 백신 접종을 받은 아이들의 비율

(1) The graph above shows / the percentage of children /
위 그래프는 보여 준다 / 아이들의 비율을 /
who received second-dose measles vaccinations /
2차 홍역 백신 접종을 받은 /
in six regions in 2000 and in 2020.
2000년과 2020년에 여섯 지역에서

①(2) The percentage of vaccinated children in the Western Pacific /
과거분사
서태평양의 백신 접종이 된 아이들의 비율은 /
was lower than that of Europe in 2000, /
=the percentage of vaccinated children
2000년의 유럽의 그것보다 낮았다 /
but the vaccination percentage in 2020 of the Western Pacific /
하지만 서태평양의 2020년의 백신 접종율은 /
exceeded that of Europe / by 3 percentage points.
=the vaccination percentage in 2020
유럽의 그것을 앞질렀다 / 3퍼센트포인트

서태평양의 백신 접종이 된 아이들의 비율은 2000년에 2퍼센트, 유럽은 48퍼센트로 유럽이 더 높았지만, 2020년에는 반대로 서태평양이 94퍼센트, 유럽이 91퍼센트로 서태평양이 3퍼센트포인트 더 높았음.

②(3) Among all regions, /
모든 지역들 중에서 /
South-East Asia achieved the second biggest increase /
동남아시아는 두 번째로 큰 증가를 이뤘다 /
in its percentage of vaccinated children / over the two decades, /
백신 접종이 된 아이들의 비율에 있어서 / 지난 20년간 /
and it ranked third / in the percentage of vaccinated children /
그리고 그것은 3위를 차지했다 / 백신 접종이 된 아이들의 비율에서 /
among the six regions in 2020.
2020년의 여섯 지역 중

동남아시아는 2000년에 비해 2020년에 백신 접종이 된 아이들의 비율이 75퍼센트포인트 증가하며 서태평양 다음으로 두 번째로 가장 큰 증가를 이뤘으며, 2020년에는 3위를 차지함.

③(4) In the Eastern Mediterranean, /
동지중해에서 /
the percentage of vaccinated children / more than doubled /
백신 접종이 된 아이들의 비율은 / 두 배 이상 증가했다 /
from 2000 to 2020, / but did not exceed that of the Americas /
=the percentage of vaccinated children
2000년에서 2020년까지 / 그러나 아메리카의 그것을 넘지는 못했다 /
in either year.
두 해 모두

✶중요 동지중해의 백신 접종이 된 아이들의 비율은 28퍼센트에서 76퍼센트로 두 배 이상 증가했으며, 2000년에는 아메리카보다 비율이 낮았지만 2020년에는 아메리카를 3퍼센트포인트 앞질렀음.

④(5) The percentage of vaccinated children in the Americas /
아메리카의 백신 접종이 된 아이들의 비율은 /
was the highest / among the six regions in 2000, /
가장 높았다 / 2000년에 여섯 지역 중에서 /
but it increased the least of all regions /
그러나 그것은 모든 지역 중 가장 적게 증가했다 /
over the two decades.
지난 20년간

2000년에 백신 접종이 된 아이들의 비율은 아메리카가 1위를 차지했지만, 2020년에 단지 8퍼센트포인트의 증가를 보이며 아메리카는 여섯 개 지역 중에 가장 적게 증가했음.

⑤(6) In Africa, / the percentage of children /
아프리카에서 / 아이들의 비율은 /
who received the vaccine in 2020 /
2020년에 백신 접종을 받은 /
was more than seven times higher than in 2000, /
2000년보다 7배 이상 높았다 /
but was still the lowest / among the six regions in 2020.
하지만 여전히 가장 낮았다 / 2020년에 여섯 지역 중에서

2000년에 비해 2020년 아프리카의 백신 접종을 받은 아이들의 비율은 7배 이상 증가했지만, 그럼에도 나머지 여섯 지역 중에서 가장 낮았음.

[전문 해석]

(1)위 그래프는 2000년과 2020년에 여섯 지역에서 2차 홍역 백신 접종을 받은 아이들의 비율을 보여 준다. ①(2)서태평양의 백신 접종이 된 아이들의 비율은 2000년의 유럽의 그것보다 낮았지만, 서태평양의 2020년의 백신 접종율은 유럽의 그것을 3퍼센트포인트 앞질렀다. ②(3)모든 지역들 중에서 동남아시아는 백신 접종이 된 아이들의 비율에 있어서 지난 20년간 두 번째로 큰 증가를 이뤘고, 그것은 2020년의 여섯 지역 중 백신 접종이 된 아이들의 비율에서 3위를 차지했다. ③(4)동지중해에서 백신 접종이 된 아이들의 비율은 2000년에서 2020년까지 두 배 이상 증가했지만, 두 해 모두 아메리카의 그것을 넘지는 못했다(→ 두 해 중 한 해만 아메리카의 그것을 넘었다). ④(5)아메리카의 백신 접종이 된 아이들의 비율은 2000년에 여섯 지역 중에서 가장 높았지만 그것은 지난 20년간 모든 지역 중 가장 적게 증가했다. ⑤(6)아프리카에서 2020년에 백신 접종을 받은 아이들의 비율은 2000년보다 7배 이상 높았지만, 2020년에 여섯 지역 중에서 여전히 가장 낮았다.

[정답 확인]

다음 도표의 내용과 일치하지 않는 것은?

Second-Dose Measles Vaccinations among Children by Region in 2000 and in 2020
2000년과 2020년 지역별 아이들의 2차 홍역 백신 접종

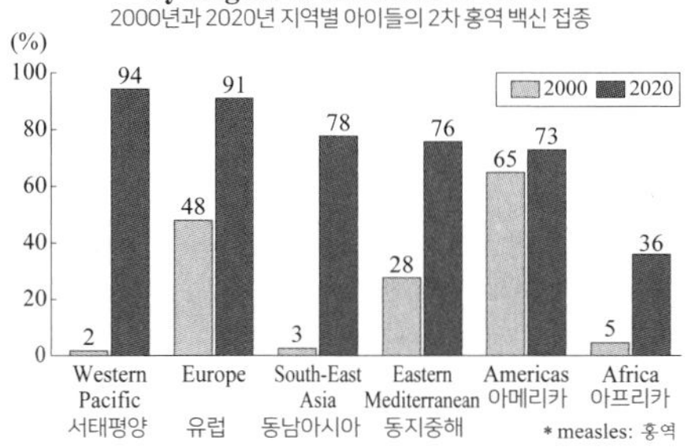

[중요 어휘]

☐ **dose**	명사 1회분, 복용량
☐ **measles**	명사 홍역
☐ **vaccination**	명사 백신 접종
☐ **vaccinate**	동사 백신 접종을 하다
☐ **Mediterranean**	명사 지중해 / 형용사 지중해의
☐ **decade**	명사 10년

16 2023년 11월 25번 (정답률 95%) 정답 ④

[지문 끊어 읽기] 표적 광고에 대한 견해

(1) The graph above shows / the results of a 2019 survey /
위 그래프는 보여 준다 / 2019년 설문 조사의 결과를 /
on the views of American age groups /
미국 연령 집단의 견해에 대한 /
on targeted online advertising.
표적 온라인 광고에 대한

①(2) In total, /
전체적으로 /
그래프 우측 '전체' 항목에 따르면 거슬린다고 말했던 응답자들의 비율은 51퍼센트, 흥미롭다고 말했던 응답자들의 비율은 27퍼센트임.
while 51% of the respondents said targeted ads were intrusive, /
51퍼센트의 응답자들이 표적 광고가 거슬린다고 말했던 반면 / said의 목적어절(that 생략)
27% said they were interesting.
=targeted ads
27퍼센트는 그것들이 흥미롭다고 말했다

②(3) The percentage of respondents /
응답자의 비율은 / S, 선행사
표적 광고가 흥미롭다고 믿은 연령 집단은 18세에서 24세가 41퍼센트로 가장 높았음.
who believed that targeted ads were interesting /
표적 광고가 흥미롭다고 믿은 / 주격 관계대명사절
was the highest / in the age group of 18 to 24.
V
가장 높았다 / 18세에서 24세의 연령 집단에서

③(4) The percentage of respondents aged 25 to 34 /
선행사 과거분사구
25세에서 34세의 응답자들의 비율은 /
표적 광고가 거슬린다고 말했던 응답자들 중 25세에서 34세의 연령 집단의 비율과 45세에서 54세의 연령 집단의 비율은 45퍼센트로 동일함.
who said that targeted ads were intrusive / was the same /
주격 관계대명사절
표적 광고가 거슬린다고 말했던 / 같았다 /
as that of respondents aged 45 to 54 / who said the same.
=the percentage 선행사 과거분사구 주격 관계대명사절
45세에서 54세의 응답자들의 그것과 / 똑같이 말했던

④(5) Among all age groups, / the gap between /
모든 연령 집단에서 / ~ 사이의 차이는 / S
✱중요 표적 광고가 흥미롭다고 말했던 응답자들과 그것이 거슬린다고 말했던 응답자들 사이의 차이는 55세 이상의 연령 집단에서 가장 컸음.
respondents who said targeted ads were interesting /
선행사 주격 관계대명사절
표적 광고가 흥미롭다고 말했던 응답자들 /
and those who believed them to be intrusive / was the largest /
선행사 주격 관계대명사절 V
그리고 그것들이 거슬린다고 믿은 사람들 / 가장 컸다 /
in the 35-to-44 age group.
35세에서 44세의 연령 집단에서

⑤(6) The age group of 55 and above was the only group /
55세 이상의 연령 집단은 유일한 집단이었다 / 선행사
55세 이상 연령 집단을 제외한 나머지 연령 집단에서 표적 광고가 거슬린다고 믿은 응답자들의 비율은 50퍼센트 미만임.
[where the percentage of respondents /
응답자들의 비율이 / S', 선행사
who believed targeted ads were intrusive / was more than 50%].
주격 관계대명사절 V' [ ]: 관계부사절
표적 광고가 거슬린다고 믿은 / 50퍼센트가 넘었다

[전문 해석]

(1)위 그래프는 표적 온라인 광고에 대한 미국 연령 집단의 견해에 대한 2019년 설문 조사의 결과를 보여 준다. ①(2)전체적으로, 51퍼센트의 응답자들이 표적 광고가 거슬린다고 말했던 반면, 27퍼센트는 그것들이 흥미롭다고 말했다. ②(3)표적 광고가 흥미롭다고 믿은 응답자들의 비율은 18세에서 24세의 연령 집단에서 가장 높았다. ③(4)표적 광고가 거슬린다고 말했던 25세에서 34세의 응답자들의 비율은 똑같이 말했던 45세에서 54세의 응답자들의 그것(비율)과 같았다. ④(5)모든 연령 집단에서, 표적 광고가 흥미롭다고 말했던 응답자들과 그것들(표적 광고)이 거슬린다고 믿은 사람들 사이의 차이는 35세에서 44세(→ 55세 이상)의 연령 집단에서 가장 컸다. ⑤(6)55세 이상의 연령 집단은 표적 광고가 거슬린다고 믿은 응답자들의 비율이 50퍼센트가 넘었던 유일한 집단이었다.

[정답 확인]

다음 도표의 내용과 일치하지 않는 것은?

연령 집단별 미국인들 사이의 표적 온라인 광고에 대한 견해
View of Targeted Online Advertising Among Americans, by Age Group

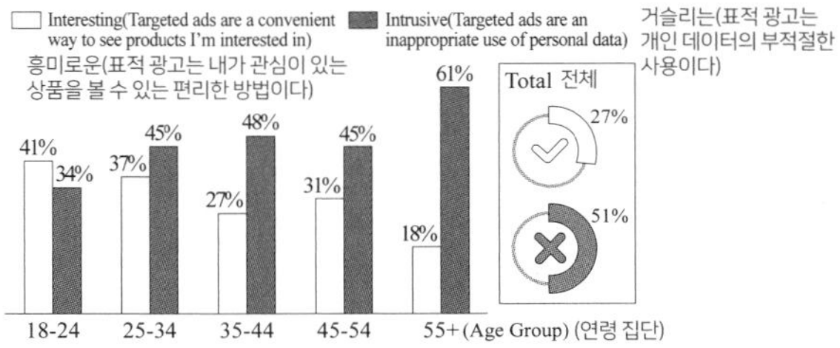

Conducted on May 1, 2019 (missing percentages to 100%: "don't know")
2019년 5월 1일에 수행됨 (100퍼센트에 누락된 비율: "잘 모르겠다")

[중요 어휘]

☐ **targeted advertising**	표적 광고
☐ **intrusive**	형용사 거슬리는, 침입하는
☐ **convenient**	형용사 편리한, 간편한
☐ **inappropriate**	형용사 부적절한, 알맞지 않은
☐ **conduct**	동사 수행하다, 행동하다

17 2024년 3월 25번 (정답률 90%) 정답 ⑤

[지문 끊어 읽기] 동물성 단백질 섭취량

(1) The graph above shows the animal protein consumption /
위 그래프는 동물성 단백질 섭취량을 보여 준다 /
[measured as the average daily supply per person /
1인당 일일 평균 공급량으로 측정된 /
in three different countries in 2020]. [ ]: 과거분사구
2020년에 세 개의 다른 국가에서

①(2) The U.S. showed the largest amount of total animal protein consumption per person /
미국은 1인당 가장 높은 양의 총 동물성 단백질 섭취량을 보여 줬다 /
미국의 1인당 동물성 단백질 섭취량의 총량은 74.8g으로 세 국가 중에 가장 높음.
among the three countries.
3개의 국가 중에서

②(3) Eggs and Dairy was the top animal protein consumption source /
계란과 유제품은 가장 높은 동물성 단백질 섭취원이었다 /
미국에서 계란과 유제품의 섭취량은 26.4g으로 가장 높은 동물성 단백질 섭취원임.
among four categories in the U.S., /
미국에서 네 가지 범주 중에서 /
followed by Meat and Poultry /
육류와 가금류가 그 뒤를 이었다 /
힌트 'A be followed by B'는 'A 뒤에 B가 오다'라는 뜻으로, 여기서 A는 계란과 유제품을, B는 육류와 가금류를 가리킴.
at 22.4g and 20.6g, respectively.
각각 22.4g과 20.6g으로

③(4) Unlike the U.S., /
미국과 달리 /

브라질에서 가장 섭취량이 높은 동물성 단백질은 육류이고 그 다음은 계란과 유제품임.

Brazil consumed the most animal protein from Meat, /
브라질은 가장 많은 동물성 단백질을 육류로부터 섭취했다 /

with Eggs and Dairy being the second most.
계란과 유제품은 두 번째로 가장 많았다

힌트 with (독립) 분사구문 (with+명사+분사 or 형용사): 명사가 ~한(인) 채로

④(5) Japan had less than 50g of the total animal protein consumption per person, /
일본은 1인당 50g 미만의 총 동물성 단백질을 섭취했다 /

which was the smallest among the three countries.
관계대명사(계속적 용법)
그리고 그것은 세 개의 국가 중에서 가장 적은 양이었다

일본의 1인당 동물성 단백질 섭취량의 총량은 49.4g으로 50g 미만이며 세 국가 중에 가장 낮은 수치임.

⑤(6) Fish and Seafood, /
S
생선과 해산물은 /

★중요 생선과 해산물이 미국과 브라질에서는 가장 적게 섭취된 동물성 단백질 섭취원인 반면, 일본에서는 가장 많이 섭취된 동물성 단백질 섭취원임.

which was the least consumed animal protein consumption source /
관계대명사 계속적 용법
이것은 가장 적게 섭취된 동물성 단백질 섭취원이었다 /

in the U.S. and Brazil, / ranked the second highest in Japan.
V
미국과 브라질에서 / 일본에서는 두 번째로 높은 순위를 차지했다

[전문 해석]

(1)위 그래프는 2020년에 세 개의 다른 국가에서 1인당 일일 평균 공급량으로 측정된 동물성 단백질 섭취량을 보여 준다. ①(2)미국은 3개 국가 중에서 1인당 가장 높은 양의 총 동물성 단백질 섭취량을 보여 줬다. ②(3)계란과 유제품은 미국에서 네 가지 범주 중에서 가장 높은 동물성 단백질 섭취원이었고, 육류와 가금류가 각각 22.4g과 20.6g으로 그 뒤를 이었다. ③(4)미국과 달리, 브라질은 가장 많은 동물성 단백질을 육류로부터 섭취했고, 계란과 유제품을 두 번째로 많이 섭취했다. ④(5)일본은 1인당 50g 미만의 총 동물성 단백질을 섭취했고, 그것은 세 개의 국가 중에서 가장 적은 양이었다. ⑤(6)생선과 해산물은 미국과 브라질에서 가장 적게 섭취된 동물성 단백질 섭취원이었는데, 일본에서는 두 번째(→ 첫 번째)로 높은 순위를 차지했다.

[정답 확인]

다음 도표의 내용과 일치하지 않는 것은?

동물성 단백질 섭취량, 2020년
Animal Protein Consumption, 2020
1인당 일일 평균 공급량으로 측정됨(단위: 그램) measured as the average daily supply per person (unit: g)

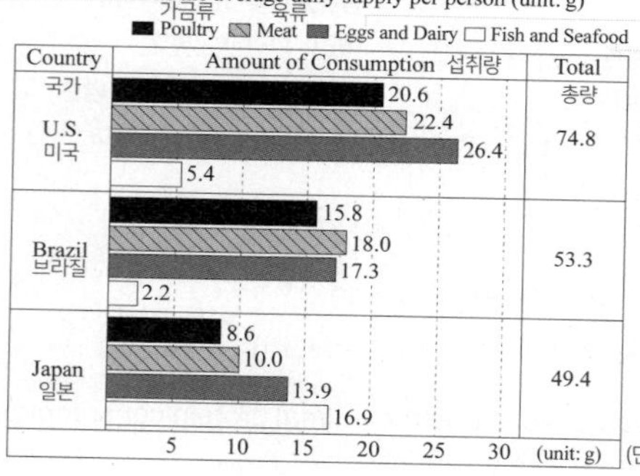

[중요 어휘]

□ protein	명사 단백질
□ consumption	명사 섭취(량), 소비(량)
□ measure	동사 측정하다, 재다
□ average	형용사 평균의, 보통의
□ daily	형용사 일일의, 매일의
□ supply	명사 공급량, 비축량
□ poultry	명사 가금류
□ respectively	부사 각각
□ consume	동사 섭취하다, 소비하다

18 2024년 6월 25번 (정답률 85%)

정답 ③

[지문 끊어 읽기]

1인당 이산화 탄소 배출량

(1) The graph above shows the amount of CO_2 emissions per person /
위 그래프는 1인당 이산화 탄소 배출량을 보여 준다 /

across selected Asian countries / in 2010 and 2020.
선택된 아시아 국가들의 / 2010년과 2020년에

①(2) All the countries except Uzbekistan /
우즈베키스탄을 제외한 모든 국가들은 /

우즈베키스탄의 1인당 이산화 탄소 배출량이 2010년 3.8톤에서 2020년 3.3톤으로 줄어든 반면, 나머지 국가들은 모두 2010년보다 2020년에 배출량이 더 증가했음.

had a greater amount of CO_2 emissions per person in 2020 /
2020년에 1인당 이산화 탄소 배출량이 더 많았다 /

than that in 2010.
=the amount of CO_2 emissions per person
2010년의 그것보다

②(3) In 2010, / the amount of CO_2 emissions per person of China /
2010년에는 / 중국의 1인당 이산화 탄소 배출량이 /

was the largest among the five countries, /
5개국 중 가장 많았다 /

2010년에는 중국의 1인당 이산화 탄소 배출량이 6.4톤으로 가장 높았고, 그 다음으로 몽골이 5.1톤으로 높았음.

[followed by that of Mongolia]. [ ]: 분사구문(being 생략)
=the amount of CO_2 emissions per person
몽골의 그것이 그 뒤를 이었다

★중요 2020년의 1인당 이산화 탄소 배출량은 몽골이 11.3톤으로 가장 높았고, 중국이 7.7톤으로 그 뒤를 이었지만, 몽골의 배출량은 중국의 배출량의 두 배를 넘지 못함.

③(4) However, / in 2020, / Mongolia surpassed China /
하지만 / 2020년에는 / 몽골이 중국을 능가했다 /

in terms of the amount of CO_2 emissions per person, /
1인당 이산화 탄소 배출량에 있어서 /

with the amount of Mongolia more than twice that of China.
몽골의 양이 중국의 그것보다 두 배 이상이었다
=the amount

④(5) In 2010, /
2010년에는 /

2010년에는 우즈베키스탄의 배출량(3.8톤)이 베트남의 배출량(1.6톤)보다 많았지만, 2020년에는 우즈베키스탄의 배출량(3.3톤)이 베트남의 배출량(3.8톤)보다 적었음.

Uzbekistan produced a larger amount of CO_2 emissions per person than Vietnam, /
우즈베키스탄이 베트남보다 1인당 더 많은 이산화 탄소 배출량을 만들어 냈다 /

while the opposite was true in 2020.
반면에 2020년에는 그 반대였다

⑤(6) Among the five countries, / India was the only one /
5개국 중에서 / 인도는 유일한 국가였다 /
선행사(=country)

where the amount of CO_2 emissions per person was less than
관계부사(=in which)

2 tons in 2020.
2020년에 1인당 이산화 탄소 배출량이 2톤 미만이었던

인도의 1인당 이산화 탄소 배출량은 2020년에 1.7톤으로 배출량이 2톤 미만인 유일한 국가였음.

[전문 해석]

(1)위 그래프는 선택된 아시아 국가들의 2010년과 2020년에 1인당 이산화 탄소 배출량을 보여 준다. ①(2)우즈베키스탄을 제외한 모든 국가들은 2010년의 배출량보다 2020년에 1인당 이산화 탄소 배출량이 더 많았다. ②(3)2010년에는 중국의 1인당 이산화 탄소 배출량이 5개국 중 가장 많았고, 몽골의 배출량이 그 뒤를 이었다. ③(4)하지만 2020년에는 1인당 이산화 탄소 배출량에 있어서 몽골이 중국을 능가했는데, 몽골의 양이 중국의 양보다 두 배 이상이었다(→ 두 배를 넘지 못했다). ④(5)2010년에는 우즈베키스탄이 베트남보다 1인당 더 많은 이산화 탄소 배출량을 만들어 낸 반면에 2020년에는 그 반대였다. ⑤(6)5개국 중에서, 인도는 2020년에 1인당 이산화 탄소 배출량이 2톤 미만이었던 유일한 국가였다.

[정답 확인]

다음 도표의 내용과 일치하지 않는 것은?

2010년과 2020년의 선택된 아시아 국가들의 1인당 이산화 탄소 배출량
CO_2 Emissions per Person across Selected Asian Countries in 2010 and 2020

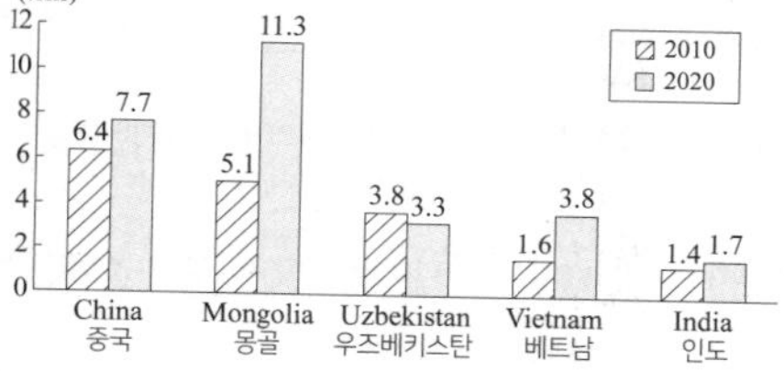

[중요 어휘]

□ emission	명사 (빛·열·가스 등의) 배출, 배출물, 배기가스
□ except	전치사 ~을 제외하고 / 접속사 ~라는 점만 제외하면
□ surpass	동사 능가하다, 뛰어넘다
□ in terms of	~에 있어서, ~에 관하여
□ opposite	명사 반대(되는 사람·것) / 형용사 반대편의, 정반대의

19 2024년 9월 25번 (정답률 90%) 정답 ④

[지문 끊어 읽기] 아동과 성인에게 무급 돌봄을 제공한 사람들의 비율

(1) The graph above shows the percentage of people /
위 그래프는 사람들의 비율을 보여 준다 / (선행사)
[who provided unpaid care to children and adults /
아동과 성인에게 무급 돌봄을 제공한 / (전치사)
by age group / in Canada in 2022]. [ ]: 주격 관계대명사절
연령 집단별로 / 2022년에 캐나다에서

① (2) Notably, / 아동에게 무급 돌봄을 제공하는 사람들의 비율이 가장 높은 연령대는 35~44세 집단으로, 59.5%를 기록했음.
특히 /
the 35-44 group had the highest percentage of individuals /
35~44세 집단은 사람들의 가장 높은 비율을 가졌다 /
providing unpaid care to children, / reaching 59.5%.
(현재분사구)
아동에게 무급 돌봄을 제공하는 / 이는 59.5%에 달했다

힌트 'reach'는 '~에 달하다'라는 뜻의 타동사로, 전치사 to 없이 뒤에 바로 목적어인 '59.5%'가 왔음에 유의해야 함. 'reach to'로 쓰면 어법상 틀림. 또한 밑줄 친 부분은 분사구문으로, 'and it reached 59.5%'로 바꾸어 쓸 수 있음.

② (3) However, /
그러나 /
the highest percentage of individuals /
사람들의 가장 높은 비율은 /
providing unpaid care to adults / was found in the 55-64 group.
(현재분사구)
성인에게 무급 돌봄을 제공하는 / 55~64세 집단에서 발견되었다

힌트 individuals가 아닌 percentage에 수 일치하여, be동사의 과거시제 단수형인 was를 썼음.

성인에게 무급 돌봄을 제공하는 사람들의 비율이 가장 높은 연령대는 55~64세 집단으로, 33.6%를 기록했음.

③ (4) Compared to the 25-34 group, /
(~에 비해)
25~34세 집단에 비해 /
the 15-24 group had a lower percentage of individuals /
15~24세 집단은 사람들의 더 낮은 비율을 가졌다 /
providing unpaid care to children /
(현재분사구)
아동에게 무급 돌봄을 제공하는 /
and a higher percentage of individuals /
그리고 사람들의 더 높은 비율을 /
providing unpaid care to adults.
(현재분사구)
성인에게 무급 돌봄을 제공하는

아동에게 무급 돌봄을 제공하는 것에 있어, 15~24세 집단(18.1%)이 25~34세 집단(34.2%)보다 더 낮은 비율을 보였고, 성인에게 무급 돌봄을 제공하는 것에 있어, 15~24세 집단(13.3%)은 25~34세 집단(11.0%)보다 더 높은 비율을 보였음.

④ (5) The percentage of people /
사람들의 비율은 /
[providing unpaid care to adults /
성인에게 무급 돌봄을 제공하는 /
in the 45-54 group] / [ ]: 현재분사구
45~54세 집단에서 /
was more than twice as high / as that in the 35-44 group.
두 배 더 높았다 / 35~44세 집단의 그것보다 (=the percentage of ~ adults)

★중요 성인에게 무급 돌봄을 제공하는 사람들의 비율은 45~54세 집단이 26.3%, 35~44세 집단이 17.2%임. 17.2%*2는 34.4%이므로 45~54세 집단에서 해당 비율(26.3%)은 35~44세 집단에서 해당 비율의 두 배(34.4%)보다 적음.

힌트 twice는 배수사로서, 밑줄 친 부분처럼 「배수사+as+원급+as+A」 형태로 쓰일 경우, 'A보다 …배 더 ~한'이라고 해석됨.

⑤ (6) The 55-64 group and the 65 and older group /
55~64세 집단과 65세 이상 집단은 /
showed a similar percentage of individuals /
사람들의 비슷한 비율을 보였다 /
providing unpaid care to children, /
(현재분사구)
아동에게 무급 돌봄을 제공하는 /
with a difference of less than 1 percentage point.
1퍼센트포인트 미만의 차이로

아동에게 무급 돌봄을 제공하는 것에 있어, 55~64세 집단(17.6%)과 65세 이상 집단(16.7%)은 단 0.9(=17.6-16.7)퍼센트포인트 차이로 비슷한 비율을 보였음.

[전문 해석]

(1)위 그래프는 2022년에 캐나다에서 아동과 성인에게 무급 돌봄을 제공한 사람들의 비율을 연령 집단별로 보여 준다. ①(2)특히, 35~44세 집단은 아동에게 무급 돌봄을 제공하는 사람들의 가장 높은 비율을 가졌으며, 이는 59.5%에 달했다. ②(3)그러나, 성인에게 무급 돌봄을 제공하는 사람들의 가장 높은 비율은 55~64세 집단에서 발견되었다. ③(4)25~34세 집단에 비해, 15~24세 집단은 아동에게 무급 돌봄을 제공하는 사람들의 더 낮은 비율과 성인에게 무급 돌봄을 제공하는 사람들의 더 높은 비율을 가졌다. ④(5)45~54세 집단에서 성인에게 무급 돌봄을 제공하는 사람들의 비율은 35~44세 집단의 비율보다 두 배 더 높았다(→ 두 배보다 더 적었다). ⑤(6)55~64세 집단과 65세 이상 집단은 1퍼센트포인트 미만의 차이로 아동에게 무급 돌봄을 제공하는 사람들의 비슷한 비율을 보였다.

[정답 확인]

다음 도표의 내용과 일치하지 않는 것은?

2022년 캐나다에서 아동과 성인에게 무급 돌봄을 제공한 사람들의 비율

Proportion of People Who Provide Unpaid Care to Children and Adults in Canada in 2022

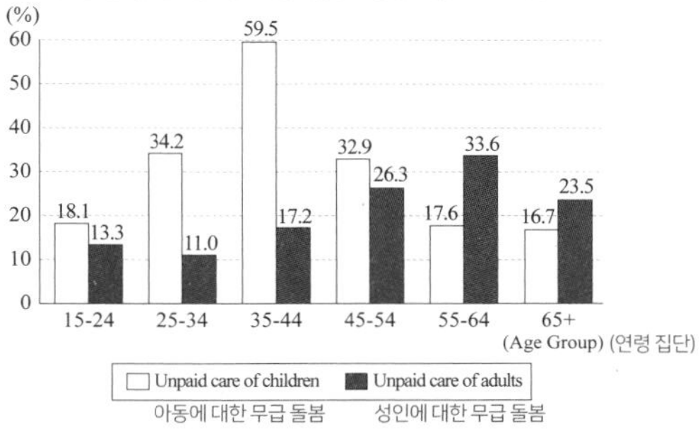

[중요 어휘]

□ unpaid	형용사 무급의, 무보수의
□ care	명사 돌봄, 보살핌
□ notably	부사 특히
□ individual	명사 사람, 개인
□ reach	동사 ~에 달하다[이르다]
□ compared to A	A에 비해, A와 비교하여

정답과 해설 08 도표의 이해

문제편 p.101

09 내용 일치 파악

01 2021년 3월 28번 (정답률 95%)

정답 ③

[지문 끊어 읽기] 영화배우 Ingrid Bergman

(1) Ingrid Bergman was born in Stockholm, Sweden /
Ingrid Bergman은 스웨덴 스톡홀름에서 태어났다 /
on August 29, 1915.
1915년 8월 29일에

힌트 등위접속사 and로 'Her mother was German'과 병렬 연결된 절로, 공통되는 요소인 동사 was가 주어 her father 뒤에 생략되었음.

(2) Her mother was German / and her father Swedish.
그녀의 어머니는 독일인이었다 / 그리고 그녀의 아버지는 스웨덴인이었다

(3) Her mother died / when she was three, /
그녀의 어머니는 돌아가셨다 / 그녀가 세 살 때 /
and her father passed away / when she was 12.
그리고 그녀의 아버지는 돌아가셨다 / 그녀가 열두 살 때

(4) Eventually / she was brought up /
결국 / 그녀는 길러졌다 /
by her Uncle Otto and Aunt Hulda.
그녀의 숙부 Otto와 숙모 Hulda에 의해

(5) She was interested in acting / from an early age.
그녀는 연기에 관심이 있었다 / 어릴 적부터

(6) When she was 17, /
그녀가 17세였을 때 /
she attended the Royal Dramatic Theater School / in Stockholm.
그녀는 Royal Dramatic Theater School에 다녔다 / 스톡홀름에 있는

(7) She made her debut on the stage / but was more interested /
그녀는 연극 무대에서 데뷔했다 / 하지만 더 관심이 있었다 /
in working in films. 정답단서
영화계에서 일하는 것에

(8) In the early 1940s, / she gained star status in Hollywood, /
1940년대 초에 / 그녀는 할리우드에서 스타의 지위를 얻었다 /
[playing many roles / as the heroine of the film].
[ ]: 분사구문(~하며)
많은 역할들을 연기하며 / 영화의 여주인공으로

힌트 '5형식V(consider)+O(Bergman)+O·C(to have~)'가 수동태로 바뀐 형태임.

(9) Bergman was considered to have /
Bergman은 가졌다고 여겨졌다 /
tremendous acting talent, an angelic natural beauty and the willingness to work hard /
형용사적 용법(~하는)
엄청난 연기 재능, 천사 같은 자연적인 미모, 그리고 열심히 일하고자 하는 의지를 /
to get the best out of films.
부사적 용법(~하기 위해서)
영화에서 가장 좋은 결과를 이끌어내기 위해서

(10) She was fluent in five languages /
그녀는 다섯 개의 언어에 유창했다 /
and appeared in a range of films, plays and TV productions.
그리고 다양한 영화, 연극, 그리고 TV 방송에 출연했다

[전문 해석]

(1)Ingrid Bergman은 1915년 8월 29일에 스웨덴 스톡홀름에서 태어났다. (2)그녀의 어머니는 독일인이었고, 아버지는 스웨덴인이었다. (3)그녀의 어머니는 그녀가 세 살 때 돌아가셨고, 그녀의 아버지는 그녀가 열두 살 때 돌아가셨다. (4)결국 그녀는 그녀의 숙부 Otto와 숙모 Hulda(의 손)에 의해 길러졌다. (5)그녀는 어릴 적부터 연기에 관심이 있었다. (6)그녀가 17세였을 때 그녀는 스톡홀름에 있는 Royal Dramatic Theater School에 다녔다. (7)그녀는 연극 무대에서 데뷔했지만 영화계에서 일하는 것에 더 관심이 있었다. (8)1940년대 초에 그녀는 영화의 여주인공으로 많은 역할들을 연기하며, 할리우드에서 스타의 지위를 얻었다. (9)Bergman은 엄청난 연기 재능, 천사 같은 자연적인 미모, 그리고 영화에서 가장 좋은 결과를 이끌어내기 위해서 열심히 일하고자 하는 의지를 가졌다고 여겨졌다. (10)그녀는 다섯 개의 언어에 유창했으며, 다양한 영화, 연극, 그리고 TV 방송에 출연했다.

[정답 확인]

Ingrid Bergman에 관한 다음 글의 내용과 일치하지 않는 것은?

① 어머니는 독일인(German)이었고 아버지는 스웨덴인(Swedish)이었다. 문장(2)
② 17세에 Royal Dramatic Theater School에 다녔다(attend). 문장(6)
③ ~~영화~~(연극 무대)를 통해 데뷔했으나 ~~연극~~(영화)(the stage)에 더 관심이 있었다. 문장(7)
④ 1940년대 초에 할리우드에서 스타의 지위를 얻었다(gain star status). 문장(8)
⑤ 다섯 개의 언어에 유창했다(be fluent in). 문장(10)

[중요 어휘]

□ pass away	돌아가시다, 사망하다
□ bring A up	A를 기르다[양육하다]
□ attend	동사 (~에) 다니다, 참석하다
□ status	명사 지위, 상태
□ tremendous	형용사 엄청난, 굉장한
□ angelic	형용사 천사 같은
□ willingness	명사 의지, 의사
□ be fluent in	~에 유창하다
□ a range of	다양한

02 2021년 11월 26번 (정답률 95%)

정답 ④

[지문 끊어 읽기] 발달 심리학자 및 정신과 의사 John Bowlby

(1) John Bowlby, /
S
John Bowlby는 /
British developmental psychologist and psychiatrist, /
영국 발달 심리학자이자 정신과 의사인 /
was born in 1907, / to an upper-middle-class family.
V
1907년에 태어났다 / 상위 중산 계급 가정에서

정답단서-① 아버지는 왕의 의료진의 일원이었음.

(2) His father, / [who was a member of the King's medical staff], /
[ ]: 주격 관계대명사절
그의 아버지는 / 왕의 의료진의 일원이었던 /
was often absent.
자주 집을 비웠다

힌트 'A nanny primarily cared for Bowlby.'라는 능동태 문장이 수동태로 바뀌어 전치사 for의 목적어 Bowlby가 주어 자리에 온 형태임.

(3) Bowlby was cared for primarily by a nanny /
V①
Bowlby는 주로 유모에 의해 돌보아졌다 /
and did not spend much time with his mother, / 정답단서-② 어머니와 많은 시간을 보내지 못했음.
V②
그리고 그의 어머니와 많은 시간을 보내지 못했다 /
as was customary at that time for his class.
이는 그 당시 그의 계급에서 관례적이었다

힌트 여기서 as는 앞 문장 전체를 선행사로 받는 관계대명사 which의 계속적 용법과 유사함(유사관계대명사). which와의 차이점은 as가 이끄는 관계대명사절은 주절의 앞에도 올 수 있지만, which가 이끄는 절은 항상 주절의 뒤에 온다는 것임.

(4) Bowlby was sent to a boarding school /
Bowlby는 기숙 학교로 보내졌다 /
at the age of seven.
7살에

(5) He later recalled this / as being traumatic to his development.
=문장(4) 전치사 동명사
그는 나중에 이것을 회상했다 / 자신의 성장에 있어 충격적인 일이었다고

정답단서-③ 여기서 '이것(this)'은 문장 (4)에 나온 기숙 학교로 보내진 일임. Bowlby는 이것을 성장에 있어 충격적인 일로 회상했음.

(6) This experience, / however, /
이 경험은 / 그러나 /
proved to have a large impact on Bowlby, /
Bowlby에게 큰 영향을 미쳤던 것으로 판명되었다 /
whose work focused on children's development.
소유격 관계대명사(계속적 용법)
그리고 그의 연구는 아동의 발달에 중점을 두었다

(7) [Following his father's suggestion], / [ ]: 분사구문
자신의 아버지의 제안을 따라 /

정답단서-④ Trinity 대학에 의학을 공부하기 위해 입학했음.

Bowlby enrolled at Trinity College, Cambridge / to study medicine, /
부사적 용법(목적)
Bowlby는 Cambridge의 Trinity 대학에 입학했다 / 의학을 공부하기 위해 /
but by his third year, / he changed his focus to psychology.
그러나 3년째 되던 해에 / 그는 자신의 관심을 심리학으로 바꿨다

(8) During the 1950s, / Bowlby briefly worked /
1950년대에 / Bowlby는 잠시 활동했다 /
as a mental health consultant / for the World Health Organization. 정답 단서-⑤ 세계 보건 기구에서 잠시 정신 건강 자문 위원으로 활동했음.
정신 건강 자문 위원으로 / 세계 보건 기구에서

(9) His attachment theory has been described /
현재완료(계속)
그의 애착 이론은 평가되어 오고 있다 /
as the dominant approach /
지배적인 접근법으로 /
to understanding early social development.
전치사 동명사
초기 사회적 발달을 이해하는 데 있어

[전문 해석]

(1)영국 발달 심리학자이자 정신과 의사인 John Bowlby는 1907년에 상위 중산 계급 가정에서 태어났다. (2)왕의 의료진의 일원이었던 그의 아버지는 자주 집을 비웠다. (3)Bowlby는 주로 유모에 의해 돌보아졌고 그의 어머니와 많은 시간을 보내지 못했는데, 이는 그 당시 그의 계급에서 관례적이었다. (4)Bowlby는 7살에 기숙 학교로 보내졌다. (5)그는 나중에 이것을 자신의 성장에 있어 충격적인 일이었다고 회상했다. (6)그러나 이 경험은 Bowlby에게 큰 영향을 미쳤던 것으로 판명되었고 그의 연구는 아동의 발달에 중점을 두었다. (7)자신의 아버지의 제안을 따라, Bowlby는 Cambridge의 Trinity 대학에 의학을 공부하기 위해 입학했으나 3년째 되던 해에 그는 자신의 관심을 심리학으로 바꿨다. (8)1950년대에 Bowlby는 잠시 세계 보건 기구에서 정신 건강 자문 위원으로 활동했다. (9)그의 애착 이론은 초기 사회적 발달을 이해하는 데 있어 지배적인 접근법으로 평가되어 오고 있다.
- attachment theory(애착 이론): 영아가 주 양육자와 형성하는 강한 정서적 결속인 애착이 영아의 생존 및 심리, 사회적 발달에 중요한 영향을 미친다는 이론

[정답 확인]

John Bowlby에 관한 다음 글의 내용과 일치하지 않는 것은?

① 아버지는 왕의 의료진(medical staff)의 일원이었다. 문장(2)
② 어머니와 많은 시간을 보내지 못했다. 문장(3)
③ 기숙 학교로 보내진 것이 성장(development)에 있어 충격적인(traumatic) 일이었다. 문장(5)
✔④ Trinity 대학에 ~~심리학~~(의학)을 공부하기 위해 입학했다(enroll). 문장(7)
⑤ 세계 보건 기구에서 정신 건강 자문 위원(consultant)으로 일했다. 문장(8)
★중요 문장 (7)에서 의학을 공부하기 위해 대학에 입학했다고 함. 심리학을 공부하기 시작한 시점은 대학 입학 후 3년째 되던 해임.

[중요 어휘]

psychiatrist	명사 정신과 의사
class	명사 계급, 계층
absent	형용사 집을 비운, 부재한, 결석한
care for	~을 돌보다[보살피다]
primarily	부사 주로
customary	형용사 관례적인, 습관적인
boarding school	명사 기숙 학교
recall	동사 회상하다, 기억해 내다
traumatic	형용사 충격적인, 정신적 외상의
development	명사 성장, 발달
prove to V	~으로 판명되다[드러나다]
enroll	동사 입학하다, 등록하다
briefly	부사 잠시, 간단히
consultant	명사 자문 위원, 상담가
dominant	형용사 지배적인, 우세한

03 2022년 3월 28번 (정답률 95%) 정답 ③

[지문 끊어 읽기] 예술가 Gordon Parks

(1) Gordon Parks was a photographer, author, film director, and musician.
Gordon Parks는 사진작가이자 작가, 영화감독, 음악가였다

(2) He documented the everyday lives of African Americans /
그는 아프리카계 미국인의 일상생활을 기록했다 /
at a time [when few people outside the black community were familiar with their lives].
선행사 [ ]: 관계부사절
흑인 사회 밖에서는 그들의 삶에 익숙한 사람이 거의 없던 시절에

(3) Parks was born the youngest of 15 children / 정답 단서-① 15명의 자녀 중 막내로 태어났음.
V①
Parks는 15명의 자녀 중 막내로 태어났다 /
and grew up on his family's farm.
V②
그리고 가족 농장에서 자랐다

(4) After the death of his mother, /
어머니가 돌아가신 후 /
he went to live with a sister in Minnesota. 정답 단서-② 어머니가 돌아가신 후 Minnesota에 있는 누나와 살러 감.
부사적 용법(목적)
그는 Minnesota에 있는 누나와 살러 갔다

(5) Parks eventually dropped out of school /
V①
Parks는 결국 학교를 중퇴했다 /
and worked at various jobs. 정답 단서-③ 학교를 중퇴하고 다양한 일자리에서 일했음.
V②
그리고 다양한 일자리에서 일했다

(6) His interest in photography was inspired /
사진에 대한 그의 관심이 생겼다 /
by a photo-essay he read / about migrant farm workers.
목적격 관계대명사절
그가 읽은 포토 에세이에 의해 / 떠돌이 농장 일꾼에 관한

(7) After he moved to Chicago, / Parks began taking photos /
동명사
그가 시카고로 옮겨간 후 / Parks는 사진을 찍기 시작했다 /
of poor African Americans.
가난한 아프리카계 미국인들의

(8) In 1949, / he became the first African American /
1949년에 / 그는 최초의 아프리카계 미국인이 되었다 /
to be a staff photographer for *Life* magazine. 정답 단서-④ 최초로 *Life* 지의 아프리카계 미국인 사진 기자가 됨.
형용사적 용법
Life 지의 사진 기자가 된

(9) He also wrote music pieces in his life / and in 1956 /
그는 또한 살아생전에 음악 작품을 작곡했다 / 그리고 1956년에 /
the Vienna Orchestra performed a piano concerto he wrote. 정답 단서-⑤ 그가 작곡한 피아노 협주곡을 1956년에 Vienna Orchestra가 연주했음.
목적격 관계대명사절
Vienna Orchestra는 그가 작곡한 피아노 협주곡을 연주했다

(10) Parks was an inspiring artist / until he died in 2006.
Parks는 영감을 주는 예술가였다 / 2006년에 사망할 때까지

[전문 해석]

(1)Gordon Parks는 사진작가이자 작가, 영화감독, 음악가였다. (2)그는 흑인 사회 밖에서는 그들의 삶에 익숙한 사람이 거의 없던 시절에 아프리카계 미국인의 일상생활을 기록했다. (3)Parks는 15명의 자녀 중 막내로 태어나 가족 농장에서 자랐다. (4)어머니가 돌아가신 후, 그는 Minnesota에 있는 누나와 살러 갔다. (5)Parks는 결국 학교를 중퇴하고 다양한 일자리에서 일했다. (6)그가 읽은 떠돌이 농장 일꾼에 관한 포토 에세이 덕분에 그는 사진에 관심이 생겼다. (7)시카고로 옮겨간 후, Parks는 가난한 아프리카계 미국인들을 사진 찍기 시작했다. (8)1949년에 그는 *Life* 지의 사진 기자가 된 최초의 아프리카계 미국인이 되었다. (9)그는 또한 살아생전에 음악 작품을 작곡했고 1956년에 Vienna Orchestra는 그가 작곡한 피아노 협주곡을 연주했다. (10)Parks는 2006년에 사망할 때까지 영감을 주는 예술가였다.

[정답 확인]

Gordon Parks에 관한 다음 글의 내용과 일치하지 않는 것은?

① 15명의 자녀 중 막내로 태어났다. 문장(3)
② 어머니가 돌아가신 후 Minnesota에 있는 누나와 살러 갔다. 문장(4)
✔③ 학교를 ~~중퇴하지 않고~~(중퇴하고) 다양한 일자리에서(at various jobs) 일했다. 문장(5)
④ *Life* 지의 사진 기자(photographer)가 된 최초의 아프리카계 미국인이었다. 문장(8)
⑤ 그가 작곡한 피아노 협주곡을 1956년에 Vienna Orchestra가 연주했다(perform). 문장(9)
★중요 문장 (5)에서 학교를 중퇴하고 다양한 일자리에서 일했다고 함.

[중요 어휘]

document	동사 기록하다 / 명사 문서
eventually	부사 결국
drop out of school	학교를 중퇴하다

문제편 p.102

□ **migrant**	명사 떠돌이, 이주자
□ **concerto**	명사 협주곡
□ **inspiring**	형용사 영감을 주는

04 2022년 6월 26번 (정답률 95%) 정답 ④

[지문 끊어 읽기] 제왕나비의 특징

(1) The monarch butterfly has lovely bright colors /
제왕나비는 예쁘고 밝은 색을 가지고 있다 /
splashed on its wings.
날개에 얼룩무늬로

(2) The wings have white spots on the outer margins. 정답 단서-① 날개의 바깥 가장자리에 흰 점들이 있음.
날개 바깥쪽 가장자리에 흰 점들이 있다

(3) The hind wings are rounded, /
뒷날개는 둥글다 /
and they are lighter in color than the front wings. 정답 단서-② 뒷날개는 앞날개보다 색이 더 밝음.
그리고 그것들은 앞날개보다 더 밝은 색을 띤다

(4) The body is black with white spots.
몸통은 검은 바탕에 흰 점이 있다

(5) The mother butterfly lays only one egg /
어미 나비는 오직 한 개의 알만 낳는다 /
on the underside of milkweed leaves, /
밀크위드 잎의 아래쪽에 /
which hatches about three to five days later. 정답 단서-③ 알은 약 3일에서 5일 후에 부화함.
그리고 그것은 약 3일에서 5일 후에 부화한다

힌트 콤마 다음의 which는 egg를 선행사로 하는 계속적 용법의 주격 관계대명사임. 선행사와 관계대명사 사이에 전치사구가 있으므로 주어와 동사 수 일치에 주의해야 함.

(6) The monarch loves to fly around in the warm sunshine, /
제왕나비는 따뜻한 햇살을 받으며 날아다니는 것을 좋아한다 /
from March through October, all across the United States.
3월부터 10월까지 미국 전역에서

(7) The monarch cannot survive /
제왕나비는 살아남을 수 없다 /
the cold winter temperatures of the northern states. 정답 단서-④ 제왕나비는 북부 주의 추운 겨울 기온에 잘 버틸 수 없음.
북부 주의 추운 겨울 기온에

(8) So, / it very wisely migrates /
그래서 / 그것은 매우 현명하게 이주한다 /
from the northern states to the south, / and hibernates.
북부 주에서 남부로 / 그리고 동면한다

(9) The monarch is the only insect / (선행사)
제왕나비는 유일한 곤충이다 /
that can fly more than four thousand kilometers / 정답 단서-⑤ 제왕나비는 4천 킬로미터 넘게 날 수 있는 유일한 곤충임.
(주격 관계대명사)
4천 킬로미터 넘게 날 수 있는 /
to a warmer climate.
더 따뜻한 지방으로

[전문 해석]

(1)제왕나비는 날개에 얼룩무늬로 예쁘고 밝은 색이 있다. (2)날개 바깥쪽 가장자리에 흰 점들이 있다. (3)뒷날개는 둥글고, 앞날개보다 더 밝은 색을 띤다. (4)몸통은 검은 바탕에 흰 점이 있다. (5)어미 나비는 밀크위드 잎의 아래쪽에 오직 한 개의 알만 낳고, 그것은 약 3일에서 5일 후에 부화한다. (6)제왕나비는 3월부터 10월까지 미국 전역에서 따뜻한 햇살을 받으며 날아다니는 것을 좋아한다. (7)제왕나비는 북부 주의 추운 겨울 기온에 살아남을 수 없다. (8)그래서, 그것은 매우 현명하게 북부 주에서 남부로 이주하여 동면한다. (9)제왕나비는 더 따뜻한 지방으로 4천 킬로미터 넘게 날 수 있는 유일한 곤충이다.

[정답 확인]

monarch butterfly에 관한 다음 글의 내용과 일치하지 않는 것은?

① 날개의 바깥 가장자리(outer margin)에 흰 점이 있다. 문장(2)
② 뒷날개(hind wing)는 앞날개(front wing)보다 색이 더 밝다. 문장(3)
③ 알은 약 3일에서 5일 후에 부화한다(hatch). 문장(5)
④ 북부 주의 추운 겨울 기온에 잘 ~~버틴다~~ 버틸 수 없다. 문장(7)
⑤ 4천 킬로미터 넘게 날 수 있다. 문장(9)

★중요 문장 (7)에서 제왕나비는 북부 주의 추운 겨울 기온에서 살아남을 수 없다고 함.

[중요 어휘]

□ **monarch**	명사 제왕, 군주
□ **margin**	명사 가장자리, 차이
□ **hind**	형용사 뒤의
□ **hatch**	동사 부화하다
□ **survive**	동사 ~에서 살아남다
□ **migrate**	동사 이주하다
□ **hibernate**	동사 동면하다

05 2022년 9월 26번 (정답률 95%) 정답 ⑤

[지문 끊어 읽기] 기상학자 Carl-Gustaf Rossby

(1) Carl-Gustaf Rossby was one of a group of notable Scandinavian researchers / (선행사)
Carl-Gustaf Rossby는 저명한 스칸디나비아 연구자들의 무리 중 한 명이었다 /
[who worked with the Norwegian meteorologist Vilhelm Bjerknes /
노르웨이 기상학자인 Vilhelm Bjerknes와 함께 일했던 /
at the University of Bergen]. [ ]: 주격 관계대명사절
University of Bergen에서

(2) While growing up in Stockholm, / (분사구문)
Stockholm에서 성장하면서 /
Rossby received a traditional education. 정답 단서-① Rossby는 Stockholm에서 전통적인 교육을 받으며 성장했음.
Rossby는 전통적인 교육을 받았다

힌트 'While growing ~ Stockholm'은 부사절과 주절의 주어가 같아 부사절의 주어인 'he'가 생략되고 동사 'grew'를 'growing'의 형태로 바꾼 분사구문임.

(3) He earned a degree in mathematical physics /
그는 수리 물리학 학위를 받았다 /
at the University of Stockholm in 1918, / 정답 단서-② Rossby는 University of Stockholm에서 수리 물리학 학위를 받았음.
1918년에 University of Stockholm에서 /
but after hearing a lecture by Bjerknes, / (분사구문①)
하지만 Bjerknes의 강의를 듣고 나서 /
and apparently bored with Stockholm, / (분사구문②)
그리고 짐작하건대 Stockholm에 지루함을 느껴 /
he moved to the newly established Geophysical Institute in Bergen.
그는 Bergen에 새로 설립된 지구 물리학 연구소로 옮겼다

(4) In 1925, / Rossby received a scholarship / 정답 단서-③ Rossby는 1925년에 장학금을 받았음.
1925년에 / Rossby는 장학금을 받았다 /
from the Sweden-America Foundation /
스웨덴-미국 재단으로부터 /
to go to the United States, /
그리고 미국으로 갔다 /
where he joined the United States Weather Bureau. (계속적 용법)
그리고 그곳에서 그는 미국 기상국에 합류했다

(5) Based in part on his practical experience /
그의 실질적인 경험을 일부 바탕으로 하여 /
in weather forecasting, /
일기 예보에 대한 /
Rossby had become a supporter of the "polar front theory," / 정답 단서-④ Rossby는 polar front theory를 지지했음.
Rossby는 'polar front theory'의 지지자가 되었다 /
which explains the cyclonic circulation / (선행사)
저기압성 순환을 설명하는 /
[that develops at the boundary between warm and cold air masses]. [ ]: 주격 관계대명사절
온난 기단과 한랭 기단 사이의 경계에서 발생하는

(6) In 1947, /
1947년에 /
Rossby accepted the chair of the Institute of Meteorology, /
Rossby는 기상 연구소의 직책을 받아들였다 /
which had been set up for him / at the University of Stockholm, / 정답 단서-⑤ Rossby는 University of Stockholm의 연구소 직책을 받아들였음.
그를 위해 마련된 / University of Stockholm에 /
where he remained / until his death ten years later. (계속적 용법)
그리고 그곳에서 그는 남아있었다 / 10년 후 그의 생을 마감할 때까지

힌트 Rossby를 위한 직책이 마련된 것이 그가 연구소 직책을 받아들인 것보다 먼저 일어났으므로 과거 완료 수동태를 사용함.

[전문 해석]

(1)Carl-Gustaf Rossby는 University of Bergen에서 노르웨이 기상학자인 Vilhelm Bjerknes와 함께 일했던 저명한 스칸디나비아 연구자들의 무리 중 한 명이었다. (2)Stockholm에서 성장하면서, Rossby는 전통적인 교육을 받았다. (3)그는 1918년에 University of Stockholm에서 수리 물리학 학위를 받았지만, Bjerknes의 강의를 듣고 나서, 짐작하건대 Stockholm에 지루함을 느껴, Bergen에 새로 설립된 지구 물리학 연구소로 옮겼다. (4)1925년에 Rossby는 스웨덴-미국 재단으로부터 장학금을 받아 미국으로 갔고, 그곳에서 미국 기상국에 합류했다. (5)일기 예보에 대한 그의 실질적인 경험을 일부 바탕으로 하여, Rossby는 온난 기단과 한랭 기단 사이의 경계에서 발생하는 저기압성 순환을 설명하는 'polar front theory(한대전선이론)'의 지지자가 되었다. (6)1947년에 Rossby는 University of Stockholm에 그를 위해 마련된 기상 연구소의 직책을 받아들였고, 그곳에서 10년 후 그의 생을 마감할 때까지 남아있었다.

- polar front theory(한대전선이론): Jacob Bjerknes가 '이동성 저기압의 구조'에 관한 논문을 발표하면서 저기압이 어떻게 발달하는지에 대해 설명한 이론임. 이 이론은 현재까지 기상학의 중요한 부분을 차지하고 있음.

[정답 확인]

Carl-Gustaf Rossby에 관한 다음 글의 내용과 일치하지 않는 것은?

① Stockholm에서 성장하면서 전통적인(traditional) 교육을 받았다. 문장(2)
② University of Stockholm에서 수리 물리학 학위(degree)를 받았다. 문장(3)
③ 1925년에 장학금(scholarship)을 받았다. 문장(4)
④ polar front theory를 지지했다(support). 문장(5)
⑤ University of Stockholm에 마련된 직책을 ~~거절했다~~ 수락했다. 문장(6)

[중요 어휘]

☐ **notable**	형용사 저명한, 유명한
☐ **meteorologist**	명사 기상학자
☐ **apparently**	부사 짐작하건대, 듣자[보아] 하니
☐ **practical**	형용사 실질적인, 실용적인
☐ **cyclonic circulation**	명사 저기압성 순환
☐ **warm air mass**	온난 기단
☐ **cold air mass**	한랭 기단

06 2022년 11월 26번 (정답률 95%) 정답 ⑤

[지문 끊어 읽기] 인도 과학자 Janaki Ammal

(1) Janaki Ammal, / one of India's most notable scientists, /
one of+최상급+복수명사
Janaki Ammal은 / 인도의 가장 유명한 과학자 중 한 명인 /
was born in 1897, / and was expected to wed /
병렬① 병렬②
1897년에 태어났다 / 그리고 결혼할 것으로 기대되었다 /
through an arranged marriage.
중매를 통해

(2) Despite living at a time /
시기에 살았음에도 불구하고 /
when literacy among women in India was less than one percent, /
관계부사
인도 여성들의 식자율이 1%보다 낮았던 /
she decided to reject tradition and attend college. 정답 단서-① Janaki Ammal은 관습을 거부하고 대학에 입학하기로 함.
병렬① 병렬②(to 생략)
그녀는 관습을 거부하고 대학에 입학하기로 결심했다

(3) In 1924, / she went to the U.S. /
1924년에 / 그녀는 미국으로 갔다 /
and eventually received a doctorate in botany /
그리고 마침내 식물학 박사 학위를 받았다 /
from the University of Michigan.
Michigan 대학에서

(4) Ammal contributed to the development /
Ammal은 개발에 기여했다 /
of the sweetest sugarcane variety in the world. 정답 단서-② Ammal은 세계에서 가장 단 사탕수수 품종의 개발에 기여함.
세계에서 가장 단 사탕수수 품종의

(5) She moved to England /
그녀는 영국으로 건너갔다 /
where she co-authored the *Chromosome Atlas of Cultivated Plants*. 정답 단서-③ Ammal은 *Chromosome Atlas of Cultivated Plants*를 공동 집필함.
그곳에서 그녀는 *Chromosome Atlas of Cultivated Plants*를 공동 집필했다

(6) Following a series of famines, / she returned to India /
연이은 기근이 있은 후 / 그녀는 인도로 돌아갔다 /
to help increase food production / 정답 단서-④ Ammal은 식량 생산을 증가시키는 데 도움을 주기 위해 인도로 돌아감.
부사적 용법
식량 생산을 증가시키는 데 도움을 주기 위해 /
힌트 'help+to V'에서 흔히 to를 생략하고 쓸 수 있음.
at the request of the Prime Minister.
수상의 요청으로

(7) However, / Ammal disagreed with the deforestation /
그러나 / Ammal은 삼림 벌채에 동의하지 않았다 /
taking place / in an effort to grow more food.
일어나는 / 더 많은 식량을 재배하기 위한 노력으로써

(8) She became an advocate / for the preservation of native plants /
병렬①
그녀는 옹호자가 되었다 / 토종 식물 보존에 대한 /
and successfully saved the Silent Valley /
병렬②
그리고 Silent Valley를 성공적으로 지켰다 /
from the construction of a hydroelectric dam. 정답 단서-⑤ Ammal은 수력 발전 댐의 건설로부터 Silent Valley를 성공적으로 지켜냄.
수력 발전 댐의 건설로부터

[전문 해석]

(1)인도의 가장 유명한 과학자 중 한 명인 Janaki Ammal은 1897년에 태어났고, 중매를 통해 결혼할 것으로 기대되었다. (2)인도 여성들의 식자율이 1%보다 낮았던 시기에 살았음에도 불구하고, 그녀는 관습을 거부하고 대학에 입학하기로 결심했다. (3)1924년에, 그녀는 미국으로 갔고 마침내 Michigan 대학에서 식물학 박사 학위를 받았다. (4)Ammal은 세계에서 가장 단 사탕수수 품종 개발에 기여했다. (5)그녀는 영국으로 건너가 그곳에서 *Chromosome Atlas of Cultivated Plants*를 공동 집필했다. (6)연이은 기근이 있은 후, 그녀는 수상의 요청으로 식량 생산을 증가시키는 데 도움을 주기 위해 인도로 돌아갔다. (7)그러나 Ammal은 더 많은 식량을 재배하기 위한 노력으로써 삼림 벌채가 일어나는 것에 동의하지 않았다. (8)그녀는 토종 식물 보존에 대한 옹호자가 되었고, 수력 발전 댐의 건설로부터 Silent Valley를 성공적으로 지켰다.

[정답 확인]

Janaki Ammal에 관한 다음 글의 내용과 일치하지 않는 것은?

① 관습을 따르지 않고(reject tradition) 대학에 입학하기로 결심했다. 문장(2)
② 세계에서 가장 단 사탕수수(sugarcane) 품종(variety) 개발에 기여했다. 문장(4)
③ *Chromosome Atlas of Cultivated Plants*를 공동 집필했다(co-author). 문장(5)
④ 식량 생산(food production)을 증가시키는 데 도움을 주기 위해 인도로 돌아갔다. 문장(6)
⑤ 수력 발전 댐(hydroelectric dam)의 건설로부터 Silent Valley를 지키는 데 ~~실패~~ 성공했다. 문장(8)

★중요 문장 (8)에서 Ammal은 수력 발전 댐의 건설로부터 Silent Valley를 성공적으로 지켜냈다고 함.

[중요 어휘]

☐ **notable**	형용사 유명한, 주목할 만한
☐ **wed**	동사 결혼하다
☐ **arranged marriage**	중매 결혼
☐ **literacy**	명사 식자율, 읽고 쓸 줄 아는 능력
☐ **reject**	동사 거부하다, 받아들이지 않다
☐ **doctorate**	명사 박사 학위
☐ **botany**	명사 식물학
☐ **sugarcane**	명사 사탕수수
☐ **variety**	명사 품종, 다양성, 변화
☐ **co-author**	동사 ~을 공동 집필하다 / 명사 공동 저자
☐ **chromosome**	명사 염색체
☐ **atlas**	명사 지도책, 도해집
☐ **famine**	명사 기근
☐ **Prime Minister**	명사 수상
☐ **deforestation**	명사 삼림 벌채
☐ **advocate**	명사 옹호자, 변호사
☐ **hydroelectric**	형용사 수력 발전의

정답과 해설 09 내용 일치 파악

문제편 p.104

07 2023년 9월 26번 (정답률 95%) 정답 ③

[지문 끊어 읽기] 프랑스인 Camille Flammarion

(1) Camille Flammarion was born / at Montigny-le-Roi, France.
Camille Flammarion은 태어났다 / 프랑스 Montigny-le-Roi에서

(2) He became interested in astronomy / at an early age, /
그는 천문학에 흥미가 생겼다 / 어린 나이에 / 정답 단서-① Flammarion은 어린 나이에 천문학에 흥미를 가짐.
and when he was only sixteen /
그리고 그가 불과 16세였을 때 /
he wrote a book on the origin of the world.
그는 세상의 기원에 관한 책을 썼다

(3) The manuscript was not published at the time, /
그 원고는 그 당시 출판되지 않았다 /
but it came to the attention of Urbain Le Verrier, /
하지만 Urbain Le Verrier의 관심을 끌게 되었다 / =
the director of the Paris Observatory.
Paris Observatory의 관리자

(4) He became an assistant to Le Verrier in 1858 / 정답 단서-②
그는 1858년에 Le Verrier의 조수가 되었다 / Flammarion은 1858년에 Le Verrier의 조수가 됨.
and worked as a calculator.
그리고 계산원으로 일했다

(5) At nineteen, / he wrote another book /
19세에 / 그는 또 다른 책을 썼다 /
called *The Plurality of Inhabited Worlds*, /
*The Plurality of Inhabited Worlds*라고 불리는 / 힌트 'in which'는 관계부사 'where'로 바꾸어 쓸 수 있음.
in which he passionately claimed /
그런데 이 책에서 그는 열정적으로 주장했다 /
[that life exists outside the planet Earth]. 정답 단서-③ Flammarion은 19세에 외계 생명체의 존재를 주장하는 책을 씀.
[ ]: claimed의 목적어절
지구 바깥에 생명체가 존재한다고

(6) His most successful work, *Popular Astronomy*, /
=
그의 가장 성공적인 저서인 *Popular Astronomy*는 /
was published in 1880, /
1880년에 출판되었다 /
and eventually sold 130,000 copies.
그리고 결국 130,000부가 판매되었다

(7) With his own funds, / he built an observatory at Juvisy / 정답 단서-④ Flammarion은 자신의 자금으로 Juvisy에 천문대를 세움.
자신의 자금으로 / 그는 Juvisy에 천문대를 세웠다 /
and spent May to November of each year there.
그리고 매년 5월에서 11월까지 그곳에서 지냈다

(8) In 1887, / he founded the French Astronomical Society / 정답 단서-⑤
1887년에 / 그는 French Astronomical Society를 설립했다 / Flammarion은 French Astronomical Society를 설립함.
and served as editor of its monthly publication.
그리고 그것의 월간 간행물의 편집자로 일했다

[전문 해석]

(1)Camille Flammarion은 프랑스 Montigny-le-Roi에서 태어났다. (2)그는 어린 나이에 천문학에 흥미가 생겼고, 그가 불과 16세였을 때 그는 세상의 기원에 관한 책을 썼다. (3)그 원고는 그 당시 출판되지 않았지만, Paris Observatory의 관리자인 Urbain Le Verrier의 관심을 끌게 되었다. (4)그는 1858년에 Le Verrier의 조수가 되었고 계산원으로 일했다. (5)19세에 그는 *The Plurality of Inhabited Worlds*라고 불리는 또 다른 책을 썼는데, 이 책에서 그는 지구 바깥(외계)에 생명체가 존재한다고 열정적으로 주장했다. (6)그의 가장 성공적인 저서인 *Popular Astronomy*는 1880년에 출판되었고, 결국 130,000부가 판매되었다. (7)자신의 자금으로 그는 Juvisy에 천문대를 세웠고, 매년 5월에서 11월까지 그곳에서 지냈다. (8)1887년에 그는 French Astronomical Society를 설립했고 그것의 월간 간행물의 편집자로 일했다.

[정답 확인]

Camille Flammarion에 관한 다음 글의 내용과 일치하지 않는 것은?

① 어린 나이에 천문학(astronomy)에 흥미가 생겼다. 문장(2)
② 1858년에 Le Verrier의 조수(assistant)가 되었다. 문장(4)
③ 19세에 쓴 책에서 외계 생명체의 존재를 ~~부인했다~~(deny). 문장(5) 주장했다
④ 자신의 자금으로 Juvisy에 천문대(observatory)를 세웠다. 문장(7)
⑤ French Astronomical Society를 설립했다(found). 문장(8)

★중요 문장 (5)에서 Flammarion은 지구 바깥(외계)에 있는 생명체의 존재를 열정적으로 주장했다고 함.

[중요 어휘]

astronomy	명사 천문학
origin	명사 기원, 유래
manuscript	명사 원고
attention	명사 관심, 주의
director	명사 관리자, 감독
assistant	명사 조수, 보조자
calculator	명사 계산원, 계산기
passionately	부사 열정적으로
copy	명사 (책을 세는 단위) 부, 사본
publication	명사 간행물, 출판

08 2019년 11월 26번 (정답률 90%) 정답 ④

[지문 끊어 읽기] 화가 Lotte Laserstein

(1) Lotte Laserstein was born into a Jewish family / in East Prussia.
Lotte Laserstein은 한 유대인 가정에서 태어났다 / 동프로이센의
힌트 과거 독일의 북동부에 있던 주(州)로, 현재는 폴란드와 러시아의 영토로 분할되어 있음.

(2) One of her relatives ran a private painting school, /
그녀의 친척 중 한 명은 사립 회화 학교를 운영했다 /
which allowed Lotte to learn painting and drawing /
5형식V O O.C(to V)
그런데 이는 Lotte가 회화와 소묘를 배울 수 있게 해주었다 /
at a young age.
어린 나이에

(3) Later, / she earned admission / to the Berlin Academy of Arts /
이후 / 그녀는 입학 허가를 받았다 / Berlin Academy of Arts에 /
and completed her master studies /
그리고 그녀의 석사 과정을 끝마쳤다 /
as one of the first women in the school.
one of 복수명사
그 학교의 첫 여성들 중 한 명으로서

(4) In 1928 / her career skyrocketed /
1928년에 / 그녀의 경력은 급상승했다 /
as she gained widespread recognition, /
그녀가 널리 인정을 받으면서 /
but after the seizure of power / by the Nazi Party, /
그러나 권력 장악 이후 / 나치당에 의한 /
she was forbidden / to exhibit her artwork / in Germany.
그녀는 금지당했다 / 그녀의 작품을 전시하는 것을 / 독일에서
힌트 'forbid A to V(A가 ~하는 것을 금지하다)'의 수동태 문장으로, 'A be동사 forbidden to V(A는 ~하는 것을 금지당하다)'가 되었음.

(5) In 1937 / she emigrated to Sweden.
1937년에 / 그녀는 스웨덴으로 이주했다

(6) She continued to work in Sweden /
그녀는 스웨덴에서 계속해서 활동했다 /
but never recaptured the fame / she had enjoyed before. 정답 단서
그러나 그 명성을 결코 되찾지 못했다 / 그녀가 이전에 누렸던
힌트 관계대명사 which/that이 생략된 목적격 관계대명사절로, the fame을 수식하고 있음. 한편 Lotte가 명성을 누렸던 시점은 그녀가 스웨덴으로 이주했던(emigrated: 과거시제) 시점보다 더 이전의 일이므로, 사건의 선후관계를 따져서 과거완료시제(had enjoyed)를 썼음.

(7) In her work, / Lotte repeatedly portrayed Gertrud Rose, /
그녀의 작품에서 / Lotte는 Gertrud Rose를 반복적으로 그렸다 /
her closest friend.
그녀의 가장 가까운 친구인

(8) To Lotte, / she embodied the type of the "New Woman" /
Lotte에게 있어 / 그녀는 '신여성'상을 구체화했다 /
and was so represented.
그리고 그렇게 표현되었다
힌트 문장 (8)의 'so'는 앞에 있는 내용을 받으며 '그렇게'라는 뜻으로 쓰였음. 여기서 'so'가 가리키는 건 the type of the "New Woman"에 해당하는 내용임.

[전문 해석]

(1)Lotte Laserstein은 동프로이센의 한 유대인 가정에서 태어났다. (2)그녀의 친척 중 한 명은 사립 회화 학교를 운영했는데, 이는 Lotte가 어린 나이에 회화와 소묘를 배울 수 있게 해주었다. (3)이후, 그녀는 Berlin Academy of Arts에 입학 허가를 받았고 그 학교의 첫 여성들 중 한 명으로서 그녀의 석사 과정을 끝마쳤다. (4)1928년에 그녀의 경력은 그녀가 널리 인정을 받으면서 급상승했으나, 나치당에 의한 권력 장악 이후, 그녀는 독일에서 그녀의 작품을 전시하는 것을 금지당했다. (5)1937년에 그녀는 스웨덴으로 이주했다. (6)그녀는 스웨덴에서 계속해서 활동했으나, 그녀가 이전에 누렸던 명성을 결코 되찾지 못했다. (7)그녀의 작품에

서 Lotte는 그녀의 가장 가까운 친구인 Gertrud Rose를 반복적으로 그렸다. (8)Lotte에게 있어 그녀는 '신여성'상을 구체화했고(구체화한 인물이었고) (그림에서도) 그렇게 표현되었다.

[정답 확인]

Lotte Laserstein에 관한 다음 글의 내용과 일치하지 않는 것은?

① 어린 나이에 회화(painting)와 소묘(drawing)를 배웠다. 문장(2)
② Berlin Academy of Arts에 입학 허가(admission)를 받았다. 문장(3)
③ 나치당의 권력 장악 이후 독일에서 작품 전시를 금지당했다(be forbidden). 문장(4)
④ 이전에 누렸던 명성(fame)을 스웨덴에서 ~~되찾았다~~ 되찾지 못했다. 문장(6)
⑤ 가장 가까운 친구인 Gertrud Rose를 그렸다(portray). 문장(7)

[중요 어휘]

□ run	동사 운영하다, 관리하다, 달리다
□ skyrocket	동사 급상승하다, 급등하다
□ recognition	명사 인정, 인식
□ seizure	명사 장악, 점령
□ exhibit	동사 전시하다, 보이다
□ emigrate	동사 이주하다, 이민 가다
□ recapture	동사 되찾다, 탈환하다
□ portray	동사 그리다, 묘사하다
□ embody	동사 구체화하다, 형상화하다, 구현하다
□ type	명사 (표)상, 전형, 본보기
□ represent	동사 표현하다, 나타내다, 대표하다

09 2020년 11월 26번 (정답률 90%) 정답 ②

[지문 끊어 읽기] 육상 선수 Alice Coachman

(1) Alice Coachman was born / in 1923, / in Albany, Georgia, U.S.A.
Alice Coachman은 태어났다 / 1923년에 / 미국 조지아주의 Albany에서

(2) Since she was unable to access athletic training facilities /
그녀가 운동 훈련 시설을 이용할 수 없었기 때문에 /
because of the racism of the time, / she trained /
당시의 인종 차별로 / 그녀는 훈련했다 /
[using what was available to her], / [running barefoot /
명사절(using의 목적어)
자신에게 이용 가능한 것을 사용하면서 / 맨발로 달리면서 /
along the dirt roads / near her home] /
비포장도로를 따라 / 그녀의 집 근처에서 /
and [using homemade equipment / to practice her jumping].
그리고 집에서 만든 장비를 사용하면서 / 그녀의 점프를 연습하기 위해

힌트 동시동작을 나타내는 분사구문 3개가 병렬을 이루고 있음.

(3) Her talent in track and field / was noticeable /
육상 경기에서 그녀의 재능은 / 눈에 띄었다 /
as early as elementary school. 정답 단서
일찍이 초등학교 때

(4) Coachman kept practicing hard / and gained attention /
Coachman은 계속 열심히 연습했다 / 그리고 주목을 받았다 /
with her achievements / in several competitions /
자신의 성취로 / 여러 대회에서 /
during her time in high school and college.
그녀의 고등학교와 대학교 시절 동안

(5) In the 1948 London Olympics, /
1948년 런던 올림픽에서 /
Coachman competed in the high jump, /
Coachman은 높이뛰기에 출전했다 /
reaching 5 feet, 6.5 inches, /
그리고 5피트 6.5인치에 도달했다 /
setting both an Olympic and an American record.
그리고 올림픽 기록과 미국 기록을 둘 다 세웠다

힌트 밑줄 친 부분은 모두 결과를 나타내는 분사구문으로, 주절의 동사 'competed'에 이어, 어떤 일이 발생했는지 순차적으로 해석하면 됨.

(6) This accomplishment made her the first black woman /
5형식V O O·C
이 성과는 그녀를 최초의 흑인 여성으로 만들었다 /
to win an Olympic gold medal.
올림픽 금메달을 딴

(7) She is in nine different Halls of Fame, /
그녀는 9개의 서로 다른 명예의 전당에 올라 있다 /
including the U.S. Olympic Hall of Fame.
미국 올림픽 명예의 전당을 포함하여

(8) Coachman died in 2014, / at the age of 90 / in Georgia /
Coachman은 2014년에 사망했다 / 90세의 나이에 / 조지아주에서 /
after she had dedicated her life to education.
그녀가 그녀의 일생을 교육에 바친 후

[전문 해석]

(1)Alice Coachman은 1923년에 미국 조지아주의 Albany에서 태어났다. (2)그녀가 당시의 인종 차별로 운동 훈련 시설을 이용할 수 없었기 때문에, 그녀는 자신에게 이용 가능한 것을 사용하여 그녀의 집 근처에서 비포장도로를 따라 맨발로 달리고, 점프를 연습하기 위해 집에서 만든 장비를 사용하면서 훈련했다. (3)육상 경기에서 그녀의 재능은 일찍이 초등학교 때(부터) 눈에 띄었다. (4)Coachman은 계속 열심히 연습했고, 그녀의 고등학교와 대학교 시절 동안 여러 대회에서 자신의 성취로 주목을 받았다. (5)1948년 런던 올림픽에서 Coachman은 높이뛰기에 출전하여 5피트 6.5인치에 도달했고, 올림픽 기록과 미국 기록을 둘 다 세웠다. (6)이 성과는 그녀를 올림픽 금메달을 딴 최초의 흑인 여성으로 만들었다. (7)그녀는 미국 올림픽 명예의 전당을 포함하여, 9개의 서로 다른 명예의 전당에 올라 있다. (8)Coachman은 그녀의 일생을 교육에 바친 후, 2014년에 조지아주에서 90세의 나이에 사망했다.

[정답 확인]

Alice Coachman에 관한 다음 글의 내용과 일치하지 않는 것은?

① 집 근처에서 맨발로(barefoot) 달리며 훈련했다. 문장(2)
② 육상 경기(track and field)에서의 재능을 ~~고등학교~~ 초등학교 때부터 보였다. 문장(3)
③ 런던 올림픽에서 높이뛰기(high jump) 올림픽 기록과 미국 기록을 세웠다. 문장(5)
④ 흑인 여성 최초로 올림픽(Olympic) 금메달리스트가 되었다. 문장(6)
⑤ 9개의 명예의 전당(Hall of Fame)에 올랐다. 문장(7)

★중요 문장 (3)에서 Alice의 재능은 초등학교 때부터 눈에 띄었다고 언급됨.

[중요 어휘]

□ access	동사 이용하다, 접근하다
□ athletic	형용사 운동의, 운동선수의
□ facility	명사 시설, 기관
□ racism	명사 인종 차별
□ barefoot	부사 맨발로 / 형용사 맨발의
□ equipment	명사 장비, 설비
□ noticeable	형용사 눈에 띄는, 주목할 만한
□ achievement	명사 성취, 업적
□ competition	명사 대회, 경기, 경쟁
□ compete in	~에 출전하다[참가하다]
□ set a record	기록을 세우다
□ accomplishment	명사 성과, 업적
□ dedicate A to B	A를 B에 바치다[헌신하다]

10 2023년 3월 26번 (정답률 90%) 정답 ④

[지문 끊어 읽기] 영국 사진가 Julia Margaret Cameron

(1) British photographer Julia Margaret Cameron /
영국의 사진가 Julia Margaret Cameron은 /
is considered one of the greatest portrait photographers of the 19th century.
19세기의 위대한 인물 사진가 중 한 명으로 여겨진다

힌트 최상급 표현인 'one of the 최상급+복수명사'는 '가장 ~한 … 중 하나'라는 뜻으로, 주어로 쓰일 때 단수 취급함.

(2) Born in Calcutta, India, into a British family, /
분사구문
인도의 Calcutta의 영국인 가정에서 태어난 /
Cameron was educated in France. 정답 단서-① Cameron은 인도에서 태어나고 프랑스에서 교육받음.
Cameron은 프랑스에서 교육받았다

(3) [Given a camera as a gift / by her daughter /
선물로 카메라를 받고 / 그녀의 딸로부터 /
in December 1863], / 정답 단서-② Cameron은 딸로부터 카메라를 선물로 받음.
1863년 12월에 / [ ]: 분사구문

she quickly and energetically devoted herself /
그녀는 빠르고 열정적으로 열중했다 /
to the art of photography.
사진술에

(4) She cleared out a chicken coop /
V①
그녀는 닭장을 비웠다 /
and converted it into studio space /
V② 선행사
그리고 그곳을 스튜디오 공간으로 바꾸었다 /
where she began to work as a photographer.
관계부사
그곳에서 그녀는 사진가로서 일하기 시작했다

(5) Cameron made illustrative studio photographs, /
Cameron은 화보 같은 스튜디오 사진을 찍었다 /
[convincing friends and family members to pose for photographs, /
병렬①
사진을 위해 친구들과 가족 구성원이 자세를 취하도록 설득하면서 /
fitting them in theatrical costumes / 정답 단서-③ Cameron은 친구들과 가족들에게 연극 의상을 입히고 촬영함.
병렬②
그들에게 연극 의상을 입히면서 /
and carefully composing them into scenes]. [ ]: 분사구문
병렬③
그리고 그들을 장면으로 신중하게 구성하면서

(6) [Criticized for her so-called bad technique /
[ ]: 분사구문
그녀의 소위 서툰 기술로 인해 비판을 받았지만 /
by art critics in her own time], / 정답 단서-④ 서툰 사진 기술로 그녀가 살던 시대의 예술 비평가들에게 비판을 받았음.
그녀가 살던 시대의 예술 비평가들에 의해 /
she ignored convention /
병렬①
그녀는 관습을 무시했다 /
and experimented with composition and focus.
병렬②
그리고 구도와 초점을 실험했다

(7) Later critics appreciated /
V①
후대의 비평가들은 높이 평가했다 /
동명사 정답 단서-⑤ 후대의 비평가들이 정신적 깊이에 가치를 둔 점을 높이 평가함.
[her valuing of spiritual depth over technical perfection] /
동명사의 의미상 주어 [ ]: O①
그녀가 기술적 완벽함보다 정신적 깊이에 가치를 둔 점을 /
and now consider her portraits /
V② O②
그리고 이제는 그녀의 인물 사진들을 생각한다 /
[to be among the finest expressions of the artistic possibilities of the medium]. [ ]: O·C②
그 표현 수단의 예술적인 가능성을 가장 뛰어나게 표현한 작품 중 하나로

[전문 해석]

(1)영국의 사진가 Julia Margaret Cameron은 19세기의 위대한 인물 사진가 중 한 명으로 여겨진다. (2)인도의 Calcutta의 영국인 가정에서 태어난 Cameron은 프랑스에서 교육받았다. (3)1863년 12월에 그녀의 딸로부터 선물로 카메라를 받고 그녀는 빠르고 열정적으로 사진술에 열중했다. (4)그녀는 닭장을 비우고 그곳을 스튜디오 공간으로 바꾸어 그곳에서 사진가로서 일하기 시작했다. (5)Cameron은 사진을 위해 친구들과 가족 구성원이 자세를 취하도록 설득하고 그들에게 연극 의상을 입히고 그들을 장면으로 신중하게 구성하면서 화보 같은 스튜디오 사진을 찍었다. (6)그녀의 소위 서툰 기술로 인해 그녀가 살던 시대의 예술 비평가들에 의해 비판 받았지만, 그녀는 관습을 무시했고 구도와 초점을 실험했다. (7)후대의 비평가들은 그녀가 기술적 완벽함보다 정신적 깊이에 가치를 둔 점을 높이 평가했고 이제는 그녀의 인물 사진들을 그 표현 수단(사진)의 예술적인 가능성을 가장 뛰어나게 표현한 작품 중 하나로 생각한다.

[정답 확인]

Julia Margaret Cameron에 관한 다음 글의 내용과 일치하지 않는 것은?

① 인도에서 태어나고 프랑스에서 교육받았다(be educated). 문장(2)
② 딸로부터 카메라를 선물로(as a gift) 받았다. 문장(3)
③ 친구들과 가족 구성원에게 연극 의상(theatrical costume)을 입히고 촬영했다. 문장(5)
④ ~~능숙한~~ 서툰 사진 기술로 자기 시대 예술 비평가(art critic)에게 ~~인정받았다~~ 받지 못했다. 문장(6)
⑤ 정신적 깊이(spiritual depth)에 가치를 둔 점을 훗날 높이 평가받았다. 문장(7)
★중요 문장 (6)에서 그녀가 살던 시대의 비평가들에게 비판을 받았다고 함.

[중요 어휘]

□ portrait	명사 인물 사진, 초상화
□ born into	(~인 가정)에서 태어난
□ devote oneself to N/V-ing	~에 열중하다[헌신하다]
□ convert	동사 바꾸다, 전환시키다
□ convince A to V	A가 ~하도록 설득하다[납득시키다]
□ fit	동사 (옷을) 입히다, (모양·크기가) 맞다
□ theatrical	형용사 연극의
□ costume	명사 의상, 복장
□ compose	동사 구성하다, 작곡하다
□ so-called	형용사 소위, 이른바
□ convention	명사 관습, 전통, 대회
□ critic	명사 비평가
□ composition	명사 구도, 구성, 작품, 작곡
□ appreciate	동사 높이 평가하다, 진가를 인정하다
□ value	동사 가치를 두다 / 명사 가치
□ spiritual	형용사 정신적인
□ depth	명사 깊이
□ medium	명사 표현 수단, 매체 (media의 단수형)

11 2017년 3월 25번 (정답률 85%) 정답 ③

[지문 끊어 읽기] 정신과 의사 Victor Frankl

(1) Victor Frankl, a famous psychiatrist, /
유명한 정신과 의사인 Victor Frankl은 /
remained head of the neurology department /
계속 신경학 과장이었다 /
at the Vienna Policlinic Hospital for twenty-five years.
Vienna Policlinic Hospital에서 25년 동안

(2) He wrote more than thirty books /
그는 책을 30권 이상 썼다 /
for both professionals and general readers.
전문가와 일반 독자 모두를 위한

(3) He met with politicians, world leaders such as Pope Paul VI, philosophers, students, teachers, and numerous individuals /
그는 정치인, 교황 바오로 6세와 같은 세계적인 지도자, 철학자, 학생, 교사, 그리고 수많은 사람들을 만났다 /
who had read and been inspired by his books.
그의 책을 읽고 영감을 받은

(4) He lectured widely in Europe, the Americas, Australia, Asia, and Africa; /
그는 유럽, 아메리카, 호주, 아시아, 그리고 아프리카에서 널리 강연했다 /
and held professorships at Harvard, Stanford, and the University of Pittsburgh. 정답 단서
그리고 하버드, 스탠퍼드, 그리고 피츠버그 대학교에서 교수직에 재직했다

(5) Even in his nineties, /
90대에도 /
Frankl continued to engage in dialogue with visitors from all over the world /
병렬①
Frankl은 전 세계에서 온 방문객과의 대화에 참여하는 것을 계속했다 /
and to respond personally to some of the hundreds of letters /
병렬②
그리고 수백 통의 편지 중 일부에는 직접 답장을 보내는 것을 /
he received every week.
매주 그가 받은

(6) Twenty-nine universities awarded him honorary degrees, /
4형식V I·O D·O
29개의 대학교가 그에게 명예 학위를 수여하였다 /
and the American Psychiatric Association honored him with the Oskar Pfister Award.
그리고 American Psychiatric Association은 그에게 Oskar Pfister Award를 수여했다

[전문 해석]

(1)유명한 정신과 의사인 Victor Frankl은 Vienna Policlinic Hospital(비엔나 외래 환자 진료부 병원)에서 25년 동안 계속 신경학 과장이었다. (2)그는 전문가와 일반 독자 모두를 위한 책을 30권 이상 썼다. (3)그는 그의 책을 읽고 영감을 받은 정치인, 교황 바오로 6세와 같은 세계적인 지도자, 철학자, 학생, 교사, 그리고 수많은 사람들을 만났다. (4)그는 유럽, 아메리카, 호주, 아시아, 그리고 아프리카에서 널리 강연했다. 그리고 하버드, 스탠퍼드, 그리고 피츠버그 대학교에서 교수직에 재직했다. (5)90대에도 Frankl은 전 세계에서 온 방문객과의 대화에 참여하는 것과 매주 자신이 받은 수백 통의 편지 중 일부에는 직접 답장을 보내는 것을 계속했다. (6)29개의 대학교가 그에게 명예 학위를 수여하였으며, American Psychiatric Association(미국 정신의학회)은 그에게 Oskar Pfister Award(오스카 피스터 상)를 수여했다.

- Victor Frankl(빅터 프랭클, 1905년~1997년): 오스트리아의 정신과 의사
- American Psychiatric Association(미국 정신의학회): 미국의 가장 큰 정신과 의사 및 교육생 전문 조직
- Oskar Pfister Award(오스카 피스터 상): 종교와 정신 의학 분야에 중대한 공헌을 한 사람들에게 영광을 베풀어 주기 위해 1983년부터 미국 정신의학회와 정신건강 성직자협회가 공동으로 수여하는 상

[정답 확인]

Victor Frankl에 관한 다음 글의 내용과 일치하지 않는 것은?

① 전문가(professionals)와 일반 독자(general readers)를 위한 책을 30권 넘게 썼다. 문장(2)
② 자신의 책에서 영감(inspiration)을 받은 많은 사람들을 만났다. 문장(3)
③ 대학교에서 강연을 ~~했지만~~(했고) 교수직(professorships)은 ~~맡지 않았다~~(을 맡았다). 문장(4)
④ 90대에도 방문객(visitors)과의 대화를 계속했다. 문장(5)
⑤ 29개의 대학교에서 명예 학위(honorary degrees)를 받았다. 문장(6)

[중요 어휘]

□ **psychiatrist**	명사 정신과 의사
□ **neurology**	명사 신경학
□ **politician**	명사 정치인
□ **pope**	명사 교황
□ **numerous**	형용사 수많은
□ **lecture**	동사 강연하다
□ **widely**	부사 널리
□ **hold**	동사 (직장·직무에) 재직하다
□ **professorship**	명사 교수직
□ **award**	동사 수여하다 / 명사 상
□ **honorary**	형용사 (학위·지위 등) 명예의
□ **association**	명사 (협)회
□ **honor**	동사 수여하다 / 명사 명예, 명성

힌트 hold는 주로 '붙잡다'의 뜻을 나타내지만 문장 (4)의 hold professorships처럼 직장·직무를 나타내는 말과 함께 쓰일 경우 '(직장·직무에) 재직하다, 있다'로 해석됨.

12 2017년 11월 25번 (정답률 85%) 정답 ④

[지문 끊어 읽기] 물리학자 및 생물학자 Francis Crick

(1) Francis Crick, /
Francis Crick은 /
the Nobel Prize-winning codiscoverer of the structure of the DNA molecule, /
DNA 분자 구조의 공동 발견자로 노벨상을 수상한 /
was born in Northampton, England in 1916.
1916년에 영국 Northampton에서 태어났다

(2) He attended University College London, /
그는 University College London을 다녔다 /
where he studied physics, /
그리고 그곳에서 그는 물리학을 공부했다 /
graduating with a Bachelor of Science degree in 1937.
그리고 1937년에 이학사 학위로 졸업했다

힌트 주절에 이어 계속적 용법의 관계사절과 분사구문(부사절)이 연달아 나옴.

(3) He soon began conducting research toward a Ph.D., /
그는 곧 박사 학위를 위한 연구를 하기 시작했다 /
but his path was interrupted / by the outbreak of World War II.
하지만 그의 계획은 중단되었다 / 제2차 세계대전의 발발로

(4) During the war, / he was involved in naval weapons research, /
전쟁 동안 / 그는 해군 무기 연구에 참여했다 /
working on the development of magnetic and acoustic mines.
자기 음향 기뢰 개발을 위해 노력하면서

(5) After the war, /
전쟁 이후 /
Dr. R. V. Jones, the head of Britain's wartime scientific intelligence, /
영국의 전시 과학 정보 부장인 R. V. Jones 박사는 /
asked Crick to continue the work, /
Crick에게 그 연구를 계속해줄 것을 부탁했다 /
but Crick decided to continue his studies, / this time in biology. (정답 단서)
하지만 Crick은 자신의 학업을 계속하기로 결정했다 / 이번에는 생물학에서

(6) In 1951, / Crick met James Watson, a young American biologist, /
1951년에 / Crick은 젊은 미국인 생물학자인 James Watson을 만났다 /
at the Strangeways Research Laboratory.
Strangeways 연구소에서

(7) They formed a collaborative working relationship /
그들은 공동 연구 관계를 형성했다 /
solving the mysteries of the structure of DNA.
DNA 구조의 비밀을 푸는

[전문 해석]

(1)DNA 분자 구조의 공동 발견자로 노벨상을 수상한 Francis Crick은 1916년에 영국 Northampton(노샘프턴)에서 태어났다. (2)그는 University College London을 다녔고, 그곳에서 물리학을 공부했으며, 1937년에 이학사 학위로 졸업했다. (3)그는 곧 박사 학위를 위한 연구를 하기 시작했지만, 그의 계획은 제2차 세계대전의 발발로 중단되었다. (4)전쟁 동안 그는 자기 음향 기뢰 개발을 위해 노력하면서 해군 무기 연구에 참여했다. (5)전쟁(이 끝난) 이후 영국의 전시 과학 정보 부장인 R. V. Jones 박사는 Crick에게 그 연구를 계속해줄 것을 부탁했지만, Crick은 이번에는 생물학에서 자신의 학업을 계속하기로 결정했다. (6)1951년에 Crick은 Strangeways 연구소에서 젊은 미국인 생물학자인 James Watson을 만났다. (7)그들은 DNA 구조의 비밀을 푸는 공동 연구 관계를 형성했다.

- magnetic and acoustic mine(자기 음향 기뢰): 적의 함선을 파괴하기 위하여 물속이나 물 위에 설치한 폭탄의 종류로 표적의 자기장, 음향 및 압력장(場)의 결합에 의하여 일정한 거리에서 폭발하도록 설계되었다.

[정답 확인]

Francis Crick에 관한 다음 글의 내용과 일치하지 않는 것은?

① University College London에서 물리학(physics)을 공부했다. 문장(2)
② 제2차 세계대전의 발발(outbreak of World War II)로 박사 학위를 위한 연구가 중단됐다. 문장(3)
③ 전쟁 중 해군 무기 연구(naval weapons research)에 참여했다. 문장(4)
④ Dr. R. V. Jones의 요청으로 전공을 생물학(biology)으로 ~~바꿨다~~(바꾼 것은 아니다). 문장(5)
⑤ James Watson과 함께 DNA 구조(the structure of DNA)의 비밀을 푸는 일을 했다. 문장(7)

★중요 Dr. R. V. Jones는 (해군 무기) 연구를 계속해줄 것을 부탁한 것이고, Crick이 스스로 생물학을 공부하기로 결정한 것임.

[중요 어휘]

□ **codiscoverer**	명사 공동 발견자
□ **conduct**	동사 (연구 등을) 하다, 행동하다
□ **outbreak**	명사 (전쟁 등의) 발발, 시작
□ **magnetic**	형용사 자기(장)의, 자석의
□ **acoustic**	형용사 음향의, 청각의
□ **wartime**	형용사 전시의(전쟁 중의)
□ **intelligence**	명사 정보, 기밀, 정보요원들
□ **collaborative**	형용사 공동의

13 2021년 9월 26번 (정답률 80%) 정답 ④

[지문 끊어 읽기] 의사 Patricia Bath

(1) Patricia Bath spent her life / advocating for eye health.
Patricia Bath는 자신의 삶을 보냈다 / 눈 건강을 옹호하는 데

(2) Born in 1942, / she was raised /
1942년에 태어난 / 그녀는 길러졌다 /

in the Harlem area of New York City.
뉴욕 시의 Harlem 지역에서

(3) She graduated / from Howard University's College of Medicine /
그녀는 졸업했다 / Howard 대학교의 의과 대학을 /
in 1968.
1968년에

힌트 'It is ~ that' 강조 구문으로 시간 부사구인 'during ~ intern'을 강조한 문장임.

힌트 여기서 see는 '보다'라기보다는 '~을 알게 되다'의 의미임.

(4) It was during her time as a medical intern / that she saw /
의과 인턴으로서의 그녀의 시간 동안이었다 / 그녀가 알게 된 것은 /
that many poor people and Black people were becoming blind /
명사절 접속사
많은 가난한 사람과 흑인이 눈이 멀게 되는 것을 /
because of the lack of eye care.
눈 관리 부족 때문에

(5) She decided / to concentrate on ophthalmology, /
그녀는 결심했다 / 안과학에 집중하기로 /
which is the branch of medicine /
계속적 용법
그것은 의학의 분야이다 /
that works with eye diseases and disorders.
주격 관계대명사
눈 질병과 장애를 연구하는

(6) As her career progressed, /
그녀의 경력이 쌓이면서 /
Bath taught students in medical schools /
Bath는 의과 대학의 학생들을 가르쳤다 /
and trained other doctors.
그리고 다른 의사들을 교육했다

(7) In 1976, / she co-founded /
1976년에 / 그녀는 공동 설립했다 /
정답단서
the American Institute for the Prevention of Blindness (AiPB) /
미국시각장애예방협회(AiPB)를 /
동격의 that
with the basic principle / that "eyesight is a basic human right."
기본 원칙으로 / '시력은 기본 인권이다'라는

(8) In the 1980s, / Bath began researching the use of lasers /
1980년대에 / Bath는 레이저의 사용을 연구하기 시작했다 /
in eye treatments.
눈 치료에서

(9) Her research led /
그녀의 연구는 이르게 했다 /

힌트 여기서 to는 전치사이고 전치사의 목적어로 동명사 becoming이 왔음. 동명사 앞에 her은 동명사의 의미상의 주어임.

to her becoming the first African-American female doctor /
의미상의 주어 동명사
그녀가 최초의 아프리카계 미국인 여성 의사가 되는 데 /
to receive a patent for a medical device.
형용사적 용법
의료 장비 특허를 받은

[전문 해석]

(1)Patricia Bath는 눈 건강을 옹호하는 데 자신의 삶을 보냈다. (2)1942년에 태어난 그녀는 뉴욕 시의 Harlem 지역에서 길러졌다. (3)그녀는 1968년에 Howard 대학교의 의과 대학을 졸업했다. (4)그녀가 많은 가난한 사람과 흑인이 눈 관리 부족 때문에 눈이 멀게 되는 것을 알게 된 것은 의과 인턴으로서의 그녀의 시간 동안이었다. (5)그녀는 안과학에 집중하기로 결심했는데, 그것은 눈 질병과 장애를 연구하는 의학의 분야이다. (6)그녀의 경력이 쌓이면서, Bath는 의과 대학의 학생들을 가르치고 다른 의사들을 교육했다. (7)1976년에 그녀는 '시력은 기본 인권이다'라는 기본 원칙으로 미국시각장애예방협회(AiPB)를 공동 설립했다. (8)1980년대에 Bath는 눈 치료에서 레이저의 사용을 연구하기 시작했다. (9)그녀의 연구는 그녀가 의료 장비 특허를 받은 최초의 아프리카계 미국인 여성 의사가 되는 데 이르게 했다.

[정답 확인]

Patricia Bath에 관한 다음 글의 내용과 일치하지 않는 것은?

① 뉴욕 시의 Harlem 지역에서 성장했다(be raised). 문장(2)
② 1968년에 의과 대학을 졸업했다(graduate from). 문장(3)
③ 의과 대학(medical schools)에서 학생을 가르쳤다. 문장(6)
④ 1976년에 AiPB를 ~~단독~~ 공동으로 설립했다(found). 문장(7)
⑤ 의료 장비 특허(patent)를 받았다. 문장(9)

★ 중요 문장 (7)에서 그녀가 AiPB를 공동 설립했다고(co-founded) 언급됨.

[중요 어휘]

□ **advocate**	동사 옹호하다, 지지하다
□ **ophthalmology**	명사 안과학
□ **branch**	명사 분야, 부서
□ **disorder**	명사 (신체 기능의) 장애, 엉망, 무질서
□ **treatment**	명사 치료, 처치, 대우
□ **patent**	명사 특허

14 2023년 6월 26번 (정답률 80%) 정답 ④

[지문 끊어 읽기] John Ray

(1) Born in 1627 / in Black Notley, Essex, England, /
1627년에 태어난 / 잉글랜드 Essex주 Black Notley에서 /
John Ray was the son of the village blacksmith. 정답 단서-① 마을 대장장이의 아들로 태어남.
John Ray는 마을 대장장이의 아들이었다

(2) At 16, / he went to Cambridge University, /
16세에 / 그는 Cambridge 대학교에 들어갔다 /
where he studied widely / and lectured on topics /
그곳에서 그는 폭넓게 공부했다 / 그리고 주제에 대해 강의를 했다 /
from Greek to mathematics, /
그리스어부터 수학에 이르는 /
before joining the priesthood in 1660. 정답 단서-② 성직자가 되기 전 Cambridge 대학에 다녔음.
1660년에 사제직으로 들어서기 전에

(3) To recover from an illness in 1650, /
1650년에 병에서 회복하기 위해 /
he had taken to nature walks / 정답 단서-③ 병에서 회복하기 위해 자연 산책을 시작함.
그는 자연을 산책하기 시작했다 /
and developed an interest in botany.
그리고 식물학에 대한 관심을 키웠다

(4) Accompanied by his wealthy student and supporter Francis Willughby, /
그의 부유한 학생이자 후원자인 Francis Willughby와 동행하며 /
Ray toured Britain and Europe in the 1660s, / 정답 단서-④ 후원자 Francis Willughby와 동행하여 여행함.
Ray는 1660년대에 영국과 유럽을 여행했다 /
studying and collecting plants and animals.
식물과 동물을 연구하고 수집하면서

(5) He married Margaret Oakley in 1673 /
병렬①
그는 1673년에 Margaret Oakley와 결혼했다 /
and, after leaving Willughby's household, /
그리고 Willughby의 집안을 떠난 후에 /
lived quietly in Black Notley / to the age of 77.
병렬②
Black Notley에서 조용히 살았다 / 77세까지

(6) He spent his later years studying samples /
그는 표본을 연구하면서 말년을 보냈다 /
in order to assemble plant and animal catalogues. 정답 단서-⑤ 동식물 목록을 만들기 위해 말년에 표본을 연구함.
동식물 목록을 정리하기 위해

(7) He wrote more than twenty works / on theology and his travels, /
그는 20편 이상의 저서를 썼다 / 신학과 그의 여행에 관해서 /
as well as on plants and their form and function.
B as well as A: A뿐만 아니라 B도
식물과 그 형태 및 기능뿐만 아니라

[전문 해석]

(1)1627년 잉글랜드 Essex주 Black Notley에서 태어난 John Ray는 마을 대장장이의 아들이었다. (2)1660년에 사제직으로 들어서기 전에, 16세에 그는 Cambridge 대학교에 들어가서 폭넓게 공부하고 그리스어부터 수학에 이르는 주제에 대해 강의를 했다. (3)1650년에 병에서 회복하기 위해, 그는 자연을 산책하기 시작했고 식물학에 대한 관심을 키웠다. (4)그의 부유한 학생이자 후원자인 Francis Willughby와 동행하며 Ray는 식물과 동물을 연구하고 수집하면서 1660년대에 영국과 유럽을 여행했다. (5)그는 1673년 Margaret Oakley와 결혼했고, Willughby의 집안을 떠난 후에는 Black Notley에서 77세까지 조용히 살았다. (6)그는 동식물 목록을 정리하기 위해 표본을 연구하면서 말년을 보냈다. (7)그는 식물과 그 형태 및 기능뿐만

아니라 신학과 그의 여행에 관해서 20편 이상의 저서를 썼다.

[정답 확인]

John Ray에 관한 다음 글의 내용과 일치하지 않는 것은?

① 마을 대장장이(blacksmith)의 아들이었다. 문장(1)
② 성직자의 길(priesthood)로 들어서기 전 Cambridge 대학에 다녔다. 문장(2)
③ 병에서 회복하기(recover) 위해 자연을 산책하기 시작했다. 문장(3)
④ Francis Willughby에게 후원받아 ~~홀로~~ 같이 유럽을 여행하였다. 문장(4)
⑤ 동식물의 목록(catalogue)을 만들기 위해 표본을 연구하며 말년을 보냈다. 문장(6)

★ 중요 문장 (4)에서 후원자인 Francis Willughby와 영국과 유럽 여행을 동행했다고 함.

[중요 어휘]

□ blacksmith	명사 대장장이
□ widely	부사 폭넓게, 널리
□ priesthood	명사 사제직, 성직
□ illness	명사 병, 질환
□ take to N	~하기 시작하다
□ botany	명사 식물학
□ accompany	동사 ~와 동행하다[동반하다]
□ household	명사 집안, 가정
□ sample	명사 표본, 샘플
□ assemble	동사 정리하다, 조립하다
□ catalogue	명사 목록, 카탈로그
□ work	명사 저서, 작품
□ theology	명사 신학

15 2023년 11월 26번 (정답률 85%) 정답 ③

[지문 끊어 읽기] 아프리카계 미국인 Maggie L. Walker

(1) Maggie L. Walker achieved national prominence /
Maggie L. Walker는 전국적인 명성을 얻었다 /
as a businesswoman and community leader.
사업가와 지역 사회 리더로서

(2) She was among the earliest Black students /
그녀는 초기 흑인 학생들 중 한 명이었다 /
to attend newly-established public schools for African Americans.
아프리카계 미국인들을 위해 새롭게 설립된 공립 학교에 다닌

정답 단서-① 아프리카계 미국인들을 위해 설립된 공립 학교에 다녔음.

(3) After graduating, / she worked as a teacher /
분사구문(=After she graduated)
졸업 후에 / 그녀는 교사로 일했다 /
for three years at the Valley School, / where she had studied.
Valley School에서 3년간 / 그녀가 공부했었던

힌트 주절의 동사 worked보다 이전에 공부한 것이므로 과거완료(대과거)를 사용함.

정답 단서-② 졸업 후에 자신이 공부했던 Valley School에서 교사로 일했음.

(4) In the early 1900s, / Virginia banks owned by white bankers /
1900년대 초반에 / 백인 은행가들에 의해 소유된 Virginia 은행들은 /
were unwilling to do business with African American organizations or individuals.
아프리카계 미국인의 단체 혹은 개인들과 거래하는 것을 꺼려했다

(5) The racial discrimination by white bankers /
백인 은행가들에 의한 인종 차별은 /
drove her to study banking and financial laws.
그녀가 은행 금융법을 공부하게 만들었다

정답 단서-③ 백인 은행가들의 인종 차별로 인해 은행 금융법 공부를 시작하게 됨.

(6) She established a newspaper /
그녀는 신문사를 설립했다 /
to promote closer communication /
부사적 용법-목적
더 긴밀한 의사소통을 장려하기 위해 /
between the charitable organization she belonged to and the public.
선행사 / 목적격 관계대명사절
그녀가 속해 있던 자선 단체와 대중들 사이에

정답 단서-④ 자선 단체와 대중 간의 소통 장려를 위해 신문사를 설립했음.

(7) Soon after, / she founded the St. Luke Penny Savings Bank, /
곧이어 / 그녀는 St. Luke Penny Savings Bank를 설립했다 /
which survived the Great Depression /
관계대명사(계속적 용법) 병렬①
그리고 그것은 대공황에서 살아남았다 /
and merged with two other banks.
병렬②
그리고 두 개의 다른 은행들과 합병했다

정답 단서-⑤ 그녀가 설립한 St. Luke Penny Savings Bank는 대공황에서 살아남아 다른 은행들과 합병했음.

(8) It thrived /
그것은 번창했다 /
as the oldest continually African American-operated bank /
지속적으로 아프리카계 미국인에 의해 운영되는 가장 오래된 은행으로 /
until 2009.
2009년까지

(9) Walker achieved successes /
Walker는 성공을 거두었다 /
with the vision to make improvements /
개선을 하고자 하는 비전으로 /
in the way of life for African Americans.
아프리카계 미국인들을 위한 삶의 방식에서

[전문 해석]

(1)Maggie L. Walker는 사업가와 지역 사회 리더로서 전국적인 명성을 얻었다. (2)그녀는 아프리카계 미국인들을 위해 새롭게 설립된 공립 학교에 다닌 초기 흑인 학생들 중 한 명이었다. (3)졸업 후에, 그녀가 공부했었던 Valley School에서 3년간 교사로 일했다. (4)1900년대 초반에 백인 은행가들에 의해 소유된 Virginia 은행들은 아프리카계 미국인의 단체 혹은 개인들과 거래하는 것을 꺼려했다. (5)백인 은행가들에 의한 인종 차별은 그녀가 은행 금융법을 공부하게 만들었다. (6)그녀는 그녀가 속해 있던 자선 단체와 대중들 사이에 더 긴밀한 의사소통을 장려하기 위해 신문사를 설립했다. (7)곧이어, 그녀는 St. Luke Penny Savings Bank를 설립했는데, 그것은 대공황에서 살아남았고 두 개의 다른 은행들과 합병했다. (8)그것은 2009년까지 지속적으로 아프리카계 미국인에 의해 운영되는 가장 오래된 은행으로 번창했다. (9)Walker는 아프리카계 미국인들을 위한 삶의 방식에서 개선을 하고자 하는 비전으로 성공을 거두었다.

[정답 확인]

Maggie L. Walker에 관한 다음 글의 내용과 일치하지 않는 것은?

① 아프리카계 미국인을 위해 설립된(be established) 학교에 다녔다. 문장(2)
② 졸업 후 자신이 공부했던 학교에서 교사로 일했다. 문장(3)
③ 인종 차별(racial discrimination)로 인해 은행 금융법 공부를 ~~시작할 수 없었다~~ 시작했다. 문장(5)
④ 자선 단체(charitable organization)와 대중 간의 소통을 장려하고자 신문사를 설립했다. 문장(6)
⑤ 그녀가 설립한(found) 은행은 대공황(the Great Depression)에서 살아남아 다른 은행들과 합병했다(merge). 문장(7)

[중요 어휘]

□ prominence	명사 명성, 유명함, 두드러짐
□ own	동사 소유하다 / 형용사 ~ 자신의
□ be unwilling to V	~하는 것을 꺼리다
□ racial discrimination	인종 차별
□ drive A to V	A가 ~하게 만들다
□ charitable	형용사 자선의, 자비로운
□ found	동사 설립하다 (found-founded-founded)
□ merge	동사 합병하다, 통합하다
□ thrive	동사 번창하다, 번영하다

16 2024년 3월 26번 (정답률 90%) 정답 ④

[지문 끊어 읽기] 헝가리계 미국인 공학자 Theodore von Kármán

(1) Theodore von Kármán, a Hungarian-American engineer, /
헝가리계 미국인 공학자 Theodore von Kármán은 /
was one of the greatest minds of the twentieth century.
20세기의 가장 위대한 지성인 중 한 명이었다

(2) He was born in Hungary / and at an early age, /
그는 헝가리에서 태어났다 / 그리고 어린 시절에 /

문제편 p.109

he showed a talent for math and science. 정답 단서-① 어린 시절에 수학과 과학에서 재능을 보였음.
그는 수학과 과학에서 재능을 보였다

(3) In 1908, / he received a doctoral degree in engineering /
1908년에 / 그는 공학 박사 학위를 받았다 /
at the University of Göttingen in Germany. 정답 단서-② University of Göttingen에서 공학 박사 학위를 받음.
독일의 University of Göttingen에서

(4) In the 1920s, / he began traveling /
1920년대에 / 그는 다니기 시작했다 /
as a lecturer and consultant to industry. 정답 단서-③ 1920년대에 업계의 강연자 겸 자문 위원으로 다니기 시작함.
업계의 강연자 겸 자문 위원으로

(5) He was invited to the United States /
그는 미국에 초청을 받았다 /
to advise engineers / on the design of a wind tunnel /
부사적 용법(결과)
공학자들에게 조언을 했다 / 윈드 터널의 설계에 관한 /
at California Institute of Technology (Caltech). 정답 단서-④ Caltech에 초청을 받아 공학자들에게 윈드 터널의 설계에 관한 조언을 했음.
캘리포니아 공과 대학(Caltech)에서

(6) He became the director /
그는 소장이 되었다 /
of the Guggenheim Aeronautical Laboratory at Caltech / in 1930.
Caltech의 Guggenheim Aeronautical Laboratory의 / 1930년에

(7) Later, / he was awarded the National Medal of Science /
이후에 / 그는 National Medal of Science를 받았다 / 정답 단서-⑤ 과학과 공학에서 National Medal of Science를 받았음.
for his leadership in science and engineering.
과학과 공학에서의 그의 리더십으로

[전문 해석]

(1)헝가리계 미국인 공학자 Theodore von Kármán은 20세기의 가장 위대한 지성인 중 한 명이었다. (2)그는 헝가리에서 태어났고 어린 시절에 수학과 과학에서 재능을 보였다. (3)1908년에 그는 독일의 University of Göttingen에서 공학 박사 학위를 받았다. (4)1920년대에 그는 업계의 강연자 겸 자문 위원으로 다니기 시작했다. (5)그는 미국에 초청을 받아 캘리포니아 공과 대학(Caltech)에서 공학자들에게 윈드 터널의 설계에 관한 조언을 했다. (6)그는 1930년에 Caltech의 Guggenheim Aeronautical Laboratory의 소장이 되었다. (7)이후에, 그는 과학과 공학에서의 그의 리더십으로 National Medal of Science를 받았다.

[정답 확인]

Theodore von Kármán에 관한 다음 글의 내용과 일치하지 않는 것은?

① 어린 시절 수학과 과학에 재능(talent)을 보였다. 문장(2)
② University of Göttingen에서 공학 박사 학위(a doctoral degree)를 받았다. 문장(3)
③ 1920년대에 강연자(lecturer) 겸 자문 위원(consultant)으로 다니기 시작했다. 문장(4)
④ Caltech~~의 공학자를 초청하여~~ 조언(advice)을 ~~구했다~~. 문장(5)
에 초청을 받아 공학자들에게 / 했다
⑤ National Medal of Science를 받았다(be awarded). 문장(7)
✱중요 문장 (5)에서 Theodore von Kármán은 미국에 초청을 받아 Caltech에서 공학자들에게 윈드 터널의 설계에 관한 조언을 했다고 함.

[중요 어휘]

☐ **mind**	명사 지성인, 마음, 정신
☐ **doctoral degree**	박사 학위
☐ **engineering**	명사 공학, 공학 기술
☐ **travel**	동사 다니다, 이동하다, 여행하다
☐ **consultant**	명사 자문 위원, 상담가
☐ **advise**	동사 조언하다, 충고하다, (정식으로) 알리다

17 2024년 6월 26번 (정답률 95%) 정답 ⑤

[지문 끊어 읽기] Henry David Thoreau

(1) Henry David Thoreau was born /
Henry David Thoreau는 태어났다 /
in Concord, Massachusetts in 1817.
1817년 Massachusetts주의 Concord에서

(2) When he was 16, / he entered Harvard College.
그가 16세가 되었을 때 / 그는 Harvard 대학에 입학했다

(3) After graduating, / Thoreau worked as a schoolteacher / 정답 단서-① Thoreau는 졸업 후에 학교 교사로 근무함.
졸업 후 / Thoreau는 학교 교사로 일했다 /
but he quit after two weeks.
하지만 그는 2주 후에 그만두었다

(4) In June of 1838 / he set up a school with his brother John.
1838년 6월에 / 그는 그의 형제 John과 학교를 세웠다

(5) However, /
하지만 /
힌트 추상명사 뒤에 쓰인 of는 추상명사의 내용을 풀어 설명하는 동명사구를 이끄는 동격의 전치사로 활용됨. 이 문장에서 'becoming a nature poet'은 앞에 언급된 'hopes'를 자세히 설명하고 있음.
he had hopes of becoming a nature poet. 정답 단서-② Thoreau는 자연 시인이 되기를 희망함.
동명사(전치사 of의 목적어)
그는 자연 시인이 되고자 하는 희망을 가지고 있었다

(6) In 1845, /
1845년 /
he moved into a small self-built house / near Walden Pond.
그는 직접 지은 작은 집으로 이사했다 / Walden 연못 근처에

(7) At Walden, / Thoreau did an incredible amount of reading.
Walden에서 / Thoreau는 엄청난 양의 독서를 했다 정답 단서-③ Thoreau는 Walden에서 엄청난 양의 독서를 함.

(8) The journal he wrote there /
S, 선행사 목적격 관계대명사절
그가 그곳에서 쓴 저널이 /
became the source of his most famous book, *Walden*.
V(2형식) S.C
그의 가장 유명한 저서인 *Walden*의 원천이 되었다

(9) In his later life, /
그의 인생 후반부에서 /
Thoreau traveled to the Maine woods, to Cape Cod, and to Canada.
Thoreau는 Maine 숲으로, Cape Cod로, 그리고 캐나다로 여행을 떠났다

정답 단서-④ Thoreau는 43세에 여행을 마치고 Concord로 돌아옴.
(10) At the age of 43, / he ended his travels and returned to Concord.
V① V②
43세의 나이에 / 그는 여행을 마치고 Concord로 돌아왔다

(11) Although his works were not widely read during his lifetime, /
비록 그의 작품이 그의 일생 동안 널리 읽히지 않았지만 / 정답 단서-⑤ Thoreau의 작품은 그의 일생 동안 널리 읽히지 않았음.
he never stopped writing, /
그는 집필을 멈추지 않았다 /
and his works fill 20 volumes.
그리고 그의 작품은 20권에 달한다

[전문 해석]

(1)Henry David Thoreau는 1817년 Massachusetts주의 Concord에서 태어났다. (2)그가 16세가 되었을 때, 그는 Harvard 대학에 입학했다. (3)졸업 후, Thoreau는 학교 교사로 일했지만 2주 후에 그만두었다. (4)1838년 6월에 그는 그의 형제 John과 학교를 세웠다. (5)하지만 그는 자연 시인이 되고자 하는 희망을 가지고 있었다. (6)1845년, 그는 Walden 연못 근처에 직접 지은 작은 집으로 이사했다. (7)Walden에서 Thoreau는 엄청난 양의 독서를 했다. (8)그가 그곳에서 쓴 저널이 그의 가장 유명한 저서인 *Walden*(숲 속의 생활)의 원천이 되었다. (9)그의 인생 후반부에서, Thoreau는 Maine 숲으로, Cape Cod로, 그리고 캐나다로 여행을 떠났다. (10)43세의 나이에, 그는 여행을 마치고 Concord로 돌아왔다. (11)비록 그의 작품이 그의 일생 동안 널리 읽히지 않았지만, 그는 집필을 멈추지 않았고, 그의 작품은 20권에 달한다.

[정답 확인]

Henry David Thoreau에 관한 다음 글의 내용과 일치하지 않는 것은?

① 졸업한 후에 교사(schoolteacher)로 일했다. 문장(3)
② 자연 시인(nature poet)이 되기를 희망했다. 문장(5)
③ Walden에서 엄청난 양의 독서(reading)를 했다. 문장(7)
④ 43세에 여행을 마치고 Concord로 돌아왔다(return). 문장(10)
⑤ 그의 작품은 그의 일생(lifetime) 동안 널리 ~~읽혔다~~. 문장(11)
읽히지 않았다
✱중요 문장 (11)에서 Thoreau의 작품은 그의 일생 동안 널리 읽히지 않았다고 함.

[중요 어휘]

☐ **quit**	동사 그만두다, (살던 곳을) 떠나다 (quit-quit-quit)
☐ **set up**	세우다, 건립하다, 설치하다 (set- set- set)
☐ **pond**	명사 연못
☐ **incredible**	형용사 엄청난, 놀랄만한, 대단한

☐ journal	명사 저널, 일기
☐ volume	명사 (전집 따위의) 권, 책, (~의) 양

18 2024년 9월 26번 (정답률 95%) 정답 ④

[지문 끊어 읽기] 현대 생태학의 선구자 Charles Elton

(1) Born in the English city of Liverpool, /
Liverpool이라는 영국의 도시에서 태어난 /
Charles Elton studied zoology /
Charles Elton은 동물학을 공부했다 / 정답 단서-① Charles Elton은 대학에서 동물학을 공부했음.
under Julian Huxley at Oxford University / from 1918 to 1922.
Oxford 대학의 Julian Huxley 아래에서 / 1918년부터 1922년까지

(2) After graduating, / he began teaching as a part-time instructor /
S V① O①
졸업 후에 / 그는 시간제 강사로서 가르치는 일을 시작했다 / 정답 단서-② 그는 대학을 졸업한 후에 가르치는 일을 시작했음.
and had a long and distinguished teaching career / at Oxford /
V② O②
그리고 장기간의 훌륭한 교수 경력을 가졌다 / Oxford 대학에서 /
from 1922 to 1967.
1922년부터 1967년까지

(3) After a series of arctic expeditions with Huxley, /
Huxley와 함께 일련의 북극 탐험 후에 /
he worked with a fur-collecting and trading company /
S V①
그는 모피 수집 및 무역 회사와 함께 일했다 /
as a biological consultant, / 정답 단서-③ 그는 생물학 컨설턴트로서 모피 수집 및 무역 회사와 함께 일했음.
생물학 컨설턴트로서 /
and examined the company's records /
V②
그리고 그 회사의 기록들을 검토했다 /
to study animal populations.
부사적 용법(목적)
동물 개체군을 연구하기 위해

(4) In 1927, / 힌트 뒤따르는 '전치사+관계대명사'로 시작하는 관계사절의 선행사로서, in which는 'and in that book(그리고 그 책에서)'의 의미로 해석할 수 있음.
1927년에 /
he wrote [his first and most important book, *Animal Ecology*], /
그는 그의 처음이자 가장 중요한 저서인 *Animal Ecology*를 썼다 / 정답 단서-④ *Animal Ecology*는 Charles Elton이 1927년에 처음으로 쓴 저서임.
in which he demonstrated the nature of food chains and cycles.
전치사+관계대명사
그리고 거기서 그는 먹이 사슬과 순환의 본질을 설명했다

(5) In 1932, / 힌트 help는 to부정사를 목적어로 취하는 것이 원칙이나, 흔히 to를 생략한 원형부정사의 형태로 쓰이기도 함.
1932년에 /
he helped [establish the Bureau of Animal Population at Oxford].
S V [ ]:O
그는 Oxford 대학에 Bureau of Animal Population을 설립하는 것을 도왔다
★중요 문장 (6)은 Elton이 동물 개체군 연구소를 설립했던 해와 같은 해인 1932년을 나타냄.

(6) In the same year / 1932년에 *Journal of Animal Ecology*의 편집자가 됨.
같은 해에 /
he became the editor of the new *Journal of Animal Ecology*. 정답 단서-⑤
S V S.C(명사구)
그는 새로운 *Journal of Animal Ecology*의 편집자가 되었다

(7) Throughout his career, / Elton wrote six books /
그의 경력 동안 / Elton은 여섯 권의 책을 썼다 / V①
and played a major role /
V②
그리고 중대한 역할을 했다 /
in [shaping the modern science of ecology]. [ ]: 동명사구
전치사
현대 생태학을 형성하는 데 있어

[전문 해석]

(1)Liverpool이라는 영국의 도시에서 태어난 Charles Elton은 1918년부터 1922년까지 Oxford 대학의 Julian Huxley 아래에서 동물학을 공부했다. (2)졸업 후에, 그는 시간제 강사로서 가르치는 일을 시작했고, 1922년부터 1967년까지 Oxford 대학에서 장기간의 훌륭한 교수 경력을 가졌다. (3)Huxley와 함께 일련의 북극 탐험 후에, 그는 생물학 컨설턴트로서 모피 수집 및 무역 회사와 함께 일했고, 동물 개체군을 연구하기 위해 그 회사의 기록들을 검토했다. (4)1927년에, 그는 그의 처음이자 가장 중요한 저서인 *Animal Ecology*를 썼고, 거기서 그는 먹이 사슬과 순환의 본질을 설명했다. (5)1932년에, 그는 Oxford 대학에 Bureau of Animal Population을 설립하는 것을 도왔다. (6)같은 해에, 그는 새로운 *Journal of Animal Ecology*의 편집자가 되었다. (7)그의 경력 동안, Elton은 여섯 권의 책을 썼고, 현대 생태학을 형성하는 데 있어 중대한 역할을 했다.

[정답 확인]

Charles Elton에 관한 다음 글의 내용과 일치하지 않는 것은?

① 대학에서 동물학(zoology)을 공부했다. 문장(1)
② 대학 졸업 후 가르치는 일(teaching)을 시작했다. 문장(2)
③ 생물학 컨설턴트(biological consultant)로서 한 회사와 함께 일했다. 문장(3)
④ ~~마지막으로~~ 처음으로 쓴 저서는 *Animal Ecology*였다. 문장(4)
⑤ 1932년에 *Journal of Animal Ecology*의 편집자(editor)가 되었다. 문장(5), (6)

[중요 어휘]

☐ zoology	명사 동물학
☐ instructor	명사 강사, 교사
☐ distinguished	형용사 훌륭한, 뛰어난
☐ career	명사 경력, 직업
☐ a series of	일련의
☐ arctic	형용사 북극의
☐ expedition	명사 탐험, 원정
☐ fur	명사 모피, 털
☐ biological	형용사 생물학의
☐ consultant	명사 컨설턴트, 고문
☐ examine	동사 검토하다, 살펴보다
☐ population	명사 개체군, 개체수
☐ demonstrate	동사 설명하다, 입증하다
☐ nature	명사 본질, 특질
☐ food chain	명사 먹이 사슬
☐ establish	동사 설립하다, 확립하다
☐ editor	명사 편집자
☐ shape	동사 형성하다, 구체화하다

10 안내문

01 2020년 11월 27번 (정답률 95%) 정답 ⑤

[중요 구문] 2020 쓰레기 없는 날 행사

(2) Zero Waste Day (ZWD) 2020 / is an opportunity / for you /
2020 쓰레기 없는 날(ZWD)은 / 기회입니다 / 여러분이 / (의미상의 주어)
[to clean out your attic and donate items for reuse]. [ ]: 형용사적 용법 (병렬① 병렬②)
여러분의 다락방을 치우고 재사용을 위한 물품을 기부할

(15) If an item isn't accepted, / please be prepared / to take it home.
만약 물품이 거절되면 / 준비를 해 주십시오 / 그것을 집으로 가져갈

(16) There is no place / for you / to drop off garbage.
장소가 없습니다 / 여러분이 / 쓰레기를 버릴 (의미상의 주어, 형용사적 용법)

[전문 해석]

(1)2020 쓰레기 없는 날
(2)2020 쓰레기 없는 날(ZWD)은 여러분이 여러분의 다락방을 치우고 재사용을 위한 물품을 기부할 기회입니다.
(3)언제 & 어디서:
(4)11월의 첫 번째 토요일 (2020년 11월 7일),
(5)오전 9시 — 오후 12시 (비가 오든, 날이 좋든) (rain or shine)
(6)400 Union 광장에서
(7)받는 물품:
(8) • 입을 수 있는 의류/신발
(9)모든 치수의 의류와 신발은 '반드시 건조된 상태여야 합니다'. All sizes of clothes and shoes MUST BE DRY.
(10) • 침구류(베개, 담요, 또는 매트리스 커버) Bedding (pillows, blankets, or mattress covers)
(11)해지거나 찢어진 것은 괜찮지만, 어떠한 기름 얼룩도 허용되지 않습니다. Worn or torn is fine, but no oil stains are allowed.
(12) • 전자 기기(컴퓨터, 노트북, 또는 휴대폰) Electronics (computers, laptops, or cell phones)
(13)기기에 저장된 모든 정보는 삭제되어야 합니다. All data on the device must be deleted.
(14)주의 사항: If an item isn't accepted, please be prepared to take it home.
(15)만약 물품이 (접수가) 거절되면, 그것을 집으로 가져갈 준비를 해 주십시오. (16)여러분이 (현장에서) 쓰레기를 버릴 장소가 없습니다. 정답 단서 There is no place for you to drop off garbage.
(17)ZWD는 모두에게 열려 있습니다!
(18)더 많은 정보를 원하시면, www.zwd.org를 방문해 주세요.

[정답 확인]

Zero Waste Day 2020에 관한 다음 안내문의 내용과 일치하지 않는 것은?
① 우천 시에도 행사가 예정대로 진행된다. 문장(5)
② 의류와 신발은 건조된(dry) 상태의 것만 받는다(accept). 문장(9)
③ 해지거나(worn) 찢어진(torn) 침구류도 기부가 가능하다. 문장(10), (11)
④ 전자 기기(electronics)에 저장된 모든 정보는 삭제되어야(must be deleted) 한다. 문장(12), (13)
⑤ 기부 물품 접수가 거절되면 현장에서 버릴(drop off) 수 ~~있다~~ 없다. 문장(15), (16)

[중요 어휘]

☐ attic	명사 다락방
☐ donate	동사 기부하다, 기증하다
☐ reuse	명사 재사용 / 동사 재사용하다
☐ wearable	형용사 입을 수 있는 / 명사 의복
☐ bedding	명사 침구류
☐ stain	명사 얼룩, 오염
☐ drop off	버리다

02 2021년 11월 27번 (정답률 95%) 정답 ④

[중요 구문] 호박 굴리기

(8) The participant / who rolls their pumpkin farthest / wins.
참가자가 / 자신의 호박을 가장 멀리 굴린 / 우승합니다 (S, 주격 관계대명사절, V)

(10) Participants must roll pumpkins / only using an underarm action.
참가자들은 호박을 굴려야 합니다 / 팔을 아래로 내린 동작만을 사용하여 (분사구문(동시동작))

[전문 해석]

(1)성대한 호박 굴리기
(2)호박들을 언덕 아래로 굴리면서 경주합시다! (3)호박들은 길을 건너 얼마나 멀리까지 갈까요?
(4)◻ 날짜: 2021년 5월의 마지막 일요일 Date: The last Sunday of May, 2021
(5)◻ 장소: Goomeri 마을의 Branford Hill
(6)◻ 등록비: 성인 10달러, 십 대 2달러
(7)◻ 규칙
(8) • 자신의 호박을 가장 멀리 굴린 참가자가 우승합니다.
(9) • 호박은 너비가 최소 15센티미터이어야만 합니다. Pumpkins must be at least 15 cm in width.
(10) • 참가자들은 팔을 아래로 내린 동작만을 사용하여 호박을 굴려야 합니다. Participants must roll pumpkins only using an underarm action.
(11) • 각 참가자는 호박을 굴릴 수 있는 기회를 단 한 번만 갖습니다. 정답 단서 Each participant has only one opportunity to roll a pumpkin.
(12)◻ 상금
(13) • 자신의 호박이 Lucky Spot에 안착한 사람에게 1,000달러 (14)(한 명보다 많은 참가자가 Lucky Spot에 자신의 호박을 안착시키면, 그 상금은 균등하게 분배될 것입니다.) (If more than one participant lands their pumpkin in the Lucky Spot, the money will be divided equally.)
(15) • 성인 우승자에게 500달러, 십 대 우승자에게 200달러
(16)www.goomeripumpkinfestival.com을 방문해 주십시오.

[정답 확인]

The Great Pumpkin Roll에 관한 다음 안내문의 내용과 일치하지 않는 것은?
① 2021년 5월의 마지막 일요일에 열린다. 문장(4)
② 경기에 사용하는 호박의 최소 너비(width)에 제한이 있다. 문장(9)
③ 참가자는 팔을 아래로 내려 호박(pumpkin)을 굴려야 한다. 문장(10)
④ 참가자에게 호박을 굴릴 수 있는 기회(opportunity)를 ~~여러 번~~ 단 한 번만 준다. 문장(11)
⑤ Lucky Spot에 호박을 넣은 모두가 상금을 균등하게(equally) 나눠 갖는다. 문장(14)

[중요 어휘]

☐ width	명사 너비, 폭
☐ underarm	형용사 팔을 아래로 내린 / 부사 팔을 아래로 내려서
☐ land	동사 안착하다, 안착시키다, 착륙하다 / 명사 육지, 땅
☐ divide	동사 분배하다, 나누다 / 명사 분할, 분배
☐ equally	부사 균등하게, 똑같이, 마찬가지로
☐ champion	명사 우승자

03 2022년 6월 27번 (정답률 95%) 정답 ③

[중요 구문] 한국어 말하기 대회

(2) Are you a foreign student / who wants to show off your Korean?
당신은 외국인 학생인가요 / 한국어를 뽐내고 싶은 (선행사, 주격 관계대명사)

(3) Make your own video / sharing your experiences / in Korea.
자신만의 영상을 만들어 보세요 / 경험을 공유하는 / 한국에서의

[전문 해석]

(1)2022 한국어 말하기 대회
(2)당신은 한국어를 뽐내고 싶은 외국인 학생인가요? (3)한국에서의 경험을 공유하는 자신만의 영상을 만들어 보세요.
(4) • 주제: "한국에서 지내는 동안의 경험" Theme: "My Experiences While Staying in Korea"
(5) • 영상 제출 마감일: 9월 5일 Video Submission Deadline: September 5th
(6) • 상품
(7)- 1등: $100 및 한국 전통차 정답 단서 1st place: $100 and traditional Korean tea
(8)- 2등: $50 및 한국 전통 인형
(9) • 세부 사항
(10)- 영상의 도입부에 이름이 언급되어야 합니다. Your name must be mentioned at the beginning of the video.
(11)- 영상은 3분에서 5분이어야 합니다.
(12)- 영상 파일을 k-speech@kcontest.com에 이메일로 보내 주십시오. Please email your video file to k-speech@kcontest.com.

[정답 확인]

2022 Korean Speech Contest에 관한 다음 안내문의 내용과 일치하지 않는 것은?

① 한국에서 지내는 동안의 경험(experience)을 주제로 한다. 문장(4)
② 영상 제출 마감일(submission deadline)은 9월 5일이다. 문장(5)
✔ 1등에게는 상금과 한국 ~~전통 인형~~(전통차)이 주어진다. 문장(7)
④ 영상 도입부에 이름이 언급되어야(be mentioned) 한다. 문장(10)
⑤ 이메일로 영상 파일을 보내야 한다. 문장(12)

[중요 어휘]

□ **speech**	명사 말하기, 연설
□ **show off**	뽐내다, 으스대다, 자랑하다
□ **submission**	명사 제출, 굴복
□ **mention**	동사 언급하다, 거론하다

04 2022년 9월 27번 (정답률 95%) 정답 ④

[중요 구문] 자선 행사

(3) You will be running through Colchester Zoo, / home to over 260 species!
당신은 Colchester 동물원을 통과하여 달릴 것입니다 / 260종 이상에게 서식지인

(10) Every runner will run 1km of the race / through the zoo / before going out to the main road.
모든 주자는 경주의 1km를 달릴 것입니다 / 동물원을 통과하여 / 주요 도로로 나가기 전에

힌트 접속사를 생략하지 않은 분사구문이며, going의 주어는 주절의 주어인 Every runner와 같음.

[전문 해석]

(1)The Colchester 동물원 자선 경주
(2)멸종 위기종을 돕기 위한 자선 행사에 참여하세요.
(3)당신은 260종 이상에게 서식지인, Colchester 동물원을 통과하여 달릴 것입니다!
(4)일자: 2022년 9월 25일 일요일
(5)시간: 오전 9시 – 오전 11시 Time: 9:00 a.m. – 11:00 a.m.
(6)등록비: 50달러 Registration fee includes a free pass to the zoo, food and drinks, and official photos.
(7) • 등록비에는 동물원 무료 입장권, 음식과 음료, 그리고 공식 사진이 포함되어 있습니다.
(8) • www.info.colchesters.com에서 등록하세요.
(9)코스 길이: 10km Course Length: 10km
(10) • 모든 주자는 주요 도로로 나가기 전에 동물원을 통과하여 경주의 1km를 달릴 것입니다.
(11)기타 정보 Only the runners who complete the race will receive a medal at the finish line.
(12) • 오직 경주를 완주한 주자만 결승선에서 메달을 받을 것입니다. 정답 단서
(13) • 행사 티셔츠는 동물원에서 구입할 수 있습니다. Event T-shirts can be purchased at the zoo.

[정답 확인]

The Colchester Zoo Charity Race에 관한 다음 안내문의 내용과 일치하지 않는 것은?

① 2시간 동안 진행된다. 문장(5)
② 등록비(registration fee)에는 음식과 음료가 포함된다. 문장(7)
③ 코스 길이(course length)는 10km이다. 문장(9)
✔ ~~모든 참가자는~~(경주를 완주한 주자만) 메달을 받는다(receive). 문장(12)
⑤ 행사 티셔츠는 동물원에서 구입할(purchase) 수 있다. 문장(13)

[중요 어휘]

□ **endangered**	형용사 멸종 위기의
□ **species**	명사 종
□ **registration fee**	명사 등록비

05 2022년 3월 26번 (정답률 95%) 정답 ⑤

[중요 구문] 온라인 자선 행사

(2) You're invited to the 2022 Bluehill Virtual Gala / [hosted by the Bluehill Community Center]. [ ]: 주격 관계대명사+be동사(which is) 생략
(수동태) (선행사)
2022 Bluehill 가상 행사에 여러분을 초대합니다 / Bluehill 커뮤니티 센터가 주최하는

(3) We'll have an online party / to raise funds / for our charity programs!
(부사적 용법(목적))
우리는 온라인 파티를 할 것입니다 / 기금을 마련하기 위해 / 자선 프로그램을 위한

[전문 해석]

(1)2022 Bluehill 가상 행사 We'll have an online party to raise funds for our charity programs!
(2)Bluehill 커뮤니티 센터가 주최하는 2022 Bluehill 가상 행사에 여러분을 초대합니다. (3)우리는 자선 프로그램 기금을 마련하기 위한 온라인 파티를 할 것입니다! (4)올해는 직접 함께 모일 수 없어서 가상으로 함께 모일 것입니다. Our Virtual Gala is on April 2 from 6 p.m. to 8 p.m.
(5)- 가상 행사는 4월 2일 오후 6시부터 오후 8시까지입니다.
(6)- 음악 공연과 특별 강연, 라이브 경매가 포함될 것입니다! It will include musical performances, special lectures, and live auctions!
(7)- 사회자는 *A Good Neighbor*의 유명한 배우인 Edward Jones일 것입니다. Our MC will be Edward Jones, the famous actor from *A Good Neighbor*.
(8)누구나 참가할 수 있습니다. (9)이 행사는 무료로 스트리밍될 것입니다! 정답 단서 This event will stream for free!
(10)파티에 참가하려면 www.bluehillgala.org를 방문하기만 하면 됩니다.

[정답 확인]

2022 Bluehill Virtual Gala에 관한 다음 안내문의 내용과 일치하지 않는 것은?

① 자선 프로그램 기금 마련(fund-raising)을 위한 온라인 파티이다. 문장(3)
② 4월 2일 오후 6시부터 8시까지 진행된다. 문장(5)
③ 음악 공연과 특별 강연(special lectures), 라이브 경매(live auctions)가 있을 것이다. 문장(6)
④ 배우 Edward Jones가 사회를 볼 것이다. 문장(7)
✔ ~~유료~~(무료)로 스트리밍될 것이다. 문장(9)

[중요 어휘]

□ **virtual**	형용사 가상의
□ **gala**	명사 행사, 축제
□ **host**	동사 주최하다
□ **virtually**	부사 가상으로, 거의, 사실상
□ **auction**	명사 경매

06 2022년 11월 27번 (정답률 95%) 정답 ④

[중요 구문] 딸기 축제

(3) This year, / we are back to hosting an in-person event / in Berry Square!
(전치사) (동명사)
올해 / 우리는 대면 행사를 다시 개최하게 되었습니다 / Berry Square에서

[전문 해석]

(1)2022 딸기 축제 This year, we are back to hosting an in-person event in Berry Square!
(2)즐거운 가족 축제에 함께하세요. (3)올해, 우리는 Berry Square에서 대면 행사를 다시 개최하게 되었습니다!
(4)□ 날짜: 2022년 11월 26일 (오전 11시-오후 5시)
(5)□ 티켓: 1인당 20달러 (6세 이하의 아이들은 무료입니다.) (Children 6 and under are FREE.)
(6)□ 특별 행사
(7) • 오전 11시 : 아이들을 위한 베이킹 클래스
(8) • 오후 1시 : 딸기파이 먹기 대회 1:00 p.m. : Strawberry Pie-Eating Contest
(9) • 오후 3시 : 딸기 의상 콘테스트
(10)□ 참고 The parking fee is $5 and includes tram service to the ticket booth.
(11) • 주차비는 5달러이며 매표소로 가는 트램 서비스를 포함합니다. 정답 단서
(12) • 여러분이 자원봉사에 관심이 있다면 신청서를 작성하여 manager@strawberryfestival.org로 이메일을 보내 주십시오. If you are interested in volunteering, complete an application form and email it to manager@strawberryfestival.org.

[정답 확인]

2022 Strawberry Festival에 관한 다음 안내문의 내용과 일치하지 않는 것은?

① 올해는 대면(in-person) 행사로 개최된다. 문장(3)
② 6세 이하의 어린이에게는 입장료를 받지 않는다. 문장(5)
③ 딸기파이 먹기 대회가 오후에 열린다. 문장(8)

✔ 매표소(ticket booth)로 가는 트램 서비스는 주차비에 ~~포함되지 않는다~~ 포함된다. 문장(11)
⑤ 자원봉사에 관심이 있다면 신청서(application form)를 이메일로 보내야 한다. 문장(12)

[중요 어휘]

☐ **in-person**	형용사 대면의, 직접
☐ **tram**	명사 트램, 전차
☐ **application**	명사 신청(서)

07 2023년 3월 27번 (정답률 95%) 정답 ⑤

[중요 구문] 수면 애플리케이션

(2) This smart app helps you have a refreshing sleep!
5형식V O O·C(동사원형/to V)
이 스마트 앱은 여러분이 상쾌한 잠을 자도록 도와줍니다

[전문 해석]

(1)Have a Good Night 앱
(2)이 스마트 앱은 여러분이 상쾌한 잠을 자도록 도와줍니다!
(3)특징들
(4)■ 수면을 위한 소리들
(5)- 수면을 위한 편안한 소리들을 제공함 Providing relaxing sounds for sleep
(6)■ 수면 녹음기
(7)- 자는 동안 기침이나 코 고는 소리 같은 소리들을 녹음함 Recording sounds such as coughing or snoring while sleeping
(8)■ 수면 패턴 추적기
(9)- 이용자의 수면 패턴을 확인하고 분석함 Checking and analyzing the user's sleep pattern
(10)■ 스트레스 없는 알람음
(11)- 이용자의 수면 패턴에 따라 알람음을 조정함 Adjusting alarm tones to the user's sleep pattern
(12)가격
(13)■ 기본 버전: 무료 정답 단서 Basic version: Free
(14)■ 프리미엄 버전 (추가 사운드트랙): 1년에 30달러
(15)앱을 다운로드하기 위해 '여기'를 클릭하세요!

[정답 확인]

Have a Good Night App에 관한 다음 안내문의 내용과 일치하지 않는 것은?
① 수면을 위한 편안한(relaxing) 소리를 제공한다. 문장(5)
② 자는 동안 기침(coughing)이나 코를 고는 소리(snoring)를 녹음한다. 문장(7)
③ 이용자의 수면 패턴을 확인하고(check) 분석한다(analyze). 문장(9)
④ 수면 패턴(sleep pattern)에 따라 알람음을 조정한다(adjust). 문장(11)
✔ 기본 버전(basic version)은 ~~1년에 30달러~~ 무료이다. 문장(13)

[중요 어휘]

☐ **refreshing**	형용사 상쾌한, 상쾌함을 주는
☐ **feature**	명사 특징 / 동사 특별히 포함하다
☐ **coughing**	명사 기침
☐ **snoring**	명사 코 고는 소리
☐ **adjust**	동사 조정하다, 조절하다

08 2023년 3월 28번 (정답률 95%) 정답 ⑤

[전문 해석] 온라인 장기 자랑

(1)2023년 온라인 재능 경연 대회
(2)여러분의 놀라운 재능을 뽐내세요!
(3)■ 부문: 노래, 춤, 악기 연주 Categories: singing, dancing, playing instruments
(4)■ 참가 방법
(5)- 여러분의 재능을 3분 길이의 비디오로 녹화하여 talent@westhigh.edu로 보내세요. Record a 3-minute video of your talent and send it to talent@westhigh.edu.
(6)- 참가작을 3월 27일과 3월 31일 사이에 제출하세요. Submit the entry between March 27 and March 31.
(7)■ 우승작 선정 방법
(8)1. 모든 비디오는 4월 5일 학교 웹사이트에 업로드될 것입니다.
(9)2. 학생들과 선생님들이 가장 좋아하는 비디오에 투표할 것입니다. Students and teachers will vote for their favorite video.
(10)3. 가장 많은 표를 받은 비디오가 우승할 것입니다.
(11)* 우승한 비디오는 학교 축제에서 상영될 것입니다. 정답 단서 The winning video will be played at the school festival.
(12)더 많은 정보를 원하시면, www.westhigh.edu를 방문하세요.

[정답 확인]

2023 Online Talent Show에 관한 다음 안내문의 내용과 일치하는 것은?
① 참가 부문(category)은 노래와 춤을 포함한 ~~네~~ 세 가지이다. 문장(3)
② 비디오의 길이에는 제한이 ~~없다~~ 있다. 문장(5)
③ 제출(submission) 기간은 3월 27일부터 ~~7일~~ 5일 동안이다. 문장(6)
④ ~~학생들만~~ 학생들과 선생님들이 우승작 선정 투표(vote)에 참여할 수 있다. 문장(9)
✔ 우승한(winning) 비디오는 학교 축제에서 상영될(be played) 것이다. 문장(11)

[중요 어휘]

☐ **talent**	명사 재능
☐ **show off**	뽐내다, 자랑하다
☐ **instrument**	명사 악기, 기구
☐ **submit**	동사 제출하다
☐ **entry**	명사 참가작

09 2023년 6월 27번 (정답률 95%) 정답 ⑤

[전문 해석] 마라톤 축제

(1)Peace 마라톤 축제
(2)Peace 마라톤 축제가 세계 평화를 장려하고 어려운 사람들에게 온정을 나누기 위해 열릴 것입니다. (3)저희와 함께 하셔서 달리기를 즐기고 더 좋은 세상을 만들어 주세요.
(4)언제 그리고 어디서
(5) • 2023년 9월 3일 일요일
(6)(출발 시각: 오전 10시) (Start time: 10 a.m.)
(7)Civic Stadium에서
(8)참가비와 자격
(9) • 풀 & 하프: 30 달러 (20세 이상)
(10) • 10km & 5km: 15 달러 (나이 제한 없음) 10 km & 5 km: $15 (No age limit)
(11)등록
(12) • 참가자 수는 1,000명으로 제한됩니다. The number of participants is limited to 1,000.
(13)(선착순입니다.) (First come, first served.)
(14) • ipmarathon.com에서 온라인으로만
(15)참고 사항
(16) • 기념품과 메달은 모든 참가자에게 주어집니다. Souvenirs and medals will be given to all participants.
(17) • 탈의실은 무료로 이용 가능합니다.
(18) • 물은 매 2.5km마다 그리고 결승선에서 제공됩니다. 정답 단서
Water will be provided every 2.5km and at the finish line.

[정답 확인]

Peace Marathon Festival에 관한 다음 안내문의 내용과 일치하지 않는 것은?
① 출발 시각(start time)은 오전 10시이다. 문장(6)
② 5 킬로미터 코스는 참가에 나이 제한(age limit)이 없다. 문장(10)
③ 참가자는 선착순 1,000명으로 제한된다(be limited). 문장(12), (13)
④ 모든 참가자들에게 기념품(souvenir)과 메달이 주어진다. 문장(16)
✔ 물은 ~~결승선(finish line)에서만~~ 매 2.5km마다 그리고 결승선에서 제공된다. 문장(18)

[중요 어휘]

☐ **promote**	동사 장려하다, 촉진하다, 홍보하다, 승진하다
☐ **compassion**	명사 온정, 동정, 연민
☐ **qualification**	명사 자격, 자질
☐ **registration**	명사 등록, 기재

10 2023년 9월 27번 (정답률 95%) 정답 ④

[중요 구문] Roselands 가상 스포츠 데이

(2) Roselands Virtual Sports Day is an athletic competition /
Roselands 가상 스포츠 데이는 운동 경기입니다 / 선행사
that you can participate in from anywhere.
목적격 관계대명사절
여러분이 어디서나 참가할 수 있는

힌트 an athletic competition을 선행사로 가지는 목적격 관계대명사절이 사용된 문장임. 이때 선행사 an athletic competition은 participate in의 목적어임.

[전문 해석]

(1)Roselands 가상 스포츠 데이
(2)Roselands 가상 스포츠 데이는 여러분이 어디서나 참가할 수 있는 운동 경기입니다.
(3)언제: 2023년 10월 16일~22일 October 16th - 22nd, 2023
(4)행사 진행 방식
(5) • 총 10개의 도전 과제가 있습니다. There are 10 challenges in total.
(6) • 여러분은 우리 학교 웹사이트에서 각 도전 과제를 설명하는 영상을 볼 수 있습니다. You can see videos explaining each challenge on our school website.
(7) • 여러분이 더 많은 도전 과제를 완성할수록, 여러분은 학급을 위해 더 많은 점수를 얻을 것입니다.
(8) • 가장 많은 점수를 가진 학급은 상을 받을 것입니다.
(9) • 학부모님들과 선생님들도 참여할 수 있습니다. 정답 단서 Parents and teachers can also participate.
(10)출품작 제출 방법
(11) • 여러분이 도전 과제들을 완성하는 영상을 virtualsportsday@roselands.com에 이메일로 보내주세요.
(12) • 영상 파일의 크기는 500MB를 초과하면 안 됩니다. The size of the video file must not exceed 500MB.

[정답 확인]

Roselands Virtual Sports Day에 관한 다음 안내문의 내용과 일치하지 않는 것은?

① 10월 16일부터 22일까지 열린다. 문장(3)
② 총 10개의 도전 과제(challenge)가 있다. 문장(5)
③ 학교 웹사이트에서 도전 과제를 설명하는(explain) 영상을 볼 수 있다. 문장(6)
✔ 학부모와 교사는 참여할(participate) 수 ~~없다~~ 있다. 문장(9)
⑤ 제출할 영상파일 용량이 500MB를 초과하면(exceed) 안 된다. 문장(12)

[중요 어휘]

□ virtual	형용사 가상의, 사실상의
□ athletic	형용사 운동의, 운동 경기의
□ complete	동사 완성하다, 끝내다 / 형용사 완전한
□ submit	동사 제출하다
□ entry	명사 출품작
□ exceed	동사 초과하다, 넘다

11 2022년 3월 27번 (정답률 90%) 정답 ④

[중요 구문] Woodside 점토 공예 워크숍

(7) Your pendants will be ready / to be picked up / from April 14.
be ready to V: ~할 준비가 되다
여러분의 펜던트는 준비될 것입니다 / 찾아가도록 / 4월 14일부터

힌트 여기서 Your pendants는 to be picked up의 의미상 주어 역할을 하고 있음.

[전문 해석]

(1)Woodside 점토 공예 워크숍
(2)2022년 3월 31일 목요일 오후 7시 7 p.m. Thursday March 31, 2022
(3)2022년 4월 7일 목요일 오후 7시 7 p.m. Thursday April 7, 2022 This is a two-session workshop for adults.
(4)성인을 위한 2차시짜리 워크숍입니다. (5)첫 번째 시간에 점토의 기본을 배우고 독특한 도자기 펜던트를 만들 것입니다. (6)두 번째 시간에는 우리가 유약을 바르고 굽기 전에 여러분이 작품을 장식할 것입니다. (7)여러분의 펜던트는 4월 14일부터 찾아가도록 준비될 것입니다.
(8)- 이 워크숍은 초보자에게 적합하므로 경험이 필요하지 않습니다. Your pendants will be ready to be picked up from April 14.
(9)- 참가비: 25파운드(모든 재료와 강습, 와인 한 잔 포함) 정답 단서 (including all materials, instruction and a glass of wine)
(10)- 자리가 한정되어 있으니 일찍 예약하십시오. (11)사전 예약만 가능합니다. Advance bookings only.
(12)더 많은 정보를 원하시면 www.woodsideclay.co.uk로 저희 웹사이트를 방문하세요.

[정답 확인]

Woodside Clay Workshop에 관한 다음 안내문의 내용과 일치하는 것은?

① 목요일 ~~오전~~ 오후에 진행된다. 문장(2), (3)
② ~~어린이~~ 성인를 대상으로 한다. 문장(4)
③ ~~두 번째 시간에~~ 두 번째 시간 이후인 4월 14일부터 펜던트를 찾아갈(pick up) 수 있다. 문장(7)
✔ 모든 재료가 참가비(fee)에 포함된다. 문장(9)
⑤ 사전 예약(advance bookings)~~을 받지 않는다~~ 만 가능하다. 문장(11)

[중요 어휘]

□ clay	명사 점토, 찰흙
□ ceramic	형용사 도자기의 / 명사 도자기
□ glaze	동사 유약을 바르다 / 명사 유약
□ be suitable for	~에게 적합하다
□ fee	명사 참가비, 요금, 사례금
□ instruction	명사 강습, 설명, 지시

12 2020년 9월 27번 (정답률 90%) 정답 ④

[중요 구문] 2020 게임 코딩 워크숍

(3) This game-coding workshop / will teach them /
이 게임 코딩 워크숍은 / 그들에게 가르칠 것입니다 / 4형식V I.O
[to use block-based coding software / to create their own games]!
[ ]: D.O(명사적 용법) 부사적 용법(목적)
블록 기반 코딩 소프트웨어를 사용하는 방법을 / 자신만의 게임을 만들기 위해

[전문 해석]

(1)2020 게임 코딩 워크숍
(2)당신의 아이들의 컴퓨터 게임에 대한 애정을 기술로 바꾸세요. (3)이 게임 코딩 워크숍은 자신만의 게임을 만들기 위해 블록 기반 코딩 소프트웨어를 사용하는 방법을 그들(아이들)에게 가르칠 것입니다!
(4)□ 날짜와 시간
(5) • 12월 12일 토요일, 오후 1시에서 오후 3시까지 Saturday, December 12th, 1:00 pm to 3:00 pm
(6)□ 등록
(7) • 11월 27일 금요일에 마감
(8) • 참가비는 30달러입니다(Lansing 키즈 클럽 회원은 무료). (free for Lansing Kids Club members)
(9) • Kid's Coding Center에서 직접 등록하거나 www.lanskidscoding.com에서 온라인으로 등록하세요. Sign up in person at Kid's Coding Center or online at www.lanskidscoding.com.
(10)□ 요구 사항
(11) • 9세에서 12세까지의 아이들만 대상으로 함.
(12) • 노트북 컴퓨터는 제공되지 않을 것입니다. (13)참가자들은 그들 자신의 것(노트북 컴퓨터)을 가져와야 합니다. Laptops will not be provided. 정답 단서
(14) • 코딩에 대한 사전 지식은 필요하지 않습니다. No prior coding knowledge is required.
(15)더 많은 정보를 위해서 우리 웹사이트를 방문해주세요.

[정답 확인]

2020 Game-Coding Workshop에 관한 다음 안내문의 내용과 일치하지 않는 것은?

① 토요일 오후에 진행된다. 문장(5)
② Lansing 키즈 클럽 회원은 참가비(participation fee)가 무료이다. 문장(8)
③ 온라인 등록(sign-up)이 가능하다. 문장(9)
✔ 참가자들에게 노트북 컴퓨터(laptop)가 제공~~된다~~ 되지 않는다. 문장(12)
⑤ 코딩에 대한 사전 지식(prior knowledge)이 필요 없다. 문장(14)

[중요 어휘]

□ turn A into B	A를 B로 바꾸다
□ in person	직접

13 2020년 11월 28번 (정답률 90%) 정답 ③

[중요 구문] 수화 수업

(2) If you've ever considered / studying sign language, /
3형식V O(V-ing)
여러분이 한번이라도 고려해본 적이 있다면 / 수화를 배우는 것을 /
our class is one of the best ways to do it!
형용사적 용법
저희 수업은 그것을 할 최고의 방법들 중 하나입니다

(15) We do not provide refunds / unless class is cancelled /
=if not
저희는 환불을 제공하지 않습니다 / 수업이 취소되지 않는 한 /
due to low registration.
저조한 등록 때문에

정답과 해설 10 안내문

[전문 해석]

(1)수화 수업
(2)여러분이 한번이라도 수화를 배우는 것을 고려해본 적이 있다면, 저희 수업은 그것을 할 최고의 방법들 중 하나입니다! (3)수업은 모든 연령의 사람들에게 열려 있지만, 모든 어린이들은 어른을 동반해야 합니다. The class is open to people of all ages, but all children must be accompanied by an adult.
(4)수업 일정
(5) • 어디서: Coorparoo 주민센터
(6) • 언제: 2020년 9월 — 10월
(7)(오후 7시 — 오후 9시)
(8)수준
(9) • 수업 #1 (월요일과 화요일) (Monday and Tuesday)
(10)- 이전의 수화 경험이 필요하지 않습니다. 정답 단서 No previous sign language experience is required.
(11) • 수업 #2 (수요일과 목요일)
(12)- 최소 1,000개의 수화 동작에 대한 지식이 필요합니다.
(13)주의 사항
(14) • 수업료는 100달러입니다. We do not provide refunds unless class is cancelled due to low registration.
(15) • 저조한 등록 때문에 수업이 취소되지 않는 한 저희는 환불을 제공하지 않습니다.
(16) • 등록은 온라인으로만, 8월 31일 이전에 가능합니다. Registration is available only online and before August 31.
(17)저희 웹사이트 www.CRsignlgs.com을 방문하세요.

[정답 확인]

Sign Language Class에 관한 다음 안내문의 내용과 일치하는 것은?

① 어린이들~~도~~(은) 어른 동반(accompany) 없이 참여할 수 ~~있다~~(없다). 문장(3)
② 수업(class)은 주 ~~3~~(2)일 진행된다. 문장(9)
✔ 수화(sign language) 경험이 없어도 참여할 수 있는 수업이 있다. 문장(10)
④ 환불(refund)은 ~~예외 없이~~(수업이 취소되지 않는 한) 불가능하다. 문장(15)
⑤ 현장 등록(registration)이 ~~가능~~(불가능)하다. 문장(16)

[중요 어휘]

□ **sign language**	명사 수화
□ **consider**	동사 고려하다, 검토하다
□ **be accompanied by**	~을 동반하다, 동행하다
□ **previous**	형용사 이전의, 사전의
□ **tuition**	명사 수업료, 수업
□ **available**	형용사 가능한, 이용할 수 있는

14 2021년 3월 26번 (정답률 90%) 정답 ⑤

[중요 구문] Grey 카운티 2021 채용 박람회

(5) Last year's was the largest ever held in this area /
=Last year's Job Fair
작년의 채용 박람회는 지금껏 이 지역에서 열린 가장 큰 행사였습니다 /
with more than 80 employers and over 1,000 job seekers.
80명이 넘는 고용주와 천 명이 넘는 구직자가 함께한

(6) This year, / we're moving to an even larger location /
올해 / 저희는 훨씬 더 넓은 장소로 옮길 것입니다 /
with plenty of space for all attendees.
모든 참가자를 위한 많은 공간이 있는

힌트 예정이나 계획된 미래의 경우는 현재진행시제로 미래를 나타낼 수 있으므로 여기서 are moving은 '옮길 것입니다'라고 해석해야 함.

[전문 해석]

(1)Grey 카운티 2021 채용 박람회
(2)4월 28일 오후 2시 - 오후 6시 April 28, 2:00 p.m. - 6:00 p.m.
(3)Bayshore 커뮤니티 센터
(4)Grey 카운티 전역의 사업체들은 지금 2021 채용 박람회 부스에 등록할 수 있습니다. (5)작년의 채용 박람회는 80명이 넘는 고용주와 천 명이 넘는 구직자가 함께한 지금껏 이 지역에서 열린 가장 큰 행사였습니다. (6)올해, 저희는 모든 참가자를 위한 많은 공간이 있는 훨씬 더 넓은 장소로 옮길 것입니다. This year, we're moving to an even larger location with plenty of space for all attendees.
(7)- 등록비: 80달러
(8)- 등록 마감 일시: 4월 14일 오후 6시 Registration Deadline: April 14, 6:00 p.m.
(9)고용주들을 위한 향상된 서비스
(10) • 5미터 × 5미터 부스 5m × 5m booth
(11) • 무료 와이파이
(12) • 고용주 전용 라운지와 다과 정답 단서 Employer-only lounge and refreshments
(13)더 많은 정보를 원하시면 www.greycountyjobfair.org를 방문하세요.

[정답 확인]

Grey County 2021 Job Fair에 관한 다음 안내문의 내용과 일치하는 것은?

① 행사 진행 시간은 ~~6~~(4)시간이다. 문장(2)
② 작년보다 더 ~~좁은~~(넓은) 장소에서 열린다. 문장(6)
③ 등록 마감일(registration deadline)은 4월 ~~28~~(14)일이다. 문장(8)
④ 가로세로 각각 ~~10~~(5)m인 부스가 제공된다. 문장(10)
✔ 고용주 전용(employer-only) 라운지와 다과(refreshments)가 제공된다. 문장(12)

★중요 간단한 지문일수록 ①처럼 총 진행 시간을 계산해야 하거나 ③처럼 행사 날짜와 등록 마감일을 구분해야 하는 선택지에 주의해야 함. ⑤에서 '고용주'가 employer인지 employee인지도 헷갈리지 않도록 신중히 확인해야 함.

[중요 어휘]

□ **county**	명사 카운티, 군(郡)
□ **job fair**	채용 박람회
□ **register**	동사 등록하다
□ **job seeker**	구직자
□ **attendee**	명사 참가자
□ **enhance**	동사 향상하다
□ **refreshment**	명사 (주로 복수) 다과

15 2022년 6월 28번 (정답률 90%) 정답 ④

[전문 해석] 휴대용 사진 프린터 설명서

(1)EZ 휴대용 사진 프린터
(2)사용자 설명서
(3)LED 표시기에 대한 유의 사항
(4) • 흰색: 전원 켜짐 White: Power on
(5) • 빨간색: 배터리 충전 중
(6)작동 방법
(7) • 프린터를 켜려면 전원 버튼을 누르시오.
(8) • 프린터를 끄려면 전원 버튼을 두 번 누르시오. Press the power button twice to turn the printer off.
(9) • 배터리를 충전하려면, 케이블을 USB 포트에 연결하시오. (10)완전 충전은 60~90분이 소요됩니다. It takes 60 - 90 minutes for a full charge.
(11) • 프린터에 무선으로 연결하기 위해서, 모바일 장치에 'EZ Printer APP'을 다운로드하시오. 정답 단서 To connect to the printer wirelessly, download the 'EZ Printer App' on your mobile device.
(12)인화지 장착 방법
(13) • 프린터의 상단 덮개를 들어 올리시오.
(14) • 인화지를 로고가 아래로 향하도록 넣으시오. Insert the photo paper with any logos facing downward.

[정답 확인]

EZ Portable Photo Printer 사용에 관한 다음 안내문의 내용과 일치하는 것은?

① LED 표시기의 흰색은 ~~충전 중~~(전원 켜짐)임을 나타낸다. 문장(4)
② 전원 버튼을 ~~한 번~~(두 번) 누르면 전원이 꺼진다. 문장(8)
③ 배터리가 완전히 충전되는(be charged) 데 ~~2시간 이상~~(60~90분) 걸린다. 문장(10)
✔ 무선 연결을 위해 앱을 다운로드해야 한다. 문장(11)
⑤ 인화지를 로고가 ~~위로~~(아래로) 향하도록(face) 넣어야 한다. 문장(14)

[중요 어휘]

□ **manual**	명사 설명서, 안내서 / 형용사 수동의
□ **note**	명사 유의 사항, 메모
□ **indicator**	명사 표시기, 지표
□ **charge**	동사 충전하다, 청구하다
□ **operate**	동사 작동시키다, 조작하다
□ **wirelessly**	부사 무선으로
□ **load**	동사 (카메라 등의 장비에 필름 등을) 넣다, (짐을) 싣다
□ **lift**	동사 들어 올리다, 올리다
□ **insert**	동사 넣다, 끼우다
□ **face**	동사 향하다, 직면하다

☐ **downward** [부사] 아래로, 아래쪽으로

16 2022년 11월 28번 (정답률 90%) 정답 ⑤

[중요 구문] 조명 예술 전시회

(3) Admire the beautiful light artwork /
명령문
아름다운 조명 예술품들을 감상하세요 /
as you walk through Maple Spring.
접속사(~하면서)
여러분이 Maple Spring을 걸으면서

[전문 해석]

(1)Maple Spring 조명 예술 전시회
(2)Maple Spring 조명 예술 전시회는 조명 예술품으로 둘러싸인 경로를 따라 당신을 비추게 될 것입니다. (3)여러분이 Maple Spring을 걸으면서 아름다운 조명 예술품들을 감상하세요.
(4)▫ 날짜: 2022년 12월 1일부터 31일까지 (5)(이달 두 번째와 네 번째 월요일은 운영하지 않음.) (closed on the 2nd and 4th Monday of the month)
(6)▫ 시간: 오후 7시부터 오후 11시까지 Time: 7 p.m. - 11 p.m.
(7)▫ 입장료: 1인당 5달러
(8)▫ 전시 경로: Maple Spring 중심부의 Bow 강을 따라 (관람 경로의 디지털 지도만 제공합니다.) (Only digital maps of the route are available.)
(9)• 기념품은 현장과 온라인에서 구매 가능합니다. Souvenirs will be available on site and online.
(10)• 지역 주민은 입장료의 10% 할인을 받을 수 있습니다. 정답단서 Local residents can get a 10% discount off the entrance fee.
(11)더 많은 정보를 위해 www.maplespringlight.com을 방문하십시오.

[정답 확인]

Maple Spring Light Art Exhibition에 관한 다음 안내문의 내용과 일치하는 것은?

① ~~매주~~ 두 번째와 네 번째 월요일은 운영하지 않는다(closed). 문장(5)
② 밤 11시 ~~이후에도~~ 까지 입장이 가능하다. 문장(6)
③ 관람 경로가 담긴 지도는 ~~종이로만~~ 디지털로만 제공한다. 문장(8)
④ 기념품(souvenir)은 현장(on site)~~에서만~~ 과 온라인에서 구매 가능하다. 문장(9)
✔ 지역 주민(resident)은 입장료의 10% 할인(discount)을 받을 수 있다. 문장(10)

[중요 어휘]

☐ **illuminate** [동사] 비추다, 밝히다
☐ **route** [명사] 경로, 길
☐ **surround** [동사] 둘러싸다, 에워싸다
☐ **admire** [동사] 감탄하다, 존경하다
☐ **souvenir** [명사] 기념품

17 2023년 6월 28번 (정답률 90%) 정답 ③

[전문 해석] 야외 점심 행사

(1)Out to Lunch
(2)맛있는 음식, 멋진 음악과 함께 오후를 즐기고 싶으신가요? (3)'Out to Lunch'는 당신의 요구를 충족시킬 완벽한 행사입니다! (4)Missoula 시내에 있는 Caras Park에서 열리는 이번 행사에 오셔서 즐기세요!
(5)날짜 및 시간
(6) • 6월 매주 수요일, 오후 12시 ~ 오후 3시 Every Wednesday in June, 12 p.m. - 3 p.m.
(7)하이라이트
(8) • 다이아몬드 아이스크림을 포함한 모든 푸드 트럭에서 10% 할인 10% discount at all food trucks including Diamond Ice Cream
(9) • 신인 그룹 Cello Brigade의 라이브 음악 공연 정답단서 Live music performance of the new group Cello Brigade
(10) • 아이들을 위한 페이스 페인팅과 물풍선 싸움
(11)공지 사항
(12) • 개인 접이식 의자와 담요를 가져오세요. Bring your own lawn chairs and blankets.
(13) • 쓰레기를 올바르게 처리하세요.
(14) • 주류를 마시는 것은 엄격하게 금지됩니다. Drinking alcoholic beverages is strictly banned.

[정답 확인]

Out to Lunch에 관한 다음 안내문의 내용과 일치하는 것은?

① ~~일 년~~ 6월 내내 수요일마다(every Wednesday) 열리는 행사이다. 문장(6)
② 푸드 트럭에서는 가격을 ~~20%~~ 10% 할인해 준다. 문장(8)
✔ 라이브 음악 공연(live music performance)이 마련되어 있다. 문장(9)
④ 개인 의자와 담요(blanket)를 가지고 올 수 ~~없다~~ 있다. 문장(12)
⑤ 주류(alcoholic beverage)~~를 포함한 음료를~~ 는 마실 수 ~~있다~~ 없다. 문장(14)

[중요 어휘]

☐ **need** [명사] 요구, 필요, 욕구
☐ **dispose of** ~을 처리하다, 없애다
☐ **properly** [부사] 올바르게, 적절히
☐ **beverage** [명사] 음료
☐ **strictly** [부사] 엄격하게
☐ **ban** [동사] 금지하다

18 2023년 9월 28번 (정답률 90%) 정답 ④

[중요 구문] 신학기 경품 행사

(3) Join us for this fun event / to help children of all ages prepare /
5형식V O O·C(동사원형)
이 즐거운 행사에 참여하세요 / 모든 연령대의 아이들이 준비할 수 있도록 도와주는 /
to go back to school / after summer vacation.
명사적 용법(목적어)
학교로 돌아가는 것을 / 여름 방학 후에

힌트 'help+O+O·C'의 5형식 구문이 사용되었음. 이때 목적격 보어로 동사원형뿐 아니라 to부정사도 사용 가능함.

[전문 해석]

(1)신학기 경품 행사
(2)Easton시는 신학기 무료 경품 행사를 개최합니다. (3)모든 연령대의 아이들이 여름 방학 후에 학교로 돌아가는 것을 준비할 수 있도록 도와주는 이 즐거운 행사에 참여하세요.
(4)언제: 9월 2일 토요일 오전 9시~오전 11시 When: Saturday, September 2nd, 9 a.m. - 11 a.m.
(5)장소: Easton시 Central Park
(6)(이 행사는 날씨에 관계없이 열릴 것입니다.) (This event will be held rain or shine.)
(7)참여 요건
(8) • Easton시 주민들에게만 열려 있음 Open to City of Easton residents only
(9) • 유효한 신분증을 반드시 가져올 것
(10)유의 사항
(11) • 선착순으로 가방 500개를 나누어 줄 것입니다. 정답단서 500 backpacks will be given out on a first-come, first-served basis.
(12) • 가방을 받기 위해서는 반드시 부모님 또는 보호자가 아이와 함께 와야 합니다. A parent or a guardian must come with their child to receive the backpack.
(13)더 많은 정보를 원하시면, 612-248-6633으로 시의회에 전화 주세요.

[정답 확인]

Back-to-school Giveaway Event에 관한 다음 안내문의 내용과 일치하는 것은?

① 토요일 ~~오후~~ 오전에 진행된다. 문장(4)
② 우천 시에~~는 취소된다~~ 도 취소되지 않는다. 문장(6)
③ Easton시 주민(resident)~~이 아니어도~~ 만 참여할 수 있다. 문장(8)
✔ 가방 500개가 선착순(first-come, first-served)으로 배부될 것이다. 문장(11)
⑤ 부모 또는 보호자~~만 와도~~ 가 아이와 함께 와야 가방을 받을(receive) 수 있다. 문장(12)

[중요 어휘]

☐ **back-to-school** [형용사] 신학기의
☐ **giveaway** [명사] 경품, 증정품
☐ **host** [동사] 개최하다, 주최하다 / [명사] 주인
☐ **rain or shine** 날씨에 관계없이, 비가 오든 화창하든
☐ **resident** [명사] 주민, 거주자
☐ **valid** [형용사] 유효한, 타당한
☐ **first-come, first-served** 선착순

정답과 해설 10 안내문

문제편 p.121

핵심 행사에 대한 세부 사항 중에서도 특히 필요조건(Requirement) 또는 우대 사항(preferred)을 바꿔놓는 경우가 많기 때문에 이 부분을 꼼꼼히 살펴봐야 함.

19 2018년 9월 27번 (정답률 85%) 정답 ③

[중요 구문] 한여름 밤의 꿈 오디션

(3) We are looking for dancers /
저희는 무용수들을 찾고 있습니다 /
for the musical *A Midsummer Night's Dream* /
선행사
뮤지컬 〈A Midsummer Night's Dream〉을 위한 /
that will open at the Elliot Arts Center / in the spring of 2019.
주격 관계대명사
Elliot 예술회관에서 열릴 / 2019년 봄에

[전문 해석]

(1)〈A Midsummer Night's Dream(한여름 밤의 꿈)〉 오디션
(2)'William Shakespeare(윌리엄 셰익스피어) 연극의 뮤지컬 각색'
(3)저희는 2019년 봄에 Elliot 예술회관에서 열릴 뮤지컬 〈A Midsummer Night's Dream(한여름 밤의 꿈)〉을 위한 무용수들을 찾고(모집하고) 있습니다. We are looking for dancers for the musical *A Midsummer Night's Dream* that will open at the Elliot Arts Center in the spring of 2019.
(4) • 언제:
(5) - 2018년 12월 15일 토요일 (오전 9시부터 오후 6시까지)
(6) - 2018년 12월 16일 일요일 (오전 9시부터 오전 11시까지) Sunday, Dec. 16, 2018 (9 a.m. until 11 a.m.)
(7) • 어디서: Vahn 스튜디오
(8)필요조건
(9) • 현대/발레 무용 경력
(10) • 가창 능력 우대
(11) • 이전 무대 경험은 요구되지 않음. 정답 단서 no prior stage experience required
(12)등록
(13) • 오디션을 보는 것에 관심이 있으시면, casting@studiovahn.com으로 저희에게 이메일을 주세요.
(14) • 당신의 이메일에 (다음 양식을) 포함해주세요:
(15) - 최근 사진과 함께(사진을 포함한) 완성된 신청서 양식
(16) - 서명된 보호자 동의서 양식 (십 대만) a signed guardian consent form (only teens)
(17) • 모든 신청서는 2018년 11월 30일 금요일까지 접수되어야 합니다. All applications must be received by Friday, Nov. 30, 2018.
(18)더 많은 정보를 위해서, www.studiovahn.com을 방문해 주세요.

- 〈A Midsummer Night's Dream(한여름 밤의 꿈)〉: 셰익스피어의 대표적인 낭만 희극으로 연인들의 사랑의 마찰과 갈등이 초자연적인 힘을 빌려 해결되는 꿈같은 이야기. 셰익스피어의 작품 중 가장 환상적이고 몽환적이며 작가의 상상력이 잘 발휘된 작품임.
- William Shakespeare(윌리엄 셰익스피어, 1564년~1616년): 희·비극을 포함한 38편의 희곡과 여러 권의 시집을 쓴 영국의 극작가

[정답 확인]

A Midsummer Night's Dream Audition에 관한 다음 안내문의 내용과 일치하지 않는 것은?

① 2019년 봄(spring)에 있을 공연을 위한 무용수들(dancers)을 모집한다. 문장(3)
② 일요일(Sunday)은 오전 오디션(audition)만 가능하다. 문장(6)
③ 이전 무대 경험(prior stage experience)이 ~~요구된다(be required)~~. 요구되지 않는다 문장(11)
④ 십 대(teens) 참가자는 보호자의 동의서(guardian consent)를 제출해야 한다. 문장(16)
⑤ 신청(application) 마감일은 2018년 11월 30일이다. 문장(17)

힌트 background는 일반적으로 배경, 배후 사정 혹은 사전지식을 뜻하지만, 본문에서는 '경력'이라는 뜻으로 사용됨. 대표적인 예로, academic background(학력)라는 표현이 있음.

[중요 어휘]

□ adaptation	명사 각색, 적응
□ play	명사 연극, 희극, 놀이 / 동사 (연극·영화 등에서) 연기하다, 배역을 맡다, 놀다
□ look for	~을 찾다, 구하다, 바라다, 기대하다
□ background	명사 경력, 전력, 배경, 배후 사정, 사전지식
□ preferred	형용사 우대되는, 우선되는
□ completed	형용사 완성된, 완전한
□ signed	형용사 서명된, 합의된

20 2019년 6월 27번 (정답률 85%) 정답 ③

[중요 구문] Flying Apron 요리 학교 수업

(11) After class, / participants can take home /
S
수업 후에 / 참가자들은 집에 가져갈 수 있습니다 /
[all recipes] / and [the meals / they cooked].
O① O②
모든 조리법을 / 그리고 식사를 / 그들이 요리한

[전문 해석]

(1)Flying Apron 요리 학교 수업
(2)저희의 아름다운 요리 학교 주방에서 여러 가지 수업을 즐기세요!
(3)수업
(4) • 프랑스식 식사: 7월 5일
(5) • 영국식 브런치: 7월 12일 British Brunch: 12th July
(6) • 멕시코의 맛: 7월 19일
(7)시간: 오후 7시 30분에서 오후 9시 30분까지
(8)수업료: 한 수업당 한 사람에 50달러 (모든 재료비 포함) Fee: $50 per person per class (including the cost of all the ingredients)
(9)*각 수업은 최소 4명의 참가자와 최대 10명을 필요로 합니다(각 수업에 최소 4명에서 최대 10명까지 받을 수 있습니다). 정답 단서 Each class requires a minimum of 4 participants and a maximum of 10.
(10)*참가자들은 그들의 수업이 시작하면 환불을 받을 수 없습니다. Participants can't get a refund once their class starts.
(11)*수업 후에, 참가자들은 모든 조리법과 그들이 요리한 식사를 집에 가져갈 수 있습니다. After class, participants can take home all recipes and the meals they cooked.

[정답 확인]

Flying Apron Cookery School Classes에 관한 다음 안내문의 내용과 일치하지 않는 것은?

① 영국식 브런치 강좌는 7월 12일에 열린다. 문장(5)
② 수업료에 모든 재료비(cost of ingredients)가 포함되어 있다. 문장(8)
③ 참가 인원이 ~~10~~명 이상이어야 강좌가 개설된다. 4 문장(9)
④ 각 수업이 시작되면 환불(refund)을 받을 수 없다. 문장(10)
⑤ 요리한 음식은 수업 이후 집으로 가져갈 수 있다. 문장(11)

★중요 문장 (9)에서 최소 4명이어야 강좌가 개설되며 10명까지만 받는다고 했음.

[중요 어휘]

□ cookery	명사 요리(법)
□ a variety of	여러 가지의
□ ingredient	명사 재료
□ refund	명사 환불(금) / 동사 환불하다

21 2021년 11월 28번 (정답률 85%) 정답 ④

[중요 구문] 플로깅 행사

(3) It comes from / the Swedish word for pick up, /
병렬①
그것은 왔습니다 / 줍는다는 의미인 스웨덴 단어에서 /
"plocka upp" / and is a combination of jogging and picking up litter.
병렬②
'plocka upp' / 그리고 조깅과 쓰레기 줍기가 결합된 말입니다

(4) In 2016, / it started in Sweden /
병렬①
2016년에 / 그것은 스웨덴에서 시작되었습니다 /
and has recently come to the UK, /
병렬②
그리고 최근 영국으로 건너왔습니다 /
[becoming a new movement for saving nature]. [ ]: 분사구문(연속동작)
그래서 자연을 보호하기 위한 새로운 운동이 되었습니다

[전문 해석]

(1)플로깅 행사
(2)플로깅에 대해 들어본 적 있으신가요? (3)그것은 줍는다는 의미인 스웨덴 단어 'plocka upp'에서 왔으며 조깅과 쓰레기 줍기가 결합된 말입니다. (4)2016년에 그것은 스웨덴에서 시작되었고 최근 영국으로 건너와 자연을 보호하기 위한 새로운 운동이 되었습니다. In 2016, it started in Sweden and has recently come to the UK, becoming a new movement for saving nature.
(5)언제 그리고 어디서
(6) • 매달 첫 번째 월요일 오전 9시 9 a.m. on the first Monday of each month
(7) • East Twickenham에 있는 ETNA 센터 밖
(8)준비해야 할 것
(9) • 여러분의 운동화만 가져오세요, 그러면 우리가 다른 모든 장비들을 지급할 것입니다. Just bring your running shoes, and we will provide all the other equipment.
(10) • 참가비는 무료이나 우리의 자연 보호 활동을 위한 기부는 기꺼이 받습니다. 정답 단서 There is no fee to participate, but you are welcome to donate toward our conservation work.
(11)※ 참가하기 위해 예약은 필요하지 않습니다. No reservations are necessary to participate.
(12)더 많은 정보를 원하시면 www.environmenttrust.org를 방문하십시오.

[정답 확인]

Plogging Event에 관한 다음 안내문의 내용과 일치하는 것은?

① 2016년에 ~~영국~~(스웨덴)에서 시작되었다. 문장(4)
② 매달 첫 번째 ~~일요일~~(월요일) 오전 9시에 열린다. 문장(6)
③ 운동화를 ~~포함한~~(제외한) 장비들(equipment)이 지급된다. 문장(9)
✔ 참가비(fee to participate)는 무료이다. 문장(10)
⑤ 참가하려면 예약(reservation)이 ~~필요하다~~(필요하지 않다). 문장(11)

[중요 어휘]

□ come from	~에서 오다, ~에서 생겨나다
□ combination	명사 결합, 조합
□ pick up	줍다, 치우다, 정리하다
□ litter	명사 쓰레기 / 동사 (쓰레기 등을) 버리다
□ movement	명사 (조직적으로 벌이는) 운동, (몸·신체 부위의) 움직임
□ equipment	명사 (불가산 명사) 장비들
□ be welcome to V	~해도 좋다
□ donate	동사 기부하다
□ conservation	명사 (자연) 보호, 보존
□ reservation	명사 예약

22 2022년 9월 28번 (정답률 85%) 정답 ②

[중요 구문] 이야기 쓰기 대회

(14) We will choose 12 finalists, / one from each genre, /
우리는 12명의 결승 진출자를 선발할 것입니다 / 각 장르에서 한 명씩 /
and the 12 entries will be published online /
병렬①
그리고 12편의 출품작들은 온라인으로 출판될 것입니다 /
and shared via social media.
병렬②
그리고 소셜 미디어를 통해 공유될 것입니다

[전문 해석]

(1)7일 이야기 쓰기 대회
(2)글쓰기가 당신의 재능인가요? (3)여기 당신을 위한 무대가 있습니다.
(4)언제: 2022년 12월 5일 월요일부터 12월 11일 일요일까지
(5)연령: 17세 이상 Age: 17 and over
(6)내용
(7)• 모든 참가자들은 동일한 주제에 대하여 글을 쓸 것입니다. 정답단서 All participants will write about the same topic.
(8)• 당신은 당신의 이야기를 위해 12가지 문학 장르 중 하나를 무작위로 배정받을 것입니다.
(9)• 당신이 이야기를 작성하고 제출하는 데 정확하게 7일이 있을 것입니다. You will be randomly assigned one of 12 literary genres for your story.
(10)제출
(11)• 1인당 한 출품작만 Only one entry per person
(12)• 당신은 마감 기한까지 출품작을 수정하여 다시 제출할 수 있습니다.
(13)시상
(14)• 우리는 각 장르에서 한 명씩 12명의 결승 진출자를 선발할 것이고, 12편의 출품작들은 온라인으로 출판되고 소셜 미디어를 통해 공유될 것입니다.
(15)• 12명의 결승 진출자들 중에서 한 명의 전체 우승자가 선발되어, 500달러를 받을 것입니다. From the 12 finalists, one overall winner will be chosen and awarded $500.
(16)※ 등록을 하거나 더 많은 정보를 위해서, www.7challenge_globestory.com을 방문하세요.

[정답 확인]

7-Day Story Writing Competition에 관한 다음 안내문의 내용과 일치하는 것은?

① 17세 ~~미만~~(이상) 누구나 참여할 수 있다. 문장(5)
✔ 참가자(participant)들은 동일한 주제에 대하여 글을 쓴다. 문장(7)
③ 참가자들은 12가지 문학 장르(literary genres) 중 하나를 ~~선택할 수 있다~~(무작위로 배정받는다). 문장(8)
④ 1인당 출품작을 ~~최대 3편까지~~(1편만) 제출할(submit) 수 있다. 문장(11)
⑤ 결승 진출자(finalist) ~~전원~~(중 우승자)에게 상금이 수여된다(be awarded). 문장(15)

[중요 어휘]

□ assign	동사 배정하다, 부과하다
□ literary	형용사 문학의
□ submit	동사 제출하다, 항복하다
□ submission	명사 제출, 항복
□ entry	명사 출품작
□ revise	동사 수정하다
□ finalist	명사 결승 진출자
□ via	전치사 (특정 시스템 등을) 통하여
□ overall	형용사 전체의, 종합적인

23 2019년 9월 28번 (정답률 80%) 정답 ④

[중요 구문] 미니 빔 프로젝터

(13) You cannot [write data to] / or [delete data from] /
당신은 ~에 데이터를 저장할 수 없습니다 / 또는 ~의 데이터를 삭제할 수 없습니다 /
the USB device.
USB 장치
힌트 write data to와 delete data from 모두 전치사의 목적어로 the USB device를 가짐.
힌트 write data: 데이터를 저장하다

[전문 해석]

(1)미니 빔 프로젝터
(2)- 설명(서) -
(3)LED 전원표시기
(4) • 빨강: 전원 대기 상태 Red: Power standby state
(5) • 녹색: 프로젝터가 켜져 있으며 작동 중
(6)작동시키는 방법
(7) • 대기 모드에서, 프로젝터를 켜기 위해 전원 버튼을 한 번 누르세요.
(8) • 프로젝터를 끄기 위해 전원 버튼을 두 번 누르세요. Press the power button twice to turn the projector off.
(9) • 조이스틱을 좌우로 움직여서 음량을 조절하세요. Adjust the volume level by moving the joystick left or right.
(10) • 포커스 링을 돌려서 이미지의 초점을 맞추세요. 정답단서 Adjust the focus of the image by rotating the focus ring.
(11)USB 장치 연결하기
(12)당신의 콘텐츠 파일을 즐기기 위해 프로젝터의 USB 포트에 USB 장치를 연결하세요.
(13)(당신은) USB 장치에 데이터를 저장하거나 USB 장치의 데이터를 삭제할 수 없습니다.
You cannot write data to or delete data from the USB device.

[정답 확인]

Mini Beam Projector 사용에 관한 다음 안내문의 내용과 일치하는 것은?

① 전원표시기의 ~~녹색~~(빨강)은 대기(standby) 상태임을 나타낸다. 문장(4)
② 전원 버튼을 ~~한 번~~(두 번)(once) 누르면 전원이 꺼진다. 문장(8)
③ 조이스틱을 ~~위아래~~(좌우)로 움직여 음량을 조절한다(adjust). 문장(9)
✔ 포커스 링을 돌려서 이미지의 초점(focus)을 맞춘다. 문장(10)
⑤ USB 장치에 있는 데이터를 삭제할(delete) 수 ~~있다~~(없다). 문장(13)

✶중요 문장 (8)에서 프로젝터를 끄려면 전원 버튼을 두 번(twice) 눌러야 한다고 했음. 반대로 프로젝터를 켜려면 전원 버튼을 한 번(once) 누르면 된다고 문장 (7)에 적혀 있음.

[중요 어휘]

□ indicator	명사 표시기, 지표
□ standby	명사 대기, 대역 / 형용사 대기의, 대역의
□ adjust	동사 조절하다, 적응하다
□ focus	명사 초점, 주목 / 동사 초점을 맞추다, 집중하다
□ port	명사 포트(기기 접속 단자), 항구

24 2020년 3월 28번 (정답률 80%) 정답 ②

[중요 구문] 빛나는 고양이 장난감

(2) Attract your cat's attention / and satisfy their hunting instincts /
당신의 고양이의 주의를 끄세요 / 그리고 그들의 사냥 본능을 충족시키세요 /
with a unique electronic cat toy.
독특한 전자 고양이 장난감으로

(6) It automatically stops running / after 8 minutes.
stop V-ing: ~하던 것을 멈추다
그것은 자동으로 작동을 멈춥니다 / 8분 후에

문제편 p.124

[전문 해석]

(1)빛나는 고양이 장난감
(2)독특한 전자 고양이 장난감으로 당신의 고양이의 주의를 끌고 (그들의) 사냥 본능을 충족시키세요.
(3)주요 이점
(4)■ 깃털이 6개의 구멍에서 무작위로 나옵니다. The feather appears randomly in the 6 holes.
(5)■ 깃털은 쉽게 교체될 수 있습니다.
(6)■ 그것은 8분 후에 자동으로 작동을 멈춥니다. 정답 단서 It automatically stops running after 8 minutes.
(7)■ 그것은 USB 케이블을 통해 30분 안에 완전히 충전되며, 5시간 동안 작동합니다. It is fully charged in 30 minutes via USB-cable, and it runs for 5 hours.
(8)사용하는 방법
(9)■ 기기의 전원을 켜거나 끄려면 버튼을 짧게 누르세요. Short press the button to power on/off the device.
(10)■ 깃털을 바꾸려면 버튼을 길게 누르세요.
(11)상자 속 내용물
(12)■ 빛나는 고양이 장난감: 1개
(13)■ 깃털: 2개(장착된 것 1개, 여분 1개) Feather: 2 pieces (1 installed, 1 extra)

[정답 확인]

Bright Cat Toy에 관한 다음 안내문의 내용과 일치하는 것은?

① 구멍에서 정해진 순서대로 깃털(feather)이 나온다. 문장(4)
② 8분 후에 자동으로(automatically) 작동을 멈춘다. 문장(6)
③ 완전히 충전하는(charge) 데 5시간이 걸린다. 문장(7)
④ 켜거나 끄려면 버튼을 길게 눌러야(press) 한다. 문장(9)
⑤ 총 세 개의 깃털이 제공된다(be provided). 문장(13)

[중요 어휘]

□ attract	동사 끌다
□ attention	명사 주의, 관심
□ instinct	명사 본능
□ via	전치사 ~을 통해
□ extra	명사 여분 / 형용사 여분의, 추가의

25 2021년 3월 27번 (정답률 80%)

정답 ③

[중요 구문]

Riverside 탈출

(3) We turn the city of Riverside / into a giant escape game /
우리는 Riverside 도시를 바꿉니다 / 하나의 거대한 탈출 게임으로 /
wherein teams must race around the city /
그리고 그곳에서 팀들은 도시를 질주해야 합니다 /
completing challenges / without getting caught.
도전 과제들을 완수하면서 / 잡히지 않은 채로

힌트 밑줄 친 분사구문 'completing challenges'는 동시동작의 의미로 쓰여서 '도전 과제들을 완수하면서'라고 해석해야 함. 관계부사인 wherein 다음에 완전한 문장이 온 것도 확인할 것.

[전문 해석]

(1)Riverside 탈출 The Riverside Escape is a city-wide escape game played on your smartphone.
(2)Riverside 탈출은 당신의 스마트폰으로 하는 도시 전역에서 벌어지는 탈출 게임입니다.
(3)우리는 Riverside 도시를 하나의 거대한 탈출 게임으로 바꾸고, 그곳(도시)에서 팀들은 잡히지 않은 채로 도전 과제들을 완수하면서 도시를 질주해야 합니다.
(4)게임하는 방법
(5) • 티켓을 구매하세요. — 최대 6인으로 이루어진 팀당 티켓 한 장 Get your ticket — one ticket per team of up to 6 players.
(6) • 게임의 시작 일자를 고르세요. (7)우리는 당신이 선택한 일자 이전에 이메일을 통해 상세한 정보를 보내 드립니다. 정답 단서 We will send you detailed information via email before your date of choice.
(8) • 그날 시작 지점에 도착해서 당신이 원하는 때에 언제든 시작하세요.
(9) • 도시를 돌아다니는 동안 퍼즐에 대한 답을 함으로써 가능한 많은 점수를 얻으세요.
(10)운영 시간
(11)2021년 3월 1일 - 2021년 5월 31일 March 1, 2021 - May 31, 2021
(12)월요일 - 일요일, 10:00 - 20:00
(13)티켓 가격
(14)티켓당 50달러 (이 가격은 매일 달라질 수 있습니다.) (This price may change on a daily basis.)
(15)탈출 모험을 위해 와서 저희와 함께하세요!

[정답 확인]

The Riverside Escape에 관한 다음 안내문의 내용과 일치하지 않는 것은?

① 도시 전역에서(city-wide) 벌어지는 탈출 게임이다. 문장(2)
② 최대(up to) 여섯 명으로 구성된 팀당 티켓 한 장을 사야 한다. 문장(5)
③ 선택한 게임 시작일 이전에 전화로 상세한 정보(detailed information)를 알려 준다. 문장(7)
④ 2021년 3월 1일부터 세 달간 열린다. 문장(11)
⑤ 티켓 가격은 매일(on a daily basis) 달라질 수 있다. 문장(14)

[중요 어휘]

□ escape	명사 탈출 / 동사 탈출하다
□ city-wide	형용사 도시 전역의
□ turn A into B	A를 B로 바꾸다
□ wherein	그곳에서
□ race	동사 질주하다, 경주하다
□ challenge	명사 도전 과제, 큰 문제
□ location	명사 지점, 장소
□ on a daily basis	매일
□ adventure	명사 모험, 모험심

26 2023년 11월 27번 (정답률 95%)

정답 ④

[중요 구문]

청소년 테니스 캠프

(2) 2024 Youth Tennis Camp is /
2024 청소년 테니스 캠프는 ~한 곳입니다 /
[where your child can get instruction from qualified tennis players /
여러분의 자녀가 자격이 있는 테니스 선수에게 지도를 받을 수 있는 /
at indoor tennis courts]. [ ]: 관계부사절(선행사 the place가 생략됨)
실내 테니스 코트에서

[전문 해석]

(1)2024 청소년 테니스 캠프
(2)2024 청소년 테니스 캠프는 여러분의 자녀가 실내 테니스 코트에서 자격이 있는 테니스 선수에게 지도를 받을 수 있는 곳입니다. (3)그것은 여러분의 자녀들에게 기본적인 테니스 기술을 제공할 것입니다! 2024 Youth Tennis Camp is where your child can get instruction from qualified tennis players at indoor tennis courts.
(4)누가: 13세에서 18세까지
(5)언제: 2024년 1월 15일부터 18일까지
(6)월요일부터 목요일까지, 오전 9시부터 오후 12시까지 Monday to Thursday
(7)등록비: 100달러(점심 식사가 포함됨) Registration Fee: $100(lunch included)
(8)취소 정책
(9) • 강습 5일 전까지: 100% 환불
(10) • 강습 1~4일 전까지: 50% 환불
(11) • 강습 당일과 그 이후: 환불 불가 정답 단서 On the day of the class and afterwards: No refund
(12)참고
(13) • 외부 음식은 허용되지 않습니다.
(14) • 참가자들은 자신의 테니스 장비를 가져와야 합니다. Participants must bring their own tennis equipment.
(15)등록은 온라인으로만 가능하며 12월 16일에 시작할 것입니다. (16)등록을 위해 우리의 웹사이트 www.ytc2024.com에 방문하세요.

[정답 확인]

2024 Youth Tennis Camp에 관한 다음 안내문의 내용과 일치하지 않는 것은?

① 자격을 가진(qualified) 테니스 선수가 지도한다. 문장(2)
② 금요일에는 강습(class)이 없다. 문장(6)
③ 등록비(registration fee)에는 점심 식사가 포함된다. 문장(7)
④ 강습 당일 취소 시 환불받을(be refunded) 수 있다. 문장(11)
⑤ 참가자들은 테니스 장비(equipment)를 가져와야 한다. 문장(14)

[중요 어휘]

□ indoor	형용사 실내의, 실내용의
□ cancellation	명사 취소, 무효화
□ policy	명사 정책, 방침
□ afterwards	부사 이후, 나중에

27 2023년 11월 28번 (정답률 95%)

정답 ④

[전문 해석] 티셔츠 디자인 대회

(1)Cherrywood 고등학교 티셔츠 디자인 대회 A panel of student council members will select the winning design.
(2)우리가 우리의 새로운 학교 티셔츠를 디자인하는 것을 도와주세요! (3)학생회 위원단이 수상 디자인을 선정할 것입니다. (4)새로운 학교 티셔츠의 디자이너가 되는 이 기회를 잡으세요.
(5)이 대회는 모든 학생들에게 열려 있습니다!
(6)제출 마감 기한: 2023년 12월 22일 16시 Submission Deadline: 16:00 on December 22, 2023
(7)수상자 발표일: 2023년 12월 29일 Winner Announcement Date: December 29, 2023
(8)제출 장소: 미술 선생님 사무실 Location for Submissions: Art Teacher's Office
(9)대회 규정
(10) • 백지 한 장에 여러분의 디자인을 스케치하세요.
(11) • 여러분의 종이에 여러분의 학번과 이름을 적으세요. 정답 단서 Write your student number and name on your paper.
(12) • 여러분의 디자인에 학교 이름과 로고를 포함시키세요.
(13) • 최대 4개의 색상이 사용될 수 있습니다. Max of 4 colors can be used.
(14)행운을 빌며 참여해 주셔서 감사합니다!

[정답 확인]

Cherrywood High School's T-shirt Design Contest에 관한 다음 안내문의 내용과 일치하는 것은?

① ~~교사들이~~(학생회 위원단이) 수상 디자인을 선정할(select) 예정이다. 문장(3)
② 수상자 발표일(announcement date)은 제출 마감일 ~~다음 날~~(7일 후)이다. 문장(6), (7)
③ 출품작은 ~~학생회실~~(미술 선생님 사무실)에 제출해야(submit) 한다. 문장(8)
✔ 종이에 자신의 학번(student number)과 이름을 써야 한다. 문장(11)
⑤ 사용 가능한 색상 수에 제한이 ~~없다~~(있다). 문장(13)

[중요 어휘]

□ panel	명사 위원단, 패널
□ student council	명사 학생회, 학생 자치위원회
□ deadline	명사 마감 기한, 마감 시간
□ announcement	명사 발표, 공고

28 2024년 3월 27번 (정답률 95%)

정답 ③

[전문 해석] 라떼 아트 수업

(1)기초 라떼 아트 수업
(2)완벽한 라떼를 만들고 그것들을 가장 아름다운 방식으로 표현해 보세요! (3)이 수업에서, 여러분은 우유를 데우고 따르는 방법을 배울 것입니다. (4)여러분은 세 가지 라떼 아트 디자인(하트, 튤립, 그리고 나뭇잎)을 스스로 만들 것입니다. You will make three latte art designs on your own: heart, tulip, and leaf.
(5)날짜: 2024년 4월 27일
(6)시간: 오전 9시부터 오후 1시까지 Time: 9 a.m. – 1 p.m.
(7)장소: Camefort 커뮤니티 센터
(8)등록 & 비용 Register online at www.camefortcc.com, from April 22 to April 24. 정답 단서
(9) • 4월 22일부터 4월 24일까지 www.camefortcc.com에서 온라인으로 등록하세요.
(10) • 1인당 60달러 (재료비 포함됨) $60 per person (cost of ingredients included)
(11)참고 Dairy alternatives will be available for non-milk drinkers.
(12) • 우유를 마시지 않는 사람은 대체 유제품을 사용할 수 있습니다.
(13) • 학생은 10% 할인을 받을 수 있습니다.

[정답 확인]

Basic Latte Art Class에 관한 다음 안내문의 내용과 일치하지 않는 것은?

① 세 가지 라떼 아트 디자인을 직접 만들 것이다. 문장(4)
② 수업(class)은 4시간 동안 진행된다. 문장(6)
✔ 등록(registration)은 4월 ~~24~~(22)일부터 시작된다. 문장(9)
④ 비용에 재료비(cost of ingredients)가 포함되어 있다. 문장(10)
⑤ 우유를 마시지 않는 사람은 대체 유제품(dairy alternatives)을 사용할 수 있다. 문장(12)

[중요 어휘]

□ pour	동사 따르다, 붓다
□ on one's own	스스로, 혼자 힘으로
□ dairy	명사 유제품 / 형용사 유제품의
□ alternative	형용사 대체의 / 명사 대체품, 대안
□ available	형용사 사용[이용]할 수 있는

29 2024년 3월 28번 (정답률 95%)

정답 ④

[전문 해석] 가족 야간 하이킹 이벤트

(1)가족 야간 하이킹 이벤트
(2)하이킹과 가족 간 유대로 즐거움이 가득한 밤을 저희와 함께하세요!
(3)날짜: 5월 4일 토요일 Date: Saturday, May 4
(4)시간: 오후 6시부터 오후 9시까지 Time: 6 p.m. – 9 p.m.
(5)장소: Skyline 보호 구역
(6)비용
(7) • 성인: 20달러 Adults: $20
(8) • 19세 미만 어린이: 10달러 Children under 19: $10
(9)지침
(10) • 어린이는 법적 보호자를 동반해야 합니다. 정답 단서 Children must be accompanied by legal guardians.
(11) • 손전등과 물 한 병을 가져오세요.
(12) • 항상 안내원의 지시를 따라 주세요.
(13)등록
(14) • www.familyhiking.com에 방문하셔서 4월 26일까지 등록하세요.
(15) • 4월 12일까지 등록을 하시는 모든 분께는 무료 구급상자가 제공됩니다. A free first aid kit is provided for all who register by April 12.

[정답 확인]

Family Night-hiking Event에 관한 다음 안내문의 내용과 일치하는 것은?

① 토요일~~과 일요일 이틀간~~(에만) 진행된다. 문장(3)
② 오후 ~~5~~(6)시에 시작된다. 문장(4)
③ 어른과 어린이의 참가비(cost)는 ~~같다~~(다르다). 문장(7), (8)
✔ 어린이는 법적 보호자(legal guardian)를 동반해야 한다. 문장(10)
⑤ ~~추첨을 통해~~(4월 12일까지 등록하는 모두에게) 구급상자(first aid kit)가 무료로 제공된다. 문장(15)

[중요 어휘]

□ bonding	명사 유대, 긴밀한 유대
□ preserve	명사 보호 구역 / 동사 보존하다, 보호하다
□ legal	형용사 법적인, 합법적인
□ guardian	명사 보호자, 후견인
□ first aid kit	구급상자

30 2024년 6월 27번 (정답률 95%)

정답 ⑤

[전문 해석] 미래 엔지니어 캠프

(1)2024 미래 엔지니어 캠프
(2)모든 젊은 크리에이터들을 초대합니다! (3)Southside Maker Space에 참여하여 흥미진진한 활동과 함께 공학 기술의 경이로움을 탐구하세요!
(4)날짜: 7월 20일 토요일 & 7월 21일 일요일
(5)시간: 오전 10시~오후 4시 Time: 10 a.m. – 4 p.m.
(6)연령: 14세~16세
(7)참가비: 100달러 Participation Fee: $100
(8)1일 차 - 로봇 공학 워크숍
(9) • 기본적인 코딩 기술을 배웁니다. Learn basic coding skills.
(10) • 팀을 이루어 미니 로봇을 만듭니다.
(11)2일 차 - 플라잉 챌린지
(12) • 장난감 비행기를 만들고 테스트합니다. Make and test toy airplanes.
(13) • 비행기 날리기 경주에 참여합니다.
(14)유의 사항
(15) • 점심 식사는 참가비에 포함되어 있습니다. 정답 단서 Lunch is included in the participation fee.
(16) • 프로젝트에 필요한 모든 도구와 재료는 제공됩니다.
(17)더 많은 정보를 위해서는 www.southsidemaker.com을 방문하세요.

[정답 확인]

2024 Future Engineers Camp에 관한 다음 안내문의 내용과 일치하지 않는 것은?

① 오전 10시부터 오후 4시까지 진행된다. 문장(5)
② 참가비(participation fee)는 100달러이다. 문장(7)
③ 기본적인 코딩 기술(basic coding skills)을 배운다. 문장(9)
④ 장난감 비행기(toy airplane)를 만들고 테스트한다. 문장(12)
✔⑤ 점심 식사는 참가비에 ~~포함되지 않는다~~(포함되어 있다). 문장(15)

[중요 어휘]

□ **explore**	동사 탐구하다, 탐험하다
□ **wonder**	명사 경이로움 / 동사 궁금해하다
□ **engineering**	명사 공학 기술
□ **robotics**	명사 로봇 공학

31 2024년 6월 28번 (정답률 95%) 정답 ③

[전문 해석] 도시 맛보기

(1)도시를 맛보세요
(2)Jamestown의 다양하고 맛있는 음식 문화를 한자리에서 모두 경험해 보세요. (3)맛있는 음식을 즐기고, 새로운 레스토랑을 발견해 보세요!
(4)언제 & 어디서
(5) • 9월 6일~8일 (오전 10시~오후 9시) September 6th - 8th (10 a.m. - 9 p.m.)
(6) • 대공원
(7)주요 사항
(8) • 현지 레스토랑에서 제공되는 음식 샘플 30종
(9) • 매일 저녁 라이브 음악 공연 Live music performances each evening
(10) • 숙련된 요리사들과의 요리 수업 정답 단서 Cooking classes with experienced chefs
(11)입장권
(12) • 성인: 15달러 Adult: $15
(13) • 어린이: 10달러 Child: $10
(14)※ 사전 예약은 필요하지 않으며, 바로 오셔서 즐기세요. No pre-reservations necessary, just show up and enjoy.

[정답 확인]

Taste the City에 관한 다음 안내문의 내용과 일치하는 것은?

① 9월 6일부터 ~~일주일~~(3일) 동안 열린다. 문장(5)
② 라이브 음악 공연(performance)이 ~~하루 종일~~(매일 저녁) 진행된다. 문장(9)
✔③ 숙련된(experienced) 요리사들과의 요리 수업이 있다. 문장(10)
④ 어른과 아이의 입장권(entry ticket) 가격은 ~~동일하다~~(다르다). 문장(12), (13)
⑤ 사전 예약(pre-reservation)이 ~~필요하다~~(필요 없다). 문장(14)

[중요 어휘]

□ **diverse**	형용사 다양한, 다른
□ **highlight**	명사 주요 사항, 하이라이트, 가장 흥미로운 부분 / 동사 강조하다
□ **local**	형용사 현지의, 지역의 / 명사 현지인
□ **chef**	명사 요리사, 주방장
□ **entry**	명사 입장

32 2024년 9월 27번 (정답률 90%) 정답 ⑤

[전문 해석] 청소의 날

(1)2024 Clifton 가을 청소의 날
(2)센트럴 파크에서 낙엽을 청소하는 올해의 연례 행사에 저희와 함께 하시고, 여러분의 이웃들과 만남을 즐기세요! Join us for this annual event to clean up the fallen leaves in Central Park, and enjoy meeting your neighbors!
(3)언제: 10월 20일 일요일 오후 1시 ~ 오후 3시
(4)세부 사항
(5) • 연령에 기반하여 10명씩 조를 이루어 청소가 될 것입니다. Clean-up will be done in groups of 10 people based on age.
(6) • 청소 후에, 여러분은 이웃들과 가벼운 모임을 즐기실 수 있습니다.
(7) • 여러분의 모임을 위한 푸드 트럭이 설치될 것입니다. Food trucks will be set up for your gathering.
(8)유의 사항
(9) • 행사 로고가 있는 티셔츠가 선물로 제공될 것입니다. A T-shirt with the event's logo will be provided as a gift.
(10) • 봉지와 장갑 같은 청소 도구들이 제공될 것이므로 여러분은 그것들을 가져올 필요가 없습니다. 정답 단서 You'll be supplied with cleaning materials, such as bags and gloves, so you don't have to bring them.
(11)저희는 그곳에서 여러분을 만나기를 고대하고 있습니다!

[정답 확인]

Clifton Fall Clean-up Day 2024에 관한 다음 안내문의 내용과 일치하지 않는 것은?

① 매년(annual) 열리는 행사이다. 문장(2)
② 10명씩 조(group)를 이루어 청소할 것이다. 문장(5)
③ 푸드 트럭이 설치될(be set up) 것이다. 문장(7)
④ 행사 로고(event's logo)가 있는 티셔츠가 제공될 것이다. 문장(9)
✔⑤ 청소 도구(cleaning material)를 ~~가져와야 한다~~(가져올 필요가 없다). 문장(10)

[중요 어휘]

□ **clean-up**	명사 청소
□ **annual**	형용사 연례의, 매년의
□ **casual**	형용사 (관계가) 가벼운, 격식을 차리지 않는
□ **gathering**	명사 모임, 집회, 수집
□ **material**	명사 도구, 재료

33 2024년 9월 28번 (정답률 95%) 정답 ④

[전문 해석] 지속 가능한 패션 페스티벌

(1)2024 지속 가능한 패션 페스티벌
(2)2024 지속 가능한 패션 페스티벌이 다가오고 있습니다! (3)멋지게 보이면서 영감을 얻고 지속 가능하게 사는 방법을 배워 보세요.
(4)언제 & 어디서
(5) • 9월 13일 금요일 오후 5시 ~ 오후 9시 Friday, September 13th, 5 p.m. - 9 p.m.
(6) • Aimes 지역 문화 센터
(7)티켓: 조기 구매 20달러 / 현장 구매 25달러
(8)(조기 구매 할인은 행사 이틀 전에 종료됩니다.) (Early purchase discount ends two days before the event.)
(9)프로그램
(10) • 지속 가능한 제품을 위한 장터: 여러분은 새 의류, 빈티지 의류 혹은 업사이클 의류를 팔거나 살 수 있습니다. You can sell or buy new, vintage, or upcycled clothing
(11) • 패션의 지속 가능한 미래를 위한 친환경 패션 전문가들의 강연
(12) • 의류 교환: 여러분은 5개 이하의 물품들을 교환할 수 있습니다. 정답 단서 You can exchange 5 or fewer items.
(13) • 지속 가능한 디자인의 패션쇼
(14)※ 장터에서 여러분의 지속 가능한 제품을 판매하기 위해서, 사전에 등록이 필요합니다. To sell your sustainable products at our marketplace, registration is required in advance.
(15)더 많은 정보를 원하시면 소셜 미디어로 저희에게 연락해 주세요.

[정답 확인]

Sustainable Fashion Festival 2024에 관한 다음 안내문의 내용과 일치하는 것은?

① 금요일 ~~오전~~(오후)에 진행된다. 문장(5)
② 티켓 조기 구매 할인(early purchase discount)은 행사 ~~사흘~~(이틀) 전 종료된다. 문장(8)
③ 장터(marketplace)에서 새 의류(new clothing)를 구입할 수 ~~없다~~(있다). 문장(10)
✔④ 5개 이하의 의류 물품(item)을 교환할(exchange) 수 있다. 문장(12)
⑤ 사전 등록(registration in advance) ~~없이도~~(을 해야만) 지속 가능 제품을 판매할 수 있다. 문장(14)

[중요 어휘]

□ **sustainable**	형용사 (환경 파괴 없이) 지속 가능한, 지탱할 수 있는
□ **inspire**	동사 영감을 주다, 고무[격려]하다
□ **fabulous**	형용사 멋진, 믿어지지 않는, 엄청난
□ **marketplace**	명사 장터, 시장
□ **upcycle**	동사 (재활용품을) 업사이클하다, 더 나은 것으로 만들다
□ **talk**	명사 강연, 연설, 이야기
□ **in advance**	사전에, 미리, 선지급으로

문제편 p.132

11 빈칸 추론(1)-어휘, 짧은 어구

핵심 Diderot Effect라는 생소한 개념이 나오므로, 새롭게 등장한 개념에 대한 파악을 중심으로 지문에 나오는 설명과 예시들을 연결해야 함.

01 2021년 6월 31번 (정답률 70%) 정답 ①

[지문 끊어 읽기] Diderot 효과

(1) The tendency for one purchase to lead to another one / (S, 의미상의 주어, 형용사적 용법, 전치사)
한 구매가 또 다른 구매로 이어지는 경향은 /
has a name: / the Diderot Effect. (V)
이름을 가지고 있다 / Diderot 효과

(2) The Diderot Effect states / that obtaining a new possession / (명사절 접속사, S')
Diderot 효과는 말한다 / 새로운 소유물을 얻는 것이 /
often creates a spiral of consumption / (V', 선행사)
종종 소비의 소용돌이를 만든다고 /
that leads to additional purchases. 정답 단서 (주격 관계대명사)
추가적인 구매들로 이어지는

(3) You can spot this pattern everywhere.
당신은 이러한 경향을 어디서든지 발견할 수 있다

(4) You buy a dress /
당신은 드레스를 산다 /
and have to get new shoes and earrings / to match. (형용사적 용법)
그리고 새 신발과 귀걸이를 사야 한다 / 어울리는

(5) You buy a toy for your child / and soon find yourself / (병렬①, 병렬②)
당신은 당신의 아이를 위해 장난감을 산다 / 그리고 곧 자신을 발견한다 /
purchasing all of the accessories / that go with it. (선행사, 주격 관계대명사)
모든 액세서리들을 구매하는 / 그것과 어울리는

(6) It's a chain reaction of purchases. 정답 단서
이것은 구매의 연쇄 반응이다

(7) Many human behaviors follow this cycle.
많은 인간의 행동들은 이 순환을 따른다

(8) You often decide / what to do next / based on /
당신은 자주 결정한다 / 다음에 무엇을 할지 / 근거하여 /
what you have just finished doing. (현재완료)
당신이 방금 하던 일을 끝낸 것에

(9) Going to the bathroom /
화장실에 가는 것은 /
leads to washing and drying your hands, / (선행사)
손을 씻고 말리는 것으로 이어진다 /
which reminds you [that / (4형식V, I·O, [ ]:D·O)
그리고 그것은 당신으로 하여금 상기시킨다 /
you need to put the dirty towels in the laundry], /
더러운 수건을 세탁실에 넣을 필요가 있다는 것을 /
so you add laundry detergent to the shopping list, / and so on. (add A to B: A를 B에 추가하다)
그래서 당신은 쇼핑 목록에 세탁 세제를 추가한다 / 그리고 기타 등등을

힌트 선행사 뒤에 콤마(,)와 관계대명사 which가 이어져 계속적 용법으로 쓰임. 선행사를 추가적으로 이어서 보충 설명하는 역할로, 앞에서부터 순차적으로 해석함.

(10) No behavior happens / in isolation.
어떤 행동도 일어나지 않는다 / 고립 상태에서

중요 빈칸이 있는 문장 (10)이 부정문이므로 '하나의 구매 행동이 또 다른 구매 행동을 유발한다'는 글의 주제와 반대되는 의미의 단어 'isolation'이 빈칸에 와야 함.

(11) Each action becomes a cue / that triggers the next behavior. 정답 단서 (선행사, 주격 관계대명사)
각 행동은 신호가 된다 / 다음 행동을 유발하는

[중요 구문]

(5) You [buy a toy for your child] and [soon find yourself purchasing all of the accessories that go with it]. (5형식V, O, O·C, 주격 관계대명사절)

힌트 5형식 동사 find의 목적격 보어로 명사, 형용사, 분사가 올 수 있는데, 목적어와 목적격 보어의 관계가 능동이므로 현재분사가 왔음. 'find oneself+목적격 보어'는 '자신이 ~하고 있음을 발견하다'라는 의미임.

[전문 해석]

(1)한 구매가 또 다른 구매로 이어지는 경향은 Diderot 효과라는 이름을 가지고 있다. (2)Diderot 효과는 새로운 소유물을 얻는 것이 종종 추가적인 구매들로 이어지는 소비의 소용돌이를 만든다고 말한다. (3)당신은 이러한 경향을 어디서든지 발견할 수 있다. (4)당신은 드레스를 사고 어울리는 새 신발과 귀걸이를 사야 한다. (5)당신은 당신의 아이를 위해 장난감을 사고 곧 그것과 어울리는 모든 액세서리들을 구매하는 자신을 발견한다. (6)이것은 구매의 연쇄 반응이다. (7)많은 인간의 행동들은 이 순환을 따른다. (8)당신은 자주 당신이 방금 하던 일을 끝낸 것에 근거하여 다음에 무엇을 할지 결정한다. (9)화장실에 가는 것은 손을 씻고 말리는 것으로 이어지고, 그것은 당신으로 하여금 더러운 수건을 세탁실에 넣을 필요가 있다는 것을 상기시키고, 그래서 당신은 쇼핑 목록에 세탁 세제를 추가하고, 기타 등등(의 행동)을 한다. (10)어떤 행동도 고립 상태에서 일어나지 않는다. (11)각 행동은 다음 행동을 유발하는 신호가 된다.

- Diderot Effect(디드로 효과): 프랑스 철학자 드니 디드로(Denis Diderot)의 에세이 <나의 오래된 가운을 버림으로 인한 후회>에 나온 일화에서 유래한 것으로, 한 물건을 구입한 후 그에 어울리는 다른 물건을 계속 구매하는 현상을 말함.

[정답 확인]

다음 빈칸에 들어갈 말로 가장 적절한 것은?

① isolation 고립 상태
② comfort 안락
③ observation 관찰
④ fairness 공정성
⑤ harmony 조화

[중요 어휘]

□ **tendency**	명사 경향, 추세
□ **purchase**	명사 구매 / 동사 구매하다
□ **obtain**	동사 얻다, 입수하다
□ **possession**	명사 소유물
□ **spiral**	명사 소용돌이, 나선
□ **consumption**	명사 소비
□ **spot**	동사 발견하다 / 명사 점, 곳
□ **go with**	~와 어울리다
□ **chain reaction**	연쇄 반응
□ **remind**	동사 상기시키다
□ **detergent**	명사 세제
□ **isolation**	명사 고립 (상태)
□ **trigger**	동사 유발하다

02 2022년 11월 31번 (정답률 65%) 정답 ②

[지문 끊어 읽기] 놀람 반응과 학습의 연관성

(1) No learning is possible / without an error signal.
어떤 학습도 가능하지 않다 / 오류 신호 없이는

(2) Organisms only learn / when events violate their expectations.
유기체는 오로지 학습한다 / 사건이 그들의 기대를 거스를 때

(3) In other words, /
다시 말해 /
surprise is one of the fundamental drivers of learning.
놀람은 학습의 근본적인 동력 중 하나이다

(4) Imagine / hearing a series of identical notes, / AAAAA. (동명사(목적어), =, 동격)
상상하라 / 일련의 동일한 음을 듣는 것을 / AAAAA인

중요 음계 '도레미파솔라시도'는 영어로 'CDEFGABC'임. 즉 A는 '라'음을 나타냄.

(5) Each note draws out a response /
각각의 음은 반응을 끌어낸다 /
in the auditory areas of your brain / — but as the notes repeat, /
여러분의 뇌의 청각 영역에서 / 하지만 음이 반복되면서 /
those responses progressively decrease. (=responses in the auditory areas of your brain)
그 반응은 점진적으로 감소한다

(6) This is called "adaptation," / a deceptively simple phenomenon / (=, 선행사)
이것은 '적응'이라고 불린다 / 현혹될 정도로 단순해 보이는 현상인 /

문제편 p.133

that shows [that your brain is learning /
주격 관계대명사 [ ]: shows의 목적어절
당신의 뇌가 배울 것임을 보여 주는 /

to anticipate the next event]. 정답 단서 적응은 다음 사건에 대한 예상을 가능하게 함.
명사적 용법(목적어)
다음 사건을 예상하는 것을

(7) Suddenly, / the note changes: / AAAAA#.
갑자기 / 그 음이 바뀐다 / AAAAA#으로

(8) Your primary auditory cortex immediately shows /
당신의 1차 청각 피질은 즉각적으로 보여 준다 /

a strong surprise reaction: /
강한 놀람의 반응을 /

not only does the adaptation fade away, /
적응이 사라질 뿐만 아니라 /

but additional neurons begin to vigorously fire /
추가적인 뉴런이 힘차게 발화하기 시작한다 /

in response to the unexpected sound. 정답 단서 예상하지 못한 소리(사건)에는 적응 반응이 사라지고 새로운 사건에 대한 놀람 반응이 일어남.
예상하지 못한 소리에 대한 반응으로

힌트 no, not, never와 같은 부정부사가 문장 맨 앞에 나올 때에는 도치가 이루어짐. 문장 (8)의 경우, 주어인 the adaptation의 수와 시제를 일치시킨 조동사 does가 주어 앞에 놓였음.

(9) And [it is not just repetition / that leads to adaptation]: /
그리고 단순한 반복이 아니다 / 적응을 유발하는 것은 / [ ]: it is ~ that 강조구문

what matters is / whether the notes are predictable.
명사절
중요한 것은 ~이다 / 그 음이 예측 가능한지

(10) For instance, / if you hear an alternating set of notes, /
예를 들어 / 만약 당신이 한 세트의 교차하는 음을 듣는다면 /

such as ABABA, / your brain gets used to this alternation, /
ABABA와 같이 / 당신의 뇌는 이 교차에 익숙해진다 /

and the activity in your auditory areas / again decreases.
그리고 당신의 청각 영역 내의 활동은 / 다시 감소한다

(11) This time, however, / [it is an unexpected repetition, /
그러나 이번에는 / 바로 예상하지 못한 반복이다 /

such as ABABB, / that triggers a surprise response]. [ ]: it is ~ that 강조구문
ABABB와 같은 / 놀람의 반응을 일으키는 것은

[전문 해석]

(1)어떤 학습도 오류 신호 없이는 가능하지 않다. (2)유기체는 오로지 사건이 그들의 기대를 거스를 때 학습한다. (3)다시 말해, 놀람은 학습의 근본적인 동력 중 하나이다. (4)일련의 동일한 음인 AAAAA를 듣는 것을 상상하라. (5)각각의 음은 여러분의 뇌의 청각 영역에서 반응을 끌어내지만 음이 반복되면서 그 반응은 점진적으로 감소한다. (6)이것은 '적응'이라고 불리며 당신의 뇌가 다음 사건을 예상하는 것을 배울 것임을 보여 주는 현혹될 정도로 단순해 보이는 현상이다. (7)갑자기 그 음이 AAAAA#으로 바뀐다. (8)당신의 1차 청각 피질은 즉각적으로 강한 놀람의 반응을 보여 주는데, 즉 적응이 사라질 뿐만 아니라 예상하지 못한 소리에 대한 반응으로 추가적인 뉴런이 힘차게 발화하기 시작한다. (9)그리고 적응을 유발하는 것은 단순한 반복이 아니라, 중요한 것은 그 음이 예측 가능한지이다. (10)예를 들어, 만약 당신이 ABABA와 같이 한 세트의 교차하는 음을 듣는다면, 당신의 뇌는 이 교차에 익숙해지고, 당신의 청각 영역 내의 활동은 다시 감소한다. (11)그러나 이번에는 놀람의 반응을 일으키는 것은 바로 ABABB와 같은 예상하지 못한 반복이다.

[정답 확인]

다음 빈칸에 들어갈 말로 가장 적절한 것은?

① audible 들을 수 있는
② predictable 예측 가능한 ✔
③ objective 객관적인
④ countable 셀 수 있는
⑤ recorded 기록되는

[문제 풀이]

필자는 학습이 놀람의 반응과 같은 자극을 동력으로 삼아 이루어진다고 말한다. 동일한 음이 일정 시간 유지되면 다음 사건을 예상할 수 있어 뇌의 청각 영역의 반응이 점차 감소한다. 이를 '적응'이라고 칭하는데, 이러한 현상은 예측하지 못한 사건으로 인해 깨지게 되고 적응 반응이 사라질 뿐만 아니라 새로운 반응을 통해 추가적인 뉴런이 발화된다. 이를 바탕으로 적응은 예측이 가능한 경우에 일어난다는 사실을 알 수 있으므로 빈칸에는 이러한 내용을 담은 ② 'predictable(예측 가능한)'이 적절하다.

[중요 어휘]

□ violate	동사 거스르다, 위반하다, 어기다
□ expectation	명사 기대, 예상
□ fundamental	형용사 근본적인, 본질적인, 필수적인
□ a series of	일련의
□ identical	형용사 동일한, 똑같은
□ note	명사 음, 음표, 메모
□ auditory	형용사 청각의, 귀의
□ progressively	부사 점진적으로, 꾸준히, 계속해서
□ adaptation	명사 적응, 각색
□ deceptively	부사 현혹될 정도로, 속여서
□ anticipate	동사 예상하다, 예측하다, 기대하다
□ primary	형용사 1차의, 첫 번째의, 주요한, 기본적인
□ cortex	명사 피질
□ fade away	사라지다
□ vigorously	부사 힘차게, 활발하게, 격렬하게
□ fire	동사 발화하다, 점화되다, 해고하다
□ matter	동사 중요하다, 문제 되다 / 명사 문제, 물질
□ alternating	형용사 교차의, 교대의
□ trigger	동사 일으키다, 촉발시키다 / 명사 방아쇠

03 2023년 6월 31번 (정답률 65%) 정답 ①

[지문 끊어 읽기] 더 엄격한 규제가 가져온 혁신

(1) In the course of his research /
그의 연구의 과정에서 /

on business strategy and the environment, /
비즈니스 전략과 환경에 대한 /

Michael Porter noticed a peculiar pattern: /
Michael Porter는 독특한 패턴을 알아차렸다 /

Businesses seemed to be profiting / from regulation.
기업들이 이익을 얻고 있는 것처럼 보였다 / 규제로부터

힌트 앞에 나온 '독특한 패턴(a peculiar pattern)'에 대한 부연 설명에 해당함.

(2) He also discovered /
그는 또한 발견했다 /

[that the stricter regulations were prompting more innovation /
더 엄격한 규제들이 더 많은 혁신을 유발하고 있다는 것을 / 비교급

than the weaker ones]. [ ]: that 명사절(목적어)
더 약한 규제들보다 =regulations

(3) The Dutch flower industry provides an illustration.
네덜란드의 꽃 산업은 한 예시를 제공한다

(4) For many years, / the companies /
수년 동안 / 회사들은 / S

[producing Holland's world-renowned tulips and other cut flowers] / [ ]: 현재분사구
네덜란드의 세계적으로 유명한 튤립과 다른 절화류의 꽃들을 생산하는 /

were also contaminating / the country's water and soil /
V
또한 오염시키고 있었다 / 그 국가의 물과 토양을 /

with fertilizers and pesticides.
비료와 농약으로

(5) In 1991, / the Dutch government adopted a policy /
1991년에 / 네덜란드 정부는 정책을 채택했다 /

[designed to cut pesticide use in half / by 2000] / [ ]: 과거분사구
농약의 사용을 절반으로 줄이도록 고안된 / 2000년까지 /

— a goal they ultimately achieved.
목적격 관계대명사절
그들이 결국 달성해 낸 목표

힌트 designed 앞에는 '주격 관계대명사+be동사'가 생략된 것으로 볼 수 있으며, 밑줄 친 부분은 「design A to V (A가 ~하도록 꾀하다[고안하다])」의 수동태인 「A+be designed+to V (A는 ~하도록 고안되다)」의 구조를 띠고 있음.

(6) [Facing increasingly strict regulation], / [ ]: 능동 분사구문
점점 더 엄격한 규제에 직면하면서 /

greenhouse growers realized /
온실 재배자들은 깨달았다 /

[they had to develop new methods /
[ ]: 명사절(접속사 that 생략)
그들이 새로운 방법들을 개발해야만 한다는 것을 /

if they were going to maintain product quality /
그들이 상품의 품질을 유지하고자 한다면 /

with fewer pesticides]. 정답 단서 더 엄격한 규제에 직면한 온실 재배자들은 더 적은 농약으로 상품 품질을 유지할 수 있는 새로운 방법을 개발할 필요성을 느끼게 됨.
더 적은 농약을 가지고

(7) In response, / they shifted to a cultivation method /
대응으로 / 그들은 재배 방식으로 전환했다 / (선행사)

[that circulates water / in closed-loop systems /
(병렬①)
물을 순환시키는 / 폐쇄 루프 체계에서 /

and grows flowers / in a rock wool substrate].
(병렬②) [ ]: 주격 관계대명사절
그리고 꽃들을 키우는 / 암면 배양판에서

★중요 문장 (7)의 '물을 폐쇄 루프 체계에서 순환시키는 것'은 문장 (4)의 '물의 오염' 문제에 대한 방안이고, 문장 (7)의 '암면 배양판에서 꽃을 키우는 것'은 문장 (4)의 '토양 오염' 문제에 대한 방안에 해당함.

힌트 「not only A but also B (A뿐만 아니라 B)」 구문으로, 'it also increased' 앞에는 접속사 but 대신 세미콜론이 왔음.

(8) The new system / not only reduced the pollution /
그 새로운 체계는 / 오염을 감소시켰을 뿐만 아니라 /

[released into the environment]; / it also increased profits /
[ ]: 과거분사구(the pollution 수식)
환경에 배출되는 / 그것은 또한 이익을 증가시켰다 /

by giving companies greater control / over growing conditions.
(4형식V) (I·O) (D·O)
회사들에게 더 큰 통제력을 줌으로써 / 재배 조건에 대한

정답 단서 새로운 체계는 환경 오염을 줄였을 뿐만 아니라 회사가 재배 조건을 더 잘 통제할 수 있게 해줌으로써 이익을 증가시킴.

[전문 해석]

(1)비즈니스 전략과 환경에 대한 그의 연구의 과정에서, Michael Porter는 기업들이 규제로부터 이익을 얻고 있는 것처럼 보인다는 독특한 패턴을 알아차렸다. (2)그는 또한 더 엄격한 규제들이 더 약한 규제들보다 더 많은 혁신을 유발하고 있다는 것을 발견했다. (3)네덜란드의 꽃 산업이 한 예시를 제공한다. (4)수년 동안, 네덜란드의 세계적으로 유명한 튤립과 다른 절화류의 꽃들을 생산하는 회사들은 또한 비료와 농약으로 그 국가의 물과 토양을 오염시키고 있었다. (5)1991년에, 네덜란드 정부는 2000년까지 농약의 사용을 절반으로 줄이도록 고안된 정책을 채택했는데, 이는 그들이 결국 달성해 낸 목표였다. (6)점점 더 엄격한 규제에 직면하면서, 온실 재배자들은 그들이 더 적은 농약을 가지고 상품의 품질을 유지하고자 한다면 그들이 새로운 방법들을 개발해야만 한다는 것을 깨달았다. (7)대응으로, 그들은 폐쇄 루프 체계에서 물을 순환시키고 암면 배양판에서 꽃들을 키우는 재배 방식으로 전환했다. (8)그 새로운 체계는 환경에 배출되는 오염을 감소시켰을 뿐만 아니라, 그것은 또한 회사들에게 재배 조건에 대한 더 큰 통제력을 줌으로써 이익을 증가시켰다.

- rock wool(암면): 덴마크에서 만든 인공무기섬유. 현무암, 안산암 등으로 만든 섬유 같은 물질로 단열재, 흡착제로 쓰임.

[정답 확인]

다음 빈칸에 들어갈 말로 가장 적절한 것은?

✔ innovation 혁신	② resistance 저항	③ fairness 공정성
④ neglect 태만	⑤ unity 단합	

[문제 풀이]

빈칸에는 더 엄격한 규제가 무엇을 유발하는지에 대한 내용이 들어가야 한다. 문장 (3)~(8)에 제시된 사례에 따르면, 네덜란드 정부는 자국의 물과 토양을 오염시키는 꽃 산업에 대해 '농약의 사용을 절반으로 줄일 것'을 요구하는 더 엄격한 규제 정책을 내놓았고, 온실 재배자들은 규제 조건에 부합하면서도 상품의 품질을 유지할 새로운 방법을 고안하게 된다. 그 결과, 폐쇄 루프 체계에서 물을 순환시킴으로써 물 오염을 줄이고 암면 배양판에서 꽃을 키움으로써 토양 오염을 줄이는 재배 방식으로의 전환이 일어나게 되고, 문장 (8)에서 알 수 있듯이 이 새로운 체계는 환경 오염을 감소시키고 회사들이 재배 조건을 더 잘 통제할 수 있게 하는 결과를 낳는다. 즉, 더 엄격한 규제가 재배 방식에 혁신을 가져옴으로써 환경과 이익이라는 두 마리 토끼를 모두 잡게 된 것이므로, 빈칸에 가장 알맞은 말은 ① 'innovation(혁신)'이다.

[중요 어휘]

□ **peculiar**	형용사 독특한, 기이한
□ **profit**	동사 이익을 얻다[주다] / 명사 이익, 수익
□ **regulation**	명사 규제, 규정
□ **illustration**	명사 예시, 실례
□ **world-renowned**	형용사 세계적으로 유명한
□ **cut flowers**	절화, 잘라 낸 꽃을 이용할 목적으로 재배되는 화훼
□ **contaminate**	동사 오염시키다, 더럽히다
□ **fertilizer**	명사 비료
□ **pesticide**	명사 농약, 살충제
□ **adopt**	동사 채택하다, 입양하다
□ **be designed to V**	~하도록 고안되다
□ **cut A in half**	A를 절반으로 줄이다
□ **ultimately**	부사 결국, 궁극적으로
□ **face**	동사 ~에 직면하다[맞서다]
□ **strict**	형용사 엄격한, 엄한
□ **method**	명사 방법, 수단
□ **maintain**	동사 유지하다, 지속하다
□ **in response**	대응으로, 반응으로
□ **shift**	동사 전환하다, 바뀌다
□ **cultivation**	명사 재배, 경작
□ **circulate**	동사 순환시키다
□ **loop**	명사 루프, 고리, 순환
□ **substrate**	명사 배양판
□ **release**	동사 배출하다, 방출하다

핵심 교향악단과 동물이라는 상관없어 보이는 소재가 어떻게 연결되는지 둘의 관계를 추론하면서 읽어야 함.

04 2021년 3월 31번 (정답률 60%) 정답 ①

[지문 끊어 읽기] 교향악단과 동물의 관계

(1) Even the most respectable of all musical institutions, / (S)
심지어 모든 음악 단체 중 가장 훌륭한 단체인 /

the symphony orchestra, /
교향악단도 /

carries / inside its DNA / the legacy of the hunt.
(V) (O)
지닌다 / 자신의 DNA 안에 / 사냥의 유산을

힌트 carries라는 동사와 연결된 목적어는 the legacy of the hunt인데, 그 사이에 'inside its DNA'라는 구가 삽입된 것에 유의해야 함.

(2) The various instruments in the orchestra /
교향악단에 있는 다양한 악기들은 /

can be traced back to these primitive origins — /
다음의 원시적인 기원으로 거슬러 올라갈 수 있다 /

their earliest forms were made /
그것들의 가장 초기 형태는 만들어졌다 /

either from the animal (horn, hide, gut, bone) /
동물(뿔, 가죽, 내장, 뼈)로 /

or the weapons employed /
(과거분사)
또는 사용된 무기로 /

in bringing the animal under control (stick, bow). 정답 단서
동물을 진압하기 위해 (막대, 활)

힌트 'either A or B'는 'A 또는 B'이며 여기서 A와 B는 from 전치사구의 형태로 병렬되어 있음. or 뒤에 from이 생략되어 있음.

(3) Are we wrong to hear this history / in the music itself, /
우리가 이러한 역사를 듣는 것이 잘못된 것인가 / 음악 그 자체에서 /

in the formidable aggression and awe-inspiring assertiveness /
강력한 공격성과 경외감을 자아내는 당당함에서 /

of those monumental symphonies /
저 기념비적인 교향곡들의 / (선행사)

[that remain the core repertoire of the world's leading orchestras]?
세계의 주요 교향악단의 핵심 레퍼토리로 남아 있는 [ ]: 주격 관계대명사절

(4) [Listening to Beethoven, Brahms, Mahler, Bruckner, Berlioz, Tchaikovsky, Shostakovich, and other great composers], / [ ]: 분사구문(동시동작)
베토벤, 브람스, 말러, 브루크너, 베를리오즈, 차이코프스키, 쇼스타코비치 및 다른 위대한 작곡가들의 음악을 들으며 /

I can easily summon up images /
나는 이미지를 쉽게 떠올릴 수 있다 /

of bands of men starting to chase animals, / 정답 단서
(현재분사)
동물을 쫓기 시작하는 사람들 무리의 /

[using sound as a source and symbol of dominance, /
소리를 지배의 원천이자 상징으로 사용하면서 /

an expression of the will to predatory power]. [ ]: 분사구문(동시동작)
공격적인 힘에 대한 의지의 표현으로

[전문 해석]

(1)심지어 모든 음악 단체 중 가장 훌륭한 단체인 교향악단도 자신의 DNA 안에 사냥의 유산을 지닌다. (2)교향악단에 있는 다양한 악기들은 다음의 원시적인 기원으로 거슬러 올라갈 수

있는데, 그것들(악기들)의 가장 초기 형태는 동물(뿔, 가죽, 내장, 뼈) 또는 동물을 진압하기 위해 사용된 무기(막대, 활)로 만들어졌다. (3)우리가 음악 그 자체에서, 세계의 주요 교향악단의 핵심 레퍼토리로 남아 있는 저 기념비적인 교향곡들의 강력한 공격성과 경외감을 자아내는 당당함에서, 이러한 역사를 듣는 것이 잘못된 것인가? (4)베토벤, 브람스, 말러, 브루크너, 베를리오즈, 차이코프스키, 쇼스타코비치 및 다른 위대한 작곡가들의 음악을 들으며, 나는 소리를 지배의 원천이자 상징으로, 공격적인 힘에 대한 의지의 표현으로 사용하면서 동물을 쫓기 시작하는 사람들 무리의 이미지를 쉽게 떠올릴 수 있다.

- repertoire(레퍼토리): 음악가나 극단 등이 무대에서 공연할 수 있도록 준비한 곡목이나 상연작의 목록

[정답 확인]

다음 빈칸에 들어갈 말로 가장 적절한 것은?

✔ hunt 사냥 ② law 법 ③ charity 자선 (행위) ④ remedy 치료법 ⑤ dance 춤

[문제 풀이]

본문은 교향악단의 기원과 그에 담긴 의미에 대한 저자의 견해를 전달하는 글이다. 문장 (2)에서 교향악단의 다양한 악기들은 동물의 일부분이나 동물을 진압하기 위한 무기로 만들어졌다고 설명한다. 또한 문장 (4)에서 저자는 교향곡을 들으면서 동물을 쫓기 시작하는 사람들의 이미지를 떠올릴 수 있음을 언급하며, 교향악단과 그 음악에는 사냥에서 유래한 유산이 담겨 있음을 암시한다. 따라서 정답은 ①이다.

[중요 어휘]

☐ **respectable**	형용사 훌륭한, 존경할 만한
☐ **institution**	명사 단체, 기관, 협회
☐ **carry**	동사 (특징을) 지니다[갖다], 나르다
☐ **trace back to**	~로 거슬러 올라가다
☐ **primitive**	형용사 원시적인
☐ **hide**	명사 가죽 / 동사 숨기다
☐ **gut**	명사 내장
☐ **formidable**	형용사 강력한, 어마어마한
☐ **aggression**	명사 공격(성)
☐ **awe-inspiring**	형용사 경외감을 자아내는
☐ **assertiveness**	명사 당당함, 자기주장
☐ **summon up**	~을 떠올리다[불러일으키다]
☐ **band**	명사 무리
☐ **dominance**	명사 지배, 우월함
☐ **predatory**	형용사 공격적인, 포식동물 같은

핵심 빈칸에 들어갈 말을 찾기 위해 우리의 정신이 결정을 내리는 데 작용하는 메커니즘이 무엇인지를 파악해야 함. 주어진 예시의 핵심을 통해 답을 추론할 수 있음.

05 2021년 9월 31번 (정답률 60%) 정답 ②

[지문 끊어 읽기] 상대성에 따른 의사 결정

(1) Relativity works / as a general mechanism for the mind, /
상대성은 작용한다 / 정신을 위한 일반적인 메커니즘으로서 /
in many ways / and across many different areas of life. 주제문
여러 방면에서 / 그리고 삶의 많은 다른 영역에 걸쳐

(2) For example, / Brian Wansink, author of *Mindless Eating*, /
예를 들어 / <Mindless Eating>의 저자 Brian Wansink는 /
showed / that it can also affect our waistlines.
=relativity
보여주었다 / 그것이 우리 허리둘레에도 영향을 미칠 수 있다는 것을

(3) We decide / how much to eat / not simply as a function /
not A but B: A가 아니라 B
우리는 결정한다 / 얼마나 먹을지를 / 단순히 함수로서가 아니라 /
of how much food we actually consume, /
우리가 실제로 얼마나 많은 음식을 소비하는지에 대한 /
but by a comparison to its alternatives. 정답단서
그것의 대안과의 비교를 통해

(4) Say / we have to choose between three burgers on a menu, /
~라고 하자 / 우리가 메뉴에 있는 버거 세 개 중 하나를 선택해야 한다 /
at 8, 10, and 12 ounces.
8온스, 10온스, 12온스의

(5) We are likely to pick the 10-ounce burger /
병렬①
우리는 10온스의 버거를 고를 것이다 /
and be perfectly satisfied / at the end of the meal.
병렬②
그리고 완벽하게 만족할 수 있을 것이다 / 식사가 끝날 때쯤에는

(6) But / if our options are instead 10, 12, and 14 ounces, /
하지만 / 만약 대신에 우리의 선택지가 10온스, 12온스, 14온스라면 /
we are likely again to choose the middle one, /
우리는 다시 중간의 것을 선택할 것이다 /
and again feel equally happy and satisfied /
그리고 다시 똑같이 행복해하고 만족해할 것이다 /
with the 12-ounce burger / at the end of the meal, /
선행사
12온스의 햄버거에 / 식사가 끝날 때쯤에는 /
even though we ate more, / which we did not need /
삽입절 목적격 관계대명사
우리가 더 많이 먹었음에도 불구하고 / 우리가 필요하지 않았던 /
in order to get our daily nourishment / or in order to feel full.
병렬① 병렬②
매일 영양분을 섭취하기 위해서 / 또는 포만감을 느끼기 위해서

[전문 해석]

(1)상대성은 여러 방면에서 그리고 삶의 많은 다른 영역에 걸쳐, 정신을 위한 일반적인 메커니즘으로서 작용한다. (2)예를 들어, <Mindless Eating>의 저자 Brian Wansink는 상대성이 우리 허리둘레에도 영향을 미칠 수 있다는 것을 보여주었다. (3)우리는 단순히 우리가 실제로 얼마나 많은 음식을 소비하는지에 대한 함수로서가 아니라, 그것의 대안과의 비교를 통해 얼마나 먹을지를 결정한다. (4)우리가 메뉴에 있는 8온스, 10온스, 12온스의 버거 세 개 중 하나를 선택해야 한다고 하자. (5)우리는 10온스의 버거를 고르고 식사가 끝날 때쯤에는 완벽하게 만족할 수 있을 것이다. (6)하지만 만약 대신에 우리의 선택지가 10온스, 12온스, 14온스라면, 우리는 다시 중간의 것을 선택할 것이고, 우리가 더 많이 먹었음에도 불구하고 식사가 끝날 때쯤에는 우리가 매일 영양분을 섭취하기 위해서나 포만감을 느끼기 위해서 필요하지 않았던 12온스의 햄버거에 다시 똑같이 행복해하고 만족해할 것이다.

[정답 확인]

다음 빈칸에 들어갈 말로 가장 적절한 것은?

① Originality 독창성 ✔ Relativity 상대성 ③ Visualization 시각화 ④ Imitation 모방 ⑤ Forgetfulness 건망증

[문제 풀이]

본문에 따르면 우리는 선택지가 주어졌을 때 중간 무게 혹은 중간 크기의 버거를 선택하는 경향이 있다. 즉, 우리는 절대적인 함수가 아닌 '상대적인' 기준에 따라 의사 결정을 내린다는 것이 본문의 핵심이므로 빈칸에는 ②가 가장 적절하다.

[중요 어휘]

☐ **relativity**	명사 상대성
☐ **mechanism**	명사 메커니즘(어떤 대상의 작동 원리나 구조)
☐ **waistline**	명사 허리둘레
☐ **function**	명사 함수, 기능
☐ **consume**	동사 소비하다
☐ **comparison**	명사 비교
☐ **alternative**	명사 대안 / 형용사 대체 가능한
☐ **nourishment**	명사 영양분, 음식물

06 2022년 9월 31번 (정답률 60%) 정답 ③

[지문 끊어 읽기] 농사 실패를 피하는 방법

(1) It is not the peasant's goal /
형식상의 주어
농부의 목표가 아니다 /
[to produce the highest possible time-averaged crop yield], /
최고로 가능한 시간 평균적인 농작물 생산량을 만드는 것은 / [ ]: 내용상의 주어

averaged over many years.
여러 해에 걸쳐서 평균 내어지는

(2) If your time-averaged yield is marvelously high /
당신의 시간 평균적인 생산량이 엄청나게 높더라도 /
as a result of the combination of nine great years and one year of crop failure, /
훌륭한 9년과 농사에 실패한 1년의 조합의 결과로 /
you will still starve to death / in that one year of crop failure /
당신은 굶어 죽을 것이다 / 농사에 실패한 그 1년에 /
before you can look back /
당신이 돌아보기 전에 /
to congratulate yourself on your great time-averaged yield.
훌륭한 시간 평균적인 생산량에 있어서 당신 자신을 축하하기 위해

(3) Instead, / the peasant's aim / is to make sure to produce a yield /
대신에 / 농부의 목표는 / 생산량을 만들어 내는 것을 확실히 하는 것이다 /
above the starvation level in every single year, /
매년 굶어 죽는 수준 이상의 /
even though the time-averaged yield may not be highest. 정답 단서
시간 평균적인 생산량이 가장 높지 않을지라도
농부는 평균적으로 가장 많은 생산량을 만들어 내기보다, 굶어 죽지 않을 수준 이상의 생산량을 매년 만들어 내는 것을 목표로 함.

(4) That's why field scattering may make sense.
그것이 바로 농지 흩어놓기가 합리적인 이유이다

(5) If you have just one big field, /
만일 당신이 그냥 하나의 큰 농지를 가지고 있다면 /
no matter how good it is on the average, / you will starve /
그것이 평균적으로 아무리 좋다고 할지라도 / 당신은 굶주리게 될 것이다 /
when the inevitable occasional year arrives /
이따금 찾아오는 피할 수 없는 해가 오면 /
in which your one field has a low yield.
당신의 유일한 농지가 낮은 생산량을 내는 정답 단서
하나의 농지만으로는 낮은 생산량을 내는 시기를 피할 수 없음.

힌트 'no matter how+형/부+S+V'는 '아무리 ~하더라도'라는 뜻의 양보의 부사절로 쓰임. 이때 no matter how 대신 however를 사용할 수 있음.

힌트 in which가 이끄는 관계사절의 선행사는 the inevitable occasional year로, 관계사절이 선행사 바로 뒤에 위치하여 주어가 너무 길어지는 경우 관계사절이 문장 뒤에 위치할 수 있음. 이때 in which 뒤에는 완전한 문장이 오며, in which를 관계부사 when으로 바꿔 쓸 수 있음.

(6) But if you have many different fields, /
그러나 만일 당신이 많은 다양한 농지들을 가지고 있다면 /
varying independently of each other, / then in any given year /
서로 독립적으로 다른 / 그렇다면 어떤 해에 /
some of your fields will produce well /
당신의 농지들 중 일부는 잘 생산할 것이다 /
even when your other fields are producing poorly. 정답 단서
당신의 다른 농지들이 빈약하게 생산하고 있을 때조차도
문장 (5)와 대조적으로 서로 다른 농지들을 가지고 있으면 다른 농지들의 생산량이 좋지 않더라도 일부 농지들의 생산량은 좋을 것이기 때문에, 굶어 죽지 않을 수준의 생산량을 매년 생산할 수 있을 것임.

[전문 해석]

(1)여러 해에 걸쳐서 평균 내어지는, 최고로 가능한 시간 평균적인 농작물 생산량을 만드는 것은 농부의 목표가 아니다. (2)당신의 시간 평균적인 생산량이 훌륭한 9년과 농사에 실패한 1년의 조합의 결과로 엄청나게 높더라도, 당신은 훌륭한 시간 평균적인 생산량에 있어서 당신 자신을 축하하기 위해 돌아보기 전에 농사에 실패한 그 1년에 굶어 죽을 것이다. (3)대신에, 농부의 목표는 시간 평균적인 생산량이 가장 높지 않을지라도, 매년 굶어 죽는 수준 이상의 생산량을 만들어 내는 것을 확실히 하는 것이다. (4)그것이 바로 농지 흩어놓기가 합리적인 이유이다. (5)만일 당신이 그냥 하나의 큰 농지를 가지고 있다면, 그것이 평균적으로 아무리 좋다고 할지라도, 당신의 유일한 농지가 낮은 생산량을 내는 이따금 찾아오는 피할 수 없는 해가 오면, 당신은 굶주리게 될 것이다. (6)그러나 만일 당신이, 서로 독립적으로 다른, 많은 다양한 농지들을 가지고 있다면, 어떤 해에 당신의 다른 농지들이 빈약하게 생산하고 있을 때조차도 당신의 농지들 중 일부는 잘 생산할 것이다.

[정답 확인]

다음 빈칸에 들어갈 말로 가장 적절한 것은?

① land leveling
땅을 평평하게 하기(땅고르기)
② weed trimming
잡초 다듬기
③ field scattering ✔
농지 흩어놓기
④ organic farming
유기 농업
⑤ soil fertilization
토양에 비료 주기

[문제 풀이]

문장 (1), (3)에서 농부의 목표는 평균적으로 가장 많은 생산량이 아니라, 매년 굶어 죽지 않을 수준 이상의 생산량을 만드는 것이라고 언급된다. 또한 문장 (5), (6)에선 하나의 큰 농지를 가지고 있는 경우와 서로 다른 농지들을 가지고 있는 경우를 비교하는데, 하나의 큰 농지의 경우 그것의 생산량이 좋지 않으면 농부는 굶주리게 되지만, 서로 다른 농지를 가지고 있으면 어느 한 농지의 생산량이 빈약하더라도 생산량이 괜찮은 일부 농지들을 통해 굶어 죽지 않을 수 있다고 말한다. 따라서 빈칸에는 '서로 다른 다양한 농지를 가지고 있는 것'을 의미하는 ③ 'field scattering(농지 흩어놓기)'이 적절하다.

[중요 어휘]

☐ peasant	명사 농부, 소작농
☐ crop	명사 농작물, 수확량
☐ yield	명사 생산량, 산출 / 동사 생산하다, 양보하다
☐ marvelously	부사 엄청나게, 놀라울 만큼
☐ starve	동사 굶주리다
☐ congratulate A on B	B에 대해 A(사람)를 축하하다
☐ level	명사 수준 / 동사 평평하게 하다
☐ scatter	동사 흩어지게 만들다, 흩어지다
☐ inevitable	형용사 피할 수 없는
☐ occasional	형용사 이따금의, 가끔의
☐ vary	동사 서로 다르다, 달라지다
☐ weed	명사 잡초 / 동사 잡초를 뽑다
☐ trim	동사 다듬다, 손질하다
☐ organic	형용사 유기농의, 유기체에서 만들어진
☐ fertilize	동사 비료를 주다, 수정시키다

07 2021년 11월 31번 (정답률 60%) 정답 ①

[지문 끊어 읽기] 동물의 맛 선호도

(1) The elements any particular animal needs /
S 목적격 관계대명사 생략
어떤 특정한 동물이 필요로 하는 요소들은 /
are relatively predictable.
V
상대적으로 예측 가능하다

(2) They are predictable based on the past: /
=The elements
그것들은 과거에 기반하여 예측이 가능하다 /
what an animal's ancestors needed /
한 동물의 조상들이 필요로 했던 것은 /
is likely to be what that animal also needs. 정답 단서
그 동물이 또한 필요로 하는 것일 가능성이 있다
한 동물의 조상이 필요했던 것을 지금의 동물도 그대로 필요로 할 가능성이 있음.

힌트 what은 선행사를 포함하는 관계대명사로 '~하는 것'으로 해석함. what이 이끄는 절은 문장에서 명사로 쓰이며 앞의 what절은 주어, 뒤의 what절은 주격 보어 역할을 하고 있음.

(3) Taste preferences, / therefore, / can be hardwired.
맛 선호도는 / 그러므로 / 타고나는 것일 수 있다

(4) Consider sodium (Na).
나트륨(Na)을 생각해 보라

(5) The bodies of terrestrial vertebrates, /
육생 척추동물의 몸은 /
including those of mammals, /
=the bodies
포유동물의 몸을 포함하여 /
tend to have a concentration of sodium /
나트륨 농도를 가지는 경향이 있다 /
nearly fifty times that of the primary producers on land, / plants.
=the concentration of sodium
육지의 주된 생산자의 그것보다 거의 50배 되는 / 식물

힌트 '배수사(e.g. twice, three times)+정관사+명사'는 '명사의 ~배'라는 뜻임. 원래 'nearly fifty times the concentration of sodium~'인데 반복되는 the concentration of sodium을 지시대명사 that으로 바꾼 것임.

(6) This is, / in part, / because vertebrates evolved in the sea /
S' V'①(자동사)
이는 / 부분적으로는 / 척추동물이 바다에서 진화했기 때문이다 /
and so evolved cells [dependent upon the ingredients /
V'②(타동사) O'(선행사) 선행사
그리고 따라서 성분들에 의존한 세포를 진화시켰기 때문이다 /
that were common in the sea], / [ ]: 주격 관계대명사+be동사 생략된 관계대명사절
주격 관계대명사절
바다에서 흔했던 /
including sodium. 정답 단서
나트륨을 포함하여
육생 척추동물은 바다에서 진화했으므로 나트륨과 같이 바다에서 흔했던 성분들에 의존한 세포를 진화시킴.

(7) To remedy the difference /
부사적 용법(목적)
격차를 해결하기 위해 /
between their needs for sodium and that available in plants, /
=herbivores' =sodium
나트륨에 대한 그것들의 욕구와 식물에서 얻을 수 있는 그것 사이의 /
herbivores can eat fifty times more plant material /
병렬①
초식 동물은 50배 더 많은 식물을 섭취할 수 있다 /
than they otherwise need / (and eliminate the excess).
부사 병렬②
그것들이 그렇지 않으면 필요로 하는 것보다 / (그리고 초과분을 배설한다)

(8) Or they can seek out / other sources of sodium.
또는 그것들은 찾아다닐 수 있다 / 나트륨의 다른 공급원을

(9) The salt taste receptor rewards animals /
짠맛 수용기는 동물에게 보상을 한다 /
for doing the latter, / seeking out salt /
=
후자의 행위에 대해 / 즉 소금을 찾아다니는 것 /
in order to satisfy their great need. 정답 단서
in order to V: ~하기 위해
그것들의 엄청난 욕구를 충족시키기 위해

★중요 지문에 따르면 바다에서 진화한 척추동물이 나트륨에 대한 욕구를 충족시키는 방법으로 문장 (7)에서 50배 더 많은 양의 식물을 섭취하는 것, 문장 (8)에서는 나트륨의 다른 공급원을 찾아다니는 것을 각각 제시했는데 문장 (9)에서 말하는 'the latter(후자)'는 문장 (8)의 내용을 가리킴. 또한 the latter 뒤에 seeking out salt ~로 the latter에 대한 내용을 한 번 더 명시해주고 있음.

육생 척추동물들은 짠맛에 대한 타고난 욕구를 충족시키기 위해 소금 공급원을 찾아다님.

[전문 해석]

(1)어떤 특정한 동물이 필요로 하는 요소들은 상대적으로 예측 가능하다. (2)그 요소들은 과거에 기반하여 예측이 가능한데, 즉 한 동물의 조상들이 필요로 했던 것은 그 동물이 또한 필요로 하는 것일 가능성이 있다. (3)그러므로 맛 선호도는 타고나는 것일 수 있다. (4)나트륨(Na)을 생각해 보라. (5)포유동물의 몸을 포함하여 육생 척추동물의 몸은 육지의 주된 생산자인 식물의 나트륨 농도보다 거의 50배 되는 나트륨 농도를 가지는 경향이 있다. (6)이는 부분적으로는 척추동물이 바다에서 진화했고 따라서 나트륨을 포함하여 바다에서 흔했던 성분들에 의존한 세포를 진화시켰기 때문이다. (7)나트륨에 대한 초식 동물들의 욕구와 식물에서 얻을 수 있는 나트륨 사이의 격차를 해결하기 위해 초식 동물들은 그것들이 그렇지 않으면 필요로 하는 것보다 50배 더 많은 식물을 섭취할 수 있다(그리고 초과분을 배설한다). (8)또는 그것들은 나트륨의 다른 공급원을 찾아다닐 수 있다. (9)짠맛 수용기는 후자의 행위, 즉 그것들의 엄청난 욕구를 충족시키기 위해 소금을 찾아다니는 것에 대해 동물에게 보상을 한다.

[정답 확인]

다음 빈칸에 들어갈 말로 가장 적절한 것은?

✔① Taste preferences
맛 선호도
② Hunting strategies
사냥 전략
③ Migration patterns
이주 패턴
④ Protective instincts
방어 본능
⑤ Periodic starvations
주기적인 굶주림

[문제 풀이]

본문에 따르면, 어떤 동물이 필요로 하는 요소는 그들의 조상들이 필요로 했던 것으로부터 예측 가능하다. 그 예시로 육생 척추동물이 등장하는데, 육생 척추동물은 바다에서 진화하여 나트륨, 즉 짠맛에 대한 욕구를 타고났고 이를 충족시키기 위해 많은 양의 식물을 섭취하거나 식물 외의 나트륨 공급원을 찾아다닌다. 따라서 이러한 '맛 선호도'는 타고나는 것이라는 내용의 ①이 빈칸의 내용으로 적절하다.

[중요 어휘]

□ need	동사 필요로 하다 / 명사 욕구, 필요
□ hardwired	형용사 타고난
□ terrestrial	형용사 육생의, 지구의
□ vertebrate	명사 척추동물
□ mammal	명사 포유동물, 포유류
□ concentration	명사 농도, 집중
□ evolve	동사 진화하다, 진화시키다
□ dependent	형용사 의존적인
□ ingredient	명사 성분, 구성 요소
□ remedy	동사 해결하다, 고치다 / 명사 약, 치료
□ herbivore	명사 초식 동물
□ eliminate	동사 배설하다, 제거하다
□ excess	명사 초과분, 과잉
□ seek out	찾아다니다
□ receptor	명사 수용기
□ reward	동사 보상하다 / 명사 보상(금)
□ periodic	형용사 주기적인
□ starvation	명사 굶주림, 기아

핵심 이 글에서는 try to V(~하려고 노력하다), attempt to V(~하려고 시도하다) 형태의 표현이 문장 (3)~(7)에 걸쳐 여러 번 반복되고 있음. 이러한 표현 반복은 글의 주제를 살리는 데 활용되기 때문에 주목해야 함.

08 2017년 9월 31번 (정답률 55%) 정답 ②

[지문 끊어 읽기] 삶의 최고 경영자

(1) We are the CEOs of our own lives. 주제문
우리는 우리 자신의 삶의 최고 경영자이다

(2) We work hard to urge ourselves / to get up and go to work / 정답 단서
우리는 우리 자신을 자극하기 위해 열심히 노력한다 / 일어나 직장에 가도록 /
and do what we must do / day after day.
그리고 우리가 반드시 해야 하는 것들을 하도록 / 매일같이

(3) We also try to encourage / the people working for and with us, / 정답 단서
우리는 또한 격려하려고 노력한다 / 우리를 위해 일하고 우리와 함께 일하는 사람들을 /
those who are doing business with us, /
우리와 거래하고 있는 사람들을 /
and even those who regulate us.
그리고 심지어 우리를 통제하는 사람들을

(4) We do this in our personal lives, too: / From a very young age, /
우리는 우리 개인의 삶에서도 이것을 한다 / 매우 어린 나이부터 /
kids try to persuade their parents / 정답 단서
아이들은 자신들의 부모를 설득하려고 노력한다 /
to do things for them / ("Dad, I'm too scared to do this!") /
자신들을 위해 어떤 것을 하도록 / ("아빠, 저는 너무 무서워서 이것을 할 수 없어요!") /
with varying degrees of success.
가지각색의 성공의 정도를 보이며

(5) As adults, / we try to encourage our significant others / 정답 단서
성인으로서 / 우리는 우리의 배우자를 격려하려고 노력한다 /
to do things for us / ("Sweetie, I had such a stressful day today, /
우리를 위해 어떤 것을 하도록 / 여보 전 오늘 너무나 스트레스가 많은 날을 보냈어요 /
can you please put the kids to bed / and do the dishes?").
아이들을 재울 수 있어요 / 그리고 설거지를 해줄 수 있어요

(6) We attempt / to get our kids to clean up their rooms. 정답 단서
우리는 시도한다 / 우리의 아이들이 자신들의 방을 치우도록 시키려고

(7) We try to induce our neighbors / 정답 단서
우리는 우리의 이웃을 유도하려고 노력한다 /
to help out with a neighborhood party.
지역 파티를 도와주도록

(8) Whatever our official job descriptions, /
우리의 공식적인 직업 설명이 무엇이든지 간에 /
we are all part-time motivators.
우리는 모두 시간제 동기부여자들이다

[전문 해석]

(1)우리는 우리 자신의 삶의 최고 경영자이다. (2)우리는 일어나 직장에 가고 우리가 반드시 해야 하는 것들을 하도록 우리 자신을 자극하기 위해 매일같이 열심히 노력한다. (3)우리는 또한 우리를 위해 일하고 우리와 함께 일하는 사람들, 우리와 거래하고 있는 사람들, 그리고 심지어 우리를 통제하는 사람들을 격려하려고 노력한다. (4)우리는 우리 개인의 삶에서도 이것을 한다. 매우 어린 나이부터 아이들은 가지각색의 성공의 정도를 보이며 부모가 자신들을 위해 어떤 것을 하도록 설득하려고 노력한다("아빠, 저는 너무 무서워서 이것을 할 수 없어요!"). (5)성인으로서 우리는 배우자가 우리를 위해 어떤 것을 하도록 격려하려고 노력한다("여보, 전 오늘 너무나 스트레스가 많은 날을 보냈어요, 아이들을 재우고 설거지를 해줄 수 있어요?"). (6)우리는 아이들이 자신들의 방을 치우도록 시키려고 시도한다. (7)우리는 이웃이 지역 파티를 도와주도록 유도하려고 노력한다. (8)우리의 공식적인 직업 설명(업무 내용)이 무엇이든지 간에, 우리는 모두 시간제 동기부여자들이다.

[정답 확인]

다음 빈칸에 들어갈 말로 가장 적절한 것은?

① judges 판사들 ✔ motivators 동기부여자들 ③ inventors 발명가들
④ analysts 분석가들 ⑤ observers 관찰자들

[문제 풀이]

본문은 우리가 삶을 경영함에 있어 자신뿐만 아니라, 어릴 때부터 성인이 된 후까지 직장과 개인적인 삶에서 타인을 설득하는 삶을 살고 있다는 점을 다양한 예를 들어 설명하고 있다. 따라서 다른 사람이 특정 행동을 하게끔 격려하는 일을 하는 ② 'motivators(동기부여자들)'가 빈칸에 들어갈 말로 가장 적절하다.

[중요 어휘]

□ **regulate**	동사 통제하다, 규제하다
□ **varying**	형용사 가지각색의, 바뀌는, 변화하는
□ **induce**	동사 유도하다
□ **part-time**	형용사 시간제의

핵심 죽음을 앞둔 한 현대의 불교 스승이 삶의 한 특징에 대해 이야기하고 있는 지문임. 그가 삶을 묘사하기 위해 사용한 단어들과 같은 맥락의 단어들을 떠올리면서 빈칸에 들어갈 말을 추론해야 함.

09 2020년 3월 31번 (정답률 55%) 정답 ①

[지문 끊어 읽기] 죽음을 앞둔 현대 불교 스승의 삶에 대한 시각

(1) When he was dying, /
그가 죽어가고 있었을 때 /
the contemporary Buddhist teacher Dainin Katagiri /
현대의 불교 스승인 Dainin Katagiri는 /
wrote a remarkable book / called *Returning to Silence*.
주목할 만한 책을 집필했다 / <침묵으로 돌아가라>라는

(2) Life, / he wrote, / "is a dangerous situation."
삽입절
삶은 / 그는 썼다 / "위험한 상황이다."

(3) It is the weakness of life / that makes it precious; / 정답단서
it is ~ that 강조구문
삶의 나약함이다 / 그것을 귀중하게 만드는 것은 /
his words are filled with the very fact / of his own life passing away.
의미상의 주어 동명사
그의 글은 바로 그 사실로 채워져 있다 / 그의 삶이 죽음을 향해가고 있다는

힌트 여기서 of는 동격의 of로 the very fact와 his ~ away가 동격임. 전치사이기 때문에 뒤에 동명사가 왔음.

(4) "The china bowl is beautiful /
도자기 그릇은 아름답다 /
because sooner or later it will break....
조만간 그것이 깨질 것이기 때문에

힌트 소문자로 쓰인 'china'는 '도자기(의)'라는 뜻임. 중국 도자기를 좋아했던 유럽인들이 질 좋은 고령토를 구할 수 없자 흰 빛깔을 내려고 동물의 뼛가루를 섞어서 만든 데서 유래한 'bone china'라는 표현도 있음.

(5) The life of the bowl is always existing / in a dangerous situation."
그 그릇의 생명은 항상 존재하고 있다 / 위험한 상황에

(6) Such is our struggle: / this unstable beauty. 정답단서
그런 것이 우리의 투쟁이다 / 이 불안정한 아름다움

(7) This inevitable wound. 정답단서
이 불가피한 상처

(8) We forget / — how easily we forget — /
우리는 잊어버린다 / 그것도 너무 쉽게 잊어버린다 /
that love and loss are intimate companions, /
사랑과 상실은 친밀한 동반자라는 것을 /
that we love the real flower /
S' V'①
우리가 진짜 꽃을 사랑한다는 것을 /
so much more than the plastic one / and love the cast of twilight /
V'②
플라스틱 꽃보다 훨씬 더 / 그리고 황혼의 색조를 사랑한다는 것을 /
across a mountainside / lasting only a moment.
산 중턱을 가로지르는 / 한 순간만 지속되는

힌트 문장 (8)은 중간에 'how+부사+S+V'의 감탄문이 삽입된 구조임. 이럴 때는 삽입된 부분을 빼고 전체적인 틀을 보는 게 도움이 됨. 여기서는 주절의 동사 'forget'에 대한 목적어로 that이 이끄는 명사절 2개가 병렬로 연결되어 있음을 확인할 수 있음.

(9) It is this very fragility / that opens our hearts.
바로 이러한 연약함이다 / 우리의 마음을 여는 것은

[전문 해석]

(1)현대의 불교 스승인 Dainin Katagiri가 죽어가고 있었을 때(죽음을 앞두고), <침묵으로 돌아가라>라는 주목할 만한 책을 집필했다. (2)그는 삶은 "위험한 상황이다."라고 썼다. (3)삶을 귀중하게 만드는 것은 (바로) 그것의 나약함이며, 그의 글은 그의 삶이 죽음을 향해가고 있다는 바로 그 사실로 채워져 있다. (4)"도자기 그릇은 조만간 깨질 것이기 때문에 아름답다…. (5)그 그릇의 생명은 항상 위험한 상황에 존재하고 있다(처해있다)." (6)그런 것이 우리의 투쟁이다(우리는 그런 것에 맞서 투쟁한다). 이 불안정한 아름다움. (7)이 불가피한 상처. (8)우리는 사랑과 상실은 친밀한 동반자라는 것을, 우리가 플라스틱 꽃보다 진짜 꽃을 훨씬 더 사랑한다는 것을, 그리고 한 순간만 지속되는 산 중턱을 가로지르는 황혼의 색조를 사랑한다는 것을 잊어버린다. 그것도 너무 쉽게 잊어버린다. (9)우리의 마음을 여는 것은 바로 이러한 연약함이다.

- Dainin Katagiri(다이닌 가타기리, 1928년~1990년): 일본에서 태어나 미국에서 선불교를 전했다. 1988년 출판된 <침묵으로 돌아가라>는 진정한 나를 찾고 삶의 의미를 깨닫는 방법에 대한 그의 설법 내용을 엮은 것이다.

[정답 확인]

다음 빈칸에 들어갈 말로 가장 적절한 것은?

✔ fragility 연약함 ② stability 안정성 ③ harmony 조화
④ satisfaction 만족감 ⑤ diversity 다양성

[문제 풀이]

지문은 죽음을 앞둔 Dainin Katagiri의 삶에 대한 철학에 대해서 설명하고 있다. 그는 삶이 깨지기 쉬운 도자기 그릇처럼 항상 위험한 상황에 처해있다고 한다. 삶은 자주 고통을 받거나 불안정한 상태에 있는데, 거기서 오히려 아름다움과 감정을 경험한다고 주장한다. 그러므로 삶은 연약하며, 우리가 마음을 열고 행복과 사랑을 느끼는 것은 바로 그러한 연약함에 있다고 할 수 있다. 따라서 정답은 ①이다.

[중요 어휘]

□ **contemporary**	형용사 현대의, 동시대의
□ **remarkable**	형용사 주목할 만한, 놀라운
□ **unstable**	형용사 불안정한
□ **inevitable**	형용사 불가피한, 필연적인
□ **intimate**	형용사 친밀한, 사적인
□ **companion**	명사 동반자
□ **fragility**	명사 연약함, 부서지기 쉬움

핵심 본문은 보조금 자본과 상업 금융 상품의 문제점을 제시하고 있음. 빈칸이 있는 마지막 문장은 위에서 언급한 내용에 대한 결론을 말하고 있으므로, 앞 문장들로부터 어떤 결론이 나와야 할지 생각하며 빈칸을 추론해야 함.

10 2020년 9월 34번 (정답률 55%) 정답 ①

[지문 끊어 읽기] 보조금 자본과 상업 금융 상품의 문제점

(1) In the current landscape, / social enterprises tend to rely /
현재 상황에서 / 사회적 기업들은 의존하는 경향이 있다 /
either on grant capital /
보조금 자본에 /
(e.g., grants, donations, or project funding) /
(예를 들어, 보조금, 기부금, 또는 프로젝트 기금) /
or commercial financing products / (e.g., bank loans).
또는 상업 금융 상품에 / (예를 들어, 은행 대출)

(2) Ironically, / many social enterprises / at the same time /
역설적이게도 / 많은 사회적 기업들은 / 동시에 /
report of significant drawbacks /
중대한 문제점들에 대해 말한다 /
related to each of these two forms of financing. 정답단서
이러한 두 형태의 자금 조달 각각에 관련된

(3) Many social enterprises / are for instance reluctant /
삽입구
많은 사회적 기업들은 / 예를 들어 꺼린다 /
to make use of traditional commercial finance products, / 정답단서
전통적인 상업 금융 상품을 이용하는 것을 /
fearing / that they might not be able to pay back the loans.
두려워하기 때문에 / 그들이 대출금을 상환하지 못할 수도 있다는 것을

힌트 밑줄 친 부분은 이유의 뜻으로 쓰인 분사구문임. that 명사절이 fearing의 목적어임.

(4) In addition, / a significant number of social enterprise leaders /
게다가 / 상당히 많은 수의 사회적 기업 리더들은 /
report / that relying too much on grant funding /
명사절 접속사 동명사S'
말한다 / 보조금 조달에 너무 많이 의존하는 것이 / 정답 단서
can be a risky strategy / since individual grants are time limited /
위험한 전략일 수 있다고 / 개별적 보조금이 시간 제한적이므로 /
and are not reliable in the long term.
그리고 장기적으로 신뢰할 수 없으므로

힌트 보조금이 특정 사회적 기업에 계속해서 지급될 것이라는 보장이 없기 때문에, 문장 (4)에서는 개별적 보조금이 '시간 제한적(time limited)'이라고 표현했음.

(5) Grant funding can also lower the incentive /
보조금 조달은 또한 동기를 낮출 수 있다 /
for leaders and employees /
리더들과 직원들이 /
to professionalize the business aspects, /
사업적인 면을 전문화하는 /
thus leading to unhealthy business behavior.
분사구문(=and thus it leads)
그리고 그로 인해 불건전한 사업 행위를 초래한다

힌트 the incentive를 수식하는 형용사적 용법의 to부정사임. 의미상의 주어로 for leaders and employees를 취함.

(6) In other words, / there seems to be a substantial need /
다시 말해서 / 상당한 필요가 있는 것처럼 보인다 /
among social enterprises /
사회적 기업들 사이에서 /
for alternatives to the traditional forms of financing. 주제문
전통적 형태의 자금 조달의 대안을 위한

[전문 해석]

(1)현재 상황에서 사회적 기업들은 보조금 자본(예를 들어, 보조금, 기부금, 또는 프로젝트 기금) 또는 상업 금융 상품(예를 들어, 은행 대출)에 의존하는 경향이 있다. (2)역설적이게도, 많은 사회적 기업들은 동시에 이러한 두 형태의 자금 조달 각각에 관련된 중대한 문제점들에 대해 말한다. (3)예를 들어, 많은 사회적 기업들은 그들이 대출금을 상환하지 못할 수도 있다는 것을 두려워하기 때문에 전통적인 상업 금융 상품을 이용하는 것을 꺼린다. (4)게다가 상당히 많은 수의 사회적 기업 리더들은 개별적 보조금이 시간 제한적이고 장기적으로 신뢰할 수 없으므로 보조금 조달에 너무 많이 의존하는 것이 위험한 전략일 수 있다고 말한다. (5)보조금 조달은 또한 리더들과 직원들이 사업적인 면을 전문화하는 동기를 낮출 수 있고, 그로 인해 불건전한 사업 행위를 초래한다. (6)다시 말해서 사회적 기업들 사이에서 전통적 형태의 자금 조달의 대안을 위한 상당한 필요가 있는 것처럼 보인다.

[정답 확인]

다음 빈칸에 들어갈 말로 가장 적절한 것은?

✔ alternatives to the traditional forms of financing
전통적 형태의 자금 조달의 대안
② guidelines for promoting employee welfare
직원 복지 증진을 위한 지침
③ measures to protect employees' privacy
직원들의 사생활을 보호하기 위한 수단
④ departments for better customer service
더 나은 고객 서비스를 위한 부서
⑤ incentives to significantly increase productivity
생산성을 상당히 높이기 위한 장려책

[문제 풀이]

본문은 사회적 기업이 자금을 조달하는 두 가지 방식으로 '보조금 자본'과 '상업 금융 상품'을 들고 있으며, 문장 (2)~(5)에서 이러한 방식들이 가지는 문제점에 대해 설명하고 있다. 따라서 문장 (6)에서는 앞서 제시된 문제점들로 인해 사회적 기업들이 새로운 자금 조달 방식을 찾을 필요가 있다고 하는 것이 자연스러우므로, 빈칸에는 ①이 들어가야 한다.

[중요 어휘]

☐ landscape	명사 상황, 풍경
☐ enterprise	명사 기업, 회사
☐ grant	명사 보조금 / 동사 주다, 승인하다
☐ capital	명사 자본(금), 수도
☐ commercial	형용사 상업의 / 명사 광고 (방송)
☐ financing	명사 금융, 자금 조달
☐ loan	명사 대출(금) / 동사 대출하다, 빌려주다
☐ significant	형용사 중대한, 상당한
☐ drawback	명사 문제점, 결점
☐ make use of	~을 이용하다, 사용하다
☐ pay back	상환하다, 되갚다
☐ incentive	명사 동기, 장려책
☐ professionalize	동사 전문화하다, 직업화하다
☐ unhealthy	형용사 불건전한, 건강하지 않은
☐ substantial	형용사 상당한, 중대한, 실질적인
☐ alternative	명사 대안 / 형용사 대안이 되는, 대체 가능한

11 2021년 11월 32번 (정답률 50%) 정답 ①

[지문 끊어 읽기] 인식에 의해 형성되는 직감

(1) We might think / that our gut instinct is just an inner feeling /
명사절 접속사
우리는 생각할지도 모른다 / 우리의 직감이 단지 내면의 느낌이라고 /
— a secret interior voice — / but in fact it is shaped /
=our gut instinct
즉 비밀스러운 내적 목소리 / 하지만 사실 그것은 형성된다 /
by a perception of something visible around us, / 정답 단서
우리 주변의 가시적인 무언가에 대한 인식에 의해 /
such as a facial expression or a visual inconsistency /
얼굴 표정 또는 시각적 불일치와 같은 /
[so fleeting / that often we're not even aware /
너무 순식간이어서 / 보통 우리가 의식하지도 못하는 /
we've noticed it].
명사절 접속사 that 생략
우리가 그것을 알아차렸음을

우리는 흔히 직감이 내면의 느낌이라고 생각하지만 실제로 직감은 인식에 의해 형성된다고 함.

힌트 'so 형용사/부사 that S V(너무 ~해서 …하다)' 구문으로 앞에 '주격 관계대명사+be동사(which is)'가 생략된 주격 관계대명사절임.

(2) Psychologists now think of this moment /
think of A as B: A를 B로 생각하다
오늘날 심리학자들은 이러한 순간을 생각한다 /
as a 'visual matching game'.
'시각적 연결시키기 게임'으로

(3) So a stressed, rushed or tired person /
그렇다면 스트레스를 받은, 서두르는 혹은 피곤한 사람이 /
is more likely to resort / to this visual matching.
의존할 가능성이 더 높다 / 이 시각적 연결시키기에

(4) When they see a situation in front of them, /
그들이 자신 앞의 상황을 볼 때 /
they quickly match it / to a sea of past experiences /
그들은 그것을 재빨리 연결한다 / 과거의 수많은 경험과 /
stored in a mental knowledge bank / and then, /
정신의 지식 저장고 안에 보관된 / 그리고 그다음에 /
based on a match, / they assign meaning /
연결에 기초하여 / 그들은 의미를 부여한다 /
to the information in front of them. 정답 단서
자신 앞에 있는 정보에

인지 처리 과정① - 사람은 자신 앞에 놓인 상황을 인식할 때 과거의 경험과 연결시키고 의미를 부여함.

(5) The brain then sends a signal to the gut, / 정답 단서
그러고 나서 뇌가 창자로 신호를 보낸다 /
which has many hundreds of nerve cells.
관계대명사(계속적 용법)
그런데 이것은 수백 개의 신경 세포를 가지고 있다

인지 처리 과정② - 뇌가 창자로 신호를 보냄.

★중요 본능적인 느낌(the visceral feeling)은 직감이라고 볼 수 있음. 즉, 빈칸에는 이 글이 직감에 대해 설명한 내용이 들어가야 함.

(6) So the visceral feeling / we get in the pit of our stomach /
S①
따라서 본능적인 느낌 / 우리가 우리의 배 속에서 얻는 /
and the butterflies / we feel /
S②
그리고 긴장감은 / 우리가 느끼는 /
are a result of our cognitive processing system.
V
우리의 인지 처리 체계의 결과이다

[전문 해석]

(1)우리는 우리의 직감이 단지 내면의 느낌, 즉 비밀스러운 내적 목소리라고 생각할지도 모르지만, 사실 그것은 얼굴 표정 또는 시각적 불일치와 같이 너무 순식간이어서 보통 우리가 그것

을 알아차렸음을 의식하지도 못하는, 우리 주변의 가시적인 무언가에 대한 인식에 의해 형성된다. (2)오늘날 심리학자들은 이러한 순간을 '시각적 연결시키기 게임'으로 생각한다. (3)그렇다면 스트레스를 받은, 서두르는 혹은 피곤한 사람이 이 시각적 연결시키기에 의존할 가능성이 더 높다. (4)그들이 자신 앞의 상황을 볼 때 그들은 정신의 지식 저장고 안에 보관된 과거의 수많은 경험과 그것을 재빨리 연결해 보고, 그다음에 연결에 기초하여 자신 앞에 있는 정보에 의미를 부여한다. (5)그리고 나서 뇌가 창자로 신호를 보내는데 이것은 수백 개의 신경 세포를 가지고 있다. (6)따라서 우리가 우리의 배 속에서 얻는 본능적인 느낌과 우리가 느끼는 긴장감은 우리의 인지 처리 체계의 결과이다.

[정답 확인]

다음 빈칸에 들어갈 말로 가장 적절한 것은?

✔ result of our cognitive processing system
우리의 인지 처리 체계의 결과
② instance of discarding negative memories
부정적인 기억들을 버리는 사례
③ mechanism of overcoming our internal conflicts
우리의 내부 갈등을 극복하는 구조
④ visual representation of our emotional vulnerability
우리의 감정적인 취약성의 시각적 표현
⑤ concrete signal of miscommunication within the brain
뇌 안에서 일어나는 잘못된 의사소통의 구체적인 신호

[문제 풀이]

본문에 따르면, 직감은 우리 주변의 무언가에 대한 인식에 의해 형성된다. 빨리 지나가는, 어떠한 정보 혹은 상황을 눈으로 인식한 우리는 그것을 과거의 경험과 연관 짓고 그것을 토대로 그 정보 혹은 상황에 의미를 부여한다. 이후 뇌가 수백 개의 신경 세포를 가지고 있는 창자에 신호를 보냄에 따라 우리는 배 속에서 어떠한 느낌을 얻게 되는데 우리는 이를 직감이라고 생각한다. 즉 본문의 핵심은 우리는 인지 처리 체계를 통해 직감을 느끼게 된다는 것이므로 빈칸에는 ①이 적절하다.

[중요 어휘]

□ **gut (instinct)**	명사 직감, 창자
□ **perception**	명사 인식, 지각
□ **inconsistency**	명사 불일치
□ **fleeting**	형용사 순식간의, 잠깐 동안의
□ **match**	동사 연결시키다, 연결하다, 어울리다 / 명사 연결, 일치하는 것
□ **resort to N/V-ing**	~에 의존하다
□ **assign**	동사 부여하다, 맡기다, 할당하다
□ **visceral**	형용사 본능적인, 강한 감정에 따른
□ **pit of one's stomach**	(긴장감 따위를 느끼게 되는) 배 속
□ **butterflies**	명사 (복수형) 긴장감, 불안한 마음
□ **discard**	동사 버리다
□ **vulnerability**	명사 취약성
□ **concrete**	형용사 구체적인

힌트 'butterflies'는 단독으로 쓰이기보다는 '긴장하다, 안절부절못하다'라는 의미로 'have/feel butterflies (in one's stomach)'라는 관용적인 표현으로 더 자주 쓰임.

12 2022년 6월 31번 (정답률 50%) 정답 ③

[지문 끊어 읽기] 목표에 따라 유동적인 추종자의 범주

(1) Followers can be defined / [by their position as subordinates] /
추종자는 정의될 수 있다 / 부하라는 직책에 의해 / (전치사) ([ ]: 병렬①)
or [by their behavior / of going along with leaders' wishes].
또는 그들의 행동에 의해 / 리더의 바람을 따르는 ([ ]: 병렬②)

(2) But followers also have power / to lead.
그러나 추종자도 힘이 있다 / 이끌 (형용사적 용법)

(3) Followers empower leaders / as well as vice versa.
(~와 마찬가지로, ~뿐만 아니라)
추종자는 리더에게 힘을 준다 / 그 반대도 마찬가지이다

(4) This has led some leadership analysts like Ronald Heifetz /
(5형식V, O)
이것은 Ronald Heifetz와 같은 일부 리더십 분석가들이 ~하게 했다 /

to avoid using the word *followers* /
(O·C①(to V))
'추종자'라는 단어를 사용하는 것을 피하게 /
and refer to the others in a power relationship /
(O·C②(to 생략))
그리고 권력 관계에 있는 다른 사람들을 지칭하게 /
as "citizens" or "constituents."
'시민' 또는 '구성원'으로

힌트 'refer to A as B'는 'A를 B라고 지칭하다, 언급하다'라고 해석함.

(5) Heifetz is correct /
Heifetz는 옳다 /
that too simple a view of followers can produce misunderstanding.
(명사절 접속사, S', V')
추종자에 대한 너무 단순한 관점이 오해를 불러일으킬 수 있다는

힌트 부사 too가 쓰일 경우, 'too+형용사+a/an+명사'의 어순에 유의할 것. 비슷한 어순을 가지는 사례로, 'so/as/how/however+형용사+a/an+명사'가 있음.

(6) In modern life, /
현대의 삶에서 /
most people wind up being both leaders and followers, / 정답단서
대부분의 사람들은 결국 리더와 추종자가 된다 /
and the categories can become quite fluid.
그리고 그 범주는 꽤 유동적일 수 있다

오늘날 대부분의 사람들은 리더와 추종자 둘 다 될 수 있음. 즉, 리더와 추종자 간의 경계가 명확하지 않음.

정답단서 목표에 따라 리더와 추종자가 결정됨.

(7) Our behavior as followers changes / as our objectives change.
(전치사(~로서), S, V, 접속사(~함에 따라))
추종자로서의 우리의 행동도 바뀐다 / 우리의 목표가 변함에 따라

(8) If I trust your judgment in music / more than my own, /
만약 내가 음악에 대한 당신의 판단을 신뢰한다면 / 나의 판단보다 더 /
I may follow your lead / on which concert we attend /
(명사절(간접의문문))
나는 당신을 따를 수 있다 / 우리가 어떤 콘서트에 참석할지에 대해서는 /
(even though you may be formally my subordinate / in position).
당신이 비록 공식적으로 나의 부하일지라도 / 지위상

(9) But if I am an expert on fishing, / you may follow my lead /
하지만 내가 낚시 전문가라면 / 당신이 나를 따를 수 있다 /
on where we fish, / regardless of our formal positions /
(명사절, 병렬①)
우리가 낚시할 장소에 대해서는 / 공식적인 지위와는 관계없이 /
or the fact / that I followed your lead on concerts yesterday.
(병렬②, =, 동격의 that)
또는 사실과는 관계없이 / 내가 어제 콘서트에 대해서는 당신을 따랐다는

[전문 해석]

(1)추종자는 부하라는 직책이나 리더의 바람을 따르는 행동에 의해 정의될 수 있다. (2)그러나 추종자도 이끌 힘이 있다. (3)추종자는 리더에게 힘을 주기도 하고 그 반대도 마찬가지이다. (4)이것은 Ronald Heifetz와 같은 일부 리더십 분석가들이 '추종자'라는 단어를 사용하는 것을 피하고 권력 관계에 있는 다른 사람들을 '시민' 또는 '구성원'으로 지칭하게 했다. (5)추종자에 대한 너무 단순한 관점이 오해를 불러일으킬 수 있다고 말하는 Heifetz는 옳다. (6)현대의 삶에서, 대부분의 사람들은 결국 리더와 추종자가 되고, 그 범주는 꽤 유동적일 수 있다. (7)우리의 목표가 변함에 따라 추종자로서의 우리의 행동도 바뀐다. (8)만약 내가 음악에 대한 나의 판단보다 당신의 판단을 더 신뢰한다면, 우리가 어떤 콘서트에 참석할지에 대해서는 당신을 따를 수 있다 (당신이 비록 공식적으로 지위상 나의 부하일지라도). (9)하지만 내가 낚시 전문가라면, 공식적인 지위나 내가 어제 콘서트에 대해서는 당신을 따랐다는 사실과는 관계없이, 우리가 낚시할 장소에 대해서는 당신이 나를 따를 수 있다.

[정답 확인]

다음 빈칸에 들어갈 말로 가장 적절한 것은?

① rigid
엄격한
② unfair
부당한
✔ fluid
유동적인
④ stable
안정된
⑤ apparent
분명한

[문제 풀이]

본문의 핵심은 부하라는 직책을 가졌거나 리더를 따르는 행동에 의해서 추종자로 정의가 되더라도 추종자도 리더처럼 이끄는 힘을 가질 수 있다는 것이다. 이는 문장 (8)~(9)의 예시를 통해 구체적으로 확인할 수 있는데, 공식적인 지위와 관계없이 목표에 따라 리더(이끄는 사람)와 추종자(따르는 사람)가 결정됨을 알 수 있다. 따라서 빈칸에는 누가 추종자가 되는지는 목표에 따라 변한다는 글의 요지가 내포되어야 하므로 문장 (7)의 change와 유사한 의미를 가진 ③이 정답이다.

[중요 어휘]

☐ **define**	동사 정의하다
☐ **subordinate**	명사 부하 / 형용사 종속된, 부수적인
☐ **go along with**	~을 따르다, ~에 동의하다, 동조하다
☐ **empower**	동사 힘·권한을 주다
☐ **vice versa**	부사 반대로, 거꾸로
☐ **analyst**	명사 분석가
☐ **constituent**	명사 구성원, 구성 성분, 유권자
☐ **wind up V-ing (=end up V-ing)**	결국 ~하게 되다
☐ **fluid**	형용사 유동적인
☐ **objective**	명사 목표, 목적 / 형용사 객관적인
☐ **follow one's lead**	~을 따르다, ~의 주도를 따르다
☐ **attend**	동사 참석하다
☐ **expert**	명사 전문가 / 형용사 전문가의
☐ **regardless of**	~와 관계없이, 상관없이
☐ **rigid**	형용사 엄격한, 뻣뻣한
☐ **stable**	형용사 안정된, 안정적인
☐ **apparent**	형용사 분명한, 명백한

13 2022년 9월 33번 (정답률 50%) 정답 ①

[지문 끊어 읽기] 도덕적 교훈을 제공하는 역사의 기능

(1) As well as making sense of events through narratives, /
이야기를 통해서 사건을 이해하는 것뿐만 아니라 /
historians in the ancient world established the tradition of history /
(S) (V)
고대 사회의 역사가들은 역사의 전통을 확립했다 /
as a source of moral lessons and reflections.
도덕적 교훈과 성찰의 근원으로서

(2) The history writing of Livy or Tacitus, /
Livy나 Tacitus의 역사적인 기술은 /
for instance, / was in part designed /
예를 들면 / 부분적으로 만들어졌다 /
to examine the behavior of heroes and villains, /
영웅과 악당의 행동을 살펴보도록 /
[meditating on the strengths and weaknesses] /
장점과 단점을 숙고하여 / [ ]: 병렬①-분사구문
in the characters of emperors and generals, /
황제와 장군들의 성격의 /
[providing exemplars / [for the virtuous to imitate or avoid]].
[ ]: 병렬②
그렇게 하여 본보기를 제공한다 / 도덕적인 사람들이 모방하거나 피해야 할

힌트 to imitate or avoid는 to부정사의 형용사적 용법으로 exemplars를 수식하며 for the virtuous를 의미상의 주어로 가짐. 또한 'the+형용사'는 사람들을 가리키는 복수 보통명사 혹은 항상 단수로 취급하는 추상명사를 나타내는데 여기서 the virtuous는 복수 보통명사 'the virtuous people(도덕적인 사람들)'로 해석됨.

정답 단서 일부 역사적 기술은 역사 속 인물들을 바탕으로 도덕적 본보기를 제공함.

(3) This continues / to be one of the functions of history.
부사적 용법(결과)
이것이 계속된다 / 그래서 역사의 기능 중 하나가 된다

(4) French chronicler Jean Froissart said /
프랑스의 연대기 학자인 Jean Froissart는 말했다 /
he had written his accounts of chivalrous knights /
과거완료
그는 기사도적인 기사들에 대한 그의 이야기를 썼다고 /
[fighting in the Hundred Years' War] / [ ]: 현재분사구
백년전쟁에서 싸운 /
"so that brave men should be inspired /
부사절 접속사(목적)
용맹스러운 자들이 영감을 받도록 /
thereby to follow such examples."
그렇게 함으로써 이러한 본보기를 따르도록

정답 단서 한 역사적 기술은 기사도적인 기사라는 본보기를 제공함.

(5) Today, /
오늘날 /
[historical studies of Lincoln, Churchill, Gandhi, or Martin Luther King, Jr.] / [ ]: S
Lincoln, Churchill, Gandhi 또는 Martin Luther King, Jr.에 대한 역사적 연구는 /
perform the same function.
(V)
같은 기능을 수행한다

[전문 해석]

(1)이야기를 통해서 사건을 이해하는 것뿐만 아니라, 고대 사회의 역사가들은 도덕적 교훈과 성찰의 근원으로서 역사의 전통을 확립했다. (2)예를 들면, Livy나 Tacitus의 역사적인 기술은 부분적으로 황제와 장군들의 성격의 장점과 단점을 숙고하여 영웅과 악당의 행동을 살펴보도록 만들어졌다. 그렇게 하여 도덕적인 사람들이 모방하거나 피해야 할 본보기를 제공한다. (3)이것이 계속되어 역사의 기능 중 하나가 된다. (4)프랑스의 연대기 학자인 Jean Froissart는 백년전쟁에서 싸운 기사도적인 기사들에 대한 이야기를 "용맹스러운 자들이 영감을 받아 이러한 본보기를 따르도록" 썼다고 말했다. (5)오늘날 Lincoln, Churchill, Gandhi 또는 Martin Luther King, Jr.에 대한 역사적 연구는 같은 기능을 수행한다.

[정답 확인]

다음 빈칸에 들어갈 말로 가장 적절한 것은?

✔ source of moral lessons and reflections
도덕적 교훈과 성찰의 근원
② record of the rise and fall of empires
제국들의 흥망성쇠에 대한 기록
③ war against violence and oppression
폭력과 억압에 반대하는 전쟁
④ means of mediating conflict
갈등을 중재하는 수단
⑤ integral part of innovation
혁신의 필수적인 부분

[문제 풀이]

문장 (2)와 문장 (4)의 예시를 통해 지문의 주제를 드러내고 있다. 문장 (2)에서는 역사적 인물들의 모습을 통해 도덕적 본보기를 제공할 수 있도록, 문장 (4)에서는 백년전쟁의 기사들의 모습을 통해 용맹스러운 자들이 기사도적인 기사라는 본보기를 따르도록 역사가 기술된다고 설명한다. 따라서 도덕적이고 용맹스러운 자들이 따라야 하는 본보기, 즉 도덕적 교훈과 성찰의 근원을 제공하는 것이 역사의 기능이라 볼 수 있으므로 정답은 ①이다.

[중요 어휘]

☐ **make sense of**	~을 이해하다
☐ **narrative**	명사 이야기, 서사
☐ **reflection**	명사 성찰, 반영
☐ **examine**	동사 살펴보다, 조사하다, 검사하다
☐ **meditate**	동사 숙고하다, 명상하다
☐ **emperor**	명사 황제
☐ **general**	명사 장군
☐ **exemplar**	명사 본보기, 모범, 표본
☐ **virtuous**	형용사 도덕적인
☐ **imitate**	동사 모방하다
☐ **chronicler**	명사 연대기 학자
☐ **account**	명사 이야기, 설명, 계좌 / 동사 간주하다
☐ **chivalrous**	형용사 기사도적인, 예의 바른
☐ **historical**	형용사 역사적인
☐ **the rise and fall**	흥망성쇠
☐ **oppression**	명사 억압, 탄압
☐ **means**	명사 수단
☐ **mediate**	동사 중재하다, 조정하다
☐ **integral**	형용사 필수적인

14 2023년 9월 31번 (정답률 50%) 정답 ①

[지문 끊어 읽기] 반항을 이용한 마케팅

(1) Rebels may think they're rebels, /
반항자들은 자신들이 반항자라고 생각할지도 모른다 /

but clever marketers influence them / just like the rest of us.
하지만 영리한 마케터들은 그들에게 영향을 준다 / 나머지 우리에게 그러듯이

(2) Saying, "Everyone is doing it" /
'모두가 그것을 하고 있다'라고 말하는 것은 /
may turn some people off from an idea.
일부 사람들을 어떠한 생각에 대해 흥미를 잃게 만들지도 모른다

(3) These people will look for alternatives, /
이 사람들은 대안을 찾을 것이다 / 선행사
which (if cleverly planned) can be exactly /
계속적 용법
그리고 그것은 (만약 영리하게 계획된다면) 정확히 ~일 수 있다 /
what a marketer or persuader wants you to believe.
선행사를 포함한 관계대명사 S 5형식V O O·C
마케터나 설득자가 당신이 믿기를 원하는 것

(4) If I want you to consider an idea, /
S' V'①
만약 내가 당신이 어떠한 아이디어를 고려하길 바란다면 /
and know you strongly reject popular opinion /
V'②
그리고 당신이 대중적인 의견을 강력히 거부한다는 것을 안다면 /
in favor of maintaining your independence and uniqueness, /
당신의 독립성과 유일성을 유지하기 위해 /
I would present the majority option first, / which you would reject /
계속적 용법
나는 대다수의 선택을 먼저 제시할 것이다 / 그리고 당신은 이를 거부할 것이다 /
in favor of my actual preference. 정답단서 당신이 대중적인 의견에 거부한다는 것을 안다면, 대다수의 선택을 먼저 제시해 당신이 거부하게 하고 내가 선호하는 아이디어를 고려하도록 유도함.
내가 실제로 선호하는 것에 맞게

(5) We are often tricked /
우리는 종종 속는다 /
when we try to maintain a position of defiance. 정답단서 우리는 반항의 입장에서 종종 속음.
우리가 반항의 입장을 유지하려고 할 때

(6) People use this reversal /
사람들은 이러한 반전을 사용한다 /
to make us "independently" choose an option /
부사적 용법(목적) 선행사
우리가 '독자적으로' 선택지를 고르도록 만들기 위해 /
which suits their purposes. 정답단서 사람들은 '빈칸'을 사용해서 우리가 사람들의 목적에 맞는 선택지를 '독자적으로' 고르도록 만듦.
주격 관계대명사절
그들의 목적에 맞는

(7) Some brands have taken full effect of our defiance /
S V①
일부 브랜드들은 우리의 반항을 완전히 활용해 왔다 /
towards the mainstream / and positioned themselves as rebels; /
V②(have 생략)
주류에 대한 / 그리고 스스로를 반항자로 자리를 잡아왔다 /
which has created even stronger brand loyalty.
그리고 이는 훨씬 더 강력한 브랜드 충성도를 만들어 왔다

[전문 해석]

(1)반항자들은 자신들이 반항자라고 생각할지도 모르지만, 영리한 마케터들은 나머지 우리에게 그러듯이 그들에게 영향을 준다. (2)'모두가 그것을 하고 있다'라고 말하는 것은 일부 사람들을 어떠한 생각에 대해 흥미를 잃게 만들지도 모른다. (3)이 사람들은 대안을 찾을 것이고, 그것은 (만약 영리하게 계획된다면) 정확히 마케터나 설득자가 당신이 믿기를 원하는 것일 수 있다. (4)만약 내가 당신이 어떠한 아이디어를 고려하길 바라고, 당신이 당신의 독립성과 유일성을 유지하기 위해 대중적인 의견을 강력히 거부한다는 것을 안다면, 나는 대다수의 선택을 먼저 제시할 것이고, 당신은 내가 실제로 선호하는 것에 맞게 이(대다수의 선택)를 거부할 것이다. (5)우리가 반항의 입장을 유지하려고 할 때 우리는 종종 속는다. (6)사람들은 우리가 '독자적으로' 그들의 목적에 맞는 선택지를 고르도록 만들기 위해 이러한 반전을 사용한다. (7)일부 브랜드들은 주류에 대한 우리의 반항을 완전히 활용하여 스스로를 반항자로 자리를 잡아왔고, 이는 훨씬 더 강력한 브랜드 충성도를 만들어 왔다.

[정답 확인]

다음 빈칸에 들어갈 말로 가장 적절한 것은?

① reversal 반전 ② imitation 모방 ③ repetition 반복
④ conformity 순응 ⑤ collaboration 협력

[문제 풀이]

빈칸을 포함한 문장 (6)은 사람들의 목적에 맞게 우리가 선택을 하면서도 우리 스스로는 독자적으로 선택한다고 믿게 만드는 '무엇'을 사용한다는 내용이다. 문장 (4)~(5)에 따르면, 당신이 독립성과 유일성 때문에 대중적인 의견에 반대한다는 것을 아는 경우, 대다수 선택을 먼저 제시하여 당신이 이를 거부하게 만드는데, 이처럼 반항의 입장을 유지할 때 종종 속는다고 한다. 이는 사람들이 우리가 반항적인 것을 이용하여 그들이 원하는 것을 얻는다는 의미이다. 따라서 빈칸에 들어갈 말로 적절한 것은 ①이다.

[중요 어휘]

rebel	명사 반항자, 반역자
turn A off	A를 흥미를 잃게 만들다
alternative	명사 대안, 양자택일 / 형용사 대체 가능한, 양자택일의
persuader	명사 설득자
independence	명사 독립성
uniqueness	명사 유일성
present	동사 제시하다
preference	명사 선호
trick	동사 속이다
defiance	명사 반항, 저항
suit	동사 맞다, 적합하다
mainstream	명사 주류(主流)

15 2018년 11월 31번 (정답률 45%) 정답 ④

[지문 끊어 읽기] 과학과 예술의 창조와 행위에 관한 유사성

(1) A good many scientists and artists /
상당히 많은 과학자들과 예술가들이 /
have noticed the universality of creativity.
창의력의 보편성에 주목해 왔다

(2) At the Sixteenth Nobel Conference, held in 1980, /
1980년에 개최된 제16차 노벨 학회에서 /
scientists, musicians, and philosophers all agreed, /
S
과학자들, 음악가들, 그리고 철학자들은 모두 동의했다 /
to quote Freeman Dyson, that /
다음과 같은 Freeman Dyson의 말을 인용하는 데 /
힌트 that절은 문장 (2)의 큰따옴표(" ")부터 문장 (4)까지 이어지는 직접인용절 전체를 포함하고 있으며, 원칙적으로는 '~라는 Freeman Dyson의 말'이라고 해석해야 하지만, 직접인용절이 너무 길게 이어져서 여기서는 that을 '다음과 같은'으로 바꾸어 해석했음.
"the analogies between science and art are very good /
과학과 예술 사이의 유사성은 매우 높다 /
as long as you are talking about the creation and the performance.
당신이 창조와 행위에 관해 이야기하고 있는 한 정답단서

(3) The creation is certainly very analogous.
창조는 확실히 매우 유사하다

(4) The aesthetic pleasure / of the craftsmanship of performance /
심미적 쾌감은 / 행위의 장인 정신에서 나오는 /
is also very strong in science."
과학에서도 매우 강하다
중요 심미적 쾌감(aesthetic pleasure)이나 장인 정신(craftsmanship) 등은 흔히 예술적인 작업과 관련이 있는 것처럼 보이지만, 본문은 이러한 요소들은 예술뿐 아니라 과학 연구와도 관련이 있다고 말하고 있음.

(5) A few years later, / at another multidisciplinary conference, /
몇 년 후 / 또 다른 여러 학문 분야에 걸친 학회에서는 /
physicist Murray Gell-Mann found that / "everybody agrees /
물리학자 Murray Gell-Mann이 다음과 같은 것을 발견했다 / 모두가 동의한다 /
on where ideas come from.
아이디어가 어디에서 오는지에 대해

(6) We had a seminar here, / about ten years ago, /
우리는 이곳에서 세미나를 했다 / 약 10년 전 /
including several painters, a poet, a couple of writers, and the physicists.
몇몇의 화가들, 시인 한 명, 두어 명의 작가들, 그리고 물리학자들을 포함하여

(7) Everybody agrees / on how it works.
모두가 동의한다 / 그것이 진행되는 방식에

문제편 p.139

(8) All of these people, /
S
이 사람들 모두는 /
whether they are doing artistic work or scientific work, /
그들이 예술적인 작업을 하고 있든 과학적인 작업을 하고 있든 /
are trying to solve a problem." 정답 단서
V
문제를 해결하려고 노력하고 있다

[전문 해석]

(1)상당히 많은 과학자들과 예술가들이 창의력의 보편성에 주목해 왔다. (2)1980년에 개최된 제16차 노벨 학회에서 과학자들, 음악가들, 그리고 철학자들은 다음과 같은 Freeman Dyson의 말을 인용하는 데 모두 동의했다. "당신이 창조와 행위에 관해 이야기하고 있는 한, 과학과 예술 사이의 유사성은 매우 높다. (3)(과학과 예술에서의) 창조는 확실히 매우 유사하다. (4)행위의 장인 정신에서 나오는 심미적 쾌감은 과학에서도 매우 강하다." (5)몇 년 후 또 다른 여러 학문 분야에 걸친(다학적) 학회에서는 물리학자 Murray Gell-Mann이 다음과 같은 것을 발견했다. "모두가 아이디어가 어디에서 오는지에 대해 동의한다. (6)약 10년 전 우리는 몇몇의 화가들, 시인 한 명, 두어 명의 작가들, 그리고 물리학자들을 포함하여 이곳에서 세미나를 했다. (7)모두가 그것이 진행되는 방식에 동의한다. (8)이 사람들 모두는 자신들이 예술적인 작업을 하고 있든 과학적인 작업을 하고 있든 문제를 해결하려고 노력하고 있다."

- Nobel Conference(노벨 학회): 미국의 Gustavus Adolphus 대학에서 1963년부터 매년 개최되는 학술대회로, 세계의 유명한 학자들이 모여 각 분야의 최신 이슈를 학생들 및 일반 대중과 공유하는 것을 목표로 하는 행사이다.
- Freeman Dyson(프리먼 다이슨, 1923년~2020년): 영국 태생의 미국인 물리학자이자 수학자이며 특히 양자 전기역학, 고체물리학, 천문학 등의 연구로 유명하다.
- Murray Gell-Mann(머리 겔만, 1927년~2019년): 미국의 물리학자이며, 물질을 구성하는 기본 입자인 쿼크(quark)를 최초로 제안 및 명명하였다. 1969년 입자물리학 연구로 노벨 물리학상을 받았다.

[정답 확인]

다음 빈칸에 들어갈 말로 가장 적절한 것은?

① formality 형식성 ② objectivity 객관성 ③ complexity 복잡성
④ universality 보편성 ⑤ uncertainty 불확실성

[문제 풀이]

본문은 과학과 예술이 서로 다른 분야임에도 불구하고 창조(creation)와 행위(performance)라는 측면에서 매우 높은 유사성을 갖는다고 말한다. 즉 창조성이 미술, 문학, 철학, 물리학 등 다양한 분야에서 공통적으로 나타난다는 것인데, 보기 중 창조성의 이러한 성질을 가장 잘 드러내주는 표현은 ④ 'universality(보편성)'이다.

[중요 어휘]

□ **a good many**	상당히 많은, 꽤 많은
□ **universality**	명사 보편성, 일반성
□ **conference**	명사 학회, 회의
□ **hold**	동사 개최하다, 열다, 잡다
□ **quote**	동사 인용하다, 전달하다
□ **analogy**	명사 유사성, 비유
□ **performance**	명사 행위, 실행
□ **analogous**	형용사 유사한, 비슷한
□ **aesthetic**	형용사 심미적인, 미학적인
□ **craftsmanship**	명사 장인 정신, 솜씨, 기예
□ **multidisciplinary**	형용사 여러 학문 분야에 걸친, 다학적인

힌트 'multi(다수의)-disciplinary(학문의, 학문에 관한)'이므로, '여러 학문 분야에 걸친'이라는 뜻임. 참고로 disciplinary는 'discipline(훈육, 규율)'의 형용사형으로, '징계의, 훈육의, 규율상의'라는 뜻으로도 자주 쓰임.

16 2023년 6월 33번 (정답률 45%) 정답 ③

[지문 끊어 읽기] 마음의 폐쇄

(1) In adolescence / many of us had the experience /
청소년기에 / 우리 중 다수는 경험이 있다 /
of falling under the sway of a great book or writer.
위대한 책이나 작가의 영향을 받은

(2) We became entranced / by the novel ideas in the book, /
우리는 매료되었다 / 책의 새로운 생각에 /
and because we were so open to influence, /
전치사
그리고 우리가 영향에 매우 열려 있었기 때문에 /
these early encounters with exciting ideas /
흥미로운 생각과의 이러한 초기의 만남은 /
sank deeply into our minds /
병렬①
우리의 마음에 깊게 가라앉았다 /
and became part of our own thought processes, /
병렬②
그리고 우리 자신의 사고 과정의 일부가 되었다 /
[affecting us decades after we absorbed them]. [ ]: 분사구문(결과)
우리가 그들을 흡수한 지 몇십 년 후에 우리에게 영향을 미쳤다

(3) Such influences enriched our mental landscape, /
그러한 영향은 우리의 정신적 풍경을 풍부하게 했다 /
and in fact our intelligence depends on the ability /
그리고 사실 우리의 지성은 능력에 의존한다 /
to absorb the lessons and ideas /
형용사적 용법
교훈과 생각을 흡수하는 /
of those [who are older and wiser].
선행사 [ ]: 주격 관계대명사절
더 나이가 많고 더 현명한 사람들의

(4) Just as the body tightens with age, /
나이가 들면서 신체가 경직되는 것처럼 /
however, / so does the mind. 정답 단서
그러나 / 마음도 그렇다
나이가 들수록 신체가 경직되는 것처럼 마음도 경직됨.

힌트 'Just as S' V', so S V(~인 것처럼, …도 그렇다)' 구문으로, so 다음에 선택적으로 도치 구문을 쓸 수 있음. 문장 (4)의 경우 조동사 does는 일반동사 tightens를 대신하며, 주어 뒤에 쓰여야 하는 'tightens with age'는 앞 문장과 반복되어 생략됨. 문장 (5)의 so 이하의 도치 이전 문장은 'so our creeping sense of superiority slowly closes us off ~ influences'가 될 수 있음.

(5) And just as our sense of weakness and vulnerability motivated the desire to learn, /
형용사적 용법
그리고 약점과 취약성에 대한 우리의 지각이 배우려는 욕망에 동기를 부여한 것처럼 /
so does our creeping sense of superiority slowly close us off /
S
슬며시 접근하는 우리의 우월성에 대한 지각은 천천히 우리를 차단한다 /
to new ideas and influences. 정답 단서
새로운 생각과 영향에 대해
약점과 취약성을 깨달을 때 배우고자 하나, 우리가 서서히 우월성을 깨달아 가면서 새로운 것을 받아들이지 않게 됨.

(6) Some may advocate /
어떤 사람들은 주장할지도 모른다 /
that we all become more skeptical in the modern world, /
우리 모두가 현대 세계에서 더 회의적으로 된다고 /
but in fact / a far greater danger comes /
비교급 강조
그러나 사실 / 훨씬 큰 위험은 온다 /
from the increasing closing of the mind /
선행사
증가하는 마음의 폐쇄에서 /
[that burdens us as individuals / as we get older, /
병렬① 전치사 접속사
개인으로서는 우리에게 부담을 주는 / 우리가 나이가 들수록 /
and seems to be burdening our culture in general]. 정답 단서
병렬② [ ]: 주격 관계대명사절
그리고 일반적으로 우리의 문화에 부담을 주는 것처럼 보이는
현대 사회의 전반적인 회의는 사실 나이가 들어가면서 닫힌 마음을 가지게 되고, 이것이 개인과 문화 전체에 부담을 주는 결과로 나타나는 것임.

[전문 해석]

(1)청소년기에 우리 중 다수는 위대한 책이나 작가의 영향을 받은 경험이 있다. (2)우리는 책의 새로운 생각에 매료되었고, 우리가 영향에 매우 열려 있었기 때문에 흥미로운 생각과의 이러한 초기의 만남은 우리의 마음에 깊게 가라앉아 우리 자신의 사고 과정의 일부가 되었고, 우리가 그들을 흡수한 지 몇십 년 후에 우리에게 영향을 미쳤다. (3)그러한 영향은 우리의 정신적 풍경을 풍부하게 했고 사실 우리의 지성은 더 나이가 많고 더 현명한 사람들의 교훈과 생각을 흡수하는 능력에 의존한다. (4)그러나, 나이가 들면서 신체가 경직되는 것처럼 마음도 그렇다. (5)그리고 약점과 취약성에 대한 우리의 지각이 배우려는 욕망에 동기를 부여한 것처럼, 슬며시 접근하는 우리의 우월성에 대한 지각은 천천히 우리를 새로운 생각과 영향에 대해 차단한다. (6)어떤 사람들은 우리 모두가 현대 세계에서 더 회의적으로 된다고 주장할지도 모르지만, 사실 훨씬 큰 위험은 우리가 나이가 들수록 개인으로서 우리에게 부담을 주고 일반적으로 우리의 문화에 부담을 주는 것처럼 보이는 증가하는 마음의 폐쇄에서 온다.

[정답 확인]

다음 빈칸에 들어갈 말로 가장 적절한 것은?

① the high dependence on others
다른 사람들에 대한 높은 의존
② the obsession with our inferiority
우리의 열등함에 대한 집착
✔ the increasing closing of the mind
증가하는 마음의 폐쇄
④ the misconception about our psychology
우리의 심리에 대한 오해
⑤ the self-destructive pattern of behavior
자기 파괴적인 행동 패턴

[문제 풀이]

문장 (1)~(3)에 따르면, 청소년기에 접하는 새로운 생각은 우리의 사고 과정을 형성하고 지성을 기르게 한다. 그러나 문장 (4)~(5)는 나이가 들수록 몸과 같이, 마음도 경직되고 슬며시 접근하는 우월함에 대한 우리의 지각은 우리를 새로운 생각으로부터 차단한다고 말한다. 따라서 빈칸에는 마음의 폐쇄가 증가한다는 내용의 ③이 적절하다.

[중요 어휘]

☐ **under the sway of**	~의 영향 아래, ~의 지배 아래
☐ **entrance**	동사 매료시키다, 황홀하게 하다 / 명사 입장
☐ **encounter**	명사 만남 / 동사 만나다, 직면하다
☐ **enrich**	동사 풍부하게 하다, 부유하게 하다
☐ **landscape**	명사 풍경
☐ **intelligence**	명사 지성, 지능
☐ **vulnerability**	명사 취약성, 상처받기 쉬움
☐ **creeping**	형용사 슬며시 접근하는, 서서히 진행되는
☐ **superiority**	명사 우월성
☐ **close off**	동사 차단시키다, 폐쇄시키다
☐ **advocate**	동사 주장하다, 지지하다 / 명사 대변인, 옹호자
☐ **skeptical**	형용사 회의적인, 의심 많은
☐ **burden**	동사 부담을 주다 / 명사 짐, 부담

17 2018년 9월 31번 (정답률 40%) 정답 ④

[지문 끊어 읽기] 온라인에서의 기록과 저장

(1) Online environments vary widely /
온라인 환경은 매우 다양하다 /
in [how easily you can save / whatever happens there], /
[ ]: 병렬①(간접의문문)
당신이 얼마나 쉽게 저장할 수 있는지에 있어서 / 거기에서 일어나는 일이 무엇이든 간에 /
[what I call its *recordability* and *preservability*]. 주제문
내가 그것의 '기록 가능성'과 '저장 가능성'이라고 부르는 것에 있어서 [ ]: 병렬②(관계대명사 what이 이끄는 명사절)

(2) Even though the design, activities, and membership of social media might change /
비록 소셜 미디어의 디자인, 활동, 그리고 멤버십이 바뀔지도 모르지만 /
over time, / the content of what people posted /
시간이 지남에 따라 / 사람들이 게시했던 것의 내용은 /
usually remains intact.
보통 온전히 남아있다

(3) Email, video, audio, and text messages can be saved.
이메일, 동영상, 음성, 그리고 문자 메시지는 저장될 수 있다

(4) When perfect preservation is possible, /
완벽한 보존이 가능할 때 /
time has been suspended.
시간은 멈춰 있다

(5) Whenever you want, / you can go back /
당신이 원할 때마다 / 당신은 되돌아갈 수 있다 /
to reexamine those events / from the past.
그러한 사건들을 다시 돌아보기 위해 / 과거로부터의

(6) In other situations, / permanency slips between our fingers, /
또 다른 상황에서 / 영속성은 우리의 손가락 사이로 빠져나간다 /
even challenging our reality testing /
심지어 우리의 현실 검증에 이의를 제기하면서 /
about whether something existed at all, / as when /
어떤 것이 어떤 식으로든 존재했었는지에 대한 / ~할 때처럼 /
an email that we seem to remember receiving /
우리가 받았다고 기억하는 것처럼 보이는 이메일이 /
mysteriously disappears from our inbox.
우리의 받은 편지함에서 불가사의하게 사라질 때

(7) The slightest accidental tap of the finger / can send /
손가락의 아주 사소한 우발적인 두드림은 / 보낼 수 있다 /
an otherwise everlasting document / into nothingness. 정답 단서
그렇게 하지 않았으면 영원히 존재할 문서를 / 무의 상태로

[전문 해석]

(1)온라인 환경은 거기에서 일어나는 일이 무엇이든 간에 당신이 얼마나 쉽게 저장할 수 있는지, (즉) 내가 온라인 환경의 '기록 가능성'과 '저장 가능성'이라고 부르는 것에 있어서 매우 다양하다. (2)비록 소셜 미디어의 디자인, 활동, 그리고 멤버십이 시간이 지남에 따라 바뀔지도 모르지만, 사람들이 게시했던 것의 내용은 보통 온전히 남아있다. (3)이메일, 동영상, 음성, 그리고 문자 메시지는 저장될 수 있다. (4)완벽한 보존이 가능할 때 시간은 멈춰 있다. (5)당신이 원할 때마다, 당신은 과거(로부터)의 그러한 사건들을 다시 돌아보기 위해 되돌아갈 수 있다. (6)또 다른 상황에서 우리가 받았다고 기억하는 것처럼 보이는 이메일이 우리의 받은 편지함에서 불가사의하게 사라질 때처럼, 심지어 어떤 것이 어떤 식으로든 존재했었는지에 대한 우리의 현실 검증에 이의를 제기하면서, 영속성은 우리의 손가락 사이로 빠져나간다. (7)손가락의 아주 사소한 우발적인 두드림은(손가락으로 우연히 살짝 톡 친 것은) 그렇게 하지 않았으면 영원히 존재할 문서를 무(無)의 상태로 보낼 수 있다.

[정답 확인]

다음 빈칸에 들어갈 말로 가장 적절한 것은?

① scarcity
결핍
② creativity
창의력
③ acceleration
가속
✔ permanency
영속성
⑤ mysteriousness
불가사의

★중요 빈칸이 있는 문장 (6)의 '손가락 사이로 빠져 나간다'와 '불가사의하게 사라진다'를 동일 선상에서 생각해 ⑤를 고르지 않도록 주의해야 함.

[문제 풀이]

지문은 온라인에서 일어나는 일들을 기록 및 저장하는 것이 다양한 수준에서 이루어지고 있음을 이메일, 동영상, 음성 등을 예시로 들어 설명하고 있다. 온라인 환경에서 우리는 과거에 게시했던 내용이나 사건들을 영원히 볼 수도 있지만, 손가락으로 툭 쳐서 삭제할 수도 있기 때문에 정답은 ④ 'permanency(영속성)'이다.

[중요 어휘]

☐ **vary in**	~이 다양하다, 여러 가지다
☐ **recordability**	명사 기록 가능성
☐ **preservability**	명사 저장 가능성
☐ **intact**	형용사 온전한, 전혀 다치지 않은
☐ **preservation**	명사 보존, 보호
☐ **suspend**	동사 멈추다, 중단하다
☐ **reexamine**	동사 다시 돌아보다, 재검토하다
☐ **slip**	동사 빠져나가다, 미끄러지다 / 명사 실수
☐ **testing**	명사 검증, 시험
☐ **mysteriously**	부사 불가사의하게, 미궁 속에
☐ **accidental**	형용사 우발적인, 우연한
☐ **everlasting**	형용사 영원히 존재하는, 변치 않는

핵심 빈칸에는 철학적 활동이 무엇에 기반을 두고 시작되는지가 포함되어야 하므로 철학적 활동의 목적에 집중해야 함.

18 2021년 9월 32번 (정답률 40%) 정답 ①

[지문 끊어 읽기] 철학적 활동의 목적

(1) Philosophical activity is based on the recognition of ignorance.
철학적 활동은 무지의 인식에 기초를 둔다

(2) The philosopher's thirst for knowledge /
지식에 대한 철학자의 갈망은 /

is shown through attempts / to find better answers to questions /
형용사적 용법
시도를 통해 보여진다 / 질문에 대해 더 나은 답을 찾으려는 /
even if those answers are never found.
그 답이 절대 발견되지 않는다 해도

(3) At the same time, / a philosopher also knows /
동시에 / 철학자는 또한 안다 /
that being too sure can hinder /
지나치게 확신하는 것이 방해할 수 있다는 것을 /
the discovery of other and better possibilities.
다르고도 더 나은 가능성의 발견을

(4) In a philosophical dialogue, / the participants are aware /
철학적 대화에서 / 참여자들은 인식한다 /
that there are things they do not know or understand. 정답단서
선행사 목적격 관계대명사절
그들이 알지 못하거나 이해하지 못하는 것이 있다는 것을

(5) The goal of the dialogue / is to arrive at a conception /
그 대화의 목표는 / 개념에 도달하는 것이다 /
that one did not know or understand beforehand. 정답단서
동격의 that
어떤 이도 미리 알지 못했거나 이해하지 못했다는
힌트 여기서 one은 부정 대명사로서, 일반적으로 불특정한 사람, 누구나를 가리킴.

(6) In traditional schools, / where philosophy is not present, /
전통적인 학교에서는 / 철학이 존재하지 않는 /
students often work with factual questions, /
학생들은 보통 사실적 질문을 공부 대상으로 한다 /
they learn specific content listed in the curriculum, /
과거분사구
그들은 교육 과정에 나열된 특정한 내용을 배운다 /
and they are not required to solve philosophical problems.
그리고 그들은 철학적 문제들을 해결하도록 요구받지 않는다

(7) However, / we know /
하지만 / 우리는 안다 /
that awareness of what one does not know /
S'
자신이 알지 못하는 것에 대한 인식이 /
can be a good way to acquire knowledge. 정답단서
V'
지식을 얻는 좋은 방법이 될 수 있다는 것을

(8) Knowledge and understanding are developed /
지식과 이해는 발달된다 /
through thinking and talking.
사색과 토론을 통해

(9) Putting things into words makes things clearer.
5형식V O O·C
생각을 말로 표현하는 것은 생각을 더 분명하게 만든다

(10) Therefore, / students must not be afraid of /
그러므로 / 학생들은 두려워해서는 안 된다 /
saying something wrong /
병렬①
잘못된 무엇인가를 말하는 것을 /
or talking without first being sure that they are right.
병렬②
혹은 자신들이 옳다는 것을 먼저 확신하지 않은 채 이야기하는 것을

[전문 해석]

(1)철학적 활동은 무지의 인식에 기초를 둔다. (2)지식에 대한 철학자의 갈망은 그 답이 절대 발견되지 않는다 해도 질문에 대해 더 나은 답을 찾으려는 시도를 통해 보여진다. (3)동시에, 철학자는 또한 지나치게 확신하는 것이 다르고도 더 나은 가능성의 발견을 방해할 수 있다는 것을 안다. (4)철학적 대화에서, 참여자들은 그들이 알지 못하거나 이해하지 못하는 것이 있다는 것을 인식한다. (5)그 대화의 목표는 어떤 이도 미리 알지 못했거나 이해하지 못했다는 개념에 도달하는 것이다. (6)철학이 존재하지 않는 전통적인 학교에서는, 학생들은 보통 사실적 질문을 공부 대상으로 하고, 교육 과정에 나열된 특정한 내용을 배우며, 철학적 문제들을 해결하도록 요구받지 않는다. (7)하지만 우리는 자신이 알지 못하는 것에 대한 인식이 지식을 얻는 좋은 방법이 될 수 있다는 것을 안다. (8)지식과 이해는 사색과 토론을 통해 발달된다. (9)생각을 말로 표현하는 것은 생각을 더 분명하게 만든다. (10)그러므로 학생들은 잘못된 무엇인가를 말하는 것이나 자신들이 옳다는 것을 먼저 확신하지 않은 채 이야기하는 것을 두려워해서는 안 된다.

[정답 확인]

다음 빈칸에 들어갈 말로 가장 적절한 것은?

✔ recognition of ignorance
무지의 인식
② emphasis on self-assurance
자신감의 강조
③ conformity to established values
확립된 가치에 대한 순응
④ achievements of ancient thinkers
고대 사상가들의 업적
⑤ comprehension of natural phenomena
자연 현상들에 대한 이해력

[문제 풀이]

본문에 따르면 사람은 철학적 대화를 통해 알지 못하는 것이나 이해하지 못하는 것이 있다는 것을 깨닫게 된다. 따라서 철학적 대화의 목적은 어떤 사람도 미리 알지 못하거나 이해하지 못했다는 그 개념 자체에 도달하는 것이다. 그러므로 정답은 철학적 대화와 같은 철학적 활동은 무지를 인식하는 것으로부터 시작된다는 내용의 ①이다.

[오답 풀이]

② - 본문에 따르면 철학적 활동에서 중요한 것은 모르는 것이 있다는 인식에 도달하는 것이다. 문장 (3)에 따르면 지나치게 확신하는 태도는 오히려 더 나은 가능성의 발견을 방해할 수 있다고 하므로 자신감 또는 자기 확신을 갖는 태도는 철학적 활동에서 지양하는 것으로 볼 수 있다. 따라서 ②는 정답이 될 수 없다.

[중요 어휘]

☐ **philosophical**	형용사 철학적인
☐ **recognition**	명사 인식
☐ **ignorance**	명사 무지
☐ **hinder**	동사 방해하다
☐ **conception**	명사 개념, 구상, 이해
☐ **beforehand**	부사 미리
☐ **work with**	~을 공부 대상으로 하다, ~와 함께 일하다
☐ **acquire**	동사 얻다
☐ **self-assurance**	명사 자신(감)
☐ **conformity**	명사 순응, 따름
☐ **thinker**	명사 사상가, 생각하는 사람
☐ **comprehension**	명사 이해력

19 2022년 3월 31번 (정답률 40%) 정답 ②

[지문 끊어 읽기] 진정한 충성심을 확인하는 방법

(1) Around the boss, / you will always find people /
우두머리 주변에서 / 여러분은 항상 사람들을 발견할 수 있다 /
[coming across as friends, good subordinates, or even great sympathizers].
친구나 좋은 부하, 심지어는 대단한 동조자라는 인상을 주는

(2) But some do not truly belong. 정답단서 일부 사람들은 우두머리 주변에 진정으로 속해 있지 않음.
그러나 몇몇은 진정으로 속해 있는 것은 아니다

(3) One day, / an incident will blow their cover, /
언젠가는 / 어떤 사건이 그들의 위장을 날려 버릴 것이다 /
and then you will know / where they truly belong.
그러면 여러분은 알게 될 것이다 / 그들이 진정으로 속한 곳을

(4) When it is all cosy and safe, / they will be there, /
모든 것이 편안하고 안전할 때 / 그들은 그곳에 있을 것이다 /
loitering the corridors / and fawning at the slightest opportunity.
분사구문① 분사구문②
복도를 서성거리면서 / 그리고 아주 작은 기회에도 알랑거리면서

(5) But as soon as difficulties arrive, /
하지만 어려움이 닥치자마자 /

힌트 5형식 문형인 'S+find+O+O·C(V-ing)'가 수동태로 바뀐 형태임.

they are the first to be found missing. 정답 단서 (형용사적 용법)
그들은 가장 먼저 보이지 않을 것이다
우두머리 주변에 진정으로 속해 있지 않은 사람들은 어려움이 닥치면 가장 먼저 사라질 것이라고 말하고 있음.

(6) And difficult times are the true test of loyalty.
그래서 어려운 시기는 충성심의 진정한 시험대이다

힌트 'A of B'에서 A 자리에 동사에서 파생된 명사가 올 경우 B는 그 행동의 주체일 수도, 대상일 수도 있음. 본문의 경우 'man'은 'test'의 대상, 즉 목적어 같은 역할을 하므로 '어떤 사람을 판단하는 궁극적인 시험대'라고 의역함.

(7) Dr. Martin Luther King said, /
Dr. Martin Luther King은 말했다 /
"The ultimate test of a man / is not where he stands / (not A but B: A가 아니라 B(B를 강조))
어떤 사람을 판단하는 궁극적인 시험대는 / 그 사람이 서 있는 곳이 아니라 /
in moments of comfort and convenience, / but where he stands /
편안함과 안락함의 순간에 / 그 사람이 서 있는 곳이다 /
at times of challenge and controversy." 정답 단서
도전과 논쟁의 시기에
어려운 시기에 그가 서 있는 곳이 진정으로 그가 속한 곳이라고 함.

(8) And so / be careful of friends / (선행사)
그러므로 / 친구를 조심하라 /
[who are always eager to take from you / (병렬①)
항상 여러분에게서 뭔가 얻어가기를 열망하는 /
but reluctant to give back / even in their little ways]. [ ]: 주격 관계대명사절 (등위접속사, 병렬②)
하지만 돌려주기를 꺼리는 / 사소하게라도

(9) If they lack the commitment /
만약 그들에게 헌신이 부족하다면 /
to sail with you through difficult weather, / 정답 단서 (형용사적 용법)
여러분과 함께 악천후를 뚫고 항해하려는 /
어려운 시기에도 함께하려는 헌신이 부족한 사람은 진정으로 속해 있는 것이 아니라고 함.
then they are more likely to abandon your ship / when it stops. (=your ship)
그들은 여러분의 배를 버릴 가능성이 더 크다 / 그것이 멈출 때

[전문 해석]

(1)우두머리 주변에서, 여러분은 항상 친구나 좋은 부하, 심지어는 대단한 동조자라는 인상을 주는 사람들을 발견할 수 있다. (2)그러나 몇몇은 진정으로 속해 있는 것은 아니다. (3)언젠가는, 어떤 사건이 그들의 위장을 날려 버릴 것이고, 여러분은 그들이 진정으로 속한 곳을 알게 될 것이다. (4)모든 것이 편안하고 안전할 때, 그들은 복도를 서성거리고 아주 작은 기회에도 알랑거리면서 그곳에 있을 것이다. (5)하지만 어려움이 닥치자마자, 그들은 가장 먼저 보이지 않을 것이다. (6)그래서 어려운 시기는 충성심의 진정한 시험대이다. (7)Dr. Martin Luther King은 "어떤 사람을 판단하는 궁극적인 시험대는 편안함과 안락함의 순간에 그 사람이 서 있는 곳이 아니라, 도전과 논쟁의 시기에 그 사람이 서 있는 곳이다."라고 말했다. (8)그러므로 항상 여러분에게서 뭔가 얻어가기를 열망하면서 사소하게라도 돌려주기를 꺼리는 친구를 조심하라. (9)만약 그들에게 여러분과 함께 악천후를 뚫고 항해하려는 헌신이 부족하다면, 여러분의 배가 멈출 때, 그것을 버릴 가능성이 더 크다.

[정답 확인]

다음 빈칸에 들어갈 말로 가장 적절한 것은?

① leadership 지도력 ✔ loyalty 충성심 ③ creativity 창의성
④ intelligence 지성 ⑤ independence 독립성

[문제 풀이]

어떤 사람이 진정으로 어디에 속하는지를 알려면 편안한 시기에 그가 어디에 있는지를 보는 것이 아니라 어려운 시기에 그가 어디에 있는지, 어려운 시기에도 그가 똑같이 헌신을 보여주는지를 보아야 한다는 것이 지문의 요지이다. 어떤 사람이 특정한 곳에 소속되어 헌신한다는 것과 가장 유사한 의미를 가진 선지는 'loyalty(충성심)'이므로, 정답은 ②이다.

[오답 풀이]

① - 지문에 'boss'라는 단어가 나와서 'leadership'을 떠올릴 수는 있다. 하지만 지문의 중심 소재는 어려운 시기에 'boss'가 무언가를 해야 한다는 내용과 관련이 없으므로 정답이 아니다.

[중요 어휘]

□ **come across as**	~라는 인상을 주다
□ **subordinate**	명사 부하, 하급자 / 형용사 종속된, 부수적인
□ **sympathizer**	명사 동조자, 지지자
□ **belong**	동사 속하다
□ **cover**	명사 위장 / 동사 씌우다, 가리다
□ **cosy(=cozy)**	형용사 편안한, 아늑한
□ **loiter**	동사 서성거리다
□ **corridor**	명사 복도
□ **fawn**	동사 알랑거리다
□ **test**	명사 시험대, 시험
□ **loyalty**	명사 충성심
□ **challenge**	명사 도전, 문제, 어려움 / 동사 도전하다, 이의를 제기하다
□ **controversy**	명사 논쟁
□ **be eager to V**	~을 열망하다
□ **reluctant**	형용사 꺼리는, 주저하는
□ **commitment**	명사 헌신, 약속

핵심 빈칸을 이해하기 위해서는 우선 문장 (2)~(4)에서 개인의 공로로 간주되는 획기적 발견의 예시가 설명되고, 문장 (5) 이후부터는 혼자가 아니라 사람들과 협업하는 모습이 언급되어 마지막에 결론을 도출하고 있음을 확인해야 함.

20 2018년 6월 34번 (정답률 35%) 정답 ⑤

[지문 끊어 읽기] 지식의 집단적 속성

(1) Appreciating the collective nature of knowledge /
지식의 집단적 속성을 이해하는 것은 /
can correct our false notions / of how we see the world. 주제문
우리의 잘못된 개념을 바로잡아 줄 수 있다 / 우리가 세상을 어떻게 바라보는가에 대한

(2) People love heroes.
사람들은 영웅을 사랑한다

(3) Individuals are given credit / for major breakthroughs.
개인들은 공로를 인정받는다 / 주요한 획기적 발견에 대한

(4) Marie Curie is treated / as if she worked alone /
마리 퀴리는 간주된다 / 마치 그녀가 홀로 연구한 것처럼 /
to discover radioactivity /
방사능을 발견하기 위해 /
힌트 동어 반복을 피하기 위해 Newton과 as if 사이의 'is treated'가 생략됨.
and Newton as if he discovered the laws of motion / by himself.
그리고 뉴턴은 운동의 법칙을 발견한 것처럼 간주된다 / 혼자 힘으로

(5) The truth is that / in the real world, / nobody operates alone. 정답 단서
진실은 ~라는 것이다 / 현실 세계에서 / 어느 누구도 홀로 일하지 않는다

(6) Scientists not only have labs with students /
과학자들은 학생들과 함께 하는 실험실이 있을 뿐만 아니라 /
who contribute critical ideas, / but also have colleagues / (not only A but also B: A뿐만 아니라 B도)
중요한 생각에 공헌하는 / 동료들도 있다 /
who are doing similar work, thinking similar thoughts, /
유사한 연구를 하고 유사한 생각을 하는 /
and without whom the scientist would get nowhere.
그리고 그들이 없다면 과학자들은 아무런 성과도 얻지 못했을
힌트 colleagues를 선행사로 취하는 두 관계대명사절 'who ~ thoughts'와 'without whom ~ nowhere'이 병렬 연결되어 있음. 후자의 경우 관계대명사가 관계사절 내에서 전치사 without의 목적어이므로 목적격 관계대명사 whom이 쓰임.

(7) And then there are other scientists /
그러고 나서 다른 과학자들이 있다 /
who are working on different problems, /
다른 문제들을 연구하는 /
sometimes in different fields, / but nevertheless set the stage /
때로는 다른 분야에서 / 그러나 그럼에도 불구하고 장을 마련해주는 /
through their own findings and ideas.
그들 자신의 발견과 생각들을 통해

(8) Once we start understanding /
일단 우리가 이해하기 시작하면 /
that knowledge isn't all in the head, /
지식이 모두 머릿속에 있지 않다는 것을 / 정답 단서
that it's shared within a community, / our heroes change.
그것이 공동체 속에서 공유된다는 것을 / 우리의 영웅은 바뀐다

(9) Instead of focusing on the individual, / we begin to focus /
개인에게 초점을 맞추는 대신에 / 우리는 초점을 맞추기 시작한다 /
on a larger group. 정답 단서
더 큰 집단에

문제편 p.142

[전문 해석]

(1)지식의 집단적 속성을 이해하는 것은 우리가 세상을 어떻게 바라보는가에 대한 우리의 잘못된 개념을 바로잡아 줄 수 있다. (2)사람들은 영웅을 사랑한다. (3)개인들은 주요한 획기적 발견에 대한 공로를 인정받는다. (4)마리 퀴리는 마치 그녀가 방사능을 발견하기 위해 홀로 연구한 것처럼 간주되며, 뉴턴은 혼자 힘으로 운동의 법칙을 발견한 것처럼 간주된다. (5)진실은 현실 세계에서 어느 누구도 홀로 일하지 않는다는 것이다. (6)과학자들은 중요한 생각에 공헌하는 학생들과 함께 하는 실험실이 있을 뿐만 아니라 유사한 연구를 하고 유사한 생각을 하는 동료들도 있으며 그들이 없다면 과학자들은 아무런 성과도 얻지 못했을 것이다. (7)그러고 나서 다른 문제들, 때로는 다른 분야에서 연구하지만 그럼에도 불구하고 그들 자신의 발견과 생각들을 통해 장을 마련해주는 다른 과학자들이 있다. (8)일단 우리가 지식이 모두 (한 명의) 머릿속에 있지 않고, 공동체 속에서 공유된다는 것을 이해하기 시작하면 우리의 영웅은 바뀐다. (9)개인에게 초점을 맞추는 대신에 우리는 더 큰 집단에 초점을 맞추기 시작한다.

[정답 확인]

다음 빈칸에 들어갈 말로 가장 적절한 것은?

① the process of trial and error
시행착오의 과정
② the changeable patterns of nature
속성의 변하기 쉬운 패턴
③ the academic superiority of scholars
학자들의 학문적 우월성
④ the diversity of scientific theories
과학 이론의 다양성
✔ the collective nature of knowledge ····★ 중요 문장 (8)의 shared within a community는 정답에서 collective라는 형용사로 표현되었음.
지식의 집단적 속성

[문제 풀이]

지문은 지식의 속성에 대해 설명하며 우리가 비슷하거나 다른 분야 혹은 다른 일을 함에도 불구하고 지식은 홀로 연구되어지는 것이 아니라 타인과 함께 공동체 속에서 연구되기 때문에 성취를 이룰 수 있는 것이라고 얘기하고 있다. 그러므로 정답은 ⑤ 'the collective nature of knowledge(지식의 집단적 속성)'이다.

[중요 어휘]

☐ **appreciate**	동사	이해하다, 감사하다, 감상하다
☐ **notion**	명사	개념, 생각
☐ **give credit for**		~에 대한 공로를 인정하다
☐ **breakthrough**	명사	획기적 발견, 돌파구
☐ **treat**	동사	간주하다, 다루다, 치료하다, 고치다
☐ **operate**	동사	일하다, 움직이다, 작용하다
☐ **get/go nowhere**		아무런 성과를 얻지 못하다
☐ **trial and error**	명사	시행착오
☐ **superiority**	명사	우월성
☐ **collective**	형용사	집단적인, 집단의

21 2019년 6월 31번 (정답률 35%) 정답 ②

[지문 끊어 읽기] 교우 관계의 형성 과정

(1) Psychologists Leon Festinger, Stanley Schachter, /
심리학자 Leon Festinger, Stanley Schachter은 /
and sociologist Kurt Back / began to wonder /
그리고 사회학자 Kurt Back은 / 궁금해하기 시작했다 /
how friendships form.
어떻게 교우 관계가 형성되는지를

(2) Why do some strangers build lasting friendships, /
왜 어떤 낯선 이들은 지속적인 교우 관계를 쌓는가 /
while others struggle / to get past basic platitudes?
다른 누군가는 어려움을 겪는 반면 / 기본적인 상투적인 말을 넘어서는 데에

(3) Some experts explained /
몇몇 전문가들은 설명했다 /
힌트 계속적 용법으로 사용된 관계부사이며 선행사로 infancy(유아기)를 취함. 이처럼 관계부사 where는 물리적인 공간뿐만 아니라 시기나 상태와 같은 추상적인 공간도 선행사로 취함.
that friendship formation could be traced to infancy, /
교우 관계 형성이 유아기로 거슬러 올라갈 수 있다고 /
where children acquired the values, beliefs, and attitudes /
그리고 그 시기에 아이들은 가치, 신념, 그리고 태도를 습득했다고 /
that would bind or separate them / later in life.
그들을 단결시키거나 분리시킬 / 훗날 삶에서

(4) But Festinger, Schachter, and Back pursued a different theory.
하지만 Festinger, Schachter, 그리고 Back은 다른 이론을 추구했다

(5) The researchers believed / that physical space was the key /
그 연구자들은 믿었다 / 물리적 공간이 핵심이라고 /
to friendship formation; / that "friendships are likely to develop /
교우 관계 형성의 / 교우 관계는 발달하는 것 같다고 /
on the basis of brief and passive contacts /
짧고 수동적인 접촉을 기반으로 /
[made / going to and from home /
p.p. 분사구문①(~하면서)
만들어지는 / 집을 오가면서
힌트 made 앞에 주격 관계대명사+be동사(which are)이 생략된 주격 관계대명사절임.
or walking about the neighborhood]." 정답단서
분사구문②
아니면 동네를 돌아다니면서

(6) In their view, / it wasn't so much that /
그들의 관점에서 / ~라기보다는 /
힌트 문장 (6)의 구조를 단순화하면, it was not so much [that ~] but rather [that ~]인데, 'not so much A as B (A라기보다는 B)'와 비슷한 의미임. 즉, '~라기보다는 오히려 ~이다'라고 해석하면 됨.
people with similar attitudes became friends, /
비슷한 태도를 가지고 있는 사람들이 친구가 되었다 /
but rather that / people who passed each other /
오히려 ~였다 / 서로를 지나쳐 갔던 사람들이 /
during the day / tended to become friends / 정답단서
그날 동안 / 친구가 되는 경향이 있었다 /
and so came to adopt similar attitudes / over time.
그래서 비슷한 태도를 취하게 되었다 / 시간이 지나면서

[전문 해석]

(1)심리학자 Leon Festinger, Stanley Schachter, 그리고 사회학자 Kurt Back은 어떻게 교우 관계가 형성되는지를 궁금해하기 시작했다. (2)다른 누군가는 (남에게 하는) 기본적인 상투적인 말을 넘어서는 데에도 어려움을 겪는 반면, 왜 어떤 낯선 이들은 지속적인 교우 관계를 쌓는가? (3)몇몇 전문가들은 교우 관계 형성이 유아기로 거슬러 올라갈 수 있으며 그 시기에 아이들은 훗날 삶에서 그들을 단결시키거나 분리시킬 가치, 신념, 그리고 태도를 습득했다고 설명했다. (4)하지만 Festinger, Schachter, 그리고 Back은 다른 이론을 추구했다. (5)그 연구자들은 물리적 공간이 교우 관계 형성의 핵심이라고 믿었다. (즉) "교우 관계는 집을 오가거나 동네를 돌아다니면서 만들어지는 짧고 수동적인 접촉을 기반으로 발달하는 것 같다."라고 믿었다. (6)그들의 관점에서 비슷한 태도를 가지고 있는 사람들이 친구가 되었다기보다는, 오히려 그날 (하루) 동안 서로를 지나쳐 갔던 사람들이 친구가 되는 경향이 있었으며, 그래서 시간이 지나면서 (그들은) 비슷한 태도를 취하게 되었다.

- Leon Festinger(레온 페스팅거, 1919년~1989년): 인지부조화 이론, 사회비교 이론, 근접성 효과 등의 개념을 최초로 제시한 미국의 사회심리학자
- Stanley Schachter(스탠리 샥터, 1922년~1997년): 정서에 관한 2요인 이론, 니코틴 중독, 집단 역동 등 다양한 분야에 대해 연구한 미국의 사회심리학자

[정답 확인]

다음 빈칸에 들어갈 말로 가장 적절한 것은?

① shared value
공유 가치
✔ physical space
물리적 공간
③ conscious effort
의식적인 노력
④ similar character
비슷한 성격
⑤ psychological support
심리적인 도움

[문제 풀이]

교우 관계가 어떻게 형성되는지에 대한 글이다. 문장 (3)에서, 몇몇 전문가들은 유아기때부터 형성된 '가치, 신념, 태도'가 이후 교우 관계 형성에 영향을 미친다고 주장한다. 그러나 문장 (4)부터는 Festinger와 같은 심리학자들의 다른 견해들이 소개되는데, 그들은 비슷한 생각을 가진 사람들이 친구가 되는 것이 아니라 친구로 지내다보니 비슷한 태도(가치관)를 취하게 되는 것이며, 결국 교우 관계는 일상의 사소한 접촉을 기반으로 형성된다고 설명한다. 문장 (5)의 빈칸은 Festinger와 같은 후자의 견해를 나타내야 하므로, 짧고 수동적인 접촉(contacts)이나, 서로 지나쳐 가는(pass each other) 상황을 나타내는 '물리적 접촉(physical contacts)'이 빈칸에 들어가는 것이 적절하다. 따라서 정답은 ②이다.

[오답 풀이]

④ - 비슷한 성격이 교우 관계를 형성하는 비결이라는 주장은 Festinger가 아닌 다른 사람들의 주장이다. Festinger, Schacter, 그리고 Back은 비슷한 성격이 교우 관계 형성의 비결이 아

니라 이미 형성된 교우 관계의 결과물이라고 설명한다. 따라서 그들의 주장을 나타내는 문장에 있는 빈칸에 ④ 'similar character(비슷한 성격)'는 적절하지 않다.

[중요 어휘]

☐ lasting	형용사 지속적인, 영속적인
☐ struggle	동사 어려움을 겪다, 애쓰다, 발버둥치다 / 명사 발버둥질, 노력
☐ be traced to	~으로 거슬러 올라가다
☐ infancy	명사 유아기
☐ bind	동사 단결시키다, 묶다
☐ pursue	동사 추구하다, 추적하다
☐ brief	형용사 짧은, 간단한
☐ passive	형용사 수동적인, 소극적인
☐ adopt	동사 취하다, 채택하다, 입양하다

핵심 필자가 뇌는 예상치 못한 사건의 특이함을 입력하도록 진화되어왔다는 사실을 설명하는 데 Judith Willis의 효과적인 학습방법에 대한 주장을 예로 들었음.

22 2021년 3월 32번 (정답률 35%) 정답 ④

[지문 끊어 읽기] 예상치 못한 사건을 기억하는 뇌

(1) Our brains have evolved /
우리의 뇌는 진화해 왔다 /
to remember unexpected events / because basic survival /
예상치 못한 사건들을 기억하도록 / 왜냐하면 기본적인 생존이 /
depends on the ability / to perceive causes and predict effects.
능력에 달려 있기 때문에 / 원인을 인식하고 결과를 예측하는

정답 단서

힌트 'the ability'를 수식하는 to부정사의 형용사적 용법으로 '동사원형+O'의 형태가 등위접속사 and로 병렬된 구조임.

(2) If the brain predicts one event and experiences another, /
만약 뇌가 어떤 사건을 예측하고 다른 사건을 경험한다면 /
the unusualness will be especially interesting /
그 특이함은 특히 흥미로울 것이다 /
and will be encoded accordingly. 정답 단서
그리고 그에 따라 입력될 것이다

힌트 '~ is one thing, … is another'은 두 개가 서로 다른 별개임을 나타내는 표현임.

(3) Neurologist and classroom teacher Judith Willis has claimed /
신경학자이자 학급 교사인 Judith Willis는 주장했다 /
that surprise in the classroom /
명사절 접속사
교실에서의 놀라움은 /
is one of the most effective ways of teaching /
가장 효과적인 교수법 중 하나라고 /
with brain stimulation in mind.
뇌 자극을 염두에 둔

(4) If students are exposed to new experiences / via demonstrations /
전치사 to
만약 학생들이 새로운 경험에 노출되면 / 실연을 통해 /
or through the unexpected enthusiasm of their teachers or peers, /
혹은 그들의 교사나 또래 친구의 예상치 못한 열의를 통해 /
they will be much more likely to connect /
그들은 연결될 가능성이 훨씬 더 클 것이다 /
with the information that follows.
뒤따르는 정보와

힌트 'be likely to V'는 '~할 가능성이 있다'는 뜻으로, 어떤 근거를 가지고 미래를 예측할 때 사용됨.

(5) Willis has written /
Willis는 기술했다 /
that encouraging active discovery in the classroom /
교실에서의 능동적인 발견을 장려하는 것이 /
allows students to interact / with new information, /
학생들로 하여금 상호 작용하게 해 준다고 / 새로운 정보와 /
moving it beyond working memory /
분사구문
그래서 그것이 작업 기억을 넘어 /
to be processed in the frontal lobe, /
to부정사-수동태 (부사적 용법-결과) 선행사
전두엽에서 처리되도록 한다고 /
which is devoted to advanced cognitive functioning.
주격 관계대명사
고도의 인지 기능을 전담하는

(6) Preference for novelty / sets us up for learning /
새로움에 대한 선호는 / 우리를 학습하도록 준비시킨다 /
by directing attention, / providing stimulation /
병렬① 병렬②
주의를 이끎으로써 / 자극을 제공함으로써 /
to developing perceptual systems, /
지각 체계를 발전시키는 데 /
and feeding curious and exploratory behavior.
병렬③
그리고 호기심 많고 탐구적인 행동을 충족함으로써

[전문 해석]

(1)우리의 뇌는 예상치 못한 사건들을 기억하도록 진화해 왔는데, 왜냐하면 기본적인 생존이 원인을 인식하고 결과를 예측하는 능력에 달려 있기 때문이다. (2)만약 뇌가 어떤 사건을 예측하고 (그것과) 다른 사건을 경험한다면, 그 특이함은 특히 흥미로울 것이고 그에 따라 (뇌 속의 정보로) 입력될 것이다. (3)신경학자이자 학급 교사인 Judith Willis는 교실에서의 놀라움은 뇌 자극을 염두에 둔 가장 효과적인 교수법 중 하나라고 주장했다. (4)만약 학생들이 실연, 혹은 교사나 또래 친구의 예상치 못한 열의를 통해 새로운 경험에 노출되면, 그들은 뒤따르는 정보와 연결될 가능성이 훨씬 더 클 것이다. (5)Willis는 교실에서의 능동적인 발견을 장려하는 것이 학생들로 하여금 새로운 정보와 상호 작용하게 해 주어서 그것(새로운 정보)이 작업 기억을 넘어 고도의 인지 기능을 전담하는 (대뇌의) 전두엽에서 처리되도록 한다고 기술했다. (6)새로움에 대한 선호는 주의를 이끌고 지각 체계를 발전시키는 데 자극을 제공하며 호기심 많고 탐구적인 행동을 충족함으로써 우리를 학습하도록 준비시킨다.

- working memory(작업 기억): 정보를 단기적으로 기억하면서 능동적으로 이해하고 조작하는 과정

[정답 확인]

다음 빈칸에 들어갈 말로 가장 적절한 것은?

① Awareness of social responsibility
사회적 책임에 대한 인식
② Memorization of historical facts
역사적 사실의 암기
③ Competition with rivals
경쟁 상대와의 경쟁
④ Preference for novelty
새로움에 대한 선호
⑤ Fear of failure
실패에 대한 두려움

[문제 풀이]

우리의 뇌는 예상치 못한 사건들, 즉 특이함을 잘 기억하도록 진화해 왔고, 이것이 교육 현장에서 응용되는 사례가 이어지고 있다. 신경학자이자 학급 교사인 Judith Willis에 따르면 교실에서의 놀라움, 즉 예상치 못한 새로운 경험을 접한 학생들과 적극적으로 새로운 발견을 하도록 권장되는 학생들은 뒤따르는 정보들을 뇌의 더 고도화된 차원에서 처리하게 된다고 한다. 따라서 주의를 끌고 자극을 제공함으로써 학습에 대한 준비를 하게 만드는 것은 ④ 'Preference for novelty(새로움에 대한 선호)'라고 할 수 있다.

[오답 풀이]

② - 본문에 따르면 교실에서의 놀라움이 뇌 자극을 염두에 둔 가장 효과적인 교수법 중 하나라고 설명한다. 즉, 우리를 학습하도록 준비시키는 것은 새로움에 대한 선호이므로 이와 대조되는 ②는 정답으로 볼 수 없다.

[중요 어휘]

☐ evolve	동사 진화하다, 발달하다
☐ perceive	동사 인식하다, 감지하다
☐ unusualness	명사 특이함, 특이성
☐ encode	동사 (정보를 특정한 형식으로) 입력하다
☐ neurologist	명사 신경학자
☐ with A in mind	A를 염두에 두고, 고려하여
☐ stimulation	명사 자극
☐ expose	동사 노출하다
☐ demonstration	명사 실연, 직접 보여 줌
☐ enthusiasm	명사 열의, 열성
☐ working memory	작업 기억
☐ devote	동사 전담하다, 전념하다, 헌신하다
☐ perceptual	형용사 지각의

문제편 p.143

- [ ] **feed** — (동사) 충족하다, 먹이를 주다
- [ ] **exploratory** — (형용사) 탐구적인

23 2022년 6월 33번 (정답률 35%)

정답 ①

[지문 끊어 읽기] 언론인의 의존성

(1) [What is unusual about journalism / as a profession] / [ ]:S
선행사를 포함하는 관계대명사
저널리즘에 관해 특이한 점은 / 직업으로서의 /
is its lack of independence.
V
그것의 독립성의 부족이다

★중요 빈칸이 지문의 첫 문장에 있을 때에는 빈칸에 들어갈 내용을 유추해가며 지문을 읽는 것이 도움이 됨. 여기서 빈칸의 내용은 '직업으로서 저널리즘이 특이한 점', 즉 '언론인의 특징'이므로 이것이 무엇인지를 파악해야 한다고 인식한 상태에서 지문을 읽는 것이 좋음. 또한 이어서 문장 (2)에서 전문직 종사자의 특징을 설명하므로 언론인의 특징을 전문직 종사자의 특징과 대조하며 글을 전개할 것을 예상할 수 있음.

(2) In theory, /
이론적으로 /
practitioners in the classic professions, /
고전적인 전문직에 종사하는 사람들은 / S
like medicine or the clergy, /
의학이나 성직자와 같은 /
contain the means of production in their heads and hands, /
V①
그들의 머리와 손에 생산 수단을 가지고 있다 /
and therefore do not have to work for a company or an employer.
V②
그러므로 회사나 고용주를 위해 일할 필요가 없다

(3) They can draw their income directly /
그들은 직접 수입을 끌어낼 수 있다 /
from their clients or patients.
고객이나 환자로부터

(4) Because the professionals hold knowledge, /
전문직 종사자들이 지식을 보유하고 있기 때문에 /
moreover, / their clients are dependent on them.
게다가 / 그들의 고객들은 그들에게 의존한다

(5) Journalists hold knowledge, / but it is not theoretical / in nature;
언론인들은 지식을 보유하고 있다 / 하지만 그것은 이론적이지 않다 / 본질적으로

(6) one might argue / that the public depends on journalists /
명사절 접속사
어떤 사람들은 주장할지도 모른다 / 대중이 언론인들에게 의존한다고 /
in the same way / that patients depend on doctors, /
같은 방식으로 / 환자들이 의사들에게 의존하는 것과 /
but in practice / a journalist can serve the public /
하지만 실제로 / 언론인은 대중들에게 봉사할 수 있다 /
usually only by working for a news organization, /
일반적으로 뉴스 기관을 위해 일해야만 / 선행사
which can fire her or him / at will. 정답 단서
관계대명사(계속적 용법)
그리고 뉴스 기관은 언론인을 해고할 수 있다 / 마음대로

힌트 방법을 나타내는 관계부사 how는 선행사 way와 함께 쓸 수 없지만(the way how는 불가능), way와 관계부사 that을 쓰는 것은 가능함.

정답 단서: 접속사 but을 통해 언론인은 그들이 속한 뉴스 기관을 위해 일해야 한다는 점에서 의사와 같은 전문직 종사자와는 대비된다는 것을 알 수 있음.

(7) Journalists' income depends /
언론인들의 수입은 의존한다 /
not on the public, but on the employing news organization, /
not A but B: A가 아니라 B / 선행사
대중이 아닌 그들을 고용한 뉴스 기관에 /
which often derives the large majority of its revenue /
관계대명사(계속적 용법)
그리고 그것은 종종 수익의 대부분을 얻는다 /
from advertisers.
광고주들로부터

정답 단서: 언론인의 수입은 그들을 고용한 뉴스 기관에 의존한다고 말함.

[전문 해석]

(1)직업으로서의 저널리즘에 관해 특이한 점은 그것의 독립성의 부족이다. (2)이론적으로, 의학이나 성직자와 같은, 고전적인 전문직에 종사하는 사람들은 그들의 머리와 손에 생산 수단을 가지고 있으므로, 회사나 고용주를 위해 일할 필요가 없다. (3)그들은 고객이나 환자로부터 직접 수입을 끌어낼 수 있다. (4)게다가, 전문직 종사자들이 지식을 보유하고 있기 때문에, 그들의 고객들은 그들에게 의존한다. (5)언론인들은 지식을 보유하고 있지만, 그것은 본질적으로 이론적이지 않다. (6)어떤 사람들은 환자들이 의사들에게 의존하는 것과 같은 방식으로 대중이 언론인들에게 의존한다고 주장할지도 모르지만, 실제로 언론인은 일반적으로 뉴스 기관을 위해 일해야만 대중들에게 봉사할 수 있으며, 뉴스 기관은 언론인을 마음대로 해고할 수 있다. (7)언론인들의 수입은 대중이 아닌, 그들을 고용한 뉴스 기관에 의존하는데, 이는 종종 광고주들로부터 수익의 대부분을 얻는다.

- journalism(저널리즘): 신문과 잡지를 통하여 대중에게 시사적인 정보와 의견을 제공하는 활동. 넓게는 라디오, 텔레비전 따위를 통하여 정보 및 오락을 제공하는 활동을 포함함.

[정답 확인]

다음 빈칸에 들어갈 말로 가장 적절한 것은?

✔ its lack of independence
그것의 독립성의 부족
② the constant search for truth
끊임없는 진실의 추구
③ the disregard of public opinion
여론의 무시
④ its balance of income and faith
그것의 수입과 신념의 균형
⑤ its overconfidence in its social influence
그것의 사회적 영향력에 대한 과신

[문제 풀이]

지문은 고전적인 전문직 종사자들과 언론인을 대비하며 내용을 전개하고 있다. 고전적인 전문직 종사자들은 회사나 고용주를 위해 일하지 않고, 수입도 그들의 고객으로부터 직접 끌어낼 수 있는 반면, 언론인은 뉴스 기관에 고용되어 뉴스 기관을 위해 일하고, 수입 역시 뉴스 기관에 의존하고 있다. 즉 전문직 종사자들에 비해 언론인은 그들의 회사 또는 고용주로부터 독립적이지 못하고 그들에게 의존적임을 말하고 있으므로 이를 보여 주는 ①이 정답이다.

[오답 풀이]

③ - 문장 (6)에서 뉴스 기관을 위해 일해야만 대중에게 봉사할 수 있다는 것이 여론을 무시한다는 뜻은 아니므로 ③은 정답이 아니다.
④ - 지문에서 언론인들의 신념에 대한 언급은 없으므로 ④는 정답이 아니다.

[중요 어휘]

- [ ] **profession** — (명사) 직업, 전문직
- [ ] **practitioner** — (명사) 전문직 종사자(특히 의사, 변호사)
- [ ] **clergy** — (명사) 성직자(들)
- [ ] **means** — (명사) (복수형으로) 수단, 방법
- [ ] **draw** — (동사) 끌어내다, 추첨하다, 인출하다, 비기다
- [ ] **in nature** — 본질적으로
- [ ] **in practice** — 실제로
- [ ] **serve** — (동사) ~에게 봉사하다, 도움이 되다, 제공하다
- [ ] **fire** — (동사) 해고하다, 발사하다
- [ ] **at will** — 마음대로
- [ ] **derive** — (동사) (이익·즐거움 등을) 얻다, 끌어내다, ~에서 유래하다
- [ ] **revenue** — (명사) 수익, 수입
- [ ] **disregard** — (명사) 무시 / (동사) 무시하다
- [ ] **public opinion** — (명사) 여론
- [ ] **overconfidence** — (명사) 과신, 지나친 자신

핵심 아이들이 어떻게 혼자 있을 수 있는 능력을 기르는지 두 가지의 예시를 들어 설명하는 글임. 주제문이 말하고자 하는 바와 두 가지 예시의 공통점을 염두에 두며 글을 읽어야 함.

24 2019년 9월 31번 (정답률 30%)

정답 ②

[지문 끊어 읽기] 아이들의 혼자 있을 수 있는 능력

(1) Children develop / the capacity for solitude /
아이들은 발달시킨다 / 혼자 있을 수 있는 능력을 /
in the presence of an attentive other. 주제문
관심을 가져주는 타인이 있을 때

(2) Consider the silences that fall / when you take a young boy /
찾아오는 고요를 생각해 보라 / 당신이 어린아이를 데리고 나갈 때 /
on a quiet walk in nature.
자연 속에서 조용한 산책을

힌트 보통 fall은 '떨어지다', '넘어지다'의 뜻으로 쓰이지만, 이 문장에서는 '찾아오다'라는 문어적인 표현으로 쓰였음. 이런 뜻의 fall은 'darkness'나 'silence'와 같은 단어들과 종종 함께 쓰임.

(3) The child comes to feel increasingly aware of /
그 아이는 점점 더 알아가는 것을 느끼게 된다 /

what it is to be alone in nature, /
형식상의 주어 내용상의 주어
자연 속에 혼자 있는 것이 무엇인지를 /
supported by being "with" someone /
누군가와 '함께' 있다는 것의 도움을 받아 / 정답단서
who is introducing him to this experience.
그를 이런 경험으로 안내하는

힌트 문장 (3)에서 what은 의문사로 쓰여서 '의문사 + 주어 + 동사'순의 간접의문문절을 이끌고 있음. what절 안은 형식상의 주어, 내용상의 주어 구문으로 이루어져 있고 what은 'it is something to be alone in nature'이라는 문장 내에서의 something에 해당한다고 볼 수 있음.

(4) Gradually, / the child takes walks alone.
점차 / 그 아이는 혼자 산책을 한다

(5) Or / imagine / a mother /
O
혹은 / 상상해 보라 / 한 엄마가 /
giving her two-year-old daughter a bath, /
O.C
두 살배기 딸을 목욕시키는 것을 /
[allowing the girl's reverie with her bath toys /
[ ]: 분사구문
그리고 그것은 소녀가 그녀의 목욕 장난감들과 함께 공상하게 하는 것을 /
as she makes up stories /
=while 병렬①
그녀가 이야기를 만들면서 /
and learns to be alone with her thoughts, /
병렬②
그리고 생각을 하며 혼자 있는 것을 배우면서 /
all the while knowing / her mother is present and available to her]. 정답단서
내내 아는 상태로 / 그녀의 엄마가 있고 그녀에게 시간을 낼 수 있다는 것을

(6) Gradually, / the bath, taken alone, / is a time /
점차 / 혼자 하는 목욕은 / 시간이 된다 /
[when the child is comfortable with her imagination]. [ ]: 관계부사절
아이가 그녀의 상상을 하기에 편안한

(7) Attachment enables solitude.
애착은 혼자 있는 것을 가능하게 한다

[전문 해석]

(1)아이들은 (자신에게) 관심을 가져주는 타인이 있을 때 혼자 있을 수 있는 능력을 발달시킨다. (2)당신이 어린아이를 데리고 자연 속에서 조용한 산책을 나갈(할) 때 찾아오는 고요를 생각해 보라. (3)그 아이는 그를 이런 경험으로 안내하는 누군가와 '함께' 있다는 것(사실)의 도움을 받아 자연 속에 혼자 있는 것이 무엇인지를 점점 더 알아가는 것을 느끼게 된다. (4)점차 그 아이는 혼자 산책을 한다. (5)혹은 한 엄마가 두 살배기 딸을 목욕시키며, 딸이 엄마와 함께 있고 엄마가 자신에게 시간을 낼 수 있다는 것을 내내 아는 상태로 이야기를 만들고 생각을 하며 혼자 있는 것을 배우면서 목욕 장난감들과 함께 공상하게 하는 것을 상상해 보라. (6)점차 혼자 하는 목욕은 아이가 (그녀의) 상상을 하기에 편안한 시간이 된다. (7)애착은 혼자 있는 것을 가능하게 한다.

[정답 확인]

다음 빈칸에 들어갈 말로 가장 적절한 것은?

① Hardship 고난 ② Attachment 애착 ③ Creativity 창의성
④ Compliment 칭찬 ⑤ Responsibility 책임

[문제 풀이]

빈칸에 들어갈 내용은 주제문과 두 가지 예시의 공통점을 찾음으로써 파악할 수 있다. 주제문인 문장 (1)에서는 주의를 기울이는 타인의 존재를 강조하며, 그 이하의 예시에서는 아이가 혼자 있지 않고 곁에 누군가 있다는 사실을 공통적으로 보여 준다. 아이와 함께 있고, 그 아이에게 언제든 시간을 내어줄 수 있다는 것은 곧 그에게 애정 내지는 애착이 있다는 것을 의미한다. 따라서 정답은 ②이다.

[중요 어휘]

☐ **capacity**	명사 능력, 용량
☐ **solitude**	명사 혼자 있음, 고독
☐ **in the presence of**	~가 있을 때, ~의 앞에서
☐ **attentive**	형용사 관심을 가져주는, 주의를 기울이는, 배려하는
☐ **fall**	동사 (어둠·침묵 등이) 찾아오다, 떨어지다
☐ **increasingly**	부사 점점 더, 갈수록 더
☐ **gradually**	부사 점차, 서서히
☐ **reverie**	명사 공상
☐ **all the while**	내내, 그동안 쭉
☐ **available**	형용사 시간을 낼 수 있는, 이용할 수 있는
☐ **attachment**	명사 애착, 부착
☐ **enable**	동사 ~을 가능하게 하다

핵심 지구의 대기 중 산소 농도가 변화해 온 과정을 생물체의 진화 발달과 함께 설명하고 있음. 시간의 흐름에 따른 대기와 생물체의 상호 작용에 유의해야 함.

25 2020년 11월 31번 (정답률 30%) 정답 ②

[지문 끊어 읽기] 지구의 대기 중 산소 농도의 변화 과정

(1) Over 4.5 billion years ago, / the Earth's primordial atmosphere /
45억 년도 더 전에 / 지구의 원시 대기는 /
was probably largely water vapour, carbon dioxide, sulfur dioxide
2형식V S.C① S.C② S.C③
and nitrogen.
S.C④
아마도 대체로 수증기, 이산화탄소, 이산화황과 질소였을 것이다

(2) The appearance and subsequent evolution /
출현과 그 후의 진화는 /
of exceedingly primitive living organisms /
극히 원시적인 살아있는 생물체의 /
(bacteria-like microbes and simple single-celled plants) /
(박테리아 같은 미생물과 단순한 단세포 식물들) /
began to change the atmosphere, / 정답단서
대기를 변화시키기 시작했다 /
liberating oxygen /
분사구문 병렬①
산소를 유리시키면서
and breaking down carbon dioxide and sulfur dioxide.
분사구문 병렬②
그리고 이산화탄소와 이산화황을 분해하면서

힌트 liberate는 주로 '자유롭게 하다, 해방하다'라는 의미로, 여기서는 화합물의 결합이 끊어져 원자나 원자단이 서로 분리되는 현상을 나타내는 '유리시키다'의 의미로 쓰임.

(3) This made it possible / for higher organisms / to develop. 정답단서
형식상의 목적어
5형식V 목적격 보어 의미상의 주어 내용상의 목적어
이것은 가능하게 했다 / 더 상위 생물체가 / 발달하는 것을

(4) When the earliest known plant cells with nuclei evolved /
S' V'
가장 최초라고 알려진 핵이 있는 식물 세포가 진화했을 때 /
about 2 billion years ago, / the atmosphere seems /
약 20억 년 전에 / 대기는 보인다 /
to have had only about 1 percent /
약 1%만을 가지고 있었던 것처럼 /
of its present content of oxygen.
그것의 현재 산소 함량의

힌트 '보이는(seems)' 시점보다 '약 20억 년 전에 대기가 현재 산소 함량의 고작 약 1%만을 가지고 있었던(to have had)' 시점이 더 과거에 해당하므로, 'seems'와의 시제 차이를 나타내기 위해 'to have p.p.'가 왔음.

(5) With the emergence of the first land plants, /
최초의 육지 식물의 출현으로 /
about 500 million years ago, / oxygen reached /
타동사
약 5억 년 전 / 산소는 도달했다 /
about one-third of its present concentration.
부사(약, 대략) reached의 목적어
그것의 현재 농도의 약 3분의 1에

(6) It had risen / to almost its present level /
그것은 증가했다 / 거의 그것의 현재 수준으로 /
by about 370 million years ago, /
약 3억 7천만 년 전까지 /
when animals first spread on to land. 정답단서
관계부사(계속적 용법)
그리고 그때 동물들이 처음 육지에 퍼졌다

(7) Today's atmosphere /
오늘날의 대기는 /
is thus not just a requirement / to sustain life /
형용사적 용법
그러므로 단지 필요조건일 뿐 아니라 / 생명체를 유지하기 위한 /
as we know it / — it is also a consequence of life.
우리가 알고 있듯 / 생명체의 결과이기도 하다

문제편 p.144

[전문 해석]

(1)45억 년도 더 전에 지구의 원시 대기는 아마도 대체로 수증기, 이산화탄소, 이산화황과 질소였을 것이다. (2)극히 원시적인 살아있는 생물체(박테리아 같은 미생물과 단순한 단세포 식물들)의 출현과 그 후의 진화는 산소를 유리(遊離)시키고(산소 원자를 분리시키고) 이산화탄소와 이산화황을 분해하면서 대기를 변화시키기 시작했다. (3)이것은 더 상위 생물체가 발달하는 것을 가능하게 했다. (4)약 20억 년 전에 가장 최초라고 알려진 핵이 있는 식물 세포가 진화했을 때, 대기는 (그것의) 현재 산소 함량의 약 1%만을 가지고 있었던 것처럼 보인다. (5)약 5억 년 전 최초의 육지 식물의 출현으로 산소는 (그것의) 현재 농도의 약 3분의 1에 도달했다. (6)산소는 약 3억 7천만 년 전까지 거의 (그것의) 현재 수준으로 증가했고 그때 동물들이 처음 육지에 퍼졌다. (7)그러므로 오늘날의 대기는 우리가 알고 있듯 단지 생명체를 유지하기 위한 필요조건일 뿐 아니라 생명체의 결과이기도 하다.

[정답 확인]

다음 빈칸에 들어갈 말로 가장 적절한 것은?

① a barrier to evolution
진화의 장애물

✔② a consequence of life
생명체의 결과

③ a record of primitive culture
원시 문화의 기록

④ a sign of the constancy of nature
자연의 불변성에 대한 흔적

⑤ a reason for cooperation among species
종(種)들 간의 협력의 이유

[문제 풀이]

45억 년 전부터 현재까지의 대기 중 산소 농도 변화 과정을 생물의 진화와 함께 설명한 글로, 본문의 과정은 '45억 년 전 대기 → 극히 원시적인 생물체의 출현과 진화 → 대기 변화 → 핵이 있는 식물 세포 진화 → 대기 변화 → 최초의 육지 식물의 출현 → 대기 변화 → 육지 동물 출현'으로 요약할 수 있다. 즉, 대기가 변화함에 따라 상위 생물체가 발달하고 이것이 다시 대기에 영향을 미치는 상호 작용 속에서 현재의 대기 상태에 이르게 되었다는 것이다. 따라서 문장 (7)에서 생명체가 있기 위해서는 대기가 뒷받침되어야 하지만, 다른 한편으로 대기는 ② 'a consequence of life(생명체의 결과)'라고 해야 옳다.

[오답 풀이]

③ - 본문에 따르면 오늘날의 대기는 원시적인 생물의 출현과 진화 과정에서 산소가 유리되고 이산화탄소와 이산화황이 분해되면서 대기의 구성 성분이 변화해 온 결과에 해당하며, 이는 인류가 등장하면서 문화가 발생하기 훨씬 전에 일어난 일이므로 대기가 원시 문화의 기록이라고 보는 것은 적절하지 않다.

④ - 본문은 생물의 진화에 따라 대기 구성 성분이 지속적으로 변화해 왔다고 설명한다. 즉, 오늘날의 대기는 자연의 불변성이 아닌 변화의 흔적으로 볼 수 있으므로 ④는 정답으로 볼 수 없다.

[중요 어휘]

☐ **primordial**	형용사 원시의, 원시적인
☐ **largely**	부사 대체로, 주로
☐ **water vapo(u)r**	명사 수증기
☐ **carbon dioxide**	명사 이산화탄소
☐ **sulfur dioxide**	명사 이산화황
☐ **nitrogen**	명사 질소
☐ **appearance**	명사 출현, 출연, 외모
☐ **subsequent**	형용사 그 후의, 뒤이은
☐ **exceedingly**	부사 극히, 몹시, 대단히
☐ **primitive**	형용사 원시적인, 발달되지 않은
☐ **organism**	명사 생물체, 유기체, 생물
☐ **microbe**	명사 미생물
☐ **liberate**	동사 (화합물에서) 유리(遊離)시키다, 해방하다
☐ **nuclei**	명사 핵 (nucleus의 복수형)
☐ **content**	명사 함량, 내용, 목차
☐ **emergence**	명사 출현, 등장
☐ **concentration**	명사 농도, 집중
☐ **requirement**	명사 필요조건, 필수품
☐ **sustain**	동사 유지하다, 지속하다, 견디다
☐ **constancy**	명사 불변성, 충성

● 지문 구조도

약 45억 년 전: 원시 대기(primordial atmosphere)
(1) 지구 대기의 대부분은 수증기, 이산화탄소, 이산화황과 질소였음.

↓

원시적인 생물체(primitive living organisms)의 출현과 진화
(2) 산소를 유리(遊離)시키고 이산화탄소와 이산화황을 분해하면서 대기를 변화시키기 시작함. → (3) 더 상위 생물체가 발달함.

↓

약 20억 년 전: 최초의 핵이 있는 식물 세포(plant cells with nuclei)의 등장
(4) 대기의 산소 함량이 현재의 약 1%에 도달함.

↓

약 5억 년 전 : 최초의 육지 식물(land plants)의 등장
(5) 대기의 산소 함량이 현재의 약 3분의 1에 도달함.

↓

약 3억 7천만 년 전: 최초의 육지 동물(land animals)의 등장
(6) 대기의 산소 함량이 현재 수준에 도달함.

↓

결론
(7) 오늘날의 대기는 우리가 알고 있듯 단지 생명체를 유지하기 위한 필요조건(a requirement to sustain life)일 뿐 아니라, 생명체의 결과(a consequence of life)이기도 함.

핵심 Bob Carlson이 일반적인 리더들과 어떤 점에서 다른지를 중점으로 지문의 내용을 이해해야 함.

26 2021년 6월 32번 (정답률 30%) 정답 ②

[지문 끊어 읽기] 다양한 문제에 인내심을 발휘하는 리더

(1) While leaders often face /
리더들은 종종 직면하지만 /
enormous pressures to make decisions quickly, / (to make: 형용사적 용법)
빠르게 결정들을 내려야 하는 거대한 압박에 /
premature decisions are / 정답 단서
섣부른 결정들은 ~이다 /
the leading cause of decision failure.
결정 실패의 주된 원인

★중요 리더들이 시간을 들이지(taking the time) 않고 너무 서둘러(premature) 결정을 내리는 것이 실패의 원인이라고 함. 정답에는 이와 반대되는 리더의 특징이 들어가야 하므로, 정답 보기에 'patience'가 쓰인 것을 볼 수 있음.

(2) This is primarily because /
이것은 주로 ~이기 때문이다 /
leaders respond to the superficial issue of a decision /
리더들이 결정의 피상적인 문제에 반응한다 /
rather than taking the time / to explore the underlying issues. (to explore: 형용사적 용법) 정답 단서
시간을 보내기보다는 / 근원적인 문제들을 탐색하는 데

(3) Bob Carlson is a good example /
Bob Carlson은 좋은 예이다 /
of a leader exercising patience / in the face of diverse issues. (exercising: 현재분사)
인내심을 발휘하는 리더의 / 다양한 문제들에 직면하여

(4) In the economic downturn of early 2001, /
2001년 초의 경기 침체기에 /
Reell Precision Manufacturing faced /
Reell Precision Manufacturing은 직면했다 /
a 30 percent drop in revenues.
총수입에서 30퍼센트 하락을

(5) Some members of the senior leadership team / favored layoffs /
몇몇의 고위 지도자 팀의 구성원들은 / 해고를 선호했다 /
and some favored salary reductions.
그리고 몇몇은 임금 삭감을 선호했다

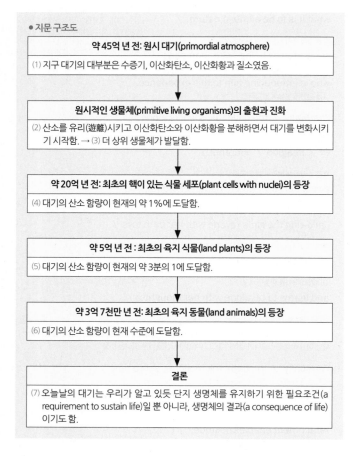

(6) While it would have been easy /
그것이 쉬웠을 테지만 /

힌트 'would+have p.p.'는 '~였을 수도 있다'의 의미로 과거에 대한 추측을 나타냄.

to push for a decision or call for a vote /
병렬① 병렬②
결정을 요구하거나 투표를 요청하는 것이 /

in order to ease the tension of the economic pressures, /
경제적 압박의 긴장 상태를 완화하기 위해서 /

as co-CEO, / Bob Carlson helped the team /
5형식V
공동 최고 경영자로서 / Bob Carlson은 그 팀을 도왔다 /

work together and examine all of the issues. **정답단서**
O·C① O·C②
함께 노력하고 모든 문제들을 검토하도록

(7) The team finally agreed on salary reductions, / [knowing that, /
그 팀은 마침내 임금 삭감에 동의했다 / 알면서 /

to the best of their ability, / they had thoroughly examined /
삽입구 과거완료: had+p.p.
그들의 능력의 최선에서 / 그들이 철저하게 검토했다는 것을 /

the implications of both possible decisions]. []:분사구문
두 가지 가능한 결정 모두의 영향을

힌트 주어의 길이가 긴 경우에 이를 뒤로 이동시키고 빈 주어 자리에 it을 삽입하는데, 이때 아무런 의미를 띠지 않는 it을 '형식상의 주어', 뒤로 이동된 주어를 '내용상의 주어'라고 함. 내용상의 주어인 'to push for a decision or (to) call for a vote'는 to부정사가 명사적 용법으로 활용된 것임.

[중요 구문]

(6) While it would have been easy
형식상의 주어
[to push for a decision or call for a vote] []:내용상의 주어(명사적 용법)

(in order to ease the tension of the economic pressures), ~,
():삽입구

Bob Carlson helped the team

힌트 준사역동사 help는 사역동사 make, have, let과는 달리 목적격 보어로 동사원형 또는 to부정사를 모두 취할 수 있음.

work together and examine all of the issues.
O·C① O·C②

[전문 해석]

(1)리더들은 종종 빠르게 결정들을 내려야 하는 거대한 압박에 직면하지만, 섣부른 결정들은 결정 실패의 주된 원인이다. (2)이것은 주로 리더들이 근원적인 문제들을 탐색하는 데 시간을 보내기보다는 결정의 피상적인 문제에 반응하기 때문이다. (3)Bob Carlson은 다양한 문제들에 직면하여(할 때) 인내심을 발휘하는 리더의 좋은 예이다. (4)2001년 초의 경기 침체기에 Reell Precision Manufacturing은 총수입에서 30퍼센트 하락을 직면했다. (5)몇몇의 고위 지도자 팀의 구성원들은 해고를 선호했고 몇몇은 임금 삭감을 선호했다. (6)경제적 압박의 긴장 상태를 완화하기 위해서 결정을 요구하거나(밀어붙이거나) 투표를 요청하는 것이 쉬웠을 테지만, 공동 최고 경영자로서 Bob Carlson은 그 팀이 함께 노력하고 모든 문제들을 검토하도록 도왔다. (7)그 팀은 마침내 그들의 능력의 최선에서, 그들이 두 가지 가능한 결정 모두의 영향을 철저하게 검토했다는 것을 알면서, 임금 삭감에 동의했다.

[정답 확인]

다음 빈칸에 들어갈 말로 가장 적절한 것은?

① justifying layoffs
해고를 정당화하는

✓ ② exercising patience
인내심을 발휘하는

③ increasing employment
고용을 증가시키는

④ sticking to his opinions
자신의 의견을 고수하는

⑤ training unskilled members
비숙련 구성원들을 훈련시키는

[문제 풀이]

본문에서는 리더들이 섣부른 결정을 하는 것이 결정 실패의 주된 원인이며, 이는 주로 그들이 근원적인 문제들을 탐색하는 데 시간을 보내지 않기 때문이라고 설명하고 있다. 반면 Bob Carlson은 공동 최고 경영자로서 회사가 어려움을 겪었을 때, 압박 속에서 바로 결정을 내리는 것이 아니라 오히려 그 팀이 함께 노력하고 모든 문제들을 검토하도록 도왔다. 즉 결정을 밀어붙이거나 투표를 요청하는 빠르고 쉬운 선택 대신, 충분한 검토 시간을 가지게 했다. 이처럼 Bob Carlson은 섣불리 결정하지 않으며 인내하며 결정에 충분한 시간을 들였으므로 정답은 ②이다.

[오답 풀이]

① - 리더들이 결정을 해야하는 순간에, 근원적인 문제들을 탐색하지 않고 종종 섣부른 결정으로 결정 실패에 이르게 된다고 한다. 문장 (3) 이후 이와 반대의 예시인 Bob Carlson에 대한 이야기를 하고 있는데, 몇몇의 고위 지도자 팀의 구성원들이 해고를 선호하긴 했지만, 팀에서 충분히 검토하면서 구성원의 해고가 아니라 임금 삭감에 동의했기 때문에 ①은 정답이 될 수 없다.

④ - Bob Carlson은 공동 최고 경영자로서 고위 지도자 팀이 철저한 검토 끝에 결정을 내릴 수

있도록 도왔을 뿐, Bob Carlson이 자신의 의견을 내거나 고집했다는 내용은 찾을 수 없다. 즉 ④는 본문과 무관한 내용이다.

[중요 어휘]

☐ enormous	형용사	거대한
☐ premature	형용사	섣부른, 시기상조의
☐ superficial	형용사	피상적인
☐ underlying	형용사	근원적인
☐ exercise	동사	발휘하다, 행사하다, 운동하다
☐ patience	명사	인내심
☐ diverse	형용사	다양한
☐ downturn	명사	침체, 하락
☐ favor	동사	선호하다
☐ layoff	명사	해고
☐ salary	명사	임금
☐ push for		~을 계속 요구하다, 추진하다
☐ call for		~을 요청하다
☐ ease	동사	완화하다
☐ tension	명사	긴장
☐ examine	동사	검토하다, 검사하다
☐ thoroughly	부사	철저하게
☐ implication	명사	영향, 암시

27 2023년 3월 31번 (정답률 30%) 정답 ④

[지문 끊어 읽기] 자유 놀이의 효과

(1) Free play is nature's means of teaching children /
자유 놀이는 아이들에게 가르치는 자연의 수단이다 /

[that they are not helpless]. []:명사절(D·O)
자신이 무력하지 않다는 것을

★중요 빈칸 앞에 not이 있을 때는 빈칸을 부정하거나 반대되는 내용이 온다는 점에서 헷갈릴 수 있으므로 주의가 필요함.

(2) In play, / away from adults, / children really do have control /
S V①(강조의 do)
놀이에서 / 어른들과 떨어져서 / 아이들은 정말로 통제력을 가진다 /

and can practice asserting it. **정답단서**
V② 동명사
그리고 그것을 행사하는 것을 연습할 수 있다

놀이를 통해 아이들은 어른들과 떨어져 독립적으로 통제력을 가지고 연습할 수 있는 기회를 얻음.

(3) In free play, / children learn to make their own decisions, /
병렬①
자유 놀이를 통해 / 아이들은 스스로 결정을 내리는 것을 배운다 /

solve their own problems, / create and follow rules, /
병렬②(to 생략) 병렬③(to 생략)
자신만의 문제를 해결하는 것을 / 규칙을 만들고 따르는 것을 /

and get along with others as equals /
병렬④(to 생략)
그리고 동등한 사람으로서 다른 사람들과 어울리는 것을 /

rather than as obedient or rebellious subordinates.
복종적이거나 반항적인 부하로서보다는

(4) In active outdoor play, / children deliberately dose themselves /
활동적인 야외 놀이에서 / 아이들은 의도적으로 스스로에게 준다 /

with moderate amounts of fear /
적정량의 두려움을 /

and they thereby learn how to control / not only their bodies, /
의문사+to부정사(명사적 용법)
그리고 그들은 그렇게 함으로써 통제하는 방법을 배운다 / 그들의 신체뿐만 아니라 /

but also their fear. **정답단서**
그들의 두려움 또한

활동적인 야외 놀이에서 아이들은 스스로 자신에게 두려움을 주고 신체와 두려움을 통제하는 법을 배움.

(5) In social play / children learn how to negotiate with others, /
사회적 놀이에서 / 아이들은 어떻게 다른 사람들과 협상하는지를 배운다 /

how to please others, /
어떻게 다른 사람들을 기쁘게 하는지를 /

and how to manage and overcome the anger /
병렬① 병렬②(to 생략) 선행사
그리고 어떻게 분노를 다스리고 극복하는지를 /

[that can arise from conflicts]. []:주격 관계대명사절
갈등으로부터 생길 수 있는

문제편 p.145

힌트 'none of'는 '~ 중 어느 것도 … 않다'의 뜻으로, 뒤에 셀 수 없는 명사가 올 때는 단수동사, 복수명사가 올 때는 복수동사로 수를 일치시킴.

(6) None of these lessons can be taught / through verbal means; /
이러한 교훈들 중 어느 것도 배울 수 없다 / 언어적 수단을 통해서는 /
they can be learned / only through experience, /
그것들은 배울 수 있다 / 오로지 경험을 통해서만 / 선행사
which free play provides.
목적격 관계대명사(계속적 용법)
그것은 자유 놀이가 제공하는 것이다

[전문 해석]

(1)자유 놀이는 아이들에게 자신이 무력하지 않다는 것을 가르치는 자연의 수단이다. (2)놀이에서 아이들은 어른들과 떨어져 정말로 통제력을 가지고 그것을 행사하는 것을 연습할 수 있다. (3)자유 놀이를 통해 아이들은 스스로 결정을 내리고, 자신만의 문제를 해결하고, 규칙을 만들고 따르며, 복종적이거나 반항적인 부하로서보다는 동등한 사람으로서 다른 사람들과 어울리는 것을 배운다. (4)활동적인 야외 놀이에서 아이들은 의도적으로 스스로에게 적정량의 두려움을 주고, 그렇게 함으로써 그들의 신체뿐만 아니라 두려움 또한 통제하는 방법을 배운다. (5)사회적 놀이에서 아이들은 어떻게 다른 사람들과 협상하는지, 어떻게 다른 사람들을 기쁘게 하는지, 그리고 어떻게 갈등으로부터 생길 수 있는 분노를 다스리고 극복하는지를 배운다. (6)이러한 교훈들 중 어느 것도 언어적 수단을 통해서는 배울 수 없고, 그것들은 오로지 경험을 통해서만 배울 수 있는데, 그것(경험)은 자유 놀이가 제공하는 것이다.

[정답 확인]

다음 빈칸에 들어갈 말로 가장 적절한 것은?

① noisy 시끄러운
② sociable 사교적인
③ complicated 복잡한
④ helpless 무력한 ✔
⑤ selective 선택적인

[문제 풀이]

필자는 자유 놀이를 통해 아이들이 어른들과 떨어진 독립적인 환경에서 통제력을 가지고 스스로 결정을 내리고 문제를 해결하는 법, 규칙을 만들고 지키는 법, 다른 사람들과 동등하게 어울리는 법을 배울 수 있다고 말한다. 이어서 스스로에게 의도적으로 두려움을 주고 자신을 통제하는 법을 배울 수 있는 활동적인 야외 놀이, 그리고 협상하는 법, 타인을 기쁘게 만드는 법, 갈등에서 오는 분노를 다스리고 극복하는 법을 습득할 수 있는 사회적 놀이에 대해 구체적으로 언급한다. 마지막으로 자유 놀이가 제공하는 경험을 통해서 이러한 것들을 배울 수 있다고 한다. 이는 아이들이 스스로 상황과 문제 해결을 위한 통제력을 가진다는 내용이므로, 아이들이 무력하지 않다는 것을 배운다는 의미가 되는 ④ 'helpless(무력한)'가 적절하다.

[오답 풀이]

② - 빈칸이 포함된 문장은 '놀이가 아이들에게 가르치는 것'이 무엇인지 설명할 수 있어야 한다. 본문은 아이들이 자유 놀이를 통해 스스로를 통제하고 자신만의 문제를 해결하는 법을 배우고 사회적인 존재로 거듭날 수 있다는 내용을 담고 있는데, ②의 sociable이 빈칸에 들어가면 '자유 놀이는 아이들에게 자신들이 사교적이지 않다는 것을 가르친다'는 의미가 되므로 어색하다. 이처럼 빈칸 앞에 'not'이 있는 경우는 의미가 헷갈리지 않도록 특별히 주의를 기울여야 한다.

[중요 어휘]

□ means	명사 (복수형으로) 수단, 방법, 방도
□ assert	동사 행사하다, 주장하다, 확고히 하다
□ get along with	~와 잘 지내다
□ equal	명사 동등한 사람 / 형용사 동일한, 평등한
□ obedient	형용사 복종하는, 말을 잘 듣는, 순종적인
□ rebellious	형용사 (규칙·일반 통념 등에 대해) 반항적인
□ subordinate	명사 부하, 하급자 / 형용사 종속된, 부차적인
□ deliberately	부사 의도적으로, 고의로, 신중하게
□ dose	동사 (약 등을) 주다, 투여하다 / 명사 1회 복용량
□ moderate	형용사 적정한, 적당한, 보통의, 중간의
□ thereby	부사 그렇게 함으로써, 그것 때문에
□ negotiate	동사 협상하다, 성사시키다, 타결하다
□ please	동사 기쁘게 하다, 만족시키다
□ overcome	동사 극복하다 (overcome-overcame-overcome)
□ arise	동사 생기다, 발생하다, (무엇의 결과로) 유발되다 (arise-arose-arisen)
□ lesson	명사 교훈, 가르침
□ verbal	형용사 언어적인, 언어의

핵심 요지를 먼저 보여주고 하나하나 예시를 들면서 근거를 밝히는 글로, 지문의 처음 문장과 마지막 문장이 의미상 서로 이어지고 있음.

28 2018년 3월 31번 (정답률 15%)

정답 ②

[지문 끊어 읽기] 돈의 예측 가능한 희소성

(1) Most importantly, / money needs to be scarce /
가장 중요한 것은 / 돈은 희소성이 있을 필요가 있다 /
in a predictable way. 주제문
예측할 수 있는 방향으로

(2) Precious metals have been desirable as money /
귀금속들은 돈으로서 바람직했다 /
across the millennia /
수천 년에 걸쳐 /
not only because they have intrinsic beauty /
내재적인 아름다움을 지니고 있기 때문일 뿐 아니라 /
but also because they exist in fixed quantities. 정답 단서
또한 그것들이 고정된 양으로 존재하기 때문에

(3) Gold and silver enter society /
금과 은은 사회에 들어간다 /
at the rate at which they are discovered and mined; /
그것들이 발견되고 채굴되는 속도로 /
additional precious metals cannot be produced, / 정답 단서
추가적인 귀금속들은 생산될 수 없다 /
at least not cheaply.
적어도 싸게는 아니다

(4) Commodities like rice and tobacco can be grown, /
쌀과 담배와 같은 상품들은 재배될 수는 있다 /
but that still takes time and resources. 정답 단서
하지만 그것은 여전히 시간과 자원을 필요로 한다

(5) A dictator like Zimbabwe's Robert Mugabe /
짐바브웨의 Robert Mugabe 같은 독재자도 /
could not order the government /
정부에 명령할 수 없었다 /
to produce 100 trillion tons of rice.
100조 톤의 쌀을 생산하라고

(6) He was able to produce and distribute /
그는 생산하고 유통시킬 수 있었다 /
trillions of new Zimbabwe dollars, /
수조의 새로운 짐바브웨 달러들을 /
which is why they eventually became more valuable /
그러나 이것은 결국에 그것들이 더 가치 있게 된 이유이다 /
as toilet paper than currency. 정답 단서
통화로서보다는 휴지로서

중요 짐바브웨에서 엄청나게 많은 달러를 찍어내는 바람에 돈이 휴지보다 가치가 떨어졌다는 것은 '희소성'이 없어졌다는 것을 드러냄.

[전문 해석]

(1)가장 중요한 것은 돈은 예측할 수 있는 방향으로 희소성이 있을 필요가 있다(는 점이다). (2)귀금속들은 내재적인 아름다움을 지니고 있을 뿐 아니라 또한 (그것들이) 고정된 양으로 존재하기 때문에 수천 년에 걸쳐 돈으로서 바람직했다. (3)금과 은은 그것들이 발견되고 채굴되는 속도로 사회에 들어간다(시장에 유입된다). 추가적인 귀금속들은 생산될 수 없고, 적어도 싸게는 아니다(생산되더라도 비용이 많이 든다). (4)쌀과 담배와 같은 상품들은 재배될 수는 있지만, 그것은 여전히 시간과 자원을 필요로 한다. (5)짐바브웨의 Robert Mugabe(로버트 무가베) 같은 독재자도 정부에 100조 톤의 쌀을 생산하라고 명령할 수 없었다. (6)그는 수조의 새로운 짐바브웨 달러들을 생산하고 유통시킬 수 있었지만, 이것이 결국에 그것들(짐바브웨달러)이 통화로서보다는 휴지로서 더 가치 있게 된 이유이다(지나친 화폐 생산으로 화폐 가치가 떨어져 휴지만도 못하게 되었다).

- Zimbabwe(짐바브웨): 아프리카 대륙 중앙 남부에 있는 나라
- Robert Mugabe(로버트 무가베, 1924년~2019년): 짐바브웨의 정치가로 1980년 4월 짐바브웨 정식 건국 당시 총리를 맡았고, 1987년부터 2017년까지 약 30년 넘게 짐바브웨를 통치함.

[정답 확인]

다음 빈칸에 들어갈 말로 가장 적절한 것은?

① invested 투자되어야 할	✔② scarce 희소성이 있을	③ transferred 양도될
④ divisible 나눌 수 있을	⑤ deposited 예치될	

[문제 풀이]

본문은 귀금속들은 고정된 양으로 존재하기 때문에, 그리고 쌀이나 담배 같은 상품들은 재배에 시간과 자원이 필요하기 때문에 돈으로서의 가치가 있음을 예로 든다. 또한 정부가 대량으로 화폐를 생산해 유통시킬 경우 인플레이션(통화 가치 하락)이 일어날 수 있음을 보여준다. 따라서 빈칸에 들어갈 말은 ② 'scarce(희소성이 있을)'이다.

[중요 어휘]

☐ **predictable**	형용사 예측할 수 있는, 예측 가능한
☐ **precious**	형용사 귀중한, 귀한
☐ **desirable**	형용사 바람직한, 가치 있는
☐ **intrinsic**	형용사 내재적인, 본질적인
☐ **fixed**	형용사 고정된
☐ **commodity**	명사 상품, 생산물
☐ **dictator**	명사 독재자
☐ **currency**	명사 통화, 화폐

● 지문 구조도

(1) **돈은 예측할 수 있는 방향으로(in a predictable way) 희소성이 있어야(scarce) 함.**

귀금속(precious metals)
(2) 내재적인 아름다움(intrinsic beauty)을 지니고 있을 뿐 아니라 고정된 양(fixed quantities)으로 존재해서 수천 년에 걸쳐 돈으로서 바람직했음.
(3) 금과 은은 발견되고 채굴되는 속도로 사회에 들어가고, 추가적인 귀금속(additional metals)은 생산될 수 없고, 적어도 싸게는 안 됨.

↔

쌀(rice), 담배(tobacco)
(4) 재배될 수는 있지만, 시간(time)과 자원(resources)을 필요로 함.

↓

(5) 짐바브웨의 Robert Mugabe 같은 독재자(dictator)도 정부에 100조 톤의 쌀을 생산하라고 명령할 수 없었음.

↓

(6) 수조의 새로운 짐바브웨 달러를 생산(produce)하고 유통(distribute)시킬 수는 있었지만, 이로 인해 통화(currency)로서보다 휴지(toilet paper)로서 더 가치 있게(valuable) 되어 버림.

29 2023년 11월 31번 (정답률 50%) 정답 ①

[지문 끊어 읽기] 기적의 근원

(1) [Coincidence that is statistically impossible] / [ ]: S
선행사 ↑ 주격 관계대명사절
통계적으로 불가능한 우연은 /
seems to us like an irrational event, /
V
우리에게 비이성적인 사건처럼 보인다 /
and some define it as a miracle.
그래서 어떤 사람들은 그것을 기적으로 정의한다

(2) But, as Montaigne has said, /
그러나 Montaigne가 말했듯이 /
"the origin of a miracle is in our ignorance, /
기적의 기원은 우리의 무지에 있다 /
at the level of our knowledge of nature, / and not in nature itself."
자연에 대한 우리의 지식 수준에 / 자연 그 자체에 있는 것이 아니라

(3) Glorious miracles have been later on discovered /
영광스러운 기적들은 추후에 밝혀졌다 / ─ 현재완료 수동태
to be [obedience to the laws of nature] / [ ]: 병렬①
자연의 법칙에 대한 순응으로 /
or [a technological development that was not widely known at the time]. [ ]: 병렬②
선행사 ↑ 주격 관계대명사절
혹은 당시에는 널리 알려지지 않은 기술적인 발전으로

(4) As the German poet, Goethe, phrased it: /
독일 시인 Goethe가 그것을 표현한 것처럼 /
"Things that are *mysterious* are *not* yet *miracles*."
S, 선행사 주격 관계대명사절 V
"'신비한' 일들은 아직 '기적'이 '아니다'."

(5) The miracle assumes the intervention of a "higher power" in its occurrence /
↑ 선행사
기적은 그것의 발생에서 '더 높은 힘'의 개입을 가정한다 /
[that is beyond human capability to grasp]. [ ]: 주격 관계대명사절
인간이 이해할 수 있는 능력을 넘어서는 ↑ 형용사적 용법

(6) Yet there are methodical and simple ways to "cause a miracle" /
그러나 '기적을 일으키는' 체계적이고 단순한 방법들이 있다 / 형용사적 용법
without divine revelation and inspiration. 정답 단서 신적인 계시와 영감 없이도 '기적을 일으킬' 체계적이고 단순한 방법들이 존재함.
신의 계시와 영감 없이

(7) Instead of checking it out, /
그것을 확인하는 것 대신에 / =
[investigating and finding the source of the event], /
병렬① 병렬②
그 사건의 근원을 조사하고 발견하는 것 /
we define it as a miracle. 정답 단서 우리는 사건의 근원을 조사하고 발견하는 대신에 그것을 기적이라고 정의함.
우리는 그것을 기적으로 정의한다

(8) The miracle, then, /
그렇다면 기적은 /
힌트 'those who ~'는 선행사 those와 who 주격 관계대명사절이 합쳐진 형태로, '~하는 사람들'로 해석함.
is the excuse of those who are too lazy to think. 정답 단서 기적은 생각하기에 너무 게으른 사람들의 변명임.
너무 게을러서 생각하지 않는 사람들의 변명이다 too+형/부+to V : 너무 ~해서 …않는

[전문 해석]

(1)통계적으로 불가능한 우연은 우리에게 비이성적인 사건처럼 보이는데, 그래서 어떤 사람들은 그것을 기적으로 정의한다. (2)그러나 Montaigne가 말했듯이, "기적의 기원은 자연 그 자체에 있는 것이 아니라, 자연에 대한 우리의 지식 수준에, 즉 우리의 무지에 있다." (3)영광스러운 기적들은 추후에 자연의 법칙에 대한 순응 혹은 당시에는 널리 알려지지 않은 기술적인 발전으로 밝혀졌다. (4)독일 시인 Goethe가 그것을 표현한 것처럼 "'신비한' 일들은 아직 '기적'이 '아니다'." (5)기적은 그것의 발생에서 인간이 이해할 수 있는 능력을 넘어서는 '더 높은 힘'의 개입을 가정한다. (6)그러나 신의 계시와 영감 없이 '기적을 일으키는' 체계적이고 단순한 방법들이 있다. (7)그것을 확인하는 것, 즉 그 사건의 근원을 조사하고 발견하는 것 대신에, 우리는 그것을 기적으로 정의한다. (8)그렇다면, 기적은 너무 게을러서 생각하지 않는 사람들의 변명이다.

[정답 확인]

다음 빈칸에 들어갈 말로 가장 적절한 것은?

✔① ignorance 무지	② flexibility 유연성	③ excellence 탁월성
④ satisfaction 만족	⑤ exaggeration 과장	

[문제 풀이]

통계적으로 불가능한 우연은 비이성적인 사건처럼 보여서 어떤 사람들은 그것을 기적이라고 정의한다. 그러나 Montaigne는 기적의 기원이 자연 그 자체가 아니라 자연에 대한 우리의 지식 수준의 정도에 있다고 한다. 빈칸이 기적의 기원을 설명하므로 이어지는 내용에서 빈칸에 해당하는 기적의 기원을 찾아야 한다. 문장 (5)에서 기적은 인간이 이해할 수 있는 능력을 넘어서는 '더 높은 힘', 즉, 신의 개입을 가정한다고 말한다. 그러나 문장 (6)~(7)에 따르면 신 없이 '기적을 일으키는' 방법들이 존재하는데, 그것은 사건의 근원을 확인하는 대신 신비한 일을 기적이라고 단순히 정의해 버리는 것이다. 그렇기에 기적으로 여겨졌던 신비한 일들 가운데는 사건 당시에는 알려지지 않은 기술이나 자연법칙 때문에 일어난 것으로 밝혀지는 경우가 있는 것이다. 따라서 기적의 기원은 자연에 대한 우리의 지식이 부족한 것에 있으므로 빈칸에는 ① 'ignorance(무지)'가 적절하다.

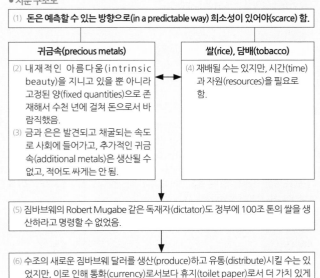

문제편 p.146

[중요 어휘]

☐ coincidence	명사 우연, 우연의 일치
☐ statistically	부사 통계적으로, 통계학상으로
☐ irrational	형용사 비이성적인, 불합리한
☐ glorious	형용사 영광스러운, 영예로운
☐ obedience	명사 순응, 복종
☐ phrase	동사 표현하다 / 명사 구, 구절
☐ mysterious	형용사 신비한, 이해하기 힘든
☐ assume	동사 가정하다, 전제하다, 추정하다
☐ intervention	명사 개입, 간섭
☐ occurrence	명사 발생, 존재, 나타남
☐ capability	명사 능력, 역량
☐ grasp	동사 이해하다, 파악하다, 손에 꽉 잡다
☐ methodical	형용사 체계적인, 꼼꼼한
☐ divine	형용사 신의, 신적인
☐ inspiration	명사 영감, 영감을 주는 사람[것]
☐ check out	확인하다, 대출하다
☐ investigate	동사 조사하다, 연구하다
☐ source	명사 근원, 출처
☐ excuse	명사 변명, 핑계 / 동사 용서하다

30 2024년 3월 31번 (정답률 60%) 정답 ③

[지문 끊어 읽기] 무용과 움직임의 제약 사이의 연관성

(1) Dancers often push themselves /
무용수는 종종 자신을 밀어붙인다 / 재귀용법
to the limits of their physical capabilities.
자신의 신체 능력의 한계까지

(2) But that push is misguided / if it is directed /
그러나 그런 밀어붙이기는 잘못 이해한 것이다 / 그것이 향하면 /
toward accomplishing something physically impossible.
물리적으로 불가능한 것을 달성하는 쪽으로

(3) For instance, / a tall dancer with long feet /
예를 들어 / 키가 크고 발이 긴 무용수가 /
may wish to perform repetitive vertical jumps / to fast music, /
반복적인 수직 점프를 수행하고 싶을 수도 있다 / 빠른 음악에 맞춰 /
[pointing his feet / while in the air] / [ ]: 병렬①(분사구문-동시동작)
발끝을 뾰족하게 하면서 / 공중에서 /
and [lowering his heels to the floor / between jumps]. [ ]: 병렬②
그리고 발뒤꿈치를 바닥에 내리면서 / 점프 사이에

(4) That may be impossible /
=문장(3)
그것은 불가능할 수 있다 /
no matter how strong the dancer is. 정답 단서 힘이 좋은 것과는 상관없이 물리적으로 제한이 있음을 언급함.
무용수가 아무리 힘이 좋을지라도

힌트 'no matter how'는 '아무리 ~일지라도, 어떻게 ~할지라도'로 해석이 가능하며, 복합관계부사인 'however'로 바꾸어 쓸 수 있음.

(5) But a short-footed dancer may have no trouble!
하지만 발이 짧은 무용수는 전혀 문제가 없을 것이다

(6) Another dancer may be struggling /
또 다른 무용수는 애쓰고 있을 수도 있다 /
to complete a half-turn in the air.
부사적 용법(목적)
공중에서 반 회전을 완성하려고

(7) [Understanding the connection / between a rapid turn rate /
연관성을 이해하는 것은 / 빠른 회전 속도와 /
and the alignment of the body close to the rotation axis] / [ ]: S
회전축에 가깝게 몸을 정렬하는 것의 /
tells her how to accomplish her turn successfully.
V
그녀에게 성공적으로 회전을 해내는 방법을 알려 준다

(8) In both of these cases, /
이 두 경우 모두에서 /
[understanding and working within the constraints /
제약을 이해하고 그 안에서 움직이는 것은 /
imposed by nature / and described by physical laws] / [ ]: S(동명사구)
병렬①(과거분사) 병렬②
선천적으로 주어진 / 그리고 물리 법칙에 의해 설명되는 /
정답 단서 선천적으로 주어진 신체 능력 내에서, 그리고 물리 법칙의 지배하에서 움직인다는 것은 어떤 식의 제약이 있다는 뜻임.
allows dancers to work efficiently, /
5형식V O O.C
무용수가 효율적으로 움직이게 해 준다 /
minimizing potential risk of injury.
분사구문(부대상황)
잠재적인 부상 위험을 최소화하면서

[전문 해석]

(1)무용수는 종종 자신의 신체 능력의 한계까지 자신을 밀어붙인다. (2)그러나 그런 밀어붙이기가 물리적으로 불가능한 것을 달성하는 쪽으로 향하면, 잘못 이해한 것이다. (3)예를 들어 키가 크고 발이 긴 무용수가 공중에서 발끝을 뾰족하게 하고 점프 사이에 발뒤꿈치를 바닥에 내리면서 빠른 음악에 맞춰 반복적인 수직 점프를 수행하고 싶을 수도 있다. (4)무용수가 아무리 힘이 좋을지라도 그것은 불가능할 수 있다. (5)하지만 발이 짧은 무용수는 전혀 문제가 없을 것이다! (6)또 다른 무용수는 공중에서 반 회전을 완성하려고 애쓰고 있을 수도 있다. (7)빠른 회전 속도와 회전축에 가깝게 몸을 정렬하는 것의 연관성을 이해하는 것은 그녀에게 성공적으로 회전을 해내는 방법을 알려 준다. (8)이 두 경우 모두에서, 선천적으로 주어지고 물리 법칙에 의해 설명되는 제약을 이해하고 그 안에서 움직이는 것은 잠재적인 부상 위험을 최소화하면서 무용수가 효율적으로 움직이게 해 준다.

[정답 확인]

다음 빈칸에 들어갈 말로 가장 적절한 것은?

① habits 습관
② cultures 문화
③ constraints 제약
④ hostilities 적대감
⑤ moralities 도덕

[문제 풀이]

지문은 무용수는 신체적 능력의 한계까지 자신을 밀어붙이지만 이는 물리적으로 불가능한 것을 이루려는 것과는 다르다는 내용으로 시작한다. 이어서 발이 긴 무용수가 빠른 수직 점프를 하려고 해도, 발이 짧은 무용수에 비해 그것을 성공하기는 힘들 것이라는 예시를 든다. 또한 공중에서 회전을 하려는 무용수가 있다면, 그 사람은 몸의 정렬과 회전 속도 등의 물리 법칙을 이해해야 할 것이다. 이러한 예시들은 모두 물리 법칙과 선천적으로 주어지는 '어떠한 사항'에 영향을 받는 것인데, 이것은 모두 '제약'에 해당한다. 결론적으로, 이런 사항을 모두 종합하여 빈칸에 들어갈 말은 ③ 'constraints(제약)'이다.

[중요 어휘]

☐ limit	명사 한계, 한도 / 동사 제한하다
☐ capability	명사 능력, 역량
☐ push	동사 밀어붙이다, 압박하다
☐ misguide	동사 잘못 이해하다, 오도하다
☐ direct	동사 향하다 / 형용사 직접적인
☐ repetitive	형용사 반복적인, 반복되는
☐ vertical	형용사 수직의, 세로의
☐ point	동사 뾰족하게 하다, 가리키다
☐ heel	명사 발뒤꿈치, 뒤꿈치
☐ rapid	형용사 빠른, 민첩한, 서두르는
☐ rate	명사 속도, 비율
☐ alignment	명사 정렬, 가지런함
☐ rotation axis	명사 회전축
☐ constraint	명사 제약, 통제
☐ impose	동사 (강제로) 주다, 부과하다
☐ minimize	동사 최소화하다, 축소하다
☐ potential	형용사 잠재적인 / 명사 가능성, 잠재력
☐ injury	명사 부상, 상처
☐ hostility	명사 적대감, 적의
☐ morality	명사 도덕, 도덕성

31 2024년 6월 31번 (정답률 65%)

정답 ①

[지문 끊어 읽기] 매력 상승의 요인

(1) We collect stamps, coins, vintage cars /
우리는 우표, 동전, 빈티지 자동차를 수집한다 /
even when they serve no practical purpose.
그것들이 실용적인 목적에는 도움이 되지 않을 때도

(2) The post office doesn't accept the old stamps, /
우체국은 오래된 우표를 받지 않는다 /
the banks don't take old coins, /
은행은 오래된 동전을 받지 않는다 /
and the vintage cars are no longer allowed on the road.
그리고 빈티지 자동차는 더 이상 도로에서 허용되지 않는다

(3) These are all side issues; /
이런 것들은 모두 부수적인 문제이다 /
the attraction is [that they are in short supply]. [ ]: 주격 보어절
그 매력은 그들이 부족한 공급에 있다는 것이다

(4) In one study, / students were asked / to arrange ten posters /
한 연구에서 / 학생들은 요청을 받았다 / 포스터 10장을 배열하라는 /
in order of attractiveness / — with the agreement /
매력 순서대로 / 합의와 함께 /
[that afterward they could keep one poster /
그들이 나중에 포스터 1장을 간직할 수 있다는 /
as a reward for their participation].
그들의 참여에 대한 보상으로

(5) Five minutes later, / they were told /
5분 후 / 그들은 들었다 / (they =students)
[that the poster with the third highest rating /
[ ]: told의 목적어절
세 번째 높은 평가의 포스터가 /
was no longer available]. **정답 단서** 실험 참여자들이 세 번째로 높게 평가된 포스터를 가져갈 수 없게 됨.
더 이상 이용 가능하지 않다고

(6) Then they were asked / to judge all ten / from scratch.
그런 다음 그들은 요청을 받았다 / 10개를 모두 평가하라는 / 처음부터

힌트 'from scratch'는 '처음부터', '아무런 준비 없이' 등의 의미로, 요리를 할 때 미리 준비된 것 없이 기본 재료부터 만들거나 컴퓨터 프로그램을 작성할 때 기존 코드를 이용하지 않고 직접 코드를 작성하는 경우처럼 어떤 것을 처음부터 시작할 때 사용함. 경주를 하기 전에 땅에 긋는 출발선을 'scratch'라고 하는 데서 유래한 표현임.

(7) The poster [that was no longer available] /
S, 선행사 [ ]: 주격 관계대명사절
더 이상 이용할 수 없는 포스터는 /
was suddenly classified /
V
갑자기 분류되었다 /
as the most beautiful. **정답 단서** 가져갈 수 없어진 포스터가 가장 좋은 것으로 평가됨.
가장 아름다운 것으로

(8) In psychology, / this phenomenon is called *reactance*: /
심리학에서 / 이러한 현상은 '리액턴스'라고 불린다 /
when we are deprived of an option, /
우리가 어떤 선택지를 빼앗길 때 /
we suddenly deem it more attractive.
5형식V O O·C
우리가 그것을 갑자기 더 매력적으로 여긴다

[전문 해석]

(1)우리는 우표, 동전, 빈티지 자동차가 실용적인 목적에는 도움이 되지 않을 때도 그것들을 수집한다. (2)우체국은 오래된 우표를 받지 않고, 은행은 오래된 동전을 받지 않으며, 그리고 빈티지 자동차는 더 이상 도로에서 허용되지 않는다. (3)이런 것들은 모두 부수적인 문제이다. 그 매력은 그들이 부족한 공급에 있다는 것이다. (4)한 연구에서, 학생들은 나중에 그들의 참여에 대한 보상으로 포스터 1장을 간직할 수 있다는 합의와 함께 포스터 10장을 매력 순서대로 배열하라는 요청을 받았다. (5)5분 후, 그들은 세 번째로 높은 평가의 포스터가 더 이상 이용 가능하지 않다고 들었다. (6)그런 다음 그들은 10개(의 포스터)를 처음부터 모두 평가하라는 요청을 받았다. (7)더 이상 이용할 수 없는 포스터는 갑자기 가장 아름다운 것으로 분류되었다. (8)심리학에서, 이러한 현상은 '리액턴스'라고 불리는데, 이것은 우리가 어떤 선택지를 빼앗길 때 우리가 그것을 갑자기 더 매력적으로 여긴다는 것이다.

[정답 확인]

다음 빈칸에 들어갈 말로 가장 적절한 것은?

✔ short supply 부족한 공급
② good shape 좋은 상태
③ current use 현재의 사용
④ great excess 엄청난 과잉
⑤ constant production 지속적인 생산

[문제 풀이]

지문은 더 이상 실용성이 없는 것들을 수집하는 근본적인 이유에 대해 설명하며 한 연구를 예로 제시한다. 빈칸에는 이후 언급되는 연구 결과와 의미가 연결될 수 있는 어구가 들어가야 한다. 연구에서 실험 참여자들이 나중에 가져갈 수 있도록 합의된 포스터 중 세 번째로 좋다고 평가한 것이 갑자기 가져갈 수 없는 것이 되었을 때, 이 말을 들은 참여자들은 그 포스터를 제일 매력적이라고 평가했다. 심리학에서 '리액턴스'라고 부르는 이러한 현상은 더 이상 선택할 수 없게 된 것을 매력적으로 판단하는 상황을 지칭한다. 공급이 충분하게 많이 이루어지지 않아 선택할 수 없게 되는 상황이 초래되므로, 빈칸에 들어갈 정답은 ① 'short supply(부족한 공급)'이다.

[중요 어휘]

☐ stamp	명사 우표 / 동사 발을 구르다
☐ serve	동사 도움이 되다, 수행하다, 제공하다
☐ practical	형용사 실용적인, 현실적인
☐ side	형용사 부수적인 / 명사 면, 쪽
☐ attraction	명사 매력, 끌림
☐ short	형용사 부족한, 짧은
☐ arrange	동사 배열하다, 정리하다
☐ agreement	명사 합의, 동의
☐ rating	명사 평가, 순위
☐ classify	동사 분류하다, 구분하다
☐ be deprived of	~을 빼앗기다
☐ deem	동사 (~로) 여기다[생각하다]
☐ excess	명사 과잉, 초과

32 2024년 9월 31번 (정답률 35%)

정답 ③

[지문 끊어 읽기] 과정의 공정성과 결과

(1) When we get an unfavorable outcome, / in some ways /
우리가 불리한 결과를 얻을 때 / 어떤 면에서 /
[the *last* thing we want to hear] / [ ]: S
우리가 '가장 듣고 싶지 않은' 말은 /
is [that the process was fair]. [ ]: S·C
V 접속사
과정이 공정했다는 것이다

힌트 the last는 '마지막의'라는 의미가 아니라 '가장[결코] ~할 것 같지 않은'이라는 의미로 해석되며, 이때 선행사 the *last* thing 뒤에 목적격 관계대명사가 생략된 형태임.

힌트 'as+형용사/부사+as+S'+V', S+V ~'는 '~이지만[~에도 불구하고], …하다'라는 양보의 의미를 나타냄.

(2) As outraging as the combination of an unfavorable outcome and an unfair process is, /
S' V'
불리한 결과와 불공정한 과정의 조합이 분노를 일으키지만 /
this combination also brings with it a consolation prize: /
S V 부사구 O
이 조합은 또한 그것과 함께 위로상을 가져온다 /
the possibility of attributing the bad outcome to something other than ourselves. **정답 단서** 불리한 결과와 불공정한 과정이 합쳐지면 분노를 일으키지만 한편으로는 나쁜 결과의 원인을 자신이 아닌 외부에 돌리는 가능성을 제공함.
~이 아닌, ~외에
나쁜 결과를 스스로가 아닌 다른 것의 탓으로 돌릴 가능성

힌트 'have ~ to do with'는 '~과 …만큼의 관련이 있다'를 의미하며, 관련된 정도에 따라 목적어 자리에 'everything/something/nothing/little' 등을 넣어 활용할 수 있음.

(3) We may reassure ourselves by believing /
우리는 믿음으로써 우리 자신을 안심시킬지도 모른다 /
that our bad outcome had [little to do with us] /
우리의 나쁜 결과가 우리와 거의 관련이 없다고 / [ ]: 병렬①
and [everything to do with the unfair process]. [ ]: 병렬②
그리고 불공정한 과정과 전적으로 관련이 있다고

힌트 'as+형용사/부사+as' 비교 구문에서 뒤에 나오는 비교 내용이 삭제되었음.

(4) If the process is fair, / however, /
과정이 공정하다면 / 그러나 /
we cannot nearly as easily externalize the outcome; /
우리는 결과를 결코 그렇게 쉽게 외적 원인으로 돌릴 수 없다 /

we got what we got "fair and square."
선행사를 포함한 관계대명사절
우리는 우리가 얻은 것을 '정정당당하게' 얻은 것이다

(5) When the process is fair /
그 과정이 공정할 때 /
we believe that our outcome is deserved, /
우리는 우리의 결과가 마땅하다고 믿는다 /
[which is another way of saying /
그런데 그것은 말하는 또 다른 방식이다 /
that there must have been something about ourselves /
우리 자신에 대한 어떤 것이 있었음에 틀림없다고 /
(what we did or who we are) / that caused the outcome].
(우리가 했던 것 또는 우리가 누구인지) / 그 결과를 야기한 주격 관계대명사절
선행사
정답 단서 과정이 공정하면 우리는 결과가 우리 자신에게서 기인한다고 생각함.
[ ]: 주격 관계대명사절 (계속적 용법)

[전문 해석]

(1)우리가 불리한 결과를 얻을 때 어떤 면에서 우리가 '가장 듣고 싶지 않은' 말은 과정이 공정했다는 것이다. (2)불리한 결과와 불공정한 과정의 조합이 분노를 일으키지만, 이 조합은 또한 그것과 함께 위로상, 즉 나쁜 결과를 스스로가 아닌 다른 것의 탓으로 돌릴 가능성을 가져온다. (3)우리는 우리의 나쁜 결과가 우리와 거의 관련이 없고 불공정한 과정과 전적으로 관련이 있다고 믿음으로써 우리 자신을 안심시킬지도 모른다. (4)그러나 과정이 공정하다면, 우리는 결과를 결코 그렇게 쉽게 외적 원인으로 돌릴 수 없으며, 우리는 우리가 얻은 것을 '정정당당하게' 얻은 것이다. (5)그 과정이 공정할 때 우리는 우리의 결과가 마땅하다고 믿는데, 그것은 그 결과를 야기한 우리 자신(우리가 했던 것 또는 우리가 누구인지)에 대한 어떤 것이 있었음에 틀림없다고 말하는 또 다른 방식이다.

[정답 확인]

다음 빈칸에 들어갈 말로 가장 적절한 것은?

① expect 예상할
② diversify 다양화할
✔ externalize 외적 원인으로 돌릴
④ generate 생성할
⑤ overestimate 과대평가할

[문제 풀이]

이 글에 따르면 우리가 불리한 결과를 얻을 때 과정이 불공정하다면 우리는 나쁜 결과에 대한 원인을 자신이 아닌 외부에서, 즉, 불공정한 과정에서 찾을 수 있다. 그러나 과정이 공정하다면 나쁜 결과에 대한 책임은 온전히 내부, 즉, 자신에게서 찾아야 한다. 빈칸은 과정이 공정한 경우를 이야기하므로 빈칸 앞에 cannot이 있음을 고려하여 ③ 'externalize(외적 원인으로 돌리다)'가 오는 것이 적절하다.

[오답 풀이]

① - 문장 (2)~(3)은 과정이 공정하지 않은 경우 나쁜 결과에 대해 외부의 탓을 하려 하며, 문장 (4)~(5)는 과정이 공정한 경우 나쁜 결과의 원인을 자신에게 있는 것으로 보고 정당한 것으로 받아들인다는 내용이다. 그러나 결과를 '예상하는' 내용은 찾을 수 없으므로 ①은 정답으로 적절하지 않다.

[중요 어휘]

☐ **unfavorable**	형용사 불리한, 호의적이 아닌
☐ **outcome**	명사 결과, 성과
☐ **outrage**	동사 분노를 일으키다 / 명사 격분, 격노
☐ **combination**	명사 조합
☐ **consolation**	명사 위로, 위안
☐ **prize**	명사 상, 포상
☐ **attribute A to B**	A를 B의 탓으로 돌리다
☐ **reassure**	동사 안심시키다
☐ **not nearly**	결코 ~가 아닌
☐ **externalize**	동사 외적 원인으로 돌리다, 외면화하다
☐ **fair and square**	정정당당하게
☐ **deserve**	동사 ~을 받을 만하다, ~을 누릴 자격이 있다

33 2024년 9월 32번 (정답률 45%) 정답 ①

[지문 끊어 읽기] 패션의 규칙성

(1) The well-known American ethnologist Alfred Louis Kroeber /
미국의 잘 알려진 민족학자인 Alfred Louis Kroeber는 /
made a rich and in-depth study /
풍부하고 심층적인 연구를 수행했다 /
of women's evening dress in the West, /
서양의 여성 이브닝 드레스에 대한 /
stretching back about three centuries /
약 3세기 전으로 거슬러 올라가 / 병렬①(분사구문)
and using reproductions of engravings.
그리고 판화 복제품을 사용하여 병렬②

힌트 'having+p.p.'의 형태를 사용하는 완료 분사구문은 주절의 시제보다 종속절의 동작이 먼저 일어난 일임을 나타냄.

(2) [Having adjusted the dimensions of these plates /
이 판들의 크기를 조정하여 /
due to their diverse origins], / [ ]: 완료 분사구문
다양한 기원 때문에 /
he was able to analyse the constant elements /
병렬①
그는 일정한 요소를 분석할 수 있었다 /
in fashion features / and to come up with a study /
패션 특징에서의 / 그리고 연구를 구상할 수 있었다 / 병렬② 선행사
[that was neither intuitive nor approximate, /
직관적이지도 대략적이지도 않은 연구를 /
but precise, mathematical and statistical].
하지만 정확하고 수학적이며 통계적인 [ ]: 주격 관계대명사절

힌트 'A도 아니고 B도 아닌'이라는 뜻의 상관접속사 'neither A nor B'에 'but'이 붙은 구조임. 'neither', 'nor', 'but' 뒤에 오는 말은 같은 어법 형태끼리 병렬 구조로 연결되어 문장 (2)에서는 모두 형용사가 쓰였음을 알 수 있음.

(3) He reduced women's clothing / to a certain number of features: /
그는 여성 의류를 정리했다 / 몇 가지 특징들로 /
length and size of the skirt, / size and depth of the neckline, /
치마의 길이와 크기 / 목선의 크기와 깊이 /
height of the waistline.
허리선의 높이

(4) He demonstrated unambiguously /
그는 분명하게 보여 주었다 /
[that fashion is a profoundly regular phenomenon /
패션이 완전히 규칙적인 현상이라는 것을 / 선행사
[which is not located at the level of annual variations /
매년 일어나는 변화의 수준에 위치하지 않는 /
but on the scale of history]].
그러나 역사의 척도에 [ ]: 주격 관계대명사절

힌트 명사절 접속사 that부터 문장 끝까지가 demonstrated의 목적어에 해당함.

힌트 상관접속사 not A but B는 'A가 아니라 B'라는 의미이며, 이때 A와 B에 같은 어법 구조가 연결되나 이 문장에서는 반복되는 어구인 located가 생략되어 쓰임.

(5) For practically 300 years, / women's dress was subject /
거의 300년 동안 / 여성 드레스는 영향을 받았다 /
to a very precise periodic cycle: /
매우 정확한 주기적인 순환의 /
forms reach the furthest point in their variations every fifty years.
형식은 50년마다 변화의 정점에 도달했다 전치사구

정답 단서 여성 드레스의 변화는 50년이라는 주기를 따라 변화함.

힌트 'every+기수+복수명사'는 '~마다'의 의미로 사용됨.

(6) If, at any one moment, skirts are at their longest, /
삽입구
어느 한 시기에 치마가 가장 길었다면 /
fifty years later / they will be at their shortest; /
=skirts
50년 후에 / 그것들은 가장 짧아질 것이다 /
thus skirts become long again / fifty years after being short /
따라서 치마는 다시 길어질 것이다 / 짧아진 데서 50년 후에 / 병렬①
and a hundred years after being long.
그리고 길어진 데서 100년 후에 병렬②

정답 단서 치마의 길이는 50년이라는 명확한 간격에 따라 변화함.

[전문 해석]

(1)미국의 잘 알려진 민족학자인 Alfred Louis Kroeber는 약 3세기 전으로 거슬러 올라가 판화 복제품을 사용하여 서양의 여성 이브닝 드레스에 대한 풍부하고 심층적인 연구를 수행했다. (2)다양한 기원 때문에 이 판들의 크기를 조정하여, 그는 패션 특징에서의 일정한 요소를 분석해서 직관적이지도 대략적이지도 않은, 정확하고 수학적이며 통계적인 연구를 구상할 수 있었다. (3)그는 여성 의류를 치마의 길이와 크기, 목선의 크기와 깊이, 허리선의 높이와 같은 몇 가지 특징들로 정리했다. (4)그는 패션이 매년 일어나는 변화의 수준에 위치하는 것이 아니라 역사의 척도에 위치하는 완전히 규칙적인 현상이라는 것을 분명하게 보여 주었다. (5)거의 300년 동안 여성 드레스는 매우 정확한 주기적인 순환의 영향을 받았는데, 형식은 50년마다

변화의 정점에 도달했다. (6)어느 한 시기에 치마가 가장 길었다면, 50년 후에 그것들은 가장 짧아질 것이고, 따라서 치마는 짧아진 데서 50년 후에 다시 길어지고, 길어진 데서 100년 후에 다시 길어진다.

[정답 확인]

다음 빈칸에 들어갈 말로 가장 적절한 것은?

✔ a profoundly regular phenomenon
완전히 규칙적인 현상
② a practical and progressive trend
실제적이고 점진적인 유행
③ an intentionally created art form
의도적으로 만들어진 예술 형식
④ a socially influenced tradition
사회적으로 영향을 받는 전통
⑤ a swiftly occurring event
재빠르게 벌어지는 사건

[문제 풀이]

지문은 한 민족학자가 여성의 이브닝 드레스의 300년간 변화를 확인한 연구를 통해 패션에 주기가 있다는 것을 설명한다. 그는 이브닝 드레스를 구성하는 패션 특징의 요소를 분석한 결과, 50년마다 변화의 정점이 있었음을 알아차렸다. 이 민족학자는 이 연구를 정확하고 통계적으로 진행했는데, 결론적으로 300년의 기간 동안 50년의 주기로 패션에 큰 변화가 있었다는 결과를 도출해냈다. 이로부터 패션이 단순히 매년 바뀌는 흐름이 아니라, 일정한 주기를 가지고 변화한다는 것을 알 수 있다. 따라서 이 내용을 모두 종합하면, 빈칸에 들어갈 정답은 ①이다.

[중요 어휘]

☐ **ethnologist**	명사 민족학자
☐ **in-depth**	형용사 심층적인, 철저하고 상세한
☐ **stretch back**	~으로 거슬러 올라가다
☐ **century**	명사 1세기, 100년
☐ **reproduction**	명사 복제(품), 재생산, 번식
☐ **engraving**	명사 판화, 조각(술)
☐ **dimension**	명사 크기, 규모, 차원
☐ **plate**	명사 판, 접시
☐ **diverse**	형용사 다양한, 다른, 별개의
☐ **origin**	명사 기원, 출신
☐ **analyse**	동사 분석하다, 조사하다
☐ **constant**	형용사 일정한, 끊임없는
☐ **element**	명사 요소, 성분
☐ **intuitive**	형용사 직관적인, 직감에 의한
☐ **approximate**	형용사 대략적인, 근사치인
☐ **precise**	형용사 정확한, 정밀한
☐ **statistical**	형용사 통계적인
☐ **reduce A to B**	A를 B로 정리하다
☐ **unambiguously**	부사 분명하게
☐ **profoundly**	부사 완전히, 매우, 깊이
☐ **scale**	명사 척도, 규모, 등급
☐ **practically**	부사 거의, 사실상
☐ **be subject to A**	A의 영향을 받다
☐ **periodic**	형용사 주기적인, 시대의, 간헐적인

문제편 p.149

12 빈칸 추론(2)-긴 어구, 문장

핵심 필자는 가장 강력한 감정적 경험은 이전의 고통과 대조함으로써 더욱 강렬해지는 행복을 느낄 수 있는 경험이라고 말함. 그리고 이러한 경험은 인간의 화학적 기록 보관소에 저장되고, 저장된 경험과 감정은 우리가 진정한 행복을 느낄 때마다 활성화되어 더 큰 기쁨을 느끼게 해준다는 것이 이 글의 요지이며, 따라서 빈칸의 내용도 이러한 내용을 담고 있어야 함.

01 2021년 9월 33번 (정답률 70%)

정답 ①

[지문 끊어 읽기] 가장 강력한 감정적 경험

(1) The most powerful emotional experiences are those / (선행사)
가장 강력한 감정적 경험은 ~것들이다 /
that bring joy, inspiration, and the kind of love / (주격 관계대명사, 선행사)
기쁨, 영감, 그리고 일종의 사랑을 가져오는 /
that makes suffering bearable. (주격 관계대명사)
고통을 견딜 수 있게 만드는

(2) These emotional experiences are the result of choices and behaviors / (선행사)
이러한 감정적 경험은 선택과 행동의 결과이다 /
that result in our feeling happy. (주격 관계대명사)
우리가 행복하다고 느끼는 것으로 이끄는

(3) When we look at happiness through a spiritual filter, / we realize /
우리가 정신적 필터를 통해 행복을 바라볼 때 / 우리는 깨닫는다 /
that it does not mean the absence of pain or heartache.
그것이 고통이나 심적 고통의 부재를 의미하지 않는다는 것을

(4) Sitting with a sick or injured child, /
아프거나 다친 아이와 함께 앉아 있으면 /
every parent gets to know the profound joy / (선행사)
모든 부모는 그 심오한 기쁨을 알게 된다 /
that bubbles over / when a son or daughter begins to heal. (주격 관계대명사)
벅차오르는 / 아들이나 딸이 회복하기 시작할 때

힌트 'As every parent sits with a sick or injured child'를 분사구문 형태로 바꾼 것임.

(5) This is a simple example of /
이것은 ~에 대한 단순한 한 예이다 /
how we can be flooded with happiness / (선행사)
어떻게 우리가 행복으로 넘쳐날 수 있는지 /
that becomes more intense / (주격 관계대명사)
더욱 강렬해지는 /
as we contrast it with previous suffering.
우리가 그것을 이전의 고통과 대조함에 따라

(6) Experiences such as this /
이와 같은 경험은 /
go into the chemical archives of the limbic system.
변연계의 화학적 기록 보관소로 간다

힌트 변연계는 해부학적 실체가 아닌 감정, 행동, 동기부여, 기억, 후각 등의 기능을 담당하는 뇌의 구조물들을 말함.

(7) Each time you experience true happiness, /
당신이 진정한 행복을 경험할 때마다 /
the stored emotions are activated /
그 저장된 감정들은 활성화된다 /
as you are flooded with even deeper joy / than you remembered. (정답 단서)
당신이 더욱 깊은 기쁨으로 넘쳐나면서 / 당신이 기억했던 것보다

(8) Your spiritual genes are, / in a sense, /
당신의 정신적 유전자들은 ~이다 / 어떤 의미에서는 /
your biological treasure map to joy.
기쁨으로 향하는 당신의 생물학적 보물지도

[전문 해석]

(1)가장 강력한 감정적 경험은 기쁨, 영감, 그리고 고통을 견딜 수 있게 만드는 일종의 사랑을 가져오는 것들이다. (2)이러한 감정적 경험은 우리가 행복하다고 느끼는 것으로 이끄는 선택과 행동의 결과이다. (3)우리가 정신적 필터를 통해 행복을 바라볼 때, 우리는 그것(행복)이 (육체적) 고통이나 심적 고통의 부재를 의미하지 않는다는 것을 깨닫는다. (4)아프거나 다친 아이와 함께 앉아 있으면, 모든 부모는 아들이나 딸이 회복하기 시작할 때 벅차오르는 그 심오한 기쁨을 알게 된다. (5)이것은 우리가 그것(행복)을 이전의 고통과 대조함에 따라 어떻게 우리가 더욱 강렬해지는 행복으로 넘쳐날 수 있는지에 대한 단순한 한 예이다. (6)이와 같은 경험은 변연계의 화학적 기록 보관소로 간다. (7)당신이 진정한 행복을 경험할 때마다 당신이 기억했던 것보다 더욱 깊은 기쁨으로 넘쳐나면서 그 저장된 감정들은 활성화된다. (8)당신의 정신적 유전자들은 어떤 의미에서는 기쁨으로 향하는 당신의 생물학적 보물지도이다.

[정답 확인]

다음 빈칸에 들어갈 말로 가장 적절한 것은?

① your biological treasure map to joy
기쁨으로 향하는 당신의 생물학적 보물지도
② your hidden key to lasting friendships
지속되는 우정의 숨겨진 열쇠(비결)
③ a mirror showing your unique personality
당신의 고유한 성격을 보여주는 거울
④ a facilitator for communication with others
다른 이들과의 소통을 위한 촉진제
⑤ a barrier to looking back to your joyful childhood
당신의 기쁜 어린 시절을 되돌아보는 것을 막는 장벽

[문제 풀이]

본문에 따르면 가장 강력한 감정적 경험인 행복함의 감정과 경험은 우리 몸의 화학적 기록 보관소에 저장된다. 이렇게 저장된 경험과 감정은 이후 우리가 행복을 느낄 때마다 활성화되어 우리는 더 큰 기쁨을 느낄 수 있다고 설명하고 있다. 화학적 기록 보관소에 저장된 행복의 경험과 감정이 마지막 문장에서 말하는 정신적 유전자에 해당한다고 볼 수 있으며, 저장된 행복의 감정을 통해 더 큰 기쁨을 느낄 수 있다고 본문에서 설명하고 있기 때문에, 정답은 ①이다.

[중요 어휘]

□ inspiration	명사 영감
□ bearable	형용사 견딜 수 있는
□ result in	~로 이끌다[야기하다]
□ spiritual	형용사 정신적인
□ absence	명사 부재, 없음, 결석
□ heartache	명사 심적 고통
□ get to know	알게 되다
□ profound	형용사 심오한
□ bubble over	(흥분·열광 등이) 벅차오르다
□ be flooded with	~로 넘쳐나다
□ contrast A with B	A와 B를 대조하다[대비시키다]
□ archive	명사 기록 보관소
□ limbic system	변연계
□ biological	형용사 생물학적(인), 생물학의
□ lasting	형용사 지속되는, 영속적인
□ facilitator	명사 촉진제, 조력자
□ barrier	명사 장벽

02 2022년 11월 32번 (정답률 65%)

정답 ①

[지문 끊어 읽기] 재정적 고통의 자기 충족성

(1) The connectedness of the global economic market /
전 세계 경제 시장의 연결성은 /
makes it vulnerable / to potential "infection." (5형식V O O·C(형용사))
그것을 취약하게 만든다 / 잠재적 '감염'에

(2) A financial failure / can make its way /
금융상의 실패는 / 나아갈 수 있다 /
from borrowers to banks to insurers, / spreading like a flu. (분사구문(~하면서))
채무자에서부터 은행, 보증인까지 / 독감처럼 퍼지면서

(3) However, / there are unexpected characteristics /
그러나 / 예상치 못한 특징들이 있다 /
when it comes to such infection / in the market. (~에 관하여)
그러한 감염에 관하여 / 시장에서의

(4) Infection can occur / even without any contact.
감염은 일어날 수 있다 / 심지어 어떤 접촉 없이도

(5) A bank might become insolvent /
은행은 지급 불능이 될 수 있다 /
even without having any of its investments fail.
전치사 동명사(사역V) O O.C(동사원형)
어떠한 투자에 실패하지 않고도

(6) Fear and uncertainty / can be damaging / to financial markets, /
두려움과 불확실성은 / 손해를 끼칠 수 있다 / 금융 시장에 /
just as cascading failures / due to bad investments. 주제문
마치 ~처럼
마치 연속된 실패처럼 / 어떤 나쁜 투자들로 인한
금융 시장에서는 두려움과 불확실성 자체가 시장에 직접적인 손해를 끼칠 수 있음.

(7) If we all woke up tomorrow and believed /
만약 우리 모두가 내일 깨어나서 믿는다면 /
[that Bank X would be insolvent], / [ ]: that 명사절(believed의 목적어)
X은행이 지급 불능이 될 것이라고 /
then it would become insolvent. 정답 단서 불확실한 상황에 대한 부정적인 예측 → 실제 손해 발생
2형식V S.C(형용사)
그것은 지급 불능이 될 것이다

(8) In fact, / it would be enough / for us / [to fear /
형식상의 주어 to부정사의 의미상의 주어 [ ]: 내용상의 주어①
사실 / 충분할 것이다 / 우리가 / 무서워하는 것은 /
that others believed / that Bank X was going to fail], /
다른 사람들이 믿고 있다는 것을 / X은행이 실패할 것이라고 /
or just to fear our collective fear! 정답 단서 금융상 실패에 대해 두려워함 → 실제 손해 발생
내용상의 주어②
혹은 단지 우리의 집단적인 두려움을 무서워하는 것은

(9) We might all even know /
우리 모두는 심지어 알고 있을지도 모른다 /
[that Bank X was well-managed with healthy investments], /
X은행이 건전한 투자로 잘 운영된다는 것을 / [ ]: that 명사절
but if we expected others to pull their money out, /
5형식V O O.C(to V)
하지만 만약 우리가 다른 사람들이 그들의 돈을 인출해 갈 것이라고 예상한다면 /
then we would fear / being the last / to pull our money out.
형용사적 용법
그러면 우리는 무서워할 것이다 / 마지막 사람이 되는 것을 / 자신의 돈을 인출하는

(10) Financial distress can be self-fulfilling /
재정적인 고통은 자기 충족적일 수 있다 /
and is a particularly troublesome aspect of financial markets.
그리고 금융 시장에서의 특히 골치 아픈 측면이다 ✶중요 재정적 고통이 'self-fulfilling(자기 충족적)'이라는 말은 재정적 고통을 예측하고 두려워하는 것만으로도 실제 재정적 고통이 발생한다는 의미임. 'self-fulfilling'이라는 단어는 본문 전체의 주제를 포괄하는 핵심적인 단어로 볼 수 있음.

[중요 구문]

(7) If we all woke up tomorrow and believed ~,
S' V'① V'②
then it would become insolvent.
S 조동사 과거형+동사원형
힌트 「If+S'+과거V' ~, S+조동사 과거형+동사원형 ~」 형태의 가정법 과거 문장임. 가정법 과거는 현재 사실의 반대 상황을 가정할 때 사용되며, 우리말로 해석할 때에도 과거 시제가 아닌 현재 시제로 해석하여야 함.

(9) ~, but if we expected others to pull their money out,
S' V'
then we would fear being the last to pull our money out.
S 조동사 과거형+동사원형

힌트 「형식상의 주어-내용상의 주어」 구문에서, 내용상의 주어에 해당하는 to부정사의 명사적 용법이 등위접속사 or을 중심으로 병렬 연결된 구조임.

(8) ~ it would be enough ~ [to fear that others believed that Bank X
형식상의 주어
was going to fail, or just to fear our collective fear]! [ ]: 내용상의 주어
힌트 'that others ~ fail'은 to fear의 목적어인 that 명사절에 해당하며, 'that Bank X was going to fail'은 동사 believed의 목적어인 that 명사절임.

[전문 해석]

(1)전 세계 경제 시장의 연결성은 그것을 잠재적 '감염'에 취약하게 만든다. (2)금융상의 실패는 독감처럼 퍼지면서 채무자에서부터 은행, 보증인까지 나아갈 수 있다. (3)그러나 시장에서의 그러한 감염에 관하여 예상치 못한 특징들이 있다. (4)감염은 심지어 어떤 접촉 없이도 일어날 수 있다. (5)은행은 어떠한 투자에 실패하지 않고도 지급 불능이 될 수 있다. (6)마치 어떤 나쁜 투자들로 인한 연속된 실패처럼, 금융 시장에 두려움과 불확실성은 손해를 끼칠 수 있다. (7)만약 우리 모두가 내일 깨어나서 X은행이 지급 불능이 될 것이라고 믿는다면, 그것은 지급 불능이 될 것이다. (8)사실 우리가 다른 사람들이 X은행이 실패할 것이라고 믿고 있다는 것을 무서워하거나 단지 우리의 집단적인 두려움을 무서워하는 것으로 충분할 것이다. (9)우리 모두는 심지어 X은행이 건전한 투자로 잘 운영된다는 것을 알고 있을지도 모르지만, 만약 우리가 다른 사람들이 그들의 돈을 인출해 갈 것이라고 예상한다면, 그러면 우리는 자신의 돈을 인출하는 마지막 사람이 되는 것을 무서워할 것이다. (10)재정적인 고통은 자기 충족적일 수 있고 금융 시장에서의 특히 골치 아픈 측면이다.

[정답 확인]

다음 빈칸에 들어갈 말로 가장 적절한 것은?

✔① Fear and uncertainty can be damaging
두려움과 불확실성은 손해를 끼칠 수 있다
② Unaffordable personal loans may pose a risk
감당할 수 없는 개인 대출은 위험을 초래한다
③ Ignorance about legal restrictions may matter
법적 제한에 대한 무지는 문제가 될 수 있다
④ Accurate knowledge of investors can be poisonous
투자자들에 대한 정확한 지식은 유해할 수 있다
⑤ Strong connections between banks can create a scare
은행들 간의 강한 유대는 불안을 만들어낼 수 있다

[문제 풀이]

빈칸 뒤에서는 반복적으로 금융 실패를 두려워하고 예측하는 상황들이 제시되고 있으며, 이러한 두려움은 실제 그러한 금융상의 실패가 발생할 가능성과는 무관하게 지급 불능의 상황을 유발한다. 즉, 불확실한 금융 시장에서의 실패 자체가 아니라 실패를 두려워하는 것만으로도 실제 손해를 발생시키는 것이므로, 빈칸에 가장 적절한 말은 ①이다.

[중요 어휘]

☐ **vulnerable**	형용사 취약한
☐ **potential**	형용사 잠재적인, 가능성이 있는 / 명사 잠재력
☐ **infection**	명사 감염, 전염
☐ **make one's way**	나아가다, 가다, 출세하다
☐ **insurer**	명사 보증인, 보험업자
☐ **contact**	명사 접촉, 연락
☐ **insolvent**	형용사 지급 불능의, 파산한
☐ **cascading**	형용사 연속적인, 폭포와 같은
☐ **collective**	형용사 집단적인, 공동의
☐ **distress**	명사 고통, 괴로움
☐ **self-fulfilling**	형용사 자기 충족적인, 자기 달성적인
☐ **troublesome**	형용사 골치 아픈, 성가신
☐ **aspect**	명사 측면

핵심 고위도에 살던 네안데르탈인들이 저조도의 환경에 진화적으로 반응하여 더 큰 망막을 갖게 되었다는 내용의 글임.

03 2016년 11월 32번 (정답률 60%) 정답 ③

[지문 끊어 읽기] 약한 빛의 환경과 시력

(1) The Neanderthals would have faced a problem /
would have p.p.: ~했을 것이다(가정법 과거완료)
네안데르탈인들은 어떤 문제에 직면했을 것이다 /
when it was daylight: /
낮에 /
the light quality is much poorer at high latitudes /
고위도에서는 빛의 질이 훨씬 더 나쁘다 /
and this would have meant /
그리고 이것은 의미했을 것이다 /
that they couldn't see things in the distance so well.
그들이 멀리 있는 물체들을 잘 볼 수 없었다는 것을

(2) For a hunter, / this is a serious problem, /
사냥꾼에게는 / 이것이 심각한 문제이다 /
because you really don't want to make the mistake /
왜냐하면 당신은 실수를 정말로 저지르고 싶지 않기 때문이다 /
of not noticing the mother rhinoceros hiding /
어미 코뿔소가 숨어있다는 것을 알아채지 못하는 /
in a dark corner of the forest edge / when trying to spear her calf.
숲 언저리의 어두운 구석에 / 그녀의 새끼 코뿔소를 창으로 찍으려고 할 때

(3) Living under low light conditions /
약한 빛의 환경에서 사는 것은 /
places a much heavier premium on vision /
시력에 훨씬 더 중요한 가치를 둔다 /
than most researchers imagine.
대부분의 연구자들이 생각하는 것보다

정답과 해설 12 빈칸 추론 (2)

(4) The evolutionary response to low light levels /
약한 빛의 정도에 대한 진화적 반응은 / 전치사
is to increase the size of the visual processing system.
시각 처리 기관의 크기를 증가시키는 것이다

(5) It is the familiar principle /
그것은 비슷한 원리이다 /
from conventional star-gazing telescopes: /
일반적인 천체 관측 망원경과 /
under the dim lighting of the night sky, /
밤하늘의 희미한 빛 아래에서 /
a larger mirror allows you to gather more of the light /
더 큰 거울은 당신이 더 많은 빛을 모으게 한다 /
from whatever you want to look at. 정답 단서
당신이 보고 싶어 하는 것이 무엇이든 간에 그것으로부터

✶중요 문장 (4)의 빈칸에 들어갈 내용을 뒷받침하기 위해 문장 (5)에서 천체 관측 망원경을 비유로 들어 설명하고 있음을 파악하는 것이 핵심임.

(6) By the same token, /
같은 이유로 /
a larger retina allows you to receive more light /
더 큰 망막은 당신이 더 많은 빛을 받아들이게 한다 /
to compensate for poor light levels.
약한 빛의 정도를 보완할 수 있도록

[전문 해석]

(1) 네안데르탈인들은 낮에 어떤 문제에 직면했을 것이다. (즉) 고위도에서는 빛의 질이 훨씬 더 나쁘고, 이것은 그들이 멀리 있는 물체들을 잘 볼 수 없었다는 것을 의미했을 것이다. (2) 사냥꾼에게는 이것이 심각한 문제인데, 왜냐하면 당신은 어미 코뿔소의 새끼 코뿔소를 창으로 찍으려고 할 때, 그녀가 숲 언저리의 어두운 구석에 숨어있다는 것을 알아채지 못하는 실수를 정말로 저지르고 싶지 않기 때문이다. (3) 대부분의 연구자들이 생각하는 것보다, 약한 빛의 환경에서 사는 것은 시력에 훨씬 더 중요한 가치를 둔다(빛이 약한 환경에서는 시력이 매우 중요하다). (4) 약한 빛의 정도에 대한 진화적 반응은 시각 처리 기관의 크기를 증가시키는 것이다. (5) 그것은 일반적인 천체 관측 망원경과 비슷한 원리이다. 밤하늘의 희미한 빛 아래에서, 더 큰 거울은 당신이 보고 싶어 하는 것이 무엇이든 간에 그것으로부터 더 많은 빛을 모으게 한다. (6) 같은 이유로, 더 큰 망막은 당신이 약한 빛의 정도를 보완할 수 있도록 더 많은 빛을 받아들이게 한다.

- Neanderthal(네안데르탈인): 유럽 지역을 중심으로 세계 전역에 분포하던 화석인류

[정답 확인]

다음 빈칸에 들어갈 말로 가장 적절한 것은?

① to get big enough to frighten animals
동물들을 겁먹게 할 만큼 충분히 커지는 것
② to move their habitats to lower latitudes
더 낮은 위도로 그들의 거주지를 옮기는 것
✔ to increase the size of the visual processing system
시각 처리 기관의 크기를 증가시키는 것
④ to develop auditory sense rather than visual system
시각 기관보다 청각을 발달시키는 것
⑤ to focus our attention on what we perceive to be the threat
우리가 위협이라고 인식하는 것에 집중하는 것

✶중요 문장 (5)의 a larger mirror의 의미가 정답에는 increase the size ~로 표현되었음.

[중요 어휘]

☐ **latitude**	명사 위도
☐ **rhinoceros**	명사 코뿔소
☐ **edge**	명사 언저리, 가장자리
☐ **spear**	동사 창으로 찍다
☐ **calf**	명사 (소·고래 등의) 새끼
☐ **processing**	명사 처리 (과정)
☐ **principle**	명사 원리
☐ **conventional**	형용사 일반적인, 전통적인
☐ **dim**	형용사 희미한
☐ **retina**	명사 망막
☐ **compensate for**	~을 보완하다[보상하다]
☐ **auditory**	형용사 청각의

04 2019년 9월 34번 (정답률 60%)

정답 ①

[지문 끊어 읽기] 경사면의 활용

(1) If you want to use the inclined plane /
만약 당신이 경사면을 사용하기를 원한다면 /
to help you move an object / (and who wouldn't?), /
당신이 물건을 움직이는 데 도움이 되도록 / (그리고 누가 안 그러겠는가?) /
then you have to move the object / over a longer distance /
그러면 당신은 물건을 옮겨야 한다 / 더 긴 거리로 /
to get to the desired height /
바라던 높이에 도달하기 위해서 /
than if you had started from directly below / and moved upward.
병렬① 병렬②
당신이 바로 밑에서부터 시작했을 때보다 / 그리고 위로 움직였을 때보다

(2) This is probably already clear to you /
이것은 아마도 당신에게는 이미 명백할 것이다 /
from a lifetime of stair climbing.
평생 계단을 올랐던 것으로 미루어 볼 때

힌트 'clear from'은 '~로 미루어 볼 때 명백하다'는 의미로, 문장 (2)는 살면서 계단을 올라본 경험으로 미루어 볼 때, 예를 들어, 아파트 한 층을 수직으로 올라가는 거리보다 계단을 타고 비스듬히 올라가는 거리가 더 멀다는 것을 우리 모두가 분명히 알 것이라는 의미임.

(3) Consider all the stairs / you climb /
모든 계단을 곰곰이 생각해 보아라 / 당신이 오르는 /
compared to the actual height / you reach /
실제 높이와 비교하여 / 당신이 도달하는 /
from where you started.
당신이 출발한 지점에서

(4) This height is always less / than the distance /
그 높이는 항상 짧다 / 거리보다 /
you climbed in stairs. 정답 단서
당신이 계단으로 올라온

(5) In other words, / more distance in stairs /
다시 말해서 / 계단에서의 더 먼 거리는 /
is traded for less force / to reach the intended height.
더 적은 힘으로 교환된다 / 목표한 높이에 도달하기 위해서

(6) Now, / if we were to pass on the stairs altogether /
이제 / 만약 우리가 계단을 완전히 지나치려고 한다면 /
and simply climb straight up to your destination /
그리고 그냥 당신의 목적지까지 곧장 올라가려고 한다면 /
(from directly below it), / it would be a shorter climb for sure, /
(그것의 바로 밑에서부터) / 그것은 틀림없이 더 짧은 오름이 될 것이다 /
but the needed force to do so / would be greater. 정답 단서
하지만 그렇게 하는 데 필요한 힘은 / 더 클 것이다

(7) Therefore, / we have stairs in our homes / rather than ladders.
그래서 / 우리는 우리의 집에 계단을 갖고 있는 것이다 / 사다리가 아니라

[전문 해석]

(1) 만약 당신이 물건을 움직이는 데 도움이 되도록 경사면을 사용하기를 원한다면 (그리고 누가 안 그러겠는가?), 당신은 바라던 높이에 도달하기 위해서 바로 밑에서부터 시작하여 위로 (수직으로) 움직였을 때보다 물건을 더 긴 거리로 옮겨야 한다. (2) 이것은 아마도 평생 계단을 올랐던 것으로 미루어 볼 때 (살면서 계단을 올라본 경험이 있는) 당신에게는 이미 명백할 것이다. (3) 당신이 출발한 지점에서 (당신이) 도달하는 실제 높이와 비교하여, 당신이 오르는 모든 계단을 곰곰이 생각해 보아라(떠올려 보아라). (4) 그 (실제) 높이는 당신이 계단으로 올라온 거리보다 항상 짧다. (5) 다시 말해서, 목표한 높이에 도달하기 위해서 계단에서의(계단을 이용했을 때의) 더 먼 거리는 더 적은 힘으로 교환된다. (6) 이제 만약 우리가 계단을 완전히 지나치려고 그냥 (당신의) 목적지까지 (그것의 바로 밑에서부터) 곧장 올라가려고 한다면, 그것은 틀림없이 더 짧은 오름이 되겠지만(실제 이동 거리는 더 짧겠지만) 그렇게 하는 데 필요한 힘은 더 클 것이다. (7) 그래서 우리는 우리의 집에 사다리가 아니라 계단을 갖고 있는 것이다.

[정답 확인]

다음 빈칸에 들어갈 말로 가장 적절한 것은?

✔ more distance in stairs is traded for less force
계단에서의(계단을 이용했을 때의) 더 먼 거리는 더 적은 힘으로 교환된다
② a ladder should be positioned at a steep angle
사다리는 가파른 각도로 두어야 한다
③ the distance needs to be measured precisely
거리는 정확하게 측정되어야 할 필요가 있다

④ an object's weight has to be reduced
물체의 무게를 줄여야 한다
⑤ slopes are often preferred to stairs
경사지는 보통 계단보다 선호된다

★중요 문장 (1)에서 'inclined plane(경사면)'이라는 언급이 있지만, 지문은 경사지와 계단을 비교하는 것이 아니라 사다리와 계단을 비교하고 있음.

[문제 풀이]

지문은 우리가 계단과 같은 경사면을 통해 목적지까지 올라가는 것과 사다리처럼 목적지 바로 밑에서 수직으로 올라가는 것을 비교하고 있다. 우리가 사다리를 이용해서 올라가면, 더 짧은 거리를 이동하지만 올라가는 데에 힘은 더 든다. 그와 반대로 우리가 계단을 통해서 올라가게 되면, 목적지의 높이보다 더 먼 거리를 이동해야 하지만 올라가는 데에 힘은 더 적게 들 것이다. 따라서 빈칸에 들어갈 정답은 ①이다.

[중요 어휘]

□ **inclined plane**	경사면
□ **desired**	형용사 바라던, 희망했던
□ **lifetime**	명사 평생, 일생, 생애
□ **trade for**	~으로[와] 교환하다
□ **intended**	형용사 목표한, 의도된
□ **steep**	형용사 가파른
□ **precisely**	부사 정확하게, 신중하게
□ **slope**	명사 경사지, 경사면

핵심 음악과 기억 간의 관계에 대해 다루고 있음. 기억이 형성되고 회복되는 과정에 음악이 어떤 방식으로 영향을 주는지에 주목해야 함.

05 2020년 11월 32번 (정답률 60%) 정답 ③

[지문 끊어 읽기] 음악과 기억의 상호 작용

(1) One of the primary ways /
단수S 선행사
주요한 방법들 중 하나는 /
by which music is able to take on significance /
전치사+관계대명사
음악이 중요성을 띨 수 있는 /
in our inner world / is by the way / it interacts with memory.
단수V
우리의 내면 세계에서 / 방식에 의해서이다 / 그것이 기억과 상호 작용하는

(2) Memories / associated with important emotions /
주격 관계대명사절(which are 생략)
기억들은 / 중요한 감정과 연관된 /
tend to be more deeply embedded / in our memory /
더욱 깊이 새겨져 있는 경향이 있다 / 우리의 기억 속에
than other events.
다른 사건들보다

(3) Emotional memories / are more likely to be vividly remembered /
감정적인 기억들은 / 생생히 기억될 가능성이 더 크다 /
and are more likely to be recalled / with the passing of time /
그리고 기억될 가능성이 더 크다 / 시간이 지나도 /
than neutral memories.
중립적인 기억들보다

(4) Since music can be extremely emotionally evocative, /
음악이 몹시 감정을 불러일으킬 수 있기 때문에 /
key life events / can be emotionally heightened /
중요한 삶의 사건들은 / 감정적으로 고조될 수 있다 /
by the presence of music, / ensuring /
음악의 존재에 의해 / 확실하게 해준다 /
that memories of the event become deeply encoded. 정답 단서
그 사건에 대한 기억들이 깊이 암호화되는 것을

(5) Retrieval of those memories / is then enhanced /
그러한 기억들의 회복은 / 그러고 나서 강화된다 /
by contextual effects, /
선행사
맥락 효과에 의해 /
계속적 용법(=and in the contextual effects)
in which a recreation of a similar context to that /
S' 선행사(=the context)
그런데 여기에서 그것과 비슷한 맥락의 재창조가 /
in which the memories were encoded /
그 기억들이 암호화되었던 /

힌트 문장 (5)는 크게 보면 주절과 '전치사+목적격 관계대명사절'이 계속적 용법으로 이루어진 문장임. 이 '전치사+목적격 관계대명사'의 주어(a recreation)와 동사(can facilitate) 사이에 또 다른 '전치사+목적격 관계대명사절'이 삽입된 형태임.

can facilitate their retrieval. 정답 단서
V'
그것들의 회복을 촉진시킬 수 있다

(6) Thus, / re-hearing the same music / associated with the event /
따라서 / 같은 음악을 다시 듣는 것이 / 그 사건과 연관된 /
can activate intensely / vivid memories of the event.
강렬하게 활성화할 수 있다 / 그 사건에 대한 생생한 기억들을

[전문 해석]

(1)음악이 우리의 내면 세계에서 중요성을 띨 수 있는 주요한 방법들 중 하나는 그것이 기억과 상호 작용하는 방식에 의해서이다. (2)중요한 감정과 연관된 기억들은 다른 사건들보다 우리의 기억 속에 더욱 깊이 새겨져 있는 경향이 있다. (3)감정적인 기억들은 생생히 기억될 가능성이 더 크고, 시간이 지나도 중립적인 기억들보다 기억될 가능성이 더 크다. (4)음악이 몹시 감정을 불러일으킬 수 있기 때문에, 중요한 삶의 사건들은 음악의 존재에 의해 감정적으로 고조될 수 있고, (이는) 그 사건에 대한 기억들이 깊이 암호화되는 것을 확실하게 해준다(확실히 깊이 암호화되게 해준다). (5)그러고 나서 그러한 기억들의 회복은 맥락 효과에 의해 강화되는데, 여기(그 맥락 효과)에서 그 기억들이 암호화되었던 그것(맥락)과 비슷한 맥락의 재창조가 그것(기억)들의 회복을 촉진시킬 수 있다. (6)따라서 그 사건과 연관된 같은 음악을 다시 듣는 것이 그 사건에 대한 생생한 기억들을 강렬하게 활성화할 수 있다.

[정답 확인]

다음 빈칸에 들어갈 말로 가장 적절한 것은?

① analyzing memories of the event thoroughly
그 사건의 기억을 철저하게 분석하는 것
② increasing storage space for recalling the event
그 사건을 기억해 내기 위한 저장 공간을 늘리는 것
✔③ re-hearing the same music associated with the event
그 사건과 연관된 같은 음악을 다시 듣는 것
④ reconstructing the event in the absence of background music
배경 음악의 부재 속에서 그 사건을 재구성하는 것
⑤ enhancing musical competence to deliver emotional messages
감정적인 메시지를 전달하기 위해 음악적 역량을 강화하는 것

[문제 풀이]

음악과 기억의 상호 작용에 대한 글이다. 문장 (2)~(4)에 따르면, 감정적인 기억은 중립적인 기억보다 더 오래 생생히 기억되는 경향이 있는데, 음악은 감정을 불러일으키므로 음악이 더해졌을 때 그 사건은 우리의 기억 속에 더욱 깊이 암호화된다. 문장 (5)는 기억의 회복을 '맥락 효과'로 설명하는데, 이는 기억들이 암호화되었던 맥락과 비슷한 맥락이 주어지면 해당 기억이 회복되는 현상을 말한다. 따라서, 그 사건과 연관된 같은 음악을 다시 들으면 사건에 대한 기억이 활성화될 것임을 추론할 수 있으므로, 정답은 ③이다.

[중요 어휘]

□ **primary**	형용사 주요한, 최초의, 근본적인
□ **take on**	(특성·특질 등을) 띠다
□ **significance**	명사 중요성, 의의
□ **embed**	동사 (마음·기억 등에) 새기다, 박아 넣다
□ **vividly**	부사 생생히, 선명하게
□ **recall**	동사 기억해 내다, 상기하다
□ **neutral**	형용사 중립적인, 감정을 자제하는
□ **heighten**	동사 고조시키다, 증가시키다
□ **presence**	명사 존재, 출석
□ **ensure**	동사 확실하게 하다, 보증하다
□ **encode**	동사 암호화하다, 부호화하다
□ **retrieval**	명사 회복, 복구
□ **context**	명사 맥락, 전후 관계
□ **facilitate**	동사 촉진시키다, 용이하게 하다
□ **reconstruct**	동사 재구성하다, 재건하다
□ **absence**	명사 부재, 결석, 없음
□ **competence**	명사 역량, 적성

문제편 p.151

06 2022년 3월 32번 (정답률 60%) 정답 ④

[지문 끊어 읽기] 서로 강력하게 얽혀 있는 뇌의 정신적, 인지적 활동

(1) When you're driving a car, /
자동차를 운전할 때 /
your memory of how to operate the vehicle /
S①
차량을 조작하는 방법에 관한 당신의 기억은 /
comes from one set of brain cells;
V①
한 세트의 뇌세포에서 나온다

힌트 세미콜론(;)으로 연결된 문장 (1)~(4)의 4개의 문장들은 모두 유사한 문장 구조를 가짐. 이를 통해 우리가 어떤 행동을 할 때의 기억, 생각, 느낌이 각각 다른 뇌세포 집단으로부터 온다는 것을 말하고 있음.

(2) the memory of how to navigate the streets /
S②
도로를 주행하는 방법에 관한 기억은 /
전치사
to get to your destination / springs from another set of neurons;
부사적 용법(목적) V②
목적지에 도착하기 위해 / 또 다른 세트의 신경 세포로부터 발생한다

(3) the memory of driving rules and following street signs /
S③
운전 규칙과 도로 표지를 따르는 것에 관한 기억은 /
originates from another family of brain cells;
V③
또 다른 뇌세포 집단으로부터 생긴다

(4) and the thoughts and feelings /
그리고 생각과 느낌은 / S④, 선행사
you have about the driving experience itself, /
목적격 관계대명사절
여러분이 운전 경험 자체에 대해 가지고 있는 /
including any close calls with other cars, /
다른 자동차와의 아슬아슬한 상황을 포함하여 /
come from yet another group of cells.
V④
또 다른 세포 집단에서 나온다

✶중요 여기서 말하는 정신적 활동(mental plays)은 문장 (1)~(4)의 운전할 때의 기억, 생각, 느낌을 말하고, 인지적 신경 활성화(cognitive neural firings)는 그에 따라 여러 뇌세포 집단이 각기 활성화되는 것을 말함.

(5) You do not have conscious awareness /
여러분은 의식적인 인지를 하고 있지는 않다 /
of all these separate mental plays and cognitive neural firings, /
이 모든 별개의 정신적 활동과 인지적 신경 활성화에 관한 /
yet they somehow work together in beautiful harmony /
=brain cells
하지만 그것들은 아름다운 조화를 이루며 어떻게든 함께 작동한다 /
to synthesize your overall experience. 정답 단서 별개의 정신적 활동과 인지적 신경 활성화를 의식적으로 인지하고 있지 않아도 그것들은 조화를 이루며 함께 작동함.
부사적 용법(목적)
여러분의 전반적인 경험을 종합하기 위해

(6) In fact, / we don't even know the real difference /
사실 / 우리는 진정한 차이를 알지도 못한다 /
between how we remember and how we think.
병렬① 병렬②
우리가 기억하는 방식과 우리가 생각하는 방식 사이의

우리가 기억하는 방식과 우리가 생각하는 방식은 강력하게 뒤얽혀 있음. 문장 (5)에서 조화를 이루며 함께 작동한다는 말과 일맥상통함.

(7) But, / we do know / they are strongly intertwined. 정답 단서
know 강조
하지만 / 우리는 정말로 알고 있다 / 그것들이 강력하게 뒤얽혀 있다는 것을

(8) That is why / truly improving memory /
그것이 바로 ~한 이유이다 / 진정으로 기억력을 향상시키는 것이 /
can never simply be about using memory tricks, /
결코 단순히 기억력 기술을 사용하는 것일 수 없는 /
although they can be helpful /
=memory tricks
그것들이 도움이 될 수 있다 하더라도 /
in strengthening certain components of memory.
기억력의 특정 구성 요소를 강화하는 데

✶중요 문장 (7)에서 말하듯이 기억과 생각의 방식은 뒤얽혀 있으나 기억력 기술은 기억력 강화의 일부에만 기여함. 따라서 이어지는 문장 (9)에서는 인지적 수준에서의 기억력 강화를 위한 더 종합적인 방법을 제시할 것을 유추할 수 있음.

(9) Here's the bottom line:
요점은 이것이다

(10) To improve and preserve memory at the cognitive level, /
병렬① 병렬②(to V의 to 생략)
인지적 수준에서 기억력을 개선하고 보존하기 위해서는 /
you have to work on all functions of your brain. 주제문 인지적 수준에서 기억력을 향상하려면 뇌의 모든 기능을 사용해야 함.
여러분은 뇌의 모든 기능을 작동시켜야 한다.

[전문 해석]

(1)자동차를 운전할 때, 차량을 조작하는 방법에 관한 기억은 한 세트의 뇌세포에서 나오고, (2)목적지에 도착하기 위해 도로를 주행하는 방법에 관한 기억은 또 다른 세트의 신경 세포로부터 발생하며, (3)운전 규칙과 도로 표지를 따르는 것에 관한 기억은 또 다른 뇌세포 집단으로부터 생긴다. (4)그리고 다른 자동차와의 아슬아슬한 상황을 포함하여 여러분이 운전 경험 자체에 대해 가지고 있는 생각과 느낌은 또 다른 세포 집단에서 나온다. (5)여러분은 이 모든 별개의 정신적 활동과 인지적 신경 활성화에 관한 의식적인 인지를 하고 있지는 않지만, 그것(뇌세포)들은 여러분의 전반적인 경험을 종합하기 위해 아름다운 조화를 이루며 어떻게든 함께 작동한다. (6)사실, 우리가 기억하는 방식과 우리가 생각하는 방식 사이의 진정한 차이를 우리는 알지도 못한다. (7)하지만, 우리는 정말로 그것들이 강력하게 뒤얽혀 있다는 것을 알고 있다. (8)그것이 바로 기억력 기술이 기억력의 특정 구성 요소를 강화하는 데 도움이 될 수 있다 하더라도, 진정으로 기억력을 향상시키는 것이 결코 단순히 그 기술을 사용하는 것일 수 없는 이유이다. (9)요점은 이것이다. (10)인지적 수준에서 기억력을 개선하고 보존하기 위해서는 뇌의 모든 기능을 작동시켜야 한다.

[정답 확인]

다음 빈칸에 들어갈 말로 가장 적절한 것은?

① keep your body and mind healthy
몸과 마음을 건강하게 유지해야
② calm your mind in stressful times
스트레스를 받을 때 마음을 가라앉혀야
③ concentrate on one thing at a time
한 번에 한 가지 일에 집중해야
④ work on all functions of your brain
뇌의 모든 기능을 작동시켜야
⑤ share what you learn with other people
배우는 것을 다른 사람과 공유해야

[문제 풀이]

운전이라는 하나의 행위를 하기 위해서도 의식적인 인지를 하지 않는 수준에서 운전과 관련된 여러 가지 기억을 떠올리고 생각해야만 한다. 이러한 모든 별개의 정신적, 인지적 활동은 뇌의 여러 세포 집단에서 벌어짐에도 불구하고 조화를 이루며 함께 작동한다고 필자는 이야기하고 있다. 즉, 이러한 다양한 정신적, 인지적 활동은 서로 강력하게 뒤엉켜 있기 때문에 진정으로 기억력을 개선하고 싶다면 관련된 정신적, 인지적 활동 모두를 강화해야 한다고 볼 수 있다. 따라서 빈칸에는 이와 가장 유사한 내용을 담은 ④가 적절하다.

[중요 어휘]

□ navigate	동사 주행하다, 항해하다, 길을 찾다
□ destination	명사 목적지, 도착지
□ spring	동사 (갑자기) 발생하다, 일어나다
□ neuron	명사 신경 세포
□ originate from	~으로부터 생기다
□ close call	아슬아슬한 상황, 위기일발
□ yet another	또 다른, 잇따라
□ conscious	형용사 의식적인
□ cognitive	형용사 인지의
□ neural	형용사 신경(계)의
□ synthesize	동사 종합하다, 합성하다
□ intertwine	동사 뒤얽다, 엮다
□ bottom line	명사 요점, 핵심
□ work on	~을 작동시키다, ~에 노력을 들이다

07 2022년 9월 34번 (정답률 60%) 정답 ③

[지문 끊어 읽기] 품성과 관련하여 말하기

(1) Psychologist Christopher Bryan finds /
심리학자인 Christopher Bryan은 알았다 /
that when we shift our emphasis / from behavior to character, /
우리가 중점을 옮길 때 / 행동에서 품성으로 /
people evaluate choices differently. 주제문 행동보다 품성에 중점을 둘 때 사람들은 선택을 다르게 평가함.
사람들은 선택을 다르게 평가한다는 것을

(2) His team was able to cut cheating / in half: /
그의 팀은 속이는 행위를 줄일 수 있었다 / 반으로 /
instead of "Please don't cheat," / they changed the appeal /
"속이지 마세요" 대신에 / 그들은 호소를 전환했다 /
to "Please don't be a cheater". 정답 단서 속이는 '행위'를 금지하는 것보다 속이는 '사람'이 되지 말라며 품성을 논하는 것이 더욱 효과적이었음.
"속이는 사람이 되지 마세요"로

(3) When you're urged / not to cheat, / you can do it /
당신이 강요받을 때 / 속이지 말라고 / 당신은 그것을 할 수 있다 / =cheating
and still see an ethical person / in the mirror.
그리고 여전히 도덕적인 사람을 볼 수 있다 / 거울 속에서

(4) But when you're told / not to be a cheater, /
하지만 당신이 들을 때는 / 속이는 사람이 되지 말라고 /
the act casts a shadow; / immorality is tied to your identity, /
그 행동이 그림자를 드리운다 / 비도덕성이 당신의 정체성과 결부된다 /
[making the behavior much less attractive]. 정답 단서 속이는 사람이 되지 말라는 말을 들으면 품성, 즉 도덕적 자질을 자신의 정체성과 연결 짓게 되어 속이는 행위를 부정적으로 보게 됨.
[ ]: 분사구문 비교급 강조
그래서 그 행동을 훨씬 덜 매력적으로 만든다

(5) Cheating is an isolated action / that gets evaluated /
속이는 것은 독립적인 행위이다 / 평가되는 /
with the logic of consequence: / Can I get away with it?
결과의 논리에 따라 / 내가 그것을 들키지 않을 수 있을까

(6) Being a cheater / evokes a sense of self, /
동명사S V
속이는 사람이 되는 것은 / 자의식을 환기한다 /
[triggering the logic of appropriateness]: / [ ]: 분사구문
그러면서 적절함에 대한 논리를 촉발한다 /
What kind of person am I, / and who do I want to be?
나는 어떤 종류의 사람인가 / 그리고 나는 누가 되고 싶은가

(7) In light of this evidence, / Bryan suggests /
이러한 증거에 비추어 볼 때 / Bryan은 제안한다 /
that we should embrace nouns / more thoughtfully.
우리가 명사를 받아들여야 한다고 / 더욱 사려 깊게

(8) "Don't Drink and Drive" / could be rephrased as: /
"음주 운전 하지 마세요"는 / ~로 바꿔 말할 수 있다 /
"Don't Be a Drunk Driver."
"음주 운전자가 되지 마세요"

(9) The same thinking can be applied / to originality.
같은 논리가 적용될 수 있다 / 독창성에도

(10) When a child draws a picture, /
아이가 그림을 그릴 때 /
instead of calling the artwork creative, /
5형식V O O·C(형용사)
작품이 창의적이라고 말하는 대신에 /
we can say "You are creative."
우리는 "너는 창의적이야"라고 말할 수 있다

[전문 해석]

(1)심리학자인 Christopher Bryan은 우리가 중점을 행동에서 품성으로 옮길 때, 사람들은 선택을 다르게 평가한다는 것을 알았다. (2)그의 팀은 속이는 행위를 반으로 줄일 수 있었다. "속이지 마세요" 대신에, 그들은 "속이는 사람이 되지 마세요"로 호소를 전환했다. (3)당신이 속이지 말라고 강요받을 때, 당신은 속이고 나서도 여전히 거울 속에서 도덕적인 사람을 마주할 수 있다. (4)하지만 당신이 속이는 사람이 되지 말라고 들을 때는 그 행동이 그림자를 드리운다. 비도덕성이 당신의 정체성과 결부되어 그 행동을 훨씬 덜 매력적으로 만든다. (5)속이는 것은 결과의 논리에 따라 평가되는 독립적인 행위이다. 내가 속인 것을 들키지 않을 수 있을까? (6)속이는 사람이 되는 것은 자의식을 환기하며 적절함에 대한 논리를 촉발한다. 나는 어떤 종류의 사람인가, 그리고 나는 누가 되고 싶은가? (7)이러한 증거에 비추어 볼 때, Bryan은 우리가 명사를 더욱 사려 깊게 받아들여야 한다고 제안한다. (8)"음주 운전 하지 마세요"는 "음주 운전자가 되지 마세요"로 바꿔 말할 수 있다. (9)같은 논리가 독창성에도 적용될 수 있다. (10)아이가 그림을 그릴 때, 작품이 창의적이라고 말하는 대신에 우리는 "너는 창의적이야"라고 말할 수 있다.

[정답 확인]

다음 빈칸에 들어갈 말로 가장 적절한 것은?

① ignore what experts say
전문가들이 말한 것을 무시할
② keep a close eye on the situation
상황을 주시할
✔③ shift our emphasis from behavior to character
중점을 행동에서 품성으로 옮길
④ focus on appealing to emotion rather than reason
이성보다는 감정에 호소하는 것에 집중할
⑤ place more importance on the individual instead of the group
집단보다 개인을 더 중요시할

[문제 풀이]

본문에 따르면, "속이지 마세요"처럼 행동을 규제하는 문구보다 "속이는 사람이 되지 마세요"처럼 품성과 연관된 문구가 사람들의 행동을 변화시키는 데 더욱 효과적이었다. 이후에 제시된 예시에서도 행위자의 품성과 관련한 명령이 행위 자체를 금지하는 명령보다 더욱 도움이 되었음을 알 수 있다. 따라서 빈칸에는 행동이 아닌 품성을 강조한다는 내용의 ③이 적절하다.

[중요 어휘]

□ **emphasis**	명사 중점, 강조
□ **character**	명사 품성, 인격
□ **appeal**	명사 호소 / 동사 호소하다
□ **urge**	동사 강요하다, 강력히 권고하다 / 명사 욕구, 충동
□ **cast**	동사 (그림자를) 드리우다, 던지다
□ **immorality**	명사 비도덕성
□ **get away with**	(나쁜 것을 하고) 들키지 않다, 그냥 넘어가다
□ **evoke**	동사 (감정·기억·이미지 등을) 환기하다, 불러일으키다
□ **trigger**	동사 촉발하다 / 명사 방아쇠
□ **appropriateness**	명사 적절함, 타당성
□ **in light of**	~에 비추어 볼 때, ~을 고려하면
□ **embrace**	동사 받아들이다, 포옹하다
□ **rephrase**	동사 바꿔 말하다
□ **originality**	명사 독창성, 창의성

핵심 첫 번째 문장부터 '가용성 휴리스틱(availability heuristic)'과 같이 어려운 어휘가 나오고 문장의 길이도 다소 길지만, 보통 어렵고 복잡한 내용이 나오면, 그 이후에 좀 더 풀어서 설명해 주거나 이해를 돕기 위한 예시를 들어주는 경우가 많음. 이 글에서도 직무 수행 평가와 관련한 예시를 들고 있음.

08

2020년 6월 34번 (정답률 55%) 정답 ④

[지문 끊어 읽기] 가용성 휴리스틱

(1) The availability heuristic refers to a common mistake /
가용성 휴리스틱은 일반적인 오류를 가리킨다 / 선행사
that our brains make / by assuming that /
목적격 관계대명사 명사절 접속사
우리의 뇌가 저지르는 / ~라고 가정함으로써 /
the instances or examples / that come to mind easily /
S'(선행사) 주격 관계대명사
사례들이나 예시들이 / 쉽게 생각나는 /
are also the most important or prevalent.
V'
또한 가장 중요하거나 널리 퍼져 있다

(2) It shows / that we make our decisions /
그것은 보여준다 / 우리가 결정한다는 것을 /
based on the recency of events. 정답 단서
사건의 최신성에 기반하여

(3) We often misjudge / the frequency and magnitude of the events /
우리는 종종 잘못 판단한다 / 사건의 빈도와 규모를 /
that have happened recently /
최근에 발생한 /
because of the limitations of our memories. 정답 단서
우리 기억의 한계 때문에

(4) According to Harvard professor, Max Bazerman, /
하버드 대학 교수 Max Bazerman에 따르면 /
managers / conducting performance appraisals /
관리자들은 / 직무 수행 평가를 수행하는 /

often fall victim / to the availability heuristic.
종종 희생양이 된다 / 가용성 휴리스틱의

(5) The recency of events highly influences / 정답단서
사건의 최신성은 크게 영향을 미친다 /
a supervisor's opinion / during performance appraisals.
관리자의 의견에 / 직무 수행 평가 동안

(6) Managers give more weight / to performance /
관리자들은 더 비중을 둔다 / 직무 수행에 /
during the three months / prior to the evaluation /
3개월 동안의 / 평가 직전의 /
than to the previous nine months of the evaluation period /
평가 기간 전 9개월보다 /
because the recent instances dominate their memories.
최근의 사례들이 그들의 기억을 지배하기 때문에

(7) The availability heuristic is influenced /
가용성 휴리스틱은 영향을 받는다 /
by the ease of recall or retrievability of information / of some event. 정답단서
병렬① 병렬②
회상의 용이함 또는 정보의 회복력에 의해 / 어떤 사건에 대한

(8) Ease of recall suggests that /
S V 명사절 접속사
회상의 용이함은 ~라는 것을 시사한다 /
if something is more easily recalled in your memory, /
만약 어떤 것이 당신의 기억 속에서 더 쉽게 회상된다면 /
you think / that it will occur with a high probability.
S' V' 명사절 접속사
당신은 생각한다 / 그것이 높은 확률로 일어날 것이라고

힌트 첫 번째 that은 문장의 동사 suggests의 목적어가 되는 명사절을 이끄는 접속사임. 이 명사절의 주어와 동사는 각각 you와 think로, 중간에 if절이 들어가 있는 구조임. 두 번째 that은 think의 목적어가 되는 명사절을 이끄는 접속사임.

[중요 구문]

힌트 첫 번째와 세 번째 that은 관계대명사이지만, 두 번째로 나온 that은 동명사 assuming의 목적어인 명사절을 이끄는 접속사임. 관계사절 안에 각각 비어 있는 선행사의 위치도 확인할 것.

(1) The availability heuristic refers to a common mistake [that our brains make ∨ by assuming [that the instances or examples (that ∨ come to mind easily) are ~]].
선행사 / 목적격 관계대명사 / 명사절 접속사 / 선행사 / 주격 관계대명사

(6) Managers give more weight to performance [during the three months prior to the evaluation] than to the previous nine months of the evaluation period ~.
비교급 / 비교대상① / [ ]: 전치사구(performance 수식) / 비교대상②

힌트 'give weight to 명사'라는 숙어 표현에 'more ~ than ~' 비교 구문이 합쳐진 문장으로, 'to+명사'에 해당하는 부분이 각각 비교대상으로서 than을 중심으로 병렬로 연결되어 있음.

[전문 해석]

(1)가용성 휴리스틱은 우리의 뇌가 (머릿속에) 쉽게 생각나는 사례들이나 예시들이 또한 가장 중요하거나 널리 퍼져 있다고 가정함으로써 저지르는 일반적인 오류를 가리킨다. (2)그것은 우리가 사건의 최신성에 기반하여 결정한다는 것을 보여준다. (3)우리는 (우리) 기억의 한계 때문에 최근에 발생한 사건의 빈도와 규모를 종종 잘못 판단한다. (4)하버드 대학 교수 Max Bazerman에 따르면, 직무 수행 평가를 수행하는 관리자들은 종종 가용성 휴리스틱의 희생양이 된다. (5)사건의 최신성은 직무 수행 평가 (기간) 동안 관리자의 의견에 크게 영향을 미친다. (6)최근의 사례들이 관리자들의 기억을 지배하기 때문에 그들은 평가 기간 전 9개월보다 평가 직전 3개월 동안의 직무 수행에 더 비중을 둔다. (7)가용성 휴리스틱은 어떤 사건에 대한 회상의 용이함 또는 정보의 회복력에 의해 영향을 받는다. (8)회상의 용이함은 만약 어떤 것이 당신의 기억 속에서 더 쉽게 회상된다면, 당신은 그것이 높은 확률로 일어날 것이라고 생각한다는 것을 시사한다.

-availability heuristic(가용성 휴리스틱): 어떤 판단을 내릴 때, 자신이 즉각적으로 떠올릴 수 있는 사건이나 상황만을 바탕으로 판단하는 것

[정답 확인]

다음 빈칸에 들어갈 말로 가장 적절한 것은?

① there is little reliable data about workers
직원들에 대해 신뢰할 만한 자료가 거의 없기
② the frequent contacts help the relationship
잦은 연락이 관계를 돕기
③ they want to evaluate employees objectively
그들은 직원들을 객관적으로 평가하기를 원하기
✔ the recent instances dominate their memories
최근의 사례들이 그들의 기억을 지배하기
⑤ distorted data have no impact on the evaluation
왜곡된 자료는 평가에 영향을 끼치지 않기

[문제 풀이]

본문은 가용성 휴리스틱, 즉 우리가 결정을 내릴 때 쉽게 생각나는 것들이 중요한 것이라고 잘못 가정함으로써 생기는 오류에 대해 다루고 있다. 문장 (2)와 (3), 그리고 (7)에서 최근에 발생한 사건일수록 회상이 용이하고 정보의 회복력이 높으므로, 우리는 최근에 발생한 사건에 기반하여 결정을 내리는 경향이 있음을 파악할 수 있다. 직무 수행 평가를 수행하는 관리자들에 대한 사례에서, 우리가 과거에 발생한 사건보다 최근에 발생한 사건에 더 비중을 두는 이유가 빈칸에 들어가야 하는데, 이는 문장 (8)에서 알 수 있듯이 최근에 발생한 사건이 기억 속에서 더 쉽게 회상되기 때문이다. 따라서 이와 같은 맥락을 얘기하고 있는 ④가 빈칸에 들어가는 것이 적절하다.

[중요 어휘]

☐ availability	명사 가용성, 유용성
☐ heuristic	명사 휴리스틱, (자기) 발견적 방법
☐ prevalent	형용사 널리 퍼져 있는, 일반적인
☐ recency	명사 최신성, 새로움
☐ frequency	명사 빈도, 주파수
☐ magnitude	명사 규모, 중요도
☐ appraisal	명사 평가, 감정
☐ fall victim to	~의 희생양이 되다, ~에 희생되다
☐ supervisor	명사 관리자, 감독관
☐ give weight to	~에 비중을 두다, ~을 중요시하다
☐ dominate	동사 지배하다, 가장 두드러지다
☐ ease	명사 용이함, 쉬움
☐ retrievability	명사 회복력, 복구 가능성
☐ probability	명사 확률, 가능성
☐ distorted	형용사 왜곡된, 비뚤어진

09 2021년 11월 33번 (정답률 55%) 정답 ③

[지문 끊어 읽기] 건조함의 원인이 되는 내륙 지역의 산

(1) When it comes to climates / in the interior areas of continents, /
~와 관련하여
기후와 관련하여 / 대륙의 내륙 지역의 /
mountains play a huge role / in stopping the flow of moisture.
산은 큰 역할을 한다 / 수분의 흐름을 막는 데

(2) A great example of this can be seen /
이것의 좋은 예가 보일 수 있다 /
along the West Coast of the United States.
미국의 서해안을 따라

(3) Air / moving from the Pacific Ocean toward the land /
S
공기는 / 태평양에서 육지로 이동하는 /
usually has a great deal of moisture in it.
V
보통 많은 수분을 그 안에 가지고 있다

(4) When this humid air moves / across the land, /
이 습한 공기가 이동할 때 / 육지를 가로질러 /
it encounters the Coast Range Mountains.
그것은 코스트산맥 산들과 마주친다

(5) As the air moves / up and over the mountains, /
공기가 이동하면서 / 상승하여 산 위로 /
it begins to cool, / which causes precipitation / 정답단서
선행사 주격 관계대명사(계속적 용법)
그것이 식기 시작한다 / 그리고 이는 강수를 발생시킨다 /
on the windward side of the mountains.
산의 풍상측에

습한 공기가 산을 따라 올라가며 강수를 발생시킴.

(6) Once the air moves down / the opposite side of the mountains /
공기가 ~으로 내려갈 때쯤이면 / 산의 반대편 /
(called the leeward side) / it has lost a great deal of moisture.
현재완료(결과)
(풍하측이라고 불리는) / 그것은 많은 수분을 잃어버린다

정답단서 그 공기가 산의 반대편으로 내려가면 수분이 없어져 건조한 공기만 남게 됨.

(7) The air continues to move / and then hits /
V① V②
공기는 계속 움직인다 / 그리고 그러고 나서 부딪친다 /
the even higher Sierra Nevada mountain range.
비교급 강조
훨씬 더 높은 시에라네바다산맥과

(8) This second uplift /
이 두 번째 상승은 /
causes most of the remaining moisture to fall out of the air, /
5형식V O O.C
남아 있는 수분 대부분을 공기로부터 빠져나오게 한다 /
so [by the time it reaches the leeward side of the Sierras], /
부사절 접속사(~할 때쯤이면, ~할 때까지) [ ]: 시간의 부사절
그래서 그것이 시에라산맥의 풍하측에 도달할 때쯤이면 /
the air is extremely dry. 정답 단서 첫 번째에 이미 수분을 많이 잃은 공기가 또 산맥과 부딪치며 더 건조해짐.
공기는 극도로 건조하다

(9) The result is / that much of the state of Nevada is a desert.
명사절 접속사
그 결과는 / 네바다주 대부분이 사막이라는 것이다

[전문 해석]

(1)대륙의 내륙 지역의 기후와 관련하여 산은 수분의 흐름을 막는 데 큰 역할을 한다. (2)이것의 좋은 예를 미국의 서해안을 따라 볼 수 있다. (3)태평양에서 육지로 이동하는 공기는 보통 많은 수분을 그 안에 가지고 있다. (4)이 습한 공기가 육지를 가로질러 이동할 때, 그것은 코스트산맥 산들과 마주친다. (5)공기가 상승하여 산 위로 이동하면서 그것이 식기 시작하고, 이는 산의 풍상측(風上側)에 강수를 발생시킨다. (6)공기가 산의 반대편, 즉 풍하측(風下側)이라고 불리는 곳으로 내려갈 때쯤이면 그것은 많은 수분을 잃어버린다. (7)공기는 계속 움직이며 그러고 나서 훨씬 더 높은 시에라네바다산맥과 부딪친다. (8)이 두 번째 상승은 남아 있는 수분 대부분을 공기로부터 빠져나오게 하며 그래서 그것이 시에라산맥의 풍하측에 도달할 때쯤이면 공기는 극도로 건조하다. (9)그 결과는 네바다주 대부분이 사막이라는 것이다.

[정답 확인]

다음 빈칸에 들어갈 말로 가장 적절한 것은?

① increase annual rainfall in dry regions
건조한 지역의 연간 강우량을 증가시킨다
② prevent drastic changes in air temperature
기온의 급격한 변화를 막는다
✔ play a huge role in stopping the flow of moisture
수분의 흐름을 막는 데 큰 역할을 한다
④ change wind speed as air ascends and descends them
공기가 산을 따라 상승하고 하강하며 풍속을 바꾼다
⑤ equalize the amount of moisture of surrounding land areas
주변 지역의 수분의 양을 균등하게 한다

[문제 풀이]

빈칸이 글의 앞부분에 있어 빈칸에는 이후 내용을 요약한 말이 들어가야 한다. 문장 (2)부터는 문장 (1)의 내용에 대한 예시이다. 문장 (2)부터 전개되는 내용에 따르면 바다로부터 불어온 수분을 가진 공기가 산을 오르면서 강수를 일으키고, 그 결과 산을 내려가는 공기는 수분이 빠져나가 건조해진다. 즉, 공기 속의 수분이 산맥 때문에 내륙 지역까지 전달되지 못하기 때문에 산맥 안쪽의 내륙 지역은 건조한 기후가 나타난다는 것이다. 따라서 이러한 예시의 핵심 내용이 두괄식으로 제시될 수 있는 ③이 정답이다.

[중요 어휘]

☐ **interior**	형용사 내륙의, 내부의 / 명사 내부
☐ **continent**	명사 대륙
☐ **play a role in V-ing**	~하는 데 역할을 하다
☐ **moisture**	명사 수분, 습기
☐ **humid**	형용사 습한
☐ **encounter**	동사 ~와 마주치다
☐ **precipitation**	명사 강수, 강수량
☐ **windward**	형용사 풍상측(風上側)의, 바람이 불어오는 쪽의
☐ **leeward**	형용사 풍하측(風下側)의, 바람이 불어가는 쪽의
☐ **uplift**	명사 상승, 증가, 희망
☐ **rainfall**	명사 강우(량)
☐ **drastic**	형용사 급격한, 극단적인
☐ **ascend**	동사 상승하다, 올라가다
☐ **descend**	동사 하강하다, 내려오다
☐ **equalize**	동사 균등하게 하다

10 2023년 3월 32번 (정답률 55%) 정답 ②

[지문 끊어 읽기] 초기 닷컴 투자자들의 수익 보고 방식

(1) Many early dot-com investors /
많은 초기의 닷컴 투자자들은 /
focused almost entirely on revenue growth /
거의 전적으로 수익 증가에만 집중했다 /
instead of net income.
순수익 대신에

(2) Many early dot-com companies / earned most of their revenue /
많은 초기의 닷컴 회사들은 / 그들의 수입의 대부분을 벌어들였다 /
from selling advertising space / on their Web sites.
전치사 동명사 O
광고 게재 공간을 판매하는 것으로부터 / 그들의 웹사이트의

(3) To boost reported revenue, / some sites began /
부사적 용법(~하기 위해서) S V
보고되는 수익을 증가시키기 위해 / 몇몇 사이트들은 시작했다 /
exchanging ad space. 주제문 초기 닷컴 투자자들은 순수익이 아니라 '보고되는 수익 증가'를 위해 서로의 광고 게재 공간을 교환했음.
O(동명사구)
광고 게재 공간을 교환하는 것을

(4) Company A would put an ad for its Web site /
A 회사는 그것의 웹사이트의 광고를 게시하곤 했다 /
on company B's Web site, /
B 회사의 웹사이트에 /
and company B would put an ad for its Web site /
그리고 B 회사는 그것의 웹사이트의 광고를 게시하곤 했다 /
on company A's Web site.
A 회사의 웹사이트에

힌트 'change hands'는 '손이 바뀌다'라는 의미로, 어떤 것을 소유한 '주인이 바뀌었음'을 뜻함.

(5) No money ever changed hands, /
어떠한 돈도 결코 주인이 바뀌지 않았다 /
but each company recorded revenue /
each + 단수N 병렬①
하지만 각각의 회사는 수익을 보고했다 /
(for the value of the space / that it gave up on its site) /
=each company
공간의 가치에 대한 / 그것이 그것의 사이트에서 내어 준 /
and expense / (for the value of its ad /
병렬②
그리고 비용을 / 그것의 광고의 가치에 대한 /
that it placed on the other company's site). 정답 단서
=each company
그것이 다른 회사의 사이트에 게재했던

실제 현금 교환이 이루어지지 않았음에도 회사들끼리 각각 웹사이트 광고 공간을 서로 내어주고 이를 비용과 수익으로 처리하여 보고함.

★중요 '이러한 관행(This practice)'이란 '현금을 교환하지 않고 서로의 광고를 각자 웹사이트에 게재해준 후 이를 수익과 비용으로 처리하여 보고되는 수익을 증가시키는 것'을 의미함.

(6) This practice did little to boost net income /
이러한 관행은 순이익을 증가시키는 데 거의 도움이 되지 않았다 /
and resulted in no additional cash inflow /
그리고 어떠한 추가적인 현금 유입을 야기하지 않았다 /
— but it did boost *reported* revenue.
강조의 do + 동사원형
하지만 그것이 정말로 '보고되는' 수익을 증가시키기는 했다

힌트 'do little to V'는 '~하기 위해 거의 아무것도 하지 않았다'라는 뜻이므로, '~하는 데 거의 도움이 되지 않다'로 의역할 수 있음.

(7) This practice was quickly put to an end /
이러한 관행은 빠르게 종결되었다 /
because accountants felt / [that it did not meet the criteria /
=this practice
왜냐하면 회계사들이 느꼈기 때문이다 / 그것이 기준을 충족시키지 않는다고 /
of the revenue recognition principle]. [ ]: that 명사절(felt의 목적어)
수익 인식에 대한 원칙의

힌트 '수익 인식에 대한 원칙(revenue recognition principle)'이란, 실제로 실현된 수익만을 회계적 관점에서 수익으로 인정한다는 원칙을 의미함.

[중요 구문]

(5) ~ but each company recorded revenue (for the value of the space
S V O① 선행사
that it gave up ∨ on its site) and expense (for the value of its ad
목적격 관계대명사 O② 선행사
that it placed ∨ on the other company's site).
목적격 관계대명사

문제편 p.154

[전문 해석]

(1)많은 초기의 닷컴 투자자들은 순수익 대신에 거의 전적으로 수익 증가에만 집중했다. (2)많은 초기의 닷컴 회사들은 그들의 수입의 대부분을 그들의 웹사이트의 광고 게재 공간을 판매하는 것으로부터 벌어들였다. (3)보고되는 수익을 증가시키기 위해, 몇몇 사이트들은 광고 게재 공간을 교환하기 시작했다. (4)A 회사는 그것의 웹사이트의 광고를 B 회사의 웹사이트에 게시하곤 했고, B 회사는 그것의 웹사이트의 광고를 A 회사의 웹사이트에 게시하곤 했다. (5)어떠한 돈도 결코 주인이 바뀌지 않았지만(돈이 실제로 넘어간 것은 아니지만), 각각의 회사는 (각 회사가 자신의 사이트에서 내어준 공간의 가치에 대한) 수익과, (각 회사가 다른 회사의 사이트에 게재했던 그것의 광고의 가치에 대한) 비용을 보고했다. (6)이러한 관행은 순이익을 증가시키는 데 거의 도움이 되지 않았으며 어떠한 추가적인 현금 유입도 야기하지 않았지만, 그것이 정말로 '보고되는' 수익을 증가시키기는 했다. (7)이러한 관행은 빠르게 종결되었는데, 왜냐하면 회계사들이 그것이 수익 인식에 대한 원칙의 기준을 충족시키지 않는다고 느꼈기 때문이다.

[정답 확인]

다음 빈칸에 들어갈 말로 가장 적절한 것은?

① simplified the Web design process
웹 디자인 과정을 간소화하였다
② resulted in no additional cash inflow
어떠한 추가적인 현금 유입도 야기하지 않았다
③ decreased the salaries of the employees
직원들의 급여를 줄였다
④ intensified competition among companies
회사들 사이의 경쟁을 심화시켰다
⑤ triggered conflicts on the content of Web ads
웹 광고의 내용에 대한 충돌을 유발했다

[문제 풀이]

문장 (1)~(3)은 많은 초기 닷컴 투자자들이 순수익이 아니라 보고되는 수익 증가에만 집중하여 광고 게재 공간을 교환하기 시작했다고 설명하고 있으며, 문장 (4)~(6)은 A 회사와 B 회사의 예시를 통해 이를 구체적으로 설명하고 있다. 특히 문장 (5)의 '어떠한 돈도 결코 주인이 바뀌지 않았다(No money ever changed hands)'라는 표현에서 알 수 있듯이, A 회사와 B 회사는 서로 현금을 교환하지 않고 서로의 광고를 자기 웹사이트에 실어주었다. 즉, 실제 돈이 오가지 않았음에도 회계상으로 각각 수익과 비용 처리를 한 것이므로, 빈칸에 가장 알맞은 말은 ② 'resulted in no additional cash inflow(어떠한 추가적인 현금 유입도 야기하지 않았다)'이다.

[중요 어휘]

☐ revenue	명사 수익
☐ net income	명사 순수익
☐ earn	동사 (돈을) 벌다, 얻다
☐ boost	동사 증가시키다, 밀어올리다
☐ exchange	동사 교환하다, 맞바꾸다
☐ change hands	주인이 바뀌다
☐ give up	~을 내어주다, ~을 포기하다
☐ expense	명사 비용, 지출
☐ practice	명사 관행, 관례, 연습, 실습
☐ result in	~을 야기하다, 결과적으로 ~이 되다
☐ additional	형용사 추가적인, 부가적인
☐ inflow	명사 유입
☐ be put to an end	종결되다, 종료되다
☐ accountant	명사 회계사
☐ meet	동사 충족시키다, 부합하다
☐ criteria	명사 기준 (criterion의 복수형)
☐ recognition	명사 인식, 인정
☐ principle	명사 원칙, 원리
☐ intensify	동사 심해지다, 격렬해지다, 강화하다
☐ trigger	동사 유발하다, 촉발하다

11 2023년 3월 33번 (정답률 55%)

정답 ①

[지문 끊어 읽기] 가상 세계의 사회적 가치

(1) Scholars of myth have long argued /
신화학자들은 오랫동안 주장해 왔다 /
that myth gives structure and meaning /
신화가 구조와 의미를 부여한다고 /
to human life; /
인간의 삶에 /
that meaning is amplified / when a myth evolves into a world.
의미가 증폭된다고 / 신화가 하나의 세상으로 진화할 때

힌트 접속사 that이 이끄는 명사절이 동사 'have argued'의 목적어 역할을 함. 세미콜론(;) 뒤에 나온 that 명사절은 앞에 나온 that 명사절을 부연 설명함.

(2) A virtual world's ability to fulfill needs grows /
형용사적 용법
욕구를 충족시키는 가상 세계의 능력은 커진다 /
when lots and lots of people believe in the world. 정답단서 가상 세계를 믿는 사람들이 많을수록 욕구를 충족시키는 가상 세계의 능력이 커짐.
수많은 사람들이 그 세상의 존재를 믿을 때 ~의 존재를 믿다

★중요 연결사 'Conversely(반대로)'를 기점으로, 문장 (2)와 문장 (3)의 상황이 대조를 이루고 있음.

(3) Conversely, /
반대로 /
a virtual world cannot be long sustained /
가상 세계는 오랫동안 지속될 수 없다 /
by a mere handful of adherents. 정답단서 지지자가 적으면 가상 세계의 능력이 줄어듦.
단지 소수의 지지자들에 의해

(4) Consider the difference / between a global sport and a game /
차이를 고려해 보라 / 세계적인 스포츠와 게임 사이의 / 선행사
[I invent with my nine friends and play regularly]. [ ]: 목적격 관계대명사절
병렬① 병렬②
내가 내 아홉 명의 친구들과 함께 만들어서 정기적으로 하는

(5) My game might be a great game, /
나의 게임은 훌륭한 게임일 수 있다 /
주격 관계대명사 주격 관계대명사
one that is completely immersive, / one that consumes /
=a game =a game
완전히 몰입하게 하는 게임 / 소모하는 게임 /
all of my group's time and attention.
내 집단의 시간과 관심 모두를

★중요 게임을 즐기는 집단의 범위가 10명뿐인 문장 (6)의 상황은 가상 세계에 단지 소수의 지지자만이 존재하는 문장 (3)의 상황에 해당함.

(6) If its reach is limited to the ten of us, /
그것의 범위가 우리 10명으로 제한된다면 /
though, / then it's ultimately just a weird hobby, /
그러나 / 그렇다면 그것은 결국 그저 이상한 취미일 뿐이다 /
and it has limited social function.
그리고 그것은 제한된 사회적 기능을 가진다

(7) For a virtual world / to provide lasting, wide-ranging value, /
의미상의 주어 부사적 용법(목적)
가상 세계가 / 지속적이고 넓은 범위에 미치는 가치를 제공하기 위해서 /
its participants must be a large enough group /
그것의 참여자들은 충분히 큰 집단이어야 한다 /
to be considered a society.
5형식 수동태(be considered+명사 보어)
하나의 사회로 여겨질 정도로

힌트 일반적으로 부사는 형용사의 앞에서 형용사를 수식하지만, 부사 enough(충분히)는 형용사를 후치 수식함. 즉, 「형용사+enough」의 어순을 따름. 또, 「enough to V」에서 to부정사는 '~할 정도로[만큼]'으로 해석됨.

(8) When that threshold is reached, /
그 기준점에 도달될 때 /
psychological value can turn / into wide-ranging social value.
심리적인 가치는 변할 수 있다 / 넓은 범위에 미치는 사회적 가치로

[전문 해석]

(1)신화학자들은 오랫동안 신화가 인간의 삶에 구조와 의미를 부여한다고, 즉 신화가 하나의 세상으로 진화할 때 의미가 증폭된다고 주장해 왔다. (2)수많은 사람들이 그 세상의 존재를 믿을 때, 욕구를 충족시키는 가상 세계의 능력은 커진다. (3)반대로, 가상 세계는 단지 소수의 지지자들에 의해 오랫동안 지속될 수 없다. (4)세계적인 스포츠와 내가 내 아홉 명의 친구들과 함께 만들어서 정기적으로 하는 게임 사이의 차이를 고려해 보라. (5)나의 게임은 훌륭한 게임, 즉 완전히 몰입하게 하는 게임이자, 내 집단의 시간과 관심 모두를 소모하는 게임일 수 있다. (6)그러나, 그것의 범위가 우리 10명으로 제한된다면, 그렇다면 그것은 결국 그저 이상한 취미일 뿐이고, 그것은 제한된 사회적 기능을 가진다. (7)가상 세계가 지속적이고 넓은 범위에 미치는 가치를 제공하기 위해서, 그것의 참여자들은 하나의 사회로 여겨질 정도로 충분히 큰 집단이어야 한다. (8)그 기준점에 도달될 때, 심리적인 가치는 넓은 범위에 미치는 사회적 가치로 변할 수 있다.

[정답 확인]

다음 빈칸에 들어갈 말로 가장 적절한 것은?

✔ be a large enough group to be considered a society
하나의 사회로 여겨질 정도로 충분히 큰 집단이어야
② have historical evidence to make it worth believing
그것을 믿을 가치가 있게 만들 역사적 증거를 가지고 있어야
③ apply their individual values to all of their affairs
그들의 개인적인 가치들을 그들의 모든 일들에 적용해야
④ follow a strict order to enhance their self-esteem
그들의 자존감을 높이기 위해 엄격한 명령을 따라야
⑤ get approval in light of the religious value system
종교적 가치 체계에 비추어 승인을 얻어야

[문제 풀이]

문장 (2)~(3)에서 가상 세계를 믿는 사람의 규모에 따라 가상 세계의 영향력이 달라진다고 했고, 문장 (4) 이후로는 가상 세계를 믿는 사람의 규모가 적은 사례로서 소수의 사람만이 참여하는 '나의 게임(My game)'을 예시로 들어 규모가 작은 경우 사회적 기능이 제한된다고 한다. 한편, 문장 (7)은 가상 세계의 영향력이 커지기 위해서는 참여자들이 어떠해야 하는지 이야기하고 있으므로, 앞 문장의 내용을 포괄할 때 빈칸에는 참여자의 규모가 '크다'는 내용이 들어가야 한다. 따라서 빈칸에 가장 적절한 것은 ① 'be a large enough group to be considered a society(하나의 사회로 여겨질 정도로 충분히 큰 집단이어야)'이다.

[중요 어휘]

□ scholar	명사 학자, 장학생
□ myth	명사 신화
□ argue	동사 주장하다, 다투다
□ amplify	동사 증폭시키다, 확대하다
□ virtual	형용사 가상의, 허상의
□ fulfill	동사 충족시키다, 실현하다
□ need	명사 욕구, 필요
□ conversely	부사 반대로, 거꾸로
□ sustain	동사 지속하다, 유지하다
□ a handful of	소수의, 한 줌의
□ adherent	명사 지지자, 추종자
□ immersive	형용사 몰입하게 하는
□ consume	동사 소모하다, 소비하다, 섭취하다
□ reach	명사 범위 / 동사 ~에 도달하다
□ though	부사 그러나, 그렇지만 / 접속사 ~이긴 하지만
□ limited	형용사 제한된, 한정된
□ A be considered B	A는 B로 여겨지다
□ threshold	명사 기준점, 한계점
□ psychological	형용사 심리적인

12 2017년 11월 33번 (정답률 50%) 정답 ⑤

[지문 끊어 읽기] 베블런재

(1) Veblen goods are named after Thorstein Veblen, /
베블런재는 Thorstein Veblen의 이름을 따서 지어졌다 /
a US economist /
미국의 경제학자인 /
who formulated the theory of "conspicuous consumption".
'과시적 소비' 이론을 만들어 낸

(2) They are strange / because demand for them increases /
그것들은 이상하다 / 그것들에 대한 수요가 증가하기 때문에 /
as their price rises.
가격이 상승함에 따라

(3) According to Veblen, / these goods must signal high status.
Veblen에 따르면 / 이러한 물건들은 높은 지위를 나타내야 한다

(4) A willingness to pay higher prices /
기꺼이 더 높은 가격을 지불하고자 하는 마음은 /
is due to a desire to advertise wealth /
부유함을 드러내 보이려는 욕구 때문이다 /
rather than to acquire better quality.
더 나은 품질을 얻기 위한 것이라기보다는

✶중요 문장 (4)에서 높은 가격을 지불하려는 마음은 부유함을 드러내려는 욕구 때문이라는 이론을 토대로 가격이 하락해서 과연 어떤 상황이 되면 부자들이 구매를 중단하는지 쉽게 추측할 수 있음.

(5) A true Veblen good, / therefore, /
진정한 베블런재는 / 그러므로 /
should not be noticeably higher quality /
두드러지게 더 높은 품질이지는 않을 것이다 /
than the lower-priced equivalents.
더 낮은 가격의 동등한 물건보다

(6) If the price falls so much / that it is no longer high enough /
만약 가격이 너무 많이 하락해서 / 더 이상 충분히 높지 않다면 /
to exclude the less well off, / the rich will stop buying it.
덜 부유한 사람들을 배제할 만큼 / 부자들은 그것을 사는 것을 멈출 것이다

힌트 문장 (6)에서 the rich와 대조를 이루는 사람들을 the less well off라고 표현했는데 well off는 원래 형용사로 '부유한'이라는 의미임.

(7) There is much evidence of this behavior /
이러한 행동에 대한 많은 증거가 있다 /
in the markets for luxury cars, champagne, watches, and certain clothing labels.
고급 차, 샴페인, 시계, 그리고 특정 의류 브랜드 시장에는

(8) A reduction in prices / might see a temporary increase in sales /
가격 하락은 / 일시적인 판매 증가를 보일 수 있다 /
for the seller, / but then sales will begin to fall. 정답단서
판매자들에게 / 하지만 그 이후에는 판매량이 하락하기 시작할 것이다

[전문 해석]

(1)베블런재는 '과시적 소비' 이론을 만들어 낸 미국의 경제학자인 Thorstein Veblen(소스타인 베블런)의 이름을 따서 지어졌다. (2)그것들(베블런재)은 가격이 상승함에 따라 그것들에 대한 수요가 증가하기 때문에 이상하다. (3)Veblen에 따르면, 이러한 물건들은 높은 지위를 나타내야 한다. (4)기꺼이 더 높은 가격을 지불하고자 하는 마음은 더 나은 품질을 얻기 위한 것이라기보다는 부유함을 드러내 보이려는 욕구 때문이다. (5)그러므로 진정한 베블런재는 더 낮은 가격의 동등한 물건보다 두드러지게 더 높은 품질이지는 않을 것이다. (6)만약 가격이 너무 많이 하락해서 더 이상 덜 부유한 사람들을 배제할 만큼 충분히 높지(비싸지) 않다면, 부자들은 그것을 사는 것을 멈출 것이다. (7)고급 차, 샴페인, 시계, 그리고 특정 의류 브랜드 시장에는 이러한 행동에 대한 많은 증거가 있다. (8)가격 하락은 판매자들에게 일시적인 판매 증가를 보일 수 있지만, 그 이후에는 판매량이 하락하기 시작할 것이다.

- Veblen goods(베블런재): 가격이 오르면 수요가 감소하는 일반 재화와 달리 오히려 선호도와 수요가 높아지는 재화를 말함. 베블런재의 가격은 일반적인 소득 수준을 가진 사람은 구입하기 어려울 정도로 충분히 높기 때문에 해당 재화를 구매한다는 것은 부유함을 나타내는 신호 효과를 발생시킴.

[정답 확인]

다음 빈칸에 들어갈 말로 가장 적절한 것은?

① the government starts to get involved in the industry
정부가 그 산업에 관여하기 시작한다면
② manufacturers finally decide not to supply the market
제조업자들이 결국 시장에 공급하지 않기로 결정한다면
③ the law of supply and demand does not work anymore
공급과 수요의 법칙이 더 이상 작용하지 않는다면
④ there is no quality competition remaining in the market
시장에서 품질 경쟁이 남아있지 않다면(사라진다면)
✔ it is no longer high enough to exclude the less well off
더 이상 덜 부유한 사람들을 배제할 만큼 충분히 높지(비싸지) 않다면

[문제 풀이]

본문의 Veblen goods(베블런재)는 과시적 소비가 발생하는 대표적인 재화로 가격이 상승할수록 수요가 증가하는데, 이는 높은 가격이 부유함을 나타내는 신호로 작용하기 때문이다. 따라서 베블런재의 가격이 하락하여 구매할 수 있는 사람이 많아지면, 부유함의 상징으로서의 가치가 떨어지므로 부자들은 더 이상 구매를 하지 않을 것이다. 그러므로 빈칸에 들어갈 답은 ⑤이다.

[중요 어휘]

□ formulate	동사 만들어 내다
□ conspicuous	형용사 과시적인, 눈에 잘 띄는

문제편 p.155

□ status	명사 (사회적) 지위, 신분, 상태, 정세
□ willingness	명사 기꺼이 ~하는 마음
□ noticeably	부사 두드러지게, 현저히
□ equivalent	명사 동등한 물건, 등가물
□ well off	부유한, 잘사는
□ reduction	명사 하락, 감소
□ temporary	형용사 일시적인
□ get involved in	~에 관여하다
□ supply	동사 공급하다 / 명사 공급

13 2022년 3월 33번 (정답률 50%)

정답 ③

[지문 끊어 읽기] 과학이 모든 것을 설명하지 못하는 이유

(1) According to many philosophers, / there is a purely logical reason / [why science will never be able to explain everything]. [ ]: 관계부사절
많은 철학자에 따르면 / 순전히 논리적인 이유가 있다 / 과학이 모든 것을 설명할 수 있는 것은 아닐 것이라는
(선행사)

(2) For in order to explain something, / whatever it is, / we need to invoke something else.
(접속사(이유)) (복합관계대명사가 이끄는 부사절)
왜냐하면 무엇을 설명하기 위해서는 / 그것이 무엇이든 간에 / 우리는 다른 무언가를 언급해야 한다

(3) But what explains the second thing? 정답 단서 무언가를 설명하는 데 필요한 무언가는 어떻게 설명할 수 있는지 묻고 있음.
(=문장 (2)의 something else)
하지만 두 번째 것은 무엇이 설명하는가

(4) To illustrate, / recall that Newton explained a diverse range of phenomena / using his law of gravity.
(명사절 접속사) (분사구문(동시동작))
예를 들어 / 뉴턴이 매우 다양한 범위의 현상을 설명했음을 떠올려 보라 / 자신의 중력 법칙을 사용하여

(5) But what explains / the law of gravity itself? 정답 단서 다른 현상을 설명하는 데 사용된 중력 법칙 그 자체는 어떤 것으로 설명할 수 있는지 묻고 있음.
하지만 무엇이 설명하는가 / 중력 법칙 자체는

(6) If someone asks / [*why* all bodies exert a gravitational attraction / on each other], / what should we tell them?
[ ]: 명사절(간접의문문)
만약 누군가가 묻는다면 / '왜' 모든 물체가 중력을 행사하는지 / 서로에게 / 우리는 그들에게 뭐라고 말해야 하는가

(7) Newton had no answer to this question. 정답 단서 뉴턴은 중력 법칙 자체에 대한 설명을 하지 못했음.
뉴턴은 이 질문에 답이 없었다

(8) In Newtonian science / the law of gravity was a fundamental principle: / it explained other things, / but could not itself be explained. 정답 단서
(V①) (등위접속사) (V②)
뉴턴의 과학에서 / 중력 법칙은 기본 원리였다 / 그것이 다른 것들을 설명했다 / 하지만 그 자체는 설명될 수 없었다
뉴턴의 중력 법칙과 같은 기본 원리는 다른 어떤 법칙과 원리에 의해 설명될 수 없음. 즉, 과학의 법칙과 원리 중에서는 설명될 수 없는 법칙과 원리가 있음.

(9) The moral generalizes.
그 교훈이 일반화된다
★중요 여기서 그 교훈(The moral)은 문장 (8)에서 말한 '뉴턴의 중력 법칙과 같은 기본 원리는 다른 어떤 법칙과 원리에 의해 설명될 수 없다'는 것을 가리킴. 그 교훈이 일반화된다는 내용을 통해 이후 과학의 법칙과 원리 중에는 설명될 수 없는 것들이 있다는 내용이 이어질 것이라고 유추할 수 있음.

(10) However much the science of the future can explain, / the explanations it gives / will have to make use / of certain fundamental laws and principles.
(선행사) (목적격 관계대명사절)
미래의 과학이 아무리 많이 설명할 수 있다 하더라도 / 그것이 제공하는 설명은 / 이용해야만 할 것이다 / 어떤 기본 법칙과 원리를
힌트 복합관계부사 'however'이 이끄는 부사절로 'However+형용사/부사+S V'는 '아무리 ~해도, 아무리 ~할지라도'라고 해석하면 됨. 이때 'However'은 'No matter how'로 바꿔 쓸 수 있음.

(11) Since nothing can explain itself, / it follows that / at least some of these laws and principles / will themselves remain unexplained.
(=fundamental laws and principles)
어떤 것도 스스로를 설명할 수 없기 때문에 / 결론적으로 / 적어도 이러한 법칙과 원리 중 일부는 / 그 자체로 설명되지 않은 채 남을 것이다
힌트 It follows that S V는 '따라서 ~라는 결론에 이르게 된다'라는 뜻임. 본문은 의역을 해서 부사처럼 '결론적으로'라고 해석함.

[전문 해석]

(1)많은 철학자에 따르면, 과학이 모든 것을 설명할 수 있는 것은 아닐 것이라는 순전히 논리적인 이유가 있다. (2)왜냐하면 무언가를 설명하기 위해서는 그것이 무엇이든 간에 우리는 다른 무언가를 언급해야 한다. (3)하지만 두 번째 것은 무엇이 설명하는가? (4)예를 들어, 뉴턴이 자신의 중력 법칙을 사용하여 매우 다양한 범위의 현상을 설명했음을 떠올려 보라. (5)하지만 중력 법칙 자체는 무엇이 설명하는가? (6)만약 누군가가 '왜' 모든 물체가 서로에게 중력을 행사하는지 묻는다면, 우리는 그들에게 뭐라고 말해야 하는가? (7)뉴턴은 이 질문에 답이 없었다. (8)뉴턴의 과학에서 중력 법칙은 기본 원리였는데, 즉 그것이 다른 것들을 설명했지만, 그 자체는 설명될 수 없었다. (9)그 교훈이 일반화된다. (10)미래의 과학이 아무리 많이 설명할 수 있다 하더라도, 그것이 제공하는 설명은 어떤 기본 법칙과 원리를 이용해야만 할 것이다. (11)어떤 것도 스스로를 설명할 수 없기 때문에, 결론적으로 적어도 이러한 법칙과 원리 중 일부는 그 자체로 설명되지 않은 채 남을 것이다.

[정답 확인]

다음 빈칸에 들어갈 말로 가장 적절한 것은?

① govern human's relationship with nature
인간의 자연과의 관계를 지배한다
② are based on objective observations
객관적인 관찰에 기초한다
③ will themselves remain unexplained ✔
그 자체로 설명되지 않은 채 남을 것이다
④ will be compared with other theories
다른 이론들과 비교될 것이다
⑤ are difficult to use to explain phenomena
현상을 설명하기 위해 사용하기 어렵다

[문제 풀이]

본문에 따르면, 과학이 모든 것을 설명할 수 있는 것은 아니다. 어떤 법칙과 원리를 설명하기 위해서는 다른 법칙과 원리를 언급해야 하는데, 다른 법칙과 원리들의 논리적 토대가 되는 기본 법칙과 원리는 어떤 다른 법칙과 원리에 의해 설명이 불가능하므로 설명되지 않은 채 남는다. 따라서 빈칸에는 일부 법칙과 원리는 설명되지 않은 상태로 존재한다는 내용의 ③이 적절하다.

[중요 어휘]

□ philosopher	명사 철학자
□ purely	부사 순전히, 순수하게
□ invoke	동사 언급하다, 호소하다
□ to illustrate	예를 들면
□ recall	동사 떠올리다, 상기하다
□ diverse	형용사 다양한
□ phenomena	명사 현상 (phenomenon의 복수형)
□ body	명사 물체
□ exert A on B	B에 A를 행사하다[가하다]
□ gravitational attraction	중력
□ moral	명사 교훈 / 형용사 도덕적인
□ generalize	동사 일반화하다
□ make use of	~을 이용하다

14 2022년 3월 34번 (정답률 50%)

정답 ②

[지문 끊어 읽기] 사회적 상황에서 웃음의 역할

(1) In one example /
한 예로 /

문제편 p.156

of the important role of laughter in social contexts, /
사회적 상황에서 웃음의 중요한 역할의 /
Devereux and Ginsburg examined frequency of laughter /
Devereux와 Ginsburg는 웃음의 빈도를 조사했다 /
in matched pairs of strangers or friends /
모르는 사람이나 친구들과 짝을 지어 / 선행사
[who watched a humorous video together] / [ ]: 주격 관계대명사절
익살스러운 동영상을 함께 본 /
compared to those who watched it alone.
~와 비교하여 주격 관계대명사절
그것을 혼자 본 사람들과 비교하여

힌트 spend+time+V-ing(~하는 데 시간을 보내다) 구문으로 목적어인 time이 선행사로 문두에 나감.

(2) The time individuals spent laughing /
S 목적격 관계대명사절
사람들이 웃는 데 보낸 시간은 /
was nearly twice as frequent in pairs / as when alone.
V 배수사 as 원급 as A: A보다 ~배 더 …한
짝을 지어 있을 때 거의 두 배 더 빈번했다 / 혼자 있을 때보다

힌트 when이 이끄는 부사절로 alone 앞에 'they(=individuals) were'이 생략됨.

(3) Frequency of laughing / was only slightly shorter for friends /
웃음의 빈도는 / 친구들의 경우가 약간 더 적었을 뿐이다 /
than strangers. 정답 단서 모르는 사람들과 함께 동영상을 봤을 때 친구들과 함께 동영상을 보는 것보다 자주 웃음.
모르는 사람들보다

(4) According to Devereux and Ginsburg, / laughing with strangers /
Devereux와 Ginsburg에 따르면 / 모르는 사람과 함께 웃는 것은 /
served to create a social bond /
선행사
사회적 유대를 형성하는 역할을 한다 /
[that made each person in the pair feel comfortable]. 정답 단서
5형식V O O·C [ ]: 주격 관계대명사절
짝을 이루는 각 사람을 편안하게 해주는

친구가 아닌 모르는 사람과 함께 웃는 것은 사회적 유대를 형성하는 데 이바지함.

(5) This explanation is supported by the fact /
이 설명은 사실에 의해 뒷받침된다 /
that in their stranger condition, / when one person laughed, /
동격의 that
모르는 사람과 함께 있는 조건에서 / 한 사람이 웃을 때 /
the other was likely to laugh as well.
상대방도 웃을 가능성이 있었다는

(6) Interestingly, / the three social conditions /
흥미롭게도 / 세 가지 사회적 조건은 / S
(alone, paired with a stranger, or paired with a friend) /
(혼자인 경우, 모르는 사람과 짝을 이룬 경우, 친구와 짝을 이룬 경우) /
did not differ in their ratings / of funniness of the video /
V 병렬①
그들의 평가에 있어서 다르지 않았다 / 동영상의 재미에 대한 /
or of feelings of happiness or anxiousness.
병렬②
혹은 행복감 또는 불안감에 대한

(7) This finding implies / that their frequency of laughter /
명사절 접속사
이 발견은 의미한다 / 그들의 웃음의 빈도는 /
was not because we find things funnier /
우리가 어떤 것이 더 재미있다고 생각하기 때문이 아니라 /
when we are with others /
다른 사람들과 함께 있을 때 /
but instead we are using laughter to connect with others.
삽입
오히려 우리가 다른 사람과 가까워지기 위해 웃음을 이용하고 있기 때문이었다는 것을

힌트 'not A but B(A가 아니라 B)' 구문으로 이 문장에서 A 자리에는 because가 이끄는 절이, B 자리에는 because가 생략된 절이 옴.

[전문 해석]

(1)사회적 상황에서 웃음의 중요한 역할의 한 예로, Devereux와 Ginsburg는 익살스러운 동영상을 혼자 본 사람들과 비교하여, 모르는 사람이나 친구들과 짝을 지어 그것을 함께 본 웃음의 빈도를 조사했다. (2)사람들이 웃는 데 보낸 시간은 혼자 있을 때보다 짝을 지어 있을 때 거의 두 배 더 빈번했다. (3)웃음의 빈도는 모르는 사람들보다 친구들의 경우가 약간 더 적었을 뿐이다. (4)Devereux와 Ginsburg에 따르면, 모르는 사람과 함께 웃는 것은 짝을 이루는 각 사람을 편안하게 해주는 사회적 유대를 형성하는 역할을 한다. (5)이 설명은 모르는 사람과 함께 있는 조건에서 한 사람이 웃을 때 상대방도 웃을 가능성이 있었다는 사실로 뒷받침된다. (6)흥미롭게도, 세 가지 사회적 조건(혼자인 경우, 모르는 사람과 짝을 이룬 경우, 친구와 짝을 이룬 경우)은 동영상의 재미나 행복감 또는 불안감에 대한 그들의 평가에 있어서 다르지 않았다. (7)이 발견은 그들의 웃음 빈도는 우리가 다른 사람들과 함께 있을 때 어떤 것이 더 재미있다고 생각하기 때문이 아니라 오히려 우리가 다른 사람과 가까워지기 위해 웃음을 이용하고 있기 때문이었다는 것을 의미한다.

[정답 확인]

다음 빈칸에 들어갈 말로 가장 적절한 것은?

① have similar tastes in comedy and humor
희극과 유머에 대한 비슷한 취향을 갖고 있기
✔ are using laughter to connect with others
다른 사람과 가까워지기 위해 웃음을 이용하고 있기
③ are reluctant to reveal our innermost feelings
우리의 가장 내밀한 감정을 드러내기를 꺼리기
④ focus on the content rather than the situation
상황보다는 내용에 집중하기
⑤ feel more comfortable around others than alone
혼자보다 다른 사람 곁에 있을 때 더 편안함을 느끼기

[문제 풀이]

본문에 따르면 웃음 빈도는 혼자 동영상을 볼 때보다 친구와 함께 볼 때, 친구와 함께 볼 때보다 모르는 사람과 함께 볼 때 더 높았다. 따라서 모르는 사람과 함께 웃는 것은 사람을 편안하게 만들어 사회적 유대를 형성한다고 한다. 세 가지 상황에서 재미나 행복감의 차이가 없었는데, 웃음 빈도에 차이를 보인 이유는 우리는 모르는 사람과 있을 때 웃음을 이용하여 상대방과 유대감을 형성하려고 하기 때문이다. 따라서 정답은 ②이다.

[중요 어휘]

☐ **examine**	동사 조사하다
☐ **frequency**	명사 빈도, 주파수
☐ **match**	동사 짝을 짓다, 어울리다
☐ **slightly**	부사 약간
☐ **serve to V**	~하는 역할을 하다, ~하는 데 도움이 되다
☐ **bond**	명사 유대 / 동사 유대감을 형성하다
☐ **rating**	명사 평가, 순위, 등급
☐ **anxiousness**	명사 불안감
☐ **imply**	동사 의미하다
☐ **reluctant**	형용사 꺼리는
☐ **innermost**	형용사 가장 내밀한, 가장 안쪽의

15 2023년 3월 34번 (정답률 50%) 정답 ④

[지문 끊어 읽기] 환경 조건의 상대성

(1) It seems natural / [to describe certain environmental conditions /
형식상의 주어 [ ]: 내용상의 주어
자연스러워 보인다 / 특정한 환경 조건을 묘사하는 것은 /
as 'extreme', 'harsh', 'benign' or 'stressful'].
'극단적인', '혹독한', '온화한' 혹은 '스트레스를 주는'이라고

(2) It may seem obvious / when conditions are 'extreme': /
그것은 명백해 보일지도 모른다 / 조건이 '극단적인' 경우에 /
the midday heat of a desert, / the cold of an Antarctic winter, /
사막의 한낮의 열기 / 남극 겨울의 추위 /
the salinity of the Great Salt Lake.
Great Salt Lake의 염도

(3) But this only means / that these conditions are extreme *for us*, /
하지만 이것은 의미할 뿐이다 / 이러한 조건이 '우리에게' 극단적이라는 것을 /
given our particular physiological characteristics and tolerances.
given+명사구: ~을 고려할 때 정답 단서 극단적인 환경은 우리에게만 극단적일 뿐임을 언급함.
우리의 특정한 생리적 특징과 내성을 고려할 때

(4) To a cactus /
선인장에게 /
there is nothing extreme about the desert conditions /
사막의 환경은 전혀 극단적이지 않다 /
in which cacti have evolved; /
선인장이 진화해 온 /

문제편 p.156

힌트 부정어 'nor'가 문장 맨 앞에 나와 있기 때문에 주어와 동사가 도치되었음. 이때 동사가 be동사이므로 'be동사+주어'의 형태로 도치되었으며, 동사가 일반동사인 경우 'do/does/did+주어+일반동사(원형)'의 형태로 도치됨.

nor are the icy lands of Antarctica / (V, S)
남극의 얼음으로 덮인 땅도 역시 ~ 아니다 /

an extreme environment for penguins. (S·C) 정답 단서 앞선 문장의 내용을 부연 설명하며 극단적인 환경이 특정 생물에게는 극단적이지 않음을 언급함.
펭귄에게 극단적인 환경이

(5) It is lazy and dangerous / for the ecologist [to assume / (형식상의 주어, 의미상의 주어, [ ]: 내용상의 주어)
나태하고 위험하다 / 생태학자가 가정하는 것은 /

that all other organisms sense the environment / in the way we do]. (=sense)
모든 다른 유기체가 환경을 느낀다고 / 우리가 느끼는 방식으로

(6) Rather, / the ecologist should try /
오히려 / 생태학자는 노력해야 한다 /

to gain a worm's-eye or plant's-eye view of the environment: /
환경에 대한 벌레의 관점이나 식물의 관점을 획득하려고 /

to see the world / as others see it. (=other organisms, =the world)
세계를 바라보기 위해 / 다른 것들이 그것을 보듯이

(7) Emotive words / like harsh and benign, / (S)
감정을 나타내는 단어들 / 혹독한, 그리고 온화한 같은 /

even relativities such as hot and cold, /
심지어 덥고 추운 것과 같은 상대적인 단어들은 /

should be used / by ecologists / only with care. (V)
사용되어야 한다 / 생태학자들에 의해 / 오로지 신중하게

[전문 해석]

(1)특정한 환경 조건을 '극단적인', '혹독한', '온화한' 혹은 '스트레스를 주는'이라고 묘사하는 것은 자연스러워 보인다. (2)사막의 한낮의 열기, 남극 겨울의 추위, Great Salt Lake의 염도와 같이 조건이 '극단적인' 경우에 그것은 명백해 보일지도 모른다. (3)하지만 이것은 우리의 특정한 생리적 특징과 내성을 고려할 때 이러한 조건이 '우리에게' 극단적이라는 것을 의미할 뿐이다. (4)선인장에게 선인장이 진화해 온 사막의 환경은 전혀 극단적이지 않으며, 펭귄에게 남극의 얼음으로 덮인 땅도 역시 극단적인 환경이 아니다. (5)생태학자가 모든 다른 유기체가 우리가 느끼는 방식으로 환경을 느낀다고 가정하는 것은 나태하고 위험하다. (6)오히려, 생태학자는 다른 유기체들이 세계를 보듯이 세계를 바라보기 위해 환경에 대한 벌레의 관점이나 식물의 관점을 획득하려고 노력해야 한다. (7)혹독한, 그리고 온화한 같은 감정을 나타내는 단어들, 심지어 덥고 추운 것과 같은 상대적인 단어들은 생태학자들에 의해 오로지 신중하게 사용되어야 한다.

[정답 확인]

다음 빈칸에 들어갈 말로 가장 적절한 것은?

① complex organisms are superior to simple ones
복잡한 유기체가 단순한 것들보다 우월하다
② technologies help us survive extreme environments
기술이 우리가 극단적인 환경에서 살아남을 수 있게 도와준다
③ ecological diversity is supported by extreme environments
생태학적 다양성이 극단적인 환경으로 뒷받침된다
✔④ all other organisms sense the environment in the way we do
모든 다른 유기체가 우리가 느끼는 방식으로 환경을 느낀다
⑤ species adapt to environmental changes in predictable ways
생물종들이 예측 가능한 방식으로 환경 변화에 적응한다

[문제 풀이]

사막이나 남극, Great Salt Lake와 같은 특정한 환경이 인간에게는 극단적이지만 다른 생물종에게는 그렇지 않다는 점에 생태학자들이 유의해야 한다는 내용의 글이다. 빈칸 이전의 문장 (3), (4)는 인간에게 극단적인 환경이지만 사막의 선인장이나 남극의 펭귄에게는 각각 사막과 남극이 생존을 어렵게 하는 환경이 아님을 설명한다. 이것은 곧 극단적인 환경이 종에 따라 상대적임을 언급하는 것으로, 모든 생물종이 인간이 느끼는 것처럼 환경을 느끼지 않는다는 의미와 같다. 따라서 빈칸에 들어갈 정답은 ④ 'all other organisms sense the environment in the way we do(모든 다른 유기체가 우리가 느끼는 방식으로 환경을 느낀다)'이다.

[중요 어휘]

☐ extreme	형용사 극단적인, 극심한 / 명사 극도, 극단
☐ harsh	형용사 혹독한, 가혹한
☐ benign	형용사 온화한, 상냥한
☐ obvious	형용사 명백한, 분명한
☐ midday	명사 한낮, 정오
☐ Antarctic	형용사 남극의
☐ salinity	명사 염도, 염분
☐ physiological	형용사 생리(학)적인
☐ tolerance	명사 내성, 관용
☐ cactus	명사 선인장 (복수형 cacti)
☐ ecologist	명사 생태학자, 생태 운동가
☐ organism	명사 유기체, 생물(체)
☐ relativity	명사 상대성, 관계 있음

16 2023년 9월 32번 (정답률 50%) 정답 ④

[지문 끊어 읽기] 실제 세상과 닮은 연속극의 추상적인 세계

(1) A typical soap opera creates an abstract world, / (S, V, O, 선행사)
전형적인 연속극은 추상적인 세계를 만들어 낸다 /

힌트 밑줄 친 부분은 '그런데 그 세계에서는(and in the abstract world)'의 의미로, in which는 where로 바꿀 수 있음.

[in which a highly complex web of relationships connects fictional characters / (S', V', O', 선행사, [ ]: 관계부사절)
그런데 그 세계에서는 매우 복잡한 관계망이 허구의 인물들을 연결한다 /

[that exist first / only in the minds of the program's creators / (병렬①)
먼저 존재하는 / 오직 프로그램 제작자들의 마음속에만 /

and are then recreated / in the minds of the viewer]]. (병렬②, [ ]: 주격 관계대명사절)
그리고 이후 재현되는 / 시청자들의 마음속에

(2) If you were to think /
만약 당신이 생각한다면 /

힌트 밑줄 친 부분은 'how 간접의문문' 내의 동사 know의 목적어의 역할을 하고, 'how 간접의문문' 전체는 명사절로서 전치사 about의 목적어 역할을 함.

about [how much human psychology, law, and even everyday physics the viewer must know / (S', V')
시청자들이 얼마나 많은 인간의 심리학, 법, 그리고 심지어 일상의 물리학을 알아야만 하는지에 대해 /

in order to follow and speculate about the plot], / (~하기 위해서, [ ]: how 간접의문문)
줄거리를 따라가고 추측하기 위해 /

힌트 대시(—) 이하로는 'much(많은)'와 'much more(훨씬 더 많은)'를 중심으로 하는 긴 형용사구가 앞에 나온 형용사 considerable(상당한)을 부연 설명함. 즉, '얼마나 상당한지'를 구체적으로 설명하고 있음.

you would discover / it is considerable /
당신은 발견할 것이다 / 그것이 상당하다는 것을 /

— at least as much as the knowledge / (병렬①)
적어도 지식만큼 많다는 것을 /

[required to follow and speculate about a piece of modern mathematics], / ([ ]: 과거분사구)
현대 수학의 한 부분을 따라가고 추측하기 위해 요구되는 /

and in most cases, much more. (병렬②)
그리고 대부분의 경우에 훨씬 더 많다는 것을

(3) Yet / viewers follow soap operas with ease. (=However, =easily)
그러나 / 시청자들은 연속극을 쉽게 따라간다

(4) How are they able to cope with such abstraction?
그들은 어떻게 그러한 추상에 대처할 수 있을까

(5) Because, of course, the abstraction is built /
물론 그 추상이 만들어져 있기 때문이다 /

on an extremely familiar framework.
아주 친숙한 틀 위에

(6) The characters in a soap opera /
연속극의 인물들은 /

and the relationships between them /
그리고 그들 사이의 관계들은 /

are very much like the real people and relationships / (선행사)
실제 사람들 및 관계와 매우 비슷하다 /

[we experience every day]. ([ ]: 목적격 관계대명사절) 정답 단서 연속극에 등장하는 인물과 그들 간의 관계는 실제 세상과 매우 비슷함.
우리가 매일 경험하는

(7) The abstraction of a soap opera / is only a step removed /
연속극의 추상은 / 고작 한 걸음 떨어져 있다 /

from the real world. 정답 단서 연속극의 추상은 실제 세상과 거의 다를 바가 없음.
실제 세상과

(8) The mental "training" / [required to follow a soap opera] /
S 부사적 용법(목적) [ ]: 과거분사구
정신적 '훈련'은 / 연속극을 따라가기 위해 요구되는 /
is provided by our everyday lives. 정답 단서 연속극을 따라가기 위해 요구되는 정신적 '훈련'이 이미 일상에서 제공되고 있음.
V
우리의 일상에 의해 제공된다

[전문 해석]

(1)전형적인 연속극은 추상적인 세계를 만들어 내는데, 그 세계에서는 매우 복잡한 관계망이 오직 프로그램 제작자들의 마음속에만 먼저 존재하고 이후 시청자들의 마음속에 재현되는 허구의 인물들을 연결한다. (2)만약 줄거리를 따라가고 추측하기 위해 시청자들이 얼마나 많은 인간의 심리학, 법, 그리고 심지어 일상의 물리학을 알아야만 하는지에 대해 생각한다면, 당신은 그것이 상당하다는 것을, 적어도 현대 수학의 한 부분을 따라가고 추측하기 위해 요구되는 지식만큼 많고 대부분의 경우에 훨씬 더 많다는 것을 발견할 것이다. (3)그러나 시청자들은 연속극을 쉽게 따라간다. (4)그들은 어떻게 그러한 추상에 대처할 수 있을까? (5)물론, 그 추상이 아주 친숙한 틀 위에 만들어져 있기 때문이다. (6)연속극의 인물들과 그들 사이의 관계들은 우리가 매일 경험하는 실제 사람들 및 관계와 매우 비슷하다. (7)연속극의 추상은 실제 세상과 고작 한 걸음 떨어져 있다. (8)연속극을 따라가기 위해 요구되는 정신적 '훈련'은 우리의 일상에 의해 제공된다.

[정답 확인]

다음 빈칸에 들어갈 말로 가장 적절한 것은?

① is separated from the dramatic contents
극적인 내용과 분리되어 있기
② is a reflection of our unrealistic desires
우리의 비현실적 욕망의 반영이기
③ demonstrates our poor taste in TV shows
TV 쇼에 대한 우리의 형편없는 취향을 보여주기
④ is built on an extremely familiar framework
아주 친숙한 틀 위에 만들어져 있기
⑤ indicates that unnecessary details are hidden
불필요한 세부 정보가 숨겨져 있음을 나타내기

[문제 풀이]

문장 (5)는 '어떻게 시청자들은 연속극의 추상에 대처하는가?'에 대한 대답으로, 빈칸에는 시청자들이 쉽게 연속극을 이해할 수 있게 하는 연속극의 추상이 가지는 특성에 대한 내용이 들어가야 한다. 그런데 문장 (6)~(8)에서, 연속극에 등장하는 인물 사이의 관계는 우리가 실제 경험하는 것들과 비슷하여 우리가 일상에서 연속극을 따라가기 위한 정신적 훈련을 이미 하고 있다고 했으므로, 시청자들이 연속극에 등장하는 추상을 무리 없이 이해할 수 있는 이유는 그 추상이 현실 세계를 반영하여 매우 친숙하기 때문임을 알 수 있다. 따라서 빈칸에 가장 적절한 말은 ④이다.

[중요 어휘]

☐ typical	형용사 전형적인, 보통의
☐ soap opera	명사 연속극, 드라마
☐ abstract	형용사 추상적인
☐ complex	형용사 복잡한, 복합의
☐ fictional	형용사 허구의, 소설의
☐ psychology	명사 심리학
☐ physics	명사 물리학
☐ speculate	동사 추측하다, 사색하다
☐ considerable	형용사 상당한, 많은
☐ with ease	쉽게
☐ cope with	~에 대처하다, ~을 다루다
☐ abstraction	명사 추상(적 개념)
☐ extremely	부사 아주, 극도로
☐ familiar	형용사 친숙한, 익숙한
☐ framework	명사 틀
☐ removed	형용사 떨어져 있는, 동떨어진

17 2018년 9월 34번 (정답률 45%) 정답 ②

[지문 끊어 읽기] 인쇄술의 발달을 통한 창의성 증가

(1) For many centuries /
수 세기 동안 /
European science, and knowledge in general, /
대체로 유럽의 과학과 지식은 /
was recorded in Latin /
라틴어로 기록되었다 /
— a language that no one spoke any longer /
더 이상 어느 누구도 사용하지 않는 언어 /
and that had to be learned in schools.
그리고 학교에서 배워야만 했던

힌트 and 앞뒤로 2개의 that 관계대명사절이 병렬을 이루고 있음. 선행사는 모두 a language이며, 각각의 that 절 안의 빈 자리를 통해 첫 번째 that은 목적격 관계대명사, 두 번째는 주격 관계대명사임을 알 수 있음.

(2) Very few individuals, / probably less than one percent, /
아주 극소수의 사람들이 / 아마 1퍼센트도 안 되는 /
had the means to study Latin enough /
충분히 라틴어를 공부할 수단을 가졌다 /
to read books in that language /
그 언어로 된 책을 읽을 만큼 /
and therefore to participate in the intellectual discourse of the times.
그래서 그 시대의 지적 담론에 참여할 만큼

중요 '지적 담론'이란 지식 또는 지성에 관련된 주제에 관한 체계적인 말이나 글을 말함.

(3) Moreover, / few people had access to books, /
게다가 / 사람들은 거의 책에 접근하지 못했다 /
which were handwritten, scarce, and expensive.
계속적 용법
그런데 그것은 손으로 쓰였고 희귀하고 비쌌다

중요 유럽에서의 창의성 폭발은 가동 활자의 사용으로 인한 갑작스러운 정보의 확산과 접근이 어려웠던 라틴어 대신 일상어가 널리 쓰인 것에서 도움을 받았다고 말하고 있음.

(4) The great explosion of scientific creativity in Europe /
유럽에서 과학적 창의성의 엄청난 폭발은 /
was certainly helped / by the sudden spread of information /
분명히 도움을 받았다 / 갑작스러운 정보의 확산에 의해서 /
brought about by Gutenberg's use of movable type in printing /
인쇄술에서 구텐베르크의 가동 활자의 사용으로 야기된 /
and by the legitimation of everyday languages, /
그리고 일상어의 합법화에 의해서 /
which rapidly replaced Latin as the medium of discourse. 정답 단서
담론의 수단으로써의 라틴어를 급속히 대체한

(5) In sixteenth-century Europe /
16세기 유럽에서 /
it became much easier to make a creative contribution /
창의적인 기여를 하는 것이 훨씬 더 쉬워졌다 /
not necessarily because more creative individuals were born then /
그 무렵 반드시 더 창의적인 사람들이 태어났기 때문이 아니라 /
than in previous centuries /
이전 세기에서보다 /
or because social supports became more favorable, /
또는 사회적 지원이 더 호의적이었기 때문이 아니라 /
but because information became more widely accessible.
정보가 더욱 널리 접근 가능하게 되었기 때문에

[전문 해석]

(1)수 세기 동안 대체로 유럽의 과학과 지식은 라틴어로 기록되었다. (그 언어는) 더 이상 어느 누구도 사용하지 않았고 학교에서 배워야만 했던 언어(였다). (2)아마 1퍼센트도 안 되는 아주 극소수의 사람들이 그 언어(라틴어)로 된 책을 읽고 그래서 그 시대의 지적 담론에 참여할 만큼 충분히 라틴어를 공부할 수단을 가졌다. (3)게다가 사람들은 거의 책에 접근하지 못했는데, 그것은 손으로 쓰였고 희귀하고 비쌌다. (4)유럽에서 과학적 창의성의 엄청난 폭발은 인쇄술에서 구텐베르크의 가동 활자의 사용으로 야기된 갑작스러운 정보의 확산과 담론의 수단으로서의 라틴어를 급속히 대체한 일상어의 합법화에 의해서 분명히 도움을 받았다. (5)16세기 유럽에서 그 무렵 반드시 이전 세기에서보다 더 창의적인 사람들이 태어났거나 사회적 지원이 더 호의적이었기 때문이 아니라 정보가 더욱 널리 접근 가능하게 되었기 때문에, 창의적인 기여를 하는 것이 훨씬 더 쉬워졌다.

-Johannes Gutenberg(요하네스 구텐베르크, 1398년~1468년): 서양 최초로 금속활자를 발명한 인쇄술의 혁신자이다. 그는 활자 설계, 활자 대량 생산 기술을 유럽에 전파했으며 이런 기술과 유성 잉크, 목판 인쇄기 사용을 결합시켰다.

문제편 p.157

[정답 확인]

다음 빈칸에 들어갈 말로 가장 적절한 것은?

① the number of rich people increased
부유한 사람들의 수가 증가했기
② information became more widely accessible
정보가 더욱 널리 접근 가능하게 되었기
③ people were able to learn Latin more easily
사람들이 더 쉽게 라틴어를 배울 수 있었기
④ education provided equal opportunities for all
교육이 모두에게 동등한 기회들을 제공했기
⑤ new methods of scientific research were introduced
과학 연구의 새로운 방법들이 도입되었기

[문제 풀이]

지문은 16세기 유럽이 어떻게 과학적 창의성에서 폭발적인 증가를 가져오게 되었는지를 설명하고 있다. 16세기 전까지 라틴어를 배울 수 있는 극소수만이 책을 읽거나 지적 담론에 참여할 수 있었는데, 구텐베르크의 인쇄술 발명과 함께 라틴어가 아닌 일상 언어를 담론에서 합법적으로 사용할 수 있게 되면서 창의성이 폭발적으로 증가했다고 한다. 즉 이러한 변화는 더 많은 사람들에게 정보의 접근이 쉬워졌기 때문에 가능한 것이었으므로 답은 ② 'information became more widely accessible(정보가 더욱 널리 접근 가능하게 되었기)'이다.

[중요 어휘]

☐ **intellectual discourse**	지적 담론
☐ **scarce**	형용사 희귀한, 드문
☐ **bring about**	야기하다, 초래하다
☐ **movable**	형용사 가동의, 움직일 수 있는
☐ **printing**	명사 인쇄술, 인쇄
☐ **legitimation**	명사 합법화, 합법적 인정
☐ **everyday language**	일상어
☐ **favorable**	형용사 호의적인, 긍정적인
☐ **accessible**	형용사 접근 가능한, 접근할 수 있는

핵심 이 글의 앞 부분은 우리가 확실성을 추구하기 때문에 불확실성에 따른 위험을 부담해야만 하는 때에도 안전한 해결책만을 선호하는 경향이 있다고 지적하고 있음. 불확실성을 기피하는 이러한 행동이 지속될 때 나타날 수 있는 결과를 빈칸 다음에 이어지는 예시를 통해 추측해야 함.

18 2020년 11월 34번 (정답률 45%) 정답 ⑤

[지문 끊어 읽기] 확실성 추구 경향

(1) In the modern world, / we look for certainty / in uncertain places.
현대 세계에서 / 우리는 확실성을 찾는다 / 불확실한 곳에서

(2) We search for order / in chaos, /
우리는 질서를 찾는다 / 혼란 속에서 /
the right answer in ambiguity, / and conviction in complexity.
모호함 속에서 정답을 / 그리고 복잡함 속에서 확신을

(3) "We spend far more time and effort /
우리는 훨씬 더 많은 시간과 노력을 쏟는다 /
on trying to control the world," /
세계를 통제하려고 하는 것에 /
best-selling writer Yuval Noah Harari says, /
베스트셀러 작가 Yuval Noah Harari는 말한다 /
"than on trying to understand it."
그것을 이해하려고 하는 것보다

(4) We look for the easy-to-follow formula.
우리는 따라하기 쉬운 공식을 찾는다

(5) Over time, / we lose our ability / to interact with the unknown.
시간이 흐르면서 / 우리는 우리의 능력을 잃어버린다 / 미지의 것과 상호 작용하는

(6) Our approach reminds me of the classic story /
우리의 접근법은 나에게 전형적인 이야기를 상기시킨다 /
of the drunk man / searching for his keys /
술 취한 남자에 대한 / 자신의 열쇠를 찾는 /
under a street lamp / at night.
가로등 아래에서 / 밤에

(7) He knows / he lost his keys /
그는 안다 / 그가 자신의 열쇠를 잃어버린 것을 /
somewhere on the dark side of the street / but looks for them /
거리의 어두운 부분 어딘가에서 / 하지만 그것을 찾는다 /
underneath the lamp, / because that's where the light is.
가로등 아래에서 / 왜냐하면 그곳이 빛이 있는 곳이기 때문이다

(8) Our yearning for certainty / leads us /
확실성에 대한 우리의 열망은 / 우리를 이끈다 /
to pursue seemingly safe solutions /
겉보기에 안전한 해결책을 추구하도록 /
— by looking for our keys / under street lamps.
우리의 열쇠를 찾음으로써 / 가로등 아래에서

(9) Instead of taking the risky walk / into the dark, /
위험한 걸음을 내딛는 대신에 / 어둠 속으로 /
we stay within our current state, / [however inferior it may be]. (정답 단서; however: 복합관계부사, inferior: S·C, it: S, may be: V)
우리는 우리의 현재 상태 안에 머무른다 / 아무리 그것이 열악하더라도 [ ]: 부사절(양보)

[전문 해석]

(1)현대 세계에서 우리는 불확실한 곳에서 확실성을 찾는다. (2)우리는 혼란 속에서 질서를, 모호함 속에서 정답을, 그리고 복잡함 속에서 확신을 찾는다. (3)베스트셀러 작가 Yuval Noah Harari는 말한다. "우리는 세계를 이해하려고 하는 것보다 그것을 통제하려고 하는 것에 더 많은 시간과 노력을 쏟는다." (4)우리는 따라하기 쉬운 공식을 찾는다. (5)시간이 흐르면서 우리는 미지의 것과 상호 작용하는 우리의 능력을 잃어버린다. (6)우리의 접근법은 나에게 밤에 가로등 아래에서 자신의 열쇠를 찾는 술 취한 남자에 대한 전형적인 이야기를 상기시킨다. (7)그는 그가 자신의 열쇠를 거리의 어두운 부분 어딘가에서 잃어버린 것을 알지만 가로등 아래에서 그것을 찾는데, 왜냐하면 그곳이 빛이 있는 곳이기 때문이다. (8)확실성에 대한 우리의 열망은 가로등 아래에서 우리의 열쇠를 찾음으로써 겉보기에 안전한 해결책을 추구하도록 우리를 이끈다. (9)어둠 속으로 위험한 걸음을 내딛는 대신에, 우리는 아무리 (그것이) 열악하더라도 우리의 현재 상태 안에 머무른다.

[정답 확인]

다음 빈칸에 들어갈 말로 가장 적절한 것은?

① weigh the pros and cons of our actions
우리 행동의 장단점을 따져 본다
② develop the patience to bear ambiguity
모호함을 견디는 인내심을 발달시킨다
③ enjoy adventure rather than settle down
정착하기보다는 모험을 즐긴다
④ gain insight from solving complex problems
복잡한 문제를 해결하는 것에서 통찰력을 얻는다
⑤ lose our ability to interact with the unknown
미지의 것과 상호 작용하는 우리의 능력을 잃어버린다

[문제 풀이]

본문은 우리가 불확실성을 특징으로 하는 현대 세계에서 확실하고 안전한 해결책만을 찾으려 한다고 설명하면서, 이러한 우리의 문제 해결법을 가로등 아래에서 열쇠를 찾는 술 취한 남자의 이야기에 비유하여 설명한다. 남자는 열쇠를 잃어버린 장소가 아닌 빛이 있는 가로등 아래에서 열쇠를 찾아 다니는데, 이는 불확실성으로 위험을 감수하는 걸음을 내딛는 대신 안전한 현재 상태 안에 머물기로 선택하는 우리의 모습을 보여준다. 따라서 빈칸에 들어갈 내용으로 적절한 것은 ⑤이다.

[오답 풀이]

④ - 가로등 아래에서 열쇠를 찾는 행위는 불확실성을 회피하는 행동으로, 이를 복잡한 문제를 해결하는 것으로 보기는 어렵다. 또한, 본문의 중심 내용은 문제를 해결할 때 확실해 보이는 해결책만을 추구하는 것이 궁극적인 해결책이 될 수 없다는 것이다. 따라서, '복잡한 문제를 해결하는 것에서 통찰력을 얻는다'는 ④의 내용은 전체적인 흐름과 어울리지 않는다.

[중요 어휘]

☐ **order**	명사 질서, 순서
☐ **chaos**	명사 혼란, 혼돈
☐ **ambiguity**	명사 모호함, 불명확함
☐ **conviction**	명사 확신, 신념, 유죄 판결
☐ **complexity**	명사 복잡함, 복잡한 것
☐ **formula**	명사 공식, 방식

☐ interact	동사 상호 작용하다, 교류하다
☐ approach	명사 접근(법) / 동사 접근하다
☐ remind A of B	A에게 B를 상기시키다
☐ underneath	전치사 ~의 아래에(서), ~의 밑에
☐ yearning	명사 열망, 동경, 간절함
☐ pursue	동사 추구하다, 쫓다
☐ seemingly	부사 겉보기에, 외견상으로
☐ risky	형용사 위험한, 무모한, 모험적인
☐ current	형용사 현재의, 지금의 / 명사 흐름, 경향
☐ state	명사 상태, 형편
☐ inferior	형용사 열악한, 열등한
☐ weigh	동사 따져 보다, ~의 무게를 달다, 무게가 ~이다
☐ patience	명사 인내심, 끈기
☐ settle down	정착하다, 몰두하다
☐ insight	명사 통찰력, 식견

핵심 고객의 구매 행동을 데이터로 수집하는 이유를 설명하는 지문임. 구매 행동을 데이터화 했을 때 고객이 그 체계 안에서 차지하는 위치를 생각하며 읽어야 함.

19 2021년 3월 34번 (정답률 45%) 정답 ④

[지문 끊어 읽기] 기업들의 고객 구매 행동 데이터 수집

(1) Even companies that sell physical products / to make profit /
that: 주격 관계대명사 / to make profit: 부사적 용법(~하기 위해)
실체가 있는 제품을 판매하는 기업들조차 / 수익을 내기 위해 /
are forced by their boards and investors /
그들의 이사회와 투자자들에게 강요받는다 /
to reconsider their underlying motives /
그들의 근본적인 동기를 다시 고려할 것을 /
and to collect as much data as possible / from consumers.
그리고 최대한 많은 정보를 모을 것을 / 소비자들로부터

(2) Supermarkets no longer make all their money /
슈퍼마켓들은 더 이상 돈을 벌지 않는다 /
selling their produce and manufactured goods.
그들의 농산물과 제조된 상품들을 파는 것으로

(3) They give you loyalty cards /
그들은 당신에게 고객 우대 카드를 준다 /
with which they track your purchasing behaviors precisely. 정답 단서
그들이 당신의 구매 행동을 정밀하게 추적하는

힌트 which는 전치사 with의 목적어로 쓰인 목적격 관계대명사로, 그 의미를 보다 정확히 전달하기 위해 전치사를 관계대명사 앞으로 도치시켜 '전치사+관계대명사'로 씀. 이처럼 '전치사+관계대명사'로 하나의 어구를 이루게 되면, 관계대명사가 목적격으로 쓰여도 생략될 수 없음.

(4) Then / supermarkets sell this purchasing behavior /
그러고 나서 / 슈퍼마켓들은 이 구매 행동을 판매한다 /
to marketing analytics companies.
마케팅 분석 기업들에

(5) The marketing analytics companies perform machine learning procedures, /
마케팅 분석 기업들은 기계 학습 절차를 수행한다 /
slicing the data / in new ways, / and resell behavioral data back /
정보를 쪼개어 / 새로운 방식으로 / 그리고 행동 정보를 되판다 /
to product manufacturers / as marketing insights. 정답 단서
제품 제조 회사에 / 마케팅 통찰력으로

(6) When data and machine learning become currencies of value /
정보와 기계 학습이 가치 있는 통화가 될 때 /
in a capitalist system, /
자본주의적인 체계 안에서 /
then every company's natural tendency is /
그렇다면 모든 기업의 자연스러운 경향은 /
[to maximize its ability / to conduct surveillance /
[ ]: 명사적 용법(보어) / to conduct surveillance: 형용사적 용법(~하는)
그들의 능력을 극대화하는 것이다 / 관찰하는 /
on its own customers] / 정답 단서
그들의 고객들을 대상으로 /
because the customers are themselves the new value-creation devices.
왜냐하면 고객들이 새로운 가치를 창조하는 장치 그 자체이기 때문이다

힌트 'of+추상명사'는 형용사의 의미를 나타냄. 따라서 'of+value'는 '가치 있는(valuable)'으로 해석할 수 있음.

힌트 문장 (6)의 'themselves'는 '그 자체'라는 의미로 'the customers'를 강조하기 위해 사용된 재귀대명사이며, 생략이 가능함.

[중요 구문]

(1) Even companies that sell ~ are forced by their boards and investors to reconsider their underlying motives and to collect as much data as possible from consumers.
(companies: S / are forced: V / to reconsider: O·C① / to collect: O·C②)

힌트 'A(S) + force(V) + B(O) + to부정사(O·C)'의 형태였던 5형식 문장이 목적어로 쓰인 B를 주어로 해서 수동태로 다시 쓰인 문장임. 목적격 보어로 쓰인 to부정사 'to reconsider~'와 'to collect~'가 접속사 'and'로 긴 병렬 구조를 이루기 때문에, 행위자 'by their boards and investors'가 목적격 보어보다 앞에 나옴.

[전문 해석]

(1)수익을 내기 위해 실체가 있는 제품을 판매하는 기업들조차 그들의 이사회와 투자자들에게 그들의 근본적인 동기를 다시 고려하고 소비자들로부터 최대한 많은 정보를 모을 것을 강요받는다. (2)슈퍼마켓들은 더 이상 그들의 농산물과 제조된 상품들을 파는 것으로 돈을 벌지 않는다. (3)그들은 그들이 당신의 구매 행동을 정밀하게 추적하는 고객 우대 카드를 당신에게 준다. (4)그러고 나서 슈퍼마켓들은 이 구매 행동을 마케팅 분석 기업들에 판매한다. (5)마케팅 분석 기업들은 새로운 방식으로 정보를 쪼개어 기계 학습 절차를 수행하고, 제품 제조 회사에 행동 정보를 마케팅 통찰력으로 되판다. (6)정보와 기계 학습이 자본주의적인 체계 안에서 가치 있는 통화가 될 때, 그렇다면 모든 기업의 자연스러운 경향은 그들의 고객들을 대상으로 관찰하는 그들의 능력을 극대화하는 것인데, 왜냐하면 고객들이 새로운 가치를 창조하는 장치 그 자체이기 때문이다.

- machine learning(기계 학습): 컴퓨터가 스스로 방대한 정보를 분석해서 미래를 예측하는 기술

[정답 확인]

다음 빈칸에 들어갈 말로 가장 적절한 것은?

① its success relies on the number of its innovative products
그것의 성공이 혁신적인 제품의 수에 달렸기
② more customers come through word-of-mouth marketing
더 많은 고객들이 입소문 마케팅을 통해 오기
③ it has come to realize the importance of offline stores
오프라인 매장의 중요성을 깨닫게 되었기
④ the customers are themselves the new value-creation devices ✔
고객들이 새로운 가치를 창조하는 장치 그 자체이기
⑤ questions are raised on the effectiveness of the capitalist system
자본주의 체계의 효율성에 대해 의문이 생겼기

[문제 풀이]

지문은 고객의 구매 행동이 기업의 수익 창출과 어떠한 연관이 있는지를 설명한다. 일례로 고객의 구매 행동은 슈퍼마켓의 고객 우대 카드를 통해 정보의 형태로 수집되어 마케팅 분석 기업으로 판매된다. 그리고 해당 기업은 그 정보를 기계 학습을 통해 분석하고, 제품 제조 회사에 분석 결과를 마케팅 통찰력, 즉 마케팅에 활용할 수 있는 정보의 형태로 되판다. 이는 결론적으로 기업이 고객의 구매 행동을 관찰하는 것과 같다. 자본주의 체계 내에서는 수익을 내는 것이 우선시되므로 고객이 제품을 많이 구매해야 더 많은 수익으로 이어지는데, 이제는 여기에 더해 고객의 구매 행동 패턴까지도 팔 수 있는 상품으로 거래되므로, 상품뿐 아니라 고객들 자체가 새로운 가치를 창조하는 장치가 되는 것이다. 따라서 정답은 ④이다.

[오답 풀이]

② – 지문은 마케팅 분석 기업들이 고객의 구매 행동에 대한 정보를 활용하는 방법에 대해 언급했다. 입소문이 마케팅에 끼치는 영향 등이 지문에서 언급된 바가 없으므로 ②는 답이 될 수 없다.

[중요 어휘]

☐ physical	형용사 실체가 있는, 물질적인, 신체의
☐ board	명사 이사회, 판자
☐ investor	명사 투자자
☐ underlying	형용사 근본적인, (다른 것의) 밑에 있는
☐ motive	명사 동기, 이유
☐ consumer	명사 소비자
☐ produce	명사 농산물, 생산물
☐ manufacture	동사 제조하다, 제작하다
☐ loyalty card	고객 우대 카드
☐ purchasing behavior	구매 행동
☐ analytics	명사 분석, 분석 정보
☐ slice	동사 쪼개다, 나누다, 가르다, 얇게 베다
☐ insight	명사 통찰력, 식견
☐ currency	명사 통화, 통용

☐ **capitalist**	형용사 자본주의적인
☐ **conduct**	동사 하다, 처리하다 / 명사 행동, 태도
☐ **surveillance**	명사 관찰, 감시
☐ **device**	명사 장치, 방법, 기기
☐ **innovative**	형용사 혁신적인, 획기적인
☐ **word-of-mouth**	형용사 입소문의, 구전의
☐ **effectiveness**	명사 효율성, 유효성

20 2022년 9월 32번 (정답률 45%) 정답 ①

[지문 끊어 읽기] 자존감을 위협하는 도움

(1) There are several reasons / why support may not be effective.
관계부사
몇몇 이유들이 있다 / 도움이 효과적이지 않을 수 있는

(2) One possible reason / is that receiving help could be a blow /
동명사S V
한 가지 가능한 이유는 / 도움을 받는 것이 타격이 될 수 있다는 것이다 /
to self-esteem. 정답 단서 타인으로부터 도움을 받는 것이 자존감에 타격을 줄 수 있음.
자존감에

(3) A recent study / by Christopher Burke and Jessica Goren /
S
최근 한 연구는 / Christopher Burke와 Jessica Goren에 의한 /
at Lehigh University / examined this possibility.
Lehigh 대학의 / 이 가능성을 조사했다 V

(4) According to the threat to self-esteem model, /
자존감 위협 모델에 따르면 /
help can be perceived / as supportive and loving, /
도움은 여겨질 수 있다 / 협력적이고 애정 있는 것으로 /
or it can be seen as threatening / if that help is interpreted /
혹은 이것은 위협적으로 보일 수 있다 / 만약 그 도움이 해석된다면 /
as implying incompetence. 정답 단서 자신이 무능해서 도움을 받는다고 생각할 경우 도움을 위협적으로 여김.
무능함을 암시하는 것으로

(5) According to Burke and Goren, /
Burke와 Goren에 따르면 /
support is especially likely to be seen as threatening /
도움은 특히 위협으로 보일 가능성이 있다 /
if it is in an area / that is self-relevant or self-defining / 정답 단서 특히 자신의 성공과 성취가 중요한 영역에서 도움을 받을 경우 도움을 위협적으로 여김.
=support 주격 관계대명사
이것이 영역 안에 있는 경우 / 자기 연관적이거나 자기 정의적인 /
— that is, / in an area /
다시 말해 / 영역 안에 /
where your own success and achievement are especially important.
관계부사
자기 자신의 성공과 성취가 특히 중요한

(6) Receiving help with a self-relevant task /
동명사S
자기 연관적인 일로 도움을 받는 것은 /
can make you feel bad about yourself, /
V(사역V) O O·C
당신이 당신 자신에 대해 나쁘게 느끼게 만들 수 있다 /
and this can undermine /
그리고 이것은 손상시킬 수 있다 /
the potential positive effects of the help.
도움의 잠재적인 긍정적 영향을

(7) For example, / if your self-concept rests, / in part, /
예를 들어 / 만약 당신의 자아 개념이 달려 있다면 / 어느 정도는 /
on your great cooking ability, / it may be a blow to your ego /
당신의 훌륭한 요리 실력에 / 이는 당신의 자아에 타격이 될 수 있다 /
when a friend helps / you prepare a meal for guests /
준사역V O O·C
친구가 도울 때 / 당신이 손님들을 위해 식사를 준비하는 것을 /
because it suggests / that you're not the master chef /
왜냐하면 이는 암시하기 때문이다 / 당신이 유능한 요리사가 아니라는 점을 /
you thought you were. 힌트 주격 보어 역할을 하는 관계대명사가 생략된 형태로, 선행사인 the master chef를 수식함.
당신이 자신이 그렇다고 생각했던

[전문 해석]

(1)도움이 효과적이지 않을 수 있는 몇몇 이유들이 있다. (2)한 가지 가능한 이유는 도움을 받는 것이 자존감에 타격이 될 수 있다는 것이다. (3)Lehigh 대학의 Christopher Burke와 Jessica Goren에 의한 최근 한 연구는 이 가능성을 조사했다. (4)자존감 위협 모델에 따르면, 도움은 협력적이고 애정 있는 것으로 여겨질 수도 있고, 혹은 만약 그 도움이 무능함을 암시하는 것으로 해석된다면 위협적으로 보일 수 있다. (5)Burke와 Goren에 따르면 도움이 자기 연관적이거나 자기 정의적인 영역, 다시 말해, 자기 자신의 성공과 성취가 특히 중요한 영역 안에 있는 경우, 그것(도움)은 특히 위협으로 보일 가능성이 있다. (6)자기 연관적인 일로 도움을 받는 것은 당신이 당신 자신에 대해 나쁘게 느끼게 만들 수 있고, 이것은 도움의 잠재적인 긍정적 영향을 손상시킬 수 있다. (7)예를 들어, 만약 당신의 자아 개념이 어느 정도는 당신의 훌륭한 요리 실력에 달려 있다면, 친구가 당신이 손님들을 위해 식사를 준비하는 것을 도울 때 이는 당신의 자아에 타격이 될 수 있는데, 왜냐하면 이는 당신이 자신이 그렇다고 생각했던 유능한 요리사가 아니라는 점을 암시하기 때문이다.

- self-esteem(자존감, 자아존중감): 자신의 능력과 가치에 대한 전반적인 평가와 태도를 말함. 사티어(V. Satir) 이론에 따르면, 인간 내면의 항상 사랑과 인정을 받고자 하는 욕구와 자아존중에 대한 원초적 욕구가 충족될 때 자존감이 학습되고 발전된다고 함.
- self-concept(자아 개념, 자기 개념): 개인이 가지고 있는 자신에 대한 견해

[정답 확인]

다음 빈칸에 들어갈 말로 가장 적절한 것은?

✔ make you feel bad about yourself
당신이 자신에 대해 나쁘게 느끼게 만들
② improve your ability to deal with challenges
도전에 대처하는 당신의 능력을 향상시킬
③ be seen as a way of asking for another favor
또 다른 부탁을 하는 방법으로 보일
④ trick you into thinking that you were successful
당신이 성공했다고 생각하도록 당신을 속일
⑤ discourage the person trying to model your behavior
당신의 행동을 본보기로 삼으려는 사람을 낙담시킬

[문제 풀이]

본문에 따르면, 도움은 상황에 따라서 자존감에 타격을 주는 위협이 되기도 한다. 예를 들어, 자신의 성공과 성취가 특히 중요한 영역에서 도움을 받을 경우, 그 도움은 자신의 무능함을 암시하는 것으로 해석될 수 있다. 즉 자신이 무능해서 도움을 받는다고 생각하여 자존감에 타격을 입게 되는 것이다. 따라서 빈칸에는 도움이 자신에 대해 나쁘게 느끼게 만들 수 있다는 내용의 ①이 적절하다.

[중요 어휘]

☐ **blow**	명사 타격, 충격
☐ **supportive**	형용사 협력적인, 지원하는
☐ **threatening**	형용사 위협적인, 협박하는
☐ **imply**	동사 암시하다
☐ **incompetence**	명사 무능함
☐ **undermine**	동사 손상시키다
☐ **rest on**	~에 달려 있다[놓여 있다]
☐ **suggest**	동사 암시하다, 제안하다

21 2022년 11월 33번 (정답률 45%) 정답 ①

[지문 끊어 읽기] 불쾌한 음수 기호(-)를 피하기 위한 전략들

(1) Negative numbers are a lot more abstract /
음수는 훨씬 더 추상적이다 /
than positive numbers /
양수보다 /
— you can't see negative 4 cookies /
여러분은 음수의 4개의 쿠키를 볼 수 없다 /
and you certainly can't eat them — /
그리고 여러분은 틀림없이 그것들을 먹을 수 없다 /
but you can think about them, / and you *have to*, /
=have to think about them
하지만 여러분은 그것들에 대해 생각할 수 있다 / 그리고 여러분은 '해야만 한다' /

힌트 비교급 표현인 '~보다 더 추상적인(more abstract than ~)'을 강조하기 위하여 비교급 강조 표현인 'a lot(훨씬)'이 사용되었음. 비교급 강조 표현으로는 'a lot, much, even, still, far' 등이 있음.

in all aspects of daily life, / from debts to contending /
일상생활의 모든 측면에서 / 채무에서부터 씨름하는 것에 이르기까지 /
with freezing temperatures and parking garages.
몹시 차가운 기온 및 주차장과

(2) Still, / many of us / haven't quite made peace /
여전히 / 우리들 중 많은 사람들은 / 잘 화해하지 못해 왔다 /
with negative numbers.
음수와

(3) People have invented / all sorts of funny little mental strategies /
사람들은 만들어 냈다 / 모든 종류의 우스꽝스럽고 사소한 정신적 전략들을 /
to sidestep the dreaded negative sign. 주제문 음수를 불쾌하게 생각해 온 사람들은 음수 기호(-)를 피하기 위한 다양한 정신적 전략들을 고안해 왔음.
부사적 용법(목적)
그 두려운 음수 기호를 피하기 위해

(4) On mutual fund statements, /
뮤추얼 펀드 보고서에서 /
losses (negative numbers) are printed in red /
손실(음수)은 빨간색으로 인쇄되어 있다 / 병렬①
or stuck in parentheses / with no negative sign to be found. 정답 단서 음수를 빨간색으로 표시하거나 음수 옆에 괄호를 쓰는 것은 사람들이 음수 기호(-)를 피하기 위한 전략에 해당함.
병렬②
혹은 괄호 안에 갇혀 있다 / 음수의 기호가 발견되지 않은 채

(5) The history books tell us / [that Julius Caesar was born /
4형식V I·O [ ]: D·O(that 명사절)
역사책은 우리에게 말한다 / Julius Caesar가 태어났다고 /
in 100 B.C., / not -100]. 정답 단서 기원전 n년이라는 표기는 음수 기호(-)를 피하기 위한 전략에 해당함.
기원전 100년에 / -100년이 아니라

(6) The underground levels in a parking garage /
주차장의 지하층은 /
often have designations / like B1 and B2. 정답 단서 지하 주차장의 B1이나 B2의 명칭은 -1층과 -2층이라는 표기를 피하기 위한 전략에 해당함.
종종 명칭을 가지고 있다 / B1과 B2와 같은

(7) Temperatures are one of the few exceptions: /
기온은 몇 안 되는 예외 중 하나이다 /
folks do say, / especially here in Ithaca, New York, /
S 강조의 do V
사람들은 분명 말한다 / 특히 여기 New York의 Ithaca에서 /
[that it's -5 degrees outside], / [ ]: O(that 명사절)
바깥의 기온이 -5도라고 /
though even then, / many prefer to say 5 below zero.
심지어 그때에도 / 많은 사람들이 영하 5도라고 말하길 선호하긴 하지만

(8) There's something / about that negative sign /
선행사
무언가가 있다 / 그 음수의 기호에 관해서는 /
that just looks so unpleasant.
주격 관계대명사 2형식V S·C(형용사)
정말 불쾌하게만 보이는

[전문 해석]

(1)음수는 양수보다 훨씬 더 추상적이어서 여러분은 음수의 4개의 쿠키를 볼 수 없고 여러분은 틀림없이 그것들을 먹을 수 없는데, 여러분은 그것들(음수)에 대해 생각할 수 있고, 채무에서부터 몹시 차가운 기온 및 주차장과 씨름하는 것에 이르기까지의 일상생활의 모든 측면에서 생각'해야만 한다'. (2)여전히, 우리들 중 많은 사람들은 음수와 잘 화해하지 못해 왔다. (3)사람들은 그 두려운 음수 기호를 피하기 위해 모든 종류의 우스꽝스럽고 사소한 정신적 전략들을 만들어 냈다. (4)뮤추얼 펀드(계약형 투자 신탁) 보고서에서 손실(음수)은 빨간색으로 인쇄되거나 음수의 기호가 발견되지 않은 채 괄호 안에 갇혀 있다. (5)역사책은 우리에게 Julius Caesar가 -100년이 아니라 기원전 100년에 태어났다고 말한다. (6)주차장의 지하층은 종종 B1과 B2와 같은 명칭을 가지고 있다. (7)기온은 몇 안 되는 예외 중 하나인데, 특히 여기 New York의 Ithaca에서, 사람들은 분명 바깥의 기온이 -5도라고 말한다. 심지어 그때에도 많은 사람들이 영하 5도라고 말하길 선호하긴 하지만. (8)그 음수의 기호에 관해서는 정말 불쾌하게만 보이는 무언가가 있다.

[정답 확인]

다음 빈칸에 들어갈 말로 가장 적절한 것은?

① sidestep the dreaded negative sign
그 두려운 음수 기호를 피하기
② resolve stock market uncertainties
주식 시장의 불확실성을 해소하기
③ compensate for complicated calculating processes
복잡한 계산 과정을 보완하기
④ unify the systems of expressing numbers below zero
0 아래의 숫자들을 표현하는 체계를 통일하기
⑤ face the truth that subtraction can create negative numbers
뺄셈이 음수를 만들어 낼 수 있다는 사실에 직면하기

[문제 풀이]

빈칸에는 사람들이 다양한 종류의 정신적 전략들을 만들어 낸 이유 및 목적이 들어가야 한다. 그런데 문장 (4)~(7)에서 언급된 '음수를 빨간색으로 표시하기, 음수 기호 없이 괄호 안에 음수를 집어넣기, 지하층을 B1, B2 등의 명칭으로 부르기, 기원전 n년이나 영하 n도와 같은 표기 사용하기'는 모두 사람들이 음수 기호(-)를 피하기 위해 고안한 다양한 전략들의 예시라고 할 수 있다. 따라서 빈칸에 가장 적절한 말은 ① 'sidestep the dreaded negative sign(그 두려운 음수 기호를 피하기)'이다.

[중요 어휘]

□ **negative**	형용사 음수의, 마이너스의, 부정적인
□ **abstract**	형용사 추상적인, 관념적인
□ **positive**	형용사 양수의, 플러스의, 긍정적인
□ **contend with**	~와 씨름하다[다투다]
□ **make peace with**	~와 화해하다
□ **sidestep**	동사 피하다, 회피하다
□ **dreaded**	형용사 두려운, 무서운
□ **statement**	명사 (사업) 보고서, 계산서, 진술, 성명
□ **parentheses**	명사 괄호 (parenthesis의 복수형)
□ **designation**	명사 명칭, 호칭, 지명, 지정
□ **exception**	명사 예외, 제외
□ **folks**	명사 (주로 복수형) 사람들
□ **resolve**	동사 해소하다, 결심하다
□ **stock market**	명사 주식 시장
□ **compensate**	동사 보완하다, 보상하다
□ **unify**	동사 통일[통합]하다
□ **subtraction**	명사 뺄셈, 삭감, 공제

22 2022년 11월 34번 (정답률 45%) 정답 ②

[지문 끊어 읽기] 교란 변수

(1) Observational studies of humans / cannot be properly controlled.
인간에 대한 관찰 연구는 / 적절하게 통제될 수 없다

(2) Humans live different lifestyles / and in different environments.
인간은 다양한 생활 방식으로 살고 있다 / 그리고 다양한 환경에서

(3) Thus, / they are insufficiently homogeneous /
따라서 / 그들은 불충분하게 동질적이다 /
to be suitable experimental subjects.
부사적 용법
적절한 실험 대상이 되기에

(4) These *confounding factors* undermine our ability /
이러한 '교란 변수'는 우리의 능력을 손상시킨다 /
to draw sound causal conclusions /
형용사적 용법
타당한 인과적 결론을 도출하는 /
from human epidemiological surveys. 정답 단서 교란 변수는 타당한 결론을 도출하는 것에 어려움을 줌.
인간 역학 조사로부터

(5) Confounding factors are variables / (known or unknown) /
선행사
교란 변수는 변수이다 / (알려지거나 알려지지 않은) /
that make it difficult / for epidemiologists [to isolate the effects /
주격 관계대명사 형식상의 목적어 to부정사의 의미상 주어 [ ]: 내용상의 목적어
어렵게 만드는 / 역학자가 영향을 분리하는 것을 /
of the specific variable being studied].
연구되고 있는 특정한 변수의

문제편 p.160

(6) For example, / Taubes argued /
예를 들어 / Taubes는 주장했다 /
that since many people who drink also smoke, /
S', 선행사 주격 관계대명사절 V'
술을 마시는 많은 사람들이 흡연도 하기 때문에 /
researchers have difficulty determining the link /
연구자들이 연관성을 결정짓는 데 어려움을 겪는다고 /
between alcohol consumption and cancer.
알코올 섭취와 암 사이의

(7) Similarly, / researchers in the famous Framingham study /
마찬가지로 / 유명한 Framingham 연구의 연구자들은 /
identified a significant correlation /
상당한 상관관계를 확인했다 /
between coffee drinking and coronary heart disease.
커피를 마시는 것과 관상 동맥성 심장 질환 사이에

(8) However, / most of this correlation disappeared /
그러나 / 이러한 상관관계의 대부분은 사라졌다 /
once researchers corrected for the fact /
접속사
연구자들이 사실을 수정하자 /
[that many coffee drinkers also smoke]. 정답단서 특정한 상관관계를 찾으려 했으나 교란 변수로 인해 상관관계가 성립되지 않음.
접속사 [ ]: the fact와 동격
커피를 마시는 많은 사람들이 흡연도 한다는

(9) If the confounding factors are known, /
교란 변수들이 알려져 있다면 /
it is often possible / to correct for them. 정답단서 연구 대상과 관련된 교란 변수를 수정하는 것도 가능함.
형식상의 주어 내용상의 주어
종종 가능하다 / 그것들을 수정하는 것이

(10) However, / if they are unknown, /
그러나 / 그것들이 알려져 있지 않다면 /
they will undermine the reliability /
그것들은 신뢰성을 손상시킬 것이다 /
of the causal conclusions / we draw /
인과적 결론의 / 우리가 도출하는 /
from epidemiological surveys.
역학 조사로부터

[전문 해석]

(1)인간에 대한 관찰 연구는 적절하게 통제될 수 없다. (2)인간은 다양한 생활 방식으로 그리고 다양한 환경에서 살고 있다. (3)따라서 그들은 적절한 실험 대상이 되기에 충분히 동질적이지 않다. (4)이러한 '교란 변수'는 인간 역학 조사로부터 타당한 인과적 결론을 도출하는 우리의 능력을 손상시킨다. (5)교란 변수는 역학자가 연구되고 있는 특정한 변수의 영향을 분리하는 것을 어렵게 만드는 (알려지거나 알려지지 않은) 변수이다. (6)예를 들어, Taubes는 술을 마시는 많은 사람들이 흡연도 하기 때문에 연구자들이 알코올 섭취와 암 사이의 연관성을 결정짓는 데 어려움을 겪는다고 주장했다. (7)마찬가지로, 유명한 Framingham 연구의 연구자들은 커피를 마시는 것과 관상 동맥성 심장 질환 사이에 상당한 상관관계를 확인했다. (8)그러나 연구자들이 커피를 마시는 많은 사람들이 흡연도 한다는 사실을 수정하자 이러한 상관관계의 대부분은 사라졌다. (9)교란 변수들이 알려져 있다면, 그것들을 수정하는 것이 종종 가능하다. (10)그러나 그것들이 알려져 있지 않다면, 그것들은 우리가 역학 조사로부터 도출하는 인과적 결론의 신뢰성을 손상시킬 것이다.

[정답 확인]

다음 빈칸에 들어갈 말로 가장 적절한 것은?

① distort the interpretation of the medical research results
의학 연구 결과의 해석을 왜곡하는
✔ isolate the effects of the specific variable being studied
연구되고 있는 특정한 변수의 영향을 분리하는
③ conceal the purpose of their research from subjects
대상에게 연구의 목적을 숨기는
④ conduct observational studies in an ethical way
윤리적인 방식으로 관찰 연구를 수행하는
⑤ refrain from intervening in their experiments
그들의 실험에 간섭하는 것을 억제하는

[문제 풀이]

문장 (1)~(3)에 따르면 인간에 대한 관찰 연구에서 연구 대상자인 인간은 저마다 생활 방식과 처한 환경이 달라 이로 인해 '교란 변수'가 발생한다. 교란 변수는 연구가 목표로 하는 특정 상관관계를 밝히고 타당한 결론을 도출하는 데 방해가 되는 요인이다. 문장 (9)~(10)을 통해 연구 목표에 개입한 교란 변수가 수정될 때 신뢰성 있는 인과적 결론을 도출하는 것이 가능함을 유추할 수 있다. 빈칸이 포함된 문장은 교란 변수가 역학자의 연구에서 무엇을 어렵게 하는지를 설명하는 내용이어야 하므로 정답은 ②이다.

[중요 어휘]

□ observational	형용사 관찰의, 감시의
□ homogeneous	형용사 동질적인, 동종의
□ suitable	형용사 적절한, 적합한
□ subject	명사 (연구) 대상, 주제, 과목
□ confounding factor	교란 변수
□ undermine	동사 손상시키다, 약화시키다
□ draw	동사 도출하다, 끌다
□ sound	형용사 타당한, 건전한
□ causal	형용사 인과 관계의
□ conclusion	명사 결론, 결말
□ epidemiological	형용사 역학의
□ variable	명사 변수 / 형용사 가변적인
□ epidemiologist	명사 역학자
□ isolate	동사 분리하다, 격리하다
□ determine	동사 결정짓다, 알아내다
□ consumption	명사 섭취, 소비
□ correlation	명사 상관관계
□ coronary	형용사 관상 동맥의
□ correct for	수정하다, 교정하다
□ reliability	명사 신뢰성
□ distort	동사 왜곡하다, 비틀다
□ interpretation	명사 해석, 이해
□ conceal	동사 숨기다, 감추다
□ conduct	동사 수행하다, 시행하다
□ refrain	동사 억제하다, 삼가다
□ intervene	동사 간섭하다, 개입하다

23 2017년 9월 33번 (정답률 40%) 정답 ②

[지문 끊어 읽기] 단순한 대상 선택의 효과

(1) One of the most curious paintings of the Renaissance /
르네상스의 가장 호기심을 끄는 그림들 중 하나는 /
is a careful depiction of a weedy patch of ground /
잡초가 무성한 한 구획의 땅의 세심한 묘사이다 /
by Albrecht Dürer.
Albrecht Dürer가 그린

(2) Dürer extracts design and harmony /
Dürer는 디자인과 조화를 끌어낸다 /
from an apparently random collection of weeds and grasses /
겉보기에 아무렇게나 모여 있는 잡초와 풀 더미로부터 /
that we would normally not think twice to look at.
우리가 보통은 다시 볼 생각하지 않을

(3) By taking such an ordinary thing, / 정답단서
그러한 평범한 사물을 취함으로써 /
he is able to convey his artistry / in a pure form.
그는 그의 예술적 재능을 전달할 수 있다 / 순수한 형태로

(4) In a similar way, / ★중요 문장 (4)의 In a similar way(유사한 방식으로)는 앞에 나온 내용과 연장선상에 있는 것을 이야기하고자 할 때 쓰는 표현이므로 빈칸 내용을 알려면 바로 앞에 있는 문장 (3)의 내용을 잘 이해해야 함.
유사한 방식으로 /
scientists often choose to study humble subjects /
과학자들은 흔히 보잘것없는 대상을 연구하기로 선택한다 /
when trying to understand the essence of a problem.
어떤 문제의 본질을 이해하려고 노력할 때

(5) Studying relatively simple systems / 정답 단서
비교적 단순한 체계를 연구하는 것은 /
avoids unnecessary complications, /
불필요한 복잡함을 피한다 /
and can allow deeper insights to be obtained.
그리고 보다 깊은 통찰력이 얻어질 수 있게 한다

(6) This is particularly true /
이것은 특히 해당된다 /
when we are trying to understand something /
우리가 어떤 것을 이해하려고 노력하고 있을 때 /
as problematic as our ability to learn.
우리의 학습 능력만큼 해결하기 어려운

(7) Human reactions are so complex /
인간의 반응은 너무 복잡하다 /
that they can be difficult to interpret objectively.
그래서 그것들은 객관적으로 해석하기에 어려울 수 있다

(8) It sometimes helps / to step back /
때때로 도움이 된다 / 한 걸음 뒤로 물러서는 것은 /
and consider how more modest creatures, /
그래서 좀 더 별것 아닌 생물들이 어떻게 ~하는지 고려하는 것은 /
like bacteria or weeds, / deal with the challenges they face. (=modest creatures)
박테리아나 잡초 같은 / 그것들이 직면하는 문제를 처리하는지

[전문 해석]

(1)르네상스의 가장 호기심을 끄는 그림들 중 하나는 Albrecht Dürer(알브레히트 뒤러)가 그린 잡초가 무성한 한 구획의 땅의 세심한 묘사이다. (2)Dürer는 우리가 보통은 다시 볼 생각하지 않을, 겉보기에 아무렇게나 모여 있는 잡초와 풀 더미로부터 디자인과 조화를 끌어낸다. (3)그러한 평범한 사물을 취함으로써, 그는 그의 예술적 재능을 순수한 형태로 전달할 수 있다. (4)유사한 방식으로, 과학자들은 어떤 문제의 본질을 이해하려고 노력할 때 흔히 보잘것없는 대상을 연구하기로 선택한다. (5)비교적 단순한 체계를 연구하는 것은 불필요한 복잡함을 피하고, 보다 깊은 통찰력이 얻어질 수 있게 한다. (6)이것은 특히 우리가 우리의 학습 능력만큼 해결하기 어려운 어떤 것을 이해하려고 노력하고 있을 때 해당된다. (7)인간의 반응은 너무 복잡해서 그것들은 객관적으로 해석하기에 어려울 수 있다. (8)때때로 한 걸음 뒤로 물러서서 박테리아나 잡초 같은 좀 더 별것 아닌 생물들이 자신들이 직면하는 문제를 어떻게 처리하는지 고려하는 것은 도움이 된다.
- Albrecht Dürer(알브레히트 뒤러, 1471년~1528년): 회화와 판화로 유명한 16세기 독일의 대표적인 화가임. 이탈리아 르네상스 미술을 경험한 선구적인 북유럽 미술가이자 지식인으로서 '르네상스인'이라는 수식어를 얻음.

[정답 확인]

다음 빈칸에 들어갈 말로 가장 적절한 것은?

① depend on personal experience
개인의 경험에 의존한다
✔② choose to study humble subjects
보잘것없는 대상을 연구하기로 선택한다
★중요 문장 (3)의 an ordinary thing, 문장 (5)의 relatively simple systems는 선택지 ②의 humble subjects에 해당함.
③ work in close cooperation with one another
서로와 긴밀히 협력하여 일한다
④ look for solutions to problems from the past
문제에 대한 해결책을 과거로부터 찾는다
⑤ test a hypothesis through lots of experiments
수많은 실험을 통해 가설을 검증한다

[문제 풀이]

본문은 박테리아나 잡초 같은 비교적 단순한 체계를 연구함으로써, 인간과 같은 더 복잡한 체계를 이해하는 데 보다 깊은 통찰력을 얻을 수 있다고 설명하는 글이다. 빈칸 다음에 이어지는 문장에서 이와 같은 요지를 분명히 밝히고 있고, 이후 지속적으로 부연 설명을 제시하고 있다. 따라서 빈칸에 들어갈 말로 가장 적절한 것은 ② 'choose to study humble subjects(보잘것없는 대상을 연구하기로 선택한다)'이다.

[중요 어휘]

□ **depiction**	명사 묘사, 서술
□ **weedy**	형용사 잡초가 무성한
□ **extract A from B**	B로부터 A를 끌어내다[추출하다]
□ **ordinary**	형용사 평범한
□ **convey**	동사 전달하다
□ **artistry**	명사 예술적 재능
□ **humble**	형용사 보잘것없는, 미천한, 겸손한
□ **relatively**	부사 비교적, 상대적으로
□ **complication**	명사 복잡함
□ **problematic**	형용사 해결하기 어려운, 문제가 있는
□ **modest**	형용사 별것 아닌, 겸손한, 신중한
□ **hypothesis**	명사 가설, 추정
□ **experiment**	명사 (과학적인) 실험

24 2019년 3월 34번 (정답률 40%) 정답 ①

[지문 끊어 읽기] 제로섬 게임

(1) Credit arrangements / of one kind or another / have existed /
신용 거래는 / 이런저런 종류의 / 존재해 왔다 /
in all known human cultures.
모든 알려진 인류 문화에

(2) The problem in previous eras / was not that /
이전 시대의 문제는 / ~라는 것이 아니었다 /
no one had the idea or knew how to use it.
아무도 그 생각을 하지 못했거나 그것을 사용하는 방법을 알지 못했다

(3) It was that / people seldom wanted /
(=The problem) (좀처럼 ~하지 않다)
그것은 ~라는 것이었다 / 사람들이 좀처럼 원하지 않았다 /
to extend much credit / because they didn't trust /
많은 신용 거래를 하는 것을 / 그들이 믿지 않았기 때문에 /
that the future would be better than the present.
미래가 현재보다 더 나으리라는 것을

(4) They generally believed / that times past had been better /
그들은 일반적으로 믿었다 / 지나간 시대가 더 나았다고 /
than their own times / and that the future would be worse.
그들 자신의 시대보다 / 그리고 미래는 더 나쁠 것이라고
힌트 두 개의 that절이 병렬로 연결되어 주절의 동사 believed의 목적어로 사용되었음.

(5) To put that in economic terms, /
이를 경제학 용어로 표현하자면 /
they believed / that the total amount of wealth was limited. 정답 단서
그들은 믿었다 / 부의 총량이 한정되어 있다고

(6) People / therefore / considered it a bad bet /
사람들은 / 그러므로 / 나쁜 선택으로 여겼다 /
to assume / that they would be producing more wealth /
추정하는 것을 / 그들이 더 많은 부를 생산할 것이라고 /
ten years down the line.
십 년 후에
힌트 시간이 평면 위에 수직으로 놓인 하나의 기다란 선이고, 이것이 위에서 아래로 흐른다고 생각하면, down the line이 '(어떠한 시점) 이후에'로 해석되는 이유를 알 수 있음.

(7) Business looked like a zero-sum game. 정답 단서
사업은 제로섬 게임처럼 보였다

(8) Of course, / the profits of one particular bakery might rise, /
물론 / 한 특정한 빵집의 수익이 오를 수는 있었다 /
but only at the expense of the bakery next door.
하지만 오직 이웃 빵집의 희생으로만

(9) The king of England / might enrich himself, /
영국 왕이 / 그 자신을 부유하게 만들 수는 있었다 /
but only by robbing the king of France.
하지만 오직 프랑스 왕을 약탈함으로써만

(10) You could cut the pie / in many different ways, /
당신은 파이를 자를 수 있었다 / 여러 가지 다양한 방법으로 /
but it never got any bigger.
하지만 그것은 결코 조금도 더 커지지 않았다
★중요 파이 하나를 어떤 비율로 자르든, 그 조각들을 다 합친 크기가 원래의 파이 크기보다 더 커질 수는 없음. 결국, 문장 (5)의 '부의 총량이 한정되어 있다'는 것, 문장 (7)의 '제로섬 게임'과 같은 맥락임.

[전문 해석]

(1)이런저런 종류의 신용 거래는 모든 알려진 인류 문화에 존재해 왔다. (2)이전 시대의 문제는 아무도 그 (신용 거래에 대한) 생각을 하지 못했거나 그것을 사용하는 방법을 알지 못했다는 것이 아니었다. (3)그것(문제)은 사람들이 미래가 현재보다 더 나으리라는 것을 믿지 않았

문제편 p.161

기 때문에, 좀처럼 많은 신용 거래를 하는 것을 원하지 않았다는 것이었다. (4)그들은 일반적으로 그들 자신의 시대보다 지나간 시대가 더 나았고, 미래는 (지금보다) 더 나쁠 것이라고 믿었다. (5)이를 경제학 용어로 표현하자면, 그들은 부의 총량이 한정되어 있다고 믿었다. (6)그러므로 사람들은 십 년 후에 그들이 더 많은 부를 생산할 것이라고 추정하는 것을 나쁜 선택으로 여겼다. (7)사업은 제로섬 게임처럼 보였다. (8)물론 한 특정한 빵집의 수익이 오를 수는 있었지만, (이는) 오직 이웃 빵집의 희생으로만 가능했다. (9)영국 왕이 그 자신을 부유하게 만들 수는 있었지만, (이는) 오직 프랑스 왕을 약탈함으로써만 가능했다. (10)당신은 파이를 여러 가지 다양한 방법으로 자를 수 있었지만, 그것(파이의 총량)은 결코 조금도 더 커지지 않았다.

- zero-sum game(제로섬 게임): 게임 이론에서 승자가 되는 쪽이 얻는 이득과 패자가 되는 쪽의 손실의 총합이 0(zero)이 되는 게임을 말함. 이 이론은 정치, 경제, 사회 등의 분야에서도 통용되는데, 무한 경쟁 속에서 승자가 있으면 승자를 제외한 나머지는 패자가 될 수밖에 없는 구조를 말함.

[정답 확인]

다음 빈칸에 들어갈 말로 가장 적절한 것은?

✔ it never got any bigger
그것은 결코 조금도 더 커지지 않았다
② its value changed in time
그것의 가치는 곧 변했다
③ it made everybody wealthier
그것은 모두를 더 부유하게 만들었다
④ there always was another pie
항상 또 다른 파이가 있었다
⑤ everyone could get an even share of it
모두가 그것의 똑같은 몫을 가질 수 있었다

[문제 풀이]

본문에서는 '빵집'과 '영국 왕'의 예시를 통해 '제로섬 게임', 즉 부의 총량이 한정되어 있어서 어느 한 명이 더 많은 부를 차지할 경우 필연적으로 다른 사람들의 부가 줄어드는 상황을 설명하고 있다. 문장 (10)은 이를 파이 자르기에 비유하는데, 여기서 빈칸에 들어갈 표현은 부의 총량, 즉 파이 전체의 크기가 고정되어 있다는 내용을 담고 있어야 한다. 따라서 정답은 ①이다.

[중요 어휘]

□ **arrangement**	명사 거래, 협정, 합의
□ **extend credit**	신용 거래를 하다, 외상을 주다
□ **bet**	명사 (도박이나 내기에서의) 선택, 추측
□ **enrich**	동사 부유하게 만들다, 풍요롭게 하다
□ **rob**	동사 약탈하다, 도둑질하다
□ **in time**	곧, 이윽고

● 지문 구조도

(1) 신용 거래(credit arrangements)는 모든 알려진 인류 문화에 존재해 왔음.

사람들이 신용 거래를 꺼렸던 이유
(2) 이전 시대에 아무도 신용 거래에 대한 생각을 하지 못했거나 그것을 사용하는 방법을 알지 못해서가 아님.
(3) 사람들은 미래가 현재보다 더 나으리라는 것을 믿지 않았음.
(4) 사람들은 그들 자신의 시대보다 지나간 시대가 더 나았으며 미래는 더 나쁠 것이라고 믿었음.

경제학적 설명
(5) 사람들은 부의 총량(total amount of wealth)이 한정되어 있다고(be limited) 믿었음.
(6) 사람들은 십 년 후에 그들이 더 많은 부를 생산할 것이라고 생각지 않았음.

(7) 사업은 제로섬 게임(zero-sum game)처럼 보였음.

제로섬 게임 1 빵집	제로섬 게임 2 영국 왕	제로섬 게임 3 파이 자르기
(8) 특정한 빵집의 수익이 오르는 것은 오직 이웃 빵집의 희생을 통해서만 가능했음.	(9) 영국 왕이 부유해지는 것은 오직 프랑스 왕을 약탈하는 것을 통해서만 가능했음.	(10) 파이를 여러 다른 방법으로 자를 수는 있지만, 파이는 결코 조금도 더 커지지 않음.

25 2019년 6월 33번 (정답률 40%) 정답 ④

[지문 끊어 읽기] '회사 무너뜨리기' 활동

(1) At the pharmaceutical giant Merck, /
제약 거대 기업 Merck에서 /
CEO Kenneth Frazier decided / to motivate his executives /
CEO Kenneth Frazier는 결정했다 / 그의 임원들에게 동기를 주기로 /
to take a more active role / in leading innovation and change.
더 적극적인 역할을 맡도록 / 혁신과 변화를 이끄는 것에

★ 중요 문장 (1)에서 Kenneth가 임원들에게 더 적극적일 수 있도록 동기를 주기로 결정하는 것을 보아 처음에 임원들이 혁신과 변화에 관심이 없었다는 것을 알 수 있음.

(2) He asked them / to do something radical: /
그는 그들에게 요청했다 / 급진적인 무언가를 하도록 /
generate ideas / that would put Merck out of business.
아이디어를 만들어내라 / Merck를 폐업하게 만들 수 있는 (폐업한)

힌트 that은 주격 관계대명사로 선행사는 ideas임.

(3) For the next two hours, / the executives worked in groups, /
다음 두 시간 동안 / 임원들은 그룹으로 일했다 /
pretending to be one of Merck's top competitors.
Merck의 주요 경쟁자 중 하나인 체하며

(4) Energy soared / as they developed ideas /
활기가 급증했다 / 그들이 아이디어를 개발함에 따라 /
for drugs that would crush theirs / (병렬①)
그들의 것을 짓밟을 수 있는 의약품을 위한 /
and key markets they had missed. (병렬②)
그리고 그들이 놓쳤던 중요한 시장들을 위한

힌트 and 앞뒤로 명사 drugs, key markets가 병렬되어 있는데, drugs는 주격 관계대명사절이 꾸미고, key markets는 목적격 관계대명사절이 관계대명사가 생략된 형태로 꾸미고 있음.

(5) Then, / their challenge was / to reverse their roles / (병렬①)
그 다음에 / 그들의 도전은 / 그들의 역할을 바꾸는 것이었다 /
and figure out / how to defend / against these threats. (병렬②) 정답 단서
그리고 알아내는 것이었다 / 방어하는 방법을 / 이러한 위협으로부터

(6) This "kill the company" exercise is powerful /
이러한 '회사 무너뜨리기' 활동은 강력하다 /
because it reframes a gain-framed activity /
그것이 수익으로 구조화된 활동을 재구조화하기 때문에 /
in terms of losses.
손실의 관점에서

★ 중요 문장 (6)의 gain-framed는 '수익'에 초점을 둔 사고의 구조화를 가리킴. 즉, 기존에 회사에서 어떻게 이익을 낼 것인지에만 초점을 두었다면, 바로 이 '회사 무너뜨리기' 활동에서는 '손실'에 기반을 두고 기존에 '수익'에만 초점을 두었던 사고의 틀을 재구조화시키는 것임.

(7) When deliberating / about innovation opportunities, /
심사숙고할 때 / 혁신 기회에 대해서 /
the leaders weren't inclined / to take risks. 정답 단서
리더들은 ~하고 싶어하지 않았다 / 위험을 감수하고

(8) When they considered /
그들이 고려할 때 /
how their competitors could put them out of business, /
어떻게 그들의 경쟁자가 그들을 폐업하게 만들 수 있는지를 /
they realized / that it was a risk / not to innovate. 정답 단서
그들은 깨달았다 / 위험이라는 것을 / 혁신하지 않는 것이

(9) The urgency of innovation was apparent.
혁신의 긴급함이 명백했다

[전문 해석]

(1)제약 거대 기업 Merck(머크)에서, CEO Kenneth Frazier는 혁신과 변화를 이끄는 것에 더 적극적인 역할을 맡도록 그의 임원들에게 동기를 주기로 결정했다. (2)그는 그들에게 급진적인 무언가를 하도록 요청했다. Merck를 폐업하게(망하게) 만들 수 있는 아이디어를 만들어내라. (3)다음 두 시간 동안, 임원들은 Merck의 주요 경쟁자 중 하나인 체하며 그룹으로 일했다. (4)그들이 그들의 것(의약품)을 짓밟을 수 있는 의약품과 그들이 놓쳤던 중요한 시장들을 위한 아이디어를 개발함에 따라, 활기가 급증했다. (5)그 다음에, 그들의 도전은 그들의 역할을 바꾸고 이러한 위협으로부터 방어하는 방법을 알아내는 것이었다. (6)이러한 '회사 무너뜨리기' 활동은 그것이 손실의 관점에서 수익으로 구조화된 활동을 재구조화하기 때문에 강력하다. (7)혁신 기회에 대해서(기회를 두고) 심사숙고할 때, 리더들은 위험을 감수하고 싶어하지 않았다. (8)그들이 어떻게 그들의 경쟁자가 그들을 폐업하게(망하게) 만들 수 있는지를 고려할 때, 그들은 혁신하지 않는 것이 (곧) 위험이라는 것을 깨달았다. (9)혁신의 긴급함(혁신이 시급하다는 것)이 명백했다.

- Merck(머크): 화이자와 함께 미국을 대표하는 글로벌 제약 회사

[정답 확인]

다음 빈칸에 들어갈 말로 가장 적절한 것은?

① the unknown is more helpful than the negative
미지의 것이 부정적인 것보다 더 도움이 되기
② it highlights the progress they've already made
그들이 이미 해왔던 진전을 강조하기
③ it is not irrational but is consumer-based practice
비논리적이지 않지만(않으면서도) 소비자에 기반을 둔 실행이기
✔ it reframes a gain-framed activity in terms of losses
그것이 손실의 관점에서 수익으로 구조화된 활동을 재구조화하기
⑤ they discuss how well it fits their profit-sharing plans
그들이 그것이 얼마나 그들의 이익 배분 계획에 잘 맞는지를 의논하기

[문제 풀이]

이 지문은 Merck의 CEO인 Kenneth Frazier의 한 일화를 담고 있다. Kenneth는 혁신의 기회가 왔을 때, 위험을 감수하고 싶어하지 않는 소극적인 모습의 임원들을 바꿔보고자 '회사 무너뜨리기' 활동을 한다. 임원들이 자신들의 역할을 바꿔 경쟁사인 체하며 Merck 기업을 짓밟을 수 있는 아이디어를 내기로 한 것인데, 이는 기존에 수익에만 초점을 두던 임원들의 사고를 전환하여 손실에 기반을 두고 위험을 감수하는 혁신이 필요하다는 것을 깨닫게 한 것이다. 따라서 정답은 ④이다.

[중요 어휘]

☐ **pharmaceutical**	형용사 제약의, 약학의
☐ **executive**	명사 임원, 경영진
☐ **innovation**	명사 혁신, 쇄신
☐ **radical**	형용사 급진적인, 근본적인
☐ **soar**	동사 급증하다, 솟구치다
☐ **crush**	동사 짓밟다, 밀어넣다
☐ **reverse**	동사 (뒤)바꾸다, 뒤집다
☐ **defend**	동사 방어하다, 옹호하다
☐ **reframe**	동사 재구조화하다, 다시 구성하다
☐ **in terms of**	~의 관점에서, (~이라는) 면에서
☐ **be inclined to V**	~하고 싶어하다, ~하는 경향이 있다
☐ **take a risk**	위험을 감수하다
☐ **urgency**	명사 긴급(함), 절박
☐ **apparent**	형용사 명백한, 분명한

핵심 지문 마지막에 빈칸이 오는 경우 지문에서 말한 내용을 요약하는 경우가 많음. 서로 다른 관점을 가진 시트콤 시청자들이 프로그램의 의도를 정반대로 해석했다는 연구 결과를 통해 글쓴이가 말하고자 한 바가 무엇인지 파악할 수 있음.

26 2020년 6월 33번 (정답률 40%) 정답 ④

[지문 끊어 읽기] 개인에 따라 달라지는 문화의 영향

(1) Sociologists have proven /
사회학자들은 증명해 왔다 /
that people bring their own views and values /
사람들이 그들 자신의 관점과 가치를 가져온다는 것을 /
to the culture / they encounter; /
문화에 / 그들이 직면하는 /
books, TV programs, movies, and music may affect everyone, /
책, TV 프로그램, 영화, 그리고 음악은 모두에게 영향을 줄지도 모른다 /
but they affect different people / in different ways. 정답 단서
하지만 그것들은 다양한 사람들에게 영향을 준다 / 다른 방식으로

힌트 관계대명사 that 혹은 which가 생략된 목적격 관계대명사절임.

(2) In a study, / Neil Vidmar and Milton Rokeach showed /
한 연구에서 / Neil Vidmar와 Milton Rokeach는 보여주었다 /
episodes of the sitcom *All in the Family* /
시트콤 <All in the Family>의 에피소드를 /
to viewers / with a range of different views / on race.
시청자들에게 / 다양한 다른 관점을 가진 / 인종에 관하여

힌트 전치사 on은 특정한 주제에 관한 것을 말할 때, '~에 관하여'라는 뜻으로 쓰기도 함.

(3) The show centers on a character / named Archie Bunker, /
그 프로그램은 인물을 중심으로 한다 / Archie Bunker라고 불리는 /
an intolerant bigot / who often gets into fights /
동격(=Archie Bunker)/선행사 주격 관계대명사
편협한 고집쟁이인 / 싸움에 종종 휘말리는 /
with his more progressive family members.
그의 더 진보적인 가족 구성원들과의

힌트 문장 (3)의 named 앞에는 '주격 관계대명사+be동사'인 'who is'가 생략되었음. 선행사는 a character이고, 수동태로 쓰였기 때문에 과거분사 named만 남았음.

(4) Vidmar and Rokeach found /
Vidmar와 Rokeach는 알아냈다 /
that viewers who didn't share Archie Bunker's views thought /
접속사 S' V'
Archie Bunker의 관점에 공감하지 않는 시청자들이 생각했다는 것을 /
the show was very funny / in the way /
그 프로그램이 굉장히 재미있다고 / 방식에 있어 /
it made fun of Archie's absurd racism / 정답 단서
그것이 Archie의 터무니없는 인종 차별주의를 조롱하는 /
— in fact, / this was the producers' intention.
사실 / 이것이 제작진의 의도였다

힌트 문장 (4)의 the way 뒤에는 관계부사 'how'가 올 수 없음. the way 뒤에 나오는 절, 즉 it made부터 racism까지가 완전한 문장이기 때문에 관계대명사가 오지 않는다는 점도 기억할 것.

(5) On the other hand, / though, /
반면에 / 그러나 /
viewers who were themselves bigots /
그들 스스로가 고집쟁이였던 시청자들은 /
thought / Archie Bunker was the hero of the show /
생각했다 / Archie Bunker가 그 프로그램의 영웅이라고 /
and that the producers meant to make fun of his foolish family! 정답 단서
그리고 제작진들이 그의 어리석은 가족을 조롱하려고 했다고

(6) This demonstrates / why it's a mistake / to assume /
이것은 입증한다 / 왜 잘못인지를 / 가정하는 것이 /
that a certain cultural product will have the same effect /
특정한 문화적 산물이 같은 영향을 줄 것이라고 /
on everyone.
모두에게

[전문 해석]

(1)사회학자들은 사람들이 그들 자신의 관점과 가치를 그들이 직면하는 문화에 가져온다는 것을 증명해 왔다. 책, TV 프로그램, 영화, 그리고 음악은 모두에게 영향을 줄지도 모르지만, 그것들은 다양한 사람들에게 다른 방식으로 영향을 준다. (2)한 연구에서, Neil Vidmar와 Milton Rokeach는 인종에 관하여 다양한 다른 관점을 가진 시청자들에게 시트콤 <All in the Family>의 에피소드를 보여주었다. (3)그 프로그램은 그의 더 진보적인 가족 구성원들과의 싸움에 종종 휘말리는 편협한 고집쟁이인 Archie Bunker라고 불리는 인물을 중심으로 한다. (4)Vidmar와 Rokeach는 Archie Bunker의 관점에 공감하지 않는 시청자들이 그 프로그램이 Archie의 터무니없는 인종 차별주의를 조롱하는 방식에 있어 굉장히 재미있다고 생각했다는 것을 알아냈는데, 사실 이것이 제작진의 의도였다. (5)그러나 반면에, 그들 스스로가 (편협한) 고집쟁이였던 시청자들은 Archie Bunker가 그 프로그램의 영웅이며, 제작진들이 그의 어리석은 가족을 조롱하려고 했다고 생각했다! (6)이것은 특정한 문화적 산물이 모두에게 같은 영향을 줄 것이라고 가정하는 것이 왜 잘못인지를 입증한다.

[정답 확인]

다음 빈칸에 들어갈 말로 가장 적절한 것은?

① can provide many valuable views
많은 가치 있는 관점들을 제공할 수 있다고
② reflects the idea of the sociologists
사회학자들의 생각을 반영한다고
③ forms prejudices to certain characters
특정한 인물들에 대한 편견을 형성한다고
✔ will have the same effect on everyone
모두에게 같은 영향을 줄 것이라고
⑤ might resolve social conflicts among people
사람들 사이의 사회적인 갈등을 해결할 수 있을 것이라고

[문제 풀이]

지문은 왜 동일한 대상이 개인에게 서로 다른 영향을 주는지에 대해 설명한다. 문장 (1)은 이 지문의 핵심으로, 이후 등장하는 연구는 문장 (1)의 예시이다. 연구에서, 사람들은 같은 시트콤을 보고도 일부는 제작진의 의도가 Archie Bunker를 조롱하는 것이라 말하는 한편, 일부는 Archie Bunker의 가족을 조롱하는 것이라 생각했는데, 이는 동일한 문화적 산물이라 하더라도 개인이 지닌 관점과 가치에 따라 그것이 사람들에게 미치는 영향이 다를 수 있음을 시사한다. 따라서 모두가 같은 감상을 느낄 수 없다는 것, 즉 모두가 같은 영향을 받을 수 없다는 것이 문장 (6)의 내용이자 전체 요약문이 되어야 하므로, 정답은 ④이다.

문제편 p.162

[오답 풀이]

① - 지문의 흐름상 빈칸에는 잘못된 가정에 대한 내용이 들어가야 한다. 지문의 내용은 동일한 문화가 사람들에게 다른 영향을 주는 것은 개인이 가지고 있는 관점과 가치가 관여하기 때문이라고 설명하는 것이지, 관점들이 가치 있는지 아닌지를 논하는 것이 아니므로, ①은 답이 될 수 없다.

[중요 어휘]

☐ **sociologist**	명사 사회학자
☐ **encounter**	동사 직면하다, 마주치다
☐ **a range of**	다양한
☐ **center on**	~을 중심으로 하다
☐ **intolerant**	형용사 편협한, 옹졸한, 견딜 수 없는
☐ **bigot**	명사 고집쟁이, 편견이 아주 심한 사람
☐ **progressive**	형용사 진보적인, 점진적인
☐ **make fun of**	조롱하다, 비웃다
☐ **absurd**	형용사 터무니없는, 말도 안 되는
☐ **intention**	명사 의도, 목적
☐ **demonstrate**	동사 입증하다, 보여주다
☐ **prejudice**	명사 편견 / 동사 편견을 갖게 하다
☐ **resolve**	동사 해결하다, 결심하다

● 지문 구조도

사회학자들의 증명

(1) 사람들이 문화(책, TV 프로그램, 영화, 음악)를 직면할(encounter) 때 개인의 관점(views)과 가치(values)가 적용되어 다른 방식으로 영향을 줌(affect).

↓

예시: Neil Vidmar와 Milton Rokeach의 연구

(2) 인종에 관하여 다양한(a range of) 다른 관점을 가진 시청자들에게 시트콤의 에피소드를 보여주었음.
(3) 시트콤 <All in the Family>: 진보적인(progressive) 가족 구성원들과 싸우는 편협한 고집쟁이(intolerant bigot) Archie Bunker를 중심으로 함.

Archie Bunker에게 공감하지 않는 시청자들

(4) 프로그램에 대한 생각: Archie의 인종 차별주의(racism)를 조롱하는 방식에 있어 재미있어 함. → 제작진의 의도였음.

Archie Bunker에게 공감하는 시청자들

(5) Archie Bunker에 대한 생각: 프로그램의 영웅
(5) 제작진의 의도에 대한 생각: 어리석은 가족을 조롱하는 것

↓

결론

(6) 특정한 문화적 산물(cultural product)이 모두에게 같은 영향을 줄(have the same effect) 것이라고 가정하는(assume) 것은 잘못임.

27 2023년 6월 32번 (정답률 40%)

정답 ③

[지문 끊어 읽기] 무능함에 대해 돈 지불하기

(1) It's hard / to pay more /
형식상의 주어 내용상의 주어
어렵다 / 더 많은 돈을 지불하는 것은 /
for the speedy but highly skilled person, /
병렬① 병렬②
빠르지만 고도로 숙련된 사람에게 /
simply because there's less effort being observed. 정답 단서
순전히 관찰되는 노력이 더 적기 때문이다

★ 중요 문장 (1)을 통해, 일을 완수하는 데 들인 '시간'이 적으면 '노력'이 적다고 보여짐을 추론할 수 있음.

일을 빠르고 숙련되게 하는 사람은 관찰되는 노력이 더 적기 때문에 돈을 많이 받기 어려움.

(2) Two researchers once did a study /
선행사
한때 두 명의 연구원이 연구를 하나 했었다 /
in which they asked people /
전치사+관계대명사 4형식V I·O
그들이 사람들에게 물어보는 /
[how much they would pay / for data recovery]. [ ]: D·O(how 간접의문문)
그들이 얼마를 지불할 것인지를 / 데이터 복구에

(3) They found / [that people would pay a little more /
S① V① [ ]: O
그들은 알아냈다 / 사람들이 약간 더 많은 돈을 지불할 것임을 /
for a greater quantity of rescued data], /
더 많은 양의 구해진 데이터에 대해 /
but [what they were most sensitive to] /
[ ]: S② =people
하지만 그들이 가장 민감했던 것은 /
was [the number of hours the technician worked]. 정답 단서
V② [ ]: S·C 목적격 관계대명사절
기술자가 일한 시간이었다

복구된 데이터 양이 많으면 사람들이 돈을 약간 더 지불하려고 하긴 했지만, 사람들이 가장 민감하게 반응했던 것은 기술자가 일한 '시간'이었음.

(4) When the data recovery took only a few minutes, /
데이터 복구가 몇 분밖에 걸리지 않았을 때는 /
willingness to pay was low, /
지불하려는 의사가 낮았다 /
but when it took more than a week /
it takes 시간 to V: ~하는 데 '시간'이 걸리다
하지만 일주일 이상이 걸렸을 때 /
to recover the same amount of data, /
같은 양의 데이터를 복구하는 데 /
people were willing to pay much more. 정답 단서
비교급 강조
사람들은 기꺼이 훨씬 더 많은 돈을 지불하려고 했다

복구된 데이터의 양이 같으면, 사람들은 일을 끝내는 데 더 많은 시간이 들었을 때 기꺼이 훨씬 더 많은 돈을 지불하려고 함.

(5) Think about it:
그것에 대해 생각해 보라

(6) They were willing to pay more / for the slower service /
그들은 기꺼이 더 많은 돈을 지불하려고 했다 / 더 느린 서비스에 /
with the same outcome. 정답 단서
같은 결과를 가지고

결과물이 같아도 더 느린 서비스, 즉 '시간'을 많이 들인 경우에 더 많은 돈을 지불하고자 함.

(7) Fundamentally, / when we value effort over outcome, /
근본적으로 / 우리가 결과보다 노력을 중시할 때 /
we're paying for incompetence.
우리는 무능함에 비용을 지불하고 있는 것이다

★ 중요 문장 (6)에서 말한 '같은 결과에서 더 느린 서비스에 더 많은 돈을 지불하는 것'이 문장 (7)에서는 '무능함에 비용을 지불하는 것'으로 이어지고 있음.

(8) Although it is actually irrational, /
=paying for incompetence
비록 그것이 실제로는 비합리적이지만 /
we *feel* more rational, and more comfortable, /
우리는 더 합리적이고 더 편안하다고 '느낀다' /
paying for incompetence.
무능함에 지불하면서

[전문 해석]

(1)빠르지만 고도로 숙련된 사람에게 더 많은 돈을 지불하는 것은 어려운데, 순전히 관찰되는 노력이 더 적기 때문이다. (2)한때 두 명의 연구원이 사람들에게 데이터 복구에 그들(사람들)이 얼마를 지불할 것인지를 물어보는 연구를 하나 했었다. (3)그들은 사람들이 더 많은 양의 구해진(복구된) 데이터에 대해 약간 더 많은 돈을 지불할 것임을 알아냈지만, 그들(사람들)이 가장 민감했던 것은 기술자가 일한 시간이었다. (4)데이터 복구가 몇 분밖에 걸리지 않았을 때는 지불하려는 의사가 낮았지만, 같은 양의 데이터를 복구하는 데 일주일 이상이 걸렸을 때 사람들은 기꺼이 훨씬 더 많은 돈을 지불하려고 했다. (5)그것에 대해 생각해 보라. (6)그들은 같은 결과를 가지고 더 느린 서비스에 기꺼이 더 많은 돈을 지불하려고 했다. (7)근본적으로, 우리가 결과보다 노력을 중시할 때, 우리는 무능함에 비용을 지불하고 있는 것이다. (8)비록 그것이 실제로는 비합리적이지만, 우리는 무능함에 지불하면서 더 합리적이고 더 편안하다고 '느낀다'.

[정답 확인]

다음 빈칸에 들어갈 말로 가장 적절한 것은?

① prefer money to time
시간보다 돈을 선호할
② ignore the hours put in
들여진 시간을 무시할
✔ value effort over outcome
결과보다 노력을 중시할
④ can't stand any malfunction
어떠한 기능 불량도 참을 수 없을
⑤ are biased toward the quality
품질 쪽으로 치우쳤을

[문제 풀이]

문장 (3)~(4)에서, 사람들은 복구된 데이터의 양(결과물)이 많으면 돈을 약간 더 지불하려고

문제편 p.162

했으나, 결과물이 좋을 때보다 일에 들인 '시간'이 더 많을 때 훨씬 더 많은 돈을 지불하고자 하는 경향이 있었다. 특히 문장 (1)에서는 일에 들이는 시간과 관찰되는 노력을 연관 짓고 있는데, 이를 연구 사례에 대입해 보면, 무능함에 돈을 지불하는 사람들은 일에 더 많은 시간을 들일수록 더 많은 노력을 들인 것으로 판단하기 때문에 기꺼이 더 많은 돈을 지불하려고 했음을 추론할 수 있다. 따라서 빈칸에 가장 알맞은 말은 ③ 'value effort over outcome(결과보다 노력을 중시할)'이다.

[오답 풀이]

① - 'prefer money to time'은 '시간보다 돈을 선호한다'는 의미이다. 그런데 '시간보다 돈을 선호하는' 사람이라면 일을 더 느리게 하더라도 값이 저렴한 사람을 고용할 것인데, 본문에 제시된 연구에 따르면, 사람들은 같은 일에 더 많은 시간을 소요한 사람에게 더 많은 돈을 지불하고 있으므로, ①은 답이 될 수 없다.

[중요 어휘]

□ **observe**	동사 관찰하다, 목격하다
□ **ask A B**	A에게 B를 묻다
□ **recovery**	명사 복구, 회복
□ **quantity**	명사 양
□ **rescue**	동사 구하다, 구제하다
□ **sensitive**	형용사 민감한, 예민한
□ **the number of A**	A의 수
□ **willingness**	명사 의사, 의지, 기꺼이 하려는 마음
□ **be willing to V**	기꺼이 ~하다, ~하기를 불사하다
□ **outcome**	명사 결과, 성과
□ **value A over B**	B보다 A를 중시하다[선호하다]
□ **incompetence**	명사 무능함
□ **irrational**	형용사 비합리적인, 비이성적인
□ **rational**	형용사 합리적인, 이성적인
□ **prefer A to B**	B보다 A를 선호하다
□ **malfunction**	명사 기능 불량, 오작동 / 동사 제대로 작동하지 않다

● 지문 구조도

(1) 빠르지만 고도로 숙련된(speedy but highly skilled) 사람들은 순전히 관찰되는 노력이 적다(less effort being observed)는 이유로 더 많은 돈을 받지 못함.

↓

연구: (2) 데이터를 복구한 기술자에게 얼마를 지불할 것인가?
→ (3) 사람들은 기술자가 복구한 '데이터의 양'보다 기술자가 일한 '시간'에 더 민감하게 반응함.

1) 복구된 데이터의 양이 다른 경우
: (3) 더 많은 양의 구해진 데이터(a greater quantity of rescued data)에 대해 약간 더 많은 돈을 지불하려고 함.

2) 복구된 데이터의 양이 같은 경우

(4) 몇 분 만(only a few minutes)에 복구한 경우 지불 의사(willingness to pay)가 낮았음(low).	(4) 일주일 이상(more than a week) 걸려 복구한 경우 기꺼이 더 많은 돈을 지불하고자 함(be willing to pay much more). (6) 더 느린 서비스(slower service)에 기꺼이 더 많은 돈을 지불하고자 함(be willing to pay more).

결론

(7)~(8) 사람들은 일의 결과물(outcome)보다 일에 들인 시간과 노력(effort)을 중시하기(value) 때문에, 무능함(incompetence)에 대해 비용을 지불하면서도 그것이 합리적(rational)이고 편안하다(comfortable)고 느낌.

28 2018년 3월 34번 (정답률 35%) 정답 ①

[지문 끊어 읽기] Theodore Roosevelt의 지능적인 홍보 활동

(1) When the late Theodore Roosevelt came back from Africa, /
고 Theodore Roosevelt는 아프리카에서 돌아왔을 때 /
just after he left the White House in 1909, /
1909년에 백악관을 떠난 직후 /
he made his first public appearance / at Madison Square Garden.
처음으로 대중 앞에 모습을 드러냈다 / Madison Square Garden에서

(2) Before he would agree to make the appearance, /
그가 모습을 드러내는 것에 동의하기 전에 /
he carefully arranged /
그는 신중하게 준비했다 /
for nearly one thousand *paid applauders* /
거의 1,000명에 달하는 '고용된 박수치는 사람들'이 /
to be scattered throughout the audience / 정답 단서
청중들 도처에 흩어져 있도록 /
to applaud his entrance on the platform.
자신이 연단 위에 입장할 때 박수갈채를 보내도록

✶중요 박수를 치는 사람을 고용해서 분위기를 조장했다면 그것은 지능적인 홍보 활동의 일환이라고 할 수 있음.

(3) For more than 15 minutes, /
15분이 넘게 /
these paid hand-clappers made the place ring /
이 고용된 박수치는 사람들은 그 장소에 울려 퍼지게 만들었다 /
with their enthusiasm.
그들의 열광이

(4) The rest of the audience took up the suggestion /
나머지 청중도 그 제안을 받아들였다 /
and joined in for another quarter hour. 정답 단서
그리고 15분 더 동참했다

(5) The newspaper men present /
참석한 신문 기자들은 /
were literally swept off their feet / by the tremendous applause / 정답 단서
문자 그대로 마음을 사로잡혔다 / 엄청난 박수갈채에 /
given the American hero, /
그 미국 영웅에게 주어진 /
and his name was emblazoned across the headlines of the newspapers /
그리고 그의 이름은 신문의 헤드라인을 가로질러 선명히 새겨졌다 /
in letters two inches high.
2인치 높이의 글자로

(6) Roosevelt understood / and made intelligent use /
Roosevelt는 이해했다 / 그리고 지능적으로 활용했다 /
of personal promotion.
개인 홍보 활동을

[전문 해석]

(1)고(故) Theodore Roosevelt(시어도어 루스벨트)는 1909년에 백악관을 떠난 직후 아프리카에서 돌아왔을 때, Madison Square Garden에서 처음으로 대중 앞에 모습을 드러냈다. (2)그가 모습을 드러내는 것에 동의하기 전에, 그는 자신이 연단 위에 입장할 때 박수갈채를 보내도록 거의 1,000명에 달하는 '고용된 박수치는 사람들'이 청중들 도처에 흩어져 있도록 신중하게 준비했다. (3)이 고용된 박수치는 사람들은 15분이 넘게 그 장소에 그들의 열광이 울려 퍼지게 만들었다. (4)나머지 청중도 그 제안을 받아들여(유도에 호응하여), 15분 더 (그 열광에) 동참했다. (5)참석한 신문 기자들은 문자 그대로 그 미국 영웅에게 주어진 엄청난 박수갈채에 마음을 사로잡혔고, 그의 이름은 2인치 높이의 글자로 신문의 헤드라인을 가로질러 선명히 새겨졌다. (6)Roosevelt는 개인 홍보 활동을 이해했고 지능적으로 활용했다.

- Theodore Roosevelt(시어도어 루스벨트, 1882년~1945년): 미국의 제26대 대통령으로 러일전쟁의 강화 알선, 모로코 분쟁 해결 공로 등으로 1906년 노벨 평화상을 수상한 인물
- Madison Square Garden(매디슨 스퀘어 가든): 미국 뉴욕시 맨해튼에 위치한 실내 경기장

[정답 확인]

다음 빈칸에 들어갈 말로 가장 적절한 것은?

✔ understood and made intelligent use of personal promotion
개인 홍보 활동을 이해했고 지능적으로 활용했다
② made public policies that were beneficial to his people
국민들에게 유익한 공공 정책을 만들었다
③ knew when was the right time for him to leave office
그가 사무실을 떠날 알맞은 때가 언제인지 알았다
④ saw the well-being of his supporters as the top priority
그의 지지자들의 행복을 우선 사항으로 여겼다
⑤ didn't appear before the public in an arranged setting
계획된(연출된) 상황에서 대중 앞에 모습을 드러내지는 않았다

✶중요 루스벨트의 이러한 지능적인 홍보 활동은 오히려 arranged setting에 해당하므로 ⑤에서 not이 없었다면 맞는 설명이 될 수 있음.

문제편 p.163

[문제 풀이]

Theodore Roosevelt(시어도어 루스벨트)는 연단에 서기 전, 미리 박수칠 사람들을 고용해 청중들 사이에 흩어져 있게 준비해두었다. 그가 등장할 때 고용된 사람들은 박수를 치기 시작했고, 다른 청중들도 그 호응에 이끌려 엄청난 박수갈채를 보냈다. 이를 목격한 신문 기자들은 Roosevelt에 대한 대중의 열정적인 반응을 신문 헤드라인으로 싣게 되었다. 즉 Roosevelt는 자신을 홍보하는 적절한 방법을 잘 활용한 것이다. 따라서 빈칸에 들어갈 말로 적절한 답은 ① 'understood and made intelligent use of personal promotion(개인 홍보 활동을 이해했고 지능적으로 활용했다)'이다.

[중요 어휘]

☐ **late**	형용사 고(故), 이미 사망한, 늦은
☐ **arrange**	동사 ~을 준비하다, 계획을 짜다, 정리하다, 배열하다
☐ **applauder**	명사 박수치는 사람, 성원을 보내는 사람
☐ **scatter**	동사 흩어지게 만들다, 흩뿌리다
☐ **applaud**	동사 박수갈채를 보내다
☐ **platform**	명사 연단, 강단, (기차역의) 플랫폼
☐ **take up**	(제의 등을) 받아들이다
☐ **literally**	부사 문자 그대로, 말 그대로
☐ **sweep off one's feet**	(~의) 마음을 사로잡다
☐ **tremendous**	형용사 엄청난
☐ **applause**	명사 박수(갈채)
☐ **emblazon**	동사 선명히 새기다
☐ **make use of**	~을 활용하다[이용하다]
☐ **promotion**	명사 홍보 (활동), 승진
☐ **priority**	명사 우선 사항

29 2019년 9월 33번 (정답률 35%) 정답 ①

[지문 끊어 읽기] 성과를 위한 적절한 집단 규모

(1) New technology tends to come / from new ventures / —startups.
신기술은 나오는 경향이 있다 / 신규 벤처 기업에서 / 스타트업과 같은

(2) From the Founding Fathers in politics /
정치계 건국의 아버지부터 /
to the Royal Society in science /
과학계 왕립학회까지 /
to Fairchild Semiconductor's "traitorous eight" in business, /
경영계 Fairchild 반도체의 '8인의 반역자'까지 /
small groups of people / bound together by a sense of mission /
소집단의 사람들이 / 사명감으로 굳게 맺어진 /
have changed the world for the better.
세상을 보다 나은 쪽으로 변화시켜왔다 정답 단서

힌트 문장 앞부분의 'from A to B to C' 형식이 생소할 수 있지만, 'A부터 B까지'의 뜻을 가진 'from A to B'에 to C를 추가해 내용을 연장한 것뿐임.

(3) The easiest explanation for this is negative: /
이것에 대한 가장 쉬운 설명은 부정적이다 /
it's hard to develop new things / in big organizations, /
새로운 것을 개발하기는 어렵다 / 큰 조직에서 /
and it's even harder / to do it by yourself. 정답 단서
그리고 훨씬 더 어렵다 / 혼자서 그것을 해내는 것은

힌트 설명이 부정적(negative)이라는 것은, 창의적이면서도 업계를 이끌어 갈 혁신을 만들어 내는 것이 소수의 집단이 아닌 대규모 집단이나 개인으로서는 힘들기 때문이라는 점에서 부정적으로 표현된다는 의미임.

(4) Bureaucratic hierarchies move slowly, /
관료주의적 계급 제도는 느리게 움직인다 /
and entrenched interests shy away from risk.
그리고 굳어진 이해관계는 위험을 피한다

(5) In the most dysfunctional organizations, /
가장 제대로 기능하지 않는 조직에서는 /
signaling that work is being done / becomes a better strategy /
일이 진행되고 있다고 나타내는 것이 / 더 나은 전략이 된다 /
for career advancement / than actually doing work.
승진을 위한 / 실제로 일을 하는 것보다

(6) At the other extreme, / a lone genius might create /
정반대로 / 한 명의 천재는 창작할지도 모른다 /
a classic work of art or literature, /
최고 수준의 예술이나 문학 작품을 /
but he could never create an entire industry.
하지만 그는 절대 산업 전체를 조성할 수 없을 것이다

(7) Startups operate on the principle /
스타트업은 원칙에 따라 작동한다 /
that you need to work with other people / to get stuff done, /
당신이 다른 사람들과 함께 일해야 한다는 / 일을 끝내려면 /
but you also need to stay small enough /
하지만 또한 당신이 충분히 작은 규모를 유지할 필요가 있다는 /
so that you actually can.
당신이 실제로 그럴 수 있도록

힌트 앞에서 천재 혼자서 산업 전체를 조성할 수는 없다고 했으므로, 본문은 무조건 집단 규모를 작게 유지하는 것이 아니라 '협업해서 일을 끝낼 수 있는' 정도의 규모를 유지하라고 말하고 있음. 따라서 can 다음에는 work with other people to get stuff done이 생략된 것으로 볼 수 있음.

[전문 해석]

(1)신기술은 스타트업과 같은 신규 벤처 기업에서 나오는 경향이 있다. (2)정치계 건국의 아버지부터 과학계 왕립학회, (그리고) 경영계 Fairchild 반도체의 '8인의 반역자'까지, 사명감으로 굳게 맺어진 소집단의 사람들이 세상을 보다 나은 쪽으로 변화시켜왔다. (3)이것에 대한 가장 쉬운 설명은 부정적이다. (즉) 큰 조직에서 새로운 것을 개발하기는 어려우며, 혼자서 그것을 해내는 것은 훨씬 더 어렵다. (4)관료주의적 계급 제도는 느리게 움직이며, 굳어진 이해관계는 위험을 피한다(피하려고 한다). (5)가장 제대로 기능하지 않는 조직에서는 실제로 일을 하는 것보다 일이 진행되고 있다고 나타내는 것이 승진을 위한 더 나은 전략이 된다. (6)정반대로, 한 명의 천재는 최고 수준의 예술이나 문학 작품을 창작할지도 모르지만, 그는 절대 (혼자서) 산업 전체를 조성할 수 없을 것이다. (7)스타트업은 (당신이) 일을 끝내려면 다른 사람들과 함께 일해야 하지만, 또한 당신이 실제로 그럴(협업하여 일을 끝낼) 수 있도록 충분히 작은 규모를 유지할 필요가 있다는 원칙에 따라 작동한다.

- Founding Fathers(건국의 아버지): 미국 독립 선언에 기여한 미국 초기 대통령과 정치인들
- Royal Society(왕립학회): 1660년에 자연 과학의 진흥을 위해 영국에서 만들어진 학자들의 모임
- Traitorous Eight(8인의 반역자): 1957년에 쇼클리 반도체 연구소에서 사직하고 페어차일드 반도체 회사를 만든 8명의 직원들로, 이들로 인해 실리콘 밸리가 전성기를 맞았음.

[정답 확인]

다음 빈칸에 들어갈 말로 가장 적절한 것은?

✔ stay small enough so that you actually can
실제로 그럴(협업하여 일을 끝낼) 수 있도록 충분히 작은 규모를 유지할
② give yourself challenges as often as possible
가능한 한 자주 스스로에게 도전 과제를 줄
③ outperform rival businesses in other countries
다른 나라의 경쟁사들을 능가할
④ employ the efficient system of big enterprises
큰 기업들의 능률적인 시스템을 이용할
⑤ control the organization with consistent policies
일관된 정책들로 조직을 관리할

[문제 풀이]

본문에 따르면, 큰 조직에서는 사람들이 위험을 피하려 하고 실제 성과를 내기보다 보여주기식 성과에 급급하다는 부작용이 있으며, 개인으로 일할 때는 최고 수준의 결과가 나오더라도 혼자서 산업 전체를 조성할 수가 없기 때문에, 대부분의 신기술이 스타트업같은 신규 벤처 기업에서 만들어진다고 한다. 스타트업은 이러한 부작용이 없을 정도의, 적지도 않고 많지도 않은 충분한 숫자의 사람들이 서로 협력하기 때문에 이러한 단점들을 보완할 수 있다는 장점이 있다. 따라서 빈칸에 들어갈 정답은 ①이다.

[오답 풀이]

② - 스타트업은 신기술을 만들기 위해 직원들에게 계속해서 도전 과제를 주는 것이 아니라 소규모 집단의 협력을 통해 최대의 능률을 이끌어내는 기업 형태이므로 보기 ②는 빈칸에 들어갈 말로 적절하지 않다.

[중요 어휘]

☐ **venture**	명사 벤처 (기업), 모험 / 동사 (위험을 무릅쓰고) 가다, 하다
☐ **startup**	명사 스타트업, 신규 업체
☐ **traitorous**	형용사 반역적인, 배반하는
☐ **bound together by**	~으로 굳게 맺어진
☐ **sense of mission**	사명감

문제편 p.163

☐	**bureaucratic**	형용사 관료주의적인
☐	**hierarchy**	명사 계급 제도, 체계
☐	**entrenched**	형용사 굳어진, 확립된, 견고한
☐	**shy away from**	~을 피하다
☐	**dysfunctional**	형용사 제대로 기능하지 않는, 고장 난
☐	**classic**	형용사 최고 수준의, 전형적인
☐	**principle**	명사 원칙, 원리
☐	**outperform**	동사 능가하다, 더 나은 결과를 내다

● 지문 구조도

(1) **신기술은 스타트업(startup)에서 나오는 경향이 있음.**

(2) **사명감(sense of mission)으로 굳게 맺어진 소집단의 사람들이 세상을 보다 나은 쪽으로 변화시켜옴.**

정치: 건국의 아버지
과학: 왕립학회
경영: Fairchild 반도체의 '8인의 반역자'

(3) **이유: 큰 조직에서 새로운 것을 개발하기는 어려우며, 혼자서 하기엔 훨씬 더 어려움.**

큰 조직	혼자서 일하기
(4) 관료적인 계급 제도(bureaucratic hierarchy)는 느리게 움직이며, 굳어진 이해관계(entrenched interests)는 위험을 피하려고 함.	(6) 절대 (혼자서) 산업 전체(entire industry)를 조성할 수 없음.

예시

(5) 실제로 일을 하는 것보다 일이 진행되고 있다고 보여주는 것이 승진(career advancement)에 도움이 됨.

↓

스타트업

(7) 일을 끝내려면 다른 사람들과 함께 일해야 하지만 실제로 그 일을 할 수 있을 만큼만 충분히 작은 규모를 유지할 필요가 있음.

핵심 첫 문장에서 태도의 네 가지 주요소들을 제시한 뒤, 글의 후반부에서는 이 네 가지의 요소들이 늑대에 대한 태도를 형성하는 데 어떻게 상호작용하는지 설명하고 있음. 이때, 각 요소의 기능을 파악하면서 빈칸을 추론할 것.

30 2019년 11월 34번 (정답률 35%) 정답 ②

[지문 끊어 읽기] 태도의 주요소

(1) Attitude has been conceptualized / into four main components: /
태도는 개념화되어 왔다 / 네 가지의 주요소로 /
affective (feelings of liking or disliking), /
정서적인(호불호의 감정) /
cognitive (beliefs and evaluation of those beliefs), /
인지적인(신념과 그러한 신념에 대한 평가) /
behavioral intention /
행동 의도 /
(a statement of how one would behave in a certain situation), /
전치사 of의 목적어인 명사절
(특정한 상황에서 누군가가 어떻게 행동할 것인지에 대한 진술) /
and behavior.
그리고 행동

(2) Public attitudes / toward a wildlife species and its management /
대중의 태도는 / 야생 동물 종과 그것의 관리에 대한 /
are generated / based on the interaction of those components.
만들어진다 / 그러한 요소들의 상호작용에 근거하여
정답 단서

(3) In forming our attitudes / toward wolves, / people strive /
in V-ing: ~할 때
우리의 태도를 형성할 때 / 늑대에 대한 / 사람들은 노력한다 /
to keep their affective components of attitude /
5형식V O
그들의 태도의 정서적인 요소를 유지하려고 /
consistent with their cognitive component.
O·C(형용사구)
그들의 인지적인 요소와 일관되게
정답 단서

힌트 여기서 keep은 5형식 동사로, 목적격 보어 자리에 형용사(구)가 왔음. 목적격 보어 자리에는 부사가 올 수 없으므로 consistent 대신에 consistently를 쓰지 않도록 유의해야 함.

(4) For example, / I could dislike wolves; / I believe /
예를 들어 / 나는 늑대를 싫어할 수도 있다 / 나는 믿는다 /
they have killed people (cognitive belief), /
그들이 사람을 죽여왔다고(인지적인 신념) /
and having people killed / is of course bad (evaluation of belief).
삽입구
그리고 사람을 죽게 하는 것은 / 당연히 나쁘다(신념에 대한 평가)

(5) The behavioral intention / that could result from this /
행동 의도는 / 이것으로부터 발생할 수 있는 /
is to support a wolf control program /
늑대 통제 프로그램을 지지하는 것이다 /
and actual behavior may be a history / of shooting wolves.
그리고 실제 행동은 이력일지도 모른다 / 늑대 사냥의

(6) In this example, / all aspects of attitude /
이 예시에서 / 태도의 모든 측면은 /
are consistent with each other, /
서로 일관되어 있다 /
producing a negative overall attitude / toward wolves.
그리고 대체로 부정적인 태도를 만들어낸다 / 늑대에 대한

[전문 해석]

(1)태도는 네 가지의 주요소로 개념화되어 왔다. 정서적인(호불호의 감정), 인지적인(신념과 그러한 신념에 대한 평가), 행동 의도(특정한 상황에서 누군가가 어떻게 행동할 것인지에 대한 진술), 그리고 행동. (2)야생 동물 종과 그것의 관리에 대한 대중의 태도는 그러한 요소들의 상호작용에 근거하여 만들어진다. (3)늑대에 대한 우리의 태도를 형성할 때, 사람들은 태도의 정서적인 요소를 인지적인 요소와 일관되게 유지하려고 노력한다. (4)예를 들어, 나는 늑대를 싫어할 수도 있다. 나는 그들이 사람을 죽여왔다고 믿는다(인지적인 신념), 그리고 사람을 죽게 하는 것은 당연히 나쁘다(신념에 대한 평가). (5)이것으로부터 발생할 수 있는 행동 의도는 늑대 통제 프로그램을 지지하는 것이며, 실제 행동은 늑대 사냥의 이력일지도 모른다. (6)이 예시에서 태도의 모든 측면은 서로 일관되어 있으며, 대체로 늑대에 대한 부정적인 태도를 만들어낸다.

[정답 확인]

다음 빈칸에 들어갈 말로 가장 적절한 것은?

① attitude drives the various forms of belief
태도는 다양한 형태의 신념을 만든다
✔ all aspects of attitude are consistent with each other
태도의 모든 측면은 서로 일관되어 있다
③ cognitive components of attitude outweigh affective ones
태도의 인지적인 요소는 정서적인 요소보다 더 크다
④ the components of attitude are not simultaneously evaluated
태도의 요소들은 동시에 평가되지 않는다
⑤ our biased attitudes get in the way of preserving biodiversity
우리의 편향된 태도는 생물의 다양성을 보존하는 데에 방해가 된다

[문제 풀이]

지문은 우리의 태도가 '정서, 인지, 행동 의도, 행동'이라는 네 가지의 요소로 나뉜다고 한다. 예를 들어, 어떤 사람의 늑대에 대한 부정적인 태도는 '늑대를 싫어하는 것(정서)', '늑대가 생명에 위협되는 위험한 동물이라고 생각하는 것(인지)', '늑대를 통제하는 것에 동의하는 것(행동 의도)', 그리고 '늑대를 사냥하는 것(행동)'의 결과물이다. 이러한 요소들은 모두 일관적으로 늑대에 대해 부정적인 측면들을 다루고 있으므로, 빈칸에 들어올 정답은 ②이다.

[오답 풀이]

① - 지문에서는 늑대들이 사람들의 생명을 위협하므로 나쁜 동물이라는 신념 외의 다른 신념은 언급되지 않으므로, 태도가 다양한 신념을 만든다고 보기 힘들다.
③ - 정서적인 요소와 인지적인 요소를 일관되게 유지하려고 노력한다는 문장 (3)의 내용은 문장 (2)에서 언급된 요소들 간의 상호작용을 '일관성'이라는 측면에서 설명하고자 한 것이지, 특정 요소가 다른 요소보다 우월하다고 말하는 것이 아니다. 따라서 ③은 정답이 될 수 없다.

문제편 p.164

[중요 어휘]

☐ attitude	명사 태도, 자세
☐ conceptualize	동사 개념화하다
☐ component	명사 요소, 부품
☐ affective	형용사 정서적인
☐ cognitive	형용사 인지적인
☐ intention	명사 의도, 목적
☐ wildlife	명사 야생 동물
☐ strive	동사 노력하다, 경쟁하다
☐ consistent	형용사 일관된, 변함없는
☐ outweigh	동사 ~보다 더 크다
☐ simultaneously	부사 동시에, 일제히
☐ biased	형용사 편향된, ~에 더 치중하는
☐ preserve	동사 보존하다, 보호하다
☐ biodiversity	명사 생물의 다양성

핵심 필자는 기름에 튀기거나 지방이 많은 음식, 즉 건강하지 않은 음식을 많이 먹는 것은 유전적으로 프로그램된 것일 수도 있다고 언급하면서 과거로부터 지금까지 이어지는 인간의 습성을 설명하고 있음. 따라서 이러한 주제와 연관지어 빈칸의 내용을 추론해야 함.

31 2021년 9월 34번 (정답률 35%) 정답 ①

[지문 끊어 읽기] 건강하지 않은 음식을 선호하는 이유

(1) Deep-fried foods are tastier than bland foods, /
기름에 튀긴 음식들은 자극적이지 않은 음식들보다 더 맛있다 /
and children and adults develop a taste for such foods.
그리고 아이들과 어른들은 그런 음식들에 대한 취향을 발달시킨다

(2) Fatty foods cause the brain to release oxytocin, /
(cause: 5형식V / the brain: O / to release: O·C(to부정사))
지방이 많은 음식들은 뇌가 옥시토신을 방출하도록 야기한다 /
a powerful hormone with a calming, antistress, and relaxing influence, /
진정, 항스트레스, 그리고 긴장을 완화시키는 효과를 가진 강력한 호르몬인 /
said to be the opposite of adrenaline, / into the blood stream; /
아드레날린의 반대로 알려진 / 혈류 속으로 /
hence the term "comfort foods."
이런 이유로 '위안 음식'이라는 용어

힌트 주격 관계대명사와 be동사(=which is)가 생략된 관계사절로 선행사인 oxytocin을 수식함.

(3) We may even be genetically programmed / to eat too much.
우리는 심지어 유전적으로 프로그램되어 있을지도 모른다 / 너무 많이 먹도록

(4) For thousands of years, food was very scarce.
수천 년 동안 음식은 매우 부족했다

(5) Food, along with salt, carbs, and fat, / was hard to get, /
소금, 탄수화물, 지방과 더불어 음식은 / 구하기 어려웠다 /
and the more you got, the better.
그리고 더 많이 구할수록 더 좋았다 정답 단서

힌트 'the 비교급+S+V, the 비교급+S+V'는 '더 ~할수록, 더 ~하다'라는 의미임. 이때 비교급 자리에는 형용사/부사의 비교급이 올 수 있으며, 이 문장에서는 뒷 문장의 S+V(it was)가 생략되었음.

(6) All of these things are necessary nutrients in the human diet, /
이것들 모두는 인간의 식단에 필수적인 영양소이다 /
and when their availability was limited, /
그리고 그것들의 이용 가능성이 제한되었을 때에는 /
you could never get too much. 정답 단서
아무리 먹어도 결코 과하지 않았다

힌트 'can + 부정어 ~ too (much)'는 '아무리 ~해도 과하지 않다'라는 뜻의 표현임. 이 문장에서는 could가 쓰였으므로 과거로 해석함.

(7) People also had to hunt down animals /
(hunt down: 병렬①)
사람들은 또한 동물들을 사냥해야 했다 /
or gather plants / for their food, / and that took a lot of calories.
(gather: 병렬②)
또는 식물을 채집해야 했다 / 그들의 음식을 위해 / 그리고 그것은 많은 칼로리를 소모했다

힌트 문장 (7)의 that은 지시대명사로, hunting down animals and gathering plants for food를 의미함.

(8) It's different / these days.
다르다 / 요즘에는

(9) We have food at every turn /
우리는 도처에 음식이 있다 /
— lots of those fast-food places and grocery stores /
많은 그러한 패스트푸드점들과 식료품점들 /
with carry-out food.
포장 음식이 있는

(10) But that ingrained "caveman mentality" says /
하지만 그 뿌리 깊은 '원시인 사고방식'은 말한다 /
that we can't ever get too much to eat.
우리가 아무리 먹을 것을 많이 구해도 결코 과하지 않다고

힌트 문장 (6)에서 나온 표현인 'could never get too much'는 'get'을 'eat(먹다, 섭취하다)'의 의미로 '아무리 먹어도 결코 과하지 않다' 정도로 해석할 수 있으나, 여기서는 말 그대로 '아무리 먹을 것을(to eat) 많이 구해도(get) 결코 과하지 않다'라고 해석하는 것이 자연스러움.

(11) So craving for "unhealthy" food may actually be our body's attempt /
그래서 '건강하지 않은' 음식에 대한 갈망은 실제로는 우리 몸의 시도일 수 있다 /
to stay healthy.
건강하게 유지하려는

[전문 해석]

(1)기름에 튀긴 음식들은 자극적이지 않은 음식들보다 더 맛있고, 아이들과 어른들은 그런 음식들에 대한 취향을 발달시킨다(그런 음식들을 점점 좋아하게 될 것이다). (2)지방이 많은 음식들은 뇌가 진정, 항스트레스, 그리고 긴장을 완화시키는 효과를 가진 강력한 호르몬인, 아드레날린의 반대로 알려진 옥시토신을 혈류 속으로 방출하도록 야기하며, 이런 이유로 '위안 음식'이라는 용어(가 있다). (3)우리는 심지어 유전적으로 너무 많이 먹도록 프로그램되어 있을지도 모른다. (4)수천 년 동안, 음식은 매우 부족했다. (5)소금, 탄수화물, 지방과 더불어 음식은 구하기 어려웠고, 더 많이 구할수록 더 좋았다. (6)이것들 모두는 인간의 식단에 필수적인 영양소이고, 그것들의 이용 가능성이 제한되었을 때에는 아무리 먹어도 결코 과하지 않았다. (7)사람들은 또한 (그들의) 음식을 위해 동물들을 사냥하거나 식물을 채집해야 했고, 그것은 많은 칼로리를 소모했다. (8)요즘에는 (상황이) 다르다. (9)포장 음식이 있는 많은 (그러한) 패스트푸드점들과 식료품점들과 같이 우리는 도처에 음식이 있다. (10)하지만 그 뿌리 깊은 '원시인 사고방식'은 우리가 아무리 먹을 것을 많이 구해도 결코 과하지 않다고 말한다. (11)그래서 '건강하지 않은' 음식에 대한 갈망은 실제로는 건강하게 유지하려는 우리 몸의 시도일 수 있다.

[정답 확인]

다음 빈칸에 들어갈 말로 가장 적절한 것은?

✔ actually be our body's attempt to stay healthy
실제로는 건강하게 유지하려는 우리 몸의 시도일
② ultimately lead to harm to the ecosystem
궁극적으로 생태계에 대한 해를 초래할
③ dramatically reduce our overall appetite
극적으로 우리의 전반적인 식욕을 감소시킬
④ simply be the result of a modern lifestyle
단순히 현대 생활 방식의 결과일
⑤ partly strengthen our preference for fresh food
부분적으로 신선 식품에 대한 우리의 선호를 강화시킬

[문제 풀이]

본문에 따르면 과거에는 음식이 매우 부족했고, 소금, 탄수화물, 지방은 필수적인 영양소임에도 구하기가 어려웠기 때문에 이러한 음식들은 아무리 많이 구해도 지나치지 않았으며 이러한 사고방식이 과거 원시인들에게 깊게 자리 잡았다. 이러한 사고방식은 음식이 매우 풍부해지고 지방이 많은 음식은 건강하지 않다고 생각되는 현재에도 작용하고 있다. 따라서 마지막 문장에서는 음식에 대한 인간의 갈망이 과거에 우리 몸에 필수적인 영양소들을 제공하는 음식들을 최대한 많이 구하려는 사고방식에서 기인한다는 글의 요지를 설명하려고 하고 있으므로 정답은 ①이다.

[오답 풀이]

④ - 본문은 과거 음식과 충분한 영양분을 섭취하기 어려웠던 원시인들의 뿌리 깊은 사고방식이 오늘날까지 현대인에게 남아있는 양상에 대해 설명한다. 음식을 향한 갈망은 과거에서 지금까지 이어지는 이러한 사고방식 때문이라고 볼 수 있으므로 과거에 대한 내용 없이 단순히 현대 생활 방식의 결과라고 보는 것은 적절하지 않다.

[중요 어휘]

☐ bland	형용사 (맛이) 자극적이지 않은, 특징 없는
☐ relaxing	형용사 긴장을 완화시키는, 느긋한
☐ blood stream	혈류
☐ hence	부사 이런 이유로
☐ comfort	명사 위안, 편안함 / 동사 위로하다
☐ genetically	부사 유전적으로, 유전학적으로
☐ scarce	형용사 부족한, 드문
☐ along with	~와 더불어, ~와 마찬가지로
☐ carbs	명사 탄수화물 (식품)

☐ at every turn	도처에, 어디에서나, 언제나
☐ carry-out	명사 포장 음식, 포장 음식 전문점
☐ ingrained	형용사 뿌리 깊은, 깊이 몸에 밴
☐ caveman	명사 원시인, 혈거인(동굴 속에 사는 사람)
☐ mentality	명사 사고방식
☐ craving	명사 갈망, 열망
☐ attempt	명사 시도 / 동사 시도하다
☐ ultimately	부사 궁극적으로
☐ appetite	명사 식욕
☐ preference	명사 선호

32 2022년 6월 32번 (정답률 35%) 정답 ⑤

[지문 끊어 읽기] 전자기 스펙트럼의 인지

(1) Color is an interpretation of wavelengths, /
색은 파장에 대한 해석이다 / 동격의 콤마(,)
one that only exists internally.
=an interpretation 주격 관계대명사절
내부에서만 존재하는 것

(2) And it gets stranger, /
그리고 그것은 더 생소하게 느껴진다 /
because the wavelengths we're talking about /
선행사(S') 목적격 관계대명사절
왜냐하면 우리가 말하고 있는 파장은 /
involve only [what we call "visible light", /
V' 선행사를 포함한 관계대명사 동격의 콤마(,)
'가시광선'이라고 부르는 것만을 포함하기 때문이다 / [ ]: involve의 목적어
a spectrum of wavelengths / that runs from red to violet].
주격 관계대명사절
파장의 스펙트럼인 / 빨간색에서 보라색까지 이어지는

(3) But visible light constitutes /
그러나 가시광선은 구성한다 /
only a tiny fraction of the electromagnetic spectrum /
전자기 스펙트럼의 극히 일부만을 /
— less than one ten-trillionth of it.
그중 10조 분의 1도 되지 않는 =the electromagnetic spectrum

힌트 대시(—)는 앞 문장에 대한 부연 설명을 할 때 사용됨. 본문의 경우 대시 뒤의 내용은 'a tiny fraction of the electromagnetic spectrum'을 부연 설명함.

(4) All the rest of the spectrum /
나머지 모든 스펙트럼이 /
— including radio waves, microwaves, X-rays, gamma rays, cell phone conversations, wi-fi, and so on — /
전파, 마이크로파, X선, 감마선, 휴대폰 통화, 와이파이 등을 포함한 /
all of this is flowing through us / right now, /
이 모든 것이 우리를 통해 흐르고 있다 / 지금 /
and we're completely unaware of it.
그리고 우리는 그것을 완전히 알지 못한다

힌트 대시(—)를 통해 삽입된 부분은 앞서 나온 'All the rest of the spectrum'의 예시임. 또한 'All the rest of the spectrum'과 'all of this', 그리고 'it'은 동일한 대상을 가리킴.

(5) This is because /
이것은 ~ 때문이다 /
we don't have any specialized biological receptors /
우리가 어떤 특별한 생물학적 수용체도 가지고 있지 않기 /
to pick up on these signals /
형용사적 용법
이러한 신호를 포착할 수 있는 /
from other parts of the spectrum. 정답단서
스펙트럼의 다른 부분으로부터

우리에게는 가시광선 외 다양한 스펙트럼을 인지할 수 있는 특별한 생물학적 수용체가 없기 때문에 전파, 마이크로파 등의 나머지 모든 스펙트럼을 인지하지 못함.

(6) [The slice of reality / that we can see] / is limited by our biology.
[ ]: S 선행사 목적격 관계대명사절 V
현실의 단면은 / 우리가 볼 수 있는 / 우리의 생명 작용에 의해 제한된다

[전문 해석]

(1)색은 파장에 대한 해석으로, 내부에서만 존재하는 것이다. (2)그리고 우리가 말하고 있는 파장은 빨간색에서 보라색까지 이어지는 파장의 스펙트럼인 '가시광선'이라고 부르는 것만을 포함하기 때문에, 더 생소하게 느껴진다. (3)그러나 가시광선은 전자기 스펙트럼의 극히 일부만을 구성하는데, 그중 10조 분의 1도 되지 않는다. (4)전파, 마이크로파, X선, 감마선, 휴대폰 통화, 와이파이 등을 포함한 나머지 모든 스펙트럼이 지금 우리를 통해 흐르고 있으며, 우리는 이 모든 것을 완전히 알지 못한다. (5)이것은 우리가 스펙트럼의 다른 부분으로부터 이러한 신호를 포착할 수 있는 어떤 특별한 생물학적 수용체도 가지고 있지 않기 때문이다. (6)우리가 볼 수 있는 현실의 단면은 우리의 생명 작용에 의해 제한된다.

[정답 확인]

다음 빈칸에 들어갈 말로 가장 적절한 것은?

① hindered by other wavelengths
다른 파장에 의해 방해된다
② derived from our imagination
우리의 상상에서 파생된다
③ perceived through all senses
모든 감각을 통해 지각된다
④ filtered by our stereotypes
우리의 고정 관념에 의해 여과된다
✔ limited by our biology
우리의 생명 작용에 의해 제한된다

[문제 풀이]

본문에 따르면, 전자기 스펙트럼 중에는 전파, 마이크로파, X선 등 다양한 스펙트럼이 있으나 우리는 전자기 스펙트럼 중 가시광선밖에 보지 못한다. 이는 우리가 나머지 스펙트럼을 포착할 수 있는 특별한 생물학적 수용체를 가지고 있지 않기 때문이다. 따라서 빈칸에는 우리의 생명 작용에 의해 세상의 모든 스펙트럼을 보지 못한다는 내용의 ⑤가 적절하다.

[중요 어휘]

☐ interpretation	명사 해석
☐ wavelength	명사 파장
☐ internally	부사 내부에서
☐ constitute	동사 구성하다
☐ fraction	명사 일부, 부분
☐ trillion	1조
☐ be unaware of	~을 알지 못하다
☐ specialized	형용사 특별한
☐ biological	형용사 생물학적인, 생물학의
☐ receptor	명사 수용체
☐ pick up on	~을 포착하다[이해하다, 알아차리다]
☐ slice	명사 단면, 조각 / 동사 썰다
☐ biology	명사 생명 작용(활동), 생물학
☐ hinder	동사 방해하다, 저해하다
☐ be derived from	~에서 파생되다[유래하다]
☐ stereotype	명사 고정 관념

33 2022년 6월 34번 (정답률 35%) 정답 ①

[지문 끊어 읽기] 자유 시장과 정부의 시장 개입

(1) In most of the world, / capitalism and free markets are accepted /
세계 대부분에서 / 자본주의와 자유 시장은 받아들여지고 있다 /
today / as constituting the best system /
전치사
오늘날 / 최고의 시스템을 구성하는 것으로 /
for allocating economic resources /
병렬①
경제적 자원을 분배하기 위한 /
and encouraging economic output.
병렬②
그리고 경제적 생산을 장려하기 위한

(2) Nations have tried other systems, /
현재완료
국가들은 다른 시스템들을 시도했다 /
such as socialism and communism, / but in many cases /
사회주의나 공산주의와 같은 / 하지만 많은 경우 /
they have either switched wholesale to /
현재완료(have p.p.) p.p.① 부사
그들은 완전히 전환했다 /
or adopted aspects of free markets.
p.p.②
혹은 자유 시장의 측면들을 받아들였다

힌트 'either A or B(A 혹은 B)' 구문으로 A와 B 자리에 'switched wholesale to (free markets)'와 'adopted aspects of free markets'가 온 형태임. 'switched wholesale to' 뒤에는 동어 반복을 피하기 위해 전치사 to의 목적어 free markets가 생략되어 있음.

(3) Despite the widespread acceptance /
전치사(~에도 불구하고)
광범위한 수용에도 불구하고 /
of the free-market system, / markets are rarely left entirely free.
자유 시장 시스템의 / 시장이 완전히 자유로운 상태로 맡겨지는 경우는 드물다

(4) Government involvement takes many forms, / [ranging /
정부의 개입은 다양한 형태를 취한다 / 이르면서 /
[ ]: 분사구문(=and it ranges~)
from the enactment and enforcement / of laws and regulations /
from A to B
제정과 집행에서부터 / 법과 규정의 /
to direct participation in the economy /
직접적인 경제 참여까지 /
through entities like the U.S.'s mortgage agencies]. 정답 단서
미국의 담보 기관과 같은 실체를 통한

오늘날 세계 대부분이 자본주의와 자유 시장 체제하에 있지만, 정부의 개입이 다양한 형태로 여전히 존재함.

(5) Perhaps / the most important form of government involvement, /
아마도 / 가장 중요한 형태의 정부 개입은 /
S
however, / comes in the attempts /
V
그러나 / 시도로 나타날 것이다 /
of central banks and national treasuries / to control and affect /
중앙은행과 국가 재무기관의 / 통제하고 영향을 미치려는 /
형용사적 용법
the ups and downs of economic cycles.
경기 주기의 흥망성쇠를

[전문 해석]

(1)오늘날 세계 대부분에서 자본주의와 자유 시장은 경제적 자원을 분배하고 경제적 생산을 장려하기 위한 최고의 시스템을 구성하는 것으로 받아들여지고 있다. (2)국가들은 사회주의나 공산주의와 같은 다른 시스템들을 시도했지만, 많은 경우 그들은 자유 시장으로 완전히 전환하거나 자유 시장의 측면들을 받아들였다. (3)자유 시장 시스템의 광범위한 수용에도 불구하고, 시장이 완전히 자유로운 상태로 맡겨지는 경우는 드물다. (4)정부의 개입은 법과 규정의 제정과 집행에서부터 미국의 담보 기관과 같은 실체를 통한 직접적인 경제 참여에 이르기까지 다양한 형태를 취한다. (5)그러나 아마도 가장 중요한 형태의 정부 개입은 중앙은행과 국가 재무기관이 경기 주기의 흥망성쇠를 통제하고 영향을 미치려는 시도로 나타날 것이다.

- capitalism(자본주의): 사유 재산제에 바탕을 두고 이윤 획득을 위해 상품의 생산과 소비가 이루어지는 경제 체제
- free market(자유 시장): 시장 활동에 대한 국가의 간섭이 배제된, 즉 개인의 경제 활동의 자유가 최대한으로 보장된 시장
- socialism(사회주의): 생산 수단의 사회적 소유와 평등을 중시하는 이데올로기
- communism(공산주의): 사유 재산제의 부정과 공유 재산제의 실현으로 빈부의 차를 없애려는 사상

[정답 확인]

다음 빈칸에 들어갈 말로 가장 적절한 것은?

✔ markets are rarely left entirely free
시장이 완전히 자유로운 상태로 맡겨지는 경우는 드물다
② governments are reluctant to intervene
정부가 개입하기를 꺼린다
③ supply and demand are not always balanced
수요와 공급이 언제나 균형을 이루지는 않는다
④ economic inequality continues to get worse
경제적 불평등이 계속 악화된다
⑤ competition does not guarantee the maximum profit
경쟁이 최대 이익을 보장하지 않는다

[문제 풀이]

본문에 따르면, 오늘날 세계 대부분에서 자본주의와 자유 시장 체제가 시행되고 있지만 문장 (4)와 (5)에서 설명하듯이 정부의 개입은 여전히 존재한다. 이는 특히 법과 규정의 제정과 집행, 미국 담보 기관을 통한 직접적인 경제 참여, 중앙은행과 국가 재무기관을 통한 경기 주기 통제 같은 구체적인 예시를 통해 확인할 수 있다. 따라서 빈칸에는 '시장이 완전히 자유로운 상태로 맡겨지는 경우는 드물다'는 내용의 ①이 적절하다.

[오답 풀이]

② - 문장 (4)와 (5)에서 정부가 법과 규정의 제정과 집행, 직접적인 경제 참여, 경기 주기의 통제 등 다양한 형태로 개입을 한다고 언급했다. 따라서 정부가 개입하기를 꺼린다는 것은 본문의 내용과 정반대이므로 답이 될 수 없다.
③ - '수요와 공급이 언제나 균형을 이루지는 않는다'는 ③은 자유 시장 시스템의 맹점에 해당하지만, 시장의 자율성과 정부 개입을 이야기하고 있는 본문의 흐름을 보았을 때 빈칸에 적절하지 않다.

[중요 어휘]

□ constitute	동사 구성하다, (단체를) 설립하다
□ allocate	동사 분배하다
□ output	명사 생산(량)
□ wholesale	부사 완전히, 대규모로 / 형용사 도매의, 대규모의 / 명사 도매
□ adopt	동사 (사상·의견·정책 등을) 받아들이다, 채택하다, 입양하다
□ widespread	형용사 광범위한
□ acceptance	명사 수용, 동의
□ involvement	명사 개입
□ range from A to B	A에서부터 B까지 이르다
□ enactment	명사 (법률의) 제정
□ enforcement	명사 집행
□ regulation	명사 규정, 규제
□ entity	명사 실체, 독립체
□ mortgage	명사 담보, (담보) 대출(금)
□ agency	명사 기관, 대리점, 단체
□ attempt	명사 시도
□ treasury	명사 재무기관, 금고
□ ups and downs	흥망성쇠
□ intervene	동사 개입하다

34 2023년 9월 34번 (정답률 35%) 정답 ②

[지문 끊어 읽기] 학습과 기억의 작동 방식

(1) Much of human thought is designed / to screen out information /
인간 사고의 대부분은 설계되었다 / 정보를 걸러내도록 /
병렬①
and to sort the rest into a manageable condition.
병렬②
그리고 나머지를 관리할 수 있는 상태로 분류하도록

(2) The inflow of data from our senses /
S
우리 감각에서 오는 데이터의 유입은 /
could create an overwhelming chaos, /
압도적인 혼란을 만들 수 있다 /
especially given the enormous amount of information /
~을 고려할 때
특히 정보의 막대한 양을 고려할 때 /
available in culture and society.
문화와 사회에서 가용할 수 있는

(3) Out of all the sensory impressions and possible information, /
모든 감각적 인상과 가능한 정보 중에서 /
it is vital / [to find a small amount /
형식상의 주어 병렬① 선행사
중요하다 / 적은 양을 찾는 것은 /
that is most relevant to our individual needs /
주격 관계대명사절
우리의 개별적인 필요에 가장 관련 있는 /
and to organize that into a usable stock of knowledge]. [ ]: 내용상의 주어
병렬②
그리고 그것을 사용할 수 있는 지식체로 정리하는 것은

(4) Expectancies accomplish some of this work, /
예상들은 이 작업의 일부를 해낸다 /
[helping to screen out information /
병렬① 선행사
정보를 걸러내는 것을 도우면서 /
that is irrelevant to what is expected, /
주격 관계대명사절
예상되는 것과 관련이 없는 /

문제편 p.166

예상은 예상되는 것과 관련이 없는 정보를 걸러내는 것을 돕고 예상되는 것과의 명백한 모순에 우리의 주의를 집중해서 정보를 정리함

and focusing our attention on clear contradictions]. 정답 단서
병렬② [ ]: 분사구문
그리고 명백한 모순에 우리의 주의를 집중하면서

(5) The processes of learning and memory are marked /
학습과 기억의 과정은 특징지어진다 /
by a steady elimination of information.
정보의 꾸준한 제거로

(6) People notice / only a part of the world around them.
사람들은 인식한다 / 그들 주위의 세계의 일부만을

(7) Then, / only a fraction of what they notice /
S
그리고 / 그들이 인식하는 것의 일부만이 /
gets processed and stored into memory. 정답 단서 사람들이 인식하는 것의 일부만이 처리되고 기억으로 저장됨.
V① V②(gets 생략)
처리되고 기억으로 저장된다

(8) And only part of what gets committed to memory /
그리고 기억에 넘겨진 것의 일부만이 / S
can be retrieved.
상기될 수 있다

[전문 해석]

(1)인간 사고의 대부분은 정보를 걸러내고 나머지를 관리할 수 있는 상태로 분류하도록 설계되었다. (2)우리 감각에서 오는 데이터의 유입은 특히 문화와 사회에서 가용할 수 있는 정보의 막대한 양을 고려할 때 압도적인 혼란을 만들 수 있다. (3)모든 감각적 인상과 가능한 정보 중에서 우리의 개별적인 필요에 가장 관련 있는 적은 양을 찾는 것과 그것을 사용할 수 있는 지식체로 정리하는 것은 중요하다. (4)예상들은 예상되는 것과 관련이 없는 정보를 걸러내는 것을 돕고 명백한 모순에 우리의 주의를 집중하면서 이 작업의 일부를 해낸다. (5)학습과 기억의 과정은 정보의 꾸준한 제거로 특징지어진다. (6)사람들은 그들 주위의 세계의 일부만을 인식한다. (7)그리고 그들이 인식하는 것의 일부만이 처리되고 기억으로 저장된다. (8)그리고 기억에 넘겨진 것의 일부만이 상기될 수 있다.

[정답 확인]

다음 빈칸에 들어갈 말로 가장 적절한 것은?

① tend to favor learners with great social skills
좋은 사회적 기술을 가진 학습자에 유리한 경향이 있다
② are marked by a steady elimination of information
정보의 꾸준한 제거로 특징지어진다
③ require an external aid to support our memory capacity
우리의 기억 용량을 지원하는 외부의 도움을 요구한다
④ are determined by the accuracy of incoming information
들어오는 정보의 정확성에 의해 결정된다
⑤ are facilitated by embracing chaotic situations as they are
있는 그대로 혼란스러운 상황을 받아들임으로써 촉진된다

[문제 풀이]

문장 (1)~(4)에 따르면, 인간의 사고는 유입되는 많은 정보들 중에서 개별적인 필요에 관련이 있는 정보를 찾아내고 그것을 정리하도록 설계되었고, 예상을 통해 그 일의 일부를 해낸다. 문장 (6)~(8)은 사람들이 그들 주위의 세계를 일부만 인식하고 그중 일부만을 처리하고 기억하며, 또 그중 일부만이 다시 상기된다고 말한다. 따라서 빈칸에는 학습과 기억의 과정이 정보의 꾸준한 제거로 특징지어진다는 내용의 ②가 적절하다.

[오답 풀이]

③ - 문장 (1)은 인간의 사고가 정보를 걸러내고 관리할 수 있는 상태로 분류하도록 설계되었다고 말하고 이후에도 인간 사고와 인지 자체에 대해 이야기하며 외부의 도움은 언급하지 않으므로 우리의 기억 용량을 지원하는 외부의 도움을 요구한다는 ③은 정답으로 적절하지 않다.

[중요 어휘]

☐ screen out	~을 걸러내다[차단하다]
☐ sort	동사 분류하다 / 명사 종류
☐ manageable	형용사 관리할 수 있는, 다루기 쉬운
☐ inflow	명사 유입
☐ chaos	명사 혼란, 혼돈
☐ sensory	형용사 감각의
☐ impression	명사 인상, 감명
☐ vital	형용사 중요한
☐ relevant	형용사 관련 있는, 적절한
☐ organize	동사 정리하다, 관리하다
☐ usable	형용사 사용할 수 있는, 편리한
☐ expectancy	명사 예상, 기대
☐ contradiction	명사 모순, 부정
☐ mark	동사 특징짓다, 표시하다 / 명사 점수, 표시
☐ steady	형용사 꾸준한, 확고한
☐ elimination	명사 제거, 삭제
☐ fraction	명사 일부, 부분
☐ process	동사 처리하다, 가공하다 / 명사 과정, 절차
☐ commit	동사 (기억·처리 등에) 넘기다[맡기다], (죄를) 범하다, 약속하다
☐ retrieve	동사 상기하다, 되찾다

35 2019년 3월 32번 (정답률 30%) 정답 ②

[지문 끊어 읽기] 청중들의 평가가 달라진 이유

(1) Sometimes / a person is acclaimed / as "the greatest" /
때때로 / 어떤 사람은 칭송된다 / '가장 위대한 사람'으로 /
because there is little basis for comparison.
비교할 기준이 거의 없기 때문에

(2) For example, /
예를 들어 /
violinist Jan Kubelik was acclaimed as "the greatest" /
바이올리니스트 Jan Kubelik는 '가장 위대한 사람'으로 칭송되었다 /
during his first tour of the United States, /
그의 첫 번째 미국 순회 공연 동안 /
but when impresario Sol Hurok brought him back /
그러나 기획자 Sol Hurok이 그를 다시 데려왔을 때 /
to the United States / in 1923, /
미국으로 / 1923년에 /
several people thought / that he had slipped a little.
몇몇 사람들은 생각했다 / 그가 실력이 조금 떨어졌다고

(3) However, / Sol Elman, /
그러나 / Sol Elman은 /
the father of violinist Mischa Elman, / thought differently.
바이올리니스트 Mischa Elman의 아버지인 / 다르게 생각했다

(4) He said, / "My dear friends, /
그는 말했다 / 친애하는 나의 친구들이여 /
Kubelik played the Paganini concerto tonight /
오늘밤 Kubelik는 Paganini 협주곡을 연주했습니다 /
as splendidly as ever he did.
그가 늘 했던 것만큼 훌륭하게

힌트 'A ~ as 형용사/부사 as B'는 'A는 B만큼 ~하다'라고 해석되는데, 이때 as 사이에 형용사가 올지 부사가 올지는 A와 B에 의해 결정됨. 문장 (4)에서 A 부분의 필수 성분은 'Kubelik(주어) played(동사) the Paganini concerto (목적어)'인데, 이는 완벽한 3형식 문장이고, '동사(played)'를 수식하므로 '부사(splendidly)'가 왔음.

(5) Today / you have a different standard. 정답 단서
오늘 / 여러분은 다른 기준을 가지고 있습니다

(6) You have Elman, Heifetz, and the rest.
여러분은 Elman, Heifetz, 그리고 나머지를 가지고 있습니다

(7) All of you have developed and grown /
여러분 모두는 발전하고 성장했습니다 /
in artistry, technique, / and, above all, /
예술성, 기법에서 / 그리고 무엇보다도 /
in knowledge and appreciation.
지식과 감상력에서

중요 문장 (6)과 (7)은 사람들이 Kubelik의 실력을 평가하는 기준이 구체적으로 어떻게 달라졌는지 설명하고 있음. 문장 (6)에서는 Elman, Heifetz 등 실력을 비교할 대상이 생겼음을, 문장 (7)에서는 사람들의 감상 능력 자체가 발전했음을 언급하고 있음.

정답 단서
(8) The point is: / you know more; / not that Kubelik plays less well."
요점은 ~입니다 / 여러분은 더 많이 압니다 / Kubelik가 연주를 잘 못한 것이 아니라

문제편 p.166

[전문 해석]

(1)때때로 어떤 사람은 비교할 기준이 거의 없기 때문에 '가장 위대한 사람'으로 칭송된다. (2)예를 들어, 바이올리니스트 Jan Kubelik(얀 쿠벨리크)는 그의 첫 번째 미국 순회 공연 동안 '가장 위대한 사람(연주자)'으로 칭송되었으나, 1923년에 기획자 Sol Hurok(솔 휴록)이 그를 미국으로 다시 데려왔을 때, 몇몇 사람들은 그(Kubelik)가 실력이 조금 떨어졌다고 생각했다. (3)그러나 바이올리니스트 Mischa Elman(미샤 엘먼)의 아버지인 Sol Elman(솔 엘먼)은 다르게 생각했다. (4)그는 (이렇게) 말했다. "친애하는 나의 친구들이여, 오늘밤 Kubelik는 Paganini(파가니니) 협주곡을 그가 늘 했던 것만큼 훌륭하게 연주했습니다. (5)오늘 여러분은 다른 기준을 가지고 있습니다. (6)여러분은 Elman, Heifetz(하이페츠), 그리고 나머지를 가지고 있습니다(여러분에게는 Elman, Heifetz, 그리고 그 밖의 연주자가 있습니다). (7)여러분 모두는 예술성, 기법에서, 그리고 무엇보다도 지식과 감상력에서 발전하고 성장했습니다. (8)요점은 (이것)입니다. 여러분은 더 많이 압니다. Kubelik가 (예전보다) 연주를 잘 못한 것이 아닙니다(요점은 Kubelik가 예전보다 연주를 잘 못한 것이 아니라, 여러분이 더 많이 알게 되었다는 것입니다)."

- Jan Kubelik(얀 쿠벨리크, 1880년~1940년): 체코의 바이올리니스트이자 작곡가로, '파가니니의 재래'라는 평을 받을 정도로 뛰어난 기교를 선보였다.

- Niccoló Paganini(니콜로 파가니니, 1782년~1840년): 이탈리아 최고로 평가되는 바이올리니스트이자 작곡가로, 탁월한 연주 실력과 자유분방한 성격으로 인해 '악마의 바이올리니스트'라는 별명을 얻었다.

- concerto(협주곡, 콘체르토): 독주 악기와 관현악이 합주하면서 독주 악기의 기교를 충분히 발휘하도록 작곡한 소나타 형식의 악곡을 가리킨다.

[정답 확인]

다음 빈칸에 들어갈 말로 가장 적절한 것은?

① there are moments of inspiration
영감의 순간들이 있기

✔② there is little basis for comparison
비교할 기준이 거의 없기

★중요 문장 (5)의 'standard(기준, 표준)'가 보기 ②에서는 유의어인 'basis(기준, 근거)'로 쓰였음.

③ he or she longs to be such a person
그 또는 그녀가 그러한 사람이 되기를 간절히 바라기

④ other people recognize his or her efforts
다른 사람들이 그 또는 그녀의 노력을 인정하기

⑤ he or she was born with great artistic talent
그 또는 그녀가 위대한 예술적 재능을 갖고 태어났기

[문제 풀이]

본문에 따르면, 바이올리니스트 Jan Kubelik에 대한 미국 청중들의 평가가 달라진 이유는 Kubelik의 연주 실력이 떨어졌기 때문이 아니라, 비교의 기준이 될 만한 다른 연주자들을 알게 되면서 청중들의 예술적인 지식과 감상력이 한층 성장했기 때문이다. 즉, Kubelik가 첫 번째 미국 순회 공연에서 '가장 위대하다'고 칭송되었던 것은 청중들이 그의 실력을 평가할 기준을 갖고 있지 못했기 때문이라고 할 수 있다. 따라서 빈칸에 들어갈 표현은 ②이다.

[중요 어휘]

□ **acclaim A (as B)**	A를 (B로) 칭송하다
□ **comparison**	명사 비교, 비유
□ **impresario**	명사 (극장 등의) 기획자, 단장
□ **slip**	동사 실력이 떨어지다, 전락하다
□ **concerto**	명사 협주곡, 콘체르토
□ **splendidly**	부사 훌륭하게, 화려하게
□ **standard**	명사 기준, 표준
□ **artistry**	명사 예술성, 예술적 기교
□ **appreciation**	명사 감상력, 음미, 비평
□ **inspiration**	명사 영감, 창조적 자극

핵심 분노에 대처하는 바람직한 방법으로 '타임아웃'을 들고 있음. 본문의 예시를 통해 타임아웃이 분노 조절에 어떤 도움을 주는지 생각해 볼 것.

36 2020년 9월 32번 (정답률 30%) 정답 ③

[지문 끊어 읽기] 분노에 대처하는 방법

(1) When we are emotionally charged, / we often use anger /
우리가 감정적으로 흥분되어 있을 때 / 우리는 종종 분노를 사용한다 /

to hide our more primary and deeper emotions, /
우리의 더 원초적이고 더 깊은 감정을 숨기기 위해 /

such as sadness and fear, / which doesn't allow /
슬픔과 공포 같은 / 그런데 그것은 허용하지 않는다 /

for true resolution to occur.
진정한 해결책이 생겨나는 것을

(2) Separating yourself / from an emotionally upsetting situation /
당신 자신을 분리하는 것은 / 감정적으로 화가 나게 하는 상황으로부터 /

gives you the space you need / to better understand /
4형식V I·O D·O
당신에게 당신이 필요로 하는 공간을 제공한다 / 더 잘 이해하기 위해 /

what you are truly feeling /
당신이 진정으로 느끼고 있는 것을 /

so you can more clearly articulate your emotions /
그래서 당신은 더 명확하게 당신의 감정을 표현할 수 있다 /

in a logical and less emotional way.
논리적이고 덜 감정적인 방법으로

★중요 여기서 '타임아웃'이란 문장 (2)의 '감정적으로 화가 나게 하는 상황으로부터 자신을 분리하는 것'을 의미함.

(3) A time-out also helps spare innocent bystanders.
타임아웃은 또한 무고한 구경꾼들을 구하는 데에도 도움이 된다

(4) When confronted with situations /
=When we are confronted
상황에 직면했을 때 /

that don't allow us to deal with our emotions /
5형식V O O·C
우리가 우리의 감정에 대처하는 것을 허용하지 않는 /

힌트 관계대명사 that이 이끄는 2개의 주격 관계대명사절은 모두 선행사인 situations를 수식하고 있음.

or that cause us to suppress them, /
5형식V O O·C
또는 우리가 그것들을 억누르도록 하는 /

we may transfer those feelings / to other people or situations /
우리는 그러한 감정을 전이할 수도 있다 / 다른 사람이나 상황에 /

at a later point.
나중에

(5) For instance, / if you had a bad day at work, /
예를 들어 / 만약 당신이 직장에서 나쁜 하루를 보냈다면 /

you may suppress your feelings at the office, / only to find /
당신은 사무실에서는 당신의 감정을 억누를 수도 있다 / 그러나 발견하게 된다 /

힌트 여기서 'only to V'는 '~하나 (결국) ~한다'라는 뜻의 결과를 나타내는 to부정사의 부사적 용법으로 사용됨.

that you release them / by getting into a fight /
당신이 그것들을 표출하는 것을 / 싸움을 시작하게 됨으로써 /

with your kids or spouse / when you get home later that evening.
당신의 아이들이나 배우자와 / 그 후 저녁에 당신이 집에 도착했을 때

(6) Clearly, / your anger didn't originate at home, / 정답 단서
분명히 / 당신의 분노는 집에서 비롯된 것이 아니다 /

but you released it there.
하지만 당신은 거기서 그것을 표출했다

(7) When you take the appropriate time /
당신이 적절한 시간을 가질 때 /

to digest and analyze your feelings, /
당신의 감정을 소화하고 분석하는 /

you can mitigate / hurting or upsetting other people /
당신은 완화시킬 수 있다 / 다른 사람들의 마음을 상하게 하거나 속상하게 하는 것을 /

who have nothing to do with the situation. 정답 단서
그 상황과 전혀 관련이 없는

[전문 해석]

(1)우리가 감정적으로 흥분되어 있을 때, 우리는 슬픔과 공포 같은 우리의 더 원초적이고 더 깊은 감정을 숨기기 위해 종종 분노를 사용하는데, 그것은 진정한 해결책이 생겨나는 것을 허용하지 않는다. (2)감정적으로 화가 나게 하는 상황으로부터 당신 자신을 분리하는 것은 당신에게 당신이 진정으로 느끼고 있는 것을 더 잘 이해하기 위해 (당신이) 필요로 하는 공간을 제공하고, 그래서 당신은 논리적이고 덜 감정적인 방법으로 더 명확하게 감정을 표현할 수 있다. (3)타임아웃은 또한 무고한 구경꾼들을 구하는 데에도 도움이 된다. (4)우리가 우리의 감정에 대처하는 것을 허용하지 않는 상황 또는 우리가 그것(감정)들을 억누르도록 하는 상황에 직면했을 때, 우리는 그러한 감정을 나중에 다른 사람이나 상황에 전이할 수도 있다. (5)예를 들어, 만약 당신이 직장에서 나쁜 하루를 보냈다면 당신은 사무실에서는 (당신의) 감정을 억누를 수도 있으나, 그 후 저녁에 당신이 집에 도착했을 때 (당신의) 아이들이나 배우자와 싸움을 시작하게 됨으로써 (당신이) 그것(감정)들을 표출하는 것을 발견하게 된다. (6)분명히 당신의 분노는 집에서 비롯된 것이 아니지만, 당신은 거기서 그것을 표출했다. (7)당신이 당신의 감정을 소화하고 분석하는 적절한 시간을 가질 때, 당신은 그 상황과 전혀 관련이 없는 다른 사람들의 마음을 상하게 하거나 속상하게 하는 것을 완화시킬 수 있다.

[정답 확인]

다음 빈칸에 들어갈 말로 가장 적절한 것은?

① restrain your curiosity
당신의 호기심을 억제하는 데
② mask your true emotions
당신의 진정한 감정을 감추는 데
✔ spare innocent bystanders
무고한 구경꾼들을 구하는 데
④ provoke emotional behavior
감정적인 행동을 유발하는 데
⑤ establish unhealthy relationships
건강하지 않은 관계를 수립하는 데

[문제 풀이]

지문은 감정적으로 화가 나는 상황에서 '타임아웃'을 통해 분노를 다스리는 법을 소개한 글이다. 문장 (4)~(6)은 화가 남에도 불구하고 분노를 드러낼 수 없는 상황일 때 그 상황과 전혀 관련이 없는 사람에게 분노가 표출될 수 있음을 보여주고, 문장 (7)은 이러한 상황에서 자기 감정을 돌아볼 혼자만의 시간을 가지는 것, 즉 '타임아웃'을 하는 것이 애꿎은 사람들의 마음을 상하게 하거나 속상하게 하지 않도록 도와준다고 설명한다. 따라서 정답은 ③이다.

[오답 풀이]

② - 본문의 요지는 감정을 억누르게 되면 이후 다른 사람이나 상황에 감정을 표출하게 되므로 타임아웃을 통해 감정에 잘 대처하자는 내용이다. 문장 (5), (6)에 사무실에서 일어난 감정을 제대로 표출하지 못하고 억누른 상태에서 퇴근하면, 집에서 비롯된 분노가 아니지만, 엄한 가족들에게 표출하게 된다는 예시가 있다. 그러므로 보기 ②와는 반대의 내용이 빈칸에 와야 하는 것을 알 수 있다.

[중요 어휘]

☐ **charge**	동사 (감정을) 흥분시키다, (요금 등을) 청구하다
☐ **primary**	형용사 원초적인, 주요한
☐ **resolution**	명사 해결책, 결단력
☐ **articulate**	동사 (분명히) 표현하다, 설명하다
☐ **spare**	동사 구하다, 살려주다 / 형용사 여분의
☐ **innocent**	형용사 무고한, 죄가 없는
☐ **bystander**	명사 구경꾼, 목격자, 행인
☐ **be confronted with**	~에 직면하다
☐ **suppress**	동사 억누르다, 진압하다
☐ **mitigate**	동사 완화시키다, 경감시키다
☐ **have nothing to do with**	~와 (전혀) 관련이 없다
☐ **restrain**	동사 억제하다, 저지하다
☐ **provoke**	동사 유발하다, 화나게 하다

37 2023년 6월 34번 (정답률 30%) 정답 ⑤

[지문 끊어 읽기] 대중적인 사고

(1) Many people look for safety and security / in popular thinking.
많은 사람이 안전과 안심을 찾는다 / 대중적인 사고에서

(2) They figure / that if a lot of people are doing something, /
명사절 접속사
그들은 생각한다 / 만약 많은 사람이 무언가를 하고 있다면 /
then it must be right.
그것은 틀림없이 옳을 것이라고

(3) It must be a good idea.
그것은 좋은 생각임이 틀림없다

(4) If most people accept it, / then it probably represents /
만약 대부분의 사람들이 그것을 받아들인다면 / 그러면 그것은 아마도 상징할 것이다 /
fairness, equality, compassion, and sensitivity, / right?
공정함, 평등함, 동정심, 그리고 민감성을 / 그러한가

(5) Not necessarily.
꼭 그렇다고 할 수는 없다

(6) Popular thinking said / the earth was the center of the universe, /
said의 목적어절
대중적인 사고는 말했다 / 지구가 우주의 중심이라고 /
yet Copernicus studied the stars and planets /
병렬①
하지만 Copernicus는 별과 행성을 연구했다 /
and proved mathematically /
병렬②
그리고 수학적으로 증명했다 /
[that the earth and the other planets in our solar system /
[ ]: proved의 목적어절
지구와 우리 태양계의 다른 행성들이 /
revolved around the sun]. 정답 단서 Copernicus는 대중적인 사고를 사실로 수용하지 않고 별과 행성을 연구하여 공전을 수학적으로 증명함.
태양 주위를 돈다는 것을

(7) Popular thinking said / surgery didn't require clean instruments, /
said의 목적어절
대중적인 사고는 말했다 / 수술이 깨끗한 도구를 필요로 하지 않는다고 /
yet Joseph Lister studied the high death rates in hospitals /
병렬①
하지만 Joseph Lister는 병원에서의 높은 사망률을 연구했다 /
and introduced antiseptic practices /
병렬② 선행사
그리고 멸균법을 소개했다 /
that immediately saved lives. 정답 단서 Joseph Lister는 대중적인 사고를 사실로 수용하지 않고 병원에서의 높은 사망률을 연구하여 멸균법을 소개함.
주격 관계대명사절
즉시 생명을 구하는

(8) Popular thinking said /
대중적인 사고는 말했다 /
that women shouldn't have the right to vote, /
명사절 접속사
여성들이 투표권을 가져서는 안 된다고 /
yet people like Emmeline Pankhurst and Susan B. Anthony /
하지만 Emmeline Pankhurst와 Susan B. Anthony 같은 사람들은 /
fought for and won that right. 정답 단서 Emmeline Pankhurst와 Susan B. Anthony는 대중적인 사고에 도전하여 여성 투표권을 쟁취함.
그 권리를 위해 싸웠고 쟁취했다

(9) We must always remember / [there is a huge difference /
우리는 항상 기억해야 한다 / 큰 차이가 있다는 것을 /
between acceptance and intelligence]. [ ]: remember의 목적어절
수용과 지성 사이에

(10) People may say / that there's safety in numbers, /
명사절 접속사
사람들은 말할지도 모른다 / 수가 많은 편이 안전하다고 /
but that's not always true. 정답 단서 대중적인 사고가 항상 사실인 것은 아님.
하지만 그것이 항상 사실인 것은 아니다

[전문 해석]

(1)많은 사람이 대중적인 사고에서 안전과 안심을 찾는다. (2)그들은 만약 많은 사람이 무언가를 하고 있다면, 그것은 틀림없이 옳을 것이라고 생각한다. (3)그것은 좋은 생각임이 틀림없다. (4)만약 대부분의 사람들이 그것을 받아들인다면, 그것은 아마도 공정함, 평등함, 동정심, 그리고 민감성을 상징할 것이다, 그러한가? (5)꼭 그렇다고 할 수는 없다. (6)대중적인 사고는 지구가 우주의 중심이라고 말했지만, Copernicus는 별과 행성을 연구했고 지구와 우리 태양계의 다른 행성들이 태양 주위를 돈다는 것을 수학적으로 증명했다. (7)대중적인 사고는 수술이 깨끗한 도구를 필요로 하지 않는다고 말했지만, Joseph Lister는 병원에서의 높은 사망률을 연구했고 즉시 생명을 구하는 멸균법을 소개했다. (8)대중적인 사고는 여성들이 투표권을 가져서는 안 된다고 말했지만, Emmeline Pankhurst와 Susan B. Anthony 같은 사람들은 그 권리를 위해 싸웠고 쟁취했다. (9)우리는 항상 수용과 지성 사이에 큰 차이가 있다는 것을 기억해야 한다. (10)사람들은 수가 많은 편이 안전하다고 말할지도 모르지만, 그것이 항상 사실인 것은 아니다.

[정답 확인]

다음 빈칸에 들어갈 말로 가장 적절한 것은?

① majority rule should be founded on fairness
다수결의 원칙은 공정성에 기초해야 한다는 것
② the crowd is generally going in the right direction
군중들은 일반적으로 옳은 방향으로 향한다는 것
③ the roles of leaders and followers can change at any time
리더와 팔로워의 역할은 언제든 바뀔 수 있다는 것
④ people behave in a different fashion to others around them
사람들은 그들 주위의 다른 사람들과 다른 방식으로 행동한다는 것
✔ there is a huge difference between acceptance and intelligence
수용과 지성 사이에 큰 차이가 있다는 것

문제편 p.167

[문제 풀이]

문장 (4)에 따르면 대부분의 사람들이 대중적인 사고를 사실이라고 받아들인다면, 그것은 공정함, 평등함, 동정심, 민감성을 상징할 것이다. 하지만 문장 (5)에서 꼭 그런 것은 아니라고 설명하면서, 문장 (6)~(8)에서 예외의 경우들을 제시한다. 언급된 각각의 예시는 대중적인 사고를 단순히 수용하지 않고 지성을 발휘하여 유의미한 결과를 얻은 경우이다. 대중적인 사고일지라도 사실이 아닐 수 있기 때문에 대중적인 사고를 사실로 받아들일 것인지 비판적으로 바라볼 것인지에 대한 두 입장 간의 차이를 유념해야 하므로, 빈칸에는 '수용과 지성 사이에 큰 차이가 있다'는 내용의 ⑤가 적절하다.

[오답 풀이]

③ - 빈칸에는 대중적인 사고와 관련하여 우리가 유념해야 할 내용이 포함되어야 하는데, 본문에서는 대중적인 사고의 수용 여부와 관련한 설명을 하고 있을 뿐 리더와 팔로워에 관한 내용은 없으므로 ③은 정답이 될 수 없다.

④ - 많은 사람들이 대중적인 사고에서 안전과 안심을 찾는다고 했으므로, 사람들이 그들 주위의 다른 사람들과 다른 방식으로 행동한다는 것은 본문의 내용과 상반된다. 따라서 ④는 정답이 될 수 없다.

[중요 어휘]

□ **figure**	동사 (~라고) 생각하다, 판단하다
□ **compassion**	명사 동정심, 연민
□ **sensitivity**	명사 민감성, 세심함
□ **revolve**	동사 돌다, 회전하다
□ **antiseptic**	형용사 멸균의
□ **practice**	명사 (변호사나 의사 등 전문직의) 일, 업무, 관습, 연습
□ **win**	동사 쟁취하다, 이기다
□ **be founded on**	~에 기초하다[기반을 두다]
□ **follower**	명사 팔로워, 추종자

● 지문 구조도

대중적인 사고(popular thinking)	
O (acceptance)	X (intelligence)
(1) 사람들은 대중적인 사고에서 안전과 안심(safety and security)을 찾음. (2)~(3) 많은 사람이 무언가를 하고 있다면, 그것은 틀림없이 옳을 것이라고 생각함(figure). (4) 대중적인 사고의 수용 → 공정함, 평등함, 동정심, 민감성(fairness, equality, compassion, and sensitivity)을 상징	(5) 꼭 그렇지는 않음(반례들 제시). (6) Copernicus: 별과 행성을 연구하여 공전을 수학적으로 증명함(prove mathematically). (7) Joseph Lister: 병원에서의 높은 사망률을 연구하여 멸균법(antiseptic practices)을 소개함. (8) Emmeline Pankhurst와 Susan B. Anthony: 여성 투표권(right to vote)을 위해 싸워서 쟁취함.
결론	
(9) 수용과 지성(acceptance and intelligence) 사이에 큰 차이가 있음. (10) 수가 많은 편이 항상 사실인 것은 아님.	

38 2023년 9월 33번 (정답률 30%) 정답 ②

[지문 끊어 읽기] 경쟁적으로 진화하는 생물

(1) As always happens with natural selection, /
자연 선택에서 항상 그렇듯이 /
bats and their prey have been engaged /
박쥐와 그 먹잇감은 참여해 왔다 /
in a life-or-death sensory arms race / for millions of years.
생사가 걸린 감각의 군비 경쟁에 / 수백만 년 동안

(2) It's believed / [that hearing in moths arose /
형식상의 주어 [ ]: 내용상의 주어
여겨진다 / 나방의 청력은 생겨났다고 /
specifically in response to the threat / of being eaten by bats].
특히 위협에 대한 반응으로 / 박쥐에게 잡아먹히는
정답 단서 나방의 청력은 박쥐에 대항하기 위해 생겼다고 여겨짐.

(3) (Not all insects can hear.)
(모든 곤충이 들을 수 있는 것은 아니다.)

(4) Over millions of years, / moths have evolved the ability /
수백만 년 동안 / 나방은 능력을 진화시켰다 /
to detect sounds at ever higher frequencies, /
형용사적 용법
계속 더 높아진 주파수의 소리를 감지하는 /
힌트 'they have'의 'they'는 moths를, 'have'는 'have evolved'를 대동사로 받았음.
and, as they have, /
그리고 그것들이 그렇게 했던 것처럼 /
the frequencies of bats' vocalizations have risen, too. 정답 단서
박쥐의 발성 주파수도 높아졌다
나방이 높은 주파수를 감지할 수 있게 진화한 만큼 박쥐도 더 높은 주파수의 소리를 내도록 진화함.

(5) Some moth species have also evolved scales on their wings /
일부 나방 종은 또한 날개의 비늘을 진화시켰다 /
and a fur-like coat on their bodies; /
그리고 몸에 모피와 같은 외피를 /
both act as "acoustic camouflage," /
=scales and a fur-like coat
둘 다 '음향 위장'의 역할을 한다 /
by absorbing sound waves in the frequencies / emitted by bats, /
주파수의 음파를 흡수함으로써 / 박쥐에 의해 방출되는 /
thereby [preventing those sound waves from bouncing back].
그 때문에 그 음파가 되돌아가는 것을 방지한다 [ ]: 분사구문

(6) The B-2 bomber and other "stealth" aircraft have fuselages /
B-2 폭격기와 그 밖의 '스텔스' 항공기는 기체를 가지고 있다 /
[made of materials /
재료로 만들어진 / 선행사
[that do something similar with radar beams]]. [ ]: 과거분사구 (made ~ beams)
레이더 전파에 대해 유사한 것을 하는 [ ]: 주격 관계대명사절

[전문 해석]

(1)자연 선택에서 항상 그렇듯이, 박쥐와 그 먹잇감은 수백만 년 동안 생사가 걸린 감각의 군비 경쟁에 참여해 왔다. (2)나방의 청력은 특히 박쥐에게 잡아먹히는 위협에 대한 반응으로 생겨났다고 여겨진다. (3)(모든 곤충이 들을 수 있는 것은 아니다.) (4)수백만 년 동안 나방은 계속 더 높아진 주파수의 소리를 감지하는 능력을 진화시켰고, 그것들(나방)이 그렇게 했던 것처럼(그렇게 함에 따라) 박쥐의 발성 주파수도 높아졌다. (5)일부 나방 종은 또한 날개의 비늘과 몸에 모피와 같은 외피를 진화시켰다. 둘 다 '음향 위장'의 역할을 하는데, 박쥐에 의해 방출되는 주파수의 음파를 흡수하고, 그 때문에 그 음파가 되돌아가는 것을 방지한다. (6)B-2 폭격기와 그 밖의 '스텔스' 항공기는 레이더 전파에 대해 유사한 것을 하는 재료로 만들어진 기체를 가지고 있다.

[정답 확인]

다음 빈칸에 들어갈 말로 가장 적절한 것은?

① been in a fierce war over scarce food sources
부족한 식량원을 두고 격렬한 전쟁을 해
② been engaged in a life-or-death sensory arms race
생사가 걸린 감각의 군비 경쟁에 참여해
③ invented weapons that are not part of their bodies
그들의 신체 일부가 아닌 무기를 발명해
④ evolved to cope with other noise-producing wildlife
또 다른 소리를 내는 야생 동물에 대처하도록 진화해
⑤ adapted to flying in night skies absent of any lights
불빛 하나 없는 밤하늘을 나는 것에 적응해

[문제 풀이]

자연 선택의 예시로 박쥐와 그 먹잇감인 나방 사이의 관계를 들어 설명하는 글이다. 나방의 청력은 박쥐에 대응하기 위해 생긴 능력이라 여겨지는데, 이 능력은 문장 (4)에서 언급한 바와 같이 더 높아진 주파수의 소리를 감지하는 것이다. 나방이 박쥐가 내는 소리를 감지해서 피하려고 할 때, 박쥐는 먹잇감을 잡기 위해 더 높은 주파수의 소리를 내도록 진화했다고 한다. 또한 나방은 그렇게 높아진 주파수의 음파가 박쥐에게 되돌아가는 것을 방지하기 위해 비늘이나 외피로 '음향 위장'을 하도록 진화했고, 이것은 박쥐가 나방의 위치를 파악하지 못하게 하는 것과 같다. 이러한 현상을 요약하는 것은 포식자와 먹잇감이 서로 살아남기 위해 경쟁적으로 무기를 만들고 대비하는 '군비 경쟁'에 빗대어 표현한 선택지 ② 'been engaged in a life-or-death sensory arms race(생사가 걸린 감각의 군비 경쟁에 참여해)'이므로 빈칸에 들어가기 가장 적절하다.

[오답 풀이]

④ - 지문에서 예시로 등장한 '감각의 군비 경쟁'이 청각적인 면에 초점을 맞추었기 때문에 이 선택지를 고르기 쉽다. 그러나 '또 다른 소리를 내는 야생 동물에 대처한다'는 것은 박쥐와 박쥐의 먹잇감인 나방 사이의 관계에 또 다른 동물이 개입할 여지가 있음을 전제로 해야 한다. 하지만 관련된 내용이 지문에 언급되지 않았으므로 답이 될 수 없다.

[중요 어휘]

☐ natural selection	명사 자연 선택, 자연 도태
☐ prey	명사 먹잇감, 피해자
☐ be engaged in	~에 참여[종사]하다
☐ life-or-death	형용사 생사가 걸린, 목숨을 건
☐ sensory	형용사 감각의
☐ arms race	명사 군비 경쟁
☐ moth	명사 나방
☐ in response to N	~에 대한 반응으로
☐ threat	명사 위협, 협박 / 동사 위협하다
☐ detect	동사 감지하다, 발견하다
☐ frequency	명사 주파수, 빈도
☐ vocalization	명사 발성
☐ scale	명사 비늘, 규모
☐ coat	명사 외피, 외투
☐ acoustic	형용사 음향의, 청각의
☐ camouflage	명사 위장 / 동사 위장하다
☐ absorb	동사 흡수하다, 빨아들이다
☐ emit	동사 방출하다, 내뿜다
☐ bounce back	되돌아가다
☐ bomber	명사 폭격기, 폭파범
☐ aircraft	명사 항공기
☐ fuselage	명사 (비행기의) 기체[동체]
☐ scarce	형용사 부족한, 드문

● 지문 구조도

자연 선택(natural selection)의 예시
(1) 박쥐와 그 먹잇감은 생사가 걸린 감각의(sensory) 군비 경쟁에 참여해(engage) 왔음.

↓

상세 내용	
[나방의 진화] (2) 나방의 청력(hearing): 포식자인 박쥐에 대항해서 생긴 것으로 여겨짐. (4) 더 높아진 주파수(frequency)의 소리를 감지하는 능력을 진화시킴. (5) 음향 위장(acoustic camouflage): 음파가 되돌아가지 않도록 주파수의 음파를 흡수하는 날개의 비늘, 모피 같은 외피를 진화시킴. ((6) 예시: '스텔스' 항공기의 기체)	[박쥐의 대응] (4) 나방이 감지하지 못할 만큼의 발성(vocalization) 주파수를 높이 내도록 진화함.

39 2021년 11월 34번 (정답률 20%) 정답 ⑤

[지문 끊어 읽기] 시장 사고방식이 관습에 끼치는 영향

(1) One vivid example /
한 생생한 예가 / S
of [how a market mindset can transform and undermine an institution] / [ ]: 간접의문문(전치사 of의 목적어절)
어떻게 시장 사고방식이 관습을 변질시키고 훼손시킬 수 있는지에 대한 /
is given by Dan Ariely / in his book *Predictably Irrational*.
V
Dan Ariely에 의해 주어진다 / 그의 저서 *Predictably Irrational*에서

(2) He tells the story / of a day care center in Israel /
그는 이야기를 들려준다 / 이스라엘의 한 어린이집에 관한 / 선행사
[that decided to fine parents /
부모들에게 벌금을 부과하기로 결정했던 /
who arrived late / to pick up their children, /
늦게 도착한 / 자신의 아이를 데리러 /
in the hope / that this would discourage them from doing so].
동격의 that(=the hope) [ ]: 주격 관계대명사절
바라서였다 / 이는 이것이 그들이 그렇게 행동하는 것을 막을 수 있기를

힌트 문맥상 뜻이 분명할 때에는 동일한 동사구를 반복하는 대신 do so를 사용할 수 있음. 문장 (2)의 doing so는 앞의 arrived late의 의미를 받은 'arriving late to pick up their children'이며 앞의 전치사 from 때문에 동명사 형태로 오게 됨. 문장 (4)의 did so는 arrived late라고 보면 됨.

(3) In fact, / the exact opposite happened.
실제로는 / 정반대의 일이 일어났다

(4) Before the imposition of fines, /
벌금 부과 전에 /
parents felt guilty about arriving late, / and guilt was effective /
부모들은 늦게 도착한 것에 대해 죄책감을 느꼈다 / 그리고 죄책감은 효과적이었다 /
in ensuring / that only a few did so.
명사절 접속사
확실히 하는 데 / 오직 몇몇만이 그렇게 하는 것을

(5) Once a fine was introduced, / it seems /
접속사(일단 ~하자) 형식상의 주어
일단 벌금이 도입되자 / ~인 것으로 보인다 /
[that in the minds of the parents /
부모들의 마음속에서 /
the entire scenario was changed /
전체 시나리오가 바뀌었던 것으로 / [ ]: 내용상의 주어
from a social contract to a market one]. 정답 단서
from A to B =contract
사회 계약에서 시장 계약으로

벌금 부과 후 사회 계약이 시장 계약으로 바뀌었음. 벌금이 죄책감을 대신하게 됨.

(6) Essentially, / they were paying for the center /
근본적으로 / 그들은 어린이집에 비용을 지불하고 있었다 /
to look after their children after hours.
방과 후에 자신의 아이를 돌보는 것에 있어

(7) Some parents thought it worth the price, /
5형식V O O·C
일부 부모들은 그것이 값어치를 한다고 생각했다 /
and the rate of late arrivals increased. 정답 단서
그리고 늦은 도착의 비율이 증가했다

일부 부모들은 어린이집에 늦게 도착하는 대신 벌금을 내는 것이 값어치를 한다고 생각했음. 따라서 어린이집에 늦게 도착하는 비율이 증가함.

(8) Significantly, / once the center abandoned the fines /
접속사(~할 때) V①
중요하게는 / 어린이집이 벌금을 그만두었을 때 /
and went back to the previous arrangement, /
V②
그리고 이전 방식으로 돌아갔을 때 /
late arrivals remained at the high level /
선행사
늦은 도착은 그 높은 수준에 머물렀다 /
[they had reached / during the period of the fines].
과거완료, 타동사 [ ]: 목적격 관계대명사절(목적격 관계대명사 생략)
그것들이 도달했었던 / 벌금 기간 동안

[전문 해석]

(1)어떻게 시장 사고방식이 관습을 변질시키고 훼손시킬 수 있는지에 대한 한 생생한 예가 Dan Ariely의 저서 *Predictably Irrational*에 나온다. (2)그는 자신의 아이를 데리러 늦게 도착한 부모들에게 벌금을 부과하기로 결정했던 이스라엘의 한 어린이집에 관한 이야기를 들려주는데, 이는 이것이 그들이 그렇게 행동하는 것을 막을 수 있기를 바라서였다. (3)실제로는 정반대의 일이 일어났다. (4)벌금 부과 전에 부모들은 늦게 도착한 것에 대해 죄책감을 느꼈고 죄책감은 오직 몇몇만이 늦게 도착하는 것을 확실히 하는 데 효과적이었다. (5)일단 벌금이 도입되자 부모들의 마음속에서 전체 시나리오가 사회 계약에서 시장 계약으로 바뀌었던 것으로 보인다. (6)근본적으로 그들은 방과 후에 자신의 아이를 돌보는 것에 있어 어린이집에 비용을 지불하고 있었다. (7)일부 부모들은 그것이 값어치를 한다고 생각했고 늦은 도착의 비율이 증가했다. (8)중요하게는 어린이집이 벌금을 그만두고 이전 방식으로 돌아갔을 때 늦은 도착은 벌금 기간 동안 그것들이 도달했었던 그 높은 수준에 머물렀다.

[정답 확인]

다음 빈칸에 들어갈 말로 가장 적절한 것은?

① people can put aside their interests for the common good 공익에 대한 내용은 언급된 적 없음.
사람들이 공익을 위해 그들의 이익을 제쳐놓을 수 있는지

② changing an existing agreement can cause a sense of guilt 문장 (4)에서
기존의 합의를 바꾸는 것이 죄책감을 유발할 수 있는지 보듯이 부모들이 죄책감을 느낀 것은 벌금을 부과하기 전, 즉 기존의 합의를 바꾸기 전임.
③ imposing a fine can compensate for broken social contracts
벌금을 부과하는 것이 깨진 사회 계약을 보상할 수 있는지
④ social bonds can be insufficient to change people's behavior
사회적 유대감이 사람의 행동을 바꾸는 데 불충분할 수 있는지 사회적 유대감에 대한 내용은 언급된 적 없음.
✔ a market mindset can transform and undermine an institution
시장 사고방식이 관습을 변질시키고 훼손시킬 수 있는지

문장 (7)에서 벌금 부과 이후 부모들의 지각 비율이 증가했다고 했으므로 벌금 부과는 깨진 사회 계약(=부모들이 지각하는 것)을 보상하지 못함.

[문제 풀이]

빈칸은 글의 가장 앞부분에 있으므로, 글의 나머지 부분을 모두 아우르는 내용이어야 한다. 필자는 한 책에 실린 예시를 들어 빈칸의 내용을 설명한다. 본문에 따르면, 기존에 부모들이 아이를 데리러 늦게 도착하는 것을 방지했던 것은 늦게 도착했을 시 느끼던 죄책감이었다. 그런데 벌금이 도입되며 부모들의 생각이 방과 후 아이들을 돌보는 것에 대한 대가를 지불하면 된다는 시장 계약의 사고방식으로 바뀌었다. 즉, 벌금 도입이라는 시장 사고방식이 아이를 데리러 늦게 도착해서는 안 된다는 기존의 관습을 약화시켰고, 그에 따라 늦게 도착하는 부모들의 비율이 증가했기 때문에 정답은 ⑤이다.

[오답 풀이]

② - 죄책감을 유발하는 것은 벌금을 부과하기 전의 방식, 즉 사회 계약의 사고 방식에 대한 내용이다. 따라서 기존의 합의를 바꿔 죄책감을 유발한다는 내용은 시장 사고방식에 대해 설명하는 글의 내용과 맞지 않으며, 빈칸에 들어가기에는 다소 지엽적이므로 정답이 아니다.
③ - 벌금 부과가 깨져버린 사회 계약을 보상할 수 있었다면, 벌금 부과를 통해 늦게 도착하는 부모의 비율이 기존 대비 줄어야 한다. 하지만 본문에서는 오히려 벌금 부과를 통해 늦게 도착하는 부모의 비율이 늘었다고 설명하고 있기 때문에 ③은 정답이 아니다.

[중요 어휘]

☐ vivid	형용사 생생한, 선명한
☐ mindset	명사 사고방식
☐ transform	동사 변질시키다, 변형시키다
☐ undermine	동사 훼손시키다, 약화시키다
☐ institution	명사 관습, 제도, 기관
☐ day care center	어린이집
☐ fine	동사 벌금을 부과하다 / 명사 벌금
☐ discourage A from V-ing	A가 ~하는 것을 막다
☐ imposition	명사 부과, 시행, 도입
☐ guilt	명사 죄책감, 유죄
☐ ensure	동사 확실히 하다, 보장하다
☐ look after	~을 돌보다
☐ after hours	근무시간 후에
☐ abandon	동사 그만두다, 버리다
☐ arrangement	명사 방식, 합의
☐ put aside	(감정·의견 차이 등을) 제쳐놓다[무시하다]
☐ common good	공익
☐ compensate	동사 보상하다
☐ bond	명사 유대(감)

● 지문 구조도

(1) 시장 사고방식(a market mindset)이 관습(institution)에 끼치는 영향
시장 사고방식은 기존의 관습을 변질시키고(transform) 훼손시킬(undermine) 수 있음.

↓

(2) 예시(Dan Ariely의 저서 속 이야기)
이스라엘의 한 어린이집은 벌금을 부과하면(fine) 아이를 늦게 데리러 오는 부모의 수가 줄어들 것이라고 예상함.

→ **(3) 반전**
예상과 반대(opposite)의 결과가 발생함.

↓

(5) 반대 결과 발생의 이유
벌금 제도를 도입하자 부모들이 시장 계약(market contract) 사고방식으로 생각하게 됨.

↓

벌금 제도 도입(the imposition of fines) 전후 부모들의 사고방식 비교

(4) **도입 전**: 사회 계약 사고방식(social contract mindset)	(6) **도입 후**: 시장 계약 사고 방식(market contract mindset)
아이를 데리러 늦게 도착하면 부모들은 죄책감(guilt)을 느꼈음.	아이를 데리러 늦게 도착해도 벌금을 내기 때문에 늦은 것에 대한 대가를 지불한다고 생각함.

↓

결과

(7) 부모들은 벌금 제도가 값어치를 한다(worth the price)고 생각했고 늦게 도착하는 부모들의 비율(the rate of late arrivals)이 증가함.	(8) 벌금 제도를 철회해도(abandon) 늦게 도착하는 비율은 증가한 상태로 유지됨.

40 2023년 11월 32번 (정답률 30%) 정답 ①

[지문 끊어 읽기] 기억의 오염

(1) [Information encountered after an event] / [ ]: S
과거분사구
사건 이후에 마주친 정보는 /
can influence subsequent remembering.
이후의 기억에 영향을 미칠 수 있다

(2) External information can easily integrate into a witness's memory, /
외부의 정보는 목격자의 기억에 쉽게 통합될 수 있다 /
especially if the event was poorly encoded /
특히 사건이 불충분하게 부호화되었다면 /
or the memory is from a distant event, /
또는 기억이 먼 사건에서 온 것이라면 /
in which case time and forgetting have degraded the original memory. 정답 단서 사건이 불충분하게 기억되거나 너무 오래전의 기억이라면, 망각이 기억을 저하시켜 외부의 정보(새로운 정보)가 목격자의 기억에 더 쉽게 통합됨.
그런 경우 시간과 망각이 원래의 기억을 저하시켜 왔을 것이다

힌트 in which case는 관계형용사구로 일반적으로 '이런 경우에'로 해석함. 이 글에서는 '앞 문장이 일어나는 경우 뒤 문장의 현상이 발생할 수 있다'라고 해석할 수 있음. 즉, 앞 문장 'especially if ~ a distant event'의 전제로 뒤 문장 'time and forgetting ~ the original memory'의 일이 발생할 수 있음을 연결해서 해석하면 됨.

힌트 With 이하는 조건절처럼 해석하는데, 'If there is reduced information available in memory with which we can confirm ~ misinformation'으로 보고 해석할 수 있음.

(3) [With reduced information available in memory /
기억에서 사용 가능한 줄어든 정보를 가지면 /
with which to confirm the validity of post-event misinformation], /
그것으로 사건 후의 잘못된 정보의 유효성을 확인할 수 있는 /
it is less likely [that this new information will be rejected].
형식상의 주어 [ ]: 내용상의 주어
이 새로운 정보가 거부될 가능성은 적다

힌트 'with+관계대명사+to V'는 관계대명사절의 주어를 생략하고 동사를 to V로 바꾼 형태임. 이때 which의 선행사는 'reduced information available in memory'이고 해석은 '사건 후의 잘못된 정보의 유효성을 확인할 수 있는 기억에서 사용 가능한 줄어든 정보'라고 할 수 있음.

(4) Instead, /
대신 /
especially when it fits the witness's current thinking /
특히 그것이 목격자의 현재 생각에 맞을 때 /
and can be used to create a story that makes sense to him or her, /
선행사 주격 관계대명사절
그리고 그나 그녀에게 말이 되는 이야기를 만드는 데 사용될 수 있을 때 /

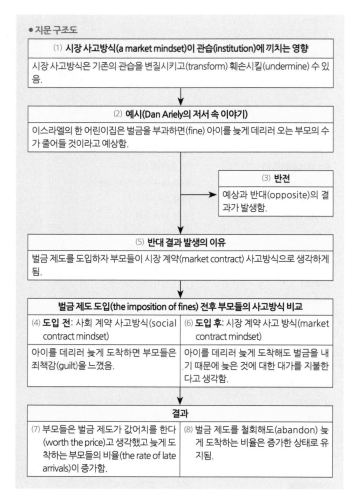

it may be integrated as part of the original experience. 정답 단서
그것은 원래의 경험의 일부로 통합될 수 있다
새로운 정보가 거부되는 대신에, 목격자의 현재 생각과 맞거나 말이 되는 이야기를 만드는 데 사용될 수 있을 때 원래 경험의 부분으로 통합됨.

(5) This process can be explicit /
이 과정은 명시적일 수 있다 /
(i.e., the witness knows it is happening), /
(즉, 목격자는 그것이 일어나고 있다는 것을 안다) /
but it is often unconscious.
그러나 그것은 흔히 무의식적이다

(6) That is, / the witness might find himself or herself /
5형식V O
즉 / 목격자는 그 자신 또는 그녀 자신을 발견할지도 모른다 /
thinking about the event differently / without awareness.
O·C(현재분사)
그 사건에 대해 다르게 생각하고 있는 / 의식하지 않은 채

(7) Over time, /
시간이 지나면서 /
the witness may not even know the source of information /
목격자는 정보의 출처조차 알지 못할지도 모른다 / 선행사
that led to the (new) memory.
주격 관계대명사절
(새로운) 기억으로 이끈

(8) Sources of misinformation in forensic contexts /
법정의 상황에서 잘못된 정보의 출처는 /
can be encountered anywhere, /
어디에서나 마주쳐질 수 있다 /
from discussions with other witnesses /
다른 목격자들과의 토론에서부터 /
to social media searches /
소셜 미디어 검색까지 /
to multiple interviews with investigators or other legal professionals, /
조사관이나 다른 법 전문가와의 다수의 인터뷰까지 /
and even in court.
그리고 심지어 법정에서까지

힌트 'from A to B'는 'A에서부터 B까지'로 해석함. 나열할 것들이 3개 이상일 경우 문장 (8)과 같이 'from A to B to C'로 표현할 수 있음.

[전문 해석]

(1)사건 이후에 마주친 정보는 이후의 기억에 영향을 미칠 수 있다. (2)외부의 정보는 목격자의 기억에 쉽게 통합될 수 있는데, 특히 사건이 불충분하게 부호화되었거나 기억이 먼 사건에서 온 것이라면, 그런 경우 시간과 망각이 원래의 기억을 저하시켜 왔을 것이다. (3)사건 후의 잘못된 정보의 유효성을 확인할 수 있는 기억에서 사용 가능한 줄어든 정보를 가지면, 이 새로운 정보가 거부될 가능성은 적다. (4)대신, 특히 그것이 목격자의 현재 생각에 맞을 때와 그나 그녀에게 말이 되는 이야기를 만드는 데 사용될 수 있을 때, 그것은 원래의 경험의 일부로 통합될 수 있다. (5)이 과정은 명시적일 수 있으나(즉, 목격자는 그것이 일어나고 있다는 것을 안다), 그것은 흔히 무의식적이다. (6)즉, 목격자는 의식하지 않은 채 그 사건에 대해 다르게 생각하고 있는 그 자신 또는 그녀 자신을 발견할지도 모른다. (7)시간이 지나면서 목격자는 (새로운) 기억으로 이끈 정보의 출처조차 알지 못할지도 모른다. (8)법정의 상황에서 잘못된 정보의 출처는 다른 목격자들과의 토론에서부터 소셜 미디어 검색, 조사관이나 다른 법 전문가와의 다수의 인터뷰, 그리고 심지어 법정에서까지 어디에서나 마주쳐질 수 있다.

[정답 확인]

다음 빈칸에 들어갈 말로 가장 적절한 것은?

① this new information will be rejected
이 새로운 정보가 거부될
② people will deny the experience of forgetting
사람들이 망각의 경험을 부인할
③ interference between conflicting data will occur
상충하는 데이터 사이의 간섭이 일어날
④ the unconscious will be involved in the recall process
무의식이 회상 과정에서 수반될
⑤ a recent event will last longer in memory than a distant one
최근 사건이 먼 것보다 기억에서 더 오래 지속될

[문제 풀이]

문장 (2)에 따르면, 사건이 불충분하게 부호화되었거나 기억이 오래된 사건에서 온 것이라면, 시간과 망각이 기억을 저하시키므로, 외부의 정보는 목격자의 기억에 쉽게 통합될 수 있다. 빈칸이 포함된 문장은 빈칸에 해당하는 내용의 가능성이 적다고 말하므로 앞뒤의 맥락에서 일어나지 않을 것이라 말하는 내용을 빈칸으로 찾아야 한다. 이어지는 문장 (4)는 빈칸 대신에 '그것'이 원래 경험의 일부로 통합될 수 있다고 말한다. 문장 (2)로 다시 돌아가보면, 문장 (4)의 '그것'은 외부의 정보, 즉, 새로운 정보라는 것을 알 수 있다. 따라서 빈칸에는 새로운 정보가 거부된다는 내용의 ①이 적절하다.

[오답 풀이]

④ - 문장 (5)~(6)에 따르면 외부의 정보가 원래의 경험의 일부로 통합되는 과정은 무의식적으로 일어날 수 있기 때문에 목격자는 의식하지 않고 사건을 다르게 기억할 수 있다. 따라서 무의식이 회상 과정에서 수반될 것이라는 ④는 일어날 가능성이 적은 것이 아니라 많은 것이므로 정답으로 적절하지 않다.

[중요 어휘]

□ encounter	동사 마주치다, 직면하다 / 명사 만남
□ subsequent	형용사 이후의, 그 다음의, 차후의
□ external	형용사 외부의, 겉면의
□ integrate	동사 통합시키다, 통합되다
□ witness	명사 목격자 / 동사 목격하다
□ poorly	부사 불충분하게, 안 좋게
□ encode	동사 부호화하다, 암호로 만들다, 표현하다
□ distant	형용사 먼, (멀리) 떨어져 있는
□ degrade	동사 저하시키다, 분해하다
□ validity	명사 유효성, 타당성
□ make sense	말이 되다, 이해하다
□ explicit	형용사 명시적인, 명백한
□ unconscious	형용사 무의식적인, 의식을 잃은
□ awareness	명사 의식, 관심
□ misinformation	명사 잘못된 정보
□ forensic	형용사 법정의, 법의학적인
□ discussion	명사 토론, 논의
□ investigator	명사 조사관, 수사관
□ legal	형용사 법의, 법적인, 합법적인
□ interference	명사 간섭, 개입, 방해

41 2023년 11월 33번 (정답률 30%) 정답 ⑤

[지문 끊어 읽기] 상관관계와 인과 관계

(1) Correlations are powerful /
상관관계는 강력하다 /
because the insights they offer are relatively clear.
그것이 제공하는 통찰력이 비교적 명확하기 때문에

(2) These insights are often covered up /
이러한 통찰력은 종종 완전히 가려진다 /
when we bring causality back into the picture. 정답 단서
우리가 인과 관계를 그 상황으로 다시 가져올 때
상관관계에 인과 관계를 적용하면 상관관계가 제공하는 통찰력은 가려짐.

(3) For instance, / a used-car dealer supplied data to statisticians /
예를 들어 / 한 중고차 매매인이 데이터를 통계학자들에게 제공했다 /
to predict / which of the vehicles /
부사적 용법(목적)
예측하기 위해 / 차량들 중 어떤 차량이 /
available for purchase at an auction / were likely to have problems.
경매에서 구입할 수 있는 / 문제가 발생할 가능성이 있는지를

(4) A correlation analysis showed /
한 상관관계 분석은 보여 주었다 / 비교급 강조
[that orange-colored cars were far less likely to have defects].
주황색 차들이 결함이 있을 가능성이 훨씬 더 적다는 것을 [ ]: 명사절(showed의 목적어절)

(5) Even as we read this, / we already think /
심지어 우리가 이것을 읽으면서도 / 우리는 이미 생각한다 /
about why it might be so: / Are orange-colored car owners /
왜 그럴지에 대해 / 주황색 차를 소유한 사람들이 /
likely to be car enthusiasts / and take better care of their vehicles?
병렬① 병렬②(to 생략)
자동차 애호가일 가능성이 있는가 / 그리고 자신들의 차량을 더 잘 관리할

(6) Or, /
아니면 /
is it because orange-colored cars are more noticeable on the road /
주황색 차들이 도로에서 더 눈에 띄기 때문인가 /
and therefore less likely to be in accidents, /
그리고 그에 따라 사고가 날 가능성이 적고 /
so they're in better condition / when resold?
그래서 그것들이 상태가 더 좋은 / 재판매될 때
힌트 접속사 when 뒤에 'they are'이 생략된 것으로 볼 수 있음.

(7) Quickly we are caught in a web / of competing causal hypotheses.
곧 우리는 거미줄에 걸린다 / 경쟁적인 인과 가설의

(8) But our attempts to illuminate things this way /
S 형용사적 용법
하지만 이런 식으로 무언가를 설명하려는 우리의 시도는 /
only make them cloudier.
V
그것들을 더 흐리게 만들 뿐이다

(9) Correlations exist; / we can show them mathematically. 정답단서
상관관계는 존재한다 / 우리는 그것들을 수학적으로 보여 줄 수 있다
상관관계는 수학적인 증명이 가능함.

(10) We can't easily do the same / for causal links. 정답단서
우리는 쉽게 똑같이 할 수 없다 / 인과 관계에 대해서는
인과 관계는 수학적인 증명을 하기 힘듦.

(11) So we would do well to hold off /
따라서 우리는 보류하는 것이 낫다 /
from trying to explain the reason / behind the correlations.
이유를 설명하기를 / 상관관계의 배후에 있는
힌트 'do well to 동사원형'은 '~하는 편이 낫다[온당하다]'라는 의미로 쓰이는 표현임.

[전문 해석]

(1)상관관계는 그것이 제공하는 통찰력이 비교적 명확하기 때문에 강력하다. (2)이러한 통찰력은 우리가 인과 관계를 그 상황으로 다시 가져올 때 종종 완전히 가려진다. (3)예를 들어, 한 중고차 매매인이 경매에서 구입할 수 있는 차량들 중 어떤 차량이 문제가 발생할 가능성이 있는지를 예측하기 위해 데이터를 통계학자들에게 제공했다. (4)한 상관관계 분석은 주황색 차들이 결함이 있을 가능성이 훨씬 더 적다는 것을 보여 주었다. (5)심지어 우리가 이것을 읽으면서도, 우리는 이미 왜 그럴지에 대해, 주황색 차를 소유한 사람들이 자동차 애호가이고 자신들의 차량을 더 잘 관리할 가능성이 있는가에 대해 생각한다. (6)아니면 주황색 차들이 도로에서 더 눈에 띄고 그에 따라 사고가 날 가능성이 적어서 그것들이 재판매될 때 상태가 더 좋기 때문인가? (7)곧 우리는 경쟁적인 인과 가설의 거미줄에 걸린다. (8)하지만 이런 식으로 무언가를 설명하려는 우리의 시도는 그것들을 더 흐리게 만들 뿐이다. (9)상관관계는 존재하며 우리는 그것들을 수학적으로 보여 줄 수 있다. (10)우리는 인과 관계에 대해서는 쉽게 똑같이 할 수 없다. (11)따라서 우리는 상관관계의 배후에 있는 이유를 설명하기를 보류하는 것이 낫다.

[정답 확인]

다음 빈칸에 들어갈 말로 가장 적절한 것은?

① stay away from simply accepting the data as they are
데이터를 있는 그대로 단순히 받아들이는 것에서 멀어지는
② point out every phenomenon in light of cause and effect
모든 현상을 원인과 결과에 비추어 지적하는
③ apply a psychological approach to color preferences
색상 선호에 심리학적 접근을 적용하는
④ admit that correlations are within the framework of causality
인과 관계의 틀 안에 상관관계가 있음을 인정하는
⑤ hold off from trying to explain the reason behind the correlations
상관관계의 배후에 있는 이유를 설명하기를 보류하는

[문제 풀이]

지문은 상관관계와 인과 관계의 차이를 중심으로 상관관계의 근거를 명확히 밝히기 어렵다는 점을 설명한다. 상관관계는 인과 관계와는 다르며, 상관관계의 근거로 인과 관계를 끌어오면 상관관계를 명확하게 설명할 수 없다. 상관관계는 서로 다른 두 사건에 연관성이 있음을 수학적인 데이터를 통해 증명 가능하지만, 그 연관성에 개입하는 변수는 여러 가지가 있다. 문장 (4)~(6)이 언급하는 것이 이러한 내용인데, 주황색 차에 결함이 적을 수 있다는 관계성은 데이터, 즉 수치를 통해 확인이 가능하지만 그 관계성의 명확한 원인은 규명하기가 어렵다. 즉 이것을 인과 관계로 설명하는 것은 거의 불가능하다. 빈칸에 들어갈 말은 상관관계와 인과 관계의 차이를 분명히 하는 내용으로, 상관관계가 인과 관계로 설명되지 않음을 짚어야 한다. 따라서 정답은 ⑤이다.

[오답 풀이]

① - 데이터를 있는 그대로 받아들이는 것은 지문에서 지적한 내용이 아니며, 그것에서 멀어지는 것 또한 상관관계와 인과 관계의 차이와 관련된 내용이 아니므로 빈칸에 들어갈 내용과 거리가 멀다.
④ - 상관관계와 인과 관계는 혼동하기 쉽지만, 지문에서는 이 두 개념이 서로 다르다는 사실을 짚는다. 어느 하나가 다른 하나의 틀 안에 있는 것이 아니라 별개의 개념으로 설명하면서, 상관관계를 인과 관계로 끌어들이지 말라고 하므로 지문의 내용과 맞지 않는다.

[중요 어휘]

□ correlation	명사 상관관계, 연관성
□ insight	명사 통찰력, 이해
□ relatively	부사 비교적, 상대적으로
□ cover up	완전히 가리다, 은폐하다
□ causality	명사 인과 관계
□ used-car dealer	중고차 매매인
□ supply	동사 제공하다, 공급하다
□ statistician	명사 통계학자
□ auction	명사 경매 / 동사 경매하다
□ defect	명사 결함, 단점, 흠
□ enthusiast	명사 애호가, 열광적인 팬
□ noticeable	형용사 눈에 띄는, 뚜렷한
□ causal	형용사 인과의, 원인이 되는
□ hypothesis	명사 가설 (복수형 hypotheses)
□ illuminate	동사 설명하다, 분명히 하다, 밝히다
□ cloudy	형용사 흐린, 탁한
□ causal link	인과 관계
□ hold off	보류하다, 미루다
□ approach	명사 접근 / 동사 접근하다
□ framework	명사 틀, 뼈대

42 2023년 11월 34번 (정답률 55%) 정답 ②

[지문 끊어 읽기] 동물의 평균 수명

(1) Most mice in the wild are eaten or die /
야생에 있는 대부분의 쥐들은 잡아 먹히거나 죽는다 /
before their life span of two years is over.
2년의 수명이 끝나기 전에

(2) They die from *external* causes, /
=Mice in the wild
그들은 '외부적인 원인들'로 죽는다 /
힌트 die from/of+질병, die from+사고 : ~로 인해 죽다
such as disease, starvation, or predators, /
질병, 굶주림 또는 포식자와 같은 /
not due to *internal* causes, such as aging. 정답단서
노화와 같은 '내부적인 원인들' 때문이 아니라
쥐의 사망 요인은 외부적 원인들 때문임.

(3) That is why nature has made mice / to live, /
그것이 자연이 쥐를 만든 이유이다 / 사는 /
on average, / for no longer than two years.
평균적으로 / 2년이 되지 않는 동안
힌트 여기서 made는 '시키다'라는 의미의 사역동사가 아니라 '만들다'라는 의미의 동사임. 따라서 뒤에는 목적어만 올 수 있으며, 목적어에 이어지는 to live는 목적격 보어가 아닌 mice를 수식하는 to부정사의 형용사적 용법으로 봐야 함.

(4) Now we have arrived at an important point:
이제 우리는 중요한 지점에 도달했다

(5) The average life span of an animal species, /
동물 종의 평균 수명 /
or the rate at which it ages, / is determined by the average time /
전치사+관계대명사절
또는 그것이 노화하는 속도는 / 평균 시간에 의해 결정된다 /
that this animal species can survive in the wild. 정답단서
이 동물 종이 야생에서 생존할 수 있는
동물 종의 평균 수명 또는 노화 속도가 '빈칸'으로 결정됨.

(6) That explains / why a bat can live to be 30 years old. 정답단서
부사적 용법(결과)
그것은 설명한다 / 왜 박쥐가 30년까지 살 수 있는지를
쥐의 수명이 평균 2년인 반면, 박쥐의 수명은 30년임.

(7) In contrast to mice, / bats can fly, /
쥐와 대조적으로 / 박쥐는 날 수 있다 /
which is why they can escape from danger much faster.
관계대명사(계속적 용법)
그리고 이것은 그들이 위험에서 훨씬 더 빨리 도망칠 수 있는 이유이다

(8) Thanks to their wings, / bats can also cover longer distances /
그들의 날개 덕분에 / 박쥐는 또한 더 긴 거리를 이동할 수 있다 /
and are better able to find food.
그리고 먹이를 더 잘 찾을 수 있다

(9) Every genetic change in the past /
S(선행사)
과거의 모든 유전적 변화는 /
[that made it possible for a bat to live longer] / [ ]: 주격 관계대명사절
형식상의 목적어 의미상의 주어 내용상의 목적어
박쥐가 더 오래 사는 것을 가능하게 했던 /
was useful, / because bats are much better able than mice /
V(2형식) S·C
유용했다 / 왜냐하면 박쥐가 쥐보다 훨씬 더 잘할 수 있기 때문이다 /
to flee from danger, find food, and survive. 정답 단서 박쥐는 날개와 같은 유전적 변화 때문에 쥐보다 더 오래 살 수 있게 되어 생존에 유리함.
위험에서 도망치고, 먹이를 찾고, 생존하는 것을

[전문 해석]

(1)야생에 있는 대부분의 쥐들은 2년의 수명이 끝나기 전에 잡아 먹히거나 죽는다. (2)그들은 노화와 같은 '내부적인 원인들' 때문이 아니라 질병, 굶주림 또는 포식자와 같은 '외부적인 원인들'로 죽는다. (3)그것이 자연이 평균적으로 2년이 되지 않는 동안 사는 쥐를 만든(쥐가 자연에서 2년 이상 살지 못하게 만든) 이유이다. (4)이제 우리는 중요한 지점에 도달했다. (5)동물 종의 평균 수명, 또는 그것이 노화하는 속도는 이 동물 종이 야생에서 생존할 수 있는 평균 시간에 의해 결정된다. (6)그것은 왜 박쥐가 30년까지 살 수 있는지를 설명한다. (7)쥐와 대조적으로 박쥐는 날 수 있는데, 이것은 그들이 위험에서 훨씬 더 빨리 도망칠 수 있는 이유이다. (8)그들의 날개 덕분에 박쥐는 또한 더 긴 거리를 이동할 수 있고 먹이를 더 잘 찾을 수 있다. (9)박쥐가 더 오래 사는 것을 가능하게 했던 과거의 모든 유전적 변화는 유용했는데, 왜냐하면 박쥐가 쥐보다 위험에서 도망치고, 먹이를 찾고, 생존하는 것을 훨씬 더 잘할 수 있기 때문이다.

[정답 확인]

다음 빈칸에 들어갈 말로 가장 적절한 것은?

① the distance that migrating species can travel for their survival
이주하는 종이 생존을 위해 이동할 수 있는 거리
② the average time that this animal species can survive in the wild
이 동물 종이 야생에서 생존할 수 있는 평균 시간
③ the amount of energy that members of the species expend in a day
그 종의 구성원이 하루에 소비하는 에너지의 양
④ the extent to which this species is able to protect its source of food
이 종이 자신의 식량 자원을 보호할 수 있는 정도
⑤ the maximum size of the habitat in which it and its neighbors coexist
자신과 이웃이 공존하는 서식지의 최대 크기

[문제 풀이]

문장 (5)는 동물 종의 평균 수명 또는 노화 속도가 빈칸에 해당하는 내용으로 결정된다는 것이다. 전반부에 나오는 쥐의 예시에서, 쥐는 자연에서 평균 수명 2년을 넘기기 힘든데, 이는 노화와 같은 '내부적 요인'이 아니라 질병, 굶주림, 포식자와 같은 '외부적 요인' 때문이라고 한다. 한편 박쥐의 수명은 30년인데, 이는 박쥐가 날 수 있기 때문에 쥐보다 위험에서 더 빨리 도망치고, 먹이를 구하는 데 있어 더 멀리 이동이 가능해 더 오래 생존할 수 있기 때문이라고 한다. 다시 말해 박쥐는 쥐와 달리 날 수 있어서 죽음에 이르게 하는 '외부적 요인'을 훨씬 더 잘 피할 수 있기 때문에 더 오래 산다고 볼 수 있다. 따라서 동물 종의 평균 수명은 '이 동물 종이 야생에서 생존할 수 있는 평균 시간'으로 보는 것이 적절하므로 정답은 ②이다.

[중요 어휘]

☐ **life span**	수명
☐ **external**	형용사 외부적인, 외부의
☐ **starvation**	명사 굶주림, 기아
☐ **predator**	명사 포식자
☐ **internal**	형용사 내부적인, 체내의, 내면의
☐ **cover**	동사 (거리를) 이동하다, 다루다, 취재하다
☐ **genetic**	형용사 유전적인, 유전학의
☐ **flee**	동사 도망치다 (flee-fled-fled)
☐ **expend**	동사 소비하다, (시간·노력 등을) 들이다

43 2024년 3월 32번 (정답률 60%) 정답 ②

[지문 끊어 읽기] 어린이 영화의 소비 실상

(1) We must explore the relationship /
우리는 관계를 탐구해야 한다 /
between children's film production and consumption habits.
어린이 영화 제작과 소비 습관 사이의

(2) The term "children's film" implies ownership by children /
'어린이 영화'라는 용어는 어린이에 의한 소유권을 암시한다 /
— *their* cinema — / but films supposedly made for children /
S 과거분사구
즉 '그들의' 영화 / 하지만 소위 어린이를 위해 만들어진 영화는 /
have always been consumed by audiences of all ages, /
V(현재완료 수동태)
항상 모든 연령대의 관객들에게 소비되어 왔다 /
particularly in commercial cinemas.
특히 상업 영화에서

(3) The considerable crossover / 힌트 'the fact' 뒤로 이어진 that절은 생략이 불가능한 동격의 접속사 that이 이끄는 명사절로, 추상명사인 the fact의 내용을 보충 설명하고 있음.
상당한 넘나듦이 /
in audience composition for children's films /
어린이 영화의 관객 구성에서의 /
can be shown / by the fact / [that, in 2007, /
= [ ]: 동격의 that절
증명될 수 있다 / 사실에 의해 / 2007년에 /
eleven Danish children's and youth films attracted 59 percent of theatrical admissions, /
11개의 덴마크 어린이 및 청소년 영화가 극장 입장의 59퍼센트를 끌어모았다 /
and in 2014, /
그리고 2014년에 /
German children's films comprised seven out of the top twenty films /
독일 어린이 영화가 상위 20개 영화 중 7개를 차지했다 /
at the national box office]. 정답 단서 어린이 영화가 과반수 이상의 입장객을 끌어모았고, 전국 극장 흥행 수익을 기준으로 보았을 때 상위 20개 영화 중 7개를 차지할 정도로 많은 사람들에게 소비됨.
전국 극장 흥행 수익에서

(4) This phenomenon corresponds /
이 현상은 일치한다 /
with a broader, international embrace of what is seemingly children's culture / 선행사를 포함한 관계대명사 (=the thing which)
겉으로 어린이 문화처럼 보이는 것을 더 광범위하고 국제적으로 수용하는 것과 /
among audiences of diverse ages. 정답 단서 다양한 연령의 관객들이 어린이 영화를 수용함.
다양한 연령대의 관객들 사이에서

(5) The old prejudice / [that children's film is some other realm, /
S = [ ]: 동격의 that절
오래된 편견은 / 어린이 영화가 다른 영역이라는 /
separate from / (and forever subordinate to) /
병렬①(which is 생략) 병렬②
~와 별개의 / (그리고 영원히 하위의) /
a more legitimate cinema for adults] /
성인을 위한 더 제대로 된 영화 /
is not supported / by the realities of consumption:
V
뒷받침되지 않는다 / 소비의 실상에 의해

(6) children's film is / at the heart of contemporary popular culture.
어린이 영화는 있다 / 현대 대중문화의 중심에

[전문 해석]

(1)우리는 어린이 영화 제작과 소비 습관 사이의 관계를 탐구해야 한다. (2)'어린이 영화'라는 용어는 어린이에 의한 소유권, 즉 '그들의' 영화를 암시하지만 소위 어린이를 위해 만들어진 영화는 특히 상업 영화에서, 항상 모든 연령대의 관객들에게 소비되어 왔다. (3)어린이 영화의 관객 구성에서의 상당한 넘나듦이 2007년에 11개의 덴마크 어린이 및 청소년 영화가 극장 입장의 59퍼센트를 끌어모았고, 2014년에 독일 어린이 영화가 전국 극장 흥행 수익에서 상위 20개 영화 중 7개를 차지했다는 사실에 의해 증명될 수 있다. (4)이 현상은 다양한 연령대의 관객들 사이에서 겉으로 어린이 문화처럼 보이는 것을 더 광범위하고 국제적으로 수용

하는 것과 일치한다. (5)어린이 영화가 성인을 위한 더 제대로 된 영화와 별개의 (그리고 영원히 하위의) 다른 영역이라는 오래된 편견은 소비의 실상에 의해 뒷받침되지 않는다. (6)어린이 영화는 현대 대중문화의 중심에 있다.

[정답 확인]

다음 빈칸에 들어갈 말로 가장 적절한 것은?

① centered on giving moral lessons
도덕적 교훈을 제공하는 데 중점이 되어 왔다
② consumed by audiences of all ages
모든 연령대의 관객들에게 소비되어 왔다
③ appreciated through an artistic view
예술적 관점을 통해 감상되어 왔다
④ produced by inexperienced directors
경험이 없는 감독에 의해 제작되어 왔다
⑤ separated from the cinema for adults
성인을 위한 영화와 분리되어 왔다

[문제 풀이]

문장 (3)~(4)에 따르면, 어린이 영화를 관람한 관객이 극장 입장의 과반수 이상을 차지하고 전국 영화 흥행 수익에서 다수의 어린이 영화가 상위권에 머물 정도로 다양한 연령대의 관객들이 어린이 영화를 소비한다. 이는 어린이 영화가 상업 영화의 측면에서 성인을 위한 영화와 별개의 영역에 존재하는 것이 아니라는 의미이다. 따라서 빈칸에는 모든 연령대의 관객들에 의해 소비된다는 내용의 ②가 적절하다.

[중요 어휘]

□ **production**	명사 (영화·연극 등의) 제작, 생산, 생산량
□ **consumption**	명사 소비, 소비량
□ **imply**	동사 암시하다, 의미하다, 함축하다
□ **supposedly**	부사 소위, 이른바, 아마도
□ **commercial**	형용사 상업의, 상업적인, 이윤을 낳는
□ **considerable**	형용사 상당한, 많은
□ **composition**	명사 구성, 구성 요소, 작곡
□ **admission**	명사 입장, 가입, 입장료
□ **comprise**	동사 차지하다, ~으로 이루어지다, 구성하다
□ **correspond with**	~와 일치하다[부합하다]
□ **diverse**	형용사 다양한, 여러 가지의
□ **prejudice**	명사 편견, 선입관
□ **realm**	명사 영역, 범위
□ **subordinate**	형용사 하위의, 종속된 / 명사 부하 직원
□ **legitimate**	형용사 제대로 된, 합리적인, 적법한
□ **contemporary**	형용사 현대의, 당대의, 동시대의

44 2024년 3월 33번 (정답률 50%)

정답 ③

[지문 끊어 읽기] 호기심과 창의성

(1) Beethoven's drive to create something novel /
S 형용사적 용법 후치수식
새로운 것을 창작하려는 베토벤의 욕구는 /
is a reflection of his state of curiosity. 정답단서 새로운 것을 창조하려는 베토벤의 욕구는 그의 호기심 상태의 반영임.
V
그의 호기심 상태의 반영이다

(2) Our brains experience a sense of reward /
우리의 뇌는 보상감을 경험한다 /
when we create something new /
우리가 새로운 것을 창작할 때 / 후치수식
in the process of exploring something uncertain, /
불확실한 것을 탐구하는 과정에서 / 후치수식
such as a musical phrase /
악절과 같은 / 선행사
that we've never played or heard before.
목적격 관계대명사절
우리가 이전에 연주한 적이나 들어본 적 없는

(3) When our curiosity leads to something novel, /
우리의 호기심이 새로운 것으로 이끌 때 / 후치수식
the resulting reward brings us a sense of pleasure.
현재분사 4형식V I·O D·O
따라오는 보상은 우리에게 기쁨을 가져다준다

힌트 a number of+복수N: 많은 ~ the number of+복수N: ~의 수

(4) A number of investigators have modeled /
S V
많은 연구자들이 모델링해 왔다 /
[how curiosity influences musical composition]. [ ]: O(간접의문문)
의문사 S' V'
호기심이 어떻게 음악 작곡에 영향을 미치는지를

힌트 computer modeling부터 thirteen까지가 주어임. 이때 후치수식하는 과거분사구를 동사와 헷갈리지 않도록 주의해야 함.

(5) In the case of Beethoven, / [computer modeling /
S
베토벤의 경우 / 컴퓨터 모델링은 /
[focused on the thirty-two piano sonatas] / [ ]: 과거분사구(후치수식)
32개 피아노 소나타에 집중한 /
written after age thirteen] / revealed /
과거분사구(후치수식) V
13살 이후에 쓰여진 / 보여 주었다 /
that [the musical patterns found in all of Beethoven's music] / [ ]: S'
명사절 접속사 과거분사구
모든 베토벤의 음악에서 발견된 음악 패턴이 /
decreased in later sonatas, / while novel patterns, /
V' 접속사(반면) S''
후기 소나타에서 줄어들었다는 것을 / 반면 새로운 패턴들은 /
[including patterns that were unique to a particular sonata], /
선행사 주격 관계대명사절 [ ]: 전치사구
특정한 소나타에만 나타나는 패턴을 포함한 /
increased. 정답단서 베토벤이 13살 이후에 작곡한 32개 피아노 소나타에 집중한 컴퓨터 모델링은 후기 소나타에서 모든 베토벤 음악에서 발견된 음악 패턴이 줄어든 반면 새로운 패턴은 증가했다는 것을 보여 줌.
V''
증가했다는 것을

(6) In other words, /
다시 말해서 /
Beethoven's music became less predictable over time /
베토벤의 음악은 시간이 지나면서 덜 예측 가능하게 되었다 /
as his curiosity drove the exploration of new musical ideas.
그의 호기심이 새로운 음악적 아이디어의 탐색을 이끌게 됨에 따라

(7) Curiosity is a powerful driver of human creativity.
호기심은 인간의 창의력의 강력한 원동력이다

[전문 해석]

(1)새로운 것을 창작하려는 베토벤의 욕구는 그의 호기심 상태의 반영이다. (2)우리의 뇌는 우리가 이전에 연주한 적이나 들어본 적 없는 악절과 같은 불확실한 것을 탐구하는 과정에서 우리가 새로운 것을 창작할 때 보상감을 경험한다. (3)우리의 호기심이 새로운 것으로 이끌 때 따라오는 보상은 우리에게 기쁨을 가져다준다. (4)많은 연구자들이 호기심이 어떻게 음악 작곡에 영향을 미치는지를 모델링해 왔다. (5)베토벤의 경우, 13살 이후에 쓰여진 32개 피아노 소나타(악곡의 한 형식)에 집중한 컴퓨터 모델링은 모든 베토벤의 음악에서 발견된 음악 패턴이 후기 소나타에서 줄어든 반면, 특정한 소나타에만 나타나는 패턴을 포함한 새로운 패턴들은 증가했다는 것을 보여 주었다. (6)다시 말해서, 베토벤의 음악은 그의 호기심이 새로운 음악적 아이디어의 탐색을 이끌게 됨에 따라 시간이 지나면서 덜 예측 가능하게 되었다. (7)호기심은 인간의 창의력의 강력한 원동력이다.

[정답 확인]

다음 빈칸에 들어갈 말로 가장 적절한 것은?

① had more standardized patterns
더 표준화된 패턴을 가졌다
② obtained more public popularity
더 대중적인 인기를 얻었다
③ became less predictable over time
시간이 지나면서 덜 예측 가능하게 되었다
④ reflected his unstable mental state
그의 불안정한 정신 상태를 반영했다
⑤ attracted less attention from the critics
비평가의 주의를 덜 끌었다

[문제 풀이]

새로운 것을 창조하려는 욕구는 호기심의 반영이며, 이 과정에서 보상감과 기쁨을 얻는다는 것을 베토벤의 예를 통해 설명한다. 호기심이 작곡에 미치는 영향을 모델링한 연구가 문장

(4)~(5)에 소개되는데, 모델링에 따르면 베토벤의 후기 소나타에서는 베토벤의 음악에서 발견되는 보편적인 패턴은 줄어들고 새로운 패턴은 증가했다고 말한다. 따라서 빈칸에는 베토벤의 음악이 시간이 지나면서 덜 예측 가능하게 되었다는 내용의 ③이 적절하다.

[중요 어휘]

□ drive	명사 욕구, 추진력 / 동사 운전하다, 이끌다
□ novel	형용사 새로운 / 명사 소설
□ reflection	명사 반영, 반사, (거울에 비친) 모습
□ state	명사 상태, 국가, 주(州)
□ curiosity	명사 호기심, 진기함, 진기한 것
□ musical phrase	악절
□ investigator	명사 연구자, 조사관
□ composition	명사 작곡, 구성
□ driver	명사 원동력, 운전사

45 2024년 3월 34번 (정답률 30%) 정답 ④

[지문 끊어 읽기] 측정 가능함과 중요함의 구분

(1) Technologists are always on the lookout for quantifiable metrics.
기술자들은 항상 정량화할 수 있는 측정 기준을 찾는다

(2) Measurable inputs to a model are their lifeblood, /
S V
모델에 측정 가능한 입력은 그들의 생명줄이다 /
and like a social scientist, / a technologist needs to identify /
그리고 사회 과학자처럼 / 기술자는 확인할 필요가 있다 /
concrete measures, or "proxies," / for assessing progress.
구체적인 측정 방법, 또는 '프록시'를 / 진척 상황을 평가하기 위해

(3) This need for quantifiable proxies produces a bias /
S V
이런 정량화할 수 있는 프록시에 대한 필요성은 편향을 생성한다 /
toward measuring things [that are easy to quantify].
선행사 [ ]: 주격 관계대명사절 부사적 용법
정량화하기 쉬운 것들을 측정하는 쪽으로

정답단서 정량화할 수 있는 프록시에 대한 필요성은 정량화하기 쉬운 것들을 측정하는 방향으로 편향을 생성함.

(4) But simple metrics can take us further away /
그러나 단순한 측정 기준은 우리를 멀어지게 할 수 있다 /
from the important goals we really care about, /
선행사 목적격 관계대명사절
우리가 정말로 신경 쓰는 중요한 목표로부터 /
병렬①
which may require complicated metrics /
계속적 용법(=and they)
그리고 이는 복잡한 측정 기준을 요구할 수도 있다 /
or be extremely difficult, or perhaps impossible, /
병렬② 병렬'①(보어) 병렬'②
또는 극도로 어렵거나 어쩌면 불가능할 수도 있다 /
to reduce to any measure.
어떤 측정 기준으로 한정하기

(5) And when we have imperfect or bad proxies, /
그리고 우리가 불완전하거나 잘못된 프록시를 가질 때 /
we can easily fall under the illusion /
우리는 착각에 쉽게 빠질 수 있다 /
[that we are solving for a good end /
동격의 접속사
우리가 좋은 목적을 위해 문제를 해결하고 있다는 /
without actually making genuine progress toward a worthy solution].
가치 있는 해결책을 향한 진정한 발전을 실제로 이루고 있지 않으면서

정답단서 우리가 불완전하거나 잘못된 프록시를 가지면 가치 있는 해결책으로 나아가고 있지 않은데도 좋은 목적을 위해 문제를 해결하고 있다는 착각에 빠지기 쉬움.

(6) The problem of proxies /
프록시의 문제는 /
results in technologists frequently [substituting /
substituting의 의미상의 주어
기술자들이 빈번하게 대체하는 결과를 낳는다 /
what is measurable for what is meaningful].
의미 있는 것을 측정 가능한 것으로

힌트 '전치사+동명사'의 구조로, 동명사의 의미상의 주어가 동명사 앞에 위치함.

힌트 'substitute B for A'는 'A를 B로 대체하다'라는 뜻임. 'substitute A with B'와 의미가 동일하지만 전치사가 달라지면 A, B의 위치가 변경되므로 해석 시 주의하여야 함.

(7) As the saying goes, /
흔히 말하듯이 /
"Not [everything that counts] can be counted, /
[ ]: S① 선행사 주격 관계대명사절 V①
중요한 모든 것이 셀 수 있는 것은 아니다 /
and not [everything that can be counted] counts."
[ ]: S② 선행사 주격 관계대명사절 V②
그리고 셀 수 있는 모든 것이 중요한 것도 아니다

정답단서 의미 있는 것을 모두 측정할 수 있는 것은 아니고 측정할 수 있는 것이 모두 의미 있는 것은 아님.

[전문 해석]

(1)기술자들은 항상 정량화할 수 있는 측정 기준을 찾는다. (2)모델에 측정 가능한 입력(을 하는 것)은 그들의 생명줄이고, 사회 과학자처럼 기술자는 진척 상황을 평가하기 위해 구체적인 측정 방법, 또는 '프록시'를 확인할 필요가 있다. (3)이런 정량화할 수 있는 프록시에 대한 필요성은 정량화하기 쉬운 것들을 측정하는 쪽으로 편향을 생성한다. (4)그러나 단순한 측정 기준은 우리가 정말로 신경 쓰는 중요한 목표로부터 우리를 멀어지게 할 수 있는데, 그 목표는 복잡한 측정 기준을 요구하거나, 또는 어떤 측정 기준으로 한정(환원)하기 극도로 어렵거나 어쩌면 불가능할 수도 있다. (5)그리고 우리가 불완전하거나 잘못된 프록시를 가질 때, 우리는 가치 있는 해결책을 향한 진정한 발전을 실제로 이루고 있지 않으면서 우리가 좋은 목적을 위해 문제를 해결하고 있다는 착각에 쉽게 빠질 수 있다. (6)프록시의 문제는 기술자들이 빈번하게 의미 있는 것을 측정 가능한 것으로 대체하는 결과를 낳는다. (7)흔히 말하듯이, "중요한 모든 것이 셀 수 있는 것은 아니고, 셀 수 있는 모든 것이 중요한 것도 아니다."

[정답 확인]

다음 빈칸에 들어갈 말로 가장 적절한 것은?

① regarding continuous progress as a valid solution
지속적인 진전을 타당한 해결책으로 고려하는
② prioritizing short-term goals over long-term visions
장기적인 비전보다 단기적인 목표를 우선시하는
③ mistaking a personal bias for an established theory
개인적인 편견을 기존의 이론으로 착각하는
✔ substituting what is measurable for what is meaningful
의미 있는 것을 측정 가능한 것으로 대체하는
⑤ focusing more on possible risks than concrete measures
구체적인 측정 방법보다 가능한 위험에 더 집중하는

[문제 풀이]

문장 (1)~(2)에 따르면, 기술자들은 항상 정량화할 수 있는 측정 기준을 찾는데, 이를 위한 구체적인 측정 방법을 '프록시'라고 부른다. 그런데 문장 (3)~(4)는 정량화할 수 있는 프록시에 대한 필요성이 정량화하기 쉬운 것들만 측정하도록 하는 편향을 생성하고, 그런 편향이 정말 중요한 목표로부터 우리를 멀어지게 할 수 있다고 말한다. 이어지는 문장 (5)는 불완전하거나 잘못된 프록시를 가질 때 우리가 가치 있는 해결책을 향해 진정한 발전을 실제로 이루고 있지 않고 있음에도 좋은 목적을 위해 문제를 해결하고 있다는 착각에 빠질 수 있다고 말한다. 이러한 프록시의 문제는 측정 가능한 것을 측정하는 것이 반드시 가치 있는 해결책으로 이어지지 않는다는 것을 암시한다. 또한 마지막 문장의 인용을 통해 측정 가능한 것과 중요한 것을 구분해야 한다고 하므로, 빈칸에는 '의미 있는 것을 측정 가능한 것으로 대체한다'라는 내용의 ④가 적절하다.

[오답 풀이]

② - 문장 (5)에 따르면 우리는 불완전하거나 잘못된 프록시를 가질 때 우리가 좋은 목적을 위해 문제를 해결하고 있다는 착각에 빠질 수 있다. 이 글에서 장기적, 단기적 목표를 구분하고 어떤 것을 우선시한다는 언급은 등장하지 않으므로 ②는 정답으로 적절하지 않다.
⑤ - 문장 (3)~(4)에 따르면 정량화할 수 있는 프록시에 대한 필요성은 쉽게 정량화할 수 있는 것을 측정하는 쪽의 편향을 생성하고, 측정 불가능한 것은 우리에게서 멀어지게 한다. 따라서 프록시의 문제는 의미 있는 해결책보다 구체적인 측정 방법에 더 집중하는 경향이 있다는 것이 이 글의 내용이므로 구체적인 측정 방법보다 가능한 위험에 더 집중한다는 ⑤는 정답으로 적절하지 않다.

[중요 어휘]

□ technologist	명사 기술자
□ be on the lookout for	~을 찾다[살피다], ~에 주의를 기울이다
□ quantifiable	형용사 정량화할 수 있는, 수량화할 수 있는
□ measurable	형용사 측정 가능한
□ input	명사 입력, 투입 / 동사 입력하다
□ lifeblood	명사 생명줄
□ identify	동사 확인하다, 동일시하다
□ concrete	형용사 구체적인, 단단한 / 명사 콘크리트

- [ ] assess — 동사 평가하다, 할당하다, 부과하다
- [ ] bias — 명사 편향, 편견
- [ ] complicated — 형용사 복잡한, 어려운
- [ ] fall under — ~에 빠지다
- [ ] illusion — 명사 착각, 환상, 환각
- [ ] end — 명사 목적, 결말
- [ ] genuine — 형용사 진정한, 진짜의, 진실된
- [ ] worthy — 형용사 가치 있는
- [ ] count — 동사 중요하다, (숫자를) 세다
- [ ] regard A as B — A를 B로 고려하다[보다]
- [ ] valid — 형용사 타당한, 유효한
- [ ] prioritize — 동사 우선시하다, 우선순위를 매기다
- [ ] short-term — 형용사 단기적인
- [ ] long-term — 형용사 장기적인
- [ ] mistake A for B — A를 B로 착각하다[오해하다]
- [ ] established — 형용사 기존의, 확립된

46 2024년 6월 32번 (정답률 60%) 정답 ③

[지문 끊어 읽기] 매몰 비용 오류

(1) If we've invested in something / that hasn't repaid us /
선행사 ↑ 주격 관계대명사절
우리가 무언가에 투자해 왔다면 / 우리에게 보답해 주지 않는 /
— be it money in a failing venture, /
실패한 사업에 투자한 돈이든 /
or time in an unhappy relationship — /
혹은 불행한 인간관계에 투자한 시간이든 간에 /
we find it very difficult to walk away.
형식상의 목적어 내용상의 목적어
우리는 벗어나기가 매우 어렵다는 것을 안다

힌트 'be it A or B'는 'A이든 B이든 간에'라는 의미로 쓰이는 표현임. 본래 'whether it (should) be A or B'인데, 'whether'가 생략되며 도치가 일어났음.

(2) This is the sunk cost fallacy.
이것은 매몰 비용 오류이다

(3) Our instinct is [to continue investing money or time] / [ ]: 명사적 용법(S·C)
S V continue+목적어(V-ing): ~를 계속하다
우리의 본능은 돈이나 시간에 투자를 계속하는 것이다 /
as we hope / [that our investment will prove to be worthwhile /
우리가 바라면서 / 우리의 투자가 가치 있는 것으로 입증될 것이라고 /
in the end]. [ ]: 명사절(hope의 목적어)
결국에는

(4) Giving up would mean acknowledging /
동명사S
포기한다는 것은 인정하는 것을 의미한다 /
that we've wasted something / we can't get back, /
접속사 선행사 ↑ 목적격 관계대명사절(관계대명사 생략)
우리가 무언가를 낭비했다고 / 우리가 되찾을 수 없는 /
and that thought is so painful / that we prefer to avoid it /
지시형용사 so ~ that …: 너무 ~해서 …하다
그리고 그 생각은 너무 고통스러워서 / 우리가 그것을 피하기를 선호한다 /
if we can.
우리가 할 수 있다면

(5) The problem, of course, is /
물론 문제는 ~이다 /
[that if something really is a bad bet, /
어떤 것이 정말 나쁜 투자라면 /
then staying with it / simply increases the amount we lose]. [ ]: S·C
동명사S' V' 선행사 ↑ 목적격 관계대명사절(관계대명사 생략)
그렇다면 그것을 계속 유지하는 것은 / 우리가 잃는 총액을 증가시킬 뿐이라는 것

정답 단서 문제는 나쁜 투자를 계속하면 잃는 것이 많아진다는 점임.

(6) Rather than walk away from a bad five-year relationship, /
5년의 나쁜 관계에서 벗어나기보다는 /
for example, / we turn it into a bad 10-year relationship; /
예를 들어 / 우리는 그것을 10년의 나쁜 관계로 바꾼다 /
rather than accept / [that we've lost a thousand dollars], /
받아들이기보다는 / 천 달러를 잃었다는 사실을 / [ ]: 명사절(accept의 목적어)

힌트 동일한 구조의 문장이 세미콜론(;)으로 연결되어 있음. 두 문장 모두 'rather than'을 포함한 절이 주절보다 앞에 배치되어 있음.

we lay down another thousand / and lose that too.
V① V②
우리는 또 다른 천 달러를 내놓는다 / 그리고 그것 또한 잃는다

(7) In the end, / by delaying the pain of admitting our problem, /
결국 / 우리의 문제를 인정하는 고통을 미룸으로써 /
we only add to it.
=our problem
우리는 그것에 보탤 뿐이다

정답 단서 문제를 인정하지 않으면 문제가 늘어나기만 하므로 문제라는 사실을 인정해야 함.

(8) Sometimes we just have to cut our losses.
때때로 우리는 손실을 끊어내야 한다

[전문 해석]

(1)실패한 사업에 투자한 돈이든 불행한 인간관계에 투자한 시간이든 간에, 우리에게 보답해 주지 않는 무언가에 투자해 왔다면, 우리는 벗어나기가 매우 어렵다는 것을 안다. (2)이것은 매몰 비용 오류이다. (3)우리의 본능은 결국에는 우리의 투자가 가치 있는 것으로 입증될 것이라고 바라면서 돈이나 시간에 투자를 계속하는 것이다. (4)포기한다는 것은 우리가 되찾을 수 없는 무언가를 낭비했다고 인정하는 것을 의미하고, 그 생각은 너무 고통스러워서 우리가 할 수 있다면 그것을 피하기를 선호한다. (5)물론 문제는 어떤 것이 정말 나쁜 투자라면, 그것을 계속 유지하는 것은 우리가 잃는 총액을 증가시킬 뿐이라는 것이다. (6)예를 들어, 5년의 나쁜 관계에서 벗어나기보다는 우리는 그것을 10년의 나쁜 관계로 바꾸고, 천 달러를 잃었다는 사실을 받아들이기보다는 우리는 또 다른 천 달러를 내놓아서 그것 또한 잃는다. (7)결국 우리의 문제를 인정하는 고통을 미룸으로써 우리는 그것(문제)에 보탤 뿐이다(문제를 더 크게 만들 뿐이다). (8)때때로 우리는 손실을 끊어내야 한다.

[정답 확인]

다음 빈칸에 들어갈 말로 가장 적절한 것은?

① reduce profit 이익을 줄여야
② offer rewards 보상을 제안해야
③ cut our losses 손실을 끊어내야
④ stick to the plan 계획을 고수해야
⑤ pay off our debt 빚을 갚아야

[문제 풀이]

지문은 매몰 비용 오류에 대해 설명한다. 매몰 비용 오류는 우리가 투자한 만큼 그에 상응하는 결과가 나오지 않으니 포기해야 한다는 것을 인정하지 않아 생기는 오류이다. 시간이나 돈을 쓰고도 나쁜 결과만을 낳는다면 그것을 포기해야 마땅한데, 그렇게 하지 않으면 오히려 나쁜 결과만 쌓이게 된다. 자신이 들인 비용에 미련을 두지 않고, 이런 문제를 인정하여 더 큰 손해를 막아야 매몰 비용 오류에서 벗어날 수 있다. 따라서 이 내용을 모두 종합하면, 빈칸에 들어갈 정답은 ③ 'cut our losses(손실을 끊어내야)'이다.

[중요 어휘]

- [ ] invest — 동사 투자하다, 출자하다
- [ ] repay — 동사 보답하다, 상환하다
- [ ] venture — 명사 (벤처) 사업, (사업상의) 모험
- [ ] sunk cost — 매몰 비용(회수할 수 없는 비용)
- [ ] fallacy — 명사 오류, 틀린 생각
- [ ] instinct — 명사 본능, 타고난 소질
- [ ] acknowledge — 동사 인정하다
- [ ] get back — 되찾다, 돌아오다
- [ ] add to N — ~에 보태다[더하다]
- [ ] offer — 동사 제안하다, 권하다
- [ ] reward — 명사 보상 / 동사 보상하다
- [ ] pay off — 갚다, 청산하다, 도움이 되다
- [ ] debt — 명사 빚, 부채

47 2024년 6월 33번 (정답률 45%) 정답 ①

[지문 끊어 읽기] 별의 소멸과 빛

(1) On our little world, / light travels, /
우리의 작은 세상에서 / 빛은 이동한다 /
for all practical purposes, instantaneously.
실제로는 순간적으로

(2) If a lightbulb is glowing, /
전구가 빛나고 있다면 /
then of course it's physically where we see it, / shining away.
당연히 그것은 물리적으로 우리가 보는 그 자리에 있다 / 빛을 내면서 (shining away: 분사구문)

(3) We reach out our hand and touch it: / It's there all right, /
우리는 우리의 손을 뻗어 그것을 만진다 / 그것은 바로 거기에 있다 /
and unpleasantly hot.
그리고 불쾌할 정도로 뜨겁다

(4) If the filament fails, / then the light goes out.
필라멘트가 끊어지면 / 그때 빛은 꺼진다

(5) We don't see it in the same place, / glowing, illuminating the room /
우리는 그것을 같은 자리에서 보지 못한다 / 빛나며 방을 비추고 있는 것을 /
years after the bulb breaks and it's removed from its socket.
전구가 고장나고 그것이 소켓에서 제거된 몇 년 후에

힌트 very는 '아주, 매우, 몹시'라는 뜻의 부사이면서 '바로 이, 바로 그'라는 뜻의 형용사로도 사용됨. 문장 (6)에서는 notion이라는 명사를 수식하는 형용사이므로 '바로 이 개념'으로 해석함.

(6) The very notion seems nonsensical.
바로 이 개념은 말이 되지 않는 것처럼 보인다

★중요 문장 (5)에서 언급된 '전구가 고장나고 그것이 소켓에서 제거된 몇 년 후에 같은 자리에서 빛나며 방을 비추고 있는 것'을 의미함.

(7) But if we're far enough away, /
그러나 만약 우리가 충분히 멀리 떨어져 있다면 /

힌트 'sun'이 정관사 'the'와 함께 올 때는 '태양'을 의미하나 문장 (7)처럼 부정관사 'a/an'과 함께 올 때는 '항성'을 의미함.

an entire sun can go out /
하나의 항성 전체가 불이 꺼질 수 있다 /

힌트 대립적 내용을 표현하는 접속사로 '그런데도, …이면서도'로 해석됨. 다음과 같은 예문에서도 확인할 수 있음. ex) He is so rich, and lives like the poor.

and we'll continue to see it shining brightly; 정답 단서 우리와 항성의 거리가 충분히 멀다면 항성의 불이 꺼져도 우리는 계속해서 그것이 밝게 빛나는 것을 볼 것임.
그런데도 우리는 계속해서 그것이 밝게 빛나는 것을 볼 것이다

(8) we won't learn of its death, / (its = a sun's)
우리는 그것의 소멸을 알지 못할 것이다 /
it may be, for ages to come / (it may be: 삽입, for: 전치사(~동안), to come: 형용사적 용법)
아마 앞으로의 오랜 시간 동안 /

힌트 기간을 나타내는 전치사 for의 목적어로 의문사절이 왔는데, 구조가 복잡하므로 해석에 유의해야 함. 우선 'for how long it takes light to V'에서 「it takes 시간 to V」가 기본 구조인데, 의문사절 내의 주어 to부정사구가 너무 길어 형식상의 주어 it을 사용하였고, '빛이 ~하는 데 얼마나 오랜 시간 동안 …'을 '빛이 ~하는 데 걸리는 시간 동안'이라고 의역하였음. 중간에 light를 수식하는 주격 관계대명사절이 삽입되었으므로 호흡을 잘 끊어 해석해야 함.

— in fact, / for [how long it takes light, / (it: 형식상의 주어, light: 선행사)
사실 / 빛이 걸리는 시간 동안 /
which travels fast but not infinitely fast, / (주격 관계대명사절)
빠르지만 무한히 빠르지는 않게 이동하는 /
to cross the intervening vastness]. (내용상의 주어)
그 사이의 광대함을 가로지르는 데

(9) The immense distances to the stars and the galaxies / (S)
별과 은하까지의 엄청난 거리는 /
mean [that we see everything in space in the past]. (mean: V, [ ]: mean의 목적어절)
우리가 우주에 있는 모든 것을 과거의 모습으로 보고 있다는 것을 의미한다

[전문 해석]

(1)우리의 작은 세상에서 빛은 실제로는 순간적으로 이동한다. (2)전구가 빛나고 있다면 당연히 그것은 빛을 내면서 물리적으로 우리가 보는 그 자리에 있다. (3)우리는 우리의 손을 뻗어 그것을 만지는데, 그것은 바로 거기에 있고 불쾌할 정도로 뜨겁다. (4)필라멘트가 끊어지면 그때 빛은 꺼진다. (5)우리는 전구가 고장나고 그것이 소켓에서 제거된 몇 년 후에 그것이 같은 자리에서 빛나며 방을 비추고 있는 것을 보지 못한다. (6)바로 이 개념은 말이 되지 않는 것처럼 보인다. (7)그러나 만약 우리가 충분히 멀리 떨어져 있다면 하나의 항성 전체가 불이 꺼질 수 있고 그런데도 우리는 계속해서 그것이 밝게 빛나는 것을 볼 것이다. (8)우리는 아마 앞으로의 오랜 시간 동안, 즉 사실, 빠르지만 무한히 빠르지는 않게 이동하는 빛이 그 사이의 광대함을 가로지르는 데 걸리는 시간 동안 그것(항성)의 소멸을 알지 못할 것이다. (9)별과 은하까지의 엄청난 거리는 우리가 우주에 있는 모든 것을 과거의 모습으로 보고 있다는 것을 의미한다.

[정답 확인]

다음 빈칸에 들어갈 말로 가장 적절한 것은?

✔ see everything in space in the past
우주에 있는 모든 것을 과거의 모습으로 보고 있다
② can predict when our sun will go out
우리의 태양이 언제 꺼질지 예측할 수 있다
③ lack evidence of life on other planets
다른 행성에 있는 생명의 증거가 부족하다
④ rely on the sun as a measure of time
시간의 척도로 태양에 의존한다
⑤ can witness the death of a star as it dies
별의 소멸을 그것이 소멸할 때 목격할 수 있다

[문제 풀이]

문장 (1)~(4)에 따르면, 전구가 빛날 때 우리는 빛이 나는 것을 볼 수 있고 전구를 만지면 뜨겁다. 그러나 문장 (5)에서 우리는 전구가 고장나고 소켓에서 제거된 후에는 전구가 빛나는 것을 보지 못한다고 말한다. 문장 (6)에 따르면 전구가 고장난 후에도 빛을 볼 수 있다는 생각이 말이 되지 않는 것처럼 보인다. 하지만 문장 (7)~(8)은 우리와 항성 사이의 거리가 충분히 멀다면 하나의 항성이 죽어서 빛이 꺼진 후에도 우리는 그 항성이 빛나는 것을 볼 수 있다고 말한다. 우리의 작은 세상에서와 달리 별과 은하까지의 거리는 엄청나게 멀어서 빛이 이동하는 데에는 시간이 걸리는 것이다. 따라서 빈칸에는 우리가 우주에 있는 모든 것을 과거의 모습으로 보고 있다는 내용의 ①이 적절하다.

[중요 어휘]

☐ for all practical purposes	실제로는, 사실상
☐ instantaneously	부사 순간적으로, 즉시
☐ lightbulb	명사 전구
☐ unpleasantly	부사 불쾌할 정도로, 불쾌하게
☐ illuminate	동사 (빛을) 비추다, 빛나다
☐ remove	동사 제거하다, 옮기다
☐ notion	명사 생각, 개념
☐ nonsensical	형용사 말이 안 되는, 터무니없는
☐ sun	명사 항성, 태양
☐ infinitely	부사 무한히, 한없이
☐ intervening	형용사 사이에 있는[오는]
☐ vastness	명사 광대함, 방대함
☐ immense	형용사 엄청난
☐ galaxy	명사 은하

48 2024년 6월 34번 (정답률 50%) 정답 ②

[지문 끊어 읽기] 유연한 소비를 가능하게 하는 금융 시장

(1) Financial markets do more / than take capital from the rich /
금융 시장은 더 많은 일을 한다 / 부자들로부터 자본을 받는 것보다 / (병렬①)
and lend it to everyone else. (병렬②)
그리고 그것을 다른 모두에게 빌려주는 것보다

(2) They enable each of us / (enable: 5형식V, each of us: O)
그것들은 우리 각자를 가능하게 한다 /
to smooth consumption over our lifetimes, / (O·C(to부정사구))
우리 평생에 걸쳐 소비를 원활하게 하는 것을 /
which is a fancy way of saying / (계속적 용법)
그리고 이는 ~을 말하는 멋진 방식이다 /
[that we don't have to spend income / ([ ]: that 명사절(saying의 목적어))
우리가 소득을 소비할 필요는 없다고 /
at the same time we earn it]. (time: 선행사, we earn it: 관계부사절) 정답 단서 금융 시장은 삶에서 소비를 원활하게 해주며, 금융 시장 덕분에 우리는 소득을 버는 동시에 소비할 필요가 없게 되었음.
우리가 그것을 버는 동시에

(3) Shakespeare may have admonished us / (may have p.p.: ~했을지도 모른다)
셰익스피어는 우리에게 충고했을지도 모른다 /
to be neither borrowers nor lenders; / the fact is / (neither A nor B: A도 B도 아닌, the fact: S, is: V)
빌리는 사람도 빌려주는 사람도 되지 말라고 / 사실은 ~이다 /
[that most of us will be both / at some point]. ([ ]: S·C(that 명사절), both = borrowers and lenders)
우리 대부분이 둘 다일 것이라는 것 / 어느 시점에는

힌트 「if+주어+과거시제V ~, 주어+조동사 과거형+동사원형」의 가정법 과거 문장으로, 형태는 과거이나 현재 사실과 반대의 상황을 가정하므로 현재시제로 해석함.

(4) If we lived in an agrarian society, /
만약 우리가 농경 사회에 산다면 /
we would have to eat our crops reasonably / (병렬①)
우리는 우리의 농작물을 합리적으로 먹어야 할 것이다 /

정답과 해설 12 빈칸 추론 (2)

soon after the harvest / or find some way to store them.
=our crops / 병렬②(to 생략) / 형용사적 용법
수확 직후에 / 혹은 그것들을 저장할 어떤 방법을 찾아야 할 것이다

(5) Financial markets /
금융 시장들은 /
are a more sophisticated way of managing the harvest.
수확을 관리하는 더 정교화된 방법이다 수식어구(전치사구)

(6) We can spend income now / that we have not yet earned /
선행사 / 목적격 관계대명사절
우리는 지금 소득을 소비할 수 있다 / 우리가 아직 벌지 않은 /
— as by borrowing for college or a home — /
~처럼
대학이나 주택을 위해 빌리는 것처럼 /
or we can earn income now and spend it later, /
병렬① 병렬②
혹은 우리는 지금 소득을 벌어서 그것을 나중에 소비할 수 있다 /
as by saving for retirement. **정답 단서** 우리는 아직 벌지 않은 소득을 지금 소비할 수도 있고, 지금 소득을 벌어서 나중에 소비할 수도 있음.
~처럼
은퇴를 위해 저축하는 것처럼

(7) The important point is /
S V
중요한 점은 ~이다 /
[that earning income has been divorced / from spending it], /
=income
소득을 버는 것이 분리되었다는 것 / 그것을 소비하는 것으로부터 / [ ]: S·C(that 명사절)
[allowing us much more flexibility in life].
비교급 강조 [ ]: 분사구문
그리고 이는 우리에게 삶에서 훨씬 더 많은 유연성을 허락해 준다

힌트 현재분사 allowing이 이끄는 능동 분사구문으로, 주절에서 언급한 내용의 결과를 나타내며「allow A B (A에게 B를 허락하다)」의 4형식 구조가 사용되었음.

[전문 해석]

(1)금융 시장은 부자들로부터 자본을 받고 그것을 다른 모두에게 빌려주는 것보다 더 많은 일을 한다. (2)그것들은 우리 각자가 우리 평생에 걸쳐 소비를 원활하게 하는 것을 가능하게 하고, 이는 우리가 소득을 버는 동시에 그것을 소비할 필요는 없다고 말하는 멋진 방식이다. (3)셰익스피어는 우리에게 빌리는 사람도 빌려주는 사람도 되지 말라고 충고했을지도 모른다. (그러나) 사실은 우리 대부분이 어느 시점에는 둘 다일 것이라는 것이다. (4)만약 우리가 농경 사회에 산다면, 우리는 수확 직후에 우리의 농작물을 합리적으로 먹거나, 그것들을 저장할 어떤 방법을 찾아야 할 것이다. (5)금융 시장들은 수확을 관리하는 더 정교화된 방법이다. (6)대학이나 주택을 위해 빌리는 것처럼 우리는 지금 우리가 아직 벌지 않은 소득을 소비할 수 있고, 혹은 은퇴를 위해 저축하는 것처럼 우리는 지금 소득을 벌어서 그것을 나중에 소비할 수 있다. (7)중요한 점은 소득을 버는 것이 그것을 소비하는 것으로부터 분리되었다는 것이며, 이는 우리에게 삶에서 훨씬 더 많은 유연성을 허락해 준다.

[정답 확인]

다음 빈칸에 들어갈 말로 가장 적절한 것은?

① we can ignore the complexity of financial markets
우리는 금융 시장의 복잡성을 무시할 수 있다
② earning income has been divorced from spending it
소득을 버는 것이 그것을 소비하는 것으로부터 분리되었다
③ financial markets can regulate our impulses
금융 시장은 우리의 충동들을 조절할 수 있다
④ we sell our crops as soon as we harvest them
우리는 우리가 그것들을 수확하자마자 우리의 작물을 판다
⑤ managing working hours has become easier than ever
근무 시간을 관리하는 것이 그 어느 때보다 쉬워졌다

[문제 풀이]

문장 (2)에서 '우리가 소득을 버는 동시에 그것을 소비할 필요가 없다'고 했고, 문장 (6)에서는 '아직 벌지 않은 소득을 지금 소비'하거나 '지금 번 소득을 나중에 소비'할 수 있다고 했다. 금융 시장을 통해 소득을 '버는(earn)' 것과 '소비하는(spend)' 것이 분리되었고, 이를 통해 인간의 소비 생활이 훨씬 더 유연해졌음을 추론할 수 있다. 따라서 빈칸에 들어갈 말로 가장 적절한 것은 ② '소득을 버는 것이 그것을 소비하는 것으로부터 분리되었다'이다.

[중요 어휘]

☐ financial	형용사 금융의, 재정의
☐ capital	명사 자본(금), 수도
☐ lend	동사 (돈을) 빌려주다, 대출하다, 부여하다
☐ enable A to V	A가 ~하는 것을 가능하게 하다
☐ smooth	동사 원활하게 하다, 매끄럽게 하다
☐ consumption	명사 소비
☐ income	명사 소득, 수입
☐ earn	동사 벌다, 얻다
☐ admonish	동사 충고하다, 권고하다, 꾸짖다
☐ lender	명사 빌려주는 사람
☐ agrarian	형용사 농경의, 농업의
☐ crop	명사 (농)작물
☐ reasonably	부사 합리적으로, 상당히, 꽤
☐ harvest	명사 수확, 추수 / 동사 수확하다, 추수하다
☐ store	동사 저장하다, 보관하다
☐ sophisticated	형용사 정교화된, 복잡한
☐ manage	동사 관리하다, 운영하다
☐ retirement	명사 은퇴, 퇴직
☐ divorce	동사 분리시키다, 이혼하다
☐ flexibility	명사 유연성, 융통성
☐ impulse	명사 충동, 자극

49 2024년 9월 33번 (정답률 60%) 정답 ①

[지문 끊어 읽기] 기술 발전으로 인한 부의 불평등한 분배

(1) Over the last few centuries, /
지난 몇 세기 동안 /
humanity's collective prosperity has skyrocketed, /
인류의 집합적 부가 급증해 왔다 /
as technological progress has made us far wealthier /
기술 발전이 우리를 훨씬 더 부유하게 만듦에 따라 /
than ever before.
그 어느 때보다

힌트 비교급 강조 부사 : far, a lot, much, even, still

(2) To share out those riches, /
부사적 용법(목적)
이러한 부를 나누기 위해 /
almost all societies have settled upon the market mechanism, /
거의 모든 사회는 시장 메커니즘을 채택했다 /
[rewarding people in various ways /
[ ]: 분사구문
사람들에게 다양한 방식으로 보상하는 /
for [the work that they do] / and [the things that they own]].
선행사 목적격 관계대명사절 선행사 목적격 관계대명사절
그들이 하는 일에 대해 / 그리고 그들이 소유한 것에 대해

힌트 괄호 친 부분은 모두 for의 목적어이고 병렬 구조로 연결되어 있음.

(3) But rising inequality, / itself often driven by technology, /
S 삽입구
그러나 증가하는 불평등은 / 그 자체가 기술로 인해 자주 생기는 /
has started to put that mechanism under strain. **정답 단서** 기술의 발전으로 인해 시장 메커니즘을 통해 부를 분배하는 메커니즘이 흔들리기 시작함.
V
그 메커니즘에 부담을 주기 시작했다

(4) Today, /
오늘날 /
markets already provide immense rewards to some people /
V①
시장은 이미 일부 사람들에게는 막대한 보상을 제공한다 /
but leave many others with very little. **정답 단서** 경제적 보상이 일부 소수에게만 편중됨.
V②
하지만 많은 다른 사람들에게는 거의 아무것도 남기지 않는다

힌트 technological unemployment는 기술 발전으로 인해 일자리가 사라지는 현상을 말함.

(5) And now, / technological unemployment threatens /
그리고 이제 / 기술 혁신이 초래한 실업은 우려가 있다 /
to become a more radical version of the same story, /
같은 이야기의 더 급진적인 형태가 될 / =문장 (4)의 내용
[taking place in the particular market /
특정 시장에서 발생하여 / 선행사
we rely upon the most: / the labor market]. **정답 단서** 노동 시장에서 불평등의 결과가 더 크게 나타날 것임.
목적격 관계대명사절(관계대명사 생략) [ ]: 분사구문
우리가 가장 의존하는 / 노동 시장

(6) As that market begins to break down, /
그 시장이 무너지기 시작함에 따라 /
more and more people will be in danger /
점점 더 많은 사람들이 위험에 처하게 될 것이다 /
of not receiving a share of society's prosperity at all.
사회의 부의 몫을 전혀 받지 않을

[전문 해석]

(1)지난 몇 세기 동안, 기술 발전이 우리를 그 어느 때보다 훨씬 더 부유하게 만듦에 따라, 인류의 집합적 부가 급증해 왔다. (2)이러한 부를 나누기 위해 거의 모든 사회는 사람들에게 그들이 하는 일과 그들이 소유한 것에 대해 다양한 방식으로 보상하는 시장 메커니즘을 채택했다. (3)그러나 증가하는 불평등은, 그 자체가 기술로 인해 자주 생기는데, 그 메커니즘에 부담을 주기 시작했다. (4)오늘날 시장은 이미 일부 사람들에게는 막대한 보상을 제공하지만 많은 다른 사람들에게는 거의 아무것도 남기지 않는다. (5)그리고 이제, 기술 혁신이 초래한 실업은 우리가 가장 의존하는 특정 시장, 즉 노동 시장에서 발생하여, 같은 이야기의 더 급진적인 형태가 될 우려가 있다. (6)그 시장이 무너지기 시작함에 따라, 점점 더 많은 사람들이 사회의 부의 몫을 전혀 받지 않을 위험에 처하게 될 것이다.

[정답 확인]

다음 빈칸에 들어갈 말로 가장 적절한 것은?

✔ not receiving a share of society's prosperity at all
사회의 부의 몫을 전혀 받지 않을
② making too large of an investment in new areas
새로운 영역에 너무 많은 투자를 할
③ not fully comprehending technological terms
기술 용어를 완전히 이해하지 못할
④ unconsciously wasting the rewards from their work
무의식적으로 그들의 업무의 보상을 낭비할
⑤ not realizing the reason to raise their cost of living
그들의 생활비를 인상해야 하는 이유를 깨닫지 못할

[문제 풀이]

지문은 기술 발전으로 인해 사람들이 지닌 전체적인 부가 증가한 이면에 대해 설명한다. 사회는 늘어난 부를 분배하기 위해 개인이 하는 일과 소유물에 대해 개인에게 보상하는 시장 메커니즘을 채택했다. 그러나 기술이 발전함에 따라 이 메커니즘은 제대로 작동하지 않았다. 이는 일부 소수에게만 막대한 보상이 돌아가고, 다른 사람들에게는 보상이 거의 돌아가지 않는 결과를 낳았다. 개인이 가장 의존하는 노동 시장에서도 같은 결과가 나타남에 따라 막대한 부를 받는 소수를 제외하고 대다수가 자신이 한 노동에 대한 보상을 받지 못하게 된다. 이는 사람들이 사회의 부를 나누어 받지 못하게 된다는 것이다. 따라서 빈칸에 들어갈 정답은 ①이다.

[중요 어휘]

□ collective	형용사 집합적인, 공동의
□ prosperity	명사 부, 번영, 번창
□ skyrocket	동사 급증하다, 급등하다
□ progress	명사 발전, 진행
□ share out	나누다, 분배하다
□ riches	명사 (복수형으로) 부, 재물
□ settle upon	채택하다, 결정하다
□ reward	동사 보상하다 / 명사 보상
□ inequality	명사 불평등, 불균등
□ drive	동사 생기다, 몰아붙이다, 운전하다
□ put A under strain	A에 부담을 주다
□ immense	형용사 막대한, 엄청난
□ threaten	동사 ~할 우려가 있다, 위협하다
□ radical	형용사 급진적인, 근본적인
□ labor market	노동 시장
□ break down	무너지다, 고장나다
□ share	명사 몫, 지분 / 동사 공유하다
□ comprehend	동사 이해하다, 포함하다
□ term	명사 용어, 말, 학기
□ cost of living	생활비

50 2024년 9월 34번 (정답률 40%) 정답 ⑤

[지문 끊어 읽기] 전문 지식의 암시성

(1) It's often said / [that those who can't do, teach]. [ ]: 내용상의 주어
형식상의 주어 / S', 선행사 / 주격 관계대명사절 / V'
흔히 말해진다 / 할 줄 모르는 사람이 가르친다고

(2) It would be more accurate /
형식상의 주어
더 정확할 것이다 /
[to say / that those who can do, can't teach the basics]. [ ]: 내용상의 주어
S', 선행사 / 주격 관계대명사절 / V'
말하는 것이 / 할 수 있는 사람은 기초를 가르칠 수 없다고

(3) A great deal of expert knowledge is implicit, / not explicit. 정답 단서
많은 전문 지식은 암시적이다 / 명시적인 것이 아니라
전문 지식은 명확하게 설명 가능한 것이 아님.

(4) The further you progress / toward mastery, /
여러분이 더 나아갈수록 / 숙련을 향해 /
the less conscious awareness you often have /
여러분은 흔히 덜 의식적인 인식을 지닌다 /
of the fundamentals.
기본에 대해
힌트 '더 ~할수록, 더 …하다'라는 의미의 'the 비교급 S+V, the 비교급 S+V' 구문이 쓰였음. '덜 ~한'이라는 의미의 열등 비교는 모든 형용사/부사 앞에 'less'를 붙임.

(5) Experiments show /
실험은 보여 준다 /
[that skilled golfers and wine aficionados have a hard time /
숙련된 골퍼와 와인 애호가는 어려움을 겪는다 /
describing their putting and tasting techniques /
자신의 퍼팅과 시음 기술을 설명하는 데 /
힌트 have a hard time[difficulty]+V-ing: ~하는 데 어려움을 겪다
— even asking them to explain their approaches /
S'(동명사구)
심지어 그들의 접근 방식을 설명해 달라고 요청하는 것은 /
is enough to interfere with their performance, /
V'
그들의 수행을 방해하기에 충분하다 / [ ]: show의 목적어절
so they often stay on autopilot]. 정답 단서 숙련된 사람들에게 그들이 사용하는 기술에 대한 설명을 요청해도, 그들은 그 기술을 자동적으로 사용하기 때문에 설명하는 것을 어려워 함.
그래서 그들은 자주 자동 조종 상태에 있다

(6) When I first saw / an elite diver do four and a half somersaults, /
5형식V(지각V) / O / O·C(동사원형)
내가 처음 봤을 때 / 한 엘리트 다이버가 공중제비를 4회 반 도는 것을 /
I asked how he managed to spin so fast.
나는 그가 어떻게 그렇게 빨리 회전할 수 있었는지 물었다

(7) His answer: / "Just go up in a ball."
그의 대답은 / "그냥 공 모양으로 올라가기만 하면 돼요."

(8) Experts often have an intuitive understanding /
전문가들은 흔히 직관적인 지식을 가지고 있다 /
of a route, / but they struggle /
방법에 대해 / 하지만 그들은 고전한다 /
to clearly express all the steps to take. 정답 단서
취해야 할 모든 단계를 분명하게 표현하는 데 형용사적 용법
전문가들은 기술 사용 방법에 대한 직관적인 지식을 가지고 있기 때문에 그 단계를 분명하게 표현하는 것은 어려워 함.

(9) Their brain dump is partially filled with garbage.
그들이 이것저것 표현하는 것은 부분적으로는 쓰레기로 차 있다
힌트 'brain dump'는 특정 주제에 대해 자신의 생각을 마구 표현하고 기록하는 것을 뜻함. 일반적으로 '브레인 덤프'라고도 쓰지만, 여기서는 보다 명확한 의미로 서술함.

[전문 해석]

(1)할 줄 모르는 사람이 가르친다고 흔히 말해진다. (2)할 수 있는 사람은 기초를 가르칠 수 없다고 말하는 것이 더 정확할 것이다. (3)많은 전문 지식은 명시적인 것이 아니라 암시적이다. (4)여러분이 숙련을 향해 더 나아갈수록, 여러분은 흔히 기본에 대해 덜 의식적인 인식을 지닌다. (5)실험은 숙련된 골퍼와 와인 애호가는 자신의 퍼팅과 시음 기술을 설명하는 데 어려움을 겪으며, 심지어 그들의 접근 방식을 설명해 달라고 요청하는 것은 그들의 수행을 방해하기에 충분해서 그들은 자주 자동 조종 상태에 있다는 것을 보여 준다. (6)내가 한 엘리트 다이버가 공중제비를 4회 반 도는 것을 처음 봤을 때, 나는 그가 어떻게 그렇게 빨리 회전할 수 있었는지 물었다. (7)그의 대답은 "그냥 공 모양으로 올라가기만 하면 돼요."였다. (8)전문가들은 흔히 방법에 대해 직관적인 지식을 가지고 있지만, 그들은 취해야 할 모든 단계를 분명하게 표현하는 데 고전한다. (9)그들이 이것저것 표현하는 것은 부분적으로는 쓰레기로 차 있다.

정답과 해설 12 빈칸 추론 (2)

문제편 p.173

[정답 확인]

다음 빈칸에 들어갈 말로 가장 적절한 것은?

① the greater efforts you have to put into your work
여러분은 작업에 더 많은 노력을 기울여야만 한다
② the smaller number of strategies you use to solve problems
여러분이 문제를 해결하기 위해 사용하는 전략의 수가 더 적다
③ the less you tend to show off your excellent skills to others
여러분은 다른 사람들에게 자신의 뛰어난 기술을 덜 뽐내는 경향이 있다
④ the more detail-oriented you are likely to be for task completion
여러분은 작업 완수를 위해 더 꼼꼼할 가능성이 있다
⑤ the less conscious awareness you often have of the fundamentals
여러분은 흔히 기본에 대해 덜 의식적인 인식을 지닌다

[문제 풀이]

이 지문은 전문가가 가지고 있는 전문 지식이 명시적이지 않고 암시적이라는 것을 바탕으로 전개된다. 숙련자들은 숙련의 단계에 오르며 직관적인 지식을 갖추게 되나, 이것을 명확한 언어로 표현하는 것은 잘 되지 않는다. 남들보다 기술이 뛰어난 사람들은 자신이 사용하는 기술을 타인에게 설명하는 것을 어려워한다. 이는 기술을 무의식에 가깝게 사용하기 때문이며, 그것을 설명해야 하는 순간 업무 수행에 방해를 받는 것이다. 빈칸에는 개인이 숙련의 단계로 나아가기 시작할 때 취하는 태도에 대한 내용이 들어가야 한다. 따라서 빈칸에 들어갈 정답은 ⑤이다.

[중요 어휘]

□ **accurate**	형용사 정확한, 정밀한
□ **a great deal of**	많은, 다량의
□ **expert**	형용사 전문적인, 숙련된 / 명사 전문가
□ **implicit**	형용사 암시적인, 내포된
□ **explicit**	형용사 명시적인, 분명한
□ **mastery**	명사 숙련, 숙달
□ **conscious**	형용사 의식적인, 의도적인
□ **awareness**	명사 인식, 의식, 관심
□ **fundamental**	명사 (주로 복수로) 기본 (원칙) / 형용사 근본적인, 핵심적인
□ **skilled**	형용사 숙련된, 노련한
□ **aficionado**	명사 애호가, 매니아
□ **approach**	명사 접근 방식 / 동사 다가가다
□ **interfere with**	~을 방해하다
□ **performance**	명사 수행, 공연
□ **autopilot**	명사 자동 조종
□ **somersault**	명사 공중제비
□ **intuitive**	형용사 직관적인, 직감에 의한
□ **understanding**	명사 지식, 이해
□ **route**	명사 방법, 길, 경로
□ **partially**	부사 부분적으로, 불완전하게

문제편 p.176

13 무관한 문장 찾기

핵심 주변 사람들의 행동이나 태도가 개인에게 미치는 영향을 말하는 '사회적 증거'가 소셜 미디어상에서도 일어나고 있으며, 컨텐츠를 추천하는 친구에 대한 신뢰도와 컨텐츠에 대한 신뢰도가 정비례한다는 것이 이 글의 내용임.

01 2021년 6월 35번 (정답률 75%)

정답 ③

[지문 끊어 읽기] 소셜 미디어의 사회적 증거

(1) An interesting phenomenon / that arose from social media /
S
흥미로운 현상은 / 소셜 미디어에서 생겨난 /
is the concept of *social proof*.
V
'사회적 증거'라는 개념이다

힌트 주어 역할을 하는 to부정사구 to accept new values or ideas가 뒤로 보내진 대신 형식상의 주어 It이 주어 자리에 온 문장임. for a person은 내용상의 주어 to accept~의 행동 주체인 의미상의 주어로 해석함.

(2) It's easier for a person to accept / new values or ideas /
사람은 받아들이기가 더 쉽다 / 새로운 가치나 아이디어를 /
when they see / that others have already done so.
부사절 접속사 / 명사절 접속사(see의 목적어) / =accepted
그들이 알 때 / 다른 사람들이 이미 그렇게 했다는 것을

①(3) If the person / they see accepting the new idea /
S'
만약 그 사람이 / 그들이 새로운 아이디어를 받아들이고 있다고 보는 /
happens to be a friend, / then social proof has even more power /
V'
우연히 친구라면 / 그때 사회적 증거는 훨씬 더 큰 힘을 가진다 /
by exerting peer pressure /
병렬①
또래 압력을 행사함으로써 /
as well as relying on the trust /
병렬②
신뢰에 의존할 뿐만 아니라 /
that people put in the judgments of their close friends.
사람들이 그들의 친한 친구들의 판단에 두는

힌트 A as well as B는 'B뿐만 아니라 A'를 의미하는 상관접속사로 A와 B는 동일한 형태를 띠어야 함. 본문에서는 동명사 exerting과 relying이 병렬로 연결됨.

②(4) For example, / a video about some issue /
S
예를 들어 / 어떤 문제에 대한 영상은 /
may be controversial on its own / but more credible /
V S·C① S·C②
그 자체로 논란이 될 수 있다 / 하지만 더 신뢰할 수 있다 /
if it got thousands of *likes*. 정답 단서
그것이 수천 개의 '좋아요'를 얻으면

③(5) When expressing feelings of liking to friends, /
친구들에게 좋아함의 감정을 표현할 때 /
you can express them / using nonverbal cues /
= feelings of liking
당신은 그것들을 표현할 수 있다 / 비언어적 신호를 이용해 /
such as facial expressions.
표정과 같은

힌트 접속사를 동반한 분사구문으로 주절의 주어와 동일하므로 'When you express'로 바꿀 수 있음.

④(6) If a friend recommends the video to you, / in many cases, /
만약에 한 친구가 당신에게 영상을 추천한다면 / 많은 경우에 있어서 /
the credibility of the idea it presents / will rise /
그것이 제시하는 아이디어의 신뢰도는 / 상승할 것이다 /
in direct proportion to the trust /
신뢰도에 정비례하여 /
you place in the friend recommending the video. 정답 단서
당신이 영상을 추천하는 친구에게 두는

힌트 목적격 관계대명사 which 또는 that이 생략된 관계대명사절로 선행사인 'the trust'를 수식함

⑤(7) This is the power of social media / and part of the reason /
이것이 소셜 미디어의 힘이다 / 그리고 이유의 일부다 /
why videos or "posts" can become "viral."
영상이나 '게시물'이 '입소문이 날' 수 있는

[중요 구문]

(3) If [the person (that) they see V accepting the new idea]
선행사 목적격 관계대명사 [ ]: S'
happens ~ , then social proof has ~ on the trust that people put V
V' 선행사 목적격 관계대명사
in the judgments ~.

힌트 If절과 주절에 각각 목적격 관계대명사절이 있는 문장임. If절을 보면, 관계사절이 목적격 관계대명사 that/whom을 생략한 채 선행사인 'the person'을 수식하고 있음. 5형식인 원래의 문장 'they see the person accepting the new idea'에서 목적어 'the person'이 선행사로 빠져있으므로 목적격 보어인 'accepting'이 동사(see) 뒤에 바로 위치함. 주절에서는 관계사절이 목적격 관계대명사 that을 표시한 채 선행사 'the trust'를 수식하고 있음. 3형식인 원래의 문장 'people put the trust in the judgments ~'에서 목적어 'the trust'가 선행사로 빠져있음.

[전문 해석]

(1)소셜 미디어에서 생겨난 흥미로운 현상은 '사회적 증거'라는 개념이다. (2)다른 사람들이 이미 그렇게 했다는(받아들였다는) 것을 알 때 사람은 새로운 가치나 아이디어를 받아들이기가 더 쉽다. ①(3)만약 그들이 새로운 아이디어를 받아들이고 있다고 보는 그 사람이 우연히 친구라면, 그때 사회적 증거는 사람들이 그들의 친한 친구들의 판단에 두는 신뢰에 의존할 뿐만 아니라 또래 압력을 행사함으로써 훨씬 더 큰 힘을 가진다. ②(4)예를 들어, 어떤 문제에 대한 영상은 그 자체로 논란이 될 수 있지만, 그것이 수천 개의 '좋아요'를 얻으면 더 신뢰할 수 있다. ③(5)친구들에게 좋아함의 감정을 표현할 때, 당신은 표정과 같은 비언어적 신호를 이용해 그것들을 표현할 수 있다. ④(6)만약에 한 친구가 당신에게 영상을 추천한다면, 많은 경우에 있어서, 그것(영상)이 제시하는 아이디어의 신뢰도는 당신이 영상을 추천하는 친구에게 두는 신뢰도에 정비례하여 상승할 것이다. ⑤(7)이것이 소셜 미디어의 힘이고 영상이나 '게시물'이 '입소문이 날' 수 있는 이유의 일부다.

- social proof(사회적 증거) : 어떠한 행동과 태도를 보여야 할지 모를 때, 주변 사람들의 행동이나 태도를 모방하게 되는 심리적·사회적 현상
- peer pressure(또래 압력): 학교, 친구들, 직장 등 특정 집단의 또래(peer) 사이에서 의사결정을 할 때, 소수 의견을 가진 사람이 다수 의견을 따르도록 명시적으로 또는 암묵적으로 가해지는 압박

[중요 어휘]

□ phenomenon	명사 현상
□ arise	동사 생겨나다, 발생하다
□ happen to V	우연히 ~하다
□ exert	동사 (영향력 등을) 행사하다, 가하다
□ peer	명사 또래
□ rely on	~에 의존하다
□ controversial	형용사 논란이 되는
□ credible	형용사 신뢰할 수 있는, 믿을 만한
□ nonverbal	형용사 비언어적인
□ cue	명사 신호, 암시
□ credibility	명사 신뢰도, 신뢰성
□ in direct proportion to	~에 정비례하여
□ viral	형용사 입소문이 나는, 바이러스성의

02 2022년 6월 35번 (정답률 70%)

정답 ④

[지문 끊어 읽기] 명목 가치와 실질 가치

(1) Inflationary risk refers to uncertainty /
인플레이션에 관한 위험성은 불확실성과 관련되어 있다 /
[regarding the future real value / of one's investments]. 정답 단서
전치사(~에 대한)
미래 실질 가치에 대한 / 개인 투자의

인플레이션에 관한 위험성은 개인 투자의 미래 실질 가치에 대한 불확실성과 관련되어 있다고 함.

(2) Say, / for instance, / that you hold $100 in a bank account /
명사절 접속사 선행사
~라고 하자 / 예를 들어 / 당신이 은행 계좌에 100달러를 가지고 있다고 /
[that has no fees and accrues no interest]. [ ]: 주격 관계대명사절
V'① V'②
수수료가 없고 이자가 생기지 않는

힌트 접속사가 있는 분사구문으로 being이 생략된 형태임. 'If it(=$100) is left untouched'로 바꿔 생각하면 이해가 쉬움.

(3) If left untouched / there will always be $100 in that bank account.
그대로 내버려 두면 / 그 은행 계좌에는 항상 100달러가 있을 것이다

①(4) If you keep that money in the bank for a year, /
선행사
만약 당신이 1년 동안 은행에 그 돈을 보관하면 /
during which inflation is 100 percent, / you've still got $100.
전치사+관계대명사(계속적 용법)
그리고 그 기간에 인플레이션이 100퍼센트라면 / 당신은 여전히 100달러만 가지고 있는 것이다

★중요 문장 (8)의 nominal value에 해당하는 값으로 화폐에 표시된 금액을 의미함.

②(5) Only now, /
이제 /
if you take it out and put it in your wallet, /
만약 당신이 그 돈을 인출해서 당신의 지갑에 넣어둔다면 /
you'll only be able to purchase half the goods /
선행사
당신은 물건들의 반만 구매할 수 있게 될 것이다 /
[you could have bought a year ago].
could have p.p.: ~할 수도 있었다 [ ]: 목적격 관계대명사절
1년 전에 당신이 살 수도 있었던

★중요 문장 (8)의 real value에 해당하는 내용으로 문장 (4)의 $100와 달리 실질 구매력을 반영한 화폐의 가치임. 문장 (4)에서 인플레이션이 100퍼센트라는 것은 물가가 2배 상승했다는 것이므로 1년 전의 100달러는 현재 50달러의 가치밖에 지니지 못함.

힌트 '배수사(half, twice, three times 등)+the+명사'는 '명사의 ~배'를 의미함.

문제편 p.177

③(6) In other words, / if inflation increases /
다시 말하자면 / 만약 인플레이션이 증가한다면 /
faster than the amount of interest you are earning, /
당신이 받고 있는 이자의 양보다 더 빨리 / 선행사 목적격 관계대명사절
this will decrease the purchasing power of your investments /
이것은 당신 투자의 구매력을 감소시킬 것이다 /
over time. 정답 단서 인플레이션이 이자의 양보다 더 빨리 증가하면, 투자의 구매력이 감소한다고 함.
시간이 지남에 따라

④(7) It would be very useful /
형식상의 주어
매우 유용할 것이다 /
[to know in advance what would happen to your firm's total revenue] / [ ]: 내용상의 주어 간접의문문
당신 회사의 총수입에 어떤 일이 일어날지를 미리 아는 것은 /
if you increased your product's price. 정답 단서 상품 가격과 총수입에 대한 내용은 언급된 적 없음.
만약 당신이 당신의 상품의 가격을 올린다면

⑤(8) That's why / ✶중요 문장 (2)~(6)의 예시를 통해 알 수 있듯이 명목 가치와 달리 실질 가치에는 인플레이션에 따른 화폐의 구매력 변화가 반영되어 있음. 즉, 실질 가치는 명목 가치에서 인플레이션에 따른 물가 상승의 영향을 제거해야 알 수 있음.
명사절 접속사
그것이 이유이다 /
we differentiate between nominal value and real value. 주제문
우리가 명목 가치와 실질 가치를 구별하는 실질 가치에는 화폐의 구매력 변화가 반영되어 있으므로 명목 가치와 실질 가치를 구별해야 함.

[전문 해석]

(1)인플레이션에 관한 위험성은 개인 투자의 미래 실질 가치에 대한 불확실성과 관련되어 있다. (2)예를 들어, 당신이 수수료가 없고 이자가 생기지 않는 은행 계좌에 100달러를 가지고 있다고 하자. (3)그대로 내버려 두면, 그 은행 계좌에는 항상 100달러가 있을 것이다. ①(4)만약 당신이 1년 동안 은행에 그 돈을 보관하고 그 기간에 인플레이션이 100퍼센트라면, 당신은 여전히 100달러만 가지고 있는 것이다. ②(5)이제, 만약 당신이 그 돈을 인출해서 당신의 지갑에 넣어둔다면, 당신은 1년 전에 당신이 살 수도 있었던 물건들의 반만 구매할 수 있게 될 것이다. ③(6)다시 말하자면, 만약 인플레이션이 당신이 받고 있는 이자의 양보다 더 빨리 증가한다면, 이것은 시간이 지남에 따라 당신 투자의 구매력을 감소시킬 것이다. ④(7)만약 당신이 당신의 상품의 가격을 올린다면 당신 회사의 총수입에 어떤 일이 일어날지를 미리 아는 것은 매우 유용할 것이다. ⑤(8)그것이 우리가 명목 가치와 실질 가치를 구별하는 이유이다.
- inflation(인플레이션): 화폐 가치가 하락하여 물가가 전반적·지속적으로 상승하는 경제 현상
- purchasing power(구매력): 1단위의 화폐로 구매할 수 있는 재화 및 용역의 수량. 물가가 오르면 같은 돈으로 구입할 수 있는 재화나 서비스의 양이 감소하므로 구매력이 감소함.

[문제 풀이]

이 지문은 명목 가치와 실질 가치의 구분에 대해 설명하는 글이다. 문장 (1)에서 인플레이션에 관한 위험성이 개인 투자의 미래 실질 가치에 대한 불확실성과 관련되어 있음을 먼저 밝히고, 문장 (2)~(6)에서 100달러가 든 은행 계좌를 가정하여 인플레이션에 따라 구매력이 어떻게 달라지는지를 보여 준다. 이러한 예시를 통해 실질 가치에는 명목 가치만으로는 파악할 수 없는 화폐의 구매력 변화가 반영되어 있다는 것을 알 수 있고, 이것이 명목 가치와 실질 가치를 구별하는 이유라고 문장 (8)에서 설명하고 있다. 반면, 문장 (7)에서는 상품의 가격을 올릴 때 회사의 총수입에 어떤 일이 일어날지를 미리 아는 것이 유용하다고 하고 있는데, 이는 상품 가격과 총수입의 관계에 대한 내용으로 인플레이션과 구매력의 관계에 대해 설명하고 있는 글의 흐름에서 벗어난다. 따라서 정답은 ④이다.

[중요 어휘]

☐ **inflationary**	형용사 인플레이션에 관한, 인플레이션의
☐ **refer to**	~와 관련 있다, ~을 참고하다
☐ **investment**	명사 투자, 투자액
☐ **account**	명사 계좌, 설명, 해석
☐ **fee**	명사 수수료, 요금
☐ **accrue**	동사 생기다, 누적되다, 축적되다
☐ **interest**	명사 이자, 관심, 흥미
☐ **untouched**	형용사 (본래) 그대로의, 훼손되지 않은
☐ **purchase**	동사 구매하다, 구입하다 / 명사 구매, 구입
☐ **earn**	동사 받다, (일을 하여 돈을) 벌다, 얻다
☐ **in advance**	미리
☐ **revenue**	명사 수입, 수익
☐ **differentiate**	동사 구별하다, 구분 짓다
☐ **nominal**	형용사 명목의, 액면(상)의

03 2019년 3월 35번 (정답률 65%) 정답 ④

핵심 본문에서는 외부적인 메시지들이 우리가 먹는 방식에 안 좋은 영향을 끼친다고 말하고 있는데, 문장 (6)은 긍정적인 효과를 언급하고 있으므로 문맥에서 벗어나 있음.

[지문 끊어 읽기] 외부적 메시지들로 인한 먹는 방식의 혼란

(1) When we were infants, / we were tuned in /
우리가 유아였을 때 / 우리는 ~에 맞춰져 있었다 /
to the signals from our body / that told us /
우리 몸으로부터의 신호에 / 우리에게 알려주는 /
when to eat and when to stop.
언제 먹어야 하는지 그리고 언제 멈추어야 하는지

힌트 'tune in A to B'는 'A를 B에 맞추다, A를 B에 맞게 조율하다'라는 뜻임. 문장 (1)에서는 이것이 수동태로 사용되어 목적어 A에 해당하던 부분이 주어(we)로 빠지면서, 'A be tuned in to B(A는 B에 맞춰지다)'가 되었음.

(2) We had an instinctive awareness /
우리는 본능적인 인식을 가지고 있었다 /
of [what foods and how much food our body needed].
우리의 몸이 어떤 음식과 얼마나 많은 음식을 필요로 하는지에 대한 [ ]: 간접의문문(of의 목적어)

힌트 what foods와 how much food는 각각 의문사를 포함하고 있는 '의문사구'로, 의문사인 동시에 needed의 목적어 역할을 함.

①(3) As we grew older / this inner wisdom became lost /
우리가 나이가 들면서 / 이 내면의 지혜는 길을 잃었다 /
in a bewildering host of outer voices /
갈피를 못 잡게 하는 다수의 외부 목소리 속에서 /
that told us / how we should eat.
4형식V I·O D·O(명사절)
우리에게 알려주는 / 우리가 어떻게 먹어야 하는지를

✶중요 지시형용사의 사용에 주목할 것. 문장 (3)의 'this inner wisdom'은 문장 (2)의 'an instinctive awareness ~ needed'를, 문장 (5)의 'these messages'는 문장 (4)의 'conflicting messages from ~ research'를 가리킴.

②(4) We received conflicting messages / from our parents, /
우리는 상충되는 메시지를 받았다 / 우리의 부모님으로부터 /
from our peers, / and from scientific research.
우리의 동료로부터 / 그리고 과학 연구로부터

③(5) These messages created /
이러한 메시지는 일으켰다 /
a confusion of desires, impulses, and aversions / 정답 단서
욕구, 충동, 그리고 혐오감의 혼란을 /
that have made us unable / to just eat and to eat just enough.
우리가 ~할 수 없게 만들어 온 / 그저 먹고 딱 필요한 만큼 먹는 것을

✶중요 이는 '욕구, 충동, 그리고 혐오감'이 뒤섞임으로써 발생한 혼란을 의미함.

④(6) They have helped us see things /
그것들은 우리가 상황을 보도록 도와주어 왔다 /
in our right perspectives, /
우리의 올바른 관점에서 /
thus having an insight into the world.
그리하여 세상에 대한 통찰력을 가지게 되었다

힌트 분사구문의 주어가 생략되기 위해서는 주절의 주어(they=messages)와 having의 주어가 일치해야 하는데, 세상에 대한 통찰을 갖게 되는 주체는 we이고 주절의 주어와 일치하지 않으므로 문법적으로 불완전한 구문임. 학교 문법으로는 설명이 안 되는 부분이므로 고민하지 말고 넘어갈 것!

⑤(7) If we are to return /
우리가 돌아가려면 /
to a healthy and balanced relationship with food, / it is essential /
음식과의 건강하고 균형 잡힌 관계로 / 필수적이다 / 형식상의 주어
[that we learn / to turn our awareness inward / and to hear again /
[ ]: 내용상의 주어
우리가 배우는 것이 / 우리의 인식을 내부로 돌리는 것을 / 그리고 다시 듣는 것을 /
what our body is always telling us]. 주제문
우리의 몸이 우리에게 늘 무엇을 말하고 있는지를

힌트 'be to V'는 문맥에 따라 '예정, 운명, 의도, 가능, 의무'의 뜻을 나타냄. 문장 (7)의 'are to return'은 문맥상 '의도'를 나타내는 '돌아가려면'으로 해석할 수 있음.

[전문 해석]

(1)우리가 유아였을 때, 우리는 언제 먹어야 하는지 그리고 언제 멈추어야 하는지 (우리에게) 알려주는 우리 몸으로부터의 신호에 맞춰져 있었다. (2)우리는 우리의 몸이 어떤 음식과 얼마나 많은 음식을 필요로 하는지에 대한 본능적인 인식을 가지고 있었다(본능적으로 인식하고 있었다). ①(3)우리가 나이가 들면서, 이 내면의 지혜는 우리가 어떻게 먹어야 하는지를 (우리에게) 알려주는, 갈피를 못 잡게 하는 다수의 외부 목소리 속에서 길을 잃었다. ②(4)우리는 우리의 부모님, 동료, 그리고 과학 연구로부터 상충되는(서로 모순되는) 메시지를 받았다. ③(5)이러한 메시지는 우리가 그저 먹고 딱 필요한 만큼 먹는 것을 할 수 없게 만들어 온 욕구, 충동, 그리고 혐오감의 혼란을 일으켰다. ④(6)그것들은 우리가 우리의 올바른 관점에서 상황을 보도록 도와주어 왔고, 그리하여 (우리는) 세상에 대한 통찰력을 가지게 되었다. ⑤(7)우리가 음식과의 건강하고 균형 잡힌 관계로 돌아가려면, 우리가 우리의 인식을 내부로 돌리고 우리의 몸이 우리에게 늘 무엇을 말하고 있는지(내면의 소리)를 다시 듣는 것을 배우는 것이 필수적이다(필수적으로 배워야 한다).

[중요 어휘]

☐ **instinctive**	형용사 본능적인, 무의식적인
☐ **awareness**	명사 인식, 관심
☐ **wisdom**	명사 지혜, 현명

☐ bewildering	형용사 갈피를 못 잡게 하는, 어리둥절하게 만드는
☐ a host of	다수의
☐ conflicting	형용사 상충되는, 모순되는
☐ confusion	명사 혼란
☐ impulse	명사 충동, 충격
☐ aversion	명사 혐오감
☐ insight	명사 통찰력, 이해

핵심 광고가 어떻게 또래 집단으로부터의 평가에 민감한 어린 소비자들의 심리를 이용해서 제품을 구매하게 만드는지에 관한 글임.

04 2021년 3월 35번 (정답률 65%) 정답 ③

[지문 끊어 읽기] 어린 소비자 대상의 광고

(1) Academics, politicians, marketers and others /
대학 교수, 정치인, 마케팅 담당자, 그리고 그 외의 사람들은 /
have in the past debated / whether or not it is ethically correct /
삽입구
지금까지 논쟁해 왔다 / 윤리적으로 옳은지 그렇지 않은지를 /
to market products and services directly / to young consumers.
제품과 서비스를 직접 판촉하는 것이 / 어린 소비자들에게

①(2) This is also a dilemma for psychologists / who have questioned /
이것은 또한 심리학자들에게도 딜레마이다 / 의문을 제기하는 /
whether they ought to help advertisers manipulate children /
광고주들이 아이들을 조종하는 것을 그들이 도와야 하는지 /
into purchasing more products /
더 많은 제품을 구매하도록 /
they have seen advertised.
그들이 광고되는 것을 본

힌트 선행사로 products를 취하는 목적격 관계대명사절임. 생략된 목적격 관계대명사가 관계대명사절에서 지각동사 see의 목적어 역할을 하고, 과거분사 advertised가 목적격 보어에 해당함.

②(3) Advertisers have admitted / to taking advantage of the fact /
광고주들은 인정했다 / 사실을 이용한 것을 /
형식상의 주어
that it is easy to make children feel / that they are losers /
동격의 that(=the fact) 내용상의 주어
아이들이 느끼게 만드는 것이 쉽다는 / 자신이 패배자라고 /
if they do not own the 'right' products. 주제문
그 '적절한' 제품을 소유하고 있지 않으면

③(4) When products become more popular, /
제품이 더 인기 있어질 때 /
more competitors enter the marketplace /
더 많은 경쟁자들이 시장에 진출한다 /
and marketers lower their marketing costs /
그리고 마케팅 담당자들은 그들의 마케팅 비용을 줄인다 /
to remain competitive.
경쟁력을 유지하기 위해

④(5) Clever advertising informs children / that they will be viewed /
영리한 광고는 아이들에게 알려 준다 / 자신들이 보일 것이라고 /
by their peers in an unfavorable way /
또래 친구들에게 부정적인 방식으로 /
if they do not have the products / that are advertised, /
그들이 제품을 갖고 있지 않으면 / 광고되는 /
thereby playing on their emotional vulnerabilities. 정답 단서
그로 인한 아이들의 정서적인 취약성을 이용한다

⑤(6) The constant feelings of inadequateness / created by advertising / 정답 단서
S
불충분하다고 끊임없이 느끼는 감정은 / 광고에 의해 만들어지는 /
have been suggested to contribute / to children becoming fixated /
V
기여한다고 언급되어 왔다 / 아이들이 집착하게 되는 데 /
with instant gratification and beliefs /
즉각적인 만족감과 믿음에 /
that material possessions are important.
동격의 that(=beliefs)
물질적 소유물이 중요하다는

힌트 '~에 기여하다'라는 뜻의 contribute to에서 to는 전치사이기 때문에 뒤에 명사나 동명사가 와야 함. 따라서 becoming의 형태가 왔고, 동명사의 의미상의 주어로 children, 보어로 fixated가 쓰인 것임.

[전문 해석]

(1)대학 교수, 정치인, 마케팅 담당자, 그리고 그 외의 사람들은 제품과 서비스를 어린 소비자들에게 직접 판촉하는 것이 윤리적으로 옳은지 그렇지 않은지를 지금까지 논쟁해 왔다. ①(2)이것은 또한 광고주들이 아이들을 조종해서 그들(아이들)이 광고되는 것을 본 제품을 더 많이 구매하도록 그들(심리학자들)이 도와야 하는지 의문을 제기하는 심리학자들에게도 딜레마이다. ②(3)광고주들은 아이들이 그 '적절한' 제품을 소유하고 있지 않으면 자신이 패배자라고 느끼게 만드는 것이 쉽다는 사실을 이용한 것을 인정했다. ③(4)제품이 더 인기 있어질 때 더 많은 경쟁자들이 시장에 진출하고 마케팅 담당자들은 경쟁력을 유지하기 위해 그들의 마케팅 비용을 줄인다. ④(5)영리한 광고는 아이들이 광고되는 제품을 갖고 있지 않으면 자신들이 또래 친구들에게 부정적인 방식으로 보일 것이라고 아이들에게 알려 주고, 그로 인한 아이들의 정서적인 취약성을 이용한다. ⑤(6)광고에 의해 만들어지는, (자신이) 불충분하다고 끊임없이 느끼는 감정은 아이들이 즉각적인 만족감과 물질적 소유물이 중요하다는 믿음에 집착하게 되는 데 기여한다고 언급되어 왔다.

[문제 풀이]

또래 집단의 평가를 중요하게 생각하는 어린 소비자들의 심리를 이용하는 광고의 특성에 관한 글이다. 문장 (3)의 'the 'right' products(그 '적절한' 제품)'라는 표현은 문장 (5)의 'the products that are advertised(광고되는 제품)'로 이어진다. 반면 문장 (4)는 시장에서 제품의 경쟁이 치열해지면 마케팅 비용이 어떻게 되는가에 관한 것으로서, 어린 소비자를 목표로 하는 광고 전략에 대한 글의 전체적인 내용과 흐름이 어긋난다. 따라서 정답은 ③이다.

[중요 어휘]

☐ academic	명사 대학 교수 / 형용사 학업의, 학문의
☐ politician	명사 정치인, 정치가
☐ ethically	부사 윤리적으로
☐ manipulate	동사 조종하다, 다루다
☐ admit to N/V-ing	~을 인정하다
☐ peer	명사 또래 (집단)
☐ unfavorable	형용사 부정적인, 호의적이지 않은
☐ play on	(감정 등을) 이용하다
☐ vulnerability	명사 취약성, 연약성
☐ inadequateness	명사 불충분함, 부적절함
☐ fixated	형용사 집착하는
☐ gratification	명사 만족(감)
☐ material	형용사 물질적인 / 명사 재료
☐ possession	명사 소유물, 소유

05 2022년 9월 35번 (정답률 65%) 정답 ④

[지문 끊어 읽기] 입장을 취하는 것의 중요성

(1) Taking a stand is important /
입장을 취하는 것은 중요하다 /
because you become a beacon for those individuals /
선행사
당신이 그 개개인들에게 횃불이 되기 때문에 /
who are your people, your tribe, and your audience.
주격 관계대명사
당신의 사람들, 당신의 부족들, 당신의 청중인

①(2) When you raise your viewpoint up like a flag, /
당신이 당신의 견해를 깃발처럼 들 때 /
people know where to find you; / it becomes a rallying point.
의문사+to V(=의문사+S+should+V)
사람들은 어디서 당신을 찾아야 할지를 안다 / 그것은 집합 지점이 된다

②(3) Displaying your perspective /
동명사S
당신의 관점을 보여주는 것은 /
lets prospective (and current) customers know /
사역V O O·C
장래의 (그리고 현재의) 고객들이 알게 한다 /
that you don't just sell your products or services.
당신이 단지 물건과 서비스만 파는 것이 아니라는 것을

③(4) The best marketing is never just about selling a product or service, /
never/not A but B: A가 아니라 B
최고의 마케팅은 결코 제품이나 서비스를 판매하는 것에 대한 것이 아니라 /
but about taking a stand / 주제문
입장을 취하는 것에 대한 것이다 /
최고의 마케팅은 제품이나 서비스를 판매하는 것에 대한 것이 아니라 입장을 취하는 것에 대한 것임.
— showing an audience /
즉 청중들에게 보여주는 것 /

정답과 해설 13 무관한 문장 찾기

[why they should believe in what you're marketing /
왜 그들이 당신이 마케팅하는 것을 믿어야 하는지를 /
enough to want it at any cost], / [ ]: 간접의문문
enough to V: ~할 만큼 충분히
어떠한 비용을 지불하더라도 그것을 원할 만큼 충분히 /
simply because they agree with what you're doing. 정답 단서
단순히 그들이 당신이 하는 것에 동의하기 때문에

'당신이 하는 것에 동의하는 것'은 문장 (6)에서 언급된 '집합 지점'에 모이는 것으로 비유할 수 있음. 따라서 문장 (4)와 문장 (6)은 자연스럽게 연결됨.

④ (5) If you want to retain your existing customers, /
만약 당신이 기존의 고객을 유지하고 싶다면 /
you need to create ways /
선행사
당신은 방법을 만들어낼 필요가 있다 /
힌트 how, where 등의 관계부사를 대신하여 that을 사용할 수 있음.
[that a customer can feel like another member of the team, /
고객이 팀의 또 다른 구성원인 것처럼 느낄 수 있는 /
participating in the process of product development]. [ ]: 관계부사절
분사구문(동시동작)
상품 개발 과정에 참여하면서

⑤ (6) Products can be changed or adjusted / if they aren't functioning, /
상품은 바꾸거나 고칠 수 있다 / 그것들이 기능하지 않으면 /
but rallying points align with the values and meaning /
하지만 집합 지점은 가치 및 의미와 같은 선상에 있다 /
behind what you do. 정답 단서 집합 지점은 당신이 하는 것의 이면에 있는 가치 및 의미와 같은 선상에 있음.
당신이 하는 것의 이면에 있는

[전문 해석]

(1)입장을 취하는 것은 당신이 당신의 사람들, 당신의 부족들, 당신의 청중인 그 개개인들에게 횃불이 되기 때문에 중요하다. ①(2)당신이 당신의 견해를 깃발처럼 들 때, 사람들은 어디서 당신을 찾아야 할지를 안다. 그것은 집합 지점이 된다. ②(3)당신의 관점을 보여주는 것은 장래의 (그리고 현재의) 고객들이 당신이 단지 물건과 서비스만 파는 것이 아니라는 것을 알게 한다. ③(4)최고의 마케팅은 결코 제품이나 서비스를 판매하는 것에 대한 것이 아니라, 입장을 취하는 것, 즉 단순히 청중들이 당신이 하는 것에 동의하기 때문에, 왜 그들이 당신이 마케팅하는 것을 어떠한 비용을 지불하더라도 그것을 원할 만큼 충분히 믿어야 하는지를 청중들에게 보여주는 것에 대한 것이다. ④(5)만약 당신이 기존의 고객을 유지하고 싶다면 당신은 고객이 상품 개발 과정에 참여하면서, 팀의 또 다른 구성원인 것처럼 느낄 수 있는 방법을 만들어낼 필요가 있다. ⑤(6)상품은 기능하지 않으면 바꾸거나 고칠 수 있지만, 집합 지점은 당신이 하는 것의 이면에 있는 가치 및 의미와 같은 선상에 있다.

[문제 풀이]

이 지문은 입장을 취하는 것의 중요성에 대해 설명하는 글이다. 문장 (1)에서 입장을 취하는 것이 중요하다고 하고, 문장 (2)에서 깃발처럼 견해를 들 때, 즉 입장을 취할 때 사람들이 모여 집합 지점이 된다고 한다. 이어지는 문장 (3)과 (4)에서는 관점을 보여주는 것, 즉 입장을 취하는 것은 당신이 단지 물건과 서비스만 파는 것이 아님을 고객들이 알게 하기 때문에 최고의 마케팅이라고 언급한다. 이에 대해 문장 (6)에서는 집합 지점이 당신이 하는 것의 이면에 있는 가치 및 의미와 같은 선상에 있음을 강조하며 입장을 취하는 것에 대해 다시 한번 언급하고 있다. 한편, 문장 (5)의 기존 고객 유지를 위한 전략에 대한 내용은 입장을 취하는 것이 중요하다고 설명하는 글 전체의 흐름과 관련이 없다. 따라서 정답은 ④이다.

[중요 어휘]

□ **stand**	명사 입장, 태도
□ **beacon**	명사 횃불
□ **tribe**	명사 부족, 집단
□ **rallying point**	집합 지점
□ **perspective**	명사 관점, 시각, 전망
□ **prospective**	형용사 장래의, 유망한, 다가오는
□ **at any cost**	어떠한 비용을 지불하더라도
□ **retain**	동사 유지하다, 간직하다
□ **align**	동사 같은 선상에 있다, 나란하다, ~을 조정하다

06 2018년 11월 35번 (정답률 60%)

정답 ④

[지문 끊어 읽기]

휘게

(1) *Hygge*, a term that comes from Danish, /
Hygge의 동격
덴마크어에서 유래한 용어인 'Hygge'는 /
is both a noun and a verb /
명사이면서 동사이기도 하다 /
and does not have a direct translation into English.
그리고 영어로의 직역을 가지고 있지 않다

(2) The closest word would have to be *coziness*, /
가장 가까운 단어는 '아늑함'일 것이다 /
but that doesn't really do it justice.
하지만 실제로 그것이 그것을 제대로 다루지는 못한다
힌트 'do A justice'라고 하면 'A를 제대로 다루다'라는 의미로 맥락에 따라 문장 (2)처럼 해석됨.

① (3) While *hygge* is centered around cozy activities, /
~이긴 하지만
'hygge'가 아늑한 활동들에 중점을 두고 있기는 하지만 /
정답 단서
it also includes a mental state / of well-being and togetherness.
그것은 정신적인 상태도 포함한다 / 행복과 연대감의

② (4) It's a holistic approach / to deliberately creating /
그것은 전체론적인 접근법이다 / 의도적으로 만들어내는 것에 대한 /
intimacy, connection, and warmth /
친밀감, 유대감, 그리고 따뜻함을 /
with ourselves and those around us.
우리 자신 그리고 우리 주변 사람들과의
힌트 여기서 'to'는 'approach to 명사'에서의 전치사 'to'이므로 뒤에 동명사 'creating'이라는 명사의 형태가 왔음.

③ (5) When we *hygge*, / we make a conscious decision /
우리가 'hygge'를 할 때 / 우리는 의식적인 결정을 내린다 /
to find joy in the simple things. 정답 단서
소박한 것에서 즐거움을 찾기 위한

④ (6) The joy in the simple things, /
소박한 것에서의 즐거움은 /
such as making a home-cooked meal, /
가정식을 요리하는 것과 같이 /
has been removed / because we perceive them /
제거되어 왔다 / 우리가 그것들을 인식하기 때문에 /
as difficult and time-consuming.
어렵고 시간이 많이 걸리는 것으로
✱중요 바로 앞 문장에 나왔던 joy in the simple things라는 표현을 그대로 사용한데다 '소박한 것'의 예시로 making a home-cooked meal을 들고 있어 마치 두 문장이 자연스럽게 연결되는 것처럼 보일 수 있지만, '소박한 것에서의 즐거움이 제거되어 왔다'라는 내용은 'hygge'를 소개하는 전체 글의 흐름과 어울리지 않음.

정답 단서
⑤ (7) For example, / [lighting candles and drinking wine /
예를 들어 / 촛불을 켜고 와인을 마시는 것 /
with a close friend you haven't seen in a while], /
선행사 목적격 관계대명사절
당신이 한동안 만나지 못했던 친한 친구와 /
or [sprawling out on a blanket /
또는 담요 위에서 팔다리를 쭉 펴고 누워있는 것은 /
while having a relaxing picnic in the park /
while V-ing(~하는 동안)
공원에서 편안한 소풍을 하며 /
with a circle of your loved ones / in the summertime] /
당신이 사랑하는 사람들의 무리와 / 여름날에 /
can both be *hygge*.
모두 'hygge'가 될 수 있다
힌트 문장 (7)을 간단히 나타내면 '[lighting and drkinking (with ~)] or [sprawling (while ~) (with ~) (in ~)] can both be *hygge*.'임. 즉 문장 전체의 주어에 해당하는 대괄호([ ]) 2개가 or로 병렬 연결되어 있는 구조임.

[전문 해석]

(1)덴마크어에서 유래한 용어인 'Hygge(휘게)'는 명사이면서 동사이기도 하며, 영어로의 직역을 가지고 있지 않다. (2)가장 가까운 단어는 '아늑함'일 것이지만, 실제로 그것('아늑함'으로의 번역)이 그것(hygge)을 제대로 다루지는(표현하지는) 못한다. ①(3)'hygge'가 아늑한 활동들에 중점을 두고 있기는 하지만, 그것은 행복과 연대감의 정신적인 상태도 포함한다. ②(4)그것은 우리 자신 그리고 우리 주변 사람들과의 친밀감, 유대감, 그리고 따뜻함을 의도적으로 만들어내는 것에 대한 전체론적인 접근법이다. ③(5)우리가 'hygge'를 할 때, 우리는 소박한 것에서 즐거움을 찾기 위한 의식적인 결정을 내린다. ④(6)가정식을 요리하는 것과 같이 소박한 것에서의 즐거움은, 우리가 그것들을 어렵고 시간이 많이 걸리는 것으로 인식하기 때문에 제거되어 왔다. ⑤(7)예를 들어, 당신이 한동안 만나지 못했던 친한 친구와 촛불을 켜고 와인을 마시는 것, 또는 여름날에 당신이 사랑하는 사람들의 무리와 공원에서 편안한 소풍을 하며 (즐기며) 담요 위에서 팔다리를 쭉 펴고 누워있는 것은 모두 'hygge'가 될 수 있다.

[중요 어휘]

□ **term**	명사 용어, 말, 학기
□ **translation**	명사 번역, 통역
□ **coziness**	명사 아늑함, 편안함
□ **do A justice**	A를 제대로 다루다[표현하다]
□ **togetherness**	명사 연대감, 단란함

- deliberately [부사] 의도적으로, 고의적으로
- intimacy [명사] 친밀감, 친교
- connection [명사] 유대감, 연결
- conscious [형용사] 의식적인, 의도적인
- perceive [동사] 인식하다, 여기다
- sprawl [동사] 팔다리를 쭉 펴고 눕다, 마구 뻗다
- circle [명사] 무리, 집단

07 2021년 9월 35번 (정답률 60%)

정답 ③

[지문 끊어 읽기] 간호사들의 역할

(1) Nurses hold a pivotal position /
V①
간호사들은 중추적인 위치를 차지하고 있다 /
in the mental health care structure /
정신 건강 관리 체계에서 /
and are placed at the centre of the communication network, / 주제문
V②
그리고 의사소통망의 중심에 놓여 있다 /
partly because of their high degree of contact with patients, /
부분적으로는 그들의 환자들과의 높은 접촉 정도 때문이다 /
but also because they have well-developed relationships with other professionals.
하지만 또한 그들이 다른 전문가들과 잘 발달된 관계를 가지고 있기 때문이기도 하다

① (2) Because of this, /
이 때문에 /
nurses play a crucial role in interdisciplinary communication.
간호사들은 학제 간의 의사소통에서 중요한 역할을 한다

✶중요 반복되는 지시대명사 this가 문맥상 무엇을 가리키는지에 주목할 것. 문장 (2)의 this는 문장 (1)의 Nurses ~ network, 문장 (5)의 this는 문장 (3)의 a mediating role ~ carer, 문장 (6)의 this는 문장 (5)의 translating communication ~ problems를 가리킴.

② (3) They have a mediating role /
그들은 중재하는 역할을 한다 /
between the various groups of professionals and the patient and carer.
다양한 집단의 전문가들과 환자 및 보호자 사이에서

③ (4) Mental healthcare professionals are legally bound /
정신 건강 관리 전문가들은 법적인 의무가 있다 /
to protect the privacy of their patients, / so they may be, /
그들의 환자들의 사생활을 보호해야 하는 / 그래서 그들은 ~일지도 모른다 /
rather than unwilling, / unable to talk about care needs.
꺼린다기보다는 / 건강 관리 필요에 대해 말할 수 없는

힌트 'be bound to V'는 보통 '~할 수밖에 없다', '반드시 ~하다' 등을 의미하는데, 여기서는 '~할 의무가 있다'라는 의미로 쓰임.

④ (5) This involves translating communication between groups
이것은 집단 간의 의사소통을 번역하는 것을 포함한다 /
into language / that is acceptable and comprehensible to people /
선행사 주격 관계대명사 선행사
언어로 / 사람들이 받아들일 수 있고 이해 가능한 /
who have different ways of understanding mental health problems.
주격 관계대명사
정신 건강상의 문제를 이해하는 다양한 방식을 가진

⑤ (6) This is a highly sensitive and skilled task, /
이것은 고도로 민감하고 숙련된 작업이다 /
requiring a high level of attention to alternative views /
분사구문 병렬①
대안적 시각에 대한 높은 수준의 관심을 요구한다 /
and a high level of understanding of communication.
병렬②
그리고 의사소통에 대한 높은 수준의 이해를

[전문 해석]

(1)간호사들은 정신 건강 관리 체계에서 중추적인 위치를 차지하고 있고 의사소통망의 중심에 놓여 있는데, 부분적으로는 그들의 환자들과의 높은 접촉 정도 때문이지만, 또한 그들이 다른 전문가들과 잘 발달된 관계를 가지고 있기 때문이기도 하다. ①(2)이 때문에 간호사들은 학제 간의 의사소통에서 중요한 역할을 한다. ②(3)그들은 다양한 집단의 전문가들과 환자 및 보호자 사이에서 중재하는 역할을 한다. ③(4)정신 건강 관리 전문가들은 환자들의 사생활을 보호해야 하는 법적인 의무가 있으므로 그들은 건강 관리 필요에 대해 (말하기를) 꺼린다기보다는 말할 수 없을지도 모른다. ④(5)이것은 정신 건강상의 문제를 이해하는 다양한 방식을 가진 사람들이 받아들일 수 있고 이해 가능한 언어로 집단 간의 의사소통을 번역하는 것을 포함한다. ⑤(6)이것은 고도로 민감하고 숙련된 작업이며, 대안적 시각에 대한 높은 수준의 관심과 의사소통에 대한 높은 수준의 이해를 요구한다.

[중요 어휘]

- hold a position 위치[지위]를 차지하다
- pivotal [형용사] 중추적인, 중요한
- degree [명사] 정도
- professional [명사] 전문가 / [형용사] 직업의, 전문적인
- interdisciplinary [형용사] 학제 간의
- mediate [동사] 중재하다, 조정하다
- carer [명사] 보호자, 간병인
- unwilling [형용사] 꺼리는, 싫어하는
- comprehensible [형용사] 이해 가능한
- alternative [형용사] 대안적인, 대체 가능한

08 2022년 3월 35번 (정답률 60%)

정답 ④

[지문 끊어 읽기] 기술 활용 능력

(1) Today's "digital natives" have grown up /
오늘날의 '디지털 원주민'들은 성장했다 / V①
immersed in digital technologies /
디지털 기술에 몰입한 채로 /
and possess the technical aptitude /
V②
그리고 기술적 소질을 가지고 있다 /
to utilize the powers of their devices fully.
형용사적 용법
자신의 기기의 힘을 충분히 활용할 수 있는

힌트 comma 없이 사용되었지만 분사구문의 일종으로 주절과 동시에 발생하는 상황을 나타냄.

① (2) But although they know /
하지만 그들이 알고 있을지라도 /
which apps to use / or which websites to visit, /
어떤 앱을 사용해야 하는지 / 혹은 어떤 웹사이트를 방문해야 하는지 /
they do not necessarily understand the workings /
부분 부정
그들이 작동 방식을 반드시 이해하는 것은 아니다 /
behind the touch screen.
터치스크린 뒤에 숨겨진

힌트 '의문사+to V' 형태의 명사구로, 풀어서 쓰면 '의문사+S+should+V'가 됨. 따라서 밑줄 친 부분을 각각 'which apps they should use', 'which websites they should visit'으로 바꿀 수 있음.

② (3) People need technological literacy /
사람들은 기술 활용 능력이 필요하다 /
if they are to understand machines' mechanics and uses. 주제문
그들이 기계의 역학과 용도를 이해하려면

기계의 역학과 용도를 이해하기 위해서는 기술 활용 능력이 필요하다고 하고 있음.

힌트 if절에서 사용된 'be to V'는 의도를 나타냄. 'if they intend to understand ~'로 바꿀 수 있음.

③ (4) In much the same way / as factory workers a hundred years ago /
~와 마찬가지로
마찬가지로 / 100년 전 공장 근로자들이 /
needed to understand the basic structures of engines, /
엔진의 기본 구조를 이해할 필요가 있었던 것과 /
we need to understand the elemental principles /
우리는 기본 원리를 이해할 필요가 있다 /
behind our devices. 정답단서 우리는 기기의 기본 원리를 이해할 필요가 있다고 하고 있음.
우리의 기기 뒤에 숨겨진

✶중요 이어지는 문장 (6)에 언급되는 소프트웨어와 하드웨어로 인해 글의 흐름과 관련 있다고 혼동하기 쉬움. 하지만 문장 (4)와 (6)에서는 기기의 기본 원리를 이해하는 것의 필요성과 효과에 대해 이야기하고 있는 것과 달리, 문장 (5)에서는 기기의 수명에 대해 설명하고 있으므로 글의 흐름에서 벗어남.

④ (5) The lifespan of devices /
기기의 수명은 /
depends on the quality of software [operating them] /
=devices
그것들을 작동하는 소프트웨어의 우수성에 달려 있다 /
as well as the structure of hardware.
B as well as A: A뿐만 아니라 B
하드웨어의 구조뿐만 아니라

정답단서 여기서 'This'는 문장 (4)에서 언급된 기기의 기본 원리를 이해하는 것을 말함.

⑤ (6) This empowers us to deploy software and hardware /
5형식V O O·C
이것은 우리가 소프트웨어와 하드웨어를 사용할 능력을 준다 /
to their fullest utility, / [maximizing our powers /
최대한 유용하게 / 우리의 능력을 극대화하면서 /
to achieve and create]. [ ]: 분사구문(동시동작)
성취하고 만들어 낼 수 있는

힌트 'by/in/to/with/without+추상명사'는 부사 역할을 할 수 있음. 따라서 '유용하게'라고 부사처럼 해석함.

[전문 해석]

(1)오늘날의 '디지털 원주민'들은 디지털 기술에 몰입한 채로 성장했고, 자신이 가진 기기의 힘을 충분히 활용할 수 있는 기술적 소질을 가지고 있다. ①(2)하지만 그들이 어떤 앱을 사용해야 하는지 혹은 어떤 웹사이트를 방문해야 하는지 알고 있을지라도, 터치스크린 뒤에 숨겨진 작동 방식을 반드시 이해하는 것은 아니다. ②(3)사람들이 기계의 역학과 용도를 이해하려면 기술 활용 능력이 필요하다. ③(4)100년 전 공장 근로자들이 엔진의 기본 구조를 이해할 필요가 있었던 것과 마찬가지로, 우리는 우리의 기기 뒤에 숨겨진 기본 원리를 이해할 필요가 있다. ④(5)기기의 수명은 하드웨어의 구조뿐만 아니라 그것들(기기)을 작동하는 소프트웨어의 우수성에 달려 있다. ⑤(6)이것은 성취하고 만들어 낼 수 있는 우리의 능력을 극대화하면서, 우리가 소프트웨어와 하드웨어를 최대한 유용하게 사용할 능력을 준다.

[문제 풀이]

이 지문은 기술 활용 능력의 필요성에 대해 강조하고 있는 글이다. 문장 (1)에 따르면 오늘날의 '디지털 원주민'들은 기기를 활용할 수 있는 기술적 소질을 가지고 있다고 했지만, 문장 (2)는 기기를 활용한다는 것이 기기의 작동 방식을 이해한다는 것은 아님을 밝히고 있다. 이어지는 문장 (3)~(4)에 따르면 기계의 역학과 용도를 이해하기 위해서는 기술 활용 능력이 필요하며, 기기의 기본 원리를 이해해야 한다. 또한 문장 (6)은 기기의 기본 원리를 이해하고 기술 활용 능력을 갖추는 것이 우리의 능력을 극대화하며, 우리로 하여금 소프트웨어와 하드웨어를 최대한 유용하게 사용할 능력을 준다고 설명한다. 한편, 문장 (5)는 기기의 수명이 하드웨어의 구조와 소프트웨어의 우수성에 따라 달라진다고 설명하는데, 이는 기술 활용 능력의 필요성을 강조하는 글의 흐름에서 벗어나므로 정답은 ④이다.

[중요 어휘]

□ **immerse**	동사 몰입하다, 몰두하다
□ **aptitude**	명사 소질, 재능
□ **utilize**	동사 활용하다
□ **not necessarily**	반드시 ~은 아닌
□ **mechanics**	명사 역학, 기계학
□ **structure**	명사 구조 / 동사 조직하다, 구조화하다
□ **elemental**	형용사 기본적인, 본질적인
□ **lifespan**	명사 수명
□ **empower**	동사 ~할 능력을 주다, 권한을 주다
□ **deploy**	동사 (효율적으로) 사용하다
□ **utility**	명사 유용성, 쓸모가 있음

09 2023년 3월 35번 (정답률 60%)

정답 ③

[지문 끊어 읽기] 인간의 행동 과정

(1) Human processes differ from rational processes /
인간의 과정은 이성적인 과정과 다르다 /
in their outcome.
그 결과에 있어서

(2) A process is *rational* / if it always does the right thing /
어떤 과정은 '이성적'이다 / 만약 그것이 항상 옳은 일을 한다면 /
based on the current information, /
현재의 정보에 근거하여 /
given an ideal performance measure.
given+명사구: ~을 고려할 때
이상적인 수행 척도를 고려할 때

(3) In short, / rational processes go by the book / and assume /
V① V②
요컨대 / 이성적인 과정은 책을 따른다 / 그리고 가정한다 /
[that the book is actually correct]. [ ]: 명사절(assume의 목적어)
그 책이 실제로 맞다는 것을

① (4) Human processes involve /
인간의 과정은 포함한다 /
instinct, intuition, and other variables /
본능, 직관, 그리고 다른 변수들을 / 선행사
that don't necessarily reflect the book /
주격 관계대명사
꼭 책을 반영하지는 않는 /

힌트 부정어 'not'과 'necessarily'가 함께 쓰이면 부분 부정의 의미를 나타내는데, 이때 해석은 '꼭(반드시) ~하는 것은 아니다'로 함.

and may not even consider the existing data.
그리고 심지어 존재하는 데이터를 고려하지 않을 수도 있다

② (5) As an example, / the rational way to drive a car /
예를 들어 / 차를 운전하는 이성적인 방식은 / S 형용사적 용법
is to always follow the laws. 정답단서 차를 운전하는 이성적인 방식을 예로 들고 있음.
명사적 용법(S·C)
항상 법규를 따르는 것이다

③ (6) Likewise, / pedestrian crossing signs vary /
비슷하게 / 보행자 횡단 신호는 서로 다르다 /
depending on the country / with differing appearances /
나라에 따라 / 다른 모습과 함께 /
of a person crossing the street.
길을 건너는 사람의

④ (7) However, / traffic isn't rational; / if you follow the laws precisely, /
그러나 / 교통은 이성적이지 않다 / 여러분이 법규를 정확히 따르더라도 /
you end up stuck somewhere /
여러분은 결국 어딘가에 갇히게 될 것이다 /
because other drivers aren't following the laws precisely. 정답단서
왜냐하면 다른 운전자들은 법규를 정확히 따르지 않기 때문이다

문장 (5)의 예시 내용의 연장선으로 법규를 정확히 지키지 않는 사람들이 많음을 지적함.

⑤ (8) To be successful, /
성공하기 위해서 /
a self-driving car must therefore act humanly, /
그러므로 자율 주행 자동차는 인간적으로 행동해야 한다 /
rather than rationally.
이성적이기보다

힌트 'rather than'으로 비교하는 대상은 병렬 관계여야 하므로 둘 다 동일한 품사(부사)로 왔음.

[전문 해석]

(1)인간의 과정은 그 결과에 있어서 이성적인 과정과 다르다. (2)이상적인 수행 척도를 고려할 때, 만약 어떤 과정이 현재의 정보에 근거하여 항상 옳은 일을 한다면 그것은 '이성적'이다. (3)요컨대, 이성적인 과정은 책을 따르고, 그 책이 실제로 맞다는 것을 가정한다. ①(4)인간의 과정은 본능, 직관 그리고 꼭 책을 반영하지는 않는 다른 변수들을 포함하고, 심지어 존재하는 데이터를 고려하지 않을 수도 있다. ②(5)예를 들어, 차를 운전하는 이성적인 방식은 항상 법규를 따르는 것이다. ③(6)비슷하게, 보행자 횡단 신호는 길을 건너는 사람의 다른 모습과 함께 나라에 따라 서로 다르다. ④(7)그러나 교통은 이성적이지 않은데, 여러분이 법규를 정확히 따르더라도 다른 운전자가 법규를 정확히 따르지 않기 때문에 여러분은 결국 어딘가에 갇히게 될 것이다. ⑤(8)성공하기 위해서, 그러므로 자율 주행 자동차는 이성적이기보다 인간적으로 행동해야 한다.

[문제 풀이]

인간의 과정, 즉 인간이 수행하는 일의 과정은 언제나 이성적이지는 않다는 내용의 글이다. 이성적인 것은 모든 것이 합리적으로, 옳은 일만 수행한다는 뜻이다. 그러나 인간이 하는 행동 과정은 본능, 직관에 따르거나 다양한 변수가 작용하여 결국 생각한 대로 되지 않는다. 필자는 이에 대한 예시로 운전을 들었고, 나 하나만 운전 법규를 지킨다고 해도 다른 사람들이 지키지 않기 때문에 교통 상황에 따라 어딘가에 갇히게 되는 결과가 나타날 수도 있다. 따라서 마지막 문장에서는 이러한 맥락에서 자율 주행 자동차가 제대로 기능하려면 이성적인 판단보다 '인간처럼' 판단하는 것이 낫다고 언급한다. 따라서 보행자 횡단 신호가 나라마다 다르다는 내용의 문장 (6)이 지문의 다른 내용과 관계가 없으므로, 정답은 ③이다.

[중요 어휘]

□ **differ from**	~과 다르다
□ **outcome**	명사 결과
□ **rational**	형용사 이성적인, 합리적인
□ **measure**	명사 척도, 측정 / 동사 재다, 측정하다
□ **go by A**	A를 따르다
□ **assume**	동사 가정하다, 추정하다
□ **instinct**	명사 본능, 타고난 소질
□ **intuition**	명사 직관, 직감
□ **variable**	명사 변수 / 형용사 변동이 심한
□ **pedestrian**	명사 보행자 / 형용사 도보의, 보행자의
□ **appearance**	명사 모습, 모양, 출현
□ **humanly**	부사 인간적으로

10 2023년 6월 35번 (정답률 60%) 정답 ④

[지문 끊어 읽기] 런던 택시 기사의 기억력

(1) Before getting licensed / to drive a cab in London, /
부사적 용법(목적)
면허를 받기 전에 / 런던에서 택시를 운전하기 위해 /
a person has to pass an incredibly difficult test /
사람은 굉장히 어려운 시험을 통과해야 한다 /
with an intimidating name — "The Knowledge."
'The Knowledge'라는 위협적인 이름의

① (2) The test involves memorizing the layout /
그 시험은 구획을 암기하는 것을 포함한다 /
of more than 20,000 streets / in the Greater London area /
2만 개 이상 거리의 / Greater London 지역의 /
— a feat that involves an incredible amount of memory resources.
엄청난 양의 기억 자원을 포함하는 재주다 **정답 단서** 런던에서 택시 기사를 하기 위해 통과해야 하는 시험은 엄청난 암기력을 필요로 함.

② (3) In fact, / fewer than 50 percent of the people /
사실 / 사람 중 50% 미만이 / 선행사(S)
[who sign up for taxi driver training] / pass the test, /
[ ]: 주격 관계대명사절 V
택시 기사 훈련에 등록한 / 시험을 통과한다 /
even after spending two or three years studying for it!
심지어 그것을 위해 2, 3년을 공부한 후에도

③ (4) And as it turns out, / the brains of London cabbies are different /
그리고 밝혀졌듯이 / 런던 택시 기사들의 두뇌는 다르다 /
from non-cab-driving humans /
택시 운전을 하지 않는 사람들과 /
in ways [that reflect their herculean memory efforts]. **정답 단서** 택시 기사의 기억력은 초인적인 수준임.
[ ]: 주격 관계대명사절
그들의 초인적인 기억 노력을 반영하는 방식에서

④ (5) In other words, / they must hold a full driving license, /
다시 말해서 / 그들은 정식 운전 면허증을 소지해야 한다 /
issued by the Driver and Vehicle Licensing Authority, /
운전 면허청에서 발급된 /
for at least a year.
최소 1년 동안

⑤ (6) In fact, / the part of the brain /
사실 / 뇌의 부분은 / S, 선행사
[that has been most frequently associated with spatial memory], /
공간 기억과 가장 자주 연관되어 온 / [ ]: 주격 관계대명사절
[the tail of the sea horse-shaped brain region /
[ ]: the part of the brain과 동격
해마 모양을 한 뇌 영역의 꼬리 부분은 /
called the hippocampus], / is *bigger* than average /
해마라 불리는 / 평균보다 '더 크다' / V
in these taxi drivers. **정답 단서** 택시 기사들의 기억력과 관련된 뇌의 부분은 일반인들에 비해 더 큼.
이들 택시 기사들에게서

[전문 해석]

(1)런던에서 택시를 운전하기 위해 면허를 받기 전에, 사람은 'The Knowledge'라는 위협적인 이름의 굉장히 어려운 시험을 통과해야 한다. ①(2)그 시험은 Greater London 지역의 2만 개 이상 거리의 구획을 암기하는 것을 포함하는데, 이것은 엄청난 양의 기억 자원을 포함하는 재주다. ②(3)사실, 심지어 그것을 위해 2, 3년을 공부한 후에도 택시 기사 훈련에 등록한 사람 중 50% 미만이 시험을 통과한다! ③(4)그리고 밝혀졌듯이, 런던 택시 기사들의 두뇌는 그들의 초인적인 기억 노력을 반영하는 방식에서 택시 운전을 하지 않는 사람들과 다르다. ④(5)다시 말해서, 그들은 운전 면허청에서 발급된 정식 운전 면허증을 최소 1년 동안 소지해야 한다. ⑤(6)사실, 공간 기억과 가장 자주 연관되어 온 뇌의 부분인, 해마라 불리는 해마 모양을 한 뇌 영역의 꼬리 부분은 이들 택시 기사들에게서 평균보다 '더 크다'.

[문제 풀이]

이 지문은 런던에서 택시 기사를 하는 사람들의 기억력에 대해 설명하는 글이다. 문장 (1)에서 런던에서 택시 기사 면허를 받기 전에 굉장히 어려운 시험을 통과해야 한다고 언급하며, 문장 (2)는 이 시험이 런던 내의 2만 개 이상 거리의 구획을 암기해야 하므로 엄청난 기억력을 요구한다고 부연 설명하고, 런던 택시 기사들의 두뇌가 택시 운전을 하지 않는 사람들과 다르다는 것을 문장 (4)에서 언급한다. 문장 (6)은 택시 기사들의 뇌에서 해마의 크기가 평균보다 크다는 것을 언급하는데, 이는 문장 (4)에서 언급한 택시 기사들의 두뇌와 택시 운전을 하지 않는 사람들의 두뇌 사이의 차이점을 이어서 설명하는 것이다. 그러나 문장 (5)는 운전 면허증을 소지해야 하는 기간을 언급했으므로, 글 전체에서 언급한 런던 택시 기사의 기억력과는 무관하다고 볼 수 있다. 따라서 정답은 ④이다.

[중요 어휘]

□ license	동사 면허를 내주다
□ intimidating	형용사 위협적인, 겁을 주는
□ layout	명사 구획, 배치
□ feat	명사 재주, 위업
□ sign up	등록하다, 참가하다
□ cabbie	명사 택시 기사
□ herculean	형용사 초인적인, 큰 힘이 드는
□ spatial memory	공간 기억
□ sea horse	명사 해마
□ hippocampus	명사 (뇌의) 해마

11 2019년 6월 35번 (정답률 55%) 정답 ④

[지문 끊어 읽기] 문화적 환경에 따른 학습의 차이

(1) People often assume erroneously /
사람들은 종종 잘못 추정한다 /
that if a Hadza adult of Tanzania does not know /
만약 어떤 탄자니아의 하드자 부족 성인이 모른다면 /
how to solve an algebraic equation, /
대수 방정식을 푸는 방법을 /
then he must be less intelligent / than we are.
그러면 그는 틀림없이 덜 똑똑할 것이라고 / 우리보다

① (2) Yet there is no evidence / to suggest /
그렇지만 증거는 없다 / 시사하는 / 형용사적 용법
that people from some cultures are fast learners /
어떤 문화의 사람들은 빠른 학습자라고 /
and people from others are slow learners.
그리고 다른 것의 사람들은 느린 학습자라고

② (3) The study of comparative cultures has taught us /
비교 문화 연구는 우리에게 가르쳐왔다 /
that people in different cultures learn different cultural content /
다른 문화의 사람들이 다른 문화적인 내용을 배운다는 것을 /
(attitudes, values, ideas, and behavioral patterns) /
(태도, 가치, 아이디어, 그리고 행동 패턴) /
and that they accomplish this / with similar efficiency. **주제문**
그리고 그들이 이것을 해낸다는 것을 / 비슷한 효율로

③ (4) The traditional Hadza hunter has not learned algebra / **정답 단서**
전통적인 하드자 부족 사냥꾼은 대수학을 학습해오지 않았다 /
because such knowledge would not particularly enhance /
그러한 지식이 특별히 향상시키지 않을 것이기 때문에 /
his adaptation to life / in the East African grasslands.
삶에 대한 그의 적응을 / 동아프리카 초원에서의

④ (5) Consequently, / he failed /
그 결과 / 그는 실패했다 /
to adapt to the environment of the grasslands /
초원의 환경에 적응하는 데 /
because he lacked survival skills.
그가 생존 기술이 부족했기 때문에

★중요 문장 (6)의 역접의 접속 부사 However를 보고 문장 (6)의 내용이 문장 (4)와 대조되는 것인지 문장 (5)와 대조되는 것인지를 파악하면 문장 (5)가 전체 흐름과 무관하다는 것을 알 수 있음.

⑤ (6) However, / he would know / **정답 단서**
역접
하지만 / 그는 알 것이다 /
how to track a wounded bush buck / that he has not seen /
다친 부시벅을 어떻게 추적하는지를 / 그가 본 적이 없는 /
for three days / and where to find groundwater.
사흘 동안 / 그리고 어디에서 지하수를 찾을 수 있는지를

[전문 해석]

(1)사람들은 종종 만약 어떤 탄자니아의 하드자 부족 성인이 대수 방정식을 푸는 방법을 모른

다면 그는 틀림없이 우리보다 덜 똑똑할 것이라고 잘못 추정한다. ①(2)그렇지만 어떤 문화의 사람들은 빠른 학습자이고 (또) 다른(어떤) 문화의 사람들은 느린 학습자라고 시사하는 증거는 없다. ②(3)비교 문화 연구는 다른 문화의 사람들이 다른 문화적인 내용(태도, 가치, 아이디어, 그리고 행동 패턴)을 배운다는 것과 그들이 비슷한 효율로 이것을 해낸다는 것을 우리에게 가르쳐왔다. ③(4)전통적인 하드자 부족 사냥꾼은 그러한 지식(대수학)이 동아프리카 초원에서의 삶에 대한 그의 적응을 특별히 향상시키지 않을 것이기 때문에 대수학을 학습해오지 않았다. ④(5)그 결과, 그는 생존 기술이 부족했기 때문에 초원의 환경에 적응하는 데 실패했다. ⑤(6)하지만 그는 그가 사흘 동안 본 적이 없는 다친 부시벅을 어떻게 추적하는지와 어디에서 지하수를 찾을 수 있는지를 알 것이다.

- Hadza(하드자 부족): 탄자니아의 중북부 지역에 거주하는 토착민 부족으로, 지구 상에서 거의 유일하게 수렵·채집 생활을 이어가고 있다.
- The study of comparative cultures(비교 문화 연구): 문화간 비교를 통해 인류의 보편적인 문화 현상과 각 문화의 고유한 특질 등을 밝혀내는 연구 분야로, 주로 cross-cultural studies라고 한다.
- bush buck(부시벅): 남아프리카에 서식하는 영양(羚羊)의 한 종류로, 흰 반점과 줄무늬가 특징이다. 수컷이 암컷보다 더 짙은 적갈색 빛을 띤다.

[문제 풀이]

본문은 대수학을 모르는 탄자니아의 하드자 부족민이 우리보다 덜 똑똑할 것이라는 통념에 반박하면서, 사람들이 습득하는 문화적 내용은 그들의 생존 환경이 무엇을 요구하는지에 달려 있을 뿐, 특정 문화권의 사람들이 다른 문화권의 사람들보다 학습 속도가 느리거나 빠른 것은 아니라고 설명한다. 문장 (4)는 하드자 부족민이 생존에 있어 대수학이 필요 없기 때문에 대수학을 배우지 않는다는 내용으로, 그들이 '먹이(부시벅)를 추적하는 방법' 또는 '지하수를 찾는 법'은 알고 있다는 문장 (6)의 내용과 역접의 접속 부사 'however'를 통해 자연스럽게 이어진다. 따라서, 하드자 부족이 대수학을 배우지 않은 '그 결과(consequently)' 생존 기술 부족으로 그들이 적응에 실패했다는 문장 (5)의 내용은 글의 흐름과 무관하다. 따라서 정답은 ④이다.

[중요 어휘]

☐ **assume**	동사 추정하다, 생각하다
☐ **erroneously**	부사 잘못(되게), 틀리게
☐ **comparative**	형용사 비교의, 상대적인
☐ **efficiency**	명사 효율, 능률
☐ **enhance**	동사 향상시키다
☐ **track**	동사 추적하다 / 명사 길, 발자국

핵심 대륙과 달리 대양은 서로 연결되어 있어서 지리적 경계가 명확하지 않고, 해양 생물 또한 물의 흐름에 따라 이동하고 분산된다는 내용의 글임. 만약 해양 생물의 이동이 제한된다는 내용이 있다면, 글의 전체적인 흐름과 맞지 않을 것이므로 이 점에 유의하면서 글을 읽어야 함.

12 2020년 9월 35번 (정답률 55%) 정답 ③

[지문 끊어 읽기] 대양의 지리적 경계와 해양 생물

(1) The major oceans are all interconnected, /
주요 대양은 모두 서로 연결되어 있다 /
so that their geographical boundaries are less clear /
그래서 그것들의 지리적 경계는 덜 명확하다 /
than those of the continents. 주제문
=the geographical boundaries
대륙의 그것들보다

(2) As a result, / their biotas show fewer clear differences /
결과적으로 / 그것들의 생물 군집은 명확한 차이를 덜 보여 준다 /
than those on land.
=the biotas
육지에서의 그것들보다

①(3) The oceans themselves are continually moving /
대양 자체가 끊임없이 움직인다 /
because the water within each ocean basin slowly rotates.
접속사 S' V'
각 대양 분지 내에서 물이 천천히 회전하기 때문에

②(4) These moving waters / carry marine organisms /
이 이동하는 물은 / 해양 생물을 운반한다 /
from place to place, / and also help the dispersal /
여기저기로 / 그리고 또한 분산을 돕는다 /
of their young or larvae. 정답 단서
그들의 새끼나 유충의

③(5) In other words, / coastal ocean currents /
즉 / 연안 해류는 /
not only move animals / much less often than expected, /
동물을 이동시킬 뿐만 아니라 / 예상보다 훨씬 덜 자주 /
but they also trap animals / within near-shore regions.
그들은 또한 동물을 가둔다 / 연안 지역 내에

④(6) Furthermore, / the gradients / between the environments /
게다가 / 변화도는 / 환경 사이에서 /
of different areas of ocean water mass / are very gradual /
다양한 지역의 해수 덩어리의 / 매우 점진적이다 / 정답 단서
and often extend over wide areas / that are inhabited /
그리고 종종 넓은 지역에 걸쳐 있다 / 서식되는 /
by a great variety of organisms / of differing ecological tolerances.
매우 다양한 종류의 유기체에 의해 / 상이한 생태학적 내성을 가진

⑤(7) There are no firm boundaries / within the open oceans /
확실한 경계는 없다 / 훤히 트인 대양 내에 /
although there may be barriers / to the movement of organisms.
비록 장애물이 있을 수 있지만 / 유기체의 이동에

[전문 해석]

(1)주요 대양은 모두 서로 연결되어 있어서, 대양의 지리적 경계는 대륙의 지리적 경계보다 덜 명확하다. (2)결과적으로, 대양의 생물 군집은 육지에서의 생물 군집보다 명확한 차이를 덜 보여 준다. ①(3)각 대양 분지 내에서 물이 천천히 회전하기 때문에 대양 자체가 끊임없이 움직인다. ②(4)이 이동하는 물은 해양 생물을 여기저기로 운반하고, 또한 그들의 새끼나 유충의 분산을 돕는다. ③(5)즉, 연안 해류는 예상보다 훨씬 덜 자주 동물을 이동시킬 뿐만 아니라 또한 연안 지역 내에 동물을 가둔다. ④(6)게다가 다양한 지역의 해수 덩어리 환경 사이에서 변화도는 매우 점진적이며, 종종 상이한 생태학적 내성을 가진 매우 다양한 종류의 유기체에 의해 서식되는 넓은 지역에 걸쳐 있다. ⑤(7)비록 유기체의 이동에 장애물이 있을 수 있지만, 훤히 트인 대양 내에 확실한 경계는 없다.

[문제 풀이]

대양의 지리적 경계가 명확하지 않다는 내용의 글이다. 특히 문장 (4)에서는 대양의 물이 끊임없이 움직이면서 해양 생물을 여기저기로 운반하고 분산시킨다고 언급하고 있으며, 문장 (6)에서는 대양 속 다양한 지역의 변화도가 넓은 지역에 걸쳐 점진적이라고 설명하므로, 본문이 대양 속 지역 간 경계가 명확하지 않고 생물의 이동이 발생한다는 점을 강조하고 있음을 알 수 있다. 그러나 문장 (5)의 경우 연안 해류에 의해서 동물의 이동이 제한된다는 점을 말하고 있으며, 이는 글의 전체적인 내용과 상반되는 내용이다. 따라서 정답은 ③이다.

[중요 어휘]

☐ **boundary**	명사 경계(선), 한계(선)
☐ **continent**	명사 대륙, 육지
☐ **basin**	명사 분지, 유역, 양푼
☐ **rotate**	동사 회전하다, 순환하다
☐ **organism**	명사 생물, 유기체
☐ **dispersal**	명사 분산, 확산
☐ **larvae**	명사 유충 (larva의 복수형)
☐ **coastal**	형용사 연안의, 해안의
☐ **ocean current**	해류(海流)
☐ **trap**	동사 가두다 / 명사 덫, 함정
☐ **near-shore**	형용사 연안의
☐ **gradient**	명사 변화도, 경사도
☐ **extend over**	~에 걸쳐있다
☐ **inhabit**	동사 서식하다, 거주하다
☐ **tolerance**	명사 내성, 관용
☐ **firm**	형용사 확실한, 단단한

13 2021년 11월 35번 (정답률 55%) 정답 ④

[지문 끊어 읽기] 판단에 있어 중요한 인간의 이성

(1) There is a pervasive idea / in Western culture /
널리 스며 있는 관념이 있다 / 서구권 문화에는 /
that humans are essentially rational, /
동격의 that
인간이 본질적으로 이성적이라는 /

[ ]: 분사구문①
skillfully [sorting fact from fiction], / and, ultimately, /
사실과 허구를 능숙하게 가려낸다는 / 그리고 최종적으로 /
[arriving at timeless truths about the world]. 정답 단서 인간을 이성적인 존재로 생각하는 서구권 문화의 관념을 언급함.
세상에 대한 영원한 진리에 도달한다는 [ ]: 분사구문②

①(2) This line of thinking holds / that humans follow the rules of logic, /
명사절 접속사 V'①
이러한 사고방식은 주장한다 / 인간은 논리의 규칙을 따른다고 /
calculate probabilities accurately, /
V'②
가능성을 정확히 계산한다고 /
and make decisions about the world /
V'③
그리고 세상에 대해 판단을 내린다고 /
that are perfectly informed by all available information.
모든 이용 가능한 정보에 의해 완벽히 정보를 갖춘

힌트 주격 관계대명사절 'that ~ information'이 바로 앞에 있는 명사 the world를 수식한다고 생각하기 쉬움. 하지만 주격 관계대명사절의 동사가 are이므로 선행사는 the world가 아니라 decisions라는 것을 알 수 있음.

②(3) Conversely, /
반대로 /
failures to make effective and well-informed decisions /
S
효과적이고 정보를 잘 갖춘 판단을 내리는 데 실패하는 것은 /
are often attributed to failures of human reasoning /
V
흔히 인간의 사고의 실패 탓으로 여겨진다 /
— resulting, say, from psychological disorders or cognitive biases.
예를 들어 심리적 장애나 인지적 편견에서 비롯되는

힌트 attribute A to B(A를 B의 탓으로 돌리다) 구문이 수동태 형태로 바뀌면서 A(failures ~ decisions)가 주어로 쓰임. 따라서 'A는 B의 탓으로 여겨진다'로 해석하면 됨.

힌트 'say'가 삽입구처럼 쓰이면 '예를 들어, 이를 테면, 말하자면'의 뜻으로 해석됨.

③(4) In this picture, /
이러한 상황에서 /
whether we succeed or fail turns out / to be a matter /
S
우리가 성공할 것인가 실패할 것인가는 판명된다 / 문제인 것으로 /
of whether individual humans are rational and intelligent. 주제문
개개인이 이성적이고 지적인지 아닌지의

힌트 밑줄 친 whether는 '~인지 아닌지'라는 뜻의 명사절을 이끄는 접속사임. 첫 번째 whether가 이끄는 명사절(whether ~ fail)은 단수 취급을 하므로 문장 (4)의 동사 'turns out'도 단수 주어에 수 일치 됨.

우리 인간이 내린 판단이 성공할 것인지(=문장 (2)) 실패할 것인지(=문장 (3))는 개개인이 가진 이성과 지적 능력에 달려 있음.

④(5) Our ability to make a reasonable decision /
S 형용사적 용법
이성적인 판단을 내리는 우리의 능력은 /
has more to do with our social interactions /
V
우리의 사회적 상호작용과 더욱 관련이 있다 /
than our individual psychology.
우리의 개인적 심리보다

정답 단서 이전 문장까지는 이성적인 판단을 내리는 인간의 능력은 개개인의 이성과 지적 능력에 달려있다고 했는데, 이 문장에서는 사회적 상호작용이 더욱 중요하다고 함.

⑤(6) And so, / if we want to achieve better outcomes /
그러므로 / 우리가 더 나은 결과를 성취하기를 원한다면 /
— truer beliefs, better decisions — / we need to focus /
더 참된 신념과 더 나은 판단과 같은 / 우리는 집중할 필요가 있다 /
on improving individual human reasoning. 정답 단서 더 나은 판단을 위해서는 개개인이 더욱 이성적이고 지적일 필요가 있다고 함.
동명사
개개인의 사고를 향상하는 것에

[전문 해석]

(1)서구권 문화에는 인간이 본질적으로 이성적이며, 사실과 허구를 능숙하게 가려내고, 최종적으로 세상에 대한 영원한 진리에 도달한다는 널리 스며 있는 관념이 있다. ①(2)이러한 사고방식은 인간은 논리의 규칙을 따르고, 가능성을 정확히 계산하며, 모든 이용 가능한 정보에 의해 완벽히 정보를 갖춘 판단을 세상에 대해 내린다고 주장한다. ②(3)반대로 효과적이고 정보를 잘 갖춘 판단을 내리는 데 실패하는 것은 흔히 인간의 사고의 실패 탓으로 여겨지는데, 예를 들어 심리적 장애나 인지적 편견에서 비롯된다고 여겨진다. ③(4)이러한 상황에서 우리가 성공할 것인가 실패할 것인가는 개개인이 이성적이고 지적인지 아닌지의 문제인 것으로 판명된다. ④(5)이성적인 판단을 내리는 우리의 능력은 우리의 개인적 심리보다 우리의 사회적 상호작용과 더욱 관련이 있다. ⑤(6)그러므로 우리가 더 참된 신념과 더 나은 판단과 같은 더 나은 결과를 성취하기를 원한다면, 우리는 개개인의 사고를 향상하는 것에 집중할 필요가 있다.

[문제 풀이]

이 지문은 인간은 이성적이고 논리적인 존재이기에 세상에 대해 판단을 내리는 데에 있어 효과적이고 정보를 잘 갖춘 판단을 내린다고 한다. 반대로 인간이 효과적인 판단을 내리는 데 실패하는 까닭은 심리적 장애나 인지적 편견으로 인한 사고의 실패 때문이라고 한다. 즉, 인간 판단의 옳고 그름은 개개인의 이성과 논리적인 사고 능력에 달려있다는 것이다. 하지만 문장 (5)는 인간의 판단이 개인의 지적 능력이 아닌, 사회적 상호작용과 더 관련이 있다고 하므로 지문의 전반적인 흐름에서 벗어난다. 따라서 정답은 ④이다.

[중요 어휘]

□ pervasive	형용사 널리 스며 있는, 널리 퍼진
□ rational	형용사 이성적인, 합리적인
□ sort	동사 가려내다, 분류하다
□ timeless	형용사 영원한, 변치 않는
□ hold	동사 주장하다, 간주하다
□ probability	명사 가능성, 확률
□ conversely	부사 반대로, 역으로
□ reasoning	명사 사고
□ result from	~에서 비롯되다, ~이 원인이다
□ disorder	명사 장애, 엉망
□ cognitive	형용사 인지적인, 인식의
□ bias	명사 편견
□ picture	명사 상황
□ turn out to be A	A로 판명되다
□ reasonable	형용사 이성적인, 타당한
□ have to do with	~와 관련이 있다

14 2022년 11월 35번 (정답률 55%) 정답 ④

[지문 끊어 읽기] 질투를 숨기려고 하는 이유

(1) Of all the human emotions, /
인간의 모든 감정 중에서 /
none is trickier or more elusive / than envy.
더 까다롭거나 더 이해하기 어려운 것은 없다 / 질투보다

(2) It is very difficult / [to actually discern the envy /
형식상의 주어 [ ]: 내용상의 주어 선행사
매우 어렵다 / 질투를 실제로 알아차리는 것은 /
that motivates people's actions].
주격 관계대명사
사람들의 행동을 자극하는

①(3) The reason for this elusiveness is simple: /
이러한 모호함의 이유는 간단하다 /
we almost never directly express the envy / we are feeling.
우리는 질투를 대부분 절대 직접적으로 표현하지 않는다 / 우리가 느끼고 있는

②(4) Envy entails the admission to ourselves /
질투는 스스로에 대한 인정을 수반한다 /
[that we are inferior to another person / in something we value].
접속사 [ ]: the admission과 동격
우리가 또 다른 사람보다 열등하다는 / 우리가 가치 있게 여기는 무언가에서

정답 단서 질투는 자신이 타인보다 열등하다는 것을 인정하게 만듦.

③(5) Not only is it painful [to admit this inferiority], /
형식상의 주어① [ ]: 내용상의 주어①
이 열등감을 인정하는 것은 고통스러울 뿐만 아니라 /
but it is even worse / for others [to see /
형식상의 주어② to부정사의 의미상 주어 [ ]: 내용상의 주어②
훨씬 더 나쁘다 / 다른 사람들이 알게 되는 것은 /
that we are feeling this]. 정답 단서 질투를 느꼈을 때의 반응은 부정적임.
우리가 이것을 느끼고 있다는 것을

힌트 'not only A but (also) B' 구문은 'A뿐만 아니라 B'라는 의미임. 이때, 'not only'가 문장 맨 앞으로 나갔기에 부정어 도치가 나왔으며 동사가 be동사이므로 'be동사+주어'의 형태인 is it으로 도치됨.

힌트 'even, far, still, much, a lot' 등은 비교급 앞에서 비교급을 강조하여 '훨씬'이라고 해석함.

④(6) Envy can cause illness /
질투는 질병을 유발할 수도 있다 /
because people with envy can cast the "evil eye" /
왜냐하면 질투하는 사람이 '증오에 찬 눈초리'를 보낼 수 있기 때문에 /
on someone they envy, / even unwittingly, /
그들이 시기하는 사람에게 / 무의식적으로라도 /
or the envious person can become ill / from the emotion.
혹은 질투심이 강한 사람이 건강이 나빠질 수 있기 때문이다 / 그 감정 때문에

⑤(7) And so /
그래서 /
almost as soon as we experience the initial feelings of envy, /
거의 우리가 최초의 질투심을 경험하자마자 /
we are motivated / to disguise it to ourselves / 정답 단서 질투를 느끼면 그것을 감추려고 함.
우리는 동기가 부여된다 / 그것을 우리 자신에게 감추도록 /

— it is not envy we feel /
그것은 우리가 느끼는 질투가 아니라 /

힌트 문장 (7)에는 'not A but B(A가 아니라 B)'의 구문이 쓰임. 문장 (5)의 'not only A but (also) B'와 의미를 구분할 것.

but unfairness at the distribution of goods or attention, /
재산의 분배나 관심에 대한 불공평함 /

resentment at this unfairness, / even anger.
이 불공평함에 대한 분개 / 심지어는 분노이다

[전문 해석]

(1)인간의 모든 감정 중에서 질투보다 더 까다롭거나 더 이해하기 어려운 것은 없다. (2)사람들의 행동을 자극하는 질투를 실제로 알아차리는 것은 매우 어렵다. ①(3)이러한 모호함의 이유는 간단한데, 우리는 우리가 느끼고 있는 질투를 대부분 절대 직접적으로 표현하지 않는다. ②(4)질투는 우리가 가치 있게 여기는 무언가에서 우리가 또 다른 사람보다 열등하다는 스스로에 대한 인정을 수반한다. ③(5)이 열등감을 인정하는 것은 고통스러울 뿐만 아니라 우리가 이것을 느끼고 있다는 것을 다른 사람들이 알게 되는 것은 훨씬 더 나쁘다. ④(6)질투는 질병을 유발할 수도 있는데 왜냐하면 질투하는 사람이 무의식적으로라도 그들이 시기하는 사람에게 '증오에 찬 눈초리'를 보낼 수 있거나 질투심이 강한 사람이 그 감정 때문에 건강이 나빠질 수 있기 때문이다. ⑤(7)그래서 거의 우리가 최초의 질투심을 경험하자마자, 우리는 그것을 우리 자신에게 감추도록 동기가 부여되는데, 즉 그것은 우리가 느끼는 질투가 아니라 재산의 분배나 관심에 대한 불공평함, 이 불공평함에 대한 분개, 심지어는 분노이다.

[문제 풀이]

지문은 인간의 감정 중 질투가 굉장히 모호한 것이라고 설명한다. 질투를 알아차리는 것은 굉장히 어려운데, 이는 사람들이 질투라는 감정을 느끼면 그것을 숨기려 하기 때문이다. 숨기는 이유는 사람들이 자신이 타인에 비해 열등하다는 것을 인정하고 싶어 하지 않고, 그러한 감정 자체가 부정적인 인식을 가지고 있어 알려져서는 안 되기 때문이다. 사람들은 주로 질투를 느꼈을 때 그것을 숨기기 위한 동기를 부여받는데, 그것은 이를테면 불공평한 상황에 대한 분개나 분노이다. 문장 (6)은 지문의 핵심 키워드인 질투와 그 부정적 측면을 다루고 있긴 하지만, 질투가 질병을 유발한다는 내용은 지문의 전체 흐름(질투를 숨기는 이유)을 벗어나므로 정답은 ④이다.

[중요 어휘]

☐ tricky	형용사 까다로운, 곤란한
☐ elusive	형용사 이해하기 어려운, 회피하는
☐ envy	명사 질투, 부러움 / 동사 시기하다, 질투하다, 부러워하다
☐ discern	동사 알아차리다, 식별하다
☐ motivate	동사 자극하다, 동기를 부여하다
☐ elusiveness	명사 모호함, 이해하기 어려움
☐ entail	동사 수반하다
☐ admission	명사 인정, 가입
☐ inferior	형용사 열등한, 하위의
☐ cast	동사 (시선·미소 등을) 보내다[던지다], (그림자를) 드리우다
☐ unwittingly	부사 무의식적으로, 무심코
☐ envious	형용사 질투심이 강한, 부러워하는
☐ disguise	동사 감추다, 변장하다
☐ resentment	명사 분개, 억울함
☐ anger	명사 분노, 화

15 2023년 9월 35번 (정답률 35%) 정답 ③

[지문 끊어 읽기] 유럽 초기 민주주의의 번영 이유

(1) The irony of early democracy in Europe /
유럽의 초기 민주주의의 아이러니는 /

is [that it thrived and prospered] / [ ]: is의 주격 보어(명사절)
그것이 번성하고 번영했다는 것이다 /

precisely because European rulers for a very long time were remarkably weak. (부사구) 주제문 유럽의 민주주의는 통치자의 권력이 약했기 때문에 번영할 수 있었음.
정확히 유럽의 통치자들이 아주 오랜 시간 동안 현저하게 약했기 때문에

① (2) For more than a millennium / after the fall of Rome, /
천 년 넘게 / 로마의 멸망 이후 /

European rulers lacked the ability /
유럽의 통치자들은 능력이 부족했다 /

to assess what their people were producing / (병렬①)
자신의 백성들이 생산하고 있었던 것을 평가할 /

and to levy substantial taxes based on this. (병렬②) (=assessment) 정답 단서 유럽 통치자들은 백성들의 생산성에 따라 세금을 부과할 능력이 부족했음.
그리고 이것을 바탕으로 상당한 세금을 부과할

② (3) The most striking way to illustrate European weakness / (형용사적 용법)
유럽의 약함을 설명하는 가장 눈에 띄는 방법은 /

is to show how little revenue they collected. (명사적 용법) 정답 단서 능력이 부족함에 따라 세입에 부정적인 결과를 낳음.
그들이 모은 세입이 얼마나 적은지를 보여 주는 것이다

힌트 'how+형용사/부사+S+V' 형태는 '얼마나 ~하는지'로, 'how+S+V'의 형태는 '어떻게 ~하는지'로 해석함.

③ (4) For this reason, /
이러한 이유로 /

tax collectors in Europe were able to collect a huge amount of revenue / (V①)
유럽의 세금 징수원은 막대한 금액의 세입을 모을 수 있었다 /

and therefore had a great influence / (V②)
그리고 따라서 큰 영향을 미쳤다 /

on how society should function.
사회가 어떻게 기능해야 하는지에 대해

④ (5) Europeans would eventually develop strong systems of revenue collection, /
유럽인들은 결국 강력한 세입 징수 시스템을 개발했다 /

but it took them an awfully long time to do so. 정답 단서 강력한 세입 징수 시스템을 개발하기까지 오랜 시간이 걸렸음.
하지만 그렇게 하는 데까지 지독하게 오랜 시간이 걸렸다

⑤ (6) In medieval times, / and for part of the early modern era, /
중세 시대에 / 그리고 초기 근대 시대의 일부 동안 /

Chinese emperors and Muslim caliphs were able to extract much more of economic production /
중국 황제와 무슬림 칼리프들은 훨씬 더 많은 경제적 생산물을 얻을 수 있었다 /

than any European ruler / with the exception of small city-states.
어떤 유럽 통치자보다 / 작은 도시 국가들을 제외하고

[전문 해석]

(1)유럽의 초기 민주주의의 아이러니는 정확히 유럽의 통치자들이 아주 오랜 시간 동안 현저하게 약했기 때문에 그것이 번성하고 번영했다는 것이다. ①(2)로마의 멸망 이후 천 년 넘게, 유럽의 통치자들은 자신의 백성들이 생산하고 있었던 것을 평가하고, 이것을 바탕으로 상당한 세금을 부과할 능력이 부족했다. ②(3)유럽의 약함을 설명하는 가장 눈에 띄는 방법은 그들이 모은 세입이 얼마나 적은지를 보여 주는 것이다. ③(4)이러한 이유로, 유럽의 세금 징수원은 막대한 금액의 세입을 모을 수 있었고, 따라서 사회가 어떻게 기능해야 하는지에 대해 큰 영향을 미쳤다. ④(5)유럽인들은 결국 강력한 세입 징수 시스템을 개발했지만, 그렇게 하는 데까지 지독하게 오랜 시간이 걸렸다. ⑤(6)중세 시대에, 그리고 초기 근대 시대의 일부 동안, 중국 황제와 무슬림 칼리프들은 작은 도시 국가들을 제외하고 어떤 유럽 통치자보다 훨씬 더 많은 경제적 생산물을 얻을 수 있었다.

[문제 풀이]

이 지문은 유럽 초기 민주주의에 대해 설명한다. 문장 (1)에서 유럽의 초기 민주주의가 번영할 수 있었던 이유가 유럽 통치자들이 약했기 때문이라고 하며, 문장 (2)에서 유럽 통치자들에게 부족했던 것은 백성들의 생산 능력 평가와 세금 부과 능력이었다고 한다. 이어지는 문장 (3), (5)에서는 유럽의 약함은 적은 세입의 양에서 명확히 드러남을 언급하며, 이러한 문제를 해결하기 위해 세입 징수 시스템을 개발했으나 그것이 개발되기까지 굉장히 오래 걸렸다고 설명한다. 이를 바탕으로 문장 (6)에서 중국 및 이슬람 국가의 통치자와 유럽 통치자의 세입 능력을 비교하며 필자는 유럽 통치자들의 약함이 오랜 시간 동안 이어졌다는 것을 강조한다. 한편, 문장 (4)에서 유럽의 세금 징수원이 막대한 세입을 모으고 사회가 기능하는 방식에 큰 영향을 끼쳤다는 내용은 유럽 통치자들의 능력 부족으로 인해 세입이 적었다는 글의 흐름과 관련이 없다. 따라서 정답은 ③이다.

[오답 풀이]

④ - 문장 (5)는 유럽에서 강력한 세입 징수 시스템이 개발되는 데 오랜 시간이 걸렸다는 내용이다. 이 문장에서 제시된 강력한 세입 징수 시스템은 문장 (3)에서 설명한 유럽의 약함, 적은 양의 세입에 대한 해결 방안으로, 앞 문장의 흐름과 자연스럽게 이어진다. 개발까지의 긴 시간 동안 유럽의 통치자들은 경제적 손실을 입을 수밖에 없었기 때문에 오랜 기간 동안 중국 황

제와 무슬림 칼리프들이 유럽 통치자보다 많은 경제적 생산물을 얻었다는 문장 (6)의 내용과 도 자연스럽게 이어진다. 따라서 ④는 정답으로 적절하지 않다.

[중요 어휘]

☐ democracy	명사 민주주의, 민주 국가, 평등
☐ thrive	동사 번성[번영]하다, 잘 자라다
☐ prosper	동사 번영[번창]하다, 성공하다
☐ precisely	부사 정확히, 바로, 꼭
☐ remarkably	부사 현저하게, 주목할 만하게
☐ assess	동사 평가하다, 재다
☐ levy	동사 부과하다, 징수하다 / 명사 (세금의) 추가 부담금
☐ substantial	형용사 상당한, 크고 튼튼한
☐ striking	형용사 눈에 띄는, 두드러진
☐ revenue	명사 세입, 수입
☐ function	동사 기능하다 / 명사 기능, 행사
☐ awfully	부사 지독하게, 정말, 몹시
☐ extract	동사 얻다, 추출하다 / 명사 추출물

16 2023년 11월 35번 (정답률 70%) 정답 ③

[지문 끊어 읽기] 도덕적 우수성을 가르치는 시기

(1) Moral excellence, / according to Aristotle, /
도덕적 우수성은 / Aristotle에 의하면 /
is the result of habit and repetition, /
습관과 반복의 결과물이다 /
though modern science would also suggest /
비록 현대 과학은 또한 주장하겠지만 /
[that it may have an innate, genetic component]. [ ]: 목적어절
그것이 선천적, 즉 유전적인 요소를 가지고 있다고

① (2) This means /
=Aristotle의 주장
이는 의미한다 /
[that moral excellence will be broadly set / early in our lives], /
도덕적 우수성이 광범위하게 설정될 것임을 / 우리의 삶에서 이른 시기에 / [ ]: 목적어절
which is why the question of how early to teach it is so important.
그리고 이것이 그것을 얼마나 일찍 가르쳐야 하는지에 대한 질문이 굉장히 중요한 이유이다

힌트 계속적 용법으로 사용된 주격 관계대명사절로, 선행사는 앞 문장 내용 전체를 가리킴. 따라서 이 관계사절은 'and this is why the question ~ is so important'의 구조로 보고 '그리고 이것이 (~라는) 질문이 굉장히 중요한 이유이다'라고 해석하면 됨.

② (3) Freud suggested /
Freud는 제시했다 /
[that we don't change our personality much /
우리가 자신의 성격을 많이 바꾸지 않는다는 것을 /
after age five or thereabouts], / [ ]: 목적어절
다섯 살 혹은 그 무렵 이후에 /
but as in many other things, / Freud was wrong. 정답단서 Freud는 다섯 살 혹은 그 무렵 이후에는 성격 변화가 이루어지지 않는다고 했으나 이는 틀렸음.
하지만 많은 다른 것들에서처럼 / Freud는 틀렸다

③ (4) A person of moral excellence /
도덕적으로 우수한 사람은 /
cannot help doing good / — it is as natural /
좋은 일을 하지 않을 수 없다 / 그것은 자연스럽다 /
as the change of seasons / or the rotation of the planets.
계절의 변화만큼 / 혹은 행성의 자전만큼

힌트 cannot help V-ing : ~하지 않을 수 없다, 어쩔 수 없이 ~하다 =cannot (help) but 동사원형 =have no choice but to V

④ (5) Recent psychological research shows /
최근의 심리 연구는 보여 준다 /
[that personality traits stabilize around age thirty /
성격 특성이 30세 무렵에 안정된다는 것을 /
in both men and women / and regardless of ethnicity /
남성과 여성 모두에서 / 그리고 민족에 상관없이 /
as the human brain continues to develop, /
인간의 뇌가 계속해서 발달함에 따라 /
both neuroanatomically and in terms of cognitive skills, /
신경 해부학적으로 그리고 인지적 기능 면에서 /
until the mid-twenties]. 정답단서 심리 연구에서 인간의 뇌는 20대 중반까지도 계속 발달하고 30세 무렵에 성격이 안정된다는 것이 밝혀짐.
20대 중반까지 [ ]: 목적어절

⑤ (6) The advantage of this new understanding is /
이 새로운 이해의 이점은 ~이다 /
[that we can be a bit more optimistic / than Aristotle and Freud /
우리가 조금 더 낙관적일 수 있다는 것 / Aristotle과 Freud보다 /
about being able to teach moral excellence]. 주제문
도덕적 우수성을 가르칠 수 있다는 점에서 [ ]: 주격 보어절

도덕적 우수성을 가르치는 것은 Aristotle과 Freud가 언급한 시기보다 느긋하게 이루어질 수 있음.

[전문 해석]

(1)비록 현대 과학은 도덕적 우수성이 선천적, 즉 유전적인 요소를 가지고 있다고 또한 주장하겠지만, Aristotle에 의하면 도덕적 우수성은 습관과 반복의 결과물이다. ①(2)이는 도덕적 우수성이 우리의 삶에서 이른 시기에 광범위하게 설정될 것임을 의미하며, 이것이 그것(도덕적 우수성)을 얼마나 일찍 가르쳐야 하는지에 대한 질문이 굉장히 중요한 이유이다. ②(3)Freud는 우리가 다섯 살 혹은 그 무렵 이후에 자신의 성격을 많이 바꾸지 않는다는 것을 제시했으나, 많은 다른 것들에서처럼 Freud는 틀렸다. ③(4)도덕적으로 우수한 사람은 좋은 일을 하지 않을 수 없고, 그것은 계절의 변화 혹은 행성의 자전만큼 자연스럽다. ④(5)최근의 심리 연구는 20대 중반까지 신경 해부학적으로 그리고 인지적 기능 면에서 인간의 뇌가 계속해서 발달함에 따라 남성과 여성 모두에서 그리고 민족에 상관없이 성격 특성이 30세 무렵에 안정된다는 것을 보여 준다. ⑤(6)이 새로운 이해의 이점은 Aristotle과 Freud보다 우리가 도덕적 우수성을 가르칠 수 있다는 점에서 조금 더 낙관적일 수 있다는 것이다.

[문제 풀이]

이 지문은 도덕적 우수성의 학습에 대해 설명하는 글이다. 문장 (1)에서 도덕적 우수성이 습관과 반복의 결과물이라는 Aristotle의 주장을 언급하면서, 문장 (2)에서 이른 시기에 도덕적 우수성을 가르칠 필요성을 제시한다. 이어지는 문장 (3)에서는 다섯 살 혹은 그 무렵 이후에는 자신의 성격을 많이 바꾸지 않는다는 Freud의 주장을 보여 주며, 그보다 이른 시기에 도덕적 우수성을 학습시켜야 함을 암시한다. 하지만 같은 문장 끝에서 Freud의 주장이 잘못되었음을 언급하면서, 문장 (5)~(6)에서 20대 중반까지 인간의 뇌가 발전한다는 결과의 최근 심리 연구를 통해 Aristotle과 Freud의 주장보다 도덕적 우수성을 느긋하게 가르칠 수 있다고 말한다. 한편, 도덕적으로 우수한 사람이 좋은 일을 하는 것은 지극히 자연스러운 일이라는 문장 (4)는 도덕적 우수성의 학습이 이루어져야 하는 시기를 논의하는 글 전체의 흐름과 관련이 없다. 따라서 정답은 ③이다.

[중요 어휘]

☐ moral	형용사 도덕적인, 도덕과 관련된
☐ excellence	명사 우수성, 탁월함, 뛰어남
☐ innate	형용사 선천적인, 타고난
☐ genetic	형용사 유전적인, 유전학의
☐ component	명사 (구성) 요소, 부품
☐ thereabouts	부사 그 무렵에, 대략, 그 근처[부근]에서
☐ rotation	명사 (천체의) 자전, 회전
☐ personality	명사 성격, 인격, 개성
☐ trait	명사 (성격상의) 특성, 이목구비, 인상
☐ stabilize	동사 안정되다, 안정시키다
☐ ethnicity	명사 민족, 민족성
☐ in terms of	~의 면에서, ~에 관하여
☐ cognitive	형용사 인지의, 인식의
☐ optimistic	형용사 낙관적인, 낙관하는

17 2024년 3월 35번 (정답률 60%) 정답 ③

[지문 끊어 읽기] 향신료 사용의 진화적 뿌리

(1) We are the only species that seasons its food, /
선행사 ↑ 주격 관계대명사절
우리는 음식에 양념을 하는 유일한 종이다 /
[deliberately altering it / with the highly flavored plant parts /
=its food 선행사
그것을 의도적으로 바꾼다 / 강한 맛을 내는 식물 부분을 이용하여 /
we call herbs and spices]. [ ]: 분사구문
목적격 관계대명사절
우리가 허브와 향신료라고 부르는

힌트 「call+목적어+목적격 보어」의 구조로, '~을 …라고 부르다'라고 해석함. 바로 앞의 선행사 'the highly flavored plant parts'가 call의 목적어에, 'herbs and spices'가 목적격 보어에 해당함.

(2) It's quite possible /
형식상의 주어
가능성이 높다 /

주제문 향신료에 대한 우리의 미각은 진화적인 뿌리를 가지고 있을 가능성이 높음.

[that our taste for spices has an evolutionary root]. [ ]: 내용상의 주어
향신료에 대한 우리의 미각은 진화적인 뿌리를 가지고 있을

①(3) Many spices have antibacterial properties / — in fact, /
많은 향신료들은 항균성을 가진다 / 실제로 /
common seasonings such as garlic, onion, and oregano /
S
마늘, 양파, 오레가노와 같은 흔한 양념은 /
inhibit the growth of almost every bacterium tested. 정답 단서
V 과거분사
거의 모든 확인된 박테리아의 성장을 저해한다

많은 향신료들은 항균성을 가지고 있고 실제로 흔한 양념은 거의 모든 확인된 박테리아의 성장을 저해함.

②(4) And [the cultures that make the heaviest use of spices] / [ ]: S
선행사 주격 관계대명사절
그리고 향신료를 가장 많이 사용하는 문화들은 /
— think of the garlic and black pepper of Thai food, the ginger and coriander of India, the chili peppers of Mexico — /
태국 음식의 마늘과 흑후추, 인도 음식의 생강과 고수, 멕시코의 고추를 생각해 보라 /
come from warmer climates, /
V 선행사
더 따뜻한 기후에서 유래한다 /
where bacterial spoilage is a bigger issue.
관계부사(계속적 용법)
그곳에서는 박테리아에 의한 부패가 더 큰 문제이다

③(5) The changing climate can have a significant impact /
변화하는 기후는 상당한 영향을 미칠 수 있다 /
on the production and availability of spices, /
향신료의 생산과 이용 가능성에 /
[influencing their growth patterns /
병렬①
그들의 성장 패턴에 영향을 미친다 /
and ultimately affecting global spice markets]. [ ]: 분사구문
병렬②
그리고 궁극적으로 전 세계의 향신료 시장에 영향을 준다

④(6) In contrast, / the most lightly spiced cuisines /
대조적으로 / 가장 약하게 양념된 요리는 / S
— those of Scandinavia and northern Europe — /
=cuisines
스칸디나비아와 북유럽의 것들 /
are from cooler climates.
V
더 시원한 기후에서 유래한다

⑤(7) [Our uniquely human attention to flavor, /
맛에 대한 우리 인간의 독특한 관심은 /
in this case the flavor of spices,] / [ ]: S
이 경우에 향신료의 맛 /
turns out to have arisen as a matter of life and death. 정답 단서
V
삶과 죽음의 문제로서 생겨난 것으로 드러난다

힌트 앞뒤에 콤마를 넣은 삽입구로, 앞에 나온 내용과 동격 혹은 구체적인 부연 설명에 해당함.

힌트 to부정사(준동사)가 have p.p.의 형태를 지닐 경우 본동사보다 더 과거임을 나타냄.

향신료의 맛에 대한 인간의 독특한 관심은 사느냐 죽느냐는 생존의 문제에서 생겨난 것임.

[전문 해석]

(1)우리는 음식에 양념을 하는 유일한 종인데, 우리가 허브와 향신료라고 부르는 강한 맛을 내는 식물 부분을 이용하여 그것(음식)을 의도적으로 바꾼다. (2)향신료에 대한 우리의 미각은 진화적인 뿌리를 가지고 있을 가능성이 높다. ①(3)많은 향신료들은 항균성을 가지며, 실제로 마늘, 양파, 오레가노와 같은 흔한 양념은 거의 모든 확인된 박테리아의 성장을 저해한다. ②(4)그리고 향신료를 가장 많이 사용하는 문화들은, 태국 음식의 마늘과 흑후추, 인도 음식의 생강과 고수, 멕시코의 고추를 생각해 보면, 더 따뜻한 기후에서 유래하는데, 그곳에서는 박테리아에 의한 부패가 더 큰 문제이다. ③(5)변화하는 기후는 향신료의 생산과 이용 가능성에 상당한 영향을 미칠 수 있는데, 그들(향신료)의 성장 패턴에 영향을 미치고 궁극적으로 전 세계의 향신료 시장에 영향을 준다. ④(6)대조적으로 스칸디나비아와 북유럽의 요리와 같은 가장 약하게 양념된 요리는 더 시원한 기후에서 유래한다. ⑤(7)맛에 대한 우리 인간의 독특한 관심, 이 경우에 향신료의 맛(에 대한 우리 인간의 독특한 관심)은 삶과 죽음의 문제로서 생겨난 것으로 드러난다.

[문제 풀이]

문장 (1)~(2)는 인간이 음식을 허브와 향신료로 양념하는 유일한 종이고 그러한 미각에는 진화적인 뿌리가 있을 가능성이 높다고 말한다. 이어지는 문장 (3)은 많은 향신료들이 항균성을 가져서 흔한 양념들이 거의 모든 확인된 박테리아의 성장을 저해한다고 말하므로, 문장 (2)에서 언급된 '진화적인 뿌리'가 향신료의 항균성과 관련된 것이라는 사실을 알 수 있다. 문장 (4)는 향신료를 가장 많이 사용하는 문화들이 박테리아에 의한 부패가 문제인 따뜻한 기후에서 유래한다고 설명하는 반면, 문장 (6)은 약하게 양념이 된 요리는 시원한 기후에서 유래한다며 문장 (4)의 내용과 대조되는 예시를 제공한다. 그에 반해 문장 (5)는 변화하는 기후가 향신료의 생산에 미치는 영향에 대해 말하고 있으므로 인간이 향신료를 이용하게 된 진화적 유래와는 관련이 없는 내용이다. 따라서 정답은 ③이다.

[중요 어휘]

□ species	명사 종, 인종
□ season	동사 양념하다 / 명사 계절
□ deliberately	부사 의도적으로, 고의로
□ alter	동사 바꾸다, 변경하다
□ highly	부사 강하게, 매우
□ flavor	동사 맛을 내다 / 명사 맛
□ spice	명사 향신료 / 동사 향신료를 사용하다
□ evolutionary	형용사 진화적인, 진화의
□ antibacterial	형용사 항균의, 항균성의
□ property	명사 속성, 재산
□ inhibit	동사 저해하다, 방해하다, 억제하다
□ bacterium	명사 박테리아 (복수형 bacteria)
□ coriander	명사 고수
□ spoilage	명사 부패, 손상
□ ultimately	부사 궁극적으로, 결국
□ uniquely	부사 독특히, 유례없이
□ turn out	~로 드러나다
□ arise	동사 생겨나다, 발생하다 (arise-arose-arisen)

18 2024년 6월 35번 (정답률 75%) 정답 ③

[지문 끊어 읽기] 유전자 배열 분석의 미래

(1) As the old joke goes: / "Software, free. User manual, $10,000."
옛 농담이 말하듯 / "소프트웨어, 무료. 사용자 매뉴얼, 10,000달러."

(2) But it's no joke.
하지만 그것은 농담이 아니다

(3) A couple of high-profile companies / make their living /
세간의 이목을 끄는 몇몇 회사들은 / 돈을 번다 /
[selling instruction and paid support / for free software]. 정답 단서 [ ]: 분사구문(~하면서)
지침과 유료 지원을 판매하면서 / 무료 소프트웨어에 대한

내로라하는 몇몇 회사들은 소프트웨어는 무료로 제공하지만 그에 대한 지침이나 지원은 유료로 판매함으로써 돈을 벎.

(4) The copy of code, / being mere bits, / is free.
S 현재분사구 V
코드 사본은 / 단지 몇 비트일 뿐인 / 무료이다

(5) The lines of free code / become valuable to you /
2형식V S·C(형용사)
무료 코드의 배열은 / 당신에게 가치 있게 된다 /
only through support and guidance.
오직 지원과 안내를 통해서만

힌트 명사의 복수형인 lines에 수를 일치시켜 동사의 현재시제 복수형인 become이 사용됨.

①(6) A lot of medical and genetic information /
많은 의료 및 유전 정보가 /
will go this route / in the coming decades. 정답 단서
이 경로를 따르게 될 것이다 / 다가올 수십 년 안에

수십 년 안에 많은 의료 및 유전 정보가 '무료 소프트웨어에 대한 유료 지원과 안내를 판매하는 것' 같은 경로를 따르게 될 것임.

②(7) Right now / [getting a full copy of all your DNA] / [ ]: S(동명사구)
지금 당장은 / 여러분의 모든 DNA의 전체 사본을 얻는 것이 /
is very expensive ($10,000), / but soon it won't be.
단수V
매우 비싸다(10,000달러) / 하지만 곧 그것은 그렇지 않을 것이다

③(8) The public exposure of people's personal genetic information /
사람들의 개인적 유전 정보의 공적인 노출은 /
will undoubtedly cause /
의심할 여지 없이 유발할 것이다 /
serious legal and ethical problems.
심각한 법적 및 윤리적 문제들을

✶중요 문장 (8)은 유전 정보의 공적인 노출이 유발할 수 있는 법적 및 윤리적 문제들에 대한 우려를 나타낸 문장으로, '유전자 배열을 밝혀주는 서비스는 무료로 제공되되 유전자 매뉴얼은 비싸게 판매될 것'이라고 예측하는 글의 전체적인 흐름과 무관함.

④(9) The price is dropping so fast, / it will be $100 soon, /
so 형용사 (that) …: 너무 ~해서 …하다
가격은 너무도 빨리 떨어지고 있다 / 그것은 곧 100달러가 될 것이다 /
and then the next year /
그리고 그런 다음 그 다음 해에는 /
insurance companies will offer to sequence you /
명사적 용법(목적어)
보험 회사들이 여러분의 유전자 배열 순서를 밝혀줄 것을 제안할 것이다 /
for free.
무료로

⑤(10) When a copy of your sequence costs nothing, / the interpretation /
여러분의 배열의 사본이 아무 비용도 들지 않을 때 / 설명은 /
of what it means, what you can do about it, and how to use it /
병렬① 병렬② 병렬③
그것이 의미하는 것, 여러분이 그것에 관해 할 수 있는 것, 그리고 그것을 사용하는 방법에 관한 /
— the manual for your genes — / will be expensive.
여러분의 유전자에 대한 매뉴얼은 / 비싸질 것이다

[전문 해석]

(1)옛 농담이 말하듯, "소프트웨어, 무료. 사용자 매뉴얼, 10,000달러." (2)하지만 그것은 농담이 아니다. (3)세간의 이목을 끄는 몇몇 회사들은 무료 소프트웨어에 대한 지침과 유료 지원을 판매하면서 돈을 번다. (4)단지 몇 비트일 뿐인 코드 사본은 무료이다. (5)무료 코드의 배열은 오직 지원과 안내를 통해서만 당신에게 가치 있게 된다. ①(6)많은 의료 및 유전 정보가 다가올 수십 년 안에 이 경로를 따르게 될 것이다. ②(7)지금 당장은 여러분의 모든 DNA의 전체 사본을 얻는 것이 매우 비싸지만(10,000달러), 곧 그것은 그렇지 않을 것이다. ③(8)사람들의 개인적 유전 정보의 공적인 노출은 의심할 여지 없이 심각한 법적 및 윤리적 문제들을 유발할 것이다. ④(9)가격은 너무도 빨리 떨어지고 있어서, 그것은 곧 100달러가 될 것이며, 그런 다음 그 다음 해에는 보험 회사들이 무료로 여러분의 유전자 배열 순서를 밝혀줄 것을 제안할 것이다. ⑤(10)여러분의 배열의 사본이 아무 비용도 들지 않을 때, 그것이 의미하는 것, 여러분이 그것에 관해 할 수 있는 것, 그리고 그것을 사용하는 방법에 관한 설명, 즉 여러분의 유전자에 대한 매뉴얼은 비싸질 것이다.

[중요 어휘]

☐ **high-profile**	형용사 세간의 이목을 끄는
☐ **make one's living**	돈을 벌다, 생계를 유지하다
☐ **instruction**	명사 지침, 설명
☐ **paid**	형용사 유료의, 유급의
☐ **support**	명사 지원 / 동사 지원하다
☐ **copy**	명사 사본 / 동사 복사하다, 베끼다
☐ **mere**	형용사 단지, 단순한
☐ **valuable**	형용사 가치 있는, 유용한
☐ **guidance**	명사 안내, 지도, 유도
☐ **medical**	형용사 의료의, 의학의
☐ **genetic**	형용사 유전의, 유전학의
☐ **route**	명사 경로, 노선
☐ **coming**	형용사 다가오는, 다음의 / 명사 시작, 도래
☐ **decade**	명사 10년
☐ **exposure**	명사 노출, 폭로
☐ **undoubtedly**	부사 의심할 여지 없이, 틀림없이
☐ **legal**	형용사 법적인, 법률과 관련된
☐ **ethical**	형용사 윤리적인, 도덕적인
☐ **insurance**	명사 보험, 보험금
☐ **sequence**	동사 (유전자의) 배열 순서를 밝히다 / 명사 배열, 순서
☐ **for free**	무료로
☐ **cost**	동사 ~의 비용이 들다 / 명사 비용, 값
☐ **interpretation**	명사 설명, 해석

19 2024년 9월 35번 (정답률 75%) 정답 ③

[지문 끊어 읽기] 최소한의 곡물 가공

(1) Minimal processing can be one of the best ways /
최소한의 가공은 가장 좋은 방법 중 하나일 수 있다 /
to keep original flavors and taste, /
형용사적 용법
본연의 풍미와 맛을 유지하는 /
without any need to add artificial flavoring or additives, or too much salt.
형용사적 용법
인공 향료나 첨가물, 또는 과도한 소금을 더할 필요 없이

(2) This would also be the efficient way / to keep most nutrients, /
형용사적 용법
이것은 또한 효율적인 방법일 것이다 / 대부분의 영양소를 유지하는 /
especially the most sensitive ones /
=nutrients
특히 가장 민감한 것들을 /
such as many vitamins and anti-oxidants. 정답 단서 가공을 최소로 하는 것은 영양소를 유지하는 효율적인 방법임.
많은 비타민과 항산화 물질과 같은

①(3) Milling of cereals is one of the most harsh processes /
곡물을 제분하는 것은 가장 가혹한 과정 중 하나이다 / 선행사
[which dramatically affect nutrient content]. [ ]: 주격 관계대명사절
영양소 함량에 크게 영향을 미치는

②(4) While grains are naturally very rich /
곡물에는 자연적으로 매우 풍부하지만 /
in micronutrients, anti-oxidants and fiber /
미량 영양소, 항산화 물질과 섬유질이 /
(i.e. in wholemeal flour or flakes), /
(즉, 통밀 가루 또는 플레이크에는) /
milling usually removes the vast majority of minerals, vitamins and fibers /
동명사S V
제분하는 것은 일반적으로 대부분의 미네랄, 비타민 그리고 섬유질을 제거한다 /
to raise white flour. 정답 단서 곡물에는 영양소가 풍부하지만, 곡물을 제분하면 곡물 안의 영양소가 제거됨.
부사적 용법(목적)
흰 밀가루를 만들기 위해

③(5) To increase grain production, /
부사적 용법(목적)
곡물 생산을 증가시키려면 /
the use of chemical fertilizers should be minimized, /
화학 비료의 사용이 최소화되어야 한다 /
and insect-resistant grain varieties should be developed.
그리고 해충에 강한 곡물 품종이 개발되어야 한다

✱중요 이 지문은 최소한의 곡물 가공이 좋다는 내용으로 전개되는데, 문장 (5)는 곡물의 생산성 증가를 위한 방법을 말하고 있으므로 지문의 흐름과 무관함.

④(6) Such a spoilage of key nutrients and fiber /
주요 영양소 및 섬유질의 그러한 손상은 /
is no longer acceptable / in the context of a sustainable diet /
더 이상 용납되지 않는다 / 지속 가능한 식단의 맥락에서 /
[aiming at an optimal nutrient density and health protection]. [ ]: 현재분사구
최적의 영양소 밀도와 건강 보호를 목표로 하는 정답 단서 제분에 의한 영양소 및 섬유질 손상은 건강한 식단에서 용납되지 않음.

⑤(7) In contrast, /
반대로 /
fermentation of various foodstuffs or germination of grains /
다양한 식품의 발효나 곡물의 발아는 /
are traditional, locally accessible, low-energy and highly nutritious processes /
전통적이고, 생산지에서 접근 가능하며, 에너지가 적게 들고, 매우 영양가가 있는 과정이다 /
of sounded interest.
알려진 관심을 받는

[전문 해석]

(1)최소한의 가공은 인공 향료나 첨가물, 또는 과도한 소금을 더할 필요 없이 본연의 풍미와 맛을 유지하는 가장 좋은 방법 중 하나일 수 있다. (2)이것은 또한 대부분의 영양소, 특히 많은 비타민과 항산화 물질과 같은 가장 민감한 것들을 유지하는 효율적인 방법일 것이다. ①(3)곡물을 제분하는 것은 영양소 함량에 크게 영향을 미치는 가장 가혹한 과정 중 하나이다. ②(4)곡물에는(즉, 통밀 가루 또는 플레이크에는) 미량 영양소, 항산화 물질과 섬유질이 자연적으로 매우 풍부하지만, 제분하는 것은 일반적으로 흰 밀가루를 만들기 위해 대부분의 미네랄, 비타민 그리고 섬유질을 제거한다. ③(5)곡물 생산을 증가시키려면, 화학 비료의 사용이 최소화되어

문제편 p.182

야 하고, 해충에 강한 곡물 품종이 개발되어야 한다. ④(6)주요 영양소 및 섬유질의 그러한 손상은 최적의 영양소 밀도와 건강 보호를 목표로 하는 지속 가능한 식단의 맥락에서 더 이상 용납되지 않는다. ⑤(7)반대로, 다양한 식품의 발효나 곡물의 발아는 알려진 관심을 받는 전통적이고, 생산지에서 접근 가능하며, 에너지가 적게 들고, 매우 영양가가 있는 과정이다.

[중요 어휘]

□ **minimal**	형용사 최소한의, 아주 적은
□ **artificial**	형용사 인공의, 인위적인
□ **additive**	명사 첨가물, 첨가제
□ **nutrient**	명사 영양소, 영양분
□ **anti-oxidant**	명사 항산화 물질
□ **mill**	동사 제분하다, 갈다 / 명사 방앗간, 제분소
□ **cereal**	명사 곡물, 곡류
□ **harsh**	형용사 가혹한, 혹독한, 눈에 거슬리는
□ **dramatically**	부사 크게, 극적으로
□ **content**	명사 함량, 함유량, 내용물
□ **fiber**	명사 섬유질, 성질, 내구성
□ **flakes**	명사 플레이크(낟알을 얇게 으깬 식품)
□ **fertilizer**	명사 비료, 거름
□ **resistant**	형용사 ~에 강한, 저항력 있는
□ **variety**	명사 품종, 다양성
□ **spoilage**	명사 (음식·식품의) 손상, 부패
□ **sustainable**	형용사 지속 가능한
□ **aim**	동사 ~을 목표로 하다 / 명사 목적, 목표
□ **optimal**	형용사 최적의, 최선의
□ **density**	명사 밀도, 농도
□ **foodstuff**	명사 식품, 식량
□ **sound**	동사 알리다, 울리다

14 문장 배열

정답과 해설 14 문장 배열

📍**핵심** 지문은 감각의 순응에 대한 글로, 예시를 통해 순응의 의미를 설명하고 있음. 연결어나 대명사에 주의하며 읽으면 글의 순서를 수월하게 파악할 수 있음.

01 2020년 9월 36번 (정답률 75%) 정답 ②

[지문 끊어 읽기] 감각의 순응

(1) When a change in the environment occurs, /
접속사 S V
환경에 변화가 일어날 때 /

there is a relative increase or decrease /
상대적인 증가나 감소가 있다 /

in the rate / at which the neurons fire, /
속도에 / 뉴런이 발화하는 /

🔖**힌트** 밑줄 친 부분은 'at which (전치사 + 관계대명사)'가 이끄는 관계사절로, 앞에 나온 'the rate'를 수식함. 원래 문장은 'The neurons fire at the rate'이기 때문에, 관계사절로 전환할 때 전치사 'at'이 생략되지 않도록 주의해야 함.

which is how intensity is coded.
명사절
그런데 이것이 강도가 부호화되는 방식이다

(2) Furthermore, / relativity operates / to calibrate our sensations.
뿐만 아니라 / 상대성은 작용한다 / 우리의 감각을 조정하기 위해서
[정답 단서-1]

(B) (5) For example, / if you place one hand in hot water /
예를 들어 / 만일 당신이 한 손을 뜨거운 물에 넣으면 / 병렬①

and the other in iced water / for some time /
병렬②
그리고 다른 한 손을 찬물에 / 일정 시간 동안 /

before immersing them both / into lukewarm water, / [정답 단서-2]
그것들 모두를 담그기 전에 / 미지근한 물에 /

you will experience conflicting sensations of temperature /
당신은 상충하는 온도 감각을 경험할 것이다 /

because of the relative change in the receptors /
감각 기관들의 상대적인 변화 때문에 /

registering hot and cold.
냉온을 인식하는

(A) (3) Although both hands are now in the same water, / [정답 단서-2]
비록 양손은 이제 같은 물에 있지만 /

one feels that it is colder / and the other feels warmer /
=the water
하나는 물이 더 차갑다고 느낀다 / 그리고 다른 하나는 더 따뜻하다고 느낀다 /

because of the relative change / from prior experience.
상대적인 변화 때문에 / 이전 경험으로부터의

(4) This process, / called adaptation, / [정답 단서-3]
이 과정은 / '순응'이라고 불리는 /

is one of the organizing principles /
구성 원리 중 하나이다 /

operating throughout the central nervous system.
중추 신경계 전반에 작용하는
[정답 단서-3]

(C) (6) It explains / why you can't see well / inside a dark room /
그것은 설명한다 / 왜 당신이 잘 볼 수 없는지를 / 어두운 방 안에서 /

if you have come in / from a sunny day.
당신이 안으로 들어오면 / 날씨가 화창한 바깥에서

(7) Your eyes have to become accustomed /
당신의 눈은 적응해야만 한다 /

to the new level of luminance.
새로운 밝기 수준에
[정답 단서-3]

(8) Adaptation explains / why apples taste sour /
순응은 설명한다 / 왜 사과가 신맛이 나는지를 /

after eating sweet chocolate /
단 초콜릿을 먹은 후에 /

and why traffic seems louder in the city /
그리고 왜 교통이 도시에서 더 시끄러운 것 같은지를 /

if you normally live in the country.
당신이 평소에 시골에 산다면

[전문 해석]

(1)환경에 변화가 일어날 때, 뉴런이 발화하는 속도에 상대적인 증가나 감소가 있는데, 이것이 강도가 부호화되는 방식이다. (2)뿐만 아니라 상대성은 우리의 감각을 조정하기 위해서 (도) 작용한다.

(B) (5)예를 들어 만일 당신이 미지근한 물에 양손 모두를 담그기 전에 일정 시간 동안 한 손을 뜨거운 물에, 그리고 다른 한 손은 찬물에 넣으면, 당신은 냉온을 인식하는 감각 기관들의 상대적인 변화 때문에 상충하는 온도 감각을 경험할 것이다.

(A) (3)비록 양손은 이제 같은 물에 있지만, 이전 경험으로부터의 상대적인 변화 때문에 하나는 물이 더 차갑다고 느끼고 다른 하나는 더 따뜻하다고 느낀다. (4)'순응'이라고 불리는 이 과정은 중추 신경계 전반에 작용하는 구성 원리 중 하나이다.

(C) (6)그것은 당신이 날씨가 화창한 바깥에서 안으로 들어오면 왜 (당신이) 어두운 방 안에서 잘 볼 수 없는지를 설명한다. (7)당신의 눈은 새로운 밝기 수준에 적응해야만 한다. (8)순응은 단 초콜릿을 먹은 후에 왜 사과가 신맛이 나는지와 당신이 평소에 시골에 산다면 왜 교통이 도시에서 더 시끄러운 것 같은지를 설명한다.

[정답 확인]

주어진 글 다음에 이어질 글의 순서로 가장 적절한 것은?

① (A) — (C) — (B) ✔② (B) — (A) — (C) ③ (B) — (C) — (A)
④ (C) — (A) — (B) ⑤ (C) — (B) — (A)

[문제 풀이]

감각의 순응(adaptation)에 관한 글로, 주어진 문장은 환경이 변화할 때 상대성이 작용한다고 설명한다. 한편, '한 손을 뜨거운 물에, 다른 한 손은 찬물에 넣는' 문장 (5)의 상황은 감각을 조정하기 위해 상대성이 작용한다는 문장 (2)에 대한 예시이므로, 주어진 글 다음에는 (B)가 와야 한다. 또, 문장 (5)와 문장 (3) 각각은 양손을 미지근한 물에 담그기 전과 후에 해당하므로, 시간의 순서상 (B) 다음에는 (A)가 와야 한다. 마지막으로, 문장 (6)의 대명사 'It'은 문장 (4)의 'adaptation'을 나타내므로 (A) 다음에는 (C)가 와야 한다. 따라서 정답은 ② '(B) — (A) — (C)'이다.

[중요 어휘]

□ relative	형용사	상대적인, 비교상의
□ fire	동사	발화하다, 발포하다
□ intensity	명사	강도, 세기
□ code	동사	부호화하다, 암호화하다
□ operate	동사	작용하다, 작동하다
□ calibrate	동사	조정하다, 눈금을 매기다
□ sensation	명사	감각, 느낌
□ immerse	동사	담그다, 몰두하게 하다
□ lukewarm	형용사	미지근한, 미온의
□ conflict	동사	상충하다 / 명사 갈등
□ receptor	명사	감각 기관, 수용체
□ register	동사	인식하다, (온도를) 가리키다
□ adaptation	명사	(생리학) 순응, 적응
□ central nervous system	명사	중추 신경계
□ become(=be) accustomed to		~에 적응하다[익숙하다]
□ luminance	명사	(빛의) 밝기

02 2021년 3월 36번 (정답률 75%) 정답 ⑤

[지문 끊어 읽기] 잘못된 원인 문제

(1) Once we recognize the false-cause issue, / we see it everywhere.
일단 우리가 잘못된 원인 문제를 인식하면 / 우리는 그것을 어디에서나 보게 된다

(2) For example, / a recent long-term study /
예를 들어 / 최근의 장기간의 연구는 /

of University of Toronto medical students / concluded /
토론토 대학교의 의과 대학 학생들에 대한 / 결론을 내렸다 /

that medical school class presidents lived an average of 2.4 years less / [정답 단서-1]
의과 대학 학년 대표들이 평균 2.4년 더 적게 살았다고 /

than other medical school graduates.
다른 의과 대학 졸업생들보다

(C) (8) At first glance, / this seemed to imply /
언뜻 보기에는 / 이것은 의미하는 것처럼 보였다 /

that being a medical school class president is bad for you. [정답 단서-1]
동명사(주어)
의과 대학 학년 대표인 것이 여러분에게 해롭다는 것을

문제편 p.186

(9) Does this mean /
이것은 의미하는가 /
that you should avoid being medical school class president /
동명사(목적어)
여러분이 의과 대학 학년 대표가 되는 것을 피해야 한다는 것을 /
at all costs? 정답 단서-2
무슨 수를 써서라도

(B) (5) Probably not. 정답 단서-2
아마도 그렇지는 않을 것이다

(6) Just because being class president is correlated with shorter life expectancy /
단지 학년 대표인 것이 더 짧은 기대 수명과 연관성이 있다고 해서 /
does not mean / that it *causes* shorter life expectancy.
=being class president
의미는 아니다 / 그것이 더 짧은 기대 수명을 '유발한다'는

(7) In fact, / it seems likely / that the sort of person /
사실 / ~인 듯하다 / 그런 부류의 사람은 / S', 선행사
[who becomes medical school class president] / [ ]: 주격 관계대명사절
의과 대학 학년 대표가 되는 /
정답 단서-3
is, on average, extremely hard-working, serious, and ambitious.
V'
평균적으로 극도로 근면하고, 진지하며, 야망을 가진다

(A) (3) Perhaps this extra stress, / 정답 단서-3
아마도 이러한 추가적인 스트레스 /
and the corresponding lack of social and relaxation time /
그리고 그에 상응하는 사교와 휴식 시간의 부족이 /
— rather than being class president per se /
학년 대표인 것 그 자체라기보다는 /
— contributes to lower life expectancy.
더 짧은 기대 수명의 원인이 된다

(4) If so, / the real lesson of the study is /
만약 그렇다면 / 이 연구의 진정한 교훈은 ~이다 /
that we should all relax a little /
V'①
우리 모두가 약간의 휴식을 취해야 한다는 것 /
and not let our work take over our lives.
V'②(=should not let) O' O·C'(동사원형)
그리고 우리의 일이 우리의 삶을 장악하게 해서는 안 된다는 것

[전문 해석]

(1)일단 우리가 잘못된 원인 문제를 인식하면, 우리는 그것을 어디에서나 보게 된다. (2)예를 들어, 토론토 대학교의 의과 대학 학생들에 대한 최근의 장기간의 연구는 의과 대학 학년 대표들이 다른 의과 대학 졸업생들보다 평균 2.4년 더 적게 살았다고 결론을 내렸다.
(C) (8)언뜻 보기에는 이것은 의과 대학 학년 대표인 것이 여러분에게 해롭다는 것을 의미하는 것처럼 보였다. (9)이것은 여러분이 무슨 수를 써서라도 의과 대학 학년 대표가 되는 것을 피해야 한다는 것을 의미하는가?
(B) (5)아마도 그렇지는 않을 것이다. (6)단지 학년 대표인 것이 더 짧은 기대 수명과 연관성이 있다고 해서 그것이 더 짧은 기대 수명을 '유발한다'는 의미는 아니다. (7)사실 의과 대학 학년 대표가 되는 그런 부류의 사람은 평균적으로 극도로 근면하고, 진지하며, 야망을 가진 듯하다.
(A) (3)학년 대표인 것 그 자체라기보다는 아마도 이러한 추가적인 스트레스와 그에 상응하는 사교와 휴식 시간의 부족이 더 짧은 기대 수명의 원인이 된다. (4)만약 그렇다면 이 연구의 진정한 교훈은 우리 모두가 약간의 휴식을 취해야 하고 우리의 일이 우리의 삶을 장악하게 해서는 안 된다는 것이다.

[정답 확인]

주어진 글 다음에 이어질 글의 순서로 가장 적절한 것은?

① (A) — (C) — (B) ② (B) — (A) — (C) ③ (B) — (C) — (A)
④ (C) — (A) — (B) ✔ (C) — (B) — (A)

[문제 풀이]

이 글은 한 연구를 예로 들며 '잘못된 원인 문제'에 대해 설명하고 있다. 문장 (8)과 (9)의 'this'는 문장 (2)에 나타난 연구 결론을 의미하므로 주어진 문장 다음으로 (C)가 온다. 또한, 문장 (9)에서 질문한 이후 문장 (5)에서 답하기 때문에 (C) 다음으로 (B)가 온다. 문장 (7)의 'extremely hard-working, serious, and ambitious(극도로 근면하고, 진지하며, 야망을 가진)'가 문장 (3)의 'this extra stress(이러한 추가적인 스트레스)'로 연결되기 때문에 (B) 다음으로 (A)가 온다. 따라서 정답은 ⑤ '(C) — (B) — (A)'이다.

[중요 어휘]

☐ **recognize**	동사 인식하다, 알아보다
☐ **medical school**	의과 대학
☐ **president**	명사 대표, 회장, 대통령
☐ **at first glance**	언뜻 보기에는, 처음에는
☐ **imply**	동사 의미하다, 넌지시 나타내다
☐ **at all costs**	무슨 수를 써서라도
☐ **A be correlated with B**	A가 B와 연관성이 있다
☐ **life expectancy**	기대 수명
☐ **hard-working**	형용사 근면한
☐ **ambitious**	형용사 야망을 가진, 야심 있는
☐ **corresponding**	형용사 (~에) 상응하는, 해당하는
☐ **relaxation**	명사 휴식
☐ **contribute to**	~의 원인이 되다
☐ **take over**	~을 장악하다

03 2023년 6월 36번 (정답률 75%) 정답 ②

[지문 끊어 읽기] 의도하지 않은 결과의 법칙

(1) When evaluating a policy, / people tend to concentrate on /
정책을 평가할 때 / 사람들은 집중하는 경향이 있다 /
[how the policy will fix some particular problem] / [ ]: 간접의문문
그 정책이 어떤 특정한 문제를 어떻게 고칠 것인지에 /
while ignoring or downplaying other effects it may have.
그것이 가질 수 있는 다른 효과들을 무시하거나 경시하면서

힌트 선행사 other effects를 목적격 관계대명사가 생략된 관계사절 it may have가 수식하고 있음.

(2) Economists often refer to this situation /
경제학자들은 종종 이런 상황을 부른다 /
as *The Law of Unintended Consequences.* 정답 단서-1
'의도하지 않은 결과의 법칙'으로

힌트 'refer to A as B'는 'A를 B라고 부르다[언급하다]'라는 의미임.

한 정책이 가지는 다른 효과는 무시하고 어떤 문제를 해결하는 것에만 집중하는 상황을 경제학자는 '의도하지 않은 결과의 법칙'이라고 부름.

(B) (6) For instance, /
예를 들어 /
suppose that you impose a tariff on imported steel /
당신이 수입된 철강에 관세를 부여한다고 가정해 보라 /
in order to protect the jobs of domestic steelworkers. 정답 단서-1
국내 철강 노동자의 일자리를 보호하기 위해

주어진 글과 관련된 예시로 수입된 철강에 관세를 부여하는 내용이 제시됨.

(7) If you impose a high enough tariff, /
당신이 충분히 높은 관세를 부여한다면 /
their jobs will indeed be protected /
그들의 일자리는 정말로 보호될 것이다 /
from competition by foreign steel companies. 정답 단서-2
외국 철강 기업에 의한 경쟁으로부터

수입된 철강에 높은 관세를 부여하면 국내 철강 노동자의 일자리는 보호됨.

(A) (3) But an unintended consequence is /
그러나 의도하지 않은 결과는 ~이다 /
that the jobs of some autoworkers will be lost /
접속사
몇몇 자동차 제조 노동자들의 일자리가 빼앗기게 된다는 것 /
to foreign competition. 정답 단서-2
외국 경쟁사에

문장 (6), (7)에 따르는 '의도하지 않은 결과'는 자동차 제조 노동자들의 일자리가 빼앗기게 된다는 것임.

(4) Why?
왜 그럴까

(5) [The tariff that protects steelworkers] / [ ]: S
선행사 주격 관계대명사절
철강 노동자를 보호하는 관세는 /
raises the price of the steel /
V 선행사
철강의 가격을 올린다 /
[that domestic automobile makers need to build their cars]. 정답 단서-3
국내 자동차 제조업체가 그들의 차를 만들기 위해 필요한 [ ]: 목적격 관계대명사절

철강 노동자를 보호하기 위해 부여한 관세는 국내 자동차 제조업에 필요한 철강의 가격을 올리는 '의도하지 않은 결과'를 가져 옴.

(C) (8) As a result, /
결과적으로 /
domestic automobile manufacturers have to raise the prices of their cars, /
국내 자동차 제조업체는 그들의 자동차 가격을 올려야 한다 / 문장 (5)의 결과로 국내 자동차 제조업체가 자동차 가격을 올려야 함.
[making them relatively less attractive than foreign cars]. 정답 단서-3
그것들을 외제 차보다 상대적으로 덜 매력적이게 만들면서 [ ]: 분사구문

(9) Raising prices tends to reduce domestic car sales, /
가격을 인상하는 것은 국산 차 판매를 줄이는 경향이 있다 /
so some domestic autoworkers lose their jobs.
그래서 몇몇 국내 자동차 제조 노동자들은 그들의 일자리를 잃는다

[전문 해석]

(1)정책을 평가할 때 사람들은 그 정책이 가질 수 있는 다른 효과들을 무시하거나 경시하면서 그것이 어떤 특정한 문제를 어떻게 고칠 것인지에 집중하는 경향이 있다. (2)경제학자들은 종종 이런 상황을 '의도하지 않은 결과의 법칙'으로 부른다.
(B) (6)예를 들어, 당신이 국내 철강 노동자의 일자리를 보호하기 위해 수입된 철강에 관세를 부여한다고 가정해 보라. (7)당신이 충분히 높은 관세를 부여한다면, 그들의 일자리는 외국 철강 기업에 의한 경쟁으로부터 정말로 보호될 것이다.
(A) (3)그러나 의도하지 않은 결과는 몇몇 자동차 제조 노동자들의 일자리가 외국 경쟁사에 빼앗기게 된다는 것이다. (4)왜 그럴까? (5)철강 노동자를 보호하는 관세는 국내 자동차 제조업체가 그들의 차를 만들기 위해 필요한 철강의 가격을 올린다.
(C) (8)결과적으로, 국내 자동차 제조업체는 그들의 자동차 가격을 올려야 하고 그것들(국산 차)을 외제 차보다 상대적으로 덜 매력적이게 만든다. (9)가격을 인상하는 것은 국산 차 판매를 줄이는 경향이 있어서 몇몇 국내 자동차 제조 노동자들은 그들의 일자리를 잃는다.

[정답 확인]

주어진 글 다음에 이어질 글의 순서로 가장 적절한 것은?

① (A) — (C) — (B)　✔② (B) — (A) — (C)　③ (B) — (C) — (A)
④ (C) — (A) — (B)　⑤ (C) — (B) — (A)

[중요 어휘]

☐ downplay	동사 경시하다, 얕보다
☐ unintended	형용사 의도하지 않은, 고의가 아닌
☐ consequence	명사 결과
☐ tariff	명사 관세
☐ import	동사 수입하다
☐ steel	명사 철강
☐ steelworker	명사 철강 노동자
☐ foreign	형용사 외국의
☐ autoworker	명사 자동차 제조 노동자
☐ manufacturer	명사 제조업체
☐ relatively	부사 상대적으로
☐ attractive	형용사 매력적인
☐ sale	명사 판매, 매출(량)

● 지문 구조도

(2) 의도하지 않은 결과의 법칙(The Law of Unintended Consequences)
(1) 정책을 평가할 때 사람들은 그 정책이 어떤 특정한 문제를 어떻게 고칠 것인지에 집중하고 그것이 가질 수 있는 다른 효과들을 무시하거나(ignore) 경시함(downplay).

↓

예시
(6) 국내 철강 노동자의 일자리 보호를 위해 수입된 철강에 관세 부여(impose a tariff) → (7) 외국 철강 기업과의 경쟁에서 국내 철강 노동자 일자리가 보호됨(be protected).

↓

위 상황의 의도하지 않은 결과
(3) 몇몇 국내 자동차 제조 노동자들(autoworkers)의 일자리가 외국 경쟁사(foreign competition)에 빼앗기게 됨.

↓

원인-1
(5) 철강 노동자(steelworkers)를 보호하는 관세 : 국내 자동차 제조업에 필요한 철강의 가격을 올림(raise).

↓

원인-2
(8) 철강 가격 상승: 국내 자동차 제조업체는 자동차 가격을 올려야 함.

↓

원인-3
(9) 국산 차 가격 상승: 국산 차 판매(domestic car sales) 감소 → 몇몇 국내 자동차 제조 노동자들이 일자리를 잃게 됨.

04 2018년 9월 35번 (정답률 70%) 정답 ②

[지문 끊어 읽기] 청바지가 파란색인 이유

(1) Calling your pants "blue jeans" / almost seems redundant /
당신의 바지를 '파란 청바지'라고 부르는 것은 / 거의 불필요한 것처럼 보인다 /
because practically all denim is blue.
실제로 모든 데님이 파란색이기 때문에

(2) While jeans are probably the most versatile pants /
청바지가 아마도 가장 다용도인 바지일 테지만 /
in your wardrobe, / blue actually isn't a particularly neutral color. 정답 단서-1
당신의 옷장 속에서 / 사실 파란색이 특별히 무난한 색은 아니다

(B) (5) Ever wonder / why it's the most commonly used hue? 정답 단서-1
궁금해 해본 적이 있는가 / 왜 그것이 가장 흔하게 사용되는 색상인지

(6) Blue was the chosen color for denim /
파란색은 데님용으로 선택된 색깔이었다 /
because of the chemical properties / of blue dye.
화학적 특성 때문에 / 청색 염료의

(7) Most dyes 정답 단서-2 will permeate fabric / in hot temperatures, /
대부분의 염료는 천에 스며든다 / 높은 온도에서 /
making the color stick.
색을 들러붙게 만든다

(A) (3) The natural indigo dye / used in the first jeans, /
천연 남색 염료는 / 최초의 청바지에 사용된 /
on the other hand, / 정답 단서-2
반면에 /
would stick only / to the outside of the threads.
~만 들러붙었다 / 실의 겉면에

(4) When the indigo-dyed denim is washed, 정답 단서-3 /
남색으로 염색된 데님을 빨 때 /
tiny amounts of that dye get washed away, /
그 염료 중 적은 양은 씻겨나간다 /
and the thread comes with them.
그리고 실은 그것들과 함께 나오게 된다

문제편 p.187

(C) (8) The more denim was washed, / the softer it would get, / 정답 단서-3
데님을 더 많이 빨수록 / 그것은 더 부드러워지게 되고 /
eventually achieving / that worn-in, made-just-for-me feeling /
결국엔 얻게 된다 / 닳고 나만을 위해 만들어졌다는 느낌을 /
you probably get with your favorite jeans.
당신이 아마도 가장 좋아하는 청바지로부터 받는

(9) That softness made jeans / the trousers of choice for laborers.
이 부드러움이 청바지를 만들었다 / 노동자용으로 선택하는 바지로

[전문 해석]

(1)실제로 모든 데님이 파란색이기 때문에 (당신의) 바지를 '파란 청바지'라고 부르는 것은 거의 (표현이) 불필요한 것처럼 보인다. (2)청바지가 아마도 당신의 옷장 속에서 가장 다용도인(활용도가 높은) 바지일 테지만, 사실 파란색이 특별히 무난한 색은 아니다.
(B) (5)왜 그것(파란색)이 (청바지를 염색할 때) 가장 흔하게 사용되는 색상인지 궁금해 해본 적이 있는가? (6)파란색은 청색 염료의 화학적 특성 때문에 데님용으로 선택된 색깔이었다(데님의 색깔로 선택되었다). (7)대부분의 염료는 높은 온도에서 천에 스며들어 색을 (천에) 들러붙게 만든다.
(A) (3)반면에 최초의 청바지에 사용된 천연 남색 염료는 실의 겉면에만 들러붙었다. (4)남색으로 염색된 데님을 빨 때, 그 염료 중 적은 양(소량)은 씻겨나가고, (옷감의) 실은 그것들(염료)과 함께 나오게 된다.
(C) (8)데님을 더 많이 빨수록 그것은 더 부드러워지게 되고, 결국엔 당신이 아마도 가장 좋아하는 청바지로부터 받는 닳고 나만을 위해 만들어졌다는 느낌을 얻게 된다. (9)이 부드러움이 청바지를 노동자용으로 선택하는 바지로 만들었다(노동자들이 가장 많이 선택하는 바지로 만들었다).
- denim(데님): 특히 청바지를 만드는 데 쓰이는 보통 푸른색의 질긴 면직물

[정답 확인]

주어진 글 다음에 이어질 글의 순서로 가장 적절한 것은?
① (A) — (C) — (B)   ✔ (B) — (A) — (C)   ③ (B) — (C) — (A)
④ (C) — (A) — (B)   ⑤ (C) — (B) — (A)

[중요 어휘]

☐ **redundant**	형용사 (표현이) 불필요한, 장황한
☐ **practically**	부사 실제로, 사실상
☐ **versatile**	형용사 다용도인, 활용도가 높은
☐ **wardrobe**	명사 옷장
☐ **neutral**	형용사 무난한, 중간색의, 중립적인, 중성의
☐ **hue**	명사 색상, 색조
☐ **property**	명사 특성, 속성, 재산, 부동산
☐ **dye**	명사 염료, 염색제 / 동사 염색하다
☐ **permeate**	동사 스며들다, 침투하다
☐ **stick to**	~에 들러붙다[달라붙다], 고수하다, 계속하다
☐ **eventually**	부사 결국(엔), 마침내
☐ **achieve**	동사 얻다, 성취하다
☐ **trousers**	명사 바지 (한 벌)
☐ **laborer**	명사 노동자

05 2021년 6월 37번 (정답률 70%)   정답 ③

[지문 끊어 읽기]   질문의 구성이 답변에 미치는 영향

(1) In one survey, / 61 percent of Americans said /
한 설문조사에서 / 61%의 미국인들이 말했다 /
that they supported the government /
그들은 정부를 지지한다고 /
spending more on 'assistance to the poor'. 정답 단서-1
후치수식
'빈곤층 지원'에 더 많이 쓰는

힌트 형용사 앞에 정관사 the를 붙여 명사처럼 사용하는 방법으로, 형용사의 특징을 가진 단체나 무리를 나타낼 때 사용함. the+poor(빈곤한)을 '빈곤층'으로 해석함.

(B) (4) But when the same population was asked /
그러나 같은 모집단이 질문을 받았을 때 /
whether they supported spending more government money on 'welfare', /
'복지'에 더 많은 정부 예산을 쓰는 것을 지지하느냐는 /
only 21 percent were in favour. 정답 단서-1
단지 21%만이 찬성했다

(5) In other words, /
다시 말해 /

★중요 '빈곤층 지원'에는 긍정적, '복지'에는 부정적인 입장을 보이는 설문조사 결과가 연결사 In other words를 기점으로 재진술되고 있음. 따라서 문장 (1) 다음에는 (B), 그 다음에는 (C)가 오는 것이 적절함.

if you ask people about individual welfare programmes /
만약 당신이 개별 복지 프로그램들에 대해 사람들에게 물어보면 /
— such as giving financial help to people /
병렬① 선행사
사람들에게 재정적 도움을 주는 것과 같은 /
who have long-term illnesses / and paying for school meals /
주격 관계대명사 병렬②
장기 질환을 가진 / 그리고 급식비를 내는 것과 같은 /
for families with low income — /
저소득 가정을 위해 /
people are broadly in favour of them. 정답 단서-2
사람들은 대체로 그것들에 찬성한다

(C) (6) But if you ask about 'welfare' /
그러나 만약 당신이 '복지'에 관해 질문한다면 /
— which refers to those exact same programmes /
선행사
정확히 동일한 프로그램을 나타내는 /
that you've just listed — / they're against it. 정답 단서-2
목적격 관계대명사
당신이 방금 열거한 것과 / 그들은 그것에 반대한다

(7) The word 'welfare' has negative connotations, /
'복지'라는 단어는 부정적인 함축된 의미를 가지고 있다 /
perhaps because of the way /
아마도 방식 때문에 /
many politicians and newspapers portray it. 정답 단서-3
많은 정치인들과 신문들이 그것을 묘사하는

힌트 관계부사 how가 생략된 관계부사절로 the way를 꾸며줌. the way how는 함께 쓸 수 없으며, 반드시 선행사(the way) 또는 관계부사(how)를 생략해서 써야 함.

(A) (2) Therefore, the framing of a question /
따라서 질문의 구성은 /
can heavily influence the answer / 정답 단서-3
답변에 크게 영향을 미칠 수 있다 /
in many ways, / which matters /
계속적 용법
여러 가지 방식으로 / 그리고 이것은 중요하다 /
if your aim is to obtain a 'true measure' / of what people think.
당신의 목표가 '진정한 척도'를 얻는 것이라면 / 사람들이 생각하는 것에 대한

(3) And next time you hear / a politician say / 'surveys prove /
그리고 다음에 당신이 듣게 될 때 / 한 정치인이 말하는 것을 / 설문조사는 입증한다 /
[that the majority of the people agree with me]', / be very wary.
대다수의 사람들이 나에게 동의한다는 것을 / 매우 조심하라 [ ]: 명사절

[전문 해석]

(1)한 설문조사에서, 61%의 미국인들이 '빈곤층 지원'에 더 많이 (돈을) 쓰는 정부를 지지한다고 말했다.
(B) (4)그러나 같은 모집단이 '복지'에 더 많은 정부 예산을 쓰는 것을 지지하느냐는 질문을 받았을 때, 단지 21%만이 찬성했다. (5)다시 말해, 만약 당신이 장기 질환을 가진 사람들에게 재정적 도움을 주고 저소득 가정을 위해 급식비를 내는(지원하는) 것과 같은 개별 복지 프로그램들에 대해 사람들에게 물어보면, 사람들은 대체로 그것들에 찬성한다.
(C) (6)그러나 만약 당신이 방금 열거한 것과 정확히 동일한 프로그램을 나타내는 '복지'에 관해 질문한다면, 그들은 그것에 반대한다. (7)'복지'라는 단어는 아마도 많은 정치인들과 신문들이 그것을 묘사하는 방식 때문인지, 부정적인 함축된 의미를 가지고 있다.
(A) (2)따라서 질문의 구성은 여러 가지 방식으로 답변에 크게 영향을 미칠 수 있으며, 이것은 당신의 목표가 사람들이 생각하는 것에 대한 '진정한 척도'를 얻는 것이라면 중요하다. (3)그리고 다음에 당신이 한 정치인이 '설문조사는 대다수의 사람들이 나에게 동의한다는 것을 입증한다'라고 말하는 것을 듣게 될 때, 매우 조심하라.

[정답 확인]

주어진 글 다음에 이어질 글의 순서로 가장 적절한 것은?
① (A) — (C) — (B)   ② (B) — (A) — (C)   ✔ (B) — (C) — (A)
④ (C) — (A) — (B)   ⑤ (C) — (B) — (A)

[중요 어휘]

☐ **spend**	동사 (돈을) 쓰다, (시간을) 보내다
☐ **assistance**	명사 지원, 도움

□ welfare	명사 복지, 후생
□ in favo(u)r (of)	~을 찬성하는, ~을 마음에 들어하는
□ broadly	부사 대체로, 대략(적으로)
□ refer to	~을 나타내다[지칭하다]
□ connotation	명사 함축(된 의미)
□ portray	동사 묘사하다, 보여주다
□ framing	명사 구성, 틀, 뼈대
□ measure	명사 척도, 측정
□ wary	형용사 조심하는, 경계하는

06 2021년 11월 36번 (정답률 70%) 정답 ②

[지문 끊어 읽기] 식품 생산 책임의 개념

(1) Regarding food production, / under the British government, /
식품 생산과 관련하여 / 영국 정부하에서는 /
there was a different conception of responsibility / 정답 단서-1 식품 생산 책임의 개념이 영국과 프랑스에서 각각 달랐음.
다른 책임의 개념이 있었다 /
from that of French government.
=the conception of responsibility
프랑스 정부의 그것과는

(2) In France, / the responsibility for producing good food /
S
프랑스에서 / 좋은 식품을 생산하는 것에 대한 책임은 /
lay with the producers. 정답 단서-1 프랑스에서는 식품 생산의 책임이 생산자들에게 있었음.
V
생산자들에게 있었다

힌트 'If+S'+should+V', S+조동사 과거+V'의 구조를 가진 가정법 미래 구문으로, 미래에 일어날 가능성이 희박한 일에 대해 가정함. 참고로 본문에서 주절의 주어는 'the state'로, 'the state would punish them'이지만 이미 앞에서 언급되었기 때문에 생략됨.

(B) (5) The state would police their activities / and, if they should fail, /
would+동사원형: ~하곤 했다 / =the producers
정부가 그들의 활동들을 감시하곤 했다 / 그리고 만약 그들이 실패했다면 /
would punish them / for neglecting the interests of its citizens.
=the state's
그들을 처벌했을 것이다 / 정부의 시민들의 이익을 등한시한 이유로

(6) By contrast, / the British government / 정답 단서-1 문장 (2)에서 프랑스 정부에 관해 설명한 것과 대조적으로 문장 (6)에서는 영국 정부에 대해 설명함.
대조적으로 / 영국 정부는 /
— except in extreme cases — /
극단적인 경우들을 제외하고 /
placed most of the responsibility / with the individual consumers. 정답 단서-2 반면 영국에서는 대부분의 경우 식품 생산의 책임이 개인 소비자들에게 있었음.
그 책임의 대부분을 두었다 / 개인 소비자들에게

(A) (3) It would be unfair /
형식상의 주어
부당했을 것이다 /
[to interfere with the shopkeeper's right / to make money]. [ ]: 내용상의 주어
가게 주인의 권리를 침해하는 것은 / 돈을 벌기 위한
정답 단서-2 영국 정부의 입장을 제시함. 영국 정부는 생산자에게 식품 생산의 책임이 있는 것을 부당하다고 봄.

(4) In the 1840s, / a patent was granted for a machine / 정답 단서-3 식품 생산의 책임이 개인 소비자에게 있을 때의 부작용을 예시로 듦.
1840년대에는 / 기계에 대해 특허권이 승인되었다 / 선행사
[designed for making fake coffee beans /
가짜 커피콩을 만들어 내기 위해 고안된 /
out of chicory, / using the same technology /
분사구문 선행사
치커리로부터 / 똑같은 기술을 이용해서 /
that went into manufacturing bullets]. [ ]: 주격 관계대명사+be동사 생략
주격 관계대명사절
총알을 제조하는 데 들어갔던

정답 단서-3 'This machine'은 문장 (4)의 'a machine designed for ~ chicory'를 지칭하므로 (C)가 (B) 뒤에 와야 자연스러움.

(C) (7) This machine was clearly designed /
이 기계는 분명히 고안되었다 /
for the purposes of swindling, /
사기의 목적으로 /
and yet the government allowed it.
그러나 정부는 그것을 허가했다

(8) A machine for forging money /
돈을 위조하기 위한 기계는 /
would never have been licensed, / so why this?
결코 허가를 받을 수 없었을 것이다 / 그렇다면 이것은 왜 그랬을까

(9) As one consumer complained, /
한 소비자가 불평했던 것처럼 /
the British system of government /
영국의 정부 체제는 /
was weighted against the consumer / in favour of the swindler.
소비자에게는 불리하도록 치우쳐져 있었다 / 사기꾼의 편을 들고

[전문 해석]

(1)식품 생산과 관련하여 영국 정부하에서는 프랑스 정부의 책임의 개념과는 다른 개념이 있었다. (2)프랑스에서 좋은 식품을 생산하는 것에 대한 책임은 생산자들에게 있었다.
(B) (5)정부가 생산자들의 활동들을 감시하곤 했고, 만약 그들이 실패했다면, 정부의 시민들의 이익을 등한시한 이유로 그들을 처벌했을 것이다. (6)대조적으로 영국 정부는 극단적인 경우들을 제외하고 그 책임의 대부분을 개인 소비자들에게 두었다.
(A) (3)돈을 벌기 위한 가게 주인의 권리를 침해하는 것은 부당했을 것이다. (4)1840년대에는 총알을 제조하는 데 들어갔던 똑같은 기술을 이용해서 치커리로부터 가짜 커피콩을 만들어 내기 위해 고안된 기계에 대해 특허권이 승인되었다.
(C) (7)이 기계는 분명히 사기의 목적으로 고안되었지만 정부는 그것을 허가했다. (8)돈을 위조하기 위한 기계는 결코 허가를 받을 수 없었을 텐데 그렇다면 이것은 왜 그랬을까? (9)한 소비자가 불평했던 것처럼 영국의 정부 체제는 사기꾼의 편을 들고 소비자에게는 불리하도록 치우쳐져 있었다.

[정답 확인]

주어진 글 다음에 이어질 글의 순서로 가장 적절한 것은?

① (A) — (C) — (B) ✔② (B) — (A) — (C) ③ (B) — (C) — (A)
④ (C) — (A) — (B) ⑤ (C) — (B) — (A)

[문제 풀이]

문장 (1)은 식품 생산 책임의 개념이 프랑스와 영국에서 각각 달랐다고 언급하고, 문장 (2)는 프랑스 정부의 경우 책임을 생산자에게 묻는다고 한다. 글의 매끄러운 전개를 위해서는 '영국 정부'가 책임을 누구에게 묻는지에 대한 내용이 이어져야 한다. 따라서 영국 정부가 대부분의 책임을 개인 소비자에게 묻는다는 문장 (6)이 있는 (B)가 주어진 문장 뒤에 와야 한다. 문장 (6) 다음으로는 영국 정부가 책임을 생산자가 아닌 소비자에게 두는 이유를 설명하는 (A)가 뒤이어 오는 것이 적절하다. 마지막으로 (A)의 문장 (4)에서 언급된 예시인 'a machine designed for making fake coffee beans out of chicory'는 문장 (7)의 'This machine'과 연결되므로 (A) 뒤에는 (C)가 온다. 따라서 정답은 ② '(B) — (A) — (C)'이다.

[중요 어휘]

□ lie	동사 있다, 놓여 있다 (lie-lay-lain)
□ police	동사 감시하다, 치안을 유지하다
□ neglect	동사 등한시하다, 방치하다, 무시하다
□ interfere	동사 침해하다, 간섭하다
□ patent	명사 특허 / 형용사 특허의
□ grant	동사 승인하다, 허락하다
□ bullet	명사 총알
□ swindle	동사 사기 치다
□ forge	동사 위조하다
□ license	동사 허가하다 / 명사 면허
□ weighted	형용사 (한쪽에 유·불리하게) 치우친, 편중된
□ in favour of(=in favor of)	~의 이익이 되도록, ~을 위하여

07 2022년 6월 37번 (정답률 70%) 정답 ③

[지문 끊어 읽기] QWERTY 키보드

(1) One interesting feature of network markets /
네트워크 시장의 한 가지 흥미로운 특징은 /
is that "history matters."
명사절 접속사 1형식V
"역사가 중요하다"라는 것이다

(2) A famous example / is the QWERTY keyboard / 정답 단서-1 네트워크 시장의 특징인 "역사가 중요하다"는 것의 유명한 예로 오늘날 사용되고 있는 QWERTY 키보드를 들었음.
한 가지 유명한 예는 / QWERTY 키보드이다 /
used with your computer.
주격 관계대명사+be동사 생략
당신의 컴퓨터에 사용되는

문제편 p.188

(B) (5) You might wonder / [why this particular configuration of keys, /
[ ]: 명사절(간접의문문) S'(=the QWERTY keyboard)
당신은 의아해할지도 모른다 / 왜 이 독특한 키의 배열이 /
with its awkward placement of the letters, / became the standard]. V'
어색한 문자 배치를 가진 / 표준이 되었는지
정답 단서-1 문장 (2) 다음에 오늘날 QWERTY 키보드가 왜 표준이 되었는지 그 이유를 이어서 설명할 것임을 예상할 수 있음.

(6) The QWERTY keyboard in the 19th century /
19세기 QWERTY 키보드는 /
was developed in the era of manual typewriters / 정답 단서-2 QWERTY 키보드는 수동 타자기의 시대인 19세기에 개발되었다고 함.
수동 타자기의 시대에 개발되었다 /
with physical keys.
물리적 키가 있는

(C) (7) The keyboard was designed / 정답 단서-2 문장 (6)에서 언급한 19세기 물리적 키가 있는 QWERTY 키보드에 대한 부연 설명임.
=The QWERTY keyboard
그 키보드는 설계되었다 /
to keep frequently used keys (like E and O) physically separated /
5형식V O O·C
(E와 O 같은) 자주 사용되는 키가 물리적으로 떨어져 있도록 /
in order to prevent them from jamming.
prevent A from V-ing: A가 ~하는 것을 막다
그것들이 걸리는 것을 막기 위해

(8) By the time the technology for electronic typing evolved, /
전자 타이핑 기술이 발전했을 때 즈음 /
millions of people had already learned / 정답 단서-3 전자 타이핑 기술이 발전했을 때는 이미 많은 사람들이 QWERTY 키보드 사용법을 익혔을 때였다고 함.
과거완료(완료)
수백만 명의 사람들이 이미 배웠다 /
to type on millions of QWERTY typewriters.
명사적 용법
수백만 개의 QWERTY 타자기에서 타자 치는 것을

(A) (3) [Replacing the QWERTY keyboard with a more efficient design] /
replace A with B: A를 B로 교체하다[대체하다] [ ]: 동명사S
QWERTY 키보드를 더 효율적인 디자인으로 교체하는 것은 /
would have been both expensive and difficult to coordinate.
would have p.p.: ~했을 것이다
비용이 많이 들고 조정하기 어려웠을 것이다
정답 단서-3 사람들이 이미 QWERTY 키보드에 익숙해진 상황에서 디자인을 교체하는 것은 오히려 비효율적일 것이라고 함.

(4) Thus, /
따라서 /
the placement of the letters stays with the obsolete QWERTY /
문자의 배치는 구식 QWERTY로 남아 있다 /
on today's English-language keyboards.
오늘날의 영어 키보드에서

[전문 해석]

(1)네트워크 시장의 한 가지 흥미로운 특징은 "역사가 중요하다"라는 것이다. (2)한 가지 유명한 예는 당신의 컴퓨터에 사용되는 QWERTY 키보드이다.
(B) (5)당신은 어색한 문자 배치를 가진, 이 독특한 키의 배열이 왜 표준이 되었는지 의아해할지도 모른다. (6)19세기 QWERTY 키보드는 물리적 키가 있는 수동 타자기의 시대에 개발되었다.
(C) (7)그 키보드는 (E와 O 같은) 자주 사용되는 키가 걸리는 것을 막기 위해 물리적으로 떨어져 있도록 설계되었다. (8)전자 타이핑 기술이 발전했을 때 즈음, 수백만 명의 사람들이 이미 수백만 개의 QWERTY 타자기에서 타자 치는 법을 배웠다.
(A) (3)QWERTY 키보드를 더 효율적인 디자인으로 교체하는 것은 비용이 많이 들고 조정하기 어려웠을 것이다. (4)따라서, 오늘날의 영어 키보드에서 문자의 배치는 구식 QWERTY로 남아 있다.

[정답 확인]

주어진 글 다음에 이어질 글의 순서로 가장 적절한 것은?

① (A) — (C) — (B) ② (B) — (A) — (C) ✔③ (B) — (C) — (A)
④ (C) — (A) — (B) ⑤ (C) — (B) — (A)

[문제 풀이]

이 지문은 네트워크 시장의 특징을 QWERTY 키보드라는 예시를 통해 설명하는 글이다. 먼저, 문장 (2)에서 "역사가 중요하다"라는 특징의 예시로 오늘날 사용되고 있는 QWERTY 키보드가 등장한다. 그런데 문장 (5)의 'this particular configuration of keys, with its awkward placement of the letters(어색한 문자 배치를 가진 이 독특한 키의 배열)'가 의미하는 것은 QWERTY 키보드이고, 이것이 오늘날 표준이 되었다고 언급하며 그 이유를 이어서 설명할 것을 예고한다. 따라서 주어진 문장 다음에 (B)가 와야 자연스럽다. 이어서 문장 (6)에서는 QWERTY 키보드가 수동 타자기의 시대인 19세기에 개발되었다고 했고, 이에 덧붙여 문장 (7)에서 그 키보드는 자주 사용되는 키가 걸리는 것을 막기 위해 물리적으로 떨어져 있도록 설계되었다고 하고 있으므로 (B) 다음에는 (C)가 온다. 다음으로, 문장 (8)에서 전자 타이핑 기술이 발전했을 때는 이미 많은 사람들이 QWERTY 키보드에 익숙해져 있을 때였다고 했고, 그래서 보다 더 효율적인 디자인으로 교체하기 어려웠을 것이라고 문장 (3)에서 설명하고 있으므로 (C) 다음에는 (A)가 온다. 따라서 정답은 ③ '(B) — (C) — (A)'이다.

[중요 어휘]

□ matter	동사 중요하다, 문제가 되다
□ wonder	동사 의아해하다, 궁금해하다
□ configuration	명사 배열
□ awkward	형용사 어색한, 곤란한, 불편한
□ placement	명사 배치
□ standard	명사 표준
□ era	명사 시대
□ manual	형용사 수동의 / 명사 설명서
□ physical	형용사 물리적인, 신체의
□ jam	동사 (기계에 무엇이) 걸리다, 작동하지 못하게 되다 / 명사 (기계에 무엇이) 걸림, 고장
□ evolve	동사 발전하다, 진화하다
□ efficient	형용사 효율적인, 능률적인
□ coordinate	동사 조정하다, 조직화하다
□ obsolete	형용사 구식의, 더 이상 쓸모가 없는

08 2023년 3월 37번 (정답률 70%) 정답 ③

[지문 끊어 읽기] 이성과 감정

(1) A common but incorrect assumption is /
일반적이지만 잘못된 가정은 ~이다 /
that we are creatures of reason /
명사절 접속사(주격 보어절을 이끎)
우리가 이성의 피조물이라는 것 /
힌트 접속사 when은 일반적으로 '~할 때'라는 시간의 접속사이지만, 여기서는 '~인데도 불구하고, ~인 것을 생각하면'이라는 양보의 의미임.
when, in fact, we are creatures of both reason and emotion.
사실 우리는 이성과 감정 둘 다의 피조물임에도 불구하고

(2) We cannot get by on reason alone /
우리는 이성만으로 살아갈 수 없다 /
since any reason always eventually leads to a feeling.
접속사(이유)
어떤 이성도 항상 결국에는 감정으로 이어지기 때문에

(3) Should I get a wholegrain cereal / or a chocolate cereal? 정답 단서-1
내가 통곡물 시리얼을 선택해야 할까 / 아니면 초콜릿 시리얼을
이성과 감정 모두에 영향을 받는다는 것을 설명하기 위한 예시임.

(B) (6) I can list all the reasons I want, /
선행사 목적격 관계대명사절
나는 내가 원하는 모든 이유를 열거할 수 있다 /
but the reasons have to be based on something.
하지만 그 이유는 무엇인가에 근거해야 한다

(7) For example, / if my goal is to eat healthy, /
조건절 접속사 명사적 용법(주격 보어)
예를 들어 / 나의 목표가 건강하게 먹는 것이라면 /
I can choose the wholegrain cereal, / 정답 단서-1 목표가 건강하게 먹는 것이라면 통곡물 시리얼을 선택할 수 있음.
나는 통곡물 시리얼을 선택할 수 있다 /
but what is my reason / for wanting to be healthy?
동명사(전치사의 목적어)
하지만 나의 이유는 무엇일까 / 건강해지기를 원하는

(C) (8) I can list more and more reasons /
나는 더 많은 이유를 열거할 수 있다 /
such as wanting to live longer, /
병렬①(동명사)
더 오래 살고 싶은 것과 같은 /
spending more quality time with loved ones, etc., / 정답 단서-2
병렬②(동명사)
사랑하는 사람들과 양질의 시간을 더 많이 보내고 싶은 것 등 /
문장 (7)에서 질문한 건강해지기를 원하는 이유에 대한 답변임.
but what are the reasons for those reasons?
하지만 그러한 이유들에 대한 이유는 무엇일까

(9) You should be able to see by now /
여러분은 이제 알 수 있을 것이다 /
that reasons are ultimately based on non-reason /
명사절 접속사(목적어절을 이끎)
이유가 궁극적으로 비이성에 근거한다는 것을 /
such as values, feelings, or emotions. 정답 단서-3 통곡물 시리얼을 선택한 이유, 건강해지기를 원하는 이유는 궁극적으로 가치, 느낌, 감정과 같은 비이성에 근거함.
가치, 느낌, 또는 감정과 같은

(A) (4) These deep-seated values, feelings, and emotions we have /
S(=선행사) 목적격 관계대명사절
우리가 가진 이러한 뿌리 깊은 가치, 느낌, 그리고 감정은 /
are rarely a result of reasoning, /
추론의 산물인 경우가 거의 없다 /
but can certainly be influenced by reasoning. 정답 단서-3 우리가 가진 비이성은 추론의 영향을 받을 수 있음.
하지만 분명히 추론의 영향을 받을 수 있다

★중요 문장 (9) 마지막의 'values, feelings, or emotions'가 문장 (4)의 'These deep-seated values, feelings, and emotions'로 그대로 쓰였음. These와 같은 지시어는 지칭하는 대상이 그 앞에 먼저 나와야 함.

(5) We have values, feelings, and emotions /
우리는 가치, 느낌, 그리고 감정을 가진다 /
before we begin to reason /
우리가 추론을 시작하기 전에 /
and long before we begin to reason effectively.
그리고 효과적으로 추론을 시작하기 훨씬 전에

[전문 해석]

(1)사실 우리는 이성과 감정 둘 다의 피조물임에도 불구하고 우리가 이성의 피조물이라는 것은 일반적이지만 잘못된 가정이다. (2)어떤 이성도 항상 결국에는 감정으로 이어지기 때문에 우리는 이성만으로 살아갈 수 없다. (3)내가 통곡물 시리얼을 선택해야 할까, 아니면 초콜릿 시리얼을 선택해야 할까?
(B) (6)나는 내가 원하는 모든 이유를 열거할 수 있지만, 그 이유는 무언인가에 근거해야 한다. (7)예를 들어, 나의 목표가 건강하게 먹는 것이라면 나는 통곡물 시리얼을 선택할 수 있지만, 건강해지기를 원하는 나의 이유는 무엇일까?
(C) (8)나는 더 오래 살고 싶은 것, 사랑하는 사람들과 양질의 시간을 더 많이 보내고 싶은 것 등과 같은 더 많은 이유를 열거할 수 있지만, 그러한 이유들에 대한 이유는 무엇일까? (9)여러분은 이유가 궁극적으로 가치, 느낌, 또는 감정과 같은 비이성에 근거한다는 것을 이제 알 수 있을 것이다.
(A) (4)우리가 가진 이러한 뿌리 깊은 가치, 느낌, 그리고 감정은 추론의 산물인 경우가 거의 없지만, 분명히 추론의 영향을 받을 수 있다. (5)우리는 우리가 추론을 시작하기 전에, 그리고 효과적으로 추론을 시작하기 훨씬 전에 가치, 느낌, 그리고 감정을 가진다.

[정답 확인]

주어진 글 다음에 이어질 글의 순서로 가장 적절한 것은?

① (A) — (C) — (B) ② (B) — (A) — (C) ✔③ (B) — (C) — (A)
④ (C) — (A) — (B) ⑤ (C) — (B) — (A)

[문제 풀이]

이 지문은 우리가 이성과 감정 둘 다에 영향을 받는다고 설명하는 글이다. 먼저, 문장 (2)에서 이성이 결국 감정으로 이어지기 때문에 우리는 이성만으로 살아갈 수 없다고 설명한다. 이어지는 문장 (3)에서 이에 대한 예시로 시리얼의 종류 선택 문제를 제시한다. 문장 (7)에서 목표가 건강하게 먹는 것이라면 통곡물 시리얼을 선택할 수 있다고 하면서 문장 (3)의 질문에 대한 답변을 제시하고 있으므로, 주어진 문장 다음에는 (B)가 온다. 문장 (7)에서 건강해지기를 원하는 이유는 무엇일지 질문하고, 이에 대한 답변으로 문장 (8)에서 더 오래 살고 싶은 것, 사랑하는 사람들과 양질의 시간을 더 많이 보내고 싶은 것 등의 예시를 들고 있으므로 (B) 다음에는 (C)가 온다. 문장 (9)에서는 예시에 대한 설명을 마무리하면서 이유가 궁극적으로 비이성에 근거하고 있음을 밝힌다. 마지막으로 문장 (4)에서 이러한 비이성이 추론의 영향을 받을 수 있다고 설명하고 있으므로 (C) 다음에는 (A)가 온다. 따라서 정답은 ③ '(B) — (C) — (A)'이다.

[중요 어휘]

☐ assumption	명사 가정, 추정
☐ creature	명사 피조물, 생물
☐ reason	명사 이성, 이유 / 동사 추론하다, 판단하다
☐ get by on	~으로 살아가다
☐ list	동사 열거하다, 목록을 작성하다 / 명사 목록
☐ be based on	~에 근거하다[기초하다]
☐ deep-seated	형용사 뿌리 깊은, 고질적인
☐ rarely	부사 거의 ~하지 않는
☐ certainly	부사 분명히, 틀림없이
☐ influence	동사 영향을 주다

핵심 잃을 것을 두려워하여 변화에 저항하기보다는 강의 흐름을 허락하는 것처럼 변화를 기꺼이 받아들이자는 내용임. 크게 보면 '변화에 저항하는 이유'와 '변화를 받아들여야 하는 이유'로 나누어 설명하고 있음.

09 2020년 9월 37번 (정답률 65%) 정답 ⑤

[지문 끊어 읽기] 변화를 받아들이는 것의 필요성

(1) When an important change takes place /
중요한 변화가 일어날 때 /
in your life, / observe your response.
당신의 삶에 / 당신의 반응을 관찰해라

(2) If you resist / accepting the change /
만약 당신이 저항한다면 / 그 변화를 받아들이는 것에 /
it is because you are afraid; / afraid of losing something. 정답 단서-1
그것은 당신이 두렵기 때문이다 / 무언가 잃는 것을 두려워하는

(C) (7) Perhaps you might lose /
어쩌면 당신은 잃을지도 모른다 /
your position, property, possession, or money. 정답 단서-1
당신의 지위, 재산, 소유물, 또는 돈을

(8) The change might mean / that you lose privileges or prestige. 정답 단서-2
그 변화는 의미할지도 모른다 / 당신이 특권이나 위신을 잃는 것을

(9) Perhaps with the change / you lose the closeness /
어쩌면 그 변화로 / 당신은 멀어지게 된다 /
of a person or a place. 정답 단서-2
어떤 사람이나 장소에서

힌트 밑줄 친 부분은 직역하면 '접근을 잃는다'이지만, 결국 무엇으로부터 '멀어지게 된다'라는 의미임.

(B) (4) In life, / all these things come and go / 정답 단서-2
인생에서 / 이러한 모든 것들은 왔다가도 사라진다 /
and then others appear, / which will also go.
그리고 그런 다음 다른 것들이 나타난다 / 그리고 그것들은 또한 사라질 것이다

(5) It is like a river / in constant movement.
그것은 강과 같다 / 끊임없는 움직임 속의

(6) If we try to stop the flow, / we create a dam; / 정답 단서-3
만약 우리가 그 흐름을 멈추려고 노력한다면 / 우리는 댐을 만든다 /
the water stagnates / and causes a pressure /
물이 고인다 / 그래서 압력을 유발한다 /
which accumulates inside us.
우리 안에 누적되는

(A) (3) To learn to let go, / [to not cling and allow the flow of the river,] / 정답 단서-3
병렬① 병렬②(to 생략)
놓아주는 법을 배우는 것은 / 매달리지 않고 강의 흐름을 허락하는 것은 /
is to live without resistances; /
저항 없이 사는 것이다 /
being the creators of constructive changes /
건설적인 변화의 창조자가 되는 것 / 선행사
that bring about improvements / and widen our horizons.
주격 관계대명사
개선을 가져오는 / 그리고 우리의 시야를 넓히는

[전문 해석]

(1)당신의 삶에 중요한 변화가 일어날 때, 당신의 반응을 관찰해라. (2)만약 당신이 그 변화를 받아들이는 것에 저항한다면, 그것은 당신이 두렵기 때문에, 즉 (당신이) 무언가 잃는 것을 두려워하기 때문이다.
(C) (7)어쩌면 당신은 (당신의) 지위, 재산, 소유물, 또는 돈을 잃을지도 모른다. (8)그 변화는 당신이 특권이나 위신을 잃는 것을 의미할지도 모른다. (9)어쩌면 그 변화로 당신은 어떤 사람이나 장소에서 멀어지게 된다.
(B) (4)인생에서 이러한 모든 것들은 왔다가도 사라지고, 그런 다음 다른 것들이 나타나고, 그것들 또한 사라질 것이다. (5)그것은 끊임없는 움직임 속의 강과 같다. (6)만약 우리가 그 흐름을 멈추려고 노력한다면, 우리는 댐을 만들고, 물이 고여서 우리 안에 누적되는 압력을 유발한다.
(A) (3)놓아주는 법을 배우는 것, 즉 매달리지 않고 강의 흐름을 허락하는 것은 저항 없이 사는 것이며, 개선을 가져오고 우리의 시야를 넓히는 건설적인 변화의 창조자가 되는 것이다.

문제편 p.189

[정답 확인]

주어진 글 다음에 이어질 글의 순서로 가장 적절한 것은?

① (A) — (C) — (B) ② (B) — (A) — (C) ③ (B) — (C) — (A)
④ (C) — (A) — (B) ✔ (C) — (B) — (A)

[문제 풀이]

지문은 변화가 일어날 때 무언가 잃을 것을 두려워하여 저항하기보다는 개선을 위해 변화를 받아들이라고 말한다. 문장 (7)~(9)는 문장 (2)의 'losing something'에 대한 구체적인 예시이므로, 주어진 글 다음에는 (C)가 오며, 문장 (7)~(9)의 예시들을 문장 (4)에서 'all these things'로 받고 있으므로 (C) 다음에는 (B)가 온다. 마지막으로, 변화에 저항하는 것이 흐르는 물을 억지로 막는 것과 같다고 설명하는 문장 (5)~(6) 다음에 변화를 저항 없이 받아들이는 것을 강의 흐름을 허락하는 것에 비유한 (A)가 와야 한다. 따라서 정답은 ⑤ '(C) — (B) — (A)'이다.

[중요 어휘]

□ observe	동사 관찰하다, 목격하다
□ resist	동사 저항하다, 반대하다
□ property	명사 재산, 소유물, 부동산
□ possession	명사 소유물, 재산
□ privilege	명사 특권, 특혜
□ prestige	명사 위신, 명망
□ constant	형용사 끊임없는, 변함없는
□ stagnate	동사 (물이) 고이다, 침체되다
□ accumulate	동사 누적되다, 축적되다
□ cling	동사 매달리다, 고수하다
□ resistance	명사 저항, 반대
□ bring about	가져오다, 초래하다
□ widen	동사 넓히다, 키우다
□ horizon	명사 시야, 수평선

10 2020년 11월 36번 (정답률 65%) 정답 ④

[지문 끊어 읽기] 유대 관계와 직업 정보

(1) Mark Granovetter / 정답 단서-1
Mark Granovetter는 /
examined the extent / to which information about jobs flowed /
(선행사 / 전치사+관계대명사 / S' / V')
정도를 조사했다 / 직업에 대한 정보가 흘러 들어오는 /
through weak versus strong ties / among a group of people.
약한 대 강한 유대 관계를 통해 / 한 무리의 사람들 사이에서

(C) (6) He found / that only a sixth of jobs / 정답 단서-1
(명사절 접속사 / S'(선행사))
그는 발견했다 / 직업의 6분의 1만이 /
that came via the network / were from strong ties, /
(주격 관계대명사 / V')
관계망을 통해 오는 / 강한 유대 관계로부터 온다는 것을 /
with the rest coming via medium or weak ties; /
그리고 나머지는 중간이나 약한 유대 관계로부터 온다는 것을 /
and with more than a quarter coming via weak ties.
그리고 4분의 1 이상은 약한 유대 관계로부터 온다는 것을

(7) Strong ties can be more homophilistic.
강한 유대 관계는 더 동족 친화적일 수 있다

(8) Our closest friends / are often those who are most like us. 정답 단서-2
우리의 가장 친한 친구들은 / 종종 우리와 가장 비슷한 사람들이다

(A) (2) This means / that they might have information / 정답 단서-2
이것은 의미한다 / 그들이 정보를 가지고 있을 수 있음을 /
that is most relevant to us, / but it also means /
우리에게 가장 의미 있는 / 하지만 그것은 또한 의미한다 /
that it is information / to which we may already be exposed.
(선행사 / 전치사+관계대명사)
그것이 정보임을 / 우리가 이미 접하고 있을지도 모르는

(3) In contrast, / our weaker relationships /
대조적으로 / 우리의 더 약한 인간 관계는 /
are often with people / who are more distant / 정답 단서-3
종종 사람들과 함께이다 / 더 멀리 떨어져 있는 /
both geographically and demographically.
지리적으로나 인구 통계학적으로나 모두

(B) (4) Their information is more novel. 정답 단서-3
그들의 정보는 더 새롭다

(5) Even though we talk to these people less frequently, /
비록 우리가 이 사람들과 덜 빈번하게 말을 하지만 /
we have so many weak ties /
(so ~ that …: 너무 ~해서 … 하다)
우리는 너무나도 많은 약한 유대 관계를 가지고 있어서 /
that they end up being a sizable source of information, /
결국 그것들은 정보의 엄청난 원천이 된다 /
especially of information /
특히 정보의 /
to which we don't otherwise have access.
우리가 다른 방법으로는 접근하지 못하는

[중요 구문]

(6) He found [that only a sixth of jobs that came via the network were from strong ties, **with** (the rest) (coming via ~); and **with** (more than a quarter) (coming via weak ties)]. [ ]: 명사절(found의 목적어절)
(명사절 접속사 / S', 선행사 / 주격 관계대명사절 / V')

힌트 밑줄 친 부분은 with 분사구문으로, 'with A V-ing'는 '그리고 A가 ~하다, A가 ~하면서'라고 해석함. 참고로 본문에서는 A가 능동적으로 행동하는 상황이므로 현재분사(V-ing)를 쓰지만 A와 행동이 수동의 관계일 때는 과거분사(-ed)를 씀.

[전문 해석]

(1)Mark Granovetter는 한 무리의 사람들 사이에서 약한 (유대 관계) 대 강한 유대 관계를 통해 직업에 대한 정보가 흘러 들어오는 정도를 조사했다.
(C) (6)그는 관계망을 통해 오는 직업 (정보)의 6분의 1만이 강한 유대 관계로부터 오며, 나머지는 중간이나 약한 유대 관계로부터 오고, 4분의 1 이상은 약한 유대 관계로부터 온다는 것을 발견했다. (7)강한 유대 관계는 더 동족 친화적일 수 있다. (8)우리의 가장 친한 친구들은 종종 우리와 가장 비슷한 사람들이다.
(A) (2)이것은 그들이 우리에게 가장 의미 있는 정보를 가지고 있을 수 있음을 의미하지만, 그것은 또한 그것이 우리가 이미 접하고 있을지도 모르는 정보임을 의미한다. (3)대조적으로 우리의 더 약한 인간 관계는 종종 지리적으로나 인구 통계학적으로나 모두 더 멀리 떨어져 있는 사람들과 함께이다.
(B) (4)그들의 정보는 더 새롭다. (5)비록 우리가 이 사람들과 덜 빈번하게 말을 하지만, 우리는 너무나도 많은 약한 유대 관계를 가지고 있어서, 결국 그것들(약한 유대 관계)은 정보의, 특히 우리가 다른 방법으로는 접근하지 못하는 정보의 엄청난 원천이 된다.

[정답 확인]

주어진 글 다음에 이어질 글의 순서로 가장 적절한 것은?

① (A) — (C) — (B) ② (B) — (A) — (C) ③ (B) — (C) — (A)
✔ (C) — (A) — (B) ⑤ (C) — (B) — (A)

[문제 풀이]

강한 유대 관계보다 약한 유대 관계를 통해 직업에 대한 정보를 더 많이 얻을 수 있다는 내용의 글이다. 먼저, 문장 (6)의 'He'는 문장 (1)의 'Mark Granovetter'를 지칭하며, 문장 (6)의 내용은 문장 (1)의 조사 결과에 해당하므로, 주어진 문장 다음에는 (C)가 온다. 다음으로, 문장 (2)의 'they'는 문장 (8)에서 언급된 '우리의 가장 친한 친구들'을 나타내므로 (C) 다음에는 (A)가 오며, 문장 (4)의 'Their'은 문장 (3)의 '지리적으로나 인구통계학적으로나 모두 더 멀리 떨어져 있는 사람들'을 나타내므로 (A) 다음에는 (B)가 온다. 따라서 정답은 ④ '(C) — (A) — (B)'이다.

[중요 어휘]

□ examine	동사 조사하다, 검사하다
□ extent	명사 정도, 범위
□ tie	명사 유대 관계 / 동사 묶다
□ via	전치사 ~을 통해(=through)
□ quarter	명사 4분의 1, 분기(3개월)
□ homophilistic	형용사 동족 친화적인
□ relevant	형용사 의미 있는, 관련된

□ expose	동사 접하게 하다, 노출시키다
□ in contrast	대조적으로
□ distant	형용사 멀리 떨어져 있는, 원격의
□ geographically	부사 지리(학)적으로
□ demographically	부사 인구 통계학적으로
□ novel	형용사 새로운, 진기한 / 명사 소설
□ frequently	부사 빈번하게, 자주
□ end up V-ing	결국 ~하게 되다
□ sizable	형용사 엄청난 (크기의), 꽤 큰
□ otherwise	부사 다른 방법으로, 그게 아니면

11 2018년 11월 37번 (정답률 60%) 정답 ⑤

[지문 끊어 읽기] 올바른 다이어트 방법

(1) Some fad diets might have you /
O
몇몇 유행하는 다이어트는 당신이 ~하게 할 수 있다 /

힌트 「have+O+V-ing/형용사」는 '~한 상황에 놓이게 하다, ~한 반응을 보이게 하다'라는 의미임.

running a caloric deficit, / 정답 단서-1
O·C
열량 부족에 시달리게 /

and while this might encourage weight loss, /
그리고 이것은 체중 감소를 촉진할 수는 있으나 /

it has no effect on improving body composition, /
이것은 체성분을 개선하는 데는 아무런 효과가 없다 /

and it could actually result in a loss of muscle mass.
그리고 이것은 실제로는 근육량의 감소를 초래할 수도 있다

(C) (6) Calorie restriction can also / 정답 단서-1
열량 제한은 또한 ~할 수도 있다 /

cause your metabolism to slow down, /
V①
당신의 신진대사를 느려지게 할 /

and significantly reduce energy levels.
V②
그리고 에너지 수준을 현저히 감소시킬

(7) Controlling caloric intake /
S
열량 섭취를 조절하는 것은 /

to deliver the proper amount of calories /
적절한 양의 열량을 전달하기 위해 /

so that the body has the energy / it needs / 정답 단서-2
신체가 에너지를 가질 수 있도록 / 그것이 필요로 하는 /

to function and heal / is the only proper approach.
V
기능하고 치유되기 위해서 / 유일한 올바른 접근법이다

정답 단서-2 정답 단서-3
(B) (4) Your body also needs / the right balance of key macronutrients /
당신의 신체는 또한 필요로 한다 / 필수 다량 영양소의 적절한 균형을 /

to heal and grow stronger.
치유되고 더 강해지기 위해서

(5) These macronutrients, /
이러한 다량 영양소는 /

which include protein, carbohydrates, and healthy fats, /
단백질, 탄수화물, 그리고 건강에 좋은 지방을 포함하는 /

can help your body maximize its ability /
5형식V O O·C
당신의 신체가 그것의 능력을 극대화하도록 도울 수 있다 /

to repair, rebuild, and grow stronger.
회복하고, 재건하고, 더 강해지기 위한

(A) (2) Timing is also important.
시기도 중요하다

중요 글의 순서를 파악하는 문제에서는 지시사와 관사를 잘 살펴봐야 함. 지시형용사 these가 사용되었다는 것은 문장 (3)의 앞부분에서 이미 key macronutrients에 관해 언급한 적이 있다는 것임.

(3) By eating the right combinations / of these key macronutrients /
알맞은 조합을 섭취함으로써 / 이러한 필수 다량 영양소의 / 정답 단서-3

at strategic intervals throughout the day, /
하루 중에 전략적인 간격으로 /

we can help our bodies / heal and grow even faster.
5형식V O O·C
우리는 우리의 신체가 ~하도록 도울 수 있다 / 훨씬 더 빠르게 치유되고 성장하도록

[전문 해석]

(1)몇몇 유행하는 다이어트는 당신이 열량 부족에 시달리게 할 수 있는데, 이것(열량 부족)은 체중 감소를 촉진할 수는 있으나, 체성분을 개선하는 데는 아무런 효과가 없으며, 실제로는 근육량의 감소를 초래할 수도 있다.
(C) (6)열량 제한은 또한 당신의 신진대사를 느려지게 할 수도 있고, 에너지 수준을 현저히 감소시킬 수도 있다. (7)신체가 (제대로) 기능하고 치유되기 위해서 그것(신체)이 필요로 하는 에너지를 가질 수 있도록, 적절한 양의 열량을 전달하기 위해 열량 섭취를 조절하는 것은 (다이어트에서) 유일한 올바른 접근법이다.
(B) (4)당신의 신체는 또한 치유되고 더 강해지기 위해서 필수 다량 영양소의 적절한 균형을 필요로 한다. (5)단백질, 탄수화물, 그리고 건강에 좋은 지방을 포함하는 이러한 다량 영양소는, 당신의 신체가 회복하고, 재건하고, 더 강해지기 위한 (그것의) 능력을 극대화하도록 도울 수 있다.
(A) (2)시기도 중요하다. (3)하루 중에 전략적인 간격으로 이러한 필수 다량 영양소의 알맞은 조합을 섭취함으로써, 우리는 우리의 신체가 훨씬 더 빠르게 치유되고 성장하도록 도울 수 있다.
- macronutrient(다량 영양소): 신체활동의 연료로 사용되는, 비교적 많은 양을 섭취해야 하는 영양소로, 일반적으로는 탄수화물, 단백질, 지방의 3대 영양소를 가리킨다.

[정답 확인]

주어진 글 다음에 이어질 글의 순서로 가장 적절한 것은?

① (A) — (C) — (B) ② (B) — (A) — (C) ③ (B) — (C) — (A)
④ (C) — (A) — (B) ✔ (C) — (B) — (A)

[문제 풀이]

주어진 문장은 열량 부족을 초래하는 다이어트의 부작용을 설명하고 있다. 따라서 열량 제한의 또 다른 문제점과 그 대안을 제시하는 (C)가 먼저 나오고, 필수 다량 영양소의 균형 잡힌 섭취도 필요하다는 점을 설명하는 (B)가 뒤따르고, 마지막으로는 그러한 영양소를 섭취하는 시기 역시 중요하다는 내용의 (A)가 오는 것이 자연스럽다. 따라서 정답은 ⑤ '(C) — (B) — (A)'이다.

[중요 어휘]

□ deficit	명사 부족, 적자
□ composition	명사 성분, 구성
□ result in	~을 초래하다, (그 결과) ~이 되다
□ mass	명사 (질)량, 크기
□ restriction	명사 제한, 제약, 구속
□ metabolism	명사 신진대사
□ significantly	부사 현저히, 상당히
□ intake	명사 섭취, 흡입
□ function	동사 (제대로) 기능하다, 작용하다 / 명사 기능, 작용
□ key	형용사 필수의, 핵심의 / 명사 열쇠, 비결
□ carbohydrate	명사 탄수화물
□ combination	명사 조합(물), 결합(물)
□ strategic	형용사 전략적인, 전략상 중요한
□ interval	명사 간격, (중간) 휴식 시간

핵심 '획기적인 발견(breakthrough)'이라는 용어가 과학이 실제 작동하는 방식에 대해 오해를 낳는다고 이야기하면서, 실제 하나의 발견이 있기까지는 수많은 과학자들의 연구와 노력이 필요하다고 설명하는 글임.

12 2019년 11월 37번 (정답률 60%) 정답 ④

[지문 끊어 읽기] 획기적인 발견에 대한 오해

(1) Like the physiological discoveries /
생리학적 발견들처럼 /

정답 단서-1
of the late nineteenth century, / today's biological breakthrough /
S
19세기 말의 / 오늘날 생물학의 획기적인 발견은 /

has fundamentally altered our understanding /
V①(have+p.p.: 현재완료시제)
우리의 이해를 근본적으로 바꾸어 왔다 /

of how the human organism works /
인체가 작동하는 방식에 대한 /

and will change medical practice / fundamentally and thoroughly.
V②(미래시제)
그리고 의료 행위를 변화시킬 것이다 / 근본적으로 그리고 완전히

(C) (6) The word "breakthrough," / however, / seems to imply / 정답 단서-1
'획기적인 발견'이라는 단어는 / 하지만 / 의미하는 것처럼 보인다 /
in many people's minds / an amazing, unprecedented revelation /
많은 이들의 마음속에서 / 놀랍고 전례 없는 발견을 /
that, in an instant, makes everything clear.
삽입구 5형식V O O·C(형용사)
순식간에 모든 것을 명백하게 만드는

(7) Science doesn't actually work that way. 정답 단서-2
실제로 과학은 그렇게 작동하지 않는다

★중요 문장 (6)에서 '획기적인 발견'에 대한 사람들의 일반적인 생각을 제시한 후, 문장 (7)에서는 그러한 통념이 잘못되었다고 말하고 있으므로 이 다음에는 문장 (6)에서 언급된 획기적인 발견에 대한 설명과 상반된 내용이 이어질 것임을 예상할 수 있음.

(A) (2) Remember the scientific method, / 정답 단서-2
과학적 방법을 기억하는가 /
which you probably first learned about /
당신이 아마 처음으로 배웠던 /
back in elementary school?
초등학교 때

(3) It has a long and difficult process /
그것은 길고도 어려운 과정을 지닌다 /
of observation, hypothesis, experiment, testing, modifying, retesting, /
관찰, 가설, 실험, 검증, 수정, 재검증의 /
and retesting again and again and again. 정답 단서-3
그리고 되풀이되는 재검증의

(B) (4) That's how science works, / 정답 단서-3
그것이 과학이 작동하는 방식이다 /
and the breakthrough understanding /
그리고 획기적인 이해는 /
of the relationship between our genes and chronic disease /
우리의 유전자와 만성질병 간의 관계에 대한 /
happened in just that way, / building on the work of scientists /
분사구문
바로 그러한 방식으로 일어났다 / 과학자들의 연구를 기반으로 하여 /
from decades — even centuries — ago.
수십 년, 심지어 수 세기 전으로부터의

(5) In fact, / it is still happening; / the story continues to unfold /
사실 / 그것은 아직도 일어나고 있다 / 그 이야기는 계속 펼쳐진다 /
as the research presses on.
연구가 계속됨에 따라

힌트 on은 무언가를 밀어붙여 앞으로 계속 나아간다는 의미가 있으므로, 여기서 'the research presses on'은 연구가 계속된다는 뜻임.

[중요 구문]

(6) The word "breakthrough," ~ seems to imply ~ an amazing, unprecedented revelation [that ~ makes everything clear].
imply의 목적어 [ ]: 주격 관계대명사절(revelation 수식)

[전문 해석]

(1)19세기 말의 생리학적 발견들처럼 오늘날 생물학의 획기적인 발견은 인체가 작동하는 방식에 대한 우리의 이해를 근본적으로 바꾸어 왔으며, 의료 행위를 근본적으로 그리고 완전히 변화시킬 것이다.
(C) (6)하지만 많은 이들의 마음속에서 '획기적인 발견'이라는 단어는 순식간에 모든 것을 명백하게 만드는 놀랍고 전례 없는 발견을 의미하는 것처럼 보인다. (7)실제로 과학은 그렇게 작동하지 않는다.
(A) (2)당신이 아마 초등학교 때 처음으로 배웠던 과학적 방법을 기억하는가? (3)그것은 관찰, 가설, 실험, 검증, 수정, 재검증, 그리고 되풀이되는 재검증의 길고도 어려운 과정을 지닌다.
(B) (4)그것이 과학이 작동하는 방식이며, 우리의 유전자와 만성질병 간의 관계에 대한 획기적인 이해는 수십 년, 심지어 수 세기 전으로부터의 과학자들의 연구를 기반으로 하여, 바로 그러한 방식으로 일어났다. (5)사실 그것은 아직도 일어나고 있으며, 연구가 계속됨에 따라 그 이야기는 계속 펼쳐진다.

[정답 확인]

주어진 글 다음에 이어질 글의 순서로 가장 적절한 것은?

① (A) — (C) — (B) ② (B) — (A) — (C) ③ (B) — (C) — (A)
✔④ (C) — (A) — (B) ⑤ (C) — (B) — (A)

[문제 풀이]

'획기적인 발견'에 대한 글로, '획기적'이라는 용어가 주는 느낌 때문에 많은 사람들이 획기적인 발견에 대해 잘못된 인식을 갖고 있다는 (C)가 먼저 오며, 실제 과학에서의 발견이 하루아침에 일어나는 것이 아니라는 내용의 (A)와 (B)가 (C) 다음에 온다. 그런데 문장 (4)의 '그것(That)'은 문장 (3)의 내용을 받은 것이므로, (A) 다음에는 (B)가 와야 한다. 따라서 정답은 ④이다.

[중요 어휘]

□ physiological	형용사 생리학적인, 생리적인
□ breakthrough	명사 획기적인 발견, 돌파구
□ fundamentally	부사 근본적으로, 완전히
□ alter	동사 바꾸다, 변하다
□ organism	명사 유기체, 생물
□ practice	명사 행위, 관행
□ thoroughly	부사 완전히, 철저히
□ imply	동사 의미하다, 암시하다
□ unprecedented	형용사 전례 없는
□ revelation	명사 발견, 폭로
□ method	명사 방법, 방식, 수단
□ observation	명사 관찰, 의견
□ hypothesis	명사 가설, 추측
□ modify	동사 수정하다, 수식하다
□ gene	명사 유전자
□ chronic	형용사 만성적인
□ build on	~을 기반으로 하다, ~을 발판으로 삼다
□ unfold	동사 펼쳐지다, 퍼지다

핵심 수렵 채집 문화 또한 현대 문명 못지 않게 가치 있는 삶의 방식이라는 점을 지적하면서, 수렵 채집 문화를 무차별적으로 제압하는 현 세태를 '자멸적'이라고 표현하며 비판하는 글임.

13 2020년 11월 37번 (정답률 60%) 정답 ⑤

[지문 끊어 읽기] 수렵 채집 문화의 가치

(1) When we think of culture, / we first think /
우리가 문화에 대해 생각할 때 / 우리는 먼저 생각한다 /
of human cultures, / of *our* culture.
인간의 문화에 대해서 / 즉 '우리의' 문화에 대해서

(2) We think / of computers, airplanes, fashions, teams, and pop stars.
우리는 생각한다 / 컴퓨터, 비행기, 패션, 팀, 그리고 팝 스타에 대해

(3) For most of human cultural history, / none of those things existed. 정답 단서-1
대부분의 인간 문화의 역사에서 / 그러한 것들은 전혀 존재하지 않았다

(C) (9) For hundreds of thousands of years, /
수십만 년 동안 /
no human culture had / a tool with moving parts. 정답 단서-1
어떠한 인간의 문화도 가지고 있지 않았다 / 움직이는 부품들이 있는 도구를

(10) Well into the twentieth century, / various human foraging cultures /
20세기까지도 / 다양한 인간의 수렵 채집 문화는 /
retained / tools of stone, wood, and bone.
보유했다 / 돌, 나무, 그리고 뼈로 된 도구들을

(11) We might pity human hunter-gatherers /
우리는 수렵 채집인들을 불쌍히 여길 수 있다 /
for their stuck simplicity, / but we would be making a mistake. 정답 단서-2
그들의 꽉 막힌 단순함 때문에 / 하지만 우리가 실수하고 있는 것일 수 있다

(B) (7) They held extensive knowledge, / 정답 단서-2
그들은 광범위한 지식을 가졌다 /
knew deep secrets of their lands and creatures.
그들의 땅과 생명체의 심오한 비밀을 알았다

(8) And they experienced rich and rewarding lives; / 정답 단서-2
그리고 그들은 풍요롭고 보람있는 삶을 경험했다 /
we know so / because when their ways were threatened, /
우리는 그렇게 알고 있다 / 왜냐하면 그들의 방식이 위협당했을 때 /
they fought / to hold on to them, / to the death. 정답 단서-3
그들이 싸웠기 때문에 / 그것을 고수하기 위해 / 죽을 때까지

(A) (4) Sadly, / this remains true / 정답 단서-3
슬프게도 / 이것은 여전히 사실이다 /

as the final tribal peoples get overwhelmed /
=when
마지막 부족민들이 제압당할 때에도 /
by those / who value money above humanity.
선행사 주격 관계대명사절
사람들에 의해 / 인간성보다 돈을 더 가치 있게 여기는

(5) We are living in their end times / and, to varying extents, /
우리는 그들의 종말의 시대에 살고 있다 / 그리고 다양한 정도로 /
we're all contributing to those endings.
우리는 모두 그러한 종말에 기여하고 있다

(6) Ultimately / our values may even prove self-defeating.
결국 / 우리의 가치는 자멸적이라는 것을 심지어 증명한 셈인지도 모른다

[전문 해석]

(1)우리가 문화에 대해 생각할 때, 우리는 먼저 인간의 문화, 즉 '우리의' 문화에 대해서 생각한다. (2)우리는 컴퓨터, 비행기, 패션, (스포츠) 팀, 그리고 팝 스타에 대해 생각한다. (3)대부분의 인간 문화의 역사에서 그러한 것들은 전혀 존재하지 않았다.
(C) (9)수십만 년 동안 어떠한 인간의 문화도 움직이는 부품들이 있는 도구를 가지고 있지 않았다. (10)20세기까지도 다양한 인간의 수렵 채집 문화는 돌, 나무, 그리고 뼈로 된 도구들을 보유했다. (11)우리는 수렵 채집인들을 그들의 꽉 막힌 단순함 때문에 불쌍히 여길 수 있지만, 우리가 실수하고 있는 것일 수 있다.
(B) (7)그들은 광범위한 지식을 가졌고, 그들의 땅과 생명체의 심오한 비밀을 알았다. (8)그리고 그들은 풍요롭고 보람있는 삶을 경험했다. (적어도) 우리는 그렇게 알고 있는데, 왜냐하면 그들의 방식이 위협당했을 때, 그들이 그것(삶의 방식)을 고수하기 위해 죽을 때까지 싸웠기 때문이다.
(A) (4)슬프게도 인간성보다 돈을 더 가치 있게 여기는 사람들에 의해 마지막 부족민들이 제압당할 때에도 이것은 여전히 사실이다. (5)우리는 그들(부족민들)의 종말의 시대에 살고 있고, 우리는 모두 다양한 정도로 그러한 종말에 기여하고 있다. (6)결국 우리의 가치는 자멸적이라는 것을 심지어 증명한 셈인지도 모른다.

[정답 확인]

주어진 글 다음에 이어질 글의 순서로 가장 적절한 것은?

① (A) — (C) — (B) ② (B) — (A) — (C) ③ (B) — (C) — (A)
④ (C) — (A) — (B) ⑤ (C) — (B) — (A)

[문제 풀이]

주어진 문장 (1)~(3)은 우리가 '문화'에 대해 생각할 때 '컴퓨터, 비행기, 패션' 등 특정한 문화만을 문화로 생각하는 경향이 있으나, 실제로 대부분의 인간 문화 역사에서 이러한 것들은 존재하지 않았다고 설명한다. 한편, 문장 (9)는 문장 (3)과 대구를 이루며, 내용상 논지와 일맥상통하므로, 주어진 글 다음에는 가장 먼저 (C)가 온다. 다음으로, 수렵 채집인들의 꽉 막힌 단순함을 불쌍히 여기는 우리의 태도가 실수일 수 있다는 문장 (11) 다음에는 그 근거로 수렵 채집인들이 문화적으로 빈곤하지 않았다는 내용이 와야 한다. 따라서 (C) 다음에는 (B)가 옴으로써 수렵 채집인들의 광범위한 지식과 가치로운 삶에 대해 언급하는 것이 자연스럽다. 마지막으로, 나름의 문화적 가치를 지닌 부족민들(수렵 채집인들)의 삶을 열등한 것으로 여기며 이러한 문화의 종말에 기여한다는 점에서 우리의 가치가 자멸적이라고 지적하는 (A)가 온다. 따라서 글의 순서로 가장 적절한 것은 ⑤ '(C) — (B) — (A)'이다.

[중요 어휘]

□ forage	동사 수렵 채집하다
□ retain	동사 보유하다, 가지다, 유지하다
□ pity	동사 불쌍히 여기다, 동정하다 / 명사 동정, 유감
□ hunter-gatherer	명사 수렵 채집인
□ stuck	형용사 꽉 막힌, 갇힌, 꼼짝 못하는
□ simplicity	명사 단순함, 간단함
□ extensive	형용사 광범위한, 넓은
□ rewarding	형용사 보람있는, 가치 있는
□ threatened	형용사 위협당한, 협박당한
□ hold on to	~을 고수하다[지키다]
□ remain	동사 여전히 ~이다, 남다, 머무르다
□ overwhelm	동사 제압하다, 압도하다
□ humanity	명사 인간성
□ contribute	동사 기여하다, 공헌하다
□ prove	동사 증명하다, 판명되다, 알려지다
□ self-defeating	형용사 (행위·계획·논의 등이 예상과는 달리) 자멸적인

14 2022년 9월 36번 (정답률 60%) 정답 ④

[지문 끊어 읽기] 환경을 통한 뇌 발달

(1) If DNA were the only thing that mattered, /
만약 DNA가 유일하게 중요한 것이라면 /
힌트 가정법 과거는 현재 사실의 반대를 가정하며, 'If+S+과거V ~, S+조동사의 과거형+동사원형'의 형태로 쓰임. 이때 if절의 동사가 be동사일 경우, 주어의 단/복수와 관계없이 주로 'were'을 씀.
there would be no particular reason /
특별한 이유가 없을 것이다 /
to build meaningful social programs / 정답 단서-1 DNA만 중요하다면 의미 있는 사회 프로그램을 만들 특별한 이유가 없음.
형용사적 용법
의미 있는 사회 프로그램을 만들 /
to pour good experiences into children /
병렬① - 형용사적 용법
아이들에게 좋은 경험을 부어주는 /
and protect them from bad experiences.
병렬②
그리고 그들을 해로운 경험들로부터 보호하는

(C) (7) But brains require the right kind of environment / 정답 단서-1 하지만 뇌가 바르게 발달하려면 적절한 종류의 환경이 필요함.
하지만 뇌는 적절한 종류의 환경을 필요로 한다 /
if they are to correctly develop.
그것이 바르게 발달하려면
힌트 if절의 be to 용법은 '~하려면'이라는 (의도의) 의미임.

(8) When the first draft of the Human Genome Project came to completion /
Human Genome Project의 첫 번째 초안이 완성되었을 때 /
at the turn of the millennium, / one of the great surprises /
새천년에 들어 / 가장 큰 놀라움 중 하나는 /
was that humans have only about twenty thousand genes. 정답 단서-2 인간은 대략 2만 개의 유전자만 갖고 있음.
명사절 접속사(주격 보어)
인간이 대략 2만 개의 유전자만 갖고 있다는 것이었다
정답 단서-2 이 숫자를 접한 생물학자들은 놀람.

(A) (2) This number came as a surprise to biologists:
이 숫자는 생물학자들에게 놀라움으로 다가왔다

(3) given the complexity of the brain and the body, / 정답 단서-3 복잡한 뇌와 신체를 위해선 수십만 개의 유전자가 필요할 것으로 추정되어 왔음.
given (that): ~을 고려할 때
뇌와 신체의 복잡성을 고려했을 때 /
it had been assumed /
형식상의 주어
추정되어 왔다 /
[that hundreds of thousands of genes would be required].
수십만 개의 유전자가 필요할 것이라고
[ ]: 내용상의 주어

(B) (4) So how does the massively complicated brain, /
그러면 어떻게 엄청나게 복잡한 뇌가 /
with its eighty-six billion neurons, /
860억 개의 뉴런을 갖고 있는 /
get built from such a small recipe book? 정답 단서-3 대략 2만 개의 적은 유전자만으로 어떻게 극도로 복잡한 뇌가 만들어질 수 있었는지에 대한 의문을 제기함.
=문장 (8)의 about twenty thousand genes
그렇게 작은 요리책으로부터 만들어질 수 있었을까

(5) The answer relies on a clever strategy /
그 해답은 한 영리한 전략에 있다 /
implemented by the genome:
게놈에 의해 실행된

(6) build incompletely / and let world experience refine.
사역V O O·C
불완전하게 만들어라 / 그리고 세상 경험이 정교하게 다듬게 하라

[전문 해석]

(1)만약 DNA가 유일하게 중요한 것이라면, 아이들에게 좋은 경험을 부어주고 그들을 해로운 경험들로부터 보호하는 의미 있는 사회 프로그램을 만들 특별한 이유가 없을 것이다.
(C) (7)하지만 뇌가 바르게 발달하려면 그것은 적절한 종류의 환경을 필요로 한다. (8)Human Genome Project의 첫 번째 초안이 새천년에 들어 완성되었을 때, 가장 큰 놀라움 중 하나는 인간이 대략 2만 개의 유전자만 갖고 있다는 것이었다.
(A) (2)이 숫자는 생물학자들에게 놀라움으로 다가왔다. (3)이는 뇌와 신체의 복잡성을 고려했을 때, 수십만 개의 유전자가 필요할 것이라고 추정되어 왔기 때문이었다.

문제편 p.192

(B) (4)그러면 860억 개의 뉴런을 갖고 있는 엄청나게 복잡한 뇌가 어떻게 그렇게 작은 요리책으로부터 만들어질 수 있었을까? (5)그 해답은 게놈에 의해 실행된 한 영리한 전략에 있다. (6)불완전하게 만들고 세상 경험이 정교하게 다듬게 하라.

- genome(게놈, 유전체): 한 개체가 가진 모든 유전 정보
- Human Genome Project(휴먼 게놈 프로젝트, 인간 유전체 사업): 2003년 완료된 인간의 유전체(게놈)를 이루는 염기 서열 전체를 밝히고자 한 프로젝트로, 의학 및 과학 분야에 많은 충격을 주었음.

[정답 확인]

주어진 글 다음에 이어질 글의 순서로 가장 적절한 것은?

① (A) — (C) — (B) ② (B) — (A) — (C) ③ (B) — (C) — (A)
✔ (C) — (A) — (B) ⑤ (C) — (B) — (A)

[문제 풀이]

이 지문은 유전자와 환경에 따른 뇌의 발달에 대해 설명하는 글이다. 먼저 문장 (1)에 따르면 DNA, 즉 유전자만이 중요하다면 아이들을 위한 의미 있는 사회 프로그램을 만들 특별한 이유가 없다고 한다. 한편 But으로 시작하는 문장 (7)에서는 뇌가 바르게 발달하려면 (사회 프로그램과 같은) 적절한 종류의 환경이 필요하다고 언급하면서 문장 (1)과 대조되는 내용을 설명하고 있으므로 주어진 문장 다음에는 (C)가 온다. 다음으로, 문장 (2)의 'This number(이 숫자)'는 문장 (8)의 'about twenty thousand genes(대략 2만 개의 유전자)'를 지칭하므로 (C) 다음에는 (A)가 온다. 이어지는 문장 (3)에서는 뇌와 신체의 복잡성에 대해 언급했고, 이를 문장 (4)의 So로 이어받아 작은 요리책으로부터, 즉 대략 2만 개의 유전자만으로 어떻게 엄청나게 복잡한 뇌가 만들어질 수 있었을지에 대한 의문을 제기하고 있으므로 (A) 다음에는 (B)가 온다. 그러므로 정답은 ④ '(C) — (A) — (B)'이다.

[중요 어휘]

☐ **matter**	동사 중요하다
☐ **require**	동사 필요로 하다, 요구하다
☐ **draft**	명사 초안, 원고 / 동사 초안을 작성하다
☐ **completion**	명사 완성, 완료
☐ **millennium**	명사 새천년
☐ **gene**	명사 유전자
☐ **assume**	동사 추정하다
☐ **massively**	부사 엄청나게, 대량으로
☐ **complicated**	형용사 복잡한
☐ **rely on**	~에 있다[의존하다]
☐ **implement**	동사 실행하다
☐ **refine**	동사 정교하게 다듬다, 개선하다

15 2023년 6월 37번 (정답률 60%) 정답 ③

[지문 끊어 읽기] 토착종 황금 두꺼비의 멸종 원인

(1) Species [that are found in only one area] /
S, 선행사 [ ]: 주격 관계대명사절
오직 한 지역에서만 발견되는 종들은 /
are called endemic species /
V①
토착종이라고 불린다 /
힌트 「call A B (A를 B라고 부르다)」의 수동형인 「A+be called+B (A는 B라고 불리다)」가 쓰였음.
and are especially vulnerable to extinction. 정답 단서-1
V②
그리고 멸종에 특히 취약하다
토착종은 한 지역에서만 발견되며 멸종에 특히 취약함.

(B) (4) They exist / on islands and in other unique small areas, /
=Endemic species
그것들은 존재한다 / 섬들과 다른 독특한 작은 지역들에 /
especially in tropical rain forests /
특히 열대 우림에 / 선행사
where most species are highly specialized. 정답 단서-1
관계부사
대부분의 종들이 매우 특화된
토착종들은 섬이나 다른 독특한 작은 지역들, 특히 열대 우림에 서식함.

(5) One example is the brilliantly colored golden toad /
하나의 예는 번쩍이는 색깔의 황금 두꺼비이다 /
[once found only in a small area of lush rain forests /
한때 푸르게 우거진 열대 우림의 작은 지역에서만 발견되었던 /
in Costa Rica's mountainous region]. 정답 단서-2
코스타리카 산악 지역에 있는 [ ]: 과거분사구
토착종의 한 예로는 한때 코스타리카 산악 지역의 열대 우림의 작은 지역에서 발견되었던 '황금 두꺼비'가 있음.

(C) (6) Despite living in the country's well-protected Monteverde Cloud Forest Reserve, /
전치사 V-ing
그 나라의 잘 보전된 Monteverde Cloud Forest Reserve에서 살았음에도 불구하고 /
by 1989, / the golden toad had apparently become extinct.
과거완료(had p.p.)
1989년쯤에 / 그 황금 두꺼비는 외관상 멸종되었다
정답 단서-2 황금 두꺼비는 잘 보전된 서식지에 살았음에도 불구하고 1989년쯤에 멸종됨.

(7) Much of the moisture / [that supported its rain forest habitat] /
선행사 [ ]: 주격 관계대명사
습기의 많은 부분은 / 그것의 열대 우림 서식지를 지탱해 주었던 /
came in the form of moisture-laden clouds /
습기를 실은 구름의 형태로 왔다 /
[blowing in from the Caribbean Sea]. 정답 단서-3
카리브해로부터 불어 들어오는 [ ]: 현재분사구
카리브해에서 불어 들어온 습기를 실은 구름이 황금 두꺼비의 서식지 환경을 지탱해 주었음.

(A) (2) But warmer air from global climate change /
S①
그러나 전 세계적인 기후 변화로 인한 더 따뜻한 공기가 /
caused these clouds to rise, /
V① O O·C
이 구름들을 상승하게 했다 /
★중요 문장 (7)에서는 황금 두꺼비의 서식지에 습기를 제공해 주었던 구름에 대해 설명하고 있고, 문장 (2)에서는 그 구름이 기후 변화로 더 이상 서식지에 습기를 제공해 주지 못한 상황을 설명하고 있으므로, 상황의 반전을 나타내기 위해 'But(그러나)'을 썼음.
depriving the forests of moisture, /
=and it deprived
숲에서 습기를 제거해버렸다 /
힌트 「deprive A of B (A에게서 B를 빼앗다[박탈하다])」라는 뜻으로, 이 문장에서는 '숲에서 습기를 제거해버렸다'라는 뜻으로 의역함.
and the habitat for the golden toad and many other species dried up. 정답 단서-3
S② V②
그리고 황금 두꺼비와 다른 많은 종들의 서식지는 말라버렸다
그러나 기후 변화로 인해 구름들이 황금 두꺼비 서식지까지 불어 들어오지 못하고 상승해 버림에 따라 서식지가 말라 버림.

(3) The golden toad appears to be /
황금 두꺼비는 ~인 것처럼 보인다 /
one of the first victims of climate change /
one of+복수N
기후 변화의 첫 번째 희생양들 중 하나 /
[caused largely by global warming]. [ ]: 과거분사구
대개 지구 온난화에 의해 유발된

[전문 해석]

(1)오직 한 지역에서만 발견되는 종들은 토착종이라고 불리며, 멸종에 특히 취약하다.
(B) (4)그것들은 섬들과 다른 독특한 작은 지역들, 특히 대부분의 종들이 매우 특화된 열대 우림에 존재한다. (5)하나의 예는 한때 코스타리카 산악 지역에 있는 푸르게 우거진 열대 우림의 작은 지역에서만 발견되었던 번쩍이는 색깔의 황금 두꺼비이다.
(C) (6)그 나라의 잘 보전된 Monteverde Cloud Forest Reserve에서 살았음에도 불구하고, 1989년쯤에 그 황금 두꺼비는 외관상 멸종되었다(멸종된 것으로 보인다). (7)그것의 열대 우림 서식지를 지탱해 주었던 습기의 많은 부분은 카리브해로부터 불어 들어오는 습기를 실은 구름의 형태로 왔다.
(A) (2)그러나 전 세계적인 기후 변화로 인한 더 따뜻한 공기가 이 구름들을 상승하게 하여 숲에서 습기를 제거해버렸으며, 황금 두꺼비와 다른 많은 종들의 서식지는 말라버렸다. (3)황금 두꺼비는 대개 지구 온난화에 의해 유발된 기후 변화의 첫 번째 희생양들 중 하나인 것처럼 보인다.

[정답 확인]

주어진 글 다음에 이어질 글의 순서로 가장 적절한 것은?

① (A) — (C) — (B) ② (B) — (A) — (C) ✔ (B) — (C) — (A)
④ (C) — (A) — (B) ⑤ (C) — (B) — (A)

[문제 풀이]

문맥상 문장 (4)의 '그것들(They)'은 문장 (1)의 '토착종(endemic species)'을 나타내며, 문장 (4)에서 제시된 장소들은 문장 (1)에서 언급한 토착종이 서식하는 '오직 한 지역'을 구체적으로 서술한 것이다. 또, (B)의 문장 (5)에는 토착종의 예시인 '황금 두꺼비'를 처음으로 소개하고 있으므로, 주어진 문장 다음에는 (B)가 가장 먼저 오는 것이 자연스럽다. 다음으로, 토착종인 황금 두꺼비가 잘 보전된 서식지에도 불구하고 결국 멸종하게 되었다는 (C)가 온 후, 황금 두꺼비 멸종의 원인을 '서식지에 습기를 제공하던 구름이 기후 변화로 더 이상 공급되지 못하여 서식지가 말라버린 것'으로 설명하는 (A)가 와야 한다. 따라서 글의 순서로 가장 적절한 것은 ③ '(B) — (C) — (A)'이다.

[중요 어휘]

☐ **species**	명사 (분류상의) 종
☐ **endemic**	형용사 (한 지역의) 토착의, 토종의, 고유의

□ vulnerable	형용사 취약한, 저항력이 없는
□ extinction	명사 멸종
□ tropical	형용사 열대의, 열대 지방의
□ rain forest	명사 (열대) 우림
□ specialized	형용사 특수화된, 분화된
□ brilliantly	부사 번쩍거리게, 눈부시게
□ lush	형용사 푸르게 우거진, 무성한
□ mountainous	형용사 산악의, 산이 많은
□ apparently	부사 외관상, 보아하니
□ extinct	형용사 멸종된, 사라진
□ habitat	명사 서식지, 자생지
□ moisture-laden	형용사 습기를 실은[머금은]
□ laden	형용사 (짐을) 실은, (~을) 잔뜩 실은, (~이) 가득한
□ cause A to V	A가 ~하게 하다
□ victim	명사 희생양, 희생자

핵심 습관이 형성되는 것의 이점과 단점을 차례로 설명하고 있는 글임. 이점과 단점에 대한 설명이 논리적으로 배열되도록 연결사와 대명사에 주의하면서 문장을 배열해야 함.

16 2020년 3월 36번 (정답률 55%) 정답 ⑤

[지문 끊어 읽기] 습관이 형성되는 것의 이점과 단점

(1) Habits create the foundation / for mastery.
습관은 기반을 만든다 / 숙달의

(2) In chess, / it is only after / the basic movements of the pieces /
체스에서 / 오직 ~ 이후이다 / 말의 기본적인 움직임이 /
have become automatic / that a player can focus /
자동화된 / 체스를 두는 사람이 집중할 수 있게 되는 것은 /
on the next level of the game.
게임의 다음 레벨에

(3) Each chunk of information / that is memorized /
each + 단수명사: 단수취급 / 선행사 / 주격 관계대명사절
각각의 정보 덩어리는 / 암기된 /
opens up the mental space / for more effortful thinking. 정답 단서-1
단수V
정신적 공간을 연다 / 더 많은 노력을 요하는 사고를 위한

정답 단서-1
(C) (10) This is true for anything / you attempt.
이것은 어느 것에든 적용된다 / 당신이 시도하는

(11) When you know the simple movements so well /
당신이 단순한 동작을 정말 잘 알고 있어서 /
that you can perform them without thinking, /
당신이 생각을 하지 않고도 그것을 수행할 수 있을 때 /
you are free to pay attention / to more advanced details. 정답 단서-2
당신은 자유롭게 집중하게 된다 / 더 높은 수준의 세부 사항에

힌트 When이 이끄는 종속절 안에 'so + 부사(well) + that S V'가 쓰였고, '정말[너무] ~해서 …하다'라고 해석하면 됨.

(12) In this way, / habits are the backbone /
이렇게 / 습관은 근간이 된다 /
of any pursuit of excellence.
어떤 탁월함의 추구에서의

(B) (7) However, / the benefits of habits come at a cost. 정답 단서-2
그러나 / 습관의 이점에는 대가가 따른다

(8) At first, / each repetition develops fluency, speed, and skill.
처음에 / 각각의 반복은 유창함, 속도, 그리고 기술을 발달시킨다

(9) But then, / as a habit becomes automatic, /
하지만 그 후 / 습관이 자동화됨에 따라 /
you become less sensitive to feedback. 정답 단서-3
당신은 피드백에 덜 민감해지게 된다

(A) (4) You fall into mindless repetition. 정답 단서-3
당신은 머리를 쓸 필요가 없는 반복에 빠진다

(5) It becomes easier / to let mistakes slide. 정답 단서-3
더 쉬워진다 / 실수를 내버려두는 것이

(6) When you can do it "good enough" automatically, /
당신이 자동적으로 '충분히 잘' 할 수 있을 때 /
you stop thinking / about how to do it better. 정답 단서-3
당신은 생각하는 것을 멈춘다 / 어떻게 그것을 더 잘 할 수 있을지에 대해

[중요 구문]

(2) In chess, it is [only after the basic movements ~ have become automatic] that a player can focus ~.
강조할 내용

힌트 only after이 이끄는 부사절을 강조하기 위해 'It is ~ that' 강조 구문이 사용됨.

[전문 해석]

(1)습관은 숙달의 기반을 만든다. (2)체스에서 체스를 두는 사람이 게임의 다음 레벨에 집중할 수 있게 되는 것은 오직 말의 기본적인 움직임이 자동화된 이후이다. (3)각각의 암기된 정보 덩어리는 더 많은 노력을 요하는 사고를 위한 정신적 공간을 연다.
(C) (10)이것은 당신이 시도하는 어느 것에든 적용된다. (11)당신이 단순한 동작을 정말 잘 알고 있어서 생각을 하지 않고도 그것을 수행할 수 있을 때, 당신은 더 높은 수준의 세부 사항에 자유롭게 집중하게 된다. (12)이렇게 습관은 어떤 탁월함의 추구에서(든 그것)의 근간이 된다.
(B) (7)그러나 습관의 이점에는 대가가 따른다. (8)처음에 각각의 반복은 유창함, 속도, 그리고 기술을 발달시킨다. (9)하지만 그 후 습관이 자동화됨에 따라 당신은 피드백에 덜 민감해지게 된다.
(A) (4)당신은 머리를 쓸 필요가 없는 반복에 빠진다. (5)실수를 내버려두는 것이 더 쉬워진다. (6)당신이 자동적으로 '충분히 잘' 할 수 있을 때, 당신은 어떻게 그것(일)을 더 잘 할 수 있을지에 대해 생각하는 것을 멈춘다.

[정답 확인]

주어진 글 다음에 이어질 글의 순서로 가장 적절한 것은?

① (A) — (C) — (B) ② (B) — (A) — (C) ③ (B) — (C) — (A)
④ (C) — (A) — (B) ✔ (C) — (B) — (A)

[문제 풀이]

지문은 습관 형성이 이점도 있지만 동시에 단점도 있다는 것을 언급한다. 주어진 글은 습관이 숙달의 기본이라고 말하며 습관의 이점으로 글을 시작한다. 어느 행동에 익숙해져서 생각을 하지 않고도 더 높은 수준의 행동을 할 수 있다는 이점을 언급하는 비슷한 맥락의 (C)가 바로 다음에 와야 한다. 그러나 (B)의 첫 문장은 지문의 흐름이 이점에서 단점으로 바뀌는 부분이므로, (B)는 이점이 모두 언급된 후인 (C) 다음에 와야 한다. (B)의 마지막 문장에 제시된 습관의 단점, 즉 습관이 자동화되어 피드백에 덜 민감해지게 된다는 것은 (A)에서 이어지므로 (B) 뒤에는 (A)가 와야 한다. 따라서 답은 ⑤이다.

[중요 어휘]

□ foundation	명사 기반, 기초, 토대
□ mastery	명사 숙달, 통달
□ chunk	명사 덩어리, 많은 양
□ effortful	형용사 노력을 요하는, 노력이 필요한
□ be free to V	자유롭게 ~하다, 마음껏 ~하다
□ backbone	명사 근간, 중추
□ pursuit	명사 추구, 추격
□ excellence	명사 탁월함, 뛰어남
□ come at a cost	대가가 따르다
□ fluency	명사 유창함
□ sensitive	형용사 민감한, 세심한
□ mindless	형용사 머리를 쓸 필요가 없는, 무심한
□ let A slide	A를 내버려두다[소홀히 하다]

17 2021년 9월 37번 (정답률 55%) 정답 ③

[지문 끊어 읽기] 생물의 크기에 따른 열 손실과 생활 방식

(1) Heat is lost at the surface, /
열은 표면에서 손실된다 /
so the more surface area you have relative to volume, /
the 비교급, the 비교급: ~할수록 더 …하다
그러므로 당신이 체적에 비례하여 더 많은 표면적을 가질수록 /
the harder you must work to stay warm.
당신은 따뜻함을 유지하기 위해 더 열심히 움직여야 한다

문제편 p.193

(2) That means /
그것은 의미한다 /
that little creatures have to produce heat more rapidly /
작은 생물들이 더 빠르게 열을 생산해야 한다는 것을 /
than large creatures. 정답 단서-1
큰 생물들보다

(B) (6) They must therefore lead / completely different lifestyles. 정답 단서-1
그러므로 그들은 이끌어야 한다 / 완전히 다른 생활 방식을

(7) An elephant's heart beats / just thirty times a minute, /
S V
코끼리의 심장은 뛴다 / 1분에 단 30회를 /
a human's sixty, / a cow's between fifty and eighty, /
인간은 60회 / 소는 50회에서 80회 사이 /
but a mouse's beats six hundred times a minute /
하지만 쥐는 1분에 600회를 뛴다 /
— ten times a second.
즉 1초에 10회

힌트 각 밑줄 친 부분 뒤에는 heart와 동사 beats가 생략되어 나열된 형태임.

(8) Every day, / just to survive, / the mouse must eat / 정답 단서-2
매일 / 단지 살아남기 위해서 / 쥐는 먹어야 한다 /
about 50 percent of its own body weight.
자신의 몸무게의 약 50퍼센트를

정답 단서-2
(C) (9) We humans, / by contrast, / need to consume /
우리 인간은 / 대조적으로 / 먹으면 된다 /
only about 2 percent of our body weight /
단지 우리 몸무게의 약 2퍼센트만 /
to supply our energy requirements.
우리의 에너지 요구량을 공급하기 위해

(10) One area / where animals are curiously uniform /
S
하나의 영역은 / 동물들이 기묘하게도 획일적인 /
is with the number of heartbeats / they have in a lifetime. 정답 단서-3
V
심장 박동의 수이다 / 그들이 평생 동안 가지는

(A) (3) Despite the vast differences in heart rates, /
심장 박동 수의 막대한 차이에도 불구하고 /
정답 단서-3
nearly all mammals have / about 800 million heartbeats in them /
거의 모든 포유동물은 가진다 / 약 8억 회의 심장 박동 수를 /
if they live an average life.
만약 그들이 평균 수명을 산다면

(4) The exception is humans.
예외는 인간이다

(5) We pass 800 million heartbeats / after twenty-five years, /
우리는 8억 회의 심장 박동 수를 넘는다 / 25년 이후에 /
and just keep on going for another fifty years /
그리고 또 다른 50년 동안 계속한다 /
and 1.6 billion heartbeats or so.
그리고 심장 박동 수가 16억 회 정도 된다

[전문 해석]

(1)열은 표면에서 손실되므로 당신이 체적에 비례하여 더 많은 표면적을 가질수록, 당신은 따뜻함을 유지하기 위해 더 열심히 움직여야 한다. (2)그것은 작은 생물들이 큰 생물들보다 더 빠르게 열을 생산해야 한다는 것을 의미한다.
(B) (6)그러므로 그들은 완전히 다른 생활 방식을 이끌어야 한다(완전히 다른 생활 방식으로 살아야 한다). (7)코끼리의 심장은 1분에 단 30회를 뛰고, 인간은 60회, 소는 50회에서 80회 사이를 뛰지만, 쥐는 1분에 600회, 즉 1초에 10회를 뛴다. (8)매일 단지 살아남기 위해서, 쥐는 자신의 몸무게의 약 50퍼센트를 먹어야 한다.
(C) (9)대조적으로, 우리 인간은 우리의 에너지 요구량을 공급하기 위해 단지 우리 몸무게의 약 2퍼센트만 먹으면 된다. (10)동물들이 기묘하게도 획일적인 하나의 영역은 그들(동물들)이 평생 동안 가지는 심장 박동의 수이다.
(A) (3)심장 박동 수의 막대한 차이에도 불구하고, 거의 모든 포유동물은 만약 그들이 평균 수명을 산다면 약 8억 회의 심장 박동 수를 가진다. (4)예외는 인간이다. (5)우리는 25년 이후에 8억 회의 심장 박동 수를 넘고, 또 다른(그 이후) 50년 동안 계속해서 심장 박동 수가 16억 회 정도 된다.

[정답 확인]

주어진 글 다음에 이어질 글의 순서로 가장 적절한 것은?
① (A) — (C) — (B) ② (B) — (A) — (C) ③ (B) — (C) — (A)
④ (C) — (A) — (B) ⑤ (C) — (B) — (A)

[문제 풀이]

생물의 크기에 따라 열 손실의 정도가 다르기 때문에 생활 방식 또한 달라지고, 그에 따라 생물들의 심장 박동 수에 차이가 있다는 내용의 글이다. 먼저, 문장 (2)에서 'little creatures(작은 생물들)'와 'large creatures(큰 생물들)'의 차이로 인해 문장 (6)의 'different lifestyles(다른 생활 방식)'가 초래되었으므로, 문장 (6)의 'They(그들)'는 문장 (2)의 'little creatures(작은 생물들)'와 'large creatures(큰 생물들)'를 지칭한다. 따라서 주어진 문장 다음에는 (B)가 온다. 다음으로, 문장 (9)에서 'by contrast(대조적으로)'를 기준으로 쥐의 에너지 요구량을 이야기하는 문장 (8)의 내용과 대조되어 인간의 에너지 요구량에 대한 내용이 전개되므로 (B) 다음에는 (C)가 온다. 마지막으로 문장 (10)의 심장 박동 수와 관련하여 추가적인 설명이 문장 (3)부터 이어지므로 (C) 다음에는 (A)가 온다. 따라서 정답은 ③이다.

[중요 어휘]

☐ **surface area**	표면적
☐ **relative to**	~에 비례하여
☐ **volume**	명사 체적
☐ **creature**	명사 생물, 사람
☐ **lead**	동사 이끌다, 살아가다
☐ **curiously**	부사 기묘하게도, 지독하게
☐ **uniform**	형용사 획일적인 / 명사 유니폼
☐ **vast**	형용사 막대한, 어마어마한
☐ **heart rate**	심장 박동 수
☐ **pass**	동사 넘다, 지나가다

18 2021년 11월 37번 (정답률 55%) 정답 ⑤

[지문 끊어 읽기] 생태계의 회복력

(1) Because we are told / that the planet is doomed, /
명사절 접속사
우리는 듣기 때문에 / 지구가 운이 다한 것이라고 /
we do not register the growing number of scientific studies /
우리는 과학적 연구의 증가하는 수를 기억하지 않는다 /
demonstrating the resilience of other species.
다른 종의 회복력을 증명하는

(2) For instance, / climate-driven disturbances are affecting /
예를 들어 / 기후로 인한 교란이 영향을 미치고 있다 /
the world's coastal marine ecosystems / 정답 단서-1 기후로 인한 교란이 세계 해안의 해양 생태계에 심각한 위기를 초래함.
세계 해안의 해양 생태계에 /
more frequently / and with greater intensity.
병렬① 병렬②
더 자주 / 그리고 더 큰 강도로

정답 단서-1 세계적인 문제인 'This'는 문장 (2)의 내용을 가리킴.
(C) (7) This is a global problem / that demands urgent action.
선행사 주격 관계대명사절
이것은 세계적인 문제이다 / 긴급한 조치를 요구하는

힌트 having been이 생략되고 접속사 as는 생략되지 않은 분사구문으로, 원문은 'as instances were detailed ~'임.

(8) Yet, / as detailed in a 2017 paper in *BioScience*, /
하지만 / *BioScience*의 2017년 논문에서 자세히 설명된 것처럼 /
there are also instances /
선행사
경우들이 또한 있다 /
where marine ecosystems show remarkable resilience /
관계부사
해양 생태계가 놀라운 회복력을 보여 주는 /
to acute climatic events. 정답 단서-2 앞서 언급된 기후로 인한 교란 문제와는 대조적으로, 해양 생태계가 놀라운 회복력을 보여 주는 경우들이 있다고 함.
극심한 기후의 사건들에

힌트 관계부사 where은 선행사로 장소를 나타내는 말 이외에 상황, 사건, 경우 등 다양한 명사가 올 수 있음.

(B) (5) In a region in Western Australia, / for instance, / 정답 단서-2 해양 생태계가 놀라운 회복력을 보여 준 예시 하나를 제시함.
Western Australia의 한 지역에서 / 예를 들어 /
up to 90 percent of live coral was lost /
살아 있는 산호의 90퍼센트까지 소실되었다 /
when ocean water temperatures rose, /
바닷물 온도가 상승했을 때 /

[causing what scientists call coral bleaching]. [ ]: 분사구문(연속동작)
그리고 과학자들이 산호 백화라 부르는 것을 야기했다

(6) Yet / in some sections of the reef surface, /
하지만 / 암초 표면의 몇몇 부분에서 /
44 percent of the corals recovered / within twelve years.
산호의 44퍼센트가 회복했다 / 12년 이내에 정답 단서-3 해양 생태계의 놀라운 회복력을 보여 주는 예시①

(A) (3) Similarly, / kelp forests / ★중요 해양 생태계가 놀라운 회복력을 보여 주는 예시 중 하나이나, 'Similarly(마찬가지로)'를 통해 앞에 다른 예시가 먼저 제시되어야 한다는 것을 알 수 있음.
마찬가지로 / 켈프 숲이 /
[hammered by intense El Niño water-temperature increases] /
극심한 엘니뇨 수온 상승에 의해 강타당한 / [ ]: 과거분사구
recovered within five years. 정답 단서-3 해양 생태계의 놀라운 회복력을 보여 주는 예시②
5년 이내에 회복했다

(4) By studying these "bright spots," /
이러한 '밝은 지점들'을 연구함으로써 /
[situations where ecosystems persist / 힌트 생태계가 지속되는 상황, 즉 어떤 공간에서 이루어지는 공간적 상황을 의미하므로, situations를 수식하는 관계부사로 where이 사용됨.
생태계가 지속되는 상황들 /
even in the face of major climatic impacts], /
중대한 기후의 영향에 직면한 순간에도 /
we can learn / [what management strategies help /
우리는 배울 수 있다 / 어떠한 관리 전략들이 도움이 되는지 / [ ]: 간접의문문(의문사+S+V)
to minimize destructive forces / and nurture resilience].
파괴적인 힘을 최소화하는 데 / 그리고 회복력을 키우는 데

[전문 해석]

(1)우리는 지구가 운이 다한 것이라고 듣기 때문에 우리는 다른 종의 회복력을 증명하는 과학적 연구의 증가하는 수를 기억하지 않는다. (2)예를 들어 기후로 인한 교란이 세계 해안의 해양 생태계에 더 자주 그리고 더 큰 강도로 영향을 미치고 있다.
(C) (7)이것은 긴급한 조치를 요구하는 세계적인 문제이다. (8)하지만 *BioScience*의 2017년 논문에서 자세히 설명된 것처럼, 해양 생태계가 극심한 기후의 사건들에 놀라운 회복력을 보여 주는 경우들이 또한 있다.
(B) (5)예를 들어 Western Australia의 한 지역에서 바닷물 온도가 상승했을 때, 살아 있는 산호의 90퍼센트까지 소실되었으며 과학자들이 산호 백화라 부르는 것을 야기했다. (6)하지만 암초 표면의 몇몇 부분에서 산호의 44퍼센트가 12년 이내에 회복했다.
(A) (3)마찬가지로 극심한 엘니뇨 수온 상승에 의해 강타당한 켈프 숲이 5년 이내에 회복했다. (4)이러한 '밝은 지점들', 즉 중대한 기후의 영향에 직면한 순간에도 생태계가 지속되는 상황들을 연구함으로써 우리는 어떠한 관리 전략들이 파괴적인 힘을 최소화하고 회복력을 키우는 데 도움이 되는지를 배울 수 있다.

[정답 확인]

주어진 글 다음에 이어질 글의 순서로 가장 적절한 것은?

① (A) — (C) — (B) ② (B) — (A) — (C) ③ (B) — (C) — (A)
④ (C) — (A) — (B) ⑤ (C) — (B) — (A)

[문제 풀이]

생태계의 회복력을 보여 주는 사례들을 연구함으로써 생태계 관리 전략 방향을 잡을 수 있다는 내용의 글이다. 먼저, 문장 (7)의 'This'는 문장 (2) 전체 내용을 지칭하므로 주어진 문장 다음에는 (C)가 온다. 다음으로, 문장 (8)에서 언급된 'instances where marine ecosystems show remarkable resilience(해양 생태계가 놀라운 회복력을 보여 주는 경우들)'에 대한 예시가 문장 (5)의 'for instance'와 이어지는 문장 (6)을 통해 설명되므로, (C) 다음에는 (B)가 온다. 마지막으로 문장 (3)이 문장 (6)의 예시를 'Similarly'로 이어받으면서 켈프 숲이 회복한 또 다른 예시를 언급하므로 (B) 다음에는 (A)가 온다. 따라서 정답은 ⑤ '(C) — (B) — (A)'이다.

[중요 어휘]

□ **doomed**	형용사 운이 다한
□ **register**	동사 기억하다(주로 부정문에서 쓰임), 등록하다
□ **demonstrate**	동사 증명하다, 행동으로 보여 주다
□ **resilience**	명사 회복력
□ **disturbance**	명사 교란, 방해, 소란
□ **intensity**	명사 강도
□ **urgent**	형용사 긴급한, 시급한
□ **detail**	동사 자세히 설명하다, 상술하다
□ **remarkable**	형용사 놀라운, 놀랄 만한
□ **acute**	형용사 극심한, 예민한
□ **coral**	명사 산호
□ **bleaching**	명사 백화, 표백
□ **reef**	명사 암초
□ **hammer**	동사 강타하다 / 명사 망치
□ **persist**	동사 지속되다, 계속하다
□ **destructive**	형용사 파괴적인
□ **nurture**	동사 키우다, 양육하다, 육성하다

19 2022년 3월 36번 (정답률 55%) 정답 ②

[지문 끊어 읽기] 상호 의존적인 logos와 mythos

(1) The ancient Greeks used to describe / used to V: ~하곤 했다
고대 그리스인들은 설명하곤 했다 / 고대 그리스인들은 'logos'와 'mythos'라는 두 가지 사고방식을 설명했음.
two very different ways of thinking / — *logos* and *mythos*. 정답 단서-1
두 가지의 매우 다른 사고방식을 / 'logos'와 'mythos'

(2) *Logos* roughly referred to the world / 정답 단서-1 'logos'와 'mythos' 중 'logos'에 대한 설명
'logos'는 대략 세계를 지칭했다 / 힌트 'the+형용사'는 명사처럼 사용할 수 있으므로 밑줄 친 부분은 전치사 of의 목적어로 사용됨.
of the logical, the empirical, the scientific. 동격의 of
논리적, 경험적, 과학적

(B) (5) *Mythos* referred to the world / 정답 단서-1 'logos'와 'mythos' 중 'mythos'에 대한 설명
'Mythos'는 세계를 지칭했다 /
of dreams, storytelling and symbols. 동격의 of
꿈, 스토리텔링, 상징의

(6) Like many rationalists today, /
오늘날의 많은 합리주의자들처럼 /
some philosophers of Greece prized *logos* / 병렬①
그리스의 일부 철학자들은 'logos'를 높이 평가했다 /
and looked down at *mythos*. 정답 단서-2 'logos'와 'mythos'에 대한 관점① 병렬②
그리고 'mythos'를 경시했다

(7) Logic and reason, / they concluded, / make us modern; / 삽입절 5형식V O O·C
논리와 이성이 / 그들은 결론지었다 / 우리를 현대적으로 만든다고 /
storytelling and mythmaking are primitive.
그리고 스토리텔링과 신화 만들기는 원시적이라고

(A) (3) But / lots of scholars / then and now /
그러나 / 많은 학자들은 / 그때나 지금이나 /
— including many anthropologists, sociologists and philosophers today — /
오늘날의 많은 인류학자, 사회학자, 그리고 철학자를 포함하여 /
see [a more complicated picture], / [ ]: 선행사
더 복잡한 상황을 이해한다 / 정답 단서-2 'logos'와 'mythos'에 대한 관점②: 서로 뒤얽혀 있고 상호 의존적임.
where *mythos* and *logos* are intertwined and interdependent. 관계부사(계속적 용법)
'mythos'와 'logos'가 뒤얽혀 있고 상호 의존적인 문장 (3)의 관점에 따르면 과학 자체(logos)는 이야기(mythos)에 의존한다고 함.

(4) Science itself, / according to this view, / relies on stories. 정답 단서-3
과학 자체가 / 이 관점에 따르면 / 이야기에 의존한다

(C) (8) The frames and metaphors / we use to understand the world / 목적격 관계대명사절(which 생략)
생각의 틀과 은유는 / 우리가 세상을 이해하기 위해 사용하는 /
shape the scientific discoveries we make; / 정답 단서-3 문장 (4)에 덧붙여 생각의 틀과 은유(mythos)는 과학적 발견(logos)을 형성한다고 함.
우리가 하는 과학적 발견을 형성한다 /
they even shape what we see.
그것들은 심지어 우리가 보는 것을 형성한다

(9) When our frames and metaphors change, /
우리의 생각의 틀과 은유가 바뀌면 /

the world itself is transformed.
세상 자체가 변한다

(10) The Copernican Revolution involved /
코페르니쿠스 혁명은 포함했다 /
more than just scientific calculation; / it involved a new story /
단순한 과학적 계산보다 더 많은 것을 / 그것은 새로운 이야기를 포함했다 /
about the place of Earth in the universe.
우주 속 지구의 위치에 관한

[전문 해석]

(1)고대 그리스인들은 'logos'와 'mythos'라는 두 가지의 매우 다른 사고방식을 설명하곤 했다. (2)'logos'는 대략 논리적, 경험적, 과학적 세계를 지칭했다.
(B) (5)'Mythos'는 꿈, 스토리텔링, 상징의 세계를 지칭했다. (6)오늘날의 많은 합리주의자들처럼, 그리스의 일부 철학자들은 'logos'를 높이 평가하고 'mythos'를 경시했다. (7)그들은 논리와 이성이 우리를 현대적으로 만들고, 스토리텔링과 신화 만들기를 원시적이라고 결론지었다.
(A) (3)그러나 오늘날의 많은 인류학자, 사회학자, 철학자를 포함하여, 많은 학자들은 그때나 지금이나 'mythos'와 'logos'가 뒤얽혀 있고 상호 의존적인, 더 복잡한 상황을 이해한다. (4)이 관점에 따르면 과학 자체가 이야기에 의존한다.
(C) (8)우리가 세상을 이해하기 위해 사용하는 생각의 틀과 은유는 우리가 하는 과학적 발견을 형성하고, 심지어 우리가 보는 것을 형성한다. (9)우리의 생각의 틀과 은유가 바뀌면 세상 자체가 변한다. (10)코페르니쿠스 혁명은 단순한 과학적 계산보다 더 많은 것을 포함하는데, 우주 속 지구의 위치에 관한 새로운 이야기를 포함했다.

[정답 확인]

주어진 글 다음에 이어질 글의 순서로 가장 적절한 것은?

① (A) — (C) — (B) ✔② (B) — (A) — (C) ③ (B) — (C) — (A)
④ (C) — (A) — (B) ⑤ (C) — (B) — (A)

[문제 풀이]

이 지문은 고대 그리스인들이 설명했던 두 가지 사고방식인 'logos'와 'mythos'를 들어 과학과 세계를 보는 관점에 대해 설명하는 글이다. 먼저, 문장 (1)은 고대 그리스인들이 설명했던 사고방식 두 가지는 'logos'와 'mythos'라고 언급하며, 문장 (2)는 그중 'logos'가 무엇을 지칭하는지 설명한다. 문장 (5)에서는 'mythos'가 무엇을 지칭하는지 설명하고 있으므로 문장 (2) 다음에는 (B)가 오는 것이 흐름상 자연스럽다. 다음으로, 문장 (6)에서 그리스의 일부 철학자들은 'logos'를 높이 평가하고 'mythos'를 경시했다고 언급한다. 역접 접속사 But으로 시작하는 문장 (3)에서는 많은 학자들이 'logos'와 'mythos'가 뒤얽혀 있고 상호 의존적이라고 하며, 'logos'와 'mythos'에 대한 다른 관점을 설명한다. 따라서 (B) 다음에는 (A)가 온다. 이어서 문장 (4)에서는 문장 (3)에서 언급된 관점에 따라 과학 자체가 이야기에 의존한다고 말하는데, 문장 (8)에서 우리가 세상을 이해하기 위해 사용하는 생각의 틀과 은유는 과학적 발견을 형성한다고 설명한다. 이는 다시 말해 과학이 이야기에 기반을 두고 있다는 것이다. 즉 문장 (8)의 내용은 문장 (4)의 내용을 구체화하고 있으므로 (A) 다음에는 (C)가 온다. 따라서 정답은 ②이다.

[중요 어휘]

□ **roughly**	부사 대략, 거의, 거칠게
□ **refer to**	~을 지칭하다, ~에 돌리다
□ **empirical**	형용사 경험적인
□ **rationalist**	명사 합리주의자
□ **prize**	동사 높이 평가하다, 소중하게 여기다 / 명사 상
□ **look down at/on**	~을 경시하다
□ **primitive**	형용사 원시적인
□ **scholar**	명사 학자
□ **anthropologist**	명사 인류학자
□ **see**	동사 이해하다, 보다
□ **picture**	명사 상황 (파악)
□ **intertwine**	동사 뒤얽히다, 밀접하게 관련되다
□ **interdependent**	형용사 상호 의존적인, 서로 의존하는
□ **frame**	명사 (생각의) 틀
□ **metaphor**	명사 은유, 비유
□ **shape**	동사 형성하다 / 명사 모양, 형태
□ **involve**	동사 포함하다, 관련시키다

20 2022년 6월 36번 (정답률 55%) 정답 ⑤

[지문 끊어 읽기] 촉감 수용체

(1) Touch receptors are spread / over all parts of the body, /
촉감 수용체는 퍼져 있다 / 신체 곳곳에 /
but they are not spread evenly.
하지만 그것들은 골고루 퍼져 있지는 않다

(2) Most of the touch receptors are found /
대부분의 촉감 수용체는 발견된다 /
in your fingertips, tongue, and lips. 정답 단서-1 대부분의 촉감 수용체가 발견되는 신체 부분으로 손가락 끝, 혀, 그리고 입술이 있음.
당신의 손가락 끝, 혀, 그리고 입술에서

정답 단서-1 촉감 수용체가 발견되는 신체 부분 중 손가락 끝에 대해 자세히 설명함.
(C) (8) On the tip of each of your fingers, / for example, /
당신의 각각의 손가락 끝에는 / 예를 들어 /
there are about five thousand separate touch receptors.
약 5천 개의 서로 떨어져 있는 촉감 수용체가 있다

(9) In other parts of the body / there are far fewer.
몸의 다른 부분에서는 / 훨씬 더 적다
(far: 비교급 강조 부사)

(10) In the skin of your back, /
당신의 등 피부에는 /
the touch receptors may be as much as 2 inches apart. 정답 단서-2 문장 (9)의 예시로 등 피부를 들었음.
(as ~ as 원급 비교)
촉감 수용체가 2인치만큼 떨어져 있을 수도 있다

정답 단서-2 등 피부의 촉감 수용체를 테스트해 보는 방법을 제시함.
(B) (5) You can test this / for yourself.
당신은 이것을 테스트해 볼 수 있다 / 스스로
★중요 여기서 this는 문장 (10) 전체, 즉 등 피부에는 촉감 수용체가 2인치만큼 떨어져 있을 수도 있다고 한 것을 나타냄.

(6) Have someone poke you in the back /
(병렬①(5형식V) O O·C)
누군가에게 당신의 등을 찌르게 하라 /
with one, two, or three fingers / and try to guess /
(병렬②)
한 손가락, 두 손가락, 또는 세 손가락으로 / 그리고 추측해 보라 /
how many fingers the person used.
(간접의문문)
그 사람이 얼마나 많은 손가락을 사용했는지

정답 단서-3 손가락들이 가까이 있을 때에는 한 개라고 생각할 것이라고 함.
(7) If the fingers are close together, / you will probably think /
만약 손가락들이 서로 가까이 붙어 있다면 / 당신은 아마 생각할 것이다 /
it was only one.
(목적어절(명사절 접속사 that 생략))
그것이 단 한 개라고

(A) (3) But if the fingers are spread far apart, / 정답 단서-3 손가락끼리 멀리 떨어져 있을 때에는 손가락들을 각각 느낄 수 있다고 함.
하지만 만약 손가락끼리 멀리 떨어져 있다면 /
you can feel them individually.
당신은 그것들을 각각 느낄 수 있다

(4) Yet if the person does the same thing / on the back of your hand /
하지만 만약 그 사람이 같은 행동을 한다면 / 당신의 손등에 /
(with your eyes closed, / so that you don't see /
(부사절 접속사(~하기 위해, ~하도록))
당신의 눈을 감은 채로 / 당신이 알지 못하게 하기 위해 /
how many fingers are being used), /
(간접의문문)
몇 개의 손가락이 사용되고 있는지 /
you probably will be able to tell easily, /
당신은 아마 쉽게 구별할 수 있을 것이다 /
even when the fingers are close together.
손가락이 서로 가까이 있을 때조차도

힌트 'with+명사+분사'는 분사구문의 일종으로 주절과 동시에 발생하는 상황을 나타내며 '~한 채로, ~하면서'로 해석함. 명사와 분사의 관계가 능동인 경우에는 현재분사, 수동인 경우에는 과거분사가 분사 자리에 옴.

[전문 해석]

(1)촉감 수용체는 신체 곳곳에 퍼져 있지만 골고루 퍼져 있지는 않다. (2)대부분의 촉감 수용체는 손가락 끝, 혀, 그리고 입술에서 발견된다.
(C) (8)예를 들어, 각각의 손가락 끝에는 약 5천 개의 서로 떨어져 있는 촉감 수용체가 있다. (9)몸의 다른 부분에서는 훨씬 더 적다. (10)당신의 등 피부에는 촉감 수용체가 2인치만큼 떨어져 있을 수도 있다.

(B) (5)당신은 스스로 이것을 테스트해 볼 수 있다. (6)누군가에게 당신의 등을 한 손가락, 두 손가락, 또는 세 손가락으로 찌르게 하고 그 사람이 얼마나 많은 손가락을 사용했는지 추측해 보라. (7)만약 손가락이 서로 가까이 붙어 있다면, 당신은 아마 그것이 단 한 개라고 생각할 것이다.
(A) (3)하지만 만약 손가락끼리 멀리 떨어져 있다면, 당신은 그것들을 각각 느낄 수 있다. (4)하지만 만약 그 사람이 당신의 손등에 같은 행동을 한다면(몇 개의 손가락이 사용되고 있는지 모르게 하기 위해, 당신의 눈을 감은 채로), 당신은 아마 손가락이 서로 가까이 있을 때조차도 쉽게 구별할 수 있을 것이다.

[정답 확인]

주어진 글 다음에 이어질 글의 순서로 가장 적절한 것은?

① (A) — (C) — (B) ② (B) — (A) — (C) ③ (B) — (C) — (A)
④ (C) — (A) — (B) ✔ (C) — (B) — (A)

[문제 풀이]

이 지문은 우리 몸의 촉감 수용체에 대해 설명하고 있는 글이다. 먼저, 문장 (2)에서 대부분의 촉감 수용체는 손가락 끝, 혀, 입술에서 발견된다고 했는데, 문장 (8)에서 언급된 신체 부분 중 손가락 끝에 있는 촉감 수용체에 대해 설명하므로 주어진 문장 다음에는 (C)가 온다. 다음으로, 문장 (10)에서 손가락 끝과 달리 촉감 수용체의 수가 적은 신체 부분의 예시로 등 피부를 들었다. 문장 (5)~(6)에서 누군가에게 손가락으로 등을 찌르게 하고 몇 개의 손가락을 사용했는지 추측해 보는 것을 통해 등 피부의 촉감 수용체를 테스트해 볼 수 있다고 하고 있으므로 (C) 다음에는 (B)가 온다. 마지막으로 문장 (7)에서는 앞서 언급한 테스트에서 사용되는 손가락들이 가까이 붙어 있을 때에는 한 개라고 생각할 것이라고 했는데, 문장 (3)에서 But으로 이어받아 손가락끼리 멀리 떨어져 있을 때에는 손가락들을 각각 느낄 수 있다고 하고 있으므로 (B) 다음에는 (A)가 온다. 따라서 정답은 ⑤ '(C) — (B) — (A)'이다.

[중요 어휘]

☐ **receptor**	명사 수용체
☐ **spread**	동사 퍼뜨리다, 펼치다, 바르다 (spread-spread-spread)
☐ **evenly**	부사 골고루, 고르게, 균등하게
☐ **tip**	명사 끝(부분), 조언
☐ **apart**	부사 떨어져, 따로, 산산이
☐ **poke**	동사 (쿡) 찌르다, (머리·손가락·막대기 등을) 내밀다
☐ **close**	형용사 가까운 / 동사 (눈을) 감다, (문을) 닫다
☐ **tell**	동사 구별하다, 말하다

21 2023년 3월 36번 (정답률 55%) 정답 ④

[지문 끊어 읽기] '습관을 부수다'라는 말의 잘못된 영향

(1) Like positive habits, / bad habits exist / on a continuum /
긍정적인 습관들과 마찬가지로 / 나쁜 습관들은 존재한다 / 연속체에 /
of easy-to-change and hard-to-change. 정답 단서-1 나쁜 습관은 변하기 쉬움과 변하기 어려움의 연속체에 있음.
병렬① 병렬②
변하기 쉬움과 변하기 어려움의

(C) (8) When you get toward the "hard" end of the spectrum, /
여러분이 그 연속체의 '어려움'의 끝에 가까워졌을 때 /
note the language you hear /
선행사 목적격 관계대명사절(that 생략)
여러분이 듣는 언어에 주목하라 /
— *breaking* bad habits / and *battling* addiction. 정답 단서-1 주어진 글에 제시된 내용의 예시를 제공함.
V-ing① V-ing②
나쁜 습관을 '부수기' / 그리고 중독과 '싸우기'

✶중요 문장 (1)에서 나쁜 습관을 'easy-to-change'와 'hard-to-change'의 양극단을 가진 연속체(a continuum)로 설명하고, 문장 (8)에서는 그 연속체(the spectrum)에서 'hard end'의 경우를 들고 있음.

(9) It's as if an unwanted behavior is a nefarious villain /
바람직하지 않은 행동은 마치 사악한 악당인 것 같다 /
to be aggressively defeated. 정답 단서-2 바람직하지 않은 행동, 즉 나쁜 습관은 반드시 없애야 할 대상인 것처럼 인식함.
형용사적 용법
격렬하게 패배시켜야 하는

(A) (2) But this kind of language / (and the approaches it spawns) /
=this kind of language
선행사 목적격 관계대명사절(that 생략)
하지만 이러한 종류의 언어는 / (그리고 그것이 낳는 접근법들) /
frames these challenges /
이러한 도전에 틀을 씌운다 /
in a way that isn't helpful or effective. 정답 단서-2 this kind of language는 문장 (8)에서 언급된 나쁜 습관을 부수고 중독과 싸워야 한다는 말(*breaking* bad habits and *battling* addiction)에 해당함.
선행사 주격 관계대명사
도움이 되지 않거나 효과적이지 않은 방식으로

(3) I specifically hope / 힌트 stop의 뒤에 to부정사와 동명사가 올 수 있음. 'stop+to V'는 '~하기 위해 멈추다', 'stop+V-ing'는 '~하는 것을 멈추다'라는 의미 차이가 있음.
나는 특히 바란다 /
we will stop using this phrase: / "break a habit."
우리가 이 구절을 그만 사용하기를 / "습관을 부수다"

(4) This language misguides people.
이 언어는 사람들을 잘못 인도한다

(5) The word "break" sets the wrong expectation /
'부수다'라는 단어는 잘못된 기대를 형성한다 /
for how you get rid of a bad habit. 정답 단서-3 '부수다'라는 단어는 잘못된 인식을 심음.
여러분이 나쁜 습관을 없애는 방법에 대한

(B) (6) This word implies / that if you input a lot of force in one moment, /
명사절 접속사(implies의 목적어절을 이끎)
이 단어는 암시한다 / 만약 여러분이 한순간에 많은 양의 힘을 가한다면 /
the habit will be gone. 정답 단서-3 This word는 문장 (5)의 "break"를 의미함.
그 습관이 사라질 것을

(7) However, / that rarely works, /
="break a habit.", 문장(6)
그러나 / 그것은 거의 작용하지 않는다 /
because you usually cannot get rid of an unwanted habit /
여러분은 대개 바람직하지 않은 습관을 제거할 수 없기 때문이다 /
by applying force one time.
by V-ing: ~함으로써
힘을 한 번 가함으로써

[전문 해석]

(1)긍정적인 습관들과 마찬가지로, 나쁜 습관들은 변하기 쉬움과 변하기 어려움의 연속체에 존재한다.
(C) (8)여러분이 그 연속체의 '어려움'의 끝에 가까워졌을 때, 여러분이 듣는 언어, 즉 나쁜 습관을 '부수기'와 중독과 '싸우기'에 주목하라. (9)바람직하지 않은 행동은 마치 격렬하게 패배시켜야 하는 사악한 악당인 것 같다.
(A) (2)하지만 이러한 종류의 언어(그리고 그것이 낳는 접근법들)는 도움이 되지 않거나 효과적이지 않은 방식으로 이러한 도전에 틀을 씌운다. (3)나는 특히 우리가 이 구절, 즉 "습관을 부수다"를 그만 사용하기를 바란다. (4)이 언어는 사람들을 잘못 인도한다. (5)'부수다'라는 단어는 여러분이 나쁜 습관을 없애는 방법에 대한 잘못된 기대를 형성한다.
(B) (6)이 단어는 만약 여러분이 한순간에 많은 양의 힘을 가한다면 그 습관이 사라질 것을 암시한다. (7)그러나 그것은 거의 작용하지 않는데, 여러분은 대개 힘을 한 번 가함으로써 바람직하지 않은 습관을 제거할 수 없기 때문이다.

[정답 확인]

주어진 글 다음에 이어질 글의 순서로 가장 적절한 것은?

① (A) — (C) — (B) ② (B) — (A) — (C) ③ (B) — (C) — (A)
✔ (C) — (A) — (B) ⑤ (C) — (B) — (A)

[문제 풀이]

이 지문은 나쁜 습관을 없애는 것에 대한 잘못된 인식에 대해 말한다. 먼저, 문장 (1)은 나쁜 습관이 '변하기 쉬움'과 '변하기 어려움'의 연속체에 존재한다고 한다. 이에 대한 설명으로, 문장 (8)에서 그 연속체에서 '어려움'에 가까울 때, 즉 나쁜 습관을 고치기 힘들 때 '부수고 싸우는' 것과 같이 우리가 나쁜 습관과 관련하여 흔히 듣는 말을 예시로 들고 있으므로, 주어진 문장 이후에는 (C)가 온다. 이어서 이런 종류의 언어와 접근법이 효과적이지 않다는 주장을 펼치며 앞 내용과 역접으로 이어지는 (A)가 오는 것이 적절하다. 이어지는 문장 (3)에서 필자는 '부수다'라는 단어를 사용해서는 안 된다고 주장하며, 문장 (4)에서 우리들에게 잘못된 인식을 심을 수 있기 때문이라고 한다. 이에 대한 구체적인 설명으로 문장 (5)에서 '부수다'라는 단어의 문제를 지적하고, (6)에서 이 단어가 손쉽게 나쁜 습관을 없앨 수 있다는 생각을 하게끔 만드는 의미를 포함하고 있다고 설명한다. 그러므로 정답은 ④ '(C) — (A) — (B)'이다.

[오답 풀이]

⑤ - 나쁜 습관을 한번에 고치기 힘들다는 내용의 문장 (7) 뒤에 '이런 종류의 언어와 그 접근법이 효과적이지 않다'는 내용이 역접으로 연결되는 것은 어색하므로 (B) 다음에는 (A)가 올 수 없다.

문제편 p.195

[중요 어휘]

□ continuum	명사 연속체
□ get toward	~에 가까워지다
□ note	동사 ~에 주목하다, 언급하다 / 명사 메모, 쪽지
□ unwanted	형용사 바람직하지 않은, 원치 않는, 반갑지 않은
□ nefarious	형용사 사악한, 비도덕적인, 범죄의
□ aggressively	부사 격렬하게, 공격적으로
□ spawn	동사 (어떤 결과 상황을) 낳다
□ frame	동사 틀을 씌우다 / 명사 틀, 액자, 뼈대
□ specifically	부사 특히, 분명히, 명확하게
□ misguide	동사 잘못 인도하다, 잘못된 길로 이끌다
□ expectation	명사 기대, 예상
□ get rid of	없애다, 제거하다
□ imply	동사 암시하다, 의미하다
□ input	동사 가하다, 투입하다 / 명사 입력, 조언, 투입
□ apply	동사 (손·발 등으로) 힘을 가하다, 적용하다, 신청하다, (연고를) 바르다

핵심 물물 교환의 문제점이 무엇인지, 그리고 돈이 어떻게 그러한 문제들을 해결해줄 수 있는지 설명하는 글임.

22 2019년 6월 36번 (정답률 50%) 정답 ⑤

[지문 끊어 읽기] 물물 교환의 문제점과 돈의 편리함

(1) Without money, / people could only barter.
돈이 없다면 / 사람들은 오직 물물 교환만 할 수 있을 것이다

(2) Many of us barter / to a small extent, / when we return favors. 정답 단서-1
to (a certain) extent: ~한 규모로, ~정도까지
우리 중 다수는 물물 교환을 한다 / 작은 규모로 / 우리가 호의에 보답할 때

(C) (9) A man might offer /
어떤 사람은 제안할지도 모른다 /
to mend his neighbor's broken door /
그의 이웃의 고장난 문을 수리해줄 것을 /
in return for / a few hours of babysitting, / for instance. 정답 단서-1
~에 대한 보답으로 / 몇 시간 동안 아이를 돌봐준 것 / 예를 들어

★중요 문장 (9)의 내용은 문장 (2)에서 언급되었던, 타인의 호의에 보답하기 위해 '작은 규모'로 이루어지는 교환의 예시임.

(10) Yet / it is hard to imagine /
그러나 / 상상하기는 어렵다 /
these personal exchanges working / on a larger scale. 정답 단서-2
이러한 개인적 교환들이 작동하는 것을 / 더 큰 규모로

힌트 5형식 동사 imagine의 목적어로 these personal exchanges, 목적격 보어로 working이 왔음.

(B) (6) What would happen / if you wanted a loaf of bread /
어떤 일이 일어날까 / 만약 당신이 빵 한 덩어리를 원한다면 /
and all you had / to trade / was your new car? 정답 단서-2
그리고 당신이 가지고 있는 전부가 / 교환하기 위해 / 당신의 새 자동차뿐이라면

(7) Barter depends on / the double coincidence of wants, /
물물 교환은 ~에 의존한다 / 욕구의 이중 부합에 /
where not only does the other person happen to have /
부정어 도치 V S
그런데 거기에서는 다른 사람이 우연히 가지고 있을 뿐만 아니라 /
what I want, / but I also have what he wants.
내가 원하는 것을 / 나 또한 그가 원하는 것을 가지고 있다

(8) Money solves all these problems. 정답 단서-3
돈은 이러한 모든 문제를 해결한다

★중요 문장 (8)은 문장 (6)과 (7)에서 언급된 물물 교환의 문제점을 돈이 해결해줄 수 있다고 했고, 문장 (3)~(5)는 해당 문제들이 구체적으로 어떻게 해결되는가에 관한 내용이 이어지고 있음.

(A) (3) There is no need to find someone /
누군가를 찾을 필요가 없다 /
who wants / what you have to trade; /
원하는 / 당신이 교환하기 위해 가지고 있는 것을 /
you simply pay for your goods / with money.
당신은 단순히 당신의 상품의 값을 치른다 / 돈으로

(4) The seller can / then / take the money /
판매자는 ~할 수 있다 / 그러면 / 돈을 받을 /
and buy from someone else.
그리고 다른 누군가로부터 구매할

(5) Money is transferable and deferrable /
돈은 이동이 가능하고 연기할 수 있다 /
— the seller can hold on to it / and buy / when the time is right. 정답 단서-3
판매자는 그것을 계속 보유할 수 있다 / 그리고 구매할 수 있다 / 시기가 적절한 때에

[전문 해석]

(1)돈이 없다면, 사람들은 오직 물물 교환만 할 수 있을 것이다. (2)우리 중 다수는, (타인의) 호의에 보답할 때 작은 규모로 물물 교환을 한다.
(C) (9)예를 들어, 어떤 사람은 몇 시간 동안 아이를 돌봐준 것에 대한 보답으로 (그의) 이웃의 고장난 문을 수리해줄 것을 제안할지도 모른다. (10)그러나, 이러한 개인적 교환들이 더 큰 규모로 작동하는 것을 상상하기는 어렵다.
(B) (6)만약 당신이 빵 한 덩어리를 원하고, 당신이 교환하기 위해 가지고 있는 전부가 당신의 새 자동차뿐이라면 어떤 일이 일어날까? (7)물물 교환은 (상호 간) 욕구의 이중 부합에 의존하는데, 거기에서는 다른 사람이 우연히 내가 원하는 것을 가지고 있을 뿐만 아니라, 나 또한 그가 원하는 것을 가지고 있다. (8)돈은 이러한 모든 문제를 해결한다.
(A) (3)(돈이 있으면) 당신이 교환하기 위해 가지고 있는 것을 원하는 누군가를 찾을 필요가 없다. 당신은 단순히 돈으로 (당신의) 상품의 값을 치른다(치르면 된다). (4)그러면 판매자는 돈을 받고 다른 누군가로부터 (또 다른 상품을) 구매할 수 있다. (5)돈은 이동이 가능하고 (지불을) 연기할 수 있는데 판매자는 그것을 계속 보유하고 있다가 (시기가) 적절한 때에 (상품을) 구매할 수 있다.
- double coincidence of wants(욕구의 이중 부합): 두 거래 당사자가 각각 서로가 원하는 물품을 가지고 있어서 중간에 매개자 없이 직접적으로 물품을 교환하는 현상

[정답 확인]

주어진 글 다음에 이어질 글의 순서로 가장 적절한 것은?

① (A) — (C) — (B) ② (B) — (A) — (C) ③ (B) — (C) — (A)
④ (C) — (A) — (B) ✔ (C) — (B) — (A)

[문제 풀이]

'작은 규모(a small extent)'의 물물 교환에 대해 언급한 문장 (2) 다음에는 그 예시인 문장 (9)가 오는 것이 자연스러우므로 주어진 글 다음에는 (C)가 오며, 문장 (6)은 문장 (10)에서 언급된 '더 큰 규모(a larger scale)'의 교환이 사실상 어렵다는 것을 보여주는 예시이므로 (C) 다음에는 (B)가 온다. 마지막으로, 거래에서의 돈의 편리함에 대해 말하는 문장 (3)~(5)는 (B)에서 언급된 물물 교환의 한계를 돈이 해결해 줄 수 있음을 보여주므로, (B) 다음에는 (A)가 온다. 따라서 정답은 ⑤ '(C) — (B) — (A)'이다.

[중요 어휘]

□ barter	동사 물물 교환하다 / 명사 물물 교환
□ extent	명사 규모, 정도
□ mend	동사 수리하다, 고치다
□ in return for	~에 대한 보답으로
□ coincidence	명사 부합, 동시 발생, 우연의 일치
□ goods	명사 상품, 재산, 소유물
□ transferable	형용사 이동이 가능한, 양도할 수 있는
□ deferrable	형용사 연기할 수 있는, 유예 가능한
□ hold on to	~을 계속 보유하다, 고수하다[지키다]

23 2022년 9월 37번 (정답률 50%) 정답 ②

[지문 끊어 읽기] 근거에 기반한 주장의 중요성

(1) One benefit of reasons and arguments /
근거와 주장의 한 가지 이점은 /
=reasons and arguments
is that they can foster humility.
명사절 접속사(주격 보어)
그것들이 겸손을 기를 수 있다는 점이다

(2) If two people disagree without arguing, / 정답 단서-1 두 사람이 논쟁 없이 의견만 다른 경우를 가정함.
만약에 두 사람이 논쟁 없이 의견만 다르다면 /
all they do is yell at each other.
그들이 하는 것은 서로에게 고함을 지르는 것뿐이다

힌트 주어 자리에 all, what, the only와 같이 명사의 의미를 한정하는 말과 동사 do가 오면 주격 보어 자리에 있는 to부정사의 to를 생략할 수 있음.
(예) All you have to do is (to) study hard.

(3) No progress is made.
어떠한 발전도 없다

정답 단서-1 문장 (2)에서 언급한 논쟁 없이 의견만 다른 사람들을 가리킴.

(B) (8) Both still think / that they are right.
양측은 여전히 생각한다 / 자신이 옳다고

(9) In contrast, / if both sides give arguments / 정답 단서-1 대조적으로, 양측이 근거를 밝히고 주장을 제시하는 경우를 가정함.
대조적으로 / 양측이 주장을 제시한다면 / 선행사
that articulate reasons for their positions, /
주격 관계대명사
자신의 입장에 대한 이유를 분명히 말하는 /
then new possibilities open up.
그러면 새로운 가능성이 열린다

(10) One of the arguments gets refuted / — that is, /
이러한 주장 중 한쪽이 반박된다 / 즉 /
it is shown to fail.
형식상의 주어 내용상의 주어
틀렸다는 것이 보여진다

(11) In that case, /
이런 경우에 /
[the person who depended on the refuted argument] learns /
선행사 주격 관계대명사 [ ]:S V
반박된 주장에 의지했던 사람은 배운다 /
that he needs to change his view. 정답 단서-2 반박된 주장에 의지했던 사람은 자신의 관점을 바꿀 필요가 있다는 것을 배움.
그가 자신의 관점을 바꿀 필요가 있다는 것을

정답 단서-2 자신의 관점을 바꿀 필요가 있다는 것을 배움으로써 겸손을 얻음.

(A) (4) That is one way to achieve humility / — on one side at least.
지시대명사 형용사적 용법
이것은 겸손을 얻는 한 방식이다 / 적어도 한쪽에서는

(5) Another possibility / is that neither argument is refuted.
명사절 접속사
또 다른 가능성은 / 어떤 주장도 반박되지 않는 것이다

(6) Both have a degree of reason / on their side.
둘 다 어느 정도 근거가 있다 / 자신의 입장에서

(7) Even if neither person involved is convinced /
관련된 사람 중 어느 누구도 설득되지 않더라도 /
by the other's argument, / 양측 중 어느 누구도 설득되지 않더라도 반대 견해를 이해하게 됨.
상대의 주장에 /
both can still come to appreciate the opposing view. 정답 단서-3
양측은 그럼에도 불구하고 반대 견해를 이해하게 된다

(C) (12) They also realize that, / even if they have some truth, /
그들은 또한 인식하게 된다 / 그들이 약간의 진실을 가지고 있다 하더라도 /
they do not have the whole truth.
그들이 완전한 진실은 가지고 있지 않다는 점을

(13) They can gain humility /
그들은 겸손을 얻을 수 있다 /
when they recognize and appreciate the reasons /
그들이 근거를 인식하고 이해할 때 /
against their own view. 정답 단서-3 자신의 견해에 반대되는 근거를 인식하고 이해할 때 겸손을 얻을 수 있음.
자신의 견해에 반대되는

[전문 해석]

(1)근거와 주장의 한 가지 이점은 겸손을 기를 수 있다는 점이다. (2)만약에 두 사람이 논쟁 없이 의견만 다르다면, 그들이 하는 것은 서로에게 고함을 지르는 것뿐이다. (3)어떠한 발전도 없다.
(B) (8)양측은 여전히 자신이 옳다고 생각한다. (9)대조적으로, 양측이 자신의 입장에 대한 이유를 분명히 말하는 주장을 제시한다면, 새로운 가능성이 열린다. (10)이러한 주장 중 한쪽이 반박된다. 즉, 틀렸다는 것이 보여진다. (11)이런 경우에 반박된 주장에 의지했던 사람은 자신의 관점을 바꿀 필요가 있다는 것을 배운다.
(A) (4)이것은 적어도 한쪽에서는 겸손을 얻는 한 방식이다. (5)또 다른 가능성은 어떤 주장도 반박되지 않는 것이다. (6)둘 다 자신의 입장에서 어느 정도 근거가 있다. (7)관련된 사람 중 어느 누구도 상대의 주장에 설득되지 않더라도, 양측은 그럼에도 불구하고 반대 견해를 이해하게 된다.
(C) (12)그들이 약간의 진실을 가지고 있다 하더라도 완전한 진실은 가지고 있지 않다는 점을 그들은 또한 인식하게 된다. (13)그들은 자신의 견해에 반대되는 근거를 인식하고 이해할 때 겸손을 얻을 수 있다.

[정답 확인]

주어진 글 다음에 이어질 글의 순서로 가장 적절한 것은?

① (A) — (C) — (B) ✔② (B) — (A) — (C) ③ (B) — (C) — (A)
④ (C) — (A) — (B) ⑤ (C) — (B) — (A)

[문제 풀이]

이 지문은 근거에 기반하여 주장을 하는 것이 중요하다고 설명한다. 먼저, 문장 (2)에서 두 사람이 논쟁 없이 의견만 다른 경우를 가정한다. 이를 문장 (9)에서는 In contrast로 이어받아 양측이 자신의 입장에 대한 이유를 분명하게 말하면서 주장하는 대조적인 경우를 가정하므로 주어진 문장 다음에는 (B)가 온다. 이어지는 문장 (11)에서 한쪽이 반박되었을 때 반박된 주장을 제시했던 사람은 자신의 관점을 바꿀 필요가 있다는 것을 배운다고 했고, 문장 (4)에서는 그러한 배움이 겸손을 얻는 한 방식이라고 설명하므로 (B) 다음에는 (A)가 온다. 이어서 문장 (7)에서 어떤 주장도 반박되지 않았을 때 양측 어느 누구도 설득되지 않더라도 반대 견해를 이해하게 된다고 했고, 문장 (13)에서는 자신의 견해에 반대되는 근거를 인식하고 이해할 때 겸손을 얻을 수 있다고 하며 문장 (7)의 내용에 대한 결론을 제시하므로 (A) 다음에는 (C)가 온다. 따라서 정답은 ② '(B) — (A) — (C)'이다.

[중요 어휘]

☐ **argument**	명사 주장, 논쟁, 논의
☐ **foster**	동사 기르다, 조성하다
☐ **humility**	명사 겸손
☐ **disagree**	동사 의견이 다르다, 동의하지 않다
☐ **yell**	동사 고함을 지르다, 외치다
☐ **still**	부사 여전히, 그럼에도 불구하고, 아직
☐ **articulate**	동사 분명히 말하다 / 형용사 분명한
☐ **refute**	동사 반박하다, 부인하다
☐ **come to V**	~하게 되다
☐ **appreciate**	동사 이해하다, 인정하다, 고마워하다
☐ **recognize**	동사 인식하다, 알아보다

24 2016년 9월 39번 (정답률 50%) 정답 ⑤

[지문 끊어 읽기] 수렵 채집인과 농부의 식단 비교

(1) The foragers' secret of success, /
수렵 채집인들의 성공 비결은 /
which protected them from starvation and malnutrition, /
굶주림과 영양실조로부터 그들을 보호했던 /
was their varied diet.
그들의 다양한 식단이었다

(2) Farmers tend to eat / a very limited and unbalanced diet. 정답 단서-1
농부들은 섭취하는 경향이 있다 / 매우 제한적이고 불균형한 식단을

(C) (9) Especially in pre-modern times, /
특히 근대 이전 시기에는 /
most of the calories feeding an agricultural population /
농업 인구를 먹여 살리던 칼로리의 대부분이 / 정답 단서-1 정답 단서-2
came from a single crop / — such as wheat, potatoes, or rice — /
단일 농작물로부터 왔다 / 밀, 감자, 또는 쌀과 같이 /
that lacks some of the vitamins, minerals, and other nutritional materials /
비타민, 미네랄, 그리고 다른 영양 성분의 일부가 결여되어 있는 /
humans need.
인간이 필요로 하는

(B) (6) The typical peasant in traditional China /
전통적인 중국의 전형적인 농부는 /
ate rice for breakfast, rice for lunch, and rice for dinner. 정답 단서-2
아침, 점심, 저녁으로 쌀을 먹었다

(7) If she was lucky, / she could expect to eat the same /
만약 그녀가 운이 좋았다면 / 그녀는 같은 것을 먹을 것이라고 기대할 수 있었다 /
on the following day.
다음 날에도

문제편 p.197

(8) By contrast, / ancient foragers regularly ate /
대조적으로 / 고대의 수렵 채집인들은 규칙적으로 먹었다 /
dozens of different foodstuffs. 정답 단서-3
수십 가지의 다른 음식물을

(A) (3) The peasant's ancient ancestor, the forager, / 정답 단서-3
농부의 고대 조상인 수렵 채집인은 /
may have eaten berries and mushrooms for breakfast; /
아침으로 딸기류와 버섯을 먹었을지도 모른다 /
fruits and snails for lunch; /
점심으로 과일과 달팽이를 /
and rabbit steak with wild onions for dinner.
그리고 저녁으로 달래를 곁들인 토끼 고기 스테이크를

(4) Tomorrow's menu might have been completely different.
다음 날의 메뉴는 완전히 달랐을지도 모른다

(5) This variety (정답 단서-3) ensured / that the ancient foragers received /
이러한 다양성은 보장해주었다 / 고대 수렵 채집인들이 얻는 것을 /
all the necessary nutrients.
모든 필요한 영양소를

[전문 해석]

(1)굶주림과 영양실조로부터 수렵 채집인들을 보호했던 그들의 성공 비결은 다양한 식단이었다. (2)농부들은 매우 제한적이고 불균형한 식단을 섭취하는 경향이 있다.
(C) (9)특히 근대 이전 시기에는 농업 인구를 먹여 살리던 칼로리의 대부분이 밀, 감자, 또는 쌀과 같이 인간이 필요로 하는 비타민, 미네랄, 그리고 다른 영양 성분의 일부가 결여되어 있는 단일 농작물로부터 왔다.
(B) (6)전통적인 중국의 전형적인 농부는 아침, 점심, 저녁으로 쌀을 먹었다. (7)만약 그녀(농부)가 운이 좋았다면, 그녀는 다음 날에도 같은 것을 먹을 것이라고 기대할 수 있었다(식량이 부족했기 때문에 쌀이라도 계속 먹을 수 있었다면 운이 좋은 것이었다). (8)대조적으로, 고대의 수렵 채집인들은 수십 가지의 다른 음식물을 규칙적으로 먹었다.
(A) (3)농부의 고대 조상인 수렵 채집인은 아침으로 딸기류와 버섯을, 점심으로 과일과 달팽이를, 저녁으로 달래를 곁들인 토끼 고기 스테이크를 먹었을지도 모른다. (4)다음 날의 메뉴는 완전히 달랐을지도 모른다. (5)이러한 (식단의) 다양성은 고대 수렵 채집인들이 모든 필요한 영양소를 얻는 것을 보장해주었다.

[정답 확인]

주어진 글 다음에 이어질 글의 순서로 가장 적절한 것은?

① (A) — (C) — (B)　② (B) — (A) — (C)　③ (B) — (C) — (A)
④ (C) — (A) — (B)　✔ (C) — (B) — (A)

[문제 풀이]

수렵 채집인에 비해 농부의 식단이 불균형한 경향이 있다는 주어진 내용에 이어서, 근대 이전 농부의 식단이 단일 농작물에 의존했다는 (C), 이에 대한 예시로 전통적인 중국의 농부의 식단을 들고, 대조적으로 수렵 채집인은 그렇지 않았다고 하는 (B), 이어서 수렵 채집인들의 다양한 식단을 예로 보여주는 (A)의 순서가 가장 적절하다. 따라서 정답은 ⑤ '(C) — (B) — (A)'이다.

[중요 어휘]

□ forager	명사 수렵 채집인
□ starvation	명사 굶주림
□ malnutrition	명사 영양실조
□ varied	형용사 다양한, 갖가지의
□ unbalanced	형용사 불균형한
□ pre-modern	형용사 근대 이전의, 전근대적인
□ single	형용사 단일의, 하나의
□ crop	명사 농작물
□ wheat	명사 밀
□ peasant	명사 농부, 소작농
□ by contrast	대조적으로
□ regularly	부사 규칙적으로, 정기적으로
□ dozens of	수십 가지의, 많은
□ ancestor	명사 조상
□ snail	명사 달팽이
□ wild onion	명사 달래
□ ensure	동사 보장해주다, 확실하게 하다

핵심 환경 보호와 일자리(경제)에 관한 관점을 문장 (1)의 business leaders and politicians의 입장과 문장 (3)의 Ecological economists의 입장으로 나누어 대조 설명하는 글로 각 입장의 차이를 파악하는 것이 중요함.

25 2016년 11월 37번 (정답률 45%) 정답 ①

[지문 끊어 읽기] 환경 보호와 일자리

(1) For years / business leaders and politicians /
수년간 / 기업가들과 정치인들은 /
have portrayed environmental protection and jobs /
환경 보호와 일자리를 묘사해왔다 /
as mutually exclusive. 정답 단서-1
상호 배타적으로

(A) (2) Pollution control, /
오염 방지가 /
protection of natural areas and endangered species, /
자연 지역과 멸종 위기에 처한 종들에 대한 보호가 /
and limits on use of nonrenewable resources, / they claim, / 정답 단서-1
그리고 재생 불가능한 자원의 사용에 대한 제한이 / 그들은 주장한다 /
will choke the economy / and throw people out of work.
경제를 질식시킬 것이라고 / 그리고 사람들을 실직시킬 것이라고

(3) Ecological economists dispute this claim, / however. 정답 단서-2
생태경제학자들은 이러한 주장에 대해 이의를 제기한다 / 그러나

(C) (7) Their studies show / 정답 단서-2
그들의 연구는 보여준다 /
that only 0.1 percent of all large-scale layoffs /
모든 대규모 해고의 0.1퍼센트만이 /
in the United States in recent years /
최근 몇 년간 미국에서 /
were due to government regulations.
정부의 규제 때문이었다는 것을

(8) Environmental protection, / they argue, /
환경 보호가 / 그들은 주장한다 /
not only is necessary for a healthy economic system, /
건강한 경제 체계를 위해 꼭 필요할 뿐만 아니라 /
but it actually creates jobs and stimulates business. 정답 단서-3
그것이 실제로 일자리를 만들어 내고 사업을 촉진한다고

(B) (4) Recycling, / for instance, / makes more new jobs / 정답 단서-3
재활용은 / 예를 들어 / 더 많은 새 일자리를 만들어 낸다 /
than extracting raw materials.
원자재를 추출해내는 것보다

(5) This doesn't necessarily mean /
이것이 반드시 의미하는 것은 아니다 /
that recycled goods are more expensive /
재활용된 상품들이 더 비싸다는 것을 /
than those from raw resources.
원자재로부터 만들어진 것들보다

(6) We're simply substituting / labor in the recycling center /
단지 우리는 대체하고 있을 뿐이다 / 재활용 센터의 노동력으로 /
for energy and huge machines /
에너지와 커다란 기계를 /
used to extract new materials in remote places.
먼 지역에서 새로운 자재를 추출하는 데 사용되는

[전문 해석]

(1)수년간 기업가들과 정치인들은 환경 보호와 일자리를 상호 배타적(인 것)으로 묘사해왔다.
(A) (2)그들(기업가들과 정치인들)은 오염 방지, 자연 지역과 멸종 위기에 처한 종들에 대한 보호, 그리고 재생 불가능한 자원의 사용에 대한 제한이 경제를 질식시키고(경제 성장을 저해하고) 사람들을 실직시킬 것이라고 주장한다. (3)그러나, 생태경제학자들은 이러한 주장에 대해 이의를 제기한다.
(C) (7)그들(생태경제학자들)의 연구는 최근 몇 년간 미국에서 (있었던) 모든 대규모 해고의 0.1퍼센트만이 정부의 (환경 보호를 위한) 규제 때문이었다는 것을 보여준다. (8)그들은 환경 보호가 건강한 경제 체계를 위해 꼭 필요할 뿐만 아니라, 그것(환경 보호)이 실제로 일자리를 만들어 내고 사업을 촉진한다고 주장한다.

(B) (4)예를 들어, 재활용은 원자재를 추출해내는 것보다 더 많은 새 일자리를 만들어 낸다. (5)이것이 반드시 재활용된 상품들이 원자재로부터 만들어진 것들(상품들)보다 더 비싸다는 것을 의미하는 것은 아니다. (6)단지 우리는 먼 지역에서 새로운 자재를 추출하는 데 사용되는 에너지와 커다란 기계를 재활용 센터의 노동력으로 대체하고 있을 뿐이다.

[정답 확인]

주어진 글 다음에 이어질 글의 순서로 가장 적절한 것은?

✔ (A) — (C) — (B)　② (B) — (A) — (C)　③ (B) — (C) — (A)
④ (C) — (A) — (B)　⑤ (C) — (B) — (A)

[문제 풀이]

주어진 글은 환경 보호와 일자리 창출에 대한 기업가와 정치인의 시각이다. 이어서 기업가와 정치인들의 주장을 부연 설명하고 그에 대해 생태경제학자가 의문을 제기한다는 (A), 생태경제학자들의 연구 내용과 주장인 (C), 생태경제학자들의 주장을 뒷받침하는 사례 (B)의 순서가 가장 적절하다. 따라서 정답은 ① '(A) — (C) — (B)'이다.

[중요 어휘]

☐ portray	동사 묘사하다
☐ protection	명사 보호
☐ mutually	부사 상호 간에, 서로
☐ exclusive	형용사 배타적인, 독점적인
☐ pollution	명사 오염, 공해
☐ endangered	형용사 멸종 위기에 처한, 위험에 처한
☐ claim	동사 주장하다 / 명사 주장, 의견
☐ choke	동사 질식시키다, 목을 조르다
☐ throw A out of work	A를 실직시키다
☐ ecological	형용사 생태의
☐ economist	명사 경제학자
☐ dispute	동사 ~에 대해 이의를 제기하다, 반박하다
☐ layoff	명사 해고
☐ argue	동사 주장하다, 언쟁하다, (말로) 다투다
☐ raw	형용사 원자재의, 가공되지 않은
☐ recycled	형용사 재활용된
☐ substitute A for B	B를 A로 대체하다
☐ remote	형용사 먼, 원격의

26 2018년 11월 36번 (정답률 45%) 정답 ②

[지문 끊어 읽기] 인쇄술의 발달이 출판물에 끼친 영향

(1) During the late 1800s, / printing became cheaper and faster, /
1800년대 후반에 / 인쇄술은 더 저렴해지고 더 빨라졌다 /
leading to an explosion / (병렬①)
그리고 폭발적인 증가로 이어졌다 /
힌트 분사인 leading은 동시동작으로 '~하면서' 라고 해석하거나, 연속동작으로 보아 and처럼 '그리고~'라고 이어지듯이 해석해도 됨.
in the number of newspapers and magazines /
신문과 잡지의 수에서의 /
and the increased use of images / in these publications. (정답 단서-1, 병렬②)
그리고 이미지의 증가된 사용으로 / 이러한 출판물들에서의

(B) (3) Photographs, / as well as woodcuts and engravings of them, / (정답 단서-1)
사진은 / 그것들에 대한 목판화와 판화뿐만 아니라 /
appeared in newspapers and magazines.
신문과 잡지에 나타났다

(4) The increased number of newspapers and magazines /
신문과 잡지의 증가된 수는 /
created greater competition / — driving some papers /
더 큰 경쟁을 일으켰다 / 몇몇 신문들이 ~하게 만들었다 /
to print more salacious articles / (정답 단서-2)
더 많은 외설스러운 기사들을 발행하도록 /
to attract readers.
부사적 용법(~하기 위해)
독자들을 유인하기 위해

(A) (2) This "yellow journalism" sometimes took the form of gossip / (정답 단서-2, 정답 단서-3)
이러한 '옐로 저널리즘'은 때때로 소문의 형태로 나타났다 /
about public figures, / as well as about socialites /
유명 인사들에 대한 / 사교계 명사들에 대해서뿐만 아니라 /
who considered themselves private figures, /
그들 자신을 사인이라고 여겼던 /
and even about those / who were not part of high society /
그리고 심지어 사람들에 대해서뿐만 아니라 / 상류 사회의 일원은 아니었던 /
but had found themselves involved in a scandal, crime, or tragedy /
하지만 스캔들, 범죄 또는 비극적인 사건에 연루되었던 /
that journalists thought would sell papers.
삽입절
기자들이 생각하기에 신문을 팔아줄

힌트 문장 (2)의 had found themselves는 '그들 자신을 찾았다'라는 뜻이 아니라 5형식 동사 find로 'O가 O·C하다는 것을 깨닫다[느끼다, 알다]'로 쓰였음. 즉, 여기서는 사건들에 휘말리게 되었다는 의미로 사용됨.

(C) (5) Gossip was of course nothing new, / but the rise of mass media / (정답 단서-3)
소문은 물론 새로운 것이 아니었다 / 하지만 대중 매체의 증가는 / S
in the form of widely distributed newspapers and magazines /
널리 배포되는 신문과 잡지 형태의 /
meant / [that gossip moved / (V, [ ]: meant의 목적어절)
의미했다 / 소문이 바뀌었음을 /
from limited (often oral only) distribution /
(주로 입으로만 전해지는) 제한된 배포에서 /
to wide, printed dissemination].
광범위한 인쇄되는 유포로

★중요 대중 매체 이전에는 소문이 입에서 입으로 구전되어 소문이 퍼지는 범위도 훨씬 제한적이었지만, 이후에는 대중 매체를 통해 소문이 인쇄물로 유포되어 그 전파 범위가 훨씬 넓어졌다는 이야기임.

힌트 결국, 핵심은 '옐로 저널리즘이 유명 인사들에 대한 소문의 형태로 나타났다'라는 것임. 이 '유명 인사들에 대한(about public figures) 소문' 이외에도, 다른 인물들에 대한 소문을 다루기도 했다는데 그 내용이 'as well as(뿐만 아니라, 게다가)' 다음에 나오는 '[about socialites who ~] and even [about those who ~]'로 이어지고 있음.

[중요 구문]

(2) This "yellow journalism" sometimes took the form of gossip (S, V)
[about public figures], as well as [about socialites who ~], (병렬①, 병렬②)
and even [about those who were not part of high society (병렬③, V'①)
but had found themselves involved in a scandal, crime, or (V'②)
tragedy that (journalists thought) would sell papers].

[전문 해석]

(1)1800년대 후반에, 인쇄술은 더 저렴해지고 더 빨라졌으며, 신문과 잡지의 수에서의 폭발적인 증가와 이러한 출판물들에서의 이미지의 증가된 사용으로 이어졌다.
(B) (3)그것들(사진들)에 대한 목판화와 판화뿐만 아니라, 사진도 신문과 잡지에 나타났다. (4)신문과 잡지의 증가된 수는 더 큰 경쟁을 일으켰는데, 몇몇 신문들이 독자들을 유인하기 위해 더 많은 외설스러운 기사들을 발행하도록 만들었다(몰아갔다).
(A) (2)이러한 '옐로 저널리즘'은 그들 자신을 (공인이 아닌) 사인(사적인 인물)이라고 여겼던 사교계 명사들, 그리고 심지어 상류 사회의 일원은 아니었지만 기자들이 생각하기에 신문을 팔아줄 (것 같은) 스캔들, 범죄 또는 비극적인 사건에 연루되었던 사람들에 대해서뿐만 아니라, 때때로 유명 인사들에 대한 소문의 형태로도 나타났다.
(C) (5)소문은(소문 자체는) 물론 새로운 것이 아니었지만, 널리 배포되는 신문과 잡지 형태의 대중 매체의 증가는 소문이 (주로 입으로만 전해지는(구전되는)) 제한된 배포에서 광범위한 (널리) 인쇄되는 유포로 바뀌었음을 의미했다.
- yellow journalism(옐로 저널리즘): 인간의 불건전한 감정을 자극하는 범죄, 괴기 사건, 성적 추문 등을 과도하게 취재, 보도하는 신문의 경향을 이르는 말이다. 이러한 선정적이고 비도덕적인 기사들은 단기적으로 독자를 끌어들이는 데 효과적이지만, 언론의 신뢰성과 공평성을 저해한다는 점에서 큰 비판을 받는다.

[정답 확인]

주어진 글 다음에 이어질 글의 순서로 가장 적절한 것은?

① (A) — (C) — (B)　✔ (B) — (A) — (C)　③ (B) — (C) — (A)
④ (C) — (A) — (B)　⑤ (C) — (B) — (A)

[문제 풀이]

본문에서는 인쇄술이 더 저렴하고 빨라지면서 신문이나 잡지 출판사에 미친 영향에 대해 설명하고 있다. 한편 (B)에서 언급된 'photographs, woodcuts, engravings' 등은 주어진 문장에서 언급된 'images'의 예시에 해당하므로, 주어진 문장 다음에는 (B)가 온다. 또, 문장 (4)의 'salacious articles(외설스러운 기사들)'은 문장 (2)의 '이러한 옐로 저널리즘'에 해당하므로, (B) 다음에는 (A)가 온다. 마지막으로, 인쇄술의 발달이 소문에 미친 영향에 대해서 정리를 해 주는 (C)가 가장 뒤에 오는 것이 적절하다. 따라서 정답은 ② '(B) — (A) — (C)'이다.

문제편 p.198

[오답 풀이]

③ - 문단 (A)는 매체의 수익을 올리기 위해 공인이 아닌 사람들의 사사로운 이야기마저 가십거리로 삼는다는 '옐로 저널리즘'에 관한 내용으로 'gossip(소문)'의 양태에 중점을 두는 반면, 문단 (C)는 인쇄물의 발달로 인해 소문이 전파되는 방식과 그 범위가 변화하였음에 중점을 두고 있으므로 (A) — (C)의 순서가 흐름상 자연스럽다. 특히 문단 (C)의 내용은 '옐로 저널리즘'과 직접적인 연관성이 없으므로, '이러한 옐로 저널리즘'을 서두로 하는 문단 (A)의 앞에 오기는 부적절하다.

[중요 어휘]

☐ **printing**	명사 인쇄술, 인쇄
☐ **explosion**	명사 폭발적인 증가, 폭발
☐ **publication**	명사 출판물, 간행물
☐ **woodcut**	명사 목판화
☐ **competition**	명사 경쟁, 대회, 시합
☐ **attract**	동사 유인하다, 끌어당기다, 매혹하다
☐ **journalism**	명사 저널리즘(기사거리를 모으고 기사를 쓰는 일)
☐ **public figure**	유명 인사, 공인
☐ **socialite**	명사 사교계 명사
☐ **private figure**	사인, 일반인(공인이 아닌 사람)
☐ **distributed**	형용사 배포[분포]되는, 광범위한
☐ **move**	동사 바뀌다, 움직이다 / 명사 변화, 이동
☐ **oral**	형용사 (입에서) 입으로 전해지는, 구두의

핵심 첫 문장에 주제를 제시하면서 예시를 보여주는 '주제-예시'의 글임. 우리가 골프를 배울 때 뇌가 어떤 과정을 거치는지에 대해서 생각하면서 읽을 것.

27 2019년 6월 37번 (정답률 45%) 정답 ③

[지문 끊어 읽기] 뇌의 운동 기술 처리 과정

(1) Brain research provides a framework / for understanding /
뇌 연구는 틀을 제공한다 / 이해하는 데에 /
how the brain processes and internalizes athletic skills. 정답 단서-1
뇌가 운동 기술을 처리하고 내면화하는 방법을

(B) (4) In practicing a complex movement / such as a golf swing, / 정답 단서-1
복잡한 움직임을 연습하는 데 있어서 / 골프 스윙과 같은 /
we experiment with different grips, positions and swing movements, / 정답 단서-2
우리는 다른 그립과 다른 자세, 그리고 다른 스윙 동작을 실험해 본다 /
analyzing each / in terms of the results / it yields.
각각을 분석하면서 / 결과에 관하여 / 그것이 산출하는

(5) This is a conscious, left-brain process.
이것은 의식적인 좌뇌 과정이다

(C) (6) Once we identify / those elements of the swing / 정답 단서-2
일단 우리가 확인하고 나면 / 스윙의 그러한 요소들을 /
that produce the desired results, /
원하는 결과를 만들어내는 /
we rehearse them over and over again /
우리는 그것들을 반복해서 연습한다 /
in an attempt to record them permanently / in "muscle memory."
그것들을 영구히 기록하기 위하여 / '근육 기억'에

★중요 문장 (6)의 those elements of the swing이 문장 (4)의 grips, positions and swing movements를 나타내는 것을 파악하면 문단 (C)가 문단 (B) 뒤로 와야 한다는 것을 알 수 있음.

(7) In this way, / we internalize the swing / as a kinesthetic feeling / 정답 단서-3
이렇게 하여 / 우리는 스윙을 내면화한다 / 운동 감각의 느낌으로서 /
that we trust / to recreate the desired swing / on demand.
우리가 믿는 / 원하던 스윙을 재현해 줄 것이라고 / 필요로 하는 즉시

(A) (2) 정답 단서-3 This internalization transfers the swing /
이러한 내면화는 스윙을 전이시킨다 /
from a consciously controlled left-brain function /
의식적으로 관리되는 좌뇌 기능에서부터 /
to a more intuitive or automatic right-brain function.
더 직관적이거나 자동적인 우뇌 기능으로

★중요 여기서 This internalization은 문장 (7)의 internalize를 명사로 받은 것임. 물론 문장 (1)에도 internalize가 나오지만, 문장 (1)은 골프 스윙에 대한 언급이 없기 때문에 문장 (2)는 문장 (7) 다음에 오는 것이 적절함.

(3) This description, / despite being an oversimplification /
이러한 설명은 / 지나친 단순화임에도 불구하고 /
of the actual processes involved, /
관련된 실제 과정의 /
serves as a model / for the interaction /
본보기의 역할을 한다 / 상호작용을 위한 /
between conscious and unconscious actions in the brain, /
뇌의 의식적이고 무의식적인 활동 간의 /
as it learns to perfect an athletic skill.
그것이 운동 기술을 완벽하게 하는 법을 배울 때

[전문 해석]

(1)뇌 연구는 뇌가 운동 기술을 처리하고 내면화(습득)하는 방법을 이해하는 데에 틀을 제공한다.
(B) (4)골프 스윙과 같은 복잡한 움직임을 연습하는 데 있어서, 우리는 그것(움직임)이 산출하는 결과에 관하여 각각을 분석하면서 다른 그립과 다른 자세, 그리고 다른 스윙 동작을 실험해(시도해) 본다. (5)이것은 의식적인 좌뇌 과정이다.
(C) (6)일단 우리가 원하는 결과를 만들어내는 스윙의 그러한 요소들을 확인하고 나면, 우리는 '근육 기억'에 그것들을 영구히 기록하기 위하여 그것들을 반복해서 연습한다. (7)이렇게 하여 우리는 우리가 필요로 하는 즉시 원하던 스윙을 재현해 줄 것이라고 믿는 운동 감각의 느낌으로서 스윙을 내면화한다.
(A) (2)이러한 내면화(습득)는 스윙을 의식적으로 관리되는 좌뇌 기능에서부터 더 직관적이거나 자동적인 우뇌 기능으로 전이(이동)시킨다. (3)이러한 설명은 관련된 실제 과정의 지나친 단순화임에도 불구하고, 그것이(뇌가) 운동 기술을 완벽하게 하는 법을 배울 때, 뇌의 의식적이고 무의식적인 활동 간의 상호작용을 위한 본보기의 역할을 한다.

[정답 확인]

주어진 글 다음에 이어질 글의 순서로 가장 적절한 것은?

① (A) — (C) — (B) ② (B) — (A) — (C) ③ (B) — (C) — (A)
④ (C) — (A) — (B) ⑤ (C) — (B) — (A)

[문제 풀이]

골프 스윙의 예를 통해 뇌의 운동 기술 처리 과정을 설명하는 글이다. 주어진 글 다음에는 복잡한 움직임의 한 예로서 골프 스윙이 처음으로 등장하는 (B)가 온다. 한편, (B)는 스윙을 배우는 초기에, 다양한 방법들을 시도해보고 각 시도의 결과를 분석하는 '좌뇌 과정'에 해당하며, (C)는 원하는 스윙을 만들어내는 요소들을 찾아내어 반복적으로 연습함으로써 각 요소들을 근육 기억에 기록하는 '우뇌 과정'에 해당한다. 또한 (A)에서는 '좌뇌'에서 '우뇌'로의 스윙 습득 과정을 종합 정리하고 있으므로 (B) 다음에는 (C)가 오고, 결론으로 (A)가 오는 것이 적절하다. 따라서 정답은 ③ '(B) — (C) — (A)'이다.

[중요 어휘]

☐ **framework**	명사 틀, 뼈대
☐ **internalize**	동사 내면화하다, 습득하다
☐ **athletic**	형용사 운동의, 체육의
☐ **yield**	동사 산출하다, 항복하다, 양보하다
☐ **conscious**	형용사 의식적인, 의식하는
☐ **rehearse**	동사 연습하다, 시연하다
☐ **in an attempt to V**	~하기 위하여, ~하려는 시도로
☐ **kinesthetic**	형용사 운동 감각(성)의
☐ **on demand**	필요로 하는 즉시, 요구만 있으면 (언제든지)
☐ **intuitive**	형용사 직관적인, 직관에 의한
☐ **oversimplification**	명사 지나친 단순화[간소화]
☐ **model**	명사 본보기, 모범

28 2020년 3월 37번 (정답률 45%) 정답 ②

[지문 끊어 읽기] 농업이 인간의 삶에 미친 영향

(1) Regardless of / whether the people existing after agriculture /
명사절 접속사 S'
~에 상관없이 / 농업 이후에 존재한 사람들이 ~인지 /
were happier, healthier, or neither, / it is undeniable /
V' 형식상의 주어
더 행복하고 더 건강했는지, 아니면 둘 다 아니었는지 / 부인할 수 없다 /
that there were more of them.
내용상의 주어
그들이 더 많이 있었다는 것은

(2) Agriculture both supports and requires / more people / 정답 단서-1
both A and B
농업은 부양하는 동시에 필요로 한다 / 더 많은 사람들을 /
to grow the crops / that sustain them.
농작물을 기르기 위해 / 그들을 살아가게 하는

(B) (5) Estimates vary, / of course, /
추정치는 다양하다 / 물론 /
but evidence points to an increase in the human population /
하지만 증거는 인구의 증가를 암시한다 /
from 1–5 million people worldwide / to a few hundred million /
전 세계적으로 1~5백만 명에서 / 수억 명으로의 /
once agriculture had become established. 정답 단서-1
일단 농업이 확립된 이후

(A) (3) And a larger population doesn't just mean / 정답 단서-2
그리고 더 많은 인구가 단지 의미하지는 않는다 /
increasing the size of everything, /
모든 것의 규모를 커지게 하는 것을 /
like buying a bigger box of cereal / for a larger family.
더 큰 시리얼 박스를 사는 것과 같이 / 더 큰 가족을 위해

★중요 문장 (3)의 첫 단어가 And인 것을 보면, 전에 larger population에 대한 내용이 이미 나왔다는 것을 알 수가 있음. 따라서 larger population에 대한 증거를 내보이는 (B)가 (A) 앞에 와야 함.

(4) It brings qualitative changes / in the way people live. 정답 단서-3
그것은 질적인 변화를 가져다준다 / 사람들이 사는 방식에

(C) (6) For example, / 정답 단서-3
예를 들어 /
more people means more kinds of diseases, /
더 많은 사람은 더 많은 종류의 질병을 의미한다 /
particularly when those people are sedentary.
특히 그러한 사람들이 한곳에 머물러 살 때

힌트 보통 people 같은 복수 명사에는 복수 동사 mean이 와야 한다고 알고 있지만 여기에서의 more people은 '많은 사람'이라는 뜻이 아니라 '사람이 많은 것'이라는 의미이기 때문에 단수 동사 means를 사용했음.

(7) Those groups of people can also store food / for long periods, /
그러한 사람들의 집단은 또한 음식을 보관할 수 있다 / 오랜 기간 /
which creates a society / with haves and have-nots.
계속적 용법(=and it) 명사① 명사②
그리고 그것은 사회를 만든다 / 가진 자들과 가지지 못한 자들이 있는

[전문 해석]

(1)농업 이후에 존재한 사람들이 더 행복하고 더 건강했는지, 아니면 둘 다 아니었는지에 상관없이, 그들이 더 많이 있었다는 것은 부인할 수 없다. (2)농업은 더 많은 사람들을 부양하는 동시에 그들을 살아가게 하는 농작물을 기르기 위해 더 많은 사람들을 필요로 한다.
(B) (5)물론 추정치는 다양하지만, 증거는 일단 농업이 확립된 이후 전 세계적으로 1~5백만 명에서 수억 명으로의 인구의 증가를(증가가 있었음을) 암시한다.
(A) (3)그리고 더 큰 가족을 위해 더 큰 시리얼 박스를 사는 것과 같이, 더 많은 인구가 단지 모든 것의 규모를 커지게 하는 것을 의미하지는 않는다. (4)그것은 사람들이 사는 방식에 질적인 변화를 가져다준다.
(C) (6)예를 들어, 더 많은 사람(사람이 많은 것)은 더 많은 종류의 질병을 의미하는데, 특히 그러한 사람들이 한곳에 머물러 살 때 (그렇다). (7)그러한 사람들의 집단은 또한 오랜 기간 음식을 보관할 수 있으며, 그것은 가진 자들과 가지지 못한 자들이 있는 사회를 만든다.

[정답 확인]

주어진 글 다음에 이어질 글의 순서로 가장 적절한 것은?

① (A) — (C) — (B) ✔② (B) — (A) — (C) ③ (B) — (C) — (A)
④ (C) — (A) — (B) ⑤ (C) — (B) — (A)

[문제 풀이]

농업이 인간의 삶에 미친 영향에 대해 설명한 글이다. 주어진 문장은 농업 이후로 인구가 증가했다고 이야기하고 있으며, 주어진 문장 다음에는 농업의 확립 이후 구체적으로 전 세계 인구가 얼마나 증가했는지에 대한 추정치를 제시한 (B)가 오는 것이 적절하다. (B)가 피상적으로 농업이 인구 수에 미친 영향을 살펴봤다면, (A)는 농업이 가져온 인간 삶의 질적인 변화에 대해 소개하므로 (B) 다음에는 (A)가 오며, 문장 (4)의 질적인 변화에 대한 예시로서 질병의 전파와 계층 분화를 언급한 (C)가 마지막에 온다. 따라서 정답은 ②이다.

[중요 어휘]

☐	agriculture	명사 농업
☐	undeniable	형용사 부인할 수 없는, 명백한
☐	sustain	동사 살아가게 하다, 지탱하다
☐	estimate	명사 추정치, 견적 / 동사 추정하다
☐	vary	동사 다양하다, 달라지다
☐	evidence	명사 증거, 흔적
☐	population	명사 인구
☐	establish	동사 확립하다, 설립하다
☐	qualitative	형용사 질적인, 성질상의
☐	sedentary	형용사 한곳에 머물러 사는, 앉아서 하는

핵심 주어진 문장은 '과세의 공정성'에 대한 화두를 던지고 있음. 이 논쟁의 예시로 언급된 다른 종류의 과세 방법들을 구별하며 글의 전후관계를 추측하면 글의 흐름이 파악될 것임.

29 2021년 3월 37번 (정답률 45%) 정답 ②

[지문 끊어 읽기] 도덕적 판단에 따른 과세

(1) We commonly argue / about the fairness of taxation / 정답 단서-1
우리는 흔히 논한다 / 과세의 공정성에 대해 /
— whether this or that tax will fall more heavily on the rich /
이런 저런 세금이 부자들에게 더 많이 부과될지 /
or the poor.
혹은 가난한 사람들에게

(B) (5) But the expressive dimension of taxation /
그러나 과세의 표현적인 차원은 /
goes beyond debates about fairness, / 정답 단서-1
공정성에 대한 토론을 넘어선다 /
to the moral judgements societies make /
사회가 내리는 도덕적 판단에까지 /
about which activities are worthy of honor and recognition, /
어떠한 활동들이 명예와 인정을 받을 가치가 있는지에 대해 /
and which ones should be discouraged. 정답 단서-2
=activities
그리고 어떠한 것들이 억제되어야 하는지

힌트 societies 앞에 목적격 관계대명사인 which/that이 생략된 목적격 관계대명사절로, 선행사인 judgements를 수식하고 있음.

힌트 'which'는 '어떠한'이라는 의미의 의문형용사로, 뒤에 오는 명사를 꾸며 주는 형태로 쓰임.

힌트 전치사 about의 목적어로 명사절 2개가 and로 병렬을 이루고 있음.

(6) Sometimes, these judgements are explicit.
가끔 이런 판단들은 노골적이다

(A) (2) Taxes on tobacco, alcohol, and casinos / are called "sin taxes" / 정답 단서-2
담배, 주류, 카지노에 대한 세금은 / '죄악세'라고 불린다 /
because they seek to discourage activities /
="sin taxes"
왜냐하면 그것들은 활동들을 억제하려 하기 때문이다 /
considered harmful or undesirable.
해롭거나 바람직하지 않다고 여겨지는

힌트 'considered' 앞에 '주격 관계대명사+be동사'가 함께 생략되어 선행사인 'activities'를 수식하는 것으로 볼 수 있음. 명사를 뒤에서 수식하는 과거분사구의 형태임.

(3) Such taxes express society's disapproval of these activities /
이와 같은 세금은 이러한 활동들에 대한 사회의 반감을 표명한다 / 정답 단서-3
by raising the cost of engaging in them.
그것들에 참여하는 비용을 올림으로써 =these activities

(4) Proposals / to tax sugary sodas / (to combat obesity) /
병렬①
제안들은 / 설탕이 든 탄산음료에 과세하는 / (비만을 방지하기 위해) /
or carbon emissions / (to address climate change) /
병렬②
혹은 탄소 배출에 과세하는 / (기후 변화 문제를 다루기 위해) /
likewise / seek to change norms and shape behavior. 정답 단서-3
마찬가지로 / 규범을 바꾸고 행동을 형성하려 한다

(C) (7) Not all taxes have this aim. 정답 단서-3
모든 세금들이 이러한 목적을 가지는 것은 아니다

힌트 'all', 'every' 등 전체를 지칭하는 단어 앞에 'no'와 같은 부정어가 오면, '모든 것이 ~는 아니다'와 같은 부분부정의 뜻으로 쓰임.

(8) We do not tax income /
우리는 소득에 과세하지 않는다 /
to express disapproval of paid employment /
부사적 용법(병렬①)
유급 고용에 대한 반감을 표명하기 위해 /
or to discourage people from engaging in it.
부사적 용법(병렬②) =paid employment
혹은 사람들이 그것에 참여하는 것을 억제하기 위해

(9) Nor is a general sales tax /
일반 판매세도 ~것이 아니다 /
intended as a deterrent / to buying things.
억제책으로서 의도된 / 물건을 구매하는 것의

힌트 여기서 to는 전치사이며 전치사의 목적어로 동명사가 왔음.

(10) These are simply ways / of raising revenue.
이것들은 단순히 방법이다 / 세수를 올리는

문제편 p.199

[전문 해석]

(1)우리는 흔히 과세의 공정성에 대해 이런 저런 세금이 부자들에게 더 많이 부과될지 혹은 가난한 사람들에게 (더 많이 부과될지) 논한다.
(B) (5)그러나 과세의 표현적인 차원은 공정성에 대한 토론을 넘어서, 어떠한 활동들이 명예와 인정을 받을 가치가 있는지, 그리고 어떠한 것들이 억제되어야 하는지에 대해 사회가 내리는 도덕적 판단에까지 이른다. (6)가끔 이런 (도덕적) 판단들은 노골적이다.
(A) (2)담배, 주류, 카지노에 대한 세금은 '죄악세'라고 불리는데, 왜냐하면 그것들은 해롭거나 바람직하지 않다고 여겨지는 활동들을 억제하려 하기 때문이다. (3)이와 같은 세금은 그것들에 참여하는 비용을 올림으로써 이러한 활동들에 대한 사회의 반감을 표명한다. (4)(비만을 방지하기 위해) 설탕이 든 탄산음료나 (기후 변화 문제를 다루기 위해) 탄소 배출에 과세하는 제안들은 마찬가지로 규범을 바꾸고 행동을 형성하려 한다.
(C) (7)모든 세금들이 이러한 목적을 가지는 것은 아니다. (8)우리는 유급 고용에 대한 반감을 표명하거나 사람들이 그것(유급 고용)에 참여하는 것을 억제하기 위해 소득에 과세하지 않는다. (9)일반 판매세도 물건을 구매하는 것의 억제책으로서 의도된 것이 아니다. (10)이것들은 단순히 세수를 올리는 방법이다.

[정답 확인]

주어진 글 다음에 이어질 글의 순서로 가장 적절한 것은?

① (A) — (C) — (B) ✔② (B) — (A) — (C) ③ (B) — (C) — (A)
④ (C) — (A) — (B) ⑤ (C) — (B) — (A)

[문제 풀이]

지문은 문장 (1)에서 언급했듯이 과세의 공정성에 대한 논의로 시작한다. (B)의 문장 (5)는 과세의 공정성 그 이상, 즉 도덕적 판단에 의해 과세하는 경우를 언급하고 있으므로 문장 (1)의 소재를 보다 확장하여 내용을 전개한다. 문장 (5)의 도덕적 판단은 결국 사회적으로 인정을 받기 어려운 행위들을 과세를 통해 억제한다는 의미인데, 이는 (A)의 문장 (2)에서 '죄악세'를 받는 것으로 예를 들 수 있으므로, (B) 다음에는 (A)가 와야 한다. 마지막으로 (C)의 문장 (7)에서 언급된 '이러한 목적'은 과세를 통해 사회적으로 특정 행동을 막는 것을 의미한다. 따라서 보기 ②와 같이 '(B) — (A) — (C)'의 순서로 이어져야 지문의 흐름이 자연스럽다.

[오답 풀이]

④ - (C)의 문장 (7)은 모든 세금이 '이러한 목적(this aim)'이 아님을 지적한다. 이에 대한 힌트는 문장 (8)에서 찾을 수 있는데, 이는 세금을 부과한다고 해서 대상에 대한 반감을 표명하는 것이 아님을 뜻한다. 그러나 이렇게 반감을 표명한다는 것은 문장 (1)의 과세의 공정성에서 이어지기에는 다소 어색한 주제다. 따라서 주어진 문장 (1)에 (C)가 이어질 수는 없다.

[중요 어휘]

☐ **fairness**	명사 공정성
☐ **taxation**	명사 과세, 조세
☐ **expressive**	형용사 표현적인, ~을 나타내는
☐ **dimension**	명사 차원, 규모
☐ **moral**	형용사 도덕적인, 도의적인
☐ **honor**	명사 명예, 영광
☐ **recognition**	명사 인정, 인식
☐ **discourage**	동사 억제하다, 막다, 좌절시키다
☐ **explicit**	형용사 노골적인, 명백한
☐ **undesirable**	형용사 바람직하지 않은, 달갑지 않은
☐ **disapproval**	명사 반감, 못마땅함
☐ **engage in**	~에 참여하다
☐ **sugary**	형용사 설탕이 든
☐ **carbon emission**	탄소 배출
☐ **address**	동사 (문제를) 다루다, 처리하다
☐ **norm**	명사 규범, 표준
☐ **shape**	동사 형성하다, (어떤) 형태로 만들다
☐ **income**	명사 소득, 수입
☐ **paid employment**	유급 고용
☐ **deterrent**	명사 억제책, 억제력
☐ **revenue**	명사 세수, 세입

30 2023년 9월 37번 (정답률 45%) 정답 ③

[지문 끊어 읽기] 알고리즘 디자인

(1) Architects might say /
건축가들은 말할지도 모른다 /
a machine can never design an innovative or impressive building /
기계는 결코 혁신적이거나 인상적인 건물을 디자인할 수 없다고 /
because a computer cannot be "creative." 정답 단서-1 컴퓨터는 '창의적'일 수 없으므로 기계가 인상적인 건물을 디자인하는 것은 불가능하다고 생각함.
컴퓨터가 '창의적'일 수 없기 때문에

(2) Yet consider the Elbphilharmonie, a new concert hall in Hamburg, /
선행사
그러나 함부르크에 있는 새로운 콘서트 홀인 Elbphilharmonie를 생각해 보자 / 정답 단서-1 문장 (1)에 대한 반례로 함부르크의 콘서트 홀인 Elbphilharmonie를 언급함.
which contains a remarkably beautiful auditorium /
주격 관계대명사
놀랍도록 아름다운 강당을 포함하는 /
composed of ten thousand interlocking acoustic panels.
1만 개의 서로 맞물리는 음향 패널로 구성된 과거분사구

(B) (5) It is the sort of space / that makes one instinctively think /
=an auditorium 선행사 주격 관계대명사 (일반적인) 사람
그것은 종류의 공간이다 / 본능적으로 생각하게 만드는 /
S'
that only a human being /
명사절 접속사(think의 목적어절을 이끎)
오직 인간만이 /
— and a human with a remarkably refined creative sensibility, at that — /
그리고 그것도 놀랍도록 세련된 창의적 감수성을 가진 인간만이 / 문장 (2)의 Elbphilharmonie의 강당에 대해 부연 설명함.
could design something so aesthetically impressive. 정답 단서-1
V'
그토록 미학적으로 인상적인 것을 디자인할 수 있다고

(6) Yet the auditorium was, in fact, designed algorithmically, / 정답 단서-2 Elbphilharmonie의 강당은 컴퓨터 알고리즘으로 디자인됨.
하지만 실제로 그 강당은 알고리즘으로 디자인되었다 /
using a technique / known as "parametric design."
기술을 사용하여 / '파라메트릭 디자인'이라고 알려진

(C) (7) The architects gave the system a set of criteria, /
4형식V I·O D·O
건축가들은 그 방식에 일련의 기준을 부여했다 /
and it generated a set of possible designs /
=the system
그리고 그것은 일련의 가능한 디자인을 만들어 냈다 /
for the architects to choose from. 정답 단서-2 문장 (6)의 알고리즘 디자인에 대해 건축가들이 그 방식에 기준을 부여해 그들이 선택할 수 있는 가능한 디자인을 만들게 했다고 함.
to부정사의 의미상의 주어 형용사적 용법
건축가들이 선택할 수 있는

(8) Similar software has been used /
유사한 소프트웨어가 사용되었다 /
to design lightweight bicycle frames and sturdier chairs, /
부사적 용법(목적)
경량 자전거 프레임과 더 튼튼한 의자를 디자인하는 데 /
among much else. 정답 단서-3 유사한 소프트웨어가 많은 제품들의 디자인 제작에 사용됨.
다른 많은 것들 중에서

(A) (3) Are these systems behaving "creatively"? 정답 단서-3 문장 (8)의 건축 디자인과 다양한 제품 디자인에도 사용되는 유사한 소프트웨어와 문장 (7)의 the system을 these systems로 지칭함.
이러한 방식들은 '창의적으로' 움직이는가

(4) No, / they are using lots of processing power /
아니다 / 그것들은 많은 처리 능력을 사용하고 있다 /
to blindly generate varied possible designs, /
부사적 용법(목적)
다양한 가능한 디자인을 무턱대고 만들기 위해 /
[working in a very different way from a human being]. [ ]: 분사구문
인간과는 매우 다른 방식으로 작동하면서

[전문 해석]

(1)건축가들은 컴퓨터가 '창의적'일 수 없기 때문에 기계는 결코 혁신적이거나 인상적인 건물을 디자인할 수 없다고 말할지도 모른다. (2)그러나 1만 개의 서로 맞물리는 음향 패널로 구성된 놀랍도록 아름다운 강당을 포함하는, 함부르크에 있는 새로운 콘서트 홀인 Elbphilharmonie를 생각해 보자.
(B) (5)그것은 오직 인간만이, 그리고 그것도 놀랍도록 세련된 창의적 감수성을 가진 인간만이 그토록 미학적으로 인상적인 것을 디자인할 수 있다고 본능적으로 생각하게 만드는 종류의 공간이다. (6)하지만 실제로 그 강당은 '파라메트릭 디자인'이라고 알려진 기술을 사용하여 알고리즘으로 디자인되었다.

(C) (7)건축가들은 그 방식에 일련의 기준을 부여했고, 그것은 건축가들이 선택할 수 있는 일련의 가능한 디자인을 만들어 냈다. (8)유사한 소프트웨어가 다른 많은 것들 중에서 경량 자전거 프레임과 더 튼튼한 의자를 디자인하는 데 사용되었다.
(A) (3)이러한 방식들은 '창의적으로' 움직이는가? (4)아니다, 그것들은 인간과는 매우 다른 방식으로 작동하면서 다양한 가능한 디자인을 무턱대고 만들기 위해 많은 처리 능력을 사용하고 있다.

[정답 확인]

주어진 글 다음에 이어질 글의 순서로 가장 적절한 것은?

① (A) — (C) — (B)　② (B) — (A) — (C)　✔ (B) — (C) — (A)
④ (C) — (A) — (B)　⑤ (C) — (B) — (A)

[문제 풀이]

이 글은 인간과는 다른 방식의 알고리즘 디자인에 관한 내용이다. 주어진 글의 문장 (1)은 창의적이지 않은 컴퓨터가 혁신적이거나 인상적인 건물을 디자인할 수 없다는 건축가들의 예상을 언급한다. 문장 (2)에서는 역접의 접속사 Yet을 시작으로 함부르크에 있는 새로운 콘서트 홀인 Elbphilharmonie를 소개한다. 문장 (5)에서 '그것'은 인간만이 디자인했을 거라 생각하게 만드는 공간이라고 설명하는데, 이는 바로 문장 (2)에서 언급한 Elbphilharmonie의 강당이다. 따라서 주어진 글 다음에는 (B)가 와야 한다. 다음으로 문장 (6)에서 그 강당이 컴퓨터 알고리즘으로 디자인되었다고 하는데, 이에 대해 문장 (7)에서 알고리즘 방식으로 건축가들이 어떻게 디자인을 만들어 냈는지 설명한다. 따라서 (B) 다음에는 (C)가 와야 한다. 문장 (7)의 그 방식(the system)에 이어, 문장 (8)에서는 유사한 소프트웨어를 통해 디자인된 자전거 프레임과 의자를 언급하고, 이는 문장 (3)의 these systems와 연결된다. 따라서 (C) 다음에 (A)가 온다. 그러므로 정답은 ③ '(B) — (C) — (A)'이다.

[중요 어휘]

☐ **innovative**	형용사 혁신적인, 획기적인
☐ **impressive**	형용사 인상적인, 강한 인상을 주는
☐ **remarkably**	부사 놀랍도록, 두드러지게
☐ **auditorium**	명사 강당, 관객석
☐ **interlock**	동사 서로 맞물리다
☐ **acoustic**	형용사 음향의, 청각의
☐ **instinctively**	부사 본능적으로, 직관적으로
☐ **refined**	형용사 세련된, 정제된
☐ **sensibility**	명사 감수성, 감성, 감각
☐ **at that**	그것도, 게다가
☐ **criteria**	명사 기준 (criterion의 복수형)
☐ **generate**	동사 만들어 내다, 발생시키다
☐ **sturdy**	형용사 튼튼한, 견고한 (sturdy-sturdier-sturdiest)
☐ **blindly**	부사 무턱대고, 맹목적으로

핵심 편견은 우리의 결정과 삶에 영향을 주므로 편견을 최대한 배제할 수 있는 전략을 선택해야 한다는 내용의 지문임. 이 전략을 선택해야 하는 이유와 선택 과정 등이 나와 있음.

31　2020년 6월 37번 (정답률 40%)　정답 ⑤

[지문 끊어 읽기]　편견 제거 전략

(1) Since we know / we can't completely eliminate our biases, /
우리는 알고 있기 때문에 / 우리가 우리의 편견들을 완전히 제거할 수 없다는 것을 /
we need to try / to limit the harmful impacts / they can have / (정답 단서-1)
우리는 노력할 필요가 있다 / 해로운 영향을 제한하기 위해 / 그것들이 미칠 수 있는 /
on the objectivity and rationality / of our decisions and judgments.
객관성과 합리성에 / 우리의 결정과 판단의

힌트 문장 (6)의 'It'은 형식상의 주어, 접속사 that부터 문장 끝까지는 하나의 명사절로 내용상의 주어가 됨.

(C) (6) It is important / that we are aware / (병렬①)
중요하다 / 우리가 자각하는 것이 /
when one of our cognitive biases is activated /
언제 우리의 인지적인 편견들 중 하나가 활성화되는지를 /
and make a conscious choice / to overcome that bias. (정답 단서-1)
(병렬②)　(형용사적 용법(~할))
그리고 의식적인 선택을 하는 것이 / 그 편견을 극복할

(7) We need to be aware of the impact / [the bias has / (정답 단서-2)
우리는 영향을 자각할 필요가 있다 / 편견이 미치는 /
on our decision making process and our life].
우리의 결정 과정과 삶에

(B) (4) Then / we can choose / an appropriate de-biasing strategy /
그러면 / 우리는 선택할 수 있다 / 적절한 편견 제거 전략을 /
to combat it. (정답 단서-2)
(=the bias)
그것과 맞서기 위해

힌트 문장 (5)의 if는 목적어 역할을 하는 명사절을 이끄는 접속사로, whether과 바꾸어 쓸 수 있고, '~인지 (아닌지)' 라는 뜻으로 쓰임. 접속사 if가 명사절로 쓰일 때는 주어 자리에 올 수 없음.

(5) After we have implemented a strategy, / we should check in again /
우리가 전략을 실행한 후 / 우리는 다시 확인해야 한다 /
to see / if it worked in the way / we had hoped. (정답 단서-3)
(부사적 용법(~하기 위해))
보기 위해 / 그것이 방식대로 작동했는지 / 우리가 바랐던

힌트 조건의 부사절의 시제가 과거이기 때문에 대동사 do를 did로 쓴 것임. 문장 (2)와 (3)의 did는 모두 문장 (5)의 'worked in the way we had hoped', 즉 '우리가 바랐던 방식대로 작동했다'를 나타냄.

(A) (2) If it did, / we can move on / (정답 단서-3)
(=a strategy)
만약 그것이 그랬다면 / 우리는 나아갈 수 있다 /
and make an objective and informed decision.
그리고 객관적이고 정보에 기반한 결정을 내릴 수 있다

(3) If it didn't, / we can try the same strategy again / (정답 단서-3)
만약 그것이 그러지 않았다면 / 우리는 같은 전략을 다시 시도해 볼 수 있다 /
or implement a new one / until we are ready /
혹은 새로운 것을 실행할 수 있다 / 우리가 준비가 될 때까지 /
to make a rational judgment.
(부사적 용법(형용사 수식))
합리적인 판단을 내릴

힌트 'the harmful impacts'를 선행사로 하는 목적격 관계대명사절에서 관계대명사 which 또는 that이 생략되었음. 관계사절 안에 비어 있는 선행사 자리를 확인하고, 'have an impact on(~에 영향을 미치다)'이라는 숙어를 활용하여 문장을 해석할 것.

[중요 구문]

(1) Since we know [(that) we can't completely eliminate our biases],
[ ]: know의 목적어인 명사절
we need to try to limit the harmful impacts [(which/that) they can have ∨ on the objectivity and rationality ~].
(선행사)　[ ]: 목적격 관계대명사절

[전문 해석]

(1)우리는 우리가 (우리의) 편견들을 완전히 제거할 수 없다는 것을 알고 있기 때문에, 우리는 그것(편견)들이 우리의 결정과 판단의 객관성과 합리성에 미칠 수 있는 해로운 영향을 제한하기 위해 노력할 필요가 있다.
(C) (6)우리가 언제 우리의 인지적인 편견들 중 하나가 활성화되는지를 자각하고 그 편견을 극복할 의식적인 선택을 하는 것이 중요하다. (7)우리는 편견이 우리의 결정 과정과 삶에 미치는 영향을 자각할 필요가 있다.
(B) (4)그러면 우리는 그것(편견)과 맞서기 위해 적절한 편견 제거 전략을 선택할 수 있다. (5)우리가 전략을 실행한 후, 우리는 그것(전략)이 우리가 바랐던 방식대로 작동했는지 (아닌지) 보기 위해 다시 확인해야 한다.
(A) (2)만약 (그것이) 그랬다면, 우리는 나아갈 수 있고, 객관적이고 정보에 기반한 결정을 내릴 수 있다. (3)만약 (그것이) 그러지 않았다면, 우리는 우리가 합리적인 판단을 내릴 준비가 될 때까지 같은 전략을 다시 시도해 보거나 혹은 새로운 것(전략)을 실행할 수 있다.

[정답 확인]

주어진 글 다음에 이어질 글의 순서로 가장 적절한 것은?

① (A) — (C) — (B)　② (B) — (A) — (C)　③ (B) — (C) — (A)
④ (C) — (A) — (B)　✔ (C) — (B) — (A)

[문제 풀이]

주어진 글은 비록 편견을 완전히 제거할 수 없지만, 편견의 해로운 영향을 제한하기 위해 노력해야 한다고 주장한다. 따라서 편견을 극복할 의식적인 선택을 강조한 (C)의 문장 (6)이 문장 (1) 다음에 이어져야 한다. 또, 문장 (4)의 편견 제거 전략은 편견이 삶에 미치는 영향을 자각했을 때 가능한 결과로, 접속 부사 Then으로 문장 (7)과 자연스럽게 연결되기 때문에 (C) 다음에는 (B)가 온다. (B)는 실행한 전략이 효과적이었는지를 확인해야 한다는 내용이며 문장 (2)와 (3)은 전략이 효과적이었을 경우와 효과적이지 않았을 경우 각각을 설명하므로, (B) 다음에는 (A)가 와야 한다. 따라서 정답은 ⑤ '(C) — (B) — (A)'이다.

[중요 어휘]

☐ **eliminate**	동사 제거하다, 삭제하다
☐ **bias**	명사 편견, 편향
☐ **have an impact on**	~에 영향을 미치다
☐ **objectivity**	명사 객관성
☐ **rationality**	명사 합리성
☐ **cognitive**	형용사 인지적인, 인지의
☐ **conscious**	형용사 의식적인, 의도적인

정답과 해설 14 문장 배열

☐ overcome	동사 극복하다
☐ appropriate	형용사 적절한, 적합한
☐ combat	동사 ~와 맞서다, 싸우다
☐ implement	동사 실행하다
☐ informed	형용사 정보에 기반한, 교양 있는
☐ rational	형용사 합리적인, 이성적인

32 2022년 11월 36번 (정답률 40%) 정답 ②

[지문 끊어 읽기] 잊힐 권리

(1) The right to be forgotten / is a right / distinct from but related to /
S 형용사적 용법 병렬① 병렬②
잊힐 권리는 / 권리이다 / 구별되지만 관련이 있는 /
a right to privacy. 정답 단서-1 '잊힐 권리'를 '사생활 권리'와 비교하여 제시하고 있음.
전치사
사생활 권리와

힌트 밑줄 친 부분은 앞에 나온 명사 a right을 수식하는 형용사구로서, 등위접속사 but을 중심으로 distinct와 related가 병렬로 연결된 구조임. distinct 앞에는 '주격 관계대명사+be동사'가 생략되어 있고, 'a right to privacy'는 distinct from과 related to의 공통 목적어임.

(2) The right to privacy / 정답 단서-1 '사생활 권리'에 관한 설명
사생활 권리는 /
is, among other things, / the right for information /
무엇보다도 / 정보에 대한 권리이다 /
traditionally regarded as protected or personal /
병렬① 병렬②
전통적으로 보호되거나 개인적인 것으로 여겨지는 /
not to be revealed.
형용사적 용법
공개되지 않아야 할

힌트 among others [other things]는 '무엇보다도, 그 중에서도, 특히'라는 뜻임.

힌트 traditionally ~ revealed는 앞에 나온 명사 information을 수식하는 형용사구로서, traditionally 앞에는 '주격 관계대명사+be동사'가 생략되어 있음.

(B) (5) The right to be forgotten, / in contrast, / 정답 단서-1 '잊힐 권리'에 대한 설명으로, '사생활 권리'를 설명하는 앞 문장과 대조의 연결사 'in contrast'로 연결되어 있음.
형용사적 용법
잊힐 권리는 / 반면에 /
can be applied to information /
정보에 적용될 수 있다 / 선행사
that has been in the public domain.
주격 관계대명사
공공의 영역에 있었던

(6) The right to be forgotten /
S 형용사적 용법
잊힐 권리는 /
broadly includes the right of an individual /
V O
개인의 권리를 광범위하게 포함한다 /
not to be forever defined /
형용사적 용법
영원히 정의되지 않아야 할 /
by information from a specific point in time. 정답 단서-2 '잊힐 권리'는 특정 시점의 정보에 의해 영원히 정의되지 않을 권리임.
어떤 시점의 정보에 의해

=the right to be forgotten
(A) (3) One motivation for such a right / is to allow individuals /
그러한 권리의 한 가지 이유는 / 개인을 허락하는 것이다 / 5형식V O
to move on with their lives / and not be defined /
O·C① O·C②(=not to be defined)
자신의 삶을 영위할 수 있도록 / 그리고 정의되지 않도록 /
by a specific event or period in their lives. 정답 단서-2 특정 사건이나 기간에 의해 정의되지 않고 자기 삶을 영위할 수 있게 하는 권리에 대한 설명으로, 문맥상 그러한 권리는 '잊힐 권리'를 의미함.
자신의 삶의 특정한 사건이나 기간에 의해

(4) For example, / it has long been recognized /
형식상의 주어
예를 들어 / 오랫동안 인식되어 왔다 /
in some countries, / such as the UK and France, /
일부 국가에서는 / 영국과 프랑스와 같은 /
[that even past criminal convictions /
과거의 범죄 유죄 판결조차도 /
should eventually be "spent" /
결국 '소모되어야' 한다고 / 병렬①
and not continue to affect a person's life]. [ ]: 내용상의 주어(=that 명사절)
병렬② 명사적 용법(continue의 목적어)
그리고 한 사람의 삶에 계속 영향을 미치지 않아야 한다고

★중요 (A)의 내용이 문장 (7)에서 말하는 '잊힐 권리를 지지하는 이유'에 해당하므로, (C)가 (A) 뒤에 와야 함.

(C) (7) Despite the reason /
그러한 이유에도 불구하고 /
for supporting the right to be forgotten, / 정답 단서-3 잊힐 권리가 분명 필요한 것은 맞지만, 때때로 잊힐 권리는 다른 권리와 충돌함.
전치사 동명사 supporting의 목적어
잊힐 권리를 지지하는 것에 대한 /
the right to be forgotten / can sometimes come into conflict /
잊힐 권리는 / 때때로 충돌할 수 있다 /
with other rights.
다른 권리와

(8) For example, / formal exceptions are sometimes made /
예를 들어 / 공식적인 예외가 때때로 만들어진다 /
for security or public health reasons.
안보 혹은 공공 보건의 이유로 인해

[중요 구문]

(3) One motivation ~ is [to allow individuals to move on ~
S V [ ]: S·C 병렬①
and not be defined ~].
병렬②

힌트 to allow 이하는 문장의 주격 보어로 'to부정사의 명사적 용법(~하는 것)'이 사용되었음. allow는 목적격 보어로 to부정사를 쓰는 5형식 동사로, allow 동사의 목적격 보어 'to move'와 'not (to) be defined'가 병렬을 이루고 있음.

[전문 해석]

(1)잊힐 권리는 사생활 권리와 구별되지만 관련이 있는 권리이다. (2)사생활 권리는 무엇보다도 전통적으로 보호되거나 개인적인 것으로 여겨지는 공개되지 않아야 할 정보에 대한 권리이다.
(B) (5)반면에, 잊힐 권리는 공공의 영역에 있었던 정보에 적용될 수 있다. (6)잊힐 권리는 어떤 시점의 정보에 의해 영원히 정의되지 않아야 할 개인의 권리를 광범위하게 포함한다.
(A) (3)그러한 권리의 한 가지 이유는 개인이 자신의 삶을 영위하고 자신의 삶의 특정한 사건이나 기간에 의해 정의되지 않도록 허락하는 것이다. (4)예를 들어, 영국과 프랑스와 같은 일부 국가에서는 과거의 범죄 유죄 판결조차도 결국 '소모되어야' 하고 한 사람의 삶에 계속 영향을 미치지 않아야 한다고 오랫동안 인식되어 왔다.
(C) (7)잊힐 권리를 지지하는 것에 대한 그러한 이유에도 불구하고 잊힐 권리는 다른 권리와 때때로 충돌할 수 있다. (8)예를 들어, 공식적인 예외가 안보 혹은 공공 보건의 이유로 인해 때때로 만들어진다.

[정답 확인]

주어진 글 다음에 이어질 글의 순서로 가장 적절한 것은?

① (A) — (C) — (B) ✔② (B) — (A) — (C) ③ (B) — (C) — (A)
④ (C) — (A) — (B) ⑤ (C) — (B) — (A)

[문제 풀이]

문장 (1)을 통해, '잊힐 권리'와 '사생활 권리'가 대조되어 설명될 것임을 알 수 있으며, 문장 (2)에서 '사생활 권리'에 대한 설명을 했으므로, 이후 대조의 연결사인 'in contrast(대조적으로)'를 통해 '잊힐 권리'에 대한 설명이 이어지는 것이 자연스럽다. 따라서 주어진 글 다음에는 가장 먼저 (B)가 온다. 다음으로, 문장 (3)의 'such a right'은 특정 사건이나 기간에 의해 개인이 정의되지 않고 자기 삶을 영위하는 것을 목표로 한다는 점에서, (B)에서 소개된 '잊힐 권리'를 나타낸다. 따라서 (B) 다음에는 (A)가 온다. 마지막으로, 잊힐 권리의 존재 이유 내지는 필요성에 대해 이야기하는 (A)의 내용은 문장 (7)의 'the reason for supporting the right to be forgotten'에 해당하므로, (A) 다음에는 (C)가 와야 한다. 따라서 글의 순서로 가장 적절한 것은 ② '(B) — (A) — (C)'이다.

[오답 풀이]

③ - (B)에는 '잊힐 권리'가 어떤 권리인지에 대한 대략적인 설명이 주어졌을 뿐, '잊힐 권리를 지지하는 이유'가 설명되지 않았기 때문에, (B) 다음에 (C)가 오면 흐름상 어색하다. (C)는 '잊힐 권리'의 존재 이유가 소개된 (A) 다음에 와야 한다.

[중요 어휘]

☐ right	명사 권리 / 형용사 옳은, 오른쪽의
☐ distinct	형용사 구별되는, (전혀) 다른
☐ related	형용사 관련이 있는, 관련된
☐ be regarded as	~이라고 여겨지다
☐ reveal	동사 공개하다, 폭로하다
☐ apply A to B	A를 B에 적용하다
☐ domain	명사 영역, 분야
☐ criminal	형용사 범죄의 / 명사 범인
☐ conviction	명사 유죄 판결
☐ come into conflict	충돌하다, 싸우다

33 2022년 11월 37번 (정답률 40%) 정답 ③

[지문 끊어 읽기] 경제학에서 인간 행동에 영향을 미치는 요인

(1) To an economist / who succeeds /
선행사 주격 관계대명사
경제학자에게는 / 성공한 /
in figuring out a person's preference structure / — understanding /
한 사람의 선호도 구조를 알아내는 것에 / 즉 이해하는 것 /
[whether the satisfaction gained from consuming one good is greater /
한 상품을 소비함으로써 얻는 만족도가 더 큰지를 /
than that of another] — / [ ]: whether 명사절(~인지 아닌지)
=the satisfaction =another good
또 다른 것에 대한 그것보다 /
explaining behavior / in terms of changes /
행동을 설명하는 것은 / 변화의 관점에서 /
in underlying likes and dislikes / is usually highly problematic.
기저에 있는 호불호의 / 일반적으로 매우 문제가 많다 정답 단서-1 경제학자들에게 있어, 사람 마음속의 '호불호'의 변화로 사람의 행동을 설명하는 것은 문제가 있음.

(B) (3) [To argue, / for instance, /
주장하는 것은 / 예를 들어 /
that the baby boom and then the baby bust resulted /
베이비 붐과 그 후의 출생률의 급락이 비롯되었다고 /
from an increase and then a decrease /
증가와 그 후의 감소에서 /
in the public's inherent taste for children, /
아이에 대한 대중의 내재적인 기호의 /
★중요 문맥상 베이비 붐이나 출생률의 급락은 인간의 행동(behavior)에 해당하고, 아이에 대한 대중의 내재적 기호는 문장 (1)의 '호불호(likes and dislikes)'와 일맥상통함.
rather than a change in relative prices /
상대적 비용의 변화보다는 /
against a background of stable preferences,] /
변동이 없는 선호도를 배경으로 한 / [ ]: S
places a social scientist / in an unsound position. 정답 단서-1
V O
사회 과학자를 놓는다 / 불안정한 입지에
아이에 대한 대중의 선호에 따라 출생률이 달라졌다고 주장하는 것은 사회 과학자들의 입지를 불안정하게 함. 즉, 문제가 있음.

(C) (4) In economics, / such an argument about birth rates /
such+a(n)+(형)+명
경제학에서 / 출생률에 대한 그러한 주장은 /
would be equivalent to saying /
~이라고 말하는 것과 같을 것이다 /
[that a rise and fall in mortality could be attributed /
사망률의 상승과 하락이 기인할 수 있다고 /
to an increase in the inherent desire change for death]. [ ]: that 명사절
죽음에 대한 내재적 욕구 변화의 증가에
정답 단서-2 아이에 대한 선호에 따라 출생률이 달라진다는 주장의 논리대로라면 죽음에 대한 욕구(호불호) 변화에 따라 사망률(행동)이 달라지게 될 것임.

(5) For an economist, / changes in income and prices, /
경제학자에게는 / 소득과 물가의 변화가 / S
rather than changes in tastes, / affect birth rates.
기호의 변화보다는 / 출생률에 영향을 미친다 V O
정답 단서-3 경제학자는 '소득과 물가 변화'가 출생률에 영향을 미친다고 봄.

(A) (2) When income rises, / for example, /
소득이 증가할 때 / 예를 들어 /
people want more children / (or, as you will see later, /
사람들은 더 많은 자녀를 원한다 / 혹은 여러분이 나중에 알게 되겠지만 /
more satisfaction derived from children), /
아이로부터 얻어지는 더 큰 만족감을 /
even if their inherent desire for children stays the same. 정답 단서-3
자녀에 대한 자신의 내재적 욕구가 그대로 유지되더라도
자녀에 대한 내재적 욕구가 똑같아도, 소득이 증가하면 사람들은 더 많은 자녀를 원할 수 있음. 즉, 소득의 변화가 출생률에 영향을 미칠 수 있음.

[중요 구문]

(1) [To an economist who succeeds in figuring out a person's preference structure — understanding [whether the satisfaction ~ is greater than that of another] —] explaining behavior ~ is usually highly problematic.
[ ]: 전치사구 선행사 주격 관계대명사 / [ ]: whether 명사절: ~인지 아닌지 / 비교급 =the satisfaction / S(동명사구) V / S·C

힌트 'understanding ~ another'은 'figuring out a person's preference structure'에 대한 부연 설명임. 전치사 in의 목적어로서 figuring과 understanding 모두 동명사의 형태를 취하고 있음.

[전문 해석]

(1)한 사람의 선호도 구조를 알아내는 것, 즉 한 상품을 소비함으로써 얻는 만족도가 또 다른 상품에 대한 만족도보다 더 큰지를 이해하는 것에 성공한 경제학자에게는, 기저에 있는 호불호의 변화의 관점에서 행동을 설명하는 것은 일반적으로 매우 문제가 많다.
(B) (3)예를 들어, 베이비 붐과 그 후의 출생률의 급락이 변동이 없는 선호도를 배경으로 한 상대적 비용의 변화보다는 아이에 대한 대중의 내재적인 기호의 증가와 그 후의 감소에서 비롯되었다고 주장하는 것은 사회 과학자를 불안정한 입지에 놓는다.
(C) (4)경제학에서, 출생률에 대한 그러한 주장은 사망률의 상승과 하락이 죽음에 대한 내재적 욕구 변화의 증가에 기인할 수 있다고 말하는 것과 같을 것이다. (5)경제학자에게는 기호의 변화보다는 소득과 물가의 변화가 출생률에 영향을 미친다.
(A) (2)예를 들어, 소득이 증가할 때 사람들은 자녀에 대한 자신의 내재적 욕구가 그대로 유지되더라도 더 많은 자녀(혹은 여러분이 나중에 알게 되겠지만, 아이로부터 얻어지는 더 큰 만족감)를 원한다.

[정답 확인]

주어진 글 다음에 이어질 글의 순서로 가장 적절한 것은?

① (A) — (C) — (B) ② (B) — (A) — (C) ③ (B) — (C) — (A)
④ (C) — (A) — (B) ⑤ (C) — (B) — (A)

[문제 풀이]

주어진 문장의 핵심은 사람 마음의 '호불호'의 변화로 '행동'을 설명하는 것이 경제학자에게는 문제가 있다는 것이다. 한편, 문장 (3)에서 언급된 '아이에 대한 대중의 내재적인 기호'가 바로 주어진 문장의 '호불호'에 해당하고, 베이비 붐과 그 후의 출생률의 급락은 인간의 '행동'을 의미하므로, 문장 (3)은 주어진 문장에 대한 구체적인 예시이다. 따라서 주어진 문장 다음에는 가장 먼저 (B)가 온다. 다음으로, 문장 (4)의 '출생률에 대한 그러한 주장'은 '아이에 대한 선호에 따라 출생률이 달라진다'는 문장 (3)의 내용을 나타내므로, (B) 다음에는 (C)가 온다. 마지막으로, '출생률'에 영향을 미치는 요인으로 '기호(= 호불호)'보다는 '소득과 물가'에 초점을 맞추는 문장 (5) 다음에는, '소득'이 변화할 때 출생률이 어떻게 변화하는지를 설명하는 (A)가 이어져야 한다. 따라서 정답은 ③ '(B) — (C) — (A)'이다.

[오답 풀이]

④ - (B) 문단은 '아이에 대한 내재적인 선호도'의 변화에 따라 '출생'이라는 인간 행동이 변화한다고 보는 관점에 대해 이야기하고 있으므로, 문장 (1)에서 언급된 '호불호의 변화의 관점에서 행동을 설명'하는 사례에 해당한다. 한편 (A)는 출생률의 변화를 '소득'의 변화로 설명하고 있으므로, (B) 문단은 (A) 다음이 아니라 주어진 문장 다음에 와야 한다. 따라서 ④ '(C) — (A) — (B)'는 답이 될 수 없다.

[중요 어휘]

□ succeed in V-ing	~하는 것에 성공하다
□ preference	명사 선호(도), 애호
□ satisfaction	명사 만족(감)
□ consume	동사 소비하다, 섭취하다
□ underlying	형용사 기저에 있는, 근본적인
□ baby bust	출생률의 급락
□ inherent	형용사 내재적인, 고유의
□ taste	명사 기호, 취향 / 동사 맛보다
□ relative	형용사 상대적인, 관계있는 / 명사 친척
□ stable	형용사 변동이 없는, 안정적인
□ unsound	형용사 불안정한, 견고하지 못한, 건강하지 않은
□ argument	명사 주장, 논거, 논쟁
□ equivalent	형용사 같은, 동등한
□ rise	명사 상승 / 동사 증가하다, 오르다 (rise-rose-risen)
□ mortality	명사 사망률
□ be attributed to	~에 기인하다, ~의 덕분으로 여겨지다
□ derived from	~에서 얻어진

34 2023년 9월 36번 (정답률 35%) 정답 ⑤

[지문 끊어 읽기] 광고의 역할

(1) If you drive down a busy street, /
만약 당신이 번화한 거리를 운전한다면 /
you will find many competing businesses, /
당신은 경쟁하는 많은 업체들을 발견할 것이다 /
often right next to one another. 정답 단서-1 번화한 거리에는 서로의 근처에서 경쟁하는 업체들이 많이 있음.
흔히 서로의 바로 옆에서

(2) For example, / in most places /
예를 들어 / 대부분의 장소에서 /
[a consumer in search of a quick meal] / has many choices, /
[ ]: S　V
빠른 식사를 찾는 소비자는 / 많은 선택권을 가지고 있다 /
and more fast-food restaurants appear all the time.
그리고 더 많은 패스트푸드 식당들이 항상 나타난다

정답 단서-1 경쟁하는 회사들은 광고를 많이 함.

(C) (7) These competing firms advertise heavily.
이 경쟁하는 회사들은 광고를 많이 한다

힌트 'The temptation is to see advertising as ~'라는 표현은 직역하면 '유혹은 광고를 ~으로 보는 것이다'라는 의미인데, 이는 '광고를 ~으로 보도록 유혹되다', 즉 '광고를 ~으로 보기 쉽다'라고 의역할 수 있음.

(8) The temptation is to see advertising /
명사적 용법
유혹은 광고를 보는 것이다 /
as driving up the price of a product /
제품의 가격을 올리는 것으로 /

힌트 'see A as B(A를 B로 보다, 여기다)'에서 B 자리에 V-ing가 왔으며, see 대신 view, think of 등으로 바꿔 쓸 수 있음.

without any benefit to the consumer. 정답 단서-2
소비자에 대한 어떤 혜택도 없이
광고는 소비자에게 아무런 혜택도 없이 단지 제품의 가격을 올리는 것으로 여겨지기 쉬움.

(B) (5) However, / this misconception doesn't account for /
그러나 / 이러한 오해는 설명하지 않는다 /
why firms advertise. 정답 단서-2 광고에 대한 오해와 달리 회사들이 광고를 하는 이유가 있음.
회사들이 광고를 하는 이유를

(6) In markets /
시장에서 /
[where competitors sell slightly differentiated products], / [ ]: 관계부사절
경쟁사들이 조금씩 차별화된 제품들을 판매하는 /
advertising enables firms to inform their customers /
동명사S　5형식V　O　O·C
광고는 회사들이 그들의 소비자들에게 알릴 수 있게 해준다 /
about new products and services. 정답 단서-3 광고는 회사들이 소비자들에게 새로운 제품과 서비스를 알리는 역할을 함.
새로운 제품과 서비스를

(A) (3) Yes, costs rise, / but consumers also gain information /
물론 가격이 오른다 / 하지만 소비자들도 정보를 얻는다 /
to help make purchasing decisions. 정답 단서-3 광고를 하면 제품의 가격이 오르게 되지만, 소비자들도 구매 결정을 돕는 정보를 얻게 됨.
형용사적 용법
구매 결정을 내리는 데 도움이 되는

(4) Consumers also benefit from added variety, /
소비자들은 또한 추가된 다양성으로부터 혜택을 얻는다 /
and we all get a product /
선행사
그리고 우리 모두는 제품을 얻는다 /
[that's pretty close to our vision of a perfect good] / [ ]: 주격 관계대명사절
완벽한 제품에 대한 우리의 상상에 매우 근접한 /
— and no other market structure delivers that outcome.
그런데 다른 어떤 시장 구조도 그러한 결과를 내놓지 않는다

[전문 해석]

(1)만약 당신이 번화한 거리를 운전한다면, 당신은 흔히 서로의 바로 옆에서 경쟁하는 많은 업체들을 발견할 것이다. (2)예를 들어, 대부분의 장소에서 빠른 식사를 찾는 소비자는 많은 선택권을 가지고 있고, 더 많은 패스트푸드 식당들이 항상 나타난다.
(C) (7)이 경쟁하는 회사들은 광고를 많이 한다. (8)광고를 소비자에 대한 어떤 혜택도 없이 제품의 가격을 올리는 것으로 보기 쉽다.
(B) (5)그러나, 이러한 오해는 회사들이 광고를 하는 이유를 설명하지 않는다. (6)경쟁사들이 조금씩 차별화된 제품들을 판매하는 시장에서, 광고는 회사들이 그들의 소비자들에게 새로운 제품과 서비스를 알릴 수 있게 해준다.
(A) (3)물론 가격이 오르지만, 소비자들도 구매 결정을 내리는 데 도움이 되는 정보를 얻는다. (4)소비자들은 또한 추가된 다양성으로부터 혜택을 얻고, 우리 모두는 완벽한 제품에 대한 우리의 상상에 매우 근접한 제품을 얻는데, 다른 어떤 시장 구조도 그러한 결과를 내놓지 않는다.

[정답 확인]

주어진 글 다음에 이어질 글의 순서로 가장 적절한 것은?

① (A) — (C) — (B)　② (B) — (A) — (C)　③ (B) — (C) — (A)
④ (C) — (A) — (B)　✔⑤ (C) — (B) — (A)

[문제 풀이]

이 지문은 기업과 소비자 양측에게 광고가 어떤 역할을 하는지를 설명하는 글이다. 먼저 문장 (1)에서 거리에는 많은 업체들이 서로의 근처에서 경쟁을 하고 있다고 언급하며, 문장 (2)에서 패스트푸드 식당을 예로 들어 설명한다. 이때 문장 (1)의 competing businesses를 문장 (7)에서 These competing firms로 지칭하고 있으므로 주어진 글 다음에는 (C)가 오는 것이 적절하다. 다음으로 문장 (8)에서는 광고를 소비자에 대한 아무런 혜택 없이 단지 제품의 가격을 올리는 것으로 여겨지기 쉽다고 언급하는데, 문장 (5)의 this misconception(이러한 오해)이 문장 (8)의 내용을 지칭하므로 (C) 다음에는 (B)가 오는 것이 적절하다. 문장 (6)에서는 기업들이 광고를 하는 이유로 그들의 제품과 서비스를 소비자들에게 알릴 수 있기 때문이라고 설명하는데, 문장 (3)에서는 이처럼 광고를 하게 되면 제품의 가격이 오르게 되겠지만 소비자들도 구매 결정에 도움이 되는 정보를 얻을 수 있다고 설명하므로 (B) 다음에는 (A)가 오는 것이 적절하다. 따라서 정답은 ⑤ '(C) — (B) — (A)'이다.

[오답 풀이]

④ - 문장 (8)에서 광고를 소비자에 대한 어떤 혜택도 없이 제품의 가격을 올리는 것으로 보기 쉽다고 설명하기 때문에, 제품의 가격이 오른다고 언급한 문장 (3)이 문장 (8) 뒤에 오는 것으로 생각할 수 있다. 하지만 문장 (3)에서 '소비자들도 정보를 얻는다(consumers also gain information)'라고 하였으므로, 문장 (3) 이전에 광고의 또 다른 역할이 언급되었어야 한다. 또한 (C) 다음에 (A)가 오게 되면 이어지는 문장 (5)의 '이러한 오해(this misconception)'가 지칭하는 것이 불분명해지게 된다. 따라서 (C) 다음에 (A)가 오는 것은 지문의 전체 흐름상 부자연스러우므로 ④는 오답이다.

[중요 어휘]

□ compete	동사 경쟁하다, (~와) 겨루다
□ temptation	명사 유혹
□ drive up	(값 등을) 끌어올리다
□ benefit	명사 혜택, 이익, 이득 / 동사 혜택을 얻다, 도움이 되다
□ misconception	명사 오해, 잘못된 생각
□ account for	~을 설명하다, 차지하다
□ competitor	명사 경쟁자
□ differentiate	동사 차별하다, 구별하다
□ enable A to V	A가 ~할 수 있게 하다
□ inform A about B	A에게 B를 알리다[통지하다]
□ variety	명사 다양성, 변화, 종류
□ vision	명사 상상, 환상, 시력
□ deliver	동사 (결과를) 내놓다[산출하다], 배달하다

핵심 두 남자의 다툼 → 다툼을 해결하기 위한 사서의 투입 → 사서의 문제 상황 파악 → 해결책 제시의 순서로 서술되어 있는 글임.

35　2021년 6월 36번 (정답률 30%)　정답 ⑤

[지문 끊어 읽기]　근원적인 이해관계를 통한 문제 해결

정답 단서-1
(1) Consider / the story of two men / quarreling in a library.
생각해 보자 / 두 남자의 이야기를 / 도서관에서 싸우는

(2) One wants the window open / and the other wants it closed.
한 명은 창문이 열려 있기를 원한다 / 그리고 다른 한 명은 그것이 닫혀 있기를 원한다

정답 단서-1
(3) They argue back and forth / about how much to leave it open: /
그들은 주고받으며 논쟁을 벌인다 / 그것을 얼마나 많이 열어 두어야 할지에 대해 /
a crack, halfway, or three-quarters of the way.
틈, 절반, 또는 4분의 3 정도

(C) (9) No solution satisfies them both. 정답 단서-1
어떤 해결책도 그들 둘 다를 만족시키지 못한다

(10) Enter the librarian.
사서를 투입하라

정답 단서-2
(11) She asks one / why he wants the window open: /
그녀는 한 명에게 묻는다 / 왜 그가 창문이 열려 있기를 원하는지 /
"To get some fresh air."
"신선한 공기를 쐬기 위해서."

정답 단서-2
(12) She asks the other / why he wants it closed: / "To avoid a draft."
그녀는 다른 사람에게 묻는다 / 왜 그는 그것이 닫혀 있기를 원하는지 / "외풍을 피하기 위해서."

(B) (6) [After thinking a minute], / [ ]: 분사구문(=After she thinks ~)
잠시 생각한 후 /
정답 단서-2
she opens wide a window in the next room, /
그녀는 옆방에서 창문을 활짝 연다 /

[bringing in fresh air / without a draft]. [ ]: 분사구문-연속동작(=and she brings ~)
신선한 공기를 들여온다 / 외풍 없이

힌트 'typical'은 형용사로 주로 '전형적인'을 의미하는데 뒤에 전치사 of가 와서 '~의 전형이다, ~의 예시이다'라고 쓰임.

(7) This story is typical / of many negotiations. 정답 단서-3
이 이야기는 전형이다 / 많은 협상들의

(8) Since the parties' problem appears / to be a conflict of positions, / 정답 단서-3
접속사(~때문에)
당사자들의 문제가 보이기 때문에 / 입장들의 충돌로 /
they naturally tend to talk about positions /
그들은 자연스럽게 입장에 대해 말하는 경향이 있다 /
— and often reach an impasse.
그리고 종종 교착 상태에 이르다

(A) (4) The librarian could not have invented the solution / she did /
사서는 해결책을 고안해 낼 수 없었을 것이다 / 자신이 한 /
if she had focused only on the two men's stated positions / 정답 단서-3
만약 그녀가 두 남자의 언급된 입장에만 집중했다면 /
of wanting the window open or closed.
창문이 열려 있거나 닫혀 있기를 원하는

힌트 'S+could+have p.p., if+S+had p.p.'의 형식이 사용된 가정법 과거완료 구문으로, 과거에 일어난 사실의 반대 상황으로 가정하고 있음.

(5) Instead, / she looked to their underlying interests /
대신 / 그녀는 그들의 근원적인 이해관계를 살펴보았다 /
of fresh air and no draft.
신선한 공기와 외풍이 없다는

[전문 해석]

(1)도서관에서 싸우는 두 남자의 이야기를 생각해 보자. (2)한 명은 창문이 열려 있기를 원하고 다른 한 명은 그것이 닫혀 있기를 원한다. (3)그들은 그것을 얼마나 많이 열어 두어야 할지에 대해 주고받으며 논쟁을 벌인다. 틈, 절반, 또는 4분의 3 정도.
(C) (9)어떤 해결책도 그들 둘 다를 만족시키지 못한다. (10)사서를 투입하라. (11)그녀는 한 명에게 왜 그가 창문이 열려 있기를 원하는지 묻는다. "신선한 공기를 쐬기 위해서." (12)그녀는 다른 사람에게 왜 그는 그것이 닫혀 있기를 원하는지 묻는다. "외풍을 피하기 위해서."
(B) (6)잠시 생각한 후 그녀는 옆방에서 창문을 활짝 열고, 외풍 없이 신선한 공기를 들여온다. (7)이 이야기는 많은 협상들의 전형이다. (8)당사자들의 문제가 입장들의 충돌로 보이기 때문에, 그들은 자연스럽게 입장에 대해 말하는 경향이 있고 종종 교착 상태(막다른 상황)에 이른다.
(A) (4)만약 사서가 창문이 열려 있거나 닫혀 있기를 원하는 두 남자의 언급된 입장에만 집중했다면, 그녀는 자신이 (실행)한 해결책을 고안해 낼 수 없었을 것이다. (5)대신 그녀는 신선한 공기와 외풍이 없다는 그들의 근원적인 이해관계를 살펴보았다.

[정답 확인]

주어진 글 다음에 이어질 글의 순서로 가장 적절한 것은?

① (A) — (C) — (B) ② (B) — (A) — (C) ③ (B) — (C) — (A)
④ (C) — (A) — (B) ✔ (C) — (B) — (A)

[문제 풀이]

문장 (3)에서 두 남자가 언쟁을 벌이지만, 어떤 방법도 해결책이 되지 못한다는 내용이 문장 (9)에 나온다. 그리고 이 문제 상황을 해결하기 위해 사서가 투입된다는 내용이 문장 (10)이고, 문장 (11), (12)에서 사서는 두 명에게 각각 원하는 것을 물어본다. 이후에는 사서가 해결책을 제시했다는 문장 (6)이 나오는 것이 자연스럽다. 문장 (7)과 (8)에서는 이러한 상황이 전형적인 갈등-협상 상황임을 보여준다. 문장 (4)와 (5)에서는 사서가 두 남자의 입장에만 집중하지 않고, 그들이 진짜 원하는 것이 무엇인지 파악했기 때문에 적절한 해결책을 제시할 수 있었다는 내용으로 글을 마무리하고 있다. 따라서 정답은 ⑤ '(C) — (B) — (A)'이다.

[오답 풀이]

④ - (C)에는 사서가 문제 상황을 파악하기 위해 언쟁의 당사자들에게 원하는 것이 무엇인지 물어본 내용만 제시되어 있다. (A)에서는 이미 상황이 정리되었고, 사서가 해결책을 생각해 낼 수 있었던 이유를 정리하고 있으므로 (C) 다음에 (A)가 오면 내용이 자연스럽지 않다.

[중요 어휘]

☐ **quarrel**	동사 싸우다, 다투다
☐ **back and forth**	주고받으며, 왔다갔다
☐ **librarian**	명사 사서
☐ **draft**	명사 외풍, 원고, 초안
☐ **negotiation**	명사 협상, 절충
☐ **party**	명사 당사자, 단체
☐ **impasse**	명사 교착 상태, 막다름
☐ **state**	동사 언급하다, 진술하다
☐ **underlying**	형용사 근원적인, 근본적인
☐ **interest**	명사 이해관계

● 지문 구조도

(1) **두 명의 남자가 도서관에서 싸우고 있는(quarreling) 상황**
(2) 한 명은 창문이 열려 있기를(open) 원하고, 다른 한 명은 창문이 닫혀 있기를(closed) 원함. (3) 두 명은 창문을 얼마나 열어 둘지 논쟁을 함(argue back and forth). (9) 논쟁을 벌였지만 두 명 모두를 만족시키는 해결책(solution)이 나오지 않음.
(10) **갈등을 중재하기 위해 사서(librarian)가 투입됨.**
(11) 한 명은 신선한 공기(fresh air)를 원한다는 것을 알아냄. / (12) 다른 한 명은 외풍(draft)을 피하고 싶어한다는 것을 알아냄.
(6) **사서의 해결책 제시: 옆방 창문을 열어 외풍 없이 신선한 공기 유입**
↓
(7) **협상(negotiation)의 전형적인(typical) 모습임.**
(8) 협상의 당사자들(the parties)은 자신의 입장(position)에 집중해서 이야기하는 경향이 있어, 해결책 없이 교착 상태(impasse)에 이르게 되는 경우가 많음. (4) 위의 이야기에서도 사서가 두 남자의 입장만 고려했다면 해결책(solution)을 제시할 수 없었을 것임. (5) 사서는 두 남자가 근본적으로 원하는 것들(underlying interests)이 무엇인지 확인해서, 그것들을 모두 제공할 수 있는 해결책을 생각해 낼 수 있었음.

36 2022년 3월 37번 (정답률 30%) 정답 ③

[지문 끊어 읽기] 발췌독의 장점과 단점

(1) There is no doubt /
의심의 여지가 없다 /
that the length of some literary works is overwhelming.
동격의 that
일부 문학 작품의 길이가 압도적이라는 데는

(2) Reading or translating a work in class, /
S
수업 시간에 작품을 읽거나 번역하는 것은 /
hour after hour, week after week, /
몇 시간, 몇 주 동안 /
can be such a boring experience / 정답 단서-1
V
너무나 지루한 경험일 수 있어서 /
that many students never want to open a foreign language book again.
많은 학생이 다시는 외국어 서적을 절대 펴고 싶어 하지 않는다

힌트 such+(a/an)+형용사+명사+that S V 구문으로 '너무 ~해서 …하다'라는 뜻임. such와 that 사이의 명사(구)가 원인, that이 이끄는 절이 결과에 해당함.

수업에서 길이가 긴 작품을 오랜 시간 동안 읽거나 번역하는 것은 지루한 경험일 수 있음.

(B) (4) Extracts provide one type of solution. 정답 단서-1 발췌본을 읽는 것이 해결책이 될 수 있다고 함.
발췌본은 한 가지 해결책을 제공한다

(5) The advantages are obvious: 정답 단서-2 발췌본을 읽는 것의 장점을 언급함.
장점은 분명하다

(6) reading a series of passages / from different works /
S
일련의 단락을 읽는 것은 / 다양한 작품에서 가져온 /
produces more variety in the classroom, /
V
교실에서 더 많은 다양성을 만들어 낸다 /
so that the teacher has a greater chance of avoiding monotony, /
부사절 접속사(결과)
그 결과 교사는 단조로움을 피할 가능성이 더 크다 /
[while still giving learners a taste /
4형식V I.O D.O
여전히 학습자에게 맛보게 하면서 /
at least of an author's special flavour].
최소한이라도 어떤 작가의 특별한 묘미를

힌트 접속사가 생략되지 않은 분사구문으로, 원래는 'while the teacher still gives learners a taste at least of an author's special flavour.'의 형태임.

(C) (7) On the other hand, / 정답 단서-2 '반면에'라고 시작하며 발췌본의 단점을 제시하므로 발췌본의 장점을 설명한 (B) 뒤에 오는 것이 자연스러움.
반면에 /
a student [who is only exposed to 'bite-sized chunks'] /
S, 선행사 [ ]: 주격 관계대명사절
'짧은 토막글'만 접한 학생은 /
will never have the satisfaction /
만족감을 결코 가질 수 없을 것이다 /
of knowing the overall pattern of a book, / 정답 단서-3 발췌본만 접한 학생은 책의 전반적인 구성을 아는 만족감을 가질 수 없다고 함.
책의 전반적인 구성을 아는 /
which is after all the satisfaction / [most of us seek /
관계대명사(계속적 용법)
그리고 그것은 결국 만족감이다 / 우리 대부분이 찾고자 하는 /
when we read something in our own language]. [ ]: 목적격 관계대명사절
우리가 모국어로 된 어떤 글을 읽을 때 '게다가'라고 시작하며 발췌본의 단점을 추가적으로 제시함.

정답 단서-3 짧은 발췌에 의해서는 충분히 설명될 수 없는 문학적 특징들이 있다고 함.
(A) (3) Moreover, / there are some literary features /
게다가 / 몇 가지 문학적인 특징이 있다 / 선행사
[that cannot be adequately illustrated by a short excerpt]: /
짧은 발췌로는 충분히 설명될 수 없는 / [ ]: 주격 관계대명사절
the development of plot or character, / for instance, /
줄거리나 등장인물의 전개 / 예를 들면 /
=the development of plot or character
with the gradual involvement of the reader / that this implies; /
독자의 점진적 몰입과 더불어 / 이것이 내포하는 /
or the unfolding of a complex theme /
또는 복잡한 주제의 전개 /
through the juxtaposition of contrasting views.
대조적인 관점의 병치를 통한

힌트 콜론(:)은 앞 문장에 대한 부연 설명을 하는 데 사용될 수 있음. 본문의 경우 발췌본에 의해 충분히 설명될 수 없는 문학적인 특징들의 예시가 나열되어 있음.

[전문 해석]

(1)일부 문학 작품의 길이가 압도적이라는 데는 의심의 여지가 없다. (2)수업 시간에 작품을 몇 시간, 몇 주 동안 읽거나 번역하는 것은 너무나 지루한 경험일 수 있어서 많은 학생이 다시는 외국어 서적을 절대 펴고 싶어 하지 않는다.
(B) (4)발췌본은 한 가지 해결책을 제공한다. (5)장점은 분명하다. (6)다양한 작품에서 가져온 일련의 단락을 읽는 것은 교실에서 더 많은 다양성을 만들어 내서 교사는 단조로움을 피할 가능성이 더 크면서도 여전히 최소한이라도 어떤 작가의 특별한 묘미를 학습자에게 맛보게 한다.
(C) (7)반면에, '짧은 토막글'만 접한 학생은 책의 전반적인 구성을 아는 만족감을 결코 가질 수 없을 것이며, 결국 그 만족감은 모국어로 된 어떤 글을 읽을 때 우리 대부분이 찾고자 하는 것이다.
(A) (3)게다가 짧은 발췌로는 충분히 설명될 수 없는 문학적인 특징이 몇 가지 있는데, 예를 들면 줄거리나 등장인물의 전개와 더불어 이것이 내포하는 독자의 점진적 몰입, 또는 대조적인 관점의 병치를 통해 복잡한 주제를 전개하는 것이다.

[정답 확인]

주어진 글 다음에 이어질 글의 순서로 가장 적절한 것은?

① (A) — (C) — (B) ② (B) — (A) — (C) ③ (B) — (C) — (A)
④ (C) — (A) — (B) ⑤ (C) — (B) — (A)

[문제 풀이]

이 지문은 발췌독의 장점과 단점에 대해 설명하는 글이다. 먼저, 문장 (2)에 따르면 길이가 긴 작품을 오랜 시간 읽거나 번역하는 것은 학생들에게 지루한 경험일 수 있는데, 문장 (4)에서 발췌본을 읽는 것이 그 해결책이 될 수 있다고 하고 있으므로 문장 (2) 다음에는 (B)가 온다. 이어지는 문장 (6)에서는 발췌본을 읽는 것이 교실에서 더 많은 다양성을 만들어 낸다며 발췌본을 읽는 것의 장점을 제시하고 있는데, 문장 (7)에서 '반면에(On the other hand)'로 문장을 시작하며 발췌독의 단점을 언급하므로 (B) 다음에는 (C)가 온다. 이후 문장 (3)에서 '게다가(Moreover)'를 통해 짧은 발췌에 의해서는 충분히 설명될 수 없는 문학적 특징들에 대해 언급하며 발췌독의 단점을 추가적으로 제시하므로 (C) 다음에는 (A)가 온다. 따라서 정답은 ③이다.

[오답 풀이]

④ - 문장 (2)에 따르면 길이가 긴 작품을 오랜 시간 읽거나 번역하는 것이 학생들에게 지루한 경험일 수 있다. 한편, 문장 (7)에 따르면 발췌본을 읽는 것만으로는 책의 전반적인 구성을 아는 만족감을 가질 수 없다. 즉, 문장 (2)에서는 길이가 긴 작품을 읽는 것의 문제점을, 문장 (7)에서는 짧은 토막글을 읽는 것, 즉 발췌독의 단점을 설명하고 있는데, 두 문장 사이에 추가적인 설명이 없다면 각 내용 간 개연성이 떨어지므로 주어진 문장 (2) 다음에는 (C)가 올 수 없다. 다음으로, 문장 (3)에서 짧은 발췌만으로는 충분히 설명될 수 없는 문학적인 특징에 대해 언급했는데, 이는 발췌독의 단점에 해당된다. 한편, 문장 (4)에서는 발췌본이 해결책이 될 수 있다고 하는데, 이는 발췌독의 단점에 대해 얘기하는 문장 (3)의 내용과 상충되므로 (A) 다음에는 (B)가 올 수 없다. 따라서 ④는 오답이다.

[중요 어휘]

☐ overwhelming	형용사 압도적인, 너무도 강력한
☐ work	명사 작품, 일
☐ extract	명사 발췌(본), 초록 / 동사 추출하다
☐ monotony	명사 단조로움
☐ flavour(=flavor)	명사 묘미, 특징, 풍미
☐ chunk	명사 토막, 덩어리
☐ adequately	부사 충분히
☐ illustrate	동사 설명하다, 예증하다
☐ excerpt	명사 발췌
☐ plot	명사 줄거리, 음모
☐ gradual	형용사 점진적인, 완만한
☐ involvement	명사 몰입, 몰두, 관련, 개입
☐ imply	동사 내포하다, 암시하다
☐ unfold	동사 (이야기·사태 등을) 전개하다, 펼치다
☐ juxtaposition	명사 병치
☐ contrasting	형용사 대조적인, 대비되는

37 2023년 11월 36번 (정답률 70%) 정답 ②

[지문 끊어 읽기] 열에 따른 생물의 크기 변동

(1) The size of a species is not accidental.
종의 크기는 우연한 것이 아니다

(2) It's a fine-tuned interaction /
그것은 미세 조정된 상호 작용이다 /
between a species and the world it inhabits.
한 종과 그것이 사는 세계 사이의 선행사 목적격 관계대명사절(관계대명사 생략)

힌트 inhabit은 live와 달리 '거주하는 곳'을 목적어로 취하는 타동사임. 즉 the world를 선행사로 하는 목적격 관계대명사가 생략되어 있음.

(3) Over large periods of time, /
오랜 시간에 걸쳐 /
size fluctuations have often signalled significant changes /
크기 변동은 상당한 변화를 자주 나타내 왔다 /
in the environment. 정답 단서-1 오랜 기간 동안 생물의 크기 변동은 상당한 변화를 보여 왔음.
환경에서

(B) (7) Generally speaking, / over the last five hundred million years, /
일반적으로 말해서 / 지난 5억 년 동안 /
the trend has been towards animals getting larger. 정답 단서-1
동명사 / 전치사 / 동명사의 의미상의 주어
그 경향은 동물들이 점점 커지는 쪽으로 되어 왔다 문장 (3)에서 언급한 크기 변동의 상당한 변화는 몸집이 커지는 경향이었음을 언급함.

(8) It's particularly notable in marine animals, /
=the trend
그것은 특히 해양 동물들에게서 두드러진다 / 문장 (7)에서 언급된 경향의 예시로 정확한 수치를 보여 주면서 생물의 거대화를 구체화시킴.
정답 단서-2
whose average body size has increased 150-fold in this time.
소유격 관계대명사(계속적 용법)
이 시기에 그들의 평균 몸 크기는 150배로 증가해 왔다

(A) (4) But we are beginning to see / changes in this trend. 정답 단서-2
하지만 우리는 관찰하기 시작하고 있다 / 이 경향에 변화를 접속사 'But'을 통해 문장 (7), (8)에서 언급된 경향에 변화가 존재함을 알 수 있음.

(5) Scientists have discovered / [that many animals are shrinking].
과학자들은 발견해 왔다 / 많은 동물들이 작아지고 있다는 것을 [ ]: 목적어절

(6) Around the world, / species in every category /
전 세계적으로 / 모든 범주의 종들은 /
have been found to be getting smaller, /
점점 작아지고 있는 것으로 발견되어 왔다 /
and one major cause appears to be the heat. 정답 단서-3
그리고 한 가지 주된 원인은 열인 것으로 보인다 열 때문에 전 세계적으로 모든 종의 크기가 점점 작아지고 있음.

(C) (9) Animals living in the Italian Alps, / for example, /
S 현재분사구
이탈리아 알프스에 사는 동물들은 / 예를 들어 /

문제편 p.203

have seen temperatures rise / by three to four degrees Celsius /
지각V O O·C(동사원형)
기온이 상승하는 것을 보아 왔다 / 섭씨 3도에서 4도까지 /
since the 1980s.
1980년대부터

(10) To avoid overheating, /
부사적 용법
과열을 피하기 위해 /
힌트 spend+시간/돈+(in) V-ing : 시간/돈을 ~하는 데 보내다[쓰다]
chamois goats now spend more of their days resting /
샤무아 염소들은 이제 쉬는 데에 더 많은 자신들의 날들을 보낸다 /
rather than searching for food, / and as a result, /
먹이를 찾는 것보다 / 그리고 그 결과 /
in just a few decades, /
불과 몇십 년 만에 /
문장 (6)의 예시로 샤무아 염소의 사례를 언급하면서 과열이 생물들의 크기 변화에 어떤 영향을 미쳤는지 보여 줌.
the new generations of chamois are 25 percent smaller. 정답 단서-3
새로운 세대의 샤무아들은 25퍼센트 더 작아져 있다

[전문 해석]

(1)종의 크기는 우연한 것이 아니다. (2)그것은 한 종과 그것(그 종)이 사는 세계 사이의 미세 조정된 상호 작용이다. (3)오랜 시간에 걸쳐, 크기 변동은 환경에서 상당한 변화를 자주 나타내 왔다.
(B) (7)일반적으로 말해서, 지난 5억 년 동안, 그 경향은 동물들이 점점 커지는 쪽으로 되어 왔다. (8)그것은 특히 해양 동물들에게서 두드러지는데, 이 시기에 그들의 평균 몸 크기는 150배로 증가해 왔다.
(A) (4)하지만 우리는 이 경향에 변화를 관찰하기 시작하고 있다. (5)과학자들은 많은 동물들이 작아지고 있다는 것을 발견해 왔다. (6)전 세계적으로, 모든 범주의 종들은 점점 작아지고 있는 것으로 발견되어 왔고, 한 가지 주된 원인은 열인 것으로 보인다.
(C) (9)예를 들어, 이탈리아 알프스에 사는 동물들은 1980년대부터 섭씨 3도에서 4도까지 기온이 상승하는 것을 보아 왔다. (10)과열을 피하기 위해, 샤무아 염소들은 이제 먹이를 찾는 것보다 쉬는 데에 더 많은 자신들의 날들을 보내고, 그 결과, 불과 몇십 년 만에 새로운 세대의 샤무아들은 25퍼센트 더 작아져 있다.

[정답 확인]

주어진 글 다음에 이어질 글의 순서로 가장 적절한 것은?

① (A) — (C) — (B) ② (B) — (A) — (C) ③ (B) — (C) — (A)
④ (C) — (A) — (B) ⑤ (C) — (B) — (A)

[문제 풀이]

이 지문은 환경에 따른 동물의 크기 변화를 설명하면서 특히 최근 기온 상승으로 모든 범주의 생물들의 크기가 작아지는 경향을 보인다고 설명한다. 먼저, 문장 (2)에 따르면 종의 크기 변화는 종과 세계의 미세 조정된 상호 작용의 결과물이라고 하며, 문장 (3)에서 상호 작용의 내용으로 환경 변화에 따라 종의 크기도 변화한다는 것을 언급한다. 이러한 주어진 문단 다음에는 (B)가 와서, 5억 년이라는 긴 시간 동안 이루어진 일반적인 종의 크기 변화 경향을 언급하면서 해양 동물은 평균 몸 크기가 150배로 증가했다는 구체적인 예시를 제시하는 것이 자연스럽다. 문장 (4)는 이러한 경향에 변화가 일어났다고 언급하는데, 이는 문장 (7)의 내용을 고려해 보았을 때 반대되는 상황으로 이어졌음을 알 수 있다. 따라서 (B) 다음에는 (A)가 온다. 이어서 문장 (6)에서 최근 전 세계적으로 모든 범주의 종의 크기가 일반적인 경향과 다르게 점차 작아지는데, 그 원인이 열이라고 설명한다. 또한 문장 (9)의 이탈리아 알프스의 샤무아 염소들이 과열로 상승한 기온으로 인해 먹이를 찾는 것보다 쉬는 데에 시간을 더 보내면서 몇십 년 만에 그 종의 크기가 25퍼센트 줄었다는 것은 현재 변화한 경향의 예시이다. 따라서 (A) 다음에는 (C)가 온다. 그러므로 정답은 ②'(B) — (A) — (C)'이다.

[중요 어휘]

☐ accidental	형용사 우연한, 돌발적인
☐ fine-tuned	형용사 미세 조정이 된
☐ inhabit	동사 살다, 거주하다, 서식하다
☐ fluctuation	명사 변동, (사람·마음의) 동요, 흥망
☐ signal	동사 나타내다, 시사하다, 암시하다 / 명사 신호
☐ significant	형용사 상당한, 중요한
☐ notable	형용사 두드러지는, 눈에 띄는, 주목할 만한
☐ shrink	동사 작아지다, 줄어들다, 수축하다
☐ major	형용사 주요한, 중대한
☐ overheat	동사 과열되다, 과열하다

38 2023년 11월 37번 (정답률 40%) 정답 ③

[지문 끊어 읽기] 전체 데이터를 갖는 것의 장점

(1) For a long time, / random sampling was a good shortcut. 정답 단서-1
오랫동안 / 무작위 추출법은 좋은 지름길이었다
무작위 추출법의 장점.
(2) It made analysis of large data problems possible /
=random sampling 5형식V O O·C
그것은 상당한 데이터 문제 분석을 가능하게 했다 /
in the pre-digital era.
디지털 시대 이전에
힌트 much as 앞에 as가 생략되었는데, 「(as) much as S'+V', S+V ~」는 'S'가 V'인 것과 마찬가지로, S가 V하다'라는 뜻임.
(B) (6) But much as converting a digital image or song into a smaller file
S'(동명사)
results in loss of data, /
V'
그러나 디지털 이미지나 노래를 더 작은 파일로 변환하는 것이 데이터 손실을 초래하는 것과 마찬가지로 /
information is lost / when sampling. 정답 단서-1
정보가 손실된다 / 추출할 때
분사구문
'추출할 때'는 문장 (1)의 추출법과 연결되는 내용임.

(7) Having the full (or close to the full) dataset /
동명사S
전체(또는 전체에 가까운) 데이터 세트를 가지는 것은 /
provides a lot more freedom to explore, /
3형식V O 병렬①(형용사적 용법)
탐색할 자유를 훨씬 더 많이 제공한다 /
to look at the data from different angles /
병렬②
다른 각도에서 데이터를 살펴보는 /
or to look closer at certain aspects of it. 정답 단서-2
병렬③ =data
또는 그것의 특정한 측면에서 더 자세하게 보게 하는
전체 데이터 세트를 가지는 것으로 다른 각도나 특정한 측면에서 데이터를 보게 되는 장점을 언급함.

(C) (8) A fitting example may be the light-field camera, / 정답 단서-2
적당한 예로 라이트 필드 카메라가 있을 수 있는데 /
문장 (7)의 전체 데이터 세트를 가지는 것의 장점의 예시로 라이트 필드 카메라를 언급함.
which captures not just a single plane of light, /
관계대명사(계속적 용법)
그것은 한 평면의 빛만 포착할 뿐만 아니라 /
힌트 'not just[only] A but (also) B' 구문으로, 'a single ~ light'와 'rays ~ field'가 병렬 구조를 이룸.
as with conventional cameras, /
기존의 카메라처럼 /
but rays from the entire light field, / some 11 million of them.
전체 라이트 필드로부터의 광선들도 / 약 1,100만 개에 달하는
=the rays from the entire light field

(9) The photographers can decide later /
사진사들은 나중에 결정할 수 있다 /
라이트 필드 카메라를 사용하는 사진사들은 이미지 초점을 나중에 맞출 수 있음.
which element of an image to focus on / in the digital file. 정답 단서-3
이미지의 어느 요소에 초점을 맞출지를 / 디지털 파일에서
힌트 「의문사+to V」의 구조로, decide의 목적어 역할을 함.
(A) (3) There is no need to focus at the beginning, / 정답 단서-3
처음에 초점을 맞출 필요는 없다 /
카메라의 초점을 초반에 맞출 필요가 없다는 것은 이미지 초점을 나중에 맞출 수 있다는 내용의 문장 (9)와 연결되는 내용임.
since collecting all the information /
동명사S
모든 정보를 수집하는 것은 ~하기 때문에 /
힌트 5형식 구조에서 목적어에 to부정사가 오는 경우, 형식상의 목적어 it을 사용하고 내용상의 목적어는 목적격 보어 뒤로 위치시킴.
[makes it possible to do that afterwards].
5형식V 형식상의 목적어 O·C 내용상의 목적어
그것을 나중에 하는 것을 가능하게 한다

(4) Because rays from the entire light field are included, /
전체 라이트 필드의 광선이 포함되기 때문에 /
it is closer to all the data.
그것은 모든 데이터에 더 가깝다

(5) As a result, /
결과적으로 /
the information is more "reuseable" than ordinary pictures, /
선행사
그 정보는 일반 사진들보다 더 '재사용 가능'하다 /
where the photographer has to decide what to focus on /
관계부사
사진사가 무엇에 초점을 맞출지를 결정해야 하는 /
before she presses the shutter.
=the photographer
그녀가 셔터를 누르기 전에

[전문 해석]

(1)오랫동안, 무작위 추출법은 좋은 지름길이었다. (2)그것은 디지털 시대 이전에 상당한 데이터 문제 분석을 가능하게 했다.
(B) (6)그러나 디지털 이미지나 노래를 더 작은 파일로 변환하는 것이 데이터 손실을 초래하는 것과 마찬가지로, 추출할 때 정보는 손실된다. (7)전체(또는 전체에 가까운) 데이터 세트를 가지는 것은 탐색하거나 다른 각도에서 데이터를 살펴보거나 그것의 특정한 측면에서 더 자세하게 보게 하는 자유를 훨씬 더 많이 제공한다.
(C) (8)적당한 예로 라이트 필드 카메라가 있을 수 있는데, 그것은 기존의 카메라처럼 한 평면의 빛만 포착할 뿐만 아니라, 약 1,100만개에 달하는 전체 라이트 필드로부터의 광선들도 포착한다. (9)사진사들은 디지털 파일에서 이미지의 어느 요소에 초점을 맞출지를 나중에 결정할 수 있다.
(A) (3)처음에 초점을 맞출 필요는 없는데, 모든 정보를 수집하는 것은 그것을 나중에 하는 것을 가능하게 하기 때문이다. (4)전체 라이트 필드의 광선이 포함되기 때문에, 그것은 모든 데이터에 더 가깝다. (5)결과적으로 그 정보는 사진사가 셔터를 누르기 전에 무엇에 초점을 맞출지를 결정해야 하는 일반 사진들보다 더 '재사용 가능'하다.

[정답 확인]

주어진 글 다음에 이어질 글의 순서로 가장 적절한 것은?

① (A) — (C) — (B) ② (B) — (A) — (C) ③ (B) — (C) — (A) ✔
④ (C) — (A) — (B) ⑤ (C) — (B) — (A)

[문제 풀이]

이 글은 무작위 추출법의 한계와 전체 데이터 세트를 갖는 것의 장점에 대한 내용이다. 주어진 문장 (1)과 (2)는 무작위 추출법의 장점으로, 디지털 시대 이전에 가능했던 데이터 문제 분석을 언급한다. 하지만 문장 (6)에서 역접의 접속사 'But'으로 시작하며 추출할 때 정보가 손실된다는 추출법의 단점을 설명하므로 주어진 문장 다음에는 (B)가 오는 것이 적절하다. 이어서 문장 (7)에서 전체 데이터 세트를 가지는 것이 데이터에 대한 다른 시각의 장점임을 설명하고, 그 예로 문장 (8)에서 라이트 필드 카메라가 나오므로 (B) 다음으로 (C)가 알맞다. 그리고 문장 (9)에서 사진사들이 이미지 초점을 나중에 맞출 수 있다는 내용이 나오는데, 문장 (3)에서 모든 정보를 수집한 후에 초점을 맞추는 것이 가능하다고 설명하므로, (C) 다음으로 (A)가 이어지는 것이 자연스럽다. 따라서 정답은 ③'(B) — (C) — (A)'이다.

[오답 풀이]

④ - (B)는 앞서 언급된 내용을 'But'으로 반박하며 추출법의 단점과 전체 데이터 세트를 가질 때의 장점을 설명하는데, (A)는 모든 데이터를 갖게 되는 라이트 필드 카메라에 대한 내용이다. (B)의 문장 (7)과 (A)의 문장 (3)~(5)는 문맥상 연결되는 내용이므로 (A) 다음으로 (B)가 오는 것은 적절하지 않다.

[중요 어휘]

☐ random	형용사 무작위의, 임의로
☐ sampling	명사 (표본, 견본의) 추출(법)
☐ shortcut	명사 지름길, 손쉬운 방법
☐ analysis	명사 분석, 분석 연구
☐ convert	동사 변환[전환]시키다, 개조하다
☐ fitting	형용사 적당한, 적절한
☐ plane	명사 평면, 수평면, 비행기
☐ as with	~와 마찬가지로
☐ conventional	형용사 기존의, 전통적인
☐ element	명사 요소, 성분

39 2024년 3월 36번 (정답률 40%) 정답 ⑤

[지문 끊어 읽기] 신체 발달 과정에서의 변이성

(1) [Development of the human body from a single cell] / [ ]:S
하나의 세포에서 인체가 발달하는 것은 /
provides many examples of the structural richness /
V 선행사
구조적 풍부함의 많은 예를 제공한다 /
that is possible /
주격 관계대명사절
가능한 /
when [the repeated production of random variation] / [ ]:S'
과거분사
무작위적인 변이의 반복적인 생산이 ~할 때 /
is combined with nonrandom selection. 정답 단서-1
V'
임의적이지 않은 선택과 결합될

하나의 세포에서 인체로 발전하는 것은 무작위적인 변이의 반복적인 생산이 임의적이지 않은 선택과 결합될 때 가능한 구조적 풍부함의 많은 예를 제공함.

(C) (7) [All phases of body development from embryo to adult] / [ ]:S
배아에서 어른까지 신체 발달의 모든 단계는 /
exhibit random activities at the cellular level, /
V
세포 수준에서 무작위적인 활동을 보여 준다 /
and body formation depends on the new possibilities /
그리고 신체 형성은 새로운 가능성에 의존한다 /
generated by these activities /
과거분사
이런 활동에 의해 생성되는 /
coupled with selection of those outcomes /
과거분사 선행사
그러한 결과의 선택과 결합하여 /
that satisfy previously built-in criteria. 정답 단서-1
주격 관계대명사절
이전에 확립된 기준을 만족시키는

모든 단계의 신체 발달은 세포 수준에서 무작위적인 활동을 보여 주고, 신체 형성은 이전에 확립된 기준을 만족시키는 결과의 선택과 더불어 이런(무작위적인) 활동으로 생성된 새로운 가능성에 의존함.

(8) Always new structure is based on old structure, /
항상 새로운 구조는 오래된 구조에 기반한다 /
and at every stage /
그리고 모든 단계에서 /
selection favors some cells and eliminates others. 정답 단서-2
S V, 병렬① 병렬② =other cells
선택은 몇몇 세포를 선호하고 다른 것들을 제거한다

새로운 구조는 항상 오래된 구조에 기반하고, 모든 단계에서 선택은 몇몇 세포를 선호하고 다른 세포들은 제거함.

(B) (5) The survivors serve to produce new cells /
생존자들은 새로운 세포를 만드는 역할을 한다 / 선행사
that undergo further rounds of selection. 정답 단서-2
주격 관계대명사절
추가적인 선택의 과정을 거치는

생존자들은 추가적인 선택의 과정을 거치는 새로운 세포를 만드는 역할을 함.

(6) Except in the immune system, / cells and extensions of cells /
면역 체계를 제외하면 / 세포와 세포의 확장은 /
are not genetically selected during development, / but rather, /
병렬①
발달 과정 동안 유전적으로 선택되지 않는다 / 그러나 오히려 /
are positionally selected. 정답 단서-3
병렬②
위치에 의해 선택된다

면역 체계를 제외하면 세포와 세포의 확장은 발달 과정 동안 유전적으로 선택되지 않고 위치에 의해 선택됨.

(A) (2) [Those in the right place / that make the right connections] /
=Cells, 선행사 주격 관계대명사절 [ ]:S①
올바른 위치에 있는 세포들은 / 올바른 연결을 만드는 /
are stimulated, / and [those that don't] /
V① 선행사 주격 관계대명사절 [ ]:S②
활성화된다 / 그리고 그렇지 않은 세포들은 /
are eliminated. 정답 단서-3
제거된다 V②

올바른 연결을 만드는 올바른 위치에 있는 세포들은 활성화되고 그렇지 않은 세포들은 제거됨.

힌트 those는 모두 cells를 가리키며, 주격 관계대명사 that이 이끄는 절의 수식을 받음. those that don't 뒤에는 반복되는 make the right connections가 생략되었음.

(3) This process is much like sculpting.
이 과정은 마치 조각을 하는 것과 같다

(4) A natural consequence of the strategy / is great variability /
S V
이 전략의 자연스러운 결과는 / 큰 변이성이다 /
from individual to individual / at the cell and molecular levels, /
개인마다 / 세포와 분자 수준에서의 /
even though large-scale structures are quite similar.
큰 규모의 구조는 꽤 비슷할지라도

[전문 해석]

(1)하나의 세포에서 인체가 발달하는 것은 무작위적인 변이의 반복적인 생산이 임의적이지 않은 선택과 결합될 때 가능한 구조적 풍부함의 많은 예를 제공한다.
(C) (7)배아에서 어른까지 신체 발달의 모든 단계는 세포 수준에서 무작위적인 활동을 보여 주고, 신체 형성은 이전에 확립된 기준을 만족시키는 그러한 결과의 선택과 결합하여 이런 활동에 의해 생성되는 새로운 가능성에 의존한다. (8)항상 새로운 구조는 오래된 구조에 기반하고, 모든 단계에서 선택은 몇몇 세포를 선호하고 다른 것들을 제거한다.
(B) (5)생존자들(생존한 세포들)은 추가적인 선택의 과정을 거치는 새로운 세포를 만드는 역할을 한다. (6)면역 체계를 제외하면 세포와 세포의 확장은 발달 과정 동안 유전적으로 선택되

지 않고 오히려 위치에 의해 선택된다.
(A) (2)올바른 연결을 만드는 올바른 위치에 있는 세포들은 활성화되고 그렇지 않은 세포들은 제거된다. (3)이 과정은 마치 조각을 하는 것과 같다. (4)이 전략의 자연스러운 결과는 큰 규모의 구조는 꽤 비슷할지라도 세포와 분자 수준에서의 개인마다 큰 변이성이다.

[정답 확인]

주어진 글 다음에 이어질 글의 순서로 가장 적절한 것은?

① (A) — (C) — (B) ② (B) — (A) — (C) ③ (B) — (C) — (A)
④ (C) — (A) — (B) ✔(C) — (B) — (A)

[문제 풀이]

주어진 문장은 인체가 하나의 세포에서부터 발달하는 과정을 무작위적인 변이와 임의적이지 않은 선택의 결합으로 설명한다. 먼저, 문장 (1)에 따르면 하나의 세포에서 성체로 발달하는 것은 무작위적인 변이의 반복적인 생산이 임의적이지 않은 선택과 결합될 때의 가능한 구조적 풍부함을 보여 준다고 말한다. 문장 (7)에서 모든 단계의 신체 발달이 세포 수준에서는 무작위적인 활동을 보여주고 신체 형성은 이전에 확립된 기준을 만족하는 선택과 무작위적인 활동에 의한 가능성의 결합으로 가능하다고 말한다. 즉, 문장 (7)은 문장 (1)을 더 구체적으로 설명하는 문장이므로 주어진 문장 다음에는 (C)가 온다. 이어지는 문장 (8)에서 모든 단계에서 선택은 몇몇 세포를 선호하고 다른 것들은 제거한다고 언급한다. 문장 (5)의 '생존자'는 문장 (8)의 선택에서 선호되는 몇몇 세포를 말한 것이다. 따라서 (C) 다음에는 (B)가 온다. 문장 (6)에서는 세포와 세포의 확장이 유전적으로 선택되지 않고 위치에 의해 선택된다고 말한다. 문장 (2)는 이에 따라 올바른 연결을 만드는 위치에 있는 세포들은 활성화되고 그렇지 않은 세포들은 제거된다고 부연 설명한다. 따라서 (B) 다음에는 (A)가 온다. 그러므로 정답은 ⑤ '(C) — (B) — (A)'이다.

[오답 풀이]

④ - 문장 (8)에서 언급하는 선택되는 몇몇 세포들은 문장 (5)에서 '생존자들'로 표현된다. 더불어 문장 (6)에서 세포와 세포의 확장이 위치에 의해 선택된다고 하였고 이는 문장 (2)의 올바른 연결을 만드는 올바른 위치에 있는 세포들은 활성화되고 그렇지 않은 세포들은 제거된다는 내용과 자연스럽게 이어지므로 (A)가 (B) 앞에 위치하는 ④는 정답으로 적절하지 않다.

[중요 어휘]

□ cell	명사 세포
□ structural	형용사 구조적인, 구조상의
□ richness	명사 풍부함, 부유함
□ random	형용사 무작위적인, 임의의
□ variation	명사 변이, 변형, 변주곡
□ phase	명사 단계, 국면, (천체의) 상
□ exhibit	동사 보여 주다, 전시하다
□ cellular	형용사 세포의, 휴대 전화의
□ formation	명사 형성, 구성
□ couple	동사 결합하다
□ previously	부사 이전에, 미리
□ built-in	형용사 확립된, 붙박이의, 타고난, 고유의
□ criteria	명사 기준 (단수형 criterion)
□ favor	동사 선호하다 / 명사 부탁, 우호
□ serve to V	~하는 역할을 하다
□ undergo	동사 거치다, 겪다
□ round	명사 과정, (정기적으로 진행되는 일의) 한 차례 / 형용사 둥근
□ immune	형용사 면역의, 면역이 된
□ extension	명사 확장, 확대
□ genetically	부사 유전적으로
□ positionally	부사 위치에 의해, 위치적으로
□ stimulate	동사 활성화하다, 자극하다
□ sculpt	동사 조각하다
□ consequence	명사 결과
□ variability	명사 변이성, 가변성, 변동성

40 2024년 3월 37번 (정답률 55%) 정답 ②

[지문 끊어 읽기] 재택 간호 관리 시스템

(1) In order to bring the ever-increasing costs of home care /
~하기 위해
재택 간호의 계속 증가하는 비용을 가져오기 위해 /
for elderly and needy persons / under control, /
노인과 빈곤층을 위한 / 통제하에 /
managers of home care providers /
재택 간호 제공 기관의 관리자들은 /
have introduced management systems. 정답 단서-1 재택 간호 제공 기관의 관리자들은 계속해서 증가하는 재택 간호 비용을 통제하기 위해 관리 시스템을 도입함.
관리 시스템을 도입해 왔다

(B) (4) These systems specify / tasks of home care workers /
이러한 시스템은 명시한다 / 재택 간호 종사자들의 업무를 / O①
and the time and budget /
O②
그리고 시간과 예산을 /
[available to perform these tasks]. 정답 단서-1 '이러한 시스템'은 재택 간호 종사자들의 업무와 시간, 예산을 명시함으로써 보다 체계화된 업무 수행을 가능하게 함. '이러한 시스템'이 가리키는 것은 문장 (1)에서 언급된 관리 시스템에 해당함.
부사적 용법
이러한 업무를 수행하는 데에 사용 가능한

(5) Electronic reporting systems require /
전자 보고 시스템은 요구한다 / 5형식V
home care workers to report on their activities and the time spent, /
O O·C
재택 간호 종사자가 자신의 활동과 소요 시간을 보고하도록 /
thus [making the distribution of time and money visible /
5형식V(현재분사) O O·C①
그러므로 시간과 비용의 분배를 잘 보이게 만든다 /
[ ]: 분사구문(결과)
and, in the perception of managers, / controllable]. 정답 단서-2 관리 시스템은 활동과 소요 시간을 보고하도록 하면서 관리자의 입장에서 통제를 원활하게 함.
삽입구 O·C②
그리고 관리자의 입장에서는 / 통제 가능하게

(A) (2) This, / in the view of managers, / 관리자의 관점에서 문제를 해결한다는 언급을 통해 '이것'이 관리자의 입장에서 원활한 통제가 가능하도록 만들어 주는 문장 (5)의 전자 보고 시스템임을 알 수 있음.
삽입구
이것이 / 관리자의 관점에서는 /
has contributed to the resolution of the problem. 정답 단서-2
문제 해결에 기여해 왔다

힌트 문장 (3)은 not A but B의 형식을 띠고 있으며, 해당 표현은 'A가 아니라 B다'로 해석함.

(3) The home care workers, / on the other hand, /
재택 간호 종사자들은 / 반면에 /
may perceive their work / not [as a set of separate tasks /
자신들의 업무를 인식할 것이다 / 일련의 분리된 업무로서가 아니라 /
to be performed as efficiently as possible], /
가능한 한 효율적으로 수행되어야 하는 / [ ]: 병렬①
but [as a service / to be provided to a client /
서비스로서 / 고객에게 제공되어야 하는 / [ ]: 병렬②
with whom they may have developed a relationship]. 정답 단서-3 재택 간호 종사자들의 관점에서는 자신의 업무를 효율적으로 수행되어야 하는 분리된 업무가 아닌 고객을 위한 서비스로 인식함.
may have p.p.: ~이었을지도 모른다
그들이 관계를 발전시켰을지도 모르는

힌트 'whom they may have ~ a relationship with'에서 전치사 with가 목적격 관계대명사 whom의 앞으로 이동한 형태임. 전치사와 함께 쓰인 목적격 관계대명사 whom은 생략이 불가능함.

(C) (6) This includes / having conversations with clients /
동명사①
이것은 포함한다 / 고객과 대화를 나누는 것을 /
and enquiring about the person's well-being. 정답 단서-3
동명사②
그리고 그 사람의 안부를 묻는 것을
'이것'은 고객과 대화를 나누고 안부를 묻는 것을 포함한다는 언급을 통해, 재택 간호 종사자들이 하는 일의 예시를 듦. 그러므로 '이것'은 문장 (3)에서 언급된 고객을 위한 서비스임을 알 수 있음.

(7) Restricted time and the requirement to report /
제한된 시간과 보고를 해야 한다는 요구 사항은 / 형용사적 용법
may be perceived as obstacles /
장애물로 인식될 수 있다 / 선행사
[that make it impossible / [to deliver the service that is needed]].
[ ]: 주격 관계대명사절
형식상의 목적어 [ ]: 내용상의 목적어 선행사 주격 관계대명사절
불가능하게 만드는 / 필요한 서비스를 제공하는 것을

(8) If the management systems are too rigid, / this may result in /
만약 관리 시스템이 너무 엄격하면 / 이것은 결과를 초래할 것이다 /
home care workers becoming overloaded and demotivated.
동명사의 의미상의 주어 동명사
재택 간호 종사자들이 너무 많은 부담을 지게 되고 의욕을 잃게 되는

[전문 해석]

(1)노인과 빈곤층을 위한 재택 간호의 계속 증가하는 비용을 통제하에 가져오기 위해(통제하기 위해) 재택 간호 제공 기관의 관리자들은 관리 시스템을 도입해 왔다.

(B) (4)이러한 시스템은 재택 간호 종사자들의 업무와 이러한 업무를 수행하는 데에 사용 가능한 시간과 예산을 명시한다. (5)전자 보고 시스템은 재택 간호 종사자가 자신의 활동과 소요 시간을 보고하도록 요구하므로, 시간과 비용의 분배를 잘 보이게 만들고 관리자의 입장에서는 통제 가능하게 만든다.
(A) (2)관리자의 관점에서는 이것이 문제 해결에 기여해 왔다. (3)반면에, 재택 간호 종사자들은 자신들의 업무를 가능한 한 효율적으로 수행되어야 하는 일련의 분리된 업무로서가 아니라 그들이 관계를 발전시켰을지도 모르는 고객에게 제공되어야 하는 서비스로서 인식할 것이다.
(C) (6)이것은 고객과 대화를 나누고 그 사람의 안부를 묻는 것을 포함한다. (7)제한된 시간과 보고를 해야 한다는 요구 사항은 필요한 서비스를 제공하는 것을 불가능하게 만드는 장애물로 인식될 수 있다. (8)만약 관리 시스템이 너무 엄격하면, 이것은 재택 간호 종사자들이 너무 많은 부담을 지게 되고 의욕을 잃게 되는 결과를 초래할 것이다.

[정답 확인]

주어진 글 다음에 이어질 글의 순서로 가장 적절한 것은?
① (A) — (C) — (B) ✔② (B) — (A) — (C) ③ (B) — (C) — (A)
④ (C) — (A) — (B) ⑤ (C) — (B) — (A)

[문제 풀이]

이 지문은 재택 간호 종사업에서의 관리 시스템이 관리자와 재택 간호 종사자의 측면에서 어떤 영향을 미치는지를 설명한다. 먼저, 문장 (1)에 따르면 노인과 빈곤층을 위한 재택 간호 비용이 계속적으로 증가하기에 이를 통제하기 위해서 관리 시스템을 도입해 왔다고 한다. 문장 (4)에서 관리 시스템이 어떤 역할을 하는지 언급하므로, 주어진 문장 다음에는 (B)가 온다. 이어지는 문장 (5)에서 해당 관리 시스템이 관리자의 입장에서 시간 및 비용 분배를 잘 보이도록 하며 통제를 가능하게 만든다는 장점을 언급한다. 이는 문장 (1)의 내용을 고려해 보았을 때 관리 시스템의 목적이 어떻게 이루어지는지를 설명한 것으로, 관리자의 관점에서 문제 해결에 기여한다는 문장 (2)와 자연스럽게 이어진다. 따라서 (B) 다음에는 (A)가 온다. 이어서 문장 (3)에서 'on the other hand'라는 역접의 접속부사를 통해 관리자와 달리 재택 간호 종사자들이 자신의 업무를 어떻게 생각하는지를 설명한다. 재택 간호 종사자들은 자신의 업무가 분리된 것이 아닌, 관계를 발전시켜 온 고객에게 제공되어야 하는 서비스로 생각한다. 또한 문장 (6)은 고객에게 제공되는 서비스의 예시이다. 따라서 (A) 다음에는 (C)가 온다. 그러므로 정답은 ②'(B) — (A) — (C)'이다.

[중요 어휘]

☐ **needy**	형용사 빈곤한, 궁핍한, 어려운
☐ **bring A under control**	A를 통제하다[제어하다]
☐ **specify**	동사 (구체적으로) 명시하다
☐ **available**	형용사 사용 가능한, 이용할 수 있는
☐ **distribution**	명사 분배, 분포
☐ **contribute to A**	A에 기여하다
☐ **resolution**	명사 해결, 결의안, 결심
☐ **perceive**	동사 인식하다, 여기다
☐ **enquire**	동사 묻다, 문의하다
☐ **obstacle**	명사 장애물, 장애
☐ **rigid**	형용사 엄격한, 융통성 없는
☐ **demotivate**	동사 의욕을 잃게 하다

41 2024년 6월 36번 (정답률 70%) 정답 ②

[지문 끊어 읽기] 우리 뇌의 제한적 정보 처리

(1) Brains are expensive / in terms of energy.
뇌는 비용이 많이 든다 / 에너지의 측면에서

(2) Twenty percent of the calories we consume /
선행사 / 목적격 관계대명사절
우리가 소비하는 칼로리의 20%는 /
are used / to power the brain. 정답 단서-1
부사적 용법(목적)
사용된다 / 뇌에 동력을 공급하기 위해
뇌에 동력을 공급하는 데에는 우리가 소비하는 칼로리의 20% 정도의 많은 에너지가 소모됨.

힌트 - be used to V : ~하기 위해 사용되다 - be used to V-ing : ~하는 데 익숙하다 - used to V: ~하곤 했다, (예전에는) ~이었다

힌트 '부분표현 of 명사'가 주어일 때, 동사의 수 일치는 of 뒤의 명사에 맞춤. 여기서는 'the calories'에 수 일치하여 복수동사 are이 왔음.

(B) (5) So brains try to operate /
그래서 뇌는 작동하려고 애쓴다 /
in the most energy-efficient way possible, / and that means /
가능한 한 가장 에너지 효율적인 방식으로 / 그리고 그것은 의미한다 /
processing only the minimum amount of information /
선행사
오직 최소한의 양의 정보만을 처리하는 것을 /
from our senses / [that we need to navigate the world]. 정답 단서-1
[ ]: 목적격 관계대명사절 부사적 용법(목적)
우리의 감각으로부터 / 우리가 세상을 항해하기 위해 필요로 하는
그에 따라 뇌는 살아가는 데 필요한 최소한의 정보만을 처리하며 가능한 한 가장 에너지 효율적인 방식으로 작동하려고 애씀.

(6) Neuroscientists weren't the first to discover /
형용사적 용법
신경과학자들은 발견한 최초가 아니었다 /
[that fixing your gaze on something / is no guarantee of seeing it].
S'(동명사구) V'
[ ]: 명사절(discover의 목적어)
무언가에 당신의 시선을 고정하는 것이 / 그것을 본다는 보장이 아니라는 것을

(7) Magicians figured this out long ago. 정답 단서-2
마술사들은 오래 전에 이것을 알아냈다
마술사들은 무언가에 시선을 고정한다고 해서 그것을 실제로 보는 것은 아님을 오래 전에 알아냈음.

(A) (3) By directing your attention, / they perform tricks with their hands /
=magicians
당신의 주의를 끎으로써 / 그들은 그들의 손으로 속임수를 행한다 /
in full view. 정답 단서-2
다 보이는 데서
마술사들은 주의를 끄는 방식을 통해 다 보이는 곳에서 손으로 속임수를 행함.

(4) Their actions should give away the game, /
(아마) ~일 것이다
그들의 행동들은 속임수를 누설할 것이다 /
but they can rest / assured that your brain processes /
하지만 그들은 그대로 있을 수 있다 / 당신의 뇌가 처리한다는 것을 확신한 채로 /
only small bits of the visual scene. 정답 단서-3
시각적 장면의 오직 작은 부분들만을
사람들의 뇌는 시각적 장면의 극히 일부만을 처리하기 때문에, 마술사들은 속임수를 안심하고 누설할 수 있음.

힌트 rest는 자동사로 '그대로 있다'의 의미이며 'assured that ~'이 주어의 상태를 설명하는 주격 보어로 쓰임. 즉, [~을 확신한 채로 그대로 있다]로 해석하면 됨.

(C) (8) This all helps /
이 모든 것은 도움이 된다 /
to explain the prevalence of traffic accidents /
선행사
교통사고들이 널리 행해지는 것을 설명하는 데 /
[in which drivers hit pedestrians in plain view, /
전치사+관계대명사 S' V'①
운전자들이 명백한 시야에 있는 보행자들을 치는 /
or collide with cars directly in front of them]. 정답 단서-3
V'② =drivers
[ ]: 관계사절
혹은 그들 바로 앞에 있는 자동차들과 충돌하는
이 모든 것은 시야가 명백함에도 운전자들이 보행자들을 치거나 바로 앞의 자동차와 충돌하는 등의 교통사고가 빈번하게 발생하는 이유를 설명해 줌.

★중요 밑줄 친 '이 모든 것'은 작동하는 데 많은 에너지를 소모하는 인간의 뇌가 최소한의 정보만을 처리하기 때문에 사람은 눈 앞에 무언가를 보고도 실제로는 인식하지 못할 수 있다는 앞 내용을 나타냄.

(9) In many of these cases, /
이러한 경우들 중 다수에서 /
the eyes are pointed in the right direction, /
그들의 눈은 올바른 방향으로 향해져 있다 /
but the brain isn't seeing / what's really out there.
=the thing which
그러나 뇌는 보고 있지 않다 / 실제로 그곳에 있는 것을

[전문 해석]

(1)뇌는 에너지의 측면에서 비용이 많이 든다. (2)우리가 소비하는 칼로리의 20%는 뇌에 동력을 공급하기 위해 사용된다.
(B) (5)그래서 뇌는 가능한 한 가장 에너지 효율적인 방식으로 작동하려고 애쓰는데, 그것은 우리의 감각으로부터 우리가 세상을 항해하기 위해 필요로 하는 오직 최소한의 양의 정보만을 처리하는 것을 의미한다. (6)신경과학자들은 무언가에 당신의 시선을 고정하는 것이 그것을 본다는 보장이 아니라는 것을 발견한 최초가 아니었다. (7)마술사들은 오래 전에 이것을 알아냈다.
(A) (3)당신의 주의를 끎으로써, 그들은 다 보이는 데서 그들의 손으로 속임수를 행한다. (4)그들의 행동들은 속임수를 누설할 것이지만, 그들은 당신의 뇌가 시각적 장면의 오직 작은 부분들만을 처리한다는 것을 확신한 채로 그대로 있을 수 있다.
(C) (8)이 모든 것은 운전자들이 명백한 시야에 있는 보행자들을 치거나, 그들 바로 앞에 있는 자동차들과 충돌하는 교통사고들이 널리 행해지는 것(빈번하게 발생함)을 설명하는 데 도움이 된다. (9)이러한 경우들 중 다수에서, 그들의 눈은 올바른 방향으로 향해져 있으나, 뇌는 실제로 그곳에 있는 것을 보고 있지 않다.

[정답 확인]

주어진 글 다음에 이어질 글의 순서로 가장 적절한 것은?
① (A) — (C) — (B) ✔② (B) — (A) — (C) ③ (B) — (C) — (A)
④ (C) — (A) — (B) ⑤ (C) — (B) — (A)

[중요 어휘]

☐ **in terms of**	~의 측면[관점]에서
☐ **consume**	동사 소비하다, 소모하다

☐ operate	동사 작동되다, 움직이다
☐ process	동사 처리하다 / 명사 과정, 절차
☐ navigate	동사 항해하다, 길을 찾다
☐ neuroscientist	명사 신경과학자
☐ fix one's gaze on	~에 시선을 고정하다, ~을 응시하다
☐ gaze	명사 시선, 눈길, 응시
☐ direct one's attention (to A)	(A로) ~의 주의를 끌다[~의 눈길을 돌리다]
☐ perform	동사 행하다, 수행하다
☐ in full view	다 보이는 데서, 바로 앞에서
☐ give away	~을 누설하다[폭로하다], ~을 나눠주다
☐ game	명사 속임수, 계략
☐ assure	동사 확신하다, 납득하다, 보장하다
☐ visual	형용사 시각적인, 시각의
☐ prevalence	명사 널리 행하여짐, 보급, 유포
☐ pedestrian	명사 보행자
☐ collide with	~와 충돌하다

42 2024년 6월 37번 (정답률 45%) 정답 ③

[지문 끊어 읽기] 소비와 투자의 차이

(1) Buying a television / is current consumption. 정답 단서-1 텔레비전을 사는 것은 '소비'에 해당함.
텔레비전을 사는 것은 / 현재의 소비이다

(2) It makes us happy today / but does nothing /
(V O O·C)
그것은 오늘 우리를 행복하게 만든다 / 하지만 아무것도 하지 않는다 /
to make us richer tomorrow. 정답 단서-1 텔레비전을 구매하면 당장은 행복하지만 미래에 더 부유해지지는 않음.
(부사적 용법(목적))
우리를 내일 더 부유하게 만들기 위해

(3) Yes, / money spent on a television / keeps workers employed /
(S↑ 과거분사구 5형식V O O·C(p.p.; 수동))
물론 / 텔레비전에 소비되는 돈은 / 노동자들이 계속 고용되게 한다 /
at the television factory.
텔레비전 공장에

✶중요 문장 (6)의 But을 기점으로, 즉각적인 만족을 제공하지만 미래의 재정적 가치를 증가시키지 않는 '소비'와, 장기적으로 미래의 재정적 가치를 증가시키는 '투자'의 사례가 대조되고 있음.

(B) (6) But if the same money were invested, /
그러나 만약 똑같은 돈이 투자된다면 /
it would create jobs somewhere else, /
그것은 다른 어딘가에서 일자리를 창출할 것이다 /
say for scientists in a laboratory /
(말하자면(=for example) 병렬①)
말하자면 실험실의 과학자들을 위해 /
or workers on a construction site, /
(병렬②)
혹은 건설 현장의 노동자들을 위해 /
[while also making us richer / in the long run]. 정답 단서-1
(5형식V O O·C(형용사) [ ]: 분사구문)
또한 우리를 더 부유하게 만들면서 / 장기적으로

🔓힌트 「if+주어+과거시제V ~, 주어+조동사 과거형+동사원형」의 가정법 과거 문장으로, 형태는 과거이나 현재 사실과 반대되는 내용을 가정하므로 현재시제로 해석함.

똑같은 돈이 '투자'된다면, 이는 일자리를 창출함으로써 장기적으로 우리를 더 부유하게 함.

(C) (7) Think about college / as an example.
대학에 관해 생각해 보자 / 예시로서

✶중요 문장 (7) 이하로는 앞에 나왔던 '텔레비전 구매하기 vs. 다른 곳에 투자하기'의 대조 관계가 '학생을 대학에 보내기 vs. 학생에게 스포츠카 사주기'의 대조 관계로 반복되어 제시됨.

(8) Sending students to college / 정답 단서-2 학생을 대학에 보내는 상황이 제시됨.
(S(동명사구))
학생들을 대학에 보내는 것은 /
creates jobs for professors.
(V)
교수들을 위한 일자리를 창출한다

(9) [Using the same money / to buy fancy sports cars /
똑같은 돈을 쓰는 것은 / 멋진 스포츠카를 사주는 데 /
for high school graduates] / 정답 단서-2 학생에게 멋진 스포츠카를 사주는 상황이 제시됨.
([ ]: S(동명사구))
고등학교 졸업생에게 /
would create jobs / for auto workers.
일자리를 창출할 것이다 / 자동차 노동자들을 위한

✶중요 문장 (4) 앞에는 '대학 교육에 돈을 들이는 사례'와 '스포츠카에 돈을 들이는 사례'가 선행되어야 함.

(A) (4) The crucial difference between these scenarios /
(S)
이러한 시나리오들의 중대한 차이점은 /
is [that a college education makes a young person
(V S' 5형식V' O')
more productive /
(O·C'(형용사))
대학 교육은 젊은이를 더 생산적이게 만든다는 것이다 /
for the rest of his or her life; / a sports car does not]. 정답 단서-3
그 또는 그녀의 남은 삶에서 / 스포츠카는 그렇지 않다
([ ]: S·C(that 명사절))
대학 교육은 장기적으로 학생들을 더 생산적이게 만들지만, 스포츠카는 그렇지 않음.

(5) Thus, / college tuition is an investment; /
따라서 / 대학 등록금은 투자이다 /
buying a sports car is consumption.
(S(동명사구) V)
스포츠카를 사는 것은 소비이다

[전문 해석]

(1)텔레비전을 사는 것은 현재의 소비이다. (2)그것은 오늘 우리를 행복하게 만들지만, 우리를 내일 더 부유하게 만들기 위해 아무것도 하지 않는다. (3)물론, 텔레비전에 소비되는 돈은 노동자들이 텔레비전 공장에 계속 고용되게 한다.
(B) (6)그러나 만약 똑같은 돈이 투자된다면, 그것은 다른 어딘가에서, 말하자면 실험실의 과학자들이나 건설 현장의 노동자들을 위해, 또한 장기적으로 우리를 더 부유하게 만들면서 일자리를 창출할 것이다.
(C) (7)예시로서 대학에 관해 생각해 보자. (8)학생들을 대학에 보내는 것은 교수들을 위한 일자리를 창출한다. (9)똑같은 돈을 고등학교 졸업생에게 멋진 스포츠카를 사주는 데 쓰는 것은 자동차 노동자들을 위한 일자리를 창출할 것이다.
(A) (4)이러한 시나리오들의 중대한 차이점은 대학 교육은 젊은이를 그 또는 그녀의 남은 삶에서 더 생산적이게 만들지만 스포츠카는 그렇지 않다는 것이다. (5)따라서, 대학 등록금은 투자이지만, 스포츠카를 사는 것은 소비이다.

[정답 확인]

주어진 글 다음에 이어질 글의 순서로 가장 적절한 것은?

① (A) — (C) — (B) ② (B) — (A) — (C) ③ (B) — (C) — (A)
④ (C) — (A) — (B) ⑤ (C) — (B) — (A)

[문제 풀이]

주어진 글에 따르면, 텔레비전을 사는 것은 '소비'로서, 이는 우리에게 즉각적인 만족감을 제공하고 텔레비전 공장 노동자들을 계속 고용하게 하지만 미래의 재정적인 가치를 증가시키지는 않는다. 한편, 텔레비전의 사례는 일자리를 창출하고 장기적으로 우리를 더 부유하게 만드는 '투자'에 대한 설명과 대조되면서 문장 (6)의 But으로 자연스럽게 연결되므로, 주어진 글 다음에는 가장 먼저 (B)가 온다. 특히, 문장 (3)과 문장 (6)의 'Yes(물론) ~. But(그러나) ~.'의 흐름은, '텔레비전에 돈을 쓰는 것이 공장 노동자들의 고용 상태를 유지시키기는 하지만 이것이 돈을 쓰는 당사자를 장기적으로 더 부유하게 하는 투자와 같지는 않다'라는 필자의 주장을 자연스럽게 전달한다. 다음으로, 문장 (7)~(9)에는 '학생을 대학에 보내는 상황(투자)'과 '학생에게 스포츠카를 사주는 상황(소비)'이 대조되고 있는데, 이는 앞서 나온 '텔레비전 구매하기(소비) vs. 다른 곳에 투자하기(투자)'의 대조 관계가 반복된 것이므로 (B) 뒤에는 (C)가 와야 한다. 마지막으로, 문장 (4)는 '학생을 대학에 보내는 상황'과 '학생에게 스포츠카를 사주는 상황'을 'these scenarios'로 받으면서 두 사례의 차이가 무엇인지 밝히고 있으며, 문장 (5)는 이러한 차이를 기반으로 '대학 등록금은 투자이며 스포츠카를 사는 것은 소비'라고 결론짓는다. 따라서 (C) 뒤에는 (A)가 와야 하므로, 정답은 ③ '(B) — (C) — (A)'이다.

[오답 풀이]

④ - 문장 (6)의 But으로 미루어 볼 때 (B) 앞에는 '투자'에 대조되는 사례인 '소비'의 사례가 제시되어야 하는데, '(C) — (A) — (B)'의 흐름이 될 경우, 이미 '대학 등록금 vs. 스포츠카 구매'라는 구체적인 사례가 '투자 vs. 소비'의 관계로 결론이 난 후에 또다시 '투자'에 대한 설명만이 이어지게 되어 But의 흐름이 다소 부자연스럽게 된다. 즉, 이 글은 문장 (7) 앞뒤로 '소비 vs. 투자'의 대조 사례가 반복되며 논의가 심화되는 구조를 가지고 있는데, ④의 흐름이 될 경우 이러한 전체적인 구조를 해치게 되므로, ④는 답이 될 수 없다.

[중요 어휘]

☐ current	형용사 현재의, 지금의
☐ consumption	명사 소비, 소모(량)
☐ invest	동사 투자하다, 쏟다, 부여하다
☐ laboratory	명사 실험실
☐ construction site	건설 현장
☐ graduate	명사 졸업생 / 동사 졸업하다
☐ crucial	형용사 중대한, 결정적인

- [ ] **productive** 형용사 생산적인, 결실이 있는
- [ ] **tuition** 명사 등록금, 수업료
- [ ] **investment** 명사 투자

43 2024년 9월 36번 (정답률 65%) 정답 ⑤

[지문 끊어 읽기] 능력자에 대한 비선호

(1) It would seem obvious / [that the more competent someone is, / the more we will like that person]. 정답 단서-1
형식상의 주어
명백해 보인다 / 누군가가 더 능력이 있을수록 / 우리가 그 사람을 더 많이 좋아할 것이다 [ ]: 내용상의 주어
힌트 '더 ~할수록, 더 …하다'의 의미인 'the 비교급 S+V, the 비교급 S'+V' 구문이 쓰였음.
우리는 능력 있는 사람을 더 좋아하는 것처럼 보임.

(2) By "competence," / I mean a cluster of qualities: /
'능력'이라는 것을 / 나는 한 무리의 특징을 뜻하는 것으로 말한다 /
smartness, the ability to get things done, wise decisions, etc.
형용사적 용법
똑똑함, 일을 수행하는 능력, 지혜로운 결정 등

(C) (7) We stand a better chance of doing well at our life tasks /
우리는 우리의 인생 과업에서 잘할 더 나은 가능성이 있다 /
if we surround ourselves with people /
우리가 사람들을 우리 주변에 둘 때 / 선행사
[who know what they're doing / and have a lot to teach us]. 정답 단서-1
병렬① 간접의문문(know의 목적어) 병렬② [ ]: 주격 관계대명사절
그들이 무엇을 하고 있는지를 아는 / 그리고 우리를 가르칠 많은 것을 갖고 있는
자신이 무엇을 하고 있는지 알고, 우리를 가르칠 것이 많은 사람들, 즉 능력 있는 사람들을 우리 주변에 둘 때 과업을 더 잘할 가능성이 있음.

(8) But the research evidence is paradoxical:
하지만 연구 증거는 역설적이다

(9) In problem-solving groups, / the participants /
문제 해결 집단에서 / 참여자들은 / S, 선행사
[who are considered the most competent /
병렬①
가장 능력이 있다고 여겨지는 /
and have the best ideas] / tend not to be the ones /
병렬② [ ]: 주격 관계대명사절 V 선행사
그리고 가장 좋은 생각을 갖고 있는 / 사람들이 아닌 경향이 있다 /
[who are best liked]. 정답 단서-2
가장 선호되는 [ ]: 주격 관계대명사절
가장 능력 있는 참여자들이 가장 선호되는 사람들이 아닌 경향이 있음.

(10) Why?
왜일까

(B) (5) One possibility is /
한 가지 가능성은 ~이다 /
[that, although we like to be around competent people, /
삽입절
비록 우리가 능력 있는 사람들 주위에 있고 싶어 하지만 /
those who are *too* competent / make us uncomfortable]. 정답 단서-2
S', 선행사 주격 관계대명사절 V'(5형식V) O' O·C' [ ]: 보어(명사절)
'너무' 능력 있는 사람들은 / 우리를 불편하게 만든다
능력 있는 사람들은 우리는 불편하게 만듦.

(6) They may seem unapproachable, distant, superhuman /
=competent people
그들은 접근할 수 없고, 멀고, 초인간적으로 보일지도 모른다 /
— and make us look bad (and feel worse) / by comparison. 정답 단서-3
사역V O O·C(동사원형)
그리고 우리를 형편없어 보이게(그리고 기분이 더 나쁘게) 만든다 / 그에 비해
능력 있는 사람들과 비교하여 우리는 형편없어 보이고 기분이 나빠지게 됨.

(A) (3) If this were true, / we might like people more /
만약 이것이 사실이라면 / 우리는 사람들을 더 좋아할 수도 있다 /
if they reveal some evidence of fallibility. 정답 단서-3
그들이 실수를 저지를 수 있다는 어떤 증거를 드러낼 때
힌트 가정법 과거(현재 사실의 반대를 가정) : If S'+동사의 과거형(were), S+조동사의 과거형+동사원형
능력 있는 사람들이 실수를 저지른다면, 우리는 그들을 더 좋아할 수도 있음. 여기서 this는 (B)의 문장 (6)의 내용을 가리킴.

(4) For example, /
예를 들어 /
if your friend is a brilliant mathematician, superb athlete, and gourmet cook, /
만약 여러분의 친구가 뛰어난 수학자, 최고의 운동선수, 그리고 미식 요리사라면 /
you might like him or her better /
여러분은 그들을 더 좋아할지도 모른다 /
if, every once in a while, they screwed up.
삽입어구
가끔 그들이 망친다면

[전문 해석]

(1)누군가가 더 능력이 있을수록, 우리가 그 사람을 더 많이 좋아할 것이 명백해 보인다. (2)나는, '능력'이라는 것을, 똑똑함, 일을 수행하는 능력, 지혜로운 결정 등과 같은 한 무리의 특징을 뜻하는 것으로 말한다.
(C) (7)그들이(자신이) 무엇을 하고 있는지를 알고, 우리를 가르칠 많은 것을 갖고 있는 사람들을 우리 주변에 둘 때 우리는 우리의 인생 과업에서 잘할 더 나은 가능성이 있다. (8)하지만 연구 증거는 역설적이다. (9)문제 해결 집단에서, 가장 능력이 있다고 여겨지고 가장 좋은 생각을 갖고 있는 참여자들은 가장 선호되는 사람들이 아닌 경향이 있다. (10)왜일까?
(B) (5)한 가지 가능성은, 비록 우리가 능력 있는 사람들 주위에 있고 싶어 하지만, '너무' 능력 있는 사람들은 우리를 불편하게 만든다는 것이다. (6)그들은 접근할 수 없고, 멀고, 초인간적으로 보일지도 모르는데, 그에 비해 우리를 형편없어 보이게(그리고 기분이 더 나쁘게) 만든다.
(A) (3)만약 이것이 사실이라면, 사람들이 실수를 저지를 수 있다는 어떤 증거를 드러낼 때 우리는 그들을 더 좋아할 수도 있다. (4)예를 들어, 만약 여러분의 친구가 뛰어난 수학자, 최고의 운동선수, 그리고 미식 요리사라면, 여러분은 가끔 그들이 망친다면 그들을 더 좋아할지도 모른다.

[정답 확인]

주어진 글 다음에 이어질 글의 순서로 가장 적절한 것은?

① (A) — (C) — (B) ② (B) — (A) — (C) ③ (B) — (C) — (A)
④ (C) — (A) — (B) ✔ (C) — (B) — (A)

[문제 풀이]

주어진 글의 문장 (1)에서 우리는 능력 있는 사람을 더 좋아할 것이라는 통념을 제시한다. 이에 대한 근거로 (C)의 문장 (7)에서 우리가 능력 있는 사람들 주변에 있을 때 과업을 더 잘할 가능성이 있다는 긍정적인 내용의 문맥으로 연결 짓는 것이 자연스러우므로 주어진 문장 다음에는 (C)가 온다. 하지만 이어지는 문장 (8)과 (9)에서 이를 반박하는 연구 증거에 대한 내용이 나오는데, 기존 통념과 다르게 가장 능력 있어 보이는 참여자들이 가장 선호되는 사람들이 아니라는 것이다. (B)의 문장 (5)에서 그 이유에 대한 한 가지 가능성으로 능력자들은 우리를 불편하게 만든다고 한다. 따라서 (C) 다음에는 (B)가 온다. 문장 (6)에서 초인적인 능력자들과 비교하여 우리가 형편없어 보여서 기분이 나빠진다고 하는데, 이와 관련하여 (A)의 문장 (3)에 능력자들이 실수를 저지른다면 우리는 그들을 더 좋아할지도 모른다는 내용으로 이어지는 것이 자연스럽다. 따라서 (B) 다음에는 (A)가 온다. 그러므로 정답은 ⑤이다.

[중요 어휘]

- [ ] **obvious** 형용사 명백한, 확실한
- [ ] **competent** 형용사 능력 있는, 능숙한, 권한이 있는
- [ ] **competence** 명사 능력, 능숙함, 권한, 기능
- [ ] **cluster** 명사 무리, (작은 열매의) 송이 / 동사 무리를 이루다
- [ ] **stand a chance of V-ing** ~할 가능성이 있다
- [ ] **paradoxical** 형용사 역설적인, 모순된
- [ ] **unapproachable** 형용사 접근할 수 없는
- [ ] **distant** 형용사 먼, 동떨어진
- [ ] **by comparison** 그에 비해
- [ ] **superb** 형용사 최고의, 최상의
- [ ] **gourmet** 형용사 미식의
- [ ] **screw up** 망치다, 엉망으로 만들다
- [ ] **(every) once in a while** 가끔, 이따금

44 2024년 9월 37번 (정답률 65%) 정답 ③

[지문 끊어 읽기] 알고리즘에서 입력의 무의미성

(1) A computational algorithm / [that takes input data /
S, 선행사 병렬①
컴퓨터를 사용하는 알고리즘은 / 입력 데이터를 받는 /
and generates some output from it] / [ ]: 주격 관계대명사절
병렬② =input data
그리고 그것으로부터 어떤 출력을 생성하는 /
doesn't really embody any notion of meaning. 정답 단서-1
V
실제로 의미라는 어떤 개념도 구현하지 않는다
컴퓨터의 알고리즘에서 입력 정보로부터 생성된 출력 정보는 실제로 의미가 있지 않음.

(2) Certainly, / such a computation does not generally have /
분명히 / 그러한 계산은 일반적으로 갖지 않는다 / 3형식V
as its purpose / its own survival and well-being.
그것의 목적으로 / 그 자체의 생존과 안녕을 O

(B) (6) It does not, in general, assign value to the inputs. 정답 단서-1
=computation
이것은 일반적으로 입력에 가치를 부여하지 않는다
컴퓨터 계산은 보통 입력 정보에 가치를 두지 않음.

힌트 compare A with B : A와 B를 비교하다

(7) Compare, for example, a computer algorithm /
예를 들어 컴퓨터 알고리즘을 비교해 보라 /
with the waggle dance of the honeybee, / 정답 단서-2 컴퓨터 알고리즘과 꿀벌의 8자 춤을 비교함.
꿀벌의 8자 춤과 /
by which means / a foraging bee conveys to others in the hive /
현재분사 3형식V' =other bees
그 수단으로 / 먹이를 찾아다니는 벌이 벌집 안에 있는 다른 벌들에게 알려준다 /
information about the source of food (such as nectar) /
O' 선행사
(꿀과 같은) 먹이의 출처에 대한 정보를 /
it has located.
목적격 관계대명사절(관계대명사 생략)
그것이 위치를 찾아낸

힌트 which는 관계형용사로, 뒤에 나온 명사인 means를 수식함. by which means는 and by this means로 바꾸어 쓸 수 있고, 위 문장에서는 '꿀벌의 8자 춤(선행사), 이 춤으로 먹이를 찾아다니는 벌이 ~ 알려준다'라고 해석 할 수 있음.

(C) (8) The "dance" / — a series of stylized movements on the comb — /
그 '춤'은 / 벌집에서의 일련의 양식화된 움직임은 /
shows the bees /
4형식V I·O
벌들에게 보여 준다 /
[how far away the food is and in which direction]. 정답 단서-2
먹이가 얼마나 멀리 있고 어느 방향으로 있는지를 의문형용사 [ ]: D·O(명사절)
The "dance"는 문장 (7)에서 나온 꿀벌의 8자 춤을 가리키고, 그 춤은 먹이의 위치 정보를 알리는 것임.

(9) But this input does not simply program /
V
그러나 이 입력은 단순히 프로그래밍하는 것이 아니다 /
other bees [to go out and look for it]. 정답 단서-3
O [ ]: O·C =the food
다른 벌들이 나가서 그것을 찾도록
먹이의 위치 정보를 입력받은 벌들이 단순히 먹이를 찾아 오는 것이 아님.

(10) Rather, / they evaluate this information, / 정답 단서-3 벌들은 입력 정보를 평가함.
=other bees
오히려 / 그들은 이 정보를 평가한다 /
[comparing it with their own knowledge of the surroundings].
=this information [ ]: 분사구문
주변 환경에 대한 그들만의 지식과 비교하며

(A) (3) Some bees might not bother to make the journey, /
어떤 벌들은 일부러 그 이동을 하지 않을 수도 있다 /
O(=the journey)
[considering it not worthwhile]. 정답 단서-3
5형식V O·C [ ]: 분사구문
그것이 가치가 없다고 생각해서
벌들은 먹이를 찾는 이동이 가치 없다고 판단하여 일부러 이동하지 않을 수도 있음.

(4) The input, / such as it is, / is processed /
S V
그 입력은 / 대단한 것은 못되지만 / 처리된다 /
in the light of the organism's own internal states and history;
유기체 자체의 내부 상태와 역사를 고려하여

(5) there is nothing prescriptive about its effects.
그 결과에 대해 규정하는 것은 없다 =the input's

[전문 해석]

(1)입력 데이터를 받아 그것으로부터 어떤 출력을 생성하는 컴퓨터를 사용하는 알고리즘은 실제로 의미라는 어떤 개념도 구현하지 않는다. (2)분명히, 그러한 (컴퓨터) 계산은 일반적으로 그 자체의 생존과 안녕을 그것의 목적으로 갖지 않는다.
(B) (6)이것은 일반적으로 입력에 가치를 부여하지 않는다. (7)예를 들어, 컴퓨터 알고리즘을, 먹이를 찾아다니는 벌이 위치를 찾아낸 (꿀과 같은) 먹이의 출처에 대한 정보를 벌집 안에 있는 다른 벌들에게 알려주는 수단인 꿀벌의 8자 춤과 비교해 보라.
(C) (8)그 '춤', 즉 벌집에서의 일련의 양식화된 움직임은 벌들에게 먹이가 얼마나 멀리 있고 어느 방향으로 있는지를 보여 준다. (9)그러나 이 입력은 단순히 다른 벌들이 나가서 그것(먹이)을 찾도록 프로그래밍하는 것이 아니다. (10)오히려 그들은 이 정보를 주변 환경에 대한 그들만의 지식과 비교하며 정보를 평가한다.
(A) (3)어떤 벌들은 그 이동이 가치가 없다고 생각해서 일부러 그 이동을 하지 않을 수도 있다. (4)그 입력은, 대단한 것은 못되지만, 유기체 자체의 내부 상태와 역사를 고려하여 처리된다. (5)그 결과에 대해 규정하는 것은 없다.
- waggle dance(8자 춤): 꿀벌이 꽃, 꿀 등이 있는 곳의 방향과 거리를 동료에게 알리는 동작

[정답 확인]

주어진 글 다음에 이어질 글의 순서로 가장 적절한 것은?

① (A) — (C) — (B)　② (B) — (A) — (C)　✔③ (B) — (C) — (A)
④ (C) — (A) — (B)　⑤ (C) — (B) — (A)

[문제 풀이]

주어진 글의 문장 (1)은 컴퓨터의 알고리즘에서 입력 데이터를 토대로 나온 출력 정보가 실제로는 어떤 의미를 담은 것이 아님을 설명한다. 이와 관련하여 입력 데이터에 가치를 두지 않는다는 (B)의 문장 (6)이 주어진 문장과 같은 맥락이다. 따라서 주어진 글 다음으로 (B)가 적절하다. 문장 (7)에서 컴퓨터 알고리즘을 꿀벌의 8자 춤과 비교하는데, 이는 (C)의 문장 (8)에서 그 '춤'이 먹이의 위치 정보를 알려준다는 내용과 연결되므로 (B) 다음으로 (C)가 적절하다. 이어서 역접의 접속사 'But'으로 시작하는 문장 (9), (10)에서 동료의 춤을 본 벌들은 곧 먹이를 찾아 나서는 것이 아니라 그 정보를 자신들이 가진 지식에 비추어 평가한다고 한다. 이는 벌들이 먹이를 찾아 이동하지 않을 수도 있다는 (A)의 문장 (3)과 인과적으로 연결되므로 (C) 다음으로 (A)가 오는 것이 알맞다. 따라서 정답은 ③이다.

[중요 어휘]

☐ computational	형용사 컴퓨터를 사용한
☐ generate	동사 생성하다, 발생시키다
☐ embody	동사 구현하다, 상징하다, 포함하다
☐ notion	명사 개념, 관념, 생각
☐ computation	명사 계산, 계량, 평가
☐ survival	명사 생존, 유물
☐ assign	동사 부여하다, 맡기다
☐ means	명사 수단, 방법, (개인이 가진) 돈, 수입
☐ forage	동사 먹이를 찾다
☐ convey	동사 알려주다, 전달하다
☐ nectar	명사 (꽃의) 꿀
☐ locate	동사 ~의 위치를 찾아내다
☐ stylize	동사 양식화하다
☐ comb	명사 벌집, 빗
☐ evaluate	동사 평가하다, ~의 수치를 구하다
☐ bother	동사 일부러 ~하다
☐ such as it is	대단한 것은 못되지만
☐ in the light of	~을 고려하여, ~에 비추어
☐ organism	명사 유기체
☐ prescriptive	형용사 규정하는, 규범적인

문제편 p.209

15 주어진 문장 위치 파악

01 2020년 3월 39번 (정답률 70%) 정답 ④

[지문 끊어 읽기] 심장 이식과 뇌사 판정의 기준

(2) Of all the medical achievements of the 1960s, /
1960년대의 모든 의학적 업적 중에서 /
the most widely known was the first heart transplant, /
가장 널리 알려져 있는 것은 최초의 심장 이식이었다 /
performed by the South African surgeon Christiaan Barnard in 1967.
1967년에 남아프리카 외과 의사 Christiaan Barnard에 의해 수행된

① (3) The patient's death / 18 days later / did not weaken the spirits /
그 환자의 사망은 / 18일 후의 / 사기를 약화시키지 않았다 /
of those who welcomed a new era of medicine.
선행사 / 주격 관계대명사절
새로운 의학의 시대를 환영하는 사람들의

② (4) The ability to perform heart transplants / was linked /
S / 형용사적 용법(~하는) / V
심장 이식을 수행하는 그 능력은 / 연관되어 있었다 /
to the development of respirators, /
인공호흡기의 개발과 /
which had been introduced to hospitals / in the 1950s.
병원에 도입되었던 / 1950년대에

③ (5) Respirators could save many lives, /
인공호흡기는 많은 생명을 살릴 수 있었다 /
but not all those / whose hearts kept beating /
S
하지만 모든 사람들이 ~하는 것은 아니었다 / 심장이 계속 뛰는 /
ever recovered any other significant functions. 정답 단서
V
항상 다른 어떤 중요한 기능을 회복하는 것은

④ (1) In some cases, /
어떤 경우에는 /
their brains had ceased / to function / altogether.
그들의 뇌가 중단했다 / 기능하는 것을 / 완전히

(6) The realization / [that such patients could be a source /
S / [ ]: The realization과 동격
그 깨달음은 / 그러한 환자들이 원천이 될 수 있다는 /
of organs for transplantation] / led /
V
이식을 위한 장기의 / 이어졌다 /
to the setting up of the Harvard Brain Death Committee, /
하버드 뇌사 위원회의 설립으로 /
and to its recommendation /
그리고 그것의 권고로 /
[that the absence of all "discernible central nervous system activity" /
모든 '식별 가능한 중추 신경계 활동'의 부재가 /
should be "a new criterion for death"]. [ ]: its recommendation과 동격
'사망의 새로운 기준'이 되어야 한다는

⑤ (7) The recommendation has since been adopted, /
부사
그 후로부터 그 권고는 받아들여졌다 /
with some modifications, / almost everywhere.
약간의 수정을 거쳐 / 거의 모든 곳에서

[전문 해석]

(2)1960년대의 모든 의학적 업적 중에서 가장 널리 알려져 있는 것은 1967년에 남아프리카 외과 의사 Christiaan Barnard에 의해 수행된 최초의 심장 이식이었다. ① (3)18일 후의 그 환자의 사망은 새로운 의학의 시대를 환영하는 사람들의 사기를 약화시키지 않았다. ② (4)심장 이식을 수행하는 그 능력은 1950년대에 병원에 도입되었던 인공호흡기의 개발과 연관되어 있었다. ③ (5)인공호흡기는 많은 생명을 살릴 수 있었지만, 심장이 계속 뛰는(인공호흡기가 살린) 모든 사람들이 항상 다른 어떤 중요한 기능을 회복하는 것은 아니었다. ④ (1)어떤 경우에는 그들의 뇌가 기능하는 것을 완전히 중단했다. (6)그러한 환자들이 이식을 위한 장기의 원천이 될 수 있다는 그 깨달음은 하버드 뇌사 위원회의 설립과 모든 '식별 가능한 중추 신경계 활동'의 부재가 '사망의 새로운 기준'이 되어야 한다는 그것(위원회)의 권고로 이어졌다. ⑤ (7)그 후로부터 그 권고는 약간의 수정을 거쳐 거의 모든 곳에서 받아들여졌다.
- central nervous system(중추 신경계): 뇌와 척수로 이루어진 신경계의 부분으로, 신경계에서 가장 많은 부위를 차지한다.

[문제 풀이]

주어진 문장은 뇌가 기능하는 것을 완전히 중단하는 경우가 있다고 하는데, 'In some cases(어떤 경우에는)'로 시작하므로 앞서 얘기한 내용의 사례를 소개하는 부분이라는 것을 알 수 있다. 문장 (5)에서 심장이 계속 뛰는 모든 사람들이 항상 다른 어떤 중요한 기능을 회복하는 것은 아니라고 하는데, 주어진 문장이 바로 이 'other significant functions'의 사례에 해당한다고 할 수 있다. 따라서 주어진 문장은 ④에 오는 것이 적절하다.

[중요 어휘]

□ **transplant**	명사 이식 / 동사 이식하다
□ **surgeon**	명사 외과 의사
□ **era**	명사 시대
□ **respirator**	명사 인공호흡기, 방독 마스크
□ **function**	명사 기능 / 동사 기능하다
□ **cease**	동사 중단하다, 그치다
□ **committee**	명사 위원회
□ **discernible**	형용사 식별 가능한, 알아볼 수 있는
□ **nervous**	형용사 신경의, 불안해하는
□ **criterion**	명사 기준, 척도 (복수형 criteria)
□ **adopt**	동사 받아들이다, 채택하다
□ **modification**	명사 수정, 변경

핵심 본문에서 언급되는 위험(risk)이 어떤 것인지 서로 구분할 필요가 있음. 주어진 문장은 내용의 전개가 달라지는 부분이므로, 문장에서 언급된 위험이 이전과 같은 것을 지칭하는지 아닌지를 파악하여 주어진 문장이 들어갈 곳을 찾아야 함.

02 2021년 6월 38번 (정답률 70%) 정답 ④

[지문 끊어 읽기] 위험의 발생과 피하는 방법

(2) Risk often arises from uncertainty /
위험은 종종 불확실성에서 발생한다 /
about how to approach a problem or situation.
문제나 상황에 접근하는 방법에 대한

① (3) One way to avoid such risk / is to contract with a party /
형용사적 용법
이러한 위험을 피하는 한 방법은 / 당사자와 계약하는 것이다 /
who is experienced / and knows how to do it. 주제문
병렬① / 병렬②
숙련된 / 그리고 그것을 하는 방법을 아는

② (4) For example, / to minimize the financial risk /
예를 들어 / 재정적인 위험을 최소화하기 위해서 /
associated with the capital cost of tooling and equipment /
세공과 장비의 자본 비용과 관련된 /
for production of a large, complex system, /
크고 복잡한 시스템의 생산을 위한 /
a manufacturer might subcontract the production /
S / V
제조업자는 생산을 하청을 줄 수도 있다 /
of the system's major components /
시스템의 주요 부품들에 대한 /
to suppliers familiar with those components.
그 부품들을 잘 아는 공급업자들에게

힌트 to부정사의 부사적 용법으로 쓰였으며 다소 길기는 하지만 내용상의 강조를 위해 주절보다 앞에 위치할 수 있음.

힌트 밑줄 친 부분들은 각각 선행사인 the financial risk와 suppliers를 수식해주며, '주격 관계대명사 + be동사'가 생략된 동일한 구조임(각각 which is / who are이 생략됨).

③ (5) This relieves the manufacturer of the financial risk /
이것이 제조업자의 재정적인 위험을 완화한다 /
associated with the tooling and equipment / 정답 단서
세공과 장비와 관련된 /
to produce these components.
이 부품들을 생산하기 위한

힌트 이 문장의 주어 This는 이전 문장에서 언급된 내용(재정적 위험의 최소화를 위한 제조업자의 하청 구조)을 의미하는 대명사임.

④ (1) However, / transfer of one kind of risk /
그러나 / 한 종류의 위험 이전은 /
often means inheriting another kind. 정답 단서
종종 다른 종류를 이어받는 것을 의미한다

힌트 another kind (of risk)를 의미함.

(6) For example, / subcontracting work for the components /
S
예를 들어 / 부품들에 대한 일을 하청을 주는 것은 /

puts the manufacturer in the position /
제조업자를 입장에 처하게 한다 /
of relying on outsiders, / which increases the risks /
외부업자에게 의지하는 / 그런데 이것은 위험을 증가시킨다 /
associated with quality control, scheduling, and the performance of the end-item system. 정답단서
품질 관리, 일정 관리, 완제품 시스템의 성능과 관련된

힌트 계속적 용법으로 쓰인 주격 관계대명사로, 앞 문장 전체를 선행사로 받으며, 하나의 문장이 선행사이므로 3인칭 단수 취급함.

⑤ (7) But these risks often can be reduced /
그러나 이런 위험은 종종 줄어들 수 있다 /
through careful management / of the suppliers.
신중한 관리를 통해 / 공급업자들의

[전문 해석]

(2)위험은 종종 문제나 상황에 접근하는 방법에 대한 불확실성에서 발생한다. ① (3)이러한 위험을 피하는 한 방법은 숙련되고 그것(문제나 상황에 접근하는 것)을 하는 방법을 아는 당사자와 계약하는 것이다. ② (4)예를 들어, 크고 복잡한 시스템의 생산을 위한 세공과 장비의 자본 비용과 관련된 재정적인 위험을 최소화하기 위해서 제조업자는 그 부품들을 잘 아는 공급업자들에게 시스템의 주요 부품들에 대한 생산을 하청을 줄 수도 있다. ③ (5)이것이 이 부품들을 생산하기 위한 세공과 장비와 관련된 제조업자의 재정적인 위험을 완화한다. ④ (1)그러나 한 종류의 위험 이전은 종종 다른 종류(의 위험)을 이어받는 것을 의미한다. (6)예를 들어, 부품들에 대한 일을 하청을 주는 것은 제조업자를 외부업자에게 의지하는 입장에 처하게 하는데, 이것은 품질 관리, 일정 관리, 완제품 시스템의 성능과 관련된 위험을 증가시킨다. ⑤ (7)그러나 이런 위험은 공급업자들의 신중한 관리를 통해 종종 줄어들 수 있다.

[중요 어휘]

☐ risk	명사 위험, 위험 요소
☐ uncertainty	명사 불확실성
☐ contract	동사 계약하다, 수축하다
☐ party	명사 당사자, 정당
☐ minimize	동사 최소화하다
☐ associated with	~와 관련된
☐ capital cost	자본 비용
☐ tooling	명사 세공, 연장을 쓰는 일
☐ manufacturer	명사 제조(업)자, 생산 회사
☐ subcontract	동사 하청을 주다
☐ major	형용사 주요한, 중대한, 심각한
☐ component	명사 부품, (구성) 요소
☐ supplier	명사 공급(업)자, 공급 회사
☐ transfer	명사 이전, 이동 / 동사 이동하다
☐ inherit	동사 이어받다, 상속받다
☐ end-item	명사 완제품

핵심 오픈 온라인 액세스로 정보에 접근하는 것이 쉬워진 것처럼 보이지만 사실은 정보가 전달되는 루트에 영향을 주는 요인이 많음을 비유를 통해 설명하고 있음. 주어진 문장의 'the same'이나 'similar'가 지칭하는 바가 무엇인지 정확히 파악해야 함.

03 2019년 9월 38번 (정답률 60%) 정답 ④

[지문 끊어 읽기] 국제적인 오픈 온라인 액세스

(2) Open international online access is understood /
국제적인 오픈 온라인 액세스는 이해될 수 있다 /
using the metaphor "flat earth."
'평평한 지구'라는 은유를 사용하여

(3) It represents a world /
이것은 세상을 나타낸다 /
where information moves across the globe / as easily /
정보가 전 세계로 이동하는 / 쉽게 /
as a hockey puck seems to slide /
하키 퍽이 미끄러지는 것만큼 /
across an ice rink's flat surface.
아이스 링크의 평평한 표면 위를

힌트 'as + 원급(형용사/부사) + as' 형태의 원급 비교구문임. 일반적으로 '~만큼 …한'으로 해석을 하는데, '~만큼'에 해당하는 두 번째 as의 뒤에는 문장 (3)처럼 주어와 동사를 다 갖춘 절이 올 수도 있음.

① (4) This framework, however, / can be misleading /
그러나 이러한 틀은 / 오해의 소지가 있을 수 있다 /
— especially if we extend the metaphor.
특히 우리가 그 은유를 확장했을 때

② (5) As anyone who has crossed an ice rink can confirm, /
아이스 링크를 가로질러 본 사람이라면 누구든 확인할 수 있듯이 /
just because the surface of the rink appears flat and open /
아이스 링크의 표면이 평평하고 트여있는 것처럼 보인다고 해서 /
does not necessarily mean / that surface is smooth or even.
반드시 의미하지는 않는다 / 그 표면이 매끄럽고 고르다는 것을

③ (6) Rather, / such surfaces tend to be covered /
오히려 / 그런 표면은 덮여 있는 경향이 있다 /
by a wide array of dips and cracks and bumps /
다수의 움푹 팬 부분과 금, 그리고 요철로 /
that create a certain degree of pull or drag or friction / 정답단서
어느 정도의 인력, 저항력 혹은 마찰력을 만드는 /
on any object / moving across it.
어떤 대상에나 / 그 위를 가로질러 움직이는

④ (1) In much the same way, /
이와 매우 유사한 방식으로 /
an array of technological, political, economic, cultural, and linguistic factors can exist /
다수의 기술적, 정치적, 경제적, 문화적, 그리고 언어적인 요인이 존재할 수 있다 /
and create a similar kind of pull or drag or friction. 정답단서
그리고 비슷한 종류의 인력이나 저항력, 혹은 마찰력을 만들 수 있다

정답단서
(7) They affect / how smoothly or directly information can move /
그것들은 영향을 준다 / 정보가 얼마나 매끄럽게 혹은 곧바로 움직일 수 있는지에 /
from point to point / in global cyberspace.
지점에서 지점으로 / 전 세계 사이버 공간 안에서

⑤ (8) Thus, / while the earth might appear to be increasingly flat /
그러므로 / 지구가 점점 더 평평하게 보일 수도 있지만 /
from the perspective of international online communication, /
국제적인 온라인 의사소통의 관점에서 /
it is far from frictionless.
그것은 마찰이 없는 것과는 거리가 멀다

[중요 구문]

힌트 문장 (5)의 구조를 요약하면, 「As S' V', S V ~」로 나타낼 수 있음. 즉, 'just because'가 이끄는 절이 주절의 주어이며, 주절은 크게 보아 '~한다고 해서 (그것이) 반드시 ~임을 의미하지는 않는다'라고 해석됨. 즉, because는 '~ 때문에'라는 부사절을 이끌기도 하지만, 이처럼 명사절로서 주어나 보어로 쓰이기도 함.

(5) As anyone [who ~] can confirm, (S' V')
[just because the surface ~ appears flat and open] [ ]:S
does not necessarily mean [that surface is smooth or even]. (V, [ ]:O)

[전문 해석]

(2)국제적인 오픈 온라인 액세스는 '평평한 지구'라는 은유를 사용하여 이해될 수 있다. (3) 이것은 하키 퍽이 아이스 링크의 평평한 표면 위를 미끄러지는 것만큼 쉽게 정보가 전 세계로 이동하는 세상을 나타낸다. ① (4)그러나 이러한 (사고의) 틀은 특히 우리가 그 은유를 확장했을 때 오해의 소지가 있을 수 있다. ② (5)아이스 링크를 가로질러 본 사람이라면 누구든 확인할 수 있듯이, 아이스 링크의 표면이 평평하고 트여있는 것처럼 보인다고 해서 (그것이) 반드시 그 표면이 매끄럽고 고르다는 것을 의미하지는 않는다. ③ (6)오히려 그런 표면은 그 위를 가로질러 움직이는 어떤 대상에나 어느 정도의 인력, 저항력 혹은 마찰력을 만드는 (가하는) 다수의 움푹 팬 부분과 금, 그리고 요철로 덮여 있는 경향이 있다. ④ (1)이와 매우 유사한 방식으로, (오픈 온라인 액세스에는) 다수의 기술적, 정치적, 경제적, 문화적, 그리고 언어적인 요인이 존재할 수 있으며 (아이스 링크의 사례와) 비슷한 종류의 인력이나 저항력, 혹은 마찰력을 만들 수 있다. (7)그것(요인)들은 정보가 전 세계 사이버 공간 안에서 지점에서 지점으로 얼마나 매끄럽게 혹은 곧바로 움직일 수 있는지에 영향을 준다. ⑤ (8)그러므로 국제적인 온라인 의사소통의 관점에서 지구가 점점 더 평평하게 보일 수도 있지만, 그것은 마찰이 없는 것과는 거리가 멀다(결코 마찰이 없는 것은 아니다).

- open online access(오픈 온라인 액세스): 온라인상에서 비용과 기술, 법의 제약을 받지 않고 일반인 또한 연구 성과물을 자유롭게 이용할 수 있게 하는 것을 가리킨다. 오픈 액세스로 누구나 무료로 정보에 접근하여 활용할 수 있다. 국내에서는 국립중앙도서관의 오픈액세스코리아(OAK)가 대표적이다.

[문제 풀이]

주어진 문장은 'the same way(유사한 방식)'나 'similar(비슷한)'의 어구를 사용하고 있다. 따라서 문장 (1)에서 말하는 '인력이나 저항력, 혹은 마찰력'이 앞에 이미 언급되었어야 하므로, 문장 (1)은 문장 (6) 이후에 들어가야 한다. 그러나 ⑤에는 들어갈 수가 없는데, 문장 (6)은 아이스 링크의 예시를 들고, 문장 (7)은 사이버 공간으로 내용이 갑자기 전환되기 때문이다. 따라서 문장 (6)과 (7)을 서로 이어주는 위치인 ④에 문장 (1)이 들어가야 가장 자연스럽다.

정답과 해설 15 주어진 문장 위치 파악

[중요 어휘]

☐ metaphor	명사 은유, 비유
☐ represent	동사 나타내다, 대표하다
☐ hockey puck	하키 퍽(아이스하키에서 공처럼 치는 고무 원반)
☐ confirm	동사 확인하다, 확정하다
☐ even	형용사 고른, 평평한
☐ an array of (= a wide array of)	다수의
☐ dip	명사 움푹 팬 부분
☐ crack	명사 (갈라져 생긴) 금
☐ bump	명사 요철, 튀어나온 부분
☐ drag	명사 저항력, 방해물 / 동사 끌다
☐ friction	명사 마찰력, (의견) 충돌
☐ linguistic	형용사 언어적인, 언어(학)의
☐ perspective	명사 관점, 시각
☐ frictionless	형용사 마찰이 없는

04 2020년 11월 38번 (정답률 60%) 정답 ④

[지문 끊어 읽기] 액체가 파괴적인 이유

(2) Liquids are destructive.
액체는 파괴적이다

힌트 'foam'은 주로 '거품'이라는 뜻의 명사이지만, 문장 (3)에서는 의자나 매트리스 등에 완충재로 쓰이는 '발포 고무'를 의미함.

(3) Foams feel soft / because they are easily compressed; /
발포 고무는 부드럽게 느껴진다 / 그것들이 쉽게 압축되기 때문에 /
if you jump on to a foam mattress, / you'll feel it give beneath you.
지각V O O·C(동사원형)
만약 당신이 발포 고무 매트리스 위로 점프한다면 / 당신은 그것이 당신 밑에서 휘어지는 것을 느낄 것이다

① (4) Liquids don't do this; / instead they flow.
액체는 이것을 하지 않는다 / 그 대신 그것은 흐른다

② (5) You see this in a river, / or when you turn on a tap, /
당신은 강에서 이것을 보게 된다 / 또는 당신이 수도꼭지를 틀 때 /
or if you use a spoon / to stir your coffee.
또는 당신이 스푼을 사용하는 경우에 / 당신의 커피를 젓기 위해

③ (6) When you jump off a diving board / and hit a body of water, /
당신이 다이빙 도약대에서 뛰어내릴 때 / 그래서 많은 양의 물을 칠 때 /
the water has to flow away from you. 정답 단서
그 물은 당신으로부터 멀리 비켜서 흘러나가야만 한다

④ (1) But the flowing takes time, / 정답 단서
그러나 흘러나가는 것은 시간이 걸린다 /
and if your speed of impact is too great, /
그리고 만약 당신의 충돌 속도가 너무 크면 /
the water won't be able to flow away / fast enough, /
물은 흘러나가지 못할 것이다 / 충분히 빠르게 /
and so it pushes back at you.
따라서 그것은 당신을 밀어낸다

(7) It's that force / that stings your skin /
정답 단서 병렬①
힌트 'It is A that ~' 강조 구문이므로, '~하는 것은 바로 A이다'라고 해석함.
바로 그 힘이다 / 당신의 피부를 얼얼하게 하는 것이 /
as you belly-flop into a pool, / and makes /
=when S' V' 병렬②
당신이 배로 수면을 치며 수영장 속으로 떨어질 때 / 그리고 만드는 것이 /
falling into water / from a great height / like landing on concrete.
물속으로 떨어지는 것을 / 굉장한 높이에서 / 콘크리트 위로 떨어지는 것처럼

⑤ (8) The incompressibility of water / is also /
물의 비압축성은 / 또한 ~이다 /
힌트 선행사 the reason이 생략된 관계부사절로, 등위접속사 and로 병렬 연결되어 있음.
why waves can have such deadly power, /
파도가 그렇게나 치명적인 힘을 가질 수 있는 이유 /
and in the case of tsunamis, /
그리고 쓰나미의 경우 /
why they can destroy buildings and cities, /
=tsunamis
그것이 건물과 도시를 부술 수 있는 이유 /
tossing cars around easily.
자동차를 이리저리 쉽게 던져버리면서

[전문 해석]

(2)액체는 파괴적이다. (3)발포 고무는 쉽게 압축되기 때문에 부드럽게 느껴진다. (따라서) 만약 당신이 발포 고무 매트리스 위로 점프한다면 당신은 그것이 당신 밑에서 휘어지는 것을 느낄 것이다. ① (4)액체는 이것(휘어지는 것)을 하지 않으며, 그 대신 그것은 흐른다. ② (5)당신은 강에서나, 당신이 수도꼭지를 틀 때나, 또는 당신이 당신의 커피를 젓기 위해 스푼을 사용하는 경우에 이것(액체가 흐르는 것)을 보게 된다. ③ (6)당신이 다이빙 도약대에서 뛰어내려 많은 양의 물(물줄기)을 칠 때, 그 물은 당신으로부터 멀리 비켜서 흘러나가야만 한다. ④ (1)그러나 흘러나가는 것은 시간이 걸리며, 만약 당신의 충돌 속도가 너무 크면 물은 충분히 빠르게 흘러나가지 못할 것이고, 따라서 그것(물)은 당신을 밀어낸다. (7)당신이 배로 수면을 치며 수영장 (물)속으로 떨어질 때 당신의 피부를 얼얼하게 하며, 굉장한 높이에서 물속으로 떨어지는 것을 콘크리트 위로 떨어지는 것처럼 만드는 것이 바로 그 힘이다. ⑤ (8)물의 비압축성은 또한 파도가 그렇게나 치명적인 힘을 가질 수 있는 이유이며, 쓰나미의 경우 그것이 자동차를 이리저리 쉽게 던져버리면서 건물과 도시를 부술 수 있는 이유이다.

[문제 풀이]

'액체가 파괴적인' 이유에 대해 설명한 글로, 문장 (3)~(4)는 충격을 받았을 때 휘어지는 발포 고무와 달리, 액체는 흐르는 속성을 가지고 있다고 주장한다. 한 예로, 문장 (6)은 다이빙을 할 때 물이 사람으로부터 멀리 비켜서 흘러나간다고 설명하는데, 이는 충돌 속도가 너무 크면 물이 흘러나갈 수 없다는 주어진 문장의 상황과 역접의 접속 부사 'But'으로 자연스럽게 연결된다. 또한, 문장 (7)에서 말하는 '그 힘(that force)'은 아주 빠르게 다이빙을 했을 때 미처 흘러나가지 못한 물이 몸을 밀어내면서 발생하는 충격을 의미하므로, 문맥상 주어진 문장이 문장 (6)과 (7) 사이에 오는 것이 자연스럽다. 따라서 정답은 ④이다.

[중요 어휘]

☐ destructive	형용사 파괴적인, 해를 끼치는
☐ compress	동사 압축하다, 꾹 누르다
☐ give	동사 (힘을 받아) 휘어지다, 구부러지다 / 명사 탄력성, 신축성
☐ tap	명사 수도꼭지 / 동사 가볍게 두드리다
☐ stir	동사 젓다, 섞다
☐ a body of	많은 양의
☐ impact	명사 충돌, 충격, 영향
☐ force	명사 힘, 군대 / 동사 강요하다, 강제하다
☐ sting	동사 얼얼하게 하다, 따끔따끔하게 하다
☐ belly-flop	동사 배로 수면을 치며 떨어지다
☐ height	명사 높이, 키, 고도
☐ concrete	명사 콘크리트 / 형용사 콘크리트로 된, 구체적인
☐ incompressibility	명사 비(非)압축성
☐ deadly	형용사 치명적인, 위험한
☐ in the case of	~의 경우에
☐ toss	동사 던지다, 토스하다

05 2021년 11월 39번 (정답률 60%) 정답 ③

[지문 끊어 읽기] 별개 환경의 조건에 묘목이 적응하는 법

(2) Scientists /
S(=선행사)
과학자들은 /
[who have observed plants growing in the dark] / have found /
지각V(5형식) O O·C [ ]: 주격 관계대명사절 V
어둠 속에서 식물이 자라는 것을 관찰해 온 / 발견해왔다 /
that they are vastly different in appearance, form, and function /
명사절 접속사
그것들이 외관, 형태 그리고 기능에서 상당히 다르다는 것을 /
from those grown in the light. 정답 단서 식물은 어둠 속에서 자랄 때와 빛 속에서 자랄 때 다른 모습으로 성장함.
=plants
빛 속에서 길러진 것들과

① (3) This is true / even when the plants in the different light conditions /
S'
이것은 적용된다 / 다른 빛 조건에 있는 식물들이 /

are genetically identical /
V'①
유전적으로 동일한 때에도 /
and are grown under identical conditions /
V'②
그리고 동일한 조건에서 길러질 때에도 /
of temperature, water, and nutrient level.
온도, 물 그리고 영양소 수준의

②(4) Seedlings grown in the dark /
S
어둠 속에서 길러진 묘목은 /
limit the amount of energy going to organs /
V① 선행사
기관으로 가는 에너지의 양을 제한한다 /
[that do not function at full capacity in the dark, /
어둠 속에서 완전한 능력으로 기능하지 않는 /
like cotyledons and roots], / [ ]: 주격 관계대명사절
떡잎이나 뿌리처럼 /
and instead initiate elongation of the seedling stem /
V②
그리고 대신 묘목 줄기의 연장을 시작한다 /
to propel the plant out of darkness. **정답 단서** 어둠 속에서 길러진 묘목은 어둠 속에서 잘 기능하지 않는 기관으로 가는 에너지의 양은 제한하고, 빛을 찾아가기 위해 줄기 연장에 더 많은 에너지를 사용함.
부사적 용법(목적)
그 식물을 어둠에서 벗어나 나아가게 하기 위하여

③(1) In full light, / seedlings reduce the amount of energy /
충분한 빛 속에서 / 묘목은 에너지의 양을 줄인다 / 선행사
they allocate to stem elongation. **정답 단서** 반면에, 충분한 빛 속에서 길러진 묘목은 줄기 연장에 배분하는 에너지를 줄임.
목적격 관계대명사절
그것들이 줄기 연장에 배분하는

(5) The energy is directed to expanding their leaves /
병렬①
그 에너지는 그것들의 잎을 확장하는 데로 향한다 /
and developing extensive root systems. **정답 단서** 그 에너지가 잎과 뿌리로 향함.
병렬②
그리고 광범위한 근계를 발달시키는 데로
힌트 '근계'는 식물의 땅속으로 뻗은 뿌리의 갈래를 말함.

④(6) This is a good example of phenotypic plasticity.
이것이 표현형 적응성의 좋은 예이다

⑤(7) The seedling adapts to distinct environmental conditions /
묘목은 별개의 환경 조건에 적응한다 /
by modifying its form and the underlying metabolic and
병렬① 병렬②
biochemical processes. **주제문** 묘목은 형태, 그리고 신진대사 및 생화학적 과정을 바꿈으로써 별개의 환경 조건에 적응함.
그것의 형태와 근원적인 신진대사 및 생화학적 과정을 바꿈으로써

[전문 해석]

(2)어둠 속에서 식물이 자라는 것을 관찰해 온 과학자들은 그것들이 빛 속에서 길러진 것들과 외관, 형태 그리고 기능에서 상당히 다르다는 것을 발견해왔다. ① (3)이것은 다른 빛 조건에 있는 식물들이 유전적으로 동일하고 온도, 물 그리고 영양소 수준의 동일한 조건에서 길러질 때에도 적용된다. ② (4)어둠 속에서 길러진 묘목은 떡잎이나 뿌리처럼, 어둠 속에서 완전한 능력으로 기능하지 않는 기관으로 가는 에너지의 양을 제한하고, 대신 그 식물을 어둠에서 벗어나 나아가게 하기 위하여 묘목 줄기의 연장을 시작한다. ③ (1)충분한 빛 속에서 묘목은 그것들이 줄기 연장에 배분하는 에너지의 양을 줄인다. (5)그 에너지는 그것들의 잎을 확장하고 광범위한 근계(根系)를 발달시키는 데로 향한다. ④ (6)이것이 표현형 적응성의 좋은 예이다. ⑤ (7)묘목은 그것의 형태와 근원적인 신진대사 및 생화학적 과정을 바꿈으로써 별개의 환경 조건에 적응한다.
- phenotypic plasticity(표현형 적응성): 변화하는 환경에 따라 다양한 표현형을 만들어 내는 능력. 표현형이란 겉으로 드러나는 생물의 특성을 말하며, 물리적, 행동적, 생화학적 특성들을 모두 포함함.

[문제 풀이]

지문은 빛의 양이 다른 조건에서 자란 식물이 서로 다른 환경에 적응하며 나타난 결과를 설명한다. 문장 (2)~(4)는 어둠 속에서 길러진 식물에 대해 설명하는데, 문장 (4)에서 구체적으로 어둠 속에서 잘 기능하지 않는 떡잎이나 뿌리와 같은 기관으로 가는 에너지의 양은 제한하고 줄기 연장에 에너지를 배분한다고 언급한다. 그런데 이어지는 문장 (5)에서는 앞의 내용과는 반대로 에너지가 잎과 뿌리로 향한다고 언급한다. 즉 문장 (4)와 문장 (5)가 서로 상반되는 내용이므로 이 둘 사이에 글의 흐름이 전환되는 문장이 와야함을 유추할 수 있다. 또한 주어진 문장을 보면 충분한 빛 속에서 길러진 묘목이 줄기 연장에 배분하는 에너지를 줄인다고 한다. 이는 어둠 속에서 길러진 식물을 설명한 문장 (2)~(4)의 내용과 상반되는 내용으로 글의 흐름을 전환시키는 문장이다. 따라서 주어진 문장은 ③에 들어가는 것이 가장 자연스럽다.

[중요 어휘]

□ vastly	부사 상당히, 굉장히, 대단히
□ function	명사 기능 / 동사 기능하다
□ identical	형용사 동일한
□ seedling	명사 묘목
□ organ	명사 기관, 장기
□ capacity	명사 능력, 용량
□ initiate	동사 시작하다, 착수시키다
□ elongation	명사 연장
□ propel	동사 나아가게 하다, 몰고 가다
□ allocate	동사 배분하다, 할당하다
□ adapt	동사 적응하다, 맞추다
□ distinct	형용사 별개의, 분명한
□ underlying	형용사 근원적인, 근본적인
□ metabolic	형용사 신진대사의

● 지문 구조도

(2) 서로 다른 빛 조건(different light conditions)에서의 식물 성장 비교
어둠 속에서(in the dark) 자란 식물 vs. 빛 속에서(in the light) 자란 식물
→ 모두 외관, 형태, 기능이 다름.

↓

결과: 어둠 속에서 자란 묘목	vs.	**결과: 빛이 가득한 곳에서 자란 묘목**
(4) 어둠 속에서 기능하지 않는 기관(ex. 떡잎, 뿌리)으로 가는 에너지가 제한(limit)되고, 묘목 줄기가 연장(stem elongation)됨.		(1) 줄기 연장에 배분하는 에너지 양을 줄임(reduce). (5) 잎이 확장(expand)되고, 광범위한 근계(root systems)가 발달함.

↓

(6) 표현형 적응성(phenotypic plasticity)
(7) 묘목이 별개의 환경 조건에 적응(adapt)하면서 형태, 그리고 신진대사 및 생화학적 과정을 바꿈(modifying).

06 2022년 6월 39번 (정답률 55%) 정답 ②

[지문 끊어 읽기] 특정 영역에 한정된 창의성

(2) [The holy grail / of the first wave of creativity research] / [ ]: S
궁극적 목표는 / 창의성 연구의 첫 번째 물결의 /
was a personality test / to measure general creativity ability, /
V 형용사적 용법
성격 검사였다 / 전반적인 창의력을 측정하는 /
in the same way / that IQ measured general intelligence.
관계부사절
같은 방식으로 / IQ가 전반적인 지능을 측정했던 것과

①(3) A person's creativity score /
한 사람의 창의성 점수는 /
should tell us his or her creative potential /
예상, 추측 4형식V I·O D·O
우리에게 그 또는 그녀의 창의적 잠재력을 말해줄 것이었다 /
in any field of endeavor, / **정답 단서** 과거에는 창의성 점수(지수)가 여러 분야에 걸친 전반적인 창의적 잠재력을 말해줄 것이라고 여김.
노력하는 어떠한 분야에서도 /
just like an IQ score is not limited to physics, math, or literature.
접속사(=as)
IQ 점수가 물리학, 수학 또는 문학에 국한되지 않는 것과 마찬가지로

②(1) But by the 1970s, / **정답 단서** 역접의 연결사 'But'을 통해 문장 (1)은 앞 문장과 대조되는 내용임을 알 수 있음.
그러나 1970년대에 /
psychologists realized / [there was no such thing /
심리학자들은 깨달았다 / 그런 것은 없다는 것을 /
as a general "creativity quotient]."
전반적인 '창의성 지수'와 같은 [ ]: 목적어절(명사절 접속사 that 생략)
힌트 'There is no such thing/person as A'는 'A와 같은 것(사람)은 없다, 존재하지 않는다'라는 뜻의 구문임. 주절의 동사가 과거 시제(realized)이므로 시제 일치를 위해 was를 사용함.

(4) Creative people aren't creative /
창의적인 사람들은 창의적인 것은 아니다 /
in a general, universal way; 정답 단서
전반적이고, 보편적으로

창의적인 사람은 전반적이고 보편적으로 창의적인 게 아니라고 함. 문장 (2)~(3)에서는 전반적인 창의력 측정에 대해 이야기하고 있으나, 문장 (4)부터는 내용이 반전되어 전반적인 창의력에 대해 부정하고 있음을 알 수 있음.

(5) they're creative /
그들은 창의적이다 /
in a specific sphere of activity, / a particular domain. 정답 단서
활동의 특정 범위에서 / 즉 특정 영역

창의적인 사람은 특정 영역에서 창의적인 것이라고 함. 문장 (4)와 마찬가지로 문장 (2)~(3)과 대조되는 내용임.

③ (6) We don't expect / a creative scientist / to also be a gifted painter.
5형식V O O·C(to V)
우리는 기대하지 않는다 / 창의적인 과학자가 / 또한 재능 있는 화가가 되는 것을

④ (7) A creative violinist may not be a creative conductor, /
창의적인 바이올린 연주자는 창의적인 지휘자가 아닐 수도 있다 /
and a creative conductor may not be very good at composing new works.
be good at V-ing: ~하는 데 뛰어나다, 잘하다
그리고 창의적인 지휘자는 새로운 곡을 작곡하는 데 매우 뛰어나지 않을 수도 있다

⑤ (8) Psychologists now know / that creativity is domain specific.
명사절 접속사
심리학자들은 이제 안다 / 창의성이 특정 영역에 한정된 것임을

[전문 해석]

(2)창의성 연구의 첫 번째 물결의 궁극적 목표는 IQ가 전반적인 지능을 측정했던 것과 같은 방식으로 전반적인 창의력을 측정하는 성격 검사였다. ① (3)한 사람의 창의성 점수는 IQ 점수가 물리학, 수학 또는 문학에 국한되지 않는 것과 마찬가지로, 노력하는 어떠한 분야에서도 우리에게 그 또는 그녀의 창의적 잠재력을 말해줄 것이었다. ② (1)그러나 1970년대에, 심리학자들은 전반적인 '창의성 지수'와 같은 것은 없다는 것을 깨달았다. (4)창의적인 사람들은 전반적이고, 보편적으로 창의적인 것은 아니다. (5)그들은 활동의 특정 범위, 즉 특정 영역에서 창의적이다. ③ (6)우리는 창의적인 과학자가 또한 재능 있는 화가가 되는 것을 기대하지 않는다. ④ (7)창의적인 바이올린 연주자는 창의적인 지휘자가 아닐 수도 있고, 창의적인 지휘자는 새로운 곡을 작곡하는 데 매우 뛰어나지 않을 수도 있다. ⑤ (8)심리학자들은 이제 창의성이 특정 영역에 한정된 것임을 안다.

[문제 풀이]

이 글은 창의적인 사람들이 전반적인 영역에 걸쳐 창의성이 두드러지는 것이 아니라 특정 영역에 한정되어서만 창의적이라는 내용이다. 문장 (1)은 연결사 But으로 시작해 전반적인 창의성 지수라는 것은 '없다'고 말한다. 따라서 문장 (1)의 앞에는 전반적인 창의성 지수가 '있다'는 내용이 나와야 할 것이다. 문장 (2)~(3)이 전반적인 창의력의 측정에 대해 이야기하고 있고, 문장 (4)부터는 이에 대해 부정하고 있으므로 지문의 내용이 반전되는 곳에 문장 (1)이 위치해야 자연스럽게 지문이 연결된다. 따라서 정답은 ②이다.

[중요 어휘]

☐ holy grail	궁극적 목표
☐ general	형용사 전반적인, 일반적인
☐ intelligence	명사 지능
☐ endeavor	명사 노력, 시도, 애씀 / 동사 노력하다, 시도하다
☐ quotient	명사 지수, (나눗셈에서) 몫
☐ universal	형용사 보편적인
☐ specific	형용사 특정한
☐ sphere	명사 범위, 영역, 구(체)
☐ particular	형용사 특정한
☐ domain	명사 영역
☐ gifted	형용사 재능 있는, 타고난
☐ conductor	명사 지휘자
☐ compose	동사 작곡하다, 구성하다

07 2022년 9월 38번 (정답률 55%)

정답 ③

[지문 끊어 읽기]

적응과 순응

(2) Adaptation involves changes in a population, /
적응은 개체군의 변화를 수반한다 /
with characteristics /
특성을 가지고 / 선행사
that are passed from one generation to the next. 주제문
주격 관계대명사
한 세대로부터 다음 세대로 전해지는

'적응'은 세대 간 유전되는 특성을 바탕으로 개체군이 변화하게 함.

(3) This is different from acclimation /
이것은 순응과는 다르다 /
— an individual organism's changes /
개별 유기체의 변화 /
in response to an altered environment.
변화된 환경에 반응한

① (4) For example, / if you spend the summer outside, /
예를 들어 / 당신이 여름을 야외에서 보낸다면 /
you may acclimate to the sunlight:
당신은 햇빛에 순응하게 될 것이다

✶중요 문장 (1)은 피부 색소를 생산하는 능력이 유전된다는 내용임. 이는 적응에 대한 설명으로, 순응의 예시를 들고 있는 문장 (4) 앞에 위치시키는 것은 자연스럽지 않으므로 ①은 정답으로 적절하지 않음.

(5) your skin will increase / its concentration of dark pigments /
당신의 피부는 증가시킬 것이다 / 어두운 색소의 농도를 / 선행사
that protect you from the sun.
주격 관계대명사
당신을 태양으로부터 보호하는

✶중요 문장 (3)~(6) 모두 순응의 특징에 대해 이야기하고 있음. 따라서 문장 (1)을 위치시켜 이러한 흐름을 깨는 것은 자연스럽지 않으므로 ②는 정답으로 적절하지 않음.

② (6) This is a temporary change, /
이것은 일시적인 변화이다 /
and you won't pass the temporary change /
그리고 당신은 그 일시적인 변화를 물려주지 않을 것이다 /
on to future generations. 정답 단서
미래 세대에

일시적인 변화는 미래 세대에 유전되지 않음.

일시적 변화와 달리 피부 색소를 생산하는 능력은 유전됨. 정답 단서

③ (1) However, / the capacity to produce skin pigments / is inherited.
S V
하지만 / 피부 색소를 생산하는 능력은 / 유전된다

(7) For populations / living in intensely sunny environments, /
사람들의 경우 / 햇빛이 몹시 내리쬐는 환경에 사는 /
individuals with a good ability to produce skin pigments /
S①
피부 색소를 생산하는 능력이 좋은 사람들이 /
are more likely to thrive, or to survive, /
V①
더 번영하거나 생존하기 쉽다 /
than people with a poor ability to produce pigments, /
색소를 생산하는 능력이 좋지 않은 사람들보다 /
and that trait becomes increasingly common /
V② S②(=the good ability to produce skin pigments)
그리고 그 특징은 더욱 흔해진다 /
in subsequent generations.
다음 세대에서

✶중요 문장 (8)이 적응의 수많은 사례를 찾을 수 있다고 이야기하고 있으므로 문장 (8) 뒤에는 적응의 사례가 소개되어야 함. 문장 (9)에서 기린을 통해 적응의 예시를 보여주고 있기 때문에 문장 (1)이 문장 (8)과 문장 (9) 사이에 들어가는 것은 자연스럽지 않음. 따라서 ⑤는 정답으로 적절하지 않음.

④ (8) If you look around, / you can find /
당신이 주변을 둘러보면 / 당신은 찾을 수 있다 /
countless examples of adaptation.
적응의 수많은 사례를

⑤ (9) The distinctive long neck of a giraffe, / for example, /
기린 특유의 긴 목은 / 예를 들어 /
developed / as individuals /
접속사 S'(=선행사)
발달했다 / 개체들이 ~함에 따라 /
that happened to have longer necks /
주격 관계대명사
우연히 더 긴 목을 갖게 된 /
had an advantage / in feeding on the leaves of tall trees.
V'
유리해짐에 따라 / 높은 나무의 잎을 먹는 데

[전문 해석]

(2)적응은 한 세대로부터 다음 세대로 전해지는 특성을 가지고 개체군의 변화를 수반한다. (3)이것은 변화된 환경에 반응한 개별 유기체의 변화인 순응과는 다르다. ① (4)예를 들어, 당신이 여름을 야외에서 보낸다면, 당신은 햇빛에 순응하게 될 것이다. (5)당신의 피부는 당신을 태양으로부터 보호하는 어두운 색소의 농도를 증가시킬 것이다. ② (6)이것은 일시적인 변화이고, 당신은 그 일시적인 변화를 미래 세대에 물려주지 않을 것이다. ③ (1)하지만 피부 색소를 생산하는 능력은 유전된다. (7)햇빛이 몹시 내리쬐는 환경에 사는 사람들의 경우, 피부 색

소를 생산하는 능력이 좋은 사람들이 색소를 생산하는 능력이 좋지 않은 사람들보다 더 번영하거나 생존하기 쉽고, 그 특징은 다음 세대에서 더욱 흔해진다. ④ (8)주변을 둘러보면, 당신은 적응의 수많은 사례를 찾을 수 있다. ⑤ (9)예를 들어, 기린 특유의 긴 목은 우연히 더 긴 목을 갖게 된 개체들이 높은 나무의 잎을 먹는 데 유리해짐에 따라 발달했다.

- adaptation(적응): 생명체가 자연선택이라는 진화의 과정을 통하여 특정 환경에서 잘 살아가게 된 모습
- acclimation(순응): 생물이 지속적인 환경 변화에 대처하여 그 생리적 기능 등을 변화시키고 생활을 유지하려고 하는 과정

[문제 풀이]

문장 (1)의 However는 역접의 의미로, 앞뒤에 상반되는 내용이 오는 것이 자연스럽다. 문장 (1)이 피부 색소 생산 능력이 다음 세대로 유전된다는 내용이므로 문장 (1) 앞에는 다음 세대로 유전되지 '않는' 특성에 대한 이야기가 나와야 한다. 문장 (6)에서 일시적 변화는 미래 세대에 유전되지 않는다고 이야기하므로 문장 (6) 이후에 문장 (1)이 이어지는 것이 자연스럽다. 또한, 문장 (7)은 색소 생산 능력이 번영과 생존 확률을 높이고, 그것이 다음 세대에서 더욱 흔해진다고 언급하며 후대에 유전되는 특성을 구체적으로 설명하고 있기 때문에 문장 (1)은 문장 (6)과 문장 (7) 사이를 연결하는 것이 적절하다. 따라서 정답은 ③이다.

[중요 어휘]

☐ **involve**	동사 수반하다, 포함하다, 관련시키다
☐ **population**	명사 개체군, 개체수, 인구
☐ **organism**	명사 유기체, 생물체
☐ **in response to**	~에 (반)응하여
☐ **alter**	동사 변하다, 달라지다, 바꾸다
☐ **acclimate(=acclimatize)**	동사 순응하다, (장소·기후 등에) 익숙해지다
☐ **concentration**	명사 농도, 집중
☐ **pigment**	명사 색소, 안료
☐ **temporary**	형용사 일시적인, 임시의
☐ **pass A on to B**	A에게 B를 물려주다
☐ **inherit**	동사 유전으로 이어받다, 상속하다
☐ **thrive**	동사 번영하다, 번창하다
☐ **trait**	명사 특징, 특성, 특색
☐ **subsequent**	형용사 다음의, 차후의
☐ **countless**	형용사 수많은, 무수한
☐ **distinctive**	형용사 특유의, 독특한
☐ **happen to V**	우연히 ~하다
☐ **have an advantage in**	~하는 데 유리하다

08 2023년 6월 38번 (정답률 55%) 정답 ④

[지문 끊어 읽기] 과학 실험에서의 조작과 통제

(2) The fundamental nature of the experimental method is manipulation and control.
실험 방법의 근본적 본질은 조작과 통제이다

(3) Scientists manipulate a variable of interest, /
V①
과학자들은 관심 변수를 조작한다 /
and see [if there's a difference].
V② [ ]: 목적어절
그리고 차이가 있는지 확인한다

(4) At the same time, / they attempt to control /
동시에 / 그들은 통제하려고 시도한다 /
for the potential effects of all other variables.
다른 모든 변수들의 잠재적 영향을

(5) [The importance of controlled experiments] / [ ]: S
통제된 실험의 중요성은 /
in identifying the underlying causes of events /
V-ing
사건의 근본적인 원인을 식별하는 것에 있어서 /
cannot be overstated.
V
아무리 강조해도 지나치지 않다

✱중요 문장 (1)은 현실 세계에서 일어나지 않는 상황을 만들어야 한다고 말함. 따라서 ①에 문장 (1)이 삽입되려면 ① 이전에 현실 세계와 동떨어져야 하는 이유에 대한 언급이 있어야 함. 하지만 이전에 그러한 언급을 찾아볼 수 없으므로 ①은 정답으로 적절하지 않음.

문제편 p.212

① (6) In the real-uncontrolled-world, / variables are often correlated.
현실의 통제되지 않은 세계에서 / 변수는 종종 상관관계가 있다

② (7) For example, / people who take vitamin supplements /
선행사 주격 관계대명사절
예를 들어 / 비타민 보충제를 섭취하는 사람들은 /
may have different eating and exercise habits /
V
다른 식습관과 운동 습관을 가지고 있을 것이다 /
than people who don't take vitamins.
선행사 주격 관계대명사절
비타민을 섭취하지 않는 사람들과

✱중요 문장 (7)~(8)은 비타민을 섭취하는 사람과 그렇지 않는 사람을 비교하는 예시를 들면서 실험을 할 때 고려해야 하는 사항들을 언급하고 있음. 따라서 ③에 문장 (1)이 삽입되는 것은 예시의 내용이 이어지는 문장 (7)과 (8)의 흐름에 방해가 되므로 ③은 정답으로 적절하지 않음.

③ (8) As a result, /
결과적으로 /
if we want to study the health effects of vitamins, /
만약 우리가 비타민의 건강에 미치는 효과를 연구하길 원한다면 /
we can't merely observe the real world, /
우리는 단지 현실 세계만을 관찰할 수 없다 /
정답 단서 비교를 하기 위한 요소 외의 것들도 영향을 미치기 때문에 현실 세계만을 관찰해서는 안 됨.
since any of these factors (the vitamins, diet, or exercise) may affect health.
이러한 요소들(비타민, 식단, 혹은 운동) 중 어떤 것이든 건강에 영향을 미칠 수 있기 때문에

④ (1) Rather, / we have to create a situation /
선행사
오히려 / 우리는 상황을 만들어야 한다 /
[that doesn't actually occur in the real world].
[ ]: 주격 관계대명사절
현실 세계에서 실제로 일어나지 않는

(9) That's just what scientific experiments do.
그것이 바로 과학 실험이 하는 일이다

✱중요 문장 (10)은 과학 실험은 다른 변수를 유지하면서 한 가지만을 조작하여 현실에서 일어날 수 없는 상황을 만들기 위해 노력한다는 사실을 정리함. 접속사 'Rather'로 시작하는 문장 (1)이 ⑤에 삽입되려면 앞선 내용을 반박해야 하는데, 문장 (9)와 연결이 부자연스러우므로 ⑤는 정답으로 적절하지 않음.

⑤ (10) They try to separate the naturally occurring relationship /
=scientific experiments
그것들은 자연스럽게 발생하는 관계를 분리하려고 노력한다 /
in the world /
세상에서 /
by manipulating one specific variable at a time, /
by V-ing: ~함으로써
한 번에 하나의 특정한 변수를 조작함으로써 /
while holding everything else constant.
5형식V O O·C
다른 모든 것들을 일정하게 유지하면서
정답 단서 자연적으로 발생하는 상관관계를 분리시킴으로써 현실 세계에서 일어나는 요소를 통제함.

힌트 'while holding everything else constant'는 분사구문으로, 주어가 주절의 주어 'they'와 같으므로 생략하고, 시제가 같은 동사를 현재분사의 형태로 변경하면서 위와 같은 형태가 되었으며, 접속사 while은 생략되지 않고 남음.

[전문 해석]

(2)실험 방법의 근본적 본질은 조작과 통제이다. (3)과학자들은 관심 변수를 조작하고 차이가 있는지 확인한다. (4)동시에, 그들은 다른 모든 변수들의 잠재적 영향을 통제하려고 시도한다. (5)사건의 근본적인 원인을 식별하는 것에 있어서 통제된 실험의 중요성은 아무리 강조해도 지나치지 않다. ① (6)현실의 통제되지 않은 세계에서 변수는 종종 상관관계가 있다. ② (7)예를 들어, 비타민 보충제를 섭취하는 사람들은 비타민을 섭취하지 않는 사람들과 다른 식습관과 운동 습관을 가지고 있을 것이다. ③ (8)결과적으로, 만약 우리가 비타민의 건강에 미치는 효과를 연구하길 원한다면, 이러한 요소들(비타민, 식단, 혹은 운동) 중 어떤 것이든 건강에 영향을 미칠 수 있기 때문에, 우리는 단지 현실 세계만을 관찰할 수 없다. ④ (1)오히려, 우리는 현실 세계에서 실제로 일어나지 않는 상황을 만들어야 한다. (9)그것이 바로 과학 실험이 하는 일이다. ⑤ (10)다른 모든 것들을 일정하게 유지하면서 한 번에 하나의 특정한 변수를 조작함으로써, 그것들은 세상에서 자연스럽게 발생하는 관계를 분리하려고 노력한다.

[문제 풀이]

문장 (1)은 Rather로 시작하면서 현실 세계에서 실제로는 일어나지 않는 상황을 만들어야 한다고 이야기하고 있다. 따라서 문장 (1)이 전복시키는 관념이 무엇인지 파악하며 지문을 읽어야 한다. 문장 (3)~(5)는 과학자들이 실험을 하는 방법과 통제의 중요성을, 문장 (6)~(8)은 현실 속 변수의 상관관계를 언급하며 비타민 보충제를 섭취하는 사람과 그렇지 않은 사람을 비교하기 위한 사항에 대한 구체적인 예시에 대해 설명하고 있다. 또한 문장 (9)는 앞선 예시를 바탕으로 과학 실험이 하는 일을 다시 한번 주장하고 있다. 현실 세계만을 관찰해서는 안 된다는 문장 (8) 이후에 현실 세계에서 일어나지 않는 일을 고려해야 한다고 주장하는 문장 (1)의 내용이 나오는 것이 자연스럽게 흐름이 이어지고, 이러한 내용의 문장 (1)은 과학 실험이 하는 일을 강조하는 문장 (9)와 이어지므로 정답은 ④이다.

[중요 어휘]

☐ **fundamental**	형용사 근본적인, 핵심적인, 필수적인
☐ **manipulation**	명사 조작, 속임수
☐ **variable**	명사 변수 / 형용사 변하기 쉬운, 가변성의

문제편 p.213

□ **attempt to V**	~하려고 시도하다
□ **potential**	형용사 잠재적인, 가능성이 있는 / 명사 가능성, 잠재력
□ **underlying**	형용사 근본적인, 근원적인, 기저에 있는
□ **correlated**	형용사 상관관계가 있는
□ **vitamin supplements**	비타민 보충제
□ **merely**	부사 단지, 그저, 한낱
□ **observe**	동사 관찰하다, 준수하다

09 2023년 9월 38번 (정답률 55%) 정답 ④

[지문 끊어 읽기] 스트레스를 받았을 때 뇌의 대응

(2) The brain is a high-energy consumer of glucose, /
뇌는 포도당의 고에너지 소비자이다 / (선행사)
which is its fuel. (=the fuel of the brain)
주격 관계대명사(계속적 용법)
그리고 그것은 그것의 연료이다

(3) Although the brain accounts for merely 3 percent of a person's body weight, /
비록 뇌는 사람 체중의 단지 3퍼센트를 차지하지만 /
it consumes 20 percent of the available fuel.
그것은 사용 가능한 연료의 20퍼센트를 소비한다

① (4) Your brain can't store fuel, / however, /
여러분의 뇌는 연료를 저장할 수 없다 / 그러나 /
so it has to "pay as it goes."
따라서 '활동하는 대로 대가를 지불'해야 한다

★중요 문장 (1)은 스트레스를 받을 때 하지 않는 일에 대해 언급함. 그러나 문장 (3)과 (4)는 뇌가 몸에서 차지하는 비율과 몸이 사용하는 연료의 비율, 그리고 연료를 사용하는 대가를 언급했기 때문에 이 사이에 문장 (1)이 들어가면 글의 흐름이 어색해짐. 따라서 ①은 정답으로 적절하지 않음.

② (5) Since your brain is incredibly adaptive, /
여러분의 뇌는 놀라울 정도로 적응력이 있기 때문에 /
it economizes its fuel resources.
그것은 그것의 연료 자원을 절약한다

★중요 문장 (4)와 (5)는 뇌가 연료를 저장하지 못하기 때문에 연료를 절약해야 한다는 내용으로 이어지며 글의 흐름이 전환되지 않음. 따라서 여기에 주어진 문장이 들어가면 어색하므로, ②는 정답으로 적절하지 않음.

③ (6) Thus, / during a period of high stress, /
그러므로 / 극심한 스트레스를 받는 기간 동안 /
it shifts away from the analysis of the nuances of a situation / (=your brain)
그것은 상황의 미묘한 차이의 분석에서 이동한다 /
to a singular and fixed focus / on the stressful situation at hand.
단일하고 고정된 초점으로 / 당면한 스트레스 상황에 대한

정답 단서 뇌가 스트레스를 받게 되면 당면한 상황에 대해서만 생각하게 됨.

★중요 문장 (6)은 극심한 스트레스를 받는 기간 동안 뇌가 취하는 행동에 대해 설명하는데, 이는 연료를 절약하기 위한 행동으로 문장 (5)에서 언급한 내용의 결과가 됨. 이는 인과의 연결사 thus를 통해 확인 가능함. 문장 (1)이 ③에 위치하면 이러한 인과 관계가 깨지므로, ③은 정답으로 적절하지 않음.

④ (1) You don't sit back / and speculate about the meaning of life /
(병렬① / 병렬②)
여러분은 편안히 앉지 않는다 / 그리고 삶의 의미에 대해 사색하지 않는다 /
when you are stressed.
여러분이 스트레스를 받을 때

(7) Instead, / you devote all your energy / to trying to figure out /
대신에 / 여러분은 모든 에너지를 쏟는다 / 알아내려고 노력하는 데 /
what action to take.
어떤 행동을 취해야 할지

정답 단서 스트레스를 받는 상황에서 취해야 할 행동에 대해 생각하게 됨.

⑤ (8) Sometimes, however, / this shift /
(S)
그러나 때때로 / 이러한 이동은 /
from the higher-thinking parts of the brain /
뇌의 고차원적 사고 영역에서 /
to the automatic and reflexive parts of the brain /
뇌의 자동적이고 반사적인 영역으로의 /
can lead you to do something too quickly, / without thinking.
(V)
여러분이 무언가를 너무 빨리하도록 이끌 수 있다 / 생각 없이

★중요 문장 (7)은 스트레스를 받은 후 뇌의 이동에 대한 내용으로, 스트레스를 받기 이전 상황(편안히 앉아서 삶의 의미를 사색하는 것)에 대한 묘사가 포함된 문장 (1)은 문장 (7) 앞에 위치해야 Instead로 시작하는 문장 (7)과의 연결이 자연스러움. 따라서 ⑤는 정답으로 적절하지 않음.

[전문 해석]

(2)뇌는 포도당의 고에너지 소비자이고, 그것(포도당)은 그것(뇌)의 연료이다. (3)비록 뇌는 사람 체중의 단지 3퍼센트를 차지하지만, 사용 가능한 연료의 20퍼센트를 소비한다. ① (4)그러나 여러분의 뇌는 연료를 저장할 수 없고, 따라서 '활동하는 대로 대가를 지불'해야 한다. ② (5)여러분의 뇌는 놀라울 정도로 적응력이 있기 때문에, 그것(여러분의 뇌)의 연료 자원을 절약한다. ③ (6)그러므로 극심한 스트레스를 받는 기간 동안, 그것(여러분의 뇌)은 상황의 미묘한 차이의 분석에서 당면한 스트레스 상황에 대한 단일하고 고정된 초점으로 이동한다. ④ (1)여러분은 스트레스를 받을 때 편안히 앉아서 삶의 의미에 대해 사색하지 않는다. (7)대신에, 여러분은 어떤 행동을 취해야 할지 알아내려고 노력하는 데 모든 에너지를 쏟는다. ⑤ (8)그러나 때때로 뇌의 고차원적 사고 영역에서 뇌의 자동적이고 반사적인 영역으로의 이러한 이동은 여러분이 무언가를 생각 없이 너무 빨리하도록 이끌 수 있다.

[문제 풀이]

뇌가 스트레스를 받았을 때 취하는 행동을 설명하는 글이다. 주어진 문장 (1)은 스트레스를 받는 상황에서 '취하지 않는 행동'을 언급한다. 문장 (6)은 스트레스를 받았을 때 뇌가 상황을 분석하기보다 상황 그 자체에 초점을 맞춘다고 했고, 문장 (7)은 특정 상황에서 취하는 행동, 즉 그 상황 속에서 '해야 할 행동'에 대해 생각한다고 말한다. 문장 (7)의 'Instead'가 문장 (1)의 '하지 않은 일' 대신 '해야 하는 일'을 언급하며 글의 흐름을 전환하고 있기 때문에, 문장 (1)을 문장 (7) 앞에 위치시켜야 한다. 따라서 정답은 ④이다.

[중요 어휘]

□ **glucose**	명사 포도당
□ **fuel**	명사 연료, 동력 에너지원
□ **account for**	~을 차지하다, ~을 설명하다
□ **adaptive**	형용사 적응력이 있는, 적응할 수 있는
□ **economize**	동사 절약하다, 아끼다
□ **shift**	동사 이동하다, 옮기다 / 명사 이동, 변경, 교대 근무 시간
□ **nuance**	명사 미묘한 차이, 뉘앙스
□ **singular**	형용사 단일한, 단수형의
□ **at hand**	당면한, 머지않아
□ **sit back**	편안히 앉다
□ **speculate**	동사 사색하다, 추측하다
□ **reflexive**	형용사 반사적인

10 2017년 6월 38번 (정답률 50%) 정답 ③

[지문 끊어 읽기] 체온과 효소의 작용

(2) It is vitally important / that wherever we go and whatever we do /
매우 중요하다 / 우리가 어디에 가든지, 무엇을 하든지 /
the body temperature is maintained at the temperature /
체온이 온도로 유지되는 것이 /
at which our enzymes work best. 주제문
우리의 효소들이 가장 잘 작용하는

힌트 형식상의 주어-내용상의 주어 구문으로, 명사절 'that ~ best'가 내용상의 주어에 해당함.

(3) It is not the temperature at the surface of the body / which matters.
몸의 표면의 온도가 아니다 / 중요한 것은

① (4) It is the temperature deep inside the body /
몸속 깊은 곳의 온도이다 /
which must be kept stable.
안정되게 유지되어야 하는 것은

② (5) At only a few degrees above or below normal body temperature /
정상적인 체온보다 단지 조금이라도 높거나 낮은 온도가 되면 /
our enzymes cannot function properly. 정답 단서
우리의 효소들은 제대로 기능할 수 없다

★중요 문장 (1)에서 죽는 상황을 초래할 수도 있다고 가정한 this에 해당하는 내용은 부정적인 내용일 것임. 따라서 문장 (5)의 cannot function properly 뒤에 오는 것이 가장 적절함.

③ (1) If this goes on for any length of time / 정답 단서
만약 이것이 어떤 긴 시간 동안 계속된다면 /
the reactions in our cells cannot continue / and we die.
우리의 세포 안에서의 반응들은 지속될 수 없다 / 그리고 우리는 죽게 된다

(6) All sorts of things can affect internal body temperature, /
모든 종류의 것들은 내부 체온에 영향을 미칠 수 있다 /
including heat generated in the muscles during exercise, /
운동 중에 근육에서 발생되는 열을 포함하여 /
fevers caused by disease, / and the external temperature.
질병으로 인한 열을 / 그리고 외부 온도를

④ (7) We can control our temperature in lots of ways: / we can change /
우리는 많은 방법으로 우리의 온도를 통제할 수 있다 / 우리는 바꿀 수 있다 /
our clothing, the way we behave and how active we are.
우리의 옷, 우리가 행동하는 방식, 그리고 우리가 얼마나 활동적인지를

⑤ (8) But we also have an internal control mechanism: /
하지만 우리는 또한 내부 통제 구조를 가지고 있다 /
when we get too hot / we start to sweat.
우리는 너무 더워지면 / 우리는 땀을 흘리기 시작한다

[전문 해석]

(2)우리가 어디에 가든지, 무엇을 하든지, 체온이 우리의(우리 몸의) 효소들이 가장 잘 작용하는 온도로 유지되는 것이 매우 중요하다. (3)중요한 것은 몸의 표면의 온도가 아니다. ① (4)안정되게 유지되어야 하는 것은 몸속 깊은 곳의 온도이다. ② (5)정상적인 체온보다 단지 조금이라도 높거나 낮은 온도가 되면, 우리의(우리 몸의) 효소들은 제대로 기능할 수 없다. ③ (1)만약 이것이 어떤 긴 시간 동안 계속된다면, 우리의 세포 안에서의 반응들은 지속될 수 없고 우리는 죽게 된다. (6)운동 중에 근육에서 발생되는 열, 질병으로 인한 열, 그리고 외부 온도를 포함하여, 모든 종류의 것들은 내부 체온에 영향을 미칠 수 있다. ④ (7)우리는 많은 방법으로 우리의 온도(체온)를 통제할 수 있다. 우리는 우리의 옷, 우리가 행동하는 방식, 그리고 우리가 얼마나 활동적인지(우리의 활동량)를 바꿀 수 있다. ⑤ (8)하지만 우리는 또한 내부 통제 구조를 가지고 있다. 우리는 너무 더워지면, 땀을 흘리기 시작한다.

[문제 풀이]

이 지문은 우리의 몸속 체온은 효소들이 가장 잘 기능하는 온도로 유지되어야 한다고 알려준다. 문장 (5)에 따르면 그렇지 않을 경우, 효소들이 제대로 기능할 수 없기 때문이다. 주어진 문장은 만약 몸속 체온이 적정 온도가 아닌 상태가 오래도록 지속된다면, 우리는 결국 죽게 된다고 설명한다. If절에서 언급한 'this(이것)'는 앞서 언급한 어떤 상태를 지칭하는데, 이는 문장 (5)에서 제시한 비정상적으로 높거나 낮은 체온을 의미한다. 따라서, 주어진 문장은 문장 (5) 뒤에 오는 것이 가장 적절하다.

[중요 어휘]

☐ **vitally**	부사 매우 중요하게, 필수적으로
☐ **wherever**	접속사 어디에(로) ~하든지, 어디든지
☐ **whatever**	접속사 무엇을 ~하든지, 무엇이든지
☐ **properly**	부사 제대로, 적절하게
☐ **internal**	형용사 내부의, 내부적인
☐ **fever**	명사 (신체의 병으로 인한) 열
☐ **external**	형용사 외부의, 외부적인

11 2019년 3월 39번 (정답률 50%) 정답 ③

[지문 끊어 읽기] 진공청소기라는 용어

(2) Hubert Cecil Booth is often credited with /
Hubert Cecil Booth는 흔히 ~로 인정받는다 /
inventing the first powered mobile vacuum cleaner.
최초의 전동 이동식 진공청소기를 발명한 것으로

① (3) In fact, / he only claimed / to be the first /
사실 / 그는 단지 주장했다 / 최초의 인물이라고 /
to coin the term "vacuum cleaner" / for devices of this nature, /
'진공청소기'라는 용어를 만든 / 이런 특징을 가진 장치들을 위한 /
which may explain / why he is so credited.
그런데 이는 설명해줄 수 있다 / 왜 그가 그렇게 인정받는지를

② (4) As we all know, / the term "vacuum" is an inappropriate name, /
우리 모두 알다시피 / '진공'이라는 용어는 부적절한 이름이다 /
because there exists no vacuum / in a vacuum cleaner. 정답단서
왜냐하면 진공이 존재하지 않기 때문에 / 진공청소기 안에는

③ (1) Rather, / it is the air moving through a small hole /
더 정확히 말하면 / 그것은 작은 구멍을 통해 움직이는 공기이다 /
into a closed container, / as a result of air being blown /
폐쇄된 용기 안으로 / 공기가 내뿜어진 결과로서 /
out of the container / by a fan on the inside.
용기 밖으로 / 내부의 환풍기로 인해

✶중요 문장 (1)의 핵심은 결국 우리가 진공이라고 믿는 것이 사실은 진공이 아니라 '공기(the air)'라는 것임.

(5) But I suppose /
하지만 나는 생각한다 /
a "rapid air movement in a closed container to create suction" cleaner / 정답단서
'흡입력을 만들어내기 위한 폐쇄된 용기에 담긴 빠른 공기의 움직임' 청소기는 /

힌트 문장 (5)를 간략히 표현하면 'I suppose (that) S (조동사)+동사원형'이 됨. that이 생략된 suppose의 목적어절의 주어는 cleaner(청소기)이고, 큰따옴표 안의 내용이 cleaner를 꾸며주고 있으며, 큰따옴표 안에 3개의 구가 있음.

would not sound as scientific or be as handy a name.
병렬① 병렬②
과학적으로 들리지 않거나 편리한 이름 같지 않다고

④ (6) Anyway, / we are stuck with it historically, / and it is hard /
그래서 / 우리는 역사상 그것을 떨쳐버리지 못한다 / 그리고 어렵다 / 형식상의 주어
[to find any references to "vacuum" / prior to Booth]. [ ]: 내용상의 주어 (to부정사구)
'진공'에 대한 어떠한 언급도 찾기가 / Booth 이전에

⑤ (7) Interestingly, / Booth himself did not use the term "vacuum" /
흥미롭게도 / 정작 Booth 자신은 '진공'이라는 용어를 쓰지 않았다 /
when he filed a provisional specification /
그가 임시 제품 설명서를 제출할 때 /
describing in general terms / his intended invention.
삽입구 describing의 목적어
일반적인 용어들로 서술하면서 / 그의 의도된 발명품을

[중요 구문]

(1) Rather, it is [the air] [moving through~container], as a result of air being blown ~.
전치사 / 의미상의 주어 / 동명사

힌트 being blown이 air를 수식하듯이 해석하면 의미가 조금 어색하고, air를 동명사의 의미상의 주어로 해석하여 '공기가 내뿜어진 결과로서'라고 해석하는 것이 더 자연스러움.

[전문 해석]

(2)Hubert Cecil Booth는 흔히 최초의 전동 이동식 진공청소기를 발명한 것으로 인정받는다. ① (3)사실 그는 단지 (자신이) 이런 특징을 가진 장치들을 위한 '진공청소기'라는 용어를 만든 최초의 인물이라고 주장했는데, 이는 왜 그가 그렇게 인정받는지를 설명해줄 수 있다. ② (4) 우리 모두 알다시피, 진공청소기 안에는 진공이 존재하지 않기 때문에, '진공'이라는 용어는 부적절한 이름이다. ③ (1)더 정확히 말하면 그것(우리가 '진공'이라고 믿는 것)은, 내부의 환풍기로 인해 공기가 용기 밖으로 내뿜어진 결과로서, 폐쇄된 용기 안으로 작은 구멍을 통해 움직이는 공기이다. (5)하지만 나는 '흡입력을 만들어내기 위한 폐쇄된 용기에 담긴 빠른 공기의 움직임' 청소기는(라는 이름은) 과학적으로 들리지 않거나 편리한 이름 같지 않다고 생각한다. ④ (6)그래서 우리는 역사상 그것('진공'이라는 이름)을 떨쳐버리지 못하고 있으며, Booth 이전에 '진공'에 대한 어떠한 언급도 찾기가 어렵다. ⑤ (7)흥미롭게도 정작 Booth 자신은 그가 그의 의도된 발명품을 일반적인 용어들로 서술하면서 임시 제품 설명서를 제출할 때 '진공'이라는 용어를 쓰지 않았다.

- Hubert Cecil Booth(휴버트 세실 부스, 1871년~1955년): 최초로 전동 진공청소기를 개발했다고 알려진 잉글랜드의 공학자

[문제 풀이]

필자는 문장 (4)에서 '진공청소기 안(in a vacuum cleaner)은 진공 상태가 아니다'라고 말하는 한편, 주어진 문장에서는 진공청소기의 작동 과정에서 청소기의 용기 내부로 흘러 들어온 '공기(air)'에 대해 설명하고 있다. 즉, 진공청소기 내부는 진공 상태가 아니라는 문장 (4)의 내용을 이어받아 '그렇다면 청소기 내부에 우리가 진공이라고 믿는 것이 무엇인지'에 대해 설명하고 있으므로, 주어진 문장은 문장 (4) 다음에 오는 것이 자연스럽다. 또한, '진공'이라는 말이 실제 청소기의 본질적 특성과 관계가 없음에도 불구하고 다른 용어로 청소기를 부르는 것은 최선이 아닌 것 같다는 문장 (5)의 필자의 견해가 주어진 문장 뒤에 역접의 접속사(but)로 자연스럽게 이어지므로, 정답은 ③이다.

[중요 어휘]

☐ **be credited with**	~라고 인정받다, 명성을 얻다
☐ **mobile**	형용사 이동식의, 기동성 있는
☐ **vacuum cleaner**	명사 진공청소기
☐ **coin**	동사 (새로운 낱말·어구를) 만들다 / 명사 동전, 주화
☐ **nature**	명사 특징, 본질, 자연, 천성
☐ **on the inside**	내부의, 안에
☐ **suction**	명사 흡입력, 흡입
☐ **handy**	형용사 편리한, 유용한
☐ **be stuck with**	~을 떨쳐버리지 못하다
☐ **reference**	명사 언급, 참조
☐ **file**	동사 제출하다, 발송하다 / 명사 파일
☐ **provisional**	형용사 임시의, 임시적인
☐ **specification**	명사 (제품) 설명서, 사양
☐ **intended**	형용사 의도된, 계획된

12 2022년 6월 38번 (정답률 50%) 정답 ④

[지문 끊어 읽기] 빛나는 물체의 색과 온도

(2) One way of measuring temperature occurs /
　　　　　　　　　　S　　　　　　　　　　　V
온도를 측정하는 한 가지 방법은 생긴다 /

🔒힌트 '형용사/부사+enough +to V' 구문으로 '…할 정도로 충분히 ~하게'라는 뜻임.

if an object is hot enough to visibly glow, / such as a metal poker /
눈에 띄게 빛이 날 정도로 물체가 충분히 뜨거울 때 / 금속 부지깽이처럼 / 선행사

that has been left in a fire.
　　주격 관계대명사절
불 속에 놓아둔

①(3) The color of a glowing object / is related to its temperature:
빛나는 물체의 색은 / 그것의 온도와 관련이 있다

(4) as the temperature rises, / the object is first red /
　접속사(~함에 따라)
온도가 상승함에 따라 / 물체는 먼저 빨간색이다 /

and then orange, / and finally it gets white, / the "hottest" color.
　　　　　　　　　　　　　　　　　　= 동격
그러고 나서 주황색 / 그리고 마지막으로 흰색이 된다 / '가장 뜨거운' 색인

②(5) [The relation /
관련성은 /

between temperature and the color of a glowing object] / []:S
　　　　　병렬①　　　　　　　　　　병렬②
온도와 빛나는 물체의 색 사이의 /

is useful to astronomers.
　V
천문학자들에게 유용하다

★중요 문장 (5)에서 '온도(temperature)'를 언급하므로 '이 온도는 (This temperature)'이라고 시작하며 별 표면의 온도에 대해 설명하는 주어진 문장이 ③에 와야 한다고 생각하기 쉬움. 하지만 주어진 문장이 ③에 오게 되면 온도와 빛나는 물체의 색 사이의 관련성을 언급한 문장 (5)와 이에 대한 부연 설명을 하는 문장 (6) 간의 흐름을 깨뜨리므로 ③은 답이 될 수 없음.

③(6) The color of stars is related to their temperature, /
별의 색은 그것들의 온도와 관련이 있다 /

and since people cannot as yet travel the great distances /
　　　접속사(~ 때문에)　　　　　　아직　　　병렬①
그리고 사람들이 아직 먼 거리를 이동할 수 없기 때문에 /

to the stars / and measure their temperature /
　병렬②
별까지의 / 그리고 그것들의 온도를 측정할 수 없기 때문에 /

별의 색은 온도와 관련이 있으며 천문학자들은 별의 색을 측정하는 데 별의 색을 사용함.

in a more precise way, / astronomers rely on their color. [정답 단서]
더 정확한 방법으로 / 천문학자들은 그것들의 색에 의존한다

🔒힌트 of 앞에 the temperature이 생략되었다고 보고 해석하면 됨.

④(1) This temperature is of the surface of the star, / [정답 단서]
이 온도는 별 표면의 온도이다 /

the part of the star /
별의 부분인　선행사

🔒힌트 'the part ~ be seen'은 앞의 the surface of the star와 동격임.

[which is emitting the light / that can be seen]. []: 주격 관계대명사절
빛을 방출하는 / 보일 수 있는　선행사↑　　주격 관계대명사절

별의 내부의 온도는 별 표면의 온도보다 훨씬 더 높음.

천문학자들이 알아내는 별의 온도를 빛을 방출하는 별의 표면 부분 온도임.

(7) The interior of the star is at a much higher temperature / [정답 단서]
별의 내부는 훨씬 더 높은 온도이다 /　비교급 강조

though it is concealed.
비록 그것은 숨겨져 있지만

★중요 이 부분은 주어진 문장의 'the surface of the star'와 대구를 이룸. 문장 (7)에서 별의 내부 온도가 더 높다고 하는데, 비교 대상이 문장 (1)의 별의 표면 온도여야 흐름이 자연스럽게 연결됨.

⑤(8) But the information /
하지만 정보는 /　S

obtained from the color of the star / is still useful.
주격 관계대명사+be동사 생략　　　　　　　　V
별의 색에서 얻은 / 여전히 유용하다

★중요 ⑤에 문장 (1)이 위치한다면 This temperature은 문장 (7)에서 말하는 별 '내부'의 온도를 가리키게 되는데, 문장 (1)에서 또다시 This temperature가 별 표면의 온도라고 말하는 것은 부자연스러우므로 ⑤는 정답이 될 수 없음.

[전문 해석]

(2)온도를 측정하는 한 가지 방법은 불 속에 놓아둔 금속 부지깽이처럼 눈에 띄게 빛이 날 정도로 물체가 충분히 뜨거울 때 생긴다. ① (3)빛나는 물체의 색은 그것(물체)의 온도와 관련이 있다. (4)온도가 상승함에 따라 물체는 먼저 빨간색 그러고 나서 주황색, 마지막으로 '가장 뜨거운' 색인 흰색이 된다. ② (5)온도와 빛나는 물체의 색 사이의 관련성은 천문학자들에게 유용하다. ③ (6)별의 색은 그것들의 온도와 관련이 있고, 사람들이 아직 별까지의 먼 거리를 이동하고 더 정확한 방법으로 그것들의 온도를 측정할 수 없기 때문에, 천문학자들은 그것들의 색에 의존한다. ④ (1)이 온도는 보일 수 있는 빛을 방출하는 별의 부분인 별 표면의 온도이다. (7)별의 내부는 비록 숨겨져 있지만, 온도가 훨씬 더 높다. ⑤ (8)하지만 별의 색에서 얻은 정보는 여전히 유용하다.

[문제 풀이]

주어진 문장의 위치를 파악하기 위해선 문장 (1)의 This temperature가 가리키는 것이 무엇인지 찾아야 한다. 우선 문장 (1)은 별 표면의 온도에 대해서 말하고 있으므로 크게 보아 별과

관련된 내용이 등장하는 문장 (6) 이후에 위치하는 것이 자연스럽다. 문장 (1)이 ④에 위치한다면 This temperature가 지칭하는 바는 별의 온도로 자연스럽게 해석이 된다. 또한 천문학자들이 별의 온도를 측정하는 데 별의 색을 사용한다는 문장 (6)에 이어 이 온도가 바로 빛을 방출함으로써 관찰 가능한 별 표면의 온도라고 부연 설명하는 문장 (1)이 오는 것이 자연스럽다. 따라서 정답은 ④이다.

[중요 어휘]

☐ temperature　　　명사 온도
☐ visibly　　　　부사 눈에 띄게, 분명히
☐ glow　　　　통사 빛나다, 타오르다 / 명사 불빛, 홍조
☐ poker　　　　명사 부지깽이, 찌르는 사람, 포커
☐ measure　　　통사 측정하다 / 명사 단위, 척도, 조치
☐ precise　　　형용사 정확한
☐ rely on　　　~에 의존하다
☐ surface　　　명사 표면
☐ emit　　　　통사 방출하다, 내뿜다
☐ interior　　　명사 내부 / 형용사 내부의
☐ conceal　　　통사 숨기다, 감추다
☐ obtain　　　　통사 얻다, 구하다

13 2022년 9월 39번 (정답률 50%) 정답 ③

[지문 끊어 읽기] 복사열 불균형

(2) On any day of the year, /
연중 어떤 날에도 /

[the tropics and the hemisphere that is experiencing its warm
season] / []: S　　　선행사　　주격 관계대명사
열대 지방과 따뜻한 계절을 겪고 있는 반구는 /

receive much more solar radiation /
　　V
훨씬 더 많은 태양 복사열을 받는다 /

🔒힌트 접속사 than 뒤에서 주어(the polar regions and the colder hemisphere)와 동사(do)가 도치된 형태임. do는 대동사로 receive solar radiation을 의미함.

than do the polar regions and the colder hemisphere.
극지방과 더 추운 반구가 받는 것보다

①(3) [Averaged over the course of the year], / []: 분사구문
일 년 중 평균적으로 /

the tropics and latitudes up to about 40° /
열대 지역과 위도 약 40도까지의 지역은 /

receive more total heat / [정답 단서] 위도 40도 이하의 지역은 복사열에 의해 잃는 열보다 받는 열이 더 많음.
더 많은 전체 열을 받는다 /

than they lose by radiation.
그들이 복사열에 의해 잃는 것보다

②(4) Latitudes above 40° receive less total heat / [정답 단서]
위도 40도를 넘는 지역은 더 적은 전체 열을 받는다 /
위도 40도보다 위에 있는 지역은 복사열에 의해 잃는 열이 받는 열보다 더 많음.

than they lose by radiation.
그들이 복사열에 의해 잃는 것보다

[정답 단서] 위도 40도를 기준으로 위 지역은 잃는 열의 양이, 아래 지역은 얻는 열의 양이 더 많은데 이를 '이러한 불균형'이라고 지칭함.

③(1) This inequality produces the necessary conditions /
이러한 불균형은 필요조건을 만들어 낸다 /

for the operation of a huge, global-scale engine /
거대한 지구적 규모의 엔진 작동을 위한 /　선행사

[that takes on heat in the tropics /
　병렬①
열대 지방에서 열을 받는 /

and gives it off in the polar regions]. []: 주격 관계대명사절
　병렬②
그래서 극지방에서 그것을 방출하는

[정답 단서] 거대한 지구적 규모의 엔진의 작동유는 대기, 특히 대기의 수분임.

(5) Its working fluid is the atmosphere, /
=a huge, global-scale engine을 지칭
그것의 작동유는 대기이다 /

🔒힌트 선행사 the moisture 뒤에 목적격 관계대명사가 생략된 형태임.

especially [the moisture it contains].
그런데 특히 그것이 품고 있는 수분　=the atmosphere

④(6) Air is heated over the warm earth of the tropics, / expands, rises, /
　　　　V①　　　　　　　　　　　　　　　　　V②　　V③
공기는 열대 지방의 따뜻한 땅에서 데워진다 / 그리고 확장되고 상승한다 /

and flows away both northward and southward at high altitudes, /
V④
그래서 높은 고도에서 북쪽과 남쪽으로 흐르게 된다 /
[cooling as it goes]. [ ]: 분사구문(연속동작)
그리고 그것은 지나가면서 식는다

✶중요 문장 (5)~(7)은 모두 문장 (1)의 a huge, global-scale engine의 작동 방식에 대하여 서술함. 문장 (1)을 위치시켜 이러한 흐름을 깨는 것은 자연스럽지 않으므로 ④, ⑤는 정답으로 적절하지 않음.

⑤ (7) It descends and flows toward the equator again /
=the air
그것은 하강해서 다시 적도를 향해 흐른다 /
from more northerly and southerly latitudes.
더 북쪽과 남쪽의 위도에서

[전문 해석]

(2)연중 어떤 날에도 열대 지방과 따뜻한 계절을 겪고 있는 반구는 극지방과 더 추운 반구가 받는 것보다 훨씬 더 많은 태양 복사열을 받는다. ① (3)일 년 중 평균적으로, 열대 지역과 위도 약 40도까지의 지역은 복사열에 의해 잃는 것보다 더 많은 전체 열을 받는다. ② (4)위도 40도를 넘는 지역은 복사열에 의해 잃는 것보다 더 적은 전체 열을 받는다. ③ (1)이러한 불균형은 열대 지방에서 열을 받아서 극지방에서 그것을 방출하는 거대한 지구적 규모의 엔진 작동을 위한 필요조건을 만들어 낸다. (5)그것의 작동유는 대기인데, 특히 대기가 품고 있는 수분이다. ④ (6) 공기는 열대 지방의 따뜻한 땅에서 데워지고, 확장되고, 상승해서 높은 고도에서 북쪽과 남쪽으로 흐르게 되고, 그것은 지나가면서 식는다. ⑤ (7)공기는 하강해서 더 북쪽과 남쪽의 위도에서 다시 적도를 향해 흐른다.

[문제 풀이]

문장 (1)은 열대 지방에서 열을 받아 극지방에서 방출하는 거대한 지구적 규모의 엔진이 '이러한 불균형'에 의해 작동한다고 말한다. 따라서 문장 (1)이 말하는 불균형이 무엇인지를 파악하며 글을 읽어야 한다. 문장 (2)에서 열대 지방과 따뜻한 계절의 반구가 그렇지 않은 지역보다 더 많은 태양 복사열을 받는다고 했으므로 '이러한 불균형'이 문장 (2)를 가리킬 수 있다. 또 문장 (3)~(4)에서 위도 40도를 기준으로 위의 지역은 잃는 열의 양이 많은 반면, 아래 지역은 얻는 열의 양이 많다고 했으므로 '이러한 불균형'이 문장 (3)~(4)를 가리킬 수 있다. 즉 '이러한 불균형'은 문장 (2)~(4)에서 설명한 내용을 가리키므로 문장 (4) 뒤에 와야 한다. 한편 문장 (5)에서 '그것의' 작동유는 대기라고 하였는데, 여기서 '그것'이 무엇을 가리키는지 또한 파악하며 글을 읽어야 한다. 이 글에서 작동하는 것은 '거대한 지구적 규모의 엔진'뿐이므로 주어진 문장은 문장 (4) 뒤에, 문장 (5) 앞에 와야 한다. 따라서 정답은 ③이다.

[중요 어휘]

☐ hemisphere	명사 (지구 또는 뇌의) 반구
☐ solar	형용사 태양의
☐ radiation	명사 복사열, 방사선
☐ over/in the course of	~중, ~동안
☐ latitude	명사 위도, 지역
☐ inequality	명사 불균형
☐ operation	명사 작동
☐ take on	받다, (일 등을) 맡다
☐ give off	(열·냄새·빛 등을) 방출하다
☐ working fluid	작동유
☐ atmosphere	명사 대기, 분위기
☐ moisture	명사 수분, 습기
☐ earth	명사 땅, 지구
☐ flow away	흐르다
☐ altitude	명사 고도
☐ descend	동사 하강하다, 내려오다
☐ equator	명사 적도
☐ northerly	형용사 북쪽의, 북쪽에 있는
☐ southerly	형용사 남쪽의, 남쪽에 있는

14 2023년 3월 39번 (정답률 50%) 정답 ④

[지문 끊어 읽기] 창의성이 생산성에 미치는 영향

(2) Creativity can have an effect / on productivity. 주제문 창의성은 생산성에 영향을 미침.
창의성은 영향을 미칠 수 있다 / 생산성에

(3) Creativity leads some individuals /
5형식V O
창의성은 몇몇 개인들을 이끈다 /
to recognize problems /
O·C(to V) 선행사
문제들을 인식하도록 /
[that others do not see], / [ ]: 목적격 관계대명사절
다른 사람들은 보지 못하는 /
but [which may be very difficult]. [ ]: 주격 관계대명사절
하지만 아주 어려울 수 있는

힌트 목적격 관계대명사인 that과 주격 관계대명사인 which가 이끄는 두 개의 관계사절이 등위접속사 but을 중심으로 병렬 연결되어 선행사인 problems를 수식함.

① (4) Charles Darwin's approach to the speciation problem /
종 분화 문제에 대한 찰스 다윈의 접근은 /
is a good example of this; /
이것의 좋은 사례이다 /

✶중요 여기서 'this'는 문장 (3)에서 말한 '창의성이 몇몇 개인으로 하여금 남들은 보지 못하지만 아주 어려울 수 있는 문제를 인식하도록 만든 것'을 의미함.

he chose a very difficult and tangled problem, speciation, /
그는 아주 어렵고 뒤얽힌 문제인 종 분화를 선택했다 /
which led him /
주격 관계대명사(계속적 용법)
그런데 이는 그를 이끌었다 /
into a long period of data collection and deliberation.
장기간의 자료 수집과 심사숙고로

② (5) This choice of problem did not allow /
이러한 문제 선택은 허용하지 않았다 /
for a quick attack or a simple experiment.
빠른 착수나 간단한 실험을

✶중요 '이러한 문제 선택(This choice of problem)'은 복잡한 문제인 '종 분화'를 선택한 찰스 다윈의 선택을 의미함.

✶중요 '그러한 경우들(such cases)'은 남들은 보지 못하지만 아주 어려울 수 있는 문제들을 선택한 경우들을 의미함.

③ (6) In such cases / creativity may actually decrease productivity /
그러한 경우들에서는 / 창의성이 실제로 생산성을 감소시킬 수 있다 /
(as measured by publication counts) /
=as (it is) measured
(출판물의 수로 측정되듯이) /
because effort is focused on difficult problems. 정답 단서 창의성이 생산성 감소로 이어질 수 있다는 문제 상황이 제시됨.
노력이 어려운 문제들에 집중되기 때문에

④ (1) For others, / [whose creativity is more focused /
선행사 소유격 관계대명사
다른 사람들에게 / 창의성이 더욱 집중된 /
on methods and technique], / creativity may lead to solutions /
선행사
방법과 기술에 / 창의성은 해결책으로 이어질 수 있다 /
[that drastically reduce the work / necessary to solve a problem].
주격 관계대명사 주격 관계대명사+be동사 생략
작업을 극적으로 줄이는 / 문제를 해결하기 위해 필요한

(7) We can see an example /
우리는 한 사례를 볼 수 있다 /
in the development of the polymerase chain reaction (PCR) /
선행사
중합 효소 연쇄 반응(PCR)의 개발에서 /
which enables us to amplify / small pieces of DNA /
주격 관계대명사 5형식V O O·C(to V)
우리가 증폭시킬 수 있게 해주는 / 작은 DNA 조각들을 /
in a short time. 정답 단서 작은 DNA 조각들을 짧은 시간 안에 증폭시키는 중합 효소 연쇄 반응(PCR) → 문장 (1)에서 언급된 '창의성이 문제 해결에 필요한 작업을 극적으로 줄이는 해결책으로 이어진' 사례에 해당함.
짧은 시간 안에

⑤ (8) This type of creativity /
이러한 유형의 창의성은 /
might reduce the number of steps /
병렬①
단계들의 수를 줄일 수 있다 /
or substitute steps / that are less likely to fail, /
병렬② 선행사 주격 관계대명사
혹은 단계들로 대체할 수 있다 / 실패할 가능성이 더 적은 /
thus increasing productivity.
분사구문(결과)
따라서 생산성을 증가시킬 수 있다

✶중요 '이러한 유형의 창의성(This type of creativity)'은 방법과 기술에 집중함으로써 문제 해결에 필요한 작업을 극적으로 줄이는 창의성을 의미함.

[전문 해석]

(2)창의성은 생산성에 영향을 미칠 수 있다. (3)창의성은 몇몇 개인들이 다른 사람들은 보지 못하지만 아주 어려울 수 있는 문제들을 인식하도록 이끈다. ① (4)종 분화 문제에 대한 찰스 다윈의 접근은 이것의 좋은 사례이다. 그는 아주 어렵고 뒤얽힌 문제인 종 분화를 선택했는데, 이는 그를 장기간의 자료 수집과 심사숙고로 이끌었다. ② (5)이러한 문제 선택은 빠른 착수나 간단한 실험을 허용하지 않았다. ③ (6)그러한 경우들에서는, 노력이 어려운 문제들에 집중되기 때문에 창의성이 (출판물의 수로 측정되듯이) 실제로 생산성을 감소시킬 수 있다. ④

(1)창의성이 방법과 기술에 더욱 집중된 다른 사람들에게, 창의성은 문제를 해결하기 위해 필요한 작업을 극적으로 줄이는 해결책으로 이어질 수 있다. (7)우리는 우리가 짧은 시간 안에 작은 DNA 조각들을 증폭시킬 수 있게 해주는 중합 효소 연쇄 반응(PCR)의 개발에서 한 사례를 볼 수 있다. ⑤ (8)이러한 유형의 창의성은 단계들의 수를 줄이거나 실패할 가능성이 더 적은 단계들로 대체할 수 있으며, 따라서 생산성을 증가시킬 수 있다.

[문제 풀이]

주어진 문장은 창의성이 문제 해결에 필요한 작업을 극적으로 줄이는 해결책으로 이어질 수 있다는 내용으로, '해결책(solutions)'이라는 말로 미루어 보아, 주어진 문장 앞에는 문제 상황이 제시되어야 한다. 이러한 문제 상황을 제시하는 부분이 바로 '창의성이 몇몇 개인들로 하여금 아주 어려운 문제를 인식하게 하여 생산성을 낮출 수 있다'는 문장 (3)~(6)의 내용이므로, 주어진 문장은 문장 (6) 이후에 와야 한다. 또, 문장 (7)은 DNA 조각들을 증폭시켜 생산성을 높이는 중합 효소 연쇄 반응(PCR)의 사례를 들고 있는데, 이는 주어진 문장에서 말한 '작업을 극적으로 줄이는 해결책'에 해당하므로, 주어진 문장은 문장 (6)과 (7) 사이인 ④에 위치하여야 한다.

[중요 어휘]

☐ **have an effect on**	~에 영향을 미치다
☐ **productivity**	명사 생산성
☐ **lead A to V**	A가 ~하도록 이끌다
☐ **individual**	명사 개인 / 형용사 각각의
☐ **speciation**	명사 종 분화, 종 형성
☐ **tangled**	형용사 뒤얽힌, 엉켜 있는, 복잡한
☐ **deliberation**	명사 심사숙고, 신중함
☐ **attack**	명사 착수, 개시, 공격
☐ **measure**	동사 측정하다, 재다 / 명사 조치, 양
☐ **publication**	명사 출판(물)
☐ **method**	명사 방법, 방식
☐ **lead to A**	A로 이어지다
☐ **drastically**	부사 극적으로, 급격히
☐ **enable A to V**	A가 ~할 수 있게 하다
☐ **amplify**	동사 증폭시키다, 확대하다
☐ **the number of**	~의 수
☐ **substitute**	동사 대체하다, 교체하다

15 2023년 9월 39번 (정답률 50%) 정답 ④

[지문 끊어 읽기] 몰입의 상황적 원인과 개인적 원인

(2) Much research has been carried out /
많은 연구가 수행되어 왔다 /
on the causes of engagement, / an issue that is important /
몰입의 원인에 대해 / 중요한 문제인 / (선행사, 주격 관계대명사절)
from both a theoretical and practical standpoint:
이론적 관점과 실제적 관점 모두에서

(3) [identifying the drivers of work engagement] / [ ]: S(동명사구)
업무 몰입의 동기를 알아내는 것은 /
may enable us [to manipulate or influence it].
(V, O, [ ]: O·C(to V), =work engagement)
우리가 그것을 조작하거나 그것에 영향을 주는 것을 가능하게 할지도 모른다

① (4) The causes of engagement / fall into two major camps: /
몰입의 원인은 / 두 가지 주된 입장으로 나뉜다 /
situational and personal. 정답단서 몰입의 원인은 '상황적인 원인'과 '개인적인 원인'으로 나뉨.
상황적인 것과 개인적인 것

② (5) The most influential situational causes /
가장 영향력 있는 상황적 원인은 /
are job resources, feedback and leadership, / 정답단서 몰입의 상황적인 원인을 설명함.
직무 자원, 피드백 그리고 리더십이다 /
[the latter, of course, being responsible / (=leadership, 현재분사)
후자는 물론 책임이 있다 /
for job resources and feedback].
직무 자원과 피드백에 대한

힌트 독립 분사구문으로, 주절의 주어와 분사구문의 주어가 일치하지 않아 분사구문에 주어를 따로 사용하였음.

③ (6) Indeed, / leaders influence engagement /
실제로 / 리더들은 몰입에 영향을 미친다 /
by giving their employees honest and constructive feedback / (병렬①, 4형식V, I·O, D·O)
그들의 직원들에게 솔직하고 건설적인 피드백을 줌으로써 /
on their performance, /
그들의 수행에 대해 /
and by providing them with the necessary resources / (병렬②, 선행사)
그리고 그들에게 필요한 자원을 제공함으로써 /
[that enable them to perform their job well]. ([ ]: 주격 관계대명사절) 정답단서 리더들이 직원들의 몰입에 영향을 끼치는 피드백과 직무 자원에 대한 설명이 이어짐.
그들이 자신의 일을 잘 수행하는 것을 가능하게 하는

★중요 문장 (5)~(6)은 리더십이 직무 자원, 피드백에 영향을 미쳐서 궁극적으로는 '몰입'에 영향을 준다는 내용으로, '몰입'의 상황적 원인에 해당함.

④ (1) It is, however, noteworthy / (형식상의 주어)
그러나 주목할 만하다 /
[that although engagement drives job performance, / ([ ]: 내용상의 주어(that 명사절))
비록 몰입이 직무 수행의 동기가 되기는 하지만 /
job performance also drives engagement]. 정답단서 직무 수행도 몰입의 동기가 됨.
직무 수행 역시 몰입의 동기가 된다

★중요 문장 (1)의 역접의 연결어 however(그러나)는 몰입의 '상황적 원인'에 대한 앞선 내용과 몰입의 '개인적 원인'에 대한 이후의 내용을 자연스럽게 연결함.

힌트 drive는 '~을 추진시키다, 작동시키다, 움직이게 하다'라는 의미로, 이 문장에서는 '~의 동기가 되다'로 의역하였음.

(7) In other words, / when employees are able to do their jobs well /
다시 말해 / 직원들이 자신의 일을 잘 할 수 있을 때 /
— to the point that they match or exceed their own expectations (선행사, 관계부사 대용)
and ambitions — /
그들이 그들 자신의 기대와 야망에 부합하거나 능가하는 정도까지 /
they will engage more, / 정답단서 직원이 직무 수행을 아주 잘 하게 되면 그들은 더 많이 몰입하게 됨. (병렬①)
그들은 더 많이 몰입할 것이다 /
be proud of their achievements, / and find work more meaningful. (병렬②(will 생략), 병렬③(will 생략))
자신의 성과를 자랑스러워할 것이다 / 그리고 일을 더 의미 있게 생각할 것이다

힌트 「find + O + O·C(형용사)」의 5형식 구조를 이루고 있음.

⑤ (8) This is especially evident /
이것은 특히 분명하다 /
when people are employed / in jobs [that align with their values]. (선행사, [ ]: 주격 관계대명사절)
사람들이 종사할 때 / 자신의 가치와 일치하는 일에

★중요 문장 (7)~(8)은 직원들이 직무를 잘 해내고 자신이 하는 일을 의미 있고 자랑스럽게 여김에 따라 '몰입'이 증가한다는 내용으로, 문장 (4)에서 말한 '몰입'의 '개인적인 원인'에 해당함.

[전문 해석]

(2)이론적 관점과 실제적 관점 모두에서 중요한 문제인 몰입의 원인에 대해 많은 연구가 수행되어 왔다. (3)업무 몰입의 동기를 알아내는 것은 우리가 그것(업무 몰입)을 조작하거나 그것(업무 몰입)에 영향을 주는 것을 가능하게 할지도 모른다. ① (4)몰입의 원인은 상황적인 것과 개인적인 것 두 가지 주된 입장으로 나뉜다. ② (5)가장 영향력 있는 상황적 원인은 직무 자원, 피드백 그리고 리더십이고, 후자(리더십)는 물론 직무 자원과 피드백에 대한 책임이 있다. ③ (6)실제로, 리더들은 그들의 직원들에게 그들의 수행에 대해 솔직하고 건설적인 피드백을 주고 그들에게 그들이 자신의 일을 잘 수행하는 것을 가능하게 하는 필요한 자원을 제공함으로써 몰입에 영향을 미친다. ④ (1)그러나, 비록 몰입이 직무 수행의 동기가 되기는 하지만, 직무 수행 역시 몰입의 동기가 된다는 것은 주목할 만하다. (7)다시 말해, 직원들이 그들 자신의 기대와 야망에 부합하거나 (그것을) 능가하는 정도까지 자신의 일을 잘 할 수 있을 때, 그들은 더 많이 몰입하고, 자신의 성과를 자랑스러워하고, 일을 더 의미 있게 생각할 것이다. ⑤ (8)이것은 사람들이 자신의 가치와 일치하는 일에 종사할 때 특히 분명하다.

[문제 풀이]

문장 (7)은 '직무 수행도 몰입의 동기가 될 수 있다'는 문장 (1)에 대한 구체적인 부연 설명으로서, 앞에 나온 말을 재진술할 때 사용되는 연결어 'In other words(다시 말해, 즉)'를 통해 문장 (1)과 자연스럽게 이어진다. 즉, 주어진 문장은 '직원들이 자신의 일을 아주 잘 하게 되면(= 직무 수행을 잘 하게 되면) 이는 몰입의 증가로 이어진다'는 문장 (7) 앞에 와야 한다. 또, 문장 (5)~(6)은 문장 (4)에서 말한 몰입의 '상황적 원인'이 몰입을 유도하여 직무 수행이 결과로 이어진다는 설명이고, 문장 (7)~(8)은 몰입의 '개인적 원인'에 해당하는 직무 수행 능력이 그 결과로 몰입을 유발한다는 설명이다. 그러므로 문장 (5)~(6)과 문장 (7)~(8) 사이에 역접의 연결어 'however(그러나)'를 수반한 주어진 문장이 들어가는 것이 글의 흐름상 가장 자연스럽다. 따라서 주어진 문장이 들어갈 자리로 가장 적절한 것은 ④이다.

[오답 풀이]

③ - 문장 (6)은 리더십이 직무 자원과 피드백에 영향을 미치고, 이것이 몰입에까지 영향을 준다는 내용으로, 문장 (5)에서 말한 '후자(=리더십)가 직무 자원과 피드백에 대해 책임이 있다'는 내용을 구체적으로 풀어 설명한 것이다. 따라서 문장 (5) 뒤에 문장 (6)이 바로 이어지는 것

이 자연스러우며, 역접의 연결어 however이 들어간 주어진 문장이 두 문장 사이에 들어갈 경우 글의 흐름이 어색해진다. 따라서 ③은 답이 될 수 없다.

[중요 어휘]

☐ carry out	~을 수행하다
☐ cause	명사 원인
☐ engagement	명사 몰입, 참여, 약속, 약혼
☐ theoretical	형용사 이론적인
☐ practical	형용사 실제적인, 실용적인
☐ standpoint	명사 관점, 견지
☐ identify	동사 알아내다, 발견하다
☐ driver	명사 동기, 동인, 추진 요인
☐ manipulate	동사 조작하다, 조종하다
☐ fall into	~으로 나뉘다
☐ camp	명사 입장, 견해, 진영, 측
☐ responsible	형용사 책임이 있는
☐ constructive	형용사 건설적인
☐ performance	명사 수행, 성과
☐ noteworthy	형용사 주목할 만한
☐ match	동사 ~에 부합하다, 일치하다
☐ exceed	동사 ~을 능가하다, 넘어서다
☐ evident	형용사 분명한, 명백한
☐ be employed in	~에 종사하다

16 2018년 11월 39번 (정답률 45%) 정답 ④

[지문 끊어 읽기] 카리스마와 인간의 상호 작용

(2) Charisma is eminently learnable and teachable, /
카리스마는 분명히 배울 수 있고 가르칠 수 있다 /
and in many ways, /
그리고 여러 면에서 /
it follows one of Newton's famed laws of motion: /
그것은 뉴턴의 유명한 운동 법칙 중 하나를 따른다 /
For every action, / there is an equal and opposite reaction.
모든 작용에 대하여 / 동등하면서 반대인 반작용이 존재한다

① (3) That is to say that / all of charisma and human interaction /
즉 ~라는 것이다 / 모든 카리스마와 인간의 상호 작용은 /
is a set of signals and cues / that lead to other signals and cues, /
일련의 신호와 단서들이다 / 다른 신호와 단서들로 이어지는 /
and there is a science to deciphering /
그리고 판독하는 데에는 과학이 있다는 /
which signals and cues work the most in your favor.
어떤 신호와 단서들이 당신에게 가장 유리하게 작용하는지

② (4) In other words, / charisma can often be simplified /
재진술
다시 말해서 / 카리스마는 종종 단순화될 수 있다 /
as a checklist / of what to do at what time.
체크리스트로 / 언제 무엇을 해야 하는지에 대한

★중요 문장 (4)의 a checklist of what to do at what time은 주어진 문장의 a logically easy set of procedures to follow에 대응하는 표현임.

③ (5) However, / it will require brief forays / out of your comfort zone.
그러나 / 그것은 일시적인 시도들을 필요로 할 것이다 / 당신의 편안한 상태를 벗어나는 정답 단서

④ (1) Even though there may be a logically easy set of procedures /
비록 논리적으로 쉬운 일련의 절차들이 있을지도 모르지만 /
to follow, / it's still an emotional battle / to change your habits /
따라야 할 / 여전히 정서적인 분투이다 / 당신의 습관을 바꾸는 것은 /
and introduce new, uncomfortable behaviors /
그리고 새롭고 불편한 행동들을 도입하는 것은 /
that you are not used to.
당신에게 익숙하지 않은

★중요 '습관을 바꾸는 것'과 '익숙하지 않은 새롭고 불편한 행동들을 도입하는 것'은 모두 문장 (5)의 brief forays out of your comfort zone에 해당함.

(6) I like to say / that it's just a matter of using muscles /
나는 ~라고 말하고 싶다 / 그것이 그저 근육들을 사용하는 문제라고 /
that have long been dormant.
오랫동안 쓰지 않았던 정답 단서

힌트 'dormant'는 '잠자고 있는, 휴면 상태의, 활동을 멈춘' 등의 뜻임. 여기서는 'dormant'가 'muscles'를 묘사하고 있으므로, '오랫동안 쓰지 않은 근육들'이라고 해석할 수 있음.

⑤ (7) It will take some time to warm them up, /
그것들을 준비시키는 데에는 다소 시간이 필요할 것이다 /
but it's only through practice and action /
it is ~ that 강조구문
하지만 오직 연습과 행동을 통해서이다 /
that you will achieve your desired goal.
당신이 바라는 목표를 성취하게 되는 것은

[전문 해석]

(2)카리스마는 분명히 배울 수 있고 가르칠 수 있으며, 여러 면에서 그것은 '모든 작용에 대하여, (크기가) 동등하면서 (방향이) 반대인 반작용이 존재한다.'라는 뉴턴의 유명한 운동 법칙 중 하나를 따른다. ① (3)즉, 모든 카리스마와 인간의 상호 작용은 다른 신호와 단서들로 이어지는 일련의 신호와 단서들이며, 어떤 신호와 단서들이 당신에게 가장 유리하게 작용하는지 판독하는 데에는 과학이 있다는 것이다. ② (4)다시 말해서 카리스마는 종종 언제 무엇을 해야 하는지에 대한 체크리스트로 단순화될 수 있다. ③ (5)그러나 그것은 당신의 편안한 상태를 벗어나는 일시적인 시도들을 필요로 할 것이다. ④ (1)비록 따라야 할, 논리적으로 쉬운 일련의 절차들이 있을지도 모르지만, 당신의 습관을 바꾸고 당신에게 익숙하지 않은 새롭고 불편한 행동들을 도입하는 것은 여전히 정서적인 분투이다. (6)나는 그것이 그저 오랫동안 쓰지 않았던 근육들을 (다시) 사용하는 문제라고 말하고 싶다. ⑤ (7)그것들을 준비시키는 데에는 다소 시간이 필요할 것이지만, 당신이 바라는 목표를 성취하게 되는 것은 오직 연습과 행동을 통해서이다.

- Newton's laws of motion(뉴턴의 운동 법칙): 아이작 뉴턴이 도입한, 물체의 운동을 다루는 세 가지의 물리 법칙을 가리키며 관성, 가속도, 작용·반작용의 법칙으로 구성되어 있다.

[문제 풀이]

주어진 문장에서, an emotional battle 이하의 내용은 문장 (5)의 'brief forays out of your comfort zone(당신의 편안한 상태를 벗어나는 일시적인 시도들)'에 대한 구체적인 부연 설명인 동시에, 문장 (6)에서 'using muscles that have long been dormant(오랫동안 활동을 중단한 근육들을 사용하는 것)'으로 비유되는 대상이다. 따라서 주어진 문장은 문장 (5)와 (6) 사이에 들어가는 것이 자연스럽다.

[중요 어휘]

☐ charisma	명사 카리스마, 통솔력
☐ eminently	부사 (긍정적인 의미에서) 분명히, 대단히
☐ famed	형용사 유명한, 널리 알려진
☐ action	명사 작용, 행동
☐ reaction	명사 반작용, 반응
☐ that is to say	즉, 다시 말해서
☐ interaction	명사 상호 작용
☐ cue	명사 단서, 신호
☐ in one's favor	~에게 유리하게, ~를 위하여
☐ procedure	명사 절차, 방법
☐ be used to	~에 익숙하다

핵심 '검증 시험'과 여러 유형의 믿음에 대한 글임. 주어진 문장의 위치를 파악하기 위해서는 'However', 'Also'와 같은 접속부사를 단서로 사용하여 글의 흐름이 달라지는 부분을 찾아내야 함. 특히 앞에 나온 '믿음'과 성격이 다른 '믿음'을 구분하는 것이 중요함.

17 2021년 3월 38번 (정답률 45%) 정답 ⑤

[지문 끊어 읽기] 검증 시험과 여러 유형의 믿음

(2) Most beliefs / — but not all — / are open to tests of verification.
대부분의 믿음은 / 전부는 아니지만 / 검증 시험에 열려 있다

(3) This means / that beliefs can be tested /
명사절 접속사
이것은 의미한다 / 믿음이 시험될 수 있다는 것을 /
to see if they are correct or false.
~인지 확인하다
그것들이 옳은지 그른지 확인하기 위해

① (4) Beliefs can be verified or falsified /
믿음은 진실임이 입증되거나 거짓임이 입증될 수 있다 /
with objective criteria / external to the person.
객관적인 기준을 통해 / 그 사람의 외부에 있는

② (5) There are people /
사람들이 있다 / 선행사
[who believe / the Earth is flat / and not a sphere]. [ ]: 주격 관계대명사절
믿는 / 지구가 평평하다고 / 그리고 구가 아니라고

③ (6) Because we have objective evidence /
우리는 객관적인 증거를 가지고 있기 때문에, /
that the Earth is in fact a sphere, /
지구가 사실은 구라는 / =
the flat Earth belief can be shown to be false. 정답단서
지구가 평평하다는 믿음은 거짓임이 증명될 수 있다

④ (7) Also, / the belief / that it will rain tomorrow /
또한 / 믿음은 / 내일 비가 올 것이라는 /
can be tested for truth / 정답단서
진실인지 시험될 수 있다 /
by waiting until tomorrow / and seeing whether it rains or not.
병렬① 병렬②
내일까지 기다림으로써 / 그리고 비가 오는지 안 오는지 봄으로써

⑤ (1) However, / some types of beliefs / cannot be tested for truth / 정답단서
하지만 / 어떤 종류의 믿음은 / 진실인지 시험될 수 없다 /
because we cannot get external evidence in our lifetimes /
우리가 일생 동안 외부 증거를 얻을 수 없기 때문에 /
(such as a belief /
믿음과 같은 / =
that the Earth will stop spinning on its axis / by the year 9999 /
동격의 that(병렬①)
지구가 지축을 중심으로 회전하는 것을 멈출 것이라는 / 9999년이 되면 /
or that there is life on a planet / 100-million light-years away).
동격의 that(병렬②)
혹은 행성에 생명체가 있을 것이라는 / 1억 광년 떨어진

(8) Also, / meta-physical beliefs /
또한 / 형이상학적 믿음은 /
(such as the existence and nature of a god) /
(신의 존재와 본질과 같은) /
present considerable challenges / in generating evidence / 정답단서
상당한 도전을 야기한다 / 증거를 만들어 내는 데 있어서 / 선행사
[that everyone is willing to use / as a truth criterion].
모든 사람이 기꺼이 사용할 / 진리 기준으로 [ ]: 목적격 관계대명사절

[전문 해석]

(2)전부는 아니지만 대부분의 믿음은 검증 시험에 열려 있다(검증 시험을 받을 수 있다). (3)이것은 믿음이 옳은지 그른지 확인하기 위해 시험될 수 있다는 것을 의미한다. ① (4)믿음은 그 사람의 외부에 있는 객관적인 기준을 통해 진실임이 입증되거나 거짓임이 입증될 수 있다. ② (5)지구가 평평하고 구(球)가 아니라고 믿는 사람들이 있다. ③ (6)우리는 지구가 사실은 구라는 객관적인 증거를 가지고 있기 때문에, 지구가 평평하다는 믿음은 거짓임이 증명될 수 있다. ④ (7)또한 내일 비가 올 것이라는 믿음은 내일까지 기다려 비가 오는지 안 오는지 봄으로써 진실인지 시험될 수 있다. ⑤ (1)하지만 (9999년이 되면 지구가 지축을 중심으로 회전하는 것을 멈출 것이라는 믿음, 혹은 1억 광년 떨어진 행성에 생명체가 있을 것이라는 믿음과 같은) 어떤 종류의 믿음은 우리가 일생 동안 외부 증거를 얻을 수 없기 때문에 진실인지 시험될 수 없다. (8)또한 (신의 존재와 본질과 같은) 형이상학적 믿음은 모든 사람이 진리 기준으로 기꺼이 사용할 증거를 만들어 내는 데 있어서 상당한 도전(어려움)을 야기한다.

[문제 풀이]

주어진 문장이 'However'로 시작하고 있고, 어떤 종류의 믿음은 진실인지 시험될 수 없다고 말한다. 그러므로 시험될 수 있는 것에 대해 이야기하다가 시험될 수 없는 것을 말하는 전환 부분에 주어진 문장을 넣어야 하는 것을 알 수 있다. 문장 (2)~(7)에서는 외부의 객관적인 기준으로 진실인지 거짓인지 입증될 수 있는 것에 대해 말하고 있고, 문장 (8)이 되어야 형이상학적 믿음이 증거를 만들어 내는 데 상당한 도전(어려움), 즉 입증하는 데 어려움을 야기한다고 하고 있으므로 주어진 문장이 들어갈 수 있는 곳은 보기 ⑤밖에 없다.

[오답 풀이]

④ - 믿음을 진실인지 거짓인지 입증하는 '검증 시험(tests of verification)'에 대해 예를 들어 설명하고 있는 글이다. 문장 (6)에 나타난 지구가 평평하다는 믿음은 거짓임이 증명될 수 있고, 문장 (7)에 나타난 내일 비가 올 것이라는 믿음은 진실 여부가 증명될 수 있다. 즉 문장 (7)은 'Also'로 시작하여 문장 (6)과 같이 검증 시험을 받을 수 있는 믿음을 예로 들고 있다. 반면, 주어진 문장은 역접의 의미를 가진 부사 'However'로 시작하여 검증 시험을 받을 수 없는 몇 가지 믿음을 설명하고 있다. 또한 문장 (8)은 'Also'로 시작하여 증거를 만드는 데 어려움을 가지는 '형이상학적 믿음'을 설명하고 있으므로, 주어진 문장이 문장 (7)과 (8) 사이에 오는 것이 문맥상 자연스럽다. 따라서 ④는 정답이 될 수 없다.

[중요 어휘]

□ verification	명사 검증, 확인, 증명
□ verify	동사 진실임을 입증하다, 확인하다
□ falsify	동사 거짓임을 입증하다
□ objective	형용사 객관적인
□ external	형용사 외부의
□ sphere	명사 구, 둥근 물체
□ evidence	명사 증거
□ lifetime	명사 일생
□ spin	동사 회전하다
□ axis	명사 축
□ meta-physical	형용사 형이상학의
□ existence	명사 존재
□ present	동사 야기하다, 주다
□ considerable	형용사 상당한
□ challenge	명사 도전, 문제 / 동사 도전하다
□ generate	동사 만들어 내다, 발생시키다
□ be willing to V	기꺼이 ~하다

18 2021년 9월 39번 (정답률 45%) 정답 ⑤

[지문 끊어 읽기] 위성 제거 방법

(2) The United Nations asks / 힌트 ask는 요구를 나타내는 동사로 'ask that 주어 (should) 동사원형 ~'으로 쓰고, 이때 조동사 should는 흔히 생략됨.
국제 연합은 요청한다 /
that all companies remove their satellites from orbit /
모든 기업들이 그들의 위성을 궤도에서 제거해 줄 것을 /
within 25 years / after the end of their mission.
25년 이내에 / 그들의 임무 종료 후

(3) This is tricky to enforce, / though, /
이것은 시행하기에 까다롭다 / 하지만 /
because satellites can (and often do) fail.
강조의 do
위성이 작동하지 않을 수 있기 (그리고 종종 정말로 작동하지 않기) 때문에

① (4) To tackle this problem, / several companies around the world /
이 문제를 해결하기 위해 / 전 세계의 몇몇 회사들이 /
have come up with novel solutions.
새로운 해결책을 내놓았다

② (5) These include / removing dead satellites from orbit /
병렬①
이것은 포함한다 / 죽은 위성을 궤도에서 제거하는 것을 /
and dragging them back into the atmosphere, /
병렬②
그리고 그것들을 대기권으로 다시 끌어들이는 것을 /
where they will burn up.
계속적 용법(=and there)
그리고 거기에서 그것들은 다 타 버리게 될 것이다

③ (6) Ways we could do this include / 힌트 문장의 목적어는 '-ing, -ing, ···, or -ing'의 형태로 병렬을 이루고 있고, 마지막에 나오는 increasing은 병렬 구조가 아닌 동시동작을 나타내는 분사구문임.
우리가 이것을 할 수 있는 방법은 포함한다 /
using a harpoon to grab a satellite, / catching it in a huge net, /
병렬① 병렬②
작살을 이용해서 위성을 잡는 것을 / 거대한 그물로 그것을 잡는 것을 /
using magnets to grab it, /
병렬③
자석을 이용해서 그것을 잡는 것을 /
or even firing lasers to heat up the satellite, /
병렬④
또는 심지어 레이저를 발사해서 위성을 가열하는 것을 /
[increasing its atmospheric drag / so that it falls out of orbit].
그것의 대기 항력을 증가시키면서 / 그것이 궤도에서 떨어져 나오도록 [ ]: 분사구문(동시동작)

④ (7) However, / these methods are only useful /
하지만 / 이러한 방법은 오직 유용하다 /

for large satellites orbiting Earth. 정답 단서
지구 궤도를 도는 큰 위성들에게만

⑤ (1) There isn't really a way / for us /
방법은 정말로 없다 / 우리가 /
to pick up smaller pieces of debris / 정답 단서
더 작은 잔해물 조각을 수거할 수 있는 /
such as bits of paint and metal.
페인트 조각이나 금속 같은

(8) We just have to wait / for them /
우리는 기다려야 할 뿐이다 / 그것들이 /
to naturally re-enter Earth's atmosphere.
자연적으로 지구의 대기권으로 다시 들어오기를

힌트 각각 for us/for them을 의미상 주어로 가지는 to부정사임. 문장 (1)의 to pick up은 형용사적 용법으로 사용되어 a way를 수식하며 문장 (8)의 to re-enter는 명사적 용법으로 사용되어 목적어 역할을 함.

[전문 해석]

(2)국제 연합은 모든 기업들이 그들의 임무 종료 후 25년 이내에 그들의 위성을 궤도에서 제거해 줄 것을 요청한다. (3)하지만 위성이 작동하지 않을 수 있기 (그리고 종종 정말로 작동하지 않기) 때문에 이것은 시행하기에 까다롭다. ① (4)이 문제를 해결하기 위해, 전 세계의 몇몇 회사들이 새로운 해결책을 내놓았다. ② (5)이것은 죽은(수명이 다한) 위성을 궤도에서 제거하고, 대기권으로 다시 끌어들이는 것을 포함하는데, 거기에서 그것들은 다 타 버리게 될 것이다. ③ (6)우리가 이것을 할 수 있는 방법은 위성이 궤도에서 떨어져 나오도록 그것의 대기 항력을 증가시키면서 작살을 이용해서 위성을 잡거나, 거대한 그물로 그것을 잡거나, 자석을 이용해서 그것을 잡거나, 또는 심지어 레이저를 발사해서 위성을 가열하는 것을 포함한다. ④ (7)하지만 이러한 방법은 오직 지구 궤도를 도는 큰 위성들에게만 유용하다. ⑤ (1)우리가 페인트 조각이나 금속 같은 더 작은 잔해물 조각을 수거할 수 있는 방법은 정말로 없다. (8)우리는 그것들이 자연적으로 지구의 대기권으로 다시 들어오기를 기다려야 할 뿐이다.

[문제 풀이]

위성을 궤도에서 제거하는 문제에 대해 설명하는 글이다. 문장 (6)에서는 위성을 궤도에서 제거할 수 있는 방법을 나열하고 있고, 문장 (7)에 따르면 이는 큰 위성들에게만 유용하다고 한다. 따라서 뒤에 작은 잔해물에 대한 내용이 나오는 것이 흐름상 자연스럽다. 또한 큰 위성은 문장 (6)에 제시된 방법을 통해 제거할 수 있으므로, 대기권으로 들어오기를 기다려야 하는 문장 (8)의 'them'은 크기가 작은 잔해물 조각을 가리킨다고 봐야 한다. 따라서 주어진 문장은 문장 (7)과 (8) 사이에 오는 것이 가장 자연스러우므로 정답은 ⑤이다.

[중요 어휘]

☐ satellite	명사 (인공)위성
☐ orbit	명사 궤도 / 동사 궤도를 돌다
☐ tricky	형용사 까다로운, 교활한
☐ enforce	동사 시행하다, 강요하다
☐ tackle	동사 해결하다, (문제 상황과) 씨름하다
☐ come up with	~를 내놓다, 생각해 내다
☐ novel	형용사 새로운 / 명사 소설
☐ drag	동사 끌다 / 명사 항력
☐ atmosphere	명사 대기(권), 분위기
☐ burn up	다 타버리다, 몹시 열이 나다
☐ fire	동사 발사하다, 불을 붙이다, 해고하다
☐ heat up	가열하다, 뜨거워지다
☐ atmospheric	형용사 대기의
☐ pick up	~을 수거하다, 집다, 획득하다
☐ debris	명사 잔해물, 쓰레기

19 2021년 11월 38번 (정답률 45%) 정답 ⑤

[지문 끊어 읽기] 소리의 밝기와 사람들의 선호도

(2) Brightness of sounds means /
소리의 밝기는 의미한다 /
much energy in higher frequencies, /
더 높은 주파수에서의 많은 에너지를 /
which can be calculated from the sounds easily.
계속적 용법
그리고 이는 소리로부터 쉽게 계산될 수 있다

(3) A violin has many more overtones / compared to a flute /
V①
바이올린은 더 많은 상음을 가지고 있다 / 플루트에 비해 /
and sounds brighter.
V②
그리고 더 밝게 들린다

① (4) An oboe is brighter than a classical guitar, /
오보에가 클래식 기타보다 더 밝다 /
and a crash cymbal brighter than a double bass.
그리고 크래시 심벌이 더블 베이스보다 더 밝다

힌트 'A is brighter than B'라는 동일한 문장 구조의 절이 'and'로 병렬 연결되어 있으며 반복되는 be동사 'is'가 'a crash cymbal'과 'brighter' 사이에서 생략됨.

② (5) This is obvious, / and indeed people like brightness.
이것은 명백하다 / 그리고 실제로 사람들은 밝음을 좋아한다

③ (6) One reason is that / it makes sound subjectively louder, /
5형식V
명사절 접속사 =brightness O O·C
한 가지 이유는 ~이다 / 그것이 소리를 주관적으로 더 크게 들리도록 만든다는 것이다 /
which is part of the loudness war / in modern electronic music, /
계속적 용법
그리고 이는 소리의 세기 전쟁의 일환이다 / 현대 전자 음악에서 /
and in the classical music of the 19th century.
그리고 19세기 클래식 음악에서

중요 문장 (6)에서 말하듯이 사람들이 밝은 소리를 선호하는 이유는 밝은 소리가 주관적으로 더 크게 들리기 때문임. 따라서 소리를 주관적으로 더 크게 들리도록 만들기 위한 경쟁이 나타났다는 것을 '소리의 세기 전쟁(the loudness war)'으로 표현함.

④ (7) All sound engineers know that /
모든 음향 기사들은 안다 / 명사절 접속사
if they play back a track to a musician /
V① 선행사
만약 그들이 음악가에게 곡을 틀어 준다면 /
that just has recorded this track /
주격 관계대명사절
방금 이 곡을 녹음한 /
and add some higher frequencies, /
V②
그리고 약간의 더 높은 주파수를 더하면 /
the musician will immediately like the track much better. 정답 단서
그 음악가는 곧바로 그 곡을 훨씬 더 좋아하게 되리라는 것을

더 높은 주파수를 더하면, 즉 노래를 더 밝게 해서 들려주면 음악가는 곧바로 그 곡을 훨씬 더 좋아할 것임.

⑤ (1) But this is a short-lived effect, / and in the long run, /
하지만 이것은 일시적인 효과이다 / 그리고 장기적으로 /
people find such sounds too bright. 정답 단서
5형식V O O·C
사람들은 그러한 소리가 너무 밝다는 것을 알게 된다

하지만 더 높은 주파수를 더하여 노래를 밝게 들려주는 것은 일시적인 효과일 뿐이고, 사람들은 노래가 너무 밝다는 것을 곧 깨닫게 될 것임.

(8) So it is wise /
형식상의 주어①
따라서 현명하다 /
[not to play back such a track with too much brightness], /
그러한 곡을 너무 밝게 틀어 주지 않는 것이 / [ ]: 내용상의 주어①
as it normally takes quite some time / [to convince the musician /
형식상의 주어②
왜냐하면 보통 꽤 상당한 시간이 걸리기 때문이다 / 그 음악가에게 납득시키는 데 /
that less brightness serves his music better in the end]. [ ]: 내용상의 주어②
명사절 접속사
더 적은 밝기가 결국 자신의 음악에 더 도움이 된다는 것을

정답 단서 노래를 너무 밝게 틀어주지 않는 것이 더 현명함.

[전문 해석]

(2)소리의 밝기는 더 높은 주파수에서의 많은 에너지를 의미하며, 이는 소리로부터 쉽게 계산될 수 있다. (3)바이올린은 플루트에 비해 더 많은 상음(上音)을 가지고 있고 더 밝게 들린다. ① (4)오보에가 클래식 기타보다 더 밝고, 크래시 심벌이 더블 베이스보다 더 밝다. ② (5)이것은 명백하고 실제로 사람들은 밝음을 좋아한다. ③ (6)한 가지 이유는 그것이 소리를 주관적으로 더 크게 들리도록 만든다는 것이며, 이는 현대 전자 음악과 19세기 클래식 음악에서 소리의 세기 전쟁의 일환이다. ④ (7)모든 음향 기사들은 만약 그들이 방금 이 곡을 녹음한 음악가에게 곡을 틀어 주고 약간의 더 높은 주파수를 더하면, 그 음악가는 곧바로 그 곡을 훨씬 더 좋아하게 되리라는 것을 안다. ⑤ (1)하지만 이것은 일시적인 효과이고 장기적으로 사람들은 그러한 소리가 너무 밝다는 것을 알게 된다. (8)따라서 그러한 곡을 너무 밝게 틀어 주지 않는 것이 현명한데 왜냐하면 그 음악가에게 더 적은 밝기가 결국 자신의 음악에 더 도움이 된다는 것을 납득시키는 데 보통 꽤 상당한 시간이 걸리기 때문이다.

- overtone(상음, 上音): 기본음보다 진동수가 크고 높은 음으로 상음의 크기에 따라 음색이 결정됨.

[문제 풀이]

본문에 따르면 소리가 밝다는 것은 주파수가 더 높고 에너지가 더 많다는 것을 의미한다. 이에 대해 문장 (5)와 (6)에서 사람들이 밝은 소리를 좋아한다는 점과 그 이유에 대해 설명하고 있다. 또한 문장 (6)의 'the loudness war(소리의 세기 전쟁)'은 사람들이 밝은 음악을 좋아하기 때문에 음악 속 소리의 세기를 경쟁적으로 키운 것을 의미하는데, 이는 문장 (7)에서 음향

기사들이 높은 주파수를 더해 곡을 조금 더 좋게 들리게 한다는 점과 연결된다. 그러나 주어진 문장은 지금까지 일관되게 이어져왔던 흐름과 상반되는 내용이다. 주어진 문장은 좋게 들리게 하는 효과, 즉 높은 주파수를 더하는 것이 일시적인 효과만 낳을 뿐 결국에는 큰 효과가 없음을 지적하고 이는 문장 (8)의 곡을 지나치게 밝게 틀어 주지 않는 편이 낫다고 하는 결론과 연결되므로, 주어진 문장은 ⑤에 들어가는 것이 가장 자연스럽다.

[오답 풀이]

③ - 주어진 문장이 ③에 들어가면 주어진 문장의 'this'가 문장 (5)의 'brightness'를 가리켜 밝음의 효과가 일시적일 뿐이고 사람들은 그런 소리를 너무 밝게 느낀다고 설명하는 것이 된다. 그런데 이는 사람들이 소리를 주관적으로 더 크게 들리도록 만든다고 하는 문장 (6)과 음악가가 더 높은 주파수를 더하여 노래를 더 밝게 들려주는 것을 더 좋아한다고 하는 문장 (7)과 자연스럽게 연결되지 않으므로 답이 될 수 없다.

[중요 어휘]

□ frequency	명사 주파수
□ calculate	동사 계산하다, 산출하다
□ obvious	형용사 명백한
□ indeed	부사 실제로, 정말
□ subjectively	부사 주관적으로
□ play back	틀어 주다
□ track	명사 곡, 길
□ short-lived	형용사 일시적인, 오래가지 못하는
□ in the long run	장기적으로, 결국
□ convince	동사 납득시키다, 설득시키다
□ serve	동사 도움이 되다, 기여하다, 제공하다

핵심 문장 (6)까지 자본 시장의 자유화의 장점을 설명하고, 문장 (7)에서는 자유화로 인한 위기를 설명하고 있음. 내용이 나뉘는 부분에 이어줄 연결 문장을 적절하게 잘 골라야 함.

20 2017년 11월 39번 (정답률 40%) 정답 ④

[지문 끊어 읽기] 자본 시장 자유화의 장점과 문제

(2) The liberalization of capital markets, /
자본 시장의 자유화는 /
where funds for investment can be borrowed, /
투자를 위한 자금이 빌려질 수 있는 /
has been an important contributor / to the pace of globalization.
중요한 기여 요인이 되어 왔다 / 세계화의 속도에

(3) Since the 1970s / there has been a trend /
1970년대 이후로 / 추세가 있어왔다 /
towards a freer flow of capital / across borders.
자본의 보다 자유로운 흐름을 향한 / 국경을 넘어선

① (4) Current economic theory suggests /
현재의 경제 이론은 주장한다 /
that this should aid development.
이것이 발전을 도와야 한다고

② (5) Developing countries / have limited domestic savings /
개발도상국들은 / 제한된 국내 자금을 갖고 있다 /
with which to invest in growth, / and liberalization allows them /
성장에 투자할 / 그리고 자유화는 그들에게 허용한다 /
to tap into a global pool of funds.
전 세계의 자금 공동 출자를 이용하도록

힌트 동사 allow는 문장 (5)에서 5형식 동사, 문장 (6)에서는 4형식 동사로 사용됨. 각각 5형식 구조 'allow(V) them(O) to tap~(O·C)'와 4형식 구조 'allow(V) investors(I·O) greater scope ~(D·O)'를 나타냄.

③ (6) A global capital market also allows investors /
전 세계 자본 시장은 또한 투자자들에게 허용한다 /
greater scope to manage and spread their risks. 정답단서
그들의 위험을 관리하고 분산시킬 보다 넓은 기회를

④ (1) However, / some say / that a freer flow of capital /
하지만 / 어떤 사람들은 말한다 / 자본의 보다 자유로운 흐름이 /
has raised the risk of financial instability. 정답단서
재정적 불안정성의 위험을 증가시켜왔다고

(7) The East Asian crisis of the late 1990s / 정답단서
1990년대 말의 동아시아 위기는 /
came in the wake of this kind of liberalization.
이러한 종류의 자유화의 결과로 시작되었다

⑤ (8) Without a strong financial system and a sound regulatory environment, /
강한 재정적 시스템과 올바른 규제 환경이 없다면 /
capital market globalization / can sow the seeds of instability /
자본 시장 세계화는 / 불안정성의 원인을 제공할 수 있다 /
in economies / rather than growth.
경제에 / 성장보다는

힌트 직역하면 '~의 씨를 뿌리다'라는 뜻이지만 보통 '~의 원인을 제공하다'라는 뜻으로 쓰이는 관용적 표현임.

[전문 해석]

(2)투자를 위한 자금이 빌려질 수 있는 자본 시장의 자유화는 세계화의 속도에 중요한 기여 요인이 되어 왔다. (3)1970년대 이후로 국경을 넘어선 자본의 보다 자유로운 흐름을 향한 추세가 있어왔다. ① (4)현재의 경제 이론은 이것(자본의 보다 자유로운 흐름)이 발전을 도와야 한다고 주장한다. ② (5)개발도상국들은 성장에 투자할 제한된 국내 자금을 갖고 있고, 자유화는 그들(개발도상국들)에게 전 세계의 자금 공동 출자를 이용하도록 허용한다. ③ (6)전 세계 자본 시장은 또한 투자자들에게 그들의 위험을 관리하고 분산시킬 보다 넓은 기회를 허용한다. ④ (1)하지만 어떤 사람들은 자본의 보다 자유로운 흐름이 재정적 불안전성의 위험을 증가시켜왔다고 말한다. (7)1990년대 말의 동아시아 위기는 이러한 종류의 자유화의 결과로 시작되었다. ⑤ (8)강한 재정적 시스템과 올바른 규제 환경이 없다면, 자본 시장 세계화는 경제에 성장보다는 불안정성의 원인을 제공할 수 있다.

[문제 풀이]

본문은 자본 시장 자유화의 두 가지 측면을 다룬다. 하나는 자본 시장 자유화가 성장에 기여한다는 긍정적인 측면, 다른 하나는 자본 시장 자유화가 경제에 불안정성을 가져다줄 수 있다는 부정적인 측면이다. 글의 흐름은 1990년대 동아시아 위기에 대한 내용이 나오며 긍정적인 내용에서 부정적인 내용으로 변화하는데, 주어진 문장은 자본 시장 자유화가 재정적 불안정성 위험을 증가시킨다는 내용으로 글 전체 흐름을 바꿔주는 문장이다. 따라서 주어진 문장은 동아시아 위기를 이야기하고 있는 문장 (7) 앞에 위치하는 것이 적절하므로 정답은 ④이다.

[중요 어휘]

□ liberalization	명사 자유화
□ capital	형용사 자본의, 주요한, 대문자의 / 명사 자본, 수도, 대문자
□ fund	명사 자금, 기금
□ investment	명사 (시간·노력 등의) 투자
□ contributor	명사 기여 요인, 공헌자
□ domestic	형용사 국내의, 가정의, 애완용의
□ tap into	~을 이용하다, 사용하다
□ scope	명사 기회, 여지, 범위
□ manage	동사 관리하다, 경영하다, 간신히 ~하다
□ spread	동사 분산시키다, 펼치다
□ instability	명사 (경제적·심리적) 불안정성
□ crisis	명사 위기, 최악의 고비 (복수형 crises)
□ in the wake of	~의 결과로, ~에 뒤이어
□ sound	형용사 올바른, 건강한
□ regulatory	형용사 규제의
□ seed	명사 (사건의) 원인, 근원, 씨앗

핵심 사람의 행동을 설명하는 원인을 '단순한' 것(기질적 귀인)과 '복잡한' 것(상황적 귀인) 두 가지로 나눠 비교하며 분석하는 글임.

21 2018년 6월 37번 (정답률 40%) 정답 ①

[지문 끊어 읽기] 사람의 행동을 설명하는 원인

(2) You may be wondering / why people prefer /
당신은 궁금해하고 있을지도 모른다 / 사람들이 왜 더 선호하는지 /
to prioritize internal disposition over external situations /
외부의 상황보다 내적인 기질을 우선시하는 것을 /
when seeking causes / to explain behaviour.
원인들을 찾고자 할 때 / 행동을 설명하기 위해서

(3) One answer is simplicity. 정답단서
하나의 답은 간편함이다

중요 문장 (3)의 One answer is simplicity는 뒤 문장의 easy와 내용상 이어지는데 '엄격=완고, 헌신=사랑'이라는 공식을 설명하기 위한 적절한 전제임.

① (1) Thinking of an internal cause /
내적인 원인을 생각해 내는 것은 /

for a person's behaviour / is easy / 정답 단서
어떤 사람의 행동에 대한 / 쉽다 /
— the strict teacher is a stubborn person, /
엄격한 선생님은 완고한 사람이다 /
the devoted parents just love their kids.
헌신적인 부모들은 그저 그들의 아이들을 사랑할 뿐이다

(4) In contrast, / situational explanations can be complex. 정답 단서
그에 반해서 / 상황적인 설명은 복잡할 수 있다

② (5) Perhaps the teacher appears stubborn / (S, V①)
그 선생님은 아마도 완고해 보이는 것일 수 있다 /
because she's seen the consequences of not trying hard /
그녀가 열심히 노력하지 않은 것에 대한 결과들을 보아왔기 때문에 /
in generations of students /
여러 세대의 학생들에게서 /
and wants to develop self-discipline in them. (V②)
그리고 그들 안에 자기 훈련을 발달시키기를 원하는 것일 수 있다

③ (6) Perhaps the parents /
아마도 부모들은 /
who're boasting of the achievements of their children /
그들의 아이들의 성취에 대해 자랑하고 있는 /
are anxious about their failures, /
그들의 실패에 대해 불안해하고 있을지도 모른다 /
and conscious of the cost of their school fees.
그리고 그들의 수업료의 비용을 의식하고 있을지도 모른다

④ (7) These situational factors require /
이러한 상황적 요인들은 필요로 한다 /
knowledge, insight, and time to think through. (형용사적 용법)
지식, 통찰력, 그리고 충분히 생각할 시간을

⑤ (8) Whereas, / jumping to a dispositional attribution / is far easier.
반면에 / 기질적 귀인으로 비약하는 것은 / 훨씬 더 쉽다

[전문 해석]

(2)당신은 (어떤) 행동을 설명하기 위해서 (그 행동의) 원인들을 찾고자 할 때, 사람들이 왜 외부의 상황보다 내적인 기질을 우선시하는 것을 더 선호하는지 궁금해하고 있을지도 모른다. (3)(이에 대한) 하나의 답은 간편함이다. ① (1)어떤 사람의 행동에 대한 내적인 원인을 생각해 내는 것은 쉽다. 엄격한 선생님은 완고한 사람이고, 헌신적인 부모들은 그저 그들의 아이들을 사랑할 뿐이다. (4)그에 반해서 상황적인 설명은 복잡할 수 있다. ② (5)그 선생님은 아마도 그녀가 여러 세대의 학생들에게서 열심히 노력하지 않은 것에 대한(노력하지 않음으로써 얻은) 결과들을 보아왔기 때문에 완고해 보이는 것일 수 있고, 그들(학생들) 안에 자기 훈련(자제력)을 발달시키기를 원하는 것일 수 있다. ③ (6)아마도 그들의 아이들의 성취에 대해 자랑하고 있는 부모들은 그들(자식들)의 실패에 대해 불안해하고 그들(자식들)의 수업료의 비용을 의식하고 있을지도 모른다. ④ (7)이러한 상황적 요인들은 (특정 상황과 사실에 대한) 지식, 통찰력, 그리고 충분히 생각할 시간을 필요로 한다. ⑤ (8)반면에 (과정을 생략하고) 기질적 귀인으로 비약하는 것은 훨씬 더 쉽다.
- dispositional attribution(기질적 귀인): 행동의 원인을 그 사람의 내적인 성향이나 기질, 고유한 특성 때문이라고 추론하는 것을 의미한다. 예를 들어, 어떤 학생이 시험을 망쳤을 때 그 원인을 자신의 노력이나 의지의 부족으로 생각한다.
- situational attribution(상황적 귀인): 행동의 원인을 그 행동이 발생한 상황이나 맥락 때문이라고 추론하는 것을 의미한다. 예를 들어, 상황적 귀인을 주로 하는 학생은 시험을 망친 원인에 대해 시험 문제가 이상했다거나, 너무 어려웠다고 생각하게 된다.

[문제 풀이]

주어진 문장은 어떤 사람의 행동을 그 사람의 개인적 성향(내적 기질)으로 돌리는 것의 간편함에 대해 말하고 있다. 따라서 문장 (3)에서 원인을 내적 기질로 돌리는 것의 간편함에 대해서 언급한 후, 주어진 문장의 '엄격한 선생님'과 '헌신적인 부모'라는 구체적인 예시가 오는 것이 적절하다. 또한 문장 (4)에서부터는 원인을 외적 상황으로 돌리는 것이 복잡하다는 내용으로 흐름이 전환되기 때문에, 주어진 문장의 위치로는 ①이 가장 적합하다.

[중요 어휘]

□	**prioritize**	동사 우선시하다
□	**disposition**	명사 (타고난) 기질, 성격
□	**seek**	동사 찾다, (추)구하다
□	**strict**	형용사 엄격한
□	**stubborn**	형용사 완고한, 고집이 센
□	**devoted**	형용사 헌신적인
□	**self-discipline**	명사 자기 훈련(자제력), 자기 수양
□	**boast of**	~을 자랑하다, 뽐내다
□	**think through**	(문제에 대해) 충분히 생각하다
□	**whereas**	접속사 반면에
□	**dispositional**	형용사 (타고난) 기질의, 성향의
□	**attribution**	명사 귀인(원인을 돌림)

핵심 사업의 세계에서 네트워크 분석의 중요성을 설명하는 글임. 지문의 어떠한 부분에서 내용이 어떻게 바뀌는지 파악하는 것이 중요함.

22 2019년 6월 39번 (정답률 40%) 정답 ③

[지문 끊어 읽기] 사업에서 네트워크 분석의 중요성

(2) You're probably already starting to see /
당신은 아마도 이미 알아보기 시작했을 것이다 /
the tremendous value of network analysis / for businesspeople.
네트워크 분석의 엄청난 가치를 / 사업가들을 위한

① (3) In the business world, / information is money: /
사업 분야에서는 / 정보가 돈이다 /
a tip about anything / from a cheap supplier / (S)
그 어떤 것에 대한 정보라도 / 값싼 공급자에서부터 /
to a competitor's marketing campaign /
경쟁자의 마케팅 캠페인까지 /
to an under-the-table merger discussion /
비밀리의 합병 논의까지 /
can inform strategic decisions / (V)
전략적인 결정들에 영향을 미칠 수 있다 /
that might yield millions of dollars in profits.
수백만 달러를 이익으로 산출할지도 모르는

힌트 문장 (3)에서의 from A to B to C는 'A에서 B까지'의 뜻을 가진 from A to B와 같은 맥락으로 사용된 것으로 그저 목록에 더 많은 것을 넣기 위해서 쓰인 것임.

② (4) You might catch it / on TV or in the newspaper, /
당신은 그것을 얻을지도 모른다 / TV에서나 신문에서 /
but that's information / everyone knows.
그러나 그것은 정보이다 / 모든 사람이 아는

③ (1) The most profitable information likely /
가장 수익성이 있는 정보는 아마 /
comes through network connections /
네트워크 연줄을 통해 들어올 것이다 /
that provide "inside" information.
'내부' 정보를 제공하는

중요 대중 매체를 통해 누구나 얻을 수 있는 문장 (4)의 정보와, 문장 (1)에서의 네트워크 연줄(연결망)을 통해 얻는 정보, 즉 특정 조직의 구성원에게 직접 받는 내부 정보가 서로 대비되고 있음.

(5) And it isn't just information / (it is ~ that 강조구문)
그리고 단지 정보뿐만이 아니다 /
that travels through network connections / — it's influence as well. 정답 단서
네트워크 연줄을 통해 이동하는 것은 / 영향력이기도 하다

④ (6) If you have a connection / at another company, /
만약 당신이 연줄이 있다면 / 다른 회사에 /
you can possibly ask your connection /
아마 당신은 당신의 연줄에게 요청할 수 있다 /
to push that company to do business with yours, /
그 회사가 당신의 회사와 함께 사업을 하도록 추진해 달라고 /
to avoid a competitor, / or to hold off on the launch of a product.
경쟁자를 피해 달라고 / 아니면 상품의 출시를 연기해 달라고

힌트 병렬 연결되어 있는 3개의 to부정사구 'to push ~', 'to avoid ~', 'to hold off ~'는 5형식 동사 ask의 목적격 보어임.

⑤ (7) So clearly, / any businessperson wants /
그러므로 분명히 / 어떤 사업가라도 원한다 /
to increase their personal network.
그들의 개인적 네트워크를 늘리기를

[전문 해석]

(2)당신은 아마도 이미 사업가들을 위한 네트워크 분석의 엄청난 가치를 알아보기 시작했을 것이다. ① (3)사업 분야에서는 정보가 돈이다. 값싼 공급자에서부터 경쟁자의 마케팅 캠페인 (그리고) 비밀리의 합병 논의까지, 그 어떤 것에 대한 정보라도 수백만 달러를 이익으로 산출

할지도 모르는 전략적인 결정들에 영향을 미칠 수 있다. ② (4)당신은 TV에서나 신문에서 그것(정보)을 얻을지도 모르나, 그것은(그렇게 얻은 정보는) 모든 사람이 아는 정보이다. ③ (1)가장 수익성이 있는 정보는 아마 '내부' 정보를 제공하는 네트워크 연줄을 통해 들어올 것이다. (5)그리고 네트워크 연줄을 통해 이동하는 것은 단지 정보뿐만이 아니라 영향력이기도 하다. ④ (6)만약 당신이 다른 회사에 연줄(인맥)이 있다면, 아마 당신은 당신의 연줄에게 그 회사가 당신의 회사와 함께 사업을 하도록 추진하거나, 경쟁자를 피하거나, 상품의 출시를 연기해 달라고 요청할 수 있다. ⑤ (7)그러므로 분명 어떤 사업가라도 그들의 개인적 네트워크를 늘리기를 원한다(원할 것이다).

- network analysis(네트워크 분석): 복수의 사람, 조직, 사물 등을 연결시키는 일정의 관계의 배치 구성을 기술하고 분석하는 것

[문제 풀이]

문장 (5)는 네트워크 연줄을 통해 정보뿐만 아니라 영향력까지도 얻을 수 있다고 말하면서 네트워크 연줄이 가져다주는 효용에 대해 부연 설명하고 있다. 이는 매체를 통해 누구나 입수할 수 있는 정보에 대해 서술하고 있는 문장 (4) 다음에 이어지기에는 부자연스러우므로, 네트워크 연줄을 통해 얻은 내부 정보가 가장 수익성이 있다는 주어진 문장이 두 문장 사이에 위치하는 것이 자연스럽다. 따라서 정답은 ③이다.

[오답 풀이]

④ - 주어진 문장이 ④에 들어갈 경우, 서로 다른 내용을 언급하는 문장 (4)와 (5)의 흐름이 부자연스러우며, 문장 (5)와 (6)에는 '영향력'에 대한 언급이 있지만 주어진 문장에는 '정보'의 언급만 있으므로 두 문장 사이에 오는 것이 자연스럽다고 보기도 어렵다. 따라서 ④는 오답이다.

[중요 어휘]

힌트 hold off의 목적어로 동명사가 오는 경우에는 주로 전치사 on 없이 바로 V-ing가 오지만, 동명사가 아닌 명사가 올 때에는 전치사 on을 주로 사용함.

☐ **tremendous**	형용사 엄청난, 굉장한
☐ **supplier**	명사 공급자, 공급 회사
☐ **under-the-table**	(거래 등이) 비밀리의, 내밀의
☐ **merger**	명사 (조직체·기업체의) 합병
☐ **inform**	동사 ~에 영향을 미치다, 알려주다
☐ **yield**	동사 산출하다, 항복하다, 양도하다
☐ **catch**	동사 얻다, 보다, 잡다
☐ **profitable**	형용사 수익성이 있는, 이득이 되는
☐ **likely**	부사 아마 / 형용사 ~할 것 같은, 적당한
☐ **hold off on A**	A를 연기하다, 미루다

핵심 주장 다음에 예시가 이어지는 두괄식 구조의 글로, '타이어'와 '내부 디자인'의 예시를 통해 '중요한(important)' 것과 '중추적인(pivotal)' 것의 차이를 설명하고 있음. 자동차 본연의 기능상 '중요한' 것은 타이어지만, 구매 결정에 '중추적인' 역할을 하는 것은 내부 디자인이라는 것임.

23 2020년 9월 38번 (정답률 40%)

정답 ④

[지문 끊어 읽기] 중요한 것과 중추적인 것의 차이

(2) Some resources, decisions, or activities are *important* /
어떤 자원, 결정, 또는 활동은 '중요'하다 /
(highly valuable on average) /
(평균적으로 매우 가치 있는) /
while others are *pivotal* / (small changes make a big difference).
반면 다른 것들은 '중추적'이다 / (작은 변화가 큰 차이를 만든다)

(3) Consider / how two components of a car relate /
의문사 S' V'
생각해 보라 / 자동차의 두 구성 요소가 어떻게 관련이 있는지 /
to a consumer's purchase decision: / tires and interior design.
소비자의 구매 결정과 / 타이어와 내부 디자인

(4) Which adds more value on average?
어떤 것이 평균적으로 더 많은 가치를 더하는가

(5) The tires.
타이어이다

① (6) They are essential / to the car's ability to move, /
그것들은 필수적이다 / 자동차의 운행 능력에 /
and they impact both safety and performance.
그리고 그것들은 안전과 성능 모두에 영향을 미친다

② (7) Yet / tires generally do not influence purchase decisions /
하지만 / 타이어는 일반적으로 구매 결정에 영향을 미치지 않는다 /
because safety standards guarantee /
왜냐하면 안전 기준들이 보장하기 때문이다 /
that all tires will be very safe and reliable.
모든 타이어가 매우 안전하고 믿을 만할 것이라고

③ (8) Differences in interior features /
S
내부 특징의 차이가 /
— optimal sound system, portable technology docks, number and location of cup holders — /
최적의 음향 시스템, 휴대용 기기 거치대, 컵 거치대의 개수와 위치 /
likely have far more effect / on the consumer's buying decision.
V O
아마도 훨씬 더 큰 영향을 미친다 / 소비자의 구매 결정에

④ (1) In terms of the overall value of an automobile, /
자동차의 전반적인 가치 측면에서 /
you can't drive without tires, / but you can drive /
당신은 타이어 없이 운전할 수 없다 / 하지만 당신은 운전할 수 있다 /
without cup holders and a portable technology dock. 정답 단서
컵 거치대와 휴대용 기기 거치대 없이

(9) Interior features, / however, / clearly have a greater impact /
내부 특징은 / 그러나 / 분명히 더 큰 영향을 미친다 /
on the purchase decision. 정답 단서
구매 결정에

⑤ (10) In our language, / the tires are important, /
우리 표현으로 하자면 / 타이어는 중요하다 /
but the interior design is pivotal.
하지만 내부 디자인은 중추적이다

힌트 밑줄 친 부분은 '우리의 언어로 바꾸어 말하자면', 즉 '우리가 알아듣기 쉽게 표현하자면'이라는 뜻임.

[전문 해석]

(2)어떤 자원, 결정, 또는 활동은 '중요한'(평균적으로 매우 가치 있는) 반면 다른 것들은 '중추적'이다(작은 변화가 큰 차이를 만든다). (3)자동차의 두 구성 요소인 타이어와 내부 디자인이 어떻게 소비자의 구매 결정과 관련이 있는지 생각해 보라. (4)어떤 것이 평균적으로 더 많은 가치를 더하는가? (5)타이어이다. ① (6)타이어들은 자동차의 운행 능력에 필수적이고 안전과 성능 모두에 영향을 미친다. ② (7)하지만 타이어는 일반적으로 구매 결정에 영향을 미치지 않는데, 왜냐하면 안전 기준들이 모든 타이어가 매우 안전하고 믿을 만할 것이라고 보장하기 때문이다. ③ (8)최적의 음향 시스템, 휴대용 기기 거치대, 컵 거치대의 개수와 위치 같은 내부 특징의 차이가 아마도 소비자의 구매 결정에 훨씬 더 큰 영향을 미친다. ④ (1)자동차의 전반적인 가치 측면에서 당신은 타이어 없이는 운전할 수 없지만 컵 거치대와 휴대용 기기 거치대 없이는 운전할 수 있다. (9)그러나 내부 특징은 분명히 구매 결정에 더 큰 영향을 미친다. ⑤ (10)우리 표현으로 하자면, 타이어는 중요하지만 내부 디자인은 중추적이다.

[문제 풀이]

문장 (8)과 (9)는 모두 '내부 특징이 구매 결정에 더 큰 영향을 미친다'는 내용으로, 문장 (8)과 (9)가 바로 이어질 경우 문장 (9)의 'however'로 인해 문장 간의 연결이 부자연스럽다. 따라서 문장 (9) 앞에는 '타이어가 더 중요하다'는 내용이 와야 하는데, 주어진 문장은 자동차의 전반적인 가치 측면에서 타이어의 중요성을 강조하고 있으므로, 주어진 문장이 문장 (8)과 (9) 사이에 오는 것이 글의 흐름상 자연스럽다. 따라서, 정답은 ④이다.

[오답 풀이]

③ - 주어진 문장은 자동차의 내부 특징으로 컵 거치대와 휴대용 기기 거치대를 언급하고 있는데, 이후 문장 (8)에서 이 특징을 새롭게 나열하는 것은 자연스럽지 않다. 따라서 주어진 문장이 문장 (8)보다 뒤에 나와야 하므로 ③은 답이 될 수 없다.

[중요 어휘]

☐ **pivotal**	형용사 중추적인, 중심이 되는
☐ **component**	명사 (구성) 요소, 부품, 성분
☐ **guarantee**	동사 보장하다 / 명사 보증
☐ **reliable**	형용사 믿을 만한, 신뢰할 수 있는
☐ **optimal**	형용사 최적의, 최선의
☐ **portable**	형용사 휴대용의, 이동식의
☐ **have an effect/impact on**	~에 영향을 미치다
☐ **overall**	형용사 전반적인 / 부사 전반적으로
☐ **automobile**	명사 자동차

24 2021년 9월 38번 (정답률 40%) 정답 ③

[지문 끊어 읽기] 아동을 사회화하는 동인

(2) Interest in ideology in children's literature / arises from a belief /
아동 문학에서의 이데올로기에 대한 관심은 / 믿음에서 비롯된다 /
[that children's literary texts are culturally formative, /
아동 문학의 텍스트가 문화적으로 형성된다는 /
and of massive importance educationally, intellectually, and socially].
그리고 교육적, 지적, 사회적으로 매우 중요하다는
[ ]: a belief와 동격
힌트 'of+추상명사'는 형용사의 뜻을 가지고 massive는 '대규모의, 거대한'을 의미하므로, 밑줄 친 부분은 '매우 중요한'으로 해석할 수 있음.

① (3) Perhaps more than any other texts, /
아마도 다른 어떤 텍스트보다도 /
they reflect society / as it wishes to be, / as it wishes to be seen, /
병렬① 병렬②
그것들은 사회를 반영한다 / 그것이 바라는 대로 / 그것이 보이고 싶은 대로 /
and as it unconsciously reveals itself to be, / at least to writers.
병렬③
그리고 그것이 무의식적으로 그것 자체를 드러내는 대로 / 적어도 작가에게는

② (4) Clearly, / literature is not the only socialising agent /
분명히 / 문학이 유일한 사회화 동인은 아니다 /
in the life of children, / even among the media. 정답 단서
아동의 삶 속에서 / 심지어 매체들 가운데에서도
힌트 for example과 today는 'It(형식상의 주어) ~ to V(내용상의 주어)' 구문 안에 포함된 삽입구이며, 이때 명사절 접속사 that 이하는 모두 argue의 목적어인 명사절임.

③ (1) It is possible to argue, / for example, /
주장할 수 있다 / 예를 들어 /
that, today, / the influence of books is vastly overshadowed /
명사절 접속사
오늘날 / 책의 영향은 크게 가려진다고 /
by that of television.
=the influence
텔레비전의 그것에 의해

(5) There is, however, a considerable degree of interaction /
그러나 상당한 수준의 상호 작용이 있다 /
between the two media. 정답 단서
두 매체 사이에는

④ (6) Many so-called children's literary classics are televised, /
소위 아동 문학 고전이라고 불리는 많은 것들이 텔레비전으로 방영되고 있다 /
and the resultant new book editions strongly suggest /
그리고 그 결과로 생긴 새로운 책 판본은 강력하게 시사한다 /
that viewing can encourage subsequent reading.
명사절 접속사
시청하는 것이 그 후의 독서를 장려할 수 있다는 것을

⑤ (7) Similarly, / some television series for children are published /
비슷하게 / 아동을 위한 몇몇 텔레비전 시리즈는 출판된다 /
in book form.
책 형태로

[전문 해석]

(2)아동 문학에서의 이데올로기에 대한 관심은 아동 문학의 텍스트가 문화적으로 형성되고, 교육적, 지적, 사회적으로 매우 중요하다는 믿음에서 비롯된다. ① (3)아마도 다른 어떤 텍스트보다도, 적어도 작가에게는, 그것들(아동 문학의 텍스트)은 사회를 그것(사회)이 바라는 대로, 보이고 싶은 대로, 그리고 무의식적으로 그것(사회) 자체를 드러내는 대로(무의식적으로 드러나 있는 그대로) 반영한다. ② (4)분명히 문학이 아동의 삶 속에서, 심지어 매체들 가운데에서도 유일한 사회화 동인(요인)은 아니다. ③ (1)예를 들어, 오늘날 책의 영향은 텔레비전의 그것(영향)에 의해 크게 가려진다고 주장할 수 있다. (5)그러나 두 매체 사이에는 상당한 수준의 상호 작용이 있다. ④ (6)소위 아동 문학 고전이라고 불리는 많은 것들이 텔레비전으로 방영되고 있고, 그 결과로 생긴 새로운 책 판본은 (텔레비전을) 시청하는 것이 그 후의 독서를 장려할 수 있다는 것을 강력하게 시사한다. ⑤ (7)비슷하게, 아동을 위한 몇몇 텔레비전 시리즈는 책 형태로 출판된다.
- agent(동인): 어떤 사태를 일으키거나 변화시키는 데 작용하는 직접적인 원인

[문제 풀이]

아동의 삶 속에서 아동을 사회화하는 동인에 대해 설명한 글이다. 문장 (4)는 문학이 매체들 가운데에서 유일한 사회화 동인은 아니라고 하므로, 뒤에 아동을 사회화하는 또 다른 매체에 대한 예시가 나올 것으로 예상된다. 또한, 문장 (5)에서 '두 매체 사이에는'이라는 말을 통해, 이 문장에 앞서 책 말고도 다른 매체에 대한 언급이 있어야 함을 알 수 있다. 이때 문장 (6)과 (7)에 텔레비전에 대한 이야기가 나오므로, 문장 (5) 앞에 텔레비전에 대한 언급이 나오는 것이 자연스럽다. 따라서 접속 부사 'for example'로 시작되고 다른 매체인 텔레비전에 대해 언급하는 주어진 문장이 문장 (4)와 (5) 사이에 위치하는 것이 문맥상 자연스러우므로, 정답은 ③이다.

[오답 풀이]

④ - 주어진 문장은 오늘날 책보다는 텔레비전의 영향이 커졌다는 주장을 나타낸다. 그러나 문장 (6)에서는 아동 문학 고전이 텔레비전으로 방영되는, 즉 주어진 문장과 반대로 책이 텔레비전에 영향을 끼친다는 구체적인 예시가 나온다. 또한, 주어진 문장이 ④에 오면 문장 (5)의 'the two media'가 나타내는 것이 무엇인지 명확하지 않기 때문에 주어진 문장 다음에 문장 (6)이 오면 지문의 흐름이 자연스럽지 않으므로 ④는 정답이 될 수 없다.

[중요 어휘]

☐	ideology	명사 이데올로기, 이념
☐	literature	명사 문학 (작품)
☐	literary	형용사 문학의, 문학적인
☐	formative	형용사 형성되는, 형성에 중요한
☐	unconsciously	부사 무의식적으로
☐	socialise(=socialize)	동사 사회화하다, 어울리다
☐	vastly	부사 크게, 막대하게
☐	overshadow	동사 가리다, 그림자를 드리우다
☐	considerable	형용사 상당한, 중요한
☐	interaction	명사 상호 작용
☐	televise	동사 텔레비전으로 방영하다
☐	resultant	형용사 그 결과로 생긴
☐	subsequent	형용사 그 후의, 다음의
☐	publish	동사 출판하다, 발표하다

25 2022년 3월 38번 (정답률 40%) 정답 ⑤

[지문 끊어 읽기] 과학자들의 의사소통 방식의 변화

(2) In the early stages of modern science, /
현대 과학의 초기 단계에서 /
scientists communicated their creative ideas /
과학자들은 그들의 창의적인 생각을 전달했다 /
largely by publishing books. 정답 단서 과학자들은 책을 통해 의사소통을 하곤 했음.
주로 책을 출판함으로써
힌트 동사 illustrate는 '(실례·도해·삽화 등을 이용해) 설명하다'라는 의미로, 예를 들 때 쓰는 표현임. 영어에서 책이나 정기 간행물의 제목을 이탤릭체로 쓴다는 점이나 단어의 의미를 모르더라도 이것들이 문장 (2)에서 언급된 books의 예시에 해당하며 모두 유명한 과학자의 저서라는 것을 알 수 있음.

① (3) This modus operandi is illustrated /
이런 작업 방식은 설명된다 /
not only by Newton's *Principia*, /
not only A but also B: A뿐만 아니라 B도
뉴턴의 *Principia*로뿐만 아니라 /
but also by Copernicus' *On the Revolutions of the Heavenly Spheres*, /
코페르니쿠스의 *On the Revolutions of the Heavenly Spheres*로도 /
Kepler's *The Harmonies of the World*, /
케플러의 *The Harmonies of the World*로도 /
and Galileo's *Dialogues Concerning the Two New Sciences*.
그리고 갈릴레오의 *Dialogues Concerning the Two New Sciences*로도

② (4) With the advent of scientific periodicals, /
과학 정기 간행물의 출현과 함께 /
such as the *Transactions of the Royal Society of London*, /
Transactions of the Royal Society of London 같은 /
books gradually yielded ground / to the technical journal article /
책은 점차 자리를 내주었다 / 전문 학술지 논문에 /
as the chief form of scientific communication. 정답 단서
전치사(~으로)
과학적 의사소통의 주요한 형식으로
과학자들의 주된 의사소통 방식이 책에서 전문 학술지 논문으로 변함.

③ (5) Of course, / books were not abandoned altogether, /
물론 / 책이 완전히 버려진 것은 아니었다 /
as Darwin's *Origin of Species* shows.
접속사(~듯이)
다윈의 *Origin of Species*가 보여 주듯이

④ (6) Even so, / it eventually became possible /
형식상의 주어
그랬다고 하더라도 / 결국 가능하게 되었다 /

for scientists [to establish a reputation /
의미상의 주어 [ ]: 내용상의 주어
과학자들은 명성을 세우는 것이 /
for their creative contributions /
그들의 창의적인 기여에 대한 /
without publishing a single book-length treatment of their ideas].
자기 생각을 다룬 책 한 권 길이의 출간물을 내지 않고도

⑤ (1) For instance, / the revolutionary ideas /
예를 들어 / 혁명적인 생각들은 / S(=선행사)
[that earned Einstein his Nobel Prize] / [ ]: 주격 관계대명사절
4형식V I·O D·O
아인슈타인에게 노벨상을 안겨 준 /
— concerning the special theory of relativity and the photoelectric effect — /
특수 상대성 이론과 광전 효과에 관한 /
appeared as papers in the *Annalen der Physik*.
V 전치사(~으로)
*Annalen der Physik*에 논문으로 등장했다

✱중요 His status는 문장 (1)에서 언급된 노벨상과 연관되어 있으므로, 문장 (1)이 문장 (7) 앞에 와야 흐름이 자연스러움.

(7) His status / as one of the greatest scientists of all time /
S 전치사(~로서)
그의 지위는 / 역사상 가장 위대한 과학자 중 한 명으로서 /
does not depend on the publication of a single book.
V
단 한 권의 책의 출간에 달려 있지는 않다

[전문 해석]

(2)현대 과학의 초기 단계에서 과학자들은 주로 책을 출판함으로써 자신의 창의적인 생각을 전달했다. ① (3)이런 작업 방식은 뉴턴의 *Principia*(자연 철학의 수학적 원리)로뿐만 아니라 코페르니쿠스의 *On the Revolutions of the Heavenly Spheres*(천체의 회전에 관하여)와 케플러의 *The Harmonies of the World*(세계의 조화), 갈릴레오의 *Dialogues Concerning the Two New Sciences*(새로운 두 과학에 대한 대화)로도 설명된다. ② (4) *Transactions of the Royal Society of London*(런던 왕립 학회 회보) 같은 과학 정기 간행물의 출현과 함께, 책은 과학적 의사소통의 주요한 형식으로 전문 학술지 논문에 점차 자리를 내주었다. ③ (5)물론 다윈의 *Origin of Species*(종의 기원)가 보여 주듯이 책이 완전히 버려진 것은 아니었다. ④ (6)그렇다고 하더라도, 과학자들은 결국, 자기 생각을 다룬 책 한 권 길이의 출간물을 내지 않고도 자신이 창의적으로 기여한 바에 대한 명성을 세우는 것이 가능하게 되었다. ⑤ (1)예를 들어, 아인슈타인에게 노벨상을 안겨 준, 특수 상대성 이론과 광전 효과에 관한 혁명적인 생각들은 *Annalen der Physik*(물리학 연보)에 논문으로 등장했다. (7)역사상 가장 위대한 과학자 중 한 명으로서 그의 지위는 단 한 권의 책의 출간에 달려 있지는 않다.

- special theory of relativity(특수 상대성 이론): 시간과 공간은 절대적인 것이 아니며 속도에 따라 상대적이라는 알베르트 아인슈타인의 이론
- photoelectric effect(광전 효과): 일정 진동수 이상의 빛을 금속에 비추면 전자가 튀어나오는 현상. 이를 통해 빛의 입자성을 설명한 공로로 아인슈타인은 노벨상을 받았음.

[문제 풀이]

문장 (2)~(3)은 과학자들이 현대 과학 초기 단계에는 주로 책을 통해 자신의 생각을 전달했다는 주장과 그 예시가 나열되어 있다. 그러나 문장 (4)부터는 과학자들의 의사소통 방식으로 책 대신 전문 학술지 논문이 대두되었다는 내용으로 전개되고 있다. 삽입해야 할 문장 (1)은 아인슈타인의 이론이 논문으로 발행되었다고 언급하므로 문장 (4) 이후인 ③~⑤로 선택지를 좁힐 수 있다. 문장 (6)에서 과학자들이 책과 같이 긴 출간물을 내지 않고도 명성을 얻는 것이 가능해졌다고 했는데, For instance로 시작하는 주어진 문장은 이에 대한 예로 볼 수 있다. 또한 문장 (7)의 His status가 지칭하는 단어가 문장 (4)~(6)에는 없다. 문장 (1)이 문장 (7) 앞에 위치하면 His status가 Einstein's status를 지칭하여 글의 흐름이 자연스럽다. 따라서 정답은 ⑤이다.

[중요 어휘]

□ communicate	동사 전달하다, 소통하다
□ advent	명사 출현
□ periodical	명사 정기 간행물
□ yield	동사 (자리를) 내주다, 양도하다, 포기하다
□ yield ground to	~에게 내주다
□ journal	명사 학술지, 신문
□ chief	형용사 주요한, 최고의 / 명사 최고위자, 우두머리
□ abandon	동사 버리다
□ altogether	부사 완전히, 총, 전체적으로 보아
□ reputation	명사 명성, 평판
□ contribution	명사 기여, 공헌
□ treatment	명사 다룸, 논의, 취급, 치료
□ revolutionary	형용사 혁명적인
□ paper	명사 논문, 종이, 신문
□ depend on	~에 달려 있다, ~에 의존하다
□ publication	명사 출간

26 2022년 3월 39번 (정답률 40%) 정답 ⑤

[지문 끊어 읽기] 스포츠 클럽의 고정된 생산 능력을 해결하는 방법

(2) A supply schedule refers to the ability of a business /
공급 일정은 업체의 능력을 말한다 /
[to change their production rates /
생산율을 바꿀 수 있는 /
to meet the demand of consumers]. [ ]: 형용사적 용법
부사적 용법(목적)
소비자의 수요를 충족하기 위해

(3) Some businesses are able to increase their production level quickly /
몇몇 업체는 조업도를 빠르게 늘릴 수 있다 /
in order to meet increased demand.
~하기 위해서
증가한 수요를 충족하기 위해

(4) However, / sporting clubs have /
그러나 / 스포츠 클럽은 가지고 있다 /
a fixed, or inflexible (inelastic) production capacity. 정답 단서
고정된 혹은 유연하지 못한(비탄력적인) 생산 능력을
스포츠 클럽은 고정된 생산 능력을 가지고 있다는 한계가 있음.

① (5) They have / what is known as a fixed supply schedule. 정답 단서
선행사를 포함한 관계대명사(=the thing which)
그들은 가지고 있다 / 고정 공급 일정이라 알려진 것을
스포츠 클럽은 고정된 공급 일정을 가지고 있음.

② (6) It is worth noting / [that this is not the case /
형식상의 주어 =the fixed supply schedule
주목할 가치가 있다 / 이것이 그렇지 않는다는 것은 /
for sales of clothing, equipment, memberships and memorabilia].
의류, 장비, 회원권, 기념품 판매에는 [ ]: 내용상의 주어

힌트 'be worth N/V-ing'는 '~할 가치가 있다'라는 뜻이고, (동)명사 자리에 to부정사나 동사원형이 오지 않음을 주의해야 함. 유사한 형태로 'be worthy of+N/V-ing'가 있음.

③ (7) But / clubs and teams can only play a certain number of times /
그러나 / 클럽과 팀은 일정 횟수만 경기할 수 있다 /
during their season. 정답 단서 스포츠 클럽은 고정된 공급 일정을 가지고 있다는 한계를 계속 언급함.
시즌 동안

④ (8) If fans and members are unable to get into a venue, /
팬과 회원이 경기장에 들어갈 수 없으면 /
that revenue is lost forever.
그 수익은 영원히 손실된다

⑤ (1) Although sport clubs and leagues may have a fixed supply schedule, /
스포츠 클럽과 리그가 고정 공급 일정을 가지고 있을지라도 /
it is possible /
형식상의 주어
가능하다 /
[to increase the number of consumers / who watch]. [ ]: 내용상의 주어
소비자의 수를 늘리는 것이 / 보는

힌트 선행사 'consumers'를 수식하는 주격 관계대명사절로 글의 맥락상 추측 가능한 목적어 'games(경기)'가 생략됨.

(9) For example, /
예를 들어 /
the supply of a sport product can be increased /
스포츠 제품의 공급을 늘릴 수 있다 /
정답 단서 앞에서는 계속해서 스포츠 클럽의 고정된 공급 일정이라는 한계에 대해 이야기했는데, 여기서는 공급을 늘릴 수 있는 해결책을 제시함.
by providing more seats, / changing the venue, /
병렬① 병렬②
더 많은 좌석을 제공함으로써 / 경기장을 바꿈으로써 /
extending the playing season /
병렬③
또는 경기 시즌을 연장함으로써 /
or even through new television, radio or Internet distribution.
또는 심지어 새로운 텔레비전, 라디오, 혹은 인터넷 배급으로

힌트 두 전치사구 'by providing~season'과 'through~distribution'이 등위 접속사 or로 병렬 연결되어 있음. 또한 by 전치사구 안에서도 동명사 'providing, changing, extending'이 병렬 연결되어 있는 구조임. 참고로 부사 'even(심지어, ~조차도)'은 단어나 구 앞에서 강조 역할을 하는데, 여기서는 through 전치사구를 강조함.

[전문 해석]

(2)공급 일정은 소비자의 수요를 충족하기 위해 생산율을 바꿀 수 있는 업체의 능력을 말한다. (3)몇몇 업체는 증가한 수요를 충족하기 위해 조업도를 빠르게 늘릴 수 있다. (4)그러나, 스포츠 클럽은 고정된, 혹은 유연하지 못한(비탄력적인) 생산 능력을 가지고 있다. ① (5)그들은 소위 고정 공급 일정이라 알려진 것을 가지고 있다. ② (6)이것이 의류, 장비, 회원권, 기념품 판매에는 그렇지 않는다는 것에 주목할 가치가 있다. ③ (7)그러나 클럽과 팀은 시즌 동안 일정 횟수만 경기할 수 있다. ④ (8)팬과 회원이 경기장에 들어갈 수 없으면, 그 수익은 영원히 손실된다. ⑤ (1)스포츠 클럽과 리그가 고정 공급 일정을 가지고 있을지라도, (경기를) 보는 소비자의 수를 늘리는 것이 가능하다. (9)예를 들어, 더 많은 좌석을 제공하거나, 경기장을 바꾸거나, 경기 시즌을 연장하거나, 심지어 새로운 텔레비전, 라디오, 혹은 인터넷 배급으로 스포츠 제품의 공급을 늘릴 수 있다.

- production level(조업도): 가능한 생산 능력에 대한 실제 생산량의 비율

[문제 풀이]

문장 (2)~(3)은 공급 일정에 대해 설명하고 있고, 문장 (4)~(8)은 스포츠 클럽이 고정된 공급 일정을 가지고 있다고 설명한다. 계속해서 스포츠 클럽의 고정된 공급 일정이라는 한계를 이야기하고 있는데 갑자기 문장 (9)에서는 스포츠 클럽이 공급을 늘릴 수 있는 해결책의 예시들을 보여 주고 있다. 이때 주어진 문장 (1)에서 스포츠 클럽의 고정된 공급 일정 해결에 대하여 처음으로 언급하고 있으므로 문장 (1)은 이에 대한 해결책 예시를 나열하는 문장 (9) 앞에 와야 한다. 따라서 정답은 ⑤이다.

[중요 어휘]

☐ supply	명사 공급 / 동사 공급하다, 제공하다
☐ meet	동사 충족하다, 만나다
☐ demand	명사 수요 / 동사 요구하다
☐ fixed	형용사 고정된
☐ inflexible	형용사 유연하지 못한
☐ inelastic	형용사 비탄력적인, 고정적인
☐ note	동사 주목하다, 언급하다
☐ memorabilia	명사 기념품, 수집품
☐ venue	명사 (콘서트·스포츠 경기·회담 등의) 장소
☐ revenue	명사 수익, 수입
☐ distribution	명사 배급, 배포

27 2022년 11월 38번 (정답률 40%) 정답 ⑤

[지문 끊어 읽기] 항영양소에 대한 신체적 반응

(2) In the natural world, / if an animal consumes a plant /
자연계에서 / 만약 동물이 식물을 섭취하면 /
with enough antinutrients to make it feel unwell, /
부사적 용법
자신의 상태를 안 좋게 하기에 충분한 항영양소가 있는 /
it won't eat that plant again.
=an animal
그것은 그 식물을 다시는 먹지 않을 것이다

(3) Intuitively, / animals also know / to stay away from these plants.
명사적 용법
직관적으로 / 동물은 또한 안다 / 이러한 식물을 멀리할 줄

(4) Years of evolution and information / being passed down /
S 현재분사구
오랜 시간의 진화와 정보는 / 전해 내려오는 /
created this innate intelligence.
V
이 타고난 지능을 만들어 냈다

✶중요 문장 (1)은 인간의 신체적 반응에 대해 이야기하고 있기 때문에, 동물뿐만 아니라 다른 존재에게서도 나타나는 직관이라고 예고하는 문장 (5) 이후에 위치하는 것이 적절하므로 ①은 정답으로 적절하지 않음.

① (5) This "intuition," though, / is not just seen in animals.
그러나 이 '직관'은 / 동물에게서만 보이는 것은 아니다

② (6) Have you ever wondered /
여러분은 궁금해한 적이 있는가 /
why most children hate vegetables?
간접의문문(의문사+S+V)
대부분의 아이들이 왜 야채를 싫어하는지

✶중요 문장 (5)에 의해 동물에서 다른 존재로 글의 흐름이 전환됨에 따라 '아이들이 야채를 싫어하는 이유'라는 구체적인 상황을 제시하고 있음. 상황에 대한 구체적인 내용의 문장 (1)은 문장 (6) 이후에 위치하는 것이 적절하므로 ②는 정답으로 적절하지 않음.

③ (7) Dr. Steven Gundry justifies this /
Dr. Steven Gundry는 이것을 정당화한다 /
as part of our genetic programming, /
우리의 유전적 프로그래밍의 일부로 /
our inner intelligence.
우리의 내적 지능

✶중요 문장 (6)에서 아이들이 야채를 싫어하는 이유에 대해 질문했고, 이에 대한 답변으로 유전적 프로그래밍의 일부라고 이야기하고 있음. 따라서 문장 (1)을 위치시켜 이러한 흐름을 깨는 것을 자연스럽지 않으므로 ③은 정답으로 적절하지 않음.

④ (8) Since many vegetables are full of antinutrients, /
접속사(이유)
많은 야채들이 항영양소로 가득 차 있기 때문에 /
your body tries to keep you away from them /
여러분의 몸은 여러분을 그것들로부터 멀리하게 하려고 노력한다 /
while you are still fragile and in development.
접속사(~할 때)
여러분이 아직 연약하고 성장 중일 때

정답 단서 성장기에 있는 몸은 항영양소로 가득한 야채를 멀리하게 함.

✶중요 유전적 프로그래밍이 작동하여 일어나는 신체적 반응이 어떤 과정을 거치는지에 대한 내용이 이어지는 게 자연스러우므로 문장 (1)은 문장 (8) 이후에 위치하는 것이 적절함. 따라서 ④는 정답으로 적절하지 않음.

⑤ (1) It does this / by making your taste buds perceive these flavors /
사역V O O·C(동사원형)
그것은 이를 수행한다 / 여러분의 미뢰로 하여금 이러한 맛을 인식하게 만듦으로써 /
as bad and even disgusting.
나쁘고 심지어 역겨운 것으로

(9) As you grow / and your body becomes stronger /
접속사
여러분이 성장하면서 / 그리고 여러분의 신체가 더 강해지면서 /
enough to tolerate these antinutrients, /
형용사+enough+to부정사: …할 만큼 충분히 ~한
이러한 항영양소를 견딜 만큼 충분히 /
suddenly they no longer taste as bad as before.
갑자기 그것들은 더 이상 이전만큼 맛이 나쁘게 느껴지지 않는다

정답 단서 성장하면서 항영양소를 견딜 만큼 강해지면 더 이상 맛이 나쁘게 느껴지지 않음.

[전문 해석]

(2)자연계에서 만약 동물이 자신의 상태를 안 좋게 하기에 충분한 항영양소가 있는 식물을 섭취하면, 그 동물은 그 식물을 다시는 먹지 않을 것이다. (3)직관적으로 동물은 또한 이러한 식물을 멀리할 줄 안다. (4)오랜 시간의 진화와 전해 내려오는 정보는 이 타고난 지능을 만들어 냈다. ① (5)그러나 이 '직관'은 동물에게서만 보이는 것은 아니다. ② (6)여러분은 대부분의 아이들이 왜 야채를 싫어하는지 궁금해한 적이 있는가? ③ (7)Dr. Steven Gundry는 이것을 우리의 유전적 프로그래밍, 즉 우리의 내적 지능의 일부로 정당화한다. ④ (8)많은 야채들이 항영양소로 가득 차 있기 때문에 여러분이 아직 연약하고 성장 중일 때 여러분의 몸은 여러분을 그것들로부터 멀리하게 하려고 노력한다. ⑤ (1)그것은 여러분의 미뢰(味蕾)로 하여금 이러한 맛을 나쁘고 심지어 역겨운 것으로 인식하게 만듦으로써 이를 수행한다. (9)여러분이 성장하고 여러분의 신체가 이러한 항영양소를 견딜 만큼 충분히 더 강해지면서, 갑자기 그것들은 더 이상 이전만큼 맛이 나쁘게 느껴지지 않는다.

- antinutrient(항영양소): 영양소의 흡수를 방해하는 물질. 식물의 경우 감염이나 포식자에 대한 방어 수단으로 항영양소 물질을 함유하고 있음.
- taste bud(미뢰, 味蕾): 혀에서 미각을 담당하는 꽃봉오리 모양의 기관

[문제 풀이]

주어진 문장 (1)은 미뢰로 하여금 맛을 나쁘게 인식하게 만듦으로써 'this(이)'를 수행한다고 이야기하고 있다. 따라서 문장 (1)의 this가 무엇을 지칭하는지 파악하면서 지문을 읽어야 한다. 문장 (2)~(4)에서 항영양소가 있는 식물을 먹고 상태가 안 좋아지는 것을 경험하게 되면 직관적으로 그러한 식물을 먹지 않는다는 동물의 예를 들면서, 오랜 시간의 진화와 전해 내려오는 정보가 그런 지능을 만들어 냈다고 설명한다. 문장 (5)에서는 이를 '직관'으로 칭하고 동물에게서만 볼 수 있는 것이 아니라고 하면서, 다른 존재에게서도 볼 수 있는 것이라고 이야기할 것을 예고하고 있다. 이에 대한 예시로, 문장 (6)~(7)에서 대부분의 아이들이 야채를 싫어하는 이유를 유전적 프로그래밍, 즉 내적 지능의 일부라고 설명한다. 이어지는 문장 (8)에 따르면, 많은 야채들이 항영양소로 가득 차 있어 성장기에 있는 몸은 야채를 멀리하게 하는데, 여기서 '몸이 야채를 멀리하게 하는 것'은 문장 (1)에서 '미뢰로 하여금 맛을 나쁘게 인식하게 만드는 것'에 의해 수행되는 'this'를 지칭하면서 내용이 연결된다. 맛을 인식한다는 내용의 문장 (1)은 성장하면서 신체가 항영양소를 견딜 만큼 강해지면 이전만큼 (야채의) 맛이 나쁘게 느껴지지 않는다고 하는 문장 (9)와 자연스럽게 이어진다. 따라서 정답은 ⑤이다.

[오답 풀이]

④ - 문장 (1)에서는 미뢰로 하여금 맛을 나쁘게 인식하게 만듦으로써 이를 수행한다고 했고, 여기서 '미뢰로 하여금 맛을 나쁘게 인식하게 만듦'은 원인으로, 수행되는 어떤 것은 결과로 볼 수 있다. 즉, 문장 (1)의 앞 문장에는 맛을 나쁘게 인식함으로써 수행되는 어떤 것이 제시되어야 한다. 이는 몸이 항영양소로 가득한 야채를 멀리하게 한다는 문장 (8)의 내용을 의미한다. 문장 (1)이 ④에 위치하게 되면, 수행되는 어떤 것에 해당하는 'this'가 지칭하는 바가 불명확하게 되므로, ④는 정답으로 적절하지 않다.

문제편 p.222

[중요 어휘]

☐ **consume**	동사 섭취하다, 소모하다
☐ **antinutrient**	명사 항영양소
☐ **intuitively**	부사 직관적으로, 직감적으로
☐ **evolution**	명사 진화, 발전
☐ **pass A down**	A를 전해주다[물려주다]
☐ **intelligence**	명사 지능, 정보
☐ **intuition**	명사 직관, 직감
☐ **justify**	동사 정당화하다, 해명하다
☐ **genetic**	형용사 유전적인, 유전(학)의
☐ **keep A away from B**	A를 B로부터 멀리하다
☐ **fragile**	형용사 연약한, 부서지기 쉬운
☐ **taste bud**	명사 미뢰(味蕾), 맛봉오리
☐ **perceive**	동사 인식하다, 인지하다
☐ **disgusting**	형용사 역겨운, 혐오스러운
☐ **tolerate**	동사 견디다, 참다, 용인하다

28 2022년 11월 39번 (정답률 40%) 정답 ③

[지문 끊어 읽기] 조수 발생의 원리

(2) The difference in the Moon's gravitational pull /
S
달 중력의 차이는 /
on different parts of our planet /
우리 행성의 서로 다른 부분들에 대한 /
effectively creates a "stretching force."
V
효과적으로 '잡아 늘이는 힘'을 만든다

①(3) It makes our planet slightly stretched out /
5형식V O O·C①
그것은 우리 행성을 약간 늘어나게 한다 /
along the line of sight to the Moon /
달을 보는 방향으로 /
and slightly compressed /
그리고 약간 눌리게 한다 / O·C②
along a line perpendicular to that.
그것에 직각을 이루는 선을 따라 =the Moon

✱중요 문장 (2)~(4)는 지구에 대한 달 중력의 차이로 '잡아 늘이는 힘'이 발생하며, 그 힘이 지구의 형태를 변형시키고 조수의 늘어남이 지구 전체에도 영향을 미친다고 설명함. ①이나 ②에 문장 (1)이 위치하려면 앞이나 뒤의 문장에 바다의 조수에 대한 언급이 있어야 함. 하지만 문장 (2)~(3)에는 이에 대한 언급이 없고 문장 (3)에서 문장 (4)로 이어지는 문맥의 흐름도 자연스러우므로, ①과 ②는 정답으로 적절하지 않음.

②(4) The tidal stretching caused by the Moon's gravity /
S 과거분사
달의 중력에 의해 발생되는 조수의 늘어남은 /
affects our entire planet, / including both land and water, /
V 현재분사구
우리의 전체 행성에 영향을 미친다 / 땅과 물을 포함한 /
inside and out. 정답 단서 조수의 늘어남은 지구의 땅과 물에 영향을 미침.
안팎으로

③(1) However, / the rigidity of rock means /
하지만 / 암석의 단단함은 의미한다 /
that land rises and falls with the tides /
명사절 접속사
땅이 조수와 함께 오르락내리락한다는 것을 /
by a much smaller amount than water, /
비교급 강조
물보다는 훨씬 더 적은 양만큼 /
which is [why we notice only the ocean tides].
주격 관계대명사(계속적 용법) [ ]: 선행사 the reason이 생략된 관계부사절
이것이 우리가 오직 바다의 조수를 알아차리는 이유이다

(5) The stretching also explains /
그 늘어남은 또한 설명한다 /
[why there are generally *two* high tides (and two low tides) /
왜 일반적으로 '두 번의' 만조(그리고 두 번의 간조)가 발생하는지 /
in the ocean each day]. 정답 단서 조수의 늘어남으로 인해 바다에서 두 번의 만조와 간조가 발생함.
매일 바다에서 [ ]: 간접의문문(의문사+S+V)

④(6) Because Earth is stretched much like a rubber band, /
접속사
지구가 고무줄처럼 늘어나기 때문에 /
the oceans bulge out /
바다는 부풀어 나간다 /
both on the side facing toward the Moon /
달을 향하는 쪽 / 현재분사구
and on the side facing away from the Moon.
현재분사구
그리고 달에서 멀어지는 쪽 모두에서

✱중요 문장 (5)에서 예고된 대로, 바다에서 두 번의 만조와 간조가 발생하는 원리에 대한 구체적인 내용이 문장 (6)에서 이어지고 있으므로 문장 (1)은 문장 (5) 이전에 위치하는 것이 적절함. 따라서 ④는 정답으로 적절하지 않음.

⑤(7) As Earth rotates, /
접속사
지구가 자전함에 따라 /
we are carried through both of these tidal bulges each day, /
우리는 매일 이 두 개의 조수 팽창부를 통과하게 된다 /
so we have high tide /
병렬①
그래서 우리는 만조를 겪는다 /
when we are in each of the two bulges /
접속사(~할 때)
우리가 각각 두 개의 팽창부에 있을 때 /
and low tide / at the midpoints in between.
병렬②
그리고 간조를 / 그 사이의 중간 지점에서

✱중요 문장 (6)에서 언급한 두 개의 조수 팽창부, 즉 달을 향하는 쪽과 달에서 멀어지는 쪽 모두에서 바다가 팽창하는 것에 대해 추가적으로 설명하고 있으므로, 문장 (1)이 ⑤에 위치하여 글의 흐름을 깨는 것은 자연스럽지 않으므로 ⑤는 정답으로 적절하지 않음.

[전문 해석]

(2)우리 행성의 서로 다른 부분들에 대한 달 중력의 차이는 효과적으로 '잡아 늘이는 힘'을 만든다. ① (3)그것은 우리 행성을 달을 보는 방향으로 약간 늘어나게 하고 그것에 직각을 이루는 선을 따라 약간 눌리게 한다. ② (4)달의 중력에 의해 발생되는 조수의 늘어남은 땅과 물을 포함한 우리의 전체 행성에 안팎으로 영향을 미친다. ③ (1)하지만 암석의 단단함은 땅이 물보다는 훨씬 더 적은 양만큼 조수와 함께 오르락내리락한다는 것을 의미하며, 이것이 우리가 오직 바다의 조수를 알아차리는 이유이다. (5)그 늘어남은 또한 왜 일반적으로 매일 바다에서 '두 번의' 만조(그리고 두 번의 간조)가 발생하는지 설명한다. ④ (6)지구가 고무줄처럼 늘어나기 때문에, 바다는 달을 향하는 쪽과 달에서 멀어지는 쪽 모두에서 부풀어 나간다. ⑤ (7)지구가 자전함에 따라 우리는 매일 이 두 개의 조수 팽창부를 통과하게 되어서, 우리가 각각 두 개의 팽창부에 있을 때 만조를 겪고 그 사이의 중간 지점에서 간조를 겪는다.

[문제 풀이]

문장 (1)은 However로 시작하면서, 암석(땅)이 단단하기 때문에 물에 비해 조수의 영향을 적게 받고, 그로 인해 우리가 바다의 조수를 알아차릴 수 있다고 한다. 문맥의 흐름이 바뀌면서 바다의 조수에 대한 설명이 자연스럽게 이어질 수 있는 구간이 어디일지 파악하면서 지문을 읽어야 한다. 문장 (2)~(3)은 지구에 대한 달 중력의 차이가 '잡아 늘이는 힘'을 만들며, 그 힘에 의해 지구의 형태가 변형되면서 조수의 늘어남이 발생한다고 설명한다. 조수의 늘어남이 땅과 물을 포함하여 지구 전체에 영향을 미친다는 문장 (4)의 내용은 암석(땅)이 물에 비해 조수의 영향을 적게 받는다는 문장 (1)의 내용과 자연스럽게 이어진다. 또한, 땅과 물이 조수에 의해 각기 다른 영향을 받기 때문에 우리가 바다의 조수를 알아차릴 수 있다는 문장 (1)의 내용은 구체적으로 바다에서 만조와 간조가 발생하는 이유에 대해 설명하는 문장 (5)~(7)과 이어지므로 정답은 ③이다.

[오답 풀이]

④ - 문장 (1)은 우리가 바다의 조수를 알아차릴 수 있는 이유에 대한 내용이다. 이는 바다에서 두 번의 만조와 간조가 발생하는 이유에 대한 설명을 예고하는 문장 (5)의 뒤에 이어지기에는 자연스럽지 않다. 또한, 바다의 팽창에 대한 문장 (6)의 내용은 우리가 바다의 조수를 알아차릴 수 있는 이유와는 관련 없는, 바다에서 발생하는 만조와 간조의 원리에 대한 것이므로 문장 (1)과 자연스럽게 이어질 수 없다. 따라서 ④는 정답으로 적절하지 않다.

[중요 어휘]

☐ **gravitational pull**	중력
☐ **stretch**	동사 잡아 늘이다, 늘이다
☐ **compress**	동사 누르다, 눌리다, 압축하다
☐ **perpendicular**	형용사 직각을 이루는, 수직적인
☐ **tidal**	형용사 조수의
☐ **rigidity**	명사 단단함, 엄격
☐ **high tide**	명사 만조(밀물)
☐ **low tide**	명사 간조(썰물)
☐ **rubber band**	명사 고무줄
☐ **bulge**	동사 부풀다 / 명사 팽창

29 2023년 6월 39번 (정답률 40%) 정답 ③

[지문 끊어 읽기] 식물의 색깔

(2) Why do people in the Mediterranean live longer /
왜 지중해 지역의 사람들은 더 오래 살까 /
and have a lower incidence of disease?
그리고 질병 발생률이 더 낮을까

(3) Some people say / [it's because of what they eat]. [ ]: say의 목적어절
선행사를 포함한 관계대명사절
몇몇 사람들은 말한다 / 그것은 그들이 먹는 것 때문이라고

(4) Their diet is full of fresh fruits, fish, vegetables, whole grains, and nuts.
그들의 식단은 신선한 과일, 생선, 채소, 통곡물, 그리고 견과류로 가득하다

(5) Individuals in these cultures / drink red wine /
이러한 문화권의 사람들은 / 적포도주를 마신다 /
and use great amounts of olive oil.
그리고 많은 양의 올리브유를 사용한다

(6) Why is that food pattern healthy?
왜 그러한 음식 패턴이 건강에 좋은가

★중요 문장 (6)은 지중해 지역 문화권 사람들의 음식 패턴이 건강에 좋은 이유에 대해 의문을 제기하고, 문장 (7)에서 이에 대한 답변으로 식단의 다양한 색깔을 제시함. 화합물에 의한 식물의 색과 기능이 인체의 건강에 도움이 된다는 내용의 문장 (1)은 오히려 문장 (7) 이후에 나오는 것이 문맥상 자연스러우므로 ①은 정답으로 적절하지 않음.

① (7) One reason is / that they are eating a palette of colors.
명사절 접속사
한 가지 이유는 ~이다 / 그들이 다양한 색깔을 먹고 있다는 것

★중요 문장 (7)에서는 지중해 지역 문화권 사람들의 음식 패턴이 건강에 좋은 이유로 식단의 다양한 색깔을 언급하고, 이에 대해 문장 (8)에서 식품에 존재하는 수천 가지의 다채로운 '식물 화학물질'의 이점에 관한 연구가 표면화되고 있다는 것을 제시하여 내용을 뒷받침함. 식물의 색과 기능이 인체의 건강에 보탬이 된다는 내용의 문장 (1)은 문장 (8)의 내용과 자연스럽게 이어질 수 있으나 문장 (8) 이후에 위치하는 것이 자연스러우므로 ②는 정답으로 적절하지 않음.

② (8) More and more research is surfacing /
선행사
점점 더 많은 연구가 표면화되고 있다 /
that shows us the benefits of the thousands of
주격 관계대명사
colorful "phytochemicals" (*phyto*=plant) /
선행사
수천 가지의 다채로운 '식물 화학물질'(*phyto*=식물)의 이점을 우리에게 보여주는 /
that exist in foods. 정답 단서 식품에 존재하는 수천 가지의 다채로운 '식물 화학물질'의 이점에 관한 연구가 표면화됨.
주격 관계대명사
식품에 존재하는

③ (1) These healthful, non-nutritive compounds in plants /
식물에 있는 건강에 좋고 영양가 없는 이 화합물들은 /
provide color and function to the plant /
식물에 색과 기능을 제공한다 /
and add to the health of the human body.
그리고 인체의 건강에 보탬이 된다

(9) Each color connects to a particular compound /
선행사
각각의 색깔은 특정 화합물과 연결된다 /
that serves a specific function in the body. 정답 단서 식물 각각의 색깔은 몸에서 특정 기능을 하는 특정 화합물과 연결됨.
주격 관계대명사
몸에서 특정 기능을 수행하는

★중요 문장 (9)에 따르면 식물 각각의 색깔은 인간의 몸에서 특정한 기능을 하는 특정 화합물과 연결될 수 있고, 이에 대한 예시로 문장 (10)에서는 보라색과 안토시아닌, 문장 (11)에서는 녹색과 엽록소에 대해 설명함. 식물의 색과 기능이 인체의 건강에 도움이 된다는 내용의 문장 (1)을 ④, ⑤에 위치시켜 이러한 흐름을 깨는 것은 자연스럽지 않으므로 ④, ⑤는 정답으로 적절하지 않음.

④ (10) For example, / if you don't eat purple foods, /
예를 들어 / 만약 당신이 보라색 음식을 먹지 않는다면 /
you are probably missing out on anthocyanins, /
당신은 아마도 안토시아닌을 놓치고 있는 것이다 /
important brain protection compounds.
중요한 뇌 보호 화합물인

⑤ (11) Similarly, / if you avoid green-colored foods, /
유사하게 / 만약 당신이 녹색 음식을 피한다면 /
you may be lacking chlorophyll, /
당신은 엽록소가 부족할 수도 있다 /
a plant antioxidant that guards your cells from damage.
선행사 주격 관계대명사
당신의 세포를 손상으로부터 막아주는 식물 산화 방지제인

힌트 두 문장 모두 콤마 이하의 내용이 각각 anthocyanins와 chlorophyll과 동격임.

[전문 해석]

(2)왜 지중해 지역의 사람들은 더 오래 살고 질병 발생률이 더 낮을까? (3)몇몇 사람들은 그것은 그들이 먹는 것 때문이라고 말한다. (4)그들의 식단은 신선한 과일, 생선, 채소, 통곡물, 그리고 견과류로 가득하다. (5)이러한 문화권의 사람들은 적포도주를 마시고 많은 양의 올리브유를 사용한다. (6)왜 그러한 음식 패턴이 건강에 좋은가? ① (7)한 가지 이유는 그들이 다양한 색깔을 먹고 있다는 것이다. ② (8)식품에 존재하는 수천 가지의 다채로운 '식물 화학물질'(*phyto*=식물)의 이점을 우리에게 보여주는 점점 더 많은 연구가 표면화되고 있다. ③ (1)식물에 있는 건강에 좋고 영양가 없는 이 화합물들은 식물에 색과 기능을 제공하고 인체의 건강에 보탬이 된다. (9)각각의 색깔은 몸에서 특정 기능을 수행하는 특정 화합물과 연결된다. ④ (10)예를 들어, 만약 당신이 보라색 음식을 먹지 않는다면, 당신은 아마도 중요한 뇌 보호 화합물인 안토시아닌을 놓치고 있는 것이다. ⑤ (11)유사하게, 만약 당신이 녹색 음식을 피한다면, 당신은 당신의 세포를 손상으로부터 막아주는 식물 산화 방지제인 엽록소가 부족할 수도 있다.

[문제 풀이]

문장 (1)은 식물 내의 어떤 화합물들이 식물에 색과 기능을 제공하고 인체의 건강에도 도움을 준다고 이야기하고 있다. 따라서 문장 (1)에서 언급된 화합물이 무엇을 말하는지에 주목하며 지문을 읽어야 한다. 문장 (2)~(7)은 지중해 지역 사람들이 더 오래 살고 질병 발생률이 더 낮은 이유가 그들의 식단 때문이라고 설명하고, 그것이 왜 건강에 좋은지에 대해 의문을 제기하면서 식품의 색깔에 대한 논의를 시작하고 있다. 이어지는 문장 (8)에 따르면 식품에 존재하는 수천 가지의 다채로운 '식물 화학물질'의 이점에 관한 연구가 표면화되고 있다. 이는 식물 내의 화합물들이 식물에 색과 기능을 제공하고 인체의 건강에도 보탬이 된다는 문장 (1)의 내용으로 자연스럽게 이어지고, 여기에서 더 나아가 식물 각각의 색깔과 인체 내의 특정 화합물이 연결될 수 있음을 설명하는 문장 (9)와도 문맥상 자연스럽게 이어지므로 정답은 ③이다.

[오답 풀이]

④ - 문장 (1)은 식물 내의 화합물에 의해 식물이 색과 기능을 얻게 되고 인체의 건강에도 보탬이 된다고 설명한다. 문장 (1)이 ④에 위치하게 되면, 식물의 색깔과 인체 내의 특정 화합물이 연결된다고 하면서 식물의 색이 인체의 건강에 보탬이 되는 구체적 과정에 대해 설명하는 문장 (9)가 문장 (1)보다 이전에 위치하게 되므로 문맥상 어색하다. 또한, 문장 (1)이 ④에 위치할 때 바로 뒤에 이어지는 문장 (10)은 문장 (9)에 대한 예시에 해당하므로 자연스럽게 이어질 수 없다. 따라서 ④는 정답으로 적절하지 않다.

[중요 어휘]

☐ incidence	명사 발생률, 영향 범위
☐ surface	동사 표면화되다, 나타나다 / 명사 표면, 지면
☐ phytochemical	명사 (식물 속에 함유된) 식물 화학물질
☐ compound	명사 화합물, 복합체 / 형용사 합성의
☐ lack	동사 부족하다 / 명사 부족, 결핍
☐ chlorophyll	명사 엽록소
☐ antioxidant	명사 산화 방지제, 방부제

30 2016년 6월 38번 (정답률 35%) 정답 ⑤

[지문 끊어 읽기] 남녀 농업 생산성의 격차

(2) In primitive agricultural systems, / the difference in productivity /
원시 농업 체제에서 / 생산성 차이는 /
between male and female agricultural labor /
남성과 여성의 농업 노동력 사이에 /
is roughly proportional to the difference / in physical strength.
차이에 대략적으로 비례했다 / 물리적인 힘에 있어서의

① (3) As agriculture becomes /
농업이 ~되면서 /
less dependent upon human muscular power, /
인간의 근력에 덜 의존하게 /
the difference in labor productivity /
노동 생산성의 차이는 /
between the two genders / might be expected to narrow.
양성 간 / 좁아질 것으로 예상될지 모른다

② (4) However, / this is far from being so.
하지만 / 이것은 전혀 그렇지 않다

③ (5) It is usually the men / who learn /
대개 남자들이다 / 배우는 것은 /
to operate new types of equipment /
새로운 종류의 장비를 조작하는 것을 /
while women continue to work / with old hand tools.
여자들이 계속 일하는 반면 / 오래된 손 도구로

힌트 it is ~ that 강조구문에서 강조하는 어구가 사람이면 that을 who로, 사물이면 which로 바꿔 쓸 수 있음. 여기서 사람인 'the men'을 강조하므로 that 대신 who가 쓰였음.

④ (6) With the introduction of improved agricultural equipment, /
향상된 농업 장비의 도입과 함께 /

there is less need / for male muscular strength. 정답 단서
필요는 줄었다 / 남성의 근력에 대한

⑤ (1) Nevertheless, / the productivity gap tends to widen / 정답 단서
그럼에도 불구하고 / 생산성 격차는 벌어지는 경향이 있다 /
because men dominate the use / of the new equipment /
남성들이 사용을 지배하기 때문에 / 새로운 장비의 /
and modern agricultural methods.
그리고 현대적인 농업 방식의

(7) Thus, / in the course of agricultural development, /
그러므로 / 농업 발전 동안 /
women's labor productivity remains unchanged / 정답 단서
여성의 노동 생산성은 그대로이다 /
compared to men's.
남성들의 것에 비해

✶중요 문장 (6)과 문장 (7)은 인과 관계가 성립하지 않기 때문에 Thus로 연결되는 것이 부자연스러움.

[전문 해석]

(2)원시 농업 체제에서 남성과 여성의 농업 노동력 사이에서 (발생하는) 생산성 차이는 물리적인 힘에 있어서의 차이에 대략적으로 비례했다. ① (3)농업이 인간의 근력에 덜 의존하게 되면서, 양성 간 노동 생산성의 차이는 좁아질 것으로 예상될지 모른다. ② (4)하지만 이것은 전혀 그렇지 않다. ③ (5)여자들이 오래된 손 도구로 계속 일하는 반면 새로운 종류의 장비를 조작하는 것을 배우는 것은 대개 남자들이다. ④ (6)향상된 농업 장비의 도입과 함께 남성의 근력에 대한 필요는 줄었다. ⑤ (1)그럼에도 불구하고 남성들이 새로운 장비와 현대적인 농업 방식의 사용을 지배하기 때문에 생산성 격차는 벌어지는 경향이 있다. (7)그러므로 농업(이) 발전(하는) 동안, 여성의 노동 생산성은 남성의 노동 생산성에 비해 그대로인 것이다.

[문제 풀이]

지문은 남녀의 농업 생산성 격차를 주된 소재로 다룬다. 장비가 발전하고 농업 수행에 있어 인간의 근력에 대한 의존도가 떨어지면서, 본래 신체적인 힘 차이에 기반을 두었던 남녀의 농업 생산성 격차도 줄어들 것으로 기대되었지만 실상은 예상과 달랐다고 말하는 글이다. 주어진 문장은 Nevertheless로 글의 흐름을 반전시키며 생산성 격차가 줄어들기는커녕 더 벌어졌다는 점을 지적하므로, 근력에 대한 필요가 줄었다고 이야기한 문장 (6) 뒤에 들어가는 것이 자연스럽다. 이어지는 문장 (7)은 여성의 노동 생산성이 남성의 노동 생산성에 비해 변하지 않고 그대로라는 말을 통해, 주어진 문장 뒷부분의 '격차가 벌어졌다'는 내용을 부연한다. 따라서 주어진 문장이 들어가기에 가장 적절한 곳은 ⑤이다.

[중요 어휘]

힌트 primitive는 modern(현대의)과 대조되어 '원시의'라는 뜻을 나타내고 있지만, 사물을 묘사할 때 쓰이는 경우에는 '소박한(simple)' 또는 '구식의(old-fashioned)'로 해석되기도 함.

□ primitive	형용사 원시의, 소박한, 구식의
□ roughly	부사 대략적으로, 거의
□ proportional	형용사 비례하는
□ physical	형용사 물리적인, 신체적인
□ muscular	형용사 근육의
□ far from	전혀 ~이 아닌
□ gap	명사 격차
□ agricultural	형용사 농업의
□ thus	부사 그러므로, 따라서
□ in the course of	~동안, ~하는 중에
□ unchanged	형용사 그대로인, 변하지 않은

핵심 본문은 인간의 아미노산 결핍 문제가 현대 사회에서뿐만 아니라 냉동 기술이 없었던 산업화 이전의 시대에도 존재했다고 이야기하면서, 자연 재해와 같은 극한의 상황 속에서 스스로 아미노산을 합성하지 못하는 인간의 무능력이 당시 인류의 생존을 더욱 힘들게 했다고 설명하고 있음.

31 2018년 11월 38번 (정답률 35%) 정답 ③

[지문 끊어 읽기] 인간의 아미노산 결핍 문제

(2) The problem of amino acid deficiency /
아미노산 결핍의 문제가 /
is not unique to the modern world / by any means.
현대 세계에 유일하지는 않다 / 결코

① (3) Preindustrial humanity probably /
산업화 이전의 인류는 아마 /
dealt with protein and amino acid insufficiency /
단백질과 아미노산의 불충분에 대처했을 것이다 /
on a regular basis.
정기적으로

힌트 동사 뒤에 ed가 붙으면 수동의 의미를 가진 과거분사(p.p.) 형태의 형용사가 됨. 해석 시 수동의 의미를 살려주어야 함.

② (4) Sure, / large hunted animals / such as mammoths /
물론 / 사냥된 큰 동물들은 / 매머드와 같은 /
provided protein and amino acids aplenty. 정답 단서
단백질과 아미노산을 많이 제공했다

✶중요 문장 (1)의 big game이 문장 (4)의 large hunted animals의 뜻을 다른 방법으로 표현한 것이니 이 두 문장이 이어진다는 것을 알 수 있음.

③ (1) However, / living off big game /
하지만 / 거대한 사냥감에 의지해서 산다는 것은 /
in the era before refrigeration / meant /
냉장 보관 전의 시대에서 / 의미했다 /
humans had to endure / alternating periods of feast and famine.
인간들이 견뎌야 했음을 / 번갈아 오는 성찬과 기근의 기간들을

(5) Droughts, forest fires, superstorms, and ice ages /
가뭄, 산불, 대폭풍, 그리고 빙하기는 /
led to long stretches of difficult conditions, /
~의 연속, 장기적인 ~
힘겨운 상황들의 연속으로 이어졌다 /
and starvation was a constant threat.
그리고 굶주림은 지속적인 위협이었다

④ (6) The human inability to synthesize /
S
합성하지 못하는 인간의 무능력은 /
such basic things as amino acids /
아미노산과 같은 그러한 기본적인 것들조차 /
certainly worsened those crises / and made surviving on /
V① V②
확실히 그러한 위기들을 악화시켰다 / 그리고 ~을 먹으며 목숨을 부지하는 것을 만들었다 /
whatever was available / that much harder.
구할 수 있는 것은 무엇이든지 / 그만큼 더 힘들게

힌트 여기서 that much harder는 'make A 형용사(A를 ~하게 만들다)'라는 5형식 용법에서의 목적격 보어임.

⑤ (7) During a famine, / it's not the lack of calories /
기근 동안에 / 칼로리의 부족이 아니다 /
that is the ultimate cause of death; /
사망의 근본적인 원인은 /
it's the lack of proteins and the essential amino acids /
단백질과 필수 아미노산의 부족이다 /
they provide.
그들이 제공하는

힌트 'it is A that ~'은 '~하는 것은 바로 A다'라는 의미의 강조 구문으로, 'it is'와 'that'을 제거하면 완전한 문장이 됨. 문장 (7)에서 'it's'와 'that'을 빼고 보면, 'The lack of calories is not the ultimate cause of death(칼로리의 부족은 사망의 근본적인 원인이 아니다)'가 됨.

[전문 해석]

(2)아미노산 결핍의 문제가 결코 현대 세계에 유일하지는 않다(현대 세계만의 고유한 문제는 아니다). ① (3)산업화 이전의 인류는 아마 정기적으로 단백질과 아미노산의 불충분에 대처(해야)했을 것이다. ② (4)물론 매머드와 같은 사냥된 큰 동물들(큰 사냥감들)은 단백질과 아미노산을 많이 제공했다. ③ (1)하지만 냉장 보관 전의 시대에서 거대한 사냥감에 의지해서 산다는 것은 인간들이 번갈아 오는 성찬과 기근의 기간들을 견뎌야 했음을 의미했다. (5)가뭄, 산불, 대폭풍, 그리고 빙하기는 힘겨운 상황들의 연속으로 이어졌으며, 굶주림은 지속적인 위협이었다. ④ (6)아미노산과 같은 그러한 기본적인 것들조차 합성하지 못하는 인간의 무능력은 확실히 그러한 위기들을 악화시켰으며 구할 수 있는 것은 무엇이든지 먹으며 목숨을 부지하는 것을 그만큼 더 힘들게 만들었다. ⑤ (7)기근 동안에, 사망의 근본적인 원인은 칼로리의 부족이 아니(었)다. 그들(동물들)이 제공하는 단백질과 필수 아미노산의 부족이(었)다.

- amino acid(아미노산): 대표적인 양성 전해질로서, 단백질을 구성하는 중요 성분
- protein(단백질): 몸에서 물 다음으로 많은 양을 차지하는 다양한 기관, 효소, 호르몬 등 신체를 이루는 주성분
- essential amino acid(필수 아미노산): 단백질의 기본 구성단위로 체내에서 합성할 수 없는 아미노산

[문제 풀이]

주어진 문장의 'big game(거대한 사냥감)'은 문장 (4)에서 언급된 'mammoths(매머드)'를 지칭한다. 또한, 매머드와 같은 큰 사냥감들로부터 부족한 아미노산을 공급받았다는 문장 (4)의 내용에 이어, 주어진 문장의 '하지만(however) 냉장 보관 기술이 없었던 시대에 거대한 사냥감을 사냥하는 것은 성찬과 기근의 반복이었다'는 전개는 자연스럽다. 따라서 주어진 문장이 ③에 들어가는 것이 가장 적절하다.

[오답 풀이]

⑤ - 거대한 사냥감에 의존하여 생존하는 것의 문제점을 설명하는 주어진 문장의 내용은, 인간이 아미노산을 합성하지 못하여 생존에 더욱 어려움을 겪었다는 내용과는 직접적인 연관성이 떨어지며, 산업화 이전 인류의 고달픈 생존기라는 점에서 두 문장의 공통점을 도출한다고 하더라도, 주어진 문장의 'however'은 대조를 나타내므로 문장 (6)과 주어진 문장을 잇기에는 부적절하다.

[중요 어휘]

□ acid	명사 산, 신맛이 나는 것 / 형용사 신맛이 나는
□ deficiency	명사 결핍, 부족
□ preindustrial	형용사 산업화 이전의
□ deal with	~에 대처하다, 해결하다 (deal-dealt-dealt)
□ insufficiency	명사 불충분, 부족
□ aplenty	부사 많이 / 형용사 많은
□ live off	~에 의지해서 살다
□ refrigeration	명사 냉장 (보관), 냉동 (보존)
□ endure	동사 견디다, 참다
□ alternating	형용사 번갈아 오는, 교차하는
□ famine	명사 기근, 굶주림
□ starvation	명사 굶주림, 기아
□ crisis	명사 위기 (복수형 crises)
□ survive on	~을 먹으며 목숨을 부지하다
□ ultimate	형용사 근본적인, 궁극적인

핵심 몸짓이나 목소리 톤과 같은 비언어적인 신호로 하는 의사소통에 대한 지문임. 주어진 문장을 알맞은 자리에 배치하기 위해서는 지시어 같은 단서들에 주목해야 함.

32 2020년 6월 39번 (정답률 35%) 정답 ①

[지문 끊어 읽기] 비언어적인 신호의 의사소통

(2) For hundreds of thousands of years /
수십만 년 동안 /
our hunter-gatherer ancestors could survive /
우리의 수렵-채집인 조상들은 살아남을 수 있었다 /
only by constantly communicating with one another /
오직 끊임없이 서로 의사소통을 함으로써 /
through nonverbal cues.
비언어적인 신호들을 통해

(3) Developed over so much time, / (분사구문)
아주 오랜 시간에 걸쳐 발달되면서 /
before the invention of language, / that is how /
언어의 발명 이전에 / 그렇게 하여 /
the human face became so expressive, /
인간의 표정은 매우 풍부해졌다 /
and gestures so elaborate. (=gestures became so elaborate)
그리고 몸짓은 매우 정교해졌다

힌트 'that is how S V'는 직역하면 '그것이 S가 V하게 된 방식이다'이지만, '그렇게 하여 S가 V하게 되었다(된 것이다)'라고 의역이 가능함. 예를 들어, 'That is how I gained weight!'는 '그렇게 해서 내가 살이 찌게 된 거야!' 정도로 해석할 수 있음.

① (1) We have a continual desire / to communicate our feelings /
우리는 끊임없는 욕구를 가지고 있다 / 우리의 감정을 전달하고자 하는 /
and yet at the same time / the need to conceal them / 정답 단서
그리고 그렇지만 동시에 / 그것들을 숨기기 위한 욕구를 /
for proper social functioning.
적절한 사회적 기능을 위해

(4) With these counterforces battling / inside us, / (정답 단서)
이 상충하는 힘들이 다투면서 / 우리 내면에서 /
we cannot completely control /
우리는 완전하게 제어할 수 없다 /
what we communicate.
우리가 전달하는 것을

힌트 'with + 명사 + 분사' 형태의 구문임. 일반적으로 분사 자리에는 명사와 분사 사이의 관계가 능동인지 수동인지에 따라 현재분사나 과거분사, 둘 중 하나가 들어가게 되는데, 여기서는 'battle(다투다, 싸우다)'이 자동사라 수동태가 불가능하기 때문에 현재분사 'battling'이 들어갔음.

② (5) Our real feelings continually leak out / in the form /
우리의 진실된 감정은 끊임없이 새어 나온다 / 형태로 /
of gestures, tones of voice, facial expressions, and posture.
몸짓, 목소리의 톤, 얼굴 표정, 그리고 자세의

③ (6) We are not trained, / however, / to pay attention /
우리는 훈련받지 않는다 / 그러나 / 주의를 기울이도록 /
to people's nonverbal cues.
사람들의 비언어적인 신호에

④ (7) By sheer habit, / we fixate on the words / people say, /
순전한 습관을 통해 / 우리는 단어에 집착한다 / 사람들이 말하는 /
while also thinking / about what we'll say next.
동시에 또한 생각한다 / 우리가 다음에 말할 것에 대해

⑤ (8) What this means is / that we are using /
(관계사절(단수 취급)) (접속사)
이것이 의미하는 바는 ~이다 / 우리가 사용하고 있다는 것 /
only a small percentage / of the potential social skills /
작은 부분만을 / 잠재적인 사회적 기술의 /
we all possess.
우리 모두가 소유한

[중요 구문]

힌트 밑줄 친 분사구문의 주어는 주절의 주어 'that'과 같고, 이 that은 문장 (2)의 'constantly communicating with one another through nonverbal cues'를 지칭하는 단수 대명사임.

(3) (Being) Developed over so much time, ~ , that(S) is(V) [how the human face(S'①) became(V'①) so expressive, and gestures(S'②) (became)(V'②) so elaborate]. [ ]: 명사절(O)

(8) What this means(명사절(S)) is(V) that we are using ~ of the potential social skills(선행사) [(that) we all possess]. [ ]: 목적격 관계대명사절

[전문 해석]

(2)수십만 년 동안 우리의 수렵-채집인 조상들은 오직 비언어적인 신호들을 통해 끊임없이 서로 의사소통을 함으로써 살아남을 수 있었다. (3)(비언어적인 신호들을 통한 끊임없는 의사소통은) 언어의 발명 이전에 아주 오랜 시간에 걸쳐 발달되었고, 그렇게 하여 인간의 표정은 매우 풍부해지고 몸짓은 매우 정교해졌다. ① (1)우리는 우리의 감정을 전달하고자 하는 끊임없는 욕구와, 그렇지만 동시에 적절한 사회적 기능을 위해 그것들을 숨기기 위한 욕구를 가지고 있다. (4)이 상충하는 힘들이 우리 내면에서 다투면서, 우리는 우리가 전달하는 것을 완전하게 제어할 수 없다. ② (5)우리의 진실된 감정은 몸짓, 목소리의 톤, 얼굴 표정, 그리고 자세의 형태로 끊임없이 새어 나온다. ③ (6)그러나 우리는 사람들의 비언어적인 신호에 주의를 기울이도록 훈련받지 않는다. ④ (7)순전한 습관을 통해 우리는 사람들이 말하는 단어에 집착하고, 동시에 또한 우리가 다음에 말할 것에 대해 생각한다. ⑤ (8)이것이 의미하는 바는 우리 모두가 소유한 잠재적인 사회적 기술의 작은 부분만을 우리가 사용하고 있다는 것이다.

[문제 풀이]

지문은 인간이 다양한 종류의 비언어적인 신호를 통해 의사소통을 해왔다는 것을 중심 내용으로 한다. 주어진 문장은 감정을 전달하려는 욕구와 감정을 숨겨야 하는 욕구가 동시에 존재한다고 하는데, 이것이 문장 (4)의 'these counterforces'에 해당하는 '상충하는 힘들'이라고 볼 수 있다. 따라서 글의 흐름상 주어진 문장은 ①에 오는 것이 가장 자연스럽다.

[오답 풀이]

② - 문장 (4)의 'these'는 가리키는 내용이 앞에서 이미 언급되어야 쓸 수 있는 지시형용사로, 주어진 문장인 문장 (1)이 문장 (4)의 뒤에 오게 되면 'these'가 지칭할 수 있는 대상이 없다. 따라서 ②는 정답이 될 수 없다.

[중요 어휘]

□ nonverbal	형용사 비언어적인
□ cue	명사 신호, 단서
□ elaborate	형용사 정교한, 정성을 들인
□ conceal	동사 숨기다, 감추다
□ proper	형용사 적절한, 제대로 된
□ counterforce	명사 상충하는 힘, 반대 세력
□ leak out	새어 나오다, 누출되다
□ posture	명사 자세, 태도
□ sheer	형용사 순전한, 완전한
□ fixate	동사 집착하다, ~을 고정시키다
□ potential	형용사 잠재적인, 가능성이 있는

핵심 일부 아프리카 부족의 음악은 악보 없이 즉흥적으로 연주되며, 그로부터 비롯되는 무작위성이 청중과 연주자에게 놀라움을 안겨준다는 내용의 글임. 맥락의 전환을 암시하는 부사인 rather가 힌트임.

33 2020년 9월 39번 (정답률 35%) 정답 ③

[지문 끊어 읽기] 아프리카 부족의 음악

(2) In the West, / an individual composer writes the music /
서양에서 / 개인 작곡가는 음악을 작곡한다 /
long before it is performed.
그것이 연주되기 오래 전에

정답과 해설 15 주어진 문장 위치 파악

(3) The patterns and melodies / we hear /
선행사 목적격 관계대명사절
패턴과 멜로디는 / 우리가 듣는 /
are pre-planned and intended.
V
사전에 계획되고 의도된다

① (4) Some African tribal music, / however, /
일부 아프리카 부족의 음악은 / 그러나 /
results from collaboration / by the players /
협연에서 비롯된다 / 연주자들의 /
on the spur of the moment.
즉흥적으로

② (5) The patterns heard, / whether they are the silences /
S 과거분사
들리는 패턴들은 / 그것들이 휴지이든 /
when all players rest on a beat / or the accented beats /
모든 연주자가 어느 한 박자에서 쉴 때의 / 아니면 강박이든 /
when all play together, / are not planned but serendipitous. 정답 단서
V S·C(not A but B)
모두가 함께 연주할 때의 / 계획된 것이 아니라 우연히 얻은 것이다

③ (1) When an overall silence appears / on beats 4 and 13, /
전반적인 휴지가 나타날 때 / 4박자와 13박자에 /
it is not because each musician is thinking, /
그것은 각각의 음악가가 생각하고 있기 때문이 아니다 /
"On beats 4 and 13, / I will rest."
4박자와 13박자에 / 나는 쉴 거야

(6) Rather, / it occurs randomly /
오히려 / 그것은 무작위로 발생한다 /
as the patterns of all the players converge /
접속사(~할 때) S' V'
모든 연주자의 패턴이 한데 모아질 때 /
upon a simultaneous rest. 정답 단서
동시의 휴식으로

④ (7) The musicians are probably as surprised / as their listeners /
감정형용사
음악가들도 아마 놀랄 것이다 / 그들의 청중만큼이나 /
to hear the silences / at beats 4 and 13.
부사적 용법-이유(~하고는, ~해서)
휴지를 듣고는 / 4박자와 13박자에

⑤ (8) Surely / that surprise is one of the joys /
한정사
확실히 / 그 놀라움은 기쁨 중 하나이다 /
tribal musicians experience / in making their music.
부족의 음악가들이 경험하는 / 그들의 음악을 연주할 때

[중요 구문]

힌트 'whether A or B(A이든 아니면 B이든)'에서 각각 A와 B에 해당하는 부분이 어디까지인지 확인할 것.

(5) The patterns heard, **whether** they are
S
[the silences (when ~)] **or** [the accented beats (when ~)],
[ ]: A [ ]: B
are not planned but serendipitous.
V S·C(not A but B)

[전문 해석]

(2)서양에서 개인 작곡가는 음악이 연주되기 오래 전에 그것을 작곡한다. (3)우리가 듣는 패턴과 멜로디는 사전에 계획되고 의도된다. ① (4)그러나 일부 아프리카 부족의 음악은 연주자들의 협연에서 즉흥적으로 비롯된다(창작된다). ② (5)들리는 패턴들은 (그것들이) 모든 연주자가 어느 한 박자에서 쉴 때의 휴지(休止)이든 아니면 모두가 함께 연주할 때의 강박이든, 계획된 것이 아니라 우연히 얻은 것이다. ③ (1)전반적인 휴지가 4박자와 13박자에 나타날 때, 그것은 각각의 음악가가 '나는 4박자와 13박자에 (연주를) 쉴 거야.'라고 생각하고 있기 때문이 아니다. (6)오히려, 그것은 모든 연주자의 패턴이 동시의 휴식으로 한데 모아질 때(모든 연주자들이 동시에 쉴 때) 무작위로 발생한다. ④ (7)음악가들도 아마 4박자와 13박자에 휴지를 듣고는 (그들의) 청중만큼이나 놀랄 것이다. ⑤ (8)확실히 그 놀라움은 부족의 음악가들이 (그들의) 음악을 연주할 때 경험하는 기쁨 중 하나이다.

[문제 풀이]

문장 (5)와 (6)은 모두 연주자의 패턴이 계획된 것이 아니라 무작위로 발생한 것이라고 한다. 연주자들이 언제 연주를 쉬어야 할지 미리 생각하고 연주를 쉬는 것이 아니라는 주어진 문장의 내용은 문장 (6)의 'rather'와 자연스럽게 이어지며, 문장 (6)의 'it' 또한 주어진 문장의 'overall silence'를 나타내는 것으로 보는 것이 타당하므로, 주어진 문장은 문장 (5)와 (6) 사이에 와야 한다. 따라서 정답은 ③이다.

[오답 풀이]

④ - 주어진 문장이 문장 (6)과 (7) 사이에 올 경우, 문장 (6)의 'Rather'로 인해 문장 (5)와 (6)의 연결이 부자연스러우므로, ④는 정답이 아니다.

[중요 어휘]

☐ **composer**	명사 작곡가
☐ **tribal**	형용사 부족의, 종족의
☐ **collaboration**	명사 협연, 공동 작업, 협력
☐ **on the spur of the moment**	즉흥적으로, 충동적으로
☐ **silence**	명사 휴지(休止), 침묵, 고요
☐ **accented**	형용사 강세가 있는
☐ **serendipitous**	형용사 우연히 얻은, 우연히 발견한
☐ **converge**	동사 (한데) 모아지다, 집중되다
☐ **simultaneous**	형용사 동시의, 동시에 일어나는

핵심 주어진 문장은 글의 흐름을 바꾸는 'But'을 포함하고 있으므로, 사람들이 가진 분류하고 일반화하려는 특성을 설명한 뒤, 그로 인해 문제가 발생할 수 있음을 서술하는 내용의 전환에 주의하여 문장 위치를 파악해야 함.

34 2021년 3월 39번 (정답률 35%) 정답 ③

[지문 끊어 읽기] 사람들의 분류하고 일반화하려는 특성

(2) Everyone automatically / categorizes and generalizes /
모든 사람들은 자동적으로 / 분류하고 일반화한다 /
all the time.
항상

(3) Unconsciously.
무의식적으로

(4) It is not a question / of being prejudiced or enlightened.
그것은 문제가 아니다 / 편견을 갖고 있다거나 계몽되어 있다는 것의

(5) Categories are absolutely necessary / for us to function.
의미상의 주어
범주는 반드시 필요하다 / 우리가 활동하는 데

① (6) They give structure / to our thoughts.
그것들은 체계를 준다 / 우리의 사고에

② (7) Imagine / if we saw every item and every scenario /
상상해 보라 / 만일 우리가 모든 품목과 모든 있을 법한 상황을 본다고 /
as truly unique / — we would not even have a language / 정답 단서
유일무이한 것으로 / 우리는 언어조차 갖지 못할 것이다 /
to describe the world around us.
우리 주변의 세계를 설명할

정답 단서
③ (1) But the necessary and useful instinct / to generalize /
그러나 필요하고 유용하기도 한 본능은 / 일반화하려는 /
can distort our world view.
우리의 세계관을 왜곡할 수 있다

(8) It can make / us mistakenly group together / 정답 단서
5형식V O O·C(동사원형)
그것은 만들 수 있다 / 우리가 하나로 잘못 묶게 /
things, or people, or countries / that are actually very different.
주격 관계대명사절
사물들이나, 사람들, 혹은 나라들을 / 실제로는 아주 다른

④ (9) It can make / us assume / everything or everyone /
S'
그것은 만들 수 있다 / 우리가 가정하게 / 모든 것이나 모든 사람이 /
in one category / is similar.
V'
하나의 범주 안에 있는 / 비슷하다고

⑤ (10) And, maybe, most unfortunate of all, / it can make us /
그리고 어쩌면 모든 것 중에서 가장 유감스러운 것은 / 그것이 우리로 하여금 만들 수 있다는 것이다 /
jump to conclusions / about a whole category /
성급하게 결론을 내리게 / 전체 범주에 대해 /
based on a few, or even just one, unusual example.
몇 가지, 또는 심지어 고작 하나의 특이한 사례를 바탕으로

[전문 해석]

(2)모든 사람들은 항상 자동적으로 분류하고 일반화한다. (3)무의식적으로 (그렇게 한다). (4)그것은 편견을 갖고 있다거나 계몽되어 있다는 것의 문제가 아니다. (5)범주는 우리가 (정상적으로) 활동하는 데 반드시 필요하다. ① (6)그것들은 우리의 사고에 체계를 준다. ② (7)만일 우리가 모든 품목과 모든 있을 법한 상황을 유일무이한 것으로 본다고 상상해보라. (그러면) 우리는 우리 주변의 세계를 설명할 언어조차 갖지 못할 것이다. ③ (1)그러나 필요하고 유용하기도 한 일반화하려는 본능은 우리의 세계관을 왜곡할 수 있다. (8)그것은 우리가 실제로는 아주 다른 사물들이나, 사람들, 혹은 나라들을 하나로 잘못 묶게 만들 수 있다. ④ (9)그것은 우리가 하나의 범주 안에 있는 모든 것이나 모든 사람이 비슷하다고 가정하게 만들 수 있다. ⑤ (10)그리고 어쩌면 모든 것 중에서 가장 유감스러운 것은, 그것이 우리로 하여금 몇 가지, 또는 심지어 고작 하나의 특이한 사례를 바탕으로 전체 범주에 대해 성급하게 결론을 내리게 만들 수 있다는 것이다.

[문제 풀이]

문장 (2)~(7)은 사람들은 무의식적으로 항상 분류하고 일반화하려는 특징이 있다고 말하며 그 현실적 필요성을 기술하고 있다. 한편, 문장 (8)~(10)은 이러한 일반화에서 발생할 수 있는 문제점들을 서술하고 있다. 따라서 필요하고 유용하기도 한 일반화의 본능이 우리의 세계관을 왜곡할 수도 있다는, 역접의 내용을 담은 주어진 문장은 내용의 전환이 필요한 문장 (7)과 (8) 사이인 ③에 위치해야 한다.

[오답 풀이]

④ - 문장 (1)과 (8)은 일반화하려는 본능이 문제가 있다는 같은 내용을 서술하고 있다. 그러나 문장 (1)에는 역접의 접속사 'But(그러나)'이 포함되어 있기 때문에 문장 (8) 뒤에 문장 (1)이 들어가면 문맥상 어색하다.

[중요 어휘]

□ categorize	동사 분류하다
□ generalize	동사 일반화하다
□ unconsciously	부사 무의식적으로
□ prejudiced	형용사 편견을 가진
□ enlightened	형용사 계몽된
□ function	동사 (제대로) 활동하다, 기능하다
□ instinct	명사 본능
□ distort	동사 왜곡하다
□ jump to a conclusion	성급하게 결론을 내리다

35 2023년 3월 38번 (정답률 30%) 정답 ②

[지문 끊어 읽기] 물고기의 전기적 의사소통

(2) Electric communication is mainly known / in fish.
전기적 의사소통은 주로 알려져 있다 / 물고기에서

(3) The electric signals are produced / in special electric organs.
전기 신호는 생성된다 / 특별한 전기 기관에서

(4) When the signal is discharged /
신호가 방출되면 /
the electric organ will be negatively loaded /
전기 기관은 음전하를 띨 것이다 /
compared to the head /
머리와 비교해서 /
and an electric field is created around the fish.
그리고 전기장이 물고기 주위에 생긴다

★중요 문장 (1)은 전기 기관과 일반 근육의 전류 강도를 비교하는 내용인데, ①에 문장 (1)이 위치하려면 ① 이전에 이미 일반 근육에서 발생하는 전류에 대한 언급이 있어야 함. 하지만 문장 (5)에서 이에 대한 언급이 나오므로, ①은 정답으로 적절하지 않음.

① (5) A weak electric current is created /
약한 전류가 발생한다 /
also in ordinary muscle cells / when they contract. 정답 단서
일반적인 근육 세포 안에서도 / 그것들이 수축할 때 (they =ordinary muscle cells)
정답 단서: 일반 근육에서도 약한 전류가 발생함.

② (1) [In the electric organ /
전기 기관 안에서 /
the muscle cells are connected / in larger chunks], / ([ ]: 선행사)
근육 세포는 연결된다 / 더 큰 덩어리로 /
which makes the total current intensity larger / (계속적 용법)
그리고 이것은 총 전류 강도를 더 크게 만든다 /

힌트 앞 문장 전체를 선행사로 가지는 계속적 용법의 관계대명사절의 동사이므로, 단수 동사가 사용되었음.

than in ordinary muscles. 정답 단서
일반 근육에서보다
정답 단서: 일반 근육에서보다 전기 기관 안의 근육 세포가 더 큰 전류를 발생시킴.

(6) The fish varies the signals / by changing /
물고기는 신호를 다양하게 한다 / 바꿈으로써 /
the form of the electric field or the frequency of discharging.
전기장의 형태 혹은 방출 주파수를

★중요 문장 (7)은 신호 체계의 작동 방식에 대한 설명으로, 문장 (6)에서 언급된 물고기의 신호 체계 내용 바로 다음에 나와야 흐름이 자연스러움. 따라서 문장 (1)은 ③에 들어갈 수 없음.

③ (7) The system is only working /
그 체계는 오직 작동한다 /
over small distances, / about one to two meters.
짧은 거리에서만 / 약 1~2미터 정도의

★중요 문장 (8)은 신호 체계를 사용하는 종들이 다른 종들과 무리를 지어서 산다는 내용으로, 문장 (1)의 내용에서 이어지는 것은 어색함.

④ (8) This is an advantage /
이것은 이점이다 /
since the species using the signal system / (S, 현재분사)
신호 체계를 사용하는 종들이 ~하기 때문이다 /
often live in large groups / with several other species. (V)
흔히 큰 무리를 지어서 살기 / 다른 여러 종들과 함께

★중요 문장 (9)는 많은 물고기가 동시에 신호를 보낼 때 그 신호의 범위가 짧으면 신호가 간섭을 받을 위험이 줄어든다고 함. 따라서 문장 (1)을 이곳에 위치시키면 흐름이 깨지므로 ⑤는 정답이 될 수 없음.

⑤ (9) If many fish send out signals / at the same time, /
만약 많은 물고기가 신호를 보내면 / 동시에 /
the short range decreases the risk of interference.
짧은 범위는 간섭의 위험을 줄여 준다

[전문 해석]

(2)전기적 의사소통은 주로 물고기에서(물고기가 한다고) 알려져 있다. (3)전기 신호는 특별한 전기 기관에서 생성된다. (4)신호가 방출되면 머리와 비교해서 전기 기관이 음전하를 띨 것이고 전기장이 물고기 주위에 생긴다. ① (5)일반적인 근육 세포가 수축할 때 약한 전류가 그 안에서도 발생한다. ② (1)전기 기관 안에서 근육 세포는 더 큰 덩어리로 연결되고, 이것은 일반 근육에서보다 총 전류 강도를 더 크게 만든다. (6)물고기는 전기장의 형태나 방출 주파수를 바꿈으로써 신호를 다양하게 한다. ③ (7)그 체계는 오직 약 1~2미터 정도의 짧은 거리에서만 작동한다. ④ (8)신호 체계를 사용하는 종들이 흔히 큰 무리를 지어서 다른 여러 종들과 함께 살기 때문에 이것은 이점이다. ⑤ (9)만약 많은 물고기가 동시에 신호를 보내면, 짧은 범위는 간섭의 위험을 줄여 준다.

[문제 풀이]

문장 (1)은 전기 기관 안에서 근육 세포가 더 큰 덩어리로 연결되어 있어 전류 강도가 일반 근육에서 발생하는 전류에 비해 크다고 이야기하고 있다. 따라서 문장 (1)이 말하는 전류 강도는 전기 기관에서 전류가 발생한다는 내용과 함께 일반 근육 세포에서도 전류가 발생한다는 내용 이후에 나와야 한다. 문장 (5)가 일반 근육 세포에서 발생하는 전류에 대해 언급을 했고, 이러한 내용을 바탕으로 문장 (1)이 ②에 들어가며 흐름이 자연스러워진다. 따라서 정답은 ②이다.

[오답 풀이]

④ - 문장 (1)은 전기 기관 안에서 근육 세포가 더 크게 연결되어 전류 강도를 더 크게 만든다는 내용이다. 그러나 문장 (1)이 ④에 위치하게 되면 바로 뒤에 이어지는 문장 (8)은 신호 체계를 사용하는 종들이 다른 여러 종과 살아서 이것(앞 문장의 내용)이 이점이 된다는 내용이므로, 문장 (1)과 자연스럽게 이어지지 못한다. 따라서 ④는 정답으로 적절하지 않다.

[중요 어휘]

□ electric	형용사 전기의, 전기를 이용하는
□ organ	명사 기관, 장기
□ discharge	동사 방출하다, 해고하다
□ negatively	부사 음전하로, 부정적으로
□ load	동사 (전하를) 띠다, 짐을 싣다
□ electric field	전기장
□ electric current	전류
□ contract	동사 수축하다, 줄어들다, 계약하다 / 명사 계약
□ chunk	명사 덩어리, 상당히 많은 양
□ intensity	명사 강도, 강렬함
□ frequency	명사 주파수, 빈도
□ range	명사 범위, 다양성 / 동사 범위가 ~에 이르다
□ interference	명사 간섭, 전파 방해, 개입

문제편 p.226

핵심 상대성 원리와 태도와 가치, 두 예시의 차이점이 무엇인지 파악할 것.

36 2019년 9월 39번 (정답률 15%) 정답 ①

[지문 끊어 읽기] 물리학의 상대성 원리

(2) In physics, / the principle of relativity requires /
물리학에서 / 상대성 원리는 요구한다 /
that all equations describing the laws of physics /
물리 법칙들을 설명하는 모든 방정식들이 /
have the same form /
동일한 형식을 가져야 한다고 /
regardless of inertial frames of reference.
관성좌표계에 상관없이

힌트 'require that S (should) V'가 적용된 문장으로, require, ask, demand와 같이 '요구하다, 요청하다' 종류의 동사들 다음에 that절이 오는 경우, that절의 동사에 '당위(~해야 한다)'의 의미가 있으면 동사 앞에 'should'가 생략된 것으로 볼 수 있음.

(3) The formulas should appear identical /
그 공식들은 동일하게 보여야 한다 /
to any two observers /
어떤 두 관찰자들에게든 /
and to the same observer / in a different time and space. 정답 단서
그리고 같은 관찰자에게든 / 다른 시공간에 있는

중요 누구에게나 그리고 심지어 다른 시공간에 있는 관찰자에게도 동일하게 보인다는 설명을 통해 상대성 원리의 공식들이 객관적임(objective)을 알 수 있음.

① (1) Attitudes and values, however, are subjective /
그러나 태도와 가치는 주관적이다 /
to begin with, / and therefore they are easily altered /
원래부터 / 그래서 그것들은 쉽게 바뀐다 /
to fit our ever-changing circumstances and goals.
늘 변화하는 우리의 상황들과 목표들에 맞추기 위해

(4) Thus, / the same task can be viewed /
따라서 / 동일한 일이 여겨질 수 있다 /
as boring one moment / and engaging the next. 정답 단서
한 순간에는 지루하게 / 그리고 그 다음에는 매력적으로

② (5) Divorce, unemployment, and cancer can seem devastating /
이혼, 실업, 그리고 암은 엄청나게 충격적으로 보일 수 있다 / 병렬①
to one person / but be perceived as an opportunity for growth /
병렬②
한 사람에게는 / 하지만 성장의 기회로 여겨질 수 있다 /
by another person, /
다른 한 사람에게는 /
depending on whether or not the person is married, employed, and healthy.
그 사람이 결혼했는지, 취직했는지, 그리고 건강한지에 따라

③ (6) It is not only beliefs, attitudes, and values / that are subjective.
it is ~ that 강조 구문
신념과 태도, 가치뿐만이 아니다 / 주관적인 것은

힌트 보통은 'not only A but also B(A뿐만 아니라 B도)'가 한 문장에 같이 오는데, 문장 (6)은 not only A에서 문장이 종결되었음. 하지만 문맥상 but also B에 해당하는 부분이 문장 (7)에서 소개되고 있는데, 즉, 신념, 태도, 가치에 이어 우리의 '인식(perceptions)' 역시 주관적임을 문맥을 통해 추론할 수 있음.

④ (7) Our brains comfortably change /
우리 뇌는 수월하게 바꾼다 / =easily alter
our perceptions of the physical world / to suit our needs.
물리적 세계에 대한 우리의 인식을 / 우리의 요구를 맞추기 위해서

⑤ (8) We will never see the same event and stimuli /
우리는 결코 동일한 사건과 자극을 보지 않을 것이다 /
in exactly the same way / at different times.
정확히 같은 방식으로 / 다른 시기에

[전문 해석]

(2)물리학에서 상대성 원리는 물리 법칙들을 설명하는 모든 방정식들이 관성좌표계에 상관없이 동일한 형식을 가져야 한다고(가질 것을) 요구한다. (3)그 공식들은 어떤 (서로 다른) 두 관찰자들에게든, (그리고) 다른 시공간에 있는 같은 관찰자에게든, 동일하게 보여야 한다. ① (1)그러나 태도와 가치는 원래(부터) 주관적이어서, 그것들은 늘 변화하는 우리의 상황들과 목표들에 맞추기 위해 쉽게 바뀐다. (4)따라서 동일한 일이 한 순간에는 지루하게, 그리고 그 다음 (순간)에는 매력적으로 여겨질 수 있다. ② (5)그 사람이 결혼했는지, 취직했는지, 그리고 건강한지에 따라, 이혼, 실업, 그리고 암은 한 사람에게는 엄청나게 충격적으로 보일 수 있지만 다른 한 사람에게는 성장의 기회로 여겨질 수 있다. ③ (6)주관적인 것은 신념과 태도, 가치뿐만이 아니다. ④ (7)우리 뇌는 우리의 요구를 맞추기 위해서 물리적 세계에 대한 우리의 인식을 수월하게 바꾼다. ⑤ (8)우리는 결코 동일한 사건과 자극을 다른 시기에 정확히 같은 방식으로 보지 않을 것이다.

[문제 풀이]

본문은 크게 '객관성(동일성)-주관성(변동 가능성)'이라는 두 가지 틀로 나누어 생각할 수 있다. 즉, 문장 (2)~(3)은 물리학에서의 방정식과 공식들의 동일성 및 일관성을 나타내는 반면, 문장 (4)~(8)은 모두 주관적이고 변화하는 것들에 대한 구체적인 설명에 해당한다. 그런데 주어진 문장은 역접의 접속 부사 however를 포함하고 있으므로, 주어진 문장은 글의 흐름이 '객관성 → 주관성'으로 변화하는 ①에 위치하는 것이 가장 자연스럽다.

[오답 풀이]

④ - 문장 (6)은 신념과 태도, 가치 이외에도 주관성을 띠는 것이 존재한다고 이야기하고 있으며, 문장 (7)은 우리의 인식이 우리의 요구에 따라 변화한다는 내용이다. 즉, 문장 (6)과 (7)은 모두 '주관성(변동 가능성)'에 대한 설명이기 때문에, 주어진 문장이 ④에 들어갈 경우 however의 연결이 매우 어색해지므로 보기 ④는 정답이 아니다.

[중요 어휘]

□ relativity	명사 상대성 (이론), 상호 의존성
□ equation	명사 방정식, 등식
□ inertial	형용사 관성의, 관성에 의한
□ formula	명사 공식, 제조법
□ identical	형용사 동일한
□ subjective	형용사 주관적인, 개인적인
□ alter	동사 바꾸다, 변하다
□ ever-changing	형용사 늘 변화하는
□ engaging	형용사 매력적인, 호감이 가는
□ devastating	형용사 엄청나게 충격적인, 파괴적인
□ perceive	동사 여기다, 감지하다
□ stimuli	명사 자극 (stimulus의 복수형)

37 2023년 11월 38번 (정답률 50%) 정답 ③

[지문 끊어 읽기] 서번트 리더십

(2) Introverted leaders do have to overcome the strong cultural presumption / 동사 강조
내향적인 리더들은 강력한 문화적 억측을 진정 극복해야 한다 /
=
[that extroverts are more effective leaders]. [ ]: 동격의 that절
외향적인 사람들이 더 유능한 리더라는

① (3) Although the population splits into almost equal parts /
비록 인구는 거의 동일한 비율로 나눠지만 /
between introverts and extroverts, /
내향적인 사람들과 외향적인 사람들 사이에서 /
more than 96 percent of managers and executives are extroverted.
관리자와 임원의 96퍼센트 이상이 외향적이다

중요 문장 (1)은 어떠한 고정 관념, 즉 글의 흐름으로 보아 내향성에 대한 고정 관념을 재검토해야 한다는 내용임. 따라서 ①에 문장 (1)이 위치하려면 ① 이전에 고정 관념이 언급되어야 함. 하지만 문장 (2)에서는 이에 대한 언급을 찾을 수 없으므로 ①은 정답으로 적절하지 않음.

힌트 '부분 표현+of+N'은 N에 수 일치함.

② (4) In a study done in 2006, /
2006년에 실시된 한 연구에서 /
65 percent of senior corporate executives viewed introversion /
기업 고위 임원의 65퍼센트가 내향성을 보았다 /
as a barrier to leadership. 정답 단서
리더십의 장애물로

중요 문장 (3)은 대부분의 관리자와 임원이 외향적이라는 이야기를, 문장 (4)는 과반수 이상의 기업 고위 임원들이 내향성이 리더십을 방해하는 요소라고 생각한다는 이야기를 하고 있으므로, 이는 내향성에 대한 고정 관념이라고 볼 수 있음. 고정 관념이 계속해서 언급되는 문장 (3)과 (4) 사이인 ②에 문장 (1)을 위치시켜 흐름을 깨는 것은 자연스럽지 않으므로 ②는 정답으로 적절하지 않음.

한 연구 결과에 따르면 기업 고위 임원의 과반수 이상이 내향성을 리더십의 장애물로 생각한다고 함.

③ (1) We must reexamine this stereotype, / however, /
=stereotype
우리는 이 고정 관념을 재검토해야 한다 / 하지만 /
as it doesn't always hold true.
~때문에
그것이 항상 맞는 건 아니기 때문에

(5) Regent University found /
Regent 대학교는 발견했다 /
[that a desire to be of service to others and to empower them to grow, /
접속사 S' 병렬①(형용사적 용법) 병렬②
다른 사람들에게 도움이 되고 그들이 성장할 수 있도록 능력을 부여하고자 하는 욕망이 /
which is more common among introverts than extroverts, /
주격 관계대명사(계속적 용법)
그리고 그것은 외향적인 사람들보다 내향적인 사람들 사이에서 더 흔하다 /
is a key factor in becoming a leader and retaining leadership]. [ ]: found의 목적어절
V' V-ing① V-ing②
리더가 되고 리더십을 유지하는 데에 핵심 요소이다

정답 단서 고정 관념과는 다르게 리더가 되고 그 리더십을 유지하는 데에 필요한 핵심 요소인 '다른 사람에게 도움이 되고 그가 성장할 수 있도록 능력을 부여하고자 하는 욕망'은 내향적인 사람들에게서 더 흔하게 나타남.

④ (6) So-called servant leadership, /
소위 서번트 리더십은 /
[dating back to ancient philosophical literature], / [ ]: 삽입구
고대 철학 문헌으로 거슬러 올라가는 /
adheres to the belief /
믿음을 고수한다 / =
[that a company's goals are best achieved /
회사의 목표가 가장 잘 달성된다는 /
by helping workers or customers achieve their goals]. [ ]: 동격의 that절
준사역V O O.C(동사원형)
근로자나 고객이 그들의 목표를 이루도록 도움으로써

⑤ (7) Such leaders do not seek attention /
V①
그런 리더들은 관심을 추구하지 않는다 /
but rather want to shine a light on others' wins and achievements; /
V②
오히려 다른 사람들의 승리와 업적에 빛을 비추고 싶어 한다 /
servant leadership requires humility, /
서번트 리더십은 겸손을 필요로 한다 /
but that humility ultimately pays off.
하지만 그 겸손은 궁극적으로 결실을 맺는다

✱중요 문장 (5)~(7)은 서번트 리더십이 무엇인지 이야기하고 있음. 고정 관념에 대한 언급이 있는 문장 (1)은 리더가 되고 리더십을 유지하는 데에 필요한 핵심 요소를 이야기하는 문장 (5)~(7) 이전에 위치하는 것이 적절함.

[전문 해석]

(2)내향적인 리더들은 외향적인 사람들이 더 유능한 리더라는 강력한 문화적 억측을 진정 극복해야 한다. ① (3)비록 인구는 내향적인 사람들과 외향적인 사람들 사이에서 거의 동일한 비율로 나뉘지만, 관리자와 임원의 96퍼센트 이상이 외향적이다. ② (4)2006년에 실시된 한 연구에서, 기업 고위 임원의 65퍼센트가 내향성을 리더십의 장애물로 보았다. ③ (1)하지만 그것이 항상 맞는 건 아니기 때문에, 우리는 이 고정 관념을 재검토해야 한다. (5)Regent 대학교는 다른 사람들에게 도움이 되고 그들이 성장할 수 있도록 능력을 부여하고자 하는 욕망이 리더가 되고 리더십을 유지하는 데에 핵심 요소이고, 그것은 외향적인 사람들보다 내향적인 사람들 사이에서 더 흔하다는 것을 발견했다. ④ (6)고대 철학 문헌으로 거슬러 올라가는 소위 서번트 리더십은 근로자나 고객이 그들의 목표를 이루도록 도움으로써 회사의 목표가 가장 잘 달성된다는 믿음을 고수한다. ⑤ (7)그런 리더들은 관심을 추구하지 않고 오히려 다른 사람들의 승리와 업적에 빛을 비추고 싶어 하고, 서번트 리더십은 겸손을 필요로 하지만 그 겸손은 궁극적으로 결실을 맺는다.

[문제 풀이]

문장 (1)은 however을 포함하면서 고정 관념이 언제나 맞는 말이 아니기에 그것을 재검토해야 한다고 이야기하고 있다. 따라서 문장 (1)이 말하는 고정 관념이 어떤 것인지를 파악하며 지문을 읽어야 한다. 문장 (3)은 관리자와 임원진의 96퍼센트가 외향적인 사람임을, 문장 (4)는 기업의 고위 임원의 65퍼센트가 내향성이 리더십을 방해하는 요소라고 생각한다는 연구 결과를 보여 준다. 그런데 문장 (5)는 리더가 되고 리더십을 유지하는 데에 필요한 핵심 요소가 외향적인 사람들보다 내향적인 사람들에게 더 흔하게 보인다고 말하며 고정 관념에 대한 시선의 전환이 있음을 보여 준다. 과반수의 사람들이 내향성은 장애물이라고 생각한다는 연구 결과를 이야기하는 문장 (4)는 고정 관념이 항상 맞는 것은 아니기에 재검토해야 한다는 문장 (1)의 내용과 자연스럽게 이어지고, 이러한 내용의 문장 (1)은 내향적인 사람들에게 오히려 리더십을 유지하는 데 필요한 핵심 요소가 더 흔하게 존재한다는 문장 (5)와 이어지므로 정답은 ③이다.

[중요 어휘]

□ **introverted**	형용사 내향적인, 내성적인
□ **presumption**	명사 억측, 추정
□ **extrovert**	명사 외향적인 사람
□ **population**	명사 인구, 주민
□ **split**	동사 나뉘다, 분열되다 / 명사 분열, 분화, 분할
□ **introvert**	명사 내향적인 사람
□ **executive**	명사 경영 간부, 경영진 / 형용사 경영의, 행정의
□ **extroverted**	형용사 외향적인, 사교적인
□ **corporate**	형용사 기업의, 법인의
□ **introversion**	명사 내향성
□ **barrier**	명사 장애물, 장벽
□ **reexamine**	동사 재검토하다, 재검사하다
□ **stereotype**	명사 고정 관념
□ **be of service to N**	~에게 도움이 되다
□ **empower**	동사 ~에게 (…하는 능력을) 부여하다, 할 수 있게 하다, 권한을 주다
□ **retain**	동사 유지하다, 보유하다
□ **adhere to N**	~을 고수하다
□ **humility**	명사 겸손, 겸양
□ **pay off**	결실을 맺다, 성공하다, 성과를 올리다

38 2023년 11월 39번 (정답률 45%) 정답 ④

[지문 끊어 읽기] 부정확성을 허용하는 것의 이점

(2) By the nineteenth century, / France had developed /
V①
19세기까지 / 프랑스는 개발했다 /
a system of precisely defined units of measurement /
정밀하게 규정된 측정 단위의 체계를 /
to capture space, time, and more, /
부사적 용법(목적)
공간, 시간, 그리고 더 많은 것을 포착하기 위해 /
and had begun to get other nations to adopt the same standards.
V② 명사적 용법(목적어)
그리고 다른 국가들이 동일한 기준을 채택하도록 만들기 시작했었다

힌트 'get'은 '~를 …하도록 만들다, ~를 …하도록 시키다'라는 의미로, 목적격 보어로 to부정사를 사용함.

① (3) Just half a century later, / in the 1920s, /
불과 반세기 후 / 1920년대에 /
the discoveries of quantum mechanics /
S
양자 역학의 발견은 /
forever destroyed the dream of comprehensive and perfect measurement.
V
포괄적이고 완벽한 측정에 대한 꿈을 영원히 깨 버렸다

② (4) And yet, / outside a relatively small circle of physicists, /
그러나 / 비교적 소수 집단의 물리학자를 제외하고는 /
[the mindset of humankind's drive to flawlessly measure] / [ ]: S
완벽하게 측정하려고 하는 인류의 추진 정신은 /
continued among engineers and scientists.
V
공학자와 과학자 사이에서 계속되었다

③ (5) In the world of business / it even expanded, /
=the mindset of ~ measure
비즈니스의 세계에서 / 그것은 심지어 확장되었다 /
as the precision-oriented sciences of mathematics and statistics /
정확성을 지향하는 수학과 통계학이라는 과학이 /
began to influence all areas of commerce. **정답 단서** 정확성의 추구가 다양한 영역에 영향을 미치며 확장됨.
상업의 모든 영역에 영향을 미치기 시작하면서

④ (1) However, / contrary to the trend of the past several decades, /
그러나 / 지난 수십 년간의 경향과 반대로 /
in many new situations that are occurring today, /
선행사 주격 관계대명사절
오늘날 발생하고 있는 많은 새로운 상황에서 /
allowing for imprecision / — for messiness — /
동명사S
부정확성을 허용하는 것은 / 즉 번잡함을 /
may be a positive feature, / not a shortcoming.
V
긍정적인 특성이 될 수도 있다 / 단점이 아니라

(6) As a tradeoff for relaxing the standards of allowable errors, /
허용되는 오류의 기준을 완화하는 것에 대한 교환으로 /
one can get a hold of much more data. **정답 단서** 더 많은 오류를 허용함으로써 더 많은 데이터를 얻을 수 있음.
비교급 강조
사람은 훨씬 더 많은 데이터를 입수할 수 있다

⑤ (7) It isn't just that "more is better than some," /
not just[only] A, but (also) B: A뿐만 아니라 B도
그것은 단순히 '더 많은 것이 조금보다 더 낫다'일뿐만 아니라 /
but that, in fact, sometimes "more is greater than better." **정답 단서** 더 많은 것이 더 좋은 것보다 더 훌륭하기도 함.
사실은 때때로 '더 많은 것이 더 좋은 것보다 더 훌륭하다'이기도 하다

문제편 p.228

[전문 해석]

(2)19세기까지, 프랑스는 공간, 시간, 그리고 더 많은 것을 포착하기 위해 정밀하게 규정된 측정 단위의 체계를 개발했고, 다른 국가들이 동일한 기준을 채택하도록 만들기 시작했었다. ① (3)불과 반세기 후, 1920년대에, 양자 역학의 발견은 포괄적이고 완벽한 측정에 대한 꿈을 영원히 깨 버렸다. ② (4)그러나, 비교적 소수 집단의 물리학자를 제외하고는, 완벽하게 측정하려고 하는 인류의 추진 정신은 공학자와 과학자 사이에서 계속되었다. ③ (5)정확성을 지향하는 수학과 통계학이라는 과학이 상업의 모든 영역에 영향을 미치기 시작하면서, 비즈니스의 세계에서 그것은 심지어 확장되었다. ④ (1)그러나, 지난 수십 년간의 경향과 반대로, 오늘날 발생하고 있는 많은 새로운 상황에서 부정확성 즉, 번잡함을 허용하는 것은 단점이 아니라 긍정적인 특성이 될 수도 있다. (6)허용되는 오류의 기준을 완화하는 것에 대한 교환으로서, 사람은 훨씬 더 많은 데이터를 입수할 수 있다. ⑤ (7)그것은 단순히 '더 많은 것이 조금보다 더 낫다'일뿐만 아니라, 사실은 때때로 '더 많은 것이 더 좋은 것보다 더 훌륭하다'이기도 하다.

[문제 풀이]

이 지문은 오늘날에는 정확하고 완벽한 측정보다 오류를 허용함으로써 더 많은 데이터를 얻는 것이 이득이 된다는 내용을 다루고 있다. 문장 (1)이 지난 수십 년간의 경향과 반대로 오늘날에는 부정확성이나 번잡함을 허용하는 것이 더 낫다는 내용이므로, 문장 (1) 이전에는 부정확성이 부정적으로 여겨졌던 경향과 관련된 내용이 오는 것이 적절하며, 문장 (1) 이후에는 오늘날 부정확성을 허용함으로써 얻게 되는 긍정적인 특성과 관련된 내용이 와야 한다. 문장 (3)에서 양자 역학의 발견으로 완벽한 측정이 불가능한 것으로 여겨지게 되었다는 언급 이후, 문장 (4), (5)에서는 그럼에도 불구하고 완벽한 측정을 추구하는 인류의 정신이 여전히 계속되었으며, 오히려 확장되었다는 내용을 다루고 있다. 반면, 문장 (6)에서는 더 많은 오류를 허용한다면 더 많은 데이터를 얻을 수 있다고 설명하며, 문장 (7)에서는 더 많은 것이 더 훌륭한 것이라고 언급한다. 따라서 문장 (5)까지는 부정확성을 기피하는 내용이 오는 반면, 문장 (6)부터는 부정확성의 긍정적인 점을 다루고 있으므로 맥락상 문장 (1)은 그 사이에 들어가는 것이 적절하다. 따라서 정답은 ④이다.

[오답 풀이]

③ - 문장 (1)은 종래의 경향과 반대로 부정확성, 번잡함을 허용하는 것이 긍정적인 특성이 될 수 있다는 내용이다. 만약 문장 (1)이 ③의 자리에 오는 경우, 그 이전 문장 (4)까지는 완벽한 측정을 추구하는 경향에 대해 다루고 있으므로, 문장 (1) 이후 이어지는 문장 (5)에서는 완벽한 측정이 아니라 부정확성을 허용하는 것의 이점과 관련된 내용이 나와야 한다. 그렇지만 문장 (5)는 정확성이 다양한 영역에 영향력을 끼친다는 내용으로, 여전히 완벽함을 추구하는 경향에 대해 다루고 있기 때문에 문장 (1)은 문장 (5) 이후에 위치하는 것이 적절하다. 따라서 ③은 오답이다.

[중요 어휘]

□ **measurement**	(명사) 측정, 측량
□ **capture**	(동사) 포착하다, 포획하다, 사로잡다
□ **adopt**	(동사) 채택하다, 입양하다
□ **standard**	(명사) 기준, 규범
□ **quantum mechanics**	양자 역학
□ **comprehensive**	(형용사) 포괄적인, 종합적인
□ **outside**	(전치사) ~을 제외하고, 빼고, 넘어서 / (명사) 바깥쪽
□ **drive**	(명사) 추진력, 투지 / (동사) ~하게 만들다
□ **flawlessly**	(부사) 완벽하게, 흠 없이
□ **oriented**	(형용사) ~을 지향하는
□ **commerce**	(명사) 상업, 무역
□ **shortcoming**	(명사) 단점, 결점
□ **tradeoff**	(명사) 교환, 거래

39 2024년 3월 38번 (정답률 50%) 정답 ③

[지문 끊어 읽기] 무리에서 벗어난 개체의 영향

(2) It is a common assumption /
형식상의 주어
일반적인 가정이다 /

[that most vagrant birds are ultimately doomed, /
[ ]: 내용상의 주어
무리에서 떨어져 헤매는 대부분의 새들은 궁극적으로 죽을 운명이다 /

aside from the rare cases /
드문 경우를 제외하고 / ↑ 선행사

[where individuals are able to reorientate /
개체들이 방향을 다시 잡을 수 있는 / 병렬①

and return to their normal ranges]].
병렬② [ ]: 관계부사절
그리고 자신들의 일반적인 범위로 돌아갈 수 있는

★중요 문장 (1)은 무리에서 떨어져 헤매는 개체가 생태계에 극적인 변화를 일으킬 수 있다는 내용임. 따라서 ①에 문장 (1)이 위치하려면 ① 이후에 어떤 변화를 일으키는지에 대한 언급이 있어야 함. 하지만 문장 (3)은 문장 (1)을 부정하는 내용이 나오므로 ①은 정답으로 적절하지 않음.

① (3) In turn, / it is also commonly assumed /
형식상의 주어
결국 / 일반적으로 여겨지기도 한다 /
강조 용법

[that vagrancy itself is a relatively unimportant biological phenomenon]. [ ]: 내용상의 주어
무리에서 떨어져 헤매는 것 자체가 상대적으로 중요하지 않은 생물학적 현상이라고

★중요 문장 (4)는 문장 (2)~(3)에서 언급한 일반적인 가정의 이유를 이야기하고 있음. 따라서 문장 (1)을 위치시켜 이러한 흐름을 깨는 것은 자연스럽지 않으므로 ②는 정답으로 적절하지 않음.

② (4) This is undoubtedly true /
이것은 의심할 여지 없이 사실이다 /

for the majority of cases, /
대부분의 경우에 /

as the most likely outcome of any given vagrancy event is /
이유
무리에서 떨어져 헤매는 어떤 경우든 가장 가능성이 있는 결과는 ~이기 때문이다 /

[that the individual will fail to find enough resources, /
[ ]: 주격 보어절 병렬①
개체가 충분한 자원을 찾는 데에 실패할 것이다 /

and/or be exposed to inhospitable environmental conditions, /
병렬②
그리고/또는 살기 힘든 환경적 조건에 노출된다 /

and perish]. 정답 단서 일반적으로 무리에서 떨어져 헤매는 개체는 생존하기 어려움.
병렬③
그리고 죽는다

③ (1) However, / there are many lines of evidence to suggest /
하지만 / 시사하는 많은 증거들이 있다 / 형용사적 용법

[that vagrancy can, / on rare occasions, /
S 삽입구
무리에서 떨어져 헤매는 것이 ~할 수 있다는 것을 / 드문 경우에 /

dramatically alter the fate /
V
운명을 극적으로 바꾼다 /

of populations, species or even whole ecosystems]. [ ]: suggest의 목적어절
개체 수, 종, 심지어 생태계 전체의

(5) Despite being infrequent, /
드물기는 하지만 /

these events can be extremely important /
이러한 경우들은 매우 중요할 수 있다 /

힌트 when 다음에 주절과 반복되는 주어인 they (=these events)와 동사 are이 생략된 부사절임.

when viewed at the timescales /
시간의 관점에서 볼 때 / ↑ 선행사

[over which ecological and evolutionary processes unfold]. 정답 단서
전치사+관계대명사(=관계부사)
생태학적이고 진화적인 과정이 진행되는

일반적인 관점과 다르게, 무리에서 떨어져 헤매는 개체가 생태학적이고 진화적인 시간의 관점에서는 매우 중요할 수 있음.

④ (6) The most profound consequences of vagrancy /
무리에서 떨어져 헤매는 것의 가장 중대한 결과는 /

relate to the establishment /
확보와 관련이 있다 /

of new breeding sites, new migration routes and wintering locations.
병렬① 병렬② 병렬③
새로운 번식지, 새 이동 경로 그리고 월동 장소

★중요 문장 (5)에서 언급된 'these events'에 대한 설명이 문장 (1)에 존재함. 따라서 문장 (1)이 ④, 혹은 ⑤에 오게 된다면 이야기의 흐름이 깨짐.

⑤ (7) Each of these can occur /
이들은 각각 발생할 수 있다 /

through different mechanisms, / and at different frequencies, /
병렬① 병렬②
다른 메커니즘을 통해 / 그리고 다른 빈도로 /

and they each have their own unique importance.
그리고 그들 각각은 자신의 고유한 중요성을 가진다

[전문 해석]

(2)무리에서 떨어져 헤매는 대부분의 새들은 개체들이 방향을 다시 잡고 자신들의 일반적인 범위로 돌아갈 수 있는 드문 경우를 제외하고, 궁극적으로 죽을 운명이라는 것이 일반적인 가정이다. ① (3)결국, 무리에서 떨어져 헤매는 것 자체가 상대적으로 중요하지 않은 생물학적 현상이라고 일반적으로 여겨지기도 한다. ② (4)이것은 의심할 여지 없이 대부분의 경우에 사실인데, 무리에서 떨어져 헤매는 어떤 경우든 가장 가능성이 있는 결과는 개체가 충분한 자원

을 찾는 데에 실패하고/하거나, 살기 힘든 환경적 조건에 노출되어 죽는 것이기 때문이다. ③ (1)하지만, 드문 경우에, 무리에서 떨어져 헤매는 것이 개체 수, 종, 심지어 생태계 전체의 운명을 극적으로 바꿀 수 있다는 것을 시사하는 많은 증거들이 있다. (5)드물기는 하지만, 이러한 경우들은 생태학적이고 진화적인 과정이 진행되는 시간의 관점에서 볼 때 매우 중요할 수 있다. ④ (6)무리에서 떨어져 헤매는 것의 가장 중대한 결과는 새로운 번식지, 새 이동 경로 그리고 월동 장소 확보와 관련이 있다. ⑤ (7)이들은 각각 다른 메커니즘 통해, 그리고 다른 빈도로 발생할 수 있고, 그들 각각은 자신의 고유한 중요성을 가진다.

[문제 풀이]

문장 (1)은 However로 시작하면서 무리에서 떨어져 헤매는 개체가 가지는 생태계적 영향에 대해 이야기하고 있다. 따라서, 문장 (1)이 말하는 증거가 어떤 것인지 파악하며 지문을 읽어야 한다. 문장 (2)~(4)는 무리에서 개체가 떨어져 헤매는 것의 일반적인 가정과 그 이유를 이야기하고 있다. 또한 문장 (5)~(6)은 무리에서 떨어져 헤매는 개체로 인해 중대한 결과를 낳는 경우를 보여 준다. 무리에서 떨어져 헤매는 것의 일반적인 결과를 설명하는 문장 (3)~(4)의 내용과, 드문 경우이지만 생태계에 극적으로 영향을 줄 수 있다며 반대의 경우를 언급하는 문장 (1)이 자연스럽게 이어지고, 이후 무리에서 떨어져 고립된 개체가 생태학적, 진화적 관점에서 바라보았을 때 중요할 수도 있다고 말하는 문장 (5)와도 이어지므로 정답은 ③이다.

[중요 어휘]

☐	**assumption**	명사 가정, 추정
☐	**doomed**	형용사 죽을 운명의, 불운한
☐	**reorientate**	동사 방향을 다시 잡다
☐	**undoubtedly**	부사 의심할 여지 없이
☐	**inhospitable**	형용사 살기 힘든, 황량한, 불친절한
☐	**perish**	동사 죽다, 소멸되다
☐	**infrequent**	형용사 드문, 흔하지 않은
☐	**timescale**	명사 시간, 기간
☐	**unfold**	동사 진행되다, 밝혀지다, 펼쳐지다
☐	**profound**	형용사 중대한, 중요한, 심오한
☐	**migration**	명사 이동, 이주

● 지문 구조도

무리에서 떨어져 헤매는 새에 대한 일반적인 가정(common assumption)

(2) 무리에서 떨어져 헤매는 새는 궁극적으로(ultimately) 죽을 운명임(be doomed).
(3) 무리에서 떨어져 헤매는 것 자체가 상대적으로 중요하지 않은 현상임.
이유: (4) 충분한 자원 확보의 실패, 살기 힘든(inhospitable) 환경적 조건에 노출되어 죽기(perish) 때문임.

↓

반박

(1) 무리에서 떨어져 헤매는 개체가 생태계에 극적인(dramatic) 영향을 미치기도 함.
(5) 생태학적(ecological)이고 진화적인(evolutionary) 관점에서 굉장히 중요한 역할을 할 수도 있음.

예시 및 설명

(6) 새로운 번식지(breeding sites) 확보(establishment), 새 이동 경로(migration routes) 확보, 월동 장소(wintering locations) 확보.
(7) 이는 서로 다른 메커니즘이나 다른 빈도로 발생할 수 있으며 각각 고유한 중요성을 가짐.

40 2024년 3월 39번 (정답률 30%) 정답 ②

[지문 끊어 읽기] 직관과 전문 지식의 연관성

(2) Intuition can be great, / but it ought to be hard-earned.
직관은 탁월할 수 있다 / 하지만 그것은 애써서 얻어야 한다

★ 중요 문장 (2)는 직관을 애써서 얻어야 한다는 내용이며, 문장 (3)은 이 내용의 연장선으로 어떻게 전문가들이 즉각적으로 생각할 수 있는지를 언급함. 문장 (1)은 전문가가 무엇을 바탕으로 행동하는지를 언급하는데, 문장 (1)이 ①에 들어가면 문장 (2)와 (3)의 흐름을 끊으므로, ①은 정답으로 적절하지 않음.

① (3) Experts, for example, /
예를 들어 전문가들은 /
are able to think on their feet /
즉각적으로 생각할 수 있다 /
because they've invested thousands of hours in learning and practice: /
그들이 학습과 실천에 수천 시간을 투자했기 때문에 /
their intuition has become data-driven. 정답단서
자신들의 직관이 데이터에서 얻어졌다
(정답단서: 전문가는 학습과 실천에 수천 시간을 쏟아서 데이터로부터 직관을 얻었기 때문에 즉각적인 생각이 가능함.)

② (1) Only then are they able to act quickly /
그래야만 그들이 빠르게 행동할 수 있다 /
(힌트: 한정사를 포함한 구 'Only then'이 문장의 맨 앞에 놓여서 주어와 be동사가 도치되었음.)
in accordance with their internalized expertise and evidence-based experience.
~에 따라서
내재화된 전문 지식과 증거에 기반한 경험에 따라서

(4) Yet most people are not experts, /
그러나 대부분의 사람들은 전문가가 아니다 /
though they often think they are. 정답단서
그들은 흔히 자신을 그렇다고 생각하지만
(정답단서: 그러나 실제로 대부분의 사람들은 전문가가 아니기 때문에 직관적으로 행동할 수 없음.)
(힌트: they are 앞에는 명사절 접속사 that이, 뒤에는 experts가 생략되었음.)

③ (5) Most of us, /
S
우리 중 대부분은 /
especially when we interact with others on social media, /
특히 우리가 소셜 미디어에서 다른 사람들과 소통할 때 /
act with expert-like speed and conviction, /
V
전문가와 같은 속도와 확신을 가지고 행동한다 /
[offering a wide range of opinions on global crises, /
국제적 위기에 대한 다양한 의견을 제시하며 /
without the substance of knowledge that supports it]. [ ]: 분사구문
그것을 뒷받침하는 지식의 실체 없이 (선행사, 주격 관계대명사절)

④ (6) And thanks to AI, / [which ensures /
(선행사, 계속적 용법)
그리고 인공 지능 덕분에 / 확실히 하는 /
[that our messages are delivered to an audience /
접속사
우리의 메시지가 독자에게 전달되도록 /
more inclined to believing it]], / [ ]: 주격 관계대명사절
그것을 믿으려는 성향이 더 있는 /
our delusions of expertise can be reinforced /
S V
전문 지식에 대한 우리의 착각이 강화될 수 있다 /
by our personal filter bubble.
개인적인 필터 버블에 의해
(힌트: ensures의 목적어절로, 'an audience'와 'more ~ it' 사이에는 「관계대명사+be동사」인 who is가 생략됨.)

⑤ (7) We have an interesting tendency /
우리는 흥미로운 경향을 가지고 있다 /
to find people more open-minded, rational, and sensible /
형용사적 용법, 5형식V O O.C
사람들을 더 개방적이고 합리적이며 분별 있다고 여기는 /
when they think just like us.
그들이 우리와 똑같이 생각할 때

[전문 해석]

(2)직관은 탁월할 수 있지만, 그것은 애써서 얻어야 한다. ① (3)예를 들어, 전문가들은 그들의 학습과 실천에 수천 시간을 투자했기 때문에, 즉 자신들의 직관이 데이터에서 얻어졌기 때문에 즉각적으로 생각할 수 있다. ② (1)그래야만 그들이 내재화된 전문 지식과 증거에 기반한 경험에 따라서 빠르게 행동할 수 있다. (4)그러나 대부분의 사람들은 흔히 자신을 그렇다고 생각하지만, 전문가가 아니다. ③ (5)우리 중 대부분은, 특히 우리가 소셜 미디어에서 다른 사람들과 소통할 때, 전문가와 같은 속도와 확신을 가지고 행동하며, 그것을 뒷받침하는 지식의 실체 없이 국제적 위기에 대한 다양한 의견을 제시한다. ④ (6)그리고 우리의 메시지가 그것을 믿으려는 성향이 더 있는 독자에게 전달되도록 확실히 하는 인공 지능 덕분에, 전문 지식에 대한 우리의 착각이 개인적인 필터 버블에 의해 강화될 수 있다. ⑤ (7)우리는 사람들이 우리와 똑같이 생각할 때 그들을 더 개방적이고 합리적이며 분별 있다고 여기는 흥미로운 경향을 가지고 있다.

- filter bubble(필터 버블): 인터넷 정보 제공자가 이용자 맞춤형 정보를 제공해 필터링된 정보만 이용자에게 도달하는 현상

[문제 풀이]

주어진 문장은 특정한 사람들이 전문 지식과 증거에 기반한 경험에 따라 행동할 수 있다는 내용이다. 또한 주어진 문장에 'they'가 있으므로, 'they'가 가리키는 대상이 무엇인지를 파악해야 한다. 문장 (2)는 직관은 쉽게 얻을 수 있는 것이 아님을 설명하며, 문장 (3)은 전문가들이 학습과 실천에 많은 시간을 쏟았기 때문에 데이터에서 직관이 얻어진 것임을 언급한다. 문장 (3)의 '학습과 실천'이 곧 주어진 문장인 문장 (1)에서 언급하는 '내재화된 전문 지식과 증거에 기반한 경험'과 연결되며, 여기서 'they'는 전문가들을 가리키는 것임을 알 수 있다. 또한 문장

문제편 p.229

(4)는 사람들 대부분이 전문가가 아님에도 자신을 전문가라고 생각한다는 내용으로 글의 흐름이 전환된다. 그렇기 때문에 주어진 문장이 문장 (4) 앞에 들어가야 이후의 글의 흐름이 전환되는 것이 자연스러우므로, 정답은 ②이다.

[오답 풀이]

③ - 내재화된 전문 지식과 경험은 전문가가 지닌 소양이다. 그러나 문장 (4)는 자신을 전문가라고 생각하는 사람들이 실제로 전문가가 아님을, 문장 (5)는 사람들이 소셜 미디어에서 지식에 근거하지 않고 마치 전문가인 것처럼 행동한다는 것을 지적한다. 이 두 문장은 비슷한 맥락을 가지고 있어 그 사이에 문장 (1)이 들어가면 'they'가 지칭하는 바가 마땅치 않고 흐름이 깨지므로 ③은 정답이 될 수 없다.

④ - 문장 (6)은 우리가 전문 지식을 가지고 있다고 생각하는 착각이 인공 지능과 필터 버블을 통해 강화될 수 있음을 언급한다. 바로 앞 문장인 문장 (5)는 사람들이 확실하지 않은 정보를 가지고 있으면서도 확신하는 태도를 보인다는 내용이므로 문장 (6)과 자연스럽게 이어진다. 따라서 문장 (1)이 이 사이에 들어가면 글의 흐름이 자연스럽지 못하므로 정답이 될 수 없다.

[중요 어휘]

□ intuition	명사 직관, 직감
□ hard-earned	형용사 애써서 얻은, 힘들게 얻은
□ expert	명사 전문가 / 형용사 전문가의
□ on one's feet	즉각적으로, 즉흥적으로
□ invest	동사 투자하다, 투입하다, 쏟다
□ practice	명사 실천, 연습
□ in accordance with	~에 따라서, ~에 부합되게
□ internalize	동사 내재화하다, 내면화하다
□ expertise	명사 전문 지식
□ conviction	명사 확신, 신념
□ substance	명사 실체, 본질, 물질
□ AI(=artificial intelligence)	명사 인공 지능
□ ensure	동사 확실히 하다, 보장하다
□ deliver	동사 전달하다, 배달하다
□ inclined	형용사 ~하는 성향이 있는, (~을) 하고 싶은
□ delusion	명사 착각, 망상
□ reinforce	동사 강화하다, 보강하다
□ tendency	명사 경향, 기질
□ open-minded	형용사 개방적인, 마음이 열린
□ rational	형용사 합리적인, 이성적인
□ sensible	형용사 분별 있는, 합리적인

41 2024년 6월 38번 (정답률 55%)

정답 ④

[지문 끊어 읽기]

인터넷의 유용성

(2) The Net differs / from most of the mass media it replaces /
선행사 / 목적격 관계대명사절
인터넷은 다르다 / 그것이 대체하는 대부분의 대중 매체와 /
in an obvious and very important way:
분명하고도 매우 중요한 방식으로

(3) it's bidirectional.
그것은 두 방향으로 작용한다

★중요 문장 (1)은 인터넷을 통해 기업과 개인의 연결뿐만 아니라 개인 대 개인의 연결 또한 가능하다는 내용임. 따라서 ①에 문장 (1)이 위치하려면 ① 이전에 개인과 기업 간의 연결에 대한 언급이 있어야 함. 하지만 문장 (2)~(3)에서 이에 대한 언급을 찾을 수 없으므로 ①은 정답으로 적절하지 않음.

① (4) We can send messages /
병렬①
우리는 메시지를 전송할 수 있다 /
through the network / as well as receive them, /
병렬②
네트워크를 통해서 / 그것들을 받을 수 있을 뿐만 아니라 /
which has made the system all the more useful.
주격 관계대명사(계속적 용법) V O O·C
그리고 이것은 그 시스템을 훨씬 더 유용하게 만들었다

② (5) The ability to exchange information online, /
S 병렬①(형용사적 용법)
온라인에서 정보를 교환하는 능력은 /
to upload as well as download, /
병렬②
다운로드뿐만 아니라 업로드하는 /
has turned the Net into a thoroughfare /
V
인터넷을 통로로 만들었다 /
for business and commerce.
기업과 상거래를 위한

★중요 문장 (5)~(6)은 기업과 상거래를 위한 인터넷 이용에 대해 이야기하고 있음. 따라서 문장 (1)을 위치시켜 이러한 흐름을 깨는 것은 자연스럽지 않으므로 ②, ③은 정답으로 적절하지 않음.

③ (6) With a few clicks, / people can search virtual catalogues, /
병렬①
몇 번의 클릭으로 / 사람들은 가상 카탈로그를 검색할 수 있다 /
place orders, / track shipments, / and update information /
병렬② 병렬③ 병렬④
주문을 할 수 있다 / 배송을 추적할 수 있다 / 그리고 정보를 업데이트할 수 있다 /
in corporate databases. 정답 단서 가상 카탈로그 검색, 주문, 배송 추적, 정보 업데이트 등 기업 및 상거래의 목적으로 인터넷을 이용할 수 있음.
기업의 데이터베이스에

④ (1) But the Net doesn't just connect us with businesses; /
하지만 인터넷은 우리를 단지 기업에 연결하는 것만은 아니다 /
it connects us with one another.
그것은 우리를 서로 연결한다

(7) It's a personal broadcasting medium /
그것은 개인 방송 매체이다 /
as well as a commercial one. 정답 단서 인터넷을 개인 매체로도 이용할 수 있음.
상업용 매체일 뿐만 아니라

★중요 개인 매체로의 인터넷 사용에 대한 이야기를 하는 문장 (7)은 그에 대한 예시를 이야기하는 문장 (8)이 이어지는 것이 자연스러우므로 문장 (1)은 오히려 문장 (6) 이후에 위치하는 것이 적절함. 따라서 ⑤는 정답으로 적절하지 않음.

⑤ (8) Millions of people use it /
수백만 명의 사람들이 그것을 이용한다 /
to distribute their own digital creations, /
부사적 용법
자신들만의 디지털 창작물을 배포하기 위해서 /
in the form of blogs, videos, photos, songs, and podcasts, /
블로그, 영상, 사진, 노래, 그리고 팟캐스트의 형식으로 /
as well as to critique, edit, or otherwise modify the creations of others.
병렬①(부사적 용법) 병렬②(to 생략) 병렬③(to 생략)
다른 사람들의 창작물을 비평하고 편집하거나 혹은 그렇지 않으면 수정하기 위해서 뿐만 아니라

힌트 문장 (5)와 (7), (8)은 'A뿐만 아니라 B도'라는 의미의 'B as well as A'의 구조를 취하고 있으며 'not only A but (also) B'의 형태로도 쓸 수 있음.

[전문 해석]

(2)인터넷은 그것이 대체하는 대부분의 대중 매체와 분명하고도 매우 중요한 방식으로 다르다. (3)그것은 두 방향으로 작용한다. ① (4)우리는 네트워크를 통해서 메시지를 받을 수 있을 뿐만 아니라 전송할 수 있고, 이것은 그 시스템을 훨씬 더 유용하게 만들었다. ② (5)온라인에서 정보를 교환하고, 다운로드뿐만 아니라 업로드하는 능력은 인터넷을 기업과 상거래를 위한 통로로 만들었다. ③ (6)몇 번의 클릭으로, 사람들은 가상 카탈로그를 검색하고, 주문을 하고, 배송을 추적하고, 기업의 데이터베이스에 정보를 업데이트할 수 있다. ④ (1)하지만 인터넷은 우리를 단지 기업에 연결하는 것만은 아니다. 그것은 우리를 서로 연결한다. (7)그것은 상업용 매체일 뿐만 아니라 개인 방송 매체이다. ⑤ (8)수백만 명의 사람들이 다른 사람들의 창작물을 비평하고 편집하거나, 혹은 그렇지 않으면 수정하기 위해서 뿐만 아니라, 블로그, 영상, 사진, 노래, 그리고 팟캐스트의 형식으로 자신들만의 디지털 창작물을 배포하기 위해서 그것을 이용한다.

[문제 풀이]

문장 (1)은 But으로 시작하면서 인터넷이 기업 대 개인의 연결뿐만 아니라 개인 대 개인의 연결 또한 가능하게 만든다는 내용이다. 따라서 문장 (1)이 말하는 개인 간의 연결이 무엇인지를 파악하며 지문을 읽어야 한다. 문장 (3)은 인터넷의 양방향적 작용을 언급하며 문장 (4)를 통해 그에 대한 예시를 든다. 문장 (5)~(6)은 기업과 개인 간의 연결에 대해 이야기하고 있다. 또한 문장 (7)은 개인 방송 매체로써 인터넷을 이용한다는 언급을 하면서 사람들이 인터넷을 통해 다양한 디지털 창작물을 창작, 비평, 수정, 배포한다는 문장 (8)로 예시를 보여 준다. 가상 카탈로그 검색, 상품 주문, 배송 추적, 기업 데이터베이스 업데이트 등 기업과 개인의 연결에 대한 구체적인 예시를 드는 문장 (6)은 기업과의 연결 외에도 개인 간의 연결 또한 가능하다는 문장 (1)의 내용과 대조를 이루며 자연스럽게 이어지고, 이러한 내용의 문장 (1)은 개인 방송 매체로써 이용되는 인터넷에 대해 이야기하는 문장 (7)과 이어지므로 정답은 ④이다.

[중요 어휘]

□ obvious	형용사 분명한, 명백한
□ bidirectional	형용사 두 방향으로 작용하는
□ thoroughfare	명사 통로, 주요[간선] 도로
□ commerce	명사 상거래, 무역, 상업
□ track	동사 추적하다 / 명사 길, 자국
□ shipment	명사 배송, 수송품, 적하물

☐ corporate	형용사 기업의, 법인의
☐ medium	명사 매체, 수단 (복수형 media)
☐ distribute	동사 배포하다, 분배하다
☐ modify	동사 수정하다, 바꾸다, 조정하다

42 2024년 6월 39번 (정답률 45%) 정답 ③

[지문 끊어 읽기] 자동화로 인한 노동의 변화

(2) Imagine /
상상해 보라 /
[that seven out of ten working Americans got fired tomorrow].
미국인 직장인 10명 중 7명이 내일 해고된다고
[ ]: 목적어절(Imagine의 목적어)

(3) What would they all do?
그들은 모두 무엇을 할까

(4) It's hard [to believe / you'd have an economy at all /
형식상의 주어 / 조금이라도
믿는 것은 어렵다 / 여러분이 조금이라도 경제를 가질 것이라고 /
if you gave pink slips / to more than half the labor force].
여러분이 해고 통지서를 보낸다면 / 노동력의 절반 이상에게
[ ]: 내용상의 주어

(5) But that is [what the industrial revolution did /
S V 목적격 관계대명사(선행사 포함)
하지만 그것은 산업혁명이 했던 것이다 /
to the workforce of the early 19th century]. [ ]: S·C
19세기 초 노동력에

(6) Two hundred years ago, /
200년 전 /
70 percent of American workers / lived on the farm.
미국 노동자의 70%는 / 농장에서 살았다

① (7) Today /
오늘날 /
✶중요 문장 (1)은 자동화로 새로운 일자리가 창출되었음을 언급함. 문장 (6)은 미국 노동자의 대부분이 농장에서 살았고, 문장 (7)은 기계가 거의 모든 일자리를 대체했다는 내용임. 이 사이에 문장 (1)이 들어가면 글의 흐름이 끊어지므로 ①은 정답으로 적절하지 않음.
automation has eliminated all but 1 percent of their jobs, /
자동화는 1%를 제외한 모든 일자리를 제거하였다 /
replacing them with machines.
분사구문
그것들을 기계로 대체하였다
✶중요 문장 (8)은 쫓겨난 노동자들이 어떤 선택을 했음을 암시하는 내용을 담고 있음. 이는 문장 (7)에서 자동화로 인해 인간 노동력이 대거 쫓겨났다는 내용과 긴밀하게 이어지므로, ②는 정답으로 적절하지 않음.

② (8) But the displaced workers / did not sit idle. 정답 단서 자동화로 인해 쫓겨난 노동자들은 가만히 있지 않았음.
하지만 쫓겨난 노동자들은 / 한가하게 앉아 있지 않았다

③ (1) Instead, / automation created hundreds of millions of jobs /
그 대신 / 자동화는 수억 개의 일자리를 창출했다 /
in entirely new fields.
완전히 새로운 분야에서

(9) Those who once farmed / were now manning the factories /
S, 선행사 주격 관계대명사절 V 선행사
한때 농사를 짓던 사람들은 / 이제 공장에서 일하고 있었다 /
[that manufactured farm equipment, cars, and other industrial products]. 정답 단서 농사를 지었던 사람들이 이제 공장에서 일하게 됨.
[ ]: 주격 관계대명사절
농기구, 자동차, 그리고 기타 산업 제품을 제조하는

④ (10) Since then, /
그 이후로 /
✶중요 문장 (10)은 자동화로 새로운 직업이 창출되었다는 내용임. 문장 (1)이 ④에 들어갈 경우, 문장 (9)에서 언급한 직업의 변화와 문장 (10)의 새로운 직업에 대한 내용으로 이어지는 흐름을 끊으므로 ④는 정답으로 적절하지 않음.
wave upon wave of new occupations have arrived /
새로운 직업의 물결이 연이어 등장했다 /
— appliance repair person, food chemist, photographer, web designer — /
가전제품 수리공, 식품 화학자, 사진작가, 웹 디자이너 /
each building on previous automation.
각각은 이전의 자동화를 기반으로 한다
힌트 each는 '각각의 새로운 직업'을 의미하는 대명사로, 이 부분은 with가 생략된 독립분사구문임.

⑤ (11) Today, /
오늘날 /
✶중요 문장 (11)은 현재의 직업은 1800년대에는 상상하지 못했던 일이 대부분임을 언급하는데, 이는 문장 (10)의 새로운 직업군이 등장한 맥락과 같음. 'Instead'로 새로운 화제를 제시하는 문장 (1)이 ⑤에 위치하면 글의 흐름이 깨지므로 ⑤는 정답으로 적절하지 않음.
the vast majority of us are doing jobs /
우리 중 대다수는 일을 하고 있다 / 선행사
[that no farmer from the 1800s could have imagined].
[ ]: 목적격 관계대명사절
1800년대의 농부들은 상상도 할 수 없었던
힌트 could have p.p.는 '~할 수도 있었을 텐데'라는 과거 상황에 대한 가정을 나타내는 표현임. 즉, 그 어떤 농부도 상상할 수 없었을 것이라는 가정을 나타냄.

[전문 해석]

(2)미국인 직장인 10명 중 7명이 내일 해고된다고 상상해 보라. (3)그들은 모두 무엇을 할까? (4)노동력의 절반 이상에게 여러분이 해고 통지서를 보낸다면, 여러분이 조금이라도 경제를 가질 것이라고(경제가 유지될 것이라고) 믿는 것은 어렵다. (5)하지만 그것은 19세기 초 노동력에 산업혁명이 했던 것이다. (6)200년 전, 미국 노동자의 70%는 농장에서 살았다. ① (7)오늘날 자동화는 1%를 제외한 모든 일자리를 제거하였고, 그것들을 기계로 대체하였다. ② (8)하지만 쫓겨난 노동자들은 한가하게 앉아 있지 않았다. ③ (1)그 대신 자동화는 완전히 새로운 분야에서 수억 개의 일자리를 창출했다. (9)한때 농사를 짓던 사람들은 이제 농기구, 자동차, 그리고 기타 산업 제품을 제조하는 공장에서 일하고 있었다. ④ (10)그 이후로, 가전제품 수리공, 식품 화학자, 사진작가, 웹 디자이너 등 새로운 직업의 물결이 연이어 등장했는데, 각각(의 직업)은 이전의 자동화를 기반으로 한다. ⑤ (11)오늘날 우리 중 대다수는 1800년대의 농부들은 상상도 할 수 없었던 일을 하고 있다.

[문제 풀이]

주어진 문장 (1)은 자동화로 새로운 일자리가 창출되었다는 내용을 담고 있는데, 'Instead'로 시작하기 때문에 앞의 내용에서 전환이 있음을 알 수 있다. 지문 앞 부분에서 갑자기 직장인 반 이상이 해고되는 상황에 경제가 제대로 돌아갈지 상상해 보라고 한 뒤, 문장 (5)부터는 19세기 산업혁명 당시 이런 상황이 실제로 벌어졌다고 하면서 구체적으로 내용을 전개한다. 당시 농장에서 살던 대다수 노동자들이 자동화 때문에 기계로 대체되면서 일자리가 없어졌다는 것이 문장 (6)~(7)의 내용이다. 그런데 문장 (8)에서 쫓겨난 노동자들은 가만히 있지 않았다고 하고, 문장 (9) 이후로는 공장을 비롯하여 자동화를 기반으로 한 새로운 직업에서 일하게 되었다고 한다. 따라서 없어진 일자리 대신 자동화로 인한 새로운 일자리가 생겨났다는 문장 (1)이 ③에 들어가야 글의 흐름이 자연스러워진다.

[오답 풀이]

④ - 문장 (9)는 농민들이 공장에서 일하게 되었고, 문장 (10)은 자동화를 기반으로 새로운 직업이 등장했다는 내용을 언급한다. 이 두 문장은 사람들이 자동화로 인해 새로운 직업을 갖게 되었다는 흐름으로 이어지므로, 이 사이에 문장 (1)을 넣으면 그 흐름이 깨진다. 새로운 일자리가 창출되었다는 내용의 문장 (1)이 오히려 문장 (9)보다 앞에 나와야 글의 흐름이 자연스러우므로, ④는 정답이 될 수 없다.

[중요 어휘]

☐ fire	동사 해고하다
☐ pink slip	해고 통지서
☐ labor force	노동력
☐ the industrial revolution	산업혁명
☐ workforce	명사 노동력, 노동자
☐ automation	명사 자동화
☐ eliminate	동사 제거하다, 없애다
☐ replace	동사 대체[대신]하다, 제자리에 놓다
☐ displaced	형용사 쫓겨난, 추방된
☐ idle	형용사 한가한, 나태한
☐ farm	동사 농사를 짓다, (동물을) 기르다 / 명사 농장
☐ man	동사 (어떤 장소에서) 일하다, ~에 인원을 배치하다
☐ manufacture	동사 제조하다, 생산하다
☐ occupation	명사 직업, 점령 (기간)
☐ appliance	명사 가전제품
☐ chemist	명사 화학자

43 2024년 9월 38번 (정답률 65%) 정답 ②

[지문 끊어 읽기] 바이러스성 전염과 행동의 전염

(2) There are deep similarities /
깊은 유사성이 있다 /
between viral contagion and behavioral contagion.
바이러스성 전염과 행동의 전염 사이에

문제편 p.230

①(3) For example, / [people in close or extended proximity /
예를 들어 / 아주 가깝게 있거나 어느 정도 근접해 있는 사람들은 /
to others infected by a virus] / [ ]: S
과거분사구
바이러스에 감염된 다른 사람들과 /
are themselves more likely to become infected, /
V 강조 용법
자신들도 감염될 가능성이 더 높다 /
just as people are more likely to drink excessively /
사람들이 술을 과도하게 많이 마실 가능성이 높은 것과 마찬가지이다 /
when they spend more time in the company of heavy drinkers.
그들이 술을 많이 마시는 사람들과 함께 시간을 많이 보낼 때

★중요 문장 (1)은 But으로 시작하며 바이러스성 전염과 행동의 전염 사이에 중요한 차이점이 있다는 내용임. 따라서 ①에 문장 (1)이 위치하려면 ① 이전에 두 종류의 전염의 유사성에 대한 설명이 선행되어야 함. 문장 (2)부터 (3)까지는 계속해서 유사성에 대한 설명을 하고 있으므로 ①이 그 사이에 들어가면 흐름을 막기 때문에 정답으로 적절하지 않음.

②(1) But there are also important differences /
하지만 중요한 차이점들도 있다 /
between the two types of contagion.
두 종류의 전염 사이에

(4) One is / [that visibility promotes behavioral contagion /
V'①
첫 번째는 ~이다 / 가시성이 행동의 전염을 촉진한다는 것이다 /
but inhibits the spread of infectious diseases]. 정답단서 첫 번째 차이점으로 가시성이 행동의 전염을 촉진하고 감염성 질병의 확산은 막는다고 설명함.
V'② [ ]: 보어(명사절)
하지만 감염성 질병의 확산은 막는다

③(5) Solar panels / that are visible from the street, / for instance, /
S, 선행사 주격 관계대명사절
태양 전지판은 / 거리에서 볼 수 있는 / 예를 들어 /
are more likely to stimulate neighboring installations.
V
이웃의 설치를 자극할 가능성이 더 높다

★중요 문장 (4)~(6)은 가시성이 행동의 전염은 촉진하고 감염성 질병의 확산은 막는다는 점을 예시를 들어 이야기하고 있음. 따라서 문장 (1)을 위치시켜 흐름을 깨는 것은 자연스럽지 않으므로 ③, ④는 정답으로 적절하지 않음.

④(6) In contrast, / we try to avoid others /
선행사
대조적으로 / 우리는 다른 사람들을 피하려고 노력한다 /
who are visibly ill.
주격 관계대명사절
눈에 띄게 아픈

★중요 또 다른 중요한 차이가 있음을 언급하면서 문장 (4)~(6)의 흐름을 이어받고 있으므로 문장 (1)이 ⑤에 위치한다면 흐름이 깨짐. 따라서 ⑤는 정답으로 적절하지 않음.

⑤(7) Another important difference is /
또 다른 중요한 차이는 ~이다 /
[that whereas viral contagion is almost always a bad thing, /
바이러스성 전염이 거의 항상 나쁜 것인 반면에 /
behavioral contagion is sometimes negative /
병렬①
행동의 전염은 때때로 부정적이다 /
— as in the case of smoking — / but sometimes positive, /
병렬②
흡연의 경우와 같이 / 하지만 때때로 긍정적이다 /
as in the case of solar installations]. 정답단서 바이러스성 전염은 항상 부정적인 반면에, 행동의 전염은 때에 따라 부정적일 수도, 긍정적일 수도 있다는 차이점을 지님.
[ ]: 보어(명사절)
태양 전지판 설치의 경우와 같이

[전문 해석]

(2)바이러스성 전염과 행동의 전염 사이에 깊은 유사성이 있다. ① (3)예를 들어, 바이러스에 감염된 다른 사람들과 아주 가깝게 있거나 어느 정도 근접해 있는 사람들은 자신들도 감염될 가능성이 더 높은데, 이는 사람들이 술을 많이 마시는 사람들과 함께 시간을 많이 보낼 때 술을 과도하게 많이 마실 가능성이 높은 것과 마찬가지이다. ② (1)하지만 두 종류의 전염 사이에 중요한 차이점들도 있다. (4)첫 번째는 가시성이 행동의 전염을 촉진하지만 감염성 질병의 확산은 막는다는 것이다. ③ (5)예를 들어, 거리에서 볼 수 있는 태양 전지판은 이웃의 설치를 자극할 가능성이 더 높다. ④ (6)대조적으로, 우리는 눈에 띄게 아픈 다른 사람들을 피하려고 노력한다. ⑤ (7)또 다른 중요한 차이는 바이러스성 전염이 거의 항상 나쁜 것인 반면에 행동의 전염은 흡연의 경우와 같이 때때로 부정적이지만 태양 전지판 설치의 경우와 같이 때때로 긍정적이라는 것이다.

[문제 풀이]

문장 (1)은 바이러스성 전염과 행동의 전염 사이에 중요한 차이점이 있다고 이야기한다. 따라서 문장 (1)이 말하는 차이점이 무엇인지를 파악하며 지문을 읽어야 한다. 문장 (3)은 두 종류의 전염 모두 거리가 가까울수록 감염될 확률이 높아진다는 이야기를 하고 있는 한편, 문장 (4)~(7)은 두 종류의 전염을 가시성과 부정적/긍정적 성격이라는 두 가지 기준으로 대조하여 보여 준다. 바이러스성 전염과 행동의 전염 사이에는 차이점이 있다는 문장 (1)의 내용은 But으로 시작하므로 차이점 이전에 두 종류의 전염의 유사성을 설명하는 문장 (2)~(3)이 선행하는 것이 적절하고, 문장 (1) 다음으로 두 전염의 차이점에 대한 설명을 시작하는 (4)가 이어지는 것이 자연스럽다. 따라서 정답은 ②이다.

[중요 어휘]

☐ contagion	명사	전염, 감염
☐ viral	형용사	바이러스성의
☐ proximity	명사	가까움, 근접
☐ excessively	부사	과도하게
☐ in the company of		~와 함께
☐ inhibit	동사	막다, 억제하다
☐ stimulate	동사	자극하다, 촉진시키다
☐ installation	명사	설치, 설비
☐ whereas	접속사	반면에

44 2024년 9월 39번 (정답률 70%) 정답 ④

[지문 끊어 읽기] 동면, 수면, 휴면의 구분

(2) Sleep is clearly about more than just resting.
수면은 분명 단지 휴식하는 것 이상이다

(3) One curious fact is / [that animals that are hibernating /
S V S', 선행사 주격 관계대명사절
한 가지 호기심을 끄는 사실은 ~이다 / 동면하고 있는 동물들은 /
also have periods of sleep]. [ ]: 보어(명사절)
V'
또한 수면 기간을 가진다

★중요 밑줄 친 it은 앞 문장의 '동면하고 있는 동물들이 수면 기간을 가지는 것'을 가리킴.

(4) It comes as a surprise to most of us, /
그것은 우리 대부분에게 놀라움으로 다가온다 /
but hibernation and sleep are not the same thing at all, /
하지만 동면과 수면은 전혀 같은 것이 아니다 / 전혀 ~이 아닌
at least not from a neurological and metabolic perspective.
적어도 신경학적이고 신진대사적인 관점에서는 아니다

힌트 「at least (they are) not (the same thing) from ~」에서 중복을 피하기 위해 괄호 부분이 생략된 것임.

①(5) Hibernating is more like being anesthetized: /
동면은 마취되는 것과 더 비슷하다 /
the subject is unconscious / but not actually asleep.
병렬① 병렬②
그 대상은 의식이 없다 / 하지만 실제로 잠들어 있지는 않다

②(6) So a hibernating animal /
그래서 동면하고 있는 동물들은 /
needs to get a few hours of conventional sleep each day /
매일 몇 시간의 전형적인 잠을 잘 필요가 있다 /
within the larger unconsciousness.
더 큰 무의식 속에서

③(7) A further surprise to most of us is /
우리 대부분에게 더욱 놀라운 점은 ~이다 /
[that bears, the most famous of wintry sleepers, /
=
겨울잠을 자는 동물들 중 가장 유명한 동물인 곰이 /
don't actually hibernate]. [ ]: 보어(명사절)
실제로는 동면하지 않는다

힌트 'wintry'는 '겨울의, 겨울 같은'이라는 뜻의 형용사로서, 'wintry sleeper'는 흔히 '겨울잠을 자는 동물'이라는 의미를 가짐.

④(1) Real hibernation involves /
실제 동면은 수반한다 /
profound unconsciousness and a dramatic fall
O① O②
in body temperature /
전치사구
깊은 무의식과 체온의 급격한 하락을 /
— often to around 32 degrees Fahrenheit.
종종 약 화씨 32도까지로의

(8) By this definition, / bears don't hibernate, /
이러한 정의에 따르면 / 곰은 동면하지 않는다 /
because their body temperature stays near normal /
왜냐하면 그들의 체온이 정상 근처를 유지하기 때문이다 /
and they are easily awakened. 정답단서 실제 동면을 깊은 무의식과 체온의 급격한 하락을 수반하는 것으로 정의할 때, 곰은 체온이 정상 근처를 유지(=체온이 급격히 하락하지 않음)하고 쉽게 잠에서 깨어나기(=깊은 무의식 상태에 들어가지 않음) 때문에 동면한다고 볼 수 없음.
그리고 그들이 쉽게 잠에서 깨어나기 때문이다

★중요 문맥상 밑줄 친 'this definition'은 '실제 동면은 깊은 무의식과 체온의 급격한 하락을 수반한다'는 문장 (1)의 내용을 나타냄.

⑤(9) Their winter sleeps /
그들의 겨울잠은 /

are more accurately called a state of torpor.
더 정확하게는 휴면 상태라고 불린다

힌트 이 문장은 5형식 동사 call이 쓰인「call A B(A를 B라고 부르다)」가 수동태 구조로 전환된 문장임. 능동태 문장에서 목적어인 A(=their winter sleeps)가 수동태 문장의 주어가 되었고, 목적격 보어인 B(=a state of torpor)는 동사구 'are ~ called' 바로 다음에 위치한 것을 확인할 수 있음.

[전문 해석]

(2)수면은 분명 단지 휴식하는 것 이상이다. (3)한 가지 호기심을 끄는 사실은 동면하고 있는 동물들은 또한 수면 기간을 가진다는 것이다. (4)그것은 우리 대부분에게 놀라움으로 다가오지만, 동면과 수면은 전혀 같은 것이 아닌데, 적어도 신경학적이고 신진대사적인 관점에서는 아니다. ① (5)동면은 마취되는 것과 더 비슷하다. 즉 그 대상은 의식이 없지만 실제로 잠들어 있지는 않다. ② (6)그래서 동면하고 있는 동물들은 매일 더 큰 무의식 속에서 몇 시간의 전형적인 잠을 잘 필요가 있다. ③ (7)우리 대부분에게 더욱 놀라운 점은 겨울잠을 자는 동물들 중 가장 유명한 동물인 곰이 실제로는 동면하지 않는다는 것이다. ④ (1)실제 동면은 깊은 무의식과 종종 약 화씨 32도까지로의 체온의 급격한 하락을 수반한다. (8)이러한 정의에 따르면, 곰은 동면하지 않는데, 왜냐하면 그들의 체온이 정상 근처를 유지하고 그들이 쉽게 잠에서 깨어나기 때문이다. ⑤ (9)그들의 겨울잠은 더 정확하게는 휴면 상태라고 불린다.

[문제 풀이]

주어진 문장은 실제 동면이 깊은 무의식과 체온의 급격한 하락을 수반한다는 내용이다. 한편, 문장 (7)~(8)은 겨울잠을 자는 것으로 가장 유명한 동물인 곰이 '체온이 정상 근처를 유지하고 쉽게 잠에서 깨어나기 때문에 동면하는 것이 아니다'라고 설명하는데, '체온이 정상 근처를 유지한다'라는 것은 문장 (1)에서 말한 '체온의 급격한 하락'에 반하는 상황이고, '쉽게 잠에서 깨어난다'는 것 또한 문장 (1)에서 말한 '깊은 무의식'에 반하는 상황이기 때문에, 문장 (8)은 문장 (1)에서 말하는 동면에 관한 정의를 바탕으로 '곰은 동면하지 않는다'라는 결론을 내렸음을 알 수 있다. 즉, 문장 (8)의 '이러한 정의'는 문장 (1)의 내용을 나타내므로, 주어진 문장이 들어가기에 가장 적절한 곳은 ④이다.

[중요 어휘]

☐ curious	형용사 호기심을 끄는, 이상한
☐ hibernate	동사 동면하다, 칩거하다
☐ hibernation	명사 동면
☐ neurological	형용사 신경학적인
☐ metabolic	형용사 신진대사적인
☐ anesthetize	동사 마취시키다, 마비시키다
☐ subject	명사 대상, 과목, 국민 / 형용사 ~될 수 있는, 종속된
☐ unconscious	형용사 의식이 없는, 무의식의
☐ conventional	형용사 전형적인, 틀에 박힌
☐ unconsciousness	명사 무의식, 인사불성
☐ involve	동사 수반하다, 포함하다
☐ profound	형용사 깊은, 심오한
☐ dramatic	형용사 급격한, 극적인
☐ fall	명사 하락, 추락
☐ temperature	명사 온도, 기온
☐ degree	명사 (온도의 단위인) 도
☐ Fahrenheit	형용사 화씨의
☐ definition	명사 정의, 의미, 선명도
☐ awaken	동사 (잠에서) 깨우다
☐ accurately	부사 정확하게
☐ state	명사 상태, 양상
☐ torpor	명사 휴면 (상태), 무기력

문제편 p.233

16 문단 요약

01 2021년 9월 40번 (정답률 80%) 정답 ②

[지문 끊어 읽기] 음악과 직원들의 협동심 간의 관계

(1) Music is used / to mold customer experience and behavior.
음악은 사용된다 / 고객의 경험과 행동을 형성하는 데

(2) A study was conducted /
선행사
연구가 수행되었다 /
that explored what impact it has on employees.
주격 관계대명사 =music
그것이 직원들에게 어떤 영향을 미치는지를 탐구하는

(3) Results from the study indicate /
연구 결과는 나타낸다 /
that participants who listen to rhythmic music /
선행사 주격 관계대명사
리듬감 있는 음악을 듣는 참가자들이 / 정답 단서
were inclined to cooperate more /
더 협력하는 경향이 있다는 것을 /
irrespective of factors like age, gender, and academic background, /
나이, 성별, 학력과 같은 요인들과 관계없이 /
compared to those who listened to less rhythmic music.
선행사 주격 관계대명사
리듬감이 덜한 음악을 들은 참가자들에 비해

(4) This positive boost / in the participants' willingness to cooperate /
이러한 긍정적인 촉진제는 / 참가자들의 협력하고자 하는 자발성의 /
was induced / regardless of whether they liked the music or not.
야기되었다 / 그들이 그 음악을 좋아했는지 그렇지 않았는지와 무관하게

(5) When people are in a more positive state of mind, /
사람들이 더 긍정적인 심리 상태에 있을 때 /
they tend to become more agreeable and creative, /
그들은 더 쾌활하고 창의적이 되는 경향이 있다 /
while those on the opposite spectrum tend to focus /
반면에 반대쪽 스펙트럼에 있는 사람들은 집중하는 경향이 있다 /
on their individual problems / rather than giving attention /
그들의 개인적인 문제에 / 주의를 기울이기보다는 /
to solving group problems.
전치사
집단의 문제들을 해결하는 데

(6) The rhythm of music has a strong pull / on people's behavior.
음악의 리듬은 강한 영향력을 가진다 / 사람들의 행동에 대해

(7) This is because / when people listen to music with a steady pulse, /
이것은 ~때문이다 / 사람들이 일정한 리듬의 음악을 들을 때 /
they tend to match their actions to the beat.
그들이 자신의 행동을 비트에 맞추는 경향이 있다

정답 단서
(8) This translates to better teamwork / when making decisions /
이것은 더 나은 팀워크로 변환된다 / 의사 결정을 할 때 /
because everyone is following one tempo.
모두가 하나의 박자를 따르고 있기 때문이다

(9) According to the study, / the music played in workplaces /
연구에 따르면 / 직장에서 연주되는 음악은 /
can lead employees to be (A)cooperative /
직원들이 (A)협동적이도록 이끌 수 있다 /
because the beat of the music creates a (B)shared rhythm for working.
음악의 비트는 업무를 위한 (B)공동의 리듬을 만들어 내기 때문에

힌트 주격 관계대명사 + be동사(=which is)가 생략된 형태로 선행사인 the music을 수식함.

[전문 해석]

(1)음악은 고객의 경험과 행동을 형성하는 데 사용된다. (2)음악이 직원들에게 어떤 영향을 미치는지를 탐구하는 연구가 수행되었다. (3)연구 결과는 리듬감 있는 음악을 듣는 참가자들이 리듬감이 덜한 음악을 들은 참가자들에 비해 나이, 성별, 학력과 같은 요인들과 관계없이 더 협력하는 경향이 있다는 것을 나타낸다. (4)참가자들의 협력하고자 하는 자발성의 이러한 긍정적인 촉진제는 그들이 그 음악을 좋아했는지 그렇지 않았는지와 무관하게 야기되었다. (5)사람들이 더 긍정적인 심리 상태에 있을 때, 그들은 더 쾌활하고 창의적이 되는 경향이 있는데, 반면에 반대쪽 스펙트럼에 있는 사람들은 집단의 문제들을 해결하는 데 주의를 기울이기보다는 그들의 개인적인 문제에 집중하는 경향이 있다. (6)음악의 리듬은 사람들의 행동에 대해 강한 영향력을 가진다. (7)이것은 사람들이 일정한 리듬의 음악을 들을 때, 자신의 행동을 비트(박자)에 맞추는 경향이 있기 때문이다. (8)이것은 모두가 하나의 박자를 따르고 있기 때문에 의사 결정을 할 때 더 나은 팀워크로 변환된다.

⬇

(9)연구에 따르면 음악의 비트(박자)는 업무를 위한 (B)공동의 리듬을 만들어 내기 때문에 직장에서 연주되는 음악은 직원들이 (A)협동적이도록 이끌 수 있다.

[정답 확인]

다음 글의 내용을 한 문장으로 요약하고자 한다. 빈칸 (A)와 (B)에 들어갈 말로 가장 적절한 것은?

	(A)		(B)
①	uncomfortable 불편한	......	competitive mood 경쟁적인 분위기
✔②	cooperative 협동적인	......	shared rhythm 공동의 리듬
③	distracted 산만해진	......	shared rhythm 공동의 리듬
④	attentive 주의를 기울이는	......	competitive mood 경쟁적인 분위기
⑤	indifferent 무관심한	......	disturbing pattern 불안감을 주는 패턴

[문제 풀이]

본문은 직장에서 연주되는 음악이 직원들의 협동심에 미칠 수 있는 영향에 대해 설명한다. 음악을 들을 때 사람들은 자신의 행동을 비트에 맞추게 되기 때문에, 모두가 하나의 동일한 박자를 따르도록 만든다면 협동심을 높일 수 있다. 그러므로 (A)에는 'cooperative(협동적인)', (B)에는 'shared rhythm(공동의 리듬)'이 와야 한다. 따라서 정답은 ②이다.

[중요 어휘]

□ **mold**	동사 형성하다, 주조하다 / 명사 거푸집
□ **conduct**	동사 수행하다, 행동하다
□ **have an impact on**	~에 영향을 미치다
□ **be inclined to V**	~하는 경향이 있다
□ **irrespective of**	~와 관계없이
□ **boost**	명사 촉진제, 부양책 / 동사 북돋우다, 신장시키다
□ **induce**	동사 야기하다, 유발하다
□ **regardless of**	~와 무관하게
□ **agreeable**	형용사 쾌활한, 선뜻 동의하는
□ **pull**	명사 영향력, 매력, 끌어당기는 힘 / 동사 끌다, 당기다
□ **pulse**	명사 리듬, 박자
□ **translate**	동사 변환되다, 변환하다

02 2021년 11월 40번 (정답률 70%) 정답 ①

[지문 끊어 읽기] 보상이 예측에 미치는 영향

(1) In a study, / Guy Mayraz, / a behavioral economist /
S =
한 연구에서 / Guy Mayraz는 / 행동 경제학자인 /
showed his experimental subjects graphs /
V(4형식V) I·O D·O
자신의 실험 대상자들에게 도표들을 보여 주었다 /
of a price rising and falling over time.
시간이 지나면서 오르내린 가격에 대한

(2) The graphs were actually of past changes / in the stock market, /
그 도표들은 사실 과거 변동에 관한 것이었다 / 주식 시장에서의 /
but Mayraz told people /
그러나 Mayraz는 사람들에게 말했다 /

문제편 p.234

that the graphs showed recent changes / in the price of wheat.
명사절 접속사
그 도표들이 최근의 변동을 보여 준다고 / 밀 가격에서의

(3) He asked each person to predict /
V①(5형식V) O O·C
그는 각각의 사람에게 예측할 것을 요청했다 /
where the price would move next /
간접의문문(의문사+S+V)
가격이 다음에 어디로 움직일지를 /
— and offered them a reward / if their forecasts came true.
V②(4형식V) I·O D·O
그리고 그들에게 보상을 제공했다 / 그들의 예측이 실현되면

(4) But / Mayraz had also divided his participants /
그러나 / Mayraz는 또한 자신의 참가자들을 나누었다 /
into two categories, / "farmers" and "bakers".
=
두 개의 범주로 / '농부'와 '제빵사'라는

(5) Farmers would be paid extra / if wheat prices were high.
농부들은 추가 보상을 받을 것이었다 / 밀 가격이 높으면

(6) Bakers would earn a bonus / if wheat was cheap.
제빵사들은 보너스를 받을 것이었다 / 밀이 저렴하면

(7) So / the subjects might earn two separate payments: /
따라서 / 실험 대상자들은 두 개의 별개 보상을 받을 수도 있었다 /
one for an accurate forecast, / and a bonus /
=a payment
정확한 예측에 대한 것 / 그리고 보너스 /
if the price of wheat moved in their direction.
밀의 가격이 자신들의 방향으로 움직이게 될 경우의

(8) Mayraz found / that the prospect of the bonus /
명사절 접속사
Mayraz는 발견했다 / 보너스에 대한 기대가 /
influenced the forecast itself. **정답 단서** 보너스에 대한 기대가 예측에 영향을 미침.
예측 자체에 영향을 미쳤음을

(9) The farmers hoped and *predicted* /
농부들은 희망했고 '예측했다' /
that the price of wheat would rise.
명사절 접속사
밀의 가격이 올라갈 것이라고

(10) The bakers hoped for / — and predicted — / the opposite.
=the price of wheat would fall
제빵사들은 희망했다 / 그리고 예측했다 / 그 반대를

(11) They let their hopes influence their reasoning. **정답 단서** 각 실험 대상자 집단이 바라는 이익에 따라 그들의 추론이 달라짐.
5형식V O O·C
그들은 자신들의 희망이 추론에 영향을 미치게 했다

(12) When participants were asked /
참가자들이 요청받았을 때 /
to predict the price change of wheat, /
밀의 가격 변동을 예측하도록 /
their (A)wish / for where the price would go, /
S 간접의문문(의문사+S+V)
그들의 (A)희망은 / 가격이 어디로 이동할 것인가에 대한 /
[which was determined by the group / they belonged to], /
집단에 의해 정해졌다 / 자신들이 속했던 /
(B)affected their predictions.
V
그들의 예측에 (B)영향을 미쳤다

힌트 주격 관계대명사절 [which ~ to]의 선행사는 'their wish for where the price would go' 전체임.

[전문 해석]

(1)한 연구에서 행동 경제학자인 Guy Mayraz는 자신의 실험 대상자들에게 시간이 지나면서 오르내린 가격에 대한 도표들을 보여 주었다. (2)그 도표들은 사실 주식 시장에서의 과거 변동에 관한 것이었으나 Mayraz는 사람들에게 그 도표들이 밀 가격에서의 최근의 변동을 보여 준다고 말했다. (3)그는 각각의 사람에게 가격이 다음에 어디로 움직일지를 예측할 것을 요청했으며, 그들의 예측이 실현되면 그들에게 보상을 제공했다. (4)그러나 Mayraz는 또한 자신의 참가자들을 '농부'와 '제빵사'라는 두 개의 범주로 나누었다. (5)농부들은 밀 가격이 높으면 추가 보상을 받을 것이었다. (6)제빵사들은 밀이 저렴하면 보너스를 받을 것이었다. (7)따라서 실험 대상자들은 두 개의 별개 보상, 즉 정확한 예측에 대한 보상과 밀의 가격이 자신들의 방향으로 움직이게 될 경우의 보너스를 받을 수도 있었다. (8)Mayraz는 보너스에 대한 기대가 예측 자체에 영향을 미쳤음을 발견했다. (9)농부들은 밀의 가격이 올라갈 것이라고 희망했고 '예측했다.' (10)제빵사들은 그 반대를 희망했고 '예측했다.' (11)그들은 자신들의 희망이 추론에 영향을 미치게 했다.

⬇

(12)참가자들이 밀의 가격 변동을 예측하도록 요청받았을 때, 가격이 어디로 이동할 것인가에 대한 그들의 (A)희망은 자신들이 속했던 집단에 의해 정해졌고 이(희망)는 그들의 예측에 (B)영향을 미쳤다.

[정답 확인]

다음 글의 내용을 한 문장으로 요약하고자 한다. 빈칸 (A)와 (B)에 들어갈 말로 가장 적절한 것은?

	(A)		(B)		(A)		(B)
✔	wish	......	affected	②	wish	......	contradicted
	희망		영향을 미쳤다		희망		모순되었다
③	disregard	......	restricted	④	disregard	......	changed
	무시		제한했다		무시		바꾸었다
⑤	assurance	......	realized				
	확언		깨달았다				

[중요 어휘]

□ **behavioral economist**	행동 경제학자
□ **subject**	명사 실험 대상자, 주제 / 형용사 ~될 수 있는, ~을 받아야 하는
□ **stock market**	명사 주식 시장
□ **reward**	명사 보상 / 동사 보상하다
□ **forecast**	명사 예측, 예보 / 동사 예측하다
□ **come true**	실현되다, 이루어지다
□ **payment**	명사 보상, 보답, 지불
□ **prospect**	명사 기대, 가능성, 예상
□ **reasoning**	명사 추론, 추리
□ **belong to**	~에 속하다
□ **contradict**	동사 모순되다, 반박하다
□ **disregard**	명사 무시, 묵살
□ **restrict**	동사 제한하다, 방해하다
□ **assurance**	명사 확언, 장담

핵심 강한 습관조차 '의도'에 기반을 두고 있으며 이렇게 다져진 습관은 마음이 산만해졌을 때에도 우리를 '안전'하게 지켜 줄 수 있다는 내용의 글임.

03 2018년 3월 40번 (정답률 65%) 정답 ①

[지문 끊어 읽기] 습관적 행동과 의도

(1) Despite all the talk /
온갖 이야기에도 불구하고 /
of how weak intentions are in the face of habits, /
습관 앞에서 의도가 얼마나 약한지에 관한 /
it's worth emphasizing / [that much of the time /
형식상의 주어 [ ]: 내용상의 주어
강조할 만한 가치가 있다 / 대부분의 시간에 /
even our strong habits / do follow our intentions]. **정답 단서**
강조의 do
우리의 강한 습관조차도 / 우리의 의도를 따른다는 것은

(2) We are mostly doing / what we intend to do, /
우리는 대체로 하고 있다 / 우리가 하려고 의도한 것을 /
even though it's happening automatically.
비록 자동적으로 일어나고 있지만

(3) This probably goes for many habits: / although we perform them /
이것은 아마 대부분의 습관에도 해당될 것이다 / 비록 우리가 그것들을 행하지만 /
without bringing the intention to consciousness, /
의도를 의식으로 가져오지 않고 /
the habits still line up / with our original intentions.
습관은 여전히 동조한다 / 우리의 본래 의도에

(4) Even better, / our automatic, unconscious habits /
한결 더 좋은 것은 / 우리의 자동적이고 무의식적인 습관들이 /
can keep us safe / **정답 단서**
우리를 안전하게 지켜줄 수 있다는 것이다 /

even when our conscious mind is distracted.
우리의 의식적인 마음이 산만해질 때조차도

(5) We look both ways before crossing the road /
우리는 길을 건너기 전에 양쪽 길을 모두 쳐다본다 /
despite thinking about a rather depressing holiday /
다소 울적한 휴일에 대해 생각하고 있음에도 불구하고 /
we took in Brazil, / and we put oven gloves on /
브라질에서 보냈던 / 그리고 우리는 오븐용 장갑을 낀다 /
before reaching into the oven / despite being preoccupied /
오븐 안으로 손을 뻗기 전에 / 몰두하고 있음에도 불구하고 /
about whether the cabbage is overcooked.
양배추가 지나치게 익었는지에 관해

(6) In both cases, / our goal of keeping ourselves alive and unburnt /
두 가지 경우 모두 / 우리 자신을 살아있게 하고 화상을 입지 않게 하려는 우리의 목표가 /
is served by our automatic, unconscious habits.
우리의 자동적이고 무의식적인 습관들에 의해 이행된다

(7) The habitual acts we automatically do /
우리가 자동적으로 하는 습관적인 행동은 /
are related to our (A)intention / and these acts can be helpful /
우리의 (A)의도와 연관되어 있다 / 그리고 이러한 행동은 도움이 될 수 있다 /
in keeping us from (B)danger in our lives.
우리의 삶에서 우리를 (B)위험으로부터 지켜주는 데

[전문 해석]

(1)습관 앞에서 의도가 얼마나 약한지에 관한 온갖 이야기에도 불구하고, 대부분의 시간(경우)에 우리의 강한 습관조차도 우리의 의도를 따른다는 것은 강조할 만한 가치가 있다. (2)비록 자동적으로 일어나고 있지만, 우리는 대체로 우리가 하려고 의도한 것을 하고 있다. (3)이것은 아마 대부분의 습관에도 해당될 것이다. 비록 우리가 의도를 의식으로 가져오지 않고 (무의식적으로) 습관들을 행하지만, 습관은 여전히 우리의 본래 의도에 동조한다. (4)한결 더 좋은 것은 우리의 자동적이고 무의식적인 습관들이 우리의 의식적인 마음(의식)이 산만해질 때조차도 우리를 안전하게 지켜줄 수 있다는 것이다. (5)우리는 브라질에서 보냈던 다소 울적한 휴일에 대해 생각하고 있음에도 불구하고 길을 건너기 전에 양쪽 길을 모두 쳐다보고, 양배추가 지나치게 익었는지에 관해 몰두하고 있음에도 불구하고 우리는 오븐 안으로 손을 뻗기 전에 오븐용 장갑을 낀다. (6)두 가지 경우 모두 우리 자신을 살아있게 하고 화상을 입지 않게 하려는 우리의 목표가 우리의 자동적이고 무의식적인 습관들에 의해 이행된다.

⬇

(7)우리가 자동적으로 하는 습관적인 행동은 우리의 (A)의도와 연관되어 있고, 이러한 행동은 우리의 삶에서 우리를 (B)위험으로부터 지켜주는 데 도움이 될 수 있다.

[정답 확인]

다음 글의 내용을 한 문장으로 요약하고자 한다. 빈칸 (A)와 (B)에 들어갈 말로 가장 적절한 것은?

	(A)		(B)
✔	intention 의도	......	danger 위험
②	intention 의도	......	ignorance 무지
③	mood 기분	......	danger 위험
④	experience 경험	......	laziness 게으름
⑤	experience 경험	......	ignorance 무지

[중요 어휘]

☐ go for	~에 해당되다, ~에도 마찬가지다
☐ line up with	~에 동조하다, ~와 함께 작용하다
☐ unconscious	형용사 무의식적인
☐ conscious	형용사 의식하고 있는, 의식적인
☐ distract	동사 산만하게 하다, 정신없게 하다
☐ depressing	형용사 울적한, 우울한
☐ preoccupied	형용사 몰두한, 열중한, 선점된
☐ overcooked	형용사 지나치게 익은, 너무 익힌
☐ habitual	형용사 습관적인
☐ helpful	형용사 도움이 되는

04 2019년 11월 40번 (정답률 65%)

정답 ①

[지문 끊어 읽기]

외부 요인에 의한 인간의 지각과 행동

(1) Psychologist John Bargh did an experiment / showing /
심리학자 John Bargh는 한 실험을 했다 / 보여주는 /
human perception and behavior can be influenced /
인간의 지각과 행동이 영향을 받을 수 있다는 것을 /
by external factors.
외부 요인에 의해

(2) He told a bunch of healthy undergraduates /
그는 다수의 건강한 대학생들에게 말했다 /
that he was testing their language abilities.
그가 그들의 언어 능력을 시험하고 있다고

(3) He presented them / with a list of words /
그는 그들에게 주었다 / 단어 목록 하나를 /
and asked them /
그리고 그들에게 요청했다 /
to create a coherent sentence / from it.
말이 되는 문장 하나를 만들어 달라고 / 그것으로부터

힌트 coherent의 사전적 의미는 '(이야기가) 말이 되는, 이치에 맞는'이라는 뜻이므로, coherent sentence라는 것은 의미가 통하는 문장을 의미함. 예를 들어, '자동차가 맛있다'라는 문장은 문법적으로는 가능하지만 'coherent'하지는 않음.

(4) One of the lists was "DOWN SAT LONELY THE MAN WRINKLED BITTERLY THE WITH FACE OLD".
one of 복수명사 / 단수V
목록 중 하나는 'DOWN SAT LONELY THE MAN WRINKLED BITTERLY THE WITH FACE OLD'였다

(5) "Bitterly, / the lonely old man / with the wrinkled face /
씁쓸하게 / 그 외로운 노인은 / 주름진 얼굴의 /
sat down" / is one possible solution.
앉았다 / 하나의 가능한 정답이다

힌트 큰따옴표 안의 문장 전체가 문장 (5)의 주어이고, is가 전체 문장의 동사임.

(6) But this was no linguistics test.
하지만 이것은 언어학 시험이 아니었다

(7) Bargh was interested / in how long it took the students /
Bargh는 관심이 있었다 / 학생들이 얼마나 오래 걸렸는지에 /
to leave the lab and walk down the hall /
실험실을 나서서 복도를 걸어가는 데 /
after they were exposed to the words.
그들이 그 단어들에 노출된 이후에

힌트 'It takes A 시간 to V(A가 ~하는 데 시간이 걸리다)'에서 '시간'에 해당하는 부분이 의문사 how와 결합한 'how long'임. 의문사 how가 이끄는 명사절이 전치사 in의 목적어 역할을 하고 있음.

(8) What he found was extraordinary.
S(명사절) / V
그가 발견한 것은 놀라웠다

(9) Those students /
그러한 학생들은 /

힌트 밑줄 친 부분은 'A take 시간 to V(A가 ~하는 데 시간이 걸리다)'라는 의미로, 문장 (7)의 'It takes A 시간 to V'와 함께 기억해둘 것.

who had been exposed / to an "elderly" mix of words /
노출되었던 / '나이 든' 단어들의 조합에 /
took almost 40 percent longer / to walk down the hall /
거의 40퍼센트나 더 오래 걸렸다 / 복도를 걸어가는 데 /
than those / who had been exposed to "random" words. 정답 단서
학생들보다 / '무작위의' 단어들에 노출되었던

(10) Some students even walked /
어떤 학생들은 심지어 걸었다 /
with their shoulders bent forwards, / dragging their feet /
with A p.p.(수동): A가 ~된 채로
그들의 어깨가 앞으로 구부러진 채로 / 그들의 발을 끌면서 /
as they left, / as if they were 50 years older /
그들이 나설 때 / 마치 그들이 50년은 더 늙은 듯이 /
than they actually were. 정답 단서
그들이 실제 그러한 것보다

(11) In an experiment / about human perception and behavior, /
한 실험에서 / 인간의 지각과 행동에 대한 /
participants / who experienced (A)exposure to words /
S
참가자들은 / 단어들에 대해 (A)노출을 경험했던 /
related to "elderly" / showed pace, /
V
'나이 든'과 관련된 / 보폭을 보여주었다 /
and some of them even showed posture, /
그리고 그들 중 일부는 심지어 자세까지도 보여주었다 /

힌트 밑줄 친 부분은 삽입절로, 밑줄 친 부분을 빼고 보면 'corresponding to ~'가 'pace'를 수식하는 구조임.

(B)corresponding to what the words suggested.
그 단어들이 암시했던 것과 (B)일치하는 명사절

[전문 해석]

(1)심리학자 John Bargh는 인간의 지각과 행동이 외부 요인에 의해 영향을 받을 수 있다는 것을 보여주는 한 실험을 했다. (2)그는 다수의 건강한 대학생들에게 그가 그들의 언어 능력을 시험하고 있다고 말했다. (3)그는 단어 목록 하나를 그들에게 주었고, 그것으로부터 말이 되는 문장 하나를 만들어 달라고 그들에게 요청했다. (4)목록 중 하나는 'DOWN SAT LONELY THE MAN WRINKLED BITTERLY THE WITH FACE OLD'였다. (5)'씁쓸하게, 주름진 얼굴의 그 외로운 노인은 (자리에) 앉았다'가 하나의 가능한 정답이다. (6)하지만 이것은 언어학 시험이 아니었다. (7)Bargh는 학생들이 그 단어들에 노출된 이후에 실험실을 나서서 복도를 걸어가는 데 얼마나 오래 걸렸는지에 관심이 있었다. (8)그가 발견한 것은 놀라웠다. (9)'나이 든' 단어들의 조합에 노출되었던 학생들은 '무작위의' 단어들에 노출되었던 학생들보다 복도를 걸어가는 데 거의 40퍼센트나 더 오래 걸렸다. (10)어떤 학생들은 심지어, 그들이 실제 그러한 것보다 마치 50년은 더 늙은 듯이, 그들이 (실험실을) 나설 때 발을 끌면서 어깨가 앞으로 구부러진 채로 걸었다.

⬇

(11)인간의 지각과 행동에 대한 한 실험에서, '나이 든'과 관련된 단어들에 대해 (A)노출을 경험했던 참가자들은 그 단어들이 암시했던 것과 (B)일치하는 보폭을 보여주었으며, 그들 중 일부는 심지어 (단어들이 암시했던 것과 일치하는) 자세까지도 보여주었다.

- John Bargh(존 바그, 1955년~현재): 예일 대학의 사회 심리학자로, 사회적 행동에 대한 이해를 위해 인간의 자동성과 무의식적 처리를 주로 연구하고 있다.

[정답 확인]

다음 글의 내용을 한 문장으로 요약하고자 한다. 빈칸 (A)와 (B)에 들어갈 말로 가장 적절한 것은?

(A)		(B)
① exposure 노출	......	corresponding 일치하는
② resistance 저항	......	irrelevant 무관한
③ exposure 노출	......	contrary 상반되는
④ resistance 저항	......	similar 비슷한
⑤ preference 선호	......	comparable 유사한

★중요 문장 (9), (10)에서 '나이 든'과 관련된 단어들의 조합을 본 학생들은 실험 직후 노인처럼 걸음이 느려지고 자세가 구부정해졌음. 즉, 학생들은 자신들이 노출되었던 단어들과 일치하는(corresponding) 행동을 보였음.

[문제 풀이]

외부 요인이 인간의 지각과 행동에 영향을 미치는지에 관한 실험을 소개한 글이다. 실험에서, 한 집단의 학생들에게는 '나이 든'과 관련된 단어들이, 다른 집단에는 무작위의 단어들이 제공되었으며, 실험 결과 '나이 든'과 관련된 단어들에 '노출(exposure)'되었던 학생들은 실험 직후 마치 노인들처럼 느리고 구부정한 자세로 걸었다. 따라서 (A)에는 exposure이 적절하다. 또한, 학생들이 보여주었던 좁은 보폭과 구부정한 자세는 '나이 든'이라는 단어가 암시하는 바와 일치하므로, 보기 중 (B)에는 'corresponding, similar, comparable'이 가능하다. 따라서 정답은 ①이다.

[중요 어휘]

☐ **perception**	명사 지각, 인식
☐ **external**	형용사 외부의, 겉의
☐ **undergraduate**	명사 대학생, 학부생
☐ **coherent**	형용사 (이야기가) 말이 되는, 이치에 맞는
☐ **wrinkled**	형용사 주름진, 쭈글쭈글한
☐ **bitterly**	부사 씁쓸하게, 비통하게
☐ **linguistics**	명사 언어학
☐ **extraordinary**	형용사 놀라운, 비범한
☐ **bend**	동사 구부리다, 휘다
☐ **corresponding**	형용사 일치하는, 상응하는
☐ **suggest**	동사 암시하다, 제안하다
☐ **irrelevant**	형용사 무관한, 상관없는
☐ **comparable**	형용사 유사한, 필적하는

05 2022년 9월 40번 (정답률 65%) 정답 ②

[지문 끊어 읽기] 그린 워싱

(1) Greenwashing involves misleading a consumer into thinking /
그린 워싱은 소비자가 생각하도록 현혹하는 것과 관련이 있다 /
[a good or service is more environmentally friendly /
재화나 서비스가 더 환경 친화적이라고 /
than it really is]. [ ]: thinking의 목적어절(명사절 접속사 that 생략)
그것이 실제로 그런 것보다

(2) Greenwashing ranges / from making environmental claims /
그린 워싱은 포함한다 / 환경적 주장을 하는 것부터 /
required by law, /
법이 요구하는 /
and therefore irrelevant (CFC-free for example), /
그리고 그러므로 무관한 것(예를 들어 염화불화탄소를 사용하지 않은 것)부터 /
to puffery (exaggerating environmental claims) to fraud.
과대 광고(환경적 주장을 과장하는 것)와 사기까지를

힌트 이 문장에는 'range from A to B (to C)' 구문이 쓰였음. 'irrelevant' 뒤에는 'claims'가 생략되었으며, 'to puffery'와 'to fraud' 사이에는 'and'가 없으나 'and'의 의미를 살려서 해석하면 됨.

(3) Researchers have shown /
연구자들은 밝혀냈다 /
that claims on products are often too vague or misleading.
명사절 접속사
제품에 대한 주장이 종종 너무 모호하거나 현혹적이라는 것을

(4) Some products are labeled "chemical-free," /
몇몇 제품들은 '화학 성분 없음'이라고 표기되어 있다 /
when the fact is everything contains chemicals, /
명사절(S·C)
사실은 모든 것이 화학 성분을 함유하고 있음에도 불구하고 /
including plants and animals.
식물과 동물을 포함하여

힌트 접속사 'when'은 문맥에 따라 '~할 때'라는 의미 대신 although와 같이 '~에도 불구하고'라는 양보의 의미를 지니기도 하므로 주의할 것.

(5) Products /
S
제품들은 /
with the highest number of misleading or unverifiable claims /
현혹적이거나 증명할 수 없는 주장을 가장 많이 포함한 /
were laundry detergents, household cleaners, and paints.
V
세탁 세제, 가정용 세제, 페인트였다

(6) Environmental advocates agree /
환경 옹호자들은 동의한다 /
[there is still a long way to go / to ensure /
[ ]: agree의 목적어절 형용사적 용법 부사적 용법(목적)
아직 갈 길이 멀다는 것에 / 확실히 하기 위해서는 /
shoppers are adequately informed /
구매자들이 정보를 적절히 알고 있다는 것을 /
about the environmental impact of the products / they buy].
제품의 환경적 영향에 대한 / 그들이 구매하는

(7) The most common reason for greenwashing /
그린 워싱의 가장 흔한 이유는 /
is to attract environmentally conscious consumers.
명사적 용법(S·C)
환경에 특별한 관심이 있는 소비자들을 끌어들이는 것이다

(8) Many consumers do not find out / about the false claims /
많은 소비자들은 알아내지 못한다 / 거짓 주장을 /
until after the purchase.
구입한 이후까지도

(9) Therefore, / greenwashing may increase sales /
그러므로 / 그린 워싱은 판매량을 증가시킬 수도 있다 /
in the short term. 정답 단서 그린 워싱으로 판매량이 단기적으로 증가할 수도 있음.
단기적으로

(10) However, / this strategy can seriously backfire /
그러나 / 이 전략은 심각한 역효과를 낳을 수도 있다 /
when consumers find out / they are being deceived. 정답 단서
소비자들이 알게 될 때 / 그들이 기만당하고 있다는 것을

그러나 소비자가 제품이 실제로는 친환경적이지 않다는 것을 알게 되면 역효과를 낳을 수 있음.

(11) While greenwashing might bring a company profits (A)temporarily /
4형식V I·O D·O
그린 워싱이 (A)일시적으로 기업에 이익을 줄 수도 있지만 /

by deceiving environmentally conscious consumers, /
환경에 특별한 관심이 있는 소비자들을 기만함으로써 /
the company will face serious trouble /
기업은 심각한 문제에 직면할 것이다 /
when the consumers figure out / they were (B)misinformed.
소비자들이 알아냈을 때 / 그들이 (B)잘못된 정보를 받았다는 것을

[전문 해석]

(1)그린 워싱은 소비자가 재화나 서비스가 실제로 그런 것보다 더 환경 친화적이라고 생각하도록 현혹하는 것과 관련이 있다. (2)그린 워싱은 법이 요구하는 환경적 주장을 하는 것과 그러므로 무관한 주장(예를 들어 염화불화탄소를 사용하지 않은 것)부터 과대 광고(환경적 주장을 과장하는 것)와 사기까지를 포함한다. (3)연구자들은 제품에 대한 주장이 종종 너무 모호하거나 현혹적이라는 것을 밝혀냈다. (4)사실은 식물과 동물을 포함하여 모든 것이 화학 성분을 함유하고 있음에도 불구하고, 몇몇 제품들은 '화학 성분 없음'이라고 표기되어 있다. (5)현혹적이거나 증명할 수 없는 주장을 가장 많이 포함한 제품들은 세탁 세제, 가정용 세제, 페인트였다. (6)환경 옹호자들은 구매자들이 자신들이 구매하는 제품의 환경적 영향에 대한 정보를 적절히 알고 있다는 것을 확실히 하기 위해서는 아직 갈 길이 멀다는 것에 동의한다. (7)그린 워싱의 가장 흔한 이유는 환경에 특별한 관심이 있는 소비자들을 끌어들이는 것이다. (8)많은 소비자들은 구입한 이후까지도 거짓 주장을 알아내지 못한다. (9)그러므로 그린 워싱은 단기적으로 판매량을 증가시킬 수도 있다. (10)그러나 이 전략은 소비자들이 그들이 기만당하고 있다는 것을 알게 될 때 심각한 역효과를 낳을 수도 있다.

⬇

(11)그린 워싱이 환경에 특별한 관심이 있는 소비자들을 기만함으로써 (A)일시적으로 기업에 이익을 줄 수도 있지만, 기업은 소비자들이 그들이 (B)잘못된 정보를 받았다는 것을 알아냈을 때 심각한 문제에 직면할 것이다.
- greenwashing(그린 워싱): 기업들의 제품이나 서비스가 실제로는 친환경적이지 않으나 친환경적인 것처럼 포장해서 홍보하는 행위

[정답 확인]

다음 글의 내용을 한 문장으로 요약하고자 한다. 빈칸 (A)와 (B)에 들어갈 말로 가장 적절한 것은?

(A)		(B)
① permanently	......	manipulated
영구적으로		조종당했다는
✔② temporarily	......	misinformed
일시적으로		잘못된 정보를 받았다는
③ momentarily	......	advocated
잠깐		옹호되었다는
④ ultimately	......	underestimated
궁극적으로		과소평가되었다는
⑤ consistently	......	analyzed
지속적으로		분석되었다는

[문제 풀이]

그린 워싱은 환경에 특별한 관심이 있는 소비자들을 끌어들이기 위해 재화나 서비스가 실제보다 더 친환경적이라고 속이는 것을 의미한다. 환경을 생각하는 소비자들은 기업들의 그린 워싱에 속아 그러한 제품을 더 많이 소비하게 되고, 이에 따라 문장 (9)에서 언급된 것처럼 단기적으로는 제품의 판매량이 증가하게 된다. 하지만 문장 (10)에서 소비자들이 그동안 친환경적인 제품이라 생각하여 구입해왔던 것들이 사실은 그렇지 않다는 것을 알게 되면 오히려 역효과가 발생한다고 언급한다. 따라서 빈칸 (A)에는 문장 (9)의 'in the short term'에 해당하는 'temporarily', 빈칸 (B)에는 문장 (10)의 'deceived'에 해당하는 'misinformed'가 오는 것이 자연스러우므로 정답은 ②이다.

[중요 어휘]

- ☐ **mislead A into V-ing** A를 ~하도록 현혹하다, 오도하다
- ☐ **good** [명사] (주로 복수형) 재화
- ☐ **puffery** [명사] 과대 광고, 과장된 칭찬
- ☐ **exaggerate** [동사] 과장하다, 부풀리다
- ☐ **fraud** [명사] 사기, 엉터리
- ☐ **vague** [형용사] 모호한, 희미한
- ☐ **label A (as) B** A를 B라고 표기하다
- ☐ **unverifiable** [형용사] 증명할 수 없는
- ☐ **detergent** [명사] 세제
- ☐ **advocate** [명사] 옹호자, 지지자 / [동사] 옹호하다
- ☐ **informed** [형용사] 정보를 알고 있는, 잘 아는
- ☐ **conscious** [형용사] (형용사/부사 뒤) 특별한 관심이 있는
- ☐ **backfire** [동사] 역효과를 낳다
- ☐ **deceive** [동사] 기만하다, 속이다
- ☐ **figure out** 알아내다
- ☐ **misinform** [동사] 잘못된 정보를 주다
- ☐ **permanently** [부사] 영구적으로
- ☐ **manipulate** [동사] 조종하다, 다루다
- ☐ **momentarily** [부사] 잠깐, 일시적으로

핵심 문단 요약 유형에서는 주제문에 쓰인 표현들을 더욱 함축적으로 나타내는 어휘들을 찾아야 함. 따라서 가장 먼저 해야 할 것은 주제문을 파악하는 것임.

06 2019년 6월 40번 (정답률 60%) 정답 ①

[지문 끊어 읽기] 집단 간 접촉과 편견

(1) Intergroup contact is more likely to /
집단 간 접촉은 ~할 가능성이 더 크다 /
reduce stereotyping and create favorable attitudes /
고정 관념 형성을 줄이고 우호적인 태도를 만들어 낼 /
if it is backed by social norms /
만약 그것이 사회적 규범에 의해 뒷받침된다면 /
that promote equality among groups. 주제문
집단 간의 평등을 장려하는

(2) If the norms support /
그 규범들이 지지하는 경우에 /
openness, friendliness, and mutual respect, /
개방성, 친밀함, 그리고 상호 존중을 /
the contact has a greater chance /
그 접촉은 더 큰 가능성을 가진다 /
of changing attitudes and reducing prejudice / than if they do not.
태도를 바꾸고 편견을 줄일 / 그것들이 그러지 않는 경우보다

(3) Institutionally supported intergroup contact /
제도적으로 지지되는 집단 간 접촉은 /
— that is, contact sanctioned by an outside authority or by established customs — /
(과거분사)
즉 외부의 권위나 기존의 관습에 의해 승인된 접촉은 /
is more likely to produce positive changes /
긍정적인 변화를 만들어 낼 가능성이 더 크다 /
than unsupported contact. 정답단서
지지되지 않는 접촉보다

(4) Without institutional support, /
제도적인 지지가 없다면 /
members of an in-group may be reluctant /
내집단의 구성원들은 꺼려할 수도 있다 /
to interact with outsiders / because they feel /
외부인들과 상호 작용하는 것을 / 왜냐하면 그들은 느끼기 때문에 /
doing so is deviant or simply inappropriate.
그렇게 하는 것이 일탈적이거나 그저 부적절하다고

(5) With the presence of institutional support, /
제도적인 지지가 존재한다면 /
however, / contact between groups / is more likely to be seen /
그러나 / 집단들 사이의 접촉은 / 여겨질 가능성이 더 크다 /
as appropriate, expected, and worthwhile.
적절하고, 기대되며, 그리고 가치 있는 것으로

(6) For instance, / with respect to desegregation /
예를 들어 / 인종 차별 폐지와 관련해서 /
in elementary schools, / there is evidence /
초등학교에서의 / 증거가 있다 /
that students were more highly motivated and learned more /
학생들이 더 많이 동기를 부여받고 더 많이 배웠다는 /
in classes conducted by teachers / (that is, authority figures) /
(과거분사)
교사들에 의해 지도된 수업에서 / (즉 권위 있는 인물들) /
who supported rather than opposed desegregation.
인종 차별 폐지를 반대하기보다 지지했던

(7) [Backed by social norms / that pursue intergroup equality], /
[ ]: 분사구문: 가정(Being 생략)
사회적 규범에 의해 뒷받침된다면 / 집단 간 평등을 추구하는 /
intergroup contact tends to weaken (A)bias more, /
집단 간 접촉은 (A)편견을 더 약화시키는 경향이 있다 /
especially when it is led by (B)organizational support.
특히 그것이 (B)조직적인 지지에 의해 이끌어질 때

[전문 해석]

(1)집단 간 접촉은, 만약 그것이 집단 간의 평등을 장려하는 사회적 규범에 의해 뒷받침된다면, 고정 관념 형성을 줄이고 우호적인 태도를 만들어 낼 가능성이 더 크다. (2)그 규범들이 개방성, 친밀함, 그리고 상호 존중을 지지하는 경우에, 그 (집단 간) 접촉은 그것들이 그러지 않는 (지지하지 않는) 경우보다 태도를 바꾸고 편견을 줄일 더 큰 가능성을 가진다. (3)제도적으로 지지되는 집단 간 접촉, 즉 외부의 권위나 기존의 관습에 의해 승인된 접촉은 지지되지 않는 접촉보다 긍정적인 변화를 만들어 낼 가능성이 더 크다. (4)제도적인 지지가 없다면, 내집단의 구성원들은 외부인들과 상호 작용하는 것을 꺼려할 수도 있는데, 왜냐하면 그들(내집단의 구성원들)은 그렇게 하는 것(외부인들과 상호 작용하는 것)이 일탈적이거나 그저 부적절하다고 느끼기 때문이다. (5)그러나 제도적인 지지가 존재한다면, 집단들 사이의 접촉은 적절하고, 기대되며, 그리고 가치 있는 것으로 여겨질 가능성이 더 크다(커진다). (6)예를 들어, 초등학교에서의 인종 차별 폐지와 관련해서, 인종 차별 폐지를 반대하기보다 지지했던 교사들(즉, 권위 있는 인물들)에 의해 지도된 수업에서 학생들이 더 많이 동기를 부여받고 더 많이 배웠다는 증거가 있다.

⬇

(7)집단 간 평등을 추구하는 사회적 규범에 의해 뒷받침된다면, 집단 간 접촉은 특히 그것(접촉)이 (B)조직적인 지지에 의해 이끌어질 때, (A)편견을 더 약화시키는 경향이 있다.

[정답 확인]

다음 글의 내용을 한 문장으로 요약하고자 한다. 빈칸 (A)와 (B)에 들어갈 말로 가장 적절한 것은?

(A)		(B)	(A)		(B)
✔ bias	......	organizational	② bias	......	individualized
편견		조직적인	편견		개인화된
③ bias	......	financial	④ balance	......	organizational
편견		재정적인	균형		조직적인
⑤ balance	......	individualized			
균형		개인화된			

✶중요 문장 (2)의 prejudice와 문장 (4)의 institutional을 각각 bias와 organizational이라는 유의어로 바꾸어 표현하고 있음.

[문제 풀이]

본문에 의하면 집단 간 접촉은 고정 관념의 형성을 줄이고 우호적인 태도를 만들어 내는 경향이 있는데, 이러한 경향은 집단 간 접촉이 외부의 권위나 기존 관습의 지지를 받을 때, 즉 제도적으로 뒷받침될 때 더욱 커지게 된다. 이를 달리 표현하면, 집단 간 접촉은 그것이 '조직적인(organizational)' 지지에 의해 이끌어질 때 '편견(bias)'을 더 약화시킬 수 있다는 것이다. 따라서 정답은 ①이다.

[중요 어휘]

☐ intergroup	형용사 집단 간의, 그룹 사이의
☐ stereotyping	명사 고정 관념 형성, 정형화
☐ back	동사 뒷받침하다, 후원하다
☐ prejudice	명사 편견, 선입관
☐ institutionally	부사 제도적으로
☐ sanction	동사 승인하다, 허가하다 / 명사 허가
☐ established	형용사 기존의, 확립된, 인정된
☐ custom	명사 관습, 관행
☐ in-group	명사 (사회학) 내집단(개인이 소속되어 공동체 의식을 느끼는 집단)
☐ deviant	형용사 일탈적인, 규범에서 벗어난
☐ worthwhile	형용사 가치 있는, 훌륭한
☐ with respect to	~과 관련해서, ~에 대해
☐ desegregation	명사 인종 차별 폐지
☐ conduct	동사 지도하다, 지휘하다, 실시하다
☐ figure	명사 인물, 사람

07 2022년 6월 40번 (정답률 60%) 정답 ②

[지문 끊어 읽기] 스포츠 심리학의 아이러니

(1) The great irony of performance psychology /
퍼포먼스 심리학의 큰 아이러니는 /
is that it teaches each sportsman to believe, /
5형식V O O.C
각 운동선수들이 믿도록 가르친다는 것이다 /
as far as he is able, / that he will win.
believe의 목적어절
그가 능력이 있는 한 / 그가 이길 것이라고

힌트 to believe와 believe의 목적어절 사이에 삽입된 부사절로 'as far as+S+V'는 '~하는 한'이라는 뜻임. 유사한 구문으로 '~이기만 하면, ~하는 한'이라는 뜻의 'as/so long as+S+V' 구문이 있음.

(2) No man doubts.
어느 누구도 의심하지 않는다

(3) No man indulges his inner skepticism.
어느 누구도 내면의 회의에 빠지지 않는다

(4) That is the logic of sports psychology.
그것이 스포츠 심리학의 논리이다

(5) But only one man *can* win.
하지만 오직 한 사람만이 이길 '수 있다'

(6) That is the logic of sport.
그것이 스포츠의 논리이다

(7) Note the difference / between a scientist and an athlete.
차이점을 주목하라 / 과학자와 운동선수의

(8) Doubt is a scientist's stock in trade.
의심은 과학자의 일상적인 업무이다

(9) Progress is made / by focusing on the evidence /
병렬① 선행사
진보는 이루어진다 / 증거에 집중함으로써 /
that refutes a theory / and by improving the theory accordingly.
주격 관계대명사절 병렬②
이론을 반박하는 / 그리고 그에 따라 이론을 개선함으로써

(10) Skepticism is the rocket fuel / of scientific advance. 정답 단서 회의론은 과학적 진보를 위해 필요함.
회의론은 추진 연료이다 / 과학적 진보의

(11) But doubt, / to an athlete, / is poison. 정답 단서 운동선수에게 의심은 치명적임.
하지만 의심은 / 운동선수에게 / 독이다

(12) Progress is made / by ignoring the evidence; /
진보는 만들어진다 / 증거를 무시함으로써 /
it is about creating a mindset /
그것은 사고방식을 만드는 것이다 / 선행사
[that is immune to doubt and uncertainty]. 정답 단서 운동선수는 의심과 불확실성에 영향을 받지 않는 사고방식을 만들어야 함.
의심과 불확실성에 영향을 받지 않는 [ ]: 주격 관계대명사절

(13) Just to reiterate: / From a rational perspective, /
다시 한번 되풀이하자면 / 이성적인 시각에서 보면 /
this is nothing less than crazy.
이건 미친 짓이나 다름없다

힌트 'nothing less than A'는 'A 미만이 아니라는', 즉 'A나 다름없는, 그야말로 A' 등으로 해석할 수 있음.

(14) Why should an athlete convince himself /
왜 운동선수는 확신해야 하는가 /
he will win / when he knows /
명사절(접속사 that 생략)
자신이 이길 것이라고 / 자신이 알면서도 /
that there is every possibility / he will lose?
명사절 접속사 = 동격의 that 생략
모든 가능성이 있다는 것을 / 자신이 질 거라는

힌트 일반적으로 접속사 when은 '~할 때'라는 시간의 의미를 나타내지만, 이 문장과 같이 '~인데도 불구하고, ~인 것을 생각하면'이라는 양보의 의미로도 쓰임.

(15) Because, / to win, / one must proportion one's belief, /
부사적 용법 =an athlete
왜냐하면 / 이기기 위해서 / 선수는 자신의 신념을 할당해야 하기 때문이다 /
not to the evidence, /
전치사
증거가 아니라 /
but to whatever the mind can usefully get away with. 정답 단서 운동선수는 성공하기 위해서 의심보다는 자신의 마음이 유용하게 할 수 있는 것에 신념을 쏟아야 함.
복합관계대명사
마음이 유용하게 해낼 수 있는 무엇이든지 간에

힌트 'A가 아닌 B'의 뜻을 가진 'not A but B' 구문임. 이때 A와 B는 운동선수가 자신의 신념을 할당할 곳을 설명하는 to 전치사구의 형태임.

(16) Unlike scientists / whose (A)skeptical attitude is needed /
소유격 관계대명사절
과학자들과는 달리 / (A)회의적인 태도가 요구되는 /

to make scientific progress, / sports psychology says /
부사적 용법
과학적 진보를 이루기 위해 / 스포츠 심리학은 말한다 /

that to succeed, /
부사적 용법
성공하기 위해서는 /

athletes must (B)eliminate feelings of uncertainty /
운동선수들이 불확실한 감정을 (B)없애야 한다고 /

about whether they can win.
명사절
그들이 이길 수 있는지에 대한

[전문 해석]

(1)퍼포먼스 심리학의 큰 아이러니는 각 운동선수들이 능력이 있는 한, 이길 것이라고 믿도록 가르친다는 것이다. (2)어느 누구도 의심하지 않는다. (3)어느 누구도 내면의 회의에 빠지지 않는다. (4)그것이 스포츠 심리학의 논리이다. (5)하지만 오직 한 사람만이 이길 '수 있다'. (6)그것이 스포츠의 논리이다. (7)과학자와 운동선수의 차이점을 주목하라. (8)의심은 과학자의 일상적인 업무이다. (9)진보는 이론을 반박하는 증거에 집중하고 그에 따라 이론을 개선함으로써 이루어진다. (10)회의론은 과학적 진보의 추진 연료이다. (11)하지만 운동선수에게 의심은 독이다. (12)진보는 증거를 무시함으로써 만들어진다. 즉 (운동선수에게) 진보란 의심과 불확실성에 영향을 받지 않는 사고방식을 만드는 것이다. (13)다시 한번 되풀이하자면, 이성적인 시각에서 보면 이건 미친 짓이나 다름없다. (14)왜 운동선수는 자신이 질 거라는 모든 가능성이 있다는 것을 알면서도 이길 것이라고 확신해야 하는가? (15)선수는 이기기 위해서 증거가 아니라 마음이 유용하게 해낼 수 있는 무엇이든지 간에 자신의 신념을 할당해야 하기 때문이다.

⬇

(16)과학적 진보를 이루기 위해 (A)회의적인 태도가 요구되는 과학자들과는 달리, 스포츠 심리학은 운동선수들이 성공하기 위해서는 그들이 이길 수 있는지에 대한 불확실한 감정을 (B)없애야 한다고 한다.

- performance psychology(퍼포먼스 심리학): 심리학의 한 분과로 인간이 무언가를 최적인 상태로 수행하는 데 영향을 미치는 심리적 요인을 분석함. 스포츠와 비즈니스 같은 분야에서 성공적인 결과를 낳기 위해 주로 사용됨.
- skepticism(회의론, 회의주의): 회의(懷疑)란 의심을 품는 것을 의미하는데, 철학에서는 보편 타당한 진리의 존재를 부정하거나 그러한 진리의 인식 가능성을 인정하지 않는 것을 말함. 한편 과학에서의 회의주의는 검증되지 않은 주장에 대하여 의심하는 태도를 일컫는데 본문의 내용이 여기 해당함.

[정답 확인]

다음 글의 내용을 한 문장으로 요약하고자 한다. 빈칸 (A)와 (B)에 들어갈 말로 가장 적절한 것은?

(A)		(B)	(A)		(B)
① confident 자신감 있는	……	keep 유지해야	✔ skeptical 회의적인	……	eliminate 없애야
③ arrogant 오만한	……	express 표현해야	④ critical 비판적인	……	keep 유지해야
⑤ stubborn 완고한	……	eliminate 없애야			

[문제 풀이]

문장 (8)~(10)에 따르면, 과학자는 언제나 의심하는 회의적인 태도를 통해서 과학적 진보를 이뤄내지만, 문장 (11)~(15)를 보면 운동선수는 스스로 이길 것이라고 믿으며 의심과 불확실성에 영향을 받지 않는 마음가짐을 통해 성공한다. 따라서 과학자들은 진보를 위해 회의적인 태도를 유지해야 하는 반면, 운동선수들은 의심과 불확실한 감정을 제거해야 한다. 그러므로 ②가 적절하다.

[중요 어휘]

☐ able	형용사 능력이 있는, 재능 있는
☐ doubt	동사 의심하다 / 명사 의심
☐ indulge	동사 ~에 빠지다, 마음껏 하다
☐ skepticism	명사 회의(감), 회의론
☐ stock in trade	일상적인 업무, 상투적인 것, 장사 수단
☐ progress	명사 진보 / 동사 나아가다
☐ refute	동사 반박하다
☐ accordingly	부사 그에 따라, 그래서
☐ advance	명사 진보, 발전, 전진
☐ mindset	명사 사고방식
☐ be immune to	~에 영향을 받지 않는, ~에 면역이 된
☐ uncertainty	명사 불확실성
☐ reiterate	동사 되풀이하다, 반복하다
☐ rational	형용사 이성적인
☐ proportion	동사 할당하다, ~에 적합하게 하다 / 명사 부분, 비율
☐ get away with	~을 (잘) 해내다, (벌 등을) 모면하다

08 2023년 3월 40번 (정답률 60%) 정답 ①

[지문 끊어 읽기] 인간의 공간 인식

(1) A young child may be puzzled /
어린아이는 당황할 수 있다 /
when asked to distinguish / between the directions of right and left.
구분하라고 요구 받을 때 / 오른쪽과 왼쪽을

힌트 때를 나타내는 종속부사절 다음에 주어와 be동사가 생략될 수 있음.

(2) But that same child may have no difficulty /
그러나 그 아이는 어려움이 없을 것이다 /
in determining the directions / of up and down or back and front.
방향을 결정하는 데에는 / 위아래 혹은 뒤와 앞의

힌트 have no difficulty in V-ing는 '~하는 데 어려움이 없다'라는 뜻임.

(3) Scientists propose / that this occurs / because, /
과학자들은 주장한다 / 이것이 일어난다고 / 왜냐하면 ~이기 때문에 /
although we experience three dimensions, /
우리가 삼차원을 경험하지만 /
only two had a strong influence on our evolution: /
오직 두 가지만이 우리의 진화에 강한 영향을 주었다 /
the vertical dimension as defined by gravity /
병렬①
중력에 의해 정의되는 수직적 차원 /
and, in mobile species, / the front/back dimension /
병렬②
그리고 이동하는 종에서 / 앞/뒤 차원 /
as defined by the positioning of sensory and feeding mechanisms.
감각과 먹이 섭취 메커니즘의 배치로 정의되는

정답단서 아이가 왼쪽과 오른쪽을 구분하기 어려운 이유는 우리의 진화에 중력에 의해 정의되는 수직적 차원과, 이동하는 종에서 감각과 먹이 섭취 메커니즘의 배치로 정의되는 앞/뒤 차원이 강한 영향을 주기 때문임.

(4) These influence [our perception /
S V [ ]:O
이것들은 우리의 인식에 영향을 준다 /
of vertical versus horizontal, / far versus close, /
수직 대 수평 / 원거리 대 근거리 /
and the search for dangers from above (such as an eagle) /
병렬①
그리고 (독수리 같은) 위로부터 오는 위험의 탐색에 /
or below (such as a snake)].
병렬②
혹은 (뱀 같은) 아래로부터 오는

(5) However, / the left-right axis is not as relevant in nature. 정답단서
그러나 / 왼쪽-오른쪽 축은 자연에서 그만큼 중요하지 않다

왼쪽-오른쪽 축은 자연에서 그만큼 중요하지 않음.

(6) A bear is equally dangerous / from its left or the right side, /
=a bear's
곰은 동일하게 위험하다 / 그것의 왼쪽이나 오른쪽에서 /
but not if it is upside down.
하지만 그것이 위아래로 뒤집혀 있다면 그렇지 않다

힌트 'but (a bear is) not (dangerous)'에서 중복되는 부분 생략됨.

(7) In fact, / when observing a scene /
사실 / 장면을 볼 때 /
containing plants, animals, and man-made objects such as cars or street signs, /
식물, 동물, 그리고 차나 도로 표지판 같은 사람이 만든 물체를 포함하는 /
we can only tell / when left and right have been inverted /
현재완료 수동태
우리는 겨우 구별할 수 있을 뿐이다 / 왼쪽과 오른쪽이 뒤집혀 있을 때 /
if we observe those artificial items.
우리가 그 인공적인 물체들을 관찰한다면

(8) Having affected the evolution of our (A)spatial perception, /
분사구문
우리의 (A)공간적 인식의 진화에 영향을 미쳐서 /
vertical and front/back dimensions are easily perceived, /
수직과 앞/뒤 차원은 쉽게 인식된다 /

but the left-right axis, / which is not (B)significant in nature, /
선행사 주격 관계대명사
그러나 왼쪽-오른쪽 축은 / 자연에서 (B)중요하지 않은 /
doesn't come instantly to us.
우리에게 즉시 이해되지 않는다

[전문 해석]

(1)어린아이는 오른쪽과 왼쪽을 구분하라고 요구 받을 때 당황할 수 있다. (2)그러나 그 아이는 위아래 혹은 뒤와 앞의 방향을 결정하는 데에는 어려움이 없을 것이다. (3)과학자들은 우리가 삼차원을 경험하지만 오직 두 가지만이 우리의 진화에 강한 영향을 주었기 때문에 이것이 일어난다고 주장하는데, (그것들은) 중력에 의해 정의되는 수직적 차원과 이동하는 종에서 감각과 먹이 섭취 메커니즘의 배치로 정의되는 앞/뒤 차원이다. (4)이것들은 우리의 수직 대 수평, 원거리 대 근거리 인식에, 그리고 (독수리 같은) 위로부터 오는 위험 혹은 (뱀 같은) 아래로부터 오는 위험의 탐색에 영향을 준다. (5)그러나 왼쪽-오른쪽 축은 자연에서 그만큼 중요하지 않다. (6)곰은 왼쪽이나 오른쪽에서 동일하게 위험하지만, 위아래로 뒤집혀 있다면 그렇지 않다. (7)사실, 식물, 동물, 그리고 차나 도로 표지판 같은 사람이 만든 물체를 포함하는 장면을 볼 때, 우리가 그 인공적인 물체들을 관찰한다면 우리는 왼쪽과 오른쪽이 뒤집혀 있을 때 겨우 구분할 수 있을 뿐이다.

⬇

(8)우리의 (A)공간적 인식의 진화에 영향을 미쳐서 수직과 앞/뒤 차원은 쉽게 인식되지만, 자연에서 (B)중요하지 않은 왼쪽-오른쪽 축은 우리에게 즉시 이해되지 않는다.

[정답 확인]

다음 글의 내용을 한 문장으로 요약하고자 한다. 빈칸 (A)와 (B)에 들어갈 말로 가장 적절한 것은?

	(A)		(B)		(A)		(B)
✔①	spatial 공간적	......	significant 중요하지	②	spatial 공간적	......	scarce 희소하지
③	auditory 청각적	......	different 다르지	④	cultural 문화적	......	accessible 접근가능하지
⑤	cultural 문화적	......	desirable 바람직하지				

[문제 풀이]

본문에 따르면, 어린아이는 오른쪽과 왼쪽은 잘 구분하지 못하지만 위와 아래, 뒤와 앞을 결정하는 데에는 어려움을 겪지 않는다. 이는 우리가 삼차원을 경험할 때 수직적 차원과 앞뒤(거리)를 구분하는 두 가지 인식 능력은 진화적으로 중요했지만 왼쪽-오른쪽 축은 자연에서 그만큼 중요하지 않았기 때문이라고 한다. 뒤이어 나오는 곰의 예시에서 곰은 좌우가 바뀌어도 위험하기는 매한가지이지만 위아래가 뒤집혀 있다면 그렇지 않다고 하며, 마지막으로 장면을 볼 때 좌우가 반전된 것은 잘 알아차리지 못한다고 한다. 따라서 우리의 공간 인식의 진화에 영향을 미쳐서 수직과 앞/뒤 차원은 쉽게 인식되지만 자연에서 중요하지 않은 왼쪽-오른쪽은 바로 이해되지 않는다는 내용의 ①이 적절하다.

[중요 어휘]

□ **puzzled**	형용사 당황하는, 어리둥절한
□ **distinguish**	동사 구분하다, 구별하다
□ **direction**	명사 쪽, 방향
□ **propose**	동사 주장하다, 제안하다
□ **dimension**	명사 차원, 규모, 치수
□ **vertical**	형용사 수직의 / 명사 수직
□ **gravity**	명사 중력
□ **mobile**	형용사 이동하는, 움직임이 자유로운
□ **species**	명사 (생물 분류의) 종
□ **position**	동사 배치하다 / 명사 위치, 자리
□ **sensory**	형용사 감각의
□ **versus**	전치사 대(對), ~에 비해
□ **horizontal**	명사 수평 / 형용사 수평의
□ **relevant**	형용사 중요한, 유의미한, 관련된, 적절한
□ **upside down**	부사 뒤집혀, 거꾸로
□ **man-made**	형용사 사람이 만든, 인공적인
□ **tell**	동사 구별하다, 알다
□ **invert**	동사 뒤집다, 거꾸로 하다
□ **artificial**	형용사 인공적인
□ **spatial**	형용사 공간적인
□ **instantly**	부사 즉시, 즉각적으로

● 지문 구조도

(1) 어린아이에게 오른쪽과 왼쪽의 방향을 구분하는 것은 어려움.	(2) 어린아이가 위아래 혹은 뒤와 앞의 방향을 결정하는(determine) 것은 어렵지 않음.
↓	↓
(5) 자연에서 왼쪽-오른쪽 축(axis)은 그렇게 중요하지 않음.	(3) 오직 수직적 차원(vertical dimension)과 앞/뒤 차원만이 우리의 진화에 강한 영향을 주었기 때문임. (4) 수직 대 수평 인식(perception)과 원거리 대 근거리 인식 및 위 혹은 아래로부터 오는 위험의 탐색에 영향을 주었음.
(7) 인공적인 물체들이 왼쪽과 오른쪽이 뒤집혀 있을(be inverted) 때 우리는 그 사실을 겨우 구분해낼(tell) 수 있음.	(6) 곰은 왼쪽이나 오른쪽 둘 다에서 위험하지만 위아래로 뒤집힌 경우에는 위험하지 않음.

09 2023년 6월 40번 (정답률 60%)

정답 ①

[지문 끊어 읽기]

행동에 영향받는 생각

(1) People behave in highly predictable ways /
사람들은 굉장히 예측 가능한 방식으로 행동한다 /
when they experience certain thoughts. 정답 단서 사람들이 특정 생각을 하면 굉장히 예측 가능한 행동을 함.
그들이 특정한 생각을 할 때

(2) When they agree, / they nod their heads.
그들은 동의할 때 / 그들은 고개를 끄덕인다

힌트 'known as'는 '~으로 알려진'으로 해석함. 전치사에 따른 해석에 차이가 있어서, 'known to'는 '~에게 알려진', 'known for'는 '(특성, 특징)으로 알려진'으로 해석하므로 유의해야 함.

(3) So far, / no surprise, / 힌트 삽입구로 쓰인 'no surprise'는 '놀랄 일은 아니다'로 해석함.
여기까지는 / 놀랄 일은 아니다 /
but according to an area of research known as "proprioceptive psychology," /
하지만 '고유 수용 심리학'으로 알려진 한 연구 분야에 따르면 /
the process also works in reverse. 정답 단서 역으로 특정 행동을 하면 예측 가능한 생각을 하게 되기도 함.
그 과정은 역으로도 작용한다

(4) Get people to behave in a certain way /
준사역V O O·C(to V)
사람들을 특정한 방식으로 행동하게 하라 /
and you cause them to have certain thoughts. 정답 단서 특정한 행동을 하게 하면 사람들은 특정한 생각을 갖게 됨.
5형식V O O·C
그러면 당신은 그들이 특정한 생각을 갖도록 한다

(5) The idea was initially controversial, / but fortunately /
그 아이디어는 처음에는 논란의 여지가 있었다 / 하지만 다행히도 /
it was supported by a compelling experiment.
설득력 있는 실험으로 뒷받침되었다

(6) Participants in a study /
한 연구에서 참가자들은 /
were asked to fixate on various products /
병렬①
다양한 제품들에 시선을 고정할 것을 요청받았다 /
moving across a large computer screen / and then indicate /
큰 컴퓨터 화면을 가로질러 움직이는 / 그러고는 나타낼 것을 / 병렬②(to 생략)
whether the items appealed to them.
그 제품들이 그들에게 매력적인지 아닌지를

(7) Some of the items moved vertically /
일부 제품은 수직으로 움직였다 /
(causing the participants to nod their heads / while watching), /
5형식V O O·C
참가자들이 고개를 끄덕이게 하면서 / 보는 동안 /

and others moved horizontally /
=other items
그리고 다른 제품은 수평으로 움직였다 /
(resulting in a side-to-side head movement).
(좌우로 고개를 움직이는 결과를 낳으면서)

(8) Participants preferred vertically moving products /
참가자들은 수직으로 움직이는 제품을 선호했다 /
without being aware /
인지하지 못한 채 /
that their "yes" and "no" head movements /
접속사
자신의 "예"와 "아니오"의 고개 움직임이 /
had played a key role in their decisions. 정답 단서
그들의 결정에 핵심적인 역할을 했다는 것을

참가자들은 자신들이 고개를 수직으로 움직였다는 것을 인지하지 못한 상태로 컴퓨터 화면에서 수직으로 움직이는 제품들을 더 선호했음.

(9) In one study, / participants responded (A)favorably /
한 연구에서 / 참가자들은 (A)호의적으로 반응했다 /
to products on a computer screen /
컴퓨터 화면에 나오는 제품들에 /
when they moved their heads up and down, / which showed /
그들의 고개를 위아래로 움직일 때 / 그리고 이것은 보여 주었다 / 계속적 용법(선행사=앞 문장 전체)
that their decisions were unconsciously influenced /
접속사
그들의 결정이 무의식적으로 영향을 받았다는 것을 /
by their (B)behavior.
그들의 (B)행동에 의해

[전문 해석]

(1)사람들은 그들이 특정한 생각을 할 때 굉장히 예측 가능한 방식으로 행동한다. (2)그들은 동의할 때, 고개를 끄덕인다. (3)여기까지는, 놀랄 일은 아니지만, '고유 수용 심리학'으로 알려진 한 연구 분야에 따르면, 그 과정은 역으로도 작용한다. (4)사람들을 특정한 방식으로 행동하게 하면, 당신은 그들이 특정한 생각을 갖도록 한다. (5)그 아이디어는 처음에는 논란의 여지가 있었지만, 다행히도 설득력 있는 실험으로 뒷받침되었다. (6)한 연구에서 참가자들은 큰 컴퓨터 화면을 가로질러 움직이는 다양한 제품들에 시선을 고정하고 그 제품들이 그들에게 매력적인지 아닌지를 나타낼 것을 요청받았다. (7)일부 제품은 (참가자들이 보는 동안 고개를 끄덕이게 하면서) 수직으로 움직였고, 다른 제품은 (좌우로 고개를 움직이는 결과를 낳으면서) 수평으로 움직였다. (8)참가자들은 자신의 "예"와 "아니오"의 고개 움직임이 그들의 결정에 핵심적인 역할을 했다는 것을 인지하지 못한 채 수직으로 움직이는 제품을 선호했다.

⬇

(9)한 연구에서, 참가자들은 그들의 고개를 위아래로 움직일 때 컴퓨터 화면에 나오는 제품들에 (A)호의적으로 반응했는데, 이것은 그들의 결정이 그들의 (B)행동에 의해 무의식적으로 영향을 받았다는 것을 보여 주었다.

[정답 확인]

다음 글의 내용을 한 문장으로 요약하고자 한다. 빈칸 (A)와 (B)에 들어갈 말로 가장 적절한 것은?

(A)		(B)	(A)		(B)
✔ favorably 호의적으로	……	behavior 행동	② favorably 호의적으로	……	instinct 본능
③ unfavorably 부정적으로	……	feeling 감정	④ unfavorably 부정적으로	……	gesture 몸짓
⑤ irrationally 비합리적으로	……	prejudice 편견			

[문제 풀이]

본문에 따르면, 사람들은 특정한 생각을 할 때 예측 가능한 방식으로 행동한다. 그러나 '고유 수용 심리학'이라는 분야에서 이것은 역으로도 작용할 수 있다고 한다. 한 실험에서 참가자들은 화면에 나오는 제품에 시선을 고정하라는 이야기를 들었고, 수직으로 움직이는 제품을 보았을 때는 자신도 모르게 고개를 끄덕이게 되었다. 반대로 제품이 수평으로 움직이면 고개를 젓게 되었는데, 이것이 제품에 대한 각각 긍정적이고 부정적인 생각으로 이어졌다. 따라서 행동이 생각에 영향을 준다는 것이 입증되었고, 요약문에는 수직으로 고개를 움직였을 때의 생각이 언급되어야 하므로 정답에는 ①이 적절하다.

[중요 어휘]

☐ highly	부사 굉장히, 매우
☐ nod	동사 (고개를) 끄덕이다
☐ area	명사 분야, 구역, 지역
☐ proprioceptive	형용사 고유 수용의, 자기 수용의
☐ in reverse	역으로, 반대로
☐ initially	부사 처음에
☐ controversial	형용사 논란의 여지가 있는
☐ compelling	형용사 설득력 있는, 강력한
☐ fixate	동사 고정하다, 응시하다
☐ indicate	동사 나타내다, 내비치다
☐ appeal	동사 매력적이다, 호소하다
☐ vertically	부사 수직으로
☐ horizontally	부사 수평으로
☐ result in	~하는 결과를 낳다, 초래하다
☐ favorably	부사 호의적으로
☐ unfavorably	부사 부정적으로, 호의적이지 않게

핵심 기억 조작을 하게 되는 외부 요인에 관한 한 실험을 다루고 있음. 참가자들에게 두 가지 다른 정보가 제시되었는데, 각각의 경우에 보인 반응이 어떻게 다른지 파악하면 요약문의 빈칸을 쉽게 채울 수 있음.

10 2020년 11월 40번 (정답률 55%)

정답 ①

[지문 끊어 읽기] 외부 요인에 의한 기억 조작

(1) In 2011, / Micah Edelson and his colleagues /
2011년에 / Micah Edelson과 그의 동료들은 /
conducted an interesting experiment /
한 흥미로운 실험을 했다 /
about external factors of memory manipulation.
기억 조작의 외부 요인에 관한

(2) In their experiment, / participants were shown /
그들의 실험에서 / 참가자들은 보았다 / be+p.p.①
a two minute documentary film / and then asked /
2분짜리 다큐멘터리 영화를 / 그리고 그런 다음에 질문을 받았다 / be+p.p.②
a series of questions / about the video.
일련의 질문을 / 그 영상에 관한

(3) Directly after viewing the videos, /
그 영상을 보고 난 직후 /
participants made few errors / in their responses /
참가자들은 거의 오류를 저지르지 않았다 / 그들의 응답에서 /
and were correctly able to recall the details.
그리고 세부 사항들을 정확하게 기억해 낼 수 있었다

힌트 few / little (거의 없는) a few / a little (약간 있는)

(4) Four days later, / they could still remember the details /
4일 후에 / 그들은 여전히 세부 사항들을 기억할 수 있었다 /
and didn't allow their memories to be swayed /
5형식V O O·C(to V)
그리고 그들의 기억이 흔들리는 것을 용납하지 않았다 /
when they were presented /
그들에게 제시되었을 때 /
with any false information about the film. 정답 단서
그 영화에 관한 어떤 잘못된 정보가

(5) This changed, / however, / when participants were shown /
이것은 바뀌었다 / 그러나 / 참가자들이 보았을 때 /
fake responses / about the film / made by other participants. 정답 단서
거짓 응답을 / 그 영화에 관해 / 다른 참가자들이 한

(6) Upon seeing the incorrect answers of others, /
upon/on V-ing: ~하자마자
다른 사람들의 옳지 않은 응답을 보자마자 /
participants were also drawn /
참가자들 또한 이끌렸다 /
toward the wrong answers themselves. 정답 단서
본인들도 잘못된 응답 쪽으로

힌트 재귀대명사인 themselves는 주어인 participants를 한 번 더 강조하기 위해 쓰임(강조 용법).

(7) Even after they found out /
심지어 그들이 발견한 이후에도 /
that the other answers had been fabricated /
명사절 접속사
다른 응답들이 조작되었다는 것을 /
and didn't have anything to do with the documentary, /
그리고 그 다큐멘터리와 아무런 관련이 없었다는 것을 /

힌트 밑줄 친 부분은 'had nothing to do with ~'와 같으므로, '~와 아무런 관련이 없었다'라고 해석함.

it was too late.
이미 너무 늦은 후였다

(8) The participants were no longer able to distinguish /
그 참가자들은 더 이상 구별할 수 없었다 /
between truth and fiction.
진실과 허구를

(9) They had already modified their memories / to fit the group.
그들은 이미 자신의 기억을 수정했다 / 그 집단에 맞게끔

(10) According to the experiment, /
실험에 따르면 /
when participants were given false information itself, /
참가자들이 잘못된 정보 자체를 받았을 때 /
their memories remained (A)stable, /
그들의 기억은 여전히 (A)안정적이었다 /
but their memories were (B)falsified /
하지만 그들의 기억은 (B)왜곡되었다 /
when they were exposed / to other participants' fake responses.
그들이 노출되었을 때 / 다른 참가자들의 거짓 응답에

[전문 해석]

(1)2011년에 Micah Edelson과 그의 동료들은 기억 조작의 외부 요인에 관한 한 흥미로운 실험을 했다. (2)그들의 실험에서 참가자들은 2분짜리 다큐멘터리 영화를 보았고 그런 다음에 그 영상에 관한 일련의 질문을 받았다. (3)그 영상을 보고 난 직후 참가자들은 그들의 응답에서 거의 오류를 저지르지 않았고 세부 사항들을 정확하게 기억해 낼 수 있었다. (4)4일 후에 그들은 여전히 세부 사항들을 기억할 수 있었고 그 영화에 관한 어떤 잘못된 정보가 그들에게 제시되었을 때에도 그들의 기억이 흔들리는 것을 용납하지 않았다. (5)그러나 참가자들이 그 영화에 관해 다른 참가자들이 한 거짓 응답을 보았을 때, 이것은 바뀌었다. (6)다른 사람들의 옳지 않은 응답을 보자마자, 참가자 본인들 또한 잘못된 응답 쪽으로 이끌렸다. (7)심지어 그들이 다른 응답들이 조작되었고 그 다큐멘터리와 아무런 관련이 없었다는 것을 발견한 이후에도 이미 너무 늦은 후였다. (8)그 참가자들은 더 이상 진실과 허구를 구별할 수 없었다. (9)그들은 이미 자신의 기억을 그 집단에 맞게끔 수정했다.

⬇

(10)실험에 따르면 참가자들이 잘못된 정보 자체를 받았을 때 그들의 기억은 여전히 (A)안정적이었지만, 그들이 다른 참가자들의 거짓 응답에 노출되었을 때 그들의 기억은 (B)왜곡되었다.

[정답 확인]

다음 글의 내용을 한 문장으로 요약하고자 한다. 빈칸 (A)와 (B)에 들어갈 말로 가장 적절한 것은?

(A)		(B)	(A)		(B)
✔ stable 안정적인	……	falsified 왜곡되었다	② fragile 손상되기 쉬운	……	modified 수정되었다
③ stable 안정적인	……	intensified 강화되었다	④ fragile 손상되기 쉬운	……	solidified 확고해졌다
⑤ concrete 구체적인	……	maintained 유지되었다			

[문제 풀이]

본문은 기억을 조작하는 외부 요인에 관한 한 실험을 소개한다. 실험 참가자들은 다큐멘터리 시청 직후에는 세부 사항을 거의 정확히 기억했다. 또한 문장 (4)에서 영상 시청 나흘 후 영화에 관한 '잘못된 정보'가 제시되었을 때에도 참가자들의 기억은 흔들리지 않았다고 하므로, (A)에는 'stable(안정적인)'이 온다. 그러나 문장 (5)의 'however'를 기점으로 반전이 일어나는데, 문장 (6)~(9)에서 알 수 있듯, 참가자들은 다른 참가자들이 한 거짓 응답을 보고 난 후, 다른 이들에게 동조하여 더 이상 진실과 허구를 구별하지 못하게 되었다고 한다. 따라서 (B)에는 영상에 대한 기존의 기억이 바뀌었다는 내용이 와야 하므로 'falsified(왜곡되었다)' 또는 'modified(수정되었다)'가 와야 한다. 따라서 정답은 ①이다.

[중요 어휘]

- ☐ **colleague** 명사 (업무상의) 동료, 동업자
- ☐ **conduct** 동사 (특정한 활동을) 하다, 지휘하다, 안내하다 / 명사 행위, 지도, 수행
- ☐ **external** 형용사 외부의, 밖의
- ☐ **manipulation** 명사 조작, 손을 씀
- ☐ **recall** 동사 기억해 내다, 상기하다
- ☐ **sway** 동사 흔들다, 동요시키다 / 명사 흔들림, 동요
- ☐ **present** 동사 제시하다, 보여주다 / 형용사 현재의, (출석해) 있는
- ☐ **fabricate** 동사 조작하다, 제작하다
- ☐ **distinguish between A and B** A와 B를 구별하다
- ☐ **modify** 동사 수정하다, 바꾸다

● 지문 구조도

(1) **기억 조작(memory manipulation)의 외부 요인(external factors)에 관한 실험**	
(2) 2분짜리의 다큐멘터리 영화를 본 참가자들이 그 비디오에 관한 질문을 받음.	
영상에 관한 잘못된 정보가 제공된 경우	**다른 참가자들의 거짓 응답이 제공된 경우**
(3) 영상을 보고 난 직후, 세부 사항들(details)을 정확하게 기억해 냄(recall).	(5) 그 영화에 관한 다른 참가자들의 거짓 응답(fake responses)을 보고서는 기억이 바뀜. (6) 다른 사람들의 옳지 않은(incorrect) 응답을 보고 자신도 잘못된 응답으로 이끌림(be drawn).
(4) 4일 후에도 여전히 세부 사항들을 기억해 냈고, 제시된 잘못된 정보에도 기억이 흔들리지(be swayed) 않음.	(7) 그 응답들이 조작되었고(be fabricated) 다큐멘터리와 무관하다는 것을 발견한(find out) 이후에도 기억 조작은 여전했음. (8) 진실(truth)과 허구(fiction)를 구분하지 못함. (9) 자신의 기억을 집단에 맞게끔(to fit the group) 수정함(modify).

↓

결론
(10) 참가자들이 잘못된 정보 자체(false information itself)를 받았을 때는 그들의 기억이 여전히 안정적(stable)이었던 반면, 그들이 다른 참가자들의 거짓 응답(fake responses)에 노출되었을(be exposed to) 때에는 그들의 기억이 왜곡되었음(be falsified).

핵심 '취미와 일의 유사성'이 자기 효능감에 미치는 영향에 대해 다룬 글임. 취미와 일이 비슷한 경우와 비슷하지 않은 경우를 비교하며 지문을 읽어볼 것.

11 2020년 9월 40번 (정답률 55%) 정답 ①

[지문 끊어 읽기] 취미와 일의 유사성이 자기 효능감에 미치는 영향

(1) Some researchers / at Sheffield University /
몇몇 연구원들은 / Sheffield 대학교의 /
recruited 129 hobbyists / to look at /
129명의 취미에 열정적인 사람들을 모집했다 / 보기 위해 /
how the time spent on their hobbies shaped / their work life.
S' V'
그들의 취미에 쓰인 시간이 어떻게 형성했는지 / 그들의 직장 생활을

(2) To begin with, / the team measured /
S V①
먼저 / 그 팀은 측정했다 /
the seriousness of each participant's hobby, /
각 참가자의 취미에 대한 진지함을 /
asking them to rate / their agreement with statements /
그들에게 평가하도록 요청하며 / 진술에 대한 그들의 동의를 /
like "I regularly train for this activity," / and also assessed /
"나는 이 활동을 위해 정기적으로 훈련한다."와 같은 / 그리고 또한 평가했다 / V②
how similar the demands of their job and hobby were.
S' V'
그들의 일과 취미에 대한 요구가 얼마나 비슷한지를

힌트 의문사 how가 동사 were의 주격 보어인 similar와 만나 의문사 덩어리를 이룸. how 이하부터 문장 끝까지는 간접의문문으로서 assessed의 목적어 역할을 함.

(3) Then, / each month for seven months, /
그 후 / 7개월 동안 매월 /
participants recorded / how many hours /
S V①
참가자들은 기록했다 / 얼마나 많은 시간을 /
they had dedicated to their activity, / and completed a scale /
그들이 자신의 활동에 전념했는지 / 그리고 평가표를 완성했다 / V②
measuring their belief in their ability /
자신의 능력에 대한 믿음을 측정하는 /

문제편 p.238

힌트 밑줄 친 부분의 or은 '동격의 or'로 '즉, 바꾸어 말하면'이라는 뜻임. 여기서 their belief in ~ job과 their "self-efficacy"가 동격임.

to effectively do their job, / or their "self-efficacy."
자신의 일을 효과적으로 수행하는 / 즉 그들의 '자기 효능감'을

(4) The researchers found that / when participants spent /
명사절 접속사
그 연구원들은 ~라는 것을 발견했다 / 참가자들이 시간을 보냈을 때 /
longer than normal / doing their leisure activity, /
보통 수준보다 더 많이 / 자신의 여가 활동을 하는 데 /
their belief in their ability / to perform their job / increased. 정답 단서
자신의 능력에 대한 그들의 믿음이 / 자신의 일을 수행하는 / 증가했다

(5) But this was only the case / when they had a serious hobby /
하지만 이는 오직 경우에만 그러했다 / 그들이 진지한 취미를 가지고 있었던 /
that was dissimilar to their job. 정답 단서
자신의 일과 다른

(6) When their hobby was both serious and similar to their job, /
both A and B: A와 B 모두
그들의 취미가 진지하면서 그들의 일과 유사했을 때 /
then spending more time on it /
그때는 그것에 더 많은 시간을 보내는 것이 /
actually decreased their self-efficacy.
실제로 그들의 자기 효능감을 감소시켰다

(7) Research suggests that / spending more time /
연구는 ~라는 것을 시사한다 / 더 많은 시간을 보내는 것이 /
on serious hobbies / can boost (A)confidence at work /
진지한 취미에 / 직장에서의 (A)자신감을 북돋울 수 있다 /
if the hobbies and the job / are sufficiently (B)different.
만약 취미와 일이 / 충분히 (B)다르다면

[전문 해석]

(1)Sheffield 대학교의 몇몇 연구원들은 취미에 쓰인 시간이 직장 생활을 어떻게 형성했는지(그 영향을) 보기 위해 129명의 취미에 열정적인 사람들을 모집했다. (2)먼저 그 (연구)팀은 그들에게 "나는 이 활동을 위해 정기적으로 훈련한다."와 같은 진술에 대한 그들의 동의(의 정도)를 평가하도록 요청하며 각 참가자의 취미에 대한 진지함을 측정했고, 또한 그들의 일과 취미에 대한 요구가 얼마나 비슷한지를 평가했다. (3)그 후 7개월 동안 매월, 참가자들은 그들이 자신의 (취미) 활동에 얼마나 많은 시간을 전념했는지 기록했고, 일을 효과적으로 수행하는 자신의 능력에 대한 믿음, 즉 '자기 효능감'을 측정하는 평가표를 완성했다. (4)그 연구원들은 참가자들이 자신의 여가 활동을 하는 데 보통 수준보다 더 많이 시간을 보냈을 때, 일을 수행하는 자신의 능력에 대한 (그들의) 믿음이 증가했다는 것을 발견했다. (5)하지만 이는 오직 그들이 자신의 일과 다른 진지한 취미를 가지고 있었던 경우에만 그러했다. (6)그들의 취미가 진지하면서 그들의 일과 유사했을 때, 취미에 더 많은 시간을 보내는 것이 실제로 그들의 자기 효능감을 감소시켰다.

⬇

(7)연구는 만약 취미와 일이 충분히 (B)다르다면 진지한 취미에 더 많은 시간을 보내는 것이 직장에서의 (A)자신감을 북돋울 수 있다는 것을 시사한다.
- self-efficacy(자기 효능감): 캐나다의 심리학자 Albert Bandura가 제시한 개념으로, 자신이 어떤 일을 성공적으로 수행할 수 있는 능력이 있다고 믿는 기대와 신념을 뜻하는 심리학 용어이다.

[정답 확인]

다음 글의 내용을 한 문장으로 요약하고자 한다. 빈칸 (A)와 (B)에 들어갈 말로 가장 적절한 것은?

	(A)		(B)
✔	confidence 자신감	......	different 다르다면
②	productivity 생산성	......	connected 연결되어 있다면
③	relationships 관계	......	balanced 균형 잡혀 있다면
④	creativity 창의성	......	separate 분리되어 있다면
⑤	dedication 헌신	......	similar 비슷하다면

[문제 풀이]

지문에 소개된 실험은 '취미와 일 사이의 유사성'과 '취미 활동에 보내는 시간'이라는 두 가지 변수에 따라 '참가자들의 자기 효능감이 어떻게 변화하는지'를 측정하였다. 실험 결과에 해당하는 문장 (4)~(6)은 취미에 더 많은 시간을 보냈을 때 자기 효능감이 증가하는 경향이 있으나 이는 취미와 일 사이의 유사성이 낮은 경우에만 유효하다고 설명하므로, (B)에는 'different(다르다면)'가 들어가는 것이 적절하다. 또한 문장 (3)에서 자기 효능감은 자신의 능력에 대한 믿음이라고 말하고 있으므로, (A)에는 'confidence(자신감)'가 들어가는 것이 적절하다. 따라서 정답은 ①이다.

[중요 어휘]

□ recruit	동사 모집하다, 채용하다
□ hobbyist	명사 취미에 열정적인 사람
□ shape	동사 형성하다 / 명사 형태, 모양
□ seriousness	명사 진지함, 심각함
□ assess	동사 평가하다, 가늠하다
□ demand	명사 요구 (사항), 수요
□ dedicate to	~에 전념하다, 헌신하다
□ scale	명사 평가표, 규모
□ dissimilar	형용사 다른, 닮지 않은
□ boost	동사 북돋우다 / 명사 격려, 증가
□ sufficiently	부사 충분히

핵심 귀여운 것을 볼 때 갖게 되는 공격성에 대해 설명하고 있는 글임. 문단 요약 문제는 일단 글의 핵심이 되는 문장을 찾아서 그 문장의 의미를 바꾸지 않는 선에서 문단을 한 문장으로 요약해야 함.

12 2019년 9월 40번 (정답률 50%) 정답 ②

[지문 끊어 읽기] 귀여운 공격성

(1) When we see an adorable creature, /
우리가 사랑스러운 생명체를 볼 때 /
we must fight an overwhelming urge / to squeeze that cuteness.
우리는 엄청난 충동과 싸워야 한다 / 그 귀여운 것을 꽉 쥐고 싶다는 형용사적 용법

(2) And pinch it, and cuddle it, and maybe even bite it.
그리고 그것을 꼬집고, 꼭 껴안고, 심지어는 깨물고 싶어하기도 한다

힌트 문장 (2)는 문장 (1)의 'urge to V'에 병렬 구조로 이어지는 문장임.

(3) This is a perfectly normal psychological tick /
이것은 완벽하게 정상적인 심리학적 행동이다 /
— an oxymoron called "cute aggression" — /
'귀여운 공격성'이라 불리는 모순 어법 /
and even though it sounds cruel, /
그리고 잔인하게 들릴지도 모르지만 /
it's not about causing harm at all.
이것은 해를 끼치는 것과는 전혀 상관이 없다

힌트 모순어법(oxymoron)이란 의미상 서로 양립할 수 없는 말을 함께 사용하는 수사법임. 대표적인 예로 'a deafening silence(귀를 먹먹하게 하는 침묵)', 'a cruel kindness(냉정한 친절)' 등이 있음.

(4) In fact, strangely enough, /
사실 충분히 이상하지만 /
this compulsion may actually make us more caring.
이 충동은 실제로 우리가 더 보살피게 할 수도 있다

(5) The first study / to look at cute aggression / in the human brain /
최초의 연구는 / 귀여운 공격성을 살펴본 / 인간 뇌에서 /
has now revealed / that this is a complex neurological response, /
이제 막 밝혀냈다 / 이것이 복잡한 신경학적인 반응이라는 것을 /
involving several parts of the brain.
뇌의 여러 부분과 연관되어 있는

힌트 'so + 형용사(부사) + that + S + V' 구문은 '너무 ~해서 …하다'는 뜻이므로 from 이하를 해석하면 '너무 감정적으로 과부하되어 굉장히 귀여운 것들을 우리가 돌볼 수 없게 된다'가 됨.

(6) The researchers propose / that cute aggression may stop us /
연구자들은 제안한다 / 귀여운 공격성이 우리가 ~하는 것을 막아 줄지도 모른다고 /
from becoming so emotionally overloaded /
너무 감정적으로 과부하되어서 /
that we are unable to look after / things that are super cute. 정답 단서
우리가 돌볼 수 없게 되는 것을 / 정말 귀여운 것들을

(7) "Cute aggression may serve / as a tempering mechanism / 정답 단서
귀여운 공격성은 역할을 할 수도 있습니다 / 조절하는 메커니즘으로서 /
that allows us to function /
병렬①
우리가 제대로 기능할 수 있도록 하는 /
and actually take care of something /
병렬②
그리고 실제로 무언가를 돌볼 수 있도록 하는 /
we might first perceive / as overwhelmingly cute," /
우리가 처음에 여길지도 모르는 / 압도적으로 귀엽다고 /
explains the lead author, Stavropoulos.
V S
대표 저자인 Stavropoulos는 설명한다

✱중요 문장 (6)과 (7)이 이 지문 속 연구의 핵심을 관통하는 내용임. 'emotionally overloaded'는 'excessive emotions'로, 'tempering'은 'regulate'로, 'look after'나 'take care of'는 'care for'와 연결되므로 정답 ②를 쉽게 찾을 수 있음.

힌트 문장 (7)의 주절은 'explains the lead author, Stavropoulos'로, 큰따옴표 안의 인용절은 모두 explains의 목적어임.

(8) According to research, / cute aggression may act /
연구에 따르면 / 귀여운 공격성은 역할을 할지도 모른다 /
as a neurological response / to (A)regulate excessive emotions /
신경학적인 반응으로서의 / 과도한 감정을 (A)조절하는 /

and make us (B)care for cute creatures.
그리고 우리가 귀여운 생명체를 (B)돌보게 하는

[중요 구문] 힌트 선행사로 mechanism을 취하는 주격 관계대명사절 'that allows ~ cute' 안에서 관계대명사가 생략된 목적격 관계대명사절 '(that) we might ~ cute'가 선행사 something을 수식하고 있음.

(7) "Cute aggression may serve as a tempering mechanism [that allows us to function and actually take care of something { (that) we might first perceive as overwhelmingly cute }]," ~.
선행사 / [ ]: 주격 관계대명사절

[전문 해석]

(1)우리가 사랑스러운 생명체를 볼 때, 우리는 그 귀여운 것을 꽉 쥐고 싶다는 엄청난 충동과 싸워야 한다. (2)그리고 그것(그 사랑스러운 생명체)을 꼬집고, 꼭 껴안고, 심지어는 깨물고 싶어하기도 한다. (3)이것은 완벽하게 정상적인 심리학적 행동, 즉 '귀여운 공격성'이라 불리는 모순 어법이며, 잔인하게 들릴지도 모르지만, 이것은 해를 끼치는 것과는 전혀 상관이 없다. (4)사실 충분히 이상하지만, 이 충동은 실제로 우리가 (다른 이를) 더 보살피게 할 수도 있다. (5)인간 뇌에서 귀여운 공격성을 살펴본 최초의 연구는 이것(귀여운 공격성)이 뇌의 여러 부분과 연관되어 있는 복잡한 신경학적인 반응이라는 것을 이제 막 밝혀냈다. (6)연구자들은 귀여운 공격성이, 우리가 너무 감정적으로 과부하되어서 (정작) 정말 귀여운 것들을 돌볼 수 없게 되는 것(상황)을 막아 줄지도 모른다고 제안한다. (7)"귀여운 공격성은 우리가 제대로 기능할 수 있도록 하고 실제로 우리가 처음에 압도적으로 귀엽다고 여길지도 모르는 무언가를 돌볼 수 있도록 하는, 조절하는 메커니즘으로서 역할을 할 수도 있습니다."라고 대표 저자인 Stavropoulos는 설명한다.

⬇

(8)연구에 따르면, 귀여운 공격성은 과도한 감정을 (A)조절하고, 우리가 귀여운 생명체를 (B)돌보게 하는 신경학적인 반응으로서의 역할을 할지도 모른다.

[정답 확인]

다음 글의 내용을 한 문장으로 요약하고자 한다. 빈칸 (A)와 (B)에 들어갈 말로 가장 적절한 것은?

	(A)		(B)
①	evaluate 평가하고	……	care 돌보게
②✔	regulate 조절하고	……	care 돌보게
③	accept 받아들이고	……	search 찾게
④	induce 유발하고	……	search 찾게
⑤	display 내보이고	……	speak 말하게

[중요 어휘]

□ adorable	형용사 사랑스러운
□ overwhelming	형용사 엄청난, 압도적인
□ squeeze	동사 꽉 쥐다, 짜내다
□ pinch	동사 꼬집다
□ cuddle	동사 꼭 껴안다
□ oxymoron	명사 모순 어법
□ aggression	명사 공격성
□ cruel	형용사 잔인한, 잔혹한
□ compulsion	명사 충동, 강요
□ reveal	동사 밝히다, 드러내다
□ neurological	형용사 신경학적인, 신경의
□ overloaded	형용사 과부하된
□ temper	동사 조절하다, 경감하다
□ perceive A as B	A를 B로 여기다

13 2023년 9월 40번 (정답률 50%) 정답 ①

[지문 끊어 읽기] 도움을 주려는 동기

(1) In 2006, / researchers conducted a study /
2006년에 / 연구자들은 연구를 수행했다 /
on the motivations for helping /
도움을 주려는 동기에 대한 /
after the September 11th terrorist attacks against the United States.
미국에 대한 9/11 테러 공격 이후에

(2) In the study, / they found /
연구에서 / 그들은 발견했다 /
that [individuals [who gave money, blood, goods, or other forms of assistance /
선행사 / [ ]: 주격 관계대명사절
돈, 혈액, 물품, 또는 다른 형태의 도움을 준 사람들이 /
because of other-focused motives /
타인 중심의 동기 때문에 /
(giving to reduce another's discomfort)]] / [ ]: S
(다른 사람의 고통을 줄이기 위한 베풂)
were almost four times more likely /
V
가능성이 거의 4배 더 높았다는 것을 /
to still be giving support one year later /
1년 후에도 여전히 도움을 줄 /
than those [whose original motivation was to reduce personal distress].
[ ]: 소유격 관계대명사절 / S.C
원래 동기가 개인적인 고통을 줄이기 위한 것이었던 사람들보다
정답 단서 연구는 타인 중심의 동기로 인해 도움을 준 사람들이 개인적인 고통을 줄이기 위해 도움을 준 사람들보다 1년 후에도 여전히 도움을 줄 가능성이 4배 더 높다고 함.

(3) This effect likely stems from differences in emotional arousal.
이 결과는 아마 감정적인 자극의 차이에서 유래하는 것 같다

(4) The events of September 11th emotionally affected /
S / V
9월 11일 사건은 감정적으로 영향을 미쳤다 /
people throughout the United States.
O
미국 전역의 사람들에게

(5) [Those who gave to reduce their own distress] / [ ]: S
선행사 / 주격 관계대명사절
그들 자신의 고통을 줄이기 위해 베푼 사람들은 /
reduced their emotional arousal with their initial gift, /
V
그들의 초기의 베풂으로 감정적인 자극을 줄였다 /
[discharging that emotional distress].
[ ]: 분사구문
그 감정적인 고통을 해소하면서
정답 단서 자신의 고통을 줄이기 위해 베푼 사람들은 초기에 베푼 것으로 감정적 자극을 줄임.

(6) However, / those who gave to reduce others' distress /
선행사 / 주격 관계대명사절
그러나 / 다른 사람들의 고통을 줄이기 위해 베푼 사람들은 /
did not stop empathizing with victims /
선행사
피해자들에게 공감하는 것을 멈추지 않았다 /
[who continued to struggle / long after the attacks]. [ ]: 주격 관계대명사절
계속해서 고군분투한 / 공격 한참 뒤에도

(7) A study found /
한 연구는 발견했다 /
that the act of giving was less likely to be (A)sustained /
베푸는 행동이 (A)지속될 가능성이 더 낮았다는 것을 /
when driven by self-centered motives /
자기중심의 동기에 의해 유도될 때 /
rather than by other-focused motives, /
타인 중심의 동기에 의해서라기보다는 /
possibly because of the (B)decline in emotional arousal.
아마 감정적인 자극의 (B)감소 때문에

[전문 해석]

(1)2006년에 연구자들은 미국에 대한 9/11 테러 공격 이후에 도움을 주려는 동기에 대한 연구를 수행했다. (2)연구에서 그들은 타인 중심의 동기(다른 사람의 고통을 줄이기 위한 베풂) 때문에 돈, 혈액, 물품, 또는 다른 형태의 도움을 준 사람들이 원래 동기가 개인적인 고통을 줄이기 위한 것이었던 사람들보다 1년 후에도 여전히 도움을 줄 가능성이 거의 4배 더 높았다는 것을 발견했다. (3)이 결과는 아마 감정적인 자극의 차이에서 유래하는 것 같다. (4)9월 11일 사건은 미국 전역의 사람들에게 감정적으로 영향을 미쳤다. (5)그들 자신의 고통을 줄이기 위해 베푼 사람들은 그들의 초기의 베풂으로 그 감정적인 고통을 해소하면서 감정적인 자극을 줄였다. (6)그러나 다른 사람들의 고통을 줄이기 위해 베푼 사람들은 공격 한참 뒤에도 계속해서 고군분투한 피해자들에게 공감하는 것을 멈추지 않았다.

⬇

(7)한 연구는 베푸는 행동이 타인 중심의 동기에 의해서라기보다는 자기중심의 동기에 의해 유도될 때 (A)지속될 가능성이 더 낮았으며, 이것은 아마 감정적인 자극의 (B)감소 때문이라는 것을 발견했다.

[정답 확인]

다음 글의 내용을 한 문장으로 요약하고자 한다. 빈칸 (A)와 (B)에 들어갈 말로 가장 적절한 것은?

(A)		(B)	(A)		(B)
✔ sustained 지속될	......	decline 감소	② sustained 지속될	......	maximization 최대화
③ indirect 간접적일	......	variation 변화	④ discouraged 좌절될	......	reduction 감소
⑤ discouraged 좌절될	......	increase 증가			

[문제 풀이]

본문에 따르면, 미국 9/11 테러 이후에 수행된 도움의 동기에 관한 연구에서 타인 중심적, 즉 타인의 고통을 줄이기 위해 베풀었던 사람들이 자신의 고통을 줄이기 위해 베풀었던 사람들보다 1년 후에도 계속해서 베풀 가능성이 4배 더 높았다고 한다. 자신의 고통을 줄이기 위해 베풀었던 사람들은 베푸는 행위로 자신의 감정적인 고통을 해소함에 따라 감정적인 자극이 줄어들게 되었고, 이에 따라 도움을 지속하지 않았다. 따라서 자신에 초점을 맞춘 동기, 즉 자기중심의 동기에 의해 베푸는 행동이 유도된 사람들은 감정적인 자극이 감소되면서 베푸는 행동이 지속되지 않는다는 내용의 ①이 적절하다.

[중요 어휘]

☐ **goods**	명사 물품, 재화, 상품
☐ **discomfort**	명사 고통, 불편
☐ **be likely to V**	~할 가능성이 있다
☐ **distress**	명사 고통, 곤란, 고난
☐ **likely**	부사 아마
☐ **stem from**	~에서 유래하다
☐ **arousal**	명사 자극, 각성
☐ **initial**	형용사 초기의, 처음의
☐ **empathize**	동사 공감하다, 감정 이입하다
☐ **struggle**	동사 고군분투하다
☐ **self-centered**	형용사 자기중심의

14 2022년 3월 40번 (정답률 40%) 정답 ①

[지문 끊어 읽기] 관계를 나타내는 지표로서의 거리

(1) Distance is a reliable indicator /
거리는 믿을 수 있는 지표이다 /
of the relationship between two people.
두 사람 간의 관계에 관한

힌트 여기서 do는 stand를 대신하는 대동사임. 또한 동사의 의미를 강조하기 위해 as, than, so 뒤에 주어와 동사가 도치될 수 있음.

(2) Strangers stand further apart / than do acquaintances, /
모르는 사람들은 더 멀리 떨어져 서 있다 / 지인들이 서 있는 것보다 /
acquaintances stand further apart / than friends, /
지인들은 더 멀리 떨어져 서 있다 / 친구들보다 /
and friends stand further apart /
그리고 친구들은 더 멀리 떨어져 서 있다 /
than romantic partners. 정답 단서 사람들 간의 거리는 모르는 사람, 지인, 친구, 연인 등 그들 간의 관계가 어떠한지에 따라 달라짐.
연인들보다

힌트 비교 구문의 접속사 than이 이끄는 절에서는 앞선 절과 공통되는 부분이 자주 생략됨. 여기서는 than friends (stand), than romantic partners (stand)처럼 동사 stand가 생략됨.

(3) Sometimes, / of course, / these rules are violated.
때때로 / 물론 / 이들 규칙은 위반된다 =문장 (2)

(4) Recall the last time / [you rode 20 stories in an elevator /
선행사
마지막 때를 떠올려 보라 / 엘리베이터를 타고 20개 층을 이동했던 /
packed with total strangers]. [ ]: 관계부사절(관계부사 생략)
완전히 모르는 사람들로 가득 찬

(5) The sardine-like experience / no doubt made the situation /
삽입구 5형식V O
승객이 빽빽이 들어찬 경험은 / 분명히 그 상황을 만들었을 것이다 /
a bit uncomfortable.
약간 불편하게 O·C

힌트 'with+명사+분사'는 부대상황을 나타내는 분사구문의 일종으로 'with+명사+현재분사'는 명사의 능동적 행위, 'with+명사+과거분사'는 명사의 수동적 행위나 상태를 나타냄.

(6) With your physical space violated, /
물리적 공간이 침범된 상태에서 /
you may have tried to create "psychological" space /
may have p.p.: ~했을 수도 있다
여러분은 '심리적' 공간을 만들어 내려고 했을 수도 있다 /
by avoiding eye contact, /
눈맞춤을 피함으로써 /
[focusing instead on the elevator buttons]. [ ]: 분사구문(동시동작)
그 대신 엘리베이터 버튼에 집중해서

(7) By reducing closeness / in one nonverbal channel (eye contact), /
가까움을 줄임으로써 / 하나의 비언어적인 채널(눈맞춤)에서의 /
one can compensate for unwanted closeness /
원치 않는 가까움을 상쇄할 수 있다 /
in another channel (proximity). 정답 단서 물리적 공간이 침범된 상태에서, 눈맞춤 등 비언어적 소통을 줄여 원치 않는 가까움을 상쇄할 수 있음.
또 다른 채널(근접성)에서의

(8) Similarly, / if you are talking with someone /
마찬가지로 / 여러분이 누군가와 이야기를 하고 있다면 /
[who is seated several feet away / at a large table], /
몇 피트 떨어져 앉아 있는 / 큰 테이블에서 / [ ]: 주격 관계대명사절
you are likely to maintain constant eye contact /
여러분은 아마도 계속 눈을 마주칠 것이다 /
— something you might feel uncomfortable doing /
목적격 관계대명사절
여러분이 하기에는 불편해할 수도 있는 것이다 /
if you were standing next to each other.
서로 옆에 서 있는 경우에

힌트 feel uncomfortable V-ing는 '~하는 것을 불편해하다, ~하는 것에 불편함을 느끼다'로 해석하면 됨.

힌트 대시(—) 뒤의 내용은 앞에서 언급된 계속 눈을 마주치는 것(to maintain constant eye contact)에 대한 부연 설명임.

(9) Physical distance between people /
사람들 사이의 물리적 거리는 /
is (A)determined by relationship status, /
관계의 상태에 의해 (A)결정된다 /
but when the distance is not appropriate, /
하지만 그 거리가 적절하지 않을 때 /
people (B)adjust their nonverbal communication /
사람들은 비언어적 의사소통을 (B)조절한다 /
to establish a comfortable psychological distance.
부사적 용법(목적)
편안한 심리적 거리를 확립하기 위해

[전문 해석]

(1)거리는 두 사람 간의 관계에 관한 믿을 수 있는 지표이다. (2)모르는 사람들은 지인들보다 더 멀리 떨어져 서 있고, 지인들은 친구들보다 더 멀리 떨어져 서 있고, 친구들은 연인들보다 더 멀리 떨어져 서 있다. (3)물론 때때로 이들 규칙은 위반된다. (4)완전히 모르는 사람들로 가득 찬 엘리베이터를 타고 20개 층을 이동했던 마지막 때를 떠올려 보라. (5)승객이 빽빽이 들어찬 경험은 분명히 그 상황을 약간 불편하게 만들었을 것이다. (6)물리적 공간이 침범된 상태에서 여러분은 눈을 마주치지 않고, 그 대신 엘리베이터 버튼에 집중해서 '심리적' 공간을 만들어 내려고 했을 수도 있다. (7)하나의 비언어적인 채널(눈맞춤)에서의 가까움을 줄임으로써, 또 다른 채널(근접성)에서의 원치 않는 가까움을 상쇄할 수 있다. (8)마찬가지로, 여러분이 큰 테이블에서 몇 피트 떨어져 앉아 있는 누군가와 이야기를 하고 있다면, 아마도 계속 눈을 마주칠 것인데, (그것은) 여러분이 서로 옆에 서 있는 경우에 하기에는 불편해할 수도 있는 것이다.

⬇

(9)사람들 사이의 물리적 거리는 관계의 상태에 의해 (A)결정되지만, 그 거리가 적절하지 않을 때 사람들은 편안한 심리적 거리를 확립하기 위해 비언어적 의사소통을 (B)조절한다.

[정답 확인]

다음 글의 내용을 한 문장으로 요약하고자 한다. 빈칸 (A)와 (B)에 들어갈 말로 가장 적절한 것은?

(A)		(B)	(A)		(B)
✔ determined 결정되지	......	adjust 조절한다	② concealed 감춰지지	......	interpret 해석한다
③ influenced 영향을 받지	......	ignore 무시한다	④ predicted 예측되지	......	stop 그만둔다
⑤ measured 측정되지	......	decrease 줄인다			

[문제 풀이]

문장 (1)~(2)에 따르면 거리는 모르는 사람, 지인, 친구, 연인 등 두 사람 간의 관계를 설명한다. 즉 사람들 간의 관계에 따라 그들 간의 물리적 거리가 달라진다. 따라서 (A)에는 물리적 거리가 관계의 상태에 의해 결정된다는 뜻의 determined가 적절하다. 다음으로, 문장 (4)~(6)의 예시가 보여주듯이 사람들은 물리적 공간이 침범된 상태를 불편하게 느낀다. 그러므로 문장 (7)에서 언급하듯이 비언어적 소통을 줄이는 등의 방법을 통해 다른 사람과의 근접성을 차단하고 거리를 확보하고자 한다. 반대로 문장 (8)의 경우처럼 거리가 멀 때에는 계속 눈을 마주치는 것으로 심리적 거리를 더 가깝게 만들기도 한다. 따라서 (B)에는 편안한 심리적 거리를 확립하기 위해 비언어적 의사소통을 조절한다는 뜻의 adjust가 적절하다.

[중요 어휘]

- **indicator** 명사 지표
- **acquaintance** 명사 지인, 아는 사람
- **violate** 동사 위반하다, 침범하다
- **packed** 형용사 가득 찬
- **channel** 명사 채널(정보의 전달 경로)
- **compensate for** ~을 상쇄하다[보상하다]
- **proximity** 명사 근접성
- **constant** 형용사 계속적인
- **adjust** 동사 조절하다, 적응하다
- **conceal** 동사 감추다, 숨기다

15 2022년 11월 40번 (정답률 40%) 정답 ①

[지문 끊어 읽기] 가정에 근거한 선입견

(1) A study investigated / the economic cost of prejudice /
한 연구는 조사했다 / 선입견의 경제적인 비용을 /
based on blind assumptions.
과거분사
맹목적인 가정에 근거한

(2) Researchers gave a group of Danish teenagers /
4형식V I·O
연구자들은 한 무리의 덴마크 십 대들에게 주었다 /
the choice of working with one of two people.
D·O
두 사람 중 한 명과 함께 일하는 선택권을

(3) The teenager had never met either of them.
십 대는 그들 중 어느 한 명과도 만난 적이 없었다

(4) One of the people had a name / [that suggested /
선행사 [ ]: 주격 관계대명사절
그 사람들 중 한 명은 이름을 가지고 있었다 / 암시하는 /
they were from a similar ethnic or religious background /
그들이 유사한 인종적 또는 종교적 배경의 출신임을 /
to the teenager].
그 십 대와

(5) The other had a name / [that suggested /
선행사 [ ]: 주격 관계대명사절
다른 한 사람은 이름을 가지고 있었다 / 암시하는 /
they were from a different ethnic or religious background].
다른 인종적 또는 종교적 배경의 출신임을

(6) The study showed /
그 연구는 보여 주었다 /
that the teenagers were prepared to earn an average of 8% less /
명사절 접속사
십 대들은 평균 8% 더 적게 벌 준비가 되어 있다는 것을 /
if they could work with someone /
선행사
만약 그들이 누군가와 함께 일할 수 있다면 /
[they thought came from the same ethnic or religious background].
삽입절 [ ]: 주격 관계대명사절
자신이 생각하기에 같은 인종적 또는 종교적 배경으로부터 온

정답 단서 연구에서 십 대들은 자신이 생각하기에 같은 인종적 또는 종교적 배경을 가진 누군가와 함께 일할 수 있다면 평균 8% 더 적게 버는 것을 감수했음.

(7) And this prejudice was evident /
그리고 이러한 선입견은 분명했다 /
among teenagers with ethnic majority names /
다수 인종의 이름을 가진 십 대들 사이에서도 /
as well as those with ethnic minority names.
=teenagers
B as well as A: A뿐만 아니라 B도
소수 인종의 이름을 가진 십 대들뿐만 아니라

(8) The teenagers were blindly making assumptions /
십 대들은 맹목적으로 가정을 했다 /
about the race of their potential colleagues.
그들의 잠재적인 동료의 인종에 대한

(9) They then applied prejudice to those assumptions, / to the point /
선행사
그들은 그러고 나서 선입견을 그 가정에 적용하였다 / 정도까지 /
where they actually allowed that prejudice to reduce *their own*
관계부사 5형식V O O·C(to V)
potential income.
그 선입견이 '그들 자신의' 잠재적인 소득을 줄이는 것을 실제로 허용할

정답 단서 십 대들은 자신의 잠재적인 소득이 실제로 줄어드는 지점까지 자신의 잠재적인 동료의 인종에 대한 가정에 선입견을 적용함.

(10) The job required the two teenagers /
그 일은 그 두 명의 십 대들에게 요구했다 /
to work together for just *90 minutes*.
단지 '90분'간만 함께 일할 것을

(11) A study / in which teenagers expressed a (A)preference /
S 전치사+관계대명사
한 연구는 / 십 대들이 (A)선호를 표현했던 /
to work with someone of a similar background, /
비슷한 배경의 누군가와 함께 일하는 것에 /
even at a financial cost to themselves, / suggests /
V
심지어 자신에게 오는 경제적인 손실에도 / 시사한다 /
that an assumption-based prejudice / can (B)outweigh rational
명사절 접속사
economic behavior.
가정에 근거한 선입견이 / 이성적인 경제 행위(B)보다 더 중요할 수 있다는 것을

[전문 해석]

(1)한 연구는 맹목적인 가정에 근거한 선입견의 경제적인 비용을 조사했다. (2)연구자들은 한 무리의 덴마크 십 대들에게 두 사람 중 한 명과 함께 일하는 선택권을 주었다. (3)십 대는 그들 중 어느 한 명과도 만난 적이 없었다. (4)그 사람들 중 한 명은 그 십 대와 유사한 인종적 또는 종교적 배경의 출신임을 암시하는 이름을 가지고 있었다. (5)다른 한 사람은 다른 인종적 또는 종교적 배경의 출신임을 암시하는 이름을 가지고 있었다. (6)그 연구는 만약 십 대들이 자신이 생각하기에 같은 인종적 또는 종교적 배경으로부터 온 누군가와 함께 일할 수 있다면 그들은 평균 8% 더 적게 벌 준비가 되어 있다는 것을 보여 주었다. (7)그리고 이러한 선입견은 소수 인종의 이름을 가진 십 대들뿐만 아니라 다수 인종의 이름을 가진 십 대들 사이에서도 분명했다. (8)십 대들은 맹목적으로 그들의 잠재적인 동료의 인종에 대한 가정을 했다. (9)그들은 그러고 나서 그 선입견이 '그들 자신의' 잠재적인 소득을 줄이는 것을 실제로 허용할 정도까지 선입견을 그 가정에 적용하였다. (10)그 일은 그 두 명의 십 대들에게 단지 '90분'간만 함께 일할 것을 요구했다.

⬇

(11)십 대들이 심지어 자신에게 오는 경제적인 손실에도 비슷한 배경의 누군가와 함께 일하는 것에 (A)선호를 표현했던 한 연구는 가정에 근거한 선입견이 이성적인 경제 행위(B)보다 더 중요할 수 있다는 것을 시사한다.

[정답 확인]

다음 글의 내용을 한 문장으로 요약하고자 한다. 빈칸 (A)와 (B)에 들어갈 말로 가장 적절한 것은?

(A)		(B)	(A)		(B)
✔ preference 선호	......	outweigh 보다 더 중요할	② hesitation 망설임	......	reinforce 강화할
③ preference 선호	......	strengthen 강화할	④ hesitation 망설임	......	overwhelm 압도할
⑤ inability 무능	......	underlie 기저를 이룰			

[문제 풀이]

본문에 따르면, 십 대들은 유사한 인종적 또는 종교적 배경을 가진 것으로 생각되는 누군가와 함께 일할 수 있다면 평균 8% 더 적게 버는 것을 감수했다. 다시 말해, 더 적게 번다고 해도 유사한 인종적 또는 종교적 배경을 가진 사람과 함께 일하고 싶어 했다. 따라서 자신에게 오는 경제적인 손실에도 불구하고 비슷한 배경의 누군가와 함께 일하는 것에 대한 선호를 표현했

문제편 p.240

던 연구로 미루어 보아 가정에 근거한 선입견이 이성적인 경제 행위보다 중요할 수 있다는 내용의 ①이 빈칸에 들어가기 적절하다.

[중요 어휘]

☐ **prejudice**	명사 선입견, 편견 / 동사 편견을 갖게 하다
☐ **blind**	형용사 맹목적인, 눈이 먼
☐ **assumption**	명사 가정, 추정
☐ **ethnic**	형용사 인종적인, 인종의
☐ **religious**	형용사 종교적인, 종교의
☐ **earn**	동사 (돈을) 벌다, 얻다
☐ **evident**	형용사 분명한, 눈에 띄는
☐ **make an assumption**	가정을 하다, 추정을 내리다
☐ **race**	명사 인종, 민족, 경주
☐ **potential**	형용사 잠재적인, 가능성이 있는 / 명사 가능성, 잠재력
☐ **apply**	동사 적용하다, 신청하다, 지원하다
☐ **rational**	형용사 이성적인, 합리적인
☐ **outweigh**	동사 ~보다 더 중요하다, ~보다 무겁다

핵심 실험에서 학생들이 암기해야 하는 숫자의 자릿수에 따라 어떤 선택을 하는지를 주목할 것. 또한 reflective와 reflexive의 의미를 파악하고 각각의 선택이 어디에 해당하는지 확인해야 함.

16 2021년 3월 40번 (정답률 30%) 정답 ④

[지문 끊어 읽기] 암기해야 하는 숫자의 자릿수에 따른 선택

(1) At the University of Iowa, / students were briefly shown /
Iowa 대학교에서 / 학생들에게 잠시 보여 주었다 /
numbers that they had to memorize.
선행사 / 목적격 관계대명사절
그들이 암기해야 하는 숫자를

(2) Then they were offered the choice /
그러고 나서 그들에게 선택하게 했다 /
of either a fruit salad or a chocolate cake.
과일 샐러드나 초콜릿 케이크 중 하나를

(3) When the number the students memorized was seven digits long, /
S'(=선행사) / 목적격 관계대명사 생략 / V'
학생들이 외운 숫자가 일곱 자리일 때 /
63% of them chose the cake.
그들 중 63%가 케이크를 선택했다

(4) When the number they were asked to remember /
S'
그들이 기억하도록 요청받은 숫자가 /
had just two digits, / however, / 59% opted for the fruit salad.
V'
두 자리밖에 되지 않았을 때 / 그러나 / 59%는 과일 샐러드를 선택했다

(5) Our reflective brains know /
우리의 숙고하는 뇌는 안다 /
that the fruit salad is better for our health, /
명사절 접속사
과일 샐러드가 우리의 건강에 더 좋다는 것을 /
but our reflexive brains desire / that soft, fattening chocolate cake.
지시형용사
하지만 우리의 반사적인 뇌는 원한다 / 그 부드럽고 살이 찌는 초콜릿 케이크를

(6) If the reflective brain is busy / figuring something else out /
만약 숙고하는 뇌가 바쁘다면 / 다른 어떤 것을 해결하느라 /
— like trying to remember a seven-digit number — /
일곱 자리 숫자를 기억하려고 애쓰는 일과 같은 /
then impulse can easily win. 정답 단서
그러면 충동이 쉽게 이길 수 있다

힌트 be busy + V-ing: ~을 하느라 바쁘다

(7) On the other hand, / if we're not thinking too hard /
한편 / 우리가 너무 열심히 생각하고 있지 않다면 /
about something else /
다른 것에 관해 /
(with only a minor distraction like memorizing two digits), /
(단지 두 자리 숫자를 외우는 것과 같은 사소한 방해만 있을 때) /
then the reflective system can deny /
그러면 숙고하는 계통은 억제할 수 있다 /
the emotional impulse of the reflexive side.
반사적인 쪽의 감정적인 충동을

(8) According to the above experiment, /
위 실험에 따르면 /
the (A)increased intellective load on the brain /
뇌에 가해지는 (A)증가된 지적 부담은 /
leads the reflexive side of the brain / to become (B)dominant.
5형식V / O / O·C
뇌의 반사적인 부분이 / (B)우세해지게 한다

힌트 '원인 lead to 결과' 순으로 사용되며, to 뒤에는 동사원형(~하게 하다)/V-ing(~로 이어지다) 모두 올 수 있음.

[전문 해석]

(1)Iowa 대학교에서 학생들에게 그들이 암기해야 하는 숫자를 잠시 보여 주었다. (2)그러고 나서 그들에게 과일 샐러드나 초콜릿 케이크 중 하나를 선택하게 했다. (3)학생들이 외운 숫자가 일곱 자리일 때, 그들 중 63%가 케이크를 선택했다. (4)그러나 그들이 기억하도록 요청받은 숫자가 두 자리밖에 되지 않았을 때, 59%는 과일 샐러드를 선택했다. (5)우리의 숙고하는 뇌는 과일 샐러드가 우리의 건강에 더 좋다는 것을 알지만, 우리의 반사적인 뇌는 그 부드럽고 살이 찌는 초콜릿 케이크를 원한다. (6)만약 숙고하는 뇌가 일곱 자리 숫자를 기억하려고 애쓰는 일과 같은 다른 어떤 것을 해결하느라 바쁘다면, 충동이 쉽게 이길 수 있다. (7)한편 우리가 다른 것에 관해 너무 열심히 생각하고 있지 않다면 (단지 두 자리 숫자를 외우는 것과 같은 사소한 방해만 있을 때), (뇌의) 숙고하는 계통은 반사적인 쪽의 감정적인 충동을 억제할 수 있다.

⬇

(8)위 실험에 따르면 뇌에 가해지는 (A)증가된 지적 부담은 뇌의 반사적인 부분이 (B)우세해지게 한다.

[정답 확인]

다음 글의 내용을 한 문장으로 요약하고자 한다. 빈칸 (A)와 (B)에 들어갈 말로 가장 적절한 것은?

(A)		(B)	(A)		(B)
① limited 제한된	......	powerful 강력하게	② limited 제한된	......	divided 분리되게
③ varied 다양한	......	passive 수동적이게	✔④ increased 증가된	......	dominant 우세해지게
⑤ increased 증가된	......	weakened 약화되게			

[문제 풀이]

본문의 실험에서, 학생들은 암기해야 하는 숫자가 더 많았을 때 과일 샐러드가 아닌 케이크를 선택했다고 한다. 즉, 우리의 숙고하는 뇌가 다른 어떤 것을 해결하느라 바쁘다면, 우리의 반사적인 뇌의 충동이 쉽게 이길 수 있다. 그러므로 실험 결과에 가장 적합하게 (A)에는 'increased(증가된)' (B)에는 'dominant(우세해지게)'가 와야 한다. 따라서 정답은 ④이다.

[오답 풀이]

① - 문장 (6)에서 설명하는 바와 같이 숙고하는 뇌가 바쁘면 충동이 우세하게 된다고 했기 때문에 (A)에 'limited(제한된)'가 쓰이면 어색하다.

[중요 어휘]

☐ **briefly**	부사 잠시, 짧게
☐ **memorize**	동사 암기하다
☐ **digit**	명사 자릿수
☐ **opt**	동사 선택하다
☐ **reflective**	형용사 숙고하는
☐ **reflexive**	형용사 반사적인
☐ **impulse**	명사 (마음의) 충동
☐ **distraction**	명사 방해, 주의를 산만하게 하는 것
☐ **intellective**	형용사 지적인
☐ **load**	명사 부담, 무거운 짐

문제편 p.241

● 지문 구조도

연구 대상 및 방법	
(1) Iowa 대학교 학생들에게 암기해야(memorize) 하는 숫자를 보여 줌. (2) 그 후 과일 샐러드나 초콜릿 케이크 중 하나를 선택하게 함.	
연구 결과	
(3) 일곱 자리 숫자(seven digits)를 외운 학생들 중 63%가 케이크를 선택함.	(4) 두 자리 숫자를 외운 학생들 중 59%가 과일 샐러드를 선택함(opt for).
연구 전제	
(5) 숙고하는(reflective) 뇌는 과일 샐러드가 우리의 건강에 더 좋다는 것을 알지만, 반사적인(reflexive) 뇌는 초콜릿 케이크를 원함.	
결론	
(6) 숙고하는 뇌가 바쁘면(일곱 자릿수 외우기) 충동(impulse)이 쉽게 이김. → 반사적인 뇌가 우위	(7) 그렇지 않으면(두 자릿수 외우기) 숙고하는 뇌는 감정적인 충동을 억제할(deny) 수 있음. → 숙고하는 뇌가 우위
(8) 뇌에 가해지는 증가된(increased) 지적 부담(intellective load)은 뇌의 반사적인 부분이 우세해지게(become dominant) 함.	

17 2023년 11월 40번 (정답률 65%) 정답 ①

[지문 끊어 읽기] 협력적인 사람에 대한 인식

(1) Multiple laboratory studies show /
여러 실험실 연구들은 보여 준다 /
[that cooperative people tend to receive social advantages from others]. [ ]: show의 목적어절 정답 단서 협력적인 사람은 사회적 혜택을 받을 가능성이 있음.
협력적인 사람들이 다른 사람들로부터 사회적 혜택을 받는 경향이 있다는 것을

(2) One way to demonstrate this / is to give people the opportunity /
S 형용사적 용법 V 4형식V I·O D·O
이것을 증명하는 한 가지 방법은 / 사람들에게 기회를 주는 것이다 /
to act positively or negatively toward contributors.
형용사적 용법
기여자들을 향해 긍정적이거나 부정적으로 행동할

(3) For example, /
예를 들어 /
Pat Barclay, a professor at the University of Guelph, /
Guelph 대학교의 Pat Barclay 교수는 /
had participants play a cooperative game /
V①(사역V) O O·C(동사원형) 선행사
참가자들로 하여금 협력적 게임을 하도록 했다 /
[where people could contribute money / toward a group fund /
관계부사(=in the cooperative game) 선행사
사람들이 돈을 기부할 수 있는 / 집단 기금에 /
which helped all group members], / [ ]: 관계부사절
주격 관계대명사절
모든 집단 구성원들을 도와주는 /
and then allowed participants to give money /
V②(5형식) O O·C(to V)
그런 다음 참가자들이 돈을 줄 수 있도록 했다 /
to other participants / based on their reputations. 정답 단서 집단 기금에 기부한 사람들이 자신들의 평판을 바탕으로 다른 참가자들에게 돈을 주게끔 함.
다른 참가자들에게 / 자신들의 평판을 바탕으로

(4) People [who contributed more to the group fund] / [ ]: 주격 관계대명사절
S, 선행사
집단 기금에 더 많이 기부한 사람들은 /
were given responsibility for more money /
V
더 많은 돈에 대한 책임이 주어졌다 /
than people [who contributed less].
선행사 [ ]: 주격 관계대명사절
덜 기부한 사람들보다

(5) Similar results have been found by other researchers.
유사한 결과들이 다른 연구자들에 의해 발견되었다

(6) People [who contribute toward their groups] / [ ]: 주격 관계대명사절
S, 선행사
그들의 집단에 기여하는 사람들은 /
are also chosen more often as interaction partners, /
V①(수동태)
또한 상호 작용 파트너로 더 자주 선택된다 /
preferred as leaders, /
V②(be동사 생략)
리더로 선호된다 /
rated as more desirable partners for long-term relationships, /
V③(be동사 생략)
장기적인 관계를 위한 더 바람직한 파트너로 평가된다 /
and are perceived to be trustworthy and have high social status.
V④ 병렬① 병렬②(to 생략) 정답 단서 집단에 기여하는 사람은 평판이 좋음.
그리고 신뢰할 수 있고 높은 사회적 지위를 가지는 것으로 인식된다

(7) Uncooperative people tend to receive /
비협조적인 사람들은 받는 경향이 있다 /
verbal criticism or even more severe punishment.
언어 비판이나 심지어 더 심한 벌을

(8) Studies suggest /
연구들은 제시한다 /
명사절 접속사
[that individuals [who act with (A)generosity toward their communities] /
S', 선행사 [ ]: 주격 관계대명사절
그들의 공동체에 (A)관대함을 가지고 행동하는 사람들이 /
are more likely to be viewed as deserving of (B)benefit /
V'
(B)혜택을 누릴 자격이 있다고 간주될 가능성이 더 크다 /
by members of that community / than those who don't]. [ ]: suggest의 목적어절
그 공동체의 구성원들에 의해 / 그렇게 하지 않는 사람들보다 선행사 주격 관계대명사절

[전문 해석]

(1)여러 실험실 연구들은 협력적인 사람들이 다른 사람들로부터 사회적 혜택을 받는 경향이 있다는 것을 보여 준다. (2)이것을 증명하는 한 가지 방법은 사람들에게 기여자들을 향해 긍정적이거나 부정적으로 행동할 기회를 주는 것이다. (3)예를 들어, Guelph 대학교의 Pat Barclay 교수는 참가자들로 하여금 모든 집단 구성원들을 도와주는 집단 기금에 사람들이 돈을 기부할 수 있는 협력적 게임을 하도록 하였고, 그런 다음 참가자들이 자신들의 평판을 바탕으로 다른 참가자들에게 돈을 줄 수 있도록 했다. (4)집단 기금에 더 많이 기부한 사람들은 덜 기부한 사람들보다 더 많은 돈에 대한 책임이 주어졌다. (5)유사한 결과들이 다른 연구자들에 의해 발견되었다. (6)그들의 집단에 기여하는 사람들은 또한 상호 작용 파트너로 더 자주 선택되고, 리더로 선호되며, 장기적인 관계를 위한 더 바람직한 파트너로 평가되고, 신뢰할 수 있고 높은 사회적 지위를 가지는 것으로 인식된다. (7)비협조적인 사람들은 언어 비판이나 심지어 더 심한 벌을 받는 경향이 있다.

⬇

(8)연구들은 그들의 공동체에 (A)관대함을 가지고 행동하는 사람들이 그렇게 하지 않는 사람들보다 그 공동체의 구성원들에 의해 (B)혜택을 누릴 자격이 있다고 간주될 가능성이 더 크다는 것을 제시한다.

[정답 확인]

다음 글의 내용을 한 문장으로 요약하고자 한다. 빈칸 (A)와 (B)에 들어갈 말로 가장 적절한 것은?

	(A)		(B)		(A)		(B)
✔①	generosity 관대함	……	benefit 혜택	②	hostility 적대감	……	support 지원
③	generosity 관대함	……	humiliation 굴욕	④	hostility 적대감	……	hospitality 환대
⑤	tolerance 관용	……	dishonor 불명예				

[문제 풀이]

문장 (1)에 따르면, 여러 실험실 연구에서 협력적인 사람들은 사회적 혜택을 받는 경향이 있다고 한다. 그리고 문장 (3)은 협력 실험에 대한 사례로, 집단 기금에 기부한 사람들이 자신들의 평판으로 참가자들에게 돈을 주게 한다는 것이다. 마찬가지로, 문장 (6)에서 집단에 기여하는 사람들은 평판이 좋다고 한다. 따라서 협력적인 사람들(=기여를 많이 한 사람들)이 혜택을 받는다는 것이 이 글의 주된 내용이므로, 정답은 ①이다.

[중요 어휘]

☐ **cooperative**	형용사 협력적인, 협동적인
☐ **demonstrate**	동사 증명하다, 보여 주다

문제편 p.241

☐ **contribute**	동사 기부하다, 기여하다
☐ **fund**	명사 기금, 자금
☐ **reputation**	명사 평판, 명성
☐ **responsibility**	명사 책임, 의무
☐ **rate**	동사 평가하다, 여기다
☐ **desirable**	형용사 바람직한, 탐나는
☐ **perceive**	동사 인식하다, 인지하다
☐ **trustworthy**	형용사 신뢰할 수 있는, 믿을 수 있는
☐ **status**	명사 지위, 신분
☐ **verbal**	형용사 언어의, 말로 하는
☐ **severe**	형용사 심한, 심각한, 엄격한
☐ **deserve**	동사 ~을 누릴 자격이 있다[받을 만하다]

18 2024년 3월 40번 (정답률 50%) 정답 ①

[지문 끊어 읽기] 데이터 활용을 위한 도구 개발의 필요성

(1) The fast-growing, tremendous amount of data, /
S
데이터의 빠르게 증가하는 엄청난 양은 /
[collected and stored in large and numerous data repositories], /
크고 많은 데이터 저장소에 수집되고 저장되는 / [ ]: 과거분사구
has far exceeded our human ability /
V
인간의 능력을 훨씬 넘어섰다 /
for understanding without powerful tools. 정답 단서 저장된 데이터의 양은 인간이 이해할 수 있는 능력을 넘어섰음.
효과적인 도구 없이도 이해할 수 있는

(2) As a result, / data collected in large data repositories /
S 과거분사구
결과적으로 / 대규모 데이터 저장소에서 수집된 데이터는 /
become "data tombs" / — data archives that are hardly visited.
V 선행사 주격 관계대명사절
'데이터 무덤'이 된다 / 찾는 사람이 거의 없는 데이터 보관소

(3) Important decisions are often made /
중요한 의사 결정은 종종 내려지기도 한다 /
based not on the information-rich data /
정보가 풍부한 데이터에 기반하지 않고 /
stored in data repositories /
데이터 저장소에 저장된 / 과거분사구
but rather on a decision maker's instinct, /
not A but rather B: A가 아니라 오히려 B
오히려 의사 결정자의 직감에 기반하여 /
simply because the decision maker does not have the tools /
단지 의사 결정자가 도구를 가지고 있지 않기 때문에 /
to extract the valuable knowledge /
형용사적 용법
가치 있는 지식을 추출하는 /
hidden in the vast amounts of data.
방대한 양의 데이터에 숨겨진 과거분사구

(4) Efforts have been made /
노력이 있었다 /
to develop expert system and knowledge-based technologies, /
형용사적 용법
전문 시스템과 지식 기반 기술을 개발하려는 /
which typically rely on users or domain experts /
계속적 용법(주격 관계대명사)
그리고 이것은 일반적으로 사용자나 분야 전문가에 의존한다 /
to *manually* input knowledge into knowledge bases.
지식을 '수동으로' 지식 베이스에 입력하는

(5) However, /
그러나 /
힌트 '-ly'로 끝나는 말이라 부사로 생각하기 쉬우나 형용사임. 형용사에 '-ly'가 붙으면 부사로 쓰이나, 명사에 '-ly'가 붙으면 형용사로 쓰임. 'costly'와 비슷하게 'lovely, friendly' 등도 명사에 '-ly'가 붙은 형태의 형용사임.
this procedure is likely to cause biases and errors /
S V①
이 방법은 편견과 오류를 일으키기 쉽다 /
and is extremely costly and time consuming.
V② 병렬①(보어) 병렬②
그리고 비용이 극도로 많이 들고 시간이 꽤 든다

(6) The widening gap between data and information /
점점 더 벌어지는 데이터와 정보 간의 격차는 /
calls for the systematic development of tools /
도구의 체계적인 개발을 요구한다 / 선행사 정답 단서 정보와 데이터 사이의 격차가 더 벌어져서 실제로 데이터를 활용할 수 있는 도구의 개발이 필요함.
[that can turn data tombs into "golden nuggets" of knowledge].
데이터 무덤을 지식의 '금괴'로 바꿀 수 있는 [ ]: 주격 관계대명사절

(7) As the vast amounts of data stored in repositories /
~때문에 S'
저장소에 저장된 방대한 양의 데이터는 ~하기 때문에 /
(A)overwhelm human understanding, /
V'
인간의 이해를 (A)압도하기 /
effective tools to (B)obtain valuable knowledge are required /
S 형용사적 용법 V
가치 있는 지식을 (B)얻기 위한 효과적인 도구가 요구된다 /
for better decision-making.
더 나은 의사 결정을 위해

[전문 해석]

(1)크고 많은 데이터 저장소에 수집되고 저장되는 데이터의 빠르게 증가하는, 엄청난 양은 효과적인 도구 없이도 이해할 수 있는 인간의 능력을 훨씬 넘어섰다. (2)결과적으로 대규모 데이터 저장소에서 수집된 데이터는 '데이터 무덤', 즉 찾는 사람이 거의 없는 데이터 보관소가 된다. (3)중요한 의사 결정은 종종 데이터 저장소에 저장된 정보가 풍부한 데이터에 기반하지 않고 오히려 의사 결정자의 직감에 기반하여 내려지기도 하는데, 이것은 단지 의사 결정자가 방대한 양의 데이터에 숨겨진 가치 있는 지식을 추출하는 도구를 가지고 있지 않기 때문이다. (4)전문 시스템과 지식 기반 기술을 개발하려는 노력이 있었는데, 이것은 일반적으로 사용자나 분야(별) 전문가가 지식을 '수동으로' 지식 베이스에 입력하는 것에 의존한다. (5)그러나 이 방법은 편견과 오류를 일으키기 쉽고, 비용이 극도로 많이 들고 시간이 꽤 든다. (6)점점 더 벌어지는 데이터와 정보 간의 격차는 데이터 무덤을 지식의 '금괴'로 바꿀 수 있는 도구의 체계적인 개발을 요구한다.

⬇

(7)저장소에 저장된 방대한 양의 데이터는 인간의 이해를 (A)압도하기 때문에, 더 나은 의사 결정을 위해 가치 있는 지식을 (B)얻기 위한 효과적인 도구가 요구된다.

[정답 확인]

다음 글의 내용을 한 문장으로 요약하고자 한다. 빈칸 (A)와 (B)에 들어갈 말로 가장 적절한 것은?

	(A)		(B)		(A)		(B)
✔	overwhelm 압도하기	......	obtain 얻기	②	overwhelm 압도하기	......	exchange 교환하기
③	enhance 강화하기	......	apply 적용하기	④	enhance 강화하기	......	discover 발견하기
⑤	fulfill 충족하기	......	access 접근하기				

[문제 풀이]

지문은 누적되는 데이터의 양이 많아질수록 인간의 능력으로 그 데이터 전부를 이해하는 것이 불가능하다는 내용으로 시작한다. 실제로 활용되지 못하는 데이터의 경우 찾는 사람이 없는 '데이터 무덤'으로 가게 되며, 또한 사람들이 데이터를 기반으로 판단하지 않고 직감을 기반으로 판단을 내리는 경우도 많아진다. 이것은 모두 유효한 데이터를 추출할 수 있는 도구가 없기 때문인데, 여기서 말하는 '데이터 추출'은 결국 자신에게 도움이 되는 데이터를 찾는 방법이 필요하다는 것과 상통한다. 따라서 문장 (6)에서 말하는 '데이터 무덤을 지식의 금괴로 바꿀 수 있는 도구'는 곧 '필요한 데이터를 얻기 위한 도구'라고 볼 수 있다. 이러한 내용을 종합하면 요약문의 (A)에는 데이터의 양이 인간의 이해를 넘어섰다는 내용이, (B)에는 도구를 통해 실제로 활용될 수 있을 가치 있는 지식을 얻는다는 내용이 들어가야 한다. 따라서 정답은 ①이다.

[중요 어휘]

☐ **fast-growing**	형용사 빠르게 증가하는, 빨리 성장하는
☐ **tremendous**	형용사 엄청난, 굉장한
☐ **store**	동사 저장하다, 보관하다
☐ **repository**	명사 저장소, 보관소
☐ **exceed**	동사 넘어서다, 초과하다
☐ **tomb**	명사 무덤
☐ **archive**	명사 (기록) 보관소

☐ **instinct**	명사 직감, 본능
☐ **extract**	동사 추출하다, 뽑다, 얻다
☐ **domain**	명사 분야, 영역, 범위
☐ **manually**	부사 수동으로, 손으로
☐ **bias**	명사 편견, 성향
☐ **costly**	형용사 비용이 많이 드는, 대가가 큰
☐ **widen**	동사 벌어지다, 넓어지다
☐ **gap**	명사 격차, 차이
☐ **systematic**	형용사 체계적인, 조직적인
☐ **golden nugget**	금괴
☐ **overwhelm**	동사 압도하다, 제압하다
☐ **obtain**	동사 얻다, 구하다

19 2024년 6월 40번 (정답률 55%) 정답 ⑤

[지문 끊어 읽기] 질투와 부러움의 차이

(1) Many things spark *envy* : /
많은 것들이 '부러움'을 촉발한다 /
ownership, status, health, youth, talent, popularity, beauty.
소유, 지위, 건강, 젊음, 재능, 인기, 아름다움

(2) It is often confused with jealousy /
이것은 종종 질투와 혼동된다 /
because the physical reactions are identical.
신체적 반응이 동일하기 때문에

(3) The difference: / the subject of *envy* is a thing /
차이점 / '부러움'의 대상은 사물이다 /
(status, money, health etc.).
(지위, 돈, 건강 등)

(4) The subject of jealousy / is the behaviour of a third person.
질투의 대상은 / 제3자의 행동이다

정답단서 질투의 대상은 사물이 아닌 제3자의 행동임.

(5) *Envy* needs two people.
'부러움'은 두 명이 필요하다

(6) Jealousy, on the other hand, requires three: /
반면에 질투는 세 명이 필요하다 /
Peter is jealous of Sam /
Peter는 Sam을 질투한다 /
because the beautiful girl next door rings him instead.
옆집의 아름다운 여자가 자기가 아니라 그에게 전화하기 때문에

(7) Paradoxically, / with envy / we direct resentments /
역설적으로 / 부러움을 가질 때 / 우리는 분노를 향하게 한다 /
toward those [who are most similar to us in age, career and residence].
선행사 [ ]: 주격 관계대명사절
나이, 직업, 거주지에서 우리와 가장 비슷한 사람들에게

정답단서 부러움을 느낀다는 것은 자신의 상황과 비슷한 사람에게 분노를 느낀다는 것임.

(8) We don't envy businesspeople / from the century before last.
우리는 사업가들을 부러워하지 않는다 / 지지난 세기의

(9) We don't envy millionaires / on the other side of the globe.
우리는 백만장자들을 부러워하지 않는다 / 지구 반대편의

(10) As a writer, / I don't envy musicians, managers or dentists, /
작가로서 / 나는 음악가, 매니저 또는 치과 의사를 부러워하지 않는다 /
but other writers.
하지만 다른 작가들을 부러워한다

(11) As a CEO / you envy other, bigger CEOs.
CEO로서 / 당신은 다른 더 잘나가는 CEO들을 부러워한다

(12) As a supermodel / you envy more successful supermodels.
슈퍼 모델로서 / 당신은 더 성공적인 슈퍼 모델들을 부러워한다

(13) Aristotle knew this: / 'Potters envy potters.'
아리스토텔레스는 이것을 알았다 / '도공은 도공을 부러워한다'

(14) Jealousy involves three parties, /
질투는 세 당사자를 포함한다 /
[focusing on the (A)actions of a third person], / [ ]: 분사구문
제3자의 (A)행위에 집중하며 /
whereas envy involves two individuals /
반면 부러움은 두 개인을 포함한다 / 선행사
[whose personal circumstances are most (B)alike], /
개인적인 상황이 가장 (B)비슷한 / [ ]: 소유격 관계대명사절
with one person resenting the other.
한 사람이 다른 사람을 불쾌하게 여기면서

힌트 「with 명사 V-ing」 분사구문은 명사와 V-ing가 능동 관계일 때 사용하고, '명사가 ~하면서/~한 채로'라는 의미로 해석함.

[전문 해석]

(1)많은 것들이 '부러움'을 촉발한다. 소유, 지위, 건강, 젊음, 재능, 인기, 아름다움. (2)이것은 신체적 반응이 동일하기 때문에 종종 질투와 혼동된다. (3)차이점: '부러움'의 대상은 사물이다(지위, 돈, 건강 등). (4)질투의 대상은 제3자의 행동이다. (5)'부러움'은 두 명이 필요하다. (6)반면에 질투는 세 명이 필요하다. Peter는 옆집의 아름다운 여자가 자기가 아니라 Sam에게 전화하기 때문에 그를 질투한다. (7)역설적으로 부러움을 가질 때 우리는 나이, 직업, 거주지에서 우리와 가장 비슷한 사람들에게 분노를 향하게 한다. (8)우리는 지지난 세기의 사업가들을 부러워하지 않는다. (9)우리는 지구 반대편의 백만장자들을 부러워하지 않는다. (10)작가로서 나는 음악가, 매니저 또는 치과 의사를 부러워하지 않지만 다른 작가들을 부러워한다. (11)CEO로서 당신은 다른 더 잘나가는 CEO들을 부러워한다. (12)슈퍼 모델로서 당신은 더 성공적인 슈퍼 모델들을 부러워한다. (13)아리스토텔레스는 이것을 알았다. '도공은 도공을 부러워한다.'

⬇

(14)질투는 제3자의 (A)행위에 집중하며 세 당사자를 포함하는 반면 부러움은 한 사람이 다른 사람을 불쾌하게 여기면서 개인적인 상황이 가장 (B)비슷한 두 개인을 포함한다.

[정답 확인]

다음 글의 내용을 한 문장으로 요약하고자 한다. 빈칸 (A)와 (B)에 들어갈 말로 가장 적절한 것은?

	(A)		(B)		(A)		(B)
①	actions 행위	……	different 다른	②	possessions 소유물	……	unique 독특한
③	goals 목표	……	ordinary 평범한	④	possessions 소유물	……	favorable 우호적인
✔⑤	actions 행위	……	alike 비슷한				

[문제 풀이]

이 글은 부러움(envy)과 질투(jealousy)의 차이를 설명한다. 이 둘은 신체적 반응이 동일하기 때문에 혼동되지만 부러움의 대상은 사물인 반면 질투의 대상은 제3자의 행동이다. 그래서 부러움에는 두 명이 필요하고 질투에는 세 명이 필요하다. 또한 부러움을 느낄 때 우리는 나이, 직업, 거주지와 같은 점에서 우리와 가장 비슷한 사람들에게 분노가 향한다. 따라서 질투는 제3자의 행위에 집중하여 세 명의 당사자를 포함하는 반면, 부러움은 한 사람이 다른 사람에게 분노하면서 개인적인 상황이 비슷한 두 명을 포함한다는 내용의 ⑤가 적절하다.

[중요 어휘]

☐ **spark**	동사 촉발하다 / 명사 불꽃
☐ **ownership**	명사 소유, 소유권
☐ **confuse**	동사 혼란시키다, 당황하게 하다
☐ **identical**	형용사 동일한, 똑같은
☐ **subject**	명사 대상, 주제, 과목
☐ **ring**	동사 전화하다 / 명사 반지
☐ **paradoxically**	부사 역설적으로
☐ **resentment**	명사 분노, 분개
☐ **residence**	명사 거주지, 주택
☐ **potter**	명사 도공, 도예가
☐ **party**	명사 당사자, 정당, 잔치
☐ **resent**	동사 분개하다, 분노하다

문제편 p.242

20 2024년 9월 40번 (정답률 60%) 정답 ①

[지문 끊어 읽기] 타인의 존재가 아이들에게 미치는 영향

(1) The concern about how we appear to others /
S about의 목적어(간접의문문)
우리가 남들에게 어떻게 보이는지에 관한 걱정은 /
can be seen in children, /
V
아이들에게서 보여질 수 있다 /
though work by the psychologist Ervin Staub suggests /
S' 전치사구 V'
다만 심리학자 Ervin Staub에 의한 연구는 시사한다 /
[that the effect may vary with age].
그 영향이 나이에 따라 다를 수도 있음을 [ ]: O'(명사절)

힌트 '우리가 남들에게 어떻게 보이는지'에 관한 걱정이 아이들에게 미치는 영향(결과)을 의미함.

(2) In a study / [where children heard another child in distress], /
선행사 [ ]: 관계부사절
한 연구에서 / 아이들이 곤경에 처한 다른 아이의 소리를 들었던 /
young children (kindergarten through second grade) /
어린아이들(유치원에서 2학년까지)은 /
were more likely to help the child in distress /
곤경에 처한 아이를 도울 가능성이 더 높았다 /
when with another child / than when alone.
비교대상① 비교대상②
다른 아이와 함께 있을 때 / 혼자 있을 때보다

힌트 접속사 when 뒤에는 각각 「주어(they)+동사(were)」가 생략되어 있으며, 밑줄 친 부분은 각각 'when they were with another child'와 'when they were alone'으로 바꿔 쓸 수 있음.

(3) But for older children / — in fourth and sixth grade — /
하지만 나이가 더 많은 아이들에게 있어서 / 4학년과 6학년에서 /
the effect reversed: /
그 결과는 뒤바뀌었다 /
they were less likely to help a child in distress /
=older children
그들은 곤경에 처한 아이를 도울 가능성이 더 낮았다 /
when they were with a peer / than when they were alone. 정답 단서
그들이 또래와 함께 있을 때 / 그들이 혼자 있을 때보다

힌트 문장 (2)와 마찬가지로, 밑줄 친 「주어(they)+동사(were)」를 생략하여, 각각 'when with a peer'과 'when alone'으로 써도 어법상 옳은 문장임.

정답 단서 나이가 더 많은 아이들은 혼자 있을 때보다 '또래와 함께 있을 때' 곤경에 처한 사람을 도울 가능성이 더 낮았음.

(4) Staub suggested /
S V
Staub는 말했다 /
[that younger children might feel more comfortable acting /
더 어린아이들은 행동하는 데 더 편안함을 느낄 수 있다고 /
when they have the company of a peer, /
그들이 또래와 함께 있을 때 /

힌트 여기서 'company'는 '동행, 함께 있음'이라는 뜻의 명사로, 「have the company of A」는 'A와 함께하다'라는 의미임.

whereas older children might feel more concern /
병렬①
반면에 나이가 더 많은 아이들은 더욱 걱정할 수도 있다고 /
about being judged by their peers /
전치사 동명사(수동)
그들의 또래들에게 판단받는 것에 대해 /
and fear feeling embarrassed by overreacting]. 정답 단서 [ ]: O(명사절)
병렬②(might 생략) 동명사구(fear의 목적어)
그리고 과잉 반응에 의해 창피함을 느끼는 것을 두려워할 수도 있다고

정답 단서 나이가 더 많은 아이들은 또래들에게 판단받는 것을 걱정하거나 과잉 반응에 의해 창피함을 느끼는 것을 두려워할 수도 있음.

(5) Staub noted /
S V
Staub는 언급했다 /

힌트 discuss는 '~에 대해 이야기하다[논하다]'라는 뜻의 타동사이므로, 전치사 없이 바로 목적어인 the distress sounds가 왔음. 전치사 about을 쓰면 어법상 틀림.

[that "older children seemed to discuss the distress sounds less /
나이가 더 많은 아이들이 곤경의 소리에 대해 덜 이야기하는 것처럼 보였다고 / 병렬①
and to react to them less openly / than younger children]."
병렬② [ ]: O(명사절)
그리고 그들에게 덜 공개적으로 반응하는 것처럼 / 더 어린아이들보다

(6) In other words, /
다시 말해서 /
the older children were deliberately putting on a poker face /
나이가 더 많은 아이들은 고의적으로 무표정한 얼굴을 하고 있었다 /
in front of their peers.
그들의 또래들 앞에서

(7) The study suggests / [that, contrary to younger children, /
S V
연구는 시사한다 / 더 어린아이들과는 상반되게 /
older children are less likely to help those in distress /
나이가 더 많은 아이들은 곤경에 처한 사람들을 도울 가능성이 더 낮다 /
in the (A)presence of others /
다른 사람들의 (A)존재 속에서 /

힌트 presence는 '존재, 함께 있음'이라는 뜻의 명사로서, 「in the presence of A」는 'A와 함께 있을 때, A가 있는 곳에서'라는 뜻으로 종종 사용됨. 비슷한 형태의 표현으로는 「in the absence of A(A가 없을 때)」나 「in the audience of A(A가 듣고 있을 때)」 등이 있음.

because they care more / about how they are (B)evaluated]. [ ]: O
왜냐하면 그들이 더 많이 신경을 쓰기 때문에 / 그들이 어떻게 (B)평가받는지에 대해

[전문 해석]

(1)우리가 남들에게 어떻게 보이는지에 관한 걱정은 아이들에게서 보여질 수 있는데, 다만 심리학자 Ervin Staub에 의한 연구는 그 영향이 나이에 따라 다를 수도 있음을 시사한다. (2)아이들이 곤경에 처한 다른 아이의 소리를 들었던 한 연구에서, 어린아이들(유치원에서 2학년까지)은 혼자 있을 때보다 다른 아이와 함께 있을 때 곤경에 처한 아이를 도울 가능성이 더 높았다. (3)하지만 4학년과 6학년에서처럼 나이가 더 많은 아이들에게 있어서, 그 결과는 뒤바뀌었는데, 그들은 그들이 혼자 있을 때보다 그들이 또래와 함께 있을 때 곤경에 처한 아이를 도울 가능성이 더 낮았다. (4)Staub는 더 어린아이들은 그들이 또래와 함께 있을 때 행동하는 데 더 편안함을 느낄 수 있는 반면에, 나이가 더 많은 아이들은 그들의 또래들에게 판단받는 것에 대해 더욱 걱정하고 과잉 반응에 의해 창피함을 느끼는 것을 두려워할 수도 있다고 말했다. (5)Staub는 "나이가 더 많은 아이들이 더 어린아이들보다 곤경(에 처한 아이들)의 소리에 대해 덜 이야기하고 그들에게 덜 공개적으로 반응하는 것처럼 보였다."라고 언급했다. (6)다시 말해서, 나이가 더 많은 아이들은 그들의 또래들 앞에서 고의적으로 무표정한 얼굴을 하고 있었다.

⬇

(7)연구는 더 어린아이들과는 상반되게, 나이가 더 많은 아이들은 다른 사람들의 (A)존재 속에서 곤경에 처한 사람들을 도울 가능성이 더 낮은데, 왜냐하면 그들이 어떻게 (B)평가받는지에 대해 더 많이 신경을 쓰기 때문이라고 시사한다.

[정답 확인]

다음 글의 내용을 한 문장으로 요약하고자 한다. 빈칸 (A)와 (B)에 들어갈 말로 가장 적절한 것은?

	(A)		(B)		(A)		(B)
✔①	presence 존재	……	evaluated 평가받는지	②	presence 존재	……	motivated 동기부여되는지
③	absence 부재	……	viewed 보여지는지	④	absence 부재	……	assisted 도움을 받는지
⑤	audience 청취	……	trained 훈련받는지				

[문제 풀이]

문장 (1)은 타인의 시선이 아이들에게 미치는 영향이 나이에 따라 다를 수도 있다고 주장한 뒤, 유치원에서 2학년까지의 어린아이들과 4학년 및 6학년과 같이 나이가 더 많은 아이들을 비교하여 문장 (1)의 주장을 뒷받침하고 있다. 한편, 문장 (3)을 통해 나이가 더 많은 아이들은 또래와 함께 있을 때, 즉 주변에 다른 사람이 '존재'할 때 곤경에 처한 사람들을 도울 가능성이 더 낮았음을 알 수 있으므로, 요약문의 빈칸 (A)에는 presence가 와야 한다. 다음으로, 문장 (4)는 나이가 더 많은 아이들이 이러한 반응을 보이는 이유로 그들이 또래들에게 '판단받는 것'에 대해 걱정한다는 사실을 들고 있으므로, 요약문의 빈칸 (B)에는 evaluated가 와야 한다. 따라서 정답은 ①이다.

[중요 어휘]

☐ concern	명사 걱정, 우려, 관심사
☐ psychologist	명사 심리학자
☐ suggest	동사 시사하다, (넌지시) 말하다, 제안하다
☐ effect	명사 영향, 결과
☐ vary	동사 다르다, 다양하다
☐ in distress	곤경에 처한, 고통받는
☐ reverse	동사 뒤바뀌다, 반대로 되다
☐ peer	명사 또래
☐ feel comfortable V-ing	~하는 데 편안함을 느끼다
☐ judge	동사 판단하다, 평가하다
☐ embarrassed	형용사 창피한, 부끄러운
☐ overreact	동사 과잉 반응하다
☐ note	동사 언급하다, 주목하다
☐ openly	부사 공개적으로, 공공연히
☐ deliberately	부사 고의적으로, 의도적으로
☐ put on a poker face	무표정한 얼굴을 하다
☐ contrary to A	A와 상반되게, A에 반해서
☐ evaluate	동사 평가하다, 감정하다

문제편 p.245

17 장문의 이해-단일지문

핵심 초반부에 일반적인 통념을 제시하고, 그 통념이 실제로는 그렇지 않음을 지적하는 구조의 글임.

01~02 2021년 9월 41~42번 (정답률 80% | 80%) 정답 ② | ③

[지문 끊어 읽기] 이메일의 에너지 사용

(1) In this day and age, / it is difficult to imagine our lives /
형식상의 주어 / 내용상의 주어
요즘 같은 시대에 / 우리의 삶을 상상하기 어렵다 /
without email.
이메일이 없는

(2) But how often do we consider /
그러나 우리는 얼마나 자주 고려하는가 /
the environmental impact of these virtual messages?
이러한 가상 메시지의 환경적 영향을

(3) At first glance, / digital messages appear to (a)save resources.
언뜻 보기에는 / 디지털 메시지가 자원을 (a)절약하는 것처럼 보인다

(4) Unlike traditional letters, / no paper or stamps are needed; /
전통적인 편지와는 달리 / 종이나 우표가 필요하지 않다 /
nothing has to be packaged or transported.
즉 어떤 것도 포장되거나 운송될 필요가 없다

(5) Many of us tend to assume / that using email requires /
명사절 접속사
우리 중 많은 사람은 추정하는 경향이 있다 / 이메일을 사용하는 것이 필요로 한다고 /
little more than the electricity / used to power our computers.
과거분사구
약간의 전기 정도만 / 컴퓨터에 전원을 공급하는 데 사용되는

(6) It's easy to (b)overlook the invisible energy usage /
보이지 않는 에너지 사용을 (b)간과하기 쉽다 /
involved in running the network /
네트워크 실행에 수반되는 /
— particularly when it comes to sending and storing data.
~에 관해
특히 데이터 전송과 저장에 관해

(7) Every single email in every single inbox in the world /
세계의 모든 받은 편지함에 있는 모든 이메일은 /
is stored on a server.
서버에 저장된다

(8) The incredible quantity of data requires huge server farms / 01번 정답 단서
엄청난 양의 데이터는 엄청난 양의 서버 팜을 필요로 한다 /
— gigantic centres with millions of computers /
수백만 대의 컴퓨터가 있는 거대한 센터 / 선행사
which store and transmit information.
주격 관계대명사
정보를 저장하고 전송하는

(9) These servers consume (c)minimum(→ massive) amounts of energy, /
병렬①
이러한 서버는 (c)최소한의(→ 상당한) 양의 에너지를 소비한다 /
24 hours a day, / and require countless litres of water, /
병렬②
하루 24시간 / 그리고 셀 수 없이 많은 리터의 물을 필요로 한다 /
or air conditioning systems, / for cooling. 02번 정답 단서
또는 에어컨 시스템을 / 냉각을 위해

(10) The more messages we send, receive and store, /
우리가 메시지를 더 많이 보내고, 받고, 저장할수록 /
the (d)more servers are needed /
(d)더 많은 서버가 필요하다 /
— which means more energy consumed, /
이는 더 많이 소비되는 에너지를 의미한다 /
and more carbon emissions. 01번 정답 단서
그리고 더 많은 탄소 배출을

힌트 'The more A, the more B'는 '더 A(하면) 할수록, 더 B하다'라고 해석함.

(11) Clearly, / sending and receiving electronic messages /
분명히 / 전자 메시지를 보내고 받는 것은 /
in an environmentally conscious manner /
환경적으로 의식하는 방식으로 /
is by no means enough to stop climate change.
결코 기후 변화를 멈추기에는 충분하지 않다

(12) But with a few careful, mindful changes, /
그러나 주의 깊고 신중한 어느 정도의 변화로 /
(e)unnecessary CO_2 emissions can easily be avoided. 01번 정답 단서
(e)불필요한 CO_2 배출은 쉽게 회피될 수 있다

[전문 해석]

(1)요즘 같은 시대에 이메일이 없는 우리의 삶을 상상하기 어렵다. (2)그러나 우리는 얼마나 자주 이러한 가상 메시지의 환경적 영향을 고려하는가? (3)언뜻 보기에는, 디지털 메시지가 자원을 (a)절약하는 것처럼 보인다. (4)전통적인 편지와는 달리, 종이나 우표가 필요하지 않다. 즉, 어떤 것도 포장되거나 운송될 필요가 없다. (5)우리 중 많은 사람은 이메일을 사용하는 것이 컴퓨터에 전원을 공급하는 데 사용되는 약간의 전기 정도만 필요로 한다고 추정하는 경향이 있다. (6)특히 데이터 전송과 저장에 관해, 네트워크 실행에 수반되는 보이지 않는 에너지 사용을 (b)간과하기 쉽다.
(7)세계의 모든 받은 편지(이메일)함에 있는 모든 이메일은 서버에 저장된다. (8)엄청난 양의 데이터는 엄청난 양의 서버 팜을 필요로 하는데, (서버 팜은) 정보를 저장하고 전송하는 수백만 대의 컴퓨터가 있는 거대한 센터(이다). (9)이러한 서버는 하루 24시간 (c)최소한의(→ 상당한) 양의 에너지를 소비하며 냉각을 위해 셀 수 없이 많은 리터의 물 또는 에어컨 시스템을 필요로 한다. (10)우리가 메시지를 더 많이 보내고, 받고, 저장할수록 (d)더 많은 서버가 필요하다. 이는 더 많이 소비되는 에너지와 더 많은 탄소 배출을 의미한다. (11)분명히 환경적으로 의식하는 방식으로 전자 메시지를 보내고 받는 것은 결코 기후 변화를 멈추기에는 충분하지 않다. (12)그러나 주의 깊고 신중한 어느 정도의 변화로 (e)불필요한 CO_2 배출은 쉽게 회피될 수 있다.

[정답 확인]

01. 윗글의 제목으로 가장 적절한 것은?

① Recycling Makes Your Life Even Better
재활용은 당신의 삶을 훨씬 더 낫게 만든다
② Eco-friendly Use of Email Saves the Earth ✔
이메일의 친환경적인 사용이 지구를 살린다
③ Traditional Letters: The Bridge Between Us
전통적 편지: 우리들 사이의 가교
④ Email Servers: Records of Past and Present
이메일 서버: 과거와 현재의 기록
⑤ Technicians Looking for Alternative Energy
대체 에너지를 찾는 기술자들

02. 밑줄 친 (a) ~ (e) 중에서 문맥상 낱말의 쓰임이 적절하지 않은 것은?

① (a) ② (b) ③ (c) ✔ ④ (d) ⑤ (e)

[문제 풀이]

01. 이메일 또는 디지털 메시지는 전통적인 편지와 달리 자원을 절약하는 것처럼 보이지만, 사실은 엄청난 양의 전기 에너지를 사용함으로써 환경에 좋지 않은 영향을 끼친다는 내용의 글이다. 따라서 디지털 메시지를 사용할 때 환경적인 영향을 고려해야 하며, 이를 통해 에너지 사용을 감축할 수 있다고 주장하고 있으므로 정답은 ②이다.

[중요 어휘]

□ impact	명사 영향, 충격
□ virtual	형용사 가상의, 사실상의
□ at first glance	언뜻 보기에는
□ overlook	동사 간과하다, 못 보고 넘어가다
□ invisible	형용사 보이지 않는, 무형의
□ run	동사 실행하다, 운영하다, 관리하다
□ incredible	형용사 엄청난, 믿을 수 없는
□ gigantic	형용사 거대한
□ transmit	동사 전송하다, 송신하다
□ countless	형용사 셀 수 없이 많은, 무수한
□ carbon	명사 탄소
□ emission	명사 배출, 배출물, 배기가스
□ conscious	형용사 의식하는, 자각하는, 의도적인
□ manner	명사 방식, 태도, 예의

문제편 p.246

□ **by no means**	결코 ~가 아닌
□ **mindful**	형용사 신중한, 의식하는, 유념하는

핵심 지문 전반부에는 우화를 통해, 후반부에는 설명을 통해 paralysis by analysis라는 개념을 설명하고 있음. 우화에 나오는 두 주인공에 어떠한 차이점이 있는지 생각하며 지문을 읽으면 쉽게 접근할 수 있음.

03~04 2021년 6월 41~42번 (정답률 75% | 60%) 정답 ④ | ⑤

[지문 끊어 읽기] 효과적인 의사 결정의 걸림돌

(1) Paralysis by analysis /
분석에 의한 마비는 /
is a state of overthinking and analyzing a particular problem, /
특정 문제를 지나치게 생각하고 분석하는 상태이다 /
but you still end up not making a decision. 03번 정답 단서
하지만 당신은 여전히 결국 결정을 내리지 못하게 된다

(2) One famous ancient fable / of the fox and the cat /
한 유명한 고대 우화는 / 여우와 고양이의 /
explains this situation of paralysis by analysis / in the simplest way.
이 분석에 의한 마비 상황을 설명한다 / 가장 간단한 방법으로

(3) In the story, / the fox and the cat discuss /
이야기에서 / 여우와 고양이는 논의한다 /
how many ways they have / to escape their hunters.
그들이 얼마나 많은 방법을 갖고 있는지 / 그들의 사냥꾼으로부터 탈출할 수 있는

힌트 간접의문문은 동사의 주어나 목적어 역할을 하는 명사절로, '의문사+S+V'의 어순으로 씀. 이 문장에서는 how many ways(의문사구)+they(S)+have(V)로 쓰여 '그들이 얼마나 많은 방법을 갖고 있는지'라는 뜻이며 동사 discuss의 목적어 역할을 하고 있음.

(4) Cat quickly climbs a tree.
고양이는 재빨리 나무에 오른다

(5) Fox, / on the other hand, / begins to analyze /
여우는 / 반면에 / 분석하기 시작한다 /
all the ways to escape / that he knows.
탈출하는 모든 방법을 / 그가 알고 있는
(형용사적 용법)

힌트 선행사 all the ways to escape를 수식하는 목적격 관계대명사절임. all the ways처럼 선행사가 all의 수식을 받을 때 일반적으로 관계대명사 that을 쓸 수 있음.

(6) But / unable to decide / which one would be the best, /
하지만 / 결정하지 못한 채 / 어떤 것이 가장 좋을지 / (간접의문문)
he (a)fails to act / and gets caught by the dogs.
그는 행동하는 데 (a)실패한다 / 그리고 개들에게 잡힌다

힌트 이 문장은 unable 앞에 being이라는 현재분사가 생략된 분사구문임.

(7) This story perfectly illustrates /
이 이야기는 완벽하게 설명한다 /
the analysis paralysis phenomenon: /
분석 마비 현상을 /
the (b)inability to act or decide / due to overthinking /
(형용사적 용법)
행동하거나 결정을 (b)할 수 없는 것 / 지나친 생각 때문에 /
about available alternatives. 04번 정답 단서
이용 가능한 대안들에 대한

(8) People experience /
사람들은 경험한다 /
that although they start with a good intention /
명사절 접속사(experience의 목적어절을 이끎)
비록 그들은 좋은 의도로 시작하지만 /
to find a solution to a problem, / they often analyze indefinitely /
형용사적 용법(~하는)
문제의 해결책을 찾으려는 / 그들은 종종 무한히 분석한다 /
about various factors / that might lead to wrong decisions.
(선행사) (주격 관계대명사절)
다양한 요인에 대해 / 잘못된 결정을 초래할지 모를

(9) They don't feel satisfied / with the available information /
그들은 만족하지 못한다 / 이용 가능한 정보에 /
and think / they still need (c)more data /
그리고 생각한다 / 그들은 여전히 (c)더 많은 데이터가 필요하다고 /
to perfect their decision.
부사적 용법(목적)
그들의 결정을 완벽하게 하기 위해

힌트 여기서 'perfect'는 '완벽한'의 형용사 의미가 아닌 '완벽하게 하다'라는 동사로 쓰임.

(10) Most often / this situation of paralysis by analysis (d)arises /
가장 자주 / 이러한 분석에 의한 마비 상황은 (d)발생한다 /
when somebody is afraid of making an erroneous decision /
(동명사) (making의 목적어(선행사))
누군가가 잘못된 결정을 내리는 것을 두려워할 때 /
[that can lead to potential catastrophic consequences]: 04번 정답 단서
잠재적인 재앙적 결과를 초래할 수 있는 / [ ]: 주격 관계대명사절
it might impact / their careers or their organizations' productivity.
그것은 영향을 미칠지도 모른다 / 그들의 경력이나 조직의 생산성에

(11) So that's why / people are generally (e)confident(→ reluctant) /
그래서 그것이 ~하는 이유이다 / 사람들이 일반적으로 (e)자신이 있는(→ 주저하는) /
in making decisions / that involve huge stakes. 03번 정답 단서
(선행사) (주격 관계대명사절)
결정을 내리는 것에 / 막대한 이해관계가 수반되는

[전문 해석]

(1)분석에 의한 마비는 특정 문제를 지나치게 생각하고 분석하는 상태이지만, 당신은 여전히 결국 결정을 내리지 못하게 된다. (2)여우와 고양이의 한 유명한 고대 우화는 이 분석에 의한 마비 상황을 가장 간단한 방법으로 설명한다. (3)이야기에서, 여우와 고양이는 그들이 그들의 사냥꾼으로부터 탈출할 수 있는 얼마나 많은 방법을 갖고 있는지 논의한다. (4)고양이는 재빨리 나무에 오른다. (5)반면에, 여우는 그가 알고 있는 탈출하는 모든 방법을 분석하기 시작한다. (6)하지만 어떤 것이 가장 좋을지 결정하지 못한 채, 그는 행동하는 데 (a)실패하고 개들에게 잡힌다. (7)이 이야기는 분석 마비 현상을 완벽하게 설명한다. 이용 가능한 대안들에 대한 지나친 생각 때문에 행동하거나 결정을 (b)할 수 없는 것(이라고 설명한다). (8)사람들은 비록 문제의 해결책을 찾으려는 좋은 의도로 시작하지만, 그들은 종종 잘못된 결정을 초래할지 모를 다양한 요인에 대해 무한히 분석한다는 것을 경험한다. (9)그들은 이용 가능한 정보에 만족하지 못하고 그들의 결정을 완벽하게 하기 위해 여전히 (c)더 많은 데이터가 필요하다고 생각한다. (10)이러한 분석에 의한 마비 상황은 누군가가 잠재적인 재앙적 결과를 초래할 수 있는 잘못된 결정을 내리는 것을 두려워할 때 가장 자주 (d)발생한다. 그것은 그들의 경력이나 조직의 생산성에 영향을 미칠지도 모른다. (11)그래서 그것이 사람들이 일반적으로 막대한 이해관계가 수반되는 결정을 내리는 것에 (e)자신이 있는(→ 주저하는) 이유이다.

[정답 확인]

03. 윗글의 제목으로 가장 적절한 것은?

① Best Ways to Keep You from Overthinking
지나친 생각을 막는 가장 좋은 방법
② Overthinking or Overdoing: Which Is Worse?
지나친 생각과 지나친 행동: 무엇이 더 나쁜가?
③ Costs and Benefits of Having Various Alternatives
다양한 대안을 가지는 것의 비용과 장점
✔④ Overthinking: A Barrier to Effective Decision-making
지나친 생각: 효과적인 의사 결정의 걸림돌
⑤ Trapped in Moral Dilemma: Harmful for Your Survival
도덕적 딜레마의 덫: 당신의 생존에 해롭다

04. 밑줄 친 (a) ~ (e) 중에서 문맥상 낱말의 쓰임이 적절하지 않은 것은?

① (a) ② (b) ③ (c) ④ (d) ✔⑤ (e)

[문제 풀이]

04. 지문은 우화를 통해 분석에 의한 마비를 소개한 후, 잇따라 그것에 대한 부가 설명을 전달하고 있다. 우화에 나오는 여우를 통해 문장 (8)에서는 이용 가능한 대안들에 대한 지나친 생각 때문에 행동하거나 결정하지 못하는 현상을 설명한다. 문장 (11)은 막대한 이해관계가 수반될 때 사람들의 행태에 대한 설명인데, 문장 (10)의 잘못된 결정을 내리는 것을 두려워하는 경우에 분석에 의한 마비 상황이 가장 자주 발생한다는 설명으로 미루어 볼 때, 사람들은 그러한 결정을 내릴 때 자신이 있는(confident) 것이 아니라 주저하는(reluctant) 것이다. 따라서 정답은 ⑤이다.

[중요 어휘]

□ **paralysis**	명사 마비
□ **analysis**	명사 분석
□ **overthink**	동사 지나치게 생각하다
□ **end up V-ing**	결국 ~하게 되다
□ **ancient**	형용사 고대의
□ **fable**	명사 우화
□ **illustrate**	동사 설명하다
□ **phenomenon**	명사 현상
□ **inability**	명사 할 수 없는 것, 무능
□ **available**	형용사 이용 가능한
□ **alternative**	명사 대안

□	**indefinitely**	부사 무한히, 무기한으로
□	**arise**	동사 발생하다
□	**erroneous**	형용사 잘못된
□	**catastrophic**	형용사 재앙적인, 큰 재해의
□	**consequence**	명사 결과
□	**stake**	명사 이해관계

핵심 글의 초반부에 전문가의 관점을 빌려 주제문을 드러냄. 사회성이 복잡한 뇌의 진화와 어떻게 관련되어 있을지 생각해보며 지문을 읽어야 함.

05~06

2020년 11월 41~42번 (정답률 65% | 65%) 정답 ① | ⑤

[지문 끊어 읽기] 사회 관계망의 진화적 이점

(1) Evolutionary biologists believe / sociability drove /
진화 생물학자들은 믿는다 / 사교성이 이끌었다고 /
the evolution of our complex brains. 05번 정답 단서
우리의 복잡한 뇌의 진화를

(2) Fossil evidence shows that / as far back as 130,000 years ago, /
화석 증거는 보여준다 / 13만 년이나 전에 /
it was not (a)unusual / for *Homo sapiens* /
형식상의 주어
(a)이상한 일이 아니었다 / '호모 사피엔스'가 /
to travel more than a hundred and fifty miles /
내용상의 주어
150마일 이상을 이동하는 것이 /
to trade, share food and, no doubt, gossip.
부사적 용법(~하기 위해)
거래하고, 음식을 공유하고, 의심의 여지 없이, 잡담하기 위해

힌트 문장 (2)의 it은 형식상의 주어이므로, 해석 시 내용상의 주어인 'to travel more than ~'을 문장의 주어로 해석해야 함. 참고로 for *Homo sapiens*는 내용상의 주어인 to 부정사(to travel)의 의미상 주어로 쓰임.

(3) Unlike the Neanderthals, / their social groups extended /
네안데르탈인과는 다르게 / 그들의 사회 집단은 뻗어 있었다 /
far beyond their own families.
그들 자신의 가족을 훨씬 넘어서

(4) Remembering all those (b)connections, /
S
모든 그런 (b)연결을 기억하는 것은 /
who was related to whom, / and where they lived /
누가 누구와 관련이 있는지 / 그리고 그들이 어디에 사는지 /
required considerable processing power. 06번 정답 단서
V
상당한 처리 능력을 필요로 했다

힌트 바로 앞에 나오는 connections의 예를 들어 구체적으로 설명하기 위해 삽입됨.

(5) It also required wayfinding savvy. 06번 정답 단서
이것은 또한 길 찾기 요령을 필요로 했다

(6) Imagine / trying to (c)maintain a social network /
상상해 보아라 / 사회 관계망을 (c)유지하려고 시도하는 것을 /
across tens or hundreds of square miles of Palaeolithic wilderness.
구석기 시대 황야의 수십 혹은 수백 제곱 마일을 가로지르는

(7) You couldn't send a text message to your friends /
여러분은 여러분의 친구들에게 메세지를 보낼 수 없었다 /
to find out / where they were /
알아내기 위해서 / 그들이 어디에 있는지 /
— you had to go out and visit them, /
병렬①
여러분은 나가서 그들을 방문해야만 했다 /
remember where you last saw them /
병렬②
여러분이 마지막으로 그들을 어디에서 봤는지 기억해야만 했다 /
or imagine where they might have gone.
병렬③
혹은 그들이 어디로 갔을지 상상해야만 했다

(8) To do this, /
이것을 하기 위해 /
you needed navigation skills, spatial awareness, a sense of direction, /
여러분은 길 찾기 능력, 공간 인식, 방향 감각이 필요했다 /
the ability to store maps of the landscape in your mind /
풍경의 지도를 여러분의 머릿속에 저장하는 능력 /
and the motivation to travel around. 05번 정답 단서
그리고 여기저기 이동할 동기

(9) Canadian anthropologist Ariane Burke believes /
캐나다인 인류학자 Ariane Burke는 믿는다 /
that our ancestors (d)developed all these attributes /
우리의 조상이 이러한 모든 특징들을 (d)발달시켰다고 /
while trying to keep in touch with their neighbours. 06번 정답 단서
=while they tried
그들의 이웃과 연락하고 지내려고 하는 동안

(10) Eventually, / our brains became primed / for wayfinding.
마침내 / 우리의 뇌는 준비가 되었다 / 길 찾기를 위한

(11) Meanwhile / the Neanderthals, / who didn't travel as far, /
한편 / 네안데르탈인은 / 그만큼 멀리 이동하지 않았다 / 주격 관계대명사절
never fostered a spatial skill set; /
다양한 공간 능력을 발전시키지 못했다 /
despite being sophisticated hunters, / well adapted to the cold /
병렬① 병렬②
수준 높은 사냥꾼임에도 불구하고 / 추위에 잘 적응했고 /
and able to see in the dark, / they went extinct.
병렬③
그리고 어둠 속에서도 볼 수 있었고 / 그들은 멸종했다

(12) In the prehistoric badlands, /
선사 시대의 불모지에서는 /
nothing was more (e)useless(→ useful) / than a circle of friends.
그 어떤 것도 (e)쓸모없는(→ 도움이 되는) 것은 없었다 / 친구 집단보다

[전문 해석]

(1)진화 생물학자들은 사교성이 우리의 복잡한 뇌의 진화를 이끌었다고 믿는다. (2)화석 증거는 13만 년이나 전에 '호모 사피엔스'가 거래하고, 음식을 공유하고, 의심의 여지 없이, 잡담하기 위해 150마일 이상을 이동하는 것이 (a)이상한 일이 아니었다는 것을 보여준다. (3)네안데르탈인과는 다르게, 그들의 사회 집단은 그들 자신의 가족을 훨씬 넘어서 뻗어 있었다. (4)누가 누구와 관련이 있는지 그리고 그들이 어디에 사는지 (등) 모든 그런 (b)연결을 기억하는 것은 상당한 처리 능력을 필요로 했다.
(5)이것은 또한 길 찾기 요령을 필요로 했다. (6)구석기 시대 황야의 수십 혹은 수백 제곱 마일을 가로지르는 사회 관계망을 (c)유지하려고 시도하는 것을 상상해 보아라. (7)여러분은 여러분의 친구들이 어디에 있는지 알아내기 위해서 그들에게 메세지를 보낼 수 없었다. 여러분은 나가서 그들을 방문하고, 마지막으로 그들을 어디에서 봤는지 기억하고, 혹은 그들이 어디로 갔을지 상상해야만 했다. (8)이것을 하기 위해 여러분은 길 찾기 능력, 공간 인식, 방향 감각, 풍경의 지도를 여러분의 머릿속에 저장하는 능력, 그리고 여기저기를 이동할 동기가 필요했다. (9)캐나다인 인류학자 Ariane Burke는 우리의 조상이 그들의 이웃과 연락하고 지내려고 하는 동안 이러한 모든 특징들을 (d)발달시켰다고 믿는다. (10)마침내 우리의 뇌는 길 찾기를 위한 준비가 되었다. (11)한편, 네안데르탈인은 그만큼 멀리 이동하지 않았고 다양한 공간 능력을 발전시키지 못했다. 수준 높은 사냥꾼이었고 추위에 잘 적응했으며 어둠 속에서도 볼 수 있었음에도 불구하고, 그들은 멸종했다. (12)선사 시대의 불모지에서는 그 어떤 것도 친구 집단보다 (e)쓸모없는(→ 도움이 되는) 것은 없었다.

[정답 확인]

05. 윗글의 제목으로 가장 적절한 것은?

① Social Networks: An Evolutionary Advantage
사회 관계망: 진화적 이점
② Our Brain Forced Us to Stay Close to Our Family!
우리의 뇌는 우리가 가족과 가까이 지내도록 강제했다!
③ How We Split from Our Way and Kept Going on My Way
우리는 어떻게 우리의 길에서 분열되었고 계속 자신의 길을 갔는가
④ Why Do Some People Have Difficulty in Social Relationships?
몇몇 사람들은 왜 사회적 관계에 어려움을 겪을까?
⑤ Being Connected to Each Other Leads to Communicative Skills
서로 연결되어 있는 것이 의사 전달 능력으로 이어진다

06. 밑줄 친 (a) ~ (e) 중에서 문맥상 낱말의 쓰임이 적절하지 않은 것은?

① (a) ② (b) ③ (c) ④ (d) ⑤ (e)

[문제 풀이]

05. 13만 년 전부터 호모 사피엔스는 사회적 교류를 위해 150마일 이상을 이동했다. 그들은 가족을 넘어서 멀리 있는 이웃과 사회적 관계를 유지하고자 했고, 이 과정에서 다양한 공간 능력을 발전시켜 뇌의 진화를 이끌었다. 반면 호모 사피엔스와 달리 네안데르탈인은 비록 높은 수준의 사냥꾼이었고 추위에 잘 적응했으며 어둠 속에서도 볼 수 있는 등 환경에 적응을 잘 했

문제편 p.248

지만 사회적 교류가 없어서 멸종하게 되었다고 말한다. 이 상반되는 예시를 통해 사회 관계망이 인간의 진화와 관련있다는 것을 알 수 있다. 따라서 정답은 ①이다.

06. 문장 (1)에서 사교성이 인간의 복잡한 뇌의 진화를 이끌었다고 말하며, 그 이후로는 호모 사피엔스와 네안데르탈인의 서로 상반되는 예시를 통해 사회성과 뇌의 발전이 어떻게 연관되어 있는지 구체적으로 보여준다. 네안데르탈인은 환경에 잘 적응했음에도 불구하고 호모 사피엔스와는 달리 사회 관계망의 유지를 위해 장거리를 이동하지 않았기 때문에 그 과정에서 발달시킬 수 있는 다양한 공간 능력을 획득하지 못했으며, 그 결과 멸종하게 되었다. 따라서 사교성을 의미하는 친구 집단은 뇌의 발전에 쓸모없는 것이 아니라 도움이 되는 것으로 볼 수 있다. 따라서 정답은 ⑤이다.

[중요 어휘]

☐ **evolutionary**	형용사 진화의, 진화론에 의한
☐ **sociability**	명사 사교성, 친목
☐ **gossip**	동사 잡담을 하다, 험담을 퍼뜨리다 / 명사 소문, 잡담
☐ **considerable**	형용사 상당한, 많은
☐ **wayfinding**	명사 길 찾기, 길 안내 표지
☐ **savvy**	명사 요령, 지식
☐ **Palaeolithic**	형용사 구석기 시대의
☐ **wilderness**	명사 황야
☐ **spatial**	형용사 공간의, 공간적인
☐ **awareness**	명사 인식, 의식
☐ **landscape**	명사 풍경, 경관
☐ **anthropologist**	명사 인류학자
☐ **attribute**	명사 특징, 특성 / 동사 원인으로 여기다
☐ **prime**	동사 준비하다 / 명사 전성기, 한창때 / 형용사 주요한, 최상의
☐ **foster**	동사 발전시키다, 조장하다
☐ **sophisticated**	형용사 수준 높은, 정교한, 복잡한
☐ **extinct**	형용사 멸종한, 사라진
☐ **badlands**	명사 불모지, 황무지
☐ **split**	동사 분열되다, 가르다, 쪼개다
☐ **communicative**	형용사 의사 전달의, 이야기하기 좋아하는

07~08 2023년 6월 41~42번 (정답률 50% | 75%) 정답 ⑤ | ⑤

[지문 끊어 읽기] 일상화된 경험과 기억의 특징

(1) [Events or experiences that are out of ordinary] / [ ]: S
선행사 주격 관계대명사절
일상을 벗어난 사건이나 경험은 /
tend to be remembered better / 07번 정답 단서 일상적이지 않은 사건이나 경험은 더 잘 기억되는 경향이 있음.
V
더 잘 기억되는 경향이 있다 /
because there is nothing competing with them /
현재분사
그것들과 경쟁하는 것이 없기 때문에 /
when your brain tries to access them /
당신의 뇌가 그것들에 접근하려고 할 때 /
from its storehouse of remembered events.
기억된 사건들의 창고에서

힌트 주어부인 'the reason it can be ~ ago'에서 the reason과 it 사이에 관계부사 why가 생략되어 있음. 이 문장의 전체적인 구조는 'the reason ~ is that ~'으로, '~인 이유는 (that절)이다'로 해석됨.

(2) In other words, / the reason it can be (a)difficult [to remember /
S 형식상의 주어 [ ]: 내용상의 주어
다시 말해 / 기억하기 (a)어려운 이유는 /
what you ate for breakfast two Thursdays ago] /
당신이 2주 전 목요일에 아침으로 무엇을 먹었는지 /
is that there was probably nothing special about that Thursday or
V
that particular breakfast /
아마도 그 목요일이나 그 특정한 아침 식사에 특별한 것이 하나도 없었기 때문이다 /
— consequently, / all your breakfast memories combine together /
결과적으로 / 당신의 모든 아침 식사 기억들은 함께 결합된다 /
into a sort of generic impression of a breakfast.
일종의 일반적인 아침 식사의 인상으로

(3) Your memory (b)merges similar events /
당신의 기억은 비슷한 사건들을 (b)합친다 /
not only because it's more efficient to do so, /
형식상의 주어 내용상의 주어
그렇게 하는 것이 더 효율적일 뿐만 아니라 /
but also because this is fundamental to how we learn things /
이것이 우리가 어떤 것을 배우는 방법에서 핵심적이기 때문이다 /
— our brains extract abstract rules /
우리 뇌는 추상적인 규칙을 추출한다 / 선행사
that tie experiences together.
주격 관계대명사절
경험을 함께 묶는

(4) This is especially true / for things that are (c)routine.
선행사 주격 관계대명사절
이것은 특히 사실이다 / (c)일상적인 것들에서

(5) If your breakfast is always the same /
당신의 아침 식사가 항상 같다면 /
— cereal with milk, a glass of orange juice, and a cup of coffee for instance — /
예를 들어 우유에 시리얼, 한 잔의 오렌지 주스, 그리고 한 잔의 커피 /
there is no easy way / for your brain to extract the details /
의미상의 주어 형용사적 용법
쉬운 방법은 없다 / 당신의 뇌가 세부 사항을 추출하는 /
from one particular breakfast.
특정한 한 아침 식사에서

(6) Ironically, then, / for behaviors that are routinized, /
선행사 주격 관계대명사절
그러면 모순적으로 / 일상화된 행동들에 대해 /
you can remember the generic content of the behavior /
당신은 그 행동의 일반적인 내용을 기억할 수 있다 /
(such as the things you ate, /
당신이 먹었던 것과 같은 것들 /
since you always eat the same thing), /
당신은 항상 같은 것을 먹기 때문에 /
but (d)particulars to that one instance /
그러나 그 한 경우에 대한 (d)세부 사항들은 /
can be very difficult to call up /
상기하기 매우 어려울 수 있다 /
(such as the sound of a garbage truck going by /
쓰레기 트럭이 지나가는 소리와 같은 것들 / 병렬①
or a bird that passed by your window) /
병렬②
혹은 당신의 창문을 지나가는 새 /
unless they were especially distinctive. 07번 정답 단서
그것들이 특별히 특이'하지 않다면'

일상화된 행동의 일반적인 내용은 기억할 수 있는 반면, 그것들이 특이한 것이 아니라면 그 세부 사항까지 상기하는 것은 쉽지 않음.

(7) On the other hand, / if you did something unique /
반면에 / 당신이 독특한 무언가를 했다면 / 선행사
that broke your routine /
주격 관계대명사절
당신의 일상을 깨뜨리는 /
— perhaps you had leftover pizza for breakfast /
아마 당신이 아침 식사로 남은 피자를 먹었다 /
and spilled tomato sauce on your dress shirt — /
그리고 당신의 와이셔츠에 토마토 소스를 흘렸다 /
you are (e)less(→ more) likely to remember it. 07번·08번 정답 단서
당신은 그것을 (e)덜(→ 더) 기억하기 쉽다

일상적이지 않은 독특한 일을 한다면 그 일을 기억할 가능성이 더 높음.

[전문 해석]

(1)일상을 벗어난 사건이나 경험은, 기억된 사건들의 창고에서 당신의 뇌가 그것들에 접근하려고 할 때 그것들과 경쟁하는 것이 없기 때문에 더 잘 기억되는 경향이 있다. (2)다시 말해, 당신이 2주 전 목요일에 아침으로 무엇을 먹었는지 기억하기 (a)어려운 이유는 아마도 그 목요일이나 그 특정한 아침 식사에 특별한 것이 하나도 없었기 때문이다. 결과적으로, 당신의 모든 아침 식사 기억들은 일종의 일반적인 아침 식사의 인상으로 함께 결합된다. (3)당신의 기억은 비슷한 사건들을 (b)합치는데, 그렇게 하는 것이 더 효율적일 뿐만 아니라 이것이 우리가 어떤 것을 배우는 방법에서 핵심적이기 때문이다. 우리 뇌는 경험을 함께 묶는 추상적인 규칙을 추출한다.
(4)이것은 (c)일상적인 것들에서 특히 사실이다. (5)당신의 아침 식사가 항상 같다면, 예를 들어, 우유에 시리얼, 한 잔의 오렌지 주스, 그리고 한 잔의 커피라면, 당신의 뇌가 특정한 한 아

문제편 p.249

침 식사에서 세부 사항을 추출하는 쉬운 방법은 없다(추출하는 것은 쉽지 않은 일이다). (6)그러면 모순적으로, 일상화된 행동들에 대해 당신은 그 행동의 일반적인 내용(당신은 항상 같은 것을 먹기 때문에 당신이 먹었던 것과 같은 것들)을 기억할 수 있지만, 그 한 경우에 대한 (d)세부 사항들(쓰레기 트럭이 지나가는 소리나 당신의 창문을 지나가는 새소리 같은 것들)은 그것들이 특별히 특이'하지 않다면' 상기하기 매우 어려울 수 있다. (7)반면에, 당신이 당신의 일상을 깨뜨리는 독특한 무언가를 했다면, 아마 당신이 아침 식사로 남은 피자를 먹었고 당신의 와이셔츠에 토마토 소스를 흘렸다면, 당신은 그것을 (e)덜(→ 더) 기억하기 쉽다.

[정답 확인]

07. 윗글의 제목으로 가장 적절한 것은?

① Repetition Makes Your Memory Sharp!
반복은 당신의 기억을 선명하게 만든다!
② How Does Your Memory Get Distorted?
당신의 기억은 어떻게 왜곡되는가?
③ What to Consider in Routinizing Your Work
당신의 일을 일상화할 때 고려해야 할 것
④ Merging Experiences: Key to Remembering Details
경험을 합치기: 세부 사항을 기억하는 비결
✔ The More Unique Events, the More Vivid Recollection
사건이 더 특이할수록, 기억이 더 선명해진다

08. 밑줄 친 (a) ~ (e) 중에서 문맥상 낱말의 쓰임이 적절하지 않은 것은?

① (a) ② (b) ③ (c) ④ (d) ✔ (e)

[문제 풀이]

07. 문장 (1)에서 설명하듯이, 일상적이지 않은 상황이나 경험은 더 잘 기억되는 경향이 있다. 가령 특이한 것이 없는 아침 식사는 다른 일상의 아침 식사와 합쳐지는데, 이것은 우리 뇌가 학습하는 기본 원리이기 때문이다. 문장 (4)와 (5)에 따르면 특히 일상적인 것, 예를 들어 아침 식사 같은 것에 이 원리가 적용된다고 한다. 이처럼 일상적인 것의 일반적인 내용은 잘 기억되는 반면, 일상의 세부 사항은 특별히 특이하지 않다면 기억하기 어렵다는 것이다. 따라서 정답은 '사건이 더 특이할수록, 기억이 더 선명해진다'는 ⑤이다.

[오답 풀이]

07. ④ - 문장 (3)에 따르면 우리는 비슷한 상황들을 합쳐서 기억하는데 이렇게 하는 것이 효율적이고 우리가 학습하는 기본이기 때문이라고 한다. 그런데 이러한 방법을 통해서는 세부 사항을 기억하기 어려우며, 반대로 일상적이지 않은 특이한 상황이나 경험의 경우가 더 세부 사항을 기억하기 쉽다는 것이 지문의 내용이므로 ④는 답이 될 수 없다.

[중요 어휘]

□ storehouse	[명사] 창고, 저장소
□ consequently	[부사] 결과적으로
□ generic	[형용사] 일반적인, 포괄적인
□ impression	[명사] 인상, 감명
□ merge	[동사] 합치다, 합병하다
□ fundamental	[형용사] 핵심적인, 근본적인
□ extract	[동사] 추출하다, 뽑다
□ abstract	[형용사] 추상적인, 관념적인
□ tie	[동사] 묶다 / [명사] 넥타이, 끈
□ routine	[형용사] 일상적인 / [명사] 일상
□ ironically	[부사] 모순적으로, 역설적이게도
□ routinize	[동사] 일상화하다
□ particulars	[명사] (주로 복수형) 세부 사항
□ call up	상기하다, (힘·용기 등을) 불러일으키다
□ distinctive	[형용사] 특이한, 독특한

핵심 조종사들이 불이익을 받을 우려 없이 자발적으로 자신의 과실을 보고할 수 있는 체계에 대한 내용임. 과실 보고서를 제출하는 주체는 누구인지, 그리고 이러한 보고 체계가 항공 안전에 어떻게 기여하였는지에 유의하면서 내용을 읽어 보면 쉽게 정답을 찾을 수 있음.

09~10

2020년 9월 41~42번 (정답률 70% | 50%) 정답 ① | ④

[지문 끊어 읽기] 익명의 보고서에 기반한 항공 안전

(1) U.S. commercial aviation / has long had /
현재완료(계속)
미국 민간 항공기 산업에는 / 오랫동안 있어 왔다 /

an extremely effective system /
매우 효과적인 체계가 /

for encouraging pilots / to submit reports of errors. 09번·10번 정답 단서
전치사 동명사(5형식V) O O·C(to V)
조종사들을 장려하기 위한 / 과실에 대한 보고서를 제출하도록

(2) The program has resulted in numerous improvements /
이 프로그램은 결과적으로 많은 개선점들을 야기해 왔다 /

to aviation safety. 09번 정답 단서
항공 안전에

(3) It wasn't easy to establish: /
그것은 확립하기 쉽지 않았다 /

pilots had severe self-induced social pressures /
조종사들은 스스로 만들어 낸 심한 사회적 압박감을 느꼈다 /

against (a)admitting to errors.
과실을 (a)인정하는 것에 대해

(4) Moreover, / to whom / would they report them?
게다가 / 누구에게 / 그들이 그것들을 보고한단 말인가

(5) Certainly not to their employers.
분명 그들의 고용주에게는 아닐 것이다

(6) Not even to the Federal Aviation Authority (FAA), /
미국 연방항공청(FAA)에게는 더욱 아닐 것이다 /

for then they would probably be punished.
=because
그러면 그들이 처벌을 받을 수도 있기 때문이다

(7) The solution was /
해결책은 ~이었다 /

to let the National Aeronautics and Space Administration (NASA)
사역V O

set up /
O·C(동사원형)
미국 항공우주국(NASA)으로 하여금 마련하도록 하는 것 /

a (b)voluntary accident reporting system /
(b)자발적인 사고 보고 체계를 /

whereby pilots could submit / semi-anonymous reports of errors /
조종사들이 제출할 수 있는 / 과실에 대한 반 익명의 보고서를 /

they had made / or observed in others. 10번 정답 단서
과거완료(had+p.p.①) p.p.②
그들이 저질렀던 / 혹은 다른 조종사에게서 목격했던

(8) Once NASA personnel had acquired the necessary information, /
일단 NASA 인사부가 필요한 정보를 얻었으면 /

they would (c)detach the contact information /
병렬①
그들은 연락처를 (c)떼어냈다 /

from the report / and mail it back to the pilot.
병렬②
보고서에서 / 그리고 그것을 조종사에게 돌려보냈다

(9) This meant / that NASA no longer knew /
이것은 의미했다 / NASA가 더 이상 알지 못한다는 것을 / 10번 정답 단서

who had reported the error, / which made it impossible /
누가 과실을 보고했는지를 / 그리고 이는 불가능하게 만들었다 /

for the airline companies or the FAA /
항공사나 FAA가 /

(which enforced penalties against errors) /
(과실에 대해 제재를 가하는) /

to find out / who had (d)rejected(→ submitted) the report.
찾아내는 것을 / 누가 그 보고서를 (d)거절했는지(→ 제출했는지)

힌트 '5형식V+형식상의 목적어(it)+목적격 보어(형용사)+for A+내용상의 목적어(to V)'의 구조로, 'A가 ~하는 것을 …하게 V하다'라고 해석해야 함.

(10) If the FAA had independently noticed the error /
FAA가 독자적으로 과실을 알아챘을 경우 /

and tried to invoke a civil penalty or certificate suspension, /
그리고 민사 처벌 또는 면허 정지를 적용하려고 시도했을 경우 /

the receipt of self-report /
자기 보고서의 접수가 /

automatically exempted the pilot from punishment.
그 조종사를 처벌로부터 자동으로 면제해 주었다

(11) When a sufficient number of similar errors had been collected, /
충분히 많은 유사한 오류가 수집되었을 때 /

NASA would analyze them /
NASA는 그것들을 분석하곤 했다 /
and issue reports and recommendations /
그리고 보고서와 권고안을 발급하곤 했다 /
to the airlines and to the FAA.
항공사와 FAA에

(12) These reports also helped the pilots realize /
5형식V O O·C(동사원형)
이러한 보고서는 또한 조종사들이 깨닫게 하는 데도 도움을 주었다 /
that their error reports were (e)valuable tools /
그들의 과실 보고서가 (e)유용한 도구라는 것을 /
for increasing safety.
안전성을 높이는 데

[중요 구문]

(7) The solution was to let the National ~ (NASA) set up
사역V O O·C(동사원형)
a ~ system [whereby pilots could submit ~].
선행사

힌트 whereby는 관계부사로, 풀어서 설명하면 'by + which(전치사 + 관계대명사)'와 같은 의미이므로, whereby부터 문장 끝까지가 'a ~ system'을 수식하듯 해석하면 됨.

[전문 해석]

(1)미국 민간 항공기 산업에는 조종사들이 과실에 대한 보고서를 제출하도록 장려하기 위한 매우 효과적인 체계가 오랫동안 있어 왔다. (2)이 프로그램은 결과적으로 항공 안전에 많은 개선점들을 야기해 왔다. (3)그것은 확립하기 쉽지 않았는데, 조종사들이 과실을 (a)인정하는 것에 대해 스스로 만들어 낸 심한 사회적 압박감을 느꼈기 때문이다. (4)게다가, 그들이 누구에게 과실을 보고한단 말인가? (5)분명 그들의 고용주에게는 아닐 것이다. (6)미국 연방항공청(FAA)에게는 더욱 아닐 것인데, 그러면 그들(조종사들)이 처벌을 받을 수도 있기 때문이다. (7)해결책은 미국 항공우주국(NASA)으로 하여금 조종사들이 그들이 저질렀거나 다른 조종사에게서 목격했던 과실에 대한 반 익명의 보고서를 제출할 수 있는 (b)자발적인 사고 보고 체계를 마련하도록 하는 것이었다.
(8)일단 NASA 인사부가 필요한 정보를 얻었으면, 그들은 보고서에서 연락처를 (c)떼어내고 그것을 조종사에게 돌려보냈다. (9)이것은 NASA가 누가 과실을 보고했는지를 더 이상 알지 못한다는 것을 의미했고, 이는 (과실에 대해 제재를 가하는) 항공사나 FAA가 누가 그 보고서를 (d)거절했는지(→ 제출했는지) 찾아내는 것을 불가능하게 만들었다. (10)(예를 들어) FAA가 독자적으로 과실을 알아채고 민사 처벌 또는 면허 정지를 적용하려고 시도했을 경우, 자기 보고서의 접수가 그 조종사를 처벌로부터 자동으로 면제해 주었다. (11)충분히 많은 유사한 오류가 수집되었을 때, NASA는 그것들을 분석하고 보고서와 권고안을 항공사와 FAA에 발급하곤 했다. (12)이러한 보고서는 또한 조종사들이 그들의 과실 보고서가 안전성을 높이는 데 (e)유용한 도구라는 것을 깨닫게 하는 데도 도움을 주었다.

[정답 확인]

09. 윗글의 제목으로 가장 적절한 것은?

① Aviation Safety Built on Anonymous Reports (✔)
익명의 보고서에 기반한 항공 안전
② More Flexible Manuals Mean Ignored Safety
보다 융통성 있는 설명서는 무시된 안전을 의미한다
③ Great Inventions from Unexpected Mistakes
예기치 않은 실수로부터의 위대한 발명
④ Controversies over New Safety Regulations
새로운 안전 규정에 대한 논란
⑤ Who Is Innovating Technology in the Air?
누가 항공 기술을 혁신하고 있는가?

10. 밑줄 친 (a) ~ (e) 중에서 문맥상 낱말의 쓰임이 적절하지 않은 것은?

① (a) ② (b) ③ (c) ④ (d) (✔) ⑤ (e)

[문제 풀이]

10. 본문은 조종사들이 과실 보고서를 제출하도록 장려하는 체계에 대한 내용임을 첫 문장에서 언급한 후, 이 체계가 확립되기 위해, 즉 조종사들이 압박감 없이 과실 보고서를 제출할 수 있게 하기 위해 낸 해결책이 무엇인가에 대해 설명하고 있다. 그 해결책은 조종사들이 반 익명의 과실 보고서를 제출할 수 있게 하는 것이었다. 즉, 항공사나 FAA에서 누가 보고서를 제출했는지 찾아낼 수 없게끔 하는 것이다. 따라서 (d)에는 누가 보고서를 '거절했는지(rejected)'가 아닌 '제출했는지(submitted)'가 오는 것이 적절하므로, 정답은 ④이다.

[중요 어휘]

□ **commercial**	형용사 민간(용)의, 상업적인, 이윤을 추구하는
□ **aviation**	명사 항공기 산업, 항공(술)
□ **improvement**	명사 개선(점)
□ **self-induced**	형용사 스스로 만들어 낸, 저절로 생긴
□ **admit**	동사 인정하다, 허가하다
□ **employer**	명사 고용주
□ **federal**	형용사 연방의
□ **voluntary**	형용사 자발적인, 자원한
□ **semi-anonymous**	형용사 반(半) 익명의
□ **personnel**	명사 인사부, 직원
□ **acquire**	동사 얻다, 습득하다
□ **detach**	동사 떼어내다, 분리하다
□ **reject**	동사 거절하다
□ **invoke**	동사 (법·규칙 등을) 적용하다, 들먹이다
□ **civil penalty**	민사 처벌
□ **suspension**	명사 정지, 보류
□ **exempt**	동사 면제해 주다 / 형용사 면제된
□ **issue**	동사 발급하다

11~12

2023년 9월 41~42번 (정답률 60% | 60%) **정답 ① | ⑤**

[지문 끊어 읽기] 노화에 대한 사회적 규범 변화

(1) In England in the 1680s, / it was unusual to live to the age of fifty.
형식상의 주어 내용상의 주어
1680년대 영국에서 / 50세까지 사는 것은 흔하지 않았다

(2) This was a period / [when knowledge was not spread (a)widely, /
선행사 [ ]: 관계부사절
이것은 시기였다 / 지식이 (a)널리 퍼지지 않았던 /
there were few books / and most people could not read]. 12번 정답 단서
책이 거의 없었던 / 그리고 대부분의 사람들은 읽을 수 없었던
책이 별로 없고 대부분의 사람들이 읽지 못하며 지식이 널리 퍼지지 않던 시기였음.

(3) As a consequence, / knowledge passed down /
결과적으로 / 지식은 전해 내려졌다 /
through the oral traditions of stories and shared experiences.
이야기와 공유된 경험의 구전 전통을 통해

(4) And since older people had accumulated more knowledge, /
과거완료
그리고 나이 든 사람들이 더 많은 지식을 축적했기 때문에 /
the social norm was / that to be over fifty was to be wise.
과거V 명사절 접속사(주격 보어)
사회적 규범은 ~이었다 / 50세가 넘는 것은 지혜롭다는 것

(5) This social perception of age began to shift /
나이에 대한 이 사회적 인식은 변화하기 시작했다 / 11번 정답 단서
나이에 대한 사회적 인식이 인쇄기와 같은 신기술의 출현으로 변함.
with the advent of new technologies / such as the printing press.
새로운 기술의 출현과 함께 / 인쇄기와 같은

(6) Over time, / as more books were printed, /
시간이 흐르면서 / 더 많은 책들이 인쇄됨에 따라 /
literacy (b)increased, /
문해력은 (b)증가했다 / 11번·12번 정답 단서
시간이 흐르면서 더 많은 책들이 인쇄되고 문해력이 올라가면서 지식 전달의 구전 전통이 사라지기 시작함.
and the oral traditions of knowledge transfer began to fade.
그리고 지식 전달의 구전 전통은 사라지기 시작했다

(7) With the fading of oral traditions, /
구전 전통이 사라지면서 /
the wisdom of the old became less important /
나이 든 사람들의 지혜는 덜 중요해졌다 /
힌트 'the+형용사'는 '~하는 사람들'이라는 뜻으로 복수명사 취급을 함.
and as a consequence / being over fifty was no longer seen /
그리고 결과적으로 / 50세가 넘는 것은 더 이상 여겨지지 않았다 /
as (c)signifying wisdom. 12번 정답 단서
지혜를 (c)의미하는 것으로
구전 전통이 사라지면서 나이 든 사람들의 지혜가 덜 중요해지고 50세가 넘는 것이 지혜를 의미하지 않게 됨.

(8) We are living in a period /
우리는 시대에 살고 있다 / 선행사
[when the gap between chronological and biological age is changing fast] / [ ]: 병렬①(관계부사절)
실제 연령과 생물학적 연령 사이의 격차가 빠르게 변하고 있는 /

and [where social norms are struggling to (d)adapt]. 12번 정답단서
[ ]: 병렬②(관계부사절)
그리고 사회적 규범이 (d)적응하기 위해 고군분투하는
우리는 실제 연령과 생물학적 연령 사이의 격차가 빠르게 변하고 사회적 규범이 적응하기 위해 고군분투하는 시대에 살고 있음.

(9) In a video /
영상에서 /
produced by the AARP (formerly the American Association of Retired Persons), /
AARP(이전의 American Association of Retired Persons)에 의해 제작된 /
young people were asked to do various activities /
젊은 사람들은 다양한 활동을 하도록 요청받았다 /
'just like an old person'.
'마치 꼭 나이 든 사람처럼'

(10) When older people joined them in the video, /
영상에서 나이 든 사람들이 그들과 합류했을 때 /
[the gap between the stereotype and the older people's actual behaviour] / [ ]: S
고정 관념과 나이 든 사람들의 실제 행동 사이의 격차는 /
was (e)unnoticeable(→ noticeable). 12번 정답단서 나이 든 사람들이 영상에서 같이 참여했을 때 고정 관념과 나이 든 사람들의 실제 행동 사이의 격차는 컸을 것임.
V
(e)눈에 띄지 않았다(→ 눈에 띄었다)

(11) It is clear / [that in today's world /
형식상의 주어 [ ]: 내용상의 주어
분명하다 / 오늘날의 세상에서 /
our social norms need to be updated quickly]. 11번 정답단서
우리의 사회적 규범이 빠르게 최신화되어야 한다는 것은
오늘날 우리의 사회적 규범은 빠르게 최신화되어야 함이 분명함.

[전문 해석]

(1)1680년대 영국에서 50세까지 사는 것은 흔하지 않았다. (2)이때는 지식이 (a)널리 퍼지지 않았고, 책이 거의 없었으며 대부분의 사람들은 읽을 수 없었던 시기였다. (3)결과적으로, 지식은 이야기와 공유된 경험의 구전 전통을 통해 전해 내려졌다. (4)그리고 나이 든 사람들이 더 많은 지식을 축적했기 때문에 사회적 규범은 50세가 넘는 것은 지혜롭다는 것이었다. (5)나이에 대한 이 사회적 인식은 인쇄기와 같은 새로운 기술의 출현과 함께 변화하기 시작했다. (6)시간이 흐르면서 더 많은 책들이 인쇄됨에 따라 문해력은 (b)증가했고, 지식 전달의 구전 전통은 사라지기 시작했다. (7)구전 전통이 사라지면서 나이 든 사람들의 지혜는 덜 중요해졌고, 결과적으로 50세가 넘는 것은 더 이상 지혜를 (c)의미하는 것으로 여겨지지 않았다. (8)우리는 실제 연령과 생물학적 연령 사이의 격차가 빠르게 변하고 있고 사회적 규범이 (d)적응하기 위해 고군분투하는 시대에 살고 있다. (9)AARP(이전의 American Association of Retired Persons)에 의해 제작된 영상에서 젊은 사람들은 '마치 꼭 나이 든 사람처럼' 다양한 활동을 하도록 요청받았다. (10)영상에서 나이 든 사람들이 그들과 합류했을 때 고정 관념과 나이 든 사람들의 실제 행동 사이의 격차는 (e)눈에 띄지 않았다(→ 눈에 띄었다). (11)오늘날의 세상에서 우리의 사회적 규범이 빠르게 최신화되어야 한다는 것은 분명하다.

[정답 확인]

11. 윗글의 제목으로 가장 적절한 것은?

✔ Our Social Norms on Aging: An Ongoing Evolution
노화에 대한 우리의 사회적 규범: 계속 진행 중인 진화
② The Power of Oral Tradition in the Modern World
현대 사회에서 구전 전통의 힘
③ Generational Differences: Not As Big As You Think
세대적 차이: 여러분이 생각하는 만큼 크지 않다
④ There's More to Aging than What the Media Shows
노화에는 매체가 보여주는 것보다 더 많은 것이 있다
⑤ How Well You Age Depends on Your Views of Aging
당신이 얼마나 잘 나이 드는지는 노화에 대한 당신의 관점에 달려 있다

12. 밑줄 친 (a) ~ (e) 중에서 문맥상 낱말의 쓰임이 적절하지 않은 것은?

① (a) ② (b) ③ (c) ④ (d) ✔ (e)

[문제 풀이]

11. 이 글은 노화에 대한 사회적 규범이 시간이 흐름에 따라 변화한다는 내용이다. 1680년대 영국에서는 50세까지 사는 것이 흔치 않았고, 책이 별로 없었으며 읽을 수 있는 사람도 많지 않았기 때문에 지식이 구전으로 전달되었다. 그러면서 50세가 넘는 것이 더 많은 지식을 축적하여 지혜로운 것이라는 사회적 규범이 있었다. 그러나 인쇄기가 등장하고 지식이 책으로 전달되면서 50세가 넘는 것이 더 이상 지혜를 의미하지 않게 되었다. AARP가 제작한 영상에서 젊은 사람들이 나이 든 사람처럼 행동하라는 요구를 받았을 때 그들이 한 행동과 실제 나이 든 사람들이 한 행동이 매우 달랐고, 우리의 사회적 규범은 이러한 차이를 줄일 수 있도록 최신화되어야 한다는 것이 이 글의 요지이다. 따라서 글의 제목은 ①이 적절하다.

12. 문장 (8)에 따르면 우리가 사는 시대에서는 생활 연령과 생물학적 연령의 격차가 빠르게 변하고 사회적 규범이 적응하기 위해 고군분투한다고 하며, 문장 (11)에서는 우리의 사회적 규범이 빠르게 최신화되어야 한다는 점을 강조한다. 그러므로 나이 든 사람들에 대한 젊은 사람들의 고정 관념과 실제 나이 든 사람들의 행동 간의 격차는 눈에 띄지 않는(unnoticeable) 것이 아니라 '눈에 띄는, 분명한(noticeable)' 것으로 보는 것이 적절하다. 따라서 정답은 ⑤이다.

[중요 어휘]

☐ oral	형용사 구전의, 구두의
☐ accumulate	동사 축적하다, 모으다
☐ norm	명사 규범, 기준
☐ shift	동사 변하다, 이동하다 / 명사 변화, 이동
☐ advent	명사 출현, 도래
☐ printing press	명사 인쇄기
☐ literacy	명사 문해력, 글을 읽고 쓰는 능력
☐ transfer	명사 전달, 전송 / 동사 전달하다, 갈아타다
☐ fade	동사 사라지다, 희미해지다
☐ signify	동사 의미하다, 중요하다
☐ chronological age	명사 실제 연령, 실제 나이
☐ biological age	명사 생물학적 연령
☐ formerly	부사 이전에
☐ stereotype	명사 고정 관념

핵심 본문은 정확한 예측이 우리 뇌의 에너지 소비를 줄이고 우리의 행동을 더 효율적이게 만든다는 장점이 있지만, 그럼에도 불구하고 우리의 뇌가 끊임없이 새로운 것을 추구한다고 주장하고 있음. 문장 (8)의 역접의 접속 부사 'But'을 기점으로 글의 논지가 어떻게 변화하는지 주의하며 읽을 것.

13~14 2019년 11월 41~42번 (정답률 60% | 50%) 정답 ③ | ④

[지문 끊어 읽기] 뇌를 만족시키는 것

(1) We're creatures / who live and die / by the energy stores /
우리는 생명체이다 / 살고 죽는 / 에너지 저장에 의해 /
we've built up in our bodies.
우리가 우리의 몸 안에 축적해온

(2) Navigating the world is a difficult job / that requires /
세상을 항해하는 것은 힘든 일이다 / 요구하는 /
moving around and using a lot of brainpower /
병렬① 병렬②
여기저기 이동하고 많은 지력을 사용하는 것을 /
— an energy-expensive endeavor.
에너지 소비가 큰 노력
힌트 밑줄 친 부분은 requires의 목적어인 'moving around and using a lot of brainpower'와 동격이므로, requires의 목적어로 해석해야 함.

(3) When we make correct (a)predictions, / that saves energy.
우리가 정확한 (a)예측을 할 때 / 그것은 에너지를 절약해준다

(4) When you know / that edible bugs can be found /
당신이 알 때 / 먹을 수 있는 곤충이 발견될 수 있다는 것을 /
beneath certain types of rocks, /
특정한 종류의 바위 아래에서 /
it saves / turning over *all* the rocks.
그것은 덜어준다 / '모든' 바위를 뒤집어보는 일을

(5) The better we predict, /
우리가 더 잘 예측할수록 /
the less energy it costs us.
그것은 우리에게 더 적은 에너지를 들게 한다
힌트 'the 비교급 S' V', the 비교급 S V'는 '~할수록, 더욱 ~하다'라고 해석함. 보통 절과 절을 연결하기 위해서는 접속사가 필요하지만, 이 구문은 접속사 없이도 두 절이 이어지는 특수한 구문임.

(6) Repetition makes us / more confident in our forecasts /
5형식V O O·C①
반복은 우리를 만든다 / 우리의 예측에 있어 더 자신감 있게 /
and more efficient in our actions.
O·C②
그리고 우리의 행동에 있어 더 효율적이게
힌트 일반적으로 형용사는 명사 앞에서 명사를 수식하지만, '-thing' 종류의 대명사들은 형용사가 명사 뒤에서 명사를 수식함. 여기서도 appealing이 something을 뒤에서 수식함.

(7) So there's something (b)appealing / about predictability.
그러므로 (b)매력적인 무언가가 있다 / 예측 가능성에 관해서는

13번 정답단서
(8) But / if our brains are going to all this effort /
하지만 / 만약 우리의 뇌가 이 모든 노력을 들이고 있는 것이라면 /

to make the world predictable, / that begs the question:
세상을 예측 가능하게 만들기 위해 / 그것은 질문을 하게 만든다

힌트 'beg the question'이라는 표현은 직역하면 '질문을 간청하다'라는 뜻이지만, '질문을 하게 만들다'라는 뜻으로 쓰임.

(9) if we love predictability so much, /
만약 우리가 예측 가능성을 그렇게 많이 좋아한다면 /
why don't we, for example, just replace our televisions /
예를 들어, 우리는 왜 우리의 텔레비전을 교체해버리지 않는가 /
with machines / that emit a rhythmic beep /
기계로 / 주기적인 신호음을 내는 /
twenty-four hours a day, / predictably?
하루 24시간 동안 / 예측 가능하게

(10) The answer is / that there's a problem with a (c)lack of surprise.
정답은 ~이다 / 놀라움의 (c)부족에는 문제가 있다는 것

힌트 예측 가능성을 매력적이라고 느끼면서도 인생의 모든 것을 예측 가능하게 바꿔버리지 않는 이유를 문장 (10)에서는 '놀라움의 부족'에서 찾고 있음. 즉, 모든 것이 예측 가능해지면 '놀라움의 부족'이라는 현상이 생기는데, 이것을 반드시 좋게만 볼 것은 아니라는 것임.

(11) The better we understand something, /
우리가 어떤 것을 더 잘 이해할수록 /
14번 정답 단서
the less effort we put / into thinking about it.
우리는 더 적은 노력을 들인다 / 그것에 대해 생각하는 데에

(12) Familiarity (d)reduces(→ increases) indifference.
친숙함은 무관심을 (d)줄인다(→ 증가시킨다)

14번 정답 단서
(13) Repetition suppression sets in / and our attention diminishes.
반복 억제가 자리를 잡는다 / 그리고 우리의 주의는 감소한다

(14) This is why /
이것이 이유이다 /
— no matter how much you enjoyed watching the World Series — /
=however
당신이 아무리 월드 시리즈를 시청하는 것을 즐긴다고 할지라도 /
you aren't going to be satisfied /
당신이 만족하지 않을 /
[watching that same game over and over]. 13번 정답 단서
같은 경기를 반복적으로 시청하면서 [ ]: 분사구문(부대상황)

(15) Although predictability is reassuring, /
비록 예측 가능성이 안도감을 줄지라도 /
the brain strives to (e)incorporate new facts /
뇌는 새로운 사실을 (e)포함시키기 위해 애를 쓴다 /
into its model of the world. 13번 정답 단서
세상에 대한 그것의 모형에

(16) It always seeks novelty. 13번 정답 단서
그것은 항상 참신함을 추구한다

[전문 해석]

(1)우리는 우리가 (우리의) 몸 안에 축적해온 에너지 저장에 의해 살고 죽는 생명체이다. (2)세상을 항해하는 것은 여기저기 이동하고 많은 지력을 사용하는 것, 즉 에너지 소비가 큰 노력을 요구하는 힘든 일이다. (3)우리가 정확한 (a)예측을 할 때, 그것은 에너지를 절약해준다. (4)당신이 먹을 수 있는 곤충이 특정한 종류의 바위 아래에서 발견될 수 있다는 것을 알 때, 그것은 '모든' 바위를 뒤집어보는 일을 덜어준다. (5)우리가 더 잘 예측할수록, 그것은 우리에게 더 적은 에너지를 들게 한다. (6)반복은 우리를 (우리의) 예측에 있어 더 자신감 있게, 그리고 (우리의) 행동에 있어 더 효율적이게 만든다. (7)그러므로 예측 가능성에 관해서는 (b)매력적인 무언가가 있다.
(8)하지만 만약 우리의 뇌가 세상을 예측 가능하게 만들기 위해 이 모든 노력을 들이고 있는 것이라면, 그것은 질문을 하게 만든다. (9)만약 우리가 예측 가능성을 그렇게 많이 좋아한다면, 예를 들어, 우리는 왜 예측 가능하게 우리의 텔레비전을 하루 24시간 동안 주기적인 신호음을 내는 기계로 교체해버리지 않는가? (10)정답은 놀라움의 (c)부족에는 문제가 있다는 것이다. (11)우리가 어떤 것을 더 잘 이해할수록, 우리는 그것에 대해 생각하는 데에 더 적은 노력을 들인다. (12)친숙함은 무관심을 (d)줄인다(→ 증가시킨다). (13)반복 억제가 자리를 잡고 우리의 주의는 감소한다. (14)이것이 (바로) 당신이 아무리 월드 시리즈를 시청하는 것을 즐긴다고 할지라도 (당신이) 같은 경기를 반복적으로 시청하면서 만족하지 않을 이유이다. (15)비록 예측 가능성이 안도감을 줄지라도, 뇌는 세상에 대한 그것의 모형에 새로운 사실을 (e)포함시키기 위해 애를 쓴다. (16)그것은 항상 참신함을 추구한다.

[정답 확인]

13. 윗글의 제목으로 가장 적절한 것은?

① Why Are Television Reruns Still Popular?
왜 텔레비전 재방송이 아직까지도 인기가 있는가?
② Predictability Is Something Not to Be Feared!
예측 가능성은 두려워할 것이 아니다!
✔ What Really Satisfies Our Brain: Familiarity or Novelty
무엇이 정말로 우리의 뇌를 만족시키는가: 친숙함 혹은 참신함
④ Repetition Gives Us Expertise at the Expense of Creativity
반복은 우리에게 창의성의 대가로 전문성을 제공한다
⑤ Our Hunter-Gatherer Ancestors Were Smart in Saving Energy
우리의 수렵채집인 조상들은 에너지를 절약하는 데 현명했다

14. 밑줄 친 (a) ~ (e) 중에서 문맥상 낱말의 쓰임이 적절하지 않은 것은?

① (a) ② (b) ③ (c) ✔ (d) ⑤ (e)

[문제 풀이]

13. 본문은 문장 (1)~(7)에서 정확한 예측과 반복을 통한 높은 예측 가능성의 효용에 관해 이야기하다가, 문장 (8)~(14)에서는 '놀라움의 부족(lack of surprise)'이 가지는 문제점을 언급하고 있다. 즉, 예측 가능성이 높아짐에 따라 어떤 것에 대한 우리의 노력과 주의는 감소하게 되며, 그 결과 아무리 좋아하는 것이라고 하더라도 그것의 단순한 반복만으로는 우리가 만족감을 얻지 못한다는 것이다. 특히 문장 (15)~(16)은 예측 가능성이 안도감을 줄지라도 우리의 뇌가 항상 참신함을 추구한다고 분명하게 말하고 있으므로, 윗글의 제목으로 가장 알맞은 것은 ③이다.
14. 문장 (11)에서 우리가 어떤 것을 더 잘 이해할수록 더 적은 노력을 들인다고 했고, 문장 (13)에서 반복 억제로 인해 우리의 주의가 감소한다고 했으므로, 친숙한 것을 접할 때 예측 가능성이 높아지게 되므로 오히려 무관심이 증가한다고 보는 것이 자연스럽다. 따라서 'reduces(줄인다)' 대신 'increases(증가시킨다)'라고 하는 것이 자연스럽다.

[오답 풀이]

14. ⑤ - 뇌가 세상에 대한 그것의 모형에 새로운 사실을 포함시킨다는 것은 곧 우리의 뇌가 세상에 대한 새로운 정보들을 받아들여 세상에 대한 우리의 인식을 계속해서 완성시켜 나간다는 의미이다. 이는 참신함을 추구한다는 문장 (16)의 내용과도 연결되므로, (e) incorporate는 문맥상 자연스럽다.

[중요 어휘]

□ **navigate**	동사 항해하다, 길을 찾다
□ **brainpower**	명사 지력, 지능
□ **endeavor**	명사 노력 / 동사 노력하다, 애쓰다
□ **edible**	형용사 먹을 수 있는, 식용의
□ **appealing**	형용사 매력적인, 호소하는
□ **predictability**	명사 예측 가능성
□ **go to the effort to V**	~하기 위해 노력을 들이다
□ **emit**	동사 내다, 내뿜다
□ **rhythmic**	형용사 주기적인, 리드미컬한
□ **familiarity**	명사 친숙함, 익숙함
□ **indifference**	명사 무관심, 무심
□ **suppression**	명사 억제, 진압
□ **diminish**	동사 감소하다, 줄어들다
□ **reassuring**	형용사 안도감을 주는, 안심시키는
□ **incorporate A into B**	A를 B에 포함시키다
□ **novelty**	명사 참신함, 새로움
□ **rerun**	명사 재방송, 재시합 / 동사 재방송하다
□ **expertise**	명사 전문성, 전문적 지식
□ **at the expense of**	~의 대가로, ~을 희생하여

15~16

2018년 9월 41~42번 (정답률 60% | 45%) **정답 ① | ④**

[지문 끊어 읽기] 의도적 합리화

(1) In 2000, / James Kuklinski of the University of Illinois /
2000년에 / Illinois 대학의 James Kuklinski는 /
led an influential experiment /
영향력 있는 실험을 이끌었다 /
in which more than 1,000 Illinois residents /
1,000명이 넘는 Illinois의 거주자들이 /
were asked questions about welfare.
복지에 대한 질문을 받았던

(2) More than half indicated / that they were confident /
절반이 넘는 사람들이 말했다 / 그들은 확신했다고 /
that their answers were correct / — but in fact, /
그들의 답이 정확하다는 것을 / 하지만 사실은 /
only three percent of the people got /
오직 그 사람들의 3퍼센트만이 맞혔다 /
more than half of the questions right.
질문의 절반 이상을 정확하게

(3) Perhaps more disturbingly, /
아마도 더 충격적인 것은 /
the ones who were the *most* confident / they were right /
S
'가장' 확신했던 사람들이 / 그들이 정확했다고 /
were generally the ones / who knew the least about the topic.
V
대체로 ~했던 사람들이었다 / 그 주제에 대해 가장 적게 알았던

(4) Kuklinski calls / this sort of response /
Kuklinski는 불렀다 / 이러한 종류의 응답을 /
the "I know I'm right" syndrome.
'내가 맞다는 것을 나는 안다'는 증후군이라고

(5) "It implies / not only that most people will resist /
이것은 나타낸다 / 대부분의 사람들이 저항할 뿐만 아니라 /
correcting their factual beliefs," / he wrote, /
그들의 사실적 믿음을 고치는 것에 / 그가 썼다 / 삽입절
"but also that the very people /
또한 바로 그 사람들이 /
who most need to correct them / will be least likely to do so."
그것들을 가장 고쳐야 할 필요가 있는 / 그렇게 할 가능성이 가장 적다는 것을

(6) How can we have things so wrong /
어떻게 우리는 그렇게 틀릴 수 있을까 /
and be so sure that we're right?
그러면서도 우리가 맞다고 그렇게 확신할 수 있을까

(7) Part of the answer lies / in the way our brains are wired.
답의 일부는 있다 / 우리의 뇌가 고정된 방식에

(8) Generally, / people tend to seek consistency.
일반적으로 / 사람들은 일관성을 추구하는 경향이 있다

(9) There is a substantial body of psychological research /
심리학 연구가 상당히 많다 /
showing that people tend to interpret information /
사람들이 정보를 해석하는 경향이 있다는 것을 보여주는 /
with an eye / toward reinforcing their preexisting views. 16번 정답 단서
시각을 가지고 / 그들의 기존의 견해들을 강화하는 쪽으로

(10) If we believe something about the world, /
만약 우리가 세상에 대해 무언가를 믿는다면 /
we are more likely to / passively accept as truth /
우리는 더 ~하는 경향이 있다 / 사실로서 소극적으로 받아들이는 /
any information that confirms our beliefs, /
우리의 믿음을 확인해 주는 어떠한 정보라도 /
and actively dismiss information / that doesn't. 15번 정답 단서
그리고 정보는 적극적으로 무시하는 / 그렇지 않은

(11) This is known / as "motivated reasoning."
이것은 알려져 있다 / '의도적 합리화'라고

16번 정답 단서
(12) Whether or not / the consistent information is accurate, /
~이든 아니든 간에 / 일관성이 있는 정보가 정확하다 /
we might accept it as fact, / as confirmation of our beliefs.
우리는 그것을 사실로 받아들일지도 모른다 / 우리의 믿음에 대한 확인으로서

(13) This makes us / more confident in said beliefs, /
5형식V O O·C①
이것은 우리를 만든다 / 앞서 언급된 믿음에 더 확신을 갖게 /
and even less likely to entertain facts / that contradict them.
O·C②
그리고 심지어 사실들은 마음에 덜 품는 경향이 있게 / 그것들에 모순되는

[전문 해석]

(1)2000년에, Illinois(일리노이) 대학의 James Kuklinski(제임스 쿠클린스키)는 1,000명이 넘는 Illinois(일리노이)의 거주자들이 복지에 대한 질문을 받았던 영향력 있는 실험을 이끌었다. (2)절반이 넘는 사람들(응답자들)이 그들의 답이 정확하다는 것을 확신했다고 말했다. 하지만 사실은, 오직 그 사람들의 3퍼센트만이 질문의 절반 이상을 정확하게 맞혔다. (3)아마도 더 충격적인 것은, 그들이 정확했다고(정확하게 알고 있다고) '가장' 확신했던 사람들이 대체로 그 주제에 대해 가장 적게 알았던 사람들이었다. (4)Kuklinski는 이러한 종류의 응답을 '내가 맞다는 것을 나는 안다'는 증후군이라고 불렀다. (5)"이것은 대부분의 사람들이 그들의 사실적 믿음을 고치는 것에 저항할 뿐만 아니라, 또한 그것들(자기가 믿고 있는 사실들)을 가장 고쳐야 할 필요가 있는 바로 그 사람들이 그렇게 할(고칠) 가능성이 가장 적다는 것을 나타낸다."라고 그가 썼다.
(6)어떻게 우리는 그렇게 틀리면서도 우리가 맞다고 그렇게 확신할 수 있을까? (7)(정)답의 일부는 우리의 뇌가 고정된 방식에 있다. (8)일반적으로, 사람들은 일관성을 추구하는 경향이 있다. (9)사람들이 그들의 기존의 견해들을 강화하는 쪽으로(의) 시각을 가지고 정보를 해석하는 경향이 있다는 것을 보여주는 심리학 연구가 상당히 많다. (10)만약 우리가 세상에 대해 무언가를 믿는다면, 우리는 우리의 믿음을 확인해 주는 어떠한 정보라도 (그것을) 사실로서 더 소극적으로 받아들이고, 그렇지 않은 정보는 더 적극적으로 무시하는 경향이 있다. (11)이것은 '의도적 합리화'라고 알려져 있다. (12)일관성이 있는 정보가 정확하든 아니든 간에, 우리는 그것을 우리의 믿음에 대한 확인으로서, 사실로 받아들일지도 모른다. (13)이것은 우리가 앞서 언급된 믿음에 더 확신을 갖게 만들고, 심지어 그 믿음에 모순되는 사실들은 마음에 덜 품는 경향이 있게 만든다.

[정답 확인]

15. 윗글의 제목으로 가장 적절한 것은?

✔ Belief Wins Over Fact
믿음은 사실을 이긴다(설득시킨다)
② Still Judge by Appearance?
아직도 겉모습으로 판단하는가?
③ All You Need Is Motivation
당신이 필요한 모든 것은 동기 부여이다
④ Facilitate Rational Reasoning
이성적인 합리화를 가능하게 하라
⑤ Correct Errors at the Right Time
맞는 순간에(적시에) 오류를 고쳐라

16. 윗글의 빈칸에 들어갈 말로 가장 적절한 것은?

① diversity 다양성
② accuracy 정확성
③ popularity 인기
✔ consistency 일관성
⑤ collaboration 협동

[문제 풀이]

16. 지문은 심리학자인 James Kuklinski(제임스 쿠클린스키)의 실험을 통해 '의도적 합리화'의 개념을 설명하며, 사람들은 정보가 정확하든 아니든 간에 우리의 믿음을 확인해주는 정보는 수용하고, 그렇지 않은 정보는 멀리하는 경향이 있다고 언급하고 있다. 또한 우리가 이전에 가지고 있던 의견을 굳히는 쪽으로 정보를 해석하기 쉽다고 했으므로 정답은 ④ 'consistency(일관성)'이다.

[중요 어휘]

힌트 '(어떤 상태에) 있다'라는 의미의 lie는 변화형이 lie-lay-lain이지만, '거짓말하다'라는 의미의 lie는 규칙 동사로 lie-lied-lied로 변화함.

☐ resident	명사 거주자
☐ welfare	명사 복지, 후생
☐ indicate	동사 말하다, 나타내다, 보여 주다
☐ disturbingly	부사 충격적인 것은, 불안하게 하여
☐ syndrome	명사 증후군, 일련의 증상
☐ factual	형용사 사실적인, 사실에 기반을 둔
☐ lie	동사 (어떤 상태로) 있다, 놓여 있다
☐ substantial	형용사 상당한
☐ reinforce	동사 강화하다, 보강하다
☐ preexist	동사 기존에 존재하다
☐ passively	부사 소극적으로, 수동적으로
☐ dismiss	동사 무시하다, 묵살하다
☐ reasoning	명사 합리화, 추론
☐ consistent	형용사 일관성 있는, 한결같은
☐ contradict	동사 모순되다, 부정하다
☐ facilitate	동사 가능하게 하다, 용이하게 하다
☐ rational	형용사 이성적인, 합리적인

문제편 p.253

17~18 2021년 11월 41~42번 (정답률 55% | 50%) 정답 ③ | ④

[지문 끊어 읽기] 이야기에 주목하는 특성

(1) Stories populate our lives.
타동사
이야기는 우리의 삶에 거주한다

(2) If you are not a fan of stories, / you might imagine /
만약 여러분이 이야기의 팬이 아니라면 / 여러분은 생각할지도 모른다 /
that the best world is a world without them, /
명사절 접속사 선행사
가장 좋은 세상이란 그것들이 없는 세상이라고 /
[where we can only see the facts / in front of us].
[ ]: 관계부사절
우리가 사실들만 볼 수 있는 / 우리 앞에 있는

힌트 여기서 쉼표(comma, 콤마)는 동격의 콤마로 의문사 how가 이끄는 명사절 'how our brains work'와 'how they are designed to work'를 동격으로 보면 됨.

(3) But / to do this / is to (a)deny how our brains work, /
그러나 / 이렇게 하는 것은 / 우리의 뇌가 어떻게 작동하는지를 (a)부인하는 것이다 /
how they are *designed* to work.
어떻게 그것들이 작동하도록 '설계되어' 있는지를

(4) Evolution has given us minds /
4형식V I·O D·O, 선행사
진화는 우리에게 머리를 주어 왔다 /
that are alert to stories and suggestion / because, /
주격 관계대명사절
이야기와 암시에 주의를 기울이는 / 왜냐하면 /
through many hundreds of thousands of years of natural selection, /
수십만 년의 자연 선택을 거쳐 /
minds that can attend to stories / have been more (b)successful /
선행사(=S') 주격 관계대명사절 V'
이야기에 주의를 기울일 수 있는 머리가 / 더 (b)성공적이었기 때문이다 /
at passing on their owners' genes. 17번 정답 단서 우리는 이야기와 암시에 주의를 기울이도록 진화했는데 그것이 생존과 번식에 유리했기 때문임.
=minds'
그들 주인의 유전자를 물려주는 것에

(5) Think about [what happens, / for example, /
의문대명사 삽입
무슨 일이 일어나는지 생각해 보라 / 예를 들어 /
when animals face one another / in conflict]. [ ]: 간접의문문: 의문사+(S)+V
동물들이 서로를 직면할 때 / 싸움에서

(6) They rarely plunge into battle / right away. 18번 정답 단서 동물들이 싸울 때 바로 전투에 뛰어들지 않음.
그것들은 좀처럼 전투에 뛰어들지 않는다 / 즉시

(7) No, / they first try to (c)signal / 18번 정답 단서 동물들은 서로에게 자신이 더 우위에 있음을 과시하는 신호를 보냄.
아니 / 그것들은 먼저 (c)신호를 보내려 애를 쓴다 /
in all kinds of ways /
온갖 종류의 방법으로 /
what the *outcome* of the battle is going to be.
전투의 '결과'가 무엇이 될지

힌트 'signal'의 목적어는 의문사 what이 이끄는 명사절, 즉 간접의문문임. 중간에 있는 전치사구 'in all kinds of ways'는 부사 역할을 하며 'signal'을 수식함.

(8) They puff up their chests, / they roar, /
그것들은 가슴을 잔뜩 부풀린다 / 그것들은 포효한다 /
and they bare their fangs.
그리고 그것들은 송곳니를 드러낸다

(9) Animals evolved / to attend to stories and signals /
부사적 용법 전치사
동물들은 진화했다 / 이야기와 신호에 주의를 기울이도록 /
because these turn out to be an efficient way /
이것들이 효율적인 방법이 되기 때문에 /
to navigate the world. 17번·18번 정답 단서 세상을 사는 효율적인 방법이 상대의 이야기나 신호에 주목하는 것이므로 동물들은 이야기와 신호에 주의를 기울이도록 진화했음.
형용사적 용법
세상을 항해하는

힌트 가정법 과거가 사용되었음. 'if'가 이끄는 조건절이 병렬로 이어져 있으며, 'it would be ~'가 주절에 해당함.

(10) If you and I were a pair of lions on the Serengeti, /
만약 여러분과 내가 세렌게티의 한 쌍의 사자라면 /
and we were trying to decide the strongest lion, /
그리고 우리가 가장 강한 사자를 결정하려 한다면 /
it would be most (d)sensible(→ unwise) /
형식상의 주어
가장 (d)분별 있는(→ 어리석은) 일일 것이다 /
— for both of us — / to plunge straight into a conflict.
의미상의 주어 내용상의 주어
우리 둘 다 / 싸움에 곧바로 뛰어드는 것이

(11) It is far better / for each of us /
비교급 강조
형식상의 주어 의미상의 주어
훨씬 낫다 / 우리 각자가 /
[to make a show of strength, / to tell *the story* /
힘을 과시하는 것이 / '이야기'를 하는 것이 /
of how our victory is inevitable]. 18번 정답 단서 자신이 우위에 있음을 이야기하는 것이 바로 싸움에 뛰어드는 것보다 훨씬 나은 선택임.
간접의문문 [ ]: 내용상의 주어
어떻게 자신의 승리가 불가피한지에 대한

힌트 문장 (3)에서와 마찬가지로 여기서 쉼표(comma, 콤마)는 동격의 콤마로 'to make a show of strength'와 'to tell ~ inevitable'을 동격으로 보면 됨.

(12) If one of those stories is much more (e)convincing /
비교급 강조
그 이야기들 중 하나가 훨씬 더 (e)설득력이 있다면 /
than the other, / we might be able to agree on the outcome /
다른 쪽보다 / 우리는 그 결과에 동의할 수 있을지도 모른다 /
without actually having the fight.
실제로 싸우지 않고도

[전문 해석]

(1)이야기는 우리의 삶에 거주한다. (2)만약 여러분이 이야기의 팬이 아니라면, 여러분은 가장 좋은 세상이란 그것들이 없는, 우리가 우리 앞에 있는 사실들만 볼 수 있는 세상이라고 생각할지도 모른다. (3)그러나 이렇게 하는 것은 우리의 뇌가 어떻게 작동하는지, 즉 어떻게 그것들이 작동하도록 '설계되어' 있는지를 (a)부인하는 것이다. (4)수십만 년의 자연 선택을 거쳐, 이야기에 주의를 기울일 수 있는 머리가 그들 주인의 유전자를 물려주는 것에 더 (b)성공적이었기(성공해 왔기) 때문에, 진화는 우리에게 이야기와 암시에 주의를 기울이는 머리를 주어 왔다.
(5)예를 들어 동물들이 싸움에서 서로를 직면할 때 무슨 일이 일어나는지 생각해 보라. (6)그것들은 좀처럼 즉시 전투에 뛰어들지 않는다. (7)아니, 그것들은 먼저 전투의 '결과'가 무엇이 될지 온갖 종류의 방법으로 (c)신호를 보내려 애를 쓴다. (8)그것들은 가슴을 잔뜩 부풀리고, 포효하며, 송곳니를 드러낸다. (9)이야기와 신호가 세상을 항해하는 효율적인 방법이 되기 때문에, 동물들은 이것들에 주의를 기울이도록 진화했다. (10)만약 여러분과 내가 세렌게티의 한 쌍의 사자이고 우리가 가장 강한 사자를 결정하려 한다면, 우리 둘 다 싸움에 곧바로 뛰어드는 것이 가장 (d)분별 있는(→ 어리석은) 일일 것이다. (11)우리 각자가 힘을 과시하는 것, 즉 어떻게 자신의 승리가 불가피한지에 대한 '이야기'를 하는 것이 훨씬 낫다. (12)그 이야기들 중 하나가 다른 쪽보다 훨씬 더 (e)설득력이 있다면, 우리는 실제로 싸우지 않고도 그 결과에 동의할 수 있을지도 모른다.

[정답 확인]

17. 윗글의 제목으로 가장 적절한 것은?
① The Light and Dark Sides of Storytelling
이야기하는 것의 밝고 어두운 면
② How to Interpret Various Signals of Animals
동물들의 다양한 신호를 해석하는 방법
③ Why Are We Built to Pay Attention to Stories? ✔
왜 우리는 이야기에 주의를 기울이도록 설계되었나?
④ Story: A Game Changer for Overturning a Losing Battle
이야기: 지고 있던 전투를 뒤집는 전환점
⑤ Evolution: A History of Human's Coexistence with Animals
진화: 동물과 공존하는 인간의 역사

18. 밑줄 친 (a) ~ (e) 중에서 문맥상 낱말의 쓰임이 적절하지 않은 것은?
① (a) ② (b) ③ (c) ④ (d) ✔ ⑤ (e)

[문제 풀이]

17. 인간이 왜 이야기에 주목하는지를 설명하는 글이다. 필자는 이야기에 주목하는 특징이 생존에 더 효과적이었기 때문에 인간을 비롯한 동물이 이야기와 암시에 주목하도록 진화했다고 설명한다. 예를 들어 동물들이 바로 전투에 뛰어들지 않고 서로에게 위협을 하는 등의 신호를 보내는 것은 자신이 더 강하다는 것을 보여 주어 싸우지 않고서도 승패를 가리기 위해서인데, 이는 즉각적으로 싸움을 시작해 서로의 생존에 위협이 되는 것보다 훨씬 나은 선택이다. 이렇게 글은 지문 전반에 걸쳐 인간을 포함한 동물들이 이야기와 신호에 주목하는 이유에 대해 설명하고 있으므로 글의 제목으로는 ③이 적절하다.
18. 문장 (5)~(8)에 따르면 동물들은 싸움에서 서로를 직면했을 때 바로 전투를 하지 않는다. 대신 가슴 부풀림, 포효 등과 같은 이야기와 신호로 자신이 상대보다 우위에 있음을 과시하는 행동을 한다. 문장 (10)에서 가정하는 내용도 이러한 상황의 연장선으로, 곧바로 싸움에 뛰어드는 것은 바람직하지 않은 행동임을 추론할 수 있다. 따라서 'sensible(분별 있는)' 대신 'unwise'와 같이 '어리석은'이라는 의미의 단어를 쓰는 것이 적절하다.

[중요 어휘]

populate	동사 거주하다, 살다
deny	동사 부인하다
alert	형용사 주의를 기울이는, 민감한
suggestion	명사 암시, 제안
attend	동사 주의를 기울이다, 참석하다
pass on	물려주다, 넘겨주다
plunge into	~에 뛰어들다, 빠지다
signal	동사 신호를 보내다, 암시하다 / 명사 신호
outcome	명사 결과
puff up	(잔뜩) 부풀리다, 부어오르다
roar	동사 포효하다, 으르렁거리다
bare	동사 드러내다, 폭로하다
fang	명사 송곳니
navigate	동사 항해하다, 길을 찾다
sensible	형용사 분별 있는, 합리적인
inevitable	형용사 불가피한, 필연적인
convincing	형용사 설득력 있는, 확실한
game changer	전환점, 승부수
overturn	동사 뒤집다, 번복시키다
coexistence	명사 공존

19~20 2022년 11월 41~42번 (정답률 50% | 50%) 정답 ③ | ②

[지문 끊어 읽기] 속임수를 쓰는 뇌

(1) A neuropsychologist, Michael Gazzaniga / conducted a study /
신경 심리학자 Michael Gazzaniga는 / 연구를 수행했다 / 선행사
[that shows /
[ ]: 주격 관계대명사절
보여 주는 /
that our brains (a)excel /
명사절 접속사(shows의 목적어절을 이끎)
우리의 뇌가 (a)탁월하다는 것을 /
at creating coherent (but not necessarily true) stories /
일관성 있는 (그러나 반드시 사실은 아닌) 이야기를 만들어 내는 데 있어 / 선행사'
that deceive us].
주격 관계대명사절'
우리를 속이는

힌트 이 문장에 세 번의 that이 등장하는데, 첫 번째 that은 선행사가 a study인 주격 관계대명사이고 문장 끝까지가 주격 관계대명사절임. 두 번째 that은 shows의 목적어절을 이끄는 명사절 접속사이며, 마지막 that은 선행사가 stories인 주격 관계대명사임.

(2) In the study, / split-brain patients were shown an image /
병렬①(be p.p.)
그 연구에서 / 분할 뇌 환자들에게 이미지를 보여 주었다 /
such that it was visible / to only their left eye /
그것이 보일 정도로 / 그들의 왼쪽 눈에만 /
and asked to select a related card / with their left hand.
병렬②(be p.p., be동사 생략됨)
그리고 관련 있는 카드를 선택하도록 요청했다 / 그들의 왼손으로

힌트 이 문장의 such that 구문은 정도를 나타내는 부사절이며, '~할 정도로'라고 해석할 수 있음.

(3) Left-eye vision and left-side body movement / are controlled /
왼쪽 눈의 시력과 왼쪽 몸의 움직임은 / 제어된다 /
by the right hemisphere.
우뇌에 의해

(4) In a split-brain patient, /
분할 뇌 환자에게 있어 /
the connection between the right and left hemispheres /
우뇌와 좌뇌 사이의 연결은
has been broken, / meaning no information can cross /
끊어졌다 / 이는 정보가 건너갈 수 없다는 것을 의미한다 / 분사구문
from one hemisphere to the other. 20번 정답 단서
한쪽 뇌에서 다른 쪽 뇌로

분할 뇌 환자는 우뇌와 좌뇌 사이의 연결이 끊어져서 우뇌와 좌뇌 간 정보가 전달될 수 없음.

(5) Therefore, in this experiment, /
따라서 이 실험에서 /
the right hemisphere was doing all of the work, / 20번 정답 단서
우뇌가 모든 작업을 수행하고 있었다 /

실험에서 우뇌가 모든 작업을 수행했음.

and the left hemisphere was (b)aware(→ unaware) /
그리고 좌뇌는 (b)알고 있었다(→ 알지 못하고 있었다) /
of what was happening.
무슨 일이 일어나고 있는지

(6) Gazzaniga then asked participants /
Gazzaniga는 그 후 참가자들에게 질문했다 /
[why they chose the card that they did]. [ ]: 간접의문문(의문사+S+V+O)
선행사 목적격 관계대명사 / =chose
그들이 선택했던 그 카드를 왜 선택했는지

(7) Because language is processed and generated /
접속사
언어는 처리되고 생성되기 때문에 /
in the left hemisphere, /
좌뇌에서 /
the left hemisphere is required to respond.
좌뇌가 응답하도록 요구된다

(8) However, / because of the experiment's design, /
전치사
그러나 / 그 실험의 설계 때문에 /
only the right hemisphere knew /
오직 우뇌만이 알고 있었다 /
why the participant selected the card.
간접의문문(의문사+S+V+O)
왜 그 참가자가 그 카드를 선택했는지

(9) As a result, /
결과적으로 /
Gazzaniga expected the participants to be (c)silent /
5형식V O O·C(to V)
Gazzaniga는 참가자들이 (c)침묵할 것이라고 예상했다 /
when asked to answer the question.
질문에 답할 것을 요청받았을 때

힌트 분사구문으로, when과 asked 사이에 they were이 생략되었음.

(10) But instead, / every subject fabricated a response.
하지만 그 대신에 / 모든 피실험자는 응답을 꾸며 냈다

(11) The left hemisphere was being asked to provide a (d)rationalization /
좌뇌는 (d)설명을 제공하라는 요청을 받고 있었다 /
for a behavior / done by the right hemisphere.
과거분사
행동에 대한 / 우뇌에 의해 행해진

(12) The left hemisphere didn't know the answer.
좌뇌는 그 답을 알지 못했다

힌트 keep A from V-ing는 'A가 ~하는 것을 막다'라는 뜻임.

(13) But that didn't keep it from fabricating an answer. 19번 정답 단서
=문장(12) 전체 =the left hemisphere
그러나 그것이 좌뇌가 답을 꾸며 내는 것을 막지는 못했다

좌뇌는 답을 알지 못했지만, 답을 꾸며 냈음.

(14) That answer, however, / had no basis in reality.
하지만 그 대답은 / 사실 근거를 가지고 있지 않았다

(15) Now if this study had been limited to split-brain patients, /
만약 이 연구가 분할 뇌 환자에게 제한됐었다면 /
it would be interesting /
그것은 흥미로울 것이다 /
but not very (e)relevant to us.
하지만 우리와 매우 (e)관련 있는 일은 아닐 것이다

힌트 'if S'+과거완료(had p.p.), S+조동사 과거+동사원형'의 형태로, 혼합 가정법이 사용된 문장임. 즉, 가정하는 사실은 이미 일어난 과거사실의 반대이므로 가정법 과거완료의 형식을, 가정의 결과는 현재 사실의 반대이므로 가정법 과거의 형식을 따르고 있음. '만약 ~했었다면, ~할 텐데'라고 해석될 수 있음.

(16) It turns out / split-brain patients aren't the only ones /
선행사
드러난다 / 분할 뇌 환자들이 유일한 사람이 아닌 것으로 /
who fabricate reasons.
주격 관계대명사
이유를 꾸며 내는

(17) We all do it.
우리 모두 그렇게 한다

(18) We all need a coherent story about ourselves, /
우리 모두는 자신에 대한 일관성 있는 이야기를 필요로 한다 /
and when information in that story is missing, /
접속사(~할 때)
그리고 그 이야기에서 정보가 빠져 있을 때 /
our brains simply fill in the details. 19번 정답 단서
우리의 뇌는 단순히 세부 사항을 채운다

우리의 뇌는 이야기에서 정보가 빠져 있을 때, 단순한 세부 사항을 채움으로써 자신에 대한 일관성 있는 이야기를 완성시킴.

문제편 p.255

[전문 해석]

(1)신경 심리학자 Michael Gazzaniga는 우리의 뇌가 우리를 속이는 일관성 있는 (그러나 반드시 사실은 아닌) 이야기를 만들어 내는 데 있어 (a)탁월하다는 것을 보여 주는 연구를 수행했다. (2)그 연구에서, 분할 뇌 환자들에게 그들의 왼쪽 눈에만 보일 정도로 이미지를 보여 주고 그들의 왼손으로 관련 있는 카드를 선택하도록 요청했다. (3)왼쪽 눈의 시력과 왼쪽 몸의 움직임은 우뇌에 의해 제어된다. (4)분할 뇌 환자에게 있어 우뇌와 좌뇌 사이의 연결은 끊어졌으며, 이는 한쪽 뇌에서 다른 쪽 뇌로 정보가 건너갈 수 없다는 것을 의미한다. (5)따라서 이 실험에서, 우뇌가 모든 작업을 수행하고 있었고, 좌뇌는 무슨 일이 일어나고 있는지 (b)알고 있었다(→ 알지 못하고 있었다).
(6)Gazzaniga는 그 후 참가자들에게 그들이 선택했던 그 카드를 왜 선택했는지 질문했다. (7)언어는 좌뇌에서 처리되고 생성되기 때문에 좌뇌가 응답하도록 요구된다. (8)그러나 그 실험의 설계 때문에, 오직 우뇌만이 왜 그 참가자가 그 카드를 선택했는지 알고 있었다. (9)결과적으로, Gazzaniga는 참가자들이 질문에 답할 것을 요청받았을 때 (c)침묵할 것이라고 예상했다. (10)하지만 그 대신에, 모든 피실험자는 응답을 꾸며 냈다. (11)좌뇌는 우뇌에 의해 행해진 행동에 대한 (d)설명을 제공하라는 요청을 받고 있었다. (12)좌뇌는 그 답을 알지 못했다. (13)그러나 그것이 좌뇌가 답을 꾸며 내는 것을 막지는 못했다. (14)하지만 그 대답은 사실 근거를 가지고 있지 않았다. (15)자, 만약 이 연구가 분할 뇌 환자에게 제한됐었다면, 그것은 흥미롭지만 우리와 매우 (e)관련 있는 일은 아닐 것이다. (16)분할 뇌 환자들이 이유를 꾸며 내는 유일한 사람이 아닌 것으로 드러난다. (17)우리 모두 그렇게 한다. (18)우리 모두는 자신에 대한 일관성 있는 이야기를 필요로 하고, 그 이야기에서 정보가 빠져 있을 때, 우리의 뇌는 단순히 세부 사항을 채운다.

[정답 확인]

19. 윗글의 제목으로 가장 적절한 것은?

① Which Side of the Brain Do We Tend to Use More?
우리는 뇌의 어느 쪽을 더 많이 사용하는 경향이 있는가?
② How Our Brain's Hemispheres Interact in Storytelling
스토리텔링에 있어서 우리 뇌의 반구들이 상호작용하는 방법
✔ The Deceptive Brain: Insights from a Split-Brain Patient Study
속임수를 쓰는 뇌: 분할 뇌 환자 연구로부터의 통찰
④ To Be Creative, Activate Both Hemispheres of Your Brain!
창의적이기 위해서는 여러분의 두 반구를 모두 활성화하라!
⑤ The Dominance of the Left Brain in Image Processing
이미지 처리에 있어서 좌뇌의 지배력

20. 밑줄 친 (a) ~ (e) 중에서 문맥상 낱말의 쓰임이 적절하지 않은 것은?

① (a) ✔ (b) ③ (c) ④ (d) ⑤ (e)

[문제 풀이]

19. 분할 뇌 환자 연구에서, 우뇌가 모든 작업을 수행했기 때문에 좌뇌는 답을 알지 못해 피실험자인 분할 뇌 환자들이 침묵할 것이라는 연구자들의 예상과 다르게 좌뇌는 답을 꾸며 냈다. 분할 뇌 환자들뿐만 아니라 우리 모두의 뇌는 이야기에서 정보가 빠져 있을 때 세부 사항을 채움으로써, 즉 속임수를 써서 이야기를 완성시킨다. 따라서 정답은 ③이다.
20. 문장 (4)에 따르면 분할 뇌 환자들의 경우 우뇌와 좌뇌 사이의 연결이 끊어져서 우뇌와 좌뇌 간 정보가 전달될 수 없다. 따라서 우뇌가 모든 작업을 수행하는 것으로 설정된 실험에서 피실험자인 분할 뇌 환자들의 좌뇌는 무슨 일이 일어나고 있는지 알고 있었다(aware)고 할 수 없고, 알지 못하고 있었다(unaware)고 하는 것이 글의 흐름상 자연스러우므로 정답은 ②이다.

[중요 어휘]

□ **neuropsychologist**	명사 신경 심리학자
□ **conduct**	동사 수행하다, 지휘하다 / 명사 행동
□ **excel**	동사 탁월하다, 뛰어나다
□ **coherent**	형용사 일관성 있는, 응집성의
□ **deceive**	동사 속이다, 기만하다
□ **split**	명사 분할, 분열 / 동사 나누다, 분열시키다
□ **visible**	형용사 보이는, 알아볼 수 있는, 뚜렷한
□ **be aware of**	~을 알다, ~을 알아 차리다
□ **process**	동사 처리하다, 가공하다 / 명사 과정
□ **silent**	형용사 침묵하는, 조용한
□ **subject**	명사 피실험자, 과목, 대상
□ **fabricate**	동사 꾸며 내다, 날조하다
□ **rationalization**	명사 (이론적) 설명, 합리화
□ **basis**	명사 근거, 기준, 기초
□ **turn out**	드러나다, 밝혀지다, 나타나다
□ **fill in**	~을 채우다, ~을 대신하다

핵심 글의 전반부에서는 인공지능의 발달로 인해 의미가 새로워진 단어(intelligence, affective)의 예를 제시하고 문장 (15)에서부터는 caring, friend, companionship 등 감성을 다루는 단어의 의미가 변하는 것에 대해 문제를 제기하고 있음.

21~22

2016년 9월 41~42번 (정답률 65% | 30%) 정답 ⑤ | ⑤

[지문 끊어 읽기] 단어의 의미의 변화

(1) We lose our words.
우리는 우리의 단어들을 잃는다

(2) *Intelligence* once meant more /
'Intelligence'는 한때 더 많은 것을 의미했다 /
than what any artificial intelligence does.
어떤 인공지능이 하는 것보다

(3) It used to include /
그것은 포함하곤 했다 /
sensibility, sensitivity, awareness, reason, wit, etc.
감각, 감성, 인지, 이성, 재치 등을

힌트 call A B는 보통 'A를 B라고 부르다'라는 뜻으로 쓰이지만 여기서는 'A를 B라고 여기다'라는 뜻임.

(4) And yet / we readily call machines intelligent now. 22번 정답 단서
그럼에도 불구하고 / 이제 우리는 주저 없이 기계가 지능적이라고 여긴다

(5) *Affective* is another word / that once meant a lot more /
'Affective'는 또 다른 단어이다 / 한때 훨씬 더 많은 것을 의미했던 /
than what any machine can deliver.
어떤 기계가 전달할 수 있는 것보다

(6) Yet / we have become used to describing machines /
하지만 / 우리는 기계를 묘사하는 것에 익숙해져 왔다 /
that portray emotional states or can sense our emotional states /
감정 상태를 표현하거나 우리의 감정 상태를 감지할 수 있는 /
as exemplars of "affective computing." 22번 정답 단서
'affective computing'의 전형으로

(7) These new meanings become our new normal, /
이러한 새로운 의미들은 우리의 새로운 표준이 된다 /
and we forget other meanings.
그리고 우리는 다른 의미들을 잊는다

(8) We have to struggle to recapture / lost language, lost meanings, /
우리는 되찾기 위해 전력을 다해야 한다 / 잃어버린 언어, 잃어버린 의미들 /
and perhaps, / in time, / lost experiences. 21번 정답 단서
그리고 아마도 / 조만간 / 잃어버린 경험들을

힌트 동사 care는 '돌보다'라는 의미뿐만 아니라 '마음(신경)을 쓰다'라는 뜻도 있음. 로봇들은 '돌보는' 행위는 해낼 수 있지만 '마음을 쓰는' 것은 불가능한데, 글쓴이는 그러한 로봇들을 caring machines라고 부르는 것이 care라는 단어의 감성적인 의미를 지운다고 이야기하고 있음.

(9) At one conference I attended, /
내가 참석했던 한 회의에서 /
the robots were called "caring machines," /
로봇들은 'caring machines'라고 불렸다 /
and when I objected, /
그리고 내가 이의를 제기했을 때 /
I was told we were using this word / not because the robots care /
나는 우리가 이 단어를 사용하고 있었다는 말을 들었다 / 로봇이 마음을 쓰기 때문이 아니라 /
but because they will take care of us.
그들이 우리를 돌볼 것이기 때문에

(10) The conference participants believed /
회의 참가자들은 생각했다 /
caring is a behavior, a function, / not a feeling.
돌보는 것은 행동, 즉 기능이라고 / 감정이 아니라고

(11) They seemed puzzled: / Why did I care so much about semantics?
그들은 당황스러워 보였다 / 왜 나는 의미론에 그렇게 신경을 썼을까

(12) What's wrong with me?
나에게 무슨 문제가 있는 것일까

(13) It is natural / for words [to change their meaning /
형식상의 주어 / 의미상의 주어 / [ ]: 내용상의 주어
당연하다 / 단어들의 의미가 변하는 것은 /
over time and with new circumstances].
시간이 흐르고 새로운 환경에서

(14) *Intelligence* and *affective* have changed their meaning /
'Intelligence'와 'affective'는 의미를 변화시켜 왔다 /
to accommodate what machines can do.
기계가 할 수 있는 것을 수용하기 위해

(15) But now /
그러나 이제 /
the words *caring, friend, companionship*, and *conversation*?
'caring', 'friend', 'companionship', 그리고 'conversation' 단어들은

(16) A lot is at stake in these words.
이러한 단어들에서 많은 것들이 위태롭다

(17) They are not yet lost.
그것들은 아직 사라지지 않았다

(18) We need to remember / these words and this conversation /
우리는 기억해야 한다 / 이러한 단어들과 이 대화를 /
before we don't know how to have it.
우리가 그것을 하는 법을 모르게 되기 전에

(19) Or before we think / we can have it with a machine.
아니면 우리가 생각하기 전에 / 우리가 기계와 그것을 할 수 있다고

[전문 해석]

(1)우리는 우리의 단어들을 잃는다. (2)'Intelligence(지능)'는 한때 어떤 인공지능이 (현재 의미)하는 것보다 더 많은 것을 의미했다. (3)그것은 감각, 감성, 인지, 이성, 재치 등을 포함하곤 했다. (4)그럼에도 불구하고 이제 우리는 주저 없이 기계가 지능적이라고 여긴다. (5)'Affective(감성적인)'는 한때 (현재) 어떤 기계가 전달할 수 있는 것보다 훨씬 더 많은 것을 의미했던 또 다른 단어이다. (6)하지만 우리는 (기계 스스로의) 감정 상태를 표현하거나 우리의 감정 상태를 감지할 수 있는 기계를 'affective computing(감성 컴퓨팅)'의 전형으로 묘사하는 것에 익숙해져 왔다. (7)이러한 새로운 의미들은 우리의 새로운 표준이 되고, 우리는 다른 의미들을 잊는다. (8)우리는 잃어버린 언어, 잃어버린 의미들, 그리고 아마도 조만간, 잃어버린(잃어버릴) 경험들을 되찾기 위해 전력을 다해야 한다.
(9)내가 참석했던 한 회의에서 로봇들은 'caring machines(돌보는 기계)'라고 불렸는데, 내가 (그렇게 부르는 것에) 이의를 제기했을 때, 나는 로봇이 마음을 쓰기 때문이 아니라 그들이 우리를 돌볼 것이기 때문에 우리가 이 단어를 사용하고 있었다는 말을 들었다. (10)회의 참가자들은 돌보는 것은 행동, 즉 기능이지 감정이 아니라고 생각했다. (11)그들은 당황스러워 보였다. 왜 나는 의미론에 그렇게 신경을 썼을까? (12)나에게 무슨 문제가 있는 것일까?
(13)시간이 흐르고 새로운 환경에서 단어들의 의미가 변하는 것은 당연하다. (14)'Intelligence(지능)'와 'affective(감성적인)'는 기계가 할 수 있는 것을 수용하기 위해 의미를 변화시켜 왔다(의미가 변해 왔다). (15)그러나 이제 'caring(돌보는)', 'friend(친구)', 'companionship(우정)', 그리고 'conversation(대화)'(같은) 단어들은 어떻게 될까?
(16)이러한 단어들에서 많은 것(단어)들이 위태롭다. (17)그것들은 아직 사라지지 않았다.
(18)우리가 대화를 하는 법을 모르게 되기 전에, 이러한 단어들과 이 대화를 기억해야 한다.
(19)아니면 우리가 기계와 대화를 할 수 있다고 생각하기 전에.
- affective computing(감성 컴퓨팅): 분위기나 감정과 관련된 신체적 특성을 감지하기 위해 생체 인식 센서를 사용하는 컴퓨터 기술로 분위기나 감정의 컴퓨터 시뮬레이션을 연구하는 분야이다.

[정답 확인]

21. 윗글의 제목으로 가장 적절한 것은?

① What's Lost When a Language Dies
한 언어가 사멸할 때 사라지는 것
② Artificial Intelligence: Good or Evil?
인공지능: 선인가 악인가?
③ Will Robots Care for You in the Future?
미래에 로봇이 당신을 돌볼 것인가?
④ Harmony Between Humans and Machines
인간과 기계 사이의 조화
✔⑤ Beware of Losing the Meaning of Words
단어의 의미를 잃는 것에 주의하라

★중요 인공지능의 발달로 인해 intelligence, affective처럼 단어의 의미가 변하면서 기존의 의미가 사라져버릴 것을 우려하는 글이므로 ⑤가 글의 제목으로 가장 적절함.

22. 윗글의 빈칸에 들어갈 말로 가장 적절한 것은?

① praise 칭찬하기
② monitor 관찰하기
③ conceal 감추기
④ restrict 제한하기
✔⑤ accommodate 수용하기

[문제 풀이]

22. 본문에 따르면 'intelligence(지능)'와 'affective(감성적인)'는 한때 더 넓은 의미를 지닌 단어였지만, 현재는 기계가 할 수 있는 것들을 가리키는 단어로 변화하면서 본래 의미의 많은 부분을 잃게 되었다. 즉, 해당 단어들의 의미가 변화한 것은 '기계가 할 수 있는 것'이라는 새로운 의미를 수용하기 위해서라는 것이다. 따라서 정답은 ⑤ 'accommodate(수용하기)'이다.

[중요 어휘]

☐ artificial	형용사 인공의
☐ sensibility	명사 감각
☐ sensitivity	명사 감성
☐ awareness	명사 인지
☐ reason	명사 이성, 이유
☐ wit	명사 재치
☐ readily	부사 주저 없이, 손쉽게
☐ affective	형용사 감성적인
☐ exemplar	명사 전형, 모범
☐ normal	명사 표준, 정상 / 형용사 보통의, 정상적인
☐ recapture	동사 되찾다
☐ in time	조만간, 이윽고
☐ caring	형용사 돌보는 / 명사 돌보는 것
☐ object	동사 이의를 제기하다, 반대하다 / 명사 물건, 물체
☐ puzzled	형용사 당황스러운, 어리둥절한
☐ semantics	명사 (언어학에서) 의미론
☐ companionship	명사 우정, 동지애
☐ at stake	위태로운, 위기에 처한

힌트 stake는 '말뚝, (내기에) 건 돈'의 의미를 나타내지만 문장 (16)처럼 at stake로 쓰이면 '위태로운'으로 해석됨.

핵심 autonomous vehicles, 즉 AV 차량의 안전성 및 선호도와 관련된 연구 조사의 결과를 분석하고 있는 글로, 두 종류의 AV 차량을 다루고 있는 만큼 이들의 차이점 및 대립 관계를 파악하는 것이 중요함.

23~24

2017년 9월 41~42번 (정답률 60% | 35%) 정답 ⑤ | ⑤

[지문 끊어 읽기] 보행자와 탑승자에 대한 AV의 딜레마

(1) A new study published in *Science* reveals /
<Science>지에 게재된 새로운 연구는 밝히고 있다 /
that people generally approve of driverless, or autonomous, cars /
운전자가 없는 즉 자율자동차에 대해 사람들은 일반적으로 찬성한다는 것을 /
programmed to sacrifice their passengers /
그들의 탑승자를 희생시키도록 프로그램이 설정된 /
in order to save pedestrians, /
보행자를 지키기 위해 /
but these same people are not enthusiastic /
하지만 이 동일한 사람들은 열광하지 않는다는 것을 /
about riding in such autonomous vehicles (AVs) / themselves.
그러한 자율자동차(AV)에 타는 것에 대해서는 / 그들 자신이

(2) In six online surveys of U.S. residents /
미국 주민들의 6개의 온라인 설문조사에서 /
conducted in 2015, / researchers asked participants /
2015년에 실시된 / 연구자들은 참여자들에게 물었다 /
how they would want their AVs to behave.
그들은 그들의 AV가 어떻게 작동하기를 원하는지

(3) The scenarios involved in the surveys /
설문조사에 포함된 시나리오들은 /
varied in the number of pedestrian and passenger lives /
보행자와 탑승자의 목숨의 수를 달리 했다 /
that could be saved, / among other factors.
구할 수 있는 / 다른 요인들 중에서

(4) For example, / participants were asked /
예를 들어 / 참여자들은 질문을 받았다 /
whether it would be more moral /
더 도덕적인지에 대해 /
for AVs to sacrifice one passenger /
AV가 한 명의 탑승자를 희생시키는 것이 /

rather than kill 10 pedestrians. 23번 정답 단서
10명의 보행자를 사망하게 하는 것보다는

(5) Survey participants said / that AVs should be programmed /
조사 참여자들은 말했다 / AV가 프로그램이 설정되어야 한다고 /
to be utilitarian and to minimize harm to pedestrians, / a position /
공리적이고 보행자에 대한 피해를 최소화하도록 / 입장 /
that would put the safety of those outside the vehicle ahead /
차량 밖에 있는 사람들의 안전을 우선시하는 /
of the driver and passengers' safety.
운전자와 탑승자의 안전보다

(6) The same respondents, however, said / they prefer to buy cars /
하지만 이 동일한 응답자들은 말했다 / 그들은 차를 사는 것을 선호한다고 /
that protect them and their passengers, /
그들과 그들의 탑승자를 보호하는 /
especially if family members are involved.
특히 가족 구성원이 관련되었을 때

✱중요 문장 (7), (8)을 같이 볼 때, 빈칸 뒤에 나오는 the good of the individual은 self-protective AVs에 해당되고, that(=the good) of the public은 utilitarian AVs에 해당됨을 알 수 있음.

(7) This suggests / that if both self-protective and utilitarian AVs /
이는 시사한다 / 만약 자기방어적인 AV와 공리적인 AV가 모두 /
were allowed on the market, /
시장에 들어오도록 허용된다면 /
few people would be willing to ride in the latter /
후자에 기꺼이 타려고 하는 사람들은 거의 없을 것이라는 것을 /
— even though they would prefer others to do so. 24번 정답 단서
그들이 다른 사람들이 그렇게 하는 것은 선호할지라도

(8) The inconsistency, / which illustrates an ethical tension /
이러한 불일치는 / 윤리적 긴장을 설명하는 /
between the good of the individual and that of the public, /
개인의 이익과 공공의 그것 사이의 /
persisted across a wide range of survey scenarios analyzed.
분석된 광범위한 설문조사 시나리오 전체에 걸쳐 지속되었다

[전문 해석]

(1)보행자를 지키기 위해 탑승자를 희생시키도록 프로그램이 설정된, 운전자가 없는, 즉 자율자동차에 대해 사람들은 일반적으로 찬성하지만, 이 동일한 사람들은 그러한 자율자동차(AV)에 그들 자신이 타는 것에 대해서는 열광하지 않는다는 것을 <Science>지에 게재된 새로운 연구는 밝히고 있다. (2)2015년에 실시된 미국 주민들의(미국 주민들을 대상으로 실시된) 6개의 온라인 설문조사에서, 연구자들은 (조사) 참여자들에게 그들의 AV가 어떻게 작동하기를 원하는지 물었다. (3)설문조사에 포함된 시나리오들은 다른 요인들 중에서, 구할 수 있는 보행자와 탑승자의 목숨의 수를 달리 했다. (4)예를 들어, (조사) 참여자들은 AV가 10명의 보행자를 사망하게 하는 것보다는 한 명의 탑승자를 희생시키는 것이 더 도덕적인지에 대해 질문을 받았다. (5)조사 참여자들은 AV가 공리적이고 보행자에 대한 피해를 최소화하도록 프로그램이 설정되어야 한다고 말했는데, (이는) 운전자와 탑승자의 안전보다 차량 밖에 있는 사람들의 안전을 우선시하는 입장이다. (6)하지만, 이 동일한 응답자들은 그들(자신)은 그들(자신)과 탑승자를 보호하는 차를 사는 것을 선호한다고, 특히 가족 구성원이 관련되었을 때 (선호한다고) 말했다. (7)이는, 만약 자기방어적인 AV와 공리적인 AV가 모두 시장에 들어오도록 허용된다면(출시된다면), 다른 사람들이 그렇게 하는(공리적인 AV에 타는) 것은 선호할지라도, 후자(공리적인 AV)에 기꺼이 타려고 하는 사람들은 거의 없을 것이라는 것을 시사한다. (8)개인의 이익과 공공의 이익 사이의 윤리적 긴장을 설명하는 이러한 불일치는 분석된 광범위한 설문조사 시나리오 전체에 걸쳐 지속되었다.
- <Science(사이언스)>: 미국과학진흥회(AAAS)에서 발행하는 과학 저널로, <네이처>, <셀>과 함께 권위 있는 과학 학술지로 꼽힘.

[정답 확인]

23. 윗글의 제목으로 가장 적절한 것은?

① Will AVs Finally End Car Accidents?
자율자동차(AV)는 드디어 자동차 사고를 끝낼 것인가?
② How Driverless Cars Cause Unemployment
운전자가 없는 자동차는 어떻게 실업을 야기하는가
③ Safety Measures Required for Driverless Cars
운전자가 없는 자동차에 요구되는 안전 조치
④ Putting Safety First: A New Trend in Car Industry
안전을 우선시하기: 자동차 산업의 새로운 경향
⑤ The Dilemma: AVs to Save Passengers or Pedestrians? ✔
딜레마: 탑승자를 지키는 AV인가 아니면 보행자를 지키는 AV인가?

✱중요 설문조사 참가자들이 AV 차량은 보행자에 대한 피해를 최소화해야 한다고 말한 문장 (5)와, 그러면서도 같은 참가자들이 막상 차를 살 때는 자신과 가족들을 보호해 줄 차량을 선호한다고 한 문장 (6)은 ⑤의 내용을 구체적으로 제시하고 있음.

24. 윗글의 빈칸에 들어갈 말로 가장 적절한 것은?

① guilt 죄책감
② inferiority 열등
③ pessimism 비관
④ ignorance 무지
⑤ inconsistency 불일치 ✔

[문제 풀이]

24. 빈칸에는 개인과 공공의 이익 사이의 긴장 즉 갈등을 설명하는 내용이 들어가야 한다. 이에 대한 내용은 본문에서 언급된 설문조사를 통해 뒷받침된다. 설문조사 참여자들은 자율자동차가 탑승자를 희생시킬 정도로 보행자의 생명을 우선시하는 것이 바람직하다고 말했지만, 막상 자신들이 자율자동차에 탄다면 보행자가 아닌 탑승자 자신의 생명을 우선시하는 자율자동차를 선호한다고 말한다. 즉 사람들이 개인과 공공의 이익 사이에서 일치되지 않은, 모순된 입장을 취하고 있는 것이다. 따라서 빈칸에는 ⑤ 'inconsistency(불일치)'가 들어가는 것이 적절하다.

[중요 어휘]

☐ **autonomous**	형용사 자율의, 자율적인
☐ **pedestrian**	명사 보행자
☐ **behave**	동사 (기계 등이) 작동하다, 움직이다, (특정한 방식으로) 행동하다
☐ **vary**	동사 달리 하다, 변화를 주다, 다르다, 변하다
☐ **factor**	명사 요인
☐ **utilitarian**	형용사 공리적인, 실리적인
☐ **put A ahead of B**	A를 B보다 우선시하다
☐ **self-protective**	형용사 자기방어적인
☐ **latter**	명사 후자, (나열된 것들 중에서) 마지막 / 형용사 후자의, 마지막의
☐ **ethical**	형용사 윤리적인, 윤리의
☐ **tension**	명사 긴장
☐ **good**	명사 이익, 가치, 선 / 형용사 좋은

25~26 2019년 6월 41~42번 (정답률 40% | 50%) 정답 ② | ③

[지문 끊어 읽기] 잘못된 실험 설계로 인한 오류

(1) One cannot take for granted /
우리는 당연하게 생각할 수 없다 /
that the findings of any given study / will have validity.
어떠한 주어진 연구의 결과가 / 타당성을 가질 것이라고

(2) Consider a situation / where an investigator is studying /
상황을 생각해보라 / 한 연구자가 연구하고 있는 /
deviant behavior.
일탈 행동을

(3) In particular, / she is investigating the extent /
특히 / 그녀는 정도를 조사하고 있다 /
to which cheating by college students occurs on exams.
(S: cheating by college students, V: occurs)
시험에서 대학생들에 의한 부정행위가 일어나는

(4) [Reasoning / that it is more (a)difficult /
[ ]: 분사구문-이유(~해서)
판단해서 / 더 (a)어려울 것이라고 /
for people monitoring an exam /
to부정사의 의미상의 주어
시험을 감독하는 사람들이 /
to keep students under surveillance / in large classes /
keep A under surveillance: A를 계속 감독하다
학생들을 계속 감독하기 / 대규모 수업에서 /
than in smaller ones], / she hypothesizes /
소규모 수업에서보다 / 그녀는 가설을 세운다 /
that a higher rate of cheating will occur /
더 높은 비율의 부정행위가 일어날 것이라고 /
on exams in large classes / than in small. 26번 정답 단서
대규모 수업에서의 시험에서 / 소규모에서보다

문제편 p.258

(5) To test this hypothesis, / she collects data /
이 가설을 시험하기 위해 / 그녀는 자료를 수집한다 /
on cheating / in both large classes and small ones /
부정행위에 관하여 / 대규모 수업과 소규모 수업 둘 다에서의 /
and then analyzes the data.
그런 다음 자료를 분석한다

(6) Her results show / that (b)more cheating / per student /
그녀의 결과는 보여준다 / (b)더 많은 부정행위가 / 학생당 /
occurs in the larger classes. 26번 정답 단서
규모가 더 큰 수업에서 일어난다는 것을

(7) Thus, / the data apparently (c)reject(→ support) /
따라서 / 그 자료는 명백히 (c)거부한다(→ 뒷받침한다) /
the investigator's research hypothesis.
연구자의 연구 가설을

★중요 문장 (6)의 연구 결과가 문장 (4)의 연구 가설과 일치하므로, 문장 (7)에서 자료가 가설을 '뒷받침한다(support)'고 해야 함.

(8) A few days later, / however, / a colleague points out /
며칠 뒤 / 하지만 / 한 동료가 지적한다 /
that all the large classes / in her study /
모든 대규모 수업이 / 그녀의 연구에서의 /
used multiple-choice exams, /
선다형 시험을 사용했다는 것을 /
whereas all the small classes used /
~에 반하여 모든 소규모 수업은 사용했다는 것을 /
short answer and essay exams.
단답형과 서술형 시험을

(9) The investigator immediately realizes /
연구자는 즉시 깨닫는다 /
that an extraneous variable (exam format) /
외부 변수(시험 형식)가 /
is interfering / with the independent variable (class size) /
방해하고 있다는 것을 / 독립 변수(수업 규모)를 /
and may be operating / as a (d)cause / in her data. 25번 정답 단서
그리고 영향을 끼칠지도 모른다는 것을 / 하나의 (d)원인으로서 / 그녀의 자료에서

★중요 문장 (9)에서 독립 변수(수업 규모)가 아닌 실험에서 통제되어야 했던 외부 변수(시험 형식)가 부정행위의 빈도에 영향을 줄 수도 있다는 것을 암시함.

(10) The apparent support / for her research hypothesis /
명백한 증거는 / 그녀의 연구 가설을 위한 /
may be nothing more than an artifact.
~에 불과한
하나의 가공물에 불과할지도 모른다

힌트 실험에서 통제되지 않은 외부 변수가 부정행위의 빈도에 영향을 주었다면, 그녀의 연구는 타당도를 잃게 되는데, 이렇게 타당도가 낮은 연구를 가공물(artifact), 즉 '원하는 목적을 위해 꾸며진 물건'이라고 표현했음.

(11) Perhaps / the true effect is / that more cheating occurs /
아마도 / 진짜 결과는 ~이다 / 더 많은 부정행위가 일어난다는 것 /
on multiple-choice exams / than on essay exams, /
선다형 시험에서 / 서술형 시험에서보다 /
regardless of class (e)size.
수업 (e)규모에 상관없이

[전문 해석]

(1)우리는 어떠한 주어진 연구 결과가 타당성을 가질 것이라고 당연하게 생각할 수 없다. (2)한 연구자가 일탈 행동을 연구하고 있는 상황을 생각해보라. (3)특히, 그녀는 시험에서 대학생들에 의한 부정행위가 일어나는 정도를 조사하고 있다. (4)소규모 수업에서보다 대규모 수업에서 시험을 감독하는 사람들이 학생들을 계속 감독하기 더 (a)어려울 것이라고 판단해서, 그녀는 소규모 (수업)에서보다 대규모 수업에서의 시험에서 더 높은 비율의 부정행위가 일어날 것이라고 가설을 세운다. (5)이 가설을 시험하기 위해, 그녀는 대규모 수업과 소규모 수업 둘 다에서의 부정행위에 관하여 자료를 수집한 다음 자료를 분석한다. (6)그녀의 결과는 학생당 (b)더 많은 부정행위가 규모가 더 큰 수업에서 일어난다는 것을 보여준다. (7)따라서 그 자료는 명백히 연구자의 연구 가설을 (c)거부한다(→ 뒷받침한다). (8)하지만 며칠 뒤, 한 동료가 그녀의 연구에서의 모든 대규모 수업이 선다형(객관식) 시험을 사용한 반면에, 모든 소규모 수업은 단답형과 서술형 시험을 사용했다는 것을 지적한다. (9)연구자는 외부 변수(시험 형식)가 독립 변수(수업 규모)를 방해하며 그녀의 자료에서 (연구 결과에 대한) 하나의 (d)원인으로서 영향을 끼칠지도 모른다는 것을 즉시 깨닫는다. (10)그녀의 연구 가설을 위한 명백한 증거는 하나의 가공물에 불과할지도 모른다. (11)아마도 진짜 결과는 수업 (e)규모에 상관없이 서술형 시험에서보다 선다형 시험에서 더 많은 부정행위가 일어난다는 것이다.

- validity(타당성): 연구자가 알고자 하는 것이 실험의 데이터가 가리키는 대상과 일치하는 정도
- extraneous variable(외부 변수): 종속 변수에 영향을 주는 독립 변수 이외의 변수
- independent variable(독립 변수): 어떠한 효과를 관찰하기 위하여 실험적으로 조작되거나 혹은 통제된 변수

[정답 확인]

★중요 문장 (11)을 보면 부정행위의 빈도에 영향을 미친 요인은 수업 규모가 아니라 시험 형식일 수도 있다는 것을 알 수 있음. 즉, 처음부터 실험을 설계할 때 문제가 있었다는 것임.

25. 윗글의 제목으로 가장 적절한 것은?

① Investigator's Attitude: Subjective vs. Objective
연구자의 태도: 주관적 vs. 객관적
✔ Research Error from Wrong Experimental Design
잘못된 실험 설계로 인한 연구 오류
③ Test Your Hypothesis to Obtain Academic Support
학업 지원을 얻기 위해 당신의 가설을 시험하라
④ Limitations of Multiple-choice Exams in Large Classes
대규모 수업에서의 선다형 시험의 한계
⑤ Is There Any Way to Discourage Students from Cheating?
학생들이 부정 행위를 단념하게 하는 방법이 있을까?

26. 밑줄 친 (a) ~ (e) 중에서 문맥상 낱말의 쓰임이 적절하지 않은 것은?

① (a) ② (b) ✔ (c) ④ (d) ⑤ (e)

[문제 풀이]

25. 지문에서는 한 연구자의 예시를 통해 연구의 타당도와 변수 통제에 대해 이야기하고 있다. 문장 (9)에서 제시된 것처럼, 변수가 제대로 통제되지 않은 실험에서는 실험의 결과가 외부 변수에 의해 변질될 수 있는데, 지문의 실험에서도 '시험 형식'과 같은 나머지 외부 변수를 통제하지 못하여 결국 실험 결과(부정행위 빈도)에 영향을 미친 독립 변수의 정체가 불분명해졌다. 즉, 이 실험의 타당도가 낮은 것은 애초에 실험 설계가 잘못되었기 때문임을 알 수 있다. 그러므로 정답은 ②이다.
26. 문장 (4)에서 연구자는 규모가 더 큰 수업에서 더 많은 부정행위가 일어날 것이라고 가설을 세웠고, 문장 (6)에서 조사 결과가 연구자의 가설과 동일했으므로 자료는 명백히 연구자의 연구 가설을 '뒷받침한다'. 따라서 '거부하다'라는 의미의 reject는 문맥상 적절하지 않은 단어이다.

[중요 어휘]

□ take for granted	당연하게 생각하다, 받아들이다
□ findings	명사 (주로 복수형) (연구) 결과
□ deviant	형용사 일탈적인, 벗어난
□ extent	명사 정도, 규모
□ monitor	동사 감독하다, 감시하다
□ surveillance	명사 감독, 감시
□ hypothesize	동사 가설을 세우다, 제기하다
□ analyze	동사 분석하다, 검토하다
□ apparently	부사 명백히, 겉보기에
□ multiple-choice	형용사 선다형(객관식)의
□ extraneous	형용사 외부의, 관련 없는
□ variable	명사 변수, 변인
□ interfere	동사 방해하다, 간섭하다
□ artifact	명사 가공물, 인공물

27~28 2022년 6월 41~42번 (정답률 50% | 40%) 정답 ⑤ | ④

[지문 끊어 읽기] 집단 양극화

(1) Common sense suggests / that discussion with others /
상식은 말한다 / 사람들과의 토론이 / 명사절 접속사
who express different opinions /
다른 의견을 내는 / 주격 관계대명사절
should produce more moderate attitudes /
가능성(~일 것이다)
좀 더 온건한 태도를 만들어 낼 것이라고 /
for everyone in the group.
그 집단 내의 모든 사람들에게

(2) Surprisingly, / this is not always the case.
놀랍게도 / 이것이 항상 사실은 아니다

(3) In group polarization, /
집단 양극화에서 /

문제편 p.258

a period of discussion pushes group members /
5형식V O
일정 기간의 토론은 집단 구성원들을 압박한다 /
to take more extreme positions /
O·C
더 극단적인 입장을 취하도록 /
27번·28번 정답 단서 집단 양극화에서 토론은 집단 구성원들이 기존의 입장에서 더 극단적인 입장을 취하도록 만든다고 함.
in the direction that they were already inclined to prefer.
선행사 목적격 관계대명사절
그들이 이미 선호하는 경향이 있던 방향으로

(4) Group polarization does not (a)reverse the direction of attitudes, /
not A but B: A가 아니라 B
집단 양극화는 태도의 방향을 (a)뒤집는 것이 아니라 /
27번·28번 정답 단서 집단 양극화는 처음에 가졌던 태도를 강화시킨다고 함.
but rather accentuates the attitudes / held at the beginning.
오히려 태도를 강화한다 / 처음에 가졌던

(5) Two pressures appear to push individuals /
5형식V O
두 가지 압력들이 개인들을 압박하는 것으로 보인다 /
to take more extreme positions / following a group discussion.
O·C 전치사(~후에)
더 극단적인 입장을 취하도록 / 집단 토론 후에

(6) First, / conformity and desire for affiliation /
첫째 / 순응과 소속 욕구는 /
contribute to group polarization.
집단 양극화에 기여한다

(7) If the majority of a group is leaning / in a particular direction, /
만약 어떤 집단의 다수가 기울어 있다면 / 특정한 방향으로 /
what could be a better way of fitting in /
더 나은 소속 방법이 무엇이겠는가 /
than (b)agreeing with that majority, /
병렬①
그 다수에게 (b)동의하는 것보다 /
and maybe even taking its argument one step farther?
병렬②
그리고 심지어 그 주장에서 한 걸음 더 나아가는 것보다

힌트 형태는 의문문이지만 답을 얻기 위해 묻는 것이 아니라 자신의 생각을 강조하기 위해 사용하는 '수사의문문'임. 앞의 문장 (6)에서 순응과 소속 욕구가 집단 양극화에 기여한다고 언급했는데, 문장 (7)에서 집단 양극화 상황에서 다수에게 동의하는 것이 집단에 소속되기 위한 좋은 방법이라며 필자의 생각을 재차 강조함.

(8) There is also a tendency / for like-minded people /
의미상의 주어
또한 경향이 있다 / 같은 생각을 가진 사람들은 /
to affiliate with one another, /
형용사적 용법
서로 뭉치는 /
27번·28번 정답 단서 집단 토론 후에 같은 생각을 가진 사람들이 서로 뭉치는 경향이 있고 이것이 기존 입장을 강화시킨다고 함.
which can provide (c)reinforcement for existing opinions, /
관계대명사(계속적 용법) V①
그런데 이는 기존 의견에 대한 (c)강화를 제공할 수 있다 /
increase people's confidence in those opinions, /
V②
그러한 의견에 대한 사람들의 신뢰를 높일 수 있다 /
lead to the discovery / [of new reasons for those opinions /
V③ 병렬①
발견으로 이어지다 / 그러한 의견에 대한 새로운 근거의 /
and counterarguments to opposing views], / [ ]: 전치사구(of+목적어)
병렬②
그리고 상반되는 관점에 대한 반론의 /
and reduce exposure to conflicting ideas.
V④
그리고 상충되는 생각에 대한 노출을 줄일 수 있다

(9) Second, / exposure to discussion on a topic /
S
둘째 / 주제에 관한 토론에 대한 노출은 /
introduces new reasons / for (d)changing(→ keeping) an attitude.
V
새로운 이유를 도입한다 / 태도를 (d)바꾸는(→ 유지하는) 것에 대한

(10) If you are already opposed to gun control /
만약 당신이 이미 총기 규제에 반대하고 있다면 /
and you listen to additional arguments / supporting your position, /
그리고 당신이 추가적인 주장을 듣는다면 / 당신의 입장을 지지하는 /
you might end up more (e)opposed / than you were originally.
추측 뒤에 opposed 생략
당신은 결국 더 (e)반대하게 될지도 모른다 / 원래보다

힌트 'end up V-ing(결국 ~하게 된다)' 구문으로 you might end up (being) more opposed에서 being이 생략된 형태임.

[전문 해석]

(1)상식은 다른 의견을 내는 사람들과의 토론이 그 집단 내의 모든 사람들에게 좀 더 온건한 태도를 만들어 낼 것이라고 말한다. (2)놀랍게도, 이것이 항상 사실은 아니다. (3)집단 양극화에서, 일정 기간의 토론은 집단 구성원들이 이미 선호하는 경향이 있던 방향으로 더 극단적인 입장을 취하도록 압박한다. (4)집단 양극화는 태도의 방향을 (a)뒤집는 것이 아니라, 오히려 처음에 가졌던 태도를 강화한다. (5)두 가지 압력들이 집단 토론 후에 개인들이 더 극단적인 입장을 취하도록 압박하는 것으로 보인다. (6)첫째, 순응과 소속 욕구는 집단 양극화에 기여한다. (7)만약 어떤 집단의 다수가 특정한 방향으로 기울어 있다면, 그 다수에게 (b)동의하는 것보다(동의하고), 심지어 그 주장에서 한 걸음 더 나아가는 것보다 더 나은 소속 방법이 무엇이겠는가? (8)또한 같은 생각을 가진 사람들은 서로 뭉치는 경향이 있는데, 이는 기존 의견에 대한 (c)강화를 제공하고, 그러한 의견에 대한 사람들의 신뢰를 높이고, 그러한 의견에 대한 새로운 근거 및 상반되는 관점에 대한 반론의 발견으로 이어지며, 상충되는 생각에 대한 노출을 줄일 수 있다. (9)둘째, 주제에 관한 토론에 대한 노출은 태도를 (d)바꾸는(→ 유지하는) 것에 대한 새로운 이유를 도입한다. (10)만약 당신이 이미 총기 규제에 반대하고 있으며 당신의 입장을 지지하는 추가적인 주장을 듣는다면, 당신은 결국 원래보다 더 (e)반대하게 될지도 모른다.

- gun control(총기 규제): 총기 소지가 합법인 미국에서 총기 규제는 찬성과 반대 입장이 첨예하게 대립되는 대표적인 논쟁거리임.

[정답 확인]

27. 윗글의 제목으로 가장 적절한 것은?

① Have More Companions and Perform Better!
동료를 더 많이 두고 일을 더 잘 수행하라!
② Group Competition: Not Necessarily Harmful
집단 경쟁: 반드시 해롭지는 않다
③ Exposure to New Ideas Weakens Group Identity
새로운 생각에의 노출은 집단 정체성을 약화시킨다
④ Sharing Ideas: The Surest Way to Foster Creativity
생각을 공유하는 것: 창의성을 기르기 위한 가장 확실한 방법
✔ Black Gets Darker, White Gets Brighter in Group Discussion
집단 토론에서 검정색은 더 어두워지고 하얀색은 더 밝아진다

28. 밑줄 친 (a) ~ (e) 중에서 문맥상 낱말의 쓰임이 적절하지 않은 것은?

① (a) ② (b) ③ (c) ✔ (d) ⑤ (e)

[문제 풀이]

27. 토론을 통해 반대 의견을 가진 사람들이 좀 더 온건한 태도를 갖게 될 것이라는 기존 상식과 달리 집단 양극화에서 토론을 통해 사람들이 더욱 극단적인 입장을 갖게 된다는 내용의 글이다. 문장 (3)에서 이러한 필자의 주장이 직접적으로 제시되는데, 집단 양극화에서 토론은 집단 구성원들이 기존의 입장에서 더 극단적인 입장을 취하도록 만든다고 한다. 이어서 문장 (4)에서 집단 양극화가 태도의 방향을 뒤집는 것이 아니라 처음에 가졌던 태도를 강화시킨다고 다시 한번 언급하며 필자의 주장을 강조한다. 따라서 집단 토론에서 구성원들이 기존에 가지고 있던 생각이 더 강해진다는 내용을 담고 있는 ⑤가 정답이다.
28. 본문에 따르면 토론 후에는 집단 양극화가 더욱 심해져 사람들은 태도의 방향을 뒤집는 것이 아니라 처음에 가졌던 태도를 강화시킨다고 한다. 또한 집단 토론 후 같은 생각을 가진 사람들끼리 서로 뭉치는 경향이 있고 이는 결국 기존 의견을 더욱더 강화시키고, 이에 대한 사람들의 신뢰를 높인다고 한다. 그러므로 문장 (9)에서 토론에 대한 노출은 태도를 바꾸는 새로운 이유를 도입하는 것이 아닌 태도를 '유지하는' 새로운 이유를 도입한다고 해야 옳다. 따라서 답은 ④이다.

[오답 풀이]

28. ⑤ - 이 지문은 계속해서 일정 기간의 토론은 집단 양극화를 더욱 강화시킨다고 한다. 그렇기에 문장 (10)에서 가정하듯이 총기 규제를 논하는 토론에서 총기 규제를 반대하는 사람이 자신의 입장을 지지하는 추가적인 주장을 듣는다면 원래 가지고 있던 입장을 더 강화시켜 총기 규제를 더욱더 '반대하게' 될 것이다. 따라서 ⑤는 정답이 될 수 없다.

[중요 어휘]

☐ **common sense**	명사 상식
☐ **moderate**	형용사 (생각·태도 등이) 온건한, 중간의 / 동사 누그러지다, 완화하다
☐ **polarization**	명사 양극화(서로 점점 더 달라지고 멀어짐)
☐ **be inclined to V**	~하는 경향이 있다
☐ **reverse**	동사 뒤집다
☐ **accentuate**	동사 강화하다, 강조하다
☐ **hold**	동사 (태도·생각·의견 등을) 가지다, 지니다 (hold-held-held)

- conformity 명사 순응
- affiliation 명사 소속
- lean 동사 기울다, ~에 기대다 (lean-leaned/leant-leaned/leant)
- like-minded 형용사 같은 생각을 가진, 생각이 비슷한
- affiliate 동사 뭉치다, 가입하다, ~와 제휴하다
- reinforcement 명사 강화
- counterargument 명사 반론
- opposing 형용사 상반되는, 대립하는
- be opposed to ~에 반대하다
- companion 명사 동료, 동반자
- foster 동사 기르다, 촉진하다

핵심 야구와 럭비, 화재 등의 예시를 들어 '우연은 그저 우연일 뿐'이라는 것을 설명하는 주제-예시 구조의 글임. 직접적인 주제문이 없으므로 예시들을 통해 주제를 추론해야 함.

29~30 2019년 3월 41~42번 (정답률 50% | 35%) 정답 ② | ④

[지문 끊어 읽기] 우연은 그저 우연일 뿐

(1) Unlike coins and dice, / humans have memories /
동전이나 주사위와는 달리 / 인간은 기억을 가지고 있다 /
and do care about wins and losses.
그리고 승리와 패배에 정말로 관심을 가진다

힌트 do가 동사 앞에 붙게 되면 문장에서 말하는 내용을 강조하기 위해서 쓰이는 조동사가 되어서 '정말로'나 '꼭'으로 해석됨.

(2) Still, / the probability of a hit in baseball / does not (a)increase /
그러나 / 야구에서 타율은 / (a)증가하지 않는다 /
just because a player has not had one lately.
현재완료(has+p.p.)
단지 한 선수가 최근에 하나를 못 쳤다고 해서

(3) Four outs in a row / may have been bad luck, /
may have p.p.(~했을 수도 있다, ~했을지도 모른다)
연이은 네 번의 아웃은 / 불운이었을 수도 있다 /
line drives hit straight into fielders' gloves.
곧장 야수의 글러브 안으로 친 직선타

힌트 여기서 hit은 과거분사로, hit이 이끄는 형용사구가 line drives를 수식함.

(4) This bad luck does not (b)ensure good luck /
이러한 불운은 행운을 (b)보장하지 않는다 /
the next time / at bat. 29번 정답 단서
다음번 / 타석에서의

(5) If it is not bad luck, /
만약 그것이 불운이 아니라면 /
then a physical problem may be causing the player / to do poorly.
신체상의 문제가 선수로 하여금 ~하게 할 수도 있다 / 잘 못하게

중요 문장 (3)의 line drives처럼, bad luck의 또 다른 예로 제시되고 있음.

(6) Either way, / a baseball player / who had four outs in a row /
어느 쪽이든 / 야구 선수는 / 연이어 네 번 아웃된 /
is not due for a hit, / nor is a player /
부정어 V S
안타를 칠 예정이 아니다 / 선수가 ~인 것도 아니다 /
who made four hits in a row / due for an out.
연이어 네 번의 안타를 친 / 아웃될 예정인

힌트 부정 부사 nor(=or not)이 이끄는 도치구문을 원래대로 바꿔보면 or a player [who ~] is not due for an out이 됨. 즉, 맨 마지막의 due for(~할 예정인)가 앞의 a player의 주격 보어인 형용사로 온 것임.

(7) If anything, / a player with four hits in a row /
오히려 / 연이어 네 번의 안타를 친 선수는 /
is probably a (c)better batter /
아마 (c)더 나은 타자일 것이다 /
than the player who made four outs in a row. 29번 정답 단서
연이어 네 번 아웃된 선수보다

(8) Likewise, / missed field goals need not be balanced /
마찬가지로 / 놓친 필드골이 균형 맞춰져야 하는 것은 아니다 /
by successes. 29번 정답 단서
성공에 의해서

(9) A poor performance may simply suggest /
저조한 실적은 단순히 암시할지도 모른다 /
that the kicker is not very good. 29번 정답 단서
공을 찬 사람이 썩 훌륭하지 않다는 것을

힌트 'make A 형용사'는 'A를 ~한 상태로 만들다'라는 5형식 용법임. likely가 부사처럼 보이지만, '가능성 있는'이라는 뜻의 형용사임.

(10) Being rejected for jobs / does not make a job offer / more likely.
일자리에서 거부당하는 것은 / 일자리 제의를 만들지 않는다 / 더 가능성 있게

(11) If anything, / the evidence is mounting /
오히려 / 증거가 증가하고 있다 /
that this person is not qualified / or interviews poorly.
이 사람이 자격이 없다는 / 혹은 면접을 형편없이 본다는

(12) Not having a fire does not increase / the chances of a fire /
S V
화재가 없다는 것은 증가시키지 않는다 / 화재의 가능성을 /
— it may just be the mark of a (d)careless(→ careful) homeowner /
그것은 단지 (d)조심성 없는(→ 신중한) 주택 소유주라는 표시일 수도 있다 /
who does not put paper or cloth near a stove, /
병렬①
난로 근처에 종이 또는 천을 놓지 않는 /
put metal in the microwave, / leave home with the stove on, /
병렬② 병렬③
전자레인지에 금속을 넣지 않는 / 난로를 켜놓고 집을 나서지 않는 /
or fall asleep smoking cigarettes. 30번 정답 단서
병렬④
아니면 담배를 피우면서 잠들지 않는

(13) Every safe airplane trip does not increase /
모든 안전한 비행기 여행이 증가시키는 것은 아니다 /
the chances [that the next trip will be a (e)crash]. [ ]: the chances와 동격
다음 여행이 (e)추락 사고가 될 가능성을

[전문 해석]

(1)동전이나 주사위와는 달리 인간은 기억을 가지고 있으며 승리와 패배에 정말로 관심을 가진다. (2)그러나 야구에서 타율은 단지 한 선수가 최근에 (안타) 하나를 못 쳤다고 해서 (a)증가하지 않는다. (3)연이은 네 번의 아웃은, 곧장 야수의 글러브 안으로 친 직선타(와 같은) 불운이었을 수도 있다. (4)이러한 불운은 다음(번) 타석에서의 행운을 (b)보장하지 않는다. (5)만약 그것이 불운이 아니라면, 신체상의 문제가 선수로 하여금 (경기를) 잘 못하게 할 수도 있다. (6)어느 쪽이든, 연이어 네 번 아웃된 야구 선수는 안타를 칠 예정이 아니며, 연이어 네 번의 안타를 친 선수가 아웃될 예정인 것도 아니다. (7)오히려 연이어 네 번의 안타를 친 선수는 아마 연이어 네 번 아웃된 선수보다 (c)더 나은 타자일 것이다. (8)마찬가지로, 놓친 필드골이 성공에 의해서 균형 맞춰져야 하는 것은 아니다(필드골을 놓쳤다고 해서, 그것이 성공에 의해 균형 맞춰지라는 법은 없다). (9)저조한 실적은 단순히 공을 찬 사람이 썩 훌륭하지 않다는 것을 암시할지도 모른다. (10)일자리에서 거부당하는 것은 일자리 제의를 더 가능성 있게 만들지 않는다(일자리에 거절당했다고 해서, 다른 일자리가 들어올 가능성이 더 높아지는 것은 아니다). (11)오히려, 이 사람이 자격이 없거나 면접을 형편없이 본다는 증거가 증가하고 있다. (12)화재가 없다는 것은 화재의 가능성을 증가시키지 않는다. 그것은 단지, 난로 근처에 종이 또는 천을 놓지 않거나, 전자레인지에 금속을 넣지 않거나, 난로를 켜놓고 집을 나서지 않거나, 담배를 피우면서 잠들지 않는, (d)조심성 없는(→ 신중한) 주택 소유주라는 표시일 수도 있다. (13)모든 안전한 비행기 여행이 다음 여행이 (e)추락 사고가 될 가능성을 증가시키는 것은 아니다.

- line drive(직선타): 야구에서 지면과 거의 수평으로 빠르게 날아가는 타구
- field goal(필드골): 럭비에서 페널티 킥이나 자유투가 아닌 방법으로 골문이나 바구니에 공을 넣어 득점하는 일

[정답 확인]

29. 윗글의 제목으로 가장 적절한 것은?

① Go with the Crowd
대세를 따르라
✔② Chance Is Only Chance
운은 단지 운일 뿐이다
③ Misfortune: A Blessing in Disguise
불행: 변장한 축복(전화위복)
④ Strike the Iron While It Is Hot
쇠는 뜨거울 때 쳐라(좋은 기회를 놓치지 마라)
⑤ No Rain from Loud Thunder
요란한 천둥에 비가 없다(빈 수레가 요란하다)

힌트 A Blessing in Disguise는 '축복이 변장해 있다'라는 뜻으로 '재앙, 근심, 걱정 등이 바뀌어 오히려 복이 된다'라는 것을 의미함.

30. 밑줄 친 (a) ~ (e) 중에서 문맥상 낱말의 쓰임이 적절하지 않은 것은?

① (a) ② (b) ③ (c) ✔④ (d) ⑤ (e)

[문제 풀이]

29. 본문은 최근 안타를 하나도 치지 못한 야구 선수의 예, 필드골을 놓치는 공을 찬 사람의 예, 일자리에서 거절당하는 구직자의 예 등을 통해, 어떤 일이 자주 발생했다고 해서 이와 균형을 맞추기 위해 그 반대의 상황이 발생할 확률이 더 높아지지는 않는다고 반복적으로 설명

한다. 오히려, 필자는 각 예시에서 발생한 사건들을 그 사람의 실력이나 자질에 의한 것으로 보고 있으므로, 정답은 ② 'Chance Is Only Chance(운은 단지 운일 뿐이다)'이다.
30. 문장 (12)에서는 주택 소유주가 난로 근처에 불에 탈 만한 종이나 천을 놓지 않고 전자레인지를 태울 금속을 넣지 않는 등, 집에 불이 나지 않도록 조심하는 경우들을 보여주므로, 보기 ④ 'careless(조심성 없는)'는 주택 소유주를 설명하는 데에 적절하지 않다. 따라서 'careful (신중한, 조심성 있는)'과 같은 어휘로 바꿔주는 것이 적절하다.

[중요 어휘]

☐ **care about**	~에 관심을 가지다
☐ **probability of a hit**	타율(야구에서 안타 수를 타격 수로 나눈 백분율)
☐ **lately**	부사 최근에, 얼마 전에
☐ **in a row**	연이어, 잇달아
☐ **ensure**	동사 보장하다, 반드시 ~하게[이게] 하다
☐ **due for**	~할 예정인
☐ **rejected**	형용사 거부당하는, 거절된
☐ **mount**	동사 증가하다, 올라가다
☐ **qualified**	형용사 자격이 있는
☐ **chances**	명사 (주로 복수형) 가능성, 확률
☐ **crash**	명사 (자동차 충돌, 항공기 추락) 사고 / 동사 충돌하다, 폭락하다

31~32

2022년 9월 41~42번 (정답률 45% | 40%) **정답 ① | ⑤**

[지문 끊어 읽기] 소외되는 것에 대한 즐거움(JOMO)

(1) The driver of FOMO (the fear of missing out) is the social pressure /
FOMO(소외되는 것에 대한 두려움)의 동인은 사회적 압박이다 /
to be at the right place with the right people, /
적재적소에 있어야 한다는 /
whether it's from a sense of duty or just trying to get ahead, /
그것이 의무감으로부터 오는 것이든지 또는 그저 앞서 나가려는 것에서 오는 것이든지 간에 /
we feel (a)obligated to attend certain events /
우리는 어떤 행사에 참석해야만 한다는 (a)의무감을 느낀다 /
for work, for family and for friends.
직장, 가족, 친구를 위해서

(2) This pressure from society / combined with FOMO /
사회로부터의 이러한 압박은 / FOMO와 결합된 / 과거분사구
can wear us down.
우리를 지치게 할 수 있다

(3) According to a recent survey, / 70 percent of employees admit /
최근 연구에 따르면 / 직원들 중 70%는 인정했다 /
that when they take a vacation, /
명사절 접속사
그들이 휴가를 가서도 /
they still don't (b)disconnect from work.
여전히 직장에서 (b)단절되지는 않는다고

(4) Our digital habits, /
S
우리의 디지털 습관은 /
which include constantly checking emails, and social media timelines, /
끊임없이 이메일과 소셜 미디어 타임라인을 확인하는 것을 포함하는 /
have become so firmly established, / it is nearly impossible /
V 형식상의 주어
아주 굳어져서 / 거의 불가능하다 /
[to simply enjoy the moment, / along with the people /
그 순간을 그저 즐기는 것은 / 사람들과 / 선행사
with whom we are sharing these moments]. [ ]: 내용상의 주어
전치사+관계대명사
우리가 그 순간을 나누고 있는

31번 정답 단서 JOMO(소외되는 것에 대한 즐거움)는 FOMO(소외되는 것에 대한 두려움)를 극복하게 해 줌.

(5) JOMO (the joy of missing out) is the emotionally intelligent antidote to FOMO /
V①
JOMO(소외되는 것에 대한 즐거움)는 FOMO에 대한 정서적으로 현명한 해독제이다 /
and is essentially about being present and [being (c)content /
V② 병렬①
그리고 본질적으로 현재에 있으면서 (c)만족하는 것에 관한 것이다 /
with where you are at in life]. [ ]: 병렬②
삶에서 당신이 있는 곳에

(6) You do not need to compare your life to others / but instead, /
당신은 다른 사람들과 자신의 삶을 비교할 필요가 없다 / 하지만 대신에 /
practice tuning out the background noise of the "shoulds" and "wants" /
병렬①
'해야 하는 것'과 '원하는 것'의 배경 소음을 무시하는 연습을 하라 /
and learn to let go of worrying /
병렬②
그리고 걱정하는 것을 버리는 법을 배워라 /
whether you are doing something wrong.
당신이 잘못된 무언가를 하고 있는 건 아닌지

(7) JOMO allows us to live life in the slow lane, /
JOMO는 우리가 느리게 가는 삶을 살도록 해 준다 /

힌트 5형식 구문 'allow+O+O·C'에서 목적격 보어 자리에 to부정사구가 병렬 연결되어 있음. 이를 통해 '소외되는 것(Missing Out)'이 우리에게 준 이점들을 나열함.

to appreciate human connections, /
인간 관계의 연결을 이해하게 해 준다 /
to be (d)intentional with our time, / to practice saying "no," /
당신의 시간에 대해서 (d)의도를 갖도록 해 준다 / "아니오"라고 말하는 연습을 하게 해 준다 /
to give ourselves "tech-free breaks," /
자신에게 '기기에서 벗어나는 시간'을 주도록 해 준다 /
and to give ourselves permission /
그리고 스스로를 허락해 준다 /
to acknowledge where we are and to feel emotions. 31번 정답 단서
병렬①-형용사적 용법 병렬②
당신이 현재 있는 곳을 인정하고 감정을 느낄 수 있도록

JOMO는 우리의 삶에 있어 다양한 이점이 있음.

(8) Instead of constantly trying to keep up with the rest of society, /
나머지 사회를 따라잡으려고 끊임없이 애쓰는 대신에 /
JOMO allows us to be who we are / in the present moment.
5형식V O O·C(to V)
JOMO는 우리가 우리 자신이 될 수 있도록 해 준다 / 현재 이 순간에

(9) When you (e)activate(→ free up) that competitive and anxious space in your brain, /
당신이 그러한 뇌 속 경쟁적이고 걱정스러운 공간을 (e)활성화할(→ 자유롭게 할) 때 /
you have so much more time, energy, and emotion /
당신은 더욱더 많은 시간, 에너지와 감정을 갖는다 /
to conquer your true priorities. 32번 정답 단서
당신의 진정한 우선순위를 얻을 수 있다

JOMO를 통해 우리는 진정한 우선순위를 위한 시간과 에너지를 가질 수 있음.

[중요 구문]

(4) Our digital habits, which include ~ timelines,
S
have become so firmly established, (that) ~ .
V(현재완료)

힌트 '너무 ~해서 …하다'라는 뜻의 'so+형용사/부사+(that)+S+V' 구문으로, that이 생략된 대신 comma가 있음.

[전문 해석]

(1)FOMO(소외되는 것에 대한 두려움)의 동인은 적재적소에 있어야 한다는 사회적 압박인데, 그것이 의무감으로부터 오는 것이든지 또는 그저 앞서 나가려는 것에서 오는 것이든지 간에, 우리는 직장, 가족, 친구를 위해서 어떤 행사에 참석해야만 한다는 (a)의무감을 느낀다. (2)FOMO와 결합된 사회로부터의 이러한 압박은 우리를 지치게 할 수 있다. (3)최근 연구에 따르면 직원들 중 70%는 휴가를 가서도 여전히 직장에서 (b)단절되지는 않는다고 인정했다. (4)끊임없이 이메일과 소셜 미디어 타임라인을 확인하는 것을 포함한 우리의 디지털 습관은 아주 굳어져서, 그 순간을 나누고 있는 사람들과 그 순간을 그저 즐기는 것은 거의 불가능하다.
(5)JOMO(소외되는 것에 대한 즐거움)는 FOMO에 대한 정서적으로 현명한 해독제이고, 본질적으로 현재에 있으면서 삶에서 당신이 있는 곳에 (c)만족하는 것에 관한 것이다. (6)당신은 다른 사람들과 자신의 삶을 비교할 필요가 없지만 대신에, '해야 하는 것'과 '원하는 것'의 배경 소음을 무시하는 연습을 하고, 당신이 잘못된 무언가를 하고 있는 건 아닌지 걱정하는 것을 버리는 법을 배워라. (7)JOMO는 우리가 느리게 가는 삶을 살도록 해 주고, 인간 관계의 연결을 이해하며, 당신의 시간에 대해서 (d)의도를 갖고, "아니오"라고 말하는 연습을 하고, 자신에게 '기기에서 벗어나는 시간'을 주며, 당신이 현재 있는 곳을 인정하고 감정을 느낄 수 있도록 스스로를 허락해 준다. (8)나머지 사회를 따라잡으려고 끊임없이 애쓰는 대신에, JOMO는 현재 이 순간에 우리가 우리 자신이 될 수 있도록 해 준다. (9)당신이 그러한 뇌 속 경쟁적이고 걱정스러운 공간을 (e)활성화할(→ 자유롭게 할) 때, 당신은 더욱더 많은 시간, 에너지와 감정을 갖고 당신의 진정한 우선순위를 얻을 수 있다.

[정답 확인]

31. 윗글의 제목으로 가장 적절한 것은?

✔ Missing Out Has Its Benefits
소외되는 것은 그만의 이점이 있다
② JOMO: Another Form of Self-Deception
JOMO: 자기기만의 또 다른 형태
③ How to Catch up with Digital Technology
디지털 기술을 따라잡는 법
④ Being Isolated from Others Makes You Lonely
다른 사람들로부터 고립되는 것이 당신을 외롭게 만든다
⑤ Using Social Media Wisely: The Dos and Don'ts
소셜 미디어 현명하게 사용하기: 해야 할 것과 하지 말아야 할 것

32. 밑줄 친 (a) ~ (e) 중에서 문맥상 낱말의 쓰임이 적절하지 않은 것은?

① (a) ② (b) ③ (c) ④ (d) ✔ (e)

[문제 풀이]

31. 문장 (5)에서 JOMO가 FOMO의 정서적 해독제라고 한 점과 문장 (7)에서 JOMO를 통해 삶 속에서 얻을 수 있는 이점들을 나열한 것을 고려하면 본문은 JOMO의 유익한 점을 설명하는 글임을 알 수 있다. 따라서 정답은 ①이다.
32. 더욱더 많은 시간과 에너지를 가지기 위해 경쟁하고 걱정하는 데 쓰는 공간을 활성화한다고 하는 것은 어색하다. 대신 그 공간을 자유롭게 함으로써 더욱 생산적인 곳에 쓸 때 우선순위를 얻을 수 있다고 하는 게 자연스럽다. 따라서 정답은 ⑤이다.

[오답 풀이]

31. ② - Self-Deception(자기기만)이란 스스로를 속인다는 뜻으로, 자신의 신조나 양심에 벗어나는 일을 하는 경우를 이르는 말이다. 본문은 FOMO와 대비하여 JOMO의 태도를 가졌을 때 얻을 수 있는 이점에 대해서 설명하고 있으며, 자기기만과는 거리가 멀다. 또한 JOMO를 긍정적인 측면에서 다루고 있으므로 JOMO를 부정적인 의미를 지니는 자기기만의 한 형태라고 하는 것은 옳지 않다.
32. ④ - be intentional with time은 '의도를 가지고 시간을 사용한다'는 뜻으로, 문장 (6)에서 말하는 '해야 하는 것'과 '원하는 것'에 집중하면서 현재의 삶에 임하는 자세를 뜻한다. 그러므로 JOMO의 이점으로 적절하다.

[중요 어휘]

☐ driver	명사 동인(어떤 사태를 일으키거나 변화시키는 데 작용하는 직접적인 원인)
☐ sense of duty	의무감
☐ obligate	동사 의무를 지우다
☐ wear down	지치게 하다, 약화시키다
☐ disconnect	동사 단절되다, 연락을 끊다
☐ intelligent	형용사 현명한, 지적인
☐ antidote	명사 해독제
☐ content	형용사 만족하는
☐ tune out	(잡음을) 무시하다
☐ let go of	버리다, ~을 손에서 놓다
☐ appreciate	동사 이해하다, 고마워하다
☐ intentional	형용사 의도적인
☐ keep up with	~을 따라잡다
☐ activate	동사 활성화하다, 작동시키다
☐ competitive	형용사 경쟁적인, 경쟁력 있는
☐ anxious	형용사 걱정스러운, 불안해하는
☐ priority	명사 우선순위
☐ deception	명사 기만, 사기
☐ catch up with	~을 따라잡다

문제편 p.261

핵심 기술적인 용어 하나하나의 의미에 집중하기보다, 첫 번째 문단에서 블록체인의 장점을 설명하는 데 사용되었던 표현들이 두 번째 문단에서는 오히려 단점을 설명하는 데 쓰였음에 주목할 것.

33~34 2018년 11월 41~42번 (정답률 45% | 35%) 정답 ② | ①

[지문 끊어 읽기] 블록체인 기술

(1) While complex, /
복잡하기는 하지만 /
blockchains exhibit a set of core characteristics, /
블록체인은 일련의 핵심적인 특징들을 보인다 /
which flow from the technology's reliance on /
계속적 용법
그런데 이는 ~에 대한 그 기술의 의존으로부터 나온다 /
a peer-to-peer network, / public-private key cryptography, /
개인 간 네트워크 / 공개-개인 키 암호화 기법 /
and consensus mechanisms.
그리고 합의 메커니즘

힌트 'While complex'는 아주 짧지만 하나의 부사절을 형성하고 있음. 원래는 'While blockchains are complex'였으나, 분사구문을 만드는 과정에서 주절의 주어와 동일한 blockchains를 생략하고 동사를 V-ing 형태로 만들면 'While (being) complex'가 되는데, 이때 'being'이 생략되어 'While complex'만 남은 것임.

(2) Blockchains are disintermediated and transnational.
블록체인은 탈중개적이며 초국가적이다

(3) They are resilient and resistant / to change, /
V①
그것은 회복 탄력성과 저항성이 있다 / 변동에 대한 /
and enable people to store nonrepudiable data, /
V②
그리고 사람들이 부인방지성의 데이터를 저장하는 것을 가능하게 한다 /
pseudonymously, / in a transparent manner.
유사 익명성을 띠고서 / 투명한 방식으로

(4) Most — if not all — blockchain-based networks /
전부는 아니더라도 대부분의 블록체인 기반 네트워크는 /
feature market-based or game-theoretical mechanisms /
선행사
시장에 기반한 또는 게임 이론적인 메커니즘을 특징으로 한다 /
for reaching consensus, /
합의에 이르기 위해 /
which can be used / to coordinate people or machines.
계속적 용법
그런데 이는 이용될 수 있다 / 사람들이나 기계들을 조직화하는 데

힌트 'be used to 명사/V-ing'는 '~에 익숙하다'이라는 뜻이지만, 'be used to V'는 '~하는 데 이용(사용)되다'라는 뜻임.

(5) These characteristics, / when combined, /
이러한 특징들은 / 결합되었을 때 /
enable the deployment of autonomous software /
자동화 소프트웨어의 배치를 가능하게 한다 /
and explain why blockchains serve as a powerful new tool /
그리고 어째서 블록체인이 강력한 새 도구의 역할을 하는지 설명한다 /
to facilitate economic and social activity /
경제적 그리고 사회적 활동을 촉진하는 /
that otherwise would be difficult to achieve. 33번 정답 단서
반대 가정
그것이 아니었다면 성취하기 어려울지도 모르는

힌트 문장 (1)의 'while complex'와 마찬가지로, 'when combined'는 'when these characteristics are combined'로 바꿀 수 있음.

(6) At the same time, / these characteristics represent /
동시에 / 이러한 특징들은 나타낸다 /
the technology's greatest limitations.
그 기술의 가장 큰 한계들을

중요 'at the same time(동시에)'은 화제를 전환하거나 이전 논의와 대조했음 직한 사실들을 언급할 때 주로 사용됨. 문장 (5)에서는 블록체인의 장점을 언급했으므로, 문장 (6)부터는 블록체인의 단점이나 한계에 대해 이야기를 할 가능성이 큼.

(7) The disintermediated and transnational nature of blockchains /
블록체인의 탈중개적이고 초국가적인 특성은 /
makes the technology difficult to govern /
그 기술을 통제하기 어렵게 만든다 /
and makes it difficult to implement changes /
형식상의 목적어 내용상의 목적어
그리고 변화를 시행하기 어렵게 만든다 /
to a blockchain's underlying software protocol. 34번 정답 단서
블록체인의 기본 소프트웨어 프로토콜에

중요 문장 (2)와 (3)에서는 블록체인의 탈중개적이고 초국가적인 특성에서 비롯되는 이점을 소개한 반면, 문장 (7)에서는 그러한 특성들로 인해 발생하는 문제점에 대해 이야기함.

(8) Because blockchains are pseudonymous /
블록체인은 유사 익명성을 띠기 때문에 /
and have a tamper-resistant data structure /
그리고 위조 방지 데이터 구조를 가지고 있기 때문에 /
supported by decentralized consensus mechanisms, /
분산적인 합의 메커니즘에 의해 지원되는 /
they can be used to coordinate /
그것은 조직화하는 데 이용될 수 있다 /
socially unacceptable or criminal conduct, / including conduct /
사회적으로 용인되지 않거나 범죄가 되는 행위를 / 행위를 포함하여 /

중요 블록체인을 이용해 조직화될 수 있는 대상이 문장 (4)에서는 '사람들이나 기계들'이었는데, 문장 (8)에서는 '사회적으로 용인되지 않는 행위' 또는 '범죄 행위'로 바뀌었음.

문제편 p.262

facilitated by autonomous software programs.
자동화 소프트웨어 프로그램에 의해 촉진된

(9) Moreover, / because blockchains are transparent and traceable, /
게다가 / 블록체인은 투명하고 추적 가능하기 때문에 /
they are prone to being co-opted /
그것들은 마음대로 사용되기 쉽다 /
by governments or corporations, /
정부나 기업들에 의해 /
transforming the technology into a powerful tool /
그 기술을 강력한 도구로 변형시키는 /
for surveillance and control. 33번 정답 단서
감시와 통제를 위한

★중요 문장 (5)에서는 블록체인이 '경제적 그리고 사회적 활동'을 촉진하는 강력한 새 도구라고 설명했는데, 문장 (9)에서는 '감시와 통제'를 위한 도구로 변질될 수 있다고 이야기함.

[전문 해석]

(1)복잡하기는 하지만, 블록체인은 일련의 핵심적인 특징들을 보이는데, 이는(이러한 핵심적인 특징들은) 개인 간 네트워크, 공개-개인 키 암호화 기법, 그리고 합의 메커니즘에 대한 그 기술(블록체인)의 의존으로부터 나온다. (2)블록체인은 탈중개적이며 초국가적이다. (3)블록체인은 변동에 대한 회복 탄력성과 저항성이 있으며, 사람들이 부인방지성의 데이터를 유사 익명성을 띠고서(가명을 사용하여) 투명한 방식으로 저장하는 것을 가능하게 한다. (4)전부는 아니더라도, 대부분의 블록체인 기반 네트워크는 합의에 이르기 위해 시장에 기반한 또는 게임 이론적인 메커니즘을 특징으로 하는데, 이는 사람들이나 기계들을 조직화하는 데 이용될 수 있다. (5)(서로) 결합되었을 때, 이러한 특징들은 자동화 소프트웨어의 배치를 가능하게 하며, 어째서 블록체인이, 그것이 아니었다면 성취하기 어려울지도 모르는 경제적 그리고 사회적 활동을 촉진하는 강력한 새 도구의 역할을 하는지 설명한다.
(6)동시에, 이러한 특징들은 그 기술(블록체인)의 가장 큰 한계들을 나타낸다. (7)블록체인의 탈중개적이고 초국가적인 특성은 그 기술을 통제하기 어렵게 만들며, 블록체인의 기본 소프트웨어 프로토콜에 변화를 시행하기 어렵게 만든다. (8)블록체인은 유사 익명성을 띠고(가명을 사용하고) 분산적인 합의 메커니즘에 의해 지원되는 위조 방지 데이터 구조를 가지고 있기 때문에, 그것은 자동화 소프트웨어 프로그램에 의해 촉진된 행위를 포함하여, 사회적으로 용인되지 않거나 범죄가 되는 행위를 조직화하는 데 이용될 수 있다. (9)게다가 블록체인은 투명하고 추적 가능하기 때문에, 그 기술을 감시와 통제를 위한 강력한 도구로 변형시키는 정부나 기업들에 의해 마음대로 사용되기 쉽다.
- blockchain(블록체인): 중앙 서버에 거래 기록을 보관하지 않고, 새로운 거래가 이루어질 때마다 해당 거래에 대한 블록(block)을 생성하여, 거래에 참여하는 모든 네트워크에 거래 정보를 투명하게 공개하고, 검증된 정보 블록만을 체인(chain)으로 연결하여 관리하는 위변조가 불가능한 분산형 데이터 저장 기술. 대부분의 암호 화폐 거래에 사용되며, 디지털 공공 거래 장부라고도 불린다.
- consensus mechanism(합의 메커니즘): 분산화된 시스템에서, 특정 데이터에 대하여 네트워크상의 모든 시스템들이 동일한 값을 유지하도록 하는 알고리즘이다.

[정답 확인]

33. 윗글의 제목으로 가장 적절한 것은?

① A Brief History of Blockchain Technology
블록체인 기술의 간략한 역사
✔② Blockchain Technology Is a Double-Edged Sword
블록체인 기술은 양날의 검이다
③ Blockchain: The Greatest Economic Breakthrough Ever
블록체인: 역대 가장 위대한 경제적 돌파구
④ Why Are People Wild About Blockchain-Based Digital Money?
왜 사람들은 블록체인 기반의 디지털 화폐에 열광하는가?
⑤ Pros & Cons of Government Regulation of Blockchain Technology
블록체인 기술의 정부 규제에 대한 찬반 의견

34. 윗글의 빈칸에 들어갈 말로 가장 적절한 것은?

✔① limitations 한계들
② stereotypes 고정 관념들
③ impacts 영향들
④ innovations 혁신들
⑤ possibilities 가능성들

[문제 풀이]

33. 본문의 첫 번째 문단은 블록체인이 지닌 탈중개성, 초국가성, 투명성 등의 특성들을 소개하고, 그러한 특성들로 인해 블록체인 기술이 경제 및 사회적 활동을 촉진하는 도구가 될 수 있다고 설명한다. 한편 두 번째 문단에서는 바로 그 특성들로 인해 발생할 수 있는 여러 문제점들에 대해 소개하고 있다. 즉 블록체인 기술의 양면성을 설명하고 있는 글이므로, 가장 적절한 제목은 ②이다.

34. 빈칸이 속한 두 번째 문단의 주된 내용은 블록체인 기술이 지닌 문제점에 관한 것이다. 따라서 빈칸에 들어갈 표현으로는 ① 'limitations(한계들)'가 가장 적절하다.

[오답 풀이]

34. ④ - 블록체인 기술의 혁신적인 측면에 관한 내용은 첫 번째 문단에 국한되어 있는데, 빈칸에 들어갈 것은 두 번째 문단을 압축해 주는 표현이므로 ④는 정답이 될 수 없다.

[중요 어휘]

☐ exhibit	동사 보이다, 드러내다, 전시하다
☐ peer-to-peer	형용사 개인 간의, P2P 방식의
☐ consensus	명사 합의, 일치된 의견
☐ disintermediated	형용사 탈중개적인, 금융기관의 중개를 벗어난
☐ transnational	형용사 초국가적인, 다국적의
☐ resilient	형용사 회복 탄력성이 있는, 탄력적인
☐ nonrepudiable	형용사 부인방지성의, 거부할 수 없는
☐ transparent	형용사 투명한, 정직한
☐ game-theoretical	게임 이론적인
☐ deployment	명사 배치, 동원
☐ autonomous	형용사 자동화된, 자립적인
☐ facilitate	동사 촉진하다, 용이하게 하다
☐ implement	동사 시행하다, 이행하다
☐ underlying	형용사 기본적인, 기초의, 기저의
☐ protocol	명사 프로토콜, 협정
☐ tamper-resistant	형용사 위조 방지의, 변경 저항적인
☐ decentralized	형용사 분산적인, 분권화된
☐ be prone to V-ing	~하기 쉽다, ~의 경향이 있다
☐ co-opt	동사 마음대로 사용하다, 억지로 끌어들이다
☐ surveillance	명사 감시, 감독
☐ double-edged	형용사 양날의, 이중적인
☐ breakthrough	명사 돌파구
☐ pros & cons	찬반 의견, 장단점
☐ regulation	명사 규제, 통제

힌트 'tamper(원문을 함부로 변경하다, 부정한 수단을 쓰다)'와 'resistant(~을 방지하는, ~에 저항하는)'가 만나, '위조를 방지하는(=위조 방지의)'이라는 의미로 사용됨.

35~36 2023년 3월 41~42번 (정답률 45% | 35%) 정답 ① | ③

[지문 끊어 읽기] 개인의 성격을 고려한 직원 관리

(1) Creative people aren't all cut from the same cloth.
창의적인 사람들이 모두 같은 부류인 것은 아니다

(2) They have (a)varying levels / of maturity and sensitivity.
그들은 (a)다양한 수준을 갖고 있다 / 성숙도와 민감성의

(3) They have different approaches to work.
그들은 일에 대해 다양한 접근법을 갖고 있다

(4) And they're each motivated / by different things.
그리고 그들은 각자 동기가 부여된다 / 다른 것들에 의해

(5) Managing people is /
사람들을 관리한다는 것은 ~이다 /
about being aware of their unique personalities. 35번·36번 정답 단서
그들의 고유한 성격을 아는 것에 대한 것
사람 관리는 개인의 고유한 성격을 아는 것임.

(6) It's also about empathy and adaptability, / and knowing /
그것은 또한 공감과 적응성과 관련 있다 / 그리고 ~을 아는 것이다 / 병렬①(동명사)
how the things you do and say will be interpreted /
선행사 목적격 관계대명사절
여러분이 하는 일과 하는 말이 어떻게 해석될지를 /
and adapting accordingly.
병렬②(동명사)
그리고 그에 따라 맞추는 것이다

(7) Who you are and what you say / may not be the (b)same /
여러분이 누구인지와 무슨 말을 하는지는 / (b)같지 않을 수도 있다 /
from one person to the next. 36번 정답 단서
개인에 따라
말하는 사람이 누구이며 무슨 말을 하는지는 그것을 듣는 개인에 따라 다를 수 있음.

(8) For instance, / if you're asking someone /
병렬①(5형식V) O
예를 들어 / 여러분이 누군가에게 요청하고 있다면 /
to work a second weekend in a row, / or telling them /
O·C 병렬②(4형식V) I·O
2주 연속으로 주말에 근무하라고 / 또는 그들에게 말하고 있다면 /
they aren't getting that deserved promotion just yet, /
D·O
그들은 마땅한 승진을 지금 당장으로서는 받지 못할 것이라고 /
you need to bear in mind the (c)group(→ individual).
여러분은 그 (c)집단(→ 개인)을 유념해야 한다

(9) Vincent will have a very different reaction to the news than Emily, /
Vincent는 그 소식에 Emily와 매우 다른 반응을 보일 것이다 /
and they will each be more receptive to the news /
그리고 그들은 각자 그 소식에 보다 더 수용적일 것이다 /
if it's bundled with different things. **36번 정답 단서** 승진 소식에 대해 개개인이 각각 다르게 반응하고 받아들일 것이라며 예시를 들고 있음
=the news
만약에 그것이 다른 것들과 묶인다면

(10) Perhaps / that promotion news will land (d)easier /
아마도 / 그 승진 소식은 (d)더 쉽게 도달할 것이다 /
if Vincent is given a few extra vacation days for the holidays, /
만약 Vincent가 연휴에 며칠의 휴가를 추가로 받는다면 /
while you can promise Emily a bigger promotion /
한편 여러분은 Emily에게는 더 큰 승진을 약속할 수 있다 /
a year from now.
지금부터 1년 후에

(11) Consider /
V
고려하라 /
each person's complex positive and negative personality traits, /
O①
사람 각각의 복잡한 긍정적이고 부정적인 성격의 특징을 /
their life circumstances, / and their mindset in the moment /
O② O③
그들의 삶의 상황을 / 그리고 그 순간의 그들의 사고방식을 /
when deciding what to say and how to say it. **주제문** 개인에게 말할 때는 그 사람의 성격, 상황, 사고 방식을 고려해야 한다는 필자의 주장을 알 수 있음.
무슨 말을 하고 그 말을 어떻게 할지 결정할 때

(12) Personal connection, compassion, and an individualized management style /
개인적인 연관, 동감, 그리고 개별화된 관리 방식은 /
are (e)key / to drawing consistent, rock star-level work /
(e)핵심이다 / 일관되고 록 스타와 같은 수준의 일을 끌어내는 데 있어 /
out of everyone. **35번 정답 단서** 개인을 고려한 관리가 일관되고, 최고의 업무 역량을 끌어내는 핵심이라고 함.
모든 사람으로부터

[전문 해석]

(1)창의적인 사람들이 모두 같은 부류인 것은 아니다. (2)그들은 (a)다양한 수준의 성숙도와 민감성을 갖고 있다. (3)그들은 일에 대해 다양한 접근법을 갖고 있다. (4)그리고 그들은 각자 다른 것들에 의해 동기가 부여된다. (5)사람들을 관리한다는 것은 그들의 고유한 성격을 아는 것에 대한 것이다. (6)그것은 또한 공감과 적응성과 관련 있고, 여러분이 하는 일과 하는 말이 어떻게 해석될지를 알고 그에 따라 맞추는 것이다. (7)여러분이 누구인지와 무슨 말을 하는지는 개인에 따라 (b)같지 않을 수도 있다. (8)예를 들어, 여러분이 누군가에게 2주 연속으로 주말에 근무하라고 요청하고 있다거나, 그들에게 마땅한 승진을 지금 당장으로서는 받지 못할 것이라고 말하고 있다면, 여러분은 그 (c)집단(→ 개인)을 유념해야 한다. (9)Vincent는 그 소식에 Emily와 매우 다른 반응을 보일 것이고, 만약에 그 소식이 다른 것들과 묶인다면 그들은 각자 그 소식에 보다 더 수용적일 것이다. (10)아마도 Vincent가 연휴에 며칠의 휴가를 추가로 받는다면 그 승진 소식은 (d)더 쉽게 도달할 것이고, 한편 여러분은 Emily에게는 지금부터 1년 후에 더 큰 승진을 약속할 수 있다. (11)무슨 말을 하고 그 말을 어떻게 할지 결정할 때, 사람 각각의 복잡한 긍정적이고 부정적인 성격의 특징, 그들의 삶의 상황, 그리고 그 순간의 그들의 사고방식을 고려하라. (12)개인적인 연관, 동감, 그리고 개별화된 관리 방식은 모든 사람으로부터 일관되고 록 스타와 같은 수준의 일을 끌어내는 데 있어 (e)핵심이다.

[정답 확인]

35. 윗글의 제목으로 가장 적절한 것은?

✔ Know Each Person to Guarantee Best Performance
최고의 기량을 보장하기 위해 사람 각각을 알라
② Flexible Hours: An Appealing Working Condition
탄력적 근무 시간: 매력적인 근로 조건
③ Talk to Employees More Often in Hard Times
힘든 시기에 좀 더 자주 직원들과 대화하라
④ How Empathy and Recognition Are Different
공감과 인정은 어떻게 다른가
⑤ Why Creativity Suffers in Competition
창의성은 경쟁에서 왜 고통받는가

36. 밑줄 친 (a) ~ (e) 중에서 문맥상 낱말의 쓰임이 적절하지 않은 것은?

① (a) ② (b) ✔(c) ④ (d) ⑤ (e)

[문제 풀이]

35. 사람들은 개인마다 모두 다르고 성숙도와 민감성이 다양하기 때문에 사람을 관리한다는 것은 그 사람의 성격을 아는 것과 관련이 있다. 사람마다 받아들이는 방식과 정도가 다르기 때문에, 무슨 말을 전하려고 할 때는 그 사람의 성격, 상황, 사고방식을 고려해야 한다. 또한 이와 같이 개별적으로 차별화된 관리 방식은 일관된 높은 업무 수준에 중요하다고 문장 (12)에 언급되었다. 따라서 글의 제목으로 적절한 것은 ①이다.
36. 문장 (5)에서 사람 관리는 그 사람의 고유한 성격을 아는 것이라고 했고, 문장 (8)은 이에 대한 예시인 연이은 주말 근무 요청이나 승진 탈락 소식을 전하는 상황이다. 이어진 문장 (9)에서 Vincent와 Emily가 그 소식에 다르게 반응하고 받아들일 것이라는 점을 미루어 보았을 때, 소식을 전할 때 기억해야 하는 것은 집단(group)이 아니라 개인(individual)이다. 따라서 정답은 ③이다.

[오답 풀이]

36. ④ - 문장 (9)에서 승진 탈락 소식이 다른 것과 묶인다면 Vincent와 Emily는 더 잘 수용할 것이라고 했다. 이어서 문장 (10)에서 Vincent는 연휴에 휴가를 추가적으로 받고 Emily는 1년 후에 더 큰 승진을 약속 받는 것은 그 승진 소식이 두 사람에게 잘 수용되도록 개인을 고려한 것이므로 '더 쉽게' 도달된다는 내용은 문맥상 적절하다.

[중요 어휘]

☐ cut from the same cloth	같은 부류인, 비슷한
☐ varying	형용사 다양한, 변화하는
☐ maturity	명사 성숙도, 성숙함
☐ sensitivity	명사 민감성, 세심함, 예민함
☐ approach	명사 접근법 / 동사 접근하다
☐ motivate	동사 동기를 부여하다
☐ be aware of	~을 알다, 알아차리다
☐ unique	형용사 고유한, 독특한
☐ personality	명사 성격, 개성
☐ empathy	명사 공감, 감정 이입
☐ adaptability	명사 적응성, 융통성
☐ interpret	동사 해석하다, 설명하다, 통역하다
☐ adapt	동사 맞추다, 적응하다
☐ accordingly	부사 그에 따라, 따라서
☐ in a row	연속하여, 연이어, 이어서
☐ deserved	형용사 마땅한, 응당한
☐ just yet	지금 당장으로서는 (~ 않다)
☐ promotion	명사 승진, 홍보, 판촉 행사
☐ bear in mind	(~을) 유념하다, 기억하다, 명심하다
☐ receptive	형용사 수용적인, 잘 받아 들이는
☐ bundle	동사 묶다 / 명사 묶음, 꾸러미
☐ complex	형용사 복잡한, 합성의 / 명사 복합 건물
☐ trait	명사 특징, 특성
☐ circumstances	명사 (주로 복수형) 상황
☐ mindset	명사 사고방식
☐ compassion	명사 동감, 연민
☐ draw	동사 끌어내다, 당기다, 그리다
☐ consistent	형용사 일관적인, 꾸준한
☐ appealing	형용사 매력적인, 호소하는

문제편 p.263

37~38

2022년 3월 41~42번 (정답률 60% | 15%) **정답 ① | ⑤**

[지문 끊어 읽기] 건설적인 갈등을 통한 창의력 증진

(1) Being able to have a good fight /
동명사S
잘 싸울 수 있다는 것은 /
doesn't just make us more civil; /
5형식V O O·C
우리를 더 정중하게 만들 뿐만 아니라 /
it also develops our creative muscles.
그것은 우리의 창의적 근력을 발달시킨다

힌트 'not just/only A but also B(A뿐만 아니라 B도)' 구문임. 세미콜론(;)으로 이어진 절의 경우 글의 맥락상 적절한 접속사를 넣어서 해석하면 되는데, 여기서는 but을 넣어서 해석하면 됨.

(2) In a classic study, / highly creative architects were more likely /
고전적인 연구에 따르면 / 매우 창의적인 건축가는 가능성이 더 크다 /
than their technically competent but less original peers /
병렬① 병렬②
기술적으로 유능하지만 덜 독창적인 그들의 동료보다 /
to come from homes with (a)plenty of friction.
충돌이 (a)많은 가정에서 나올

힌트 'be likely to V(~할 가능성이 크다)' 구문이 비교급으로 사용되었음. than이 이끄는 명사구가 be more likely와 to부정사 사이에 위치한 형태로 '~에서 나올 가능성이 더 크다'로 해석됨.

(3) They often grew up in households /
그들은 흔히 집안에서 자랐다 / 선행사
[that were "tense but secure,"] / [ ]: 주격 관계대명사절
병렬① 병렬②
'긴장감이 있지만 안전한' /
as psychologist Robert Albert notes: /
접속사
심리학자 Robert Albert가 언급하길 /
"The creative person-to-be / comes from a family /
창의적인 사람이 될 사람은 / 가정에서 나온다 / 선행사
[that is anything but (b)harmonious]." 37번·38번 정답 단서
전혀 (b)화목하지 않은 [ ]: 주격 관계대명사절

힌트 anything but은 '전혀 ~ 아닌, 결코 ~ 아닌'이라는 뜻의 관용어구로 never로 바꾸어 읽을 수 있음. 부정어구인 anything but을 모르면 문장 전체를 잘못 해석할 수 있으므로 꼭 알아두어야 함. 비슷하게 생긴 표현인 nothing but은 '오직, 단지(=only)', all but은 '거의(=almost)'를 뜻함.

창의적인 사람이 될 사람은 갈등을 피하지 않는 가정에서 나옴.

(4) The parents weren't physically or verbally abusive, /
병렬① 병렬②
그 부모들이 신체적으로나 언어적으로 학대한 것은 아니었다 /
but they didn't shy away from conflict, either.
하지만 그들은 갈등을 피하지도 않았다 not ~ either: ~도 아니다

(5) Instead of telling their children /
그들의 자녀에게 말하는 대신 /
to be seen but not heard, /
병렬① 병렬②
눈앞에 있되 아무 말도 하지 말라고 /
they (c)encouraged them / to stand up for themselves.
5형식V O O·C(to V)
그들은 그들에게 (c)권장했다 / 자신의 입장을 내세우라고

힌트 'heard' 앞에 to be가 생략되어 있음. S be heard (by ~)는 주어의 말이 누군가에게(by ~) 들리는 것임. 여기서 not heard의 의미상 주어는 their children이므로 '아이들의 말이 (부모에게) 들리지 않도록'을 뜻하며, '아무 말도 하지 말라고'로 의역함.

(6) The kids learned / to dish it out / — and take it. 38번 정답 단서
병렬① 병렬②(to 생략)
그 자녀들은 배웠다 / 남을 비판하는 것을 / 그리고 비판을 받아들이는 것을

갈등을 피하지 않는 가정에서 자란 자녀들은 남을 비판하고, 비판을 받아들이는 법을 배움.

(7) That's exactly what happened / to Wilbur and Orville Wright, /
그것이 바로 일어난 일이었다 / Wilbur와 Orville Wright 형제에게 / 선행사
[who invented the airplane]. [ ]: 주격 관계대명사절
비행기를 발명한

38번 정답 단서 Wright 형제는 가정에서 남을 비판하고 비판을 받아들이는 것을 배웠음.

(8) When the Wright brothers said / they thought together, /
S' V' O'(명사절 접속사 생략)
Wright 형제가 말했을 때 / 자기들은 함께 생각한다고 /
what they really meant / is that they fought together.
S(선행사를 포함한 관계대명사절) V S·C(that 명사절)
그들이 진짜로 의미하는 것은 / 자신들이 함께 싸웠다는 것이다

(9) When they were solving problems, / they had arguments /
그들이 문제를 풀고 있었을 때 / 그들은 논쟁을 했다 /
[that lasted not just for hours / but for weeks and months /
not just/only A but (also) B: A뿐만 아니라 B
몇 시간 동안뿐만 아니라 / 몇 주, 몇 달 동안 지속된 /
at a time]. [ ]: 주격 관계대명사절
한 번에

(10) They didn't have such (d)ceaseless fights /
그들이 그토록 (d)끊임없이 싸운 것은 아니었다 /
because they were angry.
화가 나서

(11) They kept quarreling / because they enjoyed it /
keep V-ing: 계속 ~하다 병렬①
그들은 계속 싸웠다 / 그것을 즐겼기 때문에 /
and learned from the experience. 37번·38번 정답 단서
병렬②
그리고 그 경험으로부터 배웠기 때문에

Wright 형제는 논쟁을 계속 했고 그것을 통해 배움을 얻었음.

(12) "I like scrapping with Orv," / Wilbur reflected.
"나는 Orv와 다투는 것을 좋아한다." / Wilbur는 회고했다

(13) As you'll see, /
접속사(~이듯이)
보다시피 /
it was one of their most passionate and prolonged arguments /
it is ~ that 강조구문
바로 그들의 가장 열정적이고 장기적인 논쟁 중 하나였다 /
that led them to (e)support(→ rethink) a critical assumption /
그들이 결정적인 가정을 (e)지지하도록(→ 재고하도록) 이끌었던 것은 / 선행사
[that had prevented humans / from soaring through the skies].
과거완료 [ ]: 주격 관계대명사절
인간을 막았던 / 하늘로 날아오르지 못하게

[전문 해석]

(1)잘 싸울 수 있다는 것은 우리를 더 정중하게 만들 뿐만 아니라 우리의 창의적 근력을 발달시킨다. (2)고전적인 연구에 따르면, 매우 창의적인 건축가는 기술적으로 유능하지만 덜 독창적인 그들의 동료보다 충돌이 (a)많은 가정에서 나올 가능성이 더 크다. (3)그들은 흔히 '긴장감이 있지만 안전한' 집안에서 자랐는데, 심리학자 Robert Albert는 "창의적인 사람이 될 사람은 전혀 (b)화목하지 않은 가정에서 나온다."라고 언급한다. (4)그 부모들이 신체적으로나 언어적으로 학대한 것은 아니었지만 갈등을 피하지도 않았다. (5)그들은 자녀에게 눈앞에 있되 아무 말도 하지 말라고 말하는 대신 자신의 입장을 내세우라고 (c)권장했다. (6)그 자녀들은 남을 비판하고 비판을 받아들이는 것을 배웠다. (7)그것이 바로 비행기를 발명한 Wilbur와 Orville Wright 형제에게 일어난 일이었다.
(8)Wright 형제가 자기들은 함께 생각한다고 말했을 때 그 말의 진짜 의미는 자신들이 함께 싸웠다는 것이다. (9)그들이 문제를 풀고 있었을 때 그들은 한 번에 몇 시간 동안뿐만 아니라 몇 주, 몇 달 동안 지속된 논쟁을 했다. (10)그들이 화가 나서 그토록 (d)끊임없이 싸운 것은 아니었다. (11)그들은 그것을 즐기고 그 경험으로부터 배웠기 때문에 계속 싸웠다. (12)"나는 Orv와 다투는 것을 좋아한다."라고 Wilbur는 회고했다. (13)보다시피, 인간이 하늘로 날아오르지 못하게 막았던 결정적인 가정을 그들이 (e)지지하도록(→ 재고하도록) 이끌었던 것은 바로 그들의 가장 열정적이고 장기적인 논쟁 중 하나였다.

[정답 확인]

37. 윗글의 제목으로 가장 적절한 것은?

✔ The Power of Constructive Conflict
건설적인 갈등의 힘
② Lighten Tense Moments with Humor
유머로 긴장된 순간을 가볍게 하라
③ Strategies to Cope with Family Stress
가족 스트레스에 대처하는 전략
④ Compromise: A Key to Resolving Conflict
타협: 갈등 해결의 열쇠
⑤ Rivalry Between Brothers: A Serious Crisis
형제 간의 경쟁: 심각한 위기

38. 밑줄 친 (a) ~ (e) 중에서 문맥상 낱말의 쓰임이 적절하지 않은 것은?

① (a) ② (b) ③ (c) ④ (d) ✔ (e)

[문제 풀이]

37. 지문에 따르면 건설적인 갈등을 통해 창의력을 기를 수 있다. 문장 (3)에서 창의적인 사람이 될 사람은 전혀 화목하지 않은 가정, 즉 갈등을 피하지 않고 맞서도록 가르치는 가정 속에서 자란다고 한다. 또한 문장 (6)에서 설명하듯이 이러한 가정에서 자란 사람들은 남을 비판하고 비판을 받아들이는 법을 배우게 된다. 이후 문장 (7)부터 이에 대한 예시로 Wright 형제가 등장하는데, 논쟁을 통한 배움과 갈등을 즐김으로써 창의력을 기를 수 있다는 게 예시의 핵심이다. 따라서 글의 제목으로는 갈등의 건설적인 측면을 언급하는 ①이 적절하다.
38. 지문에 따르면 좋은 논쟁은 창의력을 길러주며, 남을 비판하고 비판을 받아들이는 법을 배우도록 해 준다. Wright 형제는 이를 뒷받침하는 예시로, 비행기를 발명해 인간이 하늘을 날 수 있게 만든 인물들이다. 따라서 이들은 인간이 하늘로 날아오르지 못하게 막았던 결정적인 가정을 지지하는(support) 것이 아니라, 과연 인간은 정말 날 수 없는가 서로 끊임없이 논쟁하면서 그 가정에 대해 재고해보았을(rethink) 것이므로 정답은 ⑤이다.

[오답 풀이]

38. ② - 문장 (2)에서 창의적인 건축가는 충돌(갈등)이 많은 가정에서 나올 가능성이 높다고 설명하고 있다. 그러므로 이어지는 문장 (3)에서도 창의적인 사람이 될 사람은 전혀 화목하지 (harmonious) 않은 가정, 즉 충돌(갈등)이 많은 가정에서 나온다고 설명하는 것이 타당하다. anything but이 '전혀 ~아닌, 결코 ~아닌'이라는 뜻을 가졌음에 유의해야 한다.

38. ④ - 문장 (9)에 따르면 Wright 형제는 문제를 풀고 있었을 때 한 번에 몇 시간 동안뿐만 아니라 몇 주, 몇 달 동안 지속된 논쟁을 했다. 따라서 이들이 끊임없는(ceaseless) 싸움을 했다고 표현하는 것은 문맥상 적절하다.

[중요 어휘]

☐ **civil**	형용사 정중한, 예의 바른, 시민의
☐ **original**	형용사 독창적인, 원래의
☐ **friction**	명사 충돌, 불화, 마찰
☐ **tense**	형용사 긴장감이 있는, 긴장된, (상황 등이) 긴박한
☐ **harmonious**	형용사 화목한, 조화로운
☐ **verbally**	부사 언어적으로, 말로
☐ **abusive**	형용사 학대하는
☐ **shy away from**	~을 피하다
☐ **stand up for**	~의 입장을 내세우다, 지지(옹호)하다
☐ **dish it out**	남을 비판하다
☐ **argument**	명사 논쟁, 말다툼, 주장
☐ **ceaseless**	형용사 끊임없는
☐ **quarrel**	동사 싸우다, 말다툼하다
☐ **scrap with**	~과 다투다
☐ **prolonged**	형용사 장기적인
☐ **prevent A from V-ing**	A를 ~하지 못하게 막다
☐ **soar**	동사 날아오르다
☐ **constructive**	형용사 건설적인
☐ **compromise**	명사 타협 / 동사 타협하다, ~을 위태롭게 하다

39~40

2023년 11월 41~42번 (정답률 55% | 65%) **정답 ① | ⑤**

[지문 끊어 읽기] 청중과 공연자의 연결

(1) In Western society, /
서구 사회에서 /
many music performance settings make a clear distinction /
많은 음악 공연 상황은 뚜렷한 구분을 만든다 /
between performers and audience members: /
공연자와 청중 구성원들 사이에 /
the performers are the "doers" /
공연자들은 '행위자들'이다 /
and those in the audience take a decidedly passive role.
그리고 청중에 있는 사람들은 분명히 수동적인 역할을 맡는다

힌트 본문에서 콜론(:)은 앞 문장에 대한 부연 설명을 하기 위해 사용됨. 이 문장에서는 콜론 뒤에 공연자와 청중의 구분을 구체적으로 설명하는 내용이 이어짐.

39번 정답 단서 서구 사회 음악 공연 상황에서 공연자와 청중들은 행위자/수동적인 역할로 뚜렷하게 구분됨.

(2) The performance space itself /
강조 용법
공연 장소 그 자체는 /
may further (a)reinforce the distinction /
그 구분을 더 (a)강화할 수 있다 /
with a physical separation between the stage and audience seating.
무대와 청중 좌석 사이의 물리적인 분리로

(3) Perhaps because this distinction is so common, /
아마도 이 구분이 너무 흔하기 때문에 /
audiences seem to greatly value /
청중들은 크게 가치를 부여하는 것으로 보인다 /
opportunities to have special "access" to performers /
형용사적 용법 / 선행사
공연자들에 대한 특별한 '접근'을 가질 기회에 /
[that affords understanding about performers' style of music]. [ ]: 주격 관계대명사절
공연자의 음악 스타일에 대한 이해를 제공하는

40번 정답 단서 청중들은 공연자의 음악 스타일을 이해할 기회인 공연자들에 대한 특별한 '접근'에 큰 가치를 둠.

(4) Some performing musicians have won great approval /
몇몇 공연하는 음악가들은 엄청난 호응을 받아 왔다 /
by regularly (b)incorporating "audience participation" into their concerts.
자신들의 콘서트에 정기적으로 '청중 참여'를 (b)포함함으로써

(5) Whether by leading a sing-along activity /
함께 노래 부르는 활동을 이끌든지 / 병렬①
or teaching a rhythm to be clapped at certain points, /
병렬②(by 생략)
혹은 특정한 시점에 박수 칠 리듬을 가르치든지 /
[including audience members in the music making] / [ ]: S
음악을 연주하는 데 청중 구성원들을 포함하는 것은 /
can (c)boost the level of engagement and enjoyment for all involved.
V
참여하는 모든 이들에게 참여와 즐거움의 수준을 (c)높일 수 있다

39번 정답 단서 음악 연주에 청중들을 포함하는 것은 참여자들의 참여와 즐거움의 수준을 높임.

(6) [Performers who are uncomfortable leading audience participation] / [ ]: S
선행사 / 주격 관계대명사절
청중 참여를 이끄는 것이 불편한 공연자들은 /
can still connect with the audience /
여전히 청중들과 이어질 수 있다 /
simply by giving a special glimpse of the performer (d)perspective.
단순히 그 공연자 (d)관점을 특별히 흘끗 보여줌으로써

(7) It is quite common in classical music /
형식상의 주어
고전 음악에서 꽤 흔하다 /
[to provide audiences with program notes]. [ ]: 내용상의 주어
provide A with B: A에게 B를 제공하다
청중들에게 프로그램 해설을 제공하는 것은

(8) Typically, / this text in a program gives [background information /
전형적으로 / 프로그램에 있는 이 글은 배경 정보를 제공한다 /
about pieces of music being performed] / [ ]: 병렬①
공연되고 있는 음악 작품에 대한 /
and perhaps [biographical information /
그리고 아마도 전기적 정보를 /
about historically significant composers]. [ ]: 병렬②
역사적으로 중요한 작곡가에 대한

(9) [What may be of more interest to audience members] / [ ]: S
청중 구성원들에게 더 흥미로울 수 있는 것은 /
is background information /
V
배경 정보이다 /
about the very performers who are onstage, /
선행사 / 주격 관계대명사절
무대 위의 바로 그 공연자에 대한 /
including an explanation /
설명을 포함하는 /
of [why they have chosen the music they are presenting]. [ ]: 의문사절
그들이 표현하고 있는 그 음악을 왜 선택했는지에 대한

힌트 'of+추상명사'는 추상명사의 형용사형으로 보고 해석함. 예를 들어 'of value=valuable, of importance=important'처럼 해석할 수 있고, 여기서는 'of more interest'를 'more interesting'으로 해석하면 됨.

힌트 선행사 the music 뒤에 목적격 관계대명사가 생략된 형태임.

(10) Such insight can make audience members feel (e)distant(→ close) /
사역V / O / O.C(동사원형)
그러한 통찰은 청중 구성원들을 (e)멀게(→ 가깝게) 느끼도록 만들 수 있다 /
to the musicians onstage, / both metaphorically and emotionally.
무대에 있는 음악가들에게 / 비유적이고 정서적으로 모두

(11) This connection will likely enhance the expressive and communicative experience.
이 연결은 아마 표현하고 소통하는 경험을 향상시킬 것이다

[전문 해석]

(1)서구 사회에서 많은 음악 공연 상황은 공연자와 청중 구성원들 사이에 뚜렷한 구분을 만드는데, 즉 공연자들은 '행위자들'이고 청중에 있는 사람들은 분명히 수동적인 역할을 맡는다. (2)공연 장소 그 자체는 무대와 청중 좌석 사이의 물리적인 분리로 그런 구분을 더 (a)강화할 수 있다. (3)아마도 이 구분이 너무 흔하기 때문에 청중들은 공연자의 음악 스타일에 대한 이해를 제공하는 공연자들에 대한 특별한 '접근'을 가질 기회에 크게 가치를 부여하는 것으로 보인다. (4)몇몇 공연하는 음악가들은 자신들의 콘서트에 정기적으로 '청중 참여'를 (b)포함함으로써 엄청난 호응을 받아 왔다. (5)함께 노래 부르는 활동을 이끌든지 혹은 특정한 시점에 박수 칠 리듬을 가르치든지 음악을 연주하는 데 청중 구성원들을 포함하는 것은 참여하는 모든 이들에게 참여와 즐거움의 수준을 (c)높일 수 있다. (6)청중 참여를 이끄는 것이 불편한 공연자들은 단순히 그 공연자 (d)관점을 특별히 흘끗 보여줌으로써 여전히 청중들과 이어질 수 있

문제편 p.265

다. (7)청중들에게 프로그램 해설을 제공하는 것은 고전 음악에서 꽤 흔하다. (8)전형적으로 프로그램에 있는 이 글은 공연되고 있는 음악 작품에 대한 배경 정보와 아마도 역사적으로 중요한 작곡가에 대한 전기적 정보를 제공한다. (9)청중들에게 더 흥미로울 수 있는 것은 그들이 표현하고 있는 그 음악을 왜 선택했는지에 대한 설명을 포함하는 무대 위의 바로 그 공연자에 대한 배경 정보이다. (10)그러한 통찰은 청중 구성원들을 무대에 있는 음악가들에게 비유적이고 정서적으로 모두 (e)멀게(→ 가깝게) 느끼도록 만들 수 있다. (11)이 연결은 아마 표현하고 소통하는 경험을 향상시킬 것이다.

[정답 확인]

39. 윗글의 제목으로 가장 적절한 것은?

✔ Bridge the Divide and Get the Audience Involved
차이를 연결하고 청중을 참여시켜라
② Musical Composition Reflects the Musician's Experience
음악의 작곡은 음악가의 경험을 반영한다
③ Why a Performer's Style Changes with Each Performance
왜 공연자의 스타일이 각각의 공연과 함께 변하는가
④ Understanding Performers on Stage: An Audience's Responsibility
무대에 있는 공연자를 이해하기: 청중의 책임
⑤ The Effect of Theater Facilities on the Success of a Performance
공연의 성공에 대한 극장 시설의 영향

40. 밑줄 친 (a) ~ (e) 중에서 문맥상 낱말의 쓰임이 적절하지 않은 것은?

① (a) ② (b) ③ (c) ④ (d) ✔ (e)

[문제 풀이]

39. 문장 (1)~(2)는 서구 사회 음악 공연에서 공연자와 청중들 사이에 역할과 공간의 측면에서 분리가 일어난다고 말한다. 이러한 분리는 청중들이 공연자에 대한 특별한 '접근'을 가지는 데 큰 가치를 부여하게 하였으며, 콘서트에 '청중 참여'를 포함한 음악가들은 큰 호응을 받게 했다. 이어지는 문장들은 함께 노래 부르기, 특정한 시점에 박수 칠 리듬 가르쳐 주기와 공연자에 대한 배경 정보를 제공하는 것까지 모두 청중을 음악가에 가깝게 만들고 청중을 참여시키는 방법에 대한 예시가 되고 있다. 따라서 이 글의 제목은 ① '차이를 연결하고 청중을 참여시켜라(Bridge the Divide and Get the Audience Involved)'이다.

40. 문장 (4)~(5)에서 콘서트에 '청중 참여'를 포함시킨 음악가들은 큰 호응을 받고, 음악을 연주하는 데 여러 방식으로 청중을 포함시키는 것은 청중들의 참여와 즐거움의 수준을 높일 수 있다고 설명한다. 문장 (3)에 따르면 이러한 청중 참여는 공연자에 대한 특별한 '접근'을 제공하므로 청중들에게 큰 호응을 받는다. 따라서 문장 (9)에서 언급된 공연자에 대한 배경 정보의 제공은 청중들에게 더 흥미로울 수 있다. 그러므로 이러한 통찰은 청중들을 음악가로부터 먼(distant) 감정을 느끼게 하는 것이 아니라 가깝게(close) 느끼도록 한다는 것이 적절하다. 따라서 정답은 ⑤이다.

[중요 어휘]

□ **setting**	명사 상황, 배경
□ **distinction**	명사 구분, 분리
□ **decidedly**	부사 분명히, 확실히
□ **passive**	형용사 수동적인, 소극적인
□ **reinforce**	동사 (감정·생각 등을) 강화하다, (구조 등을) 보강하다
□ **physical**	형용사 물리적인, 신체적인
□ **separation**	명사 분리, 구분
□ **greatly**	부사 크게, 매우, 대단히
□ **value**	동사 가치를 부여하다, 소중히 여기다 / 명사 가치
□ **afford**	동사 제공하다, ~을 지불할 수 있다
□ **approval**	명사 호응, 찬성
□ **incorporate**	동사 포함하다, 합병하다 / 명사 회사
□ **sing-along**	명사 함께 노래 부르기
□ **boost**	동사 높이다, 향상하다
□ **engagement**	명사 참여, 몰입
□ **glimpse**	명사 흘끗 봄 / 동사 흘끗 보다
□ **perspective**	명사 관점, 시각
□ **biographical**	형용사 전기적인, 전기체의
□ **significant**	형용사 중요한, 상당한
□ **onstage**	형용사 무대 위의, 관객 앞에서의
□ **insight**	명사 통찰, 통찰력
□ **metaphorically**	부사 비유적으로, 은유로
□ **likely**	부사 아마 / 형용사 그럴듯한
□ **enhance**	동사 향상시키다, 높이다
□ **expressive**	형용사 표현하는, 나타내는

41~42

2024년 3월 41~42번 (정답률 80% | 50%) 정답 ① | ④

[지문 끊어 읽기] 십 대들의 멀티태스킹에 관한 진실

(1) It's untrue / that teens can focus on two things at once /
사실이 아니다 / 십 대들이 동시에 두 가지 일에 집중할 수 있다는 것은 /
— what they're doing / (S)
그들이 하고 있는 것은 /
힌트 「형식상의 주어-내용상의 주어」 구문으로, 접속사 that이 이끄는 명사절 전체가 문장의 내용상의 주어에 해당함.
is [shifting their attention from one task to another]. 41번 정답 단서
V [ ]: 주격 보어(동명사구)
그들의 주의를 한 작업에서 다른 작업으로 전환하는 것이다
십 대들은 동시에 두 가지 일에 집중할 수 없으며, 한 작업에서 다른 작업으로 주의를 전환하고 있을 뿐임.

(2) In this digital age, / teens wire their brains /
디지털 시대에 / 십 대들은 자신의 뇌를 연결한다 /
to make these shifts very quickly, / (부사적 용법(목적))
이러한 전환을 아주 빠르게 만들도록 /
but they are still, like everyone else, paying attention / (삽입구)
하지만 그들은 여전히 다른 모든 사람들과 마찬가지로 주의를 기울이고 있다 /
to one thing at a time, sequentially.
한 번에 한 가지 것에 순차적으로

(3) Common sense tells us / (S① V① I·O)
상식은 우리에게 말한다 /
[multitasking should (a)increase brain activity], /
멀티태스킹이 뇌 활동을 (a)증가시킬 것이라고 / [ ]: D·O(접속사 that이 생략된 명사절)
but Carnegie Mellon University scientists / (S②)
하지만 Carnegie Mellon 대학의 과학자들은 /
멀티태스킹이 뇌 활동을 증가시킬 것이라는 상식(통념)과 달리, 과학자들은 최신 뇌 영상 기술을 통해 그것이 사실이 아님을 발견했음. 41번 정답 단서
using the latest brain imaging technology / find it doesn't. (현재분사구, V② O(접속사 that이 생략된 명사절))
최신 뇌 영상 기술을 사용하는 / 그것이 그렇지 않다는 것을 발견했다
힌트 앞에서 반복된 동사구인 increase brain activity가 생략됨.

(4) As a matter of fact, / they discovered / (=Carnegie Mellon University scientists)
사실 / 그들은 발견했다 /
[that multitasking actually decreases brain activity]. [ ]: O(that 명사절)
멀티태스킹이 실제로는 뇌 활동을 감소시킨다는 것을

(5) Neither task is done as well / (as 원급(부사) as: ~만큼 …하게)
어떠한 작업도 잘 되지 않는다 /
as if each were performed (b)individually. 42번 정답 단서
각각의 작업이 (b)개별적으로 수행될 때만큼
모든 작업은 개별적으로 수행될 때 가장 잘 이루어짐.

(6) Fractions of a second are lost / every time we make a switch, / (=whenever)
아주 조금의 시간이 소실된다 / 우리가 전환을 할 때마다 /
and a person's interrupted task /
그리고 한 사람의 중단된 작업은 /
can take 50 percent (c)longer to finish, /
끝내는 데 50퍼센트 (c)더 오래 걸릴 수 있다 /
with 50 percent more errors. 42번 정답 단서
50퍼센트 더 많은 오류와 함께
여러 작업을 한 번에 수행하기 위해 작업을 전환할 때마다 시간은 조금씩 소실되며, 결국 작업을 끝내는 데 50퍼센트 더 많은 시간이 소요되고 50퍼센트 더 많은 오류를 낳게 됨.

(7) Turns out / [the latest brain research (d)contradicts(→ supports) / (=It turns out, [ ]: that 명사절(that 생략))
밝혀진다 / 최신 뇌 연구가 (d)반박한다(→ 뒷받침한다)는 것이 /
the old advice "one thing at a time."] 42번 정답 단서
'한 번에 하나씩'이라는 오래된 조언을
한 번에 하나의 작업을 수행하는 것이 낫다는 Carnegie Mellon 대학 과학자들의 연구 결과는 '한 번에 하나씩'이라는 오래된 조언을 뒷받침하는 내용임.

(8) It's not / [that kids can't do some tasks simultaneously]. 41번 정답 단서
형식상의 주어 [ ]: 내용상의 주어
~은 아니다 / 아이들이 몇몇 작업을 동시에 할 수 없다는 것은
아이들이 동시에 몇몇 작업을 할 수 있기는 함.

(9) But if two tasks are performed at once, /
그러나 만약 두 가지 작업이 동시에 수행된다면 /
one of them has to be familiar. **41번 정답 단서** 아이들이 두 가지 작업을 동시에 수행하려면 둘 중 하나는 익숙한 일이어야 함.
그것들 중 하나는 익숙한 것이어야 한다

(10) Our brains perform a familiar task / on "automatic pilot" /
우리의 뇌는 익숙한 작업을 수행한다 / '자동 조종' 상태로 /
[while really paying attention / to the other one].
접속사 현재분사(능동) =task
실제로는 주의를 기울이면서 / 나머지 다른 작업에

힌트 접속사가 생략되지 않은 분사구문으로, while 뒤에 각각 they(=our brains) are과 people are이 생략된 형태라고 이해할 수 있음.

(11) That's why insurance companies consider /
그것이 바로 보험 회사가 간주하는 이유이다 / 5형식V
[talking on a cell phone and driving] / [ ]: O(동명사구)
병렬① 병렬②
휴대 전화로 이야기하면서 운전하는 것을 /
[to be as (e)dangerous / as driving while drunk] / [ ]: O·C(to부정사구)
as 원급(형용사) as: ~만큼 …한
(e)위험한 것으로 / 술에 취한 상태로 운전하는 것만큼이나 /
— it's the driving / that goes on "automatic pilot" /
바로 운전이다 / '자동 조종' 상태로 가는 것은 /
while the conversation really holds our attention.
대화가 실제로 우리의 주의를 끌고 있는 동안

힌트 'the driving goes on "automatic pilot"(운전이 '자동 조종' 상태로 가게 된다)'에서 주어인 'the driving'을 강조하기 위해 「it is ~ that」 강조 구문이 사용됨.

(12) Our kids may be living in the Information Age /
우리 아이들은 정보화 시대에 살고 있을지도 모른다 /
but our brains have not been redesigned yet.
현재완료 수동(완료)
하지만 우리의 뇌는 아직 재설계되지 않았다

[전문 해석]

(1)십 대들이 동시에 두 가지 일에 집중할 수 있다는 것은 사실이 아니며, 그들이 하고 있는 것은 그들의 주의를 한 작업에서 다른 작업으로 전환하는 것이다. (2)디지털 시대에, 십 대들은 이러한 전환을 아주 빠르게 만들도록 자신의 뇌를 연결하지만, 그들은 여전히 다른 모든 사람들과 마찬가지로 한 번에 한 가지 것에 순차적으로 주의를 기울이고 있다. (3)상식은 우리에게 멀티태스킹이 뇌 활동을 (a)증가시킬 것이라고 말하지만, 최신 뇌 영상 기술을 사용하는 Carnegie Mellon 대학의 과학자들은 그것이 그렇지 않다는 것을 발견했다. (4)사실, 그들은 멀티태스킹이 실제로는 뇌 활동을 감소시킨다는 것을 발견했다. (5)어떠한 작업도 각각의 작업이 (b)개별적으로 수행될 때만큼 잘 되지 않는다. (6)우리가 전환을 할 때마다 아주 조금의 시간이 소실되며, 한 사람의 중단된 작업은 50퍼센트 더 많은 오류와 함께 끝내는 데 50퍼센트 (c)더 오래 걸릴 수 있다. (7)최신 뇌 연구가 '한 번에 하나씩'이라는 오래된 조언을 (d)반박한다(→ 뒷받침한다)는 것이 밝혀진다.
(8)아이들이 몇몇 작업을 동시에 할 수 없다는 것은 아니다. (9)그러나 만약 두 가지 작업이 동시에 수행된다면, 그것들 중 하나는 익숙한 것이어야 한다. (10)우리의 뇌는 실제로는 나머지 다른 작업에 주의를 기울이면서 익숙한 작업을 '자동 조종' 상태로 수행한다. (11)그것이 바로 보험 회사가 휴대 전화로 이야기하면서 운전하는 것을 술에 취한 상태로 운전하는 것만큼이나 (e)위험한 것으로 간주하는 이유이다. 대화가 실제로 우리의 주의를 끌고 있는 동안 '자동 조종' 상태로 가는 것은 바로 운전이다. (12)우리 아이들은 정보화 시대에 살고 있을지도 모르지만, 우리의 뇌는 아직 재설계되지 않았다.

[정답 확인]

41. 윗글의 제목으로 가장 적절한 것은?
✔ Multitasking Unveiled: What Really Happens in Teens' Brains
정체가 드러난 멀티태스킹: 십 대의 뇌에서 실제로 일어나는 일
② Optimal Ways to Expand the Attention Span of Teens
십 대의 집중 시간을 확장시키는 최적의 방법들
③ Unknown Approaches to Enhance Brain Development
뇌 발달을 향상시키기 위한 미지의 접근법들
④ Multitasking for a Balanced Life in a Busy World
분주한 세상에서 균형 잡힌 삶을 위한 멀티태스킹
⑤ How to Build Automaticity in Performing Tasks
작업을 수행할 때 자동성을 구축하는 방법

42. 밑줄 친 (a) ~ (e) 중에서 문맥상 낱말의 쓰임이 적절하지 않은 것은?
① (a) ② (b) ③ (c) ✔ (d) ⑤ (e)

[문제 풀이]

42. 문장 (3)은 멀티태스킹이 뇌 활동을 증가시킬 것이라는 통념을 제시한 후, Carnegie Mellon 대학의 연구 사례를 통해 이것이 사실이 아니라고 설명한다. 문장 (5)에서는 모든 작업이 개별적으로 수행될 때 가장 잘 된다고 설명하고 있으며, 문장 (6)은 여러 작업을 동시에 수행하려고 작업을 전환할 때마다 더 많은 시간이 소실되고 더 많은 오류가 발생한다고 말한다. 즉, Carnegie Mellon 대학의 연구를 통해, '멀티태스킹을 하기보다는 한 번에 한 작업씩 수행하는 것이 낫다'라는 결론을 도출할 수 있다. 따라서, 문장 (7)에서는 이 최신 뇌 연구가 '한 번에 하나씩'이라는 오래된 조언을 '반박하는(contradicts)' 것이 아니라 '뒷받침한다(supports)'고 하는 것이 문맥상 적절하므로, 정답은 ④이다.

[중요 어휘]

□ at once	동시에, 한꺼번에
□ shift	동사 전환하다 / 명사 전환, 변화
□ attention	명사 주의, 관심
□ sequentially	부사 순차적으로, 연속하여
□ latest	형용사 최신의, 최근의
□ as a matter of fact	사실은
□ perform	동사 수행하다, 실시하다
□ individually	부사 개별적으로, 각각 따로
□ fraction	명사 아주 조금, 파편
□ switch	명사 전환 / 동사 전환하다
□ interrupt	동사 중단시키다, 방해하다
□ contradict	동사 반박하다, 부정하다
□ advice	명사 조언, 충고
□ simultaneously	부사 동시에
□ familiar	형용사 익숙한, 친숙한
□ automatic pilot	자동 조종
□ insurance	명사 보험
□ consider A to V	A가 ~하다고 간주하다[여기다]
□ redesign	동사 재설계하다

43~44 2024년 6월 41~42번 (정답률 65% | 45%) 정답 ① | ⑤

[지문 끊어 읽기] 편견을 뒷받침하는 편견

(1) We have biases / that support our biases!
선행사 주격 관계대명사절
우리는 편견을 가진다 / 우리의 편견을 뒷받침하는

(2) If we're partial to one option /
만약 우리가 한 가지 옵션에 편향된다면 /
— perhaps because it's more memorable, /
=one option 병렬①
아마도 그것이 더 기억할 만하기 때문에 /
or framed to minimize loss, /
병렬②
혹은 손실을 최소화하기 위해 짜여진 /
or seemingly consistent with a promising pattern — /
병렬③
혹은 겉으로 보기에 유망한 패턴과 일치하는 /
we tend to search for information /
우리는 정보를 찾는 경향이 있다 / 선행사
that will (a)justify choosing that option. **43번 정답 단서** 사람은 한 가지 선택에 편향되면 그 선택을 뒷받침할 정보를 찾는 경향이 있음.
주격 관계대명사절
그 옵션을 선택한 것을 (a)정당화할

(3) On the one hand, / it's sensible [to make choices /
형식상의 주어 선행사
한편으로는 / 선택을 하는 것이 현명하다 /
that we can defend / with data and a list of reasons]. [ ]: 내용상의 주어
목적격 관계대명사절
우리가 방어할 수 있는 / 데이터와 이유들의 목록으로

(4) On the other hand, / if we're not careful, /
반면에 / 만약 우리가 주의하지 않으면 /
we're (b)likely to conduct an imbalanced analysis, /
우리는 불균형한 분석을 수행할 (b)가능성이 있다 /
[falling prey to a cluster of errors /
오류 덩어리의 희생양이 된다 /
collectively known as "confirmation biases."] **43번 정답 단서** 한 가지에 편향되면 '확증 편향'을 통해 불균형한 분석을 수행할 가능성이 있음.
총체적으로 '확증 편향'이라고 알려져 있는 [ ]: 분사구문(결과)

문제편 p.266

(5) For example, /
예를 들어 /
nearly all companies include classic "tell me about yourself" job interviews /
거의 모든 기업은 전통적인 '자기소개' 취업 면접을 포함한다 /
as part of the hiring process, /
채용 과정의 일부로 /
and many rely on these interviews alone /
그리고 많은 기업은 이러한 면접에만 의존한다 /
to evaluate applicants.
부사적 용법
지원자들을 평가하기 위해

(6) But it turns out /
형식상의 주어
하지만 판명된다 /
[that traditional interviews are actually one of the (c)least useful tools /
전통적인 면접은 실제로는 (c)가장 유용하지 않은 도구 중 하나라는 것이다 /
for predicting an employee's future success]. [ ]: 내용상의 주어
직원의 미래 성공을 예측하는 데

(7) This is because interviewers often subconsciously make up their minds about interviewees /
V'①
이것은 면접관들이 종종 잠재의식적으로 면접 대상자들에 대한 결정을 내리기 때문이다 /
based on their first few moments of interaction /
처음 몇 순간의 상호 작용을 바탕으로 /
and spend the rest of the interview / cherry-picking evidence /
V'②
그리고 면접의 나머지를 보내기 때문이다 / 증거를 선별하는 데 /
and phrasing their questions /
그리고 그들의 질문을 만드는 데 /
to (d)confirm that initial impression:
부사적 용법
그 첫인상을 (d)확인하기 위해서

힌트 「spend+N+V-ing」는 '~하는 데 (시간·돈을) 보내다[쓰다]'라는 의미로, 여기서는 V-ing 자리에 cherry-picking과 phrasing이 병렬을 이룸.

43번 정답 단서 '자기소개' 취업 면접 방식은 면접 대상자의 첫인상에 편향되어 그 '선택'을 뒷받침하는 증거를 찾기 위해 시간을 소비함.

(8) "I see here you left a good position / at your previous job.
저는 당신이 좋은 직책을 두고 나온 게 보입니다 / 당신의 이전 직장에서

(9) You must be pretty ambitious, right?" / versus /
당신은 틀림없이 꽤 야망이 있습니다, 그렇죠 / 대 /
"You must not have been very committed, huh?"
"당신은 그렇게 헌신적이지 않았음이 틀림없습니다, 그렇죠?"

힌트 과거에 대한 추측으로 「조동사+have p.p.」의 형태를 사용함. 'must have p.p.'는 '~였음에[했음에] 틀림없다'라는 의미로 해석함.

(10) This means /
이것은 의미한다 /
[that interviewers can be prone to (e)noticing(→ overlooking) significant information /
선행사
면접관들이 중요한 정보를 (e)알아차리기(→ 간과하기) 쉬운 경향이 있을 수 있다 /
[that would clearly indicate /
명확하게 보여 주는 / [ ]: 주격 관계대명사절
whether this candidate was actually the best person to hire]].
이 후보자가 실제로 고용하기 가장 좋은 사람인지 아닌지 / 형용사적 용법

힌트 명사절 접속사 that부터 문장 끝까지는 means의 목적어에 해당하는 명사절임.

(11) More structured approaches, /
S
보다 구조화된 접근 방식 /
like obtaining samples of a candidate's work /
전치사 병렬①
후보자의 업무 샘플을 확보하는 것 같은 /
or asking [how he would respond to difficult hypothetical situations], / [ ]: 의문사절(asking의 목적어)
병렬②
혹은 가정된 어려운 상황에 그가 어떻게 대응할지 묻는 것과 같은 /
are dramatically better at assessing future success, /
V
미래 성공을 평가하는 데 극적으로 더 낫다 /
with a nearly threefold advantage / over traditional interviews.
거의 세 배의 이점으로 / 전통적인 면접보다

44번 정답 단서 전통적인 면접 방식보다 면접 대상자의 업무 샘플 및 어려운 상황에 대한 대응 방식 등의 구조화된 접근 방식이 대상자를 파악하는 데에 훨씬 효과적임.

[전문 해석]

(1)우리는 우리의 편견을 뒷받침하는 편견을 가진다. (2)만약 우리가 한 가지 옵션에 편향된다면, 아마도 그것이 더 기억할 만하거나, 손실을 최소화하기 위해 짜여지거나, 혹은 겉으로 보기에 유망한 패턴과 일치하기 때문에 우리는 그 옵션을 선택한 것을 (a)정당화할 정보를 찾는 경향이 있다. (3)한편으로는, 우리가 데이터와 이유들의 목록으로 방어할 수 있는 선택을 하는 것이 현명하다. (4)반면에, 만약 우리가 주의하지 않으면, 우리는 불균형한 분석을 수행할 (b)가능성이 있으며, 총체적으로 '확증 편향'이라고 알려져 있는 오류 덩어리의 희생양이 된다.

(5)예를 들어, 거의 모든 기업은 채용 과정의 일부로 전통적인 '자기소개' 취업 면접을 포함하고, 많은 기업은 지원자들을 평가하기 위해 이러한 면접에만 의존한다. (6)하지만 전통적인 면접은 실제로는 직원의 미래 성공을 예측하는 데 (c)가장 유용하지 않은 도구 중 하나라는 것이 판명된다. (7)이것은 면접관들이 종종 잠재의식적으로 처음 몇 순간의 상호 작용을 바탕으로 면접 대상자들에 대한 결정을 내리고 그 첫인상을 (d)확인하기 위해서 증거를 선별하고 그들의 질문을 만드는 데 면접의 나머지를 보내기 때문이다. (8)"저는 당신이 이전 직장에서 좋은 직책을 두고 나온 게 보입니다. (9)당신은 틀림없이 꽤 야망이 있습니다, 그렇죠?" 대 "당신은 그렇게 헌신적이지 않았음이 틀림없습니다, 그렇죠?" (10)이것은 면접관들이 이 후보자가 실제로 고용하기 가장 좋은 사람인지 아닌지 명확하게 보여 주는 중요한 정보를 (e)알아차리기(→ 간과하기) 쉬운 경향이 있을 수 있다는 것을 의미한다. (11)후보자의 업무 샘플을 확보하는 것 혹은 가정된 어려운 상황에 그가 어떻게 대응할지 묻는 것과 같은 보다 구조화된 접근 방식은 전통적인 면접보다 거의 세 배의 이점으로 미래 성공을 평가하는 데 극적으로 더 낫다.

[정답 확인]

43. 윗글의 제목으로 가장 적절한 것은?

✔ Bias Trap: How Our Preconceptions Mislead Us
편견의 함정: 우리의 선입견이 어떻게 우리를 잘못 이끄는가
② Utilize the Power of Similar Personality Types!
비슷한 성격 유형의 힘을 활용하라!
③ More Information Adds Up to Worse Choices
더 많은 정보가 결국 더 나쁜 선택이 된다
④ Why Are You Persuaded by Others' Perspectives?
당신은 왜 다른 사람의 관점에 설득당하는가?
⑤ Interviews: The Fairest Judgment for All Applicants
면접: 모든 지원자를 위한 가장 공정한 판단

44. 밑줄 친 (a) ~ (e) 중에서 문맥상 낱말의 쓰임이 적절하지 않은 것은?

① (a) ② (b) ③ (c) ④ (d) ✔ (e)

[문제 풀이]

43. 문장 (1)에서 인간은 자신의 편견을 뒷받침하는 편견을 가진다고 이야기한다. 그러므로 문장 (1)을 통해 편견과 편견 간의 뒷받침이 무엇인지 파악하며 지문을 읽어야 한다. 문장 (2)~(3)은 인간은 한 가지의 편향에 집중하여 그것을 뒷받침할 정보를 탐색하는 경향이 있다고 말한다. 이러한 경향은 '확증 편향'을 통해 불균형한 분석을 할 수 있다고 말하는 문장 (4)로 이어지며, 기업의 전통적인 '자기소개' 면접 방식을 예시로 든 문장 (5)~(11)에서는 편향된 편견과 그 증거가 되는 편견의 관계성을 설명한다. 따라서, 이 모든 내용을 함축하는 ① 이 정답이다.

44. 문장 (1)~(4)에서 설명하듯이 사람은 한 가지 편견에 편향되어 그 증거가 되는 정보를 찾는 경향이 있다. 문장 (7)에 따르면, 전통적인 '자기소개' 면접 방식에서 면접관은 처음 행해지는 몇 번의 상호 작용만을 통해 면접 대상자의 인상을 결정짓고, 그 선입견을 뒷받침할 증거를 만들기 위해 그와 관련된 질문을 만들며 면접의 대부분의 시간을 보낸다. 그러므로 이러한 면접 방식은 면접 대상자가 고용하기 가장 좋은 사람인지 아닌지를 판명할 수 있는 가장 중요한 정보를 알아차릴(noticing) 수 있는 것이 아니라, 중요한 정보를 간과하는(overlooking) 것으로 보는 것이 적절하다. 따라서 정답은 ⑤이다.

[오답 풀이]

44. ③ - 문장 (1)에서 언급했듯이 사람은 한 가지의 편견에 편향되어 정보를 찾는 경향이 있다. 문장 (7)에 따르면 처음 행해지는 몇 번의 상호 작용이 면접 대상자에 대한 선입견을 만들고, 그에 맞추어 증거가 될 만한 질문을 만들기 때문에 전통적인 면접이 '가장 유용하지 않은' 도구라는 것은 내용의 흐름을 자연스럽게 잇는다. 따라서 ③은 정답이 아니다.

[중요 어휘]

□ bias	명사 편견, 편향
□ partial	형용사 편향된, 편파적인, 부분적인
□ promising	형용사 유망한, 촉망되는
□ justify	동사 정당화하다, 옹호하다
□ conduct	동사 수행하다, 지휘하다 / 명사 행동, 경영
□ cluster	명사 덩어리, 군집, 무리
□ collectively	부사 총체적으로, 집합적으로

- [ ] **confirmation bias** 명사 확증 편향
- [ ] **evaluate** 동사 평가하다, 어림하다
- [ ] **subconsciously** 부사 잠재의식적으로
- [ ] **cherry-pick** 동사 선별하다, 신중히 선택하다
- [ ] **be prone to N** ~하기 쉽다
- [ ] **threefold** 형용사 세 배의

45~46 2024년 9월 41~42번 (정답률 65% | 70%) 정답 ① | ④

[지문 끊어 읽기] 권위에 도전하는 아이들의 질문

(1) What makes questioning authority so hard?
S(의문사) V O(동명사구) O·C(형용사)
무엇이 권위에 의문을 제기하는 것을 그토록 어렵게 만드는가

(2) The (a)difficulties start in childhood, /
그 (a)어려움은 유년 시절에 시작한다 / 선행사
[when parents — the first and most powerful authority figures — /
S' =
그리고 이때 최초이자 가장 영향력 있는 권위자인 부모는 /
show children "the way things are."] [ ]: 관계부사절
V' I·O' D·O'
아이들에게 '사물이 존재하는 방식'을 보여 준다

★중요 문장 (1)에서 언급된 '권위에 의문을 제기하는 것의 어려움'을 받은 것이므로 문맥상 적절하게 쓰임

(3) This is a necessary element of learning language and socialization, /
이것은 언어 학습과 사회화의 필수적인 요소이다 /
and certainly most things learned in early childhood /
과거분사구
그리고 확실히 초기 유년 시절에 학습되는 대부분의 것들은 /
are (b)noncontroversial: /
(b)논쟁의 여지가 없다 /
★중요 콜론(:) 뒤에 초기 유년 시절에 학습되는 '논쟁의 여지가 없는 명백한 사실들'의 사례가 바로 제시되므로 문맥상 적절함.
the English alphabet starts with A and ends with Z, /
영어 알파벳은 A로 시작하여 Z로 끝난다 /
the numbers 1 through 10 come /
숫자 1부터 10은 온다 /
before the numbers 11 through 20, / and so on.
숫자 11부터 20 이전에 / 기타 등등

(4) Children, however, / will spontaneously question /
그러나 아이들은 / 즉흥적으로 의문을 제기할 것이다 /
things that are quite obvious to adults and even to older kids.
선행사 주격 관계대명사절
어른들과 심지어 나이가 더 많은 아이들에게는 꽤 명백한 것들에
45번 정답 단서 어른들이나 나이가 더 많은 아이들에게는 명백한 사실들도 아이들에게는 질문거리일 수도 있음.

(5) The word "why?" becomes a challenge, /
"왜요?"라는 말은 도전이 된다 /
as in, "Why is the sky blue?"
"왜 하늘은 파랄까요?"에서처럼
★중요 "그냥 그러니까" 혹은 "내가 그렇다고 하니까"와 같은 대답은 사실상 아이들에게 이유를 캐묻지 말고 그냥 받아들이라는 의미이므로 문맥상 적절함.

(6) Answers such as "because it just is" or "because I say so" /
S①
"그냥 그러니까" 혹은 "내가 그렇다고 하니까"와 같은 대답들은 /
tell children / [that they must unquestioningly (c)accept /
V① I·O
아이들에게 말한다 / 그들이 의심 없이 (c)받아들여야 한다고 /
what authorities say "just because,"] / [ ]: D·O
선행사를 포함한 관계대명사절(accept의 목적어)
권위자들이 "그냥 그러니까"라고 말하는 것을 /
and children who persist in their questioning /
S②, 선행사 주격 관계대명사절
그리고 질문하는 것을 지속하는 아이들은 /
are likely to find /
V② 5형식V
발견할 가능성이 있다 /
themselves dismissed or yelled at for "bothering" adults /
O O·C① O·C②
어른들을 '성가시게 하는 것' 때문에 스스로가 쫓겨나거나 고함을 듣는 것을 /
with "meaningless" or "unimportant" questions.
'무의미한' 혹은 '중요하지 않은' 질문들로

(7) But these questions are in fact perfectly (d)unreasonable (→ reasonable).
그러나 이러한 질문들은 실제로 완벽하게 (d)비합리적(→ 합리적)이다

(8) Why is the sky blue?
하늘은 왜 파랄까

(9) Many adults do not themselves know the answer.
재귀대명사(강조)
많은 어른들은 스스로도 그 답을 알지 못한다

(10) And who says / the sky's color needs to be called "blue," /
그리고 누가 말하는가 / 하늘의 색깔이 '파란색'이라고 불려야 한다고 /
anyway?
어쨌든
🔓힌트 선행사인 the same color가 「call+목적어+목적격 보어(~을 …라고 부르다)」의 5형식 구조에서 목적어에 해당하므로, 밑줄 친 부분은 목적격 관계대명사 that임을 알 수 있음. cf.「주어(another)+동사(calls)+목적어(the same color)+목적격 보어("blue")」

(11) How do we know / [that what one person calls "blue" /
S'(선행사를 포함한 관계대명사절)
우리는 어떻게 아는가 / 한 사람이 '파란색'이라고 부르는 것이 /
is the same color that another calls "blue"]? [ ]: know의 목적어
V' S·C', 선행사 목적격 관계대명사절
다른 사람이 '파란색'이라고 부르는 것과 동일한 색깔임을

(12) The scientific answers come from physics, /
과학적인 답은 물리학에서 나온다 /
but those are not the answers / that children are seeking.
선행사 목적격 관계대명사절
하지만 그것들은 답이 아니다 / 아이들이 찾고 있는

(13) They are trying to understand the world, /
그들은 세상을 이해하려고 노력하고 있다 /
and no matter how (e)irritating the repeated questions may become /
=however
그리고 반복되는 질문들이 아무리 (e)짜증스러워질지라도 /
to stressed and time-pressed parents, /
스트레스를 받고 시간에 쫓기는 부모들에게 있어 /
★중요 '스트레스를 받고 시간에 쫓기는 부모들'에게 아이들의 반복적인 질문은 짜증스러운 것으로 느껴질 수 있으므로 문맥상 적절함.
it is important to take them seriously /
형식상의 주어 내용상의 주어
그것들을 진지하게 받아들이는 것이 중요하다 /
to encourage kids to question authority /
부사적 용법(목적), 5형식V O O·C(to V)
아이들이 권위에 의문을 제기하도록 독려하기 위해서 /
to think for themselves.
부사적 용법(목적)
스스로 생각하도록
45번 정답 단서 아이들이 권위에 의문을 제기하여 스스로 생각할 수 있게 하기 위해서, 아이들의 반복되는 질문들이 짜증스러울지라도 그것들을 진지하게 받아들여야 함.

[전문 해석]

(1)무엇이 권위에 의문을 제기하는 것을 그토록 어렵게 만드는가? (2)그 (a)어려움은 유년 시절에 시작하는데, 이때 최초이자 가장 영향력 있는 권위자인 부모는 아이들에게 '사물이 존재하는 방식'을 보여 준다. (3)이것은 언어 학습과 사회화의 필수적인 요소이고, 확실히 초기 유년 시절에 학습되는 대부분의 것들, 즉 영어 알파벳은 A로 시작하여 Z로 끝나고, 숫자 1부터 10은 숫자 11부터 20 이전에 온다는 것, 기타 등등은 (b)논쟁의 여지가 없다. (4)그러나 아이들은 어른들과 심지어 나이가 더 많은 아이들에게는 꽤 명백한 것들에 즉흥적으로 의문을 제기할 것이다. (5)"왜 하늘은 파랄까요?"에서처럼, "왜요?"라는 말은 도전이 된다. (6)"그냥 그러니까" 혹은 "내가 그렇다고 하니까"와 같은 대답들은 권위자들이 "그냥 그러니까"라고 말하는 것을 그들(아이들)이 의심 없이 (c)받아들여야 한다고 아이들에게 말하며, 질문하는 것을 지속하는 아이들은 '무의미한' 혹은 '중요하지 않은' 질문들로 어른들을 '성가시게 하는 것' 때문에 스스로가 쫓겨나거나 고함을 듣는 것을 발견할 가능성이 있다. (7)그러나 이러한 질문들은 실제로 완벽하게 (d)비합리적(→ 합리적)이다. (8)하늘은 왜 파랄까? (9)많은 어른들은 스스로도 그 답을 알지 못한다. (10)그리고 어쨌든 누가 하늘의 색깔이 '파란색'이라고 불려야 한다고 말하는가? (11)한 사람이 '파란색'이라고 부르는 것이 다른 사람이 '파란색'이라고 부르는 것과 동일한 색깔임을 우리는 어떻게 아는가? (12)과학적인 답은 물리학에서 나오지만, 그것들은 아이들이 찾고 있는 답이 아니다. (13)그들은 세상을 이해하려고 노력하고 있고, 스트레스를 받고 시간에 쫓기는 부모들에게 있어 반복되는 질문들이 아무리 (e)짜증스러워질지라도, 아이들이 권위에 의문을 제기하여 스스로 생각하도록 독려하기 위해서 그것들을 진지하게 받아들이는 것이 중요하다.

[정답 확인]

45. 윗글의 제목으로 가장 적절한 것은?

✔① Things Plain to You Aren't to Children: Let Them Question
여러분에게 명백한 것들이 아이들에게는 그렇지 않다: 그들이 질문하게 하라
② Children's Complaints: Should Parents Accept All of Them?
아이들의 불만: 부모는 그것들 모두를 받아줘야만 할까?
③ Want More Challenges? They'll Make Your Energy Dry Up!
더 많은 도전을 원하는가? 그것들은 여러분의 에너지를 고갈시킬 것이다!

문제편 p.267

④ Authority Has Hidden Power to Nurture Children's Morality
권위는 아이들의 도덕성을 길러주는 숨겨진 힘을 가지고 있다
⑤ Answering Is More Crucial than Questioning for Quick Learning
빠른 학습을 위해서는 질문하는 것보다 답변하는 것이 더 중요하다

46. 밑줄 친 (a) ~ (e) 중에서 문맥상 낱말의 쓰임이 적절하지 않은 것은?

① (a) ② (b) ③ (c) ④ (d) ⑤ (e)

[문제 풀이]

45. 문장 (4)에 따르면, 아이들은 어른이나 나이가 좀 더 많은 아이들에게는 명백한 사실들에 대해서도 의문을 제기하는데, 문장 (6)의 설명에서처럼, 부모는 아이들에게 "그냥 그러니까" 혹은 "내가 그렇다고 하니까"와 같은 말로 대답을 얼버무리거나 질문을 고집하는 아이를 성가셔한다. 그런데 문장 (7)~(11)은 사실 아이들이 던지는 이러한 질문들이 꽤나 이유 있는 질문임을 상기시키고 있으며, 문장 (13)은 아이들이 권위에 의문을 제기하고 스스로 생각하도록 독려하기 위해 부모들이 아이들의 반복된 질문을 진지하게 받아들이고 답해주어야 한다고 충고한다. 따라서 글의 제목으로 가장 적절한 것은 ①이다.
46. 문장 (8)~(9)는 하늘이 파란 이유를 어른들 자신들조차도 모르고 있다고 말하면서, '하늘이 왜 파란지'에 대한 아이들의 질문이 타당한 것임을 보여 주고 있다. 또한 문장 (10)~(12)는 하늘의 색깔은 '파란색'이 아닐 수도 있으며 우리가 '파란색'이라고 말하는 것도 사람마다 다를 수 있음을 들어, 아이들의 질문이 타당한 것임을 나타내고 있다. 따라서 문장 (7)에서는 아이들의 '이러한 질문들'이 실제로는 완벽하게 '비합리적'인 것이 아니라 '합리적'이라고 해야 한다. 따라서 정답은 ④이다.

[중요 어휘]

□ **authority**	명사 권위, 권위자, 지휘권
□ **childhood**	명사 유년 시절, 어린 시절
□ **figure**	명사 인물, 사람, 수치, 계산, 도형
□ **element**	명사 요소, 성분
□ **socialization**	명사 사회화
□ **noncontroversial**	형용사 논쟁의 여지가 없는
□ **spontaneously**	부사 즉흥적으로, 자발적으로
□ **obvious**	형용사 명백한, 분명한
□ **unquestioningly**	부사 의심 없이, 의문을 품지 않고
□ **persist**	동사 지속하다, 고집하다
□ **dismiss**	동사 쫓아내다, 물리치다, 해고하다
□ **bother**	동사 ~을 성가시게 하다, 괴롭히다
□ **meaningless**	형용사 무의미한, 의미 없는
□ **unreasonable**	형용사 비합리적인, 부당한
□ **physics**	명사 물리학
□ **seek**	동사 찾다, 구하다, 추구하다
□ **irritating**	형용사 짜증스러운, 귀찮은
□ **time-pressed**	형용사 시간에 쫓기는
□ **seriously**	부사 진지하게, 진심으로
□ **plain**	형용사 명백한, 분명한, 소박한, 무늬가 없는

18 장문의 이해-복합지문

01~03

2021년 6월 43~45번
(정답률 90% | 85% | 90%)

정답 ② | ⑤ | ⑤

[지문 끊어 읽기] 이메일이 없어서 성공한 사업가

(A-1) Victor applied / for the position of office cleaner /
Victor는 지원했다 / 사무실 청소부 자리에 /
at a very big company.
아주 큰 회사의

(A-2) The manager interviewed him, / then gave him a test: /
매니저가 그를 인터뷰했다 / 그러고 나서 그에게 시험을 냈다 /
cleaning, / stocking, / and supplying designated facility areas.
청소하기 / 재고 채우기 / 그리고 지정된 부서에 보급하기

(A-3) After observing what (a)he was doing, / the manager said, /
(a)그(Victor)가 하고 있던 것을 지켜본 후 / 매니저는 말했다 /
"You are hired. / Give me your email address, / 01번 정답 단서
당신은 고용되었습니다 / 저에게 당신의 이메일 주소를 주세요 /
and I'll send you some documents / to fill out."
그러면 제가 당신에게 몇 가지 서류들을 보내드리겠습니다 / 작성할

* (A) 요약: Victor는 회사 청소부 자리에 지원했고, 합격 후 매니저는 이메일 주소를 요구함.

(C-1) Victor replied, / "I don't have a computer, nor an email." 01번 정답 단서
Victor는 대답했다 / "저는 컴퓨터도 이메일도 없습니다."

(C-2) "I'm sorry," said the manager.
"유감이네요."라고 매니저가 말했다

(C-3) And he added, / "If you don't have an email, /
그리고 그는 덧붙였다 / 만약 당신이 이메일이 없다면 /
how do you intend to do this job? / This job requires you /
이 일을 어떻게 하려고 합니까 / 이 일은 당신이 ~할 것을 요구합니다 /
to have an email address. / I can't hire you."
이메일 주소를 가질 것을 / 저는 당신을 고용할 수 없습니다

(C-4) Victor left / with no hope at all.
Victor는 떠났다 / 아무 희망도 없이

(C-5) (d)He didn't know what to do, / with only 10 dollars in his pocket.
(d)그(Victor)는 무엇을 해야 할지 몰랐다 / 주머니에 10달러만 가진 채

(C-6) He then decided to go to the supermarket /
그는 그러고 나서 슈퍼마켓에 가기로 결심했다 /
and bought a 10kg box of tomatoes. 01번 정답 단서
그리고 10kg짜리 토마토 한 상자를 샀다

* (C) 요약: 이메일이 없는 Victor는 고용이 취소되었고, 그가 가진 10달러로 슈퍼마켓에서 토마토를 삼.

(B-1) (b)He then sold the tomatoes / in a door to door round. 01번 정답 단서
(b)그(Victor)는 그러고 나서 토마토를 팔았다 / 집집마다 돌아다니며

(B-2) In two hours, / he succeeded / to double his capital.
두 시간 만에 / 그는 성공했다 / 자본금을 두 배로 늘리는 데

(B-3) He repeated the operation three times /
그는 그 작업을 세 번 반복했다 /
and returned home with 60 dollars.
그리고 60달러를 가지고 집으로 돌아왔다

(B-4) Victor realized / that he could survive by this way, /
Victor는 깨달았다 / 그가 이런 방법으로 살아남을 수 있다는 것을 /
and started to go every day earlier, / and returned late.
그리고 매일 더 일찍 나가기 시작했다 / 그리고 늦게 돌아왔다

(B-5) Thus, / (c)his money doubled or tripled / each day.
따라서 / (c)그(Victor)의 돈은 두 배 또는 세 배로 불었다 / 매일

(B-6) Shortly later, / he bought a cart, then a truck, /
얼마 지나지 않아 / 그는 카트 그 다음에는 트럭을 샀다 /
and then he had his own fleet of delivery vehicles.
그러고 나서 그는 자신만의 배달 차량 무리를 갖게 되었다

* (B) 요약: Victor는 살아남는 법을 배웠고, 그렇게 번 돈으로 배달 차량을 갖게 됨.

(D-1) Several years later, /
몇 년 후 /
Victor's company became the biggest food company in his city. 01번 정답 단서
Victor의 회사는 그의 도시에서 가장 큰 식품 회사가 되었다

(D-2) He started to plan his family's future, /
그는 가족의 미래를 계획하기 시작했다 /
and decided to get a life insurance.
그리고 생명 보험에 가입하기로 결심했다

(D-3) He called an insurance broker. 02번 정답 단서
그는 보험 중개인을 불렀다

(D-4) When the conversation was concluded, /
대화가 끝나자 /
(e)he asked him his email.
(e)그(an insurance broker)는 그에게 이메일을 물었다

(D-5) Victor replied: / "I don't have an email." 03번 정답 단서
Victor가 대답했다 / "저는 이메일이 없어요."

(D-6) The broker replied curiously, / "You don't have an email, /
중개인은 궁금한 듯 대답했다 / 당신은 이메일이 없습니다 /
and yet have succeeded to build an empire. / Do you imagine /
그렇지만 제국을 건설하는 데 성공했습니다 / 당신은 상상하시나요 /
what you could have been / if you had an email?"
당신이 무엇이 되었을지 / 이메일이 있었다면

힌트 'S+could+have p.p., if+S'+had p.p.'의 형식이 사용된 가정법 과거완료 구문으로, 과거에 일어난 사실을 반대 상황으로 가정하고 있음.

(D-7) He thought for a while, / and replied, /
그는 잠시 생각했다 / 그리고 대답했다 /
"An office cleaner!"
"사무실 청소부!"

* (D) 요약: 성공한 뒤 Victor는 보험에 가입하기로 하고 보험 중개사와 이메일에 대한 대화를 나눔.

[전문 해석]

(A)

(1)Victor는 아주 큰 회사의 사무실 청소부 자리에 지원했다. (2)매니저가 그를 인터뷰했고, 그러고 나서 그에게 시험을 냈다. (시험은) 청소하기, 재고 채우기 그리고 지정된 부서에 보급하기(였다). (3)(a)그(Victor)가 하고 있던 것을 지켜본 후, 매니저는 말했다, "당신은 고용되었습니다. 저에게 당신의 이메일 주소를 (알려) 주세요, 그러면 제가 당신에게 작성할 몇 가지 서류들을 보내드리겠습니다."

(C)

(1)Victor는 대답했다, "저는 컴퓨터도, 이메일도 없습니다." (2)"유감이네요."라고 매니저가 말했다. (3)그리고 그는 덧붙였다, "만약 당신이 이메일이 없다면 이 일을 어떻게 하려고 합니까? 이 일은 당신이 이메일 주소를 가질 것을 요구합니다. 저는 당신을 고용할 수 없습니다." (4)Victor는 아무 희망도 없이 떠났다. (5)주머니에 10달러만 가진 채, (d)그(Victor)는 무엇을 해야 할지 몰랐다. (6)그는 그러고 나서 슈퍼마켓에 가기로 결심했고 10kg짜리 토마토 한 상자를 샀다.

(B)

(1)(b)그(Victor)는 그러고 나서 집집마다 돌아다니며 토마토를 팔았다. (2)두 시간 만에, 그는 자본금을 두 배로 늘리는 데 성공했다. (3)그는 그 작업을 세 번 반복했고 60달러를 가지고 집으로 돌아왔다. (4)Victor는 이런 방법으로 살아남을 수 있다는 것을 깨달았고, 매일 더 일찍 나가기 시작했고 늦게 돌아왔다. (5)따라서 (c)그(Victor)의 돈은 매일 두 배 또는 세 배로 불었다. (6)얼마 지나지 않아, 그는 카트, 그 다음에는 트럭을 샀고 그러고 나서 그는 자신만의 배달 차량 무리를 갖게 되었다.

(D)

(1)몇 년 후, Victor의 회사는 그의 도시에서 가장 큰 식품 회사가 되었다. (2)그는 가족의 미래를 계획하기 시작했고, 생명 보험에 가입하기로 결심했다. (3)그는 보험 중개인을 불렀다. (4)대화가 끝나자, (e)그(an insurance broker)는 그에게 이메일을 물었다. (5)Victor가 대답했다. "저는 이메일이 없어요." (6)중개인은 궁금한 듯 대답했다, "당신은 이메일이 없지만 제국을 건설하는 데 성공했습니다. 이메일이 있었다면 당신이 무엇이 되었을지 상상하시나요(상상이 되시나요)?" (7)그는 잠시 생각하더니 대답했다, "사무실 청소부!"

[정답 확인]

01. 주어진 글 (A)에 이어질 내용을 순서에 맞게 배열한 것으로 가장 적절한 것은?

① (B) — (D) — (C)　✔② (C) — (B) — (D)　③ (C) — (D) — (B)
④ (D) — (B) — (C)　⑤ (D) — (C) — (B)

문제편 p.271

02. 밑줄 친 (a) ~ (e) 중에서 가리키는 대상이 나머지 넷과 다른 것은?

① (a) ② (b) ③ (c) ④ (d) ⑤ (e) ✔

03. 윗글의 Victor에 관한 내용으로 적절하지 않은 것은?

① 사무실 청소부(office cleaner) 자리에 지원하였다.
② 2시간 만에 자본금(capital)을 두 배로 만들었다.
③ 슈퍼마켓에 가서 토마토(tomatoes)를 샀다.
④ 그의 회사는 도시에서 가장 큰 식품 회사(the biggest food company)가 되었다.
⑤ ✔ 이메일이 ~~있다고~~ 없다고 보험 중개인(an insurance broker)에게 답했다.

[중요 어휘]

□ apply for	~에 지원하다
□ stock	동사 (재고를) 채우다 / 명사 재고
□ designated	형용사 지정된
□ fill out	작성하다
□ require	동사 요구하다, 필요로 하다
□ door to door	집집마다
□ capital	명사 자본금
□ operation	명사 작업
□ fleet	명사 무리, 함대
□ insurance broker	보험 중개인
□ empire	명사 제국

04~06

2021년 9월 43~45번
(정답률 90% | 75% | 85%)

정답 ④ | ④ | ⑤

[지문 끊어 읽기] 뒤늦게 인정받은 발레 무용수

(A-1) There once lived a girl / named Melanie.
옛날에 소녀가 살았다 / Melanie라는

(A-2) She wanted to be a ballet dancer.
그녀는 발레 무용수가 되고 싶었다

(A-3) One day, / Melanie's mother saw her dancing /
어느 날 / Melanie의 엄마는 그녀가 춤추는 것을 보았다 /
with the flawless steps and enthusiasm / of a ballerina. 06번 정답 단서
흠이 없는 스텝과 열정을 가지고 / 발레리나의

(A-4) "Isn't it strange?
놀랍지 않아요

(A-5) Melanie is dancing so well / without any formal training!" /
Melanie는 춤을 정말 잘 춰요 / 어떤 정규 교육도 받지 않고 /
her mother said.
그녀의 엄마가 말했다

(A-6) "I must get (a)her professional lessons /
나는 (a)그녀(Melanie)가 전문적인 수업을 받도록 해야겠어요 /
to help her polish her skill."
그녀가 자신의 기술을 연마하는 것을 돕기 위해

* (A) 요약: Melanie가 춤추는 것을 본 Melanie의 엄마는 Melanie가 전문적인 수업을 받는 게 좋겠다고 말함.

(D-1) The following day, / Melanie accompanied her mother /
다음 날 / Melanie는 그녀의 엄마와 동행했다 /
to a local dance institute. 06번 정답 단서
지역 댄스 학원에

(D-2) Upon meeting the dance teacher, Mr. Edler, /
(up)on V-ing: ~하자마자
댄스 교사인 Mr. Edler를 만나자마자 /
her mother requested / to admit Melanie to his institute.
그녀의 엄마는 요청했다 / Melanie를 그의 학원에 받아들여 달라고

(D-3) The teacher asked Melanie / to audition.
그 교사는 Melanie에게 요청했다 / 오디션을 보라고

(D-4) (e)She was happy /
(e)그녀(Melanie)는 기뻐했다 /
and showed him some of her favorite dance steps.
그리고 그에게 그녀가 가장 좋아하는 댄스 스텝 몇 가지를 보여 주었다

(D-5) However, / he wasn't interested in her dance. 06번 정답 단서
하지만 / 그는 그녀의 춤에 관심이 없었다

(D-6) He was busy with other tasks / in the dance room.
그는 다른 일들로 바빴다 / 댄스실에서

(D-7) "You can leave now!
이제 가셔도 됩니다

(D-8) The girl is just average.
이 소녀는 평범합니다

(D-9) Don't let her waste her time / aspiring to be a dancer," / he said.
그녀가 자신의 시간을 낭비하게 하지 마세요 / 댄서가 되길 열망하면서 / 그가 말했다

(D-10) Melanie and her mother were shocked / to hear this.
Melanie와 그녀의 엄마는 충격을 받았다 / 이 말을 듣고

* (D) 요약: 댄스 학원의 교사 Mr. Edler는 Melanie의 춤에 관심이 없었고, 그녀를 학원에 받아들이지 않음.

(B-1) Disappointed, / they returned home, /
실망하여 / 그들은 집으로 돌아왔다 /
tears rolling down Melanie's cheeks.
Melanie의 뺨에 눈물이 흘러내렸다

힌트 분사구문 'Being disappointed'에서 'Being'이 생략된 형태임. be동사 뒤에 분사, 형용사, 명사, 전치사 + 명사가 나올 때, 분사구문의 'being', 'having been'은 생략 가능함.

(B-2) With her confidence and ego hurt, / Melanie never danced again.
그녀의 자신감과 자부심에 상처를 입은 채 / Melanie는 결코 다시는 춤을 추지 않았다

(B-3) (b)She completed her studies / and became a schoolteacher.
(b)그녀(Melanie)는 학업을 마쳤다 / 그리고 학교 교사가 되었다

(B-4) One day, / the ballet instructor at her school was running late, /
어느 날 / 그녀의 학교의 발레 강사가 늦게 오는 중이었다 /
and Melanie was asked / to keep an eye on the class /
그리고 Melanie는 요청을 받았다 / 학급을 지켜봐 달라는 /
so that they wouldn't roam around the school.
그들이 학교 주변을 배회하지 않도록

(B-5) Once inside the ballet room, / she couldn't control herself.
발레실 안으로 들어가자 / 그녀는 자신을 통제할 수 없었다

(B-6) She taught the students some steps / 06번 정답 단서
그녀는 학생들에게 몇 가지 스텝을 가르쳤다 /
and kept on dancing for some time.
그리고 얼마 동안 계속해서 춤을 추었다

(B-7) Unaware of time or the people around her, / (c)she was lost /
시간과 그녀를 둘러싼 사람들을 인식하지 못한 채 / (c)그녀(Melanie)는 빠져 있었다 /
in her own little world of dancing.
그녀만의 작은 춤의 세계에

힌트 'Being unaware of time or the people around her'에서 'Being'이 생략된 형태의 분사구문임.

* (B) 요약: 춤을 그만두고 학교 교사가 된 Melanie는 학교에 늦게 오는 발레 강사를 대신해 발레실로 들어갔고 그곳에서 춤을 춤.

(C-1) Just then, / the ballet instructor entered the classroom /
바로 그때 / 발레 강사가 교실로 들어왔다 /
and was surprised / to see Melanie's incredible skill.
그리고 놀랐다 / Melanie의 놀라운 기술을 보고

(C-2) "What a performance!" / the instructor said /
"대단한 공연이에요!" / 강사가 말했다 /
with a sparkle in her eyes.
자신의 눈을 반짝이며

(C-3) Melanie was embarrassed / to see the instructor in front of her.
Melanie는 당황했다 / 자신 앞에 서 있는 강사를 보고

(C-4) "Sorry, Ma'am!" / she said.
"죄송해요, 강사님!" / 그녀는 말했다.

(C-5) "For what?" / the instructor asked.
"뭐가요?" / 강사가 물었다

(C-6) "You are a true ballerina!"
"당신은 진정한 발레리나입니다!"

(C-7) The instructor invited Melanie / to accompany (d)her /
강사는 Melanie에게 요청했다 / (d)그녀(instructor)와 동행하자고 /
to a ballet training center, /
발레 교습소로 /
and Melanie has never stopped dancing since.
그리고 Melanie는 이후 결코 무용을 그만두지 않았다

(C-8) Today, / she is a world-renowned ballet dancer. 06번 정답 단서
오늘날 / 그녀는 세계적으로 유명한 발레 무용수이다

* (C) 요약: Melanie의 춤을 보고 놀란 발레 강사는 Melanie를 발레 교습소로 데려갔고, 그 후 Melanie는 발레 무용수가 됨.

[전문 해석]

(A)

(1)옛날에 Melanie라는 소녀가 살았다. (2)그녀는 발레 무용수가 되고 싶었다. (3)어느 날 Melanie의 엄마는 그녀가 발레리나의 흠이 없는 스텝과 열정을 가지고 춤추는 것을 보았다. (4)"놀랍지 않아요? (5)Melanie는 어떤 정규 교육도 받지 않고 춤을 정말 잘 춰요!"라고 그녀의 엄마가 말했다. (6)"나는 그녀가 자신의 기술을 연마하는 것을 돕기 위해 (a)그녀(Melanie)가 전문적인 수업을 받도록 해야겠어요."

(D)

(1)다음 날 Melanie는 지역 댄스 학원에 그녀의 엄마와 동행했다. (2)댄스 교사인 Mr. Edler를 만나자마자, 그녀의 엄마는 Melanie를 그의 학원에 받아들여 달라고 요청했다. (3)그 교사는 Melanie에게 오디션을 보라고 요청했다. (4)(e)그녀(Melanie)는 기뻐하며 그에게 그녀가 가장 좋아하는 댄스 스텝 몇 가지를 보여 주었다. (5)하지만 그는 그녀의 춤에 관심이 없었다. (6)그는 댄스실에서 다른 일들로 바빴다. (7)"이제 가셔도 됩니다! (8)이 소녀는 평범합니다. (9)그녀가 댄서가 되길 열망하면서 자신의 시간을 낭비하게 하지 마세요."라고 그가 말했다. (10)Melanie와 그녀의 엄마는 이 말을 듣고 충격을 받았다.

(B)

(1)실망하여 그들은 집으로 돌아왔고, Melanie의 뺨에 눈물이 흘러내렸다. (2)그녀의 자신감과 자부심에 상처를 입은 채, Melanie는 결코 다시는 춤을 추지 않았다. (3)(b)그녀(Melanie)는 학업을 마치고 학교 교사가 되었다. (4)어느 날 그녀의 학교의 발레 강사가 (학교에) 늦게 오는 중이었고, Melanie는 그들(학생들)이 학교 주변을 배회하지 않도록 학급을 지켜봐 달라는 요청을 받았다. (5)발레실 안으로 들어가자 그녀는 자신을 통제할 수 없었다. (6)그녀는 학생들에게 몇 가지 스텝을 가르쳤고 얼마 동안 계속해서 춤을 추었다. (7)시간과 그녀를 둘러싼 사람들을 인식하지 못한 채, (c)그녀(Melanie)는 그녀만의 작은 춤의 세계에 빠져 있었다.

(C)

(1)바로 그때, 발레 강사가 교실로 들어와 Melanie의 놀라운 기술을 보고 놀랐다. (2)"대단한 공연이에요!"라고 강사가 자신의 눈을 반짝이며 말했다. (3)Melanie는 자신 앞에 서 있는 강사를 보고 당황했다. (4)"죄송해요, 강사님!" 그녀는 말했다. (5)"뭐가요?"라고 강사가 물었다. (6)"당신은 진정한 발레리나입니다!" (7)강사는 Melanie에게 발레 교습소로 (d)그녀(instructor)와 동행하자고 요청했고, Melanie는 이후 결코 무용을 그만두지 않았다. (8)오늘날 그녀는 세계적으로 유명한 발레 무용수이다.

[정답 확인]

04. 주어진 글 (A)에 이어질 내용을 순서에 맞게 배열한 것으로 가장 적절한 것은?

① (B) — (D) — (C)　② (C) — (B) — (D)　③ (C) — (D) — (B)
✔ (D) — (B) — (C)　⑤ (D) — (C) — (B)

05. 밑줄 친 (a) ~ (e) 중에서 가리키는 대상이 나머지 넷과 다른 것은?

① (a)　② (b)　③ (c)　✔ (d)　⑤ (e)

06. 윗글의 내용으로 적절하지 않은 것은?

① 엄마는 Melanie가 발레리나의 열정(enthusiasm)을 가지고 춤추는 것을 보았다.
② Melanie는 학생들에게 스텝(steps)을 가르쳤다.
③ Melanie는 세계적으로 유명한(world-renowned) 발레 댄서이다.
④ Melanie는 지역 댄스 학원에 엄마와 동행했다(accompany).
✔ Mr. Edler는 Melanie의 춤에 ~~관심을(be interested in) 보였다~~. 관심이 없었다

[중요 어휘]

□ **flawless**	형용사 흠이 없는
□ **enthusiasm**	명사 열정
□ **polish**	동사 연마하다, 윤을 내다
□ **accompany**	동사 동행하다, 동반하다
□ **institute**	명사 학원, 기관
□ **admit**	동사 받아들이다, 들어가게 하다
□ **aspire**	동사 열망하다
□ **ego**	명사 자부심, 자아
□ **roam**	동사 배회하다
□ **unaware of**	~을 인식하지 못하는
□ **be lost in**	~에 빠져 있다
□ **sparkle**	명사 반짝임 / 동사 반짝이다
□ **world-renowned**	세계적으로 유명한

07~09

2022년 11월 43~45번
(정답률 85% | 75% | 90%)

정답 ⑤ | ⑤ | ④

[지문 끊어 읽기]　팀을 우승으로 이끈 마지막 슛

(A-1) The basketball felt / like it belonged in Chanel's hands /
농구공은 느껴졌다 / 마치 그것이 Chanel의 손에 속한 것처럼 /
even though it was only a practice game.
단지 연습 경기이기는 했지만

(A-2) She decided not to pass the ball / to her twin sister, Vasha.
그녀는 공을 패스하지 않기로 결심했다 / 그녀의 쌍둥이 자매인 Vasha에게

(A-3) Instead, / (a)she stopped, jumped, /
대신에 / (a)그녀(Chanel)는 멈추고, 점프하였다 /
and shot the ball toward the basket, /
그리고 공을 골대 쪽으로 던졌다 /
but it bounced off the backboard.
그러나 그것은 백보드를 맞고 튕겨 나갔다

(A-4) Chanel could see / that her teammates were disappointed. 09번-① 정답 단서 연습 경기 중에 Chanel이 던진 공이 백보드를 맞고 튕겨 나가자 팀원들이 실망한 모습을 보였음.
Chanel은 볼 수 있었다 / 그녀의 팀원들이 실망하는 것을

(A-5) The other team got the ball /
상대 팀이 공을 가져갔다 /
and soon scored, / [ending the game]. [ ]: 분사구문-연속동작
그리고 이내 득점했다 / 경기가 끝났다

* (A) 요약: 연습 경기에서 Chanel의 실점으로 팀원들이 실망한 모습을 보였고 경기에서 지게 됨.

(D-1) When the practice game ended, / 07번 정답 단서 앞서 (A-5)에서 경기가 끝났음이 나타남.
연습 경기가 끝났을 때 /
Chanel felt her eyes sting with tears.
5형식V　O　O·C(동사원형)
Chanel은 그녀의 눈이 눈물로 따끔거리는 것을 느꼈다

(D-2) "It's okay," / Vasha said in a comforting voice.
"괜찮아." / Vasha가 위로하는 목소리로 말했다

(D-3) Chanel appreciated her, /
Chanel은 그녀에게 고마움을 느꼈다 /
but Vasha wasn't making her feel any better.
사역V　O　O·C(동사원형)
하지만 Vasha가 그녀의 기분을 더 나아지게 해 주지는 않았다

(D-4) Vasha wanted to help her twin improve.
준사역V　O　O·C(동사원형/to부정사)
Vasha는 그녀의 쌍둥이가 좋아지도록 돕고 싶었다

(D-5) She invited her twin to practice with (e)her. 08번 정답 단서 여기서 연습하기를 권유한 사람은 Vasha로, Vasha가 Chanel에게 연습을 권유함.
invite+O+O·C: ~에게 …하도록 권유하다
그녀는 그녀의 쌍둥이에게 (e)그녀(Vasha)와 함께 연습하자고 권유했다

(D-6) After school, / they got their basketball /
V①
방과 후에 / 그들은 그들의 농구공을 가졌다 /
and started practicing their basketball shots. 09번-⑤ 정답 단서 방과 후에 Vasha와 Chanel은 농구 슛을 연습하기 시작함.
V②
그리고 그들의 농구 슛을 연습하기 시작했다

* (D) 요약: 연습 경기 후 기분이 좋지 않았던 Chanel에게 쌍둥이 자매인 Vasha의 권유로 방과 후에 같이 연습을 하게 됨.

(C-1) At first, / Chanel did not like practicing with Vasha / 07번 정답 단서 (D)의 내용을 통해 Chanel과 Vasha가 연습을 시작하게 되었음을 알 수 있음.
처음에 / Chanel은 Vasha와 연습하는 것을 좋아하지 않았다 /
because every time Vasha shot the ball, / it went in.
every time S+V: S가 V할 때마다
Vasha가 슛을 할 때마다 ~이기 때문이다 / 그것이 들어갔다

정답과 해설
18 장문의 이해 - 복합지문

(C-2) But whenever it was Chanel's turn, / she missed.
~할 때마다
하지만 Chanel의 차례마다 / 그녀는 슛을 넣지 못했다

(C-3) (c)She got frustrated / at not making a shot.
동명사의 부정형
(c)그녀(Chanel)는 좌절했다 / 슛을 넣지 못한 것에

(C-4) "Don't give up!"/ Vasha shouted / after each missed shot.
"포기하지 마!" / Vasha가 외쳤다 / 각각의 실패한 슛 후에

(C-5) After twelve misses in a row, / her thirteenth shot went in /
12번의 연이은 실패 후 / 그녀의 13번째 슛이 들어갔다 / **09번-④ 정답 단서** Vasha와의 슛 연습에서 Chanel의 12번째 연이은 실패 후에 13번째에 슛이 들어감.
and she screamed, / "I finally did it!"
그리고 그녀는 외쳤다 / "마침내 내가 해냈어!"

(C-6) Her twin said, / "I knew (d)you could! /
그녀의 쌍둥이가 말했다 / 나는 (d)네(Chanel)가 해낼 줄 알았어 /
Now let's keep practicing!"
자 계속 연습하자 keep V-ing: 계속해서 ~하다

* (C) 요약: 슛이 들어가지 않아 좌절하려던 찰나에 Chanel이 13번째로 던진 슛이 마침내 들어갔음.

(B-1) The next day, / Chanel played in the championship game /
다음날 / Chanel은 챔피언십 경기에 출전했다 /
against a rival school. **09번-② 정답 단서** 라이벌 학교와의 챔피언십 경기에 출전하게 됨.
라이벌 학교와의

(B-2) It was an intense game / and the score was tied /
그것은 치열한 경기였다 / 그리고 점수는 동점이었다 /
when Chanel was passed the ball by Vasha, /
Chanel이 Vasha에게 공을 패스 받았을 때 /
with ten seconds left in the game.
경기에서 10초가 남은 상황에서

(B-3) (b)She leaped into the air / and shot the ball.
(b)그녀(Chanel)는 공중으로 뛰어올랐다 / 그리고 공을 던졌다

(B-4) It went straight into the basket!
그것은 곧바로 골대 안으로 들어갔다

(B-5) Chanel's last shot had made her team the champions. **09번-③ 정답 단서** Chanel이 던진 마지막 슛 덕분에 팀을 우승시킬 수 있었음.
5형식V O O·C(명사)
Chanel의 마지막 슛은 그녀의 팀을 우승팀으로 만들었다

(B-6) Vasha and all her other teammates cheered for her.
Vasha와 모든 다른 팀원들은 그녀에게 환호를 보냈다

* (B) 요약: 라이벌 학교와의 챔피언십 경기에서 Chanel이 던진 마지막 슛 덕분에 그녀의 팀이 우승을 하게 됨.

[전문 해석]

(A)

(1)단지 연습 경기이기는 했지만 농구공은 마치 Chanel의 손에 속한 것처럼 느껴졌다. (2)그녀는 그녀의 쌍둥이 자매인 Vasha에게 공을 패스하지 않기로 결심했다. (3)대신에 (a)그녀(Chanel)는 멈추고, 점프하여 공을 골대 쪽으로 던졌지만, 그것은 백보드를 맞고 튕겨 나갔다. (4)Chanel은 팀원들이 실망하는 것을 볼 수 있었다. (5)상대 팀이 공을 가져가서 이내 득점했고 경기가 끝났다.

(D)

(1)연습 경기가 끝났을 때, Chanel은 그녀의 눈이 눈물로 따끔거리는 것을 느꼈다. (2)"괜찮아." Vasha가 위로하는 목소리로 말했다. (3)Chanel은 그녀에게 고마움을 느꼈지만, Vasha가 그녀의 기분을 더 나아지게 해 주지는 않았다. (4)Vasha는 그녀의 쌍둥이가 좋아지도록 돕고 싶었다. (5)그녀는 그녀의 쌍둥이에게 (e)그녀(Vasha)와 함께 연습하자고 권유했다. (6)방과 후에 그들은 그들의 농구공을 가지고 그들의 농구 슛을 연습하기 시작했다.

(C)

(1)처음에 Chanel은 Vasha가 슛을 할 때마다 그것이 들어갔기 때문에 Vasha와 연습하는 것을 좋아하지 않았다. (2)하지만 Chanel의 차례마다 그녀는 슛을 넣지 못했다. (3)(c)그녀(Chanel)는 슛을 넣지 못한 것에 좌절했다. (4)"포기하지 마!" 각각의 슛이 실패한 후에 Vasha가 외쳤다. (5)12번의 연이은 실패 후, 그녀의 13번째 슛이 들어갔고, 그녀는 "마침내 내가 해냈어!"라고 외쳤다. (6)그녀의 쌍둥이가 "나는 (d)네(Chanel)가 해낼 줄 알았어! 자 계속 연습하자!"라고 말했다.

(B)

(1)다음날, Chanel은 라이벌 학교와의 챔피언십 경기에 출전했다. (2)그것은 치열한 경기였고 Chanel이 경기에서 10초가 남은 상황에서 Vasha에게 공을 패스 받았을 때 점수는 동점이었다. (3)(b)그녀(Chanel)는 공중으로 뛰어올라 공을 던졌다. (4)그것은 곧바로 골대 안으로 들어갔다! (5)Chanel의 마지막 슛은 그녀의 팀을 우승팀으로 만들었다. (6)Vasha와 모든 다른 팀원들은 그녀에게 환호를 보냈다.

[정답 확인]

07. 주어진 글 (A)에 이어질 내용을 순서에 맞게 배열한 것으로 가장 적절한 것은?

① (B) — (D) — (C) ② (C) — (B) — (D) ③ (C) — (D) — (B)
④ (D) — (B) — (C) ✔ (D) — (C) — (B)

08. 밑줄 친 (a) ~ (e) 중에서 가리키는 대상이 나머지 넷과 다른 것은?

① (a) ② (b) ③ (c) ④ (d) ✔ (e)

09. 윗글의 Chanel에 관한 내용으로 적절하지 않은 것은?

① 연습 경기 중에 팀원들의 실망한(disappointed) 모습을 보았다. 문장(A-4)
② 라이벌(rival) 학교와의 챔피언십 경기에 출전했다. 문장(B-1)
③ 팀을 우승시키는 마지막 슛을 성공했다. 문장(B-5)
✔ 슛 연습에서 연이은(in a row) 실패 후에 ~~12~~ 13번째 슛이 들어갔다. 문장(C-5)
⑤ 방과 후에 농구 슛을 연습하기 시작했다. 문장(D-6)

[중요 어휘]

☐ bounce	동사 튀다
☐ backboard	명사 (농구 골대의) 백보드
☐ sting	동사 따끔거리다, 쏘다, 찌르다
☐ frustrated	형용사 좌절감을 느끼는
☐ scream	동사 외치다, 소리치다
☐ intense	형용사 치열한, 극심한
☐ tie	동사 동점이 되다, 묶다
☐ leap	동사 뛰어오르다
☐ cheer	동사 환호하다

10~12

2022년 6월 43~45번
(정답률 85% | 80% | 85%)

정답 ④ | ⑤ | ③

[지문 끊어 읽기] 소년이 난기류에도 침착할 수 있었던 이유

(A-1) A businessman boarded a flight.
한 사업가가 비행기에 탑승했다

(A-2) Arriving at his seat, / he greeted his travel companions: /
분사구문
그의 자리에 도착한 후 / 그는 여행 동반자들과 인사를 나누었다 /
a middle-aged woman sitting at the window, /
창가에 앉아 있는 중년 여성 /
and a little boy sitting in the aisle seat.
그리고 통로 쪽 좌석에 앉아 있는 어린 소년

(A-3) After putting his bag in the overhead bin, /
가방을 머리 위 짐칸에 넣은 후 /
he took his place between them. **12번-① 정답 단서** 사업가는 중년 여성과 어린 소년 사이에 앉음.
그는 그들 사이에 앉았다

(A-4) After the flight took off, /
비행기가 이륙한 후 /
he began a conversation with the little boy. **10번 정답 단서** 사업가가 옆에 앉은 어린 소년과 대화를 함.
그는 어린 소년과 대화를 시작했다

(A-5) He appeared / to be about the same age as (a)his son /
V①
그는 보였다 / (a)그(businessman)의 아들과 나이가 비슷하게 /
and was busy with a coloring book.
V②
그리고 색칠 공부 책을 칠하느라 바빴다

* (A) 요약: 사업가가 비행기 옆 좌석에 앉은 소년과 대화를 함.

(D-1) He asked the boy a few usual questions, / **10번 정답 단서** 옆에 앉은 어린 소년과 대화하며 몇 가지 질문을 함.
4형식V I·O D·O
그는 소년에게 몇 가지 일상적인 질문을 했다 /
such as his age, his hobbies, / as well as his favorite animal.
그의 나이, 취미와 같은 / 좋아하는 동물뿐만 아니라

힌트 'B as well as A'는 'A뿐만 아니라 B도'라는 의미로, 'not only A but (also) B'로 바꾸어 쓸 수 있음. 여기서 A는 'his favorite animal', B는 'his age, his hobbies'에 해당함.

(D-2) He found it strange / (O(=형식상의 목적어), 5형식V, O·C)
그는 이상하다고 생각했다 /
[that such a young boy would be traveling alone], / [ ]: 내용상의 목적어
그런 어린 소년이 혼자 여행하는 것이 /
so he decided to keep an eye on (e)him /
그래서 그는 (e)그(a little boy)를 지켜보기로 했다 /
to make sure he was okay. 11번 정답 단서 혼자 여행하는 소년이 괜찮은지를 확인하기 위해 사업가가 소년을 지켜보기로 함.
부사적 용법(목적)
그가 괜찮은지 확인하기 위해

(D-3) About an hour into the flight, /
비행 시작 1시간여 만에 /
the plane suddenly began experiencing turbulence. 10번 정답 단서 비행기가 난기류를 타기 시작함.
비행기가 갑자기 난기류를 타기 시작했다

(D-4) The pilot told everyone / to fasten their seat belts / (5형식V, O, O·C①)
조종사는 모두에게 말했다 / 그들의 안전벨트를 매라고 / 12번-⑤ 정답 단서 조종사는 사람들에게 안전벨트를 매고 침착하라고 함.
and remain calm, / as they had encountered rough weather. (O·C②(to 생략), 접속사(이유))
그리고 침착하라고 / 그들이 악천후를 만났기 때문에

* (D) 요약: 사업가는 소년이 혼자 여행하는 것에 이상함을 느꼈고, 비행기는 난기류를 만남.

(B-1) As the plane rose and fell several times, / people got nervous /
접속사(~하자)
비행기가 여러 차례 오르락내리락하자 / 사람들은 긴장했다 /
and sat up in their seats. 10번·12번-② 정답 단서 난기류를 만난 비행기가 여러 번 흔들리자 사람들이 긴장함.
그리고 그들의 자리에 똑바로 앉았다

(B-2) The man was also nervous / and grabbing (b)his seat /
그 남자도 긴장했다 / 그리고 (b)그(businessman)의 좌석을 잡고 있었다 /
as tightly as he could.
그가 할 수 있는 만큼 최대한 꽉
힌트 '최대한 ~한/하게, 가능한 한 ~한/하게'라는 뜻의 'as 형용사/부사 as 주어 can/could' 구문으로 'as 형용사/부사 as possible'과 의미가 동일함. 여기서는 'as tightly as possible'로 바꿔 쓸 수 있음.

(B-3) Meanwhile, / the little boy was sitting quietly / beside (c)him.
그러는 동안에도 / 어린 소년은 조용히 앉아 있었다 / (c)그(businessman)의 옆에

(B-4) His coloring book and crayons were put away neatly /
그의 색칠 공부 책과 크레용은 가지런히 치워져 있었다 /
in the seat pocket in front of him, / 12번-③ 정답 단서 소년은 색칠 공부 책과 크레용을 앞 좌석 주머니에 넣었음.
그의 앞 좌석 주머니에 /
and his hands were calmly resting / on his legs.
그리고 그의 손은 차분히 놓여 있었다 / 그의 다리에

(B-5) Incredibly, / he didn't seem worried at all. (2형식V, S·C)
놀랍게도 / 그는 전혀 걱정하지 않는 것처럼 보였다

* (B) 요약: 비행기가 많이 흔들려 모두 불안해했지만 소년은 그렇지 않았음.

(C-1) Then, / suddenly, / the turbulence ended. 10번 정답 단서 난기류가 끝이 남.
그러다가 / 갑자기 / 난기류가 끝이 났다

(C-2) The pilot apologized for the bumpy ride / and announced / (V①, V②)
조종사는 험난한 비행에 대해 사과했다 / 그리고 알렸다 /
[that they would be landing soon]. [ ]: announced의 목적어절
명사절 접속사
그들이 곧 착륙할 것이라고

(C-3) As the plane began its descent, /
접속사(~할 때)
비행기가 하강하기 시작했을 때 /
힌트 부정어인 'no'나 'never'와 비교급이 함께 쓰이면 최상급과 같은 의미가 됨. 따라서 이 표현은 'I have met the bravest person'으로도 바꾸어 쓸 수 있음.
the man said to the little boy, / "You are just a little boy, /
그 남자는 어린 소년에게 말했다 / 너는 어린 소년일 뿐이다 /
but (d)I have never met a braver person / in all my life!
현재완료(경험)
하지만 (d)나(businessman)는 더 용감한 사람을 만난 적이 없었다 / 평생 동안

(C-4) Tell me, / how is it / that you remained so calm / (2형식V, S·C)
말해 주겠니 / 어떻게 / 네가 그렇게 침착하게 있었는지 /
while all of us adults were so afraid?"
어른들 모두가 두려워하는데
힌트 'How is that + S + V?'는 '어떻게/어째서 ~한 거야?, 어떻게/어째서 ~인가?'라고 해석하면 됨.

(C-5) Looking him in the eyes, / he said, / "My father is the pilot, /
분사구문(동시동작)
그의 눈을 바라보며 / 그는 말했다 / 저희 아버지께서 조종사세요 /
12번-④ 정답 단서 소년의 아버지가 조종사임.
and he's taking me home."
그리고 저를 집으로 데려가고 있는 중이에요

* (C) 요약: 사업가가 소년에게 어떻게 그렇게 침착하게 있었는지 물었고 소년이 답함.

[전문 해석]

(A)

(1)한 사업가가 비행기에 탑승했다. (2)그의 자리에 도착한 후, 그는 여행 동반자들인 창가에 앉아 있는 중년 여성과 통로 쪽 좌석에 앉아 있는 어린 소년과 인사를 나누었다. (3)가방을 머리 위 짐칸에 넣은 후, 그는 그들 사이에 앉았다. (4)비행기가 이륙한 후, 그는 어린 소년과 대화를 시작했다. (5)그는 (a)그(businessman)의 아들과 나이가 비슷하게 보였고 색칠 공부 책을 칠하느라 바빴다.

(D)

(1)그는 소년에게 좋아하는 동물뿐만 아니라 그의 나이, 취미와 같은 몇 가지 일상적인 질문을 했다. (2)그는 그런 어린 소년이 혼자 여행하는 것이 이상하다고 생각해서 그가 괜찮은지 확인하기 위해 (e)그(a little boy)를 지켜보기로 했다. (3)비행 시작 1시간여 만에 비행기가 갑자기 난기류를 타기 시작했다. (4)조종사는 악천후를 만났기 때문에, 안전벨트를 매고 침착하라고 모든 사람들에게 말했다.

(B)

(1)비행기가 여러 차례 오르락내리락하자 사람들은 긴장해 자리에 똑바로 앉았다. (2)그 남자도 긴장해서 (b)그(businessman)의 좌석을 최대한 꽉 잡고 있었다. (3)그러는 동안에도, 어린 소년은 조용히 (c)그(businessman)의 옆에 앉아 있었다. (4)그의 색칠 공부 책과 크레용은 앞 좌석 주머니에 가지런히 치워져 있었고, 그의 손은 차분히 다리에 놓여 있었다. (5)놀랍게도, 그는 전혀 걱정하지 않는 것처럼 보였다.

(C)

(1)그러다가, 갑자기, 난기류가 끝이 났다. (2)조종사는 험난한 비행에 대해 사과했고 그들이 곧 착륙할 것이라고 알렸다. (3)비행기가 하강하기 시작했을 때, 그 남자는 어린 소년에게 말했다. "너는 어린 소년일 뿐이지만, (d)나(businessman)는 평생 동안 더 용감한 사람을 만난 적이 없어! (4)어른들 모두가 두려워하는데 어떻게 그렇게 침착하게 있었는지 말해 주겠니?" (5)그의 눈을 바라보며, 그는 "저희 아버지께서 조종사신데, 아버지께서 저를 집으로 데려가고 있는 중이에요."라고 말했다.

[정답 확인]

10. 주어진 글 (A)에 이어질 내용을 순서에 맞게 배열한 것으로 가장 적절한 것은?

① (B) — (D) — (C) ② (C) — (B) — (D) ③ (C) — (D) — (B)
✔④ (D) — (B) — (C) ⑤ (D) — (C) — (B)

11. 밑줄 친 (a) ~ (e) 중에서 가리키는 대상이 나머지 넷과 다른 것은?

① (a) ② (b) ③ (c) ④ (d) ✔⑤ (e)

12. 윗글의 내용으로 적절하지 않은 것은?

① 사업가는 중년 여성과 소년 사이에 앉았다. 문장(A-3)
② 비행기가 오르락내리락하자 사람들은 긴장했다(get nervous). 문장(B-1)
✔③ 소년은 색칠 공부 책과 크레용을 ~~가방에~~ (앞 좌석 주머니에) 넣었다. 문장(B-4)
④ 소년은 자신의 아버지가 조종사(pilot)라고 말했다. 문장(C-5)
⑤ 조종사는 사람들에게 안전벨트를 매고(fasten one's seatbelt) 침착하라고 말했다. 문장(D-4)

[중요 어휘]

☐ **board**	동사 (비행기·배·차 등에) 탑승하다
☐ **flight**	명사 비행기, 항공편
☐ **greet**	동사 ~와 인사를 나누다, 환영하다
☐ **companion**	명사 동반자, 동행, 친구
☐ **aisle seat**	통로 쪽 좌석
☐ **overhead bin**	머리 위 짐칸
☐ **take off**	이륙하다
☐ **keep an eye on**	~를 지켜보다[주시하다]
☐ **turbulence**	명사 난기류, 격동
☐ **fasten one's seatbelt**	안전벨트를 매다
☐ **rough weather**	악천후
☐ **bumpy**	형용사 험난한, 울퉁불퉁한
☐ **land**	동사 착륙하다, 내려앉다
☐ **descent**	명사 하강, 내려오기

문제편 p.274

13~15 2021년 3월 43~45번 (정답률 80% | 80% | 80%)

핵심 구두 만드는 사람에게 일어난 일과 그로 인해 어떻게 그의 행동 양상이 변화하는지 확인해야 함.

정답 ⑤ | ④ | ②

[지문 끊어 읽기] 구두 만드는 사람에게 일어난 일

(A-1) Once upon a time / there lived a poor but cheerful shoemaker.
옛날 옛적에 / 가난하지만 쾌활한 구두 만드는 사람이 살았다

(A-2) He was so happy, he sang all day long.
그는 너무 행복해서 하루 종일 노래를 불렀다

(A-3) The children loved to stand around his window / to listen to (a)him.
부사적 용법(목적)
아이들은 그의 창문에 둘러서는 것을 좋아했다 / (a)그(shoemaker)가 노래하는 것을 듣기 위해

(A-4) Next door to the shoemaker / lived a rich man.
부사구 / 주어-동사 도치
구두 만드는 사람 옆집에는 / 부자가 살았다

(A-5) He used to sit up all night / to count his gold.
부사적 용법(목적)
그는 밤을 새곤 했다 / 자신의 금화를 세기 위해

(A-6) In the morning, he went to bed, / but he could not sleep /
아침에 그는 잠자리에 들었다 / 하지만 그는 잠을 잘 수 없었다 /
because of the sound of the shoemaker's singing. 13번·14번 정답 단서
구두 만드는 사람의 노랫소리 때문에

* (A) 요약: 노래 부르는 걸 좋아하는 구두 만드는 사람과 그 옆집에는 부자가 살았음.

(D-1) One day, / (d)he thought of a way of stopping the singing. 13번 정답 단서
어느 날 / (d)그(rich man)는 그 노래를 멈추는 방법을 생각해냈다

(D-2) He wrote a letter to the shoemaker / asking him to visit. 14번 정답 단서
그는 구두 만드는 사람에게 편지를 써 보냈다 / 방문해 달라고 요청하는

(D-3) The shoemaker came at once, / and to his surprise /
구두 만드는 사람은 즉시 왔다 / 그리고 놀랍게도 /
the rich man gave him a bag of gold.
부자는 그에게 금화가 든 가방을 주었다

(D-4) When he got home again, / the shoemaker opened the bag.
그가 집에 다시 돌아왔을 때 / 구두 만드는 사람은 그 가방을 열었다

(D-5) (e)He had never seen so much gold before!
과거완료
(e)그(shoemaker)는 그때까지 그렇게 많은 금화를 본 적이 없었다

힌트 옛날 이야기의 특성상 이야기가 진행되고 있는 시점이 이미 과거이기 때문에, 더 과거의 일을 나타내는 완료시제로는 과거완료가 쓰였음.

(D-6) When he sat down at his bench /
그가 의자에 앉았을 때 /
and began, carefully, to count it, /
그리고 조심스럽게 그것을 세기 시작했다 /
the children watched through the window. 13번 정답 단서
아이들이 창문을 통해서 지켜보았다

* (D) 요약: 구두 만드는 사람이 부자로부터 금화가 든 가방을 받음.

(C-1) There was so much there /
거기엔 금화가 너무 많아서 /
that the shoemaker was afraid / to let it out of his sight. 13번 정답 단서
so ~ that 구문: 너무 ~해서 …하다
구두 만드는 사람은 겁났다 / 그것을 그의 시야에서 벗어나는 곳에 두기가

(C-2) So he took it to bed with him.
그래서 그는 그것을 그와 함께 잠자리에 가져갔다

(C-3) But he could not sleep / for worrying about it.
그러나 그는 잠을 잘 수 없었다 / 그것에 대한 걱정으로

(C-4) Very early in the morning, /
매우 이른 아침에 /
he got up and brought his gold down from the bedroom.
그는 일어나서 금화를 침실에서 가지고 내려왔다

(C-5) He had decided to hide it / up the chimney instead.
과거완료
그는 그것을 숨기기로 결정했다 / 대신 굴뚝에

(C-6) But he was still uneasy, / and in a little while /
그러나 그는 여전히 불안했다 / 그리고 잠시 후에 /
he dug a hole in the garden / and buried his bag of gold in it.
그는 정원에 구멍을 팠다 / 그리고 그 안에 금화가 든 가방을 묻었다

(C-7) It was no use trying to work.
일을 해 보려고 해도 소용없었다

힌트 'It is no use V-ing'는 '~해도 소용없다'는 관용적인 표현임. use 다음에 동명사가 온다는 것에 유의해야 함.

(C-8) (c)He was too worried about the safety of his gold.
(c)그(shoemaker)는 자신의 금화의 안전이 너무나 걱정되었다

(C-9) And as for singing, / he was too miserable to utter a note.
too ~ to 구문: 너무 ~해서 …할 수 없다
그리고 노래에 관해서라면 / 그는 너무 불행해서 한 음도 낼 수 없었다

* (C) 요약: 구두 만드는 사람은 금화의 안전에 극도로 불안해짐.

(B-1) He could not sleep, or work, or sing — / and, worst of all, /
그는 잠을 잘 수도, 일을 할 수도, 노래를 부를 수도 없었다 / 그리고 최악은 /
the children no longer came to see (b)him.
아이들이 더 이상 (b)그(shoemaker)를 보러 오지 않았다

(B-2) At last, /
마침내 /
the shoemaker felt so unhappy that he seized his bag of gold /
so ~ that 구문
구두 만드는 사람은 너무 불행해져서 그의 금화가 든 가방을 움켜쥐었다 /
and ran next door to the rich man.
그리고 옆집 부자에게 달려갔다.

(B-3) "Please take back your gold," he said.
"제발 당신의 금화를 다시 가져가세요."라고 그가 말했다

(B-4) "The worry of it is making me ill, /
그것에 대한 걱정이 저를 아프게 하고 있어요 /
and I have lost all of my friends.
그리고 저는 제 친구들을 모두 잃었어요

(B-5) I would rather be a poor shoemaker, as I was before." 15번 정답 단서
저는 차라리 예전처럼 가난한 구두 만드는 사람이 되겠어요

(B-6) And so the shoemaker was happy again /
그래서 구두 만드는 사람은 다시 행복해졌고 /
and sang all day at his work.
일을 하면서 하루 종일 노래를 불렀다

* (B) 요약: 구두 만드는 사람은 부자에게 금화를 돌려주고 다시 행복하게 지낼 수 있었음.

[전문 해석]

(A)

(1)옛날 옛적에 가난하지만 쾌활한 구두 만드는 사람이 살았다. (2)그는 너무 행복해서, 하루 종일 노래를 불렀다. (3)아이들은 (a)그(shoemaker)가 노래하는 것을 듣기 위해 그의 창문에 둘러서는 것을 좋아했다. (4)구두 만드는 사람 옆집에는 부자가 살았다. (5)그는 자신의 금화를 세기 위해 밤을 새곤 했다. (6)아침에, 그는 잠자리에 들었지만, 구두 만드는 사람의 노랫소리 때문에 잠을 잘 수 없었다.

(D)

(1)어느 날, (d)그(rich man)는 그 노래를 멈추는 방법을 생각해냈다. (2)그는 구두 만드는 사람에게 방문해 달라고 요청하는 편지를 써 보냈다. (3)구두 만드는 사람은 즉시 왔고, 놀랍게도 부자는 그에게 금화가 든 가방을 주었다. (4)집에 다시 돌아왔을 때, 구두 만드는 사람은 그 가방을 열었다. (5)(e)그(shoemaker)는 그때까지 그렇게 많은 금화를 본 적이 없었다! (6)그가 의자에 앉아 조심스럽게 그것을 세기 시작했을 때, 아이들이 창문을 통해서 지켜보았다.

(C)

(1)거기엔 금화가 너무 많아서 구두 만드는 사람은 그것을 그의 시야에서 벗어나는 곳에 두기가 겁났다. (2)그래서 그는 그것을 그와 함께 잠자리에 가져갔다. (3)그러나 그는 그것에 대한 걱정으로 잠을 잘 수 없었다. (4)매우 이른 아침에, 그는 일어나서 금화를 침실에서 가지고 내려왔다. (5)그는 그것을 대신 굴뚝에 숨기기로 결정했다. (6)그러나 그는 여전히 불안했고, 잠시 후에 그는 정원에 구멍을 파고 그 안에 금화가 든 가방을 묻었다. (7)일을 해 보려고 해도 소용없었다. (8)(c)그(shoemaker)는 자신의 금화의 안전이 너무나 걱정되었다. (9)그리고 노래에 관해서라면, 그는 너무 불행해서 한 음도 낼 수 없었다.

(B)

(1)그는 잠을 잘 수도, 일을 할 수도, 노래를 부를 수도 없었고, 최악은, 아이들이 더 이상 (b)그(shoemaker)를 보러 오지 않았다(는 것이다). (2)마침내, 구두 만드는 사람은 너무 불행해져서 그의 금화가 든 가방을 움켜쥐고 옆집 부자에게 달려갔다. (3)"제발 당신의 금화를 다시 가져가세요."라고 그가 말했다. (4)"그것에 대한 걱정이 저를 아프게 하고 있고, 저는 제 친구들을 모두 잃었어요. (5)저는 차라리 예전처럼 가난한 구두 만드는 사람이 되겠어요." (6)그래서 구두 만드는 사람은 다시 행복해졌고 일을 하면서 하루 종일 노래를 불렀다.

[정답 확인]

13. 주어진 글 (A)에 이어질 내용을 순서에 맞게 배열한 것으로 가장 적절한 것은?

① (B) — (D) — (C)　② (C) — (B) — (D)　③ (C) — (D) — (B)
④ (D) — (B) — (C)　✔(D) — (C) — (B)

14. 밑줄 친 (a) ~ (e) 중에서 가리키는 대상이 나머지 넷과 다른 것은?

① (a)　② (b)　③ (c)　✔(d)　⑤ (e)

15. 윗글의 shoemaker에 관한 내용으로 적절하지 않은 것은?

① 그의 노래로 인해 옆집 사람이 잠을 잘 수 없었다(could not sleep).
✔ 예전처럼(as I was before) 가난하게 ~~살고 싶지 않다고~~ 말했다. (살겠다고)
③ 정원에 구멍을 파고(dug a hole in the garden) 금화가 든 가방을 묻었다.
④ 부자가 보낸 편지에 즉시(at once) 그를 만나러 갔다.
⑤ 금화를 셀(count the gold) 때 아이들이 그 모습을 봤다.

[문제 풀이]

14. (d)에 나오는 he는 해당 문장에서는 노래를 멈추게 하는 방법을 깨닫고, 다음 문장에서 구두 만드는 사람에게 편지를 쓰는 사람이다. 노래를 멈출 방법을 생각해 내고 구두를 만드는 사람에게 편지를 쓸 사람은 그의 노래 때문에 잠을 잘 수 없었던 옆집 부자(rich man)이다. 그 외의 보기에서 나오는 대상은 모두 구두 만드는 사람을 지칭한다. 따라서 정답은 ④이다.

[중요 어휘]

□ at once	즉시, 당장
□ out of one's sight	~의 시야에서 벗어나는, ~에게 보이지 않는 곳에
□ chimney	명사 굴뚝
□ uneasy	형용사 불안한
□ in a little while	잠시 후에
□ as for	~에 관해서라면
□ miserable	형용사 몹시 불행한, 비참한
□ utter	동사 (목소리를) 내다, 말하다
□ seize	동사 움켜쥐다

16~18

2022년 3월 43~45번
(정답률 80% | 75% | 85%)

정답 ② | ③ | ⑤

[지문 끊어 읽기]　웃음의 전염성과 John의 결심

(A-1) John was a sensitive boy.
John은 민감한 소년이었다

(A-2) Even his hair was ticklish.
심지어 그의 머리카락도 간지럼을 탔다

힌트 'would+동사원형'은 '~하곤 했다'라는 뜻으로 현재는 하지 않는 과거의 습관을 나타냄. 'used to+동사원형' 또한 '~하곤 했다'라는 뜻인데 현재는 하지 않는 과거의 습관뿐만 아니라 과거의 상태를 나타냄.

(A-3) When breeze touched his hair / he would burst out laughing.
산들바람이 그의 머리카락에 닿으면 / 그는 웃음을 터뜨리곤 했다

(A-4) And when this ticklish laughter started, /
그리고 간지럼으로 인한 웃음이 시작되면 /
no one could make him stop.
(5형식V O O·C)
아무도 그를 멈추게 할 수 없었다

(A-5) John's laughter was so contagious /
(so 형용사/부사 that S V: 너무 ~해서 …하다)
John의 웃음은 전염성이 매우 강해서 /
that when John started feeling ticklish, /
John이 간지럼을 타기 시작하면 /
everyone ended up in endless laughter.
모두가 결국 끝없이 웃게 되었다

John은 간지럼을 타지 않으려고 온갖 노력을 했음.

(A-6) He tried everything / to control his ticklishness: / 18번-① 정답 단서
(부사적 용법(목적))
그는 온갖 노력을 했다 / 간지럼을 잘 타는 것을 억제하기 위해 /

힌트 콜론(:) 뒤에 John이 간지럼을 잘 타는 것을 억제하기 위해 시도한 것들의 예시가 나열되어 있음.

wearing a thousand different hats, /
(병렬①)
수없이 많은 다양한 모자를 써 보기도 했다 /
using ultra strong hairsprays, / and shaving his head.
(병렬②　병렬③)
초강력 헤어스프레이를 사용해 보기도 했다 / 그리고 머리를 밀기도 했다

(A-7) But nothing worked.
하지만 아무것도 효과가 없었다

(A-8) One day / he met a clown in the street.
어느 날 / 그는 거리에서 어떤 광대를 만났다

(A-9) The clown was very old / and could hardly walk, /
(V① V②)
그 광대는 매우 늙었다 / 그래서 걸음도 겨우 걸었다 / 16번·17번 정답 단서 울고 있는 John을 본 광대는 그를 격려하러 감.
but when he saw John in tears, / he went to cheer (a)him up.
(부사적 용법(목적))
하지만 그는 John이 울고 있는 것을 보았을 때 / 그는 (a)그(John)를 격려하러 갔다

* (A) 요약: 간지럼을 잘 타는 John은 온갖 노력을 해도 간지럼이 억제가 안 되자 슬퍼했고, 그 모습을 광대가 봄.

(C-1) It didn't take long to make John laugh, /
(5형식V O O·C)
John을 웃게 하는 데 오래 걸리지 않았다 /
and they started to talk. 16번·17번 정답 단서 광대는 울고 있던 John을 웃게 했고, 광대와 John은 대화하기 시작함.
(명사적 용법)
그리고 그들은 이야기를 하기 시작했다

(C-2) John told (c)him / about his ticklish problem.
John은 (c)그(clown)에게 말했다 / 간지럼을 타는 자신의 문제에 관해

(C-3) Then he asked the clown /
(4형식V I·O)
그러고 나서 그는 광대에게 물었다 /　John은 광대에게 늙어서도 어떻게 계속 일할 수 있는지 물었음.
[how such an old man could carry on being a clown]. 18번-③ 정답 단서
([ ]: D·O)
그렇게 늙어서도 어떻게 광대 일을 계속할 수 있는지를

(C-4) "I have no one to replace me," / said the clown, /
"나를 대신할 사람은 없어." / 그 광대는 말했다 /
"and I have a very serious job to do."
"그리고 내게는 해야 할 매우 중요한 일이 있단다."　16번·18번-④ 정답 단서 John과 광대는 여러 병원, 보호 시설, 학교에 감.

(C-5) And then he took John / to many hospitals, shelters, and schools.
그러고 나서 그는 John을 데려갔다 / 여러 병원과 보호 시설, 학교로

* (C) 요약: John은 광대에게 어떻게 늙어서도 계속 일할 수 있는지 물었고, 광대는 이에 대한 답을 하기 위해 John을 병원, 보호 시설, 학교에 데려감.

16번 정답 단서 병원, 보호 시설, 그리고 학교는 아프거나 고아가 되었거나, 또는 심각한 문제를 가진 아이들로 가득했음.

(B-1) All were full of children / who were sick, or orphaned, /
(선행사↑　주격 관계대명사절)
모든 곳은 아이들로 가득했다 / 아프거나 고아가 된 /
children with very serious problems.
매우 심각한 문제를 가진 아이들로

힌트 문장 (C-5)에서 언급된 병원, 보호 시설, 학교 등의 모든 장소들을 지칭하는 말로, 'All' 자체가 대명사로 쓰였음. 복수의 장소들을 가리키므로 동사는 복수형(were)으로 수 일치를 해 주어야 함.

(B-2) But as soon as they saw the clown, /
하지만 그들이 그 광대를 보자마자 /
their faces changed completely / and lit up with a smile.
(병렬①　병렬②)
그들의 표정은 완전히 바뀌었다 / 그리고 미소로 밝아졌다

(B-3) That day was even more special, / because /
그날은 훨씬 더 특별했다 / 왜냐하면 /
in every show / John's contagious laughter would end up making /
(5형식V)
모든 쇼에서 / John의 전염성 있는 웃음이 결국 만들곤 했다 /
the kids laugh a lot. 17번·18번-② 정답 단서 John의 전염성 있는 웃음 때문에 아이들이 많이 웃었음.
(O O·C)
아이들이 많이 웃도록

(B-4) The old clown winked at (b)him / and said /
그 늙은 광대는 (b)그(John)에게 윙크했다 / 그리고 말했다 /
"Now do you see what a serious job it is?
이제 이 일이 얼마나 중요한 일인지 알겠니

힌트 'That's why + 결과' 구문이 쓰임. 'That's because'는 뒤에 이유가 온다는 것에 주의할 것.

(B-5) That's why I can't retire, / even at my age." 16번 정답 단서 광대는 John에게 은퇴할 수 없는 이유를 설명함.
그래서 나는 은퇴할 수가 없단다 / 내 나이에도

* (B) 요약: 광대는 어려운 처지에 놓인 아이들을 웃게 하는 일이 중요하므로 늙어서도 은퇴할 수 없다고 John에게 말함.

16번 정답 단서 광대는 늙어서도 은퇴할 수 없는 이유에 덧붙여 말함.

(D-1) And he added, / "Not everyone could do it.
(=job)
그리고 그는 덧붙여 말했다 / 아무나 그것을 할 수 있는 게 아니란다

(D-2) He or she has to have a special gift / for laughter."
그 사람은 특별한 재능이 있어야 한단다 / 웃음을 위한

정답과 해설
18 장문의 이해 - 복합지문

(D-3) This said, / the wind again set off John's ticklishness / `17번 정답 단서`
이 말을 하자 / 바람이 다시 John의 간지럼을 터지게 했다 /

바람이 불자 John은 간지럼을 타고 웃음이 터짐.

and (d)his laughter.
그리고 (d)그(John)의 웃음을

🔖**힌트** As this was said가 분사구문 This being said로 바뀐 후 being이 생략된 형태임. 참고로 여기서 분사구문의 주어 This는 주절의 주어 the wind와 다르므로 생략할 수 없음.

(D-4) After a while, / John decided / to replace the old clown.
얼마 후 / John은 결심했다 / 그 늙은 광대의 뒤를 잇기로

`17번·18번-⑤ 정답 단서`
John은 광대의 뒤를 잇기로 함.

(D-5) From that day onward, / the fact that John was different /
그날 이후로 / John이 남다르다는 사실은 /

the fact와 동격

actually made (e)him happy, / thanks to his special gift.
실제로는 (e)그(John)를 행복하게 만들었다 / 자신의 특별한 재능 덕분에

5형식V O O-C

* (D) 요약: 광대는 웃음을 주는 일은 특별한 재능이 있는 사람만이 할 수 있다고 John에게 말했고, John은 광대의 뒤를 잇기로 결심함.

[전문 해석]

(A)
(1)John은 민감한 소년이었다. (2)심지어 그의 머리카락도 간지럼을 탔다. (3)산들바람이 그의 머리카락에 닿으면 그는 웃음을 터뜨리곤 했다. (4)그리고 간지럼으로 인한 웃음이 시작되면, 아무도 그를 멈추게 할 수 없었다. (5)John의 웃음은 전염성이 매우 강해서 John이 간지럼을 타기 시작하면 모두가 결국 끝없이 웃게 되었다. (6)그는 간지럼을 잘 타는 것을 억제하기 위해 수없이 많은 다양한 모자를 써 보기도 했고, 초강력 헤어스프레이를 사용해 보기도 하며, 머리를 밀기도 하는 등 온갖 노력을 했다. (7)하지만 아무것도 효과가 없었다. (8)어느 날 그는 거리에서 어떤 광대를 만났다. (9)그 광대는 매우 늙어서 걸음도 겨우 걸었지만 John이 울고 있는 것을 보았을 때 (a)그(John)를 격려하러 갔다.

(C)
(1)John을 웃게 하는 데 오래 걸리지 않았고, 그들은 이야기를 하기 시작했다. (2)John은 (c)그(clown)에게 간지럼을 타는 자신의 문제에 관해 말했다. (3)그러고 나서 그는 광대에게 그렇게 늙어서도 어떻게 광대 일을 계속할 수 있는지 물었다. (4)"나를 대신할 사람은 없고, 내게는 해야 할 매우 중요한 일이 있단다."라고 그 광대는 말했다. (5)그러고 나서 그는 John을 여러 병원과 보호 시설, 학교로 데려갔다.

(B)
(1)모든 곳은 아프거나 고아가 된 아이들, 매우 심각한 문제를 가진 아이들로 가득했다. (2)하지만 그들이 그 광대를 보자마자, 그들의 표정은 완전히 바뀌고 미소로 밝아졌다. (3)그날은 훨씬 더 특별했는데, 모든 쇼에서 John의 전염성 있는 웃음이 결국 아이들을 많이 웃게 만들곤 했기 때문이다. (4)그 늙은 광대는 (b)그(John)에게 윙크하며 말했다. "이제 이 일이 얼마나 중요한 일인지 알겠니? (5)그래서 내 나이에도 나는 은퇴할 수가 없단다."

(D)
(1)그리고 그는 "아무나 그 일을 할 수 있는 게 아니란다. (2)웃음을 위한 특별한 재능이 있어야 한단다."라고 덧붙여 말했다. (3)이 말을 하자 바람이 다시 John의 간지럼과 (d)그(John)의 웃음을 터지게 했다. (4)얼마 후, John은 그 늙은 광대의 뒤를 잇기로 결심했다. (5)그날 이후로 자신의 특별한 재능 덕분에 John이 남다르다는 사실은 실제로는 (e)그(John)를 행복하게 만들었다.

[정답 확인]

16. 주어진 글 (A)에 이어질 내용을 순서에 맞게 배열한 것으로 가장 적절한 것은?
① (B) — (D) — (C) ✔② (C) — (B) — (D) ③ (C) — (D) — (B)
④ (D) — (B) — (C) ⑤ (D) — (C) — (B)

17. 밑줄 친 (a) ~ (e) 중에서 가리키는 대상이 나머지 넷과 다른 것은?
① (a) ② (b) ✔③ (c) ④ (d) ⑤ (e)

18. 윗글의 John에 관한 내용으로 적절하지 않은 것은?
① 간지럼을 타지 않으려고 온갖 시도를 했다(tried everything). 문장(A-6)
② 전염성 있는 웃음(contagious laughter)으로 아이들을 많이 웃게 했다. 문장(B-3)
③ 광대에게 그렇게 늙어서도 어떻게 계속 일할 수 있는지 물었다. 문장(C-3)
④ 광대와 함께 여러 병원과 보호 시설(shelters), 학교에 갔다. 문장(C-5)
✔⑤ 광대의 뒤를 잇지 않기로 했다. 문장(D-4)
잇기로

[중요 어휘]

☐ ticklish	형용사	간지럼을 타는
☐ burst out		터뜨리다, 갑자기 ~하기 시작하다
☐ contagious	형용사	전염성이 있는
☐ end up (in) N/V-ing		결국 ~하게 되다

☐ control	동사	억제하다, 조절하다
☐ shave	동사	밀다
☐ clown	명사	광대
☐ carry on N/V-ing		~을 계속하다
☐ replace	동사	~을 대신하다, ~의 뒤를 잇다
☐ shelter	명사	보호 시설, 피난처
☐ orphan	동사	고아가 되게 하다
☐ light up		밝아지다, 환해지다 (light-lighted/lit-lighted/lit)
☐ retire	동사	은퇴하다
☐ set A off		A를 터지게 하다

🔖**힌트** set off는 구동사로, 일반적으로 동사의 목적어 자리는 구동사 바로 뒤에 위치함. 그러나 전치사 뒤에 목적어가 위치하는 것도 허용함. 따라서 문장 (D-3)의 경우 John's ticklishness가 off 뒤에 위치하게 되었음. 다만 목적어가 대명사인 경우에는 무조건 구동사 바로 뒤에 위치해야 함.

19~21
2022년 9월 43~45번
(정답률 85% | 75% | 80%)
정답 ④ | ③ | ③

[지문 끊어 읽기]
부자와 수도사

(A-1) There was a very wealthy man /
한 부자가 있었다 /

who was bothered by severe eye pain. `21번-① 정답 단서` 부자는 눈 통증이 심했음.
심한 눈 통증으로 괴로워하는

`21번-① 정답 단서` 부자는 심한 눈 통증으로 인해 여러 의사들에게 치료를 받았음.

(A-2) He consulted many doctors / and was treated by several of them.
그는 많은 의사와 상담을 했다 / 그리고 그들 중 여러 명에게 치료받았다

(A-3) He did not stop / consulting a galaxy of medical experts;
그는 멈추지 않았다 / 수많은 의료 전문가들과 상담하는 것을

(A-4) he was heavily medicated /
그는 아주 많은 약을 투여받았다 /

and underwent hundreds of injections.
그리고 주사를 수백 번 맞았다

(A-5) However, / the pain persisted / and was worse than before.
하지만 / 통증은 지속되었다 / 그리고 전보다 심해졌다

(A-6) At last, / (a)he heard about a monk /
결국 / (a)그(wealthy man)는 한 수도사에 대해 듣게 되었다 /

who was famous for treating patients / with his condition.
환자들을 치료하는 것으로 유명한 / 그와 같은 상태의

`19번 정답 단서` 눈 통증을 치료하고자 부자는 수도사를 불러들였음.

(A-7) Within a few days, / the monk was called for by the suffering man.
며칠 후 / 그 고통받는 남자는 그 수도사를 불러들였다

* (A) 요약: 심한 눈 통증으로 괴로워했던 한 부자가 치료를 위해 한 수도사를 불러들였음.

`19번 정답 단서` 부자가 부른 수도사는 부자의 심한 눈 통증을 이해했음.

(D-1) The monk understood the wealthy man's problem / and said /
수도사는 그 부자의 문제를 이해하였다 / 그리고 말했다 /

that for some time (e)he should concentrate only on green colours /
V①
일정 시간동안 / (e)그(wealthy man)는 녹색에만 집중해야 한다고 /

and not let his eyes see any other colours.
V②(사역V) O O-C
그리고 그의 눈이 다른 색을 보게 해서는 안 된다고

`21번-④ 정답 단서` 부자는 수도사의 처방이 이상하다고 생각했지만 따르기로 했음.

(D-2) The wealthy man thought / it was a strange prescription, /
그 부자는 생각했다 / 그것이 이상한 처방이라고 /

but he was desperate / and decided to try it.
하지만 그는 절박했다 / 그래서 그것을 시도하기로 하였다

🔖**힌트** 명령/요구/주장/제안을 나타내는 동사가 주절에 오면 종속절에 'should+동사원형'이 쓰이는데, 이때 should가 생략되고 동사원형만 남기도 함.

(D-3) He got together a group of painters /
V①
그는 페인트공들을 모았다 /

and purchased barrels of green paint / and ordered /
V② V③
그리고 녹색 페인트 통들을 구매했다 / 그리고 지시했다 /

that every object he was likely to see be painted green /
S V'
그가 보게 될 모든 물체를 녹색으로 칠하라고 /

`19번·21번-⑤ 정답 단서` 부자는 자신이 보게 될 모든 물체를 녹색으로 칠하라고 지시했음.

just as the monk had suggested.
수도사가 제안했던 대로 과거완료

* (D) 요약: 수도사는 부자에게 녹색만 보라고 당부하였고, 부자는 녹색 페인트로 자기가 보게 될 모든 물체를 칠하라고 지시했음.

(B-1) In a few days / everything around (b)that man was green. 19번 정답 단서
S V
며칠 후 / (b)그 남자(wealthy man) 주변의 모든 것은 녹색이 되었다
부자가 지시한 대로 부자의 주변 모든 것들이 녹색이 되었음.

(B-2) The wealthy man made sure /
부자는 확실히 하였다 /
that nothing around him could be any other colour.
그의 주변의 어떤 것도 다른 색이 되지 않도록

(B-3) When the monk came to visit him / after a few days, /
수도사가 그를 찾아왔을 때 / 며칠 후 /
the wealthy man's servants ran / with buckets of green paint /
부자의 하인들은 달려왔다 / 녹색 페인트 통들을 들고 /
and poured them all over him /
그리고 그것을 그의 몸 전체에 부었다 /
because he was wearing red clothes. 20번·21번-② 정답 단서
그는 붉은 옷을 입고 있었기 때문에
며칠 뒤에 붉은 옷을 입고 부자를 다시 찾아온 수도사에게 하인들은 녹색 페인트를 쏟아부음.

(B-4) (c)He asked the servants / why they did that. 19번 정답 단서
간접의문문(의문사+S+V)
(c)그(monk)는 하인들에게 물었다 / 왜 그들이 그것을 했는지를
하인들에 의해 초록색 페인트를 뒤집어쓴 수도사는 그들에게 왜 그랬는지 물어봤음.

* (B) 요약: 부자는 주변의 모든 것을 녹색으로 칠했고, 하인들은 부자를 찾아온 수도사에게도 녹색 페인트를 부었음.

19번 정답 단서 수도사의 질문에 하인들이 대답했음.
(C-1) They replied, / "We can't let our master see any other colour."
사역V O O·C
그들은 대답했다 / "우리는 주인이 다른 어떤 색도 보게 할 수 없어요."

(C-2) Hearing this, / the monk laughed and said /
분사구문
이것을 듣고 / 수도사는 웃으며 말했다 /
"If only you had purchased a pair of green glasses / 21번-③ 정답 단서
만약에 당신들이 녹색 안경 하나만 구매했다면 /
하인들은 녹색 안경을 구매하지 않았음.
for just a few dollars, /
단돈 몇 달러밖에 하지 않는 /
힌트 해당 문장은 가정법 과거완료 표현으로, 가정법 과거완료는 과거 사실과 반대되는 상황을 가정할 때 사용함. 'If+주어+과거완료(had+p.p.), 주어+could/would+현재완료(have+p.p.)'로 나타냄.
you could have saved these walls, trees, pots, and everything else /
이러한 벽, 나무, 항아리, 그리고 다른 모든 것을 지킬 수 있었을 것입니다 /
and you could have saved a large share of (d)his fortune.
그리고 (d)그(wealthy man)의 재산의 많은 부분을 아낄 수 있었을 것입니다

(C-3) You cannot paint the whole world green."
당신들은 온 세상을 녹색으로 칠할 수는 없어요

* (C) 요약: 수도사는 녹색 안경 하나만 샀다면 이렇게 모든 것을 페인트칠 할 필요가 없었을 것이라고 말했음.

[전문 해석]

(A)

(1)심한 눈 통증으로 괴로워하는 한 부자가 있었다. (2)그는 많은 의사와 상담을 했고, 그들 중 여러 명에게 치료받았다. (3)그는 수많은 의료 전문가들과 상담하는 것을 멈추지 않았다. (4)그는 아주 많은 약을 투여받았고 주사를 수백 번 맞았다. (5)하지만 통증은 지속되었고 전보다 심해졌다. (6)결국 (a)그(wealthy man)는 그와 같은 상태의 환자들을 치료하는 것으로 유명한 한 수도사에 대해 듣게 되었다. (7)며칠 후, 그 고통받는 남자는 수도사를 불러들였다.

(D)

(1)수도사는 그 부자의 문제를 이해하였고, 일정 시간동안 (e)그(wealthy man)는 녹색에만 집중하고 그의 눈이 다른 색을 보게 해서는 안 된다고 말했다. (2)부자는 그것이 이상한 처방이라고 생각했지만, 절박해서 그것을 시도하기로 하였다. (3)그는 페인트공들을 모았고 녹색 페인트 통들을 구매하여 수도사가 제안했던 대로 그가 보게 될 모든 물체를 녹색으로 칠하라고 지시했다.

(B)

(1)며칠 후 (b)그 남자(wealthy man) 주변의 모든 것은 녹색이 되었다. (2)부자는 그의 주변의 어떤 것도 다른 색이 되지 않도록 확실히 하였다. (3)며칠 후 수도사가 그를 찾아왔을 때, 그는 붉은 옷을 입고 있었기 때문에 부자의 하인들은 녹색 페인트 통들을 들고 달려와서 그의 몸 전체에 부었다. (4)(c)그(monk)는 하인들에게 왜 그들이 그것을 했는지를 물었다.

(C)

(1)그들은 "우리는 주인이 다른 어떤 색도 보게 할 수 없어요."라고 대답했다. (2)이것을 듣고 수도사는 웃으며 말했다. "만약에 당신들이 단돈 몇 달러밖에 하지 않는 녹색 안경 하나만 구매했다면, 이러한 벽, 나무, 항아리, 그리고 다른 모든 것을 지킬 수 있었을 것이고 (d)그(wealthy man)의 재산의 많은 부분을 아낄 수 있었을 것입니다. (3)당신들은 온 세상을 녹색으로 칠할 수는 없어요."

[정답 확인]

19. 주어진 글 (A)에 이어질 내용을 순서에 맞게 배열한 것으로 가장 적절한 것은?

① (B) — (D) — (C) ② (C) — (B) — (D) ③ (C) — (D) — (B)
✔④ (D) — (B) — (C) ⑤ (D) — (C) — (B)

20. 밑줄 친 (a) ~ (e) 중에서 가리키는 대상이 나머지 넷과 다른 것은?

① (a) ② (b) ✔③ (c) ④ (d) ⑤ (e)

21. 윗글의 내용으로 적절하지 않은 것은?

① 부자는 눈 통증으로 여러 명의 의사에게 치료받았다(be treated). 문장(A-1), (A-2)
② 수도사(monk)는 붉은 옷을 입고 부자를 다시 찾아갔다. 문장(B-3)
✔③ 하인(servant)들은 녹색 안경을 ~~구입했다~~ 구입하지 않았다. 문장(C-2)
④ 부자는 수도사의 처방(prescription)이 이상하다고 생각했다. 문장(D-2)
⑤ 부자는 주변을 모두 녹색으로 칠하게 했다. 문장(D-3)

[중요 어휘]

☐ **severe**	형용사 심한, 가혹한
☐ **consult**	동사 상담하다
☐ **a galaxy of**	수많은
☐ **medicate**	동사 약을 투여하다
☐ **undergo**	동사 받다, 겪다
☐ **injection**	명사 주사, 투입
☐ **persist**	동사 지속되다
☐ **monk**	명사 수도사
☐ **call for**	불러들이다, ~를 데리러 가다
☐ **prescription**	명사 처방(전)
☐ **desperate**	형용사 절박한, 필사적인
☐ **barrel**	명사 통
☐ **servant**	명사 하인
☐ **bucket**	명사 통, 양동이
☐ **fortune**	명사 재산, 운

22~24

2023년 9월 43~45번
(정답률 80% | 75% | 85%)

정답 ③ | ② | ②

[지문 끊어 읽기] 용기 있는 삶

(A-1) When Jack was a young man /
Jack은 청년이었을 때 /
in his early twenties during the 1960s, /
1960년대에 20대 초반의 /
he had tried to work in his father's insurance business, /
그는 그의 아버지의 보험 회사에서 일하려고 노력했다 /
as was expected of him.
그에게 기대됐던 대로

(A-2) His two older brothers fit in easily /
그의 두 형은 쉽게 적응했다 / 병렬①
and seemed to enjoy their work. 24번-① 정답 단서
병렬②
그리고 자신들의 일을 즐기는 것처럼 보였다
두 형은 자신의 일을 즐기는 것으로 보임.

(A-3) But Jack was bored with the insurance industry. 22번 정답 단서
하지만 Jack은 보험 업계에 싫증이 났다
Jack은 보험 업계에 싫증이 남.

(A-4) "It was worse than being bored," he said.
"그것은 지루한 것보다 더 나빴다."라고 그는 말했다

(A-5) "I felt like I was dying inside."
"나는 내면이 죽어가는 것 같았다."

(A-6) Jack felt drawn to hair styling /
병렬①
Jack은 머리 손질에 끌림을 느꼈다 /
22번 정답 단서 Jack은 미용실을 갖기를 원함.
and dreamed of owning a hair shop with a lively environment.
병렬② 동명사(of의 목적어)
그리고 활기찬 분위기의 미용실을 갖는 것을 꿈꿨다

정답과 해설
18 장문의 이해 - 복합지문

(A-7) He was sure /
그는 확신했다 /
that (a)he would enjoy the creative and social aspects of it /
병렬① =a hair shop
(a)그(Jack)가 그것의 창의적이고 사교적인 측면을 즐길 것이라고 /
and that he'd be successful.
병렬②
그리고 그가 성공할 것이라고

* (A) 요약: Jack은 20대 초반에 아버지의 보험 회사에서 일하려고 노력했지만, 보험 업계에 싫증이 나서 자신의 미용실을 갖길 꿈꾸며 성공을 확신함.

(C-1) When he was twenty-six, / Jack approached his father /
그가 26살이었을 때 / Jack은 아버지에게 갔다 /
and expressed his intentions of leaving the business /
그리고 회사를 떠나겠다는 그의 의사를 밝혔다 / 동명사(of의 목적어)
to become a hairstylist. 22번·24번-③ 정답 단서 아버지에게 미용사가 되기 위해 회사를 떠나겠다는 의사를 밝힘.
부사적 용법(목적)
미용사가 되기 위해

(C-2) As Jack anticipated, / his father raged /
Jack이 예상했던 대로 / 그의 아버지는 몹시 화를 내었다 /
and accused Jack of being selfish, ungrateful, and unmanly.
accuse A of B: A를 B라는 이유로 비난하다
그리고 Jack을 이기적이고 배은망덕하며 남자답지 못하다는 이유로 비난했다

(C-3) In the face of his father's fury, / Jack felt confusion and fear.
아버지의 분노 앞에서 / Jack은 혼란과 두려움을 느꼈다

(C-4) His resolve became weak.
그의 결심은 약해졌다

(C-5) But then / a force filled (d)his chest /
그러나 그때 / 어떤 힘이 (d)그(Jack)의 가슴을 채웠다 /
and he stood firm in his decision. 22번 정답 단서 결심이 약해졌던 Jack은 어떤 힘으로 인해 자신의 결정을 확고히 하게 됨.
그리고 그는 자신의 결정을 확고히 했다

(C-6) In following his path, / 22번 정답 단서 자신만의 길을 가게 됨.
자신의 길을 가면서 /
Jack not only ran three flourishing hair shops, / 24번-④ 정답 단서 세 개의 번창하는 미용실을 운영함.
not only A but also B: A뿐만 아니라 B도
Jack은 세 개의 번창하는 미용실을 운영했을 뿐만 아니라 /
but also helped his clients experience their inner beauty /
또한 그의 고객들이 그들의 내면의 아름다움을 경험하도록 도왔다 /
by listening and encouraging them /
귀 기울여 듣고 그들을 격려함으로써 / =his clients
when they faced dark times.
=his clients
그들이 어두운 시기에 직면했을 때

* (C) 요약: 아버지에게 회사를 떠나겠다는 의사를 밝혔을 때 분노하는 아버지 때문에 혼란과 두려움에 그의 결심이 약해졌지만, 자신의 길을 가며 세 개의 미용실을 번창시킴.

(D-1) His love for his work / 22번 정답 단서 자신의 길을 가던 그의 일에 대한 사랑의 내용으로 이어짐.
그의 일에 대한 사랑은 /
led to donating time and talent at nursing homes, /
요양원에서 시간과 재능을 기부하는 것으로 이어졌다 /
which in turn led to becoming a hospice volunteer, /
계속적 용법 병렬①
이는 결과적으로 호스피스 자원봉사자가 되는 것으로 이어졌다 /
and eventually to starting fundraising efforts /
병렬②
그리고 마침내 모금 운동을 시작하는 것으로 /
for the hospice program in his community. 24번-⑤ 정답 단서 지역사회에서 모금 운동을 시작함.
그의 지역사회에서 호스피스 프로그램을 위한

(D-2) And all this laid a strong stepping stone /
그리고 이 모든 것은 견고한 디딤돌을 놓았다 /
for another courageous move in his life.
그의 삶에서 또 다른 용기 있는 움직임을 위한

(D-3) When, / after having two healthy children of their own, /
~할 때 / 그들 자신의 두 명의 건강한 아이를 낳은 후 /
Jack and his wife, Michele, decided /
Jack과 그의 아내 Michele이 결정했을 /
to bring an orphaned child into their family, /
고아가 된 아이를 그들의 가정에 데려오기로 /
(e)his father threatened to disown them. 22번 정답 단서 Jack과 Michele이 고아가 된 아이를 입양하려고 하자 Jack의 아버지는 이를 반대함.
(e)그(Jack)의 아버지는 그들과 의절하겠다고 위협했다

* (D) 요약: Jack은 요양원에서 봉사하며 지역사회의 호스피스 프로그램을 위한 모금 운동을 시작하였고, 고아가 된 아이를 입양하려고 아내와 결정하자 그의 아버지가 입양을 반대함.

(B-1) Jack understood / that his father feared adoption, / 22번 정답 단서 Jack의 아버지는 입양을 두려워하셨음.
Jack은 이해했다 / 자신의 아버지가 입양을 두려워한다는 것을 /
in this case especially /
이 경우에는 특히 /
because the child was of a different racial background than their family.
그 아이가 그들의 가족과 다른 인종적 배경을 가지고 있었기 때문에

(B-2) Jack and Michele risked rejection /
Jack과 Michele은 반대의 위험을 무릅썼다 /
and went ahead with the adoption. 24번-② 정답 단서 아버지의 반대에도 입양을 진행함.
그리고 입양을 진행했다

(B-3) It took years / but eventually Jack's father loved the little girl /
비인칭 주어
몇 년이 걸렸다 / 하지만 결국 Jack의 아버지는 그 어린 여자아이를 사랑했다 /
and accepted (b)his son's independent choices. 23번 정답 단서 독립적인 선택을 한 '아들'은 Jack을 가리키며, '그의 아들'이라고 했으므로 '그'는 Jack의 아버지를 가리킴.
그리고 (b)그(father)의 아들의 독립적인 선택을 받아들였다

(B-4) Jack realized / that, although he often felt fear and still does, /
Jack은 깨달았다 / 비록 그가 자주 두려움을 느꼈고 여전히 그러하지만 /
he has always had courage.
자신이 항상 용기가 있다는 것을

(B-5) In fact, / courage was the scaffolding /
사실 / 용기는 발판이었다 / 선행사
around which (c)he had built richness into his life.
전치사+목적격 관계대명사
(c)그(Jack)가 자신의 삶에 풍요로움을 쌓아온

* (B) 요약: 아버지의 반대에도 입양을 진행했고, 결국 아버지는 아들의 선택을 받아들였으며 Jack은 용기가 삶의 풍요를 쌓아온 발판이었음을 깨달음.

[전문 해석]

(A)

(1)Jack은 1960년대 20대 초반의 청년이었을 때, 그에게 기대됐던 대로 그의 아버지의 보험 회사에서 일하려고 노력했다. (2)그의 두 형은 쉽게 적응했고 자신들의 일을 즐기는 것처럼 보였다. (3)하지만 Jack은 보험 업계에 싫증이 났다. (4)"그것은 지루한 것보다 더 나빴다."라고 그는 말했다. (5)"나는 내면이 죽어가는 것 같았다." (6)Jack은 머리 손질에 끌림을 느꼈고 활기찬 분위기의 미용실을 갖는 것을 꿈꿨다. (7)그는 (a)그(Jack)가 그것의 창의적이고 사교적인 측면을 즐길 것이고 성공할 것이라고 확신했다.

(C)

(1)26살이었을 때, Jack은 아버지에게 가서 미용사가 되기 위해 회사를 떠나겠다는 의사를 밝혔다. (2)Jack이 예상했던 대로, 그의 아버지는 몹시 화를 내었고 Jack을 이기적이고, 배은망덕하며 남자답지 못하다는 이유로 비난했다. (3)아버지의 분노 앞에서, Jack은 혼란과 두려움을 느꼈다. (4)그의 결심은 약해졌다. (5)그러나 그때 어떤 힘이 (d)그(Jack)의 가슴을 채웠고 그는 자신의 결정을 확고히 했다. (6)자신의 길을 가면서, Jack은 세 개의 번창하는 미용실을 운영했을 뿐만 아니라, 또한 고객들이 어두운 시기에 직면했을 때 귀 기울여 듣고 그들을 격려함으로써 그들이 가진 내면의 아름다움을 경험하도록 도왔다

(D)

(1)그의 일에 대한 사랑은 요양원에서 시간과 재능을 기부하는 것으로 이어졌고, 이는 결과적으로 호스피스 자원봉사자가 되어 마침내 그의 지역사회에서 호스피스 프로그램을 위한 모금 운동을 시작하는 것으로 이어졌다. (2)그리고 이 모든 것은 그의 삶에서 또 다른 용기 있는 움직임을 위한 견고한 디딤돌을 놓았다. (3)그들 자신의 두 명의 건강한 아이를 낳은 후, Jack과 그의 아내 Michele이 고아가 된 아이를 그들의 가정에 데려오기로 결정했을 때, (e)그(Jack)의 아버지는 그들과 의절하겠다고 위협했다.

(B)

(1)Jack은 자신의 아버지가 입양을 두려워한다는 것을 이해했는데, 이 경우에는 특히 그 아이가 그들의 가족과 다른 인종적 배경을 가지고 있었기 때문이었다. (2) Jack과 Michele은 반대의 위험을 무릅쓰고 입양을 진행했다. (3)몇 년이 걸렸지만 결국 Jack의 아버지는 그 어린 여자아이를 사랑했고 (b)그(father)의 아들의 독립적인 선택을 받아들였다. (4)Jack은 비록 그가 자주 두려움을 느꼈고 여전히 그러하지만, 자신이 항상 용기가 있다는 것을 깨달았다. (5)사실, 용기는 (c)그(Jack)가 자신의 삶에 풍요로움을 쌓아온 발판이었다.

[정답 확인]

22. 주어진 글 (A)에 이어질 내용을 순서에 맞게 배열한 것으로 가장 적절한 것은?

① (B) — (D) — (C) ② (C) — (B) — (D) ✔③ (C) — (D) — (B)
④ (D) — (B) — (C) ⑤ (D) — (C) — (B)

23. 밑줄 친 (a) ~ (e) 중에서 가리키는 대상이 나머지 넷과 다른 것은?

① (a) ✔② (b) ③ (c) ④ (d) ⑤ (e)

24. 윗글의 Jack에 관한 내용으로 적절하지 않은 것은?

① 두 형은 자신들의 일을 즐기는(enjoy) 것으로 보였다. 문장(A-2)
✔② 아버지의 반대로 입양을 포기했다. 문장(B-2) → 포기하지 않았다
③ 아버지에게 회사를 떠나겠다는 의사(intention)를 밝혔다(express). 문장(C-1)
④ 세 개의 번창하는(flourishing) 미용실을 운영했다(run). 문장(C-6)
⑤ 지역사회에서 모금 운동(fundraising effort)을 시작했다. 문장(D-1)

[중요 어휘]

□ insurance	명사 보험
□ lively	형용사 활기찬, 생기 있는 / 부사 활발하게
□ aspect	명사 측면, 양상
□ intention	명사 의사, 의도
□ anticipate	동사 예상하다, 기대하다
□ rage	동사 몹시 화를 내다 / 명사 격렬한 분노
□ ungrateful	형용사 배은망덕한, 감사할 줄 모르는
□ fury	명사 분노, 격분
□ resolve	명사 (단호한) 결심 / 동사 결심하다, 해결하다
□ flourishing	형용사 번창하는, 무성한
□ orphan	동사 고아로 만들다 / 명사 고아
□ disown	동사 의절하다, 자기 것이 아니라고 말하다
□ adoption	명사 입양, 채택
□ courage	명사 용기
□ scaffolding	명사 발판, (건축 공사장의) 비계

핵심 이 지문은 나무를 심는 에피소드를 통해 교훈을 전달하는 글로, 할머니가 Yolanda에게 어떤 교훈을 어떻게 주는지 파악해가며 읽으면 됨.

25~27

2020년 3월 43~45번
(정답률 75% | 70% | 80%)

정답 ③ | ④ | ③

[지문 끊어 읽기]

나무를 통한 성공의 깨달음

(A-1) Eight-year-old Yolanda / went to her grandmother's /
여덟 살의 Yolanda는 / 그녀의 할머니 댁에 갔다 /
and proudly announced /
그리고 자랑스럽게 선언했다 /
that she was going to be very successful /
그녀가 크게 성공할 것이라고 /
when she grew up / and asked her grandmother /
그녀가 크면 / 그러고는 그녀의 할머니에게 물었다 /
if she could give her any tips / on how to achieve this.
그녀가 그녀에게 조언을 해 줄 수 있는지 / 이것을 성취할 방법에 대해

(A-2) The grandmother nodded, / took the girl by the hand, /
할머니는 고개를 끄덕였다 / 소녀의 손을 잡았다 /
and walked (a)her to a nearby plant nursery.
그리고 (a)그녀(Yolanda)를 가까운 식물 묘목장으로 데리고 갔다

(A-3) There, the two of them chose and purchased two small trees.
그곳에서 두 사람은 두 그루의 작은 나무를 골라서 샀다

* (A) 요약: 성공하는 방법이 궁금했던 여덟 살의 Yolanda는 할머니께 조언을 구했고, 할머니는 Yolanda와 묘목장에 가서 작은 나무 두 그루를 삼.

(C-1) They returned home /
그들은 집으로 돌아왔다 /
and planted one of them / in the back yard /
그리고 그 중 하나를 심었다 / 뒷마당에 /
and planted the other tree in a pot / and kept it indoors. 25번 정답 단서
그리고 나머지 하나의 나무는 화분에 심었다 / 그리고 그것을 실내에 두었다

✶중요 'one(하나)-the other(나머지 하나)'라는 표현이 사용됨. 'one of them'의 them은 문장 (A-3)에서 할머니와 손녀가 산 'two small trees'를 지칭하는데, (C-1)은 묘목장에서 집으로 돌아와 나무를 심는 상황이므로 (A) 다음에는 (C)가 와야 함.

(C-2) Then her grandmother asked her / which of the trees /
그런 다음 그녀의 할머니는 그녀에게 물었다 / 그 나무들 중 어느 것이 /
(c)she thought / would be more successful / in the future.
(c)그녀(Yolanda)가 생각하기에 / 더 성공적일 것인지 / 미래에

(C-3) Yolanda thought for a moment / and said /
Yolanda는 잠시 생각했다 / 그리고 말했다 /
the indoor tree would be more successful /
실내의 나무가 더 성공적일 거라고 /
because it was protected and safe, /
그것은 보호를 받고 안전하기 때문에 /
while the outdoor tree had to cope with the elements. 27번 정답 단서
집 밖의 나무는 악천후를 이겨내야 하는 반면

(C-4) Her grandmother shrugged and said, / "We'll see."
그녀의 할머니는 어깨를 으쓱하더니 말했다 / "두고 보자꾸나."

(C-5) Her grandmother took good care of both trees.
그녀의 할머니는 두 나무를 모두 정성스럽게 돌보았다

* (C) 요약: Yolanda와 할머니는 한 나무는 실내에 다른 한 나무는 뒷마당에 심었고, Yolanda는 실내에 있는 나무가 미래에 더 성공적일 것이라고 예측함.

(D-1) In a few years, / Yolanda, now a teenager, /
몇 년 후 / 이제 십 대인 Yolanda는 /
came to visit her grandmother again.
그녀의 할머니를 다시 방문했다

힌트 할머니가 Yolanda의 질문에 '대답한 적이 없었던(had never ~ answered)' 시점은 Yolanda가 여덟 살 때로, 십 대인 Yolanda가 할머니께 '상기시켰던(reminded)' 시점보다 더 과거이므로, 대과거인 'had p.p.'를 사용했음.

(D-2) Yolanda reminded her / that (d)she had never really answered /
Yolanda는 그녀에게 상기시켰다 / (d)그녀(할머니)가 딱히 대답한 적이 없었다는 것을 /
her question / from when she was a little girl /
그녀의 질문에 / 그녀가 어렸을 때의 /
about how she could become successful / when she grew up.
어떻게 하면 그녀가 성공할 수 있는지에 대한 / 그녀가 커서

(D-3) The grandmother showed Yolanda the indoor tree /
4형식V I·O D·O
할머니는 Yolanda에게 실내의 나무를 보여주었다 /
and then took (e)her outside /
그러고는 (e)그녀(Yolanda)를 밖으로 데리고 나갔다 /
to have a look at the towering tree outside.
집 밖의 높이 솟은 나무를 보도록

(D-4) "Which one is greater?" / the grandmother asked.
"어느 것이 더 크니?" / 할머니가 물었다

(D-5) Yolanda replied, / "The outside one.
Yolanda는 대답했다 / 밖에 있는 거요

(D-6) But that doesn't make sense; /
하지만 말이 되질 않아요 /
it had to cope with many more challenges / than the one inside."
그것은 더 많은 역경을 이겨내야만 했잖아요 / 실내의 것보다

* (D) 요약: 몇 년 후 할머니는 Yolanda에게 나무가 어떻게 자랐는지 보여주었는데, 집 밖의 나무가 실내의 나무보다 더 크게 자라나 있었음.

(B-1) The grandmother smiled and said, / "Remember this, /
할머니는 미소를 지으며 말했다 / 이것을 기억해라 /
and you will be successful / in whatever you do:
그러면 너는 성공할 것이다 / 네가 무엇을 하든 그 일에서

✶중요 문장 (B-1)은 (D)의 마지막에서 Yolanda가 말이 되지 않는다고 한 것에 대한 할머니의 반응임. 즉 (B)는 (D) 뒤에 이어지는 내용임.

(B-2) If you choose the safe option all of your life, /
만약 네가 평생 안전한 선택을 한다면 /
you will never grow.
너는 결코 성장하지 못할 것이다

(B-3) But if you are willing to face the world /
그러나 네가 세상에 기꺼이 맞선다면 /
with all of its challenges, / you will learn from those challenges /
모든 역경에도 불구하고 / 너는 그 역경으로부터 배우게 될 것이다 /
and grow to achieve great heights."
부사적 용법-결과
그리고 성장하여 대단히 높은 수준까지 성취하게 될 것이다

(B-4) Yolanda looked up at the tall tree, / took a deep breath, /
Yolanda는 큰 나무를 올려다봤다 / 심호흡을 했다 /

문제편 p.279

and nodded (b)her head, /
그리고 (b)그녀(Yolanda)의 머리를 끄덕였다 /
realizing that her wise grandmother was right.
분사구문
그녀의 지혜로운 할머니가 옳았다는 것을 깨닫고

*(B) 요약: 할머니는 Yolanda에게 평생 안전한 선택을 한다면 성장할 수 없으며, 모든 역경에도 불구하고 세상에 기꺼이 맞선다면, 많은 배움을 얻고 큰 성취를 할 수 있을 거라는 교훈을 줌.

[전문 해석]

(A)

(1)여덟 살의 Yolanda는 할머니 댁에 가서 그녀가 크면 크게 성공할 것이라고 자랑스럽게 선언하고는, 할머니에게 그녀(할머니)가 그녀(Yolanda)에게 이것을 성취할 방법에 대해 조언을 해 줄 수 있는지 물었다. (2)할머니는 고개를 끄덕이더니, 소녀의 손을 잡고 (a)그녀(Yolanda)를 가까운 식물 묘목장으로 데리고 갔다. (3)그곳에서 두 사람은 두 그루의 작은 나무를 골라서 샀다.

(C)

(1)그들은 집으로 돌아와 그 중 하나를 뒷마당에 심었고 나머지 하나의 나무는 화분에 심어 실내에 두었다. (2)그런 다음 그녀의 할머니는 그녀에게 (c)그녀(Yolanda)가 생각하기에 그 나무들 중 어느 것이 미래에 더 성공적일 것인지 물었다. (3)Yolanda는 잠시 생각하더니, 집 밖의 나무는 악천후를 이겨내야 하는 반면 그것(실내의 나무)은 보호를 받고 안전하기 때문에, 실내의 나무가 더 성공적일(잘 자랄) 거라고 말했다. (4)그녀의 할머니는 어깨를 으쓱하더니, "두고 보자꾸나."라고 말했다. (5)그녀의 할머니는 두 나무를 모두 정성스럽게 돌보았다.

(D)

(1)몇 년 후, 이제 십 대인 Yolanda는 그녀의 할머니를 다시 방문했다. (2)Yolanda는 어떻게 하면 그녀(Yolanda)가 커서 성공할 수 있는지에 대한 어렸을 때의 그녀의 질문에 (d)그녀(할머니)가 딱히 대답한 적이 없었다는 것을 그녀(할머니)에게 상기시켰다. (3)할머니는 Yolanda에게 실내의 나무를 보여주고는 (그녀가) 집 밖의 높이 솟은 나무를 보도록 (e)그녀(Yolanda)를 밖으로 데리고 나갔다. (4)"어느 것이 더 크니?"라고 할머니가 물었다. (5)Yolanda는 대답했다, "밖에 있는 거요. (6)하지만 말이 되질 않아요. 그것은 실내의 것보다 더 많은 역경을 이겨내야만 했잖아요."

(B)

(1)할머니는 미소를 지으며 말했다, "이것을 기억하면, 너는 네가 무엇을 하든 그 일에서 성공할 것이다. (2)만약 네가 평생 안전한 선택을 한다면, 너는 결코 성장하지 못할 것이다. (3)그러나 네가 모든 역경에도 불구하고 세상에 기꺼이 맞선다면, 너는 그 역경으로부터 배우게 될 것이고 성장하여 대단히 높은 수준까지 성취하게 될 것이다." (4)Yolanda는 큰 나무를 올려다보고, 심호흡을 하고, 그녀의 지혜로운 할머니가 옳았다는 것을 깨닫고 (b)그녀(Yolanda)의 머리를 끄덕였다.

[정답 확인]

25. 주어진 글 (A)에 이어질 내용을 순서에 맞게 배열한 것으로 가장 적절한 것은?

① (B) — (D) — (C) ② (C) — (B) — (D) ✔③ (C) — (D) — (B)
④ (D) — (B) — (C) ⑤ (D) — (C) — (B)

26. 밑줄 친 (a) ~ (e) 중에서 가리키는 대상이 나머지 넷과 다른 것은?

① (a) ② (b) ③ (c) ✔④ (d) ⑤ (e)

27. 윗글의 내용으로 적절하지 않은 것은?

① Yolanda는 자신이 크게 성공할 것(very successful)이라고 자랑스럽게 말했다.
② 할머니는 역경으로부터 배울 수 있다(learn from challenges)고 말했다.
✔③ Yolanda는 ~~집 밖에~~ 실내에 심은 나무(outdoor tree)가 더 잘 자랄 거라고 말했다.
④ 할머니는 두 나무를 정성스럽게 돌보았다(take good care).
⑤ Yolanda는 십 대(teenager)가 되어 할머니를 다시 방문했다.

[문제 풀이]

26. 첫 번째 문장에서 Yolanda가 할머니께 성공할 수 있는 방법에 대해 물어봤다고 나와 있다. 그렇다면 아직까지 그 질문에 대답하지 않은 사람도 동일 인물인 할머니일 것이다. 즉, 'she had never really answered her question'에서 'she'는 할머니(grandmother)이다. 따라서 답은 ④이다.

[중요 어휘]

□ **take A by the hand**	A의 손을 잡다
□ **nursery**	명사 묘목장
□ **indoors**	부사 실내에(서)
□ **outdoor**	형용사 집 밖의, 실외의
□ **cope with**	~을 이겨내다, ~에 대처하다
□ **elements**	명사 (복수형) 악천후
□ **shrug**	동사 어깨를 으쓱하다
□ **remind**	동사 상기시키다, 일깨워주다
□ **towering**	형용사 높이 솟은
□ **all of one's life**	평생
□ **be willing to V**	기꺼이 ~하다
□ **face**	동사 맞서다

28~30

2019년 9월 43~45번
(정답률 80% | 75% | 65%)

정답 ③ | ⑤ | ⑤

[지문 끊어 읽기] 소방관에게 구해진 아이

(A-1) It was an unbearably hot Chicago day /
it was ~ when(=that) 강조
참을 수 없을 정도로 더운 시카고의 어느 날이었다 /
when the emergency call came over the radio /
무전으로 긴급 호출이 왔던 때는 /
for Jacob's firefighting crew / to handle a fire /
to handle의 의미상의 주어
Jacob의 소방관들에게 / 화재를 진압해 달라고 /
in a downtown apartment building.
도심지 아파트의

(A-2) When they arrived, / the roaring fire was spreading /
그들이 도착했을 때 / 맹렬히 타오르는 불이 퍼지고 있었다 /
through the whole building.
건물 전체에

(A-3) Jacob thought / it was already looking pretty hopeless.
Jacob은 생각했다 / 이미 꽤 가망이 없어 보인다고

(A-4) But suddenly, / a woman came running up to (a)him /
그런데 갑자기 / 한 여성이 (a)그(Jacob)에게 뛰어왔다 /
yelling at the top of her lungs, / 28번 정답 단서
큰 소리로 외치며 /
"My baby, / my Kris is on the fifth floor!"
우리 아기 / 우리 Kris가 5층에 있어요

*(A) 요약: Jacob의 소방대가 불타고 있는 아파트에 도착하자, 한 여성이 Jacob에게 뛰어옴.

(C-1) Her desperate and urgent voice / 28번 정답 단서
그녀의 절박하고 다급한 목소리는 /
made Jacob decide / to enter the building instantly.
사역V O O·C(동사원형)
Jacob이 결심하게 만들었다 / 즉시 건물에 들어가기로

(C-2) He made his way / up to the fifth floor / with another firefighter.
그는 나아갔다 / 5층까지 / 다른 한 명의 소방관과 함께

(C-3) By the time they made it up to the fifth floor, /
그들이 5층에 도착할 무렵 /
the fire had grown so fierce, / neither could see /
불은 매우 격렬해져서 / 누구도 볼 수가 없었다 /
more than a few feet in front of them.
그들 앞 몇 피트 이상을

힌트 neither 앞에 that이 생략된 so ~ that 구문임.

(C-4) Jacob's partner looked at him / and gave him the thumbs-down.
Jacob의 동료는 그를 바라봤다 / 그리고 그에게 엄지를 내려 보였다

(C-5) As a fireman, / (c)he knew his partner was right, /
소방관으로서 / (c)그(Jacob)는 그의 동료가 옳다는 것을 알았다 /
but he just kept seeing that mother's face / in his head.
하지만 그는 계속 그 어머니의 얼굴을 봤다 / 그의 머릿속에

*(C) 요약: 여성의 아이를 구하기 위해서, Jacob은 동료와 함께 5층에 올라갔지만 불은 더 거세졌음.

(D-1) Impulsively, / Jacob ran down the hall / 28번 정답 단서
충동적으로 / Jacob은 복도를 따라 뛰었다 /
without his partner, / disappearing into the flames.
그의 동료 없이 / 그리고 화염 속으로 사라졌다

(D-2) As flames shot out of the apartment / like fireballs /
불꽃이 아파트 밖으로 분출하는 동안 / 불덩이처럼 /
(d)he could see a little boy / lying on the floor / 29번 정답 단서
(d)그(Jacob)는 어린 남자아이를 볼 수 있었다 / 바닥에 누워있는 /
in just about the only spot / that wasn't on fire.
거의 유일한 자리에서 / 불타고 있지 않는

30번 정답 단서
(D-3) He didn't even have time / to figure out / if he was alive or dead.
그는 시간조차 없었다 / 알아낼 / 그가 살았는지 죽었는지

(D-4) He just grabbed (e)him / and rushed out.
그는 바로 (e)그(Kris)를 붙잡았다 / 그리고 뛰어나갔다
★중요 누가 누구를 구하는지 생각해보면, him이 가리키는 사람이 누군지 알 수 있음.

(D-5) Jacob and the boy cleared the fifth floor landing / 28번 정답 단서
Jacob과 남자아이는 5층 층계참을 통과했다 /
just as the fireman could hear /
그 소방관이 막 들었을 때 /
the sound of the floor above collapsing.
위층이 무너지는 소리를

*(D) 요약: Jacob은 바닥에 누워있는 남자아이를 발견하고, 아이와 함께 무너지는 아파트에서 빠져나옴.

(B-1) The tense crowd below / broke into cheers /
아래쪽에서 긴장한 사람들은 / 환호하기 시작했다 /
as they saw Jacob / emerge from the building / with the boy. 28번 정답 단서
그들이 Jacob이 ~하는 것을 보자 / 건물에서 나오는 것을 / 남자아이와 함께

(B-2) Holding Kris / against (b)his chest, /
Kris를 안고 있으면서 / (b)그(Jacob)의 가슴 가까이 /
Jacob could feel the boy's heart pounding, /
Jacob은 그 남자아이의 심장이 뛰는 것을 느낄 수 있었다 /
and when he coughed from the smoke, /
그리고 그가 연기 때문에 기침했을 때 /
Jacob knew Kris would survive.
Jacob은 Kris가 살아남을 것을 알았다

(B-3) Paramedics tended to the boy /
응급 구조대원이 그 남자아이를 돌보았다 /
while Jacob himself fell to the ground.
Jacob이 땅에 쓰러지는 사이

(B-4) Two weeks after the rescue, / two people visited Jacob /
구조 2주 후에 / 두 사람이 Jacob을 찾아왔다 /
at the station / — Kris and his mother.
소방서에 / Kris와 그의 어머니

(B-5) They came to thank him / and told him /
그들은 그에게 감사를 표하기 위해 왔다 / 그리고 그에게 말했다 /
they were forever in his debt.
그들이 평생 그에게 고마운 마음을 지니고 있을 것이라고

*(B) 요약: 남자아이는 무사히 살아났고, 2주 뒤 남자아이와 엄마가 감사 인사를 하기 위해 Jacob을 찾아옴.

[전문 해석]

(A)

(1)Jacob의 소방관들에게 도심지 아파트의 화재를 진압해 달라고 무전으로 긴급 호출이 왔던 때는 (바로) 참을 수 없을 정도로 더운 시카고의 어느 날이었다. (2)그들이 도착했을 때, 맹렬히 타오르는 불이 건물 전체에 퍼지고 있었다. (3)Jacob은 (구조하기에) 이미 꽤 가망이 없어 보인다고 생각했다. (4)그런데 갑자기, 한 여성이 큰 소리로 외치며 (a)그(Jacob)에게 뛰어왔다, "우리 아기, 우리 Kris가 5층에 있어요!"

(C)

(1)그녀의 절박하고 다급한 목소리는 Jacob이 즉시 건물에 들어가기로 결심하게 만들었다. (2)그는 다른 한 명의 소방관과 함께 5층까지 나아갔다. (3)그들이 5층에 도착할 무렵, 불은 매우 격렬해져서 (둘 중) 누구도 그들 앞 몇 피트 이상을 볼 수가 없었다. (4)Jacob의 동료는 그를 바라보며 그에게 엄지를 내려 보였다(이미 가망이 없다는 사인을 보냈다). (5)소방관으로서, (c)그(Jacob)는 그의 동료가 옳다는 것을 알았지만, 그는 계속 그의 머릿속에 그 (아이) 어머니의 얼굴을 봤다(떠올렸다).

(D)

(1)충동적으로, Jacob은 그의 동료 없이 복도를 따라 뛰며 화염 속으로 사라졌다. (2)불꽃이 불덩이처럼 아파트 밖으로 분출하는 동안, (d)그(Jacob)는 불타고 있지 않는 거의 유일한 자리에서 바닥에 누워있는 어린 남자아이를 볼 수 있었다. (3)그는 그가 살았는지 죽었는지 알아낼 시간조차 없었다. (4)그는 바로 (e)그(Kris)를 붙잡고 뛰어나갔다. (5)그 소방관(Jacob)이 위층이 무너지는 소리를 막 들었을 때(듣자마자), Jacob과 남자아이는 5층 층계참을 통과했다.

(B)

(1)아래쪽에서 긴장한 사람들은 Jacob이 남자아이와 함께 건물에서 나오는 것을 보자 환호하기 시작했다. (2)(b)그(Jacob)의 가슴 가까이 Kris를 안고 있으면서, Jacob은 그 남자아이의 심장이 뛰는 것을 느낄 수 있었고, 그(남자아이)가 연기 때문에 기침했을 때 Jacob은 Kris가 살아남을 것을 알았다. (3)Jacob이 땅에 쓰러지는 사이, 응급 구조대원이 그 남자아이를 돌보았다. (4)구조 2주 후에, 두 사람이 소방서에 Jacob을 찾아왔다. Kris와 그의 어머니(였다). (5)그들은 그에게 감사를 표하기 위해 왔으며, 그들이 평생 그에게 고마운 마음을 지니고 있을 것이라고 말했다.

[정답 확인]

28. 주어진 글 (A)에 이어질 내용을 순서에 맞게 배열한 것으로 가장 적절한 것은?

① (B) — (D) — (C) ② (C) — (B) — (D) ✔③ (C) — (D) — (B)
④ (D) — (B) — (C) ⑤ (D) — (C) — (B)

29. 밑줄 친 (a) ~ (e) 중에서 가리키는 대상이 나머지 넷과 다른 것은?

① (a) ② (b) ③ (c) ④ (d) ✔⑤ (e)

30. 윗글의 내용으로 적절하지 않은 것은?

① 불이 건물 전체(whole building)로 퍼지고(spread) 있었다.
② Kris와 엄마는 소방서(fire station)에 방문했다(visit).
③ Jacob은 동료(partner)와 함께 5층으로 올라갔다.
④ 소년은 불이 붙지 않은 바닥에 누워(lying) 있었다.
✔⑤ Jacob은 소년을 ~~발견한 즉시~~ 데리고 건물에서 나온 후에 생사(alive or dead)를 확인했다.

[중요 어휘]

☐ unbearably	부사 참을 수 없을 정도로
☐ handle a fire	화재를 진압하다
☐ downtown	형용사 도심지의 / 부사 도심지에서
☐ roaring	형용사 맹렬히 타오르는, 으르렁거리는
☐ at the top of one's lungs	큰 소리로, 소리 지르며
☐ desperate	형용사 절박한, 절망적인
☐ urgent	형용사 다급한, 촉박한
☐ make one's way	나아가다, 출세하다
☐ fierce	형용사 격렬한, 사나운
☐ impulsively	부사 충동적으로
☐ collapse	동사 무너지다, 좌절하다
☐ break into	~하기 시작하다, 침입하다
☐ emerge from	~에서 나오다, 벗어나다
☐ tend to N	~을 돌보다
☐ be in one's debt	~에게 고마운 마음을 지니고 있다

31~33

2023년 3월 43~45번
(정답률 65% | 75% | 80%)

정답 ⑤ | ④ | ⑤

[지문 끊어 읽기]

팀 정신을 위한 코치의 노력

(A-1) It was a hot day / in early fall.
더운 날이었다 / 초가을의

(A-2) Wylder was heading to the school field / for his first training.
Wylder는 학교 운동장으로 향하고 있었다 / 그의 첫 훈련을 위해

(A-3) He had just joined the team / with five other students / 33번-① 정답 단서
과거완료
그는 막 팀에 합류했다 / 다섯 명의 다른 학생들과 /
Wylder는 다섯 명의 다른 학생과 팀에 합류함.
after a successful tryout.
성공적인 적격 시험 후에

(A-4) Approaching the field, / (a)he saw players getting ready, /
5형식V O O·C①(현재분사)
운동장에 가까워지면서 / (a)그(Wylder)는 선수들이 준비하는 것을 보았다 /
pulling up their socks / and strapping on shin guards.
O·C②(현재분사) O·C③(현재분사)
그들의 양말을 끌어올리는 것을 / 그리고 정강이 보호대를 착용하는 것을

정답과 해설
18 장문의 이해 - 복합지문

(A-5) But they weren't together.
그러나 그들은 함께가 아니었다

🔓힌트 팀의 선수들이 'New players'와 아닌 사람으로 나뉘어 있어서, 'New players'가 아닌 나머지 다른 사람 전부를 가리키는 'the others'가 쓰임.

(A-6) New players were sitting / in the shade by the garage, /
새로운 선수들은 앉아 있었다 / 차고 근처의 그늘에 /
while the others were standing / in the sun by the right pole.
반면에 다른 선수들은 서 있었다 / 오른쪽 기둥 옆 양지에

(A-7) Then Coach McGraw came / and watched the players. 31번 정답 단서
그 후 McGraw 코치가 왔다 / 그리고 선수들을 보았다
코치가 선수들을 보았음.

* (A) 요약: 첫 훈련에 나온 Wylder가 따로 있는 선수들을 보았고, 코치도 그 광경을 보았음.

(D-1) Coach McGraw, too, saw the pattern /
McGraw 코치도 그 패턴을 보았다 /
— new kids and others grouping separately. 31번 정답 단서
새로운 아이들과 다른 아이들이 따로 무리를 지어 있는
코치가 선수들이 서로 따로 있는 것을 확인함.

(D-2) 'This has to change,' / he thought.
'이건 바뀌어야 해.' / 그는 생각했다

(D-3) He wanted a winning team.
그는 우승하는 팀을 원했다

(D-4) To do that, / he needed to build relationships.
부사적 용법(목적)
그러기 위해서 / 그는 관계를 형성해야 했다

(D-5) "I want you guys to come over here in the middle /
5형식V O O·C①(to V)
난 너희들이 여기 중앙에 오기를 바란다 / 31번·33번-⑤ 정답 단서
McGraw 코치는 선수들에게 운동장 중앙에 와서 앉으라고 함.
and sit," / he called the players / as he walked over.
O·C②(to 생략)
그리고 앉기를 / 그는 선수들을 불렀다 / 그가 걸어가면서

(D-6) "You!" / McGraw roared, / pointing at Wylder.
"너!" / McGraw가 고함쳤다 / Wylder를 가리키며

(D-7) "Come here onto the field / and sit.
여기 운동장으로 와라 / 그리고 앉아라

(D-8) And Jonny! / You sit over there!"
그리고 Jonny / 너는 저기 앉아라

(D-9) He started pointing, / [making sure / they mixed together].
그는 가리키기 시작했다 / 그리고 확실히 했다 / 그들이 서로 섞이는 것을
[ ]: 분사구문(결과)

(D-10) Wylder realized / [what Coach was trying to do], /
Wylder는 깨달았다 / 코치가 무엇을 하려고 하는지를 /
[ ]: 간접의문문(목적어)
so (e)he hopped onto the field.
그래서 (e)그(Wylder)는 운동장으로 뛰어 올라왔다

* (D) 요약: 코치가 선수들이 서로 섞일 수 있게 자리에 앉힘.

(C-1) McGraw continued to point, / calling each player out, /
McGraw는 계속해서 가리켰다 / 각 선수를 불러내며 /
분사구문(동시동작)
until he was satisfied with the rearrangement. 31번·33번-③ 정답 단서
그가 재배열에 만족할 때까지
McGraw는 재배열에 만족할 때까지 선수들을 계속해서 불러냄.

(C-2) "Okay, / this is how it's going to be," / he began.
그래 / 이렇게 될 거다 / 그가 말을 시작했다

(C-3) "We need to learn / how to trust and work with each other.
우리는 배울 필요가 있다 / 서로를 믿고 함께 경기하는 방식을

🔓힌트 '의문사+to V'는 명사적 용법으로서 '의문사+S+should+동사원형'의 형태로 바꾸어 쓸 수 있으며, 여기서는 'how we should trust and work'의 의미로 해석할 수 있음.

(C-4) This is how a team plays.
이것이 팀이 경기하는 방식이다

(C-5) This is how I want you to be / on and off the field: / together."
이것이 내가 너희가 되길 바라는 방식이다 / 운동장 안과 밖에서 / 함께하는 것

(C-6) The players looked at each other.
선수들은 서로를 바라보았다

(C-7) Almost immediately, / McGraw noticed a change /
거의 바로 / McGraw는 변화를 알아차렸다 /
in their postures and faces. 31번·33번-④ 정답 단서
그들의 자세와 얼굴에서
McGraw는 재배열과 연설을 끝내고 선수들의 자세와 얼굴에서 변화를 알아차림.

(C-8) (d)He saw / some of them starting to smile. 32번 정답 단서
5형식V O O·C(현재분사)
(d)그(McGraw)는 보았다 / 그들 중 몇몇이 미소를 짓기 시작하는 것을
몇몇 선수들이 미소를 짓기 시작하는 것을 알아차린 사람은 McGraw 코치임.

* (C) 요약: McGraw 코치가 선수들에게 팀이 변화해야 할 방향을 말함.

(B-1) 'Wow.' / thought Wylder.
'우와.' / Wylder는 생각했다

(B-2) From his new location / on the grass, / he stretched out his legs.
그의 새로운 자리에서 / 잔디 위의 / 그는 다리를 쭉 폈다 33번-② 정답 단서
Wylder는 잔디 위의 새로운 자리에서 다리를 쭉 폈음.

(B-3) He liked / what he was hearing.
그는 마음에 들었다 / 그가 듣고 있는 것이

(B-4) A new sense of team spirit came across (b)him, /
새로운 팀 정신의 감각이 (b)그(Wylder)에게 다가왔다 /
a deeper sense of connection.
더 깊은 연대감이

(B-5) It was encouraging / [to hear Coach talk about this, /
형식상의 주어 5형식V O O·C(동사원형)
힘을 북돋아 주었다 / 코치가 이것에 대해 말하는 것을 듣는 것은 /
to see him face the challenge head-on].
그가 도전에 정면으로 맞서는 것을 보는 것은
[ ]: 내용상의 주어

🔓힌트 형식상의 주어 It과 내용상의 주어로 구성된 문장으로, 내용상의 주어인 to부정사구 2개가 병렬로 연결되어 있음. 또한 to부정사구는 각각 '지각동사+O+O·C(동사원형)'의 5형식 문장으로 구성되어 있음.

(B-6) Now / his speech was over. 31번 정답 단서
이제 / 그의 연설이 끝났다
코치가 말하던 것이 끝남.

(B-7) The players got up /
선수들은 일어났다 /
and started walking on the field / to warm up.
그리고 운동장을 걷기 시작했다 / 몸을 풀기 위해
부사적 용법(목적)

(B-8) "Good job, Coach. / That was good," / Wylder said to McGraw /
잘하셨습니다 코치님 / 그건 정말 좋았어요 / Wylder는 McGraw에게 말했다 /
in a low voice / as he walked past him, /
낮은 목소리로 / 그가 그를 지나쳐 걸으면서 /
keeping (c)his eyes down / out of respect.
(c)그(Wylder)의 시선을 아래로 한 채로 / 존경심을 담아

* (B) 요약: 코치의 연설을 듣고 Wylder는 팀 정신을 느꼈고, 코치에게 존경심을 표함.

[전문 해석]

(A)

(1)초가을의 더운 날이었다. (2)Wylder는 그의 첫 훈련을 위해 학교 운동장으로 향하고 있었다. (3)그는 성공적인 적격 시험 후에 다섯 명의 다른 학생들과 막 팀에 합류했다. (4)운동장에 가까워지면서, (a)그(Wylder)는 선수들이 준비하고, 그들의 양말을 끌어올리고 정강이 보호대를 착용하는 것을 보았다. (5)그러나 그들은 함께가 아니었다. (6)새로운 선수들은 차고 근처의 그늘에 앉아 있는 반면, 다른 선수들은 오른쪽 기둥 옆 양지에 서 있었다. (7)그 후 McGraw 코치가 왔고, 선수들을 보았다.

(D)

(1)McGraw 코치도 새로운 아이들과 다른 아이들이 따로 무리를 지어 있는 그 패턴(모습)을 보았다. (2)'이건 바뀌어야 해.'라고 그는 생각했다. (3)그는 우승하는 팀을 원했다. (4)그러기 위해서 그는 관계를 형성해야 했다. (5)"난 너희들이 여기 중앙에 와서 앉기를 바란다."라며 그는 걸어가면서 선수들을 불렀다. (6)McGraw가 Wylder를 가리키며 "너!"라고 고함쳤다. (7)"여기 운동장으로 와서 앉아라. (8)그리고 Jonny! 너는 저기 앉아라!" (9)그는 가리키기 시작했고, 그들(선수들)이 서로 섞이는 것을 확실히 했다. (10)Wylder는 코치가 무엇을 하려고 하는지를 깨달아서, (e)그(Wylder)는 운동장으로 뛰어 올라왔다.

(C)

(1)McGraw는 그가 재배열에 만족할 때까지 각 선수를 불러내며 계속해서 가리켰다. (2)"그래, 이렇게 될 거다."라고 그가 말을 시작했다. (3)"우리는 서로를 믿고 함께 경기하는 방식을 배울 필요가 있다. (4)이것이 팀이 경기하는 방식이다. (5)이것이 내가 너희가 운동장 안과 밖에서 함께하는 것이 되길(함께하기를) 바라는 방식이다." (6)선수들은 서로를 바라보았다. (7)McGraw는 그들의 자세와 얼굴에서 거의 바로 변화를 알아차렸다. (8)(d)그(McGraw)는 그들 중 몇몇이 미소를 짓기 시작하는 것을 보았다.

(B)

(1)'우와.'라고 Wylder는 생각했다. (2)잔디 위의 그의 새로운 자리에서 그는 다리를 쭉 폈다. (3)그는 그가 듣고 있는 것이 마음에 들었다. (4)새로운 팀 정신의 감각, 더 깊은 연대감이 (b)그(Wylder)에게 다가왔다. (5)코치가 이것에 대해 말하는 것을 듣는 것과 그가 도전에 정면으로 맞서는 것을 보는 것은 힘을 북돋아 주었다. (6)이제 그의 연설이 끝났다. (7)선수들은 일어나서 몸을 풀기 위해 운동장을 걷기 시작했다. (8)Wylder는 존경심을 담아 (c)그(Wylder)의 시선을 아래로 한 채로 McGraw를 지나쳐 걸으면서 그에게 "잘하셨습니다, 코치님. 그건 정말 좋았어요."라고 낮은 목소리로 말했다.

[정답 확인]

31. 주어진 글 (A)에 이어질 내용을 순서에 맞게 배열한 것으로 가장 적절한 것은?

① (B) — (D) — (C) ② (C) — (B) — (D) ③ (C) — (D) — (B)
④ (D) — (B) — (C) ✔ (D) — (C) — (B)

32. 밑줄 친 (a) ~ (e) 중에서 가리키는 대상이 나머지 넷과 다른 것은?

① (a) ② (b) ③ (c) ✔ (d) ⑤ (e)

33. 윗글의 내용으로 적절하지 않은 것은?

① Wylder는 다섯 명의 다른 학생과 팀에 합류했다(join). 문장(A-3)
② Wylder는 잔디 위의 새로운 자리에서 다리를 쭉 폈다(stretch). 문장(B-2)
③ McGraw는 재배열(rearrangement)이 마음에 들 때까지 선수들을 불러냈다. 문장(C-1)
④ McGraw는 선수들의 자세(posture)와 얼굴의 변화를 알아차렸다. 문장(C-7)
✔ McGraw는 선수들에게 운동장 ~~밖으로 나가라고~~ 말했다. 문장(D-5)
중앙에 앉으라고

[문제 풀이]

31. (A)는 Wylder가 처음으로 팀 훈련을 위해 운동장으로 가서 본 광경에 대한 내용을 담고 있다. Wylder는 팀의 신규 선수들과 기존 선수들이 각자 따로 있는 것을 보았고, 이 광경을 코치인 McGraw도 봤다는 내용으로 (A)가 마무리된다. 이 내용에서 이어지는 문단은 (D)로, 문장 (D-1)에서 코치도 새로 들어온 아이들과 기존에 있던 아이들이 따로 있다는 것을 보았다는 것이 언급된다. (D)에서 코치는 팀 선수들이 섞일 수 있도록 자리 배치를 했고, 이는 문장 (C-1)의 내용처럼 재배열이 만족스러워질 때까지 이어졌다. (C)의 마지막 문장에서 코치가 선수들 사이의 변화를 알아챘다는 것이 언급되며, 이는 (B-1)에서 Wylder의 감탄으로 이어진다. 또한 (C)에서 코치가 하는 연설은 (B-6)에서 끝났다고 언급되었으므로, (C) 다음에는 (B)가 와야 한다. 따라서 정답은 ⑤ '(D) — (C) — (B)'이다.

[중요 어휘]

☐ **head**	동사 (특정 방향으로) 향하다
☐ **training**	명사 훈련, 연수
☐ **tryout**	명사 적격 시험, 예선
☐ **approach**	동사 가까워지다, 다가가다
☐ **shin**	명사 정강이
☐ **shade**	명사 그늘, 응달
☐ **in the sun**	양지에
☐ **pole**	명사 기둥, 막대기
☐ **group**	동사 무리를 짓다, 모으다
☐ **roar**	동사 고함치다, 외치다, 으르렁거리다
☐ **call A out**	A를 불러내다
☐ **rearrangement**	명사 재배열, 재정리
☐ **posture**	명사 자세, 태도
☐ **sense of connection**	연대감
☐ **head-on**	부사 정면으로, 정통으로

34~36

2023년 6월 43~45번
(정답률 75% | 65% | 80%)

정답 ④ | ② | ③

[지문 끊어 읽기] Henrietta의 선행

(A-1) Henrietta is one of the greatest "queens of song."
Henrietta는 가장 위대한 '노래의 여왕' 중 한 명이다

(A-2) She had to go through a severe struggle /
그녀는 혹독한 시련을 겪어야 했다 /
before (a)she attained the enviable position /
접속사
(a)그녀(Henrietta)가 부러워하는 위치에 도달하기 전에 /
as the greatest singer Germany had produced.
전치사(~로서) 선행사 목적격 관계대명사절
독일이 배출한 가장 위대한 가수로서

(A-3) At the beginning of her career /
그녀의 경력 초기에 /
she was hissed off a Vienna stage /
그녀는 비엔나 무대에서 야유를 받고 퇴장당했다 /
by the friends of her rival, Amelia. 36번-① 정답 단서 Henrietta에게 Amelia는 라이벌이었음.
그녀의 라이벌인 Amelia의 친구들에 의해

(A-4) But in spite of this defeat, / Henrietta endured /
하지만 이 좌절에도 불구하고 / Henrietta는 견뎠다 /
until all Europe was at her feet. 34번 정답 단서 Henrietta는 좌절을 견뎌내고 명성을 얻음.
온 유럽이 그녀의 발밑에 있을 때까지

* (A) 요약: Henrietta는 시련과 좌절을 이겨 내고 가장 위대한 '노래의 여왕' 중 한 명이 됨.

(D-1) Many years later, /
수년 후 /
when Henrietta was at the height of her fame, / Henrietta의 명성이 절정일 때의 일화가 시작됨.
Henrietta의 명성이 절정에 달했을 때 /
one day she was riding through the streets of Berlin. 34번 정답 단서
어느 날 그녀는 베를린의 거리를 차를 타고 지나가고 있었다

(D-2) Soon she came across a little girl / leading a blind woman.
현재분사 36번-⑤ 정답 단서 Henrietta는 눈먼 여성을 데리고 가는 여자 아이와 마주침.
곧 그녀는 한 여자 아이와 마주쳤다 / 눈먼 여성을 데리고 가는

(D-3) She was touched by the woman's helplessness, /
그녀는 그 여성의 무력함에 마음이 움직였다 /
and she impulsively beckoned the child to (e)her, /
그리고 그녀는 충동적으로 아이를 (e)그녀(Henrietta)에게 오라고 손짓했다 /
[saying / "Come here, my child. /
말하면서 / 이리 와, 얘야 /
Who is that you are leading by the hand?"] 34번 정답 단서 Henrietta가 눈먼 여성을 데리고 가는 여자 아이에게 그녀가 누구인지 질문함.
네가 손을 잡고 데리고 가는 사람은 누구니 [ ]: 분사구문

* (D) 요약: Henrietta는 자신의 명성이 절정에 달했을 때, 거리에서 눈먼 여성을 데리고 가는 여자 아이를 만남.

(B-1) The answer was, / "That's my mother, Amelia Steininger. /
대답은 ~였다 / 저분은 제 어머니, Amelia Steininger입니다 /
She used to be a great singer, / but she lost her voice, /
그녀는 훌륭한 가수였습니다 / 하지만 그녀는 목소리를 잃었습니다 /
and she cried so much about it /
so+형용사/부사+that: 너무 ~해서 …하다
그리고 그녀는 그 일로 너무 많이 울어서 /
that now (b)she can't see anymore." 34번·35번 정답 단서 Henrietta의 질문에 여자 아이는 눈먼 여성이 자신의 어머니인 Amelia라고 대답함.
이제 (b)그녀(Amelia)는 더 이상 앞을 볼 수 없습니다

(B-2) Henrietta inquired their address / and then told the child, /
Henrietta는 그들의 주소를 물었다 / 그러고 나서 아이에게 말했다 /
"Tell your mother /
어머니께 말하렴 /
an old acquaintance will call on her this afternoon."
오늘 오후에 오래된 지인이 그녀를 방문할 것이라고

(B-3) She searched out their place / Henrietta는 Amelia 모녀의 거처를 찾아내 그들을 돌봄.
그녀는 그들의 거처를 찾아냈다 /
and undertook the care of both mother and daughter. 36번-② 정답 단서
그리고 모녀를 돌보았다

(B-4) At her request, / Henrietta는 예전 라이벌이었던 Amelia의 시력을 회복시키기 위해 도움을 제공했지만 Amelia의 시력은 회복되지 못했음.
그녀의 요청에 따라 / 34번·36번-③ 정답 단서
a skilled doctor tried to restore Amelia's sight, / but it was in vain.
숙련된 의사가 Amelia의 시력을 회복시키려 했다 / 하지만 그것은 허사였다

* (B) 요약: Henrietta는 예전 라이벌인 Amelia와 그녀의 딸을 돌보고 도움.

(C-1) But Henrietta's kindness to (c)her former rival /
하지만 Henrietta가 (c)그녀(Henrietta)의 예전 라이벌에게 베푼 친절은 /
did not stop here. 34번 정답 단서 Henrietta는 예전 라이벌인 Amelia와 그녀의 딸을 도운 것에 그치지 않고 친절을 더 베풂.
여기서 그치지 않았다

36번-④ 정답 단서 Henrietta는 그 불쌍한 여성을 위한 자선 콘서트를 개최함.
(C-2) The next week / she gave a benefit concert for the poor woman, /
그 다음 주에 / 그녀는 그 불쌍한 여성을 위한 자선 콘서트를 열었다 /
and it was said that on that occasion Henrietta sang /
그리고 그 자리에서 Henrietta는 노래를 불렀다고 한다 /
as (d)she had never sung before.
접속사
(d)그녀(Henrietta)가 전에 한 번도 불러본 적 없는 방식으로

(C-3) And who can doubt /
그리고 누가 의심할 수 있을까 /

that with the applause of that vast audience /
명사절 접속사
어마어마한 청중의 박수와 함께 /

there was mingled the applause of the angels in heaven /
천국에 있는 천사들의 박수가 섞여 있었다는 것을 / 선행사

who rejoice over the good deeds of those below?
주격 관계대명사
지상 사람들의 선행에 크게 기뻐하는

* (C) 요약: Henrietta는 Amelia를 돕는 것에만 그치지 않고 자선 콘서트를 개최하여 불쌍한 여성에게 친절을 베풂.

[전문 해석]

(A)

(1)Henrietta는 가장 위대한 '노래의 여왕' 중 한 명이다. (2)독일이 배출한 가장 위대한 가수로서 (a)그녀(Henrietta)가 부러워하는 위치에 도달하기 전에 그녀는 혹독한 시련을 겪어야 했다. (3)그녀의 경력 초기에, 그녀는 라이벌인 Amelia의 친구들에 의해 비엔나 무대에서 야유를 받고 퇴장당했다. (4)하지만 이 좌절에도 불구하고, Henrietta는 온 유럽이 그녀의 발밑에 있을 때까지 견뎠다.

(D)

(1)수년 후, Henrietta의 명성이 절정에 달했을 때, 어느 날 그녀는 베를린의 거리를 차를 타고 지나가고 있었다. (2)곧 그녀는 눈먼 여성을 데리고 가는 한 어린 여자 아이와 마주쳤다. (3)그녀는 그 여성의 무력함에 마음이 움직였고, 충동적으로 아이를 (e)그녀(Henrietta)에게 오라고 손짓하며, "이리 와, 얘야. 네가 손을 잡고 데리고 가는 사람은 누구니?"라고 말했다.

(B)

(1)대답은, "저분은 제 어머니, Amelia Steininger입니다. 그녀는 훌륭한 가수였지만, 목소리를 잃었고, 그 일로 너무 많이 울어서 이제 (b)그녀(Amelia)는 더 이상 앞을 볼 수 없습니다." 였다. (2)Henrietta는 그들의 주소를 묻고 나서 아이에게 "어머니께 오늘 오후에 오래된 지인이 그녀를 방문할 것이라고 말하렴."이라고 말했다. (3)그녀는 그들의 거처를 찾아내서, 모녀를 돌보았다. (4)그녀의 요청에 따라 숙련된 의사가 Amelia의 시력을 회복시키려 했지만, 그것은 허사였다.

(C)

(1)하지만 Henrietta가 (c)그녀(Henrietta)의 예전 라이벌에게 베푼 친절은 여기서 그치지 않았다. (2)그 다음 주에 그녀는 그 불쌍한 여성을 위한 자선 콘서트를 열었고, 그 자리에서 Henrietta는 (d)그녀(Henrietta)가 전에 한 번도 불러본 적 없는 방식으로 노래를 불렀다고 한다. (3)그리고 어마어마한 청중의 박수와 함께 지상 사람들의 선행에 크게 기뻐하는 천국에 있는 천사들의 박수가 섞여 있었다는 것을 누가 의심할 수 있을까?

[정답 확인]

34. 주어진 글 (A)에 이어질 내용을 순서에 맞게 배열한 것으로 가장 적절한 것은?

① (B) — (D) — (C) ② (C) — (B) — (D) ③ (C) — (D) — (B)
④ (D) — (B) — (C) ⑤ (D) — (C) — (B)

35. 밑줄 친 (a) ~ (e) 중에서 가리키는 대상이 나머지 넷과 다른 것은?

① (a) ② (b) ③ (c) ④ (d) ⑤ (e)

36. 윗글의 내용으로 적절하지 않은 것은?

① Amelia와 Henrietta는 라이벌(rival) 관계였다. 문장(A-3)
② Henrietta는 모녀의 거처를 찾아내서(search out) 그들을 돌보았다. 문장(B-3)
③ 숙련된(skilled) 의사가 Amelia의 시력(sight)을 ~~회복시켰다~~. 문장(B-4)
회복시키려 했지만 허사였다
④ 불쌍한 여성을 위해 Henrietta는 자선 콘서트(a benefit concert)를 열었다. 문장(C-2)
⑤ Henrietta는 눈먼(blind) 여성을 데리고 가는 여자 아이와 마주쳤다(come across). 문장(D-2)

[문제 풀이]

35. 문장 (B-1)은 문장 (D-3)의 Henrietta의 질문에 대한 'a little girl leading a blind woman (눈먼 여성을 데리고 가는 한 여자 아이)'의 답변으로, 눈먼 여성은 자신의 어머니, Amelia임을 밝히고 있다. 따라서 (b)는 Amelia를 지칭하며, (b)를 제외한 나머지 선택지는 Henrietta를 지칭하기 때문에 정답은 ②이다.

[중요 어휘]

☐ struggle	명사 시련, 투쟁, 싸움 / 동사 고군분투하다, 힘겹게 나아가다
☐ attain	동사 도달하다, 이루다, 획득하다
☐ enviable	형용사 부러워하는, 선망의 대상이 되는
☐ hiss off	야유하여 ~을 퇴장시키다
☐ defeat	명사 좌절, 패배 / 동사 패배시키다, 이기다
☐ endure	동사 견디다, 참다, 오래가다
☐ come across	(우연히) 마주치다, 발견하다
☐ helplessness	명사 무력함, 난감함
☐ impulsively	부사 충동적으로
☐ beckon	동사 오라고 손짓하다, 손짓으로 부르다
☐ acquaintance	명사 지인, 친분, 지식
☐ call on	방문하다, 요청하다, 촉구하다
☐ restore	동사 회복시키다, 되찾게 하다, 복원하다
☐ in vain	허사가 되어, 헛되이
☐ applause	명사 박수
☐ vast	형용사 어마어마한, 방대한, 막대한
☐ mingle	동사 섞(이)다, 어우러지다, 사람들과 어울리다
☐ rejoice over	~에 크게 기뻐하다

핵심 Maria와 그녀의 딸 Alice가 Karen 가족을 위해 벌인 크리스마스 이벤트에 대한 글임. 주요 인물인 Maria와 Alice에 주목하여 이야기를 읽을 것.

37~39

2020년 6월 43~45번
(정답률 70% | 60% | 80%)

정답 ③ | ⑤ | ④

[지문 끊어 읽기] 크리스마스 이벤트

(A-1) Maria Sutton was a social worker / in a place /
Maria Sutton은 사회복지사였다 / 지역의 /
where the average income was very low.
평균 소득이 매우 낮은

(A-2) Many of Maria's clients had lost their jobs /
Maria의 많은 고객들은 그들의 일자리를 잃었다 /
when the coal industry in a nearby town collapsed.
근처 마을의 석탄 산업이 붕괴되었을 때

(A-3) Every Christmas season, /
크리스마스 시즌마다 /
knowing / how much children loved presents at Christmas, /
분사구문-이유
알았기 때문에 / 아이들이 크리스마스에 선물을 얼마나 좋아하는지 /

힌트 생략된 분사구문의 접속사와 주어를 넣으면, 밑줄 친 부분은 'because she(=Maria) knew'로 바꿔 쓸 수 있음.

Maria tried to arrange /
Maria는 계획하려 했다 /
a special visit from Santa Claus / for one family. 37번 정답 단서
산타클로스의 특별 방문을 / 한 가족을 위해

(A-4) Alice, / the seven-year-old daughter of Maria, /
Alice는 / Maria의 일곱 살 된 딸인 /
was very enthusiastic /
매우 열정적이었다 /
about helping with (a)her mother's Christmas event.
(a)그녀(Alice)의 엄마의 크리스마스 이벤트를 돕는 것에

* (A) 요약: 사회복지사인 Maria는 크리스마스 시즌마다 한 가족을 위해 산타클로스의 특별 방문을 계획함.

(C-1) This year's lucky family / 37번 정답 단서
올해 행운의 가족은 /
was a 25-year-old mother named Karen and her 3-year-old son, /
병렬① 병렬②
Karen이라는 이름의 스물다섯 살 된 엄마와 그녀의 세 살 된 아들이었다 /
who she was raising by herself.
그리고 그녀는 혼자서 키우고 있었다

힌트 콤마(,) 뒤에 나온 who는 계속적 용법으로 쓰인 목적격 관계대명사임. 선행사는 her 3-year-old son으로, was raising에 대한 목적어가 빠져 있음. 따라서 이 관계대명사절을 'and she was raising her 3-year-old son by herself'로 풀어서 쓸 수 있음.

(C-2) However, / things went wrong.
그러나 / 상황들이 나빠졌다

(C-3) Two weeks before Christmas Day, /
크리스마스 2주 전 /
a representative from a local organization / called Maria / 39번 정답 단서
지역 단체의 대표가 / Maria에게 연락했다 /
to say that / the aid she had requested for Karen /
S' (관계사가 생략된) 목적격 관계대명사절
~라고 말하기 위해 / 그녀가 Karen을 위해 요청했던 지원이 /
had fallen through.
V'
실패했다

(C-4) No Santa Claus.
산타클로스는 없었다

(C-5) No presents.
선물도 없었다

(C-6) Maria saw the cheer disappear / from Alice's face / at the news.
지각V O O·C
Maria는 생기가 사라지는 것을 보았다 / Alice의 얼굴에서 / 그 소식에

(C-7) After hearing this, / (c)she ran to her room. 37번 정답 단서
이것을 듣고 난 뒤 / (c)그녀(Alice)는 그녀의 방으로 달려갔다

* (C) 요약: Maria는 Karen 가족을 위한 이벤트를 계획했지만, 그녀가 요청했던 지원이 성사되지 않음.

(D-1) When Alice returned, / her face was set with determination. 37번 정답 단서
Alice가 돌아왔을 때 / 그녀의 얼굴은 결의에 차 있었다

(D-2) She counted out the coins / from her piggy bank: / $4.30.
그녀는 동전들을 세면서 꺼냈다 / 그녀의 돼지 저금통에서 / 4달러 30센트

(D-3) "Mom," / she told Maria, / "(d)I know it's not much. /
"엄마," / 그녀는 Maria에게 말했다 / (d)나(Alice)는 이것이 얼마 되지 않는다는 것을 알아요 /
But maybe this will buy a present for the kid."
그렇지만 아마도 이것은 그 아이를 위한 선물을 살 거예요

(D-4) Maria gave her daughter a lovely hug.
Maria는 그녀의 딸을 사랑스럽게 안아 주었다

(D-5) The next day, / Maria told her coworkers /
그 다음 날 / Maria는 그녀의 동료들에게 말했다 /
about her daughter's latest project. 38번 정답 단서
그녀의 딸의 최근 프로젝트에 대해

(D-6) To (e)her surprise, / staff members began / to open their purses.
(e)그녀(Maria)가 놀랍게도 / 직원들은 시작했다 / 그들의 지갑을 열기

(D-7) The story of Alice's gift had spread / beyond Maria's office, /
과거완료(대과거)
Alice의 선물 이야기는 퍼졌다 / Maria의 사무실을 넘어 /
and Maria was able to raise $300 /
그리고 Maria는 300달러를 모금할 수 있었다 /
— plenty for a Christmas gift / for Karen and her son.
크리스마스 선물을 위해 충분한 / Karen과 그녀의 아들을 위한

* (D) 요약: Maria의 어린 딸 Alice가 저금통을 깨서 Karen 가족을 돕고자 한다는 이야기가 알려지자 300달러나 되는 모금액이 모임.

(B-1) On Christmas Eve, / 37번 정답 단서
크리스마스 전날 /
Maria and Alice visited Karen's house / with Christmas gifts.
Maria와 Alice는 Karen의 집을 방문했다 / 크리스마스 선물을 가지고

(B-2) When Karen opened the door, /
Karen이 문을 열었을 때 /
Maria and Alice wished the astonished woman /
Maria와 Alice는 그 깜짝 놀란 여성에게 기원해 주었다 /
a merry Christmas.
즐거운 크리스마스를

(B-3) Then / Alice began to unload the gifts from the car, /
그런 다음 / Alice는 차에서 선물을 내리기 시작했다 /
handing them to Karen / one by one.
Karen에게 그것들을 건넸다 / 하나씩

(B-4) Karen laughed in disbelief, / and said / she hoped /
Karen은 믿기지 않는다는 듯이 웃었다 / 그리고 말했다 / 그녀가 바란다고 /
she would one day be able to do / something similar /
그녀가 언젠가 할 수 있기를 / 비슷한 어떤 일을 /
for someone else in need.
어려움에 처한 다른 사람을 위해

(B-5) On her way home, / Maria said to Alice, /
그녀의 집에 가는 길에 / Maria는 Alice에게 말했다 /
"God multiplied (b)your gift."
"신이 (b)너(Alice)의 선물을 늘렸구나."

* (B) 요약: 크리스마스 전날, Maria와 Alice는 Karen의 집에 방문해 크리스마스 선물을 줌.

[전문 해석]

(A)

(1)Maria Sutton은 평균 소득이 매우 낮은 지역의 사회복지사였다. (2)Maria의 많은 고객들은 근처 마을의 석탄 산업이 붕괴되었을 때 그들의 일자리를 잃었다. (3)아이들이 크리스마스에 선물을 얼마나 좋아하는지 알았기 때문에, 크리스마스 시즌마다 Maria는 한 가족을 위해 산타클로스의 특별 방문을 계획하려 했다. (4)Maria의 일곱 살 된 딸인 Alice는 (a)그녀(Alice)의 엄마의 크리스마스 이벤트를 돕는 것에 매우 열정적이었다.

(C)

(1)올해 행운의 가족은 Karen이라는 이름의 스물다섯 살 된 엄마와 그녀의 세 살 된 아들이었고, 그녀는 (그를) 혼자서 키우고 있었다. (2)그러나 상황들이 나빠졌다. (3)크리스마스 2주 전, 지역 단체의 대표가 그녀(Maria)가 Karen을 위해 요청했던 지원이 실패했다고(성사되지 않았다고) 말하기 위해 Maria에게 연락했다. (4)산타클로스는 없었다. (5)선물도 없었다. (6)Maria는 그 소식에 Alice의 얼굴에서 생기가 사라지는 것을 보았다. (7)이것(이 소식)을 듣고 난 뒤, (c)그녀(Alice)는 그녀의 방으로 달려갔다.

(D)

(1)Alice가 돌아왔을 때, 그녀의 얼굴은 결의에 차 있었다. (2)그녀는 그녀의 돼지 저금통에서 동전들을 세면서 꺼냈다. 4달러 30센트(였다). (3)"엄마," 그녀는 Maria에게 "(d)나(Alice)는 이것이 얼마 되지 않는다는 것을 알아요. 그렇지만 아마도 이것은(이것으로) 그 아이를 위한 선물을 살 (수 있을) 거예요."라고 말했다. (4)Maria는 그녀의 딸을 사랑스럽게 안아 주었다. (5)그 다음 날, Maria는 그녀의 동료들에게 그녀의 딸의 최근 프로젝트에 대해 말했다. (6)(e)그녀(Maria)가 놀랍게도, 직원들은 그들의 지갑을 열기 시작했다. (7)Alice의 선물 이야기는 Maria의 사무실을 넘어 퍼졌고, Maria는 Karen과 그녀의 아들을 위한 크리스마스 선물을 위해 충분한 (금액인) 300달러를 모금할 수 있었다.

(B)

(1)크리스마스 전날, Maria와 Alice는 크리스마스 선물을 가지고 Karen의 집을 방문했다. (2)Karen이 문을 열었을 때, Maria와 Alice는 그 깜짝 놀란 여성(Karen)에게 즐거운 크리스마스를 기원해 주었다. (3)그런 다음 Alice는 차에서 선물을 내리기 시작했고, Karen에게 그것들을 하나씩 건넸다. (4)Karen은 믿기지 않는다는 듯이 웃었고, 그녀가 언젠가 어려움에 처한 다른 사람을 위해 비슷한 어떤 일을 할 수 있기를 바란다고 말했다. (5)(그녀의) 집에 가는 길에 Maria는 Alice에게 "신이 (b)너(Alice)의 선물을 늘렸구나."라고 말했다.

[정답 확인]

37. 주어진 글 (A)에 이어질 내용을 순서에 맞게 배열한 것으로 가장 적절한 것은?

① (B) — (D) — (C) ② (C) — (B) — (D) ✔ (C) — (D) — (B)
④ (D) — (B) — (C) ⑤ (D) — (C) — (B)

38. 밑줄 친 (a) ~ (e) 중에서 가리키는 대상이 나머지 넷과 다른 것은?

① (a) ② (b) ③ (c) ④ (d) ✔ (e)

39. 윗글의 내용으로 적절하지 않은 것은?

① Maria는 평균 소득(income)이 매우 낮은 지역의 사회복지사(social worker)였다.
② 크리스마스 전날(on Christmas Eve) Karen은 선물을 받았다.
③ Karen은 세 살 된 아들(3-year-old son)을 키우고 있었다.
✔ Maria는 지역 단체(local organization) 대표(representative)의 연락을 ~~받지 못했다~~. 받았다
⑤ Maria는 300달러를 모금할(raise) 수 있었다.

[문제 풀이]

38. 문장 (D-5)에서 Maria는 자신의 동료들에게 전날 딸이 한 말에 대해 이야기했고, Alice의 선물 이야기를 들은 후, 문장 (D-6)에서 Maria의 동료들은 모금을 하기 시작했다. 이에 놀란 '그녀'는 동료들에게 딸의 이야기를 한 Maria이다. 따라서 Alice를 가리키는 나머지 넷과 다른 것은 ⑤이다.

[중요 어휘]

☐ **social worker**	사회복지사
☐ **income**	명사 소득, 수입
☐ **coal**	명사 석탄
☐ **collapse**	동사 붕괴되다
☐ **arrange**	동사 계획하다, 배치하다, 정리하다
☐ **enthusiastic**	형용사 열정적인
☐ **raise**	동사 키우다, 모금하다
☐ **representative**	명사 대표 / 형용사 대표적인
☐ **aid**	명사 지원, 도움

□ **fall through**	실패하다, 잘 안되다
□ **cheer**	명사 생기, 환호 / 동사 환호하다
□ **determination**	명사 결의, 결심
□ **astonished**	형용사 깜짝 놀란
□ **unload**	동사 (짐을) 내리다
□ **multiply**	동사 늘리다, 증가시키다, 곱하다

40~42

2018년 6월 43~45번
(정답률 65% | 55% | 55%)

정답 ② | ③ | ④

[지문 끊어 읽기]

두 단어가 바꾼 인생

(A-1) Is it possible / that two words can change /
가능할까 / 두 단어가 바꿀 수 있는 것이 /
someone's day, / someone's life?
누군가의 하루를 / 누군가의 인생을

(A-2) What if / those same two words could change the world?
만약 ~라면 어떻게 될까 / 그 동일한 두 단어가 세상을 바꿀 수 있다면

(A-3) Well, / Cheryl Rice is on a quest / to find out.
자 / Cheryl Rice가 탐색 중이다 / 알아내기 위해

(A-4) This quest accidentally began / in November, 2016 /
이 탐색은 우연히 시작되었다 / 2016년 11월에 /
in a grocery store.
한 식료품 가게에서

(A-5) (a)She was standing / in the checkout line /
(a)그녀(Cheryl)는 서 있었다 / 계산대 줄에서 /
behind a woman / who looked to be in her 60's.
한 여자의 뒤에 / 60대로 보이는

(A-6) When it was the woman's turn to pay, /
그 여자가 계산할 차례가 되었을 때 /
the cashier greeted her by name /
계산원이 그녀의 이름을 부르며 인사했다 /
and asked her how she was doing. 40번 정답 단서
그리고 그녀에게 어떻게 지냈는지 물었다

* (A) 요약: 계산원이 Cheryl의 앞에 서 있던 60대 여성의 이름을 부르며 어떻게 지냈는지 물음.

(C-1) The woman looked down, / shook her head and said, / 41번 정답 단서
그 여자는 아래를 내려다봤다 / 그녀의 머리를 흔들며 말했다 /
"Not so good. / My husband just lost his job. 40번 정답 단서
그다지 좋지 않아요 / 제 남편이 이제 막 직장을 잃었거든요

(C-2) I don't know / how I'm going to get through the holidays."
저는 모르겠어요 / 제가 이 연휴를 어떻게 견뎌야 할지

(C-3) Then (c)she gave the cashier / some food stamps.
그러고 나서 (c)그녀(woman)는 계산원에게 주었다 / 몇 개의 푸드 스탬프를

(C-4) Cheryl's heart ached.
Cheryl의 마음은 아팠다

(C-5) She wanted to help / but didn't know how.
그녀는 돕고 싶었다 / 그러나 어떻게 할지 몰랐다

(C-6) "Should I offer to pay for her groceries, /
내가 그녀의 식료품비를 지불하겠다고 제안해야 할까 /
ask for her husband's resume?"
그녀의 남편의 이력서를 요청해야 할까

(C-7) She did nothing — yet. 42번 정답 단서
그녀는 아무것도 하지 않았다 아직까지는

(C-8) And the woman left the store.
그리고 그 여자는 가게를 떠났다

* (C) 요약: 남편이 직장을 잃어 힘든 시간을 보낸다는 이야기를 들은 Cheryl은 그녀를 돕고 싶었지만 아무것도 하지 못했음.

(B-1) As Cheryl walked into the parking lot, / she spotted the woman /
Cheryl이 주차장으로 걸어갔을 때 / 그녀는 그 여자를 발견했다 /
returning her shopping cart, / and she remembered something /
그녀의 쇼핑카트를 반납하고 있는 / 그리고 그녀는 무엇인가를 기억해냈다 /
in her purse / that could help her.
그녀의 지갑에 있는 / 그녀를 도울 수 있는

(B-2) She approached the woman and said, / "Excuse me, /
그녀는 그 여자에게 다가가서 말했다 / 실례합니다 /
I couldn't help overhearing / what you said to the cashier.
저는 엿들을 수밖에 없었어요 / 당신이 계산원에게 했던 말을

(B-3) It sounds like / you're going through a really hard time / right now.
~하는 것처럼 들리더군요 / 당신은 매우 힘든 시간을 겪고 있는 / 바로 지금

(B-4) I'm so sorry.
정말 유감이에요

(B-5) I'd like to give you something."
제가 당신에게 무엇인가를 드리고 싶어요

(B-6) And (b)she handed her / a small card. 40번 정답 단서
그리고 (b)그녀(Cheryl)는 그녀에게 건넸다 / 작은 카드를

* (B) 요약: Cheryl은 주차장에서 60대 여성을 다시 만나 작은 카드를 건넴.

(D-1) When the woman read / the card's only two words, / 40번 정답 단서
그 여자가 읽었을 때 / 카드의 단 두 단어를 /
she began to cry.
그녀는 울기 시작했다

(D-2) And through her tears, / she said, / "You have no idea /
그리고 눈물을 흘리며 / 그녀는 말했다 / 당신은 전혀 모를 거예요 /
how much this means to me."
이것이 나에게 얼마나 큰 의미인지

(D-3) (d)She was a little startled / by her reply.
(d)그녀(Cheryl)는 조금 놀랐다 / 그녀의 대답에

(D-4) Having never done anything like this before, /
이러한 일을 이전에는 해 본 적이 없었기 때문에 /
Cheryl hadn't anticipated the reaction / she might receive.
Cheryl은 그러한 반응을 예상하지 못했었다 / 그녀가 받을

(D-5) All (e)she could think to respond was, / "Oh, my. /
(e)그녀(Cheryl)가 반응하고자 생각해낼 수 있었던 전부는 ~였다 / 오 세상에 /
Would it be OK / to give you a hug?"
괜찮을까요 / 당신에게 포옹을 드려도

(D-6) After they embraced, / she walked back to her car /
그들이 껴안고 난 후 / 그녀는 그녀의 차로 걸어 돌아갔다 /
and began to cry too.
그리고 울기 시작했다

(D-7) The words on the card? / "You Matter."
그 카드에 있던 단어는 / "당신은 소중합니다."

* (D) 요약: 카드에 적힌 두 단어를 보고 여성은 눈물을 흘렸고 Cheryl과 포옹을 함.

[전문 해석]

(A)

(1)두 단어가 누군가의 하루를, 누군가의 인생을 바꿀 수 있는 것이 가능할까? (2)만약 그 동일한 두 단어가 세상을 바꿀 수 있다면 어떻게 될까? (3)자, Cheryl Rice가 (이를) 알아내기 위해 탐색 중이다. (4)이 탐색은 2016년 11월에 한 식료품 가게에서 우연히 시작되었다. (5)(a)그녀(Cheryl)는 계산대 줄에서 60대로 보이는 한 여자의 뒤에 서 있었다. (6)그 여자가 계산할 차례가 되었을 때, 계산원이 그녀의 이름을 부르며 인사했고, 그녀에게 어떻게 지냈는지 물었다.

(C)

(1)그 여자는 아래를 내려다보고, 그녀의 머리를 흔들며 말했다, "그다지 좋지 않아요. 제 남편이 이제 막 직장을 잃었거든요. (2)저는 제가 이 연휴를 어떻게 견뎌야 할지 모르겠어요." (3)그러고 나서 (c)그녀(woman)는 몇 개의 푸드 스탬프(구호 대상자용 식량 카드)를 계산원에게 주었다. (4)Cheryl의 마음은 아팠다. (5)그녀는 돕고 싶었지만 어떻게 할지 몰랐다. (6)"내가 그녀의 식료품비를 지불하겠다고 제안해야 할까? 그녀의 남편의 이력서를 요청해야 할까?" (7)그녀는 아무것도 하지 않았다. 아직까지는. (8)그리고 그 여자는 가게를 떠났다.

(B)

(1)Cheryl이 주차장으로 걸어갔을 때, 그녀는 쇼핑카트를 반납하고 있는 그 여자를 발견했고, 그녀(Cheryl)의 지갑에 있는 그녀(그 여자)를 도울 수 있는 무엇인가를 기억해냈다(자신의 지갑에 그녀를 도울 수 있는 무엇인가가 있다는 것을 기억해냈다). (2)그녀는 그 여자에게 다가가서 말했다, "실례합니다, 저는 당신이 계산원에게 했던 말을 엿들을 수밖에 없었어요.

(3)당신은 바로 지금 매우 힘든 시간을 겪고 있는 것처럼 들리더군요. (4)정말 유감이에요. (5)제가 당신에게 무엇인가를 드리고 싶어요." (6)그리고 (b)그녀(Cheryl)는 그녀에게 작은 카드를 건넸다.

(D)

(1)그 여자가 카드의(카드에 적힌) 단 두 단어를 읽었을 때, 그녀는 울기 시작했다. (2)그리고 눈물을 흘리며, 그녀는 말했다, "당신은 이것이 나에게 얼마나 큰 의미인지 전혀 모를 거예요." (3)(d)그녀(Cheryl)는 그녀의 대답에 조금 놀랐다. (4)이러한 일을 이전에는 해 본 적이 없었기 때문에, Cheryl은 그녀가 받을 그러한 반응을 예상하지 못했었다(Cheryl은 자신이 그러한 반응을 받게 될 것이라고 예상하지 못했었다). (5)(e)그녀(Cheryl)가 (재빨리) 반응하고자 생각해낼 수 있었던 전부는, "오, 세상에, 당신에게 포옹을 드려도 괜찮을까요?"였다(그녀는 "오, 세상에, 당신을 안아드려도 괜찮을까요?"라고 반응하는 것 외에는 다른 것을 생각해낼 수 없었다). (6)그들이 껴안고 난 후, 그녀는 그녀의 차로 걸어 돌아가 울기 시작했다. (7)그 카드에 있던 (두) 단어는? "당신은 소중합니다."

- food stamp(푸드 스탬프, 구호 대상자용 식량 카드): 미국에서 저소득층을 지원하기 위해 지정된 업체로부터 식품을 구매할 수 있도록 지급한 쿠폰, 할인권 및 전자카드를 통칭함.

[정답 확인]

40. 주어진 글 (A)에 이어질 내용을 순서에 맞게 배열한 것으로 가장 적절한 것은?

① (B) — (D) — (C) ✔② (C) — (B) — (D) ③ (C) — (D) — (B)
④ (D) — (B) — (C) ⑤ (D) — (C) — (B)

41. 밑줄 친 (a) ~ (e) 중에서 가리키는 대상이 나머지 넷과 다른 것은?

① (a) ② (b) ✔③ (c) ④ (d) ⑤ (e)

✱중요 밑줄 친 3인칭 여성 대명사로 지칭할 수 있는 인물이 Cheryl과 계산대에서 있던 나이 든 여자임을 파악하면 문장 (C-3)의 (c)she에 해당하는 것은 계산대에서 있던 여자임을 알 수 있음.

42. 윗글의 Cheryl Rice에 관한 내용으로 적절하지 않은 것은?

① 계산대 줄(checkout line)에 서 있었다.
② 대화를 우연히 엿들었다고(overhear) 말했다.
③ 작은 카드(small card)를 건넸다.
✔④ 식료품 구입비를 대신 ~~지불했다~~(pay for groceries). 지불하지 않았다
⑤ 차로 돌아와서(walk back) 울었다.

✱중요 문장 (C-3)에서 식료품 할인 구매권을 낸 것은 나이든 여자이며, 문장 (C-7)에서는 Cheryl이 그 여자를 돕기 위해 무언가를 하지는 않았음을 알 수 있음.

[중요 어휘]

□ on a quest	탐색 중인
□ get through	~을 견디다, ~에 닿다
□ ache	동사 (머리·마음 등이) 아프다
□ spot	동사 발견하다 / 명사 얼룩, 점
□ cannot help V-ing	~하지 않을 수 없다
□ overhear	동사 엿듣다
□ go through	~을 겪다, (시간을) 보내다
□ hand A B	A에게 B를 건네다
□ startled	형용사 놀란
□ anticipate	동사 예상하다, 기대하다
□ respond	동사 반응하다, 응답하다
□ embrace	동사 껴안다, (생각·제안을) 받아들이다

43~45

2023년 11월 43~45번
(정답률 80% | 70% | 85%)

정답 ③ | ⑤ | ⑤

[지문 끊어 읽기] 화해의 계기가 된 다리

(A-1) Once upon a time, / two brothers, Robert and James, /
S, 선행사 =
옛날 옛적에 / 두 형제인 Robert와 James가 /
who lived on neighboring farms / fell into conflict.
주격 관계대명사절 V
가까운 농장에 사는 / 갈등에 빠졌다

45번-① 정답 단서 Robert와 James는 40년 동안 나란히 농사를 지었음.

(A-2) It was the first serious fight / in 40 years of farming side by side.
그것은 최초의 심각한 싸움이었다 / 나란히 농사를 지은 지 40년 만에

(A-3) It began with a small misunderstanding /
S① V①
그것은 작은 오해로 시작했다 /
and it grew into a major argument, /
S② V②
그리고 그것은 중대한 논쟁이 되었다 /
and finally it exploded into an exchange of bitter words /
S③ V③
그리고 마침내 그것은 심한 말을 주고받는 것으로 폭발했다 /
[followed by weeks of silence]. [ ]: 과거분사구
몇 주의 침묵이 뒤따르는

(A-4) One morning there was a knock on Robert's door.
어느 날 아침 Robert의 문에 노크가 있었다

(A-5) (a)He opened it / to find a carpenter with a toolbox. 43번 정답 단서
부사적 용법(결과)
(a)그(Robert)는 그것을 열었다 / 공구 상자를 가진 목수를 발견했다
Robert는 문 앞에 목수가 와 있는 것을 확인함.

* (A) 요약: 두 형제인 Robert와 James가 크게 싸운 후 어느 날, Robert에게 한 목수가 찾아옴.

(C-1) Looking at Robert, / the carpenter said, /
분사구문(동시동작)
Robert를 바라보며 / 그 목수는 말했다 /
"I'm looking for a few days' work. 43번 정답 단서 목수가 Robert에게 말을 걸었음.
저는 며칠 동안 할 일을 찾고 있습니다

(C-2) Do (c)you have anything to repair?"
(c)당신(Robert)에게 수리해야 할 것이 있습니까

(C-3) "I have nothing to be repaired, /
수리되어야 할 것은 없습니다 /
but I have a job for you.
하지만 당신이 할 일이 있습니다

힌트 (C-2)의 'to repair'는 목수가 직접 수리해야 할 것이 있는지를 묻는 것이므로 능동의 의미로 to부정사를 사용함. 반면 (C-3)의 'to be repaired'는 Robert의 입장에서 수리공에 의해 수리되는 것이므로, 수동의 의미를 가지고 있어서 to부정사 수동 형태인 'to be+과거분사'로 쓰임. 둘 다 각각 앞의 'anything'과 'nothing'을 수식하는 형용사적 용법임.

(C-4) Look across the creek at that farm.
샛강 저편 저 농장을 보세요

(C-5) Last week, / my younger brother James took his bulldozer /
V①
지난주에 / 제 동생 James가 그의 불도저를 가지고 왔습니다 /
and put that creek in the meadow between us. 45번-③ 정답 단서
V②
그리고 우리 사이의 초원에 샛강을 만들었습니다
James가 불도저로 초원에 샛강을 만들었음.

(C-6) Well, / (d)I will do even worse.
음 / (d)저(Robert)는 훨씬 더 나쁜 일을 할 겁니다

힌트 비교급 'worse'의 의미를 강조하기 위해서 'even'을 사용함. 그 외에도 'still, much, far, a lot, way' 등이 비교급 강조 부사로 사용됨.

(C-7) I want you to build me an 8-foot tall fence / 43번 정답 단서
5형식V O O·C(동사원형, 4형식V) I·O D·O, 선행사
저는 당신이 저에게 8피트 높이의 울타리를 지어 주기를 원합니다 /
Robert가 목수에게 울타리를 지어 줄 것을 요청함.
[which will block him from seeing my place]," /
block A from V-ing: A가 ~하는 것을 막다 [ ]: 주격 관계대명사절
그가 제 장소를 보는 것으로부터 막을 /
said Robert.
Robert가 말했다

힌트 숫자와 단위 명사가 결합한 형태의 복합 형용사를 뒤에 나오는 명사를 수식하는 데 사용할 경우, 숫자와 단위 명사 사이에는 하이픈(-)을 넣고, 이때 단위 명사는 단수 형태로 써야 함.

(C-8) The carpenter seemed to understand the situation.
목수는 그 상황을 이해한 것처럼 보였다

* (C) 요약: 일을 달라고 찾아온 목수에게 Robert는 샛강에 James의 시선을 막을 만한 울타리를 만드는 일을 줌.

43번·45번-④ 정답 단서 Robert는 목수가 울타리를 만들 때 필요한 재료를 모두 준비해 줌.

(D-1) Robert prepared all the materials / the carpenter needed.
선행사 목적격 관계대명사절(관계대명사 생략)
Robert는 모든 재료를 준비했다 / 그 목수가 필요로 하는

(D-2) The next day, / Robert left to work on another farm, /
다음 날 / Robert는 또 다른 농장으로 일하러 떠났다 /
so he couldn't watch the carpenter for some days.
그래서 그는 며칠 동안 그 목수를 볼 수 없었다

(D-3) When Robert returned and saw the carpenter's work, /
Robert가 돌아와서 그 목수의 작업을 보았을 때 /
his jaw dropped.
그의 입이 쩍 벌어졌다

(D-4) Instead of a fence, / the carpenter had built a bridge /
선행사
울타리 대신에 / 그 목수는 다리 하나를 만들었다 /
[that stretched from one side of the creek to the other]. 45번-⑤ 정답 단서
[ ]: 주격 관계대명사절
샛강의 한쪽에서 다른 쪽까지 펼쳐지는
목수는 Robert가 요청한 울타리 대신 다리를 만듦.

(D-5) His brother was walking over, / [waving (e)his hand in the air]. [ ]: 분사구문
그의 동생이 걸어오고 있었다 / (e)그(James)의 손을 공중에 흔들며
44번 정답 단서 손을 공중에 흔들며 다리를 걸어오고 있던 사람은 Robert의 동생인 James임.

(D-6) Robert laughed and said to the carpenter, /
V① V②
Robert는 웃었고 목수에게 말했다 /

문제편 p.285

"You really can fix anything." 43번 정답 단서 Robert와 James가 다리를 계기로 화해의 조짐을 보임.
"당신은 정말 무엇이든 고칠 수 있군요."

* (D) 요약: Robert가 자리를 비운 며칠 사이에, 목수는 샛강에 울타리 대신 다리를 놓음.

(B-1) The two brothers stood awkwardly for a moment, / (V①)
두 형제는 잠시 어색하게 서 있었다 /
but soon met on the bridge / and shook hands. (V② V③) 43번 정답 단서 다리 위에서 만난 형제는 화해의 악수를 함.
하지만 곧 다리 위에서 만났다 / 그리고 악수를 했다

(B-2) They saw the carpenter leaving with his toolbox. (지각V, O, O.C(현재분사구))
그들은 목수가 그의 공구 상자를 가지고 떠나는 것을 보았다

(B-3) "No, wait! Stay a few more days." / Robert told him. 45번-② 정답 단서 Robert가 목수에게 더 머물러 달라고 말함.
"안 돼요, 잠깐만요! 며칠 더 머물러 주세요." / Robert가 그에게 말했다

(B-4) "Thank you for (b)your invitation.
(b)당신(Robert)의 초대에 감사드립니다

(B-5) But I need to go build more bridges.
하지만 저는 더 많은 다리를 만들러 가야 합니다

(B-6) Don't forget.
잊지 마세요

힌트 앞의 문장인 'The fence leads to isolation'과 동일한 형태가 반복되어, 'the bridge'와 'to openness' 사이에 동사 'leads'가 생략되어 있음.

(B-7) The fence leads to isolation / and the bridge to openness," /
울타리는 고립으로 이끕니다 / 그리고 다리는 관대함으로 /
said carpenter.
목수가 말했다

(B-8) The two brothers nodded at the carpenter's words.
두 형제는 그 목수의 말에 끄덕였다

* (B) 요약: 목수가 다리를 만들어 준 덕분에 두 형제가 화해함.

[전문 해석]

(A)

(1)옛날 옛적에, 가까운 농장에 사는 두 형제인 Robert와 James가 갈등에 빠졌다. (2)그것은 나란히 농사를 지은 지 40년 만에 최초의 심각한 싸움이었다. (3)그것은 작은 오해로 시작하여 중대한 논쟁이 되었고, 마침내 그것은 몇 주의 침묵이 뒤따르는 심한 말을 주고받는 것으로 폭발했다. (4)어느 날 아침 Robert의 문에 노크가 있었다. (5)(a)그(Robert)는 그것을 열어서 공구 상자를 가진 목수를 발견했다.

(C)

(1)Robert를 바라보며 그 목수는 말했다. "저는 며칠 동안 할 일을 찾고 있습니다. (2)(c)당신(Robert)에게 수리해야 할 것이 있습니까?" (3)"수리되어야 할 것은 없지만 당신이 할 일이 있습니다. (4)샛강 저편 저 농장을 보세요. (5)지난주에 제 동생 James가 그의 불도저를 가지고 우리 사이의 초원에 샛강을 만들었습니다. (6)음, (d)저(Robert)는 훨씬 더 나쁜 일을 할 겁니다. (7)저는 당신이 저에게 그가 제 장소를 보는 것으로부터 막을 8피트 높이의 울타리를 지어 주기를 원합니다."라고 Robert가 말했다. (8)목수는 그 상황을 이해한 것처럼 보였다.

(D)

(1)Robert는 그 목수가 필요로 하는 모든 재료를 준비했다. (2)다음 날, Robert는 또 다른 농장으로 일하러 떠났고, 그래서 그는 며칠 동안 그 목수를 볼 수 없었다. (3)Robert가 돌아와서 그 목수의 작업을 보았을 때, 그의 입이 쩍 벌어졌다. (4)울타리 대신에 그 목수는 샛강의 한쪽에서 다른 쪽까지 펼쳐지는 다리 하나를 만들었다. (5)그의 동생이 (e)그(James)의 손을 공중에 흔들며 걸어오고 있었다. (6)Robert는 웃었고 목수에게 "당신은 정말 무엇이든 고칠 수 있군요."라고 말했다.

(B)

(1)두 형제는 잠시 어색하게 서 있었지만, 곧 다리 위에서 만나 악수를 했다. (2)그들은 목수가 그의 공구 상자를 가지고 떠나는 것을 보았다. (3)"안 돼요, 잠깐만요! 며칠 더 머물러 주세요." 라고 Robert가 그에게 말했다. (4)"(b)당신(Robert)의 초대에 감사드립니다. (5)하지만 저는 더 많은 다리를 만들러 가야 합니다. (6)잊지 마세요. (7)울타리는 고립으로 이끌고 다리는 관대함으로 이끕니다."라고 목수가 말했다. (8)두 형제는 그 목수의 말에 끄덕였다.

[정답 확인]

43. 주어진 글 (A)에 이어질 내용을 순서에 맞게 배열한 것으로 가장 적절한 것은?

① (B) — (C) — (D) ② (C) — (B) — (D) ✔ (C) — (D) — (B)
④ (D) — (B) — (C) ⑤ (D) — (C) — (B)

44. 밑줄 친 (a) ~ (e) 중에서 가리키는 대상이 나머지 넷과 다른 것은?

① (a) ② (b) ③ (c) ④ (d) ✔ (e)

45. 윗글의 내용으로 적절하지 않은 것은?

① Robert와 James는 40년간 나란히(side by side) 농사를 지었다. 문장(A-2)
② Robert는 떠나려는 목수(carpenter)에게 더 머무르라고(stay) 말했다. 문장(B-3)
③ James는 불도저로 초원(meadow)에 샛강(creek)을 만들었다. 문장(C-5)
④ Robert는 목수가 필요로 하는 재료(material)들을 준비해 주었다. 문장(D-1)
✔ 목수는 샛강에 ~~다리~~(울타리)(bridge) 대신 ~~울타리~~(다리)(fence)를 설치했다. 문장(D-4)

[중요 어휘]

☐ **neighboring**	형용사 가까운, 이웃의, 인접한
☐ **conflict**	명사 갈등, 충돌 / 동사 상충하다
☐ **misunderstanding**	명사 오해, 착오
☐ **argument**	명사 논쟁, 주장
☐ **explode**	동사 폭발하다, 터지다
☐ **bitter**	형용사 심한, 쓴, 격렬한
☐ **carpenter**	명사 목수
☐ **creek**	명사 샛강, 개울
☐ **meadow**	명사 초원, 목초지
☐ **fence**	명사 울타리 / 동사 울타리를 치다
☐ **jaw**	명사 입, 턱
☐ **awkwardly**	부사 어색하게, 서투르게
☐ **isolation**	명사 고립, 분리, 격리
☐ **openness**	명사 관대함, 솔직함

46~48

2024년 3월 43~45번
(정답률 85% | 90% | 75%)

정답 ④ | ④ | ②

[지문 끊어 읽기] 고양이 Leo의 건강

(A-1) Christine was a cat owner / who loved her furry companion, Leo. (선행사, 주격 관계대명사절)
Christine은 고양이 주인이다 / 그녀의 털북숭이 반려동물인 Leo를 사랑하는

(A-2) One morning, / she noticed / [that Leo was not feeling well].
어느 날 아침 / 그녀는 알게 되었다 / Leo의 몸 상태가 좋지 않다는 것을 [ ]: 명사절(noticed의 목적어절)

(A-3) [Concerned for her beloved cat], / [ ]: 분사구문(Being 생략)
그녀의 사랑하는 고양이가 걱정되어서 /
Christine decided to take him to the animal hospital. (명사적 용법(목적어)) 46번 정답 단서 Christine은 Leo를 동물병원에 데려가기로 결심함.
Christine은 그를 동물병원에 데려가기로 결심했다

(A-4) As she always brought Leo to this hospital, / she was certain /
그녀가 항상 Leo를 이 병원에 데려왔기 때문에 / 그녀는 확신했다 /
that the vet knew well about Leo. (명사절 접속사) 48번-① 정답 단서 Christine은 Leo를 항상 같은 병원에 데려왔기 때문에 수의사가 Leo를 잘 알 것이라고 확신함.
수의사가 Leo에 대해 잘 알고 있을 것이라고

(A-5) (a)She desperately hoped /
(a)그녀(Christine)는 간절히 바랐다 /
[Leo got the necessary care / as soon as possible].
Leo가 필요한 보살핌을 받기를 / 가능한 한 빨리 [ ]: 목적어절(명사절 접속사 that 생략)

* (A) 요약: Christine은 그녀가 키우는 고양이인 Leo의 몸 상태가 좋지 않아 동물병원에 데려가기로 결심함.

(D-1) The waiting room was filled with other pet owners. 46번·48번-④ 정답 단서 동물병원 대기실은 다른 반려동물 주인들로 꽉 차 있었음.
대기실은 다른 반려동물의 주인들로 꽉 차 있었다

(D-2) Finally, / it was Leo's turn to see the vet. (형용사적 용법)
마침내 / Leo가 수의사에게 진찰을 받을 차례가 되었다

(D-3) Christine watched / as the vet gently examined him.
Christine은 지켜보았다 / 수의사가 조심스럽게 그를 진찰하는 모습을

(D-4) The vet said, / "(d)I think Leo has a minor infection." 47번 정답 단서 수의사는 Leo에게 경미한 감염이 있는 것 같다고 말함.
수의사가 말했다 / "(d)저(the vet)는 Leo에게 경미한 감염이 있다고 생각합니다."

(D-5) "Infection? Will he be okay?" / asked Christine.
"감염이요? 그는 괜찮을까요?" / Christine이 물었다

(D-6) "We need to do some tests / to see if he is infected. 48번-⑤ 정답 단서
부사적 용법(목적)
저희는 몇 가지 검사를 할 필요가 있습니다 / 그가 감염되었는지 알기 위해
수의사는 Leo의 감염 여부를 알기 위해 검사를 할 필요가 있다고 함.

(D-7) But for the tests, / it's best for Leo to stay here," /
형식상의 주어 의미상의 주어 내용상의 주어
하지만 그 검사를 위해서 / Leo가 여기 머무는 것이 가장 좋습니다 /
replied the vet.
수의사가 대답했다

(D-8) It was heartbreaking for Christine /
형식상의 주어 의미상의 주어
Christine에게는 가슴 아팠다 /
to leave Leo at the animal hospital, / but (e)she had to accept /
내용상의 주어
Leo를 동물병원에 두고 가는 것이 / 하지만 (e)그녀(Christine)는 받아들여야만 했다 /
[it was for the best]. 46번·47번 정답 단서
=to leave Leo ~ hospital [ ]: accept의 목적어
그것이 최선이라는 것을 (접속사 that 생략)
Christine은 수의사의 제안을 받아들여 Leo를 동물병원에 두고 가게 됨.

* (D) 요약: 수의사는 Leo가 검사를 위해 동물병원에 머무를 필요가 있다고 말하고, Christine은 이를 받아들여 Leo를 두고 돌아감.

(B-1) "I'll call (b)you with updates / as soon as we know anything," /
제가 (b)당신(Christine)에게 전화로 새로운 소식을 알려 드리겠습니다 / 저희가 뭔가 알게 되는 즉시 /
said the vet. 46번 정답 단서
수의사가 말했다
수의사는 Leo의 검사가 끝나는 대로 Christine에게 전화를 주겠다고 함.

(B-2) Throughout the day, / Christine anxiously awaited news about Leo.
그날 내내 / Christine은 초조하게 Leo에 대한 소식을 기다렸다

(B-3) Later that day, / the phone rang / and it was the vet. 48번-② 정답 단서
그날 늦게 / 전화가 울렸다 / 그리고 그것은 수의사였다
동물병원에 다녀온 당일 늦게 수의사로부터 전화가 옴.

(B-4) "The tests revealed a minor infection.
검사는 경미한 감염을 나타냈습니다

(B-5) Leo needs some medication and rest, /
Leo는 약간의 약물 치료와 휴식이 필요합니다 /
but he'll be back to his playful self soon."
하지만 그는 곧 장난기 넘치는 모습으로 돌아올 거예요

(B-6) [Relieved to hear the news], / [ ]: 분사구문
그 소식을 듣고 안도하며 /
Christine rushed back to the animal hospital / to pick up Leo.
Christine은 동물병원으로 서둘러 되돌아갔다 / Leo를 데리러
46번 정답 단서 Christine은 Leo가 금방 회복할 수 있다는 소식에 안도하며 동물병원으로 되돌아감.

* (B) 요약: 초조하게 기다리던 Christine은 수의사로부터 Leo에게 경미한 감염이 있지만 금방 나을 것이라는 소식을 듣고 안도하며 Leo를 데리러 동물병원으로 감.

(C-1) The vet provided detailed instructions /
V①
수의사는 자세한 설명을 주었다 /
on how to administer the medication /
약을 투여하는 방법에 대해 /
and shared tips for a speedy recovery. 46번·48번-③ 정답 단서
V②
그리고 빠른 회복을 위한 조언을 해주었다
수의사는 약을 투여하는 방법과 Leo가 빨리 회복할 수 있도록 조언을 해줌.

(C-2) Back at home, / Christine created a comfortable space /
집으로 돌아와서 / Christine은 편안한 공간을 만들었다 /
for Leo to rest and heal.
의미상의 주어 형용사적 용법
Leo가 쉬고 회복할 수 있는

(C-3) (c)She patted him with love and attention, /
(c)그녀(Christine)는 사랑과 관심으로 그를 쓰다듬어 주었다 /
[ensuring that he would recover in no time]. [ ]: 분사구문(동시동작)
그가 금방 회복할 수 있게 하면서

(C-4) As the days passed, /
며칠이 지나자 /
Leo gradually regained his strength and playful spirit.
Leo는 점차 그의 체력과 장난기 넘치는 활기를 되찾았다

* (C) 요약: Leo와 함께 집으로 돌아온 Christine은 Leo를 정성스레 간병했고, 곧 Leo는 건강을 되찾음.

[전문 해석]

(A)

(1)Christine은 그녀의 털북숭이 반려동물인 Leo를 사랑하는 고양이 주인이다. (2)어느 날 아침, 그녀는 Leo의 몸 상태가 좋지 않다는 것을 알게 되었다. (3)그녀의 사랑하는 고양이가 걱정되어서, Christine은 그를 동물병원에 데려가기로 결심했다. (4)그녀가 항상 Leo를 이 병원에 데려왔기 때문에, 수의사가 Leo에 대해 잘 알고 있을 것이라고 그녀는 확신했다. (5)(a)그녀(Christine)는 가능한 한 빨리 Leo가 필요한 보살핌을 받기를 간절히 바랐다.

(D)

(1)대기실은 다른 반려동물의 주인들로 꽉 차 있었다. (2)마침내, Leo가 수의사에게 진찰을 받을 차례가 되었다. (3)Christine은 수의사가 조심스럽게 그를 진찰하는 모습을 지켜보았다. (4)"(d)저(the vet)는 Leo에게 경미한 감염이 있다고 생각합니다."라고 수의사가 말했다. (5)"감염이요? 그는 괜찮을까요?"라고 Christine이 물었다. (6)"저희는 그가 감염되었는지 알기 위해 몇 가지 검사를 할 필요가 있습니다. (7)하지만 그 검사를 위해서, Leo가 여기 머무는 것이 가장 좋습니다."라고 수의사가 대답했다. (8)Leo를 동물병원에 두고 가는 것이 Christine에게는 가슴 아팠지만, (e)그녀(Christine)는 그것이 최선이라는 것을 받아들여야만 했다.

(B)

(1)"저희가 뭔가 알게 되는 즉시 제가 (b)당신(Christine)에게 전화로 새로운 소식을 알려 드리겠습니다."라고 수의사가 말했다. (2)그날 내내, Christine은 초조하게 Leo에 대한 소식을 기다렸다. (3)그날 늦게, 전화가 울렸고 그것은 수의사였다. (4)"검사는 경미한 감염을 나타냈습니다. (5)Leo는 약간의 약물 치료와 휴식이 필요하지만, 그는 곧 장난기 넘치는 모습으로 돌아올 거예요." (6)그 소식을 듣고 안도하며, Christine은 Leo를 데리러 동물병원으로 서둘러 되돌아갔다.

(C)

(1)수의사는 약을 투여하는 방법에 대해 자세한 설명을 주었고 빠른 회복을 위한 조언을 해주었다. (2)집으로 돌아와서, Christine은 Leo가 쉬고 회복할 수 있는 편안한 공간을 만들었다. (3)(c)그녀(Christine)는 그가 금방 회복할 수 있게 (하면서) 사랑과 관심으로 그를 쓰다듬어 주었다. (4)며칠이 지나자, Leo는 점차 그의 체력과 장난기 넘치는 활기를 되찾았다.

[정답 확인]

46. 주어진 글 (A)에 이어질 내용을 순서에 맞게 배열한 것으로 가장 적절한 것은?

① (B) — (D) — (C)　② (C) — (B) — (D)　③ (C) — (D) — (B)
✔④ (D) — (B) — (C)　⑤ (D) — (C) — (B)

47. 밑줄 친 (a) ~ (e) 중에서 가리키는 대상이 나머지 넷과 다른 것은?

① (a)　② (b)　③ (c)　✔④ (d)　⑤ (e)

48. 윗글의 내용으로 적절하지 않은 것은?

① Christine은 수의사(the vet)가 Leo에 대해 잘 알고 있을 거라고 확신했다. 문장(A-4)
✔② Christine은 병원을 방문한 ~~다음 날~~ 그날 늦게 수의사의 전화를 받았다. 문장(B-3)
③ 수의사는 Leo의 빠른 회복(recovery)을 위한 조언을 했다. 문장(C-1)
④ 대기실은 다른 반려동물의 주인들로 꽉 차 있었다(be filled with). 문장(D-1)
⑤ Leo의 감염(infection) 여부를 알기 위해 검사를 할 필요가 있었다. 문장(D-6)

[중요 어휘]

☐	**furry**	형용사 털북숭이의, 털로 덮인
☐	**companion**	명사 반려, 동반자, 친구
☐	**vet(=veterinarian)**	명사 수의사
☐	**examine**	동사 진찰하다, 검사하다
☐	**infection**	명사 감염, 전염병
☐	**reply**	동사 대답하다, 답장을 보내다
☐	**anxiously**	부사 초조하게, 걱정스레
☐	**medication**	명사 약물[약] (치료)
☐	**playful**	형용사 장난기 넘치는, 장난기 많은
☐	**self**	명사 (평소) 모습, 본모습, 자신
☐	**instruction**	명사 설명, 지시
☐	**administer**	동사 (약을) 투여하다, 관리하다, 운영하다
☐	**recovery**	명사 회복, 되찾음
☐	**pat**	동사 쓰다듬다, 토닥거리다
☐	**ensure**	동사 (반드시) ~하게 하다, 보장하다
☐	**spirit**	명사 활기, 정신

문제편 p.286

49~51

2024년 6월 43~45번
(정답률 75% | 75% | 80%)

정답 ② | ③ | ③

[지문 끊어 읽기] 진정한 도움

(A-1) On Saturday morning, /
토요일 아침에 /
Todd and his 5-year-old daughter Ava / walked out of the store /
Todd와 그의 5살 딸 Ava는 / 가게 밖으로 걸어 나왔다 /
with the groceries [they had just purchased]. [ ]: 목적격 관계대명사절
선행사 과거완료
그들이 방금 구매한 식료품을 가지고

(A-2) As they pushed their grocery cart through the parking lot, /
그들이 주차장에서 식료품 카트를 밀면서 갈 때 /
they saw a red car pulling into the space /
지각V O O·C(현재분사)
그들은 빨간 차가 들어오는 것을 보았다 /
next to their pick-up truck.
그들의 픽업 트럭 옆 공간에

(A-3) A young man named Greg was driving.
과거분사구
Greg라는 이름의 한 젊은 남자가 운전을 하고 있었다

(A-4) "That's a cool car," / Ava said to her dad. 51번-① 정답 단서 Ava는 멋진 차라고 그녀의 아빠에게 말함.
"멋진 차네요." / Ava가 그녀의 아빠에게 말했다

(A-5) (a)He agreed and looked at Greg, /
선행사
(a)그(Todd)는 동의하며 Greg를 쳐다보았다 /
50번 정답 단서 Todd는 Ava에게 동의하며 주차를 끝내고 문을 여는 Greg를 쳐다봄.
[who finished parking and opened his door]. [ ]: 주격 관계대명사절(계속적 용법)
그리고 그는 주차를 끝내고 그의 문을 열었다

* (A) 요약: Todd와 그의 딸 Ava는 식료품을 사고 나오면서 주차하는 Greg를 봄.

(C-1) As Todd finished loading his groceries, /
Todd가 그의 식료품을 싣는 것을 끝냈을 때 /
Greg's door remained open.
Greg의 문은 열린 채로 있었다

(C-2) Todd noticed / Greg didn't get out of his car. 49번·51번-④ 정답 단서 Todd는 Greg가 차에서 내리지 않은 것을 알아차림.
Todd는 알아차렸다 / Greg가 그의 차에서 내리지 않은 것을

(C-3) But he was pulling something from his car.
그러나 그는 그의 차에서 무언가를 꺼내고 있었다

(C-4) He put a metal frame / on the ground beside his door.
그는 금속 프레임을 두었다 / 그의 문 옆 바닥에

(C-5) Remaining in the driver's seat, /
운전석에 있는 채로 / 분사구문(부대상황)
50번 정답 단서 운전석에 있는 채로 Greg는 무언가를 잡기 위해 자신의 차 안 뒤쪽으로 손을 뻗음.
he then reached back into (c)his car to grab something else.
부사적 용법(목적)
그는 다른 무언가를 잡기 위해 (c)그(Greg)의 차 안 뒤쪽으로 손을 뻗었다

(C-6) Todd realized [what he was doing] / [ ]: 의문사절(realized의 목적어)
Todd는 그가 무엇을 하고 있는지 알아차렸다 /
and considered [whether (d)he should try to help him]. 50번 정답 단서
그리고 (d)그(Todd)가 그를 도와야 할지를 고민했다 [ ]: 명사절 (considered의 목적어)
Todd는 Greg가 무엇을 하고 있는지 알아차리고 그를 도와야 할지 고민했음.

(C-7) After a moment, / he decided to approach Greg.
잠시 후 / 그는 Greg에게 다가가기로 결심했다

* (C) 요약: Todd는 식료품을 다 실은 후 차에서 내리지 않은 Greg가 차 안에서 무언가를 꺼내려는 모습을 보고 그에게 다가가기로 결심함.

(B-1) By this time, /
그때쯤 /
V①
Greg had already pulled one thin wheel out of his car /
Greg는 이미 그의 차에서 얇은 바퀴 하나를 꺼냈다 /
and attached it to the frame. 51번-② 정답 단서 Greg는 차에서 얇은 바퀴를 하나 꺼내 프레임에 붙임.
V②
그리고 그것을 프레임에 붙였다

(B-2) He was now pulling a second wheel out /
그는 이제 두 번째 바퀴를 꺼내는 중이었다 /
when he looked up and saw Todd standing near him. 49번 정답 단서 두 번째 바퀴를 꺼내는 Greg의 옆에 Todd가 서 있었음.
지각V O O·C
그가 올려다보고 Todd가 그의 곁에 서 있는 것을 보았을 때

(B-3) Todd said, / "Hi there! Have a great weekend!"
Todd는 말했다 / "안녕하세요! 좋은 주말 보내세요!"

(B-4) Greg seemed a bit surprised, /
V①
Greg는 조금 놀란 듯 보였다 /
but replied by wishing (b)him a great weekend too. 50번 정답 단서 Greg는 조금 놀라며 Todd에게 좋은 주말을 보내라고 대답함.
V②
하지만 (b)그(Todd)에게도 좋은 주말을 보내라며 대답했다

(B-5) Then Greg added, /
그리고 Greg는 덧붙였다 /
"Thanks for letting me have my independence." 51번-③ 정답 단서 Greg는 독립성을 가질 수 있게 해주어 고맙다고 덧붙임.
사역V O O·C(동사원형)
"제가 독립성을 가질 수 있도록 해줘서 고맙습니다."

(B-6) "Of course," / Todd said.
"물론이죠." / Todd가 말했다

* (B) 요약: 바퀴를 프레임에 붙이고 있던 Greg에게 Todd가 다가가 좋은 주말을 보내라고 말했고 Greg는 독립성을 가질 수 있게 해주어 고맙다고 말함.

(D-1) After Todd and Ava climbed into their truck, / Ava became curious. 49번·51번-⑤ 정답 단서 Todd와 Ava는 트럭에 탔고 Ava는 궁금해짐.
Todd와 Ava가 그들의 트럭에 올라탄 이후에 / Ava는 궁금해졌다

(D-2) So she asked /
그래서 그녀는 물었다 /
50번 정답 단서 Ava는 왜 Todd가 휠체어를 탄 Greg에게 도움을 제공하지 않았는지 물었음.
[why (e)he didn't offer to help the man with his wheelchair].
왜 (e)그(Todd)가 휠체어를 탄 그 남자에게 도움을 제공하지 않았는지 물었다 [ ]: 의문사절 (asked의 목적어)

(D-3) Todd said, /
Todd는 말했다 /
"Why do you insist on brushing your teeth without my help?"
"왜 너는 내 도움 없이 이를 닦기를 고집하니?"

(D-4) She answered, / "Because I know how to!"
그녀는 대답했다 / "제가 어떻게 하는지 알기 때문이죠!"

(D-5) He said, / "And the man knows /
그는 말했다 / 그리고 그 남자는 알고 있지 /
how to put together his wheelchair."
그의 휠체어를 어떻게 조립하는지

힌트 to부정사의 부정은 to부정사 앞에 not을 쓰는 것이 원칙이지만, 동사의 부정을 강조하거나 의미를 명확하게 하기 위해서 분리부정사, 즉 'to not 동사원형'을 쓰기도 함.

(D-6) Ava understood /
Ava는 이해했다 /
that sometimes the best way to help someone / is to not help at all.
접속사 형용사적 용법 명사적 용법(보어)
가끔 누군가를 돕는 가장 좋은 방법은 / 전혀 돕지 않는 것임을

* (D) 요약: Ava는 Todd가 왜 휠체어를 탄 Greg에게 도움을 제공하지 않았는지 궁금해했고, Todd는 Greg가 휠체어를 혼자서 조립할 수 있었기 때문이라고 대답함.

[전문 해석]

(A)

(1)토요일 아침에 Todd와 그의 5살 딸 Ava는 그들이 방금 구매한 식료품을 가지고 가게 밖으로 걸어 나왔다. (2)그들이 주차장에서 식료품 카트를 밀면서 갈 때, 그들은 빨간 차가 그들의 픽업 트럭 옆 공간에 들어오는 것을 보았다. (3)Greg라는 이름의 한 젊은 남자가 운전을 하고 있었다. (4)"멋진 차네요."라고 Ava가 그녀의 아빠에게 말했다. (5)(a)그(Todd)는 동의하며 Greg를 쳐다보았고, 그는 주차를 끝내고 그의 문을 열었다.

(C)

(1)Todd가 그의 식료품을 싣는 것을 끝냈을 때, Greg의 문은 열린 채로 있었다. (2)Todd는 Greg가 그의 차에서 내리지 않은 것을 알아차렸다. (3)그러나 그는 그의 차에서 무언가를 꺼내고 있었다. (4)그는 그의 문 옆 바닥에 금속 프레임을 두었다. (5)운전석에 있는 채로 그는 다른 무언가를 잡기 위해 (c)그(Greg)의 차 안 뒤쪽으로 손을 뻗었다. (6)Todd는 그가 무엇을 하고 있는지 알아차렸고 (d)그(Todd)가 그를 도와야 할지를 고민했다. (7)잠시 후 그는 Greg에게 다가가기로 결심했다.

(B)

(1)그때쯤 Greg는 이미 그의 차에서 얇은 바퀴 하나를 꺼냈고 그것을 프레임에 붙였다. (2)그가 올려다보고 Todd가 그의 곁에 서 있는 것을 보았을 때 그는 이제 두 번째 바퀴를 꺼내는 중이었다. (3)Todd는 "안녕하세요! 좋은 주말 보내세요!"라고 말했다 (4)Greg는 조금 놀란 듯 보였지만 (b)그(Todd)에게도 좋은 주말을 보내라며 대답했다. (5)그리고 Greg는 "제가 독립성을 가질 수 있도록 해줘서 고맙습니다."라고 덧붙였다. (6)"물론이죠."라고 Todd가 말했다.

(D)

(1)Todd와 Ava가 그들의 트럭에 올라탄 이후에 Ava는 궁금해졌다. (2)그래서 그녀는 왜 (e)그

(Todd)가 휠체어를 탄 그 남자에게 도움을 제공하지 않았는지 물었다. (3)Todd는 "왜 너는 내 도움 없이 이를 닦기를 고집하니?"라고 말했다. (4)그녀는 "제가 어떻게 하는지 알기 때문이죠!"라고 대답했다. (5)그는 "그리고 그 남자는 그의 휠체어를 어떻게 조립하는지 알고 있지."라고 말했다. (6)Ava는 가끔 누군가를 돕는 가장 좋은 방법은 전혀 돕지 않는 것임을 이해했다.

[정답 확인]

49. 주어진 글 (A)에 이어질 내용을 순서에 맞게 배열한 것으로 가장 적절한 것은?

① (B) — (D) — (C) ✔② (C) — (B) — (D) ③ (C) — (D) — (B)
④ (D) — (B) — (C) ⑤ (D) — (C) — (B)

50. 밑줄 친 (a) ~ (e) 중에서 가리키는 대상이 나머지 넷과 다른 것은?

① (a) ② (b) ✔③ (c) ④ (d) ⑤ (e)

51. 윗글의 내용으로 적절하지 않은 것은?

① Ava는 차가 멋지다고 말했다. 문장(A-4)
② Greg는 얇은 바퀴(wheel)를 프레임(frame)에 끼웠다. 문장(B-1)
✔③ Greg는 ~~휠체어를 꺼내준~~ 것에 감사하다고 말했다. 문장(B-5) (독립성을 가질 수 있게 한)
④ Todd는 Greg가 차에서 내리지(get out of) 않은 것을 알아차렸다. 문장(C-2)
⑤ Ava는 트럭에 오른 후 호기심(curiosity)이 생겼다. 문장(D-1)

[중요 어휘]

☐ **grocery**	명사 식료품, 식료품 잡화점
☐ **metal**	명사 금속
☐ **driver's seat**	운전석
☐ **grab**	동사 잡다, 움켜잡다
☐ **wheel**	명사 바퀴, (자동차의) 핸들
☐ **independence**	명사 독립성, 독립심
☐ **insist on**	~을 고집하다[주장하다]
☐ **put together**	조립하다, 만들다
☐ **at all**	(부정문에서) 전혀, 조금도, 조금이라도

52~54

2024년 9월 43~45번
(정답률 90% | 90% | 85%)

정답 ② | ③ | ③

[지문 끊어 읽기] Benjamin과 그의 훌륭한 선생님

(A-1) My two girls grew up without challenges /
나의 두 딸은 어려움 없이 성장했다 /
with respect to development and social interaction. (~에 관해서)
발달과 사회적 상호 작용에 관해서

(A-2) My son Benjamin, / however, / was quite delayed.
나의 아들 Benjamin은 / 하지만 / 꽤 지체되었다

(A-3) He struggled through his childhood, /
그는 어린 시절 동안 고생했다 /
[not fitting in with the other children / 54번-① 정답 단서 (병렬①) Benjamin은 어린 시절 다른 아이들과 잘 어울리지 못함.
다른 아이들과 잘 어울리지 않으며 /
and wondering what he was doing wrong at every turn]. (병렬②) [ ]: 분사구문(동시동작)
그리고 언제나 그가 무엇을 잘못했는지 궁금해하며

(A-4) He was teased by the other children / (V①)
그는 다른 아이들에게 괴롭힘을 받았다 /
and frowned upon by a number of unsympathetic adults. (V②(was 생략))
그리고 인정 없는 많은 어른들의 눈살을 찌푸리게 했다

(A-5) But his Grade 1 teacher was a wonderful, caring person / (선행사)
하지만 그의 1학년 선생님은 훌륭하고 친절한 사람이었다 /
[who took the time to ask /
물어보는 시간을 갖는 / [ ]: 주격 관계대명사절
why Benjamin behaved the way (a)he did]. 52번·53번 정답 단서 선생님은 Benjamin에게 신경을 써주는 훌륭한 사람이었음.
왜 Benjamin이 (a)그(Benjamin)가 했던 방식으로 행동했는지

* (A) 요약: Benjamin은 어린 시절 다른 아이들과 어울리는 데 서툴렀지만, 그의 1학년 선생님은 Benjamin을 잘 돌봐줌.

(C-1) The teacher was determined /
그 선생님은 결심했다 /
to understand Benjamin and to accept him as he was. 52번 정답 단서 (병렬① / 병렬②) 선생님은 Benjamin을 있는 그대로 받아들이기로 결심함.
Benjamin을 이해하고 그를 있는 그대로 받아들이겠다고

(C-2) One day he came home / with a note from his teacher.
어느 날 그는 집으로 왔다 / 그의 선생님으로부터 받은 쪽지 하나를 가지고

(C-3) He suggested /
그는 제안했다 /
I go to the school library. 54번-④ 정답 단서 선생님은 나에게 학교 도서관에 방문할 것을 제안함.
내가 학교 도서관에 방문할 것을

힌트 주절에 suggest처럼 '제안, 주장, 요구, 명령, 충고 등'을 나타내는 동사가 오고, that절이 당위성을 나타낼 때 'that+S+(should)+동사원형'의 형태를 가지는데, 이때 should는 생략이 가능함.

(C-4) They were having a sale, / and (c)he thought /
그들은 판매를 하고 있었다 / 그리고 (c)그(teacher)는 생각했다 /
[my son would like one of the books]. 53번 정답 단서 선생님은 Benjamin이 도서관에서 판매하고 있는 책을 좋아할 거라고 생각함.
나의 아들이 그 책들 중 하나를 좋아할 거라고 [ ]: 명사절(thought의 목적어)

(C-5) I couldn't go for a couple of days / and was concerned / (V① / V②)
나는 며칠 동안 갈 수 없었다 / 그리고 걱정했다 /
I'd missed the opportunity.
내가 그 기회를 놓쳤을까 봐

힌트 선생님이 나에게 말한 시점보다 '판매가 끝난 것'과 '도서관이 책을 남겨둔 것'이 더 먼저 일어났으므로 과거완료 시제를 사용함.

(C-6) When I finally went to the school, / his teacher told me / (I·O)
내가 마침내 학교에 갔을 때 / 그의 선생님은 나에게 말했다 /
[that the sale had ended] / [ ]: D·O①
판매는 끝났다고 /
but [that the library had saved the book for my little boy]. 52번 정답 단서 [ ]: D·O②
하지만 도서관이 내 아이를 위해 책을 남겨 두었다고
선생님은 책 판매가 끝났지만 학교 도서관이 Benjamin을 위해 책을 남겨 두었다고 말해줌.

* (C) 요약: 선생님은 나에게 학교 도서관에서 책을 판매하고 있으니 Benjamin을 위해 방문할 것을 제안함.

(B-1) I suspected / the teacher had paid for it out of his own pocket. 52번·54번-② 정답 단서 나는 선생님이 책값을 자비로 지불했다고 짐작함.
나는 짐작했다 / 선생님이 그것을 자비로 지불했다고

(B-2) It was a story-board book / with a place for a photo.
그것은 스토리보드 책이었다 / 사진을 위한 공간이 있는

(B-3) On each page / there was an outline of an animal and a hole /
각 페이지마다 / 동물의 윤곽과 구멍이 있었다 /
[so that the face in the photo appeared to be the face of the animal]. [ ]: 부사절(결과)
그래서 사진 속의 얼굴이 그 동물의 얼굴인 것처럼 보였다

(B-4) [Wondering if Benjamin would really be interested in the book], / (=whether) [ ]: 분사구문(동시동작)
Benjamin이 그 책에 정말로 흥미가 있을지 궁금해하며 /
I brought it home.
나는 그것을 집으로 가져왔다

(B-5) He loved it! 54번-③ 정답 단서 Benjamin은 내가 도서관에서 가져온 책을 좋아함.
그는 그것을 좋아했다

(B-6) Through that book, /
그 책을 통해 /
he saw [that (b)he could be anything he wanted to be: / (선행사 / 목적격 관계대명사절)
그는 (b)그(Benjamin)가 자신이 되길 원하는 어떠한 것도 될 수 있음을 알았다 /
a cat, an octopus, a dinosaur / — even a frog]! 52번 정답 단서 Benjamin은 책을 보면서 상상력을 키우게 됨.
고양이, 문어, 공룡 / 심지어 개구리까지 [ ]: saw의 목적어절

* (B) 요약: Benjamin은 도서관에서 가져온 스토리보드 책을 마음에 들어함.

(D-1) Benjamin joyfully embarked on an imaginative journey through the book, /
Benjamin은 그 책을 통해 상상의 여행을 즐겁게 시작했다 /
and little did we know, /
그리고 우리는 거의 알지 못했다 /
it laid the groundwork for his future successes. 52번 정답 단서 그 책은 Benjamin의 미래의 성공을 위한 토대를 마련함.
그것은 그의 미래의 성공을 위한 토대를 마련했다

힌트 부정의 의미를 강조하기 위하여 부정어(little)를 문두에 둘 수 있는데, 이 경우 문장의 주어와 동사가 도치되며, 일반동사의 경우 조동사 do를 시제와 수에 맞추어 주어 앞으로 도치시키고 일반동사는 동사원형으로 주어 다음에 쓰임.

(D-2) And thankfully, /
그리고 감사하게도 /
his teacher had taken the time to observe and understand (d)him / (V① / 병렬① / 병렬②(to 생략))
그의 선생님은 (d)그(Benjamin)를 관찰하고 이해하기 위한 시간을 가졌다 /

and had discovered a way /
V②
그리고 방법을 발견했다 /

O
to help him reach out of his own world and join ours /
형용사적 용법(5형식V) O·C① O·C② =our world
그가 자신만의 세상을 벗어나 우리의 세상에 참여하도록 돕는 /

through a story-board book.
스토리보드 책을 통해

(D-3) My son later became a child actor / 54번-⑤ 정답 단서 Benjamin은 아역 배우가 되었음.
V①
내 아들은 나중에 아역 배우가 되었다 /
and performed for seven years / with a Toronto casting agency.
V②
그리고 7년 동안 공연을 했다 / Toronto에 있는 캐스팅 회사와 함께

(D-4) (e)He is now a published author /
선행사
(e)그(Benjamin)는 이제 출판 작가이다 /
[who writes fantasy and science-fiction]! [ ]: 주격 관계대명사절
판타지와 공상 과학 소설을 쓰는

(D-5) Who would have guessed?
누가 짐작이나 했을까

* (D) 요약: 선생님이 구해준 스토리보드 책 덕분에 Benjamin은 이후 아역 배우를 거쳐 소설 작가가 됨.

[전문 해석]

(A)

(1)나의 두 딸은 발달과 사회적 상호 작용에 관해서 어려움 없이 성장했다. (2)하지만, 나의 아들 Benjamin(의 성장)은 꽤 지체되었다. (3)그는 다른 아이들과 잘 어울리지 않고 언제나 그가 무엇을 잘못했는지 궁금해하며, 어린 시절 동안 고생했다. (4)그는 다른 아이들에게 괴롭힘을 받았고 인정 없는 많은 어른들의 눈살을 찌푸리게 했다. (5)하지만 그의 1학년 선생님은 왜 Benjamin이 (a)그(Benjamin)가 했던 방식으로 행동했는지 물어보는 시간을 갖는, 훌륭하고 친절한 사람이었다.

(C)

(1)그 선생님은 Benjamin을 이해하고 그를 있는 그대로 받아들이겠다고 결심했다. (2)어느 날 그는 그의 선생님으로부터 받은 쪽지 하나를 가지고 집으로 왔다. (3)그는 내가 학교 도서관에 방문할 것을 제안했다. (4)그들은 판매를 하고 있었고, (c)그(teacher)는 나의 아들이 그 책들 중 하나를 좋아할 거라고 생각했다. (5)나는 며칠 동안 갈 수 없었고, 내가 그 기회를 놓쳤을까 봐 걱정했다. (6)내가 마침내 학교에 갔을 때, 그의 선생님은 나에게 판매는 끝났지만 도서관이 내 아이를 위해 책을 남겨 두었다고 말했다.

(B)

(1)나는 선생님이 그것을 자비로 지불했다고 짐작했다. (2)그것은 사진을 위한 공간이 있는 스토리보드 책이었다. (3)각 페이지마다 동물의 윤곽과 구멍이 있어서 사진 속의 얼굴이 그 동물의 얼굴인 것처럼 보였다. (4)Benjamin이 그 책에 정말로 흥미가 있을지 궁금해하며 나는 그것을 집으로 가져왔다. (5)그는 그것을 좋아했다! (6)그 책을 통해, 그는 (b)그(Benjamin)가 자신이 되길 원하는 어떠한 것도 될 수 있음을 알았는데, 고양이, 문어, 공룡 심지어 개구리까지 말이다!

(D)

(1)Benjamin은 그 책을 통해 상상의 여행을 즐겁게 시작했고, 우리는 거의 알지 못했지만, 그것은 그의 미래의 성공을 위한 토대를 마련했다. (2)그리고 감사하게도, 그의 선생님은 (d)그(Benjamin)를 관찰하고 이해하기 위한 시간을 가졌고, 스토리보드 책을 통해 그가 자신만의 세상을 벗어나 우리의 세상에 참여하도록 돕는 방법을 발견했다. (3)내 아들은 나중에 아역 배우가 되었고 Toronto에 있는 캐스팅 회사와 함께 7년 동안 공연을 했다. (4)(e)그(Benjamin)는 이제 판타지와 공상 과학 소설을 쓰는 출판 작가이다! (5)누가 짐작이나 했을까?

[정답 확인]

52. 주어진 글 (A)에 이어질 내용을 순서에 맞게 배열한 것으로 가장 적절한 것은?

① (B) — (D) — (C) ✔ (C) — (B) — (D) ③ (C) — (D) — (B)
④ (D) — (B) — (C) ⑤ (D) — (C) — (B)

53. 밑줄 친 (a) ~ (e) 중에서 가리키는 대상이 나머지 넷과 다른 것은?

① (a) ② (b) ✔ (c) ④ (d) ⑤ (e)

54. 윗글의 내용으로 적절하지 않은 것은?

① Benjamin은 어린 시절 다른 아이들과 잘 어울리지(fit in with) 않았다. 문장(A-3)
② 'I'는 선생님이 책값을 지불했다고 짐작했다(suspect). 문장(B-1)
✔ Benjamin은 'I'가 가져온 책을 ~~좋아하지 않았다~~. 문장(B-5)
좋아했다
④ 선생님은 'I'에게 학교 도서관에 방문할 것을 제안했다(suggest). 문장(C-3)
⑤ Benjamin은 아역 배우가 되었다. 문장(D-3)

[중요 어휘]

☐ **interaction**	명사 상호 작용
☐ **delay**	동사 지체시키다, 지연시키다 / 명사 지체, 지연
☐ **fit in with**	~와 어울리다
☐ **at every turn**	언제나, 어디서나
☐ **tease**	동사 괴롭히다, 놀리다
☐ **frown upon**	~에 눈살을 찌푸리다
☐ **unsympathetic**	형용사 인정 없는, 매정한
☐ **caring**	형용사 친절한, 배려하는, 보살피는
☐ **suspect**	동사 짐작하다, 의심하다
☐ **pay out of one's own pocket**	자비로 지불하다
☐ **outline**	명사 윤곽, 개요 / 동사 윤곽을 그리다
☐ **joyfully**	부사 즐겁게, 기쁘게
☐ **embark on**	~을 시작하다[착수하다]
☐ **imaginative**	형용사 상상의, 창의적인
☐ **groundwork**	명사 토대, 초석, 기초
☐ **observe**	동사 관찰하다, (의견 등을) 말하다, 준수하다
☐ **publish**	동사 출판하다, 발행하다

1회 20분 미니모의고사

01 2020년 9월 18번 (정답률 95%) 정답 ①

[지문 끊어 읽기] 반려견이 짖는 소리 최소화 요청

(1) Dear Residents,
친애하는 주민들께

(2) We truly value and appreciate / all of our residents, /
저희는 진심으로 소중하게 생각하고 감사하고 있습니다 / 우리 주민 모두를 /
including those with pets.
=the residents
반려동물이 있는 분들을 포함하여

(3) We believe / that allowing people to live with their pets /
저희는 믿습니다 / 사람들이 그들의 반려동물과 함께 살도록 허용하는 것이 /
enriches their lives.
그들의 삶을 풍요롭게 한다고

힌트 밑줄 친 동명사구 'allowing ~ their pets'는 believe의 목적어로 쓰인 명사절 that절의 주어로, 'allow + O + O·C(to V)'의 5형식 구조임.

(4) While we encourage you to enjoy your pets, /
양보(비록 ~이지만) 5형식V O O·C(to V)
비록 저희가 여러분이 반려동물과 즐기는 것을 장려하지만 /
we also want to ensure / that you do not do so /
=enjoy your pets
저희는 또한 확실히 하고 싶습니다 / 여러분이 그렇게 하지 않는다는 것을 /
at the expense of your neighbors or your community.
여러분의 이웃이나 여러분의 지역 사회를 희생하면서

(5) We have received reports /
저희는 보고를 받아왔습니다 /
that some residents have been disturbed /
몇몇 주민들이 방해받아왔다는 /
by noise from dogs barking.
반려견이 짖는 소리로 인한 소음으로

(6) Excessive barking by dogs / disrupts everyone within hearing, /
반려견의 과도한 짖는 소리는 / 들리는 곳에 있는 모두를 방해합니다 /
particularly those / who are elderly or sick /
특히 사람들을 / 나이가 많거나 아픈 /
or who have small children.
혹은 어린아이들이 있는

힌트 반려견이 짖는 소리가 들리는 거리 '안에(within)' 있다는 의미에서 '들리는 곳에 있는'이라고 해석됨.

(7) We kindly ask / that you keep your dogs' noise levels /
저희는 정중히 요청합니다 / 여러분이 반려견의 소음 수준을 유지해 주시기를 /
to a minimum. 주제문
최소한으로

(8) Thank you for your assistance / with this.
여러분의 협조에 감사드립니다 / 이 일에 대한

(9) Regards, Conway Forest Apartments Management Office
안부를 전하며, Conway Forest 아파트 관리 사무소 (드림)

[전문 해석]

(1)친애하는 주민들께,
(2)저희는 반려동물이 있는 분들을 포함하여 우리 주민 모두를 진심으로 소중하게 생각하고 감사하고 있습니다. (3)저희는 사람들이 그들의 반려동물과 함께 살도록 허용하는 것이 그들의 삶을 풍요롭게 한다고 믿습니다. (4)비록 저희가 여러분이 반려동물과 즐기는 것을 장려하지만, 저희는 또한 여러분의 이웃이나 지역 사회를 희생하면서(까지) 여러분이 그렇게 하지 않는다는 것을 확실히 하고 싶습니다. (5)저희는 몇몇 주민들이 반려견이 짖는 소리로 인한 소음으로 방해받아왔다는 보고를 받아왔습니다. (6)반려견의 과도한 짖는 소리는 들리는 곳에 있는 모두를, 특히 나이가 많거나 아픈 사람들 혹은 어린아이들이 있는 사람들을 방해합니다. (7)저희는 여러분이 반려견의 소음 수준을 최소한으로 유지해 주시기를 정중히 요청합니다.
(8)이 일에 대한 여러분의 협조에 감사드립니다.
(9)안부를 전하며, Conway Forest 아파트 관리 사무소 (드림)

[정답 확인]

다음 글의 목적으로 가장 적절한 것은?

✔ 반려견이 짖는 소리(barking)를 최소화 해줄 것을 요청하려고
② 아파트 내 반려동물(pet) 출입 가능 구역을 안내하려고
③ 아파트 공사로 인한 소음(noise) 발생에 대해 사과하려고
④ 반려견 대소변 관련 민원처리 결과를 공지하려고
⑤ 반려동물과 외출 시 목줄 사용을 당부하려고

[중요 어휘]

☐ enrich	동사 풍요롭게 하다
☐ at the expense of	~을 희생하면서, ~에 폐를 끼치면서
☐ disturb	동사 방해하다, 건드리다
☐ excessive	형용사 과도한, 지나친
☐ disrupt	동사 방해하다, 지장을 주다

핵심 요지가 직접 드러나지 않기 때문에 전체적인 글의 전개 구조를 파악해야 함. 전반부는 어떤 상황이든 긍정적인 말로 자신을 격려하는 positive self-talk을 언급하였지만 중반에는 그에 대한 반론을 제기한 후 그와 대비되는 개념으로 상황에 따라 부정적으로도 말할 수 있는 real self-talk으로 내용이 전환되고 있음.

02 2017년 3월 20번 (정답률 65%) 정답 ⑤

[지문 끊어 읽기] 감정을 인정하는 것의 장점

(1) Much has been written and said / about positive self-talk /
많은 것들이 쓰이고 말해졌다 / 긍정적인 혼잣말에 대한 /
— for example, / repeating to ourselves /
예를 들어 / 우리 자신에게 되뇌는 것이다 /
"I am wonderful" when we feel down, /
우리가 기분이 가라앉을 때 "나는 멋져"라고 /
"I am strong" when going through a difficult time, /
어려운 시간을 겪을 때 "나는 강해"라고 /
or "I am getting better every day in every way" /
또는 "나는 매일 모든 면에서 더 나아지고 있어"라고 /
each morning in front of the mirror.
매일 아침 거울 앞에서

(2) The evidence that this sort of pep talk works / is weak, /
이러한 종류의 격려의 말이 효과가 있다는 증거는 / 빈약하다 /
and there are psychologists / who suggest /
그리고 심리학자들이 있다 / 시사하는 /
that it can actually hurt more than it can help.
그것이 사실은 도움이 될 수 있기보다 해를 더 줄 수 있다는 것을

(3) Little, unfortunately, has been written /
불행하게도 거의 쓰이지 않았다 /
about *real self-talk*, / acknowledging honestly /
'진정한 혼잣말'에 대해서는 / 솔직히 인정하는 /
what we are feeling at a given point.
우리가 어떤 주어진 시점에 느끼는 것을

힌트 문장 (3)의 acknowledging honestly에서 자신의 감정을 솔직히 받아들인다는 내용이 직접적으로 언급됨.

(4) When feeling down, / saying "I am really sad" or "I feel so torn" /
기분이 가라앉을 때 / "나는 정말 슬퍼" 또는 "나는 정말 마음이 아파"라고 말하는 것이 /
— to ourselves or to someone we trust — / is much more helpful /
우리 자신이나 우리가 신뢰하는 누군가에게 / 훨씬 더 도움이 된다 /
than declaring "I am tough" or "I am happy." 주제문
"나는 강해" 또는 "나는 행복해"라고 말하는 것보다

[전문 해석]

(1)긍정적인 혼잣말에 대한 많은 것들이 (글로) 쓰이고 말해졌다. 예를 들어, 우리가 기분이 가라앉을 때 "나는 멋져"라고, 어려운 시간을 겪을 때 "나는 강해"라고, 또는 매일 아침 거울 앞에서 "나는 매일 모든 면에서 더 나아지고 있어"라고 우리 자신에게 되뇌는 것이다. (2)이러한 종류의 격려의 말이 효과가 있다는 증거는 빈약하며, 그것이 사실은 도움이 될 수 있기보다(도움이 되기보다는) 해를 더 줄 수 있다는 것을 시사하는 심리학자들이 있다. (3)불행하게도 우리가 어떤 주어진 시점에 느끼는 것을 솔직히 인정하는 '진정한 혼잣말'에 대해서는 거의 (글로) 쓰이지 않았다. (4)기분이 가라앉을 때 우리 자신이나 우리가 신뢰하는 누군가에게 "나는 정말 슬퍼" 또는 "나는 정말 마음이 아파"라고 말하는 것이 "나는 강해" 또는 "나는 행복해"라고 말하는 것보다 훨씬 더 도움이 된다.

[정답 확인]

다음 글의 요지로 가장 적절한 것은?

① 타인에 대한 비난(criticism)은 자신의 감정도 상하게 한다.
② 우울할 때 자신에게 하는 격려의 말(pep talk)은 큰 힘이 된다.
③ 자아 성찰은 타인의 조언(advice)을 받는 것보다 효과적이다.
④ 가까운 사이일수록 말과 행동을 조심할(careful) 필요가 있다.
✔ 자신이 느끼는 감정을 솔직히 인정하는(acknowledge) 것이 도움이 된다.

문제편 p.289

[중요 어휘]

☐ **pep talk**	격려의 말
☐ **suggest**	동사 시사하다, 암시하다, 제안하다
☐ **given**	형용사 주어진
☐ **torn**	형용사 (마음이) 아픈, 슬픈
☐ **declare**	동사 (분명히) 말하다, 단언하다
☐ **tough**	형용사 강한, 굳센

핵심 북반구에 집중적으로 위치한 대규모 저수지로 인해 자전 속도가 빨라지고 자전축의 위치도 바뀌게 된 사실을 설명하는 글로, 이 변화에 영향을 준 근본적인 원인이 대규모 '저수지(reservoirs)'임을 놓치지 않는 것이 중요함.

03 2016년 11월 21번 (정답률 75%) 정답 ①

[지문 끊어 읽기] 대규모 저수지가 자전에 미치는 영향

(1) We have constructed so many large reservoirs / to hold water, /
우리는 아주 많은 대규모 저수지를 건설해 왔다 / 물을 저장하기 위해 /
and they are located primarily in the Northern Hemisphere /
그런데 그것들은 주로 북반구에 위치해 있다 /
rather than randomly around the globe.
지구 전체에 무작위로 위치해 있기보다는

(2) As a result, / enough of Earth's mass has shifted /
결과적으로 / 충분한 지구 질량이 이동해서 /
to speed up its rotation. 주제문
그것의 자전을 가속화했다

(3) Currently, / 88 huge reservoirs hold /
현재 / 88개의 거대한 저수지가 저장하고 있다 /
some 10 trillion tons of water.
약 10조 톤의 물을

(4) Before the reservoirs were built, /
저수지가 건설되기 전에 /
this water was located in the ocean, /
이 물은 바다에 있었다 /
which has most of its mass / in the Southern Hemisphere.
그것은 그것의 질량 대부분을 갖고 있다 / 남반구 내에

(5) The effect is like a whirling skater /
그 효과는 회전하는 스케이트 선수와 같다 /
who pulls her arms in / to turn faster.
자신의 팔을 안으로 당기는 / 더욱 빠르게 돌기 위해

(6) Because natural factors in the environment, /
환경의 자연적 요인들이 ~하기 때문에 /
✶중요 문장 (6)의 accidentally working의 의미가 정답에서는 Unintended Change로 제시됨.
such as the pull of tides, / are gradually slowing Earth's rotation, /
조수의 인력과 같은 / 지구의 자전을 점차 느려지게 하고 있다 /
the human influence is accidentally working /
인간의 영향은 우연히 작용하고 있다 /
against the natural rate of deceleration. 정답 단서
자연적인 감속의 속도에 반대로

(7) The shift in Earth's mass /
지구 질량의 이동은 /
정답 단서
has also changed the location of the axis / on which Earth rotates.
자전축의 위치도 바꾸어 왔다 / 지구가 중심으로 돌고 있는

[전문 해석]

(1)우리는 물을 저장하기 위해 아주 많은 대규모 저수지를 건설해 왔는데, 그것들은 지구 전체에 무작위로 위치해 있기보다는 주로 북반구에 위치해 있다. (2)결과적으로, (자전을 가속시킬 만큼) 충분한 지구 질량(물)이 이동해서 그것(지구)의 자전을 가속화했다. (3)현재, 88개의 거대한 저수지가 약 10조 톤의 물을 저장하고 있다. (4)저수지가 건설되기 전에 이 물은 바다에 있었고, 그것(바다)은 남반구 내에 그것(바다)의 질량 대부분을 갖고 있다. (5)그 효과는 더욱 빠르게 돌기 위해 자신의 팔을 안으로 당겨서 회전하는 스케이트 선수와 같다. (6)조수의 인력과 같은, 환경의 자연적 요인들이 지구의 자전을 점차 느려지게 하고 있기 때문에, 인간의 영향(저수지 건설)은 자연적인 감속의 (자전) 속도에 우연히 반대로 작용하고 있다. (7)지구 질량의 이동은 지구가 중심으로 돌고 있는 자전축의 위치도 바꾸어 왔다.

[정답 확인]

다음 글의 제목으로 가장 적절한 것은?

✔① Reservoir Effect: Unintended Change in Earth's Rotation
저수지 효과: 지구 자전에서의 의도치 않은 변화
② Why Figure Skaters Spin Faster with Their Arms in
팔을 안쪽으로 한 피겨 스케이팅 선수들이 더 빨리 회전하는 이유
③ Factors Affecting the Location of Reservoirs
저수지의 위치에 영향을 미치는 요인들
④ Eco-Friendly Water Holding Method
친환경적인 저수 방법
⑤ What Makes Earth Rotate Slower?
무엇이 지구 자전을 더 느리게 하는가?

[중요 어휘]

☐ **reservoir**	명사 저수지
☐ **mass**	명사 질량, 덩어리
☐ **shift**	동사 이동하다 / 명사 이동, 변화
☐ **whirling**	형용사 회전하는
☐ **gradually**	부사 점차, 점진적으로
☐ **deceleration**	명사 감속
☐ **unintended**	형용사 의도치 않은

04 2020년 9월 29번 | 틀린 어법 고르기 (정답률 55%) 정답 ③

[총평]

동사와 준동사의 쓰임을 구별할 수 있는지 묻는 문제이다.

[지문 끊어 읽기] 사회적 상호 작용에서의 도덕성

(1) All social interactions require some common ground /
모든 사회적 상호 작용은 공통되는 기반을 어느 정도 요구한다 / 선행사
[upon which the involved parties can coordinate their
전치사+관계대명사(+완전한 문장)
behavior].
관련 당사자들이 그에 근거해 그들의 행동을 조정할 수 있는

(2) In the interdependent groups /
선행사
상호 의존적인 집단에서 /
✶ 전치사+관계대명사(+완전한 문장) = 관계부사 where
in which humans and other primates live, /
인간 및 기타 영장류들이 사는 /
individuals must have even greater common ground /
비교급 강조 부사(훨씬) 비교급 형용사
개체들은 훨씬 더 큰 공통되는 기반을 지녀야 한다 /
to establish and maintain social relationships.
to부정사의 부사적 용법(목적)
사회적 관계를 맺고 유지하기 위해

(3) This common ground is morality.
이 공통되는 기반은 도덕성이다

✚ 주의할 표현
this(that) is because+이유
: 이것(그것)은 ~하기 때문이다
this(that) is why+결과
: 이것(그것)이 ~한 이유이다,
그래서 ~하다

(4) This is why morality often is defined /
이것은 도덕성이 흔히 정의되는 이유이다 /
as a shared set of standards /
일련의 공유된 기준으로 /
define A as B(A를 B로 정의하다)
=A be defined as B(A가 B로 정의되다)
✶ 전치사+동명사
for judging right and wrong /
옳고 그름을 판단하기 위한 /
in the conduct of social relationships.
사회적 관계의 행위 속에서

✚ 양보의 부사절을 이끄는
no matter+관계사 = 복합관계사
(~하더라도)
no matter how = however
(어떻게/아무리 ~하더라도)
no matter where = wherever
(어디에 ~하더라도)
no matter who = whoever
(누가 ~하더라도)

(5) No matter how it is conceptualized /
= However(복합관계부사)
그것이 어떤 식으로 개념화되더라도 /
— whether as trustworthiness, cooperation, justice, or caring — /
신뢰성, 협력, 정의, 또는 배려로든 /

morality is always about the treatment of people / ★ 문장 구조 파악: 동사 자리
주어(단수)
도덕성이란 늘 사람들을 대우하는 것에 관한 것이다 /
in social relationships.
사회적 관계 속에서

(6) This is likely why there is surprising agreement /
이것이 아마 놀라운 합의가 있는 까닭일 것이다 /
across a wide range of perspectives /
광범위한 시각들 전체에 걸쳐 /
★ 동격의 접속사 that
[that a shared sense of morality is necessary to social relations].
공유된 도덕관념이 사회적 관계에 필수적이라는

(7) Evolutionary biologists, sociologists, and philosophers all /
진화 생물학자, 사회학자, 그리고 철학자 모두는 /
seem to V: ~처럼 보인다, ~인 것 같다
seem to agree with social psychologists /
사회 심리학자와 뜻을 같이하는 것처럼 보인다 /
[that the interdependent relationships within groups /
명사절(agree의 목적어) 주어(복수) 전치사구
집단 내 상호 의존적 관계가 /
[that humans depend on] /
목적격 관계대명사절(the ~ relationships 수식)
인간이 의존하는 /
★ 주어와 동사의 수 일치
are not possible without a shared morality].
공유된 도덕성 없이는 가능하지 않다는 점에서

[전문 해석]

(1)모든 사회적 상호 작용은 관련 당사자들이 그에 근거해 그들의 행동을 조정할 수 있는 공통되는 기반을 어느 정도 요구한다. (2)인간 및 기타 영장류들이 사는 상호 의존적인 집단에서, 개체들은 사회적 관계를 맺고 유지하기 위해 훨씬 더 큰 공통되는 기반을 지녀야 한다. (3)이 공통되는 기반은 도덕성이다. (4)이것은 도덕성이 흔히 사회적 관계의 행위 속에서 옳고 그름을 판단하기 위한 일련의 공유된 기준으로 정의되는 이유이다. (5)그것이 어떤 식으로 개념화되더라도 — 신뢰성, 협력, 정의, 또는 배려로든 (개념화되든 간에) — 도덕성이란 늘 사회적 관계 속에서 사람들을 대우하는 것에 관한 것이다. (6)이것이 아마 광범위한 시각들 전체에 걸쳐 공유된 도덕관념이 사회적 관계에 필수적이라는 놀라운 합의가 있는 까닭일 것이다. (7)진화 생물학자, 사회학자, 그리고 철학자 모두는 인간이 의존하는 집단 내 상호 의존적 관계가 공유된 도덕성 없이는 가능하지 않다는 점에서 사회 심리학자와 뜻을 같이하는 것처럼 보인다.

[정답 풀이]

③ 문장 구조 파악: 동사 자리

(5) [No matter how it is conceptualized] — (whether as trustworthiness, cooperation, justice, or caring) — **morality** ~~to be~~ always about the treatment of people in social relationships.
(No matter how = However; 양보의 부사절; 삽입구; morality: 주어; to be → is)

주절의 주어 morality에 연결되는 본동사가 없으므로 동사를 써야 하는데, 주어가 셀 수 없는 명사로 단수 취급하고 문맥상 시제가 현재이므로 to be를 is로 고쳐야 한다.

[오답 풀이]

① 전치사+관계대명사

(2) In the interdependent groups [**in which** humans and other primates live], individuals must have even greater common ground to establish and maintain social relationships.
(the interdependent groups: 선행사; humans and other primates: 주어; live: 자동사; individuals: 주어; must have: 동사; even greater common ground: 목적어; to establish ~: to부정사구(부사적 용법))

선행사 'the interdependent groups'를 수식하는 관계사절이 1형식의 완전한 문장으로 이루어져 있으므로 「전치사+관계대명사」 형태의 in which를 쓴 것은 적절하다. 'which humans and other primates live in'에서 in이 관계대명사 앞으로 나간 형태이다.

② 전치사의 목적어로 쓰이는 동명사

(4) This is [why morality often is defined as a shared set of standards **for judging** right and wrong in the conduct of social relationships].
(morality: 주어; is defined: 동사(수동태); for: 전치사; judging: 동명사; right and wrong: 동명사의 목적어)

전치사 for의 목적어로 명사나 동명사를 써야 하는데, 뒤에 'right and wrong'이라는 명사구가 있으므로 이를 목적어로 취할 수 있는 동명사 judging을 쓴 것은 어법상 적절하다.

④ 동격의 접속사 that

(6) This is likely why there is **surprising agreement** (across a wide range of perspectives) [**that** a shared sense (of morality) is necessary to social relations].
(that: 접속사; a shared sense: 주어; is: 동사; necessary: 주격 보어)

that 뒤에 2형식의 완전한 문장이 나오므로 that이 접속사로 쓰인 것을 알 수 있다. 동격의 접속사 that이 이끄는 절은 앞에 나온 명사구 surprising agreement의 내용을 보충 설명하고 있다.

⑤ 주어와 동사의 수 일치

(7) Evolutionary biologists, sociologists, and philosophers all seem to **agree** with social psychologists [that **the interdependent relationships** (within groups) [that humans depend on] **are** not possible without a shared morality].
(that: 접속사; the interdependent relationships: 주어(복수); that: 목적격 관계대명사; are: 동사(복수))

동사 agree의 목적어절을 이끄는 접속사 that절의 주어가 복수 명사인 'the interdependent relationships'이므로 복수 동사 are를 쓴 것은 어법상 적절하다. 주어와 동사 사이에 있는 수식어구가 어디까지인지 정확히 파악하여 동사를 찾아 주어와 수 일치해야 한다.

[중요 어휘]

□ interaction	명사 상호 작용
□ common ground	명사 (사회 관계·논의·상호 이해 등의) 공통되는 기반, (관심·견해 따위의) 일치점
□ involved	형용사 관련된, 복잡한
□ party	명사 당사자, 단체, 정당, 파티
□ coordinate	동사 조정하다
□ interdependent	형용사 상호 의존적인
□ primate	명사 영장류
□ establish	동사 (관계를) 맺다, (건물이나 체계를) 확립하다
□ morality	명사 도덕성
□ define A as B	A를 B로 정의하다[규정하다]
□ conduct	명사 행위
□ conceptualize	동사 개념화하다
□ trustworthiness	명사 신뢰성, 믿을 수 있음
□ cooperation	명사 협력
□ justice	명사 정의
□ caring	명사 배려, 보살핌
□ treatment	명사 대우, 취급
□ agreement	명사 합의
□ a wide range of	광범위한
□ perspective	명사 시각, 관점
□ evolutionary	형용사 진화의
□ depend on	~에 의존[의지]하다, ~을 믿다

문제편 p.290

05 2019년 9월 30번 | 틀린 어휘 고르기 (정답률 40%) 정답 ④

[글의 내용 파악]

18세기 유럽에서 언론의 자유와 종교적 관용을 옹호했던 Voltaire가 가톨릭 교회와 귀족 세력의 억압에도 불구하고 당시 사회의 편견과 가식에 도전했다는 내용의 글이다.

[지문 끊어 읽기] Voltaire에 대한 논란

(1) A champion of free speech and religious toleration, /
동격 명사구(=Voltaire)
언론의 자유와 종교적 관용의 옹호자인 /
Voltaire was a controversial figure.
Voltaire는 논란이 많았던 인물이었다

(2) He is, / for instance, / supposed to have declared, /
그는 / 예를 들어 / 말했다고 여겨진다 /
"I hate [what you say], /
관계대명사 what이 이끄는 명사절(hate의 목적어)
나는 여러분이 하는 말을 싫어한다 /
to부정사의 형용사적 용법(명사구 수식)
but will defend (to the death) your right to say it," /
하지만 그것을 말할 여러분의 권리를 사력을 다해 옹호할 것이다 /
a powerful defense of the idea /
생각에 대한 강력한 변론 /
동격 that절(=the idea)
[that even views that you despise / deserve to be heard].
선행사 목적격 관계대명사절
여러분이 경멸하는 의견조차도 / 들려질 만하다는

(3) In eighteenth-century Europe, / however, /
18세기 유럽에서는 / 하지만 /
the Catholic Church strictly controlled / [what could be published].
의문사 what이 이끄는 명사절(controlled의 목적어)
가톨릭 교회가 엄격히 통제하였다 / 무엇이 출판될 수 있는지를

(4) Many of Voltaire's plays and books /
Voltaire의 많은 희곡들과 책들이 /
were censored and burned in public, /
과거분사① 과거분사②
검열을 받았고 공개적으로 불태워졌다 /
and he was even imprisoned in the Bastille in Paris /
그리고 그는 파리의 Bastille 감옥에 수감되기까지 하였다 /
because he had insulted a powerful aristocrat.
그가 세력이 있는 귀족을 모욕했기 때문에
stop A (from) V-ing : A가 ~하는 것을 멈추게 하다

(5) But none of this stopped him challenging /
하지만 이 중 어떤 것도 그가 도전하는 것을 멈추게 하지 못했다 /
the prejudices and pretensions of those around him.
그의 주변 사람들의 편견과 가식에

(6) In his short philosophical novel, *Candide*, /
동격 명사구(=*Candide*)
그의 철학 단편 소설인 'Candide'에서 /
he completely supported(→ undermined) /
그는 완전히 지지했다(→ 훼손했다) /
the kind of religious optimism about humanity and the universe /
선행사
인류와 우주에 대한 종교적인 낙관론을 /
[that other contemporary thinkers had expressed], /
목적격 관계대명사절
당대의 다른 사상가들이 표명했던 /
such a(an) + 형용사 + 명사 + that + 주어 + 동사 : 매우 ~해서 ...하다
and he did it in such an entertaining way /
그리고 그는 그것을 매우 재미있는 방식으로 해서 /
that the book became an instant bestseller.
그 책은 즉시 베스트셀러가 되었다

(7) Wisely, / Voltaire left his name off the title page, /
현명하게도 / Voltaire는 속표지에서 자신의 이름을 뺐다 /
otherwise its publication would have landed him in prison again /
만약 그렇지 않았다면 그것의 출판은 다시 그를 감옥에 갇히게 했을지도 모른다 /
for making fun of religious beliefs.
종교적 신념을 조롱한 이유로

[전문 해석]

(1)언론의 자유와 종교적 관용의 옹호자인 Voltaire(볼테르)는 논란이 많았던 인물이었다. (2)예를 들어, 그는 "나는 여러분이 하는 말을 싫어하지만, 그것을 말할 여러분의 권리를 사력을 다해 옹호할 것이다"라고 말했다고 여겨지는데, (그것은) 여러분이 경멸하는 의견조차도 들려질 만하다는(들려질 자격이 있다는) 생각에 대한 강력한 변론이었다. (3)하지만 18세기 유럽에서는 가톨릭 교회가 무엇이 출판될 수 있는지를 엄격히 통제하였다. (4)Voltaire의 많은 희곡들과 책들이 검열을 받았고 공개적으로 불태워졌으며, 그가 세력이 있는 귀족을 모욕했기 때문에 그는 파리의 Bastille(바스티유) 감옥에 수감되기까지 하였다. (5)하지만 이 중 어떤 것도 그가 그의 주변 사람들의 편견과 가식에 도전하는 것을 멈추게 하지 못했다. (6)그의 철학 단편 소설인 'Candide(캉디드)'에서, 그는 당대의 다른 사상가들이 표명했던 인류와 우주에 대한 종교적인 낙관론을 완전히 지지했고(→ 훼손했고), 그는 그것을 매우 재미있는 방식으로 해서 그 책은 즉시 베스트셀러가 되었다. (7)현명하게도 Voltaire는 속표지에서 자신의 이름을 뺐는데, 만약 그렇지 않았다면 그것의 출판은 종교적 신념을 조롱한 이유로 다시 그를 감옥에 갇히게 했을지도 모른다.

[정답 풀이]

(6) In his short philosophical novel, *Candide*, he completely ④ ~~supported~~ (→ undermined) the kind of religious optimism about humanity and the universe that other contemporary thinkers had expressed, and he did it in such an entertaining way that the book became an instant bestseller.

뒤 문장에 '그의 책이 종교적 신념을 조롱했다는 이유로 Voltaire가 다시 감옥에 갔을지도 모른다'는 내용이 있으므로 그가 '인류와 우주에 대한 종교적인 낙관론을 완전히 훼손했다'고 해야 문맥에 어울린다. 따라서 '지지했다'라는 의미의 supported를 '훼손했다'라는 의미의 undermined로 고쳐 써야 적절하다.

[오답 풀이]

① **defense** (n. 변론): 언론 자유의 옹호자였던 Voltaire가 사람들의 말할 권리를 지키겠다고 한 말은 사람들이 경멸하는 의견도 들을 가치가 있다는 '생각에 대한 강력한 변론(a powerful defense of the idea)'이라고 해야 문맥상 자연스럽다.
② **control** (v. 통제하다): Voltaire는 언론과 출판의 자유를 옹호했던 반면에 가톨릭 교회를 비롯한 당시 사회는 이것을 '엄격히 통제했다(strictly controlled)'라는 흐름이 적절하다.
③ **insult** (v. 모욕하다): Voltaire가 감옥에 수감된 이유는 '그가 세력이 있는 귀족을 모욕했기 때문에(because he had insulted a powerful aristocrat)'라고 해야 문맥상 자연스럽다.
⑤ **off** (prep. ~에서 제거되어): 책의 저자가 누구인지 알 수 없게 '속표지에서 그의 이름을 뺐다(left his name off the title page)'라고 해야 문맥상 적절하다.

[중요 어휘]

☐ **champion**	명사 옹호자
☐ **free speech**	명사 언론의 자유
☐ **religious**	형용사 종교적인, 종교의
☐ **toleration**	명사 관용
☐ **controversial**	형용사 논란이 많은
☐ **figure**	명사 인물
☐ **be supposed to V**	~하다고 여겨지다[생각되다]
☐ **declare**	동사 말하다, 선언하다
☐ **defend to death**	사력을 다해 옹호하다
☐ **right**	명사 권리
☐ **defense**	명사 변론, 변호, 방어
☐ **view**	명사 의견, 견해
☐ **despise**	동사 경멸하다
☐ **deserve to V**	~할 만하다, ~할 자격이 있다
☐ **strictly**	부사 엄격히
☐ **control**	동사 통제하다
☐ **publish**	동사 출판하다
☐ **play**	명사 희곡, 각본, 연극
☐ **censor**	동사 검열하다
☐ **in public**	공개적으로
☐ **imprison**	동사 수감하다, 가두다

☐ insult	동사 모욕하다
☐ aristocrat	명사 귀족, 특권 계급의 사람
☐ challenge	동사 도전하다
☐ prejudice	명사 편견, 선입관
☐ pretension	명사 가식, 허세
☐ philosophical	형용사 철학의, 철학에 관련된
☐ novel	명사 소설
☐ support	동사 지지하다
☐ undermine	동사 훼손하다
☐ optimism	명사 낙관론, 낙관주의
☐ humanity	명사 인류
☐ contemporary	형용사 당대의, 동시대의
☐ thinker	명사 사상가
☐ express	동사 표명하다, 표현하다
☐ entertaining	형용사 재미있는
☐ instant	형용사 즉시의, 즉각적인
☐ leave A off B	B에서 A를 빼다
☐ publication	명사 출판
☐ land	동사 두다, 빠트리다, 도착시키다
☐ make fun of	~을 조롱하다
☐ belief	명사 신념

06 2018년 3월 26번 (정답률 90%) 정답 ④

[중요 구문] 과학 쇼케이스 영상 대회

(2) Create a video /
선행사
영상을 만들어 보세요 /
that effectively communicates a specific aspect of science /
주격 관계대명사
과학의 특정한 측면을 효과적으로 전달하는 /
and is informative for a broad public audience.
그리고 폭넓은 대중 관객에게 유용한 정보를 주는

[전문 해석]

(1)과학 쇼케이스(공개 행사) 영상 대회
(2)과학의 특정한 측면을 효과적으로 전달하고 폭넓은 대중 관객에게 유용한 정보를 주는 영상을 만들어 보세요. (3)영상은 6월 1일에서 8월 31일 사이에 제출되어야 합니다. (4)우승자는 10월 초에 발표됩니다.
Videos should be submitted between June 1 and August 31.
(5)상금으로 2,000달러까지 (수여됩니다.) Up to $2,000 in Prize Money
Winners will be announced in early October.
(6)지침(가이드라인):
(7) ■ 개인당 한 편 또는 두 편의 출품작 정답단서 One or two entries per individual
(8) ■ 아래의 사항을 scienceshowcase@kmail.com으로 제출하세요.
(9) – 영상(물)의 제목
(10) – 이름과 전화번호
(11) – 영상으로의(영상으로 연결되는) 다운로드 링크
(12) ■ 영상의 형식에 대한 제한 없음 No restrictions on style of video
(13)더 많은 정보를 위해서 저희 웹사이트 www.scienceshowcase.org를 방문해주세요.

[정답 확인]

Science Showcase Video Contest에 관한 다음 안내문의 내용과 일치하지 않는 것은?

① 8월 31일까지 영상물을 제출해야(submit) 한다. 문장(3)
② 수상자는 10월 초에 발표한다(announce). 문장(4)
③ 상금(prize money)은 2,000달러까지 수여된다. 문장(5)
✔④ 출품작(entry)은 1인당(per individual) ~~한 편~~(두 편)으로 제한된다. 문장(7)
⑤ 영상물의 형식(type)에는 제한이 없다(no restrictions). 문장(12)

★중요 문장 (7)의 One or two entries per individual에서 개인당 출품작은 한 편으로 제한하지 않음을 확인할 수 있음.

[중요 어휘]

☐ showcase	명사 쇼케이스, 공개 행사 / 동사 소개하다
☐ effectively	부사 효과적으로
☐ communicate	동사 전달하다, 전하다
☐ aspect	명사 측면, 양상
☐ informative	형용사 유용한 정보를 주는, 유익한
☐ prize money	명사 상금
☐ guideline	명사 지침, 가이드라인
☐ restriction	명사 제한, 규제

07 2020년 3월 25번 (정답률 80%) 정답 ⑤

[지문 끊어 읽기] 내셔널 풋볼 리그 경기의 요일별 부상률

(1) The above graph shows / the injury rate by day /
위 그래프는 보여준다 / 요일별 부상률을 /
of game in the National Football League (NFL) /
내셔널 풋볼 리그 (NFL) 경기의 /
from 2014 to 2017.
2014년부터 2017년까지

①(2) The injury rate of Thursday games /
목요일 경기의 부상률은 /
was the lowest in 2014 / and the highest in 2017.
2014년에 가장 낮았다 / 그리고 2017년에 가장 높았다

②(3) The injury rate of Saturday, Sunday and Monday games /
토요일, 일요일 그리고 월요일 경기의 부상률은 /
decreased steadily / from 2014 to 2017.
꾸준하게 감소했다 / 2014년부터 2017년까지

③(4) In all the years except 2017, /
2017년을 제외한 모든 해에 /
the injury rate of Thursday games /
목요일 경기의 부상률은 /
was lower / than that of Saturday, Sunday and Monday games.
=the injury rate
더 낮았다 / 토요일, 일요일 그리고 월요일 경기의 그것보다

힌트 that은 지시대명사로 앞서 나온 명사를 반복하는 대신 사용함. 여기서는 the injury rate 대신 that을 썼음. 'that of ~' 형태로 표현되어 있으니 마찬가지로 앞에서 of가 붙어있는 명사를 찾으면 that이 무엇을 가리키는지 바로 알 수 있음.

④(5) The gap /
차이는 /
between the injury rate of Thursday games and that of Saturday,
병렬① 병렬②(=the injury rate)
Sunday and Monday games /
목요일 경기의 부상률과 토요일, 일요일 그리고 월요일 경기의 그것 간의 /
was the largest in 2014 / and the smallest in 2017.
2014년에 가장 컸다 / 그리고 2017년에 가장 작았다

⑤(6) In two years out of the four, /
4년 중 두 해에 /
the injury rate of Thursday games was higher /
목요일 경기의 부상률은 더 높았다 /
than that of the 4-year total.
=the injury rate of Thursday games
4년 전체의 그것보다

★중요 여기서 비교할 것은 좌측의 2014년~2017년 각각의 경기 부상률과 우측의 4년 전체의 경기 부상률임. 목요일 부상률은 2017년의 6.9를 제외하고는 모두 4년 전체의 경기 부상률인 5.7보다 낮았음.

[전문 해석]

(1)위 그래프는 2014년부터 2017년까지 내셔널 풋볼 리그 (NFL) 경기의 요일별 부상률을 보여준다. ①(2)목요일 경기의 부상률은 2014년에 가장 낮았고 2017년에 가장 높았다. ②(3)토요일, 일요일 그리고 월요일 경기의 부상률은 2014년부터 2017년까지 꾸준하게 감소했다. ③(4)2017년을 제외한 모든 해에 목요일 경기의 부상률은 토요일, 일요일 그리고 월요일 경기의 그것(부상률)보다 더 낮았다. ④(5)목요일 경기의 부상률과 토요일, 일요일 그리고 월요일 경기의 그것(부상률) 간의 차이는 2014년에 가장 컸고 2017년에 가장 작았다. ⑤(6)4년 중 두 해(→ 한 해)에 목요일 경기의 부상률은 4년 전체의 그것(목요일 경기의 부상률)보다 더 높았다.

- National Football League(내셔널 풋볼 리그): 내셔널 풋볼 콘퍼런스(16개 팀)와 아메리칸 풋볼 콘퍼런스(16개 팀)의 총 32개 팀이 동부·서부·남부·북부 지구로 나뉘어 치르는 미국의 미식축구리그를 말한다.

[정답 확인]

다음 도표의 내용과 일치하지 않는 것은?

Injury Rate by Day of Game in NFL (2014–2017) NFL 경기의 요일별 부상률(2014~2017년)

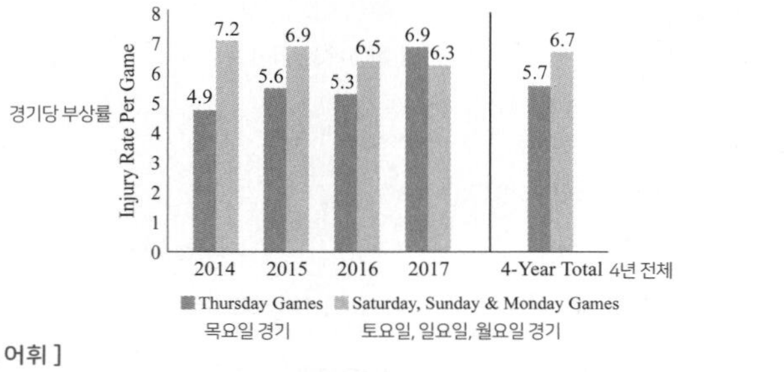

[중요 어휘]

- ☐ **injury rate** 부상률
- ☐ **steadily** [부사] 꾸준하게

핵심 '배의 모든 부분이 교체되었더라도 그 배는 여전히 그 배인가?'라는 테세우스의 배 역설을 소개하는 글임.

08 2019년 3월 33번 (정답률 40%) 정답 ②

[지문 끊어 읽기] 테세우스의 배 역설

(1) Theseus was a great hero / to the people of Athens.
테세우스는 위대한 영웅이었다 / 아테네 사람들에게

(2) When he returned home / after a war, /
그가 고향에 돌아왔을 때 / 전쟁 후에 /
the ship [that had carried him and his men] / was so treasured /
S(=선행사) [ ]: 주격 관계대명사절 V so ~ that …: 너무 ~해서 …하다
그와 그의 부하들을 태웠었던 배는 / 너무도 소중히 여겨져서 /
that the townspeople preserved it / for years and years, /
도시 주민들은 그것을 보존했다 / 수년간 /
replacing its old, rotten planks / with new pieces of wood.
그것의 낡고 썩은 나무 판자를 교체하며 / 새 나무 조각으로

(3) The question / Plutarch asks philosophers / is this: /
S(=선행사) 목적격 관계대명사절 V
질문은 / 플루타르크가 철학자들에게 물은 / 이것이다 /
is the repaired ship / still the same ship /
수리된 배는 / 여전히 바로 그 배인가 /
that Theseus had sailed? 정답단서
테세우스가 항해했었던

힌트 the same ship처럼, 선행사에 the same, the very, the only 등이 올 경우에는 관계사 which를 못 쓰고 that만 쓸 수 있음. 문장 (3)에도 the same ship을 수식하는 목적격 관계대명사절에서 관계사 that이 쓰였음.

(4) Removing one plank / and replacing it /
병렬① 병렬②
한 개의 널빤지를 제거하는 것은 / 그리고 그것을 교체하는 것은 /
might not make a difference, / but can that still be true /
차이가 안 날 수도 있다 / 하지만 그것은 여전히 그럴 수 있을까 /
once all the planks have been replaced?
모든 널빤지가 교체되었을 때도

(5) Some philosophers argue /
일부의 철학자들은 주장한다 /
that the ship must be the sum / of all its parts.
그 배가 총합이어야 한다고 / 모든 부분의

(6) But if this is true, / then as the ship got pushed around /
병렬①
하지만 만일 이것이 사실이라면 / 그렇다면 배가 이리저리 밀쳐졌을 때 /
during its journey / and lost small pieces, /
병렬②
그것의 여정 동안 / 그리고 작은 조각들을 잃었을 때 /
it would already have stopped / being the ship of Theseus. 정답단서
stop + V-ing: ~하는 것을 멈추다[그만두다]
그것은 이미 중단했을 것이다 / 테세우스의 배가 되는 것을

힌트 push A around의 과거분사(수동) 형태인 pushed around가 2형식 동사 get의 주격 보어로 왔음.

[전문 해석]

(1)테세우스는 아테네 사람들에게 위대한 영웅이었다. (2)전쟁 후에 그가 고향에 돌아왔을 때, 그와 그의 부하들을 태웠었던 배는 너무도 소중히 여겨져서 도시 주민들은 그것의 낡고 썩은 나무 판자를 새 나무 조각으로 교체하며 수년간 그것을 보존했다. (3)플루타르크가 철학자들에게 물은 질문은 이것이다. 수리된 배는 여전히 테세우스가 항해했었던 바로 그 배인가? (4)한 개의 널빤지를 제거하고 (그것을) 교체하는 것은 차이가 안 날 수도 있지만, 모든 널빤지가 교체되었을 때도 (그것은) 여전히 그럴 수 있을까? (5)일부의 철학자들은 그 배가 모든 부분의 총합이어야 한다고 주장한다. (6)하지만 만일 이것이 사실이라면, (그렇다면) 배가 (그것의) 여정 동안 이리저리 밀쳐지며 작은 조각들을 잃었을 때 그것은 이미 테세우스의 배가 되는 것을 중단했을 것이다(테세우스의 배가 아니게 되었을 것이다).

- Theseus(테세우스): 그리스 신화에서 헤라클레스에 비견되는 아테네 최고의 영웅으로, 황소 머리를 가진 반인반수의 괴물 미노타우르스를 물리친 것으로 알려져 있다.
- Plutarch(플루타르크): 그리스 출신의 철학자이자 정치가 겸 작가로, '최후의 그리스인'이라 불릴 정도로 고대 그리스 사상에 능하였으며, <모랄리아(Moralia)> 및 <영웅전(Bioi Paralleloi)> 외 다양한 저술을 남겼다.

[정답 확인]

다음 빈칸에 들어갈 말로 가장 적절한 것은?

① the reminder of victory 승리를 상기시키는 것
② the sum of all its parts 모든 부분의 총합 ✔
③ fit for the intended use 의도된 용도에 적합한
④ the property of the country 국가의 재산
⑤ around for a long period of time 오랜 기간 동안 주변에

[문제 풀이]

본문은 '보존을 위해 말끔하게 수리된 테세우스의 배'를 진정으로 '테세우스가 항해하던 바로 그 배'라고 할 수 있는지에 대한 철학적 논의를 담고 있다. 빈칸에 들어갈 말은 위 질문에 대한 일부 철학자들의 입장으로, 이어지는 문장 (6)의 '이것(this)'에 해당한다. 따라서 문장 (6)의 'if this is true(만일 이것이 사실이라면)'는 '빈칸의 내용이 전제된다면'으로 바꾸어 생각할 수 있다. 그런데 문장 (6)에서, '거친 항해 과정에서 배의 작은 조각들을 잃었을 때(잃었으므로), 그 배는 이미 테세우스의 배가 아니다'라는 결론이 성립하려면, 진정한 의미의 테세우스의 배는 '모든 (작은) 부분의 총합'이어야 한다는 전제가 필요하므로, 정답은 ② 'the sum of all its parts(모든 부분의 총합)'이다.

[중요 어휘]

- ☐ **home** [부사] 고향에, 집에
- ☐ **man** [명사] 부하, 남자
- ☐ **treasured** [형용사] 소중히[귀하게] 여겨지는
- ☐ **preserve** [동사] 보존하다, 지키다
- ☐ **replace** [동사] 교체하다, 대체하다
- ☐ **rotten** [형용사] 썩은, 부패한
- ☐ **plank** [명사] 나무 판자, 널빤지
- ☐ **philosopher** [명사] 철학자
- ☐ **repair** [동사] 수리하다, 고치다
- ☐ **sum** [명사] 총합, 전부
- ☐ **journey** [명사] 여정, 여행

핵심 빈칸이 글의 앞에 있을 때는 뒤에 오는 내용을 요약한 문장이 빈칸에 들어가는 경우가 많음. 정답을 찾기 위해서는 뒤에 나오는 사례에서 같은 유전자를 가졌다고 해도 발병 여부가 갈리는 이유를 찾는 것이 관건임.

09 2020년 3월 34번 (정답률 45%) 정답 ⑤

[지문 끊어 읽기] 유전자 발현에 대한 음식의 영향

(1) The growing field of genetics / is showing us /
발전하고 있는 유전학 분야는 / 우리에게 보여주고 있다 /
what many scientists have suspected for years /
많은 과학자들이 몇 년간 의심했던 것을 /
— foods can immediately influence the genetic blueprint.
음식이 유전자 청사진에 직접 영향을 줄 수 있다

(2) This information helps us better understand /
이 정보는 우리가 더 잘 이해할 수 있도록 돕는다 /
that genes are under our control /
S·C①
유전자가 우리의 통제하에 있음을 /
and not something we must obey.
S·C②
그리고 우리가 복종해야만 하는 무언가가 아님을

힌트 문장 (2)의 'something'과 'we must obey' 사이에는 목적격 관계대명사 'that'이 생략되었음. 관계대명사는 목적격일 때, 그리고 주격 관계대명사와 be동사가 함께 있을 때 생략이 가능함.

(3) Consider identical twins; /
일란성 쌍둥이를 생각해 보자 /

both individuals are given the same genes.
두 사람은 모두 같은 유전자를 부여받는다

힌트 문장 (4)부터 쌍둥이 두 사람을 비교할 때 반복적으로 부정대명사 'one'과 'the other'이 번갈아 나오고 있음. 두 가지의 대상에서 하나, 그리고 나머지 하나를 나타내는 경우에 쓰임.

(4) In mid-life, / one twin develops cancer, /
중년이 되었을 때 / 쌍둥이 중 한 사람은 암에 걸린다 /
and the other lives a long healthy life / without cancer.
그리고 다른 한 사람은 오래 건강한 삶을 산다 / 암 없이

(5) A specific gene instructed one twin to develop cancer, /
S V O O.C
특정한 유전자가 쌍둥이 중 한 사람이 암에 걸리도록 명령했다 /
but in the other / the same gene did not initiate the disease.
그러나 다른 한 사람에게는 / 같은 유전자가 그 질병을 일으키지 않았다

(6) One possibility is / that the healthy twin had a diet /
한 가능성은 ~이다 / 쌍둥이 중 건강한 사람이 식사를 했다는 것 / 선행사
that turned off the cancer gene / 정답 단서
주격 관계대명사
암 유전자를 차단하는 /
— the same gene / that instructed the other person to get sick.
선행사 주격 관계대명사
그 같은 유전자 / 다른 한 사람이 병에 걸리도록 명령했던

(7) For many years, / scientists have recognized /
여러 해 동안 / 과학자들은 인정해 왔다 /
other environmental factors, / such as chemical toxins /
다른 환경적인 요인들이 / 화학적 독소와 같은 /
(tobacco for example), / can contribute to cancer /
(예를 들어 담배) / 암의 원인이 될 수 있다는 것을 /
through their actions on genes.
유전자에 행하는 그것들의 작용을 통해

(8) The notion / that food has a specific influence /
생각은 / 음식이 특정한 영향을 끼친다는 /
on gene expression / is relatively new. 정답 단서
유전자 발현에 / 비교적 새롭다

[전문 해석]

(1)발전하고 있는 유전학 분야는 우리에게 많은 과학자들이 몇 년간 의심했던 것, 즉 음식이 유전자 청사진에 직접 영향을 줄 수 있다는 것을 보여주고 있다. (2)이 정보는 유전자가 우리의 통제하에 있는 것이지 우리가 복종해야만 하는 무언가가 아님을 (우리가) 더 잘 이해할 수 있도록 돕는다. (3)일란성 쌍둥이를 생각해 보자. 두 사람은 모두 같은 유전자를 부여받는다. (4)중년이 되었을 때, 쌍둥이 중 한 사람은 암에 걸리고, 다른 한 사람은 암 없이 오래 건강한 삶을 산다. (5)특정한 유전자가 쌍둥이 중 한 사람이 암에 걸리도록 명령했으나, 다른 한 사람에게는 같은 유전자가 그 질병을 일으키지 않았다. (6)한 가능성은 쌍둥이 중 건강한 사람이 암 유전자, 즉 다른 한 사람이 병에 걸리도록 명령했던 그 같은 유전자를 차단하는 식사를 했다는 것이다. (7)여러 해 동안 과학자들은 화학적 독소(예를 들어 담배)와 같은 다른 환경적인 요인들이 유전자에 행하는 (그것들의) 작용을 통해 암의 원인이 될 수 있다는 것을 인정해 왔다. (8)음식이 유전자 발현에 특정한 영향을 끼친다는 생각은 비교적 새롭다.

[정답 확인]

다음 빈칸에 들어갈 말로 가장 적절한 것은?

① identical twins have the same genetic makeup
일란성 쌍둥이는 같은 유전자 구성을 지닌다
② our preference for food is influenced by genes
우리의 음식에 대한 선호는 유전자의 영향을 받는다
③ balanced diet is essential for our mental health
균형 잡힌 식사는 우리의 정신 건강에 필수적이다
④ genetic engineering can cure some fatal diseases
유전 공학은 몇몇의 치명적인 질병을 치료할 수 있다
✔ foods can immediately influence the genetic blueprint
음식이 유전자 청사진에 직접 영향을 줄 수 있다

[문제 풀이]

두괄식 지문으로, 빈칸에는 글의 전체적인 내용에 대한 설명이 들어가는 것이 가장 자연스럽다. 따라서 정답은 지문에서 제시하는 사례 등을 일반화하거나 요약하는 내용이어야 한다. 지문에서는 유전자 구성이 같은 일란성 쌍둥이라도 암에 걸리는 양상이 다르다는 것을 예시로 들며, 그 이유가 여러 환경적 요인 중에서도 식사가 서로 달랐기 때문이라고 추측하므로, 음식이 유전자 발현에 영향을 준다는 내용이 빈칸에 들어가야 가장 자연스럽다. 따라서 정답은 ⑤이다.

[중요 어휘]

□ genetics	명사 유전학
□ suspect	동사 의심하다
□ blueprint	명사 청사진, 설계도
□ identical	형용사 일란성의, 동일한
□ develop	동사 (병에) 걸리다, 발달시키다
□ instruct	동사 명령하다, 지시하다
□ initiate	동사 일으키다, 시작하다
□ diet	명사 식사, 식습관
□ toxin	명사 독소
□ contribute to	~의 원인이 되다, ~에 기여하다
□ notion	명사 생각, 개념
□ relatively	부사 비교적, 상대적으로
□ makeup	명사 구성, 구조, 화장
□ fatal	형용사 치명적인

• 지문 구조도

(1) 음식은 유전자 청사진(genetic blueprint)에 직접 영향을 줌.

(2) 유전자는 우리가 복종해야(obey) 할 대상이 아니라 통제할(control) 수 있는 것임.
(7) 다른 환경적인 요인(other environmental factors)이 유전자에 작용하여 암의 원인이 될 수 있다는 것은 과학자들이 전부터 인정했음(recognize).
(8) 음식이 유전자 발현(gene expression)에 특정한 영향을 끼친다는 생각은 비교적 새로움.

↓

(3)~(4) 예시: 일란성 쌍둥이(identical twins)

(3) 일란성 쌍둥이는 같은 유전자(the same genes)를 부여받음.
(4) 중년(mid-life)이 되었을 때, 쌍둥이 중 한 사람(one)은 암에 걸리고(develop) 다른 한 사람(the other)은 건강하게 삶.

↓

(5)~(6) 이유

(5) 특정 유전자가 한 사람이 암에 걸리도록 명령했으나(instruct) 쌍둥이 중 다른 한 사람에게는 질병을 일으키지(initiate) 않음.
(6) 건강한 사람이 이 특정 유전자를 차단하는(turn off) 식사를 했을(have a diet) 가능성이 있음.

핵심 지구 온난화로 인한 식량 부족의 예로 아프리카의 사막화와 그 원인을 들어 설명하는 글로, 문장 (4)에 제시된 '가뭄을 극복하는 농업 체계'에 관한 내용은 글의 흐름에 어울리지 않음.

10 2017년 6월 39번 (정답률 65%) 정답 ③

[지문 끊어 읽기] 지구 온난화로 인한 식량 부족

(1) Food shortages / caused by global warming /
식량 부족은 / 지구 온난화에 의해 야기된 /
could force as many as 1 billion people to leave their homes /
10억 명만큼의 많은 사람들이 그들의 집을 떠나게 만들 수 있다 /
by 2050, / according to the Earth Institute, /
2050년까지 / Earth Institute에 따르면 /
a New York-based aid agency.
New York에 있는 구호 기관인

① (2) Hardest hit may be Africa, /
가장 강력한 타격은 아프리카일 것이다 /
which could lose two-thirds of its cropland /
그런데 경작지의 3분의 2를 잃을 수 있다 /
due to desertification, / which occurs /
사막화 때문에 / 발생하는 / 정답 단서
when the land loses its ability to produce vegetation /
땅이 초목을 생산하는 능력을 잃어버릴 때 /
and turns into deserts.
그리고 사막으로 변할 때

② (3) Although many scientists expect /
비록 많은 과학자들이 예상하지만 /

climate change to result in more rainfall, /
기후 변화가 더 많은 비를 초래할 것이라고 /
some areas could experience droughts /
어떤 지역은 가뭄을 경험할 수 있다 /
because rainfall is sporadic /
비가 산발적으로 내리기 때문에 /
or falls in concentrations in some places but misses others.
또는 어떤 곳에서는 집중하여 내리지만 다른 곳은 지나치기 때문에

③(4) Having an adequate farming system /
적절한 농업 체계를 가지는 것은 /
helps farmers overcome long-term droughts. 정답 단서
농부들이 장기적인 가뭄을 극복하도록 도와준다

④(5) Also, / desertification could occur / 정답 단서
또한 / 사막화는 발생할 수 있다 /
because warmer temperatures draw moisture / out of the soil.
더 따뜻한 기온이 습기를 빼내기 때문에 / 토양으로부터

⑤(6) When regions can no longer produce food, /
지역이 더 이상 식량을 생산해낼 수 없을 때 /
people will be forced to move to other areas, /
사람들은 다른 지역으로 이동하게 될 것이다 /
making them "climate refugees." 정답 단서
그들을 '기후 난민'이 되도록 한다

[전문 해석]

(1)New York에 있는 구호 기관인 Earth Institute에 따르면, 지구 온난화에 의해 야기된 식량 부족은 2050년까지 10억 명만큼의 많은 사람들이 그들의 집을 떠나게 만들 수 있다. ①(2)가장 강력한 타격은 아프리카일 것인데, 땅이 초목을 생산하는 능력을 잃어버리고 사막으로 변할 때 발생하는 사막화 때문에 경작지의 3분의 2를 잃을 수 있다. ②(3)비록 많은 과학자들이 기후 변화가 더 많은 비를 초래할 것이라고 예상하지만, 비가 산발적으로 내리거나, 어떤 곳에서는 집중하여 내리지만 다른 곳은 지나치기 때문에 어떤 지역은 가뭄을 경험할 수 있다. ③(4)적절한 농업 체계를 가지는 것은 농부들이 장기적인 가뭄을 극복하도록 도와준다. ④(5)또한 사막화는 더 따뜻한 기온이 토양으로부터 습기를 빼내기 때문에 발생할 수 있다. ⑤(6)지역이 더 이상 식량을 생산해낼 수 없을 때, 사람들은 다른 지역으로 이동하게 될 것이고, (결국) 그들을 '기후 난민'이 되도록 한다(그들은 '기후 난민'이 된다).

[중요 어휘]

□ shortage	명사 부족
□ force	동사 ~하게 만들다, 강요하다
□ aid	명사 구호, 원조
□ agency	명사 기관
□ cropland	명사 경작지
□ desertification	명사 사막화
□ vegetation	명사 초목, 식물
□ rainfall	명사 비, 강우
□ drought	명사 가뭄
□ in concentration	집중하여
□ farming	명사 농업, 농사
□ overcome	동사 극복하다
□ moisture	명사 습기

핵심 이 지문은 동물이 포식자의 접근을 감지했을 때 도주를 할지 공격을 할지 결정하는 거리에 대한 분석과 예시를 들고 있음.

11~12 2020년 3월 41~42번 (정답률 70% | 50%) 정답 ④ | ②

[지문 끊어 읽기] 도주나 공격의 결정 요인

(1) Animal studies have dealt with the distances /
동물 연구는 거리에 대해 다루어 왔다 /
creatures may keep /
동물들이 유지할 수도 있는 /
between themselves and members of other species.
그들 자신과 다른 종의 구성원들 사이에서

(2) These distances determine the functioning /
이러한 거리는 작용을 결정한다 /
of the so-called 'flight or fight' mechanism. 11번 정답 단서
소위 '도주 또는 공격' 메커니즘의

(3) As an animal senses / what it considers to be a predator /
5형식V O
동물은 감지하면 / 자기가 포식자라고 여기는 것이 /
approaching within its 'flight' distance, /
O·C
자신의 '도주' 거리 내로 접근하는 것을 /
it will quite simply run away. 11번 정답 단서
그것은 정말 그야말로 도망갈 것이다

(4) The distance at which this happens / is amazingly (a)consistent, /
이것이 일어나는 거리는 / 놀라울 정도로 (a)일관적이다 /
and Hediger, a Swiss biologist, /
그리고 스위스 생물학자인 Hediger는 /
claimed to have measured it / remarkably precisely /
그것을 측정했다고 주장했다 / 놀라울 만큼 정확하게 /
for some of the species that he studied.
그가 연구한 일부 종에 대해

힌트 '주장했던(claimed)' 시점보다 '측정했던(to have measured)' 시점이 더 과거이기 때문에 두 동사의 시제 차이를 'to have p.p.'로 표현했음.

(5) Naturally, / it varies from species to species, /
당연히 / 그것은 종에 따라 다르다 /
and usually the larger the animal /
그리고 보통 동물이 더 클수록 /
the (b)shorter(→ longer) its flight distance.
그것의 도주 거리는 (b)더 짧다(→ 더 길다)

힌트 'the 비교급 S' V', the 비교급 S V'는 '~하면 할수록, 더 ~하다'라는 의미로, 밑줄 친 부분은 원래 'the larger the animal (is), the shorter its flight distance (is)'임.

(6) I have had to use a long focus lens /
나는 원거리 초점 렌즈를 사용해야 했다 /
to take photographs of giraffes, /
기린의 사진을 찍기 위해서 /
which have very large flight distances. 12번 정답 단서
왜냐하면 그들은 매우 큰 도주 거리를 가지고 있기 때문이다

힌트 계속적 용법의 관계대명사는 '접속사+대명사'의 역할을 하므로, 밑줄 친 which는 'because they'로 바꿀 수 있음. 즉, 기린은 위협을 감지하는 반경 거리가 너무 넓어서 조금만 다가가도 도망가 버리기 때문에 필자가 원거리 초점 렌즈를 사용해야 했다는 것임.

(7) By contrast, /
대조적으로 /
I have several times nearly stepped on a squirrel in my garden /
have+p.p.(현재완료-경험)
나는 내 정원에서 다람쥐를 거의 밟을 뻔한 적이 여러 번 있었다 /
before it drew attention to itself / by suddenly escaping! 12번 정답 단서
그것이 그것 자신에게로 관심을 끌기 전에 / 갑자기 도망침으로써

중요 다람쥐가 갑자기 도망친 것은 다람쥐가 사람이 아주 가까이 다가올 때까지 사람을 인식하지 못했다는 것을 의미함. 그만큼 다람쥐의 도주 거리가 짧다는 것임.

(8) We can only assume /
우리는 추정할 수 있을 뿐이다 /
that this (c)variation in distance matches /
명사절 접속사 S' V'
거리에서의 이러한 (c)차이가 일치한다고 /
the animal's own assessment /
동물 자신의 평가와 /
of its ability / to accelerate and run.
그것의 능력에 대한 / 속도를 높이고 달리는

중요 문장 (8)은 동물이 자신의 달리기 능력을 높게 평가하면 누가 가까이 와도 금방 달아날 수 있을 것이라 생각하기 때문에 도주 거리가 짧고, 스스로 달리기를 못 한다고 생각하면 조금만 가까이 다가와도 미리 경계하고 도망가기 때문에 도주 거리가 길다는 의미임.

(9) The 'fight' distance is always (d)smaller / than the flight distance.
'공격' 거리는 항상 (d)더 작다 / 도주 거리보다

(10) If a perceived predator approaches / within the flight distance /
만약 인식된 포식자가 접근한다면 / 도주 거리 이내로 /
but the animal is trapped / by obstacles or other predators /
하지만 그 동물이 갇힌다면 / 장애물이나 다른 포식자들에 의해 /
and cannot (e)flee, / it must stand its ground. 11번 정답 단서
그래서 (e)달아날 수 없다면 / 그것은 물러나지 않고 버텨야 한다

(11) Eventually, / however, /
결국에는 / 하지만 /
attack becomes the best form of defence, /
공격이 가장 좋은 형태의 방어가 된다 /
and so the trapped animal will turn and fight.
그러므로 그 갇힌 동물은 돌아서서 싸울 것이다

[중요 구문]

(3) As an animal senses [what it considers ∨ to be a predator]
접속사(=when) S' V' [ ]:O'
[approaching within its 'flight' distance], it will quite simply run away.
[ ]:O·C'

힌트 여기서 what은 선행사를 포함한 관계대명사(=the thing which)로, 뒤에 불완전한 문장이 와야 함. 이 문장에서는 'consider A (to be) B' 형태에서 consider의 목적어인 A 자리가 비어 있음.

[전문 해석]

(1)동물 연구는 동물들이 그들 자신과 다른 종의 구성원들 사이에서 유지할 수도 있는 거리에 대해 다루어 왔다. (2)이러한 거리는 소위 '도주 또는 공격' 메커니즘의 작용을 결정한다. (3)동물은 자기가 포식자라고 여기는 것이 자신의 '도주' 거리 내로 접근하는 것을 감지하면, (그것은) 정말 그야말로 도망갈 것이다. (4)이것이 일어나는 거리는 놀라울 정도로 (a)일관적이며, 스위스 생물학자인 Hediger는 그가 연구한 일부 종에 대해 놀라울 만큼 정확하게 그것(거리)을 측정했다고 주장했다. (5)당연히 그것은 종에 따라 다르며, 보통 동물이 더 클수록 그것의 도주 거리는 (b)더 짧다(→ 더 길다). (6)나는 기린의 사진을 찍기 위해서 원거리 초점 렌즈를 사용해야 했는데, 왜냐하면 그들은 매우 큰 도주 거리를 가지고 있기 때문이다. (7)대조적으로, 나는 다람쥐가 갑자기 도망침으로써 그것 자신에게로 (나의) 관심을 끌기 전에 내 정원에서 그것을 거의 밟을 뻔한 적이 여러 번 있었다! (8)우리는 거리에서의 이러한 (c)차이가 속도를 높이고 달리는 (그것의) 능력에 대한 동물 자신의 평가와 일치한다고 추정할 수 있을 뿐이다.

(9)'공격' 거리는 항상 도주 거리보다 (d)더 작다. (10)만약 인식된 포식자가 도주 거리 이내로 접근하지만 그 동물이 장애물이나 다른 포식자들에 의해 갇혀서 (e)달아날 수 없다면, 그것(그 동물)은 물러나지 않고 버텨야 한다. (11)하지만, 결국에는 공격이 가장 좋은 형태의 방어가 되므로, 그 갇힌 동물은 돌아서서 싸울 것이다.

- flight distance(도주 거리): 포식자가 접근해 올 때 동물이 도피 행동을 일으키는 거리. 대개의 동물은 포식자가 다가올 때 도망가지 않다가 이 거리 이상으로 다가오면 도망간다.
- fight distance(공격 거리): 포식자가 도주 거리 이내로 접근하였으나 여건상 도망이 불가능할 때, 이 거리 이상으로 다가오면 공격 태세로 전환하여 맞서 싸우게 된다.

[정답 확인]

11. 윗글의 제목으로 가장 적절한 것은?

① How Animals Migrate Without Getting Lost
동물이 길을 잃지 않고 이동하는 방법
② Flight or Fight Mechanism: Still in Our Brain
도주 또는 공격 메커니즘: 아직도 우리의 뇌 속에
③ Why the Size Matters in the Survival of Animals
동물의 생존에서 크기가 중요한 이유
✔ Distances: A Determining Factor for Flight or Attack
거리: 도주나 공격의 결정 요인
⑤ Competition for Food Between Large and Small Animals
큰 동물과 작은 동물 사이의 먹이 경쟁

12. 밑줄 친 (a) ~ (e) 중에서 문맥상 낱말의 쓰임이 적절하지 않은 것은?

① (a) ✔ (b) ③ (c) ④ (d) ⑤ (e)

[문제 풀이]

12. 문장 (6)의 기린은 조금만 다가가도 도망가 버리기 때문에 원거리 초점 렌즈를 사용해야 할 만큼 도주 거리가 크다. 반면 문장 (7)의 다람쥐는 글쓴이가 가까이 다가올 때까지 도망가지 않아 밟을 뻔한 적이 여러 번 있었다는 것을 통해 도주 거리가 짧음을 알 수 있다. 이는 기린은 몸집이 크고 다람쥐는 몸집이 작기 때문에 발생하는 것으로, 동물이 더 클수록 도주 거리가 '더 길다(longer)'고 하는 것이 적절하다. 따라서 정답은 ②이다.

[중요 어휘]

□ **so-called**	형용사 소위, 이른바
□ **flight**	명사 도주, 도망
□ **mechanism**	명사 메커니즘, 방법
□ **predator**	명사 포식자, 포식 동물
□ **consistent**	형용사 일관적인
□ **remarkably**	부사 놀라울 만큼, 상당히
□ **precisely**	부사 정확하게
□ **draw**	동사 끌다, 당기다, 그리다
□ **assume**	동사 추정하다, 가정하다
□ **variation**	명사 차이, 변화
□ **assessment**	명사 평가
□ **accelerate**	동사 속도를 높이다, 빨라지다
□ **perceive**	동사 인식하다
□ **trap**	동사 가두다 / 명사 덫, 함정
□ **flee**	동사 달아나다, 도망하다
□ **stand one's ground**	물러나지 않고 버티다
□ **migrate**	동사 이동하다, 이주하다

문제편 p.294

2회 20분 미니모의고사

♀핵심 본문은 '레크리에이션은 다양한 개인의 욕구와 관심사를 충족시킨다'는 주제를 문장 (1)에서 먼저 제시한 후, 'Many ~, other ~', 'some ~, Others ~'라는 표현을 통해 '누구는 이렇고 누구는 저렇다'라는 식으로 서로 다른 욕구를 가진 사람들의 예시를 대조적으로 교차 제시하고 있음.

01 2020년 3월 23번 (정답률 65%) 정답 ②

[지문 끊어 읽기] 레크리에이션의 다양한 기능

(1) In addition to the varied forms / that recreation may take, /
다양한 형태 이외에도 / 레크리에이션이 취할 수 있는 /
it also meets / a wide range of individual needs and interests. 주제문
그것은 또한 충족시킨다 / 다양한 개인의 욕구와 관심사를

(2) Many participants take part in recreation / (정답단서)
많은 참여자는 레크리에이션에 참여한다 /
as a form of relaxation and release /
휴식과 분출구의 형태로 /
from work pressures or other tensions.
업무상의 압박이나 다른 긴장으로부터의

(3) Often / they may be passive spectators of entertainment /
종종 / 그들은 오락의 수동적인 구경꾼일지도 모른다 /
provided by television, movies, or other forms of electronic amusement.
텔레비전, 영화, 혹은 다른 형태의 전자 오락에 의해 제공되는

(4) However, / other significant play motivations / (정답단서)
그러나 / 다른 중요한 놀이 동기는 /
are based on the need / to express creativity, /
욕구에 기반을 두고 있다 / 창의력을 표현하고자 하는 /
discover hidden talents, / or pursue excellence /
숨겨진 재능을 발견하고자 하는 / 혹은 탁월성을 추구하고자 하는 /
in varied forms of personal expression.
다양한 형태의 개인적인 표현 속에서

힌트 the need 뒤에서 to부정사의 형용사적 용법을 사용하여 3가지 욕구에 대한 구체적인 설명이 병렬로 나왔음.

(5) For some participants, / (정답단서)
몇몇 참여자들에게 /
active, competitive recreation may offer a channel /
활동적이고 경쟁적인 레크리에이션은 통로를 제공할 수도 있다 /
[for releasing hostility and aggression] / [ ]: 병렬①
적대감과 공격성을 방출하기 위한 /
or [for struggling against others or the environment] / [ ]: 병렬②
혹은 타인이나 환경에 대항하기 위한 /
in adventurous, high-risk activities.
모험적이고 위험성이 높은 활동에서

(6) Others enjoy recreation / that is highly social / (정답단서, 병렬①)
다른 사람들은 레크리에이션을 즐긴다 / 매우 사교적인 /
and provides the opportunity / for making new friends / (병렬②)
그리고 기회를 제공하는 / 새로운 친구를 사귈 수 있는 /
or cooperating with others / in group settings.
혹은 다른 사람들과 협동할 수 있는 / 집단 환경에서

[전문 해석]

(1)레크리에이션이 취할 수 있는 다양한 형태 이외에도, 그것(레크리에이션)은 또한 다양한 개인의 욕구와 관심사를 충족시킨다. (2)많은 참여자는 업무상의 압박이나 다른 긴장으로부터의 휴식과 분출구의 형태로 레크리에이션에 참여한다. (3)종종 그들은 텔레비전, 영화, 혹은 다른 형태의 전자 오락에 의해 제공되는 오락의 수동적인 구경꾼일지도 모른다. (4)그러나 다른 중요한 놀이 동기는 창의력을 표현하거나, 숨겨진 재능을 발견하거나, 혹은 다양한 형태의 개인적인 표현 속에서 탁월성을 추구하고자 하는 욕구에 기반을 두고 있다. (5)몇몇 참여자들에게 활동적이고 경쟁적인 레크리에이션은 적대감과 공격성을 방출하거나 혹은 모험적이고 위험성이 높은 활동에서 타인이나 환경에 대항하기 위한 통로를 제공할 수도 있다. (6)다른 사람들(참여자들)은 매우 사교적이고, 새로운 친구를 사귀거나 혹은 집단 환경에서 다른 사람들과 협동할 수 있는 기회를 제공하는 레크리에이션을 즐긴다.

[정답 확인]

다음 글의 주제로 가장 적절한 것은?

① effects of recreational participation on memory
기억에 관한 레크리에이션 참여의 영향
✔② various motivations for recreational participation
레크리에이션 참여의 다양한 동기
③ importance of balance between work and leisure
일과 여가 사이의 균형의 중요성
④ social factors promoting the recreation movement
레크리에이션 운동을 장려하는 사회적 요소
⑤ economic trends affecting recreational participation
레크리에이션 참여에 영향을 주는 경제적 동향

[문제 풀이]

본문은 주제-예시 형식으로, 레크리에이션이 다양한 개인의 욕구와 관심사를 충족시킨다는 문장 (1)의 주제를 서로 다른 참여자들의 예시를 통해 뒷받침하고 있다. 예를 들어, 문장 (2)~(3)의 참여자들은 레크리에이션을 통해 긴장을 풀고 휴식하는 반면, 문장 (4)에서는 자신의 뛰어난 기량을 표출하고자 하는 목적으로 놀이에 참여하는 사람들이 소개되고 있다. 또한 문장 (5)의 참여자들은 격렬한 활동을 통해 적대감과 공격성을 분출하는 반면, 문장 (6)의 사람들은 사교적인 환경에서 다른 사람들과 소통하는 것을 즐긴다. 각각의 사례의 내용보다는, 사례의 다양성을 통해 문장 (1)의 주제를 가장 잘 표현한 보기를 고르는 것이 중요하다. 따라서 정답은 ②이다.

[중요 어휘]

☐ meet	동사 충족시키다, 만족시키다
☐ need	명사 욕구 / 동사 필요로 하다
☐ take part in	~에 참여하다
☐ relaxation	명사 휴식, 완화
☐ release	명사 분출구, 해방, 방출 / 동사 방출하다
☐ tension	명사 긴장
☐ passive	형용사 수동적인, 소극적인
☐ spectator	명사 구경꾼, 방관자, 관중
☐ channel	명사 통로, 경로
☐ hostility	명사 적대감, 적의
☐ aggression	명사 공격성
☐ cooperate	동사 협동하다, 협력하다
☐ setting	명사 환경, 설정

02 2019년 6월 21번 (정답률 70%) 정답 ②

[지문 끊어 읽기] 책임지고 할 일이 많을 때 필요한 타인의 도움

(1) If you are feeling overwhelmed / by the amount of responsibility /
만약 당신이 압도된다고 느낀다면 / 책임의 양에 의해 /
that you have to deal with / in your own life /
당신이 처리해야 하는 / 당신 자신의 삶에서 /
or your own home, / you are going to have to figure out /
또는 당신 자신의 집에서 / 당신은 알아내야 할 것이다 /
a way that you can balance out these responsibilities.
당신이 이러한 책임들의 균형을 잡을 수 있는 방법을

(2) For example, / is there somebody / that you can turn to /
예를 들어 / 누군가가 있는가 / 당신이 의지할 수 있는 /
to tell them / that you have too much on your plate /
그들에게 말할 만큼 / 당신이 해야 할 일이 너무 많다 /
and you are feeling too overwhelmed / by these responsibilities?
그리고 당신이 너무 압도된다고 느끼고 있다고 / 이러한 책임들에 의해

(3) If you can find somebody / and divide up the labor /
만약 당신이 누군가를 찾을 수 있다면 / 그리고 업무를 분담할 수 있다면 /
so that you don't feel so overwhelmed /
당신이 너무 압도된다고 느끼지 않도록 /
by everything that you are doing, / all you have to do sometimes /
당신이 하고 있는 모든 것에 의해 / 때때로 당신이 해야 할 일은 /
is to ask for help / and your life will feel that much better. 주제문
도움을 요청하는 것이다 / 그러면 당신의 삶은 그만큼 더 낫게 느껴질 것이다

(4) Many times / people will surprise you /
여러 번 / 사람들은 당신을 놀라게 할 것이다 /

with their willingness to help you out, / so never assume /
당신을 기꺼이 도와주려는 마음으로 / 그러니 결코 추정하지 마라 /
that other people don't care about your stress.
다른 사람들이 당신의 스트레스에 대해서 관심을 가지지 않는다고

(5) Let them know honestly / how you are feeling /
사역V O O·C
솔직하게 그들이 알게 하라 / 당신이 어떻게 느끼고 있는지를 /
and allow yourself some opportunities /
그리고 스스로에게 몇몇 기회들을 허용하라 /
to avoid responsibility / and give yourself a chance to relax.
책임을 피할 / 그리고 당신 자신에게 휴식을 취할 기회를 주어라

[전문 해석]

(1)만약 당신이 당신 자신의 삶이나 집에서 당신이 처리해야 하는 책임의 양에 의해 압도된다고 느낀다면, 당신은 이러한 책임들의 균형을 잡을 수 있는 방법을 알아내야 할 것이다. (2)예를 들어, 당신이 해야 할 일이 너무 많고 이러한 책임들에 의해 너무 압도된다고 느끼고 있다고 (그들에게) 말할 만큼 의지할 수 있는 누군가가 있는가? (3)만약 당신이 하고 있는 모든 것에 의해 너무 압도된다고 느끼지 않도록 (의지할 수 있는) 누군가를 찾고 업무를 분담할 수 있다면, 때때로 당신이 해야 할 일은 도움을 요청하는 것이며, 그러면 당신의 삶은 그만큼 더 낫게 느껴질 것이다. (4)여러 번 사람들은 당신을 기꺼이 도와주려는 마음으로 당신을 놀라게 할 것이니, 결코 다른 사람들이 당신의 스트레스에 대해서 관심을 가지지 않는다고 추정하지 마라. (5)솔직하게 그들이 당신이 어떻게 느끼고 있는지를 알게 하고, 스스로에게 책임을 피할 몇몇 기회를 허용하며 당신 자신에게 휴식을 취할 기회를 주어라.

[정답 확인]

다음 글에서 필자가 주장하는 바로 가장 적절한 것은?

① 자신이 맡은 일에 책임감(responsibility)을 가지고 끝까지 완수하라.
✔ 책임지고 할 일이 많을 때 타인에게 도움을 요청하라(ask for help).
③ 업무 효율성(efficiency)을 높이기 위해 스트레스를 잘 관리하라.
④ 주어진 시간을 잘 활용하기 위해 일의 우선순위(priority)를 정하라.
⑤ 갈등(conflict)을 원만하게 해결하기 위해 다양한 의견에 귀를 기울여라.

[중요 어휘]

☐ **overwhelmed**	형용사 압도된, 벅찬
☐ **responsibility**	명사 책임, 의무
☐ **deal with**	~을 처리하다, 다루다
☐ **figure out**	~을 알아내다, 계산하다
☐ **balance out**	균형을 잡다
☐ **turn to**	~에 의지하다
☐ **divide up**	분담하다, 갈리다
☐ **willingness to V**	기꺼이 ~ 하려는 마음
☐ **assume**	동사 추정하다, 당연하다고 여기다
☐ **opportunity**	명사 기회

핵심 걸작이라고 칭해지는 작품들이 나중에 작업된 변형물이 아니라 결국은 초반에 작업된 것에 기반하여 만들어졌다고 이야기하고 있음. 밑줄이 포함된 문장이 바로 앞의 문장과 역접의 관계에 있다는 것을 염두에 두고 읽을 것.

03 2020년 9월 21번 (정답률 40%) 정답 ①

[지문 끊어 읽기] 초반 작업물에 기반을 두는 걸작

(1) If creators knew / when they were on their way /
if+S'+과거V'
만약 창작자들이 안다면 / 그들이 언제 ~하는 중인지를 /
to fashioning a masterpiece, /
걸작을 만들어 내는 /
their work would progress only forward: /
S+조동사 과거형+동사원형
그들의 작품은 오직 앞으로 나아가기만 할 것이다 /
they would halt their idea-generation efforts / as they struck gold.
그들은 그들의 아이디어를 내는 노력을 멈출 것이다 / 그들이 금을 발견하자마자

힌트 문장 (1)은 가정법 과거 문장으로, 해석 시 과거가 아닌 현재로 해석함. 문장 (7)도 마찬가지임.

(2) But in fact, / they backtrack, / returning to versions /
=and they return
그러나 사실 / 그들은 되짚어간다 / 그리고 버전으로 돌아간다 /
that they had earlier discarded / as inadequate.
이전에 그들이 폐기했던 / 부적합하다고

(3) In Beethoven's most celebrated work, / the Fifth Symphony, /
베토벤의 가장 유명한 작품에서 / 제5번 교향곡 /
he scrapped the conclusion of the first movement /
그는 제1악장의 결말을 폐기했다 /
because it felt too short, / only to come back to it later. 정답 단서
부사적 용법-결과(결국 ~하다)
그것이 너무 짧게 느껴졌기 때문에 / 그러나 결국 나중에 그것으로 돌아왔다

(4) Had Beethoven been able to distinguish /
만약 베토벤이 구분할 수 있었다면 /
an extraordinary / from an ordinary work, /
=an extraordinary work
비범한 작품과 / 평범한 작품을 /
he would have accepted his composition immediately / as a hit.
그는 그의 작곡을 즉시 받아들였을 것이다 / 성공으로

(5) When Picasso was painting his famous *Guernica* /
피카소가 그의 유명한 <게르니카>를 그리고 있었을 때 /
in protest of fascism, / he produced 79 different drawings.
파시즘에 저항하여 / 그는 79개의 서로 다른 스케치를 그렸다

(6) Many of the images in the painting /
그 그림 속 많은 이미지는 /
were based on his early sketches, / not the later variations. 정답 단서
그의 초기 스케치에 기반을 두었다 / 이후의 변형물이 아니라

(7) If Picasso could judge his creations / as he produced them, /
만약 피카소가 그의 작품을 판단할 수 있다면 / 그가 그것을 그리면서 /
he would get consistently "warmer" / and use the later drawings.
그는 일관적으로 '더 뜨겁게' 될 것이다 / 그리고 이후의 스케치를 사용할 것이다

(8) But in reality, / it was just as common / that he got "colder."
그러나 실제로는 / 그만큼 흔한 일이었다 / 그가 점점 '더 차갑게' 된 것은

[중요 구문]

(4) Had Beethoven been able to distinguish ~,
=If Beethoven had been(If+S'+had+p.p.)
he would have accepted his composition ~.
S+조동사 과거형+have+p.p.

힌트 과거에 일어난 사실의 반대 상황을 가정하는 가정법 과거완료가 쓰였고, If가 생략되면서 주어와 동사가 도치되었음.

[전문 해석]

(1)만약 창작자들이 그들이 언제 걸작을 만들어 내는 중인지를 안다면, 그들의 작품은 오직 앞으로 나아가기만 할 것이며, 그들은 금을 발견하자마자(걸작을 만들자마자) 아이디어를 내는 노력을 멈출 것이다. (2)그러나 사실, 그들은 (과정을) 되짚어가며, 이전에 그들이 부적합하다고 폐기했던 버전으로 돌아간다. (3)베토벤의 가장 유명한 작품인 제5번 교향곡에서, 그는 제1악장의 결말이 너무 짧게 느껴졌기 때문에 그것을 폐기했으나, 결국 나중에 그것(폐기했던 결말)으로 돌아왔다. (4)만약 베토벤이 비범한 작품과 평범한 작품을 구분할 수 있었다면, 그는 그의 작곡을 즉시 성공으로 받아들였을 것이다. (5)피카소가 파시즘에 저항하여 그의 유명한 <게르니카>를 그리고 있었을 때, 그는 79개의 서로 다른 스케치를 그렸다. (6)그 그림 속 많은 이미지는 이후의 변형물이 아니라 그의 초기 스케치에 기반을 두었다. (7)만약 피카소가 그의 작품을 그리면서 그것을 판단할 수 있다면, 그는 일관적으로 '더 뜨겁게(바라던 결과에 가까워지게)' 될 것이고 이후의(나중에 그린) 스케치를 사용할 것이다. (8)그러나 실제로는, 그가 점점 '더 차갑게(바라던 결과에서 멀어지게)' 된 것은 그만큼 흔한 일이었다.

[정답 확인]

밑줄 친 got "colder"가 다음 글에서 의미하는 바로 가장 적절한 것은?

✔ moved away from the desired outcome
바라던 결과에서 멀어지게
② lost his reputation due to public criticism
대중의 비난 때문에 그의 명성을 잃게
③ became unwilling to follow new art trends
새로운 예술 사조를 따르기를 꺼리게
④ appreciated others' artwork with less enthusiasm
다른 사람의 작품을 덜 열정적으로 감상하게
⑤ imitated masters' styles rather than creating his own
자신만의 스타일을 만들기보다 대가들의 스타일을 모방하게

[문제 풀이]

본문은 베토벤과 피카소와 같은 거장들조차도 그들의 작품이 성공적일지 알지 못한 채 시행착오를 거쳤다고 설명한다. 한편, 밑줄이 있는 문장 (8)은 문장 (7)과 대조를 이루고 있기 때문에 밑줄 친 내용이 의미하는 바를 추론함에 있어 문장 (7)이 중요한 단서가 된다. 문장 (7)에서 피카소가 그림을 그리면서 자신의 작품을 판단할 수 있다면 그의 작품들이 더 뜨겁게

문제편 p.295

될 것이라고 했으므로, 문맥상 '더 뜨겁게 되는 것'은 피카소가 바랐을 만한 상황임을 알 수 있다. 한편 문장 (8)의 역접의 접속사 'But'으로 미루어 보아 문장 (8)의 '더 차갑게 된 것'은 그 반대를 의미하므로, 밑줄 친 부분은 '바라던 결과에서 멀어지게' 된 것을 의미한다. 따라서 정답은 ①이다.

[중요 어휘]

□ **on one's way to V-ing/N**	~하는 중에, ~로 가는 길에
□ **fashion**	동사 만들어 내다
□ **masterpiece**	명사 걸작, 대표작
□ **halt**	동사 멈추다 / 명사 중단
□ **strike**	동사 (금광·석유 등을) 발견하다
□ **backtrack**	동사 되짚어가다, 철회하다
□ **discard**	동사 폐기하다, 버리다
□ **celebrated**	형용사 유명한
□ **scrap**	동사 폐기하다, 버리다
□ **movement**	명사 (음악 작품의) 악장
□ **distinguish A from B**	A와 B를 구분하다
□ **extraordinary**	형용사 비범한, 특별한
□ **in protest of**	~에 저항하여
□ **variation**	명사 변형물, 변화
□ **creation**	명사 (예술) 작품, 창조
□ **consistently**	부사 일관적으로, 지속적으로
□ **reputation**	명사 명성, 평판
□ **criticism**	명사 비난, 비판
□ **appreciate**	동사 감상하다, 감사하다, 인정하다

04 2016년 11월 28번 | 틀린 어법 고르기 (정답률 50%) 정답 ⑤

[총평]

문장의 구조를 파악할 수 있는지 묻고 있다. 동명사나 to부정사와 같은 준동사는 문장에서 본동사 역할을 할 수 없다.

[지문 끊어 읽기] 조명 효과

(1) Why do we often feel /
우리는 왜 종종 느끼는가 /
that others are paying more attention to us / than they really are?
다른 사람들이 우리에게 더 많이 주목하고 있다고 / 실제로 그들이 그러한 것보다

(2) The spotlight effect means / seeing ourselves at center stage, /
조명 효과는 의미한다 / 우리 자신을 무대의 중앙에 있다고 보는 것을 /
thus intuitively overestimating the extent /
그러므로 정도를 직관적으로 과대평가한다는 것을 /
to which others' attention is aimed at us. 주제문
다른 사람들의 주목이 우리에게 향해 있는

(3) Timothy Lawson explored the spotlight effect /
Timothy Lawson은 조명 효과를 조사했다 /
by having college students change into a sweatshirt /
대학생들로 하여금 운동복 상의로 갈아입도록 함으로써 /
with a big popular logo on the front /
앞면에 커다란 유행하는 로고가 있는 /
before meeting a group of peers.
또래 집단을 만나기 전에

(4) Nearly 40 percent of them were sure /
그들 중 거의 40퍼센트가 확신했다 /
the other students would remember /
다른 학생들이 기억할 것이라고 /
what the shirt said, / but only 10 percent actually did.
셔츠에 무엇이 쓰여 있는지 / 하지만 단지 10퍼센트가 실제로 그러했다

(5) Most observers did not even notice /
대부분의 관찰자들은 알아차리지도 못했다 /
that the students changed sweatshirts /
학생들이 운동복 상의들을 갈아입은 것을 /
after leaving the room for a few minutes.
몇 분 동안 방을 떠난 후

(6) In another experiment, / even noticeable clothes, /
또 다른 실험에서는 / 매우 눈에 띄는 옷들조차 /
such as a T-shirt with singer Barry Manilow on it, /
가수 Barry Manilow가 새겨진 티셔츠와 같이 /
provoked only 23 percent of observers to notice /
오직 23퍼센트의 관찰자들만이 알아차리도록 자극했다 /
— far fewer than the 50 percent / estimated by the students /
50퍼센트보다 훨씬 더 적은 / 학생들이 추정한 /
sporting the 1970s soft rock singer on their chests.
그들의 가슴에 1970년대 소프트 록 가수를 자랑해 보이는

[전문 해석]

(1)우리는 왜 그들이 실제로 그러한 것보다 다른 사람들이 우리에게 더 많이 주목하고 있다고 종종 느끼는가? (2)조명 효과는 우리 자신을 무대의 중앙에 있다고 보는 것을, 그러므로 다른 사람들의 주목이 우리에게 향해 있는 정도를 직관적으로 과대평가한다는 것을 의미한다. (3)Timothy Lawson은 대학생들로 하여금 또래 집단을 만나기 전에 앞면에 커다란 유행하는 로고가 있는 운동복 상의로 갈아입도록 함으로써 조명 효과를 조사했다. (4)그들 중 거의 40퍼센트가 다른 학생들이 셔츠에 무엇이 쓰여 있는지 기억할 것이라고 확신했지만, 단지 10퍼센트가 실제로 그러했다(기억했다). (5)대부분의 관찰자들은 학생들이 몇 분 동안 방을 떠난 후 운동복 상의들을 갈아입은 것조차도 알아차리지 못했다. (6)또 다른 실험에서는, 가수 Barry Manilow가 새겨진 티셔츠와 같이 매우 눈에 띄는 옷들조차, 오직 23퍼센트 — 즉, 그들의 가슴에 1970년대 소프트 록 가수를 자랑해 보이는 학생들이 추정한 50퍼센트보다 훨씬 더 적은 관찰자들만이 알아차리도록 자극했다.

[정답 풀이]

⑤ 문장 구조 파악: 동사 자리

(6) In another experiment, **even noticeable clothes**(주어), (such as a T-shirt with singer Barry Manilow on it,)(삽입어구) ~~provoking~~ → provoked only 23 percent of observers to notice ~.

문장에 동사가 없으므로, 이 문장의 주어인 even noticeable clothes에 알맞은 본동사가 필요하다. 문맥상 시제가 과거이므로 준동사 provoking을 provoked로 고쳐야 한다.

[오답 풀이]

① 전치사 + 관계대명사

(2) ~ **the extent**(선행사) [**to which** others' attention is aimed at us](수식).

which 이하의 절이 완전한 문장이므로 관계대명사 which가 홀로 쓰이는 것은 어법상 맞지 않다. 위 문장의 원래 문장은 'others' attention is aimed at us to the extent'인데, the extent를 선행사로 하는 관계사절 'which others' attention is aimed at us to'에서 전치사 to가 관계대명사 which 앞으로 옮겨진 것이다.

② 사역동사의 목적격 보어

(3) Timothy Lawson explored the spotlight effect by **having**(사역동사) **college students**(목적어) **change**(목적격 보어(동사원형)) into a sweatshirt ~.

사역동사 have의 목적어(college students)와 목적격 보어(change)의 의미상 관계가 능동이므로 동사원형 change를 쓴 것은 어법에 맞다.

③ 주어와 동사의 수 일치

(4) Nearly 40 percent of **them**(주어) **were**(복수 동사) sure [the other students(종속절 주어) would remember(동사) ~], ~].

전체나 부분을 나타내는 표현이 주어 자리에 오면 of 뒤에 나오는 명사에 따라 동사의 수가 결정된다. 이 문장에서는 복수 대명사 them이 나왔으므로, 복수 동사 were를 쓴 것은 어법에 맞다.

④ **명사절을 이끄는 접속사 that**

(5) Most observers(주어) did not even **notice**(동사) [**that**(접속사) the students(주어) changed(동사) sweatshirts(목적어) ~].

[ ]: 목적어

that 이하의 절이 완전한 문장을 이루고 있고, 전체 문장의 동사인 did not notice의 목적어 역할을 하는 명사절을 이끌어야 하므로 접속사 that이 쓰인 것은 어법상 적절하다.

[중요 어휘]

☐ **pay attention to**	~에 주목하다
☐ **spotlight effect**	조명 효과
☐ **intuitively**	부사 직관적으로
☐ **overestimate**	동사 과대평가하다
☐ **be aimed at**	~에게 향해 있다, ~을 목표로 하다
☐ **peer**	명사 또래, 동료
☐ **nearly**	부사 거의
☐ **noticeable**	형용사 매우 눈에 띄는
☐ **provoke**	동사 자극하다

05 2016년 6월 34번 (정답률 30%) 정답 ④

[지문 끊어 읽기] 소유의 질적 수준과 환상

(1) There is no known cure / for the ills of ownership.
알려진 치료법이 없다 / 소유가 주는 병에는

(2) As Adam Smith said, / ownership is woven into our lives.
Adam Smith가 말했듯이 / 소유는 우리 삶 속에 스며들어 있다

(3) But being aware of it / might help.
하지만 그것을 알고 있는 것이 / 도움이 될지도 모른다

(4) Everywhere around us / we see the temptation /
우리 주변의 모든 곳에서 / 우리는 유혹을 보게 된다 /
to improve the quality of our lives /
우리 삶의 질을 높이려는 /
by buying a larger home, a second car, a new dishwasher, a lawn mower, and so on.
더 큰 집, 두 번째 차, 새로운 식기 세척기, 잔디 깎는 기계, 기타 등등을 구매함으로써

(5) But, / once we upgrade our possessions /
하지만 / 일단 우리가 우리의 소유물을 업그레이드하면 /
we have a very hard time going back down. 정답단서
우리는 다시 낮추는 데 매우 어려움을 겪게 된다

(6) Ownership simply changes our perspective.
소유는 우리의 관점을 간단히 바꾸어 버린다

(7) Suddenly, / moving backward to our pre-ownership state /
갑작스럽게 / 우리의 이전 소유 상태로 돌아가는 것은 /
is a loss, / one that we cannot accept.
손실이 된다 / 우리가 받아들일 수 없는 것

✶중요 문장 (7)에서 우리가 받아들일 수 없는 것은 moving backward to our pre-ownership state이고 이것이 바로 문장 (8)의 fantasy를 가리킴.

(8) And so, / while moving up in life, / we fall into the fantasy /
그래서 / 삶에서 위로 올라가는 동안 / 우리는 환상에 빠진다 /
that we can always return to the previous state, /
우리가 언제나 이전의 상태로 돌아갈 수 있다는 /
but in reality, / it's unlikely. 주제문
하지만 사실 / 그럴 것 같지 않다

(9) Downgrading to a smaller home, / for instance, /
더 작은 집으로 수준을 낮추는 것은 / 예를 들어 /
is experienced as a loss, / it is psychologically painful, /
손실로서 경험된다 / 이는 심리적으로 괴롭다 /
and we are willing to make all kinds of sacrifices /
그리고 우리는 모든 종류의 희생을 기꺼이 감수한다 /
in order to avoid such losses.
그런 손실을 피하기 위해

[전문 해석]

(1)소유가 주는 병에는 알려진 치료법이 없다. (2)Adam Smith(애덤 스미스)가 말했듯이, 소유는 우리 삶 속에 스며들어 있다. (3)하지만 그것(소유가 우리의 삶 속에 스며들었다는 사실)을 알고 있는 것이 도움이 될지도 모른다. (4)우리 주변의 모든 곳에서 우리는 더 큰 집, 두 번째 차, 새로운 식기 세척기, 잔디 깎는 기계, 기타 등등을 구매함으로써 우리 삶의 질을 높이려는 유혹을 보게 된다. (5)하지만 일단 우리가 우리의 소유물을 업그레이드하면 우리는 다시 (그 질을) 낮추는 데 매우 어려움을 겪게 된다. (6)소유는 우리의 관점을 간단히 바꾸어 버린다. (7)갑작스럽게 우리의 이전 소유 상태로 돌아가는 것은 우리가 받아들일 수 없는 것, 즉 손실이 된다. (8)그래서 삶에서 위로 올라가는 동안(삶의 질을 향상시키면서), 우리는 우리가 언제나 이전의 상태로 돌아갈 수 있다는 환상에 빠지지만, 사실 그럴 것 같지 않다. (9)예를 들어, 더 작은 집으로 수준을 낮추는 것은, (우리에게) 손실로서 경험되고, 이는 심리적으로 괴로우며, 그런 손실을 피하기 위해 우리는 모든 종류의 희생을 기꺼이 감수한다.

- Adam Smith(애덤 스미스): 고전 경제학의 창시자로서 '보이지 않는 손' 개념을 통해 자유방임주의를 주장한 것으로 유명하다.

[정답 확인]

다음 빈칸에 들어갈 말로 가장 적절한 것은?

① purchasing a house is always profitable
집을 사는 것은 언제나 이득이 된다
② everyone can improve their quality of life
모든 사람이 자신의 삶의 질을 높일 수 있다
③ we are able to deal with the loss of faith
우리는 믿음의 상실에 대처할 수 있다
✶중요 ③번의 loss of faith에서 faith의 구체적 내용은 언급된 적이 없으므로 오답임.
✔ we can always return to the previous state
우리가 언제나 이전의 상태로 돌아갈 수 있다
⑤ we are willing to sacrifice our pleasure for honor
우리는 명예를 위해 즐거움을 기꺼이 희생한다

[문제 풀이]

삶의 질을 높이기 위해 소유물의 수준을 높이기 시작하면 다시 낮추기가 어렵다는 점을 지적한 글로, 이에 따르면 언제든 이전으로 돌아갈 수 있다고 믿는 것은 실제로는 일어나기 힘든 우리의 '환상'일 뿐이다. 따라서 빈칸에 들어갈 말로 가장 적절한 것은 ④ 'we can always return to the previous state(우리가 언제나 이전의 상태로 돌아갈 수 있다)'이다.

[중요 어휘]

☐ **cure**	명사 치료(법) / 동사 치료하다
☐ **ownership**	명사 소유(권)
☐ **be woven into**	~에 스며들어 있다
☐ **be aware of**	~을 알고 있다
☐ **perspective**	명사 관점, 견해
☐ **loss**	명사 손실, 손해, 상실, 패배
☐ **downgrade**	동사 (질이나 수준을) 낮추다
☐ **sacrifice**	명사 희생 / 동사 희생하다

06 2016년 9월 31번 (정답률 50%) 정답 ②

[지문 끊어 읽기] 새로운 음식 선호의 발견

(1) Changing our food habits / is one of the hardest things /
우리의 식습관을 바꾸는 것은 / 가장 어려운 일들 중 하나이다 /
we can do, / because the impulses governing our preferences /
우리가 할 수 있는 / 왜냐하면 우리의 선호를 지배하는 충동이 /
are often hidden, / even from ourselves.
종종 숨겨져 있기 때문이다 / 심지어 우리 자신으로부터도

(2) And yet / adjusting what you eat / is entirely possible. 정답단서
그럼에도 불구하고 / 당신이 무엇을 먹을지를 조정하는 것은 / 전적으로 가능하다

(3) We do it all the time. 정답단서
우리는 항상 그것을 한다

(4) Were this not the case, / the food companies /
만약 이것이 사실이 아니라면 / 식품 회사들은 /
that launch new products each year /
매년 새 제품을 출시하는 /

would be wasting their money.
그들의 돈을 낭비하고 있는 것일 것이다

(5) After the fall of the Berlin Wall, /
Berlin Wall의 붕괴 후 /
housewives from East and West Germany /
동독과 서독 출신의 주부들은 /
tried each other's food products / for the first time in decades.
서로의 식품을 먹어보았다 / 수십 년 만에 처음으로

(6) It didn't take long / for those from the East to realize /
오래 걸리지 않았다 / 동독 출신 주부들이 깨닫는 데는 /
that they preferred Western yogurt to their own.
그들이 그들 자신들의 것보다 서독의 요거트를 선호한다는 것을

(7) Equally, / those from the West discovered /
똑같이 / 서독 출신 주부들은 발견했다 /
a liking for the honey and vanilla wafer biscuits of the East.
동독의 꿀과 바닐라 웨이퍼 비스킷에 대한 선호를

(8) From both sides of the wall, / these German housewives showed /
벽의 양쪽에서 / 이 독일인 주부들은 보여주었다 /
a remarkable flexibility / in their food preferences.
놀랄 만한 융통성을 / 그들의 음식 선호에 있어서

★중요 식습관을 바꾸는 것(changing)은 어렵지만, 먹는 것을 조정하는 것(adjusting)은 쉽다는 내용을 문장 (5)~(8)에서 동독과 서독의 주부들이 서로의 음식을 먹은 후 음식 선호를 어렵지 않게 바꾸었다는 예시 구조로 뒷받침하고 있음.

[전문 해석]

(1)우리의 식습관을 바꾸는 것은 우리가 할 수 있는 가장 어려운 일들 중 하나인데, 왜냐하면 우리의 선호를 지배하는 충동이 심지어 우리 자신으로부터도 종종 숨겨져 있기 때문이다(충동이 숨겨져 있어서 우리가 스스로 그 충동을 잘 알아차릴 수 없기 때문이다). (2)그럼에도 불구하고 당신이 무엇을 먹을지를 조정하는 것은 전적으로 가능하다. (3)우리는 항상 그것(무엇을 먹을지 조정하기)을 한다. (4)만약 이것이 사실이 아니라면, 매년 새 제품을 출시하는 식품 회사들은 그들의 돈을 낭비하고 있는 것일 것이다. (5)Berlin Wall(베를린 장벽)의 붕괴 후, 동독과 서독 출신의 주부들은 수십 년 만에 처음으로 서로의 식품을 먹어보았다. (6)동독 출신 주부들이 그들 자신들의 요거트보다 서독의 것을 선호한다는 것을 깨닫는 데는 오래 걸리지 않았다(곧 알게 되었다). (7)똑같이 서독 출신 주부들은 동독의 꿀과 바닐라 웨이퍼 비스킷에 대한 선호를 발견했다(동독의 꿀과 바닐라 웨이퍼 비스킷을 좋아했다). (8)벽의 양쪽에서(동독과 서독 모두에서), 이 독일인 주부들은 그들의 음식 선호에 있어서 놀랄 만한 융통성을 보여주었다.

- Berlin Wall(베를린 장벽): 독일이 자본주의의 서독(West Germany)과 공산주의의 동독(East Germany)으로 나누어져 있을 때 그 경계에 있던 장벽으로, 독일 분단의 상징이었다.

[정답 확인]

다음 빈칸에 들어갈 말로 가장 적절한 것은?

① simplicity 단순함
② flexibility 융통성 ✔
③ difference 차이점
④ resistance 저항
⑤ consistency 일관성

★중요 문장 (8)의 빈칸은 문장 (2)의 adjusting what you eat에 관한 예시이므로 기존의 것을 고집하지 않고 새로운 것에 맞춘다는 adjust의 의미가 flexibility로 제시되었음.

[문제 풀이]

서독과 동독의 주부들은 이전에는 서로의 음식을 알지 못했지만, 장벽이 붕괴된 이후 서로의 음식을 먹어봄으로써 새로운 선호를 발견하였다. 즉 기존에 자신들이 알던 것을 넘어서서 새로운 취향을 개발한 것이다. 이를 설명하기에 적절한 것은 ② 'flexibility(융통성)'이다.

[중요 어휘]

힌트 govern이 '(국가·국민 등을) 다스리다'의 뜻보다는 influence와 같은 의미로 쓰여서 '(행동 등을) 지배하다, 좌우하다'로 해석된다는 것에 주의해야 함.

□ **impulse**	명사 충동, 욕구
□ **govern**	동사 지배하다, 통치하다
□ **launch**	동사 출시하다, (우주선 등을) 발사하다
□ **liking**	명사 선호, 좋아함
□ **remarkable**	형용사 놀랄 만한

핵심 다소 생소한 개념이 등장하지만 지문 전체적으로 그 개념이 무엇인지 알기 쉽게 풀어서 설명하고 있음. 'demarketing(역 마케팅)'과 관련이 없는 문장을 찾으면 됨.

07 2020년 6월 35번 (정답률 65%) 정답 ③

[지문 끊어 읽기] 수요의 양에 대한 마케팅 경영

(1) Marketing management is concerned /
마케팅 경영은 관련이 있다 /
not only with finding and increasing demand /
not only A but also B: A뿐만 아니라 B도
수요를 발견하고 증가시키는 것뿐만 아니라 /
but also with changing or even reducing it.
그것을 변화시키거나 심지어 감소시키는 것과도

(2) For example, / Uluru (Ayers Rock) might have too many tourists /
예를 들어 / Uluru(Ayers Rock)에는 관광객이 너무 많이 있을지도 모른다 /
wanting to climb it, /
그것을 오르고 싶어하는 /
힌트 문장 (2)의 'wanting to climb it'이라는 분사구가 앞에 있는 'tourists'를 꾸며줌. 관광객들이 그것을 오르는 것을 능동적으로 원하는 것이기 때문에 현재분사를 사용했음.
and Daintree National Park in North Queensland /
그리고 퀸즐랜드 북부에 있는 Daintree 국립 공원은 /
can become overcrowded / in the tourist season.
과도하게 붐비게 될 수도 있다 / 관광 철에

① (3) Power companies sometimes have trouble meeting demand /
have trouble (in) V-ing: ~하는 것에 어려움을 겪다
전력 회사들은 때때로 수요를 충족시키는 것에 어려움을 겪는다 /
during peak usage periods.
최대 사용 기간 동안
힌트 문장 (4)의 'called demarketing'은 'marketing task'를 수식함. 문장 (2)의 'wanting'과 달리 '~로 불린다'라는 수동의 의미이기 때문에 과거분사를 썼음.

② (4) In these and other cases of excess demand, /
과도한 수요의 이러한 그리고 다른 경우에서 /
the needed marketing task, / called demarketing, /
요구되는 마케팅 과제는 / 역 마케팅이라 불리는 /
is to reduce demand / temporarily or permanently. 정답단서
명사적 용법(주격 보어)
수요를 감소시키는 것이다 / 일시적이거나 영구적으로

③ (5) Efforts should be made / to compensate for the losses /
노력이 이루어져야 한다 / 손해를 보상하기 위해서 /
caused by the increase in supply.
공급의 증가에 의해 발생된

④ (6) The aim of demarketing is / not to completely destroy demand, /
not A but B: A가 아니라 B
역 마케팅의 목적은 ~이다 / 수요를 완전히 없애 버리는 것이 아니라 /
but only to reduce or shift it /
단지 그것을 감소시키거나 이동시키는 것 /
정답단서
to another time, or even another product.
다른 시기로 혹은 심지어 다른 제품으로
힌트 일반적으로 관계사의 선행사로 'way'가 나오면 뒤에 올 관계사는 관계부사 'how'라고 생각하기 쉽지만, 문장 (7)의 관계대명사 that은 선행사 'a way'가 관계절 안에서 동사 helps의 주어로 쓰였으므로 관계부사가 아닌 관계대명사임에 주의해야 함.

⑤ (7) Thus, / marketing management seeks /
따라서 / 마케팅 경영은 추구한다 /
to affect the level, timing, and nature of demand / in a way /
명사적 용법(목적어)
수요의 수준, 시기와 특징에 영향을 주는 것을 / 방식으로 /
that helps the organisation achieve its objectives.
준사역V' O' O.C'
그 단체가 그것의 목적을 달성하도록 도움을 주는

[전문 해석]

(1)마케팅 경영은 수요를 발견하고 증가시키는 것뿐만 아니라 그것을 변화시키거나 심지어 감소시키는 것과도 관련이 있다. (2)예를 들어, Uluru(Ayers Rock)에는 그것을 오르고 싶어하는 관광객이 너무 많이 있을지도 모르고, 퀸즐랜드 북부에 있는 Daintree 국립 공원은 관광 철에 과도하게 붐비게 될 수도 있다. ①(3)전력 회사들은 때때로 (전력) 최대 사용 기간 동안 수요를 충족시키는 것에 어려움을 겪는다. ②(4)과도한 수요의 이러한 그리고 다른 경우에서, 역 마케팅이라 불리는 요구되는 마케팅 과제는 일시적이거나 영구적으로 수요를 감소시키는 것이다. ③(5)공급의 증가에 의해 발생된 손해를 보상하기 위해서 노력이 이루어져야 한다(노력해야 한다). ④(6)역 마케팅의 목적은 수요를 완전히 없애 버리는 것이 아니라, 단지 그것(수요)을 감소시키거나 다른 시기로, 혹은 심지어 다른 제품으로 이동시키는 것이다. ⑤(7)따라서 마케팅 경영은 그 단체가 그것의 목적을 달성하도록 도움을 주는 방식으로 수요의 수준, 시기와 특징에 영향을 주는 것을 추구한다.

- Uluru(울루루): 호주 노던 준주 남쪽에 있는 거대한 바위로, 수상의 이름을 따 Ayers Rock(에어즈 록)이라고도 불린다. 원주민들에게 신성하게 여겨졌던 곳으로, 호주의 가장 유명한 자연 지형 랜드마크이기도 하다.
- Daintree National Park(데인트리 국립 공원): 호주 동북쪽, 케언스 북쪽에 위치한 국립 공원으로 열대우림이 울창하다. 희귀한 동식물이 많아 세계유산으로 지정되어 있다.

[문제 풀이]

지문은 호주의 관광지와 전력 회사를 예로 들어, 'demarketing(역 마케팅)'이 특정한 상품에 대한 수요가 공급을 초과할 때 기업이 수요를 감소시키거나 수요의 방향을 전환하여 과잉 수요를 처리하는 전략이라고 설명한다. 반면 문장 (5)는 과잉 수요를 처리하는 전략이 아닌 과

잉 공급으로 인해 발생된 손해를 보상해야 한다는 내용이므로, 지문의 주제와 무관하다. 따라서 정답은 ③이다.

[중요 어휘]

□ be concerned with	~와 관련이 있다
□ demand	명사 수요 / 동사 요구하다
□ overcrowded	형용사 과도하게 붐비는, 초만원인
□ meet	동사 충족시키다, 만족시키다
□ peak	형용사 최대의, 최고의 / 명사 최고조, 절정
□ usage	명사 사용, 용법
□ excess	형용사 과도한, 여분의 / 명사 과다, 과잉
□ temporarily	부사 일시적으로, 임시로
□ permanently	부사 영구적으로
□ compensate for	~를 보상하다, (부족한 부분을) 메꾸다
□ supply	명사 공급 / 동사 공급하다, 제공하다
□ nature	명사 특징, 본성
□ objective	명사 목적, 목표 / 형용사 객관적인

08 2017년 11월 40번 (정답률 45%) 정답 ①

[지문 끊어 읽기] 권력 거리

(1) *Power distance* is the term / used to refer to / (정답 단서)
'권력 거리'는 용어이다 / ~를 나타내기 위해 사용되는 /
how widely an unequal distribution of power /
권력의 불평등한 분배가 얼마나 넓게 /
is accepted by the members of a culture.
한 문화의 사람들에 의해 받아들여지는지

(2) It relates to the degree /
이것은 정도와 관련이 있다 /
to which the less powerful members of a society /
전치사+관계대명사
사회에서 권력이 상대적으로 약한 구성원들이 /
accept their inequality in power / and consider it the norm. 정답 단서
권력에서의 그들의 불평등을 받아들이는 / 그리고 그것을 일반적인 것이라고 여기는

(3) In cultures / with high acceptance of power distance /
문화들에서 / 권력 거리에 대한 수용도가 높은 /
(e.g., India, Brazil, Greece, Mexico, and the Philippines), /
(예를 들어 인도, 브라질, 그리스, 멕시코, 그리고 필리핀) /
people are not viewed as equals, /
사람들은 동등한 존재로 여겨지지 않는다 /
and everyone has a clearly defined or allocated place /
그리고 모든 사람은 분명히 규정된 혹은 할당된 지위를 갖는다 /
in the social hierarchy.
사회 계급 속에서

(4) In cultures / with low acceptance of power distance / 정답 단서
문화들에서 / 권력 거리에 대한 수용도가 낮은 /
(e.g., Finland, Norway, New Zealand, and Israel), /
(예를 들어 핀란드, 노르웨이, 뉴질랜드, 그리고 이스라엘) /
people believe / inequality should be minimal, /
사람들은 믿는다 / 불평등이 최소한이어야 한다고 /
and a hierarchical division / is viewed as one of convenience only.
그리고 계급 구분은 / 오로지 편의를 위한 것으로 여겨진다

(5) In these cultures, /
이러한 문화들에서는 /
✶중요 권력 거리에 대한 수용도가 낮다는 것은 불평등을 쉽게 받아들이지 않고 개인적인 노력과 성과를 기반으로 사회 계급을 바꿀 수 있는 유동성이 있음을 의미함.
there is more fluidity within the social hierarchy, / 정답 단서
사회 계급 안에 더 많은 유동성이 있다 /
and it is relatively easy /
그리고 상대적으로 쉽다 /
힌트 형식상의 주어-내용상의 주어 구문으로, for individuals는 내용상의 주어인 [to move up ~ achievements]의 의미상의 주어임.
for individuals [to move up the social hierarchy /
개인들이 사회 계급을 상승시키는 것이 /
based on their individual efforts and achievements].
그들의 개인적 노력과 성과를 기반으로

(6) Unlike cultures with high acceptance of power distance, /
권력 거리에 대한 수용도가 높은 문화들과 달리 /
where members are more (A)willing to accept inequality, /
구성원들이 불평등을 좀 더 (A)기꺼이 받아들이는 /
cultures with low acceptance of power distance /
권력 거리에 대한 수용도가 낮은 문화들은 /
allow more (B)mobility within the social hierarchy.
사회 계급 내에서 더 많은 (B)유동성을 허용한다

[전문 해석]

(1)'권력 거리'는 권력의 불평등한 분배가 한 문화의 사람들에 의해 얼마나 넓게 받아들여지는지를 나타내기 위해 사용되는 용어이다. (2)권력 거리는 사회에서 권력이 상대적으로 약한 구성원들이 권력에서의 불평등을 받아들이고 그것을 일반적인 것이라고 여기는 정도와 관련이 있다. (3)권력 거리에 대한 수용도가 높은 문화들에서 (예를 들어 인도, 브라질, 그리스, 멕시코, 그리고 필리핀), 사람들은 동등한 존재로 여겨지지 않으며, 모든 사람은 사회 계급 속에서 분명히 규정된 혹은 할당된 지위를 갖는다. (4)권력 거리에 대한 수용도가 낮은 문화들에서 (예를 들어 핀란드, 노르웨이, 뉴질랜드, 그리고 이스라엘), 사람들은 불평등이 최소한이어야 한다고 믿으며, 계급 구분은 오로지 편의를 위한 것으로 여겨진다. (5)이러한 문화들(권력 거리에 대한 수용도가 낮은 문화들)에서는, 사회 계급 안에 더 많은 유동성이 있으며, 개인들이 그들의 개인적 노력과 성과를 기반으로 사회 계급을 상승시키는 것이 상대적으로 쉽다.

⬇

(6)구성원들이 불평등을 좀 더 (A)기꺼이 받아들이는, 권력 거리에 대한 수용도가 높은 문화들과 달리, 권력 거리에 대한 수용도가 낮은 문화들은 사회 계급 내에서 더 많은 (B)유동성을 허용한다.

[정답 확인]

다음 글의 내용을 한 문장으로 요약하고자 한다. 빈칸 (A)와 (B)에 들어갈 말로 가장 적절한 것은?

(A)		(B)	(A)		(B)
✔ willing	......	mobility	② willing	......	assistance
기꺼이 ~하는		유동성	기꺼이 ~하는		원조
③ reluctant	......	resistance	④ reluctant	......	flexibility
꺼리는		저항	꺼리는		융통성
⑤ afraid	......	openness			
두려워하는		개방			

[문제 풀이]

본문은 권력 거리에 대해 말하고 있으며, 글에 따르면 사람들은 자신들이 속한 문화에 따라 사회 계급의 불평등을 받아들이는 태도가 다르다. 권력 거리에 대한 수용도가 높은 문화들에서 사람들은 계급 구분을 일상적이고 당연한 것으로 받아들이는 반면, 권력 거리에 대한 수용도가 낮은 문화들에서 사람들은 계급 구분은 편의를 위해서 만들어진 것이며 최소화되어야 할 것으로 여긴다. 따라서 정답은 ①이 적절하다.

[중요 어휘]

□ refer to	~을 나타내다[언급하다], ~을 참고하다
□ unequal	형용사 불평등한
□ inequality	명사 불평등, 불균등
□ norm	명사 일반적인 것, 표준
□ acceptance	명사 수용, 인정
□ allocate	동사 할당하다
□ hierarchy	명사 (회사나 조직 내의) 계급, 계층
□ hierarchical	형용사 계급의, 계층의
□ convenience	명사 편의, 편리
□ fluidity	명사 유동성, 흐름

09 2021년 9월 36번 (정답률 45%) 정답 ②

[지문 끊어 읽기] 민족정신과 외부 힘으로부터의 단절

(1) When trying to sustain / an independent ethos, /
지속시키려고 할 때 / 독립적인 민족정신을 /
cultures face / a problem of critical mass.
문화는 직면한다 / 결정적 질량의 문제에

2회 20분 미니모의고사

(2) No single individual, / acting on his or her own, /
어떤 한 개인도 / 자신 혼자서 행동하는 / 삽입구
can produce an ethos. 정답 단서-1
민족정신을 만들어 낼 수 없다

(B) (6) Rather, / an ethos results /
오히려 / 민족정신은 발생한다 /
from the interdependent acts of many individuals. 정답 단서-1
많은 개인들의 상호 의존적인 행위로부터

(7) This cluster of produced meaning /
생성된 의미의 이 군집은 /
may require / some degree of insulation /
필요로 할 수 있다 / 어느 정도의 단절을 /
from larger and wealthier outside forces.
더 크고 더 부유한 외부 힘으로부터

정답 단서-2
(8) The Canadian Inuit / maintain their own ethos, /
캐나다 이누이트족은 / 그들만의 민족정신을 유지한다 /
even though they number no more than twenty-four thousand.
비록 그들이 총 2만 4천 명이 되지 않음에도 불구하고

정답 단서-2
(A) (3) They manage this feat / through a combination of trade, /
그들은 이러한 위업을 해낸다 / 무역의 조합을 통해 / 병렬①
to support their way of life, / and geographic isolation.
삽입구 병렬②
그들의 생활 방식을 지지하기 위해 / 그리고 지리적 고립의

(4) The Inuit occupy / remote territory, / 정답 단서-3
이누이트족은 차지한다 / 외딴 영토를 /
removed from major population centers of Canada.
캐나다의 주요 인구 중심지로부터 동떨어진

(5) If cross-cultural contact / were to become sufficiently close, /
만약 문화 간 접촉이 / 충분히 긴밀해진다면 /
the Inuit ethos would disappear.
이누이트족의 민족정신이 사라질 것이다

힌트 'If + S' + 과거동사(were), S + 조동사 과거+ V'의 구조를 가진 가정법 과거 구문으로, 현재 사실과 반대되는 내용을 가정함.

(C) (9) Distinct cultural groups of similar size /
비슷한 규모의 뚜렷이 다른 문화 집단은 /
정답 단서-3
do not, in the long run, persist / in downtown Toronto, Canada, /
결국에는 지속되지 않는다 / 캐나다 토론토 도심에서는 /
where they come in contact with many outside influences /
병렬①
거기에서 그들은 많은 외부 영향과 접촉하게 된다 /
and pursue essentially Western paths for their lives.
병렬②
그리고 그들의 삶을 위해 본질적으로 서구적 방식을 추구한다

[전문 해석]

(1)독립적인 민족(사회)정신을 지속시키려고 할 때, 문화는 결정적 질량(임계 질량)의 문제에 직면한다. (2)자신 혼자서 행동하는 어떤 한 개인도 민족(사회)정신을 만들어 낼 수 없다.
(B) (6)오히려, 민족(사회)정신은 많은 개인들의 상호 의존적인 행위로부터 발생한다. (7)생성된 의미의 이 군집은 더 크고 더 부유한 외부 힘으로부터 어느 정도의 단절을 필요로 할 수 있다. (8)캐나다 이누이트족은 비록 그들이 총 2만 4천 명이 되지(넘지) 않음에도 불구하고 그들만의 민족(사회)정신을 유지한다.
(A) (3)그들은 그들의 생활 방식을 지지하기 위해, 무역과 지리적 고립의 조합을 통해 이러한 위업을 해낸다. (4)이누이트족은 캐나다의 주요 인구 중심지로부터 동떨어진 외딴 영토를 차지한다. (5)만약 문화 간 접촉이 충분히 긴밀해진다면, 이누이트족의 민족(사회)정신이 사라질 것이다.
(C) (9)비슷한 규모의 뚜렷이 다른 문화 집단은 캐나다 토론토 도심에서는 결국에는 지속되지 않는데, 거기에서 그들은 많은 외부 영향과 접촉하게 되고 그들의 삶을 위해 본질적으로 서구적 방식을 추구한다.
- critical mass(임계 질량): 특정 변화나 발전이 일어나기 전에 도달해야 하는 크기나 수

[정답 확인]

주어진 글 다음에 이어질 글의 순서로 가장 적절한 것은?

① (A) — (C) — (B) ✔② (B) — (A) — (C) ③ (B) — (C) — (A)
④ (C) — (A) — (B) ⑤ (C) — (B) — (A)

[문제 풀이]

많은 개인의 상호 의존적 행위로부터 발생하는 독립적 민족(사회)정신을 지속시키기 위해서는 외부 힘으로부터의 단절이 필요할 수 있다고 설명하는 글이다. 먼저, 문장 (1)에 따르면 독립적인 민족(사회)정신을 지속시키려고 할 때, 문화는 결정적 질량(임계 질량)의 문제에 직면한다. 즉 문장 (2)에서 재진술하듯이 개인이 혼자 행동해서는 민족(사회)정신을 만들어 낼 수 없다는 것이다. 이를 문장 (6)에서 'Rather(오히려)'로 이어받아 민족(사회)정신은 많은 개인의 상호 의존적인 행위로부터 발생한다는 상반되는 내용으로 문장 (2)를 보강하고 있으므로 주어진 문장 다음에는 (B)가 온다. 다음으로, 문장 (3)의 'They(그들)'가 지칭하는 바는 문장 (8)의 'The Canadian Inuit(캐나다 이누이트족)'이므로 (B) 다음에는 (A)가 온다. 문장 (4)의 'The Inuit(이누이트족)'의 경우와 반대인 사례가 (C)에서 이어지고 있으므로 (A) 다음에는 (C)가 온다. 따라서 정답은 ②이다.

[중요 어휘]

□ sustain	동사 지속시키다
□ independent	형용사 독립적인, 독립된
□ ethos	명사 민족(사회)정신
□ rather	부사 오히려, 차라리
□ interdependent	형용사 상호 의존적인
□ cluster	명사 군집, 무리 / 동사 무리를 이루다
□ require	동사 필요로 하다, 요구하다
□ insulation	명사 단절, 단열
□ number	동사 총 ~이 되다 / 명사 수
□ feat	명사 위업
□ geographic	형용사 지리적인, 지리학의
□ remote	형용사 외딴, 외진
□ territory	명사 영토, 지역
□ sufficiently	부사 충분히
□ distinct	형용사 뚜렷이 다른, 별개의
□ in the long run	결국에는
□ persist	동사 지속되다
□ in contact with	~과 접촉하는
□ pursue	동사 추구하다
□ essentially	부사 본질적으로

핵심 수많은 사람들의 거짓말을 듣고도 왕이 만족하지 못했다는 내용의 (D)가 먼저 나오고, 십중이 나서 대회를 중단하려 할 때 가난한 남자가 나타나서 왕에게 빚을 갚으라고 요구했다는 (B)가 뒤따르고, 마지막으로 남자의 말로 인해 딜레마에 빠진 왕이 결국 황금 사과를 넘겨주었다는 (C)가 오는 것이 자연스러움.

10~12

2019년 3월 43~45번
(정답률 65% | 70% | 70%)

정답 ⑤ | ④ | ②

[지문 끊어 읽기] 거짓말의 딜레마에 빠진 왕

(A-1) Once upon a time / there was a king of Armenia, /
옛날 옛적에 / 아르메니아의 한 왕이 있었다 /
이유
who, being of a curious turn of mind /
계속적 용법
그런데 그는 호기심이 많은 성격으로 인해 /
and in need of some change, /
그리고 약간의 변화가 필요하여 /
sent (a)his men throughout the land /
(a)그(king)의 신하들을 나라 곳곳에 보냈다 /
to make the following proclamation:
다음과 같은 포고를 하기 위해

힌트 being of a curious turn of mind라는 삽입구(분사구문)와 in need of some change라는 삽입구(전치사구)가 and에 의해 연결되고 있음. 이때 전치사 in 앞에 being이 생략되었음.

(A-2) "Hear this! / Whatever man among you / can prove himself /
S
이것을 들으시오 / 여러분 중 어떤 사람이든지 / 자신이 증명할 수 있는 자는 /
the most outrageous liar in Armenia /
아르메니아에서 가장 터무니없는 거짓말쟁이임을 /
shall receive an apple / made of pure gold /
V
사과 하나를 받을 것이오 / 순금으로 만들어진 /
from the hands of His Majesty the King!"
국왕 폐하의 손으로부터

* (A) 요약: 왕이 최고의 거짓말쟁이에게 황금 사과를 주겠다고 포고함.

(D-1) People began to swarm to the palace /
사람들이 궁궐로 몰려들기 시작했다 /
from every town and village in the country, /
나라의 모든 도시와 마을로부터 /

people of all ranks and conditions, /
온갖 지위와 사정을 가진 사람들 /
princes, merchants, farmers, priests, rich and poor, tall and short, fat and thin.
제후들, 상인들, 농부들, 사제들, 부유한 사람과 가난한 사람, 키가 큰 사람과 키가 작은 사람, 뚱뚱한 사람과 마른 사람

(D-2) There was no lack of liars in the land, /
나라에는 거짓말쟁이들이 가득했다 /
and each one told his tale to the king.
그리고 각자가 자신의 이야기를 왕에게 들려 주었다

(D-3) None of those lies, / however, / convinced the king /
그 거짓말들 중 무엇도 ~하지 못하다 / 그러나 / 왕을 설득했다 /
that (e)he had listened to the best one. 10번 정답 단서
(e)그(king)가 최고의 것을 들었다고

* (D) 요약: 온갖 사람들이 몰려와 왕에게 거짓말을 했으나, 왕이 인정할 정도의 기막힌 거짓말쟁이는 없었음.

(C-1) The king was beginning / to grow tired of (c)his new sport / 10번 정답 단서
왕은 시작하고 있었다 / (c)그(king)의 새로운 장난에 싫증이 나기 /
and was thinking of calling the whole contest off /
그리고 전체 대회를 중단할 것을 생각하고 있었다 /
without declaring a winner.
승자를 발표하지 않은 채

힌트 call off는 '~을 중단하다, 취소하다'라는 뜻임. 날씨가 좋지 않아서 스포츠 경기가 취소되는 것을 '콜드 게임'이라고 하는데, 이 때 '콜드'는 called off(중단된, 취소된)에서 온 called임.

(C-2) Then / there appeared before him a poor, ragged man, / 11번 정답 단서
(V, S)
그때 / 누더기를 걸친 가난한 남자가 그의 앞에 나타났다 /
carrying a large sack / over (d)his shoulder.
커다란 자루를 들고 / (d)그(a poor, ragged man)의 어깨에

★중요 가난하고 누더기를 걸친 남자가 '그의 어깨(his shoulder)'에 자루를 메고 나타났는데, 여기서 '그'는 '가난하고 누더기를 걸친 남자' 자신이라고 보는 것이 타당함.

(C-3) "What can I do for you?" / asked His Majesty.
"무슨 용건인가?" / 왕이 물었다

(C-4) "Sire!" / said the poor man, / slightly bewildered.
"폐하!" / 그 가난한 남자가 말했다 / 다소 당혹스러워하며

(C-5) "Surely you remember?
분명히 폐하는 기억하시겠지요

(C-6) You owe me a pot of gold, / 10번 정답 단서
폐하는 제게 황금 한 항아리를 빚지셨습니다 /
and I have come to collect it."
그리고 저는 그것을 받으러 왔습니다

힌트 owe는 'owe A B(A에게 B를 빚지다)'라는 4형식 용법으로 자주 쓰임.

* (C) 요약: 왕이 싫증나려던 찰나, 허름한 차림의 한 남자가 나타나 왕이 자신에게 빚을 졌다고 주장함.

(B-1) "You are a perfect liar, sir!" / exclaimed the king.
"여보게, 자네는 완벽한 거짓말쟁이일세!" / 왕이 소리쳤다

(B-2) "I owe you no money!" 10번 정답 단서
"나는 자네에게 전혀 돈을 빚지지 않았네!"

(B-3) "A perfect liar am I?" / said the poor man.
"제가 완벽한 거짓말쟁이라고요?" / 가난한 남자가 말했다

(B-4) "Then give me the golden apple!"
"그렇다면 제게 황금 사과를 주십시오!"

(B-5) The king, / realizing that the man was trying to trick him, / said,
(S, realizing의 목적어절, V)
왕은 / 그 남자가 그를 속이려고 하고 있다는 것을 깨달은 / 말했다

(B-6) "No, no! You are not a liar!"
"아니, 아니! 자네는 거짓말쟁이가 아닐세!"

(B-7) "Then give me the pot of gold / you owe me, /
그렇다면 제게 황금 한 항아리를 주십시오 / 폐하께서 제게 빚진 /
sire," / said the man.
폐하 / 그 남자가 말했다

(B-8) The king saw the dilemma.
왕은 딜레마를 보았다

(B-9) (b)He handed over the golden apple. 12번 정답 단서
(b)그(king)는 황금 사과를 넘겨주었다

* (B) 요약: 딜레마에 빠진 왕이 결국 남자에게 황금 사과를 줌.

[전문 해석]

(A)

(1)옛날 옛적에 아르메니아의 한 왕이 있었는데, 그는 호기심이 많은 성격으로 인해(호기심이 많아서), 그리고 약간의 변화가 필요하여 다음과 같은 포고를 하기 위해 (a)그(king)의 신하들을 나라 곳곳에 보냈다. (2)"이것을 들으시오! 여러분 중 어떤 사람이든지(누구든지) 자신이 아르메니아에서 가장 터무니없는 거짓말쟁이임을 증명할 수 있는 자는 국왕 폐하의 손으로부터(국왕 폐하로부터 직접) 순금으로 만들어진 사과 하나를 받을 것이오!"

(D)

(1)나라의 모든 도시와 마을로부터 온갖 지위와 사정을 가진 사람들, (즉) 제후들, 상인들, 농부들, 사제들, 부유한 사람과 가난한 사람, 키가 큰 사람과 키가 작은 사람, 뚱뚱한 사람과 마른 사람 (등) 사람들이 궁궐로 몰려들기 시작했다. (2)나라에는 거짓말쟁이들이 가득했고, 각자가 자신의 이야기를 왕에게 들려 주었다. (3)그러나 그 거짓말들 중 무엇도 (e)그(king)가 최고의 것(거짓말)을 들었다고 왕을 설득하지 못했다.

(C)

(1)왕은 (c)그(king)의 새로운 장난에 싫증이 나기 시작하고 있었고, 승자를 발표하지 않은 채 전체 대회를 중단할 것을 생각하고 있었다. (2)그때, 누더기를 걸친 가난한 남자가 (d)그(a poor, ragged man)의 어깨에 커다란 자루를 메고 그의 앞에 나타났다. (3)"무슨 용건인가?" 왕이 물었다. (4)"폐하!" 그 가난한 남자는 다소 당혹스러워하며 말했다. (5)"분명히 폐하는 기억하시겠지요? (6)폐하는 제게 황금 한 항아리를 빚지셨고, 저는 그것을 받으러 왔습니다."

(B)

(1)"여보게, 자네는 완벽한 거짓말쟁이일세!"(라고) 왕이 소리쳤다. (2) "나는 자네에게 전혀 돈을 빚지지 않았네!" (3)"제가 완벽한 거짓말쟁이라고요?" 가난한 남자가 말했다. (4)"그렇다면 제게 황금 사과를 주십시오!" (5)그 남자가 그를(왕을) 속이려고 하고 있다는 것을 깨달은 왕은 말했다, (6)"아니, 아니! 자네는 거짓말쟁이가 아닐세!" (7)"그렇다면 제게 폐하께서 (제게) 빚진 황금 한 항아리를 주십시오, 폐하,"(라고) 그 남자가 말했다. (8)왕은 딜레마를 보았다(딜레마에 빠졌다). (9)(b)그(king)는 황금 사과를 넘겨주었다.

[정답 확인]

10. 주어진 글 (A)에 이어질 내용을 순서에 맞게 배열한 것으로 가장 적절한 것은?

① (B) — (D) — (C)　② (C) — (B) — (D)　③ (C) — (D) — (B)
④ (D) — (B) — (C)　✔⑤ (D) — (C) — (B)

11. 밑줄 친 (a) ~ (e) 중에서 가리키는 대상이 나머지 넷과 다른 것은?

① (a)　② (b)　③ (c)　✔④ (d)　⑤ (e)

12. 윗글의 내용으로 적절하지 않은 것은?

① 왕은 아르메니아 최고의 거짓말쟁이(liar)를 찾으려 했다.
✔② 왕이 가난한 남자에게 ~~황금 한 항아리~~(a pot of gold)를 하사했다. (황금 사과)
③ 왕은 승자를 발표하지(declare) 않고 대회를 중단(call off)하려고 했다.
④ 가난한 남자가 커다란 자루(a large sack)를 메고 왕 앞에 나타났다.
⑤ 온갖 부류의 사람들이 궁궐(palace)로 모여들기(swarm) 시작했다.

★중요 '황금 한 항아리(a pot of gold)'는 가난한 남자가 왕에게 요구한 것이고, 왕이 실제로 남자에게 하사한 것은 대회의 상품인 '황금 사과(the golden apple)'임.

[중요 어휘]

□ once upon a time	(이야기를 시작할 때) 옛날 옛적에
□ a ~ turn of mind	~한 성격, 사고방식
□ proclamation	명사 포고, 선언
□ outrageous	형용사 터무니없는, 충격적인
□ swarm	동사 몰려들다, 떼지어 다니다
□ prince	명사 제후, 영주, 왕자
□ no lack of	~이 가득한, 많은
□ convince	동사 설득하다, 납득시키다
□ sport	명사 장난, 오락, 스포츠
□ call off	중단하다, 철회하다
□ sire	명사 폐하, 전하
□ bewildered	형용사 당혹스러워하는, 어리둥절한
□ collect	동사 (빚·세금을) 받다, 수금하다, 모으다
□ exclaim	동사 소리치다, 외치다
□ dilemma	명사 딜레마, 진퇴양난의 상황

2회 20분 미니모의고사

문제편 p.299

3회 20분 미니모의고사

01 2019년 3월 18번 (정답률 85%) 정답 ③

[지문 끊어 읽기] 아파트 도색 작업

(1) Dear Mr. Spencer,
친애하는 Spencer 씨께

(2) I will have lived in this apartment /
저는 이 아파트에서 살아온 것이 됩니다 /
for ten years / as of this coming April.
10년 동안 / 다가오는 이번 4월부로

(3) I have enjoyed living here / and hope to continue doing so.
enjoy(3형식) + V-ing
저는 여기서 사는 것을 매우 좋아해 왔습니다 / 그리고 그렇게 하는 것을 계속하기를 희망합니다

(4) When I first moved into the Greenfield Apartments, /
제가 Greenfield Apartments로 처음 이사했을 때 /
I was told / that the apartment had been recently painted.
저는 들었습니다 / 아파트가 최근에 도색되었다고

(5) Since that time, / I have never touched the walls or the ceiling.
그때 이후로 / 저는 벽이나 천장에 손을 댄 적이 한 번도 없었습니다

(6) Looking around / over the past month /
S
둘러보는 것은 / 지난 한 달 동안 /
has made me realize / how old and dull the paint has become.
사역V O O·C(동사원형)
제가 깨닫게 만들었습니다 / 그 페인트가 얼마나 오래되고 흐려졌는지를

주제문
(7) I would like to update the apartment / with a new coat of paint.
저는 아파트를 새롭게 하고 싶습니다 / 새 페인트칠로

(8) I understand / that this would be at my own expense, /
O①
저는 알고 있습니다 / 이것이 저의 자비 부담이라는 것을 /
and that I must get permission to do so /
O②
그리고 제가 그렇게 하기 위해서는 허락을 받아야 한다는 것을 /
as per the lease agreement. 주제문
임대차 계약에 따라서

힌트 여기서 this와 to do so는 모두 문장 (7)의 to update the apartment with a new coat of paint를 대신함.

(9) Please advise / at your earliest convenience.
부디 알려주십시오 / 가능한 한 빨리

(10) Sincerely, Howard James
진심을 담아, Howard James (드림)

[전문 해석]

(1)친애하는 Spencer 씨께,
(2)다가오는 이번 4월부로, 저는 이 아파트에서 10년 동안 살아온 것이 됩니다. (3)저는 여기서 사는 것을 매우 좋아해 왔고, 그렇게 하는(여기서 사는) 것을 계속하기를 희망합니다. (4)제가 Greenfield Apartments로 처음 이사했을 때, 저는 아파트가 최근에 도색되었다고 들었습니다. (5)그때 이후로, 저는 벽이나 천장에 손을 댄 적이 한 번도 없었습니다. (6)지난 한 달 동안 (아파트를) 둘러보는 것은, 제가 그 페인트가 얼마나 오래되고 흐려졌는지를 깨닫게 만들었습니다(지난 한 달 동안 아파트를 둘러보면서 저는 그 페인트가 얼마나 오래되고 흐려졌는지를 깨달았습니다). (7)저는 새 페인트칠로 아파트를 새롭게 하고 싶습니다. (8)저는 이것(도색)이 저의 자비 부담이라는 것과, 제가 그렇게(도색 작업을) 하기 위해서는 임대차 계약에 따라서 허락을 받아야 한다는 것을 알고 있습니다. (9)부디 가능한 한 빨리 알려주십시오.
(10)진심을 담아, Howard James (드림)

[정답 확인]

다음 글의 목적으로 가장 적절한 것은?

① 아파트 안전(safety) 진단 결과를 통보하려고
② 아파트 임대차 계약(lease agreement) 연장을 논의하려고
✔ 아파트 도색(painting) 작업에 대한 허락(permission)을 받으려고
④ 아파트 수리 비용(expense) 부담에 대해 상의하려고
⑤ 아파트 도색에 대한 설문(survey) 결과를 알려 주려고

★중요 expense나 advise와 같은 어휘들로 인해 마치 집주인에게 비용에 관해 조언을 구하는 글처럼 보일 수 있지만 문장 (8)에서 도색 작업을 위해 permission이 필요하다고 했기 때문에 이에 관한 언급이 있어야 함.

[문제 풀이]

문장 (7)과 (8)을 통해 글쓴이가 아파트에 페인트칠을 새로 하고 싶어한다는 것과, 그 작업을 진행하기 위해 집주인의 허락을 받고자 한다는 것을 알 수 있다. 따라서 정답은 ③ '아파트 도색 작업에 대한 허락을 받으려고'이다.

[중요 어휘]

□ **ceiling**	명사 천장
□ **dull**	형용사 흐린, 무딘
□ **coat of paint**	페인트칠
□ **at one's own expense**	~의 자비 부담인, 사비로
□ **permission**	명사 허락, 승인
□ **lease agreement**	임대차 계약
□ **advise**	동사 알려주다, 조언하다
□ **at one's earliest convenience**	가능한 한 빨리, 되도록 일찍

핵심 자신을 계속해서 따라오는 남자가 무서워(scared) 도망가려 했지만, 사실은 그 사람이 자신이 떨어뜨린 가방을 전해주려 했다는 걸 뒤늦게 파악하고 당황했다(embarrassed)는 내용의 글임.

02 2017년 3월 19번 (정답률 90%) 정답 ①

[지문 끊어 읽기] 따라오는 남자에 대한 오해

(1) I rode my bicycle alone from work /
나는 일을 끝내고 혼자 자전거를 타고 갔다 /
on the very quiet road of my hometown.
내가 사는 동네의 아주 한적한 도로에서

(2) Suddenly, / I noticed a man with long hair /
갑자기 / 나는 머리가 긴 남자를 알아차렸다 /
secretly riding behind me.
몰래 내 뒤에서 자전거를 타고 있는 것을

(3) I felt my heart jump. 정답단서
나는 내 심장이 뛰는 것을 느꼈다

정답단서
(4) I quickened my legs pushing the pedals, / hoping to ride faster.
나는 페달을 밟는 내 다리를 더 빠르게 했다 / 더 빨리 달리기를 바라면서

(5) He kept following me through the dark, / across the field.
그는 어둠을 뚫고 계속해서 나를 따라왔다 / 벌판을 가로질러

(6) At last, / I got home and tried to reach the bell.
마침내 / 나는 집에 도착했고 초인종에 손을 뻗으려고 노력했다

(7) The man reached for me.
그 남자가 나를 향하여 손을 뻗었다

(8) I turned my head around / and saw the oddest face in the world.
나는 고개를 돌렸다 / 그리고 이 세상에서 가장 이상하게 생긴 얼굴을 보았다

(9) From deep in his throat, / I heard him say, /
그의 목구멍 깊은 곳에서부터 / 나는 그가 말하는 것을 들었다 /
"Excuse me, you dropped your bag," / giving the bag back to me.
"실례합니다만, 당신이 가방을 떨어뜨리셨습니다." / 나에게 가방을 돌려주면서

(10) I couldn't say anything, / but was full of shame and regret /
나는 아무 말도 할 수 없었다 / 하지만 부끄러움과 후회로 가득했다 /
for misunderstanding him. 정답단서
그를 오해한 것에 대한

[전문 해석]

(1)나는 일을 끝내고 내가 사는 동네의 아주 한적한 도로에서 혼자 자전거를 타고 갔다. (2)갑자기 나는 머리가 긴 남자가 몰래 내 뒤에서 자전거를 타고 있는(오는) 것을 알아차렸다. (3)나는 내 심장이 뛰는 것을 느꼈다. (4)나는 더 빨리 달리기를 바라면서 페달을 밟는 내 다리를 더 빠르게 했다(더 빠르게 움직였다). (5)그는 벌판을 가로질러 어둠을 뚫고 계속해서 나를 따라왔다. (6)마침내 나는 집에 도착했고 초인종에 손을 뻗으려고 노력했다. (7)그 남자가 나를 향하여 손을 뻗었다. (8)나는 고개를 돌렸고, 이 세상에서 가장 이상하게 생긴 얼굴을 보았다. (9)나는 그가 나에게 가방을 돌려주면서 "실례합니다만, 당신이 가방을 떨어뜨리셨습니다."라고 그의 목구멍 깊은 곳에서부터 말하는 것을 들었다. (10)나는 아무 말도 할 수 없었지만, 그를 오해한 것에 대한 부끄러움과 후회로 가득했다.

[정답 확인]

다음 글에 드러난 'I'의 심경 변화로 가장 적절한 것은?

✔ scared → embarrassed 무서워하는 → 당황한
② worried → proud 걱정하는 → 자랑스러운
③ excited → disappointed 신이 난 → 실망한
④ happy → concerned 행복한 → 염려하는
⑤ bored → moved 지루해하는 → 감동을 받은

[중요 어휘]

- ☐ **secretly** [부사] 몰래
- ☐ **quicken** [동사] 더 빠르게 하다
- ☐ **reach** [동사] 손을 뻗다
- ☐ **throat** [명사] 목구멍
- ☐ **shame** [명사] 부끄러움
- ☐ **regret** [명사] 후회
- ☐ **misunderstand** [동사] 오해하다

핵심 자신을 타인과 공유하는 것을 일컫는 '자기 개방'이라는 개념에 관해 설명하는 글로, 문장 (3)에 언급된 사적인 자아와 대조하여 개방적이고 공개적인 자아가 자신을 발견하는 데 도움을 준다는 특징을 설명하고 있음.

03 2016년 9월 24번 (정답률 70%) 정답 ②

[지문 끊어 읽기] 자기 개방

(1) People /
사람들은 /
who communicate to others about themselves rather freely, /
꽤 자유롭게 자신에 대해서 다른 사람들에게 전달하는 /
who are frank and open, /
솔직하고 개방적인 /
who express their views, opinions, knowledge, and feelings freely, /
자신의 시각, 견해, 지식, 그리고 감정을 자유롭게 표현하는 /
and who share their knowledge and personal experiences with others /
그리고 자신의 지식과 개인적인 경험을 다른 사람들과 공유하는 /
can be considered as the self-disclosing type.
자기 개방 유형으로 여겨질 수 있다

(2) These people constantly communicate with others /
이러한 사람들은 지속적으로 다른 사람들과 소통한다 /
and make an impact on them.
그리고 그들에게 영향을 준다

(3) This communication or self-disclosure /
이러한 소통이나 자기 개방은 /
helps in generating data / and such an individual has /
자료를 만들어내는 데 도움을 준다 / 그리고 그러한 개인은 지닌다 /
more of an open and public self / than private self. [정답단서]
더 개방적이고 공개적인 자아를 / 사적인 자아보다는

(4) Without an optimal amount of self-disclosure /
적절한 양의 자기 개방이 없다면 /
we deny an opportunity / for others to know us /
우리는 기회를 거절하는 것이다 / 다른 사람들이 우리에 대해 알게 되는 /
and for ourselves to get appropriate feedback. [주제문]
그리고 우리 자신이 적절한 피드백을 받을

힌트 disclosure가 외부에서 내부의 비밀을 '폭로'한다는 의미보다는 스스로 정보를 드러내는 '개방, 공개'의 의미로 쓰였음.

(5) People who don't communicate openly / are private individuals /
개방적으로 소통하지 않는 사람들은 / 사적인 개인들이다 /
who may have difficulty discovering themselves fully.
그들 자신을 완전히 발견하는 데 어려움을 겪을지도 모르는

(6) At least / it is difficult for them to see themselves fully /
적어도 / 그들은 자신을 완전하게 이해하는 것이 어렵다 /
through the eyes of others /
다른 사람들의 눈을 통해 /
and also they make limited impact on others.
그리고 그들은 또한 다른 사람들에게 제한적인 영향만 미친다

[전문 해석]

(1)꽤 자유롭게 자신에 대해서 다른 사람들에게 전달하고, 솔직하고 개방적이며, 자신의 시각, 견해, 지식, 그리고 감정을 자유롭게 표현하고, 자신의 지식과 개인적인 경험을 다른 사람들과 공유하는 사람들은 자기 개방 유형으로 여겨질 수 있다. (2)이러한 사람들은 지속적으로 다른 사람들과 소통하고 그들에게 영향을 준다. (3)이러한 소통이나 자기 개방은 (자신에 대한 이해를 돕는) 자료를 만들어내는 데 도움을 주고 그러한 개인은 사적인 자아보다는 더 개방적이고 공개적인 자아를 지닌다. (4)적절한 양의 자기 개방이 없다면, 우리는 다른 사람들이 우리에 대해 알게 되고 우리 자신이 (다른 사람들로부터) 적절한 피드백을 받을 기회를 거절하는 것이다. (5)개방적으로 소통하지 않는 사람들은 자신을 완전히 발견하는 데 어려움을 겪을지도 모르는 사적인 개인들이다. (6)적어도 그들은 다른 사람들의 눈을 통해 자신을 완전하게 이해하는 것이 어렵고, 또한 다른 사람들에게 제한적인 영향만 미친다.

[정답 확인]

다음 글의 제목으로 가장 적절한 것은?

① Why We Fear Self-disclosure
우리가 자기 개방을 두려워하는 이유
✔ Open Yourself Up for Yourself
당신 자신을 위해 스스로를 개방하라
③ How to Be Honest Without Being Harsh
가혹하지 않게 솔직해지는 방법
④ Don't Underestimate the Power of Feedback
피드백의 힘을 과소평가하지 말라
⑤ Confidence: A Key to Effective Communication
자신감: 효과적인 소통을 위한 열쇠

[중요 어휘]

- ☐ **frank** [형용사] 솔직한
- ☐ **constantly** [부사] 지속적으로, 꾸준히
- ☐ **self-disclosure** [명사] 자기 개방
- ☐ **generate** [동사] 만들어내다, 생성하다
- ☐ **public** [형용사] 공개적인, 개방적인
- ☐ **private** [형용사] 사적인, 비공개의
- ☐ **deny** [동사] 거절하다, 거부하다
- ☐ **openly** [부사] 개방적으로
- ☐ **fully** [부사] 완전히, 완전하게
- ☐ **harsh** [형용사] 가혹한, 냉혹한
- ☐ **underestimate** [동사] 과소평가하다

04 2016년 9월 28번 | 틀린 어법 고르기 (정답률 40%) 정답 ④

[총평]

앞에 나온 동사의 반복을 피하기 위해 사용하는 대동사를 아는지 묻는 문제이다.

[지문 끊어 읽기] 세탁기의 발명

(1) Before the washing machine was invented, /
세탁기가 발명되기 전에 /
people used washboards to scrub, /
사람들은 빨래를 비벼 빨기 위해 빨래판을 사용했다 /
or they carried their laundry to riverbanks and streams, /
또는 그들은 세탁물을 강기슭과 개울로 가져갔다 /
where they beat and rubbed it against rocks.
그런데 그곳에서 그들은 세탁물을 아주 세게 계속 때리거나 바위에 대고 문질렀다

(2) Such backbreaking labor /
그러한 매우 힘든 노동은 /
is still commonplace in parts of the world, /
여전히 세계의 일부에서 흔히 일어나는 일이다 /
but for most homeowners / the work is now done by a machine /
하지만 자택을 소유하고 있는 대부분의 사람들에게 / 오늘날 그 일은 기계에 의해 행해진다 /
that automatically regulates water temperature, /
자동적으로 물 온도를 조절하는 /
measures out the detergent, / washes, rinses, and spin-dries.
세제를 덜어내는 / 세탁하고, 헹구고, 원심력으로 탈수하는

(3) With its electrical and mechanical system, /
그것의 전기를 이용하고 기계로 작동되는 시스템으로 인해 /
the washing machine is one of the most technologically advanced examples /
세탁기는 가장 기술적으로 진보한 예들 중의 하나이다 /
of a large household appliance.
대형 가전제품의

(4) It not only cleans clothes, /
그것은 옷을 세탁할 뿐만 아니라 /
but it does so with far less water, detergent, and energy /
훨씬 더 적은 물과 세제, 그리고 에너지로 그렇게 한다 /
than washing by hand requires.
손빨래가 필요로 하는 것보다

(5) Compared with the old washers /
예전의 세탁기와 비교하여 /
that squeezed out excess water /
초과한 물을 짜내는 /
by feeding clothes through rollers, /
롤러에 옷을 넣어서 /
modern washers are indeed an electrical-mechanical phenomenon. 주제문
현대식의 세탁기는 정말로 전기적으로 그리고 기계적으로 경이로운 물건이다

[전문 해석]

(1)세탁기가 발명되기 전에, 사람들은 빨래를 비벼 빨기 위해 빨래판을 사용하거나 세탁물을 강기슭과 개울로 가져갔는데, 그곳에서 그들은 세탁물을 아주 세게 계속 때리거나 바위에 대고 문질렀다. (2)그러한 매우 힘든 노동은 여전히 세계의 일부에서 흔히 일어나는 일이지만, 오늘날 자택을 소유하고 있는 대부분의 사람들에게 그 일(세탁하는 일)은 자동적으로 물 온도를 조절하고, 세제를 덜어내고, 세탁하고, 헹구고, 원심력으로 탈수하는 기계에 의해 행해진다. (3)그것(세탁기)의 전기를 이용하고 기계로 작동되는 시스템으로 인해, 세탁기는 대형 가전제품의 가장 기술적으로 진보한 예들 중의 하나이다. (4)그것(세탁기)은 옷을 세탁할 뿐만 아니라, 손빨래가 필요로 하는 것보다 훨씬 더 적은 물과 세제, 그리고 에너지로 그렇게 한다(세탁한다). (5)롤러에 옷을 넣어서 초과한(남은) 물을 짜내는 예전의 세탁기와 비교하여, 현대식의 세탁기는 정말로 전기적으로 그리고 기계적으로 경이로운 물건이다.

[정답 풀이]

④ 대동사 do

(4) It not only **cleans** clothes, but it ~~is~~ so with far less water, detergent, and energy than washing by hand requires.
(It: 주어, cleans: 동사, clothes: 목적어, it: 주어, is → does)

앞에서 언급된 동사의 반복을 피하기 위해 대동사를 사용한다. be동사이면 be동사를, 일반동사이면 주어와 시제에 따라 do, does, did를 사용하는데, 여기서는 반복되고 있는 동사가 일반 동사(cleans)이고 주어(it)가 단수이므로 does를 써야 한다.

[오답 풀이]

① 관계부사 where

(1) ~ their laundry to **riverbanks and streams**, [**where** they beat and rubbed it against rocks].
(riverbanks and streams: 선행사, where: 관계부사, they beat and rubbed it against rocks: 완전한 문장)

선행사(riverbanks and streams)가 장소이고, 관계사 이하의 절이 완전한 문장이므로 관계부사 where이 와야 한다. 관계부사의 계속적 용법은 선행사와 관계사 사이에 콤마(,)가 있고, 선행사에 대한 부가적인 설명을 한다.

② 동사를 수식하는 부사

(2) ~ the work is now done by a machine that **automatically** regulates water temperature, ~
(automatically: 부사 → regulates: 동사)

부사는 동사, 형용사, 다른 부사, 그리고 문장 전체를 수식한다. 여기서는 automatically가 '자동적으로'라는 뜻으로 쓰여 동사 regulates를 수식하고 있다.

③ 대명사의 수일치

(3) With **its** electrical and mechanical system, **the washing machine** is one of the most technologically advanced examples of a large household appliance.

위 문장에서 its가 가리키는 대상은 the washing machine이다. the washing machine은 단수 명사이기 때문에 이에 상응하는 소유격 대명사 its를 써준 것은 적절하다.

⑤ 분사구문

(5) **Compared** with the old washers that squeezed out excess water by feeding clothes through rollers, **modern washers** are indeed an electrical-mechanical phenomenon.
(Compared: 수동관계, modern washers: 주어)

위 분사구문에서 생략된 주어는 주절의 주어인 modern washers인데, 주어(modern washers)와 동사(compare)의 관계가 수동이므로 과거분사 compared를 쓴 것은 어법에 맞다.

[중요 어휘]

□ washboard	명사 빨래판
□ scrub	동사 비벼 빨다
□ stream	명사 개울, 시내
□ backbreaking	형용사 매우 힘든, (체력을) 소모시키는
□ commonplace	형용사 흔히 일어나는, 아주 흔한
□ automatically	부사 자동적으로, 기계적으로
□ regulate	동사 조절하다, 조정하다
□ measure out	~을 덜어내다[떼어내다]
□ rinse	동사 헹구다, (비누 성분을) 씻어내다
□ household appliance	가전제품
□ excess	형용사 초과한, 과도한
□ indeed	부사 정말로, 참으로
□ phenomenon	명사 경이로운 물건, 진기한 물건

05 2016년 6월 36번 (정답률 40%) 정답 ⑤

[지문 끊어 읽기] 기억의 본질과 위치

(1) To learn about the nature and location of memory, /
기억의 본질과 위치에 대해 알기 위해 /
scientists in the 1940s /
1940년대의 과학자들은 /
began their search for memory / in the most obvious place: /
기억을 찾아 나서기 시작했다 / 가장 명백한 곳에서 /
within the cells of our brains / — our neurons. 정답 단서-1
우리의 뇌세포 내부 / 즉 뉴런

(C) (7) They cut out parts of rats' brains, / 정답 단서-1
그들은 쥐의 뇌 여러 부분을 잘라냈다 /
trying to make them forget a maze, / and found /
그들이 미로를 잊게 하려고 애쓰면서 / 그리고 알게 되었다 /
that it didn't matter / what part of the brain they chose; /
중요하지 않다는 점을 / 그들이 뇌의 어떤 부분을 선택했는지는 /
the rats never forgot.
쥐들은 결코 잊어버리지 않았다

(8) In 1950, / the researchers gave up, / concluding /
1950년에 / 연구자들은 포기했다 / 결론지으며 /
that memory must be somewhere else. 정답 단서-2
기억이 틀림없이 어딘가 다른 곳에 있다고

(B) (5) Researchers eventually turned / their search for memories /
연구자들은 결국 돌렸다 / 기억에 대한 연구를 /
to the wiring between neurons / 정답 단서-2
뉴런들 사이의 연결 쪽으로 /

힌트 eventually는 '결국', '마침내'라는 뜻으로 결과를 나타내기 때문에 의미적으로 내용이 시작되는 부분에서 사용할 수 없음. 그렇기 때문에 (B)가 처음 순서에서 배제됨.

rather than within the cells themselves.
세포 그 자체의 내부보다는

(6) Each of the hundred billion neurons / in our brains /
천억 개의 뉴런 각각은 / 우리 뇌 안에 있는 /
is connected to seven thousand other neurons, /
칠천 개의 다른 뉴런들과 연결되어 있다 /
in a dense web of nerve fibers.
신경 섬유의 빽빽한 망으로 정답 단서-3

★중요 문장 (6)의 a dense web이 문장 (2)의 These interconnected webs로 이어져 설명되고 있으므로 (B) 다음에 (A)가 온다는 것을 알 수 있음.

(A) (2) These interconnected webs / 정답 단서-3
이 상호 연결된 망은 /
are intricately involved / in our memories.
복잡하게 연관되어 있다 / 우리의 기억과

(3) The memory / the rats had of the maze /
기억은 / 쥐들이 미로에 대해 갖고 있던 /
was spread / throughout their brains.
퍼져 나갔다 / 그들의 뇌 전체로

(4) Whenever the scientists cut out a piece, / they damaged /
과학자들이 조각을 잘라낼 때마다 / 그들은 손상시켰다 /
only a small portion of the involved connections.
관련된 연결의 고작 작은 일부만을

[전문 해석]

(1)기억의 본질과 위치에 대해 알기 위해, 1940년대의 과학자들은 가장 명백한 곳인 우리의 뇌세포 내부, 즉 뉴런에서 기억을 찾아 나서기 시작했다.
(C) (7)그들은 그들(쥐들)이 미로를 잊게 하려고 애쓰면서 쥐의 뇌 여러 부분을 잘라냈고, 그들이 뇌의 어떤 부분을 선택했는지는(선택해서 잘랐는지는) 중요하지 않다는 점을 알게 되었다. 쥐들은 결코 (미로를) 잊어버리지 않았다. (8)1950년에, 연구자들은 기억이 틀림없이 어딘가 다른 곳에 있다고 결론지으며 (연구를) 포기했다.
(B) (5)연구자들은 결국 기억에 대한 연구를 세포 그 자체의 내부보다는 뉴런들 사이의 연결 쪽으로 돌렸다. (6)우리 뇌 안에 있는 천억 개의 뉴런 각각은 칠천 개의 다른 뉴런들과 신경 섬유의 빽빽한 망으로 연결되어 있다.
(A) (2)이 상호 연결된 망은 우리의 기억과 복잡하게 연관되어 있다. (3)쥐들이 미로에 대해 갖고 있던 기억은 그들의 뇌 전체로 퍼져 나갔다. (4)과학자들이 조각을 잘라낼 때마다, 그들은 관련된 연결(망)의 고작 작은 일부만을 손상시켰다.
- neuron(뉴런): 신경계를 구성하는 주된 세포. 다른 세포와는 달리 이온 통로를 발현하여 전기적 방법으로 신호를 전달한다.

[정답 확인]

주어진 글 다음에 이어질 글의 순서로 가장 적절한 것은?

① (A) — (C) — (B) ② (B) — (A) — (C) ③ (B) — (C) — (A)
④ (C) — (A) — (B) ✔ (C) — (B) — (A)

[문제 풀이]

과학자들이 뇌세포 안에서 기억에 대한 연구를 시작하였다는 주어진 글 뒤로, 쥐의 뇌를 대상으로 진행된 실험 과정을 구체적으로 소개하는 (C), 기억이 신경 세포 내부가 아닌 세포들 사이의 연결망에 있음을 밝히는 (B), 그리하여 어느 일부를 잘라내도 쥐들은 남은 연결망으로 기억을 유지할 수 있었음을 암시하는 (A)가 차례로 이어지는 것이 알맞다. 따라서 글의 순서로 가장 적절한 것은 ⑤ '(C) — (B) — (A)'이다.

[중요 어휘]

☐ **obvious**	형용사 명백한, 분명한
☐ **cell**	명사 세포
☐ **maze**	명사 미로
☐ **somewhere else**	어딘가 다른 곳에
☐ **eventually**	부사 결국, 마침내
☐ **wiring**	명사 연결, 배선
☐ **dense**	형용사 빽빽한, 조밀한
☐ **nerve**	명사 신경
☐ **fiber**	명사 섬유(질)
☐ **interconnected**	형용사 상호 연결된
☐ **intricately**	부사 복잡하게

문제편 p.301

핵심 Christiaan Huygens라는 인물에 대해 다룬 지문임. 인물과 관련된 사실들이 나열식으로 제시되어 있으므로 보기와 비교하며 읽으면 답을 쉽게 고를 수 있음.

06 2020년 3월 26번 (정답률 85%) 정답 ③

[지문 끊어 읽기] 수학자이자 천문학자 Christiaan Huygens

(1) Dutch mathematician and astronomer Christiaan Huygens /
네덜란드의 수학자이자 천문학자인 Christiaan Huygens는 /
was born in The Hague in 1629.
1629년 헤이그에서 태어났다

(2) He studied law and mathematics at his university, /
그는 대학에서 법과 수학을 공부했다 /
and then devoted some time to his own research, /
그런 후에 자신의 연구에 시간을 바쳤다 /
initially in mathematics / but then also in optics, /
처음에는 수학에서 / 하지만 나중에는 광학에서도 /
working on telescopes and grinding his own lenses.
분사구문① 분사구문②
망원경에 대한 작업을 하고 자신의 렌즈를 갈면서

(3) Huygens visited England several times, /
Huygens는 영국을 여러 차례 방문했다 /
and met Isaac Newton in 1689.
그리고 1689년에 Isaac Newton을 만났다

(4) In addition to his work on light, /
빛에 대한 그의 연구와 더불어 /
Huygens had studied forces and motion, /
Huygens는 힘과 운동을 연구했다 /
but he did not accept Newton's law of universal gravitation. 정답 단서
그러나 그는 뉴턴의 만유인력 법칙을 받아들이지 않았다

(5) Huygens' wide-ranging achievements /
Huygens의 광범위한 업적은 /
included some of the most accurate clocks of his time, /
당대의 가장 정확한 시계 중 몇몇을 포함했다 /
the result of his work on pendulums.
시계추에 대한 그의 연구의 결과인

(6) His astronomical work, / carried out using his own telescopes, /
그의 천문학 연구는 / 자신의 망원경을 사용하여 수행됐던 /
included the discovery of Titan, / the largest of Saturn's moons, /
Titan의 발견을 포함했다 / 토성의 위성 중 가장 큰 것인 /
and the first correct description of Saturn's rings.
그리고 토성의 고리에 대한 최초의 정확한 묘사를

[중요 구문]

(6) His astronomical work, [(which was) carried out using ~],
S 분사구문
included the discovery of Titan, the largest of Saturn's moons,
V O① =
and the first correct description of Saturn's rings.
O②

[전문 해석]

(1)네덜란드의 수학자이자 천문학자인 Christiaan Huygens는 1629년 헤이그에서 태어났다. (2)그는 대학에서 법과 수학을 공부했고, 그런 후에 처음에는 수학에서, 하지만 나중에는 망원경에 대한 작업을 하고 자신의 렌즈를 갈면서 광학에서도 (자신의) 연구에 시간을 바쳤다. (3)Huygens는 영국을 여러 차례 방문했고, 1689년에 Isaac Newton(아이작 뉴턴)을 만났다. (4)빛에 대한 (그의) 연구와 더불어, Huygens는 힘과 운동을 연구했으나, 그는 뉴턴의 만유인력 법칙을 받아들이지 않았다. (5)Huygens의 광범위한 업적은 시계추에 대한 그의 연구의 결과인, 당대의 가장 정확한 시계 중 몇몇을 포함했다. (6)자신의 망원경을 사용하여 수행됐던 그의 천문학 연구는 토성의 위성 중 가장 큰 것(위성)인 Titan의 발견과 토성의 고리에 대한 최초의 정확한 묘사를 포함했다.
- Christiaan Huygens(크리스티안 호이겐스/하위헌스, 1629년~1695년): 네덜란드의 수학자이자 천문학자로, 특히 역학과 광학의 연구로 유명하다.
- law of universal gravitation(만유인력 법칙): 질량을 가진 모든 물체들은 서로 끌어당기는 힘이 작용한다는 법칙으로, 1665년 영국의 물리학자 Isaac Newton(아이작 뉴턴)이 발견했다.

[정답 확인]

Christiaan Huygens에 관한 다음 글의 내용과 일치하지 않는 것은?

① 대학에서 법(law)과 수학(mathematics)을 공부했다.
② 1689년에 뉴턴(Newton)을 만났다.
✔ 뉴턴의 만유인력(universal gravitation) 법칙을 ~~받아들였다~~. 받아들이지 않았다

3회 20분 미니모의고사

④ 당대의 가장 정확한(accurate) 시계 중 몇몇이 업적에 포함되었다.
⑤ 자신의 망원경(telescope)을 사용하여 천문학 연구를 수행했다.

[중요 어휘]

☐ mathematician	명사 수학자
☐ astronomer	명사 천문학자
☐ devote	동사 바치다, 헌신하다
☐ initially	부사 처음에
☐ optics	명사 광학
☐ telescope	명사 망원경
☐ grind	동사 갈다 (grind-ground-ground)
☐ universal gravitation	명사 만유인력
☐ wide-ranging	형용사 광범위한
☐ achievement	명사 업적, 성취
☐ pendulum	명사 (시계)추, 진자
☐ astronomical	형용사 천문학의
☐ discovery	명사 발견
☐ moon	명사 위성, 달
☐ description	명사 묘사, 설명

07 2018년 9월 38번 (정답률 45%)

정답 ⑤

[지문 끊어 읽기] 고체가 음파를 더 잘 전달하는 이유

(2) Tap your finger / on the surface of a wooden table or desk, /
당신의 손가락으로 두드려라 / 나무 탁자나 책상의 표면을 /
and observe the loudness of the sound you hear.
그리고 당신이 듣는 그 소리의 세기를 관찰하라

(3) Then, / place your ear flat / on top of the table or desk.
그런 다음 / 당신의 귀를 바싹 대라 / 그 탁자나 책상의 표면에

① (4) With your finger / about one foot away from your ear, /
당신의 손가락으로 / 당신의 귀에서 약 1피트 떨어져서 /
tap the table top /
탁자의 표면을 두드려라 /
and observe the loudness of the sound you hear again.
그리고 다시 당신이 듣는 소리의 세기를 관찰하라

② (5) The volume of the sound you hear / with your ear on the desk /
당신이 듣는 소리의 크기는 / 책상 위에서 당신의 귀로 /
is much louder / than with it off the desk.
훨씬 더 크다 / 책상에서 떨어져 듣는 것보다

③ (6) Sound waves are capable of traveling /
음파는 이동할 수 있다 /
through many solid materials / as well as through air.
많은 고체 물질을 통해서도 / 공기를 통해서뿐만 아니라

④ (7) Solids, like wood / for example, /
나무와 같은 고체는 / 예를 들어 /
transfer the sound waves much better (정답 단서) / than air typically does /
음파를 훨씬 더 잘 전달한다 / 전형적으로 공기가 하는 것보다 /
because the molecules in a solid substance /
고체 물질 안에 있는 분자들이 ~이기 때문에 /
are much closer and more tightly packed together /
훨씬 더 촘촘하고 함께 더 꽉 묶여있기 /
than they are in air.
공기 안에 있는 그것들보다

⑤ (1) This allows the solids to carry /
이것이 고체가 전달할 수 있게 한다 /
the waves more easily and efficiently, /
파동을 더 쉽고 효과적으로 /
[resulting in a louder sound]. (정답 단서)
그래서 더 큰 소리를 만든다 [ ]: 분사구문(연속동작)

(8) The density of the air itself / also plays a determining factor /
공기 자체의 밀도도 / 또한 결정적인 요소로 작용한다 /
in the loudness of sound waves passing through it.
그것을 통과하는 음파의 크기에 있어서

[전문 해석]

(2)당신의 손가락으로 나무 탁자나 책상의 표면을 두드리고, 당신이 듣는 그 소리의 세기를 관찰하라. (3)그런 다음 당신의 귀를 그 탁자나 책상의 표면에 바싹(납작하게) 대라. ① (4)당신의 귀에서 약 1피트 떨어져서 손가락으로 탁자의 표면을 두드리고 다시 당신이 듣는 소리의 세기를 관찰하라. ② (5)책상 위에서 당신의 귀로 듣는 소리의 크기는 책상에서 떨어져 듣는 것보다 훨씬 더 크다. ③ (6)음파는 공기를 통해서뿐만 아니라 많은 고체 물질을 통해서도 이동할 수 있다. ④ (7)예를 들어, 나무와 같은 고체는 고체 물질 안에 있는 분자들이 공기 안에 있는 그것들(분자들)보다 훨씬 더 촘촘하고 함께 더 꽉 묶여있기 때문에 전형적으로 공기가 하는(음파를 전달하는) 것보다 음파를 훨씬 더 잘 전달한다. ⑤ (1)이것이 고체가(고체로 하여금) 파동을 더 쉽고 효과적으로 전달할 수 있게 해서 더 큰 소리를 만든다. (8)공기 자체의 밀도도 또한 그것을 통과하는 음파의 크기에 있어서 결정적인 요소로 작용한다.

- wave(파동): 공간이나 물질의 한 부분에서 생긴 주기적인 진동이 시간의 흐름에 따라 주위로 멀리 퍼져나가는 현상

[문제 풀이]

주어진 문장은 '이것' 때문에 고체가 더 큰 소리를 만들어 낸다고 하고 있다. 그러므로 그 앞 문장에서는 고체가 더 큰 소리를 만들어 낼 수 있는 이유에 대한 설명이 나와야 한다. 문장 (7)에서 공기가 음파를 전달하는 것보다 고체가 음파를 훨씬 잘 전달하는 이유에 대해서 설명하고 있기 때문에 정답은 ⑤이다.

[중요 어휘]

☐ tap	동사 두드리다, 치다 / 명사 두드리는 소리
☐ observe	동사 관찰하다, 지켜보다
☐ flat	부사 바싹, 납작하게 / 형용사 평평한, 납작한
☐ typically	부사 전형적으로, 일반적으로
☐ substance	명사 물질, 본질, 핵심
☐ solid	명사 고체 / 형용사 고체의, 단단한, 견고한
☐ density	명사 밀도, 농도
☐ play	동사 작용하다, 놀이를 하다 / 명사 놀이
☐ determining	형용사 결정적인

08 2016년 6월 32번 (정답률 50%)

정답 ②

[지문 끊어 읽기] 광고의 목적

(1) Although people most commonly think of persuasion /
사람들은 가장 흔히 설득을 생각하지만 /
as deep processing, / it is actually shallow processing /
깊은 사고 과정으로 / 그것은 실제로 얕은 과정이다 /
that is the more common way / to influence behavior.
보다 흔한 방법인 / 행동에 영향을 주는

(2) For example, / Facebook started inserting advertisements /
예를 들어 / Facebook은 광고를 끼워 넣기 시작했다 /
in the middle of users' webpages.
사용자의 웹 페이지 중간에

(3) Many users didn't like this change / and, on principle, /
많은 사용자들은 이러한 변화를 싫어했다 / 그리고 기본적으로는 /
refused to click on the ads.
광고를 눌러보기를 거부했다

(4) However, / this approach displays /
하지만 / 이러한 접근법은 보여준다 /
a fundamental misunderstanding of the psychology /
심리학에 대한 기본적인 오해를 /
behind the ads.
광고 뒤에 숨어 있는

(5) The truth is that / Facebook never expected /
사실 ~이다 / Facebook은 결코 기대하지 않았다 /
anyone to click on the ads.
그 누구도 광고를 클릭할 것이라

(6) All the company wants / is to expose you /
회사가 원하는 것은 단지 / 당신을 노출시키는 것이다 /
to those product brands and images.
그 상품 브랜드와 이미지에

(7) The more times you're exposed to something, /
당신이 무언가에 더 많은 시간 노출될수록 /
in general, / the more you like it. 정답 단서
일반적으로 / 그것을 더 좋아하게 된다.

(8) Everyone is influenced / by the familiarity of an image. 주제문
모든 사람은 영향을 받는다 / 이미지의 익숙함에

(9) So, / even though you can ignore the ads, /
그러므로 / 당신이 광고를 무시할 수 있다고 하더라도 /
by simply being in front of your eyes, /
당신의 눈앞에 단지 있는 것만으로 /
they're doing their work.
그것은 자기 일을 하는 것이다

힌트 빈칸이 있는 문장 (8)과 접속 부사 so로 연결되는 문장 (9)의 in front of your eyes는 우리가 눈앞에 보이는 image에 영향을 받는다는 힌트임.

[전문 해석]

(1)사람들은 가장 흔히 설득을 깊은 사고 과정이라고 생각하지만, 그것(설득)은 실제로 행동에 영향을 주는 보다 흔한 방법인 얕은 (사고) 과정이다. (2)예를 들어, Facebook(페이스북)은 사용자의 웹 페이지 중간에 광고를 끼워 넣기 시작했다. (3)많은 사용자들은 이러한 변화를 싫어했고, 기본적으로는 광고를 눌러보기를 거부했다. (4)하지만, 이러한 접근법은 광고 뒤에 숨어 있는 심리학에 대한 기본적인 오해를 보여준다. (5)사실 Facebook은 그 누구도 광고를 클릭할 것이라 결코 기대하지 않았다. (6)회사가 원하는 것은 단지 당신을 그 상품 브랜드와 이미지에 노출시키는 것이다. (7)당신이 무언가에 더 많은 시간 노출될수록, 일반적으로 그것을 더 좋아하게 된다. (8)모든 사람은 이미지의 익숙함에 영향을 받는다. (9)그러므로 당신이 광고를 무시할 수 있다고 하더라도, 당신의 눈앞에 단지 있는 것만으로 그것(광고)은 자기 일을 (충분히) 하는 것이다.

- Facebook(페이스북): 세계 최대의 소셜 네트워크 서비스 중 하나로, 월 단위 14억 9천만 명(2015년 2분기 기준)의 사용자가 활동하고 있다.

[정답 확인]

다음 빈칸에 들어갈 말로 가장 적절한 것은?

① others' opinions on the ads
광고에 대한 타인의 의견
✔ the familiarity of an image
이미지의 익숙함
③ their loyalty to a specific brand
특정 브랜드에 대한 그들의 충성
④ false information on the Internet
인터넷 상의 잘못된 정보
⑤ the deep processing of information
정보의 면밀한 처리

★중요 문장 (7)의 비교급 구문(The more times ⋯, the more ~)은 사람들이 무언가에 자주 노출되어 친숙해질수록 그 대상을 더 좋아하게 된다는 내용으로 정답에서는 familiarity(익숙함)로 표현되었음.

[문제 풀이]

Facebook 광고의 예를 들어, 광고의 목적은 사람들로 하여금 특정 브랜드와 이미지를 반복적으로 접하게 하여 그 브랜드와 이미지에 친숙해지도록 하는 데 있다는 내용을 설명하므로, 빈칸에 들어갈 말로 가장 적절한 것은 ② 'the familiarity of an image(이미지의 익숙함)'이다.

[중요 어휘]

☐ **persuasion**	명사 설득
☐ **processing**	명사 사고 과정, 처리
☐ **shallow**	형용사 얕은, 얄팍한
☐ **on principle**	기본적으로
☐ **fundamental**	형용사 기본적인, 근본적인
☐ **in general**	일반적으로
☐ **loyalty to**	~에 대한 충성

09 2016년 6월 33번 (정답률 35%)

정답 ⑤

[지문 끊어 읽기] 과학의 간접적인 증명

(1) In science, / we can never really prove / that a theory is true.
과학에서 / 우리는 절대로 증명할 수는 없다 / 어떤 이론이 참이라는 것을

(2) All we can do in science is / use evidence /
우리가 과학에서 할 수 있는 일은 단지 ~이다 / 증거를 이용하는 것 /
to reject a hypothesis.
가설을 기각하기 위해

(3) Experiments never directly prove / that a theory is right; /
실험은 결코 직접적으로 증명하지 않는다 / 어떤 이론이 옳다는 것을 /
all they can do / is provide indirect support /
그것이 할 수 있는 것은 / 간접적인 증거를 제공하는 것뿐이다 /
by rejecting all the other theories /
다른 모든 이론들을 기각함으로써 /
until only one likely theory remains.
단지 한 가지 가능성 있는 이론이 남을 때까지

(4) For example, / sometimes you hear people say things /
예를 들어 / 가끔 당신은 사람들이 말을 하는 것을 듣는다 /
like 'evolution is only a theory: / science has never proved it.'
진화는 이론일 뿐이고 / 과학은 결코 그것을 증명한 적이 없다와 같은

힌트 문장 (4)의 only a theory와 정답의 only one likely theory가 대구를 이루며 정답의 힌트를 주고 있음.

(5) Well, that's true, /
그것이 사실이다 /
but only in the sense that science never proves /
하지만 오로지 과학이 결코 증명하지 않는다는 점에서만 /
that any theory is positively true.
그 어떤 이론도 확실히 맞다고

(6) But the theory of evolution / has assembled /
하지만 진화론은 / 모아 왔다 /
an enormous amount of convincing data /
방대한 양의 설득력 있는 자료들을 /
proving that other competing theories are false.
다른 경쟁 이론들이 틀렸다는 것을 증명하는

(7) So though it hasn't been proved, / overwhelmingly, /
그래서 비록 그것이 증명된 적이 없다 하더라도 / 압도적으로 /
evolution is the best theory / that we have /
진화론은 최선의 이론이다 / 우리가 보유한 /
to explain the data we have. 정답 단서
우리가 가지고 있는 자료를 설명하기 위해

[전문 해석]

(1)과학에서, 우리는 어떤 이론이 참이라는 것을 절대로 증명할 수는 없다. (2)우리가 과학에서 할 수 있는 일은 단지 가설을 기각하기 위해 증거를 이용하는 것이다. (3)실험은 결코 어떤 이론이 옳다는 것을 직접적으로 증명하지 않으며, 그것(실험)이 할 수 있는 것은 단지 한 가지 가능성 있는 이론이 남을 때까지 다른 모든 이론들을 기각함으로써 간접적인 증거를 제공하는 것뿐이다. (4)예를 들어, 가끔 당신은 사람들이 '진화는 이론일 뿐이고, 과학은 결코 그것을 증명한 적이 없다'와 같은 말을 하는 것을 듣는다. (5)그것이 사실이긴 하지만, 오로지 과학이 결코 그 어떤 이론도 확실히 맞다고 증명하지 않는다는 점에서만 (그렇다). (6)하지만 진화론은 다른 경쟁 이론들이 틀렸다는 것을 증명하는 방대한 양의 설득력 있는 자료들을 모아 왔다. (7)그래서 비록 그것이 증명된 적이 없다 하더라도, 압도적으로 진화론은 우리가 가지고 있는 자료를 설명하기 위해 우리가 보유한 최선의 이론이다.

[정답 확인]

다음 빈칸에 들어갈 말로 가장 적절한 것은?

① scientists admit to using false data
과학자들이 잘못된 자료를 썼음을 인정할
② researchers document their methods
연구자들이 자신의 방법을 문서화할
③ people go back to their original hypothesis
사람들이 그들의 원래 가설로 돌아갈
④ the theories can be explained in words
이론들이 말로 설명될 수 있을
✔ only one likely theory remains
단지 한 가지 가능성 있는 이론이 남을

★중요 문장 (7)의 the best theory는 여럿 중 가장 뛰어난 한 가지를 의미한다는 측면에서 정답의 only one likely theory로 바뀌어 제시되었음.

3 회 20분 미니모의고사

문제편 p.303

[문제 풀이]

진화론의 예를 통해, 과학은 어떤 이론이 옳음을 직접 증명한다기보다는 가장 반박이 불가능해 보이는 이론이 남을 때까지 다른 경쟁 이론을 배제하는 방식으로 간접적인 증명을 이루어 낸다는 내용을 설명한 글이므로, 빈칸에 들어갈 말로 가장 적절한 것은 ⑤ 'only one likely theory remains(단지 한 가지 가능성 있는 이론이 남음)'이다.

[중요 어휘]

☐ **reject**	동사 기각하다, 거부하다
☐ **hypothesis**	명사 가설 (hypotheses의 단수형)
☐ **indirect**	형용사 간접적인
☐ **positively**	부사 확실히, 분명히, 긍정적으로
☐ **assemble**	동사 모으다, 수집하다
☐ **competing**	형용사 경쟁하는, 대립되는
☐ **overwhelmingly**	부사 압도적으로

10 2016년 11월 40번 (정답률 55%) 정답 ①

[지문 끊어 읽기] 과도한 정밀성과 신뢰성의 관계

(1) Inappropriate precision means /
부적절한 정밀성이란 의미한다 /
giving information or figures to a greater degree of apparent accuracy /
더 큰 정도의 명백한 정확성으로 정보나 수치를 제시하는 것을 /
than suits the context.
상황에 적절한 것보다

(2) For example, / advertisers often use the results of surveys /
예를 들어 / 광고 회사들은 종종 설문조사 결과를 사용한다 /
to prove what they say about their products.
그들의 제품에 대해 말하려는 것을 입증하기 위해서

(3) Sometimes / they claim a level of precision /
때때로 / 그들은 정밀성의 수준을 주장한다 /
not based reliably on evidence.
확실하게 증거에 근거하지 않은

(4) So, / if a company selling washing powder claims /
그러므로 / 만약 세제를 판매하는 한 회사가 주장한다면 /
95.45% of British adults agree /
95.45퍼센트의 영국 성인이 동의한다고 /
that this powder washes whiter than any other, /
이 세제가 다른 어떤 것보다 더 하얗게 세탁한다는 것에 /
then this level of precision is clearly inappropriate.
그러면 이 정밀성의 수준은 분명히 부적절한 것이다

(5) It is unlikely that all British adults were surveyed, /
모든 영국 성인이 설문조사를 받았을 수는 없다 /
so the results are based only on a sample /
그러므로 그 결과는 단지 표본에 근거한 것이다 /
and not the whole population.
전체 인구가 아니라

(6) At best / the company should be claiming /
기껏해야 / 그 회사는 주장하고 있어야 한다 /
that over 95% of *those asked* agreed /
'질문을 받은 사람들' 중 95퍼센트 이상이 동의했다고 /
that their powder washes whiter than any other.
그들의 세제가 다른 어떤 것보다 더 하얗게 세탁한다는 것에

(7) Even if the whole population had been surveyed, /
전체 인구가 설문조사를 받았다고 할지라도 /
to have given the result to two decimal points /
소수점 둘째 자리까지 결과를 제시하는 것은 /
would have been absurd.
터무니없는 것일 것이다

(8) The effect is to propose /
그 효과는 의도하려는 것이다 /
a high degree of scientific precision / in the research. 정답단서
높은 수준의 과학적 정밀성을 / 그 연구에

(9) Frequently, / however, / inappropriate precision is an attempt /
흔히 / 그러나 / 부적절한 정밀성은 시도이다 /
to mask the unscientific nature of a study.
연구의 비과학적인 본질을 감추기 위한 정답단서

✱중요 문장 (9)의 mask the unscientific nature of a study의 의미가 요약문의 conceal the lack of reliability of their research로 제시됨.

(10) Advertisers often give us information /
광고 회사들은 종종 우리에게 정보를 준다 /
with an (A)excessive precision, / but it can be considered /
(A)과도한 정밀성을 지닌 / 하지만 그것은 간주될 수 있다 /
as an intention to conceal /
숨기기 위한 의도로 /
the lack of (B)reliability of their research.
그들의 연구의 (B)신뢰성 부족을

[전문 해석]

(1)부적절한 정밀성이란 상황에 적절한 것보다 더 큰 정도의 명백한 정확성으로 정보나 수치를 제시하는 것을 의미한다. (2)예를 들어, 광고 회사들은 그들의 제품에 대해 말하려는 것을 입증하기 위해서 종종 설문조사 결과를 사용한다. (3)때때로 그들은 확실하게 증거에 근거하지 않은 정밀성의 수준을 주장한다. (4)그러므로 만약 세제를 판매하는 한 회사가 95.45퍼센트의 영국 성인이 이 세제가 다른 어떤 것(세제)보다 더 하얗게 세탁한다는 것에 동의한다고 주장한다면, (그러면) 이 정밀성의 수준은 분명히 부적절한 것이다. (5)모든 영국 성인이 설문조사를 받았을 수는 없으므로 그 결과는 (영국의) 전체 인구가 아니라 단지 표본에 근거한 것이다. (6)기껏해야 그 회사는 '질문을 받은 사람들' 중 95퍼센트 이상이 그들의 세제가 다른 어떤 것보다 더 하얗게 세탁한다는 것에 동의했다고 주장하고 있어야 한다. (7)전체 인구가 설문조사를 받았다고 할지라도, 소수점 둘째 자리까지 결과를 제시하는 것은 터무니없는 것일 것이다. (8)그 효과(소수점 둘째 자리까지 결과를 제시하는 것의 효과)는 그 연구에 높은 수준의 과학적 정밀성을 의도하려는 것이다. (9)그러나 흔히 부적절한 정밀성은 연구의 비과학적인 본질을 감추기 위한 시도이다.

⬇

(10)광고 회사들은 종종 우리에게 (A)과도한 정밀성을 지닌 정보를 주지만, 그것은 그들의 연구의 (B)신뢰성 부족을 숨기기 위한 의도로 간주될 수 있다.

[정답 확인]

다음 글의 내용을 한 문장으로 요약하고자 한다. 빈칸 (A)와 (B)에 들어갈 말로 가장 적절한 것은?

	(A)		(B)
✔	excessive 과도한	......	reliability 신뢰성
②	excessive 과도한	......	popularity 인기
③	sufficient 충분한	......	investment 투자
④	reasonable 합리적인	......	integrity 진실성
⑤	reasonable 합리적인	......	availability 유용성

✱중요 문장 (1)의 a greater degree of apparent accuracy의 예로 광고 회사의 전략을 제시하고 있으므로 (A)에 들어갈 말은 a greater degree와 비슷한 의미인 excessive로 제시되었음.

[문제 풀이]

광고에서 필요 이상으로 정확해 보이는 정보를 제시하는 것의 의도를 밝히고 있는 글이다. 그러한 정밀성은 종종 조사나 연구의 비과학적인 내용을 감추고 신뢰를 얻기 위해서 전략적으로 사용된다는 것이다. 따라서 정답은 ①이다.

[중요 어휘]

☐ **precision**	명사 정밀성
☐ **apparent**	형용사 명백한, 분명한
☐ **suit**	동사 적절하다, 들어맞다 / 명사 정장
☐ **context**	명사 상황, 문맥
☐ **prove**	동사 (사실임을) 입증하다
☐ **absurd**	형용사 터무니없는
☐ **propose**	동사 의도하다, 제안하다
☐ **intention**	명사 의도
☐ **conceal**	동사 숨기다
☐ **lack**	명사 부족, 결핍

11~12 2016년 6월 41~42번 (정답률 55% | 40%) 정답 ③ | ③

[지문 끊어 읽기] 눈 가리기의 기능

(1) Eye-blocking is a nonverbal behavior / that can occur /
Eye-blocking은 비언어적 행위이다 / 일어날 수 있는 /
when we feel threatened / or don't like what we see.
우리가 위협받는다고 느낄 때 / 혹은 우리가 보고 있는 것이 마음에 들지 않을 때

(2) Squinting and closing or shielding our eyes /
눈을 가늘게 뜨는 것과 감거나 가리는 것은 /
are actions that have evolved /
진화해온 행동들이다 /
to protect the brain from seeing undesirable images.
원하지 않는 이미지들을 뇌가 보지 못하게 하기 위해서

(3) As an investigator, / I used eye-blocking behaviors /
수사관으로서 / 나는 eye-blocking 행위를 이용했다 /
to assist in the arson investigation /
방화 수사를 돕기 위해 /
of a tragic hotel fire in Puerto Rico.
Puerto Rico의 비극적인 호텔 화재의

(4) A security guard / came under immediate suspicion /
보안 요원 한 명이 / 즉각적인 용의 선상에 올랐다 /
because the blaze broke out / in an area where he was assigned.
화재가 발생했기 때문에 / 그가 배정받은 지역에서

(5) One of the ways we determined /
우리가 밝힌 방법 중 하나는 /
he had nothing to do with starting the fire /
그는 불이 난 것과 아무 관련이 없다는 것을 /
was by asking him some specific questions /
그에게 몇 가지 구체적인 질문을 해 보는 것이었다 /
as to where he was / before the fire, /
그가 어디 있었는지에 관해 / 불이 나기 전과 /
at the time of the fire, / and whether or not he set the fire.
불이 나던 당시에 / 그리고 그가 불을 질렀는지 아닌지

(6) After each question / I observed his face /
각각의 질문 뒤에 / 나는 그의 얼굴을 관찰했다 /
for any telltale signs / of eye-blocking behavior.
어떤 숨길 수 없는 징후라도 있는지 / eye-blocking 행위의

(7) He blocked his eyes /
그는 그의 눈을 가렸다 /
only when questioned about where he was / 12번 정답 단서
그가 어디에 있었는지에 대한 질문을 받았을 때에만 /
when the fire started.
불이 났을 때

(8) Oddly, in contrast, / he did not seem troubled by the question, /
그에 반해 희한하게도 / 그는 질문에는 불안해하는 것처럼 보이지 않았다 /
"Did you set the fire?"
"당신이 불을 질렀습니까?"

(9) This told me / the real issue was his location /
이것은 내게 알려주었다 / 진짜 문제는 그의 위치였다는 점을 /
at the time of the fire.
화재 당시

(10) He was questioned further by the investigators /
그는 수사관들로부터 심도 있게 질문을 받았다 /
and eventually admitted to leaving his post /
그리고 마침내 자기 자리를 떠나 있었다는 점을 인정했다 /
to visit his girlfriend, / who also worked at the hotel.
여자 친구를 만나러 / 역시 호텔에서 일하던

(11) Unfortunately, / while he was gone, /
불행하게도 / 그가 떠나 있는 동안 /
the arsonists entered the area /
방화범들이 구역에 들어왔다 /
he should have been guarding / and started the fire.
그가 지키고 있었어야 했던 / 그리고 불을 낸 것이었다

(12) In this case, / the guard's eye-blocking behavior /
이 경우에 / 보안 요원의 eye-blocking 행위는 /
gave us the insight / we needed /
통찰력을 우리에게 주었다 / 우리가 필요한 /
to pursue a line of questioning /
일련의 심문을 계속하는 데 /
that eventually broke the case open. 11번 정답 단서
결국 사건을 해결하는

✶중요 문장 (3)에서 필자가 수사관이라는 점과 문장 (12)의 the insight we needed에서 수사관에게 필요한 것(hidden information)이 무엇인지 생각해 볼 것.

[전문 해석]

(1)Eye-blocking(눈 가리기)은 우리가 위협받는다고 느끼거나 보고 있는 것이 마음에 들지 않을 때 일어날 수 있는 비언어적 행위이다. (2)눈을 가늘게 뜨는 것과 (눈을) 감거나 가리는 것은 원하지 않는 이미지들을 뇌가 보지 못하게 하기 위해서 진화해온 행동들이다. (3)수사관으로서, 나는 Puerto Rico(푸에르토 리코)의 비극적인 호텔 화재의 방화 수사를 돕기 위해 eye-blocking 행위를 이용했다. (4)보안 요원 한 명이 그가 배정받은 지역에서 화재가 발생했기 때문에 즉각적인 용의 선상에 올랐다. (5)그는 불이 난 것과 아무 관련이 없다는 것을 (우리가) 밝힌 방법 중 하나는 불이 나기 전과, 불이 나던 당시에 그가 어디 있었는지, 그리고 그가 불을 질렀는지 아닌지에 관해 그에게 몇 가지 구체적인 질문을 해 보는 것이었다. (6)각각의 질문 뒤에 나는 eye-blocking 행위의(eye-blocking과 관련된) 어떤 숨길 수 없는 징후라도 있는지 (살펴보고자) 그의 얼굴을 관찰했다. (7)그는 불이 났을 때 그가 어디에 있었는지에 대한 질문을 받았을 때에만 그의 눈을 가렸다. (8)그에 반해, 희한하게도 그는 "당신이 불을 질렀습니까?"라는 질문에는 불안해하는 것처럼 보이지 않았다. (9)이것은 내게 진짜 문제는 화재 당시 그의 위치였다는 점을 알려주었다. (10)그는 수사관들로부터 심도 있게 질문을 받았고, 마침내 역시(같은) 호텔에서 일하던 여자 친구를 만나러 자기 자리를 떠나 있었다는 점을 인정했다. (11)불행하게도 그가 (자리를) 떠나 있는 동안, 방화범들이 그가 지키고 있었어야 했던 구역에 들어와 불을 낸 것이었다. (12)이 경우에, 보안 요원의 eye-blocking 행위는 결국 우리가 사건을 해결하는 일련의 심문을 계속하는 데 필요한 통찰력을 우리에게 주었다.
- eye-blocking(눈 가리기): 심리적으로 불편한 상황에서 눈을 감거나 손으로 가려서 눈이 노출되지 않게 하는 행위를 널리 가리킨다.

[정답 확인]

11. 윗글의 제목으로 가장 적절한 것은?

① Why Did the Man Set the Fire?
왜 남자는 불을 질렀는가?
② Factors Interrupting Eye-blocking
Eye-blocking(눈 가리기)을 방해하는 요인들
✔ Eye-blocking Reveals Hidden Information
Eye-blocking(눈 가리기)은 숨겨진 정보를 드러낸다
④ Strategies to Hide Eye-blocking Behaviors
Eye-blocking(눈 가리기) 행위를 숨기는 전략
⑤ Hiring a Security Guard to Protect a Building
건물을 지키기 위한 보안 요원 고용하기

✶중요 문장 (12)의 broke the case open의 의미가 정답에는 reveals로 표현되고 있음.

12. 윗글의 빈칸에 들어갈 말로 가장 적절한 것은?

① emotion 감정 ② judgment 판단 ✔ location 위치
④ safety 안전 ⑤ reaction 반응

✶중요 문장 (7)에서 보안 요원이 소재지 파악을 위해 물은 질문(where he was)에만 눈 가리기 증상을 보였다는 부분이 정답 location의 힌트임.

[문제 풀이]

11. 방화 사건 수사에서 보안 요원은 불이 나던 당시에 어디 있었는지를 질문 받았을 때에만 eye-blocking 행위를 보였는데, 이를 통해 수사관은 사건의 쟁점이 방화 당시 그의 위치라는 점을 파악하고 그가 여자 친구를 만나러 자리를 비운 사이에 사건이 일어났음을 알게 되었다. 따라서 글의 제목으로 가장 적절한 것은 ③ 'Eye-blocking Reveals Hidden Information(Eye-blocking은 숨겨진 정보를 드러낸다)'이다.
12. 빈칸 앞의 두 문장에서 보안 요원은 직접 불을 질렀는지를 질문 받았을 때에는 별다른 반응이 없었으나, 불이 나던 당시에 '어디에' 있었는가에 관한 질문을 받았을 때는 eye-blocking 행위를 보였다고 말하므로, 빈칸에 들어갈 말로 가장 적절한 것은 ③ 'location(위치)'이다.

[중요 어휘]

☐ **nonverbal**	형용사 비언어적인
☐ **squint**	동사 눈을 가늘게 뜨다, 눈을 찡그리다
☐ **shield**	동사 가리다, 보호하다 / 명사 방패
☐ **evolve**	동사 진화하다, 발전하다

3회 20분 미니모의고사

문제편 p.304

☐ **undesirable**	형용사 원하지 않는, 달갑지 않은
☐ **assist in**	~을 돕다
☐ **arson**	명사 방화(죄)
☐ **suspicion**	명사 용의, 혐의, 의혹
☐ **blaze**	명사 (대형) 화재, 불길
☐ **break out**	(전쟁 등 안 좋은 일이) 발생하다, 일어나다
☐ **assign**	동사 배정하다, 할당하다
☐ **determine**	동사 밝히다, 알아내다
☐ **as to**	~에 관해, ~에 대해서
☐ **observe**	동사 관찰하다, 주시하다
☐ **telltale**	형용사 숨길 수 없는
☐ **block**	동사 (시야 등을) 가리다
☐ **oddly**	부사 희한하게도, 이상하게도
☐ **troubled**	형용사 불안해하는, 걱정하는
☐ **eventually**	부사 마침내, 결국
☐ **post**	명사 자리, 위치
☐ **arsonist**	명사 방화범
☐ **insight**	명사 통찰(력), 이해
☐ **pursue**	동사 계속하다, 추구하다

힌트 post는 군인이나 보안직을 대상으로 쓰일 경우 '(근무하는) 자리, 위치, 구역', '(근무지에) 배치하다[파견하다]'의 의미로 쓰임.

최신 5개년 수능 기출 핵심 구문 60

최신 5개년 수능 기출 문제에서 영어 독해 문제를 푸는 데 도움이 되는 문장을 선별하였습니다.
핵심 구문을 익혀 빠른 독해 능력을 키워 보세요!

www.toptutor.co.kr

1. 문장의 형식

1-1) 1형식: 주어(S) + 동사(V)

전치사구, 부사 등이 뒤따르는 1형식 동사: be(~에 있다), live(살다), lie(~에 있다, 놓여 있다), stand(서 있다, ~에 존재하다), stay(~에 있다, 머무르다) 등

① Technology changes constantly. (2023학년도 수능 30번)
S V
기술은 끊임없이 변화한다.

② Many examples (of such "green taxes") exist. (2022학년도 수능 36번)
S 전치사구 V
그러한 '환경세'의 많은 예가 존재한다.

③ At last, my mind was (at peace). (2021학년도 수능 19번)
S V 전치사구
마침내, 내 마음은 평화로워졌다.

④ Yet she responded (to the hardship) (in a constructive way). (2024학년도 수능 43~45번)
S V 전치사구 전치사구
하지만 그녀는 그 고난에 건설적인 방식으로 대응했다.

1-2) 2형식: 주어(S) + 동사(V) + 주격보어(S·C)

대표적인 2형식 동사: 상태(be, remain, keep, lie, stand, stay), 상태변화(become, get, go, turn, grow, run), 인식(look, seem, appear), 감각(sound, smell, taste, feel)

① My name is Michael Brown. (상태) (2023학년도 수능 18번)
S V S·C (명사)
제 이름은 Michael Brown입니다.

② My face became reddish. (상태변화) (2021학년도 수능 19번)
S V S·C(형용사)
내 얼굴은 불그스름해졌다.

③ She seemed to be expecting someone. (인식) (2022학년도 수능 43~45번)
S V S·C(to부정사)
그녀는 누군가를 기다리고 있는 것처럼 보였다.

④ She felt ashamed (to be looking at them). (감각) (2020학년도 수능 43~45번)
S V S·C to부정사구-부사적 용법
그녀는 그들을 보고서 부끄러워졌다.

⑤ While a compliment to the person standing next to you is typically answered with a response like "Thank You," the sad fact is [that most brand compliments go unanswered]. [ ]: S·C(명사절) (상태 변화)(2024학년도 수능 22번)
S V S' V' S·C
여러분 옆에 서 있는 사람에 대한 칭찬은 보통 '감사합니다'와 같은 응답을 받지만, 슬픈 사실은 대부분의 브랜드 칭찬은 답을 받지 못한다는 것이다.

1-3) 3형식: 주어(S) + 동사(V) + 목적어(O)

① He researched a variety of subjects, (including mass media and law). (2023학년도 수능 26번)
S V O 전치사구
그는 대중 매체와 법을 포함한 다양한 주제를 연구했다.

② Values (alone) do not create and build culture. (2024학년도 수능 20번)
S 부사 V① 병렬 V② O
가치만으로는 문화가 창조되고 구축되지 않는다.

③ I hope to hear (from you) (soon). (2020학년도 수능 18번)
S V O(to부정사-명사적 용법) 전치사구 부사
저는 귀하로부터 조만간 (답변을) 듣기를 바랍니다.

④ She began (eagerly) searching (for them). (2022학년도 수능 19번)
S V 부사 O(동명사) 전치사구
그녀는 그것들을 간절히 찾기 시작했다.

1-4) 4형식: 주어(S) + 동사(V) + 간접목적어(I·O) + 직접목적어(D·O)

대표적인 4형식 동사: give, lend, pay, send, tell, show, teach, sell, write / buy, cook, get, make, find / ask

① Anna bought Cora a taekwondo uniform. (2022학년도 수능 43~45번)
S V I·O D·O
Anna는 Cora에게 태권도 도복을 사 주었다.

② (Finally), the doctor gave me the okay (to practice)." (2022학년도 수능 43~45번)
부사 S V I·O D·O to부정사-부사적 용법
마침내 의사 선생님이 연습해도 괜찮다고 허락하셨다.

③ Imagine [I tell you that Maddy is bad]. (2021학년도 수능 38번)
S' V' I·O' D·O'(that절) [ ]: Imagine의 목적어절
내가 여러분에게 Maddy가 나쁘다고 말한다고 생각해 보라.

1-5) 5형식: 주어(S) + 동사(V) + 목적어(O) + 목적격 보어(O·C)

목적격 보어의 종류: 명사/형용사(keep, find, call, make, turn), to부정사(want, tell, ask, get, allow, advise, encourage 등), 동사원형(사역동사-let, make, have), 동사원형/현재분사(지각동사-see, watch, hear, feel)

① Diaries were personal and private; one would write for oneself, or, in Habermas's formulation, one would make oneself public to oneself. (2023학년도 수능 21번)
S V O O·C(형용사)
일기는 개인적이고 사적인 것이었다. 사람들은 자신을 위해 쓰곤 했는데, Habermas의 명확한 표현을 빌리면, 자신을 자신에게 공개적으로 만들곤 했다.

② His father encouraged him to study painting. (2022학년도 수능 26번)
S V O O·C(to부정사)
그의 아버지는 그가 그림 그리기를 공부하도록 격려했다.

③ Making a good decision helps you speak faster because it provides you with more time to come up with your responses. (2024학년도 수능 35번)
S(동명사) V O O·C(동사원형)
좋은 결정을 내리면 응답을 생각해 낼 시간이 더 많아지기 때문에, 여러분은 더 빨리 말할 수 있다.

④ Then tell him [to keep his eyes closed and move his fingers over the object]. [ ]: tell의 직접목적어 (2021학년도 수능 24번)
V O O·C(과거분사)
그런 다음 그에게 그의 눈을 계속 감은 채 그 물건 위로 그의 손가락을 움직여 보라고 말하라.

⑤ (Beneath them in the water), they saw salmon slowly moving their bodies. (2020학년도 수능 43~45번)
전치사구 S V O O·C(현재분사)
그들 아래 물속에서, 그들은 천천히 몸을 움직이고 있는 연어들을 보았다.

2. 동사

2-1) 시제 – 진행

① Thus cutting down the trees is economically inefficient, and markets are not sending the correct "signal" to favor ecosystem services over extractive uses.
현재 진행형 (2024학년도 수능 23번)
따라서 나무를 베는 것은 경제적으로 비효율적인데, 시장은 채취하는 사용보다 생태계 도움을 선호하게 하는 올바른 '신호'를 **보내지 않고 있다**.

② Now, the sun was beginning to set, and her goal was still far beyond her reach. 과거 진행형 (2022학년도 수능 19번)
이제 해가 지기 **시작하고 있었고**, 그녀의 목표는 여전히 멀리 그녀의 손이 닿지 않는 곳에 있었다.

③ In learning the principles of classification, therefore, we'll be learning about the structure that lies at the core of our language. 미래 진행형 (2022학년도 수능 41~42번)
그러므로 분류의 원리를 배울 때, 우리는 언어의 핵심에 있는 구조에 대해 **배우고 있는 것이다**.

2-2) 시제 – 완료

① I have been a bird-watcher since childhood.
저는 어렸을 때부터 조류 관찰자**였습니다**. 현재완료 (2023학년도 수능 18번)

② Actually Camila, I recently found out he has long been suffering from color blindness.
현재완료 진행 (2023학년도 수능 43~45번)
사실은 Camila, 난 아빠가 오랫동안 색맹을 **앓고 있다는** 것을 최근에 알게 되었어.

③ When I learned that Linda had won, I was deeply troubled and unhappy. 과거완료 (2021학년도 수능 19번)
Linda가 **우승했다는 것을 알게 되었을** 때, 나는 매우 괴롭고 우울했다.

2-3) 수동태

① However, the expression of an idea is protected by copyright, and people who infringe on that copyright can be taken to court and prosecuted.
수동태 현재형 + 조동사 수동태 (2021학년도 수능 39번)
그러나 한 아이디어의 표현은 저작권**에 의해 보호되며**, 그 저작권을 침해하는 사람들은 법정에 **소환되어 기소될** 수 있다.

② In the 1970s, the few scientists who spoke frequently with the media were often criticized by their fellow scientists for having done so.
수동태 과거형 (2024학년도 수능 41~42번)
1970년대에는, 언론과 자주 대화하는 소수의 과학자들은 흔히 그렇게 한 것에 대해 동료 과학자들로부터 **비난을 받았다**.

2-4) 수동태 – 진행형

① Introduction of robots into factories, while employment of human workers is being reduced, creates worry and fear. 수동태 현재 진행형 (2022학년도 수능 38번)
공장에 로봇을 도입하는 것은, 인간 노동자의 고용이 **줄어들면서** 걱정과 두려움을 불러일으킨다.

2-5) 수동태 – 완료형

① Still, it is arguable that advertisers worry rather too much about this problem, as advertising in other media has always been fragmented.
수동태 현재완료 (2020학년도 수능 39번)
그렇다고 하더라도, 다른 미디어를 이용한 광고들은 늘 **단편적이었**으므로, 광고주들이 이 문제에 대해 오히려 너무 많이 걱정하는 것일 수 있다고 주장할 여지가 있다.

② Nina had been heartbroken after losing her championship belt. 수동태 과거완료 (2020학년도 수능 43~45번)
Nina는 챔피언 벨트를 잃은 뒤 **상심해 있었다**.

3. 조동사

3-1) 조동사 can

① "Dad, these glasses can help correct your red-green color blindness," said Hailey. (2023학년도 수능 43~45번)
"아빠, 이 안경은 적록색맹을 교정하는 데 도움이 될 **수 있어요**."라고 Hailey가 말했다.

② Payment can be made only by credit card.
조동사 + 수동태 (2021학년도 수능 27번)
요금 지불은 신용카드로만 **할 수 있습니다**.

3-2) 조동사 must

① Bookings must be completed no later than 2 days before the day of the tour. 조동사 + 수동태 (2024학년도 수능 27번)
예약은 늦어도 투어 당일 이틀 전에 **완료되어야 합**니다.

② As cuneiform script became more abstract, literacy must have become increasingly important to ensure one understood what he or she had agreed to.
조동사 + have p.p. (2021학년도 수능 31번)
쐐기 문자가 더욱 추상적으로 되면서, 읽고 쓰는 능력이 자신이 합의했던 것을 이해하고 있다는 것을 확실히 하기 위해 점점 더 중요**해졌음이 틀림없다**.

3-3) 조동사 should, ought to

① Participants should use the theme of "Recycling for the Future." (2023학년도 수능 28번)
참가자들은 '미래를 위한 재활용'이라는 주제를 사용**해야 합니다**.

② Submissions should be uploaded to our school website.
조동사 + 수동태 (2024학년도 수능 28번)
출품작은 우리 학교 웹사이트에 **업로드해야 합니다**.

③ For that reason, the people who monitor and control the behavior of users should also be users and/or have been given a mandate by all users.
조동사 + have p.p. (2022학년도 수능 33번)
그러한 이유로 이용자의 행동을 감시하고 통제하는 사람 또한 이용자이고/이용자이거나 모든 이용자에 의한 위임을 **받았어야 한다**.

④ As long as the user's focus is on the technology itself rather than its use in promoting learning, instruction, or performance, then one ought not to conclude that the technology has been successfully integrated — at least for that user. (2021학년도 수능 34번)
학습, 교육 또는 수행을 촉진하는 데 있어서 사용자의 초점이 기술의 사용이 아니라 기술 그 자체에 맞춰져 있는 한, 적어도 그 사용자에게는 그 기술이 성공적으로 통합되었다는 결론을 **내려서는** 안 **된다**.

3-4) 조동사 may

① Guests may use the tennis courts for free.
투숙객들은 테니스장을 무료로 이용**할 수 있습니다**. (2023학년도 수능 27번)

② Furthermore, the evaluation of past discoveries and discoverers according to present-day standards does not allow us to see how significant they may have been in their own day. 조동사 + have p.p. (2020학년도 수능 37번)
게다가, 현재의 기준에 따라 과거의 발견과 발견자들을 평가하는 것은 그것이 당시에 얼마나 중요**했을지**를 우리가 알 수 없게 한다.

3-5) 조동사 would

① These critics would listen to them well before the general public could and preview them for the rest of the world in their reviews.
과거의 불규칙적 습관·취미 (2021학년도 수능 22번)
이런 비평가들은 일반 대중들이 들을 수 있기 훨씬 전에 그것을 듣고 나머지 세상 사람들을 위해 자신의 비평에서 시사평을 쓰**곤 했다**.

3-6) 조동사 need

① Scientists need only understand *how* to use these various elements in ways that others would accept.

(2022학년도 수능 23번)

과학자들은 다른 사람들이 받아들일 방식으로 이러한 다양한 요소들을 사용하는 '방법'을 이해하기만 **하면 된다**.

4. 명사, 대명사

4-1) 명사

① An important advantage of disclosure, as opposed to more aggressive forms of regulation, is its flexibility and respect for the operation of free markets.

(2023학년도 수능 23번)

공개의 중요한 이점은 더 공세적인 형태의 규제와는 반대로 자유 시장의 작용에 대한 유연성과 존중**이다**.

② Indeed, what distinguishes a park from the broader category of public space is the representation of nature that parks are meant to embody. (2023학년도 수능 38번)

실제로 공원을 더 넓은 범주의 공공 공간과 구별하는 **것은** 공원이 구현하려는 자연의 표현**이다**.

③ Your ability to make complex use of touch, such as buttoning your shirt or unlocking your front door in the dark, depends on continuous time-varying patterns of touch sensation. (2021학년도 수능 24번)

어둠 속에서 셔츠 단추를 잠그거나 현관문을 여는 것과 같이 촉각을 복잡하게 사용하는 **능력은** 촉각이라는 감각의, 지속적인, 시간에 따라 달라지는 패턴에 **의존한다**.

④ For instance, at the aggregate level, improving the level of national energy efficiency has positive effects on macroeconomic issues such as energy dependence, climate change, health, national competitiveness and reducing fuel poverty. (2021학년도 수능 37번)

예를 들어 총체적[집합적] 차원에서, 국가의 에너지 효율 수준을 **높이는 것은** 에너지 의존도, 기후 변화, 보건, 국가 경쟁력, 연료 빈곤을 감소시키는 것과 같은 거시 경제적 문제에 긍정적인 영향을 **미친다**.

⑤ Yes, some contests are seen as world class, such as identification of the Higgs particle or the development of high temperature superconductors. (2024학년도 수능 38번)

물론, 힉스 입자의 확인 또는 고온 초전도체 개발과 같은 **몇몇 대회는** 세계적인 수준으로 **여겨진다**.

⑥ The breathtaking scene that surrounded them was beyond description. (2024학년도 수능 43~45번)

그들을 둘러싸고 있는 **숨 막히는 풍경은** 말로 표현할 수 없을 정도**였다**.

4-2) 대명사

① In the 18-34 year-olds group, the percentage of those who preferred Big/Small City was higher than that of those who preferred Suburb of Big/Small City.

(2023학년도 수능 25번)

18~34세 그룹에서는 대도시/소도시를 선호하는 비율이 대도시/소도시 근교를 선호하는 비율보다 더 높았다.

② In other words, they not only have an innate capacity for matching their own kinaesthetically experienced bodily movements with those of others that are visually perceived; they have an innate drive to do so.

(2024학년도 수능 29번)

다시 말해, 그들은 운동감각적으로 경험한 그들 자신의 신체적 움직임과 시각적으로 지각되는 다른 사람의 **신체적 움직임**을 일치시키는 타고난 능력을 가지고 있을 뿐만 아니라, 그렇게 하려는 타고난 욕구도 가지고 있다.

③ In some cases, the habitat that provides the best opportunity for survival may not be the same habitat as the one that provides for highest reproductive capacity because of requirements specific to the reproductive period. one (=habitat) (2020학년도 수능 38번)

일부의 경우, 번식기에만 특별히 요구되는 조건들 때문에, 생존을 위한 최고의 기회를 제공하는 서식지가 최고의 번식 능력을 가능하게 해주는 **서식지와** 동일한 곳이 아닐 수도 있다.

4-3) 재귀대명사

① Everyone who drives, walks, or swipes a transit card in a city views herself as a transportation expert from the moment she walks out the front door.

재귀 용법 (2024학년도 수능 34번)

도시에서 운전하거나 걷거나 교통 카드를 판독기에 통과시키는 모든 사람은 현관문을 나서는 순간부터 **자신을** 교통 전문가로 여긴다.

② Cinema is valuable not for its ability to make visible the hidden outlines of our reality, but for its ability to reveal what reality itself veils — the dimension of fantasy.

강조 (2022학년도 수능 39번)

영화는 우리 현실의 숨겨진 윤곽을 보이게 만드는 능력 때문이 아니라 현실 **자체가** 가리고 있는 것, 즉 환상의 차원을 드러내는 능력 때문에 가치가 있다.

③ In all these domains, craftsmanship focuses on objective standards, on the thing in itself.

관용적 표현 (2023학년도 수능 40번)

이 모든 영역에서 장인정신은 객관적인 기준, 즉 **그 자체의** 것에 초점을 맞춘다.

④ You can carry out an experiment to see for yourself.

직접 알아보기 위해 실험을 할 수 있다. 관용적 표현 (2021학년도 수능 24번)

5. 분사

5-1) 현재분사

① At every step in our journey through life we encounter junctions with many different pathways leading into the distance. (2023학년도 수능 20번)

평생을 두고 우리 여정의 모든 단계에서 우리는 먼 곳으로 **이어지는** 많은 다른 길들이 있는 분기점을 만난다.

② As a child learning to speak, you had to work hard to learn the system of classification your parents were trying to teach you. (2022학년도 수능 41~42번)

말하기를 **배우는** 아이로서, 여러분은 부모님이 가르쳐주려 애썼던 분류 체계를 익히기 위해 열심히 노력해야 했다.

③ Thus the individual water forager's response to unloading time (up or down) regulates water collection in response to the colony's need.

한정적 용법; 전치수식 (2023학년도 수능 33번)

따라서 (시간이 늘어나든 혹은 줄어들든 간에) 물을 **넘겨주는** 시간에 대한 개별적인 물 조달자의 반응은 군집의 수요에 맞춰서 물 수집(량)을 조절한다.

④ Each actor belonging to a specific economic class understands what the other sees as a necessity and a luxury. 한정적 용법; 후치수식 (2024학년도 수능 30번)

특정 경제 계층에 **속하는** 각 행위자는 상대방이 무엇을 필수품으로 여기고 무엇을 사치품으로 여기는지를 이해한다.

⑤ "Hailey, be careful!" Camila yelled uneasily, watching her sister carrying a huge cake to the table.

서술적 용법; 지각동사의 목적격 보어 역할 (2023학년도 수능 43~45번)

"Hailey, 조심해!" Camila는 동생이 테이블로 커다란 케이크를 **들고 오는** 것을 보며 걱정되어 소리쳤다.

⑥ Watching Clara riding beside her, Emma thought about Clara's past tragedy, which she now seemed to have overcome.

서술적 용법; 지각동사의 목적격 보어 역할 (2024학년도 수능 43~45번)

자기 옆에서 자전거를 **타고 있는** Clara를 지켜보며, Emma는 지금은 그녀가 극복한 것처럼 보이는, Clara의 과거 비극에 대해 생각했다.

5-2) 과거분사

① Parks take the shape demanded by the cultural concerns of their time. (2023학년도 수능 38번)
공원은 그것이 속한 시대의 문화적 관심사가 **요구하는** 형태를 취한다.

② The above graph shows the percentages of Americans' preferred type of place to live by age group, based on a 2020 survey. 한정적 용법; 전치수식 (2023학년도 수능 25번)
위의 그래프는 2020년 조사를 기반으로 연령대별로 미국인이 **선호하는** 거주지 유형의 비율을 보여준다.

③ Since you are an expert in online education, I would like to ask you to deliver a special lecture at the workshop scheduled for next month.
한정적 용법; 후치수식 (2022학년도 수능 18번)
귀하가 온라인 교육의 전문가이기에, 저는 다음 달에 **계획된** 워크숍에 귀하가 특별 강연을 해주시기를 부탁드리고자 합니다.

④ When your attentional spotlight is widened, you can more easily let go of stress.
서술적 용법; 주격 보어 (2024학년도 수능 21번)
여러분의 주의의 초점이 **넓어지면**, 여러분은 스트레스를 더 쉽게 해소할 수 있다.

5-3) 분사구문

① Putting all of her energy into her last steps of the running race, Jamie crossed the finish line.
동시동작 (2023학년도 수능 19번)
Jamie는 자신의 모든 에너지를 달리기 경주의 마지막 스텝에 **쏟으면서** 결승선을 통과했다.

② Fashion can also strengthen agency in various ways, opening up space for action. 연속동작 (2023학년도 수능 29번)
패션은 또한 행동을 위한 공간을 **열어주며** 다양한 방법으로 행동력을 강화할 수 있다.

③ Trusting our intuition to make the choice often ends up with us making a suboptimal choice.
with+명사+분사 (2023학년도 수능 20번)
선택을 하기 위해 우리의 직관을 믿는 것은 흔히 우리가 차선의 선택을 **하는** 것으로 결국 끝난다.

④ "Definitely! I can't wait to ride while watching those beautiful waves!" 부사절 축약 (2024학년도 수능 43~45번)
"물론이지! 나는 저 아름다운 파도를 **보면서** 어서 자전거를 타고 싶어!"

⑤ After being chosen, record a video showing you are using a tumbler. 부사절 축약 (2022학년도 수능 27번)
선택**된 후에**, 여러분이 텀블러를 사용하고 있는 동영상을 녹화하십시오.

⑥ Looking at the slowly darkening ground before her, she sighed to herself, "I can't believe I came all this way for nothing." 주절과 종속절의 주어가 같은 경우 (2022학년도 수능 19번)
천천히 어두워지는 그녀 앞의 지면을 **바라보면서** 그녀는 혼자 한숨을 쉬며 말했다. "이렇게 먼 길을 와서 아무것도 얻지 못하다니 믿을 수가 없어."

⑦ Another jumped, its body spinning until it made it over the falls. 주절과 종속절의 주어가 다른 경우 (2020학년도 수능 43~45번)
또 다른 한 마리가 뛰어올랐고, 몸이 **빙글빙글 돌더니** 마침내 폭포를 넘어가는 데 성공했다.

6. 준동사

6-1) to부정사 - 명사적 용법

① But to ask for any change in human behaviour — whether it be to cut down on consumption, alter lifestyles or decrease population growth — is seen as a violation of human rights. 주어 (2021학년도 수능 21번)
그러나 소비를 줄이는 것이든, 생활 방식을 바꾸는 것이든, 인구 증가를 줄이는 것이든, 인간의 행동에 어떤 변화든 **요구하는 것은** 인권 침해로 여겨진다.

② They need to know a little about shape, but not in great detail. 목적어 (2023학년도 수능 24번)
그것들은 모양에 대해 약간 **알아야** 하지만, 매우 자세히는 아니다.

③ In general, people post because they have something to say — and because they want to be recognized for having said it. 목적어(수동태) (2024학년도 수능 22번)
일반적으로, 사람들은 할 말이 있기 때문에, 그리고 그것을 말한 것에 대해 **인정받기를** 원하기 때문에 글을 올린다.

④ Another approach is to vary the number of ways that the principle may be applied. 보어 (2023학년도 수능 39번)
또 다른 접근법은 원칙이 적용될 수 있는 방법의 수를 **다양화하는 것**이다.

⑤ And the way to win is to figure out who you are and do your best. 보어(to 생략) (2021학년도 수능 19번)
그리고 이기는 방법은 자신이 누군가를 **알아내고** 자신의 최선을 **다하는 것**이다.

6-2) to부정사 - 형용사적 용법

① The latter have the potential to become a preferred 'last-mile' vehicle, particularly in high-density and congested areas. (2023학년도 수능 22번)
후자(자전거)는 특히 밀도가 높고 혼잡한 지역에서 선호되는 '최종 단계' 운송 수단이 **될** 잠재력이 있다.

② She pointed out, for instance, that the actors affected by the rules for the use and care of resources must have the right to participate in decisions to change the rules. (2022학년도 수능 33번)
예를 들어, 그녀는 자원의 이용 및 관리 규칙의 영향을 받는 행위자에게 규칙을 **변경하는** 결정에 **참여할** 권리가 있어야 한다고 지적했다.

③ Negotiation can be defined as an attempt to explore and (to) reconcile conflicting positions in order to reach an acceptable outcome. (2024학년도 수능 36번)
협상은 수용할 수 있는 결과에 도달하기 위해 상충하는 입장을 **탐색하고 화해시키려는** 시도라고 정의될 수 있다.

6-3) to부정사 - 부사적 용법

① We will take all possible measures to minimize noise and any other inconvenience. 목적 (2023학년도 수능 27번)
저희는 소음과 다른 불편함을 **최소화하기 위해** 가능한 모든 조치를 취할 것입니다.

② It was their dad and they were overjoyed to see him.
감정의 원인 (2023학년도 수능 43~45번)
그들의 아빠가 왔고 그들은 그를 **보고** 매우 기뻐했다.

③ The expertise that we work hard to acquire in one domain will carry over only imperfectly to related ones, and not at all to unrelated ones. 결과 (2021학년도 수능 20번)
우리가 한 영역에서 열심히 노력해서 **얻는** 전문성은 관련 영역으로 오직 불완전하게 이어질 뿐이며, 관련이 없는 영역으로는 전혀 이어지지 않을 것이다.

④ Issues that can be expressed in quantitative, measurable units are easy to slice.
형용사 수식 (2023학년도 수능 39번)
정량적이고 측정 가능한 단위로 표현될 수 있는 문제는 **나누기** 쉽다.

6-4) 다양한 to부정사의 활용

① I would like to know how to sign up for the club.
클럽에 **가입하는 법**을 알고 싶습니다. 의문사 + to부정사 (2023학년도 수능 18번)

② In order to allow these different units to cooperate successfully, the existence of a common platform is crucial. in order to V (2022학년도 수능 35번)
이 서로 다른 부문들이 성공적으로 협력할 수 있도록 **하기 위해서는** 공동 플랫폼의 존재가 매우 중요하다.

③ Although we'd like to think that our minds are sharp enough to always make good decisions with the greatest efficiency, they just aren't.
enough to V (2024학년도 수능 35번)

우리는 우리의 정신이 항상 최고의 효율로 좋은 결정을 **내릴 수 있을 정도로** 예리하다고 생각하고 싶겠지만, 그것은 정말 그렇지 않다.

6-5) 동명사

① **Studying** interactions on the dancefloor provides us with a number of illustrative examples of how individuals changing their own behavior in response to local information allow the colony to regulate its workforce. 명사적 용법; 주어 (2023학년도 수능 33번)

댄스 플로어에서의 상호 작용을 **연구하는 것은** 우리에게 지엽적인 정보에 반응하여 그것들 자신의 행동을 바꾸는 개체들이 어떻게 군집이 그것의 노동력을 조절할 수 있게 하는지에 대한 많은 예증이 되는 예들을 제공한다.

② **Developing** expertise carries costs of its own.

명사적 용법; 주어 (2021학년도 수능 20번)

전문성을 **개발하는 데는** 그 자체의 비용이 수반된다.

③ One way to avoid **contributing** to overhyping a story would be to say nothing.

명사적 용법; 목적어 (2024학년도 수능 41~42번)

이야기를 과대광고하는 것에 대한 **기여를** 피하는 한 가지 방법은 아무 말도 하지 않는 것이다.

④ Indeed, someone listening to a funny story who tries to correct the teller — 'No, he didn't spill the spaghetti on the keyboard and the monitor, just on the keyboard' — will probably be told by the other listeners to **stop interrupting**. 명사적 용법; 목적어 (2022학년도 수능 31번)

실제로, 재미있는 이야기를 듣고 있는 누군가가 '아니야, 그는 스파게티를 키보드와 모니터에 쏟은 것이 아니라 키보드에만 쏟았어.'라며 말하는 사람을 바로잡으려고 하면 그는 아마 듣고 있는 다른 사람들에게서 **방해하지 말라는** 말을 들을 것이다.

6-6) 전치사 + 동명사

① For example, **upon returning** to their hive honeybees that have collected water search out a receiver bee to unload their water to within the hive. (2023학년도 수능 33번)

예를 들어, 물을 가져온 꿀벌들은 자신들의 벌집으로 **돌아오자마자** 자신들의 물을 벌집 안으로 넘겨주기 위해 물을 받을 벌을 찾는다.

② Thus, she may prescribe the behavior to them **by uttering** the norm statement in a prescriptive manner.

(2024학년도 수능 37번)

따라서 그 사람은 지시하는 방식으로 규범 진술을 **말함으로써** 그들에게 행동을 지시할 수도 있다.

③ However, the calculation of such cost effectiveness is not easy: it is not simply a case **of looking** at private costs and **comparing** them to the reductions achieved.

(2021학년도 수능 37번)

그러나 그러한 비용 효율성의 산정은 쉽지 않은데, 그것은 단순히 사적비용을 **살펴보고** 그것을 달성한 절감액과 **비교하는** 경우가 아니기 때문이다.

④ Norms emerge in groups as a result **of** people **conforming** to the behavior of others. (2024학년도 수능 37번)

규범은 사람들이 다른 사람들의 행동에 **순응하는** 결과로 집단에서 생겨난다.

6-7) to부정사와 동명사를 모두 목적어로 취하는 동사

Negotiators should **try to find** ways to slice a large issue into smaller pieces, known as using *salami tactics*.

(2023학년도 수능 39번)

협상가들은 '살라미 전술'을 사용하는 것으로 알려진, 큰 문제를 더 작은 조각으로 나누는 방법을 **찾으려고 노력해야** 한다.

7. 관계사

7-1) 관계대명사 - 주격 관계대명사

① I was surprised and excited to find out about a community of passionate bird-watchers **who** travel annually to go birding. (2023학년도 수능 18번)

저는 조류 관찰을 하러 매년 여행**하는** 열정적인 조류 관찰자들의 공동체에 대해 알게 되어 놀랐고 신이 났습니다.

② Only that **which** survived in some form in the present was considered relevant. (2020학년도 수능 37번)

현재에 어떤 형태로 살아남은 것만이 유의미한 것으로 여겨졌다.

③ The very features **that** create expertise in a specialized domain lead to ignorance in many others.

(2022학년도 수능 21번)

전문화된 영역에서의 전문 지식을 만들어내**는** 바로 그 특징이 많은 다른 영역에서의 무지로 이어진다.

④ Parks take the shape **(which is)** demanded by the cultural concerns of their time.

주격 관계대명사 + be동사 생략 (2023학년도 수능 38번)

공원은 그것이 속한 시대의 문화적 관심사가 요구하**는** 형태를 취한다.

⑤ Just like a sports team has a playbook with specific plays **(which are) designed** to help them perform well and win, your company should have a playbook with the key shifts **(which are) needed** to transform your culture into action and turn your values into winning behaviors. 주격 관계대명사 + be동사 생략 (2024학년도 수능 20번)

스포츠 팀이 좋은 성과를 내고 승리하는 데 도움이 되도록 **고안된** 특정 플레이를 담고 있는 플레이 북을 갖고 있는 것과 마찬가지로, 여러분의 회사는 여러분의 문화를 행동으로 바꾸고 여러분의 가치를 승리하는 행동으로 바꾸는 데 **필요한** 핵심적인 변화를 담은 플레이 북을 갖고 있어야 한다.

7-2) 관계대명사 - 목적격 관계대명사

① For example, energy efficiency requirements for appliances may produce goods **that** work less well or that have characteristics that consumers do not want.

(2023학년도 수능 23번)

예를 들어, 가전제품에 대한 에너지 효율 요건은 덜 잘 작동하거나 소비자가 원하지 않**는** 특성을 가진 제품을 만들어 낼 수도 있다.

② In Delhi's bazaars, buyers and sellers can assess to a large extent the financial constraints that other actors have in their everyday life. (2024학년도 수능 30번)

델리의 상점가에서, 구매자와 판매자는 대체로 다른 행위자들이 그들의 일상생활에서 가지**는** 재정적인 제약을 평가할 수 있다.

③ However, the world **the reader encounters in literature** is already processed and filtered by another consciousness. 관계대명사 생략 (2022학년도 수능 37번)

그러나 **문학에서 독자가 접하는** 세계는 이미 또 다른 의식에 의해 처리되고 여과되어 있다.

④ We expect people to monitor machines, which means keeping alert for long periods, something **we are bad at**. 관계대명사 생략 (2021학년도 수능 23번)

우리는 사람들이 기계를 감시하기를 기대하는데, 이는 오랫동안 경계를 게을리하지 않는 것을 의미하며, 그것은 **우리가 잘하지 못하는** 어떤 것이다.

7-3) 선행사를 포함한 관계대명사 what

① That's exactly **what** will happen with information technology and its devices under human-centric computing. (2023학년도 수능 30번)

그것이 바로 정보 기술과 그 장치들이 인간 중심의 컴퓨터 사용 하에 일어날 **일**이다.

② The task of finding **what** you want would be time-consuming and extremely difficult, if not impossible.

(2022학년도 수능 41~42번)

여러분이 원하는 **것을** 찾는 일은, 불가능하지는 않더라도, 시간이 많이 걸리고 매우 어려울 것이다.

7-4) 계속적 용법

① It spreads outward, in a manner not unlike transmissible disease, **which** itself typically "takes off"

in cities. (2023학년도 수능 32번)
그것은 전염성 질병과 다르지 않은 방식으로 외부로 퍼져나가는데, **그 전염성 질병** 자체도 보통 도시에서 '이륙한다.'

② Cora was a new member, whom Anna had personally invited to join the club. (2022학년도 수능 43~45번)
Cora는 신입 회원인데, **그녀에게** Anna가 동아리에 가입하라고 직접 청했었다.

③ The Nuer are a cattle-raising people, whose everyday lives revolve around their cattle. (2020학년도 수능 26번)
Nuer족은 소를 기르는 민족으로, **그들의** 일상생활은 자신들의 소를 중심으로 돌아간다.

④ There's a direct analogy between the fovea at the center of your retina and your fingertips, both of which have high acuity. , N of which (2021학년도 수능 24번)
망막의 중심에 있는 중심와(窩)와 손가락 끝 사이에 직접적인 유사함이 있는데, **그것 둘 다** 예민함이 높다는 것이다.

⑤ Although commonsense knowledge may have merit, it also has weaknesses, not the least of which is that it often contradicts itself. , N of which (2020학년도 수능 35번)
상식적인 지식에 장점이 있을 수 있지만, 그것에는 약점도 있는데, **그중에서 중요한 것은** 그것이 모순되는 경우가 많다는 것이다.

⑥ And the species has evolved elaborate greeting behaviors, the form of which reflects the strength of the social bond between the individuals.
, N of which (2020학년도 수능 40번)
그래서 이 종은 정교한 인사 행동을 진화시켜 왔는데, **그 형태는** 개체들 사이의 사회적 유대감의 강도를 반영한다.

⑦ Some discoveries seem to entail numerous phases and discoverers, none of which can be identified as definitive. 부정대명사 of which (2020학년도 수능 37번)
몇몇 발견은 무수한 단계와 발견자들을 수반하는 것처럼 보이는데, **그중에서 어느 것도** 확정적인 것으로 확인될 수 없다.

7-5) 관계부사 where/when/how/why

① Emma and Clara jumped on their bikes and started to pedal toward the white cliff where the beach road ended. 관계부사 where (2024학년도 수능 43~45번)
Emma와 Clara는 자전거에 올라타서 해변 도로가 끝나는 하얀 절벽을 향해 페달을 밟기 시작했다.

② There are times when being able to project your voice loudly will be very useful when working in school, and knowing that you can cut through a noisy classroom, dinner hall or playground is a great skill to have.
관계부사 when (2023학년도 수능 35번)
목소리를 크게 내보낼 수 있는 것이 학교에서 일할 때 매우 유용**할** 경우가 있으며, 여러분이 시끄러운 교실, 구내식당이나 운동장을 (목소리로) 가를 수 있다는 것을 아는 것은 갖춰야 할 훌륭한 기술이다.

③ This is how you participate. 관계부사 how (2021학년도 수능 18번)
다음이 참가 **방법**입니다.

④ Since their introduction, information systems have substantially changed the way business is conducted.
관계부사 how 생략 (2022학년도 수능 35번)
정보 시스템은 도입 이래로 사업 수행 **방식**을 상당히 변화시켜왔다.

⑤ That's why we find so many well-intentioned and civic-minded citizens arguing past one another.
관계부사 why (2024학년도 수능 34번)
그런 **이유**로 우리는 선의의 시민 의식을 가진 매우 많은 사람이 서로를 지나치며 언쟁하는 것을 보게 된다.

7-6) 전치사 + 관계대명사

① This gives you a much better map of the future on which to base your decisions about which path to choose. (2023학년도 수능 20번)
이것은 여러분이 어떤 길을 선택할 것인지에 관한 결정을 내릴 때 그 근거로 삼을 수 있는 미래에 대한 훨씬 더 좋은 지도를 여러분에게 제공한다.

② They will even try to match gestures with which they have some difficulty, experimenting with their own faces until they succeed. (2024학년도 수능 29번)
심지어 그들은 자신들이 다소 어려워**하는** 제스처에 맞추려고 노력하고, 성공할 때까지 자기 자신의 얼굴로 실험한다.

③ Diaries were central media through which enlightened and free subjects could be constructed. (2023학년도 수능 21번)
일기는 **그것을 통해** 계몽되고 자유로운 주체가 구성될 수 있는 중심 매체였다.

④ If you hadn't learned to speak, the whole world would seem like the unorganized supermarket; you would be in the position of an infant, for whom every object is new and unfamiliar. (2022학년도 수능 41~42번)
만약 여러분이 말하기를 배우지 않았다면, 온 세상이 정돈되지 않은 슈퍼마켓처럼 보일 것이다. 여러분은 모든 물건이 새롭고 낯**선** 유아의 처지에 있을 것이다.

7-7) 복합관계사

① That is why we heavily depend on aphorisms whenever we face difficulties and challenges in the long journey of our lives. 복합관계부사 whenever (2020학년도 수능 35번)
그것이 우리가 삶의 긴 여정에서 어려움과 도전에 직면할 **때마다** 격언에 매우 의존하는 이유이다.

② This time, the playful and curious boy was interested in his brother Felix, who committed himself to studying no matter where he was.
복합관계부사 no matter where = wherever (2021학년도 수능 43~45번)
이번에는 그 장난기 많고 호기심 많은 아이가 형 Felix에게 관심을 보였는데, 그는 **어디에 있든지** 공부에 전념했다.

③ Whatever the nature of the outcome, which may actually favour one party more than another, the purpose of negotiation is the identification of areas of common interest and conflict.
복합관계대명사 whatever (2024학년도 수능 36번)
실제로 다른 당사자보다 한쪽 당사자에게 더 유리할 수도 있는, 그 결과의 성격이 **무엇이든**, 협상의 목적은 공통의 이익과 갈등의 영역을 밝히는 것이다.

8. 가정법

① If it weren't for the commercial enterprises that produced those records, we would know far, far less about the cultures that they came from.
가정법 과거 (2020학년도 수능 22번)
만약 그런 기록을 만들어내는 상업적 기업이 **없다면** 우리는 그런 기록이 생겨난 문화에 대해 아주 훨씬 더 적게 알 것이다.

② It's time we changed our thinking so that there is no difference between the rights of humans and the rights of the rest of the environment.
가정법 과거(It's time S 과거 V) (2021학년도 수능 21번)
인간의 권리와 나머지 환경의 권리 사이에 차이가 없도록 우리의 생각을 **바꿔야 할 때이다**.

③ His contribution is priceless because the Internet and all digital media would be unimaginable without the laser. 가정법 과거(without) (2024학년도 수능 26번)
인터넷과 모든 디지털 미디어는 레이저 **없이는** 상상할 수 없을 **것이기** 때문에 그의 공헌은 대단히 귀중하다.

④ While checking on his family, Sean interfered in their business as if it was his own. as if (2021학년도 수능 43~45번)
Sean은 가족을 확인하는 동안 그들의 일이 자기 일**인 것처럼** 그 일에 간섭했다.

⑤ If you hadn't learned to speak, the whole world would seem like the unorganized supermarket; you would be

in the position of an infant, for whom every object is new and unfamiliar. 혼합 가정법 (2022학년도 수능 41~42번)
만약 여러분이 말하기를 **배우지 않았다면**, 온 세상이 정돈되지 않은 슈퍼마켓처럼 **보일 것이다**. 여러분은 모든 물건이 새롭고 낯선 유아의 처지에 있을 것이다.

9. 비교급과 최상급

9-1) 비교급

① Each percentage of the three preferred types of place to live was higher than 20% across the three age groups. (2023학년도 수능 25번)
세 가지 선호하는 거주지 유형의 각각의 비율은 세 연령대에 걸쳐 20%보다 **더 높았다**.

② In over 100 studies across many different domains, half of all cases show simple formulas make better significant predictions than human experts, and the remainder (except a very small handful), show a tie between the two. (2023학년도 수능 41~42번)
많은 다른 영역에 걸친 100개가 넘는 연구에서, 모든 사례의 절반은 간단한 공식이 인간 전문가보다 중요한 예측을 **더 잘하고**, 그 나머지(아주 적은 소수를 제외하고)는 둘 사이의 무승부를 보여준다.

③ Thus, reading becomes a more complicated kind of interpretation than it was when children's attention was focused on the printed text, with sketches or pictures as an adjunct. (2024학년도 수능 31번)
이처럼, 읽기는 어린이들의 주의가 인쇄된 텍스트에 집중되고 스케치나 그림이 부속물일 때**보다 더 복잡한** 종류의 해석이 된다.

9-2) 동급 비교

① Services using electrically assisted delivery tricycles have been successfully implemented in France and are gradually being adopted across Europe for services as varied as parcel and catering deliveries. (2023학년도 수능 22번)
전기 보조 배달용 세발자전거를 이용하는 서비스는 프랑스에서 성공적으로 시행되었고 소포나 음식 배달**과 같은 다양한** 서비스를 위해 유럽 전역에서 점차 도입되고 있다.

② Some were trying to kick as high as they could, and some were striking the sparring pad. (2022학년도 수능 43~45번)
일부는 가능한 한 **높이** 발차기를 하려고 애쓰고 있었고, 일부는 겨루기 패드 치기를 하고 있었다.

9-3) 최상급

① In the 55 year-olds and older group, the percentage of those who chose Big/Small City among the three preferred types of place to live was the lowest.
(2023학년도 수능 25번)
55세 이상 연령층에서는 세 가지 선호하는 거주지 유형 중에서 대도시/소도시를 선택한 비율이 **가장 낮았다**.

② Among the six countries, the UK owned the largest online share of retail sales with 19.7% in 2019.
(2021학년도 수능 25번)
여섯 나라 중에서 영국은 2019년에 19.7%로 **가장 큰** 소매 판매의 온라인 점유율을 가졌다.

③ Learning to control your voice and use it for different purposes is, therefore, one of the most important skills to develop as an early career teacher. (2023학년도 수능 35번)
따라서 여러분의 목소리를 통제하고 그것을 다양한 목적을 위해 사용하는 것을 배우는 것은 경력 초기의 교사로서 개발해야 할 **가장 중요한** 기술 **중 하나**이다.

④ Charles H. Townes, one of the most influential American physicists, was born in South Carolina.
one of the 최상급 + 복수명사 (2024학년도 수능 26번)
가장 영향력 있는 미국의 **물리학자 중 한 사람인** Charles H. Townes는 South Carolina에서 태어났다.

9-4) 다양한 비교급 표현

① The more confidently you give instructions, the higher the chance of a positive class response.
the 비교급, the 비교급 (2023학년도 수능 35번)
여러분이 **더 자신 있게** 수업할수록, 긍정적인 학급의 반응이 나올 확률은 **더 높다**.

② A quiet, authoritative and measured tone has so much more impact than slightly panicked shouting.
비교급 강조 (2023학년도 수능 35번)
조용하고도 권위가 있으며 침착한 어조는 약간 당황한 고함보다 그렇게나 **훨씬 더** 큰 효과를 가진다.

③ Mending and restoring objects often require even more creativity than original production.
비교급 강조 (2022학년도 수능 24번)
물건을 고치고 복원하는 것에는 흔히 최초 제작보다 **훨씬 더 많은** 창의력이 필요하다.

10. 접속사 - 명사절 접속사 / 부사절 접속사 / 동격의 that 절

10-1) 명사절 접속사 that

① Alternately, she may communicate that conformity is desired in other ways, such as by gesturing.
목적어 (2024학년도 수능 37번)
다른 방식으로는 몸짓과 같은 것으로 순응이 요망된다는 **것을** 전달할 수도 있다.

② The most common explanation offered by my informants as to why fashion is so appealing is that it constitutes a kind of theatrical costumery.
보어 (2023학년도 수능 29번)
왜 패션이 그렇게 매력적인지에 대해 나의 정보 제공자들이 한 가장 흔한 설명은 **그것이** 일종의 연극적인 의상을 구성한다는 **것**이다.

③ I'm sure you're doing your work.
넌 틀림없이 네 일을 하고 있을 거야. that 생략 (2021학년도 수능 43~45번)

10-2) 명사절 접속사 whether(ask/wonder/question 등과 같은 불확실성을 의미하는 표현일 때)

① For example, algorithms have proved more accurate than humans in predicting whether a prisoner released on parole will go on to commit another crime, or in predicting whether a potential candidate will perform well in a job in future. (2023학년도 수능 41~42번)
예를 들어, 가석방으로 풀려난 죄수가 계속해서 다른 범죄를 저지를 **것인지** 예측하거나, 잠재적인 후보자가 장차 직장에서 일을 잘**할 것인지를** 예측하는 데 알고리즘이 인간보다 더 정확하다는 것이 입증되었다.

② As long as something is funny, we are for the moment not concerned with whether it is real or fictional, true or false. (2022학년도 수능 31번)
어떤 것이 재미있다면, 우리는 잠깐 그것이 진짜**인지** 허구**인지**, 진실**인지** 거짓**인지에** 관해 관심을 두지 않는다.

10-3) 명사절 접속사 how/when/why

① To understand how trends can ultimately give individuals power and freedom, one must first discuss fashion's importance as a basis for change.
(2023학년도 수능 29번)
유행이 궁극적으로 **어떻게** 개인에게 힘과 자유를 줄 수 있는지를 이해하기 위해서는 먼저 변화를 위한 기반으로서의 패션의 중요성에 대해 논의해야 한다.

② Each of these contradictory statements may hold true under particular conditions, but without a clear statement of when they apply and when they do not, aphorisms provide little insight into relations among people. (2020학년도 수능 35번)

이런 모순된 말들 각각은 특정한 상황에서는 사실일 수 있지만, 그것이 **언제** 적용되**는지와 언제** 적용되지 않**는지에** 관한 명확한 진술이 없으면 격언은 사람들 사이의 관계에 대한 통찰력을 거의 제공하지 못한다.

③ No doubt it is this utopian aspect of movies that accounts for **why** we enjoy them so much. (2020학년도 수능 36번)

우리가 **왜** 그렇게 많이 영화를 즐기**는지를** 설명해 주는 것은 바로 영화의 이 이상적인 측면임이 틀림없다.

10-4) 부사절 접속사 - 양보

① **Although** his books are known to be difficult to translate, they have in fact been widely translated into other languages. (2023학년도 수능 26번)

비록 그의 책들이 번역하기 어렵다고 알려져 있**지만**, 그것들은 사실 다른 언어들로 널리 번역되었다.

② Scattered attention harms your ability to let go of stress, because **even though** your attention is scattered, it is narrowly focused, for you are able to fixate only on the stressful parts of your experience. (2024학년도 수능 21번)

주의가 분산되면 스트레스를 해소하는 능력이 손상되는데, 왜냐하면 여러분의 주의가 분산되**더라도**, 여러분은 여러분의 경험 중 스트레스가 많은 부분에만 집착할 수 있으므로, 그것이 좁게 집중되기 때문이다.

③ When there are a lot of different factors involved and a situation is very uncertain, simple formulas can win out by focusing on the most important factors and being consistent, **while** human judgement is too easily influenced by particularly salient and perhaps irrelevant considerations. (2023학년도 수능 41~42번)

관련된 많은 다른 요인이 있고 상황이 매우 불확실할 때, 가장 중요한 요소에 초점을 맞추고 일관성을 유지함으로써 간단한 공식이 승리할 수 있는 **반면**, 인간의 판단은 특히 두드러지고 아마도 관련이 없는 고려 사항에 의해 너무 쉽게 영향을 받는다.

④ In 2012, the online share of retail sales in the Netherlands was larger than that in France, **whereas** the reverse was true in 2019. (2021학년도 수능 25번)

2012년에 네덜란드의 소매 판매의 온라인 점유율은 프랑스의 그것보다 더 **컸지만**, 2019년에는 그 반대였다.

10-5) 부사절 접속사 - 시간

① The water flea only expends the energy needed to produce spines and a helmet **when** it needs to. (2023학년도 수능 36번)

물벼룩은 오직 필요할 **때만** 가시 돌기와 머리 투구를 만드는 데 필요한 에너지를 소모한다.

② In this approach, lawyers do not receive fees or payment **until** the case is settled, when they are paid a percentage of the money that the client receives. (2023학년도 수능 37번)

이 방식에서 변호사는 소송이 해결될 **때까지** 수수료나 지불금을 받지 않는데, 그때 그들은 의뢰인이 받는 금액의 일정 비율을 받는다.

③ Clara's face lit up with a bright smile **as** she nodded. (2024학년도 수능 43~45번)

Clara가 고개를 끄덕일 **때** 그녀의 얼굴이 환한 미소로 밝아졌다.

④ Long **before** we had the writings of the prophets, we had the writings of the profits. (2020학년도 수능 22번)

우리가 예언자들에 관한 기록을 갖기 훨씬 **이전에** 우리는 이익에 대한 기록을 가졌다.

⑤ **After** retiring in 1952, Knight remained active in teaching and writing. (2021학년도 수능 26번)

1952년에 은퇴한 **후에도** Knight는 가르치기와 글쓰기에 여전히 적극적이었다.

10-6) 부사절 접속사 - 조건

① **If** automobile manufacturers are required to measure and publicize the safety characteristics of cars, potential car purchasers can trade safety concerns against other attributes, such as price and styling. (2023학년도 수능 23번)

자동차 제조업체가 자동차의 안전 특성을 측정하고 공개해야 한**다면**, 잠재적인 자동차 구매자는 가격과 스타일 같은 다른 속성과 안전에 대한 우려를 맞바꿀 수 있다.

② Copyright is free and is automatically invested in the author, for instance, the writer of a book or a programmer who develops a program, **unless** they sign the copyright over to someone else. (2021학년도 수능 39번)

저작권은 무료이며 저작자, 예를 들어 어떤 책의 저자나 프로그램을 개발하는 프로그래머가 저작권을 다른 누군가에게 양도하지 **않는 한** 그 저작자에게 자동으로 부여된다.

10-7) 부사절 접속사 - 이유·원인

① A narrow focus heightens the stress level of each experience, but a widened focus turns down the stress level **because** you're better able to put each situation into a broader perspective. (2024학년도 수능 21번)

초점이 좁으면 각 경험의 스트레스 수준이 높아지지만, 초점이 넓으면 여러분은 각 상황을 더 넓은 시각으로 더 잘 볼 수 있기 **때문에** 스트레스 수준이 낮아진다.

② Moments of park creation are particularly telling, however, **for** they reveal and actualize ideas about nature and its relationship to urban society. (2023학년도 수능 38번)

그러나 공원을 조성하는 순간들은 특히 의미가 있는데, 자연과 그것이 도시 사회와 갖는 관계에 대한 생각을 드러내고 실현하**기 때문이다**.

③ This means, for example, that while there are numerous smartphones all with similar functionality, this does not represent an infringement of copyright **as** the idea has been expressed in different ways and it is the expression that has been copyrighted. (2021학년도 수능 39번)

이것은 예를 들어, 모두 유사한 기능을 가진 많은 스마트폰이 있지만, 그 아이디어가 서로 다른 방식으로 표현되었고 저작권 보호를 받은 것은 그 표현이**기 때문에** 이것이 저작권 침해를 나타내지 않는다는 것을 의미한다.

④ **Since** humor can easily capture people's attention, commercials tend to contain humorous elements, such as funny faces and gestures. (2021학년도 수능 35번)

유머는 사람들의 관심을 쉽게 사로잡을 수 있**기 때문에**, 광고 방송은 웃긴 얼굴과 몸짓 같은, 유머러스한 요소들을 포함하는 경향이 있다.

10-8) 부사절 접속사 - 목적

① It may be that robots are needed to reduce manufacturing costs **so that** the company remains competitive, but planning for such cost reductions should be done jointly by labor and management. (2022학년도 수능 38번)

회사가 경쟁력을 유지**하도록** 제조원가를 낮추기 위해 로봇이 필요할 수도 있지만, 그러한 원가절감을 위한 계획은 노사가 함께해야 한다.

10-9) 동격의 접속사 that

① There is **evidence that** even very simple algorithms can outperform expert judgement on simple prediction problems. (2023학년도 수능 41~42번)

매우 간단한 알고리즘조차도 간단한 예측 문제에 대한 전문가의 판단을 능가할 수 있다는 **증거**가 있다.

② In many countries, **the fact that** some environmental hazards are difficult to avoid at the individual level is felt to be more morally egregious than those hazards that can be avoided. (2022학년도 수능 22번)

많은 국가에서, 일부 환경적 위험 요인이 개인 수준에서 피하기 어렵다는 **사실**은 피할 수 있는 그 위험 요인보다 도덕적으로 더 매우 나쁜 것으로 느껴진다.

③ A transit project that could speed travel for tens of thousands of people can be stopped by objections to the loss of a few parking spaces or by the simple fear that the project won't work. (2024학년도 수능 34번)
수만 명의 이동 속도를 높일 수 있는 교통 프로젝트는 몇 개의 주차 공간 상실에 대한 반대나 프로젝트가 효과가 없을 것이라는 단순한 **두려움** 때문에 중단될 수 있다.

11. 형식상의 주어, 형식상의 목적어

11-1) 형식상의 주어-내용상의 주어

① In the climate case, it is not that we face the facts but then deny our responsibility. (2023학년도 수능 34번)
기후의 경우, 우리가 사실을 직면하면서도 우리의 책임을 부인하는 **것이** 문제가 아니다.

② But what does it mean for a place to be full of people? (2024학년도 수능 24번)
하지만 어떤 장소가 사람으로 가득 차 **있다는 것은** 무엇을 의미하는가?

③ It was Evelyn's first time to explore the Badlands of Alberta, famous across Canada for its numerous dinosaur fossils. (2022학년도 수능 19번)
캐나다 전역에서 그곳의 수많은 공룡 화석으로 유명한 앨버타주의 Badlands를 **탐험하는 것이** Evenlyn에게는 처음이었다.

④ It is the responsibility of management to prevent or, at least, to ease these fears. (2022학년도 수능 38번)
이러한 두려움을 **예방하거나** 최소한 **완화하는 것은** 경영진의 책임이다.

11-2) 형식상의 목적어-내용상의 목적어

① Centuries ago, people found it difficult to imagine how someone could see an object without seeing what color it is. (2023학년도 수능 24번)
수 세기 전, 사람들은 어떻게 누군가가 색깔이 무엇인지 못 보면서 그 물체를 볼 수 있는지 **상상하기가** 어려웠다.

12. 특수 구문 – 도치 / 삽입 / 강조 / 동격 / 병렬 구조

12-1) 도치

① Seldom does a new brand or new campaign that solely uses other media, without using television, reach high levels of public awareness very quickly. (2020학년도 수능 39번)
텔레비전을 이용하지 않고, 다른 미디어만을 이용하는 새로운 브랜드나 새로운 캠페인이 아주 빠르게 높은 수준의 대중 인지도에 도달하는 경우는 **거의 없다**.

② Nor does the traditional view recognize the role that non-intellectual factors, especially institutional and socio-economic ones, play in scientific developments. (2020학년도 수능 37번)
전통적인 관점은 **또한** 비지성적인 요인들, 특히 제도적 요인과 사회경제적 요인이 과학 발전에서 하는 역할을 인식하**지 못한다**.

③ At no point in human history have we used *more* elements, in *more* combinations, and in increasingly refined amounts. (2020학년도 수능 33번)
인류 역사의 **어느** 지점에서도, 우리는 (지금보다) '더 많은' 조합으로, 그리고 점차 정밀한 양으로, '더 많은' 원소를 사용한 적은 **없었다**.

④ Nor does everyone leave the world in that state.
또한 모든 이가 그 상태로 세상을 떠나지**도 않는다**. (2020학년도 수능 23번)

⑤ War is never an isolated act, nor is it ever only one decision. (2021학년도 수능 36번)
전쟁은 결코 고립된 행위가 아니며, **또한 결코** 단 하나의 결정도 **아니다**.

12-2) 삽입

① Precision and determinacy are a necessary requirement for all meaningful scientific debate, and progress in the sciences is, to a large extent, the ongoing process of achieving ever greater precision. (2022학년도 수능 34번)
정확성과 확정성은 모든 의미 있는 과학 토론을 위한 필요조건이며, 과학에서의 발전은 **상당 부분**, 훨씬 더 높은 정확성을 달성하는 계속 진행 중인 과정이다.

② Places, in a similar way, are treated as stable containers with clear boundaries. (2024학년도 수능 24번)
장소는 **비슷한 방식으로**, 명확한 경계가 있는 안정적인 용기로 취급된다.

③ The existing world faced by the individual is in principle an infinite chaos of events and details before it is organized by a human mind. (2022학년도 수능 37번)
개인이 직면한 기존(현실) 세계는 **이론상으로는** 인간의 정신에 의해 조직되기 전에는 사건들과 세부 사항들의 무한한 혼돈 상태이다.

④ Today too, because of the heavy snow, Mom was doing her office work at the kitchen table. (2021학년도 수능 43~45번)
오늘 또한 **폭설로 인해** 엄마는 주방 식탁에서 사무실 업무를 보고 있었다.

12-3) 강조

① It is in that context that the idea of "the self [as] both made and explored with words" emerges. (2023학년도 수능 21번)
'말로 만들어지고 또한 탐구되는 (것으로의) 자아'라는 개념이 나타나는 **것은 바로** 그러한 맥락에서다.

② According to the market response model, it is increasing prices that drive providers to search for new sources, innovators to substitute, consumers to conserve, and alternatives to emerge. (2022학년도 수능 36번)
시장 반응 모형에 따르면, 공급자가 새로운 공급원을 찾게 하고, 혁신가가 대용하게 하고, 소비자가 아껴 쓰게 하고, 대안이 생기게 하는 **것은 바로** 가격의 인상이다.

12-4) 동격

① Niklas Luhmann, a renowned sociologist of the twentieth century, was born in Lüneburg, Germany in 1927. (2023학년도 수능 26번)
20세기의 유명한 사회학자 Niklas Luhmann은 1927년 독일 Lüneburg에서 태어났다.

② Anna, the head of the club, was teaching the new members basic moves. (2022학년도 수능 43~45번)
동아리 반장인 Anna는 신입 회원들에게 기본 동작을 가르치고 있었다.

③ He was also involved in Project Apollo, the moon landing project. (2024학년도 수능 26번)
그는 또한 **달 착륙 프로젝트인 아폴로 계획**에 관여했다.

12-5) 병렬 구조

① He slowly put them on, and stared at the birthday presents on the table. 동사 병렬 (2023학년도 수능 43~45번)
그는 천천히 그것을 **쓰고**, 테이블 위에 있는 생일 선물을 **바라보았다**.

② At the same time, other scientists continue to resist speaking with reporters, thereby preserving more time for their science and running the risk of being misquoted and the other unpleasantries associated with media coverage. 분사구문 병렬 (2024학년도 수능 41~42번)
동시에, 다른 과학자들은 기자들과의 대화를 계속 물리치며, 그렇게 함으로써 자신의 과학을 위해 더 많은 시간을 **지켜 내고**, 잘못 인용되는 위험과 언론 보도와 관련된 다른 불쾌한 상황을 **피한다**.

③ These are lost opportunities to understand what drove the compliments and (to) create a solid fan based on them. to부정사 병렬 (2024학년도 수능 22번)
이것은 무엇이 칭찬을 이끌어 냈는지 **이해하고** 그 칭찬을 바탕으로 하여 확고한 팬을 **만들어 낼 수 있는** 기회를 잃은 것이다.

④ Turning the uncertainty into numbers has proved a potent way of analyzing the paths and finding the

shortcut to your destination. 동명사 병렬 (2023학년도 수능 20번)
불확실성을 숫자로 바꾸는 것은 여러분의 목적지로 가는 길을 **분석하고** 지름길을 **찾는** 강력한 방법으로 입증되었다.

⑤ Ostrom also emphasizes the importance of democratic decision processes and that all users must be given access to local forums for solving problems and conflicts among themselves.
명사와 that절 병렬 (2022학년도 수능 33번)
Ostrom은 또한 민주적 의사결정 과정의 **중요성과** 모든 이용자에게 그들 사이의 문제와 갈등을 해결하기 위한 지역 포럼에 참여할 권한이 주어져야 **한다고** 강조한다.

⑥ Since receiver bees will only accept water if they require it, either for themselves or to pass on to other bees and brood, this unloading time is correlated with the colony's overall need of water.
either A or B(부사구 병렬) (2023학년도 수능 33번)
물을 받는 벌들은 **자신들을 위해서든** 다른 벌들과 애벌레들에게 **전해주기 위해서든**, 물이 필요할 때만 물을 받을 것이므로, 이러한 물을 넘겨주는 시간은 군집의 전반적인 물 수요와 상관관계가 있다.

⑦ Both the buyer and seller are aware of each other's restrictions. both A and B (2024학년도 수능 30번)
구매자와 판매자 둘 다 서로의 제약을 알고 있다.

⑧ Presentational styles have been subject to a tension between an informational-educational purpose and the need to engage us entertainingly.
between A and B (2022학년도 수능 32번)
표현 방식은 정보 제공 및 교육적 목적**과** 재미있게 우리의 주의를 끌 필요성 **사이의** 긴장 상태에 영향을 받아왔다.

⑨ The future of our high-tech goods may lie not in the limitations of our minds, but in our ability to secure the ingredients to produce them. not A but B (2020학년도 수능 33번)
첨단 기술 제품의 미래는 우리 생각의 제한점**에** 있는 것**이 아니라**, 그것을 생산하기 위한 재료를 확보할 수 있는 우리의 능력**에** 있을지도 모른다.

⑩ As a consequence, firms do not only need to consider their internal organization in order to ensure sustainable business performance; they also need to take into account the entire ecosystem of units surrounding them. not only A but also B (2022학년도 수능 35번)
결과적으로, 기업은 지속 가능한 사업 성과를 보장하기 위해 그들 내부 조직에 주의를 기울일 필요가 있을 **뿐만 아니라**, 자신들을 둘러싸고 있는 부문들의 전체 생태계를 고려할 필요**도** 있다.

⑪ In real life as well as in painting we do not come across just faces; we encounter people in particular situations and our understanding of people cannot somehow be precipitated and held isolated from the social and human circumstances in which they, and we, live and breathe and have our being. B as well as A (2024학년도 수능 33번)
그림에서뿐만 아니라 실생활에서도 우리는 단지 얼굴만 우연히 마주치는 것이 아니며, 우리는 특정한 상황에서 사람들을 마주치고, 사람들에 대한 우리의 이해는 그들과 우리가 살아 숨 쉬고 존재하는 사회적, 인간적 상황으로부터 괴리된 채 그럭저럭 촉발되어 보유될 수는 없다.

13. 기타 구문

13-1) 접속사 rather than, 전치사 rather than

① It therefore aims at the unmasking of previous illusions of determinacy and precision by the production of new and alternative representations, rather than at achieving truth by a careful analysis of what was right and wrong in those previous representations.
(2022학년도 수능 34번)
그러므로 그것은 이전의 진술에서 무엇이 옳고 틀렸는지에 대한 신중한 분석에 의해 진리를 획득하는 것이 **아니라**, 새롭고 대안적인 진술의 생성에 의해 확정성과 정확성에 대해 이전에 가진 환상의 정체를 드러내는 것을 목표로 한다.

② For example, owners of forest lands have a market incentive to cut down trees rather than manage the forest for carbon capture, wildlife habitat, flood protection, and other ecosystem services.
(2024학년도 수능 23번)
예를 들어, 삼림 지대의 소유자는 탄소 포집, 야생 동물 서식지, 홍수 방어 및 다른 생태계 도움을 위해 숲을 관리하기**보다는** 나무를 베어 내는 시장 인센티브를 가지고 있다.

③ For example, robots could be introduced only in new plants rather than replacing humans in existing assembly lines. (2022학년도 수능 38번)
예를 들어 로봇은 기존 조립 라인에서 인간을 대체하는 **대신** 새로운 공장에만 도입될 수 있다.

13-2) as[so] long as 구문

① As long as the irrealism of the silent black and white film predominated, one could not take filmic fantasies for representations of reality. (2022학년도 수능 39번)
무성 흑백 영화의 비현실주의가 지배하는 **동안은** 영화적 환상을 현실에 대한 묘사로 착각할 수 없었다.

② Even those with average talent can produce notable work in the various sciences, so long as they do not try to embrace all of them at once. (2024학년도 수능 40번)
평균적인 재능을 가진 사람이라도 다양한 과학 분야에서 주목할 만한 성과를 낼 수 있는데, 한 번에 그것들 모두를 수용하려고 하지 않는 **한** 그렇다.

13-3) too ~ to 구문

① Such a grouping may seem too obvious to be called a classification, but this is only because you have already mastered the word. (2022학년도 수능 41~42번)
분류라고 **하기에는** 그러한 분류가 **너무** 분명해 보일 수 있지만, 이것은 단지 여러분이 이미 그 단어를 숙달했기 때문이다.

13-4) 간접의문문

① We must know who this person is, who these other people are, what their relationship is, what is at stake in the scene, and the like. (2024학년도 수능 33번)
우리는 이 사람이 **누구인지**, 다른 이 사람들이 **누구인지**, 그들은 **어떤 관계인지**, 그 장면에서 관건이 **무엇인지** 등을 알아야 한다.